"We'll Always Have Paris"

"We'll Always Have Paris"

The Definitive Guide to Great Lines from the Movies

Robert A. Nowlan and Gwendolyn W. Nowlan

Originally published as FILM QUOTATIONS

HarperPerennial

A Division of HarperCollinsPublishers

The original hardcover edition of this book was published in 1994 by McFarland & Company, Inc., under the title *Film Quotations*.

Published by special arrangement with McFarland & Company, Inc., Publishers, Jefferson, North Carolina.

HarperCollins books may be purchased for educational, business, or sales promotional use. For information, please write: Special Markets Department, HarperCollins Publishers, Inc., 10 East 53rd Street, New York, NY 10022.

FIRST EDITION

Designed by Alma Hochhauser Orenstein

Library of Congress Cataloging-in-Publication Data
  Nowlan, Robert A.
    [Film quotations]
    We'll always have Paris : the definitive guide to great lines from the movies / Robert A. Nowlan and Gwendolyn W. Nowlan. — 1st HarperPerennial ed.
        p.   cm.
    Originally published: Film quotations. Jefferson, N.C. : McFarland & Co., 1994.
    Includes indexes.
    ISBN 0-06-272506-8 (alk. paper)
    1. Motion pictures—Quotations, maxims, etc. I. Nowlan, Gwendolyn Wright, 1945– .
II. Title.
[PN1994.9.N69   1995]
791.43—dc20   95-25203

---

95 96 97 98 99 ❖/RRD 10 9 8 7 6 5 4 3 2 1

"All speech, written or spoken,
is a dead language,
until it finds a willing
and prepared hearer."

—ROBERT LOUIS STEVENSON

This book is dedicated to all the writers and speakers of all the quotations it contains and to all of its readers.

Contents

x   **Contents**

xii   **Contents**

xiv **Contents**

xvi   **Contents**

Acknowledgments

We thank all those whose suggestions, kindness, friendship, love and understanding made the preparation of this book easier. These include Gina Acquarulo, Jerry Ainsworth, Esther Anderson, Dan Barron, Mackey Barron, Helen Bass, Claire Bennett, Augie Bessinger, Arlene Bielefield, Carmel-Lynn Brandi, Loré Brown, Tom Buckley, Linda Chojnicki, Tom Clarie, Heather Corcoran, Mary and Bill Corcoran, Mary Ann and Tony Corvi, Martin Curry, Heather Daly-Donofrio, Laura DeMartino, Ann Demsky, Roseann Diana, Don Duman, John and Gay Evans, Saeed Fakhriravari, Kenneth Florey, Rachel Garcia, Pete Golanski, Ken and Elizabeth Grant, Kerry and Sandy Grant, Bodh Gulati, Jane Hamilton-Merritt, Barbara Hanscom, Ed Harris, Ron Hekeler, Stephen Herzog, John Hill, John Iatrides, Sig and Linda Jensen, Marty and Steve Johnson, Grace Kelly, Ruth Kindersley, Lynn Kohrn, Leo Kuczynski, Louis Kuslan, Eve Kyburg, Rod and Sarah Lane, Joe Lawson, Peter Lawson, Ray and Mollie Lawson, Annabel Lee, Frances Levatino, F. E. Lowe, Jack Maselli, Gina McCaffrey, Diane McLeese, Wayne Miller, Ethel and Larry Montgomery, Paul and Marilyn Montlick, Susan Muro, Gil and Beverly Noble, Danny and Lynne Nowlan, Mary Nowlan, Michael and Kitty Nowlan, Steve Nowlan, Bob O'Brien, Rocco and Rae Orlando, Daniel and Sharon Ort, Ellen O'Sullivan, Rocco Pannella, Dave Paterson, Walter Petroskey, Kathy Pettit, Tom Porter, Elnora Potter, Diane Prunier, Kul Rai, Mike Ranfone, Barbara Reed, Rick Ricardi, Brian Russer, Martha Schaff, Ed Schoonmaker, Morton Shindell, Bruce Shattuck, Mike Shea, Diane Smith, Phil and Loretta Smith, John Splaine, Bud Stone, Tom Therriault, Sheila Wartel, Joe Williams, Martha Yandle, Irene Zaleski, Dick and Britt Zimmerman.

Our efforts are dedicated to the memories of our beloved mothers Marian Shields Nowlan and Gertrude Evans Lawson, who taught us always to do our very best. We are grateful for the love and encouragement of our fathers, Robert A. Nowlan, Sr., and Dr. Ray N. Lawson and his wife Dr. Anne Lawson; our children, Robert, Philip and Edward; Edward's wife Amy and their daughter and son, our grandchildren Alexandra and Tommy; Jennifer Nowlan; and Evan and Andrew Wright.

Preface

"By necessity, by proclivity, and by delight, we all quote. We quote not only books and proverbs, but arts, sciences, religion, customs, and laws; nay, we quote temples and houses, tables and chairs by imitation."
—AMERICAN ESSAYIST, POET AND PHILOSOPHER RALPH WALDO EMERSON.

■

"Screenwriting is what feminists call 'shit-work': if it's well done, it's ignored. If it's badly done, people call attention to it."
—AMERICAN SCREENWRITER WILLIAM GOLDMAN.

■

"The main thing is, if you talk too much, the audience won't remember anything. So say something short and memorable."
—AMERICAN FILM ACTOR STEVE MCQUEEN.

■

Ordinarily in compiling a book of quotations, ascribing a quote to its author is a fairly easy task. In preparing a book of quotations taken from motion pictures, things are a bit trickier. When the authors were young children they believed that actors made up their lines as they went along—just as did real people. Later it was discovered that the source of the words coming from actors' mouths might be many people—even, on occasion, the actors themselves. Examining movie credits, it's not unusual to find that a film is adapted by a team of screenwriters from a story by one or more writers, with additional dialogue thrown in by others for good measure. Nowadays, movies are presented as the director's picture, so certainly these auteurs have their say about the dialogue.

Our decision to credit the actor speaking a movie quotation is based on several considerations. First of all, attributing "Here's looking at you, kid" from *Casablanca* to screenwriters Julius J. and Phillip G. Epstein and Howard Koch, based on the play *Everybody Goes to Rick's* by Murray Burnett and Joan Alison, seems overkill. Everyone of a certain age who is familiar with movies knows it as Humphrey Bogart's toast to Ingrid Bergman. And with whom is the classic line "Frankly, my dear, I don't give a damn" identified, Margaret Mitchell in her novel *Gone with the Wind* or Clark Gable in the epic movie?

While we have the greatest possible respect for screenwriters and the authors of adapted material, a motion picture is not a script. It only comes alive when the words of the writers are put in the mouths of the actors on film. Writers for the movies are given more credit than speech writers for politicians who put memorable phrases in the mouths of men and women looking to convince or lead the people. Was it John F. Kennedy or one of his talented advisers who came up with the line used in his inaugural address, "And so, my fellow Americans, ask not what your country can do for you; ask what you can do for your country"? It doesn't matter, because Kennedy is remembered saying it, even though the thought did not originate with him or his speechwriters.

Wherever possible, not only is the speaker of the quotation identified but also the individual to whom the lines are spoken, and the context in which they are delivered.

The more than 11,000 quotes in the book, consecutively numbered, are listed under 900 subject categories, as for instance Bodies or Money. Within a subject category, the quotes are ordered by the year of release of the movie in which they appear, starting with the earliest released movie and progressing on to the latest. In a few instances, more than one quote in a category comes from the same movie. These are listed according to the order in which they are spoken in the film.

The speaker of a quote is identified by boldface type. If the entry is an exchange involving more than one speaker, the actors are identified in the same order their characters speak in the exchange. Occasionally, for reasons of style, we deviate from this practice if there is no chance of confusion. For each quote, the year of the film's release is provided as well as the name of the studio and or production company.

Sebastien Roch Nicolas Chamfort wrote, "The majority of those who put together collections of verses or epigrams resemble those who eat cherries or oysters, they begin by choosing the best and end by eating everything." We do not claim this book contains the "best" quotations from movies because we know of no standard for determining what "best" means in this context. With so many quotes to choose from, we leave the task of judging the relative quality of the quotations to the readers, who will have their own good reasons for deciding that certain quotes are memorable and personally meaningful.

We have by no means included everything. There are thousands of good, bad and indifferent films from which no quote is chosen. This should not be viewed as a negative comment on the films; nor does it in any way imply that these films contain nothing quotable. One of the most difficult things about completing this book was declaring it finished. We could have continued for years gathering more and more quotes. After all, hundreds of movies are released each year.

The work provides the reader with a massive collection of motion picture quotations, several times the number found in any other source. To assist readers seeking quotations suitable to their needs, each quote is assigned to a category which seems to be its primary subject or thrust. For most subject categories, readers are referred to other relevant subject categories. This practice is also followed with a number of listed subject categories to which no quotes have been assigned.

The book includes as many familiar quotations as possible, with the realization that the meaning of "familiar" is only slightly easier to define than "best." The quotations chosen are not limited to favorite lines from outstanding movies; delightful thoughts and sentiments are expressed in films of all kinds. The quotes selected are taken from movies of every genre, although drama and comedy films provide considerably more lines than do action-adventure or Western films. Most of the quotes are from English language films, but quotes from certain popular foreign language films are also included. There are a number of quotes from silent movies. While the actors did not speak the lines that appeared on title cards, it still seems that these are movie quotes and deserve some representation. Many great quotes come from so-called "B" movies, whose day ended with the arrival of television.

Quotations about specific motion pictures or ones made by those who work in the industry do not appear in the book. These are not uninteresting, but there are several such collections of quotes already available. Our enjoyable work is unfinished; we continue to gather new quotes to be included in the next edition. We welcome any suggestions from our readers.

—ROBERT A. NOWLAN, PH.D.

AND GWENDOLYN W. NOWLAN, ED.D.

Abilities and Capabilities

1 MRS. TEASDALE: "I feel you are the most able statesman in all Freedonia." RUFUS T. FIREFLY: "Well, that covers a lot of ground." Sounds like **Margaret Dumont**'s high regard for **Groucho Marx** doesn't impress him very much. After all, Freedonia is a very small country. *Duck Soup* (1933, Paramount).

2 "I am not a spectacular person; a natural ability to melt into the landscape has proved remarkably useful." Seemingly absent-minded British professor **Leslie Howard** runs a successful underground railroad for scientists and writers imprisoned in Nazi Germany. *Pimpernel Smith* (1941, GB, British National).

3 "I'm a woman completely incapable of feeling. I'll never fall in love." **Patricia Neal**'s declaration to architect Gary Cooper proves incorrect. *The Fountainhead* (1949, Warner Bros.).

4 "I want you to do something you're capable of doing. You cannot escape responsibility." **Eva Marie Saint** encourages schoolteacher Montgomery Clift to be all he can be. *Raintree County* (1958, MGM).

5 "Most people don't ever have to face the fact that in the right place, at the right time, they are capable of anything." At the wrong time in the right place, **John Huston** had an incestuous relationship with his daughter Faye Dunaway, resulting in a child—his daughter and granddaughter. *Chinatown* (1974, Paramount).

6 "I'm not sure she's capable of any real feeling. She's television generation. She learned life from Bugs Bunny." **William Holden** doesn't praise his mistress Faye Dunaway to his wife Beatrice Straight, who is very unlikely to be interested in hearing anything about Dunaway from her husband. *Network* (1976, United Artists).

7 "She's capable of putting a hole in her hand without benefit of a nail, why shouldn't she split a tiny cell in her womb?" Mother Superior **Anne Bancroft** asks court-appointed psychiatrist Jane Fonda why young nun Meg Tilly couldn't have an immaculate conception. After all, without warning Tilly acquires stigmata, with blood gushing from her hands. It would be an explanation for the child Tilly bore without any apparent contact with a man. Still there remains the question whether Tilly murdered the baby after delivering it. *Agnes of God* (1985, Columbia).

8 "The only thing that separates us from the animals is our ability to accessorize." We thought it was the ability to think, but **Olympia Dukakis** may be right. *Steel Magnolias* (1989, Tri-Star).

Abortions

9 "I assisted her in a miscarriage." Doctor **Lloyd Nolan** took pity on Hope Lange, who had been raped and impregnated by her brutish father Arthur Kennedy. At the time censors wouldn't allow Nolan to use the word abortion. *Peyton Place* (1957, 20th Century-Fox).

10 "It wasn't a miscarriage. It was an abortion, Michael, just like our marriage is an abortion, something unholy and evil." **Diane Keaton** informs her husband Al Pacino that she didn't have a miscarriage as reported. She didn't want to bring up another child in his criminal family. *The Godfather, Part II* (1974, Paramount).

Absurdities

11 "What an absurd idea! What an absurd idea! Lady, you got ten absurd ideas for my one." Gin-guzzling tugboat captain **Humphrey Bogart** and Katharine Hepburn, the refined, naïve but stubborn sister of deceased African missionary Robert Morley, are not hitting it off. *The African Queen* (1951, United Artists).

12 "It's absurd to live in this world, but it is even more ridiculous to populate it with new victims and it's most absurd of all to believe that they will have it any better than us." **Gunnar Bjornstrand** believes there is good reason to be disappointed when he learns that his wife Ingrid Thulin intends to give birth to the child she is carrying. *Wild Strawberries* (1957, Sweden, Svensk Filmindustri).

13 "Not Helen, Ellen. Helen would be an absurd name for a man." Lonely arsonist **Wallace Shawn** is named Ellen. *Nice Girls Don't Explode* (1987, New World).

Abuse *see* HARM, LANGUAGES, TREATS AND TREATMENTS, USES AND USING, WASTE AND WASTEFULNESS

Accidents

see also CHANCES, EXPECTATIONS, FATE AND DESTINY, LOSSES AND LOSING, RUINATIONS AND RUINS, TRAGEDIES

14 "Cheer up, maybe you'll have an accident." **Clark Gable** cynically consoles his wife Vivien Leigh when she finds herself with child. In the book, the line was, "Cheer up, maybe you'll have a miscarriage"—but Hollywood censors wouldn't allow that word in 1939. *Gone with the Wind* (1939, Selznick-MGM).

15 TIBOR CZERNY: "Do you always travel in an evening dress?" EVE PEABODY: "No, I was wearing this in Monte Carlo when a nasty accident occurred." TIBOR: "What happened? Fire?" EVE: "No, the roulette system I was playing collapsed under me. I left the casino with what I had on my back." Taxi driver **Don Ameche** hears of **Claudette Colbert**'s run of bad luck. *Midnight* (1939, Paramount).

16 "Well, my little pretty, I can cause accidents, too." Wicked Witch of the West **Margaret Hamilton** cackles at Judy Garland, whose house fell from the skies of Kansas onto Hamilton's sister, killing the Wicked Witch of the East. *The Wizard of Oz* (1939, MGM).

17 "Put in hours and hours of planning. Figure everything down to the last detail. Then what? Burglar alarms start going off all over the place for no sensible reason. A gun fires of its own accord and a man is shot. And a broken down old cop, no good for anything but chasing kids, has to trip over us. Blind accident. What can you do against blind accidents." Master criminal **Sam Jaffe** mutters about how the best laid plans oft go blooey. His last big heist is a big bust. *The Asphalt Jungle* (1950, MGM).

18 HOLLY MARTINS: "I don't get this. All of them there. . . his own driver, knocking him down. His own doctor passing by. No stranger at all?" ANNA SCHMIDT: "I wondered about it a hundred times—if it really was an accident." **Joseph Cotten** and **Alida**

Valli are amazed by the many coincidences in the accidental death of Orson Welles. He was conveniently killed just as the authorities were closing in on him for his black marketeering activities in bleak post-World War II Vienna. *The Third Man* (1950, GB, Korda-Selznick).

19 "I used to go to pieces. I'd see an accident like that and feel so weak inside I'd want to quit, to stop the car and get out. I could hardly make myself go past it. But I'm older now. When I see something really horrible, I put my foot down—because I know everybody else is lifting his." Experienced motor car racer **Yves Montand** points out that successful race car drivers not only can't let fear of having an accident affect their performance but must take advantage of others' misfortune. *Grand Prix* (1966, MGM).

20 "Yes sir. With me, an accident of birth. But you, you're a self-made man." Having the film's last line, **Lee Marvin** politely responds to his former employer Ralph Bellamy's oath: "You bastard!" *The Professionals* (1966, Columbia).

21 "You took a little rest-stop that wasn't on the schedule." **Jon Voight** consoles dying Dustin Hoffman, who is unable to control his bladder on a bus bound for Florida. *Midnight Cowboy* (1969, United Artists).

22 "The best thing that could happen to you would be an industrial accident." **James Belushi** feels that his friend Rob Lowe is too handsome for his own good. *About Last Night* (1986, Tri-Star).

Accusations

see also CRIMES AND CRIMINALS, INDICTMENTS, JUDGMENTS

23 "That's right Armand, no one could ever accuse you of being a great lover." **Irene Dunne** agrees with her music teacher Alexander D'Arcy, with whom she has been out all night. He tries to defuse the suspicions of Dunne's angry husband Cary Grant by claiming to be a "great teacher, not a great lover." *The Awful Truth* (1937, Columbia).

24 "You! It's you who bungled it! You and your stupid attempt to buy it! You. . . you imbecile! You bloated idiot! You stupid fat-head, you!" So outraged that he's almost in tears, **Peter Lorre** screams at Sydney Greenstreet, when they discover the black bird they've schemed and killed for is a fake. *The Maltese Falcon* (1941, Warner Bros.).

25 "If it was raining hundred dollar bills, you'd be out looking for a dime you lost someplace." Columnist **Barbara Stanwyck** accuses newspaper editor James Gleason of not recognizing the news value of a human nature story idea that she's developed. *Meet John Doe* (1941, Liberty Films).

26 "Never in my life have I been accused of any crime, sir—and if that's what you think of me, I shan't serve any dinner." Butler **Richard Haydn** seems more upset by the suggestion that he might be a criminal than by the death of his wife Queenie Leonard. She was the cook, one of the first murder victims of a vengeful executioner on a desolate island off the English coast. *And Then There Were None* (1945, Popular Pictures).

27 "Go ahead, put Christmas in your eyes and keep your voice low. Tell me about paradise and all the things I'm missing. I haven't had a good laugh since before Johnny was murdered. . . . I'm not the type that tears do anything to. . . . Maybe the trouble is my name isn't Johnny and I never taught college anywhere and I don't appreciate the finer things of life. Like looking at a doll cry, and taking the rap for a murder she committed. . . . Do you think I fell for that fancy tripe you gave me? It's not a new story, baby. . . . You killed him, why lie?" **Humphrey Bogart** accuses Lizabeth Scott of killing her former lover William Prince, Bogie's closest wartime buddy. *Dead Reckoning* (1947, Columbia).

28 "Good morning, yes, but it was good night you had on your mind." **Victor McLaglen** accuses John Wayne of an impure thought, when the latter maintains all he did was say "good morning" to McLaglen's sister Maureen O'Hara. The Duke's response ("That's a lie!") almost leads to the donneybrook, saved for the climax of the picture. *The Quiet Man* (1952, Republic).

29 "You've put a homicidal patient in 'Borderline'— a nurse could easily be killed!" Head nurse **Joan Crawford** complains to benevolent shrink Robert Stack who's added homicidal Polly Bergen to his group of "borderline maniac" patients at a mental hospital. *The Caretakers* (1963, United Artists).

30 "You're dangerous and unwholesome and children should not be exposed to you." Student **Pamela Franklin**'s accusation against her teacher Maggie Smith is on target. *The Prime of Miss Jean Brodie* (1969, 20th Century-Fox).

31 "You can't even vomit." **John Cassavetes** makes the ultimate put-down of his non-athletic friend Ben Gazzara. *Husbands* (1970, Columbia).

32 "It was you, Fredo, it was you." Sounding like Marlon Brando accusing his brother Rod Steiger in

On the Waterfront, **Al Pacino** accuses brother John Cazale of setting him up for an assassination attempt. *The Godfather, Part II* (1974, Paramount).

33 "You never stop moving! You never go anywhere!" Shouting at her sometime lover, hairdresser Warren Beatty, **Goldie Hawn** neatly sums up his life. *Shampoo* (1975, Columbia).

34 "Eight days ago you showed up half-stoned for a simple nephrectomy, botched it, put the patient in failure and damn near killed him. Then, pausing only to send in your bill, you flew off." Chief of staff **George C. Scott** reads the riot act to surgeon Richard Dysart, whom Scott has suspended from the hospital for being more interested in his investments than his patients. *The Hospital* (1971, United Artists).

35 "You have reduced me to that most contemptible of creatures—the lovesick swain." At the same time, middle-aged poet **Tom Conti** accuses and confesses to lovely young Kelly McGillis. *Reuben, Reuben* (1983, 20th Century-Fox).

36 "So you screwed another shrink?" Joe DiMaggio-like ballplayer **Gary Busey** breaks in on his wife Theresa Russell, a Marilyn Monroe-like actress, and Michael Emil, an Albert Einstein-like professor. *Insignificance* (1985, GB, Zenith).

37 "You people are cruel and dangerous. You fuck people up." After World War II, British working class stiff **Sting** turns on neurotic society woman Meryl Streep and her promiscuous Bohemian friend Tracey Ullman. *Plenty* (1985, GB, 20th Century-Fox-RKO).

38 "You've slaughtered my parents! Like cattle! My brother! My sister!" **Brigitte Nielsen** reads her lines so woodenly that by comparison, her co-star Arnold Schwarzenegger sounds like a graduate of the Royal Academy of Dramatic Arts. But of course the filmmakers expected audiences to look at Nielsen's lines, not listen to them. *Red Sonja* (1985, MGM-United Artists).

Acquaintances *see* FRIENDSHIPS AND FRIENDS, INFORMATION AND INFORMERS, KNOWLEDGE

Acting and Actors

see also ACTIONS AND ACTS, AGENTS, COMEDY AND COMEDIANS, MOTION PICTURES, PERFORMANCES, PLAYING AND PLAYERS, SHOWS, STARS, THEATERS

39 OSCAR JAFFE: "That is the way the iceman would enter, not Mary Joe." LILY GARLAND: "I wanted to be an actress, but I won't crawl on my stomach for any man!" **John Barrymore**'s direction of actress **Carole Lombard** has her in tears. *Twentieth Century* (1934, Columbia).

40 "If I can act, I want the world to know it; if I can't, I want to know." Aspiring actress **Katharine Hepburn** is pretty sure it will be the former judgment when she's given the opportunity to tread the boards. *Stage Door* (1937, RKO).

41 "It takes more than greasepaint and footlights to make an actress. It takes heartaches as well." Older thespian **Constance Collier,** who has had her share of heartaches, passes on what she's learned to aspiring actress Katharine Hepburn. *Stage Door* (1937, RKO).

42 "How do you know who's an actress and who isn't? You're an actress if you're acting. But you can't just walk up and down a room and act. Without that job and those lines to say, an actress is just like any ordinary girl trying not to look as scared as she is." Acting hopeful **Andrea Leeds** tells fellow novice Katharine Hepburn that they can't call themselves actresses until they are working at their craft. *Stage Door* (1937, RKO).

43 MARY HAINES: "He couldn't love a girl like you." CRYSTAL ALLEN: "If he couldn't he's an awful good actor." **Norma Shearer** can't see what her husband sees in cheap salesgirl **Joan Crawford**. It seems to have something to do with who makes him feel important. *The Women* (1939, MGM).

44 "This isn't the spot for the school girl act. The pair of us are sitting under the gallows." **Humphrey Bogart** is impatient with Mary Astor's lies and pretense of innocence. *The Maltese Falcon* (1941, Warner Bros.).

45 "Oh yes, I saw him once. What he did to Shakespeare, we are now doing to Poland." It's a line of very questionable taste delivered by German commandant **Sig Rumann**. He's describing Polish actor Jack Benny, to Benny disguised as a German spy. *To Be or Not to Be* (1942, United Artists).

46 "Watson, let me advise you. If you ever consider taking up another profession, never think of becoming an actor." **Basil Rathbone,** as Sherlock Holmes, gives some kindly advice to his bungling colleague and friend Nigel Bruce, as Dr. Watson. *Pursuit to Algiers* (1945, Universal).

47 "Every now and then some elder statesman of the theater or cinema assures the public that actors and actresses are just plain folks. Ignoring the fact that their greatest attraction to the public is their complete lack of resemblance to normal human

beings." **George Sanders,** as theater critic Addison DeWitt, serves as the film's Greek chorus. *All About Eve* (1950, 20th Century-Fox).

48 "Miss Caswell is an actress, a graduate of the Copacabana School of Dramatic Arts." Theater critic **George Sanders** sneeringly introduces his newest "protégée", Marilyn Monroe, to the guests at Bette Davis' party. *All About Eve* (1950, 20th Century-Fox).

49 "Dear Margo. You were an unforgettable Peter Pan. You must play it again soon." Caustic theater critic **George Sanders** tells aging Broadway actress Bette Davis to grow up. She has just informed him that she was so certain that she had removed his name from the guest list for her party to which he has just arrived. *All About Eve* (1950, 20th Century-Fox).

50 "As a physical instructor you'd lead a normal life. As an actress, you know, you'll be heading out on a pretty rough voyage." Seaman **Spencer Tracy** wants his daughter Jean Simmons to be a P.E. instructor. Simmons, who is portraying Ruth Gordon as a girl, wants to become an actress. *The Actress* (1953, MGM).

51 "I told you she was an actress. I knew she was going to do something for me. I just didn't know what." **Tyrone Power** admires the way his wife Marlene Dietrich used the judicial system and Power's barrister Charles Laughton to get him acquitted of a murder charge. *Witness for the Prosecution* (1957, United Artists).

52 "I'm not an actress. I'm a punching bag. I'm a studio prop." Title character **Carroll Baker** whines at the treatment she receives. *Harlow* (1965, Paramount).

53 LEO BLOOM: "Actors are not animals. They're human beings." MAX BIALYSTOCK: "Oh, yeah? Have you ever eaten with any?" New Broadway producer **Gene Wilder** is taught by old pro **Zero Mostel** about the theater and its people. *The Producers* (1967, MGM).

54 "He was madly overacting, as usual, but you must admit he knew how to make an exit." Theater critic **Ian Hendry**, who has survived mad Shakespearean actor Vincent Price's plot to kill all the critics who have panned his performance, reviews Price's farewell appearance. When the jig is up and his daughter Diana Rigg is killed, Price sets a chair on fire, climbs to the roof holding the body of Rigg, delivers a soliloquy from King Lear, and leaps to his death. *Theater of Blood* (1973, United Artists).

55 "I won't do this until the dancing dildoes know their steps. I'm an actress." **Alexandra Morgan**

protests about the no-talent amateurs she must work with. *The First Nudie Musical* (1976, Paramount).

56 "Don't act like you know it all. You won't get a tip that way." Brothel whore **Susan Sarandon** advises her twelve-year-old daughter Brooke Shields to act dumb on the occasion of her initiation as a prostitute. *Pretty Baby* (1978, Paramount).

57 "That's not acting. That's kissing and jumping and drinking and humping." Head TV comedy writer **Bill Macy** is not impressed with the work of guest star, fading movie star Peter O'Toole, as famous for his boozing and womanizing as he is for his swashbuckling roles. *My Favorite Year* (1982, MGM-United Artists).

58 "Live? I can't go on live! I'm a movie star—not an actor." Errol Flynn-like, alcoholic, woman-catching movie star **Peter O'Toole** panics when young television writer Mark Linn-Baker casually informs him that the TV program O'Toole is to appear on is a live broadcast. *My Favorite Year* (1982, MGM-United Artists).

59 "I'm an actor. I can do a father." **Ted Danson** believes he can perform like a responsible parent. *Three Men and a Baby* (1987, Buena Vista).

60 "How was that for a test, huh? I'm a terrific actress." **Lynn Redgrave** is an Elvira-like TV horror show hostess. *Midnight* (1989, SVS Films).

61 TOMMY NOVAK: "You just have to play that little-girl-lost routine, don't you?" LOU ANN MCGUINN: "I'm still feminine. I'm a Cosmo fighter." NOVAK: "Obviously a hardened criminal; I can tell by the kewpie-doll lips." When skip-tracer **Clint Eastwood** catches up with innocent bail-jumper **Bernadette Peters**, she pouts and flirts with him. *Pink Cadillac* (1989, Warner Bros.).

Actions and Acts

see also ACTING AND ACTORS, BEHAVIOR, INVOLVE-MENTS, JOBS, WORK AND WORKERS

62 "In this new world one does many acts one does not wholly approve. It is a question of adjustment for all of us." German physician **Eric von Stroheim** tells Russian pathologist Walter Huston that although he despises the Nazis, he does their bidding to save himself. *The North Star* (1943, RKO).

63 "Kathy and Harry and Jane and all of them. . . think they've fought the good fight for democracy in this country. They haven't got the guts to take the step from talking to action. One lit-

tle action on one little front. Sure, I know it's not the whole answer, but it's got to start somewhere. And it's got to be with action—not pamphlets, not even with your series. It's got to be with people—nice people, rich people, poor people, big and little people. It's got to be quick." **Celeste Holm** complains to crusading magazine writer Gregory Peck about "liberals" who are all talk and no action in the fight against anti-Semitism. *Gentleman's Agreement* (1947, 20th Century-Fox).

64 "Are you one of those talkers, or would you be interested in a little action?" **Judy Holliday** bluntly tests William Holden's interest. *Born Yesterday* (1951, Columbia).

65 PROSTITUTE: "Say Baby. Lookin' for some action?" FRANK HOOKS: "I don't think they got a needle big enough to kill the shit you got." PROSTITUTE: "Well, you can kiss my ass." The offer of blonde sexpot **Katherine Wallach** is turned down by black Chicago narcotics cop **Fred Williamson**. *The Big Score* (1981, Almi).

66 "I can't seem to take action. I'm like Hamlet unable to kill his uncle. I want Lee, but I can't harm Hannah. And in no other area am I a procrastinator." **Michael Caine** is having an affair with Barbara Hershey, his wife Mia Farrow's sister. *Hannah and Her Sisters* (1987, Orion).

Addiction see ALCOHOL, DRINKING AND DRUNKEN-NESS, DRUGS, HABITS, SMOKING AND SMOKERS

Admiration

see also FRIENDSHIPS AND FRIENDS, HONOR, LEADER-SHIP AND LEADERS, LOVE AND HATE, LOVE AND LOVERS, POPULARITY, RESPECT AND RESPECTABILITY, WORSHIP

67 "That's a nice pin. I'm gonna have one like it someday." **Edward G. Robinson** admires a fellow mobster's diamond stickpin. In the very next scene, Robinson is wearing the pin. *Little Caesar* (1930, Warner Bros.).

68 "You have so much life. I've always admired you so. I wish I could be more like you." It's difficult for anyone, even Vivien Leigh, to dislike kind and gentle **Olivia de Havilland**. *Gone with the Wind* (1939, Selznick-MGM).

69 "There is no room for imperfection in this world. . . . What a pity my father didn't live to see me strong—to dispose of the weak of the world whom he detested. He would have admired me for what I am going to do." Maniacal **George Brent** appears to be crediting his deceased father for the insanity that drives him to kill girls with physical or mental handicaps. *The Spiral Staircase* (1945, RKO).

70 "I like women, but I don't admire them." Contemporary Bluebeard **Charles Chaplin** makes a career out of marrying and murdering wealthy women. *Monsieur Verdoux* (1947, Chaplin-United Artists).

71 "He must be part goat. . . . Look at him go, will you." Speaking to his partner Tim Holt, puffing **Humphrey Bogart** admires old prospector Walter Huston, who is leaving them in his dust as they climb a mountain. *The Treasure of the Sierra Madre* (1948, Warner Bros.).

72 "Look, sweetie, be practical. I've got a good deal here. A long-term contract with no options. I like it that way. Maybe it's not very admirable. Well, you and Artie can be admirable." Kept man **William Holden** refuses to leave Gloria Swanson's wealth for an uncertain future with Nancy Olson. Holden suggests that she accept the marriage proposal of Jack Webb. *Sunset Boulevard* (1950, Paramount).

73 "I certainly admire people who do things. It must be pretty exciting, being so important—me, I never do anything important." **Robert Walker** feigns admiration and envy for tennis star Farley Granger. *Strangers on a Train* (1951, Warner Bros.).

74 "Look at the way he moves—like a dancer. And those fingers, those chubby fingers. And that stroke—like he's playing a violin or something." Whispering to his partner Myron McCormick, pool hustler **Paul Newman** expresses his admiration for his opponent Jackie Gleason, as the latter runs ball after ball. *The Hustler* (1961, 20th Century-Fox).

75 "One of the things I admire about you is your balance. You seem to be a truly peaceful man." Wealthy, dying **Melvyn Douglas** likes the way that slow-witted ex-gardener Peter Sellers handles himself. All the rich and powerful people believe Sellers is another Henry Kissinger. *Being There* (1979, United Artists).

76 "Get out of here. You're the terrific one. I mean you know all that deep junk and everything." At a point in her career when she was only a stunning beauty and not a stunningly beautiful actress, gum-snapping, tight-clothes-wearing, 60s teenager **Michelle Pfeiffer** shares some mutual admiration with English transfer student Maxwell Caulfield. *Grease 2* (1982, Paramount).

Adolescence see AGE AND AGING, BOYS, CHILDREN AND CHILDHOOD, GIRLS, MATURITY AND IMMATURITY, PARENTS, YOUTH

Adoration see DEVOTION, LOVE AND HATE, LOVE AND LOVERS, RESPECT AND RESPECTABILITY, WORSHIP

Adultery see INFIDELITIES, LOVE AND HATE, LOVE AND LOVERS, LUST, MARRIAGES, MEN AND WOMEN, SEX AND SEXUALITY

Advantages

see also COMPARISONS, SELFISHNESS, SUPERIORITY AND INFERIORITY, WINNERS AND LOSERS, WORTH AND VALUES

77 GROUCHO: "How about you and I passing out onto the veranda, or would you rather pass out here?" LUCILLE: "Sir, you have the advantage of me!" GROUCHO: "Not yet I haven't, but wait till I get you outside." Billed only as a "Stowaway," **Groucho Marx** comes on strongly to "Ice Cream Blonde" **Thelma Todd**. *Monkey Business* (1931, Paramount).

78 "My husband and I have decided to give the advantage of our home to one of your foundlings. . . . Of course, we wouldn't want one that cries." Wealthy **Cecil Cunningham** condescendingly confides to Greer Garson, the head of a state orphanage, that she's mother bountiful. *Blossoms in the Dust* (1941, MGM).

79 "You're a little too facile for your own good, but that can be an advantage out here." Jaded Hollywood art director **Richard A. Dysart** sees hope for altruistic art director William Atherton. *The Day of the Locust* (1975, Paramount).

80 "Someone gives me an angle, I play it. Does that mean I should die?" Looking for an advantage in making some dishonest money, Jewish bookie **John Turturro** has angled in on Italian gangster Jon Polito's angle. If the latter has his way, Turturro will die. *Miller's Crossing* (1990, 20th Century-Fox).

Adventures

see also DANGER, EXCITEMENTS, EXPERIENCES, RISKS

81 "Death is just another exciting adventure. A perfect end to an imperfect life." **Marlene Dietrich** bravely prepares to face a firing squad as a spy. *Dishonored* (1931, Paramount).

82 GERRY JEFFERS: "I might not get married again. I might become an adventuress." TOM JEFFERS: "I can just see you starting for China on a twenty-six foot sailboat." GERRY: "You're thinking of an adventurer, dear. An adventuress never goes on anything under three hundred feet with a crew of eighty." **Claudette**

Colbert and **Joel McCrea** have a civilized conversation after deciding to end their marriage. *The Palm Beach Story* (1942, Paramount).

83 "Men of our years have no business playing around with any adventure that they can avoid. We're like athletes who are out of condition. We can't handle that kind of thing anymore." District Attorney **Raymond Massey** warns his friend Professor Edward G. Robinson against "the siren call of adventure." *The Woman in the Window* (1944, RKO).

84 "For the moment, let them enjoy a calm sea, a fresh breeze and each other. The girl is pretty, and I was always sentimental. But for Jason, there are other adventures. I have not yet finished with Jason. Let us continue the game another day." The god Zeus, portrayed by **Niall MacGinnis**, blesses the love of Todd Armstrong and Nancy Kovack, but promises that Armstrong has many exciting adventures awaiting him. *Jason and the Argonauts* (1963, GB, Columbia).

85 "As I watched Holmes settle into his seat, a sudden feeling came over me, that I would most certainly be seeing him again. So ended my first adventure with Mr. Sherlock Holmes. As I watched his carriage disappear into the distance I realized that I had forgotten to thank him. He had taken a weak, frightened boy and made him into a courageous, strong man. My heart soared, I was filled with confidence. I was ready to take on the greatest and most exciting adventure of them all. And I knew it was bound to involve Sherlock Holmes." As Nicholas Rowe's carriage departs from young Alan Cox, the voice of the young John Watson, grown to be **Michael Hordern** sums up the first adventure of Holmes and Watson, when they were mere boys. *Young Sherlock Holmes* (1985, Paramount).

86 "Some other great adventure?" Having survived a series of dangerous misadventures, **Sharon Stone** is a game girl, ready for some more with title character Richard Chamberlain. *Allan Quatermain and the Lost City of Gold* (1987, Cannon).

87 "I assure you my adventures are true. . . ." **John Neville**, the notorious lying Baron, refers to his tall tales. *The Adventures of Baron Munchausen* (1989, GB, Columbia).

88 "Look at every experience as an adventure." Therapist **Brenda Bruce** advises Saskia Reeves who has been fired from her job, had an affair with the headmaster of her son's school and is quite nervous about her annual reunion with her long-time friend Imelda Staunton. *Antonia & Jane* (1991, GB, Miramax).

Advertising see ANNOUNCEMENTS, BUSINESS AND COMMERCE, BUYING AND SELLING

Advice

see also INFORMATION AND INFORMERS, INSTRUCTIONS, MESSAGES, OPINIONS, RECOMMENDATIONS, THREATS, WARNINGS, WISDOM

89 "There's a hundred million miles between us. Marry Vivian so you won't have to scratch for a living in a world you know nothing about." Despite loving him, manicurist **Carole Lombard** urges formerly wealthy Fred MacMurray to marry Astrid Allwyn, the daughter of "the Pineapple King" because he's not suited for anything else. *Hands Across the Table* (1935, Paramount).

90 "Let me give you one word of fatherly advice—never give a sucker an even break." Conniving patent-medicine salesman **W.C. Fields** bids farewell to heiress Rochelle Hudson, who always thought he was her father. *Poppy* (1936, Paramount).

91 "Let me give you a piece of advice. Don't be too wise. Don't think you know all the answers. Things have been done for people—many nice things. Remember that!" Wealthy **Edward Arnold** assures typist Jean Arthur that his offer to help her has no sinister strings attached. *Easy Living* (1937, Paramount).

92 "Whenever I'm miserable, I just sweep and sweep. You'll be surprised how quickly your troubles will disappear. And have a good cry, too. It'll make you feel better." Off to work, **Penny Singleton** has some advice for hubbie Arthur Lake, reduced to being a house husband when he's fired from his job. *Blondie Meets the Boss* (1939, Columbia).

93 "One more piece of motherly advice. Don't confide in your girl friends. . . . If you let them advise you, they'll see to it, in the name of friendship, that you lose your husband and your home." **Lucille Watson** knows her daughter's friends well. *The Women* (1939, MGM).

94 "Son, never lend money to a church. As soon as you start to close in on them, everyone thinks you're a heel." Banker **Gene Lockhart**'s advice to his son James Brown is met with the question, "Well, aren't you?" His father answers, "Yes." *Going My Way* (1944, Paramount).

95 "Veda's been here for about a month now, Mildred, and I think I know the best way to handle her. Let me give you a little advice: if you want her to do anything for you, just hit her in the head first." **Jack Carson** likens Joan Crawford's selfish, self-centered, insensitive daughter Ann Blyth to a mule—before you can get them to do anything, you first have to hit them with a two-by-four to get their attention. *Mildred Pierce* (1945, Warner Bros.).

96 DADIER: "Any tips for a rookie?" MURDOCK: "Two. Don't be a hero. And never turn your back on the class." On his first day as a teacher, **Glenn Ford** hears some discouraging words from veteran pedagogue **Louis Calhern**. *The Blackboard Jungle* (1955, MGM).

97 "You start with a blue robing bag, sir. Then if you do good work for counsel, he'll give you a red one. If at the end of seven years you haven't been given a red bag—use a suitcase." Clerk **Raymond Huntley** advises rookie barrister Ian Carmichael on how to gauge his progress as an employee of absent-minded judge Miles Malleson. *Brothers-in-Law* (1957, GB, British & Colonial).

98 "Never try to promote a promoter." **Keenan Wynn** gives some semi-friendly advice to inept dreamer Frank Sinatra, who has plans for a Florida amusement park. Wynn tells Sinatra that his plans are fine for "Disney." *A Hole in the Head* (1959, United Artists).

99 "Non-swimmers should never leap bare-assed into the sea of love." College dean **Nan Martin** lectures distraught co-ed Yvette Mimieux who has run afoul of womanizing Christopher Jones. *Three in the Attic* (1969, AIP).

100 "Jud, if you don't want to be crucified, don't stay around crosses." **Alix Wyeth** has some advice for bitter and broken returning Vietnam vet Joseph Kaufmann. *Jud* (1971, Duque-Maron).

101 "Pay close attention to the physical world. Isolate and concentrate on the details." **Steve Inwood** lectures his class on how to become actors. *Fame* (1980, MGM-United Artists).

102 "Go for the wild and crazy stuff." **Cameron Dye** advises his closest friend, Hollywood punker Nicolas Cage. *Valley Girl* (1983, Atlantic).

103 "I urge you to make an effort to be more accepting of who she is." It's an example of **Genevieve Bujold**'s glib, meaningless advice, made to a male caller to her radio call-in show for sexually troubled listeners. *Choose Me* (1983, Island Alive).

104 "Let me give you some advice. You can forget that literature. . . and philosophy. . . . You've never seen a philosopher making fifty grand a year or

driving a car like this. . . . Socrates rode around on the back of a donkey." In the 60s, automobile dealership owner **Richard Crenna,** dispensing his materialistic philosophy, discourages young Matt Dillon from going to college. *The Flamingo Kid* (1984, 20th Century-Fox).

105 "I would kill or die to make love to you'. . . You got to have eye contact first. You look. She looks. Then you say it. Don't say it like it's dirty. Say it from the heart, then it ain't dirty. . . it's passion." While in Paris on vacation, experienced **Nick Corri** offers his virginal college friend Anthony Edwards some pointers for scoring with girls. *Gotcha!* (1985, Universal).

106 "It's a jungle out there, so my advice is don't go. Live at home. Let your parents worry about it." Wealthy **Rodney Dangerfield** delivers a message to frost parents' hearts as he gives his college's commencement speech. *Back to School* (1986, Orion).

107 "Stay on your side of the street; that's what they have gutters for." Jewish mother **Blythe Danner** doesn't approve of her sister Judith Ivey's Irish suitor Alan Weeks who lives just across the street. *Brighton Beach Memoirs* (1986, Universal).

108 "Take my advice, there's money in muck." **Saeed Jaffrey** advises his nephew Gordon Warnecke. The latter and his cockney lover Daniel Day-Lewis, take the advice and refurbish a failed laundromat. *My Beautiful Laundrette* (1986, GB, Orion Classics).

109 "All you gotta do is get a nose job, get your hair fixed, get your teeth fixed, shave some hair from your hands, and be yourself." Ghetto hipster **Robert Townsend** advises title character S.L. Band, who's not very attractive. *Ratboy* (1986, Warner Bros.).

110 "Don't do anything they don't ask you for." "Old" pro **Louise Smith** gives some survival tips to Helen Nicholas on her first and last day as a prostitute in a brothel. *Working Girls* (1986, Miramax).

111 "Think repression." Seventeen-year-old **Keith Coogan** advises his cousin Jon Cryer on how to pass as a high school student. Youthful-looking Cryer plans to hide from a professional hitman hired to kill him by returning to high school. *Hiding Out* (1987, DEG).

112 "Never go against a Sicilian when death is on the line." Cackling, **Wallace Shawn** advises Cary Elwes. Shawn believes he has outwitted Elwes—he is wrong. *The Princess Bride* (1987, 20th Century-Fox).

113 "You want to catch the wild monkey, you got to climb the tree." It's **Reizl Bozyk**'s sage but nearly meaningless advice to her granddaughter Amy Irving. *Crossing Delancey* (1988, Warner Bros.).

114 "You know, Louise, a man doesn't buy the cow when he can get milk for free." For ages, mothers like **Marietta Marich** have used this old saw to advise their daughters that men will see no need to marry a woman if she sleeps with him whenever he wants. They've had about as much luck using this line with their daughters as Marich has with her spinster daughter Teri Garr, who shacks up with Gene Hackman from time to time. *Full Moon in Blue Water* (1988, Trans World).

115 "I wouldn't wait to the last moment to fill out those organ donor cards." **Leslie Nielsen**'s advice is his practical way of comforting Susan Beaubian about her critically wounded husband O.J. Simpson. *The Naked Gun* (1988, Paramount).

116 "Tess, you don't get ahead by calling your boss a pimp." Sympathetic personnel manager **Olympia Dukakis** advises Melanie Griffith. She called her boss a pimp because he was trying to fix her up with an out-of-town customer looking for a good time. *Working Girl* (1988, 20th Century-Fox).

117 "Never burn bridges. . . today's junior executive, tomorrow's senior partner." **Sigourney Weaver** shares some acumen with her secretary Melanie Griffith after the former has effectively but gently handled a man coming on very strongly at a cocktail party. *Working Girl* (1988, 20th Century-Fox).

118 "I get paid $425 an hour to talk to people and so when I offer to tell you something for nothing, I advise you to listen carefully." Divorce attorney **Danny De Vito** is so intent on telling the story of the rise and the fall of the marriage of Michael Douglas and Kathleen Turner that he informs a client that there will be no charge. Of course, this is fiction. *The War of the Roses* (1989, 20th Century-Fox).

119 "No, Oliver, you don't even want to deal with her. You avoid her. Women can be a lot meaner than we give them credit for. Never underestimate an adversary. Don't even talk to her." Counselor **Danny De Vito** gives both professional and personal advice to his client and friend Michael Douglas. The latter is in the middle of a messy custody fight with Kathleen Turner—for their house. *The War of the Roses* (1989, 20th Century-Fox).

120 "It's too bad we couldn't visit the Wizard of Oz to get good advice." **Laura Dern** recalls their favorite

movie as she and parole violator Nicolas Cage hop into a car for a trip to California. *Wild at Heart* (1990, Goldwyn).

121 "Get down off the cross, honey, someone needs the wood." **Dolly Parton** gives some glib advice to a self-pitying caller to the former's radio call-in advice show. *Straight Talk* (1992, Hollywood Pictures).

Aesthetics *see* ART AND ARTISTS, BEAUTY, MUSIC AND MUSICIANS, POETRY AND POETS, WRITING AND WRITERS

Affection *see* EMOTIONS, FEELINGS, FRIENDSHIP AND FRIENDS, LOVE AND HATE, LOVE AND LOVERS

Age and Aging

see also BIRTHS AND BIRTHDAYS, MATURITY AND IMMATURITY, TIME, YOUTH

122 "I'm fifty—I lived my life." **Lewis Stone** confuses middle-age with old-age, and even then life isn't over. *Romance* (1930, MGM).

123 "You're simply rushing at old age. I'm not ready for that yet!" Restless **Ruth Chatterton** wishes to end her marriage to industrialist Walter Huston. *Dodsworth* (1936, Goldwyn-United Artists).

124 "I was born old." Mountain woman **Beulah Bondi** describes herself in the first outdoor film shot in three-color Technicolor. The line also applies to Bondi, who usually played women much older than herself. *The Trail of the Lonesome Pine* (1936, Paramount).

125 "On account of you, I was grown up for one day. Now I know how wonderful life's gonna be when I'm 18." Sixteen-year-old **Judy Garland,** playing a twelve-year-old, thanks Mickey Rooney for taking her to a Christmas Eve dance and treating her like a "grown-up." *Love Finds Andy Hardy* (1938, MGM).

126 EDDIE BARTLETT: "He can't be more than fifteen." GEORGE HALLY: "He'll never be sixteen." Doughboy **James Cagney** doesn't approve of **Humphrey Bogart**'s enjoyment when he shoots a young German soldier. *The Roaring Twenties* (1939, Warner Bros.).

127 "It's an interesting place, full of relics, and how old are you, Mr. Connor?" While talking about the city of Brotherly Love, Philadelphia, **Katharine Hepburn** abruptly switches the subject and catches magazine writer James Stewart off guard. *The Philadelphia Story* (1940, MGM).

128 "Old age, Mr. Thompson. It's the only disease you don't look forward to being cured of." Elderly **Everett Sloane** sagely comments to reporter William Alland. *Citizen Kane* (1941, RKO).

129 DR. VENGARD: "What's your age?" JILL BAKER: "Twenty-two." DR. VENGARD: "I'm your psychiatrist." JILL: "Twenty-six." Psychiatrist **Alan Mowbray,** treating **Merle Oberon** for an uncontrollable case of hiccups, must first get her to tell him the truth. *That Uncertain Feeling* (1941, United Artists).

130 "At 21 or 22, so many things appear solid, permanent, untenable, which at 40, seems nothing but disappearing mire. Forty can't tell 20 about this. Twenty can find out only by getting to 40." **Joseph Cotten** tells Dolores Costello, the woman he loves, that her selfish son Tim Holt will have to learn things the hard way. *The Magnificent Ambersons* (1942, RKO).

131 "Anyway, I'm too old for you. 'Cold are the hands of time that creep along relentlessly, destroying slowly but without pity that which yesterday was young. Alone our memories resist that disintegration and grow more lonely with the passing years.' That's hard to say with false teeth." Hard-of-hearing "Weenie King," delightfully played by **Robert Dudley,** says a mouthful to lovely young Claudette Colbert. *The Palm Beach Story* (1942, Paramount).

132 "I shall be seven in May." Remarkable child actress **Margaret O'Brien** is Lady Jessica de Canterville. *The Canterville Ghost* (1943, MGM).

133 "Middle-aged people come in two varieties—the ones who never cared and the ones who cared too much." Crusty British air-raid warden **Roland Culver** states his opinion of middle-age to Olivia de Havilland during a London blackout. *To Each His Own* (1946, Paramount).

134 "As old as my tongue and a little bit older than my teeth." It's **Edmund Gwenn**'s answer to the question about his age on his employment card with Macy's department store where he appears as Santa Claus. *Miracle on 34th Street* (1947, 20th Century-Fox).

135 "Fifty—the old age of youth, the youth of old age." Having reached the mid-century mark, **William Powell** views it as life's mid-point. *Mr. Peabody and the Mermaid* (1948, Universal-International).

136 "Lloyd, I am not twentyish. I am not thirtyish. Three months ago I was forty years old. Forty. Four oh—That slipped out. I hadn't quite made up my mind to admit it. Now I feel as though I've suddenly taken all my clothes off." Broadway actress **Bette Davis** confesses to playwright Hugh Marlowe that she's feeling a bit old. *All About Eve* (1950, 20th Century-Fox).

137 "I've always liked older men. Look at Roosevelt, look at Churchill, look at that old fellow, what's his name in *The African Queen*—absolutely crazy about him." **Lauren Bacall,** desperate to marry millionaire William Powell, who thinks he's too old for her, praises older men—including her husband at the time, Humphrey Bogart. *How to Marry a Millionaire* (1953, 20th Century-Fox).

138 "The dangerous age. Will you be satisfied to stay home and take care of a broken-down man of sixty? No, you'll want to go out and live. And me, I'll be just around the corner from social security." **Dick Powell** has no luck trying to convince his teenage bride Debbie Reynolds that the difference in their ages will make their marriage impossible. The most difficult thing in the scene is believing 50-year-old Powell, in his last film appearance, when he claims to be 35. *Susan Slept Here* (1954, RKO).

139 "Now look, he's forty, which means he'll consider any female over eighteen too old; we might as well face it." **Agnes Moorehead** tells fortyish widow Jane Wyman to forget the attractive man she expressed interest in. *All That Heaven Allows* (1955, Universal-International).

140 "She's at that age when nothing seems to fit." **Rochelle Hudson** doesn't know how to help her troubled adolescent daughter Natalie Wood. *Rebel Without a Cause* (1955, Warner Bros.).

141 SIGNORA FIORINI: "In Italy, age is a virtue." JANE HUDSON: "If it is, I'm loaded." Innkeeper **Isa Miranda** tells American spinster **Katharine Hepburn,** vacationing in Venice, that Italians value age in a woman. *Summertime* (1955, United Artists).

142 "Well, at least age does give tone to certain things—violins, old wine, old friends to drink it with." Ancient **Edith Evans** stretches for some advantages of aging for elderly Felix Aylmer. An old fellow told us that the only advantage of aging is that there are so many more younger women. *The Chalk Garden* (1964, Universal).

143 "This is my last ascending summer—everything from now on is just downhill. . . to the grave." Thirty-five-year-old spinster school teacher **Joanne Woodward** foolishly becomes despondent and melodramatic. *Rachel, Rachel* (1968, Warner Bros.).

144 "America's greatest contribution has been to teach the world that getting old is such a drag." **Diane Varsi,** concubine of teenage President of the United States, Christopher Jones, tells it like it is to her fellow under-30 U.S. Senators. *Wild in the Streets* (1968, AIP).

145 "Being crazy about a woman... is always the right thing to do. Being a decrepit old bag of bones—that's ridiculous, getting old." **Ben Johnson** laments the passing years to young Timothy Bottoms. *The Last Picture Show* (1971, Columbia).

146 "I guess I'm getting too old for my job, too grouchy. Can't stand the aggravation." As he frisks Al Pacino, **Sterling Hayden,** as police Captain McCluskey, makes a half-hearted apology for breaking Pacino's nose the last time they met. *The Godfather* (1972, Paramount).

147 "Don't think of them as years, but carats. You're a multi-carated, blue-white diamond!" **Gene Kelly** makes a helpful suggestion that his wife Liv Ullmann count her forty years more positively. *Forty Carats* (1973, Columbia).

148 "I don't know what I'm doing here. I'm 237 years old, I should be collecting social security." **Woody Allen** is shocked and bewildered when he awakens from a 200-year sleep. *Sleeper* (1973, United Artists).

149 "I hope my age is correct; I'm always accurate about my age." **Lee Strasberg** wonders if there are the correct number of candles on his birthday cake. *The Godfather, Part II* (1974, Paramount).

150 "I've aged, Sidney. There are new lines on my face. I look like a brand-new, steel-belted radial tire." Oscar-nominated actress **Maggie Smith** complains to her husband Michael Caine before they leave for the Academy Awards ceremony. She's wrong about looking old—she only looks middle-age. *California Suite* (1978, Columbia).

151 "At 16, they call it sweet 16. At 18 you get to drink, to vote, to see dirty movies. What the hell do you get to do when you're 19?" Someone should tell **Dennis Quaid**'s character that if you're not continuing your formal education, you go to work when you're 19. *Breaking Away* (1979, 20th Century-Fox).

152 "These college kids out here, they're never gonna get old. They'll always be new ones coming along." Bloomington "townie" **Dennis Quaid** resents the University of Indiana students, whose presence constantly remind him that he has no prospects. *Breaking Away* (1979, 20th Century-Fox).

153 "Piss on them for their self-satisfying talk about old age. They think they ain't going to get old? Ha! They just have to wait a while, that's all. It don't take any talent to get old." **Melvyn Douglas** rails against the people in his home state who believe he's too old to represent them in the U.S. Senate. *The Seduction of Joe Tynan* (1979, Universal).

154 "One hundred and twenty-five years? I'll be one hundred and sixty-nine when I get out." It's **Richard Pryor**'s nonsensical reaction on being sentenced to prison for a bank robbery he didn't commit. *Stir Crazy* (1980, Columbia).

155 "Face it, you are married to a middle-aged woman with a good sense of humor and dry skin." **Carol Burnett** tries to pick a fight with her overly rational husband Alan Alda. *The Four Seasons* (1981, Universal).

156 "Middle age means the middle, Ethel. The middle of life. People don't live to be 150.... You're old and I'm ancient." Eighty-year-old **Henry Fonda** corrects the fiction of his wife Katharine Hepburn that they are middle-aged. *On Golden Pond* (1981, Universal).

157 "Well, that's what happens if you live long enough. You end up being old. It's one of the disadvantages of a long life. I still prefer it to the alternative." **Katharine Hepburn** is grateful for the longevity of herself and her 80-year-old husband Henry Fonda. *On Golden Pond* (1981, Universal).

158 "Oh, why can't we start old and get younger?" Thirtyish **Annie Potts** wishes to be like Merlin—but it also probably has some drawbacks. *Pretty in Pink* (1986, Paramount).

159 "I'm beginning to think old is a dirty word." Ex-con and one-time train robber **Burt Lancaster** finds that society disrespects him more for his age than his criminal record. *Tough Guys* (1986, Touchstone).

160 RICHARD MALONE: "I'm getting too old for this." JO BARLOW: "You're not so old." MALONE: "You have no idea." **Burt Reynolds** is a retired CIA agent who must stand up to assassins hired by fanatical right wing kook Cliff Robertson. **Cynthia Gibb** is a pert teenager who idolized Reynolds. It's an unofficial remake of *Shane. Malone* (1987, Orion).

161 "Look, I'd go out with women my own age, but there are no women my age." **George Burns** gives a geriatric reason for his affair with a buxomy gold-digger Anita Morris. Ninety-two-year-old Burns plays a younger man, a mere lad of 81. *18 Again!* (1988, New World).

162 "Hell, kid. I'm too old to grow up." Out of hiding after 20 years, legendary 60s radical **Dennis Hopper** has reached his second childhood—he's still enjoying his first. *Flashback* (1990, Paramount).

163 "I don't mind getting old—I never thought I'd live this long anyway—I mind looking old." Musical comedy actress **Shirley MacLaine** confesses her fear to daughter Meryl Streep. *Postcards from the Edge* (1990, Columbia).

164 MARTIN: "In Paris, all the women are older than the men." JULIA: "Good for them." Twenty-one-year-old **Keanu Reeves** anticipates no problems in marrying 36-year-old **Barbara Hershey**. *Tune in Tomorrow* (1990, Cinecom).

165 "I'm too young to be old and I'm too old to be young." **Kathy Bates**' complaint to 82-year-old Jessica Tandy can be appreciated by anyone who has reached the difficult age Bates is describing. *Fried Green Tomatoes* (1991, Universal).

166 "Face it, girls, I'm older and have more insurance." **Kathy Bates** is cut out of a parking place she's been waiting for at a shopping center by two young women in a small car. One of the women jeers at Bates, "Face it, lady, we're younger and faster." Having had enough of allowing people to walk over her, Bates repeatedly rams her automobile into the small car. She delivers the line when the outraged young women come running out of a store to find out what she's doing. *Fried Green Tomatoes* (1991, Universal).

Agents

see also ACTING AND ACTORS, ACTION AND ACTS, BUSINESS AND COMMERCE, BUYING AND SELLING

167 "She reminds me of an agent with one client." Former vaudevillian performer, now maid **Thelma Ritter** is suspicious of the solicitous behavior of Anne Baxter towards aging Broadway actress Bette Davis. *All About Eve* (1950, 20th Century-Fox).

168 "Think of all the people you've had ten percent of. Almost enough to make you a complete person." Egomaniacal film director **Peter Finch** insults self-sacrificing agent Milton Selzer. *The Legend of Lylah Clare* (1968, MGM).

169 "My agent tried to take 15 percent of my unemployment." Two-bit aspiring actress **Beverly D'Angelo** hasn't met many caring show biz people. *Finders Keepers* (1984, Warner Bros.).

Aggression *see* ANGER, BATTLES AND BATTLEFIELDS, COMPETITION, FORCE, HOSTILITIES, VIOLENCE, WARS

Agreements

see also ARGUMENTS, COMPROMISES, PARTNERS, UNDERSTANDINGS AND MISUNDERSTANDINGS

170 "Dot suits me down to de groun'." **Greta Garbo** bluntly replies to a sarcastic waiter, who cracks about her drink order, 'whiskey, ginger ale on the side. Shall I serve it in a pail?' *Anna Christie* (1930, MGM).

171 "I don't approve of me either." **Eve Arden** provides the comedy relief in this loose remake of *The Letter*. *The Unfaithful* (1947, Warner Bros.).

172 "You're right, you shouldn't have been deported, you should have been exterminated." Wheel-chair-bound **Lionel Barrymore** figuratively stands up to mobster Edward G. Robinson. *Key Largo* (1948, Warner Bros.).

173 "Oh, that's all right with me. I mean, I could never get my shit together till seven anyway." Covergirl **Susan Saint James** tells vampire George Hamilton that she can adjust to the life, or is that death, style. *Love at First Bite* (1979, American International Pictures).

174 "Okay, honey, I'll keep my hands off your ass if you keep your nose out of the air and wax out of your ears." In a women's prison dykish **Mackenzie Phillips** makes an agreement with 19-year-old waif Amy Madigan. *Love Child* (1982, Warner Bros.).

175 "Dear Miss Tarrant, what is most agreeable to women is to be agreeable to men!" **Christopher Reeve** doesn't score any points with feminist Madeleine Potter with this comment. *The Bostonians* (1984, GB, Almi).

176 "My idea of an agreeable person is a person who agrees with me." Street performer and ex-male prostitute **Mark Blankfield** shares his views with free-lance photographer and former teenage streetwalker Mitzi Kapture. *Angel 3: The Final Chapter* (1988, New World).

177 "Yes. . . but I also think that if you really feel you should do this. . . you should do it." Perhaps the most remarkable thing about his fantasy movie is that level-headed Midwesterner **Amy Madigan** agrees to her husband Kevin Costner's plan to plow under their corn field to build a baseball diamond on their farm. *Field of Dreams* (1989, Universal).

178 "Well, we get along all right. It's just that. . . well, I think she's an extrovert. . . I think she's loud, she probably wouldn't agree. . . she definitely wouldn't agree." Introverted and reserved **Andie MacDowell** tells James Spader about her loud, extroverted sister Laura San Giacomo. *Sex, Lies and Videotape* (1989, Miramax).

179 "Ditto. . . ." It's the way that **Patrick Swayze** affirms Demi Moore's declarations of love. She wishes he'd just say "I love you." *Ghost* (1990, Paramount).

180 "Okay, I'll be your beck and call girl." Streetwalker **Julia Roberts** accepts businessman Richard Gere's proposition that she spend a week with him. *Pretty Woman* (1990, Buena Vista-Touchstone).

Agriculture see LAND AND FARMS

Aims see ENDS AND ENDINGS, INTENTIONS, PURPOSES

Airplanes see FLYING AND FLIERS, MILITARY, TRAVEL AND TRIPS

Alcohol

see also DRINKING AND DRUNKENNESS

181 "Gimme a viskey. Ginger ale on the side. And don't be stingy, baby." History is made with **Greta Garbo**'s first spoken movie line—a drink order. *Anna Christie* (1930, MGM).

182 "Nuts to that stuff! Ain't ya got a drink in the house?" In a sour mood, **James Cagney** turns up his nose at the breakfast prepared for him by girl friend Mae Clarke. *The Public Enemy* (1930, Warner Bros.).

183 "I never drink. . . wine." However, the sight of Dwight Frye's blood is intoxicating to **Bela Lugosi**. *Dracula* (1931, Universal).

184 "It's only gin, you know gin. . . I like gin!" With a defensive decadent leer, **Ernest Thesiger** offers a drink to an unwelcome guest. *The Old Dark House* (1932, Universal).

185 "It must be a wonderful supper. . . . We may not eat it, but it must be wonderful. . . . And waiter, you see the moon?. . . I want to see that moon in the champagne. . . and you. . . I don't want to see you at all." **Herbert Marshall** instructs a waiter on the arrangements for an assignation with Miriam Hopkins. *Trouble in Paradise* (1932, Paramount).

186 PEGGY HOPKINS JOYCE: "Will you join me in a glass of wine?" PROFESSOR QUAIL: "You get in first, and if there's room enough, I'll join you." Appearing as herself, **Peggy Hopkins Joyce** plays a blonde vamp. Her offer of hospitality to **W.C. Fields** is met with a wisecrack. *International House* (1933, Paramount).

187 BARON VON MERZBACH: "To our wedding night. Come, come, drink up, drink up!" LILY CZEPANEK: "I'm not used to champagne. It will make me dizzy." VON MERZBACH: "Ha! All the better. All the better!" Having tricked her into marriage, old lecher **Lionel Atwill** takes **Marlene Dietrich** to his gloomy castle and forces her to drink champagne. *The Song of Songs* (1933, Paramount).

188 "I'll drink Scotch, hair lotion, or rat poison." Sitting in a nightclub, **Claudette Colbert** sulks because of her notoriety as the "No Girl." *The Gilded Lily* (1935, Paramount).

189 NORA CHARLES: "Darling, are you packing?" NICK CHARLES: "Just putting away the liquor." As their train pulls into the station, **Myrna Loy** calls out from the washroom to her husband **William Powell,** who is consuming what's left of a bottle of booze. *After The Thin Man* (1936, MGM).

190 "Two old-fashioneds, for two old-fashioned people." Elderly **Victor Moore** orders drinks for his equally ancient wife Beulah Bondi and himself at their final time together. *Make Way for Tomorrow* (1937, Paramount).

191 "I don't know what I'm doing here when I could be at home in bed with a hot toddy. That's a drink." **Groucho Marx** wouldn't want anyone to think he's referring to his *Horse Feathers* co-star Thelma Todd—or would he? *At the Circus* (1939, MGM).

192 "Snookums. . . you mean you've forgotten. I know you've forgotten! Those June nights at the Riviera where we sat beneath the shimmering skies, moonlight bathing in the Mediterranean. We were young, gay, reckless! That night I drank champagne from your slipper. Two quarts. It would have held more but you were wearing inner soles." **Groucho Marx** surprises Margaret Dumont in her boudoir. *At the Circus* (1939, MGM).

193 "Every time somebody orders champagne, Jacques' income bubbles. . . Jacques' family makes a very impressive income from inferior champagne." **John Barrymore** informs Claudette Colbert of the source of playboy Francis Lederer's income. *Midnight* (1939, Paramount).

194 "Champagne's funny stuff. I'm used to whiskey. Whiskey is a slap on the back and champagne's heavy mist before my eyes." **James Stewart** states his alcohol preference to Katharine Hepburn as they get drunk on champagne. *The Philadelphia Story* (1940, MGM).

195 "Henri wants us to finish this bottle, then three more. He says' he'll water his garden with champagne before he lets the Germans drink any of it." While waiting for the Germans to enter Paris, **Humphrey Bogart** pours champagne for Ingrid Bergman. *Casablanca* (1942, Warner Bros.).

196 "There is a time in every woman's life when the only thing that helps is a glass of champagne." **Bette Davis** feels the need for a touch of the bubbly after once again striking out in the arena of romance. *Old Acquaintance* (1943, Warner Bros.).

197 "It shrinks my liver, doesn't it, Nat? It pickles my kidneys, yeah. But what does it do to my mind? It tosses the sandbags overboard so the balloon can sail. Suddenly I'm above the ordinary. I'm competent, supremely competent. I'm walking a tightrope over Niagara Falls. I'm one of the great ones. I'm Michelangelo, molding the beard of Moses. I'm Van Gogh, painting pure sunlight. I'm Horowitz, playing the Emperor Concerto. I'm John Barrymore before the movies got him by the throat. I'm W. Shakespeare. And out there is not Third Avenue anymore—it's the Nile, Nat, the Nile—and down it moves the barge of Cleopatra." Before his drinking makes him morose and weepy, alcoholic **Ray Milland** poetically tells bartender Howard da Silva what liquor does for him. *The Lost Weekend* (1945, Paramount).

198 CHARLES STERNWOOD: "How do you like your brandy, sir?" PHILIP MARLOWE: "Just with brandy." STERNWOOD: "I used to like mine with champagne. The champagne as cold as Valley Forge with about three ponies of brandy under it. You may take your coat off, sir. It's too hot in here for a man with blood in his veins. You may smoke too. I can still enjoy the smell of it. The man is already dead who must enjoy his vices by proxy." Wealthy, ailing **Charles Waldron** envies **Humphrey Bogart,** as they sit in a hot house, necessary to sustain Waldron's feeble life. *The Big Sleep* (1946, Warner Bros.).

199 "It's made of grapes—like fruit juice. The Frenchman who sold it to me explained the whole thing, one night. We. . . well, I ordered a boat load." Hollywood silent screen actress **Gloria Grahame** introduces Red Skelton to champagne. *Merton of the Movies.* (1947, MGM).

200 "Champagne tastes so much better after midnight, don't you think?" Concert pianist and lothario **Louis Jourdan** seduces a willing Joan Fontaine with the help of champagne. *Letter from an Unknown Woman* (1948, Universal).

201 "Sir Wilfrid. You've forgotten your brandy." Rats! Nurse **Elsa Lanchester** knew all along that her patient Charles Laughton had alcohol in his cocoa thermos. *Witness for the Prosecution* (1957, United Artists).

202 INDUCTION CENTER DOCTOR: "For a man your age and in your profession, you're in excellent health. How do you handle it?" MICHAEL WHITEACRE: "Clean liquor." Physician **Milton Frome** is surprised by the good condition of celebrated playboy **Dean Martin,** who gives a typical wisecrack answer. *The Young Lions* (1958, 20th Century-Fox).

203 "Well, as long as I got a foot, I'll kick booze. And, as long as I got a fist, I'll punch it. And as long as I got a tooth, I'll bite it. And when I'm old and gray and toothless and bootless, I'll gum it till I go to heaven and booze goes to hell." Evangelist **Burt Lancaster** preaches against "old devil rum." He might have added that he also fought alcohol by drinking a lot of it. No, we guess not. *Elmer Gantry* (1960, United Artists).

204 "Gin was mother's milk to her." Playing Eliza Doolittle, first **Wendy Hiller,** then in the musical sequel **Audrey Hepburn,** shocks a crowd of upper-class snobs with a story about her aunt. *Pygmalion* (1938, GB, MGM); *My Fair Lady* (1964, Warner Bros.).

205 "No thanks, I'll pass. Alcohol in the middle of the day is exciting when you're thirty, but disastrous at seventy." Seventyish judge **Felix Aylmer** must have learned the lesson the hard way. *The Chalk Garden* (1964, GB, Universal-International).

206 "All right, I'd like another little nipper of brandy." Feeling no pain, **Sandy Dennis** moves on to another drink after being warned by hostess Elizabeth Taylor to watch herself. Dennis corrects Taylor for calling her husband Richard Burton a floozy. Dennis points out that a floozy refers to a female, so it must be that Taylor is the floozy. *Who's Afraid of Virginia Woolf?* (1966, Warner Bros.).

207 "Yes, but a man can't really savor a martini without an olive, otherwise it just doesn't quite make it." During the Korean war, resourceful army surgeon **Elliot Gould** pulls a jar of olives from a pocket in his parka when offered an ersatz martini by Donald Sutherland who apologizes for not having olives. *M*A*S*H* (1970, 20th Century-Fox).

208 "Best goddam drink in the world." Sailor **Jack Nicholson** extols the virtues of beer. *The Last Detail* (1974, Columbia).

209 DAD HALL: "Make me a martini." MOM HALL: "Of course, sweetheart, how would you like it, dear?" DAD HALL: "On white bread with mayonnaise." Woody Allen imagines a conversation between Diane Keaton's WASPish parents **Donald Symington** and **Colleen Dewhurst**. *Annie Hall* (1977, United Artists).

210 "Champagne gives me a headache." Playwright Al Pacino asks actress **Dyan Cannon** why she takes aspirin with her champagne. *Author! Author!* (1982, 20th Century-Fox).

211 "Bring a pitcher of beer every seven minutes until someone passes out, then bring one every ten minutes." **Rodney Dangerfield** makes a drink order for a party of college students at his table. *Back to School* (1986, Orion).

212 "Jessie, you wouldn't happen to have any good scotch?" Money-hungry, possession-driven **Alison LaPlaca** doesn't find things up to her usual standards when she's forced to move in with her sister Kirstie Alley. *Madhouse* (1990, Orion).

Alibis

see also DEFENSES, EXCUSES

213 "Alibi have habit of disappearing like hole in water." **Warner Oland,** as Charlie Chan, delivers one of his famous aphorisms. *The Black Camel* (1931, Fox).

214 "Bad alibi like dead fish—cannot stand test of time." Now it's **Sidney Toler**'s turn to introduce a bit of levity in his case with his aphorism. *Charlie Chan in Honolulu* (1938, 20th Century-Fox).

Aliens

see also FOREIGNERS, STRANGENESS AND STRANGERS

215 "[Imagine] after living in the U.S.A. for more than 30 years they called me an undesirable alien, me, Johnny Rocco! Like I was a dirty Red or something!" Mobster **Edward G. Robinson** is still outraged that he was deported. *Key Largo* (1948, Warner Bros.).

216 "This carrot, as you call it, has constructed an aircraft capable of flying millions of miles through space, propelled by a force unknown to us." Scientist **Robert Cornthwaite** corrects reporter Douglas Spencer who suggests that the visitor from outer space they have encountered at the North Pole is a form of vegetable life—"an intellectual carrot." *The Thing* (1951, RKO).

217 ELLIOTT: "Only little children can see him." GERTIE: "Gimme a break." **Henry Thomas** can't con his little sister, six-year-old **Drew Barrymore**, about their little alien visitor. *E.T., The Extra-Terrestrial* (1982, Universal).

218 "These aliens are not on ice—we gotta find 'em before they turn too much!" Wacko **Harry Dean Stanton** and his young protégé in repossessing cars, Emilio Estevez, search for a 1964 Chevy Malibu with something weird in its trunk. *Repo Man* (1984, Universal).

219 "As if things weren't bad enough, now I've been abducted by aliens." Valley girl **Geena Davis** is having one of those days. Three extra-terrestrial visitors crash-land their craft in her swimming pool. *Earth Girls Are Easy* (1989, Vestron).

Alive *see* LIVES AND LIVING

Alone *see* LONELINESS, SOLITUDE, TOGETHERNESS

Amateurs

see also EXPERTS, PROFESSIONS AND PROFESSIONALS

220 "Oh, no, no, you see, to be a kleptomaniac, you can't sell any of the stuff afterwards or you lose your amateur standing." Shoplifter **Barbara Stanwyck** refuses to accept assistant D.A. Fred MacMurray's suggestion that her taking ways are due to a mental disorder. *Remember the Night* (1940, Paramount).

221 "He was doubled up on his face in that bag of old clothes position that always meant the same thing. He had been killed by an amateur, or by somebody who wanted it to look like an amateur job. Nobody else would hit a man that many times with a sap." Private eye **Dick Powell** revives after being knocked out to find the dead body of his client Douglas Walton. *Murder, My Sweet* (1945, RKO).

222 "Mass killing. Does not the world encourage it? I am an amateur by comparison." Murder-for-profit **Charlie Chaplin** can't understand what the fuss is over killing a few women when millions were killed in World War II. *Monsieur Verdoux* (1947, Chaplin-United Artists).

223 "That's all we are—amateurs; we don't live long enough to be anything else." **Charles Chaplin** replies when an impresario tells him that he will make all the other performers at a vaudeville show look like amateurs. *Limelight* (1952, United Artists).

224 "Talk about flat-footed policemen. May the saints protect us from the gifted amateur." Scotland

Yard inspector **John Williams** is a bit put out by the know-it-all attitude of American writer Robert Cummings. *Dial M for Murder* (1954, Warner Bros.).

225 "If there is anything that burns me, it's an amateur trying to tell a professional how to do his job." American colonel **Gregory Peck** is responsible for getting young soldier Ted Avery back from the East Berlin communists who have kidnapped him. He berates the boy's interfering father Broderick Crawford, who has arrived in Berlin to kick some ass. *Night People* (1954, 20th Century-Fox).

226 "Ninety years ago I was a freak. Today I'm an amateur." **David Warner,** as Jack the Ripper, has escaped to the future in H.G. Wells' time machine. He's impressed with the violence of 1979. *Time After Time* (1979, Warner Bros.).

Amazement

see also ADMIRATION, SURPRISES, WONDERFULNESS AND WONDERS

227 DR. WATSON: "Amazing, Holmes." SHERLOCK HOLMES: "Elementary, my dear Watson, elementary." **H. Reeves-Smith** compliments modest **Clive Brook,** who responds with Holmes' classic line. *The Return of Sherlock Holmes* (1929, Paramount).

228 "Isn't it amazing how much post-graduate work goes on in this town." **Kim Novak** comments on all the married men with wives in the suburbs, who have a boy's night out, supposedly to take some self-help course, but really to be with some sexy ladies. *Boys' Night Out* (1962, MGM).

229 "How you get all that traffic without no equipment is beyond me." Heterosexual **Alex McArthur** gently teases his lesbian half-sister Patricia Charbonneau about her success with women. *Desert Bloom* (1986, Columbia).

230 "I've seen some amazing things in my life, but never anything to compare with this." We don't recall if **Richard Chamberlain** is referring to the title city or Cassandra Peterson, as the evil queen, prancing about in a golden bra that barely held her in. *Allan Quatermain and the Lost City of Gold* (1987, Cannon).

231 "You know, sometimes I even amaze myself." Mob informant **Steve Martin,** in the Witness Protection Program, is impressed with his wheeling and dealing. *My Blue Heaven* (1990, Warner Bros.).

232 "Nobody knows this yet, but I'm an amazing woman." **Kate Nelligan** has dreams and ambitions of being more than she is. *The Prince of Tides* (1991, Columbia).

Ambitions

see also DESIRES, FAME, INTENTIONS, PLANS, POWER, PURPOSES, SUCCESSES, WISHES

233 "Well! Aren't we ambitious. We want to make a lot of money, so we can buy lots of pretty clothes. Or maybe we want to put a little aside for our husband and us, in our old age." Wonder if Lana Turner feels like braining taunting **John Garfield**—don't you just hate people who speak to you in the "we-person"? *The Postman Always Rings Twice* (1946, MGM).

234 "His greatest ambition is to become immortal, then die." Novelist **Jean-Pierre Melville** speaks of a contradictory petty crook, Jean-Paul Belmondo. *Breathless* (1959, Fr., Imperia Films).

235 "I'm going up and up and up. And no one's going to pull me down." Ambitious actress **Lana Turner** tells John Gavin that she'll never be content to be an ordinary housewife as he wishes. *Imitation of Life* (1959, Universal-International).

236 "Girls like me weren't built to be educated. We were made to have children. That's my ambition—to be a walking, talking baby factory." In most quarters, **Paula Prentiss**' ambition for herself didn't seem so outrageous in 1960. *Where the Boys Are* (1960, MGM).

237 "Now I can concentrate on my ambition in life, to get married and have babies. I'm selling myself as a wife and potential mother." The fifties proclamation made by **Connie Francis** still didn't sound so out of place in the middle sixties. *Looking for Love* (1964, MGM).

238 "I really wanted to be an anarchist but I didn't know where to register." During a comedy routine, **Woody Allen** mentions an early ambition. *Annie Hall* (1977, United Artists).

239 "The great ambition of women is to inspire love." Just because **Peter Ustinov,** as Hercule Poirot, is an expert in solving murders, doesn't make him an expert on women. *Death on the Nile* (1978, Paramount).

240 "I'm not ambitious, not an artist, not a poet, not a revolutionary." Troubled **Theresa Russell** tells Art Garfunkel not to expect much from her, because she doesn't. *Bad Timing: A Sensual Obsession* (1980, GB, Rank).

241 "The trouble with ambitious men is that they aren't ready to do what's necessary." Inept lawyer William Hurt isn't ambitious, but he's willing to do whatever **Kathleen Turner** considers necessary. *Body Heat* (1981, Warner Bros.).

242 "With all there is, why settle for just a piece of the sky." In Eastern Europe in 1904, in a moving soliloquy, ambitious for an education **Barbra Streisand** questions why she can't have some of the advantages of being a male. *Yentl* (1983, GB, MGM-United Artists).

243 "All I want to do is graduate high school, go to Europe, marry Christian Slater and die." Teenage cheerleader **Kristy Swanson** has mostly modest ambitions. *Buffy, the Vampire Slayer* (1992, 20th Century-Fox).

America and Americans

see also DEMOCRACY, FREEDOMS, GOVERNMENTS, PEOPLE

244 "[I'm] an American once removed and want to see the Pacific—perhaps to drown in it." "Tourist-on-foot" **Leslie Howard** reveals his possible destination and his suicidal bent. *The Petrified Forest* (1936, Warner Bros.).

245 "He ain't a gangster, he's a real old time desperado. Gangsters is foreign. He's an American." Crazy old coot **Charley Grapewin** is proud of homegrown public enemy number one, Humphrey Bogart. *The Petrified Forest* (1936, Warner Bros.).

246 "Yes, sir. I'm a sucker for this country. I'm a sucker for the Star Spangled Banner—and I'm a sucker for this country. I like what we got here! I like it! A guy can say what he wants—and do what he wants—without having a bayonet shoved through his belly." Newspaper editor **James Gleason** confidentially tells Gary Cooper in a bar that he's glad he's an American. *Meet John Doe* (1941, Warner Bros.).

247 MAJOR STRASSER: "I strongly suspect that Señor Ugarte left the Letters of Transit with Herr Blaine. I would suggest you search the Cafe immediately and thoroughly." CAPT. RENAULT: "If Rick has the letters, he is much too smart to let us find them there." STRASSER: "You give him credit for too much cleverness. My impression was he's just another blundering American." RENAULT: "We mustn't underestimate American blundering. I was with them when they blundered into Berlin in 1918." German officer **Conrad Veidt** wants French police prefect **Claude Rains** to search Humphrey Bogart's Cafe for Letters of Transit stolen by the late unlamented Peter Lorre. Rains doesn't believe it will do any good. *Casablanca* (1942, Warner Bros.).

248 "What silly shrews American women are." German **Marlene Dietrich** bases her judgement on one American woman, Iowa congresswoman Jean Arthur. *A Foreign Affair* (1948, Paramount).

249 "I believe in America, America made my fortune. And I raised my daughter in American fashion." Funeral director **Salvatore Corsitto** has the first words of the movie. He seeks help from Godfather Marlon Brando in taking revenge against those who raped and disfigured his daughter. Before agreeing to help, Brando says, "You found paradise in America." *The Godfather* (1972, Paramount).

250 "I would like to see America—the decadence, the poverty, the crime." Robin Williams' lover **Olga Talyn** is envious of him going to the U.S. with the Moscow circus. Like other Muscovites she is frustrated with the constantly waiting in never-ending queues for "Toilet paper. . . or chickens, I'm not sure." *Moscow on the Hudson* (1984, Columbia).

251 "This is a free country welcome to almost anyone, and I hope that someday you will join me here. Of course, I'll continue to write to you every week. Yes, in America anything is possible. Good-bye for now, beloved family. I love you. Volya." Russian defector **Robin Williams** writes to his family in Moscow. *Moscow on the Hudson* (1984, Columbia).

252 "Ice cream, baseball, friendship—that's okay for America, but not what we need in the Department of Defense." Military villain **Ron Frazier** serves a higher authority than his country. *D.A.R.Y.L.* (1985, Columbia).

253 "Marry her, Charlie, just because she's a thief and a hitter doesn't mean she's not a good woman in all other departments. She's an American. She had a chance to make a buck and she grabbed it!" His former mistress, **Anjelica Huston,** advises Jack Nicholson about his new love, hitwoman Kathleen Turner. *Prizzi's Honor* (1985, ABC).

254 "Now may I extend a warm congratulations. You are now citizens of the United States of America." Judge **J. Jay Saunders** welcomes an alien family to American citizenship. *Mac and Me* (1988, Orion).

Amusements

see also COMEDY AND COMEDIANS, ENTERTAINMENTS AND ENTERTAINERS, FUN, GAMBLING, GAMES, HUMOR, LAUGHTER, MOTION PICTURES, SHOWS, SPORTS

255 "I used to live in one in New York that was old. It wasn't very amusing." **Robert Mitchum** and

Rhonda Fleming make small talk. She's just described her apartment in an old building as "amusing." *Out of the Past* (1947, RKO).

256 "When one is in town, one amuses one's self; when one is in the country, one amuses other people." English gentleman **Michael Redgrave** makes a distinction between his town and his country roles for his friend Michael Denison. *The Importance of Being Earnest* (1952, GB, Rank-Two Cities).

257 "It's the sophisticated women who get boring so quickly. . . But someone like Gigi can amuse you for months." **Maurice Chevalier** cynically comments to Louis Jourdan about the freshness and youth of Leslie Caron, as a temporary mistress. *Gigi* (1958, MGM).

258 "Men have been staring at me and rubbing up against me ever since I was twelve years old. They've been waiting for me to stumble so that they can close in. Sometimes, I get the suffocating feeling that they will. And I see myself, perhaps tomorrow, perhaps next year, being handed from man to man as if I were an amusement for men who've only really had me, never really loved me." Speaking to Richard Burton in her role as a beatnik poet, **Elizabeth Taylor** might be talking of the curse of sex symbols such as herself. *The Sandpiper* (1965, MGM).

Anachronisms

see also AGE AND AGING, TIME, YOUTH

259 "You've no place here, on the outside. We've got a job to do and you're not a part of it. You're simply a bad mistake. And what we're doing is erasing you and everyone like you and starting over again." Old seaman **George Cleveland** berates escaped con James Craig as an anachronism in an age when the U.S. is fighting totalitarian governments in World War II. *Seven Miles from Alcatraz* (1942, RKO).

260 "The world belongs to the young. Make way for them. Let them have it. I am an anachronism." In an unusual movie, **Boris Karloff,** playing himself, describes not only his character in the film, but his career as he walks out of a screening of the 1963 picture *The Terror*. *Targets* (1968, Paramount).

261 "He's an anachronism, a pure warrior. Lack of war will kill him." Near the end of World War II, German staff officer **Morgan Paull** makes an accurate prediction about George C. Scott as General George S. Patton, Jr. *Patton* (1970, 20th Century-Fox).

262 "You're a walking, friggin' combat zone. Your ideas don't fit anymore." Police captain **Bradford Dillman** berates his avenging angel, Clint Eastwood as police detective Dirty Harry Callahan. *Sudden Impact* (1983, Warner Bros.).

263 "You're an anachronism. You ought to be in a glass case with a sign saying, 'open only in case of war.'" Lieutenant **Boyd Gaines** accuses tough, old, gutsy, raspy-voiced Marine sergeant Clint Eastwood, who seems to enjoy the invasion of Grenada. *Heartbreak Ridge* (1986, Warner Bros.).

264 "You're a living charade." Corrupt Irish police chief **Richard Bradford** dismisses the honesty of Irish cop Sean Connery just before the two proceed to beat the hell out of each other in an alley. *The Untouchables* (1987, Paramount).

Analysis *see* DETECTIVES AND DEDUCTION, DIAGNOSIS, LOGIC, PROOFS, PSYCHOLOGY AND PSYCHIATRY

Ancestry *see* BIRTHS AND BIRTHDAYS, FAMILIES

Angels

see also GOD, HEAVEN, HEAVEN AND HELL, HELL, SAINTS

265 APRIL LOGAN: "Oh, Dusty! You're an angel in leather!" DUSTY RIVERS: "Heh, heh—I'd look funny with leather wings." **Madeleine Carroll** thanks Texas Ranger **Gary Cooper** for making it appear that her brother Mountie Robert Preston died a hero rather than a deserter. *Northwest Mounted Police* (1940, Paramount).

266 "Every time you hear a bell ring, it means that some angel just got his wings." Apprentice angel Clarence Goodbody, played by **Henry Travers,** shares this heavenly news with James Stewart in the wrong place—a bar filled with unfriendly and unbelieving men. Stewart's daughter Zuzu (**Karolyn Grimes**) repeats the phrase at the end of the movie. Stewart happily responds, "That's right. That's right. Attaboy, Clarence." *It's a Wonderful Life* (1946, RKO).

267 "I never before had to fight an angel, but I suggest you take off your coat and put up your dukes." Harried bishop **David Niven** is convinced that visiting angel Cary Grant is trying to steal his wife, Loretta Young. *The Bishop's Wife* (1947, RKO).

268 "I'm going to find me an angel. I'm going to find me a real hootenanny of an angel. If she gives me any trouble, she's going to find herself with them little old wings just pinned right to the ground." Naïve young cowboy **Don Murray** has come down from his remote ranch to a rodeo to compete and find a wife. *Bus Stop* (1956, 20th Century-Fox).

269 "An angel has no memory." Angel **John Phillip Law** replies to Jane Fonda when she asks how he can forgive the Black Queen Anita Pallenberg for all the terrible things she's done to him. *Barbarella* (1968, Fr.-Ital., Paramount).

270 "There are angels walking the earth masquerading as people and your mother is the best of these." **Mary Stuart Masterson,** as Idgie, comforts her dying friend Mary-Louise Parker's young son. *Fried Green Tomatoes* (1991, Universal).

Anger

see also CURSES, EXCITEMENTS, HATE AND HATRED, PROFANITY, RESENTMENTS, TEMPER

271 "I'd cut my heart out for you.... Please don't be mad at me." Cocky sailor **James Cagney** is sincerely contrite when he gets a dressing down from Pat O'Brien. *Here Comes the Navy* (1934, Warner Bros.).

272 "I'm not mad. I was just thinking I could wring your neck, that's all." Upright lawyer **Fred MacMurray** considers what to do with his fantasy-prone wife Carole Lombard. *True Confession* (1937, Paramount).

273 "She can get mad quicker than any woman I ever saw." **Carroll Nye** feels the wrath of his wife Vivien Leigh at the lumber mill when she tells him to quit bothering her and not to call her Sugar! *Gone with the Wind* (1939, Selznick-MGM).

274 "George will be mad at me." Simple-minded giant **Lon Chaney, Jr.** has accidentally killed Betty Field and is afraid that his pal Burgess Meredith will be angry. *Of Mice and Men* (1939, Roach-United Artists).

275 CHARLES, DUC DE VILLIERS: "Anger makes you very charming, mademoiselle." MARIANNE DE BEAUMANOIR: "Patronizing makes you very boring, monsieur." **Nelson Eddy**'s compliment is not well-received by **Jeanette MacDonald**. *New Moon* (1940, MGM).

276 "I'd like to break her foul, useless little neck... I said I could strangle her." **Farley Granger** angrily shouts on the phone to his new love Ruth Roman that he could kill his unfaithful wife Laura Elliott (what is he?). Elliott has refused to give him a divorce, claiming she's pregnant with someone's child. Several passersby would agree with Roman, who says, "You sound so savage, Guy." *Strangers on a Train* (1951, Warner Bros.).

277 "Don't touch my knife. That makes me mad. Very, very mad." Self-ordained preacher and psychopath **Robert Mitchum** snaps at young Sally Jane Bruce. *The Night of the Hunter* (1955, United Artists).

278 "He likes to show me off. He likes me to dress the way I do. Then, he gets furious if a man pays any attention to me." Conferring with attorney James Stewart, sexy and flirtatious **Lee Remick** speaks of her husband Ben Gazzara, who has been accused of murdering a man who paid more than a little attention to her. *Anatomy of a Murder* (1959, Columbia).

279 "I haven't lost my temper in forty years. But, pilgrim, someone ought to belt you in the mouth. But I won't. I won't...the hell I won't." **John Wayne** changes his mind about slugging Leo Gordon. *McLintock!* (1963, United Artists).

280 "They tell me I'm supposed to control my bad temper, but when I see what you've done here....I just go berserk!" Half-breed Vietnam veteran **Tom Laughlin** advances on David Roya, who has brutally beaten a young Indian pacifist, Stan Rice. Using Hapkido, Laughlin knocks the daylights out of Roya and all who come to his assistance. *Billy Jack* (1971, Warner Bros.).

281 "Stand up wherever you are, go to the nearest window and yell as loud as you can, 'I'm mad as hell, and I'm not going to take it anymore.'" When insane news anchorman **Peter Finch** instructs his audience to vent their anger, he gets quite a response. *Network* (1976, MGM-United Artists).

282 "Well, I can't get angry, okay? I mean, I have a tendency to internalize. I can't express anger. That's one of the problems I have—I grow a tumor instead." **Woody Allen** reacts to Diane Keaton's wish that he'd get angry with her as she announces she's leaving him to go back to her married lover Michael Murphy. *Manhattan* (1979, United Artists).

283 "Into the mud, scum queen!" **Steve Martin** angrily grabs his sex-crazed, sadistic wife Kathleen Turner by the scruff of her neck and flings her to the ground. *The Man with Two Brains* (1983, Warner Bros.).

284 "There's somethin' about maniacs messing with good men that always pisses me off." Retired Colonel **Louis Gossett, Jr.,** commandeers a couple of F-16s so he and Jason Gedrick can rescue the latter's father Tim Thomerson, who has been tried as a spy in Libya and is sentenced to death. *Iron Eagle* (1986, 20th Century-Fox).

285 BARBARA ROSE: "Have you ever made angry love?" GAVIN D'AMATO: "Is there any other way?" **Kathleen Turner** attempts to seduce her husband's lawyer, **Danny De Vito**, in order to secure his help in getting her house away from Michael Douglas. *The War of the Roses* (1989, 20th Century-Fox).

286 "The way I was raised it was considered bad manners to get mad—but I got mad and it felt great." **Kathy Bates** shares the excitement of expressing her anger with her friend Jessica Tandy. *Fried Green Tomatoes* (1991, Universal).

Animals

see also BIRDS, FISH AND FISHING, HUMANITY, HUMAN NATURE, INSECTS, INSTINCTS, SAVAGERY, SNAKES AND REPTILES

287 "One morning I shot an elephant in my pajamas. How he got into my pajamas I'll never know." African hunter **Groucho Marx** makes a throwaway joke during a lecture to society folk. *Animal Crackers* (1930, Paramount).

288 "I'd horsewhip you if I had a horse." **Groucho Marx** makes another empty threat. *Horse Feathers* (1932, Paramount).

289 "I tell you, if I didn't have such a splendid education I'd yield to the animal in me." **Charles Ruggles** pursues married Jeanette MacDonald. *One Hour with You* (1932, Paramount).

290 "Compared to him, an elephant's skin is tissue paper." Aspiring hoofer **Joan Crawford** refers to tough producer Clark Gable. *Dancing Lady* (1933, MGM).

291 CHICOLINI: "What is it has a trunk, but no key, weighs two thousand pounds and lives in a circus?" PROSECUTOR: "That's irrelevant." CHICOLINI: "Elephant! Hey, that's the answer." At his trial, never flustered **Chico Marx** succeeds in flustering the prosecutor **Charles B. Middleton**. *Duck Soup* (1933, Paramount).

292 "Hen squats with caution on thin egg." **Warner Oland,** in the role of the Chinese detective, uses an animal aphorism to stress the need for caution. *Charlie Chan's Courage* (1934, Fox).

293 "I coarsely gave way to the brute in me." Dignified former British butler **Charles Laughton** has a sudden urge to kiss widow ZaSu Pitts during their sedate courtship. *Ruggles of Red Gap* (1935, Paramount).

294 "Lamb bites wolf! Beautiful." Cynical press agent **Lionel Stander** takes delight in the behavior of democratic hick and heir to a fortune, Gary Cooper. *Mr. Deeds Goes to Town* (1936, Columbia).

295 "Oh, let me alone. I wish I really could die, go someplace by myself and—and die alone, like an elephant." New York takes dying **Carole Lombard** to their collective hearts and make her a heroine—but she's taking too long to die to suit some people. *Nothing Sacred* (1937, United Artists).

296 "The only thing you could follow is the trail of a lonesome horse." Screenwriter **Pat O'Brien** insults dumb cowboy star Dick Foran. *Boy Meets Girl* (1938, Warner Bros.).

297 "Don't be silly, David. You can't make a leopard stand still." **Katharine Hepburn** can't understand why Cary Grant is so upset to find a leopard in her apartment. *Bringing Up Baby* (1938, RKO).

298 "There aren't any leopards in Connecticut—are there?" Big game hunter **Charles Ruggles** hears the growling of title leopard Baby and insists it's a loon. *Bringing Up Baby* (1938, RKO).

299 "Listen, girl, I can count the great horses I ever saw on the fingers of one hand, and every one of 'em had a look in his eyes—like an eagle. You can't beat a horse with that look. You just can't beat him. And this colt's got it—the look of eagles!" Horse trainer **Walter Brennan** tells Loretta Young that he knows a Kentucky Derby winner when he sees one. *Kentucky* (1938, 20th Century-Fox).

300 "Don't be getting so uppity. Even if you is the last chicken in Atlanta." **Eddie "Rochester" Anderson** stalks a rooster that will be Christmas dinner in honor of Leslie Howard's homecoming. *Gone with the Wind* (1939, Selznick-MGM).

301 "Any of you beauties know where I can steal a horse for a good cause?" **Clark Gable** is roused from Ona Munson's bordello by Butterfly McQueen. She brings a message from Vivien Leigh who wants him to help her escape from Atlanta before the Yankees invade the city. *Gone with the Wind* (1939, Selznick-MGM).

302 "Horse make tracks." **Everett Brown,** as Big Sam, rescues Vivien Leigh from the riff-raff of Shantytown. *Gone with the Wind* (1939, Selznick-MGM).

303 "Children of the night. They howl among the Hill of the Seven Jackals when Kharis must be fed." High priest **Eduardo Ciannelli** tells his disciple and son George Zucco the meaning of the baying at the moon of a jackal far away in the desert. *The Mummy's Hand* (1940, Universal).

304 "They are incorrigible. They must be killed and boiled! Killed and boiled!" **Edna May Oliver** loathes chickens. *Pride and Prejudice* (1940, MGM).

305 "Strange how an unpleasant child can be a decent dog." Wizard **Conrad Veidt** transforms young thief Sabu into a mongrel dog. *The Thief of Bagdad* (1940, United Artists).

306 "It's all right to live on a horse—if it's your horse." **Walter Brennan,** as Judge Roy Bean, insinuates that cowboy Gary Cooper might be a horse thief. *The Westerner* (1940, United Artists).

307 MR. PENNY: "That house is doubly blest, which to our feline friends gives rest." HUBERT SMITH: "Her hats are full of bats, for spending all her dough on cats." When **Hugh Herbert** reads an inscription which seems to have influenced a rich old woman to make her dozens of cats her heirs, unimpressed **Broderick Crawford** gets into the spirit of the quote. He's a poet and doesn't know it, but his feet show it—they're Longfellows. *The Black Cat* (1941, Universal).

308 "I'm an elephant, Miss Jones. A veritable elephant. I never forget a good deed done me or an ill one. I consider myself a kind of divine justice. Other people in this world have to forget things. I do not." In order to investigate employee complaints, department store tycoon **Charles Coburn** takes a job as a clerk incognito at one of his stores where Jean Arthur works. *The Devil and Miss Jones* (1941, RKO).

309 "You're mine and you belong to me. . . . You couldn't have anything to do with that pile of southern fried chicken." **Robert Montgomery** dismisses his wife Carole Lombard's idealization of courtly southern lawyer Gene Raymond. *Mr. and Mrs. Smith* (1941, RKO).

310 "You hairy ape!" Spoiled wealthy socialite **Susan Hayward** screams the title of the film when cretinous worker William Bendix dumbly approaches her. *The Hairy Ape* (1944, United Artists).

311 VIVIAN STERNWOOD: "Speaking of horses; I like to play them myself. But I like to see them work out a little first. See if they're front-runners or come from behind. Find out what their hole card is—what makes them run." PHILIP MARLOWE: "Find out mine?" VIVIAN: "I think so. . . I'd say you don't like to be rated. You like to get out front, open up a lead, take a little breather in the back stretch, and then come home free." **Lauren Bacall** handicaps **Humphrey Bogart,** the private eye hired by her father to look after her and her zany sister Martha Vickers. *The Big Sleep* (1946, Warner Bros.)

312 "He's like an animal. He has animal's habits. There's even something subhuman about him. Thousands of years have passed him right by, and there he is, Stanley Kowalski, survivor of the Stone Age. . . ." **Vivien Leigh** maliciously classifies her sister Kim Hunter's brutish husband Marlon Brando as sub-human. She's about right. *A Streetcar Named Desire* (1951, United Artists).

313 "I don't think Little Sheba's ever coming back, Doc. I ain't going to call her anymore." By the end of the film, **Shirley Booth** is resigned to the fact that she will never see her little dog again. *Come Back Little Sheba* (1952, Paramount).

314 "Kilimanjaro is a snow-covered mountain 19,710 feet high and is said to be the highest mountain in Africa. Close to the western summit there is a dry and frozen carcass of a leopard. No one has explained what the leopard was seeking at that altitude." In the opening narration, the leopard represents Ernest Hemingway-like writer-adventurer **Gregory Peck,** who has come to the base of Kilimanjaro from where the story will be told in flashbacks. *The Snows of Kilimanjaro* (1952, 20th Century-Fox).

315 "You don't know the meaning of the word 'neighbor,' but I can't imagine any of ya bein' so low ya'd kill a helpless, friendly dog—the only thing in this whole neighborhood who liked anybody. Did ya kill him because he liked ya?" Sobbing with grief, **Sara Berner** accuses every one of her indifferent neighbors with responsibility in the strangulation death of her little dog. *Rear Window* (1954, Paramount).

316 "A horse, a horse! My kingdom for a horse." **Laurence Olivier,** as the title character, is unseated from his steed and is surrounded by the enemy. *Richard III* (1956, GB, London Films).

317 "He's big enough to learn. He's big enough to act like Old Yeller." Despondent ever since he was forced to shoot rabid Old Yeller, **Tommy Kirk** finally takes comfort from the dead dog's pup. *Old Yeller* (1957, Buena Vista).

318 "Tens of thousands of elephants are killed in Africa every year. Soon we'll be alone on this earth with nothing else to destroy but ourselves." Champion of the African elephant, **Trevor Howard** fights a losing battle to ban the hunting and poaching of elephants. *The Roots of Heaven* (1958, 20th Century-Fox).

319 "I live with them. I like looking at them and listening to them. As a matter of fact, I'd give anything to become an elephant myself." Christ-figure **Trevor Howard** tells sympathetic prostitute Juliette Greco of his dedication to preventing the slaughter of African elephants. *The Roots of Heaven* (1958, 20th Century-Fox).

320 "People have always scared me a bit, you see. They're so complicated. I suppose that's why I prefer horses." **May Hallatt** shows horse sense to Wendy Hiller in her preference of horses to people. *Separate Tables* (1958, United Artists).

321 "In canis corpore transmutto." (Translation: "I change into the body of a dog.") It's the secret spell that changes **Tommy Kirk** into the title character. *The Shaggy Dog* (1959, Buena Vista-Disney).

322 "I'm not an animal... I'm not an animal." When slave Jean Simmons is sent to the cell of gladiator-in-training **Kirk Douglas,** school owner Peter Ustinov tries to spy on their love-making. When Douglas refuses to put on a show, Ustinov orders Simmons taken to another man. Before she leaves, in reaction to Douglas' cries, she says softly, "Neither am I." *Spartacus* (1960, Universal-International).

323 "If I were a dog and somebody made me beg, I'd bite." Rich girl **Sharon Hugueny** informs Troy Donahue that she can be snappish. *Parrish* (1961, Warner Bros.).

324 "There are people in this world to whom a horse is just a horse and not a thing of beauty and culture." **Lilli Palmer** tells her husband Robert Taylor, the owner of the Spanish Riding School in Vienna, that not everyone is a horse lover. *The Miracle of the White Stallions* (1962, Walt Disney).

325 "He has every characteristic of a dog except loyalty." Presidential hopeful **Henry Fonda** is being too hard on dogs in comparing them with his opponent for the nomination, Cliff Robertson. *The Best Man* (1964, United Artists).

326 "[My paper] deals with the instincts of predators. What you might call the criminal class of the animal world. Lady animals figure very largely as predators." **Sean Connery** suggestively tells typist Tippi Hedren about his zoology paper entitled "Arboreal Predators of the Brazilian Rain Forest." *Marnie* (1964, Universal).

327 "If you smell anything like a horse, you're in." **Sean Connery** describes his kindly father Alan Napier to Tippi Hedren, who also loves horses. *Marnie* (1964, Universal).

328 "Control your animal needs or I will have them shaved within the half hour." Loony therapist **Peter Sellers** screams at a statue of King Kong menacing a fair damsel—Fay Wray, no doubt. *What's New, Pussycat?* (1965, United Artists).

329 HARMONICA: "Did you bring a horse for me?" KNUCKLES: "Well, looks like we're shy one horse." HARMONICA: "No, you brought two too many." When stranger **Charles Bronson** steps off a train, he's met by three hired killers, **Jack Elam,** Woody Strode and John Frederick. Without batting an eye Bronson guns down the three. *Once Upon a Time in the West* (1969, U.S.-Italy, Paramount).

330 "They look to me like two elephants making love to a men's glee club." **Woody Allen** takes a Rorschach inkblot test. *Take the Money and Run* (1969, Palomar).

331 "No matter what anyone says, the cat was dead when I got it from the animal shelter." Horrid young **Ellen Dano** assembled the skeleton of a cat, after boiling off its skin for an exhibit in the finals of a high school science fair. *The Effect of Gamma Rays on Man-in-the-Moon Marigolds* (1972, 20th Century-Fox).

332 "How come everybody else gets chicken and I get feathers?" Prostitute **Marsha Mason** believes life treats her unfairly. *Cinderella Liberty* (1973, 20th Century-Fox).

333 "I dislike dogs myself." **Robert De Niro,** as young Vito Corleone, quietly but effectively persuades a landlord who has evicted a widow because of her dog, to reconsider. *The Godfather, Part II* (1974, Paramount).

334 "All the animals come out at night. Sick. Venal. Someday a real rain will come and wash all the scum off the streets." As he scribbles in his diary, **Robert De Niro** dreams of becoming that cleansing rain. *Taxi Driver* (1976, Columbia).

335 "Don't worry, I promise I'll get your doggie back." L.A. police sergeant **Robert Foxworth** dries the tears of Barbara Babcock, the attractive owner of a kidnapped prize canine being held for $85,000 ransom. *The Black Marble* (1980, Avco Embassy).

336 "I'm Dr. Paul Pearlman... I did a paper on you and your films at a psychiatric convention... it was very well received, you'll be happy to know.... Have you ever had intercourse with any type of animal?" Self-serving scholar **Benjamin Rayson** reports to and questions film-maker Woody Allen. *Stardust Memories* (1980, Orion).

337 "You've got animal magnetism—You attract animals!" **Anne De Salvo** shouts to her husband Max Gail who presides over an impoverished cab company with a motley crew of drivers. *D.C. Cab* (1981, Universal).

338 "The beast that thou sawest was and is not and shall ascend out of the bottomless pit and go into perdition, and they that dwell on the earth shall wonder." Narrator **Percy Rodrigues** sums up the story of a conservative, repressive religious sect, the Hittites. *Deadly Blessing* (1981, United Artists).

339 "Isn't that a rogue elephant?" It's one of naïve young **Bo Derek**'s laughable lines to her father Richard Harris. *Tarzan, the Ape Man* (1981, MGM-United Artists).

340 "They're washing me like I was a horse." It's the pitiful wail of **Bo Derek** to her helpless father Richard Harris, as the naked beauty is washed and covered with a chalky mud to be the "bride" of a tribal leader. *Tarzan, the Ape Man* (1981, MGM-United Artists).

341 "[I feel] like a country dog in the city. If I stand still they screw me. If I run, they bite my ass." Small town sheriff **Burt Reynolds** believes he's in a no-win situation. *The Best Little Whorehouse in Texas* (1982, Universal).

342 "Wolves mate for life. There is a constant, varied display of affection." Nerd-hero-scientist **Charles Martin-Smith** lectures on misunderstood animals—the wolves. *Never Cry Wolf* (1983, Disney-Buena Vista).

343 "Now what kind of dog would hang around me?" Ruthless bookie **James Woods** seems shocked when Jeff Bridges asks him if a friendly dog with him is actually his. *Against All Odds* (1984, Columbia).

344 "Keep him out of the light. . . . Don't get him wet. . . and never, never feed him after midnight." If the instructions of San Francisco Chinese shopkeeper **Keye Luke** had been followed when Hoyt Axton purchased the cute little "Mogwai" for his son, there would have been no movie let alone the basis for a sequel. *Gremlins* (1984, Warner Bros.).

345 "Dad, Argus is the dog, I'm Henry." For perhaps the hundredth time, **Sean Penn** patiently corrects his father John Karlen when the latter calls him Argus. *Racing with the Moon* (1984, Paramount).

346 "Out of the mud of the darkness comes two ignorant animals and slowly, quite unknown to themselves, they set about the task of bringing my life and my work down, down, into the slime that bred them." **Timothy Dalton** speaks of grave-robbers and murderers, Jonathan Pryce and Stephen Rea. They portray infamous Burke and Hare types, supplying physician Dalton with fresh cadavers for his experiments—some of their own making. *The Doctor and the Devils* (1985, GB, Brooksfilm).

347 "And I looked, and Behold a Pale Horse; and the name of him that sat on him was Death. . . ." Fifteen-year-old **Sydney Penney** reads from the bible, Revelation 6, to her mother Carrie Snodgress. When she looks out of their gold mining cabin she sees Clint Eastwood sitting quietly on a pale horse. *Pale Rider* (1985, Warner Bros.).

348 "The guards are the zookeeper and you're the animals." Lesbian warden **Angel Tompkins** welcomes some new "fish" to her pen. *The Naked Cage* (1986, Cannon).

349 "I just bagged the elephant!" Young stock salesman **Charlie Sheen** tells other lowly account executives that he's landed "player" Mike Douglas as a client. *Wall Street* (1987, 20th Century-Fox).

350 "I don't know. I'd like to go home and I'd like to play with my dog." **Jodie Foster** responds to a question as what she's going to do now that the three men are convicted for inciting others to gang-rape Foster. *The Accused* (1988, Paramount).

351 "Chickens are just rats with a good reputation." **Jim Haynie** announces to his three sons that he's fed up with the business and has sold his fried chicken restaurant. *Staying Together* (1989, Hemdale).

352 "Do you know how many rich animals I had to fuck to get it?" **JoBeth Williams** snaps at a female animal rights passerby who accusingly asks: "Do you know how many poor animals had to die for you to get that coat?" *Switch* (1991, Warner Bros.).

353 "I am not a human being. I am an animal." **Danny De Vito,** as The Penguin, admits to being a crook—but a human, never. *Batman Returns* (1992, Warner Bros.).

Announcements

see also INFORMATION, INSTRUCTIONS, KNOWLEDGE, PREDICTIONS, RADIOS, TELEVISION, THREATS, WARNINGS

354 "Monday afternoon, a sailboat race will be held at the cesspool." An idiotic announcement in a German POW camp. *Stalag 17* (1953, Paramount).

355 "We interrupt this program for an announcement from American military headquarters here. The return of Corporal John J. Leatherby of Toledo, Ohio, who was picked up by the Russians ten days ago has been effected through regular channels. The promptness with which the Russians responded to diplomatic conversations is interpreted by many here as still further indication that they are now genuinely anxious for the resumption of normal peaceful relations with the Western powers." Despite the radio announcement, audiences of the film have just seen the intrigue, trickery and dangers American Colonel Gregory Peck was forced to engage in to arrange for the return of the young enlisted man. *Night People* (1954, 20th Century-Fox).

356 "He rises." **Gregory Peck** as Captain Ahab announcing the surfacing of the great white whale. *Moby Dick* (1956, GB, Warner Bros.).

357 "Ladies and gentlemen, I would like at this moment to announce that I will be retiring from this program in two weeks' time because of poor ratings. Since the show was the only thing I had going for me in my life, I have decided to kill myself. I'm going to blow my brains out right here on this program a week from today." TV news anchorman **Peter Finch** calmly announces the end of his program and himself to the few in his audience. *Network* (1976, MGM-United Artists).

358 "Attention, Camp North Star senior staff, counselors, and counselors-in-training, please rise for our national anthem." Camp counselor **Bill Murray** arouses others from their sleep early one morning. *Meatballs* (1979, Canada, Paramount).

359 "We've been together about 15 years and tonight I'd like to announce our divorce. Isn't that the kind of thing that country songs are all about?" After discovering that her always on-the-road husband, country and western singer Willie Nelson has been unfaithful with backup singer Amy Irving, **Dyan Cannon** announces the break-up of their marriage to a stadium full of stunned fans. *Honeysuckle Rose* (1980, Warner Bros.).

360 "I want the rest of you cowboys to know something. There's a new sheriff in town." Temporarily paroled black con **Eddie Murphy** flashes policeman Nick Nolte's badge in a redneck country and western bar. *48 Hours* (1982, Paramount).

361 "They're heeere!" Preschooler **Heather O'Rourke** sits before a snowy television screen, talking to the people inside. She warns her family when a strange light flashes out of the screen and onto the wall. In the sequel, she announces, "They're baaack!" *Poltergeist* (1982, MGM).

362 "The fireworks are for El Flamingo members only. Non-members don't look up." **Frank Campanella,** the snobbish owner of the fashionable Long Island El Flamingo Beach Club, announces an exclusive Fourth-of-July fireworks display—he means it. *The Flamingo Kid* (1984, 20th Century-Fox).

363 "She was at her shower, so I told her dad." In 1971, **Sam Robards,** about to be drafted, announces he's breaking his engagement to his fiancée—but not face-to-face. *Fandango* (1985, Warner Bros.).

364 "It's a sunny, woodsy day in Lumbertown. Get those chainsaws out." A radio announcer lets audiences know the kind of town that is the setting for David Lynch's story. *Blue Velvet* (1986, De Laurentiis).

365 "October the second, nineteen thirty-seven, an historic moment in the life of Eugene Morris Jerome. I have just seen the golden palace of the Himalayas. Puberty is over. Onwards and upwards." **Jonathan Silverman** has achieved his goal—to see a naked woman. *Brighton Beach Memoirs* (1986, Universal).

366 "Let's give her a shot, shall we.... You decent?... Mr. Jack Trainer to see Miss Tess McGill.... Hold all calls, Miss McGill?... Can I get you anything, Mr. Trainer: Coffee, Tea—me?" Kookie stenographer **Joan Cusack** pretends to visiting deal-maker Harrison Ford that she's personal secretary to Melanie Griffith, a personal secretary who's pretending she's a business executive. *Working Girl* (1988, 20th Century-Fox).

Answers

see also ARGUMENTS, DISCOVERIES, EXPLANATIONS, QUESTIONS, QUESTIONS AND ANSWERS

367 "Well, son, I refuse to answer without advice of counsel." Corrupt judge **Walter Huston** settles down with feminist social worker Irene Dunne. *Ann Vickers* (1933, RKO).

368 "I shall look for the answer tonight at the bottom of a large rum and coke." Shakespeare-spouting Southerner **Vincent Price** is one of a squad of American soldiers fighting the Japanese in the Philippines during World War II. *The Eve of St. Mark* (1944, 20th Century-Fox).

369 "I want answers now. I'm not interested in what I'll understand ten years from now." Alienated teenager **James Dean** rages at his weak, indecisive father Jim Backus. *Rebel Without a Cause* (1955, Warner Bros.).

370 "When are we going to have another child? You're the doctor, you have all the answers." **Doris Day** chooses a crowded Arabian market to ask the question of her physician husband James Stewart. *The Man Who Knew Too Much* (1956, Paramount).

371 RICHARD SUMMER: "You're both single minded; you go on relentlessly trying to get the answer." BUNNY WATSON: "What happens if she can't find the answer?" RICHARD: "If she becomes frustrated, her magnetic circuit is liable to go off." BUNNY: "Something like that happens to me.' Efficiency expert **Spencer Tracy** compares his computer "Emerac" to TV network research expert **Katharine Hepburn.** *Desk Set* (1957, 20th Century-Fox).

372 "Maybe in those last moments he loved life more than he ever had before. Not just his life, anybody's life. My life. . . . All he wanted were the same answers the rest of us want. Where do I come from? Where am I going? How long have I got?" Special policeman **Harrison Ford** muses after the death of replicant Rutger Hauer. *Blade Runner* (1982, Warner Bros.).

373 "Fighting war is last answer to problem." **Noriyuki "Pat" Morita** sounds like an Okinawan Charlie Chan. *The Karate Kid* (1984, Columbia).

Anticipation *see* EXPECTATIONS, WAITS AND WAITING

Anxiety *see* CONCERNS, FEARS, FUTURE, SECURITY AND INSECURITY, WORRIES

Apologies

see also CONFESSIONS, CONSCIENCES, DEFENSES, EXCUSES, JUSTIFICATIONS, PLEAS AND PLEADING, REGRETS, SORROW

374 "Miss Dobie, there's no way I can take back what I've done to you, but what little I can do—a public apology; the damage suit to be paid in full, of course; and whatever else you will be kind enough to take from me. . . ." **Alma Kruger** graciously accepts total responsibility and intends to make whatever amends she can for ruining the career of schoolmistress Miriam Hopkins when she listened to the horrid lies of her granddaughter Bonita Granville. In the remake, **Fay Bainter** makes approximately the same speech to Shirley MacLaine. *These Three* (1936, United Artists); *The Children's Hour* (1962, United Artists).

375 "You see, if I had started smacking her earlier, maybe it wouldn't have been necessary for you to do it now." **Claude Gillingwater** apologizes to Fred MacMurray after the latter slaps farmer's grand-

daughter Madeleine Carroll. Oddly, in this period of screwball comedies, there was a great deal of acceptance of slapping, spanking or punching women. *Café Society* (1939, Paramount).

376 "I'd like to apologize, Mr. Rhett, for it not being a boy." Maid **Hattie McDaniel** assumes the "blame" when Clark Gable's wife Vivien Leigh has a baby girl. *Gone with the Wind* (1939, Selznick-MGM).

377 "I seem to have offended your light of love by using a polysyllabic word." Enigmatic, alcoholic, intellectual **Van Heflin** gets the zinger in with his insecure apology, after offending one of mobster Robert Taylor's girl friends. *Johnny Eager* (1942, MGM).

378 "I apologize for the intelligence of my remarks, Sir Thomas, I had forgotten you were a Member of Parliament." Elegant heavy **George Sanders** condescendingly apologizes to Robert Greig. *The Picture of Dorian Gray* (1945, MGM).

379 "Nobody has to apologize because we both are such stinkers." Married **Rita Hayworth** believes that she and her ex-lover Glenn Ford deserve each other. *Gilda* (1946, Columbia).

380 "God should spit on me." Ernest Hemingway-like writer **Gregory Peck** apologizes to Ava Gardner for mistreating her. *The Snows of Kilimanjaro* (1952, 20th Century-Fox).

381 "If I grumbled too much at my share of the work in burying Harry, I'm sorry. I can see now it was well worth it." **Edmund Gwenn** apologizes to John Forsythe about the stiff that they have buried and dug up several times. *The Trouble with Harry* (1955, Paramount).

382 "I apologize for not being entirely honest with you. I apologize for not revealing my true feelings. I apologize for not telling you sooner that you're a degenerate, sadistic old man. And you can go to hell before I apologize to you now or ever again." French colonel **Kirk Douglas** failed to save the lives of three scapegoat soldiers in his command. The trio was sentenced to death before a firing squad to satisfy General Adolphe Menjou's need for an object lesson. *Paths of Glory* (1957, United Artists).

383 "I always tried to live free and above board like you. . . . But I just couldn't find enough elbow room." In their last meeting, chain gang prisoner **Paul Newman** apologizes to his dying mother Jo Van Fleet. *Cool Hand Luke* (1967, Warner Bros.).

384 "I'm sorry if I offended you—but it does seem a bit hard. . . that ill luck should follow a man for honestly telling a woman that she is beautiful. . . . Miss Aberdeen, you do forgive me, don't you. . . . How can you blame me for your looks—a woman like you does more damage than she can conceivably imagine." Sergeant **Terence Stamp** apologizes at his second meeting with Julie Christie for his romantic behavior at their first. *Far from the Madding Crowd* (1967, GB, MGM).

385 "I move around a lot. Not because I'm looking for anything really. But I'm getting away from things that get bad if I stay. . . the best thing that I can do is apologize. But we both know that I was really that good at it anyway. Sorry it didn't work out." **Jack Nicholson** attempts to communicate with his wheelchair-bound, stroke-paralyzed father William Challee. *Five Easy Pieces* (1970, Columbia).

386 "I don't have to apologize to a paid assassin for what I do." Jewel smuggler **Maud Adams** doesn't believe that Roger Moore, as James Bond, has any right to feel morally superior. *Octopussy* (1982, GB, MGM-United Artists).

387 "What's the statute of limitations on apologies?" Smart aleck **Billy Crystal** even wisecracks when he's apologizing to Meg Ryan. *When Harry Met Sally. . .* (1989, Columbia).

388 JOEY ADONIS: "Why don't you suck your apology out of my dick?" BEN SIEGEL: "Pull it out." When **Lewis Van Bergen** refuses to apologize to **Warren Beatty** for his unflattering characterization of Beatty's lady-love Annette Bening, Beatty nearly beats Van Bergen to death. *Bugsy* (1991, Tri-Star).

389 "I'm as embarrassed about this as you are." Obsessed with her, policeman **Ray Liotta** suddenly appears with a flashlight in the bedroom of Kurt Russell and Madeleine Stowe while they are making love. *Unlawful Entry* (1992, 20th Century-Fox).

Appearances

see also BODIES, CLOTHES, FACES, FASHIONS, HAIR, IDENTITIES, PRETENSIONS, SIGHT AND SIGHTS

390 "Take a good look, it's free." Party girl **Barbara Stanwyck,** working as a model, issues an invitation to philanderer Lowell Sherman, who tries to take a peek down a robe she's wearing. *Ladies of Leisure* (1930, Columbia).

391 "All I need is a napkin over my arm." **Edward G. Robinson** offers this quip when he looks at himself wearing his first tuxedo. *Little Caesar* (1931, Warner Bros.).

392 "I'm just telling you the truth. You know, you never were an actor. You did have looks, but they're gone now. You don't have to take my word for it. Just look in any mirror. They don't lie. Take a good look. Look at those pouches under your eyes. Look at those creases. You sag like an old woman. Get a load of yourself." Agent **Lee Tracy** is unsympathetic to his client John Barrymore who has ruined his looks and his acting chances by the excesses of his life. *Dinner at Eight* (1933, MGM).

393 "I got tired of looking like a school teacher." **Ruby Keeler** insults an entire profession while explaining why she shed her glasses and combed her hair differently. Hope she didn't need the glasses to see, contacts hadn't been perfected at the time. *Footlight Parade* (1933, Warner Bros.).

394 "I don't like his face or any part of him. He looks like a Bulgarian bald eagle mourning his firstborn." Broadway producer **Ned Sparks** characterizes backer Guy Kibbee. *42nd Street* (1933, Warner Bros.).

395 "It's better to be looked over than overlooked." **Mae West** dispenses some more of her particular feminine wisdom. *Belle of the Nineties* (1934, Paramount).

396 "He looks like the black panther in my animal book!" **Freddie Bartholomew** gives his mother Elizabeth Allan his opinion of her new husband Basil Rathbone the first time they meet. *David Copperfield* (1935, MGM).

397 "I'm a sight tonight and I wanted to look my best." **Katharine Hepburn** as the title queen, utters her first words on entering Holyrood. *Mary of Scotland* (1935, RKO).

398 "She was only thirty-six, but look at her—she looks fifty. That's what life does for you." To show the life of Charles II's mistress, former orange-seller Nell Gwynn, a framing sequence to the film had to be added in the U.S. to show Anna Neagle, as the title character, dying in the gutter. An unidentified bailiff, who finds her body, delivers the line about her looks to make certain audiences knew she suffered for her sins. *Nell Gwynn* (1935, GB, United Artists).

399 "You might from your appearance be the wife of Lucifer, yet you shall not get the better of me. I'm an Englishwoman. I'm your match." **Edna May Oliver,** as Nurse Pross, prevents frightful Blanche Yurka, as Mme. DeFarge, from harming Elizabeth Allan and her child. *A Tale of Two Cities* (1935, MGM).

400 "I always look well when I'm near death." Consumptive **Greta Garbo** responds to a compliment. *Camille* (1936, MGM).

401 "I've seen your pictures in the papers. I always wondered what you looked like." Masquerading as her ex-husband Cary Grant's sister, **Irene Dunne** speaks sense and nonsense to Molly Lamont, Grant's current fiancée. *The Awful Truth* (1937, Columbia).

402 "I'm tired. I'm sick. Can you see it? Look at me good. You've been looking at me like I used to be." Reduced to streetwalking when her ex-lover Humphrey Bogart deserted her, **Claire Trevor** forces him to see what she's become. *Dead End* (1937, Goldwyn-United Artists).

403 "I might be good looking myself when I grow out of this ugly-duckling stage." **Judy Garland** isn't happy with her appearance but she hasn't given up hope. *Babes in Arms* (1939, MGM).

404 "He looks at me like he knows what I look like without my shimmy." **Vivien Leigh**'s statement must be what passed for, "He undressed me with his eyes" in polite Southern society. *Gone with the Wind* (1939, Selznick-MGM).

405 "Were you really there? What did it look like? Does she have cut glass chandeliers, plush curtains, and dozens of mirrors?" **Leona Roberts** pesters her husband Harry Davenport for details about Ona Munson's bordello as he probes Leslie Howard's wound. *Gone with the Wind* (1939, Selznick-MGM).

406 "You looked charming, you looked bored, and you looked as though you wouldn't trump your partner's ace." **Rex O'Malley** tells Claudette Colbert why he has invited her to be a fourth at bridge in a private room. He's trying to escape a terrible concert that is being held next door. *Midnight* (1939, Paramount).

407 "I don't know what you'll look like tomorrow, but tonight you're the best looking thing I've ever seen." Having escaped from Devil's Island penal colony, **Clark Gable** knows he can't be too particular, so cheap cafe singer Joan Crawford looks good enough for one evening. *Strange Cargo* (1940, MGM).

408 "I've seen women I'd look at quicker but never one I'd look at longer." Western con man **Clark Gable** pays Lana Turner a qualified compliment. *Honky Tonk* (1941, MGM).

409 "My great Aunt Jennifer ate a box of chocolates every day of her life. She lived to be a hundred and two, and when she had been dead three days, she looked healthier than you do now." Acid-tongued patient **Monty Woolley** snaps cruelly at his harried nurse Mary Wickes. *The Man Who Came to Dinner* (1941, Warner Bros.).

410 "Well, don't stand there, Miss Preen. You look like a frozen custard." **Monty Wooley** pours another uncalled-for insult on his long-suffering nurse Mary Wickes. *The Man Who Came to Dinner* (1941, Warner Bros.).

411 JOHN L. SULLIVAN: "Don't I look like a picture director?" OLD INMATE: "You look more like a soda jerk or a plasterer." Movie director **Joel McCrea**, posing as a hobo, is thrown into jail. He reveals his identity to an unbelieving and uncaring **Chester Conklin**. *Sullivan's Travels* (1941, Paramount).

412 "He looks like a giraffe, and I love him." Nightclub entertainer **Barbara Stanwyck** speaks of shy professor Gary Cooper. *Ball of Fire* (1942, Goldwyn-RKO).

413 MARGIE STALLINGS: "Now I don't want to cause any trouble, but cold facts are cold facts. If Mr. and Mrs. Cooper come—that big, awful looking Mrs. Cooper!—he shaves." JILL BAKER: "And if he has dinner alone with his wife, he doesn't shave." MARGIE: "And if anyone should shave, it's Mrs. Cooper." **Olive Blakeney** comments on appearances, after witnessing a typically dull scene between **Merle Oberon** and her husband Melvyn Douglas. *That Uncertain Feeling* (1942, United Artists).

414 UNCLE CHARLIE: "Give me your hand, Charlie." CHARLIE: "Thank you." UNCLE CHARLIE: "You didn't even look at it." CHARLIE: "I didn't have to look at it." When he arrives for a visit, **Joseph Cotten** slips a ring on the finger of his sympatico niece **Teresa Wright**. *Shadow of a Doubt* (1943, Universal).

415 "She's beautiful but she looks as if she's been thrown off a freight train." **Tom Neal**'s thought about Ann Savage is almost on target. As a hitchhiker she was picked up and thrown out of Edmund MacDonald's car. *Detour* (1945, PRC).

416 "I choose all my friends for their good looks." It's one of many sophisticated lines from Oscar Wilde put in the mouth of decadent **George Sanders**. *The Picture of Dorian Gray* (1945, MGM).

417 "We suffer for what the gods give us, and I'm afraid Dorian Gray will pay for his good looks." **Lowell Gilmore** makes a fateful prediction of Hurd Hatfield's future. The latter's good looks limited his roles. The movies already had Tyrone Power, whom he resembled in type. *The Picture of Dorian Gray* (1945, MGM).

418 "It looked like feeding-time at the zoo. . . all you needed was money to start with and bicarbonate to finish with." In a voice-over, **Humphrey Bogart** describes a nightclub he enters, filled with moneyed customers in a luxurious setting. *Dead Reckoning* (1947, Columbia).

419 "She looked like a very special kind of dynamite, neatly wrapped in nylon and silk. Only I wasn't having any. I'd been too close to an explosion already. I was powder-shy." In voice-over, philandering husband **Robert Young** claims he can resist, but he is frozen in his tracks as he catches sight of new secretary Susan Hayward as she bends provocatively over a filing cabinet. *They Won't Believe Me* (1947, RKO).

420 "My gowns were gorgeous, very décolleté. . . I wore hardly any makeup, just some lipstick, that's all. No lights, just a baby spot. I wouldn't have an entrance—they'd play in the dark, the spot would come on, and there I'd be." One-time club singer **Claire Trevor** fondly remembers how it was before she became mobster Edward G. Robinson's mistress and a lush. *Key Largo* (1948, Warner Bros.).

421 "You're the most gorgeous first baseman I ever played against." Reporter **Bing Crosby** has to look up to six-foot Alexis Smith. *Here Comes the Groom* (1951, Paramount).

422 "Did anyone ever tell you that you look like a prince out of the Arabian Nights?" **Vivien Leigh** makes a move on a young bill collector who reminds her of her young husband who committed suicide. *A Streetcar Named Desire* (1951, MGM-20th Century-Fox).

423 "Herr Moyzisch, please do not look at me as if you had a source of income other than your salary." Impoverished Polish countess **Danielle Darrieux** puts middle-echelon German attaché Oscar Karlweis in his place when he tries to flirt with her. *Five Fingers* (1952, 20th Century-Fox).

424 "A girl with only looks to keep her from being a bum can't afford to lose them." Disfigured **Gloria Grahame** realizes she can no longer afford vanity. *The Big Heat* (1953, Columbia).

425 "We've become a race of Peeping Toms. People ought to get outside and look at themselves." Housekeeper **Thelma Ritter** doesn't approve of James Stewart spying on his neighbors from his rear window. *Rear Window* (1954, Paramount).

426 "I could see you looking very handsome and successful in a dark blue suit." Society girl **Grace Kelly** would like to revamp the identity and work of her lover, world-traveling magazine photographer James Stewart. *Rear Window* (1954, Paramount).

427 "He looks so helpless lying there smiling in his sleep just like a child." **Judy Garland** watches fading movie star James Mason sleep off a drunk. *A Star Is Born* (1954, Warner Bros.).

428 "I like the way he looks, as if he's got something to say but he won't say it. I like the way he tucks his thumbs into his belt." Plain spinster **Katharine Hepburn** admires the looks of deputy Wendell Corey, whose wife has run off and left him. *The Rainmaker* (1956, Paramount).

429 "[You look] like a giraffe with a goiter." This is **Louis Jourdan**'s unjust and inaccurate description of Leslie Caron's appearance the first time he sees the little girl he adores dressed as an adult woman. *Gigi* (1958, MGM).

430 "I see a girl who looks like a pearl. A pearl of a girl." **Keir Dullea** brightens Janet Margolin, who rewards him by allowing him to speak to her without resorting to a rhyme. *David and Lisa* (1962, Continental Distributing).

431 "Thanks for the compliment, but I know how I look. This is the way I look when I'm sober. It's enough to make a person drink, wouldn't you say?. . . You see, the world looks so dirty to me when I'm not drinking. Joe, remember Fisherman's Wharf? The water when you looked too close? That's the way the world looks to me when I'm not drinking." **Lee Remick** resists her reformed drunk husband Jack Lemmon's attempts to get her to give up alcohol. *Days of Wine and Roses* (1962, Warner Bros.).

432 "You're not looking for a wife and I'm not looking for a joy ride." Stewardess **Lois Nettleton** lets multimillionaire widower Karl Malden know she's not for sale. *Come Fly with Me* (1963, MGM).

433 "At our last meeting, I died. It alters the appearance." Governess **Deborah Kerr** speaks to judge Felix Aylmer who barely recognizes the woman he once sentenced to death. *The Chalk Garden* (1964, GB, Universal-International).

434 "When she bent over, it looked like she had her knees up under her dress." **Goldie Hawn** describes Jack Weston's buxomy girl friend Eve Bruce. *Cactus Flower* (1969, Columbia).

435 "Who the hell do you think you're dealing with? In case you didn't happen to notice it, you big

Texas longhorn bull, I'm one hellavah gorgeous chick!" **Sylvia Miles** explodes when Jon Voight wants to get paid for his stud service. *Midnight Cowboy* (1969, United Artists).

436 "You look like two decent, respectable hippies." Welfare examiner **Michael Sklar** speaks to unemployed lowlifes John Dallesandro and Holly Woodlawn in their junk-filled apartment. When he discovers that Holly really isn't pregnant, he changes his mind, saying, "You're garbage! You deserve to live here!" *Trash* (1970, Cinema 5-Andy Warhol).

437 "You look ridiculous in that makeup. Like the caricature of a whore. A little touch of mommy in the night. Fake Ophelia drowned in a bathtub. I wish you could see yourself. You'd really laugh. You're your mother's masterpiece." **Marlon Brando** addresses the corpse of his suicide wife Veronica Lazare. *Last Tango in Paris* (1972, Fr.-Italy-U.S., United Artists).

438 "You look like some kind of ice cream cone with licorice between your legs." Massage parlor proprietor **Marva Farmer** puts down black pimp John Daniels who dresses in a white suit and a white hat. *The Candy Tangerine Man* (1975, Moonstone).

439 "She threw me a look I caught in my hip pocket." Private eye Philip Marlowe, played by **Robert Mitchum,** refers to sexy Charlotte Rampling who looks him up and down. *Farewell My Lovely* (1975, Avco Embassy).

440 "Fit? You think I look fit? What an awful shit you are. I look gorgeous." **Jane Fonda** berates her ex-husband Alan Alda for the inadequacy of his compliment on her looks. *California Suite* (1978, Columbia).

441 "I realize I don't look so hot, but I thought you'd be glad to see me." Killed by a werewolf, the decomposing corpse of **Griffin Dunne** appears to warn his friend David Naughton of his fate since he also was bitten by the werewolf. *An American Werewolf in London* (1981, GB, Universal).

442 "What's the mole just above her pubic hair look like to you? To me it looks like a question mark." To get even with Dee Wallace for ending their affair, **Christopher Stone** poses the question in a note written to her husband, Daniel Hugh-Kelly. *Cujo* (1981, Warner Bros.).

443 "Are you as good as you look?" Stunningly attractive older woman **Gail Strickland** lusts after handsome, athletic teenage parking lot attendant Rob Lowe. *Oxford Blues* (1984, MGM-United Artists).

444 "I must look like hell." **Linda Kerridge** has taken a shot to the head that leaves her a bloody mess. *Mixed Blood* (1985, Fr.; Sara Films-Cinevista).

445 "My skull is too flat, my ears stick out, my mouth is too big, my belly is too round, and my buttocks are too heavy." Despite **Beatrice Dalle**'s self-proclaimed defects, she's a very good-looking woman. *Betty Blue* (1986, Fr., Alive Films).

446 "I didn't like his stinking looks." It's the reason **Sissy Spacek** gives for shooting her husband Beeson Carroll in the stomach, although she confesses she was aiming for his head. *Crimes of the Heart* (1986, De Laurentiis).

447 "I'll never look like Barbie. Barbie doesn't have bruises." **Chloe Webb,** as Nancy Spungen, screams at her sadistic lover Gary Oldman, as British punk rock singer Sid Vicious. They are engaging in an argument over their preference in dolls; his for G.I. Joe, she for Barbie. *Sid and Nancy* (1986, GB, Goldwyn).

448 EPIPHANY PROUDFOOT: "The person you're looking for could be six feet under." HARRY ANGEL: "Then I'll have to buy a shovel." Sexy **Lisa Bonet** suggests that the singer second-rate private eye **Mickey Rourke** is seeking may have had his appearance altered because he's dead and buried. *Angel Heart* (1987, Tri-Star).

449 "You looked wonderful out there." **Jerry Orbach** gives his daughter Jennifer Grey his approval of her dancing and her dance partner Patrick Swayze. *Dirty Dancing* (1987, Vestron).

450 "He has rather a large nose which he compensates for by not having much of a chin—medium homely, I'd say." Teasingly, **John Malkovich** assures his mother Joanne Woodward that the gentleman caller expected for dinner, James Naughton, isn't too handsome. *The Glass Menagerie* (1987, CineplexOdeon).

451 SUSANNA: "What does your date look like, Ray?" RAYMOND: "She's very sparkly. She looks like a holiday." **Valeria Golino** asks **Dustin Hoffman** about hooker Lucinda Jenney whom he met in a casino bar and with whom he believes he has an eleven o'clock date. *Rain Man* (1988, United Artists).

452 "You're the first woman I've ever seen at one of these damn things that dresses like a woman, not like a woman thinks a man would dress if he was a woman." **Harrison Ford** approves of the smashing appearance of Melanie Griffith at a business-oriented cocktail party. *Working Girl* (1988, 20th Century-Fox).

453 "It looks like you swallowed a tennis shoe and the laces are hanging out." Small-town police investigator **Tom Hanks** speaks to a massive ugly dog with huge floppy jowls from which run great rivers of disgusting foamy white drool. *Turner and Hooch* (1989, Touchstone).

454 RACHEL FLAX: "How do I look?" CHARLOTTE FLAX: "Like a woman about to go forth and sin." RACHEL: "Oh, good, just the look I was trying for." **Cher** seeks and gets her daughter **Winona Ryder**'s assessment of her appearance as she is about to go out on a date. *Mermaids* (1990, Orion).

455 "I'm not looking for Miss Right. I'm looking for Miss Right Now." At the time of his comment **Kenneth Branagh** isn't interested in any long term commitments—but he hasn't met Emma Thompson yet. *Dead Again* (1991, Paramount).

456 "Look at that spooky-looking guy." **Bridget Fonda** tells Andy Garcia that "The Ant," played by Vito Antuofermo, frightens her. *The Godfather, Part III* (1991, Paramount).

457 "You look like you just got banged by the dick of doom!" It's how insufferable teen **Brian Austin Green** assesses C. Thomas Howell's appearance the first time they meet. *Kid* (1991, Live).

458 "I look like Gloria fucking Swanson." Soap opera queen **Sally Field** refuses to wear a turban on the show. *Soapdish* (1991, Paramount).

459 "You know General Omar Bradley? Well, there's too strong a resemblance." Wisecracking baseball scout **Jon Lovitz** explains why he passed on one prospect because she was too homely. *A League of Their Own* (1992, Columbia).

Appetites *see* DESIRES, FOOD AND EATING, GREED, HUNGER, SATISFACTIONS

Applause

see also ACTING AND ACTORS, CHEERS, PAYMENTS, RECOGNITION, THANKS AND THANKFULNESS, THEATERS

460 "The person you should be applauding died a few hours ago. I hope that wherever she is she knows and understands and forgives." Triumphant actress **Katharine Hepburn** takes a curtain call, but acknowledges Andrea Leeds, who committed suicide when she didn't get the role that went to Hepburn. *Stage Door* (1937, RKO).

461 "I know nothing of her charms, and I care less, but I tell you this, they won't wait until the end,

they'll applaud in the middle." **Anton Walbrook** predicts a triumph for his new ballerina, Moira Shearer. *The Red Shoes* (1948, GB, Rank).

462 "So little, so little, did you say? Why if there's nothing else—there's applause. I've listened, from backstage, to people applaud. It's like—like waves of love coming over the footlights and wrapping you up. They smile. Their eyes shine. You've pleased them. They want you. You belong. Just that alone is worth everything." Aspiring actress **Anne Baxter** expresses to Celeste Holm how important applause is to a performer. *All About Eve* (1950, 20th Century-Fox).

463 "You're my audience, Father! I wish you'd give me a little applause now and then." Apprentice actress **Jane Wyman** seeks some support from her father Alastair Sim. *Stage Fright* (1950, Warner Bros.).

Appreciation *see* ENJOYMENTS, PRAISES, RECOGNITION, THANKS AND THANKFULNESS

Approval *see* ADMIRATION, BLESSINGS, POPULARITY, PRAISE, RECOMMENDATIONS

Aptitude *see* ABILITIES AND CAPABILITIES, TALENTS

Arabs

see also PEOPLE

464 "So long as the Arabs fight tribe against tribe, so long will they be a little people, a silly people—greedy, barbarous and cruel." **Peter O'Toole**, as T.E. Lawrence, characterizes the Arab people he would like to unify, by stating what he considers their weaknesses. *Lawrence of Arabia* (1962, GB, Columbia).

465 CHARLIE: "I'm pro-Palestinian. Leave the Arabs alone. Why don't you give the Arabs back the land you stole from them?" KURTZ: "Where would you have us go, back to the ghettos?" Vanessa Redgrave-like actress **Diane Keaton**, a pro-Palestinian, is recruited by **Klaus Kinski**, a high mucky-muck in Israeli intelligence. *The Little Drummer Girl* (1984, Warner Bros.).

Architecture *see* ART AND ARTISTS, BUILDINGS, PLANS

Arguments

see also AGREEMENTS, DETECTIVES AND DEDUCTION, FIGHTS AND FIGHTING, LOGIC, OPINIONS, PLEAS AND PLEADING, PRINCIPLES, PROOF, REASONS

466 "There's my argument—restrict immigration." **Groucho Marx** is frustrated by the willful stupidity of Chico Marx. *Monkey Business* (1931, Paramount).

467 "They say, when he goes out to fish, the trout jump out of the stream and into his pockets because they know there's no use arguing." **Alec Craig** exaggerates a mite about the great debater, U.S. Congressman Daniel Webster, portrayed in the movie by Edward Arnold. *All That Money Can Buy* aka: *The Devil and Daniel Webster* (1941, RKO).

468 "You're so full of persuasion—what else would you say you're full of?" **Robert Montgomery**, as private eye Philip Marlowe, is not taken in by Audrey Totter's arguments. *Lady in the Lake* (1946, MGM).

469 "I'm a book man. I believe that everything in it was put there for a purpose. Deviate from the book and you better have a half a dozen good reasons. And you'll still get an argument from me. And I don't lose arguments aboard my ship." New skipper **Humphrey Bogart** tells his officers that he expects things to be done the "Navy way." *The Caine Mutiny* (1954, Columbia).

470 "Mike and I are still together, of course. We never argue anymore, and, when we do, it never lasts more than a week or two. We're really very happily married." **Lauren Bacall** doesn't feel her fights with husband Gregory Peck are very serious. *Designing Woman* (1957, MGM).

471 "I grant you, I may become lethargic and quiescent. Happy when a nurse comes to put in a new catheter, or give me an enema, or to turn me over. These could become the high spots of my day. I might even learn to do wonderful things, like turn the pages of a book with some eyelids. And you would look at me and say: 'Wasn't it worth waiting?' and I would say: 'Yes' and be proud of my achievements. Really proud. I grant you all that, but it doesn't alter the validity of my present position." Quadriplegic **Richard Dreyfuss** argues with his doctor Christine Lahti that he should be allowed to die. *Whose Life Is It Anyway?* (1981, MGM-United Artists).

472 "Just because you can argue better doesn't mean you're right." School drop-out **Linda Griffiths** won't give a victory to her petty, mean-spirited English professor husband Jon DeVries. *Lianna* (1983, United Artists).

Armies *see* BATTLES AND BATTLEFIELDS, KILLING, MILITARY, WARS

Arms *see* BODIES, MILITARY, WEAPONS

Arrests

see also CONTROL, CRIMES AND CRIMINALS, LAWS, POLICE, PRISONS AND PRISONERS

473 "That's right. I want you to send a wire to chief of police there. Tell him to stop that train and arrest Hildy Johnson. Bring him back here. Wire him a full description. The son of a [bitch] stole my watch." After giving his watch to retiring star reporter Pat O'Brien, newspaper editor **Adolphe Menjou** instructs a subordinate on the phone to have O'Brien arrested. **Walter Matthau** says about the same thing about Jack Lemmon at the end of the 1974 remake. *The Front Page* (1931, United Artists; 1974, Universal).

474 "No mug like you will ever put the cuffs on Rico." **Edward G. Robinson** snarls at Thomas Jackson, the head of a police detective squad. *Little Caesar* (1931, Warner Bros.).

475 "You're all under arrest!. . . Her Majesty is very touchy about having her subjects strangled." Alone, **Cary Grant** brazenly announces the arrest of hundreds of Thugees in their temple of Kali. *Gunga Din* (1939, RKO).

476 "Not so fast, Louie. Nobody's going to be arrested—not for a while yet." **Humphrey Bogart** pulls a gun on police captain Claude Rains who has arrived at Bogart's club intent on arresting Resistance leader Paul Henreid. It became a popular misconception that Bogie's line was "Drop the gun, Louie." *Casablanca* (1942, Warner Bros.).

477 "How can you bust people for trying to better themselves?" Young federal agent **Bruno Kirby,** sent to the Mexican border to assist the border patrol, is horrified when he investigates the Mexican shantytowns from which the illegal aliens come. *Borderline* (1980, Associate Film Distributors).

478 "Surf's up, beach boy, but you'll be hanging ten downtown." **Dan Aykroyd,** as Sgt. Joe Friday, arrests Jack O'Halloran, after the latter crashes his limousine on the beach after a top-speed car chase. *Dragnet* (1987, Universal).

479 "What are you going to do, arrest me?" In the scene where **Sharon Stone** reveals she's not wearing any underpants by uncrossing her shapely legs, she lights a cigarette while being questioned by some nervous cops. One tells her there's no smoking in the interrogation room. *Basic Instinct* (1992, Tri-Star).

Arrogance

see also CONCEIT, DIGNITY, IMPORTANCE, INSULTS, PRIDE, VANITY

480 "All we've got is cotton and slaves, and arrogance." **Clark Gable**'s views don't sit well with excited and patriotic Southerners at the beginning of the Civil War. *Gone with the Wind* (1939, Selznick-MGM).

481 "I'm not a man that people overlook." Jaded, wealthy and flighty **Clifton Webb** makes sure that no one overlooks him. *The Razor's Edge* (1946, 20th Century-Fox).

482 "He's convinced that the world is headed for mass suicide and nothing is of importance anymore except to himself. His arrogance has become unbearable. He cares not for happiness nor success. He'd jump off a cliff if he didn't have to climb it first. What is there to do when a man deliberately works against himself and knows that he's doing it? He knows it at the moment of the act. It is an instance of premeditated disaster. He deliberately foments ill will among his fellows and gets a kind of drunken elation out of it." Vicious Broadway producer **Robert Montgomery** arrogantly describes himself for John Payne. *The Saxon Charm* (1948, Universal).

483 "I know it sounds arrogant, but I'm on my way to Nashville to become a country singer. Or a star." An assassination attempt gives **Barbara Harris** her opportunity. *Nashville* (1975, Paramount).

484 "How is it that a once arrogant young nobleman finds contentment with the salt of the earth?" **Mary Elizabeth Mastrantonio,** as Maid Marian, notes that title character Kevin Costner has changed. His answer could have been that his own class is out for his blood. *Robin Hood: Prince of Thieves* (1991, Warner Bros.).

Art and Artists

see also CREATION AND CREATURES, DRAMA AND MELODRAMA, EXPERTS, MUSIC AND MUSICIANS, PHOTOGRAPHY AND PHOTOGRAPHERS, POETRY AND POETS, SCIENCE AND SCIENTISTS, WRITING AND WRITERS

485 "I'm not a thief, I'm an artist." **Mischa Auer** is proud of his pickpocketing skills. *Seven Sinners* (1940, Universal).

486 "Sir, you rouse the artist in me." Bartender **Edgar Kennedy** is delighted with the prospects when a customer asks for the first drink of his life. *The Lady Eve* (1941, Paramount).

487 "I thought that would stop her defiling the image I created of her, stop the degrading of my work. I thought that would be the end of what she could do to me—but it wasn't. . . . Every girl I painted turned out to be Jeanette. . . and every time I painted her I had to kill her again. . . ." Nineteenth century artist **John Carradine** reveals his lurid past to his new love, Jean Parker. Ever since Carradine painted and strangled his unfaithful model and lover Anne Sterling, he's done the same with each new model. *Bluebeard* (1944, PRC).

488 "Whenever Dorian poses for me, it seems as if a power outside myself is guiding my hand. It's as if the painting had a life of its own, independent of me." Painter **Lowell Gilmore** provides the literary and film device of giving the audience a premonition of a fact about Hurd Hatfield and his portrait that is to be learned later. *The Picture of Dorian Gray* (1945, MGM).

489 "You're a painter—paint these." **Joan Bennett** sticks her bare feet into Edward G. Robinson's face, working her dominance on the meek little man by forcing him to paint her toenails. *Scarlet Street* (1945, Universal).

490 "You are the most beautiful woman I've ever painted—not because you're beautiful, but because I'm in love with you, hopelessly in love with you." Artist **Albert Lieven** is captivated by lovely pianist Ann Todd, but her guardian James Mason soon puts an end to the romance. *The Seventh Veil* (1945, GB, GED-Universal).

491 "The enjoyment of art is the only remaining ecstasy that's neither immoral or illegal." Dilettante patron of the arts **Clifton Webb** passes this nugget on to his nephew Tyrone Power. *The Razor's Edge* (1946, 20th Century-Fox).

492 "This party is like the signature of the artist." **John Dall** brags ecstatically to his murder accomplice Farley Granger, taking wicked delight in using the chest containing the body of their victim as a table for a dinner party. *Rope* (1948, Warner Bros.).

493 "Burn a city in order to create an epic? That's carrying the principle of art for art's sake too far." **Leo Genn** is shocked that mad emperor Nero, played by Peter Ustinov has torched Rome in order to inspire himself. *Quo Vadis* (1951, MGM).

494 "I wish that Italian fellow were alive. . . Leonardo. He knew how to paint a woman like you." **Stewart Granger** earns his keep as an actor, delivering this horribly embarrassing line with a straight face to lovely Jean Simmons, as young Elizabeth Tudor. *Young Bess* (1953, MGM).

495 "Of course, as far as I'm concerned, art is just a guy's name." Wealthy **Rock Hudson** proudly professes his ignorance to artist Otto Kruger. *Magnificent Obsession* (1954, Universal).

496 "There's really only three phases you need to know, 'Neo-impressionism, harmony of color, and infinity.'" **Dorothy McGuire** gives Maggie McNamara a crash course on art, when the latter becomes interested in art connoisseur Louis Jourdan. *Three Coins in the Fountain* (1954, 20th Century-Fox).

497 "Artists are better off dead—they're not so troublesome. . . . They said Van Gogh was crazy because he killed himself. He couldn't sell a painting when he was alive, and now they're worth thirty million dollars. They weren't that bad then and they're not that good now—so who's crazy?" Disturbed adolescent artist **John Kerr** makes a lot of sense with his hypothesis. *The Cobweb* (1955, MGM).

498 "He's the Cézanne of psychos." Mental patient **Oscar Levant** refers to fellow patient John Kerr who makes childlike paintings of others at the mental hospital. *The Cobweb* (1955, MGM).

499 SAM MARLOWE: "You're the most beautiful, wonderful thing I've ever seen. . . . I'd like to paint you nude." JENNIFER RODGERS: "Some other time, Mr. Marlowe." Painter **John Forsythe** hasn't been turned down completely by comely **Shirley MacLaine**. *The Trouble with Harry* (1955, Paramount).

500 GAUGUIN: "What I see when I look at your work is just you paint too fast." VAN GOGH: "You look too fast." When know-it-all **Anthony Quinn** criticizes **Kirk Douglas**'s work, the latter has the perfect squelch. *Lust for Life* (1956, MGM).

501 "I'm sweet. I'm lovely. I'm charming. And I make beautiful works of art, shrunken heads. Dummies." **Cameron Mitchell** is a disfigured mannequin maker. *Nightmare in Wax* (1969, Crown International).

502 "I must think of something quickly because before you know it the Renaissance will be here and we'll all be painting." Medieval jester **Woody Allen** has some insights into the future. *Everything You Always Wanted to Know About Sex* (*but were afraid to ask)* (1972, United Artists).

503 "Where did you grow up, in a Norman Rockwell painting?" **Woody Allen** wonders about beautiful WASP Diane Keaton. *Annie Hall* (1977, United Artists).

504 "You're always trying to get things to come out perfectly in art because it's real different in life." **Woody Allen** suggests one motivation of artists. *Annie Hall* (1977, United Artists).

505 "One day when I was about six, my parents had a row, and my mother—she threw a pickled herring at my dad—and missed. It splattered against the wall. I took one look at that pickled herring, and that's when I decided to become an abstract expressionist." **Alan Bates** tells Jill Clayburgh how he happened to choose his area of painting. *An Unmarried Woman* (1978, 20th Century-Fox).

506 "You know whenever you put 50 artists together in one room, you get a really pleasant combination of gossip, paranoia, envy, fear, trembling, hatred, lust and pretense. It's, er, wonderful." Artist **Alan Bates** tells Jill Clayburgh of his delight with his profession. *An Unmarried Woman* (1978, 20th Century-Fox).

507 "Who is the most expensive mistress in the world?. . . Art is the most expensive mistress." **Alan Bates,** as impressario Sergei Diaghilev, answers his own question. *Nijinsky* (1980, GB, Paramount).

508 "Business would adapt to art, not the other way around." Black opera singer **Wilhelmenia Wiggins Fernandez** refuses to make records, insisting that the only thing that counts is that special relationship between an artist and audience that can only occur in live performances. *Diva* (1982, Fr., United Artists Classics).

509 "The uglier the art, the more it's worth." Burglar **Cheech Marin** advises partner Tommy Chong on how to know what to steal when they break into an artist's studio. *After Hours* (1985, Warner Bros.).

510 "It closes in 15 minutes and there are 10,000 works of art to see." Ugly American **Chevy Chase** hurries his family into the Louvre for a little culture. *National Lampoon's European Vacation* (1985, Warner Bros.).

511 "Your country's one undeniable contribution to the arts. It concerns family, love, honor and courage—all that's noblest in the human spirit." **Joel Grey,** the elderly Korean mentor of intelligence agent Fred Ward, speaks of soap operas. *Remo Williams: The Adventure Begins* (1985, Orion).

512 "You're the first thing I've created in a really long time that makes me feel like an artist." Wouldbe sculptor **Andrew McCarthy** admires the department store window that he's designed and particularly the featured mannequin, who comes alive as the very lovely Kim Catrall. *Mannequin* (1987, 20th Century-Fox).

513 "I'm the world's first fully functioning homicidal artist." **Jack Nicholson,** as The Joker, knows himself well. *Batman* (1989, Warner Bros.).

514 "Remember when it was sent over here to tour all the museums? It never went back." **Penelope Ann Miller** assures Matthew Broderick that the "Mona Lisa" hanging over her Mafia boss father Marlon Brando's fireplace is the real McCoy. *The Freshman* (1990, Tri-Star).

515 "Anything can be a work of art. Sometimes you got to kill to create." Wealthy psychotic **Douglas Savant** is quite willing to steal and kill to help his artist idol Rick Rossovich, who specializes in scenes of sexual bondage. *Paint It Black* (1990, Vestron).

516 "I'd like you to meet the Olsen sisters who have made marrying well an art form." Wealthy **Richard Gere** introduces his kept-woman-for-a-week Julia Roberts to Lucinda Sue Crosby and Nancy Locke, who apparently have married often and to their advantage. *Pretty Woman* (1990, Buena Vista-Touchstone).

517 "Nobody in this town will admit that a producer is an artist." **Steve Martin**, the producer of extremely violent motion pictures, doesn't feel appreciated in Hollywood. *Grand Canyon* (1991, 20th Century-Fox).

518 "Go home. Paint something dead." **Judy Davis**, as writer George Sand, tires of her lover Ralph Brown, as artist Eugene Delacroix. *Impromptu* (1991, Hemdale).

Assessments

see also IMPORTANCE, PREDICTIONS, SIGNIFICANCE, TAXES, WORTH AND VALUES

519 "The most hard-boiled dame on the dirty white way." It's showgirl **Aline MacMahon**'s self-assessment. *Gold Diggers of 1933* (1933, Warner Bros.).

520 "I'm just a big, good-natured slob everybody thinks they can push around." Hulking cretinous killer **William Bendix** has himself pegged. *The Glass Key* (1942, Paramount).

521 "We could be having sand for supper." Passenger **Clifton Webb** makes a stiff upper lip response to a friend who questions whether the situation is serious after the new "unsinkable" luxury liner hits an iceberg. *Titanic* (1953, 20th Century-Fox).

522 "What I am is a 32-year-old, ugly, pockmarked Jew fairy, and if it takes me awhile to pull myself together, and I smoke a little grass before I get up the nerve to show my face to the world, it's nobody's goddamn business but my own." **Leonard Frey** arrives late for his birthday party, and is accused of being stoned and habitually late. *The Boys in the Band* (1970, National General).

523 "I'm about as flamboyant as a bagel." Timid Jewish **Maureen Teefy** is constantly hounded to excel by her pushy stage mother. *Fame* (1980, MGM-United Artists).

524 "I hate this Third World toilet." Small-time crook **Danny De Vito** makes an uncomplimentary assessment of the country of Colombia. *Romancing the Stone* (1984, 20th Century-Fox).

525 "You're scum, Frank, I knew that when I met you. You'll never change." Despite the fact that her assessment of Jack Nicholson is basically on target, **Jessica Lange** marries him a scene or two later. *The Postman Always Rings Twice* (1981, Lorimar-Paramount).

526 "Your mother hates your husband and she holds you in medium esteem." **Jeff Daniels** accurately assesses how much his mother-in-law Shirley MacLaine values him and his wife Debra Winger. *Terms of Endearment* (1983, Paramount).

527 "You got to have balls and you got to have brains. You got too much of one and not enough of the other." **Paul Newman** assesses his pool-hustling protégé Tom Cruise *The Color of Money* (1986, Touchstone).

528 "In this town I'm the leper with the most fingers." Private investigator **Jack Nicholson** has his problems, but he doesn't think he's as bad as his clients. *The Two Jakes* (1990, Paramount).

529 "Everybody thinks bikers are just dangerous, greasy dopeheads." We wonder what Roadmaster cyclist club member **James Belushi**'s complaint is? *Masters of Menace* (1991, Cinetel Films).

Assistance *see* GIFTS AND GIVING, HELP AND HELPING, INDEPENDENCE AND DEPENDENCE, SERVICES

Atheism and Atheists

see also BELIEFS, FAITH AND FAITHFULNESS, GOD, RELIGIONS

530 "I'm an atheist. Besides, I'm superstitious." Lost sheep **Porter Hall** resists the efforts of Bing Crosby, as Father O'Malley, to bring him back into the flock. *Going My Way* (1944, Paramount).

531 "Save us, God, and I'll give up being an atheist." With an offer like that, how can God refuse **Spike Milligan**'s prayer when atomic bombs destroy half of London. *The Bed Sitting Room* (1969, GB, United Artists).

532 "He was an atheist. I tried to beat God into him, but. . . ." **Henry Leff** confesses failure to make his son Woody Allen a believer. *Take the Money and Run* (1969, ABC).

533 "To you I'm an atheist, to God I'm the loyal opposition." Film director **Woody Allen** dismisses a studio executive who calls him an atheist. *Stardust Memories* (1980, United Artists).

Athletics and Athletes *see* COMPETITION, GAMES, PLAYING AND PLAYERS, SPORTS

Attention

see also CARES AND CARING, CONCERNS, CONSIDERATIONS

534 "How is Ashley today, Scarlett? He doesn't seem to be paying much attention to you." **Evelyn Keyes** gives her sister Vivien Leigh the needle about Leslie Howard at nap time after the barbecue at Twelve Oaks. *Gone with the Wind* (1939, Selznick-MGM).

535 "Pay no attention to the man behind the screen. . . the. . . er. . . the Great Oz has spoken!" **Frank Morgan** is exposed as a fraud when the dog Toto pulls aside the drape behind which Morgan is frantically pulling levers of an elaborate machine that projects the image of the Wizard of Oz to Judy Garland, Ray Bolger, Jack Haley and Bert Lahr. *The Wizard of Oz* (1939, MGM).

536 "You just seen me do a disgusting thing, but it got your attention." Disgusting president of Beautee Soap **Sydney Greenstreet** makes a point to his advertising advisors by spitting on a table. *The Hucksters* (1947, MGM).

537 "You try to look like an old lady and you're not. You shouldn't wear your hair like that. There are two kinds of women: those who pay too much attention to themselves and those who don't pay enough." **William Holden** makes it clear that plainly dressed Grace Kelly belongs to the second group. *The Country Girl* (1954, Paramount).

538 "Women adore small meaningless attentions like being helped with a coat." Married **Micheline Presle** will soon become the mistress of impover-

ished Dutch painter Hardy Kruger. *Blind Date* aka: *Chance Meeting* (1959, GB, Rank).

539 "Hell, man, I don't underrate him, I ignore him." Top black high school student **Brenda Sykes** is at first hesitant about the attentions of white youth John Nielson. *Honky* (1971, Harris).

540 "I will not be ignored." Married Michael Douglas finds it much harder to get rid of **Glenn Close** than to get into her bed. Come to think of it, they didn't spend much time in bed. *Fatal Attraction* (1987, Paramount).

541 "My Uncle Phil, while being one of the great men in garbage, has not always been so keen on personal hygiene. . . . So, I will now disrobe and play a Celtic classic ballad on my love flute." **Ted Danson**'s attempt to make a humorous toast at his uncle George Coe's wedding fails to get the attention of the assembled guests. *Cousins* (1989, Paramount).

Attractions

see also BEAUTY, CHARM, SEDUCTIONS, TEMPTATIONS

542 "Funny thing is, you are sort of attractive—in a corn-fed sort of way. I can see some poor girl falling for you if—well, if you threw in a set of dishes." **Bette Davis** teases local newspaper editor Richard Travis. *The Man Who Came to Dinner* (1941, Warner Bros.).

543 "Tell me why it is that every man who seems attractive these days is either married or barred on a technicality." **Celeste Holm** bemoans the lack of attractive available men. *Gentleman's Agreement* (1946, 20th Century-Fox).

544 "After the first 15 minutes, I knew I wanted to marry her. And after the first half hour, I totally gave up the idea of snatching her purse." Small-time crook **Woody Allen** recalls his first meeting with pretty laundress Janet Margolin. *Take the Money and Run* (1969, Palomar-Cinerama).

545 "I find I'm attracted to men." Doctor **Michael Ontkean** confesses to his TV executive wife Kate Jackson that he suspects he's gay. *Making Love* (1982, 20th Century-Fox).

546 "Wouldn't this be a great world if insecurity and desperation made us more attractive?" **Albert Brooks** asks a rhetorical question of Holly Hunter. *Broadcast News* (1987, 20th Century-Fox).

547 "Damn, but I'm attracted to strong-willed women." **Paul Newman**, as Louisiana governor Earl

Long, admires Lolita Davidovich as Blaze Starr. She's turned down his offer of a date, but he will persist and prevail. *Blaze* (1989, Touchstone).

548 "I don't know if it's just his body I'm attracted to or his soul. . . or if it's just me. . . . Oh, I'm feeling generally. . . attracted. . . . The truth is I'm so ripe I'm about to fall off the vine." **Cybill Shepherd** hasn't had sex since her husband died more than twenty years earlier. She is more than eager to reenter the fray with her reincarnated husband Robert Downey, Jr. *Chances Are* (1989, Tri-Star).

549 "My mom called me a bum-magnet; if there was a bum within a fifty-mile radius, I was completely attracted to him." Hooker **Julia Roberts** tells her sad story to "john" Richard Gere, who is something of a rich bum and will also use her. *Pretty Woman* (1990, Buena Vista-Touchstone).

550 "You know when I was alive, I would find her attractive." Despondent **Daniel Stern** admiringly eyes Helen Slater at a western ranch. *City Slickers* (1991, Columbia).

551 "Did you ever find Bugs Bunny attractive when he put on a dress and played a female?" It's a weird question to put to the title character Mike Myers by his strange sidekick **Dana Carvey**, as Garth. *Wayne's World* (1992, Paramount).

Authorities

see also INFLUENCES, LEADERSHIP AND LEADERS, OBEDIENCE, PERMISSIONS, POWER, RIGHTS, RULES

552 "You can't do that; you aren't authorized." The demon, possessing **Jack Magner**, complains when priest James Olsen shows up to perform an exorcism. *Amityville II: The Possession* (1982, Orion).

553 "We'll go after all of them. . . together. . . . You're going to teach me how. . . . Not only do I have the guts, I have the authority. . . . We nail them anyway we can, even your way. . . whatever it takes." But-toned-down FBI chief investigator **Willem Dafoe** tells good old boy lawman Gene Hackman that from now on they'll use any means whatever to nail those responsible for the murder of three civil rights workers. *Mississippi Burning* (1988, Orion).

554 "Now listen, boy. I was prepared to cut you a little slack because of Patty Jean; well, your time is up. So listen real good to what I'm going to tell you. This is my command here. You watch your mouth when you're here. Or I might cut off your balls and serve them for breakfast." Provost Marshal **Sean Connery** tells San Francisco police detective Mark Harmon in no uncertain terms who's running the show in the investigation of the killing of female MP Jenette Goldstein on the Frisco Presidio military installation. *The Presidio* (1988, Paramount).

555 "My boys have a real problem with authority—there's no telling what they'll do in this situation." Headmaster **Louis Gossett** worries about the teenage boys of a Virginia prep school. They are held hostage by Colombian terrorists who have seized control of the school. *Toy Soldiers* (1991, Tri-Star).

Authors *see* BOOKS, PLAYING AND PLAYERS, POETRY AND POETS, WRITING AND WRITERS

Automobiles

see also DRIVING AND DRIVERS, TRAVEL AND TRIPS

556 PETER WARNE: "Why don't you take all your clothes off? You could have stopped 40 cars." ELLIE ANDREWS: "We didn't need forty cars." **Clark Gable** is piqued because **Claudette Colbert**'s hitchhiking technique of pulling up her skirt and straightening the seams on her stocking got a car to stop and none of his inventive techniques worked. *It Happened One Night* (1934, Columbia).

557 "Automobiles are a useless nuisance. They'll never amount to anything but a nuisance. They had no business to be invented." At a dinner party **Tim Holt** not only makes another poor prediction, but he insults automobile inventor Joseph Cotten, the father of Anne Baxter, the girl Holt's trying to impress. *The Magnificent Ambersons* (1942, RKO).

558 ROSALIND: "All Ambrose seems to think about are that silly car and the other thing." WENDY: "My husband only thinks of the car." **Kay Kendall** remarks about her boyfriend Kenneth More, while **Dinah Sheridan** is speaking of her husband John Gregson. Both men are classic car freaks, but at least More still has some time for Kendall. *Genevieve* (1953, GB, General Film Distributors).

559 "I want you to check my motor. It whistles." Looking marvelous in tight short shorts, **Ann-Margret** gives orders to race car driver Elvis Presley, whom she mistakes for a garage mechanic. *Viva Las Vegas* (1964, MGM).

560 "Hey, boy, what you doin' with my momma's car?" **Faye Dunaway** yells the first line of the movie from her window to Warren Beatty, who's fixin' to steal her momma's car. *Bonnie and Clyde* (1967, Warner Bros.).

561 BONNIE PARKER: "Would you know what kind of a car this is?" C.W. MOSS: "Yeah, it's a Chevrolet 8-

cylinder coupe.' BONNIE: "No, no." C.W.: "Sure it is." BONNIE: "No, this is a stolen Chevrolet 8-cylinder coupe." **Faye Dunaway** impresses moronic service station mechanic **Michael J. Pollard.** *Bonnie and Clyde* (1967, Warner Bros.).

562 "That's it, race fans, a great day of racing. You've seen the greatest, both with cars and drivers. Turning into victory lane, Tommy Callahan, the winner. And here comes Johnny Reb carrying the traditional victory flag. And here is Tommy Callahan, the winner of the Southern Five Hundred." Race track announcer **Sandy Reed** welcomes Fabian to the winner's circle. *Thunder Alley* (1967, American International).

563 "Peel out! I just love it when boys peel out." Sexy blonde **Candy Clark** orders Charles Martin Smith to hit the gas and get his car moving fast. *American Graffiti* (1973, Universal).

564 "These days a man doesn't know if he's driving a car or an animal. Mustang, Jaguar, Cougar, Pinto.... Silly!... My first car was a Hudson... Henrik Hudson.... They should only name cars after explorers and rivers.... I'd love to drive a Mississippi... or an Amazon... a convertible Rio Grande... or an automatic Thames. A stickshift Yangtze...." Elderly **Art Carney** has most definite ideas about the names for makes of automobiles. *Harry and Tonto* (1974, 20th Century-Fox).

565 "It's a car, woman, not Lassie." **Harvey Korman** explodes at Cloris Leachman for treating her automobile as a pet. *Herbie Goes Bananas* (1980, United Artists).

566 "This is your car, man?... Looks like you bought it from one of the brothers." **Eddie Murphy** doesn't admire Nick Nolte's old beat-up powder-blue Cadillac convertible. *48 Hrs.* (1982, Paramount).

567 "Oh, man, there's nothing finer than being behind the wheel of your own car." Seventeen-year-old **Keith Gordon** is ecstatic as he barrels down a California highway. *Christine* (1983, Columbia).

568 "Could I borrow your towel? My car just hit a water buffalo!" **Chevy Chase** quips to buxom Dana Wheeler-Nicholson, who opens her door to him wearing only a towel. *Fletch* (1985, Universal).

569 "The whole world is choking in smog, and they are going to correct the situation by keeping my four cars off the road?" Hot-shot hustler **Tom Cruise** needs to sell four Lamborghinis to get the cash to bail himself out of the hole his former scams have put him in. Unfortunately for him, the cars don't have smog controls and he can't get them off the ship. *Rain Man* (1988, MGM-Universal).

570 "Volvos: They're boxy but good." Fed-up with writing exaggerating ads, top advertising executive **Dudley Moore** decides to tell the truth with candid ads. *Crazy People* (1990, Paramount).

Availability

see also EASE AND EASINESS, OPPORTUNITIES

571 "I'm hard to get—all you have to do is ask me." Wise-cracking **Jean Arthur** pronounces her availability to hard-boiled Cary Grant, chief pilot of a broken down mail and freight service in Peru. *Only Angels Have Wings* (1939, Columbia).

572 "Available? You're like an old coat that's hanging in his closet. Every time he reaches in, there you are. Don't be there once." **Joan Blondell** tells Katharine Hepburn that she makes things go easy for her sometime beau Gig Young. *Desk Set* (1957, 20th Century-Fox).

573 "She's very good in this picture. She's going to attract a lot of attention. She's got what I call, uh—it's a quality of availability. She's not particularly pretty. It's—a warmth some women have. It makes every man in the audience think he can make her if he only knew her." **Bert Freed** describes Kim Stanley's screen appeal. Most every male that meets her does make her. *The Goddess* (1958, Columbia).

574 "Well, as a matter of fact, I'm waiting for you to drive me up to London, because by a fabulous coincidence I've got the evening off." Dr. **Dirk Bogarde** just happens to be available for an evening with Samantha Eggar. *Doctor in Distress* (1963, GB, Rank).

575 "Benjamin—I want you to know I'm available to you. If you won't sleep with me this time.... If you won't sleep with me this time, Benjamin, I want you to know you can call me up any time you want, and we'll make some arrangement." In a very business-like way, **Anne Bancroft**, as Mrs. Robinson, propositions recent college graduate Dustin Hoffman. *The Graduate* (1967, United Artists).

576 "He could climb all over me any time." Art student **Candice Rialson** dreamily announces her availability for her mountain-climbing professor Clint Eastwood. *The Eiger Sanction* (1975, Universal).

Awards

see also COMPETITION, CONTESTS, GIFTS AND GIVING, HONOR, PAYMENTS

577 "This is the dining hall of the Sarah Siddons Society. The occasion is its annual banquet and presentation of the highest honor our theater knows—

the Sarah Siddons Award for Distinguished Achievement. . . . The minor awards have already been presented. . . their function is to construct a tower so the world can applaud a light which flashes on top of it, and no brighter light has ever dazzled the eye than Eve Harrington. Eve. But more of Eve later. All about Eve, in fact." Narrator **George Sanders** sets the stage for a flashback in the opening scene. *All About Eve* (1950, 20th Century-Fox).

578 "He crawled into a hole for a story and crawled out with a Pulitzer Prize." Reporter **Kirk Douglas** thinks maybe he can be as lucky with a story about a man trapped in a cave as another reporter was with a man trapped in a mine. *Ace in the Hole* aka: *The Big Carnival* (1951, Paramount).

579 "'Order of the Palm. To Lt. (J.G.) Douglas Roberts for action against the enemy, above and beyond the call of duty.'" Medical officer **William Powell** reads the citation that goes along with the farewell award to Henry Fonda, who has tossed hated captain James Cagney's palm tree overboard. *Mister Roberts* (1955, Warner Bros.).

580 "It gives me great pleasure to award this air medal, which through a regrettable error was previously awarded posthumously to Private Benjamin B. Whitledge, U.S. Army Infantry." Major General **Howard Smith** pins a medal on Nick Adams, who with sidekick Andy Griffith, fell from a plane and was presumed killed. *No Time for Sergeants* (1958, Warner Bros.).

581 "You finally made it, Frankie—Oscar night. And here you sit—on top of a glass mountain called success. You are one of the chosen five—and the whole town's holding its breath to see who'll win it. Been quite a climb, hasn't it, Frankie? Down at the bottom—scuffing for dimes at the 'smokers'—all the way to the top. Ever think about it? I do, friend Frankie, I do." Narrator **Tony Bennett** sits in the audience on the night of the Academy Awards, where his selfish friend Stephen Boyd is a nominee. It's time for a flashback, but everyone knows what the climactic scene will be. In his acting debut, Bennett proved he should stick to singing. *The Oscar* (1966, Paramount).

582 "They give awards for everything. For the World's Biggest Fascist—Adolf Hitler!" **Woody Allen** is upset when he learns that his ex-lover Diane Keaton's new lover, Paul Simon, has been nominated for Grammy Awards. *Annie Hall* (1977, United Artists).

583 "When it comes to relationships with women, I'm the winner of the August Strindberg Award." **Woody Allen** likens himself to the misogynist

Swedish novelist and playwright. *Manhattan* (1979, United Artists).

Babies

see also BIRTHS AND BIRTHDAYS, BOYS, CHILDREN AND CHILDHOOD, FATHERS, GIRLS, MOTHERS, PARENTS, YOUTH

584 "I would do anything for a quart of milk for my baby." War widow **Lillian Gish**'s title card explains why she is forced to work briefly as a prostitute. *The Enemy* (1927, Silent, MGM).

585 CONNIE BAILEY: "Is great big stwong man going to show little icky baby all about the bad football signals?" PROFESSOR WAGSTAFF: "If icky girl keep talking that way, big stwong man is going to kick her teeth wight down her thwoat." College widow **Thelma Todd** unsuccessfully uses baby talk to induce **Groucho Marx** to let her get her hands on his college football team's plays. *Horse Feathers* (1932, Paramount).

586 "Yes, I know what you mean. And some people were born to have a baby." Despite being told she was born to sing, successful opera diva **Lily Pons** slows down her career to start a family. *I Dream Too Much* (1935, RKO).

587 "Ah don' know nothin' 'bout birthin' babies." Despite her previously proclaimed expertise in delivering children, **Butterfly McQueen**, as Prissy, comes apart when it's time for Olivia de Havilland to have her child. *Gone with the Wind* (1939, Selznick-MGM).

588 "The happiest days are when babies come." **Olivia de Havilland** shares joy with Hattie McDaniel after the birth of Clark Gable and Vivien Leigh's baby girl. *Gone with the Wind* (1939, Selznick-MGM).

589 "I watched you with that baby—that other woman's baby. You looked—well, nice." Revenge-minded cowpoke **John Wayne** admires Claire Trevor, a shady lady with a heart of gold. *Stagecoach* (1939, United Artists).

590 "I congratulate you and wish you have babies, not phobias." Psychiatrist **Michael Chekhov** greets his student Ingrid Bergman and her new "husband" Gregory Peck. *Spellbound* (1945, United Artists).

591 "Believe you me, if it didn't take men to make babies I wouldn't have anything to do with any of you!" **Gena Rowlands** dismisses the male gender as she talks to her jailed husband's old friend Kirk Douglas. *Lonely Are the Brave* (1962, Universal).

592 "Well, if you're going to have a baby, I guess I better get married." When **Frank Sinatra** discovers his ex-wife Deborah Kerr is pregnant with their baby, he proposes that they re-marry, as soon as she can get a quicky divorce from Sinatra's best friend Dean Martin. *Marriage on the Rocks* (1965, MGM).

593 "I just don't understand it, Daddy. This little baby has to winky-tink all the time." Playing the helpless female, **Madeline Kahn** apologizes to Ryan O'Neal for her need of frequent pit stops as they motor along. The conversation just about turns young Tatum O'Neal's stomach. *Paper Moon* (1973, Paramount).

594 RICHARD: "Why do you have a baby?" EMMELINE: "I don't know." Shipwrecked at seven, teenagers **Christopher Atkins** and **Brooke Shields** have learned copulation—but haven't a clue of its link to their baby. *The Blue Lagoon* (1980, Columbia).

595 "Babies come from when an angel lights on their mother's chest and whispers into her ear. That makes good babies start to grow. Bad babies come from when a fallen angel squeezes in down there and they grow and grow until they come out down there. I don't know where good babies come from." Naïve novice nun **Meg Tilly** demonstrates her ignorance of sex. *Agnes of God* (1985, Columbia).

596 "The book says to feed the baby every two hours, but do you count from when you start, or when you finish? It takes me two hours to get her to eat, and by the time she's done, it's time to start again, so that I'm feeding her all the time." Bachelor **Tom Selleck** makes a case for breast feeding babies. *Three Men and a Baby* (1987, Touchstone).

597 "A dingow stole mah bibey!" That's what it sounds like **Meryl Streep** is saying with her Australian accent. She claims a wild Australian dog has carried off her baby. *A Cry in the Dark* (1988, Warner Bros.).

598 "I want to keep my baby." It's the predictable decision of unwed **Mary Stuart Masterson** who had agreed to allow childless couple Glenn Close and James Woods adopt her baby. *Immediate Family* (1989, Columbia).

599 "It's smart to have babies when you're young—before you get funky." X-ray technician **Joan Cusack**, who has no children, congratulates Jessica Lange who has two, including 16-year-old Chris O'Donnell, whom Cusack is sleeping with. *Men Don't Leave* (1990, Warner Bros.).

Bachelors

see also MARRIAGES, SPINSTERS, WEDDINGS, WIDOWS

600 OXENSTIERNA: "You cannot die an old maid." CHRISTINA: "I have no intention to. I shall die a bachelor." Swedish chancellor **Lewis Stone** isn't reassured by Swedish queen **Greta Garbo**, who believes it necessary that she be as much like a man as possible. *Queen Christina* (1933, MGM).

601 "In me you see a youth who is completely on the loose. No yens. No strings. No connections. No ties to my affections." **Fred Astaire** scoffs at the notion that he should marry, preferring his bachelorhood—but then he meets Ginger Rogers. *Top Hat* (1935, RKO).

602 "This is a bachelor establishment. It means that I don't like women about the place. I promised myself that no woman should ever enter it." Crippled and charismatic **James Mason** breaks his promise to himself by taking in talented musician Ann Todd as his ward. *The Seventh Veil* (1946, GB, GFD-Universal).

603 "Ma, when you gonna give up? You got a bachelor on your hands. I ain't never gonna get married. Whatever it is that women like, I ain't got it. . . I'm a fat, little man. . . . All that ever happened to me was girls made me feel like I was a bug." **Ernest Borgnine** pleads with his mother, Esther Minciotti, to accept that he will never find a woman to marry. *Marty* (1955, United Artists).

Badness

see also EVILNESS, GOOD AND EVIL (BAD), GOODNESS, GUILT, HARM, WRONGS AND WRONGDOINGS

604 "You're a bad boy." **Maureen O'Sullivan**, as Jane, scolds her playful and immature mate, Johnny Weissmuller, as Tarzan. *Tarzan and His Mate* (1934, MGM).

605 "You're in probably the wickedest, most corrupt, most Godless city in America. Sometimes it frightens me and I wonder what the end is going to be. But nothing can harm you if you don't allow it to. Because nothing in the world. . .no one is all bad." San Francisco priest **Spencer Tracy** mouths a few platitudes to Jeanette MacDonald and supplies a moral justification for the coming earthquake, all at the same time. *San Francisco* (1936, MGM).

606 "There isn't any such thing in the world as a bad boy. . .but a boy left alone, frightened, bewildered. . .the wrong hand reaches for him. . .he needs a friend. . . that's all he needs." The wisdom of Father Flanagan, portrayed by **Spencer Tracy**, is probably still operational today—but who will offer the right hand of friendship to the many boys with no good male role models? *Boys Town* (1938, MGM).

607 "She's a bad little girl and you should have known it." Wise old **Lionel Barrymore** chides Lew Ayres for allowing Lana Turner to seduce him. *Calling Dr. Kildare* (1939, MGM).

608 "We've got it badly, little dog, just as bad as we could get it." London artist **Ronald Colman** movingly speaks to his pet when he learns of his impending blindness. *The Light That Failed* (1939, Paramount).

609 "There are worse things than Apaches." Saloon girl **Claire Trevor** shows a bit of leg as she climbs aboard a stagecoach after being run out of town by the "decent" folks of the western town of Tonto. *Stagecoach* (1939, United Artists).

610 "Give a bad boy enough rope and he'll soon make a jackass of himself." Just to make the coachman's (voice of **Charles Judels**) assertion clear, the naughty boy Lampwick (voice of Frankie Darro) becomes a jackass and the title character (voice of Dickie Jones) just about makes it. *Pinocchio* (1940, Disney-RKO).

611 "I'm a baaad boy!" It's the wail of **Lou Costello** in several movies. *Hold That Ghost* (1941, Universal) is one.

612 "I haven't lived a good life—I've been bad." Looking for sympathy from Humphrey Bogart, **Mary Astor** makes an understated confession. *The Maltese Falcon* (1941, Warner Bros.).

613 "Things are much worse than they led me to believe." Bette Davis' callous mother **Gladys Cooper** has a negative reaction the first time she sees Davis transformed by psychiatry from a neurotic ugly duckling into a self-assured attractive young woman. *Now, Voyager* (1942, Warner Bros.).

614 "When we were married, Babe, the Justice of the Peace said something about 'for richer, for poorer, for better, for worse.' Remember? Well, this is the worse." Ever since **Dana Andrews** was mustered out of the Air Force, he's been fighting with his party-girl wife Virginia Mayo. She doesn't share his desire to settle down and have a "normal" life. *The Best Years of Our Lives* (1946, Goldwyn-RKO).

615 "That doesn't mean she's bad. Quite a number of respectable citizens get drunk and do silly things.

They're bad habits, like biting one's nails, but I don't know that they're worse than that. I call a person bad who lies and cheats and is unkind." Speaking to Gene Tierney, **Herbert Marshall**, as actor Somerset Maugham, may be morally correct that Anne Baxter isn't really bad, but he shouldn't understate her illness. She's a total lush. *The Razor's Edge* (1946, 20th Century-Fox).

616 ANN: "She can't be all bad—no one is." JEFF: "She comes the closest." **Virginia Huston** and **Robert Mitchum** are discussing double-dealing and triple-crossing femme fatale Jane Greer—a beauty almost worth the pain she causes the men in her life. *Out of the Past* (1947, RKO).

617 DADIER: "These kids, they can't be all bad. Can they?" MURDOCK: "No? Why?" On his first day of teaching at North Manual High School, **Glenn Ford** hears from experienced teacher **Louis Calhern** just how incorrigible the students are. *The Blackboard Jungle* (1955, MGM).

618 "Getting married! That'd be worse than living at the Club. I'd hate to start by getting in by one o'clock again." When Tom Ewell suggests she might get married, **Marilyn Monroe** compares the institution to the YMCA-like women's club she used to call home and hated. *The Seven Year Itch* (1955, 20th Century-Fox).

619 "We're two of a kind. Both bad." Mayor's secretary **Arlene Dahl** believes that she and John Payne, the leader of a criminal gang, are a good match. *Slightly Scarlet* (1956, RKO).

620 "Johnny, have you been bad with girls?" Teenage virgin **Sandra Dee** questions her boyfriend Troy Donahue about his behavior. *A Summer Place* (1959, Warner Bros.).

621 FREDERICK: "What a filthy job." IGOR: "It could be worse." FREDERICK: "How?" IGOR: "It could be raining." As soon as this conversation between grave robbers **Gene Wilder** and **Marty Feldman** concludes, the rains come. *Young Frankenstein* (1974, 20th Century-Fox).

622 "There are worse things than death. If you ever spent an evening with an insurance salesman, you know exactly what I mean." **Woody Allen** bravely faces death with a quip on his lips. *Love and Death* (1975, United Artists).

623 "I was going to the worst place in the world—and I didn't even know it." Military assassin **Martin Sheen** provides voice-over narration at the beginning of the film. *Apocalypse Now* (1979, United Artists).

624 "How bad does he have to be, Carla?" **Meryl Streep** questions a fearful black politician about a nominee for the Supreme Court, known for his segregationist stance. The black politician claims the prospective jurist "isn't so bad." *The Seduction of Joe Tynan* (1979, Universal).

625 "I'm getting bad." **Richard Pryor** gives a spasmodic imitation of one mean cool dude the first time he walks down a cell block corridor past hardened cons. *Stir Crazy* (1980, Columbia).

626 ARTHUR: "You know the worst part of me?" HOBSON: "I imagine your breath." Drunk **Dudley Moore** plays straight man to his valet **John Gielgud.** *Arthur* (1981, Orion).

627 "You think I'm bad. I am, and I know it, but I love you and I need you." It's difficult for William Hurt not to be impressed with **Kathleen Turner**'s sincerity as she writhes nakedly on his body. *Body Heat* (1981, Warner Bros.).

628 "Bad comes from bad." **Stacy Keach** responds when Pia Zadora, who has been trying to seduce him, claims she's his long-lost daughter. *Butterfly* (1981, Vestron).

629 HARRIET "HARRY" PURDUE: "We don't have many bad guys out here, lieutenant." RUBEN CASTLE: "Lady, there are bad guys everywhere." Tough feminist Colorado sheriff **JoBeth Williams** has a different perspective than retired New York cop **Robert Urich.** *Endangered Species* (1982, MGM-United Artists).

630 "You need people like me so you can point your fucking fingers and say 'That's the bad guy.'" Cuban Miami mobster **Al Pacino** defiantly insists he's necessary so people can distinguish good from bad. *Scarface* (1983, Universal).

631 ELI LAPP: "You know these bad men by sight? You are able to look in their hearts and see this badness?" SAMUEL: "I can see what they do. . . I have seen it." ELI: "And having seen, you become one of them. . . what you take in your hands, you take in your heart." Amish elder **Jan Rubes** tells his young grandson **Lukas Haas** that using a gun to kill is never justified. *Witness* (1985, Paramount).

632 "Blues ain't nothin' but a good man feelin' bad." Veteran blues singer and harp player **Joe Seneca**'s definition of blues seems just about perfect. *Crossroads* (1986, Columbia).

633 "You're either a romantic fool or an idiot. I don't know which is worse." Assault victim **Elizabeth McGovern** is amazed by architect Steve Gut-

tenberg. He has been discredited as a witness to her attempted murder, and is now suspected of the crime himself. Guttenberg was trying to protect his married lover Isabelle Huppert who actually witnessed the attack. *The Bedroom Window* (1987, De Laurentiis).

634 "I'm not bad. I'm just drawn that way." **Kathleen Turner**, as the voice of toon Jessica Rabbit, seductively seeks understanding from private eye Bob Hoskins. *Who Framed Roger Rabbit?* (1988, Touchstone).

635 "After the plague, things really got bad." These are the opening words of a post-apocalyptic piece of trash. *Cyborg* (1989, Cannon).

636 OLIVER ROSE: "No one who makes paté this good can be all bad." BARBARA ROSE: "It depends upon what the paté is made of." This exchange during a brief lull in the fighting of married couple **Michael Douglas** and **Kathleen Turner** is made more interesting when Douglas wonders about the whereabouts of his beloved dog and Turner smiles meaningfully. *The War of the Roses* (1989, 20th Century-Fox).

637 "I may be a lawyer, or I may be a thief—I don't know which is worse—but there are some things I will not do." Criminal defense lawyer and criminal mastermind **Andrew Stevens** risks his life to prevent some microfilm detailing special features of a top secret American jet from falling into enemy hands. *Down the Drain* (1990, Trans World).

Balance *see* EQUALITIES, COMPROMISES

Ballet *see* DANCING AND DANCERS

Banks *see* BUSINESS AND COMMERCE, MONEY, WEALTH AND RICHES

Baptism

see also BABIES, RELIGIONS

638 "Would you all like to have a mate like this? The treasures of the world are yours. In the blood of Sheila Barton, I baptize this sword." **Boris Karloff**, as Fu Manchu, stands over the white-gowned seductive body of Karen Morley bound to a sacrificial table. As he speaks, hundreds of his followers look on. He raises the ancient saber of Genghis Khan above the body of Morley, and then—. *The Mask of Fu Manchu* (1932, MGM).

639 NATALIO CURRO: "I understand Gallardo has one more contract to fulfill. I predict he will make an exit in a cloud of rotten oranges and dead cats!. . . the trouble with Gallardo is he has cats in his belly. His father was the same way. Like father, like son." JUAN GALLARDO: "That's the second time you've said things about my father. As for you, you've probably never been baptized. Well, I baptize you now! I christen you liar—and your second name is swine." Bullfight critic **Laird Cregar** is unaware that matador **Tyrone Power** is present to hear his insults. Power pours a bottle of wine into Laird's sputtering face. *Blood and Sand* (1941, 20th Century-Fox).

640 "I'm going to be baptized, damn it." With the film's final line, **William Powell** resignedly lets his wife Irene Dunne hustle him off to be baptized. *Life with Father* (1947, Warner Bros.).

Barbarians *see* ALIENS, CIVILIZATIONS, FOREIGNERS, MANNERS, SAVAGERY

Bargains

see also AGREEMENTS, COMPROMISES, COSTS, DEALS AND DEALINGS, EXPECTATIONS, MONEY, OFFERS, PRICES

641 "You're willing to pay a thousand dollars a night just for singing? Why you can get a phonograph record of 'Minnie the Moocher' for 75 cents. For a buck and a quarter you can get Minnie." **Groucho Marx** is shocked at the fee Margaret Dumont is willing to pay egotistical opera singer Walter Woolf King. *A Night at the Opera* (1935, MGM).

642 "Let you have them both for tuppence. They'd make a lovely pie, you know." Happy rat-catcher **Patrick Troughton** offers a pair of sleek rodents for sale. The locale of the famous horror story has been shifted from Paris to London. *The Phantom of the Opera* (1962, Universal-International-Hammer).

643 "Did you ever see so many men in raincoats looking for a bargain?" It's a question of a proprietor of an adult bookstore who is having a Beethoven's Birthday Sale. *Soup for One* (1982, Warner Bros.).

644 "Leave the blanket here and I'll advance all your allowances until you're forty." **William Petersen** bargains with his young daughter Katie Murray to leave her security blanket at home as they prepare to leave for a family wedding. *Cousins* (1989, Paramount).

645 "If I help you, Clarice, it will be turns for us, too. Quid pro quo. I tell you things, you tell me things. Not about the case, though. About yourself. Quid pro quo. Yes or no, Clarice? Poor little Cather-ine is waiting." **Anthony Hopkins**, as "Hannibal the Cannibal," offers a dangerous deal to FBI trainee Jodie Foster. He will help her capture a serial killer before he slaughters his latest victim if she will share her deepest secrets and fears with him. *The Silence of the Lambs* (1991, Orion).

Baseball *see* GAMES, PLAYING AND PLAYERS, SPORTS

Bashfulness *see* HUMILITY AND HUMILIATION, MODESTY

Basketball *see* GAMES, PLAYING AND PLAYERS, SPORTS

Bathing and Bathrooms

see also BODIES, CLEANLINESS, ROOMS, WATER

646 "Not since I tripped and fell into the sewer." Dirty, foul-smelling charlatan **John Barrymore** answers when asked when he last took a bath. *Svengali* (1931, Warner Bros.).

647 PEARL: "Your bath is ready, Miss Lou." LADY LOU: "You take it. I'm indisposed." Maid **Louise Beavers** interrupts **Mae West** as she's hungrily eyeing Gilbert Roland. *She Done Him Wrong* (1933, Paramount).

648 JOAN MAITLAND: "I must take my bath." TERRY RANDALL: "That might help." Theatrical boarding house resident **Ginger Rogers**' plans make her roommate **Katherine Hepburn**'s day. *Stage Door*. (1937, RKO).

649 "And another thing, I think this bathroom is perfectly ridiculous! Good night, Crystal." Young **Virginia Weidler** gets in the only shot she can think of as she leaves her stepmother Joan Crawford luxuriating in a bubble bath in an ornate bathroom. *The Women* (1939, MGM).

650 "Hot water is provided every day between the hours of two-thirty and six. When you take a bath, please sign the book behind the bedroom door." **Joyce Grenfell** firmly informs guests of the rules for bathing at her country hotel. *Genevieve* (1953, GB, GFD).

651 "Where's the little comrade's room?" Russian emissary **Cyd Charisse** asks Fred Astaire for directions to the bathroom. *Silk Stockings* (1957, MGM).

652 "She was better off in the bathroom. You hear me? Better off in the bathroom." **Walter Matthau** booms at his wife Lee Grant about their daughter Jennie Sullivan, who has finally been induced to come out of a locked bathroom on her wedding day by her long-haired groom Tom Carey. *Plaza Suite* (1971, Paramount).

653 "I don't want my brother coming out of that toilet with just his dick in his hand." **James Caan** instructs Richard Castellano to be certain that a gun is hidden in the men's room of a restaurant where Al Pacino is to have a meeting with the family's enemies, Al Lettieri and Sterling Hayden. *The Godfather* (1972, Paramount).

654 ARTHUR: "I think I'll take a bath." HOBSON: "I'll alert the media." **Dudley Moore**'s announcement generates sarcasm from his valet **John Gielgud**. *Arthur* (1981, Orion).

655 "I'm going to take a bath." Quick, here comes the smut! For those who paid their money hoping to see beautiful **Bo Derek** in the nude, their wait is over. *Tarzan, the Ape Man* (1981, MGM-United Artists).

656 "When I was growing up and we wanted a Jacuzzi, we had to fart in the tub." Street hustler **Eddie Murphy** admires his new bathroom when his life is switched with that of stockbroker Dan Aykroyd. *Trading Places* (1983, Paramount).

657 "I think about you when I go to the bathroom." Fourteen-year-old **Martha Plimpton** whispers seductively to her would-be boyfriend River Phoenix. *The Mosquito Coast* (1986, Warner Bros.).

658 MAUREEN: "I'm afraid I did leave the bathroom a mess." NORMAN BATES: "I've seen it worse." **Anthony Perkins** makes a sick in-joke out of **Diana Scarwid**'s apology. *Psycho III* (1986, Universal).

659 "He climbed on top of me and went to the bathroom." **Caroline Aaron** relates to her brother Woody Allen the disgusting result of a disastrous date with a man she met through a personal ad. *Crimes and Misdemeanors* (1989, Orion).

660 "Oh, Peter, the most awful thing has happened. The bathtub tried to eat Oscar." **Sigourney Weaver** reports to Bill Murray what almost happened to her baby in the bathroom of her weird apartment. *Ghostbusters II* (1989, Columbia).

661 "One bathroom for nine people, yes!" It's fluttery, spoiled **Shelley Long**'s response when macho Betty Thomas asks if Long believes camping at the Beverly Hills Hilton is roughing it. *Troop Beverly Hills* (1989, Weintraub).

662 "Gimme a buck and I'll let you watch my sister take a bath." **Danny Nucci** knows how to make a dollar. *Book of Love* (1991, New Line).

Battles and Battlefields

see also BRAVERY, DEATH AND DYING, HEROES, KILLINGS, MILITARY STRUGGLES, SURRENDER, VICTORIES, WARS, WINNERS AND LOSERS

663 "I can't call off the war now. I've paid a month's rent on the battlefield." Fredonia's president **Groucho Marx** figures he's invested too much to stop a war with neighboring Sylvania. *Duck Soup* (1933, Paramount).

664 "So after two hundred and forty-two days ended the siege of Tobruk. Not the biggest action of the war and far from the last one but one in which a sweating, dirty, hopelessly outnumbered garrison by its stubborn courage won for itself an unforgettable place in the world's history of battles." Narrator **Michael Rennie** speaks of the valiant men of the 9th Australian division who held off Rommel's Africa Corps. *The Desert Rats* (1953, 20th Century-Fox).

665 "All Americans love the sting of battle. That's why we never lost a war. . . . We're going to go through the enemy like crap through a goose." General George S. Patton, brilliantly portrayed by **George C. Scott**, would have hated the Korean Peace Keeping Mission and the Vietnam War. He does know his geese, however. *Patton* (1970, 20th Century-Fox).

666 "The creepy thing about battle is you always feel alone." Foot-soldier narrator **Robert Carradine** mentions the most frightening thing about wartime battles. *The Big Red One* (1980, United Artists).

Beards *see* FACE, HAIR, MEN

Beasts *see* ANIMALS, MONSTERS

Beatings *see* CORRECTIONS, DISCIPLINE, PUNISHMENTS, TORTURES

Beauty

see also APPEARANCES, ATTRACTIONS, CHARM, GLAMOUR, GOODNESS, LIVES AND LIVING, LOVE AND HATE, LOVE AND LOVERS, MEN, MEN AND WOMEN, PERFECTION, STYLES, UGLINESS, WOMEN

667 "Her beauty, so long hidden, shines out of her like a poem." A title card refers to lovely Lillian Gish. *Broken Blossoms* (1919, silent, United Artists).

668 "You're the most beautiful woman I've ever seen, which doesn't say much for you." **Groucho Marx** cracks wise to flustered Margaret Dumont. *Animal Crackers* (1930, Paramount).

669 "Her mother was pretty too, and what did it bring her but disgrace?" **Theodore von Eltz** speaks of his farm girl niece Greta Garbo. *Susan Lenox, Her Fall and Rise* (1931, MGM).

670 "Helen, you're becoming more beautiful every day. What are we going to do about it?" Bank president **Walter Huston** innocently teases his secretary Constance Cummings. Today, it might be considered sexual harassment. *American Madness* (1932, Columbia).

671 "I'd like to take you in my arms. I've never seen anything in my life as beautiful as you are. . . . Let me stay for just a little while." Hotel thief **John Barrymore** instantly falls in love with suicidal, internationally famous ballerina Greta Garbo when she discovers him in her room. *Grand Hotel* (1932, MGM).

672 JANE PARKER: "It's beautiful. Solemn and beautiful. We shouldn't be here." HARRY HOLT: "It's riches. Millions." When their safari arrives at the elephants' graveyard where the tusks and skeletons of hundreds of pachyderms are scattered across an immense plateau, **Maureen O'Sullivan** and **Neil Hamilton** react differently. *Tarzan, the Ape Man* (1932, MGM).

673 "Some hard-boiled egg gets a look at a pretty face and he cracks up and goes sappy." Promoter **Robert Armstrong** avoids intimate liaisons because he fears that the siren song of women will strip him of his masculinity. *King Kong* (1933, RKO).

674 "Oh, no, it wasn't the airplanes. It was beauty killed the beast." **Robert Armstrong** insists that the giant ape's death was a direct result of his concern for Fay Wray. The airplanes which shot him down from the top of the Empire State Building were merely instruments of his execution. *King Kong* (1933, RKO).

675 "Your beauty, Madame, is exceeded only by your wit." **Reginald Owen**, as King Louis XV of France, pays Doris Kenyon, as Mme de Pompadour, a double compliment. *Voltaire* (1933, Warner Bros.).

676 "I couldn't beat him—he was just too pretty." Title character **Barbara Stanwyck** explains why she deliberately let sharpshooter Preston Foster beat her. *Annie Oakley* (1935, RKO).

677 "Mirror , mirror, on the wall, who is the fairest of them all?" The wicked queen, voice of **Lucille La Verne**, is about to get a shock from her truthful magic mirror. *Snow White and the Seven Dwarfs* (1937, Disney-RKO).

678 MAN: "What a beautiful structure!" PEACHES: "Hey, cut that out! People'll think you know me." **Johnny Arthur** refers to the Brooklyn Bridge, but **Mae West** acts as if he's speaking of her. *Every Day's a Holiday* (1938, Paramount).

679 "You're pretty enough for all normal purposes." **Beulah Bondi** assures her daughter Martha Scott about her looks. *Our Town* (1940, Principal Artists).

680 "You're prettier than a little white kitten with a ribbon on it." Western conman **Clark Gable**, compliments Lana Turner, or is he conning her? *Honky Tonk* (1940, MGM).

681 "Mademoiselle, I was informed you were the most beautiful woman ever to visit Casablanca. That is a gross understatement." French Police Prefect **Claude Rains** flatters all the ladies, but with Ingrid Bergman, we feel he means it. *Casablanca* (1942, Warner Bros.).

682 CLEM MINIVER: "You're quite a beautiful woman." KAY MINIVER: "If you say so, darling." **Walter Pidgeon** expresses appreciation for his modest wife **Greer Garson**'s looks. *Mrs. Miniver* (1942, MGM).

683 "You are very beautiful. You corrupt and destroy men. When the evil is cut out of a beautiful thing only the beauty remains." **Laird Cregar** outlines the lofty goal of his mission of murdering beautiful women to an uncomprehending Merle Oberon. *The Lodger* (1944, 20th Century-Fox).

684 "Job says a woman is beautiful only when she is loved." This observation is one of the few things said by her dull businessman husband Claude Rains, to which selfish beauty **Bette Davis** pays any mind. *Mr. Skeffington* (1944, Warner Bros.).

685 AUGUSTIN HAUSSY: "Madame, you're very beautiful. I mean. . . beautiful!" CLIO DULAINE: "Yes, isn't it lucky?" When **Curt Bois** pays half-creole, illegitimate gold-digger **Ingrid Bergman** a compliment, she knows how to receive it. *Saratoga Trunk* (1945, Warner Bros.).

686 CISCO KID: "You are as beautiful as a butterfly." JEANNE DU BOIS: "Are you always so sure of yourself?" CISCO KID: "Always." **Gilbert Roland** leans across a breakfast table to kiss **Ramsay Ames**, who reveals herself as a woman posing as a man. *Beauty and the Bandit* (1946, Monogram).

687 "She had a homely beauty." If one recalls that "homely" means simple and unpretentious, **Tom Neal**'s assessment of despicable Ann Savage is accurate. *Detour* (1946, Producers Releasing Corporation).

688 "Whether by nature or by art, you never make a gesture without imparting beauty to it." **Herbert Marshall**, as W. Somerset Maugham, compliments Gene Tierney. *The Razor's Edge* (1946, 20th Century-Fox).

689 "You counted on your beauty with guys, even ones you were going to kill." Cargo plane pilot **Alan Ladd** accuses fragile but dangerous beauty Gail Russell of being a real femme fatale. *Calcutta* (1947, Paramount).

690 "Physical beauty is passing—a transitory possession—but beauty of the mind, richness of the spirit, tenderness of the heart—I have all these things—aren't taken away but grow! Increase with the years." Fading beauty **Vivien Leigh** desperately tries to convince herself that she's not getting older, she's getting better. *A Streetcar Named Desire* (1951, Warner Bros.).

691 "You're beautiful when you're angry." Dutch intelligence officer **Clark Gable** delivers a tired cliché to **Lana Turner.** *Betrayed* (1954, MGM).

692 BORTAI: "For me, there is no peace while you live, Mongrel!" TEMUJIN: "You're beautiful in your wrath! I shall keep you, Bortai! I shall keep you, and, in responding to my passions, your hatred will kindle into love." Even though **Susan Hayward** tries to kill him, **John Wayne** thinks she's awful cute when she's mad. Wayne really mangles the declaration. He then rapes Hayward, although as she beats at him, she is overcome with passion and finally willingly gives herself to Duke the Barbarian. *The Conqueror* (1956, RKO).

693 "What beautiful men!" Having never seen any men other than her father, **Anne Francis**, as Altaira, gushes when she first encounters newcomers to her planet Altair-4. *Forbidden Planet* (1956, MGM).

694 "Don't be afraid—look! You'll see a pretty woman, Lizzie. Lizzie, you gotta be your own lookin' glass. And then one day the lookin' glass will be the man who loves you. It'll be his eyes, maybe. And you'll look in that mirror and you'll be more than pretty—you'll be beautiful." Traveling western conman **Burt Lancaster** tries to make plain spinster Katharine Hepburn believe in her attractiveness. *The Rainmaker* (1956, Paramount).

695 "Fats, you're beautiful. All pink. . . just like a baby." Pool hustler **Paul Newman** admires Jackie Gleason as pool-great Minnesota Fats. *The Hustler* (1961, 20th Century-Fox).

696 "Isn't it odd how women of our age suddenly start looking for beauty in—well, in male partners?" Middle-aged **Coral Browne** asks the question of middle-aged Vivien Leigh. *The Roman Spring of Mrs. Stone* (1961, GB, Warner Bros.).

697 "The beautiful make their own laws." Widowed American actress **Vivien Leigh** speaks of handsome young Italian gigolo Warren Beatty. *The Roman Spring of Mrs. Stone* (1961, GB, Warner Bros.).

698 "I never met such a pretty girl, and I guess I'm just sensitive because real—real beauty makes me want to gag." Incompetent criminal **Woody Allen** has just met Janet Margolin. *Take the Money and Run* (1968, Cinerama).

699 "What happened to the old bank? It was beautiful." Outlaw **Paul Newman** is disappointed that a bank he's robbed before has been changed to deter holdups. *Butch Cassidy and the Sundance Kid* (1969, 20th Century-Fox).

700 "Little girls with sweet faces like yours always grow up pretty." Plain-looking **Patty Duke** recalls her mother Nancy Marchand's prediction of many years earlier. As she looks in a mirror, Duke says, "Mother lied." *Me, Natalie* (1969, Cinema Center).

701 "My sister is very beautiful." Young **Richard Gibson** accurately speaks of his sister Julie Christie to his 12-year-old friend Dominic Guard. The latter will become the title character, carrying love letters between farmer Alan Bates and Christie. *The Go-Between* (1970, GB, EMI-World Film Services).

702 "Where are your troubles now? Forgotten. I told you so. We have no troubles here. Here life is beautiful. The girls are beautiful. Even the orchestra is beautiful." Master of ceremonies **Joel Grey** addresses his remarks to the audience at the end of the film. *Cabaret* (1972, Allied Artists).

703 "Why ain't you beautiful? You're not even pretty." English detective **Sean Connery**, a closet sadist, rasps at his long-suffering frumpish wife Vivien Merchant. *The Offense* (1972, GB, United Artists).

704 GEORGE CONWAY: "You are more beautiful than the women of Thailand. More feminine than the women of France. More pliable than the women of Japan. More. . . ." MARIA: "Stop, stop. I don't want to hear about all these other women. What I want to hear is that you won't leave me." GEORGE: "Oh, I adore you!" **Michael York** was on a roll until stopped by **Olivia Hussey**, who is also more ancient than any woman York has ever known. *Lost Horizon* (1973, Columbia).

705 "You are beautiful when I beat you." Communist worker **Giancarlo Giannini** is the master and wealthy, obnoxious, beautiful Mariangela Melato is the slave when the two are castaway together on a deserted island. *Swept Away* (1974, Italy, Cinema 5).

706 "I think she's more beautiful now than I've ever seen her." **Burt Reynolds** speaks of Cybill Shepherd in this disastrous attempt by director Peter Bogdanovich to recreate the lush musicals of the 1930s. *At Long Last Love* (1975, 20th Century-Fox).

707 "Why do I have the feeling if my name were Fungus you'd think it beautiful?" A girl named Jane, played by **Alison Cohen**, doesn't buy Alan Abelew's pick-up line:: "That's a beautiful name—Jane." *The First Nudie Musical* (1976, Paramount).

708 "At least you're pretty. You should see some of the crones who come through here." Boss **Dabney Coleman** makes a sexist remark to Jane Fonda on her first day working in his department of a company. *Nine to Five* (1980, 20th Century-Fox).

709 "I don't know if I'm pretty." Marriage to Daniel Stern, who prefers the company of his buddies, has eroded **Ellen Barkin**'s sense of self. *Diner* (1982, MGM).

710 "You are very beautiful. . . I just didn't want you to forget." College student **Anthony Edwards** tries to pick up sultry-looking Linda Fiorentino, who tells him she knows she's beautiful. *Gotcha!* (1985, Universal).

711 "Did anyone ever tell you that you're pretty? You are and in a different way than anyone else. . . and all the nicer because of the difference. Oh, I wish you were my sister, I'd teach you to have confidence in yourself—because being different is nothing to be ashamed of—'cause other people aren't such wonderful people. Why, they're a hundred times one thousand; you're one times one. They wander all over the earth, you just stay right here. Why, they're as common as weeds, but you—you're blue roses." **James Naughton** pays shy, plain and crippled Karen Allen her first compliment from a gentleman caller. *The Glass Menagerie* (1987, Cineplex-Odeon).

712 "She's so beautiful. How can she keep from feeling herself up all the time?" Teen **Kirk Cameron** speaks lustfully of Cami Cooper to his friend Sean Astin. *Like Father, Like Son* (1987, Tri-Star).

713 "No matter what was wrong, she always looked beautiful." Owner **Maureen Stapleton** refers to her 80-year-old Catskills hotel. *Sweet Lorraine* (1988, Angelika).

714 "I just try to think beautiful thoughts, so that the beauty will come in what I write." Gothic romance novelist **Meryl Streep** shares the secret of her success with interviewer Ed Begley, Jr. *She-Devil* (1989, Orion).

715 "You're so pretty it hurts." Cute 14-year-old Elvis Presley-mad **Reese Witherspoon** envies her 17-year-old sister Emily Warfield. *The Man in the Moon* (1991, MGM).

716 "You're as pretty as a moonbeam and warm as sunlight." **Robert Duvall**'s pretty speech melts Laura Dern's heart. *Rambling Rose* (1991, Seven Arts-New Line).

717 "I've been making the most of it ever since I can remember." Stunningly beautiful **Polly Walker** responds to a tart suggestion that she make the most of her allure. *Enchanted April* (1992, GB, Miramax).

Beds

see also NIGHTS, SLEEP

718 MAVIS ARDEN: "I must be going. I'm usually in bed by this hour." AUNT KATE: "This must be one of your off nights." Here's a rare example of **Mae West** losing the last line to another performer—this time, **Elizabeth Patterson.** *Go West, Young Man* (1936, Paramount).

719 "Why do I have to go to bed? It's morning." **Mickey Kuhn**'s mother Olivia de Havilland is dying and the adults try to get the boy out of the way. *Gone with the Wind* (1939, Selznick-MGM).

720 "The bed looks like a dead animal act." Former vaudeville performer, now maid, **Thelma Ritter** eyes a bed full of furs belonging to guests at Bette Davis' party. *All About Eve* (1950, 20th Century-Fox).

721 "A man would have to be a sprinter to capture his wife in a bed like that." **Jack McGowran** is impressed with John Wayne's massive bed. *The Quiet Man* (1952, Republic).

722 "When a marriage goes on the rocks, the rocks are there—right there." **Judith Anderson** tells her daughter-in-law Elizabeth Taylor she knows that the marital troubles the latter is having with Paul Newman can be traced to their problems in bed. *Cat on a Hot Tin Roof* (1958, MGM).

723 "To be nice to you means that I should have to sleep in your bed. Then when you get tired of me I would have to go to some other gentleman's bed." **Leslie Caron** innocently rethinks entering the family profession of courtesanship when Louis Jourdan asks her to be nice to him. *Gigi* (1958, MGM).

724 "Henry's bed is Henry's province. He can people it in sheep for all I care—and often does." **Katharine Hepburn**, as Eleanor of Aquitaine, suggests that her estranged husband Peter O'Toole, as King Henry II, is into bestiality. *The Lion in Winter* (1968, GB, Avco Embassy).

725 JOE GRADY: "Look, you're just as lonely and hard-up as I am. . . ." FRAN WALKER: "I don't like that kind of talk." JOE: "Look, I don't wrestle, I don't coax. If you want to go to bed, we go. If you don't, we don't." FRAN: "Carry me?" JOE: "What?" FRAN: "Carry me into the bedroom. I like to be carried. Please." Piano player **Warren Beatty** and Las Vegas chorus girl **Elizabeth Taylor** talk each other into bed. *The Only Game in Town* (1970, 20th Century-Fox).

726 "This place is a mess. There's never any food in the house, half the time you look like you fell out of bed—you're in bed more than any other human being past the age of six that I ever heard of. . . ." **Jack Nicholson** complains about his slovenly live-in lover Ann-Margret. *Carnal Knowledge* (1971, Avco Embassy).

727 "A marriage bed is meant for two. But every damn morning it's the woman who has to make it. We have heads as well as hands. I call on man to let us use them." Visiting from the future, simian scientist **Kim Hunter** lectures women's clubs on women's liberation. *Escape from the Planet of the Apes* (1971, 20th Century-Fox).

728 "He was fantastic in bed—until I got into it." Seductive **Cathy Moriarty** complains about her husband Dan Aykroyd to her new neighbor John Belushi. *Neighbors* (1981, Columbia).

729 "Why can't I have a cup of coffee with a woman without winding up in bed?" **Tim Matheson** sees himself the victim of his promiscuity. What a curse—being the stud a bevy of beauties want to try. *A Little Sex* (1982, Universal).

730 "Take my arm, Sam. It's OK, you can touch me. A hundred and twenty pounds of pure gold, that's me. Come, children, come, let's put the Bubbie to bed." Satisfied that in pickle maker Peter Reigert, she has found the right man for her granddaughter Amy Irving, a weary **Reizl Bozyk** wishes to turn in. *Crossing Delancey* (1988, Warner Bros.).

731 "So is somebody goin' to go to bed with somebody or what?" Wildly stupid baseball pitcher **Tim Robbins** wants to know the bottom line as Susan Sarandon explains how she plans to choose between him and veteran catcher Kevin Costner as the recipient of her special treatment during the baseball season. *Bull Durham* (1988, Orion).

732 "You know, these days when everybody looks ugly and you don't know why people look at you strange, I'm better off right here in bed." **B.J. Spalding** spends most of his time in bed, drinking, and shooting at bugs on the ceiling with a hand gun. *Bail Jumper* (1990, Angelika).

733 "It's time for you to get your big, fat, extra-crispy bucket of chicken, two liter of Pepsi-Cola-drinking ass out of bed." **Denzel Washington** shouts at a sleepy Bob Hoskins. Hoskins has received deceased Washington's heart in a transplant operation, and the former dapper lawyer intends to shape up bad-living L.A. cop Hoskins. *Heart Condition* (1990, New Line).

734 "I will die in this bed. You should love in it." Near octogenarian **Sheila Florance** offers her bed to a visiting nurse friend Gosia Dobrowolska for liaisons with her lover. *A Woman's Tale* (1991, Australia, Orion Classics).

Beer *see* ALCOHOL, DRINKING AND DRUNKENNESS

Begging *see* POVERTY, PRAYERS, REQUESTS

Beginnings

see also BIRTHS AND BIRTHDAYS, ENDS AND ENDINGS, FIRSTS

735 WAITER: "Yes, Baron. What shall we start with, Baron?" MONESCU: "Mm, oh, yes. That's not easy. Beginnings are always difficult. . . . If Casanova suddenly turned out to be Romeo having supper with Juliet who might become Cleopatra—how would you start?" WAITER: "I would start with cocktails." Waiter **George Humbert** and sophisticated thief **Herbert Marshall** plan a dinner with Miriam Hopkins who also turns out to be an elegant crook. *Trouble in Paradise* (1932, Paramount).

736 "No, dear, always is just beginning for you and me." **Maureen O'Sullivan** promises her jungle lover Johnny Weissmuller that their happiness will last a long time. *Tarzan and His Mate* (1934, MGM).

737 "Were you ever raised in a small town by two maiden aunts? Have you played the organ in church since you were fifteen? No, well, I have. And right now I ask myself: 'Where did Caroline

Adams come from? How did all this start?'' Even **Irene Dunne** isn't quite able to explain how with her upbringing she was able to write the year's most shocking novel using the pseudonym Caroline Adams. *Theodora Goes Wild* (1936, Columbia).

738 "Has the war started?" **Clark Gable** arises from a couch in the library of Twelve Oaks after Vivien Leigh, angry with Leslie Howard, throws a vase against the mantle. *Gone with the Wind* (1939, Selznick-MGM).

739 "He's with her. They've only just begun to live! Goodbye, Heathcliff! Goodbye, my sweet Kathy!" Housekeeper **Flora Robson** believes that now that Laurence Olivier and Merle Oberon are dead, their souls will be together forever. *Wuthering Heights* (1939, Goldwyn-United Artists).

740 "It's a very important moment—a new chapter. In fact, for me, it's the first chapter. For what has my life been up to now? A preface? An empty foreword?" In proposing marriage to burlesque queen Barbara Stanwyck, stodgy professor **Gary Cooper** sees a new beginning to his life. *Ball of Fire* (1941, RKO).

741 "I was there before the beginning—and now I'm here after the end." **Joseph Cotten** is interviewed after the death of his one-time friend, title character Orson Welles. *Citizen Kane* (1941, RKO).

742 "Louie, I think this is the beginning of a beautiful friendship." **Humphrey Bogart** delivers the film's last line as he and sometime adversary Claude Rains leave Casablanca to join the Free-French forces. *Casablanca* (1942, Warner Bros.).

743 "You know how it is early in the morning on the water, and then you come ashore, and in no time at all you're up to your ears in trouble, and you don't know how it began." With his speech, **John Garfield**, rather nicely sums up the essence of film noir. *The Breaking Point* (1950, Warner Bros.).

744 "Let's start from the beginning again, Jeff. Tell me everything you saw. . .and what you think it means." **Grace Kelly** has just seen something that makes her think that her lover James Stewart may be correct in suspecting that neighbor Raymond Burr has murdered his wife and dismembered her body. *Rear Window* (1954, Paramount).

745 "Just one more day! I was just beginning to get into myself." Innocent prisoner **Gene Wilder** gets off a macho quip after four days in solitary confinement. *Stir Crazy* (1980, Columbia).

Behavior

see also ACTIONS AND ACTS, CAREERS, IMMORALITY, MANNERS, MORALITY, TREATS AND TREATMENTS, WAYS

746 DR. LANYON: "I thought your conduct quite disgusting, Jekyll." DR. JEKYLL: "Conduct? Why, a pretty girl kissed me. Should I call a constable? Even suppose I liked it?" **Holmes Herbert** scolds his engaged friend **Fredric March** for dallying with an obviously available strumpet, Miriam Hopkins. *Dr. Jekyll and Mr. Hyde* (1932, Paramount).

747 "Goodbye, Jennifer, be a bad girl." Warlock **Cecil Kellaway** leaves his witch daughter Veronica Lake in a burning building from which nakedly she will be rescued by Fredric March. *I Married a Witch* (1941, Paramount-United Artists).

748 "Ah, life and money both behave like loose quicksilver in a nest of cracks. When they're gone, you can't tell where or what the devil you did with them." As he departs by train, **Ray Collins** has some final words of wisdom for his nephew Tim Holt. *The Magnificent Ambersons* (1942, RKO).

749 "It would be nice to keep you, but I've got to be good—and keep my hands off children." **Vivien Leigh**, who has a weakness for young males, flirts with handsome newspaper boy Wright King. *A Streetcar Named Desire* (1951, Warner Bros.-20th Century-Fox).

750 "Until the trial is over, you're going to be a meek little housewife with horned-rimmed spectacles. You're going to stay away from men and juke joints and pinball machines. And you're going to wear a skirt and low-heeled shoes and a girdle." Attorney **James Stewart** instructs sexy, flirtatious Lee Remick on her behavior and her appearance during the trial of her husband Ben Gazzara, who killed the man who allegedly raped her. *Anatomy of a Murder* (1959, Columbia).

751 "Generally, you don't see that kind of behavior in a major appliance." **Bill Murray** quips when Sigourney Weaver's refrigerator, containing a hellhound and a gleaming apocalypse vision, begins to rumble and perk like a coffee pot. *Ghostbusters* (1984, Columbia).

752 "I know a thing or two about predatory behavior, and what once was a legitimate intelligence agency is now being used on weaker governments." American traitor and spy for the Russians **Timothy Hutton** poses as a man of conscience to his interrogators when his activities are discovered. *The Falcon and the Snowman* (1985, Orion).

753 "As our influence wanes, as our empire collapses, there is little to believe in. Behavior is all." Personnel director for the British diplomatic corps **Ian McKellen** is pragmatic. *Plenty* (1985, 20th Century-Fox-RKO).

754 "You're acting like a shit today!" Laid-back writer **Jean-Hugues Anglade** screams at his waitress mistress Beatrice Dalle. *Betty Blue* (1986, Fr., Alive Films).

755 "Why, I've just about had my fill of you trashy McGraths and your trashy ways, hangin' yourself in cellars, carryin' on with married men, shooting your husbands!" **Tess Harper** is fed up with the behavior of her cousins Diane Keaton, Jessica Lange and Sissy Spacek. *Crimes of the Heart* (1986, De Laurentiis).

756 MISS DAISY: "That car misbehaves." BOOLIE WERTHAN: "Cars don't misbehave, Mama, they have to be caused to misbehave." Having reached the age of 70, **Jessica Tandy** has all her mental facilities intact, but her son **Dan Aykroyd** has determined that she no longer is capable of driving an automobile, which she blames for her various accidents. *Driving Miss Daisy* (1989, Warner Bros.).

757 "We'd just like to know if there's been any change in Raymond's behavior lately. We're a little worried about him." Charming crooked cop **Richard Gere** pumps Nancy Travis at dinner about her husband, internal affairs investigator Andy Garcia. *Internal Affairs* (1990, Paramount).

Being see EXISTENCE, LIVES AND LIVING, OBJECTS, PEOPLE, POSSIBILITIES AND IMPOSSIBILITIES, REALITIES, THINGS, TRUTH

Beliefs

see also CERTAINTIES, CREEDS AND CREDOS, EXPECTATIONS, FAITH AND FAITHFULNESS, GOD, HUMILITY AND HUMILIATION, JEALOUSY, JUDGMENTS, KNOWLEDGE, LIVES AND LIVING, LOVE AND HATE, LOVE AND LOVERS, OPINIONS, RELIGIONS, SAINTS, SUPERNATURAL, TRUST, TRUTH, WISDOM, WORSHIP

758 "You may not believe it, but this is the best thing that ever happened to me." These are the dying words of shell-shocked World War I veteran **David Manners**. *The Last Flight* (1931, Warner Bros.).

759 ELYOT CHASE: "Don't you believe in anything?" AMANDA CHASE PAYNNE: "Oh, yes, I believe in being kind to everyone and giving money to old beggar women, and being as gay as possible." Wealthy **Robert Montgomery** and his ex-wife **Norma Shearer** always are seeking answers and finding none. *Private Lives* (1931, MGM).

760 "I'll make you believe in me." Ex-farm girl **Greta Garbo** makes a promise to big city brute Clark Gable. *Susan Lenox, Her Rise and Fall* (1931, MGM).

761 "I believe in you, not this Christ." Prefect of Rome **Fredric March** pleads with Christian Elissa Landi to renounce her belief in Christ and be saved from death in the arena. Instead, she converts him and they go to their deaths together. *The Sign of the Cross* (1932, Paramount).

762 ALICIA HATTON: "I don't suppose you believe in marriage." TIRA: "Only as a last resort." Society girl **Gertrude Michael** sneers at lion tamer **Mae West**. *I'm No Angel* (1933, Paramount).

763 "Then will you believe this, without understanding—I love you." Imposter **Ronald Colman**, impersonating a missing king, is hard-pressed to explain his actions and behavior to the king's fiancée Madeleine Carroll. In the 1952 remake, **Stewart Granger** makes the same pretty speech to Deborah Kerr. *The Prisoner of Zenda* (1937, Selznick; 1952, MGM).

764 "I like my convictions undiluted, same as I do my bourbon." Dangerous Southerner **George Brent** is a man of simple tastes and beliefs. *Jezebel* (1938, Warner Bros.).

765 "You have all sorts of unexpected gifts and qualities. . . . Believe in yourself. You can go as far as you dream." Shortly before dying in childbirth, **Greer Garson** shares a homily with her husband, Robert Donat. *Goodbye, Mr. Chips* (1939, GB, MGM).

766 "We didn't exactly believe your story, Miss O'Shaughnessy. We believed your two hundred dollars." Private investigator **Humphrey Bogart** tells client Mary Astor that he and his partner Jerome Cowan knew she was lying. They just didn't know how much. *The Maltese Falcon* (1941, Warner Bros.).

767 MAJOR STRASSER: "Captain Renault, are you entirely certain which side you're on?" CAPT. RENAULT: "Frankly, I have no convictions, if that is what you mean. I blow with the wind and the prevailing wind is blowing from Vichy." German officer **Conrad Veidt** questions **Claude Rains'** loyalty to the Third Reich. Rains, like an earlier countryman, Talleyrand, knows how to survive changing politics. *Casablanca* (1942, Warner Bros.).

768 "I don't believe in anything. If we could only get free of ourselves." Attorney **George Brent** refuses to be consoled by Olivia de Havilland after his fiancée Bette Davis runs off with de Havilland's husband Dennis Morgan. *In This Our Life* (1942, Warner Bros.).

769 "Very pretty speech—youthful, passionate, idealistic. Need I remind you that you are the fugitive from justice, not I. I'm a prominent citizen, widely respected. You are an obscure young workman wanted for committing an extremely unpopular crime. Now which of us do you think the police will believe?" Nazi fifth columnist **Otto Kruger** is confident that framed fugitive Robert Cummings is no threat. *Saboteur* (1942, Universal).

770 "I hated every part of her. I couldn't figure her out and yet I wanted to see her the way Johnny had. I wanted to hear that song of hers in Johnny's ears. Maybe she was all right—and maybe Christmas comes in July. But I didn't believe it." Narrator **Humphrey Bogart** speaks spitefully of William Prince's former girlfriend Lizabeth Scott. *Dead Reckoning* (1947, Columbia).

771 "You must believe in Mr. Kringle and keep right on doing it—you must have faith in him." Once insisting that her child have no illusions, dreams or beliefs in "fairy tales," **Maureen O'Hara** now insists to her doubting daughter Natalie Wood that she believe in Edmund Gwenn, who insists that he is the real Santa Claus. *Miracle on 34th Street* (1947, 20th Century-Fox).

772 "I don't need money. People give me things because they believe in me." It's the line of every crooked politician who's robbed the public blind. In this case, it's **Broderick Crawford** who comes to believe himself omnipotent. *All the King's Men* (1949, Columbia).

773 "He's dead for something. When I'm dead it will be for nothing, just as it will be for you. . . . He believed in something." **Sydney Greenstreet** disagrees with Spencer Tracy, who claims that his dead partner James Stewart was a fool for taking so many chances smuggling raw rubber out of Japanese-occupied Malaya for use by the U.S. armed forces. *Malaya* (1949, MGM).

774 "I believe that man ought to be made to think about the things he says." Professor **Barry Jones**, engaged in atomic research, thoughtfully comments on a man in a pub who between drinks recommends dropping atomic bombs on the Russians. *Seven Days to Noon* (1950, GB, London Films).

775 "Remember, in a pirate ship in pirate waters, in a pirate world, ask no questions; believe only what you see. . . . No!, believe half of what you see!" Before the opening credits of the film, pirate captain **Burt Lancaster** warns the audience that the adventure film is a bit of a spoof. *The Crimson Pirate* (1952, GB, Warner Bros.).

776 "Can't you believe in a love that asks for nothing?" In pre-Christian times, tavern wench **Jean Simmons** freely offers her love to physician Edmond Purdom. He's used to paying through the nose for the affection of Babylonian courtesan Bella Darvi. *The Egyptian* (1954, 20th Century-Fox).

777 "You shouldn't believe what I say when I'm with the rest of the kids." Pretty teen **Natalie Wood** confesses to James Dean that peer pressure forces her to say things she doesn't believe. *Rebel Without a Cause* (1955, Warner Bros.).

778 "The remarkable thing is that the poor creatures think the pestilence is the Lord's punishment." Church painter **Gunnar Olsson** sadly refers to the flagellants who move from town to town, beating themselves and each other during the plague. *The Seventh Seal* (1957, Sweden, Svensk Filmindustri).

779 "Oh, he talks with a twang and his suits don't fit, but he treats me as if he believes I'm the gentlest, softest woman in the world. And maybe, with enough time and tenderness, maybe I can believe it myself." Hard-as-nails magazine editor **Joan Crawford** quits her job to marry a widower with children after the break-up of her affair with a married man. She's back before the young career girls in the film get their romantic problems straightened out. Joan says, "It was too late for me." *The Best of Everything* (1959, 20th Century-Fox).

780 "I'm defending the 40 years I've lived with this man and watched him carry the burdens of people like you. If he's been wrong, at least he's stood for something. What do you stand for? Do you believe in Bertram Cates? I believe in my husband. What do you believe in?" When Donna Anderson attacks Fredric March for using her in trying to convict her boyfriend Dick York in the "Monkey Trial," March's real-life wife and his character's wife **Florence Eldridge** defends her husband. *Inherit the Wind* (1960, United Artists).

781 "All of you know what I stand for—what I believe! I believe in the truth of the Book of Genesis! Exodus! Leviticus! Numbers! Deuteronomy! Joshua! Judges! Ruth! First Samuel! Second Samuel! First Kings! Second Kings! Isaiah! Jeremiah! Lamentations! Ezekiel!" **Fredric March**, as the William Jennings Bryan character, wins his case against Spencer

Tracy as Clarence Darrow in the "monkey trial." But when the punishment doesn't satisfy him, March loses his cool and rants about his literal belief of everything in the bible. *Inherit the Wind* (1960, United Artists).

782 "When a man kills, it's the one act he does totally alone. The world isn't with him. Therefore his convictions must be tremendous. I admire people with convictions." British butler **John Mills** gives too much credit to murderers, whose convictions are probably less developed than the average person's. *The Chalk Garden* (1964, GB, Universal).

783 "We believe that human beings are more important than causes." Debating her Malaysian rebel captor, Tetsuro Tamba, **Susannah York** uses the imperial we, referring to white British imperialists. *The Seventh Dawn* (1964, United Artists).

784 CROWN PRINCE RUDOLF: "You don't believe that I love her, do you?" EMPEROR FRANZ-JOSEPH: "I don't believe it matters." Despite insisting that he loves Catherine Deneuve, **Omar Sharif** is expected to marry whomever his father **James Mason** chooses. *Mayerling* (1968, GB-Fr., MGM).

785 "I sit here and I can't believe that it happened. And yet I have to believe it. Nightmares or dreams, madness or sanity, I don't know which is which." Former mental patient **Zohra Lampert** has survived the attempts of her husband Barton Heyman to drive her mad. *Let's Scare Jessica to Death* (1971, Paramount).

786 BOGART: "Tell her your life has changed since you met her." ALLAN: "She won't fall for that." BOGART: "Oh, no? Try it and see." **Jerry Lacy** as the spirit of Humphrey Bogart advises **Woody Allen** on how to score with the lovely brunette sitting next to him on the sofa. *Play It Again, Sam* (1972, Paramount).

787 "Oh, no, I would never believe that in a million years." **Stockard Channing** won't believe that con men Warren Beatty and Jack Nicholson would try to kill her for her money. *The Fortune* (1975, Columbia).

788 EDDIE "KID NATURAL" SCANLON: "What about the ills of sex before a fight?" HILLARY KRAMER: "You don't believe that crap, do you?" Boxer **Ryan O'Neal** is afraid that having sex with his manager **Barbra Streisand**, the night before his big fight, will affect his prowess in the ring. *The Main Event* (1979, Warner Bros.).

789 LUKE SKYWALKER: "I don't believe it." YODA: "That is why you fail." **Mark Hamill** can hardly

believe it when Yoda (voice of **Frank Oz**) levitates a spaceship. *The Empire Strikes Back* (1980, 20th Century-Fox).

790 "I was brought up to believe that a woman should fall in love with the best possible provider she can stomach." Sex-kitten **Jessica Lange** is a gold-digger. *How to Beat the High Cost of Living* (1980, Filmways).

791 "You want to get home for Thanksgiving, you better believe that the guy coming at you is trying to kill you." Vietnam veteran **Steve Railsback** knows that it's kill or be killed. *The Stunt Man* (1980, 20th Century-Fox).

792 "You must be dead because I don't know how to feel. I'll believe in you all my life, every day. . . E.T., I love you." **Henry Thomas** laments the apparent death of his little alien friend. *E.T.: The Extra-Terrestrial* (1982, Universal).

793 "Do you really believe I'd stop seeing you now at a time like this just because you couldn't afford it?" **Roy Scheider** proves he's one hell of a shrink as he reassures a poor patient. *Still of the Night* (1982, MGM-United Artists).

794 "I believe virtually everything I read." So asserts nondiscriminating rock group member **Michael McKean**. *This Is Spinal Tap* (1984, Embassy).

795 "He tells me that he's anal in here (pointing to her forehead)! Do you believe that?" In bed with John Getz, **Frances McDormand** speaks derisively about her husband Dan Hedaya. *Blood Simple* (1985, River Road).

796 "I can't believe this macho bullshit." **Rae Dawn Chong** has had it with super-male Arnold Schwarzenegger. *Commando* (1985, 20th Century-Fox).

797 "I've always believed everything I was told." **Norma Aleandro** confesses to priest Leal Rey her complicity in the political tyranny of Argentina by refusing to see what was going on or speak out against it. *The Official Story* (1985, Argentina, Almi Pictures).

798 "I want to believe in you so tell me nothing." **Meryl Streep** knows how to keep from becoming disillusioned with Sting. *Plenty* (1985, 20th Century-Fox).

799 "Once I had believed in father, and the world seemed small and old. Now he was gone, and I wasn't afraid to love him anymore, and the world seemed limitless." **River Phoenix** speaks of how the death of his father Harrison Ford affected him. *The Mosquito Coast* (1986, Warner Bros.).

800 "I believe in the soul, the small of a woman's back, the hanging curve ball, high fiber, good scotch, long foreplay, show tunes. . . . I believe that Lee Harvey Oswald acted alone, that the novels of Susan Sontag are self-indulgent, overrated crap, that there should be a constitutional amendment outlawing astroturf and the designated hitter, I believe in the "sweet spot," voting every election, soft core pornography, chocolate chip cookies. . .and I believe in long, slow, deep, soft wet kisses that last three days." Journeyman baseball catcher **Kevin Costner** lists his beliefs for the benefit of baseball groupie Susan Sarandon. Guess he changed his mind when he played Jim Garrison in "JFK." *Bull Durham* (1988, Orion).

801 "You believed [me] be cause you wanted to believe—your true feelings were too gross and icky to face." **Christian Slater** tells Winona Ryder that she was an eager participant in the murders of several of the most popular people at their high school. *Heathers* (1989, New World).

802 "Look at this, the sun, the sea. Un-fucking-believable, eh?" **Andrew Dice-Clay**, playing his usual role as a vulgar, homophobic, misogynist smart-ass, ends this "Dick Tracy"-like star vehicle, intent on changing his ways and settling down with Lauren Holly and teenager Brandon Call. *The Adventures of Ford Fairlane* (1990, 20th Century-Fox).

803 "People put you down, you start to believe it. . .the bad stuff is easier to believe. . .did you ever notice that?" Hooker **Julia Roberts** has a heart-to-heart with client Richard Gere. *Pretty Woman* (1990, Buena Vista-Touchstone).

804 "They never caught who did it—but I firmly believe what goes around comes around." **Rebecca De Mornay**'s physician husband committed suicide after he was accused of sexual misconduct by Annabella Sciorra and four other female patients. De Mornay blames Sciorra for her husband's death and the subsequent loss of her baby. She has unbelievably wormed her way into Sciorra's household as a nanny. *The Hand That Rocks the Cradle* (1991, Hollywood Pictures.)

805 "And I can't believe that you'd come here tonight when everyone knows you're fucking my husband." At a dinner party, **Barbra Streisand** lets her husband Jeroen Krabbe's mistress Sandy Rowe have it when the woman condescendingly announces she can't believe that Streisand would let her teenage son, a violinist, play football and endanger his hands. *The Prince of Tides* (1991, Columbia).

Belonging

see also OWNERSHIP, PARTICIPATION, PLACES, POSSESSIONS, RELATIONSHIPS, RELATIVES

806 "You don't belong to any man now—you belong to Broadway!" Producer **Adolphe Menjou** tells his ex-lover Katharine Hepburn that now that she's a star, men must take second place to her career. *Morning Glory* (1933, RKO).

807 "You seem to belong here. As if it had been imagined for you." **Leslie Howard** lovingly speaks to his fiancée Olivia de Havilland during the barbecue at his Twelve Oaks plantation. *Gone with the Wind* (1939, Selznick-MGM).

808 "Tonight, just tonight, she belongs to me! Tonight, I want her to call me Mommy!" For once, self-sacrificing unwed mother **Bette Davis** wants the daughterly love of Jane Bryan who calls Miriam Hopkins her mother. *The Old Maid* (1939, Warner Bros.).

809 "Let her die where she belongs—in Edgar's arms! Let her die!" **Geraldine Fitzgerald** begs her husband Laurence Olivier to stay away from his dying, beloved Merle Oberon, and her husband David Niven comforts Oberon at the end. *Wuthering Heights* (1939, Goldwyn-United Artists).

810 "This is my country, and I belong here." Despite poverty and eviction from his worthless land, senile old grandpa **Charlie Grapewin** insists he has the rights due an American citizen. *The Grapes of Wrath* (1940, 20th Century-Fox).

811 "You're not marrying that cheap redhead. . . you're mine and I'm hanging on to you. . .I committed murder to get you." Having murdered her husband Alan Hale to be free for truck driver George Raft, **Ida Lupino** has no intentions of losing him to waitress Ann Sheridan. *They Drive by Night* (1940, Warner Bros.).

812 "That child is mine. Your part was finished the minute you gave that baby to me. From that day on I had only one purpose in life, to make that baby mine and forget you ever existed." **Bette Davis** ruthlessly dismisses Mary Astor's claim to her baby. *The Great Lie* (1941, Warner Bros.).

813 "The country and its institutions belong to the people who inhibit it." Ex-show girl **Judy Holliday**'s heart is in the right place, even if her vocabulary isn't. *Born Yesterday* (1950, Columbia).

814 "The house may belong to my brother, but what's in the parlor belongs to me." Irish colleen **Maureen O'Hara** proudly declares her dowry to professional matchmaker Barry Fitzgerald. *The Quiet Man* (1952, Republic).

815 "A man should have something that belongs to him." Western characters such as drifter **Randolph Scott** like to lay claim to a notion because "all men should. . . ." *The Tall T* (1957, Columbia).

816 "I was wrong. I did belong to my mother, but now she's dead, and I don't want her to live again in you. Not even in you, Miriam. I'm sure I'll never find anyone as good as you, or any love as good as yours, but I don't want to find it, because I want to be free. I don't ever want to belong to anyone again. Never any more. And perhaps I'll understand at last what it means to live. Good-bye." After his domineering mother Wendy Hiller dies, **Dean Stockwell** leaves the Nottingham area of England for London and the art career he has always dreamed of. He leaves behind Heather Sears. *Sons and Lovers* (1960, GB, 20th Century-Fox).

817 "I belong here. . . I'm home." **David Warner** as Jack the Ripper transported from 1890s London to 1979 San Francisco via H.G. Wells' time machine, finds the North Beach area to his liking. *Time After Time* (1979, Warner Bros.-Orion).

818 "Cross Creek belongs to the wind and the rain, to the sun and the seasons, to the cosmic secrecy of seed. And beyond all to time." **Mary Steenburgen**, as author Marjorie Kinnan Rawlings, pompously describes her Florida backwoods home. *Cross Creek* (1983, Universal).

819 "There are more of us than there are of them. Anyone who has ever felt excluded, left out, or unaccepted, whether you think you're a nerd or not; join us!" Head nerd **Robert Carradine** issues an invitation to fellow students to rally around the nerds rather than the so-called perfect, beautiful and popular people of their university. It's an appeal few can resist. *Revenge of the Nerds* (1984, 20th Century-Fox).

820 SISTER MIRIAM RUTH: "She belongs to God." DR. MARTHA LIVINGSTON: "And I intend to take her away from Him." Mother superior **Anne Bancroft** argues with court-appointed psychiatrist **Jane Fonda**, a lapsed Catholic, about very young and very naïve nun Meg Tilly, who has given birth to a child and may have killed it. *Agnes of God* (1985, Columbia).

821 "I'll be no man's slave and no man's whore." Speaking with great feeling, **Lana Clarkson** declares she belongs to no one but herself. *The Barbarian Queen* (1985, Concorde).

822 "A little bit of everyone belongs in hell, Lieutenant." Strong, silent type **Kris Kristofferson** offers his opinion of the human race to police detective George Kirby. *Trouble in Mind* (1986, Island Alive).

823 "I don't belong to anybody." Fiercely independent, **Karen Landry**, doesn't much care when she learns that Chris Mulkey, the father of the baby she's carrying, is married. *Patti Rocks* (1988, Filmdallas).

824 "That's my girl. And that's my boy." The ghost of pilot **Richard Dreyfuss** proudly blesses the union of his girlfriend Holly Hunter and young Brad Johnson. *Always* (1989, Universal).

Best *see* ABILITIES AND CAPABILITIES, ADVANTAGES, GOODNESS, GREATNESS, MODELS, PERFECTION, REPUTATIONS, SUPERIORITY AND INFERIORITY, VIRTUES, WORTH AND VALUES

Betrayals

see also DECEPTIONS, ENEMIES, INFORMATION AND INFORMERS, REVELATIONS, SECRETS, TREASON AND TRAITORS, TRUST

825 "Never trust or love anyone so much you can't betray him." **Montagu Love**, as King Henry VIII, advises his young son Bobby Mauch as Prince Edward. *The Prince and the Pauper* (1937, Warner Bros.).

826 ANDRE VERNE: "Who's a rat, baby?" JULIE: "You are." ANDRE: "But I'll do anyway." Always sure of himself with women, Devil's Island escapee **Clark Gable** knows **Joan Crawford** may not trust him, but she can't resist him. *Strange Cargo* (1940, MGM).

827 "Why do men always betray the strongest among them?" Old storyteller **Francis J. McDonald** raises the eternal question. He offers no answer. *Samson and Delilah* (1949, Paramount).

828 "If you want to sell your services, I'm not willing to pay the price. I loved him. You loved him. What good have we done him? Love! Look at yourself. They have a name for faces like that." **Alida Valli** accuses Joseph Cotten of betraying his friend, black marketeer Orson Welles, to keep her from falling into the hands of the Russians in post-World War II Vienna. *The Third Man* (1949, GB, British Lion-London Films-Selznick).

829 "When you give all your love and get nothing but betraying in return, it's as if your mother had slapped you in the face." After her guilt is exposed,

Marlene Dietrich tries to justify for police sergeant Ballard Berkeley her decision to murder her husband. *Stage Fright* (1950, GB, Warner Bros.).

830 "Maybe that stoolie's not an American at all. Maybe he's a German the Krauts planted in this barracks. They do that sometimes. They put an agent in on us, a trained specialist. Lots of loose information floating around a prison camp—not just whether somebody's trying to escape—what outfit we were with, where we were stationed, how our radar operates. Could be, couldn't it?" Unpopular POW **William Holden** shares with his only friend in the barracks, Gil Stratton, Jr., his theory that one of the prisoners is actually a German spy. *Stalag 17* (1953, Paramount).

831 "I certainly had him pegged wrong, didn't I? I thought he was just a rat, but he was a super rat all along—a super rat in rat's clothing." **Audrey Hepburn** is crushed that a wealthy man who she thought she had her hooks in has married another woman. *Breakfast at Tiffany's* (1961, Paramount).

832 "I didn't betray you, I simply put a stop to you." **Pamela Franklin** exposes her teacher Maggie Smith for the dangerous manipulative woman she really is. *The Prime of Miss Jean Brodie* (1969, GB, 20th Century-Fox).

833 "If my life ends because of you, that's what was meant to be. If you don't betray me, then you'll join me." Fearsome international terrorist **Harvey Keitel** speaks matter-of-factly about life and death to Natassia Kinski. *Exposed* (1983, MGM-United Artists).

834 "You have changed. You are capable of betrayal. You abuse your position as journalist and grow addicted to the risk. You attempt to draw neat lines around yourself, making a fetish of your career and making all relationships temporary lest they disturb that career." **Linda Hunt** writes in former protégé Mel Gibson's file. *The Year of Living Dangerously* (1983, Australia, MGM).

835 MICHAEL CARNES: "Stay with us, we're your family. We'll protect you." KATIE PHILLIPS-CATHY WEAVER: "The Bureau was my family. I trusted you. You used me. You betrayed me." Special FBI agent **John Heard** is unable to prevent undercover FBI agent **Debra Winger** from resigning after she is forced to kill her lover, Tom Berenger, as he's about to assassinate a political candidate. *Betrayed* (1988, MGM-United Artists).

836 "Which of us would betray the other first this time?" When title character Colin Firth asks notorious manipulator **Annette Bening** to marry him, she kisses him, tells him she still loves him, and takes him to her bed chamber to show him that she has seventeen-year-old Henry Thomas in her bed. *Valmont* (1989, Orion).

837 "I want you to sell your soul to Don Altobello. To betray me." **Al Pacino** asks his nephew Andy Garcia to convince Eli Wallach that he is angry with Pacino and wants to become Wallach's man. *The Godfather, Part III* (1991, Paramount).

Bible *see* ANGELS, BELIEFS, BOOKS, HEAVEN, HEAVEN AND HELL, HELL, RELIGIONS, SAINTS

Bigamy *see* HUSBANDS, HUSBANDS AND WIVES, MARRIAGES, WEDDINGS, WIVES

Bigness *see* GREATNESS, GROWTH AND DEVELOPMENT, IMPORTANCE, SIZES

Bigotry

see also BELIEFS, CREEDS AND CREDOS, HATE AND HATRED, OPINIONS, PREJUDICES

838 "No Vietcong ever called me nigger." Portraying himself, **Muhammed Ali** claims that he evaded the draft because he had no quarrel with the Vietcong. Of course, the same could have been said of most American soldiers sent to the war. *The Greatest* (1977, US-GB, Columbia-EMI).

839 "An old Jew woman and a nigger, taking off down the road together. What a sorry sight." In a sequence that seems to serve no purpose in an otherwise well-crafted movie, state trooper **Ray McKinnon** expresses a double-edged statement of bigotry to his partner Ashley Josey. *Driving Miss Daisy* (1989, Warner Bros.).

Birds

see also ANIMALS, FLYING AND FLIERS

840 "The stork that brought you must have been a vulture." Stranded **Ann Sheridan** flings a caustic barb at no-nonsense overseer Pat O'Brien. *Torrid Zone* (1940, Warner Bros.).

841 "Let's talk about the black bird." **Humphrey Bogart** has a business proposition for Sydney Greenstreet. *The Maltese Falcon* (1941, Warner Bros.).

842 "Pigeons marry just like people and stay that way until one of them dies." **Marlon Brando** tells Eva Marie Saint that he admires pigeons. *On the Waterfront* (1954, Columbia).

843 "Celli, you're a real cuckoo bird." Would-be kidnapper **Robert Wagner** is disappointed to discover that there's no money to pay the ransom for Neapolitan mobster Vittorio De Sica. *The Biggest Bundle of Them All* (1967, MGM).

844 "He's up on the roof with birds. He keeps birds. Dirty, disgusting, filthy, lice-ridden birds. You used to be able to sit out on the stoop like a person. Not any more. No sir. Birds! You get my drift?" "Concierge" **Madlyn Cates** snarls from the window of her tenement apartment to Zero Mostel and Gene Wilder about her tenant Kenneth Mars. *The Producers* (1968, Embassy).

845 HARRIET MACKYLE: "You shot my bird." HANDSOME JACK: "I didn't know it was a bird." At a party given by society lady **Julie Hagerty,** Damon Runyon-like character **Esai Morales** gets carried away and shoots her parrot. *Bloodhounds of Broadway* (1989, Columbia).

Births and Birthdays

see also AGE AND AGING, BABIES, BEGINNINGS, CHILDREN AND CHILDHOOD, DEATH AND DYING, FAMILIES, FATHERS, LIFE AND DEATH, LIVES AND LIVING, MOTHERS, PARENTS, YOUTH

846 ACE LAMONT: "You were born in St. Louis! What part?" RUBY CARTER: "Why all of me." **John Miljan** plays straight man for **Mae West**. *Belle of the Nineties* (1934, Paramount).

847 "I was born at home because I wanted to be near my mother. . . ." It's **William Powell**'s wisecrack to Myrna Loy when it was a new joke. *Manhattan Melodrama* (1934, MGM).

848 "I didn't want to be born, and you didn't want me to be born." **Bette Davis** finally explodes in anger at her domineering mother, Gladys Cooper. The shock kills Cooper. *Now, Voyager* (1942, Warner Bros.).

849 "I was born in Texas, but it weren't yesterday." **Gary Cooper**, very much at home in his role as the country's "most beloved illiterate," so dubbed by poet Carl Sandburg, assures Ingrid Bergman that despite his awkward and hesitant ways, he's not as dumb as he looks. *Saratoga Trunk* (1945, Warner Bros.).

850 "I was born last night when you met me in an alley; that way I'm all future and no past." Surprisingly **Glenn Ford** makes the statement to George Macready, not Rita Hayworth. He means he'd prefer to forget his unsavory past. *Gilda* (1946, Columbia).

851 "I suppose it'd been better if I'd never been born at all." Despondent **James Stewart**'s lament gives his apprentice guardian angel Clarence, played by Henry Travers, an idea. *It's a Wonderful Life* (1947, RKO).

852 "Whata ya know?. . . I just remembered somethin'. . . . It's my birthday, yeah, today. . . . I'll tell you, big man, I never spent a birthday with a better guy. . . . When I heard you spit in that judge's face, I said to myself, 'a buddy, a stand-up guy.'" Maniacal gangster **Richard Widmark** is pleased to share his natal day with Victor Mature as they are taken by train to Sing Sing penitentiary. Nobody could say "beeeg man" like Widmark. *Kiss of Death* (1947, 20th Century-Fox).

853 "I was born dead." Numbers racketeer's lawyer **John Garfield** makes one of his narrative asides in a film noir classic, directed by gifted writer Abraham Polonsky, who would be blackballed for over twenty years when he became an uncooperative witness before HUAC in 1951. *Force of Evil* (1948, MGM).

854 "I think everyone has two birthdays, the day of his physical birth and the beginning of his conscious life." **Joan Fontaine**, in voice-over, may be right, but while one knows the date of the first, the second is seldom celebrated. *Letter from an Unknown Woman* (1948, Universal).

855 "A thousand poets dreamed a thousand years, and you were born. . . ." Just before the final fadeout, **Rex Harrison** states this lovely sentiment as the camera focuses on a close-up of his beautiful wife Linda Darnell. *Unfaithfully Yours* (1948, 20th Century-Fox).

856 "I'll have a word with you. I didn't understand you. I didn't understand myself. You done a thing that numbs my belly. No man in all my life before give me things before or a kind word or a kick. Forgot it was my birthday. I wouldn't have remembered it if it weren't for you. I thank you, one and all." **Richard Todd** thanks his fellow hospital comrades for his surprise birthday party. *The Hasty Heart* (1949, Warner Bros.).

857 "He was born with the gift of laughter and a sense that the world was mad." It's the description of **Stewart Granger**'s character at the beginning of this cheerful swashbuckler set in French Revolutionary times. *Scaramouche* (1952, MGM).

858 "Yeah, I'm running, running from lies, lies like birthday congratulations and many happy returns of the day when there won't be any." Raging with self-pity, **Paul Newman** lets out the news to his father Burl Ives that he's dying. *Cat on a Hot Tin Roof* (1958, MGM).

859 "Irving F. Feldman's birthday is my own personal National Holiday. I did not open it up for the public. He is the proprietor of perhaps the most distinguished Kosher Delicatessen in our neighborhood, and as such, I hold the day of his birthday in reverence." Non-conformist writer **Jason Robards** has taken the day off from hunting for a job to honor someone important in his life. *A Thousand Clowns* (1965, United Artists).

860 "It's my birthday. I'm thirty-four years old today. I'm not prepared. I'm prepared for twenty-two. Right now, I could do a great twenty-two. I woke up this morning and all of a sudden I was not young—I was not old, but I'm all of a sudden not young." **Barbara Harris**, a singer of a very modest talent, wonders where all the years have gone. *Who Is Harry Kellerman and Why Is He Saying Those Terrible Things About Me?* (1971, National General).

861 "All I can say is thanks to everybody again for remembering me on my birthday. Only don't think, because I'm 60, I'll be a bigger damned-fool easy mark than ever." Seedy bar owner **Fredric March** expresses thanks and a warning to his patrons on the event of his birthday. *The Iceman Cometh* (1973, American Film Theater).

862 "I was born a poor black child." White **Steve Martin** begins his story. *The Jerk* (1979, Universal).

863 BILLY RAY, JR.: "I just had a birthday, too. I turned thirteen two weeks ago." NORMAN THAYER, JR.: "Oh? We're practically twins." Thirteen-year-old **Doug McKeon** and eighty-year-old **Henry Fonda** seek something to talk about. *On Golden Pond* (1981, Universal).

864 "Oh, how I do love birthday cake." The black comedy ends with **Diane Keaton**'s birthday celebration with her kooky sisters Jessica Lange and Sissy Spacek. *Crimes of the Heart* (1986, De Laurentiis).

865 "All of these guys is of woman born. They can't do shit to me." It's the confident belief of Mafioso **John Turturro**, a Macbeth character, about some rivals. Better watch out John, there's a Macduff out there. *Men of Respect* (1991, Columbia).

866 "Some people are born not to do things. I'm one of them." Nothing ever happens to **Rupert Graves**. *Where Angels Fear to Tread* (1992, GB, First Line).

Blackmail

see also CRIMES AND CRIMINALS, LAWS, PAYMENTS, THREATS

867 "Blackmail is not so pure, nor so simple. It can bring a lot of trouble to a great many people, and the blackmailer sometimes finds himself in jail at the end of it." Local magistrate **C. Aubrey Smith** pointedly warns potential blackmailer George Sanders to leave Laurence Olivier and Joan Fontaine alone. *Rebecca* (1940, United Artists).

868 NICK: "This is sheer blackmail." EDDIE KAGLE: "You ought to know, Nick, you ought to know." Calculating devil **Claude Rains** is blackmailed by gangster-turned-do-gooder **Paul Muni.** The latter demands to be made a trustee in hell with wide-ranging privileges or he'll let it be known that Rains lost a soul due to ineptitude. *Angel on My Shoulder* (1946, United Artists).

869 DETECTIVE INSPECTOR HARRIS: "Someone once called this law against homosexuality the blackmailer's charter." MELVILLE FARR: "Is that how you feel about it?" HARRIS: "I'm a policeman, sir. I don't have feelings." Policeman **John Barrie** talks to barrister **Dirk Bogarde**, who has homosexual tendencies. *Victim* (1961, GB, Pathé).

Blacks

see also APPEARANCES, HUMAN NATURE AND HUMANITY, IDENTITIES, PEOPLE, PREJUDICES, RELATIONSHIPS

870 "Anyone can convict a Negro in the South." Prosecutor **Claude Rains** isn't excited about the notion of charging a black janitor with murdering teenager Lana Turner because it wouldn't be a challenge. *They Won't Forget* (1937, Warner Bros.).

871 "Today, my friends, I find, in being black a thing of beauty, a joy, a strength, a secret cup of gladness, a native land and neither time nor place, a native land in every Negro face. Be loyal to yourself, your skin, your lips, your hair, your Southern speech, your laugh and kindness. A Negro kingdom, vast as any others. Accept therefore the sweetness of your blackness, not wishing to be red or white or yellow or any other race or thing but this. Farewell my deep and African brothers. Be brave, keep freedom in the family. Do what you can for the white folks as they in turn must do indeed for you. And now may the Constitution of the United States go with you, the Declaration of Independence stand by you, the Bill of Rights protect you, the State Commission against Discrimination keep their eyes and ears upon you, now and forever,

Amen." **Ossie Davis** as the Reverend Purlie Victorious Judson preaches black pride, black is beautiful and a hope in the American system of government. *Gone Are the Days* (1963, Hammer).

872 "We got to make them know that everytime they even think of picking up a gun against a black man, there's a black gun waiting for them." Junior high school teacher **Raymond St. Jacques** is the leader of a group of black militants. *Up Tight* (1968, Paramount).

873 "Where you been, sister? We ain't Negroes, we're black. Get it together—or get out." When black nun **Barbara McNair** refers to herself as a Negro, street tough **Ji-Tu Cumbuka** corrects McNair's choice of terms to what was then most acceptable. *Change of Habit* (1969, Universal).

874 "I was in the Black Studies program. By now I could have been black." **Woody Allen** regrets that he dropped out of college. *Bananas* (1971, United Artists).

875 "Just think, if you could only find a white girl to marry then your grandchildren would be scarcely black at all." White preacher's wife **Julie Dawson** has a solution for half-white aborigine Tommy Lewis' racial "problem." *The Chant of Jimmie Blacksmith* (1980, Australia, Film House).

876 "He's not black. He's what an interior decorator would call 'hickory bronze.' The same as your new car." **George Segal** describes his son, Denzel Washington, the product of an affair with a black girl when he was in college. *Carbon Copy* (1981, RKO).

877 "People here act like they've never seen a black man before." When **Sidney Poitier** jumps up and down and scares away a bear, it's the first mention of his race in the movie. *Shoot to Kill* (1988, Buena Vista).

878 "Blacks lead double lives—one you see and one you don't." The remark is made by vicious white Special Branch captain **Jurgen Prochnow**. *A Dry White Season* (1989, MGM-United Artists).

879 "A black man's got no place in the white man's army." **Cuba Gooding, Jr.,** quotes his father Larry Fishburne to his friend Morris Chestnut who is considering giving up his dreams to go to college and play football. He's thinking about enlisting in the army instead. *Boyz N the Hood* (1991, Columbia).

880 "The Irish are the blacks of Europe; Dubliners are the blacks of Ireland, and on our side, we're the blacks of Dublin. So say it: I'm black and I'm proud!" Band manager **Robert Arkins** encourages

his Dublin slum band when they express the fear that maybe they're too white to perform soul music. *The Commitments* (1991, 20th Century-Fox).

881 "We're probably the only two black people he knows." **Danny Glover** jokes to Alfre Woodard about Kevin Kline who has set up a blind date between Glover and Woodard. *Grand Canyon* (1991, 20th Century-Fox).

Blame

see also ACCUSATIONS, EVILNESS, FAULTS, GUILT, RESPONSIBILITIES, WRONGS AND WRONGDOINGS

882 "Here's another nice mess you've gotten me into." It's **Oliver Hardy**'s famous lament, delivered at some point to partner Stan Laurel in almost all of their talking comedies, including the 30-minute short. *The Laurel and Hardy Murder Case* (1930, Hal Roach).

883 "There is only one breast that you can pin the responsibility for this murder on. . . ." Unconventional lawyer **Lionel Barrymore** makes an impassioned speech to a jury, taking blame for his daughter Norma Shearer's predicament before falling dead in front of them. *A Free Soul* (1931, MGM).

884 TIGER KID: "If I catch some other guy foolin' 'round with you I'll bust him in half." RUBY CARTER: "Hmm, I couldn't blame you." Boxer **Roger Pryor** claims nightclub performer **Mae West** for himself. *Belle of the Nineties* (1934, Paramount).

885 "They've been blamed for every crime committed in the country." **Jean Dixon** refers to her fugitive sister Sylvia Sidney and her condemned, escaped prisoner husband Henry Fonda. *You Only Live Once* (1937, United Artists).

886 "It would've worked out if you'd been satisfied with just being editor and reporter, but not you—you had to marry me and ruin everything." Editor **Cary Grant** blames reporter Rosalind Russell and marriage for their professional split. *His Girl Friday* (1940, Columbia).

887 "I hope you had a good time because Hap paid the bill." Angry **John Wayne** rages at John Carroll and Anna Lee whose absence from their posts resulted in the death of Paul Kelly, who went on a mission for which Carroll was scheduled. *Flying Tigers* (1942, Republic).

888 "I wasn't going to do anything about it, not until I met you. You planned the whole thing, I only wanted him dead. . . . I loved you and hated him. But I didn't do anything about it until you came along. . . . And nobody's pulling out. We went in this together and we're coming out of the end together, straight down the line for both of us. . . . Remember?" **Barbara Stanwyck** shifts the blame for the murder of her husband on Fred MacMurray's broad Captain Marvel-like shoulders. *Double Indemnity* (1944, Paramount).

889 "I envy people who drink. At least they know what to blame everything on." It's an example of hypochondriac **Oscar Levant**'s "sick" humor. *Humoresque* (1947, Warner Bros.).

890 "Let him take the blame! He has it coming to him. We'll all say it was him if we have to—it was his car." After his wife Betty Field hits and kills his mistress Shelley Winters while driving Alan Ladd's roadster, **Barry Sullivan** tells her they'll claim it was Ladd who was driving the car. *The Great Gatsby* (1949, Paramount).

891 "Houston on fire. Will history blame me—or the bees?" **Richard Widmark** leads the defense of the city of Houston from an attack of African killer bees. He's not successful. *The Swarm* (1978, Warner Bros.).

892 "On account of you, I'm obstructing justice. I'm gonna get my license revoked if I don't go to jail first." Manhattan shrink **Roy Scheider** blames Meryl Streep, the mistress of a patient he's suspected of killing. *Still of the Night* (1982, MGM-United Artists).

893 FATHER DYER: "There you go, blaming God again." INSPECTOR KINDERMAN: "Who should I blame, Phil Rizzuto?" Old friends, priest **Ed Flanders** and police inspector **George C. Scott** have another of their friendly confrontational exchanges, when Scott complains about a deity who allows vicious murders. *The Exorcist III* (1990, 20th Century-Fox).

894 "I wish I was to blame for every laugh line in your face. For it just burns me to think that someone else made you smile." **Brian Wimmer** has spent 29 years in a cryonic freeze, courtesy of a benevolent mad scientist. Now Wimmer tries to reclaim the love of his wife Marcia Gay Harden. *Late for Dinner* (1991, Columbia).

Blasphemy

> *see also* CURSES, GOD, OATHS, PROFANITY, RESPECT AND RESPECTABILITY, SINS AND SINNERS

895 "You're the most blasphemous thing I've ever seen—it's a miracle you've not been struck dead." Editor **Edward G. Robinson** is disgusted with degenerate reporter Boris Karloff. *Five Star Final* (1931, Warner Bros.).

896 "If I was to punish every blasphemy, I would have no followers." **Niall MacGinnis**, as Zeus, takes a practical view of the sin of blasphemy. *Jason and the Argonauts* (1963, GB, Columbia).

897 "Blasphemer! Get him, he's a blasphemer!" In his film debut, **John Travolta** is a member of a cult of Satanists. He literally melts during the "Devil's Rain." *The Devil's Rain* (1975 U.S.-Mex., Bryanston).

Blessings

> *see also* ADMIRATION, APPLAUSE, EULOGIES, GLORY, GOD, HAPPINESS AND UNHAPPINESS, HARM, HEAVEN, LOVE AND HATE, LOVE AND LOVERS, PRAISES, PRAYERS, PROTECTION

898 "God bless us, every one." **Terry Kilburn**, as Tiny Tim, has the film's exit line. *A Christmas Carol* (1938, MGM).

899 "Go now, and heaven help you." Mother of a deceased werewolf, **Maria Ouspenskaya** gives her blessing to Lon Chaney, Jr., who killed her son, but not before Chaney was bitten. He now suffers from lycanthropy. *The Wolf Man* (1941, Universal).

900 FATHER FITZGIBBON: "Nonsense, I'll have you know that the very food before us was donated to the parish by the two boys you say have been accused of stealing. I gave them both my blessing." FATHER O'MALLEY: "And they gave you the bird." Pastor **Barry Fitzgerald** defends Stanley Clements and Carl "Alfalfa" Switzer when curate **Bing Crosby** voices suspicions that they are dishonest. He knows, but Fitzgerald doesn't, that they stole the turkey which is the center of the clerics' sumptuous meal. *Going My Way* (1944, Paramount).

901 "Blessed are those who expect nothing, for they shall not be disappointed." It's **Edmund Gwenn**'s benediction. *The Trouble with Harry* (1955, Paramount).

902 "You can ignore the blind hatred and stupid fears, or you can say 'screw all those people.'" **Spencer Tracy** finally gives his blessing to the marriage of his white daughter Katharine Houghton to black Sidney Poitier. *Guess Who's Coming to Dinner* (1967, Columbia).

903 "May all your sons be Jesuits, sister." It's **Robert Duvall**'s insulting blessing to the nun who tries to bar him access to his mother's hospital room. *True Confessions* (1981, United Artists).

Blindness *see* EYES, SIGHT AND SIGHTS

Blondes *see* BEAUTY, GIRLS, HAIR, WOMEN

Blood

see also BODIES, FAMILIES, HARM, HURT AND
HURTING, NOBILITY, PARENTS, PASSION, PUNISH-
MENTS, RELATIONSHIPS, RELATIVES, WARS

904 "Blood? You won't notice it much. The Mounted
Police wear red coats." Renegade **George Bancroft**
responds to Francis McDonald's reaction to the
Gatling gun, "Blood will run like water." *Northwest
Mounted Police* (1940, Paramount).

905 "I can feel the hot blood pounding through
your varicose veins." **Jimmy Durante** flusters nurse
Mary Wickes when he comes to visit her patient,
venomous critic Monty Woolley. *The Man Who
Came to Dinner* (1941, Warner Bros.)

906 "This Tartar woman is for me—and my blood
says 'take her.'" In a career which found **John
Wayne** forced to deliver many embarrassing lines,
this one as Genghis Khan, speaking of Susan Hayward, surely must have been difficult. *The Conqueror* (1956, RKO).

907 "Aye, it was Moby Dick that tore my soul and
body until they bled into each other." **Gregory Peck**,
as Captain Ahab, tells his crew how he lost his leg
to the great whale. *Moby Dick* (1956, Warner Bros.).

908 "How is it that you cannot stand the sight of
blood on anyone except me?" **Gregory Peck** questions his wife Lauren Bacall's concern for him.
Designing Woman (1957, MGM).

909 "O God! Mother, mother! Blood, blood!"
Anthony Perkins screams as he discovers the
naked mutilated body of Janet Leigh in a shower.
Psycho (1960, Paramount).

910 "My heart beats blood that is not my blood; but
the blood of anonymous blood donors." **Noel Coward** gazes deeply into Elizabeth Taylor's violet eyes
and says these unromantic lines. *Boom!* (1968, Universal).

911 "You give your loyalty to a Jew over your own
blood." **Michael V. Gazzo** can't understand why a
fine Sicilian godfather like Al Pacino would deal
with a Jew like Lee Strasberg. *The Godfather, Part II*
(1974, Paramount).

912 "A little adrenaline clears the blood." Vietnam
veteran and heroin smuggler **Nick Nolte** enjoys the
excitement and fear involved in his work. *Who'll
Stop the Rain?* (1978, United Artists).

913 "I bit her. I sunk my teeth in her lips so deep I
could feel the blood spurt into my mouth. It was

running down her neck when I carried her
upstairs." **Jack Nicholson** responds to Jessica
Lange's kinky plea, "Bite me! Bite me!" *The Postman
Always Rings Twice* (1981, Paramount).

914 "They drew first blood." Just like a child, who
claims someone else started the fight, **Sylvester
Stallone** justifies having destroyed a small Washington State town to his former Green Beret commander Richard Crenna. *First Blood* (1982, Orion).

915 "Maybe it was somebody whose gums are still
bleeding after $50,000." **Judith Ivey** makes a help-
ful suggestion about the murder of lecherous dentist
Joe Mantegna. *Compromising Positions* (1985,
Paramount).

916 "Do you have any idea how much blood jumps
out of a guy's throat when you cut his neck?" Psychotic hitchhiker **Rutger Hauer** holds a knife near
C. Thomas Howell's eye. *The Hitcher* (1989, Orion).

917 "No quarter asked or given.... Blood must be
answered with blood." **Nick Nolte** makes his pronouncement after Japanese soldiers massacre members of his adopted Borneo tribe. *Farewell to the
King* (1989, Orion).

918 "You know how hard it is to get blood out of
cashmere?" Tough private eye **Kathleen Turner,**
her arms pinned behind her, is undaunted when
repeatedly slugged by pudgy assailant Wayne
Knight. *V.I. Warshawski* (1991, Hollywood Pictures).

Boasts and Bragging

see also CONCEIT, GLORY, LIES AND LYING, PRAISES,
PRETENSIONS, PRIDE, SATISFACTIONS

919 "We'll show them a thing or three." It's **Ginger
Roger**'s boast as she and Fred Astaire fast-tango to
"The Carioca" in their first musical number together.
Flying Down to Rio (1933, RKO).

920 "I positively swill in their ale." Con-man **Eric
Blore** brags how he's fooled a wealthy family by
posing as an English lord. As a result they provide
him with everything he wants. *The Lady Eve* (1941,
Paramount).

921 "Ever hear of the decline and fall of the Roman
empire? That was our crowd." Witch **Veronica Lake**
does a little bragging to her new husband Fredric
March. When he says, "And the Fall of Pompeii, I
suppose that was your work too," she replies,
"Sure." *I Married a Witch* (1942, United Artists).

922 "Nobody gets the best of Fred C. Dobbs."
Born-loser **Humphrey Bogart** is trying to get

respect. *Treasure of the Sierra Madre* (1948, Warner Bros.).

923 "In vaudeville? I was vaudeville. You should see my scrapbook." Former vaudeville trooper **Kay Medford** boasts to Elizabeth Taylor and Laurence Harvey when the two drop by Medford's motel for a little heavy breathing. *Butterfield 8* (1960, MGM).

924 "We rob banks!" It's **Warren Beatty**'s proud calling-card. *Bonnie and Clyde* (1967, United Artists).

925 "Give me a girl at an impressionable age and she is mine for life." Schoolmistress **Maggie Smith** believes in indoctrinating and brain-washing her students. *The Prime of Miss Jean Brodie* (1969, GB, 20th Century-Fox).

926 "Oh, you men are all alike. Seven or eight quick ones and you're off with the boys to boast and brag. Well, you better keep your mouth shut!" Insatiable **Madeline Kahn** screams after Peter Boyle as Frankenstein's monster, as he leaves her bed and follows the strains of a mysterious violin out of the house. *Young Frankenstein* (1974, 20th Century-Fox).

927 "Hey, it's nothin'. Sinatra gives wings to hospitals. We all do what we can." Aging minor hood **Burt Lancaster** boasts to Susan Sarandon, making a big thing out of a phony gift. *Atlantic City* (1981, Canada, Paramount).

928 "Work's been kinda slow since cartoons went to color, but I still got it, Eddie." **Mae Questel**, as the voice of cartoon character Betty Boop, boasts to private eye Bob Hoskins. *Who Framed Roger Rabbit?* (1988, Touchstone-Buena Vista).

Boats and Ships

see also TRAVEL AND TRIPS

929 "Well, let's see. Look, I picked this guy up in Rio. Named him Glendale. Yeah, honey, lucky he didn't die on board. Oh, such a rough trip. On, no kidding—the third day out the wind blew off the top deck, on a great ocean liner, would you believe it? You should have seen the excitement on board. Why, they even had the passengers put on their life jackets. . . ." Con-man, gambler **Clark Gable** hasn't totally reformed as his librarian wife Carole Lombard would like. *No Man of Her Own* (1932, Paramount).

930 "Because she has a slender body. Because she is graceful. And because she goes through the roughest seas with a smile." Gay caballero **Duncan Renaldo**, as the Cisco Kid, explains when Martin Garralaga, as Pancho, asks why a ship is called "she." *The Cisco Kid Returns* (1945, Monogram).

931 "You save France. I'll save my boat." Skipper **Humphrey Bogart** rejects the appeal of Free French patriots on Martinique to use his boat to rescue an underground movement leader from Devil's Island. *To Have and Have Not* (1945, Warner Bros.).

932 "With all the unrest in the world, I don't think anybody should have a yacht that sleeps more than twelve." **Tony Curtis** puts on a rich act to impress naïve band singer Marilyn Monroe. *Some Like It Hot* (1959, United Artists).

933 "You, Bernice and I are, three of us, in a boat. Now it's my boat, and it's your lake, but Bernice has the oars." As they sit in a bathroom on his daughter's wedding day, **Gig Young** uses a not-too-clear metaphor to explain to his mistress Anne Jackson why he can't leave his wife Cloris Leachman. *Lovers and Other Strangers* (1970, ABC).

934 "We need a bigger boat." It's Sheriff **Roy Scheider**'s practical assessment to fisherman Robert Shaw when they get their first sighting of the killer shark. *Jaws* (1975, Universal).

935 JOHN PROFUMO: "You have never made love until you've made love in a gondola." CHRISTINE KEELER: "I remember a rowboat once, but never a gondola." British minister **Ian McKellan** is one-upped by party girl **Joanne Whalley-Kilmer**. *Scandal* (1989, GB, Miramax).

Bodies

see also ANIMALS, APPEARANCES, CLOTHES, DEATH AND DYING, EYES, FACES, HAIR, HUMAN NATURE, HUMANITY, LIVES AND LIVING, MEN, PEOPLE, PERSONS AND PERSONALITIES, SOULS, WOMEN

936 "How long since you had the body washed and polished?" Gangster's moll **Evelyn Brent** doesn't care much for the aroma coming from drunken bum Colin Clive. *Underworld* (1927, Paramount).

937 "I like that right arm. How about putting it around me." After a series of affairs, **Norma Shearer** returns to her ex-husband Chester Morris. *The Divorcée* (1930, MGM).

938 "Synthetic flesh! Synthetic flesh!" One-armed lab assistant **Preston Foster** is excited about growing a new extremity with which he strangles people. *Doctor X* (1932, Warner Bros.).

939 "You're not feeling well? Your arm is troubling you? Well, it's foolish to sit there in discomfort."

Lionel Atwill is sympathetic when scientist Preston Foster pulls off his artificial arm. *Doctor X* (1932, Warner Bros.).

940 "The main thing about corsets is you got to have something to put in 'em. Know what I mean?" **Mae West** extols the hourglass figure. *She Done Him Wrong* (1933, Paramount).

941 LADY LOU: "Are these absolutely necessary? You know, I wasn't born with them." CAPT. CUMMINGS: "A lot of men would have been safer if you were." LADY LOU: "I don't know. Hands ain't everything." **Cary Grant** arrests **Mae West**, putting her in handcuffs. *She Done Him Wrong* (1933, Paramount).

942 "I proved once and for all the limb is mightier than the thumb." **Claudette Colbert** is able to get a car to stop merely by straightening the seam on her stockings, after Clark Gable was unsuccessful with all his various hitch-hiking techniques. *It Happened One Night* (1934, Columbia).

943 "If her hands ever did dishwashing before, I'm an embroidery designer." **Lionel Stander**, as "Flash," tells his boss, retired racketeer Leo Carrillo, that he doubts the latter's new cook Jean Arthur has had much experience in a kitchen. *If You Could Only Cook* (1935, Columbia).

944 "I'm tired of having my own arms around me." After a brief struggle, actress **Margaret Sullavan** gives up her resistance and allows Henry Fonda to kiss her. *The Moon's Our Home* (1936, Paramount).

945 "Take care of your body, Maizie, because it's all you've got." Sexy, inept secretary **Dorothea Kent** quotes her mother's advice to her. *More Than a Secretary* (1936, Columbia).

946 WOLF VON FRANKENSTEIN: "Do you honestly know of one criminal act this poor creature committed?" INSPECTOR KROGH: "The most vivid recollection of my life. I was but a child at the time—about the age of your own son, Herr Baron. The Monster had escaped and was ravaging the countryside—maiming, killing, terrorizing. One night he burst into our house. My father took a gun and fired at him, but the savage brute sent him crashing to a corner. Then, he grabbed me by the arm. . . . One doesn't easily forget, Herr Baron, an arm torn out by the roots!" Replying to the new Baron (**Basil Rathbone**), **Lionel Atwill** memorably portrays a stiff, flamboyant one-arm police inspector. Atwill relates how a monster, owned by Rathbone's father, ripped his arm out of the socket. *Son of Frankenstein* (1939, Universal).

947 "You can't show your bosom 'fore three o'clock." Maid **Hattie McDaniel** chides Vivien Leigh for her choice of a revealing dress to wear to a party at Twelve Oaks. *Gone with the Wind* (1939, Selznick-MGM).

948 SUELLEN O'HARA: "Look at my hands! Mother always said you could always tell a lady by her hands." CARREEN O'HARA: "I guess things like hands and ladies don't matter so much any more." Both **Evelyn Keyes** and her sister **Ann Rutherford** are forced by their elder sister Vivien Leigh to work in the fields after the Civil War and their hands show the toil. *Gone with the Wind* (1939, Selznick-MGM).

949 "It's cold and I left my muff at home. Would you mind if I put my hand in your pocket?" **Vivien Leigh** flirts with Carroll Nye after lying to him. She tells him that his fiancée, her sister Evelyn Keyes, is engaged to another. *Gone with the Wind* (1939, Selznick-MGM).

950 "You ain't never again gonna be no eighteen-and-a-half inches." **Hattie McDaniel** shakes her head when Vivien Leigh can't get into an old gown after having a baby. *Gone with the Wind* (1939, Selznick-MGM).

951 "I've about as much shape as the man in the moon." Hunchback bellringer **Charles Laughton** acknowledges to Maureen O'Hara that he's no Adonis. Actor Laughton also had a low opinion of his appearance, once claiming that his face resembled an elephant's rear end. *The Hunchback of Notre Dame* (1939, RKO).

952 "You're losing your arm—you used to be able to pitch better than that." **Cary Grant** calmly ducks when his ex-wife Rosalind Russell hurls her purse at his head and misses. *His Girl Friday* (1940, Columbia).

953 "Soak them five times a day in boiling water and mustard. And go heavy on the mustard." Disguised as a doctor, **Chester Morris** as Boston Blackie, advises bungling police inspector Richard Lane who complains of occasional pains in his fingers. Later when Lane is asked how his fingers are, he mumbles, "Oh, a little mustard burned." *Confessions of Boston Blackie* (1941, Columbia).

954 "That's the hand that shook the hand of John L. Sullivan. . . . I'll never wash it again." Happily tipsy **Alan Hale** is the father of Errol Flynn, who as James J. Corbett, will take the heavyweight championship away from John L. Sullivan, played by Ward Bond. *Gentleman Jim* (1942, Warner Bros.).

955 "Your body! After all, what is it? Just a physical covering, that's all—worth chemically, thirty-two cents." Heavenly messenger **Edward Everett Horton** can't understand all the fuss Robert Montgomery is making. Horton snatched Montgomery's soul from his body long before he was to die, and Montgomery's friends had that physical covering cremated. *Here Comes Mr. Jordan* (1941, Columbia).

956 "Where is the rest of me?" It's **Ronald Reagan**'s startled question when he awakens to find his legs have been amputated unnecessarily by vindictive surgeon Charles Coburn. *Kings Row* (1941, Warner Bros.).

957 "A long, strong body is the measure of a man." Since **Clifton Webb** believes he's the most wonderful of men, and he does not have a long, strong body, this must be sarcasm. *Laura* (1944, 20th Century-Fox).

958 "My fingers looked like a bunch of bananas." **Dick Powell** considers his swollen digits which have undergone a working-over by a bunch of hoods. *Murder, My Sweet* (1944, RKO).

959 "Why don't you get a job? You look perfectly able-bodied to me—if I may use the word 'body.'" **Joseph Cotten** puts another move on Claudette Colbert, whose husband is away fighting World War II. *Since You Went Away* (1944, United Artists).

960 "Oh, I know I must be punished, of course, but not on my hands. Please, not on my hands. Today is the music scholarship, if you cane me, if my hands were—oh, please!" Young **Ann Todd** pleads in vain to prevent sadistic headmistress Compton Bennett from beating her hands. *The Seventh Veil* (1945, GB, General Films-Universal).

961 "Do you always go around leaving your fingerprints on a girl's shoulder.... It's not that I mind particularly. You've got nice strong hands." **Rhonda Fleming** shows some S&M interest when Robert Mitchum grabs her and tells her he doesn't intend to be double-crossed. *Out of the Past* (1947, RKO).

962 "There, there, Miss Cartwright. Your brother will play the violin again. I just sewed new fingers on him." In one of his many daydreams, **Danny Kaye** imagines himself as a brilliant surgeon, comforting beautiful Virginia Mayo. *The Secret Life of Walter Mitty* (1947, Goldwyn-RKO).

963 "Go ahead and kill me! Only when you do, don't lay your hands on me. Use this!" Disgusted and disheartened, **Loretta Young** offers her new husband Orson Welles a poker from the fireplace when she finally realizes that he's a Nazi war criminal posing as a professor at a small New England school. She knows he'll have to kill her to protect himself. *The Stranger* (1947, Warner Bros.).

964 "We used to shake hands a lot!" It's **Jean Hagen**'s incredible reply under oath when lawyer Katharine Hepburn asks Hagen if Tom Ewell ever touched her prior to the day his wife Judy Holliday took a shot at the two of them. *Adam's Rib* (1949, MGM).

965 "What's the matter with you? You got any idea how many times you can get hit in the stomach in a four-round bout? You know, the human body wasn't made for the sole benefit of the fight game. You hit a man in the head hard enough and long enough or just once, and you can either scramble his brains or maybe kill him. And for what? To fill a hall? To win bets for somebody you don't even know? What does it prove? Is that a way to make a living?" In trying to dissuade Kirk Douglas from making a career of boxing, **Paul Stewart** says he doesn't understand why boxing is considered a sport. *Champion* (1949, Kramer-United Artists).

966 "I suppose you know that you have a wonderful body. I'd like to do it in clay." Sculptress **Lola Albright** seductively licks her lips as she gazes at boxer Kirk Douglas. *Champion* (1949, Kramer-United Artists).

967 "Nicely packed.... Not much meat on her, but what's there is cherce." **Spencer Tracy** admires Katharine Hepburn's trim, athletic figure as the camera discreetly follows her fanny and legs. The line is fondly remembered because of the Brooklynese way that Tracy says it. *Pat and Mike* (1952, MGM).

968 "A starved body has a skinny soul." Mexican revolutionary Emiliano Zapata, played by **Marlon Brando**, insists that poor peasants must be fed before all else. *Viva Zapata!* (1952, 20th Century-Fox).

969 "Bless your big bony knees." **Ava Gardner** reacts to Clark Gable in safari shorts. *Mogambo* (1953, RKO, MGM).

970 "You look like you need a hand." Cowboy **Lee Marvin** makes a sarcastic offer to one-armed stranger Spencer Tracy who arrives on a train at a desolate one-horse town. *Bad Day at Black Rock* (1954, MGM).

971 LEONARD VOLE: "It's so weird thinking of her now lying in that living room, murdered." SIR WILFRID ROBARTS: "I assure you she's been moved by now. To leave her lying around would be unfeeling, unlawful and unsanitary." Charged with her murder,

Tyrone Power is assured by his barrister **Charles Laughton** that the authorities have taken away Norma Varden's body. *Witness for the Prosecution* (1957, United Artists).

972 "I don't want her! I've got a good figure. I want to have some fun." Marilyn Monroe-like actress **Kim Stanley** regards a baby as a ball and chain that will ruin her shapely body. *The Goddess* (1958, Columbia).

973 "You don't leave fingerprints on a piece of string." Police captain **Orson Welles** theorizes to his partner Joseph Calleia that strangling is the best way to kill a person and not be detected. *Touch of Evil* (1958, Universal-International).

974 LORA MEREDITH: "What's the matter?" STEVE ARCHER: "Your bones." LORA: "What about my bones?" STEVE: "They're perfect. I could easily imagine my camera having a love affair with you." Aspiring actress **Lana Turner** is being interviewed by photographer **John Gavin**. *Imitation of Life* (1959, Universal).

975 DAPHNE (JERRY): "I feel like everyone is staring at me." JOSEPHINE (JOE): "With those legs, are you kidding?" **Jack Lemmon** and **Tony Curtis,** disguised as female musicians, hobble along on high heels to a train. *Some Like It Hot* (1959, United Artists).

976 "Now you've done it! Now you have done it!. . . You tore off one of my chests." While both are dressed as women, Tony Curtis gets a bit rough with **Jack Lemmon**, dislodging one of his phony "breasts" in his bra. A bit later, Lemmon complains that Curtis has ripped off the other one. *Some Like It Hot* (1959, United Artists).

977 "The human body is a continent. You can spend a lifetime exploring it." Dutch painter **Hardy Kruger** speaks of his artistic specialty. *Blind Date* aka: *Chance Meeting* (1960, GB, Rank-Paramount).

978 "I'll replace it with her fine soft flesh." Janet Leigh imagines the reaction of **Frank Albertson**, whose $40,000 she has stolen. *Psycho* (1960, Paramount).

979 "A good body with a dull mind is as cheap as life itself." **Peter Ustinov** addresses newly-arrived slaves at his gladiator school. *Spartacus* (1960, Universal).

980 "I can't use my left hand at all. I got it caught in a cotton gin when I was twelve years old. All my muscles were torn loose." Small southern town defense attorney Gregory Peck uses black **Brock Peters**' testimony and the evidence that the white girl Peters is accused of beating and raping, was struck by someone who was left-handed, to show that Peters couldn't be the guilty party. Nevertheless, Peters is convicted. *To Kill a Mockingbird* (1962, United Artists).

981 ALEX MEDBOURNE: "Carl, do you think we ought to go in there?" DR. CARL HEIDEGGER: "Heh, afraid of dust and meaningless bones, Alex?" MEDBOURNE: "You're a doctor. You're used to these things." HEIDEGGER: "As a doctor, I can tell you you're not so far removed from dust and meaningless bones yourself." The longtime friendship of **Vincent Price** and **Sebastian Cabot** will be tragically and fatally altered after the two enter a tomb in the "Dr. Heidegger's Experiment" segment. *Twice Told Tales* (1963, United Artists).

982 "Your body is your only passport." **Anthony Eisley** loves prostitute Constance Towers, but refuses to believe that she can give up her unsavory life. *The Naked Kiss* (1964, F&F-Allied Artists).

983 "Oh, Mama, all they want is my body." **Carroll Baker**, as Jean Harlow, is forced to say this embarrassing line to Angela Lansbury. *Harlow* (1965, Paramount).

984 "Mother, I know I don't have any talent and I know all I have is a body and I am doing my bust exercises. . . I feel a little top heavy." **Sharon Tate**, who really wasn't all that top-heavy, talks on the phone with her ambitious mother. Later, tiring of her exercises before a mirror, Tate says, "To hell with it. . . let 'em droop." *Valley of the Dolls* (1967, 20th Century-Fox).

985 "All I've ever had is a body and now I won't even have that. Let's face it, all I know how to do is take off my clothes." **Sharon Tate** tells her troubles to Barbara Parkins. Having learned she must have a mastectomy, Tate decides to end it all. *Valley of the Dolls* (1967, 20th Century-Fox).

986 "The bones are good." Fashion magazine editor **Kay Thompson** evaluates Audrey Hepburn, whom photographer Fred Astaire wishes to make their "new face." *Funny Face* (1968, Columbia).

987 "Growing a penis." It's the smart-aleck reply of college student **Ali MacGraw** when a relative asks her what she had done the previous summer. *Goodbye, Columbus* (1969, Paramount).

988 "Look at these breasts, Mark, aren't they beautiful?" Fiftyish **Elizabeth Taylor** has undergone extensive cosmetic surgery in a "vain" attempt to win back her husband, Henry Fonda. *Ash Wednesday* (1973, Paramount).

989 "One of these days you're gonna be just as pretty as Mademoiselle, maybe prettier. You already got bone structure. When I was your age, I didn't have no bone structure. Took me years to get bone structure. And don't think bone structure's not important. Nobody started to call me Mademoiselle until I was seventeen and gettin' a little bone structure." **Madeline Kahn** unsuccessfully tries to con young Tatum O'Neal. *Paper Moon* (1973, Paramount).

990 "A hand I could have sat in took hold of my shoulder." Private eye **Robert Mitchum** describes his encounter with extra-large Jack O'Halloran. *Farewell, My Lovely* (1975, GB, Avco Embassy).

991 "She'd have decent legs way up to her bum." Young chauffeur **John Jarratt** imagines what he cannot see about Anne Lambert as the beautiful and mysterious Miranda. *Picnic at Hanging Rock* (1975, Australia, Atlantic Releasing).

992 "Not everyone in the world is after your magnificent body, lady. In the first place, it's not so magnificent. It's fair, but it ain't keepin' me up nights, ya know? I don't even think you're very pretty. Maybe if you smiled once and awhile, okay, but I don't want you to do anything against your religion. . . I don't want to jump on your bones. I don't even want to see you in the morning." **Richard Dreyfuss** lays it out for Marsha Mason with whom he reluctantly shares an apartment. *The Goodbye Girl* (1977, Warner Bros.).

993 "The legs of a woman are like the stems of a compass that measure the terrestrial globe in all directions—giving it balance and grace." The first thing that attracts lover extraordinaire **Charles Denner** to a woman is her legs. *The Man Who Loved Women* (1977, Fr., Les Films du Carrosse and Les Productions Artistes Associes).

994 "My breasts are very nice—nicer than the other girls." **Susan Sarandon**, born and raised in a Storyville whorehouse, compares favorably. *Pretty Baby* (1978, Paramount).

995 "My mum says you're a boy, but I told her you were a girl 'cos I've seen your tits." There's no fooling young **Kevin Wilson** as he talks to masculine-looking Bronwyn Mackay-Payne as Australian swimmer Dawn Fraser. *Dawn* (1979, Australia, Aquataurus-Hoyts).

996 NED RACINE: "You shouldn't dress like that." MATTY WALKER: "This is a blouse and skirt. I don't know what you're talking about." RACINE: "You shouldn't wear that body." Lawyer **William Hurt** is in heat because **Kathleen Turner** looks so hot. *Body Heat* (1981, Warner Bros.).

997 "Do you think I'm too small on top?" Sixteen-year-old **Brooke Shields** inquires about her bust to her seventeen-year-old lover Martin Hewitt in arguably the worst movie ever made. *Endless Love* (1981, Universal).

998 "His bare bottom shone white in the moonlight." **Linda Griffiths** recalls an adolescent voyeuristic experience. *Lianna* (1983, United Artists).

999 "She's got a behind you'd like to eat lunch off." **Steve Martin** refers to the very fine derriere of Kathleen Turner. *The Man with Two Brains* (1983, Warner Bros.).

1000 "They all look as though they died before they died." Lesbian beautician **Diana Scarwid** specializes in grooming dead bodies so they'll be ready for viewing. She speaks of the bodies of workers from Kerr-McGee nuclear processing plant. *Silkwood* (1983, ABC).

1001 "She broke with Freud over the concept of penis envy. He thought it was only limited to women." **Woody Allen** speaks of his psychiatrist Mia Farrow. *Zelig* (1983, Orion).

1002 "They're just like on a cow but in a more stupid place." **Matthew Modine** reacts to his friend Nicolas Cage as Cage extolls the beauty of the female breast. *Birdy* (1984, Tri-Star).

1003 DANA BARRETT: "Do you want this body?" DR. PETER VENKMAN: "Is this a trick question?" Possessed by a demon, boiling with lust **Sigourney Weaver** offers herself to parapsychologist **Bill Murray**. *Ghostbusters* (1984, Columbia).

1004 "I got a great chest. It's the most interesting thing about me." Aging sex kitten **Carol Wayne** delivers the most tragic line of the film. *Heartbreakers* (1984, Orion).

1005 "My body is overcome in frenzied spasms of delight." **Candi Milo**, secretary of a Grenada-like Caribbean medical school, speaks this line when Steve Guttenberg reaches for her. She has learned English by studying films such as *Valley of the Dolls*. *Bad Medicine* (1985, 20th Century-Fox).

1006 "With the shape my body is in, I could donate it to science fiction." Overweight **Rodney Dangerfield** has numerous bad habits that only make things worse. *Back to School* (1986, Orion).

1007 "I'm seventy-three years old. I've seen all the wonders of the world and I never laid eyes on a finer sight than, the curve of Betty Browning's breasts." Drunk again at a family Christmas celebration, patriarch **Ian Bannen** fondly remembers some of the women he's known and had in the past. *Hope and Glory* (1987, GB, Columbia).

1008 "Just think of her body parts being separated, say with a meat cleaver, and laid out. She wouldn't seem so impressive then." **Lea Thompson** makes a suggestion to her friend Victoria Jackson about blonde bombshell Valeri Breiman. *Casual Sex?* (1988, Universal).

1009 "Stretch marks are the badge of a real woman." Old-fashioned, strictly religious **Kenneth Mars** shares his views on childbearing with his son Randall Batinkoff and his pregnant girlfriend Molly Ringwald. *For Keeps* (1988, Tri-Star).

1010 "Easy with the leg, will you. . . quit staring up my gown." Broken leg in a cast, **Sigourney Weaver** yells at an attendant who's helping her into her hospital bed and helping himself to a free look up her hospital gown. *Working Girl* (1988, 20th Century-Fox).

1011 "I will not have you use the word penis in this house." **Caroline Kava** isn't a bit understanding when her paraplegic son Tom Cruise comes home drunk one night and rants about his inoperative penis. *Born on the Fourth of July* (1989, Universal).

1012 "I would give everything, Timmie, everything I've got, everything I believe, all my values, just to have my body back again, just to be whole. But I'm never going to be whole again." Bullets in Vietnam shattered the spinal cord of **Tom Cruise**, leaving him paralyzed from the chest down. He is speaking to his younger brother, Josh Evans, a war protester. *Born on the Fourth of July* (1989, Universal).

1013 "What do you expect? Your body's cream sauce all over Wisconsin Avenue." A heavenly functionary explains to recently dead Christopher McDonald why he feels funny. *Chances Are* (1989, Tri-Star).

1014 "You're wrong, he wants my body." **Cybill Shepherd** assures long-time admirer Ryan O'Neal that Robert Downey, Jr., her reincarnated husband, isn't out to get her money. *Chances Are* (1989, Tri-Star).

1015 "Looks like a penis to me—only smaller." **Bernadette Peters** has the perfect squelch when a

flasher opens his raincoat to expose himself and says "Whadda ya think?" *Pink Cadillac* (1989, Warner Bros.).

1016 "We use our breasts as weapons." Drapette (50s Baltimore slang for a female greaser) **Traci Lords** makes this declaration in a rumble with the "Squares." *Cry-Baby* (1990, Universal).

1017 "Oh, so you like large breasts." Foul-mouthed sorority leader **Mary Stuart Masterson** catches a man on an elevator staring at another woman's bust. When he denies it, Masterson (her body-double, actually) lifts her blouse and gives him an eyeful. *Funny About Love* (1990, Paramount).

1018 "You would take another body and make love to me. I don't know, it sounds kinky." **Bo Derek** mourns her deceased husband, Anthony Quinn, who has promised to return reincarnated and make love to her. In her films, Bo is usually up for kink. *Ghosts Can't Do It* (1990, Triumph).

1019 "Best tits in the Western World." It's teenage hooker **Jennifer Jason Leigh**'s proud boast. *Last Exit to Brooklyn* (1990, W. Germ. Cinecom).

1020 "Give me three." It's the high threes of the hands of four three-fingered mutant turtles. *Teenage Mutant Ninja Turtles* (1990, New Line).

1021 "I want to know and see the inside of your body. . . I'm going to become part of you." Painter **Michel Piccoli** has plans for his frequently naked model Emmanuelle Beart. *La Belle Noiseuse* (1991, Fr., MK2).

1022 "A word of caution. Guard your body well. Damage to it may result in painful metamorphosis or worse." **Richard Wharton**, a giant insectoid alien space ship pilot warns Robert Dryer, who also is an alien. Savage murderer Dryer's "horrible" punishment is to be genetically developed into human form and be abandoned on Earth. *The Borrower* (1991, Cannon).

1023 "Billy Blitton couldn't find his butt with both hands." **Gene Hackman** dismisses the talent of another lawyer to Hackman's assistant Larry Fishburne. *Class Action* (1991, 20th Century-Fox).

1024 "I'm a dumb male. . . I could never be a woman 'cause I'd just stay home and play with my breasts all day." **Steve Martin** is a dippy L.A. weatherman. *L.A. Story* (1991, Tri-Star).

1025 "Where are her breasts. . . . Is she anorexic or anything?. . . Looks like a thirteen-year-old." These are just a few of the comments that well-endowed, tart-tongued **Maureen O'Hara** makes about mortuary cosmetician Ally Sheedy, when the latter shares a first dinner with cop John Candy and his mother, O'Hara. *Only the Lonely* (1991, 20th Century-Fox).

1026 "They're nothing compared to my tits." **Teri Hatcher** issues a clear invitation to Kevin Kline who admires her beautiful eyes. Give Kline credit for looking that high with the low-cut dress that Hatcher is wearing. *Soapdish* (1991, Paramount).

1027 MAE MORDABITO: "What if my blouse pops open and my bosom is exposed?" DORIS MURPHY: "You think there are men in this country who ain't seen your bosom?" Flirtatious and promiscuous **Madonna**, who suggests that it might be good for business if she let her uniform become unbuttoned on the field, is momentarily quieted by her teammate, former dance hall bouncer **Rosie O'Donnell**. *A League of Their Own* (1992, Columbia).

1028 "My mind is alert as ever, sharpened by a sense of imminent separation. It's my body that's a bit shaky." Feisty septuagenarian **Sheila Florance** is cancer-ridden. While she is disappointed in her body letting her down, her spirit and will are unbound. *A Woman's Tale* (1992, Australia, Orion Classics).

Bombs

see also DEATH AND DYING, EXPLOSIONS, KILLINGS, MILITARY, NOISES, WARS, WEAPONS

1029 "We shall bomb Germany by day, as well as by night, in every increasing measure, casting upon them month by month a heavier discharge of bombs and making the German people taste and gulp each month a sharper dose of the miseries they have showered upon mankind. Once underway, our attack will be relentless. We will smash Cologne, Essen, Emden, Bremerhaven, Kiel, Danzig, building with increasing fury towards the day when we shall visit upon Berlin itself the complete destruction to which our preliminary raids have been but a prelude, that great day when we will strike with devastation and unconquerable strength at the detested enemy of all the free peoples of the earth." The narrator makes a promise that is carried out. *Flying Fortress* (1942, GB, Warner Bros.).

1030 "I don't like killing people, but it's a case of drop a bomb on them, or pretty soon they'll drop one on Ellen." American pilot **Van Johnson**, with the Jimmy Doolittle raid on Tokyo, tempers his regret for dropping bombs on Japan with fear of what might happen to his wife Phyllis Thaxter back on mainland U.S. He may be overestimating the range of Japanese planes and ships—but early in World War II, so did most Americans. *Thirty Seconds Over Tokyo* (1944, MGM).

1031 "I've got the power to make the atom bomb look like a firecracker." The body of nuclear physicist **John Agar** is taken over by alien Gor, a floating brain from outer space. *The Brain from the Planet Arous* (1958, Howco).

1032 "Dropping a bomb is like telling a lie." **Clark Gable** philosophizes. *The Misfits* (1961, United Artists).

1033 "Let's bomb the shit out of them. These people never give up." Brutally, insensitive colonel **Robert Duvall** orders his helicopters to attack a serene looking Vietnamese village. *Apocalypse Now* (1979, United Artists).

1034 "Drop a bomb! Drop a bomb! Wipe us all out." Middle-aged tormented writer of doggerel **Denholm Elliott** forlornly stares at the sky looking for Judgment Day. *Brimstone and Treacle* (1982, GB, United Artists Classics).

1035 "Good morning, survivors, this is radio Keno, Las Vegas. Well, the A-bomb went off and we're still here, folks. It's forty-seven degrees and six a.m." A voice on the radio announces the dawn of the Atomic Age in 1951 Nevada. *Desert Bloom* (1986, Columbia).

1036 "I never thought I'd say this to anybody, but I've got to go get an atomic bomb out of the car." Teen science genius **Christopher Collet** has produced a nuclear device. *The Manhattan Project* (1986, 20th Century-Fox).

1037 "There is no bomb in that building. I will bet vital parts of my anatomy to the fact." Police detective **Mel Gibson** talks his partner Danny Glover into entering a building where it is reported a bomb is planted before the arrival of the bomb squad. *Lethal Weapon 3* (1992, Warner Bros.).

Bones *see* BODIES, SKIN

Books

see also EDUCATION, IDEAS, LEARNING AND LESSONS, POETRY AND POETS, RULES, STUDIES AND STUDENTS, TEACHING AND TEACHERS, WORDS, WRITING AND WRITERS

1038 MAX MINCHIN: "I suppose she'll buy a book now." SADIE MINCHIN: "No, I've already got one." Chicago racketeer **Warren Hymer** comments sarcastically when he sees his wife **Marjorie White**

coming down a Hong Kong street carrying a reading lamp. *Charlie Chan Carries On* (1931, Fox).

1039 "Expert! I'm going to write a book about it. Call it *The Hitch-hiker's Hail*." Out-of-work reporter **Clark Gable** boasts to runaway heiress Claudette Colbert about his hitchhiking prowess. When all his various techniques fail to stop one car, he despondently says maybe he won't write the book. *It Happened One Night* (1934, Columbia).

1040 "What're you squawking about? When you write your book, it'll make a swell chapter: 'How It Feels to Be Starving—First Person Singular.'" Seaman **John Hodiak** snaps at Tallulah Bankhead, who complains that she's hungry. With several other survivors of the sinking of their ship by a U-boat, Hodiak and Bankhead are not quite sure what to do. *Lifeboat* (1944, 20th Century-Fox).

1041 "A book is a lovely thing—a garden stocked with beautiful flowers, a magic carpet on which to fly away to unknown climes." Smuggler **Sydney Greenstreet** praises a book as he holds a gun on writer Peter Lorre. *The Mask of Dimitrios* (1944, Warner Bros.).

1042 "I prefer books to people because a book doesn't double-cross you." Inventor **Spencer Tracy** has read more good books than he has met good people. *Without Love* (1945, MGM).

1043 "Emily Post should write a book for those thumb-riding." **Tom Neal** grumbles about his lack of success in hitchhiking. *Detour* (1946, PRC).

1044 "With a binding like you've got, people are going to want to know what's in the book." American composer **Gene Kelly** likens French gamin Leslie Caron to a book—a sexy book. *An American in Paris* (1951, MGM).

1045 "I used to go with a girl who read books. She joined the Book of the Month Club, and they had her reading books all the time. She had no more finished one than they'd shoot her another." Probably having never read a book in his life, drifter **William Holden** tries to find something in common with bright, bookish Susan Strasberg. *Picnic* (1955, Columbia).

1046 "You know something? You read too many comic books." It's all **James Dean** can think to say when punk Corey Allen slashes the tires on Dean's car. *Rebel Without a Cause* (1955, Warner Bros.).

1047 "I have no intention of leaving. I'm going to stay here, and I'm going to help rebuild the library. And if anybody ever again tries to remove a book from it, he'll have to do it over my dead body." Small town librarian **Bette Davis** pledges to supervise the building of a new library. The old one was set ablaze during a controversy between her and some politicians over a book they labeled "communistic." The politicians wanted it removed from the shelves, but Davis believed in the Bill of Rights. *Storm Center* (1956, Columbia).

1048 "I hate books." **Julie Christie** emphasizes her point by throwing them off the shelves. *Darling* (1965, GB, Anglo-Amalgamated-Vic-Appia).

1049 "A book to me means love because when you give a book about a romantic place it's like saying that all the days of your life should be as romantic as Spain and surrounded by a cover of happiness." **Diane Keaton** can't make her in-laws, Richard Castellano and Bea Arthur, understand why her husband Joseph Hindy's forgetting to get her a particular book she wanted for her birthday, signifies their marriage is doomed. *Lovers and Other Strangers* (1970, ABC-Cinerama).

1050 "Rommel, you magnificent bastard, I read your book!" Jubilant **George C. Scott**, as General George Patton, believes he's gained the upper hand in a battle with Germany's Desert Fox. *Patton* (1970, 20th Century-Fox).

1051 "I remember when I was a little boy I once stole a pornographic book that was printed in Braille. And I used to rub the dirty parts." **Woody Allen** tells of his early love of books. *Bananas* (1971, United Artists).

1052 ALVY SINGER: "Whose *Catcher in the Rye* is this?... You know, you wrote your name in all my books 'cause you knew this day was gonna come." ANNIE HALL: "Now look, all the books on death and dying are yours and all the poetry books are mine.... You only gave me books with the word 'Death' in the title." As they split up, **Woody Allen** and **Diane Keaton** sort out their books. She claims her books and reminds him of his morbid taste in reading which he tried to foster in her. *Annie Hall* (1977, United Artists).

1053 CUSTOMER: "Do you have the sequel to this one?" WILLIAM SNOW: "That is the sequel to the one before." Screenwriter **Harold Pinter** makes a cameo appearance as a pushy customer who is put in his place by polite bookstore clerk **Ben Kingsley**. *Turtle Diary* (1986, GB, Goldwyn).

1054 "Put your name in your books now while you're unpacking them, before they get all mixed up together and you can't remember whose is whose." **Billy Crystal** prepares for a future breakup when he and Meg Ryan move in together. *When Harry Met Sally. . .* (1989, Columbia).

Boredom and Bores

see also DULLNESS, FATIGUE, INTERESTS

1055 "I'm not afraid of anything, except being bored." Being a courtesan sought out by wealthy men, handsome men and sometimes wealthy handsome men, **Greta Garbo** has little time to become bored. *Camille* (1936, MGM).

1056 "You noble wives and mothers bore the brains out of me! And I'll bet you bore your husbands too!" Salesgirl **Joan Crawford** is disgusted when her lover's wife, Norma Shearer, confronts her. *The Women* (1939, MGM).

1057 "You have all the makings of an outstanding boor." American Nazi fifth columnist **Otto Kruger** grows weary of the patriotism of Robert Cummings. The latter is on the run from the police and the FBI, who wrongly believe he is the saboteur who destroyed an airplane factory. Cummings has been set up by Kruger. *Saboteur* (1942, Universal).

1058 "If I don't get out of here, I'll just die! Living here is like waiting for the funeral to begin. No, it's like waiting in the coffin for them to take you out!" Neurotic **Bette Davis** is a bored small-town doctor's wife. She counters her boredom by trying adultery, illegal abortion and murder. *Beyond the Forest* (1949, Warner Bros.).

1059 "You won't bore him, honey. You won't even get to talk." Showgirl **Marilyn Monroe** assures Anne Baxter, who expresses the opinion that famous theater critic George Sanders would find talking to her boring. *All About Eve* (1950, 20th Century-Fox).

1060 "Whenever I'm bored I always iron my money." **Bob Mitchum** explains his strange behavior to Jane Russell who has just walked in on him as he is ironing wet currency. *His Kind of Woman* (1951, RKO).

1061 "If you don't pull me out of this swamp of boredom, I'm gonna do something drastic. . . . Right now I'd welcome trouble." Confined to his apartment and a wheelchair with a broken leg, photojournalist **James Stewart** begs his editor on the phone to rescue him from his boredom. *Rear Window* (1954, Paramount).

1062 "I've discovered, Doc, that the unseen enemy of this war is the boredom that eventually becomes a faith and, therefore, a terrible sort of suicide—and

I know all the ones who refuse to surrender to it are the strongest of all." **Jack Lemmon** reads the last letter from Henry Fonda, who has been killed in action, to ship's doctor William Powell. *Mister Roberts* (1955, Warner Bros.).

1063 "One has to be as rich as you, Gaston, to be bored at Monte Carlo." **Hermione Gingold**, who has very little, finds it difficult to understand how Louis Jourdan, who has so much, always finds himself bored. *Gigi* (1958, MGM).

1064 "I suppose they're pretty to look at, the cars, otherwise it's very boring, really. It's like some people one meets. They look very interesting and after ten minutes with them you're bored speechless." Many people have had **Jessica Walter**'s experience, both with racing cars and people. *Grand Prix* (1966, MGM).

1065 RALSTON: "It ain't gonna be too exciting, but we'll get you there on time." GEORGE CALDWELL: "I just want to be bored." Railroad porter **Scatman Crothers** tells publisher **Gene Wilder** just what he wants to hear as he boards the Silver Streak luxury train heading from L.A. to Chicago. *Silver Streak* (1976, 20th Century-Fox).

1066 "It's a very little town. You might say it's boring. But that's the way we like it, and I get paid to keep it that way." Sheriff **Brian Dennehy** arrests vagrant Sylvester Stallone just before the latter breaks loose and makes certain the town isn't quiet, boring, or even existing anymore. *First Blood* (1982, Orion).

1067 "Oh, you're just saying that to bore me." **Jeff Bridges** is not taken with Claire Trevor's dinner conversation. *Kiss Me Goodbye* (1982, 20th Century-Fox).

1068 "It's like I'm totally not in love with you anymore, Tommy—I mean, it's so boring." Valley girl **Deborah Foreman** gives her old boyfriend surfer Michael Bowen the bum's rush, so she can take up with Mr. Wild, Nicolas Cage. *Valley Girl* (1983, Atlantic).

1069 "What do you think it's like sittin' in a tin trailer for weeks on end with the wind ripping through it? Waiting around for the Butane to arrive. Hiking down to the laundromat in the rain. Do you think that's thrilling or something?" **Kim Basinger** tells Sam Shepard that boredom drove her away from the trailer they shared before he went away for awhile. *Fool for Love* (1985, Cannon).

1070 "I would never have believed that a professional prostitute could be so boring." Mob hooker

Jeannie Berlin makes **Peter Falk** yawn. *In the Spirit* (1990, Castle Hill).

Borrowing and Lending *see* DEBTS

Boxing *see* BODIES, BLOOD, PUNISHMENTS, SPORTS

Boys

see also BABIES, CHILDREN AND CHILDHOOD, FAMILIES, FATHERS, GIRLS, MASCULINITY, MATURITY AND IMMATURITY, MEN, MOTHERS, PARENTS, YOUTH

1071 "Boys aren't any use to anybody. Don't you think I'm proof of that?" **Clark Gable** assures Hattie McDaniel that he's not displeased that his wife Vivien Leigh has delivered a baby girl. *Gone with the Wind* (1939, Selznick-MGM).

1072 "I have thought I heard you say, ''twas a pity I never had any children.' But I have. . . thousands of them. . . and all boys." Ancient British schoolmaster **Robert Donat** rouses himself from his deathbed to protest a comment that he had had no children. *Goodbye Mr. Chips* (1939, GB, MGM).

1073 "He was kind and gentle and lonely. In trying to be a man, he died a boy." **Deborah Kerr** fondly and sadly recalls her first husband for young John Kerr. The former was killed in the war being conspicuously brave. *Tea and Sympathy* (1956, MGM).

1074 "I like boys who are seventeen, eighteen. . . . Do not like hairy chests. . . I like smooth skin, tight eighteen-year-old bodies." Sensuous older woman **Linda Fiorentino** makes Anthony Edwards, who is eighteen, sorry he told her he was twenty-three. *Gotcha!* (1985, Universal).

1075 "Boys are like buses. You miss one; another will be along shortly." In voice-over at the end of the film, Canadian teen **Margaret Langrick** quotes her mother Jane Mortifee, with not a lot of conviction. *My American Cousin* (1986, Canada, International Spectrafilm).

Brains

see also ABILITIES AND CAPABILITIES, BODIES, HEADS AND HEADACHES, IDEAS, INSTINCTS, INTELLIGENCE, KNOWLEDGE, LEARNING AND LESSONS, MINDS, STUDIES AND STUDENTS, TALENTS, THINKING AND THOUGHTS, UNDERSTANDINGS AND MISUNDERSTANDINGS, WISDOM

1076 DR. WATSON: "Hello, what's the matter with you?" MISS PRINGLE: "That machine you brought in, Dr. Watson. It's supposed to give details of every

criminal case and the whereabouts of every criminal at any given date. You know how I worked to get it complete. And now. . . ." WATSON: "What's wrong?" SHERLOCK HOLMES: "I keep correcting it, that's all." MISS PRINGLE: "Mr. Holmes, it isn't fair. No machine can give you everything." HOLMES: "No, my dear, that's why I shall keep on using this old brain of mine." **Athole Stewart** finds a technician in **Raymond Massey**'s "computerized" study flustered and frustrated by the great detective's tinkering with the machine. Massey is delighted to triumph over the super-computer, saying, "I like a machine, Watson. It keeps me up to the mark!" *The Speckled Band* (1931, GB, British and Dominions).

1077 "I'll tell you a secret, Mr. Lane. Even though I'm a woman I have brains. I intend to use them." Turn-of-the-century feminist **Katharine Hepburn** tells her suitor Herbert Marshall that she intends to live alone and like it. *A Woman Rebels* (1936, RKO).

1078 "Crookback and Dragfoot. Misfits, eh? Well, what we lack in physical perfection we make up in brains." It's **Basil Rathbone** as the future Richard III, and his favorite torturer, Boris Karloff as Mord. *The Tower of London* (1939, Universal).

1079 "Huw is a scholar. Why take brains down a coal mine?" **Donald Crisp** finds a reason to keep his youngest son from following in his and his other sons' footsteps—working in the Welsh coal mines. *How Green Was My Valley* (1941, 20th Century-Fox).

1080 "This is the first time anybody moved in on my brain." Jazz club singer **Barbara Stanwyck** is confused when Professor Gary Cooper claims he wants to pick her brain about slang. *Ball of Fire* (1942, Goldwyn-RKO).

1081 "Some people's brains would never be missed." **Bela Lugosi**, believing that his creation could use a new brain, eyes guests at a cocktail party. *The Return of the Ape Man* (1944, Monogram).

1082 "Not only don't you have any scruples, you don't have any brains." Femme fatale **Ann Savage** easily manipulates hitchhiking stud Tom Neal. *Detour* (1945, PRC).

1083 NICK POPOLIS: "You don't have the brains of a two-year-old child!" HOPPER: "I know, look at the difference in our ages." **George Tobias** doesn't have much luck insulting **Ben Blue**. *My Wild Irish Rose* (1947, Warner Bros.).

1084 JACK JONES: "I got brains I haven't even used yet." DINKLEPUSS: "Well, don't let them go to your head." **Lou Costello** is put down by his partner **Bud Abbott**. *Jack and the Beanstalk* (1951, Universal).

1085 "He's using his brain, isn't he, Hal? Look at him. Clickety, clickety click. I can see it perking." Escaped prisoner **Humphrey Bogart** tells his brother Dewey Martin that Fredric March, the father of a family they are holding hostage, is trying to figure a way to outsmart his captors. *The Desperate Hours* (1955, Paramount).

1086 "Our duty to life is to live it to the utmost. We've been given a brain and we have to use it." Air Marshal **Michael Redgrave** is haunted by a nightmare of crashing a plane at an isolated spot off the Japanese coast. *The Night My Number Came Up* (1955, GB, Ealing).

1087 "If you had gas for brains, you couldn't back a piss-ant out of a pea shell." Professional stock car racer and moonshiner **Jeff Bridges** has a low opinion of a competitor. *The Last American Hero* aka: *Hard Driver* (1973, 20th Century-Fox).

1088 "It's like your leg—sending messages to your brain, only there's nothing there." **Lisa Eichhorn** deliberately turns that around in a harsh rebuke to her unpredictable husband John Heard. He is somewhat understandably bitter and disturbed because he lost one eye, one arm and one leg in Vietnam. *Cutter's Way* aka: *Cutter and Bone* (1981, United Artists).

1089 "I could easily kill you now, but I'm determined to have your brain." Deranged man of science **Donald O'Brian** dreams of prolonging life through brain transplants—and he needs some brains to practice with. *Doctor Butcher M.D.* (1982, Italy, Aquarius).

1090 "He's got the bod, but his brains are bad news." Valley girl **Deborah Foreman** sums up her boyfriend Michael Bowen for her girlfriends, shortly before dumping him. *Valley Girl* (1983, Atlantic).

1091 "I love you—I want to eat your brains!" **Thom Mathews**, a living corpse after whiffing deadly chemical fumes, makes an irresistible declaration to his undead sweetheart Beverly Randolph. *The Return of the Living Dead* (1985, Orion).

1092 GARY: "Should we give her a brain?" WYATT: "Yeah, we can play chess with her." Fourteen-year-old geniuses **Anthony Michael Hall** and **Ilan Mitchell-Smith** use their computer skills to build the perfect woman with specifications drawn from *Playboy* and other girlie magazines. The very acceptable result is Kelly Le Brock. *Weird Science* (1985, Universal).

1093 "The closest you'll ever get to a brainstorm is a drizzle." **Michael Caine** insults his old criminal partner Roger Moore. *Bullseye!* (1991, Columbia)

Bravery

see also COURAGE, COWARDICE AND COWARDS, FEARS, STRENGTHS, TOUGHNESS

1094 "You must be brave. You must. How else can I bear going?" **Leslie Howard** says farewell to Vivien Leigh at the end of his Christmas leave. *Gone with the Wind* (1939, Selznick-MGM).

1095 "Sat right there and took it like it was an ice cream soda." Dying **Thomas Mitchell** praises Richard Barthelmess, who brought down a crippled plane with a dangerous crash landing. *Only Angels Have Wings* (1939, Columbia).

1096 WILD BILL DONOVAN: "And I thought this man was a coward." SGT. BIG MIKE WYNN: "Coward, sir. From now on, every time I hear the name Plunkett, I'll stand to attention and salute." **George Brent** and **Alan Hale** speak of James Cagney, who dies a hero's death in World War I. *The Fighting 69th* (1940, Warner Bros.).

1097 "I don't need that spear. It's only a very young lion." Macho **Victor Mature** takes on a lion barehanded. *Samson and Delilah* (1949, Paramount).

1098 "Here are my brave bulls. They are the result of fourteen generations of breeding for bravery alone. They are born to fight. They have no other reason for existence, no other use on earth except an instinctive desire to use their horns to kill whatever disturbs them. It is that desire that dies in them last of all. The strange thing about breeding bulls is that you never know how successful you've been until a few minutes before your bull dies. A man who has bred a brave bull has a quality without measure, a spirit that may be tested only in the destruction of it." Old grandee **Ramon Diaz Meza**, speaking at his breeding ranch, talks with pride about his work. *The Brave Bulls* (1951, Columbia).

1099 "Speak not of twigs when you look at an oak." **Danny Kaye** scoffs when Angela Lansbury warns him that her brutal suitor Robert Middleton is likely to snap his neck like a twig. *The Court Jester* (1956, Paramount).

1100 "Mr. Rooster Cogburn? They tell me you are a man with true grit." Young **Kim Darby** talks in a stilted fashion, but she knows a brave man when she sees one—John Wayne. *True Grit* (1969, Paramount).

Breakfast

see also FOOD AND EATING

1101 "I see you're down early for breakfast, sir." When business tycoon Edward Arnold trips and falls down a flight of stairs, the maid laughs and butler **Robert Greig** comments dryly. *Easy Living* (1937, Paramount).

1102 "I'll bet you think an egg is something you casually order for breakfast. Well, I did once. But that was before the egg and I." **Claudette Colbert**, as author Betty MacDonald, makes an opening statement in this pleasant comedy, made memorable by the appearance of Marjorie Main and Percy Kilbride as Ma and Pa Kettle. *The Egg and I* (1947, Universal-International).

1103 "The breakfast isn't til eight, seven in the fishing season. It's not the fishing season." **Denis Lawson** called from his bed shared with Jennifer Black, and refused to accommodate visitors Peter Riegert and Peter Capaldi with any special service, when they came to his small Scottish Inn seeking food. *Local Hero* (1983, GB, Enigma-Goldcrest-Warner Bros.).

1104 "I eat Green Berets for breakfast." Rugged **Arnold Schwarzenegger** spits out the words in this silly hard action piece. *Commando* (1985, 20th Century-Fox),

1105 "How do you like your eggs?" Young divorcée and mother **Sally Field** prepares breakfast for aging pharmacist James Garner after he's spent the night. *Murphy's Romance* (1985, Columbia).

Breasts *see* BEAUTY, BODIES, GLAMOUR, MEN, MEN AND WOMEN, WOMEN

Bribery *see* CORRUPTION, TEMPTATIONS

Brothers

see also BOYS, FAMILIES, MEN, PARENTS, RELATIVES, TOGETHERNESS

1106 WARREN HAGGERTY: "Don't worry about him, he's just like my brother." GLADYS BENTON: "Maybe so, but he's not my brother." **Spencer Tracy** tells his fiancée **Jean Harlow** that she has nothing to fear from a phony marriage to William Powell in a plot to compromise wealthy Myrna Loy. *Libeled Lady* (1936, MGM).

1107 "Mike, I'm your older brother; I was stepped over." **John Cazale** complains to Al Pacino that he's been cut out of the family business. *The Godfather, Part II* (1974, Paramount).

1108 "One law of the West: Bastards have brothers." **Kathleen Turner** writes about villains in one of her gothic romances. *Romancing the Stone* (1984, 20th Century-Fox).

1109 "This is my brother, ma'am, and if he doesn't get to see *The People's Court* in exactly thirty seconds, he's going to throw a fit right here on the front porch. Now you can help me, or you can stand here and watch it happen." **Tom Cruise** squints through the screen door at a woman in an isolated farmhouse. She allows Cruise and his autistic brother Dustin Hoffman inside to watch his favorite TV show. *Rain Man* (1988, MGM-United Artists).

1110 "I like having you for my brother. . . I like having you for my big brother." In a touching scene, cynical heel **Tom Cruise** finally realizes he has affection for his autistic brother Dustin Hoffman. *Rain Man* (1988, MGM-United Artists).

1111 "Obviously! The moment I sat down I thought I was looking in a mirror." Piece of scum **Danny De Vito** thinks Arnold Schwarzenegger a nutcake when the latter introduces himself as De Vito's long lost twin brother. *Twins* (1988, Universal).

1112 "All the purity and strength went into Julius. All the leftover crap went into Vincent." Scientist **Nehemiah Persoff** explains why a scientific experiment to produce a perfect man ended up with twins Arnold Schwarzenegger and Danny De Vito. *Twins* (1988, Universal).

1113 "A toon killed my brother." Private detective **Bob Hoskins** can't get over that a cartoon creature killed his brother and partner. *Who Framed Roger Rabbit?* (1988, Touchstone).

Brunettes *see* BEAUTY, GIRLS, HAIR, WOMEN

Brutality *see* CRUELTY, SAVAGERY

Buildings

see also BUSINESS AND COMMERCE, GROWTH AND DEVELOPMENT, HOMES, HOUSES, PLANS

1114 "Say, you cover a lot of ground yourself. You'd better beat it. I hear they're going to tear you down and put up an office building where you're standing. You can leave in a taxi. If you can't leave in a taxi, you can leave in a huff. If that's too soon, you can leave in a minute and a huff." Freedonia president **Groucho Marx**'s rapid delivery of nonsense completely flusters wealthy Margaret Dumont. *Duck Soup* (1933, Paramount).

1115 "You can't build love on hate or marriage on spite!" **Myrna Loy** urges Jean Harlow to give up William Powell, her husband in name only. *Libeled Lady* (1936, MGM).

1116 "And when the day comes, I want to stand beside you and see the ships go through the canal and know you built it for all the people of the world." The spirit of half-caste **Annabella**, who died saving Tyrone Power's life in a desert wind-storm known as Black Simoon, speaks to Power as Ferdinand de Lesseps, the builder of the Suez Canal. *Suez* (1938, 20th Century-Fox).

1117 TOM MILLER: "Rome wasn't built in a day." FATS MURDOCK: "What we're talking about is already built." Talent agent **Tom Ewell** is pressed by ex-slot machine king **Edmond O'Brien** to make a star out of the latter's statuesque blonde girlfriend Jayne Mansfield. *The Girl Can't Help It* (1956, 20th Century-Fox).

1118 "Once you thought you were called to build churches of mortar and stone, but you were building chapels in the hearts of millions of men and women everywhere." **Dolores Hart**, as Sister Claire, says her farewells to Bradford Dillman, as the blind, dying founder of the Franciscans. *Francis of Assisi* (1961, 20th Century-Fox).

1119 HOMER SMITH: "I was going to build it myself. That way it will be built, slowly and carefully. I wanted to really build something. You know? Well, well, maybe if I had an education I would have been an architect or even an engineer, see? You know, and throw the Golden Gate Bridge over San Francisco Bay and even maybe build a rocket to Venus or something.... I'm not getting through to you." MOTHER MARIA: "Now the 'shapel' is being built and that's all that matters." HOMER: "I wanted to build it myself." MOTHER: "God is building out there the 'shapel' and you sit here feeling sorry for yourself because you are not He." **Sidney Poitier** is helping German nuns led by **Lilia Skala** build a chapel in the Arizona desert. *Lilies of the Field* (1963, United Artists).

1120 "Some of these buildings are over twenty years old." L.A. weatherman **Steve Martin** shows visiting British journalist Victoria Tennant the sights in the City of Angels. *L.A. Story* (1991, Tri-Star).

1121 BIG LOU KRITSKI: "What do you look for in a building?" LOUIE KRITSKI: "Death, divorce and devastation." BIG LOU: "What do you do with a building?" LOUIE: "Nothing." Slum lord **Vincent Gardenia** quizzes his son **Joe Pesci**. *The Super* (1991, 20th Century-Fox).

Bums

see also FAILURES, LOSSES AND LOSING, WASTE AND WASTEFULNESS, WINNERS AND LOSERS, WORK AND WORKERS

1122 "They always tell me I'm a bum. Well, I ain't no bum." Longshoreman **Marlon Brando** is a classic bum until he comes under the influence of pretty Eva Marie Saint and tough priest Karl Malden. *On the Waterfront* (1954, Columbia).

1123 "What's the use, baby? I'm a bum. She saw through me like an X-ray machine. There's no place in the world for a guy like me." Drifter **William Holden** tells Kim Novak that school teacher Rosalind Russell's evaluation of him is correct. *Picnic* (1955, Columbia).

1124 "I walked by the Union Square Bar, I was going to go in. Then I saw myself—my reflection in the window—and I thought, 'I wonder who that bum is.' And then I saw it was me. Now look at me. I'm a bum. Look at me. Look at you. You're a bum. Look at you. And look at us. Look at us. C'mon, look at us. See? A couple of bums." Alcoholic **Jack Lemmon** forces his dipsomaniac wife Lee Remick to look into a mirror and see what booze has done to them. *Days of Wine and Roses* (1962, Warner Bros.).

Burials *see* DEATH AND DYING, EULOGIES, FUNERALS, GRAVES AND GRAVEYARDS

Business and Commerce

see also AGENTS, BUYING AND SELLING, CAREERS, CONCERNS, CUSTOMERS, DEALS AND DEALINGS, DEBTS, MACHINERY, OCCUPATIONS, PROFESSIONS AND PROFESSIONALS, RESPONSIBILITIES, SALESMEN, SERVICES, TAXES, WORK AND WORKERS

1125 MARCUS SUPERBUS: "I'm in great haste in the Emperor's most urgent business." POPPAEA: "Come here, I'm the Emperor's most urgent business." Prefect of Rome **Fredric March**'s chariot has run into Empress **Claudette Colbert**'s carriage. She decides that he'll be just the man to ease her boredom with Emperor Charles Laughton, a man of questionable sexual orientation. *The Sign of the Cross* (1932, Paramount).

1126 "I've been in rackets all my life, and they don't pay off—except in dough... I've spent too much time in back alleys to want to go back to them." **James Cagney** joins the other side of the law for a change, becoming a government agent fighting rackets and racketeers. *G-Men* (1935, Warner Bros.).

1127 "How do you like that? Every time I get romantic with you, you want to talk business. I don't know, there's something about me that brings out the business in every woman." As usual, **Groucho Marx** is conning wealthy Margaret Dumont. *A Night at the Opera* (1935, MGM).

1128 "I hate business, stores, everything that turns people into pieces of machinery!" Efficient boss-lady **Claudette Colbert** blames her career on the failure of her marriage to department store owner Melvyn Douglas. *She Married Her Boss* (1935, Columbia).

1129 "It's so hard to be good under the capitalistic system." Wisecracking showgirl **Glenda Farrell** has set her cap for wealthy old sugar daddy Victor Moore. *Gold Diggers of 1937* (1936, Warner Bros.).

1130 "I'm telling you this is a good racket, and there isn't a racket I haven't tried." Ex-con **George Raft**, hired to work in a department store, has not totally reformed. *You and Me* (1938, Paramount).

1131 "Why don't you mind your own business?" **Ginger Rogers** plays a woman who is hired to pose as a gold digger and move into a millionaire's home. *Fifth Avenue Girl* (1939, RKO).

1132 "Our business is to mold men." Headmaster **Lyn Harding** urges young Latin master Robert Donat to have the "moral courage" to face his students again after they have mischievously disrupted his first class. *Goodbye, Mr. Chips* (1939, U.S.-GB MGM).

1133 "In the midst of life—one really hates to close these long-standing accounts. But business is business." Devil **Walter Huston** muses as he collects the soul of John Qualen with a butterfly net. *All That Money Can Buy* aka: *The Devil and Daniel Webster* (1941, RKO).

1134 "Finance is merely a matter of the heart being in the right place." Heavenly messenger **Claude Rains** glibly instructs the spirit of boxer Robert Montgomery as he's about to take over the body of a murdered financier. *Here Comes Mr. Jordan* (1941, Columbia).

1135 "You'll excuse me, gentlemen. Your business is politics. Mine is running a saloon." **Humphrey Bogart** leaves Nazi Major Conrad Veidt and French Prefect Claude Rains who have been questioning Bogie about his politics and convictions, or lack of same. *Casablanca* (1942, Warner Bros.).

1136 "For a place with a bad location and no neon sign, we're doing a heck of a business." **Rosalind Russell** notes that everyone seems to show up to stare at her sexy sister Janet Blair in their basement apartment. *My Sister Eileen* (1942, Columbia).

1137 "I'd like to know who besides me might have killed Marriott. He gave me a hundred bucks to take care of him, and I didn't. I'm just a small businessman in a very messy business, but I like to follow through on a sale." **Dick Powell**, suspected of murdering his client Douglas Walton, tells Anne Shirley that he feels responsible for solving the murder. *Murder, My Sweet* (1944, RKO).

1138 EDDIE MARS: "I could make your business my business." PHILIP MARLOWE: "You wouldn't like it, the pay's too small." Big-shot gambler **John Ridgely** and private eye **Humphrey Bogart** exchange unpleasantries. *The Big Sleep* (1946, Warner Bros.).

1139 "Well, from all I've heard about heaven, it seems to be a pretty unbusinesslike place. They could probably use a good man like me." Businessman **William Powell** lets his wife Irene Dunne handle religion in their family. She's worried that he won't get into heaven because he's never been baptized. *Life with Father* (1947, Warner Bros.).

1140 "Because it's our business to make it a hit. Tin Pan Alley is just a huge company to make people listen. Get them so used to it, they like it. Then, they buy it. Good or bad, it's our job to make it a hit anyway." Music publisher **Andrew Tombes**, who admits he knows nothing of music, can predict when a song will be a hit, while trained composer S.Z. Sakall can't. *Oh, You Beautiful Doll* (1949, 20th Century-Fox).

1141 "So did Jack the Ripper." Marine **Forrest Tucker**'s response to another grunt's comment that Sergeant John Wayne "knows his business." *The Sands of Iwo Jima* (1949, Republic).

1142 "No put money in show business!" **J. Carrol Naish**, as Sitting Bull, is willing to work in a Wild West Show, but he won't invest his money in the project. *Annie Get Your Gun* (1950, MGM).

1143 "Mankind was my business and common welfare was my business." **Michael Hordern,** as the ghost of Jacob Marley, angrily responds to Alastair Sim, as Ebeneezer Scrooge, observing that he was a "good businessman" in life. *Scrooge* aka: *A Christmas Carol* (1951, GB, Renown).

1144 "That's my business. . . mouthpiece for the mob, guardian angel for punks and gunmen. . . I'm a great believer in the easiest way." Crippled criminal lawyer **Robert Taylor**, in the hire of Al Capone-like mobster Lee J. Cobb, confesses to showgirl Cyd Charisse. *Party Girl* (1958, MGM).

1145 "Your business is a little dangerous." **Marlon Brando** says thanks, but no thanks to Al Lettieri, who wants Brando to get into the drug business. *The Godfather* (1972, Paramount).

1146 "It's war, Duddy; it's war. If you want to be a saint, go to Israel and plant some trees." Wealthy junk dealer **Joe Silver** lectures Richard Dreyfuss on the harsh realities of the business world. *The Apprenticeship of Duddy Kravitz* (1974, Canada, Paramount).

1147 "I didn't ask who gave the order, because it had nothing to do with business." **Lee Strasberg** doesn't consider an attempt on Al Pacino's life a business concern. *The Godfather, Part II* (1974, Paramount).

1148 "You know, most worshipful brother, Daniel Dravot, Esquire. Well, he became the King of Kafiristan, with a crown on his head. And that's all there is to tell. I'll be on my way now, sir. I've got urgent business in the South. I have to meet a man at Marwar Junction." Looking like an old, aged beggar, **Michael Caine** drops off Sean Connery's crowned head in the office of writer Rudyard Kipling, played by Christopher Plummer. *The Man Who Would Be King* (1975, Columbia).

1149 "There are no nations. There are no people. There are no Russians, no Arabs, no Third Worlds, no West. There is only one holistic system of systems. One vast interwoven, interacting multi-varied, multi-national dominion of dollars—petro dollars, electro dollars, Reichmarks, rubles, pounds, shekels. That's the atomic and sub-atomic and galactic structure of things today. . . . There is no democracy. There is only IBM, ITT, AT&T, DuPont, Dow, Union Carbide, Exxon—these are the nations of the world today. The world is a business, Mr. Beale. Democracy is a dying giant, a sick, sick decaying political concept. It's a nation of two-hundred million totally unnecessary human beings as replaceable as piston rods." Conglomerate president **Ned Beatty** lectures poor mad network news anchorman Peter Finch, scaring him with this grim speech about international business. *Network* (1976, MGM-United Artists).

1150 "I want to swap with you—everything—I want to stay here, run the hotel, do a little bit of business. You could go to Houston. . . I want you to leave Stella here with me, Gordon." American oil executive and trouble shooter **Peter Riegert** offers a

trade of lives and careers with Scottish innkeeper and sometimes solicitor Denis Lawson. Riegert wants the deal sweetened by Lawson leaving behind his lover Jennifer Black. Lawson isn't even momentarily tempted. *Local Hero* (1983, Enigma-Goldcrest-Warner Bros.).

1151 "It was great the way her mind worked. No doubts, no fears, just the shameless pursuit of immediate material gratification. What a capitalist." **Tom Cruise** admires prostitute Rebecca DeMornay. *Risky Business* (1983, Warner Bros.).

1152 "My name is Joel Goodsen. I deal in human fulfillment. I grossed $8,000 in one night." Upper middle class teenager **Tom Cruise** reports to the Future Enterprizers Club, whose members are kids eager to learn the art of capitalism. Cruise's business success is because he pimped for Rebecca DeMornay and other prostitutes. *Risky Business* (1983, Warner Bros.).

1153 "Have a drink. Once in Geneva, you and I and the microfilm, why don't we go into business together? Only this time not for five million dollars but for five million pounds." Kim Philby-like British spy for the Russians **Michael Caine** has a business proposal for his long-time rival Laurence Olivier. *The Jigsaw Man* (1984, United Artists).

1154 "Do you think there's something wrong with the world when a company like ours produces women's hair removal cream and nuclear warheads?" **Judge Reinhold**'s father George Coe has just bought a job for his son with a conglomerate named Inc., Inc. *Head Office* (1985, Tri-Star).

1155 "It's only business." Mafia Don **William Hickey** orders soldier Jack Nicholson to kill his hitwoman wife Kathleen Turner who has stolen money from the family. *Prizzi's Honor* (1985, 20th Century-Fox).

1156 "We're told that the business of war is killing and business is good. Well, our business is burial. . .and our business is better." Veteran of two wars, **James Caan** oversees the men who escort the many bodies to their final resting places in Arlington National Cemetery. *Gardens of Stone* (1987, TriStar).

1157 "Mr. McKussic, it seems you have been engaged in his business for purely romantic reasons, while you seem to have been involved romantically for purely business reasons. . . . Let me spell it out for you—you want to fuck your friend, fuck him—not me." **Michelle Pfeiffer** finds cop Kurt Russell's motives not as noble as those of one-time drug dealer Mel Gibson. *Tequila Sunrise* (1988, Warner Bros.).

1158 "Captains go down with their ships, not businessmen." **Martin Landau** explains why some of Jeff Bridges' backers have abandoned the Tucker Motor Company shop. *Tucker: The Man and His Dream* (1988, Paramount).

1159 "Show business is dog eat dog. It's worse than dog eat dog. It's dog doesn't return other dog's phone calls." TV documentary-maker **Woody Allen** barely makes a living in show business. *Crimes and Misdemeanors* (1989, Orion).

1160 "Your grandfather bought a boat from my grandfather, your father bought a boat from my father, and you bought a boat from someone in California! You ruined my business, you bastard!" Shipbuilder **Arthur Kennedy** screams at a former customer. *Signs of Life* (1989, Avenue Pictures).

1161 "We'll put the velour industry on full standby." Royal retainer **Peter O'Toole** is dryly sarcastic when ne'er-do-well and no-taste Las Vegas lounge singer John Goodman, by the grace of God has become King of England, and remarks that he has some ideas about redecorating Buckingham Palace. *King Ralph* (1990, Universal).

Buying and Selling

see also BARGAINS, BUSINESS AND COMMERCE, COSTS, MONEY, PAYMENTS, PRICES, SALESMEN, WORTH AND VALUES

1162 "It cures hoarseness. Who will be the first to buy a bottle?" Medicine show proprietor **W.C. Fields** offers his snake oil for sale. *The Old Fashioned Way* (1934, Paramount).

1163 "Wanna buy me a beer?" **John Garfield** radiates hard-boiled charm as he looks Priscilla Lane up and down at their first meeting. *Daughters Courageous* (1939, Warner Bros.).

1164 MAXIM DE WINTER: "Tell me is Mrs. Van Hopper a friend of yours or just a relation?" THE GIRL: "No, she's my employer. I'm what is known as a paid companion." MAX: "I didn't know that companionship could be bought." **Laurence Olivier** questions shy **Joan Fontaine** about her relationship with overbearing Florence Bates. *Rebecca* (1940, Selznick-United Artists).

1165 ILSA: "Richard, we loved each other once. If those days meant anything at all to you. . . ." RICK: "I wouldn't bring up Paris if I were you. It's poor salesmanship." **Ingrid Bergman** appeals to the memory of their love in Paris to get **Humphrey Bogart** to give up the Letters of Transit so her husband, Resistance leader Paul Henried, can escape. Since Paris was where she deserted him, Bogie doesn't think it's a good ploy. *Casablanca* (1942, Warner Bros.).

1166 "I wouldn't mind buying that for you." **Jesse Royce Landis** eyes Cary Grant, who she thinks would be just right for her daughter Grace Kelly. *To Catch a Thief* (1955, Paramount).

1167 MAJOR CLEVE SAVILLE: "The only trouble is Korea came along too soon after the real big one. It's hard to sell anyone on it." KRISTINA: "You're not sold on it?" SAVILLE: "I'm regular Air Force. I don't have to be sold." **Robert Mitchum** tells **May Britt** that he allows higher-ups to do his thinking—he just does what he's told. *The Hunters* (1958, 20th Century-Fox).

1168 "I sell myself. . . . It was free." **Gina Lollobrigida** confesses to Tony Franciosa that she's "the highest paid woman in captivity" but she loves him and to prove it, she didn't charge him. *Go Naked in the World* (1960, MGM).

1169 "I'll buy what I want, even a lover." Rich bitch **Diane McBain** is shopping for Troy Donahue. *Parrish* (1961, Warner Bros.).

1170 "Your advertising is dandy. Folks'd just never guess you don't have a thing to sell." **Faye Dunaway** angrily berates Warren Beatty who fights her off when she wants to make love. *Bonnie and Clyde* (1967, Warner Bros.).

1171 "Thirty million won't buy what it used to." World class jewel thief **Burt Reynolds** shrugs off what inflation has done to a future. *Rough Cut* (1980, GB, Paramount).

1172 "Where were you when I was selling cars?" Florist **Lou Jacobi** quips to multi-millionaire Dudley Moore, who's buying out the store for presents he plans to give to Liza Minnelli. *Arthur* (1981, Orion).

1173 "You bought the title, Baroness, you didn't buy me." **Klaus Maria Brandauer** sneers at his wife Meryl Streep, who loves his brother but settled for Brandauer's title. *Out of Africa* (1985, US-GB, Mirage-Universal).

1174 "It's just like a Tupperware party, really, but I sell sex instead of plastic containers." Incredible businesswoman and madam **Julie Walters** describes her services. *Personal Services* (1987, GB, Vestron).

1175 "I sell my body. What do you sell?" Hooker **Sally Kirkland** questions stockbroker Robert LuPone. *High Stakes* (1989, Vidmark).

Cads

see also BEHAVIOR, GENTLEMEN, MEN

1176 "I'll be quite frank with you. I suppose I'm what you call a cad." Avant-garde painter **William Powell** confesses to workaholic dress designer Myrna Loy that he doesn't believe in work, feeling life is meant to be lived to the fullest. *Double Wedding* (1937, MGM).

1177 "He wasn't a heel—he was the heel." **Kirk Douglas** amends Barry Sullivan's assessment of Douglas' father. *The Bad and the Beautiful* (1952, MGM).

Candidates

see also GOVERNMENTS, POLITICS AND POLITICIANS, VOTING AND VOTERS

1178 "Ladies and gentlemen, in all the years that I have been unsuccessfully mixed in politics, this is the first and only time that I have ever seen a candidate for office given an opportunity to prove publicly, permanently and beyond peradventure of doubt, that he was honest, courageous and veracious at being truthful." **Harry Hayden** hails Eddie Bracken as the man for the job of mayor because Bracken told the truth about his dishonesty and deception in allowing his hometown to believe he was a World War II Marine war hero. *Hail the Conquering Hero* (1944, Paramount).

1179 "Men! You say 'No thanks' to one of them and bingo! You're a candidate for the funny farm." **Tippi Hedren** explodes at her brutish husband Sean Connery, who has blackmailed her into marrying him. He's suggested that his kleptomaniac and frigid wife seek professional help. *Marnie* (1964, Universal).

1180 "He's a candidate for the canvas blazer with wrap-around arms." Hard-boiled policewoman **Paula Prentiss** makes a snap judgment about her new partner, drunken, burnt-out detective Robert Foxworth. Naturally, they fall in love. *The Black Marble* (1980, Avco Embassy).

Capitalism *see* BUSINESS AND COMMERCE, BUYING AND SELLING, GOVERNMENTS, OWNERSHIP, POSSESSIONS

Captivity *see* PRISONS AND PRISONERS, SERVANTS AND SERVITUDE, SLAVERY AND SLAVES

Cards

see also GAMBLING, GAMES, VICTORIES, WINNERS AND LOSERS

1181 "When player cannot see who deals cards, much wiser to stay out of game." It's an aphorism of **Warner Oland**, as Oriental detective Charlie Chan. *Charlie Chan Carries On* (1931, Fox).

1182 "Why, you're nothing but a pack of cards." **Charlotte Henry** recognizes the Red Queen, Edna May Oliver, for what she is. *Alice in Wonderland* (1933, Paramount).

1183 "Take a card. You can keep it: I've got fifty-one left." **Groucho Marx**'s card trick leaves something to be desired. *Duck Soup* (1933, Paramount).

1184 "Shut up and deal!" **Shirley MacLaine** delivers the film's last line to Jack Lemmon, who's been shuffling a deck of cards and talking incessantly. *The Apartment* (1960, United Artists).

1185 "After all, it's not the cards you've been dealt. It's how you play them that counts. And that's how I knew that somehow the kid was going to be OK." **Scott Hylands** reckons that half-breed William Korbut will be able to deal with the prejudice and problems life has dealt him. *Isaac Littlefeathers* (1984, Canada, Lauron).

1186 "Rain Man. . . let's play some cards." **Tom Cruise** and his autistic older brother Dustin Hoffman, who has an idiot savant talent for mental arithmetic, enter a Las Vegas casino to play blackjack. *Rain Man* (1988, United Artists).

Careers

see also JOBS, OCCUPATIONS, PROFESSIONS AND PROFESSIONALS, TRAINING, WORK AND WORKERS

1187 "This isn't just a newspaper story—it's a career." Editor **Cary Grant** tries to appeal to retiring star reporter Rosalind Russell's professional pride. *His Girl Friday* (1940, Columbia).

1188 "Really, George, I don't think being an aunt is the great career you think it is." **Ray Collins** tells selfish nephew Tim Holt that he shouldn't believe that merely being his aunt is much of a life for Agnes Moorehead. *The Magnificent Ambersons* (1942, RKO).

1189 "Funny business, a woman's career. The things you drop on your way up the ladder so you can move faster. You forget you'll need them again when you go back to being a woman."

Aging Broadway actress **Bette Davis** wonders if she's paid too much in human relationships for her success. *All About Eve* (1950, 20th Century-Fox).

1190 "I'm a 30-year man. I'm in for the whole ride." Stubborn private **Montgomery Clift** tells top kick Burt Lancaster that the army is the only home he's ever known or wants to know. *From Here to Eternity* (1953, Columbia).

1191 "I'm a much better shrink than I would have been a second baseman." **Roy Scheider** finally realizes that his psychiatrist mother Jessica Tandy was right in insisting he follow in her footsteps rather than pursuing a baseball career. *Still of the Night* (1982, MGM-United Artists).

1192 "You have changed. You are capable of betrayal. You abuse your position as a journalist and grow addicted to risk. You attempt to draw neat lines around yourself making a fetish of your career, and making all relationships temporary lest they disturb that career." **Linda Hunt**, as the male Billy Kwan, writes in his former protégé Mel Gibson's file. *The Year of Living Dangerously* (1982, Australia, MGM).

1193 "Only two things can really wreck a man's political career—being caught with a live boy or a dead girl—Don't get caught." **John Cusack** reminds James Spader of a Washington, D.C., maxim after Cusack's political career seems in ruins because he's indicted for influence peddling. *True Colors* (1991, Paramount).

1194 "I have an extensive collection of name tags and hair nets—not what I'd call a career." Title character **Mike Myers** lives with his parents and does no work to speak of. *Wayne's World* (1992, Paramount).

Carefulness

see also CARES AND CARING, CONCERNS, DANGER, RISKS, THINKING AND THOUGHTS, WORK AND WORKERS

1195 "Once I was afraid the hospital would burn down before I got here. Now I have to watch myself with matches." Ever-knowing and once eager nurse **Joan Blondell** shares her acquired feelings of anger and frustration with a new "Florence Nightingale." *Night Nurse* (1931, Warner Bros.).

1196 "You will take care of it, won't you? You won't let it get torn. Promise me." Fearful of even speaking about Leslie Howard being wounded in the war, **Olivia de Havilland** begs him to be careful with the tunic she's made him as a Christmas present. *Gone with the Wind* (1939, Selznick-MGM).

1197 "I've gotta be careful of hydrophobia." **Paulette Goddard** makes the crack after being bitten by Rosalind Russell in a cat fight over the latter's husband. *The Women* (1939, MGM).

1198 "For goodness sake, whatever you do, don't mar the coffin." **Andrew Tombes**, a mortician of questionable sincerity, exhorts Robert Armstrong as the latter crawls into a bier to capture a mad ghoul. *The Mad Ghoul* (1943, Universal).

1199 "Of course, you can't flinch from what you believe to be your duty, but certainly you don't want to act hastily." Blow-hard **Matt Briggs**, who never makes a decision if he can avoid it, comes down firmly on both sides of the issue of lynching three drifters suspected of murder and rustling. *The Ox-Bow Incident* (1943, 20th Century-Fox).

1200 "You should have been more careful." Petty crook **Jean-Paul Belmondo** puts all the responsibility on Jean Seberg when she tells him she thinks she's pregnant. *Breathless* (1959, Fr., Imperia).

1201 "Careful how you get out of a car next time." **Sean Connery** has just smashed a shattering blow to what appears to be a heavily veiled woman, dressed in black at a funeral. It becomes apparent that "she's" a he—a Spectre agent. *Thunderball* (1965, United Artists).

1202 "He wears a seatbelt in a drive-in movie." **Walter Matthau** comments on how careful his roomie Jack Lemmon is to always buckle-up. *The Odd Couple* (1968, Paramount).

1203 "You should be careful, you could get a hernia." Teen **Gary Grimes** shows more concern than knowledge of physiology when he warns "older woman" Jennifer O'Neill about shopping without a cart. *Summer of '42* (1971, Warner Bros.).

1204 "You be careful out among them, English." Amish **Jan Rubes** says good-bye to Philadelphia detective Harrison Ford who must leave lovely Kelly McGillis and her son Lukas Haas behind. *Witness* (1985, Paramount).

1205 "You can be yourself in the dark, but there's one dark place you have to be careful." **Randy Quaid**, pointing to his head, warns his son Bryan Madorsky. *Parents* (1988, Vestron).

Cares and Caring

see also ATTENTION, CAREFULNESS, CONCERNS, DESIRES, INTERESTS, LIKES AND DISLIKES, LOVE AND HATE, LOVE AND LOVERS, PROBLEMS, PROTECTION, TROUBLES, WISHES, WORRIES

1206 "I mustn't go before I tell you how much I care for you, Bert, dear!" As she says these words **Joan Blondell** slaps James Cagney at regular intervals. *Blonde Crazy* (1931, Warner Bros.).

1207 "It went all right, but I had to take care of a guy." **Edward G. Robinson** sneers to his gangland boss Maurice Black. Robinson shot the police commissioner during his first major holdup. *Little Caesar* (1931, Warner Bros.).

1208 "Take care of these men. Give them all my address." **Mae West** licks her chops when she comes across a roomful of men dressed in dinner jackets. *Belle of the Nineties* (1934, Paramount).

1209 "You think I care about money? I only care about makin' people do what I tell 'em." Jailed Lucky Luciano-like gangster **Eduardo Ciannelli** claims there's more to crime than making money. *Marked Woman* (1937, Warner Bros.).

1210 "I can take care of myself." **Katharine Hepburn** makes this proud declaration to Cary Grant just before she stumbles over a fallen tree in the woods. *Bringing Up Baby* (1938, RKO).

1211 "Nobody cares about me. You all act as though it were nothing at all." **Vivien Leigh** senses some indifference after she reports she was attacked in Shantytown. *Gone with the Wind* (1939, Selznick-MGM).

1212 SCARLETT O'HARA: "Oh, my darling, if you go, what shall I do?" RHETT BUTLER: "Frankly, my dear, I don't give a damn." When **Vivien Leigh** questions how she will manage if he leaves her, **Clark Gable** makes his famous exit line. *Gone with the Wind* (1939, Selznick-MGM).

1213 GEORGE FLAMMARION: "This means the end of Jacques as an extra man. Do you mind very much?" HELENE FLAMMARION: "Surprisingly little." **John Barrymore**'s plan to be rid of his wife **Mary Astor**'s admirer Francis Lederer has succeeded. *Midnight* (1939, Paramount).

1214 "I can get along without either one of you. I'm perfectly able to take care of myself." Dismissing ardent admirer Randolph Scott and husband Cary Grant, **Irene Dunne** promptly trips and falls, fully clothed, into a pool. *My Favorite Wife* (1940, RKO).

1215 "What do I care about a drowned dame in a lake? I got a body in here that's plenty enough for me.... Let's confine ourselves to what went on here.... That's all that's in my jurisdiction." Police captain **Tom Tully** tries to limit private eye Robert Montgomery's investigation. *Lady in the Lake* (1947, MGM).

1216 "Leave him be. A dead man is a dead man, and nobody cares." The soldiers in his squad believe that Sergeant **Gene Evans** is horribly callous when they come across the dead body of an American GI. When one soldier tries to remove the dog tags from the corpse he is instantly killed when the booby-trapped body blows up. *The Steel Helmet* (1951, Lippert).

1217 "What'd people say if I thumbed my nose at them? What'd people say if I walked down the street and showed 'em my pink panties? What do I care what people say?" When her reluctant beau Arthur O'Connell worries what people will say, old-maid school teacher **Rosalind Russell** lets him know she's too desperate to get married to care what others think. *Picnic* (1955, Columbia).

1218 "Who reads? Who cares?" Corrupt boxing promoter **Rod Steiger** doesn't feel threatened by Humphrey Bogart's intention to write a series of articles exposing the former's sleazy activities in the fight game. *The Harder They Fall* (1956, Columbia).

1219 "I don't care if he has carnal knowledge of a McCormick reaper." Former president **Lee Tracy** isn't interested in the personal shortcomings of presidential candidate Cliff Robertson. Wonder how he'd fare with the media if he was running for the nomination today? *The Best Man* (1964, United Artists).

1220 "Me? You don't care about me. All you care about is that bloody great army of children I'm supposed to work my guts out for. That's all you care about. Where the hell do I come in?. . . I can't even take a bath in peace, I can't. . . I can't even go to bed with you without one of them comes banging in in the middle, but so what, you just. . . I'm sick of living in a bloody nursery. Where the damn hell do I come in?" **Peter Finch** is Anne Bancroft's third husband and her eight kids are putting a strain on their union. *The Pumpkin Eater* (1964, GB, Columbia).

1221 "Women and children can afford to be careless; men cannot." **Marlon Brando** shares an important sexist lesson with his son Al Pacino. *The Godfather* (1972, Paramount).

1222 "Just lie there, Pop. I'll take care of you now." **Al Pacino** speaks softly to his stricken father Marlon Brando in a hospital room. Pacino has decided to enter the family business. *The Godfather* (1972, Paramount).

1223 "I don't care whether you're a man or a woman—I love you." **James Garner**'s sincere declaration as he kisses Julie Andrews would be more daring if he hadn't already discovered that the female impersonator really is a female. *Victor-Victoria* (1982, MGM-United Artists).

1224 "[He] really cares. About what, I have no idea." **Rodney Dangerfield** assesses his crazed, screaming history professor Sam Kinison. *Back to School* (1986, Orion).

1225 "Well, I thought I cared something about him, I never cared a whole lot." In 1937 North Carolina, **Lori Singer** has lost interest in her tobacco farmer husband Anthony Edwards. Hired hand Bruce Abbott is a different story. *Summer Heat* (1987, Atlantic).

1226 "Turned on the TV this morning. It had all this shit about we're livin' in a violent world, showed all these foreign places. . . . Started me thinking, either they don't know, don't show, or don't care about what's happening in the Hood. They had all this foreign shit on and nothin' on my brother—I ain't got no brother. . . I got no mother either. She loved that fool more than she loved me. . . I don't know how I feel about it, either, man. . . . Shit just goes on and on, you know. Next, you know, somebody might try to smoke me. . . . Don't matter though, we all got to go sometimes—seems like they punched the wrong clock on Rick, though. . . ." **Ice Cube** speaks eloquently to Cuba Gooding, Jr., the day after his brother Morris Chestnut was gunned down for no reason. Ice Cube and his buddies took revenge by killing those responsible. As Ice Cube starts to leave, Gooding tells him, "You still got one brother left." According to a title Ice Cube was murdered two weeks later. *Boyz N the Hood* (1991, Columbia).

1227 "What happened to caring and commitment?" Acting like the sexually insecure women he often took advantage of, **Eddie Murphy** doesn't know what to make of sexual aggressor Robin Givens. *Boomerang* (1992, Paramount).

1228 "You people really care about each other!" Street-smart New York police detective **Melanie Griffith** makes the astonishing discovery as she begins to appreciate the lives of the Hasidic Jews. *A Stranger Among Us* (1992, Hollywood Pictures).

Casualties *see* ACCIDENTS, HURT AND HURTING, VICTIMS

Cats *see* ANIMALS

Cause and Effect

see also CHANCE, CONSEQUENCES, FATE AND DESTINY, LOGIC, PROOFS, REASONS

1229 "The jugular vein has been severed." Physician **Warren William** makes the same diagnosis of cause of death each time a werewolf victim is found. *The Wolf Man* (1941, Universal).

1230 DR. BARNES: "Actually, it's the impurities that causes the laughs." INSPECTOR COCKRILL: "Just the same as in our music halls." **Trevor Howard** and **Alastair Sim** discuss laughing gas. *Green for Danger* (1946, GB, Rank).

1231 "The narcosyn then revealed the existence of earlier factors in the patient's life directly connected with the root causes of her present condition." Translation: Shrink **Leo Genn** claims to have discovered things about Olivia de Havilland's mental problems by probing her past with the help of truth serum. *The Snake Pit* (1948, 20th Century-Fox).

1232 "Only a mirage brought on by your terrible thirst." **Barry Fitzgerald** dismisses the idea when John Wayne gets his first brief glimpse of Maureen O'Hara and asks "Is that real?" *The Quiet Man* (1952, Republic).

1233 "He has 92 credit cards in his pocket. The moment he disappears America lights up." Sloppy sportswriter **Walter Matthau** isn't concerned that none of his poker cronies know the whereabouts of his fussy roommate Jack Lemmon. *The Odd Couple* (1968, Paramount).

1234 "It's a cat house on wheels. . . It's something about the movement of the train. All that motion makes a girl horny." Salesman **Ned Beatty** tells fellow passenger Gene Wilder that there's lots of good sexual pickings to be found on a train. *Silver Streak* (1976, 20th Century-Fox).

1235 "Whenever Mrs. Kissel breaks wind, we beat the dog." Minister **Max Showalter** tells Dudley Moore how he deals with his ancient flatulent housekeeper Nedra Volz and a spooked dog. *'10'* (1979, Warner Bros.).

1236 "My mother was going along the street when a procession of animals was passing by. There was a terrible crush of people to see them and unfortunately she was pushed under the elephant's feet, which frightened her very much; this occurring during a time of pregnancy was the cause of my deformity." During an interview with Anthony Hopkins' title character, **John Hurt** explains his beliefs about the cause for his condition of neurofibromatosis. *The Elephant Man* (1980, GB, EMI-Paramount).

1237 "If he had stayed home, this wouldn't have happened." Not yet radicalized, fearful and angry American businessman **Jack Lemmon** blames his missing son John Shea for his own disappearance in Chile. *Missing* (1982, Universal).

1238 "When I can't be cheerful, I go to the hospital until his affairs are over—or whatever causes me to have these headaches." **Gena Rowlands** informs a family court judge how she deals with her husband Seymour Cassel's infidelities. *Love Streams* (1984, MGM-United Artists).

1239 "Cameron's so tight if you stuck a piece of coal up his ass, in two weeks you'd have a diamond." High school truant **Matthew Broderick** makes a crude comment to the camera about his very worried friend Alan Ruck. *Ferris Bueller's Day Off* (1986, Paramount).

1240 "The last time I was happy, I got really fat; I put on 25 pounds." During a therapy session **Andie MacDowell** finds one advantage to her marital discontent. *sex, lies and videotape* (1989, Miramax).

Causes

see also BELIEFS, IDEALS, LAWS, OBJECTIVES, RIGHT AND WRONG

1241 "I believe in Rhett Butler. He's the only cause I know. The rest doesn't mean much to me." **Clark Gable** will change his mind about fighting for the cause of the Confederacy. See the next quote. *Gone with the Wind* (1939, Selznick-MGM).

1242 "The cause of living in the past is dying right in front of us. . . . I am a. . . sucker for lost causes once they're really lost." **Clark Gable** announces to Vivien Leigh that he's off to join the Confederate troops after the burning of Atlanta. *Gone with the Wind* (1939, Selznick-MGM).

1243 "Any special axes to grind, Senator?" Obnoxious reporter **Charles Lane** is suspicious of all politicians, including the newest junior senator, James Stewart. *Mr. Smith Goes to Washington* (1939, Columbia).

1244 "A man fights for what he believes in, Fernando." **Gary Cooper**'s version of "A man's gotta do what a man's gotta do" is his answer to fellow Spanish Civil War guerrilla Fortunio Bonanova, who wonders why an American school teacher blows up bridges in Spain. *For Whom the Bell Tolls* (1943, Paramount).

1245 "I love you when you get caus-y." **Spencer Tracy** won't be so delighted when he discovers that the case his wife Katharine Hepburn is so enthusiastically describing will result in the two becoming opposing counselors in a courtroom. *Adam's Rib* (1949, MGM).

1246 "It's sort of a cause. I want everybody to be smart. I want 'em to be as smart as they can be. A whole world of ignorant people is too dangerous to live in." **William Holden** explains his personal crusade to one of his clients, Judy Holliday. Unfortunately, Holden's crusade hasn't gotten very far. *Born Yesterday* (1950, Columbia).

1247 "You hold on and I don't know how. And I wish I did. . . . Maybe you were born committed. . . . I can't be negative enough. I can't get angry enough. And I can't be positive enough." In the morning after Barbra Streisand takes an exhausted **Robert Redford** into her bed, he tries to tell her why she attracts him. *The Way We Were* (1973, Columbia).

1248 "The only thing you cared about the huddled masses was standing on their bending backs." Attorney **Mary Elizabeth Mastrantonio** accuses her father, lawyer Gene Hackman, of using the causes of his clients to get his picture on the cover of *Time* magazine. *Class Action* (1990, 20th Century-Fox).

1249 "BOOM BOOM" GRAFALK: "What does it take to hire you?" V.I. WARSHAWSKI: "Money—and a just cause." "BOOM BOOM": "How much money?" WARSHAWSKI: "How just is your cause?" Sexy, tough private eye **Kathleen Turner** negotiates with potential client **Stephen Meadows**. *V.I. Warshawski* (1991, Buena Vista-Hollywood Pictures).

Caution *see* CARES AND CARING, WARNINGS

Celebrations

see also HONOR, PARTIES, PRAISES

1250 "When I heard you were alive, I drank a bottle of champagne and played Chopin's funeral march in swingtime." **Mary Astor** welcomes George Brent back to life. For the past ten months (long enough for Astor to have a baby), he was thought dead after a plane crash in the jungles of Brazil. *The Great Lie* (1941, Warner Bros.).

1251 "There are three times in a man's life when he ought to yell at the moon: when he gets married, when the kids come and when he finishes a job he was set on." Cattle buyer **Harry Carey** feels Montgomery Clift and his cowboys are entitled to a celebration for bringing a large herd of cattle all the way from Texas to the railhead in Kansas. *Red River* (1948, United Artists).

1252 "I want to celebrate. I want to be seen in your exquisite company. I want the whole world to know that I am the most fortunate of men in the possession of the most magnificent of wives. I want to swim in champagne—and paint the whole town not only red, but red, white and blue!. . . I want everybody to see how much I adore you—always have adored you, revere you, and trust you. Also how much I hope you have warmth for me. . . ." Throughout the movie, orchestra conductor **Rex Harrison** has plotted to kill his wife Linda Darnell because of his mistaken notion that she has been unfaithful. Finding he was wrong, he now changes his tune and sings her praises. *Unfaithfully Yours* (1948, 20th Century-Fox).

Certainties

see also BELIEFS, FAILURES, FAITH AND FAITHFULNESS, SECURITY AND INSECURITY

1253 "It's true, Matey. It's certain we will." **Wallace Beery**, as Long John Silver, promises weeping Jackie Cooper, as Jim Hawkins, that they will meet again. *Treasure Island* (1934, MGM).

1254 "I knew you'd come by this corner someday. . . . You'll always be my girl, Peggy." With blurred and understandably misty eyes, **James Cagney**, once a top prizefighter, is now reduced to selling newspapers on a street corner. Still smiling, he extends his hand to Ann Sheridan who is indirectly responsible for his blindness. *City for Conquest* (1941, Warner Bros.).

1255 "I always thought the best way to gentle a colt was to put a rope around it. But I'm beginning to have my doubts." **Burt Lancaster** is uncertain as to what is the best way to handle willful Lizabeth Scott. *Desert Fury* (1947, Paramount).

1256 "By informing a man about to be hanged of the exact size and location and strength of the rope, you do not remove either the hangman or the certainty of his being hanged." Valet **James Mason**, a spy for the Germans, doesn't get the fortune he expected or noblewoman Danielle Darrieux. The quote brings to mind one by Dr. Samuel Johnson who said, "When a man knows he is to be hanged. . . it concentrates his mind wonderfully." *Five Fingers* (1952, 20th Century-Fox).

1257 "I'll never be sure of anything again." The sinking of the unsinkable Titanic has a profound effect on the ship's surviving second officer, played by **Kenneth More**. *A Night to Remember* (1958, GB, Rank).

Challenges

see also ACCUSATIONS, ARGUMENTS, DARES AND DARING, DEFIANCE, EXCEPTIONS, IDENTITIES, PROOFS, WINNERS AND LOSERS

1258 "She is bad. Believe me there's one scoop you're not going to get without a little competition." Reporter **Clark Gable** challenges his main competitor Johnny Mack Brown for the affection of Jean Harlow. *The Secret Six* (1931, MGM).

1259 "Send more Japs. . . . Tell them to come and get us." Portraying gutsy Marine Commander James P. Devereaux, **Brian Donlevy** refuses to surrender to the Japanese. *Wake Island* (1942, Paramount).

1260 "C'mon, suckers, come and get me—what are you waiting for? Didn't think we were here, did you, you dirty, rotten rats! We're still here—we'll always be here." Surrounded by the graves of his 12 companions, **Robert Taylor**, the last survivor of a group of 13 soldiers ordered to hold a bridge on Bataan, shouts defiantly to the Japanese as he fires his machine gun into the mist at the end of the film. *Bataan* (1943, MGM).

1261 "You dirty nigger, get up and walk!" Psychiatrist **Jeff Corey** uses an unorthodox but successful therapy in dealing with black soldier James Edwards, who suffers paralysis as a psychological response to racism. *Home of the Brave* (1949, United Artists).

1262 TORREY: "You're a low-down, lyin' Yankee." WILSON: "Prove it." Excitable former rebel **Elisha Cook, Jr.**, is tricked into drawing on deadly gunfighter **Jack Palance**. *Shane* (1952, Paramount).

1263 FLAT NOSE CURRY: "You always told us anyone could challenge you." BUTCH CASSIDY: "That's 'cause I figured nobody'd do it." HARVEY LOGAN: "Figured wrong, Butch." **Charles Dierkop** informs **Paul Newman** that gigantic **Ted Cassidy** wants to fight Newman for control of the Hole-in-the-Wall Gang. *Butch Cassidy and the Sundance Kid* (1969, 20th Century-Fox).

1264 "Fill your hands, you son of a bitch." **John Wayne** and his horse charge across a valley to get to outlaw Robert Duvall and three members of his gang. *True Grit* (1969, Paramount).

1265 "I've never been beat. A lot of guys have tried. Seems to me there's more guys lately than there've ever been." Drag-race champ **Paul Le Mat** accepts yet another challenge, this time from Harrison Ford. *American Graffiti* (1973, Universal).

1266 "Mister, when you come to take us off the land, you better come with more than a piece of paper." **Jessica Lange** issues a challenge to an officer with an eviction notice. *Country* (1984, Touchstone).

1267 "Why work on a car when you can design one?" East Los Angeles high school mathematics teacher Jaime Escalante, portrayed by **Edward James Olmos**, challenges his students to learn calculus. *Stand and Deliver* (1988, Warner Bros.).

1268 "You know I'm a sucker for a soft dick." Stripped down to a skimpy bra and panties, **Melanie Griffith** begins to de-pants Tom Hanks, who claims he's not up for it. *Bonfire of the Vanities* (1990, Warner Bros.).

Champagne *see* ALCOHOL, DRINKING AND DRUNKENNESS

Champions

see also AWARDS, DEFENSES, FIGHTS AND FIGHTING, GAMES, PRIZES, SPORTS, VICTORIES, WINNERS AND LOSERS

1269 "I used to be marble champion of the Bronx!" **James Cagney** replies when asked where he learned to shoot a pistol so well by FBI training instructor Robert Armstrong. *G-Men* (1935, Warner Bros.).

1270 "Boy, there's a champion. She not only can give it, but look at her take it. There she goes on an assignment that's licked the best fliers in South America. We can't let her tackle this job alone. I think I've got an idea that'll get us on the next boat." Newsreel reporter **Clark Gable** has plans to help aviatrix Myrna Loy find her brother missing in the Amazon jungle—and get a big scoop for himself in the process. *Too Hot to Handle* (1938, MGM).

1271 "Eventually all things work out. There is a design in everything. You were meant to be a champion. You are." Heavenly emissary **Claude Rains** assures bodyless Robert Montgomery that his destiny will be fulfilled. *Here Comes Mr. Jordan* (1941, Columbia).

1272 "Did I say killer? I meant champion. I get my boxing terms mixed." **George Sanders** makes no mistake in calling scheming Anne Baxter a killer. *All About Eve* (1950, 20th Century-Fox).

1273 ADDISON DE WITT: "It's important right now that we talk, killer to killer." EVE HARRINGTON:

"Champion to champion." ADDISON: "Not with me, you're no champion. You're stepping way up in class." By the time **George Sanders** and **Anne Baxter** meet in New Haven's Taft Hotel, the day of an opening at the Schubert Theater, Sanders reverts to calling Baxter what he believes to be more accurate. *All About Eve* (1950, 20th Century-Fox).

1274 MARIAN STARRETT: "Are you doing this just for me?" SHANE: "For you—for Joe—and little Joey." **Jean Arthur** has just watched **Alan Ladd** knock out her husband Van Heflin to prevent him from going to a sure death facing gunfighter Jack Palance. Ladd, in his ceremonial buckskin and his guns strapped on, rides off to be Arthur's champion—and Heflin and little Brandon De Wilde's as well. *Shane* (1953, Paramount).

1275 "You fuck like a world champion—four fucking hours!" **Raul Julia** is impressed with Mel Gibson's sexual stamina while in bed with Michelle Pfeiffer. *Tequila Sunrise* (1988, Warner Bros.).

Chances

see also ACCIDENTS, CAUSE AND EFFECT, FATE AND DESTINY, GAMBLING, LUCK, PROBABILITY AND STATISTICS

1276 "If we get through this all right, is there any chance for me?" While on safari, **Neil Hamilton** becomes keenly aware of Maureen O'Sullivan's beauty, but she is noncommittal. *Tarzan, the Ape Man* (1932, MGM).

1277 "A hundred-twenty million cracked lips are straining at the leach. Where's your *patronism?* Here's a chance to do something for your country." **Jimmy Durante** makes a garbled argument that barber Buster Keaton should invest in a brewery as Prohibition is about to be repealed. *What, No Beer?* (1933, MGM).

1278 "I'll take my chances against the law. You'll take yours against the sea." Mutiny leader **Clark Gable** responds to Charles Laughton's promise that he will see Gable "hanging from the highest yardarm" as the captain and a boatload of loyal seamen are set adrift at sea by the mutineers. *Mutiny on the Bounty* (1935, MGM).

1279 "Keep shooting, you scum! You'll get a chance yet to die with your boots on!" Despicable Sgt. Markoff, played by **Brian Donlevy**, shouts at the mutinous legionnaires who are forced to defend a remote fort under attack by a desert tribe. *Beau Geste* (1939, Paramount).

1280 "You gotta look out for yourself in this world. You gotta see the main chance and grab it." Clerk **Dick Powell** states his cynical belief to his wife Ellen Drew. *Christmas in July* (1940, Paramount).

1281 "[He] should have stayed in college where he came from, but he begged for a chance and I gave it to him." Flight commander **John Wayne** expresses angry regret that he listened to young pilot Tom Neal and sent him to his death in the air against the Japanese. *Flying Tigers* (1942, Republic).

1282 JOAN: "I'll give you one last chance. Will you marry me?" EDDIE: "No." JOAN: "Let's make it two out of three." **Joan Davis** proposes marriage to a reluctant **Eddie Cantor**. *Show Business* (1944, RKO).

1283 "The generation has had its chance. The world is going up in smoke and let it come, I say, not a moment too soon." Murderous little cashiered British Major **Ivor Bernard** makes a bar room harangue in favor of Hitler and his plans. *Beat the Devil* (1954, GB, Romulus-United Artists).

1284 "A pretty girl doesn't have long—just a few years. Then she's the equal of kings. She can walk out of a shanty like this and live in a palace. But if she loses her chance when she's young she might as well throw all her prettiness away." **Betty Field**, who has been there, urges her daughter Kim Novak to parlay her looks into a secure and prosperous marriage. *Picnic* (1955, Columbia).

1285 "We ain't got a chance, guys like us, do we?" On the run from the police, little slum rat **Sal Mineo** resignedly sees no future for himself or his childhood chum Paul Newman, playing Rocky Graziano. *Somebody Up There Likes Me* (1956, MGM).

1286 FRANK RICHARDS: "You know what's between us? Hate, riots, lynching, prejudice. It won't work." JULIE CULLEN: "Somebody's got to take a chance to find out if it'll work." Initially, black **Bernie Hamilton** is reluctant to face the problems of a marriage to white **Barbara Barrie**. *One Potato, Two Potato* (1964, Cinema V).

1287 "Oh, that's unfortunate. I'm an everyday sort of man and my only chance was in being first comer." Shepherd **Alan Bates** reckons that his chances of winning Julie Christie for his wife are slim when her aunt tells him that she has dozens of suitors. *Far from the Madding Crowd* (1967, GB, EMI).

1288 "Ten years I've waited for this and I mess it up, it's back to the newsroom in Sydney, and that's a bloody graveyard." Australian correspondent **Mel Gibson** looks to make a name for himself when he arrives in Jakarta in 1965 to cover the tottering Sukarno regime. *The Year of Living Dangerously* (1973, Australia, MGM).

1289 "If this is Oz, Dorothy, I'd rather take my chances back in Kansas." **Mak Wilson**, as Billina the talking chicken, states his druthers to Fairuza Balk as Dorothy Gale. *Return to Oz* (1985, Disney-Buena Vista).

1290 "You'll only get one chance with me, sweetheart." Having had disappointing bed experiences with her husband Bryan Brown and his brother Steven Vidler, sexually frustrated **Rachel Ward** makes a cryptic remark to Don Juan-like Sam Neill. *The Good Wife* (1987, Australia, Atlantic).

1291 "I'm 36 years old. I have a wife, a child and a mortgage and I'm scared to death that I'm turning into my father. . .I never forgave him for getting old. . . . By the time he was as old as I am now, he was ancient. . . . He must've had dreams; he never did anything about them. . . . For all I know he may have heard voices too, but. . . he sure didn't listen to them. The man never did one spontaneous thing in all the years I knew him. . . . Damn, I'm afraid of what is happening to me. . . . Something tells me this may be my last chance to do something about it." **Kevin Costner** explains to his wife Amy Madigan why he believes he must build a baseball field in his Iowa cornfield. *Field of Dreams* (1989, Universal).

1292 "I know I'm just asking for the big hurt, but I thought I'd give us one last chance." Dripping with insincerity, **Bill Murray** bulls himself into the apartment of his ex-lover Sigourney Weaver. *Ghostbusters II* (1989, Columbia).

1293 "House, car, boy, girl, puppy, kitty. . . the poor bastards didn't have a chance." Lawyer **Danny De Vito** speaks of the marriage of upscale Michael Douglas and Kathleen Turner. *The War of the Roses* (1989, 20th Century-Fox).

Changes

see also DIFFERENCES, NEWNESS, PROGRESS

1294 "No one seems to realize that I am different now than when I went away. I have changed! I have seen things! I have been through hell!. . .I am out of step with everybody—all the while I was hoping to come back and start a new life—to be free—and again I find myself under orders. A drab routine, cramped, mechanical, even worse than the army. . . ." **Paul Muni** complains of his civilian existence as a menial clerk to his mother Louise Carter and his brother Hale Hamilton. Things get worse when he's innocently involved in a stickup and is sentenced to a chain gang. *I Am a Fugitive from a Chain Gang* (1932, Warner Bros.).

1295 "Everything's changed! I'll die here. I belong to the Delmonico period. A table by the windows, facing Fifth Avenue, with the flower boxes and the pink lampshades and the string orchestra. Oh, I don't know—willow plumes and Inverness capes, dry champagne and snow on the ground—God, they don't even have snow anymore!" Returning to New York after several decades in Europe, retired actress **Marie Dressler** has a romantic memory of an earlier time in the city. *Dinner at Eight* (1933, MGM).

1296 "In 1933 A.D. nothing has changed. Women are still fighters and think man's place is in the home." The 1933 whimsical comedy about Amazon women and their weak, dependent husbands, ends with this final tongue-in-cheek subtitle. *The Warrior's Husband* (1933, Fox).

1297 JULIA SCOTT BARCLAY: "Is our marriage just a bargain to you?" RICHARD BARCLAY: "You've changed. You're not the Julia Scott I know. I don't understand you any more." JULIA: "It was just my idea of being a woman." **Claudette Colbert** regrets that her insensitive husband **Melvyn Douglas** only married her because he wanted her to manage his home as efficiently and unemotionally as she did his office when she was his secretary. *She Married Her Boss* (1935, Columbia).

1298 "And of course, if things should ever get a little dull, you can always go over to Tulsa. I do think a big change like that is good for anyone." **Cary Grant** needles his ex-wife Irene Dunne about her plans to marry Oklahoma oil man Ralph Bellamy. *The Awful Truth* (1937, Columbia).

1299 "You married him for what he is and then tried to make something else out of him, but you couldn't." **Virginia Brissac** harshly scolds Patricia Neal for trying to change her husband John Wayne. *Operation Pacific* (1951, Warner Bros.).

1300 "I know you now—no friends, no woman. And now do you know what you will do? You will go to Carranza or Obregon. . . and you will never change!" **Marlon Brando** pegs emotionless professional revolutionary Joseph Wiseman. *Viva Zapata!* (1952, 20th Century-Fox).

1301 "I'm not a boy anymore. A person forms certain ways of living. Then, one day it's too late to change." Middle-aged bachelor, storekeeper **Arthur O'Connell** tells his lady friend, old maid schoolteacher Rosalind Russell, that he is too set in his ways to marry her. *Picnic* (1955, Columbia).

1302 "If we want things to stay as they are, things will have to change." **Alain Delon** is talking about the loss of the privileges of the Sicilian aristocrats in 1860 if political and economic changes aren't made. He's off to join the Redshirts of Garibaldi and do his part. *The Leopard* (1963, Italy, 20th Century-Fox).

1303 "She hasn't changed. She's the pied piper." **Bruce Davison**, as the older Patrick Dennis, happily speaks to his wife Bobbi Jordan about his aunt Lucille Ball, who is making plans for Davison's son. *Mame* (1974, Warner Bros.).

1304 "Children grow up, relations are broken off. . . love gives out." Unfaithful **Erland Josephson** attempts to explain his actions to his scorned wife Liv Ullmann. *Scenes from a Marriage* (1974, Sweden, Cinema 5).

1305 "You can't change what has always been. You have to know who you are and where you come from." Cantor **Laurence Olivier**, from a long line of cantors, argues against his son Neil Diamond leaving the world of Orthodox synagogues for that of popular entertainment. *The Jazz Singer* (1980, EMI).

1306 "I was thinking about should I change my movie? Should I change my life?" Filmmaker **Woody Allen** erases the distinction between his reel life and his real life. *Stardust Memories* (1980, United Artists).

1307 "When I was at university he was in Students for a Democratic Society. Now he's negotiating for the drilling rights to the barrier reef." Upper-class drop-out **Judy Davis** refers to a well-dressed young man engaged in a conversation with a bewigged barrister. *Heatwave* (1982, Australia, M and L Enterprises).

1308 "One day cock of the walk, next day a feather duster." Sassy **Tina Turner** eyes Mel Gibson like a cut of prime beef. *Mad Max Beyond Thunderdome* (1985, Australia, Warner Bros.).

1309 "I want to change everything and I don't know how." Restless **Meryl Streep** is headed for a nervous breakdown. *Plenty* (1985, 20th Century-Fox-RKO).

1310 "In here there are two guys killing each other, but I guess that's better than twenty million. I can change, you can change, everybody can change." **Sylvester Stallone** has a message of peace and hope for a Russian boxing audience after defeating the Soviet camp Dolph Lundgren. *Rocky IV* (1985, MGM-United Artists).

1311 VICOMTE DE VALMONT: "Do you think a man can change?" MARQUISE DE MERTEUIL: "Oh, yes, for the worse." Despoiler of women **Colin Firth** isn't encouraged by his co-conspirator **Annette Bening**, when he considers giving up his sinful ways. *Valmont* (1989, Orion).

1312 "The planet is screaming for a change. We gotta make the myths." **Val Kilmer** portrays legendary rocker Jim Morrison. *The Doors* (1991, Tri-Star).

Character

see also ACTING AND ACTORS, BEHAVIOR, ECCENTRICITIES, IDENTITIES, MORALITY, PERSONS AND PERSONALITIES, PLAYING AND PLAYERS, QUALITIES, ROLES

1313 "Have a drink—just a little one to lessen the difference in our characters." Roué **Noel Coward** successfully leads Julie Haydon astray. *The Scoundrel* (1935, Paramount).

1314 COL. PICKERING: "Are you a man of good character where women are concerned?" PROF. HENRY HIGGINS: "Have you ever known a man of good character where women are concerned?" **Scott Sunderland** and **Wilfrid Hyde-White** question **Leslie Howard** and **Rex Harrison**, respectively, about their character. *Pygmalion* (1938, GB, MGM); *My Fair Lady* (1964, Warner Bros.).

1315 "By gad, you're a chap worth knowing. An amazing character." **Sydney Greenstreet** takes the measure of Humphrey Bogart. *The Maltese Falcon* (1941, Warner Bros.).

1316 "One of the most charming characteristics of Homo-Sapiens—the wise guy on your left—is the consistency with which he has stoned, crucified, burned at the stake, and otherwise rid himself of those who consecrated their lives to his further comfort and well-being so that all his strength and cunning might be preserved for the creation of ever larger monuments, memorial shafts, triumphal arches, pyramids, and obelisks to the eternal glory of generals on horseback, tyrants, usurpers, dictators, politicians and other heroes who led him, usually from the rear, to dismemberment and death." It's **Preston Sturges**' eloquent prologue to his film about the inventor of anaesthetics. *The Great Moment* (1944, Paramount).

1317 "Madam, I am the character of my home." Wishing to hire yet another in a long line of maids for his home, **William Powell** responds indignantly to an employment office official who inquires about the character of his home. *Life with Father* (1947, Warner Bros.).

1318 ANTHONY KEANE: "We have the simple, obvious fact that Mrs. Paradine is not a murderess. She's too fine a woman." SIR SIMON FLAQUER: "Really? I was of the impression that she'd been a woman of very low estate and rather easy virtue." Because he's fallen in love with her, **Gregory Peck** will not consider the possibility that his client Alida Valli is guilty of murder. He objects angrily when his colleague **Charles Coburn** expresses a different opinion of her character. *The Paradine Case* (1947, Selznick-United Artists).

1319 "You see in business, as in everything else, there is appearance and there is reality. . . that is a reality; you are an honest man. . . but what good is that if your books make you look like a crook? All I'm going to do is make your books agree with your character." Master swindler **Humphrey Bogart** proposes to doctor Leo G. Carroll's account books so he appears to be the most successful merchant on Devil's Island. *We're No Angels* (1955, Paramount).

1320 "Miss Kubelik, one doesn't get to be a second administrative assistant around here unless he's a pretty good judge of character, and as far and I'm concerned you're the tops, I mean, decency-wise and otherwise-wise." **Jack Lemmon** reassures the elevator operator Shirley MacLaine with some business jargon. *The Apartment* (1960, United Artists).

1321 "How can I lose? Twelve ball. How can I lose? Because you were right. It's not enough to have talent. You gotta have character too. Four ball. Yeah, I sure got character now. I picked it up in a hotel room in Louisville." As he walks around a pool table, easily and efficiently making his shots in a match with Jackie Gleason, **Paul Newman** talks to George C. Scott, who is partly responsible for the suicide of Piper Laurie as Newman's girlfriend. *The Hustler* (1961, 20th Century-Fox).

1322 "Mean is a personality trait, not necessarily my character." It's hit man **Fred Williamson**'s considered response when one of the members of the "Family" tells him, "They used to call you the one-man mean machine." *Mister Mean* (1977, Lone Star-Po' Boy).

1323 "Bud, I like you, just remember something. . . . Man looks in the abyss, there's nothing staring back at him. At that moment man finds his character." **Hal Holbrook**, an older account executive, comforts young sharpie Charlie Sheen, before the latter realizes that he's being arrested for stock manipulation. *Wall Street* (1987, 20th Century-Fox).

Charity *see* GIFTS AND GIVING, HUMAN NATURE, HUMANITY, KINDNESS, LOVE AND HATE, LOVE AND LOVERS

Charm

see also ACTIONS AND ACTS, ATTRACTIONS, MAGIC, POWER

1324 "What can a Saxon hedge robber know of charm?" Before she gets to know him better, **Olivia de Havilland** as Maid Marian, is scornful of title character Errol Flynn when he turns on the soft-soap. *The Adventures of Robin Hood* (1938, Warner Bros.).

1325 "Oh, Walter's got lots of charm. He comes by it naturally. His grandfather was a snake." Reporter **Rosalind Russell** was married to editor Cary Grant and so she knows what she's talking about. *His Girl Friday* (1940, Columbia).

1326 "Oh, Leonard can be very charming. . . Leonard has a way with women. I only hope he will have an all-woman jury. They will carry him from the courtroom in triumph." **Marlene Dietrich** comments on her husband Tyrone Power's attraction for women to his barrister Charles Laughton. The latter states that a simple acquittal will suffice. *Witness for the Prosecution* (1957, United Artists).

1327 "You can turn off the charm; I'm immune." The fact that **Honor Blackman**, as Pussy Galore, is a lesbian doesn't deter Sean Connery as James Bond. *Goldfinger* (1961, GB, United Artists).

1328 "You've got all the charm going for you and it makes the youngsters want to be like you and that's the shame of it, because you don't value nothin', you don't respect nothin'. You keep no restraints on your appetites at all. . . you live just for yourself and that makes you not fit to live with." **Melvyn Douglas** condemns his selfish and self-centered son Paul Newman. *Hud* (1963, Paramount).

1329 "The one charm of marriage is that it makes a life of deception absolutely necessary for both partners." An Oscar Wilde quote serves as a caption for the film. *A Guide for the Married Man* (1967, 20th Century-Fox).

1330 "You know, you are definitely a charmer, Frank. Hey, everybody, lighten up, it's all over. Frank, go ahead and open that vermouth in two seconds." At the end of the film, **Peter Fonda**, his friend Warren Oates and their wives Lara Parker and Loretta Swit have survived attacks by a cult of Devil worshippers. *Race with the Devil* (1975, 20th Century-Fox).

1331 "Honey, when you have a little disadvantage like that, you just have to cultivate something else to take its place. You have to cultivate charm, or vivacity—or charm." **Joanne Woodward** gives well-meaning advice to her shy crippled daughter Karen Allen. *The Glass Menagerie* (1987, Cineplex-Odeon).

1332 "You're good, Charley. You use charm like a dealer uses a new deck." Movie studio owner **Robert Loggia** grudgingly compliments his daughter's fiancé, playboy Alec Baldwin. *The Marrying Man* (1991, Hollywood Pictures).

Chases see HUNTING, PURSUITS, RUNNING AND RUNNERS

Chastity see PURITY, VIRTUES

Cheats

see also DECEPTIONS, GAMES, HONESTY AND DISHONESTY, TRICKS AND TRICKERY

1333 "This is the age of chiseling. Everyone's got larceny in his heart." Sharpie **James Cagney** justifies himself to his moralizing girlfriend Joan Blondell. *Blonde Crazy* (1931, Warner Bros.).

1334 "It had to happen sooner or later, my finding out you're a cheat." **Carole Lombard** disapproves of her gambler husband Clark Gable, who married her on a bet. *No Man of Her Own* (1932, Paramount).

1335 "If a thing's worth having, it's worth cheating for." **W.C. Fields** defends himself when Mae West accuses him of being a cheat after he appears in her bedroom disguised as her lover, the Masked Bandit. *My Little Chickadee* (1940, Universal).

1336 "Every time you get a little tight, you weep on my shoulder about what a terrible thing the advertising agency business is for a sensitive soul like yourself because you make your living out of bamboozling the American public. I would say that a small part of the victimized group has now redressed the balance." **Melvyn Douglas** has little sympathy for his friend Cary Grant, who finds everyone is making a fortune on the house he's trying to build for his family. *Mr. Blandings Builds His Dream House* (1948, RKO).

1337 "Don't ever play him short. . . . You couldn't get close enough to Steve Judd to saddle his horse." Crooked **Randolph Scott** warns his young accomplice Ron Starr about honest ex-lawman Joel McCrea. *Ride the High Country* (1962, MGM).

1338 "I was thrown out of N.Y.U. my freshman year for cheating on my metaphysics final, you know. I looked into the soul of the boy sitting next to me." It's part of **Woody Allen**'s comedy act in the film. *Annie Hall* (1977, United Artists).

1339 "You can't cheat nature without paying the price." **Jose Ferrer**, as Dr. Vando, mutters about an aging Greta Garbo-like star who has miraculously kept her beauty. *Fedora* (1978, W.Ger.-Fr., Geria-SFP).

1340 "Everybody cheats. I just didn't know." Cyclist **Dennis Christopher** weeps in his father Paul Dooley's arms after discovering that his Italian cyclist heroes have wheels of clay. *Breaking Away* (1979, 20th Century-Fox).

1341 "My husband and I had our best sex during the divorce. . . it was like cheating on our lawyers." **Priscilla Lopez** shocks Tovah Feldshuh with this blushing revelation. *Cheaper to Keep Her* (1981, Regal).

1342 "Everybody gets screwed on Wall Street." **Sally Kirkland** nearly tears off Robert LuPone's clothes on the sidewalk outside his Wall Street office. *High Stakes* (1989, Vidmark).

Cheers

see also APPLAUSE, ENCOURAGEMENTS, ENTERTAINMENTS AND ENTERTAINERS, GLADNESS, HAPPINESS AND UNHAPPINESS, JOY, PRAISES

1343 "Who the hell is fighting this war—men or orders? Cheers when we left—and when we get back. But who the hell cares about this?" A title card expresses **John Gilbert**'s bitterness and despair about the treatment of the fighting men after World War I. *The Big Parade* (1925, silent, MGM).

1344 "I stood in front of this hotel when my son went by. He was going to his death and I cheered. . . ." German father **Lionel Barrymore** remorsefully confesses to a crippled World War I veteran the crime of old men against young men—sending them off to war. *The Man I Killed* aka: *Broken Lullaby* (1932, Paramount).

1345 "For the first time in my life, people cheering for me. Were you deaf? Didn't you hear them? We're not hitchhiking any more. We're riding." As he is dying, boxer **Kirk Douglas** remembers the cheers of the crowd when he was starting out as a fighter. *Champion* (1949, United Artists).

1346 "Now when the Reverend Mr. Playfair, good man that he is, comes down, I want you all to cheer like Protestants." Irish Catholic priest **Ward Bond** instructs his parishioners to cheer for vicar Arthur

Shields in order to impress the latter's visiting bishop and allow Shields to stay in the village with his small flock of Protestants. *The Quiet Man* (1952, Republic).

Chicago *see* CITIES

Chickens *see* ANIMALS

Children and Childhood

see also BABIES, BOYS, DAUGHTERS, FAMILIES, FATHERS, GIRLS, MOTHERS, PARENTS, SONS AND SONS-IN-LAW, YOUTH

1347 "Let's blow trumpets and squeakers, and enjoy the party as much as we can like very small, quite idiotic schoolchildren." **Robert Montgomery** and Norma Shearer are extremely wealthy. This comment occurs during an improbable love scene. *Private Lives* (1931, MGM).

1348 "Let that be a lesson to you. Never have any children." **Edna Best** lectures her tennis opponent when she loses her match because she's distracted by an innocent interruption by her daughter Nova Pilbeam. Best then turns to her husband Leslie Banks and says, "You take the brat. . . . You would have this child!" *The Man Who Knew Too Much* (1934, GB, Gaumont).

1349 "The world is filled with what-you-call-'em—schlemiels—and I guess somebody has to raise 'em." Speaking to his Jewish friend Maurice Moscovitch, elderly **Victor Moore** refers to his grown children who aren't much help to him and his wife. *Make Way for Tomorrow* (1937, Paramount).

1350 "You had no right. You raised five children of your own—you might at least let me raise one." **Fay Bainter** is outraged with her mother-in-law Beulah Bondi, who has interfered with Bainter's handling of her daughter's clandestine romance. *Make Way for Tomorrow* (1937, Paramount).

1351 "Cynthia was just one of the errors of my childhood." **Mickey Rooney** happily declares that he's learned his lesson after Ann Rutherford busses him enthusiastically to give him something to compare to the kisses of Lana Turner. *Love Finds Andy Hardy* (1938, MGM).

1352 "These are my children. They were born in India, poor darlings. An awful place, what with the ahays and whatnot howling around the whatdoyoucall them. I don't know how they stood it. I know I couldn't have. Of course, I've never been there myself." Introducing her children Douglas Fairbanks, Jr., and Janet Gaynor to old Minnie Dupree, flittering idiot **Billie Burke** lives up to her billing. *The Young in Heart* (1938, Selznick-United Artists).

1353 "I never seen no man, black or white, set such store in any child. . . . It's like to turn my blood cold—the things they say to one another." **Hattie McDaniel** seeks help from Olivia de Havilland for Clark Gable and Vivien Leigh after the accidental death of their only child. *Gone with the Wind* (1939, Selznick-MGM).

1354 "Only some child actors. I threw them down the stairs, and it did my heart good to hear them bounce." Publicity agent **Ned Sparks** responds to impresario Bing Crosby who asks if there were any callers while he was out. *The Star Maker* (1939, Paramount).

1355 "Every child born into this world belongs to the whole human race." These are the words of **Greer Garson** as Edna Gladney, a child welfare worker who founded the Texas Home and Society at the turn of the century. *Blossoms in the Dust* (1941, MGM).

1356 "That child is mine. Your part was finished the minute you gave that baby to me. From that day on I had only one purpose in my life, to make that baby mine and forget you ever existed." **Bette Davis** ruthlessly dismisses Mary Astor's claim to her baby. *The Great Lie* (1941, Warner Bros.).

1357 "Johnny, I'm just beginning to understand you—you're a child." **Joan Fontaine** begins to grasp the shallowness of her ne'er-do-well husband Cary Grant. *Suspicion* (1941, RKO).

1358 "I love my children, but they are not the only children in the world." Anti-fascist **Paul Lukas** responds to the charge that his activities have exposed his family to danger. *Watch on the Rhine* (1943, Warner Bros.).

1359 "So it came about that while Ling Tan left the land behind him, he did not leave hope. For he carried it with him in Jade's child, that child so truly the seed of the dragon." Narrator **Lionel Barrymore** speaks of two of the Occidentals who played Orientals in a rendition of Pearl Buck's best selling novel. Farmer Walter Huston organizes a revolt against the Japanese, vowing to leave nothing but scorched earth for the enemy before fleeing with his pregnant daughter-in-law Katharine Hepburn to the mountains to join the guerrillas. *Dragon Seed* (1944, MGM).

1360 "You're a child, Gilda, a beautiful greedy child. It amuses me to give you things because you eat

with such a good appetite." **George Macready** enjoys spoiling his selfish young wife Rita Hayworth. *Gilda* (1946, Columbia).

1361 "You're about as dependable as a four-year-old child." **Jane Greer** accuses her lover Robert Young of immaturity. He refuses to accept any responsibility for the death of another mistress, Susan Hayward, and the suicide of his wife Rita Johnson. *They Won't Believe Me* (1947, RKO).

1362 General Howard: "All are God's children." Tom Jeffords: "Suppose their skins aren't white. Are they still God's children?" The extent of **Basil Ruysdael**'s convictions are tested by frontiersman **James Stewart**, who is tired of the mutual massacre of whites and Indians. *Broken Arrow* (1950, 20th Century-Fox).

1363 "I'm a strong tree with branches for many birds, and children are mankind at his strongest, they abide." **Lillian Gish**'s words close the film. *The Night of the Hunter* (1955, United Artists).

1364 "I was an unwelcomed child in a marriage which was a nice imitation of hell. Is the old man really sure that I'm his son? Indifference, fear, infidelity and guilt feelings—these were my nurses." **Gunnar Bjornstrand** relates to his wife Ingrid Thulin the horror of his childhood with father Victor Sjostrom. *Wild Strawberries* (1957, Sweden, Svensk Filmindustri).

1365 "I think you did. I think you've had a hard tough climb. But you're a smart girl, aren't you? The careful grammar, the quiet good manners—where did you learn them?" Despite her denial that she had "a tough childhood," **Sean Connery** sees through Tippi Hedren's pose. *Marnie* (1964, Universal).

1366 "I still want a child. I just don't want *that* child." **Audrey Hepburn** is adamant after tangling with Gabrielle Middleton, a perfect little horror. Hepburn and her husband Albert Finney end a European motor trip with the little brat and her equally unbearable parents, Eleanor Bron and William Daniels. *Two for the Road* (1967, GB, 20th Century-Fox).

1367 Toni Simmons: "How do you like children?" Harvey Greenfield: "Barbecued!" **Goldie Hawn** discovers the type of fellow **Jack Weston** is. He's pretending to be the boyfriend of Ingrid Bergman who is posing as Walter Matthau's wife. Matthau is Hawn's lover. *Cactus Flower* (1969, Columbia).

1368 "Everything in [my mother's] behavior toward me as a little boy seemed to say: I'd have done better to break a leg than to give birth to this stupid child." In voice-over, **Charles Denner** explains the origins of his fruitless search for the perfect woman, as the audience sees a flashback of his childhood as an unwanted fatherless child. *The Man Who Loved Women* (1977, Fr., Les Films du Carrosse and Les Productions Artistes Associes).

1369 "You think of me as a child." Twelve-year-old prostitute **Brooke Shields** complains when photographer Keith Carradine brings her a doll. *Pretty Baby* (1978, Paramount).

1370 JOHNSON: "What kind of childhood did you have?" FRANK MORRIS: "Short." **Fred Stuthman** finds fellow con **Clint Eastwood** to be a man of few words. *Escape from Alcatraz* (1979, Paramount).

1371 "I'd like to help but I really don't like children. Especially yours." Tough-talking **Gena Rowlands** resists when a Puerto Rican couple, targeted to be rubbed out by the mob, begs her to smuggle their young son away. She develops some maternal instincts despite herself when the boy's parents are murdered and the kid, seven-year-old John Adames, is threatened. *Gloria* (1980, Columbia).

1372 "What's the point of having a dwarf if he doesn't do any chores?" Cranky 80-year-old **Henry Fonda** is not thrilled with having young Doug McKeon staying with him and his wife Katharine Hepburn. *On Golden Pond* (1981, Universal).

1373 "Think of it as a birth defect. Mother had two kids—one a scientist, the other a nymphomaniac." Primate zoologist **Edward Herrmann** speaks of himself and his womanizing younger brother Tim Matheson. The latter more properly should be called a satyr or a "Don Juan." *A Little Sex* (1982, Universal).

1374 "How is your life going to get better if you're going to keep having children with that man?" **Shirley MacLaine** disapproves of her daughter Debra Winger's husband Jeff Daniels. *Terms of Endearment* (1983, Paramount).

1375 "When I was a child, I used to race rats." It's the claim of gaunt, hollow-eyed killer **Julian Beck.** *The Cotton Club* (1984, Orion).

1376 "I was right not to want kiddies if this is what it's like." **Maggie Smith** discovers that the plump pig that she and her husband Michael Palin have kidnapped has a severe case of diarrhea. *A Private Function* (1985, GB, Handmade).

1377 "They liked the idea of having children, but they were never very interested in raising them."

Barbara Hershey refers to her ever-battling show business parents Lloyd Nolan and Maureen O'Sullivan. *Hannah and Her Sisters* (1986, Orion).

1378 THELMA CATES: "You're my child." JESSIE CATES: "I'm what became of your child." **Anne Bancroft** unsuccessfully tries to dissuade her daughter **Sissy Spacek**, who plans to commit suicide. *'Night, Mother* (1986, Universal).

1379 "My life is like death, my children are the spawn of hell." Here's the good news for amnesiac **Goldie Hawn**: Kurt Russell's undisciplined kids aren't hers. The bad news is when she regains her memory, she decides to stay with them. *Overboard* (1987, MGM).

1380 "Biology and the prejudices of others conspired to keep us childless." It's narrator **Nicolas Cage**'s folksy way of revealing that he and his wife Holly Hunter can't conceive a child and his prison record prevents them from adopting one. *Raising Arizona* (1987, 20th Century-Fox).

1381 "The only wealth is children, more than power or money." Having not been the world's best father or husband, **Al Pacino** delivers an epigram that shows he's learned something. *The Godfather, Part III* (1990, Paramount).

1382 "I was a kind of strange child." It's **Michael Moore**'s first line in his imaginative documentary. *Roger & Me* (1990, Warner Bros).

1383 "You can do anything with a child, as long as you play with him." In an unusual drama, interrogator **Alan Rickman** responds when his captive Madeleine Stowe protests that she's only a writer of children's books. *Closet Land* (1991, Universal).

Chivalry

see also COURAGE, GENEROSITY, GENTLEMEN, HEROES, HONOR, NOBILITY

1384 "He's chivalrous to the point of idiocy." **Olivia de Havilland** doesn't quite know what to make of physician-prisoner Errol Flynn. *Captain Blood* (1935, Warner Bros.).

1385 WALLY COOK: "You mean to say you stood there and let me beat up a defenseless woman?" OLIVER STONE: "I did, Mr. Cook." COOK: "Where's your sense of chivalry?" STONE: "My chivalry: Aren't you just a trifle confused, Mr. Cook? You hit her!" COOK: "That's entirely different. I love her." Newspaper reporter **Fredric March** claims to his editor **Walter Connolly** that it's all right to hit a woman if you love her. *Nothing Sacred* (1937, Selznick-UA).

1386 "Chivalry is not only dead, it's decomposing." Wealthy **Rudy Vallee** sadly comments on the passing of knightly qualities. Vallee is speaking to Claudette Colbert to whom he has been most courteous, attentive and understanding. *The Palm Beach Story* (1942, Paramount).

Choices

see also PREFERENCES

1387 "There are only two kinds, the ones in and the ones out." Factory worker **Joan Crawford**, an out, plans to become an in. *Possessed* (1931, MGM).

1388 "I'll either have a live leading lady or a dead chorus girl." **Warner Baxter**, director of Broadway's "Pretty Lady," promises that he'll push young Ruby Keeler to the limit in an effort to get her ready to go on for injured star Bebe Daniels. *42nd Street* (1933, Warner Bros.).

1389 "If I can't live the way I want, let me die the way I want." Condemned killer **Clark Gable** refuses clemency from his boyhood friend William Powell, now the governor of the state. *Manhattan Melodrama* (1934, MGM).

1390 "I wish I hadn't started this thing, but now I have to find out. All my life I'd feel that maybe he liked her better, that I was second choice. I couldn't stand that." Having exchanged places with her secretary Fay Wray, wealthy **Miriam Hopkins** has fallen in love with Joel McCrea, who makes it clear he's come to town to win the person Wray is impersonating, that is, Hopkins. Having had no luck with Wray, McCrea is now sweet on Hopkins, who he believes is poor. Hopkins has a dilemma because she wants McCrea to choose her for herself. *The Richest Girl in the World* (1934, RKO).

1391 "[She's] under a spell that can be broken only by me—or death.... Your life—or—hers. Remain here with me among the undead." Title character **Gloria Holden** tells psychiatrist Otto Kruger that the only way he can save his beautiful assistant Marguerite Churchill is to share Holden's immortality. *Dracula's Daughter* (1936, Universal).

1392 "Between two evils, I always pick the one I haven't tried before." Movie star **Mae West**, stranded in Pennsylvania when her car breaks down, probably feels local lad Randolph Scott is the evil to choose. *Go West, Young Man* (1936, Paramount).

1393 "He's either the dumbest, silliest idiot, or he's the greatest guy alive." As far as reporter **Jean Arthur** is concerned, the jury is still out on naïve man-of-integrity Gary Cooper. *Mr. Deeds Goes to Town* (1936, Columbia).

1394 "Either this man is dead or my watch has stopped." **Groucho Marx** looks at his watch as he tries to take Harpo Marx's pulse. *A Day at the Races* (1937, MGM).

1395 "If reform school did make a criminal out of him, then he chose to stay that way." Don't try to tell priest **Pat O'Brien** that society is to blame for his boyhood chum James Cagney choosing a life of crime. *Angels with Dirty Faces* (1938, Warner Bros.).

1396 "Send me shots of bombing... or send me your resignation." It's choices like this one in a cable sent by **Walter Connolly**, boss of Union Newsreel, to reporter Clark Gable in Shanghai, that makes the latter resort to staging shots. *Too Hot to Handle* (1938, MGM).

1397 "You're a slum kid who never had a chance. But so is Frank. He hates crooked cops and rotten politicians as much as you do. The only difference is you chose crime—the easy way. He's spent his life fighting." **Jane Bryan**, reporter James Cagney's fiancée, begs hardened criminal George Raft to help clear Cagney of the trumped up charge of vehicular manslaughter while drunk, which has gotten Cagney thrown into the slammer. *Each Dawn I Die* (1939, Warner Bros.).

1398 "Men like you usually have a very difficult time in the world because they do not know how to conform. You must learn, Ehrlich. It's conform or suffer." Hospital head **Sig Rumann** tells idealist scientist and physician Edward G. Robinson he must make a choice. *Dr. Ehrlich's Magic Bullet* (1940, Warner Bros.).

1399 "Madam, I was torn between Mr. Wilberforce's efforts to abolish slavery and your efforts to abolish boredom." **Robert Donat**, as British Prime Minister William Pitt, converses with a gushing hostess. *The Young Mr. Pitt* (1941, GB, 20th Century-Fox).

1400 "I can only conclude that you're a thief or you're drunk." Dutch writer **Peter Lorre** shows some guts when smuggler Sydney Greenstreet pulls a gun on him in Lorre's hotel room. *The Mask of Dimitrios* (1944, Warner Bros.).

1401 "We've been having lectures in atomic energy at school and Mr. McLaughlin, he's our physics teacher, he says that we've reached a point where the whole human race has either got to find a way to live together or else.... Because when you combine atomic energy with the jet propulsion and radar and guided missiles, just think...." Teenager

Michael Hall fills in his father Fredric March, who has just returned from fighting World War II, about the many frightening peace-time problems to be dealt with. *The Best Years of Our Lives* (1946, Goldwyn-RKO).

1402 "You know, I've never been able to understand why, when there's so much space in the world, that people should deliberately choose to live in the Middle West." Snobbish **Clifton Webb** doesn't even know the proper name for the Midwest. *The Razor's Edge* (1946, 20th Century-Fox).

1403 "When there's nothing but carbolic around, you hanker after rot." Butler **Ralph Richardson** is very tired of his nagging wife Sonia Dresdel's threats of suicide. *The Fallen Idol* (1948, GB, London Films-British Lion).

1404 "We have no choice but to submit or rule." Self-made millionaire **Raymond Massey** passes on this bit of wisdom to Patricia Neal on their first date. *The Fountainhead* (1949, Warner Bros.).

1405 "You get tough or you get killed." Aging con **Betty Garde** advises "new fish" Eleanor Parker. *Caged* (1950, Warner Bros.).

1406 "For our policeman we created a race of robots. Their function is to patrol the planets in spaceships like this one and preserve the peace. In matters of aggression we have given them absolute power over us. This power cannot be revoked. At the first signs of violence they act automatically against the aggressors. The penalty for provoking their action is too terrible to risk. The result is we live in peace without arms or armies, secure in the knowledge that we are free from aggression and war, free to pursue more profitable enterprises. Now we do not pretend to have achieved perfection, but we do have a system, and it works. I came here to give you these facts. It is no concern of ours how you run your planet, but if you threaten to extend your violence, this Earth of yours will be reduced to a burned-out cinder. Your choice is simple: join us and live in peace, or pursue your present course and face obliteration. We shall be waiting for your answer. The decision rests with you." **Michael Rennie**, as Klaatu, an envoy from the other planets of the Universe, tells the people of Earth to solve their problems or face destruction. *The Day the Earth Stood Still* (1951, 20th Century-Fox).

1407 "Choosin' a way to die, what's the difference? Choosin' a way to live—that's the hard part." Fugitive **Robert Ryan** philosophizes as he and two others are taken back by Jimmy Stewart to be hanged. *The Naked Spur* (1953, MGM).

1408 "Man has a choice, and it's a choice that makes him a man." **James Dean** shares a lesson he's learned from experience with his paralyzed father Raymond Massey. *East of Eden* (1955, Warner Bros.).

1409 "Shall we have a drink first or shall we go right to bed?" **Julie Harris**, as Sally Bowles, lays out the choices for Laurence Harvey, as writer Christopher Isherwood. *I Am a Camera* (1955, GB, Romulus-Remus).

1410 "Every man has a moment in his life when he has to choose. If he chooses right, then it's a moment of magnificence. If he chooses wrong, then it's a moment of regret that will stay with him for the rest of his life. I wish that every soldier. . . could feel the way I feel now, because if they did, they'd know what it's like to be a man who sold himself short, and who lost his moment of magnificence. I pray to God that they find theirs." **Paul Newman**, a former POW accused of collaborating with the enemy in Korea, delivers a stirring speech directly to the camera after he's found guilty. *The Rack* (1956, MGM).

1411 "Well, there's not much to choose between you two, is there? When you're together, you slash each other to pieces and when you're apart you slash yourselves to pieces. All told, it's quite a problem." **Wendy Hiller** doesn't know what to make of the continuing relationship of her lover Burt Lancaster and his ex-wife Rita Hayworth. *Separate Tables* (1958, United Artists).

1412 "I want to have a chance in life. I don't want to have to come through back doors or feel lower than other people, or apologize for my mother's color. She can't help her color but I can and will." **Susan Kohner**, a beautiful young black woman who can pass for white, chooses to do just that to escape the kind of life her mother Juanita Moore has lived. *Imitation of Life* (1959, Universal-International).

1413 "He's like a cold and there are only two things you can do with a cold. . . . You can fight it or you can go to bed with it. . . I'm going to fight it." Ever the virgin, **Doris Day** holds off womanizer Rock Hudson in *Lover Come Back*. (1961, Universal).

1414 "It is necessary to choose between two admittedly regrettable but nevertheless distinguishable postwar environments: one where you've got twenty million people killed and the other where you got one hundred and fifty million killed." General **George C. Scott** urges a follow-up strike against the communists after mad Air Force General Sterling Hayden has launched an atomic missile-laden wing of Strategic Air Command bombers to attack the U.S.S.R. *Dr. Strangelove: Or How I Learned to Stop Worrying and Love the Bomb* (1964, GB, Columbia).

1415 "I aim to kill you in one minute, Ned, or see you hang in Fort Smith at Judge Parker's convenience. Which will it be?" Old Marshal **John Wayne** gives outlaw Robert Duvall and his three remaining gang members no real choice. *True Grit* (1969, Paramount).

1416 "Christine, I've reached that realistic age when I have to choose between having fun and a heart attack." Millionaire **Joseph Cotten** recognizes that he can't keep up with his 19-year-old mistress Jacqueline Bisset who likes to live in the fast lane. *The Grasshopper* (1970, National General Pictures).

1417 "What's more important, his life or your virtue?" Army surgeon **Donald Sutherland** makes the grand sacrifice for a friend. Just before she is to be rotated back to the states, married nurse Jo Ann Pflug plans to hop in bed with Sutherland. Instead, he asks her to rejuvenate dentist John Schuck. Schuck, always a ladies' man, believes he has become a homosexual because he is having problems with impotency. As a result he has decided to commit suicide. *M*A*S*H* (1970, 20th Century-Fox).

1418 "Can you eat or do you have to get strung out all the time?" **Bruce Pecheur** condescendingly asks perpetually stoned Joe Dallesandro. *Trash* (1970, Cinema 5-Andy Warhol).

1419 "If you had your choice. . . would you rather love a girl or have her love you?" **Jack Nicholson**'s question of Art Garfunkel demonstrates his belief that love is something someone does to someone else. *Carnal Knowledge* (1971, Avco Embassy).

1420 "When a man cannot choose, he ceases to be a man. . . . The boy had no real choices. Self-interest—the fear of physical violence—drove him to that grotesque self-abasement." Prison chaplain **Godfrey Quigley** advances the argument that a truly good man needs free will. He's just seen once-vicious thug, rapist and killer, Malcolm McDowell, after psychological and physical brain-washing, lick the boots of an actor who pushed him around, and then grovel before a nude woman. *A Clockwork Orange* (1971, GB, Warner Bros.).

1421 "You can lay a bet or a broad or the base for a three-day drunk." **Ed Call** tells Joe Don Baker about the specialties of a new roadhouse. *Walking Tall* (1973, BCP-Cinerama).

1422 "Certainly. You take the blonde and I'll take the one in the turban." Servant **Marty Feldman** deliberately misunderstands Gene Wilder who asks the former to help with the bags. Feldman reaches for Madeline Kahn, leaving Teri Garr for Wilder. *Young Frankenstein* (1974, 20th Century-Fox).

1423 "You always think there's a middle you can dance around in, Howard. I'm telling you, this time there is no middle." Blacklisted writer **Michael Murphy** tells Woody Allen, a schnook who lends his non-controversial name to the work of writers who can't sell their scripts during the 1950s witch-hunts, that he must choose to betray them or be convicted of contempt of court by refusing to answer questions about his work and his friends. *The Front* (1976, Columbia).

1424 "Choosing a way to die, that's easy, it's choosing a way to live that's the difficult thing to do." Westerner **Clint Eastwood** is bent on avenging the death of his wife at the hands of bandits. *The Outlaw Josey Wales* (1976, Warner Bros.).

1425 "You know, there are three things that we could do right now: you could call a taxi and go home; or we could go on walking and I could lecture you on the real dilemma of modern art; or we could go to my place and we could thoroughly enjoy each other." Artist **Alan Bates** wonders if Jill Clayburgh would like to move on to the next plateau in their relationship. *An Unmarried Woman* (1978, 20th Century-Fox).

1426 "If you're born in the mountains you got three choices: coal mine, moonshine or movin' down the line." Just returned from his army stint, **Tommy Lee Jones** puts his options most poetically. *Coal Miner's Daughter* (1980, Universal).

1427 "You now have the option to terminate and be cremated on the premises. . . ." An omnipresent voice from a speaker system matter-of-factly ticks off Kurt Russell's options as he is led handcuffed down a bleak hallway at the debarkation center, prior to beginning his life sentence in the U.S. 1997 maximum security prison, the entire borough of Manhattan. *Escape from New York* (1981, Avco Embassy).

1428 "This war has come down to the two of us." German agent **Donald Sutherland**, attempting to escape from Great Britain with important intelligence about the Allies' invasion plans of the continent, sadly shouts to his Scottish lover Kate Nelligan, who knows him for what he is and repeatedly shoots him with an old gun. *Eye of the Needle* (1981, GB, Kings Road-United Artists).

1429 "Why would you choose someone who loves you too little over someone who loves you too much?" Obsessed **John Heard** can't understand why Mary Beth Hurt would return to her husband, Mark Metcalf. *Chilly Scenes of Winter* (1982, United Artists Classics).

1430 "I never really gave him any choice. One time he tried to discuss leaving, but I never let him discuss it. He stayed because I wanted him to stay. I stayed because. . . ." Pulitzer Prize winning journalist **Sam Waterston** feels guilty that his Cambodian go-between Haing N. Ngor, who Waterston acknowledges deserves half the award, was left behind in Cambodia to survive as best he could during the brutal reign of the Khmer Rouge. *The Killing Fields* (1984, GB, Warner Bros.).

1431 "I desperately chose celibacy after a three-year orgy with all sexes and all comers." **Zeljko Ivanek** is an idealistic young seminarian who admits to having had an unorthodox background, including having experimented with both heterosexual and homosexual lovemaking. *Mass Appeal* (1984, Universal).

1432 "It wouldn't have made any difference, I freely chose my response to this absurd world. If given the opportunity, I would be even more vigorous." After being sentenced to forty years in prison for espionage and treason, **Timothy Hutton** responds to a reporter who asks why he didn't manifest his revolutionary ideas in a more acceptable way. *The Falcon and the Snowman* (1985, Orion).

1433 "If we'd made love last night, I'd have had to stay, or you'd have had to leave." Having seen Kelly McGillis naked from the waist up the previous evening and walked away, **Harrison Ford** knows that he doesn't belong in the Amish community of which she is a member. *Witness* (1985, Paramount).

1434 JESSIE CATES: "I'm sorry about tonight, Mama, but it's exactly why I'm doing it." THELMA CATES: "If you've got the guts to kill yourself, Jessie, you've got the guts to stay alive." JESSIE: "I know that. So it's really a matter of where I'd rather be." **Sissy Spacek**, feeling that she's suffocating in the domestic routine that she shares with her mother **Anne Bancroft**, has decided to kill herself this very night. *'Night, Mother* (1986, Universal).

1435 "You can die or you can die happy." Murderess **Theresa Russell** holds a gun to the head of crooked Chinese detective James Hong. He accepts her kind offer and chooses to overdose by mainlining heroin. *Black Widow* (1987, 20th Century-Fox).

1436 "You take Sinatra and swoon, I'll take Sonny." Older woman **Talia Balsam** informs reporters that her 15-year-old husband Patrick Dempsey, the so-called "Woo Woo Kid," is all she'll ever need. *In the Mood* (1987, Lorimar).

1437 "If she's gonna die. She's gonna die with me—my way, not yours." **Danny Glover** threatens to blow up himself, his daughter and the bad guys who are holding her, with a grenade. *Lethal Weapon* (1987, Warner Bros.).

1438 "You city people, you're all warm like dishwater. That don't do nobody no good. . . I mean you don't run hot or cold. You should be one or the other—hot or cold, that's all." Bayou matriarch **Barbara Hershey** finds fault with her New York cousin Jill Clayburgh. *Shy People* (1987, Cannon).

1439 "Not quite working out the way you thought it was, huh? Live or die, asshole, your choice." Police detective **Mark Harmon** stares down a punk who has him covered with a gun in a squad room filled with cops. *The Presidio* (1988, Paramount).

1440 "You've got only one life to live. You can either make it chicken shit or chicken salad." **Lloyd Bridges** shares some hard-learned wisdom with his son Ted Danson and grandson Keith Coogan. *Cousins* (1989, Paramount).

1441 "Then I shall have a better life than all of those who doubt. . . . If necessary I will always choose God over truth." In Martin Landau's imagined Seder, his Orthodox father **David S. Howard** answers Howard's sister Anna Berger who asks what would happen if Howard's faith proves to be unfounded. *Crimes and Misdemeanors* (1989, Orion).

1442 "Because I don't think it would be a choice that you would make in a normal frame of mind." It's **James Spader**'s reason for turning down Andie MacDowell's suggestion that he make a videotape of her talking about her sex life. *sex, lies and videotape* (1989, Miramax).

1443 "Learn or be killed." We wonder if nefarious scientist **Stacey Keach**'s philosophy of education is sufficient to motivate under-achievers. *Class of 1999* (1990, Taurus-Vestron).

1444 "I am trapped between the beauty of June and the genius of Henry. Henry gives me life. June gives me death. I must choose and I cannot. . . ." **Maria de Medeiros**, as Anais Nin, writes in her diary about her relationship with Fred Ward, as author Henry Miller, and his young wife, Uma Thurman as June Miller. *Henry and June* (1990, Universal).

1445 "Eat or be eaten." Eccentric writer **Peter Falk** advises 21-year-old radio news reporter Keanu Reeves. *Tune in Tomorrow* (1990, Cinecom).

Christ *see* JESUS CHRIST

Christianity *see* BELIEFS, RELIGIONS

Christmas

see also CELEBRATIONS, JESUS CHRIST, RELIGIONS, SANTA CLAUS

1446 "Hello? Is that you? Well, this is Charlie. I just called you up not to wish you a Merry Christmas." Not in the spirit of the season, **Alan Baxter** makes a call to send his very worst. *In Name Only* (1939, RKO).

1447 "There's something swell about the spirit of Christmas, what it does to people, all kinds of people. Now why can't that spirit, that same warm Christmas spirit, last the whole year 'round?" **Gary Cooper** reads part of a radio speech written for him by reporter Barbara Stanwyck. *Meet John Doe* (1941, Warner Bros.).

1448 "Oh, Christmas isn't just a day. It's a frame of mind." **Edmund Gwenn**, as Kris Kringle, spreads his message. *Miracle on 34th Street* (1947, 20th Century-Fox).

1449 "Well, life's hard for everybody walkin' on this earth. But that doesn't mean you can't smile. Just 'cuz you know there ain't no Santa Claus don't mean you can't enjoy Christmas better than anyone else." Waitress **Diane Ladd** expresses some heartfelt, if Pollyanna-like, sentiments to discouraged Ellen Burstyn. *Alice Doesn't Live Here Anymore* (1974, Warner Bros.).

1450 "It's me. It's your daddy. And I brought you a puppy for Christmas." Ex-cop **George Peppard**, who has killed his wife's lover, breaks out of prison with only six days left to serve to see his seriously ill son. *Five Days from Home* (1979, Universal).

1451 "If this is their idea of Christmas, I gotta be here for New Year's." New York cop **Bruce Willis** deposes 12 German thieves, posing as terrorists, who occupied an L.A. skyscraper. *Die Hard* (1988, 20th Century-Fox).

1452 "She's an American and you will sit here and listen to what she wants for Christmas or I will kill you." During World War II, prejudices against Japanese-Americans ran high. **Dennis Quaid** grabs and threatens a Santa Claus who refuses to let Quaid's Japanese-American daughter sit on his lap. *Come See the Paradise* (1991, 20th Century-Fox).

Churches *see* MISSIONS AND MISSIONARIES, PRAYERS, PRIESTS, RELIGIONS, SAINTS, WORSHIP

Circumstances *see* CHANCES, FATE AND DESTINY, NEEDS AND NECESSITIES

Cities and Towns

see also COUNTRIES, HOMES, LIVES AND LIVING, LOCATIONS, PEOPLE

1453 "This town is not for softies. Rome was a Quaker village compared to this town." Reporter **Richard Barthelmess** tells his remonstrating girl friend Fay Wray the truth about the Windy City. *The Finger Points* (1931, First National-Warner Bros.).

1454 "This story is laid in a mythical kingdom—Chicago." It's an introductory title card to the movie. *The Front Page* (1931, United Artists).

1455 "I do adore Paris. It's so much like Chicago. It's such a relief when you travel to feel that you've never left home at all." The French will be happy to hear that to **Alice Brady** Paris is so much like Chicago. Of course, she doesn't elaborate on why she thinks so. *The Gay Divorcée* (1934, RKO).

1456 "[Wealthy New Yorkers] work so hard at living, they forget how to live. . . . They've created a lot of grand palaces, but they forgot about the noblemen to put in them." Mandrake Falls poet and tuba player **Gary Cooper** expresses disappointment in the Big Apple to reporter Jean Arthur. *Mr. Deeds Goes to Town* (1936, Columbia).

1457 "New York, skyscraper champion of the world, where suckers and know-it-alls peddle gold bricks to each other and where truth, crushed to earth, rises again more phony than a glass eye." The film's written introduction. *Nothing Sacred* (1937, Selznick-United Artists).

1458 "This story takes place in Paris, in the wonderful days when a siren was a brunette and not an alarm. . . and when a Frenchman turned out the lights, it wasn't because of an air raid. . . ." The film's written introduction. *Ninotchka* (1939, MGM).

1459 "I warn you, Jedediah, you're not going to like it in Chicago. The wind comes howling in off the lake, and the Lord only knows if they ever heard of Lobster Newburgh." **Orson Welles** warns Joseph Cotten when the latter requests a transfer from New York to a Chicago newspaper. *Citizen Kane* (1941, RKO).

1460 "We'll always have Paris. We didn't have it. We'd—we'd lost it until you came to Casablanca. We got it back last night." Nobly **Humphrey Bogart** insists that the love of his life Ingrid Bergman get on the Lisbon plane with her husband, Resistance leader Paul Henreid. He reminds her of their happy days in the City of Lights before it fell to the Nazis. *Casablanca* (1942, Warner Bros.)

1461 "I can't believe it. Right here where we live. Right here in St. Louis." **Judy Garland** is thrilled by the 1904 World's Fair. *Meet Me in St. Louis* (1944, MGM).

1462 "It's an odd thing, but everyone who disappears is said to be seen in San Francisco. It must be a delightful city. It has all the attractions of the next world." **George Sanders** longs to visit the wicked city, "Baghdad by the Bay." *The Picture of Dorian Gray* (1945, MGM).

1463 "I hope you like Paris, Monsieur Chopin. I'm sure Paris will like you." It's lines like **Merle Oberon**'s to Cornel Wilde that make audiences cringe. Surely French writer George Sand would never have said something so banal to Polish composer Frederic Chopin. *A Song to Remember* (1945, Columbia).

1464 "I'm a city man. I love cars and traffic lights, smoke in the lungs. What have I got? A bigmouthed nightingale under my window." Czech refugee author **Charles Boyer** is not content living in the country home of a wealthy snobbish family. *Cluny Brown* (1946, 20th Century-Fox).

1465 "This is the city as it is." Producer-narrator **Mark Hellinger** has the first line. *The Naked City* (1948, Universal).

1466 "For a painter, the mecca of the world for study, for inspiration and for living is here on this star called Paris. Just look at it. No wonder so many artists have come here and called it home. Brother, if you can't paint in Paris, you'd better give up and marry the boss' daughter." Struggling American artist **Gene Kelly** is in love with the city of Paris. *An American in Paris* (1951, MGM).

1467 "Paris? No, not this city. It's too real and too beautiful. It never lets you forget anything. It reaches in and opens you wide, and you stay that way. I know I came to Paris to study and to paint because Utrillo did, and Lautrec did, and Koualt did. I love what they created, and I thought something would happen to me, too. Well, it happened all right. Now what have I got left? Paris. Maybe that's enough for some but it isn't for me anymore because the more beautiful everything is, the more

it will hurt without you." **Gene Kelly** replies to his departing love Leslie Caron who says, "Paris has ways of making people forget." *An American in Paris* (1951, MGM).

1468 "Doors will open beyond which I shall catch a glimpse of the unknown. Let it be wonderful or let it be so awful so long as it is uncommon! And now, behold, dear Petronious: my new Rome, to rise in gleaming white beauty, master gem of the world's crown. It shall have a new name: Neropolis. City of Nero." **Peter Ustinov**, as the mad Emperor Nero, shares with his major advisor, crafty Leo Genn, Ustinov's plans to burn Rome to the ground and erect a new city in its place. *Quo Vadis* (1951, MGM).

1469 "I am the city, hub and heart of America, melting pot of every race, creed, color and religion in humanity, from my famous stockyards to my towering factories, from my tenement district to swank Lake Shore Drive. I am the voice, the heartbeat of this giant, sprawling, sordid and beautiful, poor and magnificent, citadel of civilization. And this is the story of just one night in the great city. Now meet my citizens." **Chill Wills**, who also portrays Sgt. Joe, is the voice of the city of Chicago. *City That Never Sleeps* (1953, Republic).

1470 "Chicago is a big melting pot and I got melted but good." Sultry stripper **Mala Powers** has had it with "The City of Big Shoulders." *City That Never Sleeps* (1953, Republic).

1471 "Listen, honey, let's put this house on the market and move back in the city. The country's no place to bring up kids. Our baby's going to be born in Manhattan in a normal, healthy atmosphere. And this time I hope it looks like you." **Richard Widmark** convinces his wife Doris Day to move back to the city when at long last she is able to get pregnant. *The Tunnel of Love* (1958, MGM).

1472 "The things that spell San Francisco to me are disappearing fast. I should have liked to have lived here then—color, excitement, power, freedom." While showing James Stewart old maps and woodcuts from the wild days of San Francisco, **Tom Helmore** becomes nostalgic. *Vertigo* (1958, Paramount).

1473 "Maycomb was a tired old town in 1932 when I first knew it. . . . It was hotter then. A man's shirt collar was wilted by nine o'clock in the morning." Narrator **Kim Stanley**, as the adult Scout Finch, recalls her small Alabama town. *To Kill a Mockingbird* (1962, Universal-International).

1474 "Amphibious City is only the beginning. In the future we will see other undersea colonies, great cities on the sea bottom. In truth, the great, the rich, bountiful ocean depths, cradle of all life, the world of innerspace, may provide a future home and a safe haven for mankind." Ever-hopeful, the narrator believes in the future of an undersea domed city. Unfortunately, the one in the film is more doomed than domed, collapsing, killing all but lovers William Lundigan and Julie Adams, who plan to rebuild. *The Underwater City* (1962, Columbia).

1475 "This used to be a hellava town!" **Lloyd Nolan** speaks of Los Angeles, the site of a horrible natural disaster. *Earthquake* (1974, Universal).

1476 "This is the only city in the world where there is dog shit piled on top of other dog shit. . . . Future archaeologists will learn about our civilization by examining layers of dog do. . . ." Painter **Alan Bates** speaks of the problem of dog excrement in New York City. *An Unmarried Woman* (1977, 20th Century-Fox).

1477 "New York is not the center of the goddamn universe. I grant you it's an exciting, vibrant, stimulating, fabulous city, but it's not Mecca. It just smells that way." Among the many things **Alan Alda** and his ex-wife Jane Fonda argue about is his preference for California and her belief that there is no other place on earth to live than New York City. *California Suite* (1978, Columbia).

1478 "He adored New York City. He idolized it out of proportion." In voice-over **Woody Allen**, as writer Isaac Davis, begins chapter one of his new book. *Manhattan* (1979, United Artists).

1479 "It was bad, but not as bad as New York City." **Robert Ginty** compares Vietnam to the Big Apple. *The Exterminator* (1980, Avco Embassy).

1480 "Hong Kong, a borrowed place that lives on borrowed time. The British rent it now, but in seventeen years the lease runs out, and the People's Republic is the landlord. But this is a city of survivors, and whatever happens, Hong Kong will always be the place." **Chuck Norris** expresses confidence in the future of Hong Kong. *Forced Vengeance* (1982, MGM-United Artists).

1481 "New York, like the rest of America. . . is coming apart like a cheap suit." **Robin Williams** foresees the apocalypse. *The Survivors* (1983, Columbia).

1482 "Why don't we go back to the city lights and find some of that glitter and glitz?" As they are talking in an alley in Las Vegas, **Peter MacNicol** has a suggestion for Burt Reynolds. *Heat* (1987, New Century-Vista).

1483 JAMES: "How do you like New York so far?" MIKEY: "Hey, it's my kind of town." Taxi driver **John Travolta** speaks to a baby born in his cab. **Bruce Willis** is the voice of Mikey. *Look Who's Talking* (1989, Tri-Star).

1484 "If you took away 60 percent of the buildings, Yokohama would look just like Memphis." Japanese teenager **Mashatoshi Nagase** shows his girlfriend Youki Kudoh that he's not impressed with the hometown of Elvis Presley when the two make a pilgrimage to Graceland. *Mystery Train* (1989, Orion Classics).

Citizens see CITIES AND TOWNS, CIVILIZATIONS, GOVERNMENTS, PEOPLE, VOTING AND VOTERS

Civilizations

see also PROGRESS, SOCIETIES

1485 JED WATERBURY: "[Lynnfield should learn] how people live and love in the wide awake world. You can't keep civilization out of Lynnfield forever." AUNT MARY: "If civilization is like what Caroline Adams writes about, it's best that our children do without civilization." Neither newspaper editor **Thomas Mitchell** or prim opinionated maiden aunt **Elizabeth Risdon**, realize that the racy potboiler novel they are discussing was written by Risdon's modest, demure and sensible niece Irene Dunne, using an assumed name. *Theodora Goes Wild* (1936, Columbia).

1486 GEORGE CONWAY: "We must get back to civilization." CHANG: "Are you so sure that you're away from it?" **John Howard**'s remark is insulting, but he finds Shangri-La nothing more than a lovely prison, despite the hospitality of **H.B. Warner**, the assistant to the High Lama. *Lost Horizon* (1937, Columbia).

1487 "Look here, won't you give the business a few day's consideration before you let rip? Here we all are. We've built up sort of a civilization. People fit into it, at any rate they get along. We've got the Empire. A kind of order." Somewhat deranged ex-colonel **Ralph Richardson** attempts to reason with Roland Young, a draper's assistant, who intends to use the powers given to him by some curious gods to alter the course of humanity, to prevent war and illness, and to make the world a utopia. *The Man Who Could Work Miracles* (1937, GB, London Films-United Artists).

1488 "Well, they're saved from the blessings of civilization." Alcoholic doctor **Thomas Mitchell** philosophizes as he watches outcasts John Wayne and Claire Trevor ride off at the end of the movie. *Stagecoach* (1939, United Artists).

1489 "Must be getting near civilization." **Clark Gable** casually comments to brother Cameron Mitchell as they ride by a couple of corpses strung up from a tree. *The Tall Men* (1955, 20th Century-Fox).

1490 "This was the beginning of the fall of the Roman Empire. A great civilization is not conquered from without until it has destroyed itself from within." The narrator figuratively shakes his head over the goings on in the Roman Empire after the death of philosopher-emperor Marcus Aurelius, played in little more than a cameo role by Alec Guinness. *The Fall of the Roman Empire* (1964, Paramount).

1491 "The courts are civilized. I'm not civilized." Police officer **Sylvester Stallone**'s answer to violence is more violence. *Cobra* (1986, Warner Bros.).

1492 "We did our duty to civilization. We procreated and now we can die." **Woody Allen** and his wife Bette Midler have just seen their children off on a skiing trip and are preparing to celebrate their 16th wedding anniversary. *Scenes from a Mall* (1991, Touchstone).

1493 "Once again, we've saved civilization as we know it." Wasting no words, monosyllabic **William Shatner**, as Captain Kirk, makes his claim. *Star Trek VI: The Undiscovered Country* (1991, Paramount).

1494 "I already know what I would do, I just wondered about a civilized guy like you." Police officer **Ray Liotta** sneeringly reacts when "citizen" Kurt Russell expresses the desire to beat up the burglar who broke into Russell's house and threatened his wife Madeleine Stowe with a knife. When Liotta corners the intruder and tells Russell to beat the cowering man to a pulp, Russell declines the offer. *Unlawful Entry* (1992, 20th Century-Fox).

Classes

see also DEMOCRACY, EQUALITIES, PEOPLE, SOCIETIES

1495 "The men are handsome and the women sleep in luxury." Poor young Irish girl **Nancy Carroll** has her own image of the upper class. *Personal Maid* (1932, Paramount).

1496 "You look like you got class. . . . Yessir! With a capital K. . . . And I'm the guy that knows class when he sees it, believe you me. Ask any of the boys. They'll tell ya. Shapely sure knows how to pick 'em. Yessir, Shapely's the name, and that's how I like 'em. . . ." Traveling salesman **Roscoe Karns** is a real pest to Claudette Colbert on a bus. *It Happened One Night* (1934, Columbia).

1497 HOBOKEN: "Very neat—classy, in fact, too classy. I'm running a drink and dance joint, not a kindergarten." BUBBLES: "I ain't got an ounce of class, Sugar, honest." **Harold Huber**, the swinish manager of a sleazy nightclub is unmoved by Maureen O'Hara's classical ballerina rendition of a Hawaiian dance. Loud, vulgar **Lucille Ball** offers the opinion that's she's just what he's looking for. *Dance, Girl, Dance* (1940, RKO).

1498 "Our class never lets your class down and your class never lets ours down." Valet **Edmund Gwenn** reassures gangster Robert Montgomery, who has inherited an English earldom. *The Earl of Chicago* (1940, MGM).

1499 "Grief ain't what I came after. You got class, kid. Or is it because I haven't seen any women lately?" Escaped Devil's Island prisoner **Clark Gable** likes what he sees in hardboiled dance-hall girl Joan Crawford. *Strange Cargo* (1940, MGM).

1500 "I hope you will not consider me inhospitable if I say 'sorry Mr. Van Cleve, we don't cater to your class of people. Please make your reservations somewhere else.'" Charming devil **Laird Cregar** tells Don Ameche that he doesn't merit hell after hearing the latter detail his "life of sin." *Heaven Can Wait* (1943, 20th Century-Fox).

1501 "Do you mean to stand there and tell me I ain't got class?" Show girl **Vivian Blaine** is hurt and angry when the director of a fancy musical advises her to go back to burlesque. *Cover Girl* (1945, Columbia).

1502 "Porter says Addie Ross has class. And he knows class—Like I know navigation." **Linda Darnell**, who admits to easily getting lost, speaks of her husband Paul Douglas and the unseen but influential narrator Celeste Holm. *A Letter to Three Wives* (1949, 20th Century-Fox).

1503 "I thought you were class, like a real high note you hit once in a lifetime." **Kirk Douglas** finally sees his wife, Lauren Bacall, for what she is—a selfish and self-centered woman. *Young Man with a Horn* (1950, Warner Bros.).

1504 "See! You don't understand! I could have had class. I coulda been a contender. I coulda had class and been somebody. Real class. Instead of a bum—which is what I am." Ex-boxer and longshoreman **Marlon Brando** partially blames his brother Rod Steiger for the fact that he never amounted to anything in the fight game. *On the Waterfront* (1954, Columbia).

1505 "I'll say one thing for prison; you meet a better class of people." **Humphrey Bogart** decides to return to prison on Devil's Island at the end of the film. *We're No Angels* (1955, Paramount).

1506 "I'm working class and proud of it." Perhaps so, but **Laurence Harvey**, as Joe Lampton, has ambitions to move up in class by marrying a wealthy girl. *Room at the Top* (1957, GB, Remus-Romulus).

1507 "I ain't got the class of a duck." Drifter and part-time prostitute **Debra Winger** has her own number. *Cannery Row* (1982, MGM-United Artists).

1508 "You look good. . . classy. . . whatta ya have to do—go to traffic court?" No longer appropriate boyfriend **Alec Baldwin** comments on Melanie Griffith's appearance. *Working Girl* (1988, 20th Century-Fox).

Cleanliness

see also FILTHINESS, HEALTH, PURITY

1509 GEORGE CURTIS: "I haven't got a clean shirt to my name." TOM CHAMBERS: "A clean shirt? What's up? A romance?" CURTIS: "I'm not talking pajamas. Just a clean shirt." Painter **Gary Cooper** is a bit risque in his response to apprentice playwright **Fredric March.** *Design for Living* (1933, Paramount).

1510 "I washed me face and hands before I came, I did." **Wendy Hiller** protests when Leslie Howard tells his housekeeper to give the flower girl a bath. *Pygmalion* (1938, GB, MGM).

1511 "Remember, we used to go to her house. You could eat a meal off their floor." **Thelma Ritter** tries to convince her brother-in-law **Frank Sinatra** to marry widow Eleanor Parker, who apparently keeps a very clean house. *A Hole in the Head* (1959, United Artists).

1512 JACKSON BENTLEY: "What is it, Major Lawrence, that attracts you personally to the desert." T.E. LAWRENCE: "It's clean." Lowell Thomas-like journalist **Arthur Kennedy** probably didn't get the kind of response he expected from **Peter O'Toole.** *Lawrence of Arabia* (1962, GB, Columbia).

1513 "I've seen garbage collectors who are cleaner." West Indian teacher **Sidney Poitier** is disappointed in the hygiene of his male students of a tough East End school. *To Sir with Love* (1967, GB, Columbia).

1514 "Two single men should not have a house cleaner than my mother's." **Walter Matthau**, as Oscar Madison, complains about his fussy roommate Jack Lemmon, as Felix Unger. *The Odd Couple* (1968, Paramount).

1515 "People are filthy, that's what's wrong with people. I think they wouldn't be so violent if they were clean." Obsessed with junk littering the landscape, fussy **Helena Kallianiotes** seems to believe cleanliness is next to peacefulness. *Five Easy Pieces* (1970, Columbia).

1516 "This is the cleanest and nicest police car I've ever been in in my life. . . . This thing's nicer than my apartment." Detroit police detective **Eddie Murphy** comments as he rides in a Beverly Hills patrol car. *Beverly Hills Cop* (1984, Paramount).

1517 "You clean up real nice." Prostitute **Laura San Giacomo** compliments her hooker roommate Julia Roberts, who is wearing respectable clothes for a change. *Pretty Woman* (1990, Touchstone-Buena Vista).

Clergy see MISSIONS AND MISSIONARIES, PRIESTS

Cleverness see BRAINS, INTELLIGENCE

Clichés

see also IDEAS

1518 "I told Daddy that promises don't butter the bread—the proof is in the pudding." Without clichés, **JoBeth Williams** has little to say. *Desert Bloom* (1986, Columbia).

1519 "You've got to rehearse the clichés: 'We gotta play it one day at a time. . . I'm just happy to be here. . . I just hope I can help the club. . . .'" Veteran minor leaguer **Kevin Costner** coaches brash young pitcher Tim Robbins on talking to reporters when he is called up to the "show," i.e., the major leagues. *Bull Durham* (1988, Orion).

1520 "It's such a cliché. Pretty soon a bottle will be busted over someone's head, punches will be thrown, and someone will break a chair over someone else." Seedy and world-weary police detective **Nick Nolte** makes the remark in a bar to an ex-con whom he once arrested and who wants to get even. Nolte then breaks a bottle over the ex-con's head, punches a second brawler and breaks a chair over a third. *Another 48 Hours* (1990, Paramount).

1521 TOM WINGO: "It's an art form to hate New York properly." BERNARD WOODRUFF: "No, it's a cliché." Southerner **Nick Nolte** is corrected by native New Yorker **Jason Gould**. *The Prince of Tides* (1991, Columbia).

Climates

see also HEAT, SEASONS, TEMPERATURES, WEATHER

1522 "It's all a question of climate. You cannot serenade a woman in a snowstorm. All the grace in the art of love—elaborate approaches that will make the game of love amusing—can only be practiced in those countries that quiver in the heat of the sun." Spaniard **John Gilbert** rates his country better for love than Greta Garbo's Sweden. *Queen Christina* (1933, MGM).

1523 "I always felt a little hurt when our swallows deserted us in winter for capitalistic countries. Now I know why. We have the high ideals. They have the climate." Russian Communist emissary **Greta Garbo** finds something good about Paris and the West. *Ninotchka* (1939, MGM).

1524 "The man is creating the climate for his own death." Acerbic right-wing businessman **Robert Ryan** speaks ominously about President John F. Kennedy. *Executive Action* (1973, National General).

Closeness

see also SPACE, TOGETHERNESS

1525 WALTER NEFF: "You know why you couldn't figure this one, Keyes? Because the guy you were looking for was too close—right across the desk from you." BARTON KEYES: "Closer than that, Walter." NEFF: "I love you too." **Fred MacMurray** has just confessed to claims adjuster **Edward G. Robinson** that he and Barbara Stanwyck had killed her husband in order to collect his insurance money. *Double Indemnity* (1944, Paramount).

1526 "It was as though for a time I didn't exist, as though I had no place in the world. . . I've no desire for the close contact of other people. . . I don't seem capable of being close to people." **Candace Hilligoss** tries to explain her feelings to her doctor Stanley Levitt after she has seemingly drowned. *Carnival of Souls* (1962, Herts-Lion).

1527 "We are mentally and spiritually close. Therefore, we should be physically close too." **Alan Bates** encourages Oliver Reed to join him in a little nude wrestling. *Women in Love* (1970, GB, United Artists).

1528 "Everybody that I am close to dies." **Sharon Stone** tells her sad story to police detective Michael Douglas to whom she's become very close. *Basic Instinct* (1992, Tri-Star).

Clothes

see also BODIES, FASHIONS

1529 "Let me die in the uniform in which I served, not my country, but my countrymen." Sentenced to die as a spy, **Marlene Dietrich** faces a firing squad dressed as a streetwalker. *Dishonored* (1931, Paramount).

1530 LIL ANDREWS: "Can you see through this?" SALESLADY: "I'm afraid you can, dear." LIL: "I'll take it." **Jean Harlow** knows the effect she wants her new dress to make. *Red-Headed Woman* (1932, MGM).

1531 "I wonder what you'd look like dressed. . . . Pretty good." When title character Johnny Weissmuller joins the safari, **Maureen O'Sullivan** admires his magnificent physique. *Tarzan, the Ape Man* (1932, MGM).

1532 "Perhaps you're interested in how a man undresses. Funny thing about that. Quite a study in psychology. No two men do it alike. . . I have an idiosyncracy all my own. You'll notice my coat comes first—then the tie—then the shirt— now, according to Hoyle, the pants should come next. But that's where I'm different. I go for the shoes first. After that, it's every man for himself. . . ." **Clark Gable** does a strip when Claudette Colbert refuses to go on the other side of "the Wall of Jericho" that he's rigged with a blanket and a clothesline to separate them in a bedroom. When he starts to take down the pants, she skedaddles to where she belongs. When it was discovered that Clark Gable wasn't wearing an undershirt, the sales of T-shirts plummeted across the country. *It Happened One Night* (1934, Columbia).

1533 "Do you mind taking those things off the walls of Jericho? It's tough enough as it is." **Clark Gable** makes the request of Claudette Colbert when she unthinkingly flings her undergarments on the blanket dividing the tourist camp room they are forced to share. *It Happened One Night* (1934, Columbia).

1534 "It was the busiest part of the day; damn it, I was tying my cravat." Title character **Leslie Howard** poses as a useless fop. *The Scarlet Pimpernel* (1934, GB, London Films).

1535 "Odds fish, Percy, you're brainless, spineless and useless, but you do know clothes." **Nigel Bruce**, as the Prince of Wales, underestimates Leslie Howard's capabilities as Sir Percy Blakeney. *The Scarlet Pimpernel* (1934, GB, London Films).

1536 "It's the first dress in three years that didn't make me look like a Quaker." Broadway actress **Carole Lombard** steps into a glamorous gown. *Twentieth Century* (1934, Columbia).

1537 "I might have to have it taken in a smidgeon." Well-rounded maid **Hattie McDaniel** is thrilled with the hand-me-down fitted beaded dress given to her by Jean Harlow. *China Seas* (1935, MGM).

1538 "Even the moths wouldn't eat them." Newly-rich, no-nonsense frontierswoman **Maude Eburne** orders her husband's suits be burned. *Ruggles of Red Gap* (1935, Paramount).

1539 "Tell me, little boy, did you get a whistle or a baseball bat with that suit?" **Lucille Ball** dead pans a wisecrack to a burly, gravel-voiced sailor who makes a pass at her. *Follow the Fleet* (1936, RKO).

1540 WILD BILL HICKOK: "Don't you ever wear a dress?" CALAMITY JANE: "I might if I had one." Gunfighter and frontier scout **Gary Cooper** is tired of seeing mule-skinner and stagecoach driver **Jean Arthur** in buckskin. *The Plainsman* (1936, Paramount).

1541 "Did you get two pairs of pants with that suit?" **Gypsy Rose Lee** is critical of Alice Faye's tacky, tasteless outfit. *You Can't Have Everything* (1937, 20th Century-Fox).

1542 AUNT ELIZABETH: "Well, who are you?" DAVID: "I don't know. I'm not quite myself today." ELIZABETH: "Well, you look perfectly idiotic in those clothes." DAVID: "These aren't my clothes." ELIZABETH: "Well, where are your clothes?" DAVID: "I've lost my clothes." ELIZABETH: "Why are you wearing those clothes?" DAVID: "Because I just went gay all of a sudden." **May Robson** has every right to feel that **Cary Grant** looks ridiculous wearing Katharine Hepburn's fur-edged flimsy nightgown when all his clothes are taken away from him. Some believe this is where the word "gay" as applied to homosexuals has its origin. *Bringing Up Baby* (1938, RKO).

1543 SUPERINTENDENT MORGAN: "Take this boy away and make sure the punishment fits the crime." MARK BRADEN: "Wouldn't it be better if you made the pants fit the boy?" When reform school warden **Cy Kendall** orders a guard to flog Bobby Jordan when the boy's pants fall down, Deputy Commissioner of Corrections **Humphrey Bogart** steps in. *Crime School* (1938, Warner Bros.).

1544 "Thank heaven you're not in rags. I'm sick of seeing women in rags." Needing $300 to pay the taxes on Tara, Vivien Leigh fashions a dress out of a window drape to visit **Clark Gable** in an Atlanta jail. *Gone with the Wind* (1939, Selznick-MGM).

1545 MARY HAINES: "May I suggest if you're dressing to please Stephen, get rid of that one? He doesn't like such obvious effects." CRYSTAL ALLEN: "Thanks for the tip. But when anything I'm wearing doesn't please Stephen, I take it off." Wife **Norma Shearer** confronts other woman **Joan Crawford** and insults Crawford's cheap and sexy clothes. *The Women* (1939, MGM).

1546 "It's for a friend of mine. He's waiting downstairs." **Cary Grant** holds various dresses up to himself in front of a mirror as he speaks to the psychiatrist his wife Gail Patrick has hired to find out why he won't consummate their marriage. The dresses will be taken by Randolph Scott to Grant's wife Irene Dunne who has returned after seven years on a desert island. The courts declared her legally dead moments before Grant married Patrick. *My Favorite Wife* (1940, RKO).

1547 "Say, if I had a wad of folding dough like that I'd go right out and buy an outfit that would knock this neighborhood cockeyed!" Mercenary **Susan Hayward** wishes someone—anyone, will give her some money. *Among the Living* (1941, Paramount).

1548 "Why don't you slip out of those clothes and into a dry martini?" Roué **Robert Benchley** as Mr. Osborne slyly propositions Ginger Rogers as Susan Applegate. *The Major and the Minor* (1942, Paramount).

1549 PAT O'TOOLE: "Hitler is here!" KATIE O'HARA: "I can't see him now, I'm dressing." **Cary Grant** makes an excited announcement to **Ginger Rogers** as he stares out a hotel window and witnesses the arrival of Nazi troops in Austria. Ginger is too busy with her clothes to care. *Once Upon a Honeymoon* (1942, RKO).

1550 "I've always loved very feminine clothes, but never quite dared to wear them. But I'm going to after this. I'm going to wear exactly the things that please me and you." Icy psychiatrist **Ingrid Bergman** has thawed out because of her love for Gregory Peck, who is possibly a murderer. *Spellbound* (1945, Selznick-United Artists).

1551 "You won't have to sing much in that outfit." **Humphrey Bogart** rightly implies that the predominately male audience won't pay much attention to Lauren Bacall's singing ability because of her costume. *To Have and Have Not* (1945, Warner Bros.).

1552 "I can never get a zipper to close. Maybe that stands for something, what do you think?" Promiscuous **Rita Hayworth** has a naughty thought as she asks husband George Macready to do up the back of her dress. *Gilda* (1946, Columbia).

1553 "What? This old thing? Why I only wear it when I don't care how I look." Looking like a dream in a summer frock, **Gloria Grahame** reacts to James Stewart's compliment about it. When she walks away, her wiggling hips almost cause a chain of accidents because of men ogling her. *It's a Wonderful Life* (1946, RKO).

1554 "How did you get into that dress—with a spray gun?" **Bob Hope** pants at luscious looking Dorothy Lamour. *Road to Rio* (1947, Paramount).

1555 PHOEBE FROST: "I wonder what holds up that dress?" CAPT. JOHN PRINGLE: "It must be that German willpower." Iowa Congresswoman **Jean Arthur** and U.S. Army Captain **John Lund** watch films of suspected Nazi collaborator Marlene Dietrich wearing a low-cut, strapless evening gown. *A Foreign Affair* (1948, Paramount).

1556 "It's all right. After all, I could have been the girl in the brown and white dress. Anyone could've." A very understanding **Lois Wheeler** forgives Susan Hayward for stealing her man when Hayward found herself pregnant with a dead soldier's baby. The reference is to the evening dress Hayward wore to a swanky party that put everything in motion. *My Foolish Heart* (1949, RKO).

1557 "Get me out of this Buck Rogers monkey suit!" Test pilot **Humphrey Bogart** has just made an especially dangerous flight. *Chain Lightning* (1950, Warner Bros.).

1558 EVE GILL: "I bought this dress just for today, Madam." CHARLOTTE INWOOD: "Don't confide in me, dear—just pour the tea." Acting student **Jane Wyman** poses as a dresser-maid so she can do some detective work and clear her boyfriend Richard Todd, suspected of murdering the husband of glamorous stage and singing star **Marlene Dietrich**. *Stage Fright* (1950, GB, Warner Bros.).

1559 "Couldn't we work in a little color? Or let it plunge just a little in front?" Music hall star **Marlene Dietrich** objects to the funereal black outfit she's expected to wear as a new widow. *Stage Fright* (1950, GB, Warner Bros.).

1560 "That's quite a dress you almost have on." American artist **Gene Kelly** is impressed with his would-be patron Nina Foch's one-shouldered gown. *An American in Paris* (1951, MGM).

1561 "It ain't the Taj Mahal or the Hanging Gardens of Babylon, but it'll do." It's **Robert Mitchum**'s

retort when Jane Russell asks him, "Enjoy the view?" as she catches him ogling her very low-cut gown. *Macao* (1952, RKO).

1562 "You have to start laying plans at thirteen for a dress like that." **Jean Peters** knowingly responds when her husband Casey Adams (Max Showalter) hopefully suggests that she wear a dress like the one that is clinging seductively to Marilyn Monroe's gyrating body. *Niagara* (1952, 20th Century-Fox).

1563 "It does more for you than them pants you're always wearing." Sports promoter **Spencer Tracy** compliments his client Katharine Hepburn on the dress she's wearing, which he calls "the right silks." He objects to her wearing slacks when she's playing golf. *Pat and Mike* (1952, MGM).

1564 "This is very unusual. I've never been alone with a man before—even with my dress on. With my dress off, it's most unusual." Drugged, run-away princess **Audrey Hepburn** is somewhat amused when she awakens in Gregory Peck's Rome apartment after he got stuck with her and didn't have the heart to ditch her. *Roman Holiday* (1953, Paramount).

1565 "You know when it's hot like this—you know what I do? I keep my undies in the icebox." **Marilyn Monroe** shares a cool little secret with her downstairs neighbor Tom Ewell. Showing her simple origins, she means refrigerator, of course. *The Seven Year Itch* (1955, 20th Century-Fox).

1566 "Those things have possibilities, sheriff. . . but not on you." **Angie Dickinson**, walking into a room, catches John Wayne holding a pair of red ladies bloomers. *Rio Bravo* (1959, Warner Bros.).

1567 TONY: "Your skirt's too short." VERA: "My what? That's how all the girls are wearing them. Well that's how they all wear them. . . Why? Do you think it's too short?" This exchange about the length of her skirts is ended when **James Fox** quickly embraces **Sarah Miles**. *The Servant* (1963, GB, Elstree).

1568 "Flapper skirts on a bride of Christ! I don't like undercover nuns." Father **Regis Toomey** doesn't know what the church is coming to, when three very attractive young nuns don civilian clothes to work as nurses in a ghetto clinic. *Change of Habit* (1969, Universal).

1569 "Nobody wears a beige suit to a bank robbery." Aspiring bank robber **Woody Allen** complains to his wife Janet Margolin as she sends him off to work. *Take the Money and Run* (1969, Cinerama).

1570 "I grew up wearing your things, mister. . . everything you wore out, got dirty or you outgrew. I even ate your leftovers." Angry black criminal **Fred Williamson** evicts a stunned white couple from their expensive upper East Side Manhattan apartment. *Black Caesar* (1973, American International).

1571 "Yes, I got my, my red dress and my high-heel sneakers at home waiting, baby." **Rosalind Cash** informs Sidney Poitier that she's ready for a night on the town. *Uptown Saturday Night* (1974, Warner Bros.).

1572 "I don't like the panties-drying-on-the-rod." As he inspects the bathroom, **Richard Dreyfuss** lays down his rules for sharing an apartment with Marsha Mason. *The Goodbye Girl* (1977, MGM-United Artists).

1573 "Would it kill you once in a while to wear a damn dress?" Aging private-eye **Art Carney** doesn't like Lily Tomlin in slacks. *The Late Show* (1977, Warner Bros.).

1574 "How dare you come into the room partly clothed. . . . Off with it." **Dirk Bogarde** yells at his wife Andrea Ferreol when she enters their bedroom dressed only in a black slip. *Despair* (1979, Ger., New Line).

1575 "Fruit of the Loom is doing a big ad campaign. Something tells me you could really fit into a pair of jockey shorts." With a voice that makes her sound like a drag queen, **Tammy Grimes** sizes up Bruce Jenner in his boxer shorts. *Can't Stop the Music* (1980, Associated Film Distribution).

1576 LINDA MAROLLA: "What should I wear?" HOBSON: "Steal something casual." When wealthy lush Dudley Moore proposes a date with shoplifter **Liza Minnelli**, his valet **John Gielgud** puts in his two cents. *Arthur* (1981, Warner Bros.-Orion).

1577 "No checkup is ever just a simple formality, Miss Jeremy. . . . Now get undressed." Hospital doctor **John Warner Williams** orders former Playmate of the Year and Hugh Hefner's good friend Barbi Benton to do what she does best—take off her clothes. *Hospital Massacre* (1981, Cannon).

1578 "I'd like to see you with your pants off." This is the "cute meet" of Louise Bryant, played by **Diane Keaton**, the frustrated wife of a Portland dentist, and radical journalist John Reed, impersonated by Warren Beatty. *Reds* (1981, Paramount).

1579 "How can it be? I haven't taken my clothes off." **Woody Allen** is shocked when his wife Mary Steenburgen finds his ardor for her disgusting. *A Midsummer Night's Sex Comedy* (1982, Orion-Warner Bros.).

1580 "Hey, can I try on your yellow dress?. . . What are you going to use it for?" **Jessica Lange** delivers the film's last line. She'd like to borrow a dress Dustin Hoffman wore when he masqueraded as a woman so he could get a female role in a soap opera. *Tootsie* (1982, Columbia).

1581 "I haven't had a new dress in twelve months. An' I'm not gonna get one either, not till—till I pass me first exam. Then I'll get a proper dress, the sort of dress you'd only see on an educated woman, on the sort of woman who knows the difference between Jane Austen an' Tracy Austin. . . . Let's start." Lower class hairdresser **Julie Walters** is determined to get a proper education from her university tutor Michael Caine. *Educating Rita* (1983, GB, Rank).

1582 "You are what you wear." Car dealer **Richard Crenna** imparts some sartorial advice to admiring teen Matt Dillon. *The Flamingo Kid* (1984, 20th Century-Fox).

1583 "Take your clothes off quick." Loutish soldier-of-fortune **Brent Huff** decides it's time for Tawny Kitaen to show her dramatic talents. *The Perils of Gwendoline* (1984, Fr., Goldwyn).

1584 "You can wear your understuff and all that, since it is January." Prior to going into service in World War II, **Sean Penn** tries to lure Elizabeth McGovern into skinny dipping. They're in California. *Racing with the Moon* (1984, Paramount).

1585 "I can't believe I gave my panties to a geek." Teenager **Molly Ringwald** has been talked into giving high school freshman Anthony Michael Hall a pair of her panties. He, in turn, has charged other freshmen boys a buck to see the undergarment. *Sixteen Candles* (1984, Universal).

1586 "With my help he's come a long way. He's stopped buying his clothes at Nerds-R-Us." **Joyce Hyser**, masquerading as a male, refers to Clayton Rohner, the hunk she yearns for. *Just One of the Guys* (1985, Columbia).

1587 "I never saw so much corduroy in one place." It's the reaction of Californian **John Cusack** who is a freshman at an Ivy League college. *The Sure Thing* (1985, Embassy).

1588 "If that dress had pockets, you'd look like a pool table." **Rodney Dangerfield** assesses the appearance of a rather large society matron attired in a green evening gown. *Back to School* (1986, Orion).

1589 "Not many girls could dress as casually as she did." **Jean-Hugues Anglade** comments on title character Beatrice Dalle, who shows up at his bungalow wearing only an apron and a smile. *Betty Blue* (1986, Fr., Alive Films).

1590 "Those polka dots just dripped right into the water!" Loony **Sissy Spacek** tells her sister Diane Keaton that her favorite dress was ruined in the wash. *Crimes of the Heart* (1986, De Laurentiis).

1591 "I'm really getting used to these outfits. They sell a lot of them, but I don't see anyone else wearing them." Talking Heads' **David Byrne** comments on his cowboy clothes in this satire of Texas crazies. *True Stories* (1986, Warner Bros.).

1592 "Get me out of here! I'm wearing cotton underwear!" Greedy, neurotic **Lesley Ann Warren** yells hysterically to her lawyer when she's arrested and put into jail. *Burglar* (1987, Warner Bros.).

1593 "It's only a weiner roast. Don't gild the lily. Less is more." **Dick Shawn** quips to his wife Valerie Perrine, already dressed in a metallic turban and black leotards under a gold lamé skirt. She is about to add even more jewelry to her already glittering body. *Maid to Order* (1987, New Century-Vista).

1594 "Something happens to a man when he puts on a necktie; it cuts off all the oxygen to the brain." **Michael J. Fox** isn't the first young businessman to wonder why such importance is placed on wearing neckties. *The Secret of My Success* (1987, Universal).

1595 "Well, then get yourself a decent bowling jacket, so when you take Mom out you won't look like the Roto-rooter man." **Charlie Sheen** makes a suggestion when his father Martin Sheen refuses money his son offers him to buy a new suit, claiming he doesn't need one. *Wall Street* (1987, 20th Century-Fox).

1596 LT. COL. ALAN CALDWELL: "You're not going out dressed like that, are you?" DONNA CALDWELL: "Like what?" A. CALDWELL: "Why you can see right through that dress. You might just as well go out without one." D. CALDWELL: "There's a thought." **Sean Connery** disapproves of his daughter **Meg Ryan**'s dress. It's so low cut and mini that the top and the bottom are mere inches from the waist. *The Presidio* (1988, Paramount).

1597 "It's simple, elegant, it makes a statement. . . says to people, confidence—a risk taker, not afraid to be

noticed. . . ." Secretary **Melanie Griffith** models one of her boss Sigourney Weaver's cocktail dresses for Joan Cusack, before discovering the $6,000 price tag. *Working Girl* (1988, 20th Century-Fox).

1598 "Oh, Pete,. . . girl clothes!" Air controller **Holly Hunter** usually wears shirts and jeans. She's touched when her lover Richard Dreyfuss gives her a gussy gown for her birthday. *Always* (1989, Universal).

1599 "That dress, you would wear to a hooker's wedding." Bitter Aunt Sofia, engagingly played by **Gina De Angelis**, mutters about the appearance of a wedding guest. *Cousins* (1989, Paramount).

1600 "I have more than two kinds of laundry. There's not just clean and dirty. There are more subtle levels." **Bill Murray** discovers that Sigourney Weaver has put all of his shirts into the laundry. *Ghostbusters II* (1989, Columbia).

1601 "Next time. . . wear no panties under your skirt." Injured adolescent **Regis Royer**, confined to a wheel chair, makes a breathless request of Miou-Miou, who makes her living reading to people. *The Reader* (1989, Fr., Orion).

1602 "I'm wearing black underwear." **Madonna**, as Breathless Mahoney, responds when title character Warren Beatty asks if she's grieving for her recently rubbed-out boyfriend. Madonna's fibbing—her black see-through outfit is not under anything and it hides very little. *Dick Tracy* (1990, Buena Vista-Touchstone).

1603 "Let them stay up on their own. . . . They shouldn't stay up, but they do." **Bridget Fonda**, who designs strapless evening gowns, really knows how they work. *Strapless* (1990, GB, Film Four).

1604 "It's a symbol of my individuality and my belief in personal freedom." If anyone cares, **Nicolas Cage**'s snakeskin jacket means a great deal to him. *Wild at Heart* (1990, Goldwyn).

1605 "This is my costume. I'm a homicidal maniac. They look like everyone else." **Christina Ricci**, as Wednesday, explains to her teacher why she's wearing her usual clothes to a Halloween costume party. *The Addams Family* (1991, Paramount).

1606 "Since when did you start wearing underpants?" While fleeing from killers, **Mel Gibson** finds time to comment on Goldie Hawn's underwear as he climbs up a ladder behind her just as her billowy full-skirt is blown up above his head. *Bird on a Wire* (1991, Universal).

1607 "Who's your tailor, Gus? This suit looks like the lining to a better suit." **Alec Baldwin** insults mobster Jeremy Roberts' garish tuxedo. *The Marrying Man* (1991, Hollywood Pictures).

1608 NICK CURRAN: "You seem to know a lot about me." CATHERINE TRAMELL: "You know a lot about me, too." NICK: "Everything I know about you is police business." CATHERINE: "You know I don't wear underwear, don't you, Nick?" **Michael Douglas** was caught watching **Sharon Stone** slip on a short white dress over nothing more than her luscious body. *Basic Instinct* (1992, Tri-Star).

Clues

see also CAUSE AND EFFECT, DETECTIVES AND DEDUCTION, DISCOVERIES, EXPLANATIONS, INFORMATION AND INFORMERS, MYSTERIES, PROBLEMS, RECOGNITIONS, SOLUTIONS

1609 "Look at him running around with a clue in him." This will take a bit of explaining. Someone has thrown a brick with a note attached to it through the window of **Myrna Loy** and William Powell's bedroom. Their dog, Asta, thinking it's a game, grabs the note and swallows it. *After the Thin Man* (1936, MGM).

1610 ADRIENNE FROMSETT: "I read a story once about a killer who left clues." PHILIP MARLOWE: "That was a story." Gold digger **Audrey Totter** tries to tell private eye **Robert Montgomery** how to conduct a murder investigation. *Lady in the Lake* (1947, MGM).

1611 "You can tell when Barnett's been over to my house, the toilet ain't flushed and the cat's pregnant." Cabby **Sylvester Stallone** disparages his rival Tim Thomerson. *Rhinestone* (1984, 20th Century-Fox).

Codes *see* CREEDS AND CREDOS, LAWS, RULES

Collections

see also DEBTS, HOBBIES, MONEY, PAYMENTS

1612 "I have here a collection of the world's most astonishing horrors. . . ." Sepulchral-toned traveling curator **George Zucco**'s prize possession is the skeleton of Count Dracula, complete with a stake through where the heart used to be. There ought to be a sign "Remove At Your Own Risk." *House of Frankenstein* (1944, Universal).

1613 "Tonight is collection night. The China Coast at eleven o'clock, and don't let the fog throw you. It won't bother us where we're going." Devil **Ray Milland** tells politician Thomas Mitchell that they're going to take a little trip to the island of lost souls. *Alias Nick Beal* (1949, GB, Paramount).

1614 "It is no accident that the collection comes after the sermon, it's like a Nielsen rating." Father **Jack Lemmon** criticizes young seminarian Zeljko Ivanek, who has alienated the entire congregation with his first sermon. *Mass Appeal* (1984, Universal).

Colors

see also ART AND ARTISTS, BLACKS, FLAGS, LIGHTS

1615 "I say, Thomas, look! That heavenly blue against the mauve curtains. Doesn't it excite you? That kind of blue just does something to me." Society decorator **Barry Norton** points out a shop window display to his friend Franklin Pangborn. *Only Yesterday* (1933, Universal).

1616 SYLVIA FOWLER: "Jungle Red! Isn't that divine?" NANCY BLAKE: "Looks like you've been tearing at somebody's throat." **Rosalind Russell** shows off her new nail polish to the girls. **Florence Nash** gets a chance to deliver a bitchy line. *The Women* (1939, MGM).

1617 "You know how it is just before the sun sets? You can look out and that water ain't exactly blue and it ain't exactly purple—it's a sort of a color a man can feel but he can't put a name to." **Gary Cooper**, who has never met the lady, describes actress Lillie Langtry's eyes to her greatest fan Walter Brennan as Judge Roy Bean. *The Westerner* (1940, Goldwyn).

1618 "I want to see if grass is still green." Released from prison after serving a long term, **Humphrey Bogart** takes a stroll in a park. *High Sierra* (1941, Warner Bros.).

1619 "Lettie, take an editorial. 'To the Women of America'—no, make it 'To Women Everywhere: Banish the black, burn the blue and bury the beige. From now on, girls, think pink.'" Fashion editor **Kay Thompson** dictates an editorial to secretary Ruta Lee which she hopes will dictate to fashion-conscious women to buy clothes with the primary color of pink. *Funny Face* (1957, Paramount).

1620 NICK ARNSTEIN: "That color looks wonderful with your eyes." FANNY BRICE: "Just my right eye. I hate what it does to the left." **Omar Sharif**'s compliment isn't accepted without a quip by title character **Barbra Streisand.** *Funny Girl* (1968, Columbia).

1621 "I judge a man by his deeds, not his color." White school marm **Barbara Leigh** goes ga-ga over black Sheriff Fred Williamson. *Boss Nigger* (1974, Dimension).

1622 "Gorgeous color, the smog. I wonder if they sell it in bottles. It would make lovely gifts for back home." New Yorker **Jane Fonda** breaks off another one on her laid-back Californian ex-husband Alan Alda. *California Suite* (1978, Columbia).

1623 "Excuse me, is green the only color these come in?" You'd think a spoiled Jewish American Princess like **Goldie Hawn**, who impulsively joins the army after her husband's death, would know that the color of her uniform is olive drab. *Private Benjamin* (1980, Warner Bros.).

1624 "Everyone sees shapes differently, but color is forever." Interior decorator **Anjelica Huston** states her personal career philosophy. *Prizzi's Honor* (1985, 20th Century-Fox).

1625 "Could you juice me again, the colors are starting to fade." In exchange for injecting a hallucinogen into his brain, **Rick Herbst** finds victims for the "Aylmer," a 700-year-old foot-long worm-like creature attached to Herbst. The Aylmer sucks the brains out of its victims. *Brain Damage* (1988, Palisades).

1626 "The color of the day is black." At the opening of the picture, **Sam Jackson**, as DJ Mister Señor Love Daddy, speaks ominously. *Do the Right Thing* (1989, Universal).

Combat see BATTLES AND BATTLEFIELDS, FIGHTS AND FIGHTING, WARS

Combinations

see also PURPOSES

1627 "I know a lot of smart guys and a few honest ones, but you're both." **Kirk Douglas** likes Robert Mitchum's combination of brains and honesty. That's why he's being hired to track down Douglas' mistress Jane Greer, who shot him and ran off with $40,000 of his money. *Out of the Past* (1947, RKO).

1628 "I'm afraid of you. I've discovered you have an exciting mind, something handsome men rarely have—and the combination might be too much for me." American secretary in Rome **Maggie McNamara** confesses to Louis Jourdan that she's weakening in her resolve to stay out of his bed. *Three Coins in the Fountain* (1954, 20th Century-Fox).

1629 "He said, 'Darling, we wouldn't want two Claras. You're the bright one.' That did it. I could have faced being plain, but to be plain and bright! In the high school I went to, that was a beatable combination." **Debbie Reynolds** sadly remembers her father's response to her question as to when she was going to look like her tall, beautiful sister. *Mary, Mary* (1963, Warner Bros.).

1630 "I'm insane and responsible. This is a potent combination." At bed at night, **Albert Brooks** makes an admission to his wife Julie Hagerty. *Lost in America* (1985, Warner Bros.).

1631 "You shouldn't drink and bake!" Southern Sheriff **Arnold Schwarzenegger** eggs on his wife Blanche Baker who throws a chocolate cake at him. *Raw Deal* (1986, De Laurentiis).

1632 "He's an unlovely combination of a son of a bitch and a rat's knackers." **Peter O'Toole**, the owner of an ancient Irish castle, muses about the American Croesus who holds the mortgage to the castle. The latter threatens to dismantle it, ship it to Malibu, and rebuild it as a theme park called "Irish World." *High Spirits* (1988, Tri-Star).

Comedy and Comedians

see also ENTERTAINMENTS AND ENTERTAINERS, HUMOR, SHOWS, THEATERS, TRAGEDIES

1633 "The trouble is, you're all trying to be comics. Don't you ever take anything seriously?" What heiress and aspiring actress **Katharine Hepburn** fails to comprehend is that the other would-be actresses at a hotel for women use wisecracks to mask their fear and frustration. *Stage Door* (1937, RKO).

1634 "I'm willing to admit that, to a majority of my fellow citizens, I'm a slightly comic figure—an educated man." English teacher **Kirk Douglas** wears his education like a weapon. *A Letter to Three Wives* (1949, 20th Century-Fox).

1635 "Comedy is tragedy, plus time. . . . If it bends, it's comedy. If it breaks, it isn't." Crass TV producer **Alan Alda** defines comedy in meaningless ways for an audience who likes the sound of what he says even if they don't understand what he means. *Crimes and Misdemeanors* (1989, Orion).

Comeuppance see DESERTS AND DESERVING, PUNISHMENTS

Comforts

1636 "Would you be shocked if I put on something more comfortable?" Usually misquoted as "Would you mind if I changed into something more comfortable," the now trite line was a helluva seductive question when asked by sultry **Jean Harlow** of handsome Ben Lyons. *Hell's Angels* (1930, Hughes-United Artists).

1637 "Keep your chin up; you can only die once." **Jane Darwell**'s flippant remark to doomed Dana Andrews is little comfort. *The Ox-Bow Incident* (1943, 20th Century-Fox).

1638 "God help the people who live on this earth and draw their comfort from it—and sometimes from each other." Anti-Nazi German **Spencer Tracy** leaves his message with chambermaid Signe Hasso before he departs for a boat that will take him to freedom. He is running away from the Gestapo who have promised to crucify him as they did six other escapees. *The Seventh Cross* (1944, MGM).

1639 "Tell Momma. . . tell Momma, all." Eighteen-year-old **Elizabeth Taylor**, looking more beautiful than anyone is entitled to be, comforts Montgomery Clift, pulling him close to her ample bosom. *A Place in the Sun* (1951, Paramount).

1640 "I'm sorry I made you being dead an unpleasant experience." Guru Richard Libertini accidentally transfers dying Lily Tomlin's soul into lawyer **Steve Martin**'s body and he's not at all pleased with the invasion. His remark is dripping with sarcasm. *All of Me* (1984, Universal).

1641 "Although that thought may be of great comfort to the women of the world, Mr. Moore, as a future veterinarian, you should know that every dog eventually has his day." Veterinary professor **David Wohl** quips when Anthony Edwards' lament, "I'm never going to get laid," is unfortunately spoken just as everyone stops talking in a previously noisy lecture hall, allowing his remark to be heard by all. *Gotcha!* (1985, Universal).

1642 "Fuck him. He was trash." With the film's last line, foul-mouthed, father-figure, private investigator **Robert Loggia** comforts attorney Glenn Close, who is forced to kill her client and lover Jeff Bridges in self-defense. *Jagged Edge* (1985, Columbia).

Commandments *see* COMMANDS, LAWS, RELIGIONS, RULES

Commands

1643 "It's a slaughterhouse, that's what it is, and I'm the executioner. You send men in rotten ships up to die. . . . They don't argue or revolt. . . . They just say 'Righto' and go out and do it." British squadron commander **Basil Rathbone** has had his fill of sending young pilots to their death in the air over France during World War I. *The Dawn Patrol* (1938, Warner Bros.).

1644 "A command is a lonely job. Sometimes a captain of a ship needs help." **Humphrey Bogart** obliquely asks for help, but his officers choose not to understand him. *The Caine Mutiny* (1954, Columbia).

1645 "What do you know of the soldier's code? You are unworthy of command." Japanese prison commandant **Sessue Hayakawa** has no respect for British colonel Alec Guinness who was ordered to surrender his command. *The Bridge on the River Kwai* (1957, GB, Columbia).

1646 "You know, pain is a wonderful thing. You are much too beautiful a girl to let yourself be broken into food for the royal dogs. When I command you to strip your garment off, you do as I say." Chief torturer **Victor Bo** suggests that buxomy heroine Lana Clarkson be cooperative in this T&A fantasy film. *Barbarian Queen* (1984, Vestron).

Commerce *see* BUSINESS AND COMMERCE

Commission *see* AGENTS

Common *see* HABITS, ORDINARINESS, POPULARITY

Communications *see* INFORMATION AND INFORMERS, LETTERS, MESSAGES, NOTES, RADIOS, SPEECH AND SPEAKING, TALKS AND TALKING, TELEVISION, WRITING AND WRITERS

Company *see* FRIENDSHIPS AND FRIENDS, GUESTS, RELATIONSHIPS, SOCIETIES, TOGETHERNESS, VISITS

Comparisons

1647 "Confidence is like courage of small boy at dentist—most evident after tooth extracted." **Sidney Toler** makes an interesting comparison for his son

Sen Yung. *Charlie Chan at Treasure Island* (1939, 20th Century-Fox).

1648 "She has a shoulder that would make dry ice feel like a bed-warmer." **Melvyn Douglas** confides to his attorney Allyn Joslyn about his sexless "trial marriage" with Rosalind Russell. *This Thing Called Love* (1941, Columbia).

1649 "You're about as funny as a cry for help." Tiny waitress **Jody Gilbert** sneers at W.C. Fields. *Never Give a Sucker an Even Break* (1941, Universal).

1650 "She's as complex as a Bach fugue." Musician **Oscar Levant** compares wealthy patroness Joan Crawford with the work of one of the three B's. *Humoresque* (1947, Warner Bros.).

1651 "All other women are like the second pressing of the grape." **John Wayne**, as Temujin, is deeply impressed with Susan Hayward, with whom he has had a memorable sexual encounter. *The Conqueror* (1956, RKO).

1652 "You ain't that good. If you ever listened to a Kitty Wells record, you'd go home and slit your goddamned throat." Irritated **Ed Harris** angrily attacks Jessica Lange, as country singer Patsy Cline, where she lives. *Sweet Dreams* (1985, Tri-Star).

1653 "You've become the Patty Hearst of the British Diplomatic Corps." Avaricious minister **Leonard Rossiter** sneers at Michael Caine, governor of the Caribbean British colony of Cascara. *Water* (1986, GB, Handmade).

1654 "You have to compare things all the time to get a distance on things." Twelve-year-old **Anton Glanzelius** states his philosophy. *My Life as a Dog* (1987, Sweden, Svensk Filmindustri).

1655 "Living with a Sicilian is like cooking pasta and pissing olive oil 24 hours a day." Irish career criminal **Sean Connery**'s marriage to an Italian woman, the mother of his son, Dustin Hoffman, was not joyful. *Family Business* (1989, Tri-Star).

1656 "We couldn't have been more different, but maybe we couldn't have been more alike." In voice-over American Army Captain **Beau Bridges** speaks of himself and Liem Whatley, a young Viet Cong guerrilla who captures Bridges. *The Iron Triangle* (1989, Scotti Brothers).

1657 "Marriage is like the Middle East. There's no solution. . . . Sex is like the supermarket; it's overrated." **Pauline Collins** links a couple of bromides. *Shirley Valentine* (1989, GB, Paramount).

1658 "He is to Jewish learning what Mozart is to music." An Hasidic Jew speaks respectfully of Eric Thal, son of the sect's spiritual leader. *A Stranger Among Us* (1992, Hollywood Pictures).

Compassion

see also EMPATHY, MERCY, PITY, SORROWS, SUFFERING AND SUFFERERS, SYMPATHY

1659 "Couldn't you just see her? Couldn't you stop scribbling, put down your goddamn ballpoint and see her?" **Paul Newman**, seethes at reporter Sally Field, when one of her irresponsible stories drives unfortunate Melinda Dillon to commit suicide. *Absence of Malice* (1981, Columbia).

1660 "Do you actually think that Chuck Noll has to worry if Franco Harris is gonna cry 'cause Terry Bradshaw won't talk to him? That Jack Lambert can't play 'cause Mel Blount hurt his feelings? That Lynn Swann is pregnant or that Rocky Blier forgot his Tampax?" U.S. Women's Olympic track coach **Scott Glenn** wishes he was the coach of a men's team, possibly the Pittsburgh Steelers. *Personal Best* (1982, Warner Bros.).

1661 "I see in you what Jimmy Stewart saw in Jean Arthur. . . in *Mr. Smith Goes to Washington*." **Ryan O'Neal** sees something in Shelley Long after their first trip to bed. *Irreconcilable Differences* (1984, Warner Bros.).

1662 "She didn't want tenderness." New Orleans police detective **Clint Eastwood** tells Genevieve Bujold why his wife left him—at least that's his side of the story. *Tightrope* (1984, Warner Bros.).

Competition

see also CONTESTS, GAMES, OPPOSITENESS, SPORTS, WINNERS AND LOSERS

1663 "A little healthy competition keeps a woman up to scratch." Dastardly degenerate **Dennis Price** reacts indifferently when his lovely wife Anne Crawford catches him fondling a chambermaid. *Caravan* (1946, GB, Gainsborough).

1664 "It takes more than a sudden urge to beat the Europeans. It's their whole life we're trying to beat them out of." Ski coach **Gene Hackman** tells Robert Redford that talent and desire are not enough competing against European skiers; he also must have character. *Downhill Racer* (1969, Paramount).

1665 "The only ass you need to whip is your own." Olympic swimmer **Kenny Moore** advises runner

Mariel Hemingway that her only real competition is herself. *Personal Best* (1982, Warner Bros.).

Complaints

see also ACCUSATIONS, FAULTS, PAINS, SICKNESS

1666 "I'm not complaining. I'm just wasting the best years of my life waiting for a taxi." **Myrna Loy** jumps into a cab and onto the lap of stranger William Powell. *Manhattan Melodrama* (1934, MGM).

1667 "I don't like your attitude, Roberts—all you do is bellyache." **Ann Savage** tells off sour puss Tom Neal, who feels uncomfortable assuming the identity of a dead man. *Detour* (1946, Producers Releasing Corporation).

1668 "I got no kicks. I got along." Middle-age prostitute **Mary Astor** accepts the cards life deals her. *Act of Violence* (1949, MGM).

1669 "My stream doesn't have the same force any more." As they stand at two urinals, drunken **Richard Benjamin** sobs to his friend George Segal that he can't pee like he used to. *The Last Married Couple in America* (1980, Universal).

1670 "I don't know what women are complaining about. They got half the money and all the pussy." **Mr. T** is one of the misfits working at a cab company who comes through when needed to save an ambassador's kids from kidnappers. *D.C. Cab* (1981, Universal).

1671 "We must be able to grasp the world and reality, so that we can complain of its monotony with a clear conscience." Pompous womanizer **Jarl Kulle** ends the film with a curtain speech. *Fanny and Alexander* (1983, Sweden-Fr.-W. Ger., Swedish Film Institute).

1672 "They were grooming me to be the next Vera Miles." Alcoholic movie actress **Jane Fonda** complains to her unlikely lover, down-and-out California cop Jeff Bridges. She's had the ultimate hangover, waking up with a dead body in her bed and no memory of the night before. *The Morning After* (1986, 20th Century-Fox).

1673 "You know how hot dogs come 10 to a pack and buns in packs of 8 or 12? You have to buy 9 packs to make them match up." **Swoosie Kurtz**, the laziest woman in the world, is correct if she plans to buy four packs of hot dogs and five of the eight-buns-to-the-pack. This long rock video with Talking Head David Byrne explains the eccentric lives of wierd folks who reside in the fictional town of Virgil, Texas. *True Stories* (1986, Warner Bros.).

1674 "It's sweat and sweat and sweat, and shove this stinkin' dough in and out of this hole in the wall." It seems that baker **Nicolas Cage** is telling Cher that he's not happy in his work. *Moonstruck* (1987, MGM).

1675 "As long as the Durham Bulls can't lose, I can't get laid." Baseball groupie **Susan Sarandon** complains because her stud for the summer, superstitious Tim Robbins, won't have sex with her while his team is on a winning streak. *Bull Durham* (1988, Orion).

1676 "Glasnost gives everyone the right to complain—but it doesn't make more shoes." Russian **Michelle Pfeiffer** leaves British publisher Sean Connery to wait in line for shoes. *The Russia House* (1990, MGM-United Artists).

1677 "I'm tired! I'm hungry! And I've been in these clothes for more than one dance." Unwelcomed **Lorraine Bracco** screams to Sean Connery when she arrives at his jungle camp. *Medicine Man* (1992, Buena Vista).

Compliments

see also ADMIRATION, FLATTERY, PRAISES, RESPECT AND RESPECTABILITY

1678 "You know, you'd be a pretty nice guy if you weren't around so much at the wrong time." **James Cagney** grudgingly pays Ann Sheridan a compliment. *Torrid Zone* (1940, Warner Bros.).

1679 "I could put you in my vest pocket and lose you in the small change. And me—now I've always gone for women with something to 'em. The kind that could stand up and slug it out with me toe to toe. You slug me just by looking at me." **Clark Gable** is impressed that, although quiet and refined, Lana Turner is not the shy, retiring, clinging-vine type of woman he despises. *Honky Tonk* (1941, MGM).

1680 "You're a good man, sister." **Humphrey Bogart** compliments his adoring secretary Lee Patrick. *The Maltese Falcon* (1941, Warner Bros.).

1681 "You're good. You're very good." Seems private eye **Humphrey Bogart** likes making this type of compliment. Here it's paid to Mary Astor. *The Maltese Falcon* (1941, Warner Bros.).

1682 "For me, Sir Alfred, there's nobody handles Handel like you handle Handel." Private detective **Edgar Kennedy** enthusiastically praises concert conductor Rex Harrison. *Unfaithfully Yours* (1948, 20th Century-Fox).

1683 "You'd look good in a shower curtain." Gangster-on-the-run **James Cagney** reassures his ever-whining wife, beautiful blonde Virginia Mayo, who complains she has no clothes. *White Heat* (1949, Warner Bros.)

1684 "Behold, she stands with her gown hung loose. Framed is her face in golden tresses, reflecting the milk-white beauty of her shoulders. So it was that Venus stood before Mars, welcoming her lover. Nothing do I see that is not perfection." We're trying to remember if **Robert Taylor**'s pretty speech to Deborah Kerr seemed as laughable when we saw the film at its release as it does now. *Quo Vadis* (1951, MGM).

1685 "You're just delicate." **Marilyn Monroe** awards Tom Ewell her ultimate accolade. Her favorite expression of approval in this movie is "delicate." *The Seven Year Itch* (1955, 20th Century-Fox).

1686 "I'd hate to take a bite out of you. You're a cookie full of arsenic." Coming from sleazy columnist **Burt Lancaster**, unprincipled press agent Tony Curtis can only take the comment as a compliment. *Sweet Smell of Success* (1957, United Artists).

1687 "You know, considering you're a crook and a horror, you're really very nice company." **Shirley Jones** really reaches to give corrupt dock workers union boss James Cagney a back-handed compliment. *Never Steal Anything Small* (1958, Universal-International).

1688 SCOTTIE: "We could just see a lot of each other." JUDY: "Why? Because I remind you of her? That's not very complimentary. And nothing else?" SCOTTIE: "No." JUDY: "That's not very complimentary either." **Kim Novak** figures that **James Stewart** could at least pretend he was interested in her for herself and not because she reminds him of his dead love. *Vertigo* (1958, Paramount).

1689 "You sure make fine coffee, ma'am." Bounty hunter **Randolph Scott** sweet talks buxomy young blonde Karen Steele. *Ride Lonesome* (1959, Columbia).

1690 "Fat man, you shoot a great game of pool." At the end of the film, **Paul Newman**, appreciating talent in his chosen line of work, compliments Jackie Gleason as Minnesota Fats, who replies, "So do you, Eddie." *The Hustler* (1961, 20th Century-Fox).

1691 "As far as I'm concerned a reprimand from you is the same as a compliment from any real gentleman." **Julie Christie** blasts shepherd Alan Bates for daring to criticize her. *Far from the Madding Crowd* (1967, GB, EMI).

1692 "Sex with you is a Kafkaesque experience. . . I mean that as a compliment." **Shelley Duvall**, after taking a very long time to have an orgasm, compliments sore-jawed Woody Allen. *Annie Hall* (1977, United Artists).

1693 "Your eyes are most beautiful. Your script is more beautiful." Lesbian actress **Kendal Kaldwell** looks from screenwriter Pia Zadora's breasts downward over the rest of her body. *The Lonely Lady* (1982, Universal).

1694 "You have perfection about you. . . . Your eyes have music. . . . Your heart is the best part of your body. And when you move, every man, woman and child is forced to watch." Even though **Keith Carradine**'s compliment doesn't sound quite sincere, Lesley Ann Warren can't resist it. *Choose Me* (1984, Island Alive).

1695 "You are plain." Amish farmer **Alexander Godunov** pays big city police detective Harrison Ford a compliment, meaning he's a man of no frills. *Witness* (1985, Paramount).

1696 "You are so fuckin' suave." Psychopath **Dennis Hopper** compliments kinky nightclub singer Dean Stockwell. *Blue Velvet* (1986, De Laurentiis).

1697 "You're the best looking mountain trash I've seen in a long while. I'll be seeing you around." To help establish his character, coal company detective **Kevin Tighe** pays coal miner's widow Nancy Mette a cruel compliment. *Matewan* (1987, Cinecom).

1698 "You have the face of a Botticelli and the body of a Degas." **Robert Downey, Jr.** ladles out a heavy dose of syrup to Molly Ringwald. *The Pick-Up Artist* (1987, 20th Century-Fox).

1699 "You're beautiful, you're intelligent, you're sensuous." **Michael J. Fox** butters up Margaret Whitton, the frustrated wife of his boss. It must be sincere, she's already seduced him. *The Secret of My Success* (1987, Universal).

1700 "You are as graceful as the capital letter 'S.' You will adorn our house. You will give a glow and a shine to these old walls." Southern gentleman **Robert Duvall** sweet-talks an overwhelmed Laura Dern as he welcomes her to his family's home. *Rambling Rose* (1991, Seven Arts).

1701 "By the way, I loved you in *The Wizard of Oz.*" Having drunkenly kissed the team's prim chaperon by mistake, girls' professional baseball team manager **Tom Hanks** recovers from recoiling in horror. *A League of Their Own* (1992, Columbia).

Comprehension *see* UNDERSTANDINGS AND MIS-
UNDERSTANDINGS

Compromises

see also AGREEMENTS, IDEALS, PRINCIPLES, SYSTEMS

1702 "You've had no experience—you see things in black and white—and a man as an angel or a devil. That's the young idealist in you. And that isn't how the world runs, Jeff. Certainly not government or politics. It's a question of give and take—you have to play the rules—compromise—you have to leave your ideals outside the door with your rubbers." Senior Senator **Claude Rains** does a poor job selling junior Senator James Stewart the role of compromise in getting things done. *Mr. Smith Goes to Washington* (1939, Columbia).

1703 "A woman's compromised the day she's born." It's cynicism from knowing show girl **Paulette Goddard.** *The Women* (1939, MGM).

1704 "Neal thought that life was destroyed by compromises, that was his weakness. Jack thought it was made by them, and that was his. I decided that compromises are like dental appointments. You're damned if you make them and you're damned if you don't." **Sissy Spacek** believes that she, not Nick Nolte or John Heard, has the right line on compromises. *Heart Beat* (1979, Warner Bros.).

1705 "I don't see. . . why I should have to compromise; why I should have to make some sad and decorous marriage just to have a child. I don't see why any woman should have to do that." **Meryl Streep** maintains that motherhood and marriage do not have to go together like a horse and carriage. *Plenty* (1985, 20th Century-Fox).

1706 "I'm about to compromise my values, I think." New lawyer **Judd Nelson**, somewhat shy of values or ideals, is out to make a name for himself by hook or by crook. *From the Hip* (1987, De Laurentiis).

Compulsions

see also NERVOUSNESS AND NERVES, OBSESSIONS

1707 "I can't help myself! I haven't any control over this evil thing that's inside me. . . . It's there all the time, driving me out to wander through the streets. . . . It's me, pursuing myself!. . . I want to escape. . . to escape from myself!. . . But it's impossible. . . I have to obey!" Child killer **Peter Lorre** pitifully defends himself before the city's criminals who have put him on trial because his activities give them a bad name. *M* (1933, Germany, Nero Film-Paramount).

1708 "I'm sorry. . . I don't like people touching my blue blanket. It's not important. It's a minor compulsion. I can deal with it if I want to. It's just that I've had it ever since I was a baby. . . and. . . I find it very comforting." **Gene Wilder** is calmer now after becoming hysterical when Zero Mostel snatches a piece of Wilder's baby blanket from his hands. *The Producers* (1966, MGM).

1709 "You're Macon's publisher! I'm the one who mailed you Macon's chapters. . . . Well, I'm supposed to send you some more, but first I have to buy 9 *x* 12 envelopes. All we've got left are 10 *x* 13. It's terrible when things don't fit precisely. They get all out of alignment." By her conversation with Bill Pullman, **Amy Wright** demonstrates that brother William Hurt is not the only compulsive organizer in the family. *The Accidental Tourist* (1988, Warner Bros.).

Concealment

see also HYPOCRISY

1710 "My dear, I was hiding behind screens before you were born." **Bette Davis** answers when Dolores Moran asks how Davis knew that Moran was hiding behind a screen in the apartment of roué Philip Reed. *Old Acquaintance* (1943, Warner Bros.).

1711 "This is the first place that looks like it's hiding from the world." Private detective **Martin Balsam** suspects that Janet Leigh, who has stolen $40,000 from her boss, might have stopped at the out-of-the-way Bates motel. *Psycho* (1960, Paramount).

1712 "I got some heirlooms I want to hide with you. . . those sons of bitches tried to have their way with them. . . I don't want to know where you're going. . . ." Old codger **Ben Johnson** brings virginal cuties Lea Thompson and Jennifer Grey to a guerrilla band of high school boys who are fighting the communist parachutists who have invaded their Colorado community. *Red Dawn* (1984, MGM-United Artists).

Conceit

see also BOASTS AND BRAGGING, EGOS AND EGOTISM, HUMILITY AND HUMILIATION, PRIDE, VANITIES

1713 "Laura considered me the wisest, the wittiest, the most understanding man she ever met. I was in complete accord with her on that point." WASPish intellectual **Clifton Webb**, who takes every opportunity to parade his conceit and contempt, speaks of Gene Tierney to police detective Dana Andrews. *Laura* (1944, 20th Century-Fox).

1714 "Man! I'm a volcano! A giant surrounded by ants." Ambitious black chauffeur **Sidney Poitier** clashes with his family over what should be done with his deceased father's $10,000 insurance money. *A Raisin in the Sun* (1961, Columbia).

Concerns

see also CARES AND CARING, IMPORTANCE, INTERESTS, WORRIES

1715 "I'm more or less particular about whom my wife marries." Editor **Cary Grant**, once married to his star reporter Rosalind Russell, is concerned by her decision to quit her job and marry dull Ralph Bellamy. *His Girl Friday* (1940, Columbia).

1716 "The joint looked like trouble, but that didn't bother me. Nothing bothered me. The two twenties felt nice and snug against my appendix." The time is 1944, and narrator **Dick Powell** is a cheap private eye. *Murder My Sweet* aka: *Farewell My Lovely* (1944, RKO).

1717 "It's not the going out that bothers me, it's the staying in." Businessman **Eric Portman** isn't so much concerned that his wife Greta Gynt is seen around and about with barrister Dennis Price. It's what they're doing when they're out of sight that bothers him. *Dear Murderer* (1947, GB, Gainsborough-GFD).

1718 "The source of your money has never concerned you any more than the source of your electric light. They become worrisome only when they are turned off." Valet **James Mason** recruits impoverished Polish noblewoman Danielle Darrieux as a paid spy for the Germans. *Five Fingers* (1952, 20th Century-Fox).

1719 "A proper court is concerned with law. It's a bit amateur to plead for justice." Prosecuting attorney **James Villiers** offers military lawyer Dirk Bogarde no comfort after the latter's client, World War I British private Tom Courtenay, is found guilty of desertion and sentenced to death. *King and Country* (1964, GB, BHE).

1720 "How many of those hormones you been takin', honey?" **Jessica Tandy** questions her once shy and timid friend Kathy Bates who announces that she'd machine-gun the genitals of wife-beaters, put little bombs in the copies of *Penthouse* and *Playboy* set to explode when the magazines are opened, and decree that wrinkles were sexually desirable. *Fried Green Tomatoes* (1991, Universal).

Conditions

see also LAWS, REQUIREMENTS, TREATS AND TREATMENTS

1721 "Our bodies are earth. Our thoughts are clay. And we sleep and eat with death." **Lew Ayres** describes the conditions in the trenches of World War I to some German school boys while he's home on furlough. *All Quiet on The Western Front* (1930, Universal).

1722 "We're here to investigate conditions. Drinking conditions, mostly. The drinking conditions are very bad here. The beer's so full of cinders, it makes you lay hard-boiled eggs." **Richard Barthelmess** is the spokesman for his companions when an elderly Englishman questions their motives in being in a Lisbon bar. *The Last Flight* (1931, Warner Bros.).

1723 DR. ANDRE BERTIER: "Your wife is in a very serious condition." PROF. OLIVIER: "Why shouldn't she be? Conditions are bad everywhere." Physician **Maurice Chevalier** pays too much attention to Genevieve Tobin to suit her husband **Roland Young**, who finds them together in her bedroom. *One Hour with You* (1932, Paramount).

1724 SAILOR: "Cattle ain't got it much worse than us." GLORIA: "Better. At least they feed them." **Red Buttons** and **Jane Fonda** are contestants in a marathon dance contest during the Great Depression. *They Shoot Horses, Don't They?* (1969, ABC-Cinerama).

1725 "I don't do fags and I don't do couples. I don't do kink." Male prostitute **Richard Gere** makes his living servicing Beverly Hills matrons. Later he's set up for the murder of one of his clients. *American Gigolo* (1980, Paramount).

1726 "I get $2,000 a day. I do not do animal acts. I do not do S&M or any variations of that particular bent. No water sports either. I will not shave my pussy. No fist fucking, and absolutely no coming in my face." **Melanie Griffith** as Holly Body, who when dressed, sports a white spiked haircut and wears a black lace leotard with a leather miniskirt, adamantly lists her conditions to Craig Wasson, posing as a producer who wishes to star her in a porno film. *Body Double* (1984, Columbia).

1727 "You mean we have to have sex?. . . All right, but no kissing!" **Kim Basinger** is accepting a marriage proposal from icky and unbearable attorney John Larroquette on the condition that he defend her real love Bruce Willis against a charge of assault with a deadly weapon. *Blind Date* (1987, Tri-Star).

Conduct *see* BEHAVIOR, MANNERS

Confessions

see also CRIMES AND CRIMINALS, FAITH AND FAITH-FULNESS, FAULTS, GOD, GUILT, HONESTY AND DIS-HONESTY, PRIESTS, RELIGIONS, SINS AND SINNERS

1728 "I'm going up there on that platform to tell the people the truth. To tell what a liar and cheat I've been and neither you nor anybody else is going to stop me." Phony evangelist **Barbara Stanwyck** gets some religion and tells off promoter Sam Hardy. *The Miracle Woman* (1931, Columbia).

1729 AMANDA: "What have you been doing lately?" ELYOT: "Traveling about. . . I went around the world, you know, after." AMANDA: "Yes, I know—how was it? China must be very interesting." ELYOT: "Very big, China." AMANDA: "And Japan?" ELYOT: "Very small—Darling, I love you so." AMANDA: "I never loved anyone else for an instant." Formerly married **Norma Shearer** and **Robert Montgomery** get through the small talk before stating their love for each other. Who will tell Reginald Denny and Una Merkel, their respective new spouses with whom they are honeymooning? *Private Lives* (1931, MGM).

1730 "Baron, I have a confession to make. You are a crook. You robbed the gentlemen in two-fifty-three, -five, -seven, and -nine. Would you please pass the salt?" Over a pleasant dinner, sophisticated thief **Miriam Hopkins** reveals that she knows Herbert Marshall has the same career. The two develop admiration for each other as they filch things from each other—some rather intimate. *Trouble in Paradise* (1932, Paramount).

1731 "Here's how things stand. I could have you drive me around town and then tell you I left my purse at home on the grand piano. But there's no grand piano, no home—and the purse. . . twenty-five centimes with a hole in it. . . ." Elegantly dressed **Claudette Colbert** confesses to Parisian cab driver Don Ameche that she's broke. *Midnight* (1939, Paramount).

1732 "He could get along without Mrs. Haines or Allen better than he could without me." Frustrated secretary **Ruth Hussey** confesses to a co-worker that she loves her boss and she's better for him than either his wife Norma Shearer or his mistress Joan Crawford. "Mr. Haines" never actually makes an appearance in the film. *The Women* (1939, MGM).

1733 "I don't want to understand. I don't want to know. Whatever it is, keep it to yourself. All I know is I adore you. I'll never leave you again. We'll work it out somehow." Wealthy **Henry Fonda** prevents his ex-con wife Barbara Stanwyck from confessing anything more to him. *The Lady Eve* (1941, Paramount).

1734 "Tell me, who was it you left me for? Was it Laszlo or were there others in between? Or aren't you the kind that tells?" Bitter **Humphrey Bogart** relentlessly piles abuse on Ingrid Bergman, his lover in Paris, who abandoned him when she found that her husband, Resistance leader Paul Henreid, was still alive. *Casablanca* (1942, Warner Bros.).

1735 "I'm not employed here. I took one look at you and followed you into the store. If you had gone into a restaurant, I would have become a waiter. If you had gone into a burning building, I would have become a fireman. If you had stepped into an elevator, I would have stopped it between floors and we'd have stayed there the rest of our lives." What woman could resist the sincerity of **Don Ameche**'s pick-up line? Gene Tierney can't. *Heaven Can Wait* (1943, 20th Century-Fox).

1736 "Let's take a look at that Dietrichson claim. Accident and double indemnity. You were pretty good in there for awhile, Keyes. You said it wasn't an accident. Check. You said it wasn't suicide. Check. You said it was murder. Check. You thought you had it cold, didn't you? All wrapped up in tissue paper with pink ribbons around it. It was perfect. Except it wasn't, because you made one little mistake, just one. When it came to picking the killer, you picked the wrong guy. You want to know who killed Dietrichson? Hold tight to that cheap cigar of yours, Keyes. I killed Dietrichson. Me, Walter Neff, insurance salesman, thirty-five-years old, unmarried, no visible scars—until a while ago that is. I killed him for money and a woman. I didn't get the money and I didn't get the woman." Wounded **Fred MacMurray** dictates an office memo to claims adjuster Edward G. Robinson on a dictaphone, confessing his guilt in the murder of Barbara Stanwyck's husband, Tom Powers, so they could collect his insurance money. *Double Indemnity* (1944, Paramount).

1737 "Confess it: you've been hermetically sealed most of your life." **George Brent** deduces that Barbara Stanwyck has always had her life and behavior dictated by either her mother or her late husband. *My Reputation* (1946, Warner Bros.).

1738 "Mother, I am married to an American agent." Upon discovering that his wife Ingrid Bergman is in the employ of the American government, Nazi renegade **Claude Rains** sobs out his confession to his dominating mother Leopoldine Konstantin. *Notorious* (1946, RKO).

1739 "If it gives you pleasure to know you are breaking me down, I'll give you greater satisfaction—I love you." **Patricia Neal**'s initial attempt to seduce architect Gary Cooper was ignored, but he's back to take her by force. *The Fountainhead* (1949, Warner Bros.).

1740 "You know, older woman who is well-to-do and younger man who is not doing well." Screenwriter **William Holden** confesses to Nancy Olson that he's the kept man of Gloria Swanson. *Sunset Boulevard* (1950, Paramount).

1741 "I don't know what's the matter with me. I have these black moods when I'd like to kill myself. I'd really like to kill myself. I had this nervous breakdown. . . I've been drinking heavily. I confess to the sin of drinking. Oh, my God, I was arrested twice for drunken driving, I just feel, Ma, I'm losing control of myself. I feel I'm going crazy. . . I can't bear to be alone, I can't bear it. I've taken men home with me who I didn't rightly know for more than an hour because I can't bear to be alone at night. . . . Life just seems unbearable to me. I need you, Ma. I need you to be here with me because I'm like to go insane. I feel I'm going insane." Miserable Hollywood sex-symbol **Kim Stanley** pours out her agony to her mother Betty Lou Holland. *The Goddess* (1958, Columbia).

1742 JERRY-DAPHNE: "In the first place, I'm not a natural blonde." OSGOOD E. FIELDING III: "Doesn't matter." J-D: "I smoke. I smoke all the time." OSGOOD: "I don't care." J-D: "I can never have children." OSGOOD: "We can adopt some." J-D: "You don't understand, I'm a man." OSGOOD: "Well, nobody's perfect." **Jack Lemmon**, posing as a woman, can't dissuade millionaire **Joe E. Brown** from wanting to marry "her." *Some Like It Hot* (1959, United Artists).

1743 "I like to hear dirty stories." **Mel Ferrer** confesses his motivation for becoming a psychiatrist. *Sex and the Single Girl* (1964, Warner Bros.).

1744 "I. . . ain't much of a lover boy. . . there ain't much of a percentage in it." **Warren Beatty** disappoints sexually frustrated Faye Dunaway with his confession that he feels no need for sex. *Bonnie and Clyde* (1967, Warner Bros.).

1745 "Henry, I have a confession—I don't much like our children." **Katharine Hepburn** tells her husband Peter O'Toole of her disaffection for their three unpleasant grown sons. *The Lion in Winter* (1968, GB, Embassy).

1746 MARTIN: "I'm in love with somebody else! Oh, God! I don't want to hurt you!. . . I met her in Bloomingdale's, for Christ's sake." ERICA: "You tell Patti that you're sorry. . . . Is she a good lay?" Terribly upset **Michael Murphy** blurts out that he wants a divorce from **Jill Clayburgh**. Shocked, she manages to tell him to seek forgiveness from their daughter Lisa Lucas, then walks away quickly, grabs the lamp post and vomits before running on. *An Unmarried Woman* (1978, 20th Century-Fox).

1747 "If his story really is a confession, then so is mine." Military assassin **Martin Sheen** refers to his prey, mad Colonel Marlon Brando. *Apocalypse Now* (1979, United Artists).

1748 "I, uh, I think something may be happening here that we didn't expect. . . . What do you think?. . . We don't have to do anything about it, I just don't think there's any harm in being honest. . . I don't think you have any idea how many times I've thought about you since New Orleans. . . I'm not suggesting anything. . . . However I do notice that I want this Anderson thing to go on forever. . . I think I'm infatuated with you." Married U.S. Senator **Alan Alda** confesses to married Meryl Streep, who's working with him to defeat a Supreme Court nominee, that he's fallen in love with her. *The Seduction of Joe Tynan* (1979, Universal).

1749 "I'm not ambitious, not an artist, not a poet, not a revolutionary." **Theresa Russell** confesses her lack of motivation by listing what she is not. *Bad Timing: A Sensual Obsession* (1980, GB, Northan-Rank).

1750 "I never killed anyone before. What'll I say to Father O'Brien when I go to confession?" Teenager **Michael Rubin** is turned into a zombie when his friends bring him back from the dead by dumping his body in a river contaminated with radioactive waste. Rubin is a good zombie who fights another zombie who is bad, Steve McCoy. *I Was a Teenage Zombie* (1987, Horizon).

1751 "I'm an unspeakable. . . of the Oscar Wilde sort." **James Wilby** confesses to Denholm Elliott that he has homosexual desires. *Maurice* (1987, GB, Cinecom).

1752 "I want to go to bed with you. . . . You're very sweet. Of course, you are not as clever as you think you are. You're all mixed up, nervous, and you're the worst cook. Those pancakes! Oh, I love you. I want to take care of you. I don't want pancakes." While under hypnosis, **Woody Allen** confesses his true feelings for his psychiatrist, Mia Farrow. *Zelig* (1987, Orion-Warner Bros.).

1753 "What is the use of confession if I don't repent?" Cardinal who will be a pope Raf Vallone gets **Al Pacino** to make his first confession in many years. *The Godfather, Part III* (1990, Paramount).

1754 "I have sinned, Father. I added an additional one to the thousand dollar check, because I wanted my daughter to have an $11,000 computer." **Marianne Sagebrecht** looks more for approval than absolution from her confessor Judge Reinhold. *Rosalie Goes Shopping* (1990, W. Ger., Four Seasons).

1755 "Our marriage is just a memory implant. I was written in as your wife." **Sharon Stone** confesses her part in wiping out Arnold Schwarznegger's true identity. *Total Recall* (1990, Tri-Star).

Confidence *see* BELIEFS, CERTAINTIES, SECRETS, TRUST

Conformity *see* AGREEMENTS, BEHAVIOR, NORMALITY, OPINIONS, RULES

Confusion

see also DIFFICULTIES, IDENTITIES, MISTAKES, PUZZLES

1756 "I've just been going over last month's bills, and I find that you people have confused me with the treasury department." Wealthy **Eugene Pallette**'s sarcastic comment to his family might be made by any head of family, faced with paying bills. *My Man Godfrey* (1936, Universal).

1757 "I know there's a practical world and a dream world—and I shan't mix them up." Despite her promise to her over-protective aunt Gladys Cooper, **Judy Garland** does mix them up. *The Pirate* (1948, MGM).

1758 "I'm completely happy one moment; the next I'm completely sad. . . I can't bear it." **Betsy Brantley** states the confused feelings of many young women who become involved with married men. *Five Days One Summer* (1982, Warner Bros.).

1759 "Don't you find it is confusing being a woman in the 80s?" **Jessica Lange** doesn't realize how meaningful her question is. It is addressed to Dustin Hoffman who is posing as a woman. *Tootsie* (1982, Columbia).

1760 "Some folks are always confusin' crime with sin." **Dolly Parton** is a bordello madam. *The Best Little Whorehouse in Texas* (1982, Warner Bros.).

1761 "In Russia, I knew who my enemy was. Here, it's too confusing." Russian defector **Robin Williams**

is mugged in New York City. *Moscow on the Hudson* (1984, Columbia).

1762 "I was happy he was gone and afraid he wouldn't come back." **Annabeth Gish** resents her stepfather, alcoholic World War II veteran Jon Voight, but still seeks his approval. *Desert Bloom* (1985, Columbia).

1763 "You are confusing what is important with what is impressive." Dean of Cambridge **Barry Foster** puts self-absorbed young aristocrat Mark Tandy in his place. *Maurice* (1987, GB, Cinecom).

Connections *see* RELATIONSHIPS

Consciences

see also ETHICS, GUILT, IMMORALITY, JUDGMENTS, MORALITY, PRINCIPLES, RIGHT AND WRONG, WRONGS AND WRONGDOINGS

1764 ELSA CARRINGTON: "I'd sooner see you dead than let you do this." RICHARD ASHENDEN: "Do you realize this might be the end of our forces in the East?" ELSA: "What difference does that make to me?" RICHARD: "His life against the life of thousands." ELSA: "What do I care about them? What do I care about him? He's done. We're not going to have this on our conscience." Secret agents **John Gielgud** and **Madeleine Carroll** wrestle with their conscience when they realize they must kill enemy agent Robert Young. *The Secret Agent* (1936, GB, Gaumont).

1765 "Where is the conscience of the world that allows the killing and maiming of civilians to go on?" Spanish Civil War peasant fighter **Henry Fonda** asks a rhetorical question. *Blockade* (1938, United Artists).

1766 "Well, I guess he won't need me anymore. What does an actor need with a conscience anyway?" **Cliff Edwards** as Jiminy Cricket, the conscience of puppet Pinocchio, decides to resign when the would-be boy announces he's going to become an actor. *Pinocchio* (1940, Disney-RKO).

1767 "A man just naturally can't take the law into his own hands and hang people without hurting everybody in the world, because he's not just breaking one law but all laws. Law is a lot more than words you put in a book, or judges or lawyers or sheriffs you hire to carry it out. It's everything people have ever found out about justice and what's right and wrong. It's the very conscience of humanity. There can't be any such thing as civilization unless people have got a conscience, because if people touch God anywhere, where is it except through their conscience? And what is anybody's conscience except a little piece of the conscience of all men that ever lived?" Cowpoke **Henry Fonda** reads the touching letter of farewell that **Dana Andrews** wrote to his wife just before he was unjustly lynched. *The Ox-Bow Incident* (1943, 20th Century-Fox).

1768 "There he goes—proud, stubborn, insufferable—but the keeper of my conscience." Attorney **David Brian** looks after departing, dignified black Juano Hernandez, who Brian has saved from a redneck lynch mob and a false accusation of murder. *Intruder in the Dust* (1949, MGM).

1769 "I'll buy you a new mirror and it'll be your conscience." Visitor **Michael Wilding** confronts frail Ingrid Bergman in a stuffy film set in 19th-century Australia. *Under Capricorn* (1949, GB, Warner Bros.).

1770 "What do you have in place of a conscience? Don't answer. I know: a lawyer." **Kirk Douglas** snarls at butchering abortionist George Macready. *Detective Story* (1951, Paramount).

1771 "You cannot be the conscience of the world!" **Arnold Moss** restrains Marlon Brando who gives a beating to a man who whipped a starving peasant boy who stole food from a horse. Later Brando will say, "I don't want to be the conscience of the world. I don't want to be the conscience of anybody." *Viva Zapata!* (1952, 20th Century-Fox).

1772 "I'm just his father, not his conscience. A man's life ain't worth a hill of beans—except he lives up to his conscience. I've got to give him his chance." Quaker **Gary Cooper** tells his wife Dorothy McGuire that their son Anthony Perkins must be allowed to make his own decision as to whether he will follow the dictates of his religion or fight in the Civil War. *Friendly Persuasion* (1956, Allied Artists).

1773 "I am seventy-eight years old and I want to go to my grave with a clear conscience." **Cathleen Nesbitt** feels guilt which causes troublesome nightmares about her dead sister and her lost nephew. Forty years earlier, Nesbitt forced her sister to give up her illegitimate child to spare the family a public disgrace. *Family Plot* (1976, Universal).

1774 "I don't go to sleep with no whore and I don't wake up with no whore. That's how I live with myself. I don't know how you do it." **Martin Sheen** doesn't object to his son Charlie Sheen's living with well-traveled Daryl Hannah; it's shark Michael Douglas who is the corrupting influence. *Wall Street* (1987, 20th Century-Fox).

Consequences

see also CAUSE AND EFFECT, FATE AND DESTINY, INFLUENCES

1775 OSCAR JAFFE: "I could cut my throat." LILY GARLAND: "If you did, grease paint would run out of it." No one knows more how idle producer **John Barrymore**'s threats are than actress **Carole Lombard.** *Twentieth Century* (1934, Columbia).

1776 "If you put an end to war, sir—as I believe you intend to do before teatime today—if you put an end to competition, make work unnecessary, give everyone more money than they can spend—then I ask you, what are people going to do, sir?" Deranged ex-colonel **Ralph Richardson** asks an interesting question of Roland Young, a meek draper's assistant who has been given the power to do exactly what he intends by a trio of curious gods. *The Man Who Could Work Miracles* (1937, GB, London Films-United Artists).

1777 "I am in no humor tonight to give consequence to the middle-class at play." Arrogant, rich, young bachelor **Laurence Olivier** backs out of a room because the room is filled with what he considers country hayseeds. *Pride and Prejudice* (1940, MGM).

1778 "We would stop trade and commerce if we lived up to the first, eighth and tenth. . . don't steal and don't covet. We would not see buildings housing the aged and criminals if the fifth, sixth and ninth were followed. . . . The quest for the buck, ruble or franc takes in number two. . . ." Cynical newspaper editor **Robert Ryan** dismisses the Ten Commandments as unworkable. *Lonelyhearts* (1958, United Artists).

1779 "Leave and you kill me, leave and I'm dead." **Theresa Russell**, dressed as a vampire whore, screams at Art Garfunkel when he walks out on her. *Bad Timing: A Sensual Obsession* (1980, GB, Rank).

1780 "I'm no fool. I've killed the boss. You think they're not going to fire me for a thing like that?" **Lily Tomlin** panics when she believes she has accidentally fed Dabney Coleman rat poison in his coffee. *Nine to Five* (1980, 20th Century-Fox).

1781 "Your son was a bit of a snoop. . . . If you keep on playing with fire, you get burned." Sinister American Naval Officer **Charles Cioffi** shows little sympathy for American businessman Jack Lemmon whose son John Shea is missing in an unnamed South American country. *Missing* (1982, Universal).

1782 "You should have known what would happen when you left a six-pack on a vibrating mattress." **Steve Martin** chastises John Candy in a motel room they are forced to share. *Planes, Trains and Automobiles* (1987, Paramount).

Considerations

see also ATTENTION, CONCERNS, THINKING AND THOUGHT

1783 "There's no delicacy nowadays. No consideration for others. Refinement's a thing of the past." Henry VIII, portrayed by **Charles Laughton** as an indelicate and unrefined man with no consideration for others, finds faults with others. *The Private Life of Henry VIII* (1933, GB, London Films-United Artists).

1784 "Stuffy in there, Parker? I'll give it some air." As he casually chomps on a drumstick, **James Cagney** yells to squealer Paul Guilfoyle who is locked in the trunk of a car. Cagney calmly empties six shots into the trunk, killing its captive. *White Heat* (1949, Warner Bros.).

1785 "Well, this is where you came in, back at that pool again, the one I always wanted. It's dawn now and they must have photographed me a thousand times. And then they got a couple of pruning hooks from the garden and fished me out—ever so gently. Funny, how gentle people get with you once you're dead. They beached me like a harpooned baby whale and started to check the damage just for the record." The corpse of **William Holden** appreciates the gentle consideration of the police and medical attendants who pull his body from Gloria Swanson's pool at the end of the film. *Sunset Boulevard* (1950, Paramount).

1786 "Poor kid. . . he was always cold." **James Dean** mutters sadly as he zips up his jacket on dead Sal Mineo. *Rebel Without a Cause* (1955, Warner Bros.).

1787 "Look, this boy's been kicked around all his life. He's had a pretty terrible nineteen years. I think maybe we owe him a few words, that's all." **Henry Fonda** explains to his fellow jurors why he voted not guilty in the first vote taken after the trial of John Savoca, accused of murdering his father. *12 Angry Men* (1957, United Artists).

1788 "Why don't you go to bed, honey; I'll bag the Nazi and straighten up around here." **Paul Bartel** is considerate of his tired wife, Mary Woronov. They have just killed a weirdo who fantasized that he was a Nazi beast torturing a sexy victim. It's another of their murders of swingers to make extra money so they can open a restaurant. *Eating Raoul* (1982, 20th Century-Fox).

1789 "I like you. I'll kill you last." Retired Special Forces Colonel **Arnold Schwarzenegger** sweetly promises David Patrick Kelly, a member of a gang who has kidnapped his daughter in order to force him to assassinate a South American president. He lies. *Commando* (1985, 20th Century-Fox).

1790 "This isn't so offensive, is it? I know I seem like an ass up here, but it really would help if people treated each other with more consideration—you know it as well as I do." Yuppie **Bill Murray**, having learned his lesson of Christmas, like a latter-day Ebeneezer Scrooge, interrupts his telecast of Dickens' *A Christmas Carol* to deliver the unhip message of love, so that "the miracle of Christmas can happen every day." *Scrooged* (1988, Paramount).

Consolations

see also COMFORTS

1791 "Come, my dear, your soldier won his last battle." **John Litel**, as General Phil Sheridan, consoles Olivia de Havilland, widow of Errol Flynn, as General George Custer. Flynn's "death-bed" deposition exposes the landgrabbing schemes of corrupt Washington officials. *They Died with Their Boots On* (1942, Warner Bros.).

1792 "Sir, it's the way of things, I guess I figure it's all God's making and will. Doesn't the Book say no sparrow shall fall to earth unless he first gives the nod? Well, he must have given the nod to what happened out there today." When flying minister Rock Hudson tries to console **James Edwards**, a black pilot who has accidentally strafed refugee children in Korea, he finds that Edwards has already found higher consolation. It also appears he's making a case for blaming God for everything bad that happens. *Battle Hymn* (1957, Universal).

1793 "I tried to understand Frank—not that there's much to understand. That's why I was so hurt when he strayed. But you know me. I always try to look on the bright side. I said to myself, 'Well, at least she's the one who'll be nauseous now!'" **Bea Arthur** tells her daughter-in-law Diane Keaton about the time her husband Richard Castellano had an affair. *Lovers and Other Strangers* (1970, ABC-Cinerama).

1794 "My religion, my non-violence, the kids, it's all that I have left now." **Delores Taylor** cries in Tom Laughlin's comforting arms after he arrives on the scene where she's been raped. *Billy Jack* (1971, Warner Bros.).

1795 "That's all right, dear, you can make them up after school!" Sixties high school principal **Eve Arden** is both understanding and momentarily dense when a student confides: "I've missed my last two periods." *Grease 2* (1982, Paramount).

1796 "You may not be the greatest stud in the world, but at least you've got a family." Greaser **Chris Nash** reassures virginal nerd Doug McKeon. *Mischief* (1985, 20th Century-Fox).

1797 "I must admit, you'll require more work than I'd hoped. You're unsophisticated, ignorant, and totally lacking in social grace. But I console myself with the fact that you have nice buttocks. . . . You could strap me to the throne chair with a string of pearls." It's the happy thought of **Joely Richardson** as Princess Anna of Finland, a prospective bride for John Goodman, the new uncouth American king of England. *King Ralph* (1991, Universal).

Conspiracies

see also CRIMES AND CRIMINALS, DECEPTIONS, PLANS, SECRETS

1798 "I must look my best tonight. There's dirty work afoot. I've conspiracy to do." **Louis Calhern** contemplates his image in a mirror admiringly. *Diplomaniacs* (1933, RKO).

1799 "I can no longer sit back and allow Communist infiltration, Communist indoctrination, Communist subversion and the international Communist conspiracy to sap and impurify all of our precious bodily fluids." The fluoridation of water is the final straw that pushes Air Force General **Sterling Hayden** over the edge, causing him to launch a nuclear attack on the U.S.S.R. *Dr. Strangelove: Or How I Learned to Stop Worrying and Love the Bomb* (1964, Columbia).

1800 "Me? I'm a Sicilian. To me, everything's a conspiracy. Everyone makes deals." Former O.S.S. agent **John Cassavetes** is involved in a bullion robbery attempt—and according to this movie—the elimination of General George S. Patton, who discovers the plot. *Brass Target* (1978, United Artists).

1801 "I'm not saying it's a conspiracy exactly; law enforcement is too disorganized for that." Attorney **James Woods** speaks to reporters about the case of an Asian-American who apparently was railroaded into prison some eight years earlier. *True Believer* (1989, Columbia).

Consumers *see* BUYING AND SELLING, CUSTOMERS

Contempt

see also AUTHORITIES, DIGNITY, RESPECT AND RESPECTABILITY, RIDICULE AND RIDICULOUSNESS, WORTH AND VALUES

1802 "I'll tell you briefly what I think of newspapermen. The hand of God, reaching down to the mire, couldn't elevate one of them to the depths of degradation." Small town doctor **Charles Winninger** has nothing but contempt for New York journalist Fredric March's profession. *Nothing Sacred* (1937, Selznick-United Artists).

1803 JUDGE: "Are you showing contempt for this court?" FLOWER BELLE LEE: "No, I'm doing my best to hide it." Can Judge **Addison Richards** object to **Mae West**'s truthfully answering his question? *My Little Chickadee* (1940, Universal).

1804 "I don't hate you. I have only contempt for you. I always have." **Bette Davis** turns on her dying husband Herbert Marshall. *The Little Foxes* (1941, Goldwyn-RKO).

1805 "I've been wanting to laugh in your face ever since I met you. You're old and ugly and I'm sick of you—sick, sick, sick!" After getting all she can out of him, prostitute **Joan Bennett** dismisses Edward G. Robinson, enraging him enough to kill her. *Scarlet Street* (1954, Universal).

1806 "I am not anagnostic [sic] to him. He's a shiftless rascal, but I'm not anagnostic to him." Delightful **Una O'Connor** portrays an elderly servant who doesn't know how to pronounce the word, but she knows she's not antagonistic to murder defendant Tyrone Power. However, she does despise him. *Witness for the Prosecution* (1957, United Artists).

1807 "When the preacher says, 'Do you take this woman,' he won't be kidding, will he?" Submarine Commander **Cary Grant** is contemptuous of goldbricking junior officer Tony Curtis who rattles on about his fiancée's huge fortune. *Operation Petticoat* (1959, Universal).

1808 "Took a vacation together. . . I not only don't sleep with him, I won't drink out of the same cup." **Carrie Nye** shows just the proper degree of contempt for her contemptible husband Rip Torn. *The Seduction of Joe Tynan* (1979, Universal).

Content *see* HAPPINESS AND UNHAPPINESS, SATISFACTIONS, WANTS AND WANTING

Contests

see also ARGUMENTS, FIGHTS AND FIGHTING, GAMES, LOSSES AND LOSING, SPORTS, STRUGGLES, TEAMS, VICTORIES, WINNERS AND LOSERS

1809 REFORMED SINNER: "I've wrestled the devil and thrown him. . . . I've pinned his shoulders to the mat." NICK BEAL: "I wonder if he knows it's two throws out of three?" As **Tom Dugan** tells a small crowd at a street corner gathering of the Salvation Army how he beat the devil, **Ray Milland**, Old Nick himself, doesn't believe the struggle for Dugan's soul is over quite yet. *Alias Nick Beal* (1949, Paramount).

1810 LOMAX: "Mine hit the ground first." TAW JACKSON: "Mine was taller." Friendly rivals **Kirk Douglas** and **John Wayne** have each gunned down one of greedy mine owner Bruce Cabot's henchmen. *The War Wagon* (1967, Universal).

1811 HILARY: "I dig his black ass." COCO: "It's taken, Goldilocks." HILARY: "Don't count on it." White **Antonia Franceschi** and black **Irene Cara** fight over black Gene Anthony Ray, who wears extremely tight shorts. *Fame* (1980, MGM).

Contributions *see* GIFTS AND GIVING, MONEY

Control

see also AUTHORITIES, POWER

1812 "Sometimes they both need a whip to put some sense in them. First you have to slip a bit in his mouth—and make him like it." **Barbara Stanwyck**'s prescription for controlling a man is to handle him like a horse. *Breakfast for Two* (1937, RKO).

1813 "In a world controlled by men, I have found a way to control the controllers." Power hungry **Vera Miles** cackles and gloats because she has access to a rejuvenation formula. This film is a big screen edition of episodes from the television series, "The Man from U.N.C.L.E." *One of Our Spies Is Missing* (1966, MGM).

1814 "Because I've been an unemployed actor for twenty years waiting by the phone. Then when I get the part I have no control over it." **Dustin Hoffman** decides he has a special affinity for being a woman. *Tootsie* (1982, Columbia).

1815 "'Who controls the past, controls the future. Who controls the present, controls the past.' **Richard Burton** proudly explains to John Hurt how "Big Brother" rewrites history to satisfy the ruling class. *1984* (1984, GB, Atlantic).

1816 "I can make the sky rain coconuts with pinpoint accuracy, but I still can't control men's minds." Power-hungry witch **Faye Dunaway** is frustrated. *Supergirl* (1984, GB, Tri-Star).

1817 "You made me, you control me." Delectable **Kelly LeBrock** smirks at her teenage creators, Anthony Michael Hall and Ilan Mitchell-Smith, who are like dogs who have caught an automobile and don't know what to do with it. *Weird Science* (1985, Universal).

1818 "The Third World is the last frontier. The corporation that controls the Third World in the 21st century controls the world." Conglomerate head **Eddie Albert** lectures to Judge Reinhold. *Head Office* (1986, Tri-Star).

1819 "I can't help it, I'm out of control." Psychotherapist **Lindsay Crouse** had tried to help one of her patients by getting involved in the world of gambling and con artists. She became so intrigued with the world of con man Joe Mantegna, that when she discovers she's a victim of his con, she pumps him full of bullets. *House of Games* (1987, Orion).

1820 "I'm the mother. You're the child. You're not ready for freedom. . . . You know what I'm going to do. I'm having you locked up. You're going to be locked up with the junkies in de-tox. . . . Go ahead and cry, cry and think. . . . No one will ever take you away from me again." **Jill Clayburgh** reclaims her out-of-control teenage daughter Martha Plimpton as they fly back to New York City from New Orleans. *Shy People* (1987, Cannon).

1821 "Call her up and tell her your business is going to pieces. Ask if she could just come in and get things organized. Get things under control. Put it that way. Use the words: 'Get things under control.'" **William Hurt** advises his publisher Bill Pullman on how to get his wife, Hurt's sister, compulsive organizer Amy Wright to return to him. She's left Pullman to move back in with her two other brothers, David Ogden Stiers and Ed Begley, Jr., who she believes can't function without her. *The Accidental Tourist* (1988, Warner Bros.).

1822 "It's beyond my control." After telling Michelle Pfeiffer that their affair is over, **John Malkovich** repeats over and over the phrase suggested to him by Glenn Close. *Dangerous Liaisons* (1988, Warner Bros.).

1823 "How do you get the sun on just the people who pay?" Sixties flower child **Cheech Marin** has spent the past 20 years in a Latin American jungle commune. He's intrigued when an old friend claims to run a tanning salon in New York City. *Rude Awakening* (1989, Orion).

1824 "We say who, we say when, we say how much." Hooker **Julia Roberts** is proud that she and her roommate Laura San Giacomo are independent prostitutes with no pimps. *Pretty Woman* (1990, Touchstone-Buena Vista).

Conversations

see also LISTENING AND LISTENERS, SPEECH AND SPEAKING, TALKS AND TALKING

1825 "I don't understand this conversation at all. How drunk am I?" **Paul Douglas** doesn't catch the subtle plotting and innuendos of others at a cocktail party. *A Letter to Three Wives* (1949, 20th Century-Fox).

1826 "George here doesn't cotton too much to body talk. 'Paunchy' here isn't too happy when the conversation moves to muscle." **Elizabeth Taylor** insults her husband Richard Burton in front of their guests George Segal and Sandy Dennis. *Who's Afraid of Virginia Woolf?* (1966, Warner Bros.).

1827 "Why do you always start a conversation on the most serious subjects when I'm half way out the door?" **Walter Matthau** is rather picky with his wife Maureen Stapleton. He's just confessed he's having an affair with his secretary who he is on the way to see. Understandably, Stapleton wants to discuss the situation. *Plaza Suite* (1971, Paramount).

1828 "I have to keep up my side of the conversation and your side of the conversation." **Lily Tomlin** complains about taciturn Art Carney. *The Late Show* (1977, Warner Bros.).

1829 GILBERT CHILVERS: "Well, Mrs. Rhoades' ingrown toenail has turned the corner." JOYCE CHILVERS: "Please, Gilbert, don't bring feet to the table." Dedicated Yorkshire podiatrist **Michael Palin** is reminded by his socially ambitious wife **Maggie Smith** that his work is not suitable meal time conversation. *A Private Function* (1985, GB, Island Alive).

Convictions *see* BELIEFS, OPINIONS, TRUTH

Cooking and Cooks *see* FOOD AND EATING

Corrections

see also CURES, LOGIC, PROOFS, PUNISHMENTS, RIGHT AND WRONG, TRUTH, WRONGS AND WRONG-DOINGS

1830 GERRY JEFFERS: "I'm just a milestone around your neck." TOM JEFFERS: "You mean millstone." After five years of marriage, **Claudette Colbert** loves her unsuccessful inventor husband **Joel McCrea** so much, she hatches a plot to make them money. She will divorce him, find a millionaire to marry, then use her new husband's money to help McCrea market his inventions. *The Palm Beach Story* (1942, Paramount).

1831 "That was two years ago, when he was just a cross, young man. At the time he was writing long, scholarly articles proving that Shakespeare was a homosexual." **Barry Nelson** corrects his lawyer Hiram Sherman, who refers to an English critic as "an angry young man." *Mary, Mary* (1963, Warner Bros.).

1832 "He's a man not a river." **Mark Linn-Baker** cries out a correction as his mother, Lainie Kazan, pats Peter O'Toole's character Alan Swann on the cheek and calls him "Swannie." *My Favorite Year* (1982, MGM-United Artists).

1833 "We're not old friends. . . we're acquaintances. . . very distant acquaintances." **Daphne Zuniga** corrects John Cusack who tells Tim Robbins, in whose car they are traveling across country, that they are old friends. *The Sure Thing* (1985, Embassy).

1834 "You're not with the army anymore. We had an affair, not a pitched battle." **Judy Davis**, as novelist George Sand (nee Amandine Aurore Lucie Dupin), dismisses an ex-lover and soldier who wishes to re-analyze their relationship. *Impromptu* (1991, GB, Hemdale).

Corruption

see also BADNESS, EVILNESS, GOOD AND EVIL (BAD), SINS AND SINNERS

1835 "This town is as rotten as an open grave." Police captain **Walter Huston** speaks of the corruption and moral decay of a modern city. *Beast of the City* (1932, MGM).

1836 "Everyone can be paid off with chips." Racketeer and gambler **Clark Gable** believes everyone is corrupt. *Manhattan Melodrama* (1934, MGM).

1837 "He was a talented man, but very, very corrupt." **Dudley Digges**, as Mr. Wu, speaks of savage bandit chief Akim Tamiroff, as General Yang. *The General Died at Dawn* (1936, Paramount).

1838 "They soaked me once too often in that vat of poisoned hell they keep upstate to soak men in, and I'm rotten inside." Mobster **Eduardo Ciannelli** makes the announcement to his henchmen. *Winterset* (1936, RKO).

1839 "I'm a rotter and that's all I want to be." Newspaper editor **Cary Grant** will do anything honest or dishonest to get a news story. *His Girl Friday* (1940, Columbia).

1840 "I'm only a poor corrupt official." Corrupt French Police Prefect **Claude Rains** begs for a reduction in the stake in a bet with Humphrey Bogart on whether Resistance leader Paul Henreid will be able to escape from Casablanca. *Casablanca* (1942, Warner Bros.).

1841 WALTER NEFF: "And for once I believe you, because it's just rotten enough." PHYLLIS DIETRICHSON: "We're both rotten." NEFF: "Only you're a little more rotten. You got me to take care of your husband for you." Murderers **Fred MacMurray** and **Barbara Stanwyck**'s solidarity begins to unravel as the pressure builds. *Double Indemnity* (1944, Paramount).

1842 "You stink with corruption." Crippled **Arthur Kennedy** yells at his brother Kirk Douglas and brings down his cane on the latter's head. Douglas proceeds to batter Kennedy unconscious. *Champion* (1949, United Artists).

1843 "That's. . . that's a rotten thing to say." **Robert Redford** is hurt to the quick when his wife of six days Jane Fonda accuses him of being almost perfect. *Barefoot in the Park* (1967, Paramount).

1844 "It would be a shame if a few rotten apples spoiled the whole barrel." U.S. Senator **G.D. Spradlin** makes a statement during Al Pacino's testimony before the Senate Crime Commission. Spradlin is in Pacino's pocket. *The Godfather, Part II* (1974, Paramount).

1845 "I hate purity. I hate goodness. I don't want virtue to exist anywhere. I want everyone corrupt." **John Hurt** defiantly revolts against the constant wars and bans on freedom in Oceania to his uncomprehending mistress, Suzanna Hamilton. *1984* (1984, GB, Atlantic)

Cosmetics *see* APPEARANCES, FACES, HAIR, PERFUMES

Costs

see also BUSINESS AND COMMERCE, BUYING AND SELLING, LOSSES AND LOSING, MONEY, PRICES, VICTORIES, WORTH AND VALUES

1846 "How much do you charge for the first mile?" It's nightclub entertainer **Marlene Dietrich**'s wisecracking question of a colleague known as "Taxi." *Blonde Venus* (1932, Paramount).

1847 "Anything that's different always costs more but it's worth it." Priceless **Mae West** says "no sale" to admirer William B. Davidson, who claims she's "different." *I'm No Angel* (1933, Paramount).

1848 "You couldn't even afford the headlights." Hash-house waitress **Ann Sheridan** kids in a friendly manner with a trucker who states he's prepared to pay for her in installments. *They Drive by Night* (1940, Warner Bros.).

1849 "I see you whittled them down a bit. They whittled us down, too." Tank sergeant **Humphrey Bogart** turns over the dog tags of his dead to Bruce Bennett who has brought a relief column to their rescue. *Sahara* (1943, Warner Bros.).

1850 "Here's what it cost, not much to send home, a handful of Americans." Commando Commander **Errol Flynn** fills Warner Anderson's hands with the dog tags of the soldiers who didn't make it back from their mission behind the Japanese lines. *Objective Burma* (1945, Warner Bros.).

1851 "Cheap, huh? Sure—a cigar, a drink and a couple of dirty bucks; that's all it costs to buy me—that's what she thought. Found out a little different, didn't she? Maybe I could get tired of being pushed around by cops and hotel managers and ritzy dames in bungalows. Maybe I could cost a little something just for me. And if I do end up on a slab. . . ." **Will Wright** admits he murdered Doris Dowling just before he is gunned down by the police. *The Blue Dahlia* (1946, Paramount).

1852 "Imagine. A dollar twenty just to go to the top of an old building." **Maggie McNamara** feels the fee to ride to the top of the Empire State Building is too steep. *The Moon Is Blue* (1953, United Artists).

1853 "Why don't you get off that pulpit, Wyatt? Ellsworth, Wichita, Dodge City and what have they got you but a life of misery and a woman that walked out on you. . . and the friendship of a killer." Corrupt Sheriff **Frank Faylen** tells Marshal Burt Lancaster that his dedication to honesty has cost him a great deal and gained him very little. *Gunfight at the OK Corral* (1957, Paramount).

1854 "I'll bet you paid plenty for this little piece of—sculpture. . . . She's worth every dollar, take it from me." **Cary Grant** disgustedly refers to Eva Marie Saint as he exchanges sneers with James Mason at an art auction. *North by Northwest* (1959, MGM).

1855 "I don't say we wouldn't get our hair mussed, but I say no more than ten to twenty million killed tops—that is, depending on the break." Practical

American General **George C. Scott** advises President Peter Sellers to take advantage of mad Air Force General Sterling Hayden's having sent nuclear-armed bombers to attack the U.S.S.R. *Dr. Strangelove: Or How I Learned to Stop Worrying and Love the Bomb* (1964, Columbia).

1856 "How much do you charge to give someone the rub, or whatever they say?" Aged widow **Katharine Hepburn** checks prices with hit man Nick Nolte. *Grace Quigley* aka: *The Ultimate Solution of Grace Quigley* (1984, Cannon).

1857 "Guess what? You guys will never believe. I found out that it only costs two hundred and fifty dollars to bury a cat. So I figured why don't I just put my stepmother into a large cat suit." **Demi Moore** has found a solution to a delicate problem. *St. Elmo's Fire* (1985, Columbia).

1858 KEITH NELSON: "You can't tell a book by its cover." WATTS: "Yeah, but you can tell how much it's gonna cost." **Eric Stoltz** and **Mary Stuart Masterson** discuss his dream girl, popular high school beauty Lea Thompson. *Some Kind of Wonderful* (1987, Paramount).

1859 "Joe. . . your personal battles are going to cost us the war." Superintendent of Schools **Robert Guillaume** is exasperated with unconventional principal, Morgan Freeman. *Lean on Me* (1989, Warner Bros.).

Countries

see also AMERICA AND AMERICANS, DEMOCRACY, GOVERNMENTS, LAND AND FARMS, LOCATIONS, POLITICS AND POLITICIANS

1860 "This is a fine country to live in; this is a fine country to live in. This is a bloody awful country to live in." German citizen **Raymond Huntley** uses a very British expression when he's unable to convince himself that things are good in Nazi Germany. *Night Train to Munich* (1940, GB, Gaumont-20th Century-Fox).

1861 "Our country will open like a flower once the British are gone and our country is free." Sikh **Francis Matthews**' dream and prediction doesn't seem to have come true. *Bhowani Junction* (1956, MGM).

1862 "Don't you know what country you live in? Can't you smell the bananas? You live in Guatemala with color television." Disillusioned police Lieutenant **Burt Reynolds** snaps at his prostitute girlfriend Catherine Deneuve. *Hustle* (1975, Paramount).

1863 "I thought they'd all be out drinking cider and discussing butter." Naïve London actor **Richard E. Grant** finds the country and its people not at all as he expected. *Withnail and I* (1987, GB, Cineplex Odeon).

1864 "The country is everything I hoped it would be—there can be no place like this on earth." In voice-over, narrator **Kevin Costner** falls under the spell of the endless frontier plains. *Dances with Wolves* (1990, Orion).

1865 "You're my only country now." British publisher **Sean Connery** puts his love for Russian Michelle Pfeiffer above spying for his country. *The Russia House* (1990, MGM-United Artists).

Courage

see also BRAVERY, COWARDICE AND COWARDS, DANGER, DESPAIR AND DESPERATION, FEARS, HEART AND HEARTACHES, PAINS, RIGHT AND WRONG, SPIRIT AND SPIRITS, STRENGTHS

1866 "When we go to the guillotine, will you let me hold your hand? It will give me courage, too." Poor frightened servant girl **Isabel Jewell** seeks help in facing her fate from condemned lawyer Ronald Colman. *A Tale of Two Cities* (1935, MGM).

1867 "This is a different kind of courage, the kind that only you and I and God know about. I want you to let them down. They've got to despise your memory." Priest **Pat O'Brien** asks his boyhood chum James Cagney to go to the chair a coward to kill the hero-worship of a bunch of teen punks. Cagney refuses but then goes screaming to his death. Whether it is an act or not is left to the viewer to decide. *Angels with Dirty Faces* (1938, Warner Bros.).

1868 "You haven't enough courage to be a capitalist yourself, so you try to drag everyone down to where you are." **Ginger Rogers** exposes the emptiness of the beliefs of communist chauffeur James Ellison. In this role, Rogers is posing as a gold digger who moves in with a millionaire. *Fifth Avenue Girl* (1939, RKO).

1869 "With enough courage, you can do without a reputation." **Clark Gable** assures "grieving widow" Vivien Leigh that she needn't worry about what people will think of her. Dressed all in black in memory of her young unloved husband, Rand Brooks, killed in an early Civil War battle, she's dancing with Gable at a charity bazaar in Atlanta. *Gone with the Wind* (1939, Selznick-MGM).

1870 "I love your courage and your stubbornness." It's not the sort of love Vivien Leigh is looking for from **Leslie Howard.** *Gone with the Wind* (1939, Selznick-MGM).

1871 "What makes the Hottentot so hot?. . . Courage!" **Bert Lahr**, as the Cowardly Lion, knows what he'll ask of the Wizard of Oz. *The Wizard of Oz* (1939, MGM).

1872 "I never prized safety in myself or my children. I prized courage." German professor **Frank Morgan** resists the urging that he and his family flee Nazi Germany. *The Mortal Storm* (1940, MGM).

1873 "What good is courage if you have no head." Spanish partisan **Katina Paxinou** warns that brains, not bravado, are what is needed to win their struggle. *For Whom the Bell Tolls* (1943, Paramount).

1874 "We have gone through with it, Walter. The tough part is behind us. We just have to hold on now and not go soft inside, stay close together the way we started out. . . ." **Barbara Stanwyck** tries to buck up Fred MacMurray's courage after they have murdered her husband. *Double Indemnity* (1944, Paramount).

1875 Sorrowful Jones: "You never heard my courage questioned." Gladys O'Neill: "I never heard your courage mentioned." New York bookie **Bob Hope** takes a shot from Broadway singer **Lucille Ball**. *Sorrowful Jones* (1949, Paramount).

1876 "I had courage, long ago, but I lost it." Frail **Ingrid Bergman** tells her cousin Michael Wilding that having to flee Ireland to be with her convict husband in Australia has taken a great deal out of her. *Under Capricorn* (1949, Warner Bros.).

1877 "If only Dad had the guts to knock Mom cold once." **James Dean** sighs about his henpecked father Jim Backus and his domineering mother Ann Doran. *Rebel Without a Cause* (1955, Warner Bros.).

1878 "I've got the guts to die. What I want to know is do you have the guts to live?" Dying of cancer, **Burl Ives** is sorely disappointed in his neurotic son Paul Newman, who refuses to sleep with his wife Elizabeth Taylor. *Cat on a Hot Tin Roof* (1958, MGM).

1879 "In a world of frightened people, he likes courage, whenever he finds it—even in a rude and angry woman." **Peter Chong** translates the mixed message of Chinese mandarin Robert Donat for English missionary Ingrid Bergman. *The Inn of the Sixth Happiness* (1958, 20th Century-Fox).

1880 "I would not like to die a death like I just described. Not if I had your courage." Physician **James Stewart** describes to aging gunman John Wayne the horrible pain awaiting him as his cancer worsens. Stewart suggests that Wayne find another way to die. *The Shootist* (1976, Paramount).

1881 "You are courageous to have come so far." Berber Chieftain **Ferdinand Mayne** is impressed that teenager Kelly Reno has chased his kidnapped stallion half-way round the world. *The Black Stallion Returns* (1983, 20th Century-Fox).

1882 "'Wanting only to be liked, he distorted himself beyond measure,' wrote Scott Fitzgerald. One wonders what would have happened if right at the outset he'd had the courage to speak his mind and not pretend. Near the end it was not after all the approbation of many but the love of one woman that changed his life." Narrator **Patrick Horgan** speaks of chameleon-like Woody Allen and his psychiatrist lover Mia Farrow. *Zelig* (1983, Orion).

1883 "It took every ounce of courage to walk out that door." **Eva Marie Saint** tells her son Tom Hanks about leaving his father, her husband of 30 years, Jackie Gleason. *Nothing in Common* (1986, Tri-Star).

1884 "It takes courage to feel pain. . . . You can do it. . . . Just let go." Psychiatrist **Barbra Streisand** comforts a sobbing Nick Nolte who finally lets himself feel the pain of his traumatic boyhood and the death of his beloved brother. *The Prince of Tides* (1991, Columbia).

Courts *see* Decisions, Judgments, Justice, Laws, Lawyers

Courtships *see* Flirtations, Love and Hate, Love and Lovers, Marriages, Romances, Seductions

Cowardice and Cowards

see also Bravery, Courage, Escapes, Fears

1885 "If a guy hasn't got the strength to go straight, he turns yellow inside." Honest police Captain **Walter Huston** doesn't buy the notion that society is to blame for a man choosing the life of a criminal. *Beast of the City* (1932, MGM).

1886 "I may be a coward, but, oh dear, Yankees in Georgia! How did they ever get in?" **Laura Hope Crews**, as Aunt Pittypat, flees to the country, leaving Vivien Leigh to deal with the coming of Olivia de Havilland's baby as best she can. *Gone with the Wind* (1939, Selznick-MGM).

1887 "If I could reach as high as my father's shoestrings my whole life would be justified. And I would stand before you proudly, instead of as the thief and coward that I am. A coward because I postponed until now what I should have told you a year ago when I was discharged from the Marine Corps for medical unfitness. A coward because I didn't want my mother to know. . . . A thief because I stole your admiration. I stole the ribbons I've worn. I stole the nomination [for mayor]." **Eddie Bracken**, the son of a man who heroically sacrificed his own life at Belleau Wood in World War I, confesses to all the citizens of his home town. Instead of being a disgrace, he's considered an even greater man for having told the truth and is promptly elected mayor. *Hail the Conquering Hero* (1944, Paramount).

1888 "Better be a live coward than a dead hero." **Claire Trevor** says what uncertain Humphrey Bogart is thinking. Despite his better judgment he will ultimately take on mobster Edward G. Robinson and his henchmen. *Key Largo* (1948, Warner Bros.).

1889 "You're yellow. I never saw you pick on anyone who wasn't old and sick." Bookmaker **Charlton Heston** accuses psychopath Jack Webb of cowardice. *Dark City* (1950, Paramount).

1890 "Lots of good-a'-nough men have thought they was' goin' to be great things before the fight, but when the time comes, they skedaddled." **Audie Murphy** ought to know. He panicked and ran during a Civil War battle. *Red Badge of Courage* (1951, MGM).

1891 "You're yellow. You haven't even the guts to ride a dead mule." Would-be rodeo star **Arthur Kennedy** tries to get a rise out of his mentor Robert Mitchum by questioning his courage. *The Lusty Men* (1952, RKO).

1892 LT. STEVE MARYK: "Hello, Tom. I didn't think you'd have the guts to come." LT. TOM KEEFER: "I didn't have the guts not to." **Van Johnson** is surprised and disappointed to see **Fred MacMurray** at the party celebrating Johnson's acquittal of the charge of mutiny. MacMurray's self-serving testimony almost sank Johnson. *The Caine Mutiny* (1954, Columbia).

1893 "If those little sweethearts won't face German bullets, they'll face French ones." Divisional General **George Macready** refers to a company of French soldiers who refused to leave their trenches for a suicidal charge during World War I. *Paths of Glory* (1957, United Artists).

1894 "Miss Cooper, the plain fact is that I'm far too much of a coward to stay on here now." **David Niven** speaks to hotel proprietoress Wendy Hiller when he's exposed as a phony and harasser of women in a small movie house. *Separate Tables* (1958, United Artists).

1895 "As long as valor remains a virtue, we shall have soldiers. So I preach cowardice. Cowards run like rabbits at the first shot. If everybody did, we would never get to the second shot. I'm a coward, and I say that cowardice will save the world!" Dog-robber **James Garner** thinks he's got it all figured out, but he's not fooling anyone with his phony solution to ending wars. *The Americanization of Emily* (1964, MGM).

1896 "I'm glad you're a coward. It's your most important asset, being a coward. Every man I ever loved was a hero and all he got was death." **Julie Andrews** is more practical. She doesn't preach cowardice for everyone, just the ones she loves. *The Americanization of Emily* (1964, MGM).

1897 "Get the coward out of here." Title character **George C. Scott** yells at the doctors, after he's slapped a crying battle-fatigued soldier in a field hospital. *Patton* (1970, 20th Century-Fox).

1898 "Yes, but I'm a militant coward." **Woody Allen** defends himself when he's accused of being a coward. *Love and Death* (1975, United Artists).

Cowboys

see also ANIMALS, LAND AND FARMS, RIDING AND RIDERS

1899 "I'm a cowboy. I don't know anything else." When he parts from Joan Hackett at the end of the movie, cowpuncher **Charlton Heston** is old enough to be called a cowman. *Will Penny* (1967, Paramount).

1900 "Well, I'll tell you the truth, I ain't a real cowboy, but I am one helluva stud." Dim-witted **Jon Voight** brags to a woman he hopes will pay for his special services. *Midnight Cowboy* (1969, United Artists).

1901 "You know less about these wide open spaces than I do. You're just some kind of motel cowboy." Real estate developer **Joe Don Baker** offers a job to his fading rodeo star brother Steve McQueen, a man of limited experience. *Junior Bonner* (1972, ABC-Cinerama).

1902 "I think modern men are too complicated. I told my Daddy that I go for cowboys because they represent the simple values—they're brave, strong, direct, honest. . . . 'You mean dumb,' Daddy replied. Daddy's a real scream." **Madolyn Smith** bends the ear of make-believe cowboy John Travolta. *Urban Cowboy* (1980, Paramount).

1903 Sissy: "You a real cowboy?" Bud: "Well, that depends on what you think a real cowboy is." **Debra Winger** sizes up young hardhat **John Travolta** wearing a ten gallon hat. *Urban Cowboy* (1980, Paramount).

1904 "If you ain't a cowboy, you ain't worth shit." Cowboy **Sam Shepard** is pretty certain of things. *Fool for Love* (1985, Cannon).

1905 Ed: "A cowboy doesn't leave his herd." Phil: "Aren't you a sporting goods salesman?" Ed: "Not today." When things look the worse on the cattle drive, **Bruno Kirby** is determined to do the job he came for, despite the voice of reality, **Daniel Stern.** *City Slickers* (1991, Columbia).

1906 "You came here city slickers, you're going home cowboys." Working ranch owner **Noble Willingham** congratulates a group of city dudes who met the test and passed, participating in a real cattle drive from New Mexico to Colorado. *City Slickers* (1991, Columbia).

Craziness *see* Insanity and Sanity, Minds, Psychology and Psychiatry

Creation and Creatures

see also Arts and Artists, Destruction, God, Inspirations, Inventions, Lives and Living, Men and Women, Poetry and Poets, Science and Scientists, Writing and Writers

1907 "You're a nasty creature, aren't you? But in time, I'll beat it out of you!" Newspaper editor **Henry Fonda** threatens madcap heiress Barbara Stanwyck with physical abuse. *The Mad Miss Manton* (1938, RKO).

1908 Bill Carey: "Don't the French accept the half-castes?" Father Antoine: "No, they only create them." In pre-World War II Saigon, American tourist **Robert Taylor** gets a frank answer from missionary **Ernest Cossart**. *Lady of the Tropics* (1939, MGM).

1909 "You certainly go in for mass production, don't you?" **Bette Davis** is shocked by a woman who has just given birth to her eighth child. *Beyond the Forest* (1949, Warner Bros.).

1910 "In Italy for thirty years under the Borgias, they had warfare, terror, murder and bloodshed.

But they produced Michelangelo, Leonardo Da Vinci, and the Renaissance. In Switzerland, they had brotherly love. They had five hundred years of democracy and peace. And what did they produce? The cuckoo clock." **Orson Welles** attempts to justify his dastardly actions as a black marketeer with a dubious and flawed argument for his one-time friend Joseph Cotten. For one thing, the origin of the cuckoo clock is the Black Forest in Germany. *The Third Man* (1950, GB, Korda-Selznick).

1911 "Love is a work of art and like art must be created." Once renowned courtesan **Isabel Jeans** instructs her niece Leslie Caron that love cannot be left to accidental development. *Gigi* (1958, MGM).

1912 "Answer me! You have a civil tongue in your head. I know—I sewed it there myself." **Whit Bissell**, a descendant of Dr. Frankenstein, scolds his teenage monster Gary Conway. *I Was a Teenage Frankenstein* (1958, American International Pictures).

1913 "To tell the truth, I spent the first five days thinking and created everything on the sixth." **George Burns**, as God, clears up a popular misconception about His work. *Oh, God!* (1977, Warner Bros.).

1914 "You're God's answer to Job. . . you know. You would've ended all argument between them. I mean He would've pointed to you and said, you know, 'I do a lot of terrible things, but I can also make one of these,' you know. And then Job would've said, 'Okay—well, you win.'" **Woody Allen** pays 17-year-old Mariel Hemingway a sincere compliment. *Manhattan* (1979, United Artists).

1915 "I might make the New Woman—independent, free, as bold as a man." **Sting**, as Baron Charles Frankenstein, spouts some Twentieth century feminism. *The Bride* (1985, Columbia).

1916 Eva: "You don't own me. . . . You didn't create me." Frankenstein: "As a matter of fact. . . I did." **Jennifer Beals** learns from **Sting** that she's not a "natural" girl. *The Bride* (1985, Columbia).

1917 "I want her to live! I want her to breath! I want her to aerobicize!" **Anthony Michael Hall** behaves like a young Colin Clive, when he and his buddy Ilan Mitchell-Smith create dream girl Kelly LeBrock with the help of a computer and some wild imaginations. *Weird Science* (1985, Universal).

1918 "I just created something totally illogical." **Kevin Costner**'s not alone. Sharing responsibility are director-screenwriter Phil Alden Robinson, and W.P. Kinsella, who wrote the book "Shoeless Joe" on which the film is based—and they did it so beautifully that the fantasy doesn't seem outrageous. *Field of Dreams* (1989, Universal).

1919 "I dreamed her up. I can make her vanish." **John Hurt**, as Dr. Stephen Ward, is wrong in believing that he can control the damage to the political career of Ian McKellen, as John Profumo, caused by Hurt's creation, sometime call-girl Joanne Whalley-Kilmer, as Christine Keeler. *Scandal* (1989, GB, Miramax).

1920 "This creature of yours is horny as well as psychopathic." **Gregory Hines** comments to scientist Renee Soutendijk who has created a wanton robot (also played by Soutendijk). *Eve of Destruction* (1991, Orion).

Creeds and Credos

see also BELIEFS, FAITH AND FAITHFULNESS, IDEALS, IDEAS, RELIGIONS

1921 "I shoot my way out of it. Like tonight. Sure, shoot first, argue afterwards. If you don't, the other guy gets you. The game ain't for guys that's soft." Cold-blooded killer **Edward G. Robinson** believes in "do unto others before they do unto you." *Little Caesar* (1931, Warner Bros.).

1922 "Do it first. Do it yourself. And keep doing it." It's Al Capone-like mobster **Paul Muni**'s credo. *Scarface* (1932, United Artists).

1923 "Live fast, die young and have a good looking corpse." It's the credo that **John Derek** lives by and up or down to, depending upon your point of view. *Knock on Any Door* (1949, Columbia).

1924 "Unless I suffer, how can I make the public believe me?" **James Cagney** expresses silent screen star character actor Lon Chaney's credo. *The Man of a Thousand Faces* (1957, Universal-International).

1925 "Sometimes you have to walk up to something and take what you want." Rancher **Randolph Scott** states his code as he prepares to do battle with outlaw Richard Boone and his henchmen. *The Tall T* (1957, Columbia).

1926 "Not many people got a code to live by anymore." Seedy veteran car repossessor **Harry Dean Stanton** tells neophyte Emilio Estevez that he has reason to be proud of his new profession. *Repo Man* (1984, Universal).

1927 "Once you know the world is corrupt—and you know deep down in your bones—these things become simple, clear." Narcotics agent **Kathy Shower** shares her credo. *Commando Squad* (1987, Trans World).

1928 "Live for yourself. Take it before it's too late." These are **Chad Lowe**'s principles to live by. *Apprentice to Murder* (1988, New World).

Crimes and Criminals

see also BADNESS, EVILNESS, EXECUTIONS, GOOD AND EVIL (BAD), HONESTY AND DISHONESTY, JUDGMENTS, JUSTICE, KILLING, LAWS, LAWYERS, LEGALITY AND ILLEGALITY, PRISONS AND PRISONERS, PUNISHMENTS, RIGHT AND WRONG, SINS AND SINNERS, VICES, WRONGS AND WRONGDOINGS

1929 "The state's promises didn't mean anything. It was all lies. They just wanted to get me back so they can have their revenge, to keep me here nine more years. Why, their crimes are worse than mine, worse than anybody's here. They're the ones who should be in jail, not me." When his pardon is refused, escaped chain gang convict **Paul Muni**, who returned with the assurance that its approval was a mere formality, accuses the state and its officials of being bigger criminals than any of the poor wretches shackled and mistreated on the chain gang. *I Am a Fugitive from a Chain Gang* (1932, Warner Bros.).

1930 "Remember, you are a crook, I want you as a crook, I love you as a crook. I've worshipped you as a crook. Steal, swindle, rob. . . oh, but don't become one of those useless, good-for-nothing gigolos!" **Miriam Hopkins** fears that gentleman crook Herbert Marshall is considering giving up his life of crime because of Kay Francis. *Trouble in Paradise* (1932, Paramount).

1931 MAC O'NEILL: "I had four girls chasing me down the street. . . ." "SPUD" BURKE: "What did you do, steal a pocketbook?" Sailors **Ted Healy** and **Nat Pendleton** engage in some friendly banter. *Murder in the Fleet* (1935, MGM).

1932 SHERLOCK HOLMES: "You've a magnificent brain, Moriarty. I admire it. I'd like to present it pickled in alcohol to the London Medical Society." PROFESSOR MORIARTY: "Holmes, you only now barely missed sending me to the gallows. You're the only man in England clever enough to defeat me. I'm going to bring off right under your nose the most incredible crime of the century and you'll never suspect until it's too late. It'll be the end of you, Sherlock Holmes. Then I can retire in peace. I'd like to retire;

crime no longer amuses me. I'd like to devote my remaining years to abstract science." **Basil Rathbone** and **George Zucco** share a hansom cab, after Rathbone arrives too late to present evidence in the murder trial of Zucco, who is found not guilty due to insufficient evidence. Zucco thumbs his nose at Rathbone, promising to come up with a heinous crime to show his superiority. *The Adventures of Sherlock Holmes* (1939, 20th Century-Fox).

1933 "There's your new mill hands, Mrs. Kennedy. The pick of all the best jails in Georgia." **J.M. Kerrigan** shows Vivien Leigh the convicts who will work in her lumber mill. *Gone with the Wind* (1939, Selznick-MGM).

1934 "I always thought criminals were gallant, but you've got a stupid degenerate face." **Claudette Colbert** is angry when James Stewart throws her harshly into her own car and spirits her away to an unknown fate. *It's a Wonderful World* (1939, MGM).

1935 MAYOR: "Have you seen Sheriff Hartwell?" ENDICOTT: "Well, it's so hard to tell, there's so many crooks around here." When **Clarence Kolb** sticks his head in the news room of the jail and inquires about corrupt Gene Lockhart, reporter **Cliff Edwards** has a cynical reply. *His Girl Friday* (1940, Columbia).

1936 "I'm Abu the thief, son of Abu the thief, grandson of Abu the thief, most unfortunate of ten sons, with a hunger that yearns day and night." **Sabu** tells his new friend, deposed Caliph John Justin, that he's continuing in the family business. *The Thief of Bagdad* (1940, GB, London Films).

1937 "All the A-one guys are gone, dead or in Alcatraz." Big Boss **Donald MacBride** laments the decline of quality criminals with one of the best (or should that be—one of the worst?) **Humphrey Bogart**. *High Sierra* (1941, Warner Bros.).

1938 "His only crime was that he had courage and spoke his mind. . . . The law must be engraved in our hearts." Supreme Court nominee **Ronald Colman** speaks forcefully to a mob that wishes to lynch Cary Grant. *The Talk of the Town* (1942, Columbia).

1939 "You're like the guy behind the roulette wheel, watching the customers to make sure they don't crook the house. And then one night you get to thinking how you could crook the house yourself, and do it smart because you've got the wheel right under your hands, you know every notch in it by heart, and you figure all you need is a plant out front, a shill to put down the bet. Then suddenly the doorbell rings and the whole set up is right there in the room with you." Insurance salesman **Fred MacMurray** reveals that he's been thinking for years how to carry off a perfect scam against his company. *Double Indemnity* (1944, Paramount).

1940 "You ought to pick on somebody to steal from that doesn't owe me money." Sport fishing boat skipper **Humphrey Bogart** lectures pickpocket Lauren Bacall who has lifted the wallet of Bogie's customer, Walter Sande. *To Have and Have Not* (1945, Warner Bros.).

1941 "Because any guy who could have two kids like that isn't a crook—crooked, yes. . . stupid, yes. . . on the wrong foot, yes. . . but he isn't one of those mugs that don't belong to human society. Those are two decent little human beings and no crook could make 'em that sweet." Assistant D.A. **Brian Donlevy** takes a special interest in convicted felon Victor Mature after seeing pictures of Vic's two kids. Those of a cynical bent might suggest that Donlevy is buttering up Mature because the former wants the latter to put the finger on some "real" crooks. *Kiss of Death* (1947, 20th Century-Fox).

1942 VIRGINIA CUNNINGHAM: "You're going to electrocute me! Was my crime so great?" DR. MARK KIRK: "Nobody's being electrocuted, we're your friends." Patient **Olivia de Havilland** submits with reluctance to **Leo Genn**'s electric shock treatments. *The Snake Pit* (1948, 20th Century-Fox).

1943 "There's nothing so different about them. After all, crime, my dear, is merely a left-handed form of human endeavor." Crooked lawyer **Louis Calhern** reassures his invalid wife Dorothy Tree who objects to the people he deals with. *The Asphalt Jungle* (1950, MGM).

1944 "Charlie, what are you hanging your head for? What do you got to be ashamed of? You wanted to be a burglar so be a good one. Be proud of your chosen profession. Hold up your head. There, that's better. You're a good thief, Charlie. You're no bum. They wear sweaters. Not you. You—wait a minute! Take it off, you bum. It's stolen. The name's still in it. 'Jerome Armstrong.' Where'd you get this, Charlie?" Police detective **Kirk Douglas** works on hoodlum Joseph Wiseman to confess that he's a thief and notices that Wiseman is wearing a stolen suit. *Detective Story* (1951, Paramount).

1945 "Set a thief to catch a thief." It's the source of the title of the Hitchcock movie, and a ploy to which insurance investigator **John Williams** subscribes. *To Catch a Thief* (1955, Paramount).

1946 "I never stole from anyone who would go hungry." Former cat burglar **Cary Grant** attended high society parties so he could steal from other guests. *To Catch a Thief* (1955, Paramount).

1947 AMELIE DUCOTEL: "Your friends are very obliging, especially the one who carried my daughter. How did he get into trouble?" JOSEPH: "Running after a girl." AMELIE: "Running after a girl? Is that a crime in France?" JOSEPH: "No, not exactly. . . . Unfortunately, he caught her." Devil's Island convict **Humphrey Bogart** discusses fellow convict Aldo Ray with **Joan Bennett.** At that very moment Ray is carrying Bennett's fainted daughter Gloria Talbott to her bedroom. *We're No Angels* (1955, Paramount).

1948 "I'd rather be thought of as a successful crook than a destitute monarch." Penniless European King **Charles Chaplin** is at odds with the American way of life. *A King in New York* (1957, Chaplin-Attica).

1949 "I've trapped you and caught you, and by God I'm going to keep you. I've really caught a wild thing this time—a thief!" **Sean Connery** gloats to Tippi Hedren, who supplements her earnings by robbing her various employers. *Marnie* (1964, Universal).

1950 "When I was a kid, he caught me stealin' hubcaps off his car, and he said, 'Kid, don't steal the hubcaps, steal the car.'" **Peter Falk** fondly remembers his crime mentor Edward G. Robinson, who Falk has had rubbed out. *Robin and the Seven Hoods* (1964, Warner Bros.).

1951 "I stole the candles from the chapel. Jesus won't begrudge them and the chaplain works for me." **Peter O'Toole**, as King Henry II of England, jests to his mistress Jane Merrow when they meet late at night. *The Lion in Winter* (1968, GB, Avco Embassy).

1952 "I never met a soul more affable than you, Butch, or faster than the kid, but you're still nothing but a couple of two-bit outlaws on the dodge." Friendly lawman **Jeff Corey** sizes up Paul Newman and Robert Redford. *Butch Cassidy and the Sundance Kid* (1969, 20th Century-Fox).

1953 "I robbed a butcher shop. I got away with 116 veal cutlets. Then I had to go out and rob a tremendous amount of breading." **Woody Allen** brags about his life of crime. *Take the Money and Run* (1969, Cinerama).

1954 "[I'm] busy stealing Givenchy's fall line." Divorced cut-rate fashion designer **Glenda Jackson** explains to a married American insurance executive what she's doing in Paris. *A Touch of Class* (1973, GB, Avco Embassy).

1955 MAJ. JOE DELUCA: "The war was made to order for you. You stole from both sides." SHELLY WEBBER: "What was the greater immorality, my petty crimes or the war itself?" Former O.S.S. agent **John Cassavetes** and assassin **Max von Sydow** debate morality. *Brass Target* (1978, United Artists).

1956 "Women love outlaws like a boy loves a stray dog." Sheriff **Richard Bradford** expresses the sentiment when outlaw Jack Nicholson is saved from the hangman by Mary Steenburgen's agreement to marry and reform him. *Goin' South* (1978, Paramount).

1957 "If all the men in war who committed reprisals were to be charged and tried, court-martials like this one would be in permanent session, wouldn't they?" Defense Attorney **Jack Thompson** summarizes in the court-martial of three Aussie soldiers, **Edward Woodward, Bryan Brown** and **Lewis Fitz-Gerald,** chosen by the British High Command to be scapegoats during the Boer War. They are on trial for murdering guerrilla prisoners. They don't deny it, but use as a defense that they were just following orders from higher ups. *Breaker Morant* (1980, Australia, New World).

1958 "A naked American man stole my balloons." Little **Rufus Decker** calmly reports a theft at a zoo. When he was transformed back to human form from that of a werewolf, naked David Naughton filched Decker's balloons to cover himself. *An American Werewolf in London* (1981, Universal).

1959 "I'm a thief." **James Caan**, whose personal life isn't as successful as his professional life, defiantly shouts to Tuesday Weld. *Thief* aka: *Violent Streets* (1981, United Artists).

1960 "Crime is a disease and I'm the cure." **Sylvester Stallone** hisses at the neo-Nazi criminal just before blowing away the unfortunate's head in the name of therapy. *Cobra* (1986, Warner Bros.).

1961 DAN GALLAGHER: "I don't think having dinner with anybody is a crime." ALEX FORREST: "Not yet." Married **Michael Douglas** and seductive **Glenn Close** are still in the innocent stage—but not for long. *Fatal Attraction* (1987, Paramount).

1962 "But only for inside trading and when he gets out, he'll be rich." One of Caroline Aaron's friends, **Nadia Sanford**, has found just the man for her—when he gets out of prison. *Crimes and Misdemeanors* (1989, Orion).

1963 "When you rob someone legally, that's a crime." **Sean Connery** feels his family business of robbing illegally is not such a great crime. *Family Business* (1989, Tri-Star).

1964 "There was a crime, there was a victim and there is punishment." **Harrison Ford** summarizes in voice-over. *Presumed Innocent* (1990, Warner Bros.).

1965 "Is it not a greater crime to starve a family? Now if you would be so kind to give me a name, sir, before I run you through." **Kevin Costner** rescues young Daniel Newman from Michael Wincott, as Sir Guy of Gisborne, who plans to hang the boy as a thief. *Robin Hood: Prince of Thieves* (1991, Columbia).

Crises

see also CHANGES, DANGER, SICKNESS, TROUBLES

1966 "Here, take my handkerchief. Never at any crisis of your life have I known you to have a handkerchief." **Clark Gable** offers his hankie to sniffing Vivien Leigh as he prepares to leave her for good. *Gone with the Wind* (1939, Selznick-MGM).

1967 MR. POWERS: "What do you think of the current world crisis?" JOHNNY JONES: "What crisis?" New York newspaper publisher **Harry Davenport** discovers that his star crime reporter **Joel McCrea** hasn't kept up with the events that have Europe on the brink of World War II. *Foreign Correspondent* (1940, United Artists).

1968 "You must have faced crises like this at the Stork Club when the waiter brought you the wrong wine." Charter pilot **James Cagney** sarcastically snaps at runaway heiress Bette Davis, who suffers loudly when they are stranded in the desert after crash landing unharmed. *The Bride Came C.O.D.* (1941, Warner Bros.).

1969 "It was Jules' generosity, his innocence, his vulnerability which dazzled me, conquered me. He was so different from other men. By giving him happiness, I hoped to cure him of these crises where he felt out of his depth. But I realized that these crimes are an inseparable part of him." Bohemian **Jeanne Moreau**, as Catherine, speaks lovingly of shy German Jew Oskar Werner. *Jules et Jim* (1962, Fr., Janus).

Criticism *see* ACCUSATIONS, FAULTS, JUDGMENTS

Cross-Examinations

see also JUDGMENTS, JUSTICE, LAWS, LAWYERS, QUESTIONS, QUESTIONS AND ANSWERS

1970 COL. NIKTA I. BIROSHILOV: "Where were you trained?" CPL. JOSEPH ROBERT STANTON: "In the White House where my family lived." BIROSHILOV: "Where does your family live now?" STANTON: "In Hollywood with my brothers Clark Gable and Spencer Tracy, and my sisters Esther Williams and Jane Powell." BIROSHILOV: "What's your father's occupation?" STANTON: "He's a capitalist, a monopolist, and an imperialist warmonger. And every morning he gets up and takes an autographed picture of Joe Stalin and spits it in the eye." Russian colonel **Oscar Homolka** isn't having much success with his interrogation of his American captive POW **Steve Forrest**. *Prisoner of War* (1954, MGM).

1971 DANCER: "Do you know for a fact that Barney Quill dropped the panties down the chute, or did you just assume it?" MARY PILANT: "I assumed it." DANCER: "Had you thought that perhaps someone else put the panties there?" MARY: "I hadn't thought of that." DANCER: "You wanted to crucify the dead Barney Quill, didn't you? Your pride was hurt. You were jealous. Are you Barney Quill's mistress?" MARY: "No, it's not true, Barney Quill was my—" DANCER: "Barney Quill was what, Miss Pilant? Barney Quill was what, Miss Pilant?" MARY: "Barney Quill was my father." Prosecutor **George C. Scott** commits one of the unpardonable sins of trial lawyers as he badgers **Kathryn Grant**, who is giving evidence that hurts his case—he asks a question of a witness that he doesn't know the answer to. *Anatomy of a Murder* (1959, Columbia).

Crowds

see also PEOPLE

1972 "You've got to be good in that town if you want to beat the crowd." A title card carries the ominous warning of a fellow passenger to James Murray who looks on in awe at the Manhattan skyline as the ferry brings him into the city. *The Crowd* (1928, silent, MGM).

1973 "Listen, the crowd—that's the real beast." Former matador **J. Carrol Naish** indicts the bullring crowd after Tyrone Power has been gored to death by a bull. The crowd is already cheering a new hero. *Blood and Sand* (1941, 20th Century-Fox).

1974 CECILY CARDEW: "From the top of one of the hills quite close one can see five counties." GWENDOLEN FAIRFAX: "Five counties! I don't think I should like that; I hate crowds." Country mouse **Dorothy Tutin** and city mouse **Joan Greenwood** are hysterically funny as they have tea together. *The Importance of Being Earnest* (1953, GB, Rank).

1975 "What sort of fruitcake are you?. . . Why do you have to be above the crowd? Why not part of the crowd?" **Jack Lemmon** can't understand slightly daffy New York model Judy Holiday's unquenchable yearning for fame. She rents a huge billboard and puts her name on it. She achieves some of Andy Warhol's 15 minutes of fame. *It Should Happen to You* (1954, Columbia).

Cruelty

see also HUMAN NATURE, HUMANITY, KINDNESS, MERCY, PAINS, PITY, SUFFERING AND SUFFERERS

1976 "Why, he's so mean he'd shut off the air in a baby's incubator, just to watch the little sucker squirm." **Clark Gable** tells Jack Holt about process server Edgar Kennedy who's about to prevent Jeannette MacDonald from making her San Francisco opera debut because she's under exclusive contract to work in Gable's Barbary Coast club. *San Francisco* (1936, MGM).

1977 "You've all suffered from their cruelty—the ear loppings, the beatings, the blindings and hot irons, the burning of our farms and homes, the mistreatment of our women. It's time to put an end to this." **Errol Flynn** recruits suffering peasants to his cause against Prince John and his cruel tax collectors. *The Adventures of Robin Hood* (1938, Warner Bros.).

1978 "Yes, I can be very cruel. You forget aunt, I have been taught by masters." Bitter spinster **Olivia de Havilland**, refers to her father Ralph Richardson and her one time suitor Montgomery Clift, when her aunt, Miriam Hopkins, accuses her of being cruel. *The Heiress* (1949, Paramount).

1979 "Let's have the truth for once. You think you're on the side of the angels. Well, you're not. You haven't a drop of ordinary human forgiveness in your whole nature. You're a cruel, vengeful man. You're everything you always said you hated in your own father." **Eleanor Parker** tells off her cruel and unbending husband, police detective Kirk Douglas. *Detective Story* (1951, Paramount).

1980 "You think I do not know that there are people in Rome who call me a matricide, wife-killer, call me a monster, tyrant? There is something they do not realize. A man's acts may be cruel while he himself is not cruel. And there are moments, my dear Petronius, when—when the music caresses my soul, I feel as gentle as a child in a cradle. Believe me?" **Peter Ustinov** seeks understanding for his troubled soul from Leo Genn. *Quo Vadis* (1951, MGM).

1981 "You are so much like your mother. . . I think you could be cruel. You lie to manipulate others. . . . You work me. . . to brighten your relationship with Peter." Stage director **Erland Josephson** worries that Lena Olin, daughter of his former mistress, Ingrid Thulin, has a physical interest in him. Peter is a young director with whom Olin lives. *After the Rehearsal* (1984, Sweden, Triumph).

1982 VICOMTE DE VALMONT: "I thought betrayal was your favorite word." MARQUISE DE MERTEUIL: "No, cruelty. I always think that has a nobler ring to it." Decadent **John Malkovich** and **Glenn Close** engage in some sexual gamesmanship. *Dangerous Liaisons* (1988, Warner Bros.).

1983 "I believe he must pass away in a rather cruel fashion." Actually **Sally Kirkland** plans to fix Keith Carradine's wagon by marrying him. *Cold Feet* (1989, Avenue Pictures).

1984 LILA WINGO: "Who taught you to be so cruel?" TOM WINGO: "You did mama, you did—but you also taught me that if someone almost ruins your life, you can still feel love for them." LILA: "Am I suppose to take comfort from that?" **Kate Nelligan** and her son **Nick Nolte** continue their long-standing feud. *The Prince of Tides* (1991, Columbia).

1985 "How can you be so mean to someone so meaningless?" Mousy secretary **Michelle Pfeiffer** wails to her boss, arrogant industrialist Christopher Walken, who throws an uncooperative employee out a window. *Batman Returns* (1992, Warner Bros.).

Crusades

see also CAUSES, WARS

1986 "All of my life I've tried to make this country manure-minded." In the grip of porphyria, **Raymond Lovell**, as King George III of England, bellows at title character Robert Donat. *The Young Mr. Pitt* (1941, GB, 20th Century-Fox).

1987 "In the 12th century, at the close of the Third Crusade to free the Holy Land, a Saxon knight called Wilfred of Ivanhoe undertook a private crusade of his own. . . . Richard the Lionhearted's disappearance had dealt a cruel blow to his unhappy country already in turmoil from the bitter conflict between Saxon and Norman." It's the opening narration of Sir Walter Scott's story of derring-do of medieval British knights. *Ivanhoe* (1952, MGM).

1988 "I guess I don't make a very good Joan of Arc." Unsuccessful do-gooder **Judy Davis** admits failure. *Heatwave* (1982, Australia, M and L Enterprises).

Crying and Cries

see also DESPAIR AND DESPERATION, EYES, HAPPINESS AND UNHAPPINESS, HELP AND HELPING, NEEDS AND NECESSITIES, PAINS, PLEAS AND PLEADING, SENTIMENTS AND SENTIMENTALITY, SORROWS, SOUNDS

1989 "Wait a minute, darling, you ain't gonna cry on your wedding day?" Just when con girl Jean Harlow thinks she's lost hustler **Clark Gable** for good, he proposes marriage. *Hold Your Man* (1933, MGM).

1990 "Say, you should weep—it's the first job you've had in a year." Wisecracking **Eve Arden** comforts crying Lucille Ball, who is leaving the hotel for aspiring actresses to get married. *Stage Door* (1937, RKO).

1991 "Don't cry, darling. The war'll be over in a few weeks, and I'll be coming back to you." **Rand Brooks** misinterprets the tears of his new bride Vivien Leigh as he leaves to join the Confederate troops. *Gone with the Wind* (1939, Selznick-MGM).

1992 "Don't cry. She mustn't see you've been crying." **Vivien Leigh** tells Leslie Howard to put on a brave front for dying Olivia de Havilland. *Gone with the Wind* (1939, Selznick-MGM).

1993 "What do you want me to do about it—bust out crying?" Political boss **Brian Donlevy** sheds no tears when his henchman Alan Ladd informs him that the guy who's been seeing Donlevy's sister against his wishes has just been murdered. *The Glass Key* (1942, Paramount).

1994 "Oh, fine! Here we go. The old juice. Never fails, does it? Guaranteed heart-melter. A few female tears. Stronger than the strongest acid. Well, not this time. You can cry from now until the jury comes in—it won't make you right and it won't make your silly case." **Spencer Tracy** resists the tears of opposing attorney Katharine Hepburn because he believes this time there is no doubt he's right. *Adam's Rib* (1949, MGM).

1995 "Dan Reynolds, I told you one of these days you'd make me cry." At the end of the movie, **Joan Crawford**'s tears for her husband David Brian are ones of joy. *Flamingo Road* (1949, Warner Bros.).

1996 "Cry tomorrow. You'll have the whole day to cry tomorrow." Stage mother **Jo Van Fleet** snaps when her daughter Carole Ann Campbell, portraying a young Lillian Roth, starts to cry because her mother is driving her into a stage career. *I'll Cry Tomorrow* (1955, MGM).

1997 "Whenever someone else is crying, I gotta cry too. I'm sympathetic. I've got too much heart." Truckdriver **Burt Lancaster** tells Sicilian widow Anna Magnani what a softy he is. *The Rose Tattoo* (1955, Paramount).

1998 "Don't cry about tomorrow. Wait until it's yesterday." Unfeeling, impolite and obstinate businessman **James Cagney** pontificates. *These Wilder Years* (1956, MGM).

1999 "A woman's tears are meant for women. Don't criticize a woman's tears—they're holy." **Gunnar Sjoberg** defends his crying wife Gunnel Brostrom to Ingrid Thulin. *Wild Strawberries* (1957, Sweden, Svensk Filmindustri).

2000 "What are you crying about, Anna? Don't cry, Anna. I love you. Everything will be all right. You'll like being married. You will. You'll see." **Cary Grant** comforts Ingrid Bergman with a marriage proposal. *Indiscreet* (1958, Warner Bros.).

2001 "Cry? I never knew a woman that size had so much water in her." **Tony Randall** reports to Rock Hudson on the crying of Doris Day. *Pillow Talk* (1959, Universal).

2002 "Darling, you're crying. I believe you're really sentimental after all." **Heather Sears** misinterprets her new husband Laurence Harvey's tears as they leave their wedding. He's thinking of his dead mistress Simone Signoret. *Room at the Top* (1959, GB, Remus-British Lion).

2003 "My heart is not made of granite, Madam, but I am thrifty with my tears." Retired General **Peter Sellers** addresses his complaining wife Margaret Leighton who spends most of her life in bed, complaining of one illness or another. *The Waltz of the Toreadors* (1962, GB, Rank).

2004 "I didn't cry then or ever about Finny. I didn't even cry when he was being lowered into the burial ground outside of Boston. I couldn't escape the feeling that it was my own funeral, and you don't cry in that case." In 1942, **Parker Stevenson** speaks of his prep school roommate John Heyl who dies during an operation on his leg, injured in an accident caused by Stevenson. *A Separate Peace* (1972, Paramount).

2005 "I just want to cry, I don't know what I'm supposed to be." Ex-con, former junkie, and small-time hood **Michael Moriarty** tries to hit the big time using his knowledge of the whereabouts of an ancient Aztec god, a winged serpent, known as Quetzalcoatl. *Q* aka *The Winged Serpent* (1982, United Film Distribution).

2006 "Terry, I know that you're in a world where men don't cry. But you've been crying all of your life." **Kim Cattrall** speaks to fireman Robert Urich who has been denied his pension because he was off duty and drunk when he rescued a little girl from a burning building and became disabled in the process. *Turk 182!* (1985, 20th Century-Fox).

2007 "I've been crying a lot lately. . . making up for all these years I didn't." **Isabella Rossellini** speaks to her frequently unfaithful husband William Petersen. *Cousins* (1989, Paramount).

2008 "Cry all you want, you'll pee less." Crude **Mary Wickes** advises her actress daughter and granddaughter, Shirley MacLaine and Meryl Streep, in MacLaine's hospital room. *Postcards from the Edge* (1990, Columbia).

2009 "I was already crying when it happened." After a thug smashes her car window while she's stopped at a light, **Mary-Louise Parker** explains to a handsome young police officer that her tears preceded the assault. Parker is heartbroken that her one-time married lover Kevin Kline has ended the affair. *Grand Canyon* (1991, 20th Century-Fox).

2010 "There is no crying in baseball." Over-the-hill former major league baseball player **Tom Hanks** is now the manager of a woman's professional baseball team. Many of Hanks' players have problems with which he is ill-equipped to cope. One member of the team has a particularly difficult time handling criticism—she cries. *A League of Their Own* (1992, Columbia).

Cultures *see* CIVILIZATIONS, IDEAS, KNOWLEDGE, SOCIETIES

Cures

see also DOCTORS AND DENTISTS, HABITS, HEALTH, INSANITY AND SANITY, MEDICINE, PSYCHOLOGY AND PSYCHIATRY, SICKNESS, TREATS AND TREATMENTS

2011 "I've just been to Bath to be cured of the fatigue. And now I'm so fatigued by the cure that I really think I shall have to go back to Bath to be cured of the fatigue." **Leslie Howard**, who is secretly the Scarlet Pimpernel, poses as an effeminate, foppish, useless aristocrat to throw off his French enemies. *The Scarlet Pimpernel* (1934, GB, London Films).

2012 "The past for her is quite, quite over. Her mind is clear and the clouds have been swept away, and she is no longer afraid. She will want to be with the one she loves. . . or the one she has been happiest with. . . or the one she trusts." Psychiatrist **Herbert Lom** pronounces Ann Todd is cured and is a new woman. James Mason is surprised to discover that he is all three of the men that Lom describes. *The Seventh Veil* (1945, GB, Theatrecraft-Box-Ortus).

2013 "A year in group therapy could cure your need to be a human being." **Michael Sarrazin** speaks to rejected girlfriend Jennifer Leak. *Eye of the Cat* (1969, Universal).

2014 "I'll heal the rash on his body. I'll erase the welts cut into his mind by flying manes. And when that's done, I'll set him on a metal scooter and send him puttering off onto the concrete world, and he'll never touch hide again. Hopefully, he'll feel nothing at his fork but approved flesh. I doubt, however, with much passion. Passion, you see, can be destroyed by a doctor. It cannot be created. You won't gallop anymore, Alan. Horses will be quite safe. . . . You will, however, be without pain, almost completely without pain, but not for me, it never stops, the voice of Equus, out of the cave. Why me?" Psychiatrist **Richard Burton** promises magistrate Eileen Atkins to cure Peter Firth who has blinded horses, but regrets being the one to prepare the youngster to lead a "normal" life. *Equus* (1977, United Artists).

2015 "If ever I'm happy, I go to Lourdes to get cured." Despondent **Romy Schneider** prefers it that way. *Clair de Femme* (1980, Fr., Atlantic).

Curiosity

see also DESIRES, INFORMATION AND INFORMERS, INTERESTS, KNOWLEDGE, LEARNING AND LESSONS, STUDIES AND STUDENTS, TRUTH

2016 "George, don't you ever want to know what's on the other side of the mountain?" Man-for-all-seasons **Ronald Colman** questions his uncurious brother John Howard. *Lost Horizon* (1937, Columbia).

2017 "A detective without curiosity like a glass eye at keyhole." **Sidney Toler** as the title character delivers another of his famous aphorisms. *Charlie Chan in the Secret Service* (1944, Monogram).

2018 SLADE: "You followed me." KITTY: "Do you expect to be followed?" SLADE: "No, but I know I arouse curiosity." **Laird Cregar** discovers that actress **Merle Oberon** has followed him to his alleged place of work, being curious about him because he refused to watch her perform, saying he disapproves of theaters. *The Lodger* (1944, 20th Century-Fox).

2019 "You're going to make every guy you meet a little curious." **Robert Mitchum** quips when Jane Greer claims he's a curious man. *Out of the Past* (1947, RKO).

2020 "I have no curiosity about the working classes." Stern and forceful matriarch **Gladys Cooper** dismisses a source of conversation with her dining companion peeress **Cathleen Nesbitt**. *Separate Tables* (1958, United Artists).

2021 "All three of you? Just out of curiosity, was it the same guy?" Unaware that the three "lookers" that show up at his ghetto clinic are nuns, dressed in civies, Doctor **Elvis Presley** assumes that they are Park Avenue girls who have come downtown for abortions. *Change of Habit* (1969, Universal).

2022 BART: "If it feels good, do it." ZACK: "I'm not gay, just curious." Unlike novelist **Harry Hamlin**, with whom he has an affair, Doctor **Michael Ontkean** can't admit to being a homosexual. *Making Love* (1982, 20th Century-Fox).

2023 "I assume you're watching these because you're curious about sex—or filmmaking." **Dianne Wiest** has just discovered pornographic videocassettes in her son Leaf Phoenix's room. *Parenthood* (1989, Universal).

Curses

see also BLASPHEMY, DANGER, EVILNESS, LANGUAGES, OATHS, PLEDGES, PROFANITY, PROMISES, THREATS, WARNINGS

2024 "I've been cursed for delving into the mysteries of life!" Scientist **Colin Clive**, as Dr. Frankenstein, makes a most unscientific statement. *The Bride of Frankenstein* (1935, Universal).

2025 "You dog! You dirty yellow dog, you! You ain't no son of mine!" **Marjorie Main** disowns her criminal son Humphrey Bogart. *Dead End* (1937, Goldwyn-United Artists).

2026 "There isn't anything I won't do to get you to free me of the curse of the Dracula. I am Dracula's daughter." In an excellent horror film, now all but forgotten, marvelous **Gloria Holden** begs for help from psychiatrist Otto Kruger. *Dracula's Daughter* (1938, Universal).

2027 "I wonder, Diz, if that Don Quixote hasn't got the jump on us. I wonder if it isn't a curse to go through life wised up like you and me." Cynical **Jean Arthur** muses to Washington beat reporter Thomas Mitchell about idealistic new U.S. Senator James Stewart. *Mr. Smith Goes to Washington* (1939, Columbia).

2028 "Who shall defile the temples of the ancient gods, a cruel and violent death shall be his fate, and never shall his soul rest until eternity. Such is the curse of Amon-Ra, king of all the gods." High Priest of Karnach **Eduardo Ciannelli** repeats the curse which will be carried out by Tom Tyler as Kharis the mummy. *The Mummy's Hand* (1940, Universal).

2029 "I hope you die. I hope you die soon. I'll be waiting for you to die." Ruthless, scheming **Bette Davis** shouts at her dying husband Herbert Marshall. *The Little Foxes* (1941, RKO).

2030 "I had become a reverse zombie. The world was dead and I was living." Vaudeville mentalist **Edward G. Robinson** claims he has been cursed with the gift of predicting future tragic events, most notably, deaths. *Night Has a Thousand Eyes* (1948, Paramount).

2031 "To the last I grapple with thee! From hell's heart I stab at thee! For hate's sake I spit my last breath at thee!" Captain Ahab, portrayed by **Gregory Peck**, is entangled in the many harpoon ropes covering the body of the great white whale, as they both prepare to go to their maker. *Moby Dick* (1956, Warner Bros.).

2032 "It's I who renounce you. In the name of Satan, I place a curse upon you. . . my revenge will strike down you and your accursed house. . . I shall return to torment you and to destroy throughout the nights of time." **Barbara Steele**, as the high priestess of a satanic cult, curses her brother, Enrico Olivieri, the Grand Inquisitor, who has her burned at the stake after fitting a horrible spiked mask onto her beautiful face. *Black Sunday* (1960, Ital., AIP).

2033 "As surely as the village of Arkham has risen up against me, so surely will I rise up against the village of Arkham." It's warlock **Vincent Price**'s curse as he is burnt at the stake in 1765. *The Haunted Palace* (1963, AIP).

2034 "You bastards! You finally did it! You blew it up! Damn you all to hell!" Astronaut **Charlton Heston** finally realizes that the strange planet ruled by apes upon which he has crashed is post-nuclear war Earth. *Planet of the Apes* (1968, 20th Century-Fox).

2035 "You know where you can bury your hatchet?. . . Now get your bony ass out of my sight." Angry **Melanie Griffith** is in no mood to make up with Sigourney Weaver. *Working Girl* (1988, 20th Century-Fox).

2036 "I hope your face ends up on a milk carton." It's a tasteless wish of **Thomas Brown** for his little brother Jared Rushton. *Honey, I Shrunk the Kids* (1989, Buena Vista).

Custom *see* BEHAVIOR, FASHIONS, HABITS, RULES

Customers

see also BUSINESS AND COMMERCE, BUYING AND SELLING, SALESMEN

2037 EFFIE PERINE: "There's a girl wants to see you. Her name is Wonderly." SAM SPADE: "A customer?" EFFIE: "I guess so. You'll want to see her anyway. She's a knockout." Secretary **Lee Patrick** knows what'll interest her boss, private eye **Humphrey Bogart**. *The Maltese Falcon* (1941, Warner Bros.).

2038 "The war's over. The world's going to be one big corporation—no more enemies, just customers." At the end of World War II, Army Major **Robin Clarke** displays a great deal of political and economic savvy. *The Formula* (1980, MGM).

2039 HARRIET: "Do you like working at a book store?" WILLIAM: "I love it, I love it." HARRIET: "What do you love?" WILLIAM: "All their shapes and sizes." HARRIET: "Of what?" WILLIAM: "The customers." Bookstore clerks **Harriet Walter** and **Ben Kingsley** discuss their job. *Turtle Diary* (1986, GB, Goldwyn).

Cuteness

see also ATTRACTIONS, BEAUTY, GLAMOUR

2040 "You talk too much but you're a cute little trick at that." Rubber plantation overseer **Clark Gable** finds something to like about stranded prostitute Jean Harlow. *Red Dust* (1932, MGM).

2041 "Whaddaya do that for? Something kind of cute was about to happen." **Jean Harlow** objects to be awakened at 6 a.m. from an erotic dream. *Red Dust* (1932, MGM).

2042 "You look cute, sort of boyish." **Edward Judd** makes the compliment to Janet Munro, still wet from her bath. *The Day the Earth Caught Fire* (1962, GB, Universal).

Cynicism

see also BELIEFS, GOODNESS, PHILOSOPHIES, SELF, SELFISHNESS, VIRTUES

2043 "Cynicism is an unpleasant way of telling the truth." Greedy businessman **Charles Dingle** understands his devious sister Bette Davis' use of cynicism. *The Little Foxes* (1941, RKO).

2044 "You can't go back and start again. The older you get, the worse things get." Cynical psychiatrist's secretary **Joan Bennett** discovers her boss Paul Henreid is a phony—Henreid has killed her look-alike boss and has taken his place. *Hollow Triumph* aka: *The Scar* (1948, Eagle Lion).

2045 "Let the snakes bite us, flies sting us, wild animals eat us, heathens butcher us, the wine poison us, the women give us lice, the lice devour us, the fever rot us, all for the glory of God." Cynical squire Jons, played by **Gunnar Bjornstrand**, speaks of those who participated in the Crusades. *The Seventh Seal* (1956, Sweden, Svensk Filmindustri).

Dancing and Dancers

see also ACTING AND ACTORS, ART AND ARTISTS, ENTERTAINMENTS AND ENTERTAINERS, MUSIC AND MUSICIANS, PERFORMANCES, SHOWS, SONGS AND SINGING, THEATERS

2046 "Women! Dancing! Where's it get you? I figure on making other people dance. . . . Dancin' ain't my idea of a man's game." Mobster **Edward G. Robinson** is disgusted with his buddy Douglas Fairbanks, Jr., who has given up the rackets to become Glenda Farrell's dancing partner. *Little Caesar* (1931, Warner Bros.).

2047 "When they hold the stupid asses' dance, you won't be in the orchestra." **Raimu** knows his absentminded son Pierre Fresnay. *Marius* (1931, Fr., Pagnol-Paramount).

2048 "I could dance with you till the cows come home. On second thought I'll dance with the cows and you come home." **Groucho Marx**, the incompetent president of Freedonia, badgers his country's richest citizen, Margaret Dumont. *Duck Soup* (1933, Paramount).

2049 "I'd like to try this just once—come on." **Fred Astaire**, hearing the strains of "The Carioca," leads Ginger Rogers out onto the dance floor for the first time and movie history is made. *Flying Down to Rio* (1933, RKO).

2050 "You don't have to have feet to be a dancer." No doubt some of **Mae West**'s best dancing was done when she was off her feet. *I'm No Angel* (1933, Paramount).

2051 "My soul has always yearned to express itself in the dance." Fortunately, **Edward Everett Horton** leaves the dancing to Fred Astaire and Ginger Rogers. *The Gay Divorcée* (1934, RKO).

2052 "Hey, I'm as liable to dance with those bunch of sticks as I am to buy a bucket of rusty tacks and eat 'em." Uncouth **Frank Albertson** embarrasses his sister Katharine Hepburn at a society dance. *Alice Adams* (1935, RKO).

2053 "You'd make your crippled grandmother do a fan dance." **Jean Harlow** accuses her fiancé, conniving newspaper editor Spencer Tracy, of having no ethics, morality or feelings. *Libeled Lady* (1936, MGM).

2054 "All the world loves a dancer, don't you?" Dancer and gambler **Fred Astaire** has a yen for Ginger Rogers. *Swing Time* (1936, RKO).

2055 "I've danced with you. I'm never going to dance again." Fortunately it was only **Fred Astaire**'s character who made this promise to Ginger Rogers. *Swing Time* (1936, RKO).

2056 "Tonight, I wouldn't mind dancing with Abe Lincoln himself." Young Southern widow **Vivien Leigh** is happy after Clark Gable bids for her to lead the opening reel at an Atlanta Bazaar. *Gone with the Wind* (1939, Selznick-MGM).

2057 "I think when people dance well together, it's because they're sympathetic to each other." If so, then **Fred Astaire** and Ginger Rogers are certainly simpatico. *The Story of Vernon and Irene Castle* (1939, RKO).

2058 Sir William Lucas: "Dancing is a charming amusement for young people. In my opinion, ah— it's one of the first refinements of a polished society." Mr. Darcy: "It has the added advantage, sir, of being one of the first refinements of savages. Every Hottentot can dance." Despite **E.E. Clive**'s encouragement, **Laurence Olivier** considers dancing a waste of time. *Pride and Prejudice* (1940, MGM).

2059 "Listen, sister, I don't dance and I can't take time to learn. All I want to do is get out of here." PT boat Commander **John Wayne** rebuffs nurse Donna Reed when she asks him to attend a dance when the casualty rate of World War II briefly ebbs. *They Were Expendable* (1945, MGM).

2060 "I'm all warmed up and ready to take off. . . I fly on high octane." Librarian **Greer Garson** puts on an act on a dance floor with a sailor for Clark Gable's benefit. *Adventure* (1946, MGM).

2061 "I'm not dancing. I'm trying to get my foot out of a champagne bucket." **Groucho Marx** corrects vamp Lisette Verea. *A Night in Casablanca* (1946, United Artists).

2062 "I believe this is our dance, Mother." **John Lund** approaches Olivia de Havilland whom he has just discovered is his natural mother. She was forced to put him up for adoption shortly after his birth because she was not married to his father who was killed in World War I. *To Each His Own* (1946, Paramount).

2063 Capt. John Pringle: "I guess this is where the funny man says, 'Shall we dance?'" Phoebe Frost: "You are not a funny man, Captain Pringle, but you are quite a dancer. What a waltz we had! Good night." **John Lund** tries to make light of it, when **Jean Arthur** finds him with Marlene Dietrich, but she's not in the mood for levity. *A Foreign Affair* (1948, Paramount).

2064 "I don't even like to walk." **James Cagney**, who throughout the movie never moves from his seat at a table in front of the bar, declines when he's asked to dance. *The Time of Your Life* (1948, United Artists).

2065 Morris Townsend: "We must make an arrangement, Miss Sloper. I will not kick you, if you do not kick me." Catherine Sloper: "Oh, dear. . . I am so clumsy. . . ." Morris: "No, Miss Sloper, it's only that I am wearing Arthur's boots, and he's a very bad dancer." Smooth **Montgomery Clift** makes shy, repressed **Olivia de Havilland** feel less a clod on the dance floor by making a little joke. *The Heiress* (1949, Paramount).

2066 "Oh, I can tell a lot about a man by dancing with him. You know, some boys—well, when they take a girl in their arms to dance, they— well, they make her feel sort of uncomfortable. But, with you, I,—I had the feeling you knew exactly what you were doing, and I could follow you every step of the way." **Kim Novak** compliments William Holden after their "Moonglow" dance. Holden didn't feel comfortable having to dance in the film, but he was proficient enough to make it one hell of a sexy scene. *Picnic* (1955, Columbia).

2067 "Happiness is the reward of industry and labor. Dancing is a waste of time." Special Soviet emissary **Cyd Charisse** toes to the party line, but fortunately it doesn't prevent her from later showing her great legs and dancing skills alone and with Fred Astaire. *Silk Stockings* (1957, MGM).

2068 "That fat man moves like a dancer." Pool hustler **Paul Newman**, as "Fast Eddie" Felson, admires the grace of his opponent, Jackie Gleason, the legendary pool player Minnesota Fats. *The Hustler* (1961, 20th Century-Fox).

2069 "When my little boy, Dimitri, died, everybody was crying. Me? I got up and danced. They said, 'Zorba is mad.' But it was the dancing—only the dancing—that stopped the pain. You see, he was my first. He was only three. When I'm happy, it's the same thing." **Anthony Quinn** advises Alan Bates that dancing is good therapy as well as an expression of joy. *Zorba the Greek* (1964, 20th Century-Fox).

2070 "I dance like the wind." Tipsy **Sandy Dennis** does a bit of bragging. *Who's Afraid of Virginia Woolf?* (1966, Warner Bros.).

2071 "I danced in my mother's womb." **Vanessa Redgrave** portrays celebrated dancer Isadora Duncan. *Isadora* aka: *The Loves of Isadora* (1968, GB, Universal).

2072 "To dance is to live." Title character **Vanessa Redgrave** lives life to the fullest and dances until she dies. *Isadora* (1968, GB, Universal).

2073 "Not many people knew it, but the Führer was a terrific dancer." Unreconstructed Nazi **Kenneth Mars** has written a play called "Springtime for Hitler: A Gay Romp with Adolph and Eva at Berchtesgaden." *The Producers* (1968, MGM).

2074 "The dance of destiny continues. . . ." Marathon dance contest M.C. **Gig Young** closes the picture. *They Shoot Horses, Don't They?* (1969, Palomar-ABC-Cinerama).

2075 "You make it with some of these chicks, they think you gotta dance with them." **John Travolta** gives an interesting twist on an old dating cliché. To him, fornicating and dancing are not related. *Saturday Night Fever* (1977, Paramount).

2076 "The high I get at 2001, just dancing, not just being the best. . . I wanna get, have, that high someplace else in my life, ya know what I mean?" Dancing is the only thing that gives meaning to the life of Brooklyn working class youth **John Travolta.** He feels the need of something more. *Saturday Night Fever* (1977, Paramount).

2077 "We can only dance together—but nothing more, nothing personal, no coming on to me—'Cause I don't dig guys like you no more. You're too young, you haven't any class. I'm tired of jerk-off guys who haven't got their shit together." **Karen Lynn Gorney**'s message to working-class stiff John Travolta is clear—he sure as hell can dance, but he can't do much of anything else. *Saturday Night Fever* (1977, Paramount).

2078 "I never see them. You go out there and the music starts and you begin to feel it and your body just starts to move. Something inside you just clicks. You take off and you're gone. It's like you're somebody else for a second. I just can't wait to get out there so I can disappear." **Jennifer Beals** claims that she is unfazed and almost unaware of customers ogling her exotic dancing. (Stand-in Marine Jahan did most of the dancing.) *Flashdance* (1983, Paramount).

2079 "How could anyone want to be anything but a dancer?" It's the view of Puerto Rican chorus boy **Yamil Borges.** *A Chorus Line* (1985, Columbia).

2080 "We are phantoms. We arise from the darkness and disappear again." **Marcello Mastroianni** and his long-time ballroom dancing partner Giulietta Masina briefly come out of retirement to appear on a television variety show. *Ginger and Fred* (1986, Italy, MGM-United Artists).

2081 "Can you imagine dancing like that on the main floor—home of the family fox trot? Max would close the place down first." **Cynthia Rhodes** asks Jennifer Grey what she thinks resort owner Jack Weston would think of the "dirty" dancing that the young staff enjoys after hours. *Dirty Dancing* (1987, Vestron).

2082 "Go-go is an art form; it's interpretive dance with a rock 'n' roll background." **Christina Whitaker**, the star dancer of a sleazy nightclub, is proud of her specialty. *Assault of the Killer Bimbos* (1988, Titan-Empire).

2083 "Larry Kozinski, I would love to dance with you." By accepting Ted Danson's invitation to dance, **Isabella Rossellini** ends her marriage to unfaithful William Petersen. *Cousins* (1989, Paramount).

2084 "How he loves to dance. He waltzes in and takes all my drugs, then tangos out again." Mobster **Jack Palance** sneers as he speaks of cop Sylvester Stallone. *Tango and Cash* (1989, Warner Bros.).

2085 "I promised Mom once we would dance." With the last line of the film, **Mary Elizabeth Mastrantonio** leads her father Gene Hackman onto the dance floor. *Class Action* (1991, 20th Century-Fox).

2086 "It's easy. Just grab me and squeeze." **Robin Givens** encourages Forest Whitaker to dance with her. *A Rage in Harlem* (1991, Miramax).

Danger

see also ADVENTURES, COURAGE, EXCITEMENTS, SAFETY, SECURITY AND INSECURITY, THREATS

2087 "You're considered too dangerous for local consumption." **Nancy Carroll** tempts fate by speaking to small-town rake Cary Grant. *Hot Saturday* (1932, Paramount).

2088 "Think of it, Algy! Alone, unarmed, surrounded by villains, locked in a cellar—from that, to complete mastery of the situation in ten minutes. If we can do that, we'll be magnificent." Title character **Ronald Colman** likens danger to little more than a chess problem to his assistant Charles Butterworth. *Bulldog Drummond Strikes Back* (1934, United Artists).

2089 "The most dangerous woman you'll ever meet. . . ." It's how **Lionel Atwill**, who should know, describes Marlene Dietrich for young Cesar Romero. *The Devil Is a Woman* (1935, Paramount).

2090 "It was careless of you to have a man like that in this house!. . . the world has changed, Mama, and some of the people are dangerous. It's time you knew that." **Bette Davis** berates her widowed mother Lucile Watson for taking Nazi collaborator George Coulouris into her Washington, D.C. home. *Watch on the Rhine* (1943, Warner Bros.).

2091 "I knew I had hold of a red-hot poker, and the time to drop it was before I burned my hand off." The poker is Barbara Stanwyck and a plot to murder her husband for insurance money. Unfortunately for all concerned, insurance salesman **Fred MacMurray** doesn't let go. *Double Indemnity* (1944, Paramount).

2092 "I wondered if he'd say, 'I met such a nice woman in the Kardomah: we had lunch and went to the pictures.' Then suddenly I knew he wouldn't. I knew beyond a shadow of a doubt that he wouldn't say a single word—and at that moment the first awful feeling of danger swept over me." Housewife **Celia Johnson** admits to herself that her innocent friendship with Doctor Trevor Howard has ceased to be innocent. *Brief Encounter* (1945, GB, Eagle-Lion).

2093 "You know what you're letting yourself in for? It ain't pretty. And it could be dangerous." Heroin addict **Frank Sinatra** warns Kim Novak of the risk she'll be taking in helping him kick his habit "cold turkey." *The Man with the Golden Arm* (1955, United Artists).

2094 "Look, you fools. You're in danger. Can't you see? They're after you. They're after all of us. Our wives, our children, everyone. . . . You're next!" **Kevin McCarthy** desperately tries to warn others, including the audience when he points directly into the camera near the end of the film. It's not just alien body snatchers that he's warning about in the communist witch-hunt days. *Invasion of the Body Snatchers* (1956, Allied Artists).

2095 SUGAR: "Water polo—isn't that terribly dangerous?" JUNIOR: "I'll say. I had two horses drown under me." **Marilyn Monroe** is dumb—but can she be as dumb as **Tony Curtis**, posing as a millionaire, takes her for? *Some Like It Hot* (1959, United Artists).

2096 "I don't know who's to be congratulated—kings, queens, knights, everywhere you look, and I'm the only pawn. I haven't a thing to lose. That makes me dangerous." **Jane Merrow**, content to be King Peter O'Toole's mistress, is disturbed that Henry II still plans to marry her to the one of his three sons whom he chooses to succeed him on the throne of England. *The Lion in Winter* (1968, GB, Embassy).

2097 "Danger really turns me on. Do you know how many babies were born during the blitz?" Sexually aware teenager **Joan Delaney** comes on to Ted Bessell, the bumbling son of the American ambassador to Vulgaria, a fictional country behind the Iron Curtain. American Joan Delaney and her parents have been granted asylum at the American embassy with the assistance of Bessell. *Don't Drink the Water* (1969, Avco Embassy).

2098 "I've been dangerous since I was 14. By the time they lost my records, I'd killed eight guys at least. . . . You're a pretty tough kid, but you ain't dangerous." Black inmate **Melvin Stewart** straightens out Donald Sutherland, who is serving a term for larceny, as to who is dangerous and who is not. *Steelyard Blues* (1973, Warner Bros.).

2099 DORIS THE DOMINATRIX: "You have been wicked and you're in terrible danger." RAOUL: "So is everyone who eats here." **Susan Saiger**, disguised as a blind nun with second sight, warns **Robert Beltran** while he eats in a dingy, dirty Mexican beanery. *Eating Raoul* (1982, Bartel).

2100 "What I like about you is that you don't look dangerous, even though you are." **Kelly Preston** is won over by the funny tricks of sex-obsessed teen Doug McKeon. *Mischief* (1985, 20th Century-Fox).

2101 "I know you're a brave girl, but danger is my trade." **Arnold Schwarzenegger**, as Conan, tells title character Brigitte Nielsen that maiming and killing and taking revenge is man's work. *Red Sonja* (1985, MGM-United Artists).

2102 "I think that with your I.Q., you're unarmed and still extremely dangerous." Police detective **Sylvester Stallone**, the smart one, insults his dumber partner Kurt Russell. *Tango and Cash* (1989, Warner Bros.).

2103 "You know, now that you're so respectable, Michael, you're more dangerous than you ever were. I think I preferred you when you were just a common Mafia hood." **Diane Keaton** says the M-word to her ex-husband Al Pacino. *The Godfather, Part III* (1991, Paramount).

Dares and Daring

see also BRAVERY, CHALLENGES, COURAGE, OPPO-SITENESS

2104 "How dare he make love to me when he isn't a married man." Actress **Ingrid Bergman** is indignant when she discovers that her lover, American diplomat Cary Grant, isn't married as he claimed to be. *Indiscreet* (1958, Grandon-Warner Bros.).

2105 "You dare to dicker with your pontiff." **Rex Harrison**, as Pope Julius II, is outraged with the attitude of Charlton Heston as Michelangelo. *The Agony and the Ecstasy* (1965, 20th Century-Fox).

2106 "Go ahead. Make my day." "Dirty Harry" **Clint Eastwood** urges an armed punk to make him shoot him. *Sudden Impact* (1983, Warner Bros.).

2107 "How dare you say penis to a dead person." The spirit of wealthy deceased **Lily Tomlin** lectures her lawyer, Steve Martin, whose body she is sharing. *All of Me* (1984, Universal).

Darkness

see also COLORS, LIGHTS, NIGHTS

2108 "Turn off the lights, Doyle, I can work better in the dark." Retired safecracker **William Haines**, reveals his identity to detective Lionel Barrymore when he is forced to break into a safe to rescue a child locked inside. *Alias Jimmy Valentine* (1928, MGM).

2109 "It's getting darker by the minute. Funny, I can still feel the sun on my hands." **Betty Davis** experiences the blindness that is a signal that her end is near. *Dark Victory* (1939, Warner Bros.).

2110 "I like the dark. The dark is comforting to me." Part of the reason that **Vivien Leigh**, on the brink of madness, prefers darkness, is that it hides the ravages of time on her face. *A Streetcar Named Desire* (1951, Warner Bros.).

2111 "The dark has a life of its own. In the dark, all sorts of things come alive." Hollywood producer **Kirk Douglas** invents a money-saving technique (first used by Val Lewton) of never actually showing the monsters in the movie he's making, merely suggesting their presence. *The Bad and the Beautiful* (1952, MGM).

2112 "It is early Monday morning and I'm in pain. My sisters and Anna are taking turns to sit up. Kind of them. I needn't feel so alone with the darkness." Dying of cancer, **Harriet Andersson** writes in her diary as she struggles to get through another night of agony. *Cries and Whispers* (1972, Sweden, New World).

2113 "I show him mine, he don't show me his. Come on, Rapunzel. From now on we do it in the dark." **Don Calfa** has put on some wild sex scenes with an assortment of beautiful women for the benefit of neighbor Dudley Moore, who watches the action through a telescope. Calfa is put out that Julie Andrews draws the curtains before going to bed with Moore. *'10'* (1979, Warner Bros.).

2114 "There's a darkness inside all of us. Some act it out. Some try to control it. Most of us walk a tightrope between the two." While investigating a series of sex-related murders, New Orleans cop **Clint Eastwood** discovers his own impulses aren't quite "normal." *Tightrope* (1984, Warner Bros.).

2115 BRUCE WAYNE: "You've got a kind of dark side, don't you?" SELINA KYLE: "No darker than yours, I suppose." **Michael Keaton** and **Michelle Pfeiffer** don't really know each other's secret identities—but they are suspicious. *Batman Returns* (1992, Warner Bros.).

Dates and Dating

see also AGE AND AGING, BOYS, FRIENDSHIPS AND FRIENDS, GIRLS, LOVE AND LOVERS, MEN AND WOMEN, SEASONS, SEX AND SEXUALITY, TIME

2116 "Sorry, Angel, I have a pressing date with a fat man." Private eye **Humphrey Bogart** reluctantly leaves looker Mary Astor to meet with obese Sydney Greenstreet. *The Maltese Falcon* (1941, Warner Bros.).

2117 "Well, maybe I'll still be able to keep that date with a bottle of wine, and a good-looking redhead." During the Civil War era, cowboy **Glenn Ford** lusts after Reb spy Rhonda Fleming. *The Redhead and the Cowboy* (1950, Paramount).

2118 "Comes New Year's Eve, everybody starts arranging parties. I'm the guy they got to dig up a date for." **Ernest Borgnine** despises his life because he can't interest any girl. *Marty* (1955, United Artists).

2119 "Don't tell me you never rode in a hot rod or had a late date in the balcony." Dressed in a semi-obscene outfit, cheap-looking **Mamie Van Doren** defends teenage behavior to uptight high school teacher Jan Sterling. *High School Confidential* (1958, MGM).

2120 "Let's spend one night talking to someone with higher voices than us." Divorced **Walter Matthau** suggests that he and his divorced room-mate Jack Lemmon date some girls. *The Odd Couple* (1968, Paramount).

2121 "If you got a date with him, you're gonna need a shovel." **Stuart Whitman** not-so-gently informs Elke Sommer that a Middle East leader she's seeking is dead. *The Invincible Six* aka: *The Heroes* (1970, U.S.-Iran, Moulin Rouge-Continental).

2122 "Pimps don't get you dates, cookie; they just take your money." Part-time prostitute **Jane Fonda** tells Donald Sutherland she doesn't have a pimp. *Klute* (1970, Warner Bros.).

2123 "Don't you think it was a little strange, he was married and he still couldn't get a date for New Year's Eve." **Diane Keaton** questions husband Tony Roberts about their friend Woody Allen whose wife Susan Anspach has left him. *Play It Again, Sam* (1972, Paramount).

2124 ALLAN FELIX: "What are you doing Saturday night?" DISCOTHEQUE GIRL: "Committing suicide." FELIX: "What about Friday night?" That ought to give some idea of how tough it is for **Woody Allen** to get a date as he strikes out with **Suzanne Zenor**. *Play It Again, Sam* (1972, Paramount).

2125 "I never dated Carlo. I married him. I never dated him." **Beatrice Arthur** corrects Lucille Ball about one of her husbands. *Mame* (1974, Warner Bros.).

2126 "I'm dating a girl who does homework!" **Woody Allen**'s current girlfriend is mature 17-year-old high school student Mariel Hemingway. *Manhattan* (1979, United Artists).

2127 "I had a great time tonight, really. It was like the Nuremberg trials." **Woody Allen**'s date with his ex-wife's sister Dianne Wiest is a disaster. *Hannah and Her Sisters* (1987, Orion).

2128 "I've never gone out with someone as. . . well, as basic as you." Straight A high school beauty **Ione**

Skye searches for words to describe her new boyfriend, aimless kickboxer John Cusack. *Say Anything* (1989, 20th Century-Fox).

2129 "I got married so I could quit dating." **Billy Crystal** recalls his failed marriage. *When Harry Met Sally. . .* (1989, Columbia).

2130 "Have you ever noticed that the older you get, the younger are the girls you date. Soon you'll be dating sperm." **Billy Crystal** quips about his friend Bruno Kirby's young lovers. *City Slickers* (1991, Columbia).

2131 "I wasn't dating him, I was fucking him." **Sharon Stone** speaks of one of her college professors. *Basic Instinct* (1992, Tri-Star).

Daughters

see also FATHERS, GIRLS, MOTHERS, PARENTS, WOMEN

2132 "Since I have no son, I must ask you to receive a message from my ugly and insignificant daughter." **Boris Karloff** introduces luscious Myrna Loy to his captives. *The Mask of Fu Manchu* (1932, MGM).

2133 JEFFREY GARTH: "You must be insane." COUNTESS MARYA ZALESKA: "No, desperate. There isn't anything I wouldn't do to get you to free me of the curse of the Draculas. I am Dracula's daughter." Alienist (psychiatrist) **Otto Kruger** is asked by **Gloria Holden** to cure her of her "disease of the mind"—vampirism. *Dracula's Daughter* (1936, Universal).

2134 "Think of it, Mr. Bennet—three of them married, and the other two tottering on the brink!" With the last line of the film, **Mary Boland** gushes to her husband Edmund Gwenn. She refers to their five daughters. Earlier in the film, she sang a different tune: "Look at them! Five of them without dowries! What's to become of them?" *Pride and Prejudice* (1940, MGM).

2135 "Daughters! They're a mess no matter how you look at 'em. A headache till they get married—if they get married—and after that they get worse. . . . Either they leave their husbands and come back with four kids and move in your guest room or the husband loses his job and the whole caboodle come back. Or else they're so homely that you can't get rid of them at all and they sit around like Spanish moss and shame you into an early grave." Widower **William Demarest** is not speaking from experience. His two unmarried daughters Betty Hutton and Diana Lynn cause him other types of grief. *The Miracle of Morgan's Creek* (1943, Paramount).

2136 "A nice old guy has two daughters. One of them is, well, wonderful. And the other is not so wonderful. As a result somebody gets something on her. The father hires me to pay off. Before I can get to the guy, the family chauffeur kills him! But that didn't stop things. It just starts them. And two murders later I find out somebody's got something on wonderful." Private eye **Humphrey Bogart** gives police detective Regis Toomey a vague plot summary. *The Big Sleep* (1946, Warner Bros.).

2137 "She can love whom she pleases, but she must marry the man I choose." Squire **Hugh Griffith** won't stand in the way of his daughter Susannah York's finding happiness and love with Albert Finney, but what's marriage got to do with that? *Tom Jones* (1963, GB, United Artists).

2138 "You stay away from her. I don't hand out my daughter to newlyweds." **Eddie Albert** issues a warning to honeymooning Charles Grodin who has fallen hard for Albert's beautiful daughter Cybill Shepherd. *The Heartbreak Kid* (1972, 20th Century-Fox).

2139 "Don't you ever hit her, and don't you take her away from home." **Levon Helm** issues a stern warning to Tommy Lee Jones when he gives permission for Jones to marry his 13-year-old daughter, Sissy Spacek. *Coal Miner's Daughter* (1980, Universal).

2140 "Look at this fat little girl." Eighty-year-old retired professor **Henry Fonda** refuses to acknowledge that his alienated daughter Jane Fonda is an adult. *On Golden Pond* (1981, Universal).

2141 "Polly, when I grow up I want to be just like you." Just home from what she hopes will be her last "drying-out" period, alcoholic actress **Marsha Mason** compliments her teenage daughter Kristy McNichol for her maturity and stability. *Only When I Laugh* (1981, Columbia).

2142 "I will mail your daughter to you in pieces." South American General **Dan Hedaya** has kidnapped Arnold Schwarzenegger's daughter Alyssa Milano and threatens to kill her slowly if Arnie doesn't assassinate the country's president. *Commando* (1985, 20th Century-Fox).

2143 "President Johnson today signed a highway beautification bill. Basically, the bill said that his daughters could not drive in a convertible on public highways." It's this kind of irreverent humor that gets military disk jockey Adrian Cronauer, played by **Robin Williams**, in trouble with his superiors. *Good Morning, Vietnam* (1987, Touchstone).

Days

see also NIGHTS, TIME, YEARS

2144 "I can't let him go. I can't. There must be some way to bring him back. Oh, I can't think about this now. I'll go crazy if I do. I'll think about it tomorrow. . . . But I must think about it, I must think about it. What is there to do? What is there that matters?. . . Tara. . . home. I'll go home, and I'll think of some way to get him back. After all, tomorrow is another day." In the next to last scene of the film, Clark Gable has just walked out of **Vivien Leigh**'s life. Finally aware that he's the man she really loves and has always loved, she watches as he disappears in the mist—and then Leigh decides to put off till tomorrow figuring out how to get Gable back. *Gone with the Wind* (1939, Selznick-MGM).

2145 "No looking ahead. No tomorrows. Just today." It's the timely philosophy of **Cary Grant**, the head of a small commercial airline in Latin America. *Only Angels Have Wings* (1939, Columbia).

2146 "I hate the dawn. The grass always looks as though it's been left out all night." **Clifton Webb** approximately recreates his "Laura" character, a WASPish, egotistical individual constant in his contempt of everyone and everything around him. *The Dark Corner* (1946, 20th Century-Fox).

2147 "Then the first thing that happens is I see you, and I thought this is going to be one terrific day so you better live it up, boy, 'cause tomorrow you'll be nothing." **James Dean** tells Natalie Wood she's brightened his day. *Rebel Without a Cause* (1955, Warner Bros.).

2148 ARNIE: "When is tomorrow?" SAM: "The day after today." ARNIE: "That's yesterday. Today's tomorrow." SAM: "It was." ARNIE: "When was tomorrow yesterday, Mr. Marlowe?" SAM: "Today." ARNIE: "Oh, sure, yesterday." **Jerry Mathers**, who would go on to star in TV's "Leave It to Beaver," and artist **John Forsythe** have a day's discussion. *The Trouble with Harry* (1955, Paramount).

2149 "I used to wake up in the morning and it was mine, now it all belongs to you." **Shirley Knight** calls her husband Robert Modica to tell him she's left him because she feels trapped by marriage and him. *The Rain People* (1969, Warner Bros.).

2150 "There will be days and days and days like this." Young **Meryl Streep** flings her arms wide as she breathes the fragrance of the French countryside on Armistice Day. *Plenty* (1985, 20th Century-Fox-RKO).

2151 "Oh God, not another fucking beautiful day." During the early part of World War II, **Sarah Miles** finds the never changing days in Kenya's Happy Valley monotonous. *White Mischief* (1988, GB, Columbia).

2152 "We're having a good day!" Gambler **Richard Dreyfuss** lets his accumulated day's earnings of $69,000 ride on the last race of the day. *Let It Ride* (1989, Paramount).

Dead *see* DEATH AND DYING, LIFE AND DEATH

Deals and Dealings

see also AGREEMENTS, BARGAINS, BUSINESS AND COMMERCE, BUYING AND SELLING

2153 "You can come back to work on the paper, and if we find we can't get along in a friendly fashion, we'll get married again." Newspaper editor **Cary Grant**'s proposal cuts no ice with his ex-wife and star reporter Rosalind Russell. She has turned in her notice and announces she's marrying Ralph Bellamy. *His Girl Friday* (1940, Columbia).

2154 "You have Peter's child. I have Peter's money. Let me ensure your future. Give me your child and I'll make you secure financially always." **Bette Davis** suggests an arrangement to Mary Astor, pregnant by Davis' presumed dead husband George Brent. *The Great Lie* (1941, Warner Bros.).

2155 "We made a deal and you're going to stick to it, right or wrong." Private eye **Humphrey Bogart** refuses to be bought off the case by Lauren Bacall. *The Big Sleep* (1946, Warner Bros).

2156 "I think we'll have to wait a little while. My managers are negotiating a deal of their own. If you'll excuse us, Mr. Taylor, I think this is one deal I can handle by myself." Hillbilly truck driver, turned singing sensation **Elvis Presley** tells Vernon Rich that he can handle his love affair with Dolores Hart on his own. *Loving You* (1957, Paramount).

2157 "The promise is that the deal is so good we can't refuse." **James Caan** tells Al Pacino of an offer of peace and mutual benefit made by the Tattaglia family. *The Godfather* (1972, Paramount).

2158 "How to deal with death is at least as important as how to deal with life." Admiral **William Shatner** shares some insight with half-Vulcan Kirstie Alley as she completes a training session. *Star Trek II—The Wrath of Khan* (1982, Paramount).

2159 "Actually, I'd give up writing if I could see a naked girl while I was eating ice cream." Although not risking his soul, young teen **Jonathan Silverman** (in reality Neil Simon) offers to trade something of value for something of value. *Brighton Beach Memoirs* (1986, Universal).

2160 "You think I've got an attitude?. . . I know why you like Clark. He's a guard dog, does your dirty work, keeps the black folk in line—that's fine, but you've got to be re-elected. . . . I've got enough folks lined up with me to give you a damn hard time and I will get more—I will beat the streets. . . . Appoint me to the school board, so we can vote Clark out—otherwise we'll just have to vote you out." **Lynne Thigpen** threatens Mayor Alan North with what'll happen if he doesn't help her in her crusade to get high school Principal Morgan Freeman fired. *Lean on Me* (1989, Warner Bros.).

2161 "Let's make a deal." Sounding like a contestant talking to Monty Hall, **Al Pacino** bails out crooked Archbishop Donal Donnelly who is financially embarrassed because he misappropriated $750 million in Vatican bank funds. *The Godfather, Part III* (1990, Paramount).

2162 "You've got two ways to deal with this. You got the easy way and the hard way. Do yourself a favor and make the right choice." Police captain **Delroy Lindo** warns volatile New York City homicide detective James Woods that like it or not, he will be assigned to work with actor Michael J. Fox who wants to do undercover research for an upcoming film role. *The Hard Way* (1991, Universal).

Death and Dying

see also BIRTHS AND BIRTHDAYS, ENDS AND ENDINGS, ETERNITY, EXECUTIONS, FUNERALS, GOD, HEAVEN, HEAVEN AND HELL, HELL, IMMORTALITY AND MORTALITY, KILLINGS, LASTS, LIFE AND DEATH, LIVES AND LIVING, SUICIDES, WORDS

2163 "I saw him die. I didn't know what it was to die before!" Adolescent German soldier **Lew Ayres** prays over the body of a dead friend in the trenches during World War I. *All Quiet on the Western Front* (1930, Universal).

2164 "You still think it's beautiful to die for your country. The first bombardment taught us better. When it comes to dying for your country, it's better not to die at all." While home on leave, young German soldier **Lew Ayres** visits his old school and tries to put a damper on the patriotic enthusiasm for war of the students. *All Quiet on the Western Front* (1930, Universal).

2165 "To die, to be really dead—that must be glorious!" **Bela Lugosi** finds eternal life not all it's cracked up to be. *Dracula* (1931, Universal).

2166 "It's a wonder a bolt of lightning don't come through the ceiling and strike you all dead." Clark Street hooker **Mae Clarke** denounces the newsmen assembled in the press room of the county jail, awaiting the execution of George E. Stone. *The Front Page* (1931, United Artists).

2167 AMANDA CHASE PAYNNE: "What happens if one of us dies? Does the one that's left still laugh?" ELYOT CHASE: "Yes, yes. Death's very laughable. Such a cunning little mystery. All done with mirrors." Reunited ex-spouses **Norma Shearer** and **Robert Montgomery** think ahead. *Private Lives* (1931, MGM).

2168 "Save me from that mummy! It's dead." Ordinarily this wouldn't present a problem, but the mummy **Zita Johann** refers to won't stay in its tomb. *The Mummy* (1932, Universal).

2169 "For you, my friend, they are angels of death." **Bela Lugosi**, as Murder Legendre, answers John Harron, who asks who are the zombies that Lugosi is leading. *White Zombie* (1932, United Artists).

2170 "I meddled in things that man must leave alone." Dying mad man **Claude Rains** has a bit of insight with the film's last line. As he dies, his invisibility wears off and Rains is seen for the first time in the movie. *The Invisible Man* (1933, Universal).

2171 "I'm too good for this joint." These are dancer **George Raft**'s dying words, speaking of the club in which he works. *Bolero* (1934, Paramount).

2172 "I am dying, Egypt, dying." As he lies dying at his own hands, **Henry Wilcoxon**, as Marc Antony, borrows a line from Shakespeare and speaks to Claudette Colbert as Cleopatra. *Cleopatra* (1934, Paramount).

2173 "For years men and women in this country tolerated racketeers and murderers. Because of their own hatred of Prohibition they felt in sympathy with those who broke the law they felt obsessive. Crimes and criminals became popular. Killers became heroes. But gentlemen—Prohibition has gone! And the gangsters and killers who came with it must go with it! In finding Blackie Gallagher guilty of murder we are faced with more than avenging one death. We are faced with a choice which we must make. Either we can surrender to the epidemic of crime and violence which could destroy our homes and community or we can give warning to the gangsters and murderers that they are through! In 1904, when the General Slocum burned, I made a boyish effort to save Blackie Gallagher's life. Today, I demand from you his death!" District Attorney **William Powell**'s impassioned plea to the jury, not only wins the death penalty for his boyhood friend Clark Gable, but because the summation was so inspired, even Gable is impressed and applauds it. *Manhattan Melodrama* (1934, MGM).

2174 "In an hour they'll be dying for their country. Well, I'm dying for my breakfast." With this remark, made as she watches soldiers marching off to battle, one gets the correct notion that title character **Miriam Hopkins** is an insensitive creature. *Becky Sharp* (1935, Pioneer).

2175 "I've got to have more steps. I need more steps. I've got to get higher. Higher." As he dies, the great showman, played by **William Powell**, hallucinates that he's designing one more show. *The Great Ziegfeld* (1936, MGM).

2176 "You know something, George? I think we're dead." **Constance Bennett** makes the observation to her husband Cary Grant as they step out of their bodies after a car crash. *Topper* (1937, MGM).

2177 "It's right for me to die, darling. It isn't hard. And I'm so full of love." No one died on screen more beautifully and peacefully than did **Margaret Sullavan.** She expires in the arms of her lover Robert Taylor. *Three Comrades* (1938, MGM).

2178 "Cafe society! If you'd die tomorrow, they'd have to hire half the pallbearers." Ship's reporter **Fred MacMurray** is scornful of party-mad, irresponsible heiress Madeleine Carroll. *Cafe Society* (1939, Paramount).

2179 "When death comes, it will come as an old friend." **Bette Davis** is resigned and at peace with the knowledge that her death is imminent. *Dark Victory* (1939, Warner Bros.).

2180 "The South is dead, the Yankees and the carpetbaggers have got it." **Vivien Leigh** wants Leslie Howard to run away with her to Mexico. *Gone with the Wind* (1939, Selznick-MGM).

2181 "They hanged me once. They broke my neck. They said I was dead. Then they cut me down." **Bela Lugosi**, as Ygor, a deformed, crazed shepherd, survived the gallows for stealing bodies for Basil Rathbone's father, the infamous monster-making Frankenstein. *Son of Frankenstein* (1939, Universal).

2182 "Let her die where she belongs—in Edgar's arms! Let her die!" **Geraldine Fitzgerald** begs her husband Laurence Olivier to stay from the death bed of his lifetime love Merle Oberon, married to Fitzgerald's brother David Niven. *Wuthering Heights* (1939, United Artists).

2183 "Carl didn't die. I did a little. And when I sing I hear him." When **Jeanette MacDonald** sings, the ghost of deceased Nelson Eddy, her husband, makes it a duet. *Bitter Sweet* (1940, MGM).

2184 "Death? What's my mother got to do with death? She's the liveliest person you ever saw." **Robert Taylor** reacts when he learns that his mother Alla Nazimova is in a German concentration camp, condemned to death for trying to smuggle money out of the country. *Escape* (1940, MGM).

2185 "I fear I shall not see the sun rise again over the valley of the jackals." Anticipating his imminent death, high priest **Eduardo Ciannelli** passes on his mantle to George Zucco. *The Mummy's Hand* (1940, Universal).

2186 "If this is death in the afternoon, she is death in the evening." Bullfight critic **Laird Cregar** unkindly likens femme fatale Rita Hayworth to the bull ring. *Blood and Sand* (1941, 20th Century-Fox).

2187 "Rosebud." The last word, the last thought of powerful Charles Foster Kane, played by **Orson Welles**, as he dies. *Citizen Kane* (1941, RKO).

2188 "Then, last week, as it must to all men, death came to Charles Foster Kane." The narrator of a newsreel reports on the death of fabulously rich publisher Kane, played by Orson Welles. *Citizen Kane* (1941, RKO).

2189 "Remember what Johnny Dillinger said about guys like you and him... he said you were just rushin' toward death. That's it, just rushin' toward death." Underworld sawbones **Henry Hull** cheerfully reminds habitual criminal Humphrey Bogart of his likely fate. *High Sierra* (1941, Warner Bros.).

2190 "Death is timeless." Such is a happy thought of mortician **Edward Earle**. *No Hands on the Clock* (1941, Paramount).

2191 "And now Major Amberson was engaged in the profoundest thinking of his life, and he realized that everything which had worried him or delighted him during his lifetime—all the buying and building and traveling and banking—that it was all a trifle and a waste beside what concerned him now, for the Major knew that he had no plan how to enter an unknown country where he was not even sure

of being recognized as an Amberson." Narrator **Orson Welles** speaks of Richard Bennett, who knowing death is near, prepares to meet his maker. *The Magnificent Ambersons* (1942, RKO).

2192 "These are eight men we know... we're just a little luckier than they were... I'm sorry they had to die. A lot more people are going to die." Merchant marine officer **Humphrey Bogart** prays over the dead bodies of eight of his crew, killed in battle. *Action in the North Atlantic* (1943, Warner Bros.).

2193 "I should have done away with them all... all of them.... Shoot them... shoot them...!" Dying **John Carradine**, as beastly Nazi Heydrich, rasps out his last words to Howard Freeman as Himmler after he's been assassinated by Alan Curtis. *Hitler's Madman* (1943, MGM).

2194 BETTY BENTON: "Is she ill?" DR. RICHARD MARLOWE: "No, she's dead. She has been dead for twenty-two years now." Victim-to-be **Wanda McKay** questions **Bela Lugosi** about his pale, zombie-like wife Ellen Hall. *Voodoo Man* (1944, Monogram).

2195 "For when I saw him fumble with the sheets and play with flowers and smile upon his fingers' ends, I knew there was but one way...." **Freda Jackson**, as Mistress Quickly, witnesses the death of George Robey, playing Falstaff. *Henry V* (1945, GB, Two Cities-Eagle Lion-United Artists).

2196 "Don Burnham died this weekend—of shame, the DTs, moral anemia. He wanted to kill himself." Writer **Ray Milland** tells fiancée Jane Wyman that he's killed his talent with alcohol. *The Lost Weekend* (1945, Paramount).

2197 "If you don't return I will die. After my death everything I have will belong to you. I have confidence in you." **Jean Marais**, as the Beast, gives Josette Day, as Beauty, his magic key, and allows her to visit her ailing father for a week. *La Belle et la Bete* aka: *The Beauty and the Beast* (1946, Fr., Discina-Lopert).

2198 "It's no use, Kitty, your would-be fall-guy is quite dead." Insurance investigator **Edmond O'Brien** tells Ava Gardner to quit pleading with mobster Albert Dekker to take the blame for a murder for which she's responsible. He's dead. *The Killers* (1946, Universal-International).

2199 "The dead look so terribly dead when they're dead." Ex-World War I pilot **Tyrone Power** is badly shaken by his experience in action during the war. *The Razor's Edge* (1946, 20th Century-Fox).

2200 "You're going to die, Jean, just like the others. But it won't be really dying, because you're going to live in this beautiful plant." Title character **Gale Sondergaard** has plans for Brenda Joyce's blood. *The Spider Woman Strikes Back* (1946, Universal).

2201 "I can beat 'em, the fat bellies with their stinking cigars." Boxer **Kirk Douglas** collapses in his dressing room after a hard-earned victory in the ring. *Champion* (1949, United Artists).

2202 "Custer is dead, and around the bloody guidons of the Seventh Cavalry lie the 212 officers and men he led." Narrator **Irving Pichel**'s line begins the film. *She Wore a Yellow Ribbon* (1949, RKO).

2203 "Death's at the bottom of everything, Martins. Leave Death to the professionals." British Major **Trevor Howard** tells writer Joseph Cotten to butt out of his investigation into the death of black market criminal Orson Welles. *The Third Man* (1949, GB, Selznick-London Films).

2204 "What can I do, old man. I'm dead, aren't I?" After faking his death, black marketeer **Orson Welles** insincerely apologizes to his old friend Joseph Cotten for not being able to come to the aid of his mistress, Alida Valli. *The Third Man* (1949, GB, Selznick-London Films).

2205 "Made it, Ma. Top of the world." Madman **James Cagney** goes to an uncertain glory atop an exploding oil tank, yelling to his dead mother and partner in crime Margaret Wycherly. *White Heat* (1949, Warner Bros.).

2206 "You're a dead man, Harry Fabian, a dead man." Obese **Francis L. Sullivan**, owner of a sleazy London dive, gleefully warns Richard Widmark, who has been having an affair with Sullivan's wife, Googie Withers. Sullivan entraps Widmark in a scheme that makes the latter a marked man. *Night and the City* (1950, GB, 20th Century-Fox).

2207 "Stop worrying about fear. Think of yourself as already dead." During World War II, American bomber commander **Gregory Peck** tells his men they can't worry about getting killed and fulfill their mission at the same time. He offers a solution—assume they will not survive. *Twelve O'Clock High* (1950, 20th Century-Fox).

2208 "Brave bull, it's time for one of us. Let's do it now. Only we know—they don't—what it's like to stand here and look at death right in the eye. Let's do it with courage and style. Come on, death, Brujo!" Matador **Mel Ferrer** plants his feet in the sand to receive the charge of the bull—the "recibinedo." *The Brave Bulls* (1951, Columbia).

2209 "What's a life or two, Guy? Some people are better off dead. Like your wife and my father." **Robert Walker** proposes a trade of murders with tennis star Farley Granger. *Strangers on a Train* (1951, Warner Bros.).

2210 "You've just dug your own grave. You're dead on the waterfront. You don't drive a truck or a cab. You don't push a baggage rack. You don't work no place. You're dead." Corrupt longshoreman union leader **Lee J. Cobb** spits out his words at Marlon Brando after the latter testifies against the former to a crime commission. *On the Waterfront* (1954, Columbia).

2211 "Leave him alone—can't you see he's dying?" **Jo Van Fleet**'s diagnosis of consumptive gambler Doc Holliday (played by Kirk Douglas), for Wyatt Earp (played by Burt Lancaster), is premature. Douglas gets up and joins Lancaster in a shoot-out with the Clantons. *Gunfight at the O.K. Corral* (1957, Paramount).

2212 "I am Death. . . I have been walking by your side for a long time. . . . Are you prepared?" Gaunt, mysteriously hooded **Bengt Ekerot**, as Death, introduces himself to Swedish knight Max von Sydow, whose time is nigh. *The Seventh Seal* (1958, Sweden, Svensk Filmindustri).

2213 SCOTTIE: "What are you thinking about?" MADELEINE: "All the people who were born and died while the trees went on living." SCOTTIE: "Its real name is Sequoia Semperveva." MADELEINE: "I don't like it. . . knowing I have to die!" **James Stewart** and **Kim Novak** are among the sequoia trees, the oldest living things. He sounds like someone giving a nature guide. She's much more thoughtful. *Vertigo* (1958, Paramount).

2214 "I don't want to die for Korea. What do I care for this stinking hill? You wanna see where I live back home—I sure am sure I ain't gonna die for that." Black soldier **Woody Strode** threatens Lieutenant Gregory Peck with a gun because the latter has been ordered to lead his men in an assault on a hill at the time the negotiators at Panmunjon are trying to agree on an armistice. *Pork Chop Hill* (1959, United Artists).

2215 "I've been killed already. I'm just stubborn about dying. I saw the flaming star of death. I gotta last long enough to get into the hills and die. . . . You live for me." Mortally wounded "half-breed" **Elvis Presley** rides into town to announce his epitaph for his friend Steve Forrest. *Flaming Star* (1960, 20th Century-Fox).

2216 "God bless Captain Vere!" It's naïve seaman **Terence Stamp**'s salute to Peter Ustinov as the former is hanged for killing sadistic master-of-arms Robert Ryan. *Billy Budd* (1962, GB, Anglo-Allied).

2217 "Paratus sum pro Domino mori pacem et lubertatem per sanguinem meaim goudeat Ecclesia." The last words of title character **Richard Burton** as four barons close in on him translate to: "I'm ready to die for my Lord. May the Lord's church obtain peace and liberty through my blood." *Becket* (1964, GB, Paramount).

2218 "Make his death a particularly unpleasant one." The voice of the unseen Number 1 of SPECTRE, (uncredited **Eric Pohlmann**) intones instructions to Lotte Lenya and Vladek Sheybal for dealing with Sean Connery as James Bond. *From Russia with Love* (1964, GB, United Artists).

2219 "I didn't die. Everything I loved was taken away from me and I did not die. There was nothing I could do. Nothing." Feeling guilty for having survived, **Rod Steiger** identifies with those who died in Nazi concentration camps, including his wife and children. *The Pawnbroker* (1965, Allied Artists).

2220 "Do you mind if my friend sits down? She's just dead." With tongue-in-cheek, **Sean Connery** casually parks the body of SPECTRE agent Luciana Paluzzi at a ringside table at a nightclub. Connery used Paluzzi as a shield, while they were dancing, to escape the bullets of her colleagues. *Thunderball* (1965, United Artists).

2221 "I was almost home." **Steve McQueen** stares down at the bullet hole in his chest that kills him, just when he thought he was going to find some happiness with Candice Bergen. *The Sand Pebbles* (1966, 20th Century-Fox).

2222 "No bastard ever won a war by dying for his country. He won it by making some other bastard die for his country." It's part of a speech given by title character **George C. Scott** in a prologue to the movie. *Patton* (1970, 20th Century-Fox).

2223 "I have no ties and am expendable and am ready to die for my country." Bored widow **Rosalind Russell** has journeyed to Washington to offer her services as a secret agent. *Mrs. Pollifax—Spy* (1971, United Artists).

2224 "Steve, if you read this it means I didn't make it back. It also means you've broken a filament to go to a thirteen-second-delay trigger. End of game. Bang, you're dead." Hired assassin **Charles Bronson** has a little surprise for his young apprentice Jan-Michael Vincent. *The Mechanic* (1972, United Artists).

2225 "I gotta go for broke this time. I don't wanna die in the street." Independent-minded New York racketeer Joey Gallo, played by **Peter Boyle**, is gunned down in a restaurant in Little Italy. *Crazy Joe* (1974, Columbia).

2226 "The key, I think, is to not think of death as an end, but think of it more as a very effective way to cut down on your expenses." **Woody Allen**'s character comments on one of director-writer Woody Allen's favorite topics. *Love and Death* (1975, United Artists).

2227 "[I'm] not allowed to do anything to the death." **Woody Allen** tries to avoid fighting a duel to the death. *Love and Death* (1975, United Artists).

2228 "All of a sudden, it's closer to the end than it is the beginning, and death is suddenly a perceptible thing to me—with definable features." Referring to death, **William Holden** expresses his feelings of mortality for his young, selfish mistress Faye Dunaway. *Network* (1976, MGM-United Artists).

2229 "I'm obsessed with—with, uh, with death, I think. Big—big subject with me, yeah. I've a very pessimistic view of life." **Woody Allen** confesses to Diane Keaton. *Annie Hall* (1977, United Artists).

2230 "Six weeks later the woman who called herself the Countess Sobrayanski died peacefully on the island of Corfu. The news rated one short paragraph in the local paper. The electric blanket I had sent her came back undelivered." Movie director **William Holden** speaks of Greta Garbo-like reclusive actress Hildegard Knef (Neff). *Fedora* (1978, Germany-France, United Artists).

2231 "I can't seem to shake the real implication of dying. It's terrifying. The intimacy of it embarrasses me." **Diane Keaton** finishes her long monologue sounding like a character in an Ingmar Bergman film—but that's not surprising, considering how much writer-director Woody Allen is influenced by Bergman. *Interiors* (1978, United Artists).

2232 "Funny, isn't it? One minute you're standing in the wings. Next minute, you're wearing them." It's the theatrical thought of dying Broadway producer **George C. Scott** in the "Baxter's Beauties of 1933" segment of the film. *Movie, Movie* (1978, Warner Bros.).

2233 "When there is no room in hell, the dead will walk the Earth." **Ken Foree** survives a mysterious plague that sweeps across America. The victims come back from the dead as flesh-eating zombies. *Dawn of the Dead* (1979, United Film).

2234 "The heart beats. . . . Nothing ever dies." As he is dying John Merrick, played by **John Hurt**, has a vision of his mother. *The Elephant Man* (1980, EMI).

2235 "I don't want to die in the DMZ. I don't even know where it is." **Brad Davis** has a low number in the draft lottery and fears he will end up in Vietnam. *A Small Circle of Friends* (1980, United Artists).

2236 "I've been spooked ever since I left my mother's tit—that's what keeps me from dying." Frontiersman **Harvey Keitel** knows his way around the wilderness. *Eagle's Wing* (1981, GB, Goldwyn).

2237 "Tell me, Mary, what is dead? Nobody will tell me." Retarded **Mel Gibson** questions Piper Laurie, who explains death to him as she would to a four-year-old. *Tim* (1981, Australia, Pisces-Satori).

2238 "My heart and sundry other valves have turned in their notice." It's **Jason Robards**' way of telling his daughter Marsha Mason that he's dying. *Max Dugan Returns* (1982, 20th Century-Fox).

2239 RITA: "You've got to challenge death and disease. I read this poem about fightin' death. . . ." FRANK: "Ah—Dylan Thomas." RITA: "No, Roger McGough. It was about this old man who runs away from a hospital an' goes out in the hail. He gets pissed an' stands in the street shoutin' an' challengin' death to come out and fight. It's dead good." Working class wife **Julie Walters**, who wants to better herself, teaches a thing or two to her boozy Open University professor, **Michael Caine**. *Educating Rita* (1983, GB, Rank).

2240 "In making love she was beating back death." Narrator **Peter MacNicol** divines that Polish Nazi concentration camp refugee Meryl Streep used sex to convince herself she was still alive. *Sophie's Choice* (1983, Universal).

2241 "I'm going to come back from the dead." Even though her death is imminent, wealthy **Lily Tomlin** is planning her resurrection. *All of Me* (1984, Universal).

2242 "How many corpses have to be piled up before people say it's time to go home?" Despairing and weary British doctor **Bill Paterson** tends a little girl with shrapnel in her spine. *The Killing Fields* (1984, GB, Warner Bros.).

2243 "Children shouldn't die before their parents—parents should die first." **Glenn Close** has lost a son to a hunting accident. *The Stone Boy* (1984, 20th Century-Fox).

2244 "These people are no good, they're all dead." Corrupt, world-weary cop **Ralph Foody**, guzzling cheap booze, muses as he sits atop a tombstone, surveying a graveyard. *Code of Silence* (1985, Orion).

2245 "If he dies, he dies." Machine-like, giant Russian boxer **Dolph Lundgren** shows his insensitivity after he clubs to death ex-champ Carl Weathers in an exhibition match. *Rocky IV* (1985, MGM-United Artists).

2246 "Why should I worry? If I'm unconscious I won't know it and if I'm not I'll worry about it then." Death-obsessed Woody Allen's father **Leo Postrel** is not worried about his death or what happens afterwards. *Hannah and Her Sisters* (1986, Orion).

2247 "I think he died for me. . . ." **Anjelica Huston** confesses her friendship for a delicate dark-eyed youth who used to serenade her, but whose health did not withstand a journey through the snow to her. *The Dead* (1987, Vestron).

2248 "Why should I die such a horrible death? Was I so terrible? Was this music so terrible?" Stricken with multiple sclerosis, brilliant violinist **Julie Andrews** desperately seeks a reason for her illness and fate. *Duet for One* (1987, Cannon).

2249 "No matter where you go or what you do, you're gonna die." **Olympia Dukakis** tells her husband Vincent Gardenia that a young mistress won't make him immortal. *Moonstruck* (1987, MGM).

2250 "Jesus Christ! If this man owned a funeral parlor, no one would die." Big-time Wall Street trader **Michael Douglas**'s metaphor is a reference to a competitor whom Douglas feels has no business acumen. *Wall Street* (1987, 20th Century-Fox).

2251 "How do we make it die?" Unemployed British actor **Richard E. Grant** isn't sure what to do with a chicken, the only food they have, when he and his roommate Paul McGann take a holiday in the country. *Withnail and I* (1987, GB, Cineplex Odeon).

2252 "Call my wife. . . call my wife. . . . Just let me catch my breath. . . let me catch my breath. . . ." These are the dying words of cop **Robert Duvall** who has been shot by a member of an L.A. street gang. *Colors* (1988, Orion).

2253 "For what? I told you I would not die on a cross." **Armand Assante** has survived being strapped to a cross to represent the "Christo" at the end of Lent for a Spanish-speaking splinter group of the Catholic church who believe in self-flagellation and a literal reenactment of the crucifixion. *The Penitent* (1988, New Century-Vista).

2254 "I'm going to die if I don't see you." **Kurt Russell** phones Michelle Pfeiffer to tell her the pain her beauty causes him. *Tequila Sunrise* (1988, Warner Bros.).

2255 "We have 250 freedom fighters in the United States. We seek martyrdom. Death is salvation for us." Middle East terrorist leader **Kabir Bedi** gives an interview in which he announces that suicide hit teams are in the U.S. to assassinate major political leaders. *Terminal Entry* (1988, Inter-Continental).

2256 "Now there's no point in dying." **Ron Silver** backs out of a suicide pact with his lover, Lena Olin, when he discovers she's been unfaithful to him with her husband. At least she goes through with the bargain. *Enemies, a Love Story* (1989, 20th Century-Fox).

2257 "Am I going to die in the toilet?" For a while it looks like the answer to police detective **Danny Glover**'s question is to be yes. Someone has boobytrapped his toilet. If he gets up, it goes off. His partner Mel Gibson saves the day with a perfectly timed maneuver. *Lethal Weapon 2* (1989, Warner Bros.).

2258 "I've often been threatened with death. If they kill me, I shall arise in the Salvadoran people. Let my blood be a seed of freedom and a sign that hope will soon be a reality. A bishop will die, but the church of God, which is the people, will never perish." **Raul Julia** portrays Oscar Romero, the martyred archbishop of El Salvador. *Romero* (1989, Four Seasons).

2259 "Do you think about death?. . . Sure you do. A fleeting thought that drifts in and out of the transom of your mind. I spend hours, I spend days. . . ." **Billy Crystal** is being a bit morbid for Meg Ryan. *When Harry Met Sally. . .* (1989, Columbia).

2260 "Death is the greatest kick of all. That's why they save it for last." Psychopathic Wall Street commodities trader **Ron Silver** murders at random and for pleasure. *Blue Steel* (1990, MGM-United Artists).

2261 "George is dead. . . . You might say he died in the saddle." **Virginia Madsen** phones the news of her husband Jerry Hardin's death to her reluctant lover, Don Johnson. She tied and gagged her husband who had a weak heart, told him of her affair with Johnson, climbed on top of him to have sex and told him, "George, I'm fucking you to death." *The Hot Spot* (1990, Orion).

2262 "Death is the ultimate negative—not being." **Tim Roth** likes to come up with simple and concise explanations of complicated things for his curious friend Gary Oldman. *Rosencrantz and Guildenstern Are Dead* (1990, GB, Cinecom).

2263 "Jesus Christ, he's not going to sell you insurance. Just lift him up." Autopsy technician **Clint Howard** yells at young fireman Billy Baldwin who shrinks from handling a charred corpse. *Backdraft* (1991, Universal).

2264 BARTON FINK: "Where's Audrey?" CHARLIE MEADOWS: "She's dead, if that was her name." Playwright **John Turturro** questions gregarious traveling salesman and serial killer **John Goodman** about the late Judy Davis. *Barton Fink* (1991, 20th Century-Fox).

2265 "God has chosen you to die for Him." **Marthe Tungeon**, the mother of French Jesuit Father Laforgue, sends him off to his chosen death as a martyr in New France. *Black Robe* (1991, Canada, Goldwyn).

2266 "Death is nothing to be afraid of—I'm at the jumping-off point and I'm not afraid of death." Eighty-three-year-old **Jessica Tandy** comforts middle-aged Kathy Bates. *Fried Green Tomatoes* (1991, Universal).

2267 "Death is the final frontier." Cardiologist **Martha Henry** keeps a lab in the basement of her hospital where, for unexplained reasons, she puts monkeys into a near-death state and then brings them back to life. *White Light* (1991, Academy).

Debates *see* ARGUMENTS, CONTESTS

Debauchery *see* CORRUPTION, IMMORALITY, MORALITY, PERVERSIONS

Debts

see also DUTIES, PROBLEMS, RESPONSIBILITIES

2268 "I've done my time. . . now I want my man." Parolee **Sylvia Sidney** wishes to be reunited with her husband, ex-con George Raft. *You and Me* (1938, Paramount).

2269 "No, I was in love once with a beautiful blonde. She drove me to drink—the one thing I'm indebted to her for." **W.C. Fields** tells his niece Gloria Jean of a broken romance when she asks if he ever has been married. *Never Give a Sucker an Even Break* (1941, Universal).

2270 "Look, folks, you've got to give the devil his due. We all owe him something. And you know it." Movie executive **Walter Pidgeon** makes a pitch, for a movie to be produced by Kirk Douglas, to actress

Lana Turner, screenwriter Dick Powell and director Barry Sullivan—each of whom has reasons to hate and thank Douglas. *The Bad and the Beautiful* (1952, MGM).

2271 "I don't want to leave my money, Mary. This guy threw up on our carpet, he cancelled our instant credit card, he owes us at least six hundred dollars. I'm not going to leave any money." **Paul Bartel** justifies taking all the money found in the wallet of a swinger he's killed with a heavy frying pan after the deceased attacked Bartel's wife, Mary Woronov. *Eating Raoul* (1982, Bartel).

2272 "Look at those people. I'll bet they all have bad debts. Someone should catch 'em and make 'em pay." **Harry Dean Stanton** repossesses automobiles from people who haven't paid their bills. He complains to young recruit Emilio Estevez that there are too many people in the world with bad debts for him to deal with. *Repo Man* (1984, Universal).

Decadence *see* CORRUPTION, IMMORALITY, MORALITY, PERVERSIONS

Decency

see also MODESTY, PROPRIETY

2273 "Lovin' you is the only decent thing I ever did in my life, and even that was a mistake." Dying pirate **Wallace Beery** confesses his love to promiscuous Jean Harlow. *China Seas* (1935, MGM).

2274 "Why don't you go home?. . . This is no place for you. You're halfway decent." Cynical **Jean Arthur** urges new U.S. Senator James Stewart to leave Washington before he becomes corrupt. *Mr. Smith Goes to Washington* (1939, Columbia).

2275 "I think you're a pretty decent guy. I like to talk to decent guys. They're pretty hard to find." Speakeasy entertainer **Gladys George** sizes up racketeer James Cagney. She said decent—not honest. *The Roaring Twenties* (1939, Warner Bros.).

2276 "Sure, I'm decent." It's **Rita Hayworth**'s questionable reply to gambler husband George Macready who yells into her room, "Are you decent?", as he brings home his employee Glenn Ford to meet her. Macready is unaware that they are already well acquainted. *Gilda* (1946, Columbia).

2277 "I caught a slight case of decency. It's gone to my head." **Jeff Chandler** tells his former sponsors in swindling women, Cecil Kellaway and Natalie Schafer, that he's graduated from gigolo to married man. *Female on the Beach* (1955, Universal).

2278 "You know how I got you, Marnie? There was this boy, Billy, and I wanted Billy's basketball sweater. And he said if I let him, I could have the sweater. So I let him. And then when you got started he run away. But I still got that old basketball sweater—and I got you, Marnie—and I wouldn't let them take you away from me! I promised God that if He'd let me keep you, I'd raise you different from myself—decent." **Louise Latham** tells her daughter Tippi Hedren of her conception and Latham's promise to raise her daughter as a decent woman with no need for men. *Marnie* (1964, Universal).

2279 "Decent women don't have a need for men." **Tippi Hedren** assures her mother Louise Latham that she'll never have anything to do with "men." *Marnie* (1964, Universal).

2280 "Decency is what your grandmother taught you. . . . Go home and be decent." Judge **Morgan Freeman** lectures assembled demonstrators on respect for the law. *The Bonfire of the Vanities* (1990, Warner Bros.).

Deceptions

see also HYPOCRISY

2281 SIR WILLIAM HAMILTON: "You know, Emma, there are three kinds of deceived husbands in the world: first are those who were born to be deceived; second, those who do not know; and third, those who do not care. I've wondered for some time which of the three I should be myself." EMMA HAMILTON: "Have you forgotten the fourth kind, William? The kind that is hard and empty and give nothing? You married me because you wanted a new ornament for your house, like that painting or that statue or vase. As far as you're concerned, I'm just as ornamental and just as dead." Responding to her husband **Alan Mowbray**, **Vivien Leigh** defends her affair with Laurence Olivier, claiming her husband's indifference is the cause of her unfaithfulness and deception. *That Hamilton Woman* aka: *Lady Hamilton* (1941, United Artists).

2282 KING SOLOMON: "From the first, I knew that behind those lovely eyes is the brain of a very clever woman who would never have travelled eight hundred leagues without a purpose." QUEEN OF SHEBA: "You have found me out! How could I hope to deceive you? I have been trying to entrap you with these [her arms] to bind you in soft chains so I may do with you as I will." SOLOMON: "Every woman demands a price from a man." **Yul Brynner** is being taken in by seductive **Gina Lollobrigida**. *Solomon and Sheba* (1959, United Artists).

2283 "The sea's deceitful, boy; calm above, and underneath, a world of gliding monsters preying on their fellows. Murderers, all of them. Only the sharpest teeth survive." Brutish Master-at-Arms **Robert Ryan** instructs naïve innocent seaman Terence Stamp. *Billy Budd* (1962, GB, Anglo-Allied).

2284 "People deceive themselves and that's how they stay in love." **Geraldine Chaplin** is one of a group of L.A. weirdos who realize how empty their lives have become. *Welcome to L.A.* (1976, United Artists).

2285 "I've had a lot of training in deceit. It's an occupational hazard." Aluminum siding salesman **Richard Dreyfuss** defends himself when Barbara Hershey accuses him of lying to her. *Tin Men* (1987, Touchstone).

2286 "I became a virtuoso of deceit. . . . In the end, I distilled everything to one wonderfully simple principle—win or die." **Glenn Close** shares the guiding principle of her deceitful life of sexual intrigue with equally decadent and corrupt John Malkovich. *Dangerous Liaisons* (1988, Warner Bros.).

2287 "They're a band. I won them on MTV." Quick thinking **Geena Davis** speaks with conviction to her boyfriend Charles Rocket about the three colorful aliens she's brought home. *Earth Girls Are Easy* (1989, Vestron).

Decisions

see also JUDGMENTS, MINDS

2288 "I can't decide whether to be Joan of Arc, Florence Nightingale or John L. Lewis." Wealthy, but ambitious society girl **Katharine Hepburn** considers her career options. *Holiday* (1938, Columbia).

2289 "We haven't quite decided whether he committed suicide or died trying to escape." **Claude Rains** informs Paul Henreid that Peter Lorre, the man Henreid was inquiring about at police headquarters, is dead. *Casablanca* (1942, Warner Bros.).

2290 "I think one day she just decided to go nuts because that was easier." **John Heard** envies his mother Gloria Grahame who constantly is losing her mind. *Chilly Scenes of Winter* (1982, United Artists Classics).

2291 "I keep having to make these decisions between my career, which I'm good at, and my life, which I'm not." TV reporter **Christine Lahti** looks for some understanding from the wife of her deceased lover, Ted Danson (Mary Tyler Moore). *Just Between Friends* (1986, Orion).

2292 "In America they have a thing called a manager. That is what you need. I will be your manager, because you are incapable of making decisions for yourself." **Anjelica Huston** arrives at this conclusion about her husband Ron Silver, because he currently is married to two other women besides her. *Enemies, a Love Story* (1989, 20th Century-Fox).

2293 "Whether to kill yourself is one of the most important decisions a teenager has to make." High school teacher **Betty Ramey** counsels students after the apparent suicide of three of their classmates. *Heathers* (1989, New World).

2294 "I thought about this a lot. I really don't want to be married to you anymore. . . ." After giving the matter consideration, **Kathleen Turner** has decided she wants out of her marriage to Michael Douglas. *The War of the Roses* (1989, 20th Century-Fox).

Dedications

see also DEVOTION, HONOR, PURPOSES

2295 "To those young warriors of the sky whose wings are folded about them forever." It's the dedication of the film—celebrating the exploits, adventures, sacrifices and deaths of World War I American pilots. *Wings* (1927, silent, Paramount).

2296 "With each blow you strike, you can say, 'That was for Judith, my wife.'" **Bette Davis** urges her physician husband George Brent to go on with his experiments to find a cure for whatever is killing her. *Dark Victory* (1939, Warner Bros.).

2297 "To the intrepid ones who went overseas to be the eyes and ears of America." The film is dedicated to the American journalists who covered the events in Europe just prior to World War II. *Foreign Correspondent* (1940, United Artists).

2298 "To all the funny men and clowns who have made people laugh." The dedication of Preston Sturges' movie ignores funny women, unless they're all lumped in with the clowns. *Sullivan's Travels* (1941, Paramount).

2299 "This picture is dedicated to all the beautiful women of the world who have shot their husbands full of holes out of pique. . . ." It's the written introduction to a movie spoof of the Roaring 20s. *Roxie Hart* (1942, 20th Century-Fox).

2300 "To the United States Navy, our thanks for making this picture possible. To the gallant officers and men of the silent service, to our submarines now on war patrol in hostile waters, good luck and good hunting." Narrator **Lou Marcelle** ends the movie about a submarine which entered Tokyo Bay to gather intelligence, early in World War II. *Destination Tokyo* (1943, Warner Bros.).

2301 "You've got to understand, Maria. . . I'm in this to the finish. I can't have anything serious in my life." American explosives expert **Gary Cooper** tells peasant girl Ingrid Bergman that his dedication to the cause of the partisans in the Spanish Civil War leaves him no time for romance. *For Whom the Bell Tolls* (1943, Paramount).

2302 "To the United States Marine Corps, whose exploits and valor have left a lasting impression on the world and in the hearts of their countrymen. Appreciation is gratefully acknowledged for their assistance and participation which made this picture possible." It's the dedication of the motion picture which features the historic flag raising on Mount Suribachi. *Sands of Iwo Jima* (1949, Republic).

2303 "Misty——for lonely lovers on a cool, cool night. . . and, especially for Evelyn." Disk jockey **Clint Eastwood**'s dedication gives mentally unstable Jessica Walter, as Evelyn, the misconception that she's special to him. *Play Misty for Me* (1971, Universal).

Deduction *see* DETECTIVES AND DEDUCTION, INFORMATION AND INFORMERS, KNOWLEDGE, LOGIC, PROOFS, UNDERSTANDINGS AND MISUNDERSTANDINGS

Deeds *see* ACTIONS AND ACTS, CONSEQUENCES, GOODNESS, SERVICES

Defeats

see also FAILURES, LOSSES AND LOSING, MILITARY, VICTORIES, WARS, WINNERS AND LOSERS

2304 "Many a great soldier has been defeated by a woman." Head of Russia's secret police **Purnell Pratt** warns handsome Russian officer Ivan Lebedeff, whose assignments include romancing women. *The Gay Diplomat* (1931, RKO).

2305 "Yes. . . yes, I insist, you have beaten me." Hunter of men **Leslie Banks** admits defeat at the hands of his prey Joel McCrea, just before McCrea stabs Banks to death. *The Most Dangerous Game* (1932, RKO).

2306 RUFUS T. FIREFLY: "Don't you realize we're facing disastrous defeat? What are you going to do about it?" CHICOLINI: "I've done it already. I've changed to the other side." **Groucho Marx**, president of Freedonia, is deserted by his war secretary, **Chico Marx**. *Duck Soup* (1933, Paramount).

2307 "Man is not made for defeat. Man can be destroyed but not defeated." The Ernest Hemingway words spoken by old fisherman **Spencer Tracy** sound good but unfortunately aren't true. *The Old Man and the Sea* (1958, Warner Bros.).

2308 CORNELIUS: "We will slaughter them." THE GENERAL: "Yes, but will we defeat them?" Corrupt **Curt Jurgens** is sure that feudal warlord **Eli Wallach**'s men will be able to survive an attack by the tribesmen they oppress, but Wallach is not so sure. *Lord Jim* (1965, GB, Columbia).

2309 "Can you imagine? The German nation conquered by a people who had never seen a toilet?" Aristocratic Nazi scientist **John Gielgud** is left incredulous by the defeat of the "super race" by the "barbarian Soviets." *The Formula* (1980, MGM).

2310 "You think you have won? What is light without darkness? I am part of you all. You can never defeat me. We are brothers eternal." Demon **Tim Curry** ominously warns peasant lad Tom Cruise who crusades to save the last surviving unicorns. *Legend* (1985, 20th Century-Fox).

Defenses

see also PROTECTION, SECURITY AND INSECURITY, SURVIVAL

2311 "Justifiable homicide in defense of chastity." It's the tongue-in-cheek plea entered by **Carole Lombard** when she's falsely accused of murdering a lecherous broker. *True Confession* (1937, Paramount).

2312 "I'd never turn me nose up at a fat belly, so long as he had a gold watch chain on him." **Marjorie Rhodes** deals with the effects of the Depression on her working class mill town by becoming the kept woman of a fat bookmaker. *Love on the Dole* (1940, GB, British National).

2313 "I only followed orders. I only did my duty. I am not a criminal." Nazi war-criminal **Orson Welles** echoes a familiar line shortly before he pays Hollywood's penalty for villains. *The Stranger* (1946, RKO).

2314 "You don't have to love him—just defend him." Rummy former lawyer **Arthur O'Connell** urges James Stewart, a lawyer with few clients, to take the case of Army Lieutenant Ben Gazarra, accused of murdering a man who may have raped Gazarra's wife, Lee Remick. *Anatomy of a Murder* (1959, Columbia).

2315 "I remember hearing shots. But they don't seem to be connected with me. They seemed far away. . . like somebody else was doing the shooting." With a little coaching by lawyer James Stewart, **Ben Gazzara** finds his defense for murdering the man who raped his wife, Lee Remick. *Anatomy of a Murder* (1959, Columbia).

2316 "We stayed alive because we've built up an arsenal, and we've kept the peace because we've dealt with an enemy who knew we would use that arsenal. Now we are to believe that a piece of paper will take the place of missile silos?" U.S. Air Force General **Burt Lancaster** considers a proposed disarmament treaty to be an act of "insupportable negligence." *Seven Days in May* (1964, Paramount).

2317 "Even though he roughs me up, at least he cares enough to do it." Surprisingly, **Rae Dawn Chong** defends her philandering husband Patrick Bauchau, who regularly beats her. *Choose Me* (1984, Island Alive).

2318 "Terence Mann was a warm and gentle voice of reason in a time of great madness. . . . He coined the phrase 'Make Love Not War' while other people were chanting 'Burn, Baby, Burn.' He was talking about love and peace and understanding. I cherish every one of his books and I dearly wish he had written some more and I think if you had experienced even a little bit of the 60s, you might feel the same way, too. . . . No, I think you had two 50s and moved right on to the 70s. . . . At least he's not a bookburner, you Nazi cow." **Amy Madigan** defends the writings of James Earl Jones as she takes on angry Lee Garlington at a PTA meeting. The latter wishes to ban Jones' and others' books from the school. She also makes some cracks about Madigan's "weirdo" husband Kevin Costner. *Field of Dreams* (1989, Universal).

2319 FRANKIE: "Why do we keep going from one subject I don't like to another subject?" JOHNNY: "Hey, I'm being nice, and bingo! The armor goes up." FRANKIE: "What about your own armor?" JOHNNY: "I don't have any." FRANKIE: "Everybody has armor. They'd be dead if they didn't." **Michelle Pfeiffer** has been hurt too often in the past by men to let herself be vulnerable with **Al Pacino**. *Frankie and Johnny* (1991, Paramount).

2320 "They got boys can fix your bursitis, sharpen up your game, and wipe out your campaign debt before you've got off the first tee." U.S. Senator **Richard Widmark** defends the lobbying of the American Medical Association which dictates the nation's medical policy. *True Colors* (1991, Paramount).

Defiance

see also CHALLENGES, FIGHTS AND FIGHTING

2321 "You can't discharge me. I'm my own master for the first time in my life. You can't discharge me. I'm sick. I'm going to die. Do you understand? I'm going to die, and nobody can do anything to me anymore. Nothing can happen to me anymore. Before I can be discharged, I'll be dead! Ha ha ha ha!" The knowledge that he has a fatal illness gives **Lionel Barrymore** the courage to defy his tyrannical boss, Wallace Beery. *Grand Hotel* (1932, MGM).

2322 "You can take your Bunker Hills and your bloodlines and stuff a codfish with 'em. And then you know what you can do with the codfish." Glamorous film star **Jean Harlow** tells off stuffy Bostonian Franchot Tone. *Bombshell* (1933, MGM).

2323 "I say——shit on you!" It's French student **Gerard de Bedarieux**'s defiant retort when he is ordered to publicly apologize to his repulsive, fat chemistry teacher, who has fondled the lad. *Zero de Conduite-Zero for Conduct* (1933, France, Gaumont-Franco Film).

2324 "I'm sick of it. You scolded and frightened me all I'll stand for. . . I invite the whole town to take a jump in the lake." **Irene Dunne** finally rebels against the tyranny of the two maiden aunts who have raised her. *Theodora Goes Wild* (1936, Columbia).

2325 "When the beasts like you have devoured each other, the world will belong again to the little people who give crumbs to birds." Dutch diplomat **Albert Basserman** defies his Nazi captors. *Foreign Correspondent* (1940, United Artists).

2326 SHERIFF: "Come on down. You haven't got a chance." ROY EARLE: "Come and git me, copper! Come on. Whatsa matter? Ya yellow?" Sheriff **Wade Boteler** shouts to trapped fugitive **Humphrey Bogart** to give up. Instead, Bogart races upward on Mt. Whitney. *High Sierra* (1941, Warner Bros.).

2327 "Captain, it is I—Ensign Pulver—and I just threw your stinking palm tree overboard. Now what's all this crud about no movie tonight?" Ensign **Jack Lemmon** gets up the nerve to replace Henry Fonda in standing up to tyrannical captain James Cagney. *Mister Roberts* (1955, Warner Bros.).

2328 "You will not use the excuse of that pathetic, that humorous document to blackmail me. I will not resign and you will not dismiss me, Miss McKay. . . . If one word of this outrageous calumny reaches my ears I will sue. If scandal is to your taste, Miss McKay, I shall give you a feast. . . I am a teacher, first, last, and always. I influence them to be aware of the possibilities of life, beauty, honor, courage. I have dedicated, sacrificed my life to this profession—I will not be crucified." **Maggie Smith** defies headmistress Celia Johnson, who has received a note indicating that Smith has had an affair with another teacher. *The Prime of Miss Jean Brodie* (1969, GB, 20th Century-Fox).

2329 "Hey, you bastards. I'm still here." **Steve McQueen** as the notable Devil's Island prisoner who makes numerous escapes, has the film's last words. *Papillon* (1973, Allied Artists).

2330 "You ain't broke my body, you ain't broke my mind, you ain't broke my spirit!" After serving seven years on a chain gang, **Roger E. Mosley**, as title character Huddie Ledbetter, righteously proclaims his defiance of the system. *Leadbelly* (1975, Paramount).

2331 "Come on, I love it, I love it. Bring on some more. Come on, you midgets!" U.S. Army ranger **Steve James** yells happily as he fights a horde of Ninjas. *American Ninja 2: The Confrontation* (1987, Cannon).

2332 "I wouldn't pee on him if his heart was on fire—neither of these will serve as a writ, you better get a court order." Sheriff **David Strathairn** defies coal company detectives who show him a letter from their boss who has ordered them to evict striking coal miners from their company-owned homes. *Matewan* (1987, Cinecom).

2333 "Either of you dogs lift a finger in the town limits and I'll blow you away." Sheriff **David Strathairn** continues to defy coal company detectives Kevin Tighe and Gordon Clapp when they offer him a bribe to look the other way while they deal harshly with striking coal miners. *Matewan* (1987, Cinecom.)

Democracy

see also AMERICA AND AMERICANS, CLASSES, EQUALITIES, FREEDOMS, GOVERNMENTS, LIBERTY, SOCIETIES, VOTING AND VOTERS

2334 "The only time I hate democracy is when one of you mongrels forgets his place." Unconventional lawyer **Lionel Barrymore** regrets that the laws that protect decent people also protect scum-like gangster Clark Gable, for whom Barrymore's daughter Norma Shearer has fallen. Later Shearer's fiancé kills Gable and Barrymore defends him. *A Free Soul* (1931, MGM).

2335 "I'm a firm believer in democracy, provided that it leaves me alone." Wealthy **Walter Connolly** believes in the kind of democracy found in Orwell's "Animal Farm," as interpreted by the pig Napoleon. *Soak the Rich* (1936, Paramount).

2336 "There are those who will say we have nothing to fear—that we are immune—that we are protected by vast oceans from the bacteria of aggressive dictatorships and totalitarian states. But we know and have seen the mirror of history in Europe this last year—the invasions of Poland, Norway and Denmark by Nazi Germany and Russia. . .America is not simply one of the remaining democracies, America is democracy." **Henry O'Neill**, the prosecutor of a ring of Nazi spies in the U.S. before she enters the war, summarizes for the camera, preaching against isolationism. *Confessions of a Nazi Spy* (1939, Warner Bros.).

2337 "I pay my taxes and wait for traffic lights!" Despite his criminal activities, **Humphrey Bogart** is outraged when Nazi chief Conrad Veidt questions his belief in democracy. *All Through the Night* (1941, Warner Bros.).

2338 "The Nazis and the Fascists are just as much against democracy as they are against the Communists." It's the reason Montana school teacher **Gary Cooper** gives when a guerrilla comrade asks why Coop is fighting on the side of the Spanish Loyalists. *For Whom the Bell Tolls* (1943, Paramount).

2339 "My job is to teach these natives the meaning of democracy, and they're going to learn democracy if I have to shoot every one of them." U.S. Army Colonel **Paul Ford** slightly misses the point of his mission on Okinawa in 1944. *The Teahouse of the August Moon* (1956, MGM).

2340 "Democracy is a system of self-determination. It's the—it's the right to make the wrong choice." Incompetent Army officer **Glenn Ford** struggles for a way to explain this important concept to the people of a small Okinawan village. *The Teahouse of the August Moon* (1956, MGM).

Demonstrations

see also EXPERIMENTS, EXPLANATIONS, MEETINGS, PROOFS

2341 "You're not demonstrating underwear, do you hear?" Flamboyant and conniving theatrical producer **John Barrymore** screams at budding actress Carole Lombard. *Twentieth Century* (1934, Columbia).

2342 "Demonstrations are sexy." According to graduate student **Elliott Gould** that's why college students riot. He then proves his point by seducing undergraduate Candice Bergen. *Getting Straight* (1970, Columbia).

2343 "Well, Christy, that's the nearest he'll ever come to saying I love you." **Betty Fricker** tells her son Daniel Day-Lewis that his father Ray McAnally's building Day-Lewis his own little home adjacent to his parents is a demonstration of his love—and the only one he's liable to get from his father. *My Left Foot* (1989, GB, Miramax).

Denials

see also REFUSALS AND REJECTIONS

2344 "You think I'm a fool and a spoiled brat. Well, perhaps I am, although I don't see how I can be. People who are spoiled are accustomed to having their own way. I never have. On the contrary, I've always been told what to do, how to do it, and when, and with whom. Would you believe it? This is the first time I've ever been alone with a man! It's a wonder I'm not panic-stricken." Runaway heiress **Claudette Colbert** denies Clark Gable's claim she's spoiled. She counters that she's always been completely under the thumb of her wealthy father. *It Happened One Night* (1934, Columbia).

2345 "I am neutral, you understand, I know nothing. I sell tobacco." **Jack Moss**' denial is a lie. He's actually the embodiment of evil, a vile and repulsive Nazi assassin. *Journey into Fear* (1942, RKO).

2346 JEANNIE: "Yes, mistress." HELEN HALE: "Mistress! Not yet!" British servant girl **Molly Munks** waits on American heiress **Googie Withers**. *On Approval* (1944, GB, General Film Distributors).

2347 DR. BRACK: "I think it's a pretty serious thing. . . to encourage a nurse to contradict the greatest orthopedic authorities in the world." ELIZABETH KENNY: "I'm not contradicting anybody. But I cannot deny what I saw with my own eyes." Representing the established British medical community, **Philip Merivale** expresses its disapproval with Australian nurse **Rosalind Russell**'s new treatment of infantile paralysis—even though it seems to work. *Sister Kenny* (1946, RKO).

2348 "I deny you! I give you up!" Brilliant scientist **Walter Pidgeon** screams at his own menacing subconscious, which is the invisible, terrible Id monster that prowls the planet Altair-4 in A.D. 2200. The film is a sci-fi version of William Shakespeare's "The Tempest." *Forbidden Planet* (1956, MGM).

2349 "I don't bray." **Elizabeth Taylor** brays a denial at her accusing husband Richard Burton. *Who's Afraid of Virginia Woolf?* (1966, Warner Bros.).

2350 "Repression is the father of neurosis. We should never try to deny the beast, the animal in us." These are the views of a prominent pop psychologist, **Patrick Macnee**, in a comic horror about a sanitorium of loonies surrounded by werewolves. *The Howling* (1981, Avco Embassy).

2351 MARTHA LIVINGSTON: "I am not from the Inquisition." MOTHER MIRIAM RUTH: "And I'm not from the Middle Ages." Court-appointed psychiatrist **Jane Fonda** and Mother Superior **Anne Bancroft** exchange denials. *Agnes of God* (1985, Columbia).

2352 "No, honey, not tonight, we already did it this semester." **Stephanie Sulik**, principal Mike MacDonald's leather-and-whips wife, denies him his connubial rights. *Loose Screws* (1985, Concorde).

2353 "Tess, it's not what it looks like." **Alec Baldwin** denies the obvious when his live-in lover, Melanie Griffith, walks in on him and Nora Dunn, naked in bed, making love. *Working Girl* (1988, 20th Century-Fox).

2354 "Well, he would, wouldn't he?" **Bridget Fonda**, as party-girl Mandy Rice-Davies, cheerfully reacts when told that Leslie Phillips, as married Lord Astor, has denied having had sexual intercourse with her. *Scandal* (1989, GB, Miramax).

2355 "Let's face it. I don't need to work, not for the money. And it does not necessarily make me one of these women who's married to a successful man and has dedicated her life to him and her children and then finds herself desperately trying to validate herself as a human being because the children are about to leave her." **Kathleen Turner** denies the truth as she interviews Marrianne Sagebrecht, who has asked no questions, for a job as live-in housekeeper. *The War of the Roses* (1989, 20th Century-Fox).

Dentists *see* DOCTORS AND DENTISTS

Departures and Returns

see also TRAVEL AND TRIPS

2356 "You were going away, weren't you, packing to leave. . . . Oh, honey lamb, you mustn't do that, what would father say if he came down and found you gone?. . . And I would cry—cry." **Bette Davis** with a lazy Southern accent, insincerely urges Richard Barthelmess to stay. *The Cabin in the Cotton* (1932, Warner Bros.).

2357 OSCAR JAFFE: "She's left me!" OLIVER WEBB: "Say the word, O.J., and I'll kill myself." **John Barrymore**'s associate **Walter Connolly** matter-of-factly jests when Carole Lombard leaves Broadway for Hollywood. *Twentieth Century* (1934, Columbia).

2358 "I am packing my belongings in the shawl my mother used to wear when she went to market, and I'm going from my valley and this time I shall not return. I am leaving behind me fifty years of memory." Narrator **Irving Pichel**, as the adult Huw, prepares to leave his Welsh village for the last time. *How Green Was My Valley* (1941, 20th Century-Fox).

2359 "Gentlemen, will you all leave quietly, or must I ask Miss Cutler to pass among you with a baseball bat." Wheelchair-confined radio celebrity **Monty Woolley** threatens some unwanted guests with Bette Davis. *The Man Who Came to Dinner.* (1941, Warner Bros.).

2360 "You are the best part of myself. Do you think I could leave you to a second-rate detective who thinks you are a dame?" **Clifton Webb** is prepared to kill Gene Tierney to keep her out of the arms of police detective Dana Andrews. *Laura* (1944, 20th Century-Fox).

2361 "I'll never leave you, Richard." On her death bed, maniacally possessive **Gene Tierney** threatens to stick to her husband Cornel Wilde even after her death. *Leave Her to Heaven* (1945, 20th Century-Fox).

2362 "Just get out will you, I have to sleep in this room. . . . Just leave it where it all is. Get out." **Robert Mitchum** demands that his unfaithful lover Jane Greer leave his room. *Out of the Past* (1947, RKO).

2363 "It isn't easy to leave a town like our town, to tear myself away from you three dear friends who meant so much to me. And so I consider myself extremely lucky to be able to take with me a sort of memento. Something to remind me always of the town that was my home, and of my three very dearest friends—whom I want never to forget. And I won't. You see, girls, I've run off with one of your husbands." In voice-over, never seen narrator **Celeste Holm** recites her identical letter to three women—Jeanne Crain, Linda Darnell, and Ann Sothern. *A Letter to Three Wives* (1949, 20th Century-Fox).

2364 "I'll come back, Bess. If there's any way, I'll come back. I'll come back." **Tony Curtis**, as dying escape artist Harry Houdini, promises his wife Janet Leigh to return from the grave if he can figure out how to do it. *Houdini* (1953, Paramount).

2365 "Where you guys going? Wait a minute! I'll remember this! I'll remember ever one of ya! I'll be back, don't you forget that! I'll be back!" Crooked longshoreman union boss **Lee J. Cobb** screams at longshoremen who ignore him as they walk into work with brutally beaten Marlon Brando. *On the Waterfront* (1954, Columbia).

2366 "I want you to go away with me, Frank. You don't have to marry me. You don't even have to love me." Sheriff Richard Widmark's mistress **Lena Horne** doesn't ask for much. *Death of a Gunfighter* (1969, Universal).

2367 "Right, well I have to go now, Duane, because I'm due back on planet Earth." **Woody Allen** excuses himself to escape from the company of Diane Keaton's weird brother, Christopher Walken. *Annie Hall* (1977, United Artists).

2368 "You are a master in someone else's home. You rule by humiliation. You must leave and you will leave." **Ben Kingsley**, as Mahatma Gandhi, confronts British Viceroy John Mills after the Amritsar massacre. *Gandhi* (1982, GB, Columbia).

2369 SHERRY DUNLAP: "Why did Daddy leave us?" FAITH DUNLAP: "I don't think he left you; I think he left me." **Dana Hill** asks her mother **Diane Keaton** about her father Albert Finney's leaving. *Shoot the Moon* (1982, MGM).

2370 "Distance and boredom. . . . I want you to go." Stage director **Erland Josephson**, enjoying his solitude, thinks but does not say it (a voice-over does), when his reverie is interrupted by Lena Olin. *After the Rehearsal* (1984, Sweden, Triumph).

2371 "It's time to get out. I want to touch Indians." Advertising executive **Albert Brooks** pesters his wife Julie Hagerty to give up their New York lifestyle and hit the road to find the real America. *Lost in America* (1985, Warner Bros.).

2372 "How many times is a man so taken with a woman that he leaves the screen to get her." Dashing young movie archaeologist **Jeff Daniels** bolts from the movie screen to sweep up mousy housewife Mia Farrow. *The Purple Rose of Cairo* (1985, Orion).

2373 "Nobody ever thinks of leaving this country. I do—every day. I'm the last man!" Frustrated visionary **Harrison Ford** packs up his family and moves to a remote Caribbean island where he slowly loses his mind. *The Mosquito Coast* (1986, Warner Bros.).

2374 "Elvis has left the building." Menacing **Rob Lowe** leaves James Spader's apartment where he has bludgeoned to death Lisa Zane with one of Spader's golf clubs. *Bad Influence* (1990, Epic-Triumph).

2375 "I've never gotten tired of or left anyone in my life. They've had to leave me." Widowed, health food store proprietor **Marlo Thomas** comments on her relationships. *In the Spirit* (1990, Castle Hill).

Dependence *see* CONTROL, INDEPENDENCE AND DEPENDENCE, INFLUENCES

Derrieres *see* BODIES

Descriptions

see also IDENTITIES, WORDS, WRITING AND WRITERS

2376 "Squirming with archness, being aloof and desirable, consciously alluring, snatching and grabbing, evading and surrendering, dressed and painted for victory, an object of strange contempt." It's the way **Miriam Hopkins** describes herself in the movie. *Design for Living* (1933, Paramount).

2377 "I never would have known you from his description." Anxious to win back her ex-husband Cary Grant, **Irene Dunne** dressed as a cheap hooker, shows up at the home of his fiancée Molly Lamont, posing as his sister. *The Awful Truth* (1937, Columbia).

2378 "She's. . . on the tall side. Thin ankles with one of those bracelets on one of 'em. Fair hair. . . thin eyebrows, with white marks where they was pulled out to be in fashion, you know. Her mouth—a bit thin as well, with red stuff painted round it, to make it look more; you can rub it off, I suppose. Her neck—rather thick. . . . She's—very lively." **Robert Montgomery** reveals his sly psychopathic personality, as he describes a missing woman when Dame May Whitty asks, "What's she like?" *Night Must Fall* (1937, MGM).

2379 "He's sort of a cross between a Ferris wheel and a werewolf—but with a loveable streak, if you care to blast for it." Reporter **Fredric March** describes his editor Walter Connolly for Carole Lombard. *Nothing Sacred* (1937, Selznick-United Artists).

2380 "Regular little spitfire, ain't you." Vivien Leigh's response to Yankee deserter **Paul Hurst**'s "compliment" is to shoot him in the face with a horse pistol. *Gone with the Wind* (1939, Selznick-MGM).

2381 "One who has destroyed himself a score of times. . . a veteran corpse. . . an epitaph over an ash-can." Once a famous playwright, now an alcoholic, **Thomas Mitchell** knows himself. *Angels Over Broadway* (1940, Columbia).

2382 "The prettiest woman ever tried for murder in Cook County." Silver-tongued shyster lawyer **Adolphe Menjou**, who prefers to defend guilty clients, takes one look at Ginger Rogers' legs—"her best defense"—and decides to take the case of the brassy showgirl, guilty only of wanting the publicity a murder trial will bring her. *Roxie Hart* (1942, 20th Century-Fox).

2383 "A hotheaded ape with a hair-trigger temper." News correspondent **Susan Hayward** characterizes John Wayne, the head of a construction company building an airstrip on a remote Pacific island during World War II. Of course, she loves him. *The Fighting Seabees* (1944, Republic).

2384 "She's an expensive blonde babe. . . made of cold steel, only not so clean." **Anne Shirley** describes her step-mother Claire Trevor. *Murder, My Sweet* (1945, RKO).

2385 "He's a human octopus with hands." American WAC Lieutenant **Ann Sheridan** has worked with French Captain Cary Grant before. *I Was a Male War Bride* (1949, 20th Century-Fox).

2386 "She came at me in sections. More curves than the scenic railway." **Fred Astaire** describes slinky Cyd Charisse in "The Girl Hunt" ballet. *The Band Wagon* (1953, MGM).

2387 "It drinks, it smokes, it philosophizes." **Humphrey Bogart** describes Truman Capote-like character Peter Lorre. *Beat the Devil* (1954, Romulus-United Artists).

2388 "He was a great detective, but a lousy cop." Mexican lawman **Charlton Heston** speaks of corrupt, prejudiced American cop Orson Welles after the latter is fatally shot. *Touch of Evil* (1958, Universal).

2389 "He was a poet, a scholar and a mighty warrior. He was also the most shameless exhibitionist since Barnum & Bailey." Lowell Thomas-like newspaperman **Arthur Kennedy** notes that Peter O'Toole as T.E. Lawrence had both admirable and self-serving qualities. *Lawrence of Arabia* (1962, GB, Columbia).

2390 "That was me. Braces on my teeth. Band-Aids on my knees, freckles on my nose. All elbows and shoulder blades. For two years running I got picked to play the consumptive orphan in *Michael O'Halloran*." **Debbie Reynolds** tells actor Michael Rennie what a plain, unattractive girl she was. Of course, tom-boys often develop into beauties. *Mary, Mary* (1963, Warner Bros.).

2391 "He is an arrogant, egotistical martinet with a God complex." Symphony conductor **Charlton Heston** warns his sometime mistress Kathryn Hays, wife of the orchestra's concertmaster, about music-loving Nazi General Maximillian Schell, with whom she is to have dinner later that night. Hays smiles and repeats Heston's words, adding, ". . . that should be a familiar experience." *Counterpoint* (1967, Universal).

2392 FATHER: "I heard from one of the Karamazov brothers that the nice boy next door, Raskolnikov, murdered a woman." BORIS: "He must have been 'possessed.'" FATHER: "Well, he was 'A Raw Youth.'" BORIS: "'Raw youth!' He was an 'Idiot'. . . I hear he was a 'Gambler.'" FATHER: "You know, he could be your 'Double.'" BORIS: "Really? How novel." When **Zvee Scooler** visits his son **Woody Allen** in jail they gossip about an acquaintance using Dostoyevsky titles. *Love and Death* (1975, United Artists).

2393 "I don't want to break up the meeting, or nothing, but she's something of a cunt, isn't she?" Outrageous **Jack Nicholson**'s comment about head nurse Louise Fletcher does break up the meeting of staff and mental patients. *One Flew Over the Cuckoo's Nest* (1975, United Artists).

2394 "He's fifty-four. He has a heart condition, asthma, and leans towards alcoholism. He also has the second best mind I've met in this country since Adlai Stevenson. . . . And what's with you, mate-wise?" **Jane Fonda** describes her new lover to ex-husband Alan Alda. *California Suite* (1978, Columbia).

2395 "What a brave, beautiful, extremely boring woman." **Nicol Williamson** refers to Louise Fletcher in the droll spoof of the private eye movies. *The Cheap Detective* (1978, Columbia).

2396 "Chapter One. He was as. . . tough and romantic as the city he loved. Behind his black-rimmed glasses was the coiled sexual power of a jungle cat. . . New York was his town. . . . And it always would be. . . I love this." As the film begins, **Woody Allen** in voice-over dictates the opening of a new book, describing himself. *Manhattan* (1979, United Artists).

2397 "An ex-addict from Queens who had herself surgically altered to resemble Janis Joplin." **Saul Rubinek** describes one of his typical blind dates. *Soup for One* (1982, Warner Bros.).

2398 "Spoiled, ugly, but no stranger to hard work." **Leonard Jackson** marries his 14-year-old stepdaughter Desreta Jackson to crude and brutal widower Danny Glover. *The Color Purple* (1985, Warner Bros.).

2399 "He says you're a real gourmet. . . and you're a virgin. . . . He thinks you might be gay." It's the answer "the sure thing" **Nicollette Sheridan** gives to John Cusack when he asks her what his friend Anthony Edwards told her about him. *The Sure Thing* (1985, Embassy).

2400 "A wild horse that realizes what she thought was a meadow is just a gloomy pen." It's **Jean-Hugues Anglade**'s poetic description of passionate wacko Beatrice Dalle in the title role. *Betty Blue* (1986, Fr., Alive).

2401 "You snot-looking, scrotum-cheek, donkey breath." Fourteen-year-old **Kathleen Wilhoite** uses her foul mouth to chew out tough L.A. cop Charles Bronson. *Murphy's Law* (1986, Cannon).

2402 "Monsieur Vicomte de Valmont, my child, who you very probably don't remember, except he is conspicuously charming, never opens his mouth without first calculating what damage he can do." **Swoosie Kurtz** aptly describes John Malkovich for her 16-year-old daughter Uma Thurman, whom he will deflower as a favor to Glenn Close. *Dangerous Liaisons* (1988, Warner Bros.).

2403 "You're a smart-mouth, stupid-ass, swamp-running nigger. . . that's all you'll ever be." Black Sergeant Major **Morgan Freeman** gives Private Denzel Washington a reaming-out before a battle in the Civil War. *Glory* (1989, Tri-Star).

2404 "He's a Casanova, an animal, a beatnik." Constantly complaining grandmother **Eileen Way** even goes to confession for her despised son-in-law Joseph Long. *Queen of Hearts* (1989, GB, Cinecom).

2405 "Thin, pretty, big tits. Your basic nightmare." **Carrie Fisher** describes Billy Crystal's flavor of the month. *When Harry Met Sally. . .* (1989, Columbia).

Deserts and Deserving

see also RIGHTS, WORTH AND VALUES

2406 "Any man who lets a woman like you take up on a night like this with a man like me. . . deserves it." **Roland Young** plans to make love to Jeanette MacDonald, wife of his friend Maurice Chevalier. *One Hour with You* (1932, Paramount).

2407 "You go. We belong dead." Frankenstein's monster **Boris Karloff** sends away his creator Colin Clive and his wife Valerie Hobson before pulling a lever that destroys him, weird scientist Ernest Thesiger and his uninterested monster mate, Elsa Lanchester. *The Bride of Frankenstein* (1935, Universal).

2408 "I'm one of the undeserving poor, that's what I am. Now think what that means to a man. It means he's up against middle-class morality all the time. If there's anything going and I puts in for a bit of it, it's always the same story; you're undeserving so you can't have it. But my needs is as great as the most deserving widow's that ever got money out of six different charities in one week for the death of the same husband. I don't need less than a deserving man. I need more. I don't eat less hearty than he does, and I drink—oh, a lot more." **Wilfrid Lawson** and **Stanley Holloway** as Alfred Doolittle tell of their undeserving status to Leslie Howard and Rex Harrison, as Professor Henry Higgins in the two versions of the Shaw play. *Pygmalion* (1938, GB, MGM); *My Fair Lady* (1964, Warner Bros.).

2409 "Oh, but you do Charles. If anybody ever deserved me, you do. So richly." **Barbara Stanwyck**'s words ring with double meaning for wealthy Henry Fonda, who claims he doesn't deserve her. The poor simpleton doesn't realize that she's the same lovely woman he dumped aboard a ship when he discovered she and her father Charles Coburn were swindlers after his money. She intends to punish him by marrying him. *The Lady Eve* (1941, Paramount).

2410 KATHY MOFFETT: "If you're thinking of anyone else, don't. It wouldn't work. You're no good for anyone but me. You're no good and neither am I . . . Jeff, we've been wrong a lot and unlucky. I think we deserve a lucky break." JEFF BAILEY: "We deserve each other." Evil **Jane Greer** and **Robert Mitchum** know that their destinies are intertwined. *Out of the Past* (1947, RKO).

2411 "I'm beautiful and I'm smart and I deserve better." Neurotic **Diane Keaton** protests to Woody Allen about the unfairness of life. *Manhattan* (1979, United Artists).

2412 "A man is going to die for no reason but we want him dead. He doesn't deserve it—let's not ever say that. . . ." **William Hurt** refuses to be hypocritical as he and his lover Kathleen Turner plot the murder of her husband, Richard Crenna. *Body Heat* (1981, Warner Bros.).

2413 "I want what's coming to me—the world and everything in it." **Al Pacino** has a glorified view of what he deserves. *Scarface* (1983, Universal).

2414 "We've been kicking other people's asses so long, I figure it's time we got ours kicked." Sergeant **Willem Dafoe** still has a conscience after spending a long time fighting in Vietnam. His reaction seems a little unlikely. *Platoon* (1986, Hemdale).

Desires

see also LOVE AND LOVERS, LUST, PASSION, SATISFACTIONS, WANTS AND WANTING, WISHES

2415 "It's every man's dream to find a short route to his heart's desire." Colonial artist **Robert Young** replies to Ruth Hussey, who asks if there really is a northwest passage as they watch Spencer Tracy and his rangers march away to find it. *Northwest Passage* (1940, MGM).

2416 "Three hundred and sixty-five wives were mine, but in my heart was no love: with every desire satisfied I grew empty of desire." Now a blind beggar, **John Justin** recalls when he was a bored king in need of one true love. *The Thief of Bagdad* (1940, GB, London Films).

2417 "You were unobtainable when he thought you were dead. That's when he wanted you most." Jealous **Clifton Webb** tells Gene Tierney that police detective Dana Andrews most desired her when he thought she was dead. *Laura* (1944, 20th Century-Fox).

2418 MRS. ROBINSON: "Do you find me undesirable?" BEN BRADDOCK: "Oh, no, I think you're the most attractive of my parent's friends." **Anne Bancroft**'s personal questions fluster young **Dustin Hoffman.** *The Graduate* (1967, United Artists).

2419 "A very common neurosis, particularly in this society, whereby the male child wishes to sleep with his mother. Of course, what puzzles me, Harold, is that you wish to sleep with your grandmother." Pompous and foolish psychiatrist **G. Wood** speaks to 20-year-old Bud Cort about his infatuation with 79-year-old Ruth Gordon. *Harold and Maude* (1971, Paramount).

2420 "You haven't 'provoked' me, as you put it, but you are a woman and even though I've only a piece of knotted string between my legs, I still have a man's mind. One change that I have noticed is that I now engage in sexual banter with your nurses, searching for the double-entendre in the most innocent remark. Like a sexually desperate middle-aged man. Then they leave the room and I go cold with embarrassment. It's fascinating, isn't it? Laughable? I still have tremendous sexual desire. Do you find that disgusting?" Paraplegic **Richard Dreyfuss** discusses his sexual needs with his doctor, Christine Lahti. *Whose Life Is It Anyway?* (1981, MGM).

2421 "If He did not want me to praise Him with music, why did He give me the desire." **F. Murray Abraham**, as mad old Antonio Salieri, rhetorically asks uncomprehending young priest Richard Frank, about the cruel trick God played on him. *Amadeus* (1984, Orion-Paramount).

2422 "What a fox. Dresses like Elvis Costello. Looks like the Karate Kid. I'm gonna get him." **Deborah Goodrich** is turned on and taken in by Joyce Hyser, disguised as a male. *Just One of the Guys* (1985, Columbia).

2423 "God, she's beautiful. . . . She's got the prettiest eyes, and she looks so sexy in that sweater. . . I just want to be alone with her and hold her and kiss her. . . and tell her how much I love her, and take care of her. Stop it, you idiot. She's your wife's sister. . . ." At the beginning of the film, Barbara Hershey gazes into the camera with a half-smile, while (in voice-over) her brother-in-law **Michael Caine** expresses his desire for her. *Hannah and Her Sisters* (1987, Orion).

2424 "Is it just me or do you also have this uncontrollable desire to put our lips together?" **Ted Danson** already knows what Isabella Rossellini would like. *Cousins* (1989, Paramount).

Despair and Desperation

see also COURAGE, HOPE, NEEDS AND NECESSITIES, SORROWS

2425 PATSY: "I'm going down to the bar and see Joe. Bartender or no bartender, he's still a man. Maybe he knocks off early." LUCY: "Patsy, you wouldn't." PATSY: "I wouldn't, eh? You're talking to a desperate woman." **Cecil Cunningham** lets her niece **Irene Dunne** know that she needs a man—any man. *The Awful Truth* (1937, Columbia).

2426 "Why was I not made of stone like thee?" With the last line of the film, grotesque bell-ringer **Charles Laughton** speaks to the gargoyles atop the cathedral of Notre Dame. His beloved Esmeralda, played by Maureen O'Hara, has happily gone off with poet Gringoire, played by Edmond O'Brien. *The Hunchback of Notre Dame* (1939, RKO).

2427 "Most men lead lives of quiet desperation. I can't take 'quiet desperation.'" Writer **Ray Milland** chooses alcohol instead. *The Lost Weekend* (1945, Paramount).

2428 "There goes my last lead. I feel all dead inside. I'm backed up in a dark corner and I don't know

who's hitting me." When private eye **Mark Stevens** is stumped by a case, his despair becomes the source of the title of the film. *The Dark Corner* (1946, 20th Century-Fox).

2429 "Despair is a narcotic—it blows life into indifference." **Charles Chaplin** realizes that his murderous course of marrying and then killing rich women cannot be justified, but can be explained as the act of a society-created madman. *Monsieur Verdoux* (1947, Chaplin-United Artists).

2430 "The truth is something desperate, and Maggie's got it. Believe me, it is desperate, and she has got it." **Paul Newman** refers to his wife Elizabeth Taylor. *Cat on a Hot Tin Roof* (1958, MGM).

2431 "Well, it's hard for me to take your despair very seriously, Doctor. You obviously enjoy it so much." Beautiful free-spirited **Diana Rigg** is nonplussed by physician George C. Scott's rantings about wishing to kill himself. *The Hospital* (1971, United Artists).

2432 "You are drunk with despair." Lonely and disturbed **Romy Schneider** recognizes a kindred spirit in the miserable unhappy Yves Montand. *Clair de Femme* (1980, Fr., Atlantic).

2433 "What'd I do?" What'd I do?" **Robert De Niro**, as boxer Jake LaMotta, blubbers incoherently after he's forced to take a dive in a prize fight. *Raging Bull* (1980, United Artists).

2434 "The happy, splendid life is over, and the horrible, dirty life is engulfing us." Matriarch of the Ekdahl clan, **Gunn Wallgren**, cries in despair when her beloved son Allan Edwall dies. *Fanny and Alexander* (1983, Sweden-Fr.-W. Ger., Swedish Film Institute).

2435 "It's not the despair, I can stand despair—it's the hope." Headmaster **John Cleese**, on the way to a conference, finds himself lying in a ditch after a series of misadventures. *Clockwise* (1986, GB, EMI-Moment).

2436 "Where would I go?" When title character **Natasha Richardson** is put on trial, she's asked why she didn't run away from the Symbionese Liberation Army. She despaired of ever being allowed to live after she watched on TV as authorities riddled a building containing SLA members and her, for all they knew, with bullets before they set it afire. *Patty Hearst* (1988, Atlantic).

2437 "I'm out there every day, trying to decide what I'm doing—why it is that whatever I have, it feels like nothing." Cynical radio call-in show host **Jeff Bridges** despairs. *The Fisher King* (1991, Tri-Star).

Destiny *see* FATE AND DESTINY

Destruction

see also RUINATIONS AND RUINS, VIOLENCE

2438 "You hideous yellow monster, do you mean to destroy us all?" **Karen Morley** asks her captor Boris Karloff a foolish and racist question. *The Mask of Fu Manchu* (1932, MGM).

2439 "There ain't no barn no more, Miz Scarlett. The Yankees done burned it for firewood." **Oscar Polk** fills Vivien Leigh in on the bad news when she returns to Tara after the Civil War. *Gone with the Wind* (1939, Selznick-MGM).

2440 "I'm melting! I'm melting! What a world! What a world! Who could have thought a good little girl like you could destroy my beautiful wickedness?" Wicked witch **Margaret Hamilton** cries, as she melts away after Judy Garland accidentally throws water on her. *The Wizard of Oz* (1939, MGM).

2441 "You must destroy us with that weakness you call virtue.... You can think of me as Isabella's husband." **Laurence Olivier** rejects Merle Oberon's plea that he not marry Geraldine Fitzgerald out of spite for her having married Fitzgerald's brother David Niven. *Wuthering Heights* (1939, Goldwyn-United Artists).

2442 "The end came swiftly. After all that man could do had failed, the Martians were destroyed and humanity was saved by the littlest things which God in his wisdom had put upon Earth." Narrator **Cedric Hardwicke**, wrapping things up, describes how bacteria and germs defeated invading Martians. *The War of the Worlds* (1953, Paramount-Pal).

2443 "I destroy everything I touch." Fading, alcoholic movie star **James Mason** warns Judy Garland about himself. *A Star Is Born* (1954, Warner Bros.).

2444 "You're tearing me apart." Confused teen **James Dean** yells at his bickering parents, Ann Doran and Jim Backus. *Rebel Without a Cause* (1955, Warner Bros.).

2445 "I don't want to know the man I'm trying to destroy." American destroyer Captain **Robert Mitchum** refers to Curt Jurgens, the captain of a German U-boat. *The Enemy Below* (1957, 20th Century-Fox).

2446 "Give me twelve men like Clouseau and I could destroy the world." **Herbert Lom**, as Superintendent Dreyfus, knows how destructive bungler Peter Sellers is. *A Shot in the Dark* (1964, United Artists).

2447 "When one builds to make profit, sometimes it's necessary to destroy. Yes, I think it's inevitable." Working for the sugar plantation owners, hired mercenary **Marlon Brando** puts down a revolution of natives on a Caribbean island. *Burn!* aka: *Queimada* (1970, United Artists).

2448 "If you destroy that, it may be irreparable." **Dustin Hoffman** pleads with a judge not to separate him from his son Justin Henry with whom Hoffman has built a close relationship and a good life since his ex-wife and the boy's mother Meryl Streep left them. *Kramer vs. Kramer* (1979, Columbia).

2449 "Silver bullets or fire. That's the only way to get rid of the damned things. They're worse than cock-a-roaches." Occult bookstore owner **Dick Miller** casually suggests ways to get rid of werewolves. *The Howling* (1981, Avco Embassy).

2450 "Why does the law allow her to destroy my life?" It's classical music disc jockey **John Hargreaves**' oft-repeated complaint about his unfaithful wife, Wendy Hughes. *My First Wife* (1985, Australia, Spectrafilm).

Detectives and Deduction

see also CRIMES AND CRIMINALS, DISCOVERIES, LOGIC, POLICE, PROOFS, REASONS, SECRETS, UNDERSTANDINGS AND MISUNDERSTANDINGS

2451 "I'd hate to wake up one morning and find the fortune I married you for was gone. Of course, I could always earn a living as a detective, but what worries me is, what are you and Nicky going to live on?" **William Powell** would hate to think what kind of life, he, his wealthy wife Myrna Loy and their son would have if he had to earn a living as a full-time private detective. *Another Thin Man* (1939, MGM).

2452 "Just a slight skull fracture. I'll deduct it from your salary." **Walter Abel** quips after being struck by a vase wielded by his employee Claudette Colbert when he breaks into her apartment. *Arise, My Love* (1940, Paramount).

2453 "Mr. Owen could only come to the island one way. It's perfectly clear Mr. Owen is one of us." Judge **Barry Fitzgerald** deduces that the murdering host "U.N. Owen" is one of the guests at a weekend on an isolated and deserted island. *And Then There Were None* (1945, 20th Century-Fox).

2454 "You know, Mrs. Beragon, being a detective is like—well, like making an automobile. You just take all the pieces and put them together one by one. First thing you know, you've got an automobile—or a murderer." Police detective **Moroni Olsen** tells Joan Crawford that he's a plodder, who takes a murder investigation one step at a time—but he does find the guilty party. *Mildred Pierce* (1945, Warner Bros.).

2455 "Be a detective? I could do that. I've seen enough movies." Deadbeat American punk **Dane Clark** is suspected of murder after he is paid to marry a strange girl and then blacks out. *Murder by Proxy* aka: *Blackout* (1954, GB, Hammer-Lippert).

2456 "You tint your hair and have a vitamin deficiency. You were a tomboy and an only child. Your adolescence was a nightmare, and you didn't lose your acne until your middle twenties. You can neither cook, nor sew, and your apartment needs a thorough cleaning. You suffer from insomnia and sometimes you drink yourself to sleep. You think you're homely, and you're glad you're growing old. You bite your nails; you're frightened that you're a failure; but you're lost without your work. . . . You've never been engaged. No one you've loved has ever loved you back." Respected Judge **George C. Scott** has suffered a breakdown after the death of his beloved wife. He thinks he's Sherlock Holmes and uses his powers of deduction to accurately describe psychoanalyst Joanne Woodward whom his family has hired to treat him. She does protest that she can too cook. *They Might Be Giants* (1971, Universal).

2457 "Lucky it's not a bull-shit detector or no one would get in." **Sean Young**'s comment is directed to no one in particular as a metal detector is passed over her fine body before she's allowed admittance to a presidential inaugural ball. *No Way Out* (1987, Orion).

Determination

see also DECISIONS, LIMITS AND LIMITATIONS, PROBLEMS

2458 "I've got seventeen cents and the clothes I stand in, but there's life in the old gal yet." Tough showgirl **Joan Blondell** ain't down yet. *Dames* (1934, Warner Bros.).

2459 "I'm not licked, and I'm going to stay right here and fight for this lost cause!" Junior Senator **James Stewart** filibusters while crooked politicians in his state attempt to discredit him. *Mr. Smith Goes to Washington* (1939, Columbia).

2460 "We'll never give in. . . . We won't be beaten. We won't. We just won't!" It's part of upper-class British WAAF **Joan Fontaine**'s tirade against German oppression with the bombing of Great Britain. *This Above All* (1942, 20th Century-Fox).

2461 "And it's gonna stay open. Start those trucks through. We're not stopping at Chungking. We're headed for Tokyo, Yokohama and points east. Let's go." Heroic New York cab driver **Barry Nelson** leads a caravan into Chungking, carrying medical supplies during World War II. *A Yank on the Burma Road* (1942, MGM).

2462 "When I want something I fight for it and usually get it." What wealthy **Barbara Stanwyck** wants at the moment is Burt Lancaster. *Sorry, Wrong Number* (1948, Paramount).

2463 "He came twice—I shall see to it he never comes again." Bitter **Olivia de Havilland** informs her aunt, Miriam Hopkins, that she has no intentions of answering the insistent banging at her door by insincere suitor Montgomery Clift. *The Heiress* (1949, Paramount).

2464 "Sooner or later Diablito had to be stopped. Ben was determined to do it." Indian scout **Robert Taylor** speaks of Cavalry Captain John Hodiak, who will have it out with the Apaches. *Ambush* (1950, MGM).

Devils

see also ANGELS, BADNESS, EVILNESS, GOD, GOOD AND EVIL (BAD), HEAVEN, HEAVEN AND HELL, HELL, SINS AND SINNERS, TEMPTATIONS

2465 "My boy, when the devil cannot reach us through the spirit, he creates a woman beautiful enough to reach us through the flesh." Via a title card, Pastor **George Fawcett** preaches some theological rubbish to John Gilbert. The supposed devil's accomplice is Greta Garbo. *Flesh and the Devil* (1927, silent, MGM).

2466 "The devil's got you by the shirttail, Alvin. . .rassle old Satan." Preacher **Walter Brennan** encourages backwoodsman Gary Cooper to get religion and give up his hell-raising ways. *Sergeant York* (1941, Warner Bros.).

2467 JOSEPH FOSTER: "Where's the horns and the tail? Where's the smell of sulphur and brimstone?" REV.

THOMAS GAYLORD: "Maybe the devil knows it's the twentieth century too, Joseph." Politician **Thomas Mitchell** scoffs when his friend Minister **George Macready** expresses the belief that Ray Milland, the man helping Mitchell get elected governor, is really the devil. *Alias Nick Beal* (1949, Paramount).

2468 "Satan is his father, not Guy. He came up from hell and begat a son of mortal woman. And his name is Adrian. He shall overthrow the mighty and lay waste their temples. He shall redeem the despised and reap vengeance in the name of the burned and tortured. . . God is dead. Satan lives. The heir is one." Coven leader **Sidney Blackmer** fills in Mia Farrow about her little devil of a baby. *Rosemary's Baby* (1968, Paramount).

2469 "I thought ya'll had horns." Good ol' gal, white-trash **Sally Field** meets labor organizer Ron Leibman, a New York Jew. *Norma Rae* (1979, 20th Century-Fox).

2470 "What do you think the devil is going to look like if he's around? He'll be attractive and he'll be nice and helpful and he'll get a job where he influences a great God-fearing nation and. . . he will just, bit by bit, lower standards where they are important. . . . And he will talk about all of us being salesmen. And he'll get all the great women." **Albert Brooks** makes his case to Holly Hunter on what a threat William Hurt is. *Broadcast News* (1987, 20th Century-Fox).

Devotion

see also LOVE AND HATE, LOVE AND LOVERS, LOYALTIES, RELIGIONS, WORSHIP

2471 "If he'd been a lover—a real man—he'd have taken you in his arms. He'd have been tender. Instead of that, he stalked out of the room like the Reverend Henry Davidson in *Rain*." Broadway producer **John Barrymore** questions the devotion of Ralph Forbes for actress Carole Lombard. *Twentieth Century* (1934, Columbia).

2472 "I love you, and I'm never going to leave you." **Cathy O'Donnell** refuses Harold Russell's noble offer to release her from their engagement because he's returned from World War II with two metal contraptions instead of hands. *The Best Years of Our Lives* (1946, Goldwyn-RKO).

2473 "Friendship between women, yes. But not this insane devotion. Why, it's unnatural. Just as unnatural as can be." **Miriam Hopkins** questions the relationship between schoolmistresses Audrey Hepburn and Shirley MacLaine. *The Children's Hour* (1961, United Artists).

2474 "A person should not devote himself to morbid self-attention." Cabbie **Robert De Niro** talks to himself a lot. *Taxi Driver* (1976, Columbia).

Diagnosis

see also DECISIONS, DOCTORS AND DENTISTS, EXPLANATIONS, MEDICINE, OPINIONS, SICKNESS, UNDERSTANDINGS AND MISUNDERSTANDINGS

2475 "The moment I see you with a husband whose pupils are enlarged, who has a tremor of the left hand, who is on his honeymoon with no baggage, whose name is John Brown, I know what's going on." Psychiatrist **Michael Chekhov** isn't fooled by his former student Ingrid Bergman and her new "husband" Gregory Peck. *Spellbound* (1945, United Artists).

2476 "If your chimney was shot and your sills were OK I'd say go ahead, fix her up. If your sills were shot and your chimney were OK, again I'd say go ahead, fix her up. But your sills are shot and your chimney is shot, so I say OK, you better tear her down." Construction engineer **Nestor Paiva** gives Cary Grant and Myrna Loy the bad news about the old Connecticut house they were suckers enough to buy. *Mr. Blandings Builds His Dream House* (1948, RKO).

2477 "Well, what do you think? Is she totally bananas or merely slightly off center." Mother Superior **Anne Bancroft** asks psychiatrist Jane Fonda for a diagnosis of the mental state of young nun Meg Tilly, accused of giving birth to a baby and then killing it. *Agnes of God* (1985, Columbia).

2478 GAIL: "Two months ago you thought you had a malignant melanoma." MICKEY: "Naturally, I, I—Do you know I—the sudden appearance of a black spot on my back." GAIL: "It was on your shirt." Assistant producer **Julie Kavner** tries to calm hypochondriac **Woody Allen**. *Hannah and Her Sisters* (1986, Orion).

2479 "I'm a doctor; I know an asshole when I see one." **Tom Conti** makes an astute diagnosis of his kidnappers. *Miracles* (1986, Orion).

Diaries

see also BOOKS, MEMORY AND MEMORIZATION, READING, REMINDERS, WRITING AND WRITERS

2480 "I always say, keep a diary and someday it'll keep you." Bowery confidence girl **Mae West** doesn't mind employing a little blackmail when she's not selling the Brooklyn Bridge to suckers. *Every Day's a Holiday* (1937, Paramount).

2481 "That's your father's diary, Ann. . . . There's enough in it for a hundred speeches, things people ought to hear nowadays. You be careful of it, won't you dear? It's always helped keep your father alive for me." When Barbara Stanwyck has trouble coming up with a radio speech for her "John Doe" creation Gary Cooper, her mother **Spring Byington** offers Stanwyck's deceased father's diary as a help. *Meet John Doe* (1941, Warner Bros.).

2482 "Dear Diary, nothing ever happens." The movie's first line is spoken by 12-year-old **Margaret Langrick**. *My American Cousin* (1986, Canada, Spectrafilm).

2483 "If you read this diary, all will be explained. KH. P.S. Especially the latter part." **Alfred Molina**, as Kenneth Halliwell, leaves a sad note after killing his lover Gary Oldman, as writer Joe Orton, before taking his own life. *Prick Up Your Ears* (1987, GB, Goldwyn-Zenith).

Dichotomies *see* CHOICES

Differences

see also AGREEMENTS, CHANGES, DETERMINATION

2484 "You sing Jazz, but it's different—there's a tear in it." Leading vaudeville star **May McAvoy** is impressed with new headliner Al Jolson, a cantor's son. *The Jazz Singer* (1927, part-talkie, Warner Bros.).

2485 "Me and the Kaiser, we're both fighting, with the only difference, the Kaiser isn't here." German soldier **Slim Summerville** is willing to trade places with the Kaiser. *All Quiet on the Western Front* (1930, Universal).

2486 "You are different, Tommy, very different. And I've discovered it isn't only a difference in manner and outward appearances. It's a difference in basic character. The men I know. . . and I've known dozens of them. . . oh, they're so nice, so polished, so considerate. . . . Most women like them, Tommy. I guess they're afraid of the other kind. I thought I was too. But you're so strong. You don't give, you take. Oh Tommy, I could love you to death." **Jean Harlow** caresses James Cagney's head in her arms and confesses that she prefers men who treat a dame roughly. *The Public Enemy* (1931, Warner Bros.).

2487 "I've always hated men till I met you. From now on, it'll be different." **Greta Garbo** credits Clark Gable with changing her mind about the male gender. *Susan Lenox: Her Fall and Rise* (1931, MGM).

2488 "CHINA DOLL' PORTLAND: "If you ain't decent, boyfriend, you'll do until something decent comes along." CAPT. ALAN GASKELL: "Out here, maybe, but anywhere else in the world and we'd both be a little soiled. Did you ever see an English river, Dolly?" DOLLY: "No, I'm dumb at geography, just like I am at everything else." GASKELL: "Well, it's cool, clear and clean. Put a stream like that along side any river here, dirty, yellow, muddy—you'll see the difference." It seems round-heeled **Jean Harlow** is being unfavorably, if indirectly, compared to sophisticated English girl Rosalind Russell by Harlow's old flame, **Clark Gable**, the skipper of a Hong Kong-bound tramp steamer. *China Seas* (1935, MGM).

2489 "The only difference in men is the color of their neckties." **Helen Broderick,** married to Edward Everett Horton, hasn't met too many men like Fred Astaire. *Top Hat* (1935, RKO).

2490 SARAH BROWN-'CHERRY CHESTER': "Wait a minute! Have I told you about my temper?" JOHN SMITH-'ANTHONY AMBERTON': "I've had complaints about mine." SARAH: "We'll fight every day." JOHN: "We'll make up every night." SARAH: "I'll leave you over and over again." JOHN: "I'll always find you." Movie star **Margaret Sullavan** and adventure writer **Henry Fonda** debate getting married. Sullavan and Fonda's real-life marriage was brief and stormy. They were divorced before making this movie. *The Moon's Our Home* (1936, Paramount).

2491 "The difference between a tramp and a rich man is a decent job." It seems there must be more to it than what **William Powell** claims. *My Man Godfrey* (1936, Universal).

2492 "I want to get to France to find something beautiful to look at, wine and dancing in the street. . . there's something in me that wants something different." Arizona café counter girl **Bette Davis** shares her dreams with wandering poet Leslie Howard. *The Petrified Forest* (1936, Warner Bros.).

2493 "You're wrong about things being different because they're not the same. . . . Things are very different except in a different way. . . . You're still the same. . . only I've been a fool but I'm not now. . . . As long as I'm different, don't you think that, well, maybe things could be the same again, only a little different. . . ." In his convoluted way, **Cary Grant** asks his ex-wife Irene Dunne to give him another chance, and he promises he'll be—well, different. *The Awful Truth* (1937, Columbia).

2494 ERIC: "My dear, a room in the back of the place like this!" MARGARET: "You weren't nearly so particular in Paris last autumn." ERIC: "But that was quite a different matter. Then the exhibition was at its height." **Cecil Parker** finds the bloom is a bit off the rose in his affair with **Linden Travers**. *The Lady Vanishes* (1938, GB, Gaumont-MGM).

2495 "You shoot it out with them and for some reason they get to look like heroes. You put 'em behind bars and they look little and cheap." Deputy Sheriff **James Stewart** explains to Sheriff Charles Winninger why he doesn't get into gun play with desperadoes. *Destry Rides Again* (1939, Universal).

2496 "Ain't much difference between kidnapping and marriage. You get snatched from your parents. But in marriage, nobody offers a reward." When his privacy is invaded, recluse **Harry Davenport** comforts Bette Davis, who has been kidnapped by James Cagney under orders from her wealthy father to prevent her marriage to musician Jack Carson. *The Bride Came C.O.D.* (1941, Warner Bros.).

2497 "Like most young men you greatly exaggerate the difference between one young woman and another." Munitions maker **Robert Morley** tells Rex Harrison that no woman, not even his daughter Wendy Hiller, is special enough to be preferred to another. *Major Barbara* (1941,GB, Pascal-Rank-United Artists).

2498 "Astronomy and astrology may sound alike, but that's all. Astronomy's a science. And astrology, my love, stinks!" Astronomer **William Powell** makes a distinction when his wife Hedy Lamarr takes up a diversionary interest in astrology. *The Heavenly Body* (1943, MGM).

2499 "Italians are not like Germans—only the body wears the uniform and not the soul! Mussolini is not so clever like Hitler. He can dress his Italians up only to look like thieves, cheats, murderers. He cannot, like Hitler, make them feel like that. He cannot, like Hitler, scrape from the conscience the knowledge that right is right and wrong is wrong, or dig holes in their heads to plant his own ten commandments: Steal from thy neighbor! Cheat thy neighbor! Kill thy neighbor!" Captured Italian soldier **J. Carrol Naish** makes a distinction between his countrymen and the Germans. *Sahara* (1943, Columbia).

2500 "We all come from our own little planets. That's why we're all different. That's what makes life interesting." **Cary Grant** is quite different than title character Loretta Young. He's an angel from heaven. *The Bishop's Wife* (1947, RKO).

2501 "There's a difference. If you give a hungry man a loaf of bread, that's democracy. If you leave the wrapper on it, it's imperialism." **Michael Raffetto** makes an interesting distinction with how charity is intended and perceived. *A Foreign Affair* (1948, Paramount).

2502 "Between the act and the deed lies a world of difference." Defense Attorney **Fred Clark** tries to convince a jury that Montgomery Clift is on trial for the murder of Shelley Winters, not for wanting her dead. *A Place in the Sun* (1951, Paramount).

2503 "There is a big difference between real mental illness and minor mental disturbances." Naval psychiatrist **Whit Bissell** testifies about Humphrey Bogart's mental condition at the court martial of Van Johnson. *The Caine Mutiny* (1954, Columbia).

2504 "There's a lot of people in this world who had a rougher time of it than you. . . the only difference is they don't run for cover." Reformed Western outlaw **James Cagney** tells orphan John Derek to stop his bellyaching. *Run for Cover* (1955, Paramount).

2505 "Princess, the great difference between people in this world is not between the rich and the poor or the good and the evil. The big difference between people are the ones who have had pleasure in love and those who haven't." Hollywood beach boy and would-be actor **Paul Newman** shares his opinion with neurotic has-been actress Geraldine Page. *Sweet Bird of Youth* (1962, MGM).

2506 "Even I know the difference between lovin' somebody and just goin' to bed with him. Even I know that." Lustful innkeeper **Ava Gardner** shows her smarts for wandering artist Deborah Kerr. *The Night of the Iguana* (1964, MGM).

2507 "This isn't Dallas! This is Nashville!" Legendary Country and Western singer **Henry Gibson** appeals to the crowd for calm after a crazed fan shoots singer Ronee Blakley at a political rally for a presidential candidate. *Nashville* (1975, Paramount).

2508 "I want to be different. You gotta be somebody or you might as well jump in the sea and drown." The most important thing in **Phil Daniels**' life is being a member of the Mod gang, but his parents don't approve. *Quadrophenia* (1979, GB, Polytel).

2509 "We don't murder, we kill." Snarling at soldier Mark Hamill, tough Sergeant **Lee Marvin** makes a moral distinction. *The Big Red One* (1980, United Artists).

2510 "A uterus is like absolute pitch; some have it and some don't." Newly confirmed Supreme Court Justice **Jill Clayburgh** replies when she's insultingly asked, "What's a little girl like you doing on a great big Bench?" *First Monday in October* (1981, Paramount).

2511 "I judged the risks and took my chances. War's different! It's just different." **Bill Kerr** argues when his protégé and nephew, long-distance runner **Mark Lee**, announces he's going to join the Australian army to fight in World War I. Lee counters Kerr's objections by observing that Kerr had been an adventurer as a youth. *Gallipoli* (1981, Australia, Paramount).

2512 "The only difference between you and the guy. . . with the stocking over his head is you got a badge." Junkie **Matthew Laurance** accuses his older brother, cop Treat Williams, of being merely a different kind of criminal. *Prince of the City* (1981, Warner Bros.).

2513 "You're trying to put them in jail—I'm trying to put them in a magazine." Writer **Frederic Forrest** reminds detective Peter Boyle of the difference between the two as they both minutely observe passers-by in the street. *Hammett* (1982, Orion-Warner Bros.).

2514 "No, I'm the same, the town's different." Former mental patient and perhaps compulsive liar **Keith Carradine** quips when friendly bartender John Larroquette asks, "New in town?" *Choose Me* (1984, Island Alive).

2515 ARTHUR WILLIS: "In Brooklyn you stay in school, in Long Island, you go to jail." JEFFREY WILLIS: "That's where we'd be living now if you didn't save every penny. . . but no, we have to live in that dump in Brooklyn." **Hector Elizondo** wants his son **Matt Dillon** to go to college. He blames Dillon's summer job at a beach club on Long Island for a change in his personality. Dillon rejects his father and his father's values when he comes under the influence of corrupt, wealthy businessman Richard Crenna. *The Flamingo Kid* (1984, 20th Century-Fox).

2516 "Love in a church, love in a cave, as if there is the least difference, and I held up from my business over such trifles. Nothing I say or do will make the slightest difference." **Peggy Ashcroft** refuses to testify in Victor Banerjee's rape trial. *A Passage to India* (1984, GB, EMI).

2517 PEGGY SUE: "If you could do it all over, Gramps, what would you do different?" GRANDPA ALVORG: "I'd have taken better care of my teeth." On a visit to her past, **Kathleen Turner** seeks some words of wisdom from her grandfather **Leon Ames**. *Peggy Sue Got Married* (1986, Tri-Star).

2518 "The mob is full of thieving, cheating psychopaths. . . . We work for the President of the United States." FBI agent **Matthew Modine** makes an important distinction between the good guys and the bad guys. *Married to the Mob* (1988, Trans World).

2519 "Yeah, but I didn't take a vow in front of God and everyone to be faithful to Ann." **Laura San Giacomo** notes a distinction when her lover Peter Gallagher tells her if he's a liar because of their affair, so is she. *sex, lies and videotape* (1989, Miramax).

2520 "Saturday night was for wives, but Friday at the Copa was for girlfriends." Narrator mobster **Ray Liotta** speaks of the different sexual rights and responsibilities of males in the Mafia culture. *GoodFellas* (1990, Warner Bros.).

2521 "I'm a cop, and you're. . . not." Policewoman **Ally Sheedy** explains why she can't get involved with Anthony LaPaglia, the nephew of a Mafia boss. Nevertheless, she falls in love with him. *Betsy's Wedding* (1990, Buena Vista).

2522 "I'm a BLT-down sort of person, and I think you're looking for someone more pheasant-under-glass." Waitress **Michelle Pfeiffer** uses an occupational analogy to point out to short-order cook Al Pacino that they're too different to become romantically involved. *Frankie and Johnny* (1991, Paramount).

Difficulties

see also COMPLAINTS, EFFORTS, PROBLEMS

2523 ELIZABETH BENNET: "At this moment it is difficult to believe that you are so proud." MR. DARCY: "At this moment it is difficult to believe that you are so prejudiced." Impoverished **Greer Garson** and arrogant eligible bachelor **Laurence Olivier**, don't hit it off very well in the film version of the classic Jane Austen comedy-drama. *Pride and Prejudice* (1940, MGM).

2524 ILSA: "Could we have a table very close to Sam?" LASZLO: "And as far from Major Strasser as possible." RICK: "Well, the geography might be a little difficult to arrange." **Ingrid Bergman** and **Paul Henreid**'s request for seating arrangements at his club is taken care of by **Humphrey Bogart**. *Casablanca* (1942, Warner Bros.).

2525 "I don't mind so much being killed, but you know how hard it is for me to get up in the morning." Having been challenged to a duel by Marcel Journet, the husband of deceased Joan Fontaine, lover-not-fighter **Louis Jourdan** makes a joke about the situation. *Letter from an Unknown Woman* (1948, Universal).

2526 "They say I'm difficult, they say I'm drunk, even when I'm not. Sure, I take dolls 'cause I've gotta get up at five o'clock in the morning and 'Sparkle, Neely, Sparkle!' That psychiatrist says that I'm self-destructive. So what? What do I do about it? Well, the hell with all of 'em. Even the bad publicity helps when you get as big as I am!" Night-club singer **Patty Duke** has made it big in Hollywood musicals, but is finding it difficult to deal with the stress without booze and dolls (drugs). *Valley of the Dolls* (1967, 20th Century-Fox).

2527 DOLORES GONZALES: "My friend told me to keep you occupied. Are you hard to occupy?" PHILIP MARLOWE: "As hard as getting a haircut." Sexy, seductive **Rita Moreno** is prepared to entertain private eye **James Garner**. *Marlowe* (1969, MGM).

Dignity

see also HONOR, RESPECT AND RESPECTABILITY, WORTH AND VALUES

2528 FRENCHY: "Off with your pants." BORIS: "But, Frenchy, it's undignified. I've met every king in Europe." FRENCHY: "Now you met two aces in Bottleneck." Saloon singer **Marlene Dietrich** insists that **Mischa Auer** fork over his pants after losing them in a poker game when he put them up against Dietrich's $30 bet. *Destry Rides Again* (1939, Universal).

2529 MISS CAROLINE BINGLEY: "To me, there's something so unrefined about excessive laughter." ELIZABETH BENNET: "Oh, if you want to be really refined, you have to be dead. There's no one as dignified as a mummy." **Frieda Inescort** puts on airs. **Greer Garson** deflates her balloon. *Pride and Prejudice* (1940, MGM).

2530 "We must be crooked, but never common." Con-artist **Charles Coburn** reminds his equally dishonest daughter Barbara Stanwyck that they should act dignified. *The Lady Eve* (1941, Paramount).

2531 "In Rome, dignity shortens life even more surely than disease." **Charles Laughton** warns Peter Ustinov about the intrigues of Roman politics, making those who try to do the right things by the right means vulnerable. *Spartacus* (1960, Universal).

2532 "He was entitled to a soldier's death. He asked for that. I tried to get that for him. . . just that he be permitted the dignity of a firing squad. You know what happened. He was hanged with the others." **Marlene Dietrich**, wife of a high ranking German general executed for war crimes, complains of it to American Judge Spencer Tracy. *Judgment at Nuremberg* (1961, United Artists).

2533 "You must love her tremendously. . . more even than one's dignity." **Denholm Elliott** tells Art Garfunkel of the love that Theresa Russell needs from him. *Bad Timing: A Sensual Obsession* (1980, GB, Rank).

Dilemmas *see* CHOICES

Directions

see also COMMANDS, INSTRUCTIONS, ORDERS, PLANS

2534 "The nearest bar is just down the street—You can't miss it." Librarian **Greer Garson** gives the bum's rush to seagoing roustabout Clark Gable when he blunders into her library. *Adventure* (1946, MGM).

2535 "Just head for that big star. It will take you home." **Clark Gable** directs Marilyn Monroe as they drive along. *The Misfits* (1961, United Artists).

2536 EDWARD LEWIS: "I want to find Beverly Hills. Can you give me directions?" VIVIAN WARD: "Sure. . . for five bucks." EDWARD: "You can't charge me for directions." VIVIAN: "I can do anything I want to, Babe. I ain't lost." **Richard Gere** seeks directions from streetwalker **Julia Roberts** in a "cute-meet." *Pretty Woman* (1990, Touchstone-Buena Vista).

2537 "We gladly put you at the helm of our little fleet, but our ships must all sail in the same direction." Godfather **Al Pacino** discovers that Immobliare executive Enzo Robutti is more crooked than he is. *The Godfather, Part III* (1991, Paramount).

Disadvantages *see* ADVANTAGES, LOSSES AND LOSING

Disagreements *see* AGREEMENTS

Disappearances

see also APPEARANCES, EXISTENCE, SIGHT AND SIGHTS

2538 "Oh, if I disappear someday, you'll know I ran off with the first traveling salesman who didn't have golf teeth." Bored small town girl **Carole Lombard** confides to her mother Elizabeth Patterson. *No Man of Her Own* (1932, Paramount).

2539 "The sheriff's been suddenly called out of town on urgent business. He'll be gone permanently." Dishonest Mayor **Samuel S. Hinds** announces to the assembled populace the disappearance of another sheriff. *Destry Rides Again* (1939, Universal).

2540 "We sent him up to the nursery for the baby's supper tray and we haven't seen him since." Helpful servant **Emma Dunn** ominously informs Basil Rathbone of the last sighting of the vanished butler Edgar Norton. *Son of Frankenstein* (1939, Universal).

2541 "I love her but I wish she would disappear." In segment "Oedipus Wrecks," fiftyish, successful lawyer **Woody Allen** talks about his meddlesome mother Mae Questel to his analyst Marvin Chatinover. *New York Stories* (1989, Touchstone).

Disappointments

see also EXPECTATIONS, FAILURES, HOPE, SATISFACTIONS

2542 "Anything further, Father? That can't be right. Isn't it, 'Anything farther, Further?' The idea! I married your mother because I wanted children. Imagine my disappointment when you arrived." Newly appointed college president Groucho Marx has a heart-to-heart talk with his college student son, Zeppo Marx. *Horse Feathers* (1932, Paramount).

2543 "She brought me up to be kind and thoughtful and ladylike, just like her, and I've been such a disappointment." **Vivien Leigh** gets drunk after the funeral of her second husband Carroll Nye and tells Clark Gable she's glad her mother Barbara O'Neil is dead and can't see what she has become in order to survive. *Gone with the Wind* (1939, Selznick-MGM).

2544 "You should never get married. It would disappoint so many women." **Claudette Colbert** escapes marrying playboy Francis Lederer by telling him something he'll believe. *Midnight* (1939, Paramount).

2545 "You mean I don't get to smack baby?" Thug **William Bendix** is disappointed when he's prevented from beating up Alan Ladd. *The Glass Key* (1942, Paramount).

2546 "Men marry because they are tired, women marry because they are curious, and both are disappointed." **George Sanders** could easily give a one-man show delivering Oscar Wilde's clever aphorisms. *The Picture of Dorian Gray* (1945, MGM).

2547 "You're my greatest disappointment. You lie. You shirk. You boast. . . ." **Robert Shaw**, as Lord Randolph Churchill, criticizes his son Simon Ward, as Winston Churchill. *Young Winston* (1972, GB, Columbia).

2548 "What the hell are we doing here?" Divorced **Priscilla Barnes** expresses her disappointment and confusion to George Segal after their love-making doesn't move the world for either of them. *The Last Married Couple in America* (1980, Universal).

2549 "I'm all dressed up and no place to go." Pouting **Bo Derek**, naked apart from a liberal coating of honey, complains when her Valentino-like sheik Greg Bensen falls asleep across her tummy. *Bolero* (1984, Cannon).

2550 "Where I come from people don't disappoint. They're consistent. They're always reliable." Movie character **Jeff Daniels** is an exception to his rule. He came down off the screen to be with Mia Farrow. *The Purple Rose of Cairo* (1985, Orion).

2551 "I wanted King Kong and you brought me a giant gerbil." **M. Emmet Walsh** is disappointed when his son John Lithgow makes a life-sized drawing of the Bigfoot he's encountered, and it's not very frightening. *Harry and the Hendersons* (1987, Universal).

Disasters *see* HARM, VIOLENCE, WEATHER

Discipline

see also KNOWLEDGE, LEADERSHIP AND LEADERS, LEARNING AND LESSONS, OBEDIENCE, PUNISHMENTS, STUDIES AND STUDENTS, TRAINING, TREATS AND TREATMENTS

2552 "There's one thing I do know—what this family needs is discipline. I've been a pretty patient man—but when people start riding horses up the front steps and parking them in the library that's going a bit too far." Wealthy **Eugene Pallette** tries to no avail to lay down the law to his zany out-of-control family. *My Man Godfrey* (1936, Universal).

2553 "There is no discipline problem in this school, Mr. Dadier, as long as I'm principal." Iron-willed educator **John Hoyt** lies to his newest English teacher Glenn Ford. *The Blackboard Jungle* (1955, MGM).

2554 "Never replace discipline with emotion." Fencing instructor **Anthony Higgins** lectures his student, title character Nicholas Rowe. *Young Sherlock Holmes* (1985, Paramount).

Discoveries

see also KNOWLEDGE, LEARNING AND LESSONS, REALIZATIONS

2555 "I have found that certain agents, certain chemicals have the power to disturb the trembling immateriality of the seemingly solid body in which we walk." **Fredric March**, as Dr. Jekyll, holds forth on his theory of the dualistic nature of the human psyche. *Dr. Jekyll and Mr. Hyde* (1932, Paramount).

2556 "Something big is burning. We have reason to believe they'll be boiling over soon. . . . They're sure to involve the Canal. Lorenz may or may not be the key man. It's up to you to find out." Prior to World War II, Colonel **Paul Stanton** gives undercover agent Humphrey Bogart his instructions. He's to learn the plans of Japanese agent Sydney Greenstreet. *Across the Pacific* (1942, Warner Bros.).

2557 "We'll never be more sure. We might never have found one another again." While on a two-day furlough in New York City, naïve soldier **Robert Walker** meets naïve Judy Garland, they fall in love and decide to marry. *The Clock* (1945, MGM).

2558 PHILIP MARLOWE: "You're trying to find out what your father hired me to find out and I'm trying to find out why you want to find out. . . ." VIVIAN STERNWOOD: "You could go on forever, couldn't you? Anyway, it'll give us something to talk about the next time we meet." Private eye **Humphrey Bogart** and his client's daughter **Lauren Bacall** go round one. *The Big Sleep* (1946, Warner Bros.).

2559 "You must understand, I discovered her at 16, I made her a star and I cannot let her be destroyed." Butler **Erich von Stroheim** explains to William Holden why he accepts his subservient role to wacky former silent screen star, Gloria Swanson. He was her first director in movies and her first husband. *Sunset Boulevard* (1950, Paramount).

2560 "We finally discovered that season of love. It's only found in someone else's heart. Right now, someone you know is looking everywhere for it. And it's in you." Writer **Diane Varsi** shares what she's discovered about love. *Peyton Place* (1957, 20th Century-Fox).

2561 "I have made a discovery; champagne is more fun to drink than goat's milk." Russian Communist special emissary **Cyd Charisse** gets drunk on the bubbly with Fred Astaire in Paris. *Silk Stockings* (1957, MGM).

2562 "You know, I used to live like Robinson Crusoe—shipwrecked among eight million people. Then one day I saw a footprint in the sand and there you were." Lonely, ambitious New York clerk **Jack Lemmon** marvels at his modern day Friday, Shirley MacLaine. *The Apartment* (1960, United Artists).

2563 "Bo-Bo's dead, and I had a miscarriage. But I discovered macramé." **Mary Garlington**, as

Lulu Fishpaw, has lost her punk boyfriend Stiv Bators, but has found something to ease her pain. She appears in John Waters' "Oderama" film, which no longer can be seen the way the director intended. *Polyester* (1981, New Line Cinema).

2564 "The radical discovers connections between available data and the root responsibility. Finally he connects everything. . . . Nothing is left outside the connections. At this point society becomes bored with the radical. Finally connected in the characterization, it has achieved the counter-insurgent rationale that allows it to destroy him. The radical is given the occasion for one last discovery—the connection between society and his death." **Timothy Hutton**, one of the children of executed spies, gives a discourse on radicalism. *Daniel* (1983, Paramount).

2565 "I'm 26. I don't want a baby yet. I want to discover myself." English working class hairdresser **Julie Walters** tries to make her electrician husband Malcolm Douglas understand her needs as he burns her books after discovering she's been taking birth control pills. *Educating Rita* (1983, GB, Rank).

2566 "India frees you to discover things about yourself. . . ." These are the words of old Brahman philosopher Dr. Godbole, portrayed by **Alec Guinness**. *A Passage to India* (1984, GB, EMI).

2567 "The Doobie Brothers broke up." Sitting in the fuselage of a wrecked plane in the middle of a Colombian jungle, American soldier-of-fortune **Michael Douglas** catches up with the news, reading a copy of *Rolling Stone* found in the plane. Meanwhile Kathleen Turner is menaced by a large snake. *Romancing the Stone* (1984, 20th Century-Fox).

2568 "You'll find as you go through life that great depth and smoldering sexuality doesn't always win, I'm sorry to say." **Woody Allen** shares a sad fact he's learned with his niece Jenny Nichols. *Crimes and Misdemeanors* (1989, Orion).

2569 "I've done things I didn't know I had in me." As she progresses with her self-discovery, frustrated matron **Mia Farrow** tells off her dull, unfaithful husband, William Hurt. *Alice* (1990, Orion).

2570 "I think I've found my calling. . . . Something's crossed over me. I can't go back." **Geena Davis**, as Thelma, gleefully tells Susan Sarandon, as Louise, that she's discovered she enjoys holding up convenience stores. *Thelma and Louise* (1991, Pathé-MGM-United Artists).

Diseases

see also DOCTORS AND DENTISTS, MEDICINE, SICKNESS

2571 "Measles can give a child's skin a nice polka dot effect." Prissy professional party guest **Rex O'Malley** states a rule of fashion when Claudette Colbert's fictitious children develop fictitious cases of measles. *Midnight* (1939, Paramount).

2572 "Please stand back, I have several contagious diseases." Pompous critic **Monty Woolley** shoos away people he considers beneath his contempt. *The Man Who Came to Dinner* (1942, Warner Bros.).

2573 "I hope you'll forgive my touch of epilepsy, my dear—an old family custom." **Clifton Webb** faints when he sees that Gene Tierney is alive. *Laura* (1944, 20th Century-Fox).

2574 "I bet she won't live through the night. She has four fatal diseases." Little **Margaret O'Brien** seriously discusses the fate of her doll with ice man Chill Wills. *Meet Me in St. Louis* (1944, MGM).

2575 "Delirium is the disease of night." Male nurse **Frank Faylen** informs Ray Milland, who finds himself in the drunk tank of a hospital. *The Lost Weekend* (1945, Paramount).

2576 "Susan's growing pains are rapidly becoming a major disease." The antics of teen Shirley Temple are almost more than her elder sister and guardian **Myrna Loy** can handle. *The Bachelor and the Bobbysoxer* (1947, RKO).

2577 "You're a sick girl, Amy. You'd better see a doctor." Back in the safe arms of wholesome singer Doris Day, shattered musician **Kirk Douglas** dumps his sophisticated but unloving wife Lauren Bacall. *Young Man with a Horn* (1950, Warner Bros.).

2578 "Does the Board of Health know about this epidemic?" **Peter Falk**, as Joy-Boy, walks in on a rehearsal of mobsters and gamblers practicing bows for a party to help Bette Davis, as street-beggar Apple Annie, pass as a lady for her daughter, her daughter's fiancé and his family. *Pocketful of Miracles* (1961, United Artists).

2579 "One day it will happen when I cannot hide. . . . The mob will laugh and tear me to pieces." **Rex Harrison** fears that his epilepsy will become common knowledge. It already has been noticed by a hidden Elizabeth Taylor. *Cleopatra* (1963, 20th Century-Fox).

2580 "You're driving along with a man who's been told he's dying. It was bad enough with him when he was well." Baseball pitcher **Michael Moriarty** is forced to keep the secret that his catcher and roommate Robert De Niro is dying of leukemia. *Bang the Drum Slowly* (1973, Paramount).

2581 "The poor kid! She's in Washington and her kidney is in Los Angeles." An airport attendant is touched by the plight of Linda Blair, who is making a flight in order to have her diseased kidney replaced. *Airport 75* (1974, Universal).

2582 "Disease, like God, moves in mysterious ways." Cold, emotionally unreliable Chief Nurse **Julia Blake** offers little comfort to patients or their families. *Patrick* (1979, Australia, Vanguard-Monarch).

Disgraces

see also HONOR, HUMILITY AND HUMILIATION, RESPECT AND RESPECTABILITY, SHAME

2583 "You're a disgrace to the name of Wagstaff, if such a thing is possible." College President **Groucho Marx** is ashamed of his student son, Zeppo Marx. *Horse Feathers* (1932, Paramount).

2584 "When the queen sends you home in disgrace, I'll come with you and be disgraced, too." **Vivien Leigh**, the queen's lady-in-waiting, wishes to share everything with her childhood sweetheart, British naval officer Laurence Olivier, even banishment by Queen Elizabeth, played by Flora Robson. *Fire Over England* (1937, GB, London Films-United Artists).

2585 "Yes, you squashed cabbage leaf, you disgrace to the noble architecture of these columns. . . I can pass you off as the Queen of Sheba." Phonetics professor **Leslie Howard** has plans for cockney flower girl Wendy Hiller. **Rex Harrison** expresses the same sentiments in the musical remake. *Pygmalion* (1938, GB, MGM); *My Fair Lady* (1964, Warner Bros.).

2586 "There's no disgrace in being arrested, Mr. Vole. Kings, prime ministers, archbishops, even barristers have stood in the dock." Barrister **Charles Laughton** tells his client Tyrone Power not to be downhearted just because he's been arrested for murder. It's no disgrace and quite common. *Witness for the Prosecution* (1957, United Artists).

2587 "Being vice-president isn't exactly a crime—they can't put you in jail for it—but it is a sort of disgrace, like living in a mansion with no furniture." U.S. Vice-President **Lew Ayres** tells Senator Don Murray that being vp isn't a meaningful job. *Advise and Consent* (1962, Columbia).

2588 "Yes——. He was a man I worked for and admired—till he disgraced the four stars on his uniform." Colonel **Kirk Douglas** answers megalomaniac General Burt Lancaster who asks his adjutant if he knew who Judas was. *Seven Days in May* (1964, Seven Arts).

2589 "I've done the vilest things, but I've done them superbly." **Uma Thurman**, portraying June Miller, the wife of writer Henry Miller, proudly boasts of her disgraceful behavior. *Henry and June* (1990, Universal).

Disguises *see* APPEARANCES, RECOGNITIONS

Dishonesty *see* CORRUPTION, DECEPTIONS, HONESTY AND DISHONESTY

Dislikes *see* ENEMIES, HATE AND HATRED, LIKES AND DISLIKES

Dismissals

see also ORDERS, REFUSALS AND REJECTIONS

2590 "I close the iron door on you." It's one of the temperamental Broadway producer **John Barrymore**'s more famous lines as he fires employee Charles Lane (aka Charles Levison). *Twentieth Century* (1934, Columbia).

2591 JEDEDIAH LELAND: "Hello, Charlie—I didn't know we were speaking." CHARLES FOSTER KANE: "Sure we're speaking, Jed—you're fired." Critic **Joseph Cotten** is fired by his long-time friend **Orson Welles** after the latter finished the highly critical review of Welles' mistress Dorothy Comingore's opera debut begun by Cotten. *Citizen Kane* (1941, RKO).

2592 "I don't dally much with riff-raff these days, and he's a pretty raffy type of Riff." Having been kidnapped to become Dorothy Lamour's husband, **Bob Hope** is anxious to get rid of partner Bing Crosby. *The Road to Morocco* (1942, Paramount).

2593 "I fired my secretary, my secretary got to my wife, and my wife fired me." Executive **Fred MacMurray** sums up some dismissal dominoes. When he fired his former mistress, secretary Edie Adams, she told MacMurray's wife about his new mistress Shirley MacLaine, and the wife lowered the boom on MacMurray. *The Apartment* (1960, United Artists).

2594 "I don't think you can dismiss people because they're women." Writer **Pia Zadora** fends off a lecherous admirer who isn't interested in her mind. *The Lonely Lady* (1982, Universal).

2595 "You're still here? Go on—go home." Bathrobed **Matthew Broderick** dismisses the audience after all the credits have rolled by at the end of the film. *Ferris Bueller's Day Off* (1986, Paramount).

2596 "I want all of you to take a good look at these people on the risers behind me. . . . These people have been here up to five years and have done absolutely nothing. . . they are drug dealers and drug users. . . . They have taken up space, they have disrupted the school, they have harrassed our teachers and they have intimidated you. . . . The lines are now changed. . . . You will not be bothered in Joe Clark's school. . . . These people are incorrigible and since none of them could graduate anyway—you are all expurgated. . . . You are dismissed." New principal **Morgan Freeman** expels forever all bad apples in his high school barrel as a first step toward rescuing Eastside High. His means are not appreciated by everyone. *Lean on Me* (1989, Warner Bros.).

Disobedience *see* OBEDIENCE, REBELLIONS

Disputes *see* ARGUMENTS, FIGHTS AND FIGHTING

Dissent *see* ARGUMENTS, PROTESTS, REBELLIONS, REVOLUTIONS, VIOLENCE

Distrust *see* BETRAYALS, TRUST

Disturbances

see also NORMALITY, TROUBLES, WORRIES

2597 "It's silly how upsetting a little thing like saying goodbye to one's husband can be." Sadly **Marlene Dietrich** believes her marriage to Herbert Marshall has ended. *Angel* (1937, Paramount).

2598 "I love my husband dearly, but he gets so unreasonable, so upset about the littlest things. Like the little thing in the second row." Unfaithful **Carole Lombard** likes to dally with handsome young men in her dressing room while her actor husband Jack Benny delivers Hamlet's soliloquy on stage. *To Be or Not to Be* (1941, Korda-Lubitsch-United Artists).

2599 "He'll be moving along one day and you'll be upset if you get to liking him too much." **Jean Arthur** warns her son Brandon De Wilde not to form any attachment for wanderer Alan Ladd—but he does and she does. It's always a risk to feel anything for anyone, fearing they may leave or die—but it's a risk worth taking. *Shane* (1953, Paramount).

2600 "My parents say I'm disturbed. We're all disturbed and if we're not, why not?" Quiet high school rebel **Christian Slater** gets his licks in running a late-night pirate radio station where he can let everything hang out. *Pump Up the Volume* (1990, New Line).

Divorces

see also ENDS AND ENDINGS, HATE AND HATRED, LIKES AND DISLIKES, LOVE AND HATE, MARRIAGES, MEN AND WOMEN, WEDDINGS

2601 "Madam, before I get through with you, you will have a clear case for divorce and so will my wife.... Now the first thing to do is arrange for a settlement. You take the children, your husband takes the house. Junior burns down the house, you take the insurance, and I take you." **Groucho Marx** takes advantage of a marital spat he's witnessed to make time with lovely Thelma Todd. *Monkey Business* (1931, Paramount).

2602 "You can have a divorce... Reno... a staggering settlement... and custody of your mother." Architect **George Brent** is anxious to be rid of wife Gloria Dickson and all that goes with her. *Secrets of an Actress* (1938, Warner Bros.).

2603 "The only good thing about divorce. You get to sleep with your mother." **Virginia Weidler** confides to a friend about her parent's divorce. *The Women* (1939, MGM).

2604 GERRY: "Where's the best place to get a divorce?" CABBIE: "Well, most people go to Reno, Nevada, but for my money it's Palm Beach. This time of year you get the track, you got the ocean, you got the palm trees—three months. You leave from Penn Station." When **Claudette Colbert** makes an inquiry of New York taxi driver **Frank Faylen**, he is unhesitant in making a recommendation. *The Palm Beach Story* (1942, Paramount).

2605 "Why don't you get a divorce and settle down?" **Oscar Levant** asks a relevant question of married Joan Crawford who "sponsors" talented artists and musicians like John Garfield. *Humoresque* (1947, Warner Bros.).

2606 "I guess that makes us lodge brothers now. Except that I'm paying dues while you collect them." Recently divorced **Kevin McCarthy** kids Dana Wynter, his one time sweetheart, who has also recently shed a mate. *Invasion of the Body Snatchers* (1956, Allied Artists).

2607 "When you've been married to a woman 12 years you just don't sit down to a breakfast and say 'Pass the sugar, I want a divorce.'" **Fred MacMurray** makes yet another excuse to his mistress Shirley MacLaine for not getting a divorce as he has promised. *The Apartment* (1960, United Artists).

2608 "I chose the wrong man. How many times have you heard that said, I wonder? Oh, he was the most promising, the most handsome. He had the most glorious facade. The facade was all there was. He made me the best-known wife of the best-known skirt-chaser in the community. I made life hell for him. It ended in the divorce courts. We met one day in the corridor outside the courtroom. He struck me. I took every penny he had." **Vivien Leigh** recalls her unsuccessful marriage and successful divorce. *Ship of Fools* (1965, Columbia).

2609 "I knew that divorce was too good to last." Gourmand **Robert Morley** refers to his ex, who is the answer to the title question. *Who Is Killing the Great Chefs of Europe?* (1978, Warner Bros.).

2610 "Divorce is one of America's biggest growth industries." Lecherous divorce lawyer **Bob Dishy** is extremely pleased with the phenomena. *The Last Married Couple in America* (1980, Universal).

2611 "If you were a man I'd divorce you." **Sylvia Miles** shouts at her weakling husband James Mason in the filming of an Agatha Christie mystery. *Evil Under the Sun* (1982, GB, Universal).

2612 "A civilized divorce is a contradiction in terms." Divorce lawyer **Danny De Vito** advises a client. *The War of the Roses* (1989, 20th Century-Fox).

2613 LORI QUAID: "You wouldn't hurt me. After all, we're married." DOUG QUAID: "Consider this a divorce." Devious seductress **Sharon Stone** is mistaken when she believes **Arnold Schwarzenegger** has any feelings left for her. He sends his phony wife to kingdom come with a well-placed bullet to her forehead. *Total Recall* (1990, Tri-Star).

2614 "Excuse me while I get my divorce papers to see where you have the right to ask personal questions about my life." Twice divorced from Alec Baldwin, **Kim Basinger** resents his pumping her to find out if she's become the mistress of mobster Jeremy Roberts. *The Marrying Man* (1991, Hollywood Pictures).

2615 "You try divorcing a Greek Orthodox gangster." **Kim Basinger** responds when her lover, psychiatrist Richard Gere, asks why she doesn't divorce her brutal and demeaning husband Eric Roberts. *Final Analysis* (1992, Warner Bros.).

Doctors and Dentists

see also CARES AND CARING, CURES, DISEASES, EDU-
CATION, INSANITY AND SANITY, LEARNING AND
LESSONS, MEDICINE, PSYCHOLOGY AND PSYCHIATRY,
SICKNESS, TEACHING AND TEACHERS, TREATS AND
TREATMENTS, WISDOM

2616 "I don't like doctors. They cut out little girls'
appendix and charge their papas a thousand dollars." Little **Mary Pickford** speaks her mind to her
father's medical friend Herbert Prior. *The Poor Little
Rich Girl* (1917, silent, Artcraft).

2617 "Get a doctor! Please get a doctor!" Mary Todd
Lincoln, portrayed by **Kay Hammond**, screams
after her husband Abraham Lincoln, portrayed by
Walter Huston, is assassinated by John Wilkes
Booth, played by Ian Keith. *Abraham Lincoln*
(1930, United Artists).

2618 "I am a doctor of philosophy from Edinburgh
University. I am a doctor of law from Christchurch. I
am a doctor of medicine from Harvard. My friends,
out of courtesy, call me doctor." **Boris Karloff**, as
Fu Manchu, trots out his credentials when his captor
Lawrence Grant spits out, "you fiend" at the Oriental menace. *The Mask of Fu Manchu* (1932, MGM).

2619 "I do, sir. I am supposed to have done something infamous by assisting Stillman, an unregistered
man and probably the best man in the world on this
type of case. I ask you, gentlemen, is it infamous
for a doctor to be directly instrumental in saving a
human life? Gentlemen, it's high time we started
putting our house in order. We're everlastingly saying we'll do things and we don't. Doctors have to
live but they have a responsibility to mankind, too.
If we go on trying to make out that everything's all
right inside the profession and everything's wrong
outside, it'll be the death of scientific progress. I
only ask you to remember the words of our own
Hippocratic oath, 'Into whatsoever houses I shall
enter I will work for the benefit of the sick, holding
aloof from all wrong and corruption.' How many of
us remember that? How many of us practice that? I
have made mistakes, mistakes I bitterly regret, but
Stillman isn't one of them. And if by what has been
called my infamous conduct, I have done anything
to benefit humanity, I am more than proud, gentlemen. I am profoundly grateful. Thank you, sir, for
letting me speak." After assisting non-qualified prac-
titioner Percy Parsons save a child's life, idealistic
Doctor **Robert Donat** saves his career by making
an impassioned plea to the General Medical Coun-
cil. *The Citadel* (1938, GB, MGM).

2620 DR. JAMES KILDARE: "Alice, there are two ways
of being a doctor. One is for the living you can

make out of it. Now I could marry you, settle down
and count on taking over my father's practice." ALICE
RAYMOND: "Why don't you?" KILDARE: "Because being
a doctor can be bigger than three meals a day.
Ehrlich was that kind of doctor. So was Lister. I'm
certainly no Lister. But. . . I know somehow I have to
find out where I belong in medicine. And there's no
way to do that in Dartford." Idealistic **Lew Ayres'**
ambition for life beyond that of a country doctor like
his father disappoints his longtime sweetheart
Lynne Carver. *Young Dr. Kildare* (1938, MGM).

2621 "I haven't any time for doctors." Playgirl **Bette
Davis** dismisses any suggestion of illness—but
when she falls down a flight of stairs she can no
longer ignore her problem. *Dark Victory* (1939,
Warner Bros.).

2622 "Father was a doctor. The kind who placed
ethics above collection. That speaks well for Father,
but it always left us kind of. . . ." **Jean Arthur** tells
junior U.S. Senator James Stewart that she's had to
work since she was 16, because her parents didn't
have much money. *Mr. Smith Goes to Washington*
(1939, Columbia).

2623 "One hundred and eighty thousand doctors in
the United States and I have to get you." Physician
Barry Fitzgerald bemoans the arrival of his new
assistant Bing Crosby. *Welcome Stranger* (1947,
Paramount).

2624 "I'm not a mouse and I'm not a man, I'm a
dentist." Dentist **Bob Hope** responds to Jane Russell
when she asks the usual question, "Are you a man
or a mouse?" *The Paleface* (1948, Paramount).

2625 "I always think it's nice to have a doctor in the
house. I saw a lovely film about a doctor once. He
operated on a beautiful girl and married her."
Shirley Eaton, the winsome daughter of medical
student Dirk Bogarde's landlady, operates on him
the moment he moves in. A bit later she knocks at
his door complaining of a pain in her foot. When
Eaton hikes up her skirt and proceeds to take off
her stockings, Bogarde rushes out. *Doctor in the
House* (1954, GB, Rank).

2626 "Gently, man, gently. You're not making
bread. To be a successful surgeon, you need the
eye of a hawk, the heart of a lion, and the hands of
a lady. . . ." While making rounds with medical students, Chief Surgeon **James Robertson Justice**
admonishes a student who is kneading a patient's
stomach. *Doctor in the House* (1954, GB, Rank).

2627 "My doctor says I can't have bullets enter my
body at any time." **Woody Allen** tries to ward off a
firing squad. *Casino Royale* (1967, Columbia).

2628 "I don't trust a doctor who can hardly speak English." In Cuba, mobster **Lee Strasberg** ties medical knowledge to language. *The Godfather, Part II* (1974, Paramount).

2629 "I guess it's sort of like being married to a doctor." **Margot Kidder** imagines that if she was wed to Superman, she'd have to get used to his being on call at all times of the day and night, just like a physician. *Superman II* (1980, Warner Bros.).

2630 NORMAN THAYER: "Oh, God, he'll be staring at our teeth all the time. Why does she have such a fascination with Jewish people?" ETHEL THAYER: "Who said he was Jewish?" NORMAN: "He's a dentist, isn't he? Name one dentist who isn't Jewish." ETHEL: "Your brother." NORMAN: "My brother is deceased. Name me one living dentist who isn't Jewish." Eighty-year-old **Henry Fonda** has been informed by his wife **Katharine Hepburn** that their daughter Jane Fonda is bringing her latest boyfriend, dentist Dabney Coleman, for a visit. *On Golden Pond* (1981, Universal).

2631 "Loosen up, doctor. You're not in Payne Whitney anymore." Head doctor **Donald Pleasence** warns new shrink Dwight Schultz, who has recently transferred to the open-air insane asylum, called "The Haven." *Alone in the Dark* (1982, New Line Cinema).

2632 "A dentist! God, I'd like to kill a dentist." **Edward Herrmann** only wishes it could have been him who did in dentist Joe Mantegna. *Compromising Positions* (1985, Paramount).

Dogs *see* ANIMALS

Doors

see also BUILDINGS, HOMES, HOUSES, ROOMS

2633 "A thousand doors leading to one hell." Disfigured physician **Murray Kinnell** makes a poetic description of Berlin's Grand Hotel. *Grand Hotel* (1932, MGM).

2634 "I saw him lying there, drunk, and I heard the motor running. Then I saw the doors and I heard the motor. I saw the doors. The doors made me do it. Yes, the doors made me do it." Now totally unhinged, **Ida Lupino** describes how she killed her husband Alan Hale by merely closing the garage doors and letting the exhaust from the running car do its work on the sleeping Hale. *They Drive by Night* (1940, Warner Bros.).

2635 "Remind me to nail up the board on the back fence. He's coming through the front door next winter." **Charles Ruggles** refers to the thoughtful bum Victor Moore who spends the winter in Ruggles' Fifth Avenue mansion. Moore has so positively affected the life of all the members of Ruggles' family that the wealthy mansion owner wants to repay the sweet hobo. *It Happened on Fifth Avenue* (1947, United Artists).

2636 "If I'm not here by Wednesday, chop that door down." Ham actor **Vincent Price** instructs a crony after locking Jane Russell in a closet for safekeeping. *His Kind of Woman* (1951, RKO).

2637 FRANK: "Come in! Come in." RITA: "I'm comin' in, aren't I? It's that stupid bleedin' handle on the door. You wanna get it fixed." FRANK: "Yes, I suppose, I always meant . . . ." RITA: "Well, that's no good, always meanin' to, is it? Y'should get on with it; one of these days you'll be shoutin', 'Come in' an' it'll go on forever because the poor sod on the other side won't be able to get in. And you won't be able to get out." Hairdresser **Julia Walters** makes her presence known in the office of **Michael Caine**, her tutor in the Open University. *Educating Rita* (1983, GB, Rank).

Double Entendres

see also DECENCY, PROPRIETY, SENSE AND SENSIBILITY, SEX AND SEXUALITY, SIGNIFICANCE, UNDERSTANDINGS AND MISUNDERSTANDINGS

2638 "A figure with curves offers a lot of interesting angles." **Mae West** gives a lesson in geometry. *I'm No Angel* (1933, Paramount).

2639 JACK CLAYTON: "Do you mind if I get personal?" TIRA: "I don't mind if you get familiar." **Cary Grant** is put through his paces by lion-tamer **Mae West.** *I'm No Angel* (1933, Paramount).

2640 "Well, sweet buttercup, now that I'm here and see what's to be had, I shall dally in the valley, and believe me, I can dally." **W.C. Fields** leers at larcenous blonde vamp Peggy Hopkins Joyce, as the old smoothie has a long admiring look down her very low-cut gown. *International House* (1933, Paramount).

2641 "Did you say gander? I wonder how she'd go for a goose?" **James Cagney**, being a bit naughty, speaks of Mae Clarke. *Lady Killer* (1933, Warner Bros.).

2642 "A little bit spicy, but not too raw—you know what I mean?" **Mae West** is talking about food—isn't she? *She Done Him Wrong* (1933, Paramount).

2643 ANTHONY AMBERTON: "Give me the simple primitive woman with a small high chest." CHEVY

CHESTER: "Mr. Amberton has conquered the highest peaks known to travelers." World traveler **Henry Fonda** and actress **Margaret Sullavan** are being interviewed in adjacent train compartments by reporters. The screen is split to hear and see them both at the same time. *The Moon's Our Home* (1936, Paramount).

2644 "Yeah, I always carry it with me, and put down anything that comes up." Bowery con-woman **Mae West** makes a phallic double-entendre. *Every Day's a Holiday* (1937, Paramount).

2645 "There's gold in them thar hills!" **Allen Jenkins** excitedly reacts when Marlene Dietrich drops some gold coins down the top of her dress. *Destry Rides Again* (1939, Universal).

2646 PHILIP MARLOWE: "You got a touch of class, but I don't know how you'd go over a stretch of ground." VIVIAN STERNWOOD RUTLEDGE: "A lot depends on who's in the saddle." Private eye **Humphrey Bogart** banters with **Lauren Bacall**, one of his employer's daughters. *The Big Sleep* (1946, Warner Bros.)

2647 VIVIAN STERNWOOD RUTLEDGE: "You go too far Marlowe." PHILIP MARLOWE: "Those are hard words to throw at a man, especially when he's walking out of your bedroom." **Lauren Bacall**'s meaning is deliberately misinterpreted by **Humphrey Bogart**. *The Big Sleep* (1946, Warner Bros.).

2648 "Would you like a leg or a breast?" **Grace Kelly** is outrageously seductive as she offers Cary Grant some chicken from a picnic basket. *To Catch a Thief* (1955, Paramount).

2649 "Your troubles are all behind you now." **Sean Connery**, as James Bond, makes the pronouncement to Jill St. John, as Tiffany Case, as he slips a vital weapons cassette in the back of her bikini panties. *Diamonds Are Forever* (1971, United Artists).

2650 "It ain't the size of the ship, it's the motion of the ocean that's important." Main man **Yaphet Kotto** reminds magazine photographer Pam Grier that size isn't everything. *Friday Foster* (1975, American International).

2651 "I'm the girl who works at Paramount all day and Fox all night." At 85, **Mae West** was still breaking them off. *Sextette* (1978, Crown International).

2652 "Well, I'm looking forward to saying the same thing he said. Oh, the British are coming." **Mae West** quotes Paul Revere when she marries English nobleman Timothy Dalton. *Sextette* (1978, Crown International).

2653 "Go down on the stick." Indulging in some sexual innuendo, **James Coburn** instructs a blonde on how to play pool. *The Baltimore Bullet* (1980, Avco Embassy).

2654 COCO: "Leroy ain't into vanilla." HILARY: "It might be a welcome change from black cherry." COCO: "The darker the berry, the sweeter the juice." HILARY: "Yes, but who wants diabetes!" Black **Irene Cara** and white **Antonia Franceschi** engage in a verbal sparring match over black Gene Anthony Ray. *Fame* (1980, MGM).

2655 MATTY WALKER: "My temperature runs a couple of degrees higher than normal. About a hundred. I don't mind. I guess it's the engine or something. Runs a little fast." NED RACINE: "Maybe you need a tune-up." MATTY: "Don't tell me—you've got just the right tool." If these lines of **Kathleen Turner** and **William Hurt** weren't delivered with such obvious heated passion, they would be laughable—maybe they are anyway. *Body Heat* (1981, Warner Bros.).

2656 "Say, your floors need buffing?. . . I buff it gently till it beams." **James Woods** employs a most unusual metaphor to suggest his skill in sexual foreplay. *Eyewitness* (1981, 20th Century-Fox).

2657 "How can I tell until I know what you've got?" Seventeen-year-old **Pia Zadora**, showing her all in a flimsy dress, seductively responds to silver miner Stacy Keach's question: "Want something, Miss?" *Butterfly* (1982, Analysis).

2658 "If you have pain of any kind, I'll make time for you." There's little room for misinterpreting philandering dentist **Joe Mantegna**'s meaning as he hovers over patient Susan Sarandon, trapped in a dental chair. *Compromising Positions* (1985, Paramount).

2659 "The last time I was inside a woman was when I visited the Statue of Liberty." Documentary filmmaker **Woody Allen** bemoans his lack of a sex life. *Crimes and Misdemeanors* (1989, Orion).

2660 "Would you like a little pussy?" It's **Kelly LeBrock**'s embarrassing line as she offers a small kitten to Steven Seagal, who is mercifully in a coma. *Hard to Kill* (1990, Warner Bros.).

2661 "I want you to see this special equipment I have for you. . . . Are you comfortable with a big gun?. . . Once loaded and cocked, all you need is a steady hand on the barrel." Drug Enforcement Agency team leader **Michael Shane** leers meaningfully at team members, blonde bombshells Hope Marie Carlton and Dona Speir. *Savage Beach* (1990, Columbia).

2662 "I do wish we could chat longer, but I'm having an old friend for dinner." Cannibal killer **Anthony Hopkins** cuts his call to FBI trainee Jodie Foster short when he spots doctor Anthony Heald, who treated him so cruelly when Hopkins was in the former's mental institution. *The Silence of the Lambs* (1991, Orion).

2663 "These guys look upon a woman as an object, but I look upon a woman as a whole." It's mangy dog-trainer **Jack Nicholson**'s double-entendre in a movie that disappeared from sight faster than a scrap from the table to a starving mongrel. *Man Trouble* (1992, 20th Century-Fox).

Double Standards

see also BEHAVIOR, EQUALITIES, FAIRNESS AND UNFAIRNESS, MEN AND WOMEN, TREATS AND TREATMENTS

2664 AMANDA: "How do you feel about a man who is unfaithful to his wife?" GRACE: "Not nice." AMANDA: "All right. Now, how about a woman who is unfaithful to her husband?" GRACE: "Something terrible." Attorney **Katharine Hepburn** sees what she's up against in defending Judy Holliday for taking a shot at her cheating husband Tom Ewell. Even Hepburn's assistant **Eve March** subscribes to the double-standard. *Adam's Rib* (1949, MGM).

2665 "Now look, all I'm trying to say is that there are lots of things that a man can do, and in society's eyes it's all hunky-dory. A woman does the same things—the same thing mind you—and she's an outcast. . . . All I'm saying is why let this deplorable system seep into our courts of law, where women are supposed to be equal?" Lawyer **Katharine Hepburn**'s argument against the double-standard isn't good law or good logic. She should be arguing that neither men or women should be allowed to go unpunished for shooting at philandering mates. *Adam's Rib* (1949, MGM).

2666 "All a woman has to do is to slip once and she's a tramp. A man can kill, lie, cheat. . . ." **Joan Crawford** accuses Sterling Hayden of employing the old double standard when he tries to make her feel guilty for having had many lovers. *Johnny Guitar* (1954, Republic).

Double-Talk

see also CONFUSION, NONSENSE, NON SEQUITURS, SERIOUSNESS, TALKS AND TALKING

2667 BOB GROVER: "I'm the census taker." LULU SMITH: "Oh, I lost my senses long ago." It's a bit of horse and word-play between District Attorney **Adolphe Menjou** and librarian **Barbara Stanwyck**. *Forbidden* (1932, Columbia).

2668 "Did you see that movie with Irene Dunne? Didn't you see what Dunne did?" Wonderful old vaudeville comedian **Sid Fields** confuses Lou Costello—not a very difficult trick. *In Society* (1944, Universal).

2669 CAPTAIN OVEUR: "Surely you can't be serious." DR. RUMACK: "Of course I am! And stop calling me Shirley!" Jet liner pilot **Peter Graves** questions physician **Leslie Nielsen**, pressed into service when numerous passengers and all of the flight crew become extremely ill from contaminated food. It's about par for the humor found in the movie. *Airplane!* (1980, Paramount).

Doubts *see* BELIEFS, CERTAINTIES, FAITH AND FAITHFULNESS, RELIGIONS

Drama and Melodrama

see also ACTING AND ACTORS, COMEDY AND COMEDIANS, MOTION PICTURES, PERFORMANCES, PLAYING AND PLAYERS, SHOWS, THEATERS, TRAGEDIES, WRITING AND WRITERS

2670 "There will always be a Shaw play in my repertoire as long as I remain in the theater. And of course, I shall die in the theater. My star will never set." Stagestruck **Katharine Hepburn** talks like an established luminary of the theater—but she's just a one-shot sensation, with the goal of becoming the finest actress in the world. *Morning Glory* (1933, RKO).

2671 "This may seem to you melodramatic, but indulge me, please, I love melodrama. You see I used to be a writer before the war. I now deal in living characters." **Sydney Greenstreet** is Lisbon anti-Nazi underground worker Quintanilla in an unsuccessful attempt to film a Casablanca-like sequel without Humphrey Bogart. *The Conspirators* (1944, Warner Bros.).

2672 "In a moment of supreme drama, he's trite." **Clifton Webb** dismisses Gene Tierney's fiancé Vincent Price's attempt to explain why he's found in Judith Anderson's apartment. *Laura* (1944, 20th Century-Fox).

2673 "A week? Are you kidding? This play has got to close on page four." Hollywood producer **Zero Mostel** assures his partner Gene Wilder that they have found the play so bad that they can make money from its failure. *The Producers* (1968, Embassy).

2674 "This is shaping up like a Noel Coward play. Someone should go out and make martinis." **Woody Allen** comments on the mixed-up romantic relationships of the movie's characters. *Manhattan* (1979, United Artists).

2675 MYRA BRUHL: "Is that play the young man wrote really that good?" SIDNEY BRUHL: "Darling, it's so good that it couldn't even be ruined by a gifted director." **Dyan Cannon**'s question about Christopher Reeve's play is answered by her playwright husband **Michael Caine**, but the sentiments are undoubtedly shared by Ira Levin, the author of the successful stage play. *Deathtrap* (1982, Warner Bros.).

2676 "For God's sake, Horace! Quicker and louder! The play's over when Othello dies!" **Albert Finney**, playing Othello, dying over the corpse of Desdemona, whispers impatiently to an elderly colleague, Llewellyn Rees, who is drawing out the play's final lines. *The Dresser* (1983, GB, Columbia).

2677 "The powerful play goes on, and you may contribute a verse. What will your verse be?" Teacher **Robin Williams** compares life to a drama for his students. *Dead Poets Society* (1989, Touchstone).

Dreams

see also AMBITIONS, BELIEFS, DESIRES, FANTASIES, HOPE, IDEALS, ILLUSIONS, MINDS, SENSATIONS, SLEEP, THINKING AND THOUGHTS, VISIONS AND VISUALIZATIONS

2678 "Dream lover, fold your arms around me.- Dream lover, your romance has found me. . . ." **Jeanette MacDonald** wings into her best song in a still delightful operetta blessed by the Lubitsch touch. *The Love Parade* (1929, Paramount).

2679 "Thank you, but I'd rather have exciting dreams." It's the comment of **Claudette Colbert**, as Empress Poppaea, as she walks towards her chambers, when a guard says, "May Morpheus give you deep slumber." *The Sign of the Cross* (1932, Paramount).

2680 "I seem to be spoiling everybody's brandy and cigars and dreams of victory." **Clark Gable** doesn't show the proper enthusiasm for war to satisfy the young gentlemen at Twelve Oaks. *Gone with the Wind* (1939, Selznick-MGM).

2681 "She's the only dream I ever had that didn't die in the face of reality." **Leslie Howard** speaks at the death of his beloved wife Olivia de Havilland. *Gone with the Wind* (1939, Selznick-MGM).

2682 "We were both dreaming, darling, but now, it's true." **Carole Lombard** reassures Cary Grant, who had been on the verge of death, that now that Kay Francis has been forced to give him a divorce, they can find the happiness that they have only been able to dream of. *In Name Only* (1939, RKO).

2683 "Was I part of this curious dream?" Inspector **Frank Pettingell** bursts in on Diana Wynyard who murmurs that her suspicions that her husband Anton Walbrook is trying to drive her mad must be a dream. In the American remake, police detective **Joseph Cotten** delivers the line to Ingrid Bergman, with Charles Boyer taking the husband's role. *Gaslight* aka: *Angel Street* (1940, GB, British National); (1944, MGM).

2684 "Last night I dreamt I went to Manderley again." Narrator **Joan Fontaine** has the first line of the film. *Rebecca* (1940, Selznick).

2685 "The—er—stuff that dreams are made of." **Humphrey Bogart** answers police detective Ward Bond's question about what is the black bird. *The Maltese Falcon* (1941, Warner Bros.).

2686 "In peacetime all dreams come true." The hopeful message of British Prime Minister William Pitt, portrayed by **Robert Donat**, is said to Phyllis Calvert as Eleanor Eden. *The Young Mr. Pitt* (1942, GB, 20th Century-Fox).

2687 "I dream a woman comes to my window dripping wet. She looks as if she just walked out of the sea. She looks like a woman from another time. She seems to be part of the fog that drifts through the window. She crosses to the door. And as she leaves, she turns and beckons me to follow. . . . When the dream kept coming back night after night, I began to get the feeling that I was going to follow her into the ocean. Tonight, in my sleep, I must have gone down on the beach. Look." **Nina Foch** describes her nightmare that she has in her house which overlooks craggy ocean breakers. She shows psychiatrist Warner Baxter her shoes, filled with sand. *Shadows in the Night* (1944, Columbia).

2688 "All my silly dreams disappeared and I walked home without any wings at all." Melancholy **Celia Johnson** realizes that her brief affair with married doctor Trevor Howard is over. *Brief Encounter* (1945, GB, Cineguild).

2689 "Whatever your dream was, it wasn't a very happy one was it? You've been a long way away—thank you for coming home to me." **Cyril Raymond** has noticed that his wife Celia Johnson has been preoccupied for quite a long time. But now her innocent "affair" with married doctor Trevor Howard is over. *Brief Encounter* (1945, GB, Cineguild).

2690 "Women like me find refuge in our dreams, in which we are lovely and desirable as the most beautiful woman." Plain **Dorothy McGuire**'s dream of being beautiful will come true in her marriage to disfigured Robert Young. *The Enchanted Cottage* (1945, RKO).

2691 "Elizabeth, I just had the craziest dream. You know, if you saw it in the movies, you'd never believe it." Inept third-chair orchestra trumpet player **Jack Benny** tells Alexis Smith about the dream he had in which he was the archangel chosen to blow his horn at midnight and bring about Judgment Day. *The Horn Blows at Midnight* (1945, Warner Bros.).

2692 "I remember long ago I read a book that told the meaning of dreams. If a girl dreams of a boat or ship she will reach a safe harbor. But if she dreams of daffodils she will be in great danger." In voice-over, heiress **Joan Bennett** speaks on her wedding day to moody millionaire Michael Redgrave who has a death fixation. *Secret Beyond the Door* (1948, Universal).

2693 "What good is a dream when you're too old to enjoy it?" **Burt Lancaster** tempts chemist Harold Vermilyea with the idea of stealing from the company he's worked for without much recognition or reward for 15 years. *Sorry, Wrong Number* (1948, Paramount).

2694 "Nobody ought to blame him. A salesman's got to dream. It comes with the territory." **Howard Smith**, the only mourner besides the family at the funeral of Fredric March, remembers the man to whom he was always a friend. *Death of a Salesman* (1951, Columbia).

2695 "We begin with nothing but a dream—but in the end we'll have a show." Stage director **Jack Buchanan** gives a pep-talk to the assembled cast and crew of a new Broadway show, ready to go into rehearsal. *The Band Wagon* (1953, MGM).

2696 "You think all dreams have to be your kind—golden fleece and thunder on the mountains—but there are other dreams, Starbuck, little quiet ones that come to a woman when she's shining the silverware and putting mothflakes in the closet." **Katharine Hepburn** claims that the dreams of women, well, at least one woman, are simpler than those of conman Burt Lancaster. *The Rainmaker* (1956, Paramount).

2697 "Dreams are a kind of living and lunacy a kind of dream, but life is also supposed to be a dream, isn't it. . . ?" **Victor Sjostrom** recalls the words of an old friend and classmate, a former Bishop. *Wild Strawberries* (1957, Sweden, Svensk Filmindustri).

2698 "Up the road in his shack the old man was sleeping again. He was still sleeping on his face, and the boy was sitting by him watching him. The old man was dreaming about the lions." Narrator **Spencer Tracy** speaks of the old Mexican fisherman, played by Tracy. *The Old Man and the Sea* (1958, Warner Bros.).

2699 "Could it be that dreams are ideas escaping from repression in disguise?" **Montgomery Clift**, as Dr. Sigmund Freud, asks himself a leading question. It's the screenwriter's way of showing his inspiration and insights. *Freud* (1962, GB, Universal-International).

2700 "I had a dream: me. My dream is like a nightmare, Mama. I dreamed I was a very old lady, but I was still doing the same old act. I was so ashamed of myself. I ran away, Mama—from the act, from your dreams because they only made you happy and I want a dream of my own, my very own. I have to be like you, Mama. I have to fight for it. I started toward my dream three weeks ago in between shows. I—I married—Jerry." **Natalie Wood** reads the letter her sister **Ann Jillian** has left for her mother Rosalind Russell when she runs off with her new husband for Hollywood. *Gypsy* (1962, Warner Bros.).

2701 "Nobody with a dream should come to Italy. No matter how dead and buried the dream is thought to be, in Italy it will rise and walk again." The movie's prologue reminds the audience of the magic of Italy. *Light in the Piazza* (1962, MGM).

2702 "Rallying a nation of television viewers to sweep us into the White House with powers that make martial law look like anarchy." **Angela Lansbury**, the domineering wife of dim McCarthyesque senator James Gregory, dreams of his ascent to the presidency when her programmed son kills the presidential nominee. *The Manchurian Candidate* (1962, United Artists).

2703 "How strangely awake I feel, as if living had been a long dream—someone else's dream, now finished at last—and now will begin a dream of my own which will never end. Antony—Antony will wait." Title character **Elizabeth Taylor** has taken the asp to her bosom and is expiring. *Cleopatra* (1963, 20th Century-Fox).

2704 "Man's dream of eternal youth, an illusion that begins with the first awakening of his mind and lasts until the moment he goes to his final rest. Only a dream perhaps, but what would life be without our dreams?" Narrator **Vincent Price** sums up at the end of the "Dr. Heidegger's Experiment" segment. *Twice Told Tales* (1963, United Artists).

2705 "I'll do things you never dreamed of, pawnbroker." Streetwalker **Thelma Oliver** makes enticing promises to Rod Steiger, as she bares her breasts, perhaps the first non-porno film in which such flesh was so blatantly shown. *The Pawnbroker* (1965, AIP).

2706 "When I had my heart attack, there was a dream I had. You can talk about death. I've seen it many times as a doctor, but you never know what it's like until it almost happens to you. I dreamed I had already died. I dreamed I was in a box. The sweat broke out all over my body. I wanted to cry out, 'I can't be dead—I haven't lived!'" Ship's doctor **Oskar Werner** tells Captain Charles Korvin of his frightening nightmare. *Ship of Fools* (1965, Columbia).

2707 OLD MAN: "I sure hoped you'd make it, find your dreams come true." ANTIOCHUS "TONY" WILSON: "I guess I never had a dream." OLD MAN: "Maybe that's it. That sure might have been it." It's the final conversation between **Will Geer**, the head of a company that provides aging men with new bodies and lives, and **Rock Hudson** for whom the experiment didn't work, just before Hudson is taken away to be murdered to provide a new body for the company. *Seconds* (1966, Paramount).

2708 "This isn't a dream, this is really happening!" **Mia Farrow** is raped by the devil as she sleeps. *Rosemary's Baby* (1968, Paramount).

2709 "There was a dream I used to have about you and I. It was always the same. I'd be told that you were dead, and I would run crying into the street. Someone would stop and ask, 'Why are you crying?' And I would say, 'Because my father is dead and he never said he loved me.'" **Martin Sheen** gives his father **Jack Albertson** time to rectify the situation while he's still alive—if he can. *The Subject Was Roses* (1968, MGM).

2710 "I thought of Gatsby's wonder when he first picked out the green light at the end of Daisy's dock. He had come a long way to this lawn and his dream must have seemed so close that he could hardly fail to grasp it. He did not know that it was already beyond him." Narrator **Sam Waterston** speaks of murdered Robert Redford whose fate was a direct consequence of his infatuation and obsession with flighty, married Mia Farrow. *The Great Gatsby* (1974, Paramount).

2711 "What we see and what we've seen is but a dream, a dream within a dream." It's the introductory line to the tantalizing puzzle picture that's not for folks who want all the loose ends tied up by the end of the last reel. At another time in the film, beautiful **Anne Lambert**, as Miranda, quotes Edgar Allan Poe: "What we are and what we see are but a dream, a dream within a dream." *Picnic at Hanging Rock* (1975, Australia, Australia Film Corporation).

2712 "You find me boring. I'm quite interesting. . . . My dream turns out to be your nightmare." **Fritz Weaver** leaves his wife Julie Christie because they are incompatible. *Demon Seed* (1977, MGM).

2713 "Oh, well, if one has led a fatuous life, one might as well have fatuous nightmares." It's the resigned thought of second-rate 78-year-old English novelist **John Gielgud**. *Providence* (1977, GB, Cinema 5).

2714 "I had a dream last night so boring it woke me." Assistant D.A. **Ted Danson** makes a little joke. *Body Heat* (1981, Warner Bros.).

2715 "You and Jack have a lot of middle-class dreams for a couple of radicals." **Jack Nicholson**, as playwright Eugene O'Neill, finds some inconsistencies in the behavior of revolutionaries Diane Keaton, as Louise Bryant, and Warren Beatty, as John Reed. *Reds* (1981, Paramount).

2716 "I've had my dream again: Unseen hands driving wooden stakes in my feet, and I can't move." Repertory Shakespearean actor **Albert Finney** speaks of his nightmare to his long-time dresser Tom Courtenay. *The Dresser* (1983, GB, Columbia).

2717 "When you give up your dreams, you die." **Michael Nouri** encourages welder Jennifer Beals to pursue her dreams of becoming a ballet dancer. *Flashdance* (1983, Paramount).

2718 "I'm your worst nightmare, a nigger with a badge." Temporarily furloughed con **Eddie Murphy** flashes Nick Nolte's police credentials in a redneck bar. *48 Hours* (1983, Paramount).

2719 "The dream is always the same." **Tom Cruise** opens the movie with this line. *Risky Business* (1983, Warner Bros.).

2720 "Either stop having dreams like that or clip your fingernails." Alcoholic **Ronee Blakley** is little help to her daughter Heather Langenkamp who has had her nightgown shredded by Freddy Krueger (played by Robert Englund) in her dream. *A Nightmare on Elm Street* (1984, New Line).

2721 "Me and my friends, we had a dream. Life was gonna be a great adventure and we were going to be heroes. God knows, we were dreamers. Everybody was gonna be somebody—me, I was gonna be a great writer." These are the words of struggling south side of Chicago part-time writer and full-time mailman **John Shea**. *Windy City* (1984, Warner Bros.).

2722 "Follow your heart, it's the key to everything—follow your dream." Dwarf **David Rappaport** advises his friend Clancy Brown, who portrays Frankenstein's monster, after he has fled the Baron's castle. *The Bride* (1985, Columbia).

2723 "I look into your eyes and all I see are trashy dreams." Gawky, sullen 15-year-old Laura Dern's dreams are a worry to her exasperated but kindly mother **Mary Kay Place**. *Smooth Talk* (1985, Spectrafilm).

2724 "Sometimes I have dreams about home. Like right now, I'm riding on Misty. That's my horse." While in prison for a crime she didn't commit, stupid cowgirl **Shari Shattuck** dreams of her freedom. *The Naked Cage* (1986, Cannon).

2725 "My dreams are pure rock 'n' roll." **Lou Diamond Phillips** does nicely as the ill-fated Mexican-American rock 'n' roll sensation, 17-year-old Ritchie Valens. *La Bamba* (1987, Columbia).

2726 "She's warm and vital and holds me while I sleep. That's why I don't have to dream of photons and quarks." Physicist **Jack Warden** speaks of his ex-actress wife Elaine Stritch. *September* (1987, Orion).

2727 "While armchair travelers dream of going places, traveling armchairs dream of staying put." It's the motto of the travel books written for reluctant travelers by **William Hurt.** *The Accidental Tourist* (1988, Warner Bros.).

2728 "Now's the time to go to sleep, time to slip away, time to say sweet dreams to the things that I loved today. Sweet dreams to the stars, sweet dreams to the breeze, sweet dreams to belly buttons that go in and belly buttons that go out. Sweet dreams to all the tushies in the world, little ones and the big fat ones like the waitress at the bowling alley. Sweet dreams." After the death of his alienated father Alan King, heart surgeon **Billy Crystal**, himself recovering from a heart attack, brings the picture to a close. *Memories of Me* (1988, MGM-United Artists).

2729 "How's that for a wet dream?" **Robert Englund**, as Freddy Krueger, explodes from a teen's water bed and murders him. *A Nightmare on Elm Street 4: The Dream Master* (1988, New Line Cinema).

2730 "When I was a little kid, maybe five years old in the old country, my mother used to say to me—she'd warn me—she'd say 'Don't get too close to people; you'll catch their dreams.' Years later I realized I'd misunderstood her—germs, she said, not dreams. 'You'll catch their germs.' I want you to know something Tucker, I went into this business to make money—that's all. How was I to know that if I got too close I'd catch your dream?" In a moving scene, cynical businessman **Martin Landau** confesses to Jeff Bridges that he has bought into the innovative automobile manufacturer's dream. *Tucker: The Man and His Dream* (1988, Paramount).

2731 "We'll be a great couple. . . years from now we'll be in the Guinness Book of Records. . . 'twenty years,' people will say, 'and they never had sex.'. . . And in all those years I'll be dreaming of kissing you." Married **Ted Danson** finds it difficult to resist his longing for married Isabella Rossellini. *Cousins* (1989, Paramount).

2732 "Don't dream and drive." It's the advice of **Robert Englund**, as Freddy Krueger, just before causing a deadly automobile accident. *A Nightmare on Elm Street 5: The Dream Child* (1989, New Line).

2733 "You can't sell your dreams." It's the reason **Tracy Griffith** gives for refusing to sell a gas station that was her father's dream. Instead she adds a fast food operation serving hamburgers laced with aphrodisiac sauce, causing competitors to get excited. *Fast Food* (1989, Fries Entertainment).

2734 "It was like coming this close to your dreams, and watch them walk right past with a stranger. At the time you don't think much about it. Most people don't recognize the most significant moments of our lives when they happen. There'll be other days. What we don't recognize is that is the only day." **Burt Lancaster**, the ghost of a dead physician, refers to the one-half inning he played in major league baseball some fifty years earlier—but he could be referring to anyone's dream. *Field of Dreams* (1989, Universal).

2735 "I've always dreamed of running a sophisticated place, smoking cigarettes, leaning on the bar, firing the bartender if I don't like the way he operates." Talking to Peter Coyote, disturbed **Jennifer Jason Leigh** believes that making a go of her deceased uncle's club is the only hope of learning to cope with life. Instead, it speeds her breakdown. *Heart of Midnight* (1989, Goldwyn).

2736 "Dreams are just stories people tell themselves when they're asleep." **Vincent Philip D'Onofrio** comforts Michael Lewis who is having nightmares. *Signs of Life* (1989, Avenue).

2737 "Welcome to Hollywood! What's your dream? Everybody comes here. This is Hollywood, land of dreams. Some dreams come true, some don't. But keep on dreaming. This is Hollywood, always time to dream. So keep on dreamin'." At the end of hooker Julia Roberts and corporation raider Richard Gere's fairy tale, "Happy Man," played by **Abdul Salaam El Razzac**, closes the film. *Pretty Woman* (1990, Buena Vista).

2738 "In short, I became everything I never wanted to be." **Jonathan Silverman** is forced by his disapproving parents to give up his dream of working for NASA and making a space walk. *Age Isn't Everything* (1991, Live).

2739 "This is nightmare night! All the bugs and the bats and the goblins are coming out tonight and no one can stop them!" Philandering Catholic Girls' school headmistress **Christine Amore** is hysterical when her biology teacher husband Leon Lissek goes on a killing rampage. *Bloodmoon* (1991, Australia, Live).

Dresses and Dressing *see* APPEARANCES, CLOTHES, FASHIONS, NUDITY

Drinking and Drunkenness

see also ALCOHOL, EXCESSES, FAULTS, FOOD AND EATING, TOASTS, WEAKNESS

2740 "You must drink. I'm not paying for your art." Cabaret manager **Kurt Gerron** demands that Marlene Dietrich and the other girls working in his show be B-girls. *The Blue Angel* (1930, Germany, UFA-Paramount).

2741 "May I get drunk with you?" Prostitute **Jean Harlow** gets cozy with plantation overseer Clark Gable. *Red Dust* (1932, MGM).

2742 "Drink to the war, then! I'm not going to. I can't. Rule Britannia! Send us victories, happy and glorious! Drink Joey, you're only a baby, still you're old enough for war. Drink as Germans are drinking tonight, to victory and defeat, and stupid, tragic sorrow. But don't ask me to do it, please!" Crying **Diana Wynyard** demurs when her husband Clive Brook asks his family to drink to England's success against Germany at the outbreak of World War I. *Cavalcade* (1933, Fox).

2743 NORA CHARLES: "Say, how many drinks have you had?" NICK CHARLES: "This will make six martinis." NORA: (to waiter) "All right. Will you bring me five more martinis, Leo, and line them up right here." **Myrna Loy** has some catching up to do with husband **William Powell**. *The Thin Man* (1934, MGM).

2744 "I'll drink Scotch, hair tonic or rat poison." Sulking about her notoriety, **Claudette Colbert** is not particular about what she'll have to drink. *The Gilded Lily* (1935, Paramount).

2745 "You are smug, Mr. Darnay, when you ask why people drink, but I'll tell you: so they can stand their fellow man better. After a few bottles, I might even like you." Alcoholic British barrister **Ronald Colman** will eventually make the supreme sacrifice for **Donald Woods**, whom he presently is dismissing. *A Tale of Two Cities* (1935, MGM).

2746 KING MANTRELL: "You enjoyed the cocktails, didn't you?" PRINCESS OLGA: "Oh, the first five or six. After that I was bored." Bandleader **Fred MacMurray** has been plying phony princess **Carole Lombard** with alcohol. *The Princess Comes Across* (1936, Paramount).

2747 "I had three or four before I got here, but they're beginning to wear off and you know how that is." **Irene Dunne**, acting like a cheap dame, asks for a drink, as she pretends to be her ex-husband Cary Grant's sister in the home of Grant's fiancée. *The Awful Truth* (1937, Columbia).

2748 "I've never had a headache in my life. You know it as well as I do. I never had a headache, Zan. That's a lie they tell for me. I drink. All by myself, in my room, by myself. I drink. And when they want to hide it, they say 'Birdie's got a headache.'" **Patricia Collinge** reveals to her niece Teresa Wright what everyone else in the family knows—she has a drinking problem. *The Little Foxes* (1941, RKO).

2749 OULIETTA HEMOGLOBIN: "Do you think he drinks?" MRS. HEMOGLOBIN: "He didn't get that nose from playing ping-pong." **Susan Miller** and her mother **Margaret Dumont** are discussing W.C. Fields. *Never Give a Sucker an Even Break* (1941, Universal).

2750 MAJOR STRASSER: "What is your nationality?" RICK BLAINE: "I'm a drunkard." German officer **Conrad Veidt** receives an evasive answer from saloon keeper **Humphrey Bogart**. *Casablanca* (1942, Warner Bros.).

2751 SAM CRAIG: "Make mine a double." TESS HARD-ING: "Me, too. Don't worry about me. As a diplomat's daughter, I've had to match drinks with a lot of people, from remittance men to international spies, and, I may say, I've never wound up under the table." Sports columnist **Spencer Tracy** learns that international affairs writer **Katharine Hepburn** can match him drink for drink. *Woman of the Year* (1942, MGM).

2752 "I am a drunk. A wise man gets drunk to spend his time with fools." Spanish partisan fighter **Akim Tamiroff** supplies himself with a good reason for drinking to excess. *For Whom the Bell Tolls* (1943, Paramount).

2753 "In the event of drunkenness—mine, not yours, I shall ask from you a depth of understanding that comes only from children." Philosophical telegrapher **Frank Morgan** warns his new delivery boy Mickey Rooney. *The Human Comedy* (1943, MGM).

2754 "I bet she drinks from the bottle." It's claims adjuster **Edward G. Robinson**'s disparaging remark about a supposed girlfriend of insurance salesman Fred MacMurray. Barbara Stanwyck wouldn't drink from the bottle. *Double Indemnity* (1944, Paramount).

2755 "I'll never take another drink as long as I live!" Last of the bare-knuckle heavyweight boxing champions John L. Sullivan, portrayed by **Greg McClure**, swears off after drink has driven him into the gutter. *The Great John L.* (1945, United Artists).

2756 "What I'm trying to say is, I'm not a drinker, I'm a drunk." Alcoholic writer **Ray Milland** tries to make the fine distinction for his fiancée Jane Wyman. *The Lost Weekend* (1945, Paramount).

2757 "Charming middle-aged lady with a face like a bucket of mud. I gave her a drink. She was a gal who would take a drink if she had to knock you over to get it." Private eye **Dick Powell** speaks not unkindly of blowsy widow Esther Howard. *Murder My Sweet* (1945, RKO).

2758 "If there's one thing I can't stand it's a dame who's drunk. They turn my stomach; they're no good to themselves or anybody else. She's got the shakes, see, so she has a drink to get rid of them. It tastes so good she has another one and the first thing you know, she's stinko again." **Edward G. Robinson** degrades his mistress Claire Trevor, whom he only keeps around to have someone to visit his cruelty on. *Key Largo* (1948, Warner Bros.).

2759 "Come on Oscar, let's you and me get drunk." Once famous Hollywood actress **Bette Davis** (acting more like Joan Crawford than herself) makes an offer to her symbol of past glories, her Academy Award statuette. *The Star* (1952, 20th Century-Fox).

2760 "I'd like to ask you to stay and have a drink—but I'm afraid you might accept." **Joan Crawford** can't bring herself to be hospitable to neighbor Jeff Chandler—not yet. *Female on the Beach* (1955, Universal-International).

2761 "Veronica isn't the kind of girl who's all the time got to get loaded. Uh-uh. If, ah, I get drunk and pass out, it's no fun for me, and if you get drunk and pass out, it's no fun for me." Referring to herself, **Yvonne Craig** tries to win wealthy George Hamilton. *By Love Possessed* (1961, United Artists).

2762 "Vodka martini, very dry, shaken, not stirred." It's the usual drink order of **Sean Connery**, as James Bond. *Dr. No* (1962, GB, United Artists).

2763 "Whatever you do, don't tell her you don't drink. She'll think you're a Boy Scout." **Jerry Lacy**, impersonating the spirit of Humphrey Bogart, advises Woody Allen how to win Diane Keaton. *Play It Again, Sam* (1972, Warner Bros.).

2764 "The funny thing is that I don't particularly like drinking, but I like bars. I like the people you meet in bars. I don't like the taste of liquor, but when I drink, I'm very funny. At least, that's what people tell me later." **Marsha Mason** explains to her psychiatrist Ed Moore why she drinks. *Only When I Laugh* (1981, Columbia).

2765 SUSAN: "The right girl could stop you from drinking." ARTHUR: "She'd have to be a very big woman." **Jill Eikenberry** can't get **Dudley Moore** to be serious about their engagement or his drinking problems. *Arthur* (1981, Orion).

2766 "Marry her. Poor drunks do not find love, Arthur. Poor drunks have very few teeth. They urinate outdoors. They freeze to death in summer. I can't bear to think of you that way." English valet **John Gielgud** urges his employer Dudley Moore to marry the girl his grandmother and father have chosen for him rather than be disinherited and lose a fortune. *Arthur* (1981, Orion).

2767 "Well, I know what I've got here. Come on, buy you a drink. You know a drink." After all their adventures, **Karen Allen** offers to pop for a drink for Harrison Ford. *Raiders of the Lost Ark* (1981, Paramount).

2768 "If I was plastered, could I do this?" Erroll Flynn-like movie star **Peter O'Toole**, now on the skids, shows the writers of the comedy TV program what a drunk can do. He does a somersault across a conference table—and then passes out. Head writer Bill Macy snaps, "Well, we know he can do that." *My Favorite Year* (1982, MGM-United Artists).

2769 "Why should we sip from a teacup when we can drink from a river?" Long-nosed Colorado fireman **Steve Martin** asks an intriguing question. *Roxanne* (1987, Columbia).

2770 "Ah, hell, it depends. Generally I recommend my men stay away from vodka and stick to scotch and bourbon. . . . So the bosses will know they're drunk and not stupid." Police detective **Kurt Russell** tells Michelle Pfeiffer that vodka doesn't give one tell-tale breath. *Tequila Sunrise* (1988, Warner Bros.).

2771 "Do you know what I tell an alcoholic who wants me to help them? First, stop drinking." Psychiatrist **Michael Kidd** has a sure-fire cure for John Ritter's alcoholism problem. *Skin Deep* (1989, 20th Century-Fox).

2772 "You won't let us drink from the well." **Don Costello**, one of the old dons, is disappointed with Al Pacino who is trying to sever his ties with organized crime and become a legitimate businessman. *The Godfather, Part III* (1991, Paramount).

2773 "I can't remember. I was drunk all the time." Retired gunfighter **Clint Eastwood**, trying to live down his notoriety for having "killed just about everything that walks and crawls," replies when he's asked if he was ever scared. *Unforgiven* (1992, Warner Bros.).

Driving and Drivers

see also AUTOMOBILES, FORCE, TRAVEL AND TRIPS

2774 "Left turn, Clyde." **Clint Eastwood** gives instructions to his pet orangutan who's at the wheel of a truck. *Every Which Way but Loose* (1978, Warner Bros.).

2775 "The more you drive the less intelligent you become." **Tracey Walter** has an interesting theory. *Repo Man* (1984, Universal).

2776 "Making a left turn in L.A. is one of the hardest things you're going to learn in life." **Kevin Kline** gives his son Jeremy Sisto a driving lesson in busy L.A. traffic. *Grand Canyon* (1991, 20th Century-Fox).

Drugs

see also DEATH AND DYING, HABITS, HARM, HURT AND HURTING, INDEPENDENCE AND DEPENDENCE, MEDICINE, SCIENCE AND SCIENTISTS

2777 "Monocaine. A terrible drug made from a flower that's grown in India. It draws color from everything it touches. Years ago they used it for bleaching cloth: they gave up because it destroyed the material. They tried it on a dog: it turned it dead white and sent it raving mad." Claude Rains' mentor **Henry Travers** tells of the terrible physical effects of the drug Rains uses to make himself invisible. *The Invisible Man* (1933, Universal).

2778 "Quick, Watson, the needle." **Basil Rathbone** as Sherlock Holmes demands that Nigel Bruce as Dr. Watson give him a fix after having solved the mystery of the murderous hound. *The Hound of the Baskervilles* (1939, 20th Century-Fox).

2779 "Monkey's never dead and monkey never dies. You kick him off. He just hides in a corner waiting his turn." Cynical drug dealer **Darren McGavin** tells "clean" addict Frank Sinatra that he'll be back looking for a fix. *The Man with the Golden Arm* (1955, United Artists).

2780 "If you flake around with the weed, you'll end up using the harder stuff." Undercover narcotics cop **Russ Tamblyn** tries to scare a marijuana user. *High School Confidential* (1958, MGM).

2781 "They drummed you right out of Hollywood, so you came crawling back to Broadway. Well, Broadway doesn't go for booze and dope!" When tough old battle-axe, Broadway star and fair drinker **Susan Hayward** sneers her welcome home to dope fiend Patty Duke in a ladies' room, Duke snatches the red wig off the head of Hayward and flushes it down the toilet. *Valley of the Dolls* (1967, 20th Century-Fox).

2782 "The intersection of Broadway and 72nd Street on New York's West Side is officially known as Sherman Square. To heroin addicts, it is Needle Park." The opening caption of the movie. *The Panic in Needle Park* (1971, 20th Century-Fox).

2783 DR. FREUD: "Herr Holmes' dependence on cocaine strikes me as a symptom—not an hysterical one, I grant you—but nevertheless, a symptom, an effect rather than a cause." DR. WATSON: "What makes you say that?" DR. FREUD: "Elementary, my dear fellow. Knowing something—as I do—about drugs and drug addiction, I don't believe a man succumbs to their destructive appeal out of mere boredom." Psychoanalyst **Alan Arkin** shares a diagnosis with **Robert Duvall**, regarding Nicol Williamson, as Sherlock Holmes. *The Seven-Per-Cent Solution* (1976, Universal).

2784 "[In] a world like this one, people are going to naturally want to get high." War correspondent **Nick Nolte** justifies becoming a heroin smuggler in Vietnam. *Who'll Stop the Rain?* (1978, United Artists).

2785 "Does anyone have a Valium?" It's the question **Charles Durning** asks when his brother Burt Reynolds suffers an anxiety attack in a department store. About twenty people offer the drug. *Starting Over* (1979, Paramount).

2786 "I can't get hooked if I use just a little, only once in a while. I can control my using." Young teen **Nadja Brunkhorst** experiments with alcohol and drugs, believing that she won't become an addict—she is tragically wrong. *Christiane F* (1981, Germany, New World).

2787 "He's been stoned since the third grade." It's a classmate's description of carefree teenage surfer Sean Penn. *Fast Times at Ridgemont High* (1982, Universal).

2788 "Oh, why can't you snort it like the rest of us?" Sadistic warden **John Vernon** snarls impatiently at a coke-injecting female prisoner. *Chained Heat* (1983, US-Germany, Farley).

2789 "I've never known a repo man who didn't use a lot of speed." Repossessions agent **Harry Dean Stanton** tells novice repo man **Emilio Estevez** that all the pros use drugs because their work is so filled with tension and danger. *Repo Man* (1984, Universal).

2790 "Anyone connected with drugs deserves to die." **John P. Ryan** relates to Charles Bronson the details of his daughter's death due to drugs. *Death Wish 4: The Crackdown* (1987, Cannon).

2791 "He's polluting this town with drugs and turning it into a sewer." Modern Texas Ranger **Nick Nolte** complains about drug dealer Powers Boothe ruining a border town. *Extreme Prejudice* (1987, Tri-Star).

2792 "If they give me any smack, I'll be sure and save some for you." Cop **Carl Weathers** sarcastically promises junkie Vanity a fix. *Action Jackson* (1988, Lorimar).

2793 "Let's see if I can get through one evening without chemicals." While having dinner with bright, attractive Tracy Pollan, **Michael J. Fox** steps

into the men's room for a snort of cocaine, but changes his mind. *Bright Lights, Big City* (1988, United Artists).

2794 "I didn't give her cocaine, she gave me cocaine." Philadelphia real estate salesman **Michael Keaton** wakes up to find the girl he picked up at a bar is dead. He tells the police he's not responsible. *Clean and Sober* (1988, Warner Bros.).

2795 "People use drugs to relieve the pressure of their everyday life—like having to tie their shoes." **Matt Dillon** makes a case for the use of drugs to social worker Beah Richards. *Drugstore Cowboy* (1989, Avenue).

2796 "The idea that anyone can use drugs and escape a horrible fate is anathema [to them]." Junkie priest **William S. Burroughs** predicts to Matt Dillon that in the near future the right wing will "demonize" and "scapegoat" drugs and users to set up a police state. *Drugstore Cowboy* (1989, Avenue).

2797 "This whole drug thing: It's not a black thing. It's not a white thing. It's a death thing." Undercover cop **Judd Nelson** believes the public should be color blind in dealing with the country's drug problem. *New Jack City* (1991, Warner Bros.).

2798 "If we in America don't confront the problem of crack cocaine and other drugs realistically—without empty slogans and promises, but by examining what motors the human soul on the course of spiritual destruction—then the New Jack City shall continue to thrive, and we shall forever be doomed to despair in the shadows of its demonic skyline." This was the strident epilogue of this drug-shoot-em-up. *New Jack City* (1991, Warner Bros.).

Duality

see also GOOD AND EVIL (BAD)

2799 "You go with the express disapproval of the Queen of England but take with you the grateful affection of Elizabeth." It's **Flora Robson**'s not so mixed message to Erroll Flynn who tells her of his plans to capture Spanish treasure ships. *The Sea Hawk* (1940, Warner Bros.).

2800 "There are two Don Burnhams. Don the drunk and Don the writer—I've tried to break away from that guy a lot of times, but it's no good—that other Don always wants us to have a drink." **Ray Milland** tells his fiancée Jane Wyman that he's a kind of Dr. Jekyll and Mr. Hyde. *The Lost Weekend* (1945, Paramount).

2801 "I think I was trying to say something about the duality of man." **Matthew Modine** responds to an officer who asks him to explain the meaning of a peace symbol and "born to kill" on his helmet. *Full Metal Jacket* (1987, Warner Bros.).

Dullness

see also BOREDOM AND BORES, IGNORANCE, STUPIDITY

2802 "I've been fire-fighting all afternoon down at the docks. . . . Perhaps my guests might be interested. It's been such a dull season." Merry monarch Charles II, portrayed by **George Sanders**, is an amateur fireman. *Forever Amber* (1947, 20th Century-Fox).

2803 "My wives divorced me. . . they said I led too dull a life." Even though he's wanted for murder all over the country, innocent advertising man **Cary Grant** has time to wisecrack about his marital status to lovely Eva Marie Saint. *North by Northwest* (1959, MGM).

2804 "It is widely held that too much wine will dull a man's desires. Indeed it will—in a dull man." Narrator **Michael MacLiammoir.** *Tom Jones* (1963, GB, United Artists).

Duties

see also LEGALITY AND ILLEGALITY, MORALITY, OBEDIENCE, RESPECT AND RESPECTABILITY, RESPONSIBILITIES, SERVICES

2805 "Am I a king or a breeding bull?. . . The things I do for England." Monarch **Charles Laughton** reluctantly enters the bedroom of his fourth wife, unattractive Elsa Lanchester, in the hope of producing a male heir. *The Private Life of Henry VIII* (1933, GB, London Films-United Artists).

2806 "Your dream prince, reporting for duty." This line **Nelson Eddy** is forced to deliver to Jeanette MacDonald is embarrassing enough to hear, but pitifully poor actor Eddy makes it even worse than that. *Rose Marie* (1936, MGM).

2807 "When a man's partner is killed, he's supposed to do something about it. It doesn't make any difference what you thought of him. He was your partner and you're supposed to do something about it." Private eye **Humphrey Bogart** tries to explain to Mary Astor that it's his duty to turn her in for killing his partner Jerome Cowan, even though he loves her. *The Maltese Falcon* (1941, Warner Bros.).

2808 "I ain't no hero. I'm just a guy. I'm here because someone sent me and I just want to get it over with. . . ." Marine **William Bendix** shares a thought that most fighting men would endorse, whatever the war. *Guadalcanal Diary* (1943, 20th Century-Fox).

2809 "I guess it becomes his duty to share it with the whole world." **Sara Allgood** believes her son Dennis Morgan, as Irish tenor Chauncey Olcott, has a voice that is heaven-sent and meant to be heard. *My Wild Irish Rose* (1947, Warner Bros.).

2810 "Put out of your mind any romantic notion that it's a way of glory. It's a life of suffering and hardship, an uncompromising devotion to your oath and your duty." Ramrod hard cavalry officer **John Wayne** lectures his son Claude Jarman, Jr., a new recruit in Wayne's command, whom the Duke hasn't seen in years. *Rio Grande* (1950, Republic).

2811 "A man's gotta go his own way or he's nothin'. . . a man should be what he can do." **Montgomery Clift** inarticulately explains to Donna Reed why he's a soldier. *From Here to Eternity* (1953, Columbia).

2812 "I suppose you're still on duty, Inspector?" Realizing the jig is up, **Ray Milland** pours himself a drink, but understands that Scotland Yard Inspector John Williams may not be able to join him. *Dial M for Murder* (1954, Warner Bros.).

2813 "All you're supposed to do is. . . give the boys a little tea and sympathy." Boarding school teacher **Leif Erickson** lets his wife Deborah Kerr know she's not expected to get too involved in the lives of the boys at the school. *Tea and Sympathy* (1956, MGM).

2814 "Mr. Brady, it's the duty of a newspaper to comfort the afflicted and flick the comfortable." **Gene Kelly**'s H.L. Mencken-like writer sneers at Fredric March, who stands in for William Jennings Bryan. *Inherit the Wind* (1960, United Artists).

2815 MAX BIALYSTOCK: "How can you take the last penny out of a poor man's pocket?" LANDLORD: "I have to. I'm a landlord." Failing Broadway producer **Zero Mostel** has no luck appealing to the pity and charity of his landlord—who sees his duty and does it. *The Producers* (1967, MGM).

2816 "I'm not quite sure what I'm doing here, I'm not sure what I'm doing. Perhaps it's only for the pleasure of it or maybe it's because I don't know how to do anything else. Perhaps I've nothing else to do. But I do know that whatever I do, I try to do it well and see it clearly through to the end." **Marlon Brando** is hired to crush the revolution of the inhabitants of an Antilles island. They are virtually slaves of the Greater Antilles Sugar Company. *Burn!* aka: *Queimada* (1970, Ital.-Fr.-United Artists).

2817 "You, like me, are adrift in Berlin. It's my duty to corrupt you." Bisexual German Baron **Helmut Griem** does his duty by taking both Liza Minnelli and Michael York as lovers. *Cabaret* (1972, Allied Artists).

2818 "I've lost all the venom; all the juice of youth. I've lost all the lust for women and now my mind is clear, my duty to God is clear." Despite his words, elderly don **Eli Wallach** can't be trusted, as Al Pacino will discover. *The Godfather, Part III* (1991, Paramount).

Dying Words *see* DEATH AND DYING, LIFE AND DEATH, LIVES AND LIVING

Earnings *see* MONEY

Ears *see* BODIES, FACES

Earth *see* NATURE AND NATURAL, WORLD

Ease and Easiness

see also COMFORTS, DIFFICULTIES, EFFORTS, FREEDOMS, HURRY AND HURRYING, INFLUENCES, NATURE AND NATURAL, PROBLEMS, TROUBLES

2819 "I'm hard to get, Geoff. All you have to do is ask me." Brooklyn show girl **Jean Arthur** makes herself perfectly clear to Cary Grant. She wants him to ask her to stay in a small South American town where Grant runs a flying service. *Only Angels Have Wings* (1939, Columbia).

2820 "This is going to be much easier for me than it is for you. . . . Poor sweet Jimmy." Just before their long awaited trip to the altar, **Laraine Day** is fatally injured when a truck hits her. She says her farewell to Lew Ayres. *Dr. Kildare's Wedding Day* (1941, MGM).

2821 "Look, baby, you can't get away with it. . . you want to knock him off, don't you?. . . What did you think I was anyway. . . a guy who walks into a good lookin' dame's front parlor and says, 'Good afternoon, I sell accident insurance on husbands. You got one that's been around too long, one you'd like to turn into a little hard cash? Just give me a smile and I'll help you to collect?' Boy, what a dope you must think I am." Insurance agent **Fred MacMur-**

ray lets Barbara Stanwyck know that he's not that easily drawn in when she innocently inquires if it is possible to take out an insurance policy on her husband without him knowing about it. *Double Indemnity* (1944, Paramount).

2822 "Dear Frances. We just blew a bridge and took a farmhouse. It was so easy, terribly easy." Infantryman **John Ireland** writes home at the end of the film. *A Walk in the Sun* (1946, 20th Century-Fox).

2823 CHARLOTTE MANNING: "How could you?" MIKE HAMMER: "It was easy." Sexy murderer **Peggie Castle** is fatally shot by hard-boiled private eye **Biff Elliot**, despite her seductive stripping away of all her clothes for his benefit. He did let her finish before he shot her. *I, the Jury* (1953, United Artists).

2824 "It's not so easy to raise my hand and send a boy to die without talking about it first." **Henry Fonda** explains why he voted no in the first jury vote of 11 to 1 for conviction. *12 Angry Men* (1957, United Artists).

2825 JOHNNY HOOKER: "Can you get a mob together?" HENRY GONDORFF: "After what happened to Luther, I don't think I can get more than two or three hundred guys." **Robert Redford** and **Paul Newman** plan to run a big con on mobster Robert Shaw, who had Redford's partner Robert Earl Jones murdered. *The Sting* (1973, Universal).

2826 "I'm not going to say it will be easy." **Richard Jordan** is in charge of the expedition to raise the Titanic from the waters off Newfoundland. He seriously understates the problem. *Raising the Titanic* (1980, 20th Century-Fox).

2827 "He's kind of like a strolling player. He goes from town to town entertaining people. Sometimes it isn't easy." Fast-talking female wrestlers manager **Peter Falk** speaks of Pagliacci, one of the operatic arias he is forever playing on a cassette player.. . . *All the Marbles* (1981, United Artists).

2828 TAMARA: "How do you manage it? Do you rush from one to another?" HERMAN: "I do my best. It isn't easy." **Anjelica Huston**, the first of **Ron Silver**'s three wives living in different boroughs of New York, mocks him. *Enemies, a Love Story* (1989, 20th Century-Fox).

East *see* LOCATIONS

Eating *see* FOOD AND EATING, HUNGER, OBESITY

Eccentricities

2829 "If it is eccentric to be impatient in love, sir, I am." **Fredric March** confesses that he would prefer a much shorter engagement period than suggested by his intended Rose Hobart's father Halliwell Hobbes. *Dr. Jekyll and Mr. Hyde* (1931, Paramount).

2830 "Dad makes fireworks because there's a sense of excitement about it. And mother—know why mother writes plays? Because eight years ago a typewriter was delivered to the house by mistake." **Jean Arthur** tells of some of the eccentricities of her parents Samuel S. Hinds and Spring Byington to her fiancé James Stewart. *You Can't Take It with You* (1938, Columbia).

2831 "Every family has curious little traits. What of it? My father raises orchids at ten thousand dollars a bulb. Is that sensible? My mother believes in spiritualism. That's just as bad as your mother writing plays, isn't it?" Not to be outdone, **James Stewart** tries to convince Jean Arthur that his family is every bit as strange as hers. *You Can't Take It with You* (1938, Columbia).

2832 "When I married, I didn't realize that in the Czerny family there was a streak of, shall we say, eccentricity. And yet I—I had warnings. Why else would his grandfather have sent to me, as an engagement present, one roller skate covered with thousand island dressing?" Pretender **Claudette Colbert** makes up outlandish stories about the non-existent family of her baron husband Don Ameche. He's not really a baron—he's a cab driver—and they're not married. *Midnight* (1939, Paramount).

2833 STAN: "I think Mr. Hartley is just a little bit cracked." OLLIE: "All inventors are like that, they're eccentric. They're not like you and me. They're different." During World War II, janitors **Stan Laurel** and **Oliver Hardy** are mistaken for private detectives by scientist Arthur Space, who hires them to guard a super bomb he's constructed. *The Big Noise* (1944, 20th Century-Fox).

Economy and Economics *see* BUSINESS AND COMMERCE, GOVERNMENTS, MONEY, NEEDS AND NECESSITIES, POVERTY, SCIENCE AND SCIENTISTS, SYSTEMS, TAXES, WASTE AND WASTEFULNESS, WEALTH AND RICHES

Ecstasy *see* EMOTIONS, FEELINGS, GRIEF, JOY, PASSION, POWER, RELIGIONS

Education

2834 "We're neglecting football for education." **Groucho Marx**, as Professor Wagstaff, is the president of a college with a losing football team. He wants the school to get its priorities straight. *Horse Feathers* (1932, Paramount).

2835 "I think education is terribly important. I came pretty near to getting a dose of it myself." Blonde secretary with a roving eye, **Dorothea Kent** values education for others. *More Than a Secretary* (1936, Columbia).

2836 "Either your education or your spanking has been neglected." Police lieutenant **Sam Levene** is irritated with the antics of zany socialite Barbara Stanwyck. *The Mad Miss Manton* (1938, RKO).

2837 "This will be a rare education." Sadder, but wiser, connivers **Clark Gable** and Eleanor Parker ride off into the sunset without $100,000 in gold from a stagecoach holdup. *The King and Four Queens* (1956, United Artists).

2838 "I think education is simply the process of being taken by surprise. . . ." **Richard Beymer** makes a charming point in a discussion with his father, Jack Hawkins. *Five Finger Exercise* (1962, Columbia).

2839 "Education in Britain is a nubile Cinderella, sparsely clad and often interfered with." **Peter Jeffrey**, the headmaster of a boy's public school, shares his opinion about the state of the educational process in England. *If. . .* (1968, GB, Paramount).

2840 "You never had any education, did you? All you ever had were your skis—and that's not enough." Ski coach **Gene Hackman** tells cocky skier Robert Redford that he doesn't think he's got what it takes to make the American team. *Downhill Racer* (1969, Paramount).

2841 "I am proud to think that my girls are more aware. . . to me education is simply a leading out what is already there." **Maggie Smith** sees her responsibility as a teacher is to help her students make the most of their potential—but she will decide what that means. *The Prime of Miss Jean Brodie* (1969, GB, 20th Century-Fox).

2842 "Do you know, mother, I shall have our children educated just like Lucy. Bring them up among country folk for freshness, send them to Italy for—subtlety, and then—not till then, bring them to London." Cold-fish **Daniel Day-Lewis** informs his mother Maria Britneva of his plans for the children he expects to have with fiancée Helena Bonham Carter. *A Room with a View* (1985, GB, Merchant-Ivory-Goldcrest).

2843 MISS LEVIAS: "The only reason I haven't walked out and half the staff with me, is because those children need us here. . . . You're so busy talking discipline, you forget to educate." JOE CLARK: "Is that so? Then what the hell do you think I've been doing here all this time?" MISS LEVIAS: "So you cleaned it up. That was the easy part." Vice principal **Beverly Todd** makes a valid point as she accuses controversial high school principal **Morgan Freeman** of being so concerned with restoring order to the school that he's neglected the educational goals. She believes that while it's true there can be no education without personal discipline, having discipline in a school is no guarantee that education is taking place. *Lean on Me* (1989, Warner Bros.).

Effects *see* CAUSE AND EFFECT

Efforts

see also DIFFICULTIES, ENERGY, POWER, STRENGTHS, THINKING AND THOUGHTS, WORK AND WORKERS

2844 "Mother tried to be a Seton. Then she gave up and died." Permanently tipsy **Lew Ayres** bitterly states how hard it is to measure up in his prominent family. *Holiday* (1938, Columbia).

2845 EXERCISE INSTRUCTOR: "Crawl slowly up the wall." SYLVIA FOWLER: "The way you say that makes me sound like vermin." INSTRUCTOR: "That shouldn't be much effort. . . I mean, crawling up the wall." Figure instructor **Ann Morriss** has bitchy **Rosalind Russell**'s number. *The Women* (1939, MGM).

2846 "If a man has been a good husband except for twenty-four hours, how long should he be expected to pay for it?. . . I don't suppose it will ever be the same, but we'll try." **Jane Wyatt** is willing to forgive her husband Dick Powell for his infidelity with Lizabeth Scott, but she may have difficulty forgetting. *Pitfall* (1948, United Artists).

2847 "I think it's called 'maximum effort.'" Medical officer **Paul Stewart** makes his diagnosis of Air Force General Gregory Peck. The latter has been in an almost trance-like state ever since his crews headed on yet another almost suicidal bombing run over Germany. *Twelve O'Clock High* (1949, 20th Century-Fox).

2848 CHET KEEFER: "I'd like to make a promise everything's going to be different, I mean, but how can you promise that? But I tell you what I can do. I can tell you I would certainly try." FLORENCE KEEFER: "If we could only remember not to blame each other for things going the wrong way. . . I would try, too, Chet. With the bottom of my heart." After spilling their guts in a divorce court, explaining why they want to split, **Aldo Ray** and **Judy Holliday** realize they still love each other and seek a reconciliation. *The Marrying Kind* (1952, Columbia).

2849 ADMIRAL TARRANT: "Son, whatever progress this world has made has been because of the effort of a few." LT. BRUBAKER: "I was one of the few, Admiral—New Guinea, Leyte, Okinawa. Why does it have to be me again?. . . I think we ought to pull out." TARRANT: "That's ridiculous, son, and you know it. If we did, they'd take Japan, Indo-China, The Philippines. . . ." **Fredric March** counters **William Holden**'s assertion that the U.S. shouldn't be fighting in Korea with the old "domino theory" that played better in 1955 than since. March avoids Holden's reasonable argument that he'd already done his share in World War II. *The Bridge at Toko-Ri* (1955, Paramount).

2850 "God loves triers!" Pop-philosophizing Reverend **Gene Hackman** gives a pep talk to a group of survivors he leads as they look for an escape from their cruise ship, turned upside down by a tidal wave. *The Poseidon Adventure* (1972, 20th Century-Fox).

2851 "I guess you could say that things haven't gone so well tonight, but I'm trying, Lord, I'm trying." As he escapes to safety in Brooklyn, small-time hood **Harvey Keitel** talks to God. *Mean Streets* (1973, Warner Bros.).

2852 "Try not! Do! Or do not! There is no try." **Frank Oz**, as the voice of Yoda, instructs Mark Hamill. *The Empire Strikes Back* (1980, 20th Century-Fox).

2853 "Sometimes you have to look hard at a person, and remember he's doing the best he can." **Katharine Hepburn** defends her husband Henry Fonda to their daughter Jane Fonda. *On Golden Pond* (1981, Universal).

2854 "I always try to make at least one of my characters honest and open and worried about some important interest." Aspiring writer **Pia Zadora** has a rather simplistic writing philosophy. *The Lonely Lady* (1983, Universal).

2855 "Goin' that one more round when you don't think you can—that's what makes all the difference." Boxer **Sylvester Stallone** is a success in the ring because he can take a lot of punishment, and because there are referees who won't stop the fights no matter how badly he bleeds. *Rocky IV* (1985, MGM-United Artists).

2856 "You spend nine months trying to get out, and the rest of your life trying to get back in. . . ." Taxi driver **John Travolta** has a rather crude man-to-man talk with Jason Schaller (voice of Bruce Willis) about women. *Look Who's Talking* (1989, Tri-Star).

Egos and Egotism

see also BOASTS AND BRAGGING, CONCEIT, IMPORTANCE, SELF, VANITIES

2857 "Grant likes to get upon the mountains and slap the hurricanes down." **Katharine Hepburn** notes that sometimes her husband Spencer Tracy believes he's omnipotent. *State of the Union* (1948, MGM).

2858 "We all come into this world with our little egos, equipped with individual horns. Now if we don't blow them, who else will?" Theater critic **George Sanders** sees no reason for false humility. *All About Eve* (1950, 20th Century-Fox).

2859 "You're an interesting man, Tony Rome. But I've suddenly realized I've been doing all the pursuing. Not healthy for my ego." Lovely **Jill St. John** can't tempt Miami private eye Frank Sinatra away from his job of protecting a millionaire's daughter, Sue Lyon. *Tony Rome* (1967, 20th Century-Fox).

2860 "There's no such thing as total honesty. Not with men. They're all wrapped up in sexual ego." **Kelly Bishop** believes that women have to lie to protect men from truths they can't take. *An Unmarried Woman* (1978, 20th Century-Fox).

2861 "You are an egomaniacal windbag." Vice principal **Beverly Todd** finally tells off egomaniacal windbag Morgan Freeman. *Lean on Me* (1989, Warner Bros.).

2862 "When you're an egotist, none of the harm you do is intentional. . . I'm about to go upstate to a stepmother of untrammeled malevolence." It's an epigram framed by arrogantly dissolute **Christopher Eigeman**, the leader of a group of young and privileged crew of Upper East Side New Yorkers. *Metropolitan* (1990, New Line).

Elections *see* GOVERNMENTS, POLITICS AND POLITICIANS, VOTING AND VOTERS

Electricity *see* LIGHTS, SCIENCE AND SCIENTISTS

Elegance *see* FASHIONS, STYLES, TASTES

Elephants *see* ANIMALS

Embarrassment *see* CONFUSION, DIFFICULTIES, SHAME

Emotions

see also ANGER, BELIEFS, CRYING AND CRIES, EMPATHY, EXCITEMENTS, FEARS, FEELINGS, HAPPINESS AND UNHAPPINESS, HATE AND HATRED, HEADS AND HEADACHES, HEARTS AND HEARTACHES, JEALOUSY, JOY, LIVES AND LIVING, LOVE AND HATE, LOVE AND LOVERS, LUST, PASSION, SADNESS, SENSE AND SENSIBILITY, SHAME, SORROWS, SYMPATHY, THINKING AND THOUGHTS, WORRIES

2863 "If I had ever allowed my emotions to discipline my life, I should long ago have killed Anna." Russian Count **Basil Rathbone** refers to his unfaithful wife Greta Garbo. *Anna Karenina* (1935, MGM).

2864 "You're afraid of emotion. You keep your heart in a steel safe." Secretary **Lucille Ball** accuses her boss and boyfriend, private eye Mark Stevens, of being intentionally cold. *The Dark Corner* (1946, 20th Century-Fox).

2865 "I admit the jokes could be better, but I don't see why the rest should worry you—that is, unless you plan to arrest me for lack of emotion." Screenwriter **Humphrey Bogart** responds when he's asked why he shows only annoyance and jokes while being questioned about the brutal murder of a hatcheck girl last seen alive at his bungalow. *In a Lonely Place* (1950, Columbia).

2866 "I am an old pedant, and at times quite trying, both to myself and to the people who have to be around me. I detest emotional outbursts, women's tears and the crying of children. On the whole, I find loud voices and sudden occurrences most disconcerting." As he grows older, **Victor Sjostrom** doesn't wish to be bothered with emotions of any kind. *Wild Strawberries* (1957, Sweden, Svensk Filmindustri).

2867 "You have the body of a woman and the emotions of a child." **Red Buttons** is Carroll Baker's loyal and dedicated agent. *Harlow* (1965, Paramount).

2868 "You say that we never found ecstasy—that it was like quicksilver, always promising next time. Angel, I want ecstasy. Let's find it!" **Bo Derek** enthusiastically prods her Rudolph Valentino-like matador Andrea Occhipinti into action. *Bolero* (1984, Cannon).

2869 "Why do I feel this riot of emotion?" Sophisticated **Donal McCann** thinks to himself after his wife Anjelica Huston relates a long ago brief and tragic romance with a boy now dead. *The Dead* (1987, Vestron).

2870 "Kit is always saying to me: 'Don't get emotional when you turn tricks.' That's why no kissing. . . it's too personal." Prostitute **Julia Roberts** quotes her colleague Laura San Giacomo to her trick, unemotional businessman Richard Gere. *Pretty Woman* (1990, Touchstone-Buena Vista).

2871 "You gotta take all your emotion—all your anger, love, hate—push it way down in the pit of your stomach and let it explode." Veteran ghost **Vincent Schiavelli** instructs new ghost Patrick Swayze on how to become a physical influence on the living. *Ghost* (1990, Paramount).

2872 "It must be jet lag. My emotions keep getting away from me." **Carre Otis** breathes lustfully to Mickey Rourke as they enjoy dinner at an exotic restaurant. It's her best reading of a line in the film—the beautiful lady is no actress. It's also interesting that she has flown from New York City to Rio de Janeiro, only two time zones different. *Wild Orchid* (1990, Triumph).

Empathy

see also FEELINGS, SADNESS, SYMPATHY, UNDERSTANDINGS AND MISUNDERSTANDINGS

2873 "I cry all the time. Any little thing. All my brothers, my brothers-in-law—they're—they're always telling me what a good-hearted guy I am." Butcher **Ernest Borgnine** empathizes with the pain of plain schoolteacher Betsy Blair, abandoned by her date at a dance when the latter sees someone better. *Marty* (1955, United Artists).

2874 "Well, everyone's got their own sack of rocks to carry." Poor, unemployed **Robert Preston** admits to wealthy, complaining Ken Lynch that nobody's life is easy. *The Dark at the Top of the Stairs* (1960, Warner Bros.).

2875 "Hate her? I'm afraid for her. More and more she's the child I was." Governess **Deborah Kerr**, fresh from prison for the murder of her step-sister,

fears that Hayley Mills is well down the same road that Kerr has traveled. *The Chalk Garden* (1964, GB, Universal).

2876 "Where the hell do you get off telling me how I feel? If you felt the way I do, you'd be screaming." **Kate Nelligan** scornfully rejects detective Judd Hirsch's assertion that he knows what she's going through with the disappearance of her young son. *Without a Trace* (1983, 20th Century-Fox).

Emptiness

2877 "Before she came here my house was emptier than a bullring when it rains." Cackling **Tempe Pigott** is the crotchety and deaf owner of the theater where Marlene Dietrich sings. *The Devil Is a Woman* (1935, Paramount).

2878 "You can hate a mountain because it cuts off the sun, but one morning you wake up and find that it's gone and everything's empty without it." **Anthony Perkins** makes an analogy as he contemplates the death of his widowed mother Jo Van Fleet, for whom he holds mixed feelings. *This Angry Age* (1958, Italy-Fr., Columbia).

2879 NORMAN BATES: "You've never had an empty moment in your life, have you?" MARIAN CRANE: "Only my share." **Anthony Perkins** misreads **Janet Leigh**. *Psycho* (1960, United Artists).

Encouragements

see also COURAGE, HELP AND HELPING

2880 "Go out there and be so swell you'll make me hate you." Injured star **Bebe Daniels** encourages chorus girl Ruby Keeler, who is replacing her on opening night, to "break a leg." *42nd Street* (1933, Warner Bros.).

2881 "Now go out there and show 'em who's boss, son. . . . Remember, top of the world." **Margaret Wycherly** is a brick when her psychopathic son James Cagney needs bucking up after he slowly and painfully recovers from another of his violent headache seizures. It makes no difference to her that his chosen career is robbery and murder. *White Heat* (1949, Warner Bros.).

2882 "Tomorrow will come and you will find distractions. . . a million petty things to keep you going." Speaking from experience **Diane Wiest** encourages Mia Farrow, promising her that she will find a series of minor consolations to ease the pain of her life. *September* (1987, Orion).

Endearments

see also COMPLIMENTS, GENEROSITY, LOVE AND
LOVERS, WORDS

2883 "My little shoplifter, my darling." Gentleman
thief **Herbert Marshall** lovingly addresses sophisticated lady thief Miriam Hopkins. *Trouble in Paradise* (1932, Paramount).

2884 "Oh, my barbaric Ninotchka! My divine statisti-
cal Ninotchka!" **Melvyn Douglas** is so very much in
love with lovely Russian Communist emissary Greta
Garbo. *Ninotchka* (1939, MGM).

2885 "Hello, Monkey Face!" It's **Cary Grant**'s expression of endearment for Joan Fontaine. *Suspicion*
(1941, RKO).

2886 "If I ever said anything endearing to you, it
was because I was lonely." **Leon Ames** now knows
schemer Audrey Totter for what she is. *Lady in the
Lake* (1947, MGM).

Ends and Endings

see also BEGINNINGS, CONSEQUENCES, DEATH AND
DYING, DESIRES, LASTS, PURPOSES, REASONS

2887 "In the morning of my race I have seen a
winged ship arrive, bearing the white men who are
to become the masters of our land, and before the
sunset I have seen the passing of the last of the
Mohicans." The film closes with the title card of
Theodore Lorch, as Chingachgook, lamenting the
death of his son Albert Roscoe, as Uncas, the last of
the Mohicans. *The Last of the Mohicans* (1920, silent,
Associated Pictures).

2888 PROF. MORIARTY: "You do not think this is the
end?" SHERLOCK HOLMES: "I rather hoped so, Moriarty. I start on my honeymoon tomorrow." It's the
film's final exchange between villain **Gustav von
Seyffertitz** and hero **John Barrymore**. *Sherlock
Holmes* (1922, Silent, Goldwyn).

2889 "Mother of mercy, is this the end of Rico?"
Mobster **Edward G. Robinson** is shocked when he
is fatally shot. *Little Caesar* (1931, Warner Bros.).

2890 "I'm washed up, it's all gone." Film director
Lowell Sherman despairs, shortly before he
commits suicide. *What Price Hollywood?* (1932,
RKO).

2891 "I haven't finished yet." Child murderer **Peter
Lorre** knows he will strike again. *M* (1933, Germany, Nero Film-Paramount).

2892 "So ends a partnership that should never have
begun." Pirate Captain **Errol Flynn** stands over the
body of dying Basil Rathbone, another pirate, run
through by Flynn's sword. *Captain Blood* (1935,
Warner Bros.).

2893 "I wouldn't go on living with you if you were
dipped in platinum." **Irene Dunne** calls an end to
her marriage with Cary Grant. *The Awful Truth*
(1937, Columbia).

2894 CRYSTAL WETHERBY: "Oh, if this could just go
on forever." RAYMOND DABNEY: "Well, all good
things must come to an end. You know that."
CRYSTAL: "Is that original?" RAYMOND: "No, but it's
true, unfortunately." In her penultimate screen
appearance, American widow **Jean Harlow**'s
romance with British aristocrat **Robert Taylor** has
just about run its course—at least according to the
cliché he springs on her. Each thinks the other has
money—but they're both insolvent. *Personal Property* (1937, MGM).

2985 "There is no then. There is no after." At the
end of the film, now middle-aged Emma Hamilton
(played by **Vivien Leigh**) answers her young cell-
mate's question "What happened then?" speaking of
the death of Hamilton's lover Lord Nelson, portrayed by Laurence Olivier. *That Hamilton Woman*
aka: *Lady Hamilton* (1941, United Artists).

2896 "Let's not linger on it." **Bette Davis** calmly
ends her engagement to priggish John Loder. *Now,
Voyager* (1942, Warner Bros.).

2897 "This is the end! The absolute end!" Magazine
photographer **Mischa Auer** delivers the film's last
line when he finds his editor Ginger Rogers in a
clinch with advertising manager Ray Milland. *Lady
in the Dark* (1944, Paramount).

2898 "Count the lights you can see from the window—I'll be finished before you reach 100." Young
physician **Michael Denison** comforts the frightened mother of a young boy with diphtheria, upon
whom Denison will perform a tracheotomy. *My
Brother Jonathan* (1948, GB, ABP).

2899 "If I'd known where it would end, I'd never
have let anything start." If narrator **Orson Welles**
had been able to pull that off there wouldn't be any
story to film. *The Lady from Shanghai* (1948,
Columbia).

2900 "There is no end to this story." It's the pessimistic tag line to a movie about the futility and
horror of war, any war—particularly the Korean
War. *The Steel Helmet* (1951, Lippert).

2901 SHANE: "Your kind of days are over." RYKER: "My days? What about yours, gunfighter?" SHANE: "The difference is I know it." One-time gunfighter **Alan Ladd** doesn't see any future for himself or cattle baron **Emile Meyer**. *Shane* (1953, Paramount).

2902 "Look at that sunset, Howard. . . . It's like the daytime didn't want to end, isn't it? It's like the daytime's going to put up a big scrap, set the world on fire to keep the nighttime from creeping on." Old maid school teacher **Rosalind Russell** watches the sunset of a near perfect day with her beau Arthur O'Connell. The nighttime will bring problems to all concerned. *Picnic* (1955, Columbia).

2903 "You'll end your life in the gutter, and it'll serve you right. The gutter's where you come from, and the gutter's where you belong." No longer feeling tranquil, schoolteacher **Rosalind Russell** may be right about drifter William Holden, but she's angry because she's attracted to him. *Picnic* (1955, Columbia).

2904 PLATO: "Jim, do you think the end of the world will come at nighttime?" JIM: "No, dawn." It's part of the last conversation between "child" **Sal Mineo** and "father" **James Dean**, shortly before Mineo is shot and killed just before dawn. *Rebel Without a Cause* (1955, Warner Bros.).

2905 "I thought the war was all over with." Technically, **Norman Fell** is correct—the peace talks at Panmunjon have almost concluded. Those trying to take Chinese-held Pork Chop Hill may be the last Americans killed in the Korean conflict. *Pork Chop Hill* (1959, United Artists).

2906 CAPT. WALLACE PRATT: "The war is over." PRIVATE ENDORE: "Which war?" **Charles Aidman**'s happy announcement makes little impression with weird soldier **John Saxon**. *War Hunt* (1962, United Artists).

2907 POPE JULIUS II: "When will you make an end?" MICHELANGELO: "When it is finished." **Rex Harrison** wishes **Charlton Heston** would get a move on and complete painting the ceiling of the Sistine Chapel. *The Agony and the Ecstasy* (1965, 20th Century-Fox).

2908 "Xi was beginning to think he would never find the end of the Earth. And one day, suddenly, there it was." Narrator **Paddy O'Byrne** informs us that African bushman N!xau's quest has ended. He has found the "end of the world" and is able to return the Coke bottle that the primitive Botswana natives believed came from the gods. *The Gods Must Be Crazy* (1979, Botswana, 20th Century-Fox).

2909 "I really don't want to live through every moment of another person's life. Not even yours." **Charles Grodin** touchingly explains why he and mathematics professor Jill Clayburgh should end their relationship. *It's My Turn* (1980, Columbia).

2910 "I haven't been feeling good lately. I think it's probably us. . . . This is more serious than you think. . . I think it's over." L.A. film editor **Albert Brooks** ends his relationship with bank officer Kathryn Harrold. His reason is, that although they have a great sex life, they lack communication. As soon as she angrily departs, he discovers that it's not over until it's over. *Modern Romance* (1981, Columbia).

2911 "Jean Scott Martin died on August twelfth, nineteen eighty-one. This documentary on the last year of her life is dedicated to her memory. And it is ending as she asked it to end." Valium druggie **Jill Clayburgh** has beaten her addiction and finishes a television documentary on the last year of Geraldine Page. *I'm Dancing as Fast as I Can* (1982, Paramount).

2912 "He's come to the end of his rope and found it frayed." Doctor **Guy Manning** diagnoses elderly Shakespearean actor Albert Finney, whose severe outburst of hysteria has landed him in a hospital. *The Dresser* (1983, GB, Columbia).

2913 "I just don't love you anymore." **Wendy Hughes**, not only confesses her adultery, but also announces that she wishes to leave husband John Hargreaves, who is too wrapped-up in his work to have any time for her. *My First Wife* (1984, Australia, Spectrafilm).

2914 "Draw the curtains." These are the last words of **Michelle Pfeiffer**, who dies of shame and grief over her unhappy affair with John Malkovich. *Dangerous Liaisons* (1988, Warner Bros.).

2915 "This is not the beginning of the end. It is the end of the beginning." Sherman the Robot, played by **Robert Joy** has the last words in a tale of time travellers from the future, who kidnap doomed passengers from crashing airliners. *Millennium* (1989, 20th Century-Fox).

2916 NANCY TRAINER: "We both knew this wouldn't last." BRIAN MCDERMOTT: "I didn't." Successful mayoral candidate **Stockard Channing** breaks off her affair with youngster **Tim Quill**. *Staying Together* (1989, Hemdale).

2917 "I like you Rusty, but I think it's over. . . . It's just not right for me. It's over. . . I don't want us to end enemies." Ambitious, lovely lawyer **Greta Scacchi** has got about all she can from her affair with her superior, married prosecutor Harrison Ford—and so is on to new conquests. *Presumed Innocent* (1990, Warner Bros.).

2918 "We fuck like minks, raise rug rats, and live happily after." Hard-boiled San Francisco police detective **Michael Douglas** proposes a happy ending for his affair with murder suspect Sharon Stone and the book she's writing about them. She's not so sure she wants to settle down to just one sex—or is it she wants to use her icepick on him? *Basic Instinct* (1992, Tri-Star).

Enemies

see also Friendships and Friends, Hate and Hatred, Hostilities, Revenge and Vengeance, Wars

2919 "I'm nobody's enemy but my own." Carefree cockney con-man **Cary Grant** takes to the road with some larcenous traveling actors. *Sylvia Scarlett* (1936, RKO).

2920 "Man without enemies is like dog without fleas." **Sidney Toler** investigates a murder in Honolulu, and throws out this Chanism. *Charlie Chan's Murder Cruise* (1940, 20th Century-Fox).

2921 "We shall carry the attack against the enemy. We shall hit him and hit him again, and whenever we can reach him, for we intend to bring this battle to his own home grounds." The narrator closes the movie which follows a single Flying Fortress, "Mary Ann," and her crew from December 6, 1941, to the battle of the Coral Sea. *Air Force* (1943, Warner Bros.).

2922 "I don't know. Sometimes, a dead man can be a terrible enemy." Old General **Richard Garrick** is correct in believing that merely assassinating title character Marlon Brando will not end his influence with the Mexican peasants. He was so badly riddled with bullets he could not be recognized. The peasants see his great white horse running in the mountains and believe he's there. As one puts it, "Whenever we need him, he will come." Wonder how long before they got over that idea? *Viva Zapata!* (1952, 20th Century-Fox).

2923 "Scott is not the enemy. The enemy is the nuclear age. It happens to have killed man's faith in his ability to influence what happens to him. And out of this came a sickness—a sickness, a frustration, a feeling of impotence, helplessness, weakness. And from this, this desperation, we look for a champion. . . for some it was Senator McCarthy; for some it was General Walker. Now it's Scott." It's President **Fredric March**'s eloquent response when someone refers to military coup leader Burt Lancaster as an enemy. *Seven Days in May* (1964, Paramount).

2924 "His agents may be caught and their crimes forestalled, but he—he is never so much as suspected! Until now, that is! Until I, his archenemy, managed to deduce his existence and penetrate his perimeters. And now his minions, having discovered my success, are on my track." Befuddled **Nicol Williamson**, as Sherlock Homes, refers to Laurence Olivier as Professor Moriarty. *The Seven Percent Solution* (1977, Universal).

2925 "I always credit my enemy, no matter what he may be, with equal intelligence." General **Richard Widmark** is talking about a swarm of South American killer bees heading toward the U.S. *The Swarm* (1978, Warner Bros.).

2926 "I think looking back, we did not fight the enemy, we fought ourselves. And the enemy was in us. . . ." Narrator **Charlie Sheen** represents director-screenwriter Oliver Stone in stating that U.S. soldiers in Vietnam battled as much with their own weaknesses, fears and doubts as they did with the Viet Cong. *Platoon* (1986, Orion).

Energy

see also Actions and Acts, Force, Power, Strengths, Work and Workers

2927 "The energy contained in this apple can destroy the world. And yet we cannot create one small apple." Mild-mannered physicist **Gary Cooper**'s cynical comment doesn't reflect the primary concern of true scientists. They are much too concerned with what they can do to waste time and energy worrying about what they cannot do. *Cloak and Dagger* (1946, Warner Bros.).

2928 "There's a field of measurable energy [in the house] which can be reversed. . . in essence the house is a giant battery, the residual energy of which must be tapped by all who enter it. . . ." Parapsychologist **Clive Revill** offers a scientific explanation for the strange phenomena occurring in an apparently haunted house. *The Legend of Hell House* (1973, GB, 20th Century-Fox).

2929 "You seem to have a lot of energy, and it gets stuck in your forehead." Abandoned by her husband, **Karen Black** takes up with confirmed bachelor Michael Emil. *Can She Bake a Cherry Pie?* (1983, World Wide Classics).

2930 "She's looking for a man—any man—she wants to steal some energy from him." Eccentric scientist **Frank Finlay** deduces that naked alien Mathilda May, who seduces men and then sucks the life out of them, is a vampire from outer space. *Lifeforce* (1985, Cannon-Tri-Star).

Engagements

see also ATTRACTIONS, ATTENTION, LOVE AND LOVERS, MARRIAGES, MEN AND WOMEN, PROMISES, WEDDINGS

2931 "When I put a rope round the Avenger's neck, I'll put a ring round Daisy's finger." Detective **Malcolm Kean** announces his engagement plans and that he's been assigned to the case of a mad killer who is killing young blonde women. He expects to marry his girlfriend June (Tripper) after catching the fiend. *The Lodger* (1927, silent, GB, Gainsborough).

2932 "She may be his wife, but she's engaged to me." It will take most of the picture to make sense out of newspaper editor **Spencer Tracy**'s statement. He's angry with his fiancée Jean Harlow when she shows increasing affection for Tracy's best friend, William Powell. Harlow married Powell at the behest of Tracy to set up wealthy Myrna Loy as a home-wrecker in order to ruin her slander case against the newspaper. *Libeled Lady* (1936, MGM).

2933 "It is the duty of the bride's father to give a party to announce the engagement. Apparently this is done only after everyone knows about it." **Spencer Tracy** has nothing against wedding traditions per se, but some, like an engagement party, are mighty expensive for the father of the bride. *Father of the Bride* (1950, MGM).

2934 "Pardon me! You are not engaged to anyone. When you do become engaged to someone, I or your father, should his health permit him, will inform you of the fact. An engagement should come upon a young girl as a surprise, pleasant or unpleasant as the case may be. It is hardly a matter she could be allowed to arrange for herself." **Edith Evans** corrects her daughter Joan Greenwood, who announces that she is engaged to Michael Redgrave. *The Importance of Being Earnest* (1952, GB, Two Cities-Rank).

2935 "No engagement is worth anything unless it has been broken at least once." **Dorothy Tutin** claims an engagement and one break-up of same with Michael Denison even before they met. It's because she loved the name, Earnest. *The Importance of Being Earnest* (1952, GB, Two Cities-Rank).

2936 "The disgusting way an engagement is regarded public property; all these older women smirking. . . but my point is their whole attitude is wrong—an engagement, horrid word in the first place, is a private affair and should be regarded as such." **Daniel Day-Lewis** complains to his fiancée Helena Bonham Carter about how others are nosing-in on what he, at least, considers a private matter. *A Room with a View* (1985, GB, Merchant-Ivory-Goldcrest).

England and the English

2937 "An Englishman. I lived a year with Englishmen. I hated every one of them. And how it rained." **Raymond Massey**, as King Philip II of Spain, finds fault with England and Englishmen, as he interviews **Laurence Olivier**, who is impersonating a spy. *Fire Over England* (1937, GB, London Films).

2938 DR. WATSON: "Things are looking up, Holmes. This little island is still on the map." SHERLOCK HOLMES: "Yes. This fortress built by nature for herself. This blessed plot. This earth. This realm. This England." After successfully dealing with a threat to England, **Nigel Bruce** listens as **Basil Rathbone** paraphrases Shakespeare. *Sherlock Holmes and the Secret Weapon* (1942, Universal).

2939 "Let us hope that England, having saved herself by her energy, may save Europe by her example." **Robert Donat**, appearing as British Prime Minister William Pitt, makes his last public speech. *The Young Mr. Pitt* (1942, GB, 20th Century-Fox).

2940 "I am an Englishman by birth, but I am really a citizen of the world." Smuggler **Sydney Greenstreet** introduces himself to writer Peter Lorre. *The Mask of Dimitrios* (1944, Warner Bros.).

2941 "I have loved England, dearly and deeply,- Since the first morning, shining and pure,-The white cliffs of Dover, I saw rising steeply out-Out of the sea that once made her secure. . . .-I have loved England, and still as a stranger-Here is my home, and I still am alone." The opening narration of the film quotes from Alice Duer Miller's poem on which the movie is loosely based. *The White Cliffs of Dover* (1944, MGM).

2942 "Trouble with England, it's all pomp and circumstances. You're very wise to get out of it, escape while you can." **Humphrey Bogart** teases English couple Jennifer Jones and Edward Underdown. *Beat the Devil* (1954, United Artists).

2943 "The world always underestimates the British. How could I have made the same mistake?" Wealthy

London businessman **Rex Harrison** is unsuccessful in his attempt to drive his American wife Doris Day to commit suicide. *Midnight Lace* (1960, Universal).

2944 "Wanda, do you have any idea what it's like being English? Being so correct all the time, so stilted. . . by this dread. . . of doing the wrong thing? Saying to someone 'Are you married?' and hearing 'My wife's left me this morning.' Or saying, 'Do you have any children?' and being told 'They all burned to death on Wednesday.' You see, Wanda, we're all terrified of embarrassment. That's why we're so dead. Most of my friends are dead, you know. We have these piles of corpses to dinner." Barrister **John Cleese** tells lovely American Jamie Lee Curtis what's wrong with the very proper Englishmen. *A Fish Called Wanda* (1988, GB, MGM).

2945 "You English. You're so fucking superior, aren't you? Well, would you like to know where you'd be without us to protect you? I'll tell you—the smallest fucking province in the Russian Empire. . . ." American crook **Kevin Kline** has had it with the English. *A Fish Called Wanda* (1988, GB, MGM).

Enjoyments

see also JOY, PLEASURES

2946 ADOLPH: "How I'd enjoy one hour with you." COLETTE: "You silly boy, just what would you do?" ADOLPH: "Leave that to me." COLETTE: "Now I can see what champagne can do." ADOLPH: "No, no, honestly, I'm tipsy for you." **Charles Ruggles** gets his opportunity for enjoyment with **Jeanette MacDonald** when she discovers her husband Maurice Chevalier has been unfaithful with her friend Genevieve Tobin. *One Hour with You* (1932, Paramount).

2947 "I want you to know how much I enjoyed it. If I had my way, I'll tell you, this is how I'd like to spend all my time—in the company of men like you in pursuit of knowledge." Wealthy simpleton **Henry Fonda** reluctantly leaves a group of scientists after two years on an Amazon expedition. *The Lady Eve* (1941, Paramount).

2948 "I enjoy seeing youth betray their promises." Cynical publisher **Robert Ryan** enjoys the discomfort of idealistic young journalist Montgomery Clift, who is stuck with writing an advice column. *Lonelyhearts* (1958, United Artists).

2949 "You don't think I enjoyed what we did this evening, do you? What I did tonight was for Queen and country!" **Sean Connery** plants his tongue firmly in his cheek after he seduces enemy agent Luciana Paluzzi. *Thunderball* (1965, GB, United Artists).

2950 JOAN VECCHIO: "You mean you never enjoyed sex?" BEA VECCHIO: "What's to enjoy? Love isn't physical. Love is spiritual, like—like the great love that Ingrid Bergman had for Bing Crosby in *The Bells of St. Mary's*, when she was a nun, and he was a priest and they loved each other from afar. But Frank didn't want to know from that." **Diane Keaton** is told by her mother-in-law **Bea Arthur** that she and her husband Richard Castellano have different ideas on how to show love. *Lovers and Other Strangers* (1970, ABC-Cinerama).

2951 "Susan and I do the right things. We undress in front of each other. Spend fifteen minutes in foreplay. Do it in different rooms. . . . We're considerate of each other's feelings. . . . We try to be patient, gentle with each other. . . . Maybe it's not meant to be enjoyable with women you love." **Art Garfunkel** complains to his friend Jack Nicholson that the spark has gone out of his love-making with his wife Candice Bergen. *Carnal Knowledge* (1971, Avco Embassy).

2952 "Is that a ten-gallon hat—or are you just enjoying the show?" **Madeline Kahn**, as entertaining Lili von Shtupp, questions an admirer in the audience. *Blazing Saddles* (1974, Warner Bros.).

2953 "I'm scared. It's a rat circus out there and I'm beginning to enjoy it." Fast-driving cop **Mel Gibson** tells Roger Ward that he likes his life taking on the crazies in a post-apocalypse world. *Mad Max* (1979, Australia, AIP-Filmways).

Entertainments and Entertainers

see also ACTING AND ACTORS, AMUSEMENTS, COMEDY AND COMEDIANS, HOSPITALITY, INTERESTS, MOTION PICTURES, MUSIC AND MUSICIANS, PERFORMANCES, PLEASURES, SHOWS, SONGS AND SINGING, THEATERS

2954 "Entertaining the rustics is not as difficult as I feared. Any simple, childish game seems to amuse them excessively." **Frieda Inescort** is a snobbish hostess, visited by some country relatives. *Pride and Prejudice* (1940, MGM).

2955 "They hire girls like me to entertain the visiting exhibitors. They louse you up, then they call you a louse." Starlet **Shelley Winters** complains that her job is little more than prostitution. *The Big Knife* (1955, United Artists).

2956 "Remember that while he may be a bum administrator, we have to admit two things about him. . . a terrible mayor, but a great entertainer."

Perennial mayoral candidate **Wallace Ford** harangues a crowd about his political rival, incumbent Spencer Tracy. *The Last Hurrah* (1958, Columbia).

2957 "We peddle disaster. . . . Blood and tears, football and cheers, performers, superstars. Get 'em on, get 'em off, next, next, fast, fast. We're in the entertainment business." TV news reporter **Sean Connery** fools himself as to his purpose. *Wrong Is Right* (1982, Columbia).

2958 DOLLY HARSHAW: "There's only two things to do in this town. . . . You got a TV?" HARRY MADDOX: "No." DOLLY: "Well now you're down to one. Lots of luck." **Virginia Madsen**, although married, will be happy to provide entertainment for used car salesman **Don Johnson**. *The Hot Spot* (1990, Orion).

Enthusiasm see EXCITEMENTS, INSPIRATIONS, INTERESTS

Envy see JEALOUSY, LIKES AND DISLIKES, RESENTMENTS

Epics see MOTION PICTURES, POETRY AND POETS

Epitaphs see DEATH AND DYING, EULOGIES, FUNERALS, GRAVES AND GRAVEYARDS

Equalities

see also CLASSES, DEMOCRACY, PRIVILEGES, RIGHTS

2959 ERNEST BROWN: "You know I like to get around and travel, and believe me I've been places and seen things." TIRA: "I've been things and seen places. That sorta evens us up, huh?" **William B. Davidson** is the chump **Mae West** brings to her rooms, so Ralf Harolde can break in on his "wife" and extract money from the sap. *I'm No Angel* (1933, Paramount).

2960 "Stephen and I are equals. I won't qualify that relationship now. It's wrong. Shockingly wrong." **Norma Shearer** rejects her mother's suggestion that she look the other way about her husband's peccadilloes. *The Women* (1939, MGM).

2961 "May it please the court, I submit that my entire line of defense is based upon the proposition that the female sex should be dealt with, before the law, as equals of the persons of the male sex. I submit that I cannot hope to argue this line before minds hostile to and prejudiced against the female sex." Lawyer **Katharine Hepburn** makes her argument to the court for equal treatment of the sexes under the law. *Adam's Rib* (1949, MGM).

2962 "What's good for you, is good for me and me for you, see? We're the same, we're equal, we're partners. See? Five-oh, five-oh." Sports promoter **Spencer Tracy** proposes an equal partnership with top female athlete Katharine Hepburn. *Pat and Mike* (1952, MGM).

2963 "Aurens is a sword with two edges. We are equally glad to be rid of him, are we not?" **Alec Guinness** as Prince Feisal shares a confidence with British officers and diplomats regarding Peter O'Toole as T.E. Lawrence. *Lawrence of Arabia* (1962, GB, Columbia).

2964 "A world where all men are created equal, where a man no matter how short can score with a top broad." It's **Woody Allen**'s notion of Utopia. *Casino Royale* (1967, Columbia).

2965 "I don't believe in marriage. . . a bed is the only place that offers a man and woman equal opportunity." Eccentric **Maureen Stapleton** expresses a philosophy that has led to her having affairs with many famous authors. *Lost and Found* (1979, Columbia).

2966 "If women want equality in life they have to also accept it in death." Eccentric, cat-loving, misogynist counterterrorist **Roger Moore** won't give any special consideration to female terrorists. *ffolkes* (1980, Universal).

2967 "You do not have to remind me that a man's not equal to his rhetoric." Russian mathematician and physicist **Klaus Maria Brandauer** forgives British publisher Sean Connery for not being quite as good as his words. *The Russia House* (1990, MGM-United Artists).

2968 "I like you, Iris, just as much as I love you." **Robert De Niro** shares a nice thought with Jane Fonda. *Stanley & Iris* (1990, MGM).

Eroticism see BEHAVIOR, DESIRES, EXCITEMENTS, LUST, PASSION, SEX AND SEXUALITY

Errors see MISTAKES, PERFECTION, TRUTH AND FALSEHOOD, WRONGS AND WRONGDOINGS

Escapes

see also COWARDICE AND COWARDS, EVASIONS, FEARS, FREEDOMS, ILLUSIONS, RUNNING AND RUNNERS

2969 "I thought this was going to be an escape and it turns into a yacht race." Suave thief **Ronald Colman** escapes from Devil's Island and with Ann Harding makes an improbable romp through swamps only to be caught in her state room aboard a ship sailing for France. *Condemned* (1929, United Artists).

2970 "Oh, why can't we break away from all this, just you and I, and lodge with my fleas in the hills—I mean, flee to my lodge in the hills." **Groucho Marx** wants to take Thelma Todd away from all this—whatever this is. *Monkey Business* (1931, Paramount).

2971 "I haven't escaped. They're still after me. They'll always be after me. I hide in rooms all day and travel by night. No friends, no rest, no peace. . . . Forgive me, Helen, I had to see you tonight, just to say goodbye." At the end of the film, fugitive from a chain gang **Paul Muni** speaks from the shadows to Helen Vinson, the woman he loves, detailing his struggles. *I Am a Fugitive from a Chain Gang* (1932, Warner Bros.).

2972 SLIMANE: "I'm sorry, Pepe. He thought you were trying to escape." PEPE LE MOKO: "And so I have, my friend." Native detective **Joseph Calleia** apologizes to thief **Charles Boyer** who has been fatally shot by one of Calleia's men. Since death allows Boyer to finally leave the Casbah, he is at peace. *Algiers* (1938, United Artists).

2973 "I've got to get away from it. I've got to get away from here. Instead of sitting decently at the table eating their dinners, [they're] howling and roaring at one another like a lot of banshees." Irish gardener **Barry Fitzgerald** is disgusted at Katharine Hepburn, Cary Grant, May Robson, and Charles Ruggles who are sitting around a dinner table making noises like wild animals. *Bringing Up Baby* (1938, RKO).

2974 IRENE: "Did I ever tell you about my escapes from the Soviets?" HARRY: "About eleven times. And each time it was different." IRENE: "I made several escapes. I was always making escapes." Phony Russian countess **Norma Shearer** doesn't fool vaudevillian **Clark Gable.** He knew her when. *Idiot's Delight* (1939, MGM).

2975 "I was in a tight spot, but I managed to wiggle out of it." **Mae West** gives a throaty account of her first meeting with a masked bandit. *My Little Chickadee* (1940, Universal).

2976 "You'll never make the border. . . . You'll never even make the elevator." **Edward G. Robinson** diagnoses his severely wounded friend, murderer Fred MacMurray. *Double Indemnity* (1944, Paramount).

2977 "But they learn, they must. Nobody escapes. Nobody ever really escapes." Prison doctor **Art Smith** mutters sadly after a prison breakout ends in a massacre of prisoners and the death of the brutal captain Hume Cronyn. *Brute Force* (1947, Universal).

2978 "If you don't get out of here, I'll just die! Living here is like waiting for the funeral to begin! No, it's like waiting for the coffin, for them to carry you out." **Bette Davis** is very unhappy with her small-town Wisconsin home. *Beyond the Forest* (1949, Warner Bros.)

2979 "There is no escape from the Caine, save death. We're all doing penance, sentenced to an outcast ship, manned by outcasts, and named after the greatest outcast of them all." Lieutenant **Fred MacMurray** holds forth for the benefit of new ensigns at the officers' mess. *The Caine Mutiny* (1954, Columbia).

2980 "The coffin, drowned Queequeg's coffin, was my lifebuoy. For one whole day and night it sustained me on that soft and dirge-like main. Then a sail appeared. It was the Rachel. The Rachel who in her long, melancholy search for her missing children found another orphan. The drama's done. All are departed away. The great shroud of the sea rolls over the Pequod, her crew, and Moby Dick. I only am escaped, alone, to tell thee." **Richard Basehart**, as Ishmael, is the only survivor of the sinking of the whaler Pequod by the great white, Moby Dick. *Moby Dick* (1956, Warner Bros.).

2981 "I was trying to get away from a world I had known. . . and found myself looking up its ass." **Jane Fonda** reports to her therapist Vivian Nathan about her attempt to break away from her life as a part-time prostitute. *Klute* (1971, Warner Bros.).

2982 "The whole world is breaking down. The only escapes left are art and romantic love." Director-screenwriter **James Toback** appears as an English professor, trying to make Natassja Kinski. *Exposed* (1983, MGM-United Artists).

2983 AURORA GREENWAY: "I was curious. Do you have any reaction at all to my telling you that I love you?" GARRETT BREEDLOVE: "I was just inches away from a clean getaway." **Shirley MacLaine** captures womanizer astronaut **Jack Nicholson**. *Terms of Endearment* (1983, Paramount).

2984 VALENTIN: "Your life is as trivial as your movies." MOLINA: "Unless you have the keys to that door, I will escape in my own way, thank you." Political prisoner **Raul Julia** complains about his cell-mate child-molester, homosexual **William Hurt**, who likes to relate the story of his favorite movies to pass the time. *Kiss of the Spider Woman* (1985, U.S.-Brazil, Island Alive).

2985 "This is what we talked about when we were nineteen. This is like *Easy Rider* but it's our turn." **Albert Brooks** gushes to his still dubious wife Julie Hagerty about escaping the rat race in a Winnebago. *Lost in America* (1985, Warner Bros.).

Eternity

see also BEGINNINGS, ENDS AND ENDINGS, EXISTENCE, FUTURE, IMMORTALITY AND MORTALITY, PAST, TIME

2986 "Mourn not for the brave, they live in the indestructible splendor of all eternity." British Bishop **Cedric Hardwicke** preaches to his congregation after receiving word of the death of his son George Sanders who was fighting Nazi spies in East Africa. *Sundown* (1941, United Artists).

2987 "They call these haunted shores, the southern shores of Devonshire and Cornwall and Ireland. . . there's life and death in the endless sound of waves. . . and eternity." These are the opening remarks, setting the stage for an excellent ghost story. *The Uninvited* (1944, Paramount).

2988 PROF. MORIARTY: "We've had many encounters in the past. You hope to place me on the gallows. I tell you I will never stand upon the gallows. But, if you are instrumental in any way of bringing about my destruction, you will not be alive to enjoy your satisfaction." SHERLOCK HOLMES: "Then we shall walk together through the gates of eternity hand in hand." MORIARTY: "What a charming picture that would make." HOLMES: "Yes, wouldn't it. I really think it might be worth it." **Henry Daniell** and his arch-enemy **Basil Rathbone** plan their eternity together. *The Woman in Green* (1945, Universal).

2989 "This thing will go on forever." Soldier **Chuck Connors** despairs that the Korean conflict will ever end. *Hold Back the Night* (1956, Allied Artists).

2990 "You can't stay seventeen forever." **Ron Howard** attempts to convince fellow high school graduate Richard Dreyfuss that it's time for them to grow up and go off to college. *American Graffiti* (1973, Universal).

2991 "Oh, this is a fair place to spend eternity. The air smells like honeysuckle. The wind in the pine trees makes a joysome sound. Sometimes in the wind I feel something say my name, telling me to come to some far-off place: Mary, come, Mary, come. Once I'm through raising Romey and Ima Dean, I think I'll go." When her father dies, child **Julie Gholson** assumes the role of parent figure to keep her backwoods family of three siblings together and out of an orphanage. *Where the Lilies Bloom* (1974, United Artists).

2992 "I'm not a forever person." **Shelley Hack** turned down TV jingle writer Joe Brooks in college, but he's back

2993 "The endless blacktop is my sweet eternity." Motorcyclist **Willem Dafoe** is on the way to nowhere. *The Loveless* (1984, Atlantic).

Ethics

see also IMMORALITY, MORALITY, PROFESSIONS AND PROFESSIONALS, RIGHT AND WRONG, RIGHTS

2994 "Ethics! Ethics! Who's got ethics? Am I a gentleman or ain't I?" Crooked **James Cagney** attempts to convince girlfriend Bette Davis that he's gone straight and is becoming a gentleman. *Jimmy the Gent* (1934, Warner Bros.).

2995 "Do you think it's ethical to go around the world just taking pictures of people?" **Grace Kelly** wishes globe-trotting photographer James Stewart would give up the life and marry her. Presently, he's wheelchair bound due to a leg broken on an assignment. *Rear Window* (1954, Paramount).

2996 L.B. "JEFF" JEFFRIES: "I wonder if it's ethical to watch a man with binoculars and a long focus lens. Do you suppose it's ethical even if you prove he didn't commit a crime?" LISA FREMONT: "I'm not much on rear window ethics but we're two of the most frightening ghouls I have ever known." Later in the film **James Stewart** and **Grace Kelly** speak with some shame about their "unethical" behavior in spying on Raymond Burr from Stewart's rear window. *Rear Window* (1954, Paramount).

2997 "I have done an unethical thing. I have taken your cigar and I am not taking your case." Barrister **Charles Laughton** confesses his breach of ethics to solicitor Henry Daniell who has come to get Laughton to take Tyrone Power's murder case. *Witness for the Prosecution* (1957, United Artists).

2998 "If he can do it and get away with it and he chooses not to be bothered by the ethics, then he's home free. Remember, history is written by the winners." At an imagined seder, Martin Landau's free-thinker aunt **Anna Berger** helps to salve his conscience. He's arranged to have his mistress Anjelica Huston murdered and is now trying to live with the fact. *Crimes and Misdemeanors* (1989, Orion).

Eulogies

see also BLESSINGS, DEATH AND DYING, FUNERALS, GRAVES AND GRAVEYARDS, HONOR, MEMORY AND MEMORIZATION, PRAISES, REMINDERS, SPEECH AND SPEAKING, WRITING AND WRITERS

2999 "He found what he was looking for. I know that somewhere wherever great hunters go—he's happy." **Maureen O'Sullivan** mourns her father C. Aubrey Smith who collapses and dies after reaching his goal, the great elephant graveyard. *Tarzan, the Ape Man* (1932, MGM).

3000 "O-lan, You are the Earth." **Paul Muni** cries mournfully at the grave of his wife Luise Rainer. *The Good Earth* (1937, MGM).

3001 "France is once again today a land of reason and benevolence because one of her sons through an immense work and a great action gave rise to a new order of things based on justice and the rights common to all men! Let's not pity him because he suffered and endured. Let us envy him because his great heart won him the proudest of destinies. He was a moment in the conscience of man." With the last lines of the film, **Morris Carnovsky** delivers an eulogy for his friend, title character Paul Muni. *The Life of Emile Zola* (1937, Warner Bros.).

3002 "His name is Eddie Bartlett. . . . He used to be a big shot." Mournful **Gladys George**, cradling the bullet-ridden body of James Cagney, replies to a policeman who asks who the deceased was. *The Roaring Twenties* (1939, Warner Bros.).

3003 "Jesse was an outlaw, a bandit, a criminal. Even those who loved him ain't got no answer for that. But we ain't ashamed of him. . . I don't think even America is ashamed of Jesse James. . . . Maybe because he was bold, lawless, like we all like to be sometime. . . . Or maybe it was because he was so good at what he was. . . . In Loving Remembrance— Jesse W. James. . . Murdered by a traitor whose name is not worthy to appear here." At the end of his eulogy for Jesse James, played by Tyrone Power, **Henry Hull** reads the words on the outlaw's grave marker. Because of Carl Sandburg, we know that "the dirty little coward who shot Mr. Howard and put poor Jesse in the grave" was gang member Bob Ford, impersonated in the movie by John Carradine. *Jesse James* (1939, 20th Century-Fox).

3004 "This guy could have climbed the highest mountain in the world—if he'd just started up the right one." **Van Heflin** grieves over the body of his friend, good-looking, egotistical hood Robert Taylor. *Johnny Eager* (1941, MGM).

3005 "Now she lies in 1500 fathoms and with her most of our shipmates. We have lost her, but they are still with her. Now they lie in very good company." Commander **Noel Coward** gives a valedictory for his sunken ship H.M.S. Torrin and her dead crew. *In Which We Serve* (1942, GB, Rank).

3006 "Didn't get much of a chance, did you? Maybe when we leave this country, kids like you will be able to live and grow up." **Henry Fonda**, as Wyatt Earp, delivers a solemn speech at the grave site of his murdered kid brother. *My Darling Clementine* (1946, 20th Century-Fox).

3007 "An hour ago Rudy Linnekar had this town in his pocket, now you can strain him through a sieve." It's the crude and insensitive comment of a witness commenting on the driver of a car which is a smoldering ruin after being blown up by a bomb. *Touch of Evil* (1958, Universal-International).

3008 "He was some kind of man. What does it matter what you say about people?" The movie began with the matter-of-fact eulogy of one man and ends with **Marlene Dietrich** speaking of Orson Welles after the corrupt cop has been shot to death. *Touch of Evil* (1958, Universal-International).

3009 "The dead always share the earth in peace; and that's not enough. It's time for the living to have a turn. The day will come when Arab and Jew will share the peaceful life of this land that they have always shared in death." **Paul Newman**'s prayer over the common grave of Jew Jill Haworth and Arab John Derek, has not yet been answered. *Exodus* (1960, United Artists).

3010 "He was comin' here by automobile to sing for you tonight. The doctor said his heart just stopped. So we won't be seeing Hank again, least not in this world. He was my friend. He was one of you, a poor boy, who, who never forgot you. He was on this earth twenty-nine years. Now he's gone home." **Red Buttons** announces the death of country-and-western singer Hank Williams, played by George Hamilton. *Your Cheatin' Heart* (1964, MGM).

3011 "He was a natural-born world-shaker." **George Kennedy** fondly recalls his friend, chain gang escapee Paul Newman who was killed as he tried to elude recapture. *Cool Hand Luke* (1967, Warner Bros.).

3012 "Oh, God, we pass onto you the body and soul of this nameless peckerhead. . . . Well, at least he went quick, and he ain't going to have to suffer the scurvy, the dysentery, the spotted fever, the cholera, not to mention those other maladies contracted in consorting with low women. . . ." Gold prospector **Lee Marvin** prays irreverently over the grave of a farmer killed before he could reach the gold fields. *Paint Your Wagon* (1969, Paramount).

3013 "What can you say about a twenty-five-year-old girl who died? That she was beautiful. And brilliant. That she loved Mozart and Bach. And the Beatles. And me." **Ryan O'Neal** recalls his dead wife, Ali McGraw. *Love Story* (1970, Paramount).

3014 "There's a lot I could say about this man, but I don't guess it matters now." It's **Sylvester Stallone**'s lukewarm eulogy for Carl Weathers. *Rocky IV* (1985, MGM-United Artists).

3015 "They want me to say 'Let's not forget that two white boys also died helping Negroes help themselves.' They want me to say 'we mourn with the mothers of these two white boys.' But the state of Mississippi won't even allow these white boys to be buried in the same cemetery as this Negro boy. I say I have no more love to give. I have only anger in my heart today, and I want you to be angry with me. I'm sick and I'm tired and I want you to be sick and tired with me. I. . . I. . . I'm sick and tired of going to the funeral of black men who have been murdered by white men. I. . . I am sick and tired of people of this country who continue to allow these things to happen. What is an unalienable right if you are a Negro? What does it mean 'equal treatment under the law'? What. . . what does it mean 'liberty and justice for all'? Now I say to these people 'look at the face of this young man and you will see the face of a black man, but. . . it is just like yours!'" Minister **Frankie Faison** eulogizes at the funeral of a black civil rights worker. *Mississippi Burning* (1988, Orion).

3016 "Solomon Martinson was one of us. What he suffered we all suffer. We do not mourn him, we honor him and we say the only true tribute to him is to pick up the spear from where it has fallen. Solomon is just one, one man, and when we defy them, when we resist in our hundreds, when we resist in our thousands, in our millions, then victory is certain. . . ." Priest **Jude Akuwidike** eulogizes Albee Lesotho, a murdered African National Congress political leader. *A World Apart* (1988, GB, Atlantic).

3017 "Lord we give you Curly. Try not to piss him off." Cook **Tracey Walter** eulogizes tough cowboy Jack Palance at his grave site. *City Slickers* (1991, Columbia).

Euphemisms

see also TASTES, WORDS

3018 "More marriages go on the rocks simply because people aren't better acquainted." Dolores Hart had better watch out when **George Hamilton** uses the expression "get better acquainted." He means in the sack. *Where the Boys Are* (1960, MGM).

3019 "Martha, will you show her where we keep the, er, euphemism?" **Richard Burton** asks his wife Elizabeth Taylor to show Sandy Dennis where the bathroom is. *Who's Afraid of Virginia Woolf?* (1966,Warner Bros.).

3020 "Terminate with extreme prejudice. . . ." Only the military could come up with such a swell euphemism which orders assassin Martin Sheen to kill renegade Colonel Marlon Brando. *Apocalypse Now* (1979, United Artists).

3021 "Make sure the client is completely comfortable before you take any money." The translation of prostitute **Louise Smith**'s advice to a new girl is: "Make sure the john is naked before asking for money, because then you can be sure he's not a cop." *Working Girls* (1986, Miramax).

3022 "Mr. Wiggly's been on bread and water for five years." **Mel Gibson** groans that being a fugitive is hard on his sex life. *Bird on a Wire* (1990, Universal).

Evasions

see also DECEPTIONS

3023 "Yes—and again, no." It's the line that Warren William and Bette Davis teach gubernatorial candidate **Guy Kibbee** to say any time he's questioned by the press. *The Dark Horse* (1932, Warner Bros.).

3024 "The question of Santa Claus seems to be largely a matter of opinion. Many people firmly believe in him. Others do not. The tradition of American justice demands a broad and unprejudiced view of such a controversial matter. The Court, therefore, intends to keep an open mind. We shall hear evidence on either side." Judge **Gene Lockhart** evades the political consequences of ruling on the existence of Santa Claus, demanded by prosecutor Jerome Cowan, during the sanity hearing of Edmund Gwenn, who claims to be the real Santa Claus. *Miracle on 34th Street* (1947, 20th Century-Fox).

3025 "You want to do something, you got to be where it counts. On the inside. . . . You're out—and you're a nobody." **Woody Allen** justifies his evasiveness by expressing his desire to be accepted by all groups, no matter what moral compromises he must make. *The Front* (1976, Columbia).

Evenings *see* DAYS, NIGHTS, TIME

Events *see* CONSEQUENCES

Everything

see also IMPORTANCE, THINGS

3026 "Everything I like to do is either illegal, immoral, or fattening." **W.C. Fields** delivers a line that has become a classic. *Never Give a Sucker an Even Break* (1941, Universal).

3027 "You already know everything. . . you want everything too." Troubled **Theresa Russell** rages at psychologist Art Garfunkel who has an oppressive affair with her. *Bad Timing: A Sensual Obsession* (1980, GB, Rank).

3028 "Do everything to me. Show me how I can do everything to you?" Virgin **Bo Derek** is eager to learn all there is to know about sexual pleasure. *Bolero* (1984, Cannon).

Evidence *see* PROOFS

Evilness

see also BADNESS, CORRUPTION, CRIMES AND CRIMINALS, DEVILS, GOD, GOOD AND EVIL (BAD), GOODNESS, HARM, IMMORALITY, PAINS, REPUTATIONS, SINS AND SINNERS, TROUBLES, WITCHCRAFT AND WITCHES, WRONGS AND WRONGDOINGS

3029 "It's an evil omen." As **Greta Garbo** meets Fredric March at the Moscow train station, they hear the screams of a woman who commits suicide by throwing herself under the wheels of a train. Besides being an omen, this is a Hollywood film device to predict the future. *Anna Karenina* (1935, MGM).

3030 "What a witches' sabbath. . . so incredibly evil. I didn't dream such a place existed except in my own imagination—like a half-remembered dream. Anything could happen here, at any moment." **Gene Tierney** is delighted with the decadence of an Oriental gambling den run by Ona Munson. *The Shanghai Gesture* (1941, United Artists).

3031 "Love rather than money is the root of all evil. Sometimes a thought can be like a malignant dis-

ease and start to eat away at the will power." Psychologist **Sydney Greenstreet** expounds on his theory of evil to Humphrey Bogart. *Conflict* (1945, Warner Bros.).

3032 "There will be many to say that I have done deeds of calculated and unfathomable villainy. Whether I have or not will probably remain an open verdict." Ex-Scotland Yard Superintendent **Sydney Greenstreet** confides to Peter Lorre, the illustrator of Greenstreet's book on the perfect crime. *The Verdict* (1946, Warner Bros.).

3033 "I will tell you about Mrs. Paradine. She's bad, bad to the bone. If ever there was an evil woman, she is one." **Louis Jourdan** wastes his time trying to warn barrister Gregory Peck about his client Alida Valli. Peck has already fallen in love with her. *The Paradine Case* (1947, Selznick-United Artists).

3034 "There must have been something evil in you that would take it seriously!" Professor **James Stewart** makes an unconvincing condemnation of his students John Dall and Farley Granger's premeditated murder of a classmate. Stewart preached that murders of inferiors by superiors was sometimes justified. *Rope* (1948, Warner Bros.).

3035 "This is the story of evil. Evil is headstrong—is puffed up. For our soul's sake, it is salutory for us to view it in all its ugly nakedness once in a while." It's a warning title at the beginning of the film. *Beyond the Forest* (1949, Warner Bros.).

3036 "In times like these, can a man of good conscience ask others 'protect me, kill for me, but do not ask me to stain my hands'? What must one do when a choice between two evils is all that is offered?. . . In order to save, at times we must destroy." Wise old Korean **Philip Ahn** would embrace the Vietnam War logic of destroying a village to liberate it. *Battle Hymn* (1957, Universal).

3037 "He would never rise again. After seven years he was released, ill with an incurable disease. On January twenty-fifth, nineteen forty-seven, Al Capone died. But the seeds of the evil he planted still survive. And we must continue to fight the remnants of the organization he built which still touches every one of us today." The narrator wraps up things in this film based on the evil criminal activities of Chicago's notorious Al Capone, played in this movie by Rod Steiger. *Al Capone* (1959, Allied Artists).

3038 "If you search for the evil in man expecting to find it, you certainly will." Abraham Lincoln's quote is inscribed on an amulet given to orphan Hayley Mills by her late missionary father. *Pollyanna* (1960, Buena Vista).

3039 MOHAMMED EL MAHDI: "I do not often meet with a Christian, Gordon Pasha. Is it because you are a Christian that I feel myself in the presence of evil?" GENERAL CHARLES GORDON: "I think not for I smell the same evil on your person, and you are not Christian. So it cannot be that, can it?" Negotiations of thrust and parry are made between **Laurence Olivier**, as the Mahdi, who has declared a holy war, a Jihad, intent on ridding all Sudan of infidels, and **Charlton Heston**, as paradoxical and mystical British General Sir Charles "Chinese" Gordon. Things are getting off on a bad foot. *Khartoum* (1966, GB, United Artists).

3040 "I bear no hatred, no bitterness towards the German people. People are not evil, only individuals are evil. If, after my death, this diary should be found and read, will some kind friend please say Kaddish for me." As the film ends, the voice of **Cyril Shaps**, a survivor of the Nazi death camps, who committed suicide, is heard. *The Odessa File* (1974, GB-Ger., Columbia).

3041 "Better is by evil still made better." Seen only in flashback **William Hickey** instills in his cabdriver son, Philip Bosco, the ambition to become a Shakespearean actor. *Flanagan* (1985, United Film Distributors).

3042 "You got to work at evil." Charming **Danny Glover** works at his. *To Sleep with Anger* (1990, Goldwyn).

Evolution *see* ANIMALS, BEGINNINGS, EXPLANATIONS, FISH AND FISHING, HUMAN NATURE, MEN, PROGRESS, THEORIES

Examples *see* CHOICES, MODELS, OBJECT LESSONS, WARNINGS

Excellence *see* ABILITIES AND CAPABILITIES, GENIUS, SUPERIORITY AND INFERIORITY, TALENTS

Exceptions

see also CLASSES, DIFFERENCES, PRINCIPLES, RULES

3043 "Nothing is permanent in this world except Roosevelt, dear." **Mary Astor** makes a topical joke for her brother Rudy Vallee. *The Palm Beach Story* (1942, Paramount).

3044 "If I could get back my youth, I'd do anything in the world, except get up early, take exercise or be respectable." Youth is important to **George Sanders**, but he won't pay just any price for it. *The Picture of Dorian Gray* (1944, MGM).

3045 "You know I never did anything in my life that was worthwhile except make you." Convincingly,

Gena Rowlands tells her children of her pride in them. *A Woman Under the Influence* (1974, Faces Int.).

3046 "I have heard about your lunch breaks on the set. The only thing you don't do in your dressing room is dress." Bisexual **Michael Caine** is not angry as he tells his actress wife Maggie Smith that he's well aware of her infidelities. *California Suite* (1978, Columbia).

3047 "You were the best I ever had, except for that circus fellow." **Veronica Cartwright** tries to cheer up Jack Nicholson who has been sentenced to hang. *Goin' South* (1978, Paramount).

3048 "I always knew everybody's going to die, but I really thought I'd be the exception." **Anne Bancroft**, suffering from an inoperable brain tumor, tells her son Ron Silver of her feelings about her immortality. *Garbo Talks* (1984, MGM-United Artists).

3049 "Listen, you're going to love it here. Most guys look like Paul Newman—I'm really the exception." Part-time Israeli soldier **Amos Kollek** shows the sites of Tel Aviv to reluctant American visitor Julie Hagerty. *Goodbye, New York* (1985, Israel, Castle Hill).

3050 "Larry's a failure in everything except life." **George Coe** brags to Isabella Rossellini about his nephew Ted Danson. *Cousins* (1989, Paramount).

Excesses

see also EXTRAVAGANCES, GREED

3052 "To put it simply, I would say that our general belief is in moderation. We preach the virtue of avoiding excess of all kinds, even including, if you will pardon the paradox, excess of virtue itself." **H.B. Warner** explains the "moderate" philosophy of Shangri-La to a stranded Ronald Colman. *Lost Horizon* (1937, Columbia).

3053 "I fight and fuck too much." Cheerful immoralist **Jack Nicholson** mischievously explains why, after being imprisoned for rape, he has been transferred to a mental hospital where he eventually has a forced lobotomy. *One Flew Over the Cuckoo's Nest* (1975, United Artists).

3054 "Nothing exceeds like excess." Bored **Michelle Pfeiffer**, wife of narcotics king Al Pacino, updates a cliché. *Scarface* (1983, Universal).

Excitements

see also ADVENTURES, DANGER, FEELINGS, PASSION

3055 "Yeah, there's money in the big town, all right. And the women! Good town. Somethin' doin' all the time. Excitin' things, you know. Gee, the clothes I could wear." **Douglas Fairbanks, Jr.** is excited by the plans of his pal, Edward G. Robinson, for them to move to the mobs of the big city, presumably Chicago. *Little Caesar* (1931, Warner Bros.).

3056 "Bridge at three... dinner at eight. And after dinner, bridge. Rather an amusing day, eh, Flamand?" At **C. Aubrey Smith**'s age, it doesn't take much to excite him, as he plans the day at his chateau with his butler. *Love Me Tonight* (1932, Paramount).

3057 BARBARA WILLIS: "It was just one of those excitement-for-the-moment things." VANTINE: "Well, watch out for the next moment, honey. It's longer than the first." It's an exchange between married "good" woman **Mary Astor** and tart **Jean Harlow** after Astor has yielded to Clark Gable. *Red Dust* (1932, MGM).

3058 "There's nothing more exciting than making money." Wealthy **Doris Nolan** has a heated argument with her unambitious fiancé Cary Grant. *Holiday* (1938, Columbia).

3059 "Let's make it a real rouser." Enthusiastic medium **Margaret Rutherford** begins a séance at Rex Harrison's home. *Blithe Spirit* (1945, GB, Two Cities-Cineguild).

3060 "Yes, we promised you excitement and here they are, the most exciting band in the whole country. Happy Stella Kowalski and her Schottiche Five." Title character **Bobby Van** introduces Kathleen Freeman's group. *The Affairs of Dobie Gillis* (1953, MGM).

3061 "You'd be surprised how little happens in prison. They make an effort not to have it too exciting." Escaped Devil Island's prisoner **Humphrey Bogart** tells Joan Bennett how quiet and peaceful the prison is. *We're No Angels* (1955, Paramount).

3062 "You did it to torture and excite us." Marxist thug **Giancarlo Giannini** accuses Mariangela Melato of deliberately taking off her top to lie in the sun on her yacht to perplex the crew. The two are now stranded on a deserted island with the roles of master and servant switched. *Swept Away* (1975, Italy, Cinema 5).

3063 "You're exceptional in bed because you got— you get pleasure in every part of your body when I touch you.... Like the tip of your nose, and if I stroke your teeth or your kneecaps... you get excited." **Woody Allen** believes he really turns Diane Keaton on. *Annie Hall* (1977, United Artists).

3064 "He's rich, he's powerful, he adores me, he's exciting in every way.... Someone should tell younger men about older men." **Ali MacGraw** tells Peter Weller about the appeal of Alan King, the rich man who keeps her. *Just Tell Me What You Want* (1980, Warner Bros.).

3065 "That was the most exciting sexual encounter without actually having it that I ever almost had." Brain surgeon **Steve Martin**'s beautiful, conniving, gold-digging, sadistic wife Kathleen Turner turns him on but won't deliver and consummate their marriage. *The Man with Two Brains* (1983, Warner Bros.).

3066 "Torture, murder, mutilation! Brilliant! Absolutely brilliant, and almost no production costs. Where do they get actors who can do this?... I think it's what's next." Video entrepreneur **James Woods** is stunned when he stumbles across a Malaysian television station that appears to be broadcasting pure sex and brutality. *Videodrome* (1983, Canada, Universal).

3067 "If I were, you should be my heroine and I should write, 'If Miss Honeychurch ever takes to live as she plays, it will be very exciting—both for us and for her.'" Reverend Beebe, played by **Simon Callow**, responds to Lucy Honeychurch, played by Helena Bonham Carter, when she asks him if he too is writing a novel, as he admires the way she passionately plays a piano. *A Room with a View* (1985, GB, Merchant-Ivory-Goldcrest).

3068 "I gotta admit the truth—it turned me on." Jewish princess **Lorraine Bracco** admits that she found it exciting when her Mafia date Ray Liotta viciously beat up a man who made a pass at her. *GoodFellas* (1990, Warner Bros.).

3069 "You move me, Sail, you really do. You mark me to the deepest." **Laura Dern** states her excitement as she jumps into bed with Nicolas Cage. *Wild at Heart* (1990, Goldwyn).

Excuses

see also APOLOGIES, BLAME, EXPLANATIONS, FAULTS, IMPORTANCE, JUSTIFICATIONS, PLEAS AND PLEADING, REASONS, REGRETS

3070 "My only excuse is I love you." A title card expresses the feelings of seductive temptress **Greta Garbo** for John Gilbert. *Flesh and the Devil* (1926, silent, MGM).

3071 "Ah'd love to kiss you, but Ah just washed mah hair!" **Bette Davis**, in her best Southern corn-pone voice, toys with Richard Barthelmess. *The Cabin in the Cotton* (1932, First National-Warner Bros.).

3072 "How could I? My hands were full of money!" **Claudette Colbert** replies matter-of-fact to cab driver Don Ameche's "Didn't you hit him?" when she tells him that she once attracted a millionaire but the man's father offered to buy her off. *Midnight* (1939, Paramount).

3073 "I was only trying to guess your weight." **W.C. Fields** excuses himself when a waitress complains he's too free with his hands. *Never Give a Sucker an Even Break* (1941, Universal).

3074 "You can't fix Washington. For one thing you can't find out who's in charge." Lawyer **Lloyd Corrigan** explains to his client, con-man Alan Ladd, why he's been unsuccessful in returning draftee Ladd to civilian life. *Lucky Jordan* (1943, Paramount).

3075 "Listen, when a guy's doing a job, I don't kibitz." **Elisha Cook, Jr.**, tells Humphrey Bogart why he didn't come to his aid when Bogie was being beaten up in an alley. *The Big Sleep* (1946, Warner Bros.).

3076 "I don't go to church, kneeling bags my nylons." **Jan Sterling**, the indifferent wife of Richard Benedict, trapped in a cave, sneers at self-seeking journalist Kirk Douglas who is trying to milk the public's concern for the victim into a return to the big time papers. *Ace in the Hole* aka: *The Big Carnival* (1951, Paramount).

3077 "Thank you—That's the most charming and endearing excuse for infidelity I've ever heard." **Hermione Gingold** compliments Maurice Chevalier who tells her that years ago he was so in love with her, he was going to propose, so naturally he took up with another woman until he got over the notion. *Gigi* (1958, MGM).

3078 "You know, one's awfully apt to try and excuse one's self sometimes by saying, 'Well, what I do doesn't do anybody else any harm.' But one does, you see. It's not a thought I like very much." **David Niven** confesses to Wendy Hiller that he knows his deceptions cause harm to others besides himself. *Separate Tables* (1958, United Artists).

3079 "The maid's sick—spinal meningitis." A bellboy explains to new resident Gene Hackman why his bed and room are not made up. *All Night Long* (1981, Universal).

3080 "I wish I could think of something clever to say but right now I'm in the middle of a hot flash." **Mary Steenburgen** can't think of anything clever to say to her comedy writing partner, Dudley Moore. He wishes to take their team to a new level of involvement. *Romantic Comedy* (1982, MGM-United Artists).

3081 "I can't have a baby. I have a 12:30 lunch meeting." Busy executive **Diane Keaton** panics when a relative's baby is unexpectedly dropped into her life. *Baby Boom* (1987, MGM-United Artists).

3082 "It didn't mean anything. It just kinda happened." Reporter **Christopher Reeve** gives a lame excuse to his girlfriend Mimi Rogers after he sleeps with a hooker. *Street Smart* (1987, Cannon).

3083 LARRY KOZINSKI: "Why are you always making silly excuses for your husband?" MARIA HARDY: "Because you're always making excuses for your wife." **Ted Danson** and **Isabella Rossellini** debate who's to blame when they suspect their spouses Sean Young and William Petersen are having an affair. *Cousins* (1989, Paramount).

3084 "Great paté. But I have to motor if I want to be ready for that funeral." Murderess **Winona Ryder** excuses herself for rushing away from dinner with her parents. *Heathers* (1989, New World).

3085 "I'm Italian. I'm a man. I have lots of hormones in my body." **Kevin Kline** uses an ethnic excuse for his infidelities. *I Love You to Death* (1990, Tri-Star).

Executions

see also CRIMES AND CRIMINALS, DEATH AND DYING, JUDGMENTS, JUSTICE, KILLINGS, LAWS, LAWYERS, LEGALITY AND ILLEGALITY

3086 "Did you ever see a guy die? I did. I spent eight months in that condemned cell. Believe me, kid, it's no picnic. Watching them go, one by one, and I wait day after day, week after week, month after month, wondering when it will be my turn, listening to the drone of that lousy motor and watching the lights go dim." Hard-boiled but very likeable escaped con **Spencer Tracy**'s passionate speech persuades a very young Humphrey Bogart not to kill a blackmailer. *Up the River* (1930, Fox).

3087 "No man should be late for his own hanging." **Errol Flynn**, as physician Peter Blood, scoffs at the prospect of hanging. *Captain Blood* (1935, Warner Bros.).

3088 "Well, I'll hang in the end, but they'll get their money's worth at the trial. You wait." Psychopathic killer **Robert Montgomery** is led away by the police at the end of the film. *Night Must Fall* (1937, MGM).

3089 "Hanging would be a small price to pay for the company of such a charming lady." Title character **Errol Flynn** dismisses the dangers of paying furtive court to Olivia de Havilland as Maid Marian. *The Adventures of Robin Hood* (1938, Warner Bros.).

3090 "It's like sitting in a barber chair. They're going to ask me, 'You got anything to say?' and I say, 'Sure. Give me a haircut, a shave and a massage— one of those nice new electric massages.'" **James Cagney** is still able to be macho about his coming appointment with the electric chair. *Angels with Dirty Faces* (1938, Warner Bros.).

3091 McCoy: "By the Almighty, he is going to hang." Marshal Will Wright: "Suppose Jesse doesn't want to be hanged." Railroad President **Donald Meek** refuses to honor the bargain that U.S. Marshal **Randolph Scott** made with title character Tyrone Power to get him to surrender. *Jesse James* (1939, 20th Century-Fox).

3092 "Are you going to let them hang me?" Murderess **Bette Davis** innocently questions her lawyer James Stephenson. *The Letter* (1940, Warner Bros.).

3093 Ahmad: "Another execution, Jaffar? Why had he to die?" Jaffar: "He had been thinking, O my master.... It's quite unpardonable." Prince **John Justin** and his evil grand vizer, magician **Conrad Veidt** watch a man beheaded. *The Thief of Bagdad* (1940, GB, London Films-United Artists).

3094 Ed Cornell: "I could arrest you today... but you might get some smart mouthpiece and get off with life instead of the chair. I won't be satisfied until I'm sure it's the chair." Frankie Christopher: "You're a gay dog, Cornell. You make me feel as if I'm driving a hearse." Cornell: "Oh, I know your type—I've seen hundreds of them. I don't scare you enough to make you commit suicide, but I worry you just the same. And when the day comes, they are all different. Some scream, a few faint, some light a cigarette and try a wisecrack, but it sticks in their throats—especially when they're hung." Even though macabre cop **Laird Cregar** knows promoter **Victor Mature** isn't guilty of killing actress Carole Landis, he wants him executed. *I Wake Up Screaming* (1942, 20th Century-Fox).

3095 Pa: "They're going to hang Roxie." Ma: "What did I tell you?" When **George Chandler** relays a phone message about his daughter Ginger Rogers to his wife in another room, the mother's voice responds without any surprise. *Roxie Hart* (1942, 20th Century-Fox).

3096 "Hangin's any man's business that's around.... There's always some crazy fool loses his head and starts to hang everyone in sight." Cowpoke **Henry Fonda** might be speaking of pompous ex-Confederate officer Frank Conroy who's just itching to lynch someone. *The Ox-Bow Incident* (1943, 20th Century-Fox).

3097 "The defendants and each of them are found guilty of the crime of murder as set forth into the indictment. They will be removed from the courtroom and given into the custody of the military prison until such time as the sentence of death is executed upon their bodies." **Peter Chong** reads the sentence of the Japanese court on eight bomber crew members of the Jimmy Doolittle raid against Tokyo in 1942. The men were not protected by the Geneva Convention or treated as prisoners of war. Instead they were tortured and tried as war criminals. *The Purple Heart* (1944, 20th Century-Fox).

3098 "Larkin, you're gonna get 30 days for that killin'." Then we're gonna hang you." **George "Gabby" Hayes** gives Harry Woods the "good news, bad news" bit. *Trail Street* (1947, RKO).

3099 "I want to put him in the electric chair, where he belongs. And pull the switch myself." Pathological self-righteous police detective **Kirk Douglas** refers to butchering abortionist George Macready. *Detective Story* (1951, Paramount).

3100 "I was just getting ready to take my tie off... wondering whether I should hang myself with it." Sleepy-eyed **Robert Mitchum** welcomes an assortment of thugs into his cheap hotel room. *His Kind of Woman* (1951, RKO).

3101 "Have you any idea of the average marksmanship of the army of his Majesty, King George II? Let me persuade you to be hanged." **Laurence Olivier**, as General "Gentleman Johnny" Burgoyne, encourages convicted colonial spy Kirk Douglas to accept a nice clean hanging rather than a messy end at the hands of an incompetent firing squad. Douglas accepts graciously. *The Devil's Disciple* (1959, GB, United Artists).

3102 "I die the king's good servant, but God's first." Sir Thomas More, portrayed by **Paul Scofield**, states the order of his allegiance before putting his head on the executioner's block. *A Man for All Seasons* (1966, GB, Columbia).

3103 "When's it going to end? Pretty soon you start executing people for jaywalking... or traffic violations, and then you end up executing your neighbor because his dog pisses on your lawn." **Clint Eastwood**, as Dirty Harry, is in the unfamiliar role of the voice of moderation against police vigilantes headed by police chief Hal Holbrook. *Magnum Force* (1973, Warner Bros.).

3104 "To be executed for a crime that I never committed. Of course, isn't all mankind in the same boat? Isn't all mankind ultimately executed for a crime it never committed? The difference is that all men go eventually. I'm supposed to go at 6 o'clock tomorrow morning. I was supposed to go at 5 o'clock but I've got a smart lawyer. Got leniency." In his opening voice-over narration, **Woody Allen** wonders how he got himself in his present predicament. *Love and Death* (1975, United Artists).

3105 DANIEL ISAACSON: "How will they kill you, Mommy?" ROCHELLE ISAACSON: "Well, darling, it's something called electrocution and it's very painless. How's school?" DANIEL ISAACSON: "Fine. I'm going to be a lawyer, so I can get you free." Young **Ilan Mitchell-Smith** visits his mother **Lindsay Crouse** in the death house where she and her husband will be executed for passing atomic secrets to the USSR. *Daniel* (1983, Paramount).

3106 "I've never seen an execution. It will be a new sensation." **Faye Dunaway** trills happily as she prepares to see her highwayman lover Alan Bates hanged. *Wicked Lady* (1983, GB, Cannon).

3107 "They hire a man from an ad in the personals and pay him $150 to throw the switch. He wears a hood so nobody knows who he is, and he's paid in cash so he won't have to cash a check. Twenty-two thousand volts will pass through the prisoner's body." A prison guard gives photographer Roy Scheider a tour of the electrocution chamber. *Somebody Has Got to Shoot the Picture* (1991, Warner Bros.).

Exercise *see* BODIES, HEALTH, INFLUENCES, PRACTICES, PROBLEMS, TRAINING

Exhaustion *see* FATIGUE

Existence

see also IDENTITIES, LIVES AND LIVING

3108 "There is no such person as the Baron Courtelin. I've even been through the better-class illegitimates." **Charles Butterworth** accuses Parisian tailor Maurice Chevalier, who has been introduced as a baron, of being a phony. *Love Me Tonight* (1932, Paramount).

3109 "I felt I was standing up. . . looking out at the sea. . . and someone came swimming towards me shouting something. . . something I felt I'd heard long ago. People are always thinking they know someone before, in another existence." **Evelyn Keyes** experiences déjà vu when she meets Robert Montgomery in his second reincarnation. *Here Comes Mr. Jordan* (1941, Columbia).

3110 "The man you once knew is no more. There's not a vestige of him left. Nothing." **Victor Mature**, as gambler and gunfighter Doc Holliday, tells Cathy Downs that the man she once knew, who planned to be a dentist, no longer exists. *My Darling Clementine* (1946, 20th Century-Fox).

3111 "The girl who said no, she doesn't exist anymore. She was suffocated in smoke from something on fire inside her." Confessing her life-long love for Laurence Harvey, **Geraldine Page** at last offers herself to him. *Summer and Smoke* (1961, Paramount).

3112 "I swear. . . if you existed I'd divorce you." **Elizabeth Taylor** is disgusted that she can kick around her husband Richard Burton so easily. *Who's Afraid of Virginia Woolf?* (1966, Warner Bros.).

3113 "You like to be looked at. Otherwise you won't exist." **Richard Jordan** reduces glamorous film and television actress Kristin Griffith to nothing more than a sex object. *Interiors* (1978, United Artists).

3114 "With Beirut, an old American dream disappears, that of the Orient. The Orient no longer exists. Actually, it never existed. It was only a dream of the West." War correspondent **Jean Carmet** comments on the significance or lack of same of the battles raging in Beirut. *Circle of Deceit* aka: *False Witness* (1982, Fr.,-Ger., United Artists Classics).

3115 "Nothing really exists for me. I'm a liar trying to tell the truth." Oil tanker engineer **Bruno Ganz** reports his reactions in lengthy letters to Julia Vonderlinn. *In the White City* (1983, Switzerland-Portugal, Gray City Films).

3116 "I'm poor, black. I may even be ugly, but dear God, I'm here." **Whoopi Goldberg** shouts to mean common-law husband Danny Glover from the back of a departing car. *The Color Purple* (1985, Warner Bros.).

3117 "You're now a person who doesn't exist, working for an organization that doesn't exist." **J.A. Preston** cautions Fred Ward, who has just undergone plastic surgery in order to work for an ultra-secret intelligence agency. *Remo Williams: The Adventure Begins. . .* (1985, Orion).

3118 "We went from a small infidelity to the meaning of existence." It's Rabbi **Sam Waterston**'s observation when Martin Landau takes him into his confidence and tells of his affair with Anjelica Huston without actually naming names. *Crimes and Misdemeanors* (1989, Orion).

3119 "I can't make the leap of faith necessary to believe in my own existence." Bespectacled Milquetoast **Woody Allen** is the comedy relief in a fantasy world of depression and despair. *Shadows and Fog* (1992, Orion Classics).

Expectations

see also DISAPPOINTMENTS, FUTURE, HOPE, PROBABILITY AND STATISTICS, WAITS AND WAITING

3120 PREYSING: "Are you going to be nice to me?" FLAEMMCHEN: "Yes." PREYSING: "Very nice?" FLAEMMCHEN: "That's what you expect, isn't it?" **Wallace Beery** finally gets stenographer **Joan Crawford** to give in to his innuendoes. *Grand Hotel* (1932, MGM).

3121 "I expect a very fancy profit out of it." **Clark Gable** has paid a premium price to dance the Virginia Reel with young widow Vivien Leigh at an Atlanta charity bazaar. *Gone with the Wind* (1939, Selznick-MGM).

3122 GEORGE KITTEREDGE: "Tracy, a man expects his wife—" TRACY LORD: "To behave herself, naturally." C.K. DEXTER HAVEN: "To behave herself naturally." Groom-to-be **John Howard** is demonstrated the importance of a comma by his fiancée **Katharine Hepburn** and her ex-husband **Cary Grant.** *The Philadelphia Story* (1940, MGM).

3123 "Oh, Jerry, don't let's ask for the moon. We have the stars." With the film's closing line, **Bette Davis** urges her married lover Paul Henreid not to expect too much from their relationship. *Now, Voyager* (1942, Warner Bros.).

3124 "There's small pickings in that town." **Cornel Wilde** alerts singer Ida Lupino not to expect too much from a town she's moving into. *Road House* (1948, 20th Century-Fox).

3125 "He's like a spider, and he expects me to redecorate his web." Interior decorator **Doris Day** refers to womanizer Rock Hudson, who hogs their telephone party line and hires her to redecorate his apartment which is a den of seduction. *Pillow Talk* (1959, Universal).

3126 "Shirt sleeves to shirt sleeves in three generations—at least you won't have to start where I did, from the top." Cancer-ridden, alcoholic **Arthur Kennedy** cynically expresses his low expectations of his son Troy Donahue's prospects if he marries Sandra Dee. *A Summer Place* (1959, Warner Bros.).

3127 "You see a girl a couple of times a week, just for laughs, and right away, they think you're going to divorce your wife." **Fred MacMurray**, in one of his despicable roles, is an older married man having an affair with younger single Shirley MacLaine. He strings her along with promises that eventually they'll be together forever. It's an all-too familiar story. *The Apartment* (1960, United Artists).

3128 JAMES BOND: "Suppose that when she meets me in the flesh, I don't come up to expectations." M: "See that you do." **Sean Connery** really isn't worried as he's briefed by **Bernard Lee** on his assignment with Russian cipher clerk Daniela Bianchi. She reportedly will trade a secret cryptographic device for a little loving from 007. *From Russia with Love* (1964, GB, United Artists).

3129 "Everyone cheats with their secretary. I expected more from my husband." Trying to hide her outrage and bitterness, by keeping the discussion of Walter Matthau's infidelity in a light mood, **Maureen Stapleton** expresses disappointment that he shows no more imagination than to reach for the most readily available female. *Plaza Suite* (1971, Paramount).

3130 "I may bring home a boyfriend, but only occasionally. I mean, I do feel you ought to go to a man's room if you can. I mean, it doesn't look so much as if one expected it, does it?" American singer and would-be decadent lady **Liza Minnelli**, who works in a 1930s Berlin cabaret, chats wildly with recently arrived English writer Michael York. *Cabaret* (1972, Allied Artists).

3131 "You can't take people on high places and expect them to take what's left over after that." **Betsy Brantley** reaches the decision that being the mistress of her uncle, married doctor Sean Connery, is not enough, after spending a climbing holiday with him in the purity of the Swiss Alps. *Five Days One Summer* (1982, Warner Bros.).

3132 "No matter what I do, I can never fulfill their expectations." **Peter O'Toole** sadly comments on his well-earned reputation as a lothario. *My Favorite Year* (1982, MGM-United Artists).

3133 "I expect to lose half of you before I'm finished. I will use every means at my disposal, fair or unfair, to trip you up, expose your weaknesses. . . as a potential aviator. . . and as a human being. Understand? The prize at the other end is a flight education worth one million dollars, but first you have to pass me." Drill instructor **Louis Gossett, Jr.**, describes the agony he has planned for a new class of recruits in a Naval Officers Candidate School. *An Officer and a Gentleman* (1982, Paramount).

3134 "I hope you don't expect me to save you, 'cause I don't do that nice stuff anymore." After being exposed to some synthetic Kryptonite, **Christopher Reeve** becomes an evil, selfish Superman, who has no time for damsels in distress. *Superman III* (1982, GB, Warner Bros.).

3135 "He said we made a good couple, because I had no expectations and he had too many." **Meg Tilly** quotes her dead lover Alex to his friends. *The Big Chill* (1983, Columbia).

3136 "I've forgotten what you are supposed to expect from life." Dedicated activist **Amanda Plummer** is tormented by the memory of the execution of her parents for passing atomic secrets to the Communists. *Daniel* (1983, Paramount).

3137 DOLLY HARSHAW: "Don't you ever knock?" HARRY MADDOX: "Only when it's not expected." It's a bit late for **Virginia Madsen** to play coy with **Don Johnson**, as he enters her bedroom. Her invitation was very clear. He pulls the covers off her. She pulls a derringer on him, then unzips his pants. *The Hot Spot* (1990, Orion).

3138 "By the time I'm 70, I'll be retiring to Fort Lauderdale and start eating dinner at 2:30." Despairing **Billy Crystal** finishes the depressing tale to his son's grade school class of his expectations of what life has to hold for him. *City Slickers* (1991, Columbia).

Experiences

see also INVOLVEMENTS, LEARNING AND LESSONS, LIVES AND LIVING, PARTICIPATION, SOPHISTICATION, TRAINING

3139 "Kill, then love! When you have known that, you have known everything. . . ." Maniacal human hunter **Leslie Banks** yells to his prey Joel McCrea. *The Most Dangerous Game* (1932, RKO).

3140 "Plenty!" The world-weary look says it all when **Barbara Stanwyck** makes her meaningful one word response as she's asked if she has had any experience during an application for a job at a bank. *Baby Face* (1933, Warner Bros.).

3141 "I've just been through an experience I thought would break my back and weigh me down like lead, but look at me—I'm filled with helium." **Ray Milland** is delighted that he's broken his

engagement with unsuitable Rita Johnson. It leaves him free for a relationship with Ginger Rogers, whom he first became interested in when he thought she was only 12-years-old. *The Major and the Minor* (1942, Paramount).

3142 GEORGE DOANE: "Have you any experience?" EDDIE: "I sang last week at Coney Island." GEORGE: "How did you make out?" EDDIE: "You see this bruise on my left temple?" GEORGE: "Oh, yeah. What's the one on the other side?" EDDIE: "I dance a little, too." **George Murphy** shows modest interest in the talents of **Eddie Cantor**. *Show Business* (1944, RKO).

3143 "I never dreamed any mere physical experience could be so stimulating!. . . I don't wonder you love boating, Mr. Allnut." **Katharine Hepburn** is starting to see her river trip with old sea dog Humphrey Bogart in a whole new light. *The African Queen* (1951, GB, Horizon-Romulus).

3144 "I don't know why I should act so experienced. It was only my second kiss this year." Shy **Diane Varsi** gives immature and repressed Russ Tamblyn his first kiss. *Peyton Place* (1957, 20th Century-Fox).

3145 "Experience—that's what separates the girls from the girl scouts." Ivy League smoothie **George Hamilton** will only marry a virgin and does his best to ensure that none exist. *Where the Boys Are* (1960, MGM).

3146 "I can't think of anything I've never done." **Audrey Hepburn**, as volatile and slightly crazy Holly Golightly, has had a full life. *Breakfast at Tiffany's* (1961, Paramount).

3147 ROGER DE BRIS: "What have you done?" LORENZO ST. DUBOIS: "About six months. But I'm out on probation." Incompetent stage director **Christopher Hewett** auditions pothead **Dick Shawn** for the lead in the Broadway musical "Springtime for Hitler." *The Producers* (1967, MGM).

3148 SONJA: "Sex without love is an empty experience." BORIS: "Yes, but as empty experiences go, it's one of the best." **Diane Keaton** plays straight woman for early 19th century Russian nerd **Woody Allen**. *Love and Death* (1975, United Artists).

3149 "I was utterly primal, and it was the most satisfying experience of my life." **William Hurt** solemnly shares his experience with his wife Blair Brown, the day after he slaughtered a sheep and tore at its flesh with his mouth. *Altered States* (1980, Warner Bros.).

3150 MATTY WALKER: "I could never do anything to hurt you. I love you. You've got to believe that."

NED RACINE: "Keep talking Matty. Experience has shown that I can be convinced of anything." **Kathleen Turner** and **William Hurt** both know he's not very bright, especially where a beautiful woman is concerned. He's helped her kill her husband Richard Crenna and now suspects that she's got similar plans for him. *Body Heat* (1981, Warner Bros.).

3151 "Experience good school, but sometimes fee high." Doing his turn as Chinese detective Charlie Chan, **Peter Ustinov** dishes up an aphorism. *Charlie Chan and the Curse of the Dragon Queen* (1981, American Cinema Productions).

3152 "Do you ever have the experience that people tell you they don't know what you're saying?" Confirmed bachelor **Michael Emil** gets to know recently abandoned wife Karen Black. *Can She Bake a Cherry Pie?* (1983, World Wide Classics).

3153 "I want to have a meaningful experience with a beautiful woman." **Michael J. Fox** expresses the thought as he leaves his Kansas farm home for the Big Apple. Apparently a roll in the hay with his boss's wife is a fair substitute experience. *The Secret of My Success* (1987, Universal).

3154 "I'd like to get some information about the cannibal's habits. I had thought, alongside the cannibal exhibit, you could lecture on your experiences on the island." After his rescue from an island inhabited by two cannibals, title character Aidan Quinn is offered a proposition by **Michael Higgins.** *Crusoe* (1988, Island).

3155 "I made a decision about that. I decided to write about my own experiences. I like my own experiences, all in all." At the end of a film that explores teenage suicide, loner **Michelle Meyrink** tells her friends that she's found meaning for her life in her writing. *Permanent Record* (1988, Paramount).

3156 "I've been born in peace time. I haven't been where you've been. I haven't seen what you've seen. . . ." It's the beginning of a bit of blarney concert producer **Adrian Dunbar** uses when he wants to con some older folks. It usually works. *Hear My Song* (1991, GB, Miramax).

Experiments

see also DEMONSTRATIONS, DISCOVERIES

3157 "My life is consecrated to great experiment!" Mad scientist **Bela Lugosi** plans to prove Charles Darwin's theory of natural selection by combining the blood of his pet ape with that of various young girls the creature has been trained to murder in grisly fashion. *Murders in the Rue Morgue* (1932, Universal).

3158 "[Mengele was] the chief doctor of Auschwitz, who killed 2.5 million people, experimented with children—Jewish and non-Jewish, using twins, mostly, injecting blue dyes into their eyes to make them acceptable Aryans, amputating limbs and organs from thousands without anesthetics. . . ." Nazi-hunter **Laurence Olivier** asks a European journalist to help him gather information on Gregory Peck as Mengele, who has taken refuge somewhere in South America. *The Boys from Brazil* (1978, 20th Century-Fox).

3159 "It was a little experiment, that's all. I never meant [psychoanalysis] to become an industry." **Alec Guinness**, the ghost of Sigmund Freud, consults with modern day psychiatrist Dudley Moore. *Lovesick* (1983, Warner Bros.).

Experts

see also EDUCATION, GENIUS, INTELLIGENCE, KNOWLEDGE, LEARNING AND LESSONS, SPECIALTIES, STUDIES AND STUDENTS, TRAINING, WISDOM

3160 "I've been gone over by experts, but you're the best." **Everett Sloane** admires the beating he's received from Ted de Corsia. The latter is Sloane's first recruit to a murder-for-hire organization. *The Enforcer* (1951, United States Pictures-Warner Bros.).

3161 "You can't control life, it's too messy; you can only control art and masturbation, two areas I'm an expert at." Filmmaker **Woody Allen** quacks wise at a seminar. *Stardust Memories* (1980, United Artists).

3162 "I suppose they're still learning, that's why they keep moving about. . . Mummy keeps still and Daddy moves on top of her. That's what they do when they know how." Five-year-old **Geraldine Muir** shares her knowledge of intercourse with her brother Sebastian Rice-Edwards as they spy on their older sister Sammi Davis making love with her soldier boyfriend. *Hope and Glory* (1987, GB, Columbia).

Explanations

see also EXCUSES, JUSTIFICATIONS, REASONS, UNDERSTANDINGS AND MISUNDERSTANDINGS

3163 MR. HAMMER: "Now, here is a little peninsula, and here is a viaduct leading over to the mainland." CHICO: "Why a duck?" HAMMER: "I'm all right. How are you? I say here is a little peninsula and here is a viaduct leading over to the mainland." CHICO: "All right, why a duck?" HAMMER: "I'm not playing, ask me another. I say that's a viaduct?" CHICO: "All right, why a duck? Why a duck? Why-a no chicken?" And the routine goes on and on between **Groucho Marx** and **Chico Marx.** The former is trying to explain to the latter his plan for developing the Cocoanut district in Florida. *The Cocoanuts* (1929, Paramount).

3164 INSPECTOR GUFFERT: "I didn't expect to find Chevalier del Gardo at The Blind Rat." DEL GARDO: "I came on an errand of mercy. I stayed in the interests of justice." **Robert Adair** doesn't buy **Tod Slaughter**'s explanation as to why he is found in a hangout of cutthroats and thieves. *The Face at the Window* (1939, GB, Pennant-Ambassador).

3165 GEORGE FLAMMARION: "My dear, it's amazing how little one has to explain to a man in love." EVE PEABODY: "And when he stops being in love." FLAMMARION: "Well, that's when the alimony begins." **John Barrymore** assures **Claudette Colbert** that Francis Lederer will buy without question that she is "Baroness Czerny." *Midnight* (1939, Paramount).

3166 "You're one of the ardent believers—a good American. Oh, there are millions like you. People who play along, without asking questions. I hate to use the word stupid but it seems to be the only one that applies. The great masses, the moron millions. Well, there are a few of us unwilling to troop along, a few of us who are clever enough to see that there's much more to be done than just live small complacent lives, a few of us in America who desire a more profitable type of government. When you think about it, Mr. Kane, the competence of totalitarian nations is much higher than ours. They get things done." Almost leisurely, **Otto Kruger** explains to his captive Robert Cummings his motivation for becoming a traitor to his country. It's annoying to find how willing movie villains are to go into great detail to explain their actions to movies' heroes. It's an unsatisfactory device to bring the audience quickly up to speed, rather than find a more cinematic way to inform. In real life, villains would probably just eliminate their enemies and keep their motivations to themselves. *Saboteur* (1942, Universal).

3167 "For those who believe in God, no explanation is necessary. For those who do not, no explanation is possible." The film's introduction invites audiences to take or leave the story of Bernadette of Lourdes. *The Song of Bernadette* (1943, 20th Century-Fox).

3168 "Explain! Explain! That's all I've ever done is explain. I'm tired of explaining, sick and tired of it. I don't want to have to explain—not to you. You're my son. You're in with me. My flesh and blood. You wear my clothes, eat my food, live in my home. I don't have to explain to you. If I'm guilty, then you're guilty, too. You understand me? You're guilty, too." **Edward G. Robinson** resentfully rages at his son Burt Lancaster who questions him about a wartime crime of building shoddy equipment for airplanes. *All My Sons* (1948, Universal).

3169 "Without money, I become dull, listless, and have trouble with my complexion." With tongue in cheek, **Humphrey Bogart** explains to ditzy Jennifer Jones why he's associated with the likes of crook Robert Morley. *Beat the Devil* (1954, GB, Romulus-United Artists).

3170 JEFF JEFFRIES: "You mean to say you can explain everything that's gone on over there and is still going on?" TOM DOYLE: "No, and neither can you. That's a secret, private world you're looking into out there. People do a lot of things in private that they couldn't possibly explain in public." **James Stewart**'s suspicions that a neighbor across the courtyard, Raymond Burr, has murdered and dismembered his wife are dismissed by police detective **Wendell Corey** as a lot of speculation based on inadequate and misinterpreted evidence. *Rear Window* (1954, Paramount).

3171 "If I could explain these, I wouldn't have to make them." Sculptress **Viveca Lindfors** responds when asked what her work is supposed to mean. *The Damned* (1961, GB, Columbia).

3172 "All planes fly continuously at their fail-safe points, such that, once the 'go code' is received, they are more or less beyond their fail-safe, they do not require a second order to carry out their mission, and we cannot recall them without the three letter codes which we do not have. In fifteen minutes, the Russian radar will detect our planes and they will go absolutely ape-shit and strike back with everything they've got, and we will suffer virtual annihilation." General **George C. Scott** briefs President Peter Sellers of the scenario when deranged Air Force General Sterling Hayden sends a bomber wing to attack Soviet Russia with atomic bombs. *Dr. Strangelove: Or How I Learned to Stop Worrying and Love the Bomb* (1963, GB, Columbia).

3173 "She asked me to—they shoot horses, don't they?" **Michael Sarrazin** answers the police who ask him why he honored Jane Fonda's request that he help her kill herself. *They Shoot Horses, Don't They?* (1969, Palomar-Cinerama).

3174 "She was fifteen years old, going on thirty-five, Doc, and she told me she was eighteen, and she was very willing, you know what I mean. Matter of fact, it would have had to take sewing my pants shut. But between you and me, I don't think that's crazy at all now.... No man alive could resist that, and that's why I got into jail to begin with. And now they tell me, I'm crazy over here because I don't sit there like a damn vegetable. Don't make a bit of sense to me.

If that's what being crazy is, then I'm senseless, out of it, gone-down-the-road, wacko." **Jack Nicholson**, who has feigned insanity to get himself out of prison work for the crime of statutory rape, breezily plays a charming conman for an asylum doctor. *One Flew Over the Cuckoo's Nest* (1975, United Artists).

3175 "I don't have to explain myself to a child." It's photographer **Keith Carradine**'s revealing reply as to why he spends more time with baby prostitute Brooke Shields than her whore mother Susan Sarandon. *Pretty Baby* (1978, Paramount).

3176 "Dr. Elliott was a transsexual about to make the final step, but his male side couldn't let him do it. There was Dr. Elliott and there was Bobby. Bobby came to me to get psychiatric approval for a sex reassignment operation. I thought he was unstable and Elliott confirmed my diagnosis. The sex change operation was to resolve the conflict, but as much as Bobby tried to get it, Elliott blocked it. So Bobby got even. Elliott's penis got erect and Bobby took control, trying to kill anyone who made Elliott masculinely sexual." Shrink **David Margulies** explains what drove psychiatrist Michael Caine to dress up as a woman, put on an awful wig, and take after women with a razor. *Dressed to Kill* (1980, Filmways).

3177 "I write. . . I narrate. But just what am I narrating? An ocean voyage? The voyage of life? That is not narrated, it is embarked upon. It's banal? It has already been said? And better? Well, everything's been said. . . and done." Journalist **Freddie Jones** addresses the camera as narrator of the film—but he explains he's no omnipresent omnipotent being. He will make only half-hearted attempts to explain what's going on in the movie. *And the Ship Sails On* (1983, Italy, Triumph).

3178 "Life is such a rich and frantic form that I need the drink to help me to step delicately through it." **Michael Caine** has a literary but none too convincing excuse for his heavy drinking. *Educating Rita* (1983, GB, Rank-Acorn).

3179 "I took off your shoes, I took off your dress and put you on the bed and I kept my eyes closed all the time. . . I might have peeked, I don't remember." **Harrison Ford** tells Melanie Griffith how she ended up sleeping in her underclothes in his bed after passing out from a combination of alcohol and valium. *Working Girl* (1988, 20th Century-Fox).

3180 "My mother is a complete Anglophile; anything British makes her drool like a baby so I think she heard the name in a movie or something. She's a prisoner of Public Television now." **James Spader** tells Andie MacDowell how he came to be named Graham. *sex, lies and videotape* (1989, Miramax).

3181 OLIVER ROSE: "Is there another guy?" BARBARA ROSE: "No." OLIVER: "A woman?" BARBARA: "You'd like that, wouldn't you." **Michael Douglas** can only think of two reasons **Kathleen Turner** would want a divorce after twenty years of marriage. *The War of the Roses* (1989, 20th Century-Fox).

3182 "Very deep is exactly where he wants to put it." World-wise muse **Bernadette Peters** tells naïve Mia Farrow just what her writing professor James Toback is getting at when he tells her she's deep. *Alice* (1990, Orion).

3183 "Then it was easier to fuck somebody than to explain why you didn't feel like it." **Cybill Shepherd** looks back on the sexual mores of her youth with mixed feelings. *Married to It* (1991, Orion).

Explosions

see also BATTLES AND BATTLEFIELDS, BOMBS, NOISES, WARS

3184 "Normally, to open a case like that, you move the catches to the side. If you do, the cartridge will explode in your face. Now to stop the cartridge exploding, turn the catches horizontally like that and open normally." **Desmond Llewelyn**, head of "Q" Section, lectures Sean Connery, as James Bond, on disarming a booby-trapped attaché case. *From Russia with Love* (1963, United Artists).

3185 "Animals just don't explode into flames for no reason." Dimwitted father **Clu Gulager** has no clue of the reason. *A Nightmare on Elm Street 2: Freddy's Revenge* (1985, New Line).

3186 "Well, I blew that course." **Bradley Gregg** speaks literally as he sets off an explosion in his chemistry lab. *Class of 1999* (1989, Vestron).

3187 "It's guaranteed never to wake up anyone who uses it." **Desmond Llewelyn**, as special weapons wizard "Q," shows an exploding alarm clock to Timothy Dalton as James Bond. *License to Kill* (1989, GB, MGM-United Artists).

Extinction *see* DEATH AND DYING, DESTRUCTION, EXISTENCE

Extravagances

see also COSTS, EXCESSES, LIMITS AND LIMITATIONS, WASTE AND WASTEFULNESS

3188 "Louise Bryant was hated for her extravagance in clothes. . . women whose lives have been in danger over a long period are always the most extravagant." Witness **Rebecca West** reminisces about the character portrayed by Diane Keaton. *Reds* (1981, Paramount).

3189 "Do I think you're extravagant? Of course not. Everybody goes to Switzerland to have their watches fixed." **Rodney Dangerfield** lays a bit of sarcasm on his selfish, mercenary, uncaring and unfaithful second wife Adrienne Barbeau. *Back to School* (1986, Orion).

Eyes

see also APPEARANCES, BEAUTY, BODIES, CHILDREN AND CHILDHOOD, COLORS, FACES, HEADS AND HEADACHES, HUMAN NATURE, HUMANITY, MEN, SIGHT AND SIGHTS, WOMEN

3190 "Your eyes shine like the pants of a blue serge suit." As there aren't many blue serge suits worn these days, **Groucho Marx**'s compliment to Margaret Dumont may no longer be properly appreciated. *The Cocoanuts* (1929, Paramount).

3191 "Your left eye says yes, and your right eye says no. Fifi, you're cockeyed!" **Maurice Chevalier** is confused by flirty but stand-offish Jeanette MacDonald. *The Merry Widow* (1934, MGM).

3192 BILL CHANDLER: "Your eyes. . . remind me of. . . ." CONNIE ALLENBURY: "Yes, yes, I know. Sparkling diamonds. . . pink sapphires." CHANDLER: "No. . . no. They remind me of—angry marbles." When **William Powell** is interrupted by **Myrna Loy**, he modifies his compliment. *Libeled Lady* (1936, MGM).

3193 "I like to look in those big lamps of yours. . . I'm stuck on you, kid. You know it?" **Clark Gable** is quite taken with Jeanette MacDonald's eyes and the rest of her as well. *San Francisco* (1936, MGM).

3194 "She's got those eyes that run up and down men like a searchlight." Manicurist **Dennie Moore** disapprovingly characterizes shopgirl Joan Crawford. *The Women* (1939, MGM).

3195 "Shall I spit in Crystal's eye for you. . . ? You're passing up a swell chance, honey. Where I spit, no grass grows ever." Show girl **Paulette Goddard** offers to do to Joan Crawford what Norma Shearer is too much of a lady to do. *The Women* (1939, MGM).

3196 "Here, wipe the spit out of your eye." Photographer **Ruth Hussey** offers magazine writer James Stewart a handkerchief after his first encounter with Katharine Hepburn. *The Philadelphia Story* (1940, MGM).

3197 "What good are my eyes if I cannot see her?" **John Justin** cries out as he regains his sight, realizing that this means his beloved June Duprez is in the arms of the evil Conrad Veidt. *The Thief of Bagdad* (1940, GB, London Films).

3198 "As the months went past, he came to see the light once more, as well as to feel its warmth. To see first the glory of the sun, and then mild splendor of the moon, and at last the evening star. And then one day when our first-born was put into his arms, he could see that the boy had inherited his own eyes as they once were, large, brilliant and black." Title character **Joan Fontaine** informs the audience that her husband Orson Welles, as Edward Rochester, had regained his sight. *Jane Eyre* (1943, 20th Century-Fox).

3199 "That's all I know on account of I don't see so well with my eyeballs scorched." With bandaged eyes, private eye **Dick Powell** completes telling his flashback tale of murder, blackmail and robbery, and the beatings, druggings and other indignities visited upon his body while he was investigating the case. *Murder, My Sweet* (1945, RKO).

3200 "Hug me with your eyes." **Ivan Kirov** wants Viola Essen to demonstrate her love for him without touching. *Spectre of the Rose* (1946, Republic).

3201 "Maybe this is the face that will haunt you. Maybe these are the eyes that'll drive you crazy." Assistant D.A. **Humphrey Bogart** shows Murder, Inc. founder Everett Sloane the color photograph of slain Susan Cabot. Sloane realizes that the only living witness against him has not been eliminated as he believed—the color of the eyes is wrong. *The Enforcer* (1951, United States Pictures-Warner Bros.).

3202 "All right, Miss Vetto, come out—you have a date in court tomorrow morning. I want to see that smile fade on Mendoza's face when he looks into those big blue eyes again." Assistant D.A. **Humphrey Bogart** gives the all-clear to Patricia Joiner, the only witness Everett Sloane, the head of Murder, Inc., was unable to have killed. *The Enforcer* (1951, United States Pictures-Warner Bros.).

3203 "Men aren't attentive to girls who wear glasses." Almost as blind as a bat without her glasses, **Marilyn Monroe** risks seeing very little in order to attract attentive men—preferably millionaires. *How to Marry a Millionaire* (1953, 20th Century-Fox).

3204 "One more crack, Queenie—just one—and I will not only spit in your eye, but I will punch it black and blue." **Elizabeth Taylor** threatens her sister-in-law Madeleine Sherwood, who constantly badmouths Taylor, and her marriage to Paul Newman, to his father Burl Ives. *Cat on a Hot Tin Roof* (1958, MGM).

3205 "They get those weak eyes from reading, you know—those long tiny little columns in the *Wall Street Journal.*" **Marilyn Monroe** has a theory about men who wear glasses. *Some Like It Hot* (1959, United Artists).

3206 "Life with Mary was like being in a phone booth with an open umbrella. No matter which way you turned, you got it in the eye." **Barry Nelson** and his wife Debbie Reynolds are getting a divorce. Their recollections of their marriage are sweet, funny and sad. *Mary, Mary* (1963, Warner Bros.).

3207 "You ought to see 'em from my side." Drunken gunfighter **Lee Marvin** responds when told his eyes are bloodshot. *Cat Ballou* (1965, Columbia).

3208 "They're made out of mink hairs, did you know that?" For twenty years I've been wearing animal hairs on my face." **Ellen Burstyn** refers to her false eyelashes. *The King of Marvin Gardens* (1972, Columbia).

3209 "Bags, bags, go away, come back on Doris Day." Aging movie actress **Elizabeth Taylor** chants as she examines the dark circles under her eyes in a mirror. *The Mirror Crack'd* (1981, GB, EMI).

3210 "Some guys shot him in the eyes." Mobster's moll **Mia Farrow** nonchalantly describes the demise of her first husband to talent agent Woody Allen. *Broadway Danny Rose* (1984, Orion).

3211 "I believe they're windows, but I'm not sure it's the soul I see." As he kisses his mistress Anjelica Huston, married **Martin Landau** responds to her question if he agrees that the eyes are windows of the soul. Later, after he has had her killed and has retrieved his mementoes from her apartment, he tells his brother Jerry Orbach, "There was nothing behind her eyes. All you saw is a black void." *Crimes and Misdemeanors* (1989, Orion).

3212 "How do you know how I can see, lessin' you see through my eyes." Elderly, dignified chauffeur **Morgan Freeman** replies when his ancient employer Jessica Tandy allows as how he can't see well enough to drive an automobile anymore. *Driving Miss Daisy* (1989, Warner Bros.).

3213 "I'm talking to you. You, wake up. Are you deaf? I said eyes to me. There's going to be trouble if you don't turn your head in this direction. I said eyes to me." At the end of the film in which a group of teenagers terrorize a high school biology teacher, substitute teacher **Janet Atwood** demands the attention of her class. *Hell High* (1989, MGM).

3214 "When it came to me and your dad, you had stars in your eyes." **Gwen Verdon**, the ghost of matron Mia Farrow's mother, appears to her. *Alice* (1990, Orion).

Faces

see also BEAUTY, BODIES, EYES, MOUTHS, SENSATIONS

3215 JANIE BARLOW: "I saw your face in the wings; made me feel I was doing something wrong." PATCH GALLAGHER: "I got that kind of face." Burlesque house dancer **Joan Crawford** tries to make it big in a Broadway musical directed by **Clark Gable.** She doesn't believe he appreciates her or her talent. She's right. Her lover Franchot Tone, who has an investment in the show, insists that Crawford get her chance. *Dancing Lady* (1933, MGM).

3216 "Have we been trailing Firefly? Why, my partner—he's got a nose just like a bloodhound. . . the rest of his face doesn't look so good either." **Chico Marx** and partner Harpo Marx are keeping tabs on Groucho Marx for Louis Calhern. *Duck Soup* (1933, Paramount).

3217 MYRA GALE: "I suppose you've been rubbing noses with all the female stars in the movie business." DAN QUIGLEY: "Call it noses if you like." Jealous ex-girlfriend **Mae Clarke** isn't pleased that former con-man **James Cagney** has become a movie star. *Lady Killer* (1933, Warner Bros.).

3218 "A Mongolian prince taught me this. . . . You'll never lie to a friend again—and you'll never kiss another man's wife." **Lionel Atwill** gleefully sews his victim's lips together and then leaves him to be devoured by "the cats" in an Indo-China jungle. *Murders in the Zoo* (1933, Paramount).

3219 "I kicked a guy in the face once because he was a cop." Tough con **Humphrey Bogart** tries to impress warden Pat O'Brien. *San Quentin* (1937, Warner Bros.).

3220 "Oh, please, let me see her face when he kisses her." As she watches her daughter's wedding through a window, a policeman tells **Barbara Stanwyck** to move along. Stanwyck has given up her daughter to the girl's wealthy father who can give her all the things her poor and uncouth mother can't. *Stella Dallas* (1937, United Artists).

3221 "I don't feel dressed without my lipstick." Sixteen-year-old **Lana Turner** briefly flirts with her teacher, shortly before she's brutally murdered. *They Won't Forget* (1937, Warner Bros.).

3222 "I've grown accustomed to your face!" **Leslie Howard** is surprised by his feelings for Wendy Hiller. **Rex Harrison** will break into song about Audrey Hepburn with his revelation. *Pygmalion* (1938, GB, MGM); *My Fair Lady* (1964, Warner Bros.).

3223 "I'll bet you have a lovely face under all that paint. Why don't you wipe it off some day and have a good look? And figure how you can live up to it." Only Deputy **James Stewart** complains about the amount of cosmetics dance-hall girl with a heart of gold Marlene Dietrich uses to look attractive. *Destry Rides Again* (1939, Universal).

3224 "Father, speak to me!. . . He knew who killed him! I can see it in his face!" **Marjorie Taylor** screams when she finds the body of her father Aubrey Mallalieu with a knife sticking from his back. *The Face at the Window* (1939, GB, Pennant-Ambassador).

3225 "Oh, I think it's a dream on you. You know, it—it does something for your face. It—it gives you a chin." **Claudette Colbert** is catty as she "admires" Mary Astor's new hat. *Midnight* (1939, Paramount).

3226 CHARLIE McCARTHY: "Are you eating a tomato or is that your nose?" LARSON E. WHIPSNADE: "Quiet, or I'll throw a woodpecker at you." Ventriloquist **Edgar Bergen** and **W.C. Fields** exchange some lovely insults. *You Can't Cheat an Honest Man* (1939, Universal).

3227 "Look at that face—they'll believe him!" Reporter **Barbara Stanwyck** tells her editor James Gleason that Gary Cooper will be perfect posing as her imaginary John Doe. *Meet John Doe* (1941, Warner Bros.).

3228 "Good night, dear, your nose is bleeding." **Carole Lombard** coos sweetly to her husband Robert Montgomery whom she has just slugged. *Mr. and Mrs. Smith* (1941, RKO).

3229 CHARLES PIKE: "You have a definite nose." JEAN HARRINGTON: "Do you like the rest of me?" Wealthy simpleton **Henry Fonda** is out of his depth with beautiful con-woman **Barbara Stanwyck**. *The Lady Eve* (1941, Paramount).

3230 "There are some things that are private, Mr. Dingle, and—and, when people go poking their nose in, it's just too much, that's all! And you have a very large nose, Mr. Dingle." **Jean Arthur** is correct about her tenant Charles Coburn. He's a nosy busybody trying to rearrange her life. *The More the Merrier* (1943, Columbia).

3231 "I've never seen a stronger face or a stranger one." At the beginning of the film, journalist **John Loder** is convinced that he recognizes Frenchman Humphrey Bogart, a British Bomber Command gunner, preparing to take off for a run over Berlin. And therein hangs a tale. *Passage to Marseille* (1943, Warner Bros.).

3232 "She's got a face like a Sunday School picnic." **Dick Powell** makes a sweet description of Anne Shirley's sweet face. *Murder, My Sweet* (1945, RKO).

3233 "When it bleeds—the Red Sea!" Title character **Jose Ferrer** suggests a more imaginative insult of his extremely long nose to a man whom he will kill in a duel. *Cyrano de Bergerac* (1950, United Artists).

3234 "A great nose indicates a great man." **Jose Ferrer** shows Don Beddoe, as The Meddler, that he can't win, when Beddoe claims Ferrer's nose is small. *Cyrano de Bergerac* (1950, United Artists).

3235 DIXON STEELE: "How could anyone like a face like this?" LAUREL GRAY: "I said I liked it. I didn't say I wanted to kiss it." **Humphrey Bogart** looks at himself in a mirror as Gloria Grahame looks on. *In a Lonely Place* (1950, Columbia).

3236 "We didn't need dialogue in those days. We had faces then!" Silent screen star **Gloria Swanson** proudly states the superiority of silent screen actresses to unemployed screenwriter William Holden. *Sunset Boulevard* (1950, Paramount).

3237 "It's not a pretty face, I grant you, but underneath its flabby exterior is an enormous lack of character." At the beginning of the film, in voice-over, pianist **Oscar Levant** introduces himself to the audience. *An American in Paris* (1951, MGM).

3238 "Mom's got a good nose for people. You get one, standing—year in, year out—behind a hamburger stand." Wage slave **John Lund** introduces his mother, Thelma Ritter, a woman of great good sense. *The Mating Season* (1951, Paramount).

3239 "You see her face? A real honest face. Only disgusting thing about her." Fast-talking sports promoter **Spencer Tracy** holds forth on top all-around athlete Katharine Hepburn. *Pat and Mike* (1952, MGM).

3240 "If crime showed on a man's face there wouldn't be any mirrors." **Aldo Ray** replies sagely when Gloria Talbott says he doesn't look like a criminal. *We're No Angels* (1955, Paramount).

3241 "It is the face behind the mask I seek. The malignant thing that mauls and mutilates our race." Moby Dick represents more than just a whale to **Gregory Peck** as Captain Ahab. *Moby Dick* (1956, Warner Bros.).

3242 "No one ever looks at the face of a nun." Safely back in England, dressed in her traditional habit, nun **Joan Collins** isn't recognized by Richard Burton, who fell in love with her when they were shipwrecked. *Sea Wife* (1957, GB, 20th Century-Fox).

3243 "Yes, I can see the makeup now all right. The lines that weren't there before. The beginning. And there'll be more and more and then, one day, this face will begin to decay and then there'll be nothing left to make a man grovel." **Burt Lancaster** tells his ex-wife Rita Hayworth that her aging is showing in her face. *Separate Tables* (1958, United Artists).

3244 "You're a real one-eyed Jack in this town, Dad, but I seen the other side of your face." **Marlon Brando** isn't fooled by the respectable pose of Sheriff Karl Malden. *One-Eyed Jacks* (1961, Paramount).

3245 "Your lips were made for kissin'. They are like the inner petals of a rose." Roman roué **Rossano Brazzi** pays high compliments to pretty American librarian Suzanne Pleshette. *Rome Adventure* (1962, Warner Bros.).

3246 "Read my lips." Now you know that George Bush got the line from **Clint Eastwood.** *Magnum Force* (1973, Warner Bros.).

3247 "After a rough fight, ya' nothin' but a large wound. Sometimes I feel like callin' a taxi to drive me from my bed to the bathroom. . . . Ya' eyes hurt, ya' ears hurt, ya' hair even hurts. . . . But the thing I'm proud of is I been in over sixty fights an' never had a busted nose—Bent an' twisted an' bitten but never broke—that's rare." While describing the pain he experiences after a fight to Talia Shire, **Sylvester Stallone** boasts how his snoot has stayed in one piece. *Rocky* (1976, United Artists).

3248 "You see more in a man's face than I should think of looking for." Speaking with extreme gravity, **Wesley Addy** reacts to Tim Woodward's desire to paint his portrait. *The Europeans* (1979, GB, Leavitt-Pickman).

3249 "There are only two things I dislike about you. Your face." Aging movie star **Elizabeth Taylor** lets aging movie star Kim Novak have it in the kisser. *The Mirror Crack'd* (1980, GB, EMI).

3250 "Chin up, darling—both of them." Aging movie star **Kim Novak** gets her licks in by insulting aging movie star Elizabeth Taylor on the set of the movie within a movie. *The Mirror Crack'd* (1980, GB, EMI).

3251 "You should never wear lipstick, your lips are full and generous without it. You are very beautiful, but you should never wear makeup." Dressed in all black, violinist **Rudolf Nureyev** lectures Nastassja Kinski. *Exposed* (1981, MGM-United Artists).

3252 "Her lips were warm and luscious—and so were mine." Forties private eye **Steve Martin** refers to Rachel Ward and himself. *Dead Men Don't Wear Plaid* (1982, Universal).

3253 "He was always preparing faces for the faces he met." Record producer **Paul Winfield** will never get over his love for good-looking, two-bit Hollywood hustler and amateur drug dealer, title character Mark Keyloun. *Mike's Murder* (1984, Warner Bros.).

3254 "It must be wonderful to wake up in the morning and smell the coffee—in Brazil." Fireman **Steve Martin** suggests a wisecrack witless Rick Rossovich might use to insult Martin's long nose. *Roxanne* (1987, Columbia).

3255 "Her face, the look in her eyes for all to see—there was something indecent in the explicitness of her expression." **Joan Plowright** recalls how Billie Whitelaw looked after she had been persuaded not to marry again. *The Dressmaker* (1989, GB, Euro-American Films).

3256 "Show me your face!" Twenty years after returning from Vietnam, **Bruce Willis** is an aimless, troubled man. During a thunder storm he climbs a tree and shouts to the sky—to God, perhaps, or maybe to the enemy he fought in 'Nam. *In Country* (1989, Warner Bros.).

3257 "Longest nose hairs in the western world." Ornery **Shirley MacLaine** remembers an old beau, Bill McCutcheon, who is reported to be back in town. *Steel Magnolias* (1989, Tri-Star).

3258 "Here's some money, go downtown and have a rat gnaw that growth off your face." It's an unfunny and unnecessary line delivered by **John Candy** to a grade school teacher as he flips her a quarter. *Uncle Buck* (1989, Universal).

3259 "Put on some goddamn lipstick." **Jacqueline Bisset** shouts to Carré Otis, who looks her best when wearing very little and saying nothing. *Wild Orchid* (1990, Triumph).

3260 "He looked like he walked 81 years on that face." **Danny Glover** speaks affectionately about his recently deceased, ugly 81-year-old father to his new friend Kevin Kline. *Grand Canyon* (1991, 20th Century-Fox).

3261 "When your husband makes love to you it's my face he sees." Maniacal nanny **Rebecca De Mornay** plots to ruin the life and marriage of Annabella Sciorra. *The Hand That Rocks the Cradle* (1992, Hollywood Pictures).

Facts *see* INFORMATION AND INFORMERS, PROBABILITY AND STATISTICS, THEORIES, TRUTH

Failures

see also DEFEATS, LOSSES AND LOSING, SUCCESSES, VICTORIES, WINNERS AND LOSERS

3262 "He could dish it out but he couldn't take it." Mobster **Edward G. Robinson** makes his favorite scornful comment about rivals. Ultimately, it is used against him in a newspaper article when he falls from power and is destitutely on the lam. *Little Caesar* (1931, Warner Bros.).

3263 "You'll always be behind the eight ball, and I'll always be pulling you out." Nightclub owner **Judith Anderson** must constantly rescue her bailbondsman boyfriend George Bancroft. *Blood Money* (1933, Fox-United Artists).

3264 "I knew you'd come to me. I wanted to come back to you, my darling. I failed. I meddled in things that man should leave alone." Dying invisible **Claude Rains** speaks softly to Gloria Stuart. When he's dead, he becomes visible for the first time in the movie. *The Invisible Man* (1933, Universal).

3265 MR. KIRBY: "I'm a failure as a father." GRANDPA VANDERHOF: "Mr. Kirby, you're beginning to act quite human." **Edward Arnold** is contrite and unhappy. **Lionel Barrymore** is pleased by the improvement in Arnold's attitude. *You Can't Take It with You* (1938, Columbia).

3266 "It seems almost within your grasp, but you will not attain it. Lesser men will be made president and you will be passed over." **Walter Huston**, as the devil Mr. Scratch, gleefully informs Edward Arnold, as Daniel Webster, that his presidential ambitions will not be realized. *All That Money Can Buy* aka: *The Devil and Daniel Webster* (1941, RKO).

3267 "You've been so fascinated with the glitter, you didn't bother with the gold." **Lewis Stone** makes the observation when his son Mickey Rooney fails his English course and is unable to graduate because he was too busy planning the graduation ceremony to study. *Andy Hardy's Private Secretary* (1941, MGM).

3268 "It's not our ideas that bind us together, it's failure. . . . The streets of Paris have taught you to

strike quickly and draw blood. . . I am a painter of the streets and of the gutter." **Jose Ferrer** talks over the head of his unfaithful lover Colette Marchand. *Moulin Rouge* (1952, GB, Romulus-United Artists).

3269 "You know, my wife was so twisted she once said to me, 'I hope your next play's a flop—so the whole world can see how much I love you, even though you're a failure.'" Stage director **William Holden** commiserates with actor Bing Crosby's problems with his wife Grace Kelly, by telling a tale on his own ex-spouse. *The Country Girl* (1954, Paramount).

3270 "I am disappointed in you. Not only did you do wrong, you did wrong in the wrong way. You are clearly incapable of earning a dishonest living. Why not experiment with an honest one?" Cleric detective **Alec Guinness** expresses disappointment with a captured crook. *Father Brown* (1954, GB, 20th Century-Fox).

3271 "The usual way: insufficient poison." **Isabel Jeans** tells her sister Hermione Gingold about the unsuccessful suicide attempt of Eva Gabor after she is dumped by Louis Jourdan. *Gigi* (1958, MGM).

3272 "Failure is a highly contagious disease." Aspiring actor **Paul Newman** makes a diagnosis for Shirley Knight. *Sweet Bird of Youth* (1962, MGM).

3273 "My wonderful, wonderful failure." Many-time widowed **Shirley MacLaine**, who has turned her fortune over to the IRS, has finally gotten what she's been looking for in a husband, a man who's a complete failure at making money. The man without the curse of money is Dean Martin. We suppose they live happily ever after in poverty. *What a Way to Go* (1964, 20th Century-Fox).

3274 "What we've got here is a failure to communicate." Chain gang boss **Strother Martin** stands over a broken Paul Newman, who has been given the "treatment" by the guards. *Cool Hand Luke* (1967, Warner Bros.).

3275 "I'm being sunk by a society that demands success when all I can offer is failure." Unsuccessful Broadway producer **Zero Mostel** laments his fate to accountant Gene Wilder. *The Producers* (1968, Embassy).

3276 "Virgil is an immediate failure at crime." With a touch of admiration in his voice, narrator **Jackson Beck** declares **Woody Allen**'s lack of talent for his chosen career as a crook. *Take the Money and Run* (1969, Cinerama).

3277 "I can't leave. I'm sorry. I can't leave. . . I can't seem to let go of this lamp right now. You fellas go ahead. I'll be all right soon. . . I feel like I just auditioned for the part of a human being, and I didn't get the job." **Barbara Harris** has a sinking feeling after failing an audition for a job as a singer. *Who Is Harry Kellerman and Why Is He Saying Those Terrible Things About Me?* (1971, Cinema Center).

3278 "Have I been such a failure as a mother that I've raised a son with the morals of a snake?" **Jacqueline Brookes** shouldn't blame herself for what her son James Caan has become—a compulsive gambler, with a will to lose. *The Gambler* (1974, Paramount).

3279 "I just don't bring out the man in men." **Dee Wallace** launches into an endearing account of her romantic misfortunes when Dudley Moore is unable to be aroused by her. She shouldn't take it personally, he's fantasizing about Bo Derek and during the evening he's consumed enough liquor to rival his character in *Arthur*. *'10'* (1979, Warner Bros.).

3280 "You can't even fail locally." **Shirley MacLaine** screams at her son-in-law Jeff Daniels when he takes a teaching position in a different state. *Terms of Endearment* (1983, Paramount).

3281 "Until you do right by me, everything you ever dream about will fail." **Whoopi Goldberg** predicts her brutish husband Danny Glover's fate. *The Color Purple* (1985, Warner Bros.).

3282 "How come you were never as good on your feet as you were between the sheets?" **Sally Field** questions her no-account ex-husband Brian Kerwin, who shows up to rain on her parade with James Garner. His answer, delivered at another time in the movie is, "I haven't had enough good times." *Murphy's Romance* (1985, Columbia).

3283 "You're flunking English, that's your mother tongue." **Joshua Cadman** tells his roommate John Cusack to forget Daphne Zuniga because she likes the intellectual types, which Cusack is not. *The Sure Thing* (1985, Embassy).

3284 "We are about to fail most egregiously." Valley dude **Alex Winter** reminds his friend Keanu Reeves that they are failing history. Both teens are horribly stupid, as is the movie and its sequel—but since there is a large audience of vacuous kids, they made money. *Bill and Ted's Excellent Adventure* (1989, Orion).

Faintings

see also COURAGE, HOPE, STRENGTHS, WEAKNESS

3285 "Don't be silly, I'm not going to faint. I'm not the type." **Joan Crawford** assures somewhat dullish companion Clark Gable that he has nothing to fear about her fainting. *Forsaking All Others* (1934, MGM).

3286 "Well, if I'm going to start fainting in my old age, I may as well have a doctor in the family. Think of all the money I could save on medical bills." **Alice Brady** begins to accept the idea of her daughter Gloria Stuart marrying would-be doctor, desk clerk Dick Powell. *Gold Diggers of 1935* (1935, Warner Bros.).

3287 "Just pour yourself into these, my dear, and fall into a faint!" Hat shop proprietor **Franklin Pangborn** exclaims as he shows up at Jean Arthur's hotel room carrying ladies' jewelry and hats. *Easy Living* (1937, Paramount).

3288 "Don't forget, if you feel faint, fall backwards, not across the patient." Chief Surgeon **James Robertson Justice** shares a trick of the trade with a group of medical students in an operating theater. *Doctor in the House* (1954, GB, Rank).

3289 "I do not think that will be necessary. I never faint because I'm not sure that I will fall gracefully and I never use smelling salts because they puff up the eyes. I'm Christine Vole." **Marlene Dietrich** arrives on the scene as barrister Charles Laughton suggests his colleague John Williams be prepared for fainting and screaming when she learns of her husband Tyrone Power's arrest for murder. *Witness for the Prosecution* (1957, United Artists).

3290 "Michael James, meet Tempest O'Brien. She adores me. . .[Last night] we played strip chess; she had me down to my shorts and I fainted from tension." **Woody Allen** introduces Peter O'Toole to his chess mate, stripper Nicole Karen. *What's New, Pussycat?* (1965, United Artists).

Fairies

see also FANTASIES, FICTION, IMAGINATION, STORIES

3291 PATSY: "Who's dere?" MANDIE TRIPLETT: "The fairy princess, ya mug!" Doorman **Dink Templeton** is answered by an impatient **Mae West** when he squints at her through a peephole of a speakeasy. *Night After Night* (1932, Paramount).

3292 "That fairy tale you invented to send Ilsa away with him, I know a little about women, my friend.

She went but she knew you were lying." **Claude Rains** tells Humphrey Bogart that he and Ingrid Bergman both saw through the story Bogie told her to get her to leave on the Lisbon plane with her husband Paul Henreid. *Casablanca* (1942, Warner Bros.).

3293 CAPTAIN PAUL WAGGETT: "Now, how did that get here?" FARQUHARSON: "It's the fairies. They're very active in these parts." Blimpish Home Guard Commander **Basil Radford** and officer **Henry Mollison** crash into a roadblock set up by the inhabitants of an Outer Hebrides island to prevent the authorities from finding a hidden cache of whiskey salvaged from a stranded cargo ship. *Whisky Galore* aka: *Tight Little Island* (1949, GB, Rank-Ealing).

3294 "I want the fairy tale." Hooker **Julia Roberts** rejects Richard Gere's offer to make her a kept woman. She wants love and marriage. *Pretty Woman* (1990, Touchstone-Buena Vista).

Fairness and Unfairness

see also HONESTY AND DISHONESTY, JUSTICE, PREJUDICES

3295 "For years women have been ridiculed, pampered, and chucked under the chin. I ask you to be fair to the fair sex." Attorney **Katharine Hepburn** makes a plea for fairness for defendant Judy Holliday from the jury. *Adam's Rib* (1949, MGM).

3296 HAN SUYIN: "I am so happy it frightens me. I have a feeling that heaven is unfair and is preparing for you and for me a great sadness because we have been given so much." MARK ELLIOT: "Darling, whatever happens, always remember: nothing is fair, nor unfair, under heaven." Eurasian physician **Jennifer Jones** has a premonition that something will ruin her happiness with **William Holden**. *Love Is a Many-Splendored Thing* (1955, 20th Century-Fox).

3297 "If I was bleeding out of my eyes, you'd make me go to school." **Jennifer Grey** thinks it's terribly unfair the way her folks are more considerate of her brother Matthew Broderick—for instance, allowing him to miss school each time he claims to be sick. *Ferris Bueller's Day Off* (1986, Paramount).

3298 "What kind of world do we live in where a man dressed up as a bat. . . gets all the press." Jealous **Jack Nicholson**, as the Joker, complains of the unfairness of the newspaper coverage of his battle with Michael Keaton as Batman. *Batman* (1989, Warner Bros.).

Faith and Faithfulness

see also BELIEFS, CREEDS AND CREDOS, RELIGIONS, TRUST

3299 "Anyone who has faith in me is a sucker." Cabaret singer **Marlene Dietrich** gives fair warning. *Morocco* (1930, Paramount).

3300 "You have shown faith and you will see again." As they stand in a lion cage, confidence trickster and evangelist **Barbara Stanwyck** blesses David Manners, a blind volunteer from her audience. *The Miracle Woman* (1931, Columbia).

3301 JERRY WARRINER: "I haven't any faith anymore." LUCY WARRINER: "I know just how you feel." Husband and wife **Cary Grant** and **Irene Dunne** have caught each other in lies—and probably rightfully suspect each other of infidelity. *The Awful Truth* (1937, Columbia).

3302 "I've got all the faith in the world in Johnny. Whatever he does is all right with me. If he wants to sit on his tail, he can sit on his tail. If he wants to come back and sell peanuts, Lord, how I'll believe in those peanuts." **Katharine Hepburn** gives her version of the "whither thou goest, I will go" Bible quote. She's willing to follow unambitious Cary Grant anywhere while he tries to find himself. *Holiday* (1938, Columbia).

3303 "How sad. How cruel life must have been for them. I've learned to give complete and unquestioning faith to people I love." Lovely, wealthy old **Minnie Dupree** is sympathetic and forgiving when old friend Henry Stephenson exposes Roland Young's family of frauds and fortune hunters who have taken up residence with her. *The Young in Heart* (1938, Selznick-United Artists).

3304 "You have no idea how faithful and obedient I can be." **Glenn Ford** pledges his allegiance to George Macready. *Gilda* (1946, Columbia).

3305 "Faith is believing in things when common sense tells you not to. Don't you see—it's not just Kris that's on trial, it's everything he stands for—kindness and joy and love and all the other intangibles." Idealistic lawyer **John Payne** doesn't have much luck convincing super realistic Maureen O'Hara that in defending Edmund Gwenn in a sanity hearing, when he claims to be the one and only Santa Claus, Payne is on the side of the angels. O'Hara only sees that Payne has lost his job with a law firm and is ridiculed for his fool's errand. *Miracle on 34th Street* (1947, 20th Century-Fox).

3306 "You don't even know what faith is. And I'm gonna tell you. It's believing you see white when your eyes tell you black. It's knowin' with your heart." Conman **Burt Lancaster** makes an interpretation of faith for Katharine Hepburn that Søren Kierkegaard might approve of. *The Rainmaker* (1956, Paramount).

3307 "You have no faith in anything but money." **Joseph Schildkraut** lectures his Jewish gangster son David Janssen on his lack of values. *King of the Roaring Twenties: The Story of Arnold Rothstein* (1961, Warner Bros.-Allied Artists).

3308 "I'm not counting on God; I put my faith in nuclear energy." **Kirk Douglas** is the designer of a thermonuclear power plant. *The Chosen* (1978, 20th Century-Fox).

3309 "Not everyone gets corrupted. You have to have a little faith in people." Seventeen-year-old **Mariel Hemingway** calms Woody Allen's fear that her purity will be somehow contaminated while she is away from him for several months in London. *Manhattan* (1979, United Artists).

3310 "In my religion we say 'Act as if you had faith, and faith will be given to you.' If we would have faith in justice, we must only believe in ourselves. And act with justice. And I believe there is a justice in our hearts." **Paul Newman** addresses the jury in a medical malpractice suit against the Archdiocese of Boston. *The Verdict* (1982, 20th Century-Fox).

3311 "Don't you remember their lives? They had the faith and they were prepared to suffer the passion of their faith." **John Rubinstein**, foster father to Timothy Hutton and Amanda Plummer, insists that they remember their parents who were executed in the 1950s for conspiracy to pass atomic secrets to the Russians. Yes, the Rosenbergs. *Daniel* (1983, Paramount).

Fakes

see also DECEPTIONS, REALITIES

3312 "Oh, we're both fakers. Isn't that the essence of acting?" Aspiring actress **Katharine Hepburn** coyly admits she's not totally sincere to producer Adolphe Menjou. *Stage Door* (1937, RKO).

3313 "The Cairo bazaar does a thriving business for tourists. The desert is paved with good intentions of many enthusiastic but mistaken archeologists." Fez-topped Egyptologist **George Zucco** rudely dismisses as a fake a vase that archeologist Dick Foran claims to have come from the tomb of Ananka. *The Mummy's Hand* (1940, Universal).

3314 "It's lead! It's lead! It's a fake!" **Sydney Greenstreet** discovers that his murderous quest for the falcon has ended in failure. His effeminate partner Peter Lorre, almost in tears, is beside himself with rage for Greenstreet, shouting, "You imbecile. You bloated idiot. You stupid fathead." *The Maltese Falcon* (1941, Warner Bros.).

3315 "You're a fake, John Doe, and I can prove it! You're the hero that's supposed to jump off tall buildings and things, you remember? What do you suppose your precious John Does will say when they find out that you never had any intention of doing it—that you were being paid to say so?" Fascist newspaper publisher **Edward Arnold** taunts a confused Gary Cooper. *Meet John Doe* (1941, Warner Bros.).

3316 "You're a fraud. You couldn't make spinach grow in the Garden of Eden." When his wife Rosalind Russell resists all his efforts to lure her into bed and their sexless "trial marriage," **Melvyn Douglas** resorts to placing a statue of a Mexican god of plenty and fertility in their living room—but it doesn't help. *This Thing Called Love* (1941, Columbia).

3317 "You ever see one of those brick houses? When you get close to it, the brick's not real brick at all, but just painted on. The big executive pose of hers is the same thing. Every time I see her I can't resist chipping little bits of it off to see what's underneath." **Ray Milland** explains why he never lets an opportunity pass to undermine and humiliate his boss, fashion editor Ginger Rogers. He just can't believe that any real woman would want to be boss—besides, he wants her job. *Lady in the Dark* (1944, Paramount).

3318 CATHERINE VAN OST: "Look, you played. I was honestly moved—then you made me feel embarrassed about responding to you. It wasn't necessary." ROBERT EROICA DUPEA: "Yeah, it was. Look what happened. I faked a little Chopin—you faked a big response." **Susan Anspach** is pounced on by **Jack Nicholson** after he plays the piano for her and she responds positively. *Five Easy Pieces* (1970, Columbia).

3319 "I'll tell you something, Robert—underneath that pose, there's just more pose." **Lenny Baker** tells shallow Christopher Walken that he's a fake. *Next Stop, Greenwich Village* (1976, 20th Century-Fox).

3320 "Even the bloody coffin is a fake!" Alone at night in a deserted television studio, **Beryl Reid** spots the black casket that is used for her soap opera character's funeral. She lifts the lid to discover it is made of light balsa wood. *The Killing of Sister George* (1979, Palomar).

3321 "Now I know what I've been faking all these years." **Goldie Hawn** gushes after an orgasm during intercourse with suave Frenchman Armand Assante. *Private Benjamin* (1980, Warner Bros.).

3322 "I saw Bonanza and it was not for me. The Ponderosa looked fake." **Ralph Tabakin** makes a television review. *Diner* (1982, MGM).

3323 "And I faked all those orgasms!" Outraged **Madolyn Smith** climaxes her catalogue of recriminations when Steve Martin breaks off their engagement. *All of Me* (1984, Universal).

Fame

see also GLORY, REPUTATIONS

3324 "All famous people aren't big people." **Gary Cooper** has a different notion of fame than do most people. *Mr. Deeds Goes to Town* (1936, Columbia).

3325 "This time yesterday she was just another pretty girl. Today she's the marmalade on ten thousand pieces of toast." Narrator **Mark Hellinger** callously reports the notoriety of a brutally murdered, beautiful blonde playgirl. *The Naked City* (1948, Universal).

3326 LILLIAN HELLMAN: "I like being famous. You know what happens when I go shopping for groceries now? I'm famous. I buy mayonnaise and I'm famous." DASHIELL HAMMETT: "It's only fame, Lily. It's just a paint job. Just remember, it doesn't have anything to do with writing." **Jane Fonda** is reminded by her lover **Jason Robards, Jr.** not to become too taken with fame. *Julia* (1977, 20th Century-Fox).

3327 "Then I'll be famous for having taught you. . . fuck-face." University of Chicago mathematics professor **Jill Clayburgh** understandably snaps at an obnoxious graduate student who insists he's a genius. *It's My Turn* (1980, Columbia).

3328 "I'll go shopping in a store and I'll see people going, 'Hey, that's Dorothy Stratten,' or 'Hey, can we have a picture of you, can we have an autograph?' Or even in the airport, you know, people rushing up to me to get my autograph or something. That's really exciting for me." **Mariel Hemingway**, portraying the murdered Playmate of the Year, Dorothy Stratten, enjoys her fame. *Star 80* (1983, Warner Bros.).

3329 "Fame or infamy—what does it matter?" Elderly homosexual **Rupert Everett** reflects on the pressures of his public school education as he's being interviewed in his Moscow apartment by an American journalist about his spying and defection

from Great Britain years earlier. *Another Country* (1984, GB, 20th Century-Fox).

3330 "I wonder if future generations will ever hear about us? It's not likely. After enough time, everything passes." Radio's Masked Avenger, **Wallace Shawn**, ruefully observes how transitory is fame. *Radio Days* (1987, Orion).

3331 "Famous isn't good. For Joe DiMaggio it's good. Famous for you is not good." **Ben Kingsley**, as Meyer Lansky, advises mobster Warren Beatty, as Ben Siegel, to keep a low profile. *Bugsy* (1991, Tri-Star).

Families

see also BABIES, BOYS, BROTHERS, CHILDREN AND CHILDHOOD, DAUGHTERS, FATHERS, GIRLS, MOTHERS, RELATIVES, SONS AND SONS-IN-LAW

3332 "Listen, you little piece of scum, you. . . . You can go back to that sweet-smelling family of yours, back of the railroad tracks in Passaic! And get this— if that sniveling, money grubbing, whining old mother of yours comes fooling around my office anymore, I'm going to give orders to have her thrown down those sixty flights of stairs, so help me." **Wallace Beery** uses Jean Harlow's family as a club to beat her with during an argument. *Dinner at Eight* (1933, MGM).

3333 "I shall repair to the bosom of my family, a dismal place I must admit." **W.C. Fields** takes his leave from his cronies. *The Bank Dick* (1940, Universal).

3334 "Once it was the family, whole and clear and there was some boundary to it. We were on the land and the old 'uns died and the young 'uns were born. We ain't clear no more." **Jane Darwell**, as Ma Joad, laments the lost old days and the old ways for herself and her family. *The Grapes of Wrath* (1940, 20th Century-Fox).

3335 "The same blood runs through our veins." Merry widow murderer **Joseph Cotten** reminds his niece Teresa Wright that families must stick together or perhaps that she could become as crazy as he is. *Shadow of a Doubt* (1943, Universal).

3336 "We McDonalds—we're high-tempered. We fight amongst ourselves, but let trouble come from outside and we stick together." **Agnes Moorehead** assures doctor Lew Ayres that she will help her deaf and dumb pregnant niece Jane Wyman. *Johnny Belinda* (1948, Warner Bros.).

3337 ANGELA VICKERS: "Are you worried about my family?" GEORGE EASTMAN: "Yes, I suppose I am."

ANGELA: "Don't. I've known them intimately for several years and they're quite nice. Perhaps they are a little unused to you, but that'll come in time." **Elizabeth Taylor** has faith that working class stiff **Montgomery Clift** can win over her wealthy family. *A Place in the Sun* (1951, Paramount).

3338 "Your grandfather died in Australia—in a penal colony, and your father—he was a good man, too." Irish priest **Ward Bond** welcomes American John Wayne back to his ancestral home, the village of Inisfree. *The Quiet Man* (1952, Republic).

3339 "Santino, never tell anyone from outside the Family what you're thinking." **Marlon Brando**, as Don Corleone, chides his son James Caan for speaking what was on his mind at a meeting with a rival mafioso. *The Godfather* (1972, Paramount).

3340 "Don't ever take sides with anyone against the Family again." **Al Pacino** warns his brother John Cazale that he's been too friendly with Alex Rocco, from whom Pacino plans to wrest control of the Las Vegas casinos. *The Godfather* (1972, Paramount).

3341 "Yeah, a buffer. The Family had a lot of buffers." **Joe Spinell** breaks his oath of omertà as he testifies against the Corleone Family before the Senate Crime Commission. *The Godfather, Part II* (1974, Paramount).

3342 "You come from good stock. Your grandmother snuck across the Polish border buried under sacks of potatoes. The guards put bayonets into the sacks, but she never cried out. That's where you come from." **Shelley Winters** tells her son, Lenny Baker, about his roots. *Next Stop, Greenwich Village* (1976, 20th Century-Fox).

3343 "I will not permit you to have two families no matter what their problems are!" **Shannon Wilcox** complains to her husband Dudley Moore that she and his son see very little of him because he's spending so much time with Mary Tyler Moore and her dying ten-year-old daughter Katherine Healy. *Six Weeks* (1982, Polygram-Universal).

3344 "Gaby and I continued living in the family house. We adopted a newborn baby girl and Gaby named her Alma Florencia. I take care of her upbringing and Gaby sees to her education. Gaby's writing two new books and it makes me laugh to see Almita crawling around the room. To most people we must look like a strange family, but that doesn't matter. The house is full of life again." At the end of this true story, **Norma Aleandro**, portraying nurse Florencia Morales, speaks of Rachel Levin. The latter portrays Gabriela "Gaby"

Brimmer who was stricken with severe cerebral palsy from birth, leaving her nearly immobile and mute. Nurse Morales devotes her life to Brimmer, and together they overcome the odds, with Brimmer becoming one of Mexico's most popular and celebrated authors. *Gaby—A True Story* (1987, Tri-Star).

3345 "Daddy, I know I won't stay in Tarboro my whole life. But right now my child needs her family. She needs a stable home. I'm gonna stay right here and I'm gonna ride it out, just the same as you, and Ruth, and our whole family." After taking part in a torrid romantic triangle involving her husband, Anthony Edwards, and their hired man Bruce Abbott, **Lori Singer** decides that she needs a little quieter family life with her Daddy, Clu Gulager and sister Kathy Bates. *Summer Heat* (1987, Atlantic).

3346 "One of the things I love about you is you're the kind of guy who goes back to his family." **Barbra Streisand** hugs her lover Nick Nolte who is leaving her to return to his wife and children. *The Prince of Tides* (1991, Columbia).

3347 "[You're] one generation up from white trash." Cannibal killer **Anthony Hopkins** correctly surmises FBI trainee Jodie Foster's hillbilly roots. *The Silence of the Lambs* (1991, Orion).

Fancies

see also IMAGINATION, LIKES AND DISLIKES, REALITIES

3348 "I feel like a fancy porch swing!" **Claudette Colbert** makes an announcement to a nightclub audience when she appears in an outlandish costume. *The Gilded Lily* (1935, Paramount).

3349 "In the spring a young man's fancy lightly turns to what he's been thinking about all winter." **Cary Grant** puts it nicely. *The Awful Truth* (1937, Columbia).

3350 "She hardly changed, only more fancy, cute as lace pants." Hulking **Mike Mazurki** hovers lovingly over his dead, long-lost girlfriend Velma, played by Claire Trevor. *Murder, My Sweet* (1945, RKO).

3351 DAVE: "Do you fancy me?" LYNDA: "Not half as much as you fancy yourself." Teenager **Jesse Birdsall** appears at the door of the bedroom wearing a silk dressing gown, smoking a cigarette in a holder, and doing a Ronald Colman imitation. **Emily Lloyd** just wants to get laid. *Wish You Were Here* (1987, GB, Atlantic).

Fantasies

see also DREAMS, IMAGINATION, NATURE AND NATURAL, POETRY AND POETS, WILDNESS

3352 "Why, when Tina said she wanted to come home and stay with me—well, it was like a miracle happening, like having your child, a part of you. And I even allowed myself to indulge in the fantasy that both of us loving her and doing what was best for her together would make her seem actually like our child after a while. But I see no such fantasy has occurred to you. Again, I've been just a big sentimental fool. It's a tendency I have." **Bette Davis** confesses her fantasy about Paul Henreid's daughter. *Now, Voyager* (1942, Warner Bros.).

3353 DR. RANDALL ADAMS: "Pardon me, young lady. Are you in love with anyone? And remember it's a felony to lie to a doctor." RUTH EDLY: "I'm not in love with anybody. But I like doctors. Are you available?" RANDALL: "Holy smoke! What night are we going to get together?" RUTH: "Make it easy for yourself." RANDALL: "I'm off Friday night." RUTH: "I've got a date. But I'll break it." RANDALL: "I'll buy you a swell dinner." RUTH: "Save your money. I'll give you a swell dinner at my place." RANDALL: "Then, I'll bring a bottle of gin." RUTH: "You don't have to. I've got everything you can think of in my apartment." RANDALL: "What kind of apartment have you got?" RUTH: "Only five rooms. After all, what does one girl need when she lives alone?" RANDALL: "Would you mind pinching me to see if I'm awake." RUTH: "Oh, you're awake all right. I can tell by that look in your eye." RANDALL: "I'm off at 7. I'll be there at 7:30." RUTH: "Make it 8. I want to be beautiful for you. . . I'll leave the door unlatched because it's the maid's night off." RANDALL: "Holy smoke!" Dr. **Van Johnson** can't believe his good luck with bachelor's dream, super stacked blonde nurse **Marilyn Maxwell.** For most men, it's a fantasy. *Dr. Gillespie's Criminal Case* (1943, MGM).

3354 "When we are young, we read and believe the most fantastic things. When we are older, we learn with regret that these things cannot be—we are quite, quite wrong!" The ghost story film's opening statement. *Blithe Spirit* (1945, GB, Two Cities-Cineguild).

3355 "What happened at the office? Well, I shot Mr. Brady in the head, made violent love to Miss Morris and set fire to 300,000 copies of 'Little Women.' That's what happened at the office." Book editor **Tom Ewell,** who has a Walter Mitty-type imagination, responds to his wife Evelyn Keyes' predictable question when he arrives home from work. He knows she's not listening for the answer. *The Seven Year Itch* (1955, 20th Century-Fox).

3356 "You've taken a new tack, Martha, in the last century or two which is just too much. Too much. I don't mind your dirty underthings in public—well, I do mind, but I've reconciled myself to that—but you've moved bag and baggage into your own fantasy world." **Richard Burton** feels his wife Elizabeth Taylor doesn't know the boundary of the real world and the fantasy world. *Who's Afraid of Virginia Woolf?* (1966, Warner Bros.).

3357 "Do you ever think of yourself as the sleeping beauty of a castle waiting for a prince to awaken you with a kiss?" Believe it or not, this approach works for wounded Union soldier **Clint Eastwood** with schoolgirl Elizabeth Hartman. *The Beguiled* (1971, Universal).

3358 "You play on the sexual fantasies of men like us." Mad murderer **Charles Cioffi** struggles with prostitute Jane Fonda whom he plans to kill. *Klute* (1971, Warner Bros.).

3359 "I want you to be mean to me—next time I want you to use your belt." Sickie **Susan Tyrell** parades around in front of Ben Gazzara in sexy black underwear, enjoying a rape fantasy. *Tales of Ordinary Madness* (1983, Italy-Fr., Miracle).

3360 "Love is dead. Love is a fantasy little girls have." Philandering **John Cassavetes** doesn't offer any reassurance to his distraught sister Gena Rowlands when she moves in with him after the break-up of her marriage. *Love Streams* (1984, Cannon).

3361 "I fantasize that I'm your wife and we're, like, the richest, most popular adults in town." **Liane Curtis** dreams of her life with her handsome high school senior boyfriend Michael Schoeffling. *Sixteen Candles* (1984, Universal).

3362 HERMAN: "If there were no men left, would you do it with a woman?" MASHA: "Of course. And you, would you do it with a man?" HERMAN: "Never. . . but an animal. . . ." **Ron Silver** and lover **Lena Olin** share an end-of-the-world fantasy. *Enemies, a Love Story* (1989, 20th Century-Fox).

3363 "All right. Tell me your worst paranoid fantasy. . . . Is this it? They drive off with the baby and the car, and we never see them again. Maybe they hit a couple of convenience stores on the way and we end up on the Geraldo Rivera show as the most gullible couple in America." **James Woods** shares his concern with wife Glenn Close after lending their car to an unconventional young couple, Kevin Dillon and Mary Stuart Masterson. The latter is going to have a baby for the childless couple. *Immediate Family* (1989, Columbia).

3364 "This is a fantasy. It's gone too far." **Gina Bellman** has been enlivening her marital life with Alan Bates by playing the sort of games suggested in best-selling sex manuals. *Secret Friends* (1992, GB, Briarpatch Releasing Corporation).

Farewells

see also DEPARTURES AND RETURNS

3365 "So long, it's been nice having you!" **Jean Harlow** makes a meaningful but premature farewell to Clark Gable. *Red Dust* (1932, MGM).

3366 "Goodbye, Miss Dolly, you sho' been mighty good to me even if they does hang you." Maid **Hattie McDaniel** makes a cheery farewell to **Jean Harlow** who is mixed up with Malaysian pirates. *China Seas* (1935, MGM).

3367 BARKLEY COOPER: "I figure that everyone is entitled to just so much happiness in life. In case I don't see you again, Miss Breckenridge, it's been very nice knowing you, Miss Breckenridge." LUCY COOPER: "It's been lovely, every bit of it, the whole fifty years. . . I'd rather have been your wife than anything else on earth." In one of the very few movies to deal with the hardships and heartbreaks of the elderly, **Victor Moore** and his wife of fifty years **Beulah Bondi** say their goodbyes as they part, probably forever. He's headed for a home in California; she to an old woman's home in the Northeast. It's heart wrenching. *Make Way for Tomorrow* (1937, Paramount).

3368 "Dear New York, We've had a lot of good times together—you and I—but even the best of times must end, so I have gone to face the end alone—like an elephant." **Carole Lombard** publishes her farewell to the Big Apple which took her to heart when it was believed she had only six months to live. The diagnosis was an error and now she hopes just to disappear. *Nothing Sacred* (1937, Selznick-United Artists).

3369 "This is getting too hot for me. Au revoir, play-actor." Charming villain **Douglas Fairbanks, Jr.**, runs away to fight another day. It's a rare instance in a Hollywood adventure film when the bad guy doesn't pay for his sins with his life. *The Prisoner of Zenda* (1937, Selznick-United Artists).

3370 "I'm not good at farewells. Don't be too lonely." Larcenous **Roland Young** parts from his con-man son Douglas Fairbanks, Jr., on his first day at an honest job, selling a modernistic car, the "Flying Wombat." *The Young in Heart* (1938, Selznick-United Artists).

3371 "Farewell, my little master of the universe. . . . Free, ha, ha,ha. . . . Free." Djinni **Rex Ingram**, having given Sabu his three wishes, flies off leaving the latter in the middle of nowhere. *The Thief of Bagdad* (1940, GB, London Films).

3372 "Yes, Angel, I'm going to send you over. The chances are you'll get off with life. That means if you're a good girl, you'll be out in twenty years. I'll be waiting for you. If they hang you, I'll always remember you." Private detective **Humphrey Bogart** bids farewell to Mary Astor. He's turning her over to the police for killing his partner Jerome Cowan. *The Maltese Falcon* (1941, Warner Bros.).

3373 "Oh, my darling, why do we always meet just to say goodbye." Once more, married **Vivien Leigh** must take leave of her married lover Laurence Olivier as Lord Nelson. *That Hamilton Woman* aka: *Lady Hamilton* (1941, Korda-United Artists).

3374 "I hate goodbyes!" Nevertheless **Bette Davis** must bid adieu to her shipboard lover, married Paul Henreid. *Now, Voyager* (1942, Warner Bros.).

3375 "Walking through life with you, ma'am, has been a very gracious thing." **Errol Flynn**, as General George A. Custer, takes leave of his wife Olivia de Havilland, before heading for the Little Big Horn, knowing he will never see her again. *They Died with Their Boots On* (1942, Warner Bros.).

3376 WALTER NEFF: "You can do better than that can't you, baby? Better try it again. . . . Maybe if I came a little closer. . . . How's this? Think you can do it now? Why don't you shoot again? Don't tell me it's because you've been in love with me all this time." PHYLLIS DIETRICHSON: "No, I never loved you, Walter, not you or anyone else. I'm rotten to the heart. I used you just as you said. That's all you ever meant to me. Until a minute ago. . . when I couldn't fire the second shot. I never thought it could happen to me." WALTER: "Sorry, baby, I'm not buying. . . ." PHYLLIS: "I'm not asking you to buy, just hold me close." WALTER: "Goodbye, baby." **Barbara Stanwyck** can't bring herself to finish off **Fred MacMurray**, but he's up to the task as he fatally shoots her while holding her close in his arms. *Double Indemnity* (1944, Paramount).

3377 "Good-bye for the moment, my dears. I expect we're bound to meet again one day, but until we do I'm going to enjoy myself as I've never enjoyed myself before." Delighted **Rex Harrison** takes his leave of the ghosts of his two wives, Constance Cummings and Kay Hammond. He doesn't get far. His car crashes and his ghost leaves his body and unhappily joins the women for an eternity of bickering. *Blithe Spirit* (1945, GB, Two Cities).

3378 "Hasta la vista, beautiful one. Maybe someday I'll see you again." **Gilbert Roland**, the Cisco Kid, mounts his horse and rides off alone, leaving Ramsay Ames staring after him. He doesn't look back. *Beauty and the Bandit* (1946, Monogram).

3379 "Love me for the. . . time I have left. . . . Then. . . forget me." **Montgomery Clift** meets with his beloved Elizabeth Taylor before he goes to the electric chair for the murder of his pregnant girlfriend Shelley Winters. *A Place in the Sun* (1951, Paramount).

3380 "So long. So long, you ancient pelican." Airline executive **Regis Toomey** delivers the movie's last line as he watches departing has-been pilot John Wayne saunter off. Wayne has heroically saved a crippled plane full of passengers with his know-how. *The High and the Mighty* (1954, Warner Bros.).

3381 "In a little while, we must leave our city— perhaps for years, perhaps forever. For those of us who are old, certainly forever. Elders of Wangcheng, I thank you for your help in this time of trouble, but we were born to our trouble. There is one who has taken it upon herself not from necessity but from love: Jan-Ai. We thank you for those who are not here, for the dead whose children you have taken as your own, for the poor and the sick and the afflicted, for all the people of Wangcheng, for the past and the future. I honor you for your strength. I wish to share with you the faith from which it comes. . . . It is time to go, old friends. We shall not see each other again, I think. Farewell, Jan-Ai." Chinese mandarin **Robert Donat** expresses his thanks as he says goodbye to missionary Ingrid Bergman. It's Donat's last movie speech as he ends his distinguished career. *The Inn of the Sixth Happiness* (1958, GB, 20th Century-Fox).

3382 GIL WESTRUM: "Don't worry about anything. I'll take care of it—just like you would have." STEVE JUDD: "Hell, I know that, I always did. You just forgot it for awhile, that's all. . . . So long, pardner. I'll see ya later." Slightly larcenous **Randolph Scott** assures dying **Joel McCrea** that he will deliver the gold to the bank just as McCrea promised he would. *Ride the High Country* (1962, MGM).

3383 "I'll see you in a year or so if I don't get shot." As he's off to Korea, **Jeff Bridges** says goodbye to his high school buddy Timothy Bottoms. *The Last Picture Show* (1971, Columbia).

3384 "Life and love are not easy and we have to bend a lot. I hope you find the places and the people to make you all happy as I could not. God bless you and watch over you, as I shall, until we are joined in the hereafter, sweet Leon, my Heidi, dearest Kimmy and Jimmy and my mother. Sonny." **Al Pacino** reads a statement for the TV cameras and the crowd around a bank where he's holding hostages. He realizes that his chances of surviving are minimal. *Dog Day Afternoon* (1975, Warner Bros.).

3385 "The shadows are lengthening for me, the twilight is here. My days of old have vanished, tone and tint; they have gone glimmering through the dreams of things that were. Their memory is one of wondrous beauty, watered by tears, and coaxed and caressed by the smiles of yesterday. I listened vainly, but with thirsty ears, for the witching melody of faint bugles blowing reveille, of far drums beating the long roll. In my dreams I hear the crash of drums, the rattle of musketry, the strange mournful mutter of the battlefield. But in the evening of my memory, always I return to West Point, always there echoes and re-echoes Duty, Honor, Country. Today marks my final roll call with you. I want you to know that when I cross the river, my last conscious thoughts will be one of the Corps, and the Corps, and the Corps. I bid you farewell." General Douglas MacArthur, portrayed by **Gregory Peck**, makes his farewell to the cadets of West Point. *MacArthur* (1977, Universal).

3386 "I'll be dead in a minute; just wanted to say good-bye." **Theresa Russell** calls her lover and psychologist Art Garfunkel after having swallowed a bottle of barbiturates. *Bad Timing: A Sensual Obsession* (1980, GB, Rank).

3387 "Goodbye Jennifer. Take care of yourself. Try not to play with anything sharp." **Valerie Harper** says goodbye to nubile teenager Michelle Johnson, who has had a busy time in Rio, seducing Harper's husband, Michael Caine. *Blame It on Rio* (1984, 20th Century-Fox).

3388 "We should take more care of how we say goodbye." **John Hargreaves** makes a farewell speech at his father's grave. *My First Wife* (1984, Australia, Spectrafilm).

3389 "Well, ain't we a pair. . . . Raggedy man?. . . Goodbye, Soldier." Near the end of the film, **Tina Turner** spares the life of Mel Gibson despite his having ruined her schemes. *Mad Max Beyond Thunderdome* (1985, Australia, Warner Bros.).

3390 "So long, constable. . . you won't have [me] to kick around anymore." Ex-fireman turned island club owner **Robin Williams** affects an aristocratic accent in delivering his line. *Club Paradise* (1986, Warner Bros.).

3391 "We've been saying goodbye from the beginning." English professor **Helen Shaver** tearfully ends her affair with her working class lover Patricia Charbonneau. *Desert Hearts* (1986, Goldwyn).

3392 "There's a lot of people in my life right now. I don't need this. I'll see ya around, kid." Disk jockey **Steve Shellen** is not gentle telling Virginia Madsen that he's bored with her. *Modern Girls* (1986, Atlantic).

3393 "Good-bye, Vietnam. That's right. I'm history. I'm out of here. I got the lucky ticket home, baby. Rollin', rollin', rollin', keep those wagons rollin', rawhide. Yeah, that's right, the final Adrian Kronauer broadcast, and this one is brought to you by our friends at the Pentagon. Remember the people who brought you Korea, that's right, the U.S. Army. If it's being done correctly, here or abroad, it's probably not being done by the Army. I heard that. Ha-ha, you're here, good to see you. I'm here to make sure you don't say anything controversial. Speaking of things controversial, is it true that there is a marijuana problem here in Vietnam? No, it's not a problem, everybody has it. I don't know, Adrian. Leo, Leo. Adrian, take care of yourself. I just want you to know one thing, if you're going to dress in civilian clothes, don't forget pumps. Thank you, Leo, thanks for these. They're ruby slippers, Adrian. Put these on and say 'there's no place like home,' and you can be there. Ha, ha, ha, I hope, I hope we all could." Using his array of voices and personalities, **Robin Williams** says farewell to his Vietnam radio audience before shipping home. *Good Morning, Vietnam* (1987, Buena Vista).

3394 CHARLIE BABBITT: "I'll see you soon." RAYMOND BABBITT: "Yeah, one for bad, two for good." CHARLIE: "Bet two for good." RAYMOND: "Yeah. . . . It's three minutes to Wapner." CHARLIE: "You'll make it." The words between **Tom Cruise** and autistic older brother **Dustin Hoffman** are much more than their face value as Hoffman's train pulls out, leaving Cruise behind. *Rain Man* (1988, United Artists).

3395 "See you soon." It's **Julia Roberts**' hopeful farewell as she or one of her colleagues experience brain death, hoping that they can be revived. *Flatliners* (1990, Columbia).

3396 "Hasta la vista, baby." Good terminator **Arnold Schwarzenegger** has been taught how to say goodbye when he's about to blow away the evil terminator. He must have seen the Cisco Kid movie. *Terminator 2: Judgment Day* (1991, Tri-Star).

Farms and Farming see FOOD AND EATING, GROWTH AND DEVELOPMENT, LAND AND FARMS

Fashions

see also APPEARANCES, CLOTHES, HAIR

3397 "Dashing about with a cutlass is quite out of fashion—hasn't been done since the Middle Ages." **Tyrone Power** assumes the guise of a spineless fop to put off his enemies. *The Mark of Zorro* (1940, 20th Century-Fox).

3398 "You underrate us, Mr. Wickham. Meryton is abreast of everything—everything except insolence and bad manners. Those London fashions we do not admire!" **Greer Garson** will not have her small town family viewed as bumpkins, as she puts cad soldier Edward Ashley in his place. The bounder wants to elope with Garson's sister Ann Rutherford, but not for the purpose of marriage. *Pride and Prejudice* (1940, MGM).

3399 "Is he going to do it in the normal fashion, or is he going to walk on water?" Quadriplegic **Richard Dreyfuss** inquires about messianic doctor John Cassavetes, who opposes Dreyfuss' requests to be allowed to end his life. *Whose Life Is It Anyway?* (1981, MGM).

Fast see PROMISCUITY, SPEED

Fasting see FOOD AND EATING, HUNGER, SACRIFICES

Fate and Destiny

see also CHANCES, DEATH AND DYING, LIFE AND DEATH, LIVES AND LIVING, NEEDS AND NECESSITIES, POWER

3400 "When love is more desired than riches, it is the will of Allah." With the help of a title card, **Rudolph Valentino**, all flashing eyes and flaring nostrils, makes his pitch to Agnes Ayres at his desert camp. *The Sheik* (1921, silent, Famous Players-Lasky).

3401 "When your time comes, you're going to get it." World War I aviator **Gary Cooper** expresses the thought just before going on a mission in the air. It's his time. *Wings* (1927, silent, Paramount).

3402 "Be obedient, and be worthy of a glorious destiny." **C. Aubrey Smith** gives final instructions to Marlene Dietrich who is leaving her German homeland to become the bride of the future Russian Czar. *The Scarlet Empress* (1934, Paramount).

3403 "I spend most of the time since I grew up in jail. And it looks like I spend the rest of my life dead." **Humphrey Bogart**, as mad-dog killer Duke Mantee, sees a bleak future. *The Petrified Forest* (1936, Warner Bros).

3404 "Let there be killing. All this evening I've had a feeling of destiny closing in." World-weary wandering poet **Leslie Howard** is preoccupied with death and dying. *The Petrified Forest* (1936, Warner Bros.).

3405 "You're not helping Jo by trying to keep this case alive. You know as well as I do that Eddie Taylor's been pounding on the door of the execution chamber since he was born." **Jean Dixon** believes that her sister Sylvia Sidney's husband, four-time loser Henry Fonda, is predestined for capital punishment. *You Only Live Once* (1937, United Artists).

3406 "The fates are against me. They tossed a coin—heads, I'm poor; tails, I'm rich. So what do they do? They tossed a coin with two heads." Bitter, fatalistic **John Garfield** complains about his life to Priscilla Lane. *Four Daughters* (1938, Warner Bros.).

3407 "Isn't it just possible that things we like in Johnny may be the very things that your sister can't stand? And the fate that you feel that he'll save her from may be the one fate in the whole world that she really wants?" **Edward Everett Horton** asks Katharine Hepburn if she's sure that Cary Grant is the right man for her sister Doris Nolan. *Holiday* (1938, Columbia).

3408 "By what right, señores, do the Great Powers of Europe invade the lands of simple people. . . kill all who do not make them welcome. . . destroy their fields. . . and take the fruit of their toil from those who survive?. . . The world must know the fate of any usurper who sets his foot upon this soil." Title character **Paul Muni** promises to drive the French conquerors from Mexico. *Juarez* (1939, Warner Bros.).

3409 "Each of us has a destiny for good or evil. . . I wonder if you know that you're trying to escape from yourself and you'll never succeed." Heroic Resistance leader **Paul Henreid** recognizes that bitter Humphrey Bogart has tried to withdraw from the world and its problems. *Casablanca* (1942, Warner Bros.).

3410 "I keep trying to forget what happened and wonder what my life would have been like if that car of Haskell's hadn't stopped. But one thing I don't have to wonder about—I know. Some day a car will stop to pick me up that I never thumbed. Yes, fate—or some mysterious force—can put the finger on you, for no good reason at all. . . . No matter what you do, no matter where you turn, fate sticks out its foot to trip you." **Tom Neal**'s musings about his fate provide a major premise of film noir—we're victims of chance, and there's nothing we can do to resist the end planned for us. *Detour* (1946, Producers Releasing Corporation).

3411 "If I'm hanged, all they'll be doing is rushing it." Hitchhiker **Ann Savage** believes she's destined for an early death. *Detour* (1946, Producers Releasing Corporation).

3412 "What can you do, kill me? Everybody dies." Boxer **John Garfield** isn't afraid of vengeful mobsters—so it says here. *Humoresque* (1947, Enterprise-United Artists).

3413 "The course of our lives can be changed by such little things. . . I know now that no one thing happens by chance. Every moment is measured, each step is counted." Obsessed **Joan Fontaine** writes to Louis Jourdan, the source of her obsession. *Letter from an Unknown Woman* (1948, Universal).

3414 "From the start, it all went one way. It was in the cards or it was fate or a jinx or whatever you want to call it." **Burt Lancaster** complains of his unfortunate relationship with Yvonne DeCarlo. His is a typical film noir complaint: a man or woman or both unable to alter their destiny. *Criss Cross* (1949, Universal-International).

3415 "I was sorry about the girl, but found some relief in the reflection that she had already suffered a fate worse than death in the course of the weekend." **Dennis Price** puts the best face possible upon having not only killed another of his relatives standing between him and a title, but having killed the man's female companion as well. *Kind Hearts and Coronets* (1949, GB, Ealing).

3416 "We've had this date from the beginning." Brutish **Marlon Brando** rapes his unhinged sister-in-law Vivien Leigh. *A Streetcar Named Desire* (1951, Warner Bros.-20th Century-Fox).

3417 "Destiny has held out its hand to you tonight. Take it and hold on." **James Mason**, valet to the British ambassador to Turkey during World War II, offers to sell British secrets to German embassy official Oscar Karlweis. *Five Fingers* (1952, 20th Century-Fox).

3418 "There never was a horse that couldn't be rode; there never was a cowboy that couldn't be throwed." Rodeo performer **Arthur Kennedy** repeats the line spoken earlier in the film by cowboy **Robert Mitchum**, as the latter dies after being fatally injured in a bronc-busting contest. *The Lusty Men* (1952, RKO).

3419 "A man's got to be what he is—you can't break the mold." **Alan Ladd** tells Jean Arthur that he cannot escape the fact that he has been a gunfighter all his adult life. *Shane* (1953, Paramount).

3420 MIKE FORNEY: "How'd you get out here in a smelly ditch in Korea?" LT. HARRY BRUBAKER: "That's just what I'm asking myself." Neither helicopter pilot **Mickey Rooney** nor navy jet pilot **William Holden** will live to find the answer to their fateful questions. *The Bridges at Toko-Ri* (1955, Paramount).

3421 "My life was never my own. It was charted before I was born." It's the inscription signed by alcoholic singer Lillian Roth at the opening of the film. *I'll Cry Tomorrow* (1955, MGM).

3422 "I work in haste from day to day as a miner does who knows he's facing disaster." Tormented genius Vincent Van Gogh, portrayed by **Kirk Douglas**, writes to his brother Theo, played by James Donald. *Lust for Life* (1956, MGM).

3423 "I never saw a gunslinger so tough he lived to celebrate his 35th birthday...I learned one thing about gunslingers—there's always a man faster on the draw than you are. The more you use a gun, the sooner you're gonna run into that man.... All gunfighters are lonely. They live in fear. They die without a dime, a woman or a friend." **Burt Lancaster**, as Marshal Wyatt Earp, gives some sound advice to Dennis Hopper, the youngest of the Clantons. Unfortunately for Hopper, he doesn't pay attention to the point of the heart-to-heart and suffers the fate of dying mighty young. *Gunfight at the OK Corral* (1957, Paramount).

3424 "Be wise, Judah. It's a Roman world. If you want to live in it you must become part of it... I tell you, Judah, it's no accident that one small village on the Tiber was chosen to rule the world.... It wasn't just our legions... No, it was fate that chose us to civilize the world—and we have. Our roads and our ships connect every corner of the earth, Roman law, architecture, literature and the glory of the human race." Roman Tribune **Stephen Boyd** sounds like any jingoistic defender of a tyrannical conquering nation as he argues with his boyhood friend, conquered Jew Charlton Heston. *Ben-Hur* (1959, MGM).

3425 "God always has another custard pie up His sleeve." It's fate, not the Supreme Being, who holds unpleasant surprises for **Lynn Redgrave.** *Georgy Girl* (1966, GB, Columbia).

3426 ZIRA: "What will he find there?" DR. ZAUIS: "His destiny." Simian scientist **Kim Hunter** asks skeptical orangutan **Maurice Evans** about Charlton Heston as Heston and mute Linda Harrison flee deep into the forbidden zone. *The Planet of the Apes* (1968, 20th Century-Fox).

3427 "Before you start rolling, your life makes a bee-line to the drain." Has-been boxer **Stacy Keach**'s come-back attempt is a failure. *Fat City* (1972, Columbia).

3428 "A hero can't run away from his destiny.... Sometimes you run smack into your destiny on the same road you take away from it." Hired gun **Terence Hill** stalks retired outlaw Henry Fonda. *My Name Is Nobody* (1974, Italy-Fr.-Ger., Universal).

3429 "Unless I fulfill my destiny, my mother's labor pains were pointless." In an acerbic satire on the Watergate scandal and cover-up, **Glenda Jackson** a handsome, aristocratic nun, is obsessed with power and sense of mission. She plots to become the next Abbess of the Abbey of Crewe. *Nasty Habits* (1976, GB, Brut).

3430 "He is the best and wisest man I have ever known.... And you have become his chronicler, his Boswell. Your place in the great scheme of things is to record his life, whatever happens. Your motives, thus, for coming with him to Vienna, are not pure altruism, but a sense of destiny that tells you to be at his side, always. Mixed motives." **Alan Arkin**, as Dr. Sigmund Freud, identifies the role of Robert Duvall, as Dr. Watson, to help Nicol Williamson, as Sherlock Holmes, with his cocaine and other problems. *The Seven-Per-Cent Solution* (1977, Universal).

3431 "You set your priorities and that's the way life is. Nobody said it was going to be fun." **Don Galloway**, the solid but square husband of Jo Beth Williams, doesn't fit in with her college buddies reuniting because of the funeral of their one-time leader. *The Big Chill* (1983, Columbia).

3432 If my life ends because of you, that's what was meant to be. If you betray me, then you'll join me." Terrorist **Harvey Keitel** resignedly accepts whatever fate has in store for him—and for Nastassja Kinski as well. *Exposed* (1983, MGM-United Artists).

3433 "Mr. Bond is a rare breed, soon to become extinct." Villain **Louis Jourdan** plans Roger Moore's death after he escapes Jourdan's clutches once more. *Octopussy* (1983, GB, MGM-United Artists).

3434 "There's somewhere I've got to go. I don't know where—just somewhere, out of here, and I've got to go now." As he ponders his destiny, **Aidan Quinn** sounds like an inarticulate James Dean or Marlon Brando of the 50s. *Reckless* (1984, MGM-United Artists).

3435 "And Nietzsche, with his theory of eternal recurrence; he said that the life we live we're going to live over and over again the exact same way for eternity. Great—that means I'll have to sit through the Ice Capades again." **Woody Allen** ponders his fate. *Hannah and Her Sisters* (1986, Orion).

3436 "One day we shall all become shadows." **Donal McCann** reflects on the fate of all the living as he looks out into Dublin's bleak winter dawn. *The Dead* (1987, Vestron).

3437 "I always knew I was born to decimate your sex and avenge my own." **Glenn Close** discloses her perceived mission to John Malkovich. *Dangerous Liaisons* (1988, Warner Bros.).

3438 "My road was chosen long ago—and if I'm going to hell—I'm going playing the piano." Jerry Lee Lewis, as played by **Dennis Quaid**, makes his musical stand to his cousin, evangelist Jimmy Swaggert, played by Alec Baldwin. *Great Balls of Fire!* (1989, Orion).

3439 "I'm the kind of girl who gets thrown out of cars without her clothes on." According to sexy but aging prostitute and victim **Sally Kirkland**, it's her frequent fate. *High Stakes* (1989, Vidmark).

3440 "Another elevator, another basement. . . . How can the same shit happen to the same guy twice?" Funny that **Bruce Willis** should ask. The first movie of one man taking on a gang of terrorists single-handedly made so much money a sequel was a given. Willis should have made a third film in the series rather than the career-threatening "Hudson Hawk." *Die Hard 2* aka: *Die Harder* (1990, 20th Century-Fox).

Fathers

see also BABIES, CHILDREN AND CHILDHOOD, DAUGHTERS, FAMILIES, MARRIAGES, MEN, MEN AND WOMEN, MOTHERS, PARENTS, RELATIVES, SONS AND SONS-IN-LAW

3441 "Who sent that young man out to kill Germans?. . . And who sent my boy? And your boy—and your boy? And your two boys?. . . Who gave them bullets and gas and bayonets? We—the fathers! Here and on the other side. We're too old to fight, but we're not too old to hate. . . . We're responsible. When thousands of other men's sons were killed, we called it victory, and celebrated with beer. And when thousands of our sons were killed, they called it victory and celebrated with wine. Fathers! . . . drunk to the death of sons. . . Ach! My heart isn't with you any longer, old men. My heart's with the young, dead and living . . . everywhere . . . anywhere. . ." German father **Lionel Barrymore** makes an eloquent statement about how monstrous war is, when others in this town express suspicion at the arrival of young Frenchman Phillips Holmes after World War I. *The Man I Killed* aka: *Broken Lullaby* (1931, Paramount).

3442 "I'm very like father. . . . Father is my job, not yours." **Katharine Hepburn** usurps her mother Billie Burke's role in dealing with the problems of her father, John Barrymore. He has escaped from a mental hospital, where he's spent the last 25 years, on the very day that Burke intends to divorce him. *A Bill of Divorcement* (1932, RKO).

3443 "Since when did you ask a dollar who was his father?" Cheating, cheap **Vivienne Osborne** tells her husband Edward G. Robinson that he shouldn't mind that she's borrowed money from her ex-lover J. Carrol Naish so they can pay their bills. *Two Seconds* (1932, Warner Bros.).

3444 "Dad loved Princeton. He was there nearly twenty years. If ever a man loved a place, he did—he just adored it. And he certainly kept it looking beautiful. . . . You've seen the grounds, of course." Posing as her ex-husband's ditsy sister, **Irene Dunne** puts a crimp in Cary Grant's story about his father and Princeton for the benefit of his new fiancée and her snooty society family. *The Awful Truth* (1937, Columbia).

3445 "I bet your father spent the first year of your life throwing rocks at the stork." Shyster lawyer **Groucho Marx** flings a barb at Eve Arden who is quite capable of fielding them and flinging back as good as she gets. *At the Circus* (1939, MGM).

3446 "Men like my father cannot die. They remain a living truth in my mind. . . . They are with me still—real in memory as they were real in flesh—loving and beloved forever. How green was my valley, then." Narrator **Irving Pichel**, as the grown up Huw, brings the film to its close. *How Green Was My Valley* (1941, 20th Century-Fox).

3447 NORA CHARLES: "He's more like his father every day." STELLA: "He sure is. This morning he was playing with a corkscrew." **Myrna Loy** and maid **Louise Beavers** are speaking of the former's son Dickie Hall and his often intoxicated father William Powell. *Shadow of the Thin Man* (1941, MGM).

3448 "Nobody loved him like I did." **Peggy Ann Garner** is beside herself with grief at the death of her beloved father, James Dunn. *A Tree Grows in Brooklyn* (1945, 20th Century-Fox).

3449 "You're the spittin' image of your father." With these unguarded words to his baby son, **Stephen McNally** reveals to Charles Bickford that he's the man who raped and impregnated Bickford's deaf and dumb daughter Jane Wyman. *Johnny Belinda* (1948, Warner Bros.).

3450 "Oh, yes. There was the ever present smile of my father. He was a telephone man who fell in love with long distance. The last we heard from him was a postcard containing two words—'Hello—Goodbye'—and no address." **Arthur Kennedy** comments on his long-gone father. In the 1987 version, **John Malkovich** makes a similar observation about father. *The Glass Menagerie* (1950, Warner Bros.); (1987, Cineplex Odeon).

3451 "He used to sit down on the bed at night, and I'd tug 'em off, and he'd say, 'Son, the man of the house has got to have a pair of boots because he's got to do a lot of kicking.' Then he'd say, 'Son, there'll be times when the only thing you got to be proud of is the fact that you're a man, so wear your boots so people know you're coming and keep your fists doubled up so they know you mean business when you get there.' My old man, he was a corker!" **William Holden** shares the only lesson he learned from his father. *Picnic* (1955, Columbia).

3452 "All I wanted was a father, not a boss. I wanted you to love me." **Paul Newman**, as Brick, whimpers to Burl Ives, as Big Daddy. *Cat on a Hot Tin Roof* (1958, MGM).

3453 "I heard from him last Christmas. The letter said—'Daughter, read First Kings, Chapter Twenty-one, Verse Twenty-three.' I looked it up. It said, 'And the dogs in the streets shall eat Jezebel.' Hmmm, my old man and his Bible. Tell me—how is it some people can only find hate in the Bible. . . ?" Prostitute **Shirley Jones** tells Burt Lancaster about her minister father who has disowned her. *Elmer Gantry* (1960, United Artists).

3454 "Be a father to your men. . . . Come down off your cross." Explosives expert **David Niven** defiantly ridicules Gregory Peck's unbending leadership style. *The Guns of Navarone* (1961, GB, Columbia).

3455 "Sir, I beg you not to persist in asking me to reveal the father of my baby. I promise you faithfully that one day you shall know. But I am under the most solemnities of honor, and religion, to conceal his name now. You would not want that I should sacrifice either my honor or my religion." **Joyce Redman**, as Jenny Jones, resists George Devine, as Squire Allworthy, who insists that she reveal the name of the father of the baby he found in his bed. *Tom Jones* (1963, GB, United Artists).

3456 "My father was a soldier who, after thirty years of service, was catapulted to the rank of corporal." Bungling crook and social misfit **Woody Allen** remembers his father. *Take the Money and Run* (1968, Cinerama).

3457 "I don't want you to turn out like the old man." Successful young businessman **Joe Don Baker** talks to his brother, fading rodeo star Steve McQueen, about their father, perpetual loser Robert Preston. *Junior Bonner* (1972, ABC-Cinerama).

3458 MOSE PRAY: "Just because a woman meets a man in a barroom doesn't mean he's your pa." ADDIE: "Well, then, if you ain't my pa, I want my $200." If **Ryan O'Neal** continues to deny that he's **Tatum O'Neal**'s father, she wants him to return the $200 he owes her. *Paper Moon* (1973, Paramount).

3459 "When Pop had troubles, did he ever think that maybe by trying to be strong, and trying to protect his family, that he could lose it instead?" **Al Pacino** has doubts about his role as godfather. He questions his mother, Morgana King, about his father Marlon Brando. *The Godfather, Part II* (1974, Paramount).

3460 BILLY RAY, JR.: "I hear that you turned eighty today." NORMAN THAYER: "Is that what you heard?" BILLY: "Yeah, that's really old." NORMAN: "Oh? You should meet my father." BILLY: "Your father's still alive?" NORMAN: "No, but you should meet him." Sassy 13-year-old **Doug McKeon** has an age conversation with cantankerous old **Henry Fonda**. *On Golden Pond* (1981, Universal).

3461 "I have no time for this daddy stuff." Alcoholic **Robert Loggia** has no time for his son Richard Gere. *An Officer and a Gentleman* (1982, Paramount).

3462 "The bottom line is that he's my father, and I love him." Teenager **C. Thomas Howell** refers to his father, top sergeant James Garner, who has used a tank to break his son out of a southern prison camp to which he was sent on trumped-up charges by red-necked sheriff G.D. Spradlin. *Tank* (1984, Universal).

3463 "[Our father]. . . had two separate lives. . . . He'd live with me and my mother for a while and then he'd disappear and go live with her and her mother for a while." **Sam Shepard** tells his half-sister Kim Basinger's date, Randy Quaid, about their bigamist father, Harry Dean Stanton. *Fool for Love* (1985, Cannon).

3464 "I'm looking for a father. I want to have a child. . . . Look it really is much easier than it sounds. I mean marriage is not involved. Or even looking after it. You don't even have to see the pregnancy through. I mean conception will be the end of the job." **Meryl Streep** asks Sting to father a child for her. *Plenty* (1985, 20th Century-Fox).

3465 "Because he reached in and put a string of lights around my heart." It's **Patricia Charbonneau**'s sweet response when asked why her father was so important to her. *Desert Hearts* (1986, Goldwyn).

3466 "You mean Dad used to do it?" **Jonathan Silverman** is astonished by the thought of his parents having a sexual relationship. *Brighton Beach Memoirs* (1987, Universal).

3467 "He's planning the rest of my life for me, and he's never asked me what I want. . . I can't talk with him. . . . He'll tell me that acting is a whim. . . just forget it,. . . put it out of my mind for my own good. . . I'm trapped." Teen **Robert Sean Leonard** confides in his teacher, Robin Williams, his love of acting and his father's insistence that he's not capable of planning his own life and making choices. Leonard eventually makes a chilling choice—he commits suicide. *Dead Poets Society* (1989, Touchstone).

3468 "He was born in North Dakota in 1896 and never saw a big city until he came back from France in 1918. He settled in Chicago where he quickly learned to live and die with the White Sox. . . died a little when they lost the 1919 World Series, died a lot the following summer when eight members of the team were accused of throwing that series. . . . He played in the minors for a year or two, but nothing ever came of it. . . . He moved to Brooklyn in '35 and married Mom in '38. He was already an old man working at the Naval Yards when I was born in 1952." It's part of the opening narration delivered by **Kevin Costner**. *Field of Dreams* (1989, Universal).

3469 "I'm a father, worry comes with the territory." **Steve Martin** tells his wife Diane Keaton he can't help but worry about his little girl, Kimberly Williams. It's hard for him to accept the fact she's not a little girl anymore and since she's engaged she's no longer his. *Father of the Bride* (1991, Touchstone).

3470 "My father had become the whole world to me. When he died I had nothing. I was ten years old." As part of her bargain, FBI trainee **Jodie Foster** tells criminally insane Anthony Hopkins of her worst memory—the murder of her policeman father. *The Silence of the Lambs* (1991, Orion).

Fatigue

3471 "I have never been so tired in all my life." Exhausted ballerina **Greta Garbo**'s weariness is not merely physical. *Grand Hotel* (1932, MGM).

3472 "By the time I get home to my wife, I'll be too tired to turn out the light." Weary truckdriver **Humphrey Bogart** looks forward to finishing his run. *They Drive by Night* (1940, Warner Bros.).

3473 "I'm awful tired of men talking to me man to man." **Eve Arden** complains that men don't see her as female material. *Mildred Pierce* (1945, Warner Bros.).

3474 "You're too tired. I know that feeling of exhaustion only too well. One must humor it, or it explodes." Acting head of a mental institution **Leo G. Carroll** comforts his colleague Ingrid Bergman. *Spellbound* (1945, United Artists).

3475 "I didn't say I was a gentleman. I said I was tired." **Humphrey Bogart** callously responds to police Captain Carl Benton Reid's inquiry as to why Bogie didn't ensure that murdered hatcheck girl Martha Stewart was seen safely home when she left his apartment the night before. *In a Lonely Place* (1950, Columbia).

3476 "I'm tired of people telling me what to do." **Gary Cooper** gets angry when his former deputy Lloyd Bridges joins everyone else in town insisting that Cooper run away to avoid a showdown with a vengeance-minded killer arriving on the noon train. *High Noon* (1952, United Artists).

3477 "Keep my head clear. I am a tired old man. I have killed the fish which is my brother and now I must do slave work." Old fisherman **Spencer Tracy** isn't the only one exhausted in this one-character drama. Many viewers yawned and dropped off as well. *The Old Man and the Sea* (1958, Warner Bros.).

3478 "Could you knock him off really quickly? I'm really tired." **Mary Woronov** asks her husband Paul Bartel to murder their night's victim early so she can get some rest. *Eating Raoul* (1982, 20th Century-Fox).

3479 "I'm tired of your macho bullshit." Stewardess **Rae Dawn Chong** tells off Sylvester Stallone. She's helping him rescue his daughter from some U.S. agents gone bad. *Commando* (1985, 20th Century-Fox).

3480 "I'm just hanging on here with every bit of strength that I've got. . . . God, it exhausts me." Aimless Vietnam veteran **Bruce Willis** tells his niece Emily Lloyd that he can't help her learn anything about her father who was killed in Vietnam before she was born. *In Country* (1989, Warner Bros.).

3481 "I'm so tired of being good." Well-bred nice girl **Amy Locane** sulks because she's not like the wild girls that flock around dream-boat Johnny Depp. *Cry-Baby* (1990, Universal).

3482 "I'm awful tired of being the only adult in this family." **Teri Garr** wishes some people would grow up or at least act grown up. *Waiting for the Light* (1990, Triumph).

3483 "I'm sick and tired of being treated like a piece of meat." **Ellen Barkin**, the shapely blonde reincarnation of womanizer Perry King, learns how it feels to be on the other side of the chase. *Switch* (1991, Warner Bros.).

Faults

see also CONFESSIONS, LIMITS AND LIMITATIONS, PERFECTION, VICES, VIRTUES, WEAKNESS

3484 COL. EHRHARDT: "You know there's always something wrong with a man who doesn't drink, who doesn't smoke, who doesn't eat meat." PROFESSOR SILETSKY: "You mean our Fuhrer?" Gestapo Officer **Sig Ruman** refers to his adjutant Henry Victor, but is brought up short when **Jack Benny**, disguised as a Polish spy, accuses him of an anti-Hitler remark. *To Be or Not to Be* (1942, United Artists).

3485 "If to act out a little lie to save one's mother humiliation was a fault—in other words, if tenderness toward, and consideration of, one's mother was a fault—it was a fault any man might be proud of." **Harry Hayden** defends Eddie Bracken who allowed his hometown folks to believe that he's a marine hero. *Hail the Conquering Hero* (1944, Paramount).

3486 FLO OWENS: "He's no good. He'll never be able to support you. And when he does have money, he'll spend it on drink. And then, there'll be other women." MADGE OWENS: "You don't love someone because he's perfect." Worried and experienced mother **Betty Field** warns her daughter **Kim Novak** what she can expect of a life with drifter William Holden. Novak may be correct, but Holden's only redeeming quality seems to be he looks good without a shirt. *Picnic* (1955, Columbia).

3487 "Why pick on Hud, Grandpa? Nearly everyone around here is like him." **Brandon de Wilde** sees Paul Newman's faults as pretty common. Newman's father Melvyn Douglas holds a much lower opinion of his son. *Hud* (1963, Paramount).

3488 "You don't understand anything. All you've ever done is accuse me of things and criticize me of things, analyze me, telling me why don't I have that fixed, as if it were my fault that I couldn't have them fixed." **Ali MacGraw** breaks up with librarian Richard Benjamin after their sexual activity has been discovered by her hurt and disapproving parents. *Goodbye, Columbus* (1969, Paramount).

3489 "You married an incompetent. I'm irresponsible, cruel and aimless. I hate to cook, and I'm sloppy. If you really knew me, you'd hate me." **Shirley Knight** confesses to her husband Robert Modica that she's ashamed that she hasn't fulfilled what she believes to be her wifely duties. *The Rain People* (1969, Warner Bros.).

3490 "I don't want to hear any of your anti-establishment paranoia. If he'd settled down where he belongs, none of it would have happened. . . . What stupid thing did he do?" American businessman **Jack Lemmon** angrily blames his daughter-in-law Sissy Spacek and his son John Shea for his mysterious disappearance in Chile. *Missing* (1982, Universal).

3491 REGINALD KINCAID: "How can I be expected to maintain a character when you belittle me in front of these hooligans?" DR. JOHN WATSON: "Character? Are we talking about the same man who once declared with total conviction that the late Colonel Howard had been bludgeoned to death by a blunt excrement?" KINCAID: "Is it my fault that you have such poor handwriting?" **Michael Caine** is an actor, hired by **Ben Kingsley**, to portray the latter's fictional private investigator, Sherlock Holmes. It is Kingsley's Dr. Watson who is the deductive genius. *Without a Clue* (1988, GB, Orion).

3492 "You're sick, you're filthy and you smell bad." Housewife **Lynne Adams** shouldn't be so hard on carpenter Wings Hauser. After all he's the ghost of a man executed for murder. *The Carpenter* (1989, Canada, Cinepix).

Favorites

see also LIKES AND DISLIKES, PREFERENCES

3493 SONIA: "There are many kinds of love, Boris. There's love between a man and a woman, love between a mother and a son. . . ." BORIS: "Two women, let's not forget my favorite." **Diane Keaton** tries to be serious, but **Woody Allen** wants to talk about one of his fantasies. *Love and Death* (1975, United Artists).

3494 "Why is life worth living?. . . well, there are certain things that make it worthwhile. . . like what. . . . Let's see there's Groucho Marx, Willie Mays, and. . . the second movement of the Jupiter Symphony, and. . . Louie Armstrong's recording of 'Potatohead Blues' . . . Swedish movies, naturally . . . Sentimental Education by Flaubert . . . Marlon Brando, Frank Sinatra . . . those incredible apples and pears by Cezanne . . . the crabs at Sam Wo's. . . Tracy's face." **Woody Allen** dreamily enumerates his favorite things to a dictaphone—the last makes him realize that he's in love with young Mariel Hemingway. *Manhattan* (1979, United Artists).

3495 "His favorite author is the guy who wrote 'Pull tab to open.'" Gothic romance novelist **Kathleen Turner** has a low opinion of her lover Michael Douglas' literary interests. *Jewel of the Nile* (1985, 20th Century-Fox).

3496 "'Depressing' and 'expensive.' These are two of my least favorite words. 'Peppy' and 'cheap.' These are my favorite words." Programming executive **Garry Marshall** makes himself perfectly clear to the creative staff of a television soap opera. *Soapdish* (1991, Paramount).

Favors

see also FRIENDSHIPS AND FRIENDS, GENEROSITY, GIFTS AND GIVING, KINDNESS AND SERVICES

3497 "I was just standing here and a nice gentleman came along and begged my pardon and asked if I'd mind holding his teeth for him. I think he was going to slug somebody." **Helen Chandler** is taken with the courtesy of strangers in this lost-generation film. *The Last Flight* (1931, First National).

3498 "Why should they find out? It's only two thousand dollars. Bloom, do me a favor. Move a few decimal points around. You can do it. You're an accountant. You're in a noble profession. The word count is part of your title." Down-on-his-luck Broadway producer **Zero Mostel** pleads with accountant Gene Wilder to fudge a little bit on the former's account books. *The Producers* (1968, Embassy).

3499 "Do me a favor. Will you shut up and peel?" Would-be-soldier-of-fortune **Tony Curtis** and his tough partner Charles Bronson are bunglers, who fail to escort three girls of important parentage and a shipment of coal safely out of 1920 Turkey. They have their hands full of potatoes. *You Can't Win 'Em All* (1970, Columbia).

3500 "I have a big stone in my shoe. I hope you can remove it." **Eli Wallach** hires Sicilian assassin Mario Donatone to kill Al Pacino. *The Godfather, Part III* (1991, Paramount).

Fears

see also CONCERNS, DANGER, EASE AND EASINESS, EVILNESS, FEELINGS, IMAGINATION, PAINS, TERROR

3501 "I didn't mean to, Ma. I couldn't help it. Honest, I couldn't. Don't leave me. You got to believe me. You've got to help me. I'm scared, Ma." Pathetic **James Cagney** cries to his mother, Lucille La Verne, about a murder he committed. *Sinner's Holiday* (1930, Warner Bros.).

3502 "I'm not afraid of life, although I'm not afraid of death either." Tough streetwalker **Marlene Dietrich**, a former officer's widow, shares her feelings with a policeman early in the film. *Dishonored* (1931, Paramount).

3503 "Power! To make the whole world grovel at my feet, to walk into the gold vaults of nations, the chambers of kings, into the holy of holies. Even the moon is frightened of me, frightened to death. The whole world is frightened to death." Madness is overtaking scientist **Claude Rains** who has made himself invisible. He even takes it as a sign when the moon goes behind a cloud. *The Invisible Man* (1933, Universal).

3504 "Nellie, they've all been trying to frighten me into being sensible, but they can't do it, not now, not yet. They've got to let me be as foolish as I want to be. I, I want to ride through the park. I want to. I want a white ermine coat, and I'll buy you a beautiful present, and Mr. Hedges. I'll buy Mr. Hedges a little house, and I'll have rooms full of white orchids. And they've got to tell me that I'm much more wonderful than anyone else. Oh, Nellie, Nellie, I'm not afraid. I'm not afraid of being left a morning glory. I'm not afraid. I'm not afraid. I'm not afraid. Why should I be afraid? I'm not afraid." Despite her protests to Helen Ware, hopeful young actress **Katharine Hepburn** is just a bit afraid. *Morning Glory* (1933, RKO).

3505 "It's after all better to be frightened than to be cursed." **Bela Lugosi** seeks revenge against devil-worshipper Boris Karloff who has stolen both the latter's wife and daughter. *The Black Cat* (1934, Universal).

3506 "Stabbed in the cuticle, what a way to die! If you think I should have ether, don't be afraid to say so." **Fred MacMurray** teases incompetent manicurist Carole Lombard who draws blood twice while working on his hands. *Hands Across the Table* (1935, Paramount).

3507 "There, there, now. All your terrible fears are over. Your father and Colonel Morrison are going free." **Frank McGlynn, Sr.**, as President Abraham Lincoln comforts little Shirley Temple who successfully pleaded for the lives of her father, Confederate Captain John Boles and Union officer Jack Holt, condemned as spies. *The Littlest Rebel* (1935, 20th Century-Fox).

3508 "They respect one law—fear." **Charles Laughton**, as Captain Bligh, lectures Clark Gable, as Mr. Christian, on how to deal with the crew. *Mutiny on the Bounty* (1935, MGM).

3509 "I don't think Blackie ever knew your kind of woman before. But you needn't be afraid of him...unless you're afraid of yourself." Priest **Spencer Tracy** assures Jeanette MacDonald that she has nothing to fear from amoral Clark Gable, unless she's a bit weak herself. *San Francisco* (1936, MGM).

3510 "I got goose pimples. Even my goose pimples get goose pimples." **Bob Hope** provides the comic relief in an excellent spooky house thriller. *The Cat and the Canary* (1939, Paramount).

3511 "You don't have to be afraid anymore. I'm not trying to tie you down. I don't want to plan. I don't want to change anything." **Jean Arthur** tells independent-minded Cary Grant that he has nothing to fear from her—she'll make no demands of him in their relationship. *Only Angels Have Wings* (1939, Columbia).

3512 LOIS GARLAND: "I know I should have called for an appointment. But I was afraid I wouldn't live until morning." DR. ROBERT ORDWAY: "Was tonight the first time you had an impulse to kill yourself?" LOIS: "What makes you think that's what I'm afraid of?" ORDWAY: "You're not afraid of dying from a physical illness or you would have gone to a physician. If you feared an attack on your life, you would have gone to the police. But when you come to a psychiatrist in the middle of the night with an explanation that to wait until morning would be fatal, then self-destruction is the obvious conclusion." Textile designer and heiress **Nina Foch** apologizes to **Warner Baxter** for the intrusion at three o'clock in the morning in the midst of a rainstorm. *Shadows in the Night* (1944, Columbia).

3513 "Now that I'm going home, I'm scared. I wasn't half as scared on Guadalcanal as I am now." Marine hero **John Garfield** is going home from the war against the Japanese minus his sight. *Pride of the Marines* (1945, Warner Bros.).

3514 "Don't be afraid. I don't want you should ever be afraid." These are the dying words of alcoholic singing waiter **James Dunn** to his loving daughter, Peggy Ann Garner. *A Tree Grows in Brooklyn* (1945, 20th Century-Fox).

3515 "The thing that scares me most is that everyone will want to rehabilitate me." Army Sergeant **Fredric March** is concerned as he returns home after World War II. *The Best Years of Our Lives* (1946, Goldwyn-RKO).

3516 "This is the first time I am sorry I am a scientist. Society is not ready for atomic energy. I'm scared stiff." Physics professor and O.S.S. agent **Gary Cooper** is pessimistic as to how a new discovery will be employed. *Cloak and Dagger* (1946, United States Pictures-Warner Bros.).

3517 "Come nearer. Let me look at you. Come close. Look at me. You aren't afraid of a woman who has never seen the sun since before you were born?" **Martita Hunt**, as eccentric Miss Havisham, welcomes Anthony Wager, as Pip, to the dark, dirty, and decaying great room of her uncared for mansion. *Great Expectations* (1946, GB, Rank).

3518 "Oh, it's you. You quite frightened me." **Rhonda Fleming** recognizes someone the audience doesn't see. It will be the last person she will ever see. *The Spiral Staircase* (1946, RKO).

3519 "I've been afraid of half the things I've ever done." **Robert Mitchum** boasts that fear hasn't prevented him from doing things, such as running off with mobster Kirk Douglas' mistress Jane Greer. *Out of the Past* (1947, RKO).

3520 "I'd like you to know what death looks like, then you'll not be frightened of it ever." **Irene Dunne** explains to her daughter Barbara Bel Geddes why she is being taken to visit a dying uncle. *I Remember Mama* (1948, RKO).

3521 "Henry, there's someone on the stairs." Semi-invalid **Barbara Stanwyck** talks on the phone to her husband Burt Lancaster as she hears the steps of the killer Lancaster has hired coming to get her. *Sorry, Wrong Number* (1948, Paramount).

3522 "I'm always scared." Tough marine Sergeant **John Wayne** confesses he's not fearless. *The Sands of Iwo Jima* (1949, Republic).

3523 "There's only two things in this world that scares me and a 'good woman' is both of 'em." In 1850, Indian scout **Robert Taylor** is hired by John McIntire to lead 150 "good women" to California to become wives of lonely men working there. *Westward the Women* (1951, MGM).

3524 DEATH: "Are you prepared?" KNIGHT: "The body is frightened, but I am not." DEATH: "Well, there's no shame in that." **Bengt Ekerot** has come to collect **Max von Sydow**. *The Seventh Seal* (1957, Sweden, Svensk Filmindustri).

3525 "Well, it's just that we're so frightened of other people, and we've somehow managed to forget our fright when we've been in each other's company. Speaking for myself, I'm grateful. I—I always will be." **David Niven** thanks Deborah Kerr for her company. *Separate Tables* (1958, United Artists).

3526 ANTONINUS: "Are you afraid to die, Spartacus?" SPARTACUS: "No more than I was to be born." In answering **Tony Curtis**' question about fear, **Kirk Douglas** claims that for a slave, death is nothing to fear. *Spartacus* (1960, Universal).

3527 "You're afraid to stick out your chin and say 'Okay, life's a fact.'" **George Peppard** tongue-lashes Audrey Hepburn for preferring to live in a fantasy world of her own making. *Breakfast at Tiffany's* (1961, Paramount).

3528 "Honey, we gotta go some time, reason or no reason. Dyin's as natural as livin.' Man who's afraid to die is too afraid to live, far as I've ever seen. . . I know how to live." Ironically, fearless **Clark Gable**, as the aging cowboy, has a fatal heart attack on the day the film is wrapped up, and fearful Marilyn Monroe, as the divorcee benefiting from his wisdom, never makes another released film before her death the next year. *The Misfits* (1961, United Artists).

3529 "If I'd made love to you, I'd have felt guilty—guilty of desecration. Yes, isn't that funny? I'm more afraid of your soul than you're afraid of my body." In 1916 Mississippi, young physician **Laurence Harvey** confesses to spinster Geraldine Page who is in love with him. *Summer and Smoke* (1961, Paramount).

3530 "She's not afraid of losing Mitch. She's afraid of being abandoned." **Suzanne Pleshette** tells Tippi Hedren about Rod Taylor's widowed mother Jessica Tandy. *The Birds* (1963, Universal).

3531 "Oh, people are scared, all right. But they're not scared of you. They're scared of what you represent to them, and what you represent to them is freedom. Oh, they say they're free, but talking about it, that's two different things. Being bought and sold in the marketplace, it's real hard to be free. Course, don't ever tell anybody they're not free, 'cause they're gonna get real busy killin' and maimin' just to prove to you that they are." Drunken Southern lawyer **Jack Nicholson** gives a counterculture speech to counterculture types Peter Fonda and Dennis Hopper. *Easy Rider* (1969, Columbia).

3532 MRS. HOCHEISER: "You almost scared me to death." GORDON HOCHEISER: "Almost is not good enough." **Ruth Gordon** punches her son **George Segal** in the groin when he races in her room one morning wearing a gorilla suit. *Where's Poppa?* (1970, United Artists).

3533 "I am miserly and cheap, a penny pinching. . . I enjoy looking at my face in the mirror. I am not afraid of death. . . but I am afraid of murder." Wiretap expert **Gene Hackman** muses to himself about himself. *The Conversation* (1974, Paramount).

3534 "Scared? I'm growing beak and feathers!" Russian Jewish peasant **Woody Allen** admits his fear as he awaits the entrance of Napoleon. *Love and Death* (1975, United Artists).

3535 "We're going away to another place where a man isn't crowded and can come into his own. We're not little men and there's nothing we're afraid of." **Michael Caine** boasts for himself and Sean Connery, as they take their leave of Christopher Plummer, as Rudyard Kipling. They hope to find adventure and riches in some distant part of India. *The Man Who Would Be King* (1975, Columbia).

3536 "I'm not afraid of any man, but when it comes to sharing my feelings with a woman, my stomach turns to jelly." Bare-knuckles fighter and truckdriver **Clint Eastwood** admits his fear of women to his best friend, an orangutan named Clyde. *Every Which Way But Loose* (1978, Warner Bros.).

3537 "My dick has stage fright, man." Pothead **Cheech Marin** explains to police Sergeant Stacy Keach why he's unable to relieve himself for a urinalysis test. *Up in Smoke* (1978, Paramount).

3538 "I've always been scared to death you'd get old before I grew up." **Amy Irving** tells Willie Nelson that she's loved him since she was a child. *Honeysuckle Rose* (1980, Warner Bros.).

3539 "To truly love a woman, a man must be afraid of her. . . . Woman is nature, who dispenses pleasure and pain." Nineteenth century kinky novelist Dr. Leopold von Sacher-Masoch, played by **Paolo Malco**, oversees the evolution of his wife Francesca de Sapio from a tease to a dominatrix. *Masoch* (1980, Italy, Difilm-Tierrepi).

3540 "It was fear that first brought gods into the world." **Richard Harris** likes to sprinkle little gems of wisdom as he treks through remote parts of Africa seeking the great white ape, Tarzan. *Tarzan, the Ape Man* (1981, MGM-United Artists).

3541 "Quite an experience to live in fear, isn't it? That's what it is like to be a slave." Android **Rutger Hauer** checks on Harrison Ford, sent to eliminate Hauer, as Ford clings to a building ledge by his fingers. *Blade Runner* (1982, Warner Bros.).

3542 "Now they'll know why they're afraid of the dark. Now they'll find why they're afraid of the night." Evil cult leader **James Earl Jones** vows revenge on escaping Arnold Schwarzenegger and his friends. *Conan the Barbarian* (1982, Universal).

3543 "I'm afraid—I don't want to lose what I got." **Sylvester Stallone** is afraid after losing a boxing match with Mr. T. *Rocky III* (1982, United Artists).

3544 "I was sent there because I was afraid." Catholic Polish citizen **Meryl Streep** explains why she and her children were sent to Auschwitz by the Nazis. *Sophie's Choice* (1982, Universal).

3545 "Will I die of fear? Must I be sick on the stage? I have a bucket in the wings. . . . Whether I work or 'rest.'" Alcoholic actress **Ingrid Thulin** lives in self-disgust. *After the Rehearsal* (1984, Sweden, Triumph).

3546 "If all Russians could eat moo-shoo pork, they wouldn't be afraid of the Chinese!" Russian defector **Robin Williams** makes a suggestion for improving international relations. *Moscow on the Hudson* (1984, Columbia).

3547 "I like being scared. It keeps me awake." **Aidan Quinn**, a boy from the wrong side of the tracks, shares his belief with Daryl Hannah, a girl from a "good" family. *Reckless* (1984, MGM-United Artists).

3548 "I don't even look at mens. That's the truth. I look at women, tho, cause I'm not scared of them." In all of her life, **Whoopi Goldberg**'s character never met a man who didn't use and abuse her. *The Color Purple* (1985, Warner Bros.).

3549 "These kind and likeable men. . . have another side to their nature and that is they are very limited in their ideas, they are frightened of the unknown, they want a quiet life where sex is either sport or duty but absolutely nothing in between, and they simply wouldn't agree to sleep with me if they knew it was a child I was after." **Meryl Streep** explains to Sting why she can't turn to the friends of her class to father a child for her without benefit of marriage or commitment. *Plenty* (1985, 20th Century-Fox-RKO).

3550 "There's nothing there. There's nothing to be scared of, all right. You don't have to be afraid. You don't have to be afraid anymore." Young psychiatrist **Bruce Abbott** comforts Jennifer Rubin, who 15 years earlier as a 13-year-old, survived a suicide ceremony of members of a Jim Jones—like religious cult. *Bad Dreams* (1988, 20th Century-Fox).

3551 "I tell you what you are. I have no choice, you frighten me. . . . But I guess we're stuck with each other." Talk show host **Eric Bogosian** repudiates his listeners. *Talk Radio* (1988, Universal).

3552 "No, no. I was scared because I was happy. I felt like this burden had been lifted off my shoulders." **Kathleen Turner** admits that the reason she didn't appear at the hospital where her husband Michael Douglas thought he was having a heart attack was because she was scared of her feelings of elation that she'd be rid of him. *The War of the Roses* (1989, 20th Century-Fox).

3553 "Tell me what you really desire, and what you really fear." Sadistic sociopath **Rob Lowe** "seduces" cowardly financial analyst James Spader. *Bad Influence* (1990, Triumph).

3554 CONNIE: "They fear you!" MICHAEL: "They ought to fear you." Both **Talia Shire** and her brother **Al Pacino** put the fear of God into their enemies, because they will do anything to protect the Family. *The Godfather, Part III* (1990, Paramount).

3555 "I'm not a movie star type. You'll never know the fear of losing someone like me, if you're someone like me." Sad case **Kathy Bates** tells her tale of woe to her patient and captive, romance writer James Caan. *Misery* (1990, Columbia).

3556 "You frightened me. Do it again." **Anjelica Huston** rolls her eyes at her delighted husband, Raul Julia. *The Addams Family* (1991, Paramount).

Feelings

see also ANGER, DESIRES, DESPAIR AND DESPERATION, EMOTIONS, FEARS, HAPPINESS AND UNHAPPINESS, HATE AND HATRED, LOVE AND HATE, LOVE AND LOVERS, LUST, PAINS, PASSION

3557 QUEEN CHRISTINA: "We might have been born in different centuries." DON ANTONIO DE LA PRADA: "No, I would never have permitted that. We're inevitable. Don't you feel it?" Swedish queen **Greta Garbo** and Spanish ambassador **John Gilbert** share an idyllic, but short love affair. *Queen Christina* (1933, MGM).

3558 "You know I have the strangest feeling. I feel as if I was only going to see you about five minutes all the rest of my life. . . I never had a feeling like this before. . . it's just so, that's all. . . you're never coming here again. . . . Why, it's all over isn't it?" **Katharine Hepburn** sadly realizes that her pretensions have probably driven wealthy beau Fred MacMurray away for good. In Booth Tarkington's novel, that's exactly what happened, but the film has a happy ending. *Alice Adams* (1935, RKO).

3559 "I don't know what it is that gives me a queer feeling when I look at you." **Brian Aherne**'s line to Katharine Hepburn, disguised as a boy, brings down the house. *Sylvia Scarlett* (1936, RKO).

3560 "I told myself that I was a civilized woman and it didn't matter. But you only say these things with your mind—not with your feelings." Semi-invalid **Frieda Inescort** struggles to keep her composure as she talks to Kay Francis, who is having an affair with the former's husband Patric Knowles. *Give Me Your Heart* (1936, Warner Bros.).

3561 "First you ask me, then you tell me, then you don't tell me anything at all. My feelings is hoit." Mobster **Humphrey Bogart** tells James Cagney of his growing disaffection. *The Roaring Twenties* (1939, Warner Bros.).

3562 "Did you ever get the feeling that you wanted to stay, and still get the feeling that you wanted to go?" **Jimmy Durante**, as Banjo, supposedly based on Harpo Marx, delivers one of his more famous lines. *The Man Who Came to Dinner* (1941, Warner Bros.).

3563 "The wow finish: A guy standing on a station platform in the rain with a comical look on his face, because his insides have been kicked out. . . ." **Humphrey Bogart** tells Ingrid Bergman how he felt when she stood him up at the train station in Paris. *Casablanca* (1942, Warner Bros.).

3564 KAREN BENTLEY: "Do you know how it feels to be followed and hounded and watched every second?" LARRY HAINES: "I used to, but now I pay cash for everything." Beautiful blonde spy **Madeleine Carroll** can't get a straight answer from burlesque comedian **Bob Hope**. *My Favorite Blonde* (1942, Paramount).

3565 "I've got no more feelings about it than if they had been flies on a pile of manure." **Alan Ladd** is at peace after killing Japanese soldiers who slaughtered a Chinese family, including a baby. *China* (1943, Paramount).

3566 "For one hour, I felt what it feels to be high-regarded." Gentle drifter and inept cowboy **Gary Cooper** becomes a temporary hero, even though he can't handle a gun. *Along Came Jones* (1945, RKO).

3567 "I caught the blackjack right behind my ear. A black pool opened up at my feet. I dived in. It had no bottom. I felt pretty good—like an amputated leg." Narrator **Dick Powell** describes his feelings as he's knocked out. *Murder, My Sweet* (1945, RKO).

3568 "How does it feel dying in the middle of somebody else's dirty love affair?" Tough cop **Lloyd Nolan** aims to kill Robert Montgomery who has barged in just as Nolan is finishing off Jayne Meadows, who dumped him. *Lady in the Lake* (1946, MGM).

3569 "I read in a book once, to hunt and to conquer, to kill—the savagery of it—brings emotions that are tied in with—well, the feelings that make a man a man and a woman a woman." Married **Joan Bennett** comes on strongly to African safari guide and great white hunter **Gregory Peck**. *The Macomber Affair* (1947, United Artists).

3570 "Even when I was making love to you, I had the feeling that you were wondering what time it was." Magazine writer **Robert Montgomery** bickers constantly with his colleague Bette Davis. *June Bride* (1948, Warner Bros.).

3571 JOHN FORBES: "I feel like a wheel within a wheel within a wheel." SUE FORBES: "You and fifty million others. You're John Forbes, average American, backbone of the country." JOHN: "I don't want to be. What would happen if just once, I didn't walk through the door of Olympic Insurance?" Average Joe **Dick Powell** can't get his practical wife Jane Wyatt to appreciate his feelings that his life is meaningless and he's going nowhere. Soon he will experience another life, another woman—and wish he was back the way he was. *Pitfall* (1948, United Artists).

3572 "An immaculate murder. We've killed for the sake of danger and the sake of killing. . . . How did you feel during it? I felt tremendous, exhilarated." Words rush from **John Dall** to his lover Farley Granger after they have committed a thrill murder. *Rope* (1948, Warner Bros.).

3573 "Amongst ourselves we were unendingly cheerful, but what each man feels in his heart I can only guess." In voice-over, **John Mills**, as British explorer Robert Scott, speaks lines from his diary about his small band of doomed men. *Scott of the Antarctic* (1948, GB, Ealing).

3574 "Psychologically, I'm very confused but personally I feel just wonderful." **Judy Garland** has just discovered that her pen pal whom she has come to love is none other than Van Johnson, the man she works and frequently argues with. *In the Good Old Summertime* (1949, MGM).

3575 "I don't want to have to come through back doors or feel lower than other people." Light-skinned **Susan Kohner** tells her black mother, Juanita Moore, why she's trying to pass for white. *Imitation of Life* (1959, Universal-International).

3576 "The 'blues' are because you're getting fat or maybe it's been raining too long. You're just sad, that's all. The 'mean reds' are horrible. Suddenly you're afraid, and you don't know what you're afraid of. Did you ever get that feeling?. . . Well, when I get it, the only thing that does any good is to jump into a cab and go to Tiffany's. Calms me down right away. The quietness and the proud look of it. Nothing very bad could happen to you there." **Audrey Hepburn** tells George Peppard about her color-coded feelings. *Breakfast at Tiffany's* (1961, Paramount).

3577 "It's a great feeling, boy, it's a really great feeling when you're right, and you know you're right. Like all of a sudden I got oil in my arm. Pool cue is part of me. You know pool cue has got nerves in it. It's a piece of wood, but it's got nerves in it. You can feel the roll of those balls. You don't have to look. You just know. You make shots that nobody's ever made before. And you play the game the way nobody ever played it before." **Paul Newman** describes for Piper Laurie the ecstasy one feels when something he does is just so right. *The Hustler* (1961, 20th Century-Fox).

3578 "If I could just feel complete." **Julie Christie** is starved for meaningful companionship. *Darling* (1965, GB, Anglo-Amalgamated).

3579 "Mrs. Prentice says that like her husband, I'm a burnt-out old shell of a man who cannot even remember what it's like to love a woman. . . . You're wrong as you can be. . . I know exactly how he feels about her and there's absolutely nothing that your son feels for my daughter that I don't feel for Christina. Old? Yes. Burnt-out? Certainly. But I can tell you the memories are still there. Clear. Intact. Indestructible. And they'll be there if I live to be 110. Where John made his mistake, I think, was in the attaching so much importance to what her mother and I might think. . . the only thing that matters is what they feel and how much they feel for each other. And if it's half of what we felt, then that is everything." **Spencer Tracy** strongly disagrees with Beah Richards, as he affirms his love for wife Katharine Hepburn and wishes the same for his daughter Katharine Houghton and her intended, Richards and Roy E. Glenn, Sr.'s son, black doctor Sidney Poitier. It's the romantic in us that makes us want to believe that Tracy, suspecting the end was near, wished to go on record and on film to state how much Hepburn meant to him. On another level, the film, praised for its message of racial tolerance and understanding at the time of its release, seems an embarrassment and a cop-out today. *Guess Who's Coming to Dinner* (1967, Columbia).

3580 "He'll feel a lot better once we robbed a couple of banks." **Paul Newman** notices that Robert Redford looks a mite peaked since they arrived in Bolivia. *Butch Cassidy and the Sundance Kid* (1969, 20th Century-Fox).

3581 "A person [who] has no love for himself, no respect for himself, no love for his friends, family, workers—how can he ask for love in return?" **Susan Anspach** doubts that Jack Nicholson is capable of having any real feelings for anyone or anything. *Five Easy Pieces* (1970, Columbia).

3582 ALLAN FELIX: "You were wonderful last night. . . . How do you feel now?" LINDA CHRISTIE: "I think the Pepto-Bismol helped." **Woody Allen** and **Diane Keaton** have some post-coital conversation after making love for the first time. *Play It Again, Sam* (1972, Paramount).

3583 "I think it's loathsome that we sleep together. I feel like a you-know-what." College coed **Susan Dey**'s strict upbringing makes her feel cheap when she has an affair with William Katt. *First Love* (1977, Paramount).

3584 "There's nothing wrong with feeling lonely. Or depressed. Or angry. Or anything. They're feelings. Sometimes I feel good, sometimes I feel lousy. But I'm not ashamed of how I feel." **Penelope Russianoff** shares some words of wisdom with Jill Clayburgh who claims she's lonely since her husband left her for a younger woman. *An Unmarried Woman* (1978, 20th Century-Fox).

3585 "I'm fine. I'm always fine. I'm a horse." It's **Sally Field**'s resilient answer anytime she's asked how she's feeling. Actually, she's more like a pony. *Norma Rae* (1979, 20th Century-Fox).

3586 "I feel like a walk-on in a dirty movie." **Ed Winter** arrives to find his daughter Bo Derek, her college professor lover, his wife, and her lover all sharing the same ski cottage in Vermont. *A Change of Seasons* (1980, 20th Century-Fox).

3587 "Feel the flow, feel the Force around you." **Frank Oz**, the voice of Yoda, urges on his pupil Mark Hamill. *The Empire Strikes Back* (1980, 20th Century-Fox).

3588 NED RACINE: "I like this place. It's got a nice feel." MATTY WALKER: "You were on top." Yes, **William Hurt** and **Kathleen Turner** are speaking of what you think they are. *Body Heat* (1981, Warner Bros.).

3589 "I guess I gotta feel good about something I do." Border patrolman **Jack Nicholson** answers why he goes to near fatal lengths to help Mexican Elpidia Carrillo, who has lost her baby to an adoption ring. *The Border* (1982, Universal).

3590 "Ever get the feeling there's something going on we don't know about?" **Kevin Bacon**'s heartbreakingly funny question doesn't evoke much of a response from quasi-rebel Mickey Rourke. *Diner* (1982, MGM-United Artists).

3591 "Now I know how Mr. Churchill will feel when he faces Josef Stalin." Actor **Edward Fox** plays Iago to Albert Finney's Othello. *The Dresser* (1983, GB, Columbia).

3592 "It's no secret how I feel about you. A blind person could see that." Former country and western singing star **Robert Duvall** declares his love for widow Tess Harper. *Tender Mercies* (1983, EMI-Universal).

3593 "Do you know what it is when you feel something for somebody and don't know what it is because if you knew what it was you wouldn't feel it anymore?" **Rae Dawn Chong** forms a very convoluted question for radio sex therapist Dr. Love, played by Genevieve Bujold. *Choose Me* (1984, Island Alive).

3594 "I don't feel things I want to feel anymore. I don't feel the intensity." **Marissa Chibas** tells her psychiatrist Marcia Jean Kurtz that there's something missing in her feelings. *Cold Feet* (1984, Cinecom).

3595 "Yuk! He slimed me. I feel so funky. . . I feel like the floor of a taxi cab." **Bill Murray** has been slimed by an unfriendly spirit. *Ghostbusters* (1984, Columbia).

3596 "You don't understand how I feel. I'm standing there with my pants down and my crotch hung out for all the world to see and three guys sticking it to me and a bunch of other guys yelling and clapping and you're standing there telling me that's the best you can do. If that's the best you can do, then your best sucks. Now I don't know what you got for selling me out but I sure as shit hope it's worth it." Enraged rape victim **Jodie Foster** rails at prosecutor Kelly McGillis who allowed the guys who gang raped Foster in a crowded saloon to plead guilty to a lesser charge because McGillis didn't think Foster would be believed in court because of her promiscuous past. *The Accused* (1988, Paramount).

3597 "Most people don't know how they're going to feel from one minute to the next. But a dope fiend has a pretty good idea. All you gotta do is look at the labels on the little bottles." In voice-over, **Matt Dillon** tells the good news of drug addiction. *Drugstore Cowboy* (1989, Avenue).

3598 "People think just because you're beautiful and popular, life is easy and fun. No one understood that I had feelings too." It's the suicide note that Winona Ryder writes for **Kim Walker** after Ryder and Christian Slater feed Walker a poisonous concoction. *Heathers* (1989, New World).

3599 "They tell you for the first time that you have a brother and I don't see in your face one little reaction. I'm not saying joy, I'm just saying something. You're using Raymond, Charlie. You're using me. You use everybody." **Valeria Golino** accuses her hustler lover, Tom Cruise, of having no feelings for people. *Rain Man* (1989, MGM-United Artists).

3600 "If I'd known we were going to cast our feelings into words, I'd have memorized the Song of Solomon." **Gabriel Byrne** responds when for the third or fourth time Marcia Gay Harden tells him what a heartless bastard he is. *Miller's Crossing* (1990, 20th Century-Fox).

3601 JOHNNY: "Something's going on between us, something important. Don't you feel it?" FRANKIE: "I don't know what I feel." JOHNNY: "You don't want to feel it. We're talking about two people coming together; sure it's a little scary, but it's fucking wonderful too." **Al Pacino** urges **Michelle Pfeiffer** to admit to herself and to him that she's falling in love with him. *Frankie and Johnny* (1991, Paramount).

3602 "I feel like a used pair of pantyhose at a yard sale." **Tanya Roberts** runs a bar with an illegal medium-stakes poker game running in the back room. She's also involved in the L.A. drug trade. *Legal Tender* (1991, Prism).

3603 "I feel awake. I don't ever remember feeling this awake." **Geena Davis** enjoys the moment as she and Susan Sarandon cruise along an empty canyon highway in their blue T-bird. *Thelma & Louise* (1991, MGM-Pathé).

Feet *see* BODIES, SHOES

Feminism *see* EQUALITIES, FAIRNESS AND UNFAIRNESS, MEN, MEN AND WOMEN, RIGHTS, WOMEN

Fiction

see also BOOKS, IMAGINATION, STORIES, THEATERS, TRUTH, WRITING AND WRITERS

3604 "This story of Peggy Eaton and her times is not presented as a precise account of either—rather as fiction founded upon historical fact." The meaning of this mumble-jumble, apologetic foreword is that the film is pure fiction, and no one is left alive to sue. *The Gorgeous Hussy* (1936, MGM).

3605 "If all the characters in this film were not fictitious—it would be alarming." The film's foreword. *Brothers-in-Law* (1957, GB, British Lion).

3606 "I've met the most wonderful man. Of course, he's fictional—but you can't have everything." Dewy-eyed **Mia Farrow** sighs to her sister, Stephanie Farrow, about her movie character lover, Jeff Daniels. *The Purple Rose of Cairo* (1985, Orion).

Fidelity *see* INFIDELITIES, LOVE AND LOVERS, MARRIAGES, PROMISCUITY, TRUST

Fights and Fighting

see also ARGUMENTS, BATTLES AND BATTLEFIELDS, ENEMIES, WARS, WEAPONS, WOUNDS AND SCARS

3607 MATT NOLAN: "For two cents I'd knock the ears off ya." SUE REILLY: "For less than that I'd slap your face." MATT: "Go ahead. I'll give ya the first punch." **James Cagney** is fresh with **Loretta Young**, who takes him up on his offer and slugs him. *Taxi* (1932, Warner Bros.).

3608 ELENA: "There'd be no more wars if nations would mind their own business." STEPHEN LOCKE: "And abandon their friends." ELENA: "If England had starved in the trenches as Russia had, and fought with shells filled with sawdust, I'd like to know what she'd do." STEPHEN: "Shall I tell you? She'd go on fighting—for humanity." Lenin's secretary **Kay Francis** expresses her political differences with her lover, British Consul-General **Leslie Howard**, over England's interference with Russia's plans to withdraw from World War I. *British Agent* (1934, Warner Bros.).

3609 "He starts fights and I finish them." **Fred MacMurray**, bodyguard to Robert Young, explains his duties to Claudette Colbert. *The Bride Came Home* (1935, Paramount).

3610 "Back on my ranch I've got a little red rooster and little brown hen. They fight all the time, too, but every once in awhile they make up and they're right friendly." Oklahoma rancher **Ralph Bellamy** compares the battling of Cary Grant and his ex-wife Irene Dunne to some poultry. *The Awful Truth* (1937, Columbia).

3611 "Lemme sock you just once—just once on the jaw—and I won't care what happens." **Carole Lombard** swings wildly at Fredric March just before he creams her with a solid right to the head, knocking her out. Such playful lovers. *Nothing Sacred* (1937, Selznick-United Artists).

3612 "That's when you've got to fight them." It's **Orson Welles**' stern reply to his second wife,

Dorothy Comingore, who begs to be allowed to quit trying to make it as an opera singer because the audiences "don't like me." *Citizen Kane* (1941, RKO).

3613 "Addie said there were people who ate the earth and other people who stood around and watch them do it. And just now Uncle Ben said the same thing. . . . Well, tell him for me, Mama, I'm not going to stand around and watch you do it. I'll be fighting as hard as he'll be fighting someplace else." **Teresa Wright** defiantly announces that she's leaving her mother Bette Davis and the latter's two corrupt brothers. Wright rightly suspects that Davis deliberately withheld her husband's medicine until it was too late to save him. *The Little Foxes* (1941, Goldwyn-RKO).

3614 RIO: "Let me go!" BILLY THE KID: "Hold still, lady, or you won't have much dress left." RIO: "Let me go!" **Jane Russell** tussles with **Jack Beutel.** As she tries to escape his grasp, her dress is all but torn off her. *The Outlaw* (1943, RKO).

3615 "The British will fight to the very last drop of French blood." Nazi sympathizer **Sydney Greenstreet** is bitterly and outspokenly against his country's alliance with Britain. *Passage to Marseille* (1943, Warner Bros.).

3616 "Don't make love to me! Don't be someone I like. . . . In my work I kiss without feeling. . . . When you fight scum you become scum." When American OSS Agent Gary Cooper attempts to embrace hardened Italian partisan **Lilli Palmer**, she pulls away, flaring up at him. *Cloak and Dagger* (1946, Warner Bros.).

3617 "I think maybe it's suddenly not having a lot of enemies to hate anymore. . . . Maybe it's because for four years now we've been focusing our minds on. . . on our little peanut. The 'win-the-war' peanut, that was over. Get it over, eat that peanut. All at once, no peanut. Now we start looking at each other again. We don't know what we're supposed to do. We don't know what's supposed to happen. We're too used to fighters! But we just don't know what to fight. You can feel tension in the air! A whole lot of fight and hate that doesn't know where to go. A guy like you maybe starts hatin' himself and starts likin' things again." **Sam Levene** claims that war allowed people filled with hate to fight and kill legitimate targets, and now that the war is over, these types feel lost. Levene's analysis is lost on psychoneurotically disturbed Robert Ryan. *Crossfire* (1947, RKO).

3618 "I fought for you once when I started out. I fought in many places like yours. And they're all the same—dirty holes for infirmaries, butchers instead of doctors, oxen for bulls. Drunks throwing cushions and bottles. I fought in many places like yours, and I've got the scars to prove it." Matador **Mel Ferrer** refuses small-time bull ring owner Thomas Gomez's offer of a contract. *The Brave Bulls* (1951, Columbia).

3619 "If Kane was my man, I'd never leave him. I'd get a gun and fight." Gary Cooper's former mistress **Katy Juardo** advises his young Quaker bride, Grace Kelly, to stand by her man as he faces four gunmen. *High Noon* (1952, Kramer-United Artists).

3620 "That is an emotional and ill-considered figure of speech. If I were 'the last man on the earth' and there were a million women left, you'd be fighting tooth and claw with every single one of 'em for the privilege of becoming my mate. You'd be panting to repopulate the world." Maggie McNamara tells **David Niven** that she wouldn't have him if he was the last man on the earth. He disagrees. *The Moon Is Blue* (1953, United Artists).

3621 "There's too many, Shane!" **Brandon De Wilde** begs Alan Ladd to retreat from the barroom where he's about to be given a beating by a gang of cowboys in a decidedly unfair fight. *Shane* (1953, Paramount).

3622 "It's what it was all about in the first place." **Ward Bond** and the other townspeople decide to allow Joan Crawford and Mercedes McCambridge to settle their fight in a gun-toting show-down. *Johnny Guitar* (1954, Republic).

3623 "Don't fight him down here in the jungle 'cause that's just what he wants." Priest **Karl Malden** wants longshoreman Marlon Brando to smash corrupt union leader Lee J. Cobb's stranglehold on the docks by testifying before a crime commission. Cobb's goons have just killed one of their own, Brando's brother Rod Steiger. *On the Waterfront* (1954, Columbia).

3624 "You ever try to fight thirty-five guys at the same time, Teach?" Tough punk **Vic Morrow** menacingly threatens English teacher Glenn Ford. *The Blackboard Jungle* (1955, MGM).

3625 "Yes, you are hard. You are showing your fighting face, the wounding words, barbed like arrows. . . I remember hearing Father say you were the toughest fighter in the family since Peter the Great. . . ." **Ingrid Bergman**, who claims to be the daughter of the last Czar, speaks harshly to Helen Hayes, the dowager empress. *Anastasia* (1956, 20th Century-Fox).

3626 "I wish to God someone loved me enough to hit me. You and Rubin fight. Oh, God, I'd like a good fight. Anything'd be better than this nothing. Morris and I go around being so sweet to each other, but sometimes I wonder if maybe he'd like to kill me." **Eve Arden** describes the emptiness of her marriage to Frank Overton to her younger sister, Dorothy McGuire. *The Dark at the Top of the Stairs* (1956, Warner Bros.).

3627 "All my life I've been fighting and all my life I've got into trouble from it." **Paul Newman**, as Rocky Graziano, finds it difficult to believe that he can make money from fighting. *Somebody Up There Likes Me* (1956, MGM).

3628 "I lose round one, but it's going to be a long fight, a long one." **James Cagney** confidently warns Shirley Jones who has repulsed his proposition. *Never Steal Anything Small* (1958, Universal-International).

3629 "Gentlemen, this is outrageous. I have never heard of such behavior in the War Room before!" U.S. President **Peter Sellers** scolds General George C. Scott and Russian Ambassador Peter Bull for fighting. *Dr. Strangelove: Or, How I Learned to Stop Worrying and Love the Bomb* (1963, Columbia).

3630 "Martha and I are merely exercising, that's all. We're merely walking what's left of our wits. Don't pay any attention." What **Richard Burton** and Elizabeth Taylor are doing is fighting—that's what. *Who's Afraid of Virginia Woolf?* (1966, Warner Bros.).

3631 "You can't go to sleep now. We're having a fight." Exasperated young bride **Jane Fonda** demands the attention of her new husband Robert Redford, who has decided he'd rather sleep than fight. *Barefoot in the Park* (1967, Paramount).

3632 PRINCE JOHN: "I'm vilifying you, mother. For God's sake, pay attention." QUEEN ELEANOR OF AQUITAINE: "Hush, dear, mother's fighting." **Nigel Terry** can't quite get his mother **Katharine Hepburn**'s attention. She's busy in a dispute with her husband and his father, Peter O'Toole as King Henry II. *The Lion in Winter* (1968, GB, Avco Embassy).

3633 "And don't pout. If you wanna fight, we'll fight. But don't pout. Fighting, I win. Pouting, you win." **Walter Matthau** once again is outraged by Jack Lemmon's compulsive behavior. *The Odd Couple* (1968, Paramount).

3634 "You can't fight a tidal wave." **Ryan O'Neal** knows he's no match for the romantic pursuit of kooky Barbra Streisand. *What's Up, Doc?* (1972, Warner Bros.).

3635 "You can't fight in the court. You've got to go to the streets, man the barricades, man the dynamite, blow up the cesspool.... We are in for a depression that will make the thirties seem like paradise. Maybe it's a good thing. The hard hats and the phony liberals will kill each other." Bitter old socialist **Herbert Berghof** gets fired up when Art Carney tells him that the latter is being evicted and he will have to get a lawyer to fight it. *Harry and Tonto* (1974, 20th Century-Fox).

3636 "You fight like an ape. You'll never amount to anything." Manager **Burgess Meredith** harps at boxer Sylvester Stallone whose main talent in the ring is the ability to take a lot of punishment. *Rocky* (1976, United Artists).

3637 "When they wreck everything you've got, you'll see there's no way you can win. You end up saying to yourself, what am I fighting for? That's what they count on. They figure sooner or later you'll give up. But if you're gonna do that, you might as well be dead. I can't give up. I never learned how." In a confusing bomb, convicted murderer **Gene Hackman** is recruited by a mysterious organization, bent on political assassination. *The Domino Principle* (1977, Associated General Films).

3638 "I'm fighting for this woman's life, not her temporal innocence." Mother superior **Anne Bancroft** argues with court appointed psychiatrist Jane Fonda over naïve novice nun Meg Tilly. *Agnes of God* (1985, Columbia).

3639 SALLY ANN: "Polly got in one good peck before the cat killed her." HUGH: "I didn't know Polly had such a big pecker." Actually **Candy Clark** and **James Naughton** are wrong in believing that Polly the parakeet was killed by an adorable alley cat—it was a hideous troll. *Cat's Eye* (1985, MGM-United Artists).

3640 "I'm no Red. I just fight for what I believe in." It's the time of the Great Depression and **Ray Wise** is accused of being a trouble-making communist. *The Journey of Natty Gann* (1985, Buena Vista).

3641 "We are fighting for men and women whose poetry has not yet been written." During the Civil War, **Matthew Broderick**, as the commanding officer of the 54th Regiment, the first black battalion, writes to his mother about the war to end slavery in the United States. *Glory* (1989, Tri-Star).

3642 "I want you to get this straight.... All the teachers here are here because they care... about those children out there. This is their fight, they are in it with you, they take it home at night the same as you. You are part of those children's lives. You are thoughtless and cruel... and it hurts... and none of them deserve it.... They are sick of it and so am I." Vice Principal **Beverly Todd** plays a sort of Fletcher Christian to Principal Morgan Freeman's Captain Bligh. *Lean on Me* (1989, Warner Bros.).

3643 "This ain't my life, it's yours, and if you're not going to fight for it, goddamn it, neither am I." Psychiatrist **John Heard** exhibits a decidedly unprofessional attitude toward his group therapy patients. *The End of Innocence* (1991, Skouras).

3644 "I want this brigand found! Slaughter their... livestock. I want Locksley's own people fighting to bring his head in." **Alan Rickman**, as the Sheriff of Nottingham, shouts his orders to his henchman Michael Wincott, as Guy of Gisborne. *Robin Hood: The Prince of Thieves* (1991, Warner Bros.).

Figures *see* BODIES

Filthiness

see also CORRUPTION, GARBAGE, WASTE AND WASTEFULNESS

3645 "You are the real filth, men who do the work of fascists and pretend to themselves they are better than those for whom they work." **Walter Huston** shoots Erich von Stroheim, claiming the latter is worse than any Nazi because he knows what he's doing is wrong and yet he countenances it. *The North Star* (1943, RKO).

3646 KYLE HADLEY: "You're a filthy liar." MARYLEE HADLEY: "I'm filthy, period." **Robert Stack** doesn't tell his nymphomaniac sister **Dorothy Malone** anything she doesn't already believe about herself. He attacks her for suggesting that his wife Lauren Bacall is having an affair with his friend Rock Hudson. *Written on the Wind* (1956, Universal-International).

3647 "Dirty old men seem to get away with more." **Robert Redford** is not as taken with their upstairs neighbor, debonair and strange Charles Boyer, as is his wife Jane Fonda. *Barefoot in the Park* (1967, Paramount).

3648 "It's just filthy. People are filthy. I think that's the biggest thing that's wrong with people. I think they wouldn't be as violent if they were clean because they wouldn't have anybody to pick on." **Helena Kallianiotes** may be described as a neatness freak and an ecological maniac—

but she may not be wrong. *Five Easy Pieces* (1970, Columbia).

3649 "You're rotten, Harry.... You know why? Cause you're a man. All men are filthy. All they ever want to do is get at you.... But no more... I'm not goin' to let a man's filthy hands touch me again!" Tough-as-nails prisoner **Pam Grier** tells off horny truckdriver Sid Haig who frequently makes deliveries to the prison and has his way with some of the female cons. *The Big Doll House* (1971, New World).

3650 "Can you believe that in the middle of this filth two people can find some shred of happiness?" **Mel Brooks** speaks of himself and sexy looking bag lady Lesley Ann Warren. *Life Stinks* (1991, Pathé-MGM-United Artists).

Finance *see* BUSINESS AND COMMERCE

Finishes *see* BEGINNINGS, ENDS AND ENDINGS

Fires

3651 "You have come to a place of fire—and I think you are made of fire." Priest **C. Aubrey Smith** welcomes Marlene Dietrich to the Algerian desert. *The Garden of Allah* (1936, Selznick-United Artists).

3652 "Nothing but a fire can help that parlor." Fourth-credited **Lana Turner**, the cute second daughter of a poor but proud family, rhumbas and parades around in a scanty slip to the delight of males in the audience. *Rich Man, Poor Girl* (1938, MGM).

3653 "I'm a flaming redhead. If you play with fire, you'll get burned." Vaudeville artist **Ann Sheridan** gives fair warning. *Take Me to Town* (1953, Universal-International).

3654 "Every fire is different." Firefighter **Jim Hutton** explaining the attraction of his work in fighting oil fires to his bride-to-be Katharine Ross. *Hellfighters* (1969, Universal).

3655 "He summoned the eternal fires." **Nick Mancuso** helps scientist David Warner kill vampire bats in their caves in Arizona. Seems the rabid creatures killed Warner's father. *Nightwing* (1979, Columbia).

3656 "Hey, I tried that once. Did I ever tell you guys? Eight years old and I was into arson." **Tom Cruise** makes an impression in a small role. *Endless Love* (1981, Universal).

Firsts

see also BEGINNINGS, LASTS

3657 "Tell Me, Miss Mina, when was the first time you saw Miss Lucy—after they buried her?" What a wonderful line. **Edward Van Sloan** questions Helen Chandler about her friend Frances Dade, a victim of vampire Bela Lugosi's lust for blood. *Dracula* (1931, Universal).

3658 "This is the first time I've been out in a canoe since I saw 'The American Tragedy.'" Canoeing with Thelma Todd, **Groucho Marx** refers to the first filming of the Theodore Dreiser story in which death takes place during a canoe trip. *Horse Feathers* (1932, Paramount).

3659 "I wonder if you can understand what it means to be first." Pathfinder **Randolph Scott** tells Binnie Barnes about the joys of opening new trails. *The Last of the Mohicans* (1936, United Artists).

3660 "Why didn't you starve first?" Notorious gangster **Humphrey Bogart** demands to know why his old girlfriend Claire Trevor became a streetwalker. It was the only means she had of trying to escape from the slums they both grew up in. *Dead End* (1937, United Artists).

3661 "If two men come down, let the first go on, that'll be me." **Willie Best** tells his boss Bob Hope to catch his speed if he's chased by ghosts or gangsters. *The Ghost Breakers* (1940, Paramount).

3662 "That sofa's been there for fifteen years and no one has fallen over it before." **Eugene Pallette** is disgusted by the clumsiness of his son, Henry Fonda, helped along by a trip from Barbara Stanwyck. *The Lady Eve* (1941, Paramount).

3663 ANN WINTERS: "Somebody has to do the pioneering." FLORENCE: "Bet he doesn't want to be Daniel Boone." **Rosalind Russell** arbitrarily decides to have a three-month "trial marriage" with miner and explorer Melvyn Douglas. **Gloria Dickson** has her doubts the experiment will work. *This Thing Called Love* (1941, Columbia).

3664 "I never loved anybody before. Keep the money. But keep me too." **Ramsay Ames** knows that Gilbert Roland, the Cisco Kid, has stolen her money, but he's also stolen her heart. *Beauty and the Bandit* (1946, Monogram).

3665 "You gave me my first drink, Johnny." Lush **Claire Trevor** reminds mobster Edward G. Robinson who put her on the alcoholic track. *Key Largo* (1948, Warner Bros.).

3666 "It's never a first offense. It's just the first time they get caught." Police detective **Kirk Douglas** urges James Maloney to press charges against his young clerk Craig Hill who has embezzled money to impress a girl. Maloney is reluctant because he says it's a first offense. *Detective Story* (1951, Paramount).

3667 "You gave me a look at myself I've never had before." Ascending star **Judy Garland** thanks descending star James Mason. *A Star Is Born* (1954, Warner Bros.).

3668 "It's the first time I rode shotgun for a hearse." Still that's precisely what out-of-work gunfighter **Steve McQueen** is doing. The driver is Yul Brynner, another gunfighter in need of a job. *The Magnificent Seven* (1960, MGM).

3669 "Look, Jo, one night—well, actually, it was afternoon—I loved him. I'd never really been with a man before. It was the first time. You can remember the second time and the third time and the fourth time, but there's no time like the first. It's always there." **Dora Bryan** recalls for daughter Rita Tushingham, her father who's not been there since. *A Taste of Honey* (1961, GB, Continental Distributing).

3670 "The first time is always the best." **Barbara Jefford**, as Molly Brown, remembers the day long ago when she and Milo O'Shea, as Leopold Bloom, first made love. *Ulysses* (1967, GB, Continental Distributing).

3671 "I never hit a woman in my life until I met you." **Harry Guardino** blames his wife Anna Meara for his violence towards her. *Lovers and Other Strangers* (1970, ABC-Cinerama).

3672 "The first time I do it, I want her beautiful. I don't want to waste it on some beast." College student **Jack Nicholson** is particular about the woman to whom he will present his virginity. *Carnal Knowledge* (1971, Avco Embassy).

3673 "Let me say something I've never said to a man before—help me murder Harold." **Bette Midler** enlists Ken Wahl in a plot to kill her husband Rip Torn. *Jinxed!* (1982, MGM-United Artists).

3674 "He's never done that before. . . ." **Maggie Smith** is the most apologetic when her aged husband Trevor Howard expires in the middle of Michael Palin's fund-raising pitch. *The Missionary* (1982, GB, Hand Made Films-Columbia).

3675 ALLISON CAPULETTI: "I've never been with a man before." JULIO: "Neither have I." **Jennifer Jason Leigh** is frightened on her wedding night with new husband **Taylor Negron**. *Easy Money* (1983, Orion).

3676 "Tonight is the first night of the rest of your sex life." Amateur pimp **Anthony Edwards** points his friend John Cusack in the direction of the "sure thing," Nicollette Sheridan. *The Sure Thing* (1985, Embassy).

3677 "My doc says I got cancer. Hah, I ain't never got nothin' before." Hobo **Tom Waits** makes an almost pleased announcement. *Ironweed* (1987, Tri-Star).

3678 "Don't be offended. This really doesn't have to be the greatest experience of my life. I just want to get it over with." **Matthew Broderick** assures prostitute Park Overall that his expectations for his first sexual encounter are not very high. *Biloxi Blues* (1988, Universal).

3679 "I mean, it wasn't the first time I went to bed with a man and woke up with a note." Experienced **Susan Sarandon** accepts the disappearance of her bedmate Kevin Costner with good grace. *Bull Durham* (1988, Orion).

3680 "I think that's the first time I ever saw you smile when you mentioned your father." **Amy Madigan** smiles happily at her husband Kevin Costner who has just quoted his father about Shoeless Joe Jackson. *Field of Dreams* (1989, Universal).

3681 "When he finally pulled it out and I could look at it and touch it, I completely forgot there was a guy attached to it. I remember literally being startled when the guy spoke to me. . . . He said my hand felt good. . . and then I started moving my hand and he stopped talking." **Laura San Giacomo** describes her first encounter at age 14 with a male penis for James Spader and his video camera. *sex, lies and videotape* (1989, Miramax).

3682 "My first car was a limousine." Wealthy **Richard Gere** explains to hooker Julia Roberts why he knows so little about cars, including the Lotus he's driving so badly. *Pretty Woman* (1990, Touchstone-Buena Vista).

3683 "I think you got it backwards, pal, first you go to law school, then you become a sleazeball with no respect for anyone." Law student **James Spader** kiddingly tries to set his roommate John Cusack straight. *True Colors* (1991, Paramount).

Fish and Fishing

see also ANIMALS, BOATS AND SHIPS, FOOD AND EATING

3684 "Did anyone ever tell you you look like the Prince of Wales? I don't mean the present Prince of

Wales. One of the older Wales. And, believe me, when I say Wales I mean whales. I know a whale when I see one." **Groucho Marx** gives Margaret Dumont the run around. *The Cocoanuts* (1929, Paramount).

3685 "I could jump in the seal pond. Maybe someone would throw me a fish." Hungry and jobless **Ginger Rogers** tells her tale of woe to millionaire Walter Connolly who is dejected because his family has ignored his birthday. *Fifth Avenue Girl* (1939, RKO).

3686 "Well, man, don't stand there with half the morning gone. Get the rods. Come along, boy. Wasn't it just fine of God to make all the rivers and fill them with little fishes and then send you and me here to catch them, Andrew?" With the last lines of the movie, very old missionary to China, **Gregory Peck**, prepares to go fishing with young George Nokes. *The Keys of the Kingdom* (1944, 20th Century-Fox).

3687 "She has a dead fish where her heart ought to be.... A dead fish... with a bit of perfume." Blackmailer with a conscience **Robert Montgomery** disparages a dame he doesn't admire. *Ride the Pink Horse* (1947, Universal).

3688 "Work done by hatcheries like this doesn't just mean restocking lakes and streams. It means the sportsman and the youth of America will have a chance to get away from crowded cities and their troubles, go fishing, and enjoy the privileges our forefathers had. So good luck to you, Doc." Game warden **Roy Rogers** encourages "Doc" Dale Evans. *Susanna Pass* (1949, Republic).

3689 "If God ever wanted to be a fish, He'd be a whale. Believe that, He'd be a whale." So says **Harry Andrews**, second mate of the whaler Pequod. *Moby Dick* (1956, Warner Bros.).

3690 "It's a white whale. Skin your eyes for him." **Gregory Peck**, as Captain Ahab, tells his whaling crew to be on the lookout for the leviathan that took his leg and warped his mind. *Moby Dick* (1956, Warner Bros.).

3691 "She's so helpless, such a little fish. Throw her back into the water." **Maurice Chevalier** pleads with devil-may-care lothario Gary Cooper to spare Chevalier's naïve ingenue of a daughter Audrey Hepburn. *Love in the Afternoon* (1957, Allied Artists).

3692 "Fish, I respect you and I love you." Elderly fisherman **Spencer Tracy** speaks affectionately of the fish he struggles to catch all day and all night. *The Old Man and the Sea* (1958, Warner Bros.).

3693 "Every time I would put the line down I would say a Hail Mary, and every time I said a Hail Mary, I would catch a fish." **John Cazale** tells the secret of his success as a fisherman to his nephew James Gounaris. Knowing what's coming, Cazale is taken out fishing on Lake Tahoe by Richard Bright and is executed, but not before he says one last Hail Mary. *The Godfather, Part II* (1974, Paramount).

3694 "Fish all bathe together. Although they do tend to eat one another. I often think that fish must get tired of seafood. What are your thoughts, Hobson?" Wealthy alcoholic **Dudley Moore** doesn't have his valet and companion John Gielgud's complete attention. *Arthur* (1981, Orion-Warner Bros.).

3695 "All my life I've been waiting for someone and when I find her, she's a fish." **Tom Hanks** bemoans his fate and that of his mermaid lover Daryl Hannah. *Splash* (1984, Touchstone-Buena Vista).

3696 "What are you lookin' at? You never saw a guy who slept with a fish before? Get back to work!" **John Candy** screams to the employees of his family's food wholesaling business after his brother Tom Hanks' affair with mermaid Daryl Hannah is revealed in the newspapers. *Splash* (1984, Touchstone-Buena Vista).

3697 "Now I guess I'll go in and piss on the fish." **Michael Douglas** interrupts a dinner party being held by his estranged wife, Kathleen Turner. One of the guests follows Douglas into the kitchen and returns to suggest to the other that they pass on the fish. *The War of the Roses* (1989, 20th Century-Fox).

Flags

see also AMERICA AND AMERICANS, PATRIOTISM

3698 "I guess I was born with an American flag in my hand." If George M. Cohan, portrayed by **James Cagney**, wasn't born with an American flag in his hand, he sure knew how to make flag-waving an integral part of his musical comedy career. *Yankee Doodle Dandy* (1942, Warner Bros.).

3699 "I once fought for that flag... I'll not fire on it." Cattle baron **Lionel Barrymore** backs off from a showdown with farmers over a fence across his land when the U.S. Cavalry arrives. *Duel in the Sun* (1946, Selznick).

Flattery

see also COMPLIMENTS, PRAISES, SINCERITY, VANITIES

3700 "Don't you ever tell a girl pretty things? You know, she's got hair like the west wind, eyes like limpid pools, skin like velvet. . . ." **Gloria Grahame** unsuccessfully fishes for compliments from Glenn Ford. *The Big Heat* (1953, Columbia).

3701 "Flattery'll get you anywhere." **Jane Russell** encourages Elliott Reid. *Gentlemen Prefer Blondes* (1953, 20th Century-Fox).

3702 "Flattery is cheap, Mr. Dodd—how about a little costly truth." **Grace Kelly** tells stage director William Holden to hold the banana oil and be candid with her. *The Country Girl* (1954, Paramount).

3703 "Oh, Lord Dudley, your flattery would turn a young girl's head." It's the only line that **Rosalind Russell** has in a play, but it's enough for her to have a disastrous stage debut. *Auntie Mame* (1958, Warner Bros.).

3704 "You're a heavyweight. You're the best. You're the Yoda among cops." **Michael J. Fox**, movie cop, butters up real life cop James Woods. *The Hard Way* (1991, Universal).

Flesh *see* BODIES, HUMAN NATURE, HUMANITY, LIVES AND LIVING

Flirtations

see also KISSES AND KISSING, LOVE AND LOVERS, PROMISCUITY, SEDUCTION

3705 "So you're a little stenographer. I don't suppose you'd take dictation from me sometime?" Joan Crawford would be more than happy to oblige the flirting **John Barrymore**. *Grand Hotel* (1932, MGM).

3706 "I want more from you than flirting." Southern belle Vivien Leigh isn't used to men who don't get all flustered when she flirts with them. **Clark Gable** makes his meaning all too clear for her liking. *Gone with the Wind* (1939, Selznick-MGM).

3707 NINOTCHKA: "Must you flirt?" LEON: "Well, I don't have to do it, but I find it natural." NINOTCHKA: "Suppress it. What do you do for mankind?" LEON: "For mankind, nothing. For womankind, the outlook is not so bleak." Russian special emissary **Greta Garbo** acts as if she is annoyed by the flirting of Parisian playboy **Melvyn Douglas.** *Ninotchka* (1939, MGM).

Flowers

see also PLANTS

3708 "I want you to take five dozen roses—deep red roses—and I want you to put them in a basket and send them to Mme. Colet. . . . Charge it to Mme.

Colet." In being thoughtful in arranging for a farewell gift to be sent to wealthy Kay Francis, **Herbert Marshall** almost forgets he's a crook. *Trouble in Paradise* (1932, Paramount).

3709 "You see, when one goes to lots of parties, it is so difficult to find something new and original, something no one else would think of wearing." Gamely maintaining a good front to salvage her pride, poor girl **Katharine Hepburn** gives an imaginative excuse to a florist for choosing a simple bunch of violets when she finds she can't afford a corsage to wear to a party. *Alice Adams* (1935, RKO).

3710 "The calla lilies are in bloom again." **Katharine Hepburn**'s famous stage line, delivered in a cultured Bryn Mawr accent, delighted impressionists for years. *Stage Door* (1937, RKO).

3711 "Carnation, huh? A few nights ago we had a case with roses. Turned out very nice, very nice. But once, about three months ago, we had a very sad case—with gardenias. She waited all evening and nobody came, and when we cleaned the cafe, we found underneath one of the other tables, a gardenia. Well, you can imagine. The man must have come in, taken one look at her, and said phooey, and threw away his gardenia. . . . Listen, you have nothing to worry about, a pretty girl like you. If he doesn't come, I'll put on a carnation myself." Kindly little waiter **William Edmunds** correctly sizes up that Margaret Sullavan is waiting for a man she's never met, but who will be recognized by the carnation he wears. *The Shop Around the Corner* (1940, MGM).

3712 "That—that's the blue rose of forgetfulness. If she inhales its fragrance, she'll forget everything." **John Justin** and Sabu see June Duprez in danger by looking into the all-seeing eye. *The Thief of Bagdad* (1940, GB, London Films).

3713 "What goes to make a rose, ma'am, is breeding and budding and horse manure, if you'll pardon the expression." **Henry Travers** shares his secret for growing roses with Greer Garson. He asks her permission to name a rose that he has developed after her. *Mrs. Miniver* (1942, MGM).

3714 "You are the only woman I know who can wear an orchid. Generally, it's the orchid that wears the woman." Title character **Alexander Knox** compliments Geraldine Fitzgerald, who becomes his second wife. *Wilson* (1944, 20th Century-Fox).

3715 "Pearl, who came from down along the border, and who was like a wildflower from the hard clay, quick to blossom, quick to die." Narrator

Orson Welles relates the fate of Jennifer Jones. *Duel in the Sun* (1946, Selznick).

3716 "Among the most beautiful and wonderful of the Lord's creations are the things that grow from the earth. It is strange indeed that the verdant green of grass and leaves, the myriad colors and fragrance of flowers all mean to be solace to the soul of man can be so distorted that their very essence becomes evil. Their only use, death." Narrator **Vincent Price**, sets the stage at the beginning of the segment "Rappaccini's Daughter," in which he portrays a scientist who develops a serum so deadly that even the touching of anything, flowers or his daughter Joyce Taylor, means instant death. *Twice Told Tales* (1963, United Artists).

3717 "When a flower dies in my garden, it hurts me as if a dear friend had died." Ancient **Edith Evans** tells Deborah Kerr how much she values her flowers. We share her feelings about flowers. *The Chalk Garden* (1964, GB, Universal).

3718 "With the possible exception of fresh orange juice—and music of course, there's probably nothing in the whole world I adore more than flowers. Oh, yes, massages. Massages also. Aren't these marigolds beautiful?" **Susan Anspach** describes some of her favorite things to Jack Nicholson as she arranges flowers in a vase. *Five Easy Pieces* (1970, Columbia).

3719 "They bloom till autumn, so you'll know when summer's over, because I usually wear one of the last in my hat." **Natasha Richardson** offers a white rose to Colin Firth. *A Month in the Country* (1988, GB, Orion Classics).

3720 "What do you want? Flowers?" As she gives him the brush-off, **Sharon Stone** sheds no tears as she ends her affair with Michael Douglas. *Basic Instinct* (1992, Tri-Star).

Flying and Fliers

see also BIRDS

3721 "Penny, did you ever find someone and then all of a sudden you felt like you were taking off right into space, like a propeller going round and round and round, thirty thousand revolutions a minute, and there weren't any landing fields left in the world?" **Mickey Rooney** puts an aviation spin on his declaration of love for Judy Garland. He also asks her, "Were you ever in a rainstorm, and you felt like the only person in the world that wasn't getting wet? Did you ever look up and see a full moon, and it only looked like a half-moon to you 'cause you were looking at it alone?" *Babes on Broadway* (1941, MGM).

3722 "There is one very reassuring thing about airplanes. They always come down." **Rudy Vallee**'s pointless observation seems to suggest that he's easily reassured. *Unfaithfully Yours* (1948, 20th Century-Fox).

3723 "You can fly, you can fly, you can fly!" **Bobby Driscoll** is the voice of the boy who never grew up in this animated classic. *Peter Pan* (1953, Disney-RKO).

3724 "That's our new B forty-seven wing flying the first training mission. We'll have four full new wings by the end of the year." General **Frank Lovejoy** points out a flight of bombers, capable of delivering atomic bombs wherever the President orders them dropped, to Colonel James Stewart, a once reluctant re-tread, but now won over to his patriotic duty as a pilot of an Air Force ever alert for an enemy attack. *Strategic Air Command* (1955, Paramount).

3725 "Sure beats flying, doesn't it?" As he falls into her arms, **Cary Grant** makes the hopeful observation when Eva Marie Saint opens the bed in her tiny train compartment, where he's been hiding. *North by Northwest* (1959, MGM).

3726 "I can't make a landing and I can't get up to God." Flier **Eli Wallach** moans about the death of the old west. *The Misfits* (1961, United Artists).

3727 "They say it can't fly, but that's not the point." **Dean Stockwell**, as Howard Hughes, speaking of his Spruce Goose flying machine, empathizes with Jeff Bridges, as Preston Tucker, manufacturer of a revolutionary new automobile, which may not run. *Tucker: The Man and His Dream* (1988, Paramount).

3728 "So sit back, relax, uh, we'll do what we do best. We fly." **Mel Gibson** makes a big sacrifice by dumping an accumulation of weapons he plans to sell for a fortune in order to transport Laotian refugees in his transport plane. *Air America* (1990, Tri-Star).

Following *see* ADMIRATION, LEADERSHIP AND LEADERS

Folly *see* FAULTS, STUPIDITY

Food and Eating

see also ALCOHOL, ANIMALS, BREAKFAST, DRINKING AND DRUNKENNESS, HUMAN NATURE, HUMANITY, HUNGER, LAND AND FARMS, MOUTHS, PARTIES, RESTAURANTS, SERVANTS AND SERVITUDE, TREES, VEGETABLES AND VEGETARIANS

3729 ALBERT: "We haven't eaten since breakfast, we thought maybe you could tell us what to do about it." TJADEN: "Eat without further delay." Fresh from high school, new recruit **William Bakewell** finds that he and his other replacement soldiers can't expect much help from cynical veterans like **Slim Summerville**. *All Quiet on the Western Front* (1930, Universal).

3730 "What you've been eating? Cement?" **Jean Harlow** questions the bird as she cleans out a parrot cage. *Red Dust* (1932, MGM).

3731 "It must be the most marvelous supper. We may not eat it—but it must be marvelous." **Herbert Marshall** gives instructions to a waiter, as he prepares for an assignation with Miriam Hopkins. *Trouble in Paradise* (1932, Paramount).

3732 "If it's the wolf, we'll eat it." Hungry showgirl **Aline MacMahon** responds to a knock at the door of the apartment she shares with two equally broke roommates. *Gold Diggers of 1933* (1933, Warner Bros.).

3733 "Beulah, peel me a grape." **Mae West** gives instructions to her maid Gertrude Howard. *I'm No Angel* (1933, Paramount).

3734 "I'm going to make you eat dirt, you soap bubble." Reporter **Glenda Farrell** growls at her news editor boyfriend Frank McHugh. *The Mystery of the Wax Museum* (1933, Warner Bros.).

3735 "Let not poor Nellie starve." With his last words, King Charles II of England, portrayed by **Cedric Hardwicke**, thinks of his mistress Nell Gwyn, portrayed by Anna Neagle. *Nell Gwyn* (1934, GB, British & Dominions-United Artists).

3736 "Where's the zipper on the eggplant?" Helpless but genial **Fred MacMurray** helps manicurist Carole Lombard prepare a meal. *Hands Across the Table* (1935, Paramount).

3737 "My stomach lives for good things." Retired racketeer and gourmet **Leo Carrillo** hires Jean Arthur and Herbert Marshall as his cook and butler. *If You Could Only Cook* (1935, Columbia).

3738 "I've been eating cold toast for eight years now. . . I kinda like it." **W.C. Fields** has grown used to the idea that his breakfast will consist of whatever his wife's mother and brother do not gulp down first. *The Man on the Flying Trapeze* (1935, Paramount).

3739 "Tutsi-frutsi ice cream. . . get your tutsi-frutsi ice cream. . . ." It's **Chico Marx**'s nonchalant chant as he steers a pushcart and fleeces Groucho Marx at a race track. *A Day at the Races* (1937, MGM).

3740 "Take a spoonful of food—place it on a piece of gauze and gently rub into the navel." **David Niven** reads aloud from a sacrosanct scientific book of child-rearing to Ginger Rogers on the proper way to feed a baby. He doesn't realize that two pages are stuck together. *Bachelor Mother* (1939, RKO).

3741 "Watercress! I'd just as soon eat my way across a front lawn." **Phyllis Povah** picks at her salad. *The Women* (1939, MGM).

3742 BUD: "The hot dog and the mustard go together." LOU: "Let 'em go together; I don't want to spoil any romance!" BUD: "Don't you know they spend millions of dollars every year to put up factories to manufacture mustard? Do you know those factories employ thousands and thousands of men, just to manufacture mustard? Do you know those men take care of thousands of families and homes—all on account of mustard? And you—just because you don't like mustard—what do you want them to do? Close those factories and put all those people out of work?" LOU: "Wait a minute. Do you mean to stand there and tell me just because I don't eat mustard that I'm closing down the mustard factories? Are you trying to tell me that those thousands of people are making one little jar of mustard just for me? Well, if they are, you can tell 'em not to make it any more 'cause I'm not gonna eat it! You can lay 'em off, who am I to support thousands?" Playing themselves, **Bud Abbott** is outraged when **Lou Costello** orders a hot dog without mustard. *One Night in the Tropics* (1940, Universal).

3743 MAGGIE: "Ham, onions, butter, pickles. Everything the doctor said you shouldn't have." SANDRA: "I love food. That's the way I'm made." **Bette Davis** catches pregnant **Mary Astor** raiding the refrigerator in the middle of the night. *The Great Lie* (1941, Warner Bros.).

3744 "I didn't squawk about the steak, dear. I merely said I didn't see that old horse that used to be tethered outside here." **W.C. Fields** uses some gentle sarcasm to respond to a waitress who complains he's always squawking about his food, such as the tough steak he's trying to digest. *Never Give a Sucker an Even Break* (1941, Universal).

3745 "I'd like to mix it with a little smoothage." Because of lack of funds, **Rosalind Russell** and her sister Janet Blair are forced to eat a lot of roughage in their skimpy diet. *My Sister Eileen* (1942, Columbia).

3746 "Mr. Rawitch, what you are, I wouldn't eat." Jewish Polish actor **Felix Bressart** defies Nazi collaborator Lionel Atwill. *To Be or Not to Be* (1942, United Artists).

3747 "How about some spaghetti?" **Fred MacMurray** makes a dining suggestion to his wife Joan Crawford after they cross safely over the Italian border, having escaped from 1939 Berlin where their honeymoon covered the fact they are British spies. *Above Suspicion* (1943, MGM).

3748 "They're just like a dame, if you don't feed them, they won't do anything." Sergeant **Humphrey Bogart** compares his tank, which is low on fuel, to a woman. *Sahara* (1943, Columbia).

3749 "I'm going to shoot some game. The larder's almost empty." Resourceful **Susan Hayward** leaves her wounded and melancholy husband Gregory Peck, sitting despairingly at the base of Africa's Kilimanjaro mountain. *The Snows of Kilimanjaro* (1952, 20th Century-Fox).

3750 "I wouldn't dream of eating a nut a man had cracked in his mouth." **Carroll Baker** rejects a pecan offered to her by Eli Wallach. That's about all she rejects from Wallach. *Baby Doll* (1956, Warner Bros.).

3751 "I eat like a fool—when I'm in love, I mean. My friends used to tell me they couldn't swallow a morsel, but I eat like a fool." **Lauren Bacall** is on an eating binge since she met Gregory Peck. *Designing Woman* (1957, MGM).

3752 "Fetch me a bowl of milk laced with rum." Patricia Owens recognizes the body and the voice of her husband **Al (David) Hedison**, but if she could see under the towel covering his head, she might see that he has accidentally mixed his atoms with those of a common fly, resulting in the unusual menu request. *The Fly* (1958, 20th Century-Fox).

3753 "Well, I suppose we'll have to feed the duchess. Even vultures have to eat." **Shirley MacLaine** refers to her dotty Aunt Miriam Hopkins, who had MacLaine's role in the 1936 version of the Lillian Hellman play, then called "These Three." *The Children's Hour* (1961, United Artists).

3754 "Which reminds me. I'm having nuts and whipped cream for lunch. Would you join me, please? Crew, that's lunch. One hour for the actors and seven days for the technicians. It's a movie set breaking once and for all to have lunch." Bell-hop **Jerry Lewis** has been groomed to take the place of a Hollywood comedian who was killed in an airplane crash. *The Patsy* (1964, Paramount).

3755 "Fraulein, is it to be at every meal or merely at dinner time that you intend leading us all through this rare and wonderful new world of indigestion?" Initially, Baron **Christopher Plummer** is cruelly

unimpressed with Julie Andrews' Pollyanna-like behavior and musical selections. *The Sound of Music* (1965, 20th Century-Fox).

3756 "I'm a bagel on a plate of onion rolls." **Barbra Streisand**, as Fanny Brice, uses a food metaphor to describe how out of place she feels among the tall, beautiful showgirls in the Ziegfeld Follies. *Funny Girl* (1968, Columbia).

3757 VICKI ALLESSIO: "What the hell, I mean, a girl has to eat." STEVE BLACKBURN: "This will do us both a world of good." VICKI: "You rather more than I." **Glenda Jackson** and **George Segal** plan a tryst, but not until after lunch. *A Touch of Class* (1973, GB, Avco Embassy).

3758 "A kid comes up to me in a white jacket, gives me a Ritz cracker and chopped liver. He says, 'Canapes.' I say 'Can o' peas my ass; that's a Ritz cracker and chopped liver!'" **Michael V. Gazzo** tells John Cazale that he's too food savvy to be fooled at a cocktail party. *The Godfather, Part II* (1974, Paramount).

3759 "Eating is the most important thing in the life of a cat." **Art Carney** makes the observation as he walks his cat on a leash. *Harry and Tonto* (1974, 20th Century-Fox).

3760 "Imagine your loved ones conquered by Napoleon and forced to live under French rule. Do you want them to eat all that rich food and those heavy sauces? Do you want them to have souffle every meal and croissants?" **Woody Allen** appeals to some Russian gastronomical patriotism. *Love and Death* (1975, United Artists).

3761 "Well, that's okay, 'cause we don't eat 'em, neither." It's Janis Joplin-like rock singer **Bette Midler**'s smirking response when the nervous waitress at a truck-stop cafe says, "We don't serve hippies." *The Rose* (1979, 20th Century-Fox).

3762 "This steak still has the mark of the jockey's whip on it." **Rodney Dangerfield**'s steak is tough. Dangerfield and Chevy Chase are freethinking members at a country club. *Caddyshack* (1980, Orion-Warner Bros.).

3763 "You can be in this hotel for a whole year and never have to eat the same thing twice." **Scatman Crothers** tells caretaker Jack Nicholson about the wonderful selection of food at a resort hotel, now closed for the winter. *The Shining* (1980, GB, Warner Bros.).

3764 "You should never eat fruit and starch at once." Kookie **Barbra Streisand** flicks raisins out of her Danish at an all-night hamburger joint. *All Night Long* (1981, Universal).

3765 "That old gentleman happens to mean more to me than anything else. The next time I eat, it will be with him." Schoolgirl **Tatum O'Neal** goes on a hunger strike when her parents won't let her continue to date fiftyish Toronto artist Richard Burton. *Circle of Two* (1981, Canada, Vestron).

3766 "He's able to eat things that'll make a billy goat puke." **Richard Crenna** speaks proudly of Green Berets-trained Sylvester Stallone, who's on a rampage in the Northwest. *First Blood* (1982, Orion).

3767 "I don't suppose you have a chili dog. I'd even eat it raw." **Scott Glenn** wishes he has some American junk food when he's invited to eat at Toshiro Mifune's home, where they wash down sashimi with sake. *The Challenge* (1982, Embassy).

3768 "It's amazing what you can do with a cheap piece of meat if you know how to treat it." With the film's last line, **Paul Bartel** responds to the compliment of a guest about the meat they are eating. Members of the audience are pretty sure the meat is Robert Beltran. *Eating Raoul* (1982, 20th Century-Fox).

3769 "Mom was never to know a hot meal in her home." Narrator **Jean Shepherd** notes that by the time mother Melinda Dillon had filled everyone's plate and sat down, someone was ready for seconds. *A Christmas Story* (1983, MGM-United Artists).

3770 "I've been to your wonderful Soviet markets—I've never seen anything fresh enough to bleed." American cop **Brian Dennehy** works on a case behind the then iron curtain with Russian police Officer William Hurt. *Gorky Park* (1983, Orion).

3771 "I don't know why they call this stuff Hamburger Helper. It does just fine by itself." Low life **Randy Quaid** barbecues sans hamburger meat. *National Lampoon's Vacation* (1983, Warner Bros.).

3772 "You've gained seven pounds. If you want to put something in your mouth, try a gun." Inventor **Richard Dreyfuss**' talking scale makes a sarcastic food suggestion to its creator. *The Buddy System* (1984, 20th Century-Fox).

3773 "Well, me, I'm having a hamburger, fries, a Coke and maybe a salad. How about you, Luce?" At the end of the film, there is a glimmer of hope that **Ryan O'Neal**, his ex-wife Shelley Long and their daughter Drew Barrymore who sued to divorce her parents, will get back together. *Irreconcilable Differences* (1984, Warner Bros.).

3774 JOAN RIVERS: "Did anything go wrong at lunch?" MISS PIGGY: "My frog turned on me." RIVERS: "Yeah, I had some bad tuna myself." **Joan Rivers** has found a straight woman, Miss Piggy, whose voice comes to us, compliments of **Frank Oz**. *The Muppets Take Manhattan* (1984, Tri-Star).

3775 "These guys eat too much red meat." Chatterbox stewardess **Rae Dawn Chong** pokes fun at macho Arnold Schwarzenegger and his violent adversaries. *Commando* (1985, 20th Century-Fox).

3776 "I don't know what's wrong, the zombie won't eat." Crazed scientist **Richard Liberty** is concerned for his picky walking dead. *Day of the Dead* (1985, United Artists).

3777 "Think I'll go down the street and get myself some ice cream." Having just purchased an elephant gun, street vigilante **Charles Bronson** is hungry to meet some punk prey. *Death Wish 3* (1985, Cannon).

3778 LINDA WHITE: "I'm not about to eat real sugar." BARRY STEINBERG: "All right, fine, we'll find you a Sweet 'n Low field." Yuppie **Andrea Martin** and inept womanizer **Eugene Levy** are among a lost, hungry group of resort guests who spot a field of sugarcane. *Club Paradise* (1986, Warner Bros.).

3779 "I never eat anything that hasn't been sitting on the TV for at least 24 hours. The radiation kills whatever 'they' have put in it." Nutty old **Lillian Gish** fears someone is out to get her. *Sweet Liberty* (1986, Universal).

3780 "Feed me! Feed me!" **Levi Stubbs**, the lead singer of Motown's "The Four Tops," is the voice of a man-eating plant. *Little Shop of Horrors* (1987, Warner Bros.).

3781 "Excuse me, the baby panda, is it fried in honey?" It's the question of an elegantly dressed customer in Bastard's, a smart London supper club, which has an unusual and exotic menu. *Eat the Rich* (1988, GB, New Line).

3782 "You know what you feed a dray horse in the morning if you want a day's work out of him? Just enough so he knows he's hungry." Boston smoothie **Kevin Tighe** likens baseball players of the early 20th century to plow horses. Things have certainly changed. *Eight Men Out* (1988, Orion).

3783 "You know what I'd love for lunch? Fresh asparagus, then, um, pasta, angel hair pasta with heaps of basil, garlic, olive oil, and uh, apple pie. Yeah. Uh, John, have you got the towel?" Sam Neill has rescued his wife **Nicole Kidman** from the maniacal killer Billy Zane who has kidnapped her. *Dead Calm* (1989, Australia, Warner Bros.).

3784 "Rarely do I see any Italian-Americans eating here." **Giancarlo Esposito** complains to Danny Aiello about all the photographs of Italian Americans in the latter's black ghetto pizzeria and the lack of any Black Americans' photos. *Do the Right Thing* (1989, Universal).

3785 "Sometimes I eat with Dave. . . . Dave, however, always eats alone." **Kathy Baker** notes a difference in the eating habits of herself and her brother, bitter Vietnam veteran Ed Harris. *Jackknife* (1989, Cineplex Odeon).

3786 "That's the last food I'll ever make for you, so eat it." **Melinda Dillon** dumps a pot of spaghetti on her son Dermot Mulroney's plate after he accuses her of sleeping with his boss. *Staying Together* (1989, Hemdale).

3787 "I'll have what she's having." After observing Meg Ryan simulate an orgasm for Billy Crystal in the middle of a crowded deli, **Estelle Reiner**, mother of director Rob Reiner, gives her order to her waiter. *When Harry Met Sally. . .* (1989, Columbia).

3788 "I don't eat anything with a face." Hippie **Judge Reinhold** is a very strict vegetarian. He refuses food at his fiancée Beverly D'Angelo's home. *Daddy's Dyin'. . . Who's Got the Will?* (1990, MGM-United Artists).

3789 "And that's the hardest part. Today everything is different. There's no action. I have to wait around like everyone else. Can't even get decent food. Right after I got here I ordered some spaghetti with marinara sauce and I got egg noddles and catsup. I'm an average nobody. Get to live the rest of my life like a schnook." Hoodlum **Ray Liotta** finds the Federal Witness Protection Program lacks the things that made his former life enjoyable. *GoodFellas* (1990, Warner Bros.).

3790 "I'm interested in food. . . I love food. . . I eat food. . . . Food is my life." **Jessica Lange** desperately angles for a job in a gourmet food store run by Kathy Bates. *Men Don't Leave* (1990, Warner Bros.).

3791 "He always ate everything I cooked for him, and he never hit me." Part-time hooker **Jennifer Jason Leigh** tells police detective Fred Ward that she stayed with dead Alec Baldwin even after she discovered he was a robber and a killer because he could stomach anything she cooked, even when it was intentionally awful. *Miami Blues* (1990, Orion).

3792 "Clean up your sugar and for dessert you can have some rancid trash I found in a dumpster behind the 7-11." **Stockard Channing** is the mother of a family of insects in human form. *Meet the Applegates* aka: *The Applegates* (1991, Triton).

3793 "Just because I don't know how to cook doesn't mean I don't know how to eat." Busy psychiatrist **Barbra Streisand** orders for Nick Nolte at a fancy New York French restaurant. *The Prince of Tides* (1991, Columbia).

3794 "A census taker once tried to test me. I ate his liver with some fava beans and a nice Chianti." **Anthony Hopkins** is Hannibal "The Cannibal" Lecter, a murderer who eats parts of his victims. *The Silence of the Lambs* (1991, Orion).

3795 "Hey, cowgirls, see the grass? Don't eat it." Wise-cracking, cigar-chomping baseball scout **Jon Lovitz** delivers some raw phenomenons to the training camp of the Rockford Peaches girls professional baseball team. *A League of Their Own* (1992, Columbia).

3796 "I bet the Chinese food in this town is terrible." **Marisa Tomei**, as Mona Lisa Vito, arrives from Brooklyn in a small Alabama town with her fiancé Joe Pesci, as Vinny Gambini. *My Cousin Vinny* (1992, 20th Century-Fox).

3797 "I was tastin' the soup two hours after I ate it." Sheriff **Gene Hackman** explains why he shaved off his beard. *The Unforgiven* (1992, Warner Bros.).

Fools and Foolishness *see* IGNORANCE, INSANITY AND SANITY, STUPIDITY

Football *see* SPORTS

Force

see also ENERGY, GENTLENESS, POWER, STRENGTHS, VIOLENCE

3798 "No American citizen may be forced into the service of a foreign prince." It's the law **Edward Arnold**, as Daniel Webster, cites as authority in his defense of James Craig, whose soul is at stake. *All That Money Can Buy* aka: *The Devil and Daniel Webster* (1941, RKO).

3799 "You're obvious, Munsey. . . in everything you do, you're obvious. . . . That's it, Munsey, not logic, just force, brute force." Prison doctor **Art Smith** delivers the line that gives the film its title, after being slugged by brutal prison Captain Hume Cronyn. *Brute Force* (1947, Universal-International).

3800 "They made me kill my girl." Hired killer **Lawrence Tolan** sobs as he turns himself in to the police after being forced by his associates to carry out a contract and kill Susan Cabot, the woman he loved. *The Enforcer* (1950, United States Pictures-Warner Bros.).

3801 "There is an extraordinary force piling up inside, life will not be enough to spell it." Country priest **Claude Laydu** fills his diary with his torment. *Diary of a Country Priest* (1951, Fr., Union Generale Cinematographique).

3802 "Life creates it and makes it grow, its energy surrounds us and binds us—feel the flow, feel the Force around you." **Frank Oz**, as the voice of Yoda, speaks of the "Force" to Mark Hamill. *The Empire Strikes Back* (1980, 20th Century-Fox).

Foreigners

see also COUNTRIES, NATIVES, PEOPLE

3803 "She's not an albino; she was born right here in this country." **Abner Biberman**, a pug-ugly, who works for newspaper editor Cary Grant, defends his new blonde girlfriend, when someone asks if she's an albino. *His Girl Friday* (1940, Columbia).

3804 "Foreign? Who calls me a foreigner? When the first wrong was done to the first Indian, I was here. When the first slaver put out for the Congo, I stood on the deck. True the North claimed me to be a Southerner and the South for a Northerner, but I am neither. To tell the truth, Mr. Webster, though I don't like to boast about it, my name is older in this country than yours." Devil **Walter Huston** reacts indignantly when Edward Arnold, as Daniel Webster, accuses him of being a foreigner. *All That Money Can Buy* aka: *The Devil and Daniel Webster* (1941, RKO).

3805 "So many foreigners have foreign names." Rich British buffoon **Reginald Gardiner** is a silly ass. *Cluny Brown* (1946, 20th Century-Fox).

Foreplay *see* KISSES AND KISSING, LOVE AND LOVERS, SEX

Forgetfulness and Forgetting

see also FAILURES, KNOWLEDGE, MEMORY AND MEMORIZATION, MINDS, NOSTALGIA, PAST, REMINDERS, SELF

3806 "Forget you? Not while I live, not if I die!" **John Gilbert**'s vow to Greta Garbo appears on a title card. *Flesh and the Devil* (1926, silent, MGM).

3807 "Once a man loves her—he never forgets her." A title card tells us that married **John Gilbert** has not forgotten the only woman he has ever loved, Greta Garbo. *A Woman of Affairs* (1928, silent, MGM).

3808 DR. LANYON: "Perhaps you've forgotten you're engaged to Muriel?" DR. JEKYLL: "Forgotten? Can a man dying of thirst forget water? And do you know what would happen to that thirst if it were denied water?" DR. LANYON: "If I understand you correctly, you sound almost indecent." When **Holmes Herbert** questions the interest **Fredric March** shows in sexy music hall singer Miriam Hopkins, March responds meaningfully—too meaningfully to suit Herbert. *Dr. Jekyll and Mr. Hyde* (1932, Paramount).

3809 "Boys, it's the only thing we can do. Let's forget sex!" **Miriam Hopkins** can't decide between Fredric March and Gary Cooper, so she suggests an arrangement where she tries both, without sex. *Design for Living* (1933, Paramount).

3810 KIRK LAWRENCE: "I'll never forget you." TIRA: "No one ever does." **Kent Taylor** thinks **Mae West** is unforgettable—so does West. *I'm No Angel* (1933, Paramount).

3811 "The desperate love between children—is there anything in the world forgotten so soon." **Douglass Dumbrille** couldn't be more wrong in dismissing the "puppy" love of Dickie Moore for Virginia Weidler. It will continue throughout their lives, when they grow to become Gary Cooper and Ann Harding, even till death and beyond. *Peter Ibbetson* (1935, Paramount).

3812 "If I'd forgotten myself with that girl, I'd remember it." In a silly mistaken identity plot, American dancer **Fred Astaire** is certain that nothing untoward has occurred between him and beautiful Ginger Rogers. *Top Hat* (1935, RKO).

3813 "What you want to do is to forget all about it. Just make your mind a complete blank. You know? Watch me. You can't go wrong." **Michael Redgrave** advises Margaret Lockwood to forget about the missing Dame May Whitty. *The Lady Vanishes* (1938, GB, Gaumont British-Gainsborough).

3814 "Oh, can't we go away and forget we ever said these things?" **Leslie Howard** wishes that Vivien Leigh had never declared her love for him, as he plans to wed Olivia de Havilland. *Gone with the Wind* (1939, Selznick-MGM).

3815 "You're a clever little man, little master of the universe, but mortals are weak and frail. If their stomach speaks, they forget their brain. If their brain speaks, they forget their hearts. And if their hearts speak—ha ha ha ha ha—if their hearts speak, they forget everything." Genie **Rex Ingram** notes that Sabu has wasted one of his three wishes by wishing for sausages like his mother used to make. *The Thief of Bagdad* (1940, GB, London Films-United Artists).

3816 "I shall never forget the weekend Laura died." **Clifton Webb**'s memorable first line begins a classical adult murder mystery. *Laura* (1944, 20th Century-Fox).

3817 "A big word 'innocent'—stupid's more like it. Well, everybody is somebody's fool. The only way to stay out of trouble is to grow old, so I guess I'll concentrate on that. Maybe I'll live so long that I'll forget her. Maybe I'll die trying." With the film's last line, seaman **Orson Welles** remembers homicidal, frustrated Rita Hayworth. She has just died in a fatal gunfight with her crippled husband Everett Sloane in the hall of mirrors of an amusement park. *The Lady from Shanghai* (1948, Columbia).

3818 "Don't forget to throw me over your shoulder and burp me after lunch." Talented athlete **Katharine Hepburn** sarcastically reminds her manager Spencer Tracy who has outlined a very detailed program for her. *Pat and Mike* (1952, MGM).

3819 "Don't ever forget how good you are." **James Mason**, who is about to take his own life, reminds his unsuspecting wife Judy Garland that she is extremely talented as a performer and a person. *A Star Is Born* (1954, Warner Bros.).

3820 JOHNNY GUITAR: "How many men have you forgotten?" VIENNA: "As many women as you've remembered." **Sterling Hayden** tries to make his on-and-off lover **Joan Crawford** feel guilty about her many affairs. *Johnny Guitar* (1954, Republic).

3821 "I don't want to forget a single moment of it. I think I never shall." American spinster **Katharine Hepburn** looks back fondly as her train leaves Venice and the brief romantic interlude she shared with married Italian Rossano Brazzi. *Summertime* (1955, London Films-Lopert-United Artists).

3822 "No, the boy Davy would not forget. Nor would we who stood watching as he rode away. None of us would ever forget what happened and why. For none of us were without blame. But even as we shared the guilt we shared, also the knowledge of a new hope, a new understanding. We had taken note that day that there are none who trespass against us as we trespass against ourselves." One-armed Civil War hero **Jeff Chandler** puts a stop to a gang of nomadic toughs who terrorized a peaceful western

town. Dee Pollock is a youth who is allowed to ride away. *The Plunderers* (1960, Allied Artists).

3823 "I can't dispel you from my thoughts." **Richard Burton** says it the hard way to Elizabeth Taylor. *The Sandpiper* (1965, MGM).

3824 "'There are times I simply adored you.' How like Justine to end a love affair with the only really loving thing she has ever said to me. I'll never forgive her, but I won't forget her either. I don't want to." Irish schoolmaster **Michael York** has the film's last lines about Alexandrian Jewess Anouk Aimee. *Justine* (1969, 20th Century-Fox).

3825 "He was forgotten to death." Believing he's revenging the death of God, madman **Barnard Hughes** delivers a "guilty" doctor to the emergency room, suffering from heart attack symptoms induced by a drug given to him by Hughes. The doctor is routinely examined, put in a corner of a room and forgotten—and he dies. *The Hospital* (1971, United Artists).

3826 "Forget it, Jake, it's Chinatown." **Joe Mantell**'s comment to Jack Nicholson is his way of telling his boss that nothing can or will be done now that the police shot and killed Faye Dunaway as she was fleeing from her father John Huston with their daughter Belinda Palmer. *Chinatown* (1974, Paramount).

3827 "Oh, come on, Kong. Forget about me. This thing is never going to work." **Jessica Lange** tells the giant ape that there's no future for their relationship. *King Kong* (1976, De Laurentiis).

3828 "Music, dance, champagne—the best way to forget 'til you find something to remember." **Marlene Dietrich** expresses a gay attitude towards life. *Just a Gigolo* (1979, W. Ger., United Artists).

3829 JENNIFER: "Will you forget me?" MATTHEW: "The moment I die." Their affair over, **Michael Caine** gently kisses teenager **Michelle Johnson** on the forehead. *Blame It on Rio* (1984, 20th Century-Fox).

3830 "I'm from the gutter and don't you ever forget it because I won't." Culturally deprived surrealist writer Joe Orton, portrayed by **Gary Oldman**, expresses his loathing for bourgeois respectability. *Prick Up Your Ears* (1987, GB, Goldwyn-Zenith).

Forgiveness

see also DEBTS, GOD, MERCY, PUNISHMENTS, SINS AND SINNERS

3831 "You're just a man like me and I killed you. Forgive me, comrade. Oh, God, why did they do this? We only wanted to live, you and I. . . . You have to forgive me, comrade!" Young German soldier **Lew Ayres** pleads for forgiveness from the corpse of dead French soldier Raymond Griffith. *All Quiet on the Western Front* (1930, Universal).

3832 "Frankie! Frankie! Your mother forgives me!" **Victor McLaglen** receives forgiveness from Una O'Connor, the mother of Wallace Ford, the man he betrayed to the British. Moments later McLaglen dies from the wounds inflicted by IRA members. *The Informer* (1935, RKO).

3833 "Your father's a worthless fortune hunter but I forgive you because you're only daft and I can cure you." Young Scot **Richard Carlson** chases after Janet Gaynor, the daughter of a family of confidence tricksters. *The Young in Heart* (1938, Selznick-United Artists).

3834 "If you love a person, you can forgive anything." Not everyone is as fine as **Herbert Marshall**. His convictions will be put to the test by his cheating wife Bette Davis. *The Letter* (1940, Warner Bros.).

3835 "You made me lose my poise. For that I will never forgive you." **Constance Bennett**, Melvyn Douglas' glamorous ex-girlfriend, complains to his wife Greta Garbo, posing as her own more vivacious, but imaginary sister. *Two-Faced Woman* (1942, MGM).

3836 "That's quite all right. Just pick off any little pieces that you see, will you?" **Rudy Vallee** is very understanding of Claudette Colbert after she manages to grind two pairs of his pince-nez into his face as she climbs into an upper berth of a train. *The Palm Beach Story* (1942, Paramount).

3837 "If I don't come back I forgive you. . . . If I do, it's a different matter." Polish Shakespearean actor **Jack Benny** is being noble for unfaithful wife Carole Lombard as he goes on what may be a suicidal mission against the Nazis. *To Be or Not to Be* (1942, Korda-Lubitsch).

3838 "He was a man of many follies, but he was incapable of meanness. He never bargained with God. He did good things because he enjoyed doing them. Oh, do you think that God, who understood my great-grandfather, might forgive me for having doubted?" **Tom Drake** grieves for his great grandfather Charles Coburn. *The Green Years* (1946, MGM).

3839 "I forgive you for everything." Teenage **Jane Powell** forgives Elizabeth Taylor for stealing Robert Stack. Powell is happy with her old boyfriend Scotty Beckett. *A Date with Judy* (1948, MGM).

3840 "I shall not find it so easy to forgive myself. . . . Goodbye." At the time of his retirement because of poor health, **Michael Redgrave** delivers the last words of his straightforward apology to his students for his failure as a teacher. *The Browning Version* (1951, GB, Javelin-GFD).

3841 "Oh, please, forgive me, please." **Joan Crawford** begs her husband Jeff Chandler to forgive her for believing that he killed a woman with whom he was romantically involved. *Female on the Beach* (1955, Universal).

3842 "I knew there would be no way you could ever forgive me, not with this Sicilian thing that goes back two thousand years." Al Pacino slaps the face of his wife **Diane Keaton**, telling her never to darken his door again, when she confesses that she had an abortion because she didn't want the child to grow up as corrupt as Pacino. *The Godfather, Part II* (1974, Paramount).

3843 "Can't you forgive Fredo? He's so sweet and helpless." **Talia Shire** intercedes for John Cazale with his brother Al Pacino—but to no avail. *The Godfather, Part II* (1974, Paramount).

3844 "Forgive me, I never died before." Terminal cancer patient, 17-year-old **Kathleen Beller** is understandably bitter when she is upbraided for being gloomy. *Promises in the Dark* (1979, Orion).

3845 "Funny how God can forgive you and people can't—why is that?" Brothel madam **Dolly Parton** doesn't see herself as a villain for providing a community service, but she can't abide unforgiving folks. *The Best Little Whorehouse in Texas* (1982, Universal).

3846 "Forgive you? I could ordain you. . . the way I feel tonight, I could heal people." It's **Woody Allen**'s metaphor after he and his wife Mary Steenburgen reconcile and make love in a barn. *A Midsummer Night's Sex Comedy* (1982, Orion-Warner Bros.).

3847 "The way you see him here, like this, this is the way I like to remember him. I think if you had asked Alan Swann what was the single most gratifying moment in his life, he might have said this one right here. The next day I drove up to Connecticut with him and Alfie. This time he knocked on the door, and when he and Tess saw each other it was like they'd never been apart. Like Alfie says, 'With Swann you forgive a lot, you know.' I know." In voice-over, **Mark Linn-Baker** speaks of fading movie star Peter O'Toole, who was a triumph on a comedy television program. It gave him enough confidence that O'Toole went to visit his daughter, driven by his understanding chauffeur Tony DiBenedetto. *My Favorite Year* (1982, MGM-United Artists).

3848 "I'm never going to forgive my father for calling me that—if I knew who he was." **Lesley Ann Warren** bemoans the fact that her name is Eve, because strange Keith Carradine falls in love with women of that name. *Choose Me* (1984, Island Alive).

3849 "I have forgiven David. I only wish I could have found it in my heart to forgive him when he was alive." It's part of a letter ex-prostitute **Miranda Richardson** writes to the mother of her no-account lover Rupert Everett. She shot him to death and became the last British female to be hanged. *Dance with a Stranger* (1985, GB, Goldcrest-NFFC-First Picture Co.).

3850 "Jessie, child. . . forgive me. I thought you were mine." **Anne Bancroft** begs her daughter Sissy Spacek, who is planning suicide, for forgiveness in their last anguished scene together. *'Night, Mother* (1986, Universal).

3851 "Dear Father, I'm sitting at your desk writing this. Mother is downstairs somewhere. Soon I will go back to my room and close the door for the last time. I just can't keep hating myself. I wish to God I knew where I'm going. I'm afraid. Good-bye, Father. Please forgive me as I now forgive you. May the Lord bless and keep you forever and ever. Love, Cathy." It's the note **Janet Smith** left her father James Murtaugh before hanging herself in the bedroom. He had forced the girl into incestuous relations. *The Rosary Murders* (1987, New Line).

3852 "In families there are no crimes beyond forgiveness." It's a lesson **Nick Nolte** learns by the end of the film. *The Prince of Tides* (1991, Columbia).

Fornication *see* INFIDELITIES, MEN AND WOMEN, SEX AND SEXUALITY, SINS AND SINNERS

Fortitude *see* COURAGE, COWARDICE AND COWARDS

Fortune *see* ADVANTAGES, CHANCES, FATE AND DESTINY, LOSSES AND LOSING, LUCK, WEALTH AND RICHES

Fraud *see* CHEATS, CRIMES AND CRIMINALS, DECEPTIONS, TRICKS AND TRICKERY

Free Will

see also FREEDOMS, VOLUNTEERS

3853 "No man will ever hurt me again. . . I'll never do anything that isn't of my own free will." **Gene**

Tierney is no longer a warm, wide-eyed innocent. *Laura* (1944, 20th Century-Fox).

3854 "Something to do with free will, I think." It's the response of the Supreme Being, portrayed by **Ralph Richardson**, when asked why he allows evil in the world. *Time Bandits* (1980, GB, Handmade Films).

Freedoms

see also CONTROL, DEMOCRACY, EASE AND EASINESS, INDEPENDENCE AND DEPENDENCE, LIBERTY, POWER, RIGHTS, SLAVERY AND SLAVES

3855 "Free, free at last. Deniers of life, if you could see me now what would you think?" These are the first words of Mr. Hyde played by **Fredric March**. *Dr. Jekyll and Mr. Hyde* (1932, Paramount).

3856 "An artist must be free to love, to sin, if you call it sin." Breathless, aspiring actress **Katharine Hepburn** gushes her career philosophy. *Morning Glory* (1933, RKO).

3857 "You're free, baby. Step out and be yourself." **Melvyn Douglas** advises Irene Dunne, the author of a shocking best selling novel. *Theodora Goes Wild* (1936, Columbia).

3858 "We've got to make our own lives. . . I love the feeling free inside even better than I love you." **Cary Grant** tells his wealthy fiancée Doris Nolan what she doesn't want to hear. *Holiday* (1938, Columbia).

3859 "Be glad you're rid of him, you're free. . . . Now you can go back to yourself, to your music. . . . Nothing can stop you when you do what's in your heart." After he's killed a man in the ring and broken his hand in the process, **Barbara Stanwyck** reminds ex-violinist prize-fighter William Holden that he has plenty to live for now that he's finally rid of his wily manager Adolphe Menjou. *Golden Boy* (1939, Columbia).

3860 MARIE GARSON: "Mister—what does it mean when you 'crack out'?" HEALY: "Why, it means you're free." MARIE: "He's free! He's free!" Grieving **Ida Lupino** realizes that, with his death, aging gangster Humphrey Bogart has finally escaped. Reporter **Jerome Cowan** tells her the meaning of Bogie's earlier comment to Lupino that when he was in prison, he was always wanting to "crack out." *High Sierra* (1941, Warner Bros.).

3861 "We hold the fortress of free thought and free speech in this place this afternoon." Teacher **Henry Fonda** gives a moving defense of the need to resist the suppression of ideas by reading the letter of Bartolomeo Vanzetti to his children, written shortly before he and fellow anarchist Nicola Sacco are executed for the alleged crime of murder, but possibly because of their political convictions and actions. *The Male Animal* (1942, Warner Bros.).

3862 "It doesn't matter where a man dies so long as he dies for freedom!" For patriotic **Robert Taylor** his place of death, fighting for freedom, is defending a bridge on Bataan against the Japanese. *Bataan* (1943, MGM).

3863 "Do you know why we're able to do it? Because we're stronger than they are. . . I don't mean in numbers. I mean something else. You see, those men out there never knew the dignity of freedom." Tank Sergeant **Humphrey Bogart** explains to Richard Nugent that his handful of men have an edge on a company of thirsty Germans in the desert. *Sahara* (1943, Columbia).

3864 "I am free." **Arletty**, the symbol of Paris, a beautiful survivor in the 1840s, refuses to be controlled by a dictatorial man, just as the French people refuse to be controlled by the German dictators. *Children of Paradise* (1945, Fr., Pathé).

3865 "Man's desire to be free—the greatest madness." Roman emperor Tiberius, portrayed by **Ernest Thesiger**, just doesn't get the concept. *The Robe* (1953, 20th Century-Fox).

3866 "This is your son. He is free, Spartacus. Free. He's free. He's free. He'll remember you, Spartacus, because I'll tell him. I'll tell him who his father was and what he dreamed of." Before escaping to safety, **Jean Simmons** shows crucified Kirk Douglas, the leader of the slave revolt against Rome, his son—born free. *Spartacus* (1960, Universal).

3867 RUPERT: "If you're free later this evening. . . ." GIULIETTA CAMERON: "I'm never free, sweetie." Maitre d' **John Gallaudet** has used the wrong f-word with high-cost call girl **Gina Lollobrigida**. *Go Naked in the World* (1961, MGM).

3868 "No one in love is free—or wants to be." Even though Paul Newman abandoned her, leaving her to have an abortion, **Shirley Knight** can't keep away from him when he returns to their home town. *Sweet Bird of Youth* (1962, MGM).

3869 MARK ANTONY: "Tell me. Tell me, how many have loved you since him? One? Ten? No one? Have they kissed you with Caesar's lips? Touched you with his hands? Has it been his name you cried out in the dark, and afterwards alone, has he

reproached you, and have you begged forgiveness of his memory?" CLEOPATRA: "You come here, then, running over with wine and self-pity to conquer Caesar?" ANTONY: "So long now, you've filled my life. Like a great noise that I hear everywhere in my heart. I want to be free of you, of wanting you, of being afraid. . . ." CLEOPATRA: "That Caesar would not permit it." ANTONY: "But I will never be free of you." **Richard Burton** senses that loving **Elizabeth Taylor** will lead to disaster but he can't resist her. *Cleopatra* (1963, 20th Century-Fox).

3870 "We saw her many times again, born free, and living free. But to us, she was always the same, our friend Elsa." **Virginia McKenna**, as Joy Adamson, speaks of the lioness Elsa which she raised. *Born Free* (1965, GB, Columbia).

3871 "I am the only free man on this train." Political exile **Klaus Kinski** is dying. *Doctor Zhivago* (1965, MGM).

3872 "Unless you're rich, you ain't free. I aim to be free." **Shelley Winters**, as Ma Barker, expresses a little cause and effect relation. *Bloody Mama* (1970, AIP).

3873 "The academic world dehumanizes us and we become its natural dependents. . . after which we are brainwashed, but the gods have given us freedom. . . ." Young Oxford Don **Patrick Mower** rants at a public banquet where he is delivering an important speech. *Incense for the Damned* aka: *Doctors Wear Scarlet* and *The Bloodsuckers* (1970, GB, Titan International).

3874 "If a man gives you freedom, it is not freedom. Freedom is something you take for yourself." Revolutionary leader **Evaristo Marquez** makes sense on the Portuguese controlled island of Queimada in 1854. *Burn!* aka: *Queimada!* (1970, Fr.-Ital., Les Productions Artistes Associes-Produzioni Europee Associates-United Artists).

3875 "Yes, they were free. They would still have their problems to face and dangers to meet, but they were free, living free." **Susan Hampshire**, as Joy Adamson, speaks of the lioness Elsa's cubs. *Living Free* (1972, GB, Columbia).

3876 "When you break a mirror, you free everything that it's seen." It's **Suzanna Love**'s story about a haunted mirror. *The Boogey Man* (1980, Ross).

3877 "Free me, free me. I want to return to my people." **Nastassja Kinski**, moaning with passion, undresses and stands naked before zoo curator John Heard, begging him to make love to her, even though they both know it may mean she will be transformed into a black leopard who will kill him. *Cat People* (1982, Universal).

3878 EDWARD LEWIS: "So what happened after he climbed up the tower and rescued her?" VIVIAN WARD: "She rescued him right back." **Richard Gere** and **Julia Roberts** enact her fairy tale rescue on her fire escape. *Pretty Woman* (1990, Touchstone-Buena Vista).

3879 "I used to think I'd die of suffocation when I was married. Now it's my freedom that's killing me." **Judy Davis**, as French novelist George Sand, finds things haven't gotten better for her when she lives as she pleases and with whomever pleases her. *Impromptu* (1991, Hemdale).

Friendships and Friends

see also ADMIRATION, FAMILIES, LIKES AND DISLIKES, LONELINESS, LOVE AND HATE, LOVE AND LOVERS, PROMISCUITY, RELATIONSHIPS, RELATIVES

3880 "Comradeship was all we had left; and now that's gone." **Richard Barthelmess** is the sole survivor of four friends who go to Paris after World War I rather than return to America. *The Last Flight* (1931, Warner Bros.).

3881 "I thought we might run up a a few curtains and make a batch of fudge while we decide what dress to wear to the country club dance." It's prostitute **Jean Harlow**'s sarcastic retort when Clark Gable warns her to be friendly to Mary Astor while he's away. *Red Dust* (1932, MGM).

3882 "Friend?" **Boris Karloff**, as Baron Frankenstein's monster, questions newly minted Elsa Lanchester, who isn't taken with tall, dark and gruesome. *The Bride of Frankenstein* (1935, Universal).

3883 "You and I are friends. We've had a lot of fun together. As far as I'm concerned, you're the number one girl in the archipelago. But I don't remember any vows to you, nor do I recall asking for any." **Clark Gable** makes it clear to Jean Harlow that they have no ties on each other. *China Seas* (1935, MGM).

3884 "You should understand that, like me, you're half-man and half-spectre. Just make a small sign and I'll know you're my friend." **Harry Baur** tries to make friends with the Golem played by Ferdinand Hart. *The Golem* (1936, Czechoslovakia-French).

3885 "These are the only friends I have, and I am no better than they are." Cynical Parisian courtesan **Greta Garbo** informs boyish Robert Taylor that she's no grand lady. He is shocked by an off-col-

ored joke told at the table where they are sitting. *Camille* (1937, MGM).

3886 "You can't take it with you! The only thing you can take with you is the love of your friends." "It," of course is money. Wealthy in friends, **Lionel Barrymore** teaches the lesson to wealthy-in-money Edward Arnold. *You Can't Take It with You* (1938, Columbia).

3887 "I hate the blasted army, but friendship, well, that's something else. **Douglas Fairbanks, Jr.** tells his disapproving fiancée Joan Fontaine that he re-enlisted because of Cary Grant and Victor McLaglen. *Gunga Din* (1939, RKO).

3888 "I came into your house, my dear friend, and in your unhappiness you reached out your hand for help and in my loneliness I took it. We have such a friendship that is given to very few." The friendship between 19th century governess **Bette Davis** and handsome married French nobleman Charles Boyer leads to scandal, murder and suicide. *All This and Heaven Too* (1940, Warner Bros.).

3889 "You keep me around because even Johnny Eager has to have one friend." Alcoholic **Van Heflin** knows his role in hood Robert Taylor's entourage. *Johnny Eager* (1941, MGM).

3890 "This is all I need here: drink and drugs and no friends. I had too many friends." As his dependency on alcohol and drugs grows, **Hurd Hatfield** cuts himself off from society. *The Picture of Dorian Gray* (1945, MGM).

3891 "It's a faithful and obedient friend; it is silent when I wish it to be silent and it talks when I wish it to talk." **George Macready** refers to the swordstick he uses to rescue Glenn Ford from some Argentinians who objected to Ford's cheating at gambling. *Gilda* (1946, Columbia).

3892 TOM BUCHANAN: "Since when were you a friend of Gatsby's?" NICK CARRAWAY: "Since one moment ago." When **Barry Sullivan** suggests that everyone swear that title character Alan Ladd and not Sullivan's wife Betty Field was driving the roadster that ran down and killed Sullivan's mistress, Shelley Winters, **Macdonald Carey** protests. *The Great Gatsby* (1949, Paramount).

3893 "I've shared a moment with kings." Dying **Richard Todd** warms himself in the friendship of other patients in a World War II army hospital in Burma. *The Hasty Heart* (1949, GB, ABP).

3894 "Your friendship with Margo—your deep, close friendship. What would happen to it, do you think, if she knew the cheap trick you played on her for my benefit?" **Anne Baxter** blackmails Celeste Holm into helping her win the lead in Holm's husband's new play. *All About Eve* (1950, 20th Century-Fox).

3895 "If he don't act friendly, I don't act friendly. As long as I know how to get what I want, I'm all right." **Judy Holliday** states her credo for getting along with people such as her ill-tempered lover Broderick Crawford. *Born Yesterday* (1950, Columbia).

3896 "I've arrived at the age where a platonic friendship can be sustained on the highest moral plane." **Charles Chaplin** tries to make Claire Bloom believe that she has nothing to fear from him in a romantic or sexual way. *Limelight* (1952, United Artists).

3897 SGT. 'FATSO' JUDSON: "You hit me." PVT. ANGELO MAGGIO: "Yeah, and I'm about to do it again!. . . Only my friends call me a wop." Stockade Sergeant **Ernest Borgnine** is hit with a piece of chair by **Frank Sinatra** after Borgnine makes an obscene remark while looking at a picture of Sinatra's sister. *From Here to Eternity* (1953, Columbia).

3898 "You're about as friendly as a suction pump!" **Joan Crawford** angrily faults next door gigolo Jeff Chandler. *Female on the Beach* (1955, Universal-International).

3899 "If I'm going to die, let me die with the only friend I ever had." Consumptive gambler **Kirk Douglas** insists to his mistress Jo Van Fleet that he must join Burt Lancaster in a showdown with the Clantons. *Gunfight at the OK Corral* (1957, Paramount).

3900 "If we're going to be friends, let's get one thing straight: I hate snoops." When George Peppard questions **Audrey Hepburn** about her life she sets him straight. *Breakfast at Tiffany's* (1961, Paramount).

3901 "It all pointed that way. . . ungrateful citizens, what we had coming but never got paid. I knew in my bones what you were aiming for but I wouldn't believe it. I kept telling myself you were a good man, you were my friend." Dying **Joel McCrea** still has faith in his old friend, Randolph Scott, who had planned to steal the gold shipment the two elderly ex-lawmen were hired to deliver to a bank. *Ride the High Country* (1962, MGM).

3902 "Hello, Mrs. Howard, I'm a friend of Mr. Howard." A married man's nightmare—hitchhiker **Judy Geeson**, with whom Rod Steiger has had a brief affair, shows up at his home to meet the missus, Claire Bloom. *Three Into Two Won't Go* (1969, Universal).

3903 "I do wish you weren't so friendly with Lloyd George. He has the most odious way of looking at women." **Anne Bancroft**, as Lady Jennie Churchill, objects to the friendship of her son Simon Ward, as young Winston Churchill, with Anthony Hopkins as David Lloyd George. *Young Winston* (1972, GB, Columbia).

3904 "Don't be my friend any more, I don't find it too healthy." **Fred Williamson** splits with Richard Pryor when they both find themselves on a chain gang. *Adios Amigo* (1975, Atlas).

3905 "Isn't it touching how a perfect murder has kept our friendship alive all these years?" Jewelry merchant **William Devane**, a kidnapper who "steals" prominent people and holds them for ransom, speaks to Ed Lauter who helped Devane murder his adoptive parents and make it appear that they and Devane perished in a fire. *Family Plot* (1976, Universal).

3906 "This girl, she didn't know where she was going or what she was going to do. She didn't have no money on her. Maybe she'd met up with a character. I was hoping things would work out for her. She was a good friend of mine." Resourceful young teen **Linda Manz**, on her own with no family and no prospects, thinks of her friend, Jackie Shultis. *Days of Heaven* (1978, Paramount).

3907 "Chelsea told me about you, about how you like to have a good old time with people's heads. She does too, sometimes, and sometimes I can get into it, sometimes not. I just want you to know I'm very good at recognizing crap when I see it. You know it's not imperative that you and I be friends, but it might be nice. I'm sure you're a fascinating person, and I'm sure it would be fascinating to get to know you. That's obviously not an easy task. But, it's all right, you go ahead and be as poopy as you want, to quote Chelsea, and I'll be as receptive and pleasant as I can. I just want you to bear in mind while you're jerking me around and I'm feeling like a real asshole that I know precisely what you're up to and that I can take only so much of it. Okay? Good." **Dabney Coleman** confronts his girlfriend Jane Fonda's irascible old father Henry Fonda. *On Golden Pond* (1981, Universal).

3908 "We may be friends, but every once in awhile we fuck each other." Olympic runner **Patrice Donnelly** speaks both literally and figuratively about her friend, lover and main competition, Mariel Hemingway. *Personal Best* (1982, Warner Bros.).

3909 MICKEY: "Can men and women be just friends?" VIVIANE: "It'd be nice for once." Plump disc jockey **Coluche** is friendly with tough courtesan **Isabelle Huppert**. *My Best Friend's Girl* (1984, Fr., European International).

3910 BETH WEXLER: "I thought you wanted to be my friend." LAWRENCE BOURNE III: "This is what I do with my friends." **Rita Wilson** admonishes wealthy, selfish **Tom Hanks** who makes a pass at her after sitting side-by-side with her all night on a plane headed for a Peace Corps camp in Thailand. *Volunteers* (1985, Tri-Star).

3911 "I never had any friends later on like the ones I had when I was twelve. Jesus, does anyone?" Writer **Richard Dreyfuss** recalls when he was Wil Wheaton and his best buddies were River Phoenix, Corey Feldman and Jerry O'Connell. *Stand by Me* (1986, Columbia).

3912 "You gotta be nice to your friends, Wanda. Without 'em, you're a total stranger." Just out of prison, former cop **Kris Kristofferson** offers hard-boiled advice to Genevieve Bujold, the owner of a cafe with an improbable clientele. *Trouble in Mind* (1986, Island Alive).

3913 "You're my best buddies." Grounded by his parents, **Stephen Dorff** and his friends discover the gate to hell in his suburban backyard. *The Gate* (1987, New Century).

3914 CC BLOOM: "What will I do without my best friend?" JOHN PIERCE: "You got me." CC: "It's not the same." **Bette Midler** takes no comfort from her husband **John Heard** after a rupture occurs in her life-long friendship with Barbara Hershey. *Beaches* (1988, Touchstone-Buena Vista).

3915 "This could be the end of a beautiful friendship." Police detective **Treat Williams** and his partner Joe Piscopo are decomposing zombies—but they solved their case before the rot does them in. *Dead Heat* (1988, New World.).

3916 "Oh, Frank, everyone should have a friend like you." Beautiful **Priscilla Presley** praises bumbling police Lieutenant Leslie Nielsen who has accidently prevented an assassination attempt of Queen Elizabeth II. *The Naked Gun* (1988, Paramount).

3917 "Friendship is the only choice in life you can make that's yours." Sentimental drug dealer **Raul Julia** admires Mel Gibson. *Tequila Sunrise* (1988, Warner Bros.).

3918 "Didn't you know that married men and women are only allowed to be close friends in large crowds." The reason is, of course, married men and women, like the speaker **Ted Danson** and Isabella Rossellini, and their respective spouses, Sean Young and William Petersen, become more than close friends when they are alone. *Cousins* (1989, Paramount).

3919 "It's very hard to get your head and heart to work together in life. In my case, they're not even friendly." **Woody Allen** finds it hard to understand or accept the fact that he's lost Mia Farrow to Alan Alda. He'll get over her. *Crimes and Misdemeanors* (1989, Orion).

3920 "Hoke, you're my best friend." Elderly **Jessica Tandy** expresses her feelings of friendship to her long-time chauffeur Morgan Freeman. *Driving Miss Daisy* (1989, Warner Bros.).

3921 "What I'm saying—and this is not a come-on in any way, shape or form—it's that men and women can't be friends, because the sex part always gets in the way." **Billy Crystal** is certain that any close relationship between a man and a woman would lead to bed. *When Harry Met Sally. . .* (1989, Columbia).

3922 "You know what the most important thing in life is? Friends. Best friends." **Jessica Tandy** puts it well. *Fried Green Tomatoes* (1991, Universal).

3923 "I'm sorry I can't talk longer. I'm having an old friend for dinner." Escaped **Anthony Hopkins**, as Hannibal the Cannibal, calls FBI agent Jodie Foster long distance. He speaks literally as he sees his hated former jailer and psychiatrist Anthony Heald deplaning. *The Silence of the Lambs* (1991, Orion).

Fruit *see* FOOD AND EATING, LAND AND FARMS, TREES

Frustration *see* DESIRES, DISAPPOINTMENTS, HAPPINESS AND UNHAPPINESS, HOPE, LOSSES AND LOSING

Fun

see also AMUSEMENTS, ENJOYMENTS, EXCITEMENTS, GAMES, HAPPINESS AND UNHAPPINESS, HUMOR, JOY, LAUGHTER, PLEASURES, SERIOUSNESS, SPORTS, THEATERS

3924 "Oh, I dunno, it can be fun if it's done in the right spirit." A racketeer's conniving girlfriend, **Jean Harlow**, replies seductively to young cop Wallace Ford, assigned to keep an eye on her, who asks her if she likes getting hurt. *The Beast of the City* (1932, MGM).

3925 "I like to pick my fillies. Take you, for instance. You're my type. No kidding, girlie. I could go for you in a big way. 'Fun-on-the-side Shapeley' they call me, and the accent's on the fun, believe me." Traveling salesman **Roscoe Karns** makes a big pest of himself, as he comes on to runaway heiress Claudette Colbert on a bus. *It Happened One Night* (1934, Columbia).

3926 "The only fun I get is feeding the goldfish, and they only eat once a day." To put it mildly, unstable **Bette Davis** is bored with her life, married to Eugene Pallette, the owner of a bordertown cafe. *Bordertown* (1935, Warner Bros.).

3927 "For good, clean fun, there's nothing like a wake." Reporter **Fredric March** is being cynical— but he's right about wakes, some wakes anyway. *Nothing Sacred* (1937, Selznick).

3928 "Go ahead, take a good look, you monkeys. Have a good time! Get a big kick out of it! It's fun to see an innocent man die isn't it?" **Henry Fonda** defies an angry crowd as he's led down the court-house steps, having just been sentenced to death for a crime he didn't commit. *You Only Live Once* (1937, United Artists).

3929 "We just do a little hugging and kissing, Dad. I mean, good, clean fun, just like me and Polly." **Mickey Rooney**, as Andy Hardy, assures Lewis Stone, as his father Judge Stone, that his dates with "dish" Lana Turner are as innocent as those he's had with his usual girl, Ann Rutherford. *Love Finds Andy Hardy* (1938, MGM).

3930 "I did, Norval, but some kinds of fun last longer than others, if you get what I mean." **Betty Hutton** hints of her pregnancy to Eddie Bracken, who has just said, "I thought you enjoyed yourself at the dance, Trudy." *The Miracle of Morgan's Creek* (1944, Paramount).

3931 "He's a lot of fun to fight with." American WAC officer **Ann Sheridan** speaks of French Captain Cary Grant. *I Was a Male War Bride* (1949, 20th Century-Fox).

3932 "My performance can be quite cold. I had more fun in the backseat of a '39 Ford than I can ever have in the vault at the Chase National Bank." **Elizabeth Taylor** lets wealthy Laurence Harvey know that she can be rented but not bought. *Butterfield 8* (1960, MGM).

3933 "What I'm out for is a good time—all the rest is propaganda." Brawling British working class stiff **Albert Finney** expresses his devotion to his personal pleasure in an opening work-bench soliloquy. *Saturday Night and Sunday Morning* (1960, GB, Woodfall-Continental Distributors).

3934 "Having fun, kiddies?. . . You little tramp, how dare you contaminate my pool. Here, maybe this will disinfect it." Arriving home from the studio, drinking from a bottle of booze, **Patty Duke** discovers her husband Alexander Davion in the pool with a naked girl. Duke pours the contents of the bottle into the pool. *Valley of the Dolls* (1967, 20th Century-Fox).

3935 "This life is not only sinful, it's not much fun." Once a not-so-respectable wife of a preacher, **Faye Dunaway** complains to Dustin Hoffman about her lot working in a western bordello. *Little Big Man* (1970, Cinema Center).

3936 "Oh, Bruce, we don't have fun any more. Do you know how long it is since I slept with another man?" **Jane Forth** complains to husband Joe Dallessandro as he gives himself a fix. *Trash* (1970, Cinema V-Warhol).

3937 "How can it be fun if you know I don't want it?" **Candice Bergen** asks a pertinent question of Art Garfunkel who has finally talked her into going to bed with him. He's too immature to have an answer. *Carnal Knowledge* (1971, Columbia).

3938 "Hey, you could have fun with all kinds of girls, am I right? And that's what you're doing. You go out and have fun until you meet up with your type and that's when you'll get married, am I right?" **Paul Sorvino** questions his son Joseph Bologna, a perennial loser, who's found the right girl, Renee Taylor. *Made for Each Other* (1971, 20th Century-Fox).

3939 LARRY LAPINSKY: "You're a funny lady." MRS. LAPINSKY: "My life has not been very funny." Before leaving for Hollywood, **Lenny Baker** speaks off-handedly to his long-suffering mother **Shelley Winters**. *Next Stop, Greenwich Village* (1976, 20th Century-Fox).

3940 "That was the most fun I've had without laughing." **Woody Allen**'s evaluation comes after making love with Diane Keaton for the first time. *Annie Hall* (1977, United Artists).

3941 "Fun? How would you like to go around dressed like a head waiter for the last seven hundred years?" **George Hamilton**, as Dracula, complains to his servant Arte Johnson. *Love at First Bite* (1979, AIP).

3942 "Believe me, this isn't a whole lot of fun." Decaying cadaver **Griffin Dunne** visits David Naughton to warn him that he'll turn into a werewolf at the first full moon. *An American Werewolf in London* (1981, GB, Polygram-Lycanthrope).

3943 "Are we having fun yet?" It's **Carol Burnett**'s tried and true line, sure to get things rolling. *The Four Seasons* (1981, Universal).

3944 "You can either watch me or join me. One of them's more fun." Alcoholic actor **Peter O'Toole** offers a drink to Mark Linn-Baker in the back seat of his limousine as he pours and drinks several glasses of Pinch scotch. *My Favorite Year* (1982, MGM-United Artists).

3945 "I'm gonna have fun and you're gonna have fun. We're all gonna have so much fun we'll need plastic surgery to remove our smiles." In some releases of the film, **Chevy Chase**'s declaration to his shocked family is much more earthy. *National Lampoon's Vacation* (1983, Warner Bros.).

3946 "In my heart, I know that I'm funny." The only funny thing about **Bruno Kirby**, as Lt. Hauk, is his thinking he's funny. *Good Morning, Vietnam* (1987, Touchstone-Buena Vista).

3947 "Fellas, last year I made three million dollars, but your fifty thousand was the most fun. Are you ready? Then let's go get them." **Glenne Headly** has conned con-men Michael Caine and Steve Martin, and now suggests a partnership. *Dirty Rotten Scoundrels* (1988, Orion).

3948 "All our lives are funny, babe. We're God's animated cartoons." Comedian **Tom Hanks** assures aspiring comedienne Sally Field that she can be funny, if she just examines her own life. *Punchline* (1988, Columbia).

3949 "Wow, that's about as much fun as kissing a passed-out drunk." **Don Johnson** kisses Jennifer Connelly, but she doesn't respond. *The Hot Spot* (1990, Orion).

3950 "That's more fun than eating cotton candy barefooted." **Virginia Madsen** has a way with words after Don Johnson makes oral love to her in an automobile in her husband's used car lot. Funny, Johnson never seems to sell any cars. *The Hot Spot* (1990, Orion).

Functions *see* ACTIONS AND ACTS, DUTIES, INDEPENDENCE AND DEPENDENCE, OCCUPATIONS, PURPOSES, REQUIREMENTS, USES AND USING, WORK AND WORKERS

Funerals

see also DEATH AND DYING, ENDS AND ENDING, EULOGIES, GRAVES AND GRAVEYARDS, SADNESS, SORROWS

3951 ANNABELLA: "I'd like to come home with you." HANNAY: "It's your funeral." Trying to escape from two men who want to kill her, spy **Lucie Mannheim** goes to **Robert Donat**'s rooms where his idle prophecy comes true. *The 39 Steps* (1935, GB, Gaumont).

3952 "Unto Adonai and Azriel, and in keeping with the laws of the Flame and lower pits, I consign this body to be consumed with purging fire. Let all baleful spirits that threaten the souls of men be banished. Be thou exorcised, O Dracula, and thy body long undead find destruction throughout eternity in the name of thy dark unholy master. In the name of all Holiest and through this cross, may the evil spirit be cast out until the end of time." Garbed in black and hooded, **Gloria Holden** with infinite sorrow speaks her father's obsequies, both to Satan and to God. *Dracula's Daughter* (1938, Universal).

3953 "Kind of mean for a girl to have two funerals—one for her body, one for her soul." Press agent **Fred MacMurray** pressures Lee J. Cobb to release the motion picture Alida Valli starred in before her untimely death. *The Miracle of the Bells* (1948, RKO).

3954 "Prepare a funeral for a Viking." **Tony Curtis** orders a Viking funeral after killing his half-brother Kirk Douglas. For a description of the ceremony, see the Rocket Gibraltar entry (3960). *The Vikings* (1958, United Artists).

3955 "You son of a bitch, you aim to do to me what they did with John Wesley Hardin. Lay me out and parade every damn fool in the state past me at a dollar a head, half-price for children, and then stuff me in a gunny sack and shovel me under." Dying of cancer, elderly gunfighter **John Wayne** complains when undertaker John Carradine offers to give the Duke a free funeral with all the fixings. *The Shootist* (1976, Paramount).

3956 "One funeral is just like another. And yet this one is special—not a single man. Only women. Nothing but women. Yes, definitely, I thought Bertrand would have enjoyed the sight of his own funeral." Narrator **Francois Truffaut** speaks of the late Charles Denner, whose funeral is attended by a bevy of beauties—and only women. *The Man Who Loved Women* (1977, France, Les Films de Carrosse-PAA).

3957 "You're just walking around to save funeral expenses." **Valerie Perrine** tells ex-rodeo cowboy champion Robert Redford that he's an anachronism. *The Electric Cowboy* (1979, Universal).

3958 "I don't want to sound naïve, but do you know what happens at a Jewish funeral?" **Judith Ivey** questions Susan Sarandon, as they contemplate attending the funeral of their murdered dentist Joe Mantegna. *Compromising Positions* (1985, Paramount).

3959 "If I die on a weekday, no one will come to my funeral because everybody is working." Movie extra **Alan King** expresses his fear to his son, Billy Crystal, that he will have no mourners from his profession. He is wrong. *Memories of Me* (1988, MGM).

3960 "Their whole life was the sea, the sea and their boats. And so in celebrating death (yes, you can say celebrating), they used both. The families of the great Vikings would put the body of their loved one on the ship, covered with straw, and then as the sun was setting, cast it away into the water. They would light huge bonfires on the beach, then the Vikings would light the tips of their arrows in the bonfire and shoot them at the ship. Oh, it must have been beautiful, fire on the water. Legend has it that if the color of the setting sun and the color of the burning ship were the same, then that Viking had led a good life and in the afterlife he would go to Viking heaven. Yes, all night long the Viking men, women and children watched as the ship with the body burned in the water. By dawn all that was left was ashes, complete obliteration, carried by the currents to the four corners of the earth, fresh and beautiful, vanished completely, like a dream." **Burt Lancaster** hopes for a Viking's funeral and his grandchildren make the arrangements. *Rocket Gibraltar* (1988, Columbia).

3961 "Carl and I were married just about two years when our sex life died. We had a small funeral. It was lovely." At a Boston luncheon, a bored matron tells Kim Basinger that she can empathize with Basinger, whose two-year-old marriage with Alec Baldwin is bogging down because he's too busy with his work to make love with her. *The Marrying Man* (1991, Hollywood Pictures).

Furs

see also ANIMALS, BODIES, CLOTHES, COMFORTS, HEAT, WEALTH AND RICHES

3962 NICK CHARLES: "Aren't you hot in that?" NORA CHARLES: "Yes, I'm stifling. But it's so pretty." **William Powell** doesn't understand why wife **Myrna Loy** is wearing a sumptuous full length mink coat indoors. *The Thin Man* (1934, MGM).

3963 "You know I was going to buy a fur coat. You can get it for two dollars down and one percent on the balance." **Jean Arthur**'s means of getting a fur coat is difficult. Wealthy Edward Arnold offers her an easy way to make an acquisition. *Easy Living* (1937, Paramount).

3964 "You may as well go to perdition in ermine. You're sure to come back in rags." **Katharine Hepburn** patronizes her roommate Ginger Rogers who has accepted some help in achieving her show business goals that have strings attached. *Stage Door* (1937, RKO).

3965 "A doll in Washington Heights got a fox fur out of me once." It's police detective **Dana Andrews**' non-sentimental reply when Clifton Webb asked if he had ever been in love. *Laura* (1944, 20th Century-Fox).

3966 "We're sisters under the mink." Beautiful tramp **Gloria Grahame** finds something in common with a society woman who is also wearing a mink coat. *The Big Heat* (1953, Columbia).

3967 "Take back your mink from whence it came." Showgirl **Vivian Blaine** returns a gift to her long time fiancé, gambler Frank Sinatra. *Guys and Dolls* (1955, Goldwyn-MGM).

3968 "Fur! You have fur!" Fetching **Tanya Roberts**, who has spent her life in an African jungle, raised by the Zambouli tribe, gets all excited when she sees a bare-chested white man, Ted Wass, for the first time. *Sheena* (1984, Columbia).

Future

see also EXPECTATIONS, FATE AND DESTINY, PAST, PLANS, TIME

3969 "Hoofing is all right, but there's no future in it." One can but chuckle at this character's inaccurate observation (played by Fred Astaire)—at least as far as Astaire is concerned. *Swing Time* (1936, RKO).

3970 "Posterity? What's posterity ever done for me? Why should I do anything for posterity?" Mean-spirited tycoon **Walter Connolly** shows little interest in following in the footsteps of Carnegie and Rockefeller. *Four's a Crowd* (1938, Warner Bros.).

3971 "That's the future of California, not gold. And it'll be our future, too, Jared. Isn't that something to live and work for?" Farmer's daughter **Olivia de Havilland** convinces engineer George Brent to give up his quest for gold for a farmer's life. *Gold Is Where You Find It* (1938, Warner Bros.).

3972 NINOTCHKA: "You are something we do not have in Russia." LEON: "Thank you." NINOTCHKA: "That is why I believe in the future of my country." Communist emissary **Greta Garbo** sets up Parisian playboy **Melvyn Douglas** for a zinger. *Ninotchka* (1939, MGM).

3973 "Poor Emma—what will become of her?" Told that he's dying, **Laurence Olivier**'s thoughts turn to his mistress Vivien Leigh. *That Hamilton Woman* aka: *Lady Hamilton* (1941, Korda-United Artists).

3974 "I see my future. . . a bit more burning flame-like years, and then the end." **Greta Garbo** shows a bit of Camille in her very last film role. *Two-Faced Woman* (1941, MGM).

3975 "Now for Australia and a crack at those Japs!" Having escaped from Nazi Germany, American pilot **Errol Flynn** is ready to take up the fight on a different front. *Desperate Journey* (1942, Warner Bros.).

3976 "Good old Watson—the one fixed point in a changing age. There's an east wind coming all the same, such a wind never blew on England yet. It will be cold and bitter, Watson, and a good many of us will wither before its blast. But it's God's own wind, nonetheless, and a greener, better, stronger land will be in the sunshine when the storm has cleared." **Basil Rathbone**, as the title character, lectures Nigel Bruce as Dr. Watson about the war with Nazi Germany and the ultimate triumph of truth and justice. *Sherlock Holmes and the Voice of Terror* (1942, Universal).

3977 "Forget the past, tell me the future." It's the password former mental patient **Ray Milland** innocently and unknowingly speaks to a conspirational fortune teller. She gives him information meant for another and it leads him into a future of intrigue and murder. *Ministry of Fear* (1944, Paramount).

3978 "People go out there and start polishing cuspidors." When his fiancée Claudia Drake tells **Tom Neal** that she wishes to delay their wedding plans to go to Hollywood to make it big as a singer, he tells her there's no future in it. *Detour* (1946, PRC).

3979 "Imagine, Johnny, she told me she was born the night she met me. Just think of that, the three of us with no pasts, only futures." **George Macready** introduces Glenn Ford to Macready's new wife Rita Hayworth, unaware she once was Ford's lover. *Gilda* (1946, Columbia).

3980 "You know something, Phil? I suddenly want to live to be very old. Very. I want to be around to see what happens. The world is stirring in very strange ways. Maybe this is the century for it. Maybe that's why it's so troubled. Other centuries had their driving forces. What will ours have been when men look far back to it one day? Maybe it won't be the American century after all. Or the Russian century. Or the atomic century. Wouldn't it be wonderful, Phil, if it turned out to be everybody's century? When people all over the world—free people—found a way to live together? I'd like to be around to see some of that in the beginning. I may stick around for quite awhile." Talented actress **Anne Revere** expresses a hopeful sentiment to her writer son Gregory Peck. Unfortunately for Revere, the century wouldn't be much for her. A short time later she was blacklisted because of her leftist leanings in the '30s, and perhaps for expressing thoughts similar to the one above. Today, once again we have politicians trying to put "liberals" on the defensive. Will we never learn to live by our country's own founding ideals? *Gentleman's Agreement* (1947, 20th Century-Fox).

3981 "There is hope for the future. And when the world is ready for a new, better life, all this will someday come to pass, in God's good time." The narrator sums up after Captain Nemo, his men, his submarine and his undersea city are totally destroyed. *20,000 Leagues Under the Sea* (1954, Buena Vista).

3982 "I didn't have to join up. I had a good job. . . . My girl and I decided there was a future for me in the Marines." **Chuck Connors** finds his future is fighting in a police action in Korea. *Hold Back the Night* (1956, Allied Artists).

3983 "Your future is all used up." Brothel keeper **Marlene Dietrich** correctly reads corrupt border Police Chief Orson Welles' palm near the end of the film. *Touch of Evil* (1958, Universal-International).

3984 "You're still trying to make sense out of what is laughingly referred to as the human race. Why don't you take your blinders off? Don't you know the future is already obsolete?" **Gene Kelly**'s H.L. Mencken-like character was pessimistic in the past, he's pessimistic now, and he's pessimistic about the future. *Inherit the Wind* (1960, United Artists).

3985 "I just want to say one word to you. . . . Plastics! There's a good future in plastics." **Walter Brooke** advises young college graduate Dustin Hoffman about a potential career move. *The Graduate* (1967, United Artists).

3986 "You ever sleep with a Syrian who chews tobacco?. . . Well, if anybody ever asks you, you can tell 'em there's no future in it." **Jane Fonda** explains why she left Texas *They Shoot Horses, Don't They?* (1969, ABC-Cinerama).

3987 "What do we do now?" U.S. Senate candidate **Robert Redford** asks his campaign manager Peter Boyle after he unexpectedly wins. *The Candidate* (1972, Warner Bros.).

3988 J.J. GITTES: "Why are you doing it?. . . What can you buy that you can't already afford?" NOAH CROSS: "The future, Mr. Gittes, the future." In a chilling conversation, **Jack Nicholson** learns from **John Huston** the full horror of the mystery of the movie. *Chinatown* (1974, Paramount).

3989 "I've been thinking what to do wit' my future. I could be a mud doctor. Check out the earth. Underneat'." Young **Linda Manz** is a delight with her poetic narration. *Days of Heaven* (1978, Paramount).

3990 RICHARD VERNON: "What really worries me is that when I get old, these kids will be running the country. These are the kids that will be taking care of me." CARL: "I wouldn't count on it." Teacher **Paul Gleason** fears the future with kids like the ones he's disciplining at a Saturday detention session. Janitor **John Kapelos** doesn't offer much comfort. *The Breakfast Club* (1985, Universal).

3991 "I've seen the future! It's a bald headed man from New York!" **Albert Brooks** suffers from Yuppie hysteria. *Lost in America* (1985, Warner Bros.).

3992 "The future isn't what it used to be, Mr. Angel." Devil **Robert De Niro** shares the thought with '50s New York private eye Mickey Rourke who literally descends into Hell—or at least close enough for most people. *Angel Heart* (1987, Tri-Star).

3993 "You know a cute young boy like you gotta think of a future lady friend in your life when you've finished wolfing around. Of course, I'm taken. . . ." **Sylvia Miles** is an outrageous real estate agent showing Charlie Sheen around a luxury apartment on New York's fashionable East Side. *Wall Street* (1987, 20th Century-Fox).

3994 "Music and movies are all America is good for. We build the machines, we build the future." Japanese detective **Ken Takakura** assesses the difference between the U.S. and Japan. *Black Rain* (1989, Paramount).

3995 "I wonder if future generations will ever know about us." It's probably safe to say that future generations won't have much interest in a Morton Downey, Jr. type radio talk show host like **Eric Bogosian**. *Talk Radio* (1989, Universal).

3996 "In a few years I could be prosecuting half the people here." Law student **James Spader**, who aspires to an appointment in the Justice Department, laconically comments as he listens to politicians and lobbyists at a New Year's Eve party. *True Colors* (1991, Paramount).

Gain *see* WEALTH AND RICHES, WINNERS AND LOSERS

Gallantry

see also BRAVERY, DARES AND DARING, LOVE AND HATE, LOVE AND LOVERS, NOBILITY

3997 "American women aren't accustomed to gallantry. . . ." **Irene Dunne** compliments her voice teacher Alexander D'Arcy, who has seen her to her home, after being out together all night. They are met there by suspicious husband Cary Grant. *The Awful Truth* (1937, Columbia).

3998 "No one died more gallantly—or earned more honor for his regiment." **John Wayne** tells the truth—but not all the truth about martinet cavalry officer Henry Fonda, whose arrogance and blundering led to the massacre of his troops by Apache warriors led by Geronimo. Reporters made it appear that his defeat was a great moral victory—and the public views him as a hero. Wayne knows better—but he doesn't wish to besmirch the regiment and its brave men. *Fort Apache* (1948, RKO).

3999 "You have about as much gallantry in that remark as you think I have brains." American showgirl **Ava Gardner** rails at Clark Gable who has asked her to tone down her behavior while she's around genteel Grace Kelly. *Mogambo* (1953, MGM).

Gambling

see also CARDS, CHANCES, GAMES, LOSSES AND LOSING, PROBABILITY AND STATISTICS, WINNERS AND LOSERS

4000 CONNIE RANDALL: "I'm not kidding—only—well, you just walk in and pick up a girl and walk out. . . . Is that fair?. . . Why don't you be a sport? . . . Why don't you give a girl a break?. . . Why don't you take a chance?. . . Why don't you gamble with me?. . . ." JERRY "BABE" STEWART: "All right. . . heads we do, tails we. . . ." CONNIE: "Get married!" JERRY: "All right, I never go back on a coin." Small town librarian **Carole Lombard** cons gambler **Clark Gable** into a sucker bet of whether they will have a brief fling or get married. They get married, but she still hasn't really got him. *No Man of Her Own* (1933, Paramount).

4001 LARRY CAIN: "Gee, Mabel, I lost every penny I had in the world." MABEL O'DARE: "Never mind, I bet on the other guy and I've enough for both of us." Boxer **Clark Gable** is probably glad that musical comedy star **Marion Davies** never doubted him. *Cain and Mabel* (1936, Cosmopolitan-Warner Bros.).

4002 SANDERS: "Now I give that marriage three months, and I'm laying three to one. Any takers?" HILDY JOHNSON: "I'll take that bet." Jail house reporter **Regis Toomey** doesn't see **Rosalind Russell** enter when he offers to bet his cronies that her marriage to Ralph Bellamy will go belly up. *His Girl Friday* (1940, Columbia).

4003 CAPT. LOUIS RENAULT: "I am shocked, shocked, to find that gambling is going on here." EMIL: "Your winnings, sir." RENAULT: "Oh, thank you very much." Police prefect **Claude Rains** insincerely closes down Humphrey Bogart's club just as croupier **Marcel Dalio** gives him his winnings. *Casablanca* (1942, Warner Bros.).

4004 EILEEN SHERWOOD: "What are they tossing for?" RUTH SHERWOOD: "I have a hunch it's not me." A group of Portuguese sailors match coins as they eye delectable **Janet Blair** without giving her older, more plain sister **Rosalind Russell** a second glance. *My Sister Eileen* (1942, Columbia).

4005 KATHY MOFFETT: "Is there a way to win?" JEFF BAILEY: "There's a way to lose more slowly." As they play roulette, **Jane Greer** is taught an important lesson by **Robert Mitchum.** *Out of the Past* (1947, RKO).

4006 "I'll tell you what. I'll make you a little bet. Three times 35 is, er, 105. I'll bet you $105,000 you go to sleep before I do." Greed for gold has driven **Humphrey Bogart** over the edge. He sinisterly offers to wager all their gold ore with his partner Tim Holt who has him covered with a gun because of his mad behavior. Bogie wins the bet. *The Treasure of the Sierra Madre* (1948, Warner Bros.).

4007 "One time he was sick and he wouldn't take penicillin, because he bet his fever would go to one hundred and four." Broadway character **Frank Sinatra** speaks admiringly of gambler Marlon Brando. *Guys and Dolls* (1955, Goldwyn-MGM).

4008 "Good afternoon, gentlemen. . . . What's the name of this game?" **Kirk Douglas,** as Doc Holliday, has the film's last line as he sits down at a poker table. *Gunfight at the OK Corral* (1957, Paramount).

4009 BUTCH CASSIDY: "Maybe there's a way to make a profit on this—bet on Logan." SUNDANCE KID: "I would but who'd bet on you?" Hole-in-the-wall gang leader **Paul Newman** makes an aside to his friend **Robert Redford** as he prepares to face the challenge of giant Ted Cassidy in a knife fight. *Butch Cassidy and the Sundance Kid* (1969, 20th Century-Fox).

4010 "It's out of my hands. A bad gambling debt has got to be taken care of." Friendly bookie **Paul Sorvino** tells compulsive loser James Caan that business is business. *The Gambler* (1975, Paramount).

4011 "I play in order to lose. That's what gets my juice going. If I only bet on the games I know, I could at least break even." Gambler **James Caan** understands his obsession, even though he's unable to do anything about it. *The Gambler* (1975, Paramount).

4012 "I go to a party, I bet on the hors d'oeuvres." Compulsive gambler **Burt Young** gives an idea of his illness. *Lookin' to Get Out* (1982, Paramount).

Games

see also ENJOYMENTS, ENTERTAINMENTS AND ENTERTAINING, FUN, GAMBLING, PLAYING AND PLAYERS, SPORTS, WINNERS AND LOSERS

4013 "Shoot first, argue afterwards—if you don't the other fellow gets you. . . . This game ain't for guys that's soft." **Edward G. Robinson,** speaking to old friend Douglas Fairbanks, Jr., doesn't recommend a career in the rackets for just anybody. *Little Caesar* (1930, Warner Bros.).

4014 "If this was the summer of 1894, I'd play games with you, sister. But it's much simpler now." Elderly **Tully Marshall** replies meaningfully when stranded harlot Jean Harlow asks if he knows any games. *Red Dust* (1932, MGM).

4015 "Are we not both the living dead? And now you come to me playing at being an avenging angel, childishly thirsting for my blood. We shall play a game, Vitus. A game of death, if you like." Devil worshipper **Boris Karloff** seems to be suggesting that he and his old adversary Bela Lugosi are long since dead. *The Black Cat* (1934, Universal).

4016 "Let's play a game. I will count to ten while closing my eyes, and when I open them, you will be gone." Paleontologist **Cary Grant** treats pesty Katharine Hepburn like the mindless child she is. *Bringing Up Baby* (1938, RKO).

4017 "This town's a giant dice game. . . come on, seven!" Alcoholic Broadway playwright **Thomas Mitchell** has a scheme to work a sting on big-time cardsharps. *Angels Over Broadway* (1940, Columbia).

4018 RENAULT: "Your best champagne, and put it on my bill." ILSA: "No. . . please." RENAULT: "It's a little game we play. They put it on my bill, I tear up the bill. It is most convenient." Police prefect **Claude Rains** orders drinks for **Ingrid Bergman** and Paul Henreid at Humphrey Bogart's cafe. *Casablanca* (1942, Warner Bros.).

4019 "I got a hot poker game tonight. I better go home and mark some cards. One of us has got to make a living." **James Gleason**, crony of opportunistic Broadway producer Cary Grant, notes they aren't doing very well at the moment. *Once Upon a Time* (1944, Columbia).

4020 SIR ALFRED: "Have you ever heard of Russian roulette?" DAPHNE: "I used to play it all the time with my father." SIR ALFRED: "I doubt that you played Russian roulette all the time with your father!" DAPHNE: "I most certainly did. You play it with two packs of cards and—" SIR ALFRED: "That is Russian bank. Russian roulette is a very different sort of amusement—which I could only wish your father had played continuously before he had you." Orchestra conductor **Rex Harrison** has an argument about a game with his new bride **Linda Darnell**. Throughout the film he dreams of killing her because he believes she has been unfaithful. *Unfaithfully Yours* (1948, 20th Century-Fox).

4021 "Why can't women play the game properly? Everyone knows that in love affairs only the man has the right to lie." **Clifton Webb**'s consolation of Louis Jourdan is not totally sincere. *Three Coins in the Fountain* (1954, 20th Century-Fox).

4022 "Do not worry, Nathan Detroit's crap game will float again." Promoter **Frank Sinatra** needs to find a safe place to hold his long-standing floating crap game. *Guys and Dolls* (1955, Goldwyn-MGM).

4023 "Now that we're through with Humiliate the Host—we're through with that one for this round anyway, and we don't want to play Hump the Hostess; not yet—so I know what we do: how about a little round of Get the Guests? How about a little game of Get the Guests?" **Richard Burton** proposes it's time to make his guests Sandy Dennis and George Segal squirm for a change. *Who's Afraid of Virginia Woolf?* (1966, Warner Bros.).

4024 "Tell them it was only a game." As he lays dying, **Michael Caine** bitterly advises his murderer Laurence Olivier of how to deal with the arriving police. *Sleuth* (1972, Palomar-20th Century-Fox).

4025 "When something's finished, we begin again." Recent widower **Marlon Brando** plays sexual and childish games with young Maria Schneider. *Last Tango in Paris* (1973, It.-Fr., United Artists).

4026 "There is no good or bad. . . . The object is not to win or not to lose. And the only rule is to stay in the game." Mortally wounded ex-American agent **Burt Lancaster** likens espionage to a deadly game to his former partner and assassin Alain Delon.

4027 "Greetings, Professor Falken. . . a strange game. The only winning move is not to play." WOPR, the War Operations Plan Response computer directly addresses its designer John Wood after it discovers the lesson of the game of tick-tack-toe. Its conclusion also applies to the game of nuclear war. *Wargames* (1983, MGM-United Artists).

4028 "If you take away the functions of the aristocracy, what can it do but play games too seriously?" Aristocrat without function **James Mason** holds forth with his game playing guests at his country estate. *The Shooting Party* (1985, GB, European Classics).

4029 "It's not a question of enough, pal. It's a zero-sum game. Somebody wins and somebody loses. . . ." "Player" **Michael Douglas** replies to Charlie Sheen, who asks "How much is enough?" *Wall Street* (1987, 20th Century-Fox).

4030 "Change the laws all you want, but you can't stop the game. I'll still be here. I adapt. . . . We care more for the game than the players." Corporation raider **Danny De Vito** argues that Penelope Ann Miller, lawyer for his latest victim, and he are two of a kind—ruthless, money-hungry and lovers of the game. Miller, who is fighting a takeover by "Larry the Liquidator" of a New England milling company, tells him: "Someday the laws will change to put you out of business." Miller is a beautiful woman, but she's not credible as a rough and tough lawyer—and she sure doesn't read lines with any conviction. *Other People's Money* (1991, Warner Bros.).

Garbage

see also FOOD AND EATING, WASTE AND WASTEFULNESS, WORTH AND VALUES

4031 "Garbage—but good enough for a man when he's starving—so you'll do, too, baby. . . . This is no time to be particular. Funny, a man should want something he's got no use for, and I've got no use for you. You know that, don't you?" After he escapes from the infamous Devil's Island penal colony, **Clark Gable** breaks into cafe singer Joan Crawford's dressing room and demands food. He's not very gracious when she provides some. *Strange Cargo* (1940, MGM).

4032 "This is the garbage can of the educational system. . . . They hire fools like us with college degrees to sit on their garbage can—keep them in school—so women for a few hours a day can walk around the city." Cynical veteran high school teacher **Louis Calhern** lectures the new teachers, including Glenn Ford, about the nature of their school Manual Trades, and its students. *Blackboard Jungle* (1955, MGM).

4033 "This is your neighbor speaking. I'm sure I speak for all of us when I say that something must be done about your garbage cans in the alley here. It is definitely second-rate garbage! Now, by next week, I want to see a better class of garbage. I want to see champagne bottles and caviar cans. I'm sure you're all behind me on this, so let's snap it up and get on the ball." Non-conformist writer **Jason Robards** yells from his window to his neighbors to show a little class by discarding better garbage. *A Thousand Clowns* (1965, United Artists).

4034 "My mother says the world's a garbage dump and we're just flies it attracts." **Natalie Wood**'s mother, Ruth Gordon, has a very low opinion of the world and its inhabitants. *Inside Daisy Clover* (1966, Warner Bros.).

4035 "In the twentieth century, the main product of all human endeavor is waste." In 1967, **Orson Welles'** line was laughed at. Today, it's frighteningly true. *I'll Never Forget What's 'Is Name* (1967, GB, Universal).

4036 "Looks like some garbage needs to be removed." Vietnam vet **Robert Ginty** sees some junkies hanging around Central Park. The self-proclaimed vigilante barbecues New York City drug dealers with a flamethrower. *Exterminator 2* (1984, Cannon).

4037 "Believe me, there's a future in garbage. . . . By the year 2000 there's going to be no place for human refuse. . . . Get in while the market's still open." **George Coe** urges his unambitious nephew Ted Danson to get into a growth industry. *Cousins* (1989, Paramount).

Gardening *see* FOOD AND EATING, GROWTH AND DEVELOPMENT, LAND AND FARMS

Generalizations *see* DETECTIVES AND DEDUCTION, IDEAS, LOGIC, PROOFS

Generosity

see also GIFTS AND GIVING, NOBILITY, SERVICES

4038 "She makes $45 a week and sends $100 of it home to her mother." **Una Merkel** cattily refers to another chorine who seems to augment her salary somehow. *42nd Street* (1933, Warner Bros.).

4039 SORROWFUL JONES: "I've always been generous in a quiet way." REGRET: "Practically silent." Frugal bookmaker **Adolphe Menjou** gets no respect from his raspy voiced bookkeeper **Lynne Overman**. *Little Miss Marker* (1934, Paramount).

4040 "A man wants to be met by a generous heart in a woman. An open heart. Honey, never be ashamed to say what you feel. And if you come to love a man, let him know it. Let him know all about it." **Robert Preston**'s advice to his daughter Shirley Knight is influenced by the temporary problems he's having in his marriage to Dorothy McGuire. *The Dark at the Top of the Stairs* (1960, Warner Bros.).

4041 "A generous man is merely a fool in the eyes of a thief." Narrator **Michael MacLiammoir**. *Tom Jones* (1963, GB, United Artists).

Genius

see also ABILITIES AND CAPABILITIES, INTELLIGENCE, KNOWLEDGE, LEARNING AND LESSONS, MINDS, NATURE AND NATURAL, TALENTS

4042 "I don't know. If I always knew what I meant, I'd be a genius." Private eye **Dick Powell**, up to his ears in murder and blackmail, confides to Anne Shirley that he hasn't got everything figured out yet. *Murder My Sweet* (1945, RKO).

4043 LYNN BELVEDERE: "For my work, I require an atmosphere of spartan simplicity." TACEY: "And may I ask what your profession is?" MR. BELVEDERE: "Certainly, I am a genius." Prissy **Clifton Webb** figuratively and literally looks down his nose at **Maureen O'Hara** in whose home Webb has taken a job as a live-in baby sitter and housekeeper. *Sitting Pretty* (1948, 20th Century-Fox).

4044 "You know, Oliver, I sometimes think I was born with a genius, an absolute genius for doing the wrong thing." Fading movie star **James Mason** admits to studio executive Charles Bickford that he's made some lulu mistakes. *A Star Is Born* (1954, Warner Bros.).

4045 "What we're up against is nothing less than an international black market in brains. . . scientific geniuses bought, sold, traded—if necessary, kidnapped." CIA General **Jack Warden** lays out the plot of this comedy drama. *Blindfold* (1966, Universal).

4046 "Let's pray you were the genius." **Yvette Mimieux** hopes somewhat crazy Maximilian Schell knows what he's doing in this above average science fiction film. *The Black Hole* (1979, Buena Vista).

Gentlemen

see also CHIVALRY, CLASSES, LADIES AND
GENTLEMEN, MEN, NOBILITY, SOCIETIES

4047 "If it wasn't for me, you'd still be rolling
drunks at the Silver Slipper. I made you rich. I put
those swell clothes on your back. Now, just because
you got your neck washed, you think you're a gentleman. No one can make you that. You're riffraff,
and so am I. You belong to me, and you'll stay with
me. You bet you're going to stay with me because
I'm holding on to you. Why, I committed murder to
get you." Neurotic **Bette Davis** confesses the extent
of her love for her businessman husband, Paul
Muni. *Bordertown* (1935, Warner Bros.).

4048 "No gentleman mentions a lady's name in a
bar." **George Brent** challenges to a duel the unfortunate man who commented on unconventional
Bette Davis in a southern saloon. *Jezebel* (1938,
Warner Bros.).

4049 HATFIELD: "Put out that cigar. . . . A gentleman
doesn't smoke in the presence of a lady." DR.
BOONE: "Three weeks ago I took a bullet out of a
man who was shot by a 'gentleman.' The bullet was
in the back!" Gambler **John Carradine** is concerned for the comfort of pregnant Louise Platt. Fellow stagecoach passenger Dr. **Thomas Mitchell**
isn't impressed with Carradine's kind of gentleman.
Stagecoach (1939, United Artists).

4050 "When I worked at Foeldes Brothers and
Sons, well, the sons were all right, but the brothers,
Mr. Kralik! And that's why I like it here so much.
When you say, 'Miss Novak, let's go to the stock
room and put some bags on the second shelf,' you
really want to put some bags on the second shelf.
And that's my idea of a gentleman!" Shop clerk
Margaret Sullavan feels safe with her superior
James Stewart. *The Shop Around the Corner* (1940,
MGM).

4051 "One of our gentlemen found time to say,
'How delicious.'" **Jean Adair**, one of the two sweet,
murdering old maiden aunts, fondly recalls for
nephew Cary Grant, an appreciative recipient of
their poisoned elderberry wine. *Arsenic and Old
Lace* (1944, Warner Bros.).

4052 "I realized that in becoming a gentleman, I
had only succeeded in becoming a snob." **John
Mills**, as the adult Pip, is ashamed of what a social
climber he's become as he happily sees his kindly
and always considerate brother-in-law Bernard
Miles leave after an unwelcomed and uncomfortable visit. *Great Expectations* (1946, GB, Rank-
Cineguild).

4053 "All right, Phil. Mind your manners. Be a little
gentleman. Don't let the flag touch the ground. This
sort of honorableness gets me sick." **Celeste Holm**
tells Gregory Peck that he can't fight injustice in a
gentlemanly way. *Gentleman's Agreement* (1947,
20th Century-Fox).

4054 "If my wonderful, beautiful, marvelous virtue
is still intact, it is no thanks to me, I assure you. It is
purely by courtesy of the gentleman from South
Bend." **Grace Kelly** informs her ex-husband Bing
Crosby and her fiancé John Lund, that although
willing, she did not make love with Frank Sinatra,
because he didn't want to take advantage of her
when she was loaded. *High Society* (1956, MGM).

Gentleness

see also BEHAVIOR, CLASSES, CONSIDERATIONS,
KINDNESS, NOBILITY, SOCIETIES

4055 "You are gentle and there's nothing stronger in
the world than gentleness." Eurasian doctor **Jennifer Jones** compliments lover William Holden.
Love Is a Many-Splendored Thing (1955, 20th Century-Fox).

4056 "Joe, be gentle with me." **Heather Sears**
makes the request of Laurence Harvey when he
finally has her talked into having sex with him.
Room at the Top (1958, GB, Remus).

4057 "Men who wear glasses are so much more
gentle, sweet and helpless." **Marilyn Monroe** coos
to deceitful Tony Curtis, who luckily is wearing
glasses. *Some Like It Hot* (1959, United Artists).

Geography see LAND AND FARMS, STUDIES AND
STUDENTS, WORLD

Geometry see MATHEMATICS

Gestures

see also BODIES, EMOTIONS, IDEAS, INTENTIONS

4058 "What we need right now is a stupid, futile
gesture on someone's part." **Tim Matheson** encourages his fraternity brothers after they are all thrown
out of school for low grades and unbelievably non-
academic behavior. *National Lampoon's Animal
House* (1978, Universal).

4059 "It's a gesture, not a recipe." Literary agent
Vanessa Redgrave slyly comforts Frances Barber
who is concerned that the mixture of her brother
Gary Oldman's ashes with those of his lover and
murderer Alfred Molina is not half and half. *Prick
Up Your Ears* (1987, GB, Goldwyn).

Ghosts *see* DEATH AND DYING, SPIRIT AND SPIRITS

Gifts and Giving

see also ABILITIES AND CAPABILITIES, BIRTHS AND BIRTHDAYS, CELEBRATIONS, CHRISTMAS, FRIENDSHIPS AND FRIENDS, GENEROSITY, KINDNESS, PARTIES, TALENTS, WEDDINGS

4060 ERNEST BROWN: "You're certainly givin' me the time of my life." TIRA: "Don't say givin', I don't like the word givin'." Chump **William B. Davidson** will pay dearly for his time with carnival side-show dancer **Mae West**. *I'm No Angel* (1933, Paramount).

4061 NORA CHARLES: "What are you going to give me for Christmas? I hope I don't like it." NICK CHARLES: "Well, you'll have to keep them anyway. There's a man at the aquarium who said he wouldn't take them back." **Myrna Loy** enjoys exchanging husband **William Powell**'s presents. *The Thin Man* (1934, MGM).

4062 "This is the best Christmas present you ever gave me." Clad in pajamas and a robe, **William Powell** is delighted with the air pistol given to him by his wife Myrna Loy. He stretches out on a sofa, bends his knees, props the pistol between his feet and shoots out several ornaments on the Christmas tree. *The Thin Man* (1934, MGM).

4063 "The joy of giving is indeed a pleasure—especially when you get rid of something you don't want." Pastor **Barry Fitzgerald** expresses a less than Christian thought about giving, as he confides in his curate Bing Crosby. *Going My Way* (1944, Paramount).

4064 "It shall be a wedding gift to you from the crown, for your loyalty and service to king and country." British King **Miles Mander** rewards Randolph Scott, who is to marry Barbara Britton, for ridding the seas of pirate Captain Charles Laughton. *Captain Kidd* (1945, United Artists).

4065 "Tonight I want to tell you the story of an empty stocking. Once upon a midnight clear there was a child's cry. A blazing star hung over a stable and wise men came with birthday gifts. We haven't forgotten that night down through the centuries. We celebrate it with stars on Christmas trees, with the sound of bells, and with gifts. But especially with gifts. You give me a book, I give you a tie. Aunt Martha has always wanted an orange squeezer. And Uncle Henry could do with a new pipe. Oh, we forget nobody. And our stockings are stuffed. All that is, except one, and we have even forgotten to hang up the stocking for the child born in a manger. It's his birthday we're celebrating. Don't let us ever for-

get that. Let us ask ourselves what he would wish for most, and then let each put in his share. Loving kindness, warm hearts, and a stretched out hand of tolerance. All the shining gifts make peace on earth." It's the sermon angel **Cary Grant** composed for Bishop **David Niven** to deliver on Christmas Eve. *The Bishop's Wife* (1947, RKO).

4066 "Given enough ointment, there's always a fly. Given enough presents, there's bound to be a stinker." **Spencer Tracy**'s comment is inspired by a wedding present for his daughter Elizabeth Taylor of a plaster figurine of Venus De Milo with a clock in her stomach. *Father of the Bride* (1950, MGM).

4067 "And so our Cinderella and her Prince Charming went home to their palatial estate on Long Island. But they didn't go in a coach drawn by six white horses. They went in the little gift to the bride, a solid gold Cadillac. Well, what else can you give a girl who has everything?" Narrator **George Burns** brings to an end the fairy tale story of poor little stockholder Judy Holliday and her tycoon lover Paul Douglas. *The Solid Gold Cadillac* (1956, Columbia).

4068 "If I were an Indian potentate, I'd shower you with diamonds. If I were a cobbler, I'd sew your shoe. But since I'm only a detective, all I can offer you is a detailed dossier." Detective **Maurice Chevalier** has thoroughly investigated Van Doude and his family, as an engagement gift for his daughter Audrey Hepburn. *Love in the Afternoon* (1957, Allied Artists).

4069 "I always thought I could give them life like a present, all wrapped in white with every promise of happiness.... All I can give them is life itself." **Dorothy McGuire** has mastered lessons all parents must learn as to the limitations of their ability to protect their children from the harsh realities of life. *The Dark at the Top of the Stairs* (1960, Warner Bros.).

4070 "I want to do something, though. I'd like to give you a going-away present. You may not like it, but I don't care. It's just this, you're never gonna forget me. You're gonna walk down the street of wherever you happen to be and you're gonna see me, even when you know I'm not there. And nobody in this world is ever gonna be as right for you as I was, for twelve days in Paris in autumn, 'cause that's been your gift to me." American tourist **Joanne Woodward** is seen off at a train station in Paris by American musician Paul Newman. At the last moment he changes his mind about leaving France for America with her. *Paris Blues* (1961, United Artists).

4071 "I expect that is to be your gift, Sandy—to kill without concern." **Maggie Smith** is contemptuous of her student Pamela Franklin. *The Prime of Miss Jean Brodie* (1969, 20th Century-Fox).

4072 "You call that abuse? You don't know what I'm used to. With all your carrying on—to me, Jonathan, you're a gift." Considering how badly Jack Nicholson treats his live-in lover **Ann-Margret**, the other men in her life must have been real monsters. *Carnal Knowledge* (1971, Avco Embassy).

4073 "I give you now the love you've never known. I give it feeling that you'll gain the strength to go from this house." Medium **Pamela Franklin** exorcises a ghost by making love to it. *The Legend of Hell House* (1973, GB, 20th Century-Fox).

4074 "Someone has sent me a bowel movement." Gross female impersonator **Divine** opens a gross birthday present. *Pink Flamingos* (1973, New Line).

4075 "My grandmother never gave gifts. She was too busy being raped by Cossacks." **Woody Allen** cracks a bitter joke about the hard life of Jewish Russian peasants. *Annie Hall* (1977, United Artists).

4076 "If there's one thing that I want to give my son, it's the gift of fury. . . gobble up the world. Eat life or it'll eat you." Professional warrior **Robert Duvall** has no wars to fight during peacetime, so he takes on his family, and most particularly his son Michael O'Keefe, who doesn't want to be just like dear old dad. *The Great Santini* (1979, Warner Bros.).

4077 "I can't give anymore. I have nothing more to give." **Albert Finney** howls as he contemplates his 227th performance of "King Lear." *The Dresser* (1981, GB, Columbia).

4078 "You have done with the Mogwai what your society has done with all nature's gifts. You are not ready. . . . Perhaps one day you will be ready." Ancient Chinese storekeeper **Keye Luke** decides mankind is not ready for the gremlins of the movie—at least not until the sequel. *Gremlins* (1984, Warner Bros.).

4079 "At the time I was too young to see the gift whole, to see it for what it was, and to acknowledge the love that had given it birth. I see it now, at long, long last." As an old woman, **Coral Browne** finally realizes the love that Lewis Carroll had for her as a child when he made her immortal by writing of her in "Alice in Wonderland." *Dreamchild* (1985, GB, Thorn EMI-PHF).

4080 "The kid's got a sledgehammer break. . . he's an incredible flake—but that's a gift." **Paul New-**man speaks admiringly of talented young pool player, Tom Cruise, to Helen Shaver. *The Color of Money* (1986, Touchstone-Buena Vista).

4081 "I gave her my heart and she gives me a pen." **John Cusack** can't believe how unfair life is, speaking of his beloved Ione Skye, who doesn't quite share his passion. *Say Anything. . .* (1989, 20th Century-Fox).

4082 "Dances with bikers got this for you." American Indian medicine man **Rino Thunder** presents Charlie Sheen with a leather jacket as a going away present. *Hot Shots!* (1991, 20th Century-Fox).

Girls

see also BOYS, CHILDREN AND CHILDHOOD, DAUGHTERS, WOMEN, YOUTH

4083 "I'm not a bad girl, not a good girl, just a halfway girl, half good impulses, half bad impulses." It's a title card for **Doris Kenyon**, as chorus girl Poppy La Rue, stranded in Shanghai, forced to work on infamous Malay Street. *The Half Way Girl* (1925, silent, First National).

4084 "I'm just an old-fashioned home girl—like Mae West." Tough broad **Patsy Kelly** rejects Jean Harlow's advice about trapping a wealthy man. *The Girl from Missouri* (1934, MGM).

4085 "You make out like every young girl was Jennifer Jones in the story of Bernadette." **Shirley Booth** accuses her husband of taking too much interest in the way Richard Jaeckel treats Terry Moore. *Come Back, Little Sheba* (1952, Paramount).

4086 MAJOR JEB WEBBE: "What's a girl like you doing in Korea, anyway?" LT. RUTH McCARA: "Getting in the war like everybody else." It seems to MASH Surgeon **Humphrey Bogart** that Nurse **June Allyson** is in Korea to make a play for the doctor. *Battle Circus* (1953, MGM).

4087 "If she's a girl, I don't know what my sister is." **Barry Gordon** is flabbergasted when Tom Ewell refers to Jayne Mansfield as a "girl." *The Girl Can't Help It* (1956, 20th Century-Fox).

4088 "I'm a girl. . . I'm a girl. . . I'm a girl." Posing as a girl, **Jack Lemmon** frustratingly reminds himself of his assumed gender when cuddly Marilyn Monroe climbs into a train's upper berth with him. *Some Like It Hot* (1959, United Artists).

4089 "Well, I don't know how to put it—but I have this thing about girls." In his best Cary Grant imitation, **Tony Curtis** arouses Marilyn Monroe's interest, challenging her by claiming that he's not aroused by girls. *Some Like It Hot* (1959, United Artists).

4090 "Girls like me don't fall in love." **Gina Lollobrigida** tries subtly to tell fascinated Tony Franciosa that she's a whore. *Go Naked in the World* (1960, MGM).

4091 "I see a girl who looks like a pearl. A pearl of a girl." Disturbed adolescent **Keir Dullea** brightens young schizophrenic Janet Margolin, who rewards him by allowing him to speak to her without resorting to rhyme. *David and Lisa* (1962, Continental Distributing).

4092 "Girls who feel like they are not going to be invited to dance always get on the debating team." Actor **Michael Rennie** explains how he knew Debbie Reynolds had been a member of her high school debating team. *Mary, Mary* (1963, Warner Bros.).

4093 "I'm a girl, I'm supposed to be a sissy." **Diane Baker** insists to Gregory Peck that her gender absolves her from any obligation to be brave in a dangerous situation. *Mirage* (1965, Universal).

4094 "I have always found girls fragrant in any phase of the moon." **Noel Coward**, playing an aged homosexual fortune teller, known as "The Witch of Capri," mincingly makes a perfumey declaration. *Boom!* (1968, U.S.-G.B., Universal).

4095 "When little white girls were playing with dolls in their party dresses, I was dodging drunks and praying that I wouldn't be just another nigger." Black nun **Barbara McNair** recalls how it was growing up in the ghetto. *Change of Habit* (1969, Universal).

4096 "I don't want to be a girl; I wish I were a cock." Rich girl **Andrea Feldman**'s wish seems to be a good example of penis envy. *Trash* (1970, Cinema V-Andy Warhol).

4097 "I expect to be treated with a little dignity and a little respect. Don't ever refer to me as your girl again." **Lily Tomlin** admonishes her intolerably sexist and repulsive boss, Dabney Coleman. *9 to 5* (1980, 20th Century-Fox).

4098 "You're not supposed to hit girls!" **Debra Winger** fumes at John Travolta who orders her around and slaps her when she gives him some lip. *Urban Cowboy* (1980, Paramount).

4099 "Nice, clean middle class girls do not rub elbows or anything else with nasty, dirty lower class boys." **Joanna Merlin** gives advice to her teenage daughter Rosanna Arquette about Vincent Spano, who hails from the wrong side of the tracks. *Baby, It's You* (1983, Paramount).

4100 "Oh, what are you, crazy? The Ivy League stinks. All they got there is those ugly, intellectual girls with band-aids on their knees from playing the cello. No, thank you." Californian **Anthony Edwards** rejects the notion of attending an eastern college with his buddy John Cusack. He seems to have a bias against intellectual girls who play cellos—or maybe just against ugly girls. *The Sure Thing* (1985, Embassy).

4101 "I don't know what it is—I'm usually not such a putz with the girls." Teen **Michael Rubin** can't understand why the girls at a dance wish to avoid him—maybe it has something to do with the fact that he's dead, having been thrown in a river contaminated by radioactive material and revived as a zombie. *I Was a Teenage Zombie* (1987, Horizon).

4102 "I've only met her once and already she's thinking about me. . . . It's going to happen, guys, I feel it. . . she's going to be mine." **Josh Charles** is excited after talking to the girl of his dreams, Melora Walters, on the phone. *Dead Poets Society* (1989, Touchstone).

4103 "You know me. I'm the eat-me/beat-me girl." **Samantha Mathis** identifies herself after tracking down pirate radio station host Christian Slater at the post office where he picks up fan mail from people like her. *Pump Up the Volume* (1990, New Line).

4104 "The girl strikes men like a cobra." **Robert Duvall** observes the way Laura Dern mesmerizes men. *Rambling Rose* (1991, Seven Arts-New Line).

4105 DR. RAE CRANE: "I'm not a girl!" DR. ROBERT CAMPBELL: "The hell you're not!" CRANE: "I'm your research assistant!" CAMPBELL: "The hell you are!" In this movie, the shrill exchange between **Lorraine Bracco**, with her annoying voice, and sexist **Sean Connery**, who refers to her as a "girl" is what passes for a "cute meet." *Medicine Man* (1992, Buena Vista).

4106 "She's definitely a turnoff—too overt. I mean, most girls don't fly through the air with their skirt around their waist." In voice-over **Sara Gilbert** describes hypnotically sensual Drew Barrymore. *Poison Ivy* (1992, New Line).

4107 "Girls are to sleep with after the game, not to coach during the game." Boozy former major leaguer **Tom Hanks** is the reluctant manager of the Rockford Peaches, a girls' professional baseball team. *A League of Their Own* (1992, Columbia).

Gladness

see also HAPPINESS AND UNHAPPINESS, JOY, PLEASURES

4108 "I'm Pollyanna, the glad girl." Stranded prostitute **Jean Harlow** tartly introduces herself when she arrives at an Indo-China rubber plantation. *Red Dust* (1932, MGM).

4109 "Is that a gun in your pocket or are you just glad to see me?" **Mae West**'s suggestive little line is still breaking people up today. *She Done Him Wrong* (1933, Paramount).

4110 "Now I can go, and I'm glad I'm going. Very glad." Beautiful Parisian street girl turned musical revue entertainer **Anna Sten** commits suicide to reconcile two feuding brothers, vying for her favors. *Nana* (1934, United Artists).

4111 "Yes, I killed him. And I'm glad I tell you. Glad, glad, glad!" In a controlled hysteria that would be appropriate for the climax of a Perry Mason case, **Bette Davis** admits to killing a man she says made unsolicited advances toward her. *The Letter* (1940, Warner Bros.).

4112 "I'm glad I'm not young and vulnerable any more." Observing the romantic pains of her younger secretarial colleagues Jean Peters and Maggie McNamara, **Dorothy McGuire** claims something about herself that clearly isn't so. *Three Coins in the Fountain* (1954, 20th Century-Fox).

4113 "I don't want you back, but I'm glad I had you." **Vanessa Redgrave** is determined to be free of her half-mad ex-husband David Warner. *Morgan—A Suitable Case for Treatment* (1966, GB, British Lion).

4114 "Well, I'm glad I'm not going to be at your home for the holidays." Judge **Matt Clark** quips when Gene Hackman announces as attorney for the plaintiff and his daughter Mary Elizabeth Mastrantonio announces as defense attorney in an important class action suit. *Class Action* (1991, 20th Century-Fox).

Glamour

see also APPEARANCES, ATTRACTIONS, BEAUTY, CHARM, GIRLS, MAGIC, MYSTERIES, WOMEN

4115 "I'll never be able to get a man, much less hold him. No glamour. No glamour at all." As she makes this statement, **Judy Garland** looks down at her chest, but she's not under-endowed in that region. The studios had her bosom bound because she was too buxomy for some of her kid roles. *Love Finds Andy Hardy* (1938, MGM).

4116 "I know I'm no glamour girl. . . but maybe someday you'll realize that glamour isn't the only thing in the world." Now **Judy Garland**, hopes her other fine qualities will be finally recognized, as she gazes at the photograph of her dream man, Mickey Rooney. *Babes in Arms* (1939, MGM).

4117 "You glamour girls are a drug on the market." Pilot **James Cagney** dismisses the appeal of heiress Bette Davis. *The Bride Came C.O.D.* (1941, Warner Bros.).

Glasses *see* EYES, SIGHT AND SIGHTS, SIGNS

Gloom *see* DARKNESS, DESPAIR AND DESPERATION, HOPE

Glory

see also FAME, HONOR, PRAISES, REPUTATIONS

4118 "Every year, in every theater, some young person makes a hit. Sometimes it's a big hit, sometimes a little one. It's a distinct success but how many of them keep their heads? How many of them work? Youth comes to the fore. Youth has its hour of glory. But too often it's only a morning glory—a flower that fades before the sun is very high." **C. Aubrey Smith** advises Katharine Hepburn after her triumph in a Broadway play. *Morning Glory* (1933, RKO).

4119 "In the seventeenth century Holland was a world power, her ships carried treasure to Amsterdam from all over the world, but her proudest glory was the son of a miller from Leyden. . . ." Written introduction. *Rembrandt* (1936, London Films).

4120 "To hell or glory. It depends upon your point of view." **Erroll Flynn**, as George Custer, snarls at gun and whiskey runner Arthur Kennedy, who asks where they are going, as Flynn leads his 7th Cavalry regiment to death and glorious infamy at the Little Big Horn. *They Died with Their Boots On* (1942, Warner Bros.).

4121 "Without a shred of pity, without a shred of regret, I watch you go with glory in my heart." **Ingrid Bergman** revels in her loathing for her husband, Charles Boyer, when she finally realizes he was trying to drive her mad. *Gaslight* (1944, MGM).

4122 "For over a thousand years, Roman conquerors returning from the wars enjoyed the honor of triumph, a tumultuous parade. In the procession came trumpeteers and musicians and strange animals from the conquered territories, together with carts laden with treasure and captured armaments. The conqueror rode in a triumphant chariot, the dazed prisoners walking in chains before him. Sometimes his children, robed in white, stood with him in the chariot or rode the trace horses. A slave stood behind the conqueror holding a golden crown and whispering in his ear a warning that all glory is fleeting." The last words of **George C. Scott** as General George S. Patton in the film. *Patton* (1970, 20th Century-Fox).

4123 "To be a true believer and unjustly condemned to death—that is the way to glory!" **Marlon Brando**, as the Grand Inquisitor Torquemada, sees no problems if innocent people are put to death as heretics. *Christopher Columbus: The Discovery* (1992, Warner Bros.).

Goals

see also ENDS AND ENDINGS, PURPOSES

4124 "Yes, again—again and again! Remember our aim: 'Find the microbe, kill the microbe.'" **Paul Muni**, as scientist Louis Pasteur, gives a pep talk to his workers in the laboratory regarding their goal. *The Story of Louis Pasteur* (1936, Warner Bros.).

4125 "Give me a picture that ends with a kiss and black ink on the books." Movie executive **Walter Pidgeon** names his bottom line for a film. *The Bad and the Beautiful* (1952, MGM).

4126 "What's the goal, sweetie, a nasty little love nest? That's all you'll get, if that. No cold-eyed, calculating little viper's going to do me out of a thing. Those wide, wide blue eyes turned on him like red-hot pokers, it makes me sick! He doesn't give a damn about you. . . you little tramp!" **Gene Tierney** reads the riot act to Carol Lynley, whom she's cornered in a ladies room. Lynley's fallen for Tierney's husband Brian Keith, but all she gets is a slap across the puss from Tierney. *The Pleasure Seekers* (1964, 20th Century-Fox).

4127 "I don't run to take a beating. I run to win. . . . What do I aim for now? Beating him next time." **Ben Cross** sets a goal after being defeated by Ian Charleson in a 100-meter dash. *Chariots of Fire* (1981, GB, 20th Century-Fox).

4128 "I'm not a has-been. I'm a never-was. I aspire to be a has-been." Ever since dropping a pass years earlier in the big high-school football game, **Robin Williams** has been unable to make anything of himself. He's looking for a way to redeem himself by rescheduling the game. *The Best of Times* (1986, Universal).

God

see also ANGELS, BADNESS, BELIEFS, DEVILS, CREATION AND CREATURES, EVILNESS, FATE AND DESTINY, GOOD AND EVIL (BAD), GOODNESS, HEAVEN, HEAVEN AND HELL, HELL, HELP AND HELPING, LOVE AND HATE, PEOPLE, POWER, PRAYERS, PRIESTS, RELIGIONS, SUPERNATURAL, WORSHIP

4129 "Do you know what it means to feel like God?" Egotistical scientist **Charles Laughton** transforms animals into mutant human-like creatures through a series of painful operations. *Island of Lost Souls* (1933, Paramount).

4130 "Until you stirred Him up, I had no trouble with God." **William Powell** wishes he'd never told his wife Irene Dunne that he hadn't been baptized. She's convinced he can't get into heaven unless he takes the sacrament and Powell wants nothing to do with it. *Life with Father* (1947, Warner Bros.).

4131 "Do you think that for one moment that God is interested in selling movies for me?" Film producer **Lee J. Cobb** is outraged when press agent Fred MacMurray tries to promote a so-called miracle into a campaign for a movie made by Alida Valli just before her death. *The Miracle of the Bells* (1948, RKO).

4132 "No man can ever hope to know the real nature of God, but he has given us a glimpse of his face." **Raymond Massey**, as Jewish holy man Nathan, speaks of God. *David and Bathsheba* (1951, 20th Century-Fox).

4133 NEFRETIRI: "You didn't even kill him." RAMESES: "His god is God." **Anne Baxter** sneers at her husband, Pharaoh **Yul Brynner**, who is defeated by the efforts of Charlton Heston as Moses to lead the children of Israel out of bondage in Egypt. Baxter will goad Brynner into one final effort, and he loses his chariots when Heston parts the Red Sea. *The Ten Commandments* (1956, Paramount).

4134 "Why should He hide Himself in the midst of half-spoken promises and unseen miracles? Why can't I kill God within me? Why does He live on in this painful and humiliating way even though I curse Him and want to tear Him out of my heart?" Swedish Knight **Max von Sydow** has an intense internal struggle, trying to rid himself of a belief in a merciful God. *The Seventh Seal* (1957, Sweden, Svensk Filmindustri).

4135 ANDRE: "I can transport matter." HELENE: "It's like playing God." **Al "David" Hedison** is yet another scientist whose work is questioned as being somehow sacrilegious. This time it's his wife **Patri-**

cia Owens who is critical. *The Fly* (1958, 20th Century-Fox).

4136 "Darwin was wrong. Man's still an ape. His creed's still a totem pole. When he first achieved the upright position he took a look at the stars, thought they were something to eat. When he couldn't reach them, he decided they were groceries belonging to a bigger creature. That's how Jehovah was born." Cynical H.L. Mencken-like reporter **Gene Kelly** makes an interpretation of the creation of God for Clarence Darrow-like Spencer Tracy. *Inherit the Wind* (1960, United Artists).

4137 "In my mother's house, there is still a God." It's the line that matriarch **Claudia McNeil** requires her daughter Diana Sands to repeat after she is slapped across the face by McNeil for saying she doesn't believe in God. *A Raisin in the Sun* (1961, Columbia).

4138 "Sometimes I wonder which side God's on." **John Wayne** as Col. Benjamin Vandervoort, makes a big assumption when he complains about the rain leading up to June 6, 1944: D-Day. *The Longest Day* (1962, 20th Century-Fox).

4139 "I hope you are as wise, as brilliant, a god as they say you are. You Roman generals become divine so quickly. A few victories, a few massacres. Only yesterday Pompey was a god. They murdered him, didn't they?" Speaking to Rex Harrison as Julius Caesar, Egyptian queen **Elizabeth Taylor** is rather amused at how casually divinity is proclaimed in the Roman Empire. *Cleopatra* (1963, 20th Century-Fox).

4140 "Answers to questions involving God must be carefully phrased." Judge **Felix Aylmer** addresses governess Deborah Kerr, whom he once sentenced to death. *The Chalk Garden* (1964, GB, Universal).

4141 "You have turned your back on the God of love and compassion and invented for yourself this cruel senile delinquent who blames the world and brutally punishes all He created for His own faults." Disgraced preacher **Richard Burton** screams at his fleeing parishioners. *The Night of the Iguana* (1964, MGM).

4142 "I am the absolute unknowable righteous eternal lord of hosts, king of kings, lord of lords." Mad **Peter O'Toole**, as Jack, the fourteenth Earl of Gurney, believes that he is God. *The Ruling Class* (1972, GB, Keep Films).

4143 "I'm on my way to meet my maker, but I ain't ready for Him yet." Doomed bank-robber **Lee Marvin** would like to put off meeting God for a bit longer. *The Spikes Gang* (1974, United Artists).

4144 "If it turns out there is a God, I don't think He's evil. The worst thing you can say about Him is that He's basically an underachiever." In a movie in which **Woody Allen** loses his life, he moves from atheism to agnosticism. *Love and Death* (1975, United Artists).

4145 "If God is testing us, why doesn't He give us a written?" **Woody Allen** wonders if God couldn't be a little more accommodating. *Love and Death* (1975, United Artists).

4146 "I took this form because if I showed myself to you as I am, you wouldn't be able to comprehend me." God explains to grocer John Denver why he appears to him looking like **George Burns**. *Oh, God* (1977, Warner Bros.).

4147 "Now I don't want you to consider me as just your commanding officer, I want you to look on me like I was. . . well. . . God. If I say something, you pretend it's coming from the burning bush." Crack fighter pilot **Robert Duvall** addresses his family as if he were some almighty drill instructor scaring the hell out of new recruits. *The Great Santini* (1979, Warner Bros.).

4148 "God isn't so smart. He created forty-one types of parrots and nipples for men. I would have started with lasers, eight o'clock on day one." **David Warner**, as Evil, is contemptuous of Ralph Richardson, as the Supreme Being. *Time Bandits* (1981, GB, Handmade Films).

4149 "Everything alive is God or God's thought, not only what is good but also the cruelest things." Jewish merchant and moneylender **Erland Josephson** expresses his opinion that God is the first source of everything, good or bad. *Fanny and Alexander* (1983, Sweden, Swedish Film Institute-Embassy).

4150 "This is the end for me. . . if there is a God, he is a shit." Mats Bergman startles and scares **Bertil Guve** momentarily with a towering God puppet. When he realizes what has happened Bertil formulates his bold thought about God. *Fanny and Alexander* (1983, Sweden, Swedish Film Institute-Embassy).

4151 Sister Miriam Ruth: "She belongs to God." Dr. Martha Livingston: "And I intend to take her away from Him!" Mother Superior **Anne Bancroft** argues with court-appointed psychiatrist **Jane Fonda**, a lapsed Catholic, over very young and very naïve nun Meg Tilly. The latter has given birth to a child and killed it. Later, even Tilly understands Fonda's plans to destroy her childish faith, saying, "You mean to take God away from me." *Agnes of God* (1985, Columbia).

4152 "I saw the face of God!" Awe-struck technician **Mitchell Greenberg** is beneath the subway grill where Marilyn Monroe-like actress Theresa Russell stands as her white dress is sent billowing up over her head by the cool air from below in the famous sequence from "The Seven Year Itch." *Insignificance* (1985, GB, Zenith).

4153 "My God, oh God, I want to talk to you, yes, I do. I want you to listen to me, listen. My family is dead, and we lived by your teachings. I beat it into them. I taught it to them, and what have you done? You did away with them. Well, I have news for you, I renounce you, God. I renounce you and I give my soul to Satan." No Job he, **Rod Steiger** believes God has cruelly mistreated him and so he turns his back on God. *American Gothic* (1988, Vidmark).

4154 "God is a luxury I cannot afford." **Martin Landau**, talking with Rabbi Sam Waterston, refuses to believe in a power higher than himself. To do so, he would be unable to live with the fact that he's responsible for the murder of his mistress Anjelica Huston. *Crimes and Misdemeanors* (1989, Orion).

4155 "Mr. Nolan, it's for you. It's God. He says we should have girls at Welton." **Gale Hansen** offers the receiver of a telephone that rings loudly during an assembly to headmaster Norman Lloyd. *Dead Poets Society* (1989, Touchstone).

4156 "My daddy always used to say there's a special God for children." **Mary-Louise Parker** gratefully comments after her son survived being run over by a train, losing only an arm. *Fried Green Tomatoes* (1991, Universal).

4157 "How can I love a God who let me kill my baby?" **Mimi Rogers** is devastated that she has murdered her own daughter in the name of God. After the killing, she reverts to the cynicism she held before joining a fundamentalist church group. *The Rapture* (1991, Fine Line).

Gold

see also MONEY, WEALTH AND RICHES, WORTH AND VALUES

4158 "Butter's yellow too, and you can spread it on bread—ever try doing that with gold?" **Dana Andrews**, the owner of a freight line, claims riches don't mean everything to him. His comment is rather dumb. *Canyon Passage* (1946, Universal).

4159 "Answer me this one, will you? Why's gold worth some twenty bucks per ounce? A thousand men, say, go searching for gold. After six months, one of 'em is lucky—one out of a thousand. His find represents not only his months of labor but that of nine hundred, ninety-nine others to boot. Six thousand months or fifty years of scrambling over mountains going hungry and human labor that went into the finding and getting of it." Old prospector **Walter Huston** holds court in a flophouse on the value of gold. *The Treasure of the Sierra Madre* (1948, Warner Bros.).

4160 "As long as there's no find, the noble brotherhood will last, but when the piles of gold begin to grow, that's when the trouble starts. . . I know what gold does to men's souls." Old prospector **Walter Huston** warns newcomers Humphrey Bogart and Tim Holt what gold can do to otherwise civilized men. They plan to head for the Mexican hills looking for their fortunes. *The Treasure of the Sierra Madre* (1948, Warner Bros.).

4161 "Gold don't carry any curse with it. It all depends on whether or not the guy who finds it is the right guy. The way I see it, gold can be as much of a blessing as a curse." As he and Tim Holt join old prospector Walter Huston in seeking gold, **Humphrey Bogart** believes he's the right kind of guy—but he's wrong. *The Treasure of the Sierra Madre* (1948, Warner Bros.).

4162 "Well, that's gold for ya. We haven't even struck any and already we're fighting over how to divide it up." **James Garner** sadly speaks to his none-too-bright partner, Jack Elam. *Support Your Local Sheriff* (1969, United Artists).

Good and Evil (Bad)

see also BADNESS, EVILNESS, GOODNESS

4163 "Man is not truly one, but truly two. Good and bad carry on an eternal struggle. If these two selves could be separated, the evil could be liberated." **Fredric March** expounds on his theory that each man has good and evil within him. *Dr. Jekyll and Mr. Hyde* (1932, Paramount).

4164 "Friend good. Fire bad." Monster **Boris Karloff** acquires some basic English and wisdom. *The Bride of Frankenstein* (1935, Universal).

4165 "But nobody will ever convince me that there's not a lot more good than there is bad in Blackie Norton." Priest **Spencer Tracy** refers to his amoral, atheistic friend Clark Gable. *San Francisco* (1936, MGM).

4166 "Good and Evil were invented for the ordinary man." Sneering, fastidious homosexual murderer **John Dall** believes his intelligence makes him better than anyone else. The film is a fiction inspired by the lives and crimes of Leopold and Loeb. *Rope* (1948, Warner Bros.).

4167 "You knew he was dynamite, he had to explode sometimes. . . . If you want him you got to take it all—the bad and the good." **Art Smith** wonders if Gloria Grahame would really want screenwriter Humphrey Bogart if he was "normal." *In a Lonely Place* (1950, Columbia).

4168 "Good and evil can change places like light and shadow." Vicious, insane **Charles Boyer** is behind the problems of a small French-Canadian town suffering from an outbreak of poison pen letters. *The Thirteenth Letter* (1951, 20th Century-Fox).

4169 "I'm driving good, but my life is crap." Racing driver **Paul Newman**'s life is in the pits and pit stops. *Winning* (1969, Universal).

4170 "Am I a good man or a bad man?. . . a curiosity in a hospital instead of a carnival." **Anthony Hopkins**, as compassionate Dr. Treves, struggles with his conscience, realizing that he is using John Hurt, as title character John Merrick, as a medical oddity. *The Elephant Man* (1980, EMI).

4171 "Habit. Grammar's like everything else, it gets rusty if you don't use it. Good and evil's the same thing. What's good? What's evil? Nobody knows. It doesn't get used much around here. So it gets rusty. Must be the climate." In a seedy little town in French West Africa, circa 1938, new school teacher Irene Skobline asks Chief of Police **Philippe Noiret** why he wishes to appear illiterate when she knows very well he's not. *Coup de Torchon* (1981, Fr., Quartet Films).

4172 "No, Luthor, it's as it always was, on the brink, with good fighting evil. See you in twenty." Superman **Christopher Reeve** bids adieu to master criminal Gene Hackman. *Superman IV: The Quest for Peace* (1987, Cannon).

4173 "When there's lots of tens left, tens and picture cards, it's good for us. . . . Tens are good. . . . You're gonna bet one if it's bad, two if it's good. . . . Now listen, casinos have house rules. The first one is they don't like to lose. . . . Now, you never, never show that you are counting cards. The cardinal sin, Ray. . . Ray, are you listening to me?. . . That's very, very important. . . . Counting is bad." **Tom Cruise** instructs his autistic savant brother Dustin Hoffman in playing blackjack. *Rain Man* (1988, MGM-United Artists).

4174 "Everything seems so close together. . . all the good and bad things." Life (and perhaps the movie)

has **Mary McDonnell** confused. *Grand Canyon* (1991, 20th Century-Fox).

4175 "Cheer up. We got the bad guys, and that's what we get paid for. It's like the old West out there, and we're wearing the white hats." **Loren Avedon** makes a drug bust in New York City. *The King of the Kickboxers* (1991, Hong Kong, Imperial).

Goodbyes *see* FAREWELLS

Goodness

see also BADNESS, BEAUTY, EVILNESS, GOD, GOOD AND EVIL (BAD), GREATNESS, HAPPINESS AND UNHAPPINESS, HEALTH, HONESTY AND DISHONESTY, IMMORALITY, LOVE AND HATE, LOVE AND LOVERS, LOYALTIES, MORALITY, TRUST, USES AND USING, VIRTUES, WORTH AND VALUES

4176 "You ain't so good yourself—you didn't get those medals for holding hands with the Germans." **James Cagney** is indignant when his self-righteous brother Donald Cook hurls a keg of illegal liquor, brought home by Cagney, to the ground in a rage. *The Public Enemy* (1930, Warner Bros.).

4177 "Goodness had nothing to do with it, dearie." It's **Mae West**'s classic retort when a hatcheck girl sees her diamonds and shouts "Goodness." *Night After Night* (1932, Paramount).

4178 "We make our own electricity, but we're not very good at it." **Ernest Thesiger** explains why the lights keep going on and off in the house. *The Old Dark House* (1932, Universal).

4179 BROTHER EBEN: "Are you in town for good?" RUBY CARTER: "I expect to be here, but not for good." **Sam McDaniel**'s words are twisted to a new meaning by **Mae West** as she arrives in New Orleans from St. Louis. *Belle of the Nineties* (1934, Paramount).

4180 "He's got goodness, Mabel. Do you know what that means?. . . No, of course you don't. We've forgotten. We're all too busy being smart alecks." New York reporter **Jean Arthur** is talking about country hick Gary Cooper to another tough cookie, Ruth Donnelly. *Mr. Deeds Goes to Town* (1936, Columbia).

4181 "I've never known any good to come from a concertina." **Alison Skipworth** is suspicious of Fred MacMurray's motives in serenading Carole Lombard. *The Princess Comes Across* (1936, Paramount).

4182 "There must be a great deal of good in a man who would love a child so much." **Jane Darwell**

comments to Leona Roberts about Clark Gable's love for his daughter. *Gone with the Wind* (1939, Selznick-MGM).

4183 "You see, my dear, goodness is after all the greatest force in the world, and he's got it." Narrator **Herbert Marshall**, as Somerset Maugham, makes the observation to Gene Tierney about Tyrone Power. *The Razor's Edge* (1946, 20th Century-Fox).

4184 "In brief, from now on, the best of everything is good enough for me." Slimy press agent **Tony Curtis** believes he's got it made now that famous columnist Burt Lancaster is in his debt. *Sweet Smell of Success* (1957, United Artists).

4185 "In spite of everything, I still believe that people are really good at heart." Despite her suffering, child diarist Anne Frank, portrayed by **Millie Perkins**, displays remarkable charity for the human race, not all of whose members would seem to deserve it. *The Diary of Anne Frank* (1959, 20th Century-Fox).

4186 "Wish you'd stop being so good to me, Captain." Chain gang convict **Paul Newman**'s sarcastic remark to Strother Martin earns him a violent slap to the head by the boss of the correctional farm where Newman is serving his sentence. *Cool Hand Luke* (1967, Warner Bros.).

4187 "It's going to be so good." **Greta Scacchi** whispers seductively to Harrison Ford just as they make love for the first time on the top of her desk. *Presumed Innocent* (1990, Warner Bros.).

Gossip

see also GOOD AND EVIL (BAD), PRIVACY, SECRETS, TALKS AND TALKING

4188 "Take off your clothes, get in, and tell me about it." **Claudette Colbert** as Poppaea, invites a confidant, who rushes in with unpleasant but romantic news, to join Colbert in her famous milk bath and dish the dirt. *The Sign of the Cross* (1932, Paramount).

4189 MRS. GIDEON: "I can't say anything good about her." CUTHBERT J. TWILLIE: "I can see what's good. Tell me the rest." Busybody **Margaret Hamilton** only whets **W.C. Fields**' appetite as they speak of shady lady Mae West. *My Little Chickadee* (1940, Universal).

4190 "Isn't that monstrous the way people go about saying things behind people's backs that are absolutely and entirely true?" **George Sanders**' character is in mock outrage. *The Picture of Dorian Gray* (1945, MGM).

4191 "I had lunch with Karen not three hours ago. As always with women who want to find out things, she told me more than she learned. . . ." Insufferable theater critic **George Sanders** gloats over his imagined triumph with Celeste Holm. *All About Eve* (1950, 20th Century-Fox).

4192 "Counter espionage is the highest form of gossip." Counter intelligence British agent **Michael Rennie** talks to British ambassador Walter Hampden about his career. *Five Fingers* (1952, 20th Century-Fox).

4193 "We're all prisoners of each other's gossip, killed by each other's whispers." Doctor **Lloyd Nolan** states the secret of the success of Grace Metalious' steamy novel and the film based on it. *Peyton Place* (1957, 20th Century-Fox).

4194 "The Cunningham girl is engaged. He's a doctor. Well, he's really veterinarian, but all the animals are owned by wealthy people." **Mary Davenport** spreads the news to her daughter Jennifer Salt, who she wishes would get married. *Sisters* (1973, American International).

4195 "Gossip is the new pornography. We have it in the daily newspapers." Considering all the horrible news that is reported, **Michael Murphy** shouldn't be surprised that people prefer to read about people's naughtiness. *Manhattan* (1979, United Artists).

4196 "Don't have anything nice to say about some one? Come sit by me." **Olympia Dukakis** borrows Alice Roosevelt's line. *Steel Magnolias* (1989, Tri-Star).

Governments

see also COUNTRIES, DEMOCRACY, KINGS AND QUEENS, POLITICS AND POLITICIANS, RULES, TAXES, VOTING AND VOTERS

4197 "Africa. . . . Tens of millions of natives under British rule, each tribe with its own chieftain; governed and protected by a handful of the white men whose everyday work is an unsung saga of courage and efficiency." The movie's opening title brags about the British civil servants who made imperialism run. Today, no sensible person would brag about imperialism or bureaucrats. *Sanders of the River* (1935, GB, London Films).

4198 DR. MORTON: "I hate to have it look as if I was making the government pay to relieve wounded soldiers from pain." FRANKLIN PIERCE: "The government pays for the guns, don't it?" **Joel McCrea**, the Boston dentist who introduced the use of ether to operations, has his concerns about the morality of taking pay for the use of his discovery. His worries are put to rest by the coarse and stupid president of the United States, portrayed by **Porter Hall**. *The Great Moment* (1944, Paramount).

4199 BLAZE STARR: "You know in a certain way, we're both part of show business." EARL LONG: "You are catching on to the whole idea of government." Stripper **Lolita Davidovich** and politician **Paul Newman** find they have a lot in common. *Blaze* (1989, Touchstone-Buena Vista).

Gratitude *see* THANKS AND THANKFULNESS

Graves and Graveyards

see also DEATH AND DYING, EULOGIES, FUNERALS, SPIRIT AND SPIRITS

4200 "You sag, Renault, like an old woman.... You're a corpse... go get yourself buried." Producer **Jean Hersholt** dismisses fading matinee idol John Barrymore, who has just insulted Hersholt, thus losing out on a comeback chance. *Dinner at Eight* (1933, MGM).

4201 NICK CHARLES: "How'd you like Grant's tomb?" NORA CHARLES: "It's lovely...I'm having a coffin made for you." **William Powell** introduces his wife **Myrna Loy** to the sites of New York City. *The Thin Man* (1934, MGM).

4202 "I think I shall stay here for a while. I find the atmosphere congenial." Skeletal, loony scientist Dr. Pretorius, played by **Ernest Thesiger**, pays off two grave robbers who have dug up a fresh corpse for his experiments. Thesiger pulls up a comfy gravestone and settles down to enjoy the view. *The Bride of Frankenstein* (1935, Universal).

4203 "This here's William James Joad, died of a stroke, old, old man. His folks buried him because they got no money for funerls [sic]. Nobody kilt him. Jus' a stroke and he died." **Henry Fonda** reads the marker he's put on his grandfather Charley Grapewin's simple road-side grave. *The Grapes of Wrath* (1940, 20th Century-Fox).

4204 "I'll follow you into your grave. I'll write my name on your tombstone!" Psychopathic police detective **Laird Cregar** vows his perverted lust for murdered Carole Landis. *I Wake Up Screaming* (1941, 20th Century-Fox.)

4205 "It's like exhuming a man from his grave.... They were made to capitalize on the various cravings of middle-aged glandular cases." Distinguished

college professor **Clifton Webb** accuses the TV fans of the silent movies he made as a Valentino or Fairbanks type heartthrob of suffering from some kind of necrophobia. *Dreamboat* (1952, 20th Century-Fox).

4206 "If I was buried in Potter's Field it would just about kill me." To make sure that she doesn't meet such a fate, **Thelma Ritter** saves for a fancy burial. *Pickup on South Street* (1953, 20th Century-Fox).

4207 "Walking down a long corridor... when I come to the end, there's nothing but darkness...there's a grave, an open grave. It's my grave." **Kim Novak** describes her recurring frightening dream to James Stewart as they stand near the San Francisco Bay. *Vertigo* (1958, Paramount).

4208 "Wherefore, O harlot, hear the word of the Lord. I will judge thee as women that break the wedlock and shed blood are judged." It's the ominous inscription religious fanatic **R.G. Armstrong** put on his wife's tombstone. *Ride the High Country* (1962, MGM).

4209 "They better be, 'cause I'm going to bury them." The first to reach a wagon that has gone over the cliff, **Lee Marvin** makes a practical reply when someone from above yells down to him about the passengers, "Hello... Is they dead?" *Paint Your Wagon* (1969, Paramount).

4210 "The day they lay you away what I do on your grave won't pass for flowers." **Harry Morgan** is pleased to learn that aging gunslinger John Wayne is dying of cancer. *The Shootist* (1976, Paramount).

4211 "Back in the heavy stone days when we used to stay up and talk a lot, Annie and me, we were talking about dying, how it feels and all. I said I'd never get buried, couldn't stand them shoveling dirt in my face. Like I know I'd be dead, but I still might have this strong compulsion to breathe, OK? But Annie, she said she wanted to be buried right in the ground under a pear tree, really, not in a box or anything. She said she wanted the roots going right through her, and each year they'd come along, take a pear and go. 'Hey, Annie's tasting good this year, huh?'" **Jodie Foster** recalls confidences shared with Cherie Currie. *Foxes* (1980, United Artists).

4212 "I've always seen myself as backing toward the grave, tooth by tooth, poem by poem." Scottish poet **Tom Conti** is overly melodramatic. *Reuben, Reuben* (1983, 20th Century-Fox).

Greatness

see also EXPERTS, HEROES, MINDS, NOBILITY, PURPOSES, SIZES, SUPERIORITY AND INFERIORITY

4213 "Greatness demands all." Lord Chancellor **Lewis Stone** reminds Greta Garbo that she is a queen, not merely a woman, when she tells him she is tired of being a symbol. *Queen Christina* (1933, MGM).

4214 "Manolo's the greatest of the great! The first man of the world!" Bullfight critic **Laird Cregar** has found a new "first man of the world," matador Anthony Quinn, as his former favorite Tyrone Power lies near by, dying from a goring. *Blood and Sand* (1941, 20th Century-Fox).

4215 "If I hadn't been really rich. I might have been a really great man." **Orson Welles,** as Charles Foster Kane, wonders if money got in the way of his potential. *Citizen Kane* (1941, RKO).

4216 "Of all the things in nature, great men alone reverse the laws of perspective and grow smaller as one approaches them. . . ." From the film's prologue—a variation on "familiarity breeds contempt," perhaps. *The Great Moment* (1944, Paramount).

4217 "It's what I do. Luis Bello, without bulls—nothing going back to nothing. But you only saw the bad. There is something to it, something great about it sometimes." Matador **Mel Ferrer** tries to explain to Miroslava why he has chosen bullfighting. *The Brave Bulls* (1951, Columbia).

4218 "Crap-shoot is a matter of individual enterprise. Crap-shoot makes the country great." U.S. Senate candidate **Robert Redford** makes a statement that no candidate seriously thinking of getting elected would make. *The Candidate* (1972, Warner Bros.).

4219 "This is the greatest day in the history of my life." **Sylvester Stallone** exclaims after he survives an excruciating and nearly deadly boxing match with Carl Weathers. *Rocky II* (1979, United Artists).

4220 "You have this exalted view of me and I hate it. If you think I'm that great then there must be something wrong with you." **Mary Beth Hurt**, convinced that she's no good because she left a good husband for no good reason, complains to John Heard, who thinks she's wonderful. *Chilly Scenes of Winter* aka: *Heads Over Heels* (1982, United Artists).

4221 "Is this a great country or what?" **Michael Keaton** reacts happily when Henry Winkler expresses concern that the two are living off the wages of prostitutes and call-girls. *Night Shift* (1982, Warner Bros.).

4222 "Alex and I made love the night before he died. It was fantastic!" Guileless **Meg Tilly** recalls the great sex she and her lover had the night before he committed suicide. *The Big Chill* (1983, Columbia).

4223 EDDIE WILSON: "I wanna do somethin' nobody's ever done before—Somethin' great." SAL AMATO: "We ain't great. We're just some guys from Jersey." Lead singer **Michael Pare** yearns for greatness but the group's bass player **Matthew Laurance** rains on his parade. *Eddie and the Cruisers* (1983, Embassy).

4224 "If we can't be great, then there's no point in ever playing music again." It's Jim Morrison-like working class rock star **Michael Pare**'s final declaration before disappearing, presumed dead in an automobile accident, although no body is ever found. See the sequel. *Eddie and the Cruisers* (1983, Embassy).

4225 "I think you're gonna become one of the greatest balloon folding acts of all time." Artists' agent **Woody Allen** auditions a couple who fold balloons into animal shapes. Allen specializes in offbeat acts that no one will employ. *Broadway Danny Rose* (1984, Orion).

4226 "You were great in bed last night, but you gonna have to do somethin' about those toe nails." Singer **Dee Dee Bridgewater** has spent the night with mute alien Joe Morton, who has three long toes on each foot. *The Brother from Another Planet* (1984, A-Train Films).

4227 "It's great to be young and insane." Mental patient **Michael Keaton** speaks sarcastically. *The Dream Team* (1989, Universal).

4228 "It wasn't sex—it was great." **Kirstie Alley** responds to her sister Jami Gertz's question, "How could you have sex with your brother-in-law?" It must have been great—the experience killed brother-in-law Sam Elliott. *Sibling Rivalry* (1990, Columbia).

Greed

see also DESIRES, EXCESSES, MONEY, WEALTH AND RICHES

4229 "He said 595,000 acres, Mama—and you should see the greedy look on your face." **Eliza-**

beth **Taylor** teasingly chides her mother Judith Evelyn for her reaction when she hears that Rock Hudson, who has come acourtin' the lovely Virginia beauty Taylor, owns a big chunk of Texas. *Giant* (1956, Warner Bros.).

4230 RANDOLPH DUKE: "Mother always said you were greedy." MORTIMER DUKE: "She meant it as a compliment." Rich brothers **Ralph Bellamy** and **Don Ameche** remember Mama. *Trading Places* (1983, Paramount).

4231 "I am not a destroyer of companies. I am a liberator of them. . . . The point is, ladies and gentlemen, that greed, for the lack of a better word, is good. Greed is right. Greed works. Greed clarifies, cuts through and captures the essence of the evolutionary spirit. Greed—in all of its forms—greed for life, for money, for love, for knowledge, has marked the upward surge of mankind, and greed—you mark my words—will not only save Teldar Paper, but that other malfunctioning corporation called the USA. Thank you, very much." Corporate raider **Michael Douglas** addresses stockholders of a company he has under seige. *Wall Street* (1987, 20th Century-Fox).

Greetings

see also FRIENDSHIPS AND FRIENDS, SPEECH AND SPEAKING, WRITING AND WRITERS

4232 "Comrade madame!" Communist butler **Mischa Auer** greets dizzy blonde debutante Brenda Joyce at the door of her mansion. *Public Deb No. 1* (1940, 20th Century-Fox).

4233 "Nuts to you, dope." All-American **Fred Mac-Murray** responds to a non-English speaking Nazi soldier, who greets Fred with a Heil Hitler salute. Suppose this is where General McAuliffe got the idea? *Above Suspicion* (1943, MGM).

4234 "Hello, Gorgeous." With her first line in the film, **Barbra Streisand**, as Fanny Brice, greets herself in a mirror. *Funny Girl* (1968, Columbia).

4235 "Here's Johnny!" Now maniacal, **Jack Nicholson** breaks through a door with an axe to get at his wife and child. *The Shining* (1980, GB, Warner Bros.).

4236 "Do stop standing there like a cough drop and say hello." Actress **Diana Rigg** cruelly greets her shy stepdaughter Emily Hone who has just entered the room. *Evil Under the Sun* (1982, GB, Universal).

4237 "I used to sit on our front gallery every morning and every evening just to nod hello to Ray John Murray." Elderly **Geraldine Page** recalls when she was a girl for her bus companion Rebecca De Mornay. *The Trip to Bountiful* (1985, Island).

Grief

see also EMOTIONS, LOSSES AND LOSING, PAINS, SADNESS, SORROWS, SUFFERING AND SUFFERERS

4238 "I told him you was prostrate with grief." **Hattie McDaniel** announces the arrival of Clark Gable after Vivien Leigh's husband Carroll Nye's funeral. *Gone with the Wind* (1939, Selznick-MGM).

4239 "Johnny, why don't you get rid of the grief you've got from that blonde, whoever she is? Every mile you go you sweat worse with the same pain. Didn't I tell you all females are the same with their faces washed?" **Humphrey Bogart** tries to comfort William Prince, who is suffering from female problems—namely, Lizabeth Scott. *Dead Reckoning* (1947, Columbia).

4240 "You went off in some corner, alone, never realizing that by comforting you I could have helped my own grief. You don't need anybody but yourself!" **Patricia Neal** bitterly reminds John Wayne how he emotionally deserted her when their son died. *Operation Pacific* (1951, Warner Bros.).

4241 "You're going to experience grief and woe of biblical proportions." Rebellious 23-year-old **Judd Nelson** threatens Anita Morris after returning home to investigate the murder of his father. *Blue City* (1986, Paramount).

Growth and Development

see also LEARNING AND LESSONS, MATURITY AND IMMATURITY, TRAINING

4242 EDDY HALL: "Wait till you see how I'll grow on you." RUBY ADAMS: "Yeah. . . like a carbuncle." Heel **Clark Gable** falls for hooker with a heart of gold **Jean Harlow**. *Hold Your Man* (1933, MGM).

4243 "I grow them from seed." **Ernest Thesiger**, as Dr. Pretorius, speaks of his homunculi, perfect in shape, but lacking in size. *The Bride of Frankenstein* (1935, Universal).

4244 "I've had two years to grow claws! Jungle Red!" Lady-like society woman **Norma Shearer** indicates that she's finally willing to fight like a dame to win back her ex-husband from Joan Crawford. *The Women* (1939, MGM).

4245 "I grow on people—like moss." Often married **Mary Astor** actively pursues penurious engineer Joel McCrea. *The Palm Beach Story* (1942, Paramount).

4246 "He never grew up—the world just grew up around him." **Alida Valli** sums up the character of Orson Welles for his friend Joseph Cotten. She is being too kind. *The Third Man* (1949, GB, British Lion).

4247 "You know what I mean? You're living at home, and you got your father and mother there, and you can go on like that, being a little girl all your life. But people like you and me, we got to grow up sometime." Unattractive butcher **Ernest Borgnine** talks sense to plain, scared schoolteacher Betsy Blair. *Marty* (1955, United Artists).

4248 "God, you're so opposite! I mean you write that absolutely fabulous television show. It's brilliantly funny and his view is so Scandinavian. It's bleak, my God! I mean, all that Kierkegaard, right? Real adolescent, you know, fashionable pessimism. I mean, the silence. God's silence. Okay, okay, okay, I mean, I loved it when I was at Radcliffe, but, I mean, all right, you outgrow it. You absolutely outgrow it." Pseudo- and anti-intellectual **Diane Keaton** shocks comedy writer Woody Allen with her vicious attack on Swedish movie director Ingmar Bergman. *Manhattan* (1979, United Artists).

4249 "When will we grow up—any of us?" **Barbara Harris** may be speaking of herself and her husband Alan Alda, but her question could well be asked of most people. *The Seduction of Joe Tynan* (1979, Universal).

4250 "At first we were penny ante. Then we grew." In voice-over, **Christian Slater**, as Lucky Luciano, describes how he and three other young mobsters organized crime. *Mobsters* (1991, Universal).

Guarantees see PLEDGES, PROMISES

Guesses see JUDGMENTS, PREDICTIONS, THINKING AND THOUGHTS

Guests

see also ENTERTAINMENTS AND ENTERTAINERS, FRIENDSHIPS AND FRIENDS, HOMES, HOSPITALITY, INVITATIONS, RESTAURANTS, VISITS

4251 "Excuse me while I brush the crumbs out of my bed, I'm expecting company." **Groucho Marx** tries to get rid of unwanted guests Chico and Harpo Marx before the arrival of Margaret Dumont. *Duck Soup* (1933, Paramount).

4252 "Will you serve the nuts. . . I mean, will you serve the guests the nuts?" **Myrna Loy** corrects herself to a butler, but the look on her face and the odd assortment of crooks and gun molls at her party, make one understand she meant what she said originally. *The Thin Man* (1934, MGM).

4253 "You have been guests in our home long enough. Now we want you to leave." **Ben Kingsley** as Mahatma Gandhi, politely but firmly tells British authorities that they should leave India. *Gandhi* (1983, GB, Columbia).

4254 "I think we can get her a guest shot on *The Wild Kingdom*." **Bill Murray** watches Sigourney Weaver, in the throes of demonic possession, begin to exhibit animalistic tendencies. *Ghostbusters* (1984, Columbia).

Guilt

see also CONFESSIONS, CONSCIENCES, CRIMES AND CRIMINALS, DEFENSES, JUDGMENTS, JUSTICE, LAWS, LAWYERS, SHAME, SINS AND SINNERS

4255 "I am guilty. When you make a mistake, you have to pay for it." Contrite jewel thief **Barbara Stanwyck**, in love with young Assistant District Attorney Fred MacMurray, pleads guilty at her trial. *Remember the Night* (1940, Paramount).

4256 "People often feel guilty for something they never did, and it usually goes back to something in their childhood. A child often wishes something terrible would happen to someone—and if something does happen to that person, the child believes he has caused it, and he grows up with a guilt complex over a sin that was only a child's bad dream." **Ingrid Bergman** treats patient Norman Lloyd who believes he's killed his father. *Spellbound* (1945, Selznick-United Artists).

4257 "You insist without proof that you're a murderer. You know what that is, don't you? Whoever you are, it's the guilt complex that speaks for you—a guilt fantasy that goes way back to your childhood." Psychiatrist **Ingrid Bergman** makes either a good diagnosis or a good guess about her lover Gregory Peck, who is suffering from amnesia and the certainty that he's killed the man whose identity he's taken. *Spellbound* (1945, Selznick-United Artists).

4258 "Nick Romano is guilty, and so are we, and so is that precious thing called society. . . . Knock on any door, and you may find Nick Romano." Lawyer **Humphrey Bogart** pleads mercy in court for his young cop-killer client John Derek. *Knock on Any Door* (1949, Columbia).

4259 "I know something now I didn't know before. I'm guilty of a lot of things—of most of what they say I am." Condemned **Montgomery Clift** confesses to himself that he's responsible for the death of his pregnant girlfriend Shelley Winters, even though he didn't go through with his plans to murder her. *A Place in the Sun* (1951, Paramount).

4260 "They wanted to punish me because I'd failed him, let him down. . . . They come at me from all sides. . . . They know I'm guilty." The strain proves too much for **Vera Miles**, wife of Henry Fonda, falsely accused of a crime committed by a man who looks like him. *The Wrong Man* (1956, Warner Bros.).

4261 "You come in here with your heart bleeding all over the floor about slum kids and injustice. Everyone knows the kid is guilty. He's got to burn." Self-made businessman **Lee J. Cobb** attacks Henry Fonda. Cobb wants to convict a youngster of killing his cruel father because Cobb identifies with the father. *12 Angry Men* (1957, United Artists).

4262 "Where were we when our neighbors were dragged out in the middle of the night to Dachau? If we didn't know the details, it was because we didn't want to know. If there is going to be any salvation for Germany, we who know our guilt must admit it." German jurist **Burt Lancaster** speaks of his guilt at his war crimes trial. *Judgment at Nuremberg* (1961, United Artists).

4263 ERNST JANNING: "I did not know it would come to that. You must believe it." DAN HAYWARD: "It came to that the first time you sentenced to death a man you knew to be innocent." Despite German jurist **Burt Lancaster**'s insistence that he didn't realize that following the laws of the Nazis would lead to genocide, American judge **Spencer Tracy**, who has found him guilty of war crimes, isn't buying it. *Judgment at Nuremberg* (1961, United Artists).

4264 "If I'd have made love to you, I'd have felt guilty—guilty of desecration. Yes, isn't that funny? I'm more afraid of your soul than you're afraid of my body." Doctor **Laurence Harvey** is confused by the seesaw behavior towards him of his longtime acquaintance, sexually repressed, flighty and neurotic Geraldine Page. *Summer and Smoke* (1961, Paramount).

4265 "We find the defendants incredibly guilty." Jury foreman **Bill Macy** reads the guilty verdict in the case against Zero Mostel and Gene Wilder for fleecing "little old ladies." *The Producers* (1967, Embassy).

4266 "The list is longer than anyone can imagine. It leads everywhere." **Hal Holbrook**, as "Deep Throat," tells Robert Redford, as reporter Bob Woodward, that the FBI, the CIA, the Justice Department, the Special Counsel to the President, etc., are all involved in the Watergate coverup. *All the President's Men* (1976, Warner Bros.).

4267 "I went to visit my wife today because she's in a state of depression, so depressed that my daughter flew all the way from Seattle to be with her. And I feel lousy about the pain that I've caused my wife and my kids. I feel guilty and conscience-stricken and all of those things you think sentimental but which my generation called simple human decency." Middle-aged **William Holden** tells young Faye Dunaway that he feels guilty about all the pain and suffering he's caused his wife and family. Their May-September affair is all but over, because once the sex becomes ordinary, they have nothing in common. *Network* (1976, United Artists).

4268 "I would like you to take a vacation from guilt. Stop feeling guilty for one week. Just–just say, 'Erica, turn off the guilt. Just turn it off. Don't feel guilty about feeling guilty, either.' It doesn't get you anywhere. It really prolongs the agony." Feminist analyst **Penelope Russianoff** advises Jill Clayburgh, still confused by the break-up of her marriage. *An Unmarried Woman* (1978, 20th Century–Fox).

4269 "Guilty is what the man says when your luck has run out." Low-life **Franklyn Seales** is one of two defendants accused of assassinating cop Ted Danson. *The Onion Field* (1979, Avco Embassy).

4270 "If you weren't guilty when you came in, you are now." Corrupt warden **Jill St. John** "welcomes" a new fish, 22-year-old innocent Tracy Bregman, whose dope-dealing boyfriend set her up by planting a stash of cocaine on her. *The Concrete Jungle* (1982, Pentagon).

4271 "It's important to feel guilty. Otherwise you do terrible things." **Woody Allen** is barking up the wrong tree. Tough, cheap moll Mia Farrow never has guilt feelings. *Broadway Danny Rose* (1984, Orion).

4272 "My name is a ghost to frightened children. Did I set myself up as a god over death, did I set myself up over pity? Oh, my God, I knew what I was doing." With the film's last lines, man of science **Timothy Dalton** acknowledges that he's guilty of asking too few questions when two black-guards supplied him with warm corpses for his experiments. *The Doctor and the Devils* (1985, GB, Brooksfilm).

4273 JACK FORRESTER: "How can you defend me if you think I'm guilty." EDDY BARNES: "It happens all the time. It's the way our legal system works." Murder defendant **Jeff Bridges** is assured by his lawyer Glenn Close that she'll do her best even if she does suspect he's guilty. Of course the legal ethics don't require that she fall in love and into bed with him. *The Jagged Edge* (1985, Columbia).

4274 "He looked me straight in the eye. I should have helped him." **Timothy Hutton** feels guilty for not coming to the aid of black Carl Lumbly when rednecks break up a peaceful demonstration. *Everybody's All-American* (1988, Warner Bros.).

4275 "He was guilty. Anyone is guilty who watches this happen and pretends it isn't. No, he was guilty all right. Just as guilty as the fanatics who pulled the trigger . . . maybe we all are." FBI agent **Willem Dafoe** speaks to a man who has hanged himself before he could be arrested with others for the murder of three civil rights workers. *Mississippi Burning* (1988, Orion).

4276 "People carry awful deeds around with them. What do you expect him to do, turn himself in? I mean this is reality. In reality we rationalize, we deny, or we couldn't go on living." **Martin Landau** has fictionalized his own story of having his mistress killed for Woody Allen. Allen is certain that the man's guilt won't let him live with the deed and the truth will ultimately get out. Landau doesn't think so. *Crimes and Misdemeanors* (1989, Orion).

4277 "Okay, look, I'm guilty. I didn't make enough money. Call me a hippie, send me to hell, I give up." Recently deceased **Albert Brooks** finds he's losing in a strange after-life court to decide what is to happen to him. *Defending Your Life* (1991, Warner Bros.).

Gymnasiums and Gymnastics *see* HEALTH, SPORTS, WORK AND WORKERS

Habits

see also CLOTHES, PERFORMANCES, PRACTICES

4278 "I've been drinking over 40 years; and I haven't acquired the habit yet." **Guy Kibbee** confides in Alice Brady that he doesn't consider his drinking to be a problem—yet. *Joy of Living* (1938, RKO).

4279 "At first it bothered Monte to take money from me, then it became a habit with him." In voice-over, **Joan Crawford** describes how her parasite husband Zachary Scott overcame his aversion to being kept. *Mildred Pierce* (1945, Warner Bros.).

4280 "He used to do that a lot. Not come home." **Judy Holliday** answers the question regarding the habits of her husband Tom Ewell in a strange fashion. *Adam's Rib* (1949, MGM).

4281 "You're going to have to get over this nasty habit of always losing your pants—it's undignified." **Lee Marvin** cuts down Burt Lancaster who he has rescued from a Mexican revolutionary bandit intent on cutting off Burt's head. Lancaster has been stripped to his BVDs and strung up upside down. *The Professionals* (1966, Columbia).

4282 "You know, Lottie, not all habits are bad." Assistant DA **Jeff Fahey** does wish that Theresa Russell will give up some of her dangerous ones—such as being a police decoy in murder cases. *Impulse* (1990, Warner Bros.).

Hair

see also ANIMALS, BODIES, HEADS AND HEADACHES, HUMAN NATURE, HUMANITY

4283 "I'm keen on golden hair myself, same as the Avenger." Ambitious police detective **Malcolm Keen** tells his blonde girlfriend June (Tripp)'s parents that he shares something with the madman who is terrorizing London, murdering pretty young blonde women. *The Lodger* (1926, silent, GB, Gainsborough).

4284 "I want to walk barefoot through your hair." Would-be painter **Robert Young**'s fetish could prove painful to Myrna Loy. *New Morals for Old* (1932, MGM).

4285 "So gentlemen prefer blondes, do they? Yes, they do." With her first line of the film, redheaded **Jean Harlow** dons a see-through dress and plans to test for herself what men prefer. *Red-Headed Woman* (1932, MGM).

4286 "I've known you in every ripple of moonlight I've ever seen, in every symphony I've ever heard, in every perfume I've ever smelt. . . . Your hair, your hair is like a field of silver daisies—I should like to run barefoot through your hair." Wealthy **Franchot Tone** woos glamorous film star Jean Harlow with an icky, rehearsed speech. He must have seen "New Morals for Old." *Bombshell* (1933, MGM).

4287 "I'm letting you off lightly—I was going to ask for the whole wig." **Groucho Marx** quickly amends his request for a lock of Margaret Dumont's hair. *Duck Soup* (1933, Paramount).

4288 NORA CHARLES: "You got types." NICK CHARLES: "Only you, darling, lanky brunettes with wicked jaws." When one of her husband's former cronies notes that **Myrna Loy** is not his usual type, **William Powell** is quick to assure her she's the only type that interests him. *The Thin Man* (1934, MGM).

4289 "In my day a woman with hair like that didn't come out in the daytime." **Elizabeth Patterson** lets the cat in her speak about Mae West's hair. *Go West, Young Man* (1936, Paramount).

4290 "Does you know a dyed-hair woman?" **Hattie McDaniel** questions Vivien Leigh after she sees bordello madam Ona Munson going to visit Clark Gable in the Atlanta jail. *Gone with the Wind* (1939, Selznick-MGM).

4291 "Men don't get smarter as they grow older, they just lose their hair." Having made a life's study of men, often-married **Mary Astor** may know of what she speaks. *The Palm Beach Story* (1942, Paramount).

4292 EDDIE: "Let me run my fingers through your hair." JOAN: "Because my hair is so silky?" EDDIE: "No, there are no towels in the washroom." **Eddie Cantor** sets up comedian **Joan Davis** as a straight "man." At least he didn't want to walk or run bare-footed through her hair. *Show Business* (1944, RKO).

4293 "What a curious way to do your hair—or, rather, not to do it." German cabaret singer **Marlene Dietrich** is critical of the very severe and unattractive hair style of Iowa Congresswoman Jean Arthur. *A Foreign Affair* (1948, Paramount).

4294 "Gramps, how many other people in the world have green hair?" Too bad **Dean Stockwell**'s question of Pat O'Brien wasn't made in the '90s. We've seen numerous young people with green Mohawks. *The Boy with Green Hair* (1949, RKO).

4295 "I always used to think: If a woman's got pitch-black hair, she's already half-way to being a beauty." Deputy sheriff **Wendell Corey** tells Katharine Hepburn about his ideas of hair and beauty. He's thinking of his wife who ran away from him with a traveling salesman. Spinster Hepburn, who's interested in Corey, has nondescript brown hair. *The Rainmaker* (1956, Paramount).

4296 "I've had hangovers before, but this time even my hair hurts." **Rock Hudson** admits to Tony Randall that he's over-indulged. *Pillow Talk* (1959, Universal).

4297 "Nixon would look dumb with long hair, and Ronald Reagan would look worse." It's one of the reasons that rock star **Christopher Jones** gives for running for president of the United States as a Republican. *Wild in the Streets* (1968, AIP).

4298 "I tend to notice little things like this, whether a girl is a blonde." **Sean Connery**, as 007, comments on Jill St. John's hair. She left the room a blonde and returned a moment later as a brunette. Actually, she's a redhead. *Diamonds Are Forever* (1971, GB, United Artists).

4299 "You've done well to keep so much hair when so many's after it. I hope you fare well." Mountain man **Will Geer** wishes title character Robert Redford luck in keeping his scalp. *Jeremiah Johnson* (1972, Warner Bros.).

4300 "You don't belong in Nashville. Go get your hair cut." While cutting a record tribute to the U.S. Bicentennial, country and western legendary singer **Henry Gibson** intolerantly dismisses a long-haired piano player who loses the tempo. *Nashville* (1975, Paramount).

4301 "What are these funny little hairs growing all over me?" **Christopher Atkins** is bewildered by the onset of puberty. *The Blue Lagoon* (1984, Columbia).

4302 "He went out with some cheap blonde." Cheap blonde **Mia Farrow** indignantly accuses her married lover, conceited crooner Nick Apollo Forte of two-timing her. *Broadway Danny Rose* (1984, Orion).

4303 "To me, it looks like the whole world turned blonde." Dark-haired Newark transplant **Ralph Macchio** gets a face full of sand at a Southern California beach, courtesy of a gang of Aryan-looking motorcycle bullies. *The Karate Kid* (1984, Columbia).

4304 "Why, it's the oldest trick in the world, wearing real hair." **Alan Shearman** sees through a criminal's disguise. *Bullshot* (1983, GB, Handmade).

4305 "Oh, I have napkins to match your hair." Dippy protocol officer **Goldie Hawn** gushes to Richard Romanus, an Arab dignitary visiting Washington, D.C. *Protocol* (1984, Warner Bros.).

4306 "Dry hair's for squids." It's one of the more astute observations of **Tim Thomerson**, of the 23rd century, who returns to L.A. of the '80s as his own ancestor to battle the evil "Whistler." *Trancers* aka: *Future Cop* (1985, Empire).

4307 "My God, it's me with a bad haircut." **Bette Midler** sees her long-lost twin for the first time. *Big Business* (1988, Touchstone-Buena Vista).

4308 "If you want to get ahead in business, you've got to have serious hair." While musing on her ambitions, **Melanie Griffith** makes a feeble and unintentional joke. *Working Girl* (1988, 20th Century-Fox).

4309 "Because I'm a blonde, I don't have to think. I talk like a baby and I never have to pay for drinks." A little song that sums up **Julie Brown**'s character. *Earth Girls Are Easy* (1989, Vestron).

4310 "I see split ends are universal." **Julie Brown** examines the furry bodies of aliens Jeff Goldblum, Jim Carrey and Damon Wayans. *Earth Girls Are Easy* (1989, Vestron).

4311 "I understand you work with hair." Self-made millionaire and recently elevated Knight **John Gielgud** interviews virginal 31-year-old London hairdresser Jesse Birdsall. Gielgud thinks he can buy Birdsall for his hippie daughter, Helena Bonham Carter. *Getting It Right* (1989, GB, MCEG).

4312 "How can you marry a blonde with three kids? What are you—an astronaut?" Jewish mother **Mae Questel** will be delighted when her son Woody Allen breaks up with "shiksa," Mia Farrow. "Oedipus Wrecks" segment in *New York Stories* (1989, Touchstone-Buena Vista).

4313 MRS. MILLSTEIN: "You know his father, may he rest in peace, was completely bald, too." SHELDON MILLS: "I'm not bald." MRS. MILLSTEIN: "You will be." **Mae Questel** tells her fifty-year-old son **Woody Allen**'s fiancée about an impending problem. "Oedipus Wrecks" segment in *New York Stories* (1989, Touchstone-Buena Vista).

4314 "I'm losing my hair where I want hair and getting hair where I don't." Turning 40 is traumatic for **Billy Crystal**. *City Slickers* (1991, Columbia).

4315 "My father was a very big man. And he wore a black mustache. When he grew older and it grew gray, he colored it with a pencil. The kind women use. Mascara." His father's mustache has made such an impression on polite **Christopher Walken** that he tells everyone he meets in Venice about it. *The Comfort of Strangers* (1991, Ital.-GB).

4316 "I can't think with all this hair." Womanizer Perry King is reincarnated as **Ellen Barkin**, who has quite a mane of blonde hair. *Switch* (1991, Warner Bros.).

4317 "I'm fine, but you're obviously having a bad hair day." It's **Kristy Swanson**'s reply when she's greeted nastily by 1200-year-old vampire Paul Reubens. *Buffy, The Vampire Slayer* (1992, 20th Century-Fox).

4318 "Dad, we've been through this before. I'm just expressing myself aerodynamically." **Christopher "Kid" Reid** argues with his father Meshach Taylor about his mile-high fade hairdo. *Class Act* (1992, Warner Bros.).

4319 "Dear Alfred Tennyson, who pulled my pigtails and said they were too long." Aging **Joan Plowright** is quite a name-dropper. *Enchanted April* (1992, GB, Miramax).

Hallucinations

see also EYES, IMAGINATION, SIGHT AND SIGHTS, VISIONS AND VISUALIZATIONS

4320 RUTH COLLINS: "What causes hallucinations?" DR. SCOTT ELLIOTT: "Bad nerves." **Olivia de Havilland** receives a simple answer to a potentially complicated question. *The Dark Mirror* (1946, Universal).

4321 "[She]. . . is a lush, the lady. . . after she bends the elbow a few times, she begins to see things—rats, roaches, bats, you know. . . a sock in the kisser is the only thing that will bring her out of it." Henchman **Thomas Gomez** rather enjoys the suffering of **Claire Trevor**, the boozy mistress of his boss, mobster Edward G. Robinson. *Key Largo* (1948, Warner Bros.).

4322 "After you've been working out on the desert fifteen years like I have, you hear a lot of things. See a lot of things, too. Sun in the sky. The heat. All that sand out there. Sometimes rivers and lakes that aren't real. And you think the wind gets in the wires and hums and listens." Telephone lineman **Joe Sawyer** talks of the strange effect the desert has on a person. *It Came from Outer Space* (1953, Universal-International).

Hands and Fingers *see* BODIES

Handsome *see* APPEARANCES

Hanging *see* EXECUTIONS, KILLINGS

Happiness and Unhappiness

see also EMOTIONS, FEELINGS, GLADNESS, JOY, LUCK, PLEASURE, SADNESS, SORROW

4323 "Pardon me while I have a Strange Interlude: How happy I would be with either of these two if both of them just went away." African explorer **Groucho Marx** would like to be rid of both Chico and Harpo Marx. *Animal Crackers* (1930, Paramount).

4324 BARBARA WILLIS: "Do you think I could be happy here?" DENNIS CARSON: "Do you mind if I make it my job to see that you are?" When **Mary Astor** arrives at a rubber plantation with her engineer husband Gene Raymond, overseer **Clark Gable** is very attentive. *Red Dust* (1932, MGM).

4325 GASTON MONESCU: "She must have been very happy in that bed." MARIETTE COLET: "Too happy, that's why I fired her." Con-man **Herbert Marshall** has just been hired as the new secretary of wealthy widow **Kay Francis.** They are inspecting the enormous bed once used by Francis' former secretary. *Trouble in Paradise* (1932, Paramount).

4326 "Evidently my people, who are said to love me, do not want me to be happy." **Greta Garbo** gives up her throne because her Swedish subjects object to Spaniard John Gilbert as her king. *Queen Christina* (1933, MGM).

4327 CAPT. CUMMINGS: "Haven't you ever met a man who could make you happy?" LADY LOU: "Sure, lots of times." Salvation Army-like mission Captain **Cary Grant** and Bowery saloon madam **Mae West** probably are not talking about the same kind of happiness. *She Done Him Wrong* (1933, Paramount).

4328 "Hello, Flo?. . . . Yes, this is Anna. . . . Congratulations. . . . I?. . . Oh, wonderful. . . . Never better in my whole life. . . . It's all so wonderful and I'm so happy. . . I hope you are happy too." This telephone conversation between **Luise Rainer** as Anna Held and her ex-husband William Powell as Florenz Ziegfeld, in which she congratulates him on his marriage to Myrna Loy as Billie Burke, shows only Rainer bravely fighting to control her emotions and to keep from breaking into tears. It won her an Academy Award. *The Great Ziegfeld* (1936, MGM).

4329 "He's much too happy for Sunday, if you ask me." No one asked **Elizabeth Risdon**, one of Irene Dunne's sanctimonious maiden aunts. She doesn't approve of Melvyn Douglas or anyone else for that matter. *Theodora Goes Wild* (1936, Columbia).

4330 "I don't know. You've never shown me anything other." It's **Myrna Loy**'s lovely answer to her husband Clark Gable when he asks if she's happy. Then she gets a gander at Gable's loyal and efficient secretary Jean Harlow. *Wife vs. Secretary* (1936, MGM).

4331 "Ah. . . I knew I was too happy. . . ." Courtesan **Greta Garbo** sighs when Robert Taylor's father Lionel Barrymore pleads with her to end her romance with his son for the sake of his career. *Camille* (1937, MGM).

4332 "Well, Bart, I figure that everyone is entitled to just so much happiness in life. Some get it in the beginning and some in the middle and others at the end. And then there are those that have it spread thin all through the years." It seems that **Beulah Bondi** and her husband of fifty years Victor Moore have used all their happiness up, as they are forced to be separated forever. *Make Way for Tomorrow* (1937, Paramount).

4333 "Everybody would be much happier in Europe if they knew how to make decent coffee." Ugly American, 30s-style **Clark Gable** has a recipe for a continent's contentment. *Idiot's Delight* (1939, MGM).

4334 "I wonder if happiness was ever built upon the unhappiness of others." The answer to **Ingrid Bergman**'s wistful question is "certainly," but it shouldn't be. She's concerned because she knows her affair with married Leslie Howard will make his wife and children unhappy. *Intermezzo* (1939, Selznick-United Artists).

4335 ANN RUTLEDGE: "Tell me we're going to be happy." ABE LINCOLN: "We will be happy, Ann! I know I'm not much, Ann, for a girl like you to care about. I've got less than nothing to offer you. But for whatever I am—whatever I can be—my life belongs to you—and it always will till the day I die." **Mary Howard** receives some reassurance from **Raymond Massey**, but there is to be no future for them—only remembrance in poetry. *Abe Lincoln in Illinois* (1940, RKO).

4336 "I'm not happy. I'm not happy at all." **Walter Abel**'s line loses something in print. You have to see the newspaper editor deliver it to get the full delightful effect. *Arise, My Love* (1940, Paramount).

4337 "Everything that means happiness costs money." Guess **Dick Powell** hasn't heard the one about "money can't buy happiness." *Christmas in July* (1940, Paramount).

4338 "How can I answer you when I don't know the answer myself? If you say we're happy, let's leave it at that. Happiness is something I know nothing about." **Laurence Olivier**'s reaction to his second wife Joan Fontaine's concern for their happiness isn't reassuring to the naïve, fearful girl. *Rebecca* (1940, Selznick-United Artists).

4339 "You daughters of joy are always so gloomy, why is that?" **Ruth Gordon** sees through the gay, vivacious, devil-may-care pretense of Greta Garbo. In reality, Garbo is a shy ski instructor, pretending to be her imaginary twin sister to prevent her husband Melvyn Douglas from running off with his ex-girlfriend Constance Bennett. It's easy to see why Garbo decided to retire after this turkey. *Two-Faced Woman* (1941, MGM).

4340 "And so they lived happily ever after—or did they?" It's the written introduction to the film after an opening sequence shows Joel McCrea and Claudette Colbert being married. *The Palm Beach Story* (1942, Paramount).

4341 JILL BAKER: "You could go through all of Park Avenue and not find a happier couple." DR. VENGARD: "I'm sorry, but it's my duty to explore every avenue. Especially Park Avenue." **Merle Oberon** and psychiatrist **Alan Mowbray** disagree as to whether her uncontrollable hiccups are due to her anxiety about her marriage to Melvyn Douglas. *That Uncertain Feeling* (1942, United Artists).

4342 "This is the happiest moment of my life. Is there anything I can do to make you sicker?" **Mary Astor** is delighted that Humphrey Bogart is sick from over-drinking. *Across the Pacific* (1943, Warner Bros.).

4343 "Papa, my cup runneth over." **Peggy Ann Garner** expresses her elation to her father James Dunn. *A Tree Grows in Brooklyn* (1945, 20th Century-Fox).

4344 "Listen, baby, when we first met—you and me—you thought I was common. Well, how right you was! I was common as dirt. You showed me a snapshot of the place with the columns, and I pulled you down off them columns, and you loved it! We were having them colored lights going! And wasn't we happy together? Wasn't it okay till she showed up here?" **Marlon Brando** reminds his wife Kim Hunter how happy they were until her snooty sister, Vivien Leigh, came for a visit. *A Streetcar Named Desire* (1951, Warner Bros.).

4345 "I want you to find happiness and stop having fun." To **Marilyn Monroe** finding happiness is finding a rich man to take care of her. She's worried her friend Jane Russell is squandering herself on men who don't have much to offer. *Gentlemen Prefer Blondes* (1953, 20th Century-Fox).

4346 "And so the prophecy came true, and Ella went to live in the palace. As for the fairy godmother, and she was the fairy godmother, she went back where she came from. And everybody lived happily ever after." **Walter Pidgeon** is the narrator of this musical version of the story of Cinderella starring Leslie Caron. *The Glass Slipper* (1954, MGM).

4347 MRS. LAWSON: "The Inn of the Sixth Happiness. Ah! Sounds quite Oriental, doesn't it?" GLADYS AYLWARD: "Yes. Yes. But Yang—Yang said that—that everybody in China wishes you the five happinesses: wealth, longevity, good health, virtue and a—" MRS. LAWSON: "And a peaceful death in old age." GLADYS: "Yes, but they didn't mention any more. What is the sixth happiness?" MRS. LAWSON: "That you will find out for yourself. Each person decides in his own heart what the sixth happiness is." British missionary **Athene Seyler** has an eager assistant in **Ingrid Bergman** at her inn in the North China mountains. *The Inn of the Sixth Happiness* (1958, GB, 20th Century-Fox).

4348 "I don't know if I'm unhappy because I'm not free or not free because I'm unhappy." Whore-virgin **Jean Seberg** expresses her confusion to journalist Van Doude in an existentialist classic. *Breathless* (1959, Fr., Imperia Films).

4349 CASSIDY: "Do you know what I do about unhappiness? I buy it off. Are, uh, you unhappy?" MARION CRANE: "Not inordinately." **Frank Albertson** makes a veiled proposition to **Janet Leigh.** She knocks down his pass with a polite "none of your business." *Psycho* (1960, Paramount).

4350 "Happy the man and happy he alone/He who can call today his own/He who secure within can say:/Tomorrow do thy worst! For I have lived today." Narrator **Michael MacLiammoir** brings the film to a close. *Tom Jones* (1963, GB, United Artists).

4351 "It should be easy to be happy. It should be the easiest thing in the world." It's the ironic wish for herself of dissatisfied amoral British model **Julie Christie.** *Darling* (1965, GB, Anglo-Amalgamated).

4352 EDITH LAMBERT: "I thought everybody would be so happy." HARRY LAMBERT: "There's all kinds of happiness. This is the happiness that everybody isn't too happy about." Middle-aged **Maureen O'Sullivan** has just informed her husband **Paul Ford** that she's pregnant. *Never Too Late* (1965, Warner Bros.).

4353 "We made her, Matt. We said that those who thought white people were superior were wrong. We didn't say, don't fall in love with one...I've never seen her quite so happy...I have to be happy for her." **Katharine Hepburn** encourages her husband Spencer Tracy to share her happiness with her daughter Katharine Houghton's happiness in being engaged to black physician Sidney Poitier. *Guess Who's Coming to Dinner* (1967, Columbia).

4354 LEO: "I feel so strange." MAX: "Maybe you're happy." LEO: "That's it. I'm happy." Accountant

Gene Wilder needs Broadway producer **Zero Mostel**'s help in identifying a feeling that is rare for him. *The Producers* (1967, MGM-Embassy).

4355 "We shall never again take our happiness for granted." Latin master **Peter O'Toole** continues his lecture during a bombing raid. *Goodbye, Mr. Chips* (1969, U.S.-G.B.-MGM).

4356 "If you want to really relax sometimes, just fall to rock bottom and you'll be a happy man. Most all trouble comes from having standards." It's a cynical lesson learned by **Dustin Hoffman**'s character, 121-year-old Jack Crabb. *Little Big Man* (1970, National General).

4357 "Don't look for happiness, it will only make you miserable." **Bea Arthur** advises her son Joseph Hindy who is seeking a divorce from Diane Keaton because they aren't happy together. *Lovers and Other Strangers* (1970, ABC-Cinerama).

4358 "You came out of the blue to make us happy. And we made you happy, didn't we? We trusted you with our great treasure." Aged **Julie Christie** speaks to Michael Redgrave, who as a child had been Christie's and Alan Bates' go-between. *The Go-Between* (1971, GB, EMI).

4359 "People say to me, 'He never made you happy,' and I say, 'But am I happy?' Apart from missing him. All my life I've been looking for someone courageous and resourceful. He's not it. But something. We were something." **Peter Finch** delivers a closing monologue about his lover Murray Head. *Sunday, Bloody Sunday* (1971, GB, United Artists).

4360 "You're happy? O.K. . . . clams are happy. You saved some trees. You got a clinic open. Does that make you feel good? Meanwhile Jarmon sits on his committees and carves up the land, the oil, the taxes. . . ." Professional political manager **Peter Boyle** convinces young radical activist lawyer Robert Redford to run for the U.S. Senate against incumbent Don Porter. *The Candidate* (1972, Warner Bros.).

4361 "It's easy to be happy, you know, if your one concern in life is figuring out how much saliva to dribble." **Woody Allen** is envious when he passes an idiots' convention. *Love and Death* (1975, United Artists).

4362 "It's not that I'm unhappy here. I'm fucking broke." Rock critic **Jeff Goldblum** looks for help with his financial problems from his publisher. *Between the Lines* (1977, Midwest Film).

4363 "Oh, I'm so happy for you." Wealthy **Mary Jackson** congratulates her daughter Jane Fonda on the opportunity to demonstrate her self-reliance now that her husband George Segal has lost his high-paying job. *Fun with Dick and Jane* (1977, Columbia).

4364 "Mommy left because I was bad. . . I thought that anytime I was happy, she was happy." **Dustin Hoffman** reveals to his son Justin Henry how little he understood about the needs of his wife Meryl Streep who has left them to find herself. *Kramer vs. Kramer* (1979, Columbia).

4365 "Gay used to be such a happy word." Melancholy **Paul McCrane** unburdens himself by telling his classmates that he's a homosexual. *Fame* (1980, MGM-United Artists).

4366 "I haven't met too many happy people in my life. How do they act?" **Meg Tilly** is puzzled when JoBeth Williams asks if the former's lover, Alex, who has committed suicide, was unhappy. *The Big Chill* (1983, Columbia).

4367 "You can be a real misery, can't you? I was dead happy when I came in, now I feel like I'm having a bad night at the morgue." **Julie Walters** accuses her tutor Michael Caine of bringing her down with his usual despairing manner. *Educating Rita* (1983, GB, Columbia).

4368 "I don't think there's a girl floating in any jar anywhere who's as happy as I am." **Sissy Spacek** is the voice of Brain #21, all that remains alive of a sweet young woman named Ann Uumellmahaye. *The Man with Two Brains* (1983, Warner Bros.).

4369 "See, I never trusted happiness. I never did, I never will." Former country and western singer **Robert Duvall** must have trusted happiness once, or he wouldn't be so sure that he can't find it now with new love Tess Harper. *Tender Mercies* (1983, EMI).

4370 "Why should I be happy about being a grandmother?" Snapping at her pregnant daughter Debra Winger, **Shirley MacLaine** is not quite ready for being reminded that she's aging. *Terms of Endearment* (1983, Paramount).

4371 "It's hard to believe a whole year has gone by since then. Victor finally got his divorce, and he and his wife turned around and married each other again. Victor said it was because she wanted to get the other half of everything he owned. With Karen and me it wasn't really a case of happy ever after. We were lucky to get any kind of ever after at all. I figure we're a few months away from happily. We'll make it. You only live once but it does help if you get to be young twice." **Michael Caine** provides an unnecessary summary of what happened to him, his alienated wife Valerie Harper and his friend Joseph Bologna, his wife's lover and the father of the nubile teen Michelle Johnson with whom Caine had an affair in Rio. None of the characters are interesting enough for audiences to care what happened to them. *Blame It on Rio* (1984, 20th Century-Fox).

4372 "I figure somebody's gotta be happy, might as well be me." Country and western singer Patsy Cline, portrayed by **Jessica Lange**, expresses a happy thought. *Sweet Dreams* (1985, Tri-Star).

4373 "I'd be happy with you in a Turkish prison." **Molly Ringwald** assures Andrew McCarthy that it's his company, not where they are, that's important. A girl from the wrong side of the tracks, Ringwald might be better treated in a Turkish prison than at the party of McCarthy's snobbish society friends. *Pretty in Pink* (1986, Paramount).

4374 "Do we find happiness so often that we should turn it off... when it happens to sit there?" **Denholm Elliott** fruitlessly intercedes for a carriage driver and his lusty girlfriend as a group of English gentlefolk take a ride in the countryside near Florence. *A Room with a View* (1986, GB, Merchant-Ivory-Goldcrest-Cinecom).

4375 "As I look back now, a lot of years later, I realize that my time in the army was the happiest time of my life. God knows not because I like the army, and there sure was nothing to like about a war. I liked it for the most selfish reason of all, because I was young. We all were, me and Epstein and Wykowski, Selridge, Carney, Hennessy, and even Sergeant Toomey. I didn't really like most of those guys then, but today I love every damn one of them. Life is weird, you know." Narrator **Matthew Broderick** appreciates his youthful experiences in the service from the vantage point of advancing age. As one ages, one's youth is really appreciated. *Biloxi Blues* (1988, Universal).

4376 "Those who are most worthy of love are never made happy by it.... Do you still think men love the way we do? No, men enjoy the happiness they feel. We can only enjoy the happiness we give.... They are not capable of devoting themselves exclusively to one person. So to hope to be made happy by love is a certain cause of grief." Wise old **Mildred Natwick** attempts to comfort suffering Michelle Pfeiffer by explaining why women usually get the fuzzy end of the lollipop. *Dangerous Liaisons* (1988, Warner Bros.).

4377 "Jack is dead. You can tell me, the Joker. Death's quite liberating, you have to think of it as therapy.... And as you can see I'm a lot happier." Having survived falling into a vat of acid, **Jack Nicholson** reveals himself with a mouth frozen into a rictus, his skin bleached white, and his hair turned green. *Batman* (1989, Warner Bros.).

4378 VINCE KOZINSKI: "You've made an old man very happy." EDIE COSTELLO: "You're not so old." VINCE: "I know and I'm not so happy." **Lloyd Bridges** gets in the last word with his brother's widow **Norma Aleandro** after she's agreed to have dinner with him. *Cousins* (1989, Paramount).

4379 "Human happiness does not seem to have been included in the design of creation. It is we, with our capacity for love, who give meaning to the indifferent universe. Most human beings seem to have the ability to keep trying and even to find joy from simple things like their family, their work, and from the hope that future generations might understand more." It's part of a brilliant lecture given by psychiatrist Professor Louis Levy, played by **Martin Bergmann.** *Crimes and Misdemeanors* (1989, Orion).

4380 DIANE COURT: "Why are you shaking?" LLOYD DOBLER: "I don't know, I guess I'm happy." **Ione Skye** and **John Cusack** feel the after-glow after they make love for the first time. *Say Anything...* (1989, 20th Century-Fox).

4381 "Anyway, being happy isn't all that great. The last time I was really happy, I got so fat I must have put on 25 pounds. I thought John was going to have a stroke." **Andie MacDowell** tells her therapist that happiness is relative; what makes her happy will not necessarily make husband Peter Gallagher happy. *sex, lies and videotape* (1989, Miramax).

4382 "Why are you so happy? Did you run over a small child?" **Olympia Dukakis**, needles her friend Shirley MacLaine, who is always in a bad mood. *Steel Magnolias* (1989, Tri-Star).

4383 "I've been a good girl—just one night of happiness is all I ask." WASP beauty **Amy Locane** pines for a night of bliss with bad boy Johnny Depp. *Cry-Baby* (1990, Universal).

4384 "Color me happiness, a sofa in here for two." Prostitute **Julia Roberts** is delighted as she enters a plush elevator in the Regent Beverly Wilshire Hotel with "john" Richard Gere. *Pretty Woman* (1990, Touchstone-Buena Vista).

4385 "Happiness is easy if you just take off your overcoat." **F. William Parker** makes a loose translation of an old Swedish saying at his wedding reception. *He Said, She Said* (1991, Paramount).

4386 "I was deeply unhappy, but I didn't know it because I was so happy all the time." Things could be worse for wacky L.A. weatherman **Steve Martin.** He could be happy, but not know it, because he's so unhappy. *L.A. Story* (1991, Tri-Star).

4387 GOMEZ: "Unhappy, darling?" MORTICIA: "Oh, yes, darling. Completely." It's one of the tender little romantic moments between **Raul Julia** and his beloved **Anjelica Huston**. *The Addams Family* (1991, Paramount).

Harm

see also HURT AND HURTING, PAINS, WEAPONS

4388 "There's no harm in combining a little business with pleasure is there?" Humorless **Henry Kolker** plans his daughter Doris Nolan's honeymoon with Cary Grant to include studies of European banking. *Holiday* (1938, Columbia).

4389 PA DANBY: "Why, if I'd pulled the trigger the danged thing would have blowed up in my face." JASON McCULLOUGH: "Well, it wouldn't have done my finger a bit of good, either." When **Walter Brennan** pulls a gun on him, **James Garner** sticks his finger into the barrel. *Support Your Local Sheriff* (1969, United Artists).

4390 "But Vitone is only nine, and dumb-witted. The child cannot harm you." **Maria Carta** begs Guiseppe Sillato who has already killed her husband and older son to spare her youngest son Oreste Baldini. The Sicilian mafioso chief refuses and kills Carta, but the boy escapes. Years later as Robert De Niro, he returns and kills Sillato. *The Godfather, Part II* (1974, Paramount).

4391 "Look after Mr. Bond. See that some harm befalls him." Villain **Michael Lonsdale** gives his henchman Toshiro Suga instructions for dealing with Roger Moore. *Moonraker* (1979, GB, United Artists).

4392 "Maybe I could give you an abusive phone call some night—any time that's inconvenient. The surprise element might do a lot of good—I mean harm." Using a radical new means of treatment, psychiatrist **Norman Chancer** regularly verbally abuses **Burt Lancaster**, the slightly mad head of Knox Petroleum. *Local Hero* (1983, GB, Enigma).

Hate and Hatred

see also EMOTIONS, ENEMIES, FEELINGS, LIKES AND DISLIKES, LOVE AND HATE, PREJUDICE

4393 "I've always hated men till I met you. From now on, it'll be different." Former farm girl **Greta Garbo** really isn't all that impressed with brutish Clark Gable. *Susan Lenox: Her Fall and Rise* (1931, MGM).

4394 "Say it aloud. Tell me you hate me. Please my lamb. Little bird, tell me that you hate me. . . if you don't hate me you must love me." **Fredric March**, as sadistic monster Mr. Hyde, bedevils dance-hall girl Miriam Hopkins. *Dr. Jekyll and Mr. Hyde* (1932, Paramount).

4395 "It isn't tonight. It's every night, worrying about you, hating what you do, hating who you meet." Clark Gable asks **Myrna Loy** what's the matter with her the night when she talks about marriage, children and a home with him out of the rackets. *Manhattan Melodrama* (1934, MGM).

4396 "When a woman can love a man right down to his fingertips, she can hate him just the same." **Jean Harlow** reveals why she double-crosses her former lover Clark Gable, who dumped her for Rosalind Russell. Harlow helps pirate Wallace Beery take over Gable's ship. *China Seas* (1935, MGM).

4397 "I don't dislike you—I hate you." **Helen Parrish** clears things up for Deanna Durbin, who asks, "Why do you dislike me?" *Mad About Music* (1938, Universal).

4398 "I could never hate you. And I know you must care about me. Oh, you do care, don't you. . . I'll hate you till I die. I can't think of anything bad enough to call you." **Vivien Leigh** doesn't mean it as she slaps Leslie Howard. She's just declared her love for him and he's informed her that he's going to marry her cousin, selfless Olivia de Havilland. *Gone with the Wind* (1939, Selznick-MGM).

4399 "I do hate you. You've done all you could to lower the prestige of decent people." Leslie Howard's sister **Alicia Rhett** has reasons to hate Vivien Leigh. The latter snatched Rand Brooks from her, even though Leigh didn't love the boy. *Gone with the Wind* (1939, Selznick-MGM).

4400 "All along I've been hating this kind of thing, always meeting like this, in out-of-the-way places, little dark corners, sneaking about in fear of being seen." **Ingrid Bergman** discovers the fate of young women who fall in love with older married men.

Her mentor and lover Leslie Howard replies, "Love isn't sensible." *Intermezzo* (1939, Selznick-United Artists).

4401 "I've forgotten how much that woman hates me, and how much I hate her." Tough shoplifter **Barbara Stanwyck** has her first meeting in years with her slatternly mother Georgia Caine. *Remember the Night* (1940, Paramount).

4402 "Why do any of us have to cry? You or me? What have we done? Oh, I hate it! I hate everything! I'd hate God if I could, but there's nothing you can reach." **Betty Field** is hysterically unhappy and won't be comforted by her friend Robert Cummings. *Kings Row* (1941, Warner Bros.).

4403 "I hate you so much that I would destroy myself to take you down with me." **Rita Hayworth** really despises her ex-lover Glenn Ford. *Gilda* (1946, Columbia).

4404 "I hated her so, I couldn't get her out of my mind for a minute." **Glenn Ford** realizes that when it comes to Rita Hayworth, hate and love are closely related emotions. *Gilda* (1946, Columbia).

4405 "Hate can be a very exciting emotion." **George Macready** speaks meaningfully to his employee and friend Glenn Ford, who has slept with the boss' wife Rita Hayworth. *Gilda* (1946, Columbia).

4406 "I have a home and a husband. I've got a life worth fighting for and there's nothing in the world I wouldn't do to keep it just the way it is. . . I hated my life. Okay, I wasn't strong enough to get away from it. All I could do was dream of some big pay-off that would let me quit the racket." Devious and unreliable **Ava Gardner** is still involved in a corrupt world of crime. She excuses her behavior to insurance investigator Edmond O'Brien. *The Killers* (1946, Universal-International).

4407 "My grandfather was killed just because he was an Irish Catholic. Hating is always the same, always senseless. One day it kills Irish Catholics, the next day Jews, the next day Protestants, the next day Quakers. It's hard to stop. It can end up killing people who wear striped neckties." Police detective **Robert Young** preaches about killers' blind hate and prejudices. *Crossfire* (1947, RKO).

4408 "The murderer's hate is like a gun. He had to be someone who could hate Samuels without knowing him, it had to be inside the killer." More specifically, police detective **Robert Young** is convinced that the senseless killing of Sam Levene in a barroom brawl was the work of a man who had hatred and murder in him. Levene, a Jew, was just an unfortunate victim who was in the right place at the wrong time. *Crossfire* (1947, RKO).

4409 "This business about hating Jews comes in a lot of different sizes. There's the 'can't join our country club' kind. The 'you can't live around here' kind. The 'you can't work here' kind. Because we stand for all these, we get Monty's kind. He grows out of all the rest. . . . Hating is always insane, always senseless." Now police detective **Robert Young** gets to deliver the film's final message. Bigoted, sadistic Robert Ryan killed stranger Sam Levene just because he was a Jew. *Crossfire* (1947, RKO).

4410 "You murdering little sneak. I can smell your hate. It's no different from your love." Blind artist **Charles Bickford** accuses his young wife Joan Bennett of hating him. *The Woman on the Beach* (1947, RKO).

4411 "If there's anything I hate, it's leeches—filthy little devils!" **Humphrey Bogart** comes out of the water covered with leeches. He's been pulling his boat and will have to go back in the water to finish the job. *The African Queen* (1951, United Artists).

4412 "She hates with her tongue as well as her eyes. She hates with everything. She's a real woman." French Legionnaire **George Tobias** guards captured desert princess Jody Lawrance, who has fiery daggers shooting from her eyes followed by a stream of curses. *Ten Tall Men* (1951, Columbia).

4413 "You want to hate Kirk Edwards? Then you're on the end of a long, long line." Movie director **Humphrey Bogart** talks to dancer Ava Gardner about despicable Howard Hughes-like producer Warren Stevens. *The Barefoot Contessa* (1954, United Artists).

4414 "You got what a lot of fighters don't have. Hate. Let your hate do some good for you." Prison physical education instructor **Judson Pratt** encourages young Paul Newman, appearing as Rocky Graziano, to take up boxing. *Somebody Up There Likes Me* (1956, MGM).

4415 "People who hate the light usually hate the truth." **Burt Lancaster** isn't sympathetic when his aging ex-wife Rita Hayworth doesn't wish to be seen in strong light. *Separate Tables* (1958, United Artists).

4416 "Your eyes are full of hate, Forty-one. That's good. Hate keeps a man alive. It gives him strength."

Jack Hawkins, the Roman commander of a galley ship, encourages slave Charlton Heston. *Ben-Hur* (1959, MGM).

4417 "I do hateful things for which people love me, and I do loveable things for which they hate me. I'm admired for my detestability. Now don't worry, Little Eva, I may be rancid butter, but I'm on your side of the bread." Newspaper columnist **Gene Kelly** does little to comfort Donna Anderson. Her boyfriend Dick York is on trial for teaching evolution, and her preacher father Claude Akins wants to damn York's soul to hell. *Inherit the Wind* (1960, United Artists).

4418 "I hate Raymond Ledbetter—and he's only nine years old. I didn't like him, so I tried to understand him and now that I understand him, I hate him!" Tearful **Barbara Harris** may not be cut out to be a social worker. *A Thousand Clowns* (1965, United Artists).

4419 "I hate you. I hate you. I hated you from the moment we were first married." Infantile psychoanalyst **Peter Sellers** is married to huge Valkyrie-like Eddra Gale. *What's New, Pussycat?* (1965, United Artists).

4420 "I hate the beach! I hate the sun! I'm pale and I'm a redhead! I don't tan—I stroke!" **Woody Allen** protests a visit to the beach. *Play It Again, Sam* (1972, Paramount).

4421 "The more I looked at people, the more I hated them, because I knowed there wasn't any place for me with the kind of people I knowed." **Martin Sheen** indicates a possible source of his anti-social behavior. *Badlands* (1973, Warner Bros.).

4422 "I hate a guy with a car and no sense of humor." Teen **Nancy Loomis** will have worse problems when she encounters Tony Moran as murderous madman Michael Myers. *Halloween* (1978, Falcon International-Compass).

4423 "I can't talk to her. The way she looks at me! She hates me!" **Timothy Hutton** explodes in a rage against his mother Mary Tyler Moore who has cut him out of her life ever since the death of his brother. *Ordinary People* (1980, Paramount).

4424 "His rage is terrible. I don't know how a man can live with so much hate. I saw nothing. I was too dense. He spoke to me of another life—a life of demands, of purity, of joy in the performance of duty. I had never heard such words." **Ewa Froeling** reports to her former mother-in-law Gunn Walgren about her second husband, Jan Malmsjoe, a stern

dangerous fanatic pastor. *Fanny and Alexander* (1982, Sweden-Fr.-Ger., Persona Film-Embassy).

4425 "I hate him so much because you kids think he's something he's not." The baddest cop in all the world, **William Smith**, tells Matt Dillon why it is his ambition to bring down Dillon's idolized brother Mickey Rourke. *Rumble Fish* (1983, Universal).

4426 "My teachers hated me because I was smarter than they were and kids hated me because I blew the bell curve." **Val Kilmer** assures Gabe Jarret that he is not the first child prodigy to be persecuted and misunderstood by unfeeling people. *Real Genius* (1985, Tri-Star).

4427 "That squeaking, corpulent broad, I even hate the way she licks stamps." **Danny De Vito** doesn't grieve when his wife Bette Midler is kidnapped. *Ruthless People* (1986, Touchstone-Buena Vista).

4428 "I woke up. You weren't there. I hate that." **Glenn Close** gives Michael Douglas hell for leaving her bed and heading home after they made mad, passionate love. *Fatal Attraction* (1987, Paramount).

4429 ROGER MURTAUGH: "God hates me, that's what it is." MARTIN RIGGS: "Hate Him back, it works for me." **Danny Glover** is advised by his troubled partner **Mel Gibson** on how to handle adversity. *Lethal Weapon* (1987, Warner Bros.).

4430 "I hate it when they ain't been shaved." Vampire **Adrian Pasdar** has just had a hairy bite to eat. *Near Dark* (1987, De Laurentiis).

4431 "It's ugly. This whole thing is so ugly. Do you know what it is to live with all this? People look at us and only see bigots and racists. Hatred isn't something you're born with. It gets taught. In school they said segregation is what's said in the Bible... Genesis 9, Verse 27. Seven years of age, you get told it enough times, you believe. You believe the hatred. Live it. You breathe it. You marry it." **Frances McDormand** elaborates on the *South Pacific* song, "You've Got to Be Carefully Taught." *Mississippi Burning* (1988, Orion).

4432 "This place is bullshit, man. I hate the fucking place.... If the gooks had half a brain, they'd be fighting to get out of this stinkhole instead of keeping it." Ignorant U.S. Army Sergeant **Sean Penn** doesn't think much of Vietnam. *Casualties of War* (1989, Columbia).

4433 SCOTT EDWARDS: "I thought you hated me." JOANNA SIMPSON: "I do." **Mitch Gaylord** is joined in a shower by **Victoria Prouty** for some sex. *American Rickshaw* (1991, Academy).

4434 "I hate sex and drugs but I'm always high." Cast against type, **Robert Z'dar**, usually a villain, is a new breed of law enforcer. *The Big Sweat* (1991, AIP).

4435 "If hate were people, I'd be China." **Daniel Stern** screams at his bitchy wife Karla Tamburrelli at a birthday party for Billy Crystal. *City Slickers* (1991, Columbia).

4436 "You're not going to get away with hating. You'll end up with the whole family strangling you from inside your head." Brooding eldest sibling **Vincent D'Onofrio** warns his brother Pete Berg. *Crooked Hearts* (1991, MGM-United Artists).

4437 FRANKIE: "God, why do we get involved with people it turns out hate us?" JOHNNY: "Because. . . ." FRANKIE: "Because, we hate ourselves. I know. I read the same book." JOHNNY: "I want to go upstairs, watch you get ready for bed, then climb in and make love to you for ten hours." FRANKIE: "You expect me to be fooled with a line like that?" There's no hate between **Michelle Pfeiffer** and **Al Pacino**—just fear of involvement on her side and loneliness on his. *Frankie and Johnny* (1991, Paramount).

4438 "To destroy Batman, we must first turn him into what he hates most—namely, us." **Michelle Pfeiffer**, as Catwoman, shares her plan for defeating Batman, played by Michael Keaton, with her partner in evil and crime, Danny De Vito as the Penguin. *Batman Returns* (1992, Warner Bros.).

4439 "I think you just hate men." Tramp **Ione Skye** shouts at her hard-working waitress mother Brooke Adams, who has had her own share of nowhere encounters with men. *Gas, Food, Lodging* (1992, IRS).

Hats

see also CLOTHES, HEADS AND HEADACHES

4440 COSTUME DESIGNER: "Girls! Girls! My hats! Be careful of my hats. I won't allow you to ruin them." WARDROBE MISTRESS: "I told you they were too high and too wide." COSTUME DESIGNER: "Well, big woman, I design the costumes for the show, not the doors of the theater." WARDROBE MISTRESS: "I know that. If you had, they'd have been done in lavender." The costume designer protests when a group of show girls have trouble getting out of their dressing room because they are wearing hats too large to pass through the door. The wardrobe mistress isn't sympathetic. *The Broadway Melody* (1929, MGM).

4441 "To buy a new hat." It's prostitute **Marlene Dietrich**'s flip reply when Chinese Revolutionary General Warner Oland asks her why she was traveling by train to Shanghai. *Shanghai Express* (1932, Paramount).

4442 "I once knew a man who kept his hat on until he was completely undressed. He wore a toupee." **Clark Gable** gives Claudette Colbert a lecture and a demonstration on the different ways men undress. *It Happened One Night* (1934, Columbia).

4443 "How can such a civilization survive which permits their women to put things like that on their heads?" Russian communist emissary **Greta Garbo** marvels at a chic Parisian hat which she's dying to try on. *Ninotchka* (1939, MGM).

4444 "If I throw my hat in the ring, does my head go with it?" Businessman **Spencer Tracy** asks a sensible question before deciding to make a bid for the presidency of the United States. *State of the Union* (1948, MGM).

4445 "I'm constantly amazed that women's hats don't provoke more murders." Barrister **Charles Laughton** makes the peculiar observation after his client Tyrone Power notes that the woman he's supposed to have murdered, Norma Varden, would still be alive if he hadn't met her after casually striking up a conversation with her in a millinery store. *Witness for the Prosecution* (1957, United Artists).

4446 VERNA BERNBAUM: "So you chased the hat, but when you caught up to it, it changed into something else, something wonderful." TOM REAGAN: "No, I didn't chase it. And it stayed a hat. There's nothing more foolish than a man chasing a hat." **Marcia Gay Harden** tries to predict the ending of **Gabriel Byrne**'s strange dream about a hat blowing away in a forest. *Miller's Crossing* (1990, 20th Century-Fox).

Headlines

see also NEWS AND NEWSPAPERS, REPORTERS

4447 "Rocky dies yellow; Killer coward at end." Headlines announcing James Cagney's death in the electric chair, read by hero-worshipping slum kids. *Angels with Dirty Faces* (1938, Warner Bros.).

4448 "If the headline is big enough, it makes the news big enough." It's a newspaper principle of publisher **Orson Welles.** *Citizen Kane* (1941, RKO).

4449 "Fraud at the Polls." It's the headline that Everett Sloane is forced to publish on the front page of the *New York Enquirer* when it is apparent that

Orson Welles has lost his election bid. *Citizen Kane* (1941, RKO).

4450 "Kris Kringle Krazy? Kourt Kase Koming; 'Kalamity,' Kries Kids." It's the "K" headline of the *New York Daily News* announcing that Edmund Gwenn faces a sanity hearing for claiming to be the real Santa Claus. *Miracle on 34th Street* (1947, 20th Century-Fox).

4451 "What do you think the newspapers will say when they find out about this? 'Wife Quits Miracle Worker.'" Con-man **Tyrone Power** pleads with his wife Coleen Gray not to leave him over his crooked activities as a spiritualist. *Nightmare Alley* (1947, 20th Century-Fox).

4452 "I can already see the headline: 'Wife Names Fish.'" **Clinton Sundberg** jokes that Irene Hervey will file for divorce from William Powell and name his mermaid Ann Blyth as correspondent. *Mr. Peabody and the Mermaid* (1948, Universal).

4453 "How's that for an angle: 'King Tut in New Mexico: White Man half-buried by angry Indian spirits.'" Cynical reporter **Kirk Douglas** can see the headlines now as he controls the story about a man trapped in a cave in New Mexico. *Ace in the Hole* aka: *The Big Carnival* (1951, Paramount).

4454 "Only it was you and me wearing exactly the same gown. It was an ad for Minsky. And the headline said, 'Madame Rose, and her daughter Gypsy.'" At the end of the film, **Rosalind Russell** once again shares a stage dream with her daughter Natalie Wood. *Gypsy* (1962, Warner Bros.).

4455 "It's a *New York Times*—be careful—from 1990. 'Pope's wife gives birth to twins.' Wow!" **Woody Allen** reads the headline of a newspaper, which is among the artifacts from the 20th century he's identifying for the scientists who have revived him from a 200-year sleep. *Sleeper* (1973, United Artists).

4456 "If they can make headlines with lies, we can make bigger headlines with the truth." **Joan Allen** encourages her husband Jeff Bridges during his trial for fraud. *Tucker: The Man and His Dream* (1988, Paramount).

Heads and Headaches

see also BODIES, HATS, MINDS, THINKING AND THOUGHTS

4457 "Some heads, like nuts, better if well cracked." **Warner Oland**, as Charlie Chan, sneaks in another epigram. *Charlie Chan's Chance* (1932, Fox).

4458 ALLISON: "I have a headache." JULIO: "I don't want to touch your head." **Jennifer Jason Leigh** is fearful of going to bed with her husband **Taylor Negron** on their wedding night. *Easy Money* (1983, Orion).

4459 "I had the top of her head off, but that's as far as it went." Brain surgeon **Steve Martin** complains to a colleague that his marriage to former patient Kathleen Turner hasn't been consummated. *The Man with Two Brains* (1983, Warner Bros.).

4460 "Maybe if you made love more often, you wouldn't have all those headaches." **Steve Guttenberg** has a helpful prescription for his wife Beverly D'Angelo. She is always giving him the "Not tonight, I've got a headache" excuse for not having sex with him. Both find ghosts to be better sexual partners. *High Spirits* (1988, Tri-Star).

Health

see also BODIES, CLEANLINESS, CURES, DOCTORS AND DENTISTS, HURT AND HURTING, INSANITY AND SANITY, MEDICINE, MINDS, NERVOUSNESS AND NERVES, PAINS, PSYCHOLOGY AND PSYCHIATRY, SICKNESS, WOUNDS AND SCARS

4461 "This office is a shrine—a shrine to health." Dedicated health-nut **George Brent**, the editor of *Body and Brain* magazine, insists on "correct living" when he hires Jean Arthur as his secretary. *More Than a Secretary* (1936, Columbia).

4462 "Because my real estate agent thought the altitude would be good for my asthma." **William Powell** sarcastically answers society girl Carole Lombard's dumb question as to why he's living at the city dump. *My Man Godfrey* (1936, Universal).

4463 "Health is like money, it's no good unless you spend it." Constantly under the influence of liquor, **Robert Montgomery** has a smart aleck answer when he's warned about ruining his health. *Unfinished Business* (1941, Universal).

4464 "I refuse to endanger the health of my children in a house with less than three bathrooms." Mother **Myrna Loy** worries about the effect bathroom deprivation will have on her two girls. *Mr. Blandings Builds His Dream House* (1948, RKO).

4465 "I've come to the conclusion that the world would be a healthier place if more people were sick." Stubborn Scottish soldier **Richard Todd**, having only a short time to live, thinks his nurse Patricia Neal can do anything. *The Hasty Heart* (1949, Warner Bros.).

4466 "Good health, the most important thing, more than success, more than money, more than power." Jewish mobster **Lee Strasberg** tells Al Pacino what he considers the most important gift to have. *The Godfather, Part II* (1974, Paramount).

4467 "P.S. All the above is bullshit. I'm floundering in a sea of confusion and despair, but knock on wood, I still have my health." College student **John Cusack** adds a postscript to his letter to his high school buddy Anthony Edwards. *The Sure Thing* (1985, Embassy).

4468 "I look around this town and I see John and Cynthia and you and I feel comparatively healthy." **James Spader** tells Andie MacDowell that his impotency is of small consequence compared to the problems and hangups of her, her husband Peter Gallagher, and her sister Laura San Giacomo. *sex, lies and videotape* (1989, Miramax).

4469 "Your health is everything. The treasures of the world are nothing." Al Pacino gets another lecture on the importance of health. As did Lee Strasberg before him, elderly don **Eli Wallach** wants Pacino in his grave. *The Godfather, Part III* (1991, Paramount).

Hearing

see also SENSATIONS, TALKS AND TALKING

4470 "Listen, I think I hear footprints. . . ." **Leo Carrillo** spends much of his career providing comic relief as a stereotyped Mexican as in this 15-chapter serial. *Riders of Death Valley* (1941, Universal).

4471 "You know there's something about this which is like expecting a letter you're just crazy to get, and you hang around the front door for fear you might not hear 'em ring. You never realize that he always rings twice. . . . The truth is you always hear 'em ring the second time, even if you're way out in the backyard." Murderer **John Garfield** uses an analogy to describe his situation for D.A. Leon Ames. *The Postman Always Rings Twice* (1946, MGM).

4472 BILLY GALVIN: "I thought you said you loved me." JACK GALVIN: "You've got convenient hearing." **Lenny Von Dohlen** wants to bridge the gap between himself and his construction worker father **Karl Malden**.*Billy Galvin* (1987, Vestron).

4473 "You've put part of me to ease, but I haven't heard anything yet to put my mind to ease." After years of infidelity, **Annie Potts** and her husband Jeff Bridges have once again made love, but she longs to hear what he seemingly can't say, that he loves her and wants their marriage to continue. *Texasville* (1990, Columbia).

Heart and Heartaches

see also BODIES, EMOTIONS, FEELINGS, LOVE AND HATE, LOVE AND LOVERS, MINDS, ROMANCES, SADNESS, SORROWS

4474 JERRY: "Oooh! My head's going like a pinwheel." TED: "My head's beating like a steam engine. Feel." JERRY: "When did you first start having heart trouble?" TED: "From the moment I met you." **Norma Shearer** and **Chester Morris** are either in love or falling apart physically. *The Divorcee* (1930, MGM).

4475 "I think you must have an adding machine for your heart." **Bette Davis** resents Mexican lawyer Paul Muni's indifference to her. *Bordertown* (1935, Warner Bros.).

4476 "My heart! It's not used to being happy. . . . Perhaps it's better if I live in your heart, where the world can't see me." As she expires, courtesan **Greta Garbo** bids farewell to innocent young Robert Taylor. *Camille* (1936, MGM).

4477 "Nobody but God and I know what is my heart." Self-sacrificing **Marlene Dietrich** unknowingly falls in love with moody Charles Boyer, who has broken his vows and left a Trappist monastery. The romance ends when he returns to his life of solitude. The picture wasn't among Dietrich's favorites, and she felt the line too conceitful. *The Garden of Allah* (1936, Selznick-United Artists).

4478 "He has a heart of gold—only harder." Studio head **Adolphe Menjou** introduces his new actress Janet Gaynor to publicity agent Lionel Stander. *A Star Is Born* (1937, Selznick-United Artists).

4479 "You always had my heart—you cut your teeth on it." **Leslie Howard** expresses brotherly love for Vivien Leigh. *Gone with the Wind* (1939, Selznick-MGM).

4480 "As for you, my galvanized friend, you want a heart. You don't know how lucky you are not to have one. Hearts will never be practical until they can be made unbreakable." **Frank Morgan**, as the Wizard, deals with the wish of Tin Man Jack Haley. *The Wizard of Oz* (1939, MGM).

4481 "Now I know I've got a heart, 'cause it's breaking." Tin Man, **Jack Haley**, sadly says goodbye to Judy Garland as Dorothy. *The Wizard of Oz* (1939, MGM).

4482 "You wandered off like a greedy, wanton child to break your heart and mine." **Laurence Olivier** blames Merle Oberon for their mutual unhappiness. *Wuthering Heights* (1939, Goldwyn-United Artists).

4483 "With all my heart, I still love the man I killed!" **Bette Davis** makes a double confession to her loyal husband Herbert Marshall. *The Letter* (1940, Warner Bros.).

4484 RICK BLAINE: "This gun is pointed right at your heart." CAPT. LOUIS RENAULT: "That is my least vulnerable spot." **Humphrey Bogart** turns the tables on **Claude Rains**, who believed he had a deal with Bogie to arrest resistance leader Paul Henreid. *Casablanca* (1942, Warner Bros.).

4485 "There isn't any way you can tear open the secret heart of a human being, is there, Ma?" Magazine writer **Gregory Peck** consults with his mother Anne Revere for an angle on his assignment to write a series on anti-Semitism in the U.S. *Gentleman's Agreement* (1947, 20th Century-Fox).

4486 SIR ALFRED: "You didn't do anything you shouldn't do while I was away, did you? I mean, like falling in love with anyone else or anything like that?" DAPHNE: "How could I fall in love with anyone else. . . when you took my heart with you?" SIR ALFRED: "No man ever had a better answer than that." **Rex Harrison** suspects his wife **Linda Darnell** was unfaithful while he was away on a concert tour. *Unfaithfully Yours* (1948, 20th Century-Fox).

4487 "Drain this cup as you have drained my heart." **Hedy Lamarr** offers a drink to Victor Mature with an absurd line. *Samson and Delilah* (1949, Paramount).

4488 "I wouldn't worry too much about your heart. You can always put that award where your heart ought to be." **Bette Davis** doesn't buy Anne Baxter's sincerity. Upon receiving an acting award, Baxter insists that even though she's going to Hollywood, her heart will always remain on Broadway. *All About Eve* (1950, 20th Century-Fox).

4489 "Remember the heart is the second most important organ in the human body." Sgt. **Peter Falk**, a baker before the war, brings bread to his buddies in the Ardennes Forest. He tells them that bread is very good for the heart. *Castle Keep* (1969, Columbia).

4490 "Which is worse—the heart abused or the heart unused?" Las Vegas piano player **Warren Beatty** muses on the nature of love. *The Only Game in Town* (1970, 20th Century-Fox).

4491 "You keep your heart in an ashcan." Gangster **Mark Rydell** accuses private eye Elliott Gould of being unfeeling. Sounds like the hood is British. *The Long Goodbye* (1973, United Artists).

4492 "I know it was you, Fredo; you broke my heart." **Al Pacino** tells his brother John Cazale that he knows the latter fingered Pacino for assassination. *The Godfather, Part II* (1974, Paramount).

4493 "What is essential is invisible to the eye. It's only with the heart that one can see clearly." Pilot Richard Kiley is given some advice from a fox, played by **Gene Wilder** in this so-so adaptation of the Antoine de Saint-Exupery children's classic. *The Little Prince* (1974, GB, Paramount).

4494 "You belong to an endangered species, Frank. You've got a good heart." **Pamela Stephenson** compliments bungling TV reporter Robert Hays— later, she will help frame him for the murder of his wife. *Scandalous* (1984, GB, Orion).

4495 "For all my education, accomplishments, and so-called wisdom, I can't fathom my own heart." **Michael Caine** knows one can never really understand love. *Hannah and Her Sisters* (1986, Orion).

4496 "Your rifle is only a tool. It's your heart that kills." Gunnery Sergeant **Lee Ermey** lectures his new Marine recruits. *Full Metal Jacket* (1987, Warner Bros.).

4497 "Make your heart a sword, not a spoon." Mexican cook **Edith Diaz** states a meaningless aphorism. *Scenes from the Class Struggle in Beverly Hills* (1989, Cinecom).

4498 "He has my heart. How can I live without my heart?" **Bo Derek** laments the loss of her deceased virile husband Anthony Quinn. *Ghosts Can't Do It* (1990, Triumph).

4499 "The eye does not see the same as the heart." It's an aphorism of wise old Japanese gentleman **Ryu Chishu**. *Until the End of the World* (1991, Fr.-Ger.-Australia, Warner Bros.).

Heat

see also ENERGY, EXCITEMENTS, WEATHER

4500 BUS DRIVER: "Hot, isn't it?" RUTH SHERWOOD: "Yes, but you'll cool off." At the bus station, **Bob Kellard** is given the brush by **Rosalind Russell**, as she and sister Janet Blair arrive in New York from Columbus, Ohio. *My Sister Eileen* (1942, Columbia).

4501 "Come, let me warm you." **Charlotte Rampling** makes an interesting offer to Richard Harris. *Orca—Killer Whale* (1977, Famous Films).

4502 "When it gets hot, people think the old rules aren't in effect. . . they try to kill each other." Police detective **J.A. Preston** notes a correlation between temperature and mayhem. *Body Heat* (1981, Warner Bros.).

4503 "I didn't know it would be so hot. This is Africa hot!" Recruit **Matthew Broderick** arrives in Biloxi, Mississippi for basic training. *Biloxi Blues* (1988, Universal).

Heaven

see also ANGELS, DEVILS, GOD, HEAVEN AND HELL, HELL, SPACE, UNIVERSE

4504 "Let us return to our mother's knee tonight, with the fairies and witches and gnomes and elves, and be as little children to enter a heaven of rich enjoyment." The film's foreword. *A Daughter of the Gods* (1916, silent, Fox).

4505 "Don't try to get to heaven in one night." We suspect that the heaven on **Mae West**'s mind is more physical than spiritual. *Belle of the Nineties* (1934, Paramount).

4506 "I was looking at the one hundred and second floor. It was the nearest thing to heaven. You see you were there." **Irene Dunne** refers to the Empire State building, where she was supposed to meet Charles Boyer after a six month separation to test the strength of their shipboard romance. *Love Affair* (1939, RKO).

4507 "A woman's paradise is always a fool's paradise." **Rosalind Russell** is all but bursting to be the first one to tell Norma Shearer that her husband is having an affair with Joan Crawford. *The Women* (1939, MGM).

4508 "Getting me into heaven is your business, Vinnie. If there's anything wrong with my ticket when I get there, you can fix it up. Everybody loves you so much I'm sure God does too." Businessman **William Powell** believes in division of labor—and religion is in his wife Irene Dunne's bailiwick. He sees no need for him to bother submitting to baptism. *Life with Father* (1947, Warner Bros.).

4509 HAN SUYIN: "I am so happy it frightens me. I have a feeling that heaven is unfair and is preparing for you and me with a great sadness because we have been given so much." MARK ELLIOT: "Darling, whatever happens, always remember: nothing is fair, nor unfair, under heaven." Eurasian doctor **Jennifer Jones'** premonition of disaster is not put to rest by the words of her married lover, journalist **William Holden**. *Love Is a Many-Splendored Thing* (1955, 20th Century-Fox).

4510 "I feel like we've died and gone to heaven—only we had to climb up." Exhausted **Mildred Natwick** has climbed five flights of stairs to reach her recently married daughter Jane Fonda's new apartment. *Barefoot in the Park* (1967, Paramount).

4511 "In the southeast they say if you want to go to heaven you have to change planes in Atlanta." Dog groomer **Geena Davis** talks until she thinks of something to say to unresponsive William Hurt. *The Accidental Tourist* (1989, Warner Bros.).

4512 JOHN KINSELLA: "This is so beautiful. . . I mean for me it's like a dream come true. . . . Is this heaven?" RAY KINSELLA: "It's Iowa. . . . Is there a heaven?" JOHN: "Oh, yeah, it's the place dreams come true." RAY: "Maybe this is heaven." Deceased **Dwier Brown** thinks he must be in heaven, because he's given the opportunity to play baseball with his heroes, including Shoeless Joe Jackson. His son **Kevin Costner** realizes that his baseball field in the middle of an Iowa cornfield meets his father's definition of heaven—at least for him. *Field of Dreams* (1989, Universal).

4513 "Heaven must be like coming home." Narrator **Ian Hawkes** thinks of his beloved grandfather Vittorio Duse at the end of a very special movie. *Queen of Hearts* (1989, GB, Cinecom).

4514 "Lucky heaven exists or we'd all go mad." Tall, regal, blonde **Nicole Garcia** is married to an officer in the French Navy. Life isn't all she hoped for. *Overseas* (1991, Fr., Aries Film).

4515 "It must be like this to wake up in paradise." **Max von Sydow** is awakened by his daughter on a dappled afternoon. *The Best Intentions* (1992, Denmark, Goldwyn).

Heaven and Hell

see also GOD, HEAVEN, HELL

4516 "What do they know of heaven and hell, Cathy, who know nothing of life?" Tortured and distraught **Laurence Olivier** speaks to his beloved Merle Oberon. *Wuthering Heights* (1939, Goldwyn).

4517 "Better to reign in hell than to serve in heaven." Tyrannical and mad sea captain **Edward**

G. Robinson espouses his Nietzchean superman theories to Alexander Knox. *The Sea Wolf* (1941, Warner Bros.).

4518 "As Henry Van Cleve's soul passed over the Great Divide, he realized that it was extremely unlikely that the next stop would be Heaven, and so philosophically he presented himself where quite a few people had told him to go. . . ." It's the opening lines of a delightful period fantasy film, filled with WASPish humor. *Heaven Can Wait* (1943, 20th Century-Fox).

4519 "I sent my soul through the Invisible/Some letter of that afterlife to spell/And by and by my soul returned and whispered/ I myself and heaven and hell." A title at both the beginning and the end of the film. *The Picture of Dorian Gray* (1945, MGM).

Hell

see also DEVILS, EVILNESS, FIRES, GOD, HEAVEN, HEAVEN AND HELL

4520 "I'll see you in hell." Villain **Charles Middleton** leaps to his death to avoid capture by George O'Brien. *Mystery Ranch* (1932, Fox).

4521 "How many people has he given hell to in five months?" **Pierre Fresnay** keeps tabs on his father Raimu, whom he no longer sees. *César* (1936, Fr., Pagnol-Paramount).

4522 "My dear Mr. Van Cleve, a passport to hell is not issued on generalities." His Excellency the Devil, **Laird Cregar** demands that Don Ameche be more explicit about his sins when Ameche presents himself at the portals of hell. Ameche has stated that his life "has been one continuous misdemeanor." *Heaven Can Wait* (1943, 20th Century-Fox).

4523 "Each of us has his own private hell to go to," actress **Geraldine Page** prophesies. *Sweet Bird of Youth* (1962, MGM).

4524 LORNA MELFORD: "What am I doing loose, Doctor? Go ahead, tie me up, I'm out of my head, I heard 'em talking: 'Keep her tied up, tie her up tight, tight, tight!'" DR. DONOVAN MACLEOD: "Do you know where you are?" LORNA: "In hell!" **Polly Bergen**, who blames herself for the accidental death of her child is brought to a mental hospital run by progressive shrink **Robert Stack**, when she suffers a nervous breakdown. *The Caretakers* (1963, United Artists).

4525 "I've had hell inside me, and I can spot it in others." Salesman **Lee Marvin** feels an affinity for despairing young Jeff Bridges. *The Iceman Cometh* (1973, American Film Theater).

4526 "What is this, hell week?" **Goldie Hawn** confuses the U.S. Army with a sorority rush. But Captain Eileen Brennan is no house mother as she demands Goldie give her 100 pushups. *Private Benjamin* (1980, Warner Bros.).

4527 "Hell is my natural habitat!" Alcoholic diplomat in Mexico **Albert Finney** shouts with self-pity. *Under the Volcano* (1984, Universal).

4528 "Surviving. . . coming back. . . that's the real hell." Vietnam veteran **Don Johnson** despairs after the suicide of his buddy Robert F. Lyons. *Cease Fire* (1985, Cineworld).

4529 "We're on an express elevator to hell." Marine **Bill Paxton** and others descend to the planet LV426 to rescue colonists, if any are still alive. *Aliens* (1986, 20th Century-Fox).

4530 "Somebody once wrote, 'Hell is the impossibility of reason.' That's what this place feels like—hell. I don't even know what I'm doing. . . I'm so tired. I think I made a big mistake coming here." Rich, white **Charlie Sheen** volunteered to fight in Vietnam because he didn't believe that the poor and the black had to do it all. *Platoon* (1986, Orion).

4531 "A little bit of everyone belongs in hell, Lieutenant." Strong, silent type **Kris Kristofferson** states his low opinion of humanity to police detective George Kirby. *Trouble in Mind* (1986, Island Alive).

4532 "I can't go in there. It's like yuppies from hell." **Bob Goldthwait** is frightened by a businessman's bar. *Burglar* (1987, Warner Bros).

4533 "This is hell, and I'm going to give you the guided tour." Sadistic, mad warden **Donald Sutherland** gleefully welcomes con Sylvester Stallone, whom he hates with an unrelentless passion. *Lock Up* (1989, Tri-Star).

4534 "Actually there is no hell. Although I hear L.A. is getting very near." Afterworld lawyer type **Rip Torn** answers recently dead Albert Brooks' question if he's to be sent to hell. *Defending Your Life* (1991, Warner Bros.).

Hello *see* GREETINGS

Help and Helping

see also EASE AND EASINESS, GENEROSITY, GIFTS AND GIVING, POVERTY, TROUBLES

4535 "I can't tell ya the number of men I've helped to realize themselves." **Mae West** stands prepared to help Randolph Scott, as well. *Go West, Young Man* (1936, Paramount).

4536 "Help me, I don't want to die." **James Cagney** goes to the chair screaming and crying like a coward just as Priest Pat O'Brien wanted him to do. *Angels with Dirty Faces* (1938, Warner Bros.).

4537 "Be generous, Mr. Spade. You're brave. You're strong. You can spare some of that courage and strength, surely. Help me, Mr. Spade! I need help badly. I've no right to ask you, I know I haven't, but I do ask you. Help me!" **Mary Astor** pulls out all the stops, posing as a weak female appealing to a strong male. *The Maltese Falcon* (1941, Warner Bros.).

4538 "Has it ever occurred to you that women can sometimes be of more help than men?" Well, it depends upon in what way **Vivien Leigh**, as married Lady Hamilton, plans to help Laurence Olivier as Lord Nelson. *That Hamilton Woman* aka: *Lady Hamilton* (1941, Korda-United Artists).

4539 "If any of your friends in Tokyo have trouble committing hari-kari, these boys will be glad to help them out." **Humphrey Bogart** snarls to traitor Sydney Greenstreet as the former points to U.S. planes overhead. *Across the Pacific* (1942, Warner Bros.).

4540 "It's even better when you help." **Lauren Bacall** makes the suggestion to Humphrey Bogart, after she kisses him passionately for the first time. *To Have and Have Not* (1944, Warner Bros.).

4541 "I can't count on Neeley—a boy is no good at a time like this." Widow **Dorothy McGuire**, clasping Peggy Ann Garner to her bosom, tells her she'll have to help with the birth of a new baby, because her brother Ted Donaldson will be useless. *A Tree Grows in Brooklyn* (1945, 20th Century-Fox).

4542 "You can never help anything, can you? You're like the leaf that the wind blows from one gutter to another. You can't help anything you do, even murder. . . ." **Robert Mitchum** sees lovely Jane Greer for what she is—a selfish, evil woman, who thinks only of herself. *Out of the Past* (1947, RKO).

4543 "I felt helpless, that helplessness you feel when you have no talent to offer—outside of loving your husband. How could I compete? Everything Lloyd loved about me, he had gotten used to long ago." In a voice-over, **Celeste Holm** fears she's losing her playwright husband Hugh Marlowe to conniving young actress Anne Baxter. *All About Eve* (1950, 20th Century-Fox).

4544 "All right, I'll help you. I'll help you for two reasons. . . . The first reason is I'm too young to be sent to jail. The second reason is you've got a lot of animal magnetism." Precocious seven-year-old **George Winslow**, in his fog-horn voice, comes to the aid of Marilyn Monroe who is caught coming out of a stateroom through a porthole. *Gentlemen Prefer Blondes* (1953, 20th Century-Fox).

4545 "Help me. Someone, I'm sick. I need help." Nazi concentration camp survivor **Kirk Douglas**, a famous juggler before the war, is a refugee in Israel, who believes he's killed an Israeli police officer. *The Juggler* (1953, Columbia).

4546 "Kris, help me. For God's sake, help me." Having failed to save the life of his colleague Charles Bickford, physician and surgeon **Robert Mitchum**, finally realizes that he's a man not a god, and that he needs his wife Olivia de Havilland, whom he has badly treated. *Not as a Stranger* (1955, United Artists).

4547 "I wanted your help. Now you have given it to me. By making this example of you, I discourage treason. By condemning, without hesitation, an old friend, I shall be feared." Roman Centurion **Stephen Boyd** happily puts his duty ahead of his friendship for Jewish prince Charlton Heston. *Ben-Hur* (1959, MGM).

4548 "The gods are best served by those who need their help the least." **Niall MacGinnis**, as Zeus, prefers that humans not implore him for assistance. *Jason and the Argonauts* (1963, GB, Columbia).

4549 "I realized that every bit of food I ate, every piece of clothing I wore came from them. I began hiding agitators in the chapel of the house and I ended up helping them get guns." Spanish Countess **Simone Signoret** is being sent by ship to prison for engaging in political activities in Vera Cruz. *Ship of Fools* (1965, Columbia).

4550 "Father, can you help an old altar boy? I'm a Catholic." **Mercedes McCambridge**, the voice of the demon possessing young Linda Blair, imitates the Irish brogue of an old derelict who had said the words to Priest Jason Miller on the street. *The Exorcist* (1973, Warner Bros.).

4551 "I can find you another two yards." Professional track coach **Ian Holm** will help runner Ben Cross reduce his running time. *Chariots of Fire* (1981, GB, 20th Century-Fox).

4552 "I don't think your punks need help from the outside to kill themselves." Hedonist **Bob Brady** wants to achieve sensual euphoria (junkie slang for heroin ecstasy). He is talking to government scientist Otto von Wernherr who is investigating a UFO that has landed on the roof of the apartment of Anne Carlisle, a homosexual punk model. *Liquid Sky* (1983, Z Films).

4553 "Goddamn it, I'd piss on a spark plug if I thought it would do any good." **Erik Stern** indicates to Matthew Broderick how far he'd go to avoid nuclear holocaust. *Wargames* (1983, MGM-United Artists).

4554 "I am Carlos from Algeria, have you heard of me?. . . Sh?. . . I need your help. . . I need you to walk with me to my hotel. . . I can not walk the streets of Paris alone. . . . Will you help me?. . . Sh, say no more. . . ." Dark, swarthy American **Nick Corri** picks up a blonde, named Heidi, in Paris, by letting her believe that he's a terrorist—it appears to be a very effective line. *Gotcha!* (1985, Universal).

4555 "Think of yourself as a doctor. Instead of helping those who want to live, you help those who want to die." **Katharine Hepburn** tries to cajole reluctant hit man Nick Nolte into performing his specialty on her elderly and miserable friends. *Grace Quigley* aka: *The Ultimate Solution of Grace Quigley* (1985, Canon).

4556 "A sure thing—no questions asked, no strings attached. . . . All my life, I never had a sure thing. Look kid, you pay for the traffic tickets, and I'll get you in the saddle." Trucker **Larry Hankin** offers to help John Cusack get to his date with "a sure thing." *The Sure Thing* (1985, Embassy).

4557 "It's not that I can't help these people, it's just that I don't want to." Wealthy, self-centered **Tom Hanks** hasn't quite caught the spirit of the Peace Corps while stationed in a remote part of Thailand with John Candy and Rita Wilson. *Volunteers* (1985, Tri-Star).

4558 "I'd love to help you but we can't busy the quarterback with passing out the Gatorade." **Sigourney Weaver** makes a sports allusion to justify her enjoying herself at a party while her secretary Melanie Griffith does all the work. *Working Girl* (1988, 20th Century-Fox).

4559 "Those children want to be helped. . . . They have worked their hearts out for you, Joe, done everything we've asked of them, believed what we told them. . . . But. . . they're not ready to take that test." Vice Principal **Beverly Todd** informs Principal Morgan Freeman that pep-talks, yelling and screaming, and calls for self-sacrifice and dedication are not enough to make high school students pass a basic skills test. *Lean on Me* (1989, Warner Bros.).

4560 "Hello? Hello? Is anybody there? Is anybody there?" **Joanne Woodward** is trapped in her car, unable to open the doors because the motor conked out when she tried to back out of the garage on a winter day. She'll just have to wait for her husband Paul Newman to come home to help her escape. *Mr. and Mrs. Bridge* (1990, Miramax).

4561 EVELYN COUCH: "I can't even look at my vagina!" IDGY THREADGOODE: "I can't help you there." **Kathy Bates** tells her friend **Jessica Tandy** of her failure to use a hand-held mirror to examine her genitals in a class that is supposed to help her explore her sexuality. *Fried Green Tomatoes* (1991, Universal).

4562 LOUIE KRITSKI: "When are you going to get me out of here? The rats have their own Jacuzzis." BIG LOU KRITSKI: "As soon as your mother and I get back from the Bahamas." Building supervisor **Joe Pesci**, sentenced to live 120 days in one of his apartments in a Harlem slum building, begs his slumlord father **Vincent Gardenia** for help. *The Super* (1991, 20th Century-Fox).

Heroes

see also FAME, GLORY, GREATNESS, HONOR, MILITARY, WARS

4563 "You are the life of the Fatherland, you boys—you are the iron men of Germany. You are the heroes who will repulse the enemy when you are called to do so." War-mongering teacher **Arnold Lucy**, advocating "glory for the Fatherland," rouses his entire class of young boys to enlist in the army and fight Germany's enemies. *All Quiet on the Western Front* (1930, Universal).

4564 "You see, you've been a hero to these kids and hundreds of others all through your life. And now you're going to be a glorified hero in death and I want to prevent that, Rocky. They've got to despise your memory. . . got to be ashamed of you." Priest **Pat O'Brien** asks his boyhood friend, convicted killer James Cagney, to go to the electric chair a craven coward in order to kill the hero-worship of some slum kids. *Angels with Dirty Faces* (1938, Warner Bros.).

4565 "My villain? My hero, you mean. I always think of my murderers as my heroes." Mystery writer **Auriol Lee** discusses her favorite characters with Joan Fontaine. *Suspicion* (1941, RKO).

4566 "Let me tell you about heroes, Hank. I've covered a lot of 'em, and I tell you Gehrig is the best of 'em. No front-page scandals, no daffy excitement, no horn piping in the spotlight. . . . But a guy who does his job and nothing else. He lives for his job, he gets a lot of fun out of it, and fifty million other people get a lot of fun out of him, watching him do something better than anybody ever did it before." Sports reporter **Walter Brennan** praises the heroism of Gary Cooper as Lou Gehrig to doubting reporter Dan Duryea. Years ago, in response to my question on seeing this movie, "Who is your favorite sports hero?" my Dad said that sports figures were not heroes, but the boys fighting in World War II were. *The Pride of the Yankees* (1942, RKO).

4567 "All everybody else knows is he's a hero. He's got a statue in the park and the birds sit on it. Except that I ain't got no birds on me, I'm in the same boat." Marine Sergeant **William Demarest** lectures 4-F Eddie Bracken on being a hero. *Hail the Conquering Hero* (1944, Paramount).

4568 "You can be the heroes, the guys with the fruit salad on their chest. Me? I'm staying put. I'm going to make myself as comfortable as I can, and, if it takes a little trading with the enemy to get me some food or a better mattress, that's okay by Sefton." **William Holden** tells the other sergeants in his prison barracks that he's looking out for number one. *Stalag 17* (1953, Paramount).

4569 "Made to commit acts too unspeakable to be cited here by an enemy who had captured his mind and soul. He freed himself at last, and in the end heroically and unhesitatingly gave his life to save his country. Raymond Shaw. Hell. Hell." What **Frank Sinatra** isn't saying about Laurence Harvey is that at the last moment he fought off the brainwashing of his Chinese Communist captors and assassinated his enemy agent's mother and stepfather rather than the presidential candidate. Then Harvey turned the gun on himself. *The Manchurian Candidate* (1962, United Artists).

4570 "Heroes, whatever high ideas we may have of them are mortal, not divine. We are all as God made us and many of us are much worse." Narrator **Michael MacLiammoir** sets the stage for the famous scene in which Albert Finney and Joyce Redman sit across from each other, devouring meat, fish, vegetables and fruit in a wanton orgy of passion. *Tom Jones* (1963, GB, Woodfall-Lopert-United Artists).

4571 "I'm not the heroic type. I was beaten up by Quakers." Having awakened in the future after a 200-year sleep, **Woody Allen** finds himself at the center of a plot to get rid of a dictator. *Sleeper* (1973, United Artists).

4572 "Heroes don't just shoot people. They put supper on the table." **Dabney Coleman** attempts to expand his son Henry Thomas' understanding of what makes a hero. *Cloak and Dagger* (1984, Universal).

4573 "You know, America is a funny place. We can fabricate just about anything we want now, even heroes. America tried to make a hero out of John Wisdom and found out that it was wrong. Shit, I could have told them that." These are the words of title character **Emilio Estevez**, after the modern-day Robin Hood dies in a hail of bullets. *Wisdom* (1986, 20th Century-Fox).

4574 "So far all you've done is grandstand, first for me, then for the police. From the beginning you've wanted to play the hero. You can see where it's gotten us. And I am the one with everything to lose!" Married **Isabelle Huppert** leaves her lover Steve Guttenberg in a huff after he's passed himself off as an eyewitness to an assault that she saw from his bedroom window. *The Bedroom Window* (1987, DEG).

Heterosexuality *see* HOMOSEXUALITY, LOVE AND LOVERS, MEN AND WOMEN, SEX AND SEXUALITY

Hiding *see* SECRETS

History

see also PAST, STUDIES AND STUDENTS

4575 "He ain't like the other men you done made history of." **Louise Beavers** notes that Cary Grant seems a notch above the other men that Mae West has used and discarded. *She Done Him Wrong* (1933, Paramount).

4576 "You're better than news. You're history." American reporter **Stu Erwin** puffs up Wallace Beery, portraying Mexican bandit and revolutionary Pancho Villa. *Viva Villa!* (1934, MGM).

4577 "My son, I am placing in your hands the future and destiny of Shangri-La. . . . You will preserve the fragrance of its history." Dying, ancient High Lama **Sam Jaffe** passes the torch, so to speak, to his chosen successor, British diplomat Ronald Colman. *Lost Horizon* (1937, Columbia).

4578 "Take a good look, my dear, a historic moment—you can tell your grandchildren you watched the Old South disappear." **Clark Gable** and Vivien Leigh watch Atlanta burn. *Gone with the Wind* (1939, Selznick-MGM).

4579 LEE DONLEY: "After all, that is how the Chicago fire started." GLORIA ANDERSON: "The Chicago fire was started by a cow." LEE: "History repeats itself."

Ann Sheridan reprimands **Helen Vinson** for not disposing of a cigarette properly. *Torrid Zone* (1940, Warner Bros.).

4580 "Kane helped to change the world, but Kane's world now is history, and the great yellow journalist himself lived to be history, outlived his power to make it." A newsreel narrator comments on title character **Orson Welles.** *Citizen Kane* (1941, RKO).

4581 "If history has taught us anything, it's that you can kill anyone." **Al Pacino** rejects the notion that anyone is too important to kill. *The Godfather, Part II* (1974, Paramount).

4582 "We are simply passing through history, but this is history." Crafty French archeologist **Paul Freeman** makes a nice point when he refuses to buy Harrison Ford's bluff that he will blow up the Ark of the Covenant, unless Karen Allen is released to him. *Raiders of the Lost Ark* (1981, Paramount).

4583 "When I despair, I remember that all through history the way of truth and love has always won. There have been tyrants and murderers and for a time they can seem invincible, but in the end they always fall. Think of it. Always." Saintly Mahatma Gandhi, portrayed by **Ben Kingsley**, takes comfort from history, and we don't wish to disagree with him—but it seems that even though the bad guys lose in the end, their evil lasts longer in the pages of history than goodness. *Gandhi* (1982, Columbia).

4584 "Now, who can tell me when the Magna Carta was signed?" English missionary **Michael Palin** teaches a group of primitive African natives, barely out of the Stone Age, about British history. *The Missionary* (1982, GB, Handmade Films-Columbia).

4585 MR. RYAN: "Who was Joan of Arc?" TED "THEODORE" LOGAN: "Noah's wife." History teacher **Bernie Casey** has fresh evidence that history is not one of **Keanu Reeves'** strong points. *Bill and Ted's Excellent Adventure* (1989, Orion).

4586 "My name is Ray Kinsella. Mom died when I was three and I suppose Dad did the best he could. Instead of Mother Goose, I was put to bed at night to stories of Babe Ruth, Lou Gehrig and the great Shoeless Joe Jackson. Dad was a Yankees fan then, so of course I rooted for Brooklyn. But in '58 the Dodgers moved away so we had to find other things to fight about. . . . We did. . . when it came time to go to college I picked the farthest one from home I could find. . . . This of course drove him right up the wall, which I suppose was the point. Officially my major was English, but really it was the '60s. I marched, smoked some grass, tried to

like sitar music, and I met Annie. The only thing we had in common was she came from Iowa and I had once heard of Iowa. After graduation we went to the Midwest and stayed with her family as long as we could. . . almost a full afternoon. Annie and I got married in June of '74. Dad died that fall. A few years later Karen was born. She smelled weird but we loved her anyway. Then Annie got the crazy idea that she could talk me into buying a farm. I'm 36 years old. I love my family, I love baseball, and I'm about to become a farmer." In his opening narration, **Kevin Costner** gives a brief historical sketch of his life up until he hears the "voice." *Field of Dreams* (1989, Universal).

4587 "We sail into history." Russian submarine commander **Sean Connery** takes his new nuclear sub out on its maiden voyage, fully intent on defecting to the West. *The Hunt for Red October* (1990, Paramount).

4588 "He's history. Tomorrow, he'll be geography." Mobster **Peter Boyle** speaks of a colleague who has been rubbed out and whose body will be disposed of. *Men of Respect* (1991, Columbia).

Hitchhiking *see* TRAVEL AND TRIPS, WALKS AND WALKING

Hobbies

see also ENJOYMENTS, PLEASURES, STUDIES AND STUDENTS

4589 "It's more than a hobby." **Bela Lugosi** reacts indignantly when a museum representative remarks "what a curious hobby" upon learning that Lugosi has built several torture chambers imagined by Edgar Allen Poe. *The Raven* (1935, Universal).

4590 "I've helped a lot of people. It's a hobby of mine to take a human being and give them glamour, confidence, polish." Lawyer **Edward Arnold** offers money to young police officer Gig Young, to give his life "a little dignity." *City That Never Sleeps* (1953, Republic).

Homes

see also CHILDREN AND CHILDHOOD, FAMILIES, HOSPITALITY, HOUSES

4591 "Why don't you go home to your wife? I'll tell you what. I'll go home to your wife and outside of the improvements, she'll never notice the difference." Huxley's new president, **Groucho Marx**, gives the bum's rush to retiring President Reginald Barlow. *Horse Feathers* (1932, Paramount).

4592 "I'm going home to sit on a bench and eat popcorn." After some unsuccessful living with nobleman Ray Milland, **Claudette Colbert** rushes back to down-to-earth Fred MacMurray and the bench they shared in a park. *The Gilded Lily* (1935, Paramount).

4593 "I want a home for them where they can stay and where they can learn—a town for boys, governed by boys. It's worth a shot, isn't it?" **Spencer Tracy**, as Father Flanagan, describes his dream to businessman Jonathan Hale. *Boys Town* (1938, MGM).

4594 "This room is my home—the only home I've got." **Katharine Hepburn** shows her sister's fiancé, Cary Grant, her sanctum sanctorum. *Holiday* (1938, Columbia).

4595 "Papa, I've come home." **William Holden**, who's disappointed his father Lee J. Cobb by pursuing a boxing career rather than concentrating on his violin, returns to his home at the end of the film. *Golden Boy* (1939, Columbia).

4596 "Close your eyes and tap your heels together three times. And think to yourself, there's no place like home." Good Witch of the North **Billie Burke** instructs Judy Garland so she can leave Oz and go home to Kansas. *The Wizard of Oz* (1939, MGM).

4597 "Oh, Auntie Em, there's no place like home." After she finds herself in her own bed on her Kansas farm, surrounded by familiar and loving faces, **Judy Garland** sighs to Clara Blandick. She's happy to be home after her adventures, real or imagined, in the wonderful Land of Oz. *The Wizard of Oz* (1939, MGM).

4598 "This is the story of that unconquerable fortress—the American home, 1943." The written introduction to an excellent flagwaving and tearjerking film. *Since You Went Away* (1944, Selznick-United Artists).

4599 "It's lavish, but I call it home." Insufferable writer **Clifton Webb** is being insufferable. *Laura* (1944, 20th Century-Fox).

4600 "Let them have their elephant walk. Ruth, we'll build a new place, a home somewhere else." In Ceylon, **Peter Finch** has finally come to his senses, telling his neglected wife Elizabeth Taylor, that they will rebuild their tea plantation mansion, but this time not in the path of an elephant walk. *Elephant Walk* (1954, Paramount).

4601 "It's homes like these that are the backbone of the nation—where's the spinning wheel?" Cynical musician **Frank Sinatra** wisecracks about the near perfect home of Doris Day's family. *Young at Heart* (1954, Warner Bros.).

4602 "Let's go home, Debbie." **John Wayne** has decided not to kill his niece Natalie Wood, after all. She was captured by Indians when just a child. As a teen, she became the wife of a renegade chief. *The Searchers* (1956, Warner Bros.).

4603 "That's the Australian word for people like us. A 'sundowner' is someone whose home is where the sun goes down. It's the same as saying someone who doesn't have a home." **Michael Anderson, Jr.** explains to Peter Ustinov the meaning of the term applied to people like his sheepherder father Robert Mitchum and his family. *The Sundowners* (1960, Warner Bros.).

4604 "Men think all day about what they're coming home to and one day they just don't come home." **Gloria Foster** generalizes, as she explains her husband abandoning her and their son long ago. *The Cool World* (1964, Cinema 5).

4605 "If there is a God, this is where he lives." **Jack Weston** comments to Jack Lemmon as they stand outside the United Nations Plaza apartment building. *The April Fools* (1969, National General).

4606 "You're never home. Why don't you stay home and control your son? You can't solve that murder and you're late for dinner as usual. You go in there and make him pick it up [his mess] if you can." **Barbara McNair** harangues her police detective husband Sidney Poitier about their mischievous son George Spell. *They Call Me Mister Tibbs* (1970, United Artists).

4607 "You'll always have a home here." Madam **Shirley Stoler** extends an unwanted welcome to part-time hooker Jane Fonda. *Klute* (1971, Warner Bros.).

4608 "This was a fine neighborhood. . . . Rundown. . . running down. . . it all runs down sooner or later. . . where else could I live? I still know a lot of people around here, Tonto. A lot of people. You know people, that's home. . . ." **Art Carney** confides to his best friend, a cat, about the neighborhood where he's lived so long. *Harry and Tonto* (1974, 20th Century-Fox).

4609 "I belong here. . . I'm home." **David Warner**, as Jack the Ripper, transported from 1890s London to 1979 San Francisco via H.G. Wells' time machine, finds the North Beach area to his liking. *Time After Time* (1979, Warner Bros.-Orion).

4610 "I came here to take my son home, and I realized he already is home." **Meryl Streep** has decided that although she's won custody of their son Justin Henry in a court battle, the boy is happier with his father Dustin Hoffman. *Kramer vs. Kramer* (1979, Columbia).

4611 "These boys are just waiting for a way to go back home. . . it just doesn't exist any more." Neo-nihilistic military assassin **Martin Sheen** is burnt-out, possessed by a nightmare—you can't go backwards, only forwards. *Apocalypse Now* (1979, United Artists).

4612 "The town of Castle Rock had only 1,281 residents, but to me, it was the whole world." Narrator **Richard Dreyfuss** recalls his home town when he was 12. *Stand by Me* (1986, Columbia).

4613 GEORGE CLOVERDALE: "This used to be a happy home." JACKIE CLOVERDALE: "A messy home." GEORGE: "I'd rather be happy than unmessy." JACKIE: "If it were messy again then I'd be unhappy." Wealthy New England couple **Ross Petty** and **Shelley Peterson** bicker about how things were before the arrival of their deranged housekeeper Rita Tushingham. *The Housekeeper* (1987, Canada, Castlehill-Kodiak).

4614 "I don't know anybody who has so many places to go home to." **Tony Longo** admires mob boss Rutger Hauer who has a string of mistresses. *Bloodhounds of Broadway* (1989, Columbia).

Homosexuality

see also LIVES AND LIVING, LOVE AND LOVERS, PREFERENCES, SEX AND SEXUALITY

4615 "Oh swift, what are you two guys, a couple of violets?" A nearby sailor questions Frank McHugh when the latter blows a kiss to James Cagney as the latter leaves a battleship for transfer to another ship. *Here Comes the Navy* (1934, Warner Bros.).

4616 TOLEN: "Are you a homosexual?" TOM: "No, thanks all the same." **Ray Brooks** was only seeking information. **Donal Donnelly** heard an invitation. *The Knack . . . And How to Get It* (1965, GB, Woodfall-Lopert).

4617 "Whenever there are sex crimes, the police come down on us. When you're very rich and also gay, you're very vulnerable." Rich homosexual **Hurd Hatfield** is interrogated in a gay bar by detective Henry Fonda. *The Boston Strangler* (1968, 20th Century-Fox).

4618 CHILDIE: "Not all girls are raving, bloody lesbians, you know!" JUNE BUCKRIDGE: "That's a misfortune of which I am perfectly well aware." Baby doll lover **Susannah York** snaps at butchy **Beryl Reid** when the latter questions York about a suspected affair with a co-worker. *The Killing of Sister George* (1969, Cinerama, Palomar).

4619 RATZO RIZZO: "If you wanna know the truth, that stuff is strictly for faggots! That's faggot stuff." JOE BUCK: "John Wayne! You gonna tell me that John Wayne is a fag?" RATZO: "I know enough to know that big dumb cowboy crap don't appeal to no one except every Jacky on Forty-Second Street. Fag stuff. That's all it is. Fag stuff." New York City street hustler **Dustin Hoffman** tells aspiring Texan gigolo **Jon Voight** that the only ones who'll pay him for his stud services are homosexuals. *Midnight Cowboy* (1969, United Artists).

4620 "You are a sad and pathetic man, Michael. You are a homosexual and you don't want to be, but there's nothing you can do to change it. Not all your prayers to your God. Not all the analysis your money can buy in the years you have left to live. You may one day be able to know a heterosexual life. If you want it desperately enough. If you pursue it with the fervor with which you annihilate. But you will always be homosexual as well, Michael. Always. Until the day you die." **Peter White** speaks of Kenneth Nelson's self-hatred and inability to deal with his homosexuality. *The Boys in the Band* (1970, Cinema Center).

4621 "You show me a happy homosexual and I'll show you a gay corpse." Guilt-ridden Catholic homosexual **Kenneth Nelson** makes a bitter jest. *The Boys in the Band* (1970, Cinema Center).

4622 "Forty-two percent of all liberals are queer. That's a fact. The Wallace people took a poll." Working class bigot **Peter Boyle** gets two groups that he hates with one swing of his mouth. *Joe* (1970, Cannon).

4623 "Isn't a pregnant lesbian a contradiction in terms?" Sheriff **Harry Guardino** finds it difficult to believe the combination. *They Only Kill Their Masters* (1972, MGM).

4624 "But murder? What would Socrates say? All those Greeks were homosexuals. Boy, they must have had some wild parties! I bet they all took a home together in Crete for the summer. A. Socrates is a man. B. All men are mortal. C. All men are Socrates. That means all men are homosexual. I. . . I. . . once. . . some. . . some Cossacks whistled at me. . . I. . . I. . . happen to have the kind of body that excites both persuasions." While musing on whether he should kill an unconscious Napoleon, **Woody Allen** gets sidetracked into philosophical doubts about his sexuality. *Love and Death* (1975, United Artists).

4625 McNAIR: "Are gay football players on the offense or defense?" BILLY CLYDE PUCKETT: "Defense, you can grope someone easier." Publisher **Jim McKrell** is looking for some football dirt and **Burt Reynolds** is happy to oblige. *Semi-Tough* (1977, United Artists).

4626 "I told them my father was a cultural attache; what'll they think when they find out he lives with a drag queen?" **Remy Laurent** entreats his father Ugo Tognazzi's long-time lover Michel Serrault to make himself scarce when Laurent brings his fiancée and her parents to dinner. *La Cage Aux Folles* (1979, Fr.-Italy, SPA-United Artists).

4627 "There's something to be said for the deviant life-style." It's eightyish **Henry Fonda**'s observation when someone mentions the death of a very old lesbian neighbor. *On Golden Pond* (1981, Universal).

4628 "There's nothing more inconvenient than an old queen with a head cold." Gay nightclub entertainer **Robert Preston** takes to his bed, tended by Julie Andrews. *Victor-Victoria* (1982, GB, MGM).

4629 LIANNA: "I'm gay!" SHEILA: "I'm Sheila." Recently liberated from her husband, **Linda Griffiths** introduces herself to an uncaring **Maggie Renzi** in a basement laundry room. *Lianna* (1983, United Artists).

4630 "They use their tongues, foreign instruments, eventually achieve orgasm. Then they quarrel about the condition of the room and go out to a French movie. It makes them happy." Psychiatrist **Bob Ellis** gives his opinion of the average lesbian relationship. *A Man of Flowers* (1984, Australia, International Spectrafilm).

4631 "You bet your ass, mamma! I'm a big bad bulldyke and my tongue has been places you don't even know you've got and it's great. And I don't 'deal' with it, I don't 'cope' with it. I'm fucking proud of it! What the fuck are you proud of?" When a fellow Cycle Slut (that's what they call themselves) calls **Catherine Carlin** a "twisted sister," she responds proudly. *Chopper Chicks in Zombietown* (1991, New Line).

4632 "I'm a homosexual who can't relate to gay men." **John Malkovich** puts his finger on his problem. *Queen's Logic* (1991, New Line).

4633 "Pal, if I'm gay, Clint Eastwood is a transvestite." **Ellen Barkin**, a reincarnated womanizing Perry King,

responds when his/her friend Jimmy Smits asks if she's gay as she makes a crude sexual remark about a passing female. *Switch* (1991, Warner Bros.).

4634 "Not that I'm a lesbian—well, maybe I am." Feminist **Sara Gilbert** is fascinated by the sexy mouth and lips of stranger Drew Barrymore. Gilbert has heard that the lips are supposed to be a perfect reflection of another part of a woman's anatomy. *Poison Ivy* (1992, New Line).

Honesty and Dishonesty

see also CHEATS, CRIMES AND CRIMINALS, DECEPTIONS, FAIRNESS AND UNFAIRNESS, INTEGRITY, LAWS, LAWYERS, LIES AND LYING, SINCERITY, TRUST, TRUTH, TRUTH AND FALSEHOOD

4635 "Honest men are scarcer than feathers on a frog." Conman **James Cagney** dispenses a little home-spun wisdom after he's been double-crossed. *Blonde Crazy* (1931, Warner Bros.).

4636 "If you want to keep a man honest, never call him a liar." **Clark Gable** warns his wife Myrna Loy not to misconstrue his relationship with his secretary Jean Harlow. *Wife vs. Secretary* (1936, MGM).

4637 "All women are dishonest. If they weren't, the world would be divided into two classes of people: old maids and bachelors." If we understand **Helen Broderick**'s reasoning, she claims that dishonesty keeps the world going round. This old-fashioned bit of philosophy doesn't account for men's dishonesty. *The Rage of Paris* (1938, Universal).

4638 "Do you think it would be dishonest if we went through his haversack?" **Olivia de Havilland** brings up a question of ethics in looking for anything of value in the belongings of the Yankee deserter Vivien Leigh has shot and killed. *Gone with the Wind* (1939, Selznick-MGM).

4639 "You're just the kind of honest man we want on this jury!" Title character **Henry Fonda** accepts for the jury in a murder case, town drunk Francis Ford, who freely admits to lying, laziness, and hard drinking. *The Young Mr. Lincoln* (1939, 20th Century-Fox).

4640 "This is the story of two men who met in a banana republic. One of them was honest all his life—except for one crazy moment. The other was dishonest all his life—except for one crazy moment. They both had to leave the country." It's the written introduction to a classic Preston Sturges comedy. It refers, respectively, to Louis Jean Heydt, a chief cashier for a bank who embezzled funds, and Brian

Donlevy, a former bum who became governor of a state. *The Great McGinty* (1940, Paramount).

4641 LEE LEANDER: "Supposing you were starving to death and you didn't have any food and you didn't have any place to get anything. And there were some loaves of bread out in front of a market. Now remember, you're starving to death and the man's back was turned. Would you swipe one?" JOHN SARGENT: "You bet I would." LEE: "That's because you're honest. You see, I'd have a six-course dinner at the fancy restaurant across the street and then say I forgot my purse. Get the difference?" Tough cookie **Barbara Stanwyck** lets assistant D.A. **Fred MacMurray** in on the difference between honest people and dishonest people. *Remember the Night* (1940, Paramount).

4642 "Maybe it's easy for the dying to be honest. I'm sick of you, sick of this house, sick of my unhappy life with you. I'm sick of your brothers and their dirty tricks to make a dime. There must be better ways of getting rich than building sweatshops and pounding the bones of the town to make dividends for you to spend. You'll wreck this town, you and your brothers. You'll wreck this country, you and your kind, if they let you. But not me. I'll die my own way, and I'll do it without making the world any worse. I leave that to you." Dying **Herbert Marshall** honestly tells his selfish, greedy wife Bette Davis what he thinks of her and her despicable brothers Charles Dingle and Carl Benton Reid. The only extraordinary thing is that she allows him to get it all out without interrupting. *The Little Foxes* (1941, RKO).

4643 "I'm honest because, with you, I think it's the best way to get results." **Cary Grant** wins over Joan Fontaine with his candor about his honesty. *Suspicion* (1941, RKO).

4644 GRISELDA VAUGHN: "What kind of woman are you?" KATHERINE BORG: "Honest." Well, not completely. **Constance Bennett** is not aware that **Greta Garbo** is impersonating a more glamorous fictitious sister to combat Bennett's designs on Garbo's husband, Melvyn Douglas. *Two-Faced Woman* (1941, MGM).

4645 "He's the only honest man I've come across in this town in twenty years, so naturally they wanna hang 'im." **Edgar Buchanan** refers to Cary Grant, suspected of murder. *The Talk of the Town* (1942, Columbia).

4646 JACK BURDEN: "What's so special about him?" MADISON: "They say he's an honest man." Reporter **John Ireland** is sent to the backwaters of a southern state by his editor **Houseley Stevenson** to get the low down on political hopeful Broderick Crawford. *All the King's Men* (1949, Columbia).

4647 "The difference between the honest and the dishonest is a debatable line.... We're suckers if we don't try to cram as much happiness as possible in our brief time, no matter how; everybody breaks the law." Banker **Joseph Cotten** seeks to justify his stealing half a million dollars from his own bank. *The Steel Trap* (1952, 20th Century-Fox).

4648 "These girls in love never realize they should be honestly dishonest instead of being dishonestly honest." **Clifton Webb** seems to believe he's being logical as he makes a fine point for Louis Jourdan. *Three Coins in the Fountain* (1954, 20th Century-Fox).

4649 "You don't have to spend every day of your life proving your honesty—but I do." When some jewels are stolen on the Riviera, former cat burglar **Cary Grant** indicates his predicament to insurance investigator John Williams. *To Catch a Thief* (1955, Paramount).

4650 JAMUGA: "There is no limit to her perfidy!" TEMUJIN: "She's a woman—much woman! Should her perfidy be less than that of other women?" As they watch new captive Susan Hayward, **Pedro Armendariz** and his "blood brother" **John Wayne** discuss her assumed attributes. *The Conqueror* (1956, RKO).

4651 "You make me feel like being honest, and honest women have lonely nights." Call-girl **Gina Lollobrigida** almost feels like giving up the life for naïve Tony Franciosa. *Go Naked in the World* (1960, MGM).

4652 "If only I could steal enough to become an honest man." Italian con man **Peter Sellers** tries to reach his goal by posing as a filmmaker. *After the Fox* (1966, U.S.-Italy, United Artists).

4653 "He's so full of twists. He starts to describe a doughnut and it comes out a pretzel." The trick **Jack Lemmon** claims his shyster lawyer brother-in-law Walter Matthau can carry off is topologically impossible. *The Fortune Cookie* (1966, United Artists).

4654 "Maybe the whole damn world is like Central Casting. They got it all rigged before you ever show up." Unsuccessful would-be actress **Jane Fonda** complains when she learns that the marathon dance contest she's been suffering in is fixed. *They Shoot Horses, Don't They?* (1969, ABC-Cinerama).

4655 "Hey, I'm honest. What do you want? I say what's on my mind. And if you can't take it—well, then fuck off." Neurotic **Diane Keaton** defends her candor to Woody Allen. *Manhattan* (1979, United Artists).

4656 "If that man were dying in a fire, wouldn't you do anything to save him? Well, he is dying! And we've just sold him a ticket to heaven." Vulnerable young **Nick Mancuso** accuses a fellow cult member of being dishonest. *Ticket to Heaven* (1981, Canada, United Artists).

4657 "What a fraudulent young man you are!" **Coral Browne**, as elderly Alice Liddell, who as a child was Charles Carroll's inspiration, finds young reporter Peter Gallagher to be much too brash and dishonest. *Dreamchild* (1985, GB, Universal).

4658 "Can I be totally honest with you? You're the reason I went through puberty." Teenage **Billy Jacoby** chooses pretty high school girls at random to declare his lust for. *Just One of the Guys* (1985, Columbia).

4659 "You give me this graphic harangue about the zipless fuck and then tell me you're just being honest. Well, you know what I think? I think you do that to try and keep a safe distance. . . all that jazz like you're just some poor slob who's getting led around by your cock. Well, I'm not buying it, so stop trying to sell me on it." **Brooke Adams** couldn't be more angry with Ben Masters if they were married. *Key Exchange* (1985, 20th Century-Fox).

4660 "He was so crooked he could eat soup with a corkscrew." **Annette Bening** speaks with admiration of her ex-partner J.T. Walsh to John Cusack. *The Grifters* (1990, Miramax).

4661 "Inside every honest heart is a crook trying to get out." Cynical New York police detective **Melanie Griffith** finds it hard to believe that there are any good people. *A Stranger Among Us* (1992, Hollywood Pictures-Buena Vista).

Honeymoons

see also KISSES AND KISSING, LOVE AND LOVERS, MARRIAGES, MEN AND WOMEN, WEDDINGS

4662 ELYOT CHASE: "What are you doing here?" AMANDA CHASE PAYNNE: "I'm on my honeymoon." ELYOT: "How interesting. So am I." AMANDA: "I hope you're enjoying it." ELYOT: "It hasn't started yet." AMANDA: "Neither has mine." **Robert Montgomery** and **Norma Shearer**, formerly married to each other, discover that they are honeymooning with their new spouses Una Merkel and Reginald Denny, respectively, in adjoining hotel suites. *Private Lives* (1931, MGM).

4663 IRIS: "Where are we going for our honeymoon?" GILBERT: "Somewhere quiet, with no trains." By the end of the movie, happy couple **Margaret Lockwood** and **Michael Redgrave** have had enough adventures with trains to last a lifetime. *The Lady Vanishes* (1938, GB, Gaumont British-Gainsborough).

4664 JOHN BALLANTINE: "I take it—this is your first honeymoon." DR. CONSTANCE PETERSON: "Yes, I mean, it would be—if it were." **Gregory Peck** and **Ingrid Bergman** pretend they are married while she tries to help him regain his memory and hopefully clear him of the murder of the man he has been impersonating. *Spellbound* (1945, Selznick-United Artists).

4665 JASON CORD: "What would you like to see on your honeymoon?" MONICA WINTHROP: "Lots of lovely ceilings." **George Peppard** and his bride **Elizabeth Ashley** make plans to spend a lot of their honeymoon indoors. *The Carpetbaggers* (1964, Paramount).

4666 "If the honeymoon doesn't work out, let's not get divorced, let's kill each other." New bride **Jane Fonda** almost succeeds in killing husband Robert Redford. Once they enter their suite at New York's Park Plaza, they don't budge from it for six days. *Barefoot in the Park* (1967, Paramount).

4667 "Honeymoon's over; time to get married." After six months of her affair with Walter Matthau, **Carol Burnett** decides they should get married. *Pete 'n' Tillie* (1972, Universal).

4668 "Here's your plane ticket and complete honeymoon instructions. Come out of your rooms at least once in awhile. Food is very important." **Joseph Bologna** sends his brother James Caan off on his honeymoon with Marsha Mason. *Chapter Two* (1979, Columbia).

Honor

see also FAME, GLORY, HONESTY AND DISHONESTY, INTEGRITY, TRUTH

4669 "Marius, honor is like a match: you can only use it once. . . ." **Raimu**, as Cesar, shares some fatherly wisdom with his son Pierre Fresnay, playing Marius. *Marius* (1931, Fr., Pagnol-Paramount).

4670 "Honored, ma'am, honored." In one of his best roles, **Roland Young** is a self-deluded rogue who can only murmur when his latest mark, lovely old Minnie Dupree, gives him an affectionate kiss on the cheek. *The Young in Heart* (1939, Selznick-United Artists).

4671 SCARLETT O'HARA: "There's nothing to keep us here." ASHLEY WILKES: "Nothing, except honor." **Vivien Leigh** proposes that **Leslie Howard** desert his pregnant wife Olivia de Havilland and go with Leigh to Mexico. *Gone with the Wind* (1939, Selznick-MGM).

4672 "I must remind you that among my people, honor is a sacred thing. Those who defile it can expect no mercy." Title character **Henry Brandon** is insulted when Luana Walters double-crosses him during a kidnap exchange. *Drums of Fu Manchu* (1940, Republic).

4673 "I've got a feeling you're going to graduate with honors." Miscast **George Montgomery** doesn't convince as Raymond Chandler's hard-boiled private eye Philip Marlowe. Montgomery closes the complicated case with some reassurance for frightened secretary Nancy Guild. *The Brasher Doubloon* (1947, 20th Century-Fox).

4674 "What does it matter now? Andre's dead. The man I love is dead. I thought about it day and night, but I didn't know how. I wanted to do it so that we would be free so that Andre and I could go away and live together as we should. But Andre wouldn't help me. He had his honor." **Alida Valli** admits on the witness stand to murdering her blind husband when she learns that the man she really loved, Louis Jourdan, has committed suicide. *The Paradine Case* (1947, Selznick-United Artists).

4675 "Well, on behalf of my sister Eileen and me, I, me, uh, I'd like to thank you and your wonderful country for this great honor. Actually, we didn't do anything to deserve this. All I did was say something about the conga." Every time someone mentions conga, a group of Portuguese sailors pull **Betty Garrett** and her beautiful sister Janet Leigh into a conga line. *My Sister Eileen* (1955, Columbia).

4676 "This joyful wedding can't be consummated until we pays homage to the one man who made it possible. Who romanticized this boy, who put them back the way they was, and who saved our town from being bombed? None other than that beloved man a-setting up there on an even more beloved horse, Jubilation T. Cornpone." **Stubby Kaye**, as Marrying Sam, gives credit to Dogpatch's greatest and only hero at the wedding of title character Peter Palmer and Leslie Parrish as Daisy Mae. *Li'l Abner* (1959, Paramount).

4677 "There may be honor among thieves, but there's none in politicians." Title character **Peter O'Toole** is angered that British public servant Claude Rains makes his decisions based on expediency, not principle. *Lawrence of Arabia* (1962, GB, Columbia).

4678 "Oh, Lord, how heavy Your honor is to bear." **Richard Burton**, as the soon-to-be assassinated Archbishop of Canterbury, looks sorrowfully down at the dead body of his attendant David Weston run through by Baron Niall MacGinnis in Burton's cathedral. *Becket* (1964, GB, Paramount).

4679 "It is morally honorable for the square peg to keep scraping around in the round hole rather than to discover and use the unorthodox one that would fit." Major **Marlon Brando** lectures a classroom of soldiers on leadership, strength, power and war—but his message is really a denial of his homosexuality. *Reflections in a Golden Eye* (1967, Warner Bros.).

4680 "Don Corleone, I am honored and grateful that you have invited me to your home on the wedding day of your daughter. May their first child be a masculine child." Bodyguard **Lenny Montana** rehearses the speech he will give when he sees his boss, Marlon Brando. *The Godfather* (1972, Paramount).

4681 "Honor is an appetite." **Harvey Keitel** and Keith Carradine are two Hussar officers of the early 1800s who challenge each other to a series of duels over a 16-year period. *The Duelists* (1977, GB, NFFC).

4682 "God made me for a purpose. When I run I feel His pleasure. To win is to honor Him." **Ian Charleson** dedicates his competitive running to God. *Chariots of Fire* (1981, GB, 20th Century-Fox).

4683 "What are you doing giving absolution to that mick pimp? He passed her around like a piece of Christmas candy while you were out playing golf! Catholic Layman of the Year... highest honors bestowed...." Police detective **Robert Duvall** bitterly complains in the confessional to his brother Monsignor Robert De Niro when the church honors mobster and murderer Charles Durning. *True Confessions* (1981, United Artists).

4684 "In Okinawa, honor has no time limit." **Pat Morita** explains to Ralph Macchio why his former friend Danny Kamekona still holds a grudge after 45 years and intends to fight Morita to the death over it. *The Karate Kid, Part II* (1986, Columbia).

4685 "I was roasted the other night. A friend of mine asked: 'Why are we honoring this man? Did we run out of human beings?'" Much truth is said in jest. Mover-and-shaker **Michael Douglas**, who has few friends, makes a joke at his expense. *Wall Street* (1987, 20th Century-Fox).

Hope

see also DESIRES, DESPAIR AND DESPERATION, EXPECTATIONS, OPTIMISM AND PESSIMISM, TRUST, WAITS AND WAITING

4686 "Here's hoping that Hyde rots wherever he is and burns where he ought to be. And here's hoping that Dr. Jekyll will think of Ivy once in awhile. He's an angel. Here's to you, my angel." **Miriam Hopkins** dreams lovingly of Fredric March as Dr. Jekyll, just before Fredric March as Mr. Hyde enters her room and kills her. *Dr. Jekyll and Mr. Hyde* (1932, Paramount).

4687 "Abolish despair and substitute hope. By knowing the worst in the people, bring out the best." **Ronald Colman**, as French poet and vagabond Francois Villon, lectures Basil Rathbone, as King Louis XI, on what the former would do were he the king. *If I Were King* (1938, Paramount).

4688 "If you convict him, I'll have to believe the way he does—that there's no hope for people like us." **Priscilla Lane** pleads for social misfit John Garfield, unjustly accused of murdering her mean, drunken stepfather. *Dust Be My Destiny* (1939, Warner Bros.).

4689 "I hope they don't hang you, Precious, by that pretty neck." **Humphrey Bogart** gives Mary Astor reason to worry as he prepares to turn her over to the cops for killing his partner. *The Maltese Falcon* (1941, Warner Bros.).

4690 "I don't suppose you go with the flat.... No...that'd be too much to hope for." Deaf, old Wienie King **Robert Dudley** flirts with Claudette Colbert as he inspects her apartment. *The Palm Beach Story* (1942, Paramount).

4691 "You know, Chuck, when you're young, you can keep the fires of hope burning bright, but at my age you're lucky if the pilot light doesn't go out." Pastor **Barry Fitzgerald** makes a minor analogy for curate Bing Crosby. *Going My Way* (1944, Paramount).

4692 FRANK McCLOUD: "I had hopes once but no more." JOHNNY ROCCO: "Hopes for what?" FRANK McCLOUD: "A world where there's no room for Johnny Rocco." Disillusioned ex-World War II Major **Humphrey Bogart** fought a war to rid the world of scum like vicious gangster **Edward G. Robinson**. *Key Largo* (1948, Warner Bros.).

4693 "I've been looking for you in every ditch, hopin' you was dead." **Lee Marvin** snarls at rival motorcycle gang leader Marlon Brando. *The Wild One* (1954, Columbia).

4694 "For the first time our principal subject knows that this is her life and we have her unqualified permission to tell the whole truth. It's a story of degradation and shame. But when you hear the facts you'll come to realize how much courage it took for her to come here tonight. You'll also realize that it's a story full of hope, hope for many who are living and suffering in a half world of addiction to alcohol, hope for all people wherever and whoever they are. So this is your life, Lillian Roth." **Ralph Edwards**, the host of TV's "This Is Your Life," introduces Susan Hayward as singer and former alcoholic Lillian Roth. *I'll Cry Tomorrow* (1955, MGM).

4695 "You called her an old maid. You took the last bit of hope she had. And, when you left, she took those bedcovers and ran out. I didn't ask her where she was going, but I'm glad she went because if she lost her hope in here, maybe she'll find it out there." Kindly, understanding **Cameron Prud'homme** tells insensitive and overly pragmatic Lloyd Bridges, that his sister, Prud'homme's plain spinster daughter Katharine Hepburn, has run out to the barn to be with con man Burt Lancaster. *The Rainmaker* (1956, Paramount).

4696 "Very beautiful and wonderful things do happen, and we live in the hope of them, don't we?" In Edwardian England, **William Mervyn**, as the Old Gentleman, volunteers to help some children clear their imprisoned father of the charges of treason. *The Railway Children* (1970, GB, EMI-Universal).

4697 "I hope the plane crashes! I don't want him to die. I want her to die!...Most of all, I want the Jaguar!" **Shelley Winters** rages to her divorce lawyer George Segal about her husband and his mistress. *Blume in Love* (1973, Warner Bros.).

4698 "When I get back I hope to find your clothes next to mine, and if not, we can get back to the mindfuck." Hooker **Nancy Allen** sheds her clothes and leaves shrink Michael Caine behind as she heads for the loo. *Dressed to Kill* (1980, Filmways).

4699 "Now you're on this, I hope we're going to have some gratuitous sex and violence." **Alec McCowen**, as weapons expert "Q," has come to appreciate the ways of Sean Connery as James Bond. *Never Say Never Again* (1983, Warner Bros.).

4700 "You're like Jerry Lewis, you give me hope to carry on." Once suicidal **Ellen Barkin** thanks Peter

Weller. *The Adventures of Buckaroo Banzai: Across the 8th Dimension* (1984, 20th Century-Fox).

4701 "As I watched him disappear into the green of the forest, I knew that this parting had broken their hearts. John had implored Jane to go with him, but we knew that this was an impossible course for their love. How could she survive? But I hope for their sake that the world will turn in their favor, and one day, somehow they will find each other again." **Ian Holm** has witnessed the sad parting of Christopher Lambert, as Tarzan, and Andie MacDowell as Jane Parker, who know they cannot exist in each other's world. *Greystoke: The Legend of Tarzan, Lord of the Apes* (1984, Warner Bros.).

4702 "I know 'maybe' is a very slim reed to hang your whole life on, but that's the best we have." Television comedy writer **Woody Allen**, who feared he was dying of an incurable illness, finds a new appreciation of life when he marries his former wife Mia Farrow's sister Diane Wiest. *Hannah and Her Sisters* (1986, Orion).

4703 "You're my best buddy and I love you—and if you get accepted and I don't, I hope you rot in hell." **Arye Gross** is honest about his feelings as he and fellow U.C.L.A. student C. Thomas Howell open their letters from Harvard Law School. *Soul Man* (1986, New World).

4704 "Gee, I just hope that when I'm his age I can wake up next to a woman as beautiful as you are." **Michael J. Fox** pours on the syrup to his boss Richard Jordan's predatory wife Margaret Whitton who has seduced him. *The Secret of My Success* (1987, Universal).

4705 "Think I could get him to use those on me?" Gazing wistfully at the handcuffs handsome cop Ray Liotta is demonstrating for some elementary school kids, **Deborah Offner** contemplates her chances with fellow teacher Madeleine Stowe. *Unlawful Entry* (1992, 20th Century-Fox).

Horrors

see also BADNESS, EVILNESS, FEARS, FEELINGS, LIKES AND DISLIKES, SHOCKS, TERROR, UGLINESS

4706 "Never mind, mother, to the horrid, all things are horrid." **Katharine Hepburn** tells her mother Ann Shoemaker to ignore Kate's brother Frank Albertson who has accused her of trying to steal another girl's beau. *Alice Adams* (1935, RKO).

4707 "[It] suggests an amusing kind of horror. It is like someone's tomb." **Norma Shearer** is not pleased with her hotel. *Idiot's Delight* (1939, MGM).

4708 "Veda, I think I'm really seeing you for the first time in my life—and you're cheap and horrible." **Joan Crawford** finally faces up to what a little horror her selfish and self-centered, spoiled daughter Ann Blyth is. The latter is just no good—but her permissive mother Crawford must share the blame. *Mildred Pierce* (1945, Warner Bros.).

4709 "I don't think the world has been in such a horrible mess since the Flood." **James Anderson**, the oldest inhabitant of the Hebridean outcrop of Toddy [sic], refers to the wartime shortage of the "water of life," i.e., whiskey, during World War II. *Whisky Galore* aka: *Tight Little Island* (1948, GB, Ealing).

4710 "It's impossible for words to describe what is necessary to those who do not know what horror means. Horror. Horror has a face, and you must make a friend of horror. Horror and mortal terror are your friends. If they are not, then they are enemies to fear. They are truly enemies." **Marlon Brando** philosophizes to Martin Sheen, who has been sent by military superiors to assassinate the renegade Brandon. *Apocalypse Now* (1979, Omni Zoetrope-United Artists).

4711 "The tragedy of war is that horrors are committed by normal men in abnormal situations." Defense counsel **Jack Thompson** makes a compelling point about war. *Breaker Morant* (1980, Australia, Enterprise).

4712 "The horror... the horror... the breakage!" Head researcher **Christopher Lee** is upset after gremlins trash his Splice of Life Designer Genes laboratory. *Gremlins 2: The New Batch* (1990, Warner Bros.).

Horses *see* ANIMALS

Hospitality

see also ENTERTAINMENTS AND ENTERTAINERS, GUESTS, VISITS

4713 "Wanna wash your hands or something, honey?" In her own ignorant way, **Judy Holliday** tries to be gracious to congressman's wife Barbara Brown. *Born Yesterday* (1951, Columbia).

4714 SPYROS ACEBOS: "Avail yourself of my hospitality, Mr. Harmon." SAM HARMON: "Scotch!" When mobster **Akim Tamiroff** offers, **Dean Martin** knows what will make him feel at home. *Ocean's Eleven* (1960, Warner Bros.).

4715 "We have cocaine, marijuana, vodka, gin and some prune Danish." **Dudley Moore** ushers prostitute Anne De Salvo into his limousine. *Arthur* (1981, Orion).

4716 "The unrestricted freedom of her most intimate hospitality." This lovely-stated bonus to a modest payment is the fee demanded by draughtsman **Anthony Higgins** and paid by 17th century English lady Janet Suzman. He's to make twelve drawings of her manor as a surprise for her husband. *The Draughtsman's Contract* (1983, GB, BFI).

Hostilities

see also FRIENDSHIPS AND FRIENDS, WARS

4717 SANDY: "What ya saying? Are you saying that someone like myself or Laurel and Hardy or Bob Hope are furious?" TONY: "Furious, or latent homosexuals—it's hidden beneath the joke." Filmmaker **Woody Allen** can barely believe his ears when film teacher **Tony Roberts** spouts a theory that comedians are actually hostile people. *Stardust Memories* (1980, United Artists).

4718 "Did anyone ever tell you, you have a lot of hostility?" **Rae Dawn Chong** understates the feelings of Arnold Schwarzenegger. *Commando* (1985, 20th Century-Fox).

4719 VINNY: "Your honor, may I treat Miss Vito as a hostile witness?" MONA LISA: "If you think I'm hostile now, wait until you see me tonight?" JUDGE HALLER: "Do you know each other?" VINNY: "She's my fiancée." HALLER: "Well, that would explain the hostility." **Joe Pesci** questions his P.O.'d fiancée **Marisa Tomei** in **Fred Gwynne**'s courtroom. *My Cousin Vinny* (1992, 20th Century-Fox).

Houses

see also BUILDINGS, HOMES

4720 "An empty bungalow just for you and me, where we could bill and cow—no, we could bull and cow. . . ." **Groucho Marx** gives Margaret Dumont a verbal run-around. *The Cocoanuts* (1929, Paramount).

4721 "Here's the foolish little house where I live. It is a queer little place, but you know my father is so attached to it that my family has just about given up hope to get him to build a real house farther up. You know he doesn't mind us being extravagant about anything else, but he won't let us change one single thing about his precious little house." **Katharine Hepburn** desperately puts on airs for wealthy Fred MacMurray, hoping he won't see through her and realize that she's not in his social or economic class. *Alice Adams* (1935, RKO).

4722 "When the house is filled with dread, place the beds at head to head." It's the solemn verse maid **Emma Dunn** recites as a recipe for dealing with evil. *Son of Frankenstein* (1939, Universal).

4723 "I found peace in loving you. You shall have your house in Thornton Square." **Ingrid Bergman** is cleverly conned by her new husband Charles Boyer into agreeing to take up residence in the London home where her aunt was killed ten years before. *Gaslight* (1944, MGM).

4724 TRUDY KOCKENLOCKER: "He went to sewing and cooking classes just to be near me." EMILY KOCKENLOCKER: "How perfect. He can take care of the house." Pregnant and without a husband, **Betty Hutton** considers how unfair it is to trick nerdish Eddie Bracken into marrying her as her sister **Diana Lynn** proposes. *The Miracle of Morgan's Creek* (1944, Paramount).

4725 "It had a nice front yard. Cozy for the average family, only you'd need a compass to go to the mailbox. The house was all right too, but it wasn't as big as Buckingham Palace." Narrator **Dick Powell** describes the enormous mansion home of Miles Mander. *Murder, My Sweet* aka: *Farewell, My Lovely* (1945, RKO).

4726 "What a dump!" Psychopathic slut **Bette Davis** is disgusted with her small-town house. *Beyond the Forest* (1949, Warner Bros.).

4727 "It was a great big elephant of a place, the kind of place crazy movie people built in the crazy twenties." **William Holden** describes the home of silent screen star Gloria Swanson. *Sunset Boulevard* (1950, Paramount).

4728 "It looks the way all Irish cottages should and seldom do. And only an American would think of painting it emerald green. Red is so much more practical." Gently, **Eileen Crowe** questions the improvements American John Wayne has made in the old homestead. *The Quiet Man* (1952, Republic).

4729 "Great House will live again, Mother. We'll make it live in peace and beauty." Alcoholic **Wendell Corey** pledges to his mother Carroll McComas to rebuild their mansion that has gone up in flames. *Jamaica Run* (1953, Paramount).

4730 "So this is where you live. Oh, Mother will love it here." As delighted as is former cat burglar Cary Grant to share his French Riviera villa with lovely **Grace Kelly**, he isn't anxious for her mother Jessie Royce Landis to move in with them. *To Catch a Thief* (1955, Paramount).

4731 "The house of the seven gables began its existence in the year of terror. It was in 1691 that mass hysteria gripped New England and innocent people were executed as witches. It was a time of horror and blood and left a mark on the house that would not be forgotten for more than one hundred and fifty years." **Vincent Price** narrates the opening of "The House of Seven Gables" segment. *Twice Told Tales* (1963, United Artists).

4732 "This is where I live—I will not allow violence against this house. No way." Quiet, shy mathematician **Dustin Hoffman** is ready, willing and able to adopt the violent means of his enemies to protect his Irish house and home. *Straw Dogs* (1971, GB, ABC-Cinerama).

4733 "I was so glad to be going home. I remembered the days when I sang and danced with my family on the porch of the old house. But, things change and with all the additions to the family we had to tear down the old house even though we loved it. But we built a bigger one." After seeking, finding and losing a fortune, white **Steve Martin** is back home with his black family. *The Jerk* (1979, Universal).

4734 "Maybe sports equipment and we'll have music piped in. And, darling, we'll build that dream house I always promised you, Sue. And the kids are going to help us build it. We'll do it! We're going to do it all! Everything we always dreamed of. We shouldn't have to go to sleep to dream. It's life. We can live a dream." Middle-aged **Elliott Gould**, having survived his mid-life crisis, promises his wife Susannah York to build their dream house. *Falling in Love Again* (1980, International Picture Show).

4735 "I just love housework. It's such a peaceful art." Diabolical stranger **Sting** speaks with patent falseness. *Brimstone and Treacle* (1982, GB, United Artists Classics).

4736 "This is my house!. . . I don't care about the house. I hate when these people are watching us." **Sebastian Rice-Edwards** is outraged with a sense of shame and indignation as people rummage through the remains of his house after it is hit by a German bomb during the London Blitz. *Hope and Glory* (1987, GB, Columbia).

4737 BARBARA ROSE: "I was the one who found this house. I bought everything." OLIVER ROSE: "With my money. It's a lot easier to spend it than make it, honeybun." BARBARA: "You would never have made it if it weren't for me, sweet cakes." **Kathleen Turner** and **Michael Douglas** fight over who will get the house when they divorce. *The War of the Roses* (1989, 20th Century-Fox).

4738 OLIVER ROSE: "You will never get that house. . . . Do you understand? You will never get that house." BARBARA ROSE: "We'll see." The battle lines are drawn in the divorce of **Michael Douglas** and **Kathleen Turner**, with their house and its furnishings the prize. *The War of the Roses* (1989, 20th Century-Fox).

Housewives *see* WIVES

Human Nature

see also INSTINCTS

4739 BORIS LERMONTOV: "The dancer who relies upon the doubtful comforts of human love will never be a great dancer." JULIAN CRASTER: "That's all very well, but you can't alter human nature." LERMONTOV: "No? I think you can do even better than that. You can ignore it." Impresario **Anton Walbrook** debates composer **Marius Goring** about human nature. *The Red Shoes* (1948, GB, Eagle-Lion-Rank).

4740 "Do I know human nature? Look, didn't I say that fella Quick was made for my Clara? Am I going to be a grandfather? I am! Ah, Minnie, it sure is good to be alive this summer evening—yeah, alive with friends and family and a big healthy woman to love you. Come on. I like the life, Minnie. Yeah! I like it so much I might just live forever." Large Southern landowner **Orson Welles** delivers the film's last lines to his mistress Angela Lansbury. He's delighted with the news that his daughter Joanne Woodward and her husband Paul Newman are going to have a baby. *The Long Hot Summer* (1958, 20th Century-Fox).

4741 "The same old John, throwing out the same cascade of truths, half truths and distortions. But human nature isn't as simple as you make it, John. You've left out the most important fact of all. You see, you're the only person in the world I've ever been fond of. Notice how tactfully I leave out the word love." Blowsy, social type **Rita Hayworth** is still interested in her ex-husband, reclusive American writer Burt Lancaster. *Separate Tables* (1958, United Artists).

Humanitarian *see* HUMANITY AND HUMANS

Humanity

see also BABIES, BOYS, CHILDREN, DAUGHTERS, GIRLS, FAMILIES, FATHERS, MEN, MEN AND WOMEN, MOTHERS, PEOPLE, PERSONS, SONS, WOMEN

4742 "You're a humanitarian, aren't you? You think one person is as good as another—a naïve notion so contradicted by the facts." Despicable French aristocrat **Basil Rathbone** sneers at H.B. Warner. *A Tale of Two Cities* (1935, MGM).

4743 "They are pitifully small and weak, but I like them. Their lives are so short and their efforts so futile. . . ." **Torin Thatcher**, a god, refers to earthlings. *The Man Who Could Work Miracles* (1936, GB, London Films).

4744 "You're going to find out you're a human being." **Helen Broderick** promises a revelation for boss-lady extraordinaire Madeleine Carroll. *Honeymoon in Bali* (1939, Paramount).

4745 "Every door looks like a door until you try to go through it. Every person looks like a human until you talk to him." American **Robert Taylor** tries to get his mother Nazimova out of a German concentration camp prior to World War II. *Escape* (1940, MGM).

4746 "I don't buy or sell human beings." Casablanca nightclub owner **Humphrey Bogart** refuses to do business with Sydney Greenstreet, who wishes to buy piano player Dooley Wilson for his club. *Casablanca* (1942, Warner Bros.).

4747 BARBARA MORTON: "She was a tramp." SENATOR MORTON: "She was a human being." **Patricia Hitchcock** is reminded by her father **Leo G. Carroll** that no matter what her behavior, Laura Elliott didn't deserve to be murdered. *Strangers on a Train* (1951, Warner Bros.).

4748 "I've seen how people have allowed their humanity to draw away. Only it happens slowly instead of all at once. They don't seem to mind. All of us—we harden our hearts, grow callous. Only when we have to fight to stay human do we realize how precious it is, how dear." **Kevin McCarthy**'s message to Dana Wynter about invading aliens who are taking over the bodies and souls of humans, is also a message for the audience and the risk they are facing in having someone else think for them. *Invasion of the Body Snatchers* (1956, Allied Artists).

4749 "Nothing human disgusts me, Mr. Shannon—unless it's unkind or violent." Wandering artist **Deborah Kerr** is not disgusted by defrocked Episcopalian priest Richard Burton, who now earns his keep as a tour guide in Mexico. *The Night of the Iguana* (1964, MGM).

4750 "Humans are such easy prey." Scientist Dr. Pretorius, played by **Ted Sorel**, searches for a sixth sense, but it causes everyone to go berserk. *From Beyond* (1986, Empire Pictures).

4751 PROFESSOR HENRY JONES: "Well, I'm as human as the next man." INDIANA JONES: "But I was the next man." Father and son, **Sean Connery** and **Harrison Ford** discover they both have slept with Alison Doody. *Indiana Jones and the Last Crusade* (1989, Paramount).

4752 "You didn't waken a thing, you woke a person." Having escaped from an existence as a living vegetable, **Robert De Niro** tells Doctor Robin Williams, who performed the miraculous transformation with the help of the drug L-DOPA, that De Niro wants to live as a human and experience what he's missed. *Awakenings* (1990, Columbia).

4753 "It's not just a jolt of semen; it's a human being." Widower **Jane Fonda** lectures her newly pregnant teenage daughter Martha Plimpton. *Stanley & Iris* (1990, MGM-United Artists).

4754 "After a lifetime of peeping through keyholes, you lose confidence in the human species." Retired private investigator **Bob Hoskins** now runs a pet store. *Shattered* (1991, MGM).

4755 "I just have trouble imagining her related to anyone—human." **Kevin Kline** is surprised when Elisabeth Shue tells him that self-centered soap opera star Sally Field is her aunt. There are bigger surprises in store for him involving Shue and Field. *Soapdish* (1991, Paramount).

Humility and Humiliation

see also CONCEIT, MODESTY, PRIDE

4756 "You're the spoiled brat of a rich father! The only way you can get anything is to buy it. Ever hear of the word humility?" Out-of-work reporter **Clark Gable** is offended when a runaway heiress tries to buy his silence. *It Happened One Night* (1934, Columbia).

4757 "I'm your very 'umble servant, Mr. Copperfield." **Roland Young** gives a wonderful, fawning characterization of unctuous Uriah Heep. *David Copperfield* (1935, MGM).

4758 "Humility is a virtue, Monsieur, not only in those who suffer, but in those who hope to heal." Physician **Akim Tamiroff** wants a little help from Paul Muni in Tamiroff's crusade of tearing down the establishment's resistance to the work and theories of scientist Muni. *The Story of Louis Pasteur* (1936, Warner Bros.).

4759 "I think the time has come to shed some of your humility. It's just as false not to blow your horn at all as it is to blow it too loudly." Theater critic **George Sanders** tells conniving, ambitious actress Anne Baxter that it's safe to shed some of her self-deprecating demeanor and show her true colors. *All About Eve* (1950, 20th Century-Fox).

4760 "I turned to my faith, Babs—for strength to endure. I feel I have to go through the fire for some reason. Eleanor, it's a hard way to learn humility—but I've learned it by crawling. I know what is meant—you must learn to crawl before you can walk." **Ralph Bellamy**, as polio-crippled Franklin D. Roosevelt, shares with Greer Garson, as his wife Eleanor, the lesson his illness has taught him. *Sunrise at Campobello* (1960, Warner Bros.).

4761 "God, it was so personal—like you could see right through me." **Kristy McNichol** feels only humiliation after her first sexual experience with Matt Dillon. *Little Darlings* (1980, Paramount).

Humor

see also COMEDY AND COMEDIANS, DOUBLE-TALK, LAUGHTER, NONSENSE, PUNS, RIDICULE AND RIDICULOUSNESS

4762 "Well, all the jokes can't be good! You got to expect that once in a while." **Groucho Marx** speaks directly to the camera—but he's not really apologizing for the low quality of the humor. *Animal Crackers* (1930, Paramount).

4763 "The war stopped being a joke when a girl like you doesn't know how to wear the latest fashions." **Clark Gable** has to show Vivien Leigh how to wear a Parisian hat he's bought for her. *Gone with the Wind* (1939, Selznick-MGM).

4764 "Apparently, the mind is never too ill to make jokes about psychoanalysis." Psychiatrist **Ingrid Bergman** reacts defensively when her patient and lover Gregory Peck claims he doubts all this "Freud stuff." *Spellbound* (1945, United Artists).

4765 "Laugh, Curtin, old boy! It's a great joke played on us by the Lord of fate or nature. . . whichever you prefer, but whomever or whatever played it, certainly has a sense of humor! The gold has gone back to where we got it! Laugh, my boy, laugh! It's worth ten months of labor and suffering. . . this joke's on us!" **Walter Huston** shares some irony with Tim Holt after Mexican bandits killed Huston and Holt's prospecting partner Humphrey Bogart. Not realizing the value of the gold dust carried in bags on burros, the outlaws threw it to the ground and the wind blew it back to the mountains from whence it came. *The Treasure of the Sierra Madre* (1948, Warner Bros.).

4766 "What I said about having to get out and carry the old boat was meant to be a joke. It don't look like a joke now." Because the water is so shallow, **Humphrey Bogart** has to get out of his boat and pull it to deeper water. *The African Queen* (1951, United Artists).

4767 "Among the gods, divinity, your humor is unique." **Leo Genn** knows how to placate mad emperor Peter Ustinov without saying something he doesn't really believe. *Quo Vadis* (1951, MGM).

4768 "You have a sense of humor—I don't like humor in a woman." Amazon jungle plantation owner **Charlton Heston** cruelly states his disappointment in mail-order bride Eleanor Parker, who trying to penetrate his shell, makes a small joke. *The Naked Jungle* (1953, Paramount).

4769 "You're a joke—a dirty joke, from one end of the town to the other." Married socialite **Laurence Harvey** rages at his lover, part-time model, part-time call girl, Elizabeth Taylor. *Butterfield 8* (1960, MGM).

4770 "Am I being unreasonable, Doctor? I mean, this is my life, my only life, and I'm still living in the middle of a Jewish joke—and it isn't a joke." **Richard Benjamin** still lives with his parents Lee Grant and Jack Somack, who are driving him crazy. He begs his psychiatrist D.P. Barnes for some help. *Portnoy's Complaint* (1972, Warner Bros.).

4771 "You remember that cartoon of an old Roman circus where all the lions are roaring and the page boy yells down the corridor, 'You've got five minutes, Christians'?" Former New York detective **Charles Bronson** jokes after having thwarted a Mafia-organized murder plot in L.A. *The Stone Killer* (1973, Columbia).

4772 "I'm always joking, you know that. It's a defense mechanism." **Woody Allen** explains himself to Diane Keaton whom he meets after a 200-year sleep. *Sleeper* (1973, United Artists).

4773 "You know what your trouble was, Willie? You always took the jokes too seriously. They were just jokes. We did comedy on the stage for 43 years. I don't think you enjoyed it once." **George Burns** puts his finger on the problem of his long-time comedy partner, bitter Walter Matthau. *The Sunshine Boys* (1975, MGM).

4774 "Oh, really? I heard that Commentary and Dissent had merged and formed Dysentery." **Woody**

Allen makes a joke about magazines. *Annie Hall* (1977, United Artists).

4775 "The thing that is missing here is a sense of humor. Life is a goddamn serious big deal." **Timothy Hutton** tries to find an excuse for getting out of bed and starting a new day after returning home from a mental institution to which he was confined for many months. *Ordinary People* (1980, Paramount).

4776 "What's the matter? You never seen anyone from the planet Vulcan before?" **Eric Stoltz** attempts to ease the burden for those who see his disfigured head, caused by craniodiaphyseal dyaplania which causes calcium deposits on his skull, forcing it out of shape. *Mask* (1985, Universal).

4777 "These are not really my hips. They are a cruel joke that run in my family." While being measured by an attendant at a health resort, **Victoria Jackson** makes a lame joke. *Casual Sex?* (1988, Universal).

4778 DR. BRUNER: "Hello, Raymond. Do you feel a little bit more relaxed in your favorite K-Mart clothes?" CHARLIE: "Tell him, Ray." RAYMOND: "K-Mart sucks." Raymond Babbitt, played by **Dustin Hoffman,** tells his doctor, played by **Jerry Molen,** what he's learned about K-Mart from his brother Charlie, played by **Tom Cruise.** He makes a joke that K-Mart won't appreciate. *Rain Man* (1988, United Artists).

4779 "I ran for president. . . I didn't win though." **Denzel Washington** tells his tent mates what he has been doing since he ran away from slavery years earlier. *Glory* (1989, Tri-Star).

4780 "I don't get your generation's humor half the time." **Shirley MacLaine** doesn't understand much of anything of her daughter Meryl Streep's generation. *Postcards from the Edge* (1990, Columbia).

4781 RAMADA THOMPSON: "What do you do with an elephant with three balls?" TOPPER HARLEY: "I don't know." RAMADA: "Walk him and pitch to the rhino." It's a sample of the childish humor exchanged between **Valeria Golino** and **Charlie Sheen.** *Hot Shots!* (1991, 20th Century-Fox).

4782 "Oh, you do have a sense of humor. I was beginning to believe you had it surgically removed." At a party, **Nick Nolte** is pleased to discover that serious psychiatrist Barbra Streisand can make a joke, even if it is at his expense. *The Prince of Tides* (1991, Columbia).

Hunger

see also BODIES, DESIRES, FOOD AND EATING, NEEDS AND NECESSITIES, PAINS, WEAKNESS

4783 "Hunger strike, eh? How long has this been going on?" **Walter Connolly** stomps angrily in the room of his angry daughter Claudette Colbert. *It Happened One Night* (1934, Columbia).

4784 "Hunger is an indulgence with these peasants as gout is with us." French aristocrat **Basil Rathbone**, who hasn't got a sensitive bone in his body, makes a poor analogy. *A Tale of Two Cities* (1935, MGM).

4785 "When you're hungry, no one's going to lose his job trying to feed you." **Jean Arthur** is incorrect, Ray Milland is not only willing but delivers. *Easy Living* (1937, Paramount).

4786 "Ho, varlets, bring Sir Robin food! Such insolence must support a healthy appetite." **Claude Rains**, as Prince John, briefly plays the gracious host to the uninvited Errol Flynn, as Sir Robin of Locksley—Robin Hood. *The Adventures of Robin Hood* (1938, Warner Bros.).

4787 "As God is my witness, they're not going to lick me. . . I'm going to live. . . I'm going to live through this and when it's over I'm never going to be hungry again. No, nor any of my folks! If I have to lie, steal, cheat or kill, as God is my witness, I'll never be hungry again." Hungry **Vivien Leigh** falls to her knees and plucks a radish from a garden. She tries to eat the radish but her stomach rejects it. She slowly rises and with clenched fists raised towards heaven, she makes her vow, ending Part One of the film. *Gone with the Wind* (1939, Selznick-MGM).

4788 "I'm so hungry. I'd eat anything that didn't bite me first." Waitress **Irene Dunne** needs to serve herself. *When Tomorrow Comes* (1939, Universal).

4789 AMANDA: "Now start with the day of the accident." DORIS: "No accident. I wanted to shoot him. . . so I sent the kids to school and I went out and bought a gun. So then I was hungry. . . so I went in a hamburger place and ate two. Rare. And one lemon meringue pie." AMANDA: "And then what?" DORIS: "I was still hungry. . . so then I bought two chocolate bars and I went outside of his office and I waited the whole afternoon and I kept waiting and eating the candy bars till he came out so then I followed him so then I shot him." AMANDA: "And after you shot him, how did you feel?" DORIS: "Hungry." Attorney **Katharine Hepburn** questions her client Judy Holliday on the witness stand. The latter is charged with the attempted murder of her philandering husband Tom Ewell. *Adam's Rib* (1949, MGM).

4790 "Just listen to this stomach of mine. Way it sounds, you'd think I had a hyena inside me." **Humphrey Bogart** apologizes to Katharine Hepburn and Robert Morley for the hunger pains that cause his stomach to growl. *The African Queen* (1951, United Artists).

4791 "Hunger has no conscience." Turn-of-the-century composer **Sydney Chaplin** makes a fine point in the film that is his father Charlie Chaplin's story about his career in the British music halls. *Limelight* (1952, Chaplin-United Artists).

4792 "You've got ten minutes. You're a hungry little girl. You've been starving all your life. There's a feast out there. The theater is serving you a feast. You can either take it or forever wish you had." **Henry Fonda** gives frightened aspiring actress Susan Strasberg a pep-talk. *Stage Struck* (1958, RKO).

4793 "The English have a great hunger for desolate places. I fear they hunger for Arabia." **Alec Guinness**, as Prince Feisal, tells title character Peter O'Toole that he does not believe the English are altruistic in helping the Arabs against the Turks. *Lawrence of Arabia* (1962, GB, Columbia).

4794 "[You will be] doomed to a living hell...a hunger...wild animal gnawing hunger! You will starve for an eternity.... You shall be Blacula, a living fiend doomed to never know that sweet blood which will become your only desire." In 1790, Transylvania African Prince William Marshall is cursed by **Charles Macaulay**, as Count Dracula. *Blacula* (1972, American International).

4795 "Yes, starvation is a great aphrodisiac." Photographer **Linda Hunt** responds when a foreign journalist leeringly describes Jakarta's large prostitute population. *The Year of Living Dangerously* (1982, Australia, MGM).

4796 "I'm so hungry I could eat a bowl of lard with a hair in it." Yeah, **Cheech Marin**, that's hungry all right. *Cheech & Chong's The Corsican Brothers* (1984, Orion).

4797 "But I'm a hungry man. Billy, you know that. Now come on, give up. You know I gotta have it all." **Paul Winfield** calls for revenge-minded Judd Nelson's surrender. *Blue City* (1986, Paramount).

4798 "Do you like it? Look at that. I got a leave of absence for good behavior. I guess he thought we could make some good music together. Jim, I'm starving. Do you feel well enough to take me out for some french fries?" Angel **Emmanuelle Beart** had an accident on her way to pick up dying Michael E. Knight. It prevented her from taking his soul, but gave them time to fall in love. The answer to an angel's prayer, she becomes a human, but not before curing him. *Date with an Angel* (1987, DEG).

Hunting

see also ANIMALS, KILLINGS, PURSUITS, SPORTS

4799 "Hunting is my passion. My life has been one glorious hunt.... Hunting was beginning to bore me.... When I lost my love of hunting I lost my love of life...I have invented a new sensation." Mad **Leslie Banks** informs his shipwrecked guests on his island that he now hunts humans. *The Most Dangerous Game* (1932, RKO).

4800 "I hunt griz." It's one of mountain man **Will Geer**'s longer speeches. *Jeremiah Johnson* (1972, Warner Bros.).

4801 "One shot is what hunting is all about." **Robert De Niro** wishes to make his friends understand the ritual aspects of the sport of deer hunting. *The Deer Hunter* (1978, Universal).

4802 "We ain't huntin' him, he's huntin' us." **David Caruso**, a member of a posse sent to bring in former Green Beret Sylvester Stallone, realizes that they are now Stallone's prey. *First Blood* (1982, Orion).

Hurry and Hurrying

see also FORCE, SPEED

4803 EDDIE PINK: "Did you say you can tear a telephone book in half?" PARKYAKARKUS: "Yes, sir." EDDIE: "Wait a minute, wait a minute! You're tearing one page at a time." PARKYAKARKUS: "I ain't in a hurry." **Eddie Cantor** interviews **Harry Einstein** for a job as his bodyguard. *Strike Me Pink* (1936, United Artists).

4804 "Why do you always have to hurry to a murder case? Why can't you just ooze on down to one?" **Mantan Moreland** complains to Charlie Chan's son, Benson Fong. *Dark Alibi* (1946, Monarch).

4805 "My daddy always said there's only one time a man should be in a hurry and that's when the cops are coming up the stairs." Gambler **Marlon Brando** likes to take his time and quote his old man. *Guys and Dolls* (1955, Goldwyn-MGM).

4806 "Hurry, Maitland, is the curse of civilization." **Edith Evans** shares a thought that has come to her with the passing of her years with her butler John Mills. *The Chalk Garden* (1964, GB, Universal).

4807 "If we hurry, we can catch the end of *Dynasty*." **Chevy Chase** tries to escape with Dana Wheeler-Nicholson from two gunmen anxious to kill them. *Fletch* (1985, Universal).

Hurt and Hurting

see also FEELINGS, HARM, PAINS, WOUNDS AND SCARS

4808 "Don't worry, I ain't gonna hurt him. I only wanna feel his muscles." **Mae West** fondles an amorous acrobat. *I'm No Angel* (1933, Paramount).

4809 "It's easy to make fun of someone if you don't care how much you hurt 'em." Small-town boy **Gary Cooper** is hurt by the city highbrows who have been making fun of him. Cooper was dubbed the "beloved illiterate" by poet Carl Sandburg. It always was claimed that Coop was just being himself, but as he said, "When they say I'm just being me, they don't know how hard it is to be a guy like me." *Mr. Deeds Goes to Town* (1936, Columbia).

4810 "I know why he won't defend himself. . . . He's been hurt! He's been hurt by everybody he's met since he came. Principally by me. He's been the victim of every conniving crook in town. The newspapers pounced on him—made him a target for their feeble humor. . . . Why shouldn't he keep quiet? Every time he said anything it was twisted around to sound imbecilic. . . . I found out he could never fit in with our distorted viewpoint—because he was honest and sincere and good. If that man is crazy, your Honor, the rest of us belong in straight jackets." **Jean Arthur** testifies on behalf of Gary Cooper who refuses to defend himself in his sanity hearing, brought on because he wants to give away an inherited fortune that hasn't made him happy. *Mr. Deeds Goes to Town* (1936, Columbia).

4811 "If I had a gun, why one of us might have got hurt, and it might have been me. I wouldn't have liked that, would I?" Brian Donlevy tries to pick a gunfight with new deputy **James Stewart**, only to be shown by Jimmy that he doesn't carry a gun. *Destry Rides Again* (1939, Universal).

4812 SUSAN IRELAND: "Oh, darling, you must be furious!" STEPHEN IRELAND: "No, just terribly, terribly hurt." **Myrna Loy** is sympathetic when her husband **William Powell** crashes his foot violently against the bed post. *Love Crazy* (1941, MGM).

4813 W.T.G. MORTON: "Are you the girl?. . . The girl for the leg operation?" GIRL: "Yes, sir." MORTON: "I'm terribly, terribly sorry." GIRL: "It isn't as bad as it sounds, sir. Some gentleman has made a new discovery and it doesn't hurt anymore." MORTON: "That's right. . . . It doesn't hurt anymore. . . NOW OR FOREVER." Boston dentist **Joel McCrea** realizes that he must surrender the secret of his discovery of ether anesthesia, so that servant girl **Sheila Sheldon** and others won't be merely strapped down and forced to endure the agony of having a limb amputated. *The Great Moment* (1944, Paramount).

4814 "He wasn't hurt much; he was just snapped, the way a pretty girl snaps a stalk of celery." Private eye **Dick Powell** has a poetic way of describing the appearance of the dead body of murdered Otto Kruger. *Murder, My Sweet* (1945, RKO).

4815 "Some people are going to get hurt. Want to be first?" Police Chief **Lee J. Cobb** snarls at a potential lynch mob who has come for his prisoner, Arthur Kennedy. *Boomerang* (1947, 20th Century-Fox).

4816 NICK BIANCO: "Your side of the fence is almost as dirty as mine." D'ANGELO: "With one difference. We only hurt bad people." Criminal Victor Mature believes that he and Assistant District Attorney **Brian Donlevy** have something in common. *Kiss of Death* (1947, 20th Century-Fox).

4817 "Seems like we can't do anything but hurt these people even when we try to help them." **Lionel Barrymore** mourns when two Indians are shot and killed by the sheriff while trying to flee. Mobster Edward G. Robinson murdered a cop and blamed the Indians. *Key Largo* (1948, Warner Bros.).

4818 "Everything in these forty-eight states hurts me." A man's fascination for guns leads him into a life of violence with beautiful, demanding **Peggy Cummins**. *Gun Crazy* (1949, King Brothers-United Artists).

4819 "Why should you hurt like other people hurt? Just roll up your pain into one big hurt, and then flatten it with a fix. All that you're gonna need is another and another." **Kim Novak** shows no pity for heroin addict Frank Sinatra who pleads with her to get him a fix. *The Man with the Golden Arm* (1955, United Artists).

4820 "You seem to have an infinite capacity for hurt." **Dorothy McGuire** accuses Constance Ford after the latter reveals in front of their children that she knows of McGuire's affair with her husband Richard Egan. *A Summer Place* (1959, Warner Bros.).

4821 "They'll see and they'll say, why, she wouldn't even hurt a fly." His mind completely taken over by his mother's personality, **Anthony Perkins** thinks in her voice and remains perfectly still, even when a fly lands on his face. *Psycho* (1960, Paramount).

4822 "If you're yourself, you won't get hurt." Novelist **David Pokitillow** eases the concern of twenty-year-old flirtatious and curious virgin Lelia Goldoni. *Shadows* (1960, McEndree-Cassel).

4823 "I'm Margaret De Lorca, Sergeant. As you said, Edie would never have hurt a fly." Bitter **Bette Davis** has killed and assumed the identity of her identical twin. *Dead Ringer* (1964, Warner Bros.).

4824 "Funny when people hurt your feelings they always are doing it for your own good." **Ingrid Bergman** responds when Walter Matthau hurts her feelings and tells her he's doing it for her own good. There are no willing villains, you know. *Cactus Flower* (1969, Columbia).

4825 "I don't think you'd hurt yourself." Braces gleaming, **Barbara Hershey** gives a sly reply to Richard Thomas who wonders aloud what it would be like to kiss a girl with braces on her teeth. *Last Summer* (1969, Allied Artists).

4826 "Why do you hurt me, Michael? I've always been loyal to you." Al Pacino has lost faith in his father's consigliere **Robert Duvall.** *The Godfather, Part II* (1974, Paramount).

4827 "I didn't mean any of it, boy. I just got to have someone to hurt sometimes and you're all I got." Mean drunk **Moses Gunn** beats up his son Kevin Hooks, but he's pathetically contrite each time. *Aaron Loves Angela* (1975, Columbia).

4828 "I'm a Catholic and I don't want to hurt anyone." Bisexual bankrobber **Al Pacino** assures his hostages that he has no intention of harming them—unless he's forced to do so. *Dog Day Afternoon* (1975, Warner Bros.).

4829 "I'm your wife, damn it! And, if you can't work up a winter passion for me, the least I require is respect and allegiance. I hurt! Don't you understand that? I hurt badly!" It's part of the angry, honest speech **Beatrice Straight** makes to her philandering husband William Holden. It won her an Academy Award for Best Supporting Actress. *Network* (1976, MGM-United Artists).

4830 "Anything that hurts this many people can't be right." **Amy Irving** wisely observes that her affair with married Willie Nelson is wrong. *Honeysuckle Rose* aka: *On the Road Again* (1980, Warner Bros.).

4831 "I'm red; I'm sore." **William Hurt** begs off having more sex with super hot Kathleen Turner. *Body Heat* (1981, Warner Bros.).

4832 "That's life. . . hurting and being hurt." **Lloyd Bochner** is very cynical. *The Lonely Lady* (1983, Universal).

4833 "We didn't separate to hurt each other, we were trying to stop hurting each other." **Kate Nelligan** is indignant when police detective Judd Hirsch suggests that maybe her ex-husband has something to do with the disappearance of their minor son. *Without a Trace* (1983, 20th Century-Fox).

4834 "I met her in a closet at a party. Couldn't stand her at first, but once it took, I loved her so bad it hurt." When asked what his wife was like, **Powers Boothe** declares a love so strong it hurts. *Red Dawn* (1984, MGM-United Artists).

4835 "She's not bad; I wouldn't mind hurting her a little." Sadistic murderer **John Glover** refers to Ann-Margret, wife of Roy Scheider, whom Glover is blackmailing. *52 Pick-Up* (1986, Cannon).

4836 ANTHONY CASTELO: "Do we really hurt them by killing them?" "FRANK THE FIXER" ACAVANO: "It's a great start." Mob boss **Dan Hedaya** rhetorically muses that death may be too easy for his incompetent underlings Danny De Vito and Joe Piscopo. Hedaya's muscleman **Captain Lou Albano** puts in his two cents. *Wise Guys* (1986, MGM-United Artists).

4837 "C'mon, it didn't hurt that bad. . . . Just lookin' at you hurts more." **Mel Gibson** replies when beautiful vision Michelle Pfeiffer apologizes for hurting his feelings. *Tequila Sunrise* (1988, Warner Bros.).

4838 "You hurt me very much. . . don't do it again." **Julia Roberts'** client Richard Gere has made her feel like the cheap hooker she is. *Pretty Woman* (1990, Touchstone-Buena Vista).

Husbands

see also HUSBANDS AND WIVES, MARRIAGES, MEN, WEDDINGS, WOMEN

4839 RUFUS T. FIREFLY: "What about your husband?" MRS. TEASDALE: "He's dead." FIREFLY: "He's just using that as an excuse." TEASDALE: "I was with him to the end." FIREFLY: "No wonder he passed away." TEASDALE: "I held him in my arms and kissed him." FIREFLY: "So it was murder?" It's another of the many wonderful comedy exchanges between smart alec **Groucho Marx** and his perfect foil **Margaret Dumont**. *Duck Soup* (1933, Paramount).

4840 ELLIE ANDREWS: "I just had the unpleasant sensation of hearing you referred to as my husband." PETER WARNE: "Oh, I forgot to tell you. I registered as Mr. and Mrs. . . , that's a matter of simple mathematics. These cabins cost two bucks a night and I'm very sorry to inform you, wifey dear, but the family purse won't stand for us having separate establishments." Runaway heiress **Claudette Colbert** is suspicious of the motives of her not-so-white knight, unemployed newspaper reporter **Clark Gable**, as they seek shelter for the night. *It Happened One Night* (1934, Columbia).

4841 "Sometimes, I think it's harder to raise a husband than a baby!" **Penny Singleton** always has to bail hubby Arthur Lake out of some troublesome situation. *Blondie* (1938, Columbia).

4842 DEL GARDO: "You have a very charming daughter. So charming that I am no longer content to remain a bachelor." DE BRISSON: "But the disparity of age. . . ." DEL GARDO: "An experienced man of the world makes the best husband, you know." The bank's biggest depositor, **Tod Slaughter** blackmails banker **Aubrey Mallalieu** into agreeing to the marriage of his daughter Marjorie Taylor to the old lecher. *The Face at the Window* (1939, GB, Pennant-Ambassador).

4843 "He's her husband, ain't he?" **Hattie McDaniel** prevents Vivien Leigh from running ahead of Olivia de Havilland to her husband Leslie Howard, as he limps home from the Civil War. *Gone with the Wind* (1939, Selznick-MGM).

4844 "Why do I need a husband? I don't intend to fall in love." Career woman **Madeleine Carroll** has no time for love and marriage, but both Fred MacMurray and Allan Jones will try to change her mind. *Honeymoon in Bali* (1939, Paramount).

4845 "This is awful [having two husbands] but I love it." **Jean Arthur** enjoys the attention as her new husband Melvyn Douglas and her allegedly drowned husband Fred MacMurray vie for her attentions and her decision as to which one she will remain married to. *Too Many Husbands* (1940, Columbia).

4846 "Terry was a drunken sot. But he was the best husband a woman ever had, Lord rest his soul! And in between his rasslin' bouts with John. . . Barleycorn. In between bouts I ran his job for him. A year ago he died o'. . . water poisonin'! Drank a glass o' water, thinkin' it was gin, and his stomach couldn't stand the shock. Alec let me stay in his place and I done a good job of it, too. Ain't I, Alec?" **Marjorie Rambeau** refers to her late husband (Wallace Beery, in the 1933 film with Marie Dressler as Tugboat Annie) to Clarence Kolb and Charles Halton. *Tugboat Annie Sails Again* (1940, First National-Warner Bros.).

4847 "I wonder if now would be the time to tell you about Angus with the little tight pants—and Herman—and Vernon, Herman's friend—and Cecil—and Herbert and Hubert. . . ." **Barbara Stanwyck** casually recites the names of her ex-lovers to her new husband Henry Fonda. Her litany is constantly interrupted as the train they are traveling on passes through a series of tunnels. *The Lady Eve* (1941, Paramount).

4848 STEPHEN IRELAND: "She's married now—got a husband." SUSAN IRELAND: "Yeah? Whose husband she got?" **William Powell** and his wife **Myrna Loy** discuss his old flame, siren-like Gail Patrick—Hollywood's favorite other woman. *Love Crazy* (1941, MGM).

4849 "A fine husband you'd make. Folks say you're not good 'ceptin' for fightin' and hell-raisin'." **Joan Leslie** dismisses Gary Cooper's claim that he will take her as his wife. *Sergeant York* (1941, Warner Bros.).

4850 "Stay with us, it will give the servants some experience. We can look for new husbands together. I'm thinking of an American: it seems more patriotic." Wealthy, many-times married **Mary Astor** invites once-married Claudette Colbert to join her in a hunt for new rich husbands. *The Palm Beach Story* (1942, Paramount).

4851 PHYLLIS DIETRICHSON: "Mr. Neff, why don't you drop by tomorrow around eight-thirty. He'll be in then." WALTER NEFF: "Who?" PHYLLIS: "My husband! You were anxious to talk to him, weren't you?" WALTER: "I was, but I'm sorta getting over the idea, if you know what I mean." **Barbara Stanwyck** entertains insurance agent **Fred MacMurray** when her husband Tom Powers is absent. *Double Indemnity* (1944, Paramount).

4852 "I love coming to your house, Aunt Agatha, it's one of the few places I'm likely to meet my husband." **Lisa Carpenter** speaks to Mary Forbes, sarcastically referring to George Sanders, who is present. *The Picture of Dorian Gray* (1945, MGM).

4853 "Have one husband, have eight, but you'll come back to me." Wealthy composer-conductor **Claude Rains** is confident that his long-time mistress Bette Davis will one day leave her cellist husband Paul Henreid and return to him. *Deception* (1946, Warner Bros.)

4854 "You're not chained to your husband." **Glenn Ford** advises masochistic Gloria Grahame, whose brutish husband Broderick Crawford wants her to prostitute herself to get his job back. *Human Desire* (1954, Columbia).

4855 "The streets are paved with forgotten husbands." While she's doing a strip on a stage, luscious **Rita Moreno** evades James Garner's questions from the wings, having forgotten her husband Paul Stevens will be her undoing. *Marlowe* (1969, MGM).

4856 ALDENA KITTNER: "You know, I don't think you should be seen talking to that horse's ass." JOE TYNAN: "Which one?" ALDENA: "My husband." **Carrie Nye** warns Senator **Alan Alda** about associating with her hubby, Senator Rip Torn. *The Seduction of Joe Tynan* (1979, Universal).

4857 ROBERTO TERRANOVA: "What's your husband like?" LILY WYNN: "Oh, Roberto, I don't want to talk about my marriage on such a beautiful day." ROBERTO: "I saw your husband's 'Romeo' in London. . . ." LILY: "Wasn't it a hoot? Don't you think 48 is a bit old for Romeo?" Ham actor **Christopher Plummer** has disguised himself as a young Italian actor and has fooled his wife, comedy-writer **Maggie Smith**—or has he? *Lily in Love* (1985, New Line).

4858 "This is my husband; ignore him." **Julie Walters**, as playwright Joe Orton's mother, introduces and dismisses her mate James Grant. *Prick Up Your Ears* (1987, GB, Goldwyn).

4859 "I like to daydream, but I have my two feet planted on my husband." **Julie Kavner** talks sense to her unmarried sister Dianne Wiest who constantly dreams of finding the perfect man. *Radio Days* (1987, Orion).

4860 "He was never a warm man. He ran hot. He ran cold. It's because of her that he saved us. He saved us all." **Barbara Hershey** believes that her dead husband's cruelty was why he was able to save his family from a flood when the levee collapsed. *Shy People* (1987, Cannon).

4861 LILAH KRYTSIK: "I love my husband." STEVEN GOLD: "If we're going to get married, you'll have to get over that." Even when declaring his love for **Sally Field**, aspiring comedian **Tom Hanks** makes a joke. *Punchline* (1988, Columbia).

4862 "Your husband is a boil on the butt of humanity." Eternally peeved **Shirley MacLaine** is put out with Sally Field's husband Tom Skerritt. *Steel Magnolias* (1989, Tri-Star).

4863 "In my day, husbands and beds were never spoken of in the same breath. . . husbands were taken seriously as the only real obstacles to sin." Elderly **Joan Plowright** answers contemptuously when one of the other women staying at a medieval castle asks about sleeping accommodations for her spouse. *Enchanted April* (1992, GB, Miramax).

Husbands and Wives

see also HUSBANDS, LOVE AND LOVERS, MARRIAGES, MEN, MEN AND WOMEN, TOGETHERNESS, WEDDINGS, WOMEN

4864 "What a husband doesn't know won't hurt his wife." **Carole Lombard** is infamous for her little "flirtations" with handsome young men while her actor husband Jack Benny is on stage giving Hamlet's soliloquy. *To Be or Not to Be* (1942, United Artists).

4865 "I know now that the love we should have borne each other has turned into a bitter hatred. And that's all the problem is, not a very unusual one. I venture to imagine. Nor—nor half so tragic as you seem to think it; merely the problem of an unsatisfied wife and a henpecked husband. You'll find it all over the world. It is usually, I believe, a—a subject for farce." **Michael Redgrave** explains the incompatibility of his wife Jean Kent and himself to her none-too-secret lover Nigel Patrick. *The Browning Version* (1951, GB, GFD-Universal).

4866 "Tell me, Doc, how do the wives feel about their husbands surrogatin' around wid de girls here?" Private eye Mike Hammer, played by **Armand Assante**, questions the head of a sex therapy clinic. *I, the Jury* (1982, 20th Century-Fox).

Hypocrisy

see also ACTIONS AND ACTS, DECEPTIONS, PRETENSIONS, SINCERITY

4867 "This isn't a House of God, this is a meeting place for hypocrites. . . . Get out, so I can open these windows and let some fresh air into this church." **Barbara Stanwyck** denounces her father's congregation. Firing him contributed to his death. *The Miracle Woman* (1931, Columbia).

4868 "Okay, I'm a cat, but this is dirty pool. Well, I'm intolerant of hypocrites. That's what I said, Phil—hypocrites. She'd rather let Dave lose that job than risk a fuss up there. That's it, isn't it? She's afraid. The Krays everywhere are afraid of getting the gate from their little groups of nice people. They make little clucking sounds of disapproval, but they want you and Uncle John to stand up and yell and take sides and fight. But do they fight? Oh, no!" **Celeste Holm** tells Gregory Peck that his girlfriend Dorothy McGuire, who, although insisting that discrimination is wrong, won't do anything to counter it in her own community. *Gentleman's Agreement* (1947, 20th Century-Fox).

4869 "We're all part of the same hypocrisy, Senator. But never think it applies to my family." **Al Pacino** warns U.S. Senator G.D. Spradlin. *The Godfather, Part II* (1974, Paramount).

Hysteria *see* INSANITY AND SANITY

Ice Cream *see* FOOD AND EATING

Ideals

see also IDEAS, IMAGINATION, MODELS, THINKING AND THOUGHTS, WISHES

4870 NICHETTE: "But, Marguerite, it's ideal to love—and to marry the one you love." MARGUERITE: "I have no faith in ideals." Courtesans **Elizabeth Allan** and **Greta Garbo** have different notions as to the importance of love and marriage. *Camille* (1936, MGM).

4871 "Colonel Dax, you're a disappointment to me. You've spoiled the keenness of your mind by wallowing in sentimentality. You really did want to save these men and you were not angling for Mireau's command. You're an idealist and I pity you as I would the village idiot. We're fighting a war, Dax, a war we've got to win. The men don't fight and they were shot. You brought charges against General Mireau and I insisted that he answer them. Wherein have I gone wrong." Corps Commander **Adolphe Menjou** is unable to comprehend Kirk Douglas' desire for justice and the rights of men, even in time of war. *Paths of Glory* (1957, United Artists).

4872 "Vargas will turn you into one of these starry-eyed idealists. They're the ones making all the real trouble in the world. Careful, they're worse than crooks. You can always do something with a crook." Police Captain **Orson Welles** warns his partner Joseph Calleia about the problems presented by Mexican law enforcement official Charlton Heston. *Touch of Evil* (1958, Universal-International).

4873 "Liberals are the easy answer kids with baskets of bushwah who finally harpoon themselves, and then begin to play God." Newspaper editor **Robert Ryan** damns power-crazed idealists. *Lonelyhearts* (1959, United Artists).

4874 "My psychiatrist says I suffer from the halo effect, the tendency of widows to idealize their dead husbands.... He says it keeps me from falling in love again. He has a point, but I can't imagine I'll ever stop loving Louie." **Cybill Shepherd** shares some private information with Robert Downey, Jr. Neither yet realizes he is her reincarnated husband. *Chances Are* (1989, Tri-Star).

Ideas

see also BELIEFS, IMPRESSIONS, KNOWLEDGE, LEARNING AND LESSONS, MINDS, MODELS, OPINIONS, SCHEMES, SIGNIFICANCE, THINKING AND THOUGHTS

4875 "It seemed like a good idea at the time." It's expatriate **Richard Barthelmess**' favorite line. *The Last Flight* (1931, Warner Bros.).

4876 "The world must be conquered, but not by force of arms, but by ideas that liberate." **Paul Muni**, as Emile Zola, exhorts against war on his death bed. *The Life of Emile Zola* (1937, Warner Bros.).

4877 "That's funny, I got an idea top of a bus once, got me six years." **James Cagney** makes a crack after his childhood chum Pat O'Brien claims he accepted a call to the priesthood one day while riding along on the top of a bus as it passed a cathedral. *Angels with Dirty Faces* (1938, Warner Bros.).

4878 "As soon as I saw you look at me, I had an idea you had an idea." Stranded in Paris, **Claudette Colbert**, who's been around, misinterprets John Barrymore's interest in her. *Midnight* (1939, Paramount).

4879 "Today democracy, liberty, and equality are words to fool the people. No nation can progress with such ideas. They stand in the way of action. Therefore we frankly abolish them." **Henry Daniell** is the Goebbels-like character in Charlie Chaplin's spoof of Nazi Germany. *The Great Dictator* (1940, United Artists).

4880 "The first John Doe already died to keep the good will movement alive, and he kept that idea alive for more than two thousand years.... It's [an idea] worth dying for; it's an idea worth living for.... This is no time to give up." **Barbara Stanwyck** begs Christ-figure Gary Cooper not to accept crucifixion by jumping to his death and dying for everyone's sins. *Meet John Doe* (1941, Liberty Films).

4881 "I knew the idea might not appeal to you." After manipulating Eddie Bracken into proposing, and seeing how grateful he is for accepting him,

Betty Hutton bursts into tears and tells him the truth. The reason she wants to marry him is she's pregnant and she has no idea who the father is. Bracken becomes hysterical. *The Miracle of Morgan's Creek* (1944, Paramount).

4882 "Every new idea in the world comes from the mind of some one man." Dying architect **Henry Hull** instructs his protégé Gary Cooper. Hull might have taught Cooper to be a more tolerant person, if he had added as did Isaac Newton: "If I see further than other men, it is because I stand on the shoulders of giants." *The Fountainhead* (1949, Warner Bros.).

4883 "Big Ed. . . great Big Ed. You know why they call him Big Ed? 'Cause he's got big ideas. One day he's gonna get a big idea about me. . . and it's gonna be his last." Boss **James Cagney** knows that one of his gang members, Steve Cochran, has ambitions to replace him. *White Heat* (1949, Warner Bros.).

4884 "I don't sell a piece of goods, I sell an idea." Embezzler and con man **Humphrey Bogart** demonstrates his point by selling a set of hair brushes to a bald man. *We're No Angels* (1955, Paramount).

4885 "I got no idea of love. I mean, neither of us would know what it was if we saw it coming down the street." Pool hustler **Paul Newman** feels free to include crippled Piper Laurie in the pigeonhole where he's put himself. It isn't true of either of them. *The Hustler* (1961, 20th Century-Fox).

4886 "Isn't that interesting? Where on earth do you get your ideas?" Empty-headed **Monica Evans** questions Jack Lemmon when he tells her that he writes the news for television. *The Odd Couple* (1968, Paramount).

4887 "I'm getting funny ideas. I'm getting some bad ideas in my head." Loner **Robert De Niro** has just enough control of himself to realize that he's losing control. *Taxi Driver* (1976, Columbia).

4888 "The FBI is wrong in reporting to you that I have no children. Ideas are my children and I have hundreds of them." **Jill Clayburgh** sounds somewhat pompous at her Senate confirmation hearing prior to her appointment to the U.S. Supreme Court. *First Monday in October* (1981, Paramount).

4889 "You don't like that one, I got other ideas." **Jeff Bridges** bursts into the board meeting of the world credit corporation American Success, or AmSucco, to propose credit cards for kids. *American Success* (1982, Columbia).

4890 "Now the way the system works, the loner, the dreamer, the crackpot who comes up with some crazy idea that everybody laughs at—that later turns out to revolutionize the world—is smashed from above before he gets his head out of water—because the bureaucrats—they'd rather kill a new idea than rock the boat. If Benjamin Franklin were alive today, he'd be thrown in jail for sailing a kite without a license." Automobile manufacturer **Jeff Bridges** speaks in his own behalf at his trial for fraud and misuse of funds. If he thought the bureaucrats were a problem in the '40s, he ought to see how they interfere with everyone's life today. *Tucker: The Man and His Dreams* (1988, Paramount).

Identities

see also APPEARANCES, CHARACTER, EXISTENCE, INDIVIDUALISM, NAMES, PEOPLE, PERSONS AND PERSONALITIES, SELF

4891 "It's not who you are, it's what you are that counts." We'd all like to believe **Joan Crawford**—but lately it seems that mediocrity wins out, all too often. *Dance, Fools, Dance* (1931, MGM).

4892 "I'm the whippoorwill that cries at night. . . I'm the soft morning breeze that caresses your lovely face." On his side of "the Wall of Jericho," **Clark Gable** responds to heiress Claudette Colbert's, "Who are you?" *It Happened One Night* (1934, Columbia).

4893 "He can look like a hundred people, but one thing he cannot disguise—this: half of his little finger is missing—so if ever you should meet a man with no top joint, be very careful about that." **Lucie Mannheim** tells Robert Donat how to identify the film's chief villain. *The 39 Steps* (1935, GB, Gaumont).

4894 "What would people think if it were known that I am not—how shall I put it?—what I seem?" Professor **Godfrey Tearle**, talking with Robert Donat, isn't a professor; he's a dangerous anti-British spy. *The 39 Steps* (1935, GB, Gaumont).

4895 "I'm going to break you out of this jail and give you to the world. You're a strange, sad case, girlie. Desires being strangled to death. Break loose. Be yourself." **Melvyn Douglas** encourages small-town girl Irene Dunne to be whom she wants to be and live as she wants. *Theodora Goes Wild* (1936, Columbia).

4896 "Hello, everybody—this is—Mrs. Norman Maine." In tribute to their husbands, alcoholic, failed actors Fredric March and James Mason, both suicides, **Janet Gaynor** and **Judy Garland**, respectively, address their adoring public as widows rather than as the stars they are. *A Star Is Born* (1937, United Artists), (1954, Warner Bros.).

4897 WASH DIMSDALE: "You're sure you're Destry?" TOM DESTRY: "Folks is always asking me that." Bottleneck Sheriff **Charles Winninger** finds it hard to believe that soft-spoken, milk-drinking, gunless **James Stewart** is the son of the rip-snorting brave lawman Winninger once worked for. *Destry Rides Again* (1939, Universal).

4898 "I am what I wish to be." It's menacingly spoken and meant by **Cedric Hardwicke**, the obsessed Frollo. *The Hunchback of Notre Dame* (1939, RKO).

4899 "His name is Eddie Bartlett. . . . He used to be a big shot." Brassy, blonde **Gladys George** supplies the last line of the film, when a cop asks who bullet-ridden James Cagney is. *The Roaring Twenties* (1939, Warner Bros.).

4900 "It's not enough to tell us what a man did. You've got to tell us who he was. . . . What were the last words he said on earth? Maybe he told us all about himself on his deathbed. . . . When Charles Foster Kane died he said but just one word. . . 'Rosebud'. . . . Now what does that mean?" *March of Times* editor **Philip Van Zandt** assigns William Alland the task of rooting out the significance of Orson Welles' last word. *Citizen Kane* (1941, RKO).

4901 "I'm two people—neither of them any good." Small town girl **Lana Turner** ruins her life in an attempt to become a Ziegfeld Follies star. *Ziegfeld Girl* (1941, MGM).

4902 "We were so close growing up. . . . Then you know how it is. You sort of forget you're you. You're your husband's wife." **Patricia Collinge** speaks nostalgically about her brother Joseph Cotten and herself when they were kids. *Shadow of a Doubt* (1943, Universal).

4903 "When I think of myself, I think of Uncle Charlie." **Teresa Wright** identifies emotionally and telepathically with Joseph Cotten. *Shadow of a Doubt* (1943, Universal).

4904 "There's a little Don Juan in every man and since I am Don Juan there is more of it in me." **Errol Flynn** justifies his hell-raising with women to friend Alan Hale. *The Adventures of Don Juan* (1949, Warner Bros.).

4905 ZACK: "You talk more like a dog-face than a gook." "SHORT ROUND": "I am no gook. I am Korean." ZACK: "All right, all right, all right—so you're not a

gook." As far as GI **Gene Evans** is concerned, all Koreans look alike and all are gooks, so why should young South Korean orphan William Chun be upset. *The Steel Helmet* (1951, Lippert).

4906 "Don't kid me, baby. I know a bottle by the label." **Robert Ryan** knows that Barbara Stanwyck's been around the block, and around and around. He's sure of it when she socks him before he can kiss her. *Clash by Night* (1952, RKO).

4907 PAT: "I've been around physical ed a long time." MIKE: "Physical Ed? Who's he?" Athletic **Katharine Hepburn**'s experience throws her sports manager **Spencer Tracy**. *Pat and Mike* (1952, MGM).

4908 "I am not Nijinsky. I am not Marlon Brando. I am Mrs. Hunter's little boy." **Fred Astaire** expresses his unhappiness with the way things are going in his new show by taking a shot at his dancing partner, ballerina Cyd Charisse, and director Jack Buchanan, who usually works with serious drama. *The Band Wagon* (1953, MGM).

4909 "Now look here, you stupid little broad, do you know who I am? Do you think I let dames talk that way to me?" **James Cagney**, as Martin "The Gimp" Snyder, is about to let Doris Day, as singer Ruth Etting, have one across the chops for talking out of turn. *Love Me or Leave Me* (1955, MGM).

4910 "I don't know who I am anymore. I don't know what I remember and what I've been told I remember. What is real? Am I?" Amnesia victim **Ingrid Bergman** has been stuffed with so much information about the people and events in the life of the Grand Duchess Anastasia, that she no longer knows what part of her memory is actually hers. *Anastasia* (1956, 20th Century-Fox).

4911 "Couldn't you like me the way I am?" **Kim Novak** pleads with James Stewart to love her for who she is, not for who she resembles. Stewart is trying to make her over to be his lost love. *Vertigo* (1958, Paramount).

4912 "Who do you think you are, Audie Murphy?" **Gregory Peck** is amazed at young Robert Blake who refuses to return to the rear to be treated for wounds sustained in wiping out an enemy machine gun nest. In case you didn't know, Audie Murphy was the most decorated GI in World War II. He went on to have a modest career as a movie actor. *Pork Chop Hill* (1959, United Artists).

4913 "No. I'm Spartacus. Have you come to free the slaves or something?" Drunken **Peter Sellers** responds to murder-on-his-mind James Mason who asks, "Are you guilty?" *Lolita* (1962, GB, MGM).

4914 "You Freud—me Jane?" **Tippi Hedren** contemptuously replies when Sean Connery asks her to tell him about her disturbing dreams. *Marnie* (1964, Universal).

4915 "You know who I used to be? Max Bialystock! The King of Broadway! Six shows running at once. Lunch at Delmonico's. Two hundred dollar suits. Look at me now! I'm wearing a cardboard belt!" **Zero Mostel** screams in capital letters about how the mighty have fallen to cringing accountant Gene Wilder. *The Producers* (1967, Embassy).

4916 "They're beginning to get on my nerves. Who are those guys?" **Paul Newman** repeats his rhetorical question several times, wondering the identity of the unshakeable posse chasing him and his sidekick Robert Redford. *Butch Cassidy and the Sundance Kid* (1969, 20th Century-Fox).

4917 "I have many enemies. I rarely go out unless I'm in disguise." **Dorthi Fox**, a large black woman, appears as a witness in Woody Allen's trial, claiming to be J. Edgar Hoover in disguise. *Bananas* (1971, United Artists).

4918 "Do you know who I am? I'm Moe Greene, and I made my bones while you were going out with cheerleaders." **Alex Rocco** doesn't show the proper respect for Godfather Al Pacino. He'll regret it. *The Godfather* (1972, Paramount).

4919 MABEL LONGHETTI: "I'll be whatever you want me to be." NICK LONGHETTI: "Be yourself." **Gena Rowlands** is unable to comply with her husband **Peter Falk**'s suggestion. She doesn't know who she is. *A Woman Under the Influence* (1974, Faces International).

4920 "I, the robber, you is the rob-ee." Con man thief **Richard Pryor** establishes roles. *Adios Amigo* (1975, Atlas).

4921 "Larry Lapinsky is either a sexual brute or a tender poet. Larry Lapinsky is not fine." **Lenny Baker** half-kiddingly reacts when Ellen Greene evaluates his sexual prowess by saying it's "fine." *Next Stop, Greenwich Village* (1976, 20th Century-Fox).

4922 "The time is coming for you to put away childish things and face up to who you are." **Lance Henriksen**, a sergeant at the military academy attended by little devil Damien (Jonathan Scott-Taylor), is one of the Devil's helpers who appear from time to time to give the apprentice Satan a hand. *Damien—Omen II* (1978, 20th Century-Fox).

4923 "Oh, Mr. Merrick, you're not the Elephant Man at all. You're Romeo." **Anne Bancroft** gushes to John Hurt as the two read from "Romeo and Juliet." *The Elephant Man* (1980, EMI).

4924 "Isn't this fun? Don't you wish you were me? I know I do." Constantly drunk **Dudley Moore** has some doubt as to who he is. *Arthur* (1981, Warner Bros.).

4925 "I am what I am, and I got news for you sweetheart, so are you." Ex-boxer **Tommy Lee Jones** wises-up hooker Sally Field, who angrily protests that she doesn't want to be around him if he persists in robbing people. *Back Roads* (1981, Warner Bros).

4926 "To my family I'm a doll, to my dog a chew-stick." Title character **Lily Tomlin** has some bad news and some worse news. *The Incredible Shrinking Woman* (1981, Universal).

4927 "Find out who you are or you'll never be able to love anyone else." Wealthy and beautiful **Wendy Hughes** gives some rather mature advice to her six-year-old nephew Nicholas Gledhill. *Careful, He Might Hear You* (1984, Australia, 20th Century-Fox).

4928 "I'm not God. I'm just a clown." Radio's love-torn expert **Genevieve Bujold**, as throaty Dr. Love, does not deny that she's a sham. *Choose Me* (1984, Island Alive).

4929 CEDRIC: "Do you know any good white basketball players?" BLINDMAN: "There are no good white basketball players." This exchange is the means anti-East German secret agent **Omar Sharif** uses to identify his contact, blind street peddler **Ian McNeice**. *Top Secret!* (1984, Paramount).

4930 SARAH WHEELER: "Who are you—really?" PREACHER: "It really doesn't matter, does it?" SARAH: "No." Lonely **Carrie Snodgress** and preacher-gunman **Clint Eastwood** almost make love. *Pale Rider* (1985, Warner Bros.).

4931 "Yeah, and I'm the Kumquat of Queens." Nasty little **Danny De Vito** is sarcastic and unbelieving when he's introduced to holy man Avner Eisenberg as "the jewel of the Nile." *The Jewel of the Nile* (1985, 20th Century-Fox).

4932 FITZROY WYNN: "That cantankerous piece of mozzarella is about to make love to my wife." JERRY SILBER: "Lest we forget, that cantankerous piece of mozzarella is you." **Christopher Plummer** complains to his agent **Adolph Green** about his alter ego, an Italian actor whom he impersonates. In this guise he has just about seduced his wife Maggie Smith. *Lily in Love* (1985, New Line).

4933 "Let's face it—she's not Mother Teresa. Gandhi would have strangled her." **Danny De Vito** doesn't grieve when his wife Bette Midler is kidnapped. *Ruthless People* (1986, Touchstone-Buena Vista).

4934 "I am what you are." Predator **Kevin Peter Hall** answers when guerrilla leader Arnold Schwarzenegger wonders aloud who the chameleon-like alien is. Arnie can't bring himself to finish off his wounded adversary. *The Predator* (1987, 20th Century-Fox).

4935 "Who am I?" Late at night, looking out over Manhattan from his luxurious apartment, **Charlie Sheen**, becoming rich with the help of stock market "player" Michael Douglas, has doubts. *Wall Street* (1987, 20th Century-Fox).

4936 "When I smoke a reefer, I am Odetta." Hippie **Pia Zadora** finds a personal advantage of marijuana. *Hairspray* (1988, New Line).

4937 "The Big Bopper. Maybe you know him. He's dead too." When 200-year-old ghost Daryl Hannah asks Guttenberg who wrote the song "Chantilly Lace," **Steve Guttenberg** names J.P. Richardson, who died in a plane crash along with Buddy Holly and Ritchie Valens on Feb. 3, 1959. *High Spirits* (1988, Tri-Star).

4938 "I know there has to be somebody inside there! But who? And where?" Frustrated **Tom Cruise** tries to get through to his autistic older brother, Dustin Hoffman. *Rain Man* (1988, United Artists).

4939 "The man I've been seeing for awhile. . . I think he's it and I think this could be the weekend we decide. . . . He said there was something very important he wanted to discuss with me. . . I think he's going to pop the question. . . we're in the same city now, I've indicated that I'm receptive to an offer, I've cleared the month of June. . . and I am, after all—me." Arrogant **Sigourney Weaver** is more showing off than sharing the news with her secretary Melanie Griffith that she's expecting a marriage proposal. She sounds as if she's describing a business merger. *Working Girl* (1988, 20th Century-Fox).

4940 "Do I look like Mother Teresa?" Head Heather **Kim Walker** need not fear that she will be confused with any kindly, saintly woman. *Heathers* (1989, New World).

4941 "I'm everyone and no one, everything and nothing. Call me Darkman." Having been beaten, tortured, burnt and left for dead, scientist **Liam Neeson** rises as something else indeed. *Darkman* (1990, Universal).

4942 "Oh, no, it's Cinder-fuckin'-rella." **Laura San Giacomo** reacts happily when she learns of her friend and fellow streetwalker Julia Roberts' good fortune in hooking up with wealthy business tycoon Richard Gere. *Pretty Woman* (1990, Touchstone-Buena Vista).

4943 "Your lifelong ambition is to be his exact mirror image—the opposite of everything he is, except you don't know what he is—so you don't know who you are." **Larry Fishburne**, a law associate of consumer advocate attorney Gene Hackman, puts his finger on the problem of Hackman's daughter, corporation attorney Mary Elizabeth Mastrantonio. *Class Action* (1991, 20th Century-Fox).

4944 "I don't know who you are." It's the message in the note that newlywed Colin Firth finds left with her wedding ring by his wife **Lisa Zane**. *Femme Fatale* (1991, Republic).

4945 "I am a teacher, a coach, and a well-liked man." After finally facing the horror of his childhood, **Nick Nolte** feels he has something to give back to the women in his life, his wife and daughters. *The Prince of Tides* (1991, Columbia).

4946 "Always waiting for Batman to save you. . . I am Catwoman. Hear me roar." **Michelle Pfeiffer** gives her Helen Reddy impersonation as she yells at a woman she's just rescued from an attack by a man. *Batman Returns* (1992, Warner Bros.).

4947 "Captain Kangaroo wasn't really a captain. He wasn't even a kangaroo." Opportunistic station manager **Griffin Dunne** convinces Dolly Parton to fudge her qualifications for giving advice on a radio call-in show. *Straight Talk* (1992, Hollywood Pictures-Buena Vista).

Ideology *see* CAUSES, CREEDS AND CREDOS, IDEAS

Idiots *see* STUPIDITY

Ignorance

see also DULLNESS, KNOWLEDGE, LEARNING AND LESSONS, NAÏVETÉ, SCHOOLS, STUDIES AND STUDENTS, STUPIDITY, THINKING AND THOUGHTS, WISDOM

4948 "I do not approve of anything that tampers with natural ignorance. Ignorance is like a delicate exotic fruit. Touch it and the bloom is gone. The whole theory of modern education is radically unsound. Fortunately in England, at any rate, education produces no effect whatsoever." **Edith Evans** serves as an eloquent spokesperson for playwright Oscar Wilde, flinging his sharp but amusing cynicisms in all directions. *The Importance of Being Earnest* (1952, GB, Two Cities-Rank).

4949 "Your ignorance, brother, as the great Milton says, almost subdues my patience." **Edith Evans** is exasperated with her drunken, ignorant brother Hugh Griffith. *Tom Jones* (1963, GB, Woodfall-Lopert-United Artists).

4950 "I heard what you were saying. You know nothing of my work. . . . How you can ever get to teach a course on anything is totally amazing." To squelch a pseudo-intellectual in a movie line, who claims to teach a course on TV, media and culture at Columbia University, Woody Allen brings on **Marshall McLuhan**, whom the bore quotes extensively, to put the big mouth in his place. Allen says about this obvious fantasy situation, "Boy, if life were only like this." *Annie Hall* (1977, United Artists).

4951 "I can't believe you never heard of Alice Cooper! Don't you read T-shirts?" Sixteen-year-old **Kaki Hunter**, whose mission in life is to sleep with male rock 'n' roller Alice Cooper, is incredulous when Meat Loaf asks if Alice Cooper is one of Charlie's Angels. *Roadie* (1980, United Artists).

Illegality *see* CRIMES AND CRIMINALS, LAWS, LEGALITY AND ILLEGALITY, SINS AND SINNERS

Illegitimacy *see* BIRTHS AND BIRTHDAYS, LEGITIMACY

Illiteracy *see* BOOKS, WRITING AND WRITERS

Illness *see* DISEASES, DOCTORS AND DENTISTS, MEDICINE, SICKNESS

Illusions

see also APPEARANCES, DECEPTIONS, DREAMS, ESCAPES, FANTASIES, HOPE, MYTHS, REALITIES

4952 "What's wrong with romance—and what's wrong with illusions as far as that goes, if you can keep them?" Widow **Carole Lombard** debates with Katherine Alexander about her love for Cary Grant. He's seeking a divorce from social-climber Kay Francis. *In Name Only* (1939, RKO).

4953 "I have no illusions. I know the life I lived. I know where I belong. I'd like to get it over as

quickly as possible." Recently deceased **Don Ameche** reports with resignation to devil Laird Cregar. *Heaven Can Wait* (1943, 20th Century-Fox).

4954 "Well, I think you are definitely old enough to be told the facts of life. . . I'll have to shatter your illusions, there is no Santa Claus." **Charles Coburn** blasts his 43-year-old son Louis Calhern, who demonstrates a great lack of knowledge of sexual and social realities. *Heaven Can Wait* (1943, 20th Century-Fox).

4955 "Want to buy some illusions?" Alluring ex-Nazi nightclub entertainer **Marlene Dietrich** has no takers in post-war Berlin. *A Foreign Affair* (1948, Paramount).

4956 "Yeah, grass, right? The illusion that it will make a white woman more like Billie Holiday." **Woody Allen** complains that Diane Keaton always needs a little pot before they have sex. *Annie Hall* (1977, United Artists).

4957 "I was just thinking about the illusion of safety." **Kris Kristofferson** muses as he watches Jane Fonda collapse in shock at a charity ball after being told that her husband has been murdered. *Rollover* (1981, Orion).

4958 PRIEST: "Everyday life is only an illusion behind which lies the reality of dreams." FITZCARRALDO: "I'm very interested in these ideas. I specialize in opera." Missionary **Salvador Godinez** explains the beliefs of turn-of-the-century South American Indians to obsessed dreamer **Klaus Kinski.** *Fitzcarraldo* (1982, W. Germany, New World Pictures).

Imagination

see also ART AND ARTISTS, CREATION AND CREATURES, EXPERIENCES, FANCIES, IDEAS, MINDS, THINKING AND THOUGHTS, UNDERSTANDINGS AND MISUNDERSTANDINGS

4959 "Woman's greatest weapon is a man's imagination." **Maureen O'Sullivan**'s little secret for keeping a man interested may only work with men from advanced civilizations. For Johnny Weissmuller, as Tarzan, she wears outfits that leave little to the imagination, most notably a loin cloth that leaves her midriff, hips and thighs exposed. The outfit was so skimpy and sexy, it was banned in subsequent pictures. *Tarzan and His Mate* (1934, MGM).

4960 "Oh, Alice! What an imagination!" **Ann Shoemaker** exclaims to her daughter Katharine Hepburn, who tends to allow her life to be ruled by her imagination. *Alice Adams* (1935, RKO).

4961 "The mine is dark. . . . If a light comes in the mine. . . the rivers in the mine will run fast with the voice of many women; the walls will fall in, and it will be the end of the world. . . . So the mine is dark. . . . But when I walk through the Tan—something—shaft, in the dark, I can touch with my hands the leaves of the trees underneath. . . where the corn is green." **Bette Davis**, as school mistress Miss Moffat, reads from an imaginative and eloquent composition written by sensitive, intelligent young Welsh coal miner John Dall. *The Corn Is Green* (1945, Warner Bros.).

4962 "The imagination is a place by itself. A separate country. Now, you've heard of the French nation, the British nation—well, this is the imagination. It's a wonderful place. How would you like to be able to make snowballs in the summertime? Or drive a great big bus right down Fifth Avenue? How would you like to have a ship all to yourself that makes daily trips to China? Australia? How would you like to be the Statue of Liberty in the morning and in the afternoon fly south with a flock of geese? Very simple. But it takes practice. Now, the first thing you've got to learn is how to pretend." **Edmund Gwenn** helps young Natalie Wood, who isn't allowed to join in the games of other children. Her mother Maureen O'Hara has brought her up on strict reality. *Miracle on 34th Street* (1947, 20th Century-Fox).

4963 "I never told you I was anything but what I am. You just wanted to imagine I was. That's why I left you." Selfish and self-centered **Jane Greer** denies Robert Mitchum's accusation that she betrayed him. *Out of the Past* (1947, RKO).

4964 "It's just my imagination. Some people have flat feet. Some people have dandruff. I have this appalling imagination." Summer bachelor **Tom Ewell** has several fantasies involving the girl upstairs, Marilyn Monroe. *The Seven Year Itch* (1955, 20th Century-Fox).

4965 "Imagination is just the word people use when they don't know what they're doing." Art teacher **Julia Blake** instructs her student Norman Kaye, a sexually repressed, middle-aged painter. *A Man of Flowers* (1984, Australia, International Spectrafilm).

4966 "I play this girl. She's a 'what' not a 'who.' It's just a figment of this guy's imagination. He imagines me hangin' round the place, y'know. I spend the entire movie in the kitchen, or in the bathtub, or havin' my skirt blown up—round my fuckin' ear." **Theresa Russell**, as Marilyn Monroe, answers a taxi driver's question about the part she's playing, by describing her role in "The Seven Year Itch." *Insignificance* (1985, GB, Zenith).

4967 "I'll just imagine he had an operation and the horn was removed to make him feel less freakish. And he'll feel more at home with the other horses, the ones that don't have horns." **Karen Allen** gently forgives James Naughton for accidentally breaking her favorite glass piece, a unicorn. *The Glass Menagerie* (1987, Cineplex-Odeon).

4968 VIRGINIA HILL: "Use your imagination." BEN SIEGEL: "I'm using it." VIRGINIA: "Let me know when you're finished." **Annette Bening** and **Warren Beatty** engage in some playful sexual banter at their first meeting on a movie sound stage. *Bugsy* (1991, Tri-Star).

4969 AZEEM: "In my dreams alone have I imagined such a place." LOCKSLEY: "Well then, imagine a way to cross it." Moor **Morgan Freeman** and **Kevin Costner** have come to a river near the perimeter of Sherwood Forest. *Robin Hood: The Prince of Thieves* (1991, Columbia).

Imitation

see also APPEARANCES, PRETENSIONS

4970 "Why don't you stop imitating a gorilla and start imitating a man?" **Eugene Pallette** is fed up with his wife's protégé Mischa Auer. The latter's greatest talent is making the sounds of a gorilla. *My Man Godfrey* (1936, Universal).

4971 "Oh, you must've had yourself a time with that little screwball of a Christopher! You know, she's a screwball because girls all over the country are screwballs this year. She thinks she has to be one, too." **Jessie Ralph** rates Madeleine Carroll for reporter Fred MacMurray. *Cafe Society* (1939, Paramount).

4972 "Make up your mind. You hate him and you build this shrine to him. He died over ten years ago and you've been holding a private wake for him ever since. You can't be a star in a cemetery. Because he drank, you're a drunk. Because he loved women, you're a tramp." Hollywood producer **Kirk Douglas** yells at weepy, intoxicated would-be actress Lana Turner, the daughter of a famous movie actor, perhaps John Barrymore. *The Bad and the Beautiful* (1952, MGM).

4973 JOHN ROBIE: "You know as well as I do that this necklace is an imitation." FRANCES STEVENS: "I'm not." Former cat burglar **Cary Grant** is the mouse in a cat and mouse game played by lovely **Grace Kelly**, who's testing to see what is more tempting to him, jewels or her. *To Catch a Thief* (1955, Paramount).

4974 GILLIAN BROMLEY: "Why are you doing Tony Curtis?" JACK RHODES: "I'm doing Cary Grant." GILLIAN: "No, you're not. You're doing Tony Curtis doing Cary Grant. Not even Cary Grant does Cary Grant anymore." Beautiful **Lesley-Anne Down** nicely knocks down **Burt Reynolds**' pass when he tries to imitate Cary Grant. *Rough Cut* (1980, Paramount).

4975 DAVID HOWARD: "That's everything?" MERCEDES DEALER: "Except leather." HOWARD: "For what I'm paying, I don't get leather?" DEALER: "You get Mercedes leather." HOWARD: "Mercedes leather? What's that?" DEALER: "Thick vinyl." Talking on a phone, **Albert Brooks** negotiates with Mercedes dealer **Herb Nanas**. *Lost in America* (1985, Warner Bros.).

4976 "Paris has been taken over by imitators of people who were imitators themselves." Collector **Geraldine Chaplin** concludes the City of Lights is filled with phonies. *The Moderns* (1988, Alive Films).

Immorality

see also BADNESS, EVILNESS, GOOD AND EVIL (BAD), MORALITY, SINS AND SINNERS, VICES, WRONGS AND WRONGDOINGS

4977 "Immorality may be fun, but it isn't fun enough to take the place of one hundred percent virtue and three square meals a day." Stuffed shirt **Edward Everett Horton** is appalled to learn of an earlier "ménage a trois" arrangement involving his wife Miriam Hopkins, and Fredric March and Gary Cooper. *Design for Living* (1933, Paramount).

4978 MICHAEL BRANDON: "Well, what's a man gonna do when he falls in love with a girl?" AUNT HEDWIGE: "Why, marry her and stay married." BRANDON: "And if he finds he's made a mistake? Carry on behind her back? Lie? Make excuses? Not me. I think that's immoral. Besides, I'm too busy." American millionaire **Gary Cooper**'s seven marriages and six divorces (one wife died) shocks **Elizabeth Patterson**, aunt of Claudette Colbert, whom self-righteous Cooper plans to make his eighth, but probably not his last spouse. *Bluebeard's Eighth Wife* (1938, Paramount).

4979 "Is Hiroshima the superior morality?" **Maximilian Schell**, the defense attorney for German war criminals, raises an interesting point. *Judgment at Nuremberg* (1961, United Artists).

4980 "You're an immoral man, Hud. You don't give a damn." **Melvyn Douglas** condemns his son Paul Newman for one of the greatest sins of the 20th century—indifference. *Hud* (1963, Paramount).

4981 KATE O'SULLIVAN: "It's not illegal." LAWRENCE GARFIELD: "It's immoral—a distinction lawyers ignore." Corporation lawyer **Penelope Ann Miller** must find it surprising that corporation raider **Danny De Vito** speaks of immorality when she offers him a profit, called "greenmail," to drop his unfriendly take-over bid of New England Wire and Cable. *Other People's Money* (1991, Warner Bros.).

Immortality and Mortality

see also DEATH AND DYING, ETERNITY, EXISTENCE, LIFE AND DEATH, LIVES AND LIVING

4982 IVAN IGOR: "My dear, why are you so pitifully afraid? Immortality has been the dream, the inspiration of mankind through the ages. And I am going to give you immortality." CHARLOTTE DUNCAN: "No. . . I've done nothing to hurt you. . . ." IGOR: "I have no desire to hurt you. You will always be beautiful. Think, my child. In a thousand years, you will be as lovely as you are now. Come. Come!" Mad sculptor **Lionel Atwill** can't understand **Fay Wray**'s ingratitude. She's trapped in the cellar of his museum and he's planning to turn her worthless body into a wax statue of Marie Antoinette. *Mystery of the Wax Museum* (1933, Warner Bros.).

4983 "I have the strength of a hundred men! I cannot die! I cannot be destroyed! I, Igor, will live forever!" **Bela Lugosi** shouts in exhilaration after scientist Lionel Atwill implants Lugosi's brain in the ample body of Frankenstein's monster. *The Ghost of Frankenstein* (1942, Universal).

4984 "And tomorrow morning, you will have won your beachhead on the shores of immortality." **George Sanders** predicts that Anne Baxter will become a major stage star with the opening of a new play. *All About Eve* (1950, 20th Century-Fox).

4985 "In my mind there is no difference between the magic rhythms of Bill Shakespeare's immortal verse and the major rhythms of Bill Robinson's immortal feet." Genius showman **Jack Buchanan** leads into a rousing rendition of "That's Entertainment" with Fred Astaire, Nanette Fabray and Oscar Levant. *The Band Wagon* (1953, MGM).

4986 "Once again man bestows immortality upon his fellow man." Nobel Prize Committee Chairman **Leo G. Carroll** announces the newest Nobel laureates. *The Prize* (1963, MGM).

4987 "Will you dedicate a poem to me? Maybe that will guarantee me a kind of immortality." Tom Conti is a charming drunken Irish poet who sponges off women. **E. Katherine Kerr** is one of the targets of his charms. He's on a speaking tour in New England when he meets Kelly McGillis, who decides he is worth saving. *Reuben, Reuben* (1983, 20th Century-Fox).

4988 "I'm Connor MacLeod. I was born in 1518 in the village of Glenfinnan on the shore of Loch Shul...and I'm immortal." Scotsman **Christopher Lambert** battles with his enemy Clancy Brown, the Kurgan, into the 20th century in Manhattan. *Highlander* (1986, GB-EMI, 20th Century-Fox).

4989 "You can't drown, you fool. You're immortal." **Sean Connery** gives Christopher Lambert the happy news. *Highlander* (1986, EMI-20th Century-Fox).

4990 "You should be happy to be alive, now you're asking for immortality." For Chicago Cubs fans, cop **Charles Durning**'s response to wounded Jay O. Sanders, who says as he's carried away on a stretcher, "I just don't want to die without seeing the Cubs win a pennant," is a cheap shot. *V.I. Warshawski* (1991, Hollywood-Buena Vista).

Impatience *see* PATIENCE AND IMPATIENCE

Imperialism *see* GOVERNMENTS

Imperfection *see* PERFECTION

Importance

see also AUTHORITIES, CONSEQUENCES, POWER, SIGNIFICANCE, WORTH AND VALUES

4991 "Sit in the moonlight and hold hands. A career leaves you empty. Do something really important." Disillusioned **Claudette Colbert** advises her secretary Helen Wood, who claims she wants to be just like boss-lady Colbert, saying, "My career means everything to me." *She Married Her Boss* (1935, Columbia).

4992 "I want to be the most important man in the world—a private in the United States Army." **Gene Kelly** delivers the patriotic but hardly credible line after he's learned some humility and sense of duty in this all-star extravaganza with an army camp setting. *Thousands Cheer* (1943, MGM).

4993 "Yesterday this would have meant so much to us. Now, it doesn't matter. It doesn't matter at all." Speaking glumly on a phone, **Gloria Grahame** is informed by the police that violent Humphrey Bogart, who has nearly strangled her in a rage, has been cleared of any involvement in

the murder of a hatcheck girl. *In a Lonely Place* (1950, Columbia).

4994 HAROLD MANN: "Our job is to keep the bomb at home and to apprehend the kidnappers and bring your son home safely." DR. ADDISON: "That's the order of their importance, isn't it? One, two, three. Tommy is number three." When terrorists, who want the formula for the atomic bomb, kidnap Lee Aaker, the son of nuclear physicist **Gene Barry**, the hard-nosed FBI agent in charge of the case, **Milburn Stone** lists his priorities. *The Atomic City* (1952, Paramount).

4995 "I now know the vital importance of being earnest." **Michael Redgrave** gets the last line and the title all at once. *The Importance of Being Earnest* (1952, GB, Two Cities-Rank).

4996 "A career is just fine, but it's no substitute for marriage. Don't you think a man is the most important thing in the world? A woman isn't a woman until she's been married and had children." **Debbie Reynolds** tells Frank Sinatra that her acting career is just something to do until Mr. Right comes along. *The Tender Trap* (1955, MGM).

4997 "Don't think I'm rude, but it doesn't matter to me what a critic says." Painter **John Forsythe** dismisses the criticism of a prospective buyer of his work. *The Trouble with Harry* (1955, Paramount).

4998 "What's more important, his life or your virtue?" **Donald Sutherland** induces nurse Jo Ann Pflug to cure temporarily impotent and suicidal Casanova dentist John Schuck, who has taken what he believes is poison, by making love to him. *M*A*S*H* (1970, 20th Century-Fox).

4999 "This is the most important thing to me besides you.... If I can't do this, then I'm not good for you and I'm not good for anybody." Musician **Robert De Niro** won't allow girlfriend Liza Minnelli's pregnancy to interfere with his quest to make it big as a saxophonist. *New York, New York* (1977, United Artists).

5000 "It doesn't matter. It doesn't matter what you are and what you aren't or what you think you might be. No matter what, I love you. I got to, you're the best thing I've ever done, you know." Loving father **Robert Viharo** is supportive and understanding of his son Alan Rosenberg, plagued by self-doubts regarding his sexuality. *Happy Birthday, Gemini* (1980, United Artists).

5001 "The way I figure it, there's only three people in the world that matter, Jesus Christ, Frank Sinatra and me." **Vincent Spano** proclaims a modern trinity. *Baby, It's You* (1983, Paramount).

5002 "What you do is more important than what you say. Your deeds are more important than your words." In other words, **James Wilby** is saying: "Actions speak louder than words." *Maurice* (1987, GB, Cinecom).

5003 "Chicks like her have one thing on their mind, and you don't make enough of it to matter to her." Cute tomboy **Mary Stuart Masterson**, with a crush on teen Eric Stoltz, warns him of mercenary Lea Thompson. *Some Kind of Wonderful* (1987, Paramount).

5004 JACK CRAWFORD: "Starling, when I told that sheriff we shouldn't talk in front of a woman, it really burned you up, didn't it? It was just smoke." CLARICE STARLING: "It matters, Mr. Crawford. Cops look at you to see how to act. It matters." While investigating a serial murder case at a West Virginia autopsy, FBI agent **Scott Glenn** shunts aside FBI trainee **Jodie Foster** in an obviously sexist manner. *The Silence of the Lambs* (1991, Orion).

Impossibilities *see* POSSIBILITIES AND IMPOSSIBILITIES

Impotency

see also POWER, SEX AND SEXUALITY, WEAKNESS

5005 "Unless that'll make you impotent." Newspaper reporter **Sally Field** offers to buy macho Paul Newman dinner. *Absence of Malice* (1981, Columbia).

5006 "I'm impotent. . . I can't get an erection in the presence of another person, so for all practical purposes, I'm impotent." **James Spader** tells Andie MacDowell something "personal," thus becoming a challenge she can't resist tackling. *sex, lies and videotape* (1989, Miramax).

Impressions

see also FORCE, INFLUENCES

5007 RICK: "That was some going over your men gave my place this afternoon. We just got it cleaned up in time to open." RENAULT: "I told Strasser we wouldn't find the letter here. But I told my men to be especially destructive. You know how that impresses the Germans." **Humphrey Bogart**'s cafe was torn apart by police prefect **Claude Rains**' men, looking for letters of transit. *Casablanca* (1942, Warner Bros.).

5008 "You know, Maude, someone meeting you for the first time, not knowing you were cracked, might get the wrong impression." **Rudy Vallee** knows his often-married sister Mary Astor is cracked. *The Palm Beach Story* (1942, Paramount).

5009 "It's like the first impression that's stamped in a coin. It isn't finished." **King Donovan** shows Kevin McCarthy and Dana Wynter a strange corpse-like figure, its smooth mannequin face only half-formed. *Invasion of the Body Snatchers* (1956, Allied Artists).

5010 "The extreme always seems to make an impression." Strange but appealing mental case **Christian Slater** does his best Jack Nicholson imitation as he leads Winona Ryder astray. *Heathers* (1989, New World).

Impulses

see also FORCE

5011 "The love impulse in man frequently reveals itself in terms of conflict." Quack psychiatrist **Fritz Feld** offers wacky Katharine Hepburn some useful information in understanding Cary Grant's behavior towards her. *Bringing Up Baby* (1938, RKO).

5012 "You can't shut out every decent impulse—and survive!" Desperately ill, destroyed **H.B. Warner** bitterly confronts his former business partner Edward Arnold and dies. *You Can't Take It with You* (1938, Columbia).

5013 "So sorry. But I had to leave suddenly. I was seized by an irresistible impulse." **Ben Gazarra** leaves a note for his lawyer James Stewart, fleeing the scene without paying the latter's fee. Ben uses as an excuse the legal hook that Stewart used to get Gazarra acquitted of murder. *Anatomy of a Murder* (1959, Columbia).

5014 "Spontaneity has its time and place." As they travel across country with another young couple, reserved and well-organized coed **Daphne Zuniga** snaps at John Cusack who has been lecturing her about doing everything by a timetable she's devised. When he accuses her of being repressed, Zuniga impulsively rips off her blouse and hangs out a window, yelling at a passing car of guys, whose mooning sparked the debate. *The Sure Thing* (1985, Embassy).

5015 "I had this impulse. . . I wanted to kiss your foot. It's nothing personal." Painter **Nick Nolte** confesses a possible fetish to his sometimes muse

Rosanna Arquette. "Life Lessons" segment from *New York Stories* (1989, Touchstone).

Incest *see* SEX AND SEXUALITY

Income *see* MONEY

Incompatibility

see also LOGIC, TOGETHERNESS

5016 JUDGE CARROLL: "What is it that makes you incompatible?" FLORENCE KEEFER: "Being married to each other." Divorce Judge **Madge Kennedy** asks a silly question and gets a smart answer from **Judy Holliday** who can't stand to live with husband Aldo Ray any more. *The Marrying Kind* (1952, Columbia).

5017 "I am fire, he is water. How can we ever meet?" Barabbas, portrayed by **Harry Guardino**, refers to Jesus Christ, portrayed by Jeffrey Hunter. *King of Kings* (1961, MGM).

5018 "You're a nice girl, Gloria, but you're not for me." Seven-year-old Puerto Rican boy **Juan Adames** sees no future with fiftyish Gena Rowlands, the former mobster's moll who is protecting him from the mobsters who murdered his father. *Gloria* (1980, Columbia).

5019 "Look, I'm American, you're a ghost, it would never work out." In a silly fantasy, **Steve Guttenberg** will be proven wrong. He and 200-year-old dead Daryl Hannah can find happiness together. *High Spirits* (1988, Tri-Star).

Incompetence

see also ABILITIES AND CAPABILITIES, FAILURES, KNOWLEDGE

5020 "I think I've underestimated you, Ned. You're using your incompetence as a defense." Assistant District Attorney **Ted Danson** belittles second-rate lawyer William Hurt, who with Kathleen Turner has murdered her husband Richard Crenna. *Body Heat* (1981, Warner Bros.).

5021 "The only time we doctors should accept death is when it's caused by our incompetence." During a lecture, brain surgeon **Steve Martin** makes a medical point that won't be popular with the AMA. *The Man with Two Brains* (1983, Warner Bros.).

5022 "I don't know enough to be incompetent." Nervous **Woody Allen** tries to mollify an outraged superior. *Shadows and Fog* (1992, Orion).

Independence and Dependence

see also DETERMINATION, FREEDOMS, INFLUENCES, JUDGMENTS

5023 TIGER KID: "Promise me that you'll never think of another man." RUBY CARTER: "That depends on you." Boxer **Roger Pryor** asks a great deal of nightclub entertainer **Mae West**. Pryor's not man enough to fully occupy her mind. *Belle of the Nineties* (1934, Paramount).

5024 "I'm free, white and twenty-one, and intend to work." **Ruby Keeler** defies her stuffy father Guy Kibbee, telling him that she intends to have a show business career whether he likes it or not. *Dames* (1934, Warner Bros.).

5025 "There's one thing I learned. Be independent! If you don't ask for things—if you don't let on you need things—pretty soon you don't need 'em." Bitter Deputy Sheriff **Wendell Corey** speaks of things, but everyone knows he means people. *The Rainmaker* (1956, Paramount).

5026 "I'll be no man's slave and no man's whore." Title character **Lana Clarkson** doesn't sound too convincing. Of course, none of her lines sound convincing. *Barbarian Queen* (1984, Vestron).

5027 "What am I gonna do if I don't have you to do things for?" After **Goldie Hawn**'s husband Ed Harris goes off to war, she finds diversions with work on the swing shift and 4-F musician Kurt Russell. *Swing Shift* (1984, Warner Bros.).

5028 "I do what I want when I want. I'm an independent woman." Police detective **Melanie Griffith** enters the world of Hasidic Jews in New York City, where independent women don't exist. *A Stranger Among Us* (1992, Buena Vista).

Indictments

see also CRIMES AND CRIMINALS, LAWS, LAWYERS

5029 "Every event shown in this film is based on actual experience. All the characters are portraits of actual persons, living or dead. This is an indictment of government. What are you going to do about it?" Prelude to the movie. *Quick Millions* (1931, Fox).

5030 "This picture is an indictment of gang rule in America and of the callous indifference of the government to this constantly increasing menace." We trust the indictment mentioned in the introduction to the movie is still outstanding today. *Scarface* (1932, United Artists).

5031 "The Big Three doesn't give a damn about people. . . . They should be indicted for manslaughter." Maverick automobile maker Preston Tucker, portrayed by **Jeff Bridges**, accuses the American automobile industry of "criminal neglect." *Tucker: The Man and His Dreams* (1988, Paramount).

Indifference *see* CARES AND CARING, DIFFERENCES

Indigestion *see* FOOD AND EATING

Individualism

see also CHARACTER, ECCENTRICITIES, IDENTITIES, ORIGINALITY, PERSONALITIES, SELF

5032 "You're a great apostle of rugged individualism." Death-wishing poet **Leslie Howard** admires "mad-dog" killer Humphrey Bogart. *The Petrified Forest* (1936, Warner Bros.).

5033 "Let me warn you, I say what I think. I'm a complete individualist. I'm against communism, capitalism, fascism, nazism. I'm against everything and everybody. I hate my fellow man and he hates me." Distraught musician and misanthrope **Burgess Meredith** gets up on his soapbox and makes a pronouncement. Merle Oberson observes, "Sounds rather amusing." *That Uncertain Feeling* (1942, United Artists).

Industry *see* BUSINESS AND COMMERCE

Infatuation *see* LOVE AND LOVERS

Inferiority *see* SUPERIORITY AND INFERIORITY

Infidelities

see also HUSBANDS, HUSBANDS AND WIVES, LOYALTIES, PROMISCUITY, SEX AND SEXUALITY, TRUST, WIVES

5034 SIBYL CHASE: "I bet she was. I'll bet she was unfaithful every five minutes." ELYOT CHASE: "It would take a far more concentrated woman than Amanda to be unfaithful every five minutes." New wife **Una Merkel** and **Robert Montgomery** disagree about the extent of his first wife Norma Shearer's infidelities. *Private Lives* (1931, MGM).

5035 "What most wives fail to realize is that their husband's philandering has nothing whatever to do with them." **John Halliday** maintains that a man's adultery is in no way a function of his love or lack of same for his wife. **Sidney Blackmer** makes

about the same point in the musical remake. They may be correct but it doesn't lessen the hurt and heartbreak of the wife. *The Philadelphia Story* (1940, MGM); *High Society* (1956, MGM).

5036 "What you are doing is wrong. . . I beg of you to see no more of this woman." Wheelchair bound **Halliwell Hobbes** begs his son Laurence Olivier to end his adulterous affair with married Vivien Leigh. The scene was added for U.S. audiences at the insistence of the Breen office. It was later cut. *That Hamilton Woman* aka: *Lady Hamilton* (1941, United Artists).

5037 "My affair with Maud Charters lasted exactly seven and a half weeks and she cried all the time. . . . If you wish to make an inventory of my sex life I think it only fair to tell you that you've left out several episodes. I shall consult my diary and give you a complete list after lunch." Writer **Rex Harrison** corrects his second wife Constance Cummings about the extent of his love affairs. *Blithe Spirit* (1945, GB, Two Cities-Cineguild).

5038 "Your idea of fidelity is not having more than one man in bed at the same time." **Dirk Bogarde** angrily accuses Julie Christie of being amorally promiscuous. *Darling* (1965, GB, Anglo-Amalgamated).

5039 "Two people can sleep around but stay together. We all like a change. That's what vacations are for." Tyrannical studio head **Christopher Plummer** argues to star Natalie Wood that just because her husband Robert Redford is bisexual is no reason to break up the marriage. *Inside Daisy Clover* (1965, Warner Bros.).

5040 STEVE BLACKBURN: "I have never been unfaithful to my wife. . . in the same city." VICKI ALLESSIO: "Where is your wife now?" STEVE: "Out of town." Married American insurance executive **George Segal** and divorced British fashion designer **Glenda Jackson** begin a bittersweet affair. *A Touch of Class* (1973, GB, Avco Embassy).

5041 "This is your great winter romance, isn't it? Your last roar of passion before you settle into your emeritus years. Is that what's left for me? Is that my share? She gets the winter passion, and I get the dotage? What am I supposed to do? Am I supposed to sit at home knitting and purling while you slink back like some penitent drunk? . . ." **Beatrice Straight** kicks husband William Holden out of their home when he confesses to an affair with Faye Dunaway. *Network* (1976, United Artists).

5042 "Well, I'm old-fashioned. I don't believe in extramarital relationships. I think people should mate for life, like pigeons or Catholics." **Woody Allen** champions the cause of fidelity. *Manhattan* (1979, United Artists).

5043 "We met every Tuesday at the motel. He said if we skipped lunch we'd have more time. . . to be really close." Housewife **Joan Allen** describes her affair with murdered womanizing dentist Joe Mantegna, who was too cheap to even feed her first. *Compromising Positions* (1985, Paramount).

5044 "Fool around. It's a biological function." Yuppie **Ben Masters** advises lawyer Daniel Stern, who is faithful to his wife, to have an affair. *Key Exchange* (1985, 20th Century-Fox).

5045 "What would Emily Post say about adultery with a philosophy professor at a Holiday Inn while your wife is in the hospital having her ovaries removed?" **Betty Buckley** confronts her ex-husband Ian Holm, about a past transgression. Holm is now married to that fiftyish philosophy professor, Gena Rowlands. *Another Woman* (1988, Orion).

5046 "So they drove behind a dumpster. . . in our car. . . that I made payments on by sweating my ass off. . . so he can sweat her ass off inside it. . . that car was rocking like an out-of-whack washing machine, and I went crazy. . . I decided to kill her. . . but I couldn't. . . I love her. . . so I shaved her head. . . and now see if he wants her." Distraught **Tom McBeath** describes for his lawyer how his wife's infidelity led her to suing him for divorce. *Cousins* (1989, Paramount).

5047 "Tom, if you are going to tell me about your infidelities, I will have to leave you forever." **Isabella Rossellini** prevents husband William Petersen from confessing he's cheating with Sean Young. *Cousins* (1989, Paramount).

5048 "She's on someone else's root. I can smell it on her." Junkie cop **William Baldwin** confides his suspicions of his wife's infidelity to his corrupt partner Richard Gere, who has been bedding Baldwin's wife. *Internal Affairs* (1990, Paramount).

5049 "I suppose it's fair to say that infidelity made me what I am today." In voice-over, **Jack Nicholson**, a private investigator, specializing in gathering information to be used in divorce cases, delivers the movie's first line. *The Two Jakes* (1990, Paramount).

5050 "I'm looking for a straightforward fuck. . . I'm strictly a one-man adulteress." Charming and sincere ingenue **Patsy Kensit** swears her peculiar kind of fidelity. *Twenty-One* (1991, GB, Triton).

Inflation *see* BUSINESS AND COMMERCE, BUYING AND SELLING, MONEY, WEALTH AND RICHES, WORTH AND VALUES

Influences

see also ABILITIES AND CAPABILITIES, AUTHORITIES, POWER

5051 "There's no such thing as a good influence, Mr. Gray. All influence is immoral." **George Sanders** makes another of his indefensible claims to his young protégé Hurd Hatfield. At another time, Sanders tells Hatfield, "A good influence is the worst influence of all." *The Picture of Dorian Gray* (1945, MGM).

5052 "The Force can have a strong influence on the weak-minded." **Alec Guinness** assures young Mark Hamill that the Force is a powerful weapon. *Star Wars* (1977, 20th Century-Fox).

5053 "When the two of you are together, there are tremendous influences." Spiritualist **Joie Lee** offers an interpretation of the relationship of constantly bickering B.J. Spalding and Eszter Balint. *Bail Jumper* (1990, Angelika).

Information and Informers

see also INTELLIGENCE, KNOWLEDGE, NEWS AND NEWSPAPERS

5054 "If anyone turns yellow and squeals, my gun's gonna speak its piece." **Edward G. Robinson** plays Ceasar Enrico Bardello in this classic melodrama of the rise and fall of a big city gangster. *Little Caesar* (1930, Warner Bros.).

5055 "It's easy work for an informer to be swearing oaths." Informer **Victor McLaglen** tries to convince IRA officers that protesting Donald Meek is the informer. *The Informer* (1935, RKO).

5056 "I am an informer, not a hypocrite." Stool pigeon **Gene Lockhart** assures the police that he's not a member of Charles Boyer's criminal gang. *Algiers* (1938, United Artists).

5057 "I want some facts—any kind of facts!" American newspaper publisher **Harry Davenport** sends crime reporter Joel McCrea to cover the events in Europe that are leading toward a world war. *Foreign Correspondent* (1940, United Artists).

5058 "I won't tell you what I personally thought when I read the letter. It's the duty of counsel to defend his client, not to convict her even in his own mind. I don't want you to tell me anything but what is needed to save your neck." Having violated his professional ethics by arranging for the purchase of an incriminating letter written by his married client Bette Davis, lawyer **James Stephenson** now knows she's not only guilty of murder but that the victim was her lover. *The Letter* (1940, Warner Bros.).

5059 "You know what I do with squealers? I let 'em have it in the belly so that they can move around and think it over." Moronic and maniacal gunman Tommy Udo, brilliantly portrayed by **Richard Widmark** in his film debut, giggles at his cleverness and viciousness to wheelchair bound Mildred Dunnock before pushing her down a flight of stairs to her death. *Kiss of Death* (1947, 20th Century-Fox).

5060 "Some people peddle apples, lumber, lamb chops. I peddle information." Informer **Thelma Ritter** is proud of her trade. *Pickup on South Street* (1952, 20th Century-Fox).

5061 "The canary could sing but he couldn't fly." Double-ugly-pug, union thug **Tony Galento** makes a little joke about a "squealer" who was thrown to his death from a roof. *On the Waterfront* (1954, Columbia).

5062 "All I want to know is, is he D and D or is he a canary?" Crooked longshoreman union boss **Lee J. Cobb** asks Rod Steiger if his brother Marlon Brando can be trusted to play "deaf and dumb" when he testifies before the crime commission. *On the Waterfront* (1954, Columbia).

5063 "Let me tell you what stooling is. Stooling is when you rat on your friends, the guys you're with." **Rod Steiger** tries to talk some sense into his brother Marlon Brando who is thinking of testifying at a Crime Commission investigating corruption in the longshoreman union. *On the Waterfront* (1954, Columbia).

5064 "The kid who tells on another kid is a dead kid." Snarling teen **Matt Dillon** keeps his gang of frustrated and alienated adolescents in line. *Over the Edge* (1979, Orion-Warner Bros.).

5065 "You stop sending me information, and you start getting me some!" **Michael Douglas** wants young stock broker Charlie Sheen to not bother him with prospectus and analysis; he wants inside information. *Wall Street* (1987, 20th Century-Fox).

5066 "The most valuable commodity I know of is information. . . I don't throw darts at a board. I bet on sure things. Read Sun Tzu—The Art of War: 'Every battle is won before the war is ever fought.'

Think about it. . . . Give me guys who are poor, smart and hungry—and no feelings. Win a few, you lose a few, but you keep fighting. And if you need a friend, get a dog. . . ." **Michael Douglas** instructs his protégé Charlie Sheen. *Wall Street* (1987, 20th Century-Fox).

5067 "Those who tell, don't know. Those who know, won't tell." It's **Ossie Davis**' way of telling a policeman that no one who knows will come forth as a witness to kids opening a fire hydrant and flooding a car. *Do the Right Thing* (1989, Universal).

5068 GUILDENSTERN: "There's something they're not telling us." ROSENCRANTZ: "What?" GUILDENSTERN: "There's something they're not telling us!" **Tim Roth**, who knows and understands little of what's going on at the Danish court, snaps at his friend **Gary Oldman**, who knows and understands even less. *Rosencrantz and Guildenstern Are Dead* (1990, GB, Cinecom).

Ingenuity *see* INTELLIGENCE

Injuries *see* HARM, HURT AND HURTING

Injustice *see* JUSTICE

Innocence

see also CRIMES AND CRIMINALS, GUILT, JUDGMENTS, JUSTICE, LAWS, NAÏVETÉ, PURITY, SIMPLICITY

5069 "At this solemn moment in the presence of this tribunal which is the representative of human justice, before you gentlemen of the jury, before France, before the whole world—I swear that Dreyfus is innocent! By the forty years of work, by all that I have won, by all that I have written to spread the spirit of France, I swear that Dreyfus is innocent! May all that melt away—may my name perish—if Dreyfus be not innocent! He is innocent!" Emile Zola, portrayed by **Paul Muni**, impassionately addresses the jury in his libel trial for accusing the General Staff of framing Capt. Alfred Dreyfus (played by Joseph Schildkraut) with the charge of treason, merely because he was a Jew. *The Life of Emile Zola* (1937, Warner Bros.).

5070 "You're the ones who killed him. You're the ones who stirred up all the hatred and prejudice down here. . . . You took the life of an innocent man. The kind of thing you've done is never over. It will stay with you as long as you live." **Gloria Dickson** rails at prosecuting attorney Claude Rains and newspaper reporter Allyn Joslyn after a mob lynches school teacher Edward Norris. The two show no remorse for railroading an innocent man. *They Won't Forget* (1937, Warner Bros.).

5071 "We are not alone. Every minute, every second, out there. . . thousands are dying, or sent to die, who have done no wrong." Country English doctor **Paul Muni** comforts Jane Bryan on the eve of their execution for a crime they did not commit, the murder of Muni's wife, Flora Robson. *We Are Not Alone* (1939, Warner Bros.).

5072 "That won't prevent you from going to the hot seat." Corrupt police detective **Laird Cregar** admits that he knows Victor Mature is innocent of the murder of Carol Landis. *I Wake Up Screaming* (1942, 20th Century-Fox).

5073 "You don't have to get [morally] rigid about it. It was perfectly innocent, I assure you." **Claudette Colbert** scolds her husband Joel McCrea after accepting $700 from elderly Robert Dudley to pay off their debts. *The Palm Beach Story* (1942, Paramount).

5074 "Don't you know I can see a great deal farther than you can? I can see intangible things. For example, innocence." Blind pianist **Vaughan Glaser** tells his niece Priscilla Lane that he believes that Robert Cummings, who has escaped from the police, still wearing handcuffs, is innocent of the charges of sabotage and murder made against him. *Saboteur* (1942, Universal).

5075 "How singularly innocent I look this morning. Have you ever seen such candid eyes?" Writer **Clifton Webb** is arrogantly pleased with himself while dressing. He shares his pearls of wisdom with police detective Dana Andrews, whom Webb considers less worthy than swine. *Laura* (1944, 20th Century-Fox).

5076 "The mind isn't everything. The heart can see deeper sometimes. . . I couldn't feel this way toward a man who was bad, who had committed murder. I couldn't feel the pain for someone who was evil." **Ingrid Bergman** eloquently counters her mentor Michael Chekhov's impatient view with her "woman's talk," believing that her lover Gregory Peck is innocent of any crime. She reckons her intuition is stronger than Chekhov's reasoning. *Spellbound* (1945, Selznick-United Artists).

5077 "We the jury in the above entitled action find the defendant, Lawrence Ballentine, not guilty." Court clerk **Milton Parsons** reads the jury's decision in the murder case against philandering stockbroker Robert Young, accused of killing his wife. *They Won't Believe Me* (1947, RKO).

5078 "Up here, every man claims to be innocent. But the prisoners are the hardest judges, and they believe we have only two men who don't belong here: Tomek Zaleska and Frank Wiecek." Talking to Chicago reporter James Stewart, Statesville prison warden **Richard Bishop**, speaks of prisoners George Tyne and Richard Conte, sentenced to life imprisonment for killing a cop eleven years earlier. *Call Northside 777* (1948, 20th Century-Fox).

5079 "Sooner or later, the innocence of your daughter cannot be respected if the family is going to continue." Truck driver **Burt Lancaster** tries to be practical with Anna Magnani, who is obsessed with protecting her daughter Marisa Pavan from men. *The Rose Tattoo* (1955, Paramount).

5080 "I was the perfect dupe. I believed everything anybody ever told me. I was full of the highest hopes and the most unbelievable innocence." Ship's Doctor **Oskar Werner** talks of the emptiness of his life before and after disillusionment. *Ship of Fools* (1965, Columbia).

5081 "Communism. Capitalism. It's the innocents who get slaughtered." **Richard Burton** sums up the film's despair. *The Spy Who Came in from the Cold* (1965, GB, Paramount).

5082 "When you've known innocence, when you've seen it sleep at your side, you never quite forget it. It changes you." Mythical nymphomaniac **Jeanne Moreau** wanders the seas searching for her seaman lover. *The Sailor from Gibraltar* (1967, GB, Woodfall-Lopert).

5083 "I try to save the innocent, but there aren't any. . . I just try to help people reveal their true characters." **Philippe Noiret**, police chief in a French West African town, confesses his weakness as a law-enforcement officer. *Coup de Torchon* (1982, Fr., Quartet Films).

5084 "There is no aphrodisiac like innocence." Poet **Tom Conti** confides to his recorder as he thinks of young Kelly McGillis. *Reuben, Reuben* (1983, 20th Century-Fox).

5085 "Nobody is completely innocent—we all sin." Warden's wife **Diane Keaton** shows compassion for brothers Mel Gibson and Matthew Modine, sentenced to hang for murdering a grocer during a holdup. She later proves her point by helping them escape, accompanying them in their flight, because she has fallen for Gibson. *Mrs. Soffel* (1984, MGM-United Artists).

5086 "She's an innocent. She's a slate that hasn't been touched, except by God. She was happy with us." Mother Superior **Anne Bancroft** speaks of young nun Meg Tilly to psychiatrist Jane Fonda. Bancroft is willing to accept that Tilly has had an immaculate conception. Not buying that, Fonda has been appointed by a Canadian court to determine why Tilly killed a baby to which she gave birth. *Agnes of God* (1985, Columbia).

5087 "I don't think a lot of people realize how important innocence is to innocent people." **Sam Neill** speaks of the faith in their innocence that kept him and his wife Meryl Streep going through the ordeal of accusations and trials when Streep is charged with murdering their nine-week-old baby. Streep claims a dingo stole the baby whose body was never found. *Cry in the Dark* (1988, Warner Bros.).

Innuendos

see also COMPLAINTS, GESTURES

5088 "That's what I always say. Love flies out the door when money comes innuendo." **Groucho Marx** delivers his wisecrack to Maxine Castle. *Monkey Business* (1931, Paramount).

5089 "You seem to be a man full of innuendoes." It's **Claudette Colbert**'s heavily ironic reaction when American millionaire Gary Cooper lets out an ear-piercing warwhoop in discovering that she has not remarried on the rebound nor found anyone else to love since their divorce. *Bluebeard's Eighth Wife* (1938, Paramount).

5090 "Daddy, do I look sexy by innuendo?" Cute eleven-year-old **Natalie Wood** purrs to her father Fred MacMurray during a family crisis. *Father Was a Fullback* (1949, 20th Century-Fox).

Insanity and Sanity

5091 "Crazy, am I? Well, see whether I'm crazy or not. . . I have discovered the great ray that first brought life into the world." **Colin Clive** rants and raves when his former professor Edward van Sloan scoffs at his ambition to create a living being. *Frankenstein* (1931, Universal).

5092 "Poor little crazy fellow, sitting there alone, with the Angel of Death beside him." Prostitute **Mae Clarke** upbraids reporters for their heartless indifference to the suffering of George E. Stone. The latter is but hours away from being executed at the Chicago Criminal Courts building for a crime he didn't commit. *The Front Page* (1931, United Artists).

5093 "Mad? Is one who has solved the secret of life to be considered mad? Life! Created in the laboratory! . . . Living, growing tissue. Life! That moves, pulsates, and demands food for its continued

growth! Ha! You shudder in horror. So did I the first time. . . but what are a few lives when weighed in the balance against the achievement of biological science? Think of it! I have lifted the veil! I have created life!" Fay Wray brings on his tirade when she calls mad scientist **Lionel Atwill** mad. *The Vampire Bat* (1933, Majestic).

5094 ALEXANDER ANDREWS: "Do you love her?" PETER WARNE: "Yes, but don't hold it against me—I'm a little screwy myself." Wealthy **Walter Connolly** gets out-of-work newspaperman **Clark Gable** to admit that he loves the former's zany daughter Claudette Colbert. *It Happened One Night* (1934, Columbia).

5095 "Owen, I was aiming at myself. He grabbed the gun away from me and shot me. That's the final irony; killed by a lunatic." Broadway producer **John Barrymore** suffers a flesh wound in a struggle with his associate Roscoe Karns. *Twentieth Century* (1934, Columbia).

5096 BUTLER: "It's all a simple masquerade, you must know your master like a book." JAMES BUCHANAN: "Do you think I'm out of my mind?" BUTLER: "I'm hoping for the best, sir." Automobile tycoon James Buchanan, played by **Herbert Marshall**, is so taken by out-of-work Jean Arthur that when she supposes he's also jobless and suggests that they take jobs as cook and butler in the home of retired mobster Leo Carrillo, he agrees and takes lessons in how to "buttle" from his own butler. *If You Could Only Cook* (1935, Columbia).

5097 "When a man is denied his great love, he goes mad." **Bela Lugosi** advances the theory that Edgar Allan Poe's potential for greatness was destroyed with the loss of Elenore. *The Raven* (1935, Universal).

5098 "Why everybody in Mandrake Falls is pixilated—except us." Eccentric **Margaret Seddon** gives testimony at the sanity hearing for Gary Cooper. *Mr. Deeds Goes to Town* (1936, Columbia).

5099 "Mr. Deeds, there has been a great deal of damaging testimony given against you. Your behavior, to say the least, has been most strange. But, in the opinion of the court, you are not only sane but you're the sanest man that ever walked into this courtroom." Judge **H.B. Warner** delivers his verdict in the sanity hearing of Gary Cooper. *Mr. Deeds Goes to Town* (1936, Columbia).

5100 "What's that light? There's somebody out there holding a flashlight! Somebody's watching. They've got no call to watch. I'm the one that watches! Eyes. Eyes. Hundreds of eyes. Back of each tree. Thousands of eyes. What's that? Like the sound of a big wall falling over into the sea. Everything's slipping out from under me. Can't you feel it? Starting in slow and then hundreds of miles per hour. There's a wind in my ears—a terrible rushin' wind. Everything's going past me like telegraph poles. Everything's going backward. Everything I've never seen, faster and faster back to the day I was born. I can see it coming, the day I was born." As the police close in on psychopathic killer **Robert Montgomery**, he becomes completely unhinged. *Night Must Fall* (1937, MGM).

5101 "Listen, before I knew you I disliked you intensely. When I met you, I disliked you intensely. Even now I dislike you intensely. That was the sensible, sane portion of me. But there's an insane portion of me that gets a little violent every time I think of you." Newspaperman **Henry Fonda** confesses a reluctant attraction for madcap society girl Barbara Stanwyck. *The Mad Miss Manton* (1938, RKO).

5102 "I'm going crazy. I'm standing here solidly, on my own two hands, and going crazy." **Katharine Hepburn** is a bit confused, but not crazy. *The Philadelphia Story* (1940, MGM).

5103 "Hysteria is a kind of psychic bellyache brought on by worry. The victim runs this way and that way to get out from under. He invents escapes. He invents disguises. You've seen the most effective disguise of them all. When everything is too bad, he invents a disguise so effective he doesn't know himself. Then, we say the man is crazy." Doctor **Claude Rains** teaches his student Robert Cummings about mental disorders. Rains should know, his wife went mad, his daughter is well on the way, and he's not as stable as he seems—but then few people are in the town of Kings Row. *Kings Row* (1941, Warner Bros.).

5104 DR. LAWRENCE: "Sometimes I think you're mad!" DR. RIGGS: "I am! So was Archimedes, Galileo, Newton, Pasteur, Lister and all the others who dared to dream! Fifty years ago, a man was mad to think of anaesthesia... the idea of operating on the brain was madness. Today we hold a human heart in our hands and watch it beat! Who can tell what tomorrow's madness may be." **Samuels Hinds** marvels at the plans of crazed scientist **Lionel Atwill**, who dreams of creating a race of electrical supermen. *Man Made Monster* (1941, Universal).

5105 "I suppose you think I'm nuts. But if you think you're getting married with my rock, you're nuts." When corrupt politician **Brian Donlevy** sees how it is between his fiancée Veronica Lake and his most trusted henchman Alan Ladd, he gives them his blessing, but takes back his engagement ring. *The Glass Key* (1942, Paramount).

5106 "Sharing his madness because there's grandeur in it." **Helen Walker** professes her love for mysterious, handsome young scientist Nils Asther, who in reality is a 90-year-old. He has discovered a surgical procedure for preserving his youth. *The Man in Half Moon Street* (1944, Paramount).

5107 VIRGINIA MOORE: "But you said you were crazy about me." NEAL GORDON: "Not that much." **Gail Russell** is baffled when **Alan Ladd** turns her over to the police, for bumping off his buddy. *Calcutta* (1946, Paramount).

5108 "One of our young ladies is insane. Very intelligent, but insane." Psychiatrist **Lew Ayres** has to discover which of the two twins, played by Olivia de Havilland, is the psycho. *The Dark Mirror* (1946, Universal).

5109 "You wouldn't think a woman would marry two insane men in one lifetime." Both George Macready and Glenn Ford are a bit insane, so title character **Rita Hayworth** did it. *Gilda* (1946, Columbia).

5110 "Maybe he's only a little crazy, like painters or composers or some of those men in Washington." Macy's toy Department Manager **Philip Tonge** hopes for the best when Edmund Gwenn, who has been hired as the department store's Santa Claus, insists he's the real Santa Claus. *Miracle on 34th Street* (1947, 20th Century-Fox).

5111 "I remembered once reading in a book that long ago they used to put insane people into pits of snakes. I think they figured that something which might drive normal people insane might shock an insane person back to sanity." Mental patient **Olivia de Havilland**, confined to a hellish institution, sounds normal in these lines. *The Snake Pit* (1948, 20th Century-Fox).

5112 "Hooligans—they're just like left-handed pitchers, all have a screw loose somewhere." Master criminal **Sam Jaffe** disapproves of thug Sterling Hayden. *The Asphalt Jungle* (1950, MGM).

5113 "Psychopaths sell like hot cakes." Screenwriter **William Holden** suggests that he and Nancy Olsen collaborate on a screenplay featuring a troubled soul. *Sunset Boulevard* (1950, Paramount).

5114 "Life, which can be strangely mercurial, had taken pity on Norma Desmond. The dream she had clung to so desperately had enfolded her." The corpse of **William Holden** narrates the fate of silent screen star Gloria Swanson. After she shoots and kills Holden, she goes completely bonkers, believing that the assembled reporters, police and cameramen are part of her return to the screen as a major motion picture star. *Sunset Boulevard* (1950, Paramount).

5115 "Somewhere in your blood there's a crazy bug. Get a cure or you'll get us all killed." Gang leader **Paul Stewart** orders psychopath Jack Webb to get well. *Appointment with Danger* (1951, Paramount).

5116 "A madman who almost wrecked it [the movie industry], a butcher who stole everything but the pig's whistle." Paid mourner and would-be director **Barry Sullivan** adds his comments to the eulogy for a ruthless movie producer, unaware that standing next to him at the grave site is the deceased's son, Kirk Douglas. *The Bad and the Beautiful* (1952, MGM).

5117 "What kind of fruitcake are you? Why do we have to be above the crowd? Why not part of the crowd?" **Jack Lemmon** is flabbergasted by Judy Holliday's profligacy. *It Should Happen to You* (1954, Columbia).

5118 "You think I'm mad, but you won't be able to explain away your death on the 28th of the month so easily." Playful wizard **Niall MacGinnis** threatens skeptical American psychic Dana Andrews. *Curse of the Demon* aka: *Night of the Demon* (1956, GB, Columbia).

5119 "Madness! Madness!" British POW doctor **James Donald** has the film's final words, as he watches the deaths of Alec Guinness, William Holden and Sessue Hayakawa, and the destruction of the accursed title bridge. *The Bridge on the River Kwai* (1957, GB, Columbia).

5120 NORMAN BATES: "We all go a little mad sometimes, haven't you?" MARION CRANE: "Yes, sometimes just one time can be enough." Psychopath **Anthony Perkins** makes seemingly innocent small talk with **Janet Leigh**, who impulsively has run off with $40,000 of her employer's money. *Psycho* (1960, Paramount).

5121 "Have you ever been inside one of those places? The laughter and the tears and the cruel eyes studying you." **Anthony Perkins** asks Janet Leigh if she's ever visited a lunatic asylum. *Psycho* (1960, Paramount).

5122 "I like you too much not to say it: you've got everything, except one thing—madness. A man needs a little madness, or else. . . he never dares cut the rope and be free." Gregarious Greek **Anthony Quinn** advises English writer Alan Bates to take some chances and live. *Zorba the Greek* (1964, GB, 20th Century-Fox).

5123 STANLEY MOON: "You're a nutcake." GEORGE SPIGGOT: "They said the same of Jesus, Galileo, . . ." STANLEY: "They said the same of a lot of nutcakes, too." Short order cook **Dudley Moore** questions the sanity of a very proper British Satan, Peter Cook. *Bedazzled* (1967, GB, 20th Century-Fox).

5124 "You probably think I'm crazy, but I'm not. I'm colorful: that's what happens to you when you live ten years alone in Bolivia." Crazy old coot **Strother Martin** makes a distinction for his new hired guards Paul Newman and Robert Redford. *Butch Cassidy and the Sundance Kid* (1969, 20th Century-Fox).

5125 "No sane man would wish to fly. Therefore wishing to stop cannot be insane. . . . Anyone who wants to get out of combat isn't really crazy, so I can't ground him." Employing if-then logic, military physician **Jack Gilford** sadly gives airman Alan Arkin a dose of Catch 22, when the latter tries to use an insanity argument to get out of flying any more missions during World War II. *Catch 22* (1970, Paramount).

5126 "Good morning, Mr. Beale. They tell me you're a madman." Powerful conglomerate head **Ned Beatty** seems like a messenger from God to mentally disturbed TV news anchorman Peter Finch. The latter has announced his intention of committing suicide on his low-rated show. *Network* (1976, MGM-United Artists).

5127 "They're trying to rearrange the way I think. They're trying to drive me mad." Troubled Hollywood actress Frances Farmer, convincingly portrayed by **Jessica Lange**, complains of the harsh treatment she receives in a mental facility to which she has been committed. *Frances* (1982, Universal).

5128 "They're a nation of anxious people, and they could do nothing individually, so they went mad *en masse*." British World War II POW **Tom Conti** gives his opinion of the behavior of the Japanese people. *Merry Christmas, Mr. Lawrence* (1983, Japan/GB, Universal).

5129 EVE: "You're a lunatic." MICKEY: "That's why you chose me." Ex-streetwalker, now bar owner, **Lesley Anne Warren** and pathological liar **Keith Carradine** are about to take a chance of finding happiness together. *Choose Me* (1984, Island Alive).

5130 "You're a lunatic and the church needs lunatics. The problem is they don't know how to survive. I do!" Compromising priest **Jack Lemmon** tells revolutionary young deacon Zeljko Ivanek that he can learn valuable lessons for succeeding in the priesthood from Lemmon. *Mass Appeal* (1984, Universal).

5131 DETECTIVE MOLINARI: "You think that brings the crazies out?" WES BLOCK: "No, they're always out." Police officers **Dan Hedaya** and **Clint Eastwood** discuss the effect of the moon on crime. *Tightrope* (1984, Warner Bros.).

5132 "Why, you're just as perfectly sane as anyone walking the streets of Hazelhurst, Mississippi." **Jessica Lange** reassures her nutzy sister Sissy Spacek, who is charged with the attempted murder of her husband. *Crimes of the Heart* (1986, De Laurentiis).

5133 "You're not trying to draw psycho pension. You really are crazy!" Police detective **Danny Glover** prevents his wild new partner Mel Gibson from eating a bullet from his own gun. *Lethal Weapon* (1987, Warner Bros.).

5134 "Where the hell did you get him: Psychos-R-Us?" Mobster **Ed O'Ross** questions Mitchell Ryan about weird mercenary Gary Busey, who has just proved his loyalty and ability to withstand pain by allowing Ryan to burn his arm with a cigarette lighter. *Lethal Weapon* (1987, Warner Bros.).

5135 "Well, I thought I was mad but people on the outside are just as crazy." Asylum escapee **Dan Aykroyd** impersonates a shrink on a radio call-in show. At the end of the movie, Aykroyd tells loony con man Walter Matthau, "Becker, there are worse things than being crazy." *The Couch Trip* (1988, Orion).

5136 REGINALD KINCAID: "Thank you, gentlemen, I am touched." DR. JOHN WATSON: "I can vouch for that." Actor **Michael Caine**, posing as Sherlock Holmes, the imaginary creation of genius **Ben Kingsley**, as Dr. Watson, is toasted as "the world's greatest detective" in a pub. *Without a Clue* (1988, Orion).

5137 "I ain't crazy!" It's the forthright campaign slogan of eccentric Louisiana politician Earl Long, portrayed by **Paul Newman.** *Blaze* (1989, Touchstone-Buena Vista).

5138 "Until I heard the Voice, I never done a crazy thing in my whole life." It's part of **Kevin Costner**'s opening narration. *Field of Dreams* (1989, Universal).

5139 "I'm pitching to Shoeless Joe Jackson. . . . Do you think I'm crazy?" Iowa farmer **Kevin Costner** somehow has gotten mixed up in the return of the spirits of the Black Sox players. It's a fantasy, so why should anyone think he's crazy? *Field of Dreams* (1989, Universal).

5140 "I'm the only one who can save you! Your whole family's insane." **Dylan McDermott** states the obvious to Suzy Amis. *Twister* (1990, Orion).

5141 "He's insane. In a well-organized society, he'd be institutionalized by now." Producer **George Dzundza** proclaims to screenwriter Jeff Fahey that John Huston-like director Clint Eastwood is psychologically unbalanced. *White Hunter, Black Heart* (1990, Orion).

5142 "My wife is going off the deep end. A short trip for her." Manhattan butcher **George Dzundza** shares his concerns for his lovely young wife, strange clairvoyant Demi Moore, with neighborhood psychiatrist Jeff Daniels. *The Butcher's Wife* (1991, Paramount).

5143 DEE: "Do you ever feel you're just this far from feeling hysterical 24 hours a day?" JANE: "Honey, half the people feel they're close to being hysterical 24 hours a day, the other half are hysterical 24 hours a day." Secretary **Mary-Louise Parker** shares her concerns with a friend **Alfre Woodard** who doesn't offer reassurances. *Grand Canyon* (1991, 20th Century-Fox).

5144 "Ah robbed the cradle and fell into Hell. Ah must be crazy." **Laura Dern** is remorseful after she allows curious 13-year-old Lukas Haas to explore her body and cause her to have an orgasm. *Rambling Rose* (1991, Seven Arts/New Line).

5145 "You've always been crazy. This is just the first chance you've ever had to really express yourself." **Susan Sarandon** assures her friend Geena Davis that she always had potential for weirdness. *Thelma & Louise* (1991, Pathe/MGM).

5146 "Does Elvis talk to you? Does he tell you to do things? Do you see spots?" Valley girl **Kristy Swanson** is skeptical when mysterious vampire slayer trainer Donald Sutherland tells her that she's "the Chosen One." It is her destiny to hunt down vampires and drive wooden stakes through their hearts. *Buffy, the Vampire Slayer* (1992, 20th Century-Fox).

Insects

see also ANIMALS

5147 "The spider spinning his web for the unwary fly. The blood is the life, Mr. Renfield." **Bela Lugosi**, as Count Dracula, makes Dwight Frye his abject, mad slave. *Dracula* (1931, Universal).

5148 CPL. PARIS: "You see that cockroach. Tomorrow morning we'll be dead and he'll be alive. It will have more contact with my wife and child than I will." PVT. FEROL: "Now you've got the edge on him." Condemned French soldier **Ralph Meeker** compares his life and those of Joseph Turkel and **Timothy Carey** to that of a cockroach in their cell. The three are to be executed as an object lesson to other soldiers in their regiment. Carey squashes the insect with his hand. *Paths of Glory* (1957, United Artists).

5149 "She's like a cockroach what turned into a butterfly." Likeable hood **Mickey Shaughnessy** uses a malapropism to describe the transformation of Bette Davis from an alcoholic apple-seller into a dignified-looking lady. *A Pocketful of Miracles* (1961, United Artists).

5150 "I've been killing spiders since I was 30. Okay?. . . Honey, there's a spider in your bathroom the size of a Buick." **Woody Allen** reacts when he's called from his bed with another woman to Diane Keaton's apartment in the middle of the night because she's found a spider in her bathroom. The insect is somewhat bigger than Woody expected. *Annie Hall* (1977, United Artists).

5151 "I'm going to be the first officer in the U.S. battle history to get his butt kicked by a mess of bugs." General **Richard Widmark** isn't very successful in defending Houston from an attack of killer bees. *The Swarm* (1978, Warner Bros.).

5152 "A bug is nothing! A bug does not exist. The word has no meaning. It's only used out of ignorance or malice. You know what a bug is? A bug is a colloquialism which has no basis in reality. Insects include a wide variety of living creatures that fly and crawl, but none of them can be called a bug!" **Warren Beatty**, as Ben Siegel, lectures a character who has made the mistake of calling him Bugsy. *Bugsy* (1991, Tri-Star).

Insensitivity *see* RESPONSIBILITIES, SENSITIVITY AND INSENSITIVITY

Insignificance *see* IMPORTANCE, SIGNIFICANCE

Inspirations

see also ART AND ARTISTS, CAUSE AND EFFECT, CREATION AND CREATURES, IDEAS, INFLUENCES, SUPERNATURAL

5153 "I should so love to inspire a frenzy in the men." **Katharine Hepburn** wonders if the men will adore her at a ball to which she's being taken by Franchot Tone. *Quality Street* (1937, RKO).

5154 "One percent inspiration is very important. . . . You cannot invent it. . . . You have to have it."

Elderly Thomas Alva Edison, portrayed by **Spencer Tracy**, gives an interview to two high school students. *Edison, the Man* (1940, MGM).

5155 "Mr. Rupert, we thank you, and I'll treasure this cane always and carry it in all my pictures as an inspiration to rise to the heights." New movie star **Red Skelton** accepts a gift from Leon Ames, whose career is over. *Merton of the Movies* (1947, MGM).

5156 "Monty Stratton has not won just a ball game, he's won a greater victory as he goes on pitching, winning, leading a rich, full life and stands as an inspiration to all of us as living proof of what a man can do if he has the courage, determination, to refuse to admit defeat." The narrator talks of a pitcher for the Chicago White Sox, played by James Stewart, who lost a leg in a hunting accident, but with an artificial leg came back to pitch again, albeit not at the major league level. *The Stratton Story* (1949, MGM).

5157 "This is the day, I'm sure, that inspired the poet to say that God is in His heaven and all is right with the world." Humanitarian Judge **Lee J. Cobb** is pleased by the actions of Gregory Peck and Jennifer Jones in handling their domestic problems. *The Man in the Grey Flannel Suit* (1956, 20th Century-Fox).

5158 "You're an inspiration, Lloyd. You should go on 'The 700 Club' or something." **Amy Brooks** admires John Cusack for bedding the seemingly unattainable Ione Skye. *Say Anything. . .* (1989, 20th Century-Fox).

5159 "Think of me as your inspiration." Psychopath **Kathy Bates** is writer James Caan's biggest fan and she's got him under her control. *Misery* (1990, Columbia).

Instincts

see also **Gifts and Giving**, HUMAN NATURE, TALENTS

5160 "Oh, it was all instinctive, I didn't even know I'd fired. I don't remember anything. . . just the reports one after another till there was a funny little click and the revolver was empty." Playing little Miss Innocence, **Bette Davis** has difficulty recalling shooting and killing a man she says made unwanted advances to her. The audience knows better. In the opening scene Davis is seen, calmly emptying the revolver into the man after he's already down. *The Letter* (1940, Warner Bros.).

5161 "Robbie, I've just had a most shattering experience. Did you ever look at a drop of water? All my life, I've had an instinct about that stuff. My instincts were right: look at it." **Charles Coburn**, well known for his fondness for liquor, looks at a drop of water under his great-grandson Dean Stockwell's microscope. *The Green Years* (1946, MGM).

5162 "I can't understand how anyone whose instincts are so generous could lead such a dissolute life." **Michelle Pfeiffer** is taken in by John Malkovich's careful plan to seduce her. *Dangerous Liaisons* (1988, Warner Bros.).

5163 "Your political instincts are clouded by the aroma of my perfume." Stripper Blaze Starr, portrayed by **Lolita Davidovich**, gives too much credit to her perfume. We're pretty sure it's her fine shapely body that turns on old reprobate Louisiana Governor Earl Long, portrayed by Paul Newman. *Blaze* (1989, Touchstone-Buena Vista).

Instructions

see also DIRECTIONS, EDUCATION, INFORMATION AND INFORMERS, KNOWLEDGE, LEARNING AND LESSONS, ORDERS, SCHOOLS, STUDIES AND STUDENTS, TEACHING AND TEACHERS

5164 "Tie on-a the bed, throw the rope out of the window." **Chico Marx** instructs Harpo Marx in this comedy western. *Go West* (1940, MGM).

5165 "Brake. The brake!" As a runaway train hurtles on, **Groucho Marx** yells instructions to Harpo Marx, who obliges by breaking the brake and throwing it away. *Go West* (1940, MGM).

5166 "Three of the leaves will make enough fluid to keep Kharis' heart beating. Once every night during the cycle of the full moon, you will dissolve three tanna leaves and give the fluid to Kharis." Elderly high priest of Karnack, **Eduardo Ciannelli**, gives instructions to his disciple George Zucco. Below the idol of Isis is a copper box that holds the long, thin tanna leaves which keep the mummy Kharis (Tom Tyler) alive. *The Mummy's Hand* (1940, Universal).

5167 "Find someone to type this." **Charles Coburn** barks these instructions several times to his incompetent secretary Marilyn Monroe, clearly hired for her physical attributes. *Monkey Business* (1952, 20th Century-Fox).

5168 "You will replace the bed clothes neatly. You will not walk upon any part of the floor that has been recently polished. And you will not talk to nurses on any but strictly professional matters." Fiery Head Nurse **Jean Taylor-Smith** barks instructions to medical student Dirk Bogarde. *Doctor in the House* (1954, GB, Rank).

5169 "No—beat it out on a native drum!" Dripping with sarcasm, nasty editor **Joan Crawford** snarls at Hope Lange who innocently, but dumbly, asks if Crawford wants a report typed. *The Best of Everything* (1959, 20th Century-Fox).

5170 "I read the instructions on the box." **Rae Dawn Chong** tells startled Arnold Schwarzenegger how she was able to operate a rocket launcher and rescue him during a shoot-out with the bad guys. *Commando* (1985, 20th Century-Fox).

5171 "You get him, Jack. I don't care what you have to do—just get him." Once serene **Anne Archer** frighteningly orders her husband Harrison Ford after an Irish terrorist makes a threatening phone call to their home. *Patriot Games* (1992, Paramount).

Insults

see also ARROGANCE, HURT AND HURTING, RUDENESS, TALKS AND TALKING

5172 "Why don't you bore a hole in yourself and let the sap run out?" College President **Groucho Marx** unsuccessfully tries to insult Chico Marx. *Horse Feathers* (1932, Paramount).

5173 "To have overlooked me would have been a pointed insult." WASPish egotist **Clifton Webb** is gratified that the police include him among the suspects in the supposed murder of Gene Tierney. *Laura* (1944, 20th Century-Fox).

5174 "I'd strike the sun if it insulted me!" **Gregory Peck**, as Captain Ahab, rages pridefully in a blasphemous challenge to God's power over mortal human beings. *Moby Dick* (1956, Warner Bros.).

5175 "I don't care how many dagos, guinea, wop, greaseball goombahs come out of the woodwork!" Movie studio executive **John Marley** explodes at Robert Duvall, who Marley believes is threatening him into giving Al Martino a plum part in a movie. *The Godfather* (1972, Paramount).

5176 "I don't mind an insult now and then, as long as I know it's just a little love pout." Married **Virginia Madsen** is called a tramp by Don Johnson after they've made love. *The Hot Spot* (1990, Orion).

Insurance

see also FIRES, LIFE AND DEATH, LIVES AND LIVING, LOSSES AND LOSING, PROTECTION

5177 "I want to tell you, madam, that with this insurance policy you've provided for your little ones and for your old age, which will be here in a couple of weeks now, if I'm any judge of horse flesh." While attending her society party as guest of honor, African explorer **Groucho Marx** tries to sell Margaret Dumont an insurance policy. *Animal Crackers* (1930, Paramount).

5178 WARREN HAGGERTY: "Do you want me to kill myself?" GLADYS BENTON: "Did you change your insurance?" Hard-boiled newspaper editor **Spencer Tracy** has a tiff with his fiancée **Jean Harlow.** He's conned her into marrying his best friend William Powell in a scheme to compromise wealthy Myrna Loy. *Libeled Lady* (1936, MGM).

5179 "We don't help you much when you're alive, but when you're dead, that's what counts." **Ralph Bellamy** touts the benefits of insurance to Cary Grant. *His Girl Friday* (1940, Columbia).

5180 "You might say I sell peace of mind. Fire, theft, and casualty are not things that happen to other people." Madman **John Goodman** poses as an insurance salesman. *Barton Fink* (1991, 20th Century-Fox).

Integrity

see also CHARACTER, HONESTY AND DISHONESTY, LOYALTIES, MORALITY, NOBILITY, PRINCIPLES, SINCERITY, STRENGTHS, VIRTUES

5181 "A building has integrity just like a man—and just as seldom." Idealist architect **Henry Hull** lectures his protégé Gary Cooper on his cynical views. Cooper feels the same way and repeats the aphorism to Patricia Neal. *The Fountainhead* (1949, Warner Bros.).

5182 "What's the going price on integrity this week?" Corporation owner **Orson Welles** wants to induce former hot-shot TV commercials director Oliver Reed into coming back to work for him. *I'll Never Forget What's 'Is Name* (1967, GB, Universal/Regional).

Intelligence

see also BRAINS, GENIUS, KNOWLEDGE, MINDS, REASONS, STUPIDITY, UNDERSTANDINGS AND MISUNDERSTANDINGS, WISDOM

5183 "I'm a very smart little girl." In her first talkie, **Dolores Del Rio,** playing a prostitute who falls for a client and saves him from prison, enunciates most carefully in her Mexican-American accent. *The Bad One* (1930, United Artists).

5184 "I'm too nervous to steal and too lazy to work. . . . But a smart guy can get away with any-

thing if he's got brains. And I've got 'em. I get the other jerks to work for me and I apply legitimate business methods to organizing crime. And if there's any lead thrown around—they get it—not me." Likeable mobster **Spencer Tracy** figures he's got all the angles covered in this melodrama about a truck driver who becomes Kingpin in the rackets. *Quick Millions* (1931, Fox).

5185 EDDY HALL: "Say, this is a man's robe!" RUBY ADAMS: "You don't say. Aren't you a bright little thing?" Petty criminal **Clark Gable** hides from the police in **Jean Harlow**'s apartment. When he gets his clothes wet in her tub, she lends him a robe. *Hold Your Man* (1933, MGM).

5186 "We're intellectual opposites. I'm intellectual and you're opposite." **Mae West** spots Ivan Lebedeff for the gigolo he is. *Goin' to Town* (1935, Paramount).

5187 "I belong to a vanishing race—I'm one of the intellectuals." World-weary **Leslie Howard** confesses his curse to waitress Bette Davis. *The Petrified Forest* (1936, Warner Bros.).

5188 "I'm not getting into his trap—and I'm not taking any chances of getting hit in the face with a spade either. You know we're letting ourselves in for enough as it is. Some will wind up on the short end, but not me, baby. I know all the angles and I think I'm smart enough to keep one step ahead of them till I get enough to pack it in and live on easy street the rest of my life. I know how to beat the racket." Hostess (a Hollywood euphemism for prostitute) **Bette Davis** believes she's smart enough to work for Lucky Luciano-like hoodlum Eduardo Ciannelli and not get hurt. *Marked Woman* (1937, Warner Bros.).

5189 ANDRE VERNE: "You outsmarted me." JULIE: "That's what happens when smart people get together. One of them comes out ahead." Escaped prisoner **Clark Gable** is turned in to the cops by café singer **Joan Crawford.** *Strange Cargo* (1940, MGM).

5190 "This script is an insult to a man's intelligence—even mine." Studio executive **Franklin Pangborn** explodes after hearing W.C. Fields' ideas for a screenplay. *Never Give a Sucker an Even Break* (1941, Universal).

5191 "Welcome, Holmes. . . . Just like old times, eh? A battle of wits, of superior intellects. . . valuable as your doctor and his code are to my business, I think my main interest in this affair is the chance it gives me to battle with you again." **Lionel Atwill**, as Professor Moriarty, is pleased to welcome Basil Rathbone to his hideout in a case involving a scientist's secret code and bomb sight. *Sherlock Holmes and the Secret Weapon* (1942, Universal).

5192 "Intelligent people don't marry for better or worse. They marry for better and better." Strong-willed **Joan Crawford** steers her younger sister Helen Parrish in a loveless marriage with a rich man. *They All Kissed the Bride* (1942, Columbia).

5193 "For an intelligent woman, you surround yourself with dopes." Police detective **Dana Andrews** does not approve of Gene Tierney's hoity-toity friends. *Laura* (1944, 20th Century-Fox).

5194 "Ingenuity is never a substitute for intelligence." Arch criminal **Zachary Scott** believes that blackmailing smuggler Sydney Greenstreet is no match for him. *The Mask of Dimitrios* (1944, Warner Bros.).

5195 "Oh, boy! I'm so smart, it's a disease." **Jack Carson** realizes that Joan Crawford is trying to set him up for the murder of Zachary Scott to protect her daughter Ann Blyth. *Mildred Pierce* (1945, Warner Bros.).

5196 "Intellect destroys the beauty in any face." **George Sanders'** statement is correct. When some people begin the unfamiliar act of thinking, they develop a most pained expression. *The Picture of Dorian Gray* (1945, MGM).

5197 "There's nothing to square. You're my pal. You're smart, too. I didn't know how smart until I saw you in court. You fooled me, and that takes a big man. Yeah, a big man." Psychopathic killer **Richard Widmark**'s appearance belies his words to parolee Victor Mature. Mature was forced to testify against Widmark. *Kiss of Death* (1947, 20th Century-Fox).

5198 "You're a smart fella, a college man. You could make somethin' outta nuthin' just to be important." New Orleans Police Detective **Paul Douglas** resents having to take orders from Public Health Officer Richard Widmark. They are seeking a criminal who is a bubonic plague carrier. *Panic in the Streets* (1950, 20th Century-Fox).

5199 "I can be smart when it's important, but men don't like it." Beautiful blonde **Marilyn Monroe** knows that the wealthy men she's after prefer girls who aren't too bright. *Gentlemen Prefer Blondes* (1953, 20th Century-Fox).

5200 "He is mankind developed to its ultimate intelligence. These are his slaves, existing only to do his will, as you will." Transfixed **Max Wagner** explains to other earthlings that Martians have developed into overgrown brains with vestigical body features and winky tenacles, served by mutants. *Invaders from Mars* (1953, 20th Century-Fox).

5201 "He's about as interested in your intellect as I am!" Fashion photographer **Fred Astaire** indicts both himself and Audrey Hepburn's phony existentialist philosopher hero Michel Auclair. *Funny Face* (1956, Paramount).

5202 "Go with him, Madge. For once in your life, do something bright." Bright, practical **Susan Strasberg** urges her older, beautiful but dumb sister Kim Novak to run away with drifter William Holden. *Picnic* (1955, Columbia).

5203 "Queen Cleopatra is widely read, well versed in the natural sciences and mathematics. She speaks seven languages proficiently. Were she not a woman, one would consider her to be an intellectual." **Andrew Keir,** as Agrippa, praises the intellect of Elizabeth Taylor to Rex Harrison, as Julius Caesar. The latter seems more interested in her superior physical attributes. *Cleopatra* (1963, 20th Century-Fox).

5204 "You're so damn smart. . . smarter than any white man. . . I don't think you could let an opportunity like that pass by." Southern Sheriff **Rod Steiger** tricks proud black Philadelphia police detective Sidney Poitier into helping on a murder case. *In the Heat of the Night* (1967, United Artists).

5205 "——intelligence would take the bloom off your carnality." Russian émigré **Dirk Bogarde,** who runs a German chocolate factory at the time the Nazis are about to take over, teases his plump, pretty wife Andrea Ferreol, who has a fondness for baby talk. *Despair* (1979, W. Germany/New Line).

5206 "You're too smart to do what you're doing to yourself." Union organizer **Ron Leibman** wants to shape up textile worker Sally Field, who seems bent on self-destruction with cruel men. *Norma Rae* (1979, 20th Century-Fox).

5207 "Intellectuals are like the Mafia. They only kill their own." Filmmaker **Woody Allen,** playing a filmmaker, must be referring to pseudo-intellectuals. Intellectuals are scarce. Pseudo-intellectuals can be found everywhere. *Stardust Memories* (1980, MGM-United Artists).

5208 "You're not too smart, are you? I like that in a man." **Kathleen Turner** allows dumb lawyer William Hurt to think he's pursuing her. *Body Heat* (1981, Warner Bros.).

5209 "The older I got, the smarter she got." **Carol Burnett** muses that she finally realizes that her mother was one smart lady. *Chu Chu and the Philly Flash* (1981, 20th Century-Fox).

5210 "Dorothy is smarter than I am. She doesn't argue, she just smiles and does it her way." Actor **Dustin Hoffman** refers to his female alter ego. While posing as a woman, Hoffman develops "feminine" means of survival. *Tootsie* (1982, Columbia).

5211 PAUL MOORE: "It must be nice to think you're the smartest person in the room." JANE CRAIG: "No, it's awful." Station manager **Paul Hackes** doesn't get the kind of response he expects from television news producer **Holly Hunter**. *Broadcast News* (1987, 20th Century-Fox).

5212 "Like most intellectuals, he is intensely stupid." **Glenn Close** makes an anti-intellectual observation about Keanu Reeves who portrays young Chevalier Danceny. *Dangerous Liaisons* (1988, Warner Bros.).

5213 "Now let me dispel a couple of rumors so they won't fester into facts. . . Yes! I too attended Welton and survived. And no, at the time I was not the mental giant you see before you. I was the intellectual equivalent of a 98-pound weakling. I'd go to the beach and people would kick copies of Byron in my face." English master **Robin Williams** reminisces with his students of a time when he was a literary Charles Atlas. *Dead Poets Society* (1989, Touchstone-Buena Vista).

5214 "You know when I'm not picking straw out of my teeth, I'm a very smart man." **Nick Nolte** sarcastically puts New York psychiatrist Barbra Streisand in her place for being condescending to the poor southern country boy. *The Prince of Tides* (1991, Columbia).

5215 "Just remember, breeding is no substitute for intelligence." **Sean Connery** doesn't approve of the blueblood that Bronx scientist Lorraine Bracco is engaged to. *Medicine Man* (1992, Hollywood Pictures-Buena Vista).

Intensity *see* EMOTIONS, ENERGY, STRENGTHS, VIOLENCE

Intentions

see also PLANS, PURPOSES

5216 "I meant to tell you before that I was married." **Adolphe Menjou** thinks it's about time to clear up a few things when his lover Barbara Stanwyck informs him that she's pregnant. *Forbidden* (1932, Columbia).

5217 COL. PICKERING: "I think you ought to know, Doolittle, that Mr. Higgins' intentions are entirely honorable." ALFRED DOOLITTLE: "Course, they are, guvnor. If I thought they wasn't, I'd ask for fifty." **Scott Sunderland** defends his colleague Leslie Howard when Wendy Hiller's dustman father **Wilfrid Lawson** asks five pounds for his daughter for his troubles. *Pygmalion* (1938, GB, Pascal-MGM).

5218 GRINGOIRE: "Being a poet, I'm already a vagabond and can quickly learn to be a thief." CLOPIN: "Good intentions aren't enough. They never put an onion in the soup yet." To save his life, poet **Edmond O'Brien** implores **Thomas Mitchell,** King of Paris thieves, to allow him to join their ranks. Mitchell is not impressed with the recruit. *The Hunchback of Notre Dame* (1939, RKO).

5219 "What's he up to now?" Delivering the film's first line, **Jessie Ralph** suspiciously questions her daughter Cora Witherspoon about her shiftless son-in-law, hen-pecked W.C. Fields. *The Bank Dick* (1940, Universal).

5220 "If I didn't think you meant so well, I'd feel like slapping your face." In her Academy Award-winning role, **Mary Astor** isn't certain how to take Bette Davis' "kindness." *The Great Lie* (1941, Warner Bros.).

5221 "I've been sitting here breathing cleaning fluid and ammonia for three hours. Nature didn't intend for poker to be played that way." Card player **David Sheiner** is disturbed by Jack Lemmon's constant cleaning. *The Odd Couple* (1968, Paramount).

5222 "We had such good intentions, and got so little." **Philippe Noiret** reflects on the lost hopes and intentions of the past. *Coup de Torchon* (1982, Fr., Quartet Films).

5223 "We do what we do to help people. What counts is your intentions were good." Counter-terrorist **Gregory Hines** comforts scientist Renee Soutendijk, whose creation, an android in human female form, programmed to fight evil, gets her circuits screwed up and becomes a female vengeance machine against men. *Eve of Destruction* (1991, Orion).

Interests

see also ADVANTAGES, CONCERNS, CURIOSITY, INFLUENCES, MONEY, PARTICIPATION, POWER, RIGHTS

5224 "I think you can always get people interested in the crucifixion of a woman." Secretary **Aline MacMahon** cynically reproaches her boss, Edward

G. Robinson, editor of a trashy yellow journalism newspaper. *Five Star Final* (1931, Warner Bros.).

5225 "Hey, wait a minute. Let's get something straightened out right now. If you've got any peculiar ideas that I'm interested in you, forget it. You're just a headline to me." Out-of-work reporter **Clark Gable** informs runaway heiress Claudette Colbert that he has no personal interest in her. *It Happened One Night* (1934, Columbia).

5226 "Not interested in yourself? You're fascinated, Red. You're far and away your favorite person in the world." **Cary Grant** is not fooled by his ex-wife Katharine Hepburn's claim of lack of self-interest. *The Philadelphia Story* (1940, MGM).

5227 CHARLES CONDOMINE: "Anything interesting in *The Times?*" RUTH CONDOMINE: "Don't be silly, dear." It's an example of the sparkling wit of Noel Coward found in this delightful sophisticated comedy. **Rex Harrison** and second wife **Constance Cummings** have not yet been joined by the spirit of wife number one, Kay Hammond. *Blithe Spirit* (1945, GB, Cineguild-Two Cities).

5228 "That's very interesting. You don't seem to be inhibited." Exiled Czech author **Charles Boyer** falls in love with maid Jennifer Jones who can fix anything. *Cluny Brown* (1946, 20th Century-Fox).

5229 "When an impoverished character, unendowed with any appreciable virtues, succumbs to a rich man's wife, it's to be suspected that his interest is less passionate than pecuniary." **Clifton Webb** ungallantly suggests that Kurt Krueger is more interested in Webb's money than his wife Cathy Downs' charms. *The Dark Corner* (1946, 20th Century-Fox).

5230 RICHARD SHERMAN: "Tell me, doctor, are you very expensive?" DR. BRUBAKER: "Very." SHERMAN: "I'm sure you occasionally make exceptions." BRUBAKER: "Never!" SHERMAN: "Once in a while, a case must come along that really interests you." BRUBAKER: "At $50 an hour, all my cases interest me." Paperback publisher **Tom Ewell**, who has a runaway imagination, seeks some bargain help from psychiatrist **Oscar Homolka**, whose book Ewell is publishing. *The Seven Year Itch* (1955, 20th Century-Fox).

5231 "Who will ever be interested in what a thirteen-year-old girl has to say?" It's one of the earliest entries in the diary kept by Anne Frank, portrayed by **Millie Perkins**. *The Diary of Anne Frank* (1959, 20th Century-Fox).

5232 "It was somewhere about here that I lost all interest in life." **Daniel Stern,** identifying with failure, points to a spot at the local quarry swimming hole. *Breaking Away* (1979, 20th Century-Fox).

5233 "I have gone away because I must find something interesting to do in the world." **Meryl Streep** writes to her son Justin Henry after she leaves the boy and his father Dustin Hoffman to find herself. *Kramer vs. Kramer* (1979, Columbia).

5234 "I'd really like to hear about the MIG sometime." Gorgeous astrophysicist **Kelly McGillis** coos seductively to arrogant naval fighter pilot Tom Cruise. *Top Gun* (1986, Paramount).

5235 "I came here to tell you that I'm interested in someone. . . a man, well, he's almost a man. . . he's only twenty-two years old. . . but it's not like I'm rushing into anything. I've known him for twenty-six years. . . it's a little complicated." **Cybill Shepherd** tries to explain to her analyst James Noble that she's fallen in love with Robert Downey, Jr., the reincarnation of her deceased husband. *Chances Are* (1989, Tri-Star).

5236 "You left just when you were becoming interesting." **Sean Connery** answers his son Harrison Ford, who complains, "We never talked." *Indiana Jones and the Last Crusade* (1989, Paramount).

Intimacy see CHARACTER, CLOSENESS, PRIVACY, ROMANCES, SEX AND SEXUALITY, TOGETHERNESS

Intimidation see FEARS, THREATS, WARNINGS

Introductions

see also BEGINNINGS, EXPERIENCES, FASHIONS, KNOWLEDGE, PROLOGUES

5237 "I want you all to meet a new mug what's gonna be with us." Gang boss **Stanley Fields** makes the introductions all around for new mob tough guy Edward G. Robinson. *Little Caesar* (1931, Warner Bros.).

5238 "Do you suppose I could buy back my introduction to you?" College President **Groucho Marx** snarls to brother Chico. *Horse Feathers* (1932, Paramount).

5239 "This is Miss Hambridge, our school teacher boarder from up Barrington way—she's between nervous breakdowns." Innkeeper **Margaret Hamilton** introduces actress Margaret Sullavan to fat guest Grace Hayle. *The Moon's Our Home* (1936, Paramount).

5240 "Good evening, neighbor Stone. My name is Scratch—I often go by that name in New England."

Devil **Walter Huston** introduces himself to New Hampshire farmer James Craig who has uttered the magic words about being willing to sell his soul. *All That Money Can Buy* aka: *The Devil and Daniel Webster* (1941, RKO).

5241 "I am Tondelayo." It's not what she says, it's how she looks and moves as she says it. Sexy jungle maiden **Hedy Lamarr** insinuates herself into the room, tropically and temptingly announcing her name. *White Cargo* (1942, MGM).

5242 "You're Nick Bianco, aren't you?. . . You're a big man. I'm Tommy Udo. . . Imagine me in on this cheap rap—big man like me—picked up just for shoving a guy's ears off his head—traffic ticket stuff. . . ." In a most impressive movie debut, **Richard Widmark** introduces himself to Victor Mature in a holding pen. *Kiss of Death* (1947, 20th Century-Fox).

5243 "Allow me to introduce myself. I'm the Invisible Man." At the end of a movie in which Bud Abbott and Lou Costello deal with Dracula, the Wolf Man, and Frankenstein's monster, they find themselves in a row boat with the unmistakable voice of **Vincent Price**. *Abbott and Costello Meet Frankenstein* (1948, Universal).

5244 "This boy. . . and this girl. . . were never properly introduced to the world we live in." A folksy voice-over delivers the opening lines as Farley Granger and Cathy O'Donnell, on the road to tragedy, kiss. *They Live by Night* (1948, RKO).

5245 "My name is Stryker. Sgt. John M. Stryker. You're gonna be my squad." Tough, experienced Marine Sergeant **John Wayne** introduces himself to his men. The name Stryker is very popular in action-adventure films. *Sands of Iwo Jima* (1949, Republic).

5246 "In college, I majored in geology and anthropology and running out of gas on Bunker Hill. What's your name, honey?" **Bob Hope** comes on to Jane Russell with a lousy line. *Son of Paleface* (1952, Paramount).

5247 "I am Giacomo, lover of beauty and a beauty of a lover." While under a spell, meek valet **Danny Kaye**, disguised as a court jester, announces himself and his intentions to Princess Angela Lansbury. *The Court Jester* (1956, Paramount).

5248 "Call me Ishmael." The novel's and the film's first line, is delivered in the movie by narrator **Richard Basehart**. *Moby Dick* (1956, Warner Bros.).

5249 "Lovely ladies, kind gentlemen, pleased to introduce myself: Sakini by name, interpreter by profession, education by the ancient dictionary, Okinawan by the whim of gods." Okinawan narrator **Marlon Brando**, bowing politely, speaks directly to the audience at the beginning of the film. *The Teahouse of the August Moon* (1956, MGM).

5250 OSGOOD: "I'm Osgood Fielding the Third." DAPHNE: "I'm Cinderella the Second." Millionaire **Joe E. Brown** introduces himself to "new" girl in town, **Jack Lemmon**. *Some Like It Hot* (1959, United Artists).

5251 "Excuse me. . . my name's Barrett, sir." With the film's first line, **Dirk Bogarde** introduces himself as rich, ineffectual James Fox's new manservant. Ultimately, Bogarde debases Fox and rules him and his home. *The Servant* (1963, GB, Landau).

5252 "I am Ayesha, who some call 'She-Who-Waits.' And you, do you know who you are?" Queen **Ursula Andress**, who cannot die unless she falls in love, makes the acquaintance of Professor John Richardson. *She* (1965, GB, Hammer).

5253 "Allow me to introduce myself. I am Ernst Stavro Blofeld. They told me you were assassinated. You only live twice, Mr. Bond." SPECTRE chief **Donald Pleasence** introduces himself to agent Sean Connery, as 007. This time, Pleasence means for Connery to stay dead. *You Only Live Twice* (1967, GB, United Artists).

5254 "My name is Mattie Ross. We are located in Yell County near Dardanelle. My mother is at home looking after my sister Victoria and my brother Little Frank." It's how **Kim Darby** introduces herself to anyone and everyone she happens to meet. *True Grit* (1969, Paramount).

5255 "There was me, that is Alex, and my three droogs, that is Pete, Georgie and Dim. . . ." **Malcolm McDowell** introduces himself and his gang with the first line of a movie which seems more pretentious and trite with each passing year. *A Clockwork Orange* (1971, GB, Warner Bros.).

5256 SASHA: "You must be Manolo." MANOLO: "You must be Sasha." JONATHAN: "You must be going." After meeting **Linda Fiorentino, Nick Corri** is hurried out of the Paris hotel room he shares with **Anthony Edwards,** who is anxious to have his first sexual experience ever with "older woman" Fiorentino. *Gotcha!* (1985, Universal).

5257 "Direct from the wasteland, he's bad, he's beautiful, he's crazy. He's the Man With No Name."

Thunderdome emcee **Edwin Hodgeman** introduces Mel Gibson to the crowd. *Mad Max Beyond Thunderdome* (1985, Australia, Warner Bros.).

5258 "Tom Tuttle from Tacoma." **John Candy**'s character, who talks like he's reading from a government manual, introduces himself with this line to everyone he encounters. *Volunteers* (1985, Tri-Star).

5259 "My name is Inigo Montoya. You killed my father. Prepare to die." **Mandy Patinkin** challenges villain Chris Sarandon to a duel. *The Princess Bride* (1987, 20th Century-Fox).

5260 "I'm Batman." **Michael Keaton** rather formally introduces himself to friend and foe alike, as if they wouldn't guess from his weird costume. *Batman* (1989, Warner Bros.).

5261 "Folks call me Marina and I'm a clairvoyant." Blonde **Demi Moore** identifies herself. *The Butcher's Wife* (1991, Paramount).

5262 "Hello, I'm Rose. I come to live with you and your family." **Laura Dern** introduces herself to 13-year-old Lukas Haas who has watched with interest as Dern ambles toward his house across a wooden bridge. She wears a diaphanous dress, prim hat and gloves. *Rambling Rose* (1991, Seven Arts-New Line).

Intuition *see* EMOTIONS, SENSE AND SENSIBILITY

Inventions

see also CREATION AND CREATURES, EXPERIMENTS, THINKING AND THOUGHTS

5263 "I beg your pardon. I realize they haven't been invented yet, but do you have a match?" Traveling magician **Hans Conried** makes a request of a guard at a slave market. *Siren of Bagdad* (1953, Columbia).

5264 "I often wondered how you chanced to invent yourself." Oily, amoral **John Malkovich** admires scheming manipulator Glenn Close. *Dangerous Liaisons* (1988, Warner Bros.).

Invitations

see also GUESTS, MESSAGES, NOTES, PARTIES, VISITS

5265 "You know when you blow out the match, it's an invitation to kiss you." **John Gilbert**'s title card announces his intention as Greta Garbo inhales sensuously and blows out the fire after he lights her cigarette. *Flesh and the Devil* (1926, silent, MGM).

5266 MYRA GALE: "Won't you come in for a moment?" DAN QUIGLEY: "Who could say no?" **Mae Clarke** invites **James Cagney** into her apartment when he appears at the door with her lost purse. He has quite a gleam in his eyes as he walks through the door. *Lady Killer* (1933, Warner Bros.).

5267 "Why don't you come up sometime, see me? Come up, I'll tell your fortune." It's **Mae West**'s famous, albeit misquoted, come-on line to Cary Grant. *She Done Him Wrong* (1933, Paramount).

5268 "When spider send invitation to house, fly better beware." Unfortunately, British Prime Minister Neville Chamberlain probably never heard Chinese detective **Sidney Toler**'s aphorism before visiting Adolf Hitler. *City of Darkness* (1939, 20th Century-Fox).

5269 "My colleagues wish to know respectfully if the young ladies will join them in a little drink?" Army Commandant **Joseph Schildkraut** inquires about the show girls that work with Clark Gable. *Idiot's Delight* (1939, MGM).

5270 "You must come down with me after the show to the lumberyard and ride piggy-back on the buzz saw." **W.C. Fields** gets in his at-bats with wisecracking Charlie McCarthy. *You Can't Cheat an Honest Man* (1939, Universal).

5271 "Anytime you got nothin' to do—and lots of time to do it—come on up." Shady lady **Mae West** is now hospitable to Dick Foran. *My Little Chickadee* (1939, Universal).

5272 "Is your invitation to spread a little fertilizer still open?" **Gregory Peck**'s question of Ava Gardner requires no comment. *On the Beach* (1959, United Artists).

5273 "You need lookin' after, c'mon to my room, it's warmer. I got the end stopped up. Besides, you don't look like someone'd take 'vantage of a girl. C'mon, I won't bite. Besides I got twin beds." Homeless **Jane Fonda** offers to share her drain pipe with drifter Laurence Harvey. *Walk on the Wild Side* (1962, Columbia).

5274 "Won't you come in for a minute? I don't bite, you know, unless it's called for." **Audrey Hepburn** makes an open-ended invitation to Cary Grant. *Charade* (1963, Universal).

5275 "Charlie, uh, I'd like to invite you over to your home for dinner on Sunday with your kids. I'll make a strudel." Having returned from her past, **Kathleen Turner** moves towards resurrecting her marriage to Nicolas Cage. *Peggy Sue Got Married* (1986, Tri-Star).

5276 "Come and get some." Fresh from a seven-year coma, martial arts expert and ex-cop **Steven Seagal** challenges the villains who thought they had put him away for good a long time ago. *Hard to Kill* (1990, Warner Bros.).

5277 "Come to my bed. You will never leave." Ancient Greek **Anthony Quinn** besieges his resistant next-door neighbor Maureen O'Hara with passionate promises. *Only the Lonely* (1991, MGM).

5278 KATE: "Do you shower once a week?" DOUG: "Is that an invitation?" Figure skater **Moira Kelly** and hockey player **D.B. Sweeney** team up for pairs competition. *The Cutting Edge* (1992, MGM).

Involvements

see also ACTIONS AND ACTS, EXPERIENCES

5279 "A woman like you could never become involved with any man, sane or insane." Slimeball shrink **John Emery** disparages his colleague Ingrid Bergman when she doesn't respond to his crude overtures. *Spellbound* (1945, United Artists).

5280 "[I don't like] getting mixed up with tricky females who want to knock off the boss' wife and marry him for herself." **Robert Montgomery** becomes involved with Audrey Totter despite his protests. *Lady in the Lake* (1947, MGM).

5281 "Let's level with each other, sir. If you hadn't been personally involved in this unfortunate incident, you'd be sitting at home complacent and more or less oblivious to all this." U.S. Ambassador **Richard Venture** takes a strange tack with American businessman Jack Lemmon, whose son John Shea was taken into custody by the Chilean officials and killed. It would seem that Venture's comment is a message for a complacent audience. *Missing* (1982, Universal).

5282 "I gotta say what's on my mind, and I think I'm gettin' involved here." Tough-talking New York cabbie **Sylvester Stallone** makes a confession to Dolly Parton. She's trying to transform him into a country singer in two weeks' time to win a bet from her loudmouth manager Ron Leibman. *Rhinestone* (1984, 20th Century-Fox).

5283 "I want to get him. I want to tell you how much it means to me to see someone like you who's not afraid to get involved." **Elizabeth McGovern** thanks Steve Guttenberg, who claims to

have witnessed an attempted assault on McGovern. Actually, it was Guttenberg's married lover Isabelle Huppert who saw the attack. *The Bedroom Window* (1987, DEG).

Irritations

5284 "I'm not a feminist, but the expression, 'It's a man's world,' irritates me." Department store head **Madeleine Carroll** doesn't intend to choose marriage as a career, but she's not going to do without romance either. *Honeymoon in Bali* (1939, Paramount).

5285 "If I irritate you, you can imagine how much I irritate myself!" Idle rich **Susan Kohner** and hubby Robert Wagner aren't compatible. *All the Fine Young Cannibals* (1960, MGM).

5286 "When you're forced to sit a lot—and watch others move about—you feel apart—lonely—because you can't get up and pace around. I find myself irritated when people come in here and parade all over the place. I have to keep exercising self-control to prevent from screaming at them to sit down—quiet down—stand still." Paralyzed Franklin Delano Roosevelt, portrayed by **Ralph Bellamy,** finds it difficult to accept his disability while others innocently show off what they can do and he can not. *Sunrise at Campobello* (1960, Warner Bros.).

5287 "I'm sure you're irritable because your colon is clinched." **Alison Steadman** scoffs when her husband Griff Rhys-Jones complains to her. *The Misadventures of Mr. Wilt* (1990, GB, Goldwyn).

Jealousy

see also EMOTIONS, FEELINGS, LOVE AND HATE, LOVE AND LOVERS, RESENTMENTS

5288 "Never be jealous again. Never doubt that I love you more than the world. More than myself." Courtesan **Greta Garbo** pledges her love to young Robert Taylor. *Camille* (1936, MGM).

5289 "'Jealous' is a disease of the flesh." Ghost **Rex Harrison** insists to Gene Tierney that he's not capable of being jealous. *The Ghost and Mrs. Muir* (1947, 20th Century-Fox).

5290 "I don't believe in jealousy. It's dumb. One thing though. Touch his dick and he's dead." Dumb **Kevin Kline** gives his girl friend Jamie Lee Curtis some instructions. She plans to romance barrister John Cleese to get information that will help them find some hidden stolen jewels. *A Fish Called Wanda* (1988, MGM-United Artists).

Jesus Christ

see also BELIEFS, CHRISTMAS, GOD, RELIGIONS, WORSHIP

5291 "If you don't think Christ is down here on the waterfront, you've got another guess coming! Every morning when the hiring boss blows his whistle, Jesus stands along side you in the shape-up. He sees why some of you get picked and why some get passed over." Priest **Karl Malden** tries to convince longshoremen to testify against their crooked union leaders. *On the Waterfront* (1954, Columbia).

5292 "Life is pain and sin and torment, and Jesus Christ absolves you, and there ain't no pain, and there ain't no sin, and there ain't no torment because your body is filled with His eternal love and His eternal compassion. Just open your arms and let Christ come in to every part of you." **Betty Lou Holland** tells her unhappy sex goddess daughter Kim Stanley that all her problems will be taken care of if she just accepts Jesus Christ as her savior. *The Goddess* (1958, Columbia).

5293 "Jesus had guts! He wasn't afraid of the whole Roman army. Think that quarterback's hot stuff? Well, let me tell you, Jesus would have made the best little All-American quarterback in the history of football. Jesus was a real fighter—the best little scrapper, pound for pound, that you ever saw. And why, gentlemen? Love! Jesus had love in both fists!" **Burt Lancaster** gives a demonstration of his preaching ability in a speakeasy on Christmas Eve. *Elmer Gantry* (1960, United Artists).

5294 "If Jesus was a carpenter I wonder how much he charged for bookshelves." Probably there were some people not amused by what they might consider an irreverent wisecrack from **Woody Allen.** But Jesus was a carpenter and before his public life, he made his living that way. *Love and Death* (1975, United Artists).

5295 "You believe in Jesus?. . . Well, you're going to meet him." These are the last words heard by one of five punks who gang-raped and impaled urban vigilante **Charles Bronson**'s daughter, resulting in her death. Just before blowing him away, Bronson notices his victim is wearing a crucifix on a chain. *Death Wish II* (1982, Columbia-EMI-Warner Bros.).

5296 "I just want to know: are you the anti-Christ?" Super straight attorney **Griffin Dunne** is appalled by the dishonesty and disregard for property and social etiquette exhibited by ex-convict Madonna as they search for the men who framed her. *Who's That Girl?* (1987, Warner Bros.).

5297 "Jesus loves you—everyone else thinks you're an asshole." Smart-aleck Jesuit priest **Ed Flanders** admits to his superior that he gave this blessing to one of the Catholic university's most generous benefactors. *The Exorcist III* (1990, 20th Century-Fox).

Jewelry

see also APPEARANCES, CLOTHES, WORTH AND VALUES

5298 "This is just my summer jewelry. You should see my winter stuff." **Mae West** tells a gawking visitor to her room that the latter hasn't seen the best of West's glittering sparklers. *She Done Him Wrong* (1933, Paramount).

5299 "Ze roo-bies, Bella. . . give me ze roo-bies." Victorian schizophrenic **Anton Walbrook** demands that his wife Diana Wynyard hand over the rubies for which he has murdered and tried to drive her crazy. In the American remake, after being caught, **Charles Boyer** confesses to Ingrid Bergman why he tried to drive her insane, "Between us all the time were those jewels, like a fire—a fire in my brain that separated us—those jewels which I wanted all my life." *Gaslight* aka: *Angel Street* (1939, GB, British National); (1944, MGM).

5300 "I can recommend the bait. I ought to know—I bit on it myself." Stranded in a lifeboat with other survivors of a U-boat attack, **Tallulah Bankhead** offers her diamond necklace for fish bait. *Lifeboat* (1944, 20th Century-Fox).

5301 "I always say a kiss on the hand might feel very good, but a diamond tiara lasts forever." Not so dumb blonde **Marilyn Monroe** pouts to wealthy Charles Coburn whose wife owns a diamond tiara. *Gentlemen Prefer Blondes* (1953, 20th Century-Fox).

5302 "Here, hold them. . . they're the most beautiful things in the world, the one thing you can't resist." If you listen to **Grace Kelly**'s words, she's tempting the one-time cat thief with her necklace, but the camera seems to be looking at her fetchingly displayed decolletage. *To Catch a Thief* (1955, Paramount).

5303 "It, uh, it seems that one of the crowns was adorned with a great jewel, a diamond as big as a gull's egg. Now the three crowns have been lost for many, many years, but I feel, sire, that if we organized a proper expedition it would be quite possible to follow those. . . ." Viking adventurer **Richard Widmark** is in there pitching again, after butting heads with Moorish chieftain Sidney Poitier over a golden bell. *The Long Ships* (1964, GB-Yugo., Columbia).

5304 "James, how the hell do we get those diamonds down again?" **Jill St. John,** as Tiffany Case, questions Sean Connery, as James Bond, about a diamond-powered laser that has been launched into space. *Diamonds Are Forever* (1971, GB, United Artists).

5305 "I could never be intimate with anyone who wore a pinky ring." **Susan Sarandon** explains one of her reasons for rejecting an affair with lustful dentist Joe Mantegna. *Compromising Positions* (1985, Paramount).

5306 "They're in the business to sell jewelry. They use gold cigarette cases as loss-leaders." **Madonna** insists that Cartier expects her to shoplift a gold cigarette case lying on a counter. *Who's That Girl?* (1987, Warner Bros.).

Jews

5307 "[Karl] Marx wasn't a German. Marx was a Jew." **Orson Welles,** posing as a teacher in a small Connecticut town, gives himself away with his racial remark to Edward G. Robinson. The latter has been trailing the Nazi war criminal, whose identity and appearance he did not know. *The Stranger* (1946, International/RKO).

5308 "My best friend, a Jew, is lying back in a fox-hole at Guadalcanal. I'm gonna spit in your eye for him, because we don't have room for people like you in this country." **Robert Mitchum** screams at the leader of a semi-fascist veterans group who claims his association represents everybody except "niggers, Jews and Catholics." *Till the End of Time* (1946, RKO).

5309 "Oh, God, I've got it. It's the only way. It's the only way. I'll be Jewish." Looking for an angle on a series of articles exposing America's anti-Semitism, crusading journalist **Gregory Peck** gets the idea to pretend he's Jewish and experience the prejudice first hand. *Gentleman's Agreement* (1947, 20th Century-Fox).

5310 "I have no religion, so I am not Jewish by religion. I am a scientist, so I must rely on science which tells me I am not Jewish by race, since there's no such thing as a Jewish type. . . I remain a Jew because the world makes it an advantage not to be one. So, for many of us, it becomes a matter of pride to call ourselves Jews." World famous physicist **Sam Jaffe** tells Gregory Peck and Dorothy McGuire that he resents the evasions of Jewish intellectuals to publicly identify with their heritage. *Gentleman's Agreement* (1947, 20th Century-Fox).

5311 "I've come to see that lots of nice people who aren't [anti-Semites]—people who despise it and deplore it and protest their innocence—help it along and then wonder why it grows. People who'd never beat up a Jew, or yell 'kike' at a child, people who think that anti-Semitism is something away off in some dark crackpot place with low-class morons. That's the biggest discovery I've made about this whole business, Kathy, the good people, the nice people." In order to write a series on anti-Semitism, Christian writer **Gregory Peck** pretends to be a Jew so he can experience first-hand the subtle and not-so-subtle prejudices. He is most shocked to find "nice people" like his girl friend Dorothy McGuire passively prejudiced against Jews. *Gentleman's Agreement* (1947, 20th Century-Fox).

5312 "There are nearly a million Jews in Germany. What are they going to do? Kill us all?" German Jewish businessman **Heinz Ruehmann** dismisses the threat of the Nazis because he is unable to think the unthinkable. *Ship of Fools* (1965, Columbia).

5313 "They're different. They don't even seem to be Jewish." In 1938, **Romolo Valli** refers to the wealthy Italian Jewish family, the Finzi-Continis. *The Garden of the Finzi-Continis* (1970, Italy-W. Germany, Documento Film-CCC Filmkunst).

5314 "I am a retired investor on a pension, and I wished to live there as a Jew in the twilight of my life." Mobster **Lee Strasberg** wishes to emigrate to Israel, but he's not welcome. *The Godfather, Part II* (1974, Paramount).

5315 "Jewish women don't believe in sex after marriage." At the time of Napoleon's invasion, **Woody Allen** is a 19th century Russian stand-up comedian. *Love and Death* (1975, United Artists). [MPL]

5316 "So I said, 'Did you eat yet or what?' And Tom Christie said, 'No, JEW?' Not 'Did you?'. . . JEW eat? JEW?" Paranoid **Woody Allen** explains to Tony Roberts that he thinks an acquaintance has made an ethnic remark. *Annie Hall* (1977, United Artists).

5317 ANNIE HALL: "Well, you are what Grammy Hall calls a 'real Jew.'" ALVY SINGER: "Thank you." Before their relationship takes off, WASP **Diane Keaton** makes a bizarre comment to a startled **Woody Allen**. *Annie Hall* (1977, United Artists).

5318 "That was a regime. Now all we have is a government. . . Better to gas 100,000 Jews than to have a pig like that messing around with my daughter." When German truck driver **Jorg von Liebenfels** discovers that his 14-year-old daughter Eva Mattes has willingly given her virginity to 19-year-old Jew

Harry Baer, von Liebenfels misses the Nazis. *Jail Bait* aka: *Wild Game* (1977, W. Germany, Interfel-New Yorker).

5319 "Jews know two things: suffering and where to find great Chinese food." **Mark Linn-Baker** shares a secret with cute little WASP Jessica Harper. *My Favorite Year* (1982, MGM-United Artists).

5320 "There are 40,000 Italian Jews—they are all our Jews. We are responsible for them." Catholic priest **Ben Cross** spearheads the efforts to find safe passage out of Italy for Jews traveling to freedom as Christian pilgrims. *The Assisi Underground* (1985, Cannon).

5321 "There are six million Jews in Europe for whom the world is divided into two parts, places in which they are not allowed to live and places in which they cannot enter." **Peter Ustinov,** as detective Hercule Poirot, makes an ironic observation while on holiday in Palestine in the 1930s. *Appointment with Death* (1988, Golan-Globus/Cannon).

Jinx *see* LUCK

Jobs

see also CAREERS, OCCUPATIONS, WORK AND WORKERS

5322 "As long as they have sidewalks, you've got a job." **Joan Blondell**'s catty remark is directed to gold-digger Claire Dodd. *Footlight Parade* (1933, Warner Bros.).

5323 "Well, sir, in three months I could pass her off as a duchess at an ambassador's reception. . . Yes. . . I could even get her a job as a lady's maid or shop assistant, which required better English." Phonetics professor **Leslie Howard** brags to Scott Sunderland what he can do for Cockney flower girl Wendy Hiller. *Pygmalion* (1938, GB, MGM).

5324 "I'm gonna stay here and do the job I came for. My pa did it the old way, and I'm gonna do it the new way." Despite his protest, when things get tough, Deputy Sheriff **James Stewart** straps on his six-guns and shoots down the bad guys, the same way his famous lawman father did. *Destry Rides Again* (1939, Universal).

5325 "Our task is to present Turkey with a match that will inflame the people against Russia." During World War II, **Sydney Greenstreet**'s job as one of Germany's top agents is to involve Turkey in a war with Russia. *Background to Danger* (1943, Warner Bros.).

5326 "To me a claims man is a surgeon. That desk is an operating table, and those pencils are scalpels and bone chisels, and those papers are not just forms and statistics and claims for compensation, they're alive, they're packed with drama, with twisted hopes and crooked dreams. A claims man, Walter, is a. . . is a doctor and a bloodhound and a cop and a judge and a jury and a father confessor, all in one." In a staccato delivery, insurance claims man **Edward G. Robinson** insists to insurance salesman Fred MacMurray how important Robinson's job is. *Double Indemnity* (1944, Paramount).

5327 "Every man must do what he does best—and what he does best can be done best in Guadalcanal." Mayor **Raymond Walburn** prepares a speech suggesting that his "marine hero" opponent Eddie Bracken go back to war and leave politics to civilians. *Hail the Conquering Hero* (1944, Paramount).

5328 "Kissing is nice, but your father didn't hire me to sleep with you." Private eye Philip Marlowe, played by **Humphrey Bogart,** does his best to resist Lauren Bacall and keep his mind on what he was hired for. *The Big Sleep* (1946, Warner Bros.).

5329 "Plenty of jobs here, even for the unlucky ones—and no prejudices." Narrator **Coleen Gray** refers to the penitentiary to which Victor Mature is sent. *Kiss of Death* (1947, 20th Century-Fox).

5330 "I've never been an idler or a parasite." Self-proclaimed genius **Clifton Webb** answers exasperated Robert Young's question, "Is there anything you haven't been?" Webb has run through a long list of his accomplishments. His words sound suspiciously like an accusation. *Sitting Pretty* (1948, 20th Century-Fox).

5331 LINDA DE CALDERON: "Why did you do it, Luis? How can you go on doing that Sunday after Sunday?" LUIS BELLO: "It's what I do. Luis Bello without bulls—nothing going back to nothing. But you saw only the bad. There is something great about it sometimes." **Miroslava** can't understand why **Mel Ferrer** persists as a matador. But he sees it as a job which can, on occasion, be an art in defying death with grace and courage. *The Brave Bulls* (1951, Columbia).

5332 "I'm not in a popularity contest. We've got a job to do." Marine Officer **John Wayne** is a strict disciplinarian, who doesn't care if his troops on Guadalcanal like him or not. *Flying Leathernecks* (1951, RKO).

5333 MAJ. JEB WEBBE: "Maybe the war's catching up with me. Its ugliness, its stupidity, futility." LT. COL.

HILARY WHALTERS: "It's a job, that's all." WEBBE: "Yeah, but other jobs get done." Surgeon **Humphrey Bogart** knows that his commanding officer **Robert Keith** isn't right about war being just another job. *Battle Circus* (1953, MGM).

5334 "Well, my job's finished when I get you there." Desperately in need of money, farmer **Van Heflin** takes a job of escorting notorious killer Glenn Ford to Yuma prison. Ford's gang intends to prevent Heflin from collecting his fee. *3:10 to Yuma* (1957, Columbia).

5335 "There are plenty of soldiers that don't like war. It's a dirty job enforcing the law, but it's what we're supposed to be doing." Mexican narcotics investigator **Charlton Heston** uses a cliché to respond to U.S. Police Detective Orson Welles, who accuses Heston of seeming to not like being a lawman. *Touch of Evil* (1958, Universal-International).

5336 "You want a job? I got a job for you—fix up this goddamn pigsty. Listen, you've got a pretty good salary for testing out that bed all day. You want another fifty a week? Try vacuuming. You want an extra hundred. Try making the bed. Try opening the windows! That's why you can hardly stand up. The goddamn place smells like a coffin." **Jack Nicholson** yells at his live-in love, lazy Ann-Margret. Looks like the honeymoon's over. *Carnal Knowledge* (1971, Avco Embassy).

5337 "You think because I'm black, I'll blow the whistle on you. I want your job on my terms. When are you going to start looking at me on my terms?" Cultured black Police Detective **Yaphet Kotto** is put in charge of a robbery and murder case at a Harlem numbers bank instead of a veteran, tough, aging white cop Anthony Quinn. *Across 110th Street* (1972, United Artists).

5338 LORNA: "I think you're the most selfish man in the world!" BENSINGTON: "So why do you work for me?" LORNA: "Because jobs for lady bacteriologists are not easy to find." Scientist **Pamela Franklin** doesn't like working for greedy businessman **Ralph Meeker.** He hopes to market an ambrosia-like substance discovered on a remote island. *Food of the Gods* (1976, AIP).

5339 LINDA MAROLLA: "What does he do?" ARTHUR BACH: "He helps me." LINDA: "What do you do?" ARTHUR: "Nothing." LINDA: "You've got a good job." **Liza Minnelli** questions **Dudley Moore** about John Gielgud's duties. *Arthur* (1981, Orion-Warner Bros.).

5340 "Hi, lady. You know, Millie, I'm sure we're doing the right thing, but since we only work days at a college, I could moonlight and pick up some extra bucks. I can't decide what to do. It's a toss-up. It'll either be brain surgery or trying for that opening at the nuclear plant." Former circus clown **Jerry Lewis** tells Deanna Lund that he's still trying to adjust to real life. *Hardly Working* (1981, 20th Century-Fox).

5341 "It's part of my job to get people. The rich and powerful won't allow that, so, I came down twice as hard on the Negroes and the poor." French West African Police Chief **Philippe Noiret** explains his work. *Coup de Torchon* (1982, Fr., Quartet Films).

5342 MICHAEL DORSEY: "You mean nobody in New York wants to hire me?" GEORGE FIELDS: "I'd go farther than that, Michael. Nobody in Hollywood wants to hire you either." Agent **Sydney Pollack** tells his difficult client **Dustin Hoffman** that he can't find him an acting job on either coast. *Tootsie* (1982, Columbia).

5343 "Then get a job in a bakery." **Mr. T** advises a hooker who claims she needs "bread." *D.C. Cab* (1983, Universal).

5344 "Every morning I wake up and thank God for drugs and subversion and murder—because without them we'd be out of a job." Government agent **Kurtwood Smith** looks on the bright side of a crime for border patrol Officer Kris Kristofferson. *Flashpoint* (1984, Tri-Star).

5345 "Help, I hate this job." Whiny waitress **Teri Garr** scribbles the message on the back of Griffin Dunne's bill. He doesn't know if he's expected to tip her or rescue her. *After Hours* (1985, Warner Bros.).

5346 "I thought this Christmas season was going to be, you know, the kind you see in movies. Me and Rina in front of a warm fire. Instead, you know the rest. Here I am driving fifty miles out into the suburbs because some guy offers me $100,000 to kill his wife. I want to meet the woman that's worth $100,000. After all, I did take the down payment." To unlicensed private eye **Billy Dee Williams** a job is a job—and this is a particularly well-paying job. *Deadly Illusions* (1987, Cinetel).

5347 WESLEY: "I ain't got no fixed job. I just do what comes by. That's what we do back home." RITA: "Could you be a businessman?" WESLEY: "I guess, if it comes by." American soldier **Tim Ransom,** with only one thing on his mind, is asked what he does in civilian life by pretty romantic 17-year-old British **Jane Horrocks.** *The Dressmaker* (1989, GB, Euro-American Films).

5348 "We've never held a day job in our lives." **Beau Bridges** brags to singer Michelle Pfeiffer, referring to himself and his brother Jeff Bridges, both lounge piano players. *The Fabulous Baker Boys* (1989, 20th Century-Fox).

5349 TOM REAGAN: "Intimidating helpless women is part of my job." VERNA: "Then why don't you find one and intimidate her?" Irish hood **Gabriel Byrne** has just cornered tough broad **Marcia Gay Harden** in a ladies' room. *Miller's Crossing* (1990, 20th Century-Fox).

5350 "Why don't they get a real job and live like everyone else? Then they could do their painting on the weekends. That's how I'd handle it." It's Babbitt-like **Paul Newman**'s predictable opinion and indignation when an artist asks for real money for a painting. *Mr. and Mrs. Bridge* (1990, Miramax).

5351 "My job was to bring back the bad news and keep the body count." **Sharon Stone** recalls her cub-reporter experience in Vietnam for journalist Andrew McCarthy. *Year of the Gun* (1991, Triumph).

5352 "I'm going to be a buyer. . . I don't know, it's just a job I heard of, sounded pretty cool." Teen **Kristy Swanson** has a career goal. *Buffy, the Vampire Slayer* (1992, 20th Century-Fox).

Joinings *see* PARTICIPATIONS, TOGETHERNESS

Jokes and Joking *see* FUN, HUMOR, LAUGHTER, RIDICULE, TAUNTS

Journalism *see* HEADLINES, NEWSPAPERS, REPORTERS, WRITING AND WRITERS

Journeys *see* TRAVELS AND TRIPS, TOURS AND TOURISM

Joy

see also ENJOYMENT, HAPPINESS, PLEASURE

5353 "Let joy be unconfined. Let there be dancing in the streets, drinking in the saloons and necking in the park." Tacky promoter **Groucho Marx** tries to impress wealthy Margaret Dumont. *A Night at the Opera* (1935, MGM).

5354 "All my life nothing ever quite matched the perfect joy of that moment. My school lay in ruins with a beckoning of stolen days." In voice-over, director and screenwriter **John Boorman,** as the adult Bill Rohan, recalls how happy he was when his school was destroyed by a German bomb during World War II, thereby extending his vacation indefinitely. *Hope and Glory* (1987, GB, Columbia).

Judgments

see also DECISIONS, JUSTICE, LEGALITIES, OPINIONS, PUNISHMENTS

5355 "Remember my sentimental friend, you will be judged not by how much you love, but by how much you are loved." **Frank Morgan,** as the Wizard of Oz, imparts a bit of homespun wisdom to Jack Haley, as the Tin Man, who wants a heart. *The Wizard of Oz* (1939, MGM).

5356 "The man who kills in self-defense must not be judged by the same standards as the man who kills in anger." Professor **Edward G. Robinson** makes this observation when his opinion is merely academic. *The Woman in the Window* (1944, International/RKO).

5357 "That boy you trained personally shows a substantial lacking of good judgment." Honest, aging ex-lawman **Joel McCrea** is suspicious of his larcenous friend Randolph Scott, who is like a Mephistopheles to young Ron Starr. *Ride the High Country* (1962, MGM).

5358 "Cancel my order! My patient has developed some instabilities which make his judgment questionable." Psychiatrist **Alan Hewitt** regularly gets stock tips from Gig Young. When he mistakenly gets the impression that Young is in love with his boss Cary Grant, Hewitt no longer values the information. *That Touch of Mink* (1962, Universal-International).

5359 "You have to have men who are moral and at the same time are able to utilize their primordial instincts to kill without feeling; without passion, without judgment—without judgment. Because it's judgment that defeats us." Mad Colonel **Marlon Brando** converses with just such a man, military assassin Martin Sheen, sent to kill him. *Apocalypse Now* (1979, Omni Zoetrope-United Artists).

5360 "Soldiers at war should not be judged by civilian rules even though they may commit acts, which when calmly viewed afterwards, could be seen as un-Christian and brutal." Defense counsel **Jack Thompson** makes a point in the court martial trial of three Australian officers accused of murdering prisoners of war during the Boer War. *Breaker Morant* (1980, Australia, South Australian Film Corporation).

5361 "What is this, a Pauline Kael review?" **George Segal** is put out when his bed partner Priscilla Barnes judges his performance as disappointing. *The Last Married Couple in America* (1980, Universal).

5362 "Never hate your enemies. It affects your judgment." Godfather **Al Pacino** instructs his nephew and successor-in-training Andy Garcia. *The Godfather, Part III* (1990, Paramount).

5363 "Why don't you just pull 'em out and I'll judge which one is bigger?" **Laurie Metcalf** responds to the rivalry between Richard Gere and Andy Garcia with a challenge. *Internal Affairs* (1990, Paramount).

Judges *see* JUDGMENTS, JUSTICE, LAWS, LAWYERS, LEGALITIES, OPINIONS

Jumping

see also ACTION AND ACTS, FEARS

5364 "I will so jump. I can jump better than ever because I've grown. And I moved the bar higher." **Cammie King** defies her father Clark Gable, and jumps her pony, but doesn't make it and is killed. *Gone with the Wind* (1939, Selznick-MGM).

5365 "Trying to improve the world by jumping off buildings. You couldn't improve the world if the building jumped on you!" **Walter Brennan**, as "The Colonel," dismisses Gary Cooper's job playing "John Doe," who has announced he plans to jump off the courthouse on Christmas Eve to protest the conditions in the U.S. *Meet John Doe* (1941, Warner Bros.).

5366 "I knew a girl once who told me to jump in the lake and when I came back she was gone." Naïve **Eddie Bracken** allows girls to take advantage of him, especially Betty Hutton. *The Miracle of Morgan's Creek* (1944, Paramount).

5367 BUTCH CASSIDY: "I'll jump first." SUNDANCE KID: "No." BUTCH: "Then you jump first." KID: "No, I said." BUTCH: "What's the matter with you?" KID: "I can't swim." BUTCH: "Why you're crazy! The fall will probably kill you." It's an amusing exchange between outlaws **Paul Newman** and **Robert Redford** who are trapped by a posse. The only way to escape is to jump from a high ledge into a river far below. *Butch Cassidy and the Sundance Kid* (1969, 20th Century-Fox).

Jungles *see* ANIMALS, LAND, TREES

Justice

see also FAIRNESS AND UNFAIRNESS, JUDGMENTS, LAWS, LAWYERS, LEGALITIES, RIGHT AND WRONG, RIGHTS, WRONG AND WRONGDOINGS

5368 "I'll tell the world who's a fake! You are! I taught you everything you know. Even your name, Lily Garland—I gave you that. If there's any justice in the world, Mildred Plotka, you'll end up where you belong—in a burlesque house!" Temperamental Broadway producer **John Barrymore** damns his former protégé, star actress Carole Lombard, for her lack of appreciation. *Twentieth Century* (1934, Columbia).

5369 "I know that by coming here I've saved these people. But that isn't why I'm here. I don't care about saving them. The law doesn't know that a lot of things that were important to me, silly things, maybe, like a belief in justice and the idea that men were civilized, and a feeling of pride that this country of mine was different from all others. . . the law doesn't know that these things were burned to death with me that night." **Spencer Tracy** addresses the court at the trial of the leaders of the lynch mob that set afire the jail, in which he was being held, mistaken for a murderer. Although his body survived, the ordeal has changed him into a bitter, vengeful man. *Fury* (1936, MGM).

5370 "What does it matter if an individual is shattered if only Justice is resurrected?" **Paul Muni,** as the title character, raises a vital question, arguing the innocence of Joseph Schildkraut as Jewish Captain Dreyfus. *The Life of Emile Zola* (1937, Warner Bros.).

5371 "Not only is an innocent man crying out for justice; but more, much more—a great nation is in desperate danger of forfeiting her honor!" Title character **Paul Muni** pleads before a court not only for the falsely accused, convicted and imprisoned Joseph Schildkraut, as Captain Dreyfus, but for the nation of France itself. *The Life of Emile Zola* (1937, Warner Bros.).

5372 "What happened this afternoon was just what you deserved. And if there was any justice, you'd have gotten worse." **Alicia Rhett** believes that Vivien Leigh's close call with several men who waylaid her in Shantytown was well warranted. Rhett has hated Leigh since the latter stole the former's fiancé for her first husband. *Gone with the Wind* (1939, Selznick-MGM).

5373 "Aim this only at injustice and you cannot fail." **Morton Selten,** the ancient ruler of the Land of Legend, presents Sabu with a magic crossbow. *The Thief of Bagdad* (1940, GB, London Films).

5374 "So much for those bandits. You know, you got to hand it to the Mexicans when it comes to swift justice. Once the Federales get their mitts on a criminal, they know just what to do with him. They hand him a shovel, tell him where to dig, and when he's dug enough, they tell him to put the shovel down, smoke a cigarette and say his prayers. In another five minutes, he's being covered over with the earth he dug up." **Bruce Bennett** explains to Tim Holt that there's very little delay in dispensing justice in Mexico. *The Treasure of the Sierra Madre* (1948, Warner Bros.).

5375 "Sign that, and Roman justice will receive a blow from which it may never recover. Condemn these Christians, and you make martyrs of them and assure their immortality. Condemn them, and, in the eyes of history, you condemn yourself." In trying to advise mad Emperor Nero, played by Peter Ustinov, **Leo Genn** sounds like he has the advantage of hind-sight. *Quo Vadis* (1951, MGM).

5376 "I come from a very old country where it's traditional for each man to make his own justice." Sicilian **Eli Wallach** claims to have his own personal moral code. *Baby Doll* (1956, Warner Bros.).

5377 "The wheels of justice grind slowly, but they grind finely." Realizing that he has succeeded in getting his guilty client Tyrone Power acquitted of murder, barrister **Charles Laughton** warns Power that justice will be served. *Witness for the Prosecution* (1957, United Artists).

5378 "In this country our courts are the great levelers, and in our courts all men are created equal. I'm no idealist to believe firmly in the integrity of our courts and the jury system. That is no ideal to me. . . it is a living, working reality. Gentlemen, a court is no better than each one of you sitting before me on the jury. A court is only as sound as its jury, and a jury is only as sound as the men who make it up. I am confident that you gentlemen will review without passion the evidence you have heard, come to a decision and restore this defendant to his family. In the name of God, do your duty. In the name of God, believe Tom Robinson." Despite the elegant pleas of defense counsel **Gregory Peck** and the evidence of innocence, the jury in a small Southern town in the 30s convicts black man Brock Peters of raping white woman Collin Wilcox. *To Kill a Mockingbird* (1962, Universal).

5379 GEORGE BECKWORTH: "There is still such a thing as due process." COL. MIKE KIRBY: "Out here due process is a bullet." Sickened and angry, reporter **David Janssen** complains to Green Berets Colonel **John Wayne** after witnessing the torture of a Viet Cong prisoner. *The Green Berets* (1968, Warner Bros.).

5380 DR. TAYLOR: "I came here for justice. I'm going to get it. I don't want a policeman's idea of justice. I want a victim's idea of justice, from the bottom looking up, not from the top looking down." COMMISSIONER RUSSELL: "I think you're talking about

revenge, not justice." TAYLOR: "Commissioner, during the Harlem riots, I, well, I was called an Uncle Tom for using whatever influence I had to bring about peace and understanding. Was I wrong?" RUSSELL: "You were right, doctor." TAYLOR: "Prove it, commissioner, you prove it to me." Black clergyman **Raymond St. Jacques'** son has been picked up by the police for interrogation about a crime of which he is innocent. When his son is released, St. Jacques seeks Police Commissioner **Henry Fonda**'s guarantee that the officers involved in the false arrest will be punished. *Madigan* (1968, Universal).

5381 "What good is the law if it prevents me from receiving justice?" **Martin Landau** justifies the murder of his mistress Anjelica Huston by putting his rights and interests above hers. *Crimes and Misdemeanors* (1989, Orion).

5382 "[I will take the case] if only to prove that justice in South Africa is misapplied when it concerns the question of race. . . Law and justice are just not on speaking terms at all in South Africa." Liberal lawyer **Marlon Brando** agrees to take a human rights case. *A Dry White Season* (1989, MGM).

5383 "Poetic justice." **Charles Bronson** is pleased when pimp and child molester Juan Fernandez is placed in a cell with a huge brute waiting to sodomize his new roommate. *Kinjite: Forbidden Subjects* (1989, Cannon).

5384 "Sweetheart, if there's any justice on this planet, they'll never make you give back that red dress." **Clint Eastwood** thinks Bernadette Peters looks especially nice in a dress she "borrowed." *Pink Cadillac* (1989, Warner Bros.).

5385 "I'm a prosecutor. I'm part of the business of accusing, judging and punishing. I explore the evidence of a crime, and determine who is charged, who is brought to this room to be tried before his peers. I present my evidence to the jury and they deliberate upon it. They must determine what really happened. If they cannot, we will not know whether the accused deserves to be freed or should be punished. If they cannot find the truth, what is our hope of justice?" In voice-over, **Harrison Ford** sets the stage as the camera focuses on a large empty courtroom at the beginning of the movie. *Presumed Innocent* (1990, Warner Bros.).

5386 "Will you go next door and remind them justice is blind, not deaf?" Judge **Abigail Van Alyn** sends her bailiff from her courtroom, where lawyer Mary Elizabeth Mastrantonio is making her summation, to the court next door where spectators are cheering Mastrantonio's lawyer father Gene Hackman. *Class Action* (1991, 20th Century-Fox).

5387 "Let justice be done though the heavens may fall." This quote to reporters is **Kevin Costner**'s way of saying "let the chips fall where they may." He portrays New Orleans District Attorney Jim Garrison investigating the John F. Kennedy assassination. *JFK* (1991, Warner Bros.).

Justifications

see also DEFENSES, RIGHT AND WRONG

5388 "Look what I've done with what it left me— I've given to charity, built schools, hospitals. I've given thousands of people work." **Barbara Stanwyck** admits to Van Heflin that she killed her wealthy aunt years ago, but firmly believes that the end justifies the means. *The Strange Love of Martha Ivers* (1946, Paramount).

5389 "Listen, stupe, the first week I was in this joint somebody stole my Red Cross package, my blanket, and my left shoe. Well, since then I've wised up. This ain't no Salvation Army. This is everybody for himself, dog eat dog." POW **William Holden** justifies his sharp trading with the Germans that allows him to live a life of relative luxury compared to that of the other prisoners. *Stalag 17* (1953, Paramount).

5390 "Oh, Mark, we both know that even the fat, ugly people of this world believe that being in love makes them beautiful and justifies everything." Eurasian physician **Jennifer Jones** doesn't fool herself into believing that because she's in love with married William Holden and he's in love with her, that makes everything okay. *Love Is a Many-Splendored Thing* (1955, 20th Century-Fox).

5391 "All I want is to enter my house justified." Honorable and honest **Joel McCrea** stays that way despite the attempts of his old friend Randolph Scott to corrupt him. *Ride the High Country* (1962, MGM).

5392 "The end justifies the means." Sinister mad scientist **Maximilian Schell** is determined to plumb the depths of a black hole in space. *The Black Hole* (1979, Buena Vista).

5393 "I think I finally saw one too many bodies." Photographer **Nick Nolte** justifies his breach of journalistic neutrality in Nicaragua. *Under Fire* (1983, Orion).

5394 "It was the same love. It just got split in half, that's all." Bigamist **Harry Dean Stanton** defends his two-wives, two-family arrangements. *Fool for Love* (1985, Cannon).

5395 "If you ain't better than a nigger, who are you better than?" **Gene Hackman** quotes his poor white trash father's justification for poisoning a black man's mule. The latter was better off than he. *Mississippi Burning* (1988, Orion).

Juvenile Delinquency *see* CHILDREN AND CHILDHOOD, CRIMES AND CRIMINALS, YOUTH

Kidnappings

see also CRIMES AND CRIMINALS, FORCE, MONEY

5396 "Do I understand this correctly? I've been marked down? I've been kidnapped by K-Mart?" **Bette Midler** is outraged to learn that when her husband Danny De Vito refuses to pay the ransom for her, kidnappers Judge Reinhold and Helen Shaver lower their demand. *Ruthless People* (1986, Touchstone/ Buena Vista).

5397 "We're going to requisition a girl for a little portable R & R." Squad leader Sergeant **Sean Penn** and his men kidnap a Vietnamese girl and repeatedly rape her while on patrol. When they are finished with her, they kill her. *Casualties of War* (1989, Columbia).

Killings

see also DEATH AND DYING, DESTRUCTION, ENDS AND ENDINGS, EXECUTIONS, VIOLENCE, WARS, WEAPONS

5398 "I'm going to kill you with my own hands." Crooked gold commissioner **Tom Santschi** threatens gold miner William Farnum just before they start the climactic fight sequence of this often-filmed western. *The Spoilers* (1914, silent, Selig).

5399 "It's murder and you call it fun." Reluctant spy **John Gielgud** corrects Madeleine Carroll, who is delighted with the thought of mayhem. She is disappointed when she's not allowed to assist in the assassination of suspected enemy agent Percy Marmont. *Secret Agent* (1935, GB, Gaumont British).

5400 "I don't like murder in close quarters as much as I expected." Secret agent **Madeleine Carroll** changes her tune when she finds political assassination is not all the fun she expected. *Secret Agent* (1935, GB, Gaumont British).

5401 "It's murder. I'd sooner see you dead than see you do this. What do I care about them or him? It's us! I'm not going to have this on our consciences!" When John Gielgud moves in for the kill of real enemy agent Robert Young, **Madeleine Carroll** changes her mind about the whole spy business. *Secret Agent* (1935, GB, Gaumont British).

5402 "They're murderers. I know the law says they're not, because I'm still alive, but that's not their fault." **Spencer Tracy** angrily denounces the lynch mob leaders, on trial for killing him when they burned down the jail holding him. *Fury* (1936, MGM).

5403 "They made me a murderer. . . I'm through." After killing kindly Chaplain William Gargan while escaping from prison, **Henry Fonda** tells his wife Sylvia Sidney that there's no hope for him. *You Only Live Once* (1937, United Artists).

5404 "That wasn't surgery. It was murder." Physician **Robert Donat** accuses Cecil Parker of blundering in operating on Ralph Richardson, resulting in the latter's death. *The Citadel* (1938, MGM).

5405 "Well, I guess I've done murder. Oh, I won't think about that now. I'll think about that tomorrow." Forced to shoot and kill Yankee deserter Paul Hurst, **Vivien Leigh** expresses her firm belief in "never worry today about something you can put off worrying about until tomorrow." *Gone with the Wind* (1939, Selznick-MGM).

5406 "She's a mighty cold woman. Prancing about Atlanta by herself. She killed her husband same as if she shot him." **Ona Munson** speaks of Vivien Leigh as Olivia de Havilland thanks Munson for saving her husband Leslie Howard's life. *Gone with the Wind* (1939, Selznick-MGM).

5407 "Kill for the love of killing! Kill for the love of Kali! Kill! Kill! Kill!" Indian guru **Eduardo Ciannelli** rouses the followers of the goddess Kali to a fever pitch, thirsting for blood. *Gunga Din* (1939, RKO).

5408 "You should've seen 'em, he jumped up like a board." Doughboy **Humphrey Bogart** relishes a kill as he shoots a German soldier. *The Roaring Twenties* (1939, Warner Bros.).

5409 VALERIE TRAVERS: "Simon Templar, I have often wondered why someone, in the course of your brazen existence, hasn't killed you." SIMON TEMPLAR: "They have often tried, my dear. But somehow, they have never yet succeeded." **Wendy Barrie** is both repelled by and attracted to reformed British crook **George Sanders** who now fights crime in his own inimitable way. *The Saint Strikes Back* (1939, RKO).

5410 "I've never killed in hot blood. It must be different, more. . . more exciting." Deformed executioner and torturer **Boris Karloff** pleads with Basil Rathbone to allow him to kill as a soldier. *Tower of London* (1939, Universal).

5411 "Madrid: when the Spanish Empire encompassed the globe, and young Spanish blades were taught the fine and fashionable art of killing." The film's foreword. *The Mark of Zorro* (1940, 20th Century-Fox).

5412 "You're not marrying that cheap redhead. . . you're mine and I'm hanging on to you. . . I committed murder to get you." **Ida Lupino** murdered her older husband Alan Hale to be free for truck driver George Raft and she's not going to let waitress Ann Sheridan get her hands on him. *They Drive by Night* (1940, Warner Bros.).

5413 "I'm as much agin' killin' as ever but when I heard them machine guns. . . well, them guns was killin' hundreds, maybe thousands, and there weren't nothin' anybody could do to stop them guns. That's what I done." Title character **Gary Cooper,** a conscientious objector, explains that he fought and killed in World War I to put an end to fighting and killing. *Sergeant York* (1941, Warner Bros.).

5414 "I've seen this happen before. It'll either kill him or it'll go away by itself. . . . One of these days it will kill him." **Cary Grant** explains to Joan Fontaine about his friend Nigel Bruce who has collapsed in a near-fit of toxic reaction from just one sip of brandy. *Suspicion* (1941, RKO).

5415 "Whoever is bitten by a werewolf and lives becomes a werewolf himself. A werewolf can be killed only with a silver bullet or a silver knife or a stick with a silver handle. Go now. Heaven help you." Besides being the mother of the werewolf that bit Lon Chaney, Jr., before Chaney was able to kill the beast with a silver-headed walking cane, **Maria Ouspenskaya** dispenses needed information to the audience. Chaney discovers the five-pointed star—the pentagram, over his heart. *The Wolf Man* (1941, Universal).

5416 "I picked up a knife and I let her have it—in the throat. They put a label on me, 'Killer,' and sent me to reform school, and they beat me there, too." Hired killer **Alan Ladd** fails to impress or shock Veronica Lake with the details of his first murder and hard childhood. *This Gun for Hire* (1942, Paramount).

5417 "Don't let's go off half-cocked and do something we'll be sorry for. . . . If we hang these men ourselves. . . we'll be worse than murderers." Storekeeper **Harry Davenport** pleads with members of a posse not to take the law into their hands and lynch three men they suspect of rustling and murder. *The Ox-Bow Incident* (1943, 20th Century-Fox).

5418 "You rotten insane brute. Do you think you can go on murdering?" Dutch novelist **Peter Lorre** is outraged with notorious scoundrel Zachary Scott. *The Mask of Dimitrios* (1944, Warner Bros.).

5419 "Come back! Or do you want this carrion to kill me?" **Zachary Scott** begs Peter Lorre not to leave him alone with Sydney Greenstreet. Lorre leaves and Greenstreet shoots and kills Scott with his own gun. *The Mask of Dimitrios* (1944, Warner Bros.).

5420 "I plead no mitigating circumstances. They deserved to die, as I deserve to die, for I long since killed a person much superior to either of them: myself. I killed that person the day I gave my family name to the woman who became my wife. And since I believe the punishment should fit the crime, I suggest that you hang me until I'm dead." **Herbert Marshall** shows no remorse for having killed his Indian dancer wife Tilly Losch and her lover Sidney Blackmer. Marshall gets his wish to leave the world of which he has grown weary. *Duel in the Sun* (1946, Selznick).

5421 "Bright boy wants to know what it's all about. . . We're gonna kill a Swede. We're killing him for a friend." Killer **William Conrad,** hired with Charles McGraw to rub out Burt Lancaster, is candid with a counter man at a diner who asks what they want with Lancaster when they inquire about him. *The Killers* (1946, Universal).

5422 "You kill a man and that's not a pleasant thing to live with the rest of your life." District Attorney **John Litel** is sympathetic to Dick Powell, whose boredom with his life led him to an involvement with beautiful blonde Lizabeth Scott, sleazy lawyer Raymond Burr, and escaped bank robber Byron Barr. Powell killed Barr to protect his family. *Pitfall* (1948, United Artists).

5423 "Murder is a crime for most men, but a privilege for the few." Professor **James Stewart** postulates that he does not oppose contemplating murder for those who are superior, but he does oppose the actual performance of the murder. *Rope* (1948, Warner Bros.).

5424 "We killed for the sake of danger and the sake of killing." **John Dall** considers himself a Nietzschean superman who has the privilege of killing lesser folks. *Rope* (1948, Warner Bros.).

5425 "Get killed somewhere else. . . ." Sheriff **Millard Mitchell** chases Skip Homeier out of town after the latter shoots gunfighter Gregory Peck in the back. Before he dies, Peck claims he was shot in a fair fight. He wants Homeier to have to live with the reputation of being the fastest gun alive. *The Gunfighter* (1950, 20th Century-Fox).

5426 "If you die, I'll kill you." **Gene Evans,** as Sgt. Zack, threatens a North Korean major. *The Steel Helmet* (1950, Lippert).

5427 "She is, as you rightly say, 'out to kill me.' That is only another fact I have managed to face, as indeed I have faced the more important fact, that she succeeded in her purpose long ago." **Michael Redgrave** acknowledges to his vicious wife Jean Kent's lover Nigel Patrick that he has a bad marriage. *The Browning Version* (1951, GB, Universal).

5428 "All my life I heard of black men being killed because of white girls." Author **Richard Wright,** portraying his creation Bigger Thomas, desperately tries to cover up the fact that he has accidentally smothered his white employer's daughter. *Native Son* (1951, U.S.-Argentina, Argentina Sono-Classic).

5429 "There's no overlooking the fact that murder is at our doorstep, so I wish you wouldn't drag it into the living room." **Leo G. Carroll** wishes his younger daughter Patricia Hitchcock would not discuss the murder of Laura Elliott—the wife of Farley Granger. Granger is Carroll's eldest daughter's boyfriend. *Strangers on a Train* (1951, Warner Bros.).

5430 "I hate killers. . . and when I hate, I hate hard. Killers have to die. . . she was bad. . . she was dangerous. I wouldn't trust her any further than I could throw her. But she was my kind of woman." Mike Hammer-like private eye **Fred Astaire** says goodbye to sexy but bad Cyd Charisse in the "Girl Hunt Ballet." *The Band Wagon* (1953, MGM).

5431 "People don't commit murder on credit." Tennis bum **Ray Milland** has had to save for a long time to come up with the money to hire Anthony Dawson to kill his wife Grace Kelly. *Dial M for Murder* (1954, Warner Bros.).

5432 ROGER THORNHILL: "How did a girl like you get to be a girl like you?" EVE KENDALL: "Lucky, I guess." THORNHILL: "Not lucky—wicked. . . naughty. . . up to no good. . . Ever kill anyone? Bet you could tease a man to death without even trying. . . so stop trying." After returning from an Illinois cornfield, where he was almost killed by a crop-dusting plane, **Cary Grant** is aware that beautiful **Eva Marie Saint** sent him to his intended death—but she doesn't know he knows. *North by Northwest* (1959, MGM).

5433 "My husband and I hated Hitler. What did my husband know of the crimes they convicted him for?. . . He was part of the revenge the victors always take on the vanquished. It was political murder." **Marlene Dietrich**, the widow of a German general executed for war crimes, complains to American jurist Spencer Tracy. *Judgment at Nuremberg* (1961, United Artists).

5434 "If these murderers were monsters, this event would have no more moral significance than an earthquake.... How easily it can happen." American jurist **Spencer Tracy** convicts four German judges of war crimes, because he believes that they knew what they were doing when they served the Nazis, rather than justice, and as such should be held responsible for their actions. *Judgment at Nuremberg* (1961, United Artists).

5435 "It don't take long to kill things, not like it does to grow." **Melvyn Douglas** sadly comments after he and other men herd his diseased cattle into a pit and shoot them all. It takes just a few minutes to kill a couple hundred head. *Hud* (1963, Paramount).

5436 "People don't kill reasonably. They kill unreasonably." **Deborah Kerr,** having committed and been punished for murder, knows what she's talking about. *The Chalk Garden* (1964, GB, Universal).

5437 "About ten minutes ago I tried to kill a cat with a cabbage." Brooding Victorian **Vincent Price** metamorphoses his dead wife into a cat. *The Tomb of Ligeia* (1964, GB, American International).

5438 "Killing is an excellent way of dealing with a hostility problem." Psychoanalyst **James Coburn** makes no moral judgments. *The President's Analyst* (1967, Paramount).

5439 "It's garlic.... If the bullets don't kill ya, ya die of blood poisoning." In a small role, **Jack Nicholson,** one of Capone's henchmen, responds to the question, "What are you rubbing on those bullets?" *The St. Valentine's Day Massacre* (1967, 20th Century-Fox).

5440 "You've done too much for amnesty and you're too well known to disguise; you should have got yourself killed a long time ago when you had the chance." When Paul Newman and Robert Redford are unable to shake a posse trailing them, they get patriotic and seek help from an old friend Sheriff **Jeff Corey** so they can enlist in the army and fight in the Spanish-American war. *Butch Cassidy and the Sundance Kid* (1969, 20th Century-Fox).

5441 "There'll be no killin' around this church unless I do the killin'." Gunslinger-turned-preacher **Glenn Ford** is a peace-loving man who, if necessary, is able to give men eternal peace. *Heaven with a Gun* (1969, MGM).

5442 "The only man I ever murdered is standing before you, with a gun in his hand, defending his corpse to the bitter end." In a film similar to *Seven Samurai/ The Magnificent Seven* **Curt Jurgens** is one of a gang of thieves who protect Iranian villagers from bandit attacks. *The Invincible Six* aka: *The Heroes* (1970, U.S.-Iran, Moulin Rouge-Continental).

5443 "I figured they'd never kill you, at least not until after they found the money." Hamburg whore **Goldie Hawn** never doubted for a minute that security expert Warren Beatty would survive criminals wishing to kill him for stealing their ill-gotten gains from their Hamburg safe deposit boxes. *Dollars* aka: *$ (Dollars)* (1971, Columbia).

5444 "Murder is only killing without a license and everybody kills... the Army, the police...." Antihero **Charles Bronson** justifies his work as a hired assassin. *The Mechanic* (1972, United Artists).

5445 "When you do my dirty laundry ain't gonna help you. And all them honky big partners you got ain't gonna be able to protect your ass, either, because in case you're thinking I'm trying to pull some of that old-time legal shit on you, Captain, I think you ought to know something. I hired the very best killers there are. White killers. White ones, baby, so you better take good care of me. Nothing, nothing better happen to one hair of my gorgeous head. Can you dig it?" Harlem cocaine pusher **Ron O'Neal** threatens his white connection in the corrupt police force. *Superfly* (1972, Warner Bros.).

5446 MIKE: "I've always wondered. I mean, was it hard? All that killing?" DANNY: "Yeah. In the beginning.... But I got better at it." **Timothy Scott** questions his brother-in-law **Joe Don Baker** about his experiences in Vietnam. *Welcome Home, Soldier Boys* (1972, 20th Century-Fox).

5447 GIRL: "You become what you do." DANNY: "I'll tell you what I've done. The only thing I've ever done." GIRL: "What?" DANNY: "I've killed one hundred and thirteen people... maybe more. That's the official count." GIRL: "Then you're a killer. A—killer." DANNY: "That's kinda what I've been thinking." **Jennifer Billingsley** discusses **Joe Don Baker**'s identity with him after he returns from Vietnam. *Welcome Home, Soldier Boys* (1972, 20th Century-Fox).

5448 "I killed them because they were bounty hunters who wanted the reward money. If they was policeman, just being paid to do their job, that would have been different." **Martin Sheen**'s justification for killing two deputies who tried to capture them satisfies none-too-bright Sissy Spacek. *Badlands* (1973, Columbia).

5449 "I mean, they gonna kill you. They gonna tear your heart out if you keep on. They gonna walk on your soul, girl. . . . They gonna kill you in this town, girl." **Robert DoQui** tries to warn waitress Gwen Welles that she's got no future as a singer. She's got a fine shape but a lousy voice. *Nashville* (1975, Paramount).

5450 "When things get a little rough, I just go and kill a few people—that's all." Schizophrenic paranoid Deputy Sheriff **Stacy Keach** has a remedy for dealing with stress. *The Killer Inside Me* (1976, Warner Bros.).

5451 "You would think it would take quite a while to make up your mind to kill someone and then do it. I'm just an ignorant black man but take my word for it, it just takes a second." Aborigine mass murderer **Tommy Lewis** comments at his trial. *The Chant of Jimmie Blacksmith* (1978, Australia, Film House).

5452 "Charging a man with murder in this place is like handing out speeding tickets at the Indy 500." Military assassin **Martin Sheen** laughs at the trumped-up murder charges that military intelligence uses for an excuse to have renegade Colonel Marlon Brando killed. *Apocalypse Now* (1979, United Artists).

5453 "Did I kill the guy that killed me?" It's the dying question of soldier **Perry Lang** about the sniper who shot him. *The Big Red One* (1980, United Artists).

5454 "It is customary during war to kill as many of the enemy as possible." Title character **Edward Woodward** speaks on his own behalf in his trial for war atrocities in the Boer War. He readily admits to having killed unarmed prisoners—but justifies it by the nature of the war and the fact that he was given orders to do so. *Breaker Morant* (1980, Australia, South Australian Film Corporation).

5455 "You should never kill a man unless it's absolutely necessary." **Clint Eastwood,** the feature attraction of a rundown wild west show, passes on some profound advice to the kiddies at his performances. *Bronco Billy* (1980, Warner Bros.).

5456 "I'll kill anybody that's tryin' ta kill me." **Gena Rowlands** is armed and not afraid to use her weapon to protect herself and a seven-year-old boy targeted for assassination by the mob. *Gloria* (1980, Columbia).

5457 "Where are you going to be killed?" It's the heart-wrenching question wide-eyed seven-year-old **Jena Greco** asks her condemned parents Mandy Patinkin and Lindsay Crouse when she visits them in prison. The pair are called Paul and Rochelle Isaacson in the movie, but it's clear they are Julius and Ethel Rosenberg, who were executed for espionage in the fifties. *Daniel* (1981, Paramount).

5458 "This hospital will kill no quadriplegic before his time." In a sick parody of Orson Welles' TV pitch for a wine company, quadriplegic **Richard Dreyfuss,** wishing to be allowed to die, sasses his physician Christine Lahti with some gallows humor. *Whose Life Is It Anyway?* (1981, MGM).

5459 "It's not just crazy ones who kill when we must." Dangerous escaped mental patient **Jack Palance** surveys his slain comrades, frenzied psychos all. *Alone in the Dark* (1982, New Line Cinema).

5460 "Guns don't kill detectives, love does." In a spoof of the hard-boiled private eye movies, **Steve Martin** gives his version of an NRA motto. *Dead Men Don't Wear Plaid* (1982, Universal).

5461 "Try not to kill more than two or three people today, okay?" Police Captain **Paul Sorvino** makes a sarcastic request of private eye Mike Hammer, played by Armand Assante. *I, the Jury* (1982, America Cinema).

5462 "A filthy child murderer who killed at least twenty children in the neighborhood. . . the lawyers got fat and the judge got famous. . . but somebody forgot to sign the search warrant in the right place and he was freed just like that." **Ronee Blakley** tells her daughter Heather Langenkamp how Robert Englund, as Freddy Krueger, escaped legal justice. However, he was then set afire by a mob of outraged parents. Unfortunately, his evil spirit survived to take revenge. *A Nightmare on Elm Street* (1984, New Line).

5463 "I've terminated you, fucker!" No longer a meek housewife, **Linda Hamilton** uses a hydraulic press to crush what remains of terminator from the future, Arnold Schwarzenegger. *The Terminator* (1984, Orion).

5464 TRACY: "We should stick together." SCARLET: "Even if it kills us." TRACY: "Even if it doesn't." In a *Defiant Ones* clone, upper-crust black girl **Irene Cara** and tough white street girl **Tatum O'Neal** are being chased by the police. They don't like each other, but learn they need each other. *Certain Fury* (1985, New World).

5465 "It's like killing roaches—you have to kill 'em all, otherwise what's the use?" Modern-day vigilante **Charles Bronson** sees it as his job to eliminate all the scum that infest the streets with their crime and degeneracy. *Death Wish 3* (1985, GB, Cannon).

5466 "I used to kill in the name of science. Now I kill because I'm addicted. It's the only way I can feel alive." Dr. **Klaus Kinski,** the son of a Nazi war criminal, is a sadistic landlord. *Crawlspace* (1986, Trans World).

5467 "You ever met anyone you didn't kill?" Police detective **Danny Glover** believes his new partner Mel Gibson is trigger-happy. *Lethal Weapon* (1987, Warner Bros.).

5468 "The hard part, the part I'm not looking forward to. . . the fact of the matter is I've never killed a woman before." As pained as he feels about the matter, Kim Basinger can be sure that, if necessary, **Rip Torn** will find the strength to kill her as well as her husband Jeff Bridges. *Nadine* (1987, Tri-Star).

5469 MATT: "Why did you kill her?" JOHN: "She was talking shit." **Keanu Reeves** asks teen **Daniel Roebuck** why he strangled his girl friend. It's a disturbing film. *River's Edge* (1987, Hemdale-Island).

5470 "I killed a girl once; it was no accident. Put the gun right to the back of her head, blew her brains right out the front. I was in love." One-armed ex-biker **Dennis Hopper** exchanges stories about killing girl friends with teenager Daniel Roebuck, who claims he strangled his by accident. *River's Edge* (1987, Hemdale-Island).

5471 "Hey, I liked Johnny, but not enough to kill him." **Madonna** has just been released from prison after serving four years for killing her boyfriend, a small-time hood—but she was framed. *Who's That Girl?* (1987, Warner Bros.).

5472 LT. COL. ICEAL HAMBLETON: "Bird Dog, I killed a man today. . . . He wasn't even a soldier, he just kept coming. I couldn't stop him. I didn't want to do it. I never had to do anything like that before in my life." CAPT. BARTHOLOMEW CLARK: "Listen here, Bat 21, I never met you, but you don't sound like a killer to me. I'm sure you couldn't stop it from happening." Shot down behind Viet Cong lines, **Gene Hackman** tells helicopter pilot **Danny Glover,** who's trying to rescue him, that he was forced to kill in self-defense. *Bat 21* (1988, Tri-Star).

5473 NICK: "Did you see the killer leave?" JOYCE: "Yeah, sure, and he wrote his name and address on the back of my dress." American police detective **Michael Douglas** questions **Kate Capshaw,** an American hostess in a Japanese club where a murder has taken place. *Black Rain* (1989, Paramount).

5474 "Thou shalt not kill, Mom! Thou shalt not kill women and children." Embittered paraplegic **Tom Cruise,** sobbing, yells at his unsympathetic mother Caroline Kava. He confesses that while in Vietnam, he killed civilians and a fellow soldier. *Born on the Fourth of July* (1989, Universal).

5475 "If there is one thing I can tell you, it's that a crazy killer is crazy and he will kill you." Detective **Joe Don Baker** is remarkably redundant. *Criminal Law* (1989, Hemdale).

5476 "I'm gonna kill somebody today." **Danny Aiello**'s warning to his squabbling sons John Turturro and Richard Edson is an omen of tragedy to come. *Do the Right Thing* (1989, Universal).

5477 "Mercenaries kill for money, sadists kill for fun, paratroopers kill for both." **Christopher Burgard** and six others are on a jungle reconnaissance mission in Vietnam. *84 Charlie Mopic* (1989, New Century-Vista).

5478 "In this country, they kill each other left and right and nobody gets caught." Yugoslavian mother **Joan Plowright** tells her daughter Tracey Ullman not to worry as she makes up her mind to have her cheating husband Kevin Kline murdered. *I Love You to Death* (1990, Tri-Star).

5479 "Fifteen years later the Hurons, having accepted Christianity, were killed by their enemies, the Iroquois." The terse epilogue to the movie suggests a shaky cause and effect relationship. *Black Robe* (1991, Canada-Australia, Goldwyn).

5480 MITCH ROBBINS: "Hello, Curly, kill anybody today?" CURLY: "The day ain't over yet." City-boy wrangler **Billy Crystal** trades morning pleasantries with tough trail boss **Jack Palance**. *City Slickers* (1991, Columbia).

5481 "All I ask is, if they are going to kill me that they have the guts to look me in the eye when they do it." Condemned **Arliss Howard** wants full TV coverage of his execution, but settles for free-lance photographer Roy Scheider. *Somebody Has to Shoot the Picture* (1991, Warner Bros.).

5482 "Killing isn't like smoking—you can quit." **Sharon Stone** is such a tease as she offers a cigarette to Michael Douglas, who claims he's trying to quit. *Basic Instinct* (1992, Tri-Star).

5483 "Kill him a lot." Twelve-hundred-year-old vampire leader **Paul Reubens** hisses instructions to his squad of living dead. *Buffy, the Vampire Slayer* (1992, 20th Century-Fox).

5484 WILL MUNNY: "It's a hell of a thing, killin' a man. . . . You take away all he's got and all he's ever gonna." THE SCHOFIELD KID: "I guess he had it comin'." MUNNY: "We all have it comin'." Former gunman **Clint Eastwood** instructs young **Jaimz Woolvett** on killing. *Unforgiven* (1992, Warner Bros.).

Kindness

see also CRUELTY, FEELINGS, GENEROSITY, GENTLENESS, GIFTS AND GIVING, LOVE AND LOVERS, TREATS AND TREATMENTS

5485 "We have one simple rule here: be kind." Dying ancient High Lama **Sam Jaffe** tells his chosen successor, Ronald Colman, the secret of the success of the peaceful community of Shangri-La. *Lost Horizon* (1937, Columbia).

5486 "I hope you'll find this, Mr. O'Hara. I am Janos. You remember the fire at the Excelsior Palace? You were kind to me and I never forgot. Those you find here were unkind and I did not forget them either. Janos Szabo. P.S., Here is the five dollars I owe you." Hungarian refugee **Peter Lorre** is hideously burned. To cover the cost of his expressionless mask, he becomes involved with the mob. Lorre falls in love with blind girl Evelyn Keyes. When she is killed by a car bomb meant for him, Lorre takes his revenge, but he doesn't forget the kindness of Don Beddoe. *The Face Behind the Mask* (1941, Columbia).

5487 "There's not enough kindness in the world. If only men would live as brothers without hatred, seeing only the beautiful things, but no, there are always people who look on the black side." Calculating smuggler **Sydney Greenstreet** preaches brotherhood as he has writer Peter Lorre covered with a gun. *The Mask of Dimitrios* (1944, Warner Bros.).

5488 "Whoever you are—I have always depended on the kindness of strangers." Pitiful **Vivien Leigh,** driven over the edge by her brutal rape at the hands of her brother-in-law Marlon Brando, is offered an arm by doctor Richard Garrick as she's taken away to a mental institution. *A Streetcar Named Desire* (1951, Feldman-Kazan/Warner Brothers/20th Century-Fox).

5489 "I have abused your kindness. You who gave my wife and me a home—even friendship, so wonderful a thing for a refugee, a German, a man without a home." **O.E. Hasse** confesses to a murder to Father Montgomery Clift, but it is the priest who will be accused of the crime. *I Confess* (1953, Warner Bros.).

5490 "I'd like to see you again very much. The reason I didn't let you kiss me was because I just didn't know how to handle the situation. You're the kindest man I've ever met. The reason I tell you this is because I want to see you again very much. I know that when you take me home I'm just going to lie on my bed and think about you. I want very much to see you again." Shy **Betsy Blair** soothes butcher Ernest Borgnine's hurt feelings. *Marty* (1955, United Artists).

5491 "When you speak of this in future years—and you will—be kind." Understanding housemaster's wife **Deborah Kerr** patiently introduces sensitive youngster John Kerr to love and loving at the end of the film. *Tea and Sympathy* (1956, MGM).

5492 "Simple kindness is so rare in this house that it's instantly mistaken for passion." **John Mills** corrects Hayley Mills' impression of his interest in new governess Deborah Kerr. *The Chalk Garden* (1964, GB, Universal-International).

5493 HENRIK VOGLER: "You are always in my thoughts." RAKEL EGERMAN: "Kindly said." As he prepares to leave, theater director **Erland Josephson** attempts to soothe the hurt he has caused tearful actress **Ingrid Thulin**. *After the Rehearsal* (1984, Sweden, Triumph).

5494 "Stores are never kind to people. They're kind to credit cards." Wealthy **Richard Gere** tells hooker Julia Roberts that the key to service is "plastic." *Pretty Woman* (1990, Touchstone/Buena Vista).

5495 "There was no trace of harm in her, a kinder or more good-hearted girl never lived." As an adult, **John Heard** remembers promiscuous Laura Dern, who helped raise him when he was Lukas Haas. *Rambling Rose* (1991, Seven Arts-New Line).

Kinds

see also CLASSES

5496 "I've been lookin' at her kind since my voice changed." **Clark Gable**'s initial reaction to likeable tramp Jean Harlow is negative. *Red Dust* (1932, MGM).

5497 "That's the kind of woman that makes whole civilizations topple." Housekeeper **Kathleen Howard** sneers at burlesque queen Barbara Stanwyck. Howard informs professor Gary Cooper that either Stanwyck goes or Howard quits. *Ball of Fire* (1941, Goldwyn/RKO).

5498 "There are two kinds of people: those who don't do what they want to do, so they write down in a diary about what they haven't done, and those who haven't the time to write about it because they're out doing it." There's no mistaking which group **Charles Coburn** feels Jean Arthur should belong to. *The More, the Merrier* (1943, Columbia).

5499 "[She's] the kind of girl a guy brings four bottles of beer to. . . ." **Gene Kelly,** not unkindly, comments on Brooklyn-born waitress Renie Riano, who works in a Mexican restaurant in Hollywood. *Anchors Aweigh* (1945, MGM).

5500 "There are two kinds of people in the world: those who walk into a room and immediately turn the TV on and those who immediately turn it off." Brainwashed **Laurence Harvey** notes that he and his bride Leslie Parrish are not in the same subset of this partition. *The Manchurian Candidate* (1962, United Artists).

5501 "There are two kinds of people: my kind and assholes." A lot would probably agree with **Mink Stole**'s dichotomy. *Pink Flamingos* (1973, New Line).

Kings and Queens

see also ENGLAND AND THE ENGLISH, NOBILITY

5502 "He was a king in the world he knew, but now he comes to civilization merely a captive, a show to gratify your curiosity. Ladies and gentlemen, look at Kong." **Robert Armstrong** addresses an audience of men and women in evening clothes before the curtains part of a giant stage to reveal the mammoth ape in chains. *King Kong* (1933, RKO).

5503 OLLIE: "Every man should be the king in his own castle. Do you have to ask your wife everything?" STAN: "Well, if I didn't I wouldn't know what she wanted me to do." Neither **Oliver Hardy** or **Stan Laurel** are kings in their castles, but at least henpecked Laurel knows his place. *Sons of the Desert* (1933, Roach-MGM).

5504 CHARLES II: "The king is father to his people." NELL GWYN: "Well, a good many of them." British monarch **Cedric Hardwicke** speaks figuratively, while his mistress **Anna Neagle** replies literally. *Nell Gwyn* (1934, GB, B & D).

5505 "I have the body of a weak and feeble woman, but I have the heart and valor of a king, and a king of England too!" **Flora Robson**, as Queen Elizabeth I, addresses her captains who will face the great Spanish Armada. *Fire Over England* (1936, GB, London Films).

5506 "Do you know, it wasn't until I was a married woman that I learned that kings don't sleep with their crowns on." **Alison Skipworth,** as Lady Gertrude, confides to Carole Lombard, as the phony Princess Olga. *The Princess Comes Across* (1936, Paramount).

5507 "I haven't lived like a king; perhaps I can die like one." **Ronald Colman** is a "real" pretender to the throne of Ruritania. **Stewart Granger** echoes the sentiments in the remake. *The Prisoner of Zorro* (1937, Selznick-United Artists); (1952, MGM).

5508 "Just think, Mama, . . . I shall be queen. I shall be queen of France!" Title character **Norma Shearer** bubbles to her mother Alma Kruger, as Empress Maria Theresa of Austria, before Shearer journeys to France to become the bride of Robert Morley, the heir to the French throne, the future Louis XVI. *Marie Antoinette* (1938, MGM).

5509 "Cathy, you're still my queen." **Laurence Olivier** pledges eternal love for Merle Oberon, even though they have married others. *Wuthering Heights* (1939, Goldwyn/United Artists).

5510 ANGHARAD MORGAN: "You are the king of the chapel, but I will be queen in my own kitchen." MR. GRUFFYDD: "You will be queen wherever you walk." Even though they love each other, **Maureen O'Hara** and local preacher **Walter Pidgeon** will not marry because he refuses to tie her to a life of poverty. *How Green Was My Valley* (1941, 20th Century-Fox).

5511 "My king? I'm an Irishman, and every Irishman is a king!" Nineteenth century Irishman **Douglas Fairbanks, Jr.** makes his proclamation when asked by Helena Carter, "Are you loyal to your king?" *The Fighting O'Flynn* (1949, Universal-International).

5512 "Don't you ever talk that way to me! 'Pig,' 'disgusting,' 'vulgar,' 'greasy'—those kind of words have been on your tongue and your sister's tongue too much around here. What do you think you are? A pair of queens? Now, just remember what Huey Long said—that every man's a king—and I'm king around here, and don't you forget it." **Marlon Brando** crowns himself as he tells off his wife Kim Hunter, referring to her sister Vivien Leigh. *A Streetcar Named Desire* (1951, Warner Bros.).

5513 "You're going to Africa to become a king and you need a beautiful blonde queen." Married **Jennifer Jones,** who has allowed her imagination to replace reality, is certain that she fits the bill for married Humphrey Bogart. *Beat the Devil* (1954, GB, Romulus-United Artists).

5514 "I don't think that Matt would have made a great president, but I would have voted for him for king—just to have you as queen." **Spencer Tracy** pays a nice compliment to Florence Eldridge, the wife of Tracy's adversary Fredric March in the infamous "monkey trial." *Inherit the Wind* (1960, United Artists).

5515 "If he can free the Jews without spilling blood, he deserves the crown. I'll shape the crown myself and place it on his brow." Jewish revolutionary criminal Barabbas, played by **Harry Guardino,** speaks of Jesus Christ, played by Jeffrey Hunter. *King of Kings* (1961, MGM).

5516 "Elizabeth shall be a greater queen than any king of yours. She shall rule a greater England than you could ever have built. My Elizabeth shall be queen and my life will have been well spent." **Genevieve Bujold,** as Anne Boleyn, makes an unlikely prediction about her daughter, before facing the executioner's sword. *Anne of the Thousand Days* (1969, Universal).

5517 "Better to be king for a night than a schmuck for a lifetime." Wannabe comedian **Robert De Niro** is willing to risk anything for just one taste of the success he so dearly yearns for. *King of Comedy* (1982, 20th Century-Fox).

5518 "Do not forget your dying king." **Kevin Costner,** as New Orleans D.A. Jim Garrison, makes his final statement to the jury in the trial of Tommy Lee Jones as Clay Shaw. *JFK* (1991, Warner Bros.).

Kisses and Kissing

see also BODIES, LOVE AND LOVERS, MARRIAGES, MEN AND WOMEN, MOUTHS, ROMANCES, SEDUCTIONS, SEX AND SEXUALITY, TOUCHES

5519 "Kiss me, my fool!" Vamp **Theda Bara** shocked and delighted audiences with this zinger that appears on a title card as she scatters rose petals over the drained body of a dead lover. *A Fool There Was* (1915, silent, Fox).

5520 GAVIN: "I've never kissed a woman before." BABBIE: "Before what?" As **John Beal** advances their courtship to the love-making stage, **Katharine Hepburn** becomes a bit fearful. *The Little Minister* (1934, RKO).

5521 "You old mug. Take off your shoes and kiss me." **Claudette Colbert** leaves her titled Englishman Ray Milland for plain old Fred MacMurray. *The Gilded Lily* (1935, Paramount).

5522 "This is one kiss you won't be able to wipe off." Usually when **Jean Arthur,** as Calamity Jane, kisses Gary Cooper as Wild Bill Hickok, he wipes it off. This time the Indians have him bound and are planning to kill him. *The Plainsman* (1936, Paramount).

5523 "I've been kissed by a tunnel." **Bob Hope** reacts after a smooch from bigmouth Martha Raye. *The Big Broadcast of 1938* (1937, Paramount).

5524 "D'ya think there's anything wrong with a guy that don't want a girl to kiss him all the time?. . . Cynthia. . . oh, she'll let you kiss her whenever you want. She doesn't want to swim. She doesn't want to play tennis, go for walks. All she wants to do is kiss you. I'm a nervous wreck!" A lot of men of the time would have liked to have been in **Mickey Rooney**'s shoes. He's seeking advice from his father Lewis Stone about fast flirt Lana Turner. *Love Finds Andy Hardy* (1938, MGM).

5525 "No, I don't think I will kiss you—although you need kissing badly. That's what's wrong with you. You should be kissed and often and by someone who knows how." Just when she's ready for his kiss, **Clark Gable** changes his mind about kissing Vivien Leigh. *Gone with the Wind* (1939, Selznick-MGM).

5526 AUGUSTA NASH: "There's an ant crawling up your cheek." TOM MARTIN: "I'd rather have a kiss. [She kisses him.]. . . That's an awful small kiss." AUGUSTA: "It was a small ant." TOM: "I wish it had been an elephant." American reporter stationed in France **Claudette Colbert** and noted rebel pilot **Ray Milland** get better acquainted after she rescues him from a Spanish prison. *Arise, My Love* (1940, Paramount).

5527 "I had one of those Frenchmen living here last year. Honest to goodness, every time you turned around that Frenchman was a-grabbing for your hand and kissing until he'd like to pull the skin off." **Maude Eburne** is not turned on by the gallantry of Frenchmen. *Among the Living* (1941, Paramount).

5528 "Kiss your mammy and pappy and say goodbye to the lady." **Bette Davis** instructs "her" son with regard to his father George Brent and his natural mother Mary Astor, who has given him up to Davis. *The Great Lie* (1941, Warner Bros.).

5529 "When I want to kiss my wife, I'll kiss her anytime, any place, anywhere. That's the kind of hairpin I am." Dentist **James Cagney** busses blushing Olivia de Havilland in public. *The Strawberry Blonde* (1941, Warner Bros.).

5530 "Now I've kissed you through two centuries." As 1800 arrives, Lord Nelson, portrayed by **Laurence Olivier** kisses his mistress Lady Hamilton, impersonated by Vivien Leigh. Guess he didn't know that the 19th century began in 1801. *That Hamilton Woman* aka: *Lady Hamilton* (1941, Korda Films).

5531 PAULA: "Darling, you've proposed to me, and I've accepted you. . . ." CHARLES: "What's wrong? What's wrong?" PAULA: "Smithy, do I always have to take the initiative? You're supposed to kiss me." CHARLES: "Oh, my." **Greer Garson** has to take the lead when her intended **Ronald Colman** is a bit slow on the uptake. He finally kisses her. *Random Harvest* (1942, MGM).

5532 "I don't know how to kiss, or I would kiss you. Where do the noses go?" Having been gang-raped and tortured by Spanish fascists, **Ingrid Bergman** is still inexperienced in the ways of showing affection. *For Whom the Bell Tolls* (1943, Paramount).

5533 "Did I ever tell you that a fella in my state of mind is apt to kiss a girl in your state of mind?" **Mickey Rooney** warns Judy Garland, who responds, "I double-dare you." *Girl Crazy* (1943, MGM).

5534 "Kiss is like candy. You eat candy for the beautiful taste and this is enough reason to eat candy." Vivacious French tutor **Signe Hasso** instructs young Dickie Moore about a new permissive age. *Heaven Can Wait* (1943, 20th Century-Fox).

5535 "I, uh, I hope you don't draw any wrong conclusions from that conversation. This, this girl, I, I'm not in love with her and she's not in love with me, but I think she's a very nice person and that's what she thinks of me. I'm good for her and she's good for me. This girl's past the silly stage of casual kissing and smooching. This girl, if she ever let a fella kiss her, it would be because at that particular moment in that particular place she'd want that particular fella to kiss her. And, oh, boy, I'm that fella." **Mickey Rooney** gets himself in trouble when he goes to his father Lewis Stone's alma mater, where he pays too much attention to too many girls including Bonita Granville and the Wilde Twins, Lee and Lyn. Stone arrives and puts his son back on course. *Andy Hardy's Blonde Trouble* (1944, MGM).

5536 "It's even better when you help." Having kissed Humphrey Bogart, **Lauren Bacall** observes that it takes the efforts of two to make the sparks fly. *To Have and Have Not* (1944, Warner Bros.).

5537 "You shouldn't kiss a girl when you're wearing a gun—it leaves a bruise." Tough dame **Claire Trevor** isn't too badly hurt by private eye Dick Powell. *Murder, My Sweet* (1945, RKO).

5538 MAN ON PORCH: "Why don't you kiss her instead of talking her to death?" GEORGE BAILEY: "How's that?" MAN: "Why don't you kiss her instead of talking her to death?" GEORGE: "You want me to kiss her, huh?" MAN: "Oh! Youth is wasted on the wrong people!" GEORGE: "Hey, hey, mister! Come back out here! I'll show you a kiss that'll put hair back on your head." Bald older man **Dick Elliott** challenges **James Stewart** to show less talking and more action as he talks and walks Donna Reed home. *It's a Wonderful Life* (1946, RKO).

5539 "Give me a kiss or I'll sock you." **John Garfield** sweet-talks Lana Turner. *The Postman Always Rings Twice* (1946, MGM).

5540 "Kisses that come from life, not death." That's the kind of smooching **Lana Turner** seeks from John Garfield after they've murdered her husband Cecil Kellaway. *The Postman Always Rings Twice* (1946, MGM).

5541 "Don't tell me it's subversive to kiss a Republican." Army Captain **John Lund** romances visiting Congresswoman Jean Arthur in Germany after World War II. *A Foreign Affair* (1948, Paramount).

5542 "A kiss like that could kill a guy." Lucille Ball plants a good one on **Bob Hope** at the end of the film. *Fancy Pants* (1950, Paramount).

5543 "You're a bold one. Who gave you the right to kiss me?" **Maureen O'Hara** slugs John Wayne after he impulsively kisses her. *The Quiet Man* (1952, Republic).

5544 "Frankly, my child. I had a sudden, powerful and very ignoble desire to kiss you till your lips were somewhat bruised." Middle-aged roué **David Niven** works on seducing young Maggie McNamara. *The Moon Is Blue* (1953, United Artists).

5545 "Don't wipe it off. If she thinks that's cranberry sauce, tell her she's got cherry pits in her head." Model **Marilyn Monroe** gives Tom Ewell a big kiss before sending him back to his wife Evelyn Keyes who rather takes him for granted. *The Seven Year Itch* (1955, 20th Century-Fox).

5546 JUNIOR: "They told me I was kaput, finished, all washed up. And here you are making a chump out of all those experts. . . . Where did you learn to kiss like that?" SUGAR: "I used to sell kisses for the milk fund." JUNIOR: "Tomorrow, remind me to send a check for a hundred thousand dollars to the milk fund." **Tony Curtis**' plot to get some loving from **Marilyn Monroe** has worked well. *Some Like It Hot* (1959, United Artists).

5547 "I want a big sloppy kiss." Even with **Elizabeth Taylor,** the prospect seems unappealing. *Who's Afraid of Virginia Woolf?* (1966, Warner Bros.).

5548 "Kiss my butterfly!" Hippie **Leigh Taylor-Young**'s offer is very tempting to smitten Peter Sellers. She's referring to a tattoo high up on her thigh. *I Love You, Alice B. Toklas* (1968, Warner Bros.).

5549 "Would you like a kiss on account?" It's twinkly little **Kirby Furlong**'s icky question to his aunt Lucille Ball. *Mame* (1974, Warner Bros.).

5550 "Kiss me, pig. . . . When I'm getting fucked, I like to be kissed a lot." Trapped bank robber **Al Pacino** isn't buying the deal of Charles Durning, the police detective who is trying to negotiate a release of Pacino's hostages. *Dog Day Afternoon* (1975, Warner Bros.).

5551 "By taking the pressure off the moment, we'll digest our food better." On their first date, **Woody Allen** suggests to Diane Keaton that they kiss at the beginning of the date, so they won't have to worry all evening if they should kiss at the end of the night. *Annie Hall* (1977, United Artists).

5552 "Down deep, I'm not evil or anything. I'm just floundering. . . . A huge, big, wet kiss would go a long way to selling this idea." **Woody Allen** allows his anger with both his critics and his fans show in this film. It's based on his personal experiences as a comedy director who moves on to other things and isn't appreciated for his attempts. *Stardust Memories* (1980, United Artists).

5553 "My mother-in-law. For years I wouldn't kiss her face. I ended up kissing her ass." **Rodney Dangerfield**'s mother-in-law Geraldine Fitzgerald's will specifies that he will receive her millions if he loses weight, quits smoking, drinking, gambling and girl-chasing. *Easy Money* (1983, Orion).

5554 "I French kiss, and Daddy says I'm the best." Randy Quaid's 13-year-old daughter **Jane Krakowski** brags to her visiting cousin Dana Barron. *National Lampoon's Vacation* (1983, Warner Bros.).

5555 "I only kiss women that I'd marry." That restriction doesn't cut down much on **Keith Carradine**'s smooching. *Choose Me* (1984, Island Alive).

5556 "Is this story going to have a lot of kissing in it?" **Fred Savage** questions his grandfather Peter Falk who is reading a story to the sick boy. *The Princess Bride* (1987, 20th Century-Fox).

5557 SUSANNA: "Iris missed a beautiful dance. . . . Ray, have you ever kissed a girl?. . . Open your mouth. . . . You will taste something very good and very soft. . . like this, close your eyes. . . how was that?" RAYMOND: "Wet!" **Valeria Golino** gives autistic **Dustin Hoffman** his first kiss as he dances with her in a stopped elevator to the strains of Fred Astaire singing, "They Can't Take That Away From Me" on Hoffman's portable television. *Rain Man* (1988, United Artists).

5558 "Kiss me where the sun doesn't shine. . . . I'll show you where." **George Coe** answers a heckler at his wedding reception as he drops his pants and moons the assemblage. *Cousins* (1989, Paramount).

5559 BEN SIEGEL: "Do you want to kiss me as much as I want to kiss you?" VIRGINIA HILL: "What makes you think I want to kiss you?" **Warren Beatty** and **Annette Bening** haven't had their first kiss yet. *Bugsy* (1991, Tri-Star).

5560 "A kiss may not be true, but at least it's what we wish were true." It's L.A. weatherman **Steve Martin**'s profound message for the day. *L.A. Story* (1991, Tri-Star).

5561 "I hear you go out to the cemetery to kiss where Bugsy's ass used to be." Playboy **Alec Baldwin** does his best to insult mobster Jeremy Roberts, referring to his former boss Bugsy Siegel, played by Armand Assante. *The Marrying Man* (1991, Hollywood Pictures/Buena Vista).

5562 "Kiss nose." Jewelry jangling **Candy Clark** bids her daughter Kristy Swanson goodbye. *Buffy, the Vampire Slayer* (1992, 20th Century-Fox).

Knives *see* WEAPONS

Knowledge

see also BOOKS, CERTAINTIES, EDUCATION, GENIUS, IDEAS, IGNORANCE, INTELLIGENCE, LEARNING AND LESSONS, STUDIES AND STUDENTS, TEACHING AND TEACHERS, UNDERSTANDINGS AND MISUNDERSTANDINGS, WISDOM

5563 "Every time he opens his mouth he subtracts from the total sum of human knowledge. . . . We're going to convince the voters that we've got someone of their level." Cynical campaign manager **Warren William** refers to his political candidate Guy Kibbee. *The Dark Horse* (1932, Warner Bros.).

5564 "All I know about you is you stole my car and I'm insane about you." American automobile designer **Gary Cooper** coos dreamily to beautiful jewel thief Marlene Dietrich. *Desire* (1936, Paramount).

5565 "I'm a dame from Newark and I know a dozen ways." **Barbara Stanwyck** is sure she can convince William Holden to do things her way. *Golden Boy* (1939, Columbia).

5566 "Well to hardly know him is to know him well." **Cary Grant** claims that his ex-wife Katharine Hepburn's fiancé, John Howard is not very deep. *The Philadelphia Story* (1940, MGM).

5567 "Knowledge can be more terrible than ignorance if one can do nothing." As **John Justin** and Sabu look into the All-Seeing Eye, Justin realizes that he is hopeless in finding a way to save his lady-love June Duprez. *The Thief of Bagdad* (1940, GB, London Films-United Artists).

5568 FERRARI: "The news about Ugarte upsets me very much." RICK: "You're a fat hypocrite. You don't feel any sorrier for Ugarte than I do." FERRARI: "Of course not. What upsets me is the fact that Ugarte died and no one knows where those Letters of Transit are." RICK: "Practically no one." **Sydney Greenstreet** knows that the late Peter Lorre left the Letters of Transit with **Humphrey Bogart,** and Bogie knows he knows. *Casablanca* (1942, Warner Bros.).

5569 "If a gnat had broken into your pool of knowledge, it would have broken its neck." World War II American radio war correspondent **Cary Grant** gives his first impression of the intelligence of ex-American burlesque queen Ginger Rogers, now married to an "Austrian Nazi" baron. *Once Upon a Honeymoon* (1942, RKO).

5570 "You know a lot about boats, Steve, but you don't know anything about people." First Mate **Humphrey Bogart** corrects an impression his idealist merchant marine Skipper Raymond Massey holds. Julie Bishop isn't Bogie's latest trollop, she's his wife. *Action in the North Atlantic* (1943, Warner Bros.).

5571 "You take the torch of knowledge, and behold the palace of the future." Elderly Marie Curie, portrayed by **Greer Garson**, gives a rousing address to a gathering of research scientists at the University of Paris, urging them to move ahead with their work. *Madame Curie* (1943, MGM).

5572 "I'm the Whistler. I know many things, for I walk by night. . . . I know many strange tales hidden in the hearts of men and women who have stepped into the shadows. Yes. . . I know the nameless terror of which they dare not speak." Identified by a mournful whistling of the theme music, **Otto Forrest**, who never actually participates in the drama, is the Whistler who observes the action of the players and comments on the ironies of life throughout the picture. *The Whistler* (1944, Columbia).

5573 "The more I know about you, the more I want to know; I want to know everything about you." Psychologist **Lew Ayres** falls in love with one of the twin sisters played by Olivia de Havilland. Is she the one who is a murderer? *The Dark Mirror* (1946, Universal).

5574 CHICK YOUNG: "I know there's no such person as Dracula. You know there's no such person as Dracula." WILBUR GREY: "But does Dracula know it?" **Bud Abbott** tries to reassure fellow railroad porter **Lou Costello** as they deliver the "undead" bodies of Frankenstein's monster and Dracula in a wax museum. *Abbott and Costello Meet Frankenstein* (1948, Universal).

5575 "Is it really true, Dad, 'If you wanna know, ask Joe'?" Eventually this stock remark made by Edward G. Robinson's workers will make his son **Burt Lancaster** wonder why his father wouldn't know about some defective airplane engine parts manufactured by his company that caused the deaths of many airmen in World War II. *All My Sons* (1948, Universal).

5576 "We know so little about the ways of providence; but now I know a little more." Painter **Joseph Cotten** loved and lost Jennifer Jones, the spirit of a young woman who had died long before they met. *Portrait of Jennie* (1948, Selznick).

5577 "I know he's a good man—you know he's a good man. My bad days are when he knows he's a good man." **Katharine Hepburn** speaks of her decent, talented and sometimes insufferable husband Spencer Tracy. *State of the Union* (1948, Liberty Films-MGM).

5578 "Maybe I'm just a dame and didn't know it." Murder suspect **Barbara Stanwyck** becomes introspective. *The File on Thelma Jordan* (1949, Paramount).

5579 "Then you must ask Miss Harrington how to get one. Miss Harrington knows all about it." Theater critic **George Sanders** advises young Barbara Bates how to win an acting award like Anne Baxter's. Bates admits to Sanders that she'd love to become a star actress. *All About Eve* (1950, 20th Century-Fox).

5580 "I know everything but what is commonly known as how to make a buck." **Ronald Colman** can't find a job despite having encyclopedic knowledge. It's not how many facts you know, but how you can relate them. *Champagne for Caesar* (1950, United Artists).

5581 "Behind me there was nothing, in front of me, a wall, a black wall. . . . I know nothing about people, I never shall know anything." **Claude Laydu** feels sadness and a powerlessness to heal either the souls or the bodies of his parishioners. *Diary of a Country Priest* (1951, Fr., Union General Cinematographique).

5582 "Knowledge is more important than life, Captain. It doesn't matter what happens to us, nothing counts except our thinking. We owe it to the species of our brain to stand here and die without destroying a source of wisdom. Civilization has given us an order." Scientist **Robert Cornthwaite** insists to Air Force Captain Kenneth Tobey that they must not kill alien James Arness no matter what the risk. *The Thing* (1951, RKO).

5583 "I'm a scientist also, I know the value of the cold light of reason. But I also know the deep shadows that light can cast. It can blind us to the truth." **Liam Redmond** warns Dana Andrews that his explorations and research may lead to problems. *Curse of the Demon* aka: *Night of the Demon* (1956, GB, Columbia).

5584 SAN QUENTIN CAPTAIN: "Take a deep breath, it's easier that way." BARBARA GRAHAM: "How would you know?" **Dabbs Greer** tries to be compassionate at **Susan Hayward**'s execution in the gas chamber, but she asks a pertinent question. *I Want to Live* (1958, United Artists).

5585 "It seems to me the only people who really know each other are people in love." **Carol Lynley**'s teen wisdom may contain a few flaws. *Blue Denim* (1959, 20th Century-Fox).

5586 EVE KENDALL: "I'm twenty-six and unmarried. Now you know everything. . . . I ought to know more about you." ROGER THORNHILL: "Well, what more could you know?" EVE: "You're an advertising man. That's all I know." ROGER: "What else do you know?" EVE: "You've got taste in clothes, taste in food. . . ." ROGER: "And taste in women. I like your flavor." EVE: "You're very clever with women. You can probably make them do anything for you. . . sell people things they don't need, make women who don't know you fall in love with you. . . ." ROGER: "I'm beginning to think I'm underpaid." This conversation is interspersed with some very serious and sexy kisses between **Eva Marie Saint** and **Cary Grant** in her train compartment. *North by Northwest* (1959, MGM).

5587 "Love? We're talking about rent! There's a dozen men in this room who know that girl better than you—including me, you dumb kid." **Ernest Borgnine** rages at his son Tony Franciosa who

introduces call girl Gina Lollobrigida as the woman he loves. *Go Naked in the World* (1960, MGM).

5588 "The brutality was brought about by a few extremists, the criminals, and very few Germans knew about what was going on." Defense Attorney **Maximilian Schell** uses the line popular in Germany after the war that the extermination of millions was the responsibility of the Nazis, a small percentage of the Germans. In defending his client, German jurist Burt Lancaster, Schell sees the case as one in which all Germans are accused of complicity with the Nazis. *Judgment at Nuremburg* (1961, United Artists).

5589 "It isn't. It just isn't like that. I mean if I knew where I was going I wouldn't have to go there, would I? I'd be there already." **Richard Beymer** makes some kind of sense, explaining he doesn't know what he's going to be or where he's going, when his father Jack Hawkins insists on discussing the subject. *Five Finger Exercise* (1962, Columbia).

5590 ANNIE SULLIVAN: "That little head is dying to know." JAMES KELLER: "Know what?" ANNIE: "Anything." Half-blind teacher **Anne Bancroft** tells cynical **Andrew Prine** that his younger sister, blind, deaf and mute Patty Duke, has a mind that craves knowledge. *The Miracle Worker* (1962, United Artists).

5591 "Everyone takes you seriously until they get to know you." Not unkindly, **Vanessa Redgrave** speaks to her ex-husband, talented but half-mad artist, David Warner. *Morgan* (1966, GB, British Lion).

5592 "I know. You know I know. I know you know I know. We know Henry knows, and Henry knows we know it. We're a pretty knowledgeable family." **John Castle** tells his mother Katharine Hepburn that everyone in the family knows of the maneuvering of the others to name a successor to the king, Peter O'Toole. *The Lion in Winter* (1968, GB, Avco Embassy).

5593 "I knowed General George Armstrong Custer for what he was and I also knowed the Indians for what they was. . . ." One-hundred-twenty-one-year-old Jack Crabb, played by **Dustin Hoffman,** reminisces for a reporter about his days with Custer and the Indians. *Little Big Man* (1970, National General).

5594 COMMITTEE CHAIRMAN: "Do you know Alfred Miller?" HOWARD PRINCE: "How do you mean?. . . In the Biblical sense?" McCarthyist Committee Chairman **M. Josef Sommer** gets an evasive answer from **Woody Allen** when he asks about blacklisted Michael Murphy. *The Front* (1976, Columbia).

5595 "I know her as one knows a woman who's staying at the same hotel." Amnesiac **Alan Bates** has no recollection of his wife Julie Christie. *The Return of the Soldier* (1982, GB, 20th Century-Fox).

5596 FRANK: "What do you want to know?" RITA: "Everything." Dissipated English professor **Michael Caine** learns that his working class Open University student **Julie Walters** has extensive ambitions. *Educating Rita* (1983, GB, Rank).

5597 GUY BENNETT: "I will never love a woman." TOMMY JUDD: "That's ridiculous. How can you possibly know something like that about yourself?" BENNETT: "You didn't become a communist because you read Karl Marx. You read Karl Marx because you know you are a communist." **Rupert Everett** tells his roommate **Colin Firth**, a committed Marxist, that he's fallen in love with another boy. *Another Country* (1984, GB, Drion Classics).

5598 "The first step to knowing who we are is knowing where we are and when we are." Punctilious Headmaster **John Cleese** has forgotten to tell his students they must also know what, why and how we are. *Clockwise* (1986, GB, Universal).

5599 "You know when to say 'Yes,' when to say 'No,' and everybody goes home in a limousine." Pool hustler **Paul Newman** advises his protégé Tom Cruise. In poker jargon, it would be, "You have to know when to hold and you have to know when to fold." *The Color of Money* (1986, Touchstone/Buena Vista).

5600 ELIZABETH: "How did you know I'd respond to you?" JOHN: "I saw myself in you." Sultry art gallery entrepreneur **Kim Basinger** and commodities broker **Mickey Rourke** have a sadomasochistic affair. *9 1/2 Weeks* (1986, MGM-United Artists).

5601 MARY: "Do you think he knew I didn't like it?" MOLLY: "Mary, he doesn't want to know." **Helen Nicholas** wonders if the "john" who paid extra for her and **Louise Smith** to put on a lesbian performance recognized that her heart wasn't in it. *Working Girls* (1986, Miramax).

5602 REGINALD KINCAID: "Dr. Moriarty!. . . You didn't tell me that homicidal maniac was involved in this. . . ." DR. WATSON: "Moriarty knows I am the only match for his evil genius." KINCAID: "You're sure he's not trying to kill me?" WATSON: "Of course not, he knows you're an idiot." KINCAID: "Thank God!" Terrorized actor **Michael Caine**, posing as Sherlock Holmes, the creation of the true genius **Ben Kingsley**, stops a train on which they are traveling when he learns that evil mastermind Paul Freeman is involved in their latest case. *Without a Clue* (1988, GB, Orion).

5603 HERMAN: "I didn't know you were alive." TAMARA: "You never knew." **Ron Silver** is shocked when he encounters his wife **Anjelica Huston**, who he believed perished with their children in a concentration camp. She's not lost her sharp tongue. *Enemies, a Love Story* (1989, 20th Century-Fox).

5604 "He held her in his arms and kissed her long and hard. He felt he understood this woman completely now. Not a part of her existed that he didn't know. Except of course what she didn't want him to know." **Tom Selleck** claims to know everything about drop-dead beauty Paulina Porizkova that she will allow him to know. Well, at least he no longer suspects she's trying to kill him. *Her Alibi* (1989, Warner Bros.).

5605 "The older I get, the less I know." Once puritanical **Rebecca Jenkins** has grown non-judgmental as World War II drags on. Her decline in knowledge is offset by an increase in wisdom. *Bye, Bye Blues* (1990, Canada-U.S., Circle).

5606 "When you get where I am, you will know the rest." In voice-over, **Glenn Close,** the voice of comatose Sunny von Bulow, says that no one of this world will ever know the whole story of how she got to be the way she is. *Reversal of Fortune* (1990, Warner Bros.).

5607 "What I know about you I love. What I don't terrifies me." **Leah Pinsent,** a resident of a small Canadian town confesses her feelings to stranded mobster Nick Mancuso. *Double Identity* (1991, Canada-Fr., Monarch).

5608 "I think it would be quite something to know you in private life." Brilliant psychopath **Anthony Hopkins** shows a bit of personal interest in FBI trainee Jodie Foster. *The Silence of the Lambs* (1991, Orion).

5609 "Excuse me for not knowing about El Salvador—like I'm ever going to Spain anyway." Val-speaking **Kristy Swanson** is in a snit at a mall. She's just another teen ignorant of geography. *Buffy, the Vampire Slayer* (1992, 20th Century-Fox).

Labor see WORK AND WORKERS

Ladies

see also SOCIETIES, WOMEN

5610 "I'm going to be a lady if it kills me!" Shrill and brassy **Jean Harlow** has a long way to go, and she's not going to get much help from her boorish husband Wallace Beery. *Dinner at Eight* (1933, MGM).

5611 "Hey, you ain't no lady!" Sheriff **Walter Catlett** is disappointed in Katharine Hepburn's behavior. *Bringing Up Baby* (1938, RKO).

5612 "What's to become of me. Now that you've made a lady out of me, I'm not fit for anything else!" **Wendy Hiller**, as Eliza Doolittle, angrily accuses Leslie Howard, as Professor Henry Higgins, of meddling in her life, giving her a new identity, but doing her more harm than good. *Pygmalion* (1938, GB, MGM).

5613 "That lady all dressed in blue." It is test pilot **Clark Gable's** personification of the sky. *Test Pilot* (1938, MGM).

5614 "Go on, you tramp. Don't you be pestering the ladies." **Eddie "Rochester" Anderson** chases bordello madam Ona Munson away from Olivia de Havilland and the other fine ladies on the steps of an Atlanta hospital. *Gone with the Wind* (1939, Selznick-MGM).

5615 "Maria, in the garden of a convent in Peru, there's a beautiful statue. The Spanish nuns call it Nuestra Senora de Las Rosas. This is how I'll remember you. . . as the Lady of the Roses." Notice how cleverly Englishman **Errol Flynn** gets in a translation of the Spanish phrase when he expresses his love for Brenda Marshall, the beautiful niece of the Spanish ambassador to England. *The Sea Hawk* (1940, Warner Bros.).

5616 CINDY LOU BETHANY: "Who is that?" LLOYD: "General Sherman on a horse." CINDY: "Who is the lady in front?" LLOYD: "That's 'Victory.'" CINDY: "Isn't that just like a Yankee to let a lady walk?" Southern belle **Mary Martin** asks **Don Ameche** about some statues. *Kiss the Boys Goodbye* (1941, Paramount).

5617 "I got a date with a lady. You know what a lady is? Naw, how could you?" Boxer **Kirk Douglas** dumps sexy blonde Marilyn Maxwell for fight manipulator Luis Van Rooten's wife Lola Albright. *Champion* (1949, United Artists).

5618 "Listen, Paolo, there is no such thing as a great American lady. Great ladies do not occur in a nation less than 200 years old." Ruthless procurer **Lotte Lenya** informs Italian gigolo Warren Beatty that American widow Vivien Leigh is not a great lady because she comes from a johnny-come-lately country. *The Roman Spring of Mrs. Stone* (1961, U.S., GB, Warner Bros.).

5619 THOMAS: "I thought you said she was a tart." GEORGE: "She is, but she's also a lady." **Robbie Coltrane** checks with his mate **Bob Hoskins** who tells Robbie that his beautiful, reed-thin, black call girl Cathy Tyson is a lady. *Mona Lisa* (1986, GB, Island Pictures).

5620 "Miss Ruth was a lady and a lady always knows when to leave." **Cicely Tyson** comforts Mary Stuart Masterson as Mary-Louise Parker dies from cancer. *Fried Green Tomatoes* (1991, Universal).

Ladies and Gentlemen

see also MEN AND WOMEN

5621 SCARLETT O'HARA: "Sir, you are no gentleman." RHETT BUTLER: "And you, miss, are no lady." It's the first encounter of **Vivien Leigh** and **Clark Gable** in the movie. He has innocently overheard her conversation with the man she loves, Leslie Howard. *Gone with the Wind* (1939, Selznick-MGM).

5622 VICTORIA WARE: "I'm no lady." JAMES J. CORBETT: "I'm no gentleman." **Alexis Smith** and **Errol Flynn** must be just ordinary folks. *Gentleman Jim* (1942, Warner Bros.).

5623 "I do not accept gifts from disapproving gentlemen—especially not disapproving gentlemen who are kept by other ladies. So take it. You should be used to taking money from ladies by now." **Audrey Hepburn** pays George Peppard for her drink, scorching him for his relationship with "patroness" Patricia Neal. *Breakfast at Tiffany's* (1961, Paramount).

Lamentations

see also COMPLAINTS, GRIEF, SADNESS, SORROWS

5624 "The old town ain't what it used to be. Cops pick up a man, got two guns and a butcher's knife in one pocket, and a powder-puff and lipstick in the other." Murder suspect **Humphrey Bogart** bemoans the lack of tough guys in his town of late. *Big City Blues* (1932, Warner Bros.).

5625 "Of all the gin joints in all the towns in all the world, she walks into mine." **Humphrey Bogart** is right. It is a pretty big coincidence that former lover Ingrid Bergman and her resistance hero husband Paul Henreid would show up in Rick's Cafe in Casablanca. *Casablanca* (1942, Warner Bros.).

5626 "They come here. They all come here. How do they find me?" Broadway producer **Zero Mostel** mumbles about all the fruitcakes that make their way to his office, including the very nervous and obsessive accountant Gene Wilder. *The Producers* (1966, Embassy).

5627 "Everything's disposable, nothing's permanent. Neighbors split up, friends split up." Sadly **Natalie Wood** laments the marriage breakups of so many of their friends to her husband George Segal. *The Last Married Couple in America* (1980, Universal).

5628 "I've been reduced to old men, cripples and nancy boys." It's the complaint of confused old actor **Albert Finney**, the star of a seedy 1940 British repertory company. *The Dresser* (1983, GB, Columbia-Goldcrest).

Land and Farms

see also AMERICA AND AMERICANS, COUNTRIES, ENGLAND AND THE ENGLISH, FOOD AND EATING, GROWTH AND DEVELOPMENT, HOMES, HOUSES, WATER, WORLD

5629 "Land is the only thing in the world worth working for, worth fighting for, worth dying for, because it's the only thing that lasts." Plantation owner **Thomas Mitchell** imparts an important lesson to his daughter Vivien Leigh. It's one that she never forgets. *Gone with the Wind* (1939, Selznick-MGM).

5630 "We finished plowing the creek bottom today. What do you want me to start on tomorrow?" Overseer **Victor Jory** is about to get his walking papers, when Barbara O'Neil, playing Mrs. O'Hara, returns from the bedside of his pregnant mistress Isabel Jewell. *Gone with the Wind* (1939, Selznick-MGM).

5631 "It's my dirt, it's no good, but it's mine." Wild-eyed farmer **John Qualen** whines with heart-breaking affection for his worthless dust bowl farm. *The Grapes of Wrath* (1940, 20th Century-Fox).

5632 "What'd I tell you? They're coming back, wagons by the score. It's the promised land. Jane Ellen, someday Texas is going to be biggest and the finest." With the help of scriptwriters, drifter **Gary Cooper** peers into the future for Doris Davenport. *The Westerner* (1940, Goldwyn/United Artists).

5633 "I'm goin' to get us a piece of bottom land." Poor Tennessee farmer **Gary Cooper** shares with his mother Margaret Wycherly his plans to better their lot. *Sergeant York* (1941, Warner Bros.).

5634 "Our farm was in the family for generations. One hundred sixty acres, thirty in bluegrass, and the rest in crops." Delirious hooligan **Sterling Hayden** muses nostalgically to Jean Hagen as he bleeds to death. *The Asphalt Jungle* (1950, MGM).

5635 "Piece by piece, our improvident grandfathers exchanged the land for their epic debauches, to put it mildly, till finally all that was left—and Stella can verify that!—was the house itself and about 20 acres of ground including a graveyard to which now all but Stella and I have retreated." **Vivien Leigh** relates to her brother-in-law Marlon Brando the fate of the family estate. *A Streetcar Named Desire* (1951, Warner Bros.).

5636 "Time! Time is one thing to a lawmaker, but, to a farmer, there is a time to plant and a time to harvest—and you cannot plant at harvest time." **Marlon Brando** expresses the impatience of the farming peasants who seek justice and land reform from their government officials. *Viva Zapata!* (1952, 20th Century-Fox).

5637 "We can't give up this valley and we ain't going to do it. This is farming country, a place where people can come and bring up their families. Who is Ruff Ryker or anyone else to run us away from our homes? He only wants to grow beef and what we grow is families, to grow 'em good and grow 'em strong, the way they were meant to be. God didn't make this country just for one man like Ryker." Farmer **Van Heflin**'s simple eloquence holds together the small community of homesteaders against the threats of cattleman Emile Meyer. *Shane* (1953, Paramount).

5638 "There's only one thing on this earth more important than money, and that's land. Why, I've heard Luz say it a thousand times. Pa said it, and Bick Benedict says it, and it's true." **Jane Withers** is one of the Texas landed class who knows more money can be produced, but not more land. *Giant* (1956, Warner Bros.).

5639 "I've got to do what Roy said. I've got to find a place with my own name on it. I've got to find my promised land." Due to the influence of wizened John Marley, young gunslinger **Robby Benson** forsakes the life to become a rancher. *Jory* (1972, Avco Embassy).

5640 "A man without land is a nobody." Richard Dreyfuss quotes his grandfather **Zvee Scooler**. *The Apprenticeship of Duddy Kravitz* (1974, Canada, Paramount).

5641 "On June thirtieth, eighteen sixty-four, President Lincoln signed the historic bill providing for protection of twenty thousand acres in the California mountains. It was the first step ever taken toward preserving our country's great wilderness, and it brought about the formation of America's national park system. The doctor had told Galen he would die at the age of fifty-two, but he lived on to be ninety-six years old. He always wanted to do something special, and I knew he wouldn't give up until he did. To me he became an example of what a man can really accomplish if he believes in himself. It was through Galen's hard work and far-sighted efforts that the land he loved and fought for would remain forever exactly as it was when he first saw it, for all future generations to enjoy. Oh, he names this magnificent valley for the bear that was his lifelong friend and protector, Yosemite." Narrator **John Dehner** speaks of the efforts and accomplishments of Galen Clark, played by Denver Pyle, to save the Sequoia Forest of California. *Guardian of the Wilderness* (1977, Sunn Classic).

5642 "The sound barrier is a farm you can buy in the sky." **Sam Shepard,** as test pilot Chuck Yeager, knows that trying to break the sound barrier in the air may prove fatal to him. *The Right Stuff* (1983, Warner Bros.).

5643 "They can't sell the land, can they? It's been in the family for over a hundred years." **Jessica Lange** protests the imminent loss of her family's farm. *Country* (1984, Touchstone-Buena Vista).

5644 GIL IVY: "You can't look on this thing short term. Hell, this is a way of life." TOM MCMULLEN: "No, Gil, it's a business. Farming is a business." Farmer **Sam Shepard** and **Matt Clark,** the local administrator of the Farmers Home Administration that holds the mortgage on Shepard's land, differ on the nature of farming. *Country* (1984, Touchstone-Buena Vista).

5645 "Sooner or later, you'll have to. The river will flood again, or there'll be a drought, or a surplus." Banker **Scott Glenn** reckons that Mel Gibson and Sissy Spacek will be forced to sell their family farm despite their desperate attempts to hold on to it. *The River* (1984, Universal).

5646 "I had a farm in Africa. . . ." **Meryl Streep** delivers the film's opening line. *Out of Africa* (1985, Mirage-Universal).

5647 "Gotta get back and smell that salt air and work that dirt. . . . I haven't had my hands in dirt in 20 years." **Geraldine Page** tells her fellow bus passenger Rebecca De Mornay of her desire to return to her old country home. *The Trip to Bountiful* (1985, Island Alive).

5648 "Eight hundred square yards, not a weed on it. When I'm out here in the middle nothing else matters. People come to sit on the edge, just to drink it in." Elderly groundskeeper **Jimmy Jewel** has tended the same cricket field for nearly half a century. *Arthur's Hallowed Ground* (1986, GB, Cinecom).

Languages

see also DOUBLE ENTENDRES, DOUBLE-TALK, SPEECH AND SPEAKING, WORDS, WRITING AND WRITERS

5649 "Remember that you are a human being with a soul, the divine gift of articulate speech, and that your language is the language of Milton, Shakespeare and the Bible, and don't sit there crooning like a bilious pigeon." **Leslie Howard** as Professor Henry Higgins, lectures Wendy Hiller, as Eliza Doolittle, on the sounds that she makes. *Pygmalion* (1938, GB, Pascal-MGM).

5650 "I can make love in 12 languages." Home from the army, **Tony Franciosa** brags that he's quite a linguist of love. *Go Naked in the World* (1960, MGM).

5651 "Think what you're trying to accomplish. Just think what you're dealing with. The majesty and grandeur of the English language. It's the greatest possession we have. The noblest thoughts that ever flowed through the hearts of men are contained in its extraordinary, imaginative and musical mixtures of sounds. And that's what you've set yourself out to conquer, Eliza. And conquer it you will." **Rex Harrison** gives a pep talk to Cockney flower girl Audrey Hepburn before beginning his instruction to have her speak like a real lady. *My Fair Lady* (1964, Warner Bros.).

5652 "I can speak their language, but I don't really know what they mean." Polish contractor **Jeremy Irons** voices his frustration with English manners and customs. *Moonlighting* (1982, GB, Miracle-Universal).

5653 "And just think, a week in Paree and he'll come back sounding just like. . . Marcel Marceau." **Marla Adams** supports her son Anthony Edwards' plans to go to Paris during spring break—and her prediction is probably correct. *Gotcha!* (1985, Universal).

Lasts

see also BEGINNINGS, ENDS AND ENDINGS, EXPECTATIONS, FIRSTS, NEWNESS

5654 "The last stage we were on was held up by Jesse James." Wisecracking vaudevillian **Joan Davis** admits to a long layoff between show business jobs. *Show Business* (1944, RKO).

5655 "Neither do I, baby, but if I have to, I'm going to die last." **Robert Mitchum** responds to vicious but beautiful Jane Greer, who says she doesn't want to die. *Out of the Past* (1947, RKO).

5656 "This is the day, this is the day, the last time I shall drive up to these gates, three iron bars that keep the man I love away from me." Gun moll **Claire Trevor** arrives at the prison where she helps break out her man Dennis O'Keefe, a gangster serving life for a crime he didn't commit. *Raw Deal* (1948, Reliance-Eagle-Lion).

5657 "The last time anyone was nice to me was in 1891." Escaped Devil's Island prisoner **Peter Ustinov** is touched by the kindness shown him by Leo G. Carroll's family. *We're No Angels* (1955, Paramount).

5658 "I was wrong—this war's going to last a long time." **Robert Ryan** comes to the conclusion when his platoon is cut off from headquarters as they try to take an enemy-held hill in Korea in 1950. *Men in War* (1957, United Artists).

5659 HARRY: "When did you last sleep with a woman?" JACOB: "Saturday night—March, 1951." Two old codgers, **Art Carney** and **Herbert Berghof** can still talk about it. *Harry and Tonto* (1974, 20th Century-Fox).

5660 "You gotta be one of the last cowboys left in Texas." **Amy Madigan** is bemused as she sees Vietnamese Ho Nguyen dressed in boots and a ten gallon hat. *Alamo Bay* (1985, Tri-Star).

5661 "The last time I did this I got more than a patch for it." Scout troop leader **Shelley Long** obeys a CPR instructor's command to lie down and open her mouth. *Troop Beverly Hills* (1989, Weintraub).

Lateness

see also TIME

5662 "Oh, well, it's late. I've got to be getting into my straight jacket. I'll call a broom." Humorist **Robert Benchley** makes light of claims of witchcraft being practiced in the 20th century. *I Married a Witch* (1942, Paramount-United Artists).

5663 "No matter how early I get in—it's too late." Eighteen-year-old **Jean Heather** complains to Bing Crosby, as Father O'Malley, that she and her parents don't agree on anything. *Going My Way* (1944, Paramount).

5664 "It's too late. It is, I tell you. I destroy everything I touch. You've come too late." Washed-up movie actor **James Mason** despairs to his wife, Judy Garland, a rising star. *A Star Is Born* (1954, Warner Bros.).

5665 "It's too late, there's something I must do. It shouldn't have happened this way." Despite having fallen in love with him, **Kim Novak** pulls away from James Stewart to fulfill her role in a complicated plot. She runs up the stairs to a church's bell tower, knowing he is unable to follow because of his fear of heights. *Vertigo* (1958, Paramount).

5666 "I must say she keeps late hours for a decorator." **Audrey Hepburn** meows about Patricia Neal, who Hepburn has just seen leaving some money in the apartment of her kept man George Peppard. *Breakfast at Tiffany's* (1961, Paramount).

Laughter

see also AMUSEMENTS, COMEDY AND COMEDIANS, CONTEMPT, ENTERTAINMENTS AND ENTERTAINERS, FUN, HUMOR, PLEASURES, RIDICULE AND RIDICULOUSNESS, SMILES, SOUNDS

5667 "You were born for laughter. Nothing in this life of yours now is as important as that. Laughter can take this whole life of yours—that home, those people, those jewels—and blow them to pieces. You're rich. You're dirty rich. And only laughter can make you clean. . . ." Composer **Fredric March** offers his former lover Nancy Carroll, now married to multi-millionaire Frank Morgan who denies her nothing, the cleansing power of laughter. *Laughter* (1930, Paramount).

5668 "That's been his downfall, everybody always laughing at him, saying 'He's a case. Oh, he's a caution.' He's gone on. We're all responsible. We're all to blame. All we do is laugh." **Aline MacMahon** accuses Wallace Beery's family of being too tolerant of his very serious drinking problem. **Agnes Moorehead** holds the same opinion regarding Frank Morgan in the remake. *Ah, Wilderness* (1935, MGM); *Summer Holiday* (1948, MGM).

5669 "Laugh now, Heathcliff. There's no laughter in Hell." Drunken **Hugh Williams** aims a pistol at his tormentor Laurence Olivier. He can't or won't pull the trigger, perhaps because the miserable Olivier encourages him to do so. *Wuthering Heights* (1939, Goldwyn/United Artists).

5670 RAVELLI: "Look at me and laugh." WOLF J. FLYWHEEL: "I've been doing that for years." **Chico Marx** poses **Groucho Marx** for a photograph. *The Big Store* (1941, MGM).

5671 "You know the nice thing about buying food for a man is that you don't have to laugh at his jokes." Dressed in evening clothes, starlet **Veronica Lake** buys breakfast for Joel McCrea, a movie director who she believes is a hobo. *Sullivan's Travels* (1941, Paramount).

5672 "There's a lot to be said for making people laugh. Did you know that's all some people have? It isn't much, but it's better than nothing in this cock-eyed caravan." Hollywood comedy director **Joel McCrea** relates the important lesson he's learned while traveling as a bum across the country trying to discover real life. *Sullivan's Travels* (1941, Paramount).

5673 "You always give me the feeling that you're laughing at me." Mousey **Joan Fontaine** doesn't quite know what to make of handsome, charming Cary Grant who is paying court to her. *Suspicion* (1941, RKO).

5674 "She was convalescing from pneumonia and one evening began to laugh helplessly at one of the BBC musical programmes and died of a heart attack." Writer **Rex Harrison** describes the circumstances of the death of his first wife Kay Hammond. She will soon make a spiritual visit with him and his second wife Constance Cummings. *Blithe Spirit* (1945, GB, Cineguild-Two Cities).

5675 "You make it sound so sacred and holy when all the time it's just a gag with you. . . . You're just laughing your head off at these chumps. You think God's going to stand for that?" **Coleen Gray** accuses her con man husband Tyrone Power of sacrilege. *Nightmare Alley* (1947, 20th Century-Fox).

5676 SIR ALFRED: "[The cymbals] are my favorite instrument in the entire orchestra, but I can't hear you." DR. SCHULTZ: "I was afraid of being a little loud, Sir Alfred. You know, vulgar. As a small boy, I was always taught never to be vulgar." SIR ALFRED: "Be vulgar by all means, but let me hear that brazen laugh." Orchestra conductor **Rex Harrison** tries to coax just the sound he wants from cymbals player **Torben Meyer**. *Unfaithfully Yours* (1948, 20th Century-Fox).

5677 "I knew a girl that collapsed a lung, [laughing] like that." Songwriter **David Wayne** issues a warning to Katharine Hepburn when he's laughed at. *Adam's Rib* (1949, MGM).

5678 "I wish I could find something to laugh about. This used to be such a happy home." Teenager **William Reynolds** suspects his milquetoast father Fred MacMurray is having an affair with old flame Barbara Stanwyck. *There's Always Tomorrow* (1956, Universal).

5679 BRIDEY MAE: "He likes me, I can tell." ELMA: "That'd make a cat laugh." **Nancy Mette** thinks

union organizer Chris Cooper is interested in her. **Mary McDonnell** doubts it. *Matewan* (1987, Cinecom).

5680 "Down here girls marry the first boy in high school who makes them laugh." **Frances McDormand** sounds like she wishes she had waited to hear a second boy's joke rather than having married redneck Brad Dourif. *Mississippi Burning* (1988, Orion).

5681 "A laugh can be a very powerful thing. Why, sometimes laughter is the only weapon we have." Roger Rabbit, the voice of **Charles Fleischer,** makes sense to private eye Bob Hoskins. *Who Framed Roger Rabbit?* (1988, Touchstone-Buena Vista).

5682 "What are you laughing at?" **Jack Nicholson,** as The Joker, snarls at a stone gargoyle after Batman gets the upper hand in their battle of evil versus good. *Batman* (1989, Warner Bros.).

5683 "It's like you're the one who makes them laugh." Sicilian movie projectionist **Philippe Noiret** sums up the good part of his lonely job. *Cinema Paradiso* (1990, It., Fr., Miramax).

Laws

see also COUNTRIES, CRIMES AND CRIMINALS, GOVERNMENTS, JUDGMENTS, JUSTICE, LAWYERS, LEGALITY AND ILLEGALITY, RULES

5684 "In Switzerland, we have a very peculiar law. If the husband shoots his wife, they put him in jail." Professor **Roland Young** hires detective Richard Carle to shadow his duplicitous wife Genevieve Tobin. *One Hour with You* (1932, Paramount).

5685 "Now this is the law of Pancho Villa's court: two for one. Understand? One peon is killed, I kill two majordomos or the best that I can find." Revolutionary bandit **Wallace Beery** makes his legal proclamation. *Viva Villa!* (1934, MGM).

5686 "It's about time you rebels learned you can't take the law into your own hands?" Yankee Captain **Ward Bond** interrupts the women's evening sewing circle looking for the men who raided Shantytown. *Gone with the Wind* (1939, Selznick-MGM).

5687 "Not enough to hurt me." **Henry Fonda** responds smartly to a bystander who asks young Abe Lincoln what he knows about the law. *Young Mr. Lincoln* (1939, 20th Century-Fox).

5688 "The law is a jealous mistress and a stern mistress." **Erskine Sanford** greets his new apprentice

Tim Holt with a lawyer's old bromide. *The Magnificent Ambersons* (1942, RKO).

5689 "Article six. The law is the expression of the will of the people. All citizens have the right to assist personally, or through their elected representatives, in its formation. It ought to be the same for all whether it protects or whether it punishes. All citizens being equal in the eyes of the law have equal rights to all dignities, places and public positions according to their capacity and without any other distinction than those of their virtues and talents." Somewhere in France, school teacher **Maureen O'Hara** continues reading from "A Declaration of Rights" that teacher Charles Laughton was reading to his students when he was hauled away by German soldiers to be executed. *This Land Is Mine* (1943, RKO).

5690 "The only law a sailor's ever known is the personal decision of his captain. If a sailor objects, he's sentenced to starvation, flogging or even death. Gentlemen, they'll keep it that way as long as the government will let them. Whether sailors die or not, that decision is up to you. If you believe that we've told the truth, that the things we did were justified, we beg you to make just laws to protect the lives of the men who serve our country on the high seas. Thank you very much." **Alan Ladd**, the spoiled son of an American ship owner, is shanghaied to work on his father's ship. Conditions on the ship are appalling. The captain, Howard da Silva, ruthlessly mistreats the men. Ultimately, the men mutiny. They sail back to Boston and are put on trial. The sensational details of the case reach Congress, which influenced by the book on the subject written by intelligent sailor Richard Henry Dana, passes legislation guaranteeing the rights of seamen. *Two Years Before The Mast* (1946, Paramount).

5691 "Law, like men, is composed of two parts. . . Just as man is body and soul, so is the law, letter and spirit. . . . An unwritten law stands back of a man who fights to defend his home. Apply the same to this maltreated wife and neglected mother. We ask you no more." **Katharine Hepburn** makes her summation to the jury in the attempted murder case against Judy Holliday. *Adam's Rib* (1949, MGM).

5692 "You're shaking the tail of the law, Amanda, and I don't like it." Prosecuting attorney **Spencer Tracy** disapproves of the tactics of his wife, Katharine Hepburn, the defense attorney in a case they are trying. *Adam's Rib* (1949, MGM).

5693 "I say that you cannot administer a wicked law impartially. You can only destroy. You can only punish. I warn you that a wicked law, like cholera, destroys everyone it touches—its upholders as well as its defilers." Attorney **Spencer Tracy** addresses the court in the infamous "monkey trial." *Inherit the Wind* (1960, United Artists).

5694 "I always say the law was meant to be interpreted in a lenient manner." **Paul Newman** proposes selling diseased cattle before the law forces them to be destroyed. *Hud* (1963, Paramount).

5695 "The law's here to protect the little guy like you, McCabe, and I tell you, you don't have to pay me nothing. . . . Until people stop dying for freedom, they aren't gonna be free." Lawyer **William Devane** reassures mining town gambler and brothel keeper Warren Beatty when the latter protests he doesn't want to get killed. *McCabe and Mrs. Miller* (1971, Warner Bros.).

5696 "You see any law around here? We're the law. What we decide is the way things are. So let's vote on it." **Burt Reynolds** tells his canoeing chums that it's up to them to decide what to do with a dead mountain man who Reynolds killed with a bow and arrow after the man sodomized Ned Beatty. *Deliverance* (1972, Warner Bros.).

5697 "What law is it that says a woman is a better parent simply by virtue of her sex? . . . I've had to think a lot about whatever it is that makes somebody a good parent: constancy, patience, understanding. . . love. Where is it written that a man has less of those qualities than a woman?" **Dustin Hoffman** testifies in a custody suit brought by his ex-wife Meryl Streep for their son Justin Henry. *Kramer vs. Kramer* (1979, Columbia).

5698 "With this scum, you gotta take the law into your own hands. You don't just book these guys, you kill 'em." Avenging angel **Strother Martin** describes how he feels about the gangsters chasing Jill Ireland. *Love and Bullets* (1979, Associated Film Distribution).

5699 "I'll see you in small claims court." College coed **Lynn-Holly Johnson** refuses to pay gigolo Frank Zagarino's fee after seeing his wares. *Where the Boys Are '84* (1984, Tri-Star).

5700 "I don't know anything about the law, but I think this is a violation of my civil liberties." Reporter **Chevy Chase** warns villainous Police Chief Joe Don Baker who announces his intention to kill Chase. *Fletch* (1985, Universal).

5701 "This is where the law stops and I begin." Police detective **Sylvester Stallone** has no qualms about violating due process and the rights of suspects. The one he shoots will never cost the state a trial. *Cobra* (1986, Warner Bros.).

5702 "Whenever you have a group of individuals beyond any investigation, who can manipulate the press, the judges, members of Congress—you are always going to have those who are above the law. . . . Not one CIA agent has ever been accused, much less tried of any crime. You guys think you're above the law. Well, you're not above mine!" Tough Chicago cop **Steven Seagal** snarls at some corrupt CIA creeps. *Above the Law* (1988, Warner Bros.).

Lawyers

see also CAREERS, CRIMES AND CRIMINALS, JUSTICE, LAWS, LEGALITY AND ILLEGALITY, OCCUPATIONS, PROFESSIONS AND PROFESSIONALS

5703 LUCILLE: "I didn't know you were a lawyer. You're awfully shy for a lawyer." GROUCHO: "You bet I'm shy. I'm a shyster lawyer." **Thelma Todd** can't set up a line for **Groucho Marx** the way Margaret Dumont did—but she tries. *Monkey Business* (1931, Paramount).

5704 "If there is ever to be law and order in the West, the first thing we've got to do is take all lawyers out and shoot 'em down like dogs." Missouri newspaper editor **Henry Hull** expresses a wishful sentiment about the people who have made laws that allow land to be stolen from poor folk legally. *Jesse James* (1939, 20th Century-Fox).

5705 "When you brought me this case, did I ask is she innocent or is she guilty? All I said was, have you got five thousand dollars." Crafty attorney **Adolphe Menjou** is more interested in his fee than the guilt or innocence of his client—sassy, gum-snapping dance hall girl Ginger Rogers who has confessed to a murder for the publicity. *Roxie Hart* (1942, 20th Century-Fox).

5706 MISS PLIMSOLL: "How lucky you lawyers are. . . I almost married a lawyer once. I was in attendance when he had his appendectomy and we became engaged as soon as he could sit up. Then peritonitis set in and he went like that." SIR WILFRID ROBARTS: "He certainly was a lucky lawyer." Pesty private nurse **Elsa Lanchester** makes small talk with her charge, recuperating irascible barrister **Charles Laughton** but ignores his many digs. *Witness for the Prosecution* (1957, United Artists).

5707 "A lawyer, all a lawyer cares about is the law." Tired, old Police Captain **Orson Welles** is annoyed by the short-sightedness of attorneys. *Touch of Evil* (1958, Universal-International).

5708 "Of course he's upset. He's a lawyer. He's paid to be upset." **Jack Lemmon** speaks of his shyster brother-in-law Walter Matthau. *The Fortune Cookie* (1966, United Artists).

5709 "You come in here with a skull full of mush and you leave thinking like a lawyer." Law professor **John Houseman,** who teaches using the Socratic method, lectures his intimidated students. *The Paper Chase* (1973, 20th Century-Fox).

5710 "Call your mother and tell her you will never be a lawyer." Law professor **John Houseman** gives law student Timothy Bottoms a dime and the brush; but he will soon forget Bottoms as he forgets all his other students. *The Paper Chase* (1973, 20th Century-Fox).

5711 "Some men are heterosexual; some men are bisexual; some men don't think about sex at all—they become lawyers." **Woody Allen** questions the level of interest attorneys have with regard to sex. *Love and Death* (1975, United Artists).

5712 NEAL PAGE: "You're a thief!" MAN: "Close, I'm a lawyer." **Steve Martin** has just paid **Nicholas Wyman** $100 in the latter's taxi in busy downtown Manhattan. While he's making the transaction, John Candy jumps in the cab and speeds off. *Planes, Trains and Automobiles* (1987, Paramount).

5713 "What's 500 lawyers at the bottom of the ocean?. . . A start!" Attorney **Danny De Vito** makes a joke at the expense of his profession for a client. *The War of the Roses* (1989, 20th Century-Fox).

5714 "I don't need tough guys. I need more lawyers." Mobster **Al Pacino** realizes that the rackets have reached a point where a new breed of musclemen and killers is needed. *The Godfather, Part III* (1990, Paramount).

5715 "There are one hundred and fifty lawyers down there. Couldn't they find someone who didn't fuck her to handle the case?" **Bonnie Bedelia** bitterly questions her husband, assistant prosecutor Harrison Ford, when he tells her he's been assigned to the case of the murder of beautiful, sexy, ambitious and heartless lawyer Greta Scacchi, once his mistress. *Presumed Innocent* (1990, Warner Bros.).

5716 "I'm going to need a lawyer, a very, very good lawyer, an expensive lawyer. It could break us." **Harrison Ford** confides to his wife Bonnie Bedelia when it becomes apparent that he will be arrested and charged with the murder of his one-time mistress Greta Scacchi. *Presumed Innocent* (1990, Warner Bros.).

5717 "You've got that sharp, useless look about you." It's hooker **Julia Roberts**' reason for thinking her wealthy client, business tycoon Richard Gere is a lawyer. *Pretty Woman* (1990, Touchstone-Buena Vista).

5718 "I'm a professional killer. . . . I'm a lawyer." A bit in her cups, **Mary Elizabeth Mastrantonio** identifies her profession to a flirtatious bartender the day she used brutal tactics to break down a crippled witness. *Class Action* (1991, 20th Century-Fox).

5719 "Scientists are now using lawyers instead of rats for their experiments. There are two reasons for this. The scientists don't become attached to the lawyers and there are some things rats won't do." Lawyer **Robin Williams,** the grown-up Peter Pan, repeats an old joke to a gathering of grown-up "lost boys" assembled to honor the original Wendy Darling, now ancient Maggie Smith. The sentiments are worth hearing again and again. *Hook* (1991, Tri-Star).

5720 "I'm going to be a lawyer, not a cop." **James Spader** responds when John Cusack accuses him of not being sufficiently ambitious. *True Colors* (1991, Paramount).

Laziness

see also SLOWNESS, WORK AND WORKERS

5721 "I've no respect for a man who was born lazy. It took me a long time to get where I am." Success school founder **Don Ameche** thinks he's the best advertisement for his methods. *The Magnificent Dope* (1942, 20th Century-Fox).

5722 "I loaf—but in a decorative and highly charming manner. . . . With me, loafing is a science." Apparently being charming is the only trick socially prominent, land-poor **Zachary Scott** has learned. *Mildred Pierce* (1945, Warner Bros.).

5723 "You were probably frightened by a callus at an early age." **Eve Arden** correctly spots Zachary Scott as a lazy parasite. *Mildred Pierce* (1945, Warner Bros.).

5724 "It's not that I shouldn't, it's not that I wouldn't, and you know it's simply because I'm the laziest gal in town." **Marlene Dietrich**'s song is a tip-off of the resolution of the film's plot. *Stage Fright* (1950, Warner Bros.).

5725 "Lazy—gets tired of selling his gun all over, and decides to sell it in one place." **John Wayne** explains to Angie Dickinson what makes a gunman become a lawman. *Rio Bravo* (1959, Warner Bros.).

Leadership and Leaders

see also AUTHORITIES, COMMANDS, OBEDIENCE, RULES

5726 "All right, you guys, I'm boss here. See!" Having eliminated his competitor and mentor Stanley Fields, **Edward G. Robinson** takes over the gang. *Little Caesar* (1931, Warner Bros.).

5727 "L'amour! L'amour! Where love leads, I always follow." It's many-times married **Mary Boland**'s battle cry. *The Women* (1939, MGM).

5728 "As leader of all the illegal activities in Casablanca, I'm a very influential and respected man, but it would not be worth my life to do anything for M'sieur Laszlo. You, however, are a different matter." **Sydney Greenstreet** informs Paul Henreid and Ingrid Bergman that even he is unable to get an exit visa from Casablanca for resistance leader Henreid, but he may be able to help Bergman escape. *Casablanca* (1942, Warner Bros.).

5729 LASZLO: "You must know that it's very important I get out of Casablanca." RICK: "Why you more than any of the other thousands who are stuck here?" LASZLO: "Whether Victor Laszlo, the man, gets out is not important at all. But it's my privilege to be one of the leaders of a great movement. You know what it means to the work—to the lives of thousands and thousands of little people that I be free to reach America and continue my work." **Paul Henreid**'s appeal to **Humphrey Bogart**'s patriotism doesn't work at the moment. Bogie is still hurting because he was dumped by Henreid's wife Ingrid Bergman back in Paris. *Casablanca* (1942, Warner Bros.).

5730 "I'd follow him right into the Mikado's bathtub." Veteran sailor **Tom Tully** has a great deal of respect for submarine commander Cary Grant. *Destination Tokyo* (1943, Warner Bros.).

5731 "I'd follow him down the barrel of a cannon!" Not to be outdone in the area of respect for a commanding officer, parachutist **George Tobias** has extreme confidence in mission leader Errol Flynn. *Objective Burma* (1945, Warner Bros.).

5732 "I took her hand in mine, and we went out of the ruined place. . . and in all the broad expanse of tranquil light. . . I saw the shadow part of her." **John Mills,** as the adult Pip, leads Valerie Hobson, as the adult Estella, out of the squalor of Miss Havisham's home. There as a girl, played by Jean Simmons, Estella was trained to be the instrument of the old woman's revenge on men. *Great*

Expectations (1946, GB, Cineguild-Universal-International).

5733 "You've looked for leaders. For strong men without faults. There aren't any. There are only men like yourselves.... There's no leader but yourselves." **Marlon Brando,** as Mexican revolutionary Emiliano Zapata, tries with little success to convince the peasants that they shouldn't expect too much from those who would be their leaders. The truth of his statement applies to all countries and all forms of government. *Viva Zapata!* (1952, 20th Century-Fox).

5734 "And that's the difference. I'm a leader because someone pins crowns on me. You're a leader because God made you one, I suppose. There's nothing you can do about it." **Jack Hawkins,** as General Allenby, speaks of the duty of command to title character Peter O'Toole. *Lawrence of Arabia* (1962, Columbia.)

5735 "A teacher or a leader? The dangerous Miss Brodie and her troops! Well, where you lead, I cannot follow." **Robert Stephens** walks out on his impossible lover Maggie Smith. *The Prime of Miss Jean Brodie* (1969, GB, 20th Century-Fox).

5736 "We lead the world in hernias." **Woody Allen,** the president of San Marcos, states his small country's major claim to fame. *Bananas* (1971, United Artists).

5737 "When I die... in the newspapers they'll write that the sons of bitches of the world have lost their leader." Baseball manager **Vincent Gardenia** accepts the fact that he's not well liked. *Bang the Drum Slowly* (1973, Paramount).

5738 "The sole function of any international cartel is to insure political harmony. The first obligation of power is to lead. Now that's been the Holy Grail since the Industrial Revolution." Billionaire oil tycoon **Marlon Brando** educates George C. Scott, who is investigating the death of his best friend. Scott learns that a formula for synthetic fuel is behind everything. *The Formula* (1980, MGM).

5739 "It's hard to lead people anywhere when you don't know where you're going." Motorcycle rat **Mickey Rourke** rejects the notion of his brother Matt Dillon that he's anyone to follow or emulate. *Rumble Fish* (1982, Universal).

5740 "The endless staircase will lead us to the center of the earth. Follow me." Title character **Lou Ferrigno** rallies his followers. *Hercules* (1983, MGM-Cannon).

Learning and Lessons

see also EDUCATION, EXPERIENCES, GROWTH AND DEVELOPMENT, INFORMATION AND INFORMERS, KNOWLEDGE, PRACTICES, SCHOOLS, STUDIES AND STUDENTS, TEACHING AND TEACHERS, WISDOM

5741 "We have been fighting death itself and have learned what is truly precious. There is enough left for the life we are going to lead." **Charles Wellesley,** who until now has mostly ignored his daughter Mary Pickford, comes to his senses after spending a night with the child until her delirium ended. *A Poor Little Rich Girl* (1917, silent, Artcraft).

5742 "I can learn to live, after all." Staid banker **Roland Young** breaks out of his shell with a small dance step. *Topper* (1937, MGM).

5743 "If I ever go looking for my heart's desire again, I won't look any further than my own backyard, because if it isn't there, I never really lost it to begin with." It's the sorta garbled lesson **Judy Garland** learns from her exploits in the Land of Oz. *The Wizard of Oz* (1939, MGM).

5744 "I've had a lot of luck to have had such a good life. I wish there was some way to pass on what I've learned. I was learning fast there at the end." **Gary Cooper,** Ernest Hemingway's hero Robert Jordan, realizes near the conclusion of the film that he will not survive. His only regret is that he can't pass on something of himself to someone else. *For Whom the Bell Tolls* (1943, Paramount).

5745 "If you want to win a girl you have to have a lot of beetles." In voice-over **Don Ameche** states the lesson he learned when he was nine years old. He had to give a girl two beetles for the privilege of walking with her. *Heaven Can Wait* (1943, 20th Century-Fox).

5746 "Don't treat me to any more lessons in tolerance. I'm sick of it." **Dorothy McGuire** is fed up with her fiancé Gregory Peck who lectures her on her passive prejudice while he's writing a magazine series on anti-Semitism. *Gentlemen's Agreement* (1947, 20th Century-Fox).

5747 "I'm learning what it is to be a soldier's wife." French Captain **Cary Grant** tells his new wife American WAC Lieutenant Ann Sheridan of his frustrations with bureaucratic red tape which keeps them from consummating their marriage. *I Was a Male War Bride* (1949, 20th Century-Fox).

5748 "You never know when you're well off until you aren't." **Betty Warren,** one of the inhabitants of a small section of London that briefly secedes from

Great Britain, utters the final message and lesson of the film. *Passport to Pimlico* (1949, GB, Ealing).

5749 "Myrtle Mae, you have a lot to learn; and I hope you never learn it." Most parents can identify with **Josephine Hull**'s wish for her daughter Victoria Horne, but everyone has to learn some harsh facts of life. *Harvey* (1950, Universal-International).

5750 "I've learned something today, and it's that, well, there comes a time in a man's life when he's got to quit rolling around like a pin ball. Maybe a—a little town like this is it. A place to settle down where people are easy-going and sincere." It's a nice thought for drifter **William Holden**—but stealing the heart of Kim Novak, the best girl of Cliff Robertson, the son of the town's leading citizen, doesn't earn him a warm welcome. *Picnic* (1955, Columbia).

5751 "I'm going to tell you something, Miz Thornton—something you can teach your class someday. The minute they walk out that there door, they walk into a dog-eat-dog world. It's 'Crawl in front of the big dogs if you want to eat.' 'Get a job.' I won't do it! I won't do it! That's—that's why I'm washing windows, scrubbing walls, emptying ashes." Janitor **Arthur Kennedy** tells teacher Mildred Dunnock that the reason he holds such a lowly position is that he won't betray his principles—whatever they may be. *Peyton Place* (1957, 20th Century-Fox).

5752 "No, no, no—is that all they taught you in school? They give a course in, 'yes,' you know." Diane Baker falls for the reasoning of playboy **Bob Evans**. *The Best of Everything* (1959, 20th Century-Fox).

5753 "You want me to be corny and say this has taught me a lesson. O.K., it's taught me a lesson." Badly shaken by a fight in which he's picked up some nasty wounds, **Ben Carruthers** confesses to his friends. *Shadows* (1960, McEndree-Cassel).

5754 "Oh, Jo, why can't you learn from my mistakes? It takes half your lifetime to learn from your own." **Dora Bryan** unsuccessfully urges her daughter Rita Tushingham to listen and benefit from her experiences and errors. *A Taste of Honey* (1961, GB, Continental Distributing).

5755 CAROL BREWSTER: "That's cheap!" DONNA STUART: "Cheap? I'll tell you what's cheap: make-believe mink, synthetic sable. Sweetie Pie, there are ins and outs, have and have-nots. Me? I want in. Any questions? Class dismissed." New stewardess **Pamela Tiffin** is given one of life's lessons when she expresses shock that fellow stewardess **Dolores Hart** has made a date with a passenger. *Come Fly with Me* (1963, MGM).

5756 "Haven't you learned the lesson of the show? You can be anything you want. All you have to do is go out and become it." **Clint Eastwood,** owner and chief attraction of a seedy traveling Wild West show, shares his optimism with runaway heiress Sondra Locke. *Bronco Billy* (1980, Warner Bros.).

5757 "Even with all the accumulated knowledge, when will these dummies learn to use the doorknob?" **Gene Hackman,** as Lex Luthor, is disgusted when aliens Terence Stamp, Jack O'Halloran and Sarah Douglas crash through the walls to enter the office of Jackie Cooper, editor of the Daily Planet. *Superman II* (1981, Warner Bros.).

5758 "Listen, you know what I learned this summer? How to kill usin' just my thumbs." Good-hearted bruiser **Rick Rossovich** shares the fruits of his summer vacation with other cadets at the Carolina Military Institute. *The Lords of Discipline* (1983, Paramount).

5759 "You can't learn to be real. It's like learning to be a midget. It's not something you can learn." Movie actor **Jeff Daniels** tries to talk some sense into his movie character (also Daniels), who has come down off the screen to be with Mia Farrow. *The Purple Rose of Cairo* (1985, Orion).

5760 "Tess, you don't get anywhere in this world by waiting for what you want to come to you. . . . You make it happen. Watch me, Tess, learn from me." **Sigourney Weaver**'s advice and example will be taken by her secretary Melanie Griffith much further than Weaver would ever anticipate or appreciate. *Working Girl* (1988, 20th Century-Fox).

5761 "Times change. These days, we learn from the philanthropists like the Rockefellers. First you rob everybody, then you give to the poor." **Al Pacino** tells his lawyer George Hamilton that he's just another robber baron. *The Godfather, Part III* (1991, Paramount).

Leaving *see* DEPARTURES AND RETURNS

Legality and Illegality

see also LAWS, LAWYERS, LEGITIMACY

5762 "We just found out that anybody who got married between 1936 and now with an Idaho license in Nevada—well, they're not legally married." Lawyer **Charles Halton** informs Robert Montgomery and Carole Lombard that due to a technicality, they are living in sin. *Mr. and Mrs. Smith* (1941, RKO).

5763 "Everything that's illegal is illegal because it makes more money for people that way." Drug dealer **Carl Lee** offers no apologies for his criminal profession. *The Connection* (1962, Allen-Clarke).

5764 "I believe my mental situation is extremely illegal." Loveable British Marxist **David Warner** has fixations for gorillas and his former wife Vanessa Redgrave. He's delightfully insane. *Morgan—A Suitable Case for Treatment* (1966, GB, British Lion).

5765 "Damn it all, why is everything we're good at illegal?" **Paul Newman** bemoans the fact that the talents of his partner Robert Redford and he are not appreciated by lawful folks. *Butch Cassidy and the Sundance Kid* (1969, 20th Century-Fox).

5766 "I remember when legal meant lawful. Now it means loophole." Cop **Charles Bronson** is angry because Richard Speck-like psychopath Gene Davis is literally getting away with murder due to bureaucratic bungling. *10 to Midnight* (1983, Cannon).

5767 "This is a wonderful country, my boy, but our legal system doesn't work the way it's supposed to." **Wilfred Brimley** recruits New York cop Fred Ward to become a U.S. agent and political assassin. *Remo Williams: The Adventure Begins* (1985, Orion).

5768 JUNE EDWARDS: "You could borrow it from a bank." BUSTER EDWARDS: "That's what I do for a living." JUNE: "I mean legally." **Julie Walters** would like a nice bungalow for herself, her daughter and her criminal husband **Phil Collins**. *Buster* (1988, GB, Tri-Star).

Legends

see also FAME, MYTHS, POPULARITY, STORIES

5769 SIR JOHN TALBOT: "It's an old legend. You'll find something like it in the folklore of nearly every nation. The scientific name for it is lycanthropy. It's a variety of schizophrenia." LARRY TALBOT: "That's Greek to me." SIR JOHN: "It is Greek. It's a technical explanation for something simple. There's good and evil in every man's soul. In this case, evil takes the form of an animal." **Claude Rains** lectures his son **Lon Chaney, Jr.** and the audience on the nature of werewolf-ness. *The Wolf Man* (1941, Universal).

5770 "In 1877, a young man rode out of the West and overnight his name became a household world. He was not a great general, or a great statesman, or a great scientist. Yet, even now more than sixty years later, the legends which surround him are as vivid as they were then. His name was William Frederick Cody. But to the young and old,

rich and poor, king and commoner, he's known as Buffalo Bill. This is the story of his life." The anonymous narrator's claim that the film tells the story of Buffalo Bill Cody's life shouldn't be taken too seriously. *Buffalo Bill* (1944, 20th Century-Fox).

5771 "Deep among the lonely sunbaked hills of Texas, the great and weather-beaten stone still stands. The Comanches call it Squaw's Head Rock. Time cannot change its impassive face, nor dim the legend of Pearl, who was herself a wildflower, sprung from the hard clay, quick to blossom and early to die." At the beginning of the movie, narrator **Orson Welles** sets the stage. *Duel in the Sun* (1946, Selznick).

5772 "Here I am having reached the age of forty and I have never known what it is like to be loved. It is like the legend of the sleeping princess, only here it is the prince that sleeps and awaits the kiss of a beautiful young maiden that will bring him back to life." Regent **Laurence Olivier**'s obvious ploy to bed showgirl Marilyn Monroe is doomed to failure. *The Prince and the Showgirl* (1957, Warner Bros.).

5773 "This is the West, sir. When the legend becomes the fact, print the legend." Newspaper editor **Edmond O'Brien** knows what's news and what's not. *The Man Who Shot Liberty Valance* (1962, Paramount).

5774 "And so ended the Jonas Cord legend, leaving its aspirations and scars on those who lived under his creative genius, as well as his tyranny." As George Peppard's role was clearly drawn from the life of Howard Hughes, the narrator is wrong to declare his legend is over at the end of the movie. There were many more fascinating chapters. *The Carpetbaggers* (1964, Paramount).

5775 "Once in a generation, a hero becomes a legend." It's the opening statement of the surprising trendy radical hit. *Billy Jack* (1971, Warner Bros.).

5776 "She lived in a savage world in an age of violence. . . A fierce warrior with flaming red hair in the Hyborian kingdom. Her quest for justice and vengeance became a legend. This is how the legend began." The opening lines of the fantasy adventure starring Brigitte Nielsen. *Red Sonja* (1985, MGM-United Artists).

5777 "He was always ready to go off at the drop of a legend." Title character **Richard Chamberlain** seeks his brother who has disappeared in quest of the title city. *Allan Quatermain and the Lost City of Gold* (1987, Cannon).

Legitimacy

see also CORRECTIONS, LEGALITIES AND ILLEGALITY, PROFESSIONS AND PROFESSIONALS

5778 "There are no illegitimate children, there are only illegitimate parents." Appearing before the Texas legislature, child welfare worker **Greer Garson** pleads for the passage of a bill to protect adopted children. *Blossoms in the Dust* (1941, MGM).

5779 "So, you've gone legitimate, eh? I knew you'd come to no good." **Robert Preston** disapproves of his old con man crony Buddy Hackett who is reduced to working for a living. *The Music Man* (1962, Warner Bros.).

5780 "Kay, my father's way of doing things is over. It's finished. Even he knows that, I mean, in five years the Corleone family is going to be completely legitimate. Trust me—that's all I can tell you about my business." Those who have seen "The Godfather, Part III" know that **Al Pacino** was never able to keep his promise to his wife Diane Keaton. *The Godfather* (1972, Paramount).

Legs *see* BODIES

Letters

see also MESSAGES, NOTES, SPEECH AND SPEAKING, SYMBOLS, WORDS, WRITING AND WRITERS

5781 "Dear Mr. Gable: I am writing this to you, and I hope that you read it so you'll know. My heart beats like a hammer, and I stutter and I stammer every time I see you at the picture show. I guess I'm just another fan of yours, and I thought I'd write and tell you so. . . . You made me love you, I didn't want to do it. I didn't want to do it. You made me love you. . . ." While gazing at his photograph, **Judy Garland** writes a fan letter to Clark Gable that leads her into singing, "You Made Me Love You." *Broadway Melody of 1938* (1938, MGM).

5782 PHILLS: "Do you think they're becoming stereotyped?" MAJOR BRAND: "No matter how you write it, it will break his mother's heart just the same." Adjutant **Donald Crisp** must write letters of sympathy to bereaved parents and wives of young pilots sent to their death in World War I air battles by commander **Basil Rathbone**. *The Dawn Patrol* (1938, Warner Bros.).

5783 "Robert will be away for the night. I absolutely must see you. I am desperate, and, if you don't come, I won't answer for the consequences. Don't drive up." Lawyer **James Stephenson** reads to Bette Davis part of the letter she wrote to the man

she killed, claiming he had made unwanted advances to her. *The Letter* (1940, Warner Bros.).

5784 "My heart was trembling as I walked into the post office, and there you were, lying in box 237. I took you out of your envelope and read you—read you right there—oh, my dear friend." Leather goods clerk **James Stewart** reads a portion of a letter from his lady pen pal to his co-worker Felix Bressart. Stewart is unaware that his "dear friend" is none other than another co-worker Margaret Sullavan, who also doesn't know his identity. The two secret lovers don't get along very well. A similar scene took place in a 1949 remake with Van Johnson reading to Buster Keaton about unknown pen pal Judy Garland. *The Shop Around the Corner* (1940, MGM); *In the Good Old Summertime* (1949, MGM).

5785 "If it had not been for these things, I might have lived out of my life talking at street corners to scorning men. I might have died unmarked, unknown, a failure. Now, we are not a failure. Never in our full life could we hope to do so much for tolerance, for justice, for man's understanding of man, as now we do by accident. Our words, our lives, our pain, nothing! The taking of our lives, the lives of a good shoemaker and a poor fish peddler, all! That last moment belongs to us—that agony is our triumph." Teacher **Henry Fonda** starts a controversy when he reads to his class an eloquent letter from anarchist Bartolomeo Vanzetti to his children, written shortly before he and Nicola Sacco were executed, supposedly for murder and robbery, but more likely because of their political views. *The Male Animal* (1942, Warner Bros.).

5786 "By the time you read this letter, I may be dead. I have so much to tell you and perhaps so very little time. Will I ever send it? I don't know. I must find the strength to write now before it's too late. And as I write, it may become clear that what has happened to us had its own reason beyond our poor understanding. If this reaches you, you'll know how I became yours when you didn't even know who I was, or even that I existed." In voice-over, **Joan Fontaine,** as Louis Jourdan reads her letter, sets the stage for a flashback of the story of her obsessive love for musician Jourdan. In this three hanky picture, Fontaine loves not wisely, but too well. *Letter from an Unknown Woman* (1948, Universal).

5787 MATT BRENNAN: "I wrote you a couple of times." JO HOLLOWAY: "I never got them." MATT: "I never mailed them." Ex-World War II bomber pilot and now civilian test pilot **Humphrey Bogart** mentions the extent of his efforts to keep in touch with ex-girl friend **Eleanor Parker**. *Chain Lightning* (1950, Warner Bros.).

5788 "These are love letters, yellowing with antiquity, all from one boy. Give them back to me! . . . The touch of your hand insults them!. . . Now that you've touched them I'll burn them. . . . Poems a dead boy wrote. I hurt him the way that you would like to hurt me, but you can't! I'm not young and vulnerable any more. But my young husband was. . . ." **Vivien Leigh** tries to reclaim her letters from her brutish brother-in-law, Marlon Brando, who has snatched them from her hands. *A Streetcar Named Desire* (1951, Warner Bros.-20th Century-Fox).

5789 "There is much we both can do for our people. Many things we have learned from each we can teach to them, patience, kindness and the wisdom to know the truth. You would not have let me say these things to you, but in your heart you will know they are true. You will be sad as I am sad, and you will think of me as I will think of you many times in the years to come, when you see the river of white water dancing in the sun or clouds hanging high above the mountains. But soon the memories will grow dim as memories should and there will be others to take their place. May they be happy ones for you, my love, as happy as those we shared together, all the days of your life." It's part of a letter **Donna Reed,** as Indian maiden Sacajawea, leaves for Charlton Heston, as William Clark. She realizes that their lives and cultures are too different to sustain their love in either's world. *The Far Horizons* (1955, Paramount).

5790 "I never answer letters from large organizations." Eccentric **Jason Robards, Jr.** includes the various utilities under the heading of large organizations. *A Thousand Clowns* (1965, United Artists).

5791 "What's with him—I gotta get a letter of introduction to have a 'sitdown'?" **Michael V. Gazzo** complains to John Cazale about his brother Al Pacino's inaccessibility. *The Godfather, Part II* (1974, Paramount).

5792 "I wrote her love letters, and she corrected them." **Rodney Dangerfield** claims he used to date an English teacher. *Back to School* (1986, Orion).

5793 "Dear Noodle, I had a little accident last week and I was in a hospital for three days, but everything is fine now. Anna had a nervous breakdown, but it is a common thing with actors in America. With the money I made from the film, I'm going to take Anna and myself to Hawaii. Well, dear Noodle, blue ocean, and a lot of flowers and palm trees. They don't have that in New York. Anna thinks she may get more work if she looks younger so I want to pay for her facelift. That's normal here too. I'm very sorry I couldn't attend Grandpa's funeral, but I was filming, and I couldn't possibly make it. I sent flowers through a special agency. Did you get them? I hope you did because they cost me a fortune. Please send my childhood photos because a man wants to write a book about me. Boy, I love America. Yours, Krystyna." At the beginning of the film, **Paulina Porizkova** was a poor little Czech waif, who arrives at the New York apartment of a Czech superstar Sally Kirkland, exiled during the 1968 Russian invasion. Porizkova has become a very much in demand actress. She writes home to her mother, as she does periodically in the movie. *Anna* (1987, Vestron).

5794 "I wrote a letter to the president of the United States to send no more arms in this country." **Raul Julia** portrays the soon-to-be martyred archbishop of El Salvador. *Romero* (1989, Four Seasons-Vidmark).

Liberty

see also DEMOCRACY, FREEDOMS, RIGHTS, SERVANTS AND SERVITUDE, SLAVERY AND SLAVES

5795 "Liberty is too precious a thing to be buried in books. . . . Men should hold it up in front of them every single day of their lives and say 'I'm free—to think and to speak. My ancestors couldn't. I can and my children will.'" Junior Senator **James Stewart** holds liberty dear at a time in the world when it was disappearing at an alarming rate. *Mr. Smith Goes to Washington* (1939, Columbia).

5796 "There's no compromising with human liberty. Graft, lies, self-seeking—and that kind of mad scrambling for money and power no matter who or how many he grinds on the way—all those things—they can't live if democracy is going to live too!" Late in the film, exhausted U.S. Junior Senator **James Stewart** puts his reputation and his credo on the line as he haltingly rasps out his words after a 23-hour filibuster to prevent his state's political boss Edward Arnold milking a great deal of graft from a bill to build a useless dam. *Mr. Smith Goes to Washington* (1939, Columbia).

5797 MAXIMO: "I'm sorry I didn't learn to spell liberty." MISS BERTHA BARNES: "Who ever learned it better?" In an obvious ploy to move the audience to tears, young **"Ducky" Louie** apologizes for his lack of studiousness to his teacher Beulah Bondi as he dies a Filipino hero. *Back to Bataan* (1945, RKO).

5798 "Go, proclaim liberty throughout all the lands and to all the inhabitants thereof." **Charlton Heston,** as Moses, sends out a proclamation. *The Ten Commandments* (1956, Paramount).

Lies and Lying

see also DECEPTIONS, IMPRESSIONS, TRUTH, TRUTH AND FALSEHOOD

5799 "A better dame than you called me a liar and they had to sew her up in twelve different places." Once **Mae West** spit a mouthful of water at her upper-class rival Gertrude Michael. Now she threatens to cut up the frightened girl who had the temerity to suggest that West wasn't entirely truthful. *I'm No Angel* (1933, Paramount).

5800 "Any lie will find believers as long as you tell it with force." **Greta Garbo**'s claim to John Gilbert reminds one of Nazi propagandist Joseph Goebbels' claim for the Big Lie. *Queen Christina* (1933, MGM).

5801 "I don't distort the truth. I heighten the composition." No matter how he says it, newsreel reporter **Clark Gable** will do just about anything to get a news scoop—including manufacturing the story. *Too Hot to Handle* (1938, MGM).

5802 "A lie grows and grows until it's as plain as the nose on your face." Pinocchio (voice of Dickie Jones) will learn most painfully the meaning of the Blue Fairy's (voice of **Evelyn Venable**) warning when his nose grows and grows when he tells a lie. *Pinocchio* (1940, Disney-RKO).

5803 "The woman that washed up at Edgecoombe—the woman that is now buried in the family crypt—that was not Rebecca. That was the body of some unknown woman, unclaimed, belonging nowhere. I identified it, but I knew it wasn't Rebecca. It was all a lie. I knew where Rebecca's body was! Lying on the cabin floor on the bottom of the sea.... Because I put it there!" **Laurence Olivier** tells his second wife that he told a pack of lies about the death of his hated first wife. *Rebecca* (1940, Selznick-United Artists).

5804 "I live in a small town and we eat at the drugstore but we leave a tip just the same. The lies I told were not too much to pay for one week of happiness." Bitter school teacher **Olivia de Havilland** confronts refugee Charles Boyer when she discovers he only married her so he could get into the U.S. *Hold Back the Dawn* (1941, Paramount).

5805 "I've always been a liar.... I'm so tired, so tired of lying and making up lies...not knowing what is a lie and what's the truth." **Mary Astor** is still lying as she tells Humphrey Bogart the truth about herself. *The Maltese Falcon* (1941, Warner Bros.).

5806 "Don't you know that the best men in the world have told lies and let things be misunderstood if it was useful to them? Didn't you ever hear of campaign promises?" **Claudette Colbert** excuses her deceptions by pointing out that she's in good company. *The Palm Beach Story* (1942, Paramount).

5807 "Here was a girl lying to her mother. Naturally, that interested me at once." In voice-over **Don Ameche** recalls his first glimpse of his wife-to-be Gene Tierney, who is on the telephone to her mother, misrepresenting where she is. *Heaven Can Wait* (1943, 20th Century-Fox).

5808 "If you want to believe other people, you'd better give up lying yourself." **Claude Rains'** advice to Bette Davis is on target. *Deception* (1946, Warner Bros.).

5809 "To be a real prize fathead, you've got to swallow whole all the lies you can think to tell yourself." Narrator **Orson Welles** hasn't quite been able to accomplish this. *Lady from Shanghai* (1948, Columbia).

5810 "I have been thirty-eight years on the force, but in a lifetime of investigation, you are probably the biggest and most willing liar I have ever met." Police Captain **Barry Fitzgerald** accuses murder suspect Howard Duff of major league mendacity. *The Naked City* (1948, Universal).

5811 "Course, I lied. How could I have friends? No education. Being as poor as a church mouse. I had no money to squander. And there was always the fact that I was—there are a lot of reasons why—so I kept to myself. Though no one liked me and that there was no one I liked." Dying Scot soldier **Richard Todd** confesses to using lying as a defense mechanism. *The Hasty Heart* (1949, Warner Bros.).

5812 "People will believe any lie if it is fantastic enough." **Leo Genn** is yet another echoing Adolph Hitler and Joseph Goebbels—or since Genn is a character in the court of Nero, maybe the Nazis stole it from Genn's character. *Quo Vadis* (1951, MGM).

5813 "Untruthful? My nephew Algernon untruthful? Impossible! He was at Oxford." Delightful **Edith Evans** defends her nephew Michael Denison against a charge of telling a fib. *The Importance of Being Earnest* (1952, GB, Two Cities-Rank).

5814 "I've done a lot of lying in my time. I've lied to men who wear belts. I've lied to men who wear suspenders. But I'd never be as stupid as to lie to a man who wears both belt and suspenders. He doesn't even trust his own trousers." Out-of-work big-time reporter **Kirk Douglas** applies for a job on a small town newspaper, edited by Porter Hall, a careful man. *Ace in the Hole* aka: *The Big Carnival* (1951, Paramount).

5815 JOHNNY GUITAR: "Tell me lies." VIENNA: "I have waited for you, Johnny." **Sterling Hayden** gets what he asked for if not what he wanted from **Joan Crawford**. *Johnny Guitar* (1954, Republic).

5816 "White man's tongue is forked." We don't claim that **Carol Thurston,** as Princess Yellow Flower, was the first or last movie character to utter this line. *Yukon Vengeance* (1954, Allied Artists).

5817 "The only people who make love all the time are liars." **Louis Jourdan** tells Leslie Caron not to believe that the idle rich idle away all their time in each other's beds. *Gigi* (1958, MGM).

5818 "You know something, Ann? No one I know of lies with such sincerity." **Burt Lancaster** pays his ex-wife Rita Hayworth something of a compliment. *Separate Tables* (1958, United Artists).

5819 "Maggie, you ought to know that in the world of advertising there's no such thing as a lie—there's only the expedient exaggeration." **Cary Grant** lectures his secretary Doreen Lang after he displaces a man from a taxi with a lie that makes her blanch. *North by Northwest* (1959, MGM).

5820 "Son, this is a Washington, D.C. kind of lie— that's where the other person knows you're lying and he knows you know." Secretary of State nominee **Henry Fonda** has had his son Eddie Hodges tell someone on the phone that he wasn't at home. *Advise and Consent* (1962, Columbia).

5821 TONI SIMMONS: "A man who lies cannot love." STEPHANIE DICKINSON: "That sounds like something out of a fortune cookie." **Goldie Hawn** is young and idealistic. **Ingrid Bergman** is older and wiser. *Cactus Flower* (1969, Columbia).

5822 "Lie to yourself, not to me. You got married because you knew you were second-rate. You got pregnant because Wayne was a ballet dancer, and that meant queer!" Ballet star **Anne Bancroft** isn't buying into Shirley MacLaine's belief that she might have been just as big a star if she hadn't quit dancing to raise a family. *The Turning Point* (1977, 20th Century-Fox).

5823 "At least I won't have to lie to you anymore." On his deathbed, Bob Fosse clone **Roy Scheider** bids farewell to the women in his life. *All That Jazz* (1979, 20th Century-Fox).

5824 "They are lying. That's what advertising is— lying. He sells his name and his picture to the cereal company for money. But he's a worker. . . . And the fact that he plays baseball makes him no different. . . than a man who works in the factory, and do you now why? Because he doesn't own the team. And there are Negro players who can't play and do you know why? Jim Crow. No matter how good they are." **Mandy Patinkin** lectures his young son Ilan Mitchell-Smith about an athlete whose picture appears on a box of Wheaties. *Daniel* (1983, Paramount).

5825 "I lie the facts. I lie the truth until I am no longer sure if it happened or not." Alcoholic homosexual writer **Jeroen Krabbe** reveals his secret during a lecture on his creative process—he fictionalizes real events through exaggeration. *The 4th Man* (1979, The Netherlands, Spectrafilm).

5826 "This is the second lie, Jonathan. . . . Do not let there be a third." **Linda Fiorentino,** who's not who she claims to be, has a lot of nerve complaining about lying, even if Anthony Edwards did fib to her about his age and sexual experience. *Gotcha!* (1985, Universal).

5827 "I just wanted you to know everything's 100 percent okay." Struggling for control, tears in his eyes, **Jack Nicholson** lies to his wife Kathleen Turner on the phone. He's been ordered by godfather William Hickey to kill Turner. *Prizzi's Honor* (1985, 20th Century-Fox).

5828 CHELSEA DEARDON: "Do you always cross-examine people?" TOM LOGAN: "Only when they lie to me." **Daryl Hannah** is a strange, beautiful girl, and Assistant D.A. **Robert Redford** knows he shouldn't get involved with her but he does. *Legal Eagles* (1986, Universal).

5829 "But you lied too. You told me everyone's alike and deserves a fair shake. But you meant everyone who was like you." Caught in a lie about what she did with money given to her by her father Jerry Orbach, **Jennifer Grey** is disillusioned when she finds that her physician father's liberal views don't apply when she uses the money to help a girl in trouble get an abortion. *Dirty Dancing* (1987, Vestron).

5830 "Do you know, Vicomte, why I never married again? It was certainly not for the lack of advantageous matches: it was solely so that no one should have the right to object to anything I might do. It was not even for fear that I might no longer be able to have my way, for I should always succeed in that end; but I should have found it irksome if anyone had so much as a right to complain. In short, I wished to lie only when I wanted to, not when I had to." **Glenn Close,** as a widowed Marquise, reprimands John Malkovich in a letter for his "connubial" manner with her. *Dangerous Liaisons* (1988, Warner Bros.).

5831 "That's a goddamn lie! I never bought a congressman in my life! I rent 'em. It's cheaper!" **Paul Newman**, as Louisiana Governor Earl Long, corrects a critic's accusation of corruption. *Blaze* (1989, Touchstone/Buena Vista).

5832 "If we are lovers, I'd have to lie. . . I don't think I can do that." Despite her desire for married Ted Danson, married **Isabella Rossellini** rues the consequences of an affair with him. *Cousins* (1989, Paramount).

5833 "If, in this case, the truth won't set you free— then lie." **Donald Moffat,** who has always preached high morals, ethics, honesty and truth, advises his son Tom Hanks to save himself from a hell of a mess by lying. *The Bonfire of the Vanities* (1990, Warner Bros.).

5834 "You're not being straight with me. I can smell a lie like a fart in a car." **Christian Slater** reacts with disbelief to a yarn of seduction of one of the listeners to his pirate radio station. *Pump Up the Volume* (1990, New Line).

5835 "We've been totally lied to by our album covers." It's **Alex Winter**'s reaction when he and Keanu Reeves visit Hell. *Bill & Ted's Bogus Journey* (1991, Orion).

5836 "Are you a politician or does lying just run in your family?" Tomboyish **Mary Stuart Masterson** snaps at Nick Searcy who tells her she's looking very attractive. *Fried Green Tomatoes* (1991, Universal).

5837 "You're the Ernest Hemingway of bullshit!" **Steve Martin** is steamed over another lie told by Goldie Hawn who has already told everyone she's his wife. *Housesitter* (1992, Universal).

Life and Death

see also DEATH AND DYING, LIVES AND LIVING

5838 "Believe me, if a man doesn't know death, he doesn't know life." **Lionel Barrymore,** who is dying, knows both. *Grand Hotel* (1932, MGM).

5839 "Oh! Amon-Ra, Oh! God of Gods! Death is but the doorway to new life. We live today—we shall live again. In many forms shall we return. Oh, Mighty One!" It's from "The Scroll of Thoth." *The Mummy* (1932, Universal).

5840 "If I can't live the way I want, let me die the way I want." **Clark Gable** refuses a reduction of his death sentence to life imprisonment from his childhood friend, Governor William Powell. *Manhattan Melodrama* (1934, MGM).

5841 "Keep your chin up and your nose clean, kid. Forget about that commutation. You don't want it anyway. Die the way you lived, all of a sudden, that's the way to go. Don't drag it out—living like that don't mean a thing." Having made his decision to not seek a commutation of his death sentence, **Clark Gable** swaggers along the last mile in the Death House, giving similar advice along with his farewell to another candidate for the hot seat. *Manhattan Melodrama* (1934, MGM).

5842 "And so she lived as she wished, and died as she must. . . ." The narrator announces the death of former orange seller and English Charles II's mistress Nell Gwyn, played by Anna Neagle. *Nell Gwyn* (1934, GB, B and D-Wilcox).

5843 "If Cathy died, I might begin to live." **Geraldine Fitzgerald** wishes Merle Oberon would die, thinking then maybe her husband Laurence Olivier would love her. *Wuthering Heights* (1939, Goldwyn/United Artists).

5844 "I have become a reverse zombie. The world was dead and I was living." Vaudeville mentalist **Edward G. Robinson** finds the power to predict the future is a curse rather than a gift. *Night Has a Thousand Eyes* (1948, Paramount).

5845 EBEN ADAMS: "I want you, not dreams of you." JENNIE APPLETON: "There is no life, my darling, until you love and have been loved and then there is no death." **Joseph Cotten** is comforted by long dead **Jennifer Jones,** when he finds a love affair with a ghost something less than ideal. *Portrait of Jennie* (1948, Vanguard-Selznick).

5846 "Somewhere in here I was born, and there I died. It was only a moment for you, you took no notice." **Kim Novak** traces her gloved finger across a cross section of an ancient giant redwood, indicating a span of an earlier century. Talking absently to James Stewart, she is speaking of the woman of whom she is the reincarnation. *Vertigo* (1958, Paramount).

5847 "There's right, and there's wrong. You gotta do one or the other. You do the one, and you're living. You do the other, and you may be walking around, but you're dead as a beaver hat." **John Wayne,** as Davy Crockett, convinces his Tennessee volunteers to help defend the Alamo against Santa Anna's troops. *The Alamo* (1960, United Artists).

5848 "It's quite possible, Octavian, that when you die, you will die without ever having been alive." Mark Antony, portrayed by **Richard Burton**, disapproves of his brother-in-law and future enemy Octavian, portrayed by Roddy McDowall. *Cleopatra* (1963, 20th Century-Fox).

5849 "She didn't die of pneumonia—she died of life." Agent **Red Buttons** makes a meaningless eulogy of the late, lamented title character Carroll Baker. *Harlow* (1965, Paramount).

5850 "Sorry, but this man's still alive and that one's dead, and that's a fact." Surgeon **Tom Skerritt** commandeers the assistance of Chaplain Rene Auberjonois, who is giving last rites to a dead patient. *M*A*S*H* (1970, 20th Century-Fox).

5851 "I don't want to die. . . I want to live, though it's been a disgusting life so far. I've been miserable with it, but I don't want it to come to an end. I'm not going to let them end it." Gaunt Italian concentration camp inmate **Giancarlo Giannini** cries as he watches his fellow prisoners being led to their deaths by Nazi guards. He'll do anything to survive—and does. *Seven Beauties* (1975, Italy, Cinema 5).

5852 "I come here to die with you, or live with you. Dyin' ain't hard for people like you and me. It's the livin' that's hard." Mediator **Clint Eastwood** attempts to arrange a peace treaty with stern Comanche chief, Will Sampson. *The Outlaw Josey Wales* (1976, Warner Bros.).

5853 "The earth is the only country I belong to. When I die, that's the end of it. I live now." **Giancarlo Giannini** is a rich, handsome, arrogant, self-confident and cruel atheist of the turn-of-the-century world. *The Innocent* (1977, Italy, Analysis Film Releasing Corp.).

5854 "Only the living need each other. Only the living can carry life on. Part of me was trying to die because I thought I owed that to Jenny. I owe her something else, something much harder to give: a new life, another try. A setting free." Having found someone new, namely Candice Bergen, young widower **Ryan O'Neal** gives up the ghost of his first wife Ali MacGraw from *Love Story*. *Oliver's Story* (1978, Paramount).

5855 "Us dead people sure know how to live." Former slave **Sherman Hemsley** is a guide through the spiritual world for the newly dead. *Ghost Fever* (1987, Miramax).

5856 "Kathleen, my love, you asked me a question once: was it instinct to save a life or to take it? I don't know, my darling. All I do know is that we are free to choose. I hope to God we choose life over death. Not because I believe the implacable universe cares a damn, but because as I look at you, my darling, I realize how glorious, how magical, life can be." Young scientist **John Cusack**'s affair with nurse Laura Dern is left unconsummated because he is accidentally exposed to a high dose of radiation, causing him a slow, agonizing death. *Fat Man and Little Boy* (1989, Paramount).

5857 "His body may be dead, but his spirit is released." Psychic **Tracy Griffith** explains to police detective Lou Diamond Phillips about executed serial killer Jeff Kober who still seems capable of causing a lot of trouble. *The First Power* (1990, Orion).

5858 "The only thing worse than thinking about dying is thinking you might have a chance to live." **Arliss Howard** is granted a governor's reprieve after he's been strapped into the electric chair. *Somebody Has Got to Shoot the Picture* (1991, Warner Bros.).

Lights

see also DAYS, EYES, FIRES, INSPIRATIONS, MOON AND MOONLIGHT, NIGHTS, SENSE AND SENSIBILITY, SENSITIVITY AND INSENSITIVITY, SIGHT AND SIGHTS, SMOKING AND SMOKERS

5859 "Don't forget to stand in the light when you're talking to a producer." Showgirl **Aline MacMahon** gives sexist advice to Ruby Keeler who is off to an audition wearing a filmy dress. *Gold Diggers of 1933* (1933, Warner Bros.).

5860 "Hello, America. . . I've been watching a part of the world blown to pieces. . . I can't read the rest of my speech because the lights have gone out. Yours are the only lights left burning. Cover them with steel, ring them with guns. Hang on to your lights, America, they're the only lights left in the world!" War correspondent **Joel McCrea,** broadcasting from London, urges America to join the fight against the fascists. *Foreign Correspondent* (1940, United Artists).

5861 "Anybody got a match?" Sexy **Lauren Bacall** slouches across the screen for the first time. *To Have and Have Not* (1944, Warner Bros.).

5862 "Hey, Randy, light these torches over here." At the end of the film, the sheriff and his posse arrive at the house where Duane Jones is hiding. They shoot every zombie in sight. Unfortunately, before he can identify himself, Jones is also shot and killed. *Night of the Living Dead* (1968, Continental).

5863 "Have you ever seen her when the light hits her face just right? She looks very beautiful. Of course, you can't depend on that light." **Dudley Moore** speaks of Jill Eikenberry, the girl his father Thomas Barbour demands he marry or lose an inheritance of $750 million. *Arthur* (1981, Orion-Warner Bros.).

5864 Garrett Breedlove: "I like the lights on." Aurora Greenway: "Then go home and turn them on." **Jack Nicholson** learns that in her house, in her bed, **Shirley MacLaine** calls the shots during love-making. *Terms of Endearment* (1983, Paramount).

5865 "Love is like this beautiful light that lets you see things that no one else can see." **Mariel Hemingway** instructs professor Peter O'Toole, for whom she has set her cap. *Creator* (1985, Universal).

5866 The Actress: "Light travels at. . . a hundred and eighty-six thousand miles a second." The Professor: "Point three nine seven." Actress: "It got faster?" Professor: "We got more accurate." Actress: "Then don't confuse me." Marilyn Monroe-like actress **Theresa Russell** discusses relativity with Albert Einstein-like professor **Michael Emil**. *Insignificance* (1985, GB, Island Alive).

5867 "I didn't ask for a fucking psychological lecture. I only asked for a fucking light." **Daniel Day-Lewis,** as cerebral palsy sufferer and Irish writer and painter Christy Brown, snaps at hired nurse Ruth McCabe who advises him that smoking is not good for him. *My Left Foot* (1989, Irish, Miramax).

Likeness *see* Equalities, Resemblances

Likes and Dislikes

see also Love and Hate, Love and Lovers, Pleasures, Preferences, Tastes, Wants and Wanting, Wishes

5868 "Nothin' I like better than to meet a high-class mama that can snap 'em back at you. Cause the colder they are, the hotter they get. . . ." Traveling salesman **Roscoe Karns** uses all of his questionable charm to make time with runaway heiress Claudette Colbert. *It Happened One Night* (1934, Columbia).

5869 Gavin: "Can a man like a woman against her will?" Babbie: "Of course he can. That's the very nicest way to be liked." Pastor **John Beal** is encouraged by gypsy girl **Katharine Hepburn**. *The Little Minister* (1934, RKO).

5870 "Are you sure you don't still like that fella?" Nerdish **Ralph Bellamy** is suspicious that his fiancée Irene Dunne hasn't quite gotten over her ex-husband, Cary Grant. *The Awful Truth* (1937, Columbia).

5871 "Imagine Aunt Elizabeth coming to this apartment and running smack into a leopard. If you had an aunt who would give you a million dollars if she liked you, and you knew she wouldn't like you if she found a leopard in your apartment, what would you do?" The rapidity with which **Katharine Hepburn** puts this question to Cary Grant almost makes him believe she's making sense. *Bringing Up Baby* (1938, RKO).

5872 "Wahoo, I finally found something you like to do." **Mickey Rooney** comes up for air from a long impassioned clinch with Lana Turner, who doesn't want to walk, swim, play tennis, etc. *Love Finds Andy Hardy* (1938, MGM).

5873 "I've got my claws in plush and I like it." Unemployed **Ginger Rogers** enjoys posing as a gold digger to help millionaire Walter Connolly annoy his family. *Fifth Avenue Girl* (1939, RKO).

5874 "I like men who reach for a slice of fame." **Barbara Stanwyck** accuses William Holden of being a whiner rather than a doer. He grabs her and kisses her. She remains unimpressed. *Golden Boy* (1939, Columbia).

5875 "My Johnnie doesn't like Sylvia's 'Jungle Red.' He says he'd like to do her nails right down to the wrist with a buzz saw." **Joan Fontaine**'s never-seen husband must dislike a lot more than the color of bitchy Rosalind Russell's nail polish. *The Women* (1939, MGM).

5876 "I'm testing the air. I like it, but it doesn't like me." **James Stewart** suffers from a hangover. *The Philadelphia Story* (1940, MGM).

5877 "When you're slapped, you'll take it and like it." Cool, cunning private eye **Humphrey Bogart** advises cringing gunman Peter Lorre. *The Maltese Falcon* (1941, Warner Bros.).

5878 "I don't like being an average girl from an average family." **Teresa Wright** believes she should be more than ordinary. *Shadow of a Doubt* (1943, Universal).

5879 "You want to bargain with me at a time like this? I don't like your insinuations about my husband and I don't like your methods. In fact, I don't like you, Mr. Norton." Doing a fine acting job as the outraged, grieving widow, murderess **Barbara Stanwyck** blasts Richard Gaines, the foolish president of Pacific All Risk Insurance Company, who claims her husband's death was not an accident but that he had committed suicide. *Double Indemnity* (1944, Paramount).

5880 "Maybe because I like you, and I don't like them." **Humphrey Bogart** answers when he's asked why he's changed his mind about helping a French resistance fighter escape from Vichy-controlled Devil's Island. *To Have and Have Not* (1944, Warner Bros.).

5881 "Yes, I take money from you. But not enough to make me like kitchens or cooks. They smell of grease." Caddish, ne'er-do-well **Zachary Scott** represents a lifetime of endless taking and no giving. He dismisses his wife Joan Crawford for her lack of class because she works for a living, running a restaurant, to support him and her hellish, selfish daughter Ann Blyth. *Mildred Pierce* (1945, Warner Bros.).

5882 "How is tall, dark and obnoxious?" Clearly, nurse **Marjorie Davies** doesn't care for Donna Reed's troublesome patient, PT Commander John Wayne. *They Were Expendable* (1945, MGM).

5883 "It seems funny to say, but I don't like you, Benjamin. I don't like any of my children. I just feel sorry for you." **Florence Eldridge** makes a painful admission to her heartless and dishonest son Edmond O'Brien. *Another Part of the Forest* (1948, Universal).

5884 CHIP: "What are you doing driving a cab? The war's over." BRUNHILDE: "I never give up anything I like. Come up to my place." Sailor **Frank Sinatra** believes that women only took jobs during World War II because there weren't enough men to go around. **Betty Garrett** likes the freedom to be the chaser rather than the chasee. *On the Town* (1949, MGM).

5885 "I still like the way you are—attractive and average." **Jeff Donnell** assures her police detective husband Frank Lovejoy that she prefers him to Humphrey Bogart, a violent, paranoid genius. *In a Lonely Place* (1950, Columbia).

5886 "It's not what you say, it's how you say it—personality always wins the day. Start big and you'll end up big. It's important not only to be liked but to be well-liked." Salesman **Fredric March** shares his philosophy of successful selling with his sons. *Death of a Salesman* (1952, Columbia).

5887 "There's something about working the streets I like. It's the tramp in me, I suppose." "The Little Tramp" **Charles Chaplin** is a street entertainer. *Limelight* (1952, United Artists).

5888 "I don't like lobsters. I have a long list of dislikes. It's getting longer." **Joan Crawford** is about to add gigolo Jeff Chandler to her list, but later she'll erase it. *Female on the Beach* (1955, Universal).

5889 DRUMMOND HALL: "People like me." LYNN MARKHAM: "Not everybody." **Jeff Chandler** is introduced to **Joan Crawford**'s deep-freeze, but he thaws her out. *Female on the Beach* (1955, Universal).

5890 "You don't like her. My mother doesn't like her. She's a dog. And I'm a fat, ugly man. Well, all I know is I had a good time last night. I'm going to have a good time tonight. If we have enough good times together, I'm going to get down on my knees and beg that girl to marry me. . . . You don't like it, that's too bad." Brooklyn butcher **Ernest Borgnine** sets his buddy Joe Mantell straight about how he stands with respect to Betsy Blair, a shy plain girl Borgnine met the night before. *Marty* (1955, United Artists).

5891 "He don't like nobody—not even himself." **Valerie French** refers to her old flame, cold-blooded Rod Steiger, so mean he makes Jud in *Oklahoma* look like a humanitarian. *Jubal* (1956, Columbia).

5892 "Well, you like me a lot better than I like you." Former bank robber turned marshal **Robert Taylor** wipes out the gang of his former partner Richard Widmark, saving the last shot for Widmark. *The Law and Jake Wade* (1958, MGM).

5893 "If I don't like her and you do, you marry her and take care of me!" Widower **Frank Sinatra** has a suggestion for his young son Eddie Hodges about the wealthy widow Sinatra's brother Edward G. Robinson has picked for him to marry. *A Hole in the Head* (1959, United Artists).

5894 "I'd like to be faceless and bodiless and be left alone." Part-time model and actress, part-time call girl **Jane Fonda** delivers her version of Greta Garbo's famous line. *Klute* (1971, Warner Bros.).

5895 MEADOWS: "I know it was an act for her, but I think she really liked me." BUDDUSKY: "She probably did, kid. They have feelings like everyone else." **Randy Quaid** and **Jack Nicholson** are speaking of prostitute Carol Kane with whom Quaid had his first sexual experience. Career sailors Nicholson and Otis Young have been assigned to take Quaid from their West Virginia base to a prison in Massachusetts where teenage Quaid will serve eight years for stealing forty dollars. Nicholson and Young try to make the trip as memorable for Quaid as possible. *The Last Detail* (1973, Columbia).

5896 "I don't like your kind of people. I don't like to see you come out to this clean country in—oily hair, and dressed up in those silk suits, and try to pass yourselves off as decent Americans. . . . I despise your masquerade—the dishonest way you pose yourself, and your fucking family." U.S. Senator **G.D. Spradlin** tells off Al Pacino. Pacino sets it up to appear that Spradlin has killed a prostitute and the politician is in the Family bag. *The Godfather, Part II* (1974, Paramount).

5897 MILES KENDIG: "Does he bite?" ISOBEL VON SCHMIDT: "Only people he doesn't like." MILES: "I only bite people I like." Leering **Walter Matthau** eyes **Glenda Jackson** and her Doberman. *Hopscotch* (1980, Avco Embassy).

5898 "Perhaps you'd like me to come in and wash your dick for you, you little shit." Looking up from his newspaper, **John Gielgud** mutters sarcastically when Dudley Moore yells from his bath. In some releases of the movie, neck and twit were substituted for dick and shit. *Arthur* (1981, Orion).

5899 MATTY WALKER: "You're not too smart. I like that in a man." NED RACINE: "What else do you like? Lazy. Ugly. Horny. I got them all." MATTY: "You don't look lazy." **Kathleen Turner** finds **William Hurt** to be just the man she's looking for to help murder her husband. *Body Heat* (1981, Warner Bros.).

5900 "I've always liked Jerry. To be honest, I've always liked him rather more than I've liked you." **Ben Kingsley** prefers his best friend Jeremy Irons even when he discovers that his wife Patricia Hodge and Irons have been lovers for years. *Betrayal* (1983, 20th Century-Fox).

5901 "Everybody liked me. I liked myself. Until he came. . . ." Elderly Antonio Salieri, portrayed by **F. Murray Abraham,** traces his discontent from the time of the arrival of Wolfgang Amadeus Mozart, played by Tom Hulce, at the Austrian Court. *Amadeus* (1984, Orion).

5902 "Why do I like you so much? You could be anybody." Jazz singer **Dee Dee Bridgewater** doesn't quite know what she sees in mute alien Joe Morton whom she has taken as a lover. *The Brother from Another Planet* (1984, Cinecom).

5903 "I like the way you look at the world. . . the way you make me smile." **Virginia Madsen** explains to Lenny Von Dohlen why she loves him. *Electric Dreams* (1984, MGM-United Artists).

5904 "These things are good: ice cream and cake, a ride on a Harley, seeing monkeys in the trees, the rain on my tongue and the sun shining on my face. These things are a drag: dust in my hair, holes in my shoes, no money in my pocket, and the sun shining on my face." Loose living biker and druggie, but fighter and survivor, **Cher** ticks off her favorite and not so favorite things. *Mask* (1985, Universal).

5905 "I like me, my wife likes me, my customers like me." Overbearing loutish salesman **John Candy** shames persnickety businessman Steve Martin who has bombarded Candy with complaints about his shortcomings. *Planes, Trains and Automobiles* (1987, Paramount).

5906 TESS MCGILL: "You know, maybe I just don't like you." JACK TRAINER: "Me?. . . Nah." **Melanie Griffith**'s reason why they shouldn't become romantically involved is rejected by **Harrison Ford** just as they are separated by a closing elevator door. *Working Girl* (1988, 20th Century-Fox).

5907 "Girls like guitar players. They like to see them wiggle around. You can't wiggle behind a piano." **Trey Wilson,** as record producer Sam Phillips, gives Dennis Quaid, as rocker Jerry Lee Lewis, an idea that will become his trademark. *Great Balls of Fire* (1989, Orion).

5908 "Leave me alone! I don't like fast women." Shortly after making his protest to Alison Doody, **Harrison Ford** falls into bed with her. *Indiana Jones and the Last Crusade* (1989, Paramount).

5909 "He likes his women bad—not cheap." **Ricki Lake** speaks in behalf of her brother Johnny Depp to a busty teen who's hot for him, offering him her all. *Cry-Baby* (1990, Universal).

5910 "You know something, Tracy, I kind of like that dame." **Charlie Korsmo,** as "Kid," tells title character Warren Beatty that he's growing accustomed to Glenne Headly as Tess Trueheart. *Dick Tracy* (1990, Touchstone-Buena Vista).

5911 "We don't have to like each other. We just have to be married." **Andie MacDowell** and Frenchman Gerard Depardieu marry to get her a special apartment and him a green card. She doesn't see any reason for them to have any feelings for each other. *Green Card* (1990, Australia-Fr., Touchstone/Buena Vista).

5912 "I like girls." **Elizabeth McGovern** reveals to Natasha Richardson that her crime, which got her condemned to whoredom in a totalitarian state, is that she is a "gender traitor." (She's a lesbian.) *The Handmaid's Tale* (1990, Cinecom).

5913 "You know what we're going to do here. First, we're going to need a few more people helping us out. I'll tell you why. We're going to be spending an obscene amount of money in here... so we're going to need a lot more help sucking up to us, because that's what we really like." **Richard Gere** expects more fawning from Larry Miller, the manager of a Rodeo Drive boutique, where he has taken Julia Roberts to buy her an expensive wardrobe. *Pretty Woman* (1990, Touchstone/Buena Vista).

5914 JEDIDIAH WARD: "She used to like ice cream." ESTELLE WARD: "She used to like you." **Gene Hackman,** a lawyer champion of the little guy, and his wife **Joanna Merlin** are talking about their daughter Mary Elizabeth Mastrantonio, a member of a firm that defends large corporations against class action suits brought by lawyers like Hackman. *Class Action* (1991, 20th Century-Fox).

Limits and Limitations

see also ENDS AND ENDINGS, FAULTS, MATHEMATICS, MATURITY AND IMMATURITY

5915 CARMEN: "You're a mess, aren't you?" MARLOWE: "I'm not very tall either. Next time I'll come on stilts." Blackmailed **Martha Vickers** is not much impressed with private eye **Humphrey Bogart.** He has been hired by her dying father Charles Waldron to look after her. *The Big Sleep* (1946, Warner Bros.).

5916 "To God, there is no zero!" Perhaps not, but **Grant Williams** is shrinking asymptotically toward the limit. *The Incredible Shrinking Man* (1957, Universal-International).

5917 "There is an endless supply of white men, but there has always been a limited number of human beings." **Chief Dan George,** as Old Lodge Skins, gently speaks to his adopted grandson, white man Dustin Hoffman. George says more than he realizes, referring to the struggles of his people, the Cheyenne, with the white man. *Little Big Man* (1970, National General).

5918 "A man's got to know his limitations." San Francisco police detective **Clint Eastwood** rids the city of a gang of young cops who acted as a right wing death squad. Working under the direction of Police Lieutenant Hal Holbrook, they assassinated people they considered scum and garbage. *Magnum Force* (1973, Warner Bros.).

Lips and Lipstick *see* FACES, MOUTHS

Listening and Listeners

see also CONVERSATIONS, TALKS AND TALKING

5919 "I never found out much listening to myself." It's **Robert Mitchum**'s way of telling mobster Kirk Douglas to get to the point at their first meeting. *Out of the Past* (1947, RKO).

5920 "Now, shut up! Shut up, all of you. Now, listen to me, you hicks.... Yeah, you're hicks too, and they fooled you a thousand times, just like they fooled me. But this time, I'm going to fool somebody. I'm going to stay in this race. I'm on my own and I'm out for blood. Listen to me, you hicks...." **Broderick Crawford** discovers his constituency as he addresses a crowd of country folks during his campaign for election. *All the King's Men* (1949, Columbia).

5921 "Avidly, avidly." Broadway flake **Tony Curtis** replies absent-mindedly when bedazzled cigarette girl Barbara Nichols asks if he's listening to her tale of woe. *Sweet Smell of Success* (1957, United Artists).

5922 "I'm sitting here listening to some cracker asshole who lives in a trailer court compare his life to mine." **Jack Nicholson** may share many things with co-worker Billy Green Bush, but his ego won't allow him to accept them as equals. *Five Easy Pieces* (1970, Columbia).

5923 "Would you listen to me?" At the end of the movie, **Alan Alda** still can't get his wife Carol Burnett to pay attention to what he has to say. *The Four Seasons* (1981, Universal).

5924 "Just listening is an obsessively intimate act." **Jacqueline Bisset** makes the observation to Rolling Stone reporter Hart Bochner, who claims he's just listening to her when he's supposed to be interviewing her. *Rich and Famous* (1981, MGM-United Artists).

5925 "Join the sideshow. You're a talking head. Who'll listen to you?" Mad young scientist **Jeffrey Combs** works on a serum that can revive the dead. He snaps to mad old scientist David Gale, who loses his composure and his head—literally. *Re-Animator* (1985, Vestron).

5926 "You will listen! You will stay here and listen to these accusations.... The past several months you've been flapping your mouth and you haven't heard a thing. You haven't even seen what's painfully obvious.... No, I'm talking, now let me finish!... Everybody here may not like you as a person, but we all applaud your efforts.... But what you don't understand is that the same people who are supporting you are the ones you're beating up. . . . No thank you for a job well done, nothing, you just step on their necks, constantly abuse them." Vice Principal **Beverly Todd** tells off controversial high school Principal Morgan Freeman, who treats students, teachers and parents all the same—badly. *Lean on Me* (1989, Warner Bros.).

5927 "If you listened to me, I wouldn't have to repeat myself like a fucking radio." Strident **Rosie Perez** intimidates meek Spike Lee, the father of her son. *Do the Right Thing* (1989, Universal).

5928 "My nephew is a nice boy, but he talks when he should be listening." **Al Pacino** is talking about Andy Garcia to family lawyer George Hamilton. Pacino sounds like his father Marlon Brando, who made a similar remark about Brando's other son James Caan. *The Godfather, Part III* (1991, Paramount).

Literature *see* BOOKS, POETRY AND POETS, WRITING AND WRITERS

Littleness *see* SIZES

Lives and Living

see also ABORTIONS, ACCIDENTS, AGE AND AGING, ALIENS, BABIES, BACHELORS, BADNESS, BAPTISM, BIRTHS AND BIRTHDAYS, BLOOD, BODIES, BOYS, BROTHERS, BUMS, CHILDREN AND CHILDHOOD, DAUGHTERS, DEATH AND DYING, DISEASES, FAMILIES, FATHERS, GENTLEMEN, GIRLS, GOODNESS, HEARTS AND HEARTACHE, HUMAN NATURE, HUMANITY, HUSBANDS, HUSBANDS AND WIVES, LADIES, LADIES AND GENTLEMEN, LIFE AND DEATH, LOVE AND HATE, LOVE AND LOVERS, MARRIAGES, MEN, MEN AND WOMEN, MIDGETS, MODELS, MONSTERS, MOTHERS, PARENTS, PEOPLE, PERSONS AND PERSONALITIES, RELATIONSHIPS, RELATIVES, SICKNESS, SKIN, SONS AND SONS-IN-LAW, SPIRIT AND SPIRITS, UNIQUENESS, VAMPIRES, VEGETABLES AND VEGETARIANS, WIDOWS, WITCHCRAFT AND WITCHES, YOUTH

5929 "This is not a play. This is life!" **Herbert Marshall** is a member of a jury that convicts actress Norah Baring of murder. Now he's trying to prove her innocence. *Murder* (1930, GB, British International).

5930 "It's alive! It's alive! (In the name of God, now I know what it feels to be God!)" The parenthetical part of **Colin Clive**'s excited exclamation, when his monster comes to life, was censored from his speech, leaving a noticeable jump cut in the film. *Frankenstein* (1931, Universal).

5931 "Of course, it had to be. I felt it. A presence. Oh, life can be so gloriously improbable." **John Gilbert** remarks excitedly when Greta Garbo reveals to him that the young lad he is sharing a room with is a woman. *Queen Christina* (1933, MGM).

5932 "I've seen a luau, and heard you sing. I guess life has practically nothing more to offer me." **Ruby Keeler**'s confession to Dick Powell shows that her character has very modest life expectations. *Flirtation Walk* (1934, Warner Bros.).

5933 "All I ask is to live with your forgiveness and your help and your love." **Fredric March** chooses to join Anna Sten who has been sentenced to exile in Siberia. *We Live Again* (1934, Goldwyn-United Artists).

5934 "Do I want to live this foolish life if I can't have you?" Colonial **Nelson Eddy** doesn't believe he wants to live if he can't have Princess Jeanette MacDonald. *Naughty Marietta* (1935, MGM).

5935 "People who live to themselves are generally left to themselves." **Alma Kruger**'s Words of wisdom make little impression on her niece-in-law Rosalind Russell. The latter makes it very clear that she wishes to keep to herself and finds having people close to her stifling. *Craig's Wife* (1936, Columbia).

5936 "I was fighting for life—you can't drag me back!" **Ruth Chatterton** pleads with her husband Walter Huston to release her from their uneventful marriage. *Dodsworth* (1936, Goldwyn-United Artists).

5937 "The Parkes were never educated to face life. We've been puppets for ten generations." Butler **William Powell** isn't really an ex-tramp. He's a Harvard graduate from a wealthy family. He tells friend Alan Mowbray that he withdrew from society after an abortive romance. *My Man Godfrey* (1936, Universal).

5938 "I say this to the modern young girl—to be free, express yourself. Take your life in your own hands and mold it." In 1936, **Irene Dunne**'s advice seemed radical to many in the audience, but they knew she just needed a good man to straighten her out. *Theodora Goes Wild* (1936, Columbia).

5939 "I try to make his life smooth and pleasant. The opposite of all that back there—worry and action and achievement. I want to be the refuge from that, to laugh or just be quiet with him." **Myrna Loy** is certain she knows her role as a perfect wife in her marriage to businessman Clark Gable. *Wife vs. Secretary* (1936, MGM).

5940 "Until you have lived at the Hotel Louis, you ain't!" **Luis Alberni** is the proud proprietor of the very posh Hotel Louis. *Easy Living* (1937, Paramount).

5941 "You're still alive!" It dawns on British diplomat **Ronald Colman** that High Lama Sam Jaffe is the same priest who founded Shangri-La more than 200 years earlier. *Lost Horizon* (1937, Columbia).

5942 "It's kind of startling to be brought to life twice, and each time in Warsaw." Warsaw, Vermont native **Carole Lombard** has mixed feelings when she learns that befuddled doctor Charles Winninger has mixed up her X-rays and she's not dying as he originally thought. *Nothing Sacred* (1937, Selznick-United Artists).

5943 WALLY COOK: "You've lived here all your life." HAZEL FLAGG: "Twice as long." In response to reporter **Fredric March**'s question, **Carole Lombard** answers that living in Warsaw, Vermont is not her idea of living. *Nothing Sacred* (1937, Selznick-United Artists).

5944 "Life has only one great moment left for me—when they make Shirley Temple president of a bank." **Joan Blondell** kids about the nine-year-old wunderkind. *Stand-In* (1937, United Artists).

5945 "I'm dead until you come down. Is he alive? Like a clock ticking. . . still alive. . . still alive. . . still alive." **Myrna Loy** is a nervous wreck each time her lover test pilot Clark Gable takes to the sky. *Test Pilot* (1938, MGM).

5946 "You never had an idea in your life. You've done nothing all your life except give parties, each one sillier than the rest." **Claude Gillingwater** accuses his granddaughter Madeleine Carroll of living an empty, useless life. *Cafe Society* (1939, Paramount).

5947 "My life is over. Nothing will ever happen to me anymore." **Vivien Leigh** isn't mourning the death of her unloved husband Rand Brooks, but she doesn't see much future for a young widow. *Gone with the Wind* (1939, Selznick-MGM).

5948 "I killed you! Haunt me then! Haunt your murderer! I cannot live without my life! I cannot live without my soul!" **Laurence Olivier,** as Heathcliff, won't suffer a long separation from his dead beloved Merle Oberon as Cathy. *Wuthering Heights* (1939, Goldwyn-United Artists).

5949 "If unbelievers seek to desecrate the tomb of Ananka, you will use nine [tanna] leaves each night to give life and movement to Kharis. Thus, you will enable him to bring vengeance on the heads of those who try to enter." Dying High Priest **Eduardo Ciannelli** passes on instructions to George Zucco on what to do if anything happens to the inviolate temple of Ananka. *The Mummy's Hand* (1940, Universal).

5950 LINA MCLAIDLAW: "You wouldn't actually want to live on your wife's allowance, would you?" JOHNNIE AYSGARTH: "Of course not, darling." Protected spinster **Joan Fontaine** can't imagine that charming rogue **Cary Grant** would marry her for her money—why not? *Suspicion* (1941, RKO).

5951 "Perhaps the best way to tell you the story of my life is to tell you about the women in my life." **Don Ameche** prepares to confess all his sins to devil Laird Cregar. *Heaven Can Wait* (1943, 20th Century-Fox).

5952 "We're alive, Ann, alive. Oh, there is so much to do, we know that now. There is so much to live for. Ann, Ann, we're alive." Despondent **Paul Henreid** and Eleanor Parker decide to commit suicide and turn on the gas. They come to and board the ship of the dead. Unlike others aboard, they are "betweeners," not yet dead. Their experience aboard ship changes them and they are given a chance to try life again. *Between Two Worlds* (1944, Warner Bros.).

5953 "Now that I've met you I feel I've lived a full life. I think I'll go home and kill myself." **Joan Davis** is a trifle sarcastic with Eddie Cantor in this story of vaudeville people. *Show Business* (1944, RKO).

5954 "When a man says he has exhausted life, you may be sure life has exhausted him." Manipulative and hedonistic **George Sanders** lays a good line on his impressionable and evil 19th century London aristocratic protégé Hurd Hatfield. *The Picture of Dorian Gray* (1945, MGM).

5955 "Strange, isn't it? Each man's life touches so many other lives—and when he isn't around he leaves an awful hole, doesn't he?. . . You see, George, you really had a wonderful life. Don't you see what a mistake it would be to throw it away?" Wise apprentice angel Clarence Peabody, beautifully portrayed by **Henry Travers,** has shown James Stewart how much his life mattered. *It's a Wonderful Life* (1946, RKO).

5956 VIRGINIA MOORE: "[You're] sadistic and egotistical." NEALE GORDON: "Maybe, but I'm still alive." **Gail Russell** snaps at **Alan Ladd** who shrugs and gives her a thin smile. *Calcutta* (1947, Paramount).

5957 "You look as if you've lived." Plastic surgeon **Houseley Stevenson** guesses correctly about escaped convict Humphrey Bogart. *Dark Passage* (1947, Warner Bros.).

5958 "You wouldn't like being on the inside of my life. . . there's nothing there but a few mathematical equations and a lot of question marks." Engineer **Van Heflin** tries to turn off Joan Crawford who is obsessed with being an important variable in his life. *Possessed* (1947, Warner Bros.).

5959 "Ah, you young people, making the most out of life. . . while it lasts." **Bela Lugosi** as Dracula licks his chops as he stares at corpulent Lou Costello. *Abbott and Costello Meet Frankenstein* (1948, Universal).

5960 "I want you to see how it is to live like a big tough gunnie." Rather than opt for quick punishment for fatally shooting him in the back, dying gunfighter **Gregory Peck** claims Skip Homeier beat him in a fair fight. Peck wants Homeier to live with the reputation of being the fastest gun—a title every young punk good with a gun will want to challenge, no matter where he goes. *The Gunfighter* (1950, 20th Century-Fox).

5961 "I lived a few weeks while you loved me. Goodbye, Dix." **Gloria Grahame** quotes one of writer Humphrey Bogart's lines as she leaves him at the end of the film. *In a Lonely Place* (1950, Columbia).

5962 "I used to live in a sewer. Now I live in a swamp. I've come up in the world." Poor white trash **Linda Darnell** is bitter. *No Way Out* (1950, 20th Century-Fox).

5963 "Don't cry, white boy. You're gonna live." True to his Hippocratic oath, black physician **Sidney Poitier** tends to racist Richard Widmark, who has been badly injured in a riot he engineered. *No Way Out* (1950, 20th Century-Fox).

5964 "What is there to fight for? Everything! Life itself! Isn't that enough? To have lived, suffered, enjoyed. What is there to fight for? Life is a beautiful, magnificent thing—even to a jellyfish. . . . The trouble is you won't fight. You've given up. But there's something just as inevitable as death. And that's life. Think of the power of the universe—turning the earth, growing the trees. That's the same power within you—if you'll only have the courage and the will to use it." One-time British music hall great **Charles Chaplin** takes in depressed young dancer Claire Bloom, who speaks of the futility of living and the meaningless of her life, after her attempted suicide. *Limelight* (1952, Chaplin-United Artists).

5965 "Life, every now and then, behaves as though it had seen too many bad movies, when everything fits too well—the beginning, the middle, the end—from fade-in to fade-out. In a nutshell, the plot is that life louses up the script." Has-been movie director **Humphrey Bogart** may be correct, but this film about the life of glamorous barefoot dancer Ava Gardner who becomes a Hollywood star is not a bad movie. *The Barefoot Contessa* (1954, United Artists).

5966 "Our duty to life is to live it to the utmost. We've been given a brain and we have to use it." Air Marshal **Michael Redgrave**'s final remarks are an assertion of the appropriateness of his ignoring a dream of an air disaster. *The Night My Number Came Up* (1954, GB, Ealing).

5967 "If you want to give me a present, give me a good life. That's something I can value." Stern, Bible-reading **Raymond Massey** refuses the gift of money that his troubled and troublesome son James Dean has earned. *East of Eden* (1955, Warner Bros.).

5968 "Not everyone wears their lives on their faces." **Angie Dickinson,** as prostitute "Lucky Legs," doesn't tell everyone her woes. *China Gate* (1957, 20th Century-Fox).

5969 "Life's never quite interesting enough, somehow. You people who come to the movies know that." **Shirley Booth** addresses the movie audiences directly. *The Matchmaker* (1958, Paramount).

5970 "Live, live, live. Life is a banquet and most poor suckers are starving to death." **Rosalind Russell** shouts her optimistic philosophy in 1958. **Lucille Ball** echoes the sentiments in 1974. *Auntie Mame* (1958, Warner Bros.); *Mame* (1974, Warner Bros.).

5971 "I did just what she told me. I lived! I've got to find out what to do now." Once shy and retiring Rosalind Russell's secretary **Peggy Cass** is now pregnant. *Auntie Mame* (1958, Warner Bros.).

5972 "I'm not living with you. We occupy the same cage, that's all." **Elizabeth Taylor** disagrees with her husband Paul Newman, who always is negative with her and is a major disappointment in bed—mainly because he won't get in it with her. *Cat on a Hot Tin Roof* (1958, MGM).

5973 "Maggie the Cat is alive." **Elizabeth Taylor** screams at her husband Paul Newman, who wants nothing to do with her, dead or alive. *Cat on a Hot Tin Roof* (1958, MGM).

5974 "A life that is planned is a closed life. . . It can be endured, perhaps. It cannot be lived." **Robert Donat** makes his last screen appearance as a wise old Chinese mandarin. He advises ill educated, but most sincere missionary Ingrid Bergman and her lover, Chinese army officer Curt Jurgens. *The Inn of the Sixth Happiness* (1958, GB, 20th Century-Fox).

5975 "Well, life is very long and full of salesmanship, Miss Clara. You might buy something yet." **Paul Newman** allows as how spinsterish Joanne Woodward may yet find herself talked out of her chosen lifestyle. *The Long Hot Summer* (1958, 20th Century-Fox).

5976 "Life is like a battle. Someone has to get a bloody nose." **Anna Lee** holds a bleak view of life. *The Crimson Kimono* (1959, Columbia).

5977 BRAD ALLEN: "She's always listening in to brighten up a drab, empty life." JAN MORROW: "If I could get a call through once in awhile, my life wouldn't be so drab." **Rock Hudson** speaks unkindly of **Doris Day** who shares a phone party line with him. He's on the phone to one of his many girl friends with whom he ties up the line. *Pillow Talk* (1959, Universal-International).

5978 "I always thought I could give them life like a present, all wrapped in white with every promise of happiness. . . . All I can promise them is life itself." **Dorothy McGuire** learns a lesson about raising children that all parents should mind. *The Dark at the Top of the Stairs* (1960, Warner Bros.).

5979 "Life is a beastly mess." It's the view of third-rate vaudevillian **Laurence Olivier**. *The Entertainer* (1960, GB, British-Lion).

5980 "Is there nothing more in life than what my mom and dad got—a telly and a packet of fags?" British working-class stiff **Albert Finney** wonders if there's more to life for him than what his parents settled for. *Saturday Night and Sunday Morning* (1960, GB, Continental Distributing).

5981 "I feel like I'll never be smart and I'll never get the things I want in life." Twenty-year-old virgin **Lelia Goldoni** believes life is passing her by. *Shadows* (1960, McEndree-Cassel).

5982 "It's your life. Ruin it in your own way." **Dora Bryan** isn't a perfect mother, so she doesn't try too hard to guide her daughter Rita Tushingham on the proper path. *A Taste of Honey* (1961, GB, British Lion).

5983 "[Women] sense my power and they seek the life essence. I do not avoid women. . . but I, I do deny them my essence." Off his rocker, **Sterling Hayden** tells Peter Sellers he doesn't give women everything. *Dr. Strangelove* (1964, GB, Columbia).

5984 "You good people can't even exist without your prejudices, and the worst thing is, you can't even recognize what you are. . . I wonder if it's true that life is really as stupid and meaningless as it seems to be on this ship." Ship's doctor **Oskar Werner** is outraged with anti-Semitic seating charts and cold stabs at vanity. *Ship of Fools* (1965, Columbia).

5985 "Life is all memory." So says **Elizabeth Taylor,** the richest woman in the world. *Boom!* (1968, Universal).

5986 NANCY BARKER: "Did you ever kill anybody? I mean, you were in the army. You were in Vietnam, weren't you?" JACK RYAN: "Yeah, for awhile." NANCY: "Well, did you kill anybody?" JACK: "I suppose so." NANCY: "Was it fun?" JACK: "I never hung around long enough to find out. Listen, I wasn't trying to win any goddamn war, you understand. I just wanted to stay alive." Sexy psychopath **Leigh Taylor-Young** has a morbid interest in **Ryan O'Neal**'s war-time experiences. *The Big Bounce* (1969, Warner Bros.).

5987 "The two basic items necessary to sustain life are sunshine and coconut milk. That's a known fact. In Florida, your only problem is, diet-wise, you gotta lift your arm to wipe warm milk off your chin—tough? And chicks! Statistically, Miami has more rich chicks than any resort in the U.S.A. You can't scratch yourself without you brush against a bare belly button." Crippled New York street hustler **Dustin Hoffman** convinces stud wannabe Jon Voight that the only place for the two of them to live is in Miami, Florida. *Midnight Cowboy* (1969, United Artists).

5988 "An enemy had saved my life by shooting my best friend." **Dustin Hoffman,** as ancient Jack Crabb, recalls when an American soldier shot a member of Hoffman's Cheyenne family who was attacking Dustin because he didn't recognize him. *Little Big Man* (1970, Cinema Center).

5989 "A lot of people enjoy being dead. But they are not dead really. They're just backing away from life. They're players—but they sit on the bench. The game goes on without them. At any moment they can join in. Reach out! Take a chance! Get hurt maybe. But play as well as you can. Go team, go! Give me an 'L.' Give me an 'I.' Give me a 'V.' Give me an 'E.' LIVE!! Otherwise, you'll have nothing to talk about in the locker room." Elderly **Ruth Gordon** uses a sports analogy to encourage young Bud

Cort to participate in life. *Harold and Maude* (1971, Paramount).

5990 "Life is made up of small comings and goings, and for everything that we take with us there is something that we leave behind." Narrator and director **Robert Mulligan,** as the older Hermie, is profound. *Summer of '42* (1971, Warner Bros.).

5991 "He's saying life is bullshit, and it is, so what are you screaming about?" **William Holden** defends his friend, network news anchorman Peter Finch, who uses an obscenity on the air. *Network* (1976, United Artists).

5992 "That's essentially how I feel about life. Full of loneliness and misery and suffering and unhappiness, and it's all over much too quickly." Having just told a story about two little old ladies who complain about how bad the food is at the Catskills resorts and how small the portions are, **Woody Allen** expresses a healthy appreciation for life and its shortcomings. *Annie Hall* (1977, United Artists).

5993 "Leave your troubles outside. Life is disappointing? In here, life is beautiful." During the period just before the Nazis come to power, demonic-looking Master of Ceremonies **Joel Grey** addresses the audience of the film as the audience of the decadent Kit Kat Club in depression-plagued Berlin. *Cabaret* (1977, Allied Artists).

5994 "These women here, they live life like it's a can of Coke and they're afraid to drink it too fast or it'll be all gone. Life isn't a can of Coke." Hairdresser **Craig Russell** complains about his customers. *Outrageous!* (1977, Canada, Cinema 5).

5995 "I don't have a lifestyle. I have a life." Restless New Yorker **Jane Fonda** corrects her laid-back California ex-husband Alan Alda. *California Suite* (1978, Columbia).

5996 "I am old. And I know one thing: Life is very long." It's the impression of cynical New Orleans brothel keeper **Frances Faye**. *Pretty Baby* (1978, Paramount).

5997 "It's not the men in my life, but the life in my men that counts." Amazingly, at 86, **Mae West** is still in there pitching. *Sextette* (1978, Crown International).

5998 "Life is like a railway station. The train of life brings us in, the train of death will carry us away." Poetess **Stevie Smith**, portrayed by **Glenda Jackson**, views life and death as a coming and going, both of which she fears. *Stevie* (1978, GB, First Artists).

5999 TANYA: "Your whole life has been disrupted—discombobulated—and it's a new life right now." ERICA: "I mean, you can't live my life for me, can you?" TANYA: "No, no, I certainly can't live your life for you. It's your life." Therapist **Penelope Russianoff** pushes recently divorced **Jill Clayburgh** to find her new life. *An Unmarried Woman* (1978, 20th Century-Fox).

6000 "To be on the wire is life. . . the rest is waiting." **Roy Scheider** tells his Angel of Death Jessica Lange that he doesn't wish to change his excessive lifestyle. *All That Jazz* (1979, Columbia-20th Century-Fox).

6001 "I'm sorry that I'm late, but I was trying to make a living, O.K.?" **Dustin Hoffman** bitterly defends himself when his wife Meryl Streep tells him that she's leaving him and their son, in part because he's always too busy to have any time for them. *Kramer vs. Kramer* (1979, Columbia).

6002 "It's life, Captain, but not life as we know it." **Leonard Nimoy**, as Dr. Spock, speaks to William Shatner as Capt. Kirk about the mysterious alien force with which they must contend. *Star Trek: The Motion Picture* (1979, Paramount).

6003 "Life doesn't have truths." Physical anthropology doctoral candidate **Blair Brown** believes that psychophysiologist William Hurt will sell his soul for truth. *Altered States* (1980, Warner Bros.).

6004 "Life as I know it is over!" Monogamous-minded 20-year-old **Mary Beth Hurt** confronts her philandering parents Shirley MacLaine and Anthony Hopkins. *A Change of Seasons* (1980, 20th Century-Fox).

6005 LYDIA: "I have no desire to live anymore." MICHEL: "That is the oldest way of living." **Romy Schneider** grieves for her daughter killed in an automobile accident that left her husband in a semi-catatonic state. **Yves Montand**'s beloved wife committed suicide while in the last stages of cancer. *Clair de Femme* (1980, Fr., Atlantic).

6006 "Poor fool, he's dead and he never really found out the meaning of life." After Woody Allen's imagined "death," nurse **Alice Spivak**, chomping on an apple, sadly comments on his failure. *Stardust Memories* (1980, United Artists).

6007 "We will never surrender. We win or we die. We will have the next generation to fight, and after that the next, the next. As for me, I will live longer than my hangman." **Anthony Quinn**, as the famed Arab hero Omar Mukhtar who led the fight in Libya against Mussolini's fascists during World War II, defiantly goes to his execution. *Lion of the Desert* (1981, Libya-GB, United Film Distribution).

6008 "There must be more to life than meets the eye or else I weep." It's **Woody Allen**'s thoughtful observation to his wife Mary Steenburgen. *A Midsummer Night's Sex Comedy* (1982, Warner Bros.-Orion).

6009 "I don't know how you can live with that. . . man." **Geraldine Fitzgerald** questions her daughter Candy Azzara about Rodney Dangerfield who has problems with booze, broads, drugs and gambling. *Easy Money* (1983, Orion).

6010 "The truth is he was alive when I buried him." **John Getz** informs his lover Frances McDormand that her husband Dan Hedaya was a hard man to kill, so Getz buried him while he was still fighting to stay alive. *Blood Simple* (1983, River Road/Circle).

6011 "All life is madness. . . the defeated, the demented, and the damned are the real people of the world, and I'm proud to be in their company." Aging Beat poet **Ben Gazzara** examines life. *Tales of Ordinary Madness* (1983, Italy, Miracle).

6012 "I just have to see that he gets this—floral delivery is my life." Police detective **Eddie Murphy** uses one of his several impersonations to get his foot in the door and past a receptionist who is there to bar all unwanted entries. *Beverly Hills Cop* (1984, Paramount).

6013 "Life is a fairy tale. . . so we dream on—a lost sister, saintly mother, a heroic father." In the final scene, **Rob Lowe**, in voice-over, sums up as the dead return, wearing dreamy white, dancing and cavorting around the grounds of the title hotel. *The Hotel New Hampshire* (1984, Orion).

6014 "Life is a series of divorces, suicides, promises broken, children abandoned." Philandering **John Cassevetes** might have added that life is a series of minor triumphs and major disasters. *Love Streams* (1984, Cannon).

6015 "I mate for life—one day at a time." African hunter **Robert Redford** hates confinements and commitments, especially marriage, even with Meryl Streep. *Out of Africa* (1985, Universal).

6016 "I'm the kind of guy that likes to live on the edge." **John Cusack** makes a more hopeful than accurate self-appraisal. *The Sure Thing* (1985, Embassy).

6017 "Life goes by so fast that if you don't stop and look around, you might miss it." It's high school truant **Matthew Broderick**'s version of "stop and smell the roses." *Ferris Bueller's Day Off* (1986, Paramount).

6018 "I'm watching these people on the screen and I started getting hooked on the film, you know, and I started to feel, how could you even think of killing yourself? I mean. . . look at all the people up there on the screen. They're real funny, and, what if the worst is true? What if there is no God, and you only go around once, and that's it? Well, don't you want to be part of the experience?" While watching a Marx Brothers film, hypochondriac **Woody Allen**, who fears he may have a fatal disease, talks himself out of his suicidal funk. *Hannah and Her Sisters* (1986, Orion).

6019 "Why should my life be turned upside down just because I happened to look out the window?" Married **Isabelle Huppert** pouts to lover Steve Guttenberg when he calls the police to report an attempted murder that she witnessed from his bedroom window. *The Bedroom Window* (1987, De Laurentiis).

6020 "How poor a part I played in your life. What were you like then?" **Donal McCann** laments the emptiness of his marriage to Anjelica Huston who still grieves for a 17-year-old boy of years gone by, of whom she says, "I think he died for me." *The Dead* (1987, Vestron).

6021 "My thoughts drift back to erect-nipple wet dreams, about Mary Jane Rottencrotch, and the great homecoming fuck fantasy. I'm so happy that I am alive, in one piece, and short. I am in a world of shit. But I'm alive and I'm not afraid." Narrator Marine **Matthew Modine** closes the Vietnam War film, as he and other grunts march past exploding flares and burning buildings to the theme from the Mickey Mouse television show. *Full Metal Jacket* (1987, Warner Bros.).

6022 "You can lead your life any way you want, but stay the hell out of mine." Wealthy **Nicholas Pryor** banishes his drug-addicted son Robert Downey, Jr. from his home. *Less Than Zero* (1987, 20th Century-Fox).

6023 "Seize the day! Gather ye rosebuds while ye may. . . . Why do the writers use these lines?. . . Because we are food for worms, lads. . . . Everyone in this room is one day going to stop breathing, turn cold and die. . . Look at them. . . invincible, just like you feel. . . the world is their oyster. They believe they are destined for great things, just like many of you. Their eyes are full of hope, just like you. . . . Did they wait until it was too late to make their lives even one iota of what they were capable? For you see, gentlemen, these boys are now fertilizing daffodils. . . if you listen real close, you can hear them whisper their legacy to you. . . . Seize the days, boys. Make your life extraordinary.'" **Robin Williams** teaches an important lesson as his prep school literature class looks in the display case containing photographs of boys who attended the school decades and decades earlier. *Dead Poets Society* (1989, Touchstone/Buena Vista).

6024 "You two have something in common. You both knew me when I was alive." **Anjelica Huston**'s survival of the Nazi death camps complicates things for her husband Ron Silver and his new wife Margaret Sophie Stein. *Enemies, a Love Story* (1989, 20th Century-Fox).

6025 "When you realize you want to spend the rest of your life with somebody, you want the rest of your life to start as soon as possible." **Billy Crystal** finally realizes that Meg Ryan is the one for him. *When Harry Met Sally. . .* (1989, Columbia).

6026 Roy Dillon: "I guess I owe you my life." Lily Dillon: "You always did." **John Cusack** grudgingly thanks his mother **Anjelica Huston** who saves his life by getting him to a hospital in time when he was internally bleeding to death. *The Grifters* (1990, Miramax).

6027 "I don't intend to spend the rest of my life raising children in the suburbs. You can say it was good enough for Mother, but it's not good enough for me." **Kyra Sedgwick** defiantly tells her WASPish father Paul Newman that she plans to leave her upper-middle-class Kansas City life for New York City, where she will try to become an actress. *Mr. & Mrs. Bridge* (1990, Miramax).

6028 "Do you know what it's like for me every morning to wake up and look to see if you're still alive?" Nurse-companion **Julia Roberts** is in love with her wealthy patient Campbell Scott, who is suffering from leukemia. *Dying Young* (1991, 20th Century-Fox).

6029 "Life's a bitch, now so am I." Mousy, lonely secretary **Michelle Pfeiffer** transforms herself into powerful, nasty Catwoman. *Batman Returns* (1992, Warner Bros.).

6030 "That's life, my friends. It's give and take and mix it up, and that's what I'm good at." Title character **Jack Nicholson** announces proudly. *Hoffa* (1992, 20th Century-Fox).

Loans *see* Debts

Loathing *see* Hate and Hatred, Likes and Dislikes

Locations

see also Losses and Losing, Searches and Searching, Space

6031 Miss Novak: "Mr. Kralik, it's true we're in the same room, but we're not on the same planet." Mr. Kralik: "Why, Miss Novak. . . you certainly know how to put a man in his planet." Neither **Margaret Sullavan** nor **James Stewart** knows the other is his or her secret pen-pal with whom they are falling in love. *The Shop Around the Corner* (1939, MGM).

6032 "To the highest peak of the highest mountain of the world, where earth meets the sky; and there is the temple of the gods; and in the great wall of the temple is the Goddess of Light; and in the head of the Goddess is the All-Seeing Eye." Djinni **Rex Ingram** tells Sabu where he must fly to if he wishes to discover the whereabouts of his friend John Justin. *The Thief of Bagdad* (1940, GB, London Films).

6033 "You will find the dinghy by the jetty." Stiff-backed shrew **Beatrice Lillie** delivers what has been acclaimed as the perfect Lillie line. *On Approval* (1943, GB, GFD).

6034 "This is a Halloween tale of Brooklyn, where anything can happen, and it usually does. . . ." A narrator begins the black comedy. *Arsenic and Old Lace* (1944, Warner Bros.).

6035 "No bar, no pinball machine. Just pool. This here is Ames, son." **Michael Constantine** condescendingly answers when Paul Newman asks about a bar in Ames, the most prestigious pool hall in America. *The Hustler* (1961, 20th Century-Fox).

6036 "The Caribbean! That's in the Great Lakes, isn't it?" **Jill St. John**, reportedly with an IQ of 162, is reduced to another of her dumb-redhead roles. *Who's Been Sleeping in My Bed?* (1963, Paramount).

6037 "Don't worry, Mother Parker. When this is all over, Bonnie and I will settle down not three miles from you." **Warren Beatty** reassures Faye Dunaway's mother **Mabel Cavitt** at a family picnic. The old lady knows better, telling him: "Try to live three miles from me and you'll be dead, Clyde Barrow." *Bonnie and Clyde* (1967, Warner Bros.).

6038 "Well, he'll be working on it, wherever he is." **Terry-Thomas** knows the world hasn't heard the last of maniacal surgeon Dr. Anton Phibes, played by ham **Vincent Price**. *The Abominable Dr. Phibes* (1971, GB, AIP).

6039 NANCY: "Have you ever been to Denmark?" FIELDING: "Yes, I've been to the Vatican." NANCY: "But the Vatican is in Rome." FIELDING: "They were doing so well that they opened a branch in Denmark." **Louise Lasser** is put through the paces by Woody Allen. *Bananas* (1971, United Artists).

6040 "Where am I? I never know where the fuck I am." Rock singer **Bette Midler** hasn't a clue where she is as her private plane heads for her next concert date. *The Rose* (1979, 20th Century-Fox).

6041 "I don't know what you're looking for, but it's a little to the right." Blind **Richard Pryor** hopefully makes a suggestion to luscious murderer Joan Severance as she checks his pockets for a valuable gold coin. *See No Evil, Hear No Evil* (1989, Tri-Star).

6042 "You know how you said you wanted to have sex with me in some weird place? How about Detroit?" Lonely divorced New York lawyer **Goldie Hawn** hopefully phones her boy friend from the Motor City. *Bird on a Wire* (1990, Universal).

6043 "You can always tell where you are by the way the road looks." **River Phoenix** is in the middle of nowhere when he delivers the film's opening line. *My Own Private Idaho* (1991, First Line).

6044 "We're not in the middle of nowhere, but we can see it from here." As she speaks on the phone to Arkansas cop Harvey Keitel, **Susan Sarandon** answers his query as to where she is. *Thelma and Louise* (1991, MGM).

Locks

see also DOORS, SAFETY, PRISONS AND PRISONERS

6045 "Why bother? If I wanted to come in, no lock could keep me out." Vivien Leigh locks the door to her bedroom. Her husband **Clark Gable** breaks it down. *Gone with the Wind* (1939, Selznick-MGM).

6046 "There'll be no locks between us, Mary Kate—except those in your own mercenary little heart." **John Wayne** shouts to his new bride Maureen O'Hara after breaking down the door of their bedroom which she locked to keep him out. She's ashamed of him because he wouldn't fight her brother Victor McLaglen to get her dowry. *The Quiet Man* (1952, Republic).

6047 "Maggie, we're through with lies and liars in this house. Lock the door." At the end of the film, **Paul Newman** reconciles with his wife Elizabeth Taylor and deigns to go to bed with her, something they haven't done for a long time. *Cat on a Hot Tin Roof* (1958, MGM).

6048 MADRIGAL: "I don't care much for locks." MAITLAND: "Nevertheless, they're the principal reason for whatever honesty still exists in our society today." Governess **Deborah Kerr**'s aversion to locks is understandable. She's been in prison. Butler **John Mills** believes locks are quite functional in discouraging the larcenous. *The Chalk Garden* (1964, GB, Universal).

Logic

see also DETECTIVES AND DEDUCTION, MATHEMATICS, PRINCIPLES, PROOFS, REASONS

6049 "You came back and caught me in the truth, and there's nothing less logical than the truth." **Irene Dunne** realizes the truth about what she was doing all night with her music teacher **Alex D'Arcy** is not believed by her husband Cary Grant. *The Awful Truth* (1937, Columbia).

6050 "I've talked with the prisoner. He's a friend of Lily Langtry's. It stands to reason no friend of Lily Langtry goes around stealing horses—leastways, there's a reasonable doubt." Gary Cooper's neck is saved from a rope stretching when frontier Judge **Walter Brennan,** a great admirer of Lily Langtry, rules favorably for Coop, using a bit of "Would an angel lie?" type of logic. *The Westerner* (1940, Goldwyn/United Artists).

6051 "My dear Mr. Marlowe, I notice in you an unpleasant tendency toward abrupt transitions. A characteristic of your generation, but in this case, I must ask you to follow some sort of logical progression." **Otto Kruger** is critical of the way private eye Dick Powell's mind works. *Murder, My Sweet* (1944, RKO).

6052 "I'm a friend to no one and nothing except logic." Professional revolutionary **Joseph Wiseman** makes it clear that he's untrustworthy to have as a friend. *Viva Zapata!* (1952, 20th Century-Fox).

6053 "A man being rich is like a girl being pretty. You might not marry her just because she's pretty, but my goodness, doesn't it help?" With perfect logic, **Marilyn Monroe** explains to Taylor Holmes, the wealthy father of the young man she plans to marry, why blondes prefer millionaires. *Gentlemen Prefer Blondes* (1953, 20th Century-Fox).

6054 "It has been said that the logic of this story is the logic of a dream. Do you feel lost in a labyrinth? Do not look for a way out. You will not be able to find one. . . . There's no way out." Narrator **Orson Welles** speaks directly to the audience in the film based on Franz Kafka's story of Joseph K, tried and condemned for an unspecified crime. *The Trial* (1962, Fr.-Italy-W. Ger., Europa-Fi-C-It-Hisa-Astor).

6055 "What V-ger needs in order to evolve. . . is our capacity to leap beyond logic." Practical Captain Kirk, played by **William Shatner**, speaks of the strange alien craft that is gobbling up everything in its path as it voyages towards earth. *Star Trek: The Motion Picture* (1979, Paramount).

6056 "Love is apples, marriage is oranges; not everyone can stomach fruit cocktail." **Edward Herrmann** tries to form a syllogism for his womanizing younger brother Tim Matheson. *A Little Sex* (1982, Universal).

6057 "If you're going to use logic, I'll lose my edge." **Michael Caine** wishes to convince his best friend's teenage daughter, Michelle Johnson, that he's much too old to marry her. She brings up the examples of Picasso and Chaplin who married much younger women. *Blame It on Rio* (1984, 20th Century-Fox).

6058 "I make the illogical logical." Rube Goldberg-like inventor **Hoyt Axton** explains his profession. *Gremlins* (1984, Warner Bros.).

6059 "When school's in session, you get an education. When it's not in session, you get a job." **Alex Rocco** takes what he considers a most logical position in opposing his son Anthony Edwards' plan to go to Paris during spring break instead of working. *Gotcha!* (1985, Universal).

6060 "If there hadn't been a Columbus, we'd all be Indians," states ballplayer **Gary Busey**. *Insignificance* (1985, GB, Zenith).

6061 "Why was Carmen Miranda always smiling?. . . Because she was the Abraham Lincoln of Brazil and she knew it?" Fiery Brazilian drug dealer **Marilia Pera** displays her own peculiar brand of logic. *Mixed Blood* (1985, Sara Films-Cinevista).

6062 "Because, if later I found out you were lying, I wouldn't have the pleasure of killing you then." When a rival thug is shot in the leg by sociopath **J.E. Freeman**, he asks reasonably, "How do I know you won't kill me anyway once I've told you?" When Freeman insists he give him the information he seeks, Freeman answers with a logic that convinces the thug to tell what he knows. Freeman then fires a bullet through the thug's brain, saying, "You know what, I believe you!" *Miller's Crossing* (1990, 20th Century-Fox).

6063 "Logic is the beginning of wisdom, not the end." These are the words of **Leonard Nimoy,** as

the ever rational Mr. Spock. *Star Trek VI: The Undiscovered Country* (1991, Paramount).

6064 "My heart does not know from logic." This **Woody Allen** character's comment sounds like Woody himself, who, speaking of the love he feels for Mia Farrow's adopted daughter Soon-Yi, said: "The heart wants what it wants. There's no logic to these things." *Husbands and Wives* (1992, Tri-Star).

Loneliness

see also HAPPINESS AND UNHAPPINESS, INDEPENDENCE AND DEPENDENCE, SOLITUDE

6065 "I'm not a machine. Come on home with me. I'm lonesome." Broadway director **Warner Baxter** wants the company of his stage manager George E. Stone after a long, tiring rehearsal. Stone has plans with chorus girl Una Merkel. *42nd Street* (1933, Warner Bros.).

6066 "Forty-nine acres of nothing but scenery and statues. I'm lonesome." Orson Welles' second wife **Dorothy Comingore** finds life in the museum-like Xanadu to be cold and lonely. *Citizen Kane* (1941, RKO).

6067 "You see me surrounded by thousands of subjects, and yet I'm lonely, Marquis, I'm lonely." **Tallulah Bankhead**, here complaining to Vincent Price, chews up the scenery as Catherine the Great of Russia. *A Royal Scandal* (1945, 20th Century-Fox).

6068 "They call me a great man, but it's the loneliest animal in the world." Famous composer **Claude Rains** looks for some sympathy from his long time mistress, struggling pianist Bette Davis. *Deception* (1946, Warner Bros.).

6069 "I'll never be lonely again." Even though her love George Brent is leaving on a train, he has told **Barbara Stanwyck** that he will return to her after the war. *My Reputation* (1946, Warner Bros.).

6070 "I was born lonely, I guess." Escaped convict **Humphrey Bogart** confides in Lauren Bacall who is hiding him. *Dark Passage* (1947, Warner Bros.).

6071 "I just couldn't go to heaven without Clare. Why, I get lonesome for him even when I go to Ohio." **Irene Dunne** speaks from the heart about her husband William Powell, who she fears she won't see in heaven because he refuses to be baptized. *Life with Father* (1947, Warner Bros.).

6072 "No, Ben. You'll always be busy. You'll have to be busy because you're a lonely man. All your life you're going to be lonely. An empty man." **Florence Eldridge** has no use for her son Edmond O'Brien. She believes he deserves to be lonely. *Another Part of the Forest* (1948, Universal).

6073 STEFAN BRAND: "Are you lonely out there?" LISA BERNDLE: "Yes. Very lonely." **Louis Jourdan** interprets **Joan Fontaine**'s visit as a willingness for another of his endless dalliances. He's gone to another room to get some champagne and calls out to her. Fontaine's answer is not limited to the moment at hand. *Letter from an Unknown Woman* (1948, Universal).

6074 "I should think that loneliness would be unknown to a lovely woman." **Jose Ferrer,** as Parisian painter Henri de Toulouse-Lautrec, pays a compliment to model Suzanne Flon. *Moulin Rouge* (1952, United Artists).

6075 "Help me. . . I'm dying of loneliness." Cynical, bitter **Robert Ryan** pleads on the phone to disillusioned Barbara Stanwyck, the wife of his good friend Paul Douglas. *Clash by Night* (1952, RKO).

6076 "I always thought the one thing I would never be anymore when I ever got married was lonesome. But the funny thing—you can be it even in the same bedroom if he seems to be thinking about different things except you." **Judy Holliday** gives one of her major reasons for seeking a divorce from Aldo Ray. *The Marrying Kind* (1952, Columbia).

6077 "Nobody ever lies about being lonely." Lonely **Montgomery Clift** confesses to "hostess" Donna Reed. *From Here to Eternity* (1953, Columbia).

6078 "What did I ever get out of this company— except loneliness and sudden death?" **Barbara Stanwyck** reacts bitterly when her lover, the president of the furniture manufacturing company her family owns, collapses and dies from the strain. *Executive Suite* (1954, MGM).

6079 "You know, maybe he likes to be lonely. . . . He never asks any favors for himself, never trusts anybody so he doesn't get hurt, that's not a bad way to live. Maybe you'll learn that when you grow up." **James Stewart** uses a howling coyote as an object lesson for Corinne Calvet. *The Far Country* (1955, Universal).

6080 "A great many mistakes are made in the name of loneliness." American newspaperman **William Holden** tells Eurasian doctor Jennifer Jones he married his wife even though he didn't love her. *Love Is a Many-Splendored Thing* (1955, 20th Century-Fox).

6081 "I know all about loneliness—only I don't whine about it." **Anthony Quinn**, as painter Paul Gauguin, tells unhappy Kirk Douglas, as painter Vincent Van Gogh, to be more of a man. *Lust for Life* (1956, MGM).

6082 "You know, my first husband used to tell me about how lonely he felt. Now, I know what he meant. It's like the whole world's off someplace else, like an echo." Marilyn Monroe-like screen actress **Kim Stanley** finds that it's possible to be terribly lonely when surrounded by people. *The Goddess* (1958, Columbia).

6083 "It's hard to believe, but you can be more lonely in New York than this hotel. Even with their separate tables, they can talk back and forth. But being alone in a crowd is worse. It's more painful, more frightening, oh so frightening, so frightening. I'm an awful coward, you see. I—I've never been able to face anything alone." **Rita Hayworth** admits her vulnerability and fear of loneliness to her ex-husband Burt Lancaster. *Separate Tables* (1958, United Artists).

6084 "You know I used to live like Robinson Crusoe—shipwrecked among eight million people. Then one day I saw a footprint in the sand and there you were. It's a wonderful thing, dinner for two." Lonely New Yorker **Jack Lemmon** is delighted to have elevator operator Shirley MacLaine's company for dinner. *The Apartment* (1960, United Artists).

6085 "Young lady, I know what Bert is going through. It's the loneliest feeling in the world. It's like walking down an empty street and listening to your own footsteps. But all you have to do is knock on any door and say, 'If you let me in, I'll live the way you want me to live and I'll think the way you want me to think.' And all the blinds'll go up and all the doors'll open and you'll never be lonely ever again." **Spencer Tracy** tells Donna Anderson that if her fiancé Dick York wishes to think for himself, he'll have to put up with a certain amount of loneliness. *Inherit the Wind* (1960, United Artists).

6086 HENRY DRUMMOND: "What touches you? What warms you? Every man has a dream. What do you dream about? What—what do you need? You don't need anything, do you? People love an idea just to cling to them. You poor slob! You're all alone. Where will your loneliness lead you? When you go to your grave, there won't be anyone to pull the grass over your head. Nobody to mourn you. Nobody to give a damn. You're all alone." E.K. HORNBECK: "You're wrong, Henry. You'll be there. . . . Who else would defend my right to be lonely?"

Spencer Tracy as the Clarence Darrow character sadly reproaches cynical **Gene Kelly**, and H.L. Mencken-like reporter. Kelly, as always, has the last word. *Inherit the Wind* (1960, United Artists).

6087 "Y'know, Roslyn, I don't think I've known a woman I'd grieve about if she left. I've always enjoyed saying goodbye. But there's somethin' about you—I don't know what it is—I'd be lonesome. For a long time." **Clark Gable** tells Marilyn Monroe she's different—he'd miss her if she was gone. *The Misfits* (1961, United Artists).

6088 "Loneliness is a curse, isn't it?" Wealthy widower **Karl Malden** thrills gold-digging stewardess Lois Nettleton with his insights. *Come Fly with Me* (1963, MGM).

6089 "A bedroom with only one person in it is the loneliest place in the world." It's an epigram delivered by platinum blonde Jean Harlow, portrayed by **Carroll Baker**. *Harlow* (1965, Paramount).

6090 "You know me. I'm just like you. It's two in the morning, and I don't know anybody." **Robert Redford** knocks on the door of waitress Dimitra Arliss, talking himself in and into her bed. *The Sting* (1973, Universal).

6091 "Loneliness has followed me my whole life everywhere." **Robert De Niro** sadly feels the loneliness that is affecting his mind. *Taxi Driver* (1976, Columbia).

6092 "God, I feel so lonesome." Teenager **Kristy McNichol** feels desolate after giving her virginity to Matt Dillon. *Little Darlings* (1980, Paramount).

6093 "Have you ever talked to a corpse? It's boring. I'm lonely." The rotting ripped-up carcass of **Griffin Dunne,** relegated to the ranks of the undead after being bitten by a werewolf, complains about his "existence" to his friend David Naughton. The latter, also bitten, merely becomes a monster once a month. *An American Werewolf in London* (1981, GB, Polygram-Lycanthrope-Universal).

6094 KADY: "I like doing things for a man." JEFF: "What do you plan to do?" KADY: "Keep you from being lonely." Lolita-like **Pia Zadora** gets her daddy **Stacy Keach** all hot for her. *Butterfly* (1982, Analysis).

6095 "I'm not a liberal. . . I was just lonely!" Southern gal **Sissy Spacek** gives her real reason for seducing a teenage black boy when her sister Jessica Lange says she didn't know Sissy was a "liberal." *Crimes of the Heart* (1986, De Laurentiis).

6096 "I'm at a dead end. . . I've wasted my life. . . I've got no place to live. I'm going to get wiped out in the divorce because I committed adultery, so I may never even see my kids again. I'm alone." Sitting in a tent, gun in hand, **Daniel Stern** sobs as he contemplates suicide. *City Slickers* (1991, Columbia).

6097 "It's lonely, isn't it, when you're a freak?" CIA agent **Sam Neill** chides stockbroker Chevy Chase who becomes invisible in a freak industrial accident. *Memoirs of an Invisible Man* (1992, Warner Bros.).

Looks and Looking see APPEARANCES, BEAUTY, SIGHT AND SIGHTS

Losses and Losing

see also ACCIDENTS, FAILURES, MISSING, NOSTALGIA, RUINATIONS AND RUINS, WASTE AND WASTEFULNESS, WINNERS AND LOSERS

6098 "Something seems to have gone out of all of us, and I'm not sure I like what's left." **Diana Wynyard**'s prescient line is from a 1918 scene of the movie that chronicles the lives of two British families from the eve of the 20th century to the 1930s. *Cavalcade* (1931, Fox).

6099 PROFESSOR QUAIL: "Is this Kansas City, Missouri or Kansas City, Kansas?" HOTEL MANAGER: "This Wuhu." QUAIL: "Then what is Wuhu doing where Kansas City ought to be?" MANAGER: "Maybe you're lost." QUAIL: "Kansas City is lost. I am here." **W.C. Fields** has just landed his autogyro on the roof of the International House, a hotel in the mythical land of Wuhu, China. His exchange with the hotel manager **Franklin Pangborn** is a lulu. *International House* (1933, Paramount).

6100 PRESIDENT MALLOY: "It must be difficult to lose your mother-in-law." AMBROSE WOLFINGER: "It is very hard. . . almost impossible." **Oscar Apfel** commiserates with **W.C. Fields,** who wishing to attend a big wrestling match, asks for the day off from his boss, suggesting that his mother-in-law has passed away. *The Man on the Flying Trapeze* (1935, Paramount).

6101 "Nothing lost, Mr. Christian." Ship's surgeon **Dudley Digges**' dying words are the same expression the drunken physician used whenever he was in danger of spilling his drinks. *Mutiny on the Bounty* (1935, MGM).

6102 "Say, wait a minute. Don't anyone leave this room. I've lost my purse." **Irene Dunne,** posing as the sister of her ex-husband Cary Grant, dressed like a streetwalker, acts low-class and trampish in the home of Grant's new fiancée, socialite Molly Lamont. *The Awful Truth* (1937, Columbia).

6103 "It's hard to be strict with a man who loses money so pleasantly." Yankee Major **Robert Elliott** enjoys playing poker with Clark Gable, because the latter always makes sure he loses. *Gone with the Wind* (1939, Selznick-MGM).

6104 "This 'Rosebud' you're trying to find out about.... Maybe that was something he lost. Mr. Kane was a man who lost almost everything he had." **Everett Sloane** sadly tries to be helpful when interviewed by a reporter about Orson Welles as Charles Foster Kane and the meaning of his dying word. *Citizen Kane* (1941, RKO).

6105 "We'll never give in.... We won't be beaten. We won't. We just won't!" Upper-British class WAAF **Joan Fontaine**'s blistering tirade against losing to the German aggressors, inspires conscientious objector and army deserter Tyrone Power to show his bravery during an air raid. *This Above All* (1942, 20th Century-Fox).

6106 "You are inclined to lose things, Paula." It's part of **Charles Boyer**'s campaign to make his wife Ingrid Bergman believe that she is going insane. *Gaslight* (1944, MGM).

6107 "It's not easy to face the thought of losing you.... I've lain awake night after night... and I've come to a conclusion, Tony. I want her to live. I want very much for her to live, and I hope she gets free... not for any noble reason, but because I want all this business over and done with, and an end to your being part lawyer, part frustrated lover.... If she dies, you're lost to me forever. I know you'd go on thinking that you love her, you'd go on imagining her as your great lost love." **Ann Todd** is a pretty smart lady. Her husband, barrister Gregory Peck, has fallen obsessively in love with his client Alida Valli, on trial for the murder of her blind older husband. *The Paradine Case* (1947, Selznick-United Artists).

6108 "A lost lamb loose in our stone jungle." It's how Broadway actress **Bette Davis** views Anne Baxter when Davis invites Baxter into her home. *All About Eve* (1950, 20th Century-Fox).

6109 "When you lose something you thought was valuable, you bleed a little and forget it." Disappointed **Alan Ladd** discovers that former O.S.S. agent Wanda Hendrix, whom he loved and thought dead, is alive and married to Francis Lederer. *Captain Carey, U.S.A.* (1950, Paramount).

6110 "We've lost him. No use wasting any more time around here." Northern secret agent **Alex Nicol** allows Rebel sympathizer Robert Stack to escape. *Great Day in the Morning* (1956, RKO).

6111 "The dashing Kyle Hadley! I saw him dash through the office recently. It seems he misplaced his money belt." His money belt is not the only thing wealthy Robert Stack has lost—he's lost the respect of his wife **Lauren Bacall**. *Written on the Wind* (1956, Universal).

6112 "I don't lose, because I have nothing to lose—including my life." Consumptive ex-dentist Doc Holliday, played by **Kirk Douglas,** reveals the secret of his success with gambling. *Gunfight at the OK Corral* (1957, Paramount).

6113 "Well, what have I got to lose?... Don't answer that." **Janet Leigh** gives a slight shudder as she agrees to accompany a sinister-looking Mexican tough who eyes her appreciatively. He claims to have something for her law enforcement officer husband Charlton Heston. *Touch of Evil* (1958, Universal-International).

6114 "If you fellows can't lick the Vandamms without asking girls like her to bed down with them and fly away with them and probably never come back alive, maybe you better start learning to lose a few cold wars." Translation: **Cary Grant** growls to secret government agency head Leo G. Carroll that using young beautiful girls like Eva Marie Saint to get the goods on the likes of James Mason is too high a price to pay, especially when it seems likely she'll get killed. *North by Northwest* (1959, MGM).

6115 "As long as we live we must stay true to ourselves. I do know that we're brothers, and I know that we're free.... A free man dies, he loses the pleasures of life; a slave dies, he loses the pain. That's why we will win." Title character **Kirk Douglas** addresses his slave army just before a battle with the Roman legions. *Spartacus* (1960, Universal-International).

6116 "Stay with this kid. He's a born loser." Gambler **George C. Scott** sizes up pool hustler Paul Newman for Jackie Gleason as Minnesota Fats. *The Hustler* (1961, 20th Century-Fox).

6117 "You don't know what winnin' is, Bert. You're a loser. 'Cause you're dead inside, and you can't live unless you make everything else dead around you." Near the end of the picture, **Paul Newman** returns the compliment to George C. Scott. Scott has driven Newman's love Piper Laurie to commit suicide. *The Hustler* (1961, 20th Century-Fox).

6118 "We haven't lost a war yet, but we sure are pussy-footing our way through this one." A soldier since 1937, Private **Tony Ray** doesn't understand the no-win approach dictated by politics during the Korean Police Action. *War Hunt* (1962, United Artists).

6119 "I want you to get straight back to the gallery—start your motor. When you get there, go into the office and make out a check for $5,000 because you deserve it. Then take the check for $5,000 and get permanently lost, because I feel we are not the kind of people you can afford to be associated with." **Katharine Hepburn** pushes her soon-to-be ex-employee Virginia Christine back into her car, and slams the door. Christine has revealed her prejudice upon learning of Hepburn's daughter's engagement to a black man. *Guess Who's Coming to Dinner* (1967, Columbia).

6120 "No, Billy, we blew it." Drop-out motorcycle rider **Peter Fonda**'s line to Dennis Hopper makes about as much sense as does the rest of the movie. *Easy Rider* (1969, Columbia).

6121 "Sometimes a man has to lose something before he finds himself." Here's some wisdom from he-man **Burt Reynolds**. *Deliverance* (1972, Warner Bros.).

6122 "But that's you, Marlowe. . . . You'll never learn, you're a born loser." Former New York Yankee pitcher **Jim Bouton**, in the role of a wife-killer, mutters to his former friend Elliott Gould, just before Gould kills Bouton. *The Long Goodbye* (1973, United Artists).

6123 "Lose? Well, lose is a four-letter word and I don't use those." **Susan Anton** has been transformed into a tall, beautiful track star by her father Curt Jurgens. He formerly worked for Hitler to produce a super race. *Goldengirl* (1979, Avco Embassy).

6124 "Joan of Arc was burned for hearing voices. I was almost killed for not hearing them. Seems you can't win for losing." Faith healer **Ellen Burstyn** makes a feeble joke after her one-time lover Sam Shepard tries to assassinate her. *Resurrection* (1980, Universal).

6125 "Guys like you and me, they strike oil under our gardens and all we get is dead tomatoes." Sideman **Matthew Laurance** tells the rock band's wordsman Tom Berenger that they're losers. *Eddie and the Cruisers* (1983, Embassy).

6126 "When I lost touch with the group, I lost my idea of what I should be. . . . We expected something from each other; we needed that." College radical now TV star, **Tom Berenger** lives in a superficial, world compared to his college days when he had some pride in who he was and what he did. *The Big Chill* (1983, Columbia).

6127 "If you really think that you're going over the edge, the first thing you lose is your sense of time." Police helicopter pilot **Roy Scheider** is constantly monitoring his mental equilibrium, matching his sense of time with his high-tech watch. *Blue Thunder* (1983, Columbia).

6128 "I just figured out why we are going broke. We're losing 75 cents on every bushel of corn we produce." **Jessica Lange** has spent the night going over the books of her and her husband Sam Shepard's farm. *Country* (1984, Touchstone/Buena Vista).

6129 "You know, if you shoot me you'll lose all those humanitarian awards." Even facing death at the hands of Tim Matheson, **Chevy Chase** makes a joke. *Fletch* (1985, Universal).

6130 "Hey, look friend. . . we both know why I was transferred. Everyone thinks I'm suicidal, in which case I'm fucked and nobody wants to work with me. Or they think I'm faking it to draw a psycho pension, in which case I'm fucked and nobody wants to work with me. Basically, I'm fucked." Suicidal, nutty cop **Mel Gibson** levels with his new partner Danny Glover. *Lethal Weapon* (1987, Warner Bros.).

6131 "Sometimes you just get lost in the dumbness of it all. . . ." Rural Minnesota mother and radio journalist **Pamela Reed** speaks for us all. *Rachel River* (1987, American Playhouse Theatrical Films).

6132 "We're not losers, we're not gonna be losers. So don't revert." Ex-San Quentin lifer playwright **Nick Nolte** gives a pep talk to his cast of ex-cons. *Weeds* (1987, De Laurentiis).

6133 "The bank took my farm, and Vietnam took my son." White extremist **John Mahoney** explains to Debra Winger how he got that way. *Betrayed* (1988, United Artists).

6134 "Being thrown out of baseball. . . like having part of me amputated. . . I heard that some men wake up to scratch itchy legs that have been gone for over fifty years. . . . That was me. . . . I'd wake up at night with the smell of the ballpark in my nose. . . the cool of the grass on my feet. . . the thrill of the grass." The ghost of Shoeless Joe Jackson, portrayed by **Ray Liotta,** still feels the loss more than sixty years after being banned from baseball for being part of the "Black Sox" scandal of 1919. *Field of Dreams* (1989, Universal).

6135 "The disadvantage is that they tend to get lost in the tall grass." **Harry Dean Stanton** sees a few problems with investing in miniature cows. *Twister* (1989, Vestron).

6136 "This is Sherman, who started with so much, lost everything, but he gained his soul. Whereas I, you see, who started with so little, gained everything. But what does it profit a man if he gains the whole world and loses? Ah, well, there are compensations." Journalist **Bruce Willis** compares himself to stockbroker Tom Hanks. *The Bonfire of the Vanities* (1990, Warner Bros.).

6137 "I dream of my wife and children and how I lost them." Older and wiser **Al Pacino** has many regrets. *The Godfather, Part III* (1990, Paramount).

Love and Hate

see also HATE AND HATRED, LOVE AND LOVERS

6138 "We hate the people we love because they're the only ones who can hurt us." **Samuel S. Hinds,** as fatherly Dr. Arnold, explains the paradox to Claudette Colbert, as Dr. Jane Everest. *Private Worlds* (1935, Paramount).

6139 "You thought I loved Rebecca? You thought that? I hated her!. . . Oh, I was carried away by her—enchanted by her, as everyone was. And when I was married, I was told I was the luckiest man in the world. She was so lovely—so accomplished—so amusing. 'She's got three things that really matter in a wife,' everybody said: breeding, brains and beauty. And I believed them—completely. But I never had a moment's happiness with her. She was incapable of love, or tenderness, or decency." **Laurence Harvey** tells his second wife of the love and hate he felt for his first wife. *Rebecca* (1940, Selznick-United Artists).

6140 "Love and hate are horns on the same goat." A bit of wisdom from rune woman **Eileen Way.** *The Vikings* (1958, United Artists).

6141 "Is that what love is? Using people? And maybe that's what hate is—not being able to use people." **Elizabeth Taylor** recites the lesson she's learned from her relatives. *Suddenly, Last Summer* (1959, Columbia).

6142 "If you love someone, you don't do that to them, even if you hate them." **Anthony Perkins** reacts to Janet Leigh's suggestion that his mother should be in an institution. *Psycho* (1960, Paramount).

Love and Lovers

see also ADMIRATION, ATTRACTIONS, BEAUTY, BEDS, BEHAVIOR, BELIEFS, BELONGING, BETRAYALS, BODIES, CHARM, COMPASSION, COMPLIMENTS, CRUELTY, CRYING AND CRIES, CUTENESS, DATES AND DATING, DECENCY, DENIALS, DESIRES, DEVOTION, DIARIES, DIVORCES, DOUBLE ENTENDRES, DREAMS, EMOTIONS, EMPATHY, EULOGIES, EXCITEMENTS, EYES, FACES, FAINTINGS, FAIRNESS AND UNFAIRNESS, FAKES, FANTASIES, FAVORITES, FEELINGS, FLATTERY, FRIENDSHIPS AND FRIENDS, GENTLENESS, GESTURES, HAPPINESS AND UNHAPPINESS, HATE AND HATRED, HEART AND HEARTACHES, HELP AND HELPING, HOMOSEXUALITY, HONEYMOONS, HOPE, HUSBANDS, HUSBANDS AND WIVES, IDEALS, IMAGINATION, IMMORTALITY AND MORTALITY, IMPOTENCY, INCOMPATIBILITY, INDEPENDENCE AND DEPENDENCE, INVOLVEMENTS, KINDNESS, KISSES AND KISSING, LIKES AND DISLIKES, LONELINESS, LOVE AND HATE, LUST, MARRIAGES, MEETINGS, MEMORY AND MEMORIZATION, MEN, MEN AND WOMEN, MOODS, MYSTERIES, NARCISSISM, ORGASMS, PASSION, PLEDGES, POETRY AND POETS, PROPOSALS, PURITY, RELATIONSHIPS, ROMANCES, SACRIFICES, SELF, SEX AND SEXUALITY, THE SEXES, SMILES, SOULS, SURRENDER, SWEETNESS, TEAMS, TEMPTATIONS, THRILLS, TOASTS, TOGETHERNESS, UNIQUENESS, VIRGINITY AND VIRGINS, WEDDINGS, WIVES, WORSHIP

6143 CHILD: "Mama, is a cross a sign of love?" MOTHER: "Yes, and love often means a cross." **May Allison** questions **Mabel Fremyear** who has learned of her husband Edward Jose's indiscretions with vamp Theda Bara. *A Fool There Was* (1915, silent, Fox).

6144 "There were two great loves in Johnny Gray's life: his engine and his girl." It's the opening to Buster Keaton's silent classic. *The General* (1926, silent, United Artists).

6145 "I love you, little fellow, I love you. I'd do murder for you." In his own sincere way, gangster **Robert Ellis** pledges his troth to chorus girl Merna Kennedy. *Broadway* (1929, Universal).

6146 "Love! That's soft stuff. You move and it's suicide for both of you." Though gangster **Edward G. Robinson** claims no interest in love, his relationship with Douglas Fairbanks, Jr. is suspicious. *Little Caesar* (1930, Warner Bros.).

6147 ACE WILFONG: "How much do you love me?" JAN ASHE: "How much? Let me see how much. Well, it's about ten feet high and about seven feet wide." ACE: "Never mind that." JAN: "Oh, I can measure it now. It's a storm at sea." ACE: "You do love me, don't you?" JAN: "It's madness, nothing else." No-good gangster **Clark Gable** doesn't get an articulate answer to his question from his attorney's flapper daughter **Norma Shearer.** *A Free Soul* (1931, MGM).

6148 JAN ASHE: "You're swine walking with swine." ACE WILFONG: "You're talking to the man you love." **Norma Shearer** sees no reason to accept gangster **Clark Gable**'s marriage proposal—her clothes are already hanging in his closet. *A Free Soul* (1931, MGM).

6149 "My love has lasted longer than the temples of your gods. No man ever suffered as I did for you." **Boris Karloff,** as Im-Ho-Tep, declares his love and devotion to Zita Johann, the reincarnation of an ancient Egyptian princess. *The Mummy* (1932, Universal).

6150 "Love makes everything difficult and dangerous." Married **Joan Barry** remarks to Percy Marmont with whom she is infatuated. *Rich and Strange* (1932, GB, BIP).

6151 "Then there is love which casts out fear, and I have found it. And love is greater than illusion, and as strong as death." Title character **Fredric March,** posing as Prince Sirki, learns about love from Evelyn Venable. *Death Takes a Holiday* (1934, Paramount).

6152 TARZAN: "Good morning. I love you." JANE: "Good morning. I love you. You never forget, do you, Tarzan?" TARZAN: "Never forget I love you." JANE: "Love who?" TARZAN: "Love Jane." JANE: "Love my. . . ." TARZAN: "Love my. . . ? Wife! My wife!" The studio uses this scene to suggest that sometime between the filming of *Tarzan, the Ape Man* in 1932 and this movie, **Johnny Weissmuller** and **Maureen O'Sullivan** tied the knot. *Tarzan and His Mate* (1934, MGM).

6153 "I love you because you know such lovely people." **Myrna Loy** purrs to her husband William Powell as she surveys the assorted low-lifes that he has invited to their Christmas party. *The Thin Man* (1934, MGM).

6154 "When I love a woman, I'm an Oriental. It never goes. It never dies." **John Barrymore**'s statement, whatever it means, is probably racist. *Twentieth Century* (1934, Columbia).

6155 "Hard-boiled Hannah was going to fall in love with a bankroll. You can't run away from love!" **Carole Lombard** has money on her mind, but penniless Fred MacMurray in her heart. *Hands Across the Table* (1935, Paramount).

6156 ARMAND DUVAL: "No one has ever loved you as I love you!" MARGUERITE GAUTIER: "That may be true, but what can I do about it?" **Greta Garbo** takes no responsibility for **Robert Taylor**'s infatuation with her. *Camille* (1936, MGM).

6157 "I'll love you all my life. I know that now. All my life." Later **Robert Taylor** professes love for a dying Greta Garbo. *Camille* (1936, MGM).

6158 "Love has got to stop someplace short of suicide." American businessman **Walter Huston** informs his restless wife Ruth Chatterton that there are limitations to what one can expect from love. *Dodsworth* (1936, Goldwyn/United Artists).

6159 "You can't build love on hate or marriage on spite." **Myrna Loy** pleads with Jean Harlow to give up her husband-in-name-only William Powell. *Libeled Lady* (1936, MGM).

6160 "There's only one way I could ever fall in love. . . . Not as Cherry Chester the actress—but as a plain ordinary girl. . . . I'd only fall in love with a man I didn't know." Headstrong actress **Margaret Sullavan** marries novelist Henry Fonda on impulse. *The Moon's Our Home* (1936, Paramount).

6161 "It's easy to tell when a girl's ready for love." Then clumsy **Dick Foran** should be able to tell that Bette Davis is not ready for love with him. *The Petrified Forest* (1936, Warner Bros.).

6162 "That isn't love. It isn't love to let him drag you down to his level." Priest **Spencer Tracy** is outraged that his amoral friend, Barbary Coast dive owner Clark Gable, plans to exploit his new love Jeanette MacDonald by showing off her body in a review at his club. *San Francisco* (1936, MGM).

6163 "I'm still in love with that crazy lunatic and there's nothing I can do about it." **Irene Dunne** confesses to her aunt Cecil Cunningham that she's breaking off her engagement to Oklahoma oil man Ralph Bellamy because she still loves her ex-husband Cary Grant. *The Awful Truth* (1937, Columbia).

6164 "It's the old, old story: 'Boy Meets Girl'— Romeo and Juliet—Minneapolis and St. Paul." **Groucho Marx** declares his love for wealthy Margaret Dumont—for her money, that is. *A Day at the Races* (1937, MGM).

6165 "There is one thing that moves me deeply: the bravery and generosity of love. It is because these qualities are so evident in this room that has seen so much of qualities far different, that you are pardoned." Czar of all the Russias, **William Stack** pardons lovers William Powell, a Polish secret agent, and Luise Rainer, a Russian spy. *The Emperor's Candlesticks* (1937, MGM).

6166 "I'll love all the women in Vienna if I want, and you can do nothing! Nothing!" **Charles Boyer,** the heir to the Hapsburg Empire, screams at his real love, Danielle Darrieux, after she returns to him, despite the efforts of their parents to keep them apart. *Mayerling* (1937, Fr., Corona-Winchester).

6167 "I love you. . . . I love you more than truth or life or honor. In all else I've been an imposter, but never in that." **Ronald Colman** has been impersonating his look-alike cousin, the heir to the throne of Ruritania. Colman declares his love for Madeleine Carroll, the intended of the future king. **Stewart Granger** makes the same pretty speech to Deborah Kerr in the remake. *The Prisoner of Zenda* (1937, Selznick-United Artists); (1952, MGM).

6168 "Love is wonderful but it can't survive seven people for one bathtub." Jitterbugging **Lana Turner** tosses off a wisecrack. *Rich Man, Poor Girl* (1938, MGM).

6169 "I love you, Peter, but I'm not in love with you." Actress **Kay Francis** rejects her wealthy suitor, architect Ian Hunter, by making a subtle distinction. *Secrets of an Actress* (1938, Warner Bros.).

6170 "To the party of the first part—I love you. The party of the second part." **James Stewart** demonstrates for his wife Carole Lombard that lawyers can be romantic. *Made for Each Other* (1939, United Artists).

6171 "Why must you bring in wrong values? Love is a romantic designation for a most ordinary biological, or shall we say, chemical process, and chemically we are quite sympathetic." **Greta Garbo** offers an evasive and scientific answer when Melvyn Douglas asks if she's in love with him. *Ninotchka* (1939, MGM).

6172 "She's just a sour old maid who hates me because I'm young and attractive and in love, while she's old and hideous and dried up and has never known anything about love." Young **Jane Bryan** cruelly lambasts Bette Davis unaware that Bette is her real mother. *The Old Maid* (1939, Warner Bros.).

6173 "Clem didn't love you. He loved me. I loved him. She should have been ours. I am her mother!" **Miriam Hopkins** speaks of George Brent and the child he fathered with Bette Davis before he died. *The Old Maid* (1939, Warner Bros.).

6174 "Because I love you. . . . But don't let's get sticky about it. . . . I also love fireflies, mockingbirds and pink sunsets. I think, however, we could find each other more diverting than a pink sunset." **George Sanders,** as Simon Templar, doesn't overwhelm Wendy Barrie, as Valerie Travers, with emotion. *The Saint Strikes Back* (1939, RKO).

6175 "Henriette, there are many kinds of love possible between a man and a woman. And peace, gentleness and companionship are not the least of these. I promised you once that you would find heaven on this earth. I'm going to keep that promise if it takes a lifetime of devotion." The Reverend **Jeffrey Lynn** isn't as exciting as French nobleman Charles Boyer, but at least he's not a murderer and is alive to marry governess Bette Davis. *All This and Heaven Too* (1940, Warner Bros.).

6176 "Two lovers in moonlight cast only one shadow. One shadow now—many shadows later." That's what must have happened to **Sidney Toler** as the Oriental detective with many children. *Charlie Chan at the Wax Museum* (1940, 20th Century-Fox).

6177 JOHNNY JONES: "I'm in love with you and I want to marry you!" CAROL FISHER: "I'm in love with you and I want to marry you!" JONES: "That cuts down our love scene quite a bit, doesn't it?" **Joel McCrea** and **Laraine Day** are in complete agreement. *Foreign Correspondent* (1940, United Artists).

6178 "I love the shimmer of satins and silks, the matching of scents and lotions. As to ornaments and jewels. . . ." **Tyrone Power,** in reality the fearless masked avenger Zorro, pretends to be a sissy. *The Mark of Zorro* (1940, 20th Century-Fox).

6179 TRACY LORD: "All of a sudden I've got the shakes." MIKE CONNOR: "It can't be anything like love, can it?" TRACY: "No, no, it mustn't be. It can't." MIKE: "Would it be inconvenient?" TRACY: "Terribly. Anyway, I know it isn't. Oh, Mike, we're out of our minds. . . ." MIKE: "And right into our hearts. . . Tracy, you're tremendous." TRACY: "That's funny, because I feel very small. Put me in your pocket, Mike." **Katharine Hepburn** and **James Stewart** better sort things out fast. She's scheduled to marry John Howard in the morning and she's certainly not over her first husband Cary Grant. *The Philadelphia Story* (1940, MGM).

6180 "You hit hard, baby, so you love hard." **Clark Gable** makes the observation after Joan Crawford hits him in the head. *Strange Cargo* (1940, MGM).

6181 "I loved you. I've never loved anyone else. I never shall. That's the truth, Roy. I never shall." The words of his dead World War I lover **Vivien Leigh**

haunt Robert Taylor during an air raid in World War II. *Waterloo Bridge* (1940, MGM).

6182 "Doggone it, Peter. If this is what it's like to be in love, I'm glad I'm only going to be in love once." Tomboy **Jean Arthur**'s love affair with wanderer William Holden has not run smoothly. *Arizona* (1940, Columbia).

6183 "Scientists can write all the books they like about love being a trap of nature. I remember reading that—that it's biology and the chemistry inside of her that fools her. But all that scientists are going to convince are other scientists, not women in love." **Jean Arthur** doesn't want love to be reduced to a mere scientific inquiry. *The Devil and Miss Jones* (1941, RKO).

6184 "I love you, I worship you, I am used to you." In declaring his love and intention of marrying Carole Lombard again after their marriage is proven to be illegal, **Robert Montgomery** gets down to his bottom line. *Mr. and Mrs. Smith* (1941, RKO).

6185 "Yes, I love him. I love the hick shirts he wears and the boiled cuffs and the way he always has his vest buttoned wrong. He looks like a giraffe, and I love him. I love him because he's the kind of guy who gets drunk on a glass of buttermilk, and I love the way he blushes right up over his ears. I love him because he doesn't know how to kiss—the jerk! I love him, Joe. That's what I'm trying to tell ya." Burlesque dancer Sugarpuss O'Shea, played by **Barbara Stanwyck,** counts the ways she loves stodgy linguist Gary Cooper for her gangster fiancé Dana Andrews. *Ball of Fire* (1941, Goldwyn-RKO).

6186 "The truth is, Charlie, you just don't care about anything except you. You just want to convince people that you love them so much that they should love you back. Only you want love on your terms. It's something to be played your way—according to your rules. And if anything goes wrong and you're hurt—then the game stops, and you've got to be soothed and nursed, no matter what else is happening—and no matter who else is hurt." **Joseph Cotten** ends his friendship with Orson Welles, when he tells the tycoon that his love is the selfish, hurtful type. *Citizen Kane* (1941, RKO).

6187 CHARLES FOSTER KANE: "You can't do this to me." SUSAN ALEXANDER KANE: "I see, it's you this is being done to. It's not me at all. Not what it means to me. You don't love me. You want me to love you. Sure, I'm Charles Foster Kane. Whatever you want, you just name it, and it's yours. But you gotta love me." **Orson Welles** is more insulted than hurt when

his second wife **Dorothy Comingore** announces she's leaving him. *Citizen Kane* (1941, RKO).

6188 "Now I know you still love me—and it won't die, what's between us. Do what you will. Ignore it. Neglect it. Starve it. It's stronger than both of us." Unhappily married **Paul Henreid** is reunited with his love Bette Davis, although the two can't have all their dreams. But maybe Henreid's wife will somehow depart the picture. *Now, Voyager* (1942, Warner Bros.).

6189 TESS HARDING: "[Will you love me] even when I'm sober?" SAM CRAIG: "Even when you're brilliant." Late in the film, sports columnist **Spencer Tracy** reaffirms his love for his important international affairs writer wife **Katharine Hepburn**. *Woman of the Year* (1942, MGM).

6190 "I'm doing a very bad job of saying I love you, Commander." You can tell that fiery **Susan Hayward** and tough John Wayne are in love. They fight all the time. *The Fighting Seabees* (1944, Republic).

6191 "Love is eternal. It has been the strongest motivation for human action throughout the centuries. Love is stronger than life. It reaches beyond the dark shadow of death." If his radio broadcast were about self-love, **Clifton Webb** would have more expertise. *Laura* (1944, 20th Century-Fox).

6192 "He's infatuated with you—in some peculiar way." Police detective **Dana Andrews** tells Gene Tierney that vicious writer Clifton Webb's all-consuming passion for her is a bit sick. *Laura* (1944, 20th Century-Fox).

6193 "Love rather than money is the root of all evil. Sometimes a thought can be like a malignant disease and start to eat away at the will power." Psychologist **Sydney Greenstreet** lectures Humphrey Bogart who is haunted by the wife he's murdered. *Conflict* (1945, Warner Bros.).

6194 "I love you so I can't bear to share you with anybody." **Gene Tierney** is insanely jealous of her husband's former girl friend Jeanne Crain. *Leave Her to Heaven* (1945, 20th Century-Fox).

6195 "Something has happened to us. . . . like lightning striking. . . . it strikes rarely. . . ." Amnesiac **Gregory Peck** rises and moves towards lovesick shrink Ingrid Bergman when she confesses her feelings for him. *Spellbound* (1945, Selznick-United Artists).

6196 "To rob a bank, to hold up a stagecoach is play for a child. But to make love to two senoritas, ah, that is a job for a man." It's **Gilbert Roland** as the Cisco Kid. *Beauty and the Bandit* (1946, Monogram).

6197 "Love is not the exclusive province of adolescence, my dear. It's a heart ailment that strikes all age groups. Like my love for you. My love for you is the only malady I've contracted since the usual childhood diseases, and it's incurable." **Clifton Webb** tells his unfaithful wife Cathy Downs that he can't stop loving her. *The Dark Corner* (1946, 20th Century-Fox).

6198 "Nothing is stronger than the law in the universe, but on earth nothing is stronger than love!" In a heavenly court, physician **Roger Livesey** ends his summation in his case to allow David Niven to live and share his love with Kim Hunter. *A Matter of Life and Death* aka: *Stairway to Heaven* (1946, GB, Archers-Universal).

6199 "A loving look alone could save me. Love can make a man a beast. Love can make a man ugly." **Jean Marais,** now a handsome prince, is at last able to tell Josette Day that she needed her love to be transformed from the beast he was. *La Belle et la Bête* aka: *Beauty and the Beast* (1947, Fr., Discina-Lopert).

6200 CORAL: "Rip, can't we put the past behind us? Can't you forget?" RIP: "The trouble is, I can't forget that I might die tomorrow.... A guy's pal was killed, he ought to do something about it." CORAL: "Don't you love me?" RIP: "That's the tough part of it. But it'll pass. These things do in time. But there's one other thing. I loved him more." **Lizabeth Scott** is about to suffer the same fate as Mary Astor in *The Maltese Falcon.* **Humphrey Bogart** can't ignore the fact that Scott killed his best friend William Prince. *Dead Reckoning* (1947, Columbia).

6201 "But, George, I've heard you say love is largely nonsense." **Richard Haydn** is surprised by his friend, Boston Brahmin Ronald Colman's attitude. *The Late George Apley* (1947, 20th Century-Fox).

6202 "Listen to me. I'm no good—I never pretended to be—but I love you. I'm a hustler—I've always been one—but I love you. I may be the thief of the world, but with you I've always been on the level. You've done a lot of talking about love. I never mentioned it before, but I guess you get the general idea. If you want to walk out on that, it's okay with me." Con artist **Tyrone Power** does the best he can to prevent his wife Coleen Gray from leaving him because she no longer can stand the kind of life they share. *Nightmare Alley* (1947, 20th Century-Fox).

6203 "Don't bring the subject around to marriage again. I like all kinds of music, except a little number called 'Promise me.' It's a duet and I want to play solo. Why is it when a man gets interested in his work, or a book or something, a woman always has to start acting like a woman? See that curve? It's a parabola. Now that's something a mathematician could fall in love with." Engineer **Van Heflin** refuses to allow Joan Crawford to monopolize him. *Possessed* (1947, Warner Bros.).

6204 "Love, your magic spell is everywhere." Physician **Charles Boyer** makes a cynical observation after he unsuccessfully operates on a young girl who dies as a result of a botched illegal abortion. *Arch of Triumph* (1948, United Artists).

6205 CHARLIE: "Have you ever made love to a woman?" HAVEN: "Only from the doorway." CHARLIE: "You haven't made love to me." HAVEN: "Come over to the doorway." Gambling den owner **Jane Greer** questions investigator **Dick Powell.** *Station West* (1948, RKO).

6206 DON JUAN: "I have loved you since the beginning of time." CATHERINE: "But you only met me yesterday." DON JUAN: "That was when time began." CATHERINE: "But you made love to so many women." DON JUAN: "Catherine, an artist may paint a thousand canvases before achieving one work of art. Would you deny a lover the same practice?" **Errol Flynn** cons a gullible and willing **Mary Stuart** after he climbs to her moonlit balcony to take her in his arms. *The Adventures of Don Juan* (1949, Warner Bros.).

6207 "Love isn't anything you can put on or take off like an overcoat, you know." **Arthur Kennedy** tells Ruth Roman he can't change his feelings toward his brother Kirk Douglas, even though the latter is a heartless user of people. *Champion* (1949, United Artists).

6208 "Look here, old sport. Daisy doesn't love you. She has loved me since eleven years ago." **Alan Ladd** confronts Barry Sullivan about his wife Betty Field. *The Great Gatsby* (1949, Paramount).

6209 "From now on, her love would be doled out like a farmer's wife tossing scraps to the family rooster." **Spencer Tracy** uses the simile to make the point that once his daughter Elizabeth Taylor announces her engagement, he's lost forever the little girl he adored. *Father of the Bride* (1950, MGM).

6210 "I suppose I shouldn't have seen him as often as I did, but I didn't realize how madly infatuated he was with me. I just didn't realize. You'll never know how much I blame myself for all this. When my husband came back from New York last week and I told Johnny I couldn't see him, he kept phoning me. He wouldn't let me alone. Oh, maybe if I'd agreed to see him he wouldn't have done this dreadful thing." **Marlene Dietrich** implicates Richard Todd as the murderer of her husband. *Stage Fright* (1950, Warner Bros.).

6211 "Sure I do, it's something that goes on between a man and a .45 that won't jam." Hired killer **Alan Ladd** responds to Phyllis Calvert's question if he knows what love is. *Appointment with Danger* (1951, Paramount).

6212 "Two kinds of love, hers and mine, worlds apart, as I know now, though when I married her I did not think they were incompatible. Now, I suppose she did. In those days I had not thought that her kind of love, that the kind of love she requires and which I seemed unable to give her, was so important that its absence would drive out the other kind of love, the kind of love I required and—and which I had thought in my folly was a far greater part of love." **Michael Redgrave,** an instructor of classic languages at an English public school, discusses his marriage with his wife Jean Kent's lover Nigel Patrick. *The Browning Version* (1951, GB, GFD).

6213 "I love you. I've loved you since the first moment I saw you. I guess maybe I even loved you before I saw you." **Montgomery Clift** had an ideal woman in mind to love who turns out to be Elizabeth Taylor. *A Place in the Sun* (1951, Paramount).

6214 GEORGE EASTMAN: "Oh, Angela, if I could only tell you how much I love you!" ANGELA VICKERS: "Tell mama. Tell mama all." This scene between **Montgomery Clift** and **Elizabeth Taylor** is done in extreme close-up, making it seem all the more intense. *A Place in the Sun* (1951, Paramount).

6215 "Really foolish, vulgar, a clown—but not to me. To me, he was a man like a rock. Nothing could shake his love. It was from him that I learned what love really was, not a frail little fancy to be smashed and broken by pride and vanity and self-pity—that's for children, that's for high school kids—but a rock as strong as life itself, indestructible and determined." **Bette Davis** tells Gary Merrill what a great guy her husband Keenan Wynn is. *Phone Call from a Stranger* (1952, 20th Century-Fox).

6216 "Well, we were so busy raising a family I guess I just didn't have time. But I happen to love you very much, Mrs. Rose." What with their own three children, and the troubled children they take into their home, there isn't much time for **Cary Grant** to tell his wife Betsy Drake that he loves her. *Room for One More* (1952, Warner Bros.).

6217 EDIE DOYLE: "You just stay away from me." TERRY MALLOY: "Edie, I—Edie, you love me." EDIE: "I didn't say I didn't love you. I said stay away from me." TERRY: "I want you to say it to me." EDIE: "Stay away from me." **Marlon Brando** breaks through the door of **Eva Marie Saint** to get to her. The exchange ends with a kiss. *On the Waterfront* (1954, Columbia).

6218 "Love is like the measles. You only get it once. The older you are, the tougher it goes." Recently married, and in his own mind an expert on the subject, **Howard Keel** sympathizes with his lovesick six younger brothers. *Seven Brides for Seven Brothers* (1954, MGM).

6219 "Mr. Trask, it's awful not to be loved. It's the worst thing in the world. Don't ask me—even if you could—how I know that. I just know it. It makes you mean—and violent—and cruel. And that's the way Cal has always felt, Mr. Trask. All his life! Maybe you didn't mean it that way—but it's true. You never gave him your love. You never asked for his. You never asked him for one thing. . . . Cal did something very bad and I'm not asking you to forgive him—or bless him or anything like that. Cal has got to forgive you—for not having loved him— or for not having shown your love. And he has forgiven you. I know he has. . . . But you must give him some sign, Mr. Trask, some sign that you love him—or he'll never be a man. All his life he'll feel guilty and alone unless you release him." **Julie Harris** as Abra pleads with stroke-paralyzed Raymond Massey to reconcile with his son James Dean. *East of Eden* (1955, Warner Bros.).

6220 "I haven't got the price. Around here, love has a very low cash-surrender value." **Jan Sterling** isn't sincere when she claims she'll pass on love. *Female on the Beach* (1955, Universal).

6221 "I'll always love him. But I've discovered there's a big difference between loving someone and being in love." **Susan Hayward** loves her husband Gene Barry, a photographer missing in the Far East, but she's in love with soldier of fortune Clark Gable, who she's hired to smuggle Barry out of Communist China. *Soldier of Fortune* (1955, 20th Century-Fox).

6222 "Oh, love is like a glass of sparkling wine. Enjoy it while it lasts." Strong-willed, passionate **Melina Mercouri** dumps her lovers when they become serious and propose marriage. *Stella* (1955, Greece, Millas Films).

6223 "Marry him, stop running away. Stop living by the opinions, the smiles and frowns of others. You were ready for a love affair but you weren't ready for love." **Conrad Nagel** tells Jane Wyman to follow her heart and marry much younger Rock Hudson. *All That Heaven Allows* (1955, Universal).

6224 "I loved you, Julie. Know that. I loved you." On a return visit to earth, deceased carousel barker **Gordon MacRae** makes his wife Shirley Jones feel what he's saying to her. *Carousel* (1956, 20th Century-Fox).

6225 "Just say you love me. You don't have to mean it." Greenwich Village existentialist **Carolyn Jones** will go to bed with Don Murray if he will just lie to her. *The Bachelor Party* (1957, United Artists).

6226 "I love thee with the breath, smiles, tears of all my life. And if God chooses, I shall but love thee better after death." **Jennifer Jones,** as Elizabeth Barrett Browning, pledges her love to Bill Travers, as Robert Browning. *The Barretts of Wimpole Street* (1957, U.S.-G.B. MGM).

6227 "I am not allowed to love. But I will love you if that is your wish." Beautiful Japanese Matsubayashi dancer **Miiko Taka** offers herself to American Army Major Marlon Brando. *Sayonara* (1957, Warner Bros.).

6228 "I love you now. In half an hour, I'll wonder how I ever got into this. You have a passion for respectability, and I have a horror of loneliness— that's love." **Steven Hill**'s notion of love won't do for neurotic movie sex goddess Kim Stanley. *The Goddess* (1958, Columbia).

6229 "I love you because you love me and because you're warm and soft." Young newspaper columnist **Montgomery Clift** pledges his love to cuddly Dolores Hart. *Lonelyhearts* (1958, United Artists).

6230 "It wasn't supposed to happen this way. . . . If you love me, you'll know I loved you and I wanted to go on loving you. . . ." **Kim Novak** makes a declaration of love for James Stewart just before her fall to her death. *Vertigo* (1958, Paramount).

6231 CAROLINE: "[If I'm not married] by the time I'm 26, I may have to take a lover." APRIL: "If you're that old, you have a right to live." **Hope Lange** and **Diane Baker** believe in being working girls, until they catch Mr. Right. *The Best of Everything* (1959, 20th Century-Fox).

6232 MIKE: "Get out quick—and love happily ever after." CAROLINE: "Please make love to me, even if you don't love me—26 is too far ahead." Before **Stephen Boyd** can act on **Hope Lange**'s request, she passes out. *The Best of Everything* (1959, 20th Century-Fox).

6233 "And what is love? Love is the mornin' and the evenin' star. It shines on the cradle of the babe. Hey, ye sinners! Love is the inspiration of poets and philosophers. Love is the voice of music. I'm talking about divine love. . . not carnal love." Born preacher and con man **Burt Lancaster** takes in the flock. *Elmer Gantry* (1960, United Artists).

6234 NICK STRATTON: "How many? Did you ever count?" GIULIETTA CAMERON: "Why count waves in the ocean?" **Tony Franciosa** is curious how many men his call-girl lover **Gina Lollobrigida** has made it with. *Go Naked in the World* (1960, MGM).

6235 "A lot of people loved my husband, but he never loved anybody. That's why he's dead." **Karen Steele** speaks of her murdered mobster husband Ray Danton. *The Rise and Fall of Legs Diamond* (1960, Warner Bros.).

6236 RYDER SMITH: "You'd never lose your grip. You're a pretty strong girl, Merritt." MERRITT ANDREWS: "Not really. No girl is when it comes to love. What she thinks is love. How do you know the difference? Do you love me, Ryder?" In one of the classic clichés, **George Hamilton** is something of a bounder who tries to sweet-talk **Dolores Hart**. *Where the Boys Are* (1960, MGM).

6237 "By your example I have been called. All my life I have longed to find to what I could give my whole devotion. Love has been a confused thing in me, until I saw your love of all life, and all God's creatures. I wish to be devoted to that love." **Dolores Hart,** as Clare Scefi, founder of a religious order of nuns, took these lines to title character, Bradford Dillman, to heart. Two years after the film was produced, Hart entered a convent and is now known as Mother Dolores. *Francis of Assisi* (1961, 20th Century-Fox).

6238 "I fall in love too easily. I shatter too easily." British **Julie Andrews** resists American James Garner's advances. *The Americanization of Emily* (1964, MGM).

6239 MARNIE: "You must have loved me, Momma— you must have loved me." BERNICE: "Why sugar pop, you're the only thing I ever loved!" **Tippi Hedren** and her mother **Louise Latham** have a happy, tearful reunion at the end of the film. *Marnie* (1964, Universal).

6240 "If you have such a fervent, evangelical affection for your country, why, in the name of God. . . don't you try to get it through the normal democratic channels the flag represents?" President **Fredric March** confronts General Burt Lancaster, who heads a planned military coup. *Seven Days in May* (1964, Paramount).

6241 "Never fall in love during a total eclipse." **Michael Hordern,** eyeing his witch of a wife, Patricia Jessel, warns his son Michael Crawford. *A Funny Thing Happened on the Way to the Forum* (1966, United Artists).

6242 "Whatever there was between us, Frankie, you could never call it love! Because 'to love' means 'to commit yourself' and 'to belong.' And you never belonged to anybody but yourself, Frankie! You don't belong—nothing belongs to you. So you may have your Oscar—and you may have everything—but you'll have nothing! Bye, Frankie! And I do hope the Oscar keeps you warm on cold nights." **Elke Sommer** gets in her licks as her marriage to self-centered actor Stephen Boyd collapses. *The Oscar* (1966, Embassy).

6243 "I love you more than common." Plain speaking shepherd **Alan Bates** declares his love to Julie Christie. *Far from the Madding Crowd* (1967, GB, EMI).

6244 "Do you think that you are Providence, that you can order love?" **Pamela Franklin** stands up to her strong-willed teacher Maggie Smith. *The Prime of Miss Jean Brodie* (1969, GB, 20th Century-Fox).

6245 "A person [who] has no love for himself, no respect for himself, no love for his friends, family, workers—how can he ask for love in return?" **Susan Anspach** accuses Jack Nicholson of being incapable of having any real loving feelings. *Five Easy Pieces* (1970, Columbia).

6246 "Besides sex—and my wife's very good at it—I love you guys best." **Ben Gazzara** made this remark about his lifetime buddies Peter Falk and John Cassavetes. *Husbands* (1970, Columbia).

6247 "Love means never having to say you're sorry." Both **Ali MacGraw** and **Ryan O'Neal** say the deathless line, but he's quoting her. *Love Story* (1970, Paramount).

6248 "Love means never having to say you're ugly." **Vincent Price** has his own interpretation of the deathless line. *The Abominable Dr. Phibes* (1971, GB, AIP).

6249 "I love yoga. I love Eastern philosophy. It's metaphysical and redundant and absolutely pedantic." **Woody Allen** tries to impress Louise Lasser into bed. *Bananas* (1971, United Artists).

6250 "Is this love or only infatuation of the body?" German Jew **Marisa Berenson** asks this question of Fritz Wepper when he tells her he loves her. Born-to-be-bad Liza Minnelli pipes in with, "Does it really matter as long as we're having fun?" *Cabaret* (1972, Allied Artists).

6251 "Love is a miracle. It's like a birthmark. You can't hide it." **George Segal** interprets the most tender emotion. *Blume in Love* (1973, Warner Bros.).

6252 "You see, Evelyn loved me. And I loved her. And that was the trouble. Oh, it would have been easy to find a way out if she hadn't loved me so much. Or if I hadn't loved her. But, as it was, there was only one possible way. I had to kill her." The drunks of Fredric March's saloon always enjoyed salesman **Lee Marvin**'s visits and his stories about his wife and the iceman—but this time he admits he's killed her. *The Iceman Cometh* (1973, American Film Theater).

6253 "Do you love her enough to give her up?" **Paul Sorvino** asks his married friend George Segal about the depth of his love for divorcée Glenda Jackson. *A Touch of Class* (1973, GB, Avco Embassy).

6254 "When you love somebody, you go deaf, dumb and blind." This is **Robert Redford**'s assessment of love for Barbra Streisand. *The Way We Were* (1973, Columbia).

6255 "First love, what a change it makes in a lad. What a magnificent secret it is that he carries about with him. The tender passion gushes instinctively out of a man's heart; he loves as a bird sings, as a wind blows, from nature." Narrator **Michael Hordern** reflects on Ryan O'Neal's crush on Gay Hamilton. *Barry Lyndon* (1975, GB, Warner Bros.).

6256 "I could never love a man who wasn't criminally handsome." Part-time actress, full-time slut **Karen Black** dismisses the marriage proposal of earnest William Atherton. *The Day of the Locust* (1975, Paramount).

6257 "Boris, I just don't love you. Oh, I mean I love you, but I'm not in love with you." **Diane Keaton** makes things perfectly clear to Woody Allen as she climbs into bed with him on their wedding night. At another time she tells him, "Love is everything, Boris." *Love and Death* (1975, United Artists).

6258 "You must learn to love someone else apart from me, Sara. I won't be here much longer." School girl **Anne Lambert,** who has been compared to a Botticelli angel by one of her teachers, prophesizes her mysterious disappearance to her closest friend Margaret Nelson. *Picnic at Hanging Rock* (1975, Australia, Atlantic Releasing).

6259 "True love is erection not orgasm." It's part of aging rou **Alain Cuny**'s instruction to 19-year-old Sylvia Kristel. He has been entrusted with the task of turning her into a sexual animal. *Emmanuelle* (1976, France, Trinacra-Orphee).

6260 "This may sound crazy to you, but I want you to make love to me." **Pamela Franklin** confesses to Marjoe Gortner. *Food of the Gods* (1976, AIP).

6261 "I just want you to love me, primal doubts and all." The more **William Holden** lets Faye Dunaway know he needs her, the less she wants him. *Network* (1976, United Artists).

6262 "Love is too weak a word for what I feel. I lurve you. I luff you." Words fail **Woody Allen** when he tries to make Diane Keaton know what she means to him. *Annie Hall* (1977, United Artists).

6263 "People think that because I have never married I know nothing about love. . . . But I love Aunt and Aunt loves me." **Glenda Jackson,** as the English poet Stevie Smith, speaks of Mona Washburne, whom she calls "The Lion Aunt." *Stevie* (1978, U.S.-G.B., First Artists).

6264 "Relax, I know that you and Saul are lovers." Trying to act older than her years, teen **Lisa Lucas** calms her mother Jill Clayburgh, nervous when Alan Bates comes to dinner for the first time. *An Unmarried Woman* (1978, 20th Century-Fox).

6265 "You can love without it; that's why they gave you two!" Practical Sergeant **Lee Marvin** practices rough bedside manners on a young replacement soldier who has a testicle blown off by a booby trap. *The Big Red One* (1980, United Artists).

6266 "I love a man I no longer love, so I try to love him more." **Romy Schneider** makes a kind of sense, confessing to Yves Montand her feelings for her husband who is in a semi-catatonic state since an automobile accident that also took their daughter's life. *Clair de Femme* (1980, Fr., Atlantic).

6267 "If we could just love each other. . . . I suspect there wouldn't be the bother in the world there is." Elderly **Eva LeGallienne** gushes her version of the Golden Rule. *Resurrection* (1980, Universal).

6268 "If there's anything holy here, it's only love." **Ellen Burstyn** can't explain her healing powers, but knows they aren't evil. *Resurrection* (1980), Universal).

6269 "Hitler would have loved the IRS." Mailman **Edward Herrmann** is beaten but not bowed in his fight with the tax man. *Harry's War* (1981, Taft International).

6270 "God, I have so many great albums. I love 'em, I love 'em." Compulsive film editor **Albert Brooks** isn't quite as sure about his feelings for his on-again, off-again lover Kathryn Harrold. *Modern Romance* (1981, Columbia).

6271 "I love money! I love power! I love capitalism! I don't love children!" **Albert Finney,** as Daddy Warbucks, makes himself perfectly clear before being charmed by little moppet Aileen Quinn whom he then adopts. *Annie* (1982, Columbia).

6272 "How does it happen that people I love keep telling me to go away?" Married politician **Dudley Moore** asks an unanswerable question of businesswoman Mary Tyler Moore, mother of ten-year-old Katherine Healy who is dying of leukemia. *Six Weeks* (1982, Universal).

6273 "I don't think we don't love each other." **Jeremy Irons** makes a double-negative declaration of love for Patricia Hodge. *Betrayal* (1983, GB, Horizon).

6274 "What then must we do? We must give love to whomever God has placed in our path." **Linda Hunt,** as male Billy Kwan, voices her version of love thy neighbor. *The Year of Living Dangerously* (1983, Australia, MGM).

6275 "In the way of love, we're kindergarten toddlers." Virginal 1920s schoolgirl **Bo Derek** complains to her classmate Ana Obregon. *Bolero* (1984, Cannon).

6276 "Love is a stream. It doesn't stop." With **Gena Rowlands**' help, we know where the title of her movie comes from. *Love Streams* (1984, Cannon).

6277 "I'll never love anybody but Laura, never. I'll never make love to anyone again. That's almost definite." Sixteen-year-old photographer **Jon Cryer** leaves himself the smallest out when his crush on 23-year-old singer Demi Moore doesn't pan out. *No Small Affair* (1984, Columbia).

6278 "Love is an emotion that has always frightened me, but I have always recognized it when I see it." As a child, **Coral Browne**'s character Alice Liddell, inspired Charles Dodgson (Lewis Carroll) to write *Alice in Wonderland. Dreamchild* (1985, GB, Thorn EMI-PFH).

6279 "Extend love to the enemy so that love might unite them." It's one of the messages in the *Talmut,* a small book Drac **Lou Gossett, Jr.** wears around his neck. *Enemy Mine* (1985, 20th Century-Fox).

6280 "We all love you, Preacher!" In a scene reminiscent of *Shane* when Brandon de Wilde called out to Alan Ladd to come back, fourteen-year-old **Sydney Penny** runs after Clint Eastwood as he rides away after ridding the area of bad guys. *Pale Rider* (1985, Warner Bros.).

6281 "I look at you. I see what I want to see. That's what love is." Mafioso **Jack Nicholson** has a simple definition. *Prizzi's Honor* (1985, ABC).

6282 "I'm hopelessly, head over heels in love with Cecilia. . . . Every breath she takes makes my heart dance." After coming off the screen to be with Mia Farrow, screen character **Jeff Daniels** turns down a freebie from some whores. *The Purple Rose of Cairo* (1985, Orion).

6283 "As she leaned over, she whispers in his ear: 'Do you love me?'. . . Thoughts raced through his mind. . . . Did she really want him?. . . What did he do to deserve this bounty?. . . Does God exist?. . . Who invented liquid soap and why?. . . 'Do you love me?'. . . Staring in her eyes, he knew that she really didn't need to hear it. . . . For the first time in his life he knew. . . these were no longer just words. . . . If he said it, it would be a lie. . . .'Do you love me?' she whispered. 'Do you love me. . . love me tonight?' The answer was, 'No!'" As creative writing professor **Viveca Lindfors** comes to the end of John Cusack's composition entitled, "The Sure Thing," there are groans from some of the males in the class. But Daphne Zuniga knows that Cusack didn't sleep with luscious Nicollette Sheridan, the girl he traveled three thousand miles to bed, because he loves Zuniga. *The Sure Thing* (1985, Embassy).

6284 MR. EMERSON: "There's only one thing impossible—that's to love and to part. . . . You love George. . . you love the boy, body and soul—as he loves you." LUCY HONEYCHURCH: "But of course I do. . . what did you think?" **Denholm Elliott** urges **Helena Bonham Carter** to admit her love for his son Julian Sands, which she readily does. *A Room with a View* (1985, GB, Merchant Ivory-Goldcrest).

6285 "I love you guys." Small town Indiana high school basketball coach **Gene Hackman** loves his players who have worked so hard to succeed. *Hoosiers* (1986, Orion).

6286 "If might is right, then love has no place in the world." Missionary Father Gabriel, played by **Jeremy Irons,** refuses to fight to save his mission. *The Mission* (1986, GB, Goldcrest-Kingsmere-Enigma-Ghia).

6287 "Generous tears filled Gabriel's eyes. He had never felt like that himself toward any woman, but he knew that such a feeling must be love." These are the words of James Joyce, as Donal McCann realizes that there is a large part of his sleeping wife Anjelica Huston's life that he doesn't even suspect. What **Donal McCann** actually says is, "I had never felt like that myself toward any woman, but I know such a feeling must be love." He makes the statement as he contemplates the boy who many years earlier died rather than lose Huston. *The Dead* (1987, Vestron).

6288 "Not loving enough! It's a terrible thing to do to someone. I suppose I did it to Clive. I always held something back. . . ." **Sarah Miles** confesses to Derrick O'Connor that she wishes he had asked her to marry him rather than her husband David Hayman. *Hope and Glory* (1987, GB, Columbia).

6289 "Oh, yes, I love you. I always have. I always will. I just have to keep learning how." Bayou matriarch **Barbara Hershey,** who has some strange ways of showing it, confesses her love for her wild, ignorant sons. *Shy People* (1987, Cannon).

6290 "I'm in love. I have to face up to my heterosexuality, but don't worry, you'll be provided for." Police detective **Richard Dreyfuss** quips to Emilio Estevez when he announces that he's fallen in love with Madeleine Stowe, a woman they have had under surveillance. *Stakeout* (1987, Touchstone/Buena Vista).

6291 "I love you, TM, you really are too much." Adorable little **Bridgette Andersen** loves her cute little robot friend Masato Fukazama, known as "Too Much." *Too Much* (1987, Cannon).

6292 "Makin' love is like hittin' a baseball. You just gotta relax and concentrate." **Susan Sarandon** instructs Kevin Costner at a batting cage. She looks good taking swings in a tight skirt. *Bull Durham* (1988, Orion).

6293 "I love you, baby. I love you." **Harrison Ford** is elated his wife Betty Buckley is safely back after she disappeared from their Paris hotel room. *Frantic* (1988, Warner Bros.).

6294 "Would you still love me if I had little tits and worked in a fish house?" **Lolita Davidovich,** as stripper Blaze Starr, turns the table on Paul Newman, as Louisiana Governor Earl Long, when he asks if she'd still love him if he weren't governor. *Blaze* (1989, Touchstone/Buena Vista).

6295 "Who's gonna love me? Who's ever gonna love me, Dad?" Drunken paraplegic **Tom Cruise** begs his father Raymond J. Barry for an answer. *Born on the Fourth of July* (1989, Universal).

6296 "I'm going to find out once and for all what it feels like to hold the woman I love, have always loved, and will always love until the day I die." **Ryan O'Neal** is a man who has faithfully waited for over twenty years for Cybill Shepherd to get over the death of her husband. *Chances Are* (1989, Tri-Star).

6297 "I would have played for food money. . . it was the game, the sounds, the smells. . . . Did you ever hold a ball or a glove to your face?. . . I used to love traveling on the trains from town to town. . . the hotels, brass spittoons in the lobby, brass beds in the rooms. . . the crowd, rising to its feet when the ball is hit deep. . . . Shoot, I'd play for nothing." The ghost of Shoeless Joe Jackson, portrayed by **Ray Liotta**, a simple country illiterate, speaks eloquently. *Field of Dreams* (1989, Universal).

6298 "It's funny. You wake up one morning and suddenly you're out of love." Jewish lawyer **Woody Allen** realizes that he no longer loves his fickle gentile fiancée Mia Farrow. "Oedipus Wrecks," *New York Stories* (1989, Touchstone-Buena Vista).

6299 "You've had sex every day of your life; you've never made love." **Steve Irlen** exaggerates a bit about his friend Mark McKelvey. The latter does have sex once too often, contracts AIDS and dies. *On the Make* (1989, Taurus).

6300 "If love is blind, marriage is like having a stroke." Divorce lawyer **Danny De Vito** shares some questionable wisdom with a client. *The War of the Roses* (1989, 20th Century-Fox).

6301 "Love is a most complex emotion. No rational thought. . . much romance, but much suffering." In his farewell appearance, **Keye Luke,** as Chinese herbalist Dr. Yang, advises Mia Farrow. *Alice* (1990, Orion).

6302 "I love you, cousin." Hopelessly miscast **Sofia Coppola** declares her love for Andy Garcia. *The Godfather, Part III* (1990, Paramount).

6303 "When they come, they'll come at what you love." **Al Pacino** is ready to turn control of the Family over to his nephew Andy Garcia, but only if Garcia will give up Pacino's daughter Sofia Coppola. *The Godfather, Part III* (1990, Paramount).

6304 BARBARA SABICH: "You're still in love with her." RUSTY SABICH: "It was never love." BARBARA: "Then what was it?" RUSTY: "It was never love." **Bonnie Bedelia** comes across her husband **Harrison Ford** in tears as he looks at the pictures of the bludgeoned body of his one-time mistress

Greta Scacchi. *Presumed Innocent* (1990, Warner Bros.).

6305 GRACE: "They seemed so in love." MIKE: "Well, those are the people who usually kill each other." **Emma Thompson** and **Kenneth Branagh** are speaking of a couple that years earlier looked just like them. The man was executed for murdering his wife. *Dead Again* (1991, Paramount).

6306 "I'm not so loveable." Irish immigrant widow **Maureen O'Hara** confesses to her son, Chicago policeman John Candy, who agrees. *Only the Lonely* (1991, 20th Century-Fox).

6307 SUSAN LOWENSTEIN: Admit it, you love her more." TOM WINGO: "No, just longer." **Barbra Streisand** is corrected by her lover **Nick Nolte** who is leaving her to return to his wife Blythe Danner and his children. *The Prince of Tides* (1991, Columbia).

6308 "Sex. . . ain't nothin' but a mosquito bite. . . . I'm going to tell you a secret: Girls don't want sex, girls want love." What sweet, sexy **Laura Dern** tells young Lukas Haas may be true, but Dern attracts men like bugs to light and she usually seems in some sexual frenzy. *Rambling Rose* (1991, Seven Arts-New Line).

6309 NICK: "I'll nail you." CATHERINE: "You'll fall in love with me." NICK: "I'm already in love with you, but I'll nail you anyway." Police detective **Michael Douglas** is convinced that **Sharon Stone** is a brilliant, beautiful murderer—and, oh, yes, he loves her. *Basic Instinct* (1992, Tri-Star).

6310 "Love should have brought your ass home last night." **Halle Berry** lays down the law to Eddie Murphy. *Boomerang* (1992, Paramount).

6311 "No one could ever love you like I love you." On her death bed, **Anne Bancroft** gets her son Nicolas Cage to promise that he will never marry. *Honeymoon in Vegas* (1992, Columbia).

Loyalties

see also DEFENSES, DUTIES, FAITH AND UNFAITHFULNESS, IDEALS

6312 "We are touched by this man's expression of loyalty. We will give him another chance." Grand Duchess **Florence Vidor** allows clumsy waiter Adolphe Menjou to continue to serve her. In reality, Menjou is a wealthy man, who, infatuated with Vidor's loveliness, has taken the role of a servant to be near her. *The Grand Duchess and the Waiter* (1926, silent, Paramount).

6313 "I don't mind admitting that I'm loyal." Secretary of State nominee **Henry Fonda** responds to a senator's questions: is it true he does not believe in war; did he belong to communist associations while in school; is he loyal to the United States of America? *Advise and Consent* (1962, Columbia).

6314 "Peyton, there's only one woman for me." **Matt McCoy** proves his loyalty to his wife Annabella Sciorra by holding off panting, full-lipped, hot and ready nanny Rebecca De Mornay. *The Hand That Rocks the Cradle* (1992, Touchstone-Buena Vista).

Luck

see also CHANCES, FATE AND DESTINY

6315 "I wish you all the luck in the world—name the first one after me." **James Cagney** wishes his secretary Joan Blondell all the best as she leaves him to marry a respectable businessman. *Blonde Crazy* (1931, Warner Bros.).

6316 "And tell her not to try to thank me for it. It's, uh, it's bad luck." Because he loves Jeanette MacDonald, Sheriff **Walter Pidgeon** steps aside so she can be with her dashing outlaw, Nelson Eddy. *The Girl of the Golden West* (1938, MGM).

6317 "Some people say I've had a bad break, but today. . . I consider myself the luckiest man on the face of the earth." With his words echoing throughout Yankee Stadium, **Gary Cooper** as Lou Gehrig says goodbye to his fans on his day. The "Iron Man" who played in 2,310 consecutive games dies at age 37 from amyotropic lateral sclerosis, ever after known as "Lou Gehrig's disease." *The Pride of the Yankees* (1942, Goldwyn-RKO).

6318 "Cats bring luck. . . I killed it, I killed my luck." Superstitious hired murderer **Alan Ladd** strangles a cat he gently picked up and caressed when its purring threatened to expose him to the police. *This Gun for Hire* (1942, Paramount).

6319 "Okinawa very fortunate. Culture brought to us, not have to leave home for it." **Marlon Brando,** an Okinawan interpreter for the U.S. Army, puts the best possible face on the various invasions of his homeland over the centuries. *The Teahouse of the August Moon* (1956, MGM).

6320 "Oh, Sebastian. What a lovely summer it's been. Just the two of us. Sebastian and Violet. Violet and Sebastian. Just the way it's always going to be. Oh, we are lucky, my darling, to have one another and need no one else ever." Near the end of the movie, **Katharine Hepburn** retreats into a fantasy with her late son. *Suddenly, Last Summer* (1959, Columbia).

6321 MATTIE ROSS: "Have you heard of a robber called Lucky Ned Pepper?" ROOSTER COGBURN: "I know him well. I shot him in the lip last August down in the Winding Stair Mountain. He was plenty lucky that day." **Kim Darby** and Marshal **John Wayne** discuss Robert Duvall. *True Grit* (1969, Paramount).

6322 "I know what you're thinkin'. Did he fire six shots or only five? Well, to tell the truth, I kinda forgot myself in all the excitement. But bein' this is a .44 Magnum, the most powerful handgun in the world, and will blow your head clean off, there's only one question you should ask yourself. . . 'Do I feel lucky?' Well, do ya, punk?" **Clint Eastwood** has a robber covered with his .44 Magnum, having cornered him after a bloody shootout. The punk, Andy Robinson, doesn't take a chance, but Eastwood satisfies his curiosity by pulling the trigger while pointing the gun at Robinson's head, resulting in a resounding click. *Dirty Harry* (1971, Warner Bros.).

6323 "I don't know, but I think I know what he'd have said. It doesn't make any sense, Admiral Yamamoto had everything going for him: power, experience, confidence. Were we better than the Japanese or just luckier?" **Henry Fonda,** as Admiral Chester W. Nimitz, knows he was lucky to defeat Japanese Admiral Isoroku Yamamoto, played by Toshiro Mifune, at the decisive WWII battle of Midway. *Midway* (1976, Universal).

6324 "Guilty is what the man says when your luck runs out." Lowlife **Franklyn Seales** takes a cynical view of his drawn-out trial for the murder of a cop. *The Onion Field* (1979, Avco Embassy).

6325 "I got lucky with one of these phone-for-sex gals." **Michael Hagerty** covers up for Kurt Russell to amnesiac Goldie Hawn when she finds a pair of panties (hers, but she doesn't know it) in the family truck. *Overboard* (1987, MGM).

6326 "The wolf isn't bad—he's just unlucky." **Sally Kirkland** places her own slant on the wolf when she tells Keith Carradine's daughter Kathleen York the Little Red Riding Hood story. *Cold Feet* (1989, Avenue Pictures).

6327 "I had Miss All-America in my bed and I couldn't believe my luck." Psychiatrist **Jeff Bridges** has an amicable divorce from Farrah Fawcett. *See You in the Morning* (1989, Warner Bros.).

6328 "Luckily, they turned out to be drug dealers." Police detective **Leslie Nielsen** is relieved that two pedestrians he killed deserved to die when he ran over them as he backed out of a parking place. *The Naked Gun 2½: The Smell of Fear* (1991, Paramount).

6329 DEATH'S HEAD: "Don't you find me strangely attractive?" FRANCESCA: "Deep sea fishermen throw back better looking faces than yours. . . sit down. You're lucky I'm a nymphomaniac." Sinister **Christopher Adamson** gets lucky with **Deborah Leng**. *Bullseye!* (1991, 21st Century Productions).

Luggage

see also TRAVEL AND TRIPS

6330 "I am not part of your luggage. Whatever I am, I am not part of your luggage." **Paul Newman** doesn't usually mind being a kept man of actress Geraldine Page. *Sweet Bird of Youth* (1962, MGM).

6331 "I hate my luggage more than life itself." No one really cares about what high powered agent **Dyan Cannon** hates as she arrives for a yacht trip with five other people. They are all suspects in the hit-and-run death of host James Coburn's wife sometime earlier. *The Last of Sheila* (1973, Warner Bros.).

6332 "The business traveler should bring only what fits in a carry-on bag. Checking your luggage is asking for trouble." **William Hurt** speaks in voice-over as hands carefully pack a carry-on bag at the opening of the film. *The Accidental Tourist* (1988, Warner Bros.).

Lunacy and Lunatics *see* INSANITY AND SANITY

Lust

see also DESIRES, LOVE AND LOVERS, SEX AND SEXUALITY, PROMISCUITY

6333 "You have a very hot hand—for an aunt." **Michael Sarrazin** leers at his beautiful aunt, Eleanor Parker. *Eye of the Cat* (1969, Universal).

6334 "They are so horny. . . sometimes at night you can hear them honking." **Sid Haig** tells fellow truck driver Jerry Francks about the frustrated lust of the female cons at the prison to which they make deliveries. *The Big Doll House* (1971, New World).

6335 "I can feel the steam coming right through my dress." Angelic 12-year-old prostitute-to-be **Brooke Shields** whispers seductively to the "lucky" customer who makes the winning bid for her virginity. *Pretty Baby* (1978, Paramount).

6336 ARIEL: "Tell me something. If you lusted after me so, why weren't you in love with me? Can the two feelings be separate?" ANDREW: "Sometimes I think the two are totally different. Sex alleviates tension and love causes it." **Mia Farrow** is instructed in the difference between lust and love by her one-time lover **Woody Allen**. *A Midsummer Night's Sex Comedy* (1982, Orion/Warner Bros.).

6337 "My lust was insatiable." **Peter MacNicol** recalls his lovemaking with Polish refugee Meryl Streep after she tells him the horrible choice she had to make at Auschwitz. *Sophie's Choice* (1982, Universal).

6338 DR. EMMETT BROWN: "Apparently your mother is amorously infatuated with you instead of your father." MARTY MCFLY: "Are you trying to tell me my mom has the hots for me?" **Christopher Lloyd**'s meaning is translated into teen jargon by **Michael J. Fox.** Fox finds himself 30 years in the past, thanks to a time machine made from a DeLorean automobile by weird scientist Lloyd. His mother, Lea Thompson, is just a teenager who finds Fox awfully cute. The problem is, if she doesn't transfer her affection to Fox's dad, Crispin Glover, Fox won't be born. *Back to the Future* (1985, Universal).

6339 "It's the beast that wants to spit you into the eternal fires of hell, where for all eternity your flesh will be ripped from your body by serpents with razor-sharp teeth." Priest **Wallace Shawn** admonishes students at a school mixer on lust. *Heaven Help Us* (1985, Tri-Star).

6340 DAWN: "I want him. I want him so much. I'll kill myself if I don't have him." GRACE: "Oh, my baby. . . . Go, if you want to. . . what does it matter, we may all be dead tomorrow. . . . You better bring him home if you really do love him. Don't kill love. You'll regret it for the rest of your life." DAWN: "Who said anything about love?" **Sammi Davis** and her mother **Sarah Miles** are speaking of two very different things, as Miles comforts Davis about her need for her soldier boy friend Jean-Marc Barr. *Hope and Glory* (1986, GB, Columbia).

6341 "You is the horniest bunch of white folks I's ever seen." Black maid **Pearl Jones** stumbles across grappling teens all over the house. *Shag* (1989, Hemdale).

Machinery

see also BUSINESS AND COMMERCE, WORK AND WORKERS

6342 "Are you meaning to infer, sir, that I am not a cog in the wheel?" Independent-minded pilot **James**

Cagney kids his friend, Ground Commander Pat O'Brien, about Cagney's lack of concern for team work. *Ceiling Zero* (1935, Warner Bros.).

6343 "You're the most adorable cog I ever saw in my life." Gay blade **Melvyn Douglas** lauds Soviet special emissary Greta Garbo, who claims to be a tiny cog in the wheel of revolution. *Ninotchka* (1939, MGM).

6344 "You're a machine—not a woman." Bohemian journalist **Melvyn Douglas** flings a nasty accusation at boss-lady Joan Crawford, who proves him wrong. *They All Kissed the Bride* (1942, Columbia).

6345 "Abominable things, these machines. You can't reason with them." **Anthony Hopkins** operates on a man mutilated in an industrial accident. *The Elephant Man* (1980, GB, EMI).

6346 "Inside I'm a lean, mean fighting machine." On the outside, **John Candy** is an overweight soldier called "Ox." *Stripes* (1981, Columbia).

6347 "He's a wreckin' machine and he's hungry." Manager **Burgess Meredith** warns Sylvester Stallone about boxer Mr. T. *Rocky III* (1982, United Artists).

6348 "If a machine can learn the value of human life, then maybe we can too." **Linda Hamilton** takes hope from a friendlier version of terminator Arnold Schwarzenegger. *Terminator 2: Judgment Day* (1991, Tri-Star).

Madness see INSANITY AND SANITY, MINDS, PSYCHOLOGY AND PSYCHIATRY

Magic

see also CONTROL, ILLUSIONS, MYSTERIES, WITCHCRAFT AND WITCHES

6349 "I don't want real. . . I want magic!" Aging neurotic Blanche DuBois, played by **Vivien Leigh,** prefers the joys of a make-believe world. *A Streetcar Named Desire* (1951, Warner Bros.-20th Century-Fox).

6350 "You ought to sleep with him a few times. Then you'd see there isn't any magic in it." **Ellen Burstyn** urges her daughter Cybill Shepherd to experiment sexually with Jeff Bridges, not marry him. *The Last Picture Show* (1971, Columbia).

6351 "Are women magical creatures?" The answer to **Jean-Pierre Leaud**'s question is undoubtedly, "Yes!" *Day for Night* (1973, Fr.-Italy, Films du Carrosse-PECF-PIC).

Magnificence

see also BEAUTY, GREATNESS, NOBILITY, WEALTH AND RICHES

6352 "Those movies you were in! It's sacrilege, throwing you away on things like that. When I left that movie house, I felt some magnificent ruby had been thrown into a platter of lard. You set yourself back ten years—but we can mend all that. You'll be greater than ever, Lily Garland." Theater director **John Barrymore** wishes to discourage his protégé Carole Lombard's film career and lure her back to Broadway. *Twentieth Century* (1934, Columbia).

6353 "There's a magnificence in you, Tracy. A magnificence that comes out of your eyes, in your voice, in the way you stand there, in the way you walk. You're lit from within, Tracy! You've got fires banked down in you, hearth-fires and holocausts! . . . Oh, you're the golden girl, Tracy, full of life and warmth and delight. . . ." **James Stewart** pays Katharine Hepburn a major compliment. *The Philadelphia Story* (1940, MGM).

6354 "You're maudlin and full of self-pity. You're magnificent." Theater critic **George Sanders** admires stage actress Bette Davis. *All About Eve* (1950, 20th Century-Fox).

6355 "I try to be careful, Mr. Dodd, but being an actor's wife is not the easiest of jobs. If I tell him he's magnificent, he says I'm not being honest. If I tell him he's not magnificent, he says I don't love him." **Grace Kelly** tells theater director William Holden of her situation with alcoholic performer Bing Crosby, who is attempting a comeback. *The Country Girl* (1954, Paramount).

Manners

see also ACTIONS AND ACTS, BEHAVIOR, GENTLEMEN, LADIES, LADIES AND GENTLEMEN, SOCIETIES, WAYS

6356 "It's a pity her manners don't match her looks." Title character **Errol Flynn** has just been treated to a tirade by Olivia de Havilland, as Maid Marian. *The Adventures of Robin Hood* (1938, Warner Bros.).

6357 "We are not questioning your authority, sir, but if manners prevent our speaking the truth, we will be without manners." **John Loder** acts as the spokesman for the adult sons of the Morgan family in standing up to the tyranny of their father Donald Crisp. *How Green Was My Valley* (1941, 20th Century-Fox).

6358 "Young woman, either you have been raised in some incredibly rustic community where good manners aren't known or you suffer from the common feminine delusion that the mere fact of being a woman exempts you from the rules of civilized conduct." Writer **Clifton Webb** chastises Gene Tierney who interrupts him dining out to get him to endorse a pen. *Laura* (1944, 20th Century-Fox).

6359 "I've always been a man of the world. There's no reason why I should forget my manners as I am leaving it." Dying, wealthy dilettante **Clifton Webb** finds time to dictate his regrets to a party invitation. *The Razor's Age* (1946, 20th Century-Fox).

6360 "Bad manners. . . an infallible sign of talent." **Joan Crawford** may be arguing from the converse in speaking of John Garfield. He has bad manners and he is talented. *Humoresque* (1947, Warner Bros.).

6361 ADRIENNE FROMSETT: "I don't like your manner." PHILIP MARLOWE: "I'm not selling it." Book editor **Audrey Totter** can see writer, ex-private eye **Robert Montgomery,** but because the camera sees things from his point of view, the audience only sees him when he's reflected in a mirror. *The Lady in the Lake* (1947, MGM).

6362 "You lose your manners when you're poor." **Betsy Blair** insincerely apologizes to Fredric March. *Another Part of the Forest* (1948, Universal-International).

6363 "Low as my opinion has always been of you, August, little as I ever expected of chivalry or even common dignity, today you've sunk below even yourself! This is the sewer, the nadir of good manners." Orchestra conductor **Rex Harrison** is outraged with his dismal brother-in-law Rudy Vallee. The latter so misunderstood Harrison's request, "keep an eye on my wife" while Rex was on a concert tour, that Rudy hired a private detective to trail the conductor's wife Linda Darnell. *Unfaithfully Yours* (1948, 20th Century-Fox).

6364 "You eat terrible. You got no manners. Taking your shoes off—that's another thing—picking your teeth. You're just not couth." Brassy blonde **Judy Holliday,** having developed some class through the instructions of her tutor William Holden, berates her unloveable lover Broderick Crawford. *Born Yesterday* (1950, Columbia).

6365 META: "Haven't you any manners at all?" VARIUS: "No, I'm a barbarian." **Marge Champion** asks a silly question of one of Hannibal's followers **Gower Champion**. *Jupiter's Darling* (1955, MGM).

6366 "Bad manners have broken up more households than infidelity." Still proud ex-courtesan **Isabel Jeans** stresses the importance of etiquette to her niece Leslie Caron who is in training to enter the family business. *Gigi* (1958, MGM).

6367 "Good manners spoil good food." **David Kossoff,** Ingrid Bergman's chauffeur, poses as her lover to make Cary Grant jealous. *Indiscreet* (1958, Warner Bros.).

6368 "Just because you have good manners doesn't mean I suddenly turn into Dale Evans." Widowed **Ellen Burstyn** is suspicious of gentle, well-meaning rancher, Kris Kristofferson. *Alice Doesn't Live Here Anymore* (1975, Warner Bros.).

Marines *see* MILITARY

Marriages

see also BACHELORS, CHILDREN AND CHILDHOOD, DIVORCES, FAMILIES, HUSBANDS, HUSBANDS AND WIVES, INFIDELITIES, LOVE AND LOVERS, PARENTS, SEX AND SEXUALITY, SPINSTERS, WEDDINGS, WIVES

6369 MRS. POTTER: "My dear Mr. Hammer, I shall never marry before my daughter." HAMMER: "You did once." **Margaret Dumont** may reject **Groucho Marx**'s marriage proposal but she can't refute his logic. *The Cocoanuts* (1929, Paramount).

6370 "Unless you are well-mated, this business of marriage is overrated." **Genevieve Tobin** shares her thoughts with friend Jeanette MacDonald. *The Love Parade* (1929, Paramount).

6371 CAPTAIN JEFFREY SPAULDING: "Shall we get married?" MRS. RITTENHOUSE: "That's bigamy." SPAULDING: "Of course it's big of me." African explorer **Groucho Marx** can't resist flustering poor **Margaret Dumont** with a pun. *Animal Crackers* (1930, Paramount).

6372 "Marriage makes a respectable citizen out of a man." For reporter **Walter Catlett**, marriage represents the ultimate surrender to convention. *The Front Page* (1931, United Artists).

6373 "Make sure they're not in love. Get a married couple." Producer **James Cagney** instructs his secretary Joan Blondell to hire a dance team for his new show. *Footlight Parade* (1933, Warner Bros.).

6374 "We're practically marrying a pauper. We're throwing ourselves away just for spite—we don't love that mug, we love you!" **Ruth Donnelly,** who thinks of her daughter Mary Brian as an extension of herself, changes her tune about marrying a twenty-five-thousand-a-year man, when Brian's former suitor James Cagney suddenly becomes rich. *Hard to Handle* (1933, Warner Bros.).

6375 "For as much as Robert and Elizabeth have consented together in holy wedlock, and have witnessed the same before God and this company, I pronounce they be man and wife together. In the name of the Father and of the Son and of the Holy Ghost. Amen. God the Father, God the Son, God the Holy Ghost, bless, preserve and keep that ye may so live together in this life that in the world to come ye may have life everlasting. Amen." Minister **Winter Hall** does the honors for Fredric March as Robert Browning and Norma Shearer as Elizabeth Barrett. *The Barretts of Wimpole Street* (1934, MGM).

6376 "Marriage should be like a ski jump—sudden, swift, reckless! Starting on the heights, leaping into the void! Never knowing the end, never caring!" Swathed in a satin white dressing gown trimmed in mink, movie actress **Margaret Sullavan** gives an interview of questionable sincerity to a movie magazine writer. *The Moon's Our Home* (1936, Paramount).

6377 "I told you I haven't even met her yet, but I'd kind of like to marry her." Falling in love at first glance, **Fred Astaire** informs Edward Everett Horton he's thinking of dancing down the aisle with Ginger Rogers. *Shall We Dance* (1937, RKO).

6378 "I've been everywhere and done everything. . . what's left for me except marriage." **Margaret Lockwood** resignedly entrains for a trip back to England and her fiancé. *The Lady Vanishes* (1938, GB, Gaumont-MGM).

6379 "Mingle with plumbers and you'll marry one, mingle with millionaires and you'll marry one." Posing as a wealthy woman, **Loretta Young** figures it's just as easy to love a rich man as a poor man—but first you have to meet one. *Three Blind Mice* (1938, 20th Century-Fox).

6380 "Well, what difference does it make who you marry—so long as he's a Southerner and thinks like you." **Thomas Mitchell** knows the qualities important in a prospective mate for his daughter Vivien Leigh. *Gone with the Wind* (1939, Selznick-MGM).

6381 "Do you ever shrink from marrying men you don't love?" **Clark Gable** questions Vivien Leigh after she has married her sister Evelyn Keyes' beau Carroll Nye because he owns a store. It's her second marriage of convenience. Conveniently, both men die. *Gone with the Wind* (1939, Selznick-MGM).

6382 "You kissed me. You'll have to marry me now." Shy schoolmaster **Robert Donat** shouts a kind of marriage proposal to Greer Garson at a noisy train station. She accepts. *Goodbye Mr. Chips* (1939, GB, MGM).

6383 "Marriage is no longer the answer to a maiden's prayer." Professional bachelor girl **Loretta Young** writes a popular book entitled, *Spinsters Aren't Spinach. The Doctor Takes a Wife* (1940, Columbia).

6384 "Women got the vote now. . . they don't like bachelors. . . . Marriage has always been the most beautiful setup between the sexes. I know all about it. My parents were married." Bachelor political boss **Akim Tamiroff** urges gubernatorial candidate Brian Donlevy to take a wife for political reasons. *The Great McGinty* (1940, Paramount).

6385 "I had no say in my father's marriage, so why should he in mine?" **Tyrone Power,** being something of a smart aleck, resists the urgings of his mother Janet Beecher to accept his father Montagu Love's wishes and abandon his plans to marry Linda Darnell, the niece of the local tyrant, J. Edward Bromberg. *The Mark of Zorro* (1940, 20th Century-Fox).

6386 "Think of it, Mr. Bennet—three of them married and the other two trembling on the brink!" With the last line of the film, ecstatic mother **Mary Boland** gushes to husband Edmund Gwenn as she takes pleasure in her handiwork of finding husbands for her dowry-less daughters. Earlier in the movie she sang a different tune, lamenting, "Look at them! Five of them without dowries! What's to become of them?" *Pride and Prejudice* (1940, MGM).

6387 "Getting married is serious business. It's kinda formal, like funerals or playing stud poker." Foreman **William Gargan** shares his views on marriage with his boss Charles Laughton, a California-Italian vineyard owner, who has sent away for a mail-order bride. *They Knew What They Wanted* (1940, RKO).

6388 CHARLES PIKE: "I have no right to be in your cabin. . .because I'm married." JEAN HARRINGTON: "But so am I, darling, so am I." **Henry Fonda** and **Barbara Stanwyck** are married to each other, although only Barbara knows it for sure. *The Lady Eve* (1941, Paramount).

6389 "Darling, if you had it all to do over again, would you marry me?" **Carole Lombard** asks a fateful question of Robert Montgomery. Since she always demands complete honesty, he answers, "No." *Mr. and Mrs. Smith* (1941, RKO).

6390 Biff Grimes: "So you don't believe in the institution of marriage?... Don't you want to meet a nice man and have children someday?" Amy Lind: "What's marriage anyhow?... Just a tradition started by cavemen and encouraged by florists and jewelers." **James Cagney** is shocked by **Olivia de Havilland**'s stance. *The Strawberry Blonde* (1941, Warner Bros.).

6391 "I've always heard that the ideal marriage should be something of a mystery." **Merle Oberon**'s marriage to Melvyn Douglas is a mystery to her. So are her hiccups. *That Uncertain Feeling* (1941, United Artists).

6392 "I see marriage as a sort of permanent welding, a growing together of two trees... into a permanent mixed... mass, like a permanent grafting of two trees, like a permanent... graft." Wealthy **Rudy Vallee** seems to be confusing marriage with horticulture. *The Palm Beach Story* (1942, Paramount).

6393 "Always swore I wouldn't. The frightening idea of getting tied down.... Guess there's one thing I didn't figure on—you." Feminist columnist **Katharine Hepburn** accepts when sportswriter Spencer Tracy proposes. *Woman of the Year* (1942, MGM).

6394 Sam Craig: "The outstanding woman of the year isn't a woman at all." Tess Harding: "I thought we had a perfect marriage." Sam: "It wasn't perfect or a marriage." Sports columnist **Spencer Tracy** puts the blame for failure of his marriage to political columnist **Katharine Hepburn** on her career and ineptness at being the "little woman." *Woman of the Year* (1942, MGM).

6395 "Marriage is an agreeable state, is it not?" Passive, sweet **Phyllis Calvert** hopefully asks a maid on her wedding night with James Mason. *The Man in Grey* (1943, GB, Gainsborough-GFD).

6396 "You can bring a minister in the morning if it'll make you feel better about it." When Jack Buetel, as Billy the Kid, is wounded and suffering from chills, **Jane Russell** climbs into bed with him and uses her body to warm him up. After nursing him back to health in her very sweet way, the two fall in love and marry in a secret ceremony. *The Outlaw* (1943, RKO).

6397 "The responsibility for recording a marriage has always been up to the woman. If it wasn't for her, marriage would have disappeared long ago. No man is going to jeopardize his present or poison his future with a lot of little brats hollering around the house unless he's forced to. It's up to the woman to knock him down, hog-tie him and drag him in front of two witnesses immediately, if not sooner." **Alan Bridge** pontificates to man-crazy blonde Betty Hutton and her bitchy younger sister Diana Lynn. *The Miracle of Morgan's Creek* (1944, Paramount).

6398 "No, your look is cordial—not connubial. I've married you, Fanny, but I haven't won you." The only reason selfish beauty Bette Davis married dull businessman **Claude Rains** was to save her beloved brother Richard Waring, who embezzled funds from Rains. *Mr. Skeffington* (1944, Warner Bros.).

6399 "Tell me, Mrs. Wright, does your husband interfere with your marriage?" **Oscar Levant** gets personal with wealthy dilettante Joan Crawford who is trapped in a loveless marriage with Paul Cavanagh. *Humoresque* (1946, Warner Bros.).

6400 Felipe: "Baines, why did you come back from Africa?" Baines: "Oh, to get married, for one thing." Felipe: "Was there no one to marry over there?" Baines: "Plenty, but they weren't white." Felipe: "Must they be white?" Butler **Ralph Richardson** has filled the head of the French ambassador's young son **Bobby Henrey** with stories of his exploits in Africa. *The Fallen Idol* (1948, GB, London Films-British Lion).

6401 "Marriage, what's it supposed to be?... What makes it work out perfect... balance, equality, mutual everything. There's no room in marriage for what used to be known as the little woman. She's got to be as big as the man is... sharing... that's what it takes to make a marriage, keep a marriage from getting sick of all the duties and responsibilities and troubles.... Listen, no part of marriage is the exclusive province of any one sex...." Lawyer **Katharine Hepburn** makes an important point about marriage to her lawyer husband Spencer Tracy. *Adam's Rib* (1949, MGM).

6402 "It's been a rather perfect marriage." Fatally ill **Greer Garson** rhapsodizes about her rather perfect marriage to Walter Pidgeon. *The Miniver Story* (1950, GB, MGM).

6403 "And then I knew what people meant when they said their heart was broken. All that was left of George and me and our marriage was that little pile of ashes. I knew that some way or somehow I had to begin to live again. But right then, all I could do was pray to lose that one day, that one terrifying day." **Loretta Young** burns the letter to the district attorney, sent by her crazed husband Barry Sullivan, who promptly dies of a heart attack. He unjustly accuses her of infidelity with his physician Bruce Cowling and of planning to murder him. The letter was returned to sender because of lack of postage. *Cause for Alarm* (1951, MGM).

6404 "You married? Me neither. Everybody tells you, 'Why don't you get married? You should be married.' My mother. My father. My sister. 'Try and get married.' As if I didn't want to get married! Where do you find a man? You get me a man, and I'll marry him—anything as long as it's got pants." Neurotic shoplifter **Lee Grant** pathetically deplores her single status to captive audience Cathy O'Donnell. *Detective Story* (1951, Paramount).

6405 "Marrying the boss' daughter—the short cut to a career." **Robert Walker** refers to Farley Granger, who wishes to be rid of his tramp of a wife, Laura Elliott, so he can marry Ruth Roman, the daughter of U.S. Senator Leo G. Carroll. *Strangers on a Train* (1951, Warner Bros.).

6406 "Marriage is like a dull meal, with the dessert at the beginning." It seems to be a practiced aphorism of French painter Toulouse Lautrec, played by **Jose Ferrer.** The artist never partook of the meal of marriage. *Moulin Rouge* (1952, GB, Romulus).

6407 "If you'd told me you'd quit your job, we never would've got married." Newlywed **Rand Harper** shouts at her husband Harris Davenport. The honeymoon for the randy couple, who have spent the entire movie in bed, would seem to be over. *Rear Window* (1954, Paramount).

6408 "I now pronounce you men and wives." Preacher **Ian Wolfe** marries six mountain brothers to six town girls in a shotgun marriage with twelve happy participants. *Seven Brides for Seven Brothers* (1954, MGM).

6409 "What is she anyway, a nymphomaniac or something? What'd you marry her for, to wear your label?" Patient **John Kerr** rages at shrink Richard Widmark about his wife Gloria Grahame. *The Cobweb* (1955, MGM).

6410 "Marriage is a funny business. . . . We can starve or we can look for 'it' outside." Discontented married **Gloria Grahame** murmurs to married psychiatrist Charles Boyer. *The Cobweb* (1955, MGM).

6411 MISS ADELAIDE: "In Rhode Island people do not remain engaged for fourteen years. They get married." NATHAN DETROIT: "So how come it's such a small state?" New York showgirl **Vivian Blaine** has been engaged to Broadway hustler **Frank Sinatra** for fourteen years. *Guys and Dolls* (1955, MGM).

6412 "Marriage is a comfortable way to spend the winter." **Edmund Gwenn** congratulates John Forsythe who plans to marry Shirley MacLaine. Gwenn has his

eye on Mildred Natwick. *The Trouble with Harry* (1955, Paramount).

6413 "I just got to feel that whomever I marry has some real regard for me, aside from all that lovin' stuff." The sad comment of her character Cherie could have been made by **Marilyn Monroe** as well. *Bus Stop* (1956, 20th Century-Fox).

6414 "I wanted to marry her when I first saw the moonlight shining on the barrel of her father's shotgun." Syrian peddler **Eddie Albert** tells Gordon MacRae that his love for farmer's daughter Gloria Grahame was heightened by her father James Whitmore's weapon. *Oklahoma!* (1956, Magna).

6415 "Used to have a boyfriend was a cowboy. Met him in Colorado. He was in love with me because I was an older woman and had some sense. . . . Took me up in the mountains one night and wanted to marry me, right there on the mountain top. He said the stars'd be our preacher and the moon our best man. Did you ever hear such talk?" Spinster school teacher **Rosalind Russell** entertains boarding house regulars with romantic tales that probably were just that. *Picnic* (1955, Columbia).

6416 "I didn't marry a man, did I? I married a middleweight." **Pier Angeli** sighs to her husband Paul Newman, portraying middleweight boxer Rocky Graziano. *Somebody Up There Likes Me* (1956, MGM).

6417 "On Monday, August twenty-fourth of this year, the case of Frank Flannagan and Ariane Chavasse came up before the superior judge in Cannes. They are now married, serving a life sentence in New York, state of New York, U.S.A." French private investigator **Maurice Chevalier** announces the marriage of his young daughter Audrey Hepburn to one-time roué Gary Cooper, looking every bit old enough to be her father—maybe her grandfather. *Love in the Afternoon* (1957, Allied Artists).

6418 BERT: "She's different. The first kiss and she'll expect an engagement ring." ARTHUR: "I take my tip from the fishes. Never bite unless the bait is good. I won't get married until I'm good and ready." As they fish along a lonely canal, **Norman Rossington** warns his cousin **Albert Finney** that Shirley Anne Field is not a girl who can be trifled with. *Saturday Night and Sunday Morning* (1960, GB, Woodfall-Continental Distribution).

6419 "Marriage is forever. It's like cement." **Peter O'Toole** dreads the thought of marriage, even to lovely Romy Schneider. *What's New, Pussycat?* (1965, United Artists).

6420 CLYDE BARROW: "Hey, you're fillin' out there. Must be that prison food." BUCK BARROW: "Hell, no! It's married life. You know what they say, it's the face powder that gets a man interested, but it's the baking powder that keeps him at home." **Warren Beatty** learns that marriage to Estelle Parsons agrees with brother **Gene Hackman**. *Bonnie and Clyde* (1967, Warner Bros.).

6421 MARK WALLACE: "Did we get married?" JOANNA WALLACE: "Yes, don't you remember? When the sex stopped being fun?" MARK: "Oh, yeah, when it got official." The marriage of **Albert Finney** and **Audrey Hepburn** is in trouble. *Two for the Road* (1967, GB, 20th Century-Fox).

6422 "Marriage is not a pleasing institution but right now it's the only game in town, and we're gonna play it." At the end of the movie, **Warren Beatty** announces to Elizabeth Taylor that he's hers. *The Only Game in Town* (1970, 20th Century-Fox).

6423 "I'd get married in a minute if I could find the right girl." Poor **Jack Nicholson,** seeking perfect sex, will never find a woman who loves him as much as he does. *Carnal Knowledge* (1971, Avco Embassy).

6424 LEO: "Why don't you marry Ted?" MARIAN: "Because I can't." LEO: "Then why are you marrying Trimmington?" MARIAN: "Because I must." Go-between **Dominic Guard** is too young to understand why **Julie Christie** cannot marry her lover, farmer Alan Bates, but must marry the more suitable Edward Fox. *The Go-Between* (1971, GB, MGM-EMI-Columbia).

6425 "Never marry a wop—they treat their wives like shit." Over-the-hill actress **Marianna Hill** can't be controlled by her husband John Cazale. *The Godfather, Part II* (1974, Paramount).

6426 "You marry it the way a nun marries Jesus." Music teacher **Lee Remick** points her pupil Amy Irving toward a piano. Her meaning is probably lost on the nice Jewish girl. *The Competition* (1980, Columbia).

6427 "Everything seems disposable. I feel that we must be the last married couple in America." **Natalie Wood** deplores the situation to her husband George Segal as all their closest friends split, even the homosexual couple down the street. *The Last Married Couple in America* (1980, Universal).

6428 "If I'm not going to be married I don't know what I'm supposed to do with myself. . . . I've never belonged to someone. . . . Did you see that movie, *An Unmarried Woman?* I didn't get it. If I'd been that woman, I'd have been Mrs. Alan Bates so fast that guy wouldn't know what hit him." **Goldie Hawn**'s bridegroom, Albert Brooks, dies of a heart attack as they are having sex in an automobile while their wedding reception is being held nearby. She explains her ideas of marriage to a call-in radio talk show host. Apparently Goldie's character and that of Jill Clayburgh have different notions of independence. *Private Benjamin* (1980, Warner Bros.).

6429 "I'm a married woman. . . meaning I'm not looking for company." **Kathleen Turner** brushes off the advances of lawyer William Hurt. *Body Heat* (1981, Warner Bros.).

6430 GEORGIA: "Why don't we get married?" JIMMY: "Because I'm gay and you're an alcoholic and we'd have trouble getting our kids in a decent school." Reformed lush **Marsha Mason** is given sound reasons by aspiring actor **James Coco** for why they shouldn't become Mr. and Mrs. *Only When I Laugh* (1981, Columbia).

6431 "We were a very good marriage. Everyone said so, and not just the magazines, even our friends." Trashy novelist **Candice Bergen** speaks of her marriage with her ex, David Selby, to her long-time friend, "serious" writer Jacqueline Bisset. *Rich and Famous* (1981, MGM-United Artists).

6432 "I was once married. Now I just lease." Hit man **Walter Matthau**'s job is hampered by Jack Lemmon, who, because of his miserable marriage, wants to kill himself. *Buddy, Buddy* (1982, MGM-United Artists).

6433 "I don't know, but it's good." **Daniel Stern** gives a qualified answer when Steve Guttenberg asks him if he's happy with his marriage to Ellen Barkin. *Diner* (1982, MGM-United Artists).

6434 ARIEL: "How is your marriage?" ANDREW: "It's fine. It's not working, but it's fine." **Mia Farrow** questions **Woody Allen** about his marriage to Mary Steenburgen. *A Midsummer Night's Sex Comedy* (1982, Orion/Warner Bros.).

6435 "Marriage is the death of hope." Physician **Tony Roberts** explains why he has remained a bachelor. *A Midsummer Night's Sex Comedy* (1982, Orion/Warner Bros.).

6436 "I asked her to marry me once. She turned me down." Diminutive **Linda Hunt,** playing a male photographer, speaks of stunning Sigourney Weaver to Australian journalist Mel Gibson. *The Year of Living Dangerously* (1983, Australia, MGM).

6437 "I've ruined too many marriages to ever have one of my own." Bar owner and former streetwalker **Lesley Ann Warren** has what she considers a good reason for never having married. *Choose Me* (1984, Island Alive).

6438 "We started talking and it stopped working." **Rae Dawn Chong**'s marriage to Patrick Bauchau started to go down the drain when their sexual activity slowed down. *Choose Me* (1984, Island Alive).

6439 LIZ GARCIA: "When are we going to get married, Rudy?" RUDY VELOZ: "We're going to get married. There's no escaping it." LIZ: "I have nothing but you, Rudy." RUDY: "You're a very lucky person." **Elizabeth Pena** wants more than just being Latino musician **Ruben Blades**' girl friend. *Crossover Dreams* (1985, New Films).

6440 "I guess something in our marriage just died. I didn't know it—he did." **Ellen Burstyn** resignedly rationalizes when her husband of thirty years, Gene Hackman, wants out of their marriage. *Twice in a Lifetime* (1985, Yorkin).

6441 "We got a good life, me and her. We don't talk much, we don't go out much, but I can't complain." **Jason Miller** doesn't expect much from his marriage to Gena Rowlands. *Light of Day* (1987, Tri-Star).

6442 "You know what these small towns are like. A girl spends her entire time in high school trying to marry some guy and spends the rest of her life trying to figure out why." **Gene Hackman** accounts for Willem Dafoe how someone as decent and sensitive as Frances McDormand could marry sadistic, ignorant, bigoted sheriff's deputy Brad Dourif. *Mississippi Burning* (1988, Orion).

6443 "Do you like marriage? What do you like about it?" The first time he meets her, **James Spader** questions Andie MacDowell almost as if he were a nosy reporter, determined to get a story. *sex, lies and videotape* (1989, Miramax).

6444 "If love is blind. . . marriage is like having a stroke." To divorce lawyer **Danny De Vito** marriage is an affliction. *The War of the Roses* (1989, 20th Century-Fox).

6445 "What did they do to make him get married this time? Stick a cannon up his ass?" Motion picture executive **Robert Loggia** is outraged that for the second time Alec Baldwin has stood up Loggia's daughter to marry Kim Basinger. *The Marrying Man* (1991, Hollywood Pictures/Buena Vista).

Martyrs *see* RELIGIONS, SACRIFICES, SAINTS

Masculinity

see also BOYS, MEN

6446 SALA POST: "You left your boyhood behind you." PARRISH MCLEAN: "Yes, one night under the ice at the North Pole. . . it separated the men from the boys." Tobacco farmer **Dean Jagger** welcomes back **Troy Donahue** to the Connecticut River Valley tobacco region after the latter spends two years in the navy. The experience didn't loosen Donahue up. He's as wooden as ever. *Parrish* (1961, Warner Bros.).

6447 "Honey, I'm more man than you'll ever be and more woman than you'll ever get." Black transvestite **Antonio Fargas** tells off a black militant who claims Fargas is just one more example of how the white man has corrupted the black man, robbing him of his masculinity. *Car Wash* (1976, Universal).

6448 "I was a better man with you as a woman than I ever was for a woman as a man. I just have to learn to do it without a dress." **Dustin Hoffman** assesses his masculinity for Jessica Lange after his stint masquerading as a woman in a television soap is exposed. *Tootsie* (1982, Columbia).

6449 VALENTIN ARREGUI: "And what's masculine in your terms?" LUIS MOLINA: "It's a lot of things, but for me. . . to be marvelous-looking and strong, but without making any fuss about it, and also walking very tall. . . walking absolutely straight, not afraid to say anything. And it's knowing what you want, where you're going." VALENTIN: "That's pure fantasy, that type doesn't exist." Political prisoner **Raul Julia** rejects homosexual prisoner **William Hurt**'s notion of masculinity. *The Kiss of the Spider Woman* (1985, U.S.-Brazil, Island Alive).

Masochism *see* HURT AND HURTING, PAINS, PERVERSIONS, PLEASURES, SEX AND SEXUALITY

Masters

see also CONTROL, LEADERSHIP AND LEADERS, LEARNING AND LESSONS, OWNERSHIP, SLAVERY AND SLAVES, TEACHING AND TEACHERS, VICTORIES

6450 "I am Mata Hari, my own master." World War I spy **Greta Garbo** only thinks she's her own master. *Mata Hari* (1932, MGM).

6451 "Here on the quiet page I am master, just as I'm master in the darkroom. . . . I shuffle like cards the lives I deal with, people who will become other people, people who will become old, become ghosts, betray their dreams." As he types, dwarf cameraman Billy Kwan, played by **Linda Hunt,**

muses on his role as puppet master. *The Year of Living Dangerously* (1983, Australia, MGM).

6452 "All you have to do is command me. You created me. You are my master." Luscious **Kelly LeBrock** is the fantasy woman created by horny teenagers Anthony Michael Hall and Ilan Mitchell-Smith. *Weird Science* (1985, Universal).

Masturbation *see* SEX AND SEXUALITY

Mathematics

see also ARGUMENTS, DETECTIVES AND DEDUCTION, LOGIC, PROBABILITY AND STATISTICS, PROOFS, RELATIONSHIPS, SCIENCE AND SCIENTISTS, TIME

6453 "In international diplomacy the shortest distance between two points is never a straight line." Malevolent Nazi spy **Sydney Greenstreet** makes a geometric comparison to his work. Except in a Euclidean plane, the shortest distance between two points is seldom a straight line. *Background to Danger* (1943, Warner Bros.).

6454 "Numbers sanctify." Elegant serial killer of foolish women, **Charles Chaplin** calls people hypocritical for being outraged with his few murders while extolling genocide by warring nations. *Monsieur Verdoux* (1947, United Artists).

6455 TED HIGGINS: "What would you have if you had ten dollars in one pants' pocket and five dollars in the other?" HOMER HINCHCLIFFE: "Somebody else's pants on." **Bud Abbott** finds that **Lou Costello** doesn't know his arithmetic but he knows his finances. *The Noose Hangs High* (1948, Eagle-Lion).

6456 ALVY SINGER: "Hardly ever, maybe three times a week." ANNIE HALL: "Constantly, I'd say three times a week." In a split screen, **Woody Allen** and **Diane Keaton** respond to the questions of their analysts about the frequency of their lovemaking. It demonstrates that the same number can represent different amounts depending on one's perspective. *Annie Hall* (1977, United Artists).

6457 "A line has length, but no breadth. If you could see it, it wouldn't be a line." In 1930, Russian emigré **Dirk Bogarde** gives an accurate geometry lesson. *Despair* (1979, West Germany, New Line).

6458 "There is a sixth dimension beyond that which is known to man. It is a dimension as vast as space and timeless as infinity. It is an area that we call the Twilight Zone." Narrator **Burgess Meredith** launches into the late Rod Serling's famous monologue at the beginning of the film based on the classic television series. There is no mathematical significance to Serling's description. *Twilight Zone—The Movie* (1983, Warner Bros.).

6459 "Tonight I'm going for No. 100." **Mark McKelvey** brags to his friend Steve Irlen about his numerous sexual conquests. The callous young man, who sees women as mere numbers, pays the ultimate penalty for indiscriminate sex—he contracts AIDS and dies. The film seems to suggest that some people deserve to die from AIDS. No one deserves to die from AIDS. *On the Make* (1989, Taurus).

Matters *see* SIGNIFICANCE

Maturity and Immaturity

see also AGE AND AGING, CHILDREN AND CHILDHOOD, GROWTH AND DEVELOPMENT, YOUTH

6460 "He never grew up—the world just grew up around him." **Alida Valli** excuses monstrous black marketeer Orson Welles' crimes for his one-time friend, pulp-fiction writer Joseph Cotten. *The Third Man* (1949, GB, Korda-Selznick).

6461 "I come from such a different world. You and I would only end in nothing. All my life I've stayed at parties too long because I didn't know when to go. Now, with you, I've grown up. I think I do know when to." American spinster **Katharine Hepburn** leaves Venice and her married Italian lover Rossano Brazzi. *Summertime* (1955, Lopert-Korda).

6462 "You and Skipper and millions like you live in a kid's world, playing games, touchdowns, no responsibilities." **Burl Ives,** as Big Daddy, dismisses the younger generation for their preoccupation with games. *Cat on a Hot Tin Roof* (1958, MGM).

6463 "You just haven't managed to grow up, Mrs. Treadwell of Murray Hill, Virginia. You can paint your toenails green. You know how it ends, don't you? Alone—sitting in a cafe, with a paid escort." **Vivien Leigh** speaks of her immaturity to her reflection in a mirror. *Ship of Fools* (1965, Columbia).

6464 FIELDING MELLISH: "How am I immature?" NANCY: "Emotionally, sexually and intellectually." FIELDING: "Yeah, but in what other ways?" **Woody Allen** tries to prevent girl friend **Louise Lasser** from giving him the brush-off. *Bananas* (1971, United Artists).

6465 "His gun made him older." Police detective **Charles Bronson** gives an excuse for killing a fleeing 17-year-old suspect. *The Stone Killer* (1973, Columbia).

6466 "You're the winner of the Zelda Fitzgerald Emotional Maturity Award." **Woody Allen** makes the presentation to Diane Keaton, who lives in a world of her own making. *Manhattan* (1979, United Artists).

6467 "Don't be so mature." Finally knowing that he loves and wants to marry her, **Woody Allen** wistfully speaks to 17-year-old Mariel Hemingway who assures him that a six-month separation while she's in England won't end what they have. *Manhattan* (1979, United Artists).

6468 "You're so immature." Whining **Fran Drescher** yells at Robert Wuhl when he experiences premature ejaculation. *The Hollywood Knights* (1980, Columbia).

6469 "Oh, George, you're so much more mature." Married housewife **Barbra Streisand** prefers Gene Hackman over his son Dennis Quaid, with whom she was having an affair. *All Night Long* (1981, Universal).

6470 "Ten years old—with the body of a woman of 13!" Adolescent **Douglas Sannachan** makes a mature observation about the physical "maturity" of young Allison Forster. *Gregory's Girl* (1982, Scottish, Lake Film Production-Goldwyn).

6471 "I don't take any of them seriously. They still got their mother's milk dribbling down their chins." Bored barmaid **Joanne Whalley** pays no attention to the crude propositions of male customers in a tawdry London nightclub. *Dance with a Stranger* (1985, GB, First Film-Goldwyn).

6472 VICOMTE DE VALMONT: "Why do you suppose we only feel compelled to chase the ones who run away?" MARQUISE DE MERTEUIL: "Immaturity?" Unscrupulous colleagues in sexual deceit **Glenn Close** and **John Malkovich** compare notes. *Dangerous Liaisons* (1988, Warner Bros.).

Maxims *see* PROVERBS AND SAYINGS, QUOTATIONS

Meanings *see* ABSURDITIES, EXPLANATIONS, SENSE AND SENSIBILITY, SIGNIFICANCE, UNDERSTANDINGS AND MISUNDERSTANDINGS

Measurements *see* MATHEMATICS

Medicine

see also DIAGNOSIS, DISEASES, DOCTORS AND DENTISTS, HEALTH, PATIENTS, PSYCHOLOGY AND PSYCHIATRY, SICKNESS

6473 "Hazel, you've got what is known in medicine as a hangover." Physician **Charles Winninger** diag-

noses a hurting Carole Lombard. *Nothing Sacred* (1937, Selznick/United Artists).

6474 "You act on me just like a tonic." **Carroll Nye** believes that Vivien Leigh is good medicine following her tour of his Atlanta store and lumber mill, and her invitation to dinner and a visit. *Gone with the Wind* (1939, Selznick-MGM).

6475 CISCO KID: "What do you call the [animal's] sickness?" DR. VALEGRA: "We have not completed our diagnosis." CISCO KID: "Ah, you do not know the sickness, but you know the remedy." When **Gilbert Roland** sees a child crying because his goat is sick, he pays a visit to the doctor, **Martin Garralaga.** The latter offers to sell Roland medicine for the goat that he says is costly. Roland takes the medicine without paying. *Beauty and the Bandit* (1946, Monogram).

6476 "Ever see any botched plastic jobs?" Taxi driver **Tom D'Andrea** has arranged for escaped con Humphrey Bogart to be given a new face by discredited plastic surgeon Houseley Stevenson. *Dark Passage* (1947, Warner Bros.).

6477 "White Man's medicine is strong. Nothing can stop them." Apparently the Indians were too polite to laugh in the face of **Gary Cooper** when he delivered this condescending line in their camp. *Unconquered* (1947, Paramount).

6478 "Out here we have three cures for everything: quinine, iodine and castor oil." It is African big game hunter **Clark Gable**'s reply when an angry Grace Kelly asks if he's not going to do anything else for her husband Donald Sinden who has passed out due to a reaction to a tsetse fly innoculation. *Mogambo* (1953, MGM).

6479 "I practice good medicine on good people, bad medicine on bad people." Native American medicine man **Chief Dan George** explains his work to Art Carney. *Harry and Tonto* (1974, 20th Century-Fox).

6480 "Don't sew up anything that belongs open." **Billy Crystal** pleads with a Spanish doctor who doesn't understand English. Crystal has been gored by a bull in the rear while running with the bulls in the streets of Pamplona. *City Slickers* (1991, Columbia).

Mediocrity

see also ORDINARINESS, SUPERIORITY AND INFERIORITY

6481 "How is it one becomes second-rate, can you answer me that? How does the dust fall? When has one lost? First, I'm a prince, the heir to the kingdom. Suddenly, before I know it, I am deposed. Death taps me on the shoulder. The room is cold and we can't pay for the wood. I'm ugly and unkind. And I'm unkindest to the one person who cares for me. You can never forgive me. I'm a shitter and a rotter." Mediocre academic **Boerje Ahlstedt** laments to his wife Christina Schollin. *Fanny and Alexander* (1983, Sweden-Fr.-Ger., Embassy).

6482 "Mediocrities everywhere—now and to come, I absolve you all." Antonio Salieri, played by **F. Murray Abraham,** feels God has made him unfairly inferior to Wolfgang Amadeus Mozart, played by Tom Hulce. Salieri was not a mediocre talent. *Amadeus* (1984, Orion).

Meditation *see* MINDS, THINKING AND THOUGHTS

Meetings

see also MEN AND WOMEN, PEOPLE

6483 GENERAL VON HINDAU: "What a charming evening we might have had if you had not been a spy and I a traitor." X-27: "Then we might never have met." Exposed as a traitor working for the Russians, Austrian General **Warner Oland** politely excuses himself to Austrian agent **Marlene Dietrich** and goes into the next room and blows out his brains. *Dishonored* (1931, Paramount).

6484 OLLIE: "You never met my wife, did you?" STAN: "Yes, I never did." A gentle exchange between **Oliver Hardy** and **Stan Laurel**. *Helpmates* (1932, Roach).

6485 "Next time you drop in, bring your folks." It's the cute meet of **Clark Gable** and Claudette Colbert when she trips and falls into his lap while maneuvering down the aisle of a moving bus. *It Happened One Night* (1934, Columbia).

6486 "I hate meeting like this, in out-of-the-way places and dark corners." **Ingrid Bergman**'s cliché might be the lament of any young woman having an affair with an older married man. Hers is spoken to Leslie Howard. *Intermezzo* (1939, Selznick-United Artists).

6487 "I'd like to meet the man who wouldn't take orders from me." **Googie Withers** is the indomitable owner of a sheep farm on Romney Marshes. *The Loves of Joanna Godden* (1946, GB, Ealing-GFD).

6488 "Every night I went to meet her. How did I know she'd ever show up? I didn't. What stopped her from taking a boat to Chile or Guatemala? Nothing. How big a chump can you get to be? I was

finding out. And then she'd come along like school was out, and everything else was just smooth sailing on the sea." While in Acapulco, **Robert Mitchum** falls for Jane Greer, mobster Kirk Douglas' mistress who Mitchum has been hired to find and return to Douglas. *Out of the Past* (1947, RKO).

6489 "I'd just helped Ed Hickey into a taxi. Ed had been mixing his drinks, and I felt he needed conveying. I started to walk down the street when I heard a voice saying: 'Good evening, Mr. Dowd.' I turned, and there was this big white rabbit leaning against a lamppost. Well, I thought nothing of that! Because when you lived in a town as long as I've lived in this one, you get used to the fact that everybody knows your name. . . ." **James Stewart,** masterfully playing gentle madman Elwood P. Dowd, describes for Dr. Charles Drake and nurse Peggy Dow how he first met his best friend, a six-foot three-inch white rabbit named Harvey. *Harvey* (1950, Universal-International).

6490 ROOM CLERK: "Can I help you, sir!" BEN BRADDOCK: "What? Oh—no—I'm just. . . ." CLERK: "Are you here for an affair, sir?" Does room clerk **Buck Henry** read **Dustin Hoffman**'s mind? No, he's merely asking if Hoffman is at the hotel to attend one of the several meetings or parties being held there. *The Graduate* (1967, Embassy).

6491 "It was like standing in an enchanted world." **Beryl Reid** recalls the first time she met Susannah York, who became her lover. *The Killing of Sister George* (1969, Palomar).

6492 JENNY CAVILLERI BARRETT: "Dying is like falling off a cliff.You've never fallen off a cliff in your life, have you, Olllie?" OLIVER BARRETT IV: "Yes, I did. When I met you." Dying **Ali MacGraw** makes an analogy but seems to feel her husband **Ryan O'Neal** won't understand it. *Love Story* (1970, Paramount).

6493 MILENA FLAHERTY: "If we're gonna meet, it might as well be now." DR. ALEX LINDEN: "If we don't meet, there could always be the possibility that it would have been perfect." Licking her lips, American divorcée **Theresa Russell** relentlessly pursues Vienna psychoanalyst and voyeur **Art Garfunkel.** She blocks his exit from a party by buttressing her body across a doorway. *Bad Timing: A Sensual Obsession* (1980, GB, Rank).

6494 "How nice to meet you. Usually we must go to a bowling alley to meet a woman of your calibre." Valet **John Gielgud** flings a tart zinger when his master Dudley Moore introduces him to shoplifter Liza Minnelli that he's just met. *Arthur* (1981, Warner Bros.).

6495 "I met Ethel when I was a principal and she was a substitute teacher. She was about the prettiest thing I'd ever seen. So I told her she made my heart go pitter-pat. She fell in love with me immediately." Eighty-year-old **Henry Fonda** tells teenager Doug McKeon how he met his wife Katharine Hepburn. *On Golden Pond* (1981, Universal).

6496 "Look at that guy. He's got a girl. He wasn't born with his arm around her—he must have met her somewhere." Lonely **Steve Martin** grouses to lonely Charles Grodin about meeting girls. *The Lonely Guy* (1984, Universal).

6497 "I want to meet a total bonehead with the most incredible bod." Florida bound co-ed **Lynn-Holly Johnson** is not looking for a meaningful relationship during her spring break vacation. *Where the Boys Are '84* (1984, ITC).

6498 "And then through the doorway...I see this girl...she just appears. She's just standing there, staring at me and I'm staring back at her and we can't take our eyes off each other. It was like we knew each other from somewhere but we couldn't place where. But the second we saw each other, the very second, we knew we'd never stop being in love." **Sam Shepard** describes his first sighting of Kim Basinger, who becomes the love of his life. Only later will he learn that she is his half-sister. *Fool for Love* (1985, Cannon).

6499 "Holy cow, Charlie, just tell me where you want to meet!" With the film's last line, **Anjelica Huston** jumps at the chance to get back together with one-time lover Jack Nicholson. *Prizzi's Honor* (1985, 20th Century-Fox).

6500 "I don't want to be without you either. Do you think that we could find a place where we can meet, not in silence and not in sound?" The place that **William Hurt** seeks to be with deaf Marlee Matlin is not necessarily a physical place. *Children of a Lesser God* (1986, Paramount).

6501 "I'll meet you at the place near the thing where we went that time." Holly Hunter knows precisely what location **Albert Brooks** is talking about. *Broadcast News* (1987, 20th Century-Fox).

6502 "Tomas was sent to a spatown to perform an operation. It was there that Tomas meets the exceptional young woman who changes the course of his existence, forever altering one aspect of what has seemed to be his lightness of being." A title card tells of Daniel Day-Lewis' encounter with Juliette Binoche. *The Unbearable Lightness of Being* (1988, Orion).

6503 "If there's a God, I'd like to meet the dude." **Mickey Rourke**'s character delivers this line. *Harley Davidson and the Marlboro Man* (1991, MGM).

Melodrama *see* DRAMA AND MELODRAMA, EMOTIONS, EXTRAVAGANCES, ROMANCES, THEATERS

Memory and Memorization

see also FORGETFULNESS AND FORGETTING, NOSTALGIA, PAST, REMINDERS

6504 "You will not remember what I show you now. Yet I shall awaken memories of love and crime and death." In his commanding sepulchral voice, High Priest **Boris Karloff** instructs Zita Johann, the reincarnation of a long dead Egyptian princess. *The Mummy* (1932, Universal).

6505 "I have been memorizing this room. In the future, in my memory, I shall live a great deal in this room." Swedish queen **Greta Garbo** refers to the room where she and John Gilbert spend many happy hours making love. *Queen Christina* (1933, MGM).

6506 "Remember me? I'm the fellow you slept with last night." Claudette Colbert awakens to find that during the night she snuggled into the arms of fellow passenger **Clark Gable** who sat next to her on a bus. *It Happened One Night* (1934, Columbia).

6507 "I remember thinking how hot it was and wondering how long we'd been away—when it happened...I heard a crack—like a stick breaking—and all of a sudden the fellow next to me stopped talking and fell over on his side...." A wounded **Henry Fonda** tells his wife Claudette Colbert of the historic moment the battle with the Indians in upstate New York began. *Drums Along the Mohawk* (1939, 20th Century-Fox).

6508 "I will never forget your faces. In my mind you remain boys. Remember me sometimes. I shall remember you." Retiring Latin master **Robert Donat** says farewell to his assembled students. In the musical remake, **Peter O'Toole** put it as follows: "When you come to see me in the after years, as I hope some of you will, and you're all very grand and grown up, I may well not recognize you. And you'll say, 'Poor old boy, his memory's gone!' But, you see, I will remember you all perfectly well, because I'll remember you as you are now. That's the point. In my mind you never grow up at all. I get older.... But you will always stay the same, and you always will, and in that I shall find great comfort in days to come. So you see, this isn't really goodbye at all. Simply au revoir." *Goodbye Mr. Chips* (1939, MGM); (1969, MGM).

6509 "I'm trying to memorize your face. I'm trying to memorize everything about you so that, no matter what happens, I won't forget you." **Robert Montgomery** knows that the body he's inhabiting is only a temporary home. He wills it that his love for Evelyn Keyes be so strong that it will survive when he finds his permanent physical home. *Here Comes Mr. Jordan* (1941, Columbia).

6510 "Memory. Strange that the mind will forget so much of what only this moment has passed and yet hold clear and bright the memory of what happened years ago—of men and women long since dead. Who shall say what is real and what is not?" Narrator **Irving Pichel,** as the adult Huw Morgan, believes that memory is often a function of intensity, whether it be love, happiness, pain or sorrow. *How Green Was My Valley* (1941, 20th Century-Fox).

6511 "I remember every detail. The Germans wore grey. You wore blue." **Humphrey Bogart** sarcastically recalls how Ingrid Bergman deserted him just as they were planning to escape together before the Nazis entered Paris. *Casablanca* (1942, Warner Bros.).

6512 "I was thinking: 'Now I won't have to say goodbye to Johnny.' I remembered him in Berlin, crazy song he always sang. I used to say, 'You drive me nuts with it.' Yeah, I used to say to him. . . well, let's just say I remember Johnny—laughing, tough and lonesome. Let's just say that. But I knew all at once I had a job. They don't give the Congressional Medal to dead guys wanted for murder, but he was gonna get it even if he got it on his grave. And I was going after whoever tries to gyp him out of it." In voice-over, **Humphrey Bogart** makes a pledge regarding his close friend William Prince, who disappeared before he could be decorated in Washington, D.C. after World War II. *Dead Reckoning* (1947, Columbia).

6513 "Try to remember that though ignorance becomes a Southern gentleman, cowardice does not." **Fredric March** advises his cowardly, stupid son Dan Duryea to show some fortitude. *Another Part of the Forest* (1948, Universal).

6514 "He draws from the left, so lean to the right./There's a wind from the east, so aim to the west./He crouches when he shoots, so stand on your toes." These are three bits of contradictory and confusing advice **Bob Hope** tries to remember as he prepares to face a gunfighter. *The Paleface* (1948, Paramount).

6515 "My memoirs. My memoirs. My memoirs. My memoirs." Having been reprieved and freed just before he is to be executed for murder, **Dennis Price** realizes that he's left his memoirs in his cell. In them he proudly details how he murdered his relatives who stood between him and a dukeship. *Kind Hearts and Coronets* (1949, GB, Eagle-Lion-GFD).

6516 "Ever have a tune running through your head and you can't remember the words?" Assistant District Attorney **Humphrey Bogart** racks his brain, certain that he's overlooked a crucial fact that he can use in his case against Everett Sloane, founder of Murder, Inc. *The Enforcer* (1950, United States Pictures).

6517 "I don't remember a lot of things." **Barbara Stanwyck** demonstrates how valuable she can be. *Clash by Night* (1952, RKO).

6518 "Well, here, here we are, Rachel. Look at them. Some of those good people feel sorry for me. More fools, they. They don't know what memories I've brought with me. They can't see the way you looked that first day when we met when our whole lives lay ahead of us. I remember the way the wind blew your hair back sittin' there in the prow of that old riverboat, and the look of trust that was always there when there was danger to face. What a vision you were at the top of those stairs. And the way you looked with Lincoya crowdin' his poor little life into a few short years. And the way you always ran to me when I came home again. The way you ran to me. Why, I have enough memories to sustain me all the days of my life." **Charlton Heston** portrays Andrew Jackson, who must enter the White House without his beloved wife played by Susan Hayward. She died between the time of the election and his inauguration. *The President's Lady* (1953, 20th Century-Fox).

6519 "The pellet with the poison is in the chalice from the palace. The vessel with the pestle has the brew that is true." It's the mnemonic taught to Danny Kaye by **Mildred Natwick.** Just when he learns it, the vessel with the pestle is replaced by "the flagon with a dragon." *The Court Jester* (1956, Paramount).

6520 "This is the way I remember it—definitely." **Rocky Graziano**'s voice introduces the story of his life and career as a boxer. He is portrayed with gusto by Paul Newman. James Dean was slated to play the role. *Somebody Up There Likes Me* (1956, MGM).

6521 "Winter must be cold for those with no warm memories. We've already missed the spring." **Debo-**

rah **Kerr** refers to her mid-life affair with Cary Grant. *An Affair to Remember* (1957, 20th Century-Fox).

6522 "I'll remember you, honey. You're the one that got away." **Paul Newman** salutes cook and housekeeper Patricia Neal who leaves the ranch after he tries to rape her. *Hud* (1963, Paramount).

6523 "I'm sorry. I never remember a face." Parisian streetwalker **Shirley MacLaine** disappoints a former customer who asks if she remembers him. *Irma la Douce* (1963, United Artists).

6524 "Remember the Spanish word for 'No' is 'No.'" Career girl **Ann-Margret** offers some friendly advice to Carol Lynley and Pamela Tiffin who have recently arrived in Madrid. *The Pleasure Seekers* (1964, 20th Century-Fox).

6525 "That's the easiest piece I could remember. I think I first played it when I was about eight years old. In this room. The whole family gathered. Plus their friends. Plus people from town. I was all got up in this suit and bow tie. If I remember correctly. . . that time I let go a resounding fart at the end." **Jack Nicholson** recalls a past musical triumph for Susan Anspach. *Five Easy Pieces* (1970, Columbia).

6526 "Some of us are cursed with memories like fly-paper." **Robert Stephens,** as Sherlock Holmes, reveals to Colin Blakely, as Dr. Watson, how painful memory is to him. *The Private Life of Sherlock Holmes* (1970, GB, United Artists).

6527 "I will not try to explain what happened last night because I know that in time you will find a proper way in which to remember it." It's part of a note left by **Jennifer O'Neill** for 15-year-old Gary Grimes, who she took to her bed in a moment of vulnerability upon learning of the death of her young soldier husband. *Summer of '42* (1971, Warner Bros.).

6528 "My father was a. . . a drunk, whore-fucker, bar fighter, super masculine, and he was tough. . . . My mother was. . . very poetic, also drunk, and my memories 'bout when I was a kid was of her being arrested nude." **Marlon Brando** wistfully remembers his parents and childhood which in part helps explain his bizarre behavior. *Last Tango in Paris* (1972, Fr.-Italy-U.S., Les Artistes Associes-PEA-United Artists).

6529 "Remember the cross is a plus sign." Pastor **Thayer David** preaches the profit motive to his parishioners. *Fun with Dick and Jane* (1977, Columbia).

6530 "You went through a very trying ordeal and your mind is bogged down with a closetful of memories." Her psychiatrist explains why Sallee Elyse is having trouble coping after a traumatic gang rape. When her mind snaps, she gets even. *Demented* (1980, Four Features Partners).

6531 "I treated myself to a taxi. I rode through the city streets. There wasn't a street, there wasn't a building that wasn't connected to some memory in my mind. There I was buying a suit with my father. There I was having an ice cream soda after school. When I finally came in, Debby was home from work. I told her everything about my dinner with Andre." Playwright/actor **Wallace Shawn** goes home from his dinner with his old friend, theater director Andre Gregory. *My Dinner with Andre* (1981, New Yorker).

6532 "The memory dims like a camp fire at sunrise." Slightly kookie old street person **Rory Calhoun** thinks he's old-time Western scout Kit Carson. *Angel* (1983, New World).

6533 "I remember your hand as a boy. It was small and firm and dry." Ancient **Gunn Wallgren** holds the hand of the ghost of her deceased son Allan Edwall. *Fanny and Alexander* (1983, Sweden-Fr.-Ger., Persona Film-Embassy).

6534 "We finally got our revenge. We managed to make it on our own. I got a job to help put Chris through medical school. Little Carrie grew up but she was never truly healthy. I even started dancing again. We left the past behind, all except the memories, my mother, grandmother, and the attic. I sometimes wonder if grandmother is still alive, still presiding over Foxworth Hall, still awaiting my return." **Kristy Swanson** reflects on her fortune-hunting mother Victoria Tennant and her evil grandmother Louise Fletcher in a film version of the V.C. Andrews' horror story, popular with adolescent girls. *Flowers in the Attic* (1987, New World).

6535 "I knew him. I won't forget." **James Caan** eulogizes idealistic young D.B. Sweeney at the latter's military funeral at Arlington National Cemetery. *Gardens of Stone* (1987, Tri-Star).

6536 "That's a thing you gotta remember about WASPs; they love animals, they can't stand people." **Michael Douglas,** thinking of competitor Terence Stamp, makes an unfair generalization—the problem isn't limited to WASPs. *Wall Street* (1987, 20th Century-Fox).

6537 "I wondered if memory is something you have or something you lost." Fiftyish philosophy professor **Gena Rowlands** sifts her broken relationships through her mind. *Another Woman* (1988, Orion).

6538 "Someday, Lilah. . .you'll remember that the people in this house loved you whether you were funny or not." Kindly, wise **John Goodman** gently reminds his wife Sally Field, obsessed with becoming a stand-up comedienne, that she already has a very appreciative audience—her family. *Punchline* (1988, Columbia).

6539 TED: "Remember when we were freshmen and she was a senior?" BILL: "Shut up, Dude." **Keanu Reeves** unnecessarily reminds **Alex Winter** that the latter's sexy stepmother Amy Stock-Poynton is only three years their senior. *Bill and Ted's Excellent Adventure* (1989, Orion).

6540 "If I should fall, remember what you see here." Just before leading his black Civil War troops into history and a suicidal charge against a Confederate fort, **Matthew Broderick** asks a reporter to note their valor. *Glory* (1989, Tri-Star).

6541 "Honey, I married him four weeks before he left for the war. I was nineteen. I hardly even remember him." **Joan Allen** can't help Emily Lloyd learn about her father who was killed in Vietnam before Lloyd was born. *In Country* (1989, Warner Bros.).

6542 "He told me I would forget. But how could I not remember? The young general who wanted to change the world. The old writer who wanted to bid it farewell. I am the one who will live to remember them both." **Jane Fonda** remembers Mexican revolutionary General Jimmy Smits, ordered executed by Pancho Villa for killing Gregory Peck who portrayed writer Ambrose Bierce. *Old Gringo* (1989, Columbia).

6543 "The jury is going to remember Caroline tortured to death. They'll want someone to pay for the crime." Prosecutor **Harrison Ford**, on trial for the brutal murder of his former colleague and mistress Greta Scacchi, confides to his wife Bonnie Bedelia that even though he's innocent, the jury might convict him because they'll want to punish someone. *Presumed Innocent* (1990, Warner Bros.).

6544 "Memory is what I have instead of a view." Brilliantly insane **Anthony Hopkins** as Dr. Hannibal "The Cannibal" Lecter, talks to FBI trainee Jodie Foster from his windowless dungeon-like cell in a Dickensesque insane asylum. *The Silence of the Lambs* (1991, Orion).

Men

see also BACHELORS, BOYS, FATHERS, GENTLEMEN, HUSBANDS, HUSBANDS AND WIVES, MEN AND WOMEN, WOMEN

6545 MADAME LUCY: "You're impossible! You walk almost like a man." IRENE: "So do you." Effeminate dressmaker **George K. Arthur** throws his hands up in disgust with **Colleen Moore** who is modeling one of Arthur's latest creations. *Irene* (1926, silent, First National).

6546 "I'm no beauty. But under this exterior you'll find the flower of a man." **Fredric March**, as hideous Mr. Hyde, presses his attentions on prostitute Miriam Hopkins. *Dr. Jekyll and Mr. Hyde* (1932, Paramount).

6547 "If there's one thing I know, it's men. I ought to. It's been my life's work." Down-on-her-luck former stage star **Marie Dressler** has enough pluck left to advise Madge Evans, whose affair with fading matinee idol John Barrymore will end badly. *Dinner at Eight* (1933, MGM).

6548 ACE LAMONT: "What kind of men do you like?" RUBY CARTER: "Just two, domestic and imported." **John Miljan** plays straight man for **Mae West**. *Belle of the Nineties* (1934, Paramount).

6549 CHAN LO: "It is written that there are only two perfectly good men—one dead, the other unborn." FRISCO DOLL: "Which one are you?" Chinese **Harold Huber** is jealous of his mistress **Mae West**, a girl he took in off the streets. *Klondike Annie* (1936, Paramount).

6550 "What man's mind can conceive, man's character can control." **Spencer Tracy**, as 82-year-old Thomas Alva Edison, disputes a speaker at a banquet honoring Edison, who claims that mankind is at risk of destroying itself with its own inventive genius. *Edison, the Man* (1940, MGM).

6551 "Whatever I am, men made me!" Scarred and embittered **Joan Crawford** justifies becoming part of a blackmail ring to seek retribution for her misfortunes. She changes when plastic surgeon Melvyn Douglas makes her beautiful. *A Woman's Face* (1941, MGM).

6552 "Man was in the forest." In a scene that frightened young children, Bambi's mother tells the young deer of the danger in their forest homeland. *Bambi* (1942, Disney).

6553 "You're going to start college. That means you're a man. Well, your father's only a man. Now if there's anything between you, you go right up and talk to him." **Fay Holden** urges her son Mickey Rooney to settle any differences he has with his father Lewis Stone. *Andy Hardy's Double Life* (1942, MGM).

6554 TOM JEFFERS: "And where are these men who are going to faint at your feet?" GERRY JEFFERS: "They're always there, and they make new ones every year." **Joel McCrea**'s opinion that his soon to be ex-wife **Claudette Colbert** won't find herself surrounded by men, preferably rich men, is not shared by Colbert. *The Palm Beach Story* (1942, Paramount).

6555 "Papa wrote it years ago. Papa said the only men on earth worth their time on earth were the men who would fight for other men. Papa said, 'We have struggled through from darkness. But man moves forward with each day and each hour to a better, freer life. That desire to go forward—that willingness to fight for it—cannot be put in a man. But when it is there. . .!'" **Bette Davis** is married to such a man, anti-fascist fighter Paul Muni. *Watch on the Rhine* (1943, Warner Bros.).

6556 "Man is the only animal that blushes—or needs to." **Fredric March,** as Samuel Clemens, repeats Mark Twain's famous line. *The Adventures of Mark Twain* (1944, Warner Bros.).

6557 "Fanny cannot live by oxygen alone. She must be surrounded by men." **Claude Rains** states the needs of his vain selfish wife Bette Davis. *Mr. Skeffington* (1944, Warner Bros.).

6558 FATHER O'MALLEY: "Naturally, I like to see a man who can take care of himself. On the outside, it's—it's a man's world." SISTER BENEDICT: "How are they doing, Father?" FATHER: "They're not doing too good, but you know what I mean. There are some times a man has to fight his way through." SISTER: "Wouldn't it be better to—to think your way through?" Friendly rivals, pastor **Bing Crosby** and Mother Superior **Ingrid Bergman,** discuss choices men face in the outside world. *The Bells of St. Mary's* (1945, RKO).

6559 "Oh, men! I never yet met one of them who didn't have the instincts of a heel. Sometimes I wish I could get along without them." During the period of this movie, **Eve Arden**'s character was too independent and too opinionated to hold a man for very long. *Mildred Pierce* (1945, Warner Bros.).

6560 "It's a man's world. Yeah. See something you want, go after it. Get it. That's nature. Why we're

made strong and women weak. That's what a man's for. Teach our kids more of that, be more men." Wealthy self-made man **Paul Douglas** believes he's the perfect role model for would-be men. *A Letter to Three Wives* (1948, 20th Century-Fox).

6561 "You're just like any other man only a little more so. You have a feeling of being trapped, hemmed in, and you don't know whether or not you like it." **Pamela Britton** outlines her fiancé Edmond O'Brien's dilemma as she sees it. Things get somewhat worse when he is effectively murdered by a slow action poison. *D.O.A.* (1949, United Artists).

6562 "This is the story of a land. . .and a people. . .and a man, whose name was. . .Cochise." It's the introduction to a movie that called itself "The first major Hollywood movie to renounce time-worn clichés and. . .portray Indians as full-blooded human beings." Jeff Chandler portrays Apache chief Cochise as a wise, sensitive man whose people were bedeviled by whites and the American government. The major full-blooded native American characters were portrayed by full-blooded Caucasians. *Broken Arrow* (1950, 20th Century-Fox).

6563 "That's the kind of man I'd like to talk to!" Unfortunately, outer space alien **Michael Rennie** came about a century too late to talk to the author of the Gettysburg address, Abraham Lincoln. *The Day the Earth Stood Still* (1951, 20th Century-Fox).

6564 "This was the noblest Roman of them all. All the conspirators, save only he, did what they did in envy of great Caesar. He only, in a general honest thought and common good to all, made one of them. His life was gentle and the elements so mixed in him that nature might stand up and say to all the world, this was a man." Marc Antony, played by **Marlon Brando,** believes that in assassinating Julius Caesar, played by Louis Calhern, only Brutus, played by James Mason, acted from noble motives. *Julius Caesar* (1953, MGM).

6565 "Where do we find such men?" Fatherly admiral **Fredric March** asks a rhetorical question, after several pilots, including William Holden, die valiantly in battle over the skies of Korea. *The Bridges at Toko-Ri* (1955, Paramount).

6566 "I never belong to any one man—I belong to all men." **Lana Turner,** as Samarra, the wicked High Priestess of Astarte, tells title character Edmund Purdom that she can't be his exclusively. *The Prodigal* (1955, MGM).

6567 "What do you do when you have to be a man?" Confused teenager **James Dean** desperately and unsuccessfully seeks an answer to his question from his pathetically henpecked father Jim Backus. *Rebel Without a Cause* (1955, Warner Brothers).

6568 "I am not witty or brilliant, but I am a man." Married Italian **Rossano Brazzi** hopes that one out of three will be enough for American spinster Katharine Hepburn. *Summertime* (1955, Lopert/Korda).

6569 "We wouldn't be caught dead with men. Rough hairy beasts! Eight hands!" In drag, **Jack Lemmon** insists to bandleader Joan Shawlee that "she" and "girlfriend" Tony Curtis have no use for men. *Some Like It Hot* (1959, United Artists).

6570 "You have to play a man like a fish." **Constance Ford** gives some motherly mis-advice to her daughter, teen Sandra Dee. *A Summer Place* (1959, Warner Brothers).

6571 "He's a delicious man and all man from the top of his head to the tip of his toes." **Joanne Woodward** describes her new husband Paul Newman to a friend. *From the Terrace* (1960, 20th Century-Fox).

6572 "Because the 9th Cavalry was my home, my real freedom, and my self-respect. The way I was deserting it, I was nothin' but a swamp-running nigger and I ain't that. Do you hear me? I'm a man!" Title character **Woody Strode** defiantly explains why he has returned to face a charge of raping a white woman after first having escaped. *Sergeant Rutledge* (1960, Warner Brothers).

6573 "And if there's a future for man, insensitive as he is, proud and defiant in his pursuit of power, let him resolve to live it lovingly, for he knows well how to do so. Then he may say once more, truly the light is sweet and what a pleasant thing it is for the eyes to see the sun." **Edward Judd** gives the benediction in this Armageddon film in which the earth is knocked off its axis by nuclear bomb tests conducted on the same day at opposite poles of the planet by the Americans and the Russians. Because of the different orbit, earth moves towards the sun. *The Day the Earth Caught Fire* (1961, GB, Universal).

6574 "You can never tell about people. I've known men. . . so-called happily married, y'know? And the night before their wedding they are calling me up. I mean calling me up." **Marilyn Monroe** has had experience with men looking to set up their own bachelor party. *The Misfits* (1961, United Artists).

6575 "You know why the world is in such a mess? Men. It's a man's world and all men are alike." Stewardess **Pamela Tiffin** may have consulted only a small sample, womanizer pilot Hugh O'Brian, but she knows what she knows. *Come Fly with Me* (1963, GB, MGM).

6576 "Am I not a man? And is not a man stupid? I'm a man, so I married. Wife, children, house, everything, the full catastrophe." **Anthony Quinn** equates his gender with stupidity. *Zorba the Greek* (1964, 20th Century-Fox).

6577 "What kind of man is he? There's grace in the line and color, but it doesn't emerge pure. It pushes at the edge of something still tentative, unresolved—as if somewhere in the man there is still a key unturned." "Reborn" Rock Hudson overhears **Salome Jens**' impression of him. *Seconds* (1966, Paramount).

6578 "Dad, you're my father. I'm your son. I love you. I always have, and I always will. But you think of yourself as a colored man. I think of myself as a man." Physician **Sidney Poitier** favorably compares himself to his father Roy Glenn, who questions the wisdom of Poitier marrying white Katharine Houghton. *Guess Who's Coming to Dinner* (1967, Columbia).

6579 "A man who doesn't spend time with his family can never be a real man." Godfather **Marlon Brando** doesn't approve of his married godson, singing star Al Martino's involvement with movie actresses. *The Godfather* (1972, Paramount).

6580 TYRONE TACKETT: "I know how you like your men. Proud and erect." LAURAL: "You ain't the only one who fits the description." TYRONE: "I'm the only one here." LAURAL: "Give me a dime for a phone call. I'll fill the room." Small-time criminal **Bernie Casey** is put in his place by motel clerk **Lisa Moore**. *Hit Man* (1972, MGM).

6581 "I wish I had been born a man. . . . The concerns are so simple: money and death. Making ends meet until they met—the end, if they do." **Katharine Hepburn** tells her daughter, Lee Remick, that she believes it would have been easier to have been her father. *A Delicate Balance* (1973, American Film Theater).

6582 "You are a man as he must have existed in nature." If **Mariangela Melato** means that Giancarlo Giannini behaves much like an animal—she's right. *Swept Away* (1974, Italy, Cinema 5).

6583 "I don't have the answers for you. I can tell you what I would do if I were in your situation. I'd do a lot of what you're doing already. . . . Get back into the stream of life. Don't be scared of going out with guys. Risk it with some new men. They're people, you know. Take a chance." Psychiatrist **Penelope Russianoff** advises recently divorced Jill Clayburgh. *An Unmarried Woman* (1978, 20th Century-Fox).

6584 ISABELLE: "You pilots are such—men!" PATRONI: "They don't call it a cockpit for nothing." **Sylvia Kristel** is impressed with pilots. **George Kennedy** isn't a pilot—but Kristel does not know that. *The Concorde—Airport '79* (1979, Universal).

6585 "Men go to seed early. They go to bars and sit in front of their TVs. Men at 40 already have pot bellies." **Vera Alentova**'s lament is certainly not restricted to men of the U.S.S.R. *Moscow Does Not Believe in Tears* (1979, USSR, Mosfilm).

6586 "I am not an elephant, I am not an animal. I am a man!" Horribly disfigured **John Hurt** shouts to a curious crowd that has trapped him. *The Elephant Man* (1980, GB, EMI-Brooksfilm).

6587 "C'mon, please, we're men—can we have a bond?" Film editor **Albert Brooks** seeks a little support from his best friend, assistant editor Bruno Kirby. *Modern Romance* (1981, Columbia).

6588 "You want somethin', you gotta go get it. Men have got to be bolder, more dashing. We could have been great pirates." Even as he's dying of some unnamed disease, **Josh Mostel** still has a dream. *Windy City* (1984, Warner Bros.).

6589 "Men are just a bunch of titless females if you ask me." Elderly **Burgess Meredith** does not seem impressed with either gender. *Full Moon in Blue Water* (1988, Trans World).

6590 "When it comes to marriage, one man is as good as the next; and even the least accommodating is less trouble than a mother." Devious **Glenn Close** advises sixteen-year-old Uma Thurman on men, marriage and mothers. *Dangerous Liaisons* (1988, Warner Bros.).

6591 "Aren't men full of shit?" **Pauline Collins**' question is addressed to the camera, when one of the men in her life tries to feed her an outrageous and obvious lie. *Shirley Valentine* (1988, Paramount).

6592 "Every fool with a dick can make a baby, but only a man can raise his children." Good father **Larry Fishburne** speaks of parental responsibility to his son Cuba Gooding, Jr. *Boyz N the Hood* (1991, Columbia).

6593 "Married men suck by definition." Secretary **Mary-Louise Parker,** who has had a disappointing affair with her married boss Kevin Kline, springs the line on a friendly young cop who comes to her rescue when a mugger tries to break into her car. *Grand Canyon* (1991, 20th Century-Fox).

6594 "It's definitely men you've got to watch. . . in my life, sex and love have come in different packages. . . and never, never show you care what they say!" Lovely young **Patsy Kensit** lectures the camera. *Twenty-One* (1991, GB, Cine-Triton).

6595 TEEN-AGE BOY: "What say we get in the back of the car and you make a man of me?" DOTTIE HINSON: "What say I smack you around?" BOY: "Can't we do both?" A teen-age boy comes on to sexy six-foot tall catcher for the Rockford Peaches, **Geena Davis**. *A League of Their Own* (1992, Columbia).

6596 "Men are pigs; I don't care how nice they seem." **Jennifer Jason Leigh** tells her new roommate Bridget Fonda her opinion of men. *Single White Female* (1992, Columbia).

Men and Women

see also LADIES AND GENTLEMEN, MEN, WOMEN

6597 "I need a woman who knows how to deal with men." Austrian Intelligence Chief **Gustav von Seyffertitz** recruits Marlene Dietrich, an officer's widow and prostitute, to be a spy as she plies her trade on the dark streets of Vienna. *Dishonored* (1931, Paramount).

6598 "You are right, Mr. Kringelein: a man who is not with a woman is a dead man." Doctor **Lewis Stone** agrees with dying Lionel Barrymore. *Grand Hotel* (1932, MGM).

6599 "I ain't a one-woman man, I never have been and I never will be." Rubber plantation overseer **Clark Gable** lets stranded prostitute Jean Harlow know that she can't expect an exclusive relationship. *Red Dust* (1932, MGM).

6600 "A thing happened to me that usually happens to men. You see a man can meet two, three or four women and fall in love with all of them, and then, by a process of—er—interesting elimination, he is able to decide which he prefers; but a woman must decide purely on instinct, guesswork, if she wants to be considered nice. . . ." **Miriam Hopkins** tells Fredric March and Gary Cooper that she's in love with both of them and would like to set up an innocent procedure to try both men before making her choice between them. *Design for Living* (1933, Paramount).

6601 "If you were free. . . and if I was free. I don't think any man has ever understood any woman since the beginning of things. You don't understand our imagination. How wild our imagination can be. I wish I were a man. . . . Oh, if I were a man! . . . Does any man realize what the life of a woman is? How trivial we have to be. We have to please. We are obliged to please. . . ." **Margaretta Scott** expresses a complaint that many women and thoughtful men can and must understand. *Things to Come* (1936, GB, London Films/ United Artists).

6602 "Men use their heads. Women use their emotions." **Fred MacMurray** chooses his weapon and assigns Madeleine Carroll hers in the continuing battle of the sexes. *Honeymoon in Bali* (1939, Paramount).

6603 "A woman's not supposed to be a boss. Your kind of boss-woman needs a boss-man." Opera singer **Allan Jones** stands aside, advising department store head Madeleine Carroll to chase after Fred MacMurray and submit to him. *Honeymoon in Bali* (1939, Paramount).

6604 "Just say no to the men, and the girls probably won't speak to you anyway." Wealthy department-store owner's son, **David Niven**, instructs sales girl Ginger Rogers who wonders what she'll have to say to his fancy friends when he takes her to a nightclub on a date. *Bachelor Mother* (1939, RKO).

6605 VALERIE TRAVERS: "I dislike you intensely." SIMON TEMPLAR: "Oh, no, you don't. You're really very fond of me." VAL: "Why should I be fond of you?" SIMON: "Tell me and you'll answer the riddle of the world. My dear Val, that's what made history, literature, even chemistry. A man and a woman." The murder of **Wendy Barrie**'s father is being investigated by Robin Hood-like sleuth The Saint, played by **George Sanders**. *The Saint Strikes Back* (1939, RKO)

6606 "We women are so much more sensible! When we tire of ourselves, we change the way we do our hair, or hire a new cook. Or redecorate the house. I suppose a man could do his office, but he never thinks of anything so simple. No, dear, a man has only one escape from his own self—to see a different self in the mirror of some women's eyes." Wise **Lucille Watson** consoles her daughter Norma Shearer whose husband has taken up with salesgirl Joan Crawford in this drama about the interconnecting lives of a group of women. *The Women* (1939, MGM).

6607 "Sometimes a woman's intuition is better than a man's brains." **Judy Garland** helps Mickey Rooney save face when he gets put through the wringer by glamour girl Diana Lewis. Is Garland suggesting that only women have intuition and only men have brains? *Andy Hardy Meets Debutante* (1940, MGM).

6608 "Women can change better'n a man. Man lives in jerks—baby born or somebody dies, that's a jerk—gets a farm, or loses one, an' that's a jerk. With a woman it's all one flow, like a stream, little eddies, little waterfalls, but the river goes right on. Woman looks at it like that." Dear ole Ma Joad, played by **Jane Darwell,** makes her interpretation of the difference between men and women to her husband Russell Simpson. *The Grapes of Wrath* (1940, 20th Century-Fox).

6609 "All men marry the wrong woman." Warlock **Cecil Kellaway** scoffs at his daughter, witch Veronica Lake, who takes satisfaction in finding that the curse she issued when they were burned at the stake in 17th century Salem, Massachusetts, has resulted in all male descendants of her chief accuser having miserable marriages. *I Married a Witch* (1942, United Artists).

6610 "Oh, darling, I'm almost sorry for you, having such a nice quiet peaceful time when things were really happening, but that's what men are for, isn't it? To go out and do things while you womenfolk look after the house." Having returned from helping to evacuate troops from Dunkirk, **Walter Pidgeon** muses chauvinistically, unaware that while he was away his wife Greer Garson captured a downed German pilot. *Mrs. Miniver* (1942, MGM).

6611 "I'm analyzing women at present. The subject is less difficult than I was led to believe. Women represent the triumph of matter over mind just as men represent the triumph of the mind over morals." **George Sanders** enjoys summing up important things in tidy, concise generalizations. *The Picture of Dorian Gray* (1945, MGM).

6612 MRS. PARADINE: "I am—what would you say? A woman who has seen a great deal of life. . . . When I was still at school in Naples, it began. I was sixteen, or so I said—actually, I was younger." ANTHONY KEANE: "Tragic." MRS. PARADINE: "Yes, perhaps, but I didn't think so then. I ran away with a man—Istanbul, Athens, Cairo." KEANE: "He was much older, of course—rich, he took advantage of your youth." MRS. PARADINE: "He was married, respected. I took advantage of him! Then, as suddenly as it began, it ended. He wearied of me, I wearied of him—what difference does it make?" KEANE: "There were others?" MRS. PARADINE: "Of course, there were others! We cannot hide these things!" **Alida Valli** refuses to allow her smitten, married Defense Attorney **Gregory Peck** to find excuses for her having used and been used by numerous men. *The Paradine Case* (1947, Selznick-United Artists).

6613 "What is it that makes a man and a woman know that of all of the men and the women in the world they were meant for each other?" Struggling artist **Joseph Cotten** believes that he has found the one girl meant for him. *Portrait of Jennie* (1948, Selznick).

6614 "You like to get hurt. Always picking the wrong guy. It's a sickness with a lot of women. Always looking for a new way to get hurt by a new man. Get smart: there hasn't been a new man since Adam." Bitter **Richard Conte,** betrayed by his brothers, writes off the males of the species for his one-time lover Susan Hayward. *House of Strangers* (1949, 20th Century-Fox).

6615 CATHERINE WINSLOW: "I have a confession and an apology to make to you." SIR ROBERT MORTON: "My dear lady, I am sure the one is rash and the other is superfluous. I should make neither. . . [they go on to speak of feminism]. It's a lost cause, you know." CATHERINE: "How little you know of women. . . I doubt we shall meet again." SIR ROBERT: "Oh—do you really think so? How little you know of men, Miss Winslow." The final exchange between **Margaret Leighton** and **Robert Donat** suggests that their relationship is to take on a more personal flavor, now that Donat has successfully induced a court to find in favor of Leighton's 14-year-old brother Neil North. The latter was expelled from a naval college for allegedly stealing a postal order. *The Winslow Boy* (1950, GB, London Films-Eagle Lion).

6616 "Men are so disgustingly prompt. . . . I think they do it just to put us women in a bad light. . . ." **Elizabeth Taylor** teasingly welcomes an on-time Montgomery Clift. *A Place in the Sun* (1951, Paramount).

6617 "Thank heavens I'm a woman, a man couldn't take it." State department Protocol Officer **Deborah Kerr** comes to the rescue of her ex-fiancé Cary Grant. He plans to marry Betta St. John, a sheik's daughter schooled in the art of pleasing a man. *Dream Wife* (1953, MGM).

6618 BERNIE DODD: "Why is it that women always think they understand men better than men do?" GEORGIE ELGIN: "Maybe because they live with them." **William Holden**'s exasperated question is nicely answered by **Grace Kelly**. *The Country Girl* (1954, Paramount).

6619 "Why can't a woman be more like a man?" It's the lament of **Rex Harrison** as Professor Henry Higgins. *My Fair Lady* (1964, Warner Bros.).

6620 "It takes a true woman to understand that the purest form of love is to love a man who denies himself to her. A man who inspires worship, because he has no need for any woman because he has himself. . . . You're getting hard and strong, virile, domineering, more irresistible. It's up. It's in the air." Prostitute **Rita Moreno** mouths the lines taught to her by Jack Nicholson that are necessary to restore his fading manhood. *Carnal Knowledge* (1971, Avco Embassy).

6621 "I want to go back to being a man. I don't like being a woman in this country." Aging homosexual and transvestite **Michel Serrault** tells his lover Ugo Tognazzi that he's too old to be an effective female—especially after he has been put to work like a peasant woman in the Northern Italy home of Tognazzi's widowed mother. *La Cage aux Folles II* (1981, France-Italy, United Artists).

6622 "It's a man's world. . . women aren't allowed to be participants. I don't dislike men, I envy their freedom. I resent not having the same." Victorian **Bo Derek** chafes at the inferior status of women. *Tarzan, the Ape Man* (1981, MGM).

6623 "Any man with any style at all can make a mess of his love life. . . and any woman with any gumption at all can make a shambles of her marriage." Scottish poet **Tom Conti** addresses a group of middle-aged suburban matrons at a country club. *Reuben, Reuben* (1983, 20th Century-Fox).

6624 "If there's a beast in men, it meets its match in women, too." It's **Tusse Silberg**'s evasive answer when her young daughter Sarah Patterson, having witnessed her parents making love, asks her mother if her father David Warner was hurting her. *The Company of Wolves* (1984, GB, Cannon).

6625 "I don't ask you to stop being a woman. Don't ask me to stop being a man." **Sylvester Stallone** makes a less than perfect analogy for his wife Talia Shire who wants him to give up boxing. *Rocky IV* (1985, MGM-United Artists).

6626 "Earthmen will fall to their knees, betray their country, and give away real estate for a desirable woman." Planet elders dispatch an emissary, who has taken the form of desirable Kim Basinger, to Earth to find a way to save their world. *My Stepmother Is an Alien* (1988, Columbia).

6627 "If men had their way a woman would lie down a prostitute and get up a virgin." Set in 1949

Brooklyn, Ron Silver suddenly discovers he has three wives to contend with, one of which is **Anjelica Huston** who was thought to have died in a Nazi death camp. *Enemies, a Love Story* (1989, 20th Century-Fox).

6628 PAM BOUVIER: "It's Ms. Kennedy, and why can't you be my executive secretary?" JAMES BOND: "It's south of the border; it's a man's world." Working together on a case, **Carey Lowell** objects to **Timothy Dalton** forcing her to assume the subservient role, posing as his executive secretary, who he introduces as Miss Kennedy. Though it's not much, Lowell's role is the most assertive non-villain female in the 007 series. *License to Kill* (1989, GB, United Artists).

6629 "I remember reading somewhere that men learn to love the person they are attracted to and that women become more and more attracted to the person that they love." Although impotent, **James Spader** gets his sexual kicks from making videotapes of women discussing their sex lives. *sex, lies and videotape* (1989, Miramax).

6630 "The biggest jerk you ever knew has a woman somewhere who's nuts over him. Women are perfect." World weary **Alan Arkin** expresses the belief that for every man there's a woman. *Havana* (1990, Universal).

6631 "If it had been a younger man, I could at least have gone to the gym more often. But another woman. . . .!" Doctor **Michael Davenport** is fed up with his young, long-haired photographer lover Stephen Gatta, who has taken up with Erica Nagy. *Hearing Voices* (1991, Phoenix).

6632 "Never underestimate a man's ability to underestimate a woman." Private detective **Kathleen Turner** shares some universal feminine wisdom with 13-year-old Angela Goethals. *V.I. Warshawski* (1991, Hollywood Pictures-Buena Vista).

Mercy

see also COMPASSION, FORGIVENESS, KINDNESS, PITY

6633 "With Major Lawrence, mercy is a passion. With me, it is merely good manners. You may judge which motive is more reliable." **Alec Guinness,** as Prince Feisal, speaks to journalist Arthur Kennedy about title character Peter O'Toole. *Lawrence of Arabia* (1962, GB, Columbia).

6634 "That's the problem with mercy, kid. It just ain't professional." **Paul Newman** scolds pool shark Tom Cruise when the latter passes up an opportunity to make a quick buck because he feels sorry for his opponent. *The Color of Money* (1986, Touchstone/Buena Vista).

Messages

see also NOTES, SPEECH AND SPEAKING, WRITING AND WRITERS

6635 "I'm sick of messages from the front. Don't we ever get messages from the side?" **Groucho Marx** grumbles at his headquarters during the war between his country of Freedonia and neighboring Sylvania. *Duck Soup* (1933, Paramount).

6636 "Thank you. This message means the liberation of our people." **Enrique Acosta,** the leader of the Cuban insurgents, thanks John Boles for bringing a message of support from President McKinley. *A Message to Garcia* (1936, 20th Century-Fox).

6637 "Elaine communicates with my brother and myself entirely by rumor." Out-of-work writer **Jason Robards**' sister dropped off her illegitimate son at Robards' home seven years earlier and vanished. *A Thousand Clowns* (1965, United Artists).

6638 "I'm gonna deliver a Valentine to Bugs so he will never forget." **Jason Robards, Jr.** makes a threat against Ralph Meeker that Al Capone probably never said about Bugs Moran. *The St. Valentine's Day Massacre* (1967, 20th Century-Fox).

6639 "We communicate with him Indian-style; when we need him, somehow he's there." Alternate society teacher **Delores Taylor** knows that she can depend on Tom Laughlin to be around when there's trouble. *Billy Jack* (1971, Warner Bros.).

6640 "It's a Sicilian message—means Luca Brasci sleeps with the fish." **Richard Castellano** interprets the arrival of a package containing a fish and the bullet proof vest of Lenny Montana. *The Godfather* (1972, Paramount).

6641 "I've got a special message for you little partners out there. I want you to finish your oatmeal at breakfast and do as your mom and pa tell you because they know best. Don't ever tell a lie and say your prayers at night before you go to bed. And as our friends south of the border say, adios, amigos." **Clint Eastwood,** the owner and chief attraction of a shoddy traveling Wild West show, says goodbye with advice for his audience of children and their parents. *Bronco Billy* (1980, Warner Bros.).

6642 "My life is my message." Mahatma Gandhi, portrayed by **Ben Kingsley,** makes a simple but profound statement. *Gandhi* (1982, GB, Goldcrest-Columbia).

6643 "Well, ma'am, if I see him, I'll sure give him the message." Dying, slimy private eye **M. Emmet Walsh** sees some irony in the fact that Frances McDormand who has fatally shot him, mistakes him for her already murdered husband, Dan Hedaya. She shouts, "I'm not afraid of you, Marty." *Blood Simple* (1984, River Road-Circle).

6644 "Go the distance." It's the third message of the Voice to Iowa farmer Kevin Costner. *Field of Dreams* (1989, Universal).

Middle Age *see* AGE AND AGING

Midgets

6645 BUD JONES: "What's the idea of teaching midgets to wrestle?" LOU HOTCHKISS: "They're for those small television sets." In a scene deleted from most prints, **Bud Abbott** comes across **Lou Costello** with two midgets grappling in a small ring. *Abbott and Costello in the Foreign Legion* (1950, Universal).

6646 "We're breeding a race of moral midgets." It's part of megalomaniac school teacher **James Mason**'s tirade at a PTA meeting. *Bigger Than Life* (1956, 20th Century-Fox).

6647 "Who's the midget?" **Jack Nicholson**'s reward for playing it tough when cornered by two thugs is to have his nose slit by the "midget," director Roman Polanski. *Chinatown* (1974, Paramount).

Midnight *see* DREAMS, NIGHTS

Military

see also BATTLES AND BATTLEFIELDS, BOMBS, FIGHTS AND FIGHTING, KILLINGS, WARS, WEAPONS

6648 "Our bodies are earth. Our thoughts are clay. And we sleep and eat with death." World War I German soldier **Lew Ayres** refers to himself, his comrades and also the enemy, the French soldiers. *All Quiet on the Western Front* (1930, Universal).

6649 "Yeah, you made a soldier out of him. You gave him a gun and told him how to be a hero. Why don't you pin a medal on him now, Sergeant Meadowlark? He was your star pupil." Circus owner **Spencer Tracy** blames Army Sergeant Edgar Dearing for the fact that his World War I buddy Franchot Tone was so indoctrinated in killing that after the war he becomes a murdering racketeer. *They Gave Him a Gun* (1937, MGM).

6650 "He's the best soldier we'll ever see." **Gary Cooper** grudgingly admires beastly French Foreign Legion Sergeant Brian Donlevy for his military acumen. *Beau Geste* (1939, Paramount).

6651 "The whole Confederate Army's got the same troubles—crawlin' clothes and dysentery." **Hattie McDaniel** adds Carroll Nye's trousers to a boiling pot. *Gone with the Wind* (1939, Selznick-MGM).

6652 "If ever a man deserved the name and rank of soldier, it was he. His name will be written on the rolls of our honored dead." Colonel **Montagu Love** speaks at the grave of Indian water bearer Sam Jaffe, who in death achieves his dream of becoming a soldier with the occupying British Army. *Gunga Din* (1939, RKO).

6653 "The Marines fought a great fight. They wrote history. But this is not the end. There are other leathernecks, other fighting Americans, a hundred and forty million of them, whose blood and sweat and fury will exact a just and terrible vengeance." Narrator **Bill Goodwin** speaks of the valiant men who gave their lives in the first battle against the Japanese after Pearl Harbor. *Wake Island* (1942, Paramount).

6654 "I think so, sir. The PT boats are swell. They do a grand job, and they'll play their part in winning the war. But not without submarines. They've got their job to do in all the seven seas, and boy, how they're doing it. And the carriers that bring the planes that drop the bombs that sink the enemy ships. And the cruisers that protect the airplane carriers. And the battleships, the dreadnoughts and super dreadnoughts, the big shots of the fleet. They're in there punching too. They're all in there doing their job, working together. I found that out, sir. It isn't one branch of the service, it's all branches. And it isn't all ships, it's men. The men behind the guns of the PT boats and the submarines and the Coast Guard ships and the mine layers and the tenders and the tankers and the troop ships. The men that take them out, who fight their way over and land them there. That's the Navy. The United States Navy." Former PT boat commander, turned submarine executive officer, **Tyrone Power** is a team player. *Crash Dive* (1943, 20th Century-Fox).

6655 "They aren't forgotten because they haven't died. They're living out there. . . and they'll keep on living as long as the regiment lives. . . . The faces may change. Names. But they're there. They're the regiment—the regular army—now and fifty years from now." Cavalry Officer **John Wayne** nostalgically and proudly recalls his fallen comrades and thinks of those who will join the regiment in years to come. *Fort Apache* (1948, RKO).

6656 "The army is always the same. The sun and the moon may change, but the army knows no season." Cavalry Officer **John Wayne** contemplates his imminent forced retirement from the army. *She Wore a Yellow Ribbon* (1949, RKO).

6657 "Looks to me like you're trying to acquire the reputation of a lone wolf. You should know that in the army, it's not the individual that counts." Incompetent Captain **Philip Ober** is outraged when Private Montgomery Clift refuses to join the company boxing team. *From Here to Eternity* (1953, Columbia).

6658 "This is the infantry. But you poor, miserable young people, you will never make it. My name is Sergeant Ryan. Pick up your bags. Left face. Forward double time. Hup, two, three, four. Hup, two, three, four. Hup, two, three, four." Drill instructor **Richard Widmark** welcomes some new army recruits fresh off the buses that bring them to camp. *Take the High Ground* (1953, MGM).

6659 ENSIGN KEITH: "Well, he's certainly Navy." LT. KEEFER: "So was Captain Bligh." Ever hopeful **Robert Francis** and ever cynical **Fred MacMurray** exchange views on new skipper Humphrey Bogart. *The Caine Mutiny* (1954, Columbia).

6660 "They call me Mac. The name's not important. It's January, 1942. Marine outposts all over the world have fallen to the Japanese. Our ranks are empty and ill equipped. We need help. And from every part of the country, kids are answering the call." Some of today's isolationists may wish for marine gunnery Sergeant **James Whitmore** to make another call for young men and women to resist the invasion of Japanese automobiles, televisions, cameras, computers, and to reclaim American golf courses and movie companies. *Battle Cry* (1955, Warner Bros.).

6661 "You know, a year from now the army comes and says, 'O.K., Artie West. You get in uniform, you're a soldier. You save the world and you get your lousy head blown off.' Well, maybe I get a year in jail and maybe the army doesn't want Artie West to be a soldier no more. Maybe what I get is out. . . ." Juvenile delinquent **Vic Morrow** has a well-conceived reason for rejecting teacher Glenn Ford's warning that if he continues stealing he might end up in prison. *The Blackboard Jungle* (1955, MGM).

6662 "I'd rather be a captain in the army than president of France." Jewish **Jose Ferrer,** as Captain Alfred Dreyfus, realizes that he must do everything twice as well as his fellow officers. But his patriotism remains strong. *I Accuse!* (1958, GB, MGM).

6663 "If sailors didn't exist, we would have to invent them." It's **Jeanne Moreau**'s tag line at the end of the movie. *The Sailor from Gibraltar* (1967, GB, WoodfallLopert).

6664 MARGARET HOULIHAN: "How did a degenerate person like that ever reach a responsible position in the regular army?" RADAR O'REILLY: "He was drafted." Head nurse **Sally Kellerman**'s disapproving rhetorical question about Army Surgeon Donald Sutherland is answered by company clerk **Gary Burghoff**. *M*A*S*H* (1970, 20th Century-Fox).

6665 "You know what they say, 'If the Marines wanted you to have a wife, they'd have issued you one.'" **Mary Jackson** reminds fellow leatherneck wife Jane Fonda how important they are to the Corps. *Coming Home* (1978, United Artists).

6666 "I think they sent me to the wrong place. I joined a different army." Jewish American princess **Goldie Hawn** confides her doubts about her army enlistment to hard-as-nails Captain Eileen Brennan. *Private Benjamin* (1980, Warner Bros.).

6667 "An army without leaders is like a foot without a big toe." **Bill Murray**'s simile needs work. *Stripes* (1981, Columbia).

6668 "Looks like the Russian Army stopped for lunch today." **Teri Garr** reacts when her son Christopher Collet brings home his buddies after school. *Firstborn* (1984, Paramount).

Minds

see also BRAINS, HEADS AND HEADACHES, IMAGINATION, INTELLIGENCE, THINKING AND THOUGHTS, UNDERSTANDINGS AND MISUNDERSTANDINGS, WISDOM

6669 "It would be a terrific innovation if you could get your mind to stretch a little further than the next wisecrack." Eve Arden's jibes are getting to aspiring actress **Katharine Hepburn.** Eve has the last word, responding, "You know I tried that once, but it didn't snap back into place." *Stage Door* (1937, RKO).

6670 "Trouble is, Ann, when I'm standing up, my mind's lying down. When I'm lying down, my mind's standing—course, allowing I got a mind." Title character **Henry Fonda** joshes with Pauline Moore as Ann Rutledge. *Young Mr. Lincoln* (1939, 20th Century-Fox).

6671 "Mind like parachute—only function when open." Charlie Chan, played by **Sidney Toler** shares some wisdom with one of his 14 kids. *Charlie Chan's Murder Cruise* (1940, 20th Century-Fox).

6672 "He looks as though his mind could stand a little laundering." **John McGuire** is disgusted when he catches his next door neighbor Charles Halton leering at young girls in a diner. *The Stranger on the Third Floor* (1940, RKO).

6673 "Why don't you have that mind of yours sent out and dry cleaned?" Central American banana plantation manager **James Cagney** is annoyed when stranded showgirl Ann Sheridan questions Cagney's interest in married Helen Vinson. *Torrid Zone* (1940, Warner Bros.).

6674 "She tries to read my mind, and, if she can't read my mind, she reads my mail." Nazi **Walter Slezak** teases about his Brooklyn-born wife Ginger Rogers. She poses as a society lady, but most of her experience is in stripping off her clothes in front of bald-headed men. *Once Upon a Honeymoon* (1942, RKO).

6675 "If you don't mind my mentioning it, father, I think you have a mind like a swamp." Sharp-tongued teen **Diana Lynn** lets her crude, opinionated widower father William Demarest have it. *The Miracle of Morgan's Creek* (1943, Paramount).

6676 "The way I stood in there, packing my suitcase. Only my mind wasn't on the suitcase and it wasn't on the weekend. Nor was it on the shirts I was putting in the suitcase either. My mind was hanging outside the window. It was suspended just about eighteen inches below. And out there in that great big concrete jungle, I wonder how many others there are like me. Those poor bedeviled guys on fire with thirst. Such comical figures to the rest of the world as they stagger blindly towards another binge, another bender, another spree." Drunk and alcoholic writer **Ray Milland** has the film's last lines. *The Lost Weekend* (1945, Paramount).

6677 "What is there for you to say? We both know that the mind of a woman in love is operating on the lowest level of the intellect." Psychiatrist **Michael Chekhov** tells his former student Ingrid Bergman that she can't be objective in treating Gregory Peck if she's in love with him. The way he puts it, we can't be sure if he feels the same about a male analyst with a female patient. *Spellbound* (1945, Selznick-United Artists).

6678 "The human mind is like Salome at the beginning of her dance. Salome, hidden from the world by seven veils. Veils of reserve, shyness, fear. With friends, the average person will drop first one veil, then another...maybe three or four altogether. With a lover, she will take off five or even six. But never the seventh. Never!" Psychiatrist **Herbert Lom** helps pianist Ann Todd lift the veils of memory and find the reason for her fits of depression and self-destructive urges. *The Seventh Veil* (1946, GB, Theatrecraft-Ortus/GFD-Universal).

6679 "Now there's a guy who never goes out of a girl's mind. He just stays there like a heavy meal." **Veda Ann Borg** has an unusual way of expressing her infatuation with playboy Cary Grant. *The Bachelor and the Bobbysoxer* (1947, RKO).

6680 "Boston's not just a city. It's a state of mind. You can't move away from a state of mind." **Ronald Colman** can't understand why anyone would wish to live any place other than Beantown. *The Late George Apley* (1947, 20th Century-Fox).

6681 "Dave. Stop. Stop.... My mind is going...I can feel it. There is no question about it. I can feel it. I'm afraid." **Douglas Rain,** as the voice of supercomputer HAL 9000 reacts humanly as Keir Dullea manually lobotomizes the fussy robot that's gone berserk. *2001: A Space Odyssey* (1968, GB, MGM).

6682 "You gotta get your mind out of that white woman's dream." Black criminal **Paul Benjamin** reminds his girl friend Norma Donaldson who she is and who she is not. *Across 110th Street* (1972, United Artists).

6683 "When I stepped out into the bright sunshine from the darkness of the movie house, I had only two things on my mind...." **Matt Dillon** is the leader of a gang of rebellious young punks who have "adventures." *The Outsiders* (1983, Warner Bros.).

6684 "Come, amigo, throw away your mind." Courtly Mexican doctor **Ignacio Lopez Tarso** makes an appealing invitation to his English drinking companion Albert Finney. *Under the Volcano* (1984, Universal).

6685 "I am the feminine in your mind." Space alien **Mathilda May** identifies with space ship Commander Steve Railsback. *Lifeforce* (1985, Cannon/ Tri-Star).

6686 "I love you.... Of course, I mean your mind." **Kathy Bates** can't quite bring herself to say what's on her mind to injured writer James Caan. *Misery* (1990, Columbia).

6687 "Ultimate mastery comes not of the body, but of the mind." Ninja master Splinter (voice of **Kevin Clagh**), a large animatronic rat, is the mentor and father figure to four superhero turtles. *Teenage Mutant Ninja Turtles* (1990, New Line).

6688 "The fiercest weapon is the human mind." Zen master **Michel Qissi** mumbles to martial arts expert Sasha Mitchell. *Kickboxer 2* (1991, Trimark).

Minorities *see* BLACKS, JEWS, PREJUDICES

Miracles

see also FAITH AND UNFAITHFULNESS, GOD, JESUS CHRIST, RELIGIONS, SUPERNATURAL

6689 "Get this for a miracle. See I come up to Sister like this. She lays the heating mitts and I sees the light and wham—hallelujah!" A fake cripple demonstrates a scam for con woman, evangelist Barbara Stanwyck and her manager Sam Hardy. *The Miracle Woman* (1931, Columbia).

6690 "Ah, to have found anyone in this wilderness would have been miracle enough, but to have found you—this is too improbable. I don't believe in you. You're an illusion. You'll vanish before my eyes." Spanish emissary **John Gilbert** can't believe his good fortune when he discovers the young man he is to share a room with for three snowbound days is lovely Greta Garbo. He has another surprise coming. She's the queen of Sweden. *Queen Christina* (1933, MGM).

6691 "Stay a moment. When the door closes upon you. I shall doubt that all this really happened. You're here beside me. If I bend my head, I can feel your cheek against my lips and I can hear your voice saying incredible things. Have you ever thought that people to whom miracles happen must be a little dazed? The blind man to whom sight is suddenly given must be startled by the strange new world. So it is with me. I came here hoping to catch a glimpse of you at court. You might have flung a word, gracious and indifferent, as you passed. Instead. . . ." Handsome **Tyrone Power** makes a lengthy pretty speech before finally kissing French Queen Norma Shearer. *Marie Antoinette* (1938, MGM).

6692 "Enjoy it—it's a miracle. Accept your blessing and don't talk about it." Blind poet **Herbert Marshall** admonishes disfigured World War I veteran Robert Young and his decidedly plain wife Dorothy McGuire not to question the small miracle that occurs when they are alone in their honeymoon cottage. He regains his handsome features and she becomes a beautiful woman. *The Enchanted Cottage* (1945, RKO).

6693 "You could make miracles of music in Majorca." **Merle Oberon,** as French writer George Sand, tempts Cornel Wilde, as composer Frederic Chopin. *A Song to Remember* (1945, Columbia).

6694 "You should not be too surprised. I told you if you love someone deeply enough anything is possible, even miracles." **Barry Jones** welcomes 20th century American Gene Kelly to the Scottish village that only appears one day in each century. Kelly will share its fate so he can be with his beloved Cyd Charisse. *Brigadoon* (1954, MGM).

6695 "In a child's power to master the multiplication table, there is more sanctity than in all your shouted 'amens' and 'holy holies' and 'hosannas.' An idea is a greater monument than a cathedral, and the advance of man's knowledge is a greater miracle than all the sticks turned to snakes or the parting of the waters. But, now, are we to forego all the progress because Mr. Brady now frightens us with a fable?" Defending the teaching of Darwin's theory of evolution in the Tennessee schools, Clarence Darrow-like attorney **Spencer Tracy** rejects William Jennings Bryan-like prosecutor Fredric March's notions that the only miracles are the ones described in the Bible and precisely as they are described in the Bible. *Inherit the Wind* (1960, United Artists).

6696 "The Egyptians must remain in Khartoum, for I shall take it in blood and the streets must flow with blood; and the Nile must taste of blood for a thousand miles downstream so that the whole of Islam will learn that my miracle is a great and terrible thing, and no man will stand against me." **Laurence Olivier,** as The Mahdi, shares his plan for domination of the Arab world with his adversary, Charlton Heston, as General Charles "China" Gordon. *Khartoum* (1966, United Artists).

6697 "I will not leave Khartoum, for I too, perform miracles. And you shall witness one. While I may die for your miracle, you will certainly die of mine." **Charlton Heston,** as General Charles "China" Gordon, promises The Mahdi, portrayed by Laurence Olivier, that he's in for a fight if he attempts to take Khartoum. *Khartoum* (1966, United Artists).

6698 "Oh, Torvald, I don't believe in miracles anymore. We would have to change so much." Ibsen's filmed play comes to an end with **Jane Fonda**'s declaration to her husband David Warner. *A Doll's House* (1973, GB, World Film Services).

6699 "Do you thing God was planning to waste a miracle on us?" Postulant **Genevieve Bujold** questions her priest lover Christopher Reeve. *Monsignor* (1982, 20th Century-Fox).

6700 "I don't know the meaning behind the song she sang. Perhaps it was a song of seduction, and the father was a field hand. Perhaps the song was some lullaby that she remembered from many years ago, and the father was hope and love and desire, the belief in miracles. I want to believe that she was blessed, and I do miss her, and hope she's left some little part of herself with me. That would be miracle enough, wouldn't it?" Psychiatrist **Jane Fonda** speaks of young novitiate Meg Tilly who seems to have had an immaculate conception and killed the consequences. *Agnes of God* (1985, Columbia).

6701 "Maybe because we don't have any experience with miracles is why we don't recognize them." **Mary McDonnell** tries to convince her husband Kevin Kline that some dramatic coincidences provided by the screen writer and director are miracles. *Grand Canyon* (1991, 20th Century-Fox).

6702 "A miracle without proof is just a miracle." Brazilian scientist **Jose Wilker** tells Lorraine Bracco that he can't accept that Sean Connery has found a cure for cancer since the latter can't replicate his earlier successes. *Medicine Man* (1992, Hollywood Pictures-Buena Vista).

Mischief *see* EVILNESS, TROUBLES

Misery *see* DESPAIR AND DESPERATION, SUFFERING AND SUFFERERS

Misfortune *see* FATE AND DESTINY, PROBLEMS, TROUBLES

Missed Things and Persons

see also ESCAPES, FAILURES, REGRETS

6703 "Why isn't there the smell of heather in your hair? Why are your eyes always empty?" **Laurence Olivier** refuses to love his wife Geraldine Fitzgerald because she isn't his beloved Merle Oberon. *Wuthering Heights* (1939, Goldwyn-United Artists).

6704 "Ricky, I'm going to miss you. Apparently you're the only one in Casablanca who has even less scruples than I." **Claude Rains** compliments Humphrey Bogart. Bogie allows Rains to believe that he plans to get the goods on Paul Henreid that will "chuck him in a concentration camp for years," while Bogie flies off with Henreid's wife Ingrid Bergman. *Casablanca* (1942, Warner Bros.).

6705 "No more than I would miss my eyes." **Robert Mitchum** replies to Jane Greer who asks, "Did you miss me?" *Out of the Past* (1947, RKO).

6706 "We have not missed, you and I—we have not missed that many-splendored thing." It's part of married U.S. war correspondent **William Holden**'s posthumous letter to his Eurasian lover Jennifer Jones. *Love Is a Many-Splendored Thing* (1955, 20th Century-Fox).

6707 "If you don't know what you're missin', then you're missin' it." Alcoholic maid **Thelma Ritter** believes career woman Doris Day needs a man. *Pillow Talk* (1959, Universal).

6708 "Oh, my God! I knew something was missing." **Louise Lasser** reacts when Woody Allen, disguised as the leader of a newly liberated Central American country, makes love to her, and then triumphantly reveals that he is the guy she dumped in New York City some time earlier. *Bananas* (1971, United Artists).

6709 "Sometimes I miss you even though we're together." Teenage rock 'n' roller **Adam Tonsberg** is completely consumed with love for Camila Soeberg. *Twist and Shout* (1986, Denmark-Cannon).

6710 "You know, sometimes I miss you, Gordon. You're really twisted." **Daryl Hannah** finds something to admire in her sometimes lover Michael Douglas—his self absorption, self-centeredness, indifference of other, greed,.... *Wall Street* (1987, 20th Century-Fox).

6711 "There was Watergate and Three Mile Island, acid rain, pollution. . . we blew a hole in the atmosphere. . . . Contra-gate. . . then crack came along to give marijuana a badname. . . ." **Julie Hagerty** ticks off some of the things 60s radicals Eric Roberts and Cheech Marin missed when they dropped out to live in a Central American jungle for 20 years. *Rude Awakening* (1989, Orion).

Missions and Missionaries

see also DUTIES, PRIESTS

6712 "I was born backwards. That is why I work in Africa as missionary, teaching little brown babies more backward than myself." While being questioned by Albert Finney as detective Hercule Poirot, investigating the murder of Richard Widmark aboard the Orient Express, **Ingrid Bergman** tells him she dedicates her life to helping those worse off than herself. *Murder on the Orient Express* (1974, GB, Paramount).

6713 "We're on a mission from God." At various times, both **James Belushi** and **Dan Aykroyd** announce their special errand. *The Blues Brothers* (1980, Universal).

6714 "Go out amongst the prostitutes, Fortescue. Find out what they do and why they do it, and stop them from doing it." Bishop **Denholm Elliott** assigns former African missionary Michael Palin to a London slum mission for "fallen women." *The Missionary* (1983, GB, Columbia).

Mistakes

see also CORRECTIONS, UNDERSTANDINGS AND MISUNDERSTANDINGS

6715 "We all make mistakes. Michelangelo painted Adam with a navel." Former World War I flyer **Richard Barthelmess** believes we're all born with human frailties. *The Last Flight* (1931, Warner Bros.).

6716 "I've made a mistake. I've stumbled and fallen, but I'm not throwing myself away." **Joan Crawford,** a girl with a past, joins the Salvation Army. *Laughing Sinners* (1931, MGM).

6717 "No, you're wrong, girls, you're wrong. In the first place, Gary Cooper is much taller than I am." Surrounded by pretty girls, **Groucho Marx** doth protest too much. *Monkey Business* (1931, Paramount).

6718 "Ejaculations!" **Joe E. Brown** means to say "Exaltations." *The Tenderfoot* (1931, Warner Bros.).

6719 "Don't make the same mistake twice—unless it pays." **Mae West** advises us to learn from our mistakes and repeat them if there's value in it. *Belle of the Nineties* (1934, Paramount).

6720 "We taught you how to think, your mother and I, and if you make a mistake, it's our mistake too." **Lionel Barrymore,** as Judge Hardy, shares the blame with his son Mickey Rooney, as Andy Hardy. *A Family Affair* (1937, MGM).

6721 "That's the first mistake we've made since that guy sold us the Brooklyn Bridge." **Stan Laurel** discovers that he and Oliver Hardy have handed over the deed to a gold mine to a phony heir. *Way Out West* (1937, Roach, MGM).

6722 "I've been waiting here two whole days. And I got to tell her that I was wrong about something." **Alicia Rhett** begs doctor Harry Davenport to see her sister-in-law Olivia de Havilland who is on her death bed. *Gone with the Wind* (1939, Selznick-MGM).

6723 "I can't help but think that there's been a big mistake made somehow." **James Stewart**'s first words in the film are at a banquet honoring him after the corrupt governor of the state appoints him to fill the unexpired term of a U.S. senator who has died. *Mr. Smith Goes to Washington* (1939, Columbia).

6724 "I debated before sending these. With these on, you might be mistaken for a girl." **Melvyn Dou-**glas' crude sentiment accompanies a corsage for Joan Crawford. *They All Kissed the Bride* (1942, Columbia).

6725 "If you think I'm going to stand there and let Dr. Lloyd splash me with water, you're mistaken." **William Powell** adamantly tells his wife Irene Dunne that he will not allow Minister Edmund Gwenn or anyone else baptize him. *Life with Father* (1947, Warner Bros.).

6726 "My mother wanted to make a priest out of me. I never wanted to do a decent thing until I met you. . . . Don't make the same mistake my mother did." Blackmailer **James Mason** admits that Joan Bennett invokes in him the memory and hopes his mother had for him. *The Reckless Moment* (1949, Columbia).

6727 "A lot of guys make mistakes, I guess, but every one we make, a whole stack of chips goes with it. We make a mistake, and some guy don't walk away—forever more, he don't walk away." Veteran Marine Sergeant **John Wayne** makes a strong point to gyrene Forrest Tucker that there's no margin for error in their work. *Sands of Iwo Jima* (1949, Republic).

6728 "They are like all rebel leaders. They mistake their own bitterness and frustration and hatred for devotion to cause." Priest **John Hoyt** speaks to John Barrymore, Jr. about his dead parents, French Canadians Patric Knowles and Corrine Calvert, who conspired to overthrow British rule in the 1830s. The question still has not been resolved. *Quebec* (1951, Paramount).

6729 "When I was new on this job, we brought in two boys caught stealing from a car. They looked like babies. They cried. I let them go. Two nights later—two nights! One of them held up a butcher in Harlem and shot him through the head and killed him. Yes, I made a mistake—and I'm not going to make it again." Police detective **Kirk Douglas** replies to Cathy O'Donnell, who while pleading that Craig Hill, who has stolen from his employer, be given another chance, asks if Douglas ever made a mistake. *Detective Story* (1951, Paramount).

6730 "I once thought you were a woman. I was wrong—you're nothing but a career." **Sterling Hayden** loses patience with Bette Davis who is obsessed with regaining her movie stardom. *The Star* (1952, 20th Century-Fox).

6731 "I should have anticipated this. Twenty years ago, I made the pardonable mistake of thinking I could civilize a girl who bought her hats out of a

Sears Roebuck catalogue." While crossing the ocean on the Titanic, **Clifton Webb** is told by his wife Barbara Stanwyck that she is leaving him and his snobbish, socialite ways, and that Harper Carter, whom he adores and adores him, is not his natural son. *Titanic* (1953, 20th Century-Fox).

6732 "They're making a mistake scraping this ship. The only thing keeping water out is the rust." Lazy sailor **Lee Marvin** finds good reason for not scraping the rust from the aging destroyer—mine sweeper U.S. Caine. *The Caine Mutiny* (1954, Columbia).

6733 "We're out in the middle of nowhere looking for nothing in the wrong season." **John Wayne**'s evaluation of seeking a lost city in the Sahara could as easily be applied to the film. *Legend of the Lost* (1957, United Artists).

6734 "I made the big mistake about five days ago. When I say big, I mean Radio City Music Hall big." New York Jew **Charles Grodin** confesses to midwestern WASP goddess Cybill Shepherd that his marriage to Jeannie Berlin is a mistake. He intends to get out of it so that he may pursue Shepherd. *The Heartbreak Kid* (1972, 20th Century-Fox).

6735 "I made the seeds too big." **George Burns,** as God, admits to fallibility or poor judgment in his creation of avocados. *Oh, God* (1977, Warner Bros.).

6736 NORMAN ROBBINS: "Remember, next week, China." CLAUDE EASTMAN: "I told you, no China." ROBBINS: "What? Shrugging off a whole continent. That's 800 million people. You get 200 million people to see you by mistake just because they are looking for a restaurant." **Albert Brooks** tries to convince his brother-in-law, orchestra conductor **Dudley Moore**, that he should make a tour of China. *Unfaithfully Yours* (1984, 20th Century-Fox).

6737 "What's that girl doing? What is she doing, taking pictures? Oh, no, give me a break. She is cute, though. Look at those legs. Hey, come on now, stop it, none of that stuff. I made a mistake. I learned my lesson, and I will never do it again." It's hard to believe that **Gene Wilder** won't make the same mistake again. After crawling out on the ledge of Kelly LeBrock's bedroom window when her husband comes home, married Wilder is thought to be a potential suicide. As he leaps to a safety net brought by the rescue squad he can only think of beautiful blonde Sandra Wilder who is photographing his descent. *The Woman in Red* (1984, Orion).

6738 "Oh, Lisa, I hear you, I hear what you're saying. Half of me says sure, do it, she's a great dame and you're crazy about her and this could surely be IT, boyo, and the other half says, sure, go ahead, but realize that somewhere down the line one of you will meet someone else, or it won't work out, and there will be tears and hurt and the whole shebang because you had a perfectly good thing going and go off and hinge everything on it, and wear it down with keys and commitments and all, because we couldn't leave well enough alone." **Ben Masters** gushes out his belief that any closer relationship with Brooke Adams will lead to disaster. *Key Exchange* (1985, 20th Century-Fox).

6739 "Decent people make mistakes sometimes." Liberal reporter **Anjelica Huston** comforts confused career soldier James Caan. *Gardens of Stone* (1987, Tri-Star).

6740 "Look, you've been thoroughly decent from first to last. So decent that I mistook your friendliness. . . . I thought it was something else. I'm sorry to have insulted you. . . . It's like the good blundering creature you are to try and comfort me, but there are limits. . . . I'm thankful that it was into your hands I fell. Most men would have reported me to the dean or the police." When **Hugh Grant** tells James Wilby that he loves him, he is initially rebuffed, but then Wilby confesses his love for Grant. *Maurice* (1987, GB, Cinecom).

6741 "Hector, I shouldn't be telling you this but you would find it out sooner or later. Ya father ain't no real father. He's a bum, a two-bit bum in a hundred dollar world. Your father is to the curb. You're smart. I see that look in ya face. You're saying if he's such a bum why am I with him? Good question. Like I said before, you're no dummy. He talked his way into my panties. I thought being a mother would make me happy, make me whole. He's a mistake, but you are not." **Rosie Perez,** holding her baby tightly to her breasts, demeans the boy's father Spike Lee. *Do the Right Thing* (1989, Universal).

Misunderstandings *see* UNDERSTANDINGS AND MISUNDERSTANDINGS

Mixtures

see also COMBINATIONS

6742 "Music and fighting don't mix." By the end of the film, **William Holden** faces a future without either. *Golden Boy* (1939, Columbia).

6743 "The Hill and The Coast are like champagne and beer. They don't mix." **George Raft** tells Joan

Bennett that a Nob Hill lady like her and a Barbary Coast gent such as himself have nothing in common. *Nob Hill* (1945, 20th Century-Fox).

6744 "For me, sex and money don't mix." **Molly Ringwald** rejects a gangster's suggestion that she sleep with a very rich Columbian drug dealer who has the hots for her. For Molly, it's not a question of morality, but one of attraction. *The Pickup Artist* (1987, 20th Century-Fox).

Models

6745 "Whatever I teach them, you show me up. You show them the easy way." **Pat O'Brien,** as Father Connelly, asks James Cagney, as mobster Rocky Sullivan, to give up his life of crime because he's a poor model for the neighborhood kids. *Angels with Dirty Faces* (1938, Warner Bros.).

6746 "He was a lantern. He helped me see things clear." **Henry Fonda** speaks eloquently of his martyred friend John Carradine. *The Grapes of Wrath* (1940, 20th Century-Fox).

6747 "You don't really do anything in modeling. People just sort of. . . use you." **Lana Turner** finds the modeling business not very glamorous. *A Life of Her Own* (1950, MGM).

6748 "Let me tell you I am not a father figure. I am not a brother figure or an uncle figure or a cousin figure. In fact, the only figure I intend being is a total stranger figure." During World War II, South Seas beachcomber **Cary Grant** unsuccessfully rejects an Australian request that he become the protector of stranded school mistress Leslie Caron and her six refugee students. *Father Goose* (1964, Universal-International).

6749 YALE: "You think you're God." ISAAC DAVIS: "I've got to model myself after someone." Professor **Michael Murphy** doesn't get a serious response from his friend, television writer **Woody Allen.** *Manhattan* (1979, United Artists).

6750 "If I could unzip myself and step out and be somebody else, I'd wanna be you." **Burt Young** is trying to pay his brother-in-law Sylvester Stallone a compliment. *Rocky IV* (1985, MGM-United Artists).

6751 "Except for socially, you're my role model." "Gofer" **Joan Cusack** wishes to emulate TV producer Holly Hunter up to a point. *Broadcast News* (1987, 20th Century-Fox).

Moderation *see* EXCESSES, SUFFICIENCY

Modesty

see also BEHAVIOR, BOASTS AND BRAGGING, HUMILITY AND HUMILIATION, PROPRIETY, VANITIES

6752 "That's very generous of you but the diamond was there. I merely applied a little polish." **John Barrymore** expresses some false modesty about directing actress Carole Lombard. *Twentieth Century* (1934, Columbia).

6753 "Your husband has a great deal to be modest about." Self-proclaimed genius **Clifton Webb** sort of agrees with Maureen O'Hara, who has complimented her husband Robert Young for being modest. *Sitting Pretty* (1948, 20th Century-Fox).

6754 "You're Roger Thornhill of Madison Avenue and you're wanted for murder on every front page in America—don't be so modest." **Eva Marie Saint** coolly tells Cary Grant she knows precisely who he is as they share a dining car table on a train from New York to Chicago. *North by Northwest* (1959, MGM).

6755 "She pulled her skirt down on her knees as if they were a national treasure." Businessman **Martin Gabel** betrays himself in describing his employee Tippi Hedren who has robbed him. He had eyes for more than just her knees. *Marnie* (1964, Universal).

Moments

see also TIME

6756 "But these moments are so precious. I want to keep them. I want to think of this old room and all the places where we've been happy. I want to remember you as you are tonight." Promiscuous Parisian model **Greta Garbo** slips away while her lover Robert Montgomery sleeps. She's being very noble, leaving him because of her dissolute life and the realization that she'll never be faithful to just one man. *Inspiration* (1931, MGM).

6757 SABIEN PASTAL: "I want this moment to last." PRINCESS NADYA: "How long?" PASTAL: "At least until breakfast." Commoner **Fredric March** attempts to seduce **Claudette Colbert,** princess of a small mythical middle-European country. *Tonight Is Ours* (1932, Paramount).

6758 ACE LAMONT: "It won't be all work. You will have moments of your own." RUBY CARTER: "Well, I do have my moments." ACE: "You have?" RUBY: "Yeah, but they're all weak ones." **John Miljan** shows **Mae West** around his establishment, "The

Sensation House" where he wants her to work. *Belle of the Nineties* (1934, Paramount).

6759 "Right in the moment when you're sure you've got me buffaloed, that's when you'll die." Waitress **Kim Basinger** wants to destroy her obsession for her cowboy half-brother Sam Shepard by killing him. *Fool for Love* (1985, Cannon).

Monarchy *see* KINGS AND QUEENS

Money

see also BUSINESS AND COMMERCE, BUYING AND SELLING, GOLD, PAYMENTS, PRICES, WEALTH AND RICHES

6760 "No, my friends, no, money will never make you happy—and happy will never make you money. That might be a wise crack, but I doubt it." Hotel manager **Groucho Marx** cons the bellboys and bellgirls out of their back pay. *The Cocoanuts* (1929, Paramount).

6761 "Get outta here, small change, you don't look like big money to me." Beautiful young black dancer **Nina Mae McKinney** hasn't time for poor cotton picker Daniel L. Haynes. *Hallelujah!* (1929, MGM).

6762 "You've got beauty, style, money. . . you have got money, haven't you? If not, we can quit right now." In the midst of a romantic scene, **Groucho Marx** makes no bones about which of Margaret Dumont's attributes are most important to him. *Animal Crackers* (1930, Paramount).

6763 "He has everything a woman wants. . . nothing but money." Countess **Jeannette MacDonald** has run out on her wedding to silly-ass-duke Claud Allister. She slips out of her wedding dress, throws a coat over her underwear, and boards the first train out of town. *Monte Carlo* (1930, Paramount).

6764 "Money's all right, but it ain't everything. No, be somebody, know that a bunch of guys will do anything you tell 'em, have your own way or nothin'." Mobster **Edward G. Robinson** knows that control is more valuable than money. *Little Caesar* (1931, Warner Bros.).

6765 "Unemployed money leads to unemployed men. . . . The answer is bank money, fuel to start industry's wheels turning again. Hoarding money in vaults makes as much sense as pouring oil back into oil wells." Populist **Walter Huston** appears in one of the few movies in which a banker is a hero—a misunderstood and put-upon hero at that. *American Madness* (1932, Columbia).

6766 "She makes forty-five dollars a week and sends her mother a hundred of it." **Una Merkel** marvels at the financial acumen and generosity of another chorus girl. *42nd Street* (1933, Warner Bros.).

6767 E. "EDDY" HUNTINGTON HALL: "That reminds me. I left something in my pants pocket. Say, listen, I had two tens when I came in here. What could've happened to the other one." RUBY ADAMS: "That must be awful hard for you to figure out." While hiding from the police in **Jean Harlow**'s apartment, **Clark Gable** gets his clothes wet in her tub. He notices something missing while she's ironing his clothes. *Hold Your Man* (1933, MGM).

6768 JIMMY CORRIGAN: "Look, baby, what would you do for five hundred bucks?" MABEL: "I'd do my best." **James Cagney** gets the kind of answer he hoped for from **Alice White**. *Jimmy the Gent* (1934, Warner Bros.).

6769 LOTTA MORGAN: "Do you think money grows on trees?" BARNEY GLASGOW: "Mine did." Tough saloon girl **Frances Farmer** is barking up the wrong tree with her financial line to timber tycoon **Edward Arnold**. *Come and Get It* (1936, Goldwyn/United Artists).

6770 "Money, money! The Frankenstein monster that destroys souls!" Free-loader **Mischa Auer** has nothing but disgust for money. As long as he's Alice Brady's "protégé" he doesn't need any. *My Man Godfrey* (1936, Universal).

6771 "I'm not allowed to take money. Internes can't do that while they're serving time at a hospital." **Joel McCrea,** as Jimmie Kildare, refuses a $1000 gift from mob boss Lloyd Nolan. McCrea skillfully wields a scalpel and saves Nolan's life after he was shot in a bar. One of Nolan's henchmen, impressed by McCrea's technique says: "The kid's got eyes in his fingers." *Internes Can't Take Money* (1937, Paramount).

6772 "We do not seek personal fortunes. We have no money as you know it." **H.B. Warner** tells Ronald Colman that the people of Shangri-La have no need for money. *Lost Horizon* (1937, Columbia).

6773 MELSA MANTON: "Can you afford it?" PETER AMES: "No, but you can." MELSA: "Isn't there a drop of red blood in your veins? I wanted to live on your income." PETER: "That's foolish. Who's going to live on yours?" Wealthy socialite **Barbara Stanwyck** can't believe that newspaper man **Henry Fonda** suggests they spend her money on a honeymoon to South America. This is at a time before pre-nuptial agreements. *The Mad Miss Manton* (1938, RKO).

6774 "You might as well take my money, Miz Wilkes. It's good money even if it's mine." **Ona Munson,** who runs an Atlanta brothel, offers money to Olivia de Havilland for the hospital. *Gone with the Wind* (1939, Selznick-MGM).

6775 PENNY COOPER: "I'm afraid the revolution is over. You're probably just marrying me for my money." ALAN BLAKE: "Sure I am, but it's nice you're good-lookin' too, cutie pants." Soup heiress **Brenda Joyce** drops her communistic sympathies after Russia invades Finland. She plans to marry waiter **George Murphy,** who gave her a public spanking. *Public Deb No. 1* (1940, 20th Century-Fox).

6776 "A girl's best friend is a dollar." Selfish night-club singer **Lucille Ball** has a better friend in busboy Henry Fonda, but she doesn't appreciate it. It was one of the famous redhead's few roles as an unlikable person. *The Big Street* (1942, RKO).

6777 "You live in a dream. You're a sleepwalker, blind. How do you know what the world is like? Do you know that the world is a foul sty? Do you know if you rip the fronts off houses you find swine. . . silly wives. . . and what do these women do? You see them in the best hotels. Eating the money. Drinking the money. Losing at bridge. Smelling of money. Proud of it but of nothing else. Fat, wheezing animals. And what do we do to such animals when they get too lazy and too fat?" **Joseph Cotten**'s tirade arouses the suspicion of his niece Teresa Wright that he is the "Merry Widow" murderer. *Shadow of a Doubt* (1943, Universal).

6778 "For money, some men will allow the innocent to hang. . . ." The movie's foreword. *The Mask of Dimitrios* (1944, Warner Bros.).

6779 "Money talks, they say. All it ever said to me was 'good-bye.'" Cockney drifter **Cary Grant** is always short of funds. *None But the Lonely Heart* (1944, RKO).

6780 "It's a piece of paper crawling with germs. . . . Money causes problems in the world simply because there's too little of it." Night club pianist **Tom Neal** is one of the have-nots. *Detour* (1945, Producers Releasing Corporation).

6781 "It was Dandy Gow's hope, Robert, that you'd spend the sum wisely on your education. But I seem to mind him saying—oh, sort of an afterthought, it was—that if you preferred to invest it in wine, women and song, that was your privilege." Lawyer **Lumsden Hare** tells Tom Drake of his great-grandfather's wishes with respect to the insurance money Drake inherits. *The Green Years* (1946, MGM).

6782 "You throw money around like it was money." Out-of-work **John Ireland** comments to politician Broderick Crawford who hires Ireland for $400 a month and expenses to do "research," i.e., dig up dirt on Crawford's opponents. *All the King's Men* (1949, Columbia).

6783 "Money is the only thing that counts." **Henry Hull** informs Alan Ladd that his sensuous young wife Carole Mathews will never leave Hull for Ladd, because the former has lots of money and the latter doesn't. Ladd takes this shallow philosophy to heart and makes the pursuit of wealth his life's work. *The Great Gatsby* (1949, Paramount).

6784 "Money, what is money but the vulgar implement to tempt man's soul?" **S.Z. "Cuddles" Sakall** is unable to support his family as a "serious musician," but is quite a success writing popular ballads. *Oh, You Beautiful Doll* (1949, 20th Century-Fox).

6785 "All right, stop it, Kristo. There you are, Kristo. Give her the blood money. She cut my throat for you." Trying to save his one true love, Gene Tierney, conniving **Richard Widmark** shouts to Herbert Lom that she's led them to him. Widmark tries to run but runs right into Mike Mazurki, who kills him. *Night and the City* (1950, 20th Century-Fox).

6786 "I'm awfully sorry, but I don't have anything smaller." Shabby-looking **Gregory Peck** casually presents a million pound banknote to pay for a meal at a fancy restaurant. *The Million Pound Note* aka: *Man with a Million* (1954, GB, GFD).

6787 "Money isn't dirty, just people." Gun moll **Kim Novak** defends the money she makes in unprincipled ways. *Pushover* (1954, Columbia).

6788 "What has she got more than me, except money?" Sexy French girl **Brigitte Auber** pouts to Cary Grant about his interest in elegant beauty Grace Kelly. *To Catch a Thief* (1955, Paramount).

6789 LESLIE BENEDICT: "Money isn't all, you know, Jett." JETT RINK: "Not when you got it." It's always easier for wealthy people like **Elizabeth Taylor** to discount the importance of money than it is for dirt poor folks like **James Dean**. *Giant* (1956, Warner Bros.).

6790 "A man that gives away twenty-six thousand dollars you can't talk to. I want to tell you one more thing. I wouldn't give you twenty-six cents for your future." Corrupt boxing promoter **Rod**

Steiger threatens sportswriter Humphrey Bogart, who plans to expose Steiger. *The Harder They Fall* (1956, Columbia).

6791 "That's what I like—everything in contrasting shades of money." Neurotic cartoonist **Bob Hope** takes in the luxurious apartment of his new boss George Sanders. *That Certain Feeling* (1956, Paramount).

6792 "You can be young without money, but you can't be old without it." **Elizabeth Taylor** makes the need for money a function of age. *Cat on a Hot Tin Roof* (1958, MGM).

6793 "Money seems to have lost its value these days. With $200,000 my grandfather cornered the wheat market and started a panic in Omaha. Today, you can't even frighten songwriters with it." Millionaire **Tony Randall** complains to songwriter Rock Hudson. *Pillow Talk* (1959, Universal).

6794 "You started out with nothing and you've really made something of yourself. Me? I started out in college with eight million dollars and I've still got eight million dollars. I just can't get ahead." **Tony Randall** envies Rock Hudson's success. *Pillow Talk* (1959, Universal).

6795 "I never carry more money than I can afford to lose." Slightly tipsy **Frank Albertson** flashes $40,000 in cash in front of a desperate Janet Leigh, almost begging her to steal it. *Psycho* (1960, Paramount).

6796 "Not much money. It's all I can afford." Starving painter **Woody Allen** has a job helping strippers dress between numbers for which he pays twenty francs a week. *What's New, Pussycat?* (1965, United Artists).

6797 "What's wrong? Insurance companies have too much, they have to microfilm it!" Shyster lawyer **Walter Matthau** justifies cheating an insurance company by pretending that Jack Lemmon is more hurt in an accident than he really is. *The Fortune Cookie* (1966, United Artists).

6798 "Money is like fertilizer. It does more good if you spread it around." **Barbra Streisand**'s economics lesson is lost on cheap businessman Walter Matthau. *Hello, Dolly!* (1968, 20th Century-Fox).

6799 BUTCH CASSIDY: "It's not as bad as it might be—you get more for your money in Bolivia than anywhere—I checked." SUNDANCE KID: "What could they sell here you could possibly want to buy?" **Paul Newman, Robert Redford** and Katharine Ross arrive in the middle of nowhere in Bolivia. *Butch Cassidy and the Sundance Kid* (1969, 20th Century-Fox).

6800 "I don't want to spend the rest of my life grubbing around for money as if nothing else in the world existed." As a librarian, **Richard Benjamin** won't have a lot of money to worry about. *Goodbye, Columbus* (1969, Paramount).

6801 "We don't have to steal nothing no more, boy. I got nine bucks left and twenty more Thursday and before you know it we're gonna be riding on Easy Street." Homeless dumb New York City hustler **Jon Voight** tries to cheer up his only friend, crippled and sick street person Dustin Hoffman. *Midnight Cowboy* (1969, United Artists).

6802 "A bankroll so big that when you walk down the street it's gonna look like your pockets have the mumps. . . . Being rich and black means something." Black pimp **Max Julien** has ambition. *The Mack* (1973, Cinerama).

6803 "Money buys dignity. Poverty is a crime. Nobody asks you where you got your dollars, they ask do you have it." Black soul brother gone bad, **Rod Perry** figures the almighty dollar is almighty important. *The Black Godfather* (1974, Cinemation).

6804 "Hyman Roth always makes money for his partners." **Dominic Chianese** encourages Al Pacino to make a criminal alliance with Jewish mobster Lee Strasberg. *The Godfather, Part II* (1974, Paramount).

6805 MISS ANAHEIM: "Boys get money for making touchdowns, why shouldn't girls get money for being cute?" MISS ANTELOPE VALLEY: "Yeah, but maybe boys shouldn't get money for playing football." **Annette O'Toole** responds with a kind of logic when **Joan Prather** remarks that perhaps beauty pageants are a little demeaning. Actually football and beauty pageants are both absurd, but can be entertaining. *Smile* (1975, United Artists).

6806 "Follow the money." **Hal Holbrook** as "Deep Throat" advises Robert Redford as Washington Post reporter Bob Woodward how to get the goods on the Watergate scandal and cover-up. *All the President's Men* (1976, Warner Bros.).

6807 "There's money to be made from rich hippies who like to spread polyurethane all over their houses." Rural Texas dreamer **Lou Perry** is ready to risk his fortune on a polyurethane business. *The Whole Shootin' Match* (1978, Cinema Perspectives).

6808 "I think that girl can make herself fifty dollars real easy tonight. . . if she can get up the stairs ten or twelve times. Bitchy **Carrie Nye** rips a cheap, sexy-looking woman dancing at a political party. *The Seduction of Joe Tynan* (1979, Universal).

6809 "Money, capital has a life of its own." Banking tycoon **Hume Cronyn** makes a financial statement. *Rollover* (1981, Warner Bros.).

6810 "I wish I had a dime for every dime I have." Wealthy alcoholic **Dudley Moore** makes sense to himself. *Arthur* (1981, Orion).

6811 "If you had a job, you would have the money to help your friend out yourself! I'm going to ask father to lower your stipend." **Richard Pierson** refuses his brother Kevin Bacon's request for money to help out his friend Mickey Rourke. *Diner* (1982, MGM).

6812 "My father left me forty million dollars. In those days that was a lot of money." **Albert Finney,** as Daddy Warbucks, tells how he got his start on his way to real wealth. *Annie* (1983, Columbia).

6813 "Do you want to accomplish anything or just make money?" When teenager **Tom Cruise** puts this question to his high school friends, their answer is unhesitantly, "Make money." The age of youthful idealism is over. *Risky Business* (1983, Warner Bros.).

6814 "Money is God's Music." It's the title of marketing ace Eric Roberts' master thesis. *The Coca-Cola Kid* (1985, Australia, Cinecom).

6815 "It's not about pool, it's about money. Money won is twice as sweet as money earned. . . the best is the guy with the most." Old pool hustler **Paul Newman** instructs young pool hustler Tom Cruise. *The Color of Money* (1986, Touchstone/Buena Vista).

6816 "Well, sir, like a lot of people who make a lot of money, you don't seem to have any." Blackmailer **John Glover** is disappointed as he goes over the account books of his victim Roy Scheider. *52 Pick-Up* (1986, Cannon).

6817 "Money really means nothing to me. Do you think I'd treat my parents' house this way if it did?" Effete, rich snob **James Spader** gestures to a household full of kids drinking and making out. *Pretty in Pink* (1986, Paramount).

6818 "Money never sleeps, pal. Just made $800,000 in Hong Kong gold; it's been wired to you. Play with it. You done good, but you gotta keep doing good. I showed you how the game works. Now school's out. . . I want to be surprised. Astonish me, pal. . . I'm going to make you rich, Buddy Fox. Rich

enough that you can afford a girl like Darien. This is your wake up call, pal. Go to work." Stock manipulator **Michael Douglas** calls Charlie Sheen at daybreak with the "good news" that he's to become a "player." *Wall Street* (1987, 20th Century-Fox).

6819 "Money is only something you need in case you don't die tomorrow." Coming with a different view of wealth, **Martin Sheen** asserts to his greedy son Charlie Sheen that the quest for money shouldn't rule one's life. *Wall Street* (1987, 20th Century-Fox).

6820 "I like older men. They have more money." Older men with money tend to like beautiful sexy **Greta Scacchi**. *White Mischief* (1988, GB, Columbia).

6821 SUZIE WAGGONER: "Kinda like Robin Hood?" FREDERICK J. FRENGER, JR.: "Yeah, except I don't give the money to the poor." Novice hooker **Jennifer Jason Leigh** questions **Alec Baldwin** about his hard day fleecing shoppers at a Miami mall. *Miami Blues* (1990, Orion).

6822 "You and I are similar creatures; we both screw people for money." Prostitute Julia Roberts' occupation is probably less distasteful than that of businessman **Richard Gere**, who makes unfriendly take-overs of companies, then sells off their assets. *Pretty Woman* (1990, Touchstone-Buena Vista).

6823 "I love money more than the things it can buy. . . but what I love more than money is other people's money." Before the opening credits have rolled across the screen, **Danny De Vito,** as Louie the Liquidator, has already told the audience what makes him tick. *Other People's Money* (1991, Warner Bros.).

6824 "A man who travels with two servants and claims he's without money is either a fool or a liar." **Nick Brimble,** as Little John, demands that Kevin Costner and his two companions pay for the privilege of crossing a river near Sherwood Forest. *Robin Hood: Prince of Thieves* (1991, Warner Bros.).

Monotony *see* BOREDOM AND BORES

Monsters

see also ANIMALS, CRUELTY, HUMANITY, HUMAN NATURE, IMAGINATION

6825 "He makes Frankenstein look like a lily." Wisecracking reporter **Glenda Farrell** has briefly seen disfigured monster Lionel Atwill. *The Mystery of the Wax Museum* (1933, Warner Bros.).

6826 "There's a monster afoot and you know it! He's in your control! By heaven, I think you're a worse fiend than your father! Where is the monster?. . . I'll stay by your side until you confess. And if you don't, I'll feed you to the villagers like the Romans fed the Christians to the lions." One-armed Police Inspector **Lionel Atwill** hounds Basil Rathbone who has revived his father's monster. The creature is once again on a killing spree. *Son of Frankenstein* (1939, Universal).

6827 "My heart is good, but I am a monster." **Jean Marais** assures Josette Day that his terrifying appearance doesn't mean he's a terrible person. *La Belle et la Bête* aka: *Beauty and the Beast* (1946, Fr., Discina-Lopert).

6828 "You can print it if you want to. Karl Schneider was a monster who murdered two girls and got away with it. High time somebody put the fear of God in him. The law wouldn't, so I did." Police detective **Kirk Douglas** proudly addresses a reporter after the former slugs hated abortionist George Macready. *Detective Story* (1951, Paramount).

6829 "We're all part monsters in our unconscious. That's why we have laws and religion." Commander **Leslie Nielsen** warns innocent Anne Francis who has never seen a monster or a man other than her father before. *Forbidden Planet* (1956, MGM).

6830 "You dirty, filthy, perverted monster! You are the meanest, cruelest, most loathsome thing I've ever met." **Carroll Baker** just about says it all about her former lover and stepson Howard Hughes—like George Peppard. *The Carpetbaggers* (1964, Paramount).

6831 "I'm loud and I'm vulgar and I wear the pants in the house because somebody's got to, but I'm not a monster." Shrewish **Elizabeth Taylor** tries to defend herself. *Who's Afraid of Virginia Woolf?* (1966, Warner Bros.).

6832 "[You're] a wretched, grotesque, ridiculous, insignificant little monster." Naked **Daliah Lavi** lashes out at Woody Allen who has her strapped down to a table with shiny aluminum bands. *Casino Royale* (1967, GB, Columbia).

6833 "It wouldn't be the first time in history a monster was mistaken for a god. I guess that's why I have to kill it. If you can kill it, it's not a god, just a good old-fashioned monster." Detective **David Carradine** uses the same reasoning as did the Romans and Jewish high priests with Jesus. *Q: Quetzalcoatl* (1982, UFD).

6834 "He's not a psychopath! He's an iceman. He's a monster." Prosecutor **Peter Coyote** tries to make Defense Attorney Glenn Close recognize the kind of guy her client and lover Jeff Bridges is. *Jagged Edge* (1985, Ransohoff Columbia).

6835 "My mommy said there are no monsters, no real monsters, but there are." Terrified little **Carrie Henn,** clutching a headless doll, is not at all reassured by Sigourney Weaver that everything is going to be all right. *Aliens* (1986, 20th Century-Fox).

6836 "I really like you, Tomas. You are the most complete opposite of kitsch. In the Kingdom of Kitsch, you would be a monster." **Lena Olin** compliments Daniel Day-Lewis in an unusual manner. *The Unbearable Lightness of Being* (1988, Orion).

6837 "We're both perceived as monsters, but you're a well-respected monster and I—to date—am not." **Danny De Vito,** as the Penguin, wants to alter his image and be like ruthless industrialist Christopher Walken. *Batman Returns* (1992, Warner Bros.).

Monuments *see* BUILDINGS, RUINATION AND RUINS

Moods

see also ANGER, COURAGE, EMOTIONS, FEELINGS, HATE AND HATRED, JEALOUSY, LOVE AND HATE, SPIRIT AND SPIRITS

6838 "Now listen, I'm in a very ugly mood. I put up a stiff battle for that seat. So if it's just the same with you—scram." Out-of-work, reporter **Clark Gable** angrily dismisses runaway heiress Claudette Colbert on a cross country bus. *It Happened One Night* (1934, Columbia).

6839 "Now, Sonia, if you feel in the mood for a banker, the door is not locked." Womanizer **Maurice Chevalier** offers Jeanette MacDonald the opportunity to leave, when she says she prefers rich men. He believes her to be a courtesan, but in fact she's an immensely wealthy widow from his country, whom he has been ordered to woo. *The Merry Widow* (1934, MGM).

6840 "How hard is it to decide to be in a good mood and just be in a good mood?" **John Cusack** asks a difficult question. *Say Anything. . .* (1989, 20th Century-Fox).

6841 "I'm not crazy, I've just been in a really bad mood for 40 years." And it looks as if **Shirley MacLaine** will be in a bad mood for the next 40 years as well. *Steel Magnolias* (1989, Tri-Star).

Moon and Moonlight

see also NIGHTS

6842 "Just think—tonight, tonight when the moon is sneaking around the clouds, I'll be sneaking around you. I'll meet you tonight under the moon. Oh, I can see you now—you and the moon. You wear a necktie so I'll know you." Hotel manager **Groucho Marx** courts wealthy guest Margaret Dumont with a bit of double-talk. *The Cocoanuts* (1929, Paramount).

6843 "The moonlight's so terrible." **Martha Scott** exchanges teenage confidences with William Holden from the windows of their facing bedrooms. *Our Town* (1940, United Artists).

6844 GEORGE BAILEY: "What is it you want, Mary? What do you want? You—you want the moon? Just say the word, and I'll throw a lasso around it and pull it down. Hey, that's a pretty good idea. I'll give you the moon." MARY HATCH: "I'll take it." Coming home from a dance in a weird assortment of clothes after they fell in the pool, **James Stewart** and **Donna Reed** are falling in love. The mood and the love will have to wait—news comes that Stewart's father Samuel S. Hinds has had a heart attack and died. *It's a Wonderful Life* (1946, RKO).

6845 "It's the moon, that's what it is." **Ernest Borgnine** believes his son Tony Franciosa is a lunatic when he announces that he's decided to marry Gina Lollobrigida, despite her history as a high-priced call girl. *Go Naked in the World* (1960, MGM).

6846 "I'll bet there's a lover's moon out tonight." The last words of the film belong to **Cindy Fisher**, who in one ending of the movie, dies after a botched abortion. In another version, she survives. *Liar's Moon* (1982, Crown International).

Morality

see also BEHAVIOR, CONSCIENCES, GOOD AND EVIL, GOODNESS, IMMORALITY, INTEGRITY, VIRTUES

6847 "My morality—my religion—must have a place for cannons and torpedoes in it." Munitions manufacturer **Robert Morley** isn't interested in salvation that requires him to change his business. *Major Barbara* (1941, GB, Pascal-Rank-United Artists).

6848 "And if that isn't a moral story, I don't know what is." Scot narrator **Finlay Currie** sums up in an epilogue to a movie in which the scarcity of whisky caused inhabitants of an Outer Hebrides island to resort to desperate measures during World War II. *Whisky Galore* aka: *Tight Little Island* (1949, GB, Ealing-Universal).

6849 DR. OTTO HASSLEIN: "We have evidence that one day talking apes will dominate the earth and destroy it by 3950." THE PRESIDENT: "Given the power to alter the future, have we the right to use it?" HASSLEIN: "I don't know. . . . If I urge the destruction of these apes, am I defying God's will or obeying it?" PRESIDENT: "Do you approve of assassination?" HASSLEIN: "Mr. President, we condoned the attempted assassination of Hitler because he was evil." PRESIDENT: "Yes, but would we have approved killing him in babyhood when he was still innocent? Or killing his mother when he was still in her womb? Or slaughtering his remote ancestors?" **Eric Braeden**, President **William Windom**'s science advisor, warns that intelligent apes from the future, Roddy McDowall and Kim Hunter, pose a threat to mankind and they should be prevented from breeding. *Escape from the Planet of the Apes* (1971, 20th Century-Fox).

6850 "Vice? Virtue? It's best not to be too moral. You cheat yourself out of too much life. Aim above morality. As Confucius says, 'Don't simply be good, make good things happen.'" **Ruth Gordon** puts her words in Confucius' mouth for the benefit of young Bud Cort. *Harold and Maude* (1971, Paramount).

6851 "Might makes right. . . . For those who want morality there's morality. Nothing's handed down in stone." At a family seder that Martin Landau imagines, his Aunt **Anna Berger** argues the Holocaust proves there is no absolute moral structure. *Crimes and Misdemeanors* (1989, Orion).

Morning *see* DAYS

Mothers

see also CHILDREN AND CHILDHOOD, DAUGHTERS, FATHERS, PARENTS, SONS AND SONS-IN-LAW

6852 "And my own dear mama, wherever she is, God bless her and keep her safe from harm." Young **Buster Phelps** prays for his mother Ann Dvorak who sacrificed her life to save his. *Three on a Match* (1932, Warner Bros.).

6853 "That's the trouble with mothers. You get to like them and they die." **Kay Francis** struggles for words of comfort when she learns that Miriam Hopkins' mother is no longer alive. *Trouble in Paradise* (1932, Paramount).

6854 TED DREW: "You're as good as my mother. Mother used to kiss me good night." REGI ALLEN: "I'm almost as good as your mother was." When

Fred MacMurray tumbles out of bed and awakens **Carole Lombard**, he asks her to tuck him in, which she does. *Hands Across the Table* (1935, Paramount).

6855 "I'm not the marrying kind. What do I need with a wife? I've got you, haven't I?" **James Cagney** feigns disinterest in a girl friend as he jokes with his mother Mary Gordon. *The Irish in Us* (1935, First National-Warner Bros.).

6856 "I'm my mother's girl." **Barbara Stanwyck** snaps when mobster Joseph Calleia asks prizefight promoter Adolphe Menjou, "This your girl?" *Golden Boy* (1939, Columbia).

6857 "Where is my mother going away to, and why can't I go along, please?" Young **Mickey Kuhn** doesn't understand that his mother Olivia de Havilland is dying. *Gone with the Wind* (1939, Selznick-MGM).

6858 "Tonight, just tonight, she belongs to me! Tonight, I want her to call me Mommy!" Self-sacrificing, unwed mother **Bette Davis** just once wishes to receive the daughterly love of Jane Bryan, who considers Miriam Hopkins her mother and Davis an old maid aunt. *The Old Maid* (1939, Warner Bros.).

6859 "You are the mother she wants and needs tonight. She is not mine—just as her father was never really mine. At least she was mine—when she was little." Later spinster **Bette Davis** is finally resigned to the fact that her daughter Jane Bryan, who calls Davis "aunt," will always think of Davis' cousin Miriam Hopkins, who raised Bryan, as her mother. Davis urges Hopkins to go to Bryan on the eve of the latter's wedding. *The Old Maid* (1939, Warner Bros.).

6860 "You mustn't kid mother, dear. I was a married woman before you were born." **Lucile Watson** comforts her daughter Norma Shearer, whose husband is having an affair with Joan Crawford. *The Women* (1939, MGM).

6861 "My mother told me always to count to ten. And if that doesn't do the trick, start over again." Burlesque queen **Lucille Ball** passes on some advice to newcomer Maureen O'Hara on dealing with the indignities of their profession. *Dance, Girl, Dance* (1940, RKO).

6862 "You're no more my mother than a toad." **Gene Tierney** vehemently refuses to accept that Oriental Ona Munson, the twisted criminal proprietor of a Shanghai gambling den, is her mother. *The Shanghai Gesture* (1941, United Artists).

6863 "Don't disgrace me, Ma, this is your son, Ernie Mott. Ma! This is the boy who loves you, needs you, wants you." Shiftless Cockney lad **Cary Grant** finally pleases his mother Ethel Barrymore after she is arrested for being a fence to get money for him. *None But the Lonely Heart* (1944, RKO).

6864 "So much for Mrs. Hollis' nine months of pain and 20 years of hope." Parachutist **John Whitney** bitterly mutters after finding William Hudson's body during a mission behind Japanese lines in World War II. *Objective Burma* (1944, Warner Bros.).

6865 "You know, I've got a mother that's anxious to meet you." After solving the case of a murdered composer, Police Lieutenant **George Raft** decides Lynn Bari is the girl to take home to mother. *Nocturne* (1946, RKO).

6866 "I'm not his mother, not really. Just bringing a child into the world doesn't make you that. It's being there always, nursing him. . . all the things I've missed." Biological mother **Olivia de Havilland** comes to the conclusion after a traumatic meeting with the child who is unaware of their relationship. *To Each His Own* (1946, Paramount).

6867 "What is a mother?" In post World War II Germany, fleeting Czech refugee boy **Ivan Jandl** asks a heart-rending question of his new friend, American G.I. Montgomery Clift. *The Search* (1948, U.S.-Switzerland, MGM-Praesens Film).

6868 "All I ever had is Ma." Violent gangster **James Cagney** admits his Oedipus complex. *White Heat* (1949, Warner Bros.).

6869 "That was a good feeling out there, talking to Ma. . . . Maybe I am nuts." Psychopathic criminal **James Cagney** expresses some doubts about his sanity when he confesses to Edmond O'Brien that he has been walking around having a conversation with his dead mother. *White Heat* (1949, Warner Bros.).

6870 "My mother said men are born evil and cruel." **David Wayne** makes a case for his mother being to blame that he's a child killer. *M* (1951, Columbia).

6871 "Trouble with you, Phyllis, is you don't know what it means to be a mother! I do." Widower **Van Heflin** knows that hot-shot TV personality Virginia Field is not the one to raise his children. *Weekend with Father* (1951, Universal).

6872 "I put a crimp in her career. It slows her down, having a growing boy around the house, but that's all right because she gives me two big weeks at home—Christmas and Easter—plus an autographed picture of herself for my birthday, signed 'Sincerely, Gertrude Vanderhof.' It comes out of the studio mailing room. It seems they've got me mixed up with one of her fans." **Lee Kinsolving** sadly tells Shirley Knight that he has no life with his movie actress mother, who barely knows he's alive-or cares. *The Dark at the Top of the Stairs* (1960, Warner Bros.).

6873 "A boy's best friend is his mother." **Anthony Perkins**'s insincerity is clear to motel guest Janet Leigh. *Psycho* (1960, Paramount).

6874 "Mother—what is the phrase? Isn't quite herself today." **Anthony Perkins** apologizes to motel guest Janet Leigh, who has overheard a shrill exchange between Perkins and his mother, coming from their house, with Leigh the subject of the argument. *Psycho* (1960, Paramount).

6875 "It's all part of your contempt for the family unit. You think mother is a dirty word." Ordinarily tolerant **Angela Lansbury** shouts contemptuously at her narcissistic and callous son Warren Beatty. *All Fall Down* (1962, MGM).

6876 "My momma loved me, but she died." Drunken **Paul Newman** has come home to a scathing denunciation of his evil ways by his father Melvyn Douglas. *Hud* (1963, Paramount).

6877 "My mother's a Jezebel. She's so overloaded with sex that it sparkles! She's golden and striped like something in the jungle!" Feeling unloved, young **Hayley Mills** has unkind words for her mother Elizabeth Sellars, who remarried and dumped Mills with her grandmother. *The Chalk Garden* (1964, GB, Universal).

6878 "Momma, why don't you love me?" Frigid amnesiac and kleptomaniac **Tippi Hedren** pitifully pleads with unyielding Louise Latham. *Marnie* (1964, Universal).

6879 "You're all flops. I am the Earth Mother, and you're all flops." **Elizabeth Taylor** shouts to George Segal that he and all men are failures. *Who's Afraid of Virginia Woolf?* (1966, Warner Bros.).

6880 MAYOR OLLY PERKINS: "She takes after her dear departed mother." JASON McCULLOUGH: "Her mother is dead?" PERKINS: "No, she just departed." Mayor **Harry Morgan** and his new Sheriff **James Garner** are discussing Morgan's accident-prone daughter Joan Hackett. *Support Your Local Sheriff* (1969, United Artists).

6881 "Your mother sucks cock in hell." The voice of **Mercedes McCambridge,** as the demon possessing young Linda Blair, screams at priest Jason Miller. *The Exorcist* (1973, Warner Bros.).

6882 "You're not a mother, you're a telephone operator." **Henry Thomas** believes his mother Sissy Spacek's work comes ahead of her children. *Raggedy Man* (1981, Universal).

6883 SPENCER: "So my old lady's a dyke. Big deal." LIANNA: "I'm not your old lady, I'm your mother." **Jesse Solomon**'s mother **Linda Griffiths** corrects a portion of her son's observation. *Lianna* (1983, United Artists).

6884 "I remember in high school her saying, 'Now what'd you want to take that science class for? There's no girls in that science class. You take home ec, why don't you? That's the way to meet the nice boys.' 'Mom,' I said, 'There ain't no boys in home ec. The boys are in the science class.' She hated when I said 'ain't.'" **Meryl Streep** recalls discussing her studies with her mother. *Silkwood* (1983, 20th Century-Fox-ABC).

6885 "It sure would be nice to have a mother that somebody liked." **Debra Winger** doesn't feel her mother Shirley MacLaine qualifies, although the feisty redhead does attract a lot of male suitors. *Terms of Endearment* (1983, Paramount).

6886 "I didn't have a mother—Dutch found me in a garbage pail." **Julian Beck** is one of Dutch Schultz's (James Remar) henchmen. *The Cotton Club* (1984, Orion).

6887 "Marty, don't be such a square. You're beginning to sound just like my mother." **Lea Thompson** is all over Michael J. Fox. He is her son from the future. He is having a heck of a time holding off her sexually aggressive behavior. *Back to the Future* (1985, Universal).

6888 "My mother's away for Christmas. She's spending it at the plastic surgeon's." **Jonathan Pryce** refers to his mother Katherine Helmond who is constantly having something lifted, tucked or augmented. *Brazil* (1985, Universal).

6889 "You must live. You have something wonderful to look forward to. . . . It's such a joy to be a mother. It's such a joy and I thank God for letting me know it." **Kate Nelligan** portrays a Greek woman sentenced to death by the communists. She says goodbye to her daughter at their final meeting. *Eleni* (1985, Warner Bros.).

6890 "Finding new and preferably disgusting ways to describe a friend's mother was always held in high regard." Narrator **Richard Dreyfuss** recalls when he and his 12-year-old friends exchanged insults and wisecracks. *Stand by Me* (1986, Columbia).

6891 "Yeah! I almost had one, too, but your mother beat me to him." **Whoppi Goldberg** responds to the crack that she's late for a function because she stopped to pick up a sailor. *Fatal Beauty* (1987, MGM-United Artists).

6892 "Dirk Bogarde never distempered his mother's bedspread." **Julie Walters** is angry with her homosexual son Gary Oldman. *Prick Up Your Ears* (1987, GB, Goldwyn).

6893 "You're a two-bit pirate. . . . Not only would you sell your mother to make a deal, you'd send her C.O.D." Corporate raider **Terence Stamp** insults his competitor Michael Douglas. The mention of the latter's mother will cost Stamp money. *Wall Street* (1987, 20th Century-Fox).

6894 "I see Molly every second weekend and during school vacations and we try to make the most of our time together. Sometimes I'm all right, but other times the pain of the loss is terrible. And then I, I think of something that Gram said to me when my losing Molly seemed unthinkable, something that could never come to pass. She said, 'Everybody knows you're a good mother, Anna.'" We don't debate the question as to whether **Diane Keaton** is a good mother to Asia Vieira as grandmother Teresa Wright claims, but we do insist she's a dumb one—almost as dumb as this annoying movie about a woman who loses custody of her daughter because of the actions of her lover. *The Good Mother* (1988, Touchstone-Buena Vista).

6895 "He'd be five inches taller with a Scots mother." **Sean Connery** blames his son Dustin Hoffman for having an Italian mother. *Family Business* (1989, Tri-Star).

6896 "I'm fifty years old. . . and I still haven't resolved my relationship with my mother." Dignified lawyer **Woody Allen** complains to his analyst about his demon of a mother, Mae Questel, in the "Oedipus Wreck" segment of the movie. *New York Stories* (1989, Touchstone-Buena Vista).

6897 "Your mother did it to you, and her mother did it to her—back to Eve." Director and father-figure **Gene Hackman** comforts actress Meryl Streep, advising her to say, "Fuck it! I start with me!" *Postcards from the Edge* (1990, Columbia).

6898 "My mother should have raised cobras, not children." **Nick Nolte** questions the suitability of Kate Nelligan as a mother. *The Prince of Tides* (1991, Columbia).

Motion Pictures

see also ACTING AND ACTORS, DRAMA AND MELODRAMA, ENTERTAINMENTS AND ENTERTAINERS, PHOTOGRAPHY AND PHOTOGRAPHERS, STARS

6899 "I want to be in the movies." Stenographer **Joan Crawford** responds when Wallace Beery asks her what kind of job she really wants. *Grand Hotel* (1932, MGM).

6900 "Ed hates anything that keeps him from going to the movies every night I guess I'm what you call a Garbo widow." We suppose **Louise Closser Hale** could attend the movies with her husband Grant Mitchell. After all, Garbo movies were essentially "women" movies. *Dinner at Eight* (1933, MGM).

6901 "I've been to the movies. I saw a very long picture about a dog, the moral of which was that a dog is man's best friend, and a companion feature which questioned the necessity of marriage for eight reels and then concluded it was essential in the ninth." Orchestra conductor **Rex Harrison** describes a boring evening at the movies. *Unfaithfully Yours* (1948, Warner Bros.).

6902 DIXON STEELE: "And what do you call an epic?" MILDRED ATKINSON: "You know, a picture that's real long and has lots of things going on." Screenwriter **Humphrey Bogart** asks for clarification from hat check girl Martha Stewart, who tells him about a novel he hasn't time to read. She claims it's an epic. *In a Lonely Place* (1950, Columbia).

6903 JOE GILLIS: "You're Norma Desmond. You used to be in silent pictures. You used to be big." NORMA DESMOND: "I am big! It's the pictures that got small." GILLIS: "I knew there was something wrong with them." DESMOND: "They're dead, they're finished! There was a time they had the eyes of the whole world on them. But, oh, no, they had to have the ears of the world too! They opened their big mouths and out came talk, talk, talk!" GILLIS: "That's when the popcorn business came in. You buy yourself a bag and plug up your ears." Unsuccessful screenwriter **William Holden** exchanges views on the effect of sound on movies with silent star **Gloria Swanson**. *Sunset Boulevard* (1950, Paramount).

6904 "I don't go to the movies much—if you've seen one you've seen them all. Oh, they are all right for the masses." Young would-be stage actress **Debbie Reynolds** puts on airs, as she casually dismisses the films of silent screen star Gene Kelly at their first meeting. *Singin' in the Rain* (1951, MGM).

6905 "Shall I get dressed or is this foreign movie time?" **Romy Schneider** raises the question when fully-clothed Peter O'Toole joins her in her shower. *What's New, Pussycat?* (1965, United Artists).

6906 "French subtitles over a bare bottom doesn't necessarily make it art." **Sharon Tate** is unhappy making French porno films. *Valley of the Dolls* (1967, 20th Century-Fox).

6907 "You know, I think movies are a conspiracy. They set you up to believe everything." Unhappily involved with a married man, **Gena Rowlands** believes that real life can never stack up to reel life. *Minnie and Moskowitz* (1971, Universal).

6908 "You like movies because you're one of life's watchers." **Susan Anspach** accuses her husband Woody Allen of being a non-participant in life when she informs him she's leaving him. *Play It Again, Sam* (1972, Paramount).

6909 "When I begin a film, I want to make a great film. Halfway through, I just hope to finish the film." Director **Francois Truffaut** appears as the director of the film within a film. *Day for Night* (1973, Fr.-Italy, Films du Carrosse-PECF-PIC).

6910 "I'd leave a guy for a film, but I'd never leave a film for a guy!" Spirited young director's assistant **Nathalie Baye** has her priorities. *Day for Night* (1973, Fr.-Italy, Films du Carrosse-PECF-PIC).

6911 "I owe my life to a movie. They were showing this film I refused to watch and that's why I was on deck by myself when the yacht exploded. Did you ever meet anyone before whose life was saved by *Deep Throat?*" **Jessica Lange** relates the story of how she survived the sinking of a yacht after she's rescued from a lifeboat at sea. *King Kong* (1976, De Laurentiis).

6912 "I don't like the way this script of ours is turning out. It's turning into a seedy little drama. Middle-aged man leaves wife and family for young heartless woman, goes to pot. *The Blue Angel* with Marlene Dietrich and Emil Jannings. I—I don't like it." Heartless young woman **Faye Dunaway** is growing weary of her older lover William Holden's whining about the pain he's caused his wife and family when he took up with Dunaway. *Network* (1976, United Artists).

6913 "I have to see a movie from start to finish 'cause I'm anal." **Woody Allen** refuses to stay for a movie when his date Diane Keaton arrives late because they've missed the opening credits. Keaton wails, "But they're in Swedish." *Annie Hall* (1977, United Artists).

6914 "Do you like gladiator movies, Tommy?" Deviant airplane pilot **Peter Graves** begins to put some moves on Rossie Harris, a youngster brought into the cockpit for a visit. Graves also asks the lad if he's ever seen a grown man naked and if he's ever been in a Turkish prison. True to the nuttiness of the movie, the boy pays no attention to the questions, nor does anyone else in the cockpit. *Airplane* (1980, Paramount).

6915 "I could eat a can of Kodak and puke better movies." Temperamental actress **Kim Novak** snarls as she clashes with her director Rock Hudson. *The Mirror Crack'd* (1980, GB, EMI).

6916 "You've made a Valium movie—a movie about death without any death in it." **Geraldine Page** screams at Jill Clayburgh who has made a documentary movie about Page, a poet dying of cancer. *I'm Dancing as Fast as I Can* (1982, Paramount).

6917 "I haven't been to a movie since the Duke died." And it looks like druggist **James Garner** won't be going to any others soon, as he walks out of a screening of "Friday the 13th" to which he has been dragged by Sally Field. *Murphy's Romance* (1985, Columbia).

6918 "I promised your father on his death bed that I would give you a rounded education, so we probably shouldn't go to the movies every day." Movie lover **Woody Allen** kids his niece Jenny Nichols. *Crimes and Misdemeanors* (1989, Orion).

6919 DAVIS: "Mack, did you ever see a movie called *Sullivan's Travels?*" MACK: "No." DAVIS: "That's part of your problem. You haven't seen enough movies. All of life's riddles are answered in the movies. It's a story about a man who loses his way. He forgets for a moment just what he was set on earth to do." **Steve Martin**'s statement to **Kevin Kline** may be wrong, but it is certainly true that movies ask all of life's important questions—the answers are sometimes elusive. *Grand Canyon* (1991, 20th Century-Fox).

6920 "When are you going to come to see me with something with a little relevance, something with a little social conscience, something that doesn't have a goddamn Roman numeral in the title? You ever hear of Hamlet III? Midsummer Night's IV?" Movie actor **Michael J. Fox** has had it with sequels. *The Hard Way* (1991, Tri-Star).

Motives and Motivation see ENDS AND END-INGS, GOALS, PURPOSES, REASONS

Mottos

see also BEHAVIOR, GOALS, PRINCIPLES

6921 "Do it first, do it yourself, and keep doing it." **Paul Muni** has a simple formula for surviving in prohibition gangland. *Scarface* (1932, Hughes-United Artists).

6922 "Remember our motto—'It's all in fun.' Always keep your sense of humor and you can't miss." Inebriated film director **Lowell Sherman** encourages waitress Constance Bennett, who is determined to break into the movies as an actress. *What Price Hollywood?* (1932, RKO).

6923 "Find 'em, fool 'em, and forget 'em." Gold digging **Mae West** explains how she nabs rich men in this spicy comedy. *I'm No Angel* (1933, Paramount).

6924 "Your wife is safe with Tonetti, he prefers spaghetti. . . ." Lovable professional correspondent **Erik Rhodes** reassures one and all. *The Gay Divorcée* (1934, RKO).

6925 "For the man, the sword; for the woman, the kiss." It is Italian dress designer **Erik Rhodes**' motto. *Top Hat* (1935, RKO).

6926 "Damn the torpedoes, full speed ahead." Congressional consultant **Charles Coburn** takes his motto from Admiral Farragut. *The More the Merrier* (1943, Columbia).

6927 "Live fast, die young, and have a good looking corpse." Slum kid **John Derek** lives down to his motto. *Knock on Any Door* (1949, Columbia).

6928 "Dignity—always dignity." **Gene Kelly** tells a Louella Parsons–like Madge Blake his family's motto for living. *Singin' in the Rain* (1952, MGM).

6929 "First is first and second is nobody." Racketeer **Richard Conte** states his motivating motto. *The Big Combo* (1955, Allied Artists).

6930 "It takes all kinds of critters. . . to make Farmer Vincent's fritters." It's the cheerful motto of **Rory Calhoun**. He waylays travelers, knocks them out, buries them up to their necks in his secret garden, fattens them up with cattle feed, slaughters them, smokes them in his smokehouse, and sells them as sausage at his roadside stand. *Motel Hell* (1980, United Artist).

6931 "We don't put out." It's the motto of the female singing group, The Fabulous Stains, whose trademark is skunk style dyed hair. *Ladies and Gentlemen, the Fabulous Stains* (1982, Paramount).

6932 "We're ready to relieve you." It's the motto of the Ghostbusters. *Ghostbusters* (1984, Columbia).

6933 "If you don't go out with us, you probably won't come back." It's the motto of **Paul Hogan**'s small Australian safari business for tourists to the outback. *Crocodile Dundee* (1986, Australia, Paramount).

6934 "If you can't do the time, don't do the crime." Professional thief **Sean Connery** advises his grandson Matthew Broderick, who is considering entering the family business. *Family Business* (1989, Tri-Star).

6935 "We come from Beverly Hills. Shopping is our greatest skill. We will fight and try real hard, leave behind our credit cards. Beverly Hills, what a thrill." The chant taught by troop leader **Shelley Long** to the Beverly Hills chapter of the Wilderness Girls reflects their privileged background. *Troop Beverly Hills* (1989, Weintraub).

6936 "'We feast on those who would subdue us.'—not just pretty words." **Anjelica Huston** recites the Addams' family motto. *The Addams Family* (1991, Paramount).

Mouths

see also BODIES, FACES, SPEECH AND SPEAKING, TALKS AND TALKING, TONGUE TWISTERS

6937 "I hope all your teeth have cavities, and don't forget abscess makes the heart grow fonder." Chiseling Florida hotel manager **Groucho Marx** slaps a pun on Chico Marx. *The Cocoanuts* (1929, Paramount).

6938 "You talk too much. I think I'll cut you a new mouth." As she says this to communist chauffeur James Ellison, shop girl **Ginger Rogers** calmly picks up a kitchen knife. *Fifth Avenue Girl* (1939, RKO).

6939 "I feel as if somebody stepped on my tongue with muddy feet." **W.C. Fields** makes an excuse for needing a drink—not that he ever needed an excuse for a drink. *Never Give a Sucker an Even Break* (1941, Universal).

6940 "I think if I got the bit between your teeth I wouldn't have any trouble handling you at all." **Joan Fontaine** replies in the equestrian spirit of Cary Grant's question when he asks what she thinks of him in contrast to her fine horse. *Suspicion* (1941, RKO).

6941 "If I loved a man again I could bear anything. . . he could have my teeth for watch fobs." Disillusioned **Barbara Stanwyck** arrives from the big city, looking for a new life in a northern California fishing village. *Clash by Night* (1952, RKO).

6942 "Every time I show my teeth on television, more people see me than ever saw Sarah Bernhardt. It's something to think about, isn't it?" Model and TV commercials actress **Marilyn Monroe** muses to Tom Ewell on how strange are the ways of fame. *The Seven Year Itch* (1955, 20th Century-Fox).

6943 "I know you have a civil tongue in your head. I sewed it there myself." **Whit Bissell**, a descendant of Dr. Frankenstein, scolds his teenage monster Gary Conway. *I Was a Teenage Frankenstein* (1958, AIP).

6944 "Big mouth don't make a big man." **John Wayne** snaps at one of the boys who applies for a job as a wrangler with the Duke, that actions, not talk is necessary. *The Cowboys* (1972, Warner Bros.).

6945 "My mouth is so dry they could shoot *Lawrence of Arabia* in it." Wise-cracking talent agent **Dyan Cannon** desperately needs a drink. *The Last of Sheila* (1973, Warner Bros.).

6946 "I have the tears in the play. . . . Serve the playwright and keep your teeth in." Acting troupe head **Albert Finney** plays Lear and Lockwood West is the fool. *The Dresser* (1983, GB, Columbia).

6947 "Put your tongue in my mouth." **Harvey Keitel** instructs Marilyn Jones, a girl he meets in a bordello. *The Men's Club* (1986, Atlantic).

6948 "Close your mouth, dear." Impeccably dressed middle-aged woman admonishes her shocked husband as he gawks at hooker Julia Roberts wearing hip high boots, a mini skirt and a skimpy top in the lobby of the Regent Wilshire Hotel. *Pretty Woman* (1990, Touchstone-Buena Vista).

6949 "Sometimes my mouth just runs off without checking with my brain first." Radio call-in show advisor **Dolly Parton** fesses up. *Straight Talk* (1992, Hollywood Pictures-Buena Vista).

Movies *see* MOTION PICTURES

Murders *see* DEATH AND DYING, EXECUTIONS, KILLINGS

Music and Musicians

see also ENTERTAINMENTS AND ENTERTAINERS, SONGS AND SINGING, SOUNDS

6950 COUNTESS VON CONTI: "Have I missed very much?" PRINCE OTTO VON SEIBENHEIM: "Oh, no, no. Only the first and second acts." When **Jeanette MacDonald** finally shows up for the opera "Monsieur Beaucaire" about a nobleman posing as a hairdresser winning the love of a noblewoman, her suitor **Claude Allister** is most understanding. MacDonald has just come from the man she loves, Jack Buchanan, a count posing as a hairdresser. *Monte Carlo* (1930, Paramount).

6951 "Listen to them—children of the night. What music they make." **Bela Lugosi** enjoys the howling of wolves. *Dracula* (1931, Universal).

6952 "We could have made beautiful music together." Research shows that **Gary Cooper**, speaking to Madeleine Carroll, is the first one in a movie to use this line before it became a cliché. *The General Died at Dawn* (1936, Paramount).

6953 SUSAN: "He also adores music. Particularly that song. 'I Can't Give You Anything But Love, Baby.'" DAVID: "Oh, that's absurd." SUSAN: "No, it isn't, David. Really—listen." DAVID: "This is probably the silliest thing that ever happened to me." SUSAN: "I know it's silly, but it's true. He absolutely adores the tune." DAVID: "What's the difference whether he adores the tune or not?" SUSAN: "It's funny that he should love such an old tune, isn't it, but I imagine that down in Brazil. . . ." **Katharine Hepburn** acquaints **Cary Grant** with the musical preference of her pet leopard. The song turns the animal into a real pussy cat. *Bringing Up Baby* (1938, RKO).

6954 "I've paid the penalty. Now let's have some music." **Greta Garbo**, in a happy state of inebriation, demands that she be "shot" as a traitor for her betraying the Russian ideal. Melvyn Douglas blindfolds her, stands her against a wall, and as a cork pops from a champagne bottle, she sinks gracefully to the floor. *Ninotchka* (1939, MGM).

6955 "I might have known. Every time I try to see *The Magic Flute* something happens." Harassed newspaper editor **Walter Abel**, dressed in top hat and tuxedo, rushes into his Paris newsroom after the Nazis invade Poland. *Arise, My Love* (1940, Paramount).

6956 "You've delighted us long enough." **Edmund Gwenn** dismisses one of his five daughters who has given a wretched piano recital. *Pride and Prejudice* (1940, MGM).

6957 "Hey, kids! Let's start a band." It's a show biz cliché if we ever heard one. It's introduced by **Mickey Rooney**. *Strike Up the Band* (1940, MGM).

6958 "That ain't mine. That's gonna be everybody's blue music." Dixieland singer, band leader and clarinetist **Bing Crosby** rightly doesn't take credit for inventing the "blues." That happened in the black culture. *Birth of the Blues* (1941, Paramount).

6959 "I don't mind having a fortune-hunter in the family, but I don't want a piano player." Oil magnate **Eugene Pallette** draws the line when his daughter Bette Davis makes plans to marry musician Jack Carson. *The Bride Came C.O.D.* (1941, Warner Bros.).

6960 "I think tunes jump from head to head." **Teresa Wright,** who shares a special affinity with her uncle Joseph Cotten, gets the tune of the "Merry Widow Waltz" in her head when he comes for a visit. She doesn't know he's the Merry Widow murderer. *Shadow of a Doubt* (1943, Universal).

6961 "On what corner do you wish me to beat my tambourine?" **Audrey Totter** is bitter when Robert Montgomery ruins her mercenary wedding plans. *Lady in the Lake* (1947, MGM).

6962 KAREN DUNCAN: "There have been many men in my life—Bach, Brahms, Beethoven." DR. ANTHONY STANTON: "Your music belongs to the world. You've got to get better for that." Tuberculosis-stricken concert pianist **Barbara Stanwyck** immediately is attracted to **David Niven,** the chief physician at a Swiss sanitarium. *The Other Love* (1947, United Artists).

6963 "Making love to the piano—one of my more attractive minor accomplishments." Engineer **Van Heflin** plays a Schumann piece on the piano for Joan Crawford. *Possessed* (1947, Warner Bros.).

6964 "You see, Papa, good music is good music. Some people like it played slower, some people like it played faster." Know-it-all **Charlotte Greenwood** takes a simplistic view of the dilemma her husband S.Z. Sakall faces—whether to concentrate on classical music, where he's a failure, or on Tin Pan Alley ballads, where he's a success. *Oh, You Beautiful Doll* (1949, 20th Century-Fox).

6965 LT. COL. KIRBY YORKE: "This music. . . is not of my choosing." KATHLEEN YORKE: "I wish it had been." **John Wayne** tells his estranged wife **Maureen O'Hara** that he had not arranged for the regimental

singers to serenade her with "I'll Take You Home Again, Kathleen." *Rio Grande* (1950, Republic).

6966 "I'm a concert pianist. That's a pretentious way of saying I'm unemployed at the moment." **Oscar Levant** speaks of his favorite subject—himself. *An American in Paris* (1951, MGM).

6967 "Music opens up new worlds for me, draws back the veil from new delights. I can see Olympus, and a breeze blows on me from the olive fields. And in those moments, I, a god, feel as diminutive as dust." **Peter Ustinov,** as Emperor Nero, proclaims his feelings for music. *Quo Vadis* (1951, MGM).

6968 "Suddenly, all the pieces fit together. I knew how the crime had been done. The high note on the trumpet had shattered the glass." During the "Girl Hunt" ballet, **Fred Astaire,** as a dancing Mike Hammer, solves the case. *The Band Wagon* (1953, MGM).

6969 "This is the wonderful thing about music, it is never quite new and never quite the same. And just when you love it best, you think that you have heard it before. And who knows, maybe you have, deep in your heart." **Jose Ferrer,** as composer Sigmund Romberg introduces an orchestra to his latest composition. *Deep in My Heart* (1954, MGM).

6970 "Music is essential for parades." Special Russian Emissary **Cyd Charisse** sees little use for music—but she changes. *Silk Stockings* (1957, MGM).

6971 "You see, I have this thing about saxophone players. . . . Especially tenor sax. I don't know what it is, but they just curdle me. All they have to do is play eight bars of 'Come to Me, My Melancholy Baby,' and my spine turns to custard, I get goose pimply all over and I come to 'em." Band singer **Marilyn Monroe** tells tenor saxophonist Tony Curtis, masquerading as a woman, that she's a pushover for male saxophonists. *Some Like It Hot* (1959, United Artists).

6972 JUNIOR: "Syncopators—does that mean you play that fast music—jazz?" SUGAR: "Yaaaah, real hot." JUNIOR: "Oh, well, I guess some like it hot. But personally, I prefer classical music." Saxophone player **Tony Curtis** takes time out from impersonating a girl saxophone player to impersonate a millionaire for naïve, round heeled band singer **Marilyn Monroe**. *Some Like It Hot* (1959, United Artists).

6973 "Do you ever do it to Ravel's Bolero? My uncle turned me on to it." **Bo Derek** coos to Dudley

Moore as his dream girl puts on music to have sex by. *"10"* (1979, Warner Bros.).

6974 "If a woman listens to music alone, it's an emergency." **Yves Montand** offers an aphorism as he arrives at Romy Schneider's apartment where gloomy Peruvian flute music is on the record player. *Clair de Femme* (1980, Fr., Atlantic).

6975 "I don't know much about classical music. For years I thought the 'Goldberg Variations' were something Mr. and Mrs. Goldberg tried on their wedding night." Melancholy comedian **Woody Allen** muses in the writer-director's "8½." *Stardust Memories* (1980, United Artists).

6976 "The best music. You got to be joking. I spent a week in Boston once, and I don't think I heard a decent mariachi player in the city." California caballero **George Hamilton** finds the music of Beantown wanting. *Zorro, the Gay Blade* (1981, 20th Century-Fox).

6977 SHREVIE: "How could you file my James Brown under J?" BETH: "It's just music. It's not that big a deal." SHREVIE: "It is to me.... You never ask me what's on the flip side." **Daniel Stern** is disappointed that his wife **Ellen Barkin** neither shares his interest in his record collection or treats it with the reverence he feels it deserves. *Diner* (1982, MGM).

6978 "When it comes to making out, this is most important: put on side one of Led Zepplin IV." Slick **Robert Romanus** sells everything and gives advice on dealing with chicks to his shy friend Brian Backer. *Fast Times at Ridgemont High* (1982, Universal).

6979 "I'm missin' the music. I may not be any good anymore, but that doesn't keep me from missin' it." Reformed alcoholic and has-been country and western singer **Robert Duvall** still misses his songs. *Tender Mercies* (1982, EMI-Universal).

6980 "God, I hate rock and roll." **Alexandra Paul** shouldn't worry too much, her boy friend Keith Gordon's demonic '58 Plymouth Fury probably will make its own decision as to what music will play on its radio. *Christine* (1983, Columbia).

6981 "This was music I'd never heard before. It seemed to be the voice of God." **F. Murray Abraham** as Antonio Salieri, recalls the first time he heard the music of prodigy Wolfgang Amadeus Mozart, played by Tom Hulce. *Amadeus* (1984, Orion-Paramount).

6982 "There are too many notes." **Jeffrey Jones,** the well-meaning but musically illiterate Emperor of

Austria, tells Tom Hulce, as Mozart, that his latest work is too long. *Amadeus* (1984, Orion).

6983 "Music is about death. It always has been. . . . Music is the highest of the arts. It needs to reference to the figurative or to the corportium. It is therefore of all the arts the closest to death." Unpleasant, opinionated British university student of the 1910s, **Mark Tandy** holds forth for his classmates in the filming of the E.M. Forster story of coming to terms with one's homosexuality. *Maurice* (1987, GB, Cinecom).

6984 "That's my theme music. Every good hero should have some. See you around." **Keenen Ivory Wayans** is surrounded by a lot of aging former black heroes in this spoof of the blaxploitation films of the 70s. *I'm Gonna Git You Sucka* (1988, United Artists).

6985 "I brought them music and they made me king." U.S. Army deserter **Nick Nolte** modestly explains why a primitive Borneo tribe of headhunters made him their king in 1942. *Farewell to the King* (1989, Orion).

6986 "It's the devil's music, I can feel it." Evangelist Jimmy Swaggart, portrayed by **Alec Baldwin,** reacts negatively to the raucous "black" music that his cousin Jerry Lee Lewis, played by Dennis Quaid, admires. *Great Balls of Fire!* (1989, Orion).

6987 "You take a white right hand a black left hand and what do you get? You get rock 'n' roll." **Trey Wilson,** as the legendary Sam Phillips of Sun Records, makes a musical definition. *Great Balls of Fire!* (1989, Orion).

6988 "It's parsley. Take it away and no one would know the difference." Singer **Michelle Pfeiffer** insists that the shopworn standard "Feelings" should be dropped from the repertoire of the act she has with pianists Beau and Jeff Bridges. *The Fabulous Baker Boys* (1989, 20th Century-Fox).

6989 KATE: "Did I make bells ring for you?" FAUSTO: "You make the whole world ring for me." Lovely **Bo Derek** coos in the ear of her new husband **Leo Damien,** the promised reincarnation of her deceased husband Anthony Quinn. *Ghosts Can't Do It* (1990, Triumph).

6990 "Play some rap music." It's **Bruce Willis'** macho reply to Taylor Negron who has covered him with a gun and says, "I want to hear you scream." *The Last Boy Scout* (1991, Warner Bros.).

Mutiny *see* BOATS AND SHIPS, REBELLIONS, REVOLUTIONS

Mysteries

see also CURIOSITY, FICTION, KNOWLEDGE, SECRETS, UNKNOWNS

6991 DON ANTONIO DE LA PRADA: "There's a mystery in you." QUEEN CHRISTINA: "Is there not in every human being?" Spanish ambassador **John Gilbert** has not yet learned that **Greta Garbo,** his lover for two glorious days and nights in a room at the snowed-in inn, is the Queen of Sweden. *Queen Christina* (1933, MGM).

6992 NICK CHARLES: "Darling, you don't need mystery, you have something more alluring." NORA CHARLES: "What?" NICK: "Me." **William Powell** and **Myrna Loy** are excellent as a happily married couple. *After the Thin Man* (1936, MGM).

6993 "I spent more time at the morgue than at my office. You and your mysteries were making a wreck out of me." Prominent surgeon **William Powell** blames the break-up of his marriage to Jean Arthur on her career as a mystery writer. *The Ex-Mrs. Bradford* (1936, RKO).

6994 "If there were no mystery left to explain, life would be rather dull, wouldn't it?" Heavenly agent **Claude Rains** comments to Robert Montgomery who is owed a return to earth and a new body. *Here Comes Mr. Jordan* (1941, Columbia).

6995 "In 1539 the Knights Templar of Malta paid tribute to Charles V of Spain by sending him a Golden Falcon encrusted from the beak to claw with rarest jewels—but pirates seized the galley carrying the priceless token and the fate of the Maltese Falcon remains a mystery to this day." **Sydney Greenstreet** gives the history of the fabled treasure that he and others are seeking and killing for. *The Maltese Falcon* (1941, Warner Bros.).

6996 "I've always heard that the ideal marriage should be something of a mystery." **Merle Oberon** is so bored with her marriage to inattentive Melvyn Douglas that she develops a hiccup problem. *That Uncertain Feeling* (1941, United Artists).

6997 "So that's what they mean when they say the Lord moves in mysterious ways." Poor sharecropper **Paul Robeson** finds a fancy tail coat thrown out an airplane window by crook J. Carrol Naish. In the pockets Robeson finds $40,000, which he gives to preacher Eddie Anderson. *Tales of Manhattan* (1942, 20th Century-Fox).

6998 "It is said that no man is a hero to his valet. It is also true that no woman is a mystery to her husband's valet." Suave valet **James Mason** tells Danielle Darrieux that he can read her like a book. *Five Fingers* (1952, 20th Century-Fox).

6999 "I'm just a girl from the country. The theater and the people in it have always been a complete mystery to me. They still are." **Grace Kelly**, the wife of has-been alcoholic actor Bing Crosby, responds to stage director William Holden's question as to whether she had ever been in the theater herself. *The Country Girl* (1954, Paramount).

7000 "There was something mysterious going on and I plunged in over my head." Anachronistic Beat Generation existentialist **Ben Gazzara** sounds like a second-rate Mickey Spillane. *Tales of Ordinary Madness* (1982, Italy, Miracle).

Myths

see also FICTION, HISTORY, ILLUSIONS, STORIES

7001 "The unwritten law is a myth, Lieutenant. Anyone who commits murder under this belief is reserving himself room and board in the state penitentiary. . . maybe for life." Attorney **James Stewart** advises his client Ben Gazzara, who is confident that he will be acquitted of murder because the deceased raped his wife Lee Remick. *Anatomy of a Murder* (1959, Columbia).

7002 "You and I are the same, Darien. You're smart enough not to buy into the oldest myth running—love. A fiction created by people to keep them from jumping out windows." Business mover-and-shaker **Michael Douglas** compliments interior decorator Daryl Hannah on her practical nature. *Wall Street* (1987, 20th Century-Fox).

Naïveté

see also IGNORANCE, INNOCENCE

7003 "Now that you've got the mine, I'll bet you'll be a swell gold digger." **Stan Laurel** and Oliver Hardy hand over the deed of a gold mine entrusted to them to imposter Sharon Lynne, posing as the deceased owner's daughter. Laurel delivers an on-target but unintentional double-entendre. *Way Out West* (1937, Roach-MGM).

7004 "I was a different girl then. I was really rather naïve. . . . All my knowledge came from books." **Margaret Sullavan** explains to James Stewart why she initially treated him so badly. *The Shop Around the Corner* (1940, MGM).

7005 "There's as fine a specimen of Sucker Sapiens as I've ever seen." Delighted con man **Charles Coburn** points out wealthy, naïve-looking Henry Fonda to his partner and daughter Barbara Stanwyck. *The Lady Eve* (1941, Paramount).

7006 "I'm green as grass." Naïve soldier **Robert Walker** wanders around Grand Central Station in New York like a lovable lost puppy. *The Clock* (1945, MGM).

7007 "That your cigar in here, honey?" **Steve Martin** isn't being sarcastic with Judith Ivey, just naïve and innocent. *The Lonely Guy* (1984, Universal).

Nakedness *see* NUDITY

Names

see also IDENTITIES

7008 "They call me Lola." Tawdry cabaret singer **Marlene Dietrich** identifies herself for fuddy-duddy teacher Emil Jannings. *The Blue Angel* (1930, Germany, UFA).

7009 "Love? Why don't you call it by its real name?" Shop girl Jean Harlow's prey **Chester Morris** is all for calling a spade a spade. *Red-Headed Woman* (1932, MGM).

7010 "Tugboat Annie Brennan! That's what the waterfront calls me. And I didn't get the name pushin' toy boats around the bath tub either!" **Marie Dressler** introduces herself to her new boss Oscar Apfel who doesn't want a woman running one of his tugs. *Tugboat Annie* (1933, MGM).

7011 "Ever since I was a golden-haired little tot, paddling about the ancestral home in pale pink pajamas." **Edward Everett Horton** tells how he picked up the name "Pinky." *The Gay Divorcée* (1934, RKO).

7012 "From now on they'll spell mutiny with my name." **Clark Gable,** as Fletcher Christian, realizes that by taking the ship *H.M.S. Bounty* from its legal master, Charles Laughton, as Captain Bligh, he is doomed to be an outcast for eternity. *Mutiny on the Bounty* (1935, MGM).

7013 JERRY WARRINER: "But Dixie Belle Lee isn't her real name. No, no, she changed it you see. Her family objected to her going into show business." LUCY WARRINER: "I guess that is easier than all of them changing theirs." **Cary Grant** and ex-wife **Irene Dunne** discuss Joyce Compton, the sexy nightclub singer he's passing off as his new flame to make Dunne jealous. *The Awful Truth* (1937, Columbia).

7014 JERRY WARRINER: "Oklahoma! Ever since I was a small boy, that name has been filled with magic for me." DANIEL LEESON: "We're going to live in Oklahoma City." JERRY: "Not in Oklahoma City itself? Lucy, you're a lucky girl." **Cary Grant** makes his former wife Irene Dunne wince as he goes on about her life with Oklahoma oilman **Ralph Bellamy** once they marry. Grant rolls the name Ok-la-ho-ma across his tongue. *The Awful Truth* (1937, Columbia).

7015 "I call everyone Babe." Perhaps **Clark Gable** is like Babe Ruth, who supposedly got his nickname "Babe" because that's what he called everyone rather than bother to learn their name. *Idiot's Delight* (1939, MGM).

7016 "Don't start calling names, you Park Avenue play girl.... I know more words than you do!" Showgirl **Paulette Goddard** snaps at Rosalind Russell whose soon-to-be ex-husband will be Goddard's next spouse. *The Women* (1939, MGM).

7017 "Well, girls, looks like it's back to the perfume counter for me. By the way, there's a name for you ladies, but it isn't used in high society—outside of a kennel." Realizing that she's been put in her place by society dames Norma Shearer, Mary Boland and others, former salesgirl **Joan Crawford** gets in a final shot. *The Women* (1939, MGM).

7018 "The girls call me Pilgrim because every time I dance with one I make a little progress." Wisecracking radio commentator **Bob Hope** alludes to John Bunyan's "Pilgrim's Progress." *The Ghost Breakers* (1940, Paramount).

7019 "Look at the tag they put on me! 'Mad Dog Roy Earle'—those newspaper rats!" Fugitive **Humphrey Bogart** roars when he sees his photograph on the front page of a newspaper. *High Sierra* (1941, Warner Bros.).

7020 "Good names are always useful." **Carl Benton Reid** suggests to his son Dan Duryea that marrying someone from a respected or wealthy family is good business. That's why Reid married Patricia Collinge. *The Little Foxes* (1941, Goldwyn-RKO).

7021 "Good name! Look, nobody has a good name in a bad house. Nobody has a good name in a silly house, either." **Ray Collins** tries to put his selfish, spoiled nephew Tim Holt straight about the danger of gossip about their family's proud name. *The Magnificent Ambersons* (1942, RKO).

7022 "There's a name for such reptiles, but I won't sully this sweet ocean breeze by saying it." Wealthy **Rudy Vallee** is contemptuous of Claudette Colbert's ex-husband Joel McCrea. *The Palm Beach Story* (1942, Paramount).

7023 "Millie remembers the same things I do. That's important. For one thing, she's the only one I know who remembers when I used to be called Chunky." It would seem the recollection of that particular nickname would be enough reason for **Bette Davis** to wish an end to her long friendship with Miriam Hopkins. *Old Acquaintance* (1943, Warner Bros.).

7024 "Good morning, Mary Sunshine! I'm a nurse. Name of Nolan, but my friends call me Bim. You can call me Bim." Male nurse **Frank Faylen** attends Ray Milland at the drunk tank during his delirium. *The Lost Weekend* (1945, Paramount).

7025 DEXTER BROADHURST: "You know, these days they give ballplayers very peculiar names. Take the St. Louis team: Who's on first. What's on second. I Don't Know is on third...." SEBASTIAN DINWIDDIE: "That's what I want to find out. I want you to tell me the names of the fellows on the St. Louis team." DEXTER: "I'm telling you. Who's on first, What's on second. I Don't Know is on third." SEBASTIAN: "Who's playing first?" DEXTER: "Yes." SEBASTIAN: "I mean, the fellow's name on first base." DEXTER: "Who." SEBASTIAN: "The fellow playing first base." DEXTER: "Who." SEBASTIAN: "The guy on first base." DEXTER: "Who is on first." SEBASTIAN: "Well, what are you asking me for?" DEXTER: "I'm not asking you. I'm telling you. Who is on first." SEBASTIAN: "I'm asking you—who's on first?" DEXTER: "That's the man's name." SEBASTIAN: "That's who's name?" DEXTER: "Yes." SEBASTIAN: "Well, go ahead, tell me." DEXTER: "Who!" SEBASTIAN: "All I'm trying to find out is, what's the guy's name on first base." DEXTER: "Oh, no, What is on second." SEBASTIAN: "I'm not asking you who's on second." DEXTER: "Who's on first." SEBASTIAN: "That's what I'm trying to find out. What's the guy's name on first base." DEXTER: "What's the guy's name on second base." SEBASTIAN: "I'm not asking who's on second." DEXTER: "Who's on first." SEBASTIAN: "I don't know." DEXTER: "He's on third." **Bud Abbott** gives **Lou Costello** the lowdown on the unusual names of the players on the St. Louis Wolves baseball team. The catcher was "Today," the pitcher was "Tomorrow," the left-fielder was "Why," the center-fielder was "Because," the shortstop (the last mentioned) was "I don't give a darn (damn)." No right-fielder is mentioned in the routine. *The Naughty Nineties* (1945, Universal).

7026 JOHNNY: "Such a hard name to remember and such an easy one to forget." **Rita Hayworth** gets in a little dig, meaningful only to Glenn Ford, a former lover, who has just been introduced to her by her husband George Macready. *Gilda* (1946, Columbia).

7027 "Ma'am, I sure like that name Clementine." **Henry Fonda** as Marshal Wyatt Earp admires more than Cathy Downs' name. *My Darling Clementine* (1946, 20th Century-Fox).

7028 BERNICE REINER: "My name is Bernice Reiner. I stop at the hotel." RONALD KORNBLOW: "My name is Ronald Kornblow. I stop at nothing." Slinky hotel guest **Lisette Verea**'s introduction is easily topped by hotel manager **Groucho Marx**. *A Night in Casablanca* (1946, United Artists).

7029 THE GHOST OF CAPTAIN GREGG: "And I shall call you Lucia." LUCY MUIR: "My name is Lucy." GREGG: "It doesn't do you justice, my dear. Women named Lucy are always imposed upon. But Lucia! Now there's a name for an Amazon, for a queen." Lively spirit **Rex Harrison** imposes his will on **Gene Tierney.** *The Ghost and Mrs. Muir* (1947, 20th Century-Fox).

7030 "They say the day you die your name is written on a cloud." **Virginia Huston** can be expecting to read Robert Mitchum's name in the sky very soon. *Out of the Past* (1947, RKO).

7031 "Names are unimportant—never bother with names." Illegal alien, physician **Charles Boyer** calms frightened and confused Ingrid Bergman as they walk by the Seine in Paris in the winter of 1938. *Arch of Triumph* (1948, United Artists).

7032 NICK HELMAR: "Jassy Woodroffe? Woodroffe? I seem to know that name." JASSY WOODROFFE: "You are thinking of my father. You shot him outside that door." Is it any wonder that **Margaret Lockwood** is a bit cool while talking to evil squire **Basil Sydney**? *Jassy* (1948, GB, Gainsborough-Universal).

7033 "A pretty masculine handle for such a feminine pile of goods." **Bob Hope** makes a chauvinistic remark about Jane Russell's alias "Mike." *The Paleface* (1948, Paramount).

7034 DR. SANDERSON: "Think carefully, Dowd. Didn't you ever know someone named Harvey?" ELWOOD P. DOWD: "No, not one, doctor. Maybe that's why I had such high hopes for it." Psychiatrist **Charles Drake** asks **James Stewart** to think into his past for anyone who was important to him with the name Harvey. Harvey is the name of Stewart's best friend, a six-foot three-inch rabbit that only he can see. *Harvey* (1950, Universal International).

7035 "The Himmler of the Lower Fifth! I suppose that will become my epitaph." Stuffy English master **Michael Redgrave** prepares to retire from his school, well aware that his students despise him. *The Browning Version* (1951, GB, Universal).

7036 "It's a French name. It means wood, and Blanche means white, so the two together means white woods. Like an orchard in spring. You can remember that, if you care to." **Vivien Leigh** is a coquettish Blanche Du Bois as she explains the meaning of her name to new beau Karl Malden. *A Streetcar Named Desire* (1951, Warner Bros.-20th Century-Fox).

7037 "Mr. Allnut, dear. There's something I must know. What's your first name?" **Katharine Hepburn** and Humphrey Bogart have survived a great deal and have fallen in love. She thinks it's time to be a bit less formal. His name is Charlie. *The African Queen* (1952, GB, Horizon-Romulus).

7038 "We live. . . as I hope you know, Mr. Worthing—in an age of ideas. . . and my idea has always been to love someone of the name Earnest. There is something in that name that inspires absolute confidence. The moment Algernon first mentioned that he had a friend named Earnest, I knew I was destined to love you." **Joan Greenwood**, in her plummiest voice, pledges her love first for Michael Redgrave's name and then him. *The Importance of Being Earnest* (1952, Two Cities-Rank).

7039 "My name doesn't matter. I'm any wife, any daughter, any sister, mother or sweetheart." Off-camera narrator **Ann Blyth** claims to be "Any-woman," but in the film about Korean refugees, she's the love interest for American Colonel Robert Mitchum. *One Minute to Zero* (1952, RKO).

7040 "You must have been born with that name. You couldn't have made it up." **James Mason** is sure Judy Garland wouldn't choose the name Esther Blodgett. *A Star Is Born* (1954, Warner Bros.).

7041 "You know what name I was born with? Smith, for the love of Mike, Smith! Now what kind of name is that for a fella like me? I need a name with a whole sky in it, and the power of a man. Starbuck. Now there's a name, and it's mine." **Burt Lancaster** tells Katharine Hepburn that you don't have to settle for what you're born with, name or anything else. *The Rainmaker* (1956, Paramount).

7042 "No, I gotta be Lizzie. Melisande is a name for one night only, but Lizzie can do me my whole life long." At long last, plain, spinster **Katharine Hepburn** has two men who want her. She chooses steady Deputy Sheriff Wendell Corey over drifter Burt Lancaster who has renamed her Melisande. *The Rainmaker* (1956, Paramount).

7043 "Do you know what Quick means in this country? Hellfire. Ashes and char. Flames follow that man around like a dog. He's a barn burner!" **Orson Welles** refers to hot-tempered Paul Newman. Newman's father settled disputes by burning down his opponent's barns—and it looks like his boy is following in his footsteps. *The Long Hot Summer* (1958, 20th Century-Fox).

7044 "I want to be like the others. I want to have a hard time remembering your name!" When **Tony Franciosa** finally catches on to the obvious, he pelts his lover, call girl Gina Lollobrigida with dollar bills. *Go Naked in the World* (1960, MGM).

7045 LISA: "Me, the same, Lisa's the name." DAVID: "Me, the same, David's the name." For a time, disturbed teenagers **Janet Margolin** and **Keir Dullea** communicate only in rhyme. *David and Lisa* (1962, Continental Distributing).

7046 TATIANA ROMANOVA: "My friends call me Tanya." JAMES BOND: "Mine call me James Bond." Lovely Russian agent **Daniela Bianchi** and **Sean Connery** get acquainted before becoming very, very friendly. *From Russia with Love* (1963, GB, United Artists).

7047 "Oh, kiss me, Frank, kiss my hot lips!" While in a passionate embrace with Robert Duvall, **Sally Kellerman**'s words are broadcast all over the MASH unit, thus earning her the nickname "Hot Lips." *M*A*S*H* (1970, 20th Century-Fox).

7048 "Felix? Your name is Felix? That's sort of an ooghie name." Prostitute **Barbra Streisand** doesn't think much of bookstore salesman George Segal's first name. *The Owl and the Pussycat* (1970, Columbia).

7049 "No, No, I don't—I don't want to know your name. You don't have a name, and I don't have a name either. No names here. Not one name." **Marlon Brando** tells Maria Schneider that he wants their affair to be zipperless. *Last Tango in Paris* (1972, Fr.-Ital.-U.S., United Artists).

7050 "Tom is my slave name. Makimba is my real name." Angry young black **Tom Johnigarn** snarls at white Vietnam veteran Greydon Clark. The latter arrives in Watts to tell Johnigarn's father that his best friend, the man's son, had died bravely in combat and to deliver a letter to the deceased wrote before he was killed. *The Bad Bunch* (1976, Dimension)

7051 "I'm Dwan. D-W-A-N, Dwan. That's my name. You know—like Dawn except I switched two letters to make it more memorable." Sexy **Jessica Lange** isn't as naïve as she seems. *King Kong* (1976, De Laurentiis).

7052 "Why are you calling me a nigger, huh? You don't know me well enough to call me nigger. I'll slap the taste out of your mouth. You don't know my name. I'll whup your ass. . . beat the white off your ass." When villain Patrick McGoohan makes a disparaging remark about **Richard Pryor,** posing as a railroad porter, the latter whips out a gun and threatens McGoohan. *Silver Streak* (1976, 20th Century-Fox).

7053 "Just don't expect miracles. I'm changing my name to Susan B. Anthony. Let's go." **Mary Steenburgen** agrees to return to London of 100 years ago with her lover from the past, Malcolm McDowell, as H.G. Wells. *Time After Time* (1979, GB, Warner Bros.).

7054 "The Mother Superior of Orange County." It's the title liberal Supreme Court Judge **Walter Matthau** lays on Jill Clayburgh, a conservative female jurist recently appointed to the high court. *First Monday in October* (1981, Paramount).

7055 "Sushi: That's what my ex-wife used to call me. Cold fish." Licensed-to-kill L.A. policeman **Harrison Ford,** circa 2019, recalls his ex's pet name for him. *Blade Runner* (1982, Warner Bros.).

7056 "Cayahuari Yacu, the jungle Indians call the country 'the land where God did not finish His creation.' Only after man has disappeared, they think, He will return to finish His work." An opening title of the movie. *Fitzcarraldo* (1982, Germany, New World).

7057 "Fitzcarraldo—Conquistador of the Useless." It's the taunting title rubber exporters and local dignitaries anoint Klaus Kinski with because of his obsession with building an opera house in the Peruvian jungle. *Fitzcarraldo* (1982, Germany, New World).

7058 "It's a pet, not an animal. It had a name. You don't eat things with a name. This is horrific." **Peter Riegert** is shocked with Denis Lawson who has just served for dinner the injured rabbit the former had picked up along the road. *Local Hero* (1983, GB, Enigma).

7059 "It's animals like you who give Cubans a bad name." **Miriam Colon** refuses money from her son, Miami mobster Al Pacino. *Scarface* (1983, Universal).

7060 "You don't know what it's like when they call you names like Airhead, Ding-a-ling, Yoyo, Bimbo—there's no way you can know that, Scotty." Blond hardbody **Teal Roberts** sobs to Grant Cramer as she tells him how much it hurts to be treated as a dumb, cheap piece of meat. *Hardbodies* (1984, Columbia).

7061 "Did you know your last name's an adverb?" Showgirl **Marilu Henner** proves her education wasn't wasted when she meets title character Johnny Dangerously, played by Michael Keaton. *Johnny Dangerously* (1984, 20th Century-Fox).

7062 "When we make love, she calls out her own name." **Rodney Dangerfield** claims his surly wife Adrienne Barbeau is totally self-absorbed. *Back to School* (1986, Orion).

7063 "Catchy name, isn't it?" At the end of the film, killing machine police officer **Sylvester Stallone** tells Brigitte Nielsen his full name: Marion Cobretti. *Cobra* (1986, Warner Bros.).

7064 "My name's Edna, but the girls just call me Eddie." Gross, buxomy prison matron **Pat Ast**, the obligatory dyke in these kinds of movies, munches on chocolates and checks out the new arrivals at Pridemore Juvenile Facilities. *Reform School Girls* (1986, New World).

7065 "That was the summer of 1963, when everybody called me 'Baby' and it didn't occur to me to mind." At the beginning of the film, in voice-over, **Jennifer Grey** recalls a past time. *Dirty Dancing* (1987, Vestron).

7066 "I was out of school a little while with pleurosis. When I came back you asked me what was the matter. I said I had pleurosis and you thought I said Blue Roses. So that's what you always called me after that." **Karen Allen** reminisces with her gentleman caller James Naughton. *The Glass Menagerie* (1987, Cineplex Odeon).

7067 "Even after settling on fifty percent, Yano complained about the name for days. We couldn't agree so we left it as it was, the Blue Iguana. Funny thing is, Yano was right about Diablo becoming the next big thing. Six months later they built a Club Med right next door." Bounty hunter **Dylan McDermott** makes some accommodations with a South American on ownership of a club. *The Blue Iguana* (1988, Paramount).

7068 "Wow, that really felt great. What's your name again?" **Lea Thompson** has had sex with a virtual stranger. *Casual Sex?* (1988, Universal).

7069 "Was I trying to say Raymond and it came out Rain Man?. . . You, you're the Rain Man?" **Tom Cruise** realizes that his autistic older brother Dustin Hoffman was the vaguely remembered "Rain Man" of his early childhood. *Rain Man* (1988, United Artists).

7070 "Did you used to be Eddie Valiant or did you change your name to Jack Daniels?" Smart alec Police Lieutenant **Richard Le Parmentier** makes sport of frequently drunk private eye Bob Hoskins. *Who Framed Roger Rabbit?* (1988, Touchstone-Buena Vista).

7071 "In this class you can either call me Mr. Keating or if you are slightly more daring, Oh Captain, My Captain!" Instructor **Robin Williams** introduces himself to his English class at their first meeting. *Dead Poets Society* (1989, Touchstone-Buena Vista).

7072 "Don't call me Junior." **Harrison Ford** repeats the demand several times to his father Sean Connery. *Indiana Jones and the Last Crusade* (1989, Paramount).

7073 "Hi, my name's Mae, and that's more than a name—it's an attitude." Outrageous **Madonna** portrays an outrageous female baseball player. *A League of Their Own* (1992, Columbia).

Narcissism

see also LOVE AND LOVERS, PLEASURES, SELF, SELF-ISHNESS

7074 "It's only me—that must be the understatement of the year!" Incompetent war correspondent **Bob Hope** polishes his role as a man who thinks more of himself than anyone else in the world. *They Got Me Covered* (1943, RKO).

7075 "Your love affair with yourself has reached heroic proportions. It doesn't seem to leave much room for me. Are you sure you can get along without somebody to help you admire yourself?" **Joan Crawford**'s unrequited love for womanizer Van Heflin becomes so obsessive that she loses her perception of reality. *Possessed* (1947, Warner Bros.).

7076 "It would take a great woman to make Crassus fall out of love with himself." Roman Senator **Charles Laughton** doubts that slave Jean Simmons is the woman for the job of taming ambitious Roman General Laurence Olivier. *Spartacus* (1960, Universal).

7077 "It isn't easy to be a fat narcissist." Top Sergeant **Jackie Gleason** is a man of many dreams that don't come true. *Soldier in the Rain* (1963, Allied Artists).

7078 "He longed to be an artist but balked at the necessary sacrifice. In his most private moments, he spoke of his fear of death, which he elevated to tragic heights when, in fact, it was mere narcissism."

The lines are from the book written by **Meryl Streep,** lesbian ex-wife of Woody Allen. *Manhattan* (1979, United Artists).

7079 "I wasn't the only one who couldn't keep his eyes off; she couldn't either." **Jeff Bridges** refers to his narcissistic wife Belinda Bauer. *The American Success Company* aka: *Success* (1980, Columbia).

7080 "It would be narcissistic of us to feel that we're alone in the universe." **Lindsay Crouse** comforts her husband Christopher Walken who believes he's encountered aliens from another world. Once he says, "The world is getting so small that it would be nice to meet someone new." *Communion* (1989, Vestron).

Narration and Narrators *see* EXPLANATIONS, INTRODUCTIONS

Nations and Nationalism *see* AMERICA AND AMERICANS, PATRIOTISM

Natives

see also BIRTHS AND BIRTHDAYS, NATURE AND NATURAL

7081 "The natives are restless tonight." Before it became a cliché, **Charles Laughton** said it of the animals on a remote South Sea island that he has transformed into humans by vivisection. *Island of Lost Souls* (1932, Paramount).

7082 "I'm the most displaced of all displaced persons, your native son in a nuclear town." Chicken farmer and self-styled philosopher **Roberts Blossom** identifies himself for visiting poet Tom Conti. *Reuben, Reuben* (1983, 20th Century-Fox).

Nature and Natural

see also FLOWERS, HUMAN NATURE, INSECTS, INSTINCTS, RIVERS, SEAS, SEASONS, TREES, WATER, WEATHER, WINDS

7083 "I want to be clean not only in conduct but in my innermost thoughts and desires. There is one way to do it. . . . By separating the two natures in us." **Fredric March**, as Dr. Jekyll, tells his friend Holmes Herbert that he doesn't even wish to sin in his thoughts and he will have out his evil nature. *Dr. Jekyll and Mr. Hyde* (1931, Paramount).

7084 "Fryer-less cookers! Seems like it's goin' against nature somehow." **Elizabeth Patterson,** as small town Aunt Ella, is suspicious of new things and new people. *Men Without Names* (1935, Paramount).

7085 "Nature is far too subtle to repeat itself." Scientist **Paul Muni** makes an interesting observation about the seemingly infinite variety found in nature. *The Story of Louis Pasteur* (1936, Warner Bros.).

7086 "Nature is so natural." Spinster **Elsa Lanchester** has a way of getting to the essence of an idea. *The Beachcomber* aka: *Vessel of Wrath* (1938, GB, Mayflower-Paramount).

7087 "She shouldn't try to be top man. She's not built for it. She's flying in the face of nature." Sexist **Ray Milland** refers to his boss, Ginger Rogers, editor of a fashion magazine. *Lady in the Dark* (1944, Paramount).

7088 "I wish I could borrow your nature for awhile, Captain. . . the word failure does not even exist for you." French resistance leader **Walter Molnar** admires Humphrey Bogart's resilience. *To Have and Have Not* (1944, Warner Bros.).

7089 "Nature, Mr. Allnut, is what we are put into this world to rise above." **Katharine Hepburn** lectures alcoholic riverboat captain Humphrey Bogart. *The African Queen* (1951, GB, Horizon-Romulus).

7090 "I happen to like women. I have a promiscuous nature, and unlike these aristocrats, I will not take a marriage vow which I know that my nature will prevent me from keeping." Roman Senator **Charles Laughton** makes a virtue out of his habit of keeping numerous female slaves and servants for his pleasure. *Spartacus* (1960, Universal).

7091 "Honey, you're not Sarah Bernhardt. Make the most of what nature gave you." Assistant director **Peter Hansen** advises title character Carroll Baker, who doesn't wish to sleep her way to success. *Harlow* (1965, Paramount).

7092 "I have an extravagant nature. Surely you've discovered that about me by now." Eccentric character dancer Isadora Duncan, portrayed by **Vanessa Redgrave** *is* extravagant. *Isadora* (1968, GB, Universal).

7093 "I've been sitting here breathing cleaning fluid and ammonia for three hours. Nature didn't intend for poker to be played like that." Card player **David Sheiner** is disturbed by Jack Lemmon's constant cleaning. *The Odd Couple* (1968, Paramount).

7094 BUDDUSKY SM1: "Was it in the nature of a serious offense? For example, was it in the nature of a felony or a misdemeanor?" MEADOWS SN: "Well, it was in the nature of shoplifting." Career sailor **Jack Nicholson** is one of the escorts taking **Randy Quaid** from West Virginia to prison in Massachusetts. Quaid has been sentenced to eight years in jail for stealing from a polio charity box. *The Last Detail* (1973, Columbia).

7095 SONJA: "Boris, look at this leaf, isn't it perfect? And this one, too. Yes, I definitely think this is the best of all possible worlds." BORIS: "It's certainly the most expensive." SONJA: "Isn't nature incredible?" BORIS: "To me, nature is. . . I don't know, spiders and bugs and then big fish eating little fish and the plants eating plants, and animals eating. . . . It's like an enormous restaurant in the way I see it." In 1812 Russia, cousins **Diane Keaton** and **Woody Allen**, are plotting to assassinate Napoleon in this comedy. *Love and Death* (1975, United Artists).

7096 "It's not right, it's not natural. It doesn't look nice. If women were meant to play football they'd have their tits somewhere else." Scottish teen **Gordon John Sinclair** objects when extremely attractive blonde Dee Hepburn joins the soccer team. *Gregory's Girl* (1980, GB, Lake-NFFC-STV).

7097 "You messed up before and you'll mess up again. It's your nature." Police Officer **J.A. Preston** warns incompetent, womanizing lawyer William Hurt to steer clear of Kathleen Turner, who is suspected of murdering her husband. *Body Heat* (1981, Warner Bros.).

7098 "I'll keep her at home and have a good time with her there. . . . It is much more natural to give herself to a man instead of a movement." Impoverished lawyer and anti-feminist **Christopher Reeve** is sure he can win Madeleine Potter and cure of her crusading for women's rights. *The Bostonians* (1984, GB, Almi).

7099 "You know, Nature has a way of reminding man just how puny we are, whether it tells us in the form of a tornado, an earthquake, or a Godzilla." The narrator of a film welcomes back the giant monster that threatens Tokyo. *Godzilla 85* (1985, Japan, Toho-New World).

7100 "They are not naturally animals, they are naturally spiritual. . . . We are going to make Christians of these people." Missionary **Jeremy Irons** speaks of the Portuguese adventurers about the Indians at the San Carlos Mission in the South American wilderness. *The Mission* (1986, GB, Warner Bros.).

7101 "There is no such thing as natural beauty." Beautician **Dolly Parton** insists one must work at looking beautiful. *Steel Magnolias* (1989, Tri-Star).

7102 "Heresy by nature is insidious." So speaks **Marlon Brando** as Torquemada, the Grand Inquisitor. *Christopher Columbus: The Discovery* (1992, Warner Bros.).

Naughtiness

see also BADNESS, BEHAVIOR, EVILNESS, OBEDIENCE

7103 THE HAWK: "You're gonna be my prisoner for a long time. . . you naughty girl." LADY LOU: "You'll find out." **Cary Grant**'s warning is less threatening than **Mae West**'s as he carries her off at the end of the picture. *She Done Him Wrong* (1933, Paramount).

7104 "You have a very naughty mind, ah'm happy to say." Southern belle **Gloria Grahame** gently chides her writer husband Dick Powell. *The Bad and the Beautiful* (1952, MGM).

Navigation *see* BOATS AND SHIPS, RIVERS, SEAS

Navy *see* BOATS AND SHIPS, MILITARY, RIVERS, SEAS

Nazis

7105 "Wake me up when you get to the part where he claims Milwaukee." Fascist fighting pilot **Ray Milland** quips to reporter Claudette Colbert who settles down to read Hitler's *Mein Kampf. Arise, My Love* (1940, Paramount).

7106 "These guys [Nazi agents] make you and I look like Little Bo-Peep." Racketeer **Humphrey Bogart** tells his erstwhile rival Barton MacLane that compared to the Nazis, they're the good guys. *All Through the Night* (1941, Warner Bros.).

7107 "Perhaps publishing a pro-Nazi paper in the United States isn't the best of occupations. There may be no future in it." Prior to the United States entry in World War II, **Erwin Kalser** warns fascist George Coulouris that Americans may not take to Nazi causes. *Watch on the Rhine* (1943, Warner Bros.).

7108 "Some of you boys I know are wondering whether or not you'll chicken out under fire. Don't worry about it. I assure you that you will do your duty. The Nazis are the enemy. Wade into them. Spill their blood. Shoot them in the belly. When you put your hands into a bunch of goo that a moment before was your best friend's face, you'll know what to do." **George C. Scott**, as General George Patton, addresses his troops before a big battle with the Germans. *Patton* (1970, 20th Century-Fox).

7109 MICKEY: "But if there's a God, then why is there so much evil in the world?. . . Why were there Nazis?" MOTHER: "Tell him, Max." FATHER: "How the hell do I know why there were Nazis? I don't even know how the can opener works."

Woody Allen has a discussion about God and religion and Nazis with his parents **Helen Miller** and **Leo Postrel**. *Hannah and Her Sisters* (1986, Orion).

7110 "Where are the Nazis? What kind of world is this without Nazis?" **Lena Olin** questions Ron Silver as the two holocaust survivors visit a sylvan lake at a resort hotel in the Catskills in 1949. *Enemies, a Love Story* (1989, 20th Century-Fox).

7111 "Nazis! I hate those guys." **Harrison Ford** is disgusted when he discovers that his father Sean Connery is being held captive by Nazis. *Indiana Jones and the Last Crusade* (1989, Paramount).

Needs and Necessities

see also FATE AND DESTINY, POVERTY, REQUIREMENTS

7112 "All you need to start an asylum is an empty room and the right kind of people." **Eugene Pallette** eyes his family and assorted free-loaders that his wealth supports in the living room of his home. *My Man Godfrey* (1936, Universal).

7113 "I need you as much as I need a giraffe." **William Powell** remarries his ex-wife Jean Arthur. *The Ex-Mrs. Bradford* (1936, MGM).

7114 "Your kind of woman needs a guy—not a fine gentleman." Friendly, philosophical window washer **Akim Tamiroff** offers some free advice to Madeleine Carroll, who can't decide between down-to-earth Fred MacMurray and opera singer Allan Jones. *Honeymoon in Bali* (1939, Paramount).

7115 "I kept crying for Rosie and you. A husband and children are necessary to make me complete." Typical of the movie message of the era, brooding and unhappy career woman **Madeleine Carroll** abjectly surrenders to Fred MacMurray. *Honeymoon in Bali* (1939, Paramount).

7116 "He ought to have his brakes relined." **Claudette Colbert** refers to Parisian playboy Francis Lederer who doggedly pursues her. *Midnight* (1939, Paramount).

7117 "What we need in California now is an angel with a flaming sword." Friar **Eugene Pallette** gives young caballero Tyrone Power an idea. *The Mark of Zorro* (1940, 20th Century-Fox).

7118 "I need him like the axe needs the turkey." Con artist **Barbara Stanwyck** sharpens her hatchet for pigeon Henry Fonda. *The Lady Eve* (1941, Paramount).

7119 "As you grow older, my dear, you will learn that conventions are there because there is a need for them." **Lucile Watson** scolds her widowed daughter Barbara Stanwyck about the gossip that has arisen due to her involvement with George Brent. *My Reputation* (1946, Warner Bros.).

7120 "He needs me. And all the rest of us need him. . . . It's not just Kris that's on trial. It's everything he stands for. It's kindness and joy and love and all the other. . . lovely intangibles that are the only things that are worthwhile." Attorney **John Payne** attempts to make cynical Maureen O'Hara see why he's defending Edmund Gwenn in a sanity hearing, brought on by his insistence that he's the real Santa Claus. Payne's law firm feels the case undignified and fires him. *Miracle on 34th Street* (1947, 20th Century-Fox).

7121 "Oh, you'll need me. You'll need a woman. Need what a woman can give you. To do what you have to do. The sun only shines half the time." **Coleen Gray** breathlessly argues with John Wayne who refuses to take her with him when he leaves a wagon train heading further west. *Red River* (1948, United Artists).

7122 "Was this trip necessary? Thousands died because they thought it wasn't, till there was nothing left to do but fight. We must never let force impose itself on a free world. Yes, this trip was necessary. Don't let anyone say you were a sucker for fighting in a war against fascism." Chaplain **Leon Ames** gives a rousing justification of American involvement in the war against the Nazis. *Battleground* (1949, MGM).

7123 "You need me almost as much as I need you, Danny. I know I can make you happy." Nightclub singer **Lizabeth Scott** assures bookmaker Charlton Heston that he's in good hands with her. *Dark City* (1950, Paramount).

7124 "Do you know why I put up with it? I need the money." Beautiful but hard-boiled **Mari Aldon** is frank about why she puts up with arrogant millionaire filmmaker Warren Stevens. *The Barefoot Contessa* (1954, United Artists).

7125 "My dear, you have a neurotic need to be needed, and your Mr. Bronte obviously needs no one—except his violin, of course." **Louis Calhern** advises his daughter Elizabeth Taylor that violinist Vittorio Gassman loves his music more than he does Taylor. *Rhapsody* (1954, MGM).

7126 "Whoever I am, kiddo, I'm what makes you tick." Brutish mobster Martin "The Gimp" Snyder, impersonated by **James Cagney**, uses strongarm tactics to further the career of his wife Ruth Etting, portrayed by Doris Day. *Love Me or Leave Me* (1955, MGM).

7127 "Like it? I've got to. I've saved up for such a long time." Spinster American school teacher **Katharine Hepburn** tells another train passenger as they arrive in Venice that she has no choice but to like it. *Summertime* (1955, Lopert-Korda).

7128 "You give me powders, pills, baths, injections, and enemas—when all I need is love." What **William Holden** wants from nurse Ann Sears is not love. *The Bridge on the River Kwai* (1957, GB, Columbia).

7129 "I want to be needed, I want to be necessary. It's your world. It used to be ours. Now I'm just looking on. Just a sidewalk superintendent." **Ginger Rogers** complains to Tony Randall that the spark has gone from their marriage. *Oh, Men! Oh, Women!* (1957, 20th Century-Fox).

7130 "No, thanks, I've had one cold-hearted bastard in my life. I don't need another." **Joanne Woodward** delivers the socko put-down to Paul Newman. Director Martin Ritt and screenwriters Irving Ravetch and Harriet Frank liked the line so much they had **Patricia Neal** lay it on Newman five years later. *The Long Hot Summer* (1958, 20th Century-Fox); *Hud* (1963, Paramount).

7131 "You need the words?" **Paul Newman** confesses to crippled Piper Laurie that he can only go so far in their relationship. *The Hustler* (1961, 20th Century-Fox).

7132 "I need a cake with a gun in it. And I need a dozen chocolate chip cookies with a bullet in each." Jailed **Woody Allen** gives baking instructions to his wife Janet Margolin. *Take the Money and Run* (1969, Palomar).

7133 "People just don't understand that people need love." Sensitive but oafish accountant **Donald Sutherland** loves the sluttish would-be actress Karen Black from afar. *The Day of the Locust* (1975, Paramount).

7134 "I feel a real need to express something but I don't know what to express or how to express it." **Mary Beth Hurt** has ambitions to become some kind of an artist, but has no talent for it. *Interiors* (1978, United Artists).

7135 "I'm divorced—third time. But I just got married again. I need to be in love. I can't live without the aggravation." **Dom De Luise**, who has just married a working prostitute, tells George Segal of his need for the wedded life. *The Last Married Couple in America* (1980, Universal).

7136 "You gotta know the bottom line. That's what counts. . . . You gotta do what's necessary." Kathleen Turner's sinister husband **Richard Crenna** is marked for death for underrating her. *Body Heat* (1981, Warner Bros.).

7137 "I don't need you. . . . I don't need anybody." **Richard Gere** rejects Debra Winger's attempts to comfort him with her love and sympathy when they find the nude corpse of David Keith, who had hanged himself partly because Winger's friend, Lisa Blount, used him to escape her factory life. *An Officer and a Gentleman* (1982, Paramount).

7138 "I need a Valium the size of a hockey puck." Talent agent **Woody Allen** has another of those bad days trying to place his talentless talents. *Broadway Danny Rose* (1984, Orion).

7139 "You need four inches of bod and a great birthday." Insecure teen **Molly Ringwald** examines herself in a mirror. *Sixteen Candles* (1984, Universal).

7140 "Roads? Where we're going we don't need roads." Pointing towards a sequel, **Christopher Lloyd,** as Doc Brown, tells Michael J. Fox that he's needed in his future to straighten out some family problems. *Back to the Future* (1985, Universal).

7141 "I wanna be just like you—all I need is a lobotomy and some tights." Hoodish **Judd Nelson** sneers sarcastically at high school wrestler Emilio Estevez. *The Breakfast Club* (1985, Universal).

7142 "We need an adult lifeform who is a fearless soldier with the strength of a thousand men." Villainous U.S. General **Ron Frazier** should put out a call for Sylvester Stallone or Arnold Schwarzenegger. *D.A.R.Y.L.* (1985, Paramount).

7143 "There are very few necessities in the world that do not come in travel-size packets." Travel advisor **William Hurt** drones on in voice-over on how to pack efficiently when traveling. *The Accidental Tourist* (1988, Warner Bros.).

7144 BILLY: "It's a rush—man, I need that." EDDIE: "But do they need you?" BILLY: "Who cares?" Womanizer **Chris Mulkey** is questioned about his numerous sexual conquests by his friend **John Jenkins**. *Patti Rocks* (1988, Filmdallas).

7145 "All it needs is a little spackling and some napalm to turn it into a really nice mausoleum."

Chevy Chase is disappointed when he catches his first sight of his crumbling inheritance in the old South. *Fletch Lives* (1989, Universal).

7146 "I need food; I need a manicure; I need my therapist." Screaming **Goldie Hawn** whines about lost luxuries as she and Mel Gibson flee killers. *Bird on a Wire* (1990, Universal).

7147 "We had different needs. I needed to be treated decently and he needed to empty my bank account." **Helen Slater** recalls a guy she once lived with. *City Slickers* (1991, Columbia).

7148 "Women need a reason to have sex; men just need a place." **Billy Crystal** oversimplifies as he shares some questionable male wisdom with his cronies Daniel Stern and Bruno Kirby. They have been speculating about Helen Slater. *City Slickers* (1991, Columbia).

7149 "There are three things you need in life: respect for all kinds of life, a nice bowel movement on a regular basis and a blue blazer." Traumatized **Robin Williams** ticks off the bare necessities of life. *The Fisher King* (1991, Tri-Star).

7150 "I need to admire you. Don't let me down." **Nicole Garcia** tries to buck up her husband Philippe Galland when he shows a moment of weakness. *Overseas* (1991, Fr., Aries Films).

Neglect *see* CARES AND CARING

Nervousness and Nerves

see also COURAGE, FEARS, FEELINGS, SPIRIT AND SPIRITS

7151 "Well, there they go to face life. And their training was to face death. They fell six thousand meters. Like dropping a fine Swiss watch on the pavement. Their nervous systems are shattered." It's the pessimistic diagnosis of one of the doctors who has been treating four shell-shocked World War I American pilots. *The Last Flight* (1931, Warner Bros.).

7152 "A petticoat for any length of time is smallpox to the nerves." Indian scout **Nelson Eddy** claims to have no interest in Jeanette MacDonald, a French princess posing as a servant girl in America. *Naughty Marietta* (1935, MGM).

7153 "Ever since I had my nervous breakdown, I've been a psychic." Vacuous **Everly Gregg** enters the conversation at a dinner held in Robert Donat's Scottish castle. *The Ghost Goes West* (1936, United Artists).

7154 "You have the Reno jumpsie-wumpsies!" Countess **Mary Boland** comforts Norma Shearer, new to divorce. *The Women* (1939, MGM).

7155 "You mistake me, my dear. I have a high respect for your nerves. They are my old friends. I have heard you mention them with consideration these twenty years at least." Impoverished gentlemen-of-the-old-school **Edmund Gwenn** gently reassures his wife Mary Boland. *Pride and Prejudice* (1940, MGM).

7156 GEORGE CUSTER: "They outnumber us three to one." JEB STUART: "Well, if it makes you nervous, don't count." **Ronald Reagan**, as the young Custer, is comforted by **Errol Flynn** as the young Stuart, when their troops face a far superior number. *Santa Fe Trail* (1940, Warner Bros.).

7157 "Dr. Jacquith says our secretiveness and fits of crying indicate you're on the verge of a nervous breakdown. Is that what you're trying to achieve?" Domineering and insensitive **Gladys Cooper** suggests that her fortyish, ugly duckling daughter Bette Davis is deliberately choosing to be mentally unstable. *Now, Voyager* (1942, Warner Bros.).

7158 "I always cough when I'm nervous." **Ingrid Bergman** convinces Empress Helen Hayes that she is the older woman's granddaughter and the only survivor from the massacred royal Russian family. *Anastasia* (1956, 20th Century-Fox).

7159 "There's a chemical in our bodies that makes it so we get on each other's nerves sooner or later." **Woody Allen** explains why meaningful relationships between men and women don't last. *Sleeper* (1973, United Artists).

7160 "You know what hymns do to my nerves." **Carlin Glynn**, aging Geraldine Page's obnoxious, bossy, daughter-in-law, denies Page one of her simple pleasures—singing hymns. *The Trip to Bountiful* (1985, Island Alive).

7161 "That's the second time he dropped the Bible since she's been in there." **Rosie O'Donnell** cracks as she watches teammate Madonna emerge from a confessional followed by a priest in a cold sweat. *A League of Their Own* (1992, Columbia).

Neurosis and Neurotics see FEELINGS, INSANITY AND SANITY, PSYCHOLOGY AND PSYCHIATRY TROUBLES

New York City see CITIES AND TOWNS

Newness

see also EXISTENCE, ORIGINALITY, TIME

7162 "You're a new kind of man in a new kind of world." Socialite **Norma Shearer** makes an incorrect and unfortunate evaluation of gangster Clark Gable. *A Free Soul* (1931, MGM).

7163 "You don't know what it means to us to see something that's not new." **Jean Parker**, the daughter of a wealthy, acquisitive American Eugene Pallette, attempts to show the proper reverence for antiquity as Robert Donat shows her around his Scottish castle. *The Ghost Goes West* (1936, United Artists).

7164 MR. JORDAN: "Unpardonable presumption. What territory do you cover?" MESSENGER 7073: "It's a place called New Jersey, and if it can be arranged, sir, I should very much like to be transferred." MR. JORDAN: "You're new, aren't you?" 7073: "I am, yes sir, first trip. I was put on only this morning." JORDAN: "I thought so. Over-zealousness, out for record collections. This happens right along with the unexperienced." **Claude Rains** reprimands heavenly messenger **Edward Everett Horton** who, wishing to spare Robert Montgomery the agony of crashing in a plane, snatched his soul a moment or two before his time and then discovers Montgomery was to survive. *Here Comes Mr. Jordan* (1941, Columbia).

7165 "All of a sudden I don't like being married to what is known as a new woman." Prosecutor **Spencer Tracy** objects to the attitudes and tactics of his wife Katharine Hepburn who is the opposing counsel in the trial of Judy Holliday. *Adam's Rib* (1949, MGM).

7166 JOSEPHINE (JOE): "We're the new girls." DAPHNE (JERRY): "Brand new." Hiding from gangsters, musicians **Tony Curtis** and **Jack Lemmon**, posing as female musicians, report to band leader Joan Shawlee as Sweet Sue. *Some Like It Hot* (1959, United Artists).

7167 "I heard there was a new student. Are you it?" **Michelle Meyrink** has her first meeting with 14-year-old genius Gabe Jarret at Pacific Tech, a school for scientific brains. *Real Genius* (1985, Tri-Star).

7168 "You've never been like that before." Therapist **Jeanne Tripplehorn** understates the situation after cop, patient, and lover Michael Douglas slams her against a wall, kisses her roughly, rips apart her underwear, kisses her violently again, pushes her face down onto a chair, and takes her from behind. *Basic Instinct* (1992, Tri-Star).

News and Newspapers

see also INFORMATION AND INFORMERS, PHOTOGRA-
PHY AND PHOTOGRAPHERS, RADIOS, REPORTERS,
TELEVISION

7169 "I never did like the idea of sitting on a newspaper. I did it once, and all the headlines came off
on my white pants. On the level! It actually happened. Nobody bought a paper that day. They just
followed me around all over town and read the
news off the seat of my pants." Reporter **Clark
Gable** provides evidence that fishermen aren't the
only ones who tell tall tales. *It Happened One Night*
(1934, Columbia).

7170 "She's the star reporter of the *Mail!* Every time
you opened your kisser, you gave her another story.
She's the dame who slapped that moniker on you!
Cinderella Man! You've been making love to a double dose of cyanide." **Lionel Stander** exposes Jean
Arthur to Gary Cooper. Arthur saw the naïve young
man with a large inheritance as a great news story.
She wormed her way into Cooper's confidence, and
used his obvious infatuation with her to get more
material for her stories—but then she fell in love,
too. *Mr. Deeds Goes to Town* (1936, Columbia).

7171 "Write a piece about me. I like my name in the
paper." On the train to the Big House, smooth
crook **George Raft** kids reporter James Cagney,
framed for manslaughter. *Each Dawn I Die* (1939,
Warner Bros.).

7172 "News is what happens. . . . Time is only an
illusion." Elderly newspaper librarian **John Philliber**
talks about yesterday's news to Dick Powell who
has just been promoted from obituary writer to cub
reporter. *It Happened Tomorrow* (1944, United
Artists).

7173 "Why don't they have all the good news on
one station and all the bad news on another station?
Now why wouldn't that be good?" **Katharine Hepburn** acts ditzy as her husband Spencer Tracy tunes
in the radio. *Adam's Rib* (1949, MGM).

7174 "I can handle big news, and little news, and if
there's no news, I'll go out and bite a dog." One
time ace New York reporter **Kirk Douglas** applies
for a job with a small New Mexico newspaper run
by Porter Hall. *Ace in the Hole* aka:. *The Big Carnival* (1951, Paramount).

7175 "Me? I didn't go to any college, but I know
what makes a good story, because before I ever
worked on a paper, I sold 'em on a street corner.
You know the first thing I found out? Bad news
sells best because good news is no news." Cynical

reporter **Kirk Douglas** instructs young photographer Robert Arthur. *Ace in the Hole* aka: *The Big
Carnival* (1951, Paramount).

7176 "When it comes to newspapermen, give me a
reformed lush every time. Your solid citizen writes
the facts and watches the clock. The ex-dipso lets
himself go. Work takes the place of liquor. He's
dedicated, Julian." Former alcoholic **James Cagney**
has reformed himself and earned back his job as
editor of a newspaper. He tells Larry Keating that he
prefers to hire guys like himself who know they are
"one drink away from destruction," as reporters.
Come Fill the Cup (1951, Warner Bros.).

7177 "Hang on to your swabs, gentlemen. You can
cut the patient's throat while he's under an anes-
thetic and nobody will mind. But if you leave anything inside, you will be in the Sunday papers in no
time." Chief Surgeon **James Robertson Justice**
confides to medical students as he makes the first
incision on a patient. *Doctor in the House* (1954,
GB, Rank).

7178 WALLY HILL: "Do you know what a sex maniac
does?" BEN HARVEY: "N-n-n-no." WALLY: "He sells
newspapers." Sensation-seeking newspaper editor
Clark Gordon sends novice newsman **Beau
Bridges** to get a photograph of an alleged sex
maniac. *Gaily, Gaily* (1969, United Artists).

7179 "Mr. Corleone is a man who insists on hearing
bad news immediately." Consigliari **Robert Duvall**
tells movie mogul John Marley that he must take the
red-eye flight from L.A. back to New York to tell
godfather Marlon Brando that Marley refuses to give
Al Martino the movie role he seeks. *The Godfather*
(1972, Paramount).

7180 "Dear Channel Two News. I have got a solid-
gold, guaranteed, sure-fire story just for you: news
film of the Bobby Ogden wedding in Mexico. Now
it can be yours on an absolutely exclusive basis, no
radio or other TV. The price is eight hundred dollars
for color, six hundred dollars for black and white.
But hurry because we're going with the first offer.
Also extend our warmest congratulations to Mayor
Cavanaugh. See you all soon. Mrs. Tina Waters
Ogden. P.S. Hope Gar's other leg heals real soon."
Band singer **Susan Saint James** continues her publicity blitz in making ex-con, country and western
singer Peter Fonda a folk legend. *Outlaw Blues*
(1977, Warner Bros.).

7181 "A lot of news is bad news for somebody. . . .
After a while, the somebodies start adding up."
Newspaper editor **Josef Sommer** admits that news
stories often hurt people—even innocent people.
Absence of Malice (1981, Columbia).

7182 MALCOLM ANDERSON: "I don't want to see my name in the paper next to pictures of dead bodies anymore." BILL NOLAN: "We're not the manufacturers, we just retail. News gets made somewhere else, we just sell it." Burnt-out big city reporter **Kurt Russell** is tired of covering stories of violence and sordid crimes. His editor **Richard Masur** doesn't want to lose his star reporter to retirement at a small Colorado town weekly. *The Mean Season* (1985, Orion).

7183 "Well, I got some good news and some bad news. The good news is that, yes, I am a cop and I do have to take you in. The bad news is, I just got suspended and I don't give a fuck." **James Woods** takes time to make a poor joke just before he blows off the head of a psycho killer. *Cop* aka: *Blood on the Moon* (1988, Atlantic).

7184 "There are no small jobs here. A newspaper is a daily miracle." Obituary writer **Kevin Bacon** consoles Elizabeth Perkins, who has an equally unexciting job on the newspaper where they both work. *He Said, She Said* (1991, Paramount).

Niceties

see also ATTRACTIONS, CONSIDERATIONS, KINDNESS, MANNERS, PROPRIETY

7185 "I'm not a nice girl." Flapper **Bette Davis** briefly steals George Brent from the nominal lead of this soap opera, Ruth Chatterton. *The Rich Are Always with Us* (1932, First National-Warner Bros.).

7186 "I'm never nice." It's the truth about famous writer **Noel Coward**, but he needn't brag about it. Coward dies and is sent back to earth to find the meaning of love. *The Scoundrel* (1935, Paramount).

7187 "There ain't never been a lady in this town nice to me like you was." Bordello owner **Ona Munson** is happy she is about to save Olivia de Havilland's husband Leslie Howard's life. *Gone with the Wind* (1939, Selznick-MGM).

7188 "Why don't you love me like that? I'm a lot nicer than a girder." **Joan Crawford** whispers seductively to engineer Van Heflin, who, in a moment of technological ecstasy, finds a girder he designed more beautiful than Crawford. *Possessed* (1947, Warner Bros.).

7189 "Nice clean world, no drunks to roll, no salesmen to listen to." Dance hall girl **Betty Grable** finds herself in new surroundings where she's mistaken for the new school marm. *The Beautiful Blonde from Bashful Bend* (1949, 20th Century-Fox).

7190 "Nice guys don't make money." Prizefighter **Kirk Douglas** alienates everybody. *Champion* (1949, Kramer-United Artists).

7191 "I don't think that's very nice." Crazy **Robert Walker** thinks it's distasteful when a park attendant tells him that crowds flock to see the site where Walker murdered Laura Elliott. *Strangers on a Train* (1951, Warner Bros.).

7192 "I'm nice to people when it pays to be nice!" Despicable public relations man **Tony Curtis** doesn't show his nice side at any point. *Sweet Smell of Success* (1957, United Artists).

7193 "Kid, any day the war ends is a nice day." Sergeant **Kirk Douglas** shares the thought with Private Robert Walker, Jr., when they learn that an armistice has been signed in Korea. *The Hook* (1962, MGM).

7194 "The bottom's full of nice people; only cream and bastards rise." Private eye **Paul Newman** holds a cynical view of the world and its people. *Harper* (1966, Warner Bros.).

7195 "Toni, you're a kook, but a nice kook." Writer **Rick Lenz** compliments Goldie Hawn. She has decided to send the mink coat given to her by her lover, Walter Matthau, to his poor "wife" Ingrid Bergman. *Cactus Flower* (1969, Columbia).

7196 "I'm a nice person. I have healthy life drives and good goals. I don't drink, I don't smoke and I would never force myself sexually on a blind person." **Woody Allen** stresses his good points. *Sleeper* (1973, United Artists).

7197 "It's a nice building. You get a—a better class of cockroaches." Garbage man **James Earl Jones** compliments mother of six Diahann Carroll on her apartment building. *Claudine* (1974, 20th Century-Fox).

7198 "You're real nice—If I didn't have puke breath, I'd kiss you." Lynne Griffin must be glad that **Rick Moranis** is so thoughtful. *Strange Brew* (1983, MGM-United Artists).

7199 "It was nice but let's not make a Wagnerian opera out of it." Sexy **Sela Ward** befuddles Tom Hanks after a one-night stand. *Nothing in Common* (1986, Tri-Star).

7200 "One day you'll be nice to me. We might both be dead and buried, but you'll be nice. At least civil." **Ossie Davis,** as Da Mayor, talks to Ruby Dee as Mother Sister, who delights in berating him. *Do the Right Thing* (1989, Universal).

Nicknames and Titles *see* NAMES

Nightmares *see* DREAMS, NIGHTS

Nights

see also DARKNESS, DAYS, DREAMS, SLEEP

7201 "It's never going to strike twelve for us, is it, Bob?" Worried that she's too happy, **Barbara Stanwyck** seeks reassurance from lover Adolphe Menjou that she won't face Cinderella's fate. *Forbidden* (1932, Columbia).

7202 "At this time of night, I'm not looking for needlepoint." No wide-eyed innocent, stranded **Claudette Colbert** confides to Paris taxi-driver Don Ameche. *Midnight* (1939, Paramount).

7203 "Every Cinderella has her midnight." **Claudette Colbert** realizes her masquerade as an aristocrat can't go undiscovered forever. *Midnight* (1939, Paramount).

7204 "This is the night I dreamed about when I was a child. . . the night when I'm waiting to hear that my husband has become president of the United States. And even if he does—it's ruined for me." **Ruth Gordon** as Mary Todd Lincoln is not happy with her marriage or her life. *Abe Lincoln in Illinois* (1940, RKO).

7205 "I don't like to be alone at night. I guess everybody in the world's got a time they don't like. Me, it's right before I go to sleep. And now it's going to be for always. All the rest of my life." Sadly, **Bette Davis** speaks with resignation after her husband Paul Lukas is forced to flee to Mexico to continue his fight against fascists, leaving her and their three children behind. *Watch on the Rhine* (1943, Warner Bros.).

7206 "In the morning when the sun rises, sometimes it's hard to believe there ever was a night. You'll find that, too." Police detective **Joseph Cotten** comforts Ingrid Bergman, whose ordeal of her husband Charles Boyer's trying to drive her crazy is over. *Gaslight* (1944, MGM).

7207 "It's nights like this that drive men like me to women like you for nights like this." Impersonating an international spy, burlesque comic **Bob Hope** has a romantic evening with lovely Hedy Lamarr. *My Favorite Spy* (1951, Paramount).

7208 "It's going to be a long night, and I don't particularly like the book I started. . . know what I mean?" In a sly suggestive way, beautiful **Eva Marie Saint** seems to be offering Cary Grant a night of sex without commitment as they travel by train from New York to Chicago—but this was 1959 and times weren't yet that permissive. *North by Northwest* (1959, MGM).

7209 "Night is the new frontier." Ditzy **Barbra Streisand** tells Gene Hackman that he's a brave pioneer when he is demoted to a lowly night manager at one of his corporations' super-drugstores, frequented by a wide assortment of weirdos. *All Night Long* (1985, Universal).

Nobility

see also CHARACTER, MORALITY, SUPERIORITY AND INFERIORITY, VIRTUES

7210 "Every man, at birth, is endowed with the nobility of a king. The strain of the world soon makes him forget even his birthright. Perhaps, that's why they invented death. Just to give us another chance at remembering who we were before we are born again." Sympathetic prison Chaplain **William Gargan** repudiates the warden's wife's assertion that condemned convict Henry Fonda was "born bad." *You Only Live Once* (1937, United Artists).

7211 "You needn't look so noble. Tea is only a little hot water." Angry young **John Garfield** is ungracious when May Robson offers him a cup of tea. *Four Daughters* (1938, Warner Bros.).

7212 "You noble wives and mothers bore the brains out of me." Gold-digger **Joan Crawford** has no maternal instincts. *The Women* (1939, MGM).

7213 "I know it's considered noble to accept apologies, but I'm afraid I'm not the noble type." **Joan Crawford** rejects Jan Sterling and her apologies. *Female on the Beach* (1955, Universal-International).

7214 "There's no nobility in poverty anymore, Dad." **Charlie Sheen** tries to make his honest laborer father Martin Sheen understand why the younger man can't make it in New York City on a mere $50,000 a year salary. *Wall Street* (1987, 20th Century-Fox).

Noises

see also MUSIC AND MUSICIANS, SHOOTINGS, SOUNDS

7215 RUPERT OF HENTZAU: "Why don't you let me kill you quietly?" RUDOLPH RASSENDYL: "Oh, noise always adds a little cheer." **Douglas Fairbanks, Jr.** and **Ronald Colman** playfully banter in a deadly duel. *The Prisoner of Zenda* (1937, Selznick-United Artists).

7216 "I don't mind a little noise, we'll be dead soon enough." **Joel McCrea** is despondent. *The Palm Beach Story* (1942, Paramount).

7217 "She makes a lot of pretty noises, but she can't come. Like her books: all lovesick posturing. . . ." Poet Alfred de Musset, portrayed by **Mandy Patinkin**, accuses his one-time lover, novelist George Sand, portrayed by Judy Davis, of being sexually vapid. *Impromptu* (1990, GB, Hemdale).

Non Sequiturs

see also LOGIC, PROOFS

7218 "That's my wife. When I married her she was a brunette. Now you can't believe a word she says." Professor **Roland Young** correctly suspects his wife Genevieve Tobin has a roving eye. *One Hour with You* (1932, Paramount).

7219 WYATT EARP: "Mac, have you ever been in love?" MAC: "No, I've been a bartender all my life." **Henry Fonda** isn't about to learn anything about love by questioning bartender **J. Farrell MacDonald.** *My Darling Clementine* (1946, 20th Century-Fox).

7220 "People! I ain't people! I'm a shimmering glowing star in the cinema firm-a-mint! . . . What do they think I am—dumb or somethin'? Why I make more money than Calvin Coolidge put together." Crass movie actress **Jean Hagen,** believing her own publicity, makes some kind of point about her contractual rights. *Singin' in the Rain* (1952, MGM).

7221 "Did you ever pick your toes in Poughkeepsie?" It's New York police detective **Gene Hackman**'s favorite nonsense question of suspects. *The French Connection* (1971, 20th Century-Fox).

7222 "Oh, no, he's been in the school orchestra for over a year now." One Scottish teenage girl responds to another who wonders about classmate Gordon John Sinclair: "Do you think he's a virgin?" *Gregory's Girl* (1982, GB, Lake Film-Goldwyn).

7223 "It's a shame, isn't it, a good looking guy like you locked up in a bathroom? I guess you like rock music." It's sadistic policeman **Harvey Keitel**'s idiotic non sequitur to demented, suspected cop killer, John Lydon. The brutal cop keeps Lydon locked up in his bathroom, only to be taken out on occasion to receive a vicious beating, which Lydon seems to enjoy. *Corrupt* (1984, Italy, Vigo-New Line).

7224 "Remember, no matter where you are—there you are." Cop killer **Robert Grubb** momentarily distracts guard Angry Anderson who is then pummeled by a falling grain shoot. *Mad Max Beyond Thunderdome* (1985, Australia, Warner Bros.).

7225 LOUIS CYPHRE: "Are you an atheist?" HARRY ANGEL: "Yes, I'm from Brooklyn." Mysterious and sinister **Robert DeNiro** is reassured by down-and-out private investigator **Mickey Rourke** that Rourke will have no moral scruples in investigating the disappearance of a singer DeNiro is seeking. *Angel Heart* (1987, Tri-Star).

7226 "I screwed the debate team in high school." Hooker **Julia Roberts** explains to Richard Gere how she learned to tie a tie so well. *Pretty Woman* (1990, Touchstone-Buena Vista).

7227 "Close—you want close? Close is a lingerie shop without windows." Mel Gibson doesn't understand what **Rene Russo** means by this, but because they are becoming intimate, he doesn't care. *Lethal Weapon 3* (1992, Warner Bros.).

Nonsense

see also SENSE AND SENSIBILITY, STUPIDITY

7228 "I ask you as one lady to another—isn't that a load of clams?" Having concluded an interview with a gossip columnist about her scandalous publicity, glamorous film star **Jean Harlow** admits it's all nonsense. *Bombshell* (1933, MGM).

7229 "Was you there, Charley?" **James Cagney**'s nonsense question is the last line of the film. *Picture Snatcher* (1933, Warner Bros.).

7230 "Such nonsense. What do you take me for— Little Nell from the country? Been my understudy for over a week without my knowing, carefully hidden no doubt." Broadway actress **Bette Davis** is furious, railing at her director-fiancé Gary Merrill when he informs her that ambitious Anne Baxter is her new understudy. *All About Eve* (1950, 20th Century-Fox).

7231 "The future is always nonsense until it becomes the past." **Tony Randall,** as Appolonius, dispenses wisdom to the uncomprehending inhabitants of a small western town. *7 Faces of Dr. Lao* (1964, MGM).

7232 "Just give me the money, my dear boy, and let's be done with this nonsense." Con artist **John Geilgud** blackmails reporter Robert Hays. *Scandalous* (1984, Orion).

Normality

see also NATURE AND NATURAL

7233 "I can have a normal life. Think normal things. Even play normal music." Now that she has disposed of her father's body, title character **Gloria Holden** tries to convince herself that she is free of the curse of vampirism. *Dracula's Daughter* (1936, Universal).

7234 "Isn't it wonderful to see our lives so settled. . . temporarily?" Countess **Mary Boland** doesn't hold out any hope that her life and the lives of her friends will remain tranquil over the long run. *The Women* (1939, MGM).

7235 "Not after this he won't be. After this he'll be a perfectly normal human being—and you know what stinkers they are!" Taxi driver **Wallace Ford** disagrees with Josephine Hull that her rumpot brother James Stewart will be just as generous after he's given a personality-altering serum at Chumley's Sanitarium as before. *Harvey* (1950, Universal-International).

7236 "You're supposed to be making me fit for normal life. What's normal? Yours? If it's a question of values, your values stink. Lousy middle-class, well-fed, smug existence. All you care about is a paycheck you don't earn and a beautiful thing to go home to every night." Patient **John Kerr** is uncooperative and accusatory with his psychiatrist Richard Widmark. *The Cobweb* (1955, MGM).

7237 "I never met an ordinary person. To me all people are extraordinary. I meet all sorts here, you know, in my job, and the one thing I've learnt in five years is that the word normal, applied to any human being, is utterly meaningless. In a sort of way it's an insult to our Maker, don't you think, to suppose that He could possibly work to any set pattern?" **Wendy Hiller,** the manager of a British seaside guest house, talks to shy, mother-dominated Deborah Kerr about normality. *Separate Tables* (1958, United Artists).

7238 "He wasn't like you and me. He was a normal person." **Sue Lyon** shares her estimation of Peter Sellers with her step-father and lover James Mason. She would seem to be wrong. *Lolita* (1962, GB, MGM).

7239 "You've seen these women: disturbed, psychotic, miserable. But I want you to realize—they are basically normal people who are sick." Calmly, psychiatrist **Robert Stack** explains to a group of nurses who are watching a cat fight between ex-hooker Janis Paige and homicidal Polly Bergen on a video

hook-up. The fight began when Bergen snarled at Paige, "You're the filth of the world, you prostitute, you whore!" *The Caretakers* (1963, United Artists).

7240 "If you're normal, who wants to be normal?" Deeply troubled young **Keir Dullea** shouts when one of the neighbors of a suburban sanitarium school for "exceptional" teens, yells tactlessly about "a bunch of screwballs spoiling the town." *David and Lisa* (1963, Continental).

7241 "Our life will be a paradise because we are both abnormal." Sex pervert **Anthony Eisley** sees a rosy future together with former prostitute Constance Towers. *The Naked Kiss* (1963, Allied Artists).

7242 "She cut off her nipples with garden shears. You call that normal?" **Elizabeth Taylor** wonders what Marlon Brando's definition of normal is as applied to Julie Harris' behavior after she gave birth to a deformed child. *Reflections in a Golden Eye* (1967, Warner Bros.).

7243 "I want to construct my normalcy." **Jean-Louis Trintignant** is hired by Mussolini's fascists to hunt down subversives. *The Conformist* (1970, Italy-Fr.-W. Ger., Mars-Marianne-Maran).

7244 "What sexual problem? I'm relatively normal for a guy raised in Brooklyn." **Woody Allen** corrects Diane Keaton who talks loudly about their sexual problems as they stand in a movie line. *Annie Hall* (1977, United Artists).

7245 "I'm not being precocious. I'm just a normal 15-year-old. Actually, I'm not normal. I'm still a virgin." **Lisa Lucas** wishes to appear precocious to her mother Jill Clayburgh's boy friend Alan Bates by acting in a way she thinks is shocking. *An Unmarried Woman* (1978, 20th Century-Fox).

7246 "I've spent a lot of time trying to figure out what normal means." Psychiatrist **Art Garfunkel** tells police inspector Harvey Keitel that he's still looking for an answer. *Bad Timing: A Sensual Obsession* (1980, GB, World Northal-Rank).

7247 "I look weird, but otherwise I'm real normal." Even though **Eric Stoltz** is disfigured by a rare disease that gives his face a hideous build-up of bone and tissue, he has a normal teen's interest in blond Laura Dern. *Mask* (1985, Universal).

7248 "Mom is many things. . . normal isn't one of them." **Winona Ryder** speaks of her eccentric mother Cher. *Mermaids* (1990, Orion).

7249 "I'm trying to turn her neurotic misery into general misery, so she can be like the rest of us." Psychiatrist **Richard Gere** answers Kim Basinger's question as to what he's treating her sister Uma Thurman for. He tells her that miserable is a normal state for humans. *Final Analysis* (1992, Warner Bros.).

Noses *see* APPEARANCES, BODIES, FACES

Nostalgia

see also LOSSES AND LOSING, MEMORY AND MEMORIZATION, PAST, REMINDERS

7250 "It is possible to feel nostalgia for a place one has never seen." **Greta Garbo** informs lover John Gilbert that there is something inside her that will not allow her to rest. *Queen Christina* (1933, MGM).

7251 "A fellow will remember things you wouldn't think he'd remember. You take me. One day, back in 1896, I was crossing over to Jersey on a ferry and as we pulled out there was another ferry pulling in—and on it there was a girl waiting to get off. A white dress she had on—and she was carrying a white parasol—and I only saw her for a second and she didn't see me at all—but I'll bet a month hasn't gone by since that I haven't thought of that girl." Elderly **Everett Sloane** gives an example of long-lasting memories to reporter William Alland who is investigating the meaning of Orson Welles' last word on his deathbed, "Rosebud." *Citizen Kane* (1941, RKO).

7252 "Once I stood where we're standing now to say good-bye to a pretty girl. . . . We knew we wouldn't see each other again for almost a year. I thought I couldn't live through it, and she stood there crying—don't even know where she lives now, or if she is living. If she ever thinks of me, she probably imagines I'm still dancing in the ballroom of the Amberson mansion. She probably thinks of the mansion as still beautiful—still the finest house in town." Waiting for a train at the railroad station, **Ray Collins** recalls an old love as he says good-bye to his nephew Tim Holt, now that the Amberson wealth is gone. *The Magnificent Ambersons* (1942, RKO).

7253 "I keep remembering things—all the old things. Everybody was sweet and pretty then, the whole world. A wonderful world. Not like the world today. Not like the world now. It was great to be young then." As in all cases of nostalgia, **Joseph Cotten** remembers only the good things about the past, not the bad. *Shadow of a Doubt* (1943, Universal).

7254 "For as long as I can remember, the house on Larkin Street had been home. Papa and Mama had both been born in Norway, but they came to San Francisco because Mama's sisters were here. . . . I remember it all. . . . But first and foremost I remember Mama." **Barbara Bel Geddes** narrates as the film fades to a flashback when she was young Katrin living with her family and their boarders at the turn of the century. Irene Dunne is flawless in the role of the hardworking, understanding and wise mother. *I Remember Mama* (1948, RKO).

7255 "God. . . remember that Ebbets Field game? The championship of the city? When that team came out. . . he was the tallest, remember? Like a young god. Hercules. . . something like that. And the sun, the sun all around him. . . . Remember how he waved to me? Right up from the field, with the representatives of three colleges standing by? And the buyers I brought and the cheers when he came out—Loman, Loman, Loman! God Almighty, he'll be great yet. A star like that, magnificent, can never really fade away!" Salesman **Fredric March** recalls for his wife Mildred Dunnock the days when his now 34-year-old, ne're-do-well son Kevin McCarthy was a high school football star and the world seemed to be his oyster. *Death of a Salesman* (1951, Columbia).

7256 "Gee, when you tipped one seventy-five you were beautiful. You should've been another Billy Conn. That skunk I got to manage you brought you along too fast." **Rod Steiger** nostalgically misremembers his brother Marlon Brando's boxing career. *On the Waterfront* (1954, Columbia).

7257 "Do you remember Uvalde. . . eleven thousand dollars. . . you held him, I took off the top of his head." **Lee J. Cobb** fondly recalls the good old days with his nephew Gary Cooper, who is reluctant to take up outlawing again. *Man of the West* (1958, United Artists).

7258 "When I was your age I couldn't get enough of anything. I dunno which we ran the hardest, them cars or the country girls. . . we do-si-doed and chased a lot of girlish butts around that summer." **Paul Newman** fondly recalls his lost youth with his brother, Brandon de Wilde's deceased father. *Hud* (1963, Paramount).

7259 "I brought a young lady swimming down here once. Me and this lady was pretty wild. . . . We used to come down on horseback and go swimming without no bathing suits. . . . She bet me a silver dollar she could beat me across. She did." **Ben Johnson,** as Sam the Lion, reminisces at the old swimming hole. *The Last Picture Show* (1971, Columbia).

7260 "Rackets, whoring, guns—it used to be beautiful. The Atlantic was something then." Aging, retired small-time hood **Burt Lancaster** rhapsodizes about the good old days in Atlantic City. *Atlantic City* (1981, Fr.-Canada, Paramount).

7261 "When I listen to my records they take me back to certain periods in my life." **Daniel Stern** is obsessed with his record collection. This collection means more to him than does his wife Ellen Barkin. *Diner* (1982, MGM).

7262 "I used to sit on our front gallery every morning and every evening just to nod hello to Roy John Murray." **Geraldine Page** fondly recalls a shy romance that didn't go very far to her bus companion Rebecca De Mornay. *The Trip to Bountiful* (1985, Island).

7263 "Laura, Laura. . . I tried so hard to leave you behind me. . . Laura, I am more faithful than I intended to be. . . . I reach for a cigarette, I cross a street. I run to movies or a bar. I buy a drink. I speak to the nearest stranger. Anything that will blow the candle out. . . . For nowadays, the world is lit by lightning. . . . Blow out the candles, Laura. . . Goodbye." **John Malkovich** tries to put aside the ghost of his sister Karen Allen at the end of the film. Arthur Kennedy has made a somewhat similar statement at the end of the 1950 Warner Brothers film. *The Glass Menagerie* (1987, Cineplex-Odeon).

7264 "A painful nostalgia gripped me for the South itself. . . [and for] the first person I ever loved outside my family." Returning to his family's home, **John Heard** recalls when he was 13-year-old Lukas Haas and fell in love with Laura Dern. *Rambling Rose* (1991, Seven Arts-New Line).

Notes

see also MESSAGES

7265 "Don't bother to read the note. I'll tell you what it says: 'Eleven roses, and the twelfth is you.'" It's **Gail Patrick**'s subtle way of letting Ginger Rogers know that Adolphe Menjou uses the same line with each of his new conquests. *Stage Door* (1937, RKO).

7266 "Hosannahs to the high gods for throwing us together." It's the note that playboy **Francis Lederer** sends with flowers to Claudette Colbert. John Barrymore, who has hired Colbert to distract Lederer's attention from his wife Mary Astor, observes: "I should resent that. To my wife he only wrote, 'So glad we met.'" *Midnight* (1939, Paramount).

7267 "I can't take it anymore, Felix. I'm crackin' up. . . . You leave me little notes on my pillow. I told you 158 times I cannot stand little notes on my pillow. 'We're all out of corn flakes, F.U.' It took me three hours to figure out F.U. was Felix Unger." Sloppy, disorganized **Walter Matthau** is slowly being driven mad by his compulsively clean and efficient roommate Jack Lemmon. *The Odd Couple* (1968, Paramount).

7268 "Please put $15,000 into this bag and act naturally. I am pointing a gub [sic] at you." At least that's what a very unshakeable teller thinks the illegible note that would-be bank robber **Woody Allen** has passed him, says. When the teller asks for an interpretation from a colleague, the second teller has trouble as well, saying, 'Place $50,000 in the bag. Act matural [sic].' What's that mean?" When Allen finally gets them to understand the stickup note, they tell him he must have the note signed by an officer of the bank before they can give him the money. *Take the Money and Run* (1969, Cinerama).

7269 "Dear Mr. Blakely: Congratulations on your forthcoming marriage. Please return the front door key immediately." It's the note **Miranda Richardson** includes with the flowers she sends lover Rupert Everett when she learns of his engagement. *Dance with a Stranger* (1985, GB, Goldcrest-NFFC-First Picture Co.).

7270 "Why don't you get some Chinese food for dinner? I've left your father. Love, Mom." **Veronica Cartwright** leaves a note for her son Barry Tubb when she's finally had it with her philandering husband Frederic Forrest. *Valentino Returns* (1989, Skouras).

Nothingness

see also EXISTENCE, WORTH AND VALUES

7271 "No friends, no rest, no peace. . . keep moving, that's all that's left!" An escapee from a Georgia chain gang, **Paul Muni** has nothing and he's certainly not free. *I Am a Fugitive from a Chain Gang* (1932, Warner Bros.).

7272 MRS. CLAYPOOL: "Mr. Driftwood, three months ago you promised to put me in society. In all that time, you've done nothing but draw a very handsome salary." OTIS P. DRIFTWOOD: "You think that's nothing, huh? How many men do you suppose are drawing a handsome salary nowadays? Why, you can count them on the fingers of one hand, my good woman." **Margaret Dumont** is not convinced that she's getting her money's worth from fast-talking con man **Groucho Marx**. *A Night at the Opera* (1935, MGM).

7273 "We have nothing to reproach ourselves for." After they are rescued, muscular nature boy **Randolph Scott** assures Irene Dunne, with whom he has spent seven years shipwrecked on a desert island, that they need not apologize to anyone, not even her husband Cary Grant, for anything that went on between them. *My Favorite Wife* (1940, RKO).

7274 VERA: "It's nothing." ROBERTS: "That's what Camille said." When **Ann Savage** dismisses her cough, her reluctant partner in deception **Tom Neal** responds hopefully. *Detour* (1946, PRC).

7275 "Now we're starting out with exactly an even nothing in the world. It's neater that way." Having quit his job as an advertising executive by dumping a pitcher of water over the head of loathsome soap company owner Sidney Greenstreet, yelling, "You're all wet!," **Clark Gable** tells his love Deborah Kerr that they'll have to start life at the bottom and work their way back up. That's fine with her. *The Hucksters* (1947, MGM).

7276 "It's nothing, just a broken arm." Mother's boy **Danny Kaye** engages in one of his daydreams of derring-do. *The Secret Life of Walter Mitty* (1947, Goldwyn-RKO).

7277 "I wanted to be the one woman who asked him for nothing." That's precisely what **Joan Fontaine** got from her selfish sometime lover Louis Jourdan. There was a child however. *Letter from an Unknown Woman* (1948, Universal).

7278 JIM CONOVER: "What's your stake in all this?" KAY THORNDYKE: "I want nothing." CONOVER: "People who want nothing worry me. The price isn't right." Political expert **Adolphe Menjou** doesn't believe that wealthy newspaper publisher **Angela Lansbury** has only altruistic motives for financing her lover Spencer Tracy's bid for the presidential nomination. *State of the Union* (1948, MGM).

7279 "I like it. Early nothing." **Gloria Grahame** comments when she visits Glenn Ford's seedy hotel room. *The Big Heat* (1953, Columbia).

7280 "O stands for nothing—it's my trademark ROT." **Cary Grant** charmingly admits to Eva Marie Saint that his middle initial represents nothing, but taken together the three letters may be significant. *North by Northwest* (1959, MGM).

7281 "What can I do? What? I'm nobody. A zero." Collaborator **Josef Kroner** cries with guilt and impotency as the Jews of his Slovakian village are rounded up. *The Shop on Main Street* (1965, Czech, Narrandov-Prominent).

7282 "Sometimes nothing is a very cool hand." **Paul Newman** makes the observation after winning a big poker pot with a bust hand, thus earning a nickname given to him by George Kennedy. *Cool Hand Luke* (1967, Warner Bros.).

7283 "Everything is flat here. There is nothing to do." **Ellen Burstyn** refers to the dusty, windblown Texas town of Anarene. *The Last Picture Show* (1971, Columbia).

7284 LAURA BAXTER: "One of your children has posed a curious question: 'If the world is round, why is a frozen pond flat?'" JOHN BAXTER: "Nothing is what it seems." **Julie Christie** may conclude that father **Donald Sutherland** doesn't know best if he keeps giving evasive answers like that. *Don't Look Now* (1973, GB-Italy, Paramount).

7285 "You're nothing to me now, Fredo, not a brother, not a friend. I don't want to know you, or what happens to you. I don't want to see you in the hotels, or near my home. When you visit our mother I want to know a day in advance, so I won't be there." **Al Pacino** ostracizes his brother John Cazale, who has worked with Lee Strasberg to set up an assassination attempt on Pacino at his Lake Tahoe estate. *The Godfather, Part II* (1974, Paramount).

7286 FRANZ: "Why are you getting dressed?" HANNI: "There's nothing else to do." Nineteen-year-old Jewish **Harry Baer** is surprised that 14-year-old German **Eva Mattes**, a well-developed, full-breasted Rubenesque girl, is matter-of-factly putting on her clothes after he has deflowered her. *Jail Bait* aka: *Wild Game* (1977, Germany, Interel-New Yorker).

7287 "You're nothing going nowhere." Ambitious public relations secretary **Karen Lynn Gorney** likes paint store clerk John Travolta but realizes that he's content being a big fish in a small pond as top dancer at a local Brooklyn disco. *Saturday Night Fever* (1977, Paramount).

7288 "I know that you think what I do for a living is nothing. It really isn't nothing. I just did it badly." Reporter **Sally Field** apologizes to Paul Newman, an innocent businessman who has been badly hurt by news stories written by Field. *Absence of Malice* (1981, Columbia).

7289 FRANCOIS: "Don't you ever think of something?" ANNE: "No, because then nothing is something." Post office worker and evening law student **Philippe Marlaud** is given something to think about by **Marie Riviere**. *The Aviator's Wife* (1981 Fr., Gaumont-Films du Losange).

7290 "I've been out of Mercury, and there's nothing out there." Because he doesn't want his girlfriend Kathleen Quinlan to pursue an art school scholarship in Los Angeles, **David Keith** dismisses all the world outside of their home town Mercury, New Mexico. *Independence Day* (1983, Warner Bros.).

7191 "The reason people treat me like nothing is because I am nothing." Except for his dancing ability, working class stiff **Patrick Swayze** hasn't got much going for him. But Jennifer Grey sees more than he does. *Dirty Dancing* (1987, Vestron).

7292 "I always think there's more to the world than meets the eye. It never works. . . . You're right, I am nothing. It beats being a waitress." **Julie Kavner** admits to Woody Allen that she's an incompetent psychic. "Oedipus Wrecks" in *New York Stories* (1989, Touchstone-Buena Vista).

7293 "I'm more afraid of being nothing than I am of being hurt." Stock car racer **Tom Cruise** tells Nicole Kidman why he's willing to take the risks of his profession. *Days of Thunder* (1990, Paramount).

7294 MICKEY: "What have I ever done to you?" FINTAN: "Nothing, but it doesn't matter." Once again, **Adrian Dunbar** has taken advantage of his friend **James Nesbitt**. *Hear My Song* (1991, GB, Miramax).

Nudity

see also ART AND ARTISTS, BODIES, PROPRIETY, SEX AND SEXUALITY, SHAME

7295 "When I get hot I sleep raw." **Connie Stevens** draws a nice picture for Troy Donahue. *Parrish* (1961, Warner Bros.).

7296 "Oh, my! A naked man chained to a tree! Am I dreaming?" An aging homosexual leading a pink poodle comes across naked cop Tim McIntire, who has been chained to a tree in a park and abandoned by his buddies. *The Choirboys* (1977, Universal).

7297 "Have you ever seen a grown man naked? **Peter Graves,** as pilot Captain Oveur, comes on to Tommy, a young boy visiting the cockpit. *Airplane* (1980, Paramount).

7298 "Now it's time for some gratuitous nudity." **Penn Jillette** could be cueing the audience of an obligatory scene in films of this type. He's a hustler for wealthy Arab Teller. Jillette induces three young women to doff their clothes in the back seat of Teller's limousine. *My Chauffeur* (1986, Crown International).

7299 "He did a whole series of nudes of me. It's a funny feeling to know you're being hung naked in some stranger's living room." **Barbara Hershey** confesses to her sister Mia Farrow that Hershey's artist lover Max von Sydow has sold some paintings of Hershey. *Hannah and Her Sisters* (1987, Orion).

7300 HERBIE: "Take away the clothes and makeup and what'd ya got?" STAN: "A gorgeous naked woman?" Wedding guests **Alex Bruhanski** and **Stephen E. Miller,** enjoying themselves by commenting on passing females, assess Sean Young. *Cousins* (1989, Paramount).

7301 "I only had one dream about her when she was naked, and she was vacuuming. It wasn't about sex, it was about cleanliness." Four years after his mother's death, **Nicolas Cage** tells his impatient girl friend Sarah Jessica Parker that once again he's dreamt about his mother Anne Bancroft. Parker asks if Bancroft was naked. *Honeymoon in Vegas* (1992, Columbia).

Numbers *see* MATHEMATICS, PROBABILITY AND STATISTICS

Nurses

see also DISEASES, DOCTORS AND DENTISTS, HEALTH, MEDICINE, SICKNESS

7302 "It's gonna be nice having a nurse in the family." FBI agent **James Cagney** rescues girl friend Margaret Lindsay from Barton MacLane and his gang. *G-Men* (1935, Warner Bros.)

7303 "This is it. And if you're looking for his nurse, she's ready to go to work." **Dianne Foster** is an altruistic nurse that society doctor Charlton Heston finally realizes is better for him than Lizabeth Scott. *Bad for Each Other* (1954, Columbia).

7304 "All right, Frank. Doug and I made the scotch. The nurse is your department." **William Powell** and Henry Fonda concoct some ersatz scotch from Coke, hair tonic, and various other liquids to help Jack Lemmon seduce scotch-loving nurse Betsy Palmer. *Mister Roberts* (1955, Warner Bros.).

7305 "Where did you train your nurses, Mrs. Christie—Dachau?" **George C. Scott,** the hospital's chief resident, is flabbergasted when Head Nurse Nancy Marchand reports on the disastrous treatment of some of the hospital's patients due to inefficiency and indifference. *The Hospital* (1971, United Artists).

7306 "If you nurse as good as your sense of humor, I won't make it to Thursday." Grouchy as ever, **Walter Matthau,** who has suffered a stroke, complains to his black nurse Rosetta LeNoire. *The Sunshine Boys* (1975, MGM).

Oaths

see also CURSES, PLEDGES, PROFANITY, PROMISES

7307 "Say, 'From now on, I, Rosalie Wells, am the vassal of Mary Tilford and will do and say whatever she tells me under the solemn oath of a knight.'" Horrid child **Bonita Granville** blackmails frightened Marcia Mae Jones into becoming her slave. *These Three* (1936, Goldwyn-United Artists).

7308 "As God is my witness, they're not going to lick me. . . . I'm going to live through this and when it's over, I'll never be hungry again. No, nor any of my folks! If I have to lie, steal, cheat, kill—as God is my witness, I'll never be hungry again." **Vivien Leigh** as Scarlett O'Hara displays the grit that will see her through the hard times in the South after the Civil War. *Gone with the Wind* (1939, Selznick-MGM).

7309 "I figure a man's only good for one oath at a time. I still got my saber. . . . Didn't turn it into no plowshare, neither." **John Wayne** tells his brother Walter Coy that he never rejoined the Union after General Lee surrendered the Confederacy to General Grant, and still considers himself a Rebel. *The Searchers* (1956, Warner Bros.).

7310 HERMAN: "You swore a holy oath!" MASHA: "I swore falsely." **Ron Silver** is upset when he discovers that **Lena Olin** has lied to him when she swore she hadn't slept with her husband Paul Mazursky. *Enemies, a Love Story* (1989, 20th Century-Fox).

Obedience

see also AUTHORITIES, LEADERSHIP AND LEADERS, SERVANTS AND SERVITUDE, SLAVERY AND SLAVES

7311 "To hear is to obey, little master of the universe." Djinni **Rex Ingram** bows down to Sabu after the latter has tricked the former. *The Thief of Bagdad* (1940, GB, London Films).

7312 "If you're to become my wife, you must learn to obey me!" **Stewart Granger** responds to Phyllis Calvert, who complains she can't bear a year's enforced separation from him. *The Man in Grey* (1943, GB, Gainsborough-GFD).

7313 "I cannot disobey the king." **Anita Louise**, as Lady Catherine Maitland, happily obeys King Maurice R. Tauzin, who orders her to marry Cornel Wilde, the son of Robin Hood. *The Bandit of Sherwood Forest* (1946, Columbia).

7314 "Obedience without understanding is a blindness too—is that all I wished on her?" **Anne Bancroft**, as Annie Sullivan, contemplates the fate of her student Patty Duke, who portrays a young deaf, mute and blind Helen Keller. Bancroft has successfully helped Duke overcome some behavior problems. *The Miracle Worker* (1962, United Artists).

7315 "They can have my dead body—but not my obedience." **Ben Kingsley** as Mahatma Gandhi refers to the British Imperialists. *Gandhi* (1982, GB, Columbia).

Obesity

see also FOOD AND EATING, SIZES

7316 "Darling, you're a mess. You should lay off the candy bars." Brothel keeper **Marlene Dietrich** weighs the appearance of grossly obese police detective Orson Welles. *Touch of Evil* (1958, Universal-International).

7317 "You and I have a tendency towards corpulence. Corpulence makes a man reasonable, pleasant and phlegmatic." Scheming Roman Senator **Charles Laughton** shares a confidence with equally chubby gladiator school owner Peter Ustinov. *Spartacus* (1960, Universal).

7318 "Well, come see a fat old man sometime." **John Wayne,** as Rooster Cogburn, takes his leave of Kim Darby, as Mattie Ross, by jumping his horse over a cemetery wall. Darby is tending her father's grave and indicates that there's plenty of room for Wayne in the plot. *True Grit* (1969, Paramount).

Object Lessons

see also LEARNING AND LESSONS, PRINCIPLES

7319 "Mrs. King, throughout this grisly meal your son has been pelting me with cereal. I have taught him an object lesson, and, as you will observe, he doesn't like it. I guarantee that he will never throw cereal at me or anyone else again. Ever." **Clifton Webb** has just poured a bowl of cereal over the head of Maureen O'Hara's youngest son Roddy McCaskill. *Sitting Pretty* (1948, 20th Century-Fox).

7320 "This execution will be a perfect tonic for the entire division. There are few things more fundamentally encouraging and stimulating than seeing someone else die. You see, Colonel, troops are like children. Just as a child wants his father to be firm, troops crave discipline. And one way to maintain discipline is to shoot a man now and then." Callous French General **Adolphe Menjou** patiently explains to Kirk Douglas why the execution of three soldiers chosen at random from a division will have a positive effect on the survivors. *Paths of Glory* (1957, United Artists).

7321 "Now that's someone I love. Think what would happen to you." Gangster **Mark Rydell** makes a point to Elliott Gould by smacking his girl friend with a pop bottle. *The Long Goodbye* (1973, United Artists).

7322 "He took my thumb!" **Eric Roberts** screams and sobs at the top of his lungs after mobsters cut off his thumb as an object lesson to remind him not to chisel in on their turf. *The Pope of Greenwich Village* (1984, MGM-United Artists).

7323 "You see that building. . . I bought that building ten years ago—my first real estate deal. Sold it two years later—made an $800,000 profit. It's better than any sex. . . . At the time I thought it was all the money in the world. Now it's a day's pay." High roller **Michael Douglas** tries to teach young hot shot Charlie Sheen that money is merely the chips played in the high stakes game of investments. *Wall Street* (1987, 20th Century-Fox).

Objections

see also AGREEMENTS, OPPOSITENESS, REASONS

7324 "Wait a minute, I'll decide with whom my wife is going to have dinner and who she's going to kill." Polish actor **Jack Benny** objects to plans that will have his wife Carole Lombard meet traitor Stanley Ridges for a quiet dinner, at which time she is to kill him. *To Be or Not to Be* (1942, Korda-Lubitsch-United Artists).

7325 "I won't be looked at in this merciless glare." **Vivien Leigh** objects to her sister Kim Hunter about the lighting, fearful someone might see how her looks have faded. *A Streetcar Named Desire* (1951, Warner Bros.-20th Century-Fox).

7326 "You didn't object to my pom-poms then!" Pouting **Jill St. John,** as Toby Tyler, reminds ex-lover Dean Martin of happier times together. *Who's Been Sleeping in My Bed?* (1963, Paramount).

Objects

see also INTENTIONS, THINGS

7327 "It's like being a gourmet all my life, and now I'm a lamb chop." When a skirt-chasing male Harry Madden is killed and comes back to life as **Debbie Reynolds,** he/she learns what it feels like to be treated as a sexual object. *Goodbye Charlie* (1964, 20th Century-Fox).

7328 "You're treating me like an object. You think I'm a girl?" Boxer **Ryan O'Neal** rails at manager Barbra Streisand, who promotes him as if he were a bottle of perfume. *The Main Event* (1979, Warner Bros.).

7329 "I'm not steak. You cannot just order me." **Melanie Griffith** tries to get her fisherman boy friend Alec Baldwin to treat her with more respect. *Working Girl* (1988, 20th Century-Fox).

7330 "I'm not a piece of steak for you two to fight over." Despite **Sean Young**'s protests, Nicolas Cage and Tommy Lee Jones do fight over her. Young and Griffith should get together. *Firebirds* (1990, Touchstone-Buena Vista).

Obsessions

see also COMPULSIONS, EMOTIONS, FEELINGS, NERVOUSNESS AND NERVES

7331 PRINCESS JEANETTE: "Don't you think of anything but men?" COUNTESS VALENTINE: "Oh, yes, dear, schoolboys." Sickly widow **Jeanette MacDonald,** who needs a man, converses with her healthy and lusty cousin **Myrna Loy,** who is never without one. *Love Me Tonight* (1932, Paramount).

7332 "I must have it, I must have it." Mechanical toy-obsessed **Miles Malleson** agrees to give his daughter June Duprez's hand in marriage to Grand Vizier Conrad Veidt in exchange for a mechanical winged horse. *The Thief of Bagdad* (1940, GB, London Films).

7333 BORIS LERMONTOV: "Why do you want to dance?" VICTORIA PAGE: "Why do you want to live?" LERMONTOV: "I don't know exactly, but I must." PAGE: "That's my answer too." Ballet impresario **Anton Walbrook** and young ballerina **Moira Shearer** find they share something in common. *The Red Shoes* (1948, GB, Rank-Eagle-Lion).

7334 "Did you ever have one of those nightmares in which you try to run from danger and can't move?" Banker **Joseph Cotten** is obsessed with the idea of stealing money from his bank. *The Steel Trap* (1952, 20th Century-Fox).

7335 "Once you find the way you'll be bound. It'll obsess you. But believe me, it'll be a magnificent obsession." Physician **Paul Cavanagh** believes that medicine is a "magnificent obsession." *Magnificent Obsession* (1954, Universal).

7336 "I'm going to get my balance. Then I can go back to being obsessed with my family." **Gena Rowlands** confides to her psychiatrist David Rowlands. *Love Streams* (1984, MGM-United Artists).

7337 "All the jocks think about is football. All we nerds think about is sex." Nerdish **Robert Carradine** explains to gorgeous Julie Montgomery why he's such a good sex partner. *Revenge of the Nerds* (1984, 20th Century-Fox).

7338 "Well, if you think about it, I think you'll see that the object of your obsession is invariably something negative which you have no control over." Therapist **Ron Vawter** sums up Andie MacDowell's problem. *sex, lies and videotape* (1989, Miramax).

Obviousness

see also UNDERSTANDINGS AND MISUNDERSTANDINGS

7339 "I know you hate the obvious. Would you mind for a moment if I'm not the least subtle?" Although he hates to seem direct or unsophisticated, **Melvyn Douglas** wants to just come out and tell Greta Garbo that he loves her. *Ninotchka* (1939, MGM).

7340 "When faced with the obvious, look elsewhere." It's **Peter Ustinov**'s aphorism in what is arguably the worst Charlie Chan movie ever made. *Charlie Chan and the Curse of the Dragon Queen* (1981, American Cinema).

Occupations

see also CAREERS, JOBS, WORK AND WORKERS

7341 "I run a couple of newspapers. What do you do?" Publishing magnate **Orson Welles** low-keys his answer to Dorothy Comingore whom he has just met. *Citizen Kane* (1941, RKO).

7342 "I'm an anti-fascist and to answer your question, no, that does not pay well." German **Paul Lukas** responds to the questions asked and unasked of his American mother-in-law Lucile Watson about his work. *Watch on the Rhine* (1943, Warner Bros.).

7343 LADY BRACKNELL: "Do you smoke?" JACK WORTHING: "Well, yes, I must admit I smoke." LADY BRACKNELL: "I'm glad to hear it; a man should have an occupation of some kind." **Edith Evans** questions gentleman **Michael Redgrave** to determine his suitability to be her daughter's husband. *The Importance of Being Earnest* (1952, GB, Rank-Two Cities).

7344 "I get 'em coming and goin'." Town physician and mortician **Walter Brennan** tells stranger Spencer Tracy that his dual occupations keep him pretty busy. Wonder if he has any conflicts of interest? *Bad Day at Black Rock* (1954, MGM).

7345 "A press agent is many things, most of them punishable by law." Director **Humphrey Bogart** comments on Edmond O'Brien's profession. *The Barefoot Contessa* (1954, United Artists).

7346 "There's not much call for human flies these days." Looks like schizoid, out-of-work circus performer **Peter Boyle** will have to find a new gimmick. *Steelyard Blues* (1973, Warner Bros.).

7347 "He watches television." It is hulking teenager **Adam Baldwin**'s reply when asked what his father does. *My Bodyguard* (1980, 20th Century-Fox).

7348 "You got it, a great spender of other people's money." **Daryl Hannah** answers in the affirmative when Charlie Sheen asks if she's an interior decorator. *Wall Street* (1987, 20th Century-Fox).

Odd *see* STRANGENESS AND STRANGERS

Odds *see* PROBABILITY AND STATISTICS

Offers

see also MARRIAGES, PROPOSALS, REFUSALS AND REJECTIONS, VOLUNTEERS

7349 "Come and live with me in my gutter." Mobster **Robert Alda** doesn't offer nightclub singer Ida Lupino a reduction in her living conditions. *The Man I Love* (1946, Warner Bros.).

7350 "I came to offer you my whole life—and you don't even remember me." It's a passage from **Joan Fontaine**'s letter to rakish pianist Louis Jourdan on whom she has wasted her life loving. *Letter from an Unknown Woman* (1948, Universal).

7351 "Offer me friendship or marriage, but not an affair—I wouldn't be very good at it." **Claudette Colbert** limits tobacco baron Karl Malden's options. *Parrish* (1961, Warner Bros.).

7352 "I can offer you a comfortable home. . . a sunny garden. . . a congenial atmosphere. . . my cherry pies. . . ." Insufferable **Shelley Winters** induces James Mason to board in her home. He accepts with pleasure when he sees her nubile 14-year-old daughter Sue Lyon. *Lolita* (1962, GB, MGM).

7353 "Would you like me to massage your think muscles?" **Jill St. John** makes an offer to Frank Sinatra. *Come Blow Your Horn* (1963, Paramount).

7354 "Oh, Forio, if you want to bite somebody, bite me!" **Tippi Hedren** offers herself to her horse, her substitute object for her repressed sexual impulses. *Marnie* (1964, Universal).

7355 "Boys who wear sandals probably don't get many offers." **Edy Williams** responds to David Gurian, who jokingly claims he's looking for a woman who will lick him between his toes. *Beyond the Valley of the Dolls* (1970, 20th Century-Fox).

7356 "Why don't we shack up?" The results are disastrous when swinging bachelor and "swordsman" Jack Nicholson takes voluptuous 29-year-old TV model **Ann-Margret** up on her offer. *Carnal Knowledge* (1971, Avco Embassy).

7357 "He's a businessman. I'll make him an offer he can't refuse." **Marlon Brando** as Don Corleone speaks of movie producer John Marley, who has refused to give the don's godson Al Martino the part in a film he desperately wants. *The Godfather* (1972, Paramount).

7358 "My father made him [the band leader] an offer he couldn't refuse. Luca Brasci held a gun to his head, and my father assured him that either his brains or his signature would be on the contract. . . . That's my family, Kay, it's not me." **Al Pacino** tells Diane Keaton how his father Marlon Brando used Lenny Montana to convince a band leader to release singer Al Martino from a personal-services contract. *The Godfather* (1972, Paramount).

7359 "I'm going to make him an offer he can't refuse." The new godfather **Al Pacino** tells his brother John Cazale that the Family is buying out Alex Rocco's interest in the Las Vegas casinos. *The Godfather* (1972, Paramount).

7360 "How about coming up to my place for a spot of heavy breathing?" **Walter Matthau** makes a tempting offer to Carol Burnett—she accepts. *Pete 'n' Tillie* (1972, Universal).

7361 "You wanna fuck?" In her first screen role playing a seventeen-year-old nymphet, **Carrie Fisher** makes an offer to hairdresser Warren Beatty that he doesn't refuse. *Shampoo* (1975, Columbia).

7362 "Things are not fine. [My husband] gave me one of his whiz-bang specials and I'm mad at him. . . . Would you want to sleep with me?" Beautiful, unsatisfied **Angie Dickinson** takes her very personal problems to her analyst Michael Caine. Caine is interested. *Dressed to Kill* (1980, Filmways).

7363 "You could have the room where I first violated Ethel." **Henry Fonda** hectors Dabney Coleman with his offer of a room for Coleman to share with Henry's daughter Jane Fonda at their lakeside cottage. *On Golden Pond* (1981, Universal).

7364 "They offered me one hundred grand. . . . But you know something? When I found out I'd be getting my hands on you, I told them I'd do it for nothing." **Vernon Wells,** once a member of retired Commando Arnold Schwarzenegger's team, is happy to kill Arnie for free. *Commando* (1985, 20th Century-Fox).

7365 "How would you like a sexual encounter so intense it could conceivably change your political views?" This line doesn't work for **John Cusack.** He strikes out with a coed who looks at him like he was nuts. *The Sure Thing* (1985, Embassy).

7366 MICHAEL KELLAM: "I think it's your turn to change." PETER MITCHELL: "I'll give you a thousand dollars if you do it." **Steve Guttenberg** and **Tom Selleck** argue over who will change a baby's dirty diaper. *Three Men and a Baby* (1987, Touchstone-Buena Vista).

7367 "They had nothing to offer the school but date rapes and AIDS jokes." Psychopath **Christian Slater** justifies to Winona Ryder their killing two macho high school football players and making it appear that it was a double suicide of gay lovers. *Heathers* (1989, New World).

7368 "Most of the time you're just another good-looking, sweet-talking, charm-oozing, fuck-happy fella with nothing to offer but some dialogue. Dialogue is cheap in Hollywood. . . . Why don't you go outside and jerk yourself a milk shake?" Bit actress Virginia Hill, played by **Annette Bening**, makes a crude suggestion to Ben Siegel, played by Warren Beatty, when he approaches her on a movie set he's visiting. *Bugsy* (1991, Tri-Star).

Old Age see AGE AND AGING, LIVES AND LIVING, MATURITY AND IMMATURITY, RETIREMENT, YOUTH

Omens see EVILNESS

Opera see MUSIC AND MUSICIANS

Opinions

see also AGREEMENTS, BELIEFS, FEELINGS, IDEAS, IMPRESSIONS, JUDGMENTS, SENTIMENTS AND SENTIMENTALITY

7369 "I wish someone would tell you what I really think of you." In an oblique way **Claudette Colbert** gets her wish that Gary Cooper learn of her low opinion of him. *Bluebeard's Eighth Wife* (1938, Paramount).

7370 "Now that you have seen me, what do you

think of me?" Nouveau riche title character **Alan Ladd** tells obvious lies to MacDonald Carey, then abruptly asks him for his opinion of Ladd. *The Great Gatsby* (1949, Paramount).

7371 VIKTOR: "In my opinion, a modern man looks at insignificance straight in the eye and believes in himself and his biological death. Everything else is nonsense." ANDERS: "And in my opinion, modern man exists only in your imagination. Because man looks at his death with horror and can't bear his own insignificance." **Bjorn Bjelvenstam**, studying to be a physician, and **Folke Lundquist**, studying to be a minister, debate man's insignificance. *Wild Strawberries* (1957, Sweden, Svensk Filmindustri).

7372 "It is my professional opinion, as the man who invented psychoanalysis, that you are not Fagin." **Alec Guinness**, charming as the spirit of Sigmund Freud, counsels psychiatrist Dudley Moore who has fallen in love with his patient Elizabeth McGovern. *Lovesick* (1983, Warner Bros.).

7373 "When I want your opinion, I'll beat it out of you." A Chicago version of *Dirty Harry*, played by **Chuck Norris**, who threatens a punk who opens his mouth at the wrong time. *Code of Silence* (1985, Orion).

7374 "If I'd wanted your opinion, I'd have beaten it out of you." Campy Mistress of the Macabre, buxomy vamp **Elvira** (**Cassandra Peterson**) snaps at one of her slaves. *Elvira, Mistress of the Dark* (1988, New World).

Opportunities

see also CHANCES

7375 "The reason you're alive and walking around in that horse blanket is because I like you. . . . This is the land of opportunity. Everybody lives by chiseling everybody else." Political boss **Akim Tamiroff** takes an immediate liking to brash bum Brian Donlevy, instructing the latter on how things work before making him an alderman. *The Great McGinty* (1940, Paramount).

7376 "They say opportunity's only got one hair on its head and you got to grasp it while it's going by." Crusty Marine Sergeant **William Demarest** advises Eddie Bracken to take advantage of the opportunity facing him when the folks in his hometown mistakenly believe he's a war hero. *Hail the Conquering Hero* (1944, Paramount).

7377 "Six feet four inches of opportunity doesn't

come along every day, you now." **Thelma Ritter** advises Doris Day not to turn up her nose at Rock Hudson. *Pillow Talk* (1959, Universal).

7378 "Two adults who saw an opportunity and took advantage of it." That's how **Michael Douglas** views his weekend affair with Glenn Close. She sees it differently. *Fatal Attraction* (1987, Paramount).

Oppositeness

7379 "I ask myself what General Motors would do and do the opposite." Free-spirited, unambitious **Cary Grant** disappoints his society fiancée Doris Nolan with his views. *Holiday* (1938, Columbia).

7380 "Chain them to opposite walls; in the morning they die the death of a thousand cuts." Evil **Conrad Veidt** passes judgments on lovers John Justin and June Duprez. *The Thief of Bagdad* (1940, GB, London Films).

7381 "We're like flying buttresses leaning on opposite sides of a Gothic church to keep it from falling." Liberal jurist **Walter Matthau** eulogizes his deceased conservative colleague on the U.S. Supreme Court. *First Monday in October* (1981, Paramount).

Optimism and Pessimism

see also BELIEFS, EXPECTATIONS, GOOD AND EVIL, POSSIBILITIES AND IMPOSSIBILITIES

7382 "I've a very pessimistic view of life. You should know this about me if we're gonna go out, you know. I feel that life is divided into the horrible and the miserable." **Woody Allen** gives Diane Keaton fair warning. She should remember the rule: "Never sleep with someone whose problems are worse than yours." *Annie Hall* (1977, United Artists).

7383 "Oh, there's got to be a phone or a gas station around here somewhere." Ever optimistic **Chevy Chase** sets out to find one when he and his family find themselves stranded in the middle of Monument Valley. *National Lampoon's Vacation* (1983, Warner Bros.).

7384 "Nobody's going to get caught. You have to look optimistic. Grieving, but optimistic." **Demi Moore** counsels friend Glenne Headly in the restroom of a funeral home after the latter's brutish husband Bruce Willis is killed. *Mortal Thoughts* (1991, Columbia).

Order *see* LAWS, LAWYERS, PLANS, ROUTINES, SYSTEMS

Orders

see also COMMANDS, INSTRUCTIONS, REQUESTS

7385 "This is the only thing that gives orders." Al Capone-like mobster **Paul Muni** lovingly pats his machine gun. *Scarface* (1932, United Artists).

7386 "Sing, Mister, or I'll have you thrown into the guard house for flagrant disrespect of my orders." **Ruby Keeler,** the daughter of the regiment commander, puts cadet Dick Powell through her drill. *Flirtation Walk* (1934, Warner Bros.).

7387 "All correspondence school players will kindly leave the stage—also those who play by ear." Temperamental conductor **Charles Boyer** dictates to members of his orchestra. *Break of Hearts* (1935, RKO).

7388 "Get on the belt line and keep 'em coming." It's seething, jealous **Jean Harlow**'s drink order to a waiter. *China Seas* (1935, MGM).

7389 "Mr. Christian, come here!" As one of the screen's most hissable villains, Captain Bligh, **Charles Laughton** demands the immediate presence of Clark Gable as Fletcher Christian. *Mutiny on the Bounty* (1935, MGM).

7390 "If that door is forced, you're not to be alive to tell it." **C. Aubrey Smith** gives David Niven orders to prevent the King's evil brother Raymond Massey from discovering that the monarch is missing from this room. The loyal Niven replies, "Do you think I would be, sir?" **Louis Calhern** gives the same orders to Robert Coote in the remake, who replies as did Niven. *The Prisoner of Zenda* (1937, Selznick-United Artists); (1952, MGM).

7391 "You will please clasp your hands behind your head." **Peter Lorre**, as Joel Cairo, momentarily has the drop on Humphrey Bogart as Sam Spade. *The Maltese Falcon* (1941, Warner Bros.).

7392 "Get out, Veda. Get your things out of this house right now before I throw them into the street and you with them. Get out before I kill you." **Joan Crawford** finally gets wise to her horrible teenage daughter Ann Blyth. The final straw is that the selfish and self-centered little brat goes after her mother's equally worthless second husband Zachary Scott. *Mildred Pierce* (1945, Warner Bros.).

7393 "Don't tell me what to think. I'll take your orders about work but not about what to think." **Montgomery Clift** stands up to dictatorial John Wayne who believes he should do all the thinking for those working for him. *Red River* (1948, United Artists).

7394 "Get killed somewhere else!" Sheriff **Millard Mitchell** orders Skip Homeier out of town after the latter has ambushed gunfighter Gregory Peck. Dying Peck, wishing to give Homeier a slower punishment, claims he was killed in a fair fight. *The Gunfighter* (1950, 20th Century-Fox).

7395 "Gort! Klaatu barada nikto." **Patricia Neal** speaks the words taught her by alien Michael Rennie. They stop Rennie's robot from incinerating Washington, D.C. *The Day the Earth Stood Still* (1951, 20th Century-Fox).

7396 "There's a stagecoach for Abilene in the morning. I want you to be on it." Marshal **Burt Lancaster** orders gambler Kirk Douglas out of town. *The Gunfight at the OK Corral* (1957, Paramount).

7397 "Were you ordered to find out whether he was innocent or guilty before you killed him?" Underground contact **Irene Worth** questions young British agent Paul Massie, whose mission is to assassinate a French resistance fighter suspected of being a traitor. *Orders to Kill* (1958, GB, British Lion).

7398 "Take him out and shoot him." It's the solution of **Orson Welles,** as General Dreedle, for people he thinks are stupid and have disobeyed him. *Catch 22* (1970, Paramount).

7399 "Stranger, when you find us lying here, go tell the Spartans we obeyed their orders." It's the translation of a sign at a French cemetery gate in Vietnam. It is a quote from 5th century B.C. Greek historian Herodotus, writing about the Battle of Thermopylae in 480 B.C. in which 300 Spartans died defending a pass against a far superior force of Persians. The quote is used in the movie as the source of its title. *Go Tell the Spartans* (1978, Avco Embassy).

7400 "Children of the night—shut up!" **George Hamilton**, as Dracula, yells at howling wolves drowning out his piano playing. *Love at First Bite* (1979, AIP).

7401 "The only thing that gives orders in this world is balls." Miami-based Cuban mobster **Al Pacino**, who has worked his way up from a refugee to a drug kingpin, believes it takes guts to be in charge of things. *Scarface* (1983, Universal).

7402 "Mr. Emerson, go out of this house as long as I live here. . . no discussion. . . go please. I don't want to call Mr. Vyse." Innocent Edwardian girl **Helena Bonham-Carter** sends away Julian Sands, whom she really loves, because she's already engaged to Daniel Day-Lewis. *A Room with a View* (1985, GB, Merchant-Goldcrest).

7403 "He thinks love is something you order on a phone like pizza." **Daphne Zuniga** wails after John Cusack escorts sure thing Nicollette Sheridan upstairs to a bedroom. *The Sure Thing* (1985, Embassy).

7404 "You've got an hour to clear out. Don't be here when I get back." **Robin Williams** orders a couple of mice from his motel room. *The Best of Times* (1986, Universal).

7405 "You're on the state payroll. Now wake up!" **Paul Newman** as Louisiana Governor Earl Long, lectures his rebellious member when he fails to achieve an erection while trying to make love to Lolita Davidovich as stripper Blaze Starr. *Blaze* (1989, Touchstone-Buena Vista).

7406 "Get up, Rose, and put that tit back in your dress." **Robert Duvall** resists promiscuous Laura Dern's attempts to seduce him. *Rambling Rose* (1991, Seven Arts-New Line).

7407 "No more humane beheadings. . . cancel the table scraps for lepers and orphans. . . . And call off Christmas." Arch-villain Sheriff of Nottingham, beautifully played by **Alan Rickman**, snarls to his scribe when his problems with Robin Hood exacerbate. *Robin Hood: Prince of Thieves* (1991, Warner Bros.).

Ordinariness

see also NORMALITY

7408 NICOLE: "Here's to our agreement. No love-making, no quarrels." MICHAEL: "Just like an ordinary married couple." NICOLE: "I said no quarrels." French aristocrat's daughter **Claudette Colbert** toasts her agreement with many-times married American millionaire **Gary Cooper** on the no-no's of their marriage. *Bluebeard's Eighth Wife* (1938, Paramount).

7409 "You've got to get a classy name. That 'George Raft' is too ordinary." Showgirl **Iris Adrian** advises nightclub hoofer George Raft, who is playing himself, on how to get ahead in show business. His real name happens to be George Ranft. *Broadway* (1942, Universal).

7410 "Oh, don't turn ordinary on me. I get tired of ordinary dames, and I don't want to ever get tired of you." Mobster **Robert Taylor** insists that society girl Lana Turner not change one iota. *Johnny Eager* (1942, MGM).

7411 "You think you know something, don't you? You think you're the clever little girl who knows something. There's so much you don't know. What do you know, really? You're just an ordinary little girl living in an ordinary little town. You wake up each morning of your life and you know perfectly well that there's nothing in the world to trouble you. You go through your ordinary little day and at night you sleep your untroubled ordinary little sleep filled with peaceful stupid dreams. And I brought you nightmares. . . ." **Joseph Cotten**, the Merry Widower murderer of wealthy women, berates his niece Teresa Wright, who has begun to suspect that her beloved favorite uncle, with whom she has a special affinity, is not as great as she always felt. Ordinary she may be—but she'll be his downfall. *Shadow of a Doubt* (1943, Universal).

7412 PHILIP: "Brandon, you don't think the party is a mistake, do you?" BRANDON: "Being weak is a mistake." PHILIP: "Because it's human?" BRANDON: "Because it's ordinary." Homosexual lovers **Farley Granger** and **John Dall** have cooly executed a long-time friend and stuffed his body in an antique chest that sits in the center of the room in which they plan to hold a cocktail party. *Rope* (1948, Warner Bros.).

7413 "Palaces are for royalty. We're just common folk with a bank account." Soon after completion of the movie in which wealthy young American **Grace Kelly** delivers this line to retired cat burglar Cary Grant, she moved into a palace as the wife of Prince Rainier of Monaco. *To Catch a Thief* (1955, Paramount).

7414 "Back in the forties this town was crawling with dollies like you, screwing up their lives just the same." Aging California private eye **Art Carney** tells actress, talent agent, astrologer and part-time drug dealer Lily Tomlin that she's not as unique or hip as she seems to think she is. *The Late Show* (1977, Warner Bros.).

7415 "Everybody else around here is eccentric or colorful or charismatic. And I'm perfectly ordinary!" **Maureen Teefy** is afraid that she doesn't fit in at Manhattan's High School for the Performing Arts. *Fame* (1980, MGM).

7416 "I have a realistic opinion of myself. I'm an ordinary person—I can't live up to this thing that you have about me. . . . In fact, I'm worse than an ordinary person since I left a perfectly decent man for no good reason. . . . I don't deserve to be happy." **Mary Beth Hurt** denies John Heard's suggestion that she has an unnaturally low opinion of herself. *Chilly Scenes of Winter* aka: *Head Over Heels* (1982, United Artists Classics).

7417 "We're changing—we're alike, turning into ordinary people." **Sylvester Stallone** as Rocky need never worry about becoming ordinary. *Rocky IV* (1985, MGM).

7418 "The future of the world isn't worked out on a grand scale. It's worked out by ordinary people doing ordinary jobs." Australian Army lawyer **Bryan Brown** is charged with prosecuting Japanese soldiers responsible for the massacre of Australian soldiers at a POW camp. *Blood Oath* aka: *Prisoners of the Sun* (1991, Australia, Skouras).

Orgasms

see also EXCITEMENTS, PERVERSIONS, PROMISCUITY, PROSTITUTION AND PROSTITUTES, SEX AND SEXUALITY

7419 "Do you mean to tell me that a girl drinking blood from your neck will give you an orgasm?" Retired Greek army Major **Patrick Macnee**'s incredulous question is put to willing vampire victim Patrick Mower. *Incense for the Damned* (1970, GB, Lucinda-Titan International).

7420 "I wonder if she had a real orgasm in the two years we were married or was she faking that night?" **Woody Allen** is filled with self-doubt about his prowess with his wife Susan Anspach. *Play It Again, Sam* (1972, Paramount).

7421 MARY WILKE: "I finally had an orgasm and my doctor told me it was the wrong kind." ISAAC DAVIS: "I've never had the wrong kind. All of mine have been the right kind." Neurotic **Diane Keaton** and insecure **Woody Allen** compare notes. *Manhattan* (1979, United Artists).

7422 ANN MILLANEY: "I thought about you. Have you thought about me?" GRAHAM DALTON: "Yes." ANN: "What did you think?" GRAHAM: "I thought about what you'd look like having an orgasm." ANN: "I think I'd like to know what I look like having an orgasm. . . . Can you do that? Give a woman an orgasm?" GRAHAM: "Yes." ANN: "Could you do that for me?" GRAHAM: "No." ANN: "Why not?" GRAHAM: "Because I can't." ANN: "Can't or won't." GRAHAM: "I can't because I won't." **Andie MacDowell** and **James Spader** make talking about sex quite erotic. *sex, lies and videotape* (1989, Miramax).

7423 "I won't tell you all my secrets just because I had an orgasm." Murder suspect, novelist **Sharon Stone** tells police detective Michael Douglas that even though they had, as he puts it, "the fuck of the century," she's not inclined to confess to anything. *Basic Instinct* (1992, Tri-Star).

Orgies *see* PARTIES, PERVERSIONS, SEX AND SEXUALITY

Originality

see also ECCENTRICITIES, IMITATION, UNIQUENESS

7424 "Don't go, little girl, you're too original and charming." Ditzy matron **Alice Brady** prevents Deanna Durbin from leaving the society party that Durbin has crashed. *100 Men and a Girl* (1937, Universal).

7425 "Be yourself. The world worships the original." Faded Countess **Ingrid Bergman** tutors country chambermaid Liza Minnelli. *A Matter of Time* (1976, U.S.-Ital., AIP).

Outlaws *see* CRIMES AND CRIMINALS

Ownership

see also BELONGING, POSSESSIONS

7426 "You're mine, do you understand me? Mine to do with as I please." **Errol Flynn,** who has been a slave owned by Olivia de Havilland's family, turns the tables on her. *Captain Blood* (1935, Warner Bros.).

7427 "There are hundreds of Hubbards sitting in rooms like this throughout the country. All their names aren't Hubbard, but they are all Hubbards and they will own this country someday." **Charles Dingle** makes a frightening prediction about the selfish merchant class. *The Little Foxes* (1941, Goldwyn-RKO).

7428 "I own you. . . I bought you, your house, your kid, business. . . I own a paper on your whole life. I'll wipe out your whole family. People will be eatin' 'em for lunch tomorrow in their burgers and not even know it. You're working for me until you are burned out, busted, or dead. Got it?" Crime syndicate chief **Robert Prosky** stakes his ownership claim on professional thief James Caan. *Thief* (1981, United Artists).

7429 "We're not owners here, Karen. We're just passin' through." Mysterious white hunter **Robert Redford** reminds farm owner Meryl Streep that Africa is not theirs to shape. *Out of Africa* (1985, Universal).

Pacifists *see* FORCE, PEACE

Pains

see also COMPLAINTS, HURT AND HURTING, INSANITY AND SANITY, PLEASURES, PUNISHMENTS, SICKNESS, SORROWS, SUFFERING AND SUFFERERS, TROUBLES

7430 "It's foolish to kill people you hate, because then they are beyond pain." Empress **Patricia Laf-**

fan tries both to seduce victorious Roman Commander Robert Taylor and warn him of what awaits him if he disappoints her. *Quo Vadis* (1951, MGM).

7431 "I can stand anything but pain." Hypochondriac **Oscar Levant** is in pain after accidentally being knocked down. *The Band Wagon* (1953, MGM).

7432 "There is a pain beyond pain, an agony so intense, it shocks the mind into instant beauty." Madman **Vincent Price** gleefully informs bound and gagged Phyllis Kirk that he plans to make her immortal by covering her body with boiling wax. *House of Wax* (1953, Warner Bros.).

7433 "You get kicked around enough, you get to be a real professor of pain." Homely Brooklyn butcher **Ernest Borgnine** empathizes with plain school teacher Betsy Blair. *Marty* (1955, United Artists).

7434 "I'm too tired to scream from the pain you just caused me." **Tom Hanks** speaks to a female jogger he's just tripped on purpose. *He Knows You're Alone* (1980, MGM-United Artists).

7435 "If you can't feel pain, then you're not going to feel anything else either." Psychiatrist **Judd Hirsch** soothingly counsels emotionally drained Timothy Hutton, who finally understands his feelings of guilt in the death of his brother. *Ordinary People* (1980, Paramount).

7436 "I am the future. . . . Life is pain, pain is everything." Defiant nihilist **Timothy Van Patten,** a bright psychotic mid-western high school student, terrorizes students and faculty alike. He runs a drug and prostitution ring. *Class of 1984* (1981, Canada, United Film Distribution).

7437 ETHEL THAYER: "How are you feeling, Norman?" NORMAN THAYER: "Oh, pretty good. How are you?" ETHEL: "How's the pain, dammit?" NORMAN: "Pretty good, as pain goes." **Katharine Hepburn** desperately tries to get the telephone operator when her husband **Henry Fonda** keels over and falls to the floor with an apparent heart attack. *On Golden Pond* (1981, Universal).

7438 "The whole thing with girls is painful, and it seems like it keeps getting more painful." **Timothy Daly** is not comfortable dealing with females. *Diner* (1982, MGM).

7439 PRINCESS JEHNNA: "I suppose nothing hurts you." CONAN: "Only pain." **Olivia D'Abo**'s question is given some serious thought before being answered by **Arnold Schwarzenegger**. *Conan the Destroyer* (1984, Universal).

7440 "I hurt therefore I am. . . . Pain is the principal condition of all existence." **Athol Fugard**, as the South African poet, naturalist and morphine addict Eugene Marais, gives a twist to the Rene Descartes quote as he tries to understand his drug addiction. *The Guest* (1984, GB, RM Productions).

7441 "You can take it—you're a stunt man, right?" **Kim Basinger** asks sweetly, as she violently knees Sam Shepard in the groin. *Fool for Love* (1985, Cannon).

7442 "I see you are no stranger to pain." Russian officer **Steven Berkoff** tortures captive Sylvester Stallone in the steamy jungles of Southeast Asia. *Rambo: First Blood II* (1985, Tri-Star).

7443 "When you have to explore every night, even the most beautiful things you find can be the most painful." Jazz saxophonist **Dexter Gordon** narrates. *'Round Midnight* (1986, Warner Bros.).

7444 "Endo here has forgotten more about dispensing pain than you and I will ever know. . . . Now if you would kindly tell me everything you know, I promise I'll kill you quickly. . . ." Villain **Gary Busey** makes a no-win offer to trussed-up for torture Mel Gibson. *Lethal Weapon* (1987, Warner Bros.).

7445 "Ease his pain." Kevin Costner interprets the second message of the Voice in his Iowa corn field to be referring to sixties writer James Earl Jones. *Field of Dreams* (1989, Universal).

7446 "Let's go, it's all right. You can let go now. . . Let go of the pain." **Bruce Davison** holds the hand of Campbell Scott, dying of AIDS. Davison encourages the suffering patient to quit fighting the disease and die. *Longtime Companion* (1990, American Playhouse-Goldwyn).

Painting and Painters *see* ART AND ARTISTS, COLORS

Panic *see* FEARS, SUSPICIONS AND SUSPECTS, TRUST

Paradise *see* HEAVEN, HEAVEN AND HELL

Parasites

see also GROWTH AND DEVELOPMENT

7447 "My grandfather used to drive a team of mules. I'm afraid he'd think you a parasite." Luscious society girl **Marguerite Churchill** puts down racketeer Spencer Tracy. *Quick Millions* (1931, Fox).

7448 "I don't mind a parasite. I object to a cut-rate one." **Humphrey Bogart** is contemptuous of Peter Lorre. *Casablanca* (1942, Warner Bros.).

Parents

see also Babies, Boys, Children and Childhood, Daughter, Families, Fathers, Girls, Mothers, Relatives, Sons and Sons-in-Law

7449 "I don't care who the father is. I'm the grandfather." Department store owner **Charles Coburn** all but confirms that his son David Niven is the father of an abandoned baby who everyone believes has Ginger Rogers for a mother. *Bachelor Mother* (1939, RKO).

7450 Ygor: "You have same father." Wolf Von Frankenstein: "You mean to imply that he is my brother." Ygor: "Yes, but his mother is lightning." **Bela Lugosi** informs **Basil Rathbone** that his father's monster still lives but is in need of repairs. *Son of Frankenstein* (1939, Universal).

7451 "When my folks moved here from Europe they settled in Iowa." Liberated **Hedy Lamarr**'s line is included in the movie to explain her Viennese accent. *H.M. Pulham, Esq.* (1941, MGM).

7452 "If my father was the head of our house, my mother was its heart." Narrator **Irving Pichel**, as the grown-up Huw, recalls the division of responsibility in his happy home. *How Green Was My Valley* (1941, 20th Century-Fox).

7453 "I left home at the age of four and I haven't been back since. They can hear me on the radio and that's enough for them." With a slight bit of exaggeration, acerbic columnist and radio commentator **Monty Woolley** speaks of his parents. *The Man Who Came to Dinner* (1941, Warner Bros.).

7454 "Your father was Frankenstein, but your mother was the lightning." **Bela Lugosi,** as the hunchback Ygor, informs Lon Chaney, Jr., as the monster, of his parentage. Seems we've heard Lugosi's line before. *The Ghost of Frankenstein* (1942, Universal).

7455 "You think just because you made a little money you can get yourself a new hairdo and some expensive clothes and turn yourself into a lady, but you can't because you'll never be anything but a common frump, whose father lived over a grocery store and whose mother took in washing." Now let's see if we understand **Ann Blyth**'s logic. Her mother Joan Crawford is of little value because of her parents. Ann holds a low opinion of her mother, and it's a given that her father Bruce Bennett is a loser. Therefore, what right does Blyth have to be putting on airs? *Mildred Pierce* (1945, Warner Bros.).

7456 "If I seem a bit sinister as a parent, Mr. Marlowe, it's because my hold on life is too slight to include any Victorian hypocrisy. I need hardly add that any man who has lived as I have and indulges for the first time at parenthood at the age of 55 deserves all he gets." **Charles Waldron,** as aging and ailing General Sternwood, speaks to Humphrey Bogart, as private detective Philip Marlowe. Waldron hires Bogart to protect his two wild daughters, Lauren Bacall and Martha Vickers. *The Big Sleep* (1946, Warner Bros.).

7457 "There'll be $1,000 on that table for you by six in the morning. Get on the early train. Send a Christmas card each year to an aging parent who now wishes you to stop talking." The time is after the American Civil War. Tyrannically, cruel **Fredric March** has nothing but contempt for his whining, spineless, cowardly son Dan Duryea, who is being sent away. *Another Part of the Forest* (1948, Universal).

7458 Jack Worthing: "I have lost both my parents." Lady Bracknell: "To lose one parent may be regarded as a misfortune, to lose both looks like carelessness." **Michael Redgrave**'s claim of being an orphan cuts little ice with **Edith Evans**. *The Importance of Being Earnest* (1952, GB, Two Cities-Rank).

7459 "I had the chance to choose my own parents." Through love and sincerity, emotionally scarred crippled **Clifford Tatum, Jr.** finds happiness with his foster parents Cary Grant and Betsy Drake. *Room for One More* aka: *The Easy Way* (1952, Warner Bros.).

7460 "Be a parent, not a policeman." Housekeeper **Sophia Loren** encourages widower Cary Grant to be more loving to his three kids. *Houseboat* (1958, Paramount).

7461 "My home is hell. We've got a 23-year-old boy. I threw him out of the house last year. Shaggy haired Maoist! I don't know where he is—presumably building bombs in basements as an expression of his universal brotherhood. We've got a 17-year-old daughter who's had two abortions in two years. Got arrested last week at a rock festival for pushing drugs. They let her go. A typical affluent American family. I don't mean to be facile about this. I blame myself for those two useless young people. I never exercised parental authority. I'm no good at that." Physician **George C. Scott** confesses to stranger Diana Rigg that he hasn't been a good parent in this black satire about a doctor torn between his duty to the hospital and his involvement with the daughter of a crazy patient. *The Hospital* (1971, United Artists).

7462 "I fart in your direction. Your mother was a hamster and your father smelled of elderberries." **John Cleese,** an extraordinarily rude guard at a French castle, gives Graham Chapman as King Arthur the crudest of insults. *Monty Python and the Holy Grail* (1974, GB, Cinema 5).

7463 "My mother and father together are like a bad car wreck." Bank robber **Al Pacino** observed his parents' stormy marriage from a close vantage point. *Dog Day Afternoon* (1975, Warner Bros.).

7464 "Why is a woman a better parent by virtue of her sex?" Engaged in a bitter custody battle for his son, **Dustin Hoffman** doesn't understand why it should be assumed that a child is always better off with his mother. *Kramer vs. Kramer* (1979, Columbia).

7465 NORMAN THAYER: "Do you visit your folks, young man?" BILL RAY: "No. My parents have both passed away." NORMAN: "I see. Then you have a good excuse, don't you?" Eighty-year-old **Henry Fonda** checks on **Dabney Coleman**'s attention to his parents. *On Golden Pond* (1981, Universal).

7466 "My parents got divorced. My father's living in California with a young girl. My mother's in analysis again. And I'm fine...." Apparently **Nancy Kagler** is under the mistaken notion that Marsha Mason really wants an answer when she asks how Kagler has been. *Only When I Laugh* (1981, Columbia).

7467 "Mother goes to a seance every Friday night since my father died just so she can still yell at him." **Henry Winkler** is the second male in his family to be under the domineering thumb of his mother. *Night Shift* (1982, Warner Bros.).

7468 "Part of being a parent is trying to learn to kill your kids." **Christopher Walken** gloomily bases his claim on his parents Sean Sullivan and Jackie Burroughs. *The Dead Zone* (1983, Paramount).

7469 "Such a bother over a few drops of semen!" **Jill Clayburgh** dismisses Gabriel Byrne's concern for the paternity of "their" child. *Hanna K* (1983, France, Gaumont-Universal).

7470 "My mother couldn't even spell, but they fried her, too." **Johnny Depp** sadly recalls that his parents were sent to the electric chair because his father was the notorious Alphabet Bomber. *Cry-Baby* (1990, Universal).

Paris *see* CITIES AND TOWNS

Participation

see also WAITS AND WAITING, WATCHING AND WATCHERS

7471 "You could stand by and watch forever. There comes a time when you have to do something." At the close of this fantasy film, disgusted ex-journalist **Michael Redgrave** relates what he's learned while living in a lighthouse on Lake Michigan that is haunted by ghosts. *Thunder Rock* (1942, GB, Charter Films-MGM-EFI).

7472 "There are two kinds of people: those who don't do what they want to do so they write down in a diary about what they haven't done; and those who haven't time to write about it because they're out doing it." **Charles Coburn** gives a pep-talk to non-participant Jean Arthur. He wants her to break out of her shell. *The More the Merrier* (1943, Columbia).

7473 "Do you know what you are? You're a watcher. There are watchers in the world and there are do-ers. And the watchers sit around watching the do-ers. Well, tonight you watched and I did." Uninhibited **Jane Fonda** blasts her young husband Robert Redford for not participating in the unusual activities of the evening. *Barefoot in the Park* (1967, Paramount).

7474 "You're one of life's great watchers. I'm not like that. I'm a doer." **Susan Anspach** tells her husband Woody Allen that they are incompatible and she wants a divorce. *Play It Again Sam* (1972, Paramount).

7475 "They lead me to water, but they won't let me drink." Jewish **Ben Cross** runs competitively to get back at the Christian world that denies him access to upper levels of power. *Chariots of Fire* (1981, GB, 20th Century-Fox).

Parties

see also ENTERTAINMENTS AND ENTERTAINERS, TOGETHERNESS

7476 "You call this a party? The beer is warm, the women are cold, and I'm hot under the collar. In fact, a more poisonous little barbecue I've never attended." Ungracious and uninvited guest **Groucho Marx** complains at a society party. *Monkey Business* (1931, Paramount).

7477 "Let's blow trumpets and squeakers and enjoy the party as much as we can, like very small, quite idiotic school children.... Let's be superficial."

Robert Montgomery encourages Norma Shearer to shed her cares. *Private Lives* (1931, MGM).

7478 ADOLPH: "Marcel, why did you tell me it was a costume party?" MARCEL: "Oh, sir, I did so want to see you in tights." Dressed as Romeo, **Charles Ruggles** discovers the party he's to attend is not a costume party as he was informed by his butler **Charles Coleman**. *One Hour with You* (1932, Paramount).

7479 "Scusi! Scusi! I'm also very good at parties." Professional correspondent **Erik Rhodes** has the last line in the first of the Fred Astaire-Ginger Rogers' co-starring vehicles. *The Gay Divorcée* (1934, RKO).

7480 "Gentlemen, keep the war going, please. We're off to roll in a few gutters." World War I British fliers **Errol Flynn** and David Niven steal a motor bike to paint the town red before returning to death in the skies. *The Dawn Patrol* (1938, Warner Bros.).

7481 "My best friend! My own wife! I feel like an unwanted corpse at a party." Mistakenly reported drowned, **Fred MacMurray** comes back to find that his wife Jean Arthur has married his best friend Melvyn Douglas. *Too Many Husbands* (1940, Columbia).

7482 "Darling, I was afraid you might be angry or resent my coming here, but—but I had to take that chance. Why, right in the middle of everything, suddenly I knew one thing so clearly; the party's where you are." Her first starring movie a grand success, actress **Lana Turner** leaves her premiere party to be with her lover, producer Kirk Douglas. He's not pleased to see her—he's having a small intimate party with Elaine Stewart. *The Bad and the Beautiful* (1952, MGM).

7483 "You know, I've been to so many wonderful parties here, Mame. Now, I'm going to find out how they all ended." Actress **Coral Browne** usually gets roaring drunk at Rosalind Russell's parties and passes out. She hasn't taken the pledge. She's going to read Russell's autobiography. *Auntie Mame* (1958, Warner Bros.).

7484 "I want a sit down orgy for forty." **Leon Greene** places an order at Phil Silvers' elaborate Roman brothel. *A Funny Thing Happened on the Way to the Forum* (1966, United Artists).

7485 "The party didn't slow down till dawn. The crew of San Pedro tuna boat showed up at one and was routed. The police came by at two and stayed to join the party. Mack used their squad car to go get more wine. A woman called the police to complain about the noise and couldn't get anybody. The crew of the tuna boat came back about three and was welcomed with open arms. The police reported their own car stolen and found it later on the beach. Things were finally back to normal in Cannery Row. Once again the world was spinning in greased grooves." Narrator **John Huston** sums up at the end of this John Steinbeck story of ex-baseball player Nick Nolte and young hooker Debra Winger and the down-and-outers they live among. *Cannery Row* (1982, United Artists-MGM).

7486 "It's some tradition. They throw a great party for you on the one day they know you can't enjoy it." **Jeff Goldblum** confides to William Hurt about the funeral of their old friend who has committed suicide. *The Big Chill* (1983, Columbia).

Partners

see also BUSINESS AND COMMERCE, FRIENDSHIPS AND FRIENDS, MARRIAGES, MEN AND WOMEN

7487 "Bailey, Bailey. That's it, Barnum and Bailey. That's right. Take a partner. You know, a hundred years from now people are likely to be talking about us. Barnum and Bailey, the greatest show on earth." Title character **Wallace Beery** takes Adolphe Menjou, as Bailey Walsh, as a partner in his circus. *The Mighty Barnum* (1934, 20th Century-Fox-United Artists).

7488 "The cat has a new kitten. When do we start?" **Grace Kelly** is an unwanted enlistee in the efforts of retired cat burglar Cary Grant to discover who has been impersonating him on the French Riviera. *To Catch a Thief* (1955, Paramount).

7489 "I'm going to take a nap. When I wake up, if the money is on the table, I'll know I have a partner. If it isn't, I'll know I don't." Meyer Lansky-like mobster **Lee Strasberg** concludes negotiations with Al Pacino. *The Godfather, Part II* (1974, Paramount).

7490 "I sleep with my wife but I live with my partners." Cop **Treat Williams** refuses to turn informant against his fellow officers who have gone bad. *Prince of the City* (1981, Warner Bros.).

7491 "I've had plenty of sex; I'd just like to try it with a partner." Very horny 15-year-old **Billy Jacoby** is in lust for a girl—any girl. *Just One of the Guys* (1985, Columbia).

7492 "Well, my daughter's got a husband, I got a partner. You know, he really ain't half bad, except when he's got that rotten milk on his breath." Alcoholic cop **James Caan** refers to his partner Mandy Patinkin, one of the 100,000 aliens whose space ship landed in the Mojave desert in the 1980s. *Alien Nation* (1988, 20th Century-Fox).

7493 "He's not just a dog. He's my partner." Police detective **James Belushi** insists that a hospital physician treat his wounded dog Jerry Lee. *K-9* (1989, Universal).

7494 "If somebody shoots your partner, you don't wait for the lawyers to sort things out." Narcotics cop **Jason Patric** explains to his new partner Jennifer Jason Leigh his sense of obligation—and hers. *Rush* (1991, MGM-Pathé).

Passion

see also ANGER, DESIRES, EMOTIONS, HATE AND HATRED, JEALOUSY, LOVE AND LOVERS, LUST, SEX AND SEXUALITY

7495 "The blood is quickened by the kill. One passion builds upon another. Kill, then love! When you have known this, you have known ecstasy!" Mad Russian Count **Leslie Banks** gives his shipwrecked guests on his island home a warning of what is to come. He will track them with bow and arrow, henchmen and vicious dogs as if they were wild animals. *The Most Dangerous Game* (1932, RKO).

7496 "How could I help loving you? You who have all the passion for life that I lack!" Wimpish **Leslie Howard** vicariously envies Vivien Leigh's zest for life. *Gone with the Wind* (1939, Selznick-MGM).

7497 "I'm sorry, Louise. You watch temperatures go down and then go up again. In love there are no relapses. Once you're out of it, the fever never comes back." Engineer **Van Heflin** doesn't want to fan the flames of passion that have burned out between him and jealous, possessive nurse Joan Crawford. *Possessed* (1947, Warner Bros.).

7498 "I was married for nine years. The first eight were very passionate. Passion is probably too mild a word. It was more like war. . . . Almost once a month, regularly, she would toss all my paintings out on the street and I would come running out and pick them up. . . . Then we'd make up. . . passionately." Artist **Alan Bates** entertains his new lover Jill Clayburgh with recollections of his first marriage. *An Unmarried Woman* (1978, 20th Century-Fox).

7499 "What passion today with Lee. She's a volcano." **Michael Caine** recalls his love-making with his lover Barbara Hershey. She's the sister of his wife Mia Farrow. *Hannah and Her Sisters* (1986, Orion).

7500 "One by one they were becoming shades. Better pass boldly into that other world, in the full glory of some passion, than fade and wither dismally with age." **Donal McCann,** noting how paltry his life seems, speaks of the assemblage at a lively holiday dinner party. He envies the youth who loved his wife Anjelica Huston and died for her at a young age. *The Dead* (1987, Vestron).

7501 "I wish I had your passion, Ray. Misguided as it is, it's still a passion." World-weary voice of the 60s, **James Earl Jones** envies Kevin Costner who hasn't lost his enthusiasm for life. *Field of Dreams* (1989, Universal).

Past

see also FUTURE, HISTORY, MEMORY AND MEMORIZATION, NOSTALGIA, REMINDERS, TIME

7502 "Don't look back, don't look back. It'll drag at your heart until there's nothing you can do but look back." **Vivien Leigh** tries to bring Leslie Howard back to the present. He's lost in nostalgia for gentility, speaking of "its golden warm security." *Gone with the Wind* (1939, Selznick-MGM).

7503 "I have seen the old traditions dying. Grace, dignity, feeling for the past. . . . Modern methods—poppycock!" Elderly pedagogue **Robert Donat** resents his impending retirement and changes in education. *Goodbye, Mr. Chips* (1939, U.S.-GB, MGM).

7504 "Everybody was sweet and pretty, the whole world—not like today." Mad murderer **Joseph Cotten** shares a romantic notion of the past with his worried niece Teresa Wright. *Shadow of a Doubt* (1943, Universal).

7505 "I'll try to keep all the good things as they were. I'll keep the past alive. Like a warm room for you to come back to." Hugging the empty bathrobe of her husband who is away at war, **Claudette Colbert** pledges to be true and brave until he returns. *Since You Went Away* (1944, Selznick-United Artists).

7506 "The waxworks, dim figures from the silent days." It's **William Holden**'s rather cruel description of a bridge foursome consisting of Gloria Swanson, Buster Keaton, Anna Q. Nilsson and H.B. Warner. *Sunset Boulevard* (1950, Paramount).

7507 "I am the past. I like it. It's sweet and familiar, and the present is cold and foreign, and the future—fortunately, I don't need to concern myself with that. But you do. It's yours." **Helen Hayes,** portraying the Dowager Empress of Russia, comments to Ingrid Bergman. The latter claims to be

Hayes' granddaughter, daughter of the last Tsar, presumed to have been executed ten years earlier, in 1918. *Anastasia* (1956, 20th Century-Fox).

7508 "I believe I am past my prime. I had reckoned my prime lasting till I was at least 50." **Maggie Smith** admits to her student and romantic rival Pamela Franklin that she's seen better days. *The Prime of Miss Jean Brodie* (1969, 20th Century-Fox).

7509 "The past is foreign country. They do things differently there." Narrator **Michael Redgrave** sets the stage for a flashback to the time when as a 12-year-old (Dominic Guard), he carried love letters back and forth from farmer Alan Bates and his friend's sister Julie Christie. *The Go-Between* (1970, GB, EMI Productions).

7510 "You know, Richie, the best thing about the past is you figure out what it was that could have made you happy." **Richard Castellano** tells his son Joseph Hindy that there's something to be said for hindsight. *Lovers and Other Strangers* (1970, Cinerama).

7511 "Talk about the pot calling the kettle black. The day I got an earful of your checkered past, I felt like a celibate." Satyr **Jack Nicholson** feels morally superior to his live-in lover Ann-Margret, who has had round heels most of her life. *Carnal Knowledge* (1971, Avco Embassy).

7512 "To do that, I'd have to send the girl back to the sixteenth century." Doubting Jesuit **Jason Miller** is reluctant to encourage the performance of the ritual of exorcism on Linda Blair, who appears possessed by a devil. *The Exorcist* (1973, Warner Bros.).

7513 "We're like two junkies getting a fix from the past—you with your war and me with my farm." Neurotic New York housewife **Joanne Woodward** spends a great deal of time thinking of her early life on a farm. She speaks to her husband, who is obsessed with a French battlefield where he spent the scariest moments of his life. *Summer Wishes, Winter Dreams* (1973, Columbia).

7514 "Talking about the past bothers everyone who works in Chinatown because you can't always tell what's going on. . . ." Private investigator **Jack Nicholson** recalls that when he was a cop, things were done differently in Chinatown than in any other part of L.A. *Chinatown* (1974, Paramount).

7515 "A long time ago, in a galaxy far, far away. . . ." The movie's opening crawl. *Star Wars* (1977, 20th Century-Fox).

7516 "I'm the only one here who doesn't have a past." In 1962, the summer before she starts college, blossoming **Elizabeth Edmonds** is a lonely student working as a waitress in a Welch seaside hotel. *Experience Preferred . . . But Not Essential* (1983, GB, Enigma-Goldwyn).

7517 "Oh, my God!. . . You're from the 60s. . . out! Back to the 60s. Back! There's no place for you here in the future. Get back while you still can." J.D. Salinger-like writer **James Earl Jones** chases Kevin Costner from his apartment. *Field of Dreams* (1989, Universal).

7518 "Politics is out, sex is out. All the great themes have been done: they've been turned into theme parks." Pirate radio station host **Christian Slater** jeers after playing The Youngbloods' 60s hit, "Get Together," Slater bills himself as "Happy Harry Hard-On." *Pump Up the Volume* (1990, New Line).

7519 "You can't fight the past any more than you can change it." Private eye **Jack Nicholson** reflects sadly. *The Two Jakes* (1990, Paramount).

7520 "You close your eyes. You cast your mind back 30 years and you see and hear what you want to hear." **Gladys Sheehan**, as Grandma Ryan, expresses one of the themes of the movie. *Hear My Song* (1991, GB-Ireland, Film Four).

Patience and Impatience

see also RESIGNATIONS, UNDERSTANDINGS AND MISUNDERSTANDINGS, WAITS AND WAITING

7521 "Stand still, Godfrey, it'll be all over in a minute." **Carole Lombard** tries to calm her somewhat confused bridegroom William Powell. *My Man Godfrey* (1936, Universal).

7522 "There's more than one Kingsby on the Christmas tree and I'll shake one loose yet." When private eye Robert Montgomery's investigation queries hard-boiled **Audrey Totter**'s plans to marry millionaire Leon Ames, she announces that she hasn't given up on her goal to snag a wealthy husband. *Lady in the Lake* (1947, MGM).

7523 "Being with you is wonderful, Baby. You make me feel important—no—you make me feel patient." Does that mean that drifter **William Holden** might even consider settling down and developing some ambition for Kim Kovak? Not a chance. *Picnic* (1955, Columbia).

7524 "Remember, impatient boys sometimes miss dessert." **Shirley MacLaine** fends off the crude advances of womanizing ex-astronaut Jack Nicholson. *Terms of Endearment* (1983, Paramount).

Patients

see also DISEASES, DOCTORS AND DENTISTS, PAINS, SICKNESS, SUFFERING AND SUFFERERS

7525 "You would be the first patient who fell in love with a corpse." **Clifton Webb** recommends that police detective Dana Andrews see a psychiatrist about his growing affection for deceased Gene Tierney. Actually Webb misspeaks; Andrews is not a necrophile, it's the lovely Tierney's portrait, not her body, whose face has been obliterated by a shotgun blast, that attracts his interest. *Laura* (1944, 20th Century-Fox).

7526 STEVEN W. HOLTE: "Everybody's tilted around here. That's why you didn't know who I was. You can't tell the patients from the doctors." KAREN MCIVER: "Yes, I can, the patients get well." New patient **John Kerr,** suffering from suicidal tendencies, is mistaken for a doctor by **Gloria Grahame**, the neglected wife of the head of the psychiatric clinic, Richard Widmark. *The Cobweb* (1955, MGM).

7527 "Yesterday at school they asked Rosie what she wanted to be when she grew up. Like to know what she answered? 'A patient.'" **Gloria Grahame** accuses her shrink husband Richard Widmark of not paying enough attention to his kids. *The Cobweb* (1955, MGM).

7528 "If you're treated like a patient, you're apt to act like one." **Jessica Lange,** as high-strung actress Frances Farmer, defends her bizarre behavior. *Frances* (1982, EMI-Universal).

7529 "Nymphomaniacs in bus three with me." Escaped mental patient **Dan Aykroyd**, posing as a radio psychiatrist, separates patients according to their sexual dysfunctions. He's taking them all to a baseball game as part of their therapy. *The Couch Trip* (1988, Orion).

Patriotism

see also AMERICA AND AMERICANS, ENGLAND AND THE ENGLISH, LOVE AND HATE

7530 "I have been a bad friend and lover—but I have been a patriot." It's **Lewis Stone**'s title card, as he lays dying, shot by a fellow conspirator in the plot to assassinate Stone's friend and monarch, Emil Jannings, the stark raving mad Czar of Russia. *The Patriot* (1928, silent, Paramount).

7531 "Through discipline and hunger, hunger and discipline, we shall rise again." **Emilia Unda**, the principal of a girls' boarding school in pre-Hitler Germany, teaches that life is not meant to be easy and that her girls will become soldiers' wives and mothers. *Maedchen in Uniform* (1932, Ger., Deutsche Film).

7532 "A young patriot turned loose in our nation's capitol—I can handle him." Corrupt senior Senator **Claude Rains** warms to the idea of idealistic and naïve young James Stewart's being appointed to the unfinished term of a deceased U.S. senator. *Mr. Smith Goes to Washington* (1939, Columbia).

7533 CAPTAIN RENAULT: "You're not only a sentimentalist, but you've become a patriot." RICK BLAINE: "Maybe, but it seemed like a good time to start." **Claude Rains** accuses **Humphrey Bogart** of patriotism when he helps Resistance leader Paul Henreid to escape the Nazis and fly away with his wife Ingrid Bergman on a plane to Lisbon. *Casablanca* (1942, Warner Bros.).

7534 "We're hoodlums, but we're American hoodlums." Even escaped con **Frank Jenks** feels the pull of patriotism with the coming of World War II. *Seven Miles from Alcatraz* (1942, RKO).

7535 "First you walk out on my soliloquy, then you walk into my slippers, now you question my patriotism. I love my country and I love my slippers." Polish actor **Jack Benny** takes umbrage with young Polish officer Robert Stack's inattention to Benny's performance, his attention to Benny's wife Carole Lombard and his questioning of Benny's concern for his country. *To Be or Not to Be* (1942, Korda-Lubitsch-United Artists).

7536 "You're not going to let a woman have the last word, are you? Where is your sense of honor, your male patriotism?" **Maurice Chevalier** urges his nephew Louis Jourdan to take some action when he discovers that his mistress Eva Gabor is having an affair with skating instructor Jacques Bergerac. *Gigi* (1958, MGM).

7537 "The Marxists are denying third-world people the right to eat Mr. Chicken. When that right is compromised, it undermines everything this country stands for. . . . We are protecting the entire concept of internationally franchised chicken." Ruthless businessman **Eddie Albert**, the president of Inc., Inc., has been accused of choreographing third-world coups to stabilize business interests. *Head Office* (1985, Tri-Star).

7538 "I want what every guy who came out here to spill his guts wants—for our country to love us as much as we love it." Vietnam veteran, killing machine **Sylvester Stallone** feels, probably rightfully, that soldiers who fought in Nam were not given the respect and appreciation they deserved. *Rambo: First Blood II* (1985, Tri-Star).

7539 "Now it's patriotic to be poor." World War II British working class housewife **Sarah Miles** sighs as she chooses some second-hand clothes from a rack. *Hope and Glory* (1987, GB, Columbia).

Payments

see also COSTS, GIFTS AND GIVING, MONEY, PRICES

7540 "You're going to pay for everything I lose in life." Bitter shop girl **Joan Crawford** shouts to the world in general as she exits the courtroom where she's been sentenced to three years in prison for a crime she didn't commit. *Paid* (1930, MGM).

7541 "It pays to be good—but it doesn't pay much." Saloon entertainer **Mae West** is in love with two men. *Belle of the Nineties* (1934, Paramount).

7542 "It's not because I love England but because it will pay me better that way." Beautiful, mysterious spy **Lucie Mannheim** admits to Robert Donat that she works for the highest bidder. *The 39 Steps* (1935, GB, Gaumont).

7543 "Oh, don't think it's going to be easy. Nothing you really want is ever given away free. You have to pay for it—and usually with your heart." Studio executive **Adolphe Menjou** warns his new actress Janet Gaynor of the heartache that goes with stardom. *A Star Is Born* (1937, Selznick-United Artists).

7544 "I made him pay for what he wants. You made him pay for what he doesn't." **Paulette Goddard** tells Rosalind Russell why her husband left her for Goddard. *The Women* (1939, MGM).

7545 "Young man, a red is any fellow that wants thirty cents an hour when I'm paying twenty-five." Orchard owner **John Arledge** answers when asked by a migrant worker, "What's a red?" *The Grapes of Wrath* (1940, 20th Century-Fox).

7546 "Is this for my beauty and talent—or is it payment in advance?" Dancer **Vanessa Redgrave** is suspicious of Jason Robards' motives when he gives her diamonds. *Isadora* (1968, GB, Universal).

7547 "You got a long way to go before anybody gonna pay $2 for an hour of your time." Madam **Isabel Sanford** doesn't think Diana Ross has much future as a whore. *Lady Sings the Blues* (1972, Paramount).

7548 "You pay your way through life as though every relationship was a tollbooth. Every time you go someplace, you bring something." **Sylvia Sidney** criticizes her daughter Joanne Woodward's generosity, noting that Woodward feels she must pay to be welcomed. *Summer Wishes, Winter Dreams* (1973, Columbia).

7549 "Some of us never pay the piper because some of us are the piper." Shady cop **Dabney Coleman** collects kickbacks from everyone. *Black Fist* (1977, Worldwide).

7550 "You don't have to thank me—you have to pay me." Immigration attorney **Alejandro Rey** expects to be reimbursed for helping Russian defector Robin Williams get official status in the U.S. *Moscow on the Hudson* (1984, Columbia).

7551 "If we're gonna waste the dude, we ought to get paid for it, man." Druggies **Keanu Reeves** and William Hurt have been hired by Tracey Ullman to kill her cheating husband Kevin Kline. *I Love You to Death* (1990, Tri-Star).

7552 "Am I behind in my Sony payments again?" Ditzy but spunky **Judith Hoag** quips when she finds herself surrounded by Japanese martial arts hoods in a dark alley. *Teenage Mutant Ninja Turtles* (1990, New Line).

Peace

see also DEATH, DEFEATS, FIGHTS AND FIGHTING, VICTORIES, WARS, WINNERS AND LOSERS

7553 "Spoil, glory, flags, trumpets—what is behind these words? Cripples, dead men! I want for my people security and happiness. I want to cultivate the arts of happiness. I want a peace, and peace I will have." Title character **Greta Garbo** wants an end to war and conquest. *Queen Christina* (1933, MGM).

7554 DR. EVAN BEAUMONT: "What is death?" JOHN ELLMAN: "Peace." **Edmund Gwenn**, having reanimated unjustly executed **Boris Karloff**, seeks any supernatural knowledge the latter has when he dies for the second time. *The Walking Dead* (1936, Warner Bros.).

7555 "Very well then, think of Kaye. Are you going to let her down? You've got to give the performance she wanted you to give. Then, perhaps, wherever she is, it might bring her peace." **Constance Collier** insists that Katharine Hepburn must go on the stage and give a performance for herself and for Andrea Leeds who committed suicide when she lost the role to Hepburn. *Stage Door* (1937, RKO).

7556 "You can't make peace with a dictator." **Laurence Olivier**, as Lord Nelson, warns the admiralty of making peace with the French. It's an obvious reference to contemporary politics and England's dealings with Nazi Germany. *That Hamilton Woman* aka: *Lady Hamilton* (1941, London Films).

7557 "The way you walked was thorny, through no fault of your own. But as the rain enters the soil, the river enters the sea, so tears run to a predestined end. Your suffering is over. Now you will find peace, for eternity." After Claude Rains has beaten a werewolf to death with his silver-tipped cane, the beast is transformed into Rains' son Lon Chaney, Jr. Gypsy **Maria Ouspenskaya** recites a final prayer over his body, declaring his suffering has come to an end. *The Wolf Man* (1941, Universal).

7558 "Laddie, I've never gone any place peacefully in my life." **Victor McLaglen** tells a squad of cavalry men who have come to arrest him for being intoxicated that they will have a fight on their hands. *She Wore a Yellow Ribbon* (1949, RKO).

7559 EMILIANO ZAPATA: "I've been fighting so long I don't understand peace." FRANCISCO MADERO: "Peace is the hard problem. Any man can be honest in war, but peace—! I often wonder how a man can stay honest under the pressure of peace." In a brief respite from civil war, Mexican revolutionary General **Marlon Brando** rests under a tree with **Harold Gordon**, the man Brando has fought to make president. *Viva Zapata!* (1952, 20th Century-Fox.).

7560 "I learned in Tobiki the wisdom of gracious acceptance. You see, I don't want to be a world leader. I've made peace with myself somewhere between my ambitions and my limitations. . . . It's a step backward in the right direction." Incompetent Army Officer **Glenn Ford** learns a valuable lesson from the Okinawans—one everyone should learn—when to be content with what he or she is. *The Teahouse of the August Moon* (1956, MGM).

7561 "I've got everything I want but peace of mind. And if you ain't got peace of mind, you ain't got nothing." Cockney Lothario **Michael Caine** ruminates aloud to the audience. *Alfie* (1966, GB, Paramount).

7562 "I want peace—and I don't care who I have to kill to get it." Judge Roy Bean, portrayed by **Paul Newman**, sees nothing incongruous in his statement. *The Life and Times of Judge Roy Bean* (1972, National General).

7563 "You're a pacifist!" **Kevin Costner** yells a reminder to writer James Earl Jones who threatens to beat the former with a crowbar. *Field of Dreams* (1989, Universal).

7564 "Call a meeting. . . we will make the peace." **Al Pacino** asks his father's old advisor Eli Wallach to call together the dons and family heads so he can make peace with hot-headed Joe Mantegna. *The Godfather, Part III* (1990, Paramount).

7565 "Increase the peace." These words that appear at the end of the closing credits are the simple message and urgent plea of talented young writer and director **John Singleton,** who brilliantly portrays a catastrophe in the making. *Boyz N the Hood* (1991, Columbia).

7566 "Peace is worth a great many personal risks." The message of **Leonard Nimoy**, as Mr. Spock, is lost on many people who would turn away from situations threatening peace in the world. *Star Trek VI: The Undiscovered Country* (1991, Paramount).

Peculiarities

see also ECCENTRICITIES, STRANGENESS AND STRANGERS

7567 "Don't you think it's rather peculiar that she's wearing high heel shoes?" **Michael Redgrave** suspiciously questions Paul Lukas about a supposedly deaf-and-dumb nun (Catherine Lacey) attending Lucas' patient aboard a train traveling across Europe. *The Lady Vanishes* (1938, GB, Gainsborough-Gaumont British).

7568 "We all have our little foibles and mine is the prompt settlement of accounts." Poor cousin **Maggie Smith** fumbles in her purse to find the money to pay for her carriage ride to the estate of her wealthy relatives. *A Room with a View* (1985, GB, Merchant-Ivory).

Penises *see* BODIES

People

see also CLASSES, CROWDS, DEMOCRACY, HUMANITY, MEN AND WOMEN, PERSONS AND PERSONALITIES, SOCIETIES

7569 "When a man dies, people weep. When an attitude dies, people shrug." **Edwardo Ciannelli** makes a distinction between feelings for most men and someone like the not-so-late Noel Coward, who must find someone to cry for him in order to save his soul. *The Scoundrel* (1935, Paramount).

7570 TERRY RANDALL: "Certainly you must have heard of Hamlet?" EVE: "Well, I meet so many people." Wealthy debutante **Katharine Hepburn** is put-on by wisecracking **Eve Arden**. Hepburn tells the other aspiring actress at the theatrical boarding house for women that she wishes to play Shakespeare. *Stage Door* (1937, RKO).

7571 "Why should I save people who don't want to be saved, so they can go out and exterminate each other?" At the outbreak of World War II, physician **Charles Coburn**'s frustration is somewhat understandable. *Idiot's Delight* (1939, MGM).

7572 "Can't nobody lick us, Pa. We're the people." Indomitable **Jane Darwell** assures husband Russell Simpson that they will survive their current hardships. *The Grapes of Wrath* (1940, 20th Century-Fox).

7573 "There you are, Norton, the people! Try and lick that!" At the end of the film, honest newspaper editor **James Gleason** turns his back on fascist publisher Edward Arnold. *Meet John Doe* (1941, Liberty Films).

7574 "You talk about the people as though they belong to you. As long as I can remember you've talked about giving the people their rights as though you could make a present of liberty—in reward for services rendered. You remember the working man? You used to write an awful lot about the working man. Well, he's turning into something called organized labor, and you're not going to like that a bit when you find it means that he thinks he's entitled to something as his right and not your gift. . . . And listen, Charles. When your precious underprivileged really do get together—that's going to add up to something bigger than your privilege— and then I don't know what you'll do. Sail away to a desert island, and lord it over the monkeys." Long-time friend **Joseph Cotten** really lets noblesse oblige publisher Orson Welles have it. *Citizen Kane* (1941, RKO).

7575 "I find this is a convenient vantage point. From here I can see people as they really are." Lavatory attendant Uncle Pio, played by **Steven Geray**, sits on the floor to shine shoes. *Gilda* (1946, Columbia).

7576 "People like the Salters [homesteaders] can never be stopped. . . . Indians can kill them and run them off, but more will keep coming. The Salters are the New World, unconquered, unconquerable because they're strong and free—because they have faith in themselves and in God." Producer-director Cecil B. De Mille's mouthpiece **Gary Cooper** could just as well be speaking of the Indians as he justifies homesteaders pushing them off their land. *Unconquered* (1947, Paramount).

7577 "You and me's the same sort of people. . . we're mongrels." **Karl Malden** proposes marriage to his foster-daughter Jennifer Jones, arguing that

they are a perfect match. *Ruby Gentry* (1952, 20th Century-Fox).

7578 KITTY FREMONT: "People are the same no matter what they're called." ARI BEN CANAAN: "Don't believe it. People have a right to be different." **Eva Marie Saint** lectures Jewish **Paul Newman** who recognizes that mixed-faith romances face special problems. *Exodus* (1960, United Artists).

7579 "It was as though for a time I didn't exist, as though I had no place in the world. . . . I've no desire for a close contact of other people.". . . I don't seem to be capable of being close to people." **Candace Hilligoss** tells her haunted feelings to doctor Stanley Levitt. *Carnival of Souls* (1962, Herts-Lion).

7580 JOANNA WALLACE: "What kind of people just sit like that without a word to say to each other?" MARK WALLACE: "Married people." Before they are married, **Audrey Hepburn** finds it difficult to understand the people sitting at a nearby table, effectively ignoring each other as they have their meal. Her husband to be, **Albert Finney**, understands. *Two for the Road* (1967, GB, 20th Century-Fox).

7581 "We subsidize trains, we subsidize planes, why not subsidize people?" U.S. Senate candidate **Robert Redford** makes a case for the government helping people directly. *The Candidate* (1972, Warner Bros.).

7582 "Maybe WASPs outgrow people. Italians outgrow clothes, not people." **Mickey Rourke** angrily replies when WASPish Daryl Hannah asks why he hasn't outgrown his troublesome cousin Eric Roberts. *The Pope of Greenwich Village* (1984, MGM-United Artists).

7583 "I think of France more than I tell you. I was seventeen and I was thrown into the war. I often think of it. . . . The most unlikely people. People I met only for an hour or two. Astonishing kindness. Bravery. The fact that you could meet someone for an hour and see the very best of them and then move on." British subject **Meryl Streep** pines for the emotional charges and purity of purpose she experienced during World War II working with the resistance in France. *Plenty* (1985, GB, 20th Century-Fox).

7584 "You've got to think of the people first. In the name of human decency, something we Americans are supposed to believe in, you got to at least try to make something of a just society here." Protagonist journalist **James Woods** begs U.S. Embassy officials to do something to help the Salvadorian people. *Salvador* (1986, Hemdale).

7585 "No, but I feel better when they're not around." Boozy, macho writer **Mickey Rourke** responds when his bar stool companion Faye Dunaway asks if he hates people. *Barfly* (1987, Cannon).

7586 "The lake must be full of people. I've heard stories all my life. You can bet there were a lot of people on the train nobody knew about." Speaking to her two orphaned nieces for whom she is caring, eccentric and charming **Christine Lahti** refers to a train accident in a lake in the mountainous interior of the Pacific Northwest. *Housekeeping* (1987, Columbia).

7587 "No. You see, I'm, I'm, not very good with people." Shy scientist **John Malkovich** will just have to take lessons from the affable android he's created that looks just like him. *Making Mr. Right* (1987, Orion).

7588 "Ray, people will come. . . . They'll come to Iowa for reasons they can't even fathom. . . . They will turn in your driveway, not really sure why they're doing it. They'll arrive at your door, as innocent as children, longing for the past. 'Of course, we won't mind if you look around,' you'll say, 'it's only $20 a person.' They'll pass over the money without even thinking about it. Money they have; it's peace they'd like. . . . They'll walk out to the bleachers, sit in the shirtsleeves on a perfect afternoon. . . they'll find they have reserved seats somewhere along the baselines. . . they'll settle in with the children and cheer their heroes. . . and they'll watch the game and it'll be as if they dipped themselves in magic waters. . . the memories will be so thick they'll have to brush them away from their faces. . . . People will come, Ray. . . . Oh, people will come, Ray. People will most definitely come." **James Earl Jones** gives a benediction as he helps Kevin Costner understand why he followed the directions of a mysterious voice to build a baseball diamond in the middle of the corn field, so that the likes of Shoeless Joe Jackson and the other "Black Sox" could once again play baseball. *Field of Dreams* (1989, Universal).

Pep Talks

see also ENCOURAGEMENTS, SPORTS

7589 "No matter what I may say, no matter what I may do on this stage during our work, I love you all." Broadway theatrical impresario **John Barrymore** addresses the cast of his new play with patent insincerity. *Twentieth Century* (1934, Columbia).

7590 "I've called you here as freeborn Englishmen, loyal to our king. While he reigned over us, we lived in peace. But since Prince John has seized the regency, Guy of Gisbourne and the rest of the traitors have murdered and pillaged. You've all suffered from their cruelty—the ear loppings, the beatings, the blindings with hot irons, the burning of our farms and homes, the mistreatment of our women. It's time we put an end to this! Now, this forest is wide. It can shelter and clothe and feed a band of good determined men—good swordsmen, good archers, good fighters. Men, if you're willing to fight for our people, I want you! Are you with me, men?" **Errol Flynn**, as Sir Robin of Locksley, whips up the passions of the oppressed to fight the tyranny of Claude Rains, a usurping prince, and his chief supporter, Basil Rathbone. The men enthusiastically rally to his call as he becomes Robin Hood and they, his merry men of Sherwood Forest. *The Adventures of Robin Hood* (1938, Warner Bros.).

7591 "I'm going to tell you something I've kept to myself for years. None of you ever knew George Gipp. He was long before your time, but you all know what a tradition he is at Notre Dame. And the last thing he said to me, 'Rock,' he said, 'some time when the team is up against it and the breaks are beating the boys, tell them to go out there with all they got and win just one for the Gipper. I don't know where I'll be then, Rock,' he said, 'but I'll know about it, and I'll be happy.'" All of us who have ever been associated in one way or another with the University of Notre Dame know the story of how that master motivator Knute Rockne, played in the movie by **Pat O'Brien,** charged up a mediocre team at half time in a big game. They all but ran through the walls to defeat their opponent. *Knute Rockne—All American* (1940, Warner Bros.).

7592 "You don't need to be number one as you amble down life's highway. But don't be last!" **Gig Young** serves as a sort of Greek Chorus for a group of marathon dance competitors. *They Shoot Horses, Don't They?* (1969, ABC-Cinerama).

7593 "We sink, we swim, we rise, we fall, we meet our fate together." Principal **Morgan Freeman** gives a pep talk to the students of Eastside High School before they take the basic skills test which will decide the future of their high school. *Lean on Me* (1989, Warner Bros.).

Perceptions *see* EYES, INSTINCTS, SENSATIONS, SENSE AND SENSIBILITY, SIGHT AND SIGHTS, UNDERSTANDINGS AND MISUNDERSTANDINGS, VISIONS AND VISUALIZATIONS

Perfection

see also PURITY, TALENTS

7594 "Goodness, why because she's perfectly perfect. . . . Yes, we all fairly adore her. You know she's like some big noble cold statue, way up above the rest of us. She hardly ever does anything mean or treacherous. Of all the girls I know, I think she plays the fewest mean tricks." **Katharine Hepburn**'s faint praise of Evelyn Venable to the latter's beau Fred MacMurray, whom Hepburn would like to steal, makes Venable seem less than perfect. *Alice Adams* (1935, RKO).

7595 "Tracy sets exceptionally high standards for herself." **Mary Nash** half-heartedly defends her daughter Katharine Hepburn to Kate's sister Virginia Weidler. Hepburn views herself as just about perfect and expects her notion of perfection from everyone else. *The Philadelphia Story* (1940, MGM).

7596 "Oh, hello, Mr. President. This is Mary Peppertree. I wanted you to know that everything is perfect. Just perfect." **Deanna Durbin** is a White House switchboard operator who enlisted the help of the President of the United States to sort out her romantic problems. *For the Love of Mary* (1948, Universal).

7597 "I'm practically perfect in every way." **Julie Andrews** is compelled to tell the truth about herself when she is interviewed for a position as nanny to David Tomlinson and Glynis Johns' children. *Mary Poppins* (1964, Buena Vista).

7598 "There are women who reach a perfect time of life, when the face will never be as good, the body as graceful or powerful. It had happened that year to Julia." **Jane Fonda,** as Lillian Hellman, speaks of her friend Vanessa Redgrave. *Julia* (1977, 20th Century-Fox).

7599 "Your tan is perfect. I always wondered how you got the back of your ears so dark." The way **Jane Fonda** disapproves of everything about her ex-husband Alan Alda, it's difficult to imagine they were ever in love. *California Suite* (1978, Columbia).

7600 "Nobody's perfect. There was never a perfect person around. You just have half-angel and half-devil in you." In a beautifully photographed period piece, young narrator **Linda Manz** wisely reflects on people in 1916 Texas. *Days of Heaven* (1978, Paramount).

7601 ARTHUR: "It's a perfect crime." HOBSON: "If she murdered the tie, it would be a perfect crime." **Dudley Moore** and his valet **John Gielgud** watch as Liza Minnelli sneaks a tie into her purse at Bergdorf's. *Arthur* (1981, Orion).

7602 "I can't believe it. I love you. Now you watch. It's going to be perfect. I promise. Oh, Mary. Perfect. Perfect." Neurotic film editor **Albert Brooks** has once again made up with his girl friend Kathryn Harrold. *Modern Romance* (1981, Columbia).

7603 "Perfection is a road, not a destination." Elderly Korean mentor **Joel Grey** lectures his student Fred Ward. *Remo Williams: The Adventure Begins* (1985, Orion).

7604 "The beautiful, the perfect Ann is a lousy lay." **Laura San Giacomo** gleefully shares with James Spader that her sister Andie MacDowell is hopeless in bed. San Giacomo has the information on the best authority. She is having a wild, passionate affair with MacDowell's husband Peter Gallagher. *sex, lies and videotape* (1989, Miramax).

7605 "You didn't blink an eye when you killed him, you were perfect." Psychopath **Ron Silver** admires rookie New York cop Jamie Lee Curtis, who on her first night of duty, shoots and kills an armed thief in a busy convenience store. Silver is more turned on by Curtis' gun than by her—he really is sick. *Blue Steel* (1990, Vestron).

7606 "Nobody's perfect. I realize this is embarrassing, but who were you exposed to, dear?" Kindly, **Diane Ladd** takes over the questioning of Laura Dern from Ladd's husband Robert Duvall when it appears that Dern is pregnant. *Rambling Rose* (1991, New Line).

Performances

see also ACTING AND ACTORS, MUSIC AND MUSICIANS

7607 "You've been giving those apple knockers too much for their money." Cynical promoter **Sam Hardy** tells evangelist Barbara Stanwyck that her "performance" for her audiences is needlessly exhausting her. *The Miracle Woman* (1931, Columbia).

7608 "It wasn't a reading. It was a performance. Brilliant, vivid, something made of music and fire." Theater critic **George Sanders** takes perverse pleasure in telling aging stage actress Bette Davis that her conniving understudy Anne Baxter has given a brilliant reading. *All About Eve* (1950, 20th Century-Fox).

7609 "Substandard performance is not permitted to exist; that I warn you." New commander of the Caine, **Humphrey Bogart**, as Captain Queeg, lays down the law to his officers. *The Caine Mutiny* (1954, Columbia).

7610 LUNA: "Do you want to perform sex with me?" MILES: "Perform sex? I don't think I'm up to a performance, but I'll rehearse with you if you like." **Diane Keaton**, a girl of the future, casually suggests sex with **Woody Allen** who recently has awakened from a 200-year sleep. *Sleeper* (1973, United Artists).

Perfumes

see also ATTRACTIONS, SEX AND SEXUALITY, SMELLS, WOMEN

7611 BUD NORTON: "Perfume's a lovely thing. But you know they make it out of the darndest things: horses' hooves, potato peelings, coal tar. . . ." MAVIS: "I always say science is golden." Farm boy **Randolph Scott** may be concerned with the source of perfume, but **Mae West** is only interested in its effect. *Go West, Young Man* (1936, Paramount).

7612 "In these days of greater equality between the sexes, perfume should not be the privilege of the lady only." Senior shop assistant **Charles Halton** tries to convince wealthy Gary Cooper to buy some perfume for himself. *Bluebeard's Eighth Wife* (1938, Paramount).

7613 "Mom has been gone two years now. It's all right to have a little perfume in your life." Free-spirit **Robby Benson** encourages his widower father Paul Newman to seek some female companionship. *Harry and Son* (1984, Orion).

Permissions

see also AUTHORITIES, OPPORTUNITIES

7614 "Ya gotta ask permission for everything, even to wipe the sweat away." Grizzled old con **Edward Ellis** explains the rules to new fish Paul Muni on a southern chain gang. *I Am a Fugitive from a Chain Gang* (1932, Warner Bros.).

7615 "You gotta go, you gotta go." At a meet with ambitious Mafioso Al Lettieri, the latter's bodyguard, corrupt Police Captain **Sterling Hayden** gives Al Pacino permission to go to the men's room. There Pacino hopes he'll find a hidden gun with which to kill Lettieri and Hayden. *The Godfather* (1972, Paramount).

7616 BROR BLIXEN-FINECKE: "You should have asked permission." DENYS FINCH-HATTON: "I did. She said yes." **Klaus Maria Brandauer** is mildly annoyed when **Robert Redford** moves in with his wife Meryl Streep during his absence. *Out of Africa* (1985, Universal).

Persons and Personalities

see also CHARACTER, IDENTITIES, ROLES

7617 "When the mind houses two personalities, there is always a conflict, a battle." At the end of the movie, psychiatrist **Simon Oakland** summarizes Anthony Perkins' problems for the police and the audience. *Psycho* (1960, Paramount).

7618 "Your brother has the same personality as the Boston Strangler." **Dom De Luise** complains to his wife Leigh French about her brother, ex-Marine Glenn Campbell, recently returned from Vietnam. *Norwood* (1970, Paramount).

7619 DR. MCCOY: "Spock, you haven't changed a bit—you're just as personable as ever." MR. SPOCK: "Nor have you, Doctor, as your continued predilection for irrelevancy demonstrates." **DeForest Kelley** sarcastically responds to **Leonard Nimoy**'s cold reception to the former's greeting after not having seen each other for a long time. *Star Trek: The Motion Picture* (1979, Paramount).

7620 "He has the personality of a pimp." **Cliff Robertson,** as Hugh Hefner, privately characterizes her boyfriend-manager Eric Roberts, as Paul Snider, for Mariel Hemingway, as Playmate of the Year Dorothy Stratten. *Star 80* (1983, Warner Bros.).

7621 "Why are you always one inch from becoming a good person?" Petty thief Mickey Rourke has no answer for **Daryl Hannah**. *The Pope of Greenwich Village* (1984, MGM-United Artists).

7622 "Between the two of you there's almost a whole person." Loony man-hating **Genevieve Bujold** snarls at Kris Kristofferson and Lori Singer. *Trouble in Mind* (1986, Atlantic).

7623 "You have a nice personality and you know sweaters." It's the best thing **William Hurt** can think to say about his wife, unhappy, ever-shopping society matron Mia Farrow. *Alice* (1990, Orion).

Persuasion *see* ARGUMENTS, INFLUENCES, TEMPTATIONS

Perversions

7624 "Such delicious debauchery." **Charles Laughton,** made up as effeminate Nero, with rouged cheeks, lipstick, plucked eyebrows and a contralto voice, lisps about an orgy of sex and brutality. *The Sign of the Cross* (1932, Paramount).

7625 "I may not be a paragon of virtue, but I'm not a drooling sex fiend." Drooling sex fiend pilot **Hugh O'Brian** snows naïve stewardess Pamela Tiffin. *Come Fly with Me* (1963, MGM).

7626 "I think you're some kind of deviated prevert [sic]. I think General Ripper found out about your preversions and that you were organizing some kind of mutiny of preverts." **Keenan Wynn,** as Colonel "Bat" Guano, is very suspicious of Peter Sellers, as Group Captain Lionel Mandrake. *Dr. Strangelove, or How I Learned to Stop Worrying and Love the Bomb* (1963, GB, Columbia).

7627 "Then account for yourself! Do you believe in God? Do you believe in gold? Why are you looking up old ladies' dresses? Bit of a pervert, eh?" Broadway producer **Zero Mostel** completely flusters accountant Gene Wilder who walks in on Mostel while he's romancing one of his ancient female backers. *The Producers* (1966, Embassy).

7628 "There was that dumper once, he sounded like that dumper —dumpers? They get their kicks beating you up. A man hired me once, then tried to really kill me... he wasn't kidding. Usually it's a fakeout. You probably know. They pretend to tie you up and you wear a dress with a cloth belt, and they pretend to whip you. Hell, it's their money. I'll hang from the shower rod and whistle 'Maytime.' Except this guy was really tripped out on it...." Part-time New York City hooker **Jane Fonda** recalls for small town cop Donald Sutherland, a sadist with whom she once got involved. *Klute* (1971, Warner Bros.).

7629 "Klute, tell me, what's your bag? Are you a talker, or a button man or a doubler, or maybe you like very young—children—or get your chest walked around with high heel shoes, or have us watch you tinkle. Or—You want to wear women's clothes, or you get off ripping things—you perverted hypocrite square bastards." In listing perversions that might appeal to Donald Sutherland, prostitute **Jane Fonda** rages at all of her customers. *Klute* (1971, Warner Bros.).

7630 "My wife divorced me. She said I was a pervert... because I drank the water bed." After awakening from a 200-year sleep, **Woody Allen** is questioned about his past life. *Sleeper* (1973, United Artists).

7631 "Whores, queens, fairies, dopers, junkies... all the animals come out at night." Restless, alienated taxi driver **Robert De Niro** complains about the perverts and deviant people that roam the streets of New York City at night. *Taxi Driver* (1976, Columbia).

7632 "Oh, that's so kinky. Are you biting me?" Sexually liberated cover girl **Susan Saint James** is in bed with George Hamilton as Dracula. *Love at First Bite* (1979, AIP).

7633 "Mr. Raoul, are you at all familiar with handcuffs?... Well, how much would it cost to put a set of handcuffs in the wall?... Just as a decorative motif." **Mary Woronov** attempts to make her request of locksmith Robert Beltran seem innocent and light-hearted in this black comedy. *Eating Raoul* (1982, 20th Century-Fox).

7634 "She ate me up like an enchilada and spit me into a police car." **Ben Gazzara** refers to sleazy blonde Susan Tyrrell whom he met on a Venice beach. He followed her home where she ravished him and then had him arrested for unspeakable acts. *Tales of Ordinary Madness* (1982, Italy-Fr., Giugno-Ginis-Miracle).

7635 "Have you ever had sex with an animal?" Bailjumper **Charles Grodin** tries to make conversation with modern bounty hunter Robert De Niro who is transporting his prisoner across country from New York to Los Angeles. *Midnight Run* (1988, Universal).

7636 "You know, I'd like to do it in your house sometime.... I must confess the idea of doing it in my sister's bed gives me a perverse thrill...." **Laura San Giacomo** tells her lover Peter Gallagher she'd like to have sex with him right in her sister Andie MacDowell's marriage bed. Her interest in Gallagher seems to be competition with her "perfect" sister instead of passion for him. *sex, lies and videotape* (1989, Miramax).

7637 "You marry me for my money, then you want to work. You're the prince of perversion." **Glenn Close,** as Sunny von Bulow, doesn't want her husband Jeremy Irons, as Claus, to work. *Reversal of Fortune* (1990, Warner Bros.).

Pessimism *see* OPTIMISM AND PESSIMISM

Pet Expressions

see also MOTTOS, PROVERBS AND SAYINGS

7638 "I'll take vanilla." It's **Helen Chandler**'s oft-repeated cynical expression indicating her preference to the available options. *The Last Flight* (1931, Warner Bros.).

7639 "Why, I should write a book!" It's the frequent assertion of know-it-all newspaper man in this Oscar-winning romance. **Clark Gable**. *It Happened One Night* (1934, Columbia).

7640 "Yur durn tootin', Hoppy." Gravel-voiced sidekick **George "Gabby" Hayes** could be counted upon to say this to William Boyd, as Hopalong Cassidy, in each of their movies together. *Hills of Old Wyoming* (1937, Paramount).

7641 "Do you mind if I take one more look?" It's **Fredric March**'s exit line to his love Janet Gaynor each time he leaves her, including just before he walks into the ocean and drowns himself. *A Star Is Born* (1937, Selznick-United Artists).

7642 "Blond-dee. Oh, Blond-eeeeee!" Whenever **Arthur Lake,** as Dagwood Bumstead, is in trouble, which is his usual situation, he calls for his wife, played by Penny Singleton, to bail him out. *Blondie* (1938, Columbia).

7643 "I'll go home—and I'll think of some way to get him back. After all, tomorrow is another day." **Vivien Leigh** as Scarlett O'Hara decides she can wait until another day to get back her departed husband Clark Gable as Rhett Butler. It's a wise person who realizes that one should put off till tomorrow that which can be done tomorrow. *Gone with the Wind* (1939, Selznick-MGM).

7644 "I haven't had a busy day since yesterday." It's thirty-year cop **Barry Fitzgerald**'s oft-repeated sigh that probably doesn't endear him to those working with or for him. *The Naked City* (1948, Universal).

7645 "What d'ya know!" It's **Judy Holliday**'s usual expression of surprise. *Born Yesterday* (1950, Columbia).

7646 "I kid you not." It's a pet expression of **Humphrey Bogart**, the humorless commander of the mine-sweeper Caine. *The Caine Mutiny* (1954, Columbia).

7647 "So it is written, so it shall be done." The words frequently repeated by some Egyptian official, including **Yul Brynner,** when the Pharaoh makes a decree. It's also used in place of The End at the conclusion of the film. *The Ten Commandments* (1956, Paramount).

7648 "Cross my heart and kiss my elbow." It's the favorite line of Holly Golightly, played by **Audrey Hepburn**. *Breakfast at Tiffany's* (1961, Paramount).

7649 "But that's another story." **Lou Jacobi**, as bartender "Moustache," has a million of them. *Irma la Douce* (1963, United Artists).

7650 "So what's the story?" **Richard Castellano**'s oft-repeated query is never answered to his satisfaction. *Lovers and Other Strangers* (1970, ABC-Cinerama).

7651 "Not hardly!" **John Wayne**'s response when various people see him and say "Jacob McCandles! I thought you was dead." *Big Jake* (1971, Batjac-National General).

7652 "Come on. We're burning daylight." It's cattleman **John Wayne**'s frequent orders to the eleven school boys who are his drovers. *The Cowboys* (1972, Warner Bros.).

7653 "Hey, Bud, let's party." It's the favorite line of pot-smoking teen surfer Jeff Spicoli, played by **Sean Penn**. *Fast Times at Ridgemont High* (1982, Universal).

7654 "The game is afoot!" The cry is used frequently by young Sherlock Holmes, played by **Nicholas Rowe**. **Robert Stephens**, as the adult detective says it also, but more as a jibe at his friend and biographer Colin Blakely, playing Dr. Watson. *Young Sherlock Holmes* (1985, Paramount); *The Private Life of Sherlock Holmes* (1970, GB, United Artists).

7655 "Up your bum." It's the irreverent favorite line of 15-year-old **Emily Lloyd**, a sexually spunky girl who fancies she has legs like Betty Grable. She has a mouth to make a sailor blush. *Wish You Were Here* (1987, GB, Atlantic).

7656 "There's your boyfriend." The in-joke is shared by good friends **Lea Thompson** and **Victoria Jackson** every time they see a male loser. *Casual Sex?* (1988, Universal).

7657 "Uh-oh, fifteen minutes to Wapner." Technically autistic **Dustin Hoffman**'s announcement that it's almost time for TV's "The People's Court" isn't a pet expression; but he uses it often enough for it to qualify for inclusion here. *Rain Man* (1988, MGM-United Artists).

7658 "Fuck me gently with a chainsaw." An echo line of **Kim Walker,** beautiful but nasty leader of a group of popular high school girls. *Heathers* (1989, New World).

7659 "Tish, kiss my squirrel." Teen **Keith Coogan** yells something obviously obscene to his stepmother Sean Young each time he becomes exasperated with her. *Cousins* (1989, Paramount).

7660 "I came to America in 1914." Russian Jewish immigrant **Armin Mueller-Stahl** as Sam Krichinsky, a Baltimore paper hanger, proudly repeats the line to all who will listen. The film is based on the experiences of the family of writer-director Barry Levinson. *Avalon* (1990, Tri-Star).

7661 "Let's party, dudes." The likely suggestion of any one of the four "bodacious, awesome, gnarly" mutant superhero turtles. *Teenage Mutant Ninja Turtles* (1990, New Line).

7662 "Talk hard." So, teenager **Christian Slater,** who runs a pirate radio station, regularly advises his listeners. *Pump Up the Volume* (1990, Canada-U.S., New Line.)

7663 "Sometimes it's good to be a cop." Each time he enjoys one of the perks of being a Chicago police officer, **John Candy** repeats the line. *Only the Lonely* (1991, 20th Century-Fox).

Petting *see* DATES AND DATING, KISSES AND KISSING, SEX AND SEXUALITY

Phantasy *see* DREAMS, FANTASIES, ILLUSIONS, IMAGINATION, SPIRIT AND SPIRITS

Philosophies

see also BELIEFS, CREEDS AND CREDOS, REASONS, THEORIES, THINKING AND THOUGHTS

7664 "Okay, I'm a juvenile cornball. But I know the kind of man I want—not a lazy catfish floating with the tide, no sirree. I want me a red-blooded salmon who fights his way upstream, yes, and gets there, if it kills him. That's my juvenile cornball philosophy and if you don't like it, you can just plain go to hell!" Stewardess **Pamela Tiffin** charges into the cockpit during flight and roars her fishy philosophy to womanizing pilot Hugh O'Brian whom she'd like to net exclusively. *Come Fly with Me* (1963, MGM).

7665 SONIA: "Immortality is subjective." BORIS: "Yes, but subjectivity is objective." SONIA: "Not in any rational scheme of perception." BORIS: "Perception is irrational, it implies the imminence." SONIA: "But the judgment of any system is a priori relation for phenomena exists in any rational or metaphysical or at least epistemological contradiction to be an abstract and empirical concept such as being or to be, or to occur in the thing itself or of the thing itself." **Diane Keaton** and **Woody Allen** share some philosophical mumbo jumbo. *Love and Death* (1975, United Artists).

7666 "I guess everybody does what they got to do." It's the philosophy of black **John Daniels** who dreams of making it big in the music industry. *Getting Over* (1976, Maverick International).

7667 MICHAEL MCPHEE: "Can you make any money in philosophy?" MAX DUGAN: "It depends on which one you have." **Matthew Broderick** is being steered towards the study of philosophy by his grandfather **Jason Robards** when he goes to college. *Max Dugan Returns* (1983, 20th Century-Fox).

7668 TINA VITALE: "You know what my philosophy of life is? It's over quick so have a good time. You see what you want, go for it. Don't pay attention to anybody else. And do it to the other guy first, 'cause if you don't he'll do it to you." DANNY ROSE: "This is a philosophy of life? It sounds like the screenplay of Murder, Incorporated." Talent agent **Woody Allen** expresses disbelief with the views of cheap bimbo **Mia Farrow**. *Broadway Danny Rose* (1984, United Artists).

Phonies

see also DECEPTIONS, FAKES

7669 JOHNNY: "You know, there's something awful phony about all of this." MARY: "You're just beginning to figure that out?" In a farcical romantic comedy, **Ray Milland** is the son of tycoon Edward Arnold. Both father and son become involved with unemployed stenographer **Jean Arthur**. *Easy Living* (1937, Paramount).

7670 "You're so beautifully phony." Dancer **Clark Gable** sizes up old flame Norma Shearer who is posing as a Russian countess. *Idiot's Delight* (1939, MGM).

7671 "Every month hundreds of claims come to this desk and some of them are phonies and I know which ones. How do I know? Because my little man tells me. . . the little man in here. . . every time one of these phonies comes along he ties knots in my stomach." Claims adjustor **Edward G. Robinson** tells insurance salesman Fred MacMurray that he has help in deciding which claims are legit and which are bogus. *Double Indemnity* (1944, Paramount).

7672 "Oh, no—no, you want him wholly and utterly dependent. You realized long ago, with all your fine background and breeding, you were a failure—but it gave you a reason for being, a feeling of power to control and manipulate someone else's life. And, worst of all, you do it in the name of love. You're as phony to me as an opera soprano." **William Holden** accuses Grace Kelly of trying to keep her alcoholic husband Bing Crosby under her control. *The Country Girl* (1954, Paramount).

7673 "You're wrong, she is, but on the other hand, you're right, because she's a real phony. You know why? Because she honestly believes all this phony junk she believes in." **Martin Balsam** sort of cleans up things for George Peppard, who questions if ding-a-ling Audrey Hepburn is a phony. *Breakfast at Tiffany's* (1961, Paramount).

Photography and Photographers

see also MOTION PICTURES, NEWS AND NEWSPAPERS, REPORTERS

7674 "You're the lowest thing on a newspaper, a picture snatcher, stealing pictures from folks who are so down in the mouth they can't fight back—just a thug doing the same thing you always did." **Patricia Ellis** accuses James Cagney of having an unscrupulous job. The way he works, she's correct. *Picture Snatcher* (1933, Warner Bros.).

7675 "It was me. . . eight years ago. A fella in the States saw that picture. He wrote me. I was lonely so I answered. There were a lot of letters—beautiful letters—and then last month I agreed to marry him. I never got around to telling him the picture was eight years old." **Jan Sterling** shows a fellow airplane passenger an old photograph of herself. *The High and the Mighty* (1954, Warner Bros.).

7676 "We were just playing a game called Photography. You turn off the lights and see what develops." Puritanical Lana Turner is not amused with **Barry Coe**'s explanation when she walks in on her daughter Diane Varsi's teenage friends in a petting party in her living room. *Peyton Place* (1957, 20th Century-Fox).

7677 "You know, Mom sent my picture in to the Seventeen National Smiling Contest and I won runner-up. Everybody said I should have been first of course. Everybody has got to love me. Everybody." Whatever **Tuesday Weld** wants, Tuesday Weld will get with the help of brilliant high school senior Roddy McDowall in this wacky black comedy. *Lord Love a Duck* (1966, Universal).

7678 "You give me back my pictures, too. I don't want you showing them to all the boys and telling them how hot I am." **Sharon Taggart** isn't too broken up when her high school boy friend Timothy Bottoms tells her he wants them to break up. *The Last Picture Show* (1971, Columbia).

7679 "Here, read this magazine. There—are—many—pictures." **John Gielgud** treats Dudley Moore like a dull child as Moore waits nervously in his father's outer office. *Arthur* (1981, Orion).

7680 "Hey, I almost forgot, uh, this picture of Mom. I think she'd like you to have it." **Denzel Washington** is the result of a college liaison between George Segal and a black coed. After his mother's death, Washington shows up to complicate Segal's life. *Carbon Copy* (1981, Avco Embassy).

7681 "The picture doesn't do her justice. She's suffering from water buildup." **Henry Winkler** shows a photograph of his fiancée Nita Talbot to Michael Keaton. *Night Shift* (1982, Warner Bros.).

7682 "I don't take sides, I take pictures." It's photojournalist **Nick Nolte**'s neutral position before he is radicalized by conditions in Nicaragua. *Under Fire* (1983, Orion).

7683 "Uh, I'll just be a second. You can take your prints out of the fixer now. I think they've been in long enough." Glasgow photography assistant **David McKay** has fallen in love with an unknown girl in a picture. *The Girl in the Picture* (1985, GB, Rank).

7684 "You take my picture, I'll strangle you with your own brassiere—you got me?" Philadelphia police detective **Harrison Ford**, posing as a member of an Amish community, threatens a thoughtless tourist who asks to take his picture because he's "quaint." *Witness* (1985, Paramount).

7685 "If I can get some good combat shots for AP, I can make some money." Cynical freelance photojournalist **James Woods** sees the misery of others as a money-maker. *Salvador* (1986, Hemdale).

Pictures *see* PHOTOGRAPHY AND PHOTOGRAPHERS

Pity

see also COMPASSION, CONCERNS, EMPATHY, GRIEF, MERCY, SORROWS, SYMPATHY, UNDERSTANDINGS AND MISUNDERSTANDINGS

7686 "It's a pity we couldn't have fought the war out in a poker game. You'd have done better than General Grant with far less effort." **Clark Gable**

compliments George Meeker, a Yankee captain to whom he regularly loses in poker games held in his jail cell. *Gone with the Wind* (1939, Selznick-MGM).

7687 TIBOR CZERNY: "What you went through!" EVE PEABODY: "How far do you think 'through' is for a woman these days." Taxi driver **Don Ameche** is horrified at **Claudette Colbert**'s pathetic recent history. *Midnight* (1939, Paramount).

7688 "You have a lovely head and neck, milady. It would be a pity to separate them." **Henry Daniell** makes a not-so-subtle threat to Olivia de Havilland. *The Private Lives of Elizabeth and Essex* (1939, Warner Bros.).

7689 "His bath was tepid. . . . Poor Lolita, I'm afraid her wedded life will be the same." **Basil Rathbone** sneers in speaking of foppish Tyrone Power and his intended Linda Darnell. *The Mark of Zorro* (1940, 20th Century-Fox).

7690 "I do pity her! Who needs pity more than a woman who's sinned?" Good-hearted **Ethel Barrymore** has sympathy for murderess Valli who is being tried before Barrymore's insensitive and cruel husband judge Charles Laughton. *The Paradine Case* (1947, Selznick-United Artists).

7691 "What a lovely evening. Pity we couldn't have done it with the curtains open, in bright sunlight." The 'it' **John Dall** refers to is the carefully planned thrill killing of a long-time acquaintance carried out by Dall and his lover Farley Granger. *Rope* (1948, Warner Bros.).

7692 "But you tricked and cheated me. You didn't give me friendship. You gave me pity." Arrogant young Scot **Richard Todd**, who has only a few weeks to live, turns on his friends in an army hospital in Burma. *The Hasty Heart* (1949, GB, ABP-Warner Bros.).

7693 "You don't yell at a sleepwalker. That's it, she was still sleepwalking among the dizzy heights of her lost career, one subject: her celluloid self. The great Norma Desmond! How could she breath in that house so crowded with Norma Desmond?" **William Holden** feels pity for Gloria Swanson, a great silent screen star unable to live in the reality of life after the end of her career. *Sunset Boulevard* (1950, Paramount).

7694 "Have pity, miss. . . I'll perish without a hair of the dog." Suffering from a hangover, **Humphrey Bogart** pleads with Katharine Hepburn as she pours his booze overboard. *The African Queen* (1951, United Artists).

7695 "I'd rather be dead than living with you. I don't hate you. I pity you." **Susan Harrison** walks out of the life and apartment of her manipulative Broadway columnist brother Burt Lancaster. *Sweet Smell of Success* (1957, United Artists).

7696 "You're the most pathetic person I've ever met. Because you could be so much and you won't do anything." Pregnant **Carol Androsky**, claiming she pities him, tells off Olympic boxing hopeful Jon Voight. He is unwilling to commit himself to anything or any person. *The All American Boy* (1973, Warner Bros.).

7697 HICKEY: "Of course, I have pity. But now that I've seen the light, it's not my old kind of pity—the kind yours is. The kind that lets itself off easy by encouraging some poor guy to go on kidding himself with a lie. The kind that leaves the poor slob worse off because he feels guiltier than ever. The kind that makes his lying hopes nag at him and reproach him until he's a rotten skunk in his own eyes. No sir, the kind of pity I feel now is after final results that really helped save the poor guy, make him contented with what he is and quit battling himself so he can find peace for the rest of his life." SLADE: "Don't waste your pity. They manage to stay drunk and keep their pipe dreams, and that's all they ask out of life. It isn't often that men attain the true goal of their heart's desire." Hardware salesman **Lee Marvin** and radical **Robert Ryan** hold different opinions of the has-beens and drunks that are the denizens of a seedy saloon. *The Iceman Cometh* (1973, American Film Theater).

7698 "Do I look a pathetic wretch and figure of fun?" Middle-aged Celtic poet **Tom Conti** asks a dangerous question of young Kelly McGillis. Frankly, the answer should be yes. *Reuben, Reuben* (1982, 20th Century-Fox).

Places

see also LOCATIONS, SPACE, TRAVEL AND TRIPS

7699 "Some place where there isn't any trouble. . . behind the moon, beyond the rain. . . somewhere over the rainbow." Forlorn **Judy Garland** speaks longingly before breaking into the haunting song, "Somewhere Over the Rainbow." *The Wizard of Oz* (1939, MGM).

7700 "This is the place." **Dean Jagger**, as Mormon leader Brigham Young, announces that the Great Salt Lake is the new home that he and his followers have been seeking. *Brigham Young—Frontiersman* (1940, 20th Century-Fox).

7701 "One place or another, some place I've never been." Drifter **Alan Ladd** replies when farmer Van Heflin asks him where he's headed. *Shane* (1953, Paramount).

7702 "I don't want to take your place, but you can't take mine either. I can't be a guest in my husband's house." New wife **Elizabeth Taylor** lays down the law to her dominating sister-in-law Mercedes McCambridge. *Giant* (1956, Warner Bros.).

7703 "It's not a person, it's a place." Desperate to find her kidnapped son, **Doris Day** finally realizes that the name "Ambrose Chapel," a dying Frenchman whispered to her husband James Stewart in a Moroccan bazaar, refers to a place in London, not a person. *The Man Who Knew Too Much* (1956, Paramount).

7704 "If you look in this place tomorrow, and it's gone, you mustn't be sad, because you know it still exists, not very far away." It's the voice of blind **Audrey Hepburn**, who may or may not have survived a fire in a hollow tree in a Venezuelan jungle, where she was hiding from Indians who consider her an evil spirit. *Green Mansions* (1959, MGM).

7705 SUNSHINE: "We'll go someplace where it doesn't have to be like this." MARTIN: "Oh, really? Tell me, where is that place? In what remote corner of this country—no, the entire goddamn planet—is there such a place where men really care about one another and really love each other? Just one place!" Tired of being subjected to racist attacks, **Susan Sosa** and **Stan Rice** share a pessimistic exchange. *Billy Jack* (1971, Warner Bros.).

7706 "I had two grand inside my breast pocket that needed a home, and I knew just the place." At the end of the film, private detective **Robert Mitchum** happily contemplates what he'll do with his fee. *Farewell, My Lovely* (1975, Avco Embassy).

7707 "It's a silly place." It's the reason **Graham Chapman**, as King Arthur, gives for not returning to Camelot. *Monty Python and the Holy Grail* (1975, GB, EMI).

7708 "I have a white cubicle for my screams, my prayers, my vomit and my fears." Actress **Ingrid Thulin** has been hospitalized for her alcoholism. *After the Rehearsal* (1984, Sweden, Triumph).

7709 "I've had people die that are close to me. I want to make sure they've gone to a nice place." It's the idiotic reason medical student **Julia Roberts** gives for experimenting with rendering herself brain-dead and then being revived. *Flatliners* (1990, Columbia).

7710 MICKEY O'NEILL: "What is this place?" JOSEF LOCKE: "It used to be the edge of the world. Now the next parish is New York City." Concert promoter **Adrian Dunbar** questions **Ned Beatty** about the stone tower on the Irish coast to which the latter has brought him. *Hear My Song* (1991, GB, Miramax).

Plans

see also DESIRES, INTENTIONS, OBJECTIVES, OBJECTS, PREPARATIONS, SCHEMES

7711 SHEP: "Well, the old war is fini." CARY: "What are you going to do now, Shep?" SHEP: "Get tight." CARY: "And then what?" SHEP: "Stay tight." World War I American fliers **David Manners** and **Richard Barthelmess** make post-war plans on Armistice Day. *The Last Flight* (1931, Warner Bros.).

7712 "Sitting or reclining?" **Mae West** wants to know what to plan for when a fortune teller gazes into a crystal ball and sees "a change in position" for Mae. *I'm No Angel* (1933, Paramount).

7713 "Maybe they're planning a double suicide." Secretary **Johnny Arthur** sarcastically replies to naïve Ruby Keeler who wonders what Dick Powell and Joan Blondell are doing closeted in an inner office. *Dames* (1934, Warner Bros.).

7714 "Did you ever know a woman who didn't want to make plans?" **Colin Clive** refers to his wife Jean Arthur, whom he suspects of having taken Charles Boyer as a lover. Actually, he shoves her into it. *History Is Made at Night* (1937, United Artists).

7715 "Make it look as if the girl flew serum to Shanghai. . . . She'll be a bonanza for us, a gold mine. . . I'm coming home. . . with Alma herself. Yeah, she's a comic little dame who thinks she's a man flying around the world with grease on her face and her hands in her pocket. But maybe I can show her how it feels to be a woman. I'll make her the darling of Union Newsreel. . . .[There'll be a] million dollar melon that you and I and the stockholders can split three ways." Cynical newsreel reporter **Clark Gable** specializes in managed news. He cables his corrupt boss Walter Connolly about his plans, both publicly and privately, for Amelia Earhart-like aviatrix Myrna Loy. *Too Hot to Handle* (1938, MGM).

7716 "I love Russians! I've been fascinated by your Five-Year Plan for the past fifteen years." French playboy **Melvyn Douglas** teases Russian Communist emissary Greta Garbo. *Ninotchka* (1939, MGM).

7717 "Well, we're going to marry and raise fat children and watch our vineyards grow." Having disposed of the California tyrant, **Tyrone Power** contemplates married life with Linda Darnell. *The Mark of Zorro* (1940, 20th Century-Fox).

7718 YVONNE: "Where were you last night?" RICK: "That's so long ago I can't remember." YVONNE: "Will I see you tonight?" RICK: "I never make plans so far in advance." It slowly dawns on **Madeleine LeBeau** that she no longer figures in Humphrey Bogart's plans. *Casablanca* (1942, Warner Bros.).

7719 "I always planned that as soon as we got a few dollars ahead I'd go back to the old country to see my mother—would you believe it, that was forty-five years ago?" Wistfully **Barry Fitzgerald**, as pastor Father Fitzgibbon, reveals an unfulfilled dream to his curate Bing Crosby, as Father O'Malley. *Going My Way* (1944, Paramount).

7720 "You should be grateful to me for having the foresight to think ahead. To survive one must have a plan. But there's nothing to worry about. Soon we will reach the supply ship and then we'll all have food and water. Too bad Schmidt couldn't have waited." Lifeboat survivors have just discovered that German U-Boat Captain **Walter Slezak** has a private supply of water, a compass, and is responsible for the death of William Bendix. All, men and women, except black steward Canada Lee, fall upon him and beat Slezak to death. *Lifeboat* (1944, 20th Century-Fox).

7721 "It's been all set for next Tuesday for the last ten years and it'll still be set for next Tuesday in the next ten years." **Charles Bickford** points to an old con who has been dreaming and planning a prison break for years. *Brute Force* (1947, Universal-International).

7722 "The way I see it, the Lord went to an awful lot of trouble to put those people in our way. . . and if I were Him, I wouldn't want anybody messing up my plans!" Wagonmaster **Ward Bond** forcefully speaks to Russell Simpson, the leader of a group of Mormon settlers who are concerned about the members of a traveling medicine show who have asked to join the wagon train. *Wagonmaster* (1950, RKO).

7723 "We'll bash their heads in, gouge their eyes out, cut their throats. . . after we wash the dishes." **Humphrey Bogart** is only kidding as he outlines his plans for Leo G. Carroll and his family to his fellow Devil's Island escapees Peter Ustinov and Aldo Ray. *We're No Angels* (1955, Paramount).

7724 ANGIE: "What do you wanna do tonight?" MARTY: "I dunno, Angie. What do you wanna do?"

Joe Mantell and **Ernest Borgnine** go through a familiar daily routine. *Marty* (1955, United Artists).

7725 "You lousy trash. You no-count, two-faced dog. I'm gonna watch you cringe, then I'm gonna put a bullet in your belly." **Robert Stack** threatens his one-time friend Rock Hudson who is having an affair with Stack's wife Lauren Bacall, but that is not what makes Stack really mad at Hudson. *Written on the Wind* (1956, Universal-International).

7726 "I plan to assemble a human being using parts and organs from different cadavers. I'm carrying the principle of selective breeding one step higher. . . . Where Baron Frankenstein created a monster, I shall bring forth a perfectly healthy normal human being." Perhaps **Whit Bissell** forgets that his infamous ancestor had exactly the same intention. *I Was a Teenage Frankenstein* (1958, American International).

7727 "I planned a ceiling, he plans a miracle." **Rex Harrison**, as Pope Julius II, refers to the ceiling of the Sistine Chapel and painter Michelangelo, portrayed by Charlton Heston. *The Agony and the Ecstasy* (1965, 20th Century-Fox).

7728 DRAGLINE: "All the time you were planning on running again." LUKE: "I never planned anything in my life." **George Kennedy** admires **Paul Newman**'s foresight as they jump into a pickup truck and run away from a chain gang. It's Newman's third escape attempt. *Cool Hand Luke* (1967, Warner Bros.).

7729 "I don't need you. Just get me on that bus. I don't want nothing more from you. I got other plans for my life than dragging around some dumb cowboy who thinks he's God's gift to women. One twenty-buck trick and he's already the biggest stud in New York City. It's laughable." **Dustin Hoffman**, as Ratso Rizzo, shouts to Jon Voight, as Joe Buck, that he doesn't figure in Hoffman's future plans. *Midnight Cowboy* (1969, United Artists).

7730 POSNER: "You really think those Green Beret karate tricks gonna help you against all these boys." BILLY JACK: "Well, it doesn't look to me like I really have any choice, now does it?" POSNER: "That's right, you don't." BILLY JACK: "You know what I think I'm going to do then, just for the hell of it?" POSNER: "Tell me." BILLY JACK: "I'm going to take this right foot and I'm going to whop you on that side of your face—and you want to know something? There's not a damn thing you're going to be able to do about it." Brutal racist **Bert Freed** and a dozen men form a circle around **Tom Laughlin**, but Laughlin does precisely what he said he would do. *Billy Jack* (1971, Warner Bros.).

7731 "To hell with it. If I can't dance, I'll switch to the drama department." Changing her plans, **Laura Dean** reconsiders committing suicide when she's drummed out of her dance class by hard-as-nails teacher Debbie Allen. *Fame* (1980, MGM).

7732 "I'm just making this up as I go." **Harrison Ford** as Indiana Jones admits that he has no master plan to recover the Ark of the Covenant. *Raiders of the Lost Ark* (1981, Paramount).

7733 "I got plans. If you don't have good dreams, Bagel, you have nightmares." **Mickey Rourke** talks it up to Michael Tucker as the two plan to get into the home improvement business. *Diner* (1982, MGM-United Artists).

7734 "You tell me another gang that's got a dental plan." Thirties gangster **Michael Keaton** proudly speaks of his mob. *Johnny Dangerously* (1984, 20th Century-Fox).

7735 "I'm considering nothing less than world domination." Nasty villain **Faye Dunaway** has big bad plans. *Supergirl* (1984, GB, Tri-Star).

7736 "You don't know what you want. One minute you like me and the next you don't. One minute you're ashamed to be seen with me. The next, you think I'm the best thing that ever happened to you. You think you can just go along like this. No plans...maybe tomorrow you'll be here, maybe you won't." Not unreasonably, **Geena Davis** wants to know what plans William Hurt has for them. Why Davis wants a future with boring Hurt is perplexing. He doesn't seem to wish to participate in life. *The Accidental Tourist* (1988, Warner Bros.).

7737 "We wanted to go to the beach and meet boys and go to wild parties and make out and dance." About to be married, sixties coed **Phoebe Cates** plans one final fling with three of her girlfriends. *Shag* (1989, Hemdale).

7738 "She's is going to marry someone she met in a hotel!" **Barbara Jefford** is alarmed about the plans of her widowed daughter-in-law Helen Mirren, who is about to drag the family's good English name through the Italian mud. *Where Angels Fear to Tread* (1992, Fine Line).

Plants

see also FLOWERS, LAND AND FARMS, NATURE AND NATURAL, TREES

7739 "Remember, a man is never so tall as when he stoops to pet a plant." Loony panhandler **Walter Matthau** solicits funds on behalf of "People for the Ethical Treatment of Plants." *The Couch Trip* (1988, Orion).

7740 "Mistletoe! Many a maid has lost her resolve to me thanks to this little plant." It's hard to imagine **Kevin Costner** as Robin Hood mouthing this trite line—it's even harder to watch him do it. *Robin Hood: Prince of Thieves* (1991, Warner Bros.).

Playing and Players

see also ACTING AND ACTORS, AMUSEMENTS, GAMES, MUSIC AND MUSICIANS, SPORTS

7741 GARRY MADISON: "I'd like to play hearts with you sometime." LADY LEE: "I kinda figured that!" Reading what's on **Joel McCrea**'s mind is no trick for gambler **Barbara Stanwyck**. *Gambling Lady* (1934, Warner Bros.).

7742 "Go ahead and stare. I'm not ashamed. Go ahead and laugh, get your money's worth. We're not going to hurt you. I know you want me to tear my clothes off so you can get your fifty cents worth. Fifty cents for the privilege of staring at a girl the way your wife won't let you. What do you think we think of you up here with your silly smirks your mother would be ashamed of? It's a thing of the moment for the dress suits to come and laugh at us. We'd laugh, too, only we're paid to let you sit there and roll your eyes and make your screaming clever remarks. What's it all for? So you can go home and strut before your wives and sweethearts...play at being the stronger sex for a minute! I'm sure they see through you like we do!" Dancer **Maureen O'Hara** scolds the hecklers in a burlesque audience. Most of the dancers just look bored and act is if no one is watching them. Everyone, dancers and men in the audience, is playing at being something they are not. *Dance, Girl, Dance* (1940, RKO).

7743 "Most men have objects they play with. Churchmen have their beads...I toy with my sword." **Basil Rathbone** gestures menacingly with his sword in the direction of Tyrone Power. *The Mark of Zorro* (1940, 20th Century-Fox).

7744 "I thought I told you never to play it." **Humphrey Bogart** angrily chides piano player Dooley Wilson, who reluctantly has accommodated Ingrid Bergman's request for "As Time Goes By." *Casablanca* (1942, Warner Bros.).

7745 "If you won't play for me, then you won't play for anyone else!" **James Mason** cruelly brings down a stick on the knuckles of his ward, pianist Ann Todd. *The Seventh Veil* (1945, GB, GFD-Universal).

7746 "Why don't you kids go play on the freeway?" Shyster lawyer **Walter Matthau** yells at his two kids who are causing a racket roller skating through the house. *The Fortune Cookie* (1966, United Artists).

7747 "Yes. I understand. A lot of people enjoy being dead. But they are not dead really. They're just backing away from life. They're players—but they sit on the bench. The game goes on before them. At any moment they can join in. Reach out! Take a chance! Get hurt maybe. But play as well as you can. Go, team! Give me an 'L.' Give me an 'I.' Give me a 'V.' Give me an 'E' LIVE!!!!!! Otherwise you have nothing to talk about in the locker room." Eighty-year-old **Ruth Gordon** uses a sports analogy to encourage young withdrawn Bud Cort to participate in life. *Harold and Maude* (1971, Paramount).

7748 "I'm going to play this thing like Charlie Parker." **John Heard**, as "beat" writer Jack Kerouac, compares his typewriter to the saxophone of jazz great Charlie "Bird" Parker. *Heart Beat* (1980, Orion-Warner Bros.).

7749 ARTHUR BACH: "Remember how we would play hide-and-seek and you couldn't find me." HOBSON: "I couldn't find you, because I didn't look for you." Dissolute playboy—**Dudley Moore**—wishes to reminisce with his valet **John Gielgud**. *Arthur* (1981, Orion-Warner Bros.).

7750 "Don't play hard to get." **Bill Murray** doesn't think his roommate Dustin Hoffman is very attractive, dressed as a woman. Hoffman is disguised so he can apply for a female role in a soap opera. *Tootsie* (1982, Columbia).

7751 "What else can you play so beautifully?" **Nastassja Kinski** playfully asks violinist Rudolf Nureyev, who responds by sawing away with his bow on her fine body. *Exposed* (1983, MGM-United Artists).

7752 "I'd have played for food money, I'd have played for nothing." **Ray Liotta**, as the ghost of Shoeless Joe Jackson, is grateful to once again be playing baseball, the game he loves. *Field of Dreams* (1989, Universal).

7753 RAY KINSELLA: "Hey, Dad. . . you want to have a catch?" JOHN KINSELLA: "I'd like that." **Kevin Costner** reestablishes a bond with his long dead father **Dwier Brown** by offering to play catch with him, something he refused to do when he was young and his father was alive. *Field of Dreams* (1989, Universal)

Plays *see* DRAMA AND MELODRAMA, THEATERS

Pleas and Pleading

see also ARGUMENTS, DEFENSES, JUSTIFICATIONS

7754 "Don't leave me—Marguerite, come back, come back." **Robert Taylor** pleads to no avail to beautifully expired Greta Garbo. *Camille* (1936, MGM).

7755 "Come back, Shane. . . come back." Heartbroken **Brandon de Wilde** begs Alan Ladd, who is riding out of the valley, to stay with him and his parents Van Heflin and Jean Arthur. *Shane* (1953, Paramount).

7756 "Please lock me up. I'm gonna hit someone, do something. . . are you going to keep me from going?" Teenager **James Dean** pleads with his wimpish father Jim Backus for some parental guidance and some sense of limits—but the latter only says, "When did I ever stop you from doing anything?" *Rebel Without a Cause* (1955, Warner Bros.).

7757 "It's no good living in a rented room. Each year, I tell myself it's the last. Something will happen. It never does. You gotta marry me, Howard. Please marry me, Howard, please!" Desperate old-maid school teacher **Rosalind Russell** pitifully begs reluctant boy friend Arthur O'Connell to marry her. *Picnic* (1956, Columbia).

7758 "Times are hard. . . . Now, if you fool around on the hill up here, then you don't get nothin', I don't get nothin', he don't get nothin'. So, how about it, honey? Just for a little while. Let old Trixie sit up front with her big tits." **Madeline Kahn** pleads with Tatum O'Neal to let her sit up front in Ryan O'Neal's coupe. *Paper Moon* (1973, Paramount).

7759 "No, not the bore worms." The pleadings of **Ornella Muti**, the naughty but fetching and amorous Princess Aura, that Flash Gordon and his companions not be tortured are not totally sincere. *Flash Gordon* (1980, GB, EMI).

7760 "Please, Joel, do as they say. Just. . . get off the baby-sitter." **Tom Cruise** fantasizes about making love to a girl on a table. But a commando squad arrives and his mother Janet Carroll pleads with him. *Risky Business* (1983, Warner Bros.).

7761 "What do you want from me? What have I done? I'm just a word processor, for Christ's sake." **Griffin Dunne** sinks to his knees in a New York street and looks up for some heavenly help, after a rough night in SoHo. *After Hours* (1985, Warner Bros.).

7762 "Don't kill me. I'm basically a good kid." **Corey Haim** pleads with his older brother Jason Patric, who has become a vampire, to spare him. *The Lost Boys* (1987, Warner Bros.).

Pleasures

see also ENJOYMENTS, FUN, HAPPINESS AND SUFFERERS, JOY, PAINS, SUFFERING AND UNHAPPINESS

7763 "He won't shoot himself. It would please too many people." Agent **Roscoe Karns** does not take seriously producer John Barrymore's threats to kill himself. *Twentieth Century* (1934, Columbia).

7764 "No civilized man ever regrets a pleasure, and no uncivilized man ever knows what the pleasure is." Here are more smug words of wisdom from Oscar Wilde through **George Sanders**. *The Picture of Dorian Gray* (1945, MGM).

7765 "I have never allowed my duty as a gentleman to interfere with my pleasures to the smallest degree." Completely useless but charming gentleman **Michael Denison** defends his position to equally redundant Michael Redgrave. *The Importance of Being Earnest* (1952, GB, Rank-Two Cities).

7766 "My pleasure is physical; my men call me the Beast." Brutish Marine Colonel **William Holden** announces proudly and, perhaps, profanely. *The Proud and the Profane* (1956, Paramount).

7767 "The pleasure does not lie in the end itself. It's the pleasurable steps to that end." A bit of Oriental wisdom that translates to "Getting there is half the fun," is quoted in voice-over in the movie. *Sayonara* (1957, Warner Bros.).

7768 "Look, I know perfectly well the pleasures of music and dancing, but pleasure itself is an indulgence. Only by denying selfish interests can one properly serve the state." Communist emissary to Paris, **Cyd Charisse** quotes the party line, but she's turned on by silk stockings and Fred Astaire. *Silk Stockings* (1957, MGM).

7769 "It's always a pleasure to watch the rich enjoy the comforts of the poor." **Hermione Gingold** mocks with gentle sarcasm as she invites wealthy Louis Jourdan to partake of the simple meal she has cooked for herself and her granddaughter Leslie Caron. *Gigi* (1958, MGM).

7770 "With Jan you look forward to having your branches cut off." Wealthy **Tony Randall** tells his friend Rock Hudson about the new woman in his life, Doris Day. *Pillow Talk* (1959, Universal).

7771 "Look into my eyes. I can bring you pleasure mortals cannot know." Resurrected burnt witch **Barbara Steele** purrs hypnotically to John Richardson. *Black Sunday* (1960, Italy, AIP).

7772 "Looking at you became one of the biggest pleasures of my life—maybe the biggest. Got so I had you memorized. . . not only your face. Everything. Even the way the back of your legs look when you walk away." **Ben Gazzara** is driven wild by wealthy nymphomaniac Suzanne Pleshette. *A Rage to Live* (1965, United Artists).

7773 "Inhibitions are always nice, because they're so nice to overcome." Call girl **Jane Fonda** knows just what to say to put a "john" at ease. *Klute* (1971, Warner Bros.).

7774 BLUME: "What would you like to have?" NINA: "Sex!" It's not on the menu, but as soon as **George Segal** can get **Susan Anspach** away from the restaurant, he'd be pleased to accommodate her request. *Blume in Love* (1973, Warner Bros.).

7775 "I can't take no pleasure in killin'. There's some things you gotta do. Don't mean you gotta like it." Gas man **Jim Siedow** notes that a job is a job. *The Texas Chainsaw Massacre* (1974, Vortex).

7776 "I don't respond well to mellow." **Woody Allen** admits his inability to experience pleasure. *Annie Hall* (1977, United Artists).

7777 DORIS: "What's your pleasure: a walk by the ocean, or a good book, or me?" GEORGE: "You." DORIS: "Oh, I thought you would never ask." Married, but not to each other, **Ellen Burstyn** and **Alan Alda** maintain their affair for over twenty years by meeting for a weekend at the same lodge each year. *Same Time, Next Year* (1978, Universal).

7778 "It's pleasure that I care for, pleasure and amusement." European-raised American **Lee Remick** has returned to her stuffy Boston relatives. *The Europeans* (1979, GB, Leavitt-Pickman).

7779 "I don't mind pleasure. . . pressure." Drugstore night manager **Gene Hackman** makes a Freudian slip while talking to married housewife Barbra Streisand. *All Night Long* (1981, Universal).

7780 "There are no innocent pleasures." Enigmatic **Richard Bohringer** makes a wise observation. *Diva* (1982, Fr., United Artists Classics).

7781 "It is necessary and not in the least bit shameful to take pleasure in a little world—good food, gentle smiles, fruit trees in bloom, waltzes." Slightly drunk **Jarl Kulle** lectures for the audience's benefit in the final sequence of the film. *Fanny and Alexander* (1983, Sweden, Persona Film-Tobis).

7782 "Think of sticking your knife into my flesh. . . and twisting it. You don't want to deny yourself that pleasure." **Arnold Schwarzenegger** cons Vernon Wells into throwing aside his gun to engage in some hand-to-hand combat. *Commando* (1985, 20th Century-Fox).

7783 HENRY MILLER: "I want to vulgarize you." ANAIS NIN: "I want pleasure." This priceless prose is spoken by literary giants played respectively by **Fred Ward** and **Maria de Medeiros** as the two get down to the business of love-making under a Parisian bridge—what she calls "the process of becoming a woman." *Henry & June* (1990, Universal).

7784 QUENTIN HAPSBURG: "I want the pleasure of killing him myself." FRANK DREBIN: "The pleasure is all mine." Villain **Robert Goulet** has plans for polite but dumb police detective **Leslie Nielsen**. *The Naked Gun 2½: The Smell of Fear* (1991, Paramount).

Pledges

see also PROMISES

7785 "Forget you? Not while I live. . . not if I die." Via a title card, **John Gilbert** pledges eternal love for Greta Garbo. *Flesh and the Devil* (1926, silent, MGM).

7786 "I wouldn't fall for another man if he were the biggest crook on earth." Sophisticated thief **Miriam Hopkins** is furious that Kay Francis has taken crooked Herbert Marshall as a lover. *Trouble in Paradise* (1932, Paramount).

7787 "I'm going to flirt and lie and cheat and swindle—right through to our golden wedding anniversary." Newspaper reporter **Fredric March** makes an uninspiring if honest pledge to Carole Lombard. *Nothing Sacred* (1937, Selznick-United Artists).

7788 BISHOP LAMPTON: "Will thou love her?" JACK, 14TH EARL OF GURNEY: "From the bottom of my soul to the tip of my penis—like a sun in its brightness, the moon in its glory!" **Alastair Sim** gets a sincere reply from **Peter O'Toole**, a royal British madman, who believes he's Christ, at his marriage to Carolyn Seymour. *The Ruling Class* (1972, GB, Avco Embassy).

7789 LARRY LAPINSKY: "I'll always love you, Sarah." SARAH: "No, you won't." When they part, **Lenny Baker**'s pledge of love is seen for what it is by his some-time lover **Ellen Greene**. *Next Stop, Greenwich Village* (1976, 20th Century-Fox).

7790 "I came through and I will return." **Gregory Peck**, appearing as General Douglas MacArthur, makes his famous pledge to the people of the Philippines when he leaves their islands as they are conquered by the Japanese. *MacArthur* (1977, Universal).

7791 "We agree to be married for now because there is no always. We will remember the pledge until we can no longer remember. . . . I now pronounce us man, child and wife." Ten-year-old leukemia victim **Katherine Healy** stages a mock wedding ceremony for herself, married politician Dudley Moore and her mother, cosmetics tycoon Mary Tyler Moore. *Six Weeks* (1982, Polygram).

7792 "My brothers, I promise you blood for blood." **Henry Silva** pledges revenge to his massacred gangland buddies. *Code of Silence* (1985, Orion).

7793 "From this day forward, I will raise my hand against no man." Army deserter **Nick Nolte**, who has become the leader of a Borneo tribe during World War II, sounds something like a latter-day Chief Joseph of the Nez Pierce who pledged, "I will fight no more forever." *Farewell to the King* (1989, Vestron-Orion).

Plots *see* SCHEMES

Poetry and Poets

see also CREATION AND CREATURES, LANGUAGES, SONGS AND SINGING, WRITING AND WRITERS

7794 ROSALIND: "Are you so much a man as your rhymes speak?" ORLANDO: "Neither rhyme nor reason can express how much." **Elisabeth Bergner** seeks reassurance. She does not know whether to believe the pledges of love from lovesick **Laurence Olivier**. *As You Like It* (1936, GB, Inter-Allied-20th Century-Fox).

7795 TENNY: "A bit on the feathery side, don't you think, sir?" BULLDOG DRUMMOND: "Nonsense, what rhymes with married?" TENNY: "Harried, sir." Butler **E.E. Clive** is called upon to give **John Howard** some help with a poem the latter is writing to his lady love. *Bulldog Drummond Comes Back* (1937, Paramount).

7796 "Well, all I can say is, I just thought of a poem. Uh, roses are red, violets are blue, I get a hundred grand for this, but I want you." Lady poet Claudette Colbert has fallen in love with her gentle kidnapper, bungling private eye **James Stewart**, who tries to prove his innocence in a murder case. *It's a Wonderful World* (1939, MGM).

7797 "It is easy to understand why the most beautiful poems about England in the spring were written by poets living in Italy at the time." Cynical **George Sanders** makes a valid point to widow writer Gene Tierney. *The Ghost and Mrs. Muir* (1947, 20th Century-Fox).

7798 "I shot an arrow in the air; she fell to earth in Berkeley Square." **Dennis Price** recites a bit of doggerel after he dispatches dear Aunt Agatha, played by Alec Guinness, by shooting down the air balloon she's riding in. *Kind Hearts and Coronets* (1949, GB, Ealing-GFD).

7799 "Strictly speaking, his life was his occupation. Yes, yes, Sebastian was a poet. That's what I meant when I said his life was his work because the work of a poet is the life of a poet, and, vice versa, the life of a poet is the work of a poet. I mean, you can't separate them. I mean, a poet's life is his work, and his work is his life in a special sense." **Katharine Hepburn** has some of the worst cases of excessive mother love seen in movies. She's speaking of her deceased son—whom she holds in greater awe than anyone or anything else. *Suddenly, Last Summer* (1959, Columbia).

7800 "'Because you took advantage/Because you took/Because you took advantage of my disadvantage.' Gee, that's a dang-blasted durn good poem you done there. . . .'When I stood Adam naked. . .' Oh, Adam-naked: You should be ashamed of yourself, captain. 'Before a Federal Law and its stinging stars.' Tarnation, you old horned toad, that's a mighty pretty. . . that's a pretty poem. 'Because you took advantage. . . ' Gee, it's getting repetitious, isn't it? 'Because. . . ' Here's another one—'Because you cheated me/ Because you took her at an age. . . when young lads. . . .'" **Peter Sellers** isn't very serious as he reads a poem that James Mason has forced into his hands, but the latter is deadly serious. *Lolita* (1962, GB, MGM).

7801 "Someday, they'll go down together;/They'll bury them side by side;/To few it'll be grief—/To the law a relief—/But it's death for Bonnie and Clyde." **Faye Dunaway** finishes reading her prophetic poem "The Story Of Bonnie and Clyde" to Warren Beatty. *Bonnie and Clyde* (1967, Warner Bros.).

7802 "This is really too poetic a way to die." Title character **Jane Fonda** is locked in a cage with starving birds. *Barbarella* (1968, Fr.-Ital., Paramount).

7803 "Well, I'll ya somethin', I got poetry in me. I do. . . she's frozen my soul, nothing but a whore, but what the hell, never was so much of a percentage man. A whore's about the only kind of woman I could have." Referring to Julie Christie, **Warren Beatty** delivers his final eloquent monologue. *McCabe and Mrs. Miller* (1971, Warner Bros.).

7804 LOU FRIEDLANDER: "We can walk on the moon and turn garbage into roses." SARAH GANTZ: "You're a poet!" New York columnist **Paul Sorvino** is complimented by ailing dancer **Anne Ditchburn** who has just moved into his building. *Slow Dancing in the Big City* (1978, United Artists).

7805 "Everyone who drinks is not a poet. Some of us drink because we are not poets." Alcoholic **Dudley Moore** corrects Jill Eikenberry who tries to put his drinking problem in a better light. *Arthur* (1981, Orion).

7806 "You probably won't think it's any good. . . It's the sort of poetry you can understand." Lower-class London hairdresser **Julie Walters** offers to bring her Open University tutor Michael Caine a book that she's been reading. *Educating Rita* (1983, GB, Rank).

7807 "Oh, it means getting the rhyme wrong." **Julie Walters** draws her own conclusion as to the meaning of the term assonance after being given examples by her tutor Michael Caine. (Assonance is a partial rhyme in which the accented vowel sounds correspond but the consonances differ as in swan and stone.) *Educating Rita* (1983, GB, Rank).

7808 "Excrement!. . . That's what I think of Mr. J. Evans Pritchard. . . . We're not laying pipe, we're talking about poetry. How can you describe poetry like 'American Bandstand'? 'I like Byron, I gave him a 42, but I can't dance to him.'. . . Now, I want you to rip out that page. . . go on, rip out the entire page. . . rip it out. . . I'll tell you what, don't just tear out that page, tear out the entire introduction. I want it gone, history, leave nothing of it. . . . Be gone, J. Evans Pritchard." Innovative, caring teacher **Robin Williams** tells his students to rip out the pompous and condescending introductory pages of their literature anthology. He could have told them to ignore it. Students don't read the introductions to texts anyway. *Dead Poets Society* (1989, Touchstone-Buena Vista).

7809 "We don't read and write poetry because it's cute. . . . We read and write poetry because we are members of the human race, and the human race is filled with passion. Medicine, law, business, engineering, these are noble pursuits and necessary to sustain life. . . but poetry, beauty, romance, love. . . these are what we stay alive for. To quote from Whitman, 'Oh, me, oh life of the questions of these recurring, of the endless trains of the faithless, of cities filled with the foolish; what good amid these. Oh, me, oh life?' The answer that you are here, and life exists and identity, and the powerful play goes on and you may contribute a verse... the powerful play goes on and you may contribute a verse...." As only exceptional teachers can, **Robin Williams** inspires his students by making them understand how important not only what they are learning is, but what they are contributing. *Dead Poets Society* (1989, Touchstone-Buena Vista).

7810 "Like a blanket that always leaves your feet cold... you kick, push it, stretch it, it'll never be enough. You kick at it, beat it, it'll never cover any of us, from the moment we enter crying to the moment we leave dying, it will just cover your face as you wail and cry and scream...." It's part of a spontaneous poem delivered in a frenzy by **Ethan Hawke**. *Dead Poets Society* (1989, Touchstone-Buena Vista).

Poisons

see also CURES, DEATH AND DYING, HARM, KILLINGS, SICKNESS

7811 "You're the sweetest poison that ever got into a man's blood. I love you! I want you!" Later, Mountie **Robert Preston** will want to kill half-breed Paulette Goddard. She demonstrates her love for him by tying him up and preventing him from warning or joining his comrades and being massacred by warring Indians. *Northwest Mounted Police* (1940, Paramount).

7812 "They're all poison sooner or later. Almost all." Goon **Don Costello** has no use for women—except for Veronica Lake with her "peek-a-boo" hairdo. *The Blue Dahlia* (1946, Paramount).

7813 "I'm poison—to myself and everybody around me!" Alluring, treacherous, immoral, femme fatale **Ava Gardner** gets that right in a tale of cross and double-cross. *The Killers* (1946, Universal-International).

7814 "Someone oughta put poison in her Epsom salts." **James Dean** doesn't love his nosy grandmother. *Rebel Without a Cause* (1955, Warner Bros.).

7815 "Never came poison from so sweet a place." Having murdered her husband, title character **Laurence Olivier** tries to woo Claire Bloom as Lady Anne. She spits in his face, wishing it was poison. *Richard III* (1956, GB, London Films).

7816 "I wonder what subtle form of manslaughter is next on the program. Am I going to be dropped into a vat of molten steel and become part of some

new skyscraper... or are you going to ask this... female to kiss me again and poison me to death?" **Cary Grant**'s anger with Eva Marie Saint almost blows her cover as an American agent to her villainous lover James Mason. *North by Northwest* (1959, MGM).

7817 MARGARET: "If you were my husband, I'd give you poison." BILLY: "If I were your husband, I'd take it." **Margaret Hamilton** and **Billy Gilbert** are among the inhabitants of a sleazy boarding house in a Grade-ZZZ film, produced, written, directed and starring Hugo Haas. *Paradise Alley* aka: *Stars in Your Backyard* (1962, Pathé-American).

7818 "At one time! At one time it was great what we had. The kidding around. It can't have a natural time span? Affairs can't dissolve in a good way? There's always got to be poison? I don't see why—I really don't see why." **Jack Nicholson** complains to his live-in lover Ann-Margret that the magic of their affair has turned poisonous. *Carnal Knowledge* (1971, Avco Embassy).

7819 "Yes, dear, I took the tablets an hour ago. I'll be gone by midnight." Eighty-year-old **Ruth Gordon** confides to her twenty-year-old lover Bud Cort that she has taken a fatal dose of poison. *Harold and Maude* (1971, Paramount).

Police

see also CRIME AND CRIMINALS, DETECTIVES AND DEDUCTION, LAWS

7820 "Either there are cops in *La Traviata* or the jig is up." Sitting in an opera box watching the performance, **Groucho Marx** comments when a horde of policeman suddenly descend on the stage. *A Night at the Opera* (1935, MGM).

7821 CRIMP: "Looks like we're taking the same plane, sister." PEGGY: "I don't talk to cops." CRIMP: "They been botherin' you lately?" Looks like police detective **John Carradine** and **Lucille Ball** won't be sitting next to each other on the clipper ship they are boarding. *Five Came Back* (1939, RKO).

7822 "The police force hasn't a monopoly on fallen arches, Dr. Barnes. Ask any chiropodist." **Alastair Sim**, as Inspector Cockrill, responds to surgeon Trevor Howard, who accuses the former of being "as insensitive as any flatfoot on the beat." *Green for Danger* (1946, GB, Rank).

7823 "A policeman's job is only easy in a police state." It's Mexican lawman **Charlton Heston**'s response to police detective Orson Welles' complaint that a policeman's job is tough enough without having to worry about the fine points of the law. *Touch of Evil* (1958, Universal-International).

7824 "Who ever heard of a Jewish cop? Everyone knows you gotta be Irish to get ahead on the force." **Eileen Heckart** berates her police detective son, George Segal. *No Way to Treat a Lady* (1968, Paramount).

7825 "Damn it, Dorothy, it's not just a uniform, it's a state of mind." Young cop **Stacy Keach** angrily answers his wife Jane Alexander who has had it with the demands of his career and spits out accusingly, "You like being a cop." *The New Centurions* (1972, Columbia).

7826 "You know the old story: when St. Patrick drove the snakes out of Ireland, they swam to New York and joined the police force." Saloon keeper **Fredric March** insults an Irish policeman. *The Iceman Cometh* (1973, American Film Theater).

7827 "If I say you're gonna be a cop, you're gonna be a cop." Reinstated to the police force, security guard **John Candy** insists that his partner Eugene Levy join him. *Armed and Dangerous* (1986, Columbia).

7828 "Tonight I'm not a cop—this is personal." After Patsy Kensit is murdered by South African drug dealers, **Mel Gibson** vows vengeance. *Lethal Weapon 2* (1989, Warner Bros.).

7829 "I want to be known as the environmental police lieutenant." As Lt. Frank Drebin, **Leslie Nielsen** wages war against the coal, oil and nuclear power companies. *The Naked Gun 2½ The Smell of Fear* (1991, Paramount).

7830 "I never really saw myself as a cop. I'm more like the bad guy. . . . I'm only going to stick around till I clean up the neighborhood." Smirking **Christian Slater** is recruited to a private law enforcement corps that works under the direction of the San Francisco police. *Kuffs* (1992, Universal).

Politeness *see* MANNERS

Politics and Politicians

see also GOVERNMENT, VOTING AND VOTERS

7831 "Politics? You couldn't get into politics. You couldn't get in anywhere. You couldn't get into the men's room at the Astor." **Jean Harlow** doesn't seem to be the kind of supportive, helpful wife Wallace Beery will need to succeed in politics. *Dinner at Eight* (1933, MGM).

7832 "Politics isn't women's business." **Edna May Oliver** advises Claudette Colbert to let men think of things like politics. *Drums Along the Mohawk* (1939, 20th Century-Fox).

7833 "Gentlemen and fellow citizens, I presume you know who I am. I'm plain Abraham Lincoln. My politics are short and sweet, like the old woman's dance." **Henry Fonda**, as the young Abe Lincoln, is on the campaign stump. *Young Mr. Lincoln* (1939, 20th Century-Fox).

7834 "They forget if it weren't for graft, you'd get a very low type of people in politics. Men with no ambition." Political flunky **William Demarest** defends the spoils system. *The Great McGinty* (1940, Paramount).

7835 "Peasants have no politics. We keep cows." **James Stewart** refuses Robert Young's demand that he become part of the "new Germany" and join the Nazi party. *The Mortal Storm* (1940, MGM).

7836 "Politics is a very peculiar thing, Woodrow. If they want you, they want you. They don't need reasons anymore. They find their own reasons. It's just like when a girl wants a man." Wise old **Harry Hayden** explains the peculiar nature of politics to young Eddie Bracken. All politicians wish they knew the trick of getting the people to want them. *Hail the Conquering Hero* (1944, Paramount).

7837 "What does it matter, a woman's politics? Women pick out what's in fashion and change it like a spring hat. Everything is forgiven the eternal female." As the German mistress of American Captain John Lund, **Marlene Dietrich** makes a biting reply when she's confronted with her notorious past affairs with high ranking Nazis. *A Foreign Affair* (1948, Paramount).

7838 "The only difference between Democrats and Republicans is that they're in and we're out." Cynical political hack **Adolphe Menjou** introduces would-be presidential candidate Spencer Tracy to political reality. It's more true today than ever. *State of the Union* (1948, MGM).

7839 "When I'm through with tennis, I'm going into politics." **Farley Granger** confides to the detectives assigned to keep an eye on him of his career plans. *Strangers on a Train* (1951, Warner Bros.).

7840 LADY BRACKNELL: "What are your politics?" JACK WORTHING: "Well, I'm afraid I have none—I'm a liberal." An exchange between **Edith Evans** and **Michael Redgrave** gets in Oscar Wilde's dig at the Liberal political party. *The Importance of Being Earnest* (1952, GB, Two Cities-Rank).

7841 "Politics is the greatest spectator sport in the country." Boston Mayor **Spencer Tracy** wants his nephew Jeffrey Hunter to experience an old fashioned political campaign. *The Last Hurrah* (1958, Columbia).

7842 "Now don't be stiff-necked about it. Politics is a practical profession. If a criminal has what you want, you do business with him." Roman Senator **Charles Laughton** sounds like a ward heeler talking to an idealistic young candidate as he tells young John Gavin, as Julius Caesar, how the game of politics is played. *Spartacus* (1960, Universal).

7843 "There is nothing like a dirty low-down political fight to put the roses in your cheeks." Former U.S. President **Lee Tracy** enjoys the fight between president hopefuls Henry Fonda and Cliff Robertson. *The Best Man* (1964, United Artists).

7844 "I need, Don Corleone, those politicians that you carry in your pocket like so many nickels and dimes." **Al Lettieri** seeks Marlon Brando's political clout for his planned excursion into the drugs racket. *The Godfather* (1972, Paramount).

7845 HUBBELL GARDINER: "I don't see how you do it." KATIE MOROSKY: "I don't know how you can't." The 'it' **Robert Redford** and **Barbra Streisand** are discussing is politics and the various causes so dear to Streisand's heart. *The Way We Were* (1973, Columbia).

7846 DR. EMMETT BROWN: "So, who's president of the U.S. in 1985?" MARTY MCFLY: "Ronald Reagan." BROWN: "Ronald Reagan, the actor? And who's vice president, Jerry Lewis?" **Christopher Lloyd** believes his visitor from the future **Michael J. Fox** is putting him on. *Back to the Future* (1985, Universal).

7847 "I detest politics, but I'm mad about the leading man." Drag queen **William Hurt** refers to the Nazi propaganda film he's describing to his cellmate Raul Julia. *Kiss of the Spider Woman* (1985, U.S.-Brazil, Island Alive).

7848 "Well, that's something I thought I'd never live to see, a politician with his hands in his own pockets." Innovative automobile manufacturer Preston Tucker, portrayed by **Jeff Bridges,** sneers at Senator Ferguson, played by Lloyd Bridges. The politician is in the pockets of the established automobile companies. *Tucker: The Man and His Dream* (1988, Paramount).

7849 "Finance is a gun. Politics is knowing when to pull the trigger." Powerful, corrupt businessman **Enzo Robutti** instructs Andy Garcia. *The Godfather, Part III* (1991, Paramount).

Popularity

see also APPLAUSE, LIKES AND DISLIKES

7850 JASMINE: "I never knew a woman who had so many gentlemen friends. You certainly know the way to a man's heart." RUBY CARTER: "Funny, too, because I don't know how to cook." Maid **Libby Taylor** admires **Mae West**'s popularity with men. *Belle of the Nineties* (1934, Paramount).

7851 "I was voted the boy most likely to succeed; you were the prettiest girl in the class. Something should happen to people like us." Insurance man **Dick Powell** complains to his wife Jane Wyatt about their averageness—they were so popular in high school. *Pitfall* (1948, United Artists).

7852 "Kit wanted to work in the feed lot, while I carried on with my studies. Little by little we fell in love. As I've never been popular in school and didn't have a lot of personality, I was surprised that he took such a liking to me, especially when he could have had any other girl if he'd given it half a try. . . I wasn't popular at school on account of having no personality and not being pretty." **Sissy Spacek**'s character isn't very bright either. Maybe garbage collector and mass murderer Martin Sheen likes her for her freckles. *Badlands* (1973, Columbia).

7853 "Popular? Nixon was popular. Hula hoops were popular. An epidemic of typhus is popular. Quantity doesn't imply quality." **Woody Allen** is on his soapbox again. *Annie Hall* (1977, United Artists).

7854 "I could name twenty guys that would kill to love me." Beautiful high school senior **Haviland Morris** has a high price for her favors. *Sixteen Candles* (1984, Universal).

7855 "We've been seeing a lot of each other lately, and I really think it's in my best interest if I went out with someone more popular." Fickle teen **Amanda Wyss** gives boy friend John Cusack the old heave-ho. *Better Off Dead* (1985, Warner Bros.).

7856 "I like art. I'm working at a gas station. My best friend is a tomboy. These things don't fly too high in the American high school." **Eric Stoltz** explains to his father John Ashton why he's not very popular. *Some Kind of Wonderful* (1987, Paramount).

7857 "These are the people I work with, and our job is being popular and shit." Teenager **Winona Ryder** informs rebellious hipster Christian Slater of the expectations of the leading girls in the high school. *Heathers* (1989, New World).

Possession (Supernatural)

see also DEATH AND DYING, DEVILS, LIFE AND DEATH, LIVES AND LIVING, SPIRIT AND SPIRITS

7858 "Do you believe that someone dead, someone out of the past, can take possession of a living person?" **Tom Helmore** sets up James Stewart. *Vertigo* (1958, Paramount).

7859 DANA BARRETT: "I want you inside me." PETER VENKMAN: "It seems there are at least two people inside you already." Possessed by a demon and dripping with lust, **Sigourney Weaver** demands that **Bill Murray** take her. *Ghostbusters* (1984, Columbia).

Possessions

see also BELONGING, OWNERSHIP

7860 "Bonds. They're all we saved. All we have left. Bonds!" Half-mad **Thomas Mitchell** shows his daughter Vivien Leigh his worthless Southern bonds, about all that's left of his beloved, ravaged plantation Tara. *Gone with the Wind* (1939, Selznick-MGM).

7861 "You brought nothing into the world and you're certainly taking nothing out." Cattleman and trail boss **John Wayne** wistfully eulogizes drover Noah Beery, Jr., killed in a cattle stampede. *Red River* (1948, United Artists).

7862 "The thought of you marrying that man. . . . Oh, I would have held back if your Cecil had been a different person—but he's the sort who can't know anyone intimately, least of all a woman. . . he doesn't know what a woman is. . . he wants you for a possession, something to look at, like a painting in an ivory box. . . something to own and display. . . he doesn't want you to be real and to think, and to live. . . he doesn't love you. . . but I love you. . . I want you to have thoughts and ideas and feelings, even when I hold you in my arms." **Julian Sands** makes an assessment of the appropriateness of himself and Helena Bonham Carter's fiancé Daniel Day-Lewis to become her husband. *A Room with a View* (1985, GB, Merchant-Ivory-Goldcrest).

7863 "Ah —they're only things. We still have each other." Lower-class Mrs. Miniver, **Sarah Miles** comforts her family after their home and possessions are destroyed by a German bomb during the London Blitz. *Hope and Glory* (1987, GB, Columbia).

Possibilities and Impossibilities

see also OPPORTUNITIES

7864 "As I live and hemstitch, she's impossible! Even I cannot make a peach melba from a prune." Dressmaker **George K. Arthur** gets his first look at Irish immigrant slum girl Colleen Moore. *Irene* (1926, silent, First National).

7865 "It can't be done. . . writing your name upside down and backwards without stopping." Bored **Cary Grant** complains at a bank board meeting. *Topper* (1937, MGM).

7866 "Are you hinting, Mr. Butler, that the Yankees can lick us?" **Rand Brooks** becomes indignant with Clark Gable during the discussion of the possibility of war as the gentlemen enjoy their cigars and brandy at a barbecue at Twelve Oaks. *Gone with the Wind* (1939, Selznick-MGM).

7867 "You mustn't think unkindly of her. She's made it possible for us to keep Tara always." **Ann Rutherford** gently chastises her sister Evelyn Keyes, who complains about their sister Vivien Leigh, who drives them like farm hands to bring back Tara to its pre-War eminence. *Gone with the Wind* (1939, Selznick-MGM).

7868 "I'm going to have to do the impossible. I'm going to have to surpass myself." Second-rate, but not in his own mind, Polish actor **Jack Benny** accepts a role which he realizes if not played perfectly could result in his death. He must impersonate a German spy. *To Be or Not to Be* (1942, United Artists).

7869 "I don't know if we will, but it's possible. Anything's possible!" As the steamer they are traveling on slowly sinks, hysterical Jennifer Jones asks **Humphrey Bogart** if they are going to survive. *Beat the Devil* (1954, United Artists).

7870 "L. Bernstein—seventy-eight dollars. That's impossible. The only L. Bernstein I know is Leonard Bernstein and I don't know Leonard Bernstein." **Debbie Reynolds** expresses shock to her ex-husband Barry Nelson as they review canceled checks. *Mary, Mary* (1963, Warner Bros.).

7871 "Impossible, I'm afraid. If I go I shall. . . drag you with me, and if I leave you here, well, I'm actually bound to stay and keep you company." Soldier **Terence Stamp** jests with Julie Christie at their first meeting. The hem of her gown is caught on his spur. She demands that he leave her alone. *Far from the Madding Crowd* (1967, GB, EMI).

7872 "Impossible is a word I don't retain you to use." Imperiously, **Eleanor Parker** demands that her attorney make a quick change in her will. *Eye of the Cat* (1969, Universal).

7873 "Is it possible for a woman to be Jewish and psychedelic at the same time?" **Maggie Thrett** says something profoundly meaningless. *Three in the Attic* (1969, AIP).

7874 "It's impossible to experience one's own death objectively and still carry a tune." It's difficult to argue with **Woody Allen**'s observation. *Love and Death* (1975, United Artists).

7875 "I don't know if this is a good time to ask, but would it be possible for me to get my briefcase back?" After the credits have rolled, "mad bomber" **Sonny Bono** makes an inquiry about the briefcase that held the bomb that put a space ship on a course to the sun. *Airplane II: The Sequel* (1982, Paramount).

Posterity *see* FUTURE

Poverty

see also HUNGER, MONEY, NEEDS AND NECESSITIES, WANTS AND WANTING, WEALTH AND RICHES

7876 "Oh, I realize it's a penny here and a penny there, but look at me. I've worked myself up from nothing to a state of extreme poverty." **Groucho Marx** brags about his financial prowess. *Monkey Business* (1931, Paramount).

7877 "Once I was so poor that I didn't know where my next husband was coming from." Gay Nineties saloon keeper **Mae West** quips. *She Done Him Wrong* (1933, Paramount).

7878 "I'm practically flat broke, not including the silverware." Heiress **Claudette Colbert** is wiped out by the stock market crash. *The Bride Comes Home* (1935, Paramount).

7879 "When you're poor, love flies out the window." Taxi driver **Don Ameche** sounds as if he's speaking from experience. *Midnight* (1939, Paramount).

7880 "To wit, that the greatest of our evils, and the worst of our crimes is poverty, and that our first duty, to which every other consideration must be sacrificed, is not to be poor." The movie's preface reflects author George Bernard Shaw's Fabian socialism. *Major Barbara* (1941, Pascal-Rank-United Artists).

7881 "Have you ever been in love with poverty like St. Francis? Have you ever been in love with dirt like St. Simeon? Have you ever been in love with disease and suffering like our nurses and philanthropists? Such passions are unnatural. This love of the common people may please an earl's granddaughter and a university professor, but I'm a poor man and a common man, and it has no romance for me. Leave it to the poor to pretend that poverty is a blessing. We know better than that. We three must stand together above the common people and help their children climb up beside us. Barbara must belong to us, not the Salvation Army." **Robert Morley** serves as playwright George Bernard Shaw's mouthpiece. In speaking to Rex Harrison and Wendy Hiller, he delivers Shaw's message to the audience. *Major Barbara* (1941, GB, Pascal-Rank-United Artists).

7882 "If you'll permit me to say so, the subject is not an interesting one. The poor know all about poverty, and only the morbid rich find the subject glamorous. You see, sir, rich people and theorists, who are usually rich people, think of poverty in the negative, as the lack of riches—as disease might be called the lack of health. But it isn't, sir. Poverty is not the lack of anything, but a positive plague, virulent in itself, contagious as cholera, with filth, criminality, vice and despair as only a few of its symptoms. It is to be stayed away from, even for the purpose of study. It is to be shunned." Butler **Robert Greig**, stand-in for writer-director Preston Sturges, elegantly corrects Joel McCrea's notion that there is nobility in poverty. *Sullivan's Travels* (1941, Paramount).

7883 "My sidekick—he's eccentric, he's poor." Having inherited wealth, **Robert Stack** seems to believe that his friend Rock Hudson has chosen his financial condition. *Written on the Wind* (1956, Universal-International).

7884 "Leo, he who hesitates is poor." Broadway producer **Zero Mostel** urges accountant Gene Wilder to join in a beautiful scheme to make money from a flop show. *The Producers* (1967, Embassy).

7885 "It's no shame to be poor, but it's no great honor either." Poor Jewish milkman **Topol** knows of where he speaks. *Fiddler on the Roof* (1971, United Artists).

7886 "I don't mind living in Watts, but do we have to live in the poorer section?" White **George Segal** quips to his mulatto son Denzel Washington, the product of a college romance with a now dead black woman. *Carbon Copy* (1981, RKO).

7887 "I was so poor, I had hand-me-down lunches." Romantic steel executive **Michael Nouri** fondly reminisces about his poverty. *Flashdance* (1983, Paramount).

7888 "I've always been sheltered and special. I just want to be anonymous, like everyone else. Well, here I am, anonymous, with guys nobody really cares about. . . . They are poor, they are the bottom of the barrel, and they know it. Maybe that's why they call themselves 'grunts.'" In a letter home, privileged **Charlie Sheen** writes of the typical American soldier in Vietnam, poor, black, uneducated, without any way to avoid doing his duty. *Platoon* (1986, Orion).

7889 "I am a rich man's son. But today I am as poor as any man. And when I killed the sheriff's men, I too became an outlaw." Poverty and a price on one's head being the prerequisites for joining the men of Sherwood Forest, **Kevin Costner** is qualified. *Robin Hood: The Prince of Thieves* (1991, Columbia).

7890 "The poor are poor, and one's sorry for them, but there it is." **Anthony Hopkin**s compassion for poor Sam West doesn't extend to helping him find a job. *Howards End* (1992, GB, Sony Pictures Classics).

Power

see also ABILITIES AND CAPABILITIES, AUTHORITIES, CONTROL, INFLUENCES AND TYRANTS, STRENGTHS, TYRANNY

7891 "The drugs I took seemed to light up my brain. Soon I realized the power I hold—the power to rule. . . . Power to walk into the gold vaults of the nations. . . into the secrets of kings. . . into the holy of holies. Power to make multitudes run screaming in terror at the touch of my little invisible finger. Even the moon's frightened of me—frightened to death, the whole world is frightened to death. . . . We'll begin with a reign of terror—a few murders here and there—murders of big men, murders of little men, just to show them that we make no distinctions. We might even wreck a train or two—just these fingers round a signalman's throat—that's all." **Claude Rains** uses the imperial "we" as the serum he takes to make him invisible turns him into a madman. *The Invisible Man* (1933, Universal).

7892 "I believe that a man lost in the mazes of his mind may imagine he's anything. Science has found many examples of the mind's power over the body, the case of stigmata appearing in the skin of

zealots." Dr. **Warren William** doesn't rule out anything when Lon Chaney, Jr. asks if he believes werewolves really exist. *The Wolf Man* (1941, Universal).

7893 "The power to kill can be just as satisfying as the power to create. You know I'd never do anything unless I did it perfectly." Psychopath **John Dall** easily manipulates his weak-willed lover Farley Granger. *Rope* (1948, Warner Bros.).

7894 LT. HEARN: "How do you think the enlisted men feel when they see us eating meat?" GEN. CUMMINGS: "They don't hate us; they fear us. The morality of the future is power morality. Power can only flow from the top down." Idealistic **Cliff Robertson** is taught an object lesson by **Raymond Massey** who throws a cigarette to the ground and orders Robertson to pick it up or be court-martialed. Robertson picks up the butt. *The Naked and the Dead* (1958, Warner Bros.).

7895 "Power is as exciting as love, I discover." Anne Boleyn, portrayed by **Genevieve Bujold** would have been better off if she hadn't made the discovery. *Anne of the Thousand Days* (1969, Universal).

7896 "Well, you have a choice. You can either feel lonely—you know, the hate—or—so you take a call and you go to a hotel room and there's some John you've never seen before, but he wants you. He must, he's paying for it. And usually they're nervous and that's all right too, because you're not; you know this thing. And then for awhile, boy, they really pay attention, you're all there is. And it's not real and you don't even like them—you can even hate them, it's all right, it's safe—you know?" Call girl **Jane Fonda** describes the power and control she feels in her work to her psychiatrist Vivian Nathan. *Klute* (1971, Warner Bros.).

7897 "If you strike me down, I shall become more powerful than you can possibly imagine. . . ." Jedi Knight Ben Kenobi, played by **Alec Guinness**, duels with Darth Vader. *Star Wars* (1977, 20th Century-Fox).

7898 "We are not interested in the good of others; we are interested solely in power. . . . The object of power is power." Interrogator **Richard Burton**, in his last role, levels with victim John Hurt. *1984* (1984, GB, Umbrella-Rosenblum-Virgin).

7899 "Without power in this country, no man is a real man." Revolutionary prisoner **Raul Julia** warms to his homosexual cellmate John Hurt. *Kiss* *of the Spider Woman* (1985, U.S.-Brazil, Island Alive).

7900 "Stock and real estate speculation. It's bull shit. You got ninety percent of the American public out there with little or no net worth. I create nothing. . . I own. . . . We make the rules, pal. The news, war, peace, famine, upheaval, a plant for paper clips. . . you're not naïve enough to think we're living in a democracy, are you, buddy?" Wall Street manipulator **Michael Douglas** boasts that people like him run the world. *Wall Street* (1987, 20th Century-Fox).

7901 "In today's world, it seems the power to absolve debt is greater than the power of forgiveness." Dishonest Vatican bank Archbishop **Donal Donnelly** confides to Mafia don Al Pacino. *The Godfather, Part III* (1990, Paramount).

7902 "Never, ever let an attractive woman hold a power position in your home." There would be no movie or suspense if Annabella Sciorra paid attention to **Julianne Moore**'s warning about hiring attractive Rebecca De Mornay as a nanny. *The Hand That Rocks the Cradle* (1992, Hollywood Pictures-Buena Vista).

Practices

see also HABITS, LEARNING AND LESSONS, PERFORMANCES, USES AND USING

7903 "I haven't had much practice, but I can kiss a man." At the time that twenty-year-old **Lana Turner** said this to Clark Gable, millions of men would have volunteered to practice with her. *Honky Tonk* (1941, MGM).

7904 MICKEY: "How can you be such a tramp?" VIVIANE: "I've had lots of practice. I was lucky enough to start very young, so it's become second nature." Disc jockey **Coluche** questions ever flirtatious adorable **Isabelle Huppert**. *My Best Friend's Girl* (1984, Fr., European International).

7905 "Percy and Byron preach free love—I practice it." In 1818 England, lovely, enticing **Bridget Fonda** as Mary Godwin, soon to be the author of *Frankenstein,* seduces John Hurt, a visitor from the future. *Frankenstein Unbound* (1990, 20th Century-Fox).

7906 "Can't get the hang of it, eh?" Private detective **Kathleen Turner** zaps Charles McCaughan who boasts he's slept with over 500 women. *V.I. Warshawski* (1991, Hollywood Pictures-Buena Vista).

Praises

see also APPLAUSE, BOASTS AND BRAGGING, COMPLIMENTS, FLATTERY

7907 "Father, talk to him about me—you know me so well, it will not be immodest of you to praise me a little." Plain, shy **Olivia de Havilland** begs her stern, insensitive father Ralph Richardson to say something nice about her to her suitor Montgomery Clift in this drama about a woman embittered by love. Poor de Havilland doesn't know her father very well—he holds her in low regard. *The Heiress* (1949, Paramount).

7908 "Praise the Lord—another convert." Religious fanatic and medical whiz **Danny Nelson** runs a "body shop" where he lops off parts of humans and sells them to broker Ray Walston. He's just chloroformed his latest victim. *Blood Salvage* (1990, Magnum).

Prayers

see also CONFESSIONS, GOD, RELIGIONS, REQUESTS, THANKS AND THANKFULNESS, WORSHIP

7909 "Even as thine arms were spread upon the cross, so receive me into the arms of mercy, and forgive my sins." Title character **Katharine Hepburn** prays before laying her head on the executioner's block. *Mary of Scotland* (1936, RKO).

7910 "I want to thank God, Tim. What do I say?" Barbary Coast saloon keeper **Clark Gable** asks priest Spencer Tracy how to pray after he discovers that his love Jeanette MacDonald has survived the San Francisco earthquake of 1906. *San Francisco* (1936, MGM).

7911 "And please make every little boy and girl in the world as happy as I am." At the end of the film, **Shirley Temple** offers an unselfish prayer. *Heidi* (1937, 20th Century-Fox).

7912 "Okay, boys. Let's go say a prayer for a boy who couldn't run as fast as I could." Priest **Pat O'Brien** leads a group of down-cast juvenile delinquent would-bes to church to pray for their hero, James Cagney, who went to the electric chair screaming and begging for mercy. *Angels with Dirty Faces* (1938, Warner Bros.)

7913 "Well, Sir, here we are again." **Lionel Barrymore** respectfully begins his prayer to the Lord. *You Can't Take It with You* (1938, Columbia).

7914 "Father, I have been talking to your boss." Dying agnostic soldier **James Cagney** tells Chaplain

Pat O'Brien that he's been praying. *The Fighting 69th* (1940, Warner Bros.).

7915 "I lost the call. But, boy, I sure used to have it. I'd get an irrigation ditch so squirmin' full of repented sinners I pretty near drowned half of 'em. But not no more. I lost the spirit. At the meetin's I used to get the girls glory-shoutin' till they about passed out. Then I go to comfort 'em. . . and end up by lovin' 'em. I'd feel bad, and pray, an' pray, but it didn't do no good. Next time, do it again. I figured there just warn't no hope for me." Self-ordained preacher **John Carradine** recalls some occupational hazards. *The Grapes of Wrath* (1940, 20th Century-Fox).

7916 "Don't bother me, I'm praying." As he stares at six glasses of straight Scotch set before him, financier **Charles Ruggles** has no time for the problems of actress Rosalind Russell. *No Time for Comedy* (1940, Warner Bros.).

7917 "By prayer, I don't mean shouting and mumbling and wallowing like a hog in religious sentiment. Prayer is only another name for good, clean, direct thinking. When you pray, think. Think well what you're saying, and make your thoughts into things that are solid. In that way, your prayer will have strength, and that strength will become a part of you in body, mind and spirit." Welsh preacher **Walter Pidgeon** sounds like a good Unitarian as he instructs Roddy McDowall in how to pray. *How Green Was My Valley* (1941, 20th Century-Fox).

7918 "Bernadette, pray for me." Atheistic village prosecutor **Vincent Price**, who once tried to have Jennifer Jones as Bernadette of Lourdes confined to a madhouse, gets religion when he learns he's dying of cancer. *The Song of Bernadette* (1943, 20th Century-Fox).

7919 "I pray for guidance and blush when I get it." Washington, D.C. widow **Katharine Hepburn** suggests a platonic marriage to misogynous scientist Spencer Tracy because of the wartime housing shortage. The results are predictable. *Without Love* (1945, MGM).

7920 "Get me back. Get me back. I don't care what happens to me. Get me back to my wife and kids. Help me, Clarence. Please. Please. I want to live again. I want to live again. I want to live again. Please, God, let me live again." Having seen the consequences of having never existed, **James Stewart** prays for the chance to appreciate his life for what it was rather than worry about what it was not. *It's a Wonderful Life* (1946, RKO)

7921 "Father, could you send up a prayer for me and Cora and if you can find it in your heart, make it so we're together. . . wherever it is?" Waiting in his death cell, **John Garfield** makes a final request of the prison chaplain. *The Postman Always Rings Twice* (1946, MGM).

7922 "Dear God, we've come to the end of our journey. In a little while, we will stand before You. I pray for You to be merciful. Judge us not for our weakness but for our love, and open the doors of heaven for Charlie and me." **Katharine Hepburn** prays for herself and Humphrey Bogart prior to their expected hanging by the Germans. *The African Queen* (1951, United Artists).

7923 "'God, grant me the serenity to accept the things I cannot change, courage to change the things I can and wisdom to know the difference.'" Alcoholic **Burt Lancaster** quotes the prayer of Alcoholic's Anonymous for his wife Shirley Booth. *Come Back, Little Sheba* (1952, Paramount).

7924 "We all have a secret prayer that the other fellow will crash so that we can get on top." Monte Carlo rally racer **Kirk Douglas** and his colleagues have unworthy prayers. *The Racers* (1955, 20th Century-Fox).

7925 "And Jesus said, 'I am the resurrection and the life. He that believeth in me though he were dead yet shall he live and whosoever liveth and believeth in me shall never die.' Blessed be the God and Father of our Lord Jesus Christ. Father of mercies and God of all comforts. Comfort us in all our afflictions that we may be able to comfort them that are in any affliction with the comfort wherewith we ourselves are comforted. Hear my prayer, oh, Lord, and with thine eyes consider my calling." Cavalry scout **Jeff Chandler,** a literal voice in the wilderness, prays to God when his words of reason are ignored and bloodshed occurs on Indian territory. *Pillars of the Sky* (1956, Universal).

7926 "Because we are small and frightened and ignorant." When death comes to his castle to collect him, Knight Antonius Block, portrayed by **Max von Sydow** prays to God for mercy. *The Seventh Seal* (1956, Sweden, Svensk Filmindustri).

7927 "Hey, Lord! Can you hear me up there, Jesus? You didn't think we'd forget your birthday, did you, boy? There you are, Jesus—and if I had any more you'd be welcome to it." Drunken salesman **Burt Lancaster** helps collect money from other speakeasy customers on Christmas Eve for nuns begging funds for an orphanage. *Elmer Gantry* (1960, United Artists).

7928 "Thinking is a kind of prayer, isn't it?" **Eva Marie Saint** inquires of her Episcopal minister husband Richard Burton. *The Sandpiper* (1965, MGM).

7929 "Almighty God, look down with pity on this miserable company of sinners, conceived in lust, delivered in evil and slaves to every loathing appetite the flesh is heir to. We have held fast against atheism, Romanism, Unitarianism and a score of lesser evils, and we thank thee that thou has chosen one of us to carry the holy word and precious light of John Calvin to the wicked and benighted heathen of Hawaii." **Carroll O'Connor** intones a proud prayer before his daughter Julie Andrews and her missionary husband Max von Sydow sail for Hawaii and their mission to convert the heathen. Von Sydow is one of the few such missionaries to remain true to his calling. Many others are said to have gone to Hawaii to do good and did well by becoming wealthy landowners. *Hawaii* (1966, United Artists).

7930 "Hey, old man, you home tonight?. . . I know I ain't got no call to ask for much. But even so, you got to admit you ain't dealt me no cards in a long time. You got things fixed so I can't never win. . . . You made me like I am. Just where am I supposed to fit in? What you got in mind for me? What do I do now?" Prisoner **Paul Newman** uses a familiar tone in addressing God, whom he seems to blame for his troubles and the way he is. *Cool Hand Luke* (1967, Warner Bros.).

7931 "I musta said a million 'Hail Marys' to get out of a neighborhood just like this." **Barbara McNair** has bad recollections as she wanders into a ghetto neighborhood to work as a nurse with two other undercover nuns. *Change of Habit* (1969, Universal).

7932 "You have decided that the human beings will not walk a road that leads nowhere." **Chief Dan George** believes that the Great Spirit will guide his tribe of Cheyenne. *Little Big Man* (1970, National General).

7933 "It hurts very bad to leave you. My prayer for ya is that the river is good to you in the crossing." Teacher **Jon Voight** says farewell to the black students he taught on a small island off the coast of South Carolina. *Conrack* (1974, 20th Century-Fox).

7934 "Oh, God, please let me get hit by a rich man in a Rolls-Royce." Out-of-work dancer **Marsha Mason** looks for a good break. *The Goodbye Girl* (1977, Warner Bros.).

7935 "We've come full circle, Lord. I'd like to believe there's some higher purpose in all this. . . . It would certainly reflect well on you." Sly young 13th century thief **Matthew Broderick** respectfully prays to God, but lets a hint of impatience creep in. *Ladyhawke* (1985, Warner Bros.).

7936 "When the gods want to punish you, they answer your prayers." **Meryl Streep** expresses her concern at the time that Robert Redford agrees to move in with her at her farm. *Out of Africa* (1985, Universal).

7937 "Lord, bless this clock, keep it accurate. Thank you for sending us a man who believed he could make such a thing and in the making of it, could inspire and unite us. Thank you for suggesting to him that he could make my daughter happy. One is as silly as the other, Lord. Neither one of them does anything the regular way, so help them, Lord. These two need more help than most to find in each other a future to cherish." **Lloyd Bridges** prays for clockmaker Kurt Russell and his daughter Kellie McGillis. *Winter People* (1989, Columbia).

Preaching *see* PRAYERS, PRIESTS, RELIGIONS, TEACHING AND TEACHERS

Predestination *see* FATE AND DESTINY

Predicaments *see* PROBLEMS

Predictions

see also FUTURE, PROPHECIES AND PROPHETS, VISIONS AND VISUALIZATIONS

7938 ALAN: "How long do I have to live?" CESARE: "Until dawn." **Hans Heinz von Twardowski** doesn't care for the answer to the question he puts to somnambulist **Conrad Veidt**, but the prediction is accurate. *The Cabinet of Dr. Caligari* (1919, Germany, Delca-Bioscop).

7939 "You're me forty years from now." Prostitute **Greta Garbo** sees her future in the face of old wreck Marie Dressler. *Anna Christie* (1930, MGM).

7940 "And if Fu Manchu wields the gold scimitar and puts the golden mask across his face, he will declare himself Genghis Khan come to life again, and all Asia will rise." **Lewis Stone** warns of the "yellow menace" in the person of Boris Karloff as the evil Oriental genius Fu Manchu. *The Mask of Fu Manchu* (1932, MGM).

7941 "Someday you're going to fall down in the gutter—right where the horses have been standing—right where you belong!" Police inspector **C. Henry Gordon** makes a prediction for mobster Paul Muni. *Scarface* (1932, United Artists).

7942 "Carnage is imminent and I'm due to be among the fallen." World-weary traveling poet **Leslie Howard** prophesizes his death. *The Petrified Forest* (1936, Warner Bros.).

7943 "If the cops nail him, he'll get a hundred years. . . maybe life." Gun moll **Ann Sothern** speaks of mobster Humphrey Bogart. *Brother Orchid* (1940, Warner Bros.).

7944 "One day, two weeks from now, we'll be riding in the hills. . . and the sunset will be so beautiful I'll be overcome and have to get off my horse to admire it." Con woman **Barbara Stanwyck** anticipates the moment she will arrange for rich sucker Henry Fonda to propose to her. *The Lady Eve* (1941, Paramount).

7945 "She'll be back!" Sympathetic warden **Agnes Moorehead** sadly comments on Eleanor Parker who is leaving prison, where she changed from an innocent 19-year-old to a hardened con. *Caged* (1950, Warner Bros.).

7946 "I'll probably walk down an aisle and wind up in a suburb with a husband, a mortgage, and children." **Lauren Bacall** makes the prediction for herself at her initial meeting with wealthy Texas oil baron Robert Stack. She marries Stack, but can't forget friend of the family Rock Hudson. *Written on the Wind* (1957, Universal).

7947 "Men without faces tend to get elected president, and power or responsibility or personal honor fill in the features." Unsuccessful in his attempt to win his party's nomination for president of the United States, **Henry Fonda** makes a hopeful statement as he watches the dark horse who has won the endorsement enter the convention center. *The Best Man* (1964, United Artists).

7948 "Hyman Roth will never see the New Year." **Al Pacino**'s prediction to his brother John Cazale is correct. Lee Strasberg is gunned down at an airport by Pacino's goons. *The Godfather, Part II* (1974, Paramount).

7949 "You're nowhere on your way to no place." Upwardly mobile **Karen Lynn Gorney** sizes up teenage Brooklyn paint store clerk John Travolta. *Saturday Night Fever* (1977, Paramount).

7950 "Some day your dick is going to lead you into a very big hassle." Attorney **Ted Danson** makes an accurate prediction in the case of his friend, dimwitted lawyer William Hurt. *Body Heat* (1981, Warner Bros.).

7951 "You are not special enough to overcome a bad marriage." Plain speaking **Shirley MacLaine** disapproves of her daughter Debra Winger's marriage to teacher Jeff Daniels. *Terms of Endearment* (1983, Paramount).

7952 "I guess you guys aren't ready for that yet, but your kids are gonna love it." While visiting thirty years into the past, teenager **Michael J. Fox** essentially invents rock 'n' roll a few years before its time. *Back to the Future* (1985, Universal).

7953 "You'll be dead in a year. . . . You hear what I'm saying. . . you'll be dead within a year." Principal Joe Clark, portrayed by **Morgan Freeman** predicts the dismal future of an amicable student who's dropping out of school to pursue a career as a drug dealer. *Lean on Me* (1989, Warner Bros.).

7954 "I'll give 'em six months, four if she cooks." **Dianne Wiest** estimates the duration of her teenage daughter Martha Plimpton's marriage to shiftless Keanu Reeves. *Parenthood* (1989, Universal).

7955 "I would be all right for a while. But then you'd just end up calling me a self-centered bastard and scream and pull your hair out and say 'I never want to see you again.'" **Tom Hanks** looks to the future for reasons for not getting involved with Mare Winningham. *Turner and Hooch* (1989, Touchstone-Buena Vista).

Preferences

see also OFFERS, PRIORITIES, WORTH AND VALUES

7956 "No, thank you, I prefer being in distress." Having taken shelter in a deserted band pavilion when caught in a rain storm, **Ginger Rogers** refuses to be rescued by Fred Astaire, who offers to pick her up in his cab. *Top Hat* (1935, RKO).

7957 "I do so prefer these things to my subjects. I have only to turn a key and they do what I want. So often my subjects refuse to do what I want and I have to have their heads cut off." Sultan **Miles Malleson** tells evil wizard Conrad Veidt that he prefers his mechanical toys to his people. *The Thief of Bagdad* (1940, GB, London Films).

7958 "I'd rather do anything than keep still." **Bette Davis** refuses to sit through a movie with George Brent and Olivia de Havilland. *In This Our Life* (1942, Warner Bros.).

7959 "I guess you can't blame a girl for preferring soldiers to civilians. Maybe it would be different if we had uniforms." Four-F **Eddie Bracken** tries to be understanding of Betty Hutton's preference for the military. *The Miracle of Morgan's Creek* (1944, Paramount).

7960 "I'd rather be digging egg shells out of garbage cans than try to get information out of you. . . . You're not a detective, you're a slot machine. You'd slit your own throat for six bits, plus tax." Police detective **Don Douglas** doesn't have a high opinion of private eye Dick Powell. *Murder, My Sweet* (1945, RKO).

7961 "A few minutes ago I liked Jerry better, but now I like you better. It's funny how men change." Teenager **Shirley Temple** finds men to be so fickle. First there was young Johnny Sands that made her heart go pitter-patter and now it's older man Cary Grant. *The Bachelor and the Bobbysoxer* (1947, RKO).

7962 "Well, thank you, Harvey. I prefer you, too." At the end of the movie, lovable lunatic **James Stewart** is reunited with his best friend, an imaginary six-foot-three rabbit. *Harvey* (1950, Universal).

7963 "My immaculate wife. I thought you were everything good and pure. I'd rather go to jail for twenty years than find my wife was a tramp." Pathological self-righteous police detective **Kirk Douglas** discovers he was not his wife Eleanor Parker's first man. *Detective Story* (1951, Paramount).

7964 "I'd much rather prosecute. . . ." Naval lawyer **Jose Ferrer** sees little glory in defending Van Johnson and Robert Francis against a charge of mutiny, but he reluctantly takes the case. *The Caine Mutiny* (1954, Columbia).

7965 "You'd rather kill a man than love a girl." Sheriff **Sterling Hayden** accuses hired presidential assassin Frank Sinatra of making a strange choice. *Suddenly* (1954, United Artists).

7966 "I'd rather have a hundred Jeremiahs. You can't cuddle up to diamonds." **Jesse Royce Landis** speaks to her daughter Grace Kelly about her deceased husband for whom she'd gladly trade all her jewels. *To Catch a Thief* (1955, Paramount).

7967 "I don't want to go to jail. I'd rather stay with you." Thief and embezzler **Tippi Hedren** chooses the lesser of two evils, Sean Connery, who tricked her into marrying him and attempted to cure her frigidity by rape. *Marnie* (1964, Universal).

7968 "Some of us prefer Austrian voices raised in song to ugly German threats." Austrian baron **Christopher Plummer** refuses to go along with the Nazi sympathizers in his country. *The Sound of Music* (1965, 20th Century-Fox).

7969 "This woman is more to me, dead as she is. . . than you ever were, or are, or could be." **Ter-ence Stamp** tells his wife Julie Christie that even in death he prefers his mistress Prunella Ransome, who lies in a coffin with their baby. *Far from the Madding Crowd* (1967, GB, MGM).

7970 "How do you want to make it—like this?" Thirteen-year-old streetwalker **Jodie Foster**, wearing hot pants, halter top, and platform shoes, is anxious to get down to business with customer Robert De Niro. He only wants to protect her. *Taxi Driver* (1976, Columbia).

7971 NELL POTTER: "Why can't you have a nice office and treat ordinary neurotics like everyone else?" DAN POTTER: "I guess I just prefer psychopaths." Shrink's wife **Deborah Hedwall** and husband **Dwight Schultz** have a little spat about his work. *Alone in the Dark* (1982, New Line Cinema).

7972 "I'd rather be a killer than a victim." Reluctant cop of the future, **Harrison Ford** speaks his mind at the beginning of the film. His assignment is to track down and kill a group of human-like robots whose usefulness has come to an end. *Blade Runner* (1982, Warner Bros.).

7973 "The monologue is his preferred mode of discourse." **Sonja Smits** refers to TV programmer James Woods, a closet voyeur of sex and violence. *Videodrome* (1983, Canada, Universal).

7974 "I'd rather be a thief than do what you do for a living." Iowa farm wife **Jessica Lange** sneers disgustingly to a banker. For some of the savings and loan officials, the terms thief and banker seem synonymous. *Country* (1984, Touchstone-Buena Vista).

7975 "You mean you'd rather do nothing than go out with me?" **Anthony Edwards** has a hard time accepting the rejection of a date offer by pretty coed Christie Claridge, who admits she has no plans for Saturday night. *Gotcha!* (1985, Universal).

7976 "We'd rather eat our children than part with money." **Jack Nicholson** convinces Kathleen Turner to return the money she's stolen from a Mafia family. *Prizzi's Honor* (1985, ABC-20th Century-Fox).

7977 "I'd stick pins in my eyeballs before I'd let that woman fool with me." **Christopher Walken** expresses his doubts about shrink Frances Sternhagen to his wife Lindsay Crouse. *Communion* (1989, Vestron).

7978 "Let's put it to you this way, I'd rather have a case of clap than a case of this wine." **Lloyd Bridges** is quite candid in responding to William

Petersen, who asks him how he likes a wine ordered by Petersen. *Cousins* (1989, Paramount).

7979 SHIRLEY: "What would you rather have. . . a boy or a girl?" CYRIL: "I'd rather have a hot poker up my arse." **Ruth Sheen** and **Philip Davis** have made contraceptiveless love and have different hopes for the outcome. *High Hopes* (1989, GB, Skouras).

7980 "I'd rather you cut straighter and care less." Physician **William Hurt**, claims empathy for patients interferes with the technical demands of a surgeon. He tells a colleague what he'd say if he needed surgery. Shortly thereafter he gets the opportunity to test his convictions when he is diagnosed with life-threatening cancer. He finds being treated as no more than a number to be demeaning and believes that it jeopardizes his chances of recovery. *The Doctor* (1991, Touchstone-Buena Vista).

7981 "I'd rather chew glass." **Mandy Patinkin**, as French poet and dramatist Alfred de Musset, states his preference when someone suggests that he still lusts after Judy Davis as novelist George Sand. *Impromptu* (1991, Hemdale).

7982 "One day with the top down is better than a lifetime in a box." Sexy teen **Drew Barrymore** tells Cheryl Ladd why she drives her red Corvette in the rain with the top down. *Poison Ivy* (1992, New Line).

Pregnancies

see also BABIES, CHILDREN AND CHILDHOOD, MARRIAGES, MEN AND WOMEN, MOTHERS, PARENTS, PROBLEMS, WOMEN

7983 "I get pregnant if we drink from the same cup." **Ellen Burstyn** tells her once-a-year lover Alan Alda that with her husband she's very fertile. *Same Time, Next Year* (1978, Universal).

7984 "I'm pregnant." **Dianne Wiest** makes a happy announcement to a delighted Woody Allen. *Hannah and Her Sisters* (1985, Orion).

7985 "This is no reflection on you, but I'm not ready to cash in my chips. Don't worry, I'll split all the costs right down the line—50-50." Shortly after learning that Rosanna Arquette is pregnant, **Jim Youngs** does split. *Nobody's Fool* (1986, Island Pictures).

7986 "She ain't pregnant, she's just fat." **Burt Young** denies that his fat daughter Ricki Lake is pregnant—even though she's in her eighth month. *Last Exit to Brooklyn* (1990, W. German-Cinecom).

Prejudices

see also BLACKS, HATE AND HATRED, JEWS, JUDGMENTS, RELIGION, SUSPICIONS AND SUSPECTS

7987 "We're the victims of a foul disease called social prejudice, my child. . . . These dear ladies of the Law And Order League are scouring out the dregs of town. Come on, be a proud, glorified dreg like me." Alcoholic doctor **Thomas Mitchell** greets prostitute Claire Trevor, who is being escorted by a committee of unhappy looking townswomen to the stagecoach that will take them both from Tonto, New Mexico. *Stagecoach* (1939, United Artists).

7988 "It's detestable, but that's the way it is. It's even worse in New Canaan. There, nobody can sell or rent to a Jew. And even in Darien where Jane's house is and my house is, there's sort of a gentlemen's agreement when you. . . ." **Dorothy McGuire** represents the otherwise good people who contribute to prejudicial behavior by accepting it in others, without speaking out against it. *Gentlemen's Agreement* (1947, 20th Century-Fox).

Preparations

7989 "Put it on his ears, his nose, his mouth, put it every place on him, every place." Brutal title character **Wallace Beery** orders Joseph Schildkraut be covered with honey and staked out for ants to eat. *Viva Villa!* (1934, Selznick-MGM).

7990 "Something tells me you weren't ready to leave Columbus!" **Rosalind Russell** sighs to her dewy-eyed, innocent-looking sister Janet Blair, who attracts every man in sight. *My Sister Eileen* (1942, Columbia).

7991 KAREN HOLMES: "I've got a bathing suit under my dress." MILTON WARDEN: "Me too." It's a bit of dialogue leading up to one of the most spectacular kissing scenes in the movies. **Deborah Kerr** and **Burt Lancaster** get into a stretched-out embrace and kiss as the waves roll over them. *From Here to Eternity* (1953, Columbia).

7992 "Remove the earth woman; prepare her for our pleasure." **Max von Sydow**, as Ming the Merciless, orders Melody Anderson, as Dale Arden, to be made ready for some sexual shenanigans. *Flash Gordon* (1980, GB, EMI).

7993 "Here I am, ready for another disaster!" Postulant **Genevieve Bujold** shows up for another tryst with her lover Christopher Reeve. She doesn't know he's a priest. *Monsignor* (1982, 20th Century-Fox).

7994 "Are you ready for me?" Beautiful young underwearless hooker **Rebecca De Mornay** asks a silly question of horny seventeen-year-old Tom Cruise. The two later go into business, bringing together Cruise's affluent teenage friends and De Mornay's coterie of hookers. *Risky Business* (1983, Warner Bros.).

Prerequisites

see also CONDITIONS, FIRSTS, NEEDS AND NECESSITIES

7995 "You can't have a wedding without a reiteach, and you can't have a reiteach without the whisky." **Wylie Watson** gives Bruce Seton an ultimatum: if he wishes to marry Watson's daughter Joan Greenwood, there must be a traditional betrothal feast for which a seven-gallon jug of whisky is required. Constable Seton is guarding the only available whisky that was salvaged from a ship stranded off the Hebrides island of Todday [sic]. *Whisky Galore* aka: *Tight Little Island* (1949, GB, Ealing-Rank).

7996 "If I am to continue my work, human bodies must be obtained—at any cost." Early 19th century London physician **Timothy Dalton** makes deals with grave robbers to obtain cadavers for his experiments. *The Doctor and the Devils* (1985, GB, 20th Century-Fox).

7997 "When you know how to love, you'll know how to pitch." Baseball groupie **Susan Sarandon** imparts her quirky and self-serving wisdom to erratic minor league baseball pitcher Tim Robbins, who is as undisciplined in bed as he is on the pitcher's mound. *Bull Durham* (1988, Orion).

7998 "I'll put a tie on the day they machine gun the royal family." What would it take to get scraggly **Philip Davis** to get a haircut and trim his beard? *High Hopes* (1989, GB, Skouras).

Presents *see* GIFTS AND GIVING

Pressures *see* INFLUENCES

Pretensions

see also DECEPTIONS, FAKES, HYPOCRISY, IMAGINATION

7999 "I'm a regular knight-errant. These gowns are my coat of female." **Julian Eltinge** disguises himself as Countess Raffelski to retaliate against a family that has prevented him from seeing their daughter. *The Countess Charming* (1917, silent, Paramount).

8000 "When you're seventy... about all the fun you have left is pretending there aren't any facts to face." **Beulah Bondi** responds poignantly to her granddaughter Barbara Read who tells her to "face facts." *Make Way for Tomorrow* (1937, Paramount).

8001 "I never believe in making pretenses. Lots of men who have separated from their wives simply let it be understood that they are not married. I believe, in this day and age, that a man can have a home on the one hand and still live his own life—that is, any man of character." Broadway producer **Adolphe Menjou** feels that being open about his selfish ways justifies his lecherous life. *Stage Door* (1937, RKO).

8002 "Listen to them. Bluffing themselves, pretending death doesn't mean anything to them, trying to live just for the minute, the hour, pretending they don't care if they go up tomorrow and never come back." Squadron Commander **Basil Rathbone** speaks of his young World War I pilots waiting for their next and perhaps last mission. *The Dawn Patrol* (1938, Warner Bros.).

8003 "Hey, flatfoot! I'm gonna unbutton my puss and shoot the woiks. An' I wouldn't be squealin' if he hadn't a give me the runaround for another twist." **Katharine Hepburn** affects a tough Brooklyn accent and claims that Cary Grant is a much wanted criminal. *Bringing Up Baby* (1938, RKO).

8004 "Maybe you think it's improper for an old man to have a young, desirable wife. I've played a little game with myself. I—I've pretended that she would have become my wife, even if I'd been unable to give her wealth. I've enjoyed pretending that. It's given me great happiness." **Miles Mander** admits to Dick Powell that he must pretend about Claire Trevor's love. *Murder, My Sweet* (1944, RKO).

8005 "I want you to like me. I want you to think I'm nineteen, with a white dress, a girl who has never been kissed before." Hardened Resistance fighter **Lilli Palmer** wants to experience a fantasy with O.S.S. agent Gary Cooper. *Cloak and Dagger* (1946, United States Pictures).

8006 "If I ever run into any of you bums on a street corner, just pretend we never met before." Unpopular **William Holden** flings the farewell to his fellow POWs as he begins his escape from a German camp. *Stalag 17* (1953, Paramount).

8007 "We put up a wonderful front. In private it was different." Fading beauty **Vivien Leigh** regrets a famous marriage that failed. *Ship of Fools* (1965, Columbia).

8008 "We keep up a front for everyone else. Why can't we do it for ourselves?" The marriage of bisexual **Michael Caine** and aging, promiscuous actress Maggie Smith is a farce. *California Suite* (1978, Columbia).

8009 "You can pretend I'm crazy. . . but you can't pretend that I love you, because I don't." **Jessica Lange,** as troubled actress Frances Farmer, spits the words angrily at her mother Kim Stanley, who once again has had her daughter committed to a mental hospital. *Frances* (1982, Universal).

8010 "There's a kidney in Kansas City that ain't gettin' any fresher." Needing to get to Kansas City and having no money, **Bette Midler** is able to bluff her way on a plane by pretending to be a nurse taking Shelley Long to a transplant operation. *Outrageous Fortune* (1987, Touchstone-Buena Vista).

8011 "I'll be a virgin and you be Michael Douglas." **Heather Tobias** suggests a favorite fantasy to her husband Philip Jackson. *High Hopes* (1989, GB, Skouras).

8012 "I'm just tired. I'm not going to pretend anymore." **Gina Bellman** is weary of the sex-games she is forced to play with husband Alan Bates. *Secret Friends* (1992, Briarpatch Releasing Corporation).

Prices

see also COSTS, MONEY, WORTH AND VALUES

8013 "How much would you want to run into an open manhole?. . . Stand at the wrong end of a shooting gallery?" **Groucho Marx** will never get the best of Chico Marx. *Animal Crackers* (1930, Paramount).

8014 "Every time a man has helped me there was a price. What's yours?" Having no illusions left, cabaret singer **Marlene Dietrich** questions Adolphe Menjou's motives. *Morocco* (1930, Paramount).

8015 WOMAN CUSTOMER: "How much is that belt in the window? The one that's marked 2.95?" KRALIK: "Er. . . 2.95." WOMAN (DISAPPEARING)**:** "Oh, no. . . ." Shopper **Gertrude Simpson** offers clerk **James Stewart** the opportunity to bargain and he blows it. *The Shop Around the Corner* (1940, MGM).

8016 "They told me of your victories, but not the price you paid." **Vivien Leigh**, as Lady Hamilton, is shocked to see Laurence Olivier, as Lord Nelson. He has returned from victory at the Battle of the Nile minus an arm and an eye. *That Hamilton Woman* aka: *Lady Hamilton* (1941, U.S., London Films).

8017 "What else is there I can buy you with?" **Mary Astor** asks Humphrey Bogart to name his price. He does. *The Maltese Falcon* (1941, Warner Bros.).

8018 "Right now, they're probably haggling over the price for us with Murder, Incorporated." **Robert Cummings** confides to Priscilla Lane as they dance in a mansion owned by Nazi sympathizers and spies. *Saboteur* (1942, Universal).

8019 "Look at that cheap squirt, passin' up and down. . . . For a nickel, I'd grab him, stick both thumbs in his eyes, hang on till he drops dead." Psychopath Tommy Udo, brilliantly played by **Richard Widmark** in his screen debut, stares contemptuously at a prison guard. *Kiss of Death* (1947, 20th Century-Fox).

8020 "I admit I may have seen better days, but I am still not to be had for the price of a cocktail—like a salted peanut." **Bette Davis** rages at her fiancé Gary Merrill, whom she believes is taking her for granted. She fears he prefers someone younger. *All About Eve* (1950, 20th Century-Fox).

8021 "Poor kid! Maybe this is the price you pay for sleeping together." Ambulance driver **Rock Hudson** is forced to make this ludicrous comment after the death of his lover, nurse Jennifer Jones, who has delivered a dead child. *A Farewell to Arms* (1957, 20th Century-Fox).

8022 "If the price is right, the job is right." It's the motto of black hit man **Fred Williamson.** *Mister Mean* (1977, Lone Star-Po' Boy).

8023 "If we obtain our freedom by murder and bloodshed, then I want no part of it." **Ben Kingsley**, as Mahatma Gandhi, insists on nonviolence in India's fight to be rid of British rule. *Gandhi* (1982, GB, Goldcrest-Columbia).

8024 "I'll let you have her at the old price, which is anything you want to give her." Talent agent **Woody Allen** offers the services of one of his less than stellar clients. *Broadway Danny Rose* (1984, Orion).

8025 "Six thousand dollars—it's not even leather!" **Joan Cusack** is shocked by the price tag on a cocktail dress belonging to Sigourney Weaver that Melanie Griffith borrows to wear to a party. *Working Girl* (1988, 20th Century-Fox).

Pride

see also BOASTS AND BRAGGING, CONCEIT, HUMIL-
ITY AND HUMILIATION, OPINIONS, RESPECT AND
RESPECTABILITY, SELF, SELFISHNESS, SPIRIT AND SPIR-
ITS, VANITIES, WORK AND WORKERS

8026 "I shall be proud to speak to you. Proud to be
under obligation to you." **Olivia de Havilland**
thanks bordello owner Ona Munson for saving her
husband Leslie Howard's life. *Gone with the Wind*
(1939, Selznick-MGM).

8027 "Take him to the tower and teach him the
error of false pride." Scary Indian guru **Eduardo
Ciannelli** orders British Sergeant Cary Grant tortured when he stumbles into the temple of a sect of
fanatical Thugees. *Gunga Din* (1939, RKO).

8028 "Reno's full of women who have their pride,
sweetheart—a pretty chilly exchange for the guy
you're stuck on." Street smart **Paulette Goddard**
advises mousy housewife Joan Fontaine. *The
Women* (1939, MGM).

8029 "A woman in love has no pride." Divorced
Norma Shearer makes her plans to win her ex-
husband back from Joan Crawford. *The Women*
(1939, MGM).

8030 "When you told me that you loved me,
I was so proud; I could have walked into a den
of lions; in fact, I did, and the lion didn't hurt
me." Once repressed spinster **Bette Davis** has
a remarkable reaction to married Paul Henreid's
pledge of love. *Now, Voyager* (1942, Warner
Bros.).

8031 "He just swallowed his pride. It'll take him a
moment or two to digest it." Nurse **Patricia Neal**
alludes to suddenly humbled Scot Richard Todd.
The Hasty Heart (1949, Warner Bros.).

8032 "Yes, Dad, Gilbreth and Company will go on.
Mother and your even dozen will see to that.
Mother will go to Europe and you'll be proud of
the way she delivers those speeches for you. And
she'll go right on following in your footsteps to
become the foremost woman industrial engineer
in the world. And by nineteen forty-eight, America's Woman Of the Year. But wherever you are,
Dad, somehow I'm sure you know that, and never
doubted it for a moment." In this true story, **Barbara Bates** speaks of her mother Myrna Loy to
the spirit of her dead father Clifton Webb. Her
purpose is to fill in the movie audiences of Loy's
activities and achievements after the loss of her
husband. *Cheaper by the Dozen* (1950, 20th Century-
Fox).

8033 "Great stars have great pride." Once famous
silent screen actress **Gloria Swanson** confesses to
younger kept man William Holden after she has
attempted suicide because he left her alone. *Sunset
Boulevard* (1950, Paramount).

8034 "I want to be able to face my children when
they ask, 'What were you doing when the world
was shaking, Daddy?'" World War II veteran **Dana
Andrews** explains to his wife Dorothy McGuire
why he decided to re-enlist and volunteer for service in Korea. *I Want You* (1951, RKO).

8035 MRS. KINGSHEAD: "You ought to be proud of
your heritage. Our family came out to California in
a covered wagon." LEE KINGSHEAD: "Now that I've
seen them I know why the wagon was covered."
Spring Byington has no luck in getting her daughter **Piper Laurie** to feel any pride for her mother's
motley relatives. *No Room for the Groom* (1951, Universal-International).

8036 "Did I forget to tell you I'm proud?" **Grace
Kelly** snaps angrily at William Holden. Later, Kelly,
the wife of alcoholic has-been actor Bing Crosby,
realizes that their constant fighting is just masking
the fact that they are falling in love. *The Country
Girl* (1954, Paramount).

8037 "I'm proud—I don't make love to the dead."
Robert Mitchum pulls back from Rita Hayworth
who doesn't respond when he kisses her. *Fire
Down Below* (1957, U.S.-GB, Columbia).

8038 "Oh, Father, how proud I am of you—how
proud." Ruthless army officer Yul Brynner apologizes to David Opatoshu, making the poverty-
stricken captain important in his young son **Miko
Oscard**'s eyes. *The Brothers Karamazov* (1958,
MGM).

8039 "Emily, I'm going out looking for my pride—
alone. When I find it, if you're here, I'll come back
and we'll see if it'll have any value to either of us."
After the death of his mistress, a shaken and repen-
tant **Laurence Harvey** leaves his wife Dina Merrill
with some hope he will return to her. *Butterfield 8*
(1960, MGM).

8040 "I'm a great one for race pride except I don't
need it much in my line of work." Domestic **Ruby
Dee** can't get too excited when Ossie Davis tries to
invoke a spirit of racial pride in her. *Gone Are the
Days* aka: *Purlie Victorious* (1963, Hammer).

8041 "Our love was a beautiful thing, wasn't it? Tell
him he can feel proud to be descended from our
union, a child of so much happiness and beauty.
Tell him." Ancient **Julie Christie** ends the movie

thinking of her love for Alan Bates. *The Go-Between* (1970, GB, Columbia).

8042 "I ain't spittin' on my whole life." Aging cowboy **Lee Marvin** is too proud to compromise himself by accepting a needed job with a Wild West show. *Monte Walsh* (1970, Cinema Center).

8043 "Anybody who could swallow two Snow Balls and a Ding-Dong shouldn't have any trouble with pride." Composer **Steve Guttenberg** shares this deep thought with Valerie Perrine, a very chunky "Garbo of models." *Can't Stop the Music* (1980, EMI).

8044 "Twenty years ago I came to this town with less than $43 million in my pocket, and now I own all this—that's America." **Eddie Albert**, CEO of a major conglomerate, proudly relates his own personal Horatio Alger story to new employee Judge Reinhold, the son of a prominent U.S. senator. *Head Office* (1986, Tri-Star).

8045 "You have to have something to point to." Construction worker **Karl Malden** tries to talk some sense to his college-age son Lenny Von Dohlen who wants to follow in his father's line of work. *Billy Galvin* (1987, Vestron).

8046 "I never had no trouble with these people. They grew up on my food and I'm very proud of that." Italian pizzeria owner **Danny Aiello** rails at his stupid, angry son John Turturro. Aiello refers to the blacks in whose neighborhood his establishment is located. *Do the Right Thing* (1989, Universal).

8047 "Your folks must be real proud, huh?" Under-schooled streetwalker **Julia Roberts** injects when her wealthy "john" Richard Gere admits that he finished high school. *Pretty Woman* (1990, Touchstone-Buena Vista).

Priests

see also RELIGIONS

8048 "Young man, as a—as a matter of curiosity, what made you become a priest?" Elderly priest **Barry Fitzgerald** doesn't believe young Bing Crosby's behavior fits Fitzgerald's notion of that of a priest. *Going My Way* (1944, Paramount).

8049 "I never thought of the priesthood as offering a hiding place." On trial for murdering an attorney, Canadian priest **Montgomery Clift** answers the Crown Prosecutor Brian Aherne, who wonders if Clift felt he could hide his crime under his clerical robes. *I Confess* (1953, Warner Bros.).

8050 "Will no one rid me of this troublesome priest?" **Peter O'Toole**, as Henry II of England, asks a rhetorical question about his one-time friend Richard Burton, the Archbishop of Canterbury. Three of his barons take the hint and murder Burton in his cathedral. *Becket* (1964, GB, Paramount).

8051 "Who will be the one among you to rid me of this Romero?" Being a bit more obvious than Henry II, **Tony Plana**, the leader of the Salvadorian right wing, encourages his henchmen to assassinate critic Archbishop Romero, portrayed by Jose Carlos Ruiz. *Salvador* (1986, Hemdale).

8052 "I didn't know that priests hung out with assholes." It's a hooker's remark to Father Tom Berenger, son of a Mafia boss. *Last Rites* (1988, MGM-United Artists).

8053 "Somebody around here just hates priests. . . you could be number three." Police detective **Ned Beatty** warns priest Ben Cross after two clerics have been murdered. *The Unholy* (1988, Vestron).

8054 "No priest died during the potato famine." Poor Irish tenant farmer **Richard Harris** has nothing but contempt for the clergy. *The Field* (1990, Ireland, Avenue).

Principles

see also ETHICS, INTEGRITY, LAWS, MORALITY, RIGHTS, RULES, TRUTH AND FALSEHOOD

8055 "I like persons better than principles. A person with no principles is better than anything else in the world." **George Sanders**' text today for protégé Hurt Hatfield is hedonism. *The Picture of Dorian Gray* (1945, MGM).

8056 "I know I'm different from the others. I'm here out of principle. All my life I've lived according to principles, and I couldn't change even if I wanted to." Police detective **Kirk Douglas** believes his motives are purer than those of his colleagues. *Detective Story* (1951, Paramount).

8057 "If a man don't go his way, he's nothin'." **Montgomery Clift** is a highly principled soldier—at least with respect to his personal set of principles. *From Here to Eternity* (1953, Columbia).

8058 "If we give in, there'll be no end to it. It's a matter of principle." **Alec Guinness** stiffly tells doctor James Donald that he refuses to give in to Japanese prison camp Commander Sessue Hayakawa. The latter insists that the captured British officers work along side the enlisted men on building a bridge. Guinness prefers to stay in the kennel-sized punishment hut of corrugated iron set in the blazing sun, to which he is confined. *The Bridge on the River Kwai* (1957, GB, Columbia).

8059 "Despite my rejection of most Judeo-Christian ethics, I am, within the framework of a baseball season, monogamous.... I won't sleep with a ballplayer hitting under .250 unless he has a lot of RBIs or a great glove man up the middle. A woman's got to have standards." **Susan Sarandon** lays her cards on the table to Tim Robbins and Kevin Costner. She's offering to be one of the two player's exclusive sexual groupie for the season. *Bull Durham* (1988, Orion).

8060 "I've distilled everything to one simple principle—win or die!" Unscrupulous **Glenn Close** reveals her principle to libertine John Malkovich. *Dangerous Liaisons* (1988, Warner Bros.).

8061 "It'd be against my principles—if I had any." It's **Robert Redford**'s cynical reaction to Lena Olin's attempt to bribe him. *Havana* (1990, Universal).

Priorities

see also ORDERS, RIGHTS, TIME

8062 "First the hunt, then the revels." Mad hunter **Leslie Banks** gleefully eyes his quarry Joel McCrea. *The Most Dangerous Game* (1932, RKO).

8063 "I'll have supper and then the Duchess of Portsmouth." **Cedric Hardwicke**, as King Charles II of England, fixes his evening's schedule with Jeanne de Casalis saved for dessert. *Nell Gwyn* (1934, GB, United Artists).

8064 "I'll do anything for these kids, anything.... Those kids come first in this house, before either of us." **Joan Crawford** lays down the law to her wimpy husband Bruce Bennett. Joan's character is one of the movies' first "permissive parents." *Mildred Pierce* (1945, Warner Bros.).

8065 "First, I'm going to kiss my girl like she's never been kissed before.... Then I'm going to take off my parachute." **George Tobias** answers enthusiastically when asked what will be the first thing he'll do after getting back home from his mission behind Japanese lines in World War II. *Objective Burma!* (1945, Warner Bros.).

8066 "You made me small in my father's eyes. You made my sister spit at me. Then you stole my wife." **Robert Stack** lists in his order of importance the alleged crimes of his one-time friend Rock Hudson. *Written on the Wind* (1956, Universal-International).

8067 "You set your priorities and that's the way life is. Nobody said it was going to be fun." Serious-minded **Don Galloway** makes sense as he sees it to his complaining wife JoBeth Williams. *The Big Chill* (1983, Columbia).

8068 "We spent a lotta money going to the moon. We shoulda tried to go to heaven." Dying **Josh Mostel** regrets lost opportunities. *Windy City* (1984, Warner Bros.).

8069 "I'm doing the best I can right now.... Having an affair is not too high on my priorities.... If you don't get it, well, that's too bad." Widow **Jessica Lange** makes it clear to Arliss Howard that she's not ready to get emotionally involved with him. *Men Don't Leave* (1990, Warner Bros.).

Prisons and Prisoners

see also CRIMES AND CRIMINALS, FREEDOMS, LAWS, LAWYERS

8070 "There ain't any jail made of steel or stone that can hold a body prisoner as tight as one built of old age and lack of money." Poor, elderly **May Robson** is confined to a miserable nursing home where the old ladies are denied everything that would make them want to go on living. When Robson receives a check for a million dollars from eccentric Richard Bennett, she changes all that. *If I Had a Million* (1932, Paramount).

8071 RUFUS T. FIREFLY: "I suggest we give him ten years in Leavenworth or eleven years in Twelveworth." CHICOLINI: "I tell you what I'll do. I'll take five and ten in Woolworth." President of Freedonia **Groucho Marx** exchanges cracks with his War Secretary **Chico Marx** at the latter's trial for treason. *Duck Soup* (1933, Paramount).

8072 "King Solomon imprisoned me in that bottle 3,000 years ago." Djinni **Rex Ingram** tells Sabu how he came to be trapped in the bottle from which the young thief released him. *The Thief of Bagdad* (1940, GB, London Films).

8073 "Yeah, I've been a lot of places and no place. To tell you the truth, Danny, I've been sightseeing. I spent a year and a day on a sweet little island they call Blackwell's. And I took a little trip up the Hudson, too. Hey, there's a beautiful view up there from a certain window, and I ought to know because I looked at it for 36 months." Before becoming a respected director, **Elia Kazan** acted in several films, including this one for which he's an ex-con visiting boxing contender James Cagney. *City for Conquest* (1941, Warner Bros.).

8074 "Nothing's all right. It'll never be all right until we're out." Con **Burt Lancaster** formulates a plan to break out of the prison run by brutal Captain Hume Cronyn. *Brute Force* (1947, Universal-International).

8075 "It always makes me sore when I see those war pictures, all about flying leathernecks and submarine patrols and frogmen and guerrillas in the Philippines. What gets to me is that there was never a movie about POWs, about prisoners of war." Narrator **Gil Stratton, Jr.** introduces a war picture about prisoners of war. *Stalag 17* (1953, Paramount).

8076 "I always thought it was a ridiculous name for a prison—Sing Sing. I mean. Sounds more like it should be an opera house or something." **Audrey Hepburn** is right about the New York State prison. With one more "Sing" it could be the great swing hit of Benny Goodman. *Breakfast at Tiffany's* (1961, Paramount).

8077 "No. No. That would be letting you off too easy, too fast. Your words, do you remember? I do. No. We're gonna take good care of you, gonna nurse you back to health. You're strong, Cady. You're gonna live a long life. In a cage. That's where you belong. That's where you're going. And this time for life. Bang your head against the walls. Count the years, the months, the hours. Until the day you rot." **Gregory Peck** doesn't want to kill psychopath Robert Mitchum who has been terrorizing Peck's family. He wants to see him suffer in prison. *Cape Fear* (1962, Universal).

8078 "We have put all our rotten eggs in one basket and we intend to watch that basket very carefully. With your cooperation, we may all sit out the war very comfortably." Stalag Commandant **Hannes Messemer**, a Luftwaffe colonel, seeks agreement from senior British officer James Donald that no escapes will be attempted from a new German POW camp. It's filled with Allied prisoners who have made numerous previous escape attempts. *The Great Escape* (1963, United Artists).

8079 ELEANOR OF AQUITAINE: "How dear of you to let me out of jail." KING HENRY II: "It's only for the holidays." **Katharine Hepburn**, who has been confined by her husband **Peter O'Toole** to a remote castle to prevent her from meddling with his empire, is allowed a reunion of his politically ambitious family. *The Lion in Winter* (1968, GB, Avco Embassy).

8080 "This place is not a prison. You can get a release, y'know." Ghetto clinic doctor **Elvis Presley** follows nurse-nun Mary Tyler Moore into her convent to propose marriage. *Change of Habit* (1969, Universal).

8081 "The prison hasn't been built that can hold me. I'll get out of this one if it means spending my entire life here." Con **Woody Allen** expresses false bravado. *Take the Money and Run* (1969, United Artists).

8082 NURSE: "Doctor, this man is a prisoner of war." TRAPPER JOHN: "So are you, nurse. You just don't know it." One of the nurses is shocked that surgeon **Elliott Gould** would work so diligently to save the life of a wounded Communist soldier. *M*A*S*H* (1970, 20th Century-Fox).

8083 "We don't make good citizens. We make good prisoners." Warden **Patrick McGoohan** explains that Alcatraz has no rehabilitation program because it only caters to incorrigibles. *Escape from Alcatraz* (1979, Paramount).

8084 "There are no guards inside the prison. Only prisoners and the world they made.... Once you go in, you don't come out." The film's opening narration reveals that in 1997 Manhattan has become the country's maximum security prison. *Escape from New York* (1981, Avco Embassy).

8085 "I saw a prison near Plymouth Rock. It was overgrown with weeds, ragweed and thistles, milkweed and vetch. They sprang from every crack. Someday their roots will pry the walls apart. I won't be around, but I saw them last summer and they were in bloom. They were springing up from the wall with all the strength they were given to tell the world they were there. And bees came and drank from them. Just like any garden flower, they have nectar to give, too." After winning a pardon, prisoner **Nick Nolte** forms a group of traveling actors who perform in prisons. *Weeds* (1987, DEG).

8086 "Prison is very structured—more than most people care for." Having served several terms in prison, **Nicolas Cage** knows whereof he speaks. *Raising Arizona* (1988, 20th Century-Fox).

8087 "You're a prisoner of the system, like I am." Abbie Hoffman-like 60s radical **Dennis Hopper** addresses a bewildered black porter as "soul brother." *Flashback* (1990, Paramount).

8088 "When you think of prison you have this image from movies.... It wasn't like that for wise guys. We owned the joint." **Ray Liotta** describes life in the pen for organized crime members as rather jolly. *GoodFellas* (1990, Warner Bros.).

Privacy

see also PUBLIC, SECRETS

8089 "I like privacy when I retire. I'm very delicate in that respect. Prying eyes annoy me. Behold the walls of Jericho! Maybe not as thick as the one that Joshua blew down with his trumpet, but a lot safer. You see I have no trumpet." Reporter **Clark Gable** separates the room he must share with runaway heiress Claudette Colbert by hanging a blanket over a string between two beds. *It Happened One Night* (1934, Columbia).

8090 "Life without a room to oneself is a barbarity." **Edith Evans** sees to it that governess Deborah Kerr escapes barbarity by being given a private room. *The Chalk Garden* (1964, GB, Universal).

8091 "He has to learn to do it in private like the rest of us." Glasgow parochial school teacher **Tom Conti** defends a boy caught masturbating. *The Gospel According to Vic* (1987, GB, Skouras).

8092 "I don't have any privacy. It's like having children in the house." Elderly Southern Jewish woman **Jessica Tandy** complains to her son Dan Aykroyd about having servants around. *Driving Miss Daisy* (1989, Warner Bros.).

Privileges

see also ADVANTAGES, FAVORS, RIGHTS

8093 "I am a woman and it is the privilege of a woman not to make sense. Men who expect women to be logical are likely to be failures in love." **Marlene Dietrich** counters her English diplomat husband Herbert Marshall's claim that she makes no sense. *Angel* (1937, Paramount).

8094 "It used to be the privilege of class. . . but it, like all else, has been lost to the masses." French soldier **Pierre Fresnay** refers to venereal disease. *Grand Illusion* aka: *La Grande Illusion* (1937, Fr., RAC).

8095 "I ask only the privilege of looking after you. . . ." Wealthy farmer **Peter Finch** pressures Julie Christie to pledge she will marry him in six years if her missing husband Terence Stamp doesn't show up. *Far from the Madding Crowd* (1967, GB, EMI).

8096 "Going nowhere is the privilege of youth." Not yet a star, **Kevin Costner** appears as one of five college students who wander aimlessly in the summer of 1971, under the specter of graduation and the Vietnam war. *Fandango* (1985, Warner Bros.).

Prizes

see also AWARDS, CHANCES, GAMES, SPORTS, WINNERS AND LOSERS, WORTH AND VALUES

8097 "You know, the first man that can think up a good explanation how he can be in love with his wife and another woman is going to win that prize they're always giving out of Sweden." **Mary Cecil** suggests a Nobel Prize for justifying infidelity. *The Women* (1939, MGM).

8098 "You can't live alone forever. I'm tired of winning prizes—they're cold comfort. For once, I'd like to be the prize." Feminist **Fay Bainter** explains to sophisticated columnist Katharine Hepburn that she's fed up with being alone, just before she marries Hepburn's widower father. *Woman of the Year* (1942, MGM).

8099 BOBBY JO PEPPERDINE: "I guess I ain't such a prize, am I?" M/SGT. MAXWELL SLAUGHTER: "Who is, Miss Pepperdine? Who is?" Callous teen **Tuesday Weld** has second thoughts after calling **Jackie Gleason** "a fat Randolph Scott." *Soldier in the Rain* (1963, Allied Artists).

Probability and Statistics

see also MATHEMATICS

8100 "Statistics show that there are more women in the world than anything else—except insects." As do about ninety percent of the people in the world, **Glenn Ford** manufactures statistics to suit his own purpose. *Gilda* (1946, Columbia).

8101 MARY: "God bless you, sergeant, you're a fine man." STRYKER: "You'd get odds on that in the Marine Corps." Forced into prostitution to support her baby, **Julie Bishop** admires tough gyrene **John Wayne**, who dumps all his dough in the baby's crib and leaves without availing himself of Bishop's services. *Sands of Iwo Jima* (1949, Republic).

8102 "That I should want you at all suddenly seems to me the height of improbability. But that in itself is probably the reason. You're an improbable person, Eve, and so am I. We have that in common. Also a contempt for humanity, an inability to love or be loved, insatiable emotion. . . and talent. We deserve each other. In his own way, acerbic theater critic **George Sanders** answers the question, "How do I love thee. . . let me count the ways," as he claims ruthless actress Anne Baxter as his woman. *All About Eve* (1950, 20th Century-Fox).

8103 "Make him feel important. If you do that, you'll have a happy and wonderful marriage—like two out of every ten couples." **Mildred Natwick** expresses a realistic but not terribly hopeful prediction for her newlywed daughter Jane Fonda's marriage to Robert Redford. Natwick could have reduced her fraction to lowest terms, one in five. *Barefoot in the Park* (1967, Paramount).

8104 "I suppose all cowboys dream of going back to the land. Well, I'm probably full of shit." **John Travolta**'s self-assessment seems on target. *Urban Cowboy* (1980, Paramount).

8105 "It's enough to make a man re-examine his life or at least the laws of probability." **Tim Roth** tries to comprehend how a coin flipped several hundred times always comes up heads. *Rosencrantz and Guildenstern Are Dead* (1990, GB, Cinecom).

8106 DR. CAMPBELL: "Sweet dreams." DR. CRANE: "Go to hell!" DR. CAMPBELL: "Probably." Scientists **Sean Connery** and **Lorraine Bracco** come to the end of an imperfect day together at his Amazon rain forest laboratory. *Medicine Man* (1992, Hollywood Pictures-Buena Vista).

Problems

see also DIFFICULTIES, QUESTIONS, TROUBLES

8107 MARIA: "What's the matter, darling? Is it France?" SIR FREDERICK: "No, no. Yugoslavia." MARIA: "Oh, I see." **Marlene Dietrich**'s diplomat husband **Herbert Marshall** hasn't much time for her. *Angel* (1937, Paramount).

8108 "You would be surprised, Conway, how a little courtesy all round helps to smooth out the most complicated problems." Assistant to the High Lama, **H.B. Warner** tells Ronald Colman why things work so well in Shangri-La. *Lost Horizon* (1937, Columbia).

8109 "Ilsa, I'm no good at being noble, but it doesn't take much to see that the problems of three little people don't amount to a hill of beans in this crazy world." **Humphrey Bogart** successfully induces his beloved Ingrid Bergman to escape from Casablanca and the Nazis by flying to Lisbon with her Resistance leader husband Paul Henreid. *Casablanca* (1942, Warner Bros.).

8110 "Did you ever have one of those days when just nothing seems to go right?" **Fredric March**'s problems are the work of witch Veronica Lake, who pledged to trouble all the descendants of the man who had her burned at a stake during the Salem witch trials. March is the latest in a long line of men who have suffered from her curse. *I Married a Witch* (1942, United Artists).

8111 "Money causes problems in the world simply because there's too little of it." Being one of those with too little, **Tom Neal** isn't just whistling Dixie. *Detour* (1946, Producers Releasing Corporation).

8112 "I know men. Somehow they always seem to be more interested in the problems of young wives with older husbands." **Lana Turner**, who meets the conditions of her proposition, shares her problems with interested drifter John Garfield. *The Postman Always Rings Twice* (1946, MGM).

8113 RIP: "Say, when you get on again as a professor at some college and I'm back running my cab at St. Louis, send me a problem in algebra once in a while." JOHNNY: "Blonde or brunette?" RIP: "A redhead in a sloppy-joe sweater." **Humphrey Bogart** and **William Prince** pass time as they travel to Washington, D.C., where Prince is to be decorated for his heroism in World War II. *Dead Reckoning* (1947, Columbia).

8114 "Well, gentlemen, I suppose you're wondering why I've asked you here. Well, uh, let's put it this way. Your problems are my problems. Artie, tell me something about yourself. What are you and what do you want to be?" Having found the courage to face a tough street gang, once shy and cowardly janitor **Jerry Lewis** now tries to change them. *The Delicate Delinquent* (1957, Paramount).

8115 "I don't have any bedroom problems. There's nothing in my bedroom that bothers me." **Doris Day** responds angrily, and perhaps revealingly, to Rock Hudson, the womanizer who shares her party line. He accuses her of being repressed because she has "bedroom problems." *Pillow Talk* (1959, Universal).

8116 "And so, ladies and gentlemen, you, too, like this satisfied customer, can solve all your problems by subscribing to an answering service." A narrator speaks of a telephone answering service, which has solved all of composer Dean Martin's problems and won him operator Judy Holliday. *Bells Are Ringing* (1960, MGM).

8117 "You're two wonderful people who happened to fall in love and happen to have a pigmentation problem." **Spencer Tracy** avoids direct reference to the fact that his daughter Katharine Houghton is white and her fiancé Sidney Poitier is black. *Guess Who's Coming to Dinner* (1967, Columbia).

8118 "You know, even as a kid, I always went for the wrong woman. I think that's my problem. When my mother took me to see *Snow White,* everybody fell in love with Snow White. I immediately fell for the Wicked Queen." In voice-over, **Woody Allen**

discusses his problems with women. *Annie Hall* (1977, United Artists).

8119 "My problem is I'm both attracted and repelled by the male organ." **Diane Keaton** identifies her hang-up for Woody Allen. *Manhattan* (1979, United Artists).

8120 BATTY: "It's not easy to meet your maker. Could the maker repair what he makes?" TYRELL: "What seems to be the problem?" BATTY: "Death." Replicant **Rutger Hauer** confronts his creator **Joe Turkel.** When the latter tells the former that there is no way to change the android's termination date, Hauer kisses Turkel and then crushes his skull. *Blade Runner* (1982, Warner Bros.).

8121 "My problem is I look at my work and I think it's ugly." Gum-snapping bimbo interior decorator **Mia Farrow** speaks of her ugly work. *Broadway Danny Rose* (1984, Orion).

8122 "Every path has its puddles, Daddy." **JoBeth Williams** gives out with one of her many clichés to comfort husband Jon Voight. *Desert Bloom* (1986, Columbia).

8123 "What do I do? Do I ice her? Do I marry her?" Mafia soldier **Jack Nicholson**'s predicament is what to do with his lady-love Kathleen Turner, a hit woman for hire. *Prizzi's Honor* (1986, 20th Century-Fox).

8124 "Got a problem and the problem is you." The credo of the Sex Pistols is expressed by **Drew Schofield** as Johnny Rotten. *Sid & Nancy* (1986, GB, Goldwyn).

8125 "Did you ever try to put panty hose on with wet nails?" **Sean Young** has an excellent excuse for being late getting dressed to attend a wedding. *Cousins* (1989, Paramount).

8126 "What's your damage, Heather? Did you have a brain tumor for breakfast?" Head teenage bitch Heather Chandler, played by **Kim Walker**, snaps at Heather McNamara, played by Lisanne Falk. *Heathers* (1989, New World).

8127 "My problem is that I can have anything I want, but I don't know what I want." Criminal **Alec Baldwin**, masquerading as a cop, states his dilemma to simple-minded hooker Jennifer Jason Leigh. *Miami Blues* (1990, Orion).

8128 "If you are hundreds or thousands of dollars in debt, it's your problem. If you're a million in debt, it's the bank's." Portly, appealing **Marianne Sagebrecht** understands the S&L bail-out plan. *Rosalie*

Goes Shopping (1990, W. German-Four Seasons Entertainment).

8129 "My problem is real simple. I've got a cop who wants me out of the way so he can get my wife." **Kurt Russell** feels helpless knowing that cop **Ray Liotta** is obsessed with Russell's wife Madeline Stowe. *Unlawful Entry* (1992, 20th Century-Fox).

8130 "The only problem I have is sleazy, low-life whores like you." L.A. cop **Ray Liotta** shoves Sherrie Rose out of his squad car after a sexual encounter. When he didn't seem to be enjoying the afterglow of sex because his mind is on Madeline Stowe, she asks him if he has a problem. *Unlawful Entry* (1992, 20th Century-Fox).

Processes see ACTIONS AND ACTS, ENDS AND ENDINGS, PREPARATIONS, SYSTEMS

Productions see BUILDINGS, CREATION AND CREATURES, WORK AND WORKERS

Profanity

see also BLASPHEMY, CONTEMPT, CURSES, VULGARITIES

8131 "I don't swear just for the hell of it. Language is a poor enough means of communications. I think we should all use the words we've got. Besides there are damn few words that anybody understands." **Spencer Tracy**, as a Clarence Darrow-like lawyer, makes an eloquent defense of profanity. *Inherit the Wind* (1960, United Artists).

8132 "Don't use profanity in this house. What the hell's he gonna think?" Concerned with what Ryan O'Neal may think, "Do as I say, not as I do" **John Marley** instructs his daughter Ali MacGraw. *Love Story* (1970, Paramount).

8133 "You know what you can do with your contract. You can take your contract and shove it up your ass." Having slept with just about anyone to further her country and western singing career, now successful **Monica Gayle** realizes the sacrifices she's made are not worth it. *New Girl in Town* (1977, New World).

Professions and Professionals

see also AMATEURS, PAYMENTS, TRAINING

8134 KITTY PACKARD: "I was reading a book the other day." CARLOTTA VANCE: "Reading a book?" KITTY: "Yes, it's all about civilization or something— a nutty kind of book. Do you know that the guy said that machinery is going to take the place of every profession?" CARLOTTA: "Oh, my dear. That's something you need never worry about." In an exchange that must be seen to be fully appreciated, **Jean Harlow** surprises the great comic actress **Marie Dressler** into one of the greatest doubletakes ever seen. Dressler recovers and zings the uncomprehending Harlow with her wisecrack. *Dinner at Eight* (1933, MGM).

8135 "Men have been buzzing around me since I was fourteen years old. I'm not interested. All I want is a chance to be somebody. To work. To have my own profession." **Lana Turner** is ambitious—to little avail. She becomes a model. *A Life of Her Own* (1950, MGM).

8136 "It may not be the oldest profession, but it's the best." **Humphrey Bogart**, the managing editor of a dying metropolitan daily, is proud of the newspaper business. *Deadline U.S.A.* (1951, 20th Century-Fox).

8137 "Booth! Ha, I'm no actor. Bustin' my leg on a stage so I can yell 'Down with the tyrant!' If Booth wasn't such a ham he might've made it." Hired presidential assassin **Frank Sinatra** objects when Sterling Hayden likens him to an amateur like John Wilkes Booth—he's a professional. *Suddenly* (1954, United Artists).

8138 "This isn't just a job; it's a profession." Well, it's certain that streetwalker **Shirley MacLaine** is no amateur in the world's oldest profession. *Irma la Douce* (1963, United Artists).

8139 "The less said about our professions, the better, for we have been most things in our times. We have been all over India. We know her cities and her jungles, her palaces and her jails." British Sergeant **Sean Connery** speaks for himself and Michael Caine to Christopher Plummer as Rudyard Kipling. *The Man Who Would Be King* (1975, Columbia).

8140 "Like the man said, I'm Ralph Garcy and I'm a professional asshole." **Barry Miller** begins his stand-up comedy routine. *Fame* (1980, MGM).

8141 "A professional always specializes." Gentleman bandit **Richard Farnsworth** has his standards when he takes up robbing trains after spending many years in prison for robbing stagecoaches. *The Grey Fox* (1982, Canada, United Artists).

8142 "The moment you accepted money, you became professionals. It's just beginning." KGB agent **David Suchet** refuses to allow Americans Timothy Hutton and Sean Penn, who sell military secrets, to believe that they are anything other than

paid traitors. *The Falcon and the Snowman* (1985, Orion).

Professors *see* TEACHING AND TEACHERS

Profit *see* BUSINESS AND COMMERCE, BUYING AND SELLING, PAYMENTS

Progress

see also GOALS, GROWTH AND DEVELOPMENT

8143 "Three years ago I came to Florida without a nickel in my pocket. Now I have a nickel in my pocket." Chiseling **Groucho Marx**, the manager of a seedy hotel, wants to get in on the Florida land boom. *The Cocoanuts* (1929, Paramount).

8144 "What is this progress? What is the good of all this progress onward and onward? We demand a rest. . . . An end to progress! Make an end to this progress now! Let this be the last day of the scientific age." **Cedric Hardwicke** wishes the future to be the past. *Things to Come* (1936, GB, London Films-United Artists).

8145 IDA REUTER: "Julius, progress can't destroy us, can it?" JULIUS REUTER: "Of course not. It killed my pigeon post, but at the same time it makes another step toward making the world a little smaller. I believe in progress, just as I believe in a smaller world where men may come closer to each other, get to know each other. That's the ultimate objective of all progress—knowledge and, through knowledge, the truth." Loyal and dutiful wife **Edna Best** gives **Edward G. Robinson** a chance to be profound when telegraphy makes his carrier pigeons, used to transmit news between cities, obsolete. *A Dispatch from Reuters* (1940, Warner Bros.).

8146 "Look at me. I started as a file clerk. In two years I became a secretary." **Dolores Hart** holds out hope for Montgomery Clift, stuck in the role of a sob-sister columnist. *Lonelyhearts* (1958, United Artists).

8147 "He's very progressive. He has all sorts of ideas about artificial insemination and all that sort of thing. He breeds all over the world." **Debbie Reynolds**' revelation about her fiancé Tab Hunter is not exactly comforting to her father Fred Astaire. *The Pleasure of His Company* (1961, Paramount).

8148 "Sunya means and progress is. . . like a train. You either get on, get out of the way, or get crushed." **Robby Benson** issues a warning in a film dealing with youth gangs fighting in a post-apocalypse world. *City Limits* (1985, SHO-Videoform).

8149 "Look, they're coming this way. The future on the march. I curse you volts, watts and amps." Elderly **Ian Bannen** resents the advance of progress to his quiet home on the river at the time of World War II. *Hope and Glory* (1987, GB, Columbia).

Prologues

see also INTRODUCTIONS

8150 "After the tragic war between the states, America turned to the winning of the West. The symbol of this era was the building of the transcontinental railroads. The advance of the railroads was, in some cases, predatory and unscrupulous. . . . It was this uncertain and lawless age that gave the world, for good or ill, the most famous outlaws, the brothers Frank and Jesse James." Prologue to *Jesse James* (1939, 20th Century-Fox).

8151 "The United States Military Academy—West Point. When the gray cradle of the American Army was only a small garrison with a few cadets, but under a brilliant commandant, named Robert E. Lee, it was already building for the defense of a newly-born nation in a new world." Prologue to *Santa Fe Trail* (1940, Warner Bros.).

8152 "We are proud to present this picture and are grateful to the many heroic figures still living, who have generously consented to be portrayed in its story. To their faith and ours that a day will come when men will live in peace on earth, this picture is humbly dedicated." Prologue to *Sergeant York* (1941, Warner Bros.).

8153 "The story of the average English middle-class family begins with the summer of 1939; when the sun shone down on a happy, careless people, who worked and played, reared their children and tended their gardens in that happy, easy going England that was soon to be fighting desperately for her way of life and for life itself." Written introduction to *Mrs. Miniver* (1942, MGM).

8154 "Out of the humble cabin, out of the singing heart of the Old South, have come the tales of Uncle Remus, rich in simple truths, forever fresh and new." Prologue to *Song of the South* (1946, Disney-RKO).

8155 "At the forks of the Ohio stands an American city, a colossus of steel, whose mills and furnaces bring forth bone and sinew for a nation. Not so long ago a lonely outpost guarded this very spot. It was called Fort Pitt. . . men kept coming west, some to build their own fortunes, even at the price of Indian wars—others to build a nation—

even at the price of their own lives. These are the unconquered, who push ever forward the frontiers of man's freedom." The prologue, spoken by director **Cecil B. DeMille**, to *Unconquered* (1947, Paramount).

8156 "Before the dawn of history, ever since the first man discovered his soul, he has struggled against the forces that sought to enslave him. . . ." Part of the prologue, read by **Cecil B. DeMille**, to *Samson and Delilah* (1949, Paramount).

8157 "Three thousand years ago, David and Bathsheba ruled over the united tribes of Israel. This story of King David's reign is based on one of the world's oldest historical narratives written by an anonymous chronicler in the Second Book of Samuel of the Old Testament." Prologue to *David and Bathsheba* (1951, 20th Century-Fox).

8158 "This is the story of the biggest of the big tops and the men and women who fight to make it the greatest show on earth." Opening narration by **Cecil B. DeMille** in *The Greatest Show on Earth* (1952, Paramount).

8159 "Rome, master of the earth, in the eighteenth year of the Emperor Tiberius, our legions stand guard on the boundaries of civilization. . . we have reached the point where there are more slaves in Rome than citizens. . . ." The opening narration of *The Robe* (1953, 20th Century-Fox).

8160 "There has never been a mutiny on a ship of the United States Navy. The truths of this film lie not in its incidents but in the way a few men meet the crisis of their lives. . . ." Prologue to *The Caine Mutiny* (1954, Columbia).

Promiscuity

see also INFIDELITIES, PROSTITUTION AND PROSTITUTES, SEDUCTIONS, SEX AND SEXUALITY

8161 "I changed my name. . . . No, it took more than one man to change my name to Shanghai Lily." **Marlene Dietrich** corrects the impression of former lover Colin Clive who asks if her name change is due to marriage. *Shanghai Express* (1932, Paramount).

8162 "Not Anytime Annie! Say, who could forget her? She only said 'no' once and then she didn't hear the question." Stage manager **George E. Stone** comments on the easy availability of show girl Ginger Rogers. *42nd Street* (1933, Warner Bros.).

8163 "If I'd been a ranch, they'd have named me the Bar Nothing." **Rita Hayworth** jokingly admits that when it came to lovers she hasn't been too particular. *Gilda* (1946, Columbia).

8164 "I have a heart like an artichoke—a leaf for everyone." **Joan Blondell** allows that she's promiscuous. *Nightmare Alley* (1947, 20th Century-Fox).

8165 "Seven isn't a few. Did they give you money?. . . Did they give you presents?. . . Expensive ones? I'd rather go to jail for twenty years than find my wife was a tramp." Police detective **Kirk Douglas** discovers that his wife Eleanor Parker, who he thought was a virgin before their marriage, had a few men before him. The straw that breaks his unbending back is that she became pregnant with the child of small-time crook and gambler Gerald Mohr and went to abortionist George Macready, whom Douglas hates more than anyone else in the world. *Detective Story* (1951, Paramount).

8166 "Armies have marched over me." **Rita Hayworth** knows the kind of lady she is. *Fire Down Below* (1957, GB, Columbia).

8167 "Mama, face it. I was the slut of all time." Up till this time, **Elizabeth Taylor** and her mother Mildred Dunnock haven't faced up to Taylor's promiscuity. *Butterfield 8* (1960, MGM).

8168 "She's been around more in her twenty years than the man in the moon in millions." Attorney **Everett Sloane** describes decidedly loose young Yvonne Craig. *By Love Possessed* (1961, United Artists).

8169 ELAINE NAVAZIO: "Aren't you appalled at the promiscuity you find everywhere?" BARNEY CASHMAN: "I haven't found it everywhere." **Sally Kellerman** is one of three women with whom married middle-aged **Alan Arkin** attempts to have an affair. *Last of the Red Hot Lovers* (1972, Paramount).

8170 "I'm no one-nighter." **Jill Clayburgh** is really steamed when she wakes up and finds Burt Reynolds has left her bed and apartment after they make love for the first time. *Starting Over* (1979, Paramount).

8171 "I slept with over 300 men in Paducah, Kentucky—and it wasn't easy to find that many." **Beverly D'Angelo** and an odd assortment of characters are trying to get an exit ramp built in a small Florida town. *Honky Tonk Freeway* (1981, EMI).

8172 "Everybody does, why should you be any different?" Ex-prostitute **Miranda Richardson** has a flip response when Rupert Everett tells her he loves her as they are making love in her bed. *Dance with a Stranger* (1985, GB, Goldwyn).

8173 "I can't do casual anymore." Gorgeous television producer **Brooke Adams** wants more than a fling with detective story writer Ben Masters. *Key Exchange* (1985, 20th Century-Fox).

8174 "He says, 'She's been following me around since I've got here. She's been trailing me like a bitch in heat. She doesn't wear any drawers so she'll be ready to do it with anyone who comes down the pike.' He said she did it with one of the niggers." Coal company undercover agent **Bob Gunton** lies to lonely widow Nancy Mette, claiming union organizer Chris Cooper ridiculed her and her attraction for him to a group of coal miners. *Matewan* (1987, Cinecom).

Promises

see also AGREEMENTS, EXPECTATIONS, OATHS, PLEDGES

8175 "I'll take the snap out of your garters." Through a title card, sassy working class flapper **Clara Bow** makes a snappy promise to Antonio Moreno, the owner of the department store where she sells ribbons. *It* (1927, silent, Famous Players-Paramount).

8176 "And you, Prince Alfred. . . do you promise to be an obedient and docile husband. . . .?" Maurice Chevalier finds the words of Priest **Winter Hall** humiliating. They are part of the wedding ceremony when he marries Jeanette MacDonald, queen of Sylvania. *The Love Parade* (1929, Paramount).

8177 "I'm gonna lay off the booze—word of honor. I'm not gonna gamble anymore." Drunken washed-up prizefighter **Wallace Beery** makes a promise to his weepy son Jackie Cooper which he means, but won't keep. *The Champ* (1931, MGM).

8178 "The world shall hear from me again. . . ." The voice of Fu Manchu, played by **Boris Karloff**, reverberates across the wide ocean at the end of the film. **Christopher Lee** as the "Yellow Menace" makes the same promise in the 1965 film. *The Mask of Fu Manchu* (1932, MGM); *The Face of Fu Manchu* (1965, GB, Anglo-EMI).

8179 "I'll live to see all of you hanging from the highest yardarm in England." **Charles Laughton** as Captain William Bligh yells from his new command, a longboat, to Clark Gable and the other mutineers aboard HMS Bounty. *Mutiny on the Bounty* (1935, MGM).

8180 "It was a city of wood—and now it's ashes—but out of fire'll be comin' steel. . . . We O'Learys are a strange tribe, but there's strength in us, and what we set out to do we'll finish." **Alice Brady** as Molly O'Leary, watches the burning city of Chicago as she speaks with resolution about the future of her family and their city. *In Old Chicago* (1937, 20th Century-Fox).

8181 "I may kill half of you in training... but the half that lives will be soldiers, I promise you!" Brutal French Foreign Legion Sergeant **Brian Donlevy** sounds like most basic training non-coms speaking to the new recruits assigned to them—only Donlevy means the part about killing half. *Beau Geste* (1939, Paramount).

8182 "I'll be all around in the dark. I'll be everywhere.... Whenever there's a fight so hungry people can eat, I'll be there. Whenever there's a cop beatin' up a guy I'll be there.... And when people are eatin' the stuff they raise and livin' in the house they build, I'll be there, too." Before he flees because the authorities are after him, **Henry Fonda** resolves to his Ma, Jane Darwell, to be committed in fighting social injustice, wherever he finds it. *The Grapes of Wrath* (1940, 20th Century-Fox).

8183 "Please promise me never to wear black satin or pearls or to be thirty-six years old." **Laurence Olivier** seeks a pledge of youth from his second wife Joan Fontaine. *Rebecca* (1940, United Artists).

8184 "You'll sit right down at that table and draw up a document promising never to bother Jabez Stone or his heirs or assignees or any other New Hampshireman till doomsday! For any Hades we want to raise in this state, we can raise ourselves, without assistance from strangers." **Edward Arnold** as Daniel Webster, dictates terms to defeated Walter Huston as the devil, Mr. Scratch. *All That Money Can Buy* aka: *The Devil and Daniel Webster* (1941, RKO).

8185 "I shall be back. We shall all be back." British professor **Leslie Howard**'s quiet voice from the shadows makes a promise to Nazi General Francis L. Sullivan as Howard escapes across the border. *Pimpernel Smith* (1941, GB, British National).

8186 "Those aren't lies. Those are campaign promises. They expect 'em." Practical Marine **William Demarest** advises reluctant mayoral candidate Eddie Bracken. *Hail the Conquering Hero* (1944, Paramount).

8187 "Some day you'll turn around and I'll be there.... I'm gonna kill ya, Matt." **John Wayne** promises to kill his adopted son Montgomery Clift, when the latter mutinies and takes control of brutal Wayne's cattle drive. *Red River* (1948, United Artists).

8188 "I'll plead for you as hard as ever I can. Better than that, I'll come tomorrow and cut you down from the tree myself and bury you with grief and respect." **Edmond O'Brien**, as ruthless as his tyrannical father Fredric March, promises what he will do when the lynch mob comes for March. O'Brien threatens to reveal that his father was directly responsible for the deaths of many confederate troops. O'Brien will spare his father this indignity if the old man will just turn the family fortune over to him. *Another Part of the Forest* (1948, Universal).

8189 CALAMITY JANE: "Remember, you promised to love, honor and obey." "PAINLESS" PETE POTTER: "Yeah, let's do it in the order named." **Jane Russell** will make sure her husband in name only, **Bob Hope**, stays that way. *The Paleface* (1948, Paramount).

8190 "You butcher one more patient, and law or no law—I'll find you. I'll put a bullet in the back of your head, and I'll drop your body in the East River. And I'll go home—and I'll sleep sweetly." Police detective **Kirk Douglas** tells George Macready that his conscience will not be troubled by killing an abortionist. *The Detective Story* (1951, Paramount).

8191 "I'll be any way you want me to be. From the beginning, I knew you were the best. Don't leave. I was in a hotel room once, the night before he flew away for the last time." Neurotic babysitter **Marilyn Monroe** promises pick-up lover Richard Widmark that she'll do whatever he wants. She lives in a fantasy world ever since she was traumatized when her pilot fiancé was killed in a World War II plane crash. Confusing Widmark with her fiancé, Monroe tries to kill her charge, Donna Corcoran, when the child interrupts their love making. *Don't Bother to Knock* (1952, 20th Century-Fox).

8192 "Have you forgotten what he is, how he promised to come back and kill you? He sat in that chair and said, 'I'll come back, Will Kane. I'll come back and I'll kill you.'" Judge **Otto Kruger** skedaddles out of town and recommends that lawman Gary Cooper do the same before fierce killer Ian MacDonald arrives on the noon train to take his revenge. *High Noon* (1952, United Artists).

8193 RICK MCALLISTER: "Money's nice but it doesn't make the world go around." PAUL SHERIDAN: "Don't it?... I promised myself as a kid that I'd have a lot of dough." Police officers **Phil Carey** and **Fred MacMurray** differ on the importance of money. *Pushover* (1954, Columbia).

8194 "You fall for them and you love 'em—you think it's going to be the biggest thing since the Graf Zeppelin—and the next thing you know, they're borrowing money from you and spending it on other dames and betting the horses.... Then one morning... the saxophone is gone and the guy is gone, and all that's left behind is a pair of socks and a tube of toothpaste, all squeezed out.... I can tell you one thing—it's not going to happen to me again. Ever. I'm tired of getting the fuzzy end of the lollipop." **Marilyn Monroe** tells saxophonist Tony Curtis, posing as a female musician, that she's had nothing but bad experiences with her lovers—all saxophonists. She promises herself that she has learned her lesson. She hasn't. *Some Like It Hot* (1959, United Artists).

8195 "Do you promise to give up all women, except me?" Cosmetics firm spy **Doris Day** seeks a promise from rival agent Richard Harris. *Caprice* (1967, 20th Century-Fox).

8196 "I don't yet know my powers nor my talents in farming, but I shall do my best—and if you serve me well, so I shall serve you. And don't suppose that because I am a woman I don't understand the difference between bad goings on and good. I shall be up before you are awake. I shall be afield before you're up, and I shall have breakfasted before you're afield. In short, I shall astonish you all." **Julie Christie**, the new mistress of a large farm, gives a pep talk to the hired help. *Far from the Madding Crowd* (1967, GB, EMI).

8197 "I'll do all the things you like." Hooker **Jamie Lee Curtis**, wearing a tight fitting pink mini dress and red wig, passionately kisses Dan Aykroyd and begs him for drugs on the front steps of police headquarters in front of his shocked fiancée, society girl Kristin Holby. *Trading Places* (1983, Paramount).

8198 "I promise you, if your wife never wakes up again, I'll take you to the restaurant of your choice. Do you like Chinese food?" Talent agent **Woody Allen** tries to calm a man whose wife has been put in a trance by Woody's client, an incompetent hypnotist, and she won't snap out of it. *Broadway Danny Rose* (1984, Orion).

8199 "Nighttime is a promise broken." Mute black alien Joe Morton, who lands in Harlem, has no more clue of Rastafarian **Yves Rene**'s meaning than do audiences. *The Brother from Another Planet* (1984, A-Train Films-Cinecom).

8200 "I'll be back...." Although his character didn't mean it that way, was there ever a doubt that **Arnold Schwarzenegger** would return in a sequel to this blockbuster hit? *The Terminator* (1984, Orion).

8201 "I'll fuck you so good." Would-be dancer and hooker **Rosanna Arquette** promises a potential customer a good time. *8 Million Ways to Die* (1986, Tri-Star).

8202 "When you sign with me, you get three people." In an unbilled appearance, **Martin Short** is a strange talent agent. When he makes this promise to aspiring movie director Kevin Bacon, Short holds up four fingers. *The Big Picture* (1989, Columbia).

8203 "If you build it, he will come." It's the voice that only Iowa farmer Kevin Costner can hear, but not necessarily understand. *Field of Dreams* (1989, Universal).

8204 "Every word I say is by definition a promise." Dead-pan Mafioso don **Marlon Brando** drolly upholds the fiction of honor among thieves. *The Freshman* (1990, Tri-Star).

8205 "I love you. I won't let you down." British publisher **Sean Connery** assures his Russian lover Michelle Pfeiffer that he won't desert her. *The Russia House* (1990, MGM-United Artists).

8206 "Stick with me, Baby, and you'll be farting through silk." It's **Adrian Dunbar**'s charming thought to his girl friend Tara Fitzgerald just before all of his grand dreams and plans fall apart. *Hear My Song* (1991, GB, Miramax).

8207 "Get rid of her, and Mr. Fuzzy is yours." Soap opera performer **Cathy Moriarty** holds out a promise of her sexual delights if TV executive Robert Downey, Jr. will dump her rival Sally Field. *Soapdish* (1991, Paramount).

Proofs

see also ARGUMENTS, DEMONSTRATIONS, LOGIC, MATHEMATICS, REASONS

8208 "I proved once and for all the limb is mightier than the thumb." **Claudette Colbert** is rather proud of herself after she pulls up the back of her dress to straighten her hem and gets a car to stop after all of Clark Gable's fancy hitchhiking ploys fail. *It Happened One Night* (1934, Columbia).

8209 "Oh, Mother, Godfrey loves me—he put me in the shower!" For ditzy **Carole Lombard**, William Powell's action is a sure sigh of his affection. *My Man Godfrey* (1936, Universal).

8210 FRED GAILEY: "Your honor, every one of these letters is addressed to Santa Claus. The post office has delivered them. The post office is a branch of the federal government. Therefore, the United States government recognizes this man, Kris Kringle, as the one and only Santa Claus." JUDGE HARPER: "Since the United States of America believes this man to be Santa Claus, this court will not dispute it." **John Payne**, attorney for Edmund Gwenn, who claims to be Santa Claus, piles bags full of letters addressed to Santa Claus on the desk of Judge **Gene Lockhart**. *Miracle on 34th Street* (1947, 20th Century-Fox).

8211 "The purpose of radio writing. . . is to prove to the masses that a deodorant can bring happiness, a mouthwash guarantees success and a laxative attracts romance." Poorly paid high school English teacher **Kirk Douglas** holds a high opinion of himself, but belittles the source of his soap opera writer wife Ann Sothern's income. *A Letter to Three Wives* (1949, 20th Century-Fox).

8212 "They were all disloyal. I wanted to run the ship properly. . . . They fought me at every turn. . . . Aha, the strawberries. That's where I had them. They laughed at me. But I proved beyond a shadow of doubt and with geometric logic that a duplicate key to the wardroom icebox did exist. I'd have produced that key if they didn't pull the Caine out of action." War weary **Humphrey Bogart**'s paranoid babbling clears Van Johnson and Robert Francis of mutiny. *The Caine Mutiny* (1954, Columbia).

8213 "Look at me! Can you face it? Look at this drippy fat of the land. Could you ever know that all my life I yearned for a world and people to call out the best in me? How can life be so empty? But it can't be! It can't! It's proven—statistics and graphs prove it—we are the world's happiest, earth's best. . . ." Depressed Hollywood star **Jack Palance** laments his lost potential. *The Big Knife* (1955, United Artists).

8214 "What a shame we haven't a scalpel with us. I'd make a slight incision to convince you." Eurasian **Jennifer Jones** puts up the defenses when brash William Holden tries to pick her up at a cocktail party with the sexist line that he can't believe she's a doctor. *Love Is a Many-Splendored Thing* (1955, 20th Century-Fox).

8215 "A man doesn't travel 4,000 miles just to prove he's a louse. He'd do that in a letter." By convict **Aldo Ray**'s reasoning, the man of Gloria Talbott's dreams, John Baer, has come all the way from France to Devil's Island to elope with her. *We're No Angels* (1955, Paramount).

8216 "He's so good he doesn't feel he's got to prove it." **John Wayne** refers to Ricky Nelson's skills with a six-gun, not his acting ability. *Rio Bravo* (1959, Warner Bros.).

8217 "I just wanna prove somethin'—I ain't no bum. . . . It don't matter if I lose. . . don't matter if he opens my head. . . . The only thing I wanna do is go the distance—That's all." **Sylvester Stallone**, a boxer who bleeds a lot, but can take the punishment, explains his goals for an upcoming fight with champion Carl Weathers. *Rocky* (1976, United Artists).

8218 "You see what I mean? Takin' over! Look at that!" In what may be the first of the recent Japanese-bashing movies, L.A. police detective **Charles Bronson** has a thorough dislike and fear of the Japanese. When he finds a large group of Japanese guests outside the L.A. Hilton, he takes it as proof of what he's been telling his partner about their intentions. *Kinjite: Forbidden Subjects* (1989, Cannon).

Propaganda *see* IDEAS, INTERESTS, NEWS AND NEWSPAPERS, OPINIONS

Property *see* BUILDINGS, HOMES, HOUSES, LAND AND FARMS, MONEY, POVERTY, WEALTH AND RICHES

Prophecies and Prophets

see also PREDICTIONS, RELIGIONS, TEACHING AND TEACHERS

8219 "We may be witnessing a biblical prophecy come true. . . . The beasts will reign over the earth." Scientist **Edmund Gwenn** refers to the giant ants threatening the world. *Them!* (1954, Warner Bros.).

8220 DR. ERASMUS CRAVEN: "Prophet! Thing of evil! Profit still, if bird or devil!. . . Tell this soul with sorrow laden if, within the distance Aidenn, it shall clasp a sainted maiden whom the angels named Leonore." THE RAVEN: "How the hell should I know? Whaddaya think I am, huh, a fortune teller?" Recently retired wizard **Vincent Price** seeks information about his beloved deceased wife from an obnoxious talking raven with the unmistakable voice of **Peter Lorre**. *The Raven* (1963, AIP).

8221 "I am a prophet." Symbionese Liberation Army's black General Field Marshal Cinque, played by **Ving Rhames**, introduces himself to his petrified captive, title character Natasha Richardson. *Patty Hearst* (1988, Atlantic).

8222 "Money is like the sun. Trust the coins, but beware the King of Swords." **Joseph Long** correctly interprets the prophecy of a roast pig in a dream, making him successful in his new country. *Queen of Hearts* (1989, GB, Cinecom).

Proposals

see also MARRIAGES, OFFERS, PLANS, TOASTS

8223 ACE LAMONT: "I must have your golden hair, your fascinating eyes, alluring smile and lovely arms, your form divine." RUBY CARTER: "Hold on, is this a proposal or are you taking inventory?" **John Miljan** is quite taken with **Mae West**'s physical allure, but she's not carried away by his sweet talk. *Belle of the Nineties* (1934, Paramount).

8224 "Marry me and I'll never look at another horse." **Groucho Marx** proposes to Margaret Dumont. He is a veterinarian, which explains somewhat his reference to an animal. *A Day at the Races* (1937, MGM).

8225 FLORENZ ZIEGFELD: "I haven't anything to offer you because there's nothing you really seem to need. You've made the most of yourself unassisted and that's grand. You're a great star already, so there's little I can offer you. Nothing I can give you except love." BILLIE BURKE: "That isn't enough. I expect part of your ambition, half of your troubles, two-thirds of your worries, and all of your respect." **William Powell** as the great showman proposes to **Myrna Loy**, as the famed actress who is best remembered for her flighty roles in several movies. She sounds pretty bright with this response. *The Great Ziegfeld* (1938, MGM).

8226 "Well, who's asking you to be rational? Listen, when I was courting your grandmother, it took me two years to propose. Know why? The moment she'd walk into a room, my knees would buckle, blood'd rush up into my head and—and the walls'd start to dance. Why, twice I keeled over in a dead faint.... She finally dragged it out of me when I was in bed with a 104 degree fever—and in a state of hysteria. The moment she accepted, the fever went down to normal—and I hopped out of bed. Oh, the case was written up in all the medical journals as the phenomenon of the times. There was nothing phenomenal about it. I just had it bad, that's all, and I never got over it." **Lionel Barrymore** offers the case of his marriage proposal as evidence to convince his granddaughter Jean Arthur that loving a person and rationality may be mutually exclusive. *You Can't Take It with You* (1938, Columbia).

8227 "What gentlemens say and what they thinks is two different things. And I ain't notices Mist' Ashley asking for to marry you." **Hattie McDaniel** tells Vivien Leigh that she might as well give up on winning Leslie Howard away from his wife Olivia de Havilland. *Gone with the Wind* (1939, Selznick-MGM).

8228 "I can't go through all my life waiting to catch you between husbands." **Clark Gable** proposes marriage to Vivien Leigh—recently widowed for the second time. *Gone with the Wind* (1939, Selznick-MGM).

8229 "I never wanted to see you again. But you pulled me here with a two-inch cable. I'm taking you out of the side show.... You're coming with me as my wife... in the eyes of God, and man, and the United States Passport Bureau." American playboy **Robert Taylor** rather forcefully proposes marriage to beautiful Saigon half-caste Hedy Lamarr. *Lady of the Tropics* (1939, MGM).

8230 "I'm asking you to marry me, you little fool." **Laurence Olivier** sweet-talks shy, naïve Joan Fontaine, who thinks he wants to hire her for some purpose. *Rebecca* (1940, Selznick-United Artists).

8231 PETER VAN ALLEN: "I'm asking you to marry me." SANDRA: "You were much more amusing the first time." PETER: "Well, I'm sober now." Having discovered that their marriage is illegal because it occurred before her divorce decree became final, **George Brent** isn't so excited about marrying **Mary Astor** again. *The Great Lie* (1941, Warner Bros.).

8232 "You'll never want for food, and you'll never worry about rent. I've worked since I was seven.... I'm 21. I'm not legitimate. I've got good teeth. I'm not tattooed." Young Scot soldier **Richard Todd** tells older nurse Patricia Neal what she'll get if she marries him. *The Hasty Heart* (1949, Warner Bros.).

8233 "Uh, that is, I mean, uh. I'll pick you up. We could go to the license bureau and get married and then have a baby and have another baby in the country, and oh, Julie." After a stumbling beginning, **Frank Sinatra** gets ahead of himself with his proposal of marriage to Debbie Reynolds. *The Tender Trap* (1955, MGM).

8234 "Better Wed Than Dead." It's the sign **Steve McQueen** holds up near the end of the movie, proposing to his pregnant girl friend Natalie Wood. *Love with the Proper Stranger* (1963, Paramount).

8235 "When we are married, I shall work twice as hard as I do now.... I know I can make you happy.... And at night by the fire, whenever I look up, there you will be... and whenever you look up, there I shall be." Plain-speaking but earnest shepherd **Alan Bates** pledges his troth to Julie Christie. *Far from the Madding Crowd* (1967, GB, EMI).

Propositions

see also BARGAINS, DEALS AND DEALINGS, LOGIC,
OFFERS, PLANS, PROPOSALS, SEX AND SEXUALITY

8236 "Tell you what. I got a proposition for you.
Now you sing us your song, and you can have a
drink." **Edward G. Robinson** cruelly offers to trade
booze for Claire Trevor's pitiful rendition of
"Moanin' Low." *Key Largo* (1948, Warner Bros.).

8237 "Your wife, my father—crisscross." Psychotic
Robert Walker proposes exchanging murders with
tennis star Farley Granger. *Strangers on a Train*
(1951, Warner Bros.).

8238 "You made a business proposition. I agree to
that part of it. As for the rest of the proposition, it's
not an impossibility, it's merely an improbability,
and, above all, an impertinence." Down-and-out
noblewoman **Danielle Darrieux** slaps valet James
Mason, letting him know that they may be partners
as spies, but his being a servant makes him unsuitable as a lover. *Five Fingers* (1952, 20th Century-
Fox).

8239 "Mr. Allen, this may come as a shock to you;
but there are some men who don't end every sentence with a proposition." Interior decorator **Doris
Day** is indignant with playboy composer Rock Hudson who shares her party line. *Pillow Talk* (1959,
Universal).

8240 "Remember when I said I'd never really let you
make love to me until I was married? Well, I'm married now." **Jessica Walter** makes an amusing offer
to uninterested Warren Beatty after her husband
Gene Hackman departs. *Lilith* (1964, Columbia).

8241 MATTIE ROSS: "What about my proposition?"
ROOSTER COGBURN: "I am thinking on it." MATTIE: "It
sounds like a mighty easy way to make fifty dollars
to me. You would just be doing your job anyway,
and getting extra pay besides." ROOSTER: "Don't
crowd me. I am thinking about expenses. If I am
going up against Ned Pepper I will need a hundred
dollars. I have figured out that much. I will want
fifty dollars in advance." Young **Kim Darby** bargains with Marshal **John Wayne** to go into outlaw
territory to bring out Jeff Corey, who murdered
Darby's father. Corey is now riding with Robert
Duvall's gang. *True Grit* (1969, Paramount).

8242 "You always wanted my body. Now you've
killed my husband. Take me." Half-naked **Mary
Elizabeth Mastrantonio** offers herself to her hoodlum brother Al Pacino as she shoots inexpertly at
him with a pistol. *Scarface* (1983, Universal).

8243 "It's possible we make jig-a-jig." Italian POW
Giovanni Mauriello may not know how to say it
in English, but he knows what he wants from love-
starved Scottish farmer's wife Phyllis Logan, and so
does she. *Another Time, Another Place* (1984, GB,
Umbrella-Goldwyn).

8244 "Let's do it. Right here on the Oriental." **Anjelica Huston** makes Mafioso soldier Jack Nicholson
an offer he can't refuse. *Prizzi's Honor* (1985, 20th
Century-Fox).

Propriety

see also BEHAVIOR, CONDITIONS, CORRECTIONS,
RIGHT AND WRONG, WRONGS AND WRONGDOINGS

8245 "I can't behave properly. I can't paint properly,
but I can live my life properly." **Charles Laughton**
is the Dutch painter Rembrandt Harmensz van Rijn,
whose paintings may not have been proper when
painted, but are memorable. *Rembrandt* (1936, GB,
London Films-United Artists).

8246 "A girl should never kiss a man she doesn't
intend to marry." **Judy Garland** is a very proper
and old-fashioned girl in a sentimental New York
City period piece. *Little Nellie Kelly* (1940, MGM).

8247 "I'm not sure of the protocol in a case like this,
but. . . ." U.S. Representative **Joseph Cotten** is in
love with new U.S. Representative Loretta Young,
formerly a maid in his mother's home. *The Farmer's
Daughter* (1947, RKO).

8248 "You, my dear chap, have the habit of over-
charging yourself with emotion when facing the jury,
and I'm bound to confess that it does not particularly appeal to my sense of what's proper in court."
At a dinner party, Judge **Charles Laughton** finds
fault with the conduct of Barrister Gregory Peck. *The
Paradine Case* (1947, Selznick-United Artists).

8249 "I want to be proper. I want to meet the
proper man with the proper position and make a
proper wife and raise proper children." Prostitute
Donna Reed turns down Montgomery Clift's marriage proposal. She plans to work at her profession long enough to save enough money so she
can leave Hawaii for the mainland with a tidy nest
egg for the future. *From Here to Eternity* (1953,
Columbia).

8250 "There shall be no bowing like toad nor
crouching nor crawling. This does not mean, however, you do not show respect for king. You will
stand with shoulders back and chin high like this.
You will face king with proud expression showing

pride in self as well as in king. This is proper way for men to show esteem for one another. By looking upon each other's faces with kindness of spirit, eyes meeting eyes in equal gaze. Bodies upright, standing as men were meant to stand with dignity. . . ." At the death of his father Yul Brynner, Crown Prince **Patrick Adiarte** of Siam, shows the influence of his English tutor Deborah Kerr in changing the way his subjects will meet him. *The King and I* (1956, 20th Century-Fox).

8251 "There's only one proper way for a professional soldier to die. That's from the last bullet of the last battle of the last war." Title character **George C. Scott** states his preferred end. He doesn't get it. *Patton* (1970, 20th Century-Fox).

8252 "I had so many years of being so very proper. I had good-girl claustrophobia." **Bo Derek** explains to her chauffeur George Kennedy why she mooned the teachers and students of her private girls' boarding school after graduation exercises. *Bolero* (1984, Cannon).

8253 "The war's put an end to decent things. . . we did the proper things and we lost love." **Sarah Miles** sadly confesses to Derrick O'Connor, the man she didn't marry, but now realizes she should have. *Hope and Glory* (1987, GB, Columbia).

Prospects *see* CHANCES, EXPECTATIONS

Prostitution and Prostitutes

see also KISSES AND KISSING, LOVE AND LOVERS, LUST, PERVERSIONS, PROMISCUITY, SEDUCTIONS, SEX AND SEXUALITY

8254 "Confound it, sir, that's Shanghai Lily. For the last fortnight I've been treating a man who went out of his mind after spending a day with her." Parson **Lawrence Grant** gives Clive Brook the low-down on his former lover Marlene Dietrich in this drama about the events on a train as it passes through war-torn China. *Shanghai Express* (1932, Paramount).

8255 "I'm a girl you met at the New Congress Club. That's two steps up from the pavement." **Donna Reed** reminds soldier Montgomery Clift that she's little more than a streetwalker. The film called her a "hostess"—a pseudonym for prostitute. *From Here to Eternity* (1953, Columbia).

8256 "I'm hooked on a hooker!" **Tony Franciosa** laments his love for prostitute Gina Lollobrigida. *Go Naked in the World* (1960, MGM).

8257 "She's enough to make a bulldog bust its chain." Small town Sheriff **Anthony Eisley** admires

ex-prostitute Constance Towers. *The Naked Kiss* (1964, Allied Artists).

8258 "I don't take whores in taxis." Angry **Dirk Bogarde** lashes his unfaithful lover Julie Christie with his tongue. *Darling* (1965, GB, Anglo-Amalgamated).

8259 "Look at it this way, you had sex with your husband in exchange for your bed and board. Now you're a harlot and you take money. Small difference." Opium-addicted madam **Julie Christie** rationalizes for whore Shelley Duvall. *McCabe and Mrs. Miller* (1971, Warner Bros.).

8260 "At least I know where she is at night." Unlikely porno star **Dom De Luise** finds something positive about his wife being a hooker. *The Last Married Couple in America* (1980, Universal).

8261 "My God, you're a hooker? I thought I was making out so well!" Drunken **Dudley Moore** makes a scene for the benefit of patrons of the Oak Room of New York's Plaza Hotel, where he has taken streetwalker Anne DeSalvo dressed to kill in red hot pants. Having seen everything in her trade, DeSalvo isn't taken aback in the least by his behavior. *Arthur* (1981, Warner Bros.).

8262 "I don't know why. That little tart could save you a fortune in prostitutes." **John Gielgud** doesn't understand why Dudley Moore should break up with Liza Minnelli just because his family is blackmailing him into marrying Jill Eikenberry or lose his huge inheritance. *Arthur* (1981, Warner Bros.).

8263 "Whores are high school girls doing it for nothing." Twenty dollar hooker **Sally Field** complains about amateurs. *Back Roads* (1981, Meta Films-Warner Bros.).

8264 "I was a very sinful whore until I found Christ my Redeemer." Former child prostitute **Lydia Lei** begs Frederic Forrest to hide her for a few hours, cajoling him by kissing his fingers. Her redemption doesn't seem complete. *Hammett* (1983, Orion-Warner Bros.).

8265 "She was a whore of an angel who flew too close to the ground and crashed." Drunken poet **Ben Gazzara** refers to low-life Ornella Muti, who is supposed to be a symbol for mutilation. *Tales of Ordinary Madness* (1983, Italy, Giugno-Ginis-Miracle).

8266 "You know what happens to used up whores? They don't go to Leisure World, baby." Cop **Cliff Gorman** seems to believe lines like that will get baby hookers like Donna Wilkes off the streets. *Angel* (1984, New World).

8267 "It's not a prom date, sweetie. I'm a hooker, you're a trick. Why ruin a perfect relationship." It's the reply of sultry, cheap-looking prostitute **Kathleen Turner** when customer John Laughlin asks her, "Who are you?" *Crimes of Passion* (1984, New World).

8268 "Prostitution isn't just spreading your legs." Prostitute **Christine Moore** insists her profession isn't as simple as it seems. *Alexa* (1989, Platinum-B Tru).

8269 "If you're going to work in a whorehouse, there's only one thing to be—the best whore in the house." Writer **Bruce Willis** figures he's prostituting his talents—but the pay is excellent. *The Bonfire of the Vanities* (1990, Warner Bros.).

8270 "If you want to be a whore, you can be one for the rest of your life." **Anthony Quinn** delivers his unfaithful wife Madeleine Stowe to a bordello. *Revenge* (1990, Columbia).

Protection

see also DEFENSES, HARM, HURT AND HURTING

8271 "I'm just a guy with a one-ton brain who's too nervous to steal and too lazy to work. I do other people's thinking for them and make them like it. I realize that human beings have their weakness and all the man-made laws in the country were made to protect honest people. And how many people will admit that they're not honest? Racketeering is just getting what the other guy's got in a nice way." Mobster **Spencer Tracy** establishes a protection racket for garage owners. *Quick Millions* (1931, Fox).

8272 "You'll be coming back, Harry. I can see a huge safari with you at the head bearing ivory down to the coast. Only this time there'll be no danger. Because we'll be there to protect you every stop of the way." **Maureen O'Sullivan** consoles Neal Hamilton as she sends him on his way, having decided to stay behind in the jungle with title character Johnny Weissmuller. *Tarzan, the Ape Man* (1932, MGM).

8273 "We're off for Hollywood where dear Mr. Hays will protect me." In an in-joke, aging countess and former showgirl **Mary Boland**, who has been married many times, speaks of the former postmaster general of the United States who served as the movie industry's own censor. *The Women* (1939, MGM).

8274 "You want to be at the mercy of every slug who wears a uniform? You need someone to protect you from human greed." **Brian Donlevy** gives a sales pitch for a protection racket run by crooked politicians. *The Great McGinty* (1940, Paramount).

8275 "Every man I meet wants to protect me. I can't figure out what from." **Mae West**, as Flower Belle Lee, muses about men. *My Little Chickadee* (1940, Universal).

8276 "I get paid to protect people. I don't have to like them." And Police Captain **Dean Jagger** doesn't particularly like small-time hood and con man Charlton Heston. *Dark City* (1950, Paramount).

8277 "Protecting the prisoner, because if he escaped you would be forced to shoot him in the back." **Lou Gilbert** is one of thousands of Mexican peasants who fall into line as two policemen march Marlon Brando off to jail. He responds to their question, "What are you doing?" *Viva Zapata!* (1952, 20th Century-Fox).

8278 "When a girl's under 21, she's protected by the law; when she's over 65 she's protected by nature. Anywhere in between, she's fair game." When told that Dina Merrill is messing with womanizer Tony Curtis, submarine Commander **Cary Grant** makes an extremely insensitive comment. *Operation Petticoat* (1959, Universal).

8279 "When I was fourteen I knew I should carry around an emergency contraceptive. By the time I got around to using it, it was dust." **Woody Allen** believed in being protected—he just had nothing to be protected from. *Annie Hall* (1977, United Artists).

8280 "You got to treat us different. We're the only thing between you and the jungle." New York cop **Treat Williams** speaks of an elite group of cops, the Special Investigations Unit, of which he is a member. He claims it is the first line of defense for the public against the criminal scum of the city. *Prince of the City* (1981, Warner Bros.).

Protests

see also REBELLIONS, REVOLUTIONS

8281 BARBARA WILLIS: "We shouldn't have done that." DENNIS CARSON: "We did." **Mary Astor** feebly protests the kiss she shares with **Clark Gable**, the head of a rubber plantation in the Far East. When her engineer husband is out of the way, they will be naughtier. *Red Dust* (1932, MGM).

8282 "I protest against collapse of decency in the world. I protest against corruption in local politics. I protest against civic heads being in league with crime. I protest against state relief being used as political football. I protest against County Hospital's shutting out the needy. I protest against all the brutality and slaughter in the world." The things that "John Doe," played by **Gary Cooper**, protests against are written by reporter Barbara Stanwyck. *Meet John Doe* (1941, Warner Bros.).

8283 "How can you make a Yale man a private?" Wealthy socialite **Nella Walker** protests the treatment of her son Lee Bowman after he's been drafted. *Buck Privates* (1941, Universal).

8284 "But Muffy hasn't been in an institution for three years; she's been at Vassar!" Collegian **Deborah Goodrich** protests on behalf of her friend Deborah Foreman in a spoof of holiday horror films. *April Fool's Day* (1986, Paramount).

8285 "Can't things be just what they are on the surface sometimes?" **Woody Allen** protests that his wife Bette Midler looks for too many hidden meanings. *Scenes from a Mall* (1991, Touchstone-Buena Vista).

Proverbs and Sayings

8286 "Oh, no, there is an old saying, all is fair in love and war, but no slingshot." **Luis Alberni** has the last line in this oater featuring John Wayne as the new sheriff who must take on vicious cattle rustler Noah Beery. *The Big Stampede* (1932, Warner Bros.).

8287 "And the people said: 'Lo! The beast looked upon the face of beauty and it stayed its hand from killing.' And from that day it was as one dead." An African proverb opens the film. *King Kong* (1933, RKO).

8288 "The colder they are, the hotter I get, is what I always say." Persistent and annoying traveling salesman **Roscoe Karns** proudly quotes himself to an uninterested Claudette Colbert. *It Happened One Night* (1934, Columbia).

8289 "'Mon amour dure après la mort (My love endures after death).' That was written for us, and for everyone on earth who will ever feel as we do." Married violinist **Leslie Howard** reads the words carved in stone at the ruins of a Mediterranean village to his protégé and lover Ingrid Bergman. *Intermezzo* (1939, Selznick-United Artists).

8290 "There is an old Russian saying: 'The cat who has cream on his whiskers had better find good excuses.'" Special Russian Communist emissary **Greta Garbo** invents an appropriate proverb to warn Sig Rumann, Alexander Granach and Felix

Bressart that they had better have a good explanation for living like capitalists in Paris. *Ninotchka* (1939, MGM).

8291 TORCHY BLANE: "There's an old Chinese saying: 'What's sauce for the goose is sauce for the gander.'" STEVE MCBRIDE: "And it's a wise goose that doesn't stick her neck out." TORCHY: "Don't worry about me. I can always duck." Reporter **Glenda Farrell** always gets the last word with her tough cop boy friend **Barton MacLane**. *Torchy Blane in Chinatown* (1939, Warner Bros.).

8292 "Don't forget the old proverb, Doctor: never trust a man who doesn't drink." Judge **Barry Fitzgerald** warns physician Walter Huston. *And Then There Were None* (1945, 20th Century-Fox).

8293 "The Argentineans say, 'three days of sowing wild oats, and then the harvest.'" Married **Rita Hayworth** expects retribution for her affair with Glenn Ford. *Gilda* (1946, Columbia).

8294 "Man who trust woman walk on duckweed over pond." **Alan Ladd** quotes a Gurkha saying for treacherous Gail Russell. *Calcutta* (1947, Paramount).

8295 "The Somalis have a proverb. . . 'A brave man is afraid of a lion three times: when he first sees its track, when he first hears its roar and when he first looks it in the eye.'" White hunter **Gregory Peck** shares some native wisdom with his safari client Robert Preston. *The Macomber Affair* (1947, United Artists).

8296 HAN SUYIN: "There is an old Chinese proverb: 'Do not wake a sleeping tiger.'" MARK ELLIOT: "Certainly not in a small boat." Eurasian doctor **Jennifer Jones** has little luck getting lover **William Holden** to take the old Chinese proverbs seriously. *Love Is a Many-Splendored Thing* (1955, 20th Century-Fox).

8297 "I come from a long line of Swedes. We have a saying too: 'When the cat's away, why should the mouse act like a rat?'" Magazine photographer **Celeste Holm** manufactures a proverb to fit her straying boy friend, writer Frank Sinatra. *High Society* (1956, MGM).

8298 "Tears are good. You know what they say in Turkey? They say, 'Tears wash the eyes that one can see better.'" **Heinz Ruehmann** makes up a proverb to help him console tearful Gila Golan, who believes herself to be an ugly duckling. *Ship of Fools* (1965, Columbia).

8299 LINDA CHRISTIE: "That's beautiful." ALLAN FELIX: "It's from *Casablanca*. I waited my whole life to say it." **Diane Keaton** and **Woody Allen** have just replayed the final scene of *Casablanca* between Ingrid Bergman and Humphrey Bogart, almost verbatim. *Play It Again, Sam* (1972, Paramount).

8300 "He who has two lovers loses his heart; he who has two houses loses his mind." The proverb introduces the film. *Full Moon in Paris* (1984, Fr., Les Films Arione).

8301 "Some people say freeways are the cathedrals of our time—not me." Talking Heads' **David Byrne** states in rock-video about the eccentric lives of the weird folks who reside in Virgil, Texas. *True Stories* (1986, Warner Bros.).

8302 "Here in L.A., we have a saying: 'A friend is someone who stabs you in the front.'" Narcotics agent **Kathy Shower** narrates over the titles. *Commando Squad* (1987, Trans World).

8303 "Twenty dwarfs took turns doing handstands on the carpet." It's the mantra-like saying **Warren Beatty**, as Ben "Bugsy" Siegel, repeats time and time again to improve his diction. *Bugsy* (1991, Tri-Star).

Providence *see* FATE AND DESTINY

Psychology and Psychiatry

see also CARES AND CARING, CURES, DISEASES, DOCTORS AND DENTISTS, MEDICINE, MINDS, NERVOUSNESS AND NERVES

8304 "I wanted to be a dancer. Psychiatry showed me I was wrong." **Fred Astaire** is an unusual psychiatrist to whom Ginger Rogers comes for help in making up her mind about Ralph Bellamy. The musical numbers aren't up to the standards of other teamings of Astaire and Rogers. *Carefree* (1938, RKO).

8305 "There's nothing shameful about my work but frightening ideas. It's very simple really what I try to do. People walk along a road. They come to a fork in the road. They're confused. They don't know which way to take. I just put up a signpost: 'Not that way—this way.'" Psychiatrist **Claude Rains** gives a simplistic explanation of his work in this drama about a repressed spinister who is brought out by a psychiatrist. *Now, Voyager* (1942, Warner Bros.).

8306 "Good night and sweet dreams. . . which we will analyze at breakfast." Psychology professor **Michael Chekhov** wishes Gregory Peck and Ingrid Bergman interesting and revealing dreams. *Spellbound* (1945, United Artists).

8307 "I have a great respect for psychiatry—and great contempt for meddling amateurs who go around practicing it." Department store Santa Claus **Edmund Gwenn** tells off store personnel counselor Porter Hall. Hall comes off as one of the movies' great villains, the man who tried to have the real Santa Claus committed. *Miracle on 34th Street* (1947, 20th Century-Fox).

8308 "Maybe someday some autopsy will analyze that mind." Head shrink **Stephen McNally** refers to bigoted Richard Widmark, who has sworn he'll kill young black doctor Sidney Poitier. *No Way Out* (1950, 20th Century-Fox).

8309 "Why don't you analyze my Oedipus complex or my lousy father?" Young mental patient **John Kerr** questions Richard Widmark, the head of a psychiatric clinic. *The Cobweb* (1955, MGM).

8310 "I should have listened to my psychiatrist. He told me never to trust anyone but him." **Tony Randall** reacts when he discovers that his best pal Rock Hudson is after his best gal Doris Day. *Pillow Talk* (1959, Universal).

8311 "I have to tell my psychiatrist everything that happens to me. We're down to the smaller, starker details." Promiscuous **Elizabeth Taylor** tells latest lover Laurence Harvey that their love-making is discussed with her analyst. *Butterfield 8* (1960, MGM).

8312 "A psychiatrist doesn't lay the ground work; he merely tries to explain it." Psychiatrist **Simon Oakland** clears up the loose ends regarding the behavior of Anthony Perkins as Norman Bates. *Psycho* (1960, Paramount).

8313 "Who ever heard of a Negro psychiatrist anyway? Don't you people have enough trouble? Boy, you must be a real masochist." Black prison psychiatrist Sidney Poitier is baited by violent racist **Bobby Darin**. *Pressure Point* (1962, United Artists).

8314 "The man who polices my psyche." It's how **Inger Stevens** describes her psychiatrist. *House of Cards* (1969, Universal).

8315 "I was in analysis for years. Nothing happened. My poor analyst got so frustrated, the guy finally put in a salad bar." **Woody Allen**'s years in psychoanalysis didn't help rid him of his hypochondria. *Hannah and Her Sisters* (1987, Orion).

8316 "He's not hallucinating in a manner characteristic of psychosis. . . . He appears to have adapted very well to life at a high level of uncertainty." Psychiatrist **Frances Sternhagen** testifies at the sanity hearing of author Christopher Walken. The latter claims to have been visited by extraterrestrials who tell him, "you are the chosen one." *Communion* (1989, Vestron).

8317 "I'm offering you a psychological profile of Buffalo Bill based on case evidence. I'll help you catch him, Clarice." **Anthony Hopkins**, as mad psychologist Dr. Hannibal "The Cannibal" Lecter, offers to help FBI trainee Jodie Foster catch a serial killer who skins his victims. *The Silence of the Lambs* (1991, Orion).

Public

see also PEOPLE

8318 "The public is like a cow, bellowing—bellowing to be milked." Press agent **James Cagney** promotes rigged contests and trick products. *Hard to Handle* (1933, Warner Bros.).

8319 "The public doesn't give a damn about integrity. A town that won't defend itself deserves no help. Get out, Will. It's all for nothing." Aged and arthritic ex-marshal **Lon Chaney, Jr.** advises retiring peacemaker Gary Cooper to leave Hadleyville and not face the gunman who wants to kill Cooper. The villain arrives on the noon train and with three henchmen comes looking for Cooper. *High Noon* (1952, United Artists).

8320 "The world is full of Allesandros and Anglos. They are your public. You owe them something—your voice." **Johanna von Koczian** encourages opera singer Mario Lanza to go on with his career. *For the First Time* (1959, US-Ger.-Italy, MGM).

Punishments

see also CRIMES AND CRIMINALS, DISCIPLINES, EXECUTIONS, JUDGMENTS, JUSTICE, LAWS, LAWYERS, PAINS, PRISONS AND PRISONERS

8321 "I have been whipped. Now can I have the milk?" Caught and punished for stealing milk for a baby, **Mary Pickford** believes she's entitled to her booty. *Tess of the Storm Country* (1914, silent, Famous Players).

8322 VRONSKY: "You're trembling. Are you cold?" ANNA: "We'll be punished." VRONSKY: "Punished?" ANNA: "For being so happy." **Fredric March** is not punished for his affair with married **Greta Garbo**, but she is. *Anna Karenina* (1935, MGM).

8323 "There is punishment for those who emulate God." **Elsa Lanchester**, as Mary Wollstonecraft Shelley, expresses an oft-repeated anti-intellectual warning found in movies featuring scientists who develop some kind of madness. *The Bride of Frankenstein* (1935, Universal).

8324 "David, come here. If I have an obstinate horse or dog to deal with, what do you think I do?. . . I beat him! I make him wince and smart! I say to myself, 'I'll conquer that fellow'—and if it were to cost him all the blood he had—I'd do it." **Basil Rathbone**, as Mr. Murdstone, thrashes his stepson title character Freddie Bartholomew. Rathbone hated giving the young actor the beating, even though Freddie's bottom was well-protected. *David Copperfield* (1935, MGM).

8325 "You big bully, why are you hitting that little bully?" **Groucho Marx** chastises Sig Rumann for cuffing Harpo Marx. *A Night at the Opera* (1935, MGM).

8326 "Dr. Mudd? I've been waitin' for you. So all they gave you was life?. . . Couldn't hang ya, eh? Well by Judas, you're gonna wish they had before I'm through with ya!. . . Take a look at him, you filthy rats. Take a look at the man who killed Abe Lincoln, the greatest man who ever lived! Look at him! Watch him get what's coming to him!" Sadistic sergeant of the guards **John Carradine** punches title character Warner Baxter in the face, knocking him to the ground. Carradine tells the other prisoners of the hellish Tortugas to look at the man Carradine holds personally responsible for Lincoln's assassination. *The Prisoner of Shark Island* (1936, 20th Century-Fox).

8327 "I was going to thrash them within an inch of their lives but I didn't have a tape measure." His brothers Chico and Harpo are getting on **Groucho Marx**'s nerves again. *At the Circus* (1939, MGM).

8328 "You know, Christopher's grandmother was never any good 'til one night I spanked her with her own hairbrush. . . and so after that she was all right. We had no more trouble with her at all." **Claude Gillingwater** recommends to Fred MacMurray that he whip the old man's granddaughter Madeleine Carroll into shape. *Cafe Society* (1939, Paramount).

8329 "I've always thought a good lashing with a buggy whip would benefit you immensely." **Clark Gable** threatens Vivien Leigh with what he might do if she doesn't get their daughter's things packed for a trip to London as he insists. *Gone with the Wind* (1939, Selznick-MGM).

8330 "It's permissible for a wife to be beaten, as long as she's struck not more than nine times with an instrument not larger than a broomstick." Judge **Monty Woolley** quotes an alleged French law that allows wife abuse. *Midnight* (1939, Paramount).

8331 "Somebody must have given you an awful beating once." Falling in love with cynical Cary Grant, **Jean Arthur** correctly surmises that some dame did him wrong, making him the way he is. *Only Angels Have Wings* (1939, Columbia).

8332 "A bunch of lazy people trying to get something for nothin'.... What you need is a good spanking." Incompetent waiter **George Murphy** is angry with debutante Brenda Joyce, who he believes has been duped by the communists. Murphy turns her over his knee and to the tune of "Ta-Ra-Ra-Boom-De-Ay" paddles her fanny. Spanking women in the movies at the time was often seen as a move towards romance. *Public Deb No. 1* (1940, 20th Century-Fox).

8333 "Something had happened. A thing which years ago had been the eagerest hope of many good citizens of the town. And now it had come at last; George Amberson Minafer had got his comeuppance. He got it three times filled and running over. But those who had longed for it were not there to see it, and they never knew it. Those who were still living had forgotten all about it and all about him." Narrator **Orson Welles** speaks of the deserved fall of the proud, selfish Tim Holt, scion of a once most prominent and influential family that has lost its wealth. Over the years, many in the community, stung by the young man's arrogant and insensitive behavior, prayed for the punishment he was now experiencing. *The Magnificent Ambersons* (1942, RKO).

8334 "You will see that the woman is punished. Death that comes quickly is not punishment. There are other forms that must be more painfully absorbed." As he prepares to commit ritual suicide for his failure, **John Emery**, as Premier Tanaka, gives orders to Robert Armstrong, as Colonel Tojo, to be sure that interfering Chinese woman Sylvia Sidney is punished for upsetting their plans. *Blood on the Sun* (1945, United Artists).

8335 "You forgot—in your imbecilic devotion to your patient—that the punishment for two murders is the same as for one." **Leo G. Carroll** threatens Ingrid Bergman, who has discovered that he's guilty of the murder of which her lover and patient Gregory Peck was suspected. *Spellbound* (1945, United Artists).

8336 ROUSTABOUT: "How can a guy get so low?" CARNIVAL MANAGER: "He reached too high." In the movie's final scene, insisted upon by the Hays office, the degradation of irreverent con man Tyrone Power is discussed on the fairgrounds. Power has been reduced to appearing as a geek in a tawdry carnival. *Nightmare Alley* (1947, 20th Century-Fox).

8337 "Prew, listen, Fatso done it, Prew. He liked to whack me in the gut. He asks me if it hurts and I spit at him like always—only yesterday it was bad. He hit me. He hit me." **Frank Sinatra**'s death scene ensures him an Oscar. He tells Montgomery Clift that sadistic stockade Sergeant Ernest Borgnine has beaten him to death. *From Here to Eternity* (1953, Columbia).

8338 "Our life was too good and we were satisfied with ourselves. The Lord wanted to punish us for our complacency." Squire **Gunnar Bjornstrand** tries to find a reason for the bad times in his world. *The Seventh Seal* (1956, Sweden, Svensk Filmindustri).

8339 "Three years in the Marine Corps. Five years in the ring. He has to come home to get half-killed." **Elizabeth Hartman** refers to living legend Joe Don Baker, who can take punishment. He's been carved up so badly by a gang of goons that he requires 200 stitches. *Walking Tall* (1973, BCP-Cinerama).

8340 "Pimples are the Lord's way of chastising you." **Piper Laurie** uses God as a weapon against her daughter Sissy Spacek. *Carrie* (1976, Paramount).

8341 "You don't punish me enough." **Paolo Malco**, as Dr. Leopold von Sacher-Masoch, complains that his wife Francesca de Sapio doesn't torment him enough. Later, when she gets the swing of it, he complains, "Your behavior is impairing my work." There's just no pleasing men. *Masoch* (1980, Italy, Difilm-Tierrepi).

8342 "You wouldn't want me to have to pull down your pants and spank your buns, would you?" New neighbor **Cathy Moriarty** seductively drapes herself all over John Belushi. His expression leads one to believe that the prospect both shocks and excites him. *Neighbors* (1981, Columbia).

8343 "You can just sit there in the dark and think about what you have done." Wacky scientist **Richard Liberty** attempts to civilize a captive zombie. *Day of the Dead* (1985, United Film-Laurel).

Puns

see also COMEDY AND COMEDIANS, HUMOR, WORDS

8344 JOHN KENT: "They tell me in Paris, if you don't buy your gown from Roberta, you're not dressed at all." HUCK HAINES: "I see, nude if you don't and nude if you do." Football player **Randolph Scott** and band leader **Fred Astaire** comment on the work of Parisian dress designer Helen Westley. *Roberta* (1935, RKO)

8345 "Don't take gravity too lightly or it will pull you down." **Karl Swenson**, the voice of Merlin, gives punnish advice to Ricky Sorenson, the voice of Wart. *The Sword in the Stone* (1963, Disney-Buena Vista).

8346 DR. ORMSBY: "We want you to feel a member of our congregation." GOWAN MCGLAND: "Who is she?" Even in responding to the hospitality of the local minister **Ed Grady**, visiting poet **Tom Conti** feels obliged to be irreverent. *Reuben, Reuben* (1983, 20th Century-Fox).

8347 "He disagreed with something that ate him." Vicious drug king **Robert Davi** makes a pun in referring to American agent David Hedison, whom Davi partially fed to sharks. *Licence to Kill* (1989, GB, United Artists).

Purity

see also INNOCENCE

8348 "A girl may look as pure as a freshly fallen snow—and then you find the footprints of a hundred men." Middle-age philanderer **Gary Cooper** is always searching for an "untouched" woman but he touches all he can get his hands on. *Love in the Afternoon* (1957, Allied Artists).

8349 "Boys with impure minds come out in acne, you know." Housekeeper **Patricia Neal** teases teen Brandon De Wilde when she discovers dirty pictures in his room. *Hud* (1963, Paramount).

8350 GEORGE: "I think you'll enjoy this. Type double O positive. The type is rare." COUNT DRACULA: "Beautiful." COUNTESS DRACULA: "Pure?" COUNT: "Oh, that is too much to hope for." In order to serve champagne glasses filled with blood to his master, **Alex D'Arcy** and mistress **Paula Raymond**, evil butler **John Carradine** has tapped the veins of some beautiful girls the Draculas have chained in their cellar. *Blood of Dracula's Castle* (1969, Crown International).

8351 "To the pure in heart, all things are pure." It's the sentiment expressed on the grave stone of young Nicholas Gledhill's mother. *Careful, He Might Hear You* (1983, Australia, TLC Films).

8352 "I haven't had anything this pure since the Vienna Boys Choir hit town." Beautiful 400-year-old vampire **Lauren Hutton** licks her chops when she sees horny 18-year-old virgin Jim Carrey. *Once Bitten* (1985, Goldwyn).

8353 "We must be pure.... Let's do some good." Special federal law enforcement agent **Kevin Cost**ner gives a pep talk to his team, whose assignment is to get Al Capone without being bought off. *The Untouchables* (1987, Paramount).

Purposes

see also DECISIONS, ENDS AND ENDINGS, INTENTIONS, RESOLUTIONS

8354 "The purpose of this film is to depict an environment, rather than glorify the criminal." It's the preface of a movie starring James Cagney and Edward Woods as two slum boys who begin as bootleggers. Their climb up the criminal ladders ends with a fall to their deaths. *The Public Enemy* (1931, Warner Bros.).

8355 MCQUARG: "You been smelling rubber and sweating to get it and you'll die that way." DENNIS CARSON: "Yeah, just so some old woman can take a hot water bottle to bed with her." MCQUARG: "Yeah, and so some baby can suck on a rubber nipple." **Tully Marshall** and **Clark Gable** discuss the purpose of their hard work on a rubber plantation. *Red Dust* (1932, MGM).

8356 "The purpose of life is to work and eat and sleep and screw and drink and to keep goin'—that's all there is." **Henry Fonda** reduces the purpose of life to fundamental appetites. *Sometimes a Great Notion* (1971, Universal).

8357 "A surprising number of human beings are without purpose, though it is probable that they are performing some function unknown to themselves." It's the thought of **Jane Vallis**, a student at an Australian girls school in the backland at the turn of the century. *Picnic at Hanging Rock* (1975, Australia, Atlantic Releasing).

8358 "Jennie, I believe God made me for a purpose. He also made me fast. And when I run I feel his pleasure." **Ian Charleson**, as Scottish missionary Eric Liddell, assures his sister, played by Cheryl Campbell, that he's not wasting God's time with his running. *Chariots of Fire* (1981, GB, 20th Century-Fox).

8359/60 JOHN KEATING: "That was an exercise to prove a point, the dangers of conformity." MR. NOLAN: "But, John, the curriculum is set, it's proven, it works. If you question it, what's to prevent them from doing the same?" KEATING: "I always thought the purpose of education was to learn to think for yourself." NOLAN: "At these boys' ages? Not on your life.... Tradition, John, discipline...." English master **Robin Williams** and headmaster **Norman Lloyd** disagree on the purpose of education. Unfortunately, Lloyd is such an obvious strawman, defending indoctrination, and Williams, the noble champion of free inquiry, that the argument is a contrivance to get the audience to comfortably come down on the "right" side. More unfortunate is that most special interest groups wish the young to be indoctrinated, not free to find their own way. *Dead Poets Society* (1989, Touchstone-Buena Vista).

8361 "Do you want a fence to keep things in or to keep things out?" Slightly retarded handyman **Ernie Hudson** asks Annabella Sciorra what he considers a pertinent question. She answers, "Well, both I guess." *The Hand That Rocks the Cradle* (1992, Hollywood Pictures-Buena Vista).

Pursuits

see also CAREERS, DEVOTION, WORK AND WORKERS

8362 "From now on I'm going to be the one doing the chasing, and believe me, you'll know you've been chased." **Myrna Loy** gives fair warning to her once dull husband William Powell, who is a changed man due to amnesia. *I Love You Again* (1940, MGM).

8363 "Where there is a pursued, there is a pursuer." When **Louis Jourdan** meets Joan Fontaine outside an opera house, it isn't clear who is the pursued and who is the pursuer. *Letter from an Unknown Woman* (1948, Universal).

8364 "You're not getting away from me, Bandit. I'll chase you in hot pursuit. To the ends of the earth, you son of a bitch." Sheriff **Jackie Gleason** is determined to capture Burt Reynolds. *Smokey and the Bandit II* (1980, Universal).

8365 "Why do men chase women?" Surely **Olympia Dukakis** isn't so old that she's forgotten. What she's really asking is why her husband Vincent Gardenia is philandering. *Moonstruck* (1987, MGM).

Puzzles

see also GAMES, GENIUS, PROBLEMS

8366 LONGFELLOW DEEDS: "Puzzles me why these people all want to work for nothing." CORNELIUS COBB: "Why do mice go where there is cheese?" **Gary Cooper** can't understand why his deeply envious cousin Douglas Dumbrille, who considers Cooper "the most naïve fellow I have ever seen," asks for power of attorney. He offers to take care of all the legal details for his recently wealthy cousin for no charge. **Lionel Stander** answers the rhetorical question with a rhetorical question. *Mr. Deeds Goes to Town* (1936, Columbia).

8367 "I guess Rosebud is just a piece in a jigsaw puzzle. . . a missing piece." Reporter **William Alland** is unable to determine the significance of Orson Welles' dying word, despite interviewing everyone who knew the tycoon. To make certain audiences don't meet with the same failure, the film ends focusing on the destruction by fire of Welles' boyhood sled with the name Rosebud printed on it. *Citizen Kane* (1941, RKO).

8368 "I'd love to think I was a puzzle. A woman of mystery. Smiling and enigmatic on the surface—but underneath, a tigress. . . . I hate to admit it, but what you see is all there is. Underneath this plain, girlish exterior, there's a very plain girl." Matinee idol Michael Rennie, who has called **Debbie Reynolds** a puzzle, holds a different opinion of her. *Mary, Mary* (1963, Warner Bros.).

Qualifications

see also PREPARATIONS, QUALITIES, RIGHT AND WRONG

8369 "I submit, your Highness, that the Court of the Inquisition is not qualified to pass fair judgment on English seamen or to subject them to the cruel indignities of the Spanish galleys." English privateer **Errol Flynn** defends his attack on a Spanish ship, with an ends justifies the means argument, telling Flora Robson as Elizabeth I that he freed twenty Englishmen who were galley slaves on the ship. *The Sea Hawk* (1940, Warners).

8370 "I was a shoplifter for three years." **Groucho Marx** states his qualifications to be a department store floorwalker to manager Douglas Dumbrille. *The Big Store* (1941, MGM).

8371 "It takes courage, brains and a gun to be a detective. I've got the gun." Even so, the bullets keep falling out of baby photographer **Bob Hope**'s revolver. *My Favorite Brunette* (1947, Paramount).

8372 "Mister, I was made for it." **Tyrone Power**, who has fallen on bad times, tells a carnival manager that he's perfectly suited for the job of a geek. *Nightmare Alley* (1947, 20th Century-Fox).

8373 "I give good phone." As they travel across country by train, art expert Stefan Gierasch's assistant **Jill Clayburgh** states her qualifications for the job to Gene Wilder. *The Silver Streak* (1976, 20th Century-Fox).

8374 "I got out of Nam in one piece—that's a great stunt." Running from the police, Vietnam veteran **Steve Railsback** takes a job as a movie stunt man. *The Stunt Man* (1980, 20th Century-Fox).

8375 STEDMAN: "Are you executive material?" JACK ISSEL: "Do you mean can I play hardball?" STEDMAN: "No, I mean can you kiss ass." **Danny De Vito** checks the qualifications of recent college graduate **Judge Reinhold**, who has just joined a major corporation as an executive trainee. *Head Office* (1985, Tri-Star).

8376 "I've got a head for business and a bod for sin. . . . Is there anything wrong with that?" Slightly tipsy career woman **Melanie Griffith** lists her talents for Harrison Ford. *Working Girl* (1988, 20th Century-Fox).

Qualities

see also CHARACTER, NATURE AND NATURAL, PERSONS AND PERSONALITIES

8377 "Augusta, I always said you were the best." **Ray Milland** recognizes the qualities of Claudette Colbert. *Arise, My Love* (1940, Paramount).

8378 "When you're on the screen, no matter who you're with, whatever you're doing, the audience is looking at you. That's star quality." Producer **Kirk Douglas** tells Lana Turner why he's willing to take a gamble and star her, an unknown with little experience, in one of his movies. *The Bad and the Beautiful* (1952, MGM).

8379 "Regarding love, you know, what can you say? It's not the quantity of your sexual relations that count. It's the quality. On the other hand, if the quantity drops below once every eight months, I would definitely look into it." **Woody Allen** holds forth on a subject on which he's an expert. *Love and Death* (1975, United Artists).

8380 "One of the nicest qualities about you is that you always recognize your weaknesses; don't lose that quality when you need it most." **Shirley MacLaine** shapes up her son-in-law Jeff Daniels while her daughter Debra Winger is dying of cancer. *Terms of Endearment* (1983, Paramount).

8381 "I don't take drugs and I've never had an abortion." Promiscuous high school cheerleader **Daryl Hannah** ticks off her good points to her mother Lois Smith. *Reckless* (1984, MGM–United Artists).

Quantities *see* MATHEMATICS, PROBABILITY AND STATISTICS, QUALITIES

Questions

see also ANSWERS, QUESTIONS AND ANSWERS

8382 "Yes, I'd like to ask you one question. . . . Do you think girls think less of a boy if he lets himself be kissed? I mean, don't you think that although girls go out with boys like me they always marry the other kind?" Harry Woods asks **Groucho Marx** if there's anything he'd like to say before he's killed. *Monkey Business* (1931, Paramount).

8383 "People should not ask that question on their wedding night. It's either too late or too early." **Miriam Hopkins**, who has married for money rather than love, replied to her new husband Edward Everett Horton's question, "Do you love me?" *Design for Living* (1933, Paramount).

8384 RUFUS T. FIREFLY: "What is it that has four pairs of pants, lives in Philadelphia, and it never rains but it pours?" CHICOLINI: "That's a good question. I give you three guesses." Once again, **Groucho Marx** fails in a battle of wits with **Chico Marx**. *Duck Soup* (1933, Paramount).

8385 "And that night as I left Germany I thought lots of things weren't quite the same. True, the fires were still burning in the hills, and Hitler's children were still swearing to die for him. But to me, the fires didn't seem to burn so brightly and the voices didn't come up quite so bravely. And perhaps all over Germany people were beginning to ask themselves the same question you might ask yourself tonight as you go home. Can we stop Hitler's children before it's too late? Well, you and I at least know the answer to that question. So long as we have boys like Karl and girls like Anna, the light will always outshine the dark. For as the prophets of old used to say, the memory of virtue is immortal, and we have a long, long memory." Professor **Kent Smith** leaves Germany, remembering the sacrifices of Tim Holt and Bonita Granville, who went to their deaths resisting the Third Reich. *Hitler's Children* (1940, RKO).

8386 "Every evening at seven I will ask the same question. Will you marry me?" **Jean Marais** as the beast looks to wed Josette Day as Beauty. *La Belle et la Bête* aka: *Beauty and the Beast* (1946, Fr., Discina-Lopert).

8387 "All right, let's play Twenty Questions. If you answer them correctly, maybe I won't knock your teeth out." Probably, private eye **Mark Stevens'** first question to pug William Bendix will be, "Are you animal, vegetable or mineral?" *The Dark Corner* (1946, 20th Century-Fox).

8388 "Since time began man has looked into the awesome reaches of infinity and asked the eternal questions: What is time? What is life? What is space? What is death? Through a hundred civilizations, philosophers and scientists have come with answers, but the bewilderment remains. . . . Science tells us that nothing ever dies but only changes; that time itself does not pass but curves around us; and that the past and the future are together at our side forever. Out of the shadows of knowledge, and out of a painting that hung on a museum wall comes our story, the truth of which lies not on our screen but in your hearts." It's the highly philosophical and pretentious opening statement of the film. *Portrait of Jennie* (1948, Selznick).

8389 "Quo vadis, Domini? (Whither goest Thou, Lord?)" As Simon Peter, portrayed by **Finlay Currie**, flees Rome, he has a vision of Christ and mutters the question that is the source of the movie's title. *Quo Vadis* (1951, MGM).

8390 "Blessed Rachel, only you can know now this burden that I must carry to the end of my days. This question that I must ask myself again and again every day of my life, never to be answered now until we meet at last in Purgatory. Were you innocent or were you guilty? Release my torment. My blessed, blessed torment." After the death of his beloved Olivia de Havilland, **Richard Burton** still doesn't know if his suspicions are correct that she murdered his cousin and best friend. *My Cousin Rachel* (1952, 20th Century-Fox).

8391 "The only question I ever ask a woman is: 'What time is your husband coming home?'" **Paul Newman** doesn't feel the need to talk with the women he beds with. *Hud* (1963, Paramount).

8392 "I haven't answered so many idiotic questions since I tried to open a charge account at Saks! . . . There must be a genteel, lady-like way of telling you that's none of your damn business." **Debbie Reynolds** has had enough of Michael Rennie's ever-increasing personal questions. *Mary, Mary* (1963, Warner Bros.).

8393 "'Why?' Will no man ever do something without a 'why?,' just like that, for the hell of it?" **Anthony Quinn** believes in doing things without worrying about one's reasons. *Zorba, the Greek* (1964, 20th Century-Fox).

8394 "Each person who tries to see beyond his own time must face questions for which there are no absolute answers." Futuristic witch **Clare Bloom** instructs Rod Steiger. *The Illustrated Man* (1969, Warner Bros.).

8395 "Fellows, I don't recognize the right of this committee to ask me these kind of questions. And, furthermore, you can all go fuck yourself." **Woody Allen**, who "fronts" for writers who are blacklisted because of their earlier political affiliations, tells off the Red-hunting congressional committee. *The Front* (1976, Columbia).

8396 "I don't answer questions. I'm allergic to them. They make me break out." Enigmatic sculptress **Ali MacGraw** doesn't wish to talk about her past with her new young lover, tennis star Dean-Paul Martin. *Players* (1979, Paramount).

8397 "Why not?" **Max von Sydow**, as Ming the Merciless, answers a question with a question when asked why he's attacking Earth. *Flash Gordon* (1981, GB, Universal).

8398 "The reason why they could never answer the question, 'How could it possibly happen?' is that it's the wrong question. Given what people are, the question is, 'Why doesn't it happen more often?' Of course it does, in subtler forms." Artist **Max von Sydow** talks to his live-in lover Barbara Hershey about the Holocaust. *Hannah and Her Sisters* (1986, Orion).

8399 "Are you drying your nails or do you have a question?" Mean and nasty chief troop leader **Betty Thomas** acknowledges Shelley Long's hand at a meeting of the Wilderness Girls' troop leaders. *Troop Beverly Hills* (1989, Weintraub).

8400 "If I don't answer his questions, he handcuffs me to the radiator." Reforming hooker and porno star **Jeannie Berlin** bitches about her new boy friend. *In the Spirit* (1990, Castle Hill).

8401 "There are questions that cannot be resolved. Not in this court." **John Bach** refers to the questions of guilt and responsibility that come up during the 1945 trial of Japanese soldiers accused of massacring Australian POWs held in an Indonesia camp. *Blood Oath* (1991, Australia, Skouras).

8402 "If you want a simple yes or no, you'll have to finish the question." It's **Annette Bening**'s meaningful response when mobster Warren Beatty offers to light her cigarette by asking, "May I?" *Bugsy* (1991, Tri-Star).

8403 "Her questions made me as dizzy as her perfume." In voice-over, **Nick Nolte** describes the effect Barbra Streisand has on him. *The Prince of Tides* (1991, Columbia).

Questions and Answers

see also ANSWERS, QUESTIONS

8404 EDWARD FITZPATRICK: "Are you bright enough to answer some questions?" DAISY: "Sure, if you don't ask them in Yiddish." Police detective **Wallace Ford** questions gun moll **Jean Harlow**. *The Beast of the City* (1932, MGM).

8405 CORA MOORE: "Don't you ever love me any-more?" ANTHONY MALLARE: "That is an ungallant question that women always want answered gallantly." Young author **Julie Haydon** shouldn't expect much from charming heel **Noel Coward**. *The Scoundrel* (1935, Paramount).

8406 ELIZABETH I: "Crooked answers, crooked answers!" CYNTHIA: "Yes, madame, to cross questions." English Queen **Flora Robson**'s lady-in-waiting **Vivien Leigh** is a bit careless in speaking to her monarch. *Fire Over England* (1936, GB, London Films-United Artists).

8407 ELLEN GORDON: "Wouldn't that be gay?" JOHN CLEVES: "Oh, no! I never answer questions like that without my lawyer at my side." **Jane Fonda** is **Jason Robards'** once-a-week mistress. She's just told him that her fantasy is a room full of balloons. *Any Wednesday* (1966, Warner Bros.).

8408 "Never ask a question unless you have an answer." **Jack Warden** accuses attorney Paul Newman of forgetting a fundamental piece of legal wisdom. *The Verdict* (1982, 20th Century-Fox).

Quietness

see also NOISES, PEACE, SILENCE

8409 "I demand quiet during the ceremony." Slow-burn artist **Edgar Kennedy** is an harassed justice of the peace whose flowery marriage ceremony between Claudette Colbert and Fred MacMurray is continuously interrupted. Kennedy moves from mild annoyance to a towering rage. *The Bride Comes Home* (1935, Paramount).

8410 "Shut up, the both of you! It is love that counts." Confined to a wheelchair, aviator **Ralph Bellamy** shouts at Carole Lombard and Fred MacMurray, who are bickering as usual. *Hands Across the Table* (1935, Paramount).

8411 LAWYER: "Think it over. Marriage is a beautiful thing." LUCY WARRINER: "Shut your mouth." Attorney **Edward Mortimer** makes a feeble attempt to save **Irene Dunne**'s marriage to Cary Grant. *The Awful Truth* (1937, Columbia).

8412 "In moments of quiet, I'm strangely drawn to you, but–well . . . there haven't been any quiet moments." Absentminded scientist **Cary Grant** confesses a limited attraction for madcap Katharine Hepburn. *Bringing Up Baby* (1938, RKO).

8413 "I've been quiet, oh, ever so quiet. I hardly move, yet it keeps coming all the time, closer and closer." Consumptive prostitute **Elizabeth Russell** anticipates her death. *The Seventh Victim* (1943, RKO).

8414 CHARLIE BURNS: "It's quiet." EDDIE FELSON: "Yeah, like a church. The church of the good hustler." **Myron McCormick** and **Paul Newman** are almost in awe as they walk into New York's Ames Pool Hall where Minnesota Fats (Jackie Gleason) holds sway. *The Hustler* (1961, 20th Century-Fox).

8415 "Martha, in my mind, you are buried in cement right up to the neck. Now, up to the nose, it's much quieter." Henpecked professor **Richard Burton** briefly stands up on his hind legs and tells his bossy, talky wife that he'd like her to be quiet. *Who's Afraid of Virginia Woolf?* (1966, Warner Bros.).

8416 "All right, Curley, enough's enough. You can't eat the venetian blinds. I just had 'em installed on Wednesday." Private investigator **Jack Nicholson** attempts to quiet down his client Burt Young who has just been shown photographic evidence of his wife's infidelity. *Chinatown* (1974, Paramount).

Quitting and Quitters

see also DEPARTURES AND RETURNS, ENDS AND ENDINGS

8417 "I'm not working here anymore. No, Hinchecliffe has to get himself a new head butcher. I've had ten years of filth and blood. I'm splashed with it, drenched with it! I've had all I can stand! Plenty of it! Take your . . . killings to Hinchecliffe with my compliments! And tell him to shove it up his. . . ." Scandal sheet editor **Edward G. Robinson** finally has had enough when his paper's stories result in the suicide of an elderly couple. Robinson refers to his publisher Oscar Apfel. *Five Star Final* (1931, Warner Bros.).

8418 "You can't quit on me any more than I can quit on you and you can kiss a stack of cookbooks on that." It's **Jean Harlow**'s colorful way of informing Clark Gable that they are meant for each other. *China Seas* (1935, MGM).

8419 "Well, give me patience. No, this is too much. I can't stand it. . . . And then they say keep away from the bottle. Don't drink. No, not even a wee drop to steady a man's nerves. If one more thing happens I'll quit. And where Aloysius Gogarty goes, Mrs. Gogarty goes too." Gardener **Barry Fitzgerald** thinks his employer May Robson and her guests, niece Katharine Hepburn, Cary Grant and Charles Ruggles, have gone mad as they sit around a dinner table imitating animals and birds, and every once in awhile jumping up to chase all over the grounds. *Bringing Up Baby* (1938, RKO).

8420 "So many worries, so many quarrels–they just gave up. They didn't even hate each other." **Claudette Colbert** tells Parisian taxi driver Don Ameche about the dissolution of her parents' marriage. *Midnight* (1939, Paramount).

8421 "I'm not only walking on this case, Mr. Whiteside, I am leaving the nursing profession. I became a nurse because all my life, ever since I was a little girl, I was filled with the idea of serving a suffering humanity. After one month with you, Mr. Whiteside, I am going to work in a munitions plant. From now on, anything I can do to exterminate the human race will fill me with the greatest of pleasure. If Florence Nightingale had ever nursed you, Mr. Whiteside, she would have married Jack the Ripper instead of founding the Red Cross." Having acid-tongued radio celebrity Monty Woolley as a patient has a profound effect on **Mary Wickes**. The wonder is that self-absorbed Woolley allowed her to get her entire speech in. *The Man Who Came to Dinner* (1941, Warner Bros.).

8422 "You're wrong. I fire people, but nobody quits me. You started this and you'll end it." Mobster **Kirk Douglas** refuses Robert Mitchum's resignation offer from the job of locating Douglas' beautiful mistress Jane Greer. Mitchum has already tracked her down and fallen in love with her. *Out of the Past* (1947, RKO).

8423 "All right. My closing chorus. You know, in show business you gotta quit when you can't top yourself, and I can't because now I've got the billing I've always really wanted, Mrs. Benny Fields." **Betty Hutton**, as singer Blossom Seeley, tells her audience of her happiness in being married to Ralph Meeker. *Somebody Loves Me* (1952, Paramount).

8424 "Just this once, Kirk, why don't you empty your own ashtrays?" It's press agent **Edmond O'Brien**'s way of telling Howard Hughes–like tycoon Warren Stevens that he's quitting. *The Barefoot Contessa* (1954, United Artists).

8425 "I've been beaten up, but I'm not beaten. And I'm not quitting." High school English teacher **Glenn Ford**, who has been waylaid in an alley by a bunch of his students, insists to his pregnant wife Anne Francis that he won't be scared out of his job. *The Blackboard Jungle* (1955, MGM).

8426 "It's all Bud's fault. He walked out on me. Quit. Threw that key right in my face. ... Said I couldn't bring anyone to the apartment. Especially Miss Kubelik." **Fred MacMurray**'s complaint lets Shirley MacLaine know that Jack Lemmon loves her. *The Apartment* (1960, United Artists).

8427 DRAGLINE: "Stay Down. You're beat." LUKE: "You're going to have to kill me." Time after time, con **George Kennedy** drops **Paul Newman** with blow after blow, and each time Newman struggles to his feet for more. *Cool Hand Luke* (1967, Warner Bros.).

8428 "I'd like to make one good score and back off." **William Holden** realizes that the glory days for western bandits is over and would like to quit. His friend and colleague Ernest Borgnine sagely asks, "Back off to where?" *The Wild Bunch* (1969, Warner Bros.).

8429 "You don't think I'd come here peddling any brand of temperance bunk, do you? Just 'cause I quit the stuff don't mean I'm going prohibition. I'm not that ungrateful. It's given me too many good times. So, if anybody wants to get drunk–if that's the only way they can be happy and feel at peace with themselves–why the hell shouldn't they? Don't I know that game from soup to nuts. I wrote the book. The only reason I quit is–well, I finally had the guts to face myself and throw overboard that damned lying pipe dream that was making me miserable and do what I had to do for the happiness of all concerned. Then, all at once, I was at peace with myself, and I didn't need the booze anymore." **Lee Marvin** has quit alcohol and makes a subtle pitch to his barfly friends to do the same. *The Iceman Cometh* (1973, American Film Theater).

8430 "You never quit, do you? You just keep on coming." **William Hurt** is forced to admire Kathleen Turner's determination to have her way. *Body Heat* (1981, Warner Bros.).

8431 "No, thanks, I'm trying to taper off." **Frederic Forrest** quips to the whores of Chinatown who want to do some business with him. *Hammett* (1982, Orion-Warner Bros.).

8432 "Nobody wants me to quit. The cops wanna bust me. The Colombians want my connections. My wife, she wants my money. Her lawyer agrees, and mine likes getting paid to agree with them. ... I haven't even mentioned my customers. You know they don't want me to quit." Former drug dealer **Mel Gibson** makes fun of how hard it is to stay out of the drug trade to Michelle Pfeiffer. *Tequila Sunrise* (1988, Warner Bros.).

Quotations

see also ADVICE, PROVERBS AND SAYINGS

8433 "What shall it profit a man if he gains the whole world and suffers the loss of his soul?" The words of Jesus Christ appear on the opening title card. *The Manxman* (1929, silent, GB, British International).

8434 "My father always said, 'Never desert a lady in trouble'—he took it to the point of marrying my mother." Looks like **Michael Redgrave** just escaped being born out of wedlock. *The Lady Vanishes* (1938, GB, Gainsborough-Gaumont).

8435 "Ma says that if you puts a knife under the bed it cuts the pain in half." **Butterfly McQueen**, who alternates from knowing nothing and being a know-it-all about birthin' babies, quotes her own mother during Olivia de Havilland's labor. *Gone with the Wind* (1939, Selznick-MGM).

8436 "Arise, my love, my fair one, come away." Pilot **Ray Milland** quotes from the Song of Solomon. It's a prayer he makes every time he takes an airplane into the sky. *Arise, My Love* (1940, Paramount).

8437 "We live, not as we wish to—but as we can." The quote from Menander that prefaces the movie. *The Primrose Path* (1940, RKO).

8438 "Now, voyager, sail forth to seek and find." Psychiatrist **Claude Rains** quotes Walt Whitman as he sends his patient Bette Davis on an ocean voyage in order to learn to manage her own life. *Now, Voyager* (1942, Warner Bros.).

8439 "I run to death and death meets me as fast, and all my pleasures are like yesterday." A John Donne quote opens the film. *The Seventh Victim* (1943, RKO).

8440 "Here I stand. I can do nothing else. God help me. Amen." Fascist fighter **Paul Lukas** quotes Martin Luther. *Watch on the Rhine* (1943, Warner Bros.).

8441 "I'm the most widely misquoted man in America. When my friends do it, I resent it. From Sergeant McAvity and Schultz, I should find it intolerable." Arrogant, elitist writer **Clifton Webb** has nothing but contempt for investigating Police Sergeants James Flavin and Harold Schlickenmayer. *Laura* (1944, 20th Century-Fox).

8442 "A strange woman lyeth in wait for her prey. She increases transgressions among men. It was the evil of woman that led my brother to his destruction. There is evil in beauty, but if the evil is cut out. . . ." Jack the Ripper–like murderer **Laird Cregar** quotes Solomon to intended victim, beautiful Merle Oberon. *The Lodger* (1944, 20th Century-Fox).

8443 "I sent my soul through the Invisible/Some letter of that after-life to spell/And by and by my soul

returned and whispered/'I myself am heaven and hell.'" It's a verse from Omar which both opens and ends the film. *The Picture of Dorian Gray* (1945, MGM).

8444 "Home is the Sailor/Home from the Sea/And the Hunter home from the Hill." U.S. Naval Lieutenant **John Wayne** recites from Robert Louis Stevenson's "Requiem" over the bodies of two of his men who were killed in action. *They Were Expendable* (1945, MGM).

8445 "Nothing's really changed, has it? You know what they say: my son's my son till he gets him a wife, but my daughter's my daughter all of her life. All of our life." **Spencer Tracy** consoles himself with the belief that he's not lost a daughter but gained a son when Elizabeth Taylor marries Don Taylor. *Father of the Bride* (1950, MGM).

8446 "A house divided against itself cannot stand. Your president said that. Our president." Former Rebel Captain **Alan Ladd** rejoins the Union. *Red Mountain* (1951, Paramount).

8447 "Half the people on earth would be ruined at once if everyone told what they knew." Dingbat **Jennifer Jones** quotes her old nurse. *Beat the Devil* (1954, GB, Romulus-United Artists).

8448 "Tis ye, tis your estranged face that miss the many splendored thing." War correspondent **William Holden** quotes from poet Francis Thompson to Eurasian physician Jennifer Jones. *Love Is a Many-Splendored Thing* (1955, 20th Century-Fox).

8449 "Ducotel says to give credit is exactly the same as giving a present." Convict **Humphrey Bogart** makes up a quote for merchant Leo G. Carroll to impress stingy businessman Basil Rathbone. *We're No Angels* (1955, Paramount).

8450 "I fooled my lawyer. I fooled that head shrinker. And I'll fool all the corn cobs on the jury." Prisoner **Don Russ** gives testimony, allegedly quoting murder defendant Ben Gazzara, whose defense rests on the premise that he acted under "an irresistible impulse." *Anatomy of a Murder* (1959, Columbia).

8451 "Sebastian said, 'Truth is the bottom of a bottomless well.'" Wealthy **Katherine Hepburn** quotes her homosexual son who was ripped apart by a pack of poor, hungry and angry young men with whom he was debauching. *Suddenly, Last Summer* (1959, GB, Columbia).

8452 "He that troubleth his own house shall inherit the wind." **Fredric March**, in his William Jennings

Bryan role, quotes from Solomon in the Book of Proverbs to fundamentalist minister Claude Akins, who has asked God's damnation for all supporters of Dick York, the John T. Scopes–like school teacher, and even his own daughter, Donna Anderson. *Inherit the Wind* (1960, United Artists).

8453 "The heart has reasons that reason itself never knows about." **Thomas Mitchell,** as Judge Blake, quotes Blaise Pascal for Apple Annie, played by Bette Davis. *Pocketful of Miracles* (1961, United Artists).

8454 "What happens to a dream deferred/Does it dry up/Like a raisin in the sun?" The Langston Hughes line about a dream deferred provides the title for the Lorraine Hansberry play and movie. *A Raisin in the Sun* (1961, Columbia).

8455 "The Reverend Mother always says, 'When the Lord closes a door somewhere, He opens a window.'" **Julie Andrews** quotes Peggy Wood, mother superior of a convent of nuns where Andrews once was a novitiate. *The Sound of Music* (1965, 20th Century-Fox).

8456 "'Do not go gentle into that good night/Old age should burn and rage at close of day;/Rage, rage against the dying of the light./Though mere men at their end know dark is right,/Because when words had formed no lightning they/Do not go gentle into that good night.'" One evening, on a deserted Brooklyn street, aspiring actor **Lenny Baker** does his imitation of Dylan Thomas. *Next Stop, Greenwich Village* (1975, 20th Century-Fox).

8457 "The woods are lovely, dark and deep/But I have promises to keep/And miles to go before I sleep." Brainwashed Americans are activated by the KGB, when someone recites the Robert Frost passage to them over the phone. *Telefon* (1977, MGM-United Artists).

8458 "I was further out than you thought/And not waving but drowning." **Glenda Jackson**, as poet Stevie Smith, quotes from her best known poem. *Stevie* (1978, US-GB, First Artists).

8459 "Is all that we see or seem/But a dream within a dream?" A quote from Edgar Allen Poe prefaces the opening of the film. *The Fog* (1980, Avco Embassy).

8460 "One thing I know that, whereas I was blind, now I see." A quote from the Gospel according to St. John ends the picture. *Raging Bull* (1980, United Artists).

8461 "It says in the old book: 'He that honors me, I will honor.' Good Luck." It's the contents of a note

American Olympian Jack Scholz, portrayed by **Brad Davis**, passes to Scotsman Eric Liddell, portrayed by Ian Charleson, shortly before they compete in the 440-meter race. *Chariots of Fire* (1981, GB, 20th Century-Fox).

8462 "Love looks not with the eyes, but with the mind. And therefore is a winged cupid painted blind." Old queen **Robert Preston** quotes from Shakespeare's "A Midsummer Night's Dream" when he awakens to find his boy friend Malcolm Jamieson sneaking money out of Preston's wallet. *Victor/Victoria* (1982, MGM-United Artists).

8463 "Dying is easy; comedy is hard." Errol Flynn–like **Peter O'Toole** quotes the great British stage actor Edmund Kean's dying remark. *My Favorite Year* (1982, MGM-United Artists).

8464 "She used to say it's a big melting pot, because when you bring it to a boil, all the scum rises to the top." **Billie Neal** recalls her mother's analysis of America. *Down by Law* (1986, Island Pictures).

8465 "'All warfare is based on deception.'—Sun Tzu—'If your enemy is inferior, invade him; if angry, irritate him; if equally matched, fight, and if not, split . . . reevaluate it.'" **Charlie Sheen** proves he's learning by paraphrasing wheeler-dealer Michael Douglas' favorite author. *Wall Street* (1987, 20th Century-Fox).

8466 "Carpe diem—Seize the day." **Robin Williams** quotes the epigram attributed to Horace and exhorts his students to lead full and creative lives. *Dead Poets Society* (1989, Touchstone/Buena Vista).

8467 "Only in their dreams may men be truly free/It was always thus and always will be." English master John Keating, portrayed by **Robin Williams**, quotes one of his own verses. *Dead Poets Society* (1989, Touchstone-Buena Vista).

8468 "You once wrote: 'There comes a time when all the cosmic tumblers have clicked into place and the universe opens itself up for a few seconds to show you what is possible.'" **Kevin Costner** quotes 60s guru James Earl Jones to himself. *Field of Dreams* (1989, Universal).

8469 "'Never let them see you sweat.' That's what Mr. Mayer always said—or was it 'Never let them see your ass?'" Aging former movie star **Shirley MacLaine** quotes studio head Louis B. Mayer to her daughter, troubled actress Meryl Streep. *Postcards from the Edge* (1990, Columbia).

8470 "'Ah, Constantine, how much misfortune you caused. Not by becoming Christian, but by the dowry which the first rich pope accepted for you.'" Corrupt Archbishop **Donal Donnelly** quotes Dante for Al Pacino. *The Godfather, Part III* (1991, Paramount).

8471 "Let your mind go and your body will follow." L.A. weatherman **Steve Martin** quotes his mentor—an electronic freeway sign—to Victoria Tennant. *L.A. Story* (1991, Tri-Star).

Rackets *see* BUSINESS AND COMMERCE, HONESTY AND DISHONESTY, NOISES, SCHEMES

Radicalism and Radicals *see* CHANGES, POLITICS AND POLITICIANS, REBELLIONS, REVOLUTIONS

Radios

see also ENTERTAINMENTS AND ENTERTAINERS, NEWS AND NEWSPAPERS, TELEVISION

8472 SGT. COLLINS: "Who's playing that radio?" HERBIE BROWN: "Nobody, it's playin' by itself." **Nat Pendleton** bursts into an army tent where **Lou Costello** has absent-mindedly turned on a radio. *Buck Privates* (1941, Universal).

8473 "I am now going upstairs to disconnect my radio, so that not even accidentally will I ever hear your voice again!" **Grant Mitchell** has had all he can take of the terrorizing antics of his unwanted guest, Monty Woolley. The latter is recuperating from an injury suffered after slipping on ice outside Mitchell's house. *The Man Who Came to Dinner* (1942, Warner Bros.).

8474 "I thought I told you to stay off the radio. . . . If that radio is dead, it's gonna have company." **James Cagney** slugs a member of his gang who reports that he's heard on the car radio that a big storm is coming in the direction of their hide-out. *White Heat* (1949, Warner Bros.).

8475 "Do it on the radio." **Julie Waters** has a one-line solution to an English exam question on how to stage Henrik Ibsen's difficult play, "Peer Gynt." *Educating Rita* (1983, GB, Rank).

8476 MOTHER: "Turn off the radio." JOE: "Why should I? You listen to it." MOTHER: "That's the difference. Our lives are ruined anyway." Disenchanted **Julie Kavner** instructs her son **Seth Green**, apparently the young Woody Allen. *Radio Days* (1987, Orion).

8477 "I never forget that New Year's Eve, when Aunt Bea awakened me to watch 1944 come in. And I've never forgotten any of those people or any of the voices we used to hear on the radio. Although the truth is, with the passing of each New Year's Eve, those voices do seem to grow dimmer and dimmer." Narrator **Woody Allen** fondly recalls a time when the radio and the voices heard on it were at the center of everyone's life. *Radio Days* (1987, Orion).

8478 "Hey, Mook, it's the Mook man. I see you walkin' down the block. Go on home to your kids. Now the news and weather. Our mayor has commissioned a blue-ribbon panel and I quote, to get to the bottom of last night's disturbance. The City of New York will not let property be destroyed by anyone end quote. His honor plans to visit our block today. Maybe he should hook up with our own Da Mayor, buy him a beer. Your Love Daddy says register to vote. The election is coming up. There's no end in sight from this heat wave so today the cash money word is chill. That's right C-H-I-L-L. When you hear 'chill' call 555-L-O-V-E, and you'll win cash money, honey. This is Mister Senor Love Daddy coming at you from what's last on your dial but first in your hearts, and that's the quintessential truth, Ruth. The next record goes out to Radio Raheem. We love you, brother." Disc jockey **Sam Jackson** closes Spike Lee's story of a day of racism in Brooklyn's Bedford-Stuyvesant neighborhood. *Do the Right Thing* (1989, Universal).

Rage *see* ANGER

Rain *see* WEATHER

Rape

see also CRIMES AND CRIMINALS, SEX AND SEXUALITY, VIOLENCE

8479 PAUL BIEGLER: "Tell the court how Lieutenant Manion described the trouble his wife had had with Barney Quill." SGT. DURGO: "He told me that Quill had raped his wife." Defense Attorney **James Stewart** is able to get mention of an alleged rape of Lee Remick into the proceedings. Stewart is questioning Police Sergeant **Ken Lunch** during the murder trial of Remick's husband Ben Gazzara. *Anatomy of a Murder* (1959, Columbia).

8480 "Fie upon it, have more resolution. Are you frightened by the word rape? All women love a man of spirit. Remember the story of the Sabine ladies. I believe they made tolerably good wives afterward." **Joan Greenwood** encourages David Tomlinson to rape Susannah York. *Tom Jones* (1963, GB, United Artists).

8481 "I have mixed feelings about rape." British Police Inspector **Michael Bates** shrugs off the seriousness of the crime. *Bedazzled* (1967, GB, 20th Century-Fox).

8482 "Is this your first rape?" In a black comedy, **Joe Keyes, Jr.**, the leader of a group of black toughs, forces Ron Leibman, dressed in a gorilla suit, to join in a gang rape of what turns out to be a male policeman in drag. *Where's Poppa?* (1970, United Artists).

8483 DR. PHIL SNEIDERMAN: "He felt like a man?" CARLA MORAN: "A big man." SNEIDERMAN: "Did he ejaculate?" CARLA: "I think so." Psychiatrist **Ron Silver** presses young mother **Barbara Hershey** who has been repeatedly raped by an invisible entity. *The Entity* (1983, 20th Century-Fox).

8484 "Whatever happened to the raping and pillaging?" It's the approximate question of a pirate during a battle scene. *The Ice Pirates* (1984, MGM-United Artists).

8485 "After a few times, you'll be the one in control." Well-around-the-bend **Anthony Zerbe**, commander of a mock enemy force, tells captive U.S. Army Officer Lisa Eichhorn that he's raping her for her own good. *Opposing Force* (1987, Orion).

8486 "Have you ever been a woman, counselor? Some fat, hairy hillbilly's wet dream? I learned to get in touch with the feminine side of myself–the soft nurturing side." Ex-con **Robert DeNiro** speaks of his own rape in prison to lawyer Nick Nolte. *Cape Fear* (1991, Universal).

8487 "I didn't rape you, Charley. I just left the window open a little." **Kim Basinger** tells Alec Baldwin not to put all the blame on her when her gangster lover Armand Assante forces them to get married for punishment after he found them together in bed. *The Marrying Man* (1991, Hollywood Pictures-Buena Vista).

Rationality *see* REASONS, SENSE AND SENSIBILITY, THINKING AND THOUGHTS

Reading *see* BOOKS, WRITING AND WRITERS

Realities

see also EXISTENCE, FICTION, IDEAS, ILLUSIONS, TRUTH

8488 "Are you real, or born of a snow drift?" **Charles Boyer**, as Napoleon Bonaparte, is stuck with this question to Greta Garbo, as Marie Walewska. *Conquest* (1937, MGM).

8489 "What you've read and what you've heard is one thing. The real thing is something else." In the prologue of the movie, narrator **Robert Montgomery** sets the stage for the unfolding of the story in which the audience sees everything through his eyes. *The Lady in the Lake* (1947, MGM).

8490 "We all have dreams, Mrs. Smith-bad dreams sometimes, but we wake up, and we say, 'That was a bad dream.' Occasionally, however, we find a patient who can't wake up. He or she lacks insight, the ability to distinguish between what is real and what isn't. Now that may be true in your case." Psychiatrist **Stanley Ridges** kindly tells Joan Crawford that she suffers from schizophrenia. *Possessed* (1947, Warner Bros.).

8491 BART: "Everything's going so fast. It's . . . it's all in such high gear. It sometimes . . . it . . . doesn't . . . feel like me. Does that make sense? . . . It's as if none of it really happened. As if nothing was real anymore?" LAURIE: "Next time you wake up, Bart, look over at me lying there beside you. I'm yours. And I'm real." BART: "Yes, but you're the only thing that is, Laurie. The rest is a nightmare." **John Dall** and **Peggy Cummins** have left a trail of robbery and murder behind them. Dall appears to be denying any responsibility. Cummins is more realistic. *Gun Crazy* aka: *Deadly Is the Female* (1950, United Artists).

8492 "I wrestled with reality for 35 years, and I'm happy, Doctor. I finally won out over it." Middle-aged **James Stewart** makes dipsomania seem a proud accomplishment when doctor Charles Drake tries to get him to be realistic about the existence of his invisible friend, a giant rabbit. *Harvey* (1950, Universal-International).

8493 "Is he mechanical or is he real? Watch him walk, watch him move, then guess whether he's made of wax, metal and putty, or is he flesh and blood." Nightclub barker **Ron Hagerthy** poses a question about Walley Cassell, who makes his living as a mechanical man. *City That Never Sleeps* (1953, Republic).

8494 "What's so wonderful about reality?" **Warren Beatty** exhibits some of his emerging madness early in the film. *Lilith* (1964, Columbia).

8495 "Too much reality is not what the people want." One of Woody Allen's bullying producers yells that Allen is losing touch with what audiences want from his pictures. *Stardust Memories* (1980, United Artists).

8496 "You see reality too clearly." Woody Allen's psychiatrist **Leonardo Cimino** echoes the movie producer. *Stardust Memories* (1980, United Artists).

8497 "You're just like a statue in a museum, only you're real." **Bo Derek** gushes over the body of

Miles O'Keeffe as the title character. *Tarzan, the Ape Man* (1981, MGM).

8498 GREG: "Can't he just beam himself up?" ELLIOTT: "This is reality, Greg." Neighborhood kid **K.C. Martel** asks **Henry Thomas** if E.T. can't just beam up out of danger as done on "Star Trek." *E.T., the Extra-Terrestrial* (1982, Universal).

8499 "I'm a real person and no matter how tempted I am, I have to choose the real world." Mousy housewife **Mia Farrow** rejects her handsome but imaginary screen character Jeff Daniels' proposal that she live with him in his movie. *The Purple Rose of Cairo* (1984, Orion).

8500 "Why should I think about reality in a stink hole like this?" Homosexual **William Hurt** rejects his cell-mate Raul Julia's suggestion that Hurt not live in the dream world of the movies he recalls for Julia. *Kiss of the Spider Woman* (1985, U.S.-Brazil-Island Alive).

8501 "Yes, but this is the real life. . . . You've seen too many movies. . . . If you want a happy ending, go see a Hollywood movie." **Martin Landau** hypothetically describes how he has gotten away with the murder of his mistress Anjelica Huston to an uncomprehending Woody Allen. The latter wonders if the murderer of the story won't suffer from a guilty conscience. *Crimes and Misdemeanors* (1989, Orion).

Realizations

see also IDEALS, PLANS, UNDERSTANDINGS AND MIS-UNDERSTANDINGS

8502 "Girls who start with breakfasts usually don't end up with supper." **Claudette Colbert** realizes she may have been a bit too easy to get to keep Maurice Chevalier. *The Smiling Lieutenant* (1931, Paramount).

8503 "You realize what that means, that you must like me a little bit?" Cary Grant has made the mistake of betraying his feelings for screwy **Katherine Hepburn**. *Bringing Up Baby* (1938, RKO).

8504 DICK ORR: "And I thought I hated you." RAY CARTER: "It's ridiculous. This is so sudden." ORR: "Lightning never struck faster." Architect **George Brent** kisses actress **Kay Francis** as they realize they are in love. *Secrets of an Actress* (1938, Warner Bros.).

8505 "I ate everything the doctor forbade. And then . . . shall we say I fell asleep without realizing it? When I was awakened, there were my rela-tives, saying nothing but the kindest things about me. And then I knew I was dead." Elderly play-boy **Don Ameche** recounts for Satan, played charmingly by Laird Cregar, the events of his peaceful death. *Heaven Can Wait* (1943, 20th Century-Fox).

8506 "It's about time that the piano realized it has not written the concerto!" Playwright **Hugh Marlowe** unsuccessfully attempts to put temperamental actress Bette Davis in her place by comparing her to a musical instrument for whom he has written a composition. *All About Eve* (1950, 20th Century-Fox).

8507 "Just now I realized something. The trouble with me is that for a long time I have been just an 'I' person. All other people can say 'we.' When Bernice says 'we' she means her lodge and church and colored people. Soldiers can say 'we' and mean the army. All people belong to the 'we' except me. . . . Not to belong to a 'we' makes you too lonesome." **Julie Harris** as 12-year-old Frankie realizes what's been missing from her life. *The Member of the Wedding* (1952, Columbia).

8508 "I walked and walked and realized with each step what it meant to be a thief, a man without honor or self-respect, a man without a wife, a daughter, a home." Banker **Joseph Cotten**'s conscience haunts him after he's stolen half a million dollars from his bank vault. *The Steel Trap* (1952, 20th Century-Fox).

8509 "I never realized that the Third Reich meant Germany. The whole play is just drenched with historical goodies like that. . . . That whole third act has to go. They're losing the war! It's too depressing!" The theater's worst director **Christopher Hewett** critiques "Springtime for Hitler," a nostalgic romance written by maniacal Kenneth Mars, as ex-German soldier Franz Liebkind. *The Producers* (1967, Embassy).

8510 "I'm just an odd girl to fill up an odd month that you don't know what to do with!" American in Paris **Karen Allen** correctly surmises that married Frenchman Thierry Lhermitte wants a brief fling until his wife returns from vacation. She agrees to the arrangement. *Until September* (1984, MGM-United Artists).

8511 "They're just as paranoid and dangerous as we are. I don't know why I ever thought any differ-ently." After he visits Mexico to meet the Russians he's been selling classified information to, **Timothy Hutton** realizes that they're just as bad as he believes American government agents are. *The Fal-con and the Snowman* (1985, Orion).

8512 "My poor boy has brains but he's very muddled. . . . Think how he's been brought up: free from all superstition that leads men to hate one another in the name of God. . . . Make my boy realize that at the side of the Everlasting Why, there is a Yes! and a Yes, and a Yes!" **Denholm Elliott** implores Helena Bonham Carter to help his son Julian Sands. *A Room with a View* (1985, GB, Merchant-Ivory-Goldcrest).

8513 "I'm beginning to think that maybe it's not just how much you love someone—maybe what matters is who you are when you're with them." **William Hurt** finally realizes that his future belongs with Geena Davis, not his ex-wife Kathleen Turner. *The Accidental Tourist* (1988, Warner Bros.).

8514 "They didn't even try to take us alive. . . . They think I'm dead. I am dead." As she watches the destruction of the headquarters of the Symbionese Liberation Army and its six inhabitants on television, title character **Natasha Richardson** concludes that the police want her dead too. *Patty Hearst* (1988, Atlantic).

8515 "And in the end, I realized that I took more than I gave, that I was trusted more than I trusted, that I was loved more than I loved. And what I was looking for was not to be found but to be made." **Kevin Bacon** is growing up in his marriage to Elizabeth McGovern. *She's Having a Baby* (1988, Paramount).

8516 TED: "Do you realize you've stranded one of history's greatest personages?" RANDALF: "He was a dick." **Keanu Reeves** berates his younger brother **Steve Shepherd** for abandoning Napoleon Bonaparte (Terry Camilleri), brought back from the past by Reeves and Alex Winter, in a bowling alley. *Bill and Ted's Excellent Adventure* (1989, Orion).

8517 "Rose, I'm sure you realize it's the 90s. I'm not sure you realize it's the 1990s." **Marvin J. McIntyre** hears the confession of mean-spirited, bigoted Maureen O'Hara. *Only the Lonely* (1991, 20th Century-Fox).

Reasons

see also ARGUMENTS, FAITH AND UNFAITHFULNESS, INTELLIGENCE, PROOFS, PURPOSES, THEORIES, THINKING AND THOUGHTS

8518 CAPT. RENAULT: "There are many exit visas sold in this cafe, but we know that you have never sold them. That is the reason we permit you to remain open." RICK BLAINE: "I thought it was because we let you win at roulette." RENAULT: "That is another reason." French police prefect **Claude Rains** regularly takes bribes from cafe owner **Humphrey Bogart**. *Casablanca* (1942, Warner Bros.).

8519 "Would you tell us, Miss Baxter, how you happened to take up banditry? Was it an inferiority complex or would you call yourself a thrill slayer?" Newspaper sob-sister Little Mary Sunshine, played by **Spring Byington**, questions Two-Gun Gertie, played by Iris Adrian. *Roxie Hart* (1942, 20th Century-Fox).

8520 "I can only think of fifteen or twenty reasons why you shouldn't be happy." Lawyer **Hume Cronyn** makes the caustic quip at the wedding of murderers Lana Turner and John Garfield. *The Postman Always Rings Twice* (1946, MGM).

8521 "I'm going home with him. And you know why? Because I'm a tramp." Blonde starlet **Mari Aldon** has no illusions when she accepts wealthy movie producer Warren Steven's proposition. *The Barefoot Contessa* (1954, United Artists).

8522 "A man needs a reason to ride this country. When people feel the morning sun on them, they want to get up and start over." Bounty hunter **Randolph Scott** has his reason—vengeance. *Ride Lonesome* (1959, Columbia).

8523 "I only picked you up in the first place because I thought I wanted to make it with someone new, and I end up with a freak!" **Shirley Knight** gives her reason for picking up hitchhiker, brain-damaged football player James Caan—but finds he isn't all she hoped for. *The Rain People* (1969, Warner Bros.).

8524 BUTCH CASSIDY: "I swear, Etta, I don't know. I've been working like a dog all my life and I can't get a penny ahead." ETTA PLACE: "Sundance says it's because you're a soft touch and you're always taking expensive vacations and buying drinks for everybody, and you're a rotten gambler." BUTCH: "Well, I guess that has something to do with it." Outlaw **Paul Newman** can't understand why he can't save any of the money he's stolen. **Katharine Ross** tells him that his partner Robert Redford can think of several reasons. *Butch Cassidy and the Sundance Kid* (1969, 20th Century-Fox).

8525 "Nobody honors nothin', but that's no reason to blow up the whole world." **Paul Winfield** stops renegade ex-general Burt Lancaster from firing a missile at Russia. *Twilight's Last Gleaming* (1977, U.S.-W. Ger., Warner Bros.).

8526 "It wasn't just insanity or murder. There was enough of that to go around. . . ." **Martin Sheen**

wonders what's the real reason high-ranking intelligence officers order him to assassinate demented maverick Green Beret Officer Marlon Brando. *Apocalypse Now* (1979, United Artists).

8527 "Because we spend too much time arguing, and not enough time making love." **Julie Andrews** turns down Dudley Moore's marriage proposal. *"10"* (1979, Warner Bros.).

8528 "When things go wrong there's not one reason, but a million reasons." It's the assertion of **Philippe Noiret**, the police chief of a small French African town in 1938. *Coup de Torchon* (1982, Fr., Quartet).

Rebellions

see also REVOLUTIONS, VIOLENCE

8529 "What've ya got?" Motorcycle gang leader **Marlon Brando** answers waitress Mary Murphy's question, "What are you rebelling against?" *The Wild One* (1953, Columbia).

8530 "I don't have to be anything. I'm a Rebel because I choose to be." Ex-Civil War veteran **Rod Steiger** has no plans in this violent and bloody western. *Run of the Arrow* (1956, RKO).

8531 "You're right. I am a rebel, but I funnel it into the system. Deep down, I've got what it takes." Super straight businessman **Jeff Daniels** enthusiastically agrees with kookie Melanie Griffith who wishes to open him up. *Something Wild* (1986, Orion).

Rebounds

see also MARRIAGES

8532 HELEN "WHITEY" WILSON: "If you leave him now, you'll never get him back. . . . He's going to be lonely. His life won't end with you, you know, and when the rebound sets in, he's going to turn to the woman nearest him. You know who it will be." LINDA STANHOPE: "I'm sure I do." WHITEY: "Tomorrow he's taking me to Bermuda, as a friend, but it won't go on like this . . . if he ever turns to me, I won't turn around. . . . I'll take him second best but he'll be fairly happy. Not as happy as he was, not as happy as you could make him, but as happy as anybody else could make him. You're still going?" LINDA: "Yes." WHITEY: "You're a fool, for which I'm grateful." Secretary **Jean Harlow** is unbelievably fair in telling **Myrna Loy** that she will take the latter's husband, Clark Gable, on the rebound. Loy is leaving Gable because she wrongly feels he's been having an affair with Harlow. *Wife vs. Secretary* (1936, MGM).

8533 "There is the first bounce, the second bounce; well, look at me—you wind up like an old tennis ball." **Cecil Cunningham**, who has been through it all before, warns her niece Irene Dunne against love on the rebound. *The Awful Truth* (1937, Columbia).

8534 "I think now I shall pay a call on Yvonne—maybe get her on the rebound, eh?" **Claude Rains** has plans for Humphrey Bogart's discarded girl friend Madeleine LeBeau. *Casablanca* (1942, Warner Bros.).

Recognitions

see also ATTENTION, KNOWLEDGE

8535 "Why, don't you recognize your own 'bog trottin' mug?" **Colleen Moore** is a bit put out when Kenneth Harlan asks her who's the subject of the portrait she's painted after taking art lessons by mail. *April Showers* (1923, silent, Preferred).

8536 LIL ANDREWS: "Why, you son of a sea snake. Have you got on my pajamas? . . . Well, you shake right out of 'em, Hortense. . . . I'm too important to sleep informally. What if there'd be a fire?" SALLY: "You'd have to cover up to keep from being recognized." Sinful redhead **Jean Harlow** exchanges snappy comebacks with **Una Merkel**. *Red Headed Woman* (1932, MGM).

8537 "No one would recognize me from that—doesn't catch the spirit." Murder suspect **Cary Grant** reacts when he sees his picture on a wanted poster. *The Talk of the Town* (1942, Columbia).

8538 "I knew darn well it was the same fella. 'Course, he's changed some. Being buried in the earth does it." Town character **Billy House** comments on one-time Nazi Konstantin Shayne, a stranger in the New England town, whose strangled body has been found in a shallow grave. *The Stranger* (1946, RKO).

8539 "It's been four years since I saw you, Sorrowful, but I recognize the suit." Broadway singer **Lucille Ball** manages to get in a dig at New York bookie Bob Hope. *Sorrowful Jones* (1949, Paramount).

8540 "Give me a girl at an impressionable age and she is mine for life. I am dedicated to you in your prime. . . you little girls must be on the alert to recognize the prime at whatever time it might occur and live it to the full." School mistress **Maggie Smith** believes that her influence on her impressionable students rivals the Jesuits, who it is said, claim they'll answer for a person's soul if they can mold his or her thinking as a child. *The*

Prime of Miss Jean Brodie (1968, 20th Century-Fox).

8541 "The Americans won't recognize us 'cause they think we're communists. The communists won't recognize us 'cause they think we're American puppets. The only person in the world who recognizes us was arrested yesterday on a morals charge." **Woody Allen** is the president of the new government of the Caribbean country of San Marco. *Bananas* (1971, United Artists).

8542 "I almost didn't recognize you without a starlet on your face." Feeling guilty for his behavior, would-be movie director Kevin Bacon fantasizes what his sexy girl friend **Emily Longstreth** would say to him. *The Big Picture* (1989, Columbia).

8543 "I'm easy to recognize. I look like a large unmade bed with a shopping bag attached." Speaking on the phone, British **Sean Connery** arranges a luncheon rendevous with Russian Michelle Pfeiffer who's never seen him before. *The Russia House* (1990, MGM-United Artists).

Recommendations

see also ADVICE, IMPRESSIONS

8544 "Why don't you try stout, Mr. Dodsworth?" **Mary Astor**'s voice comes from the dark recesses of a deck chair, as Walter Huston asks a steward to bring him a drink to steady his nerves. His life is unalterably changed. *Dodsworth* (1936, Goldwyn-United Artists).

8545 "Miss Bradbury... you on the other hand... you express your ideas very clearly... except your paper is... dry... there's not enough of you coming through. Loosen up, Alison, have some fun... eat, sleep when you feel like it, not when you think you should... eat food that is bad for you just once in awhile... have conversations with people whose clothes are not color-coordinated.... Make love in a hammock...." English professor **Viveca Lindfors** recommends Daphne Zuniga be less rigid in her writing. Her suggestions sound better than they really are. *The Sure Thing* (1985, Embassy).

8546 "Very attractive, average yield, very attractive, rising profits, strong balance sheet... it's ready to take off... I'd jump all over it." Stock broker **Charlie Sheen** advises call girl Lisa Zebro in Michael Douglas' limousine. She's asked Sheen about a stock. As he reports on it, she loosens his belt, unzips his pants and does as he recommends. *Wall Street* (1987, 20th Century-Fox).

Reforms and Reformers

see also CHANGES, IDEALS, JUSTICE, REBELLION, RESPONSIBILITIES, REVOLUTIONS

8547 "I am the Reform party, who do you think?... In this town, I'm all the parties." Political boss **Akim Tamiroff** tells mayoral candidate Brian Donlevy that he really controls the town. *The Great McGinty* (1940, Paramount).

8548 "What makes the sacred cause of reform so sacred? Why does the sacred cause of reform have to be exempt from all the other facts of life? Why do the laws of this state have to be executed by a man on a white charger?" **Orson Welles**' outburst is caused when his long-time friend Joseph Cotten expresses his disappointment in Welles for losing the gubernatorial race because of a sex scandal. *Citizen Kane* (1941, RKO).

8549 "The trouble with people who reform is that they always want to rain on everyone else's parade. Children don't have respect for their parents anymore." Con man **Charles Coburn** is irritated with his daughter and partner Barbara Stanwyck, who plans to go straight. *The Lady Eve* (1941, Paramount).

8550 "This is just the first step in a reform package that will take the government of this state back to the people." **Larry Gates** expresses an unlikely outcome of the program of highly-principled Governor Dean Martin, and his ex-whore wife Susan Hayward. She steps in and runs the show when Martin has a near-fatal car accident. *Ada* (1961, MGM).

8551 "You can't reform the system if you're not in it." **Jane Alexander** unsuccessfully tries to persuade penologist Robert Redford to "go along, to get along" if he wishes to accomplish his goal of reforming a corrupt prison system. *Brubaker* (1980, 20th Century-Fox).

8552 NORMA: "I think the right woman could reform you." TODDY: "I think the right girl could do the same for you." Dumb blond show girl **Lesley Ann Warren** comes on to homosexual **Robert Preston**. *Victor/Victoria* (1982, MGM-United Artists).

8553 "I am beginning to be intolerant of reformers—I am beginning to be nauseated by men of good will. We are dealing here with a failure to make convictions. The failure to make convictions is complicity. Reform is complicity." Angry **Timothy Hutton**, whose parents were executed for passing atomic secrets to the Russians, is fed up with those hoping to make a better world. *Daniel* (1983, Paramount).

8554 "I ain't like that anymore. I gave up drink and wickedness." Whenever someone regales **Clint Eastwood** with tales of his former glory as a vicious killer, he claims to have reformed. *Unforgiven* (1992, Warner Bros.).

Refusals and Rejections

see also DENIALS, DISMISSALS

3555 "It's so soon after dinner." **Norma Shearer** flauntingly rejects Robert Montgomery's attempts at love making. *Private Lives* (1931, MGM).

8556 "It's not the kind of girl I am—especially before tea." **Jessie Matthews** softens her refusal to make love to John Gielgud. *The Good Companions* (1933, GB, Gaumont).

8557 "You're asking me to crawl on my belly—the last thing I'd do in my life. Nothing doing." Condemned killer **James Cagney** refuses priest Pat O'Brien's plea that he go to the chair as a cringing coward to kill the hero worship of some slum kids. Whether Cagney changes his mind isn't clear, but he does go to his death crying and pleading to live when he sees the electric chair. *Angels with Dirty Faces* (1938, Warner Bros.).

8558 "This is one night you're not turning me out." Having lost patience with his wife Vivien Leigh, **Clark Gable** kisses her fiercely and carries her upstairs to the bedroom, two steps at a time. The next scene is the next morning. Leigh is smiling happily. *Gone with the Wind* (1939, Selznick-MGM).

8559 "I ain't proud of what I done over there. What we done in France is something we had to do. Some fellows done it ain't a-comin' back. So the way I figure, things like that ain't for buyin' and sellin' —I reckon I'll have to refuse them." Title character **Gary Cooper**, the most decorated hero of World War I and a pacifist, refuses to commercialize what he did. *Sergeant York* (1941, Warner Bros.).

8560 "I'm here as a rejected manuscript dropped by a mysterious postman." **Lionel Stander** serves as screenwriter Ben Hecht's alter ego. *Spectre of the Rose* (1946, Republic).

8561 "I talked to a couple of yes men at Metro. To me they said no." Hollywood scriptwriter **William Holden** finds no takers for his services. *Sunset Boulevard* (1950, Paramount).

8562 "If he were the last man on earth and my sister the last woman, I'd still say no." **Victor McLaglen** rejects a match of his sister Maureen O'Hara with John Wayne. *The Quiet Man* (1952, Republic).

8563 "I wouldn't have you if you were hung with diamonds—upside down." Wealthy widow **Joan Crawford** is just being peevish. She falls for gigolo Jeff Chandler. *Female on the Beach* (1955, Universal-International).

8564 "What can I do with a bunch of rotten oil wells?. . . I can't ride out and prowl among them like I can with cattle. I can't breed 'em or tend them or rope them or chase them or nothin', I can't feel a smidgen of pride in 'em because they ain't none of my doin'. I don't want that kind of money." **Melvyn Douglas** rejects his son Paul Newman's suggestion that they drill for oil on their cattle ranch. *Hud* (1963, Paramount).

8565 "Man was without pets. To man, this was intolerable. . . . So humans took primitive apes as pets, primitive and dumb, but 20 times more intelligent than dogs and cats. They were quartered in cages. But they lived and moved freely in human homes. They became responsive to human speech. In the course of less than three centuries, they progressed from performing mere tricks to performing mere services. . . . After more than three centuries, they turned the tables on their owners. Then they became alert to the concept of slavery. And when their numbers grew they became alert to slavery's antidote, which is, of course, unity. At first, they began assembling in small groups. Then they learned the art of corporate and militant action. They learned to refuse. Of course, they just grunted their refusal. But then on a historic day which is commemorated by my species and which is fully documented in the sacred scrolls, there came Aldo. He did not grunt. He articulated. He spoke a word. . . . He said, 'No!'" Proudly, simian **Roddy McDowall**, who has returned to the past, relates the events leading to the domination of humans by apes—started when a plague wiped out the world's dogs and cats. *Escape from the Planet of the Apes* (1971, 20th Century-Fox).

8566 "No Sicilian can refuse any request on his daughter's wedding day." At the wedding of Marlon Brando's daughter Talia Shire, consigliere **Robert Duvall** shares this information with his wife Tere Livrano, who being Sicilian herself, should already know it. *The Godfather* (1972, Paramount).

8567 "No, not here." **Diane Keaton** refuses her husband Woody Allen who reaches for her in their bed at night. *Love and Death* (1972, United Artists).

8568 "I done some lousy things for money in my life, but I ain't gonna do this." Escaped convict **Gene Hackman** draws the line at assassinating the president of the U.S. or even the governor of California. *The Domino Principle* (1977, Avco Embassy).

8569 "I've been ignoring the fact that I'm fallin' apart." Professional football player **Nick Nolte** refuses to allow his numerous injuries to prevent him from playing. *North Dallas Forty* (1979, Paramount).

8570 "I wouldn't call that bitch a taxi to take her to hell." **Alan King** makes an immoderate response to the suggestion by Myrna Loy that he call his ex-mistress Ali MacGraw. *Just Tell Me What You Want* (1980, Warner Bros.).

8571 "The woman I love is not you but another woman in your shape." **Peter Firth** rejects his new wife Nastassja Kinski when she honestly confesses her unfortunate past. *Tess* (1980, Fr.-GB, Renn-Burill-Columbia).

8572 "Do you know what it feels like to be rejected for a hemorrhoid commercial?" Gay actor **James Coco** has trouble finding work in his profession. *Only When I Laugh* (1981, Columbia).

8573 "Stop, we just got cable." **Annie Potts**, who doesn't like sex, has found a new reason to put off her husband John Laughlin. *Crimes of Passion* (1984, New World).

8574 "Wyoming? Are you crazy? I'm not moving to Wyoming. What's up there? Marlboro Men?" **Kim Basinger** refuses to move to Wyoming with her some-time lover and half-brother Sam Shepard. *Fool for Love* (1985, Cannon).

8575 "We could plod on—everyone else does—but I'm not gonna do it." **Gene Hackman** announces to his wife of 30 years, Ellen Burstyn, that he doesn't want to hang on to a marriage that no longer holds any meaning for him. *Twice in a Lifetime* (1985, Yorkin).

8576 "After 12 years in the minors, I don't try out." Veteran minor league baseball catcher **Kevin Costner** refuses to compete with wild young pitcher Tim Robbins for the honor of being baseball groupie Susan Sarandon's season-long bed mate. *Bull Durham* (1988, Orion).

Regrets

see also APOLOGIES, DISAPPOINTMENTS, GRIEF, SORROWS

8577 "If I thought you were going to be on this train, I'd have stayed another week in the hotel."

Michael Redgrave regrets that he's taken the same train as Margaret Lockwood. She shares his regret, but they both get over it and fall in love. *The Lady Vanishes* (1938, GB, Gainsborough-Gaumont British).

8578 "The Dutch bought New York from the Indians in 1626 and in May 1941 there wasn't an Indian left who regretted it." It's an opening title of the film. *The Major and the Minor* (1942, Paramount).

8579 "I hope you'll never regret what promises to be a disgustingly earthy relationship." **Clifton Webb** makes a caustic farewell, seeing Gene Tierney and Dana Andrews in an embrace. *Laura* (1944, 20th Century-Fox).

8580 "As you grow older, you'll find that the only things you regret are the things you didn't do." Parasite **Zachary Scott**'s philosophy justifies just about anything he does or to be more accurate, doesn't do. *Mildred Pierce* (1945, Warner Bros.).

8581 "He'll regret it to his dying day...if ever he lives that long." Irish squire **Victor McLaglen** speaks contemptuously of newcomer John Wayne. *The Quiet Man* (1952, Republic.)

8582 "I've been married for forty years and I don't regret a day of it. The one day I don't regret is Aug. 2, 1936; my wife was visiting her ailing mother." **Eddie Mayehoff** must have quite a marriage with Claire Trevor. *How to Murder Your Wife* (1964, United Artists).

8583 "And I will now say something I will soon regret. . . . Okay, Corrie, maybe we have nothing in common. Maybe we rushed into marriage a little too fast. Maybe love isn't enough. Maybe two people should have to take more than a blood test. Maybe they should be checked for common sense, understanding and emotional maturity." Tired and over-wrought **Robert Redford** indeed does say something he will regret to his wife of one week, Jane Fonda, in their first married argument. *Barefoot in the Park* (1967, Paramount).

8584 "Oh, Harry, I just want to go around apologizing to everybody. I just want to thank everybody for being so patient with me. Oh, Harry, regret hurts so much. I never could—I never could tell Mama I loved her. I never could tell anybody. I wanted to tell Bobby so bad. I don't want to die without saying it to somebody. Harry, just because I'm not demonstrative doesn't mean I don't feel. I just—I can't show anything to the ones that mean the most to me." **Joanne Woodward** tells her husband Martin Balsam how much she regrets her inability to show her true feelings. Perhaps she's only fooling herself. Perhaps she really is demonstrating her true feelings. *Summer Wishes, Winter Dreams* (1973, Columbia).

8585 "Even if I manage to win her over, there's going to be many times I'm going to regret it." Marine biologist **Nick Nolte** realizes that life with part-time prostitute Debra Winger will be no Tupperware party. *Cannery Row* (1982, MGM-United Artists).

8586 ROBIN HOOD: "Well, Friar Tuck, are these not here the meek of the Earth? We have need of an honest man of God to minister to them. What say you, Friar?" FRIAR TUCK: "The Lord moves in mysterious ways. I accept." ROBIN: "You won't regret it." TUCK: "Aye, but you may." **Kevin Costner** recruits earthy Friar **Michael McShane** to the ranks of his merry men. *Robin Hood: Prince of Thieves* (1991, Columbia).

Relationships

see also MARRIAGES, RELATIVES, UNDERSTANDINGS AND MISUNDERSTANDINGS

8587 "Have you ever had diplomatic relations with a woman?" Ambassador **Edward Everett Horton** sends playboy Maurice Chevalier to Paris to woo and wed wealthy widow Jeanette MacDonald, and to bring her and her fortune back to her near bankrupt country of Marshovia. *The Merry Widow* (1934, MGM).

8588 "Our relationship has been a series of misadventures." **Cary Grant** is nevertheless falling in love with Katharine Hepburn. *Bringing Up Baby* (1938, RKO).

8589 "I'd be glad to explain that any connection between you and me is revolting." For almost the only time in the film, **Cary Grant** has the last line with Ann Sheridan who insists that he retract any intimation that there is a romantic relationship between them. *I Was a Male War Bride* (1949, 20th Century-Fox).

8590 "Susie's all I got and I want my relationship with her to remain on par." Powerful Broadway gossip columnist Burt Lancaster tells nervous press agent Tony Curtis that he wants the latter to discredit the lover of his sister Susan Harrison. There's something unhealthy about Lancaster's relationship with his sister. *Sweet Smell of Success* (1957, United Artists).

8591 "Death ends a life. But it does not end a relationship which struggles on in the survivor's mind toward some resolution which it may never find." In voice-over, **Gene Hackman** refers to his troubled

relationship with his elderly cantankerous father Melvyn Douglas. *I Never Sang for My Father* (1969, Columbia).

8592 "I know we just met a couple of hours ago, but just what do I mean to you? I mean, am I just a passing train you want to board for the night, or are you attracted to my inner being and this night could be the start of a meaningful relationship?" **Marian Hailey** seeks an excuse to go to bed with her new date Bob Dishy. They are at cross-purposes, but at least she's giving him the opportunity to make a correct response to her question. *Lovers and Other Strangers* (1970, ABC-Cinerama).

8593 "Mr. Corleone is Johnny's godfather. To the Italian people, that is a very religious, sacred, close relationship." Consigliere **Robert Duvall** explains, to movie mogul John Marley, Marlon Brando's interest in securing the motion picture role Al Martino is seeking. *The Godfather* (1972, Paramount).

8594 "Relationship! Where did you get that word? From one of your Park Avenue head-shrinkers?" **Jerry Lacy**, as the ghost of Humphrey Bogart, snarls at Woody Allen when the latter speaks of having a relationship with a woman. *Play It Again Sam* (1972, Paramount).

8595 "Meaningful relationships between men and women don't last. You see, there's a chemical in our bodies that makes it so that we all get on each other's nerves sooner or later." **Diane Keaton** shares some modernistic wisdom with Woody Allen, fresh from a 200-year sleep. *Sleeper* (1973, United Artists).

8596 "A relationship, I think, is—is like a shark. You know, it has to constantly move forward or it dies, and I think what we got on our hands is a dead shark." **Woody Allen** analyzes his failing romance with Diane Keaton. Toward the end of the movie he will say, "Annie and I broke up. . . I keep sifting the pieces of the relationship through my mind. . . ." *Annie Hall* (1977, United Artists).

8597 "There must be something wrong with me because I've never had a relationship that's lasted longer than the one between Hitler and Eva Braun." **Woody Allen** laments his romantic failures. *Manhattan* (1979, United Artists).

8598 "Any idiot can have a long-term relationship; all you have to do is smile a lot." **Josh Mostel** wisecracks at a dinner party. *Almost You* (1984, 20th Century-Fox).

8599 "Gib, you want a relationship? Fine. Just remember that every relationship starts with a one-night stand." **Anthony Edwards** is able to separate sex and the girl he has sex with. John Cusack cannot. *The Sure Thing* (1985, Embassy).

8600 "Let's get the basic relationship down. . . . I'm the lifeguard, you're the drowning man. If you relax I can bring you to shore. If you fight me, then I'll have to slap you around." By radio, helicopter pilot **Danny Glover** lays down the law to military mastermind Gene Hackman, whose plane crashed behind enemy lines in Vietnam. *Bat 21* (1988, Tri-Star).

8601 "When we started out together, he was my brother in name. . . and now. . . and this morning we had pancakes. . . You see, we. . . I made a connection. . . ." **Tom Cruise** tries to make psychiatrist Barry Levinson and doctor Jerry Molen realize that his autistic brother Dustin Hoffman has come to mean a great deal to him. *Rain Man* (1988, United Artists).

8602 "I met her in a mall. I should have known our relationship was doomed!" High school loner **John Cusack** is not surprised that his relationship with class brain Ione Skye isn't proceeding smoothly. *Say Anything* (1989, 20th Century-Fox).

8603 "If this relationship lasts this will have been the most romantic moment of my life. If it doesn't, I'm a complete slut." **Kathleen Turner** finds herself in bed with Michael Douglas, whom she has just met. *The War of the Roses* (1989, 20th Century-Fox).

8604 "What kind of foundation for a relationship is that, calling your wife a lying bitch-whore?" Car salesman **Robin Williams** bravely confronts heavily armed and out-of-control Tim Robbins who has called his adulterous wife Annabella Sciorra a lying bitch-whore. *Cadillac Man* (1990, Orion).

Relatives

see also BROTHERS, DAUGHTERS, FAMILIES, FATHERS, MOTHERS, RELATIONSHIPS, SONS AND SONS-IN-LAW

8605 "Man without relatives is man without trouble." We all know that Charlie Chan, here played by **Sidney Toler,** had many children. *Charlie Chan in Panama* (1940, 20th Century-Fox).

8606 "The sheriff has just put two hundred more relatives on the payroll to protect the city from the Red Army, which is leaving Moscow in a couple of moments." Reporter **Roscoe Karns** kids the actions of crooked Sheriff Gene Lockhart, his nepotism and his favorite whipping boys. *His Girl Friday* (1940, Columbia).

8607 GERRY JEFFERS: "You're not a burglar or something?" J.D. HACKENSACKER III: "Oh, no, that was my grandfather." GERRY: "I keep feeling that two men with butterfly nets are going to creep up behind you and lead you away." HACKENSACKER: "You're thinking of my uncle." It's part of an exchange between gal-on-the-make **Claudette Colbert** and eccentric millionaire **Rudy Vallee** when they first meet aboard a train headed for Palm Beach. *The Palm Beach Story* (1942, Paramount).

8608 "That's not fair, Vinnie. When I talk about my relatives, I criticize them." If **William Powell** had his way, there would be no visits from his wife Irene Dunne's family. *Life with Father* (1947, Warner Bros.).

8609 "Don't ever again, as long as you live, dare to call me uncle. By no stretch of the imagination could I possibly be a relative of yours. My name is Mr. Belvedere. Is that clear?" **Clifton Webb** reads the riot act to young Anthony Sydes, who had the audacity to call the self-centered, self-proclaimed genius, uncle. *Sitting Pretty* (1948, 20th Century-Fox).

8610 "I'll tell you who lives in New Jersey! Cousins live in New Jersey!" Fast-talking millionaire **Alan King** dismisses the Garden State as of no great importance. *Just Tell Me What You Want* (1980, Warner Bros.).

8611 "This show 'Bonanza' is about a fifty-year old father and his three forty-seven-year old sons. What kind of show is that?" Aluminum siding salesman **Jackie Gayle** is baffled by the ages of Lorne Greene and the three actors Dan Blocker, Pernell Roberts and Michael Landon who play his three sons on the popular TV western. *Tin Men* (1987, Touchstone-Buena Vista).

8612 "My drug fiend thief of a son and his crazy little nymphomaniac wife." It is **Grace Zabriskie**'s less than gracious greeting when her son Matt Dillon and his wife Kelly Lynch show up at Zabriskie's home unexpectedly. *Drugstore Cowboy* (1989, Avenue).

8613 "I just have trouble imagining her related to anyone—human." **Kevin Kline** is a bit taken back when Elisabeth Shue tells him that Sally Field is her aunt. *Soapdish* (1991, Paramount).

Religions

see also BELIEFS, CREEDS AND CREDOS, DEVILS, GOD, HEAVEN, HEAVEN AND HELL, HELL, PRAYERS, PRIESTS, SAINTS, WORSHIP

8614 "Religion's like anything else. It's great if you can sell it, no good if you give it away." Promoter

Sam Hardy has a mercenary but interesting theory about religion that he's trying to sell to preacher's daughter Barbara Stanwyck. *The Miracle Woman* (1931, Columbia).

8615 OLLIE: "Why did you get a veterinarian?" STAN: "Well, I didn't think his religion would make a difference." **Stan Laurel** has fetched a doctor who prescribes an ocean voyage for **Oliver Hardy**. *Sons of the Desert* (1933, Roach-MGM).

8616 "Any time you take religion as a joke, the laugh's on you." Disguised as a nun, **Mae West** does a bit of preaching. *Klondike Annie* (1936, Paramount).

8617 "I don't go for that Holy Joe stuff." Tough little World War I Irish recruit **James Cagney** tells Chaplain Pat O'Brien that he has no need for God or religion. *The Fighting 69th* (1940, Warner Bros.).

8618 "Strength is her religion, Mr. Connor. She finds imperfection unforgivable." **Cary Grant** tells James Stewart that his "perfect" ex-wife Katharine Hepburn isn't perfect. *The Philadelphia Story* (1940, MGM).

8619 "I've swallowed twenty religions. It's my life's work." **Rex Harrison** admits he's easily converted but not easily convinced. *Major Barbara* (1941, GB, Pascal-Rank-United Artists).

8620 "I am a millionaire. That is my religion." Munitions manufacturer **Robert Morley** asserts that money gives him all the spiritual comfort he needs. *Major Barbara* (1941, GB, Pascal-Rank-United Artists).

8621 "It always worries me when these hoodlums get religion." Assistant District Attorney **Humphrey Bogart** is suspicious when Zero Mostel, as Big Babe Lazich, is rescued screaming from a church confessional. *The Enforcer* (1950, United States Pictures-Warner Bros.).

8622 "When I was a child I was stuffed with religion as a Strasbourg goose with grain. I have no appetite left." Master thief **Peter Finch** warns Priest Alec Guinness that a religious appeal to him will be useless. *Father Brown* (1954, GB, Columbia).

8623 "Are you a religious fanatic, or something?" Aging American lothario **Gary Cooper** can't understand why young French girl Audrey Hepburn is resisting his seduction pitch. *Love in the Afternoon* (1957, Allied Artists).

8624 "It's my religion to play the winning streak." Gambler **Omar Sharif** tells Barbra Streisand what is holy to him. *Funny Girl* (1968, Columbia).

8625 "Frank, were you on this religious kick at home, or did you crack up over here?" **Donald Sutherland** bedevils religious fanatic Robert Duvall. The two are surgeons with a M.A.S.H unit in Korea. *M*A*S*H* (1970, 20th Century-Fox).

8626 "I can't get with any religion that advertises in *Popular Mechanics*." **Woody Allen** must be referring to the Rosicrucians. *Annie Hall* (1977, United Artists).

8627 "I was born Jewish, you know, but last winter I tried to become a Catholic. . . and it didn't work for me. I studied and tried and I gave it everything, but, you know, Catholicism for me was die now, pay later, you know. And I just couldn't get with it." **Woody Allen** is being interviewed by Hare Krishna leader Daniel Haber. *Hannah and Her Sisters* (1987, Orion).

Remembrances *see* MEMORY AND MEMORIZATION, REMINDERS

Reminders

see also MEMORY AND MEMORIZATION, NOSTALGIA, PAST

8628 "You thought of him when you thought of her. A woman never stops thinking of the man she loves; she thinks of him in all sorts of unconscious ways—a sunset, an old song, a cameo and a chain." **Bette Davis** speaks of long dead George Brent to her cousin Miriam Hopkins. *The Old Maid* (1939, First National-Warner Bros.).

8629 "This will remind you that I have been here once and can return." **Tyrone Power**, as Zorro, carves a Z with his sword in the wall of the office of California Governor J. Edward Bromberg. *The Mark of Zorro* (1940, 20th Century-Fox).

8630 "That reminds me, I must get my watch fixed." **Groucho Marx** ogles sexy Lisette Verea. *A Night in Casablanca* (1946, United Artists).

8631 "You see, some men just naturally make you think of brut champagne. With others, you think of prune juice." **Barbara Lawrence** comments to her husband Rudy Vallee as they watch Rex Harrison greet his wife Linda Darnell with a passionate kiss. When Vallee laughs at Lawrence's remark, she adds, "You have nothing to laugh about." *Unfaithfully Yours* (1948, Columbia).

8632 "Remind me to tell you about the time I looked into the heart of an artichoke." **Bette Davis** breaks up a conversation between her fiancé, director Gary Merrill and her "assistant" Anne Baxter as

Merrill tells Baxter about the time he looked into the wrong end of a movie camera. *All About Eve* (1950, 20th Century-Fox).

8633 "Remember thou art only a man." The reminder is constantly repeated to victorious Roman Commander Robert Taylor, by a slave standing behind him in a chariot as Taylor receives the tribute of the crowd while he drives triumphantly through the city. *Quo Vadis* (1951, MGM).

8634 "I'll always keep it a half hour slow to remind me of the fouled-up crew of the Caine." Captain **Tom Tully** refers to the watch given to him as a going away present by his crew as he leaves the minesweeper U.S.S. Caine. *The Caine Mutiny* (1954, Columbia).

8635 "She reminds Jules of his youth, me of the home and family I never had, and Albert. . . Albert is a swine." Devil's Island escaped convict **Humphrey Bogart** explains to Joan Bennett why he and two fellow convicts Peter Ustinov and Aldo Ray have been so good to her and her pretty young daughter Gloria Talbott. *We're No Angels* (1955, Paramount).

8636 "I thought it would serve to remind people that they must die. . . . Why should one always make people happy? It might not be a bad idea to scare them a little once in a while." Church painter **Gunnar Olsson** explains to squire Gunnar Bjornstrand why he paints such depressing subjects. *The Seventh Seal* (1956, Sweden, Svensk Filmindustri).

8637 "Well, that's all for tonight, folks. This is Sweet Sue reminding all you daddy-Os out there that every girl in my band is a virtuoso, and I intend to keep it that way." **Joan Shawlee**, leader of an all-girl band, closes her show with a warning. *Some Like It Hot* (1959, United Artists).

8638 "She reminds me of me." One-eyed marshal **John Wayne** pays teenage Kim Darby the ultimate compliment. *True Grit* (1969, Paramount).

8639 JOE TYNAN: "You remind me of John F. Kennedy. . . . If you looked just behind his eyes you could see his intelligence, his wit, his compassion—just like yours." KAREN TRAYNOR: "Did you make a pass at Kennedy?" Kennedy-like U.S. Senator **Alan Alda** gives lover **Meryl Streep** the highest praise he can think of. *The Seduction of Joe Tynan* (1979, Universal).

8640 "What this place reminds me of is the war. . . . It's England, man, everything except Glenn Miller." It falls to **John Goodman** to remind the audience

that the film about flying forest fire fighters is a remake of the World War II film about American pilots stationed in England, *A Guy Named Joe*. *Always* (1989, Universal-United Artists).

8641 "I stand on my desk to remind myself that we must constantly look at things in different ways. . . ." English teacher **Robin Williams** jumps up on the top of his classroom desk to make a point. *Dead Poets Society* (1989, Touchstone-Buena Vista).

8642 "This field, this team, is part of our past. It reminds us of what was good and what can be again." J.D. Salinger-like writer **James Earl Jones** makes a Capraesque speech near the end of the film. *Field of Dreams* (1989, Universal).

8643 "He reminds me of dolls hanging from suction cups staring out from behind car windows." Villain **John Glover** refers to gremlin Gizmo (voice of Howie Mandel). *Gremlins 2: The New Batch* (1990, Warner Bros.).

Remorse *see* CONSCIENCES, GUILT

Reporters

see also NEWS, NEWSPAPERS, PHOTOGRAPHY AND PHOTOGRAPHERS, RADIOS, TELEVISION

8644 LOUIS BLANCO: "I want to give you a little advice: lay off." BRECKENRIDGE LEE: "You're not talking to a chump; you're talking to a representative of the press. Quite a few people believe in it." Bigshot gangster **Clark Gable** has reporter **Richard Barthelmess** on his payroll. Barthelmess mistakenly believes that Gable won't have a newspaperman killed. *The Finger Points* (1931, First National-Warner Bros.).

8645 "It's peeking through keyholes. It's running after fire engines, waking up people in the middle of the night to ask them what they thought of Mussolini and stealing pictures off little old ladies after their daughters get attacked in Grove Park. And for what—so a million hired girls and motormen's wives will know what's going on?" **Pat O'Brien**, who scoops rival reporters by exercising greater cunning and telling bigger lies, isn't proud of his profession and wants to quit. *The Front Page* (1931, United Artists).

8646 "When you fired me, you fired the best newshound your filthy scandal sheet ever had—you gashouse palooka!" Reporter **Clark Gable** tells off his former editor Wallis Clark over the phone. Actually, Clark has already hung up, but Gable makes the statement to impress other reporters hanging around the phone. *It Happened One Night* (1934, Columbia).

8647 ELLEN GARFIELD: "Why not? I'm a reporter." CURT DEVLIN: "No, you're not, you're just a sweet little kid whose family let her read too many newspaper novels." When cub reporter **Bette Davis** arrives at a prison to cover her first execution, **George Brent**, a writer for a rival paper, smiles pityingly at her. *Front Page Woman* (1935, Warner Bros.).

8648 "Holdups and murders are my meat. I'm Torchy Blane of *The Star*." Brash and brassy newspaper reporter **Glenda Farrell** pushes by cops sealing off a bank. One tells her, "You can't go in there, lady, there's been a holdup and a murder." *Smart Blonde* (1936, Warner Bros.).

8649 "You're a newspaperman. I can smell 'em. I've always been able to smell 'em. Excuse me while I open a window." New Hampshire physician **Charles Winninger** turns up his nose at New York reporter Fredric March. *Nothing Sacred* (1937, Selznick-United Artists).

8650 NORA CHARLES: "I got rid of those reporters." NICK CHARLES: "What did you tell them?" NORA: "We're out of scotch." NICK: "What a gruesome idea." **Myrna Loy** knows that both her husband **William Powell** and reporters can't function without booze. *Another Thin Man* (1939, MGM).

8651 "You're all cast iron and all fish." **Ray Milland** thinks of Claudette Colbert only as a reporter—for the moment. *Arise, My Love* (1940, Paramount).

8652 "Just give me an expense account and I'll cover anything." New York crime reporter **Joel McCrea** is sent to Europe by his publisher to get the scoop on impending World War II. *Foreign Correspondent* (1940, United Artists).

8653 WALTER BURNS: "You can't quit, you're a newspaperman." HILDY JOHNSON: "That's why I'm getting out. I want to go some place where I can be a woman." Newspaper editor **Cary Grant** hits the wrong note trying to induce his ex-wife and star reporter **Rosalind Russell** to abandon her plans to quit the paper and marry Ralph Bellamy. *His Girl Friday* (1940, Columbia).

8654 "If I ever get to buy another newspaper, I'll remember what a few cents can buy." Parachutist Commander **Errol Flynn** pays tribute and says farewell to war correspondent Henry Hull who expires during a mission behind Japanese lines in World War II. *Objective Burma* (1945, Warner Bros.).

8655 MR. WINSLOW: "What shall I say?" SIR ROBERT MORTON: "I hardly think it matters, sir, whatever you say will have very little bearing on what they write." **Cedric Hardwicke** is cynically, but probably correctly advised, by politician **Robert Donat**, on talking to reporters. *The Winslow Boy* (1948, GB, London Films).

8656 "You journalists, I envy you. The world's in flames, you stand apart as if you were gods. The folly of man is no more to you than a news item." Anti-fascist Greek patriot **Donald Wolfit** muses about Robert Mitchum's profession and detachment. *The Angry Hills* (1959, GB, MGM).

8657 "'Catwoman is thought to weigh 140 pounds'— I don't know how these hacks sleep at night." **Michelle Pfeiffer** gets her fur up when she reads what a reporter has written about the weight of her alter ego. *Batman Returns* (1992, Warner Bros.).

Repulsion

see also LIKES AND DISLIKES

8658 "You're the one man in the world I could never get low enough to touch!" Cheap café entertainer **Joan Crawford** tells informer Peter Lorre that his desire for her repulses her. *Strange Cargo* (1940, MGM).

8659 "I don't find you any fun; I feel you suffocate me; I don't feel rapport with you, and I don't dig you physically." **Susan Anspach** gives Woody Allen more reasons than he wants to hear her desire to end their marriage. *Play It Again, Sam* (1972, Paramount).

8660 "I'm beginning to repel people I'm trying to seduce." **Holly Hunter**, despite obvious efforts, is unable to get William Hurt into her bed. *Broadcast News* (1987, 20th Century-Fox).

8661 "Because. . . when I watch you eat, when I see you asleep, whenever I look at you lately I just want to smash your face in." It may not be the best grounds for divorce, but it's **Kathleen Turner**'s reason for wishing to divorce Michael Douglas. *The War of the Roses* (1989, 20th Century-Fox).

Reputations

see also FAME

8662 "You like me. In fact, you're crazy about me. Otherwise you wouldn't worry about my reputation. Isn't that so?. . . But I don't like you. I don't like you at all! I wouldn't hesitate one instant to ruin your reputation." Even if she meant it, which she doesn't, rich Parisian **Kay Francis** couldn't do much to ruin jewel thief Herbert Marshall's reputation. *Trouble in Paradise* (1932, Paramount).

8663 "My dear, don't you know? That's Rhett Butler. He's from Charleston. He has the most terrible reputation." **Marcella Martin** identifies Clark Gable for Vivien Leigh as they stand on the staircase at Twelve Oaks. *Gone with the Wind* (1939, Selznick-MGM).

8664 BRIGID O'SHAUGHNESSY: "Would you have done this to me if the falcon had been real, and you'd got your money?" SAM SPADE: "Don't be too sure I'm as crooked as I'm supposed to be. That sort of reputation might be good business—bringing high priced jobs and making it easier to deal with the enemy but a lot more money would have been one more item on your side of the ledger." **Mary Astor** has been told by **Humphrey Bogart** that he's turning her over to the police for the murder of his partner Jerome Cowan. He admits that it's a close call. *The Maltese Falcon* (1941, Warner Bros.).

8665 "I have a reputation of knowing about good clothes, good food and good wine. Do you like martinis? They are an acquired taste, like Ravel." Bored society dame **Joan Crawford** puts on the dog for violinist John Garfield. *Humoresque* (1947, Warner Bros.).

8666 LINDA NORDLEY: "Doesn't a woman's reputation mean anything to you?" VICTOR MARSWELL: "Not unless I'm personally involved." Married **Grace Kelly** finds herself falling for safari leader **Clark Gable**. *Mogambo* (1953, MGM).

Requests

see also DESIRES, REFUSALS AND REJECTION

8667 "Nomination's in the bag. I made a special request to be seated behind you. I wanted to see how a four-flusher behaves when he has a full house." **Ralph Bellamy** torments Adolphe Menjou at a political convention with a poker insult. *Forbidden* (1932, Columbia).

8668 "I'd like to see Paris before I die. . . Philadelphia will do." **W.C. Fields** amends his last request as he's about to be strung up by an angry lynch mob. *My Little Chickadee* (1940, Universal).

8669 "Alex, will you come in, please? I wish to talk to you." Nazi renegade leader **Ivan Triesault** calls Claude Rains to his doom when it becomes clear that Rains has married an American agent, Ingrid

Bergman, now being rescued by her contact Cary Grant. *Notorious* (1946, RKO).

8670 "Will you please not bark at me?" **Jane House** makes the request of werewolf Dean Stockwell, with whom she'd like to become amorous after he locks himself in a lavatory and is about to metamorphize. *The Werewolf of Washington* (1973, Diplomat).

8671 "Hey, if you guys ever have kids and one of them when he's eight years old accidentally sets fire to the living room rug—go easy on him, will ya?" While visiting the recent past, **Michael J. Fox** asks his parents-to-be, Lea Thompson and Crispin Glover, to be understanding when he makes one of his bigger childhood mistakes. *Back to the Future* (1985, Universal).

8672 "If anything happens to me tell every woman I've ever gone out with I was talking about her at the end. That way they'll have to re-evaluate me." While covering a story during a battle in Central America, TV reporter **Albert Brooks** makes the request of producer Holly Hunter. *Broadcast News* (1987, 20th Century-Fox).

8673 MORTICIA: "Gomez, you were a desperate howling demon last night." GOMEZ: "Yes." MORTICIA: "Do it again." **Anjelica Huston** requests an encore from husband **Raul Julia**. *The Addams Family* (1991, Orion-Paramount).

8674 "Could you just not breathe?" Beautiful, dead **Meryl Streep** hisses a request of her middle-aged husband Bruce Willis. *Death Becomes Her* (1992, Universal).

Requirements

see also AUTHORITIES, COMMANDS, ORDERS

8675 DR. WATSON: "Good heavens, Holmes! It's a long drop." SHERLOCK HOLMES: "Yes, rather more than is required by law, my dear Watson, but equally effective." **Ian Fleming** as Dr. Watson, has just witnessed maniacal Lyn Harding as Professor Moriarty dash up a castle's ruined tower and topple, screaming, "Curse you, Holmes!" **Arthur Wontner**, as Sherlock Holmes, refers to the drop at the end of a rope when one is hanged. *The Triumph of Sherlock Holmes* (1935, GB, Gaumont-British).

8676 "We ain't got no badges. We don't need no badges. . . I don't have to show you no stinkin' badges." Mexican bandit **Alfonso Bedoya**, becoming increasingly angry, growls at hidden Humphrey Bogart. Bogie has challenged Bedoya's assertion that he and his men are federales by asking to see their badges. *The Treasure of the Sierra Madre* (1948, Warner Bros.).

8677 "Agatha Christie should be required reading for the police force." In an in-joke, Agatha Christie's amateur detective Miss Marple creation, portrayed by **Margaret Rutherford**, insists the police could learn from the author. *Murder at the Gallop* (1963, GB, MGM).

Resemblances

see also APPEARANCES

8678 "A slight resemblance or do I flatter myself?" **Ernest Thesiger**, as Dr. Praetorious, fancies that he looks like the devil. *The Bride of Frankenstein* (1935, Universal).

8679 "Any resemblance to you or me might be purely intentional." Unseen narrator **Celeste Holm** speaks to the characters of the movie and the audience. *A Letter to Three Wives* (1949, 20th Century-Fox).

Resentments

see also HURT AND HURTING

8680 TRIXIE LORRAINE: "Start walking and keep walking—and if you ever come near him again I'll break both your legs." FAY FORTUNE: "I could easily resent that." Showgirl **Aline MacMahon** warns haughty gold digger **Ginger Rogers** not to make a play for sugar daddy Guy Kibbee. *Gold Diggers of 1933* (1933, Warner Bros.).

8681 "I don't mind being killed, but I resent hearing about it from a character whose head comes to a point." **Groucho Marx** reacts when Chico Marx tells him his life is in danger. *A Night in Casablanca* (1946, United Artists).

8682 "My cunt has teeth." Lesbian punker **Anne Carlisle** (who also portrays a gay male model) resents Bob Brady wanting her to dress and behave like a sweet housewife. *Liquid Sky* (1983, Cine Vista).

Resignations

see also FATE AND DESTINY, NEEDS AND NECESSITIES, PATIENCE AND IMPATIENCE

8683 "The only way to resign from our profession is to die." **Lewis Stone** warns Greta Garbo, who believes she can quit being a spy. *Mata Hari* (1932, MGM).

8684 "After we had all been resigned to his death, his sudden return seems to me particularly depressing." Spinster **Margaret Rutherford** reacts to the news that the imaginary brother Earnest that Michael Redgrave invented and then killed off has survived and arrives in the person of Redgrave's friend Michael Denison. *The Importance of Being Earnest* (1952, GB, Two Cities-Rank).

8685 "Well, that's the way of it sometimes." It's the chief stoker's calm and resigned response when Brian Aherne, the captain of the Titanic, asks him to keep the engine running as long as possible. Aherne offers the man no hope, saying, "I suppose you know you may not get out of here." *Titanic* (1953, 20th Century-Fox).

8686 "There it goes. Every day it goes and somebody goes with it. Today it's me." **Richard Widmark** comments on the burning red sun and his imminent demise. He loses in drawing lots to see who will stay behind to hold off the savages, while the other whisks Susan Hayward to safety. *Garden of Evil* (1954, 20th Century-Fox).

8687 "What can't be remedied must be endured." Fugitive from his wife and family for thirty years, fabled outlaw **Willie Nelson** makes like Nietzsche. *Barbarosa* (1982, Universal).

8688 "What can you do? The world spins around." **Susan Sarandon** wastes no tears when James Spader tells her he's recently lost his wife. She's lost a son a bit earlier. *White Palace* (1990, Universal).

Resistances

see also REBELLIONS

8689 SISTER ANNIE ALDEN: "Too many girls follow the line of least resistance." ROSE CARLTON: "Yeah, but a good line is hard to resist." Missionary **Helen Jerome Eddy** and escaping accused murderer **Mae West** have slightly different slants on the word "line." *Klondike Annie* (1936, Paramount).

8690 "The Communist underground was ready to turn genuine passive resistance into a bloodbath." English Colonel **Stewart Granger** sets the stage for the movie in voice-over narration. *Bhowani Junction* (1956, MGM).

8691 "When just one man says 'No,' Rome begins to fear." Title character **Kirk Douglas** insists that resistance itself is the power of his slave army. *Spartacus* (1960, Universal-International).

Resolutions

see also PROMISES, PURPOSES

8692 NICK CHARLES: "Make any New Year's resolutions?" NORA CHARLES: "Not yet. Any complaints or suggestions?" NICK: "Few." NORA: "Which?" NICK: "Complaints." NORA: "All right, shoot." NICK: "Well, you don't scold, you don't nag, and you look far too pretty in the mornings." NORA: "All right. I'll remember: must scold, must nag, mustn't be too pretty in the morning." **William Powell** and **Myrna Loy** are playful as the movies' favorite married couple. *After the Thin Man* (1936, MGM).

8693 "I made a resolution never again to take up with any hell-bent types." Teenager **Sissy Spacek** finally wises up to the fact that mass murderer Martin Sheen was the wrong kind of guy to hook up with. *Badlands* (1974, Warner Bros.).

8694 REGINALD KINCAID: "Mrs. Hudson, an occasional libation enables me to stiffen my resolve." MRS. HUDSON: "Your resolve should be pickled by now." Actor **Michael Caine**, posing as private investigator Sherlock Holmes, exchanges views on his drinking with housekeeper **Pat Keen**. *Without a Clue* (1988, GB, Orion).

Respect and Respectability

see also ADMIRATION, HONOR, LOVE AND HATE, LOVE AND LOVERS

8695 "I've heard all the questions and I know all the answers—and I've kept myself fairly respectable through it all." Torch singer **Barbara Stanwyck**, grown weary of the life and the city, speaks to her bootlegger boyfriend Lyle Talbot. *The Purchase Price* (1932, Warner Bros.).

8696 "Oh, you wouldn't know them, darling; they're respectable people." **Myrna Loy** sees no reason to identify some people she waved to for her husband William Powell. *After the Thin Man* (1936, MGM).

8697 "There are but three things that men respect: the lash that descends, the yoke that breaks, and the sword that slays. By the power and terror of these you may rule the world." **Conrad Veidt** wasn't the first or the last megalomaniac to believe that respect can be won by mistreatment of slaves. *The Thief of Bagdad* (1940, GB, London Films-United Artists).

8698 "I haven't any respect for a man who was born lazy; it took me a long time to get where I am." **Don Ameche** is the head of a school created to transform pathetic losers and failures into self-confident successes. *The Magnificent Dope* (1942, 20th Century-Fox).

8699 SAM GRIGGS: "All you left Ma and me was a fifteen dollar saloon bill." BEN GRIGGS: "I'll thank you to treat your father with somewhat more respect." SAM: "Respect? Why I'm twice as old as you are!" Ghosts **Frank Morgan** and his father **Keenan Wynn,** having returned to earth to set their family straight, go off to their eternal rest still arguing. *The Cockeyed Miracle* (1946, MGM).

8700 "Attention must be finally paid to such a man. He's not to be allowed to fall into his grave like an old dog." **Mildred Dunnock** demands that her sons Kevin McCarthy and Cameron Mitchell show some respect for their despondent father Fredric March. *Death of a Salesman* (1951, Columbia).

8701 "Miss Jean Louise, stand up. Your father's passing." Elderly black minister **Bill Walker** tells Mary Badham to join the blacks consigned to the balcony of a courtroom in standing to show respect for Badham's father, white lawyer Gregory Peck. With dignity and eloquence, Peck demonstrated that black Brock Peters was innocent of the charges of the rape and assault of white Collin Wilcox—nevertheless, his client was convicted by the prejudiced jury. *To Kill a Mockingbird* (1962, Universal).

8702 "I respect anybody who has to fight and howl for his decency." **Deborah Kerr** consoles defrocked priest-turned tour guide Richard Burton. *The Night of the Iguana* (1964, MGM).

8703 "You have exactly ten seconds to change that disgusting look of pity into one of enormous respect. One...two...." Has-been Broadway producer **Zero Mostel** orders accountant Gene Wilder to change his expression. *The Producers* (1966, Embassy).

8704 "I want to get back on welfare, be respectable, and have a decent place." Transvestite **Holly Woodlawn** pretends to be pregnant. *Trash* (1970, Cinema 5-Andy Warhol).

8705 "Young people don't respect anything these days. Times are changing for the worse." Undertaker **Salvatore Corsitto** complains about the younger generation to Godfather Marlon Brando on the latter's daughter's wedding day. *The Godfather* (1972, Paramount).

8706 "If you're a boy kid, you better learn to respect women. And if you're a girl kid, I'm gonna teach you to respect yourself." **Susan Anspach** talks to her unborn child. *Blume in Love* (1973, Warner Bros.).

8707 "Course I'm respectable. I'm old. Politicians, ugly buildings and whores are all respectable if they last long enough." Wealthy, conniving old **John Huston** says his piece to private investigator Jack Nicholson. *Chinatown* (1974, Paramount).

8708 "I won't be wronged. I won't be insulted, and I won't be laid a hand on. I don't do these things to other people and I expect the same from them." Aging gunslinger **John Wayne**'s demand for respect is tied to his version of the golden rule. *The Shootist* (1976, Paramount).

8709 "Well, even the most primitive society has an innate respect for the insane." Former gang-leader **Mickey Rourke** lectures his hero-worshiping brother Matt Dillon. *Rumble Fish* (1983, Universal).

8710 "You've come thousands of miles just to get laid. I really respect that." One of the male party-goers expresses admiration for John Cusack, who is about to hook up with "the sure thing." *The Sure Thing* (1985, Embassy).

Responsibilities

see also CAUSE AND EFFECT, DECISIONS, REQUIRE-MENTS, TRUST

8711 "You're my responsibility now. See you in church." **Carole Lombard** establishes bum William Powell as the butler in her wealthy family's home. She has romantic plans for him. *My Man Godfrey* (1936, Universal).

8712 "Special hair like mine is a responsibility." Carvel High vamp **Lana Turner** won't swim because it would wet her beautiful hair. *Love Finds Andy Hardy* (1938, MGM).

8713 "You saved my life. You're responsible for me." **Leslie Banks** dies in the arms of his wife Marie Ney, offering his regrets for having caused her so much pain for so long. *Jamaica Inn* (1939, GB, Mayflower-Paramount).

8714 "There are some things a man can't run away from." For **John Wayne** that means killing three brothers who murdered his father and brother. *Stagecoach* (1939, United Artists).

8715 "Ever hear of the decline and fall of the Roman Empire? That was our crowd." Beautiful witch **Veronica Lake** brags to her mortal husband Fredric March. *I Married a Witch* (1941, United Artists).

8716 "We lived in a five-room house and I did the laundry. And I never went anywhere because I had a kid to look after. I don't have a kid to look after anymore. And the people I go around with now don't use a kiss as an excuse to sock people." **Doris Dowling** states her independence to her husband Alan Ladd, just back from World War II. Dowling has been unfaithful to Ladd. During a drunken binge, she had an automobile accident that killed their son. *The Blue Dahlia* (1946, Paramount).

8717 "I am leaving soon and you'll forgive me if I speak bluntly. The universe grows smaller every day and the threat of aggression by any group anywhere can no longer be tolerated. There must be security for all or no one is secure. Now this does not mean giving up any freedom, except the freedom to act irresponsibly. Your ancestors knew this when they made laws to govern themselves and hired policemen to enforce them. We, of the other planets, have long accepted this principle. We have an organization for the mutual protection of all planets and for the complete elimination of aggression. The test of all such higher authority is, of course, the police force that supports us." Before leaving earth, alien **Michael Rennie** tries to talk some sense to its inhabitants, demanding that they join their neighbors in outer space and act responsibly. *The Day the Earth Stood Still* (1951, 20th Century-Fox).

8718 MRS. ANTONY: "Sometimes he's terribly irresponsible." ANNE MORTON: "He's responsible for a woman's death." **Marion Lorne** refuses to comprehend what **Ruth Roman** is saying about her psychopathic son Robert Walker. *Strangers on a Train* (1951, Warner Bros.).

8719 "The lid's off the garbage can, and I did it." Disfigured **Gloria Grahame** sets in motion her revenge by killing Jeanette Nolan, thereby ensuring a letter will be mailed that will destroy Lee Marvin, who threw scalding coffee in her face. *The Big Heat* (1953, Columbia).

8720 "A man's gotta do what a man's gotta do." **Alan Ladd** reduces the code of the west to a manageable cliché. *Shane* (1953, Paramount).

8721 "You don't know what it's like to stand out there on that stage all alone, with the whole show on your shoulders. If I'm no good, the show's no good." Unlike his own laid-back approach to performing, **Bing Crosby**'s alcoholic character sweats all the responsibility. *The Country Girl* (1954, Paramount).

8722 "And that's the difference between us, Mr. Dodd. You want him to become the actor he once was. I'm his wife! I want him just once more as the man he once was—able to stand on his own two feet and face responsibility. And—and you don't do that by bending the truth!" **Grace Kelly** has different ambitions for her husband, entertainer Bing Crosby's comeback than does producer-director William Holden. *The Country Girl* (1954, Paramount).

8723 "A man must do what he must do." **Louis Calhern**, impersonating James A. Michener, delivers the message of the film. *Men of the Fighting Lady* (1954, MGM).

8724 "There are some things a man can't ride around." It's rancher **Randolph Scott**'s version of "a man's gotta do what a man's gotta do." *The Tall T* (1957, Columbia).

8725 "Gooper is your first-born. Why, he's always had to carry a bigger load of the responsibility than Brick. Brick never carried anything in his life but a football or a highball." **Madeleine Sherwood** can't understand why her in-laws, Burl Ives and Judith Anderson, prefer their younger son Paul Newman to her husband, Jack Carson. It could have something to do with her and her brood of ill-mannered kids. *Cat on a Hot Tin Roof* (1958, MGM).

8726 "It was my responsibility. I shouldn't have got you involved. . . . Goodbye, Scottie. There's no way for them to understand. You and I know who killed Madeleine." **Tom Helmore** consoles James Stewart after a coroner concludes that Helmore's wife Kim Novak killed herself while in "a state of unsound mind." *Vertigo* (1958, Paramount).

8727 "I want you to listen tight. I'm talkin' about all the people everywhere. . . that's what's important. . . to feel useful in this old world, to hit a lick against what's wrong or to say a word for what's right even tho' ya get walloped for saying that word. Now I may sound like a Bible-beater yellin' up a revival at a river crossing camp. But that don't change the truth none. There's right and there's wrong, and ya gotta do one or the other. Ya do the one and yer living; ya do the other and ya may be walkin' around, but you're dead as a beaver hat." **John Wayne**, as Davy Crockett, uses his eloquence to get his Tennessee volunteers to take on a suicide mission at the Alamo. *The Alamo* (1960, United Artists).

8728 "If Ernst Janning is to be found guilty, certain implications must arise. . . . A judge does not make the law. He carries out the laws of his country. . . . He carries out the laws of his country. . . . The statement, 'My country right or wrong,' was expressed by a great American patriot. It is no less true for a German patriot. . . . Should Ernst Janning have carried out the laws of his country? Or should he have refused to carry them out and become a traitor? This is the crux of the issue at the bottom of the trial. . . . The defense is as dedicated to finding responsibility as the prosecution. For it is not only Ernst Janning who is on trial here. It is the German people." Defense Attorney **Maximilian Schell** addresses the court with his opening statement in the war crimes cases of German jurists, including Burt Lancaster as Ernst Janning. *Judgment at Nuremberg* (1961, United Artists).

8729 "The band makes it rock but the roadies make it roll." **Kaki Hunter** refers to touring rock bands and the roadies who set up the stages and equipment at each new site. *Roadie* (1980, United Artists).

8730 "We've got a responsibility to people in our lives. It's the only thing that separates us from the goddamned animals." Caring and sensitive **David Keith** implores his friend Richard Gere, who is afraid of getting close to people. *An Officer and a Gentleman* (1982, Paramount).

8731 "Your job is to get them through school and keep them out of trouble." Vice principal **Judd Hirsch** expresses the unexpressed view of far too many high school administrators and teachers to Nick Nolte, a caring teacher. *Teachers* (1984, MGM-United Artists).

8732 "I just gotta do what I gotta do." **Sylvester Stallone**'s line to his wife Talia Shire sounds vaguely familiar. *Rocky IV* (1985, MGM-United Artists).

Rest see EASE AND EASINESS, PEACE, SLEEP

Restaurants

see also BREAKFAST, FOOD AND EATING

8733 "Madame, this is a restaurant, not a meadow." Waiter **Armand Kaliz** turns up his nose to Communist emissary Greta Garbo when she requests some raw beets and carrots. *Ninotchka* (1939, MGM).

8734 "The International House of Pancakes is the one consistent thing in my life." Waitress **Beverly D'Angelo** finds I-HOP a revolving door of men looking just for her. *Honky Tonk Freeway* (1981, EMI).

8735 "This is the House of Pancakes, Ma'am!" Waitress **Lois DeBanzie** tries to restrain customer Mariangela Melato, who begins to behave lewdly. *So Fine* (1981, Warner Bros.).

8736 "I busted this joint fourteen times when I was in Vice. Now I eat here every day." It's homicide detective **Robert Duvall**'s ironic remark to his cleric brother Robert De Niro as they have a bite to eat in a disreputable eatery. *True Confessions* (1981, United Artists).

8737 "Younger men are like fast food restaurants; it's quick, but not all that good. But with you, it's like dining in the most expensive restaurant in the world. Of course, the service may be a little slow. . . ." Young **Nastassja Kinski** favorably compares her older husband Dudley Moore to younger lovers, but not without a catch. *Unfaithfully Yours* (1984, 20th Century-Fox).

Retirement

see also BEDS, DEPARTURES AND RETURNS, ENDS AND ENDINGS, QUITTING AND QUITTERS

8738 PROF. MORIARTY: "Mr. Holmes, it has been an intellectual treat to cross swords with you, and I say unaffectedly it would have been a great grief to me to have been forced to take any extreme measures." SHERLOCK HOLMES: "Danger happens to be part of my trade, Professor." MORIARTY: "Danger? It isn't a question of danger but of inevitable destruction! Therefore I say again you are wise to retire! When you once get to the country, take my advice and stay there!" HOLMES: "And suppose I should reconsider my decision?" MORIARTY: "You have my warning. I wish you a pleasant and permanent retirement." When **Arthur Wontner**, as Holmes, announces his retirement, the Napoleon of crime, **Lyn Harding**, as Moriarty, makes a surprise visit to Baker Street. *The Triumph of Sherlock Holmes* (1935, GB, Gaumont-British).

8739 "Well, Mary, only six more days and your old Nathan will be out of the army." Cavalry officer **John Wayne** addresses the grave site of his wife. He stops when the shadow of Joanne Dru crosses the tombstone. *She Wore a Yellow Ribbon* (1949, RKO).

8740 "Harry, I'm fifty-seven years old. All I want to do is get out in a boat and smell the sea. Thirty-eight years in this business. All I want to do is catch a fish. Am I being unreasonable? Is that too much to ask?" **Jack Gilford** tells his partner Jack Lemmon that he'd like to retire from the rat race of the garment industry. *Save the Tiger* (1973, Paramount).

8741 "I'm officially retired now." Who's going to believe that bleeder **Sylvester Stallone** will refuse to challenge the brutal slugger Mr. T and the others to follow in III, IV, and V? *Rocky II* (1979, United Artists).

Retreat *see* ESCAPES

Retribution *see* CAUSE AND EFFECT, CONSEQUENCES, JUSTICE, PUNISHMENTS, REVENGE AND VENGEANCE

Returning *see* DEPARTURES AND RETURNS

Revelations

see also GOD, TRUTH

8742 JOHNNY: "Get this straight. I don't care what you do. But I'm going to see to it that it looks all right to him. From now on, you go anywhere you please, with anyone you please. But I'm going to take you there and I'm going to bring you home. Get that? Exactly the way I pick up his laundry." GILDA: "Shame on you, Johnny. Any psychiatrist would tell you your thought associations are very revealing. All to protect Ballin—who do you think you're kidding, Johnny?" **Glenn Ford** doesn't fool **Rita Hayworth.** She knows that he's not interested in protecting his boss George Macready from her cheating ways. She knows he wants her for himself. *Gilda* (1946, Columbia).

8743 "I have lived in the theater as a Trappist monk lives in his faith. I have no other world; no other life—and once in a great while I experience that moment of revelation for which all true believers wait and pray. You are one. Jeanne Eagels another. . . there are others, three or four, Eve Harrington will be among them." Acerbic theater critic **George Sanders** is almost reverent in speaking to Bette Davis of the acting talents of truly great thespians, past and present, and one of the future, Anne Baxter. *All About Eve* (1950, 20th Century-Fox).

8744 LISL: "My nightie is slipping." JAMES BOND: "So is your accent, Countess." **Roger Moore**'s spy conquest **Cassandra Harris** is revealed in more ways than one. *For Your Eyes Only* (1981, United Artists).

Revenge and Vengeance

see also HATE AND HATRED, KILLINGS, PAINS, PUNISHMENTS

8745 "I'm going to get even with you, you dirty stiff—I'll do it." Tough-talking reporter **Glenda Farrell** figures the best possible way to punish Frank McHugh is to accept his marriage proposal. *The Mystery of the Wax Museum* (1933, Warner Bros.).

8746 "I'll get even if I have to crawl back from the grave to do it." Clip-joint hostess (prostitute) **Bette Davis** threatens Eduardo Ciannelli, a Lucky Luciano-like mobster, who is responsible for Bette's kid sister Jane Bryan entering the profession and getting killed. *Marked Woman* (1937, Warner Bros.).

8747 "The United States doesn't settle for a deal. . . . Forgive your enemies, but first get even." In Japan of the 30s, newspaperman **James Cagney** spits his words defiantly at Japanese official Marvin Miller as Cagney stumbles to safety into the courtyard of the U.S. Embassy. Now that Cagney is safe, Miller looks to smooth over the fact that the Japanese police tried to kill Cagney. He asks for Cagney's forgiveness. *Blood on the Sun* (1945, Cagney-United Artists).

8748 "That moment when he thinks he has me, he'll lose everything." **Teresa Wright** offers herself as the instrument of revenge for her parents Dean Jagger and Judith Anderson against Robert Mitchum. She plans to marry him and murder him on their wedding night. *Pursued* (1947, Warner Bros.).

8749 "You see, Ralls, I'm not one of those eye-for-an-eye men. I always take two eyes." It's not perfectly clear whether it's the loss of Gail Russell or of a fortune in pearls that is the major motivating factor for **Luther Adler**'s desire for revenge against John Wayne. *Wake of the Red Witch* (1948, Republic).

8750 "Revenge is the dish which most people of taste prefer to eat cold. . . . Because she married for love, instead of for rank, or money, or land, they condemned her to a life of poverty and slavery, in a world with which they had not equipped her to deal." Genteel **Dennis Price** relates that he is avenging his mother who was abandoned by her family, just before he shoots the eighth and last relative who stands between him and a dukedom. All of Price's victims are played by Alec Guinness. *Kind Hearts and Coronets* (1949, GB, Ealing-GFD).

8751 "No mob ever wants justice. They want revenge." Mad Emperor Nero, portrayed by **Peter Ustinov**, knows his mobs. He placates the citizens by putting the blame on the Christians when he burns Rome. *Quo Vadis* (1951, MGM).

8752 "I am the sword of vengeance. . . whereby the wrong shall be righted and the truth be told." Vindictive ex-Civil War veteran **Joseph Wiseman** shouts his message from the sand-swept hilltops. *The Unforgiven* (1960, United Artists).

8753 "I'm sick and tired of being your dishrag and I'm gonna get even." Ditzy country and western singer **Bette Midler** has grown tired of her gambler lover Rip Torn. Unfortunately for the movie, she and casino dealer Ken Wahl get rid of Torn, the only interesting character in the film. *Jinxed!* (1982, MGM-United Artists).

8754 "All this revenge stuff. It's such a letdown." **Jodie Foster** cries out as Nastassja Kinski and Dorsey Wright perform a ritual rape of Matthew Modine, one of the boys who gang-raped Foster. *The Hotel New Hampshire* (1984, Orion).

8755 "Justice isn't good enough. You gotta exact a biblical revenge." Police Captain **Gerald Castillo** accuses Lieutenant Charles Bronson of going too far. Bronson hates pimps so much he forces one, Juan Fernandez, to swallow a gold pocket watch. *Kinjite: Forbidden Subjects* (1989, Cannon).

8756 "Revenge is the only justice. I and others not of this world can help." Necromancer **Lois Masten** offers help to Elizabeth Kaitan who seeks revenge against a trio of low-lifes who have raped her and are blackmailing her to keep quiet. *Necromancer* (1989, Bonaire-Spectrum).

8757 "They wouldn't put me on a pedestal, so I'm laying 'em on a slab!" Fiendish **Danny De Vito**, as the Penguin, seeks revenge when Christopher Walken's attempts to get him elected mayor of Gotham City fail. *Batman Returns* (1992, Warner Bros.).

Revolutions

see also BATTLES AND BATTLEFIELDS, FIGHTS AND FIGHTING, REBELLIONS, TYRANNY AND TYRANTS, VIOLENCE, WAR

8758 "There's a strange new spirit in the world today. A spirit of revolt. I don't understand it—and I don't like it." Wealthy businessman **Henry Kolker** is profoundly upset by the ideas of his daughter Doris Nolan's fiancé Cary Grant. *Holiday* (1938, Columbia).

8759 "Maybe there's only one revolution. The big revolution. The good guys versus the bad guys. The question is who are the good guys?" **Burt Lancaster** answers Robert Ryan who asks what Americans were doing in the Mexican Revolution. *The Professionals* (1966, Columbia).

8760 "You've heard of the sexual revolution? Well, I'm one of the first casualties." Not everyone would feel sorry for **Christopher Jones**, who is kidnapped by three lovely coeds and forced to have sex with each of them until he's willing to settle for just one of them. *Three in the Attic* (1968, AIP).

8761 "If only we had more women like her. What a revolution we could have." Revolutionary **Vic Diaz** admires machine-gun wielding Philippines nightclub singer Pam Grier. *The Big Bird Cage* (1972, New World).

8762 "You can't fight in the court. You've got to go to the streets, man the barricades, man the dynamite, blow up the cesspool. . . . We are in for a depression that will make the thirties seem like paradise. Maybe it's a good thing. The hard hats and the phony liberals will kill each other." Bitter old socialist **Herbert Berghof** gets fired up when Art Carney tells him that he's being evicted and will have to find a lawyer to fight it. *Harry and Tonto* (1974, 20th Century-Fox).

8763 "What kind of revolution is it that doesn't allow you to eat an avocado?" **William Hurt** offers his revolutionary cellmate Raul Julia some food and gets a lecture on what revolutionaries should and should not do. *Kiss of the Spider Woman* (1985, U.S.-Brazil-Island Alive).

8764 "Hi, we're starting a people's uprising. Do you fancy joining us?" Transsexual **Lanah Pellay** tries to recruit members for his planned revolution. *Eat the Rich* (1987, GB, New Line).

Rhymes see MUSIC AND MUSICIANS, POETRY AND POETS, SONGS AND SINGING

Riches see GOLD, MONEY, POSSESSIONS, POVERTY, WEALTH AND RICHES

Ridicule and Ridiculousness

see also ABSURDITIES, FEELINGS, LAUGHTER, TAUNTS, WORDS

8765 "Your boys should see you now." **Marlene Dietrich** ridicules once stuffy professor Emil Jannings, dressed in a clown's outfit. *The Blue Angel* (1930, Germany, UFA).

8766 "I know I must look funny to you. Maybe if you came to Mandrake Falls, you'd look just as funny to us. But nobody would laugh at you and make you feel ridiculous. . . cause that wouldn't be good manners." "Cinderella Man" **Gary Cooper** responds to the vicious lampoon of him and his poetry by a group of reporters. *Mr. Deeds Goes to Town* (1936, Columbia).

8767 MRS. VAN HOPPER: "Most girls would give their eyes to see Monte." MAXIM DE WINTER: "Wouldn't that rather defeat the purpose?" Delightful **Florence Bates** is grotesquely coquettish with **Laurence Olivier** on the Riviera. *Rebecca* (1940, Selznick-United Artists).

8768 "Oh, Harry, you look so ridiculous—like a knight questing for the Holy Grail." **Hildegarde Neff** doesn't mind when her lover Gregory Peck prepares to leave her. *The Snows of Kilimanjaro* (1952, 20th Century-Fox).

8769 "That's a ridiculous thing to say." It's **Cary Grant**'s surprised reaction when lovely Grace Kelly tells him she loves him. *To Catch a Thief* (1955, Paramount).

Riding and Riders

see also ANIMALS, AUTOMOBILES, TRAINS, TRAVEL AND TRIPS

8770 "Stick around and let the Germans mop you up and spend the rest of the war in a prison camp in Berlin. But when I go to Berlin, I'm gonna be riding that tank, the same one you see standing there with the name Lulubelle written on her!" American Tank Sergeant **Humphrey Bogart** offers a group of British stragglers in the Sahara desert the opportunity to join him and his tank and get back into the war. *Sahara* (1943, Columbia).

8771 "Just knack. Down with your head, up with your heart, and you're over the top like a flash and skimming down the other side like a dragonfly." **Margaret Rutherford** reveals her secret when Joyce Carey expresses amazement that Rutherford can ride her bicycle everywhere without tiring. *Blithe Spirit* (1945, GB, Two Cities-Cineguild).

8772 "The old guard, still in the saddle, they'd rather ride two to a horse than give up riding. But if you give them a shove, they make room." Social climbing British playboy **Alan Bates**, will commit any act, including murder, to get ahead. *Nothing But the Best* (1964, GB, Anglo Amalgamated).

8773 "Whenever I get sick, I get on a horse and ride myself better." It's **Elizabeth Taylor**'s prescription for bed-ridden Julie Harris. *Reflections in a Golden Eye* (1967, Warner Bros.).

8774 "When you ride with a man, you stay with him. Otherwise, you're an animal. We started together—we'll end together." Expressing a version of the Code of the West, **William Holden** angrily responds to the suggestion that his gang split up in order to escape a posse of men out to capture or kill them. *The Wild Bunch* (1969, Warner Bros.).

8775 "May you ride long and hard." Oklahoma badman **Burt Lancaster** shouts after departing teens, Amanda Plummer and Diane Lane, who ride off after spending some time with Lancaster's outlaw gang. *Cattle Annie and Little Britches* (1981, Universal).

8776 "Can I have a ride to the airport?" Nerdish insomniac Jeff Goldblum helps beautiful **Michelle Pfeiffer** who's chased by killers when she smuggles six perfect emeralds into the country from Iran. *Into the Night* (1985, Universal).

8777 "You're like one of those crazed cops who no one wants to ride with." **Harrison Ford** states some reservations about working with ambitious Melanie Griffith. *Working Girl* (1988, 20th Century-Fox).

Right and Wrong

see also CORRECTIONS, GOOD AND EVIL (BAD), GOODNESS, RIGHTS, WRONGS AND WRONGDOINGS

8778 "You know what's right and what's wrong. You know better, but you just won't do anything about it. You choose to think that you can get through the world by outsmarting it. But I've learned that those kind of people generally end up by outsmarting themselves. And that's what's going to happen to you. And I don't feel a bit sorry about it because, lady, you've got it coming to you." District Attorney **Humphrey Bogart** tells off "hostess" Bette Davis for refusing to testify against crime boss Eduardo Ciannelli. *Marked Woman* (1937, Warner Bros.).

8779 "I may not know much about law, but I know what is right and what is wrong." Title character **Henry Fonda** claims some powerful knowledge. Life might be a lot easier if there were some absolute rights and wrongs that everyone could know. *Young Mr. Lincoln* (1939, 20th Century-Fox).

8780 "Terry's a paranoiac. A paranoiac has no more sense of right and wrong than a two-year-old." Psychiatrist **Lew Ayres** speaks of "bad" twin Olivia de Havilland. *The Dark Mirror* (1946, Universal).

8781 "You're sick. You don't even know what's right and what's wrong." **Van Heflin**'s accusation of murderer Barbara Stanwyck will give her a swell insanity defense if she chooses to use it. *The Strange Love of Martha Ivers* (1946, Paramount).

8782 "I don't care who's right and who's wrong. There's got to be some better way for people to live." On her wedding day, Quaker **Grace Kelly** tries to convince her new husband, retiring Sheriff Gary Cooper, that resorting to violence against gunmen who are coming for him, isn't the right way to start their life together. *High Noon* (1952, United Artists).

8783 "There is nothing which can be called right or wrong. One functions according to one's needs; you can read that in an elementary school textbook." **Gunner Bjorstrand** replies to his wife Ingrid Thulin who claims he's wrong in believing that life is disgusting. *Wild Strawberries* (1957, Sweden, Svensk Filmindustri).

8784 BRENDA: "You know the trouble with you is that you don't know the difference between right and wrong. I don't think you ever will." ARTHUR: "Maybe I don't. But I don't want anybody teaching me, either." Married **Rachel Roberts** scolds an unrepentant **Albert Finney**, with whom she's having an affair. *Saturday Night and Sunday Morning* (1960, GB, Continental Distribution).

8785 "Little by little, the look of the country changes because of men we admire. . . . You're just going to have to make up your mind one day about what's right and wrong." **Melvyn Douglas** would like to destroy the hero-worship his grandson Brandon de Wilde has for his hell-raising, selfish uncle, Paul Newman. *Hud* (1963, Paramount).

8786 "It was just like we were back in Nam. It didn't matter whether it was right or wrong. I just did it." Vietnam vet **Robert Ginty** describes a New York street gang that attacked and paralyzed his buddy Steve James, causing Ginty to go on a murderous rampage. *The Exterminator* (1980, Interstar-Avco Embassy).

8787 "I got to have you. I'm tired of what's right or wrong." Unhappily married **Jessica Lange** gives in to her passion for drifter Jack Nicholson. *The Postman Always Rings Twice* (1981, Paramount).

8788 JEFF TYLER: "It ain't right." KADY: "It's right if it's good." JEFF: "You're my daughter, Kady." KADY: "I'm a woman, too." **Stacy Keach** is talked into **Pia Zadora**'s bed. *Butterfly* (1982, Analysis).

8789 "Sometimes it's right to do the wrong thing, isn't it?" **Jamie Lee Curtis** wonders aloud to her friend Amy Madigan, as she considers infidelity with a situation ethics justification. *Love Letters* (1983, New World).

Rights

see also JUSTICE, LAWS, MORALITY, PRIVILEGES, PROPRIETY, SATISFACTIONS

8790 "What do you know about it? What are you saying? If it comes to that, who are you? What right do you have to speak?" Child murderer **Peter Lorre** defies the crowd of criminals who have put him on trial. *M* (1931, Germany, Nero Film-Paramount).

8791 "I'm just dumb enough to want to get the right fall guy." Police Captain **Tom Powers** isn't willing to arrest just any handy scapegoat for the murder of Doris Dowling. *The Blue Dahlia* (1946, Paramount).

8792 "We've been a long time getting here. We're tired, but we're here. We've got a right to be happy." Doctor Sidney Poitier's wife, **Mildred Joanne Smith**, believes that she, her husband and other blacks have earned the right to be treated as well as white folks. *No Way Out* (1950, 20th Century-Fox).

8793 "Let right be done." Famed British attorney **Robert Donat** addresses parliament in the case of 14-year-old Neil North, expelled from a naval college for an alleged theft of stealing a five-shilling postal order. *The Winslow Boy* (1950, London Films-Eagle-Lion).

8794 "A man ought to do what he thinks is right." It's another of **John Wayne**'s "a man's gotta do what a man's gotta do" lines. *Hondo* (1953, Warner Bros.).

8795 "The trouble about being on the side of right as one sees it, is that one often finds one's self in the company of some very questionable allies." Even though he's sided with others who choose to expel David Niven from a seaside hotel, **Felix Aylmer** doesn't feel good about it. *Separate Tables* (1958, United Artists).

8796 "We've got a right to climb out of the sewer and live like other people." **Dolores Dorn** says so to young gangster Cliff Robertson, who is bent on avenging his father's killing. *Underworld U.S.A.* (1960, Columbia).

8797 "What difference does it make if a few political extremists lost their rights? What difference does it make if a few racial minorities lose their rights? It's only a passing phase. It's only a stage we are going through. It will be discarded sooner or later. Hitler will be discarded sooner or later—the country was in danger. . . . What was going to be a passing phase became a way of life." Convicted of war crimes, German Judge **Burt Lancaster** tries to make American Judge Spencer Tracy understand how he thought when he went along with the Nazis and denied rights to certain people. It's a lesson that anyone who believes that "criminals and other low lives" don't deserve the same rights as decent people should learn. *Judgment at Nuremberg* (1961, United Artists).

8798 "Yes, actually, Stella. What's right is right. Let's split." Nutty chemistry professor **Jerry Lewis** no longer needs his Jekyll and Hyde concoction to turn him into dashing and obnoxious singer Buddy Love to win the love of Stella Stevens. *The Nutty Professor* (1963, Paramount).

8799 "For years, private citizens have been deprived of their rights. But now I'm afraid the pendulum has swung too far the other way." Police Chief **Charles McGraw** makes an incongruous statement. It seems that he is suggesting that there's a point at which private citizens should be deprived of their rights. *Pendulum* (1969, Columbia).

8800 "Oh, quit preening. I don't think you did it right anyway." **Cybill Shepherd** deflates Jeff Bridges after they leave a motel, having made love for the first time. *The Last Picture Show* (1971, Columbia).

8801 "Everything begins at exactly the right time and place." **Anne Lambert** is Miranda, a strange beautiful girl, one of those who disappears without a trace at Hanging Rock. *Picnic at Hanging Rock* (1975, Australia, Austalia Film Corporation).

8802 "You got no right to call me a murderer. You have the right to kill me—you have the right to do that—but you have no right to judge me." Mad maverick Green Beret Colonel **Marlon Brando** denies that his military assassin Martin Sheen has any moral right to judge his actions and behavior. *Apocalypse Now* (1979, United Artists).

8803 "Federation will make no difference to black bastards like you. You'll still have the same rights—none." Constable **Ray Barrett** tells mixed-race aborigine Tommy Lewis not to expect any improvement in conditions with a change of government in Australia. *The Chant of Jimmie Blacksmith* (1980, Australia, Film House).

8804 "Crap has a right to be crap." William Douglas-like liberal Supreme Court Justice **Walter Matthau** defends the right of people to make and see trash if they want to. *First Monday in October* (1981, Paramount).

8805 "Who gave you the right to judge who is fit to be a Negro and who is not?" Black Investigating Officer **Howard E. Rollins, Jr.** roars at the killers of tough non-com Adolph Caesar at a 1944 Louisiana Army post. *A Soldier's Story* (1984, Columbia).

8806 "[She]. . . has a right to know that there is a world out there filled with people who don't believe in God. . . people who fall in love, and make babies, and occasionally are very happy. . . . But you, and your order, and your church have kept her ignorant." Lapsed Catholic **Jane Fonda**, a psychiatrist whose sister died in a convent, accuses Mother Superior Anne Bancroft of deliberately keeping novice nun Meg Tilly ignorant of the world. *Agnes of God* (1985, Columbia).

8807 "Can't you admit that just once I was right about something?" **Timothy Hutton** gloats to his politically conservative father Pat Hingle as the latter watches the Watergate hearings with disgust. *The Falcon and the Snowman* (1985, Orion).

8808 "I have no profession. My attitude is quite an indefensible one, that as long as I'm no trouble to anyone, I have the right to do as I like. It is, I dare say, an example of my decadence." It also helps that Helena Bonham Carter's stuffy fiancé **Daniel Day-Lewis** is extremely wealthy. *A Room with a View* (1985, GB, Merchant-Ivory-Goldcrest).

8809 "You can't do this to me. I'm very rich and I have certain rights." Preppie **Tom Hanks** buys his way into the Peace Corps to escape his gambling debts and the gamblers who wish to do him bodily harm. Now he is threatened by a Thai warlord who wishes to do him bodily harm. *Volunteers* (1985, Tri-Star).

8810 "That's right, you're not a cocaine dealer, you're an importer—and your brother's not a scum-sucking pimp, he's a talent agent." Police detective **Charles Bronson** snarls at his natural enemy, a drug dealer. *Murphy's Law* (1986, Cannon).

8811 "I'm not going anywhere. I'm staying. This is my home. I was born here. . . probably die here. . . . If I wanted to leave I'd done it a long time ago. Things will work out. There's enough good people around here know what I did was right. Enough ladies like the way I fix their hair. . . ." Badly beaten **Frances McDormand** refuses to leave her small home town, even though her marriage is over and her house has been trashed because she helped Gene Hackman find the murderers of three civil rights workers. *Mississippi Burning* (1988, Orion).

8812 "Being miserable and treating other people like dirt is every New Yorker's God-given right." Ed Koch-like New York City Mayor **David Margulies** defends his constituents' rights to be rude and hostile. *Ghostbusters II* (1989, Columbia).

8813 "We're not communists here, ya know. We're Americans who got a right to make a living." Spaced-out druggie **William Hurt** negotiates for himself and Keanu Reeves with Tracey Ullman over the price of "hitting" unfaithful husband Kevin Kline. *I Love You to Death* (1990, Tri-Star).

8814 "I am a person. I have a right to the ball." Babbling psychological jargon basketball coach **Mark De Carlo** instructs his players. *Buffy, The Vampire Slayer* (1992, 20th CenturyFox).

8815 "You're a patient's sister. It doesn't feel right." Psychiatrist **Richard Gere** momentarily thinks of his

ethics before thrashing around naked in bed with beautiful Kim Basinger, sister of his patient Uma Thurman. *Final Analysis* (1992, Warner Bros.).

8816 "You have the right to remain unconscious." Cop **Mel Gibson** facetiously advises an unconscious felon passed out on an armored car. When the man starts to come to, Gibson knocks him out again. *Lethal Weapon 3* (1992, Warner Bros.).

Risks

see also CHANCES, LOSSES AND LOSING

8817 TRACY LORD: "Dexter, are you sure?" DEXTER HAVEN: "Not in the least, but I'll risk it. Will you?" TRACY: "You bet. You didn't do it just to soften the blow?" DEXTER: "No, Tracy." TRACY: "Nor to save my face?" DEXTER: "Oh, it's a nice little face." TRACY: "Never in my life have I been so full of love before." **Katharine Hepburn** is delighted when her ex-husband **Cary Grant** agrees to replace John Howard in a wedding ceremony. *The Philadelphia Story* (1940, MGM).

8818 "I stick my neck out for nobody." **Humphrey Bogart** responds to Creighton Hale, who expresses his disgust that Bogart ignored Peter Lorre's plea to help him escape from the police who arrest him. *Casablanca* (1942, Warner Bros.).

8819 "Anytime you take a chance, make sure the risks are worth the payoff." Ex-con **Sterling Hayden** gets it backwards on purpose. *The Killing* (1956, United Artists).

8820 "They have risked their lives to be here. . . . They have given up their freedom." **Matthew Broderick**, as Col. Robert Gould Shaw, refers to the black troops he commands in the Civil War, as he talks to an unfeeling superior officer. *Glory* (1989, Tri-Star).

Rituals

see also RELIGIONS

8821 "Ritual slaughter to preserve a fixed society, to rid it of mutations." **Andrew Keir** as Professor Bernard Quatermass describes what happened to the ancient Martians. *Five Million Years to Earth* (1968, GB, Hammer-20th Century-Fox).

8822 "Have you ever heard of exorcism? It's a stylized ritual in which the rabbi or the priest tries to drive out the so-called invading spirit." Doctors cryptically suggest to Ellen Burstyn a new, but very old treatment for her tormented daughter Linda Blair. *The Exorcist* (1973, Warner Bros.).

Rivers

see also SEAS, WATER

8823 TOM GRAYSON: "How long have you been navigating the river?" CMDR. ORLANDO JACKSON: "Ever since I took it away from the Indians." Showboat singer **Bing Crosby** checks on riverboat master **W.C. Fields**' qualifications. *Mississippi* (1935, Paramount).

8824 "Now, for the last time, Miss. Just try and listen, won't you. Try to understand. It's sure death a dozen times over down this river. I hate to disappoint you, Miss. But don't blame me. Blame the river." **Humphrey Bogart** unsuccessfully tries to dissuade Katharine Hepburn from forcing him to take her down a treacherous African river on his ancient tug. *The African Queen* (1951, United Artists).

8825 ED: "We beat it, didn't we?" LEWIS: "You don't beat it. You don't beat the river." **Jon Voight**'s delight that he and Burt Reynolds have made it through a section of white water rapids of the river on which they are canoeing is tempered by the latter's ominous comment. Up to this point the two and their companions Ned Beatty and Ronny Cox have had a picnic compared to what awaits them further down the river. *Deliverance* (1972, Warner Bros.).

Roles

see also ACTING AND ACTORS, BEHAVIOR, EXPECTATIONS

8826 "A lot of people think I am a stooge for you. They don't know I am a modern Boswell, meticulously recording for posterity the doings of a unique individual—an individual out of the Medicis—and I'm your Boswell. The story of Johnny Eager. The next forty generations will find it required reading along with the works of Machiavelli." Drunken stooge **Van Heflin** romanticizes his role with unscrupulous racketeer Robert Taylor. *Johnny Eager* (1941, MGM).

8827 "You're the nellie!. . . not me, I'm a pitcher, not a catcher! Don't you ever forget that." In an ugly and offensive sequence **Tom Berenger** screams at his homosexual lover in a parking lot. *Looking for Mr. Goodbar* (1977, Paramount).

8828 "Isn't it a little early to start imposing roles?" **Graham Chapman** replies when a mother asks the sex of her newborn child. *Monty Python's the Meaning of Life* (1983, GB, Universal).

8829 "Since I'm stealthy, you must be agile." Police Lieutenant **Clint Eastwood** assigns private eye Burt Reynolds the task of climbing a building. *City Heat* (1984, Warner Bros.).

8830 "How poor a part I played in your life. What were you like then?" **Donal McCann** laments on the emptiness of his marriage to Anjelica Huston who still grieves for a 17-year-old boy of whom she says, "I think he died for me." *The Dead* (1987, Vestron).

Romances

see also ADVENTURES, FICTION, KISSES AND KISSING, LOVE AND LOVERS, LUST, SEDUCTIONS, SEX AND SEXUALITY, WRITING AND WRITERS

8831 "Hi, baby. How's business? Listen, if you're going to fall for anybody, make it me. I'm dependable. I even could take you around to meet my Aunt Emma." Reporter **Clark Gable** tries to promote a romance with cigarette counter girl Jean Harlow. *The Secret Six* (1931, MGM).

8832 "I've passed that romantic nonsense of adolescence." Widowed department store owner **Melvyn Douglas** makes an unromantic, very business-like marriage proposal to his efficient assistant Claudette Colbert. *She Married Her Boss* (1935, Columbia).

8833 "Don't be an idiot, Harry. If you love her and she loves you, don't let your mother or anybody else in the world come between you. Don't lose it, my boy. It's the greatest thing in the world, romance." Elderly Bishop **Gavin Gordon** advises his grandson Elliott Nugent not to make the same mistake that he made when as a young curate he fell in love with opera diva Greta Garbo, but due to misunderstandings he left her forever. *Romance* (1939, MGM).

8834 "How did you manage it? He's normally stiffer than a plank. This romance must have done him a power of good." **Mary Astor** congratulates Claudette Colbert for her effect on Astor's overly-rational brother Rudy Vallee. *The Palm Beach Story* (1942, Paramount).

8835 "The very essence of romance is uncertainty." It is for **Michael Denison** until he meets fetching Dorothy Tutin, and then he's certain she's the one for him. *The Importance of Being Earnest* (1952, GB, Two Cities-Rank).

8836 "You're worse than a hopeless romantic. You're a hopeful one." Cynical **Jane Fonda** dismisses her ex-husband Alan Alda, who thinks things are not all bad. *California Suite* (1974, Columbia).

8837 "It's just a romance, but it's so beautiful." Aging drag queen **William Hurt** is thrilled by the movie which he is describing to his cell mate, revolutionary Raul Julia. *The Kiss of the Spider Woman* (1985, U.S.-Brazil, Island Alive).

8838 "The Dead Poets Society was dedicated to sucking the marrow out of life. . . . We were romantics, we didn't just read poetry, we let it drip from our tongues like honey. Spirits soared, women swooned and gods were created, gentlemen. Not a bad way to spend an evening, eh?" **Robin Williams** recalls for his students the secret society to which he belonged when he was a student. *Dead Poets Society* (1989, Touchstone-Buena Vista).

8839 "I suspect your idea of romance is whatever will separate me from my panties." Small-town girl **Julie Warner** has pegged passing-through doctor Michael J. Fox about right when he says that her local boyfriend doesn't sound very romantic. Of course, by this time he's already seen her emerge naked from a pond. *Doc Hollywood* (1991, Warner Bros.).

Rome *see* CITIES AND TOWNS

Rooms

see also BUILDINGS, HOMES, HOUSES, SPACE

8840 "This is the Rose Room. We call it that on account of the roses!" Innkeeper **Margaret Hamilton** has a way with the obvious as she leads actress Margaret Sullavan to a floral-printed room. *The Moon's Our Home* (1936, Paramount).

8841 "It's not that I'm prudish. It's just that my mother told me never to enter any man's room in months ending in R." **Irene Dunne** sidesteps a possible compromising situation with Charles Boyer. *Love Affair* (1939, RKO).

8842 "Which part of the room is mine?" Russian community emissary **Greta Garbo** enters the lavish suite prepared for her in a top Parisian hotel. *Ninotchka* (1939, MGM).

8843 "Say, who decorated this piece—the mug that shot Lincoln?" Jazz club singer **Barbara Stanwyck** enters the musty-looking Victorian living room in the home of eight eccentric professors. *Ball of Fire* (1942, Goldwyn-RKO).

8844 ADRIAN: "Do you want a roommate?" ROCKY: "Absolutely." Sitting tearful and crumpled in her bedroom after her brother Burt Young has wrecked the living room with a baseball bat, **Talia Shire** whispers to **Sylvester Stallone**. *Rocky* (1976, United Artists).

8845 "When you know this room, you'll know me." **Susan Dey** leads William Katt through her childhood room. *First Love* (1977, Paramount).

8846 "Nice place. I like a living room you can land a plane in." Uninvited guest **Liza Minnelli** surveys the room in which Dudley Moore's engagement party to Jill Eickenberry is held. *Arthur* (1981, Warner Bros.-Orion).

8847 "I think if Liberace had children, this would be their room." **Albert Brooks** cracks about the twin heart-shaped beds in the bridal suite of a Las Vegas hotel. *Lost in America* (1985, Warner Bros.)

8848 "I would have given the larger room to you, but I happen to know it was the young man's. . . . In a small way I am a woman of the world and I know where things can lead to." **Maggie Smith**'s concern for propriety for her young traveling companion Helena Bonham Carter is a bit suspect. Having the larger and more comfortable room for herself seems more likely the reason she assigns Bonham Carter to the smaller room, once occupied by Denholm Elliott, rather than any concern that some compromising of the girl might occur had she slept in the room previously used by Elliott's son, Julian Sands. *A Room with a View* (1985, GB, Merchant-Ivory-Goldcrest).

Rotten *see* CORRUPTION

Routines

see also HABITS, ORDERS

8849 "The first morning saw us up at six, breakfasted, and back in bed at seven—this was our routine for the first three months." African explorer Captain Spaulding, played by **Groucho Marx**, regales party guests with tales of his adventures. *Animal Crackers* (1930, Paramount).

8850 "People coming, going. Nothing ever happens." Hotel manager **Lewis Stone** takes no note of the drama of the lives of his guests. *Grand Hotel* (1932, MGM).

8851 "Ask a question, get an answer, ask another." Narrator **Mark Hellinger** sums up tedious police procedures. *The Naked City* (1948, Universal).

Rudeness

see also BEHAVIOR, INSULTS, MANNERS

8852 "A cow does that and gives milk besides." **Frank McHugh** zings his sometime girl friend, brassy reporter Glenda Farrell, when she makes an indescribably rude sound. *The Mystery of the Wax Museum* (1933, Warner Bros.).

8853 "If you're going to be rude to my daughter, you might as well at least take your hat off." Feather-brained **Alice Brady** insists on some semblance of manners from William Powell when he deals with Carole Lombard. *My Man Godfrey* (1936, Universal).

8854 "We do not tolerate rudeness. There's still a place for the rich of New York City!" Frazer-Morris manager **Ed Crowley** instructs newly hired delivery man Ron Silver. *Garbo Talks* (1984, MGM-United Artists).

8855 "Lecter wouldn't come after me. He'd think it to be rude." Gutsy FBI trainee **Jodie Foster** assures her superiors that she has nothing to fear from deceptively intelligent and heartless cannibalistic killer Anthony Hopkins, who has escaped. *The Silence of the Lambs* (1991, Orion).

Ruinations and Ruins

see also BUILDINGS, DESTRUCTION, LOSSES AND LOSING

8856 "See what you have made of me—and still you prosper, you hellcat." At a dockside, vamp Theda Bara encounters one of her past victims, **Victor Benoit**, now an elderly derelict. *A Fool There Was* (1915, silent, Fox).

8857 "The last man nearly ruined this place/He didn't know what to do with it/If you think the country's bad enough now/Just wait until I get through with it." It's **Groucho Marx**'s unabashed manifesto as he assumes the presidency of Freedonia. *Duck Soup* (1933, Paramount).

8858 "She ruined my life. She has me looking for a job." Formerly wealthy playboy **Fred MacMurray** lightly complains about manicurist Carole Lombard to aviator Ralph Bellamy. *Hands Across the Table* (1935, Paramount).

8859 "They tried to ruin me, but they are ruined. They tried to ruin me because they didn't like what I have done. Do you like what I have done?" Governor **Broderick Crawford** addresses a crowd of cheering "hicks" after he successfully wins an impeachment trial in the state senate. *All the King's Men* (1949, Columbia).

8860 "Daylight has never exposed so total a ruin." **Vivien Leigh** checks her morning appearance and finds it wanting. *A Streetcar Named Desire* (1951, MGM-20th Century-Fox).

8861 "If you like ruins, take a look at my business when you get back." Newark kosher caterer **Jackie Gleason**, reluctantly traveling with his wife Estelle Parsons and daughter Joan Delaney in Europe, mutters about a planned stop in Greece to see the "ruins." *Don't Drink the Water* (1969, Avco Embassy).

8862 "Maybe they should leave it as it is, as a kind of monument to all the bullshit in the world." After a devastating fire in the world's tallest skyscraper, caused by fraud and greed, bitter architect **Paul Newman** surveys the ruins. *The Towering Inferno* (1974, 20th Century-Fox).

8863 "The sacrifices I've made because of that man. He's ruined me with his ego, his philandering, his, his, his, his mediocrity!" **Maureen O'Sullivan** sputters out her complaints about her husband Lloyd Nolan. *Hannah and Her Sisters* (1987, Orion).

Rules

see also AUTHORITIES, GOVERNMENTS, LEADERSHIP AND LEADERS

8864 "There isn't any rules that a G-Man can't kiss an old friend goodbye, is there?" Dying **Ann Dvorak** makes a final request of FBI agent James Cagney. *G-Men* (1935, Warner Bros.).

8865 TRACY LORD: "Why? Was I so unattractive, so distant, so forbidding?" MIKE CONNOR: "You were extremely attractive. And as for distant and forbidding, quite the reverse, but you were also a little the worse, or better, for wine, and there are rules about that." **Katharine Hepburn** asks and **James Stewart** explains why he didn't make love to her when she was intoxicated. *The Philadelphia Story* (1940, MGM).

8866 "You are not allowed to leave the bedroom after a quarrel unless you've made up. . . . We must never change that rule. You know if every couple had it, there'd be no divorce." **Carole Lombard** likes to make up rules to guide her marriage to Robert Montgomery—they're not enough. *Mr. & Mrs. Smith* (1941, RKO).

8867 "An American is a good sport, he plays by the rules. No secret agent is. Years of decency and honest living—forget all about that or turn in your suits—because the enemy has." **James Cagney** tells a class of American spies in training that in their occupation they can't afford any rules of fair play. *13 Rue Madeleine* (1946, 20th Century-Fox).

8868 "There's a rule in our state—if you can't beat 'em, bribe 'em." Foolish U.S. Senator **William Pow-**

ell's claim earned the film the charge by Senator Joe McCarthy that it was communistic propaganda. *The Senator Was Indiscreet* (1947, Universal-International).

8869 "A long time ago I made me a rule. I let people do what they want to do." Tough wanderer **John Wayne** tells Geraldine Page of his accommodating ways. *Hondo* (1953, Warner Bros.).

8870 "I never shake hands with a left-handed gun." Drifter **Sterling Hayden**'s rule is a sign of good sense. He refuses leftie outlaw Scott Brady's outstretched hand, seeing as how both men are interested in saloon owner Joan Crawford. *Johnny Guitar* (1954, Republic).

8871 "Course, we all grasp at happiness—but there are such things as rules." **Clifton Webb** pretends to console lothario Louis Jourdan, who isn't getting what he expected from American secretary Maggie McNamara. *Three Coins in the Fountain* (1954, 20th Century-Fox).

8872 "I'm rather old-fashioned. I have just two rules. I want this school to teach the truth, as far as we know it. I don't want any teacher making a fairy tale out of life. . . . And rule two. . . teaching a minimum of facts and a maximum of ideas. . . if war comes, these kids shouldn't fight for historical dates, but the ideas behind them." New high school principal **Lee Philips** rightly impresses teacher Mildred Dunnock, who expected to be given the job. *Peyton Place* (1957, 20th Century-Fox).

8873 "Either you go by the rules or you lose." Sheriff **Walter Matthau** mutters sadly about aging, noncompromising cowboy Kirk Douglas, who loses all. *Lonely Are the Brave* (1962, Universal-International).

8874 "There's only one rule—expedience." British agent **Richard Burton** explains the essence of his profession to Claire Bloom. *The Spy Who Came in from the Cold* (1965, Paramount).

8875 "We caught them and we shot them under rule .303." Title character **Edward Woodward** refers to captured Boers who were executed under the authority of rule which is the calibre of the English rifles. *Breaker Morant* (1980, Australia, South Australian Film Corporation).

8876 "I keep thinking there must be rules to decide what I'm supposed to be doing." Reporter **Sally Field** muses wistfully, after she's been set up with a phony story for the second time. Guess she's never heard of common sense, integrity and a degree of cynicism. *Absence of Malice* (1981, Columbia).

8877 "I make it a rule never to get involved with possessed people. . . . Actually, it's more of a guideline than a rule." **Bill Murray**'s resolve weakens as possessed Sigourney Weaver writhes against him. *Ghostbusters* (1984, Columbia).

8878 "Different rules apply when it gets this late, you know what I mean? It's like. . . after hours." **Dick Miller**, a counterman in an all-night diner, welcomes office worker Griffin Dunne to a world he's never seen before and doesn't understand. *After Hours* (1985, Warner Bros.).

8879 "In Vietnam they changed the rules halfway through play and no one lowered the flag." Vietnam veteran **Robert F. Lyons** complains. *Cease Fire* (1985, Cineworld).

8880 "You know the rules; there are no rules." Master of Ceremonies Dr. Dealgood (**Edwin Hodgeman**) acts as an unneeded referee in the fight to the death between Mel Gibson as "Mad Max" and Paul Larsson as "The Blaster" in the Thunderdome. *Mad Max Beyond Thunderdome* (1985, Australia, Warner Bros.).

8881 "You never call a broad more than once a week." Self-proclaimed male-female relationship expert and male chauvinist, **James Belushi**, advises Rob Lowe on how to keep women like Demi Moore in line. *About Last Night. . .* (1986, Tri-Star).

8882 "The first working rule of business: 'Don't get emotional about stock, it clouds your judgment.'" **Michael Douglas** instructs young stockbroker Charlie Sheen. *Wall Street* (1987, 20th Century-Fox).

8883 "I'm trying to make it better. I'm not going to spend the rest of my life working my ass off and getting nowhere just because I follow rules that I had nothing to do with setting up. . . ." Secretary **Melanie Griffith** tells her friend Joan Cusack why she's masquerading as a wheeler-dealer businesswoman. *Working Girl* (1988, 20th Century-Fox).

8884 "When you get a bunch of rich fat people who are determined to get thin at any cost, some of them are going to die. It's a rule of thumb." Quack doctor **Paul Bartel**, a thinologist, justifies the fact that not all of his clients survive his treatment. *Scenes from the Class Struggle in Beverly Hills* (1989, Cinecom).

8885 BETH MACAULEY: "Dad isn't here and I'm making the rules now." CHRIS MACAULEY: "I wish it were the other way around." When widow **Jessica Lange** tries to set some ground rules for her rebellious teenage son **Chris O'Donnell**, he cruelly and unthinkingly lashes out at her. *Men Don't Leave* (1990, Triumph).

Rumors *see* GOSSIP

Running and Runners

see also SPORTS, VICTORIES, WINNERS AND LOSERS

8886 "I can run faster in red shoes." **Helen Chandler** stops to change her shoes. *The Last Flight* (1931, Warner Bros.).

8887 "Hard-boiled Hannah was going to fall in love with a bankroll. You can't run away from love." Manicurist **Carole Lombard** talks to herself about herself when her plans to catch a rich man hits a snag named Fred MacMurray. *Hands Across the Table* (1935, Paramount).

8888 "Working for your father is like running in a dream. No matter how hard you try, you know you'll never get anywhere." **Burt Lancaster** is not happy with the job given to him by his wife Barbara Stanwyck's father. *Sorry, Wrong Number* (1948, Paramount).

8889 "It's no good. I've got to go back, Amy. They're making me run. I've never run before." Ex-marshal **Gary Cooper** tells his new Quaker bride Grace Kelly that he must return to face the man who's coming on the noon train planning to kill him. *High Noon* (1952, United Artists).

8890 "I like a man who can run faster than I can." **Jane Russell** tells Marilyn Monroe that she likes men who can catch her. *Gentlemen Prefer Blondes* (1953, 20th Century-Fox).

8891 "All right, then run, lady—and you keep on running. Buy yourself a bus ticket and disappear. Change your name. Dye your hair. Get lost. And then maybe—just maybe—you're gonna be safe from me." **Paul Newman** propositions Joanne Woodward by telling her she can run but she can't hide. *The Long Hot Summer* (1958, 20th Century-Fox).

8892 "Sonny, I think you're going to have to learn how to fight. Running's no good. You run now, you'll be doing it when you're a grown man." **Robert Preston** advises his son Robert Eyer that he'll have to meet his fears and fight for his rights. *The Dark at the Top of the Stairs* (1960, Warner Bros.).

8893 "My family has been running ever since I can remember and what we have usually been running from is the police." **Tom Courtenay** tells it like it

is to Michael Redgrave, governor of the reform school to which Courtenay is sentenced. *The Loneliness of the Long Distance Runner* (1962, GB, British Lion).

8894 "You run one time, you get one set of chains. You run twice, you get two sets. You ain't gonna need a third set 'cause you going to get your mind right." Prison camp boss **Strother Martin** lectures Paul Newman after he's been recaptured for a second time. *Cool Hand Luke* (1967, Warner Bros.).

8895 "Running feels good, like a love affair. It's like a relationship—you get out of it what you put in it." Marathon runner **Michael Douglas** makes an interesting analogy. *Running* (1979, Canada, Universal).

8896 "I'm going to take them on, all of them, one by one, and run them off their feet." **Ben Cross**, the son of a wealthy Lithuanian Jew, refers to "proper Englishmen." *Chariots of Fire* (1981, GB, 20th Century-Fox).

8897 "When they stop laughing, I start running." Black college student **Spike Lee** feels safer when women are laughing at his antics and jokes. *She's Gotta Have It* (1986, Island Pictures).

8898 "Go ahead and run, sweetie. I'll track down all you whores." Marcia Gay Harden escapes the murderous clutches of psychopathic brute **J.E. Freeman** by ducking out a window. *Miller's Crossing* (1990, 20th Century-Fox).

Sacrifices

see also GIFTS AND GIVING, SERVICE, WORTH AND VALUES

8899 "It's a far, far better thing that I do than I have ever done; it is a far, far better rest that I go to than I have ever known." Charles Dickens' noble words are delivered eloquently by **Ronald Colman** in 1935 before the blade of the guillotine falls. **Dirk Bogarde** did the honors in 1958. *A Tale of Two Cities* (1935, MGM); (1958, GB, Rank).

8900 "Listen, son. . . you and I are professionals. If a manager says 'Sacrifice,' we lay down a bunt and let somebody else hit the home runs. Our job is to lay down that sacrifice. That's what we were trained for and that's what we'll do." **Charles Trowbridge**, as Admiral Blackwell, uses a baseball analogy to explain their duties to Robert Montgomery. *They Were Expendable* (1945, MGM).

8901 "I gave up the best years of my life." "Girls-just-want-to-have-fun" **Virginia Mayo** angrily splits from her husband Dana Andrews after World War II.

She finds him not as dashing or exciting as when he was in uniform. *The Best Years of Our Lives* (1946, Goldwyn).

8902 ANTHONY KEANE: "We will have answers for everything. You loved [your blind] husband and he needed you." ANNA PARADINE: "You know that?" KEANE: "Weren't you his eyes?. . . It was a voluntary service. You devoted your entire life to this fellow, freely, gladly. . . ." ANNA: "Yes, I see what you mean." KEANE: "It was a sacrifice, a sublime sacrifice—and it was the more tremendous that Paradine could not understand, could not possibly understand the sacrifice you were making. He'd never seen you—he'd never, as I say, seen you." Barrister **Gregory Peck** has fallen in love with his client **Alida Valli**, accused of murdering her blind husband. *The Paradine Case* (1947, Selznick-United Artists).

8903 "I'm just going outside and may be some time." **Derek Bond**, as Captain L.E.G. Oates, suffering from frost bite, believes he's endangering Captain Robert Falcon Scott's Antarctic expedition's chances of reaching safety. He chooses to sacrifice his life. It is to no avail—all perish. *Scott of the Antarctic* (1948, GB, Ealing).

8904 "The world is perishing in an orgy of self-sacrifice." Architect Howard Roark, played by **Gary Cooper** rejects collectivism as he delivers a long didactic speech in which he insists that all creators must stand alone and that their ideas are their personal property to do with as they please. Cooper is on trial for dynamiting a housing project based on his ideas but which he considers were perverted when changes were made in his original plans. *The Fountainhead* (1949, Warner Bros.).

8905 "Poor boy. I'm afraid he gets rather upset down here. He's essentially a town person, really like me. And I get it from my mother. Being French, of course, like all Parisians she detested the country. She used to say, 'Fields are for cows. Drawing rooms are for ladies.' Of course, it sounds better in French. If I had my way I'd never stir from London. I did all this for Mr. Harrington. He's what we call here an open-air type, you know." Snobbish **Rosalind Russell** tells German refugee Maximilian Schell that living in a country cottage is a great sacrifice. *Five-Finger Exercise* (1962, Columbia).

8906 "I thought you did it for me, Mama!" **Natalie Wood** bitterly complains to her obsessed stage mother Rosalind Russell who wonders why she made so many sacrifices in her life. *Gypsy* (1962, Warner Bros.).

8907 MRS. RENFREW: "Women in my day were willing to make sacrifices for love, or for some ideal, like the vote or Lucy Stonerism." DOTTIE RENFREW: "That was your day, Mother. Sacrifices aren't necessary anymore. . . . Sacrifice is a dated idea." **Leora Dana** and her Depression era college graduate daughter **Joan Hackett** don't see eye-to-eye on things. *The Group* (1966, United Artists).

8908 "Fertility rites were practiced here. When the seasons and the cycles of the moon were right, then they came, one by one, and gathered among these stones. Then they selected a beautiful girl like you. And then placed the girl's virginal body upon the altar naked to the elements and their black robes blending into the night they lighted candles and gathered around to relish her nakedness. Then they waited for the moment when she would allow the power of darkness to enter, the moment when the gate would open and the old one would come through. . . ." **Dean Stockwell** describes to Sandra Dee the devil-worship once practiced at a mysterious cliffside place called Devil's Hopyard to which he has brought her. *The Dunwich Horror* (1969, American International Pictures).

8909 "How much more blood? How many more lives? You want another life? Then take mine!" Pop Minister **Gene Hackman** challenges God and God responds by preventing this "Moses" from escaping from the upside-down ship Poseidon with his surviving followers. *The Poseidon Adventure* (1972, 20th Century-Fox).

8910 "You're willing to sacrifice a solid future for a bicycle race. It's very self-destructive." **Talia Shire** doesn't understand her son Bill Allen, an entrant in a BMX bike race. *Rad* (1986, Tri-Star).

Sadness

see also HAPPINESS AND UNHAPPINESS, SORROWS, SPIRIT AND SPIRITS

8911 "I think I was just being sadly happy. . . don't you know only children can be just happily happy. I think when we get older some of the happiest moments are the sad ones." It's **Katharine Hepburn**'s profound reply when Fred MacMurray asks her what she's thinking about. *Alice Adams* (1935, RKO).

8912 "Yes. My brother always drank too much. He was sad, the saddest of us all. He needed so much, and had so little." Nymphomaniac **Dorothy Malone** recalls her wealthy brother Robert Stack, whom she accidentally shoots and kills as she tries to wrestle a gun out of his hand. *Written on the Wind* (1956, Universal).

8913 "Ghosts of thousands of kids who came down here for Easter week, fall in love, and when it's over they go out there to say goodbye. They write their initials in the sand. It always seems so sad to me to come by later after the wind has swept the sand smooth again. Jim, what's gonna happen to us?" **Stefanie Powers** hopes that her spring break affair with Troy Donahue will last longer than most such romances. *Palm Springs Weekend* (1963, Warner Bros.).

8914 "I think fireworks are the saddest thing in the whole world. The way they just disappear. They should make 'em so they just hang up there all night." Teenager **Tuesday Weld** hates to see the glow disappear. *Soldier in the Rain* (1963, Allied Artists).

Safety

see also DANGER, EVILNESS, LOCKS, PROTECTION, SECURITY AND INSECURITY

8915 "They may think it's twice as safe because they're two of 'em, but it isn't twice as safe—it's ten times twice as dangerous." Without realizing that his friend Fred MacMurray is Barbara Stanwyck's accomplice in the murder of her husband, insurance claims chief **Edward G. Robinson** observes that Barbara and her unknown boyfriend are bound to make a mistake and reveal their guilt. *Double Indemnity* (1944, Paramount).

8916 "A wife doesn't feel safe until her husband turns the 'fifty corner.'" **Irene Hervey**'s problems with husband William Powell really begin after his fiftieth birthday—then he meets mermaid Ann Blyth. Hervey's assertion seems like a challenge for over-fifty men. *Mr. Peabody and the Mermaid* (1948, Universal).

8917 "Is it safe? Safest thing in the world—would you mind paying me now?" **Bob Hope**, as dentist "Painless Peter" Potter, assures a patient that his extraction work is painless and safe. *The Paleface* (1948, Paramount).

8918 "No matter what happens he can't ask you to marry him." Model **Marilyn Monroe** is relieved when Tom Ewell lets it slip that he's married—she considers married men less dangerous. She says nothing can get "drastic" with a married man. Things get pretty "drastic" if a girl falls in love with a married man. *The Seven Year Itch* (1955, 20th Century-Fox).

8919 "While I live, while my blood runs hot, your daughter is not safe in her tent." Mongol **John Wayne** warns Tartar ruler Ted DeCorsia of his lust for the latter's daughter Susan Hayward. *The Conqueror* (1956, RKO).

8920 EMILY FITZJOHN: "I tried to kill myself, you monster, isn't that enough for you?" GEN. LEO FITZJOHN: "You were stretched out on the tracks in an awkward position, but quite safe. The train had already passed." **Margaret Leighton**'s suicide attempt doesn't seem sincere to her unfaithful husband, retired General **Peter Sellers**. *Waltz of the Toreadors* (1962, GB, Independent Artists).

8921 "I was scared to death—that's why I came running back. To see your pretty face, to feel safe." Elderly **Henry Fonda** is relieved to be back with his wife Katharine Hepburn after becoming confused and lost when he's sent out to pick berries. *On Golden Pond* (1981, Universal).

8922 "I don't see why not; I'm on the pill." **Michelle Phillips** knows where things lead when she accepts a drink invitation. *Let It Ride* (1989, Paramount).

8923 "She'll be all right; silicone is buoyant." It's **Shelley Long**'s catty comment when her ex-husband's buxomy date falls overboard. *Troop Beverly Hills* (1989, Weintraub).

8924 "Pick one. I got red, I got green, I got yellow, I'm out of purple, but I do have one circle coin left, the condom of champions, the one and only, nothing is getting through this sucker. . . I'm a safety girl." Hooker **Julia Roberts** offers "John" Richard Gere his choice of condoms when she decides it's time to get down to business. *Pretty Woman* (1990, Touchstone-Buena Vista).

8925 "That's all right, what can't get up can't get out." Drunken **John Goodman** is nonplussed, when told by Trini Alvarado that his fly is open. *Stella* (1990, Touchstone-Buena Vista).

Sailors *see* MILITARY

Saints

see also GOD, HEAVEN, RELIGIONS

8926 ROMEO: "If I profane with my unworthiest hand this holy shrine, the gentle sin is this: my lips, two blushing pilgrims, ready stand to smooth that rough touch with a tender kiss." JULIET: "Good pilgrim, you do wrong your hand too much, for saints have hands that pilgrims' hands do touch, and palm to palm, is holy palmer's kiss." ROMEO: "Have no saints lips, and holy palmers, too?" JULIET: "Ay, pilgrim, lips that they must use in prayer." ROMEO: "Oh, then, dear saint, let lips do what hands do; they pray, grant thou, lest faith turn to despair." JULIET: "Saints do not move, though grant for prayers' sake." ROMEO: "They move not, while my prayer's effect I take. Thus from my lips, by thine, my sin is purged." JULIET: "Then have my lips the sin they have took." ROMEO: "Sin from my lips? O trespass sweetly urged! Give me my sin again." **Leslie Howard** and **Norma Shearer** talk a great deal before getting around to a couple of kisses. *Romeo and Juliet* (1936, MGM).

8927 "Oh, I forgot. I am putting these bottles out for the milkman. The Russian saints won't do it for me." Grand Duchess **Claudette Colbert** and Prince Charles Boyer, survivors of the Bolshevik revolution, having turned over the Czar's fortune they smuggled out of Russia to the new government, settle in as servants for a wealthy Parisian family. *Tovarich* (1937, Warner Bros.).

8928 YALE: "Well, I'm not a saint, okay?" ISAAC: "You're being too easy on yourself." **Michael Murphy** is confronted by **Woody Allen** when Murphy ruins his friendship with Allen by resuming his affair with flighty Diane Keaton whom Allen had been romancing. *Manhattan* (1979, United Artists).

8929 "Hey, honey, it's tough being a saint." It's **Nick Nolte**'s rather barbed compliment to his wife Blythe Danner who expresses weariness with their life. *The Prince of Tides* (1991, Columbia).

Salesmen

see also BUSINESS AND COMMERCE, BUYING AND SELLING, WORK AND WORKERS

8930 "A salesman is somebody way up there in the blue, riding a smile and a shoeshine." **Fredric March** recommends his profession to his sons. *Death of a Salesman* (1951, Columbia).

8931 "My God, you must be the best salesman in the world! You've sold them a policy that pays double for falling off a choo-choo and nothing from an airplane." What insurance claims investigator **Charles Durning** doesn't know is that salesman Alan Arkin has sold a life policy to Peter Falk, who has only a week to live. *Big Trouble* (1986, Columbia).

8932 "You get on the phone and ask strangers for money—right! . . . You're a salesman." **Martin Sheen** corrects his son Charlie Sheen who insists he's not a salesman, he's an account executive. *Wall Street* (1987, 20th Century-Fox).

Salutations

see also PRAISES

8933 "Dear friend. . . ." It's the ritual salutation used in the letters exchanged by **James Stewart** and

Margaret Sullavan in the 1940 film, and by **Van Johnson** and **Judy Garland** in the 1949 remake. *The Shop Around the Corner* (1940, MGM); *In the Good Old Summertime* (1949, MGM).

8934 "Oh Captain, My captain." One by one, **Ethan Hawke** and other members of the fired Robin Williams' literature class jump to the tops of their desks to salute their departing teacher. *Dead Poets Society* (1989, Touchstone-Buena Vista).

San Francisco *see* CITIES AND TOWNS

Sanctuaries

see also GOD, PROTECTION

8935 "Against that time is why I avoided death and am here and why you were brought here. For when that day comes, the world must begin to look for a new life and it is our hope that they may find it here. For here we shall be with their books and their music and a way of life based on one simple rule—'be kind.' When that day comes it is our hope that the brotherly love of Shangri-la will spread throughout the world." Ancient Hyh Laua **Sam Jaffe** softly speaks to his chosen successor Ronald Colman of the coming devastation of the world and the hope that Shangri-La will serve as a safe haven for those wishing to preserve ideas and all the best of civilization. *Lost Horizon* (1937, Columbia).

8936 "Sanctuary! Sanctuary!" Monstrous hunchback **Charles Laughton** bellows cheerfully as he triumphantly holds aloft Maureen O'Hara, who he has rescued from her executioners and carried to the top of the Notre Dame Cathedral. *The Hunchback of Notre Dame* (1939, RKO).

Sanity *see* INSANITY AND SANITY, HEALTH, PSYCHOLOGY AND PSYCHIATRY

Santa Claus

see also CHRISTMAS

8937 DORIS WALKER: "You've got to help me out—please." KRIS KRINGLE: "Madam, I am not in the habit of substituting for spurious Santa Clauses; however, the children must not be disappointed. I'll do it." **Maureen O'Hara** begs **Edmund Gwenn** to take the place of the drunk she's hired to portray Santa Claus in the Macy's Thanksgiving Parade. *Miracle on 34th Street* (1947, 20th Century-Fox).

8938 "Your honor, we request an immediate ruling from this court: is there or is there not a Santa Claus?" Attorney **John Payne** puts Judge Gene Lockhart on the spot during the sanity hearing of

Edmund Gwenn, who claims he's Santa Claus. *Miracle on 34th Street* (1947, 20 Century-Fox).

8939 "Now, wait a minute, Susie. Just because every child can't get its wish, that doesn't mean there isn't a Santa Claus." **Edmund Gwenn** consoles Natalie Wood, who hasn't got the home she was hoping for—but then Christmas isn't over yet. *Miracle on 34th Street* (1947, 20th Century-Fox).

8940 "Once there was a credulous people who believed in Santa Claus, but Santa Claus turned out to be the gas man!" On his third birthday, now twelve-year-old **David Bennent** decided never to grow up. He beats out a constant tattoo on his tin drum as he observes the hypocrisy of adults, and acts as the film's crazed voice of reason as the Nazis come to power in Germany. *The Tin Drum* (1979, W. Ger.-Fr., United Artists).

8941 "That's how I found out there is no Santa Claus." **Phoebe Cates** confesses that she hates Christmas because as a child her father disappeared on Christmas Eve, only to be found some days later, decomposing halfway down the chimney in a Santa Claus suit. *Gremlins* (1984, Warner Bros.)

Satire see FUN, LAUGHTER, RIDICULE AND RIDICULOUSNESS, WRITING AND WRITERS

Satisfactions

see also DESIRES, EXPECTATIONS, NEEDS AND NECESSITIES, PLEASURES

8942 "I made you what you are today—I hope you're satisfied." Drunken director **Lowell Sherman** has been instrumental in making waitress Constance Bennett a film star. *What Price Hollywood?* (1932, RKO).

8943 HOWARD JOYCE: "Ong Chi Seng, what are you getting out of this?" ONG CHI SENG: "Two hundred dollars, sir, and the great satisfaction of being of service to you and our client." Attorney **James Stephenson** (who just about stole the picture, even with Bette Davis giving a superb performance) questions his Chinese assistant **Victor Sen Yung**, who acts as the intermediary for Gale Sondergaard, the Eurasian wife of the man Bette Davis shot and killed, supposedly defending her honor. Sondergaard has a letter from Davis to her husband that indicates he and Davis were lovers. *The Letter* (1940, Warner Bros.).

8944 "Seven children I've had with her, Father. And I've never even seen her navel. I'm a vigorous man. How can I find satisfaction with a woman who makes the sign of the cross before every embrace

and cries 'Gesumaria!'" Aging 1860s Sicilian aristocrat **Burt Lancaster** complains to his confessor Romolo Valli about the lack of response of his wife Rina Morelli. *The Leopard* (1963, Italy, 20th Century-Fox).

8945 "Boy, it would give me a whirl of satisfaction to horse whip you, Virgil." Bigoted Southern Sheriff **Rod Steiger** must turn to black Philadelphia police detective Sidney Poitier for help solving a murder. *In the Heat of the Night* (1967, United Artists).

8946 "Any position under you would be just fine." **Cyd Belliveau**, as French teacher Mona Lott, will be satisfied with whatever job Mike McDonald, as Principal Arsenault, gives her. *Loose Screws* (1985, Concorde).

Savagery

see also CIVILIZATIONS, CRUELTY, MANNERS, RUDENESS

8947/48/49 PARKER: "Were you very frightened?" JANE: "At first. I thought he was a savage. But I found out he wasn't." PARKER: "Oh, my dear, he's not like us...." **C. Aubrey Smith** embraces his daughter **Maureen O'Sullivan** whom he had given up for dead. She's been quite safe with title character Johnny Weissmuller. *Tarzan, the Ape Man* (1932, MGM).

8950 "You're a savage, Louvette! A vicious, cruel savage. Plotting revenge is all you know—not love." Prim English nurse **Madeleine Carroll** confronts "hot-blooded" half-breed (Metis) Paulette Goddard. The Metis get a raw deal in Cecil B. DeMille's convoluted and inaccurate version of Canadian history. *Northwest Mounted Police* (1940, Paramount).

8951 "He's rather what you find in a Van Gogh painting, a touch of the savage." **Joan Crawford**'s description of angry and violinist John Garfield. *Humoresque* (1946, Warner Bros.).

8952 "You make me think your Cochise has studied under Alexander the Great or Bonaparte at least.... He's a breech-clothed savage, uncivilized murderer and a treaty breaker...." Not only is martinet cavalry officer **Henry Fonda** a racist, he underestimates his enemy, the great Apache chief Cochise, played by Miguel Inclan. Fonda dismisses the Apaches as "the gnat stings and flea bites of a few digger Indians" to his more experienced second-incommand John Wayne. *Fort Apache* (1948, RKO).

8953 "When I said that we were savages, well, there are savages and savages...." **Tom Ewell** can't deal with having one of his fantasies come true. Marilyn Monroe tells him she wants to spend the night in his apartment because he has air conditioning. *The Seven Year Itch* (1955, 20th Century-Fox).

8954 "You're a descendant of generations of inbred, incestuous mental defectives—how dare you call anyone barbarian!" It's unlikely that Egyptian Queen Elizabeth Taylor would have called **Rex Harrison**, as Julius Caesar, a barbarian. That's the word the Romans used to describe non-Romans or non-Greeks. *Cleopatra* (1963, 20th Century-Fox).

8955 "Why is it that a woman always thinks that the most savage thing she can say to a man is to impugn his cockmanship?" This is **William Holden**'s question of Faye Dunaway as their affair fizzles. *Network* (1976, United Artists).

Save and Savings *see* CARES AND CARING, DANGER, EXCEPTIONS, HARM, MONEY

Sayings *see* PROVERBS AND SAYINGS

Scandals

see also DISGRACES, GOSSIP, IMMORALITY, MORALITY, SINS AND SINNERS

8956 MRS. POTTER: "One who clerks, Polly, is a clerk. And I want you to remember that no Potter has ever been involved in a single scandal." POLLY POTTER: "What about Uncle Dick?" MRS. POTTER: "Polly, it's a well-known fact that your uncle was drunk at the time." Snooty **Margaret Dumont** doesn't approve of her daughter **Mary Eaton**'s interest in hotel clerk Oscar Shaw, who hopes to become an architect. *The Cocoanuts* (1929, Paramount).

8957 "Towards the close of the last century, when history still wore a rose and politics had not yet outgrown the waltz, a royal scandal was whispered in the anterooms of Europe. . . ." It's the introduction to a nearly perfect adventure film. *The Prisoner of Zenda* (1937, Selznick-United Artists).

8958 "You mean I'm not white? This is a scandal. Why didn't you tell me before. . . you're my sister." Blind **Richard Pryor** puts on an act for his sister Kirsten Childs, as he makes a scene in a subway. *See No Evil, Hear No Evil* (1989, Tri-Star).

Scars *see* WOUNDS AND SCARS

Schemes

see also ACTIONS AND ACTS, PLANS, VISIONS AND VISUALIZATIONS

8959 "I left the same house at the same time for eleven years. Of course, I wasn't serious about this wild scheme, but I had an uncontrollable urge to probe its possibilities. . . ." In voice-over narration, **Joseph Cotten** considers a scheme to steal from his own bank. *The Steel Trap* (1952, 20th Century-Fox).

8960 "Just keep in mind that the day you first scheme. . . you marry the scheme and the scheme's children." Oily press agent **Wendell Corey** pressures movie star Jack Palance to sign a new seven-year contract with Hollywood mogul Rod Steiger or face exposure of his role in a hit-and-run accident, some years earlier. *The Big Knife* (1955, United Artists).

8961 "Do you realize that fluoridation is the most monstrously conceived and dangerous Communist plot we have ever had to face?" **Sterling Hayden**, as mad General Jack D. Ripper, explains to Peter Sellers, as Group Captain Lionel Mandrake, why Hayden ordered an atomic attack on the Soviet Union. *Dr. Strangelove, or How I Learned to Stop Worrying and Love the Bomb* (1963, GB, Columbia).

Schools

see also EDUCATION, LEARNING AND LESSONS, STUDIES AND STUDENTS, TEACHING AND TEACHERS

8962 "Yes, you really do. I know what Roger meant about Eton and the great things that have stood for a thousand years, the traditions that belong to both countries. I've learned some of them here. I guess you'll learn some more in America. Only remind me to get rid of this before I show up at Notre Dame, will you?" Brash American **Mickey Rooney** has finished his stay at England's Eton Academy, where he has difficulty adjusting to the very proper British ways, but eventually becomes friends with Freddie Bartholomew. *A Yank at Eton* (1942, MGM).

8963 "I don't take kindly to kids playin' hooky from school. . . I think every kid in America ought to go to school at least up through the eighth grade." **Clint Eastwood** believes his own legend as he lectures some youngsters on staying in school. *Bronco Billy* (1980, Warner Bros.).

8964 "I can't see it, signin' on for four more years of this garbage." Greasy street kid **Vincent Spano** ridicules Rosanna Arquette's talk about going to college after high school. *Baby, It's You* (1983, Paramount).

8965 DR. GERALD MARX: "I did it! I found a school that will take him!" JEFF MARX: "Where? Miami?" DR. MARX: "Farther south." **Bill Macy** finally finds a medical school that will accept his average college student son **Steve Guttenberg**, the scion of a long line of doctors. It's a Grenada-like medical school "somewhere in Central America." *Bad Medicine* (1985, 20th Century-Fox).

8966 "I did not spend six years in junior college to be a maid." Despite being educationally overqualified, a maid is precisely what **Ally Sheedy** becomes. *Maid to Order* (1987, New Century-Vista).

8967 "What is this, some sort of Lord of the Flies preschool?" **Robin Williams**, as the grown up Peter Pan, quips about the home of the Lost Boys in Never Never Land. *Hook* (1991, Tri-Star).

Science and Scientists

see also ART AND ARTISTS, CAUSE AND EFFECT, CREATION AND CREATURE, DISCIPLINE, EXPERIENCES, EXPERIMENTS, KNOWLEDGE, LEARNING AND LESSONS, MATHEMATICS, SENSE, STUDIES AND STUDENTS, TEACHING AND TEACHERS

8968 "This isn't science! It's more like black magic." **Colin Clive** rejects Ernest Thesiger's contribution to the art of creating life, which consists of six miniature people living in jars. *The Bride of Frankenstein* (1935, Universal).

8969 "If you think there is no science in a cat-o'-nine tails, you should see my bos'n." **Charles Laughton**, captain of the HMS Bounty, boasts proudly to a visitor prior to sailing. *Mutiny on the Bounty* (1935, MGM).

8970 "The benefits of science are not for scientists, Marie. They're for humanity." One night in their bed, **Paul Muni** preaches to his wife Josephine Hutchinson. *The Story of Louis Pasteur* (1936, Warner Bros.).

8971 "You young men, doctors and scientists of the future, do not let yourselves be tainted by barren skepticism nor discouraged by the sadness of certain hours that creep over nations. Do not become angry at your opponents for no scientific theory has ever been accepted without opposition. Live in the serene peace of libraries and laboratories. Say to yourselves first, 'What have I done for my instruction?' and as you gradually advance, 'What am I accomplishing?' until the time comes when you have the immense happiness of thinking that you have contributed in some way to the welfare and progress of mankind." An elderly Louis Pasteur, authored by **Paul Muni**, addresses an assemblage of medical and scientific students and neophytes. *The Story of Louis Pasteur* (1936, Warner Bros.).

8972 "Simple phonetics. The science of speech. That's my profession, also my hobby. Anybody can spot an Irishman or a Yorkshire man by his brogue.

I can place a man within six miles. I can place him within two miles of London, sometimes within two streets." First **Leslie Howard** and then **Rex Harrison** boast of their prowess. *Pygmalion* (1938, GB, MGM); *My Fair Lady* (1964, Warner Bros.).

8973 "It's just a matter of chemistry, see? Anodes attract cathodes." Professor **James Stewart** explains his fascination with flashy show girl Ginger Rogers. An anode is a positively charged electrode and a cathode is one that is negatively charged. *Vivacious Lady* (1938, RKO).

8974 "Scientists can write all the books they like about love being a trap of nature. I remember reading that—that it's biology and the chemistry inside of [a woman] that fools her. But all the scientists are going to convince are scientists, not women in love." Department store salesgirl **Jean Arthur** doesn't buy scientific attempts to define love. *The Devil and Miss Jones* (1941, RKO).

8975 "Women and science are incompatible. No true scientist can have anything to do with a woman." Not only does scientist **Walter Pidgeon** change his tune, he marries Greer Garson and helps her discover radium. *Madame Curie* (1943, MGM).

8976 DR. KURT VAN BRUECKEN: "We are no longer scientists. Now we are murderers." JULIAN KARELL: "What is one life to science—or a dozen?" Ailing, aged Doctor **Reinhold Schunzel** aids **Nils Asther** in surgery needed to prolong the latter's life. Medical student Morton Lowry has just succumbed to an excessive dosage of drugs. *The Man in Half-Moon Street* (1944, Paramount).

8977 "A true scientist is married to his profession." Mad scientist **Bela Lugosi** and his colleague John Carradine thaw out a prehistoric man frozen in ice. When Carradine complains that Lugosi is going too far with his prize, Bela kills John and transplants his brain into the creature. *Return of the Ape Man* (1944, Monogram).

8978 "God have mercy on us if we ever thought we could really keep science secret—or wanted to. God have mercy on us if we haven't the sense to keep the world in peace." This speech of scientist and O.S.S. agent **Gary Cooper** was deleted from the final version of the film. Only one year after the end of World War II, the U.S. had decided it could not trust its wartime allies with some of its scientific secrets. *Cloak and Dagger* (1946, United States Pictures).

8979 JOHN: "I'm a scientist." SHAWN: "One of those atomic bomb fellas?" Stricken with epilepsy, biochemist **Ronald Reagan** settles in a secluded area of the Gulf Coast to convalesce. **Broderick Crawford** is a new friend. *Night Unto Night* (1949, Warner Bros.).

8980 "I use a number of sciences in my experiments with the human family." Bizarre hypnotist **Jose Ferrer** offers to help psychiatrist's wife Gene Tierney cure her habitual kleptomania. *Whirlpool* (1949, 20th Century-Fox).

8981 "Why can't scientists leave things alone? What about my bit of washing when there's no washing to do?" Frail 70-year-old washerwoman **Edie Martin** complains to Alec Guinness, who has invented an incredible fabric that never gets dirty. *The Man in the White Suit* (1951, GB, Ealing).

8982 NED "SCOTTY" SCOTT: "If you were for sale, I could get a million bucks for you from any foreign government." DR. ARTHUR CARRINGTON: "There are no enemies in science, just phenomena to study." Reporter **Douglas Spencer** can't tempt Nobel Prize winning scientist **Robert Cornthwaite**, who has no time or interest in politics. *The Thing* (1951, RKO).

8983 "You should have seen that man's apartment. He's got it down to a science. He pushes a button, and the couch becomes a bed with baby blue sheets." **Doris Day** is shocked that Rock Hudson has his apartment rigged for seduction and sex. *Pillow Talk* (1959, Universal).

8984 "How the hell did they get ahead of us? Our German scientists are better than their German scientists." As Senator Lyndon Johnson, **Donald Moffat** sums up the government's surprise when the Soviets launched Sputnik in 1957. *The Right Stuff* (1983, Warner Bros.).

8985 "[You seem] less a scientist and more a game show host." **Sigourney Weaver** finds parapsychologist Bill Murray too flippant to meet her notion of a scientist. Scientists, like every other group of individuals, have weaknesses and peculiar behavior patterns which have nothing to do with their work. *Ghostbusters* (1984, Columbia).

8986 "You got somethin' I haven't seen before, we'll donate it to science." Hooker **Liza Minnelli** dismisses cop Burt Reynolds' request that she look the other way while he gets dressed. *Rent-A-Cop* (1988, Kings Road).

8987 "Five thousand scientists and I get Dr. Mengele with a pony tail." Recently arrived in the Amazon rain forest, scientist **Lorraine Bracco** is not warmly received by eccentric chemist Sean Connery. *Medicine Man* (1992, Hollywood Pictures-Buena Vista).

Screams

see also CRYING AND CRIES, FEARS, NOISES, PAINS, SOUNDS, VOICES

8988 "It's horrible but you can't look away. . . you're helpless. . . . If only you could scream. . .. Cover your eyes and scream, Ann, scream for your life." Movie maker **Robert Armstrong** directs Fay Wray on a ship headed for Skull Island and her encounter with a tall, dark leading man. And, boy, can she ever scream. *King Kong* (1933, RKO).

8989 "If you touch my garter, I'll scream." Lovely clothes-horse **Kay Francis**, who has a speech defect, has only two r's to worry about in delivering this short warning to bogus Oriental Warner Oland in a Rangoon nightspot. *Mandalay* (1934, Warner Bros.).

8990 "I heard a scream, and I didn't know if it was me who screamed or not—if it was I or not." She may be in a mental institution, but **Olivia de Havilland** wishes to get her pronouns correct. *The Snake Pit* (1948, 20th Century-Fox).

8991 "A good many dramatic situations begin with screaming." **Jane Fonda**, as the title character, reacts thusly upon hearing a scream. *Barbarella* (1968, Fr.-Ital., Paramount).

8992 "I'm so close to my menstrual cycle that I could just scream." **Madeline Kahn** has a severe case of pre-menstrual syndrome. *High Anxiety* (1977, 20th Century-Fox).

8993 "It's a good scream. It's a good scream." Movie sound effects man **John Travolta** is back at work after becoming involved in a politically motivated murder. *Blow Out* (1981, Filmways).

8994 "I heard someone screaming, and it was me." **Jodie Foster** recalls the horror of her gang rape. *The Accused* (1988, Paramount).

Searches and Searching

see also LEARNING AND LESSONS

8995 "At this time of night, I'm not looking for needlepoint." **Claudette Colbert**, no wide-eyed innocent, gets cabbie Don Ameche to drive her around Paris looking for a singing job. *Midnight* (1939, Paramount).

8996 "Why is it necessary to search through so many people looking for what our education tells us can be found in one person?" **Brigette Fossey** muses at the funeral of Charles Denner, a man with an insatiable appetite for new female conquests. *The Man Who Loved Women* (1977, Fr., Les Films de Carrose-PAA).

8997 "I looked for you in my closet tonight." Her closet was where beautiful masochistic **Isabella Rossellini** found Kyle MacLachlan before. *Blue Velvet* (1986, De Laurentiis).

8998 "I will search for a woman who will engage my intellect as well as my loins." African Prince **Eddie Murphy** rejects the foxy bride his royal parents have picked out to be his wife, because he wants to search for a wife with whom he can have a meaningful relationship. *Coming to America* (1988, Paramount).

8999 "Once upon a time, men and women were part of the same being. But they were so incredibly powerful that the gods tore them apart. Now they say that everyone, men and women, women and women, men and men, are still looking for the other half." It's **Christopher Walken**'s interesting interpretation of the love urge. *Homeboy* (1988, 20th Century-Fox).

9000 "You're just the kind of pussy I've been looking for." The way **Danny De Vito**, as the Penguin, says this and leers at Michelle Pfeiffer, as Catwoman, he makes it clear that this is no double-entendre. *Batman Returns* (1992, Warner Bros.).

Seas

see also BOATS AND SHIPS, FISH AND FISHING, MILITARY, WATER

9001 "Fog, fog all the time. You can't tell where you was going. Only that old devil sea, she knows." Old seaman **George F. Marion** has the film's last line. *Anna Christie* (1930, MGM).

9002 "This is a story of the Battle of the Atlantic, the story of an ocean. Two ships and a handful of men. The men are the heroes. The heroines are the ships. The only villain is the sea—the cruel sea—that man has made more cruel." In voice-over, **Jack Hawkins** sets the stage for a remarkable sea film. *The Cruel Sea* (1953, GB, Universal).

9003 "We searched for survivors but all that we found was a riddle of the sea. . . . Had the sea taken them or had they reached the nearby shore where the fjords could hide a secret?. . . Who can say? There are only two people who can answer that, wherever they are. . . but knowing Karl Ehrlich as I do, I have my opinion. . . ." Narrator **David Farrar** holds out hope that German sea Captain John Wayne and his lover Lana Turner may have sur-

vived the sinking of a German freighter. *The Sea Chase* (1955, Warner Bros.).

9004 "Choose any path you please and tend to one that carries you down to water. There's a magic in water that draws all men away from the land, that leads them over the hills, down creeks and streams and rivers to the sea—the sea, where each man, as in a mirror, finds himself." **Richard Basehart**, as the narrator and protagonist, delivers this wonderful line from Herman Melville's book. *Moby Dick* (1956, Warner Bros.).

9005 "Listen to that bitch—the sea—the maker of widows." Gregarious Greek **Anthony Quinn** speaks to young English writer Alan Bates on Crete about all the sailing men who have been lost at sea. *Zorba the Greek* (1964, U.S.-Gr., 20th Century-Fox).

Seasons

see also TIME, WEATHER

9006 "You get pretty used to it after you've had nothin' else for forty years." Innkeeper **Margaret Hamilton** reacts bluntly to Margaret Sullavan's admiration for the peaceful quality of a New England winter. *The Moon's Our Home* (1936, Paramount).

9007 "In the spring a young man's fancy turns pretty fancy." **Burt Lancaster** is reminded of his younger days by Richard Jaeckel and Terry Moore. *Come Back, Little Sheba* (1952, Paramount).

9008 "Winter must be cold for those with no warm memories. We've already missed the spring." Permanently crippled **Deborah Kerr** has warm memories of Cary Grant in this remake of the tear-jerker *Love Affair*. *An Affair to Remember* (1957, 20th Century-Fox).

9009 "Your piss would freeze before it hit the ground." Elderly **Herbert Berghof** remembers the winters in his native Poland when he was a boy. *Harry and Tonto* (1974, 20th Century-Fox).

9010 "Spring is the time for planting." It's one of simple-minded gardener **Peter Sellers**' innocent observations that is taken for an audaciously clever metaphor by the rich and powerful people who mistake him for a political pundit. *Being There* (1979, United Artists).

Secrets

see also CONCEALMENT, MYSTERIES, PRIVACY, SECURITY AND INSECURITY

9011 "It's easy, really, if you're clever. A few chemicals mixed together, that's all. And flesh and blood and bone just fade away. A little of this injected under the skin of the arm for a month. . . . An invisible man can rule the world. Nobody will see him come. Nobody will see him go. He can hear every secret. He can rob the rich and kill." The voice of invisible **Claude Rains** breaks into a hysterical laugh as he reveals his secret. *The Invisible Man* (1933, Universal).

9012 "I shall offer my secret to the world. . . . The nations of the world will bid for it—thousands, millions. The nation that wins my secret can sweep the world with invisible armies." **Claude Rains** pays no attention to his fiancée Gloria Stuart, who warns him that the monocaine he's used is warping his mind. *The Invisible Man* (1933, Universal).

9013 "They've got secrets, funny secrets. I can't say them out loud. I've got to whisper them." Lying school girl **Bonita Granville** is about to make false accusations about the relationships of Joel McCrea, Merle Oberon and Miriam Hopkins to her grandmother Alma Kruger. *These Three* (1936, Goldwyn-United Artists).

9014 "The studio is keeping her under wraps, but those who've peeked tell me that she just couldn't be more divine." Radio gossip **Franklin Pangborn** confides to his audience in a conspiratial whisper about promising new film face Janet Gaynor. *A Star Is Born* (1937, Selznick-United Artists).

9015 "Poor Philip. Too many people have looked into his secrets. We must let him rest now." **Ingrid Bergman** is most forgiving of her maniacal husband Robert Montgomery, who almost succeeded in getting George Sanders executed for Montgomery's death, which was really a suicide. *Rage in Heaven* (1941, MGM).

9016 "I'm glad that mother named me after you, and that she thinks we're both alike. I think we are too. I know it. . . . We're not just an Uncle and a niece. It's something else. I know it. I know you don't tell people a lot of things. I don't either. I have a feeling that inside you somewhere there's something nobody knows about. . . something secret and wonderful. I'll find out. . . we're sort of like twins, don't you see? We have to know." **Teresa Wright**'s instincts about her uncle Joseph Cotten are on target. He does have a secret but it's not wonderful. Her comments worry Cotten. He fears that she'll discover that he's a murderer. *Shadow of a Doubt* (1943, Universal).

9017 DEATH: "Now I'll be leaving you. When we meet again you and your companions' time will be up." KNIGHT: "And you will divulge your secrets." DEATH: "I have no secrets." KNIGHT: "So you know

nothing." DEATH: "I have nothing to tell." Death, portrayed by **Bengt Ekerot**, announces that knight Antonius Block, played by **Max von Sydow**, will be mated with the next move and at that time Death will collect the Knight and six others. *The Seventh Seal* (1958, Sweden, Svensk Filmindustri).

9018 "I hate secrets. . . never knew one that was kept." **John Wayne** informs his son Patrick Wayne why they aren't trying to disguise their mission or the strong box filled with money they are carrying as they ride into a town. *Big Jake* (1971, National General).

9019 "The secret's not being you, it's being me. True, you're not too tall and kind of ugly, but, what the hell, I'm short enough and ugly enough myself to succeed on my own." By the end of the film, **Woody Allen** realizes that he doesn't need the spirit of Humphrey Bogart, played by Jerry Lacy, to help him romance the ladies. *Play It Again, Sam* (1972, Paramount).

9020 GROCERY CLERK: "My grandfather is eighty-two and he never stops screwing." HARRY: "What's his secret?" CLERK: "Maybe it's because he eats bananas, maybe because he doesn't know he's eighty-two." Puerto Rican grocer **Rene Enriquez** tells 72-year-old widower **Art Carney** of a possible aphrodisiac. Later, Carney will be seen eating a banana. *Harry and Tonto* (1974, 20th Century-Fox).

9021 "It isn't always being fast, or even accurate, that counts. It's being willing. I found out early that most men, regardless of cause or need, aren't willing. They blink an eye or draw a breath before they pull the trigger. I won't." **John Wayne** shares the secret of his longevity as a successful (i.e., living) gunfighter. *The Shootist* (1976, Paramount).

9022 "Whenever I meet a beautiful woman, I ask her to give me her secret." **John Cassavetes** frequently uses the line in the film. *Love Streams* (1984, Cannon).

9023 "I'll let you into a secret, Miss Bartlett. I have my eyes on your cousin Miss Honeychurch. . . a young English girl transfigured by Italy—and why should she not be transfigured? It happened to the Goths." Author **Judi Dench** informs Maggie Smith that Dench is considering using Helena Bonham Carter as a character in one of her novels. *A Room with a View* (1985, GB, Merchant-Ivory-Goldcrest).

9024 "What happens in the bush stays in the bush." Sergeant **Sean Penn** reminds the men in his squad that no one is to report on their activities while they are on patrol in Vietnam. Especially, they must keep secret the fact that they kidnapped a Vietnamese girl, brutally gang raped her and then murdered her. *Casualties of War* (1989, Columbia).

9025 CURLY: "One thing. You stick to it and nothing else means shit." MITCH: "What is it?" CURLY: "You figure it out." Trail boss **Jack Palance,** "leathery like a saddlebag with eyes," tells tenderfoot **Billy Crystal** that he has to discover the secret of life for himself. *City Slickers* (1991, Columbia).

Security and Insecurity

see also DANGER, FEARS, FREEDOMS, LOSSES AND LOSING, SAFETY

9026 "I want security. You're as irresponsible as a two-month old kitten." Fashion designer **Claudette Colbert** rejects philanderer Robert Young's marriage proposal. *I Met Him in Paris* (1937, Paramount).

9027 JOE/JOSEPHINE: "You're a guy. Why should a guy want to marry a guy?" JERRY/DAPHNE: "Security." **Tony Curtis** and **Jack Lemmon** are hiding from mobsters. They disguise themselves as members of a girl's band. Millionaire Joe E. Brown proposes marriage to Lemmon. *Some Like It Hot* (1959, United Artists).

9028 "He who is secure within can say: Tomorrow, do thy worst! For I have lived today." Narrator **Michael MacLiammoir** ends the film with another of Henry Fielding's pithy sayings. *Tom Jones* (1963, GB, United Artists).

9029 "You know who's not insecure? Bogie. . . well, look, if I'm going to identify, who am I going to pick? My rabbi? I mean, Bogart's a perfect image." **Woody Allen** disagrees with Diane Keaton who remarks that in trying to be like Bogart, he's setting too high a standard for himself. *Play It Again, Sam* (1972, Paramount).

9030 "Put me down! You male chauvinistic pig ape!. . . I didn't mean that! I swear I didn't! Sometimes I get too physical; it's a sign of insecurity, you know? Like when you knock down trees." Brave **Jessica Lange** yells when she's captured by the gigantic gorilla. She apologizes when he loses his temper. *King Kong* (1976, De Laurentiis).

Seductions

see also KISSES AND KISSING, LOVE AND LOVERS, ROMANCES, SEX AND SEXUALITY, TEMPTATIONS, VIRGINITY AND VIRGINS, WINNERS AND LOSERS

9031 ERIC GORMAN: "You don't think I sat there all evening with an eight-foot mamba in my pocket, do you? Why, it would be an injustice to my tailor. . . . I never saw you more beautiful." EVELYN GORMAN: "Yes, Eric. . . I know. Now, you're going to make love to me. You're not human." ERIC: "I'm not going to kiss you. You're going to kiss me." Having once again murdered one of his wife's lovers, this time with the help of the poison of the deadly green mamba snake, zoologist **Lionel Atwill** is aroused and passionately clutches the grieving **Kathleen Burke**. *Murders in the Zoo* (1933, Paramount).

9032 RITA HUSSMAN: "I see glimpses of a strange world. . . a world of people who are dead and yet alive." COUNT DRACULA: "It is the place from which I've just returned." RITA: "It frightens me." DRACULA: "Wear it. It will drive away your fears. . . I will call for you before dawn." Vampire **John Carradine** hypnotically seduces **Anne Gwynne** with the help of his strange ring. *House of Frankenstein* (1944, Universal).

9033 "This face that haunts me, drugs me. . . these hands that were designed for a thousand pleasures. . . these lips. . . were they meant to speak of love or grocery lists?" **Louis Jourdan**, as Rodolphe, seduces Jennifer Jones as Emma Bovary. *Madame Bovary* (1949, MGM).

9034 "For God's sake, Mrs. Robinson, here we are. You've got me in your house. You give me a drink. You put on music, now you start opening up your personal life to me and tell me your husband won't be home for hours. . . . Mrs. Robinson, you are trying to seduce me." Recent college graduate **Dustin Hoffman** can hardly believe the message he's getting from laughing Anne Bancroft, who shows him a great deal of thigh. *The Graduate* (1967, United Artists).

9035 "Okay, Valentino. Hit it." Having thrown off all her clothes in a motel room, **Liza Minnelli** yells at stupid, sexually naïve Wendell Burton, who just stands there with his heavy coat buttoned all the way up to the top. *The Sterile Cuckoo* (1969, Paramount).

9036 "Well, Max, here we are—middle-aged man reaffirming his middle-aged manhood and a terrified young woman with a father complex. What sort of script do you think we can make of this?" Television idea woman **Faye Dunaway** seduces TV news executive William Holden. *Network* (1976, MGM-United Artists).

9037 "You're different; I watch you on TV. I know how good I could make you feel. . . I want to give you something." Werewolf **Robert Picardo** tells Dee Wallace that the undead have more fun. *The Howling* (1981, Avco Embassy).

9038 "You're a hard man to seduce." Beautiful **Bo Derek** has a hard time arousing Spanish matador Andrea Occhipinti, even when she rides her horse around the bull ring bareback all over. *Bolero* (1984, Cannon).

9039 "To seduce a woman famous for strict morals, religious fervor and the happiness of her marriage; what could possibly be more prestigious?" **John Malkovich** explains to Glenn Close why he has chosen virtuous Michelle Pfeiffer to be his next sexual conquest. *Dangerous Liaisons* (1988, Warner Bros.).

9040 "The way I see it, we can do this either of two ways. We can sit here and talk for a couple of hours and wonder what it'll be like to be alone together—or we can just cut to the chase." **Meg Ryan** fast forwards the seduction schedule on her first date with Mark Harmon with her version of "Your place, my place, or any place?" *The Presidio* (1988, Paramount).

9041 "For the past few weeks I've heard this funny little sound way deep down inside. . . tick-tock, tick-tock, tick-tock. . . my biological clock. . . and I've been thinking. . . . Let's merge. . . you and I. . . . Think of it, darling. . . . Mr. and Mrs. Fabulously Happy. . . . Can Big Jack come out to play?. . . ." **Sigourney Weaver** proposes marriage and a little bit on account as she paws reluctant Harrison Ford as she lies seductively underdressed in her bed. *Working Girl* (1988, 20th Century-Fox).

9042 "I appreciate this whole seduction thing you got going, but let me give you a tip: I'm a sure thing." Streetwalker **Julia Roberts** assures "john" Richard Gere that his payment has guaranteed that he's going to "get lucky" with her. *Pretty Woman* (1990, Touchstone-Buena Vista).

Self

see also APPEARANCES, CHARACTER, IDENTITIES, INDIVIDUALISM, NAMES, PEOPLE, PERSONALITIES

9043 "Adolphus, I have something very serious to discuss with you. When you meet lady dogs on the street who are not dachshunds, you must exercise self-control." **John Barrymore** lectures his dachshund. *Grand Hotel* (1932, MGM).

9044 "He's tired of himself. A man has only one escape from his old self, to see a different self in the mirror of another woman's eyes." **Lucile Watson** makes an astute observation to her daughter Norma Shearer on why men are unfaithful. *The Women* (1939, MGM).

9045 "That's what I always tell my drivers. No telephone pole ever hit a truck unless it was in self-defense." Trucking firm owner **Alan Hale** boozily dispenses bromides at a party. *They Drive by Night* (1940, Warner Bros.).

9046 "Don't tell me how you are, Sherry, I want none of the tiresome details. I've very little time, and so the conversation will be entirely about me, and I shall love it. Shall I tell you how I glittered through the South Seas like a silver scimitar, or would you rather hear how I finished a three-act play with one hand and made love to a maharajah's daughter with the other?" Noel Coward-like **Reginald Gardiner** proves more than a match for self-centered Monty Woolley. *The Man Who Came to Dinner* (1941, Warner Bros.).

9047 DR. VENGARD: "Now what I'm trying to do is introduce you to your real self. I want you to get acquainted with yourself. Wouldn't you like to meet you?" JILL BAKER: "No! You see, I'm a little shy." Psychiatrist **Alan Mowbray** treats neurotic patient **Merle Oberon**, suffering from uncontrollable hiccups. She is resistant to his attempts to cure her. *That Uncertain Feeling* (1942, United Artists).

9048 "In my case, self-absorption is completely justified. I have never discovered any other subject quite so worthy of my attention." Holy terror columnist **Clifton Webb** takes second place to no one in admiration of himself. *Laura* (1944, 20th Century-Fox).

9049 "You don't yell at a sleepwalker. That's it, she was still sleepwalking along the dizzy heights of her lost career. One subject: her celluloid self. The great Norma Desmond! How could she breathe in that house so crowded with Norma Desmond?" Narrator **William Holden** speaks of slightly mad former silent screen star Gloria Swanson. *Sunset Boulevard* (1950, Paramount).

9050 "They always tell me I'm a bum. Well, I ain't a bum." Until this point in the movie, **Marlon Brando** also thought of himself as a bum, but the love of Eva Marie Saint and standing up to crooked union leader Lee J. Cobb gives him some self-esteem. *On the Waterfront* (1954, Columbia).

9051 "I'm a prima donna—I know it!" **George C. Scott** is the vain American general George S. Patton. *Patton* (1970, 20th Century-Fox).

9052 "He's done a great job on you, you know. Your—your self-esteem is like a notch below Kafka's." **Woody Allen** sarcastically compliments Diane Keaton on the progress she's making with her analyst. *Manhattan* (1979, United Artists).

9053 "I'll get over it because I'm shallow and self-centered." Egotistical symphony conductor **Alexander Godunov** comforts Shelley Long about the break-up of their marriage. *The Money Pit* (1986, Universal).

9054 "The world is made for people who aren't cursed with self-awareness." **Susan Sarandon** has dumb baseball pitcher Tim Robbins in mind when he's called up to the major leagues. *Bull Durham* (1988, Orion).

9055 "You selfish, self-centered swine! I am your woman!" **Kim Thompson** as Heloise, bitterly speaks to her lover Derek de Lint as Abelard when the latter says he will give her up and enter a monastery. *Stealing Heaven* (1988, GB-Yugo., Scotti Bros.).

9056 "At times I sing and dance around the house in my underwear. . . . It doesn't make me Madonna." Stenographer **Joan Cusack** knows the difference between make-believe and reality, but she's not so sure her friend Melanie Griffith does. *Working Girl* (1988, 20th Century-Fox).

9057 "Wait until they get a load of me." A vat of waste has recently changed mobster **Jack Nicholson** into a white-faced, green-haired Joker. *Batman* (1989, Warner Bros.).

9058 "Never look at the backside of a mirror, because you're looking at your inner self and you don't recognize it, because you've never seen it before." Reforming junkie and armed robber **Matt Dillon** shares some wisdom that may have been induced by drugs. *Drugstore Cowboy* (1989, Avenue).

9059 "I see somebody who is extremely aware of people looking at you." **James Spader** tells Andie MacDowell that he has studied her and finds her very self-conscious. *sex, lies and videotape* (1989, Miramax).

Self-Absorption *see* SELF

Self-Assessment *see* ASSESSMENTS, SELF

Self-Awareness *see* SELF

Self-Centered *see* SELF

Self-Consciousness *see* SELF

Self-Control *see* CONTROL, SELF

Self-Defense *see* DEFENSES, SELF

Self-Esteem *see* SELF

Self-Indulgence *see* SELF

Selfishness

see also EGOS AND EGOTISM, INTERESTS, SELF

9060 "Selfish to the end, aren't you? Thinking only of your own precious hide with never a thought for the noble Cause. . . . There's one thing I do know and that is that I love you, Scarlett. In spite of you and me and the whole silly world going to pieces around us, I love you, because we're alike—bad lots, both of us. Selfish and true and able to look things in the eye and call them by their right names." Having rescued Vivien Leigh from burning Atlanta, **Clark Gable** leaves her at a safe point. She calls the Southern soldiers fools for starting a war they couldn't win. He goes off to join the Confederates. *Gone with the Wind* (1939, Selznick-MGM).

9061 "I'm no good. I was only thinking of myself, not how to help him." Richard Barthelmess' wife **Rita Hayworth** condemns herself for her unfaithfulness. *Only Angels Have Wings* (1939, Columbia).

9062 "I told you once that I've done a very selfish thing in marrying you. You can understand now what I meant. I loved you, my darling—I shall always love you—but I've known all along that Rebecca would win in the end." **Laurence Olivier** apologizes to second wife Joan Fontaine when the circumstances of the death of his first wife threaten their happiness. *Rebecca* (1940, Selznick).

9063 "Harry's a menace. The whole history of the world is the story of the struggle between the selfish and the unselfish. . . . All that's bad around us is bred by selfishness. Sometimes selfishness is a cause, an organized force, even a government and then it's called fascism." **William Holden** holds up selfish Broderick Crawford to his mistress Judy Holliday as an example of the causes of the misery in the world. *Born Yesterday* (1950, Columbia).

Self-Love *see* NARCISSISM, SELF, VANITIES

Self-Pity *see* PITY, SELF

Self-Respect *see* RESPECT AND RESPECTABILITY, SELF

Self-Sacrifice *see* SACRIFICES, SELF

Self-Sufficient *see* HELP AND HELPING, SELF

Selling *see* BUYING AND SELLING, SALESMEN

Sensations

see also EXCITEMENTS, FEELINGS, IMPRESSIONS, SENSES AND SENSIBILITY

9064 SUGAR: "Have you ever tried American girls?. . . Was it anything?" JUNIOR: "I'm not sure. Can we try again?. . . I've got a funny sensation in my toes, like someone was barbecuing them with a slow flame." SUGAR: "Let's throw another log on the fire." JUNIOR: "I think you're on the right track." SUGAR: "I must be. Your glasses are beginning to steam up." **Marilyn Monroe** accepts the challenge when **Tony Curtis** pretends to be a millionaire who cannot be aroused by girls. Curtis tries to play down the effect of her kisses. *Some Like It Hot* (1959, United Artists).

9065 "It's not a breakdown. I have never felt so orderly in my life! It is a shattering and beautiful sensation! It is the exalted flow of the space-time continuum, save that it is spaceless and timeless and of such loveliness! I feel on the verge of some great ultimate truth." Television news anchorman **Peter Finch**, intoxicated with his madness, speaks of a Voice that puts words into his mouth. *Network* (1976, MGM-United Artists).

Sense and Sensibility

see also EYES, FACES, FEELINGS, HEARING, MINDS, NONSENSE, SIGHT AND SIGHTS, SMELLS, TALKS, TASTES, THINKING AND THOUGHTS, TOUCHES, UNDERSTANDINGS AND MISUNDERSTANDINGS

9066 "I can still sense death in the air." **Bela Lugosi** comments happily as he's shown secret passages and spiral staircases through a mausoleum. *The Black Cat* (1934, Universal).

9067 "When you get inside my head, see if you can find any sense there." Good-time society girl **Bette Davis** teases George Brent who is to perform brain surgery on her. *Dark Victory* (1939, Warner Bros.).

9068 "I ain't afraid, but my feets ain't gonna stay around and see my body abused." **Willie Best** displays some sense, but he also demonstrates the stereotyping of blacks as being afraid of their shadows, typical of the time. *The Smiling Ghost* (1941, Warner Bros.).

9069 LAURA JESSON: "We must be sensible." ALEC HARVEY: "It's too late to be sensible." Married, but not to each other, **Celia Johnson** and **Trevor Howard**, fall in love. *Brief Encounter* (1945, GB, Cineguild-Eagle Lion).

9070 "Going to a man's apartment always ends in one of two ways: either a girl is willing to lose her virtue, or she fights for it. I don't want to lose mine, and I think it's vulgar to fight for it, so I always put my cards on the table. Don't you think that's sensible?" Candid **Maggie McNamara** heads off William Holden's advances. Plain speaking in the movie put it at the center of a major censorship storm at the time of its release. *The Moon Is Blue* (1953, United Artists).

9071 "Kirk was wrong when he said I didn't know where movie scripts left off and life began. A movie script has to make sense, and life doesn't." Fading director-screenwriter **Humphrey Bogart** refers to Howard Hughes-like movie producer Warren Stevens. *The Barefoot Contessa* (1954, United Artists).

9072 "You know, since I started taking lithium, I feel more sensible than this month's *Good House-keeping*." **Kelly Bishop** informs Jill Clayburgh that her calmness is chemically induced. *An Unmarried Woman* (1978, 20th Century-Fox).

9073 "It's ridiculous these niceties; they go against common sense—any kind of sense. I don't care what I see outside. My vision is within. Here is where the bird sings. Here is where the sky is blue." **Denholm Elliott** taps his forehead. *A Room with a View* (1985, GB, Merchant-Ivory-Goldcrest).

Sensitivity and Insensitivity

see also DISTURBANCES, IMPRESSIONS, SENSE AND SENSIBILITY

9074 "It's extraordinary to me that you people cannot take care of yourselves and your children. One or the other of you is forever in the way. How do you know what injury you might do to the horses?" **Basil Rathbone**, as the cruel Marquis St. Evremonde, demonstrates the insensitivity of some French aristocrats that helped spark the French Revolution. Rathbone's speeding carriage strikes and kills a young boy. Rathbone disdainfully lectures the child's father who cradles the boy's lifeless body in his arms. *A Tale of Two Cities* (1935, MGM).

9075 "You know, it's a curious fact, that ever since my earliest experiments with rabbits and guinea pigs, I always found the female of the species was more sensitive to electrical impulse than was the male. It's fortunate that we met here. Shall I show you how it was done?" Mad scientist **Lionel Atwill** leers chillingly at Anne Nagel, who has entered his laboratory wearing a negligee. He quickly pins her to his operating table. *Man Made Monster* (1941, Universal).

9076 "I don't need a crack like that any more than I need your dough, which is what I've been telling you. I missed her. The dame caught a boat south. . . . Look, I got along before this job. I ate good and grew as big as you did and if there is something you don't like, you can say so." **Robert Mitchum** is sensitive to his employer mobster Kirk Douglas' casual question about progress on finding Douglas' mistress Jane Greer. The reason is that Mitchum has fallen in love with Greer and is trying to get away with her. *Out of the Past* (1947, RKO).

9077 AMANDA BONNER: "I know your touch. I know a slap from a slug." ADAM BONNER: "Okay, okay." AMANDA: "I'm not so sure it is. I'm not so sure I want to be subjected to a typical, instinctive, masculine brutality. And it felt not only as though you meant to but as though you thought you had a right to. I can tell." ADAM: "What you got back there, radar equipment?" It's the exchange between **Katharine Hepburn** and **Spencer Tracy** after he gives her a bit more than a playful slap on the rear. He is giving her a massage as they discuss the merits of the legal case they are arguing from opposing sides. *Adam's Rib* (1949, MGM).

9078 "He was sweeping! That's what he was doing in the streets, you heartless bastards." **Timothy Bottoms** screams at the insensitive townspeople who coldly comment on the death of Sam Bottoms, a mentally incompetent youngster struck by a truck. *The Last Picture Show* (1971, Columbia).

9079 "Sidney, I have just thrown up in front of the best people in Hollywood. Now is no time to be sensitive." British actress **Maggie Smith**'s nervousness proves too much for her at the Academy Awards ceremonies. She shares her after-sickness recollections with her husband Michael Caine. *California Suite* (1978, Columbia).

9080 "It took me three hours to get her off. When it was over, I thought I'd done something worthwhile—who else would have taken the time?" Male hustler **Richard Gere** congratulates himself for his sensitivity with a woman customer who has a difficult time achieving an orgasm. *American Gigolo* (1980, Paramount).

9081 "Paul, do you think you could buy another frying pan? I'm just a little squeamish about cooking in the one we use to kill people." **Mary Woronov** makes a reasonable shopping request of husband Paul Bartel. Their weapon of choice for killing swingers for their money is a cast iron frying pan. *Eating Raoul* (1982, Bartel Film).

9082 "Be careful what you call my car. She's real sensitive." **Keith Gordon** gives sound advice to his best friend John Stockwell about his vindictive 1958 Plymouth Fury. *Christine* (1983, Columbia).

9083 "Your opinion of Larry is a tribute to your insensitivity to other human beings. Larry would never have sex with anyone like your wife." **Sean Young** ridicules her lover William Petersen's suspicion that her husband Ted Danson is having an affair with his wife Isabella Rosselini. At the time, she's correct. *Cousins* (1989, Paramount).

Sentiments and Sentimentality

see also EMOTIONS, FEELINGS, MINDS, NOSTALGIA, OPINIONS, ROMANCES, THINKING AND THOUGHTS

9084 "Let me love you. Let me live for you. Don't let's ask for more from Heaven than that—God might get angry. . . . I don't suppose you can understand, Monsieur, how someone, unprotected as you say I am, can be lifted above selfishness by sentiments so delicate and pure. . . ." Courtesan **Greta Garbo**, who has been loved by many men, experiences true love for the first time with Robert Taylor. *Camille* (1936, MGM).

9085 "The sentiment comes easy at fifty cents a word." Egomaniac writer **Clifton Webb** names his price. *Laura* (1944, 20th Century-Fox).

9086 "Schmaltz? You want schmaltz?" It's cynical pianist **Oscar Levant**'s reaction to a musical request. *Humoresque* (1947, Warner Bros.).

9087 "Sentiment has no cash values." Miserly businessman **John Baer** echoes the sentiments of his deceased uncle Basil Rathbone for whom he has no tears to shed. *We're No Angels* (1955, Paramount).

9088 "Practically perfect people never permit sentiment to muddle their feelings." Practically perfect nanny **Julie Andrews** instructs her charges Karen Dotrice and Matthew Garber. *Mary Poppins* (1964, Disney-Buena Vista).

9089 "No, I—I don't have the sentiment on my side. You've got to have a sentimental reason for them to vote for me. Any decent actress can give a good performance, but a dying husband—that would have ensured everything!" Actress **Maggie Smith** lightly suggests that her husband Michael Caine didn't do all he could have to support her efforts to win an Academy Award. *California Suite* (1978, Columbia).

9090 "I like you people, but you are sentimental shits. You fall in love with the poets, the people fall in love with the Marxists, the Marxists fall in love with themselves. The country is destroyed with rhetoric, and the end is we are stuck with tyrants." French CIA operative **Jean-Louis Trintignant** scolds journalists Nick Nolte and Joanna Cassidy for faking a photograph of a rebel leader to give a boost to the Sandinista revolution in Nicaragua. *Under Fire* (1983, Orion).

Separations

see also COMBINATIONS, DIVORCES, MIXTURES

9091 LORD NELSON: "You shouldn't have come. People will see you, they'll talk." EMMA HAMILTON: "Oh, let them talk. I don't care. Do you? Are you sorry?" NELSON: "I'm only sorry for all the wasted years I've been without you. For all the years I shall have to be without you." EMMA: "You'll come back, won't you?" NELSON: "I wonder if I shall. I feel that I should not. You are married and I am married. In the magic and music of the ballroom, these things become rather blurred. But they stand out very clearly in the dawn. Your life is here, my life is there. We must obey the creed and codes that we've sworn our lives to. I know that I must not come back, and I know that nothing in this world can keep me away." Once more, **Laurence Olivier** reluctantly leaves his mistress **Vivien Leigh** as he goes off to battle. *That Hamilton Woman* aka: *Lady Hamilton* (1941, GB, London Films-United Artists).

9092 "This is the moment I've dreaded. . . coming back to our house alone. . . . Darling, darling, I've tried to understand. I've held myself together through all our goodbyes. . . . I'll try to remember what you said—that this will be the greatest adventure we ever had, even though we had it separately." **Claudette Colbert** wistfully talks to her husband's photograph after leaving him at the train station, as he goes to war. *Since You Went Away* (1944, Selznick-United Artists).

9093 "If you walk out that door, Howard, I will consider it a trial separation." **Sally Kellerman** makes a feeble threat when her husband, Jack Lemmon, announces that he's leaving to fly to Paris with Catherine Deneuve. *The April Fools* (1969, National General).

9094 "They do not separate." It's **Diane Venora**'s response to a Bellevue doctor's question regarding Forest Whitaker, "Do you want a husband or a musician?" *Bird* (1988, Warner Bros.).

Serenity *see* QUIETNESS

Seriousness

see also CONSIDERATIONS, DIFFICULTIES, EFFORTS, IMPORTANCE

9095 "If you think I won't pull the trigger, you don't know me." Escaped criminal **Humphrey Bogart** has his gun pointed at the head of his hostage, Fredric March's son Richard Eyer. *The Desperate Hours* (1955, Paramount).

9096 "Shut up. You and I have a different idea about what 'serious' is. You think it's making a choice, don't you? Deciding you want to play, going at it eight hours a day and taking hot baths. Let me tell you what serious is. . . when you inherit it from a father. . . who only responds to your musical accomplishments, and nothing else. Then what you get is my sister Tita, who has more ability than anyone in the house, and no assurance—none—and as a result, is an incomplete, totally unhappy woman. And you've got Carl who has the conceit of assurance, without any notable ability, so he coaches somebody to do what he can't. The only serious musician that isn't faking something in the family is Herbert, and you can't talk to the man about anything that goes on beyond the top row of the orchestra. . . . And if you want to complete your judgement on me, I came last to this predetermined heritage. . . . And I worked at it every day. . . from the age of three to the age of twenty-eight, hating it. . . playing without assurance, without ability, without satisfaction. And their approval, their applause, their enthusiasm—or yours—doesn't mean crap to me. I don't feel it." **Jack Nicholson** angrily explains in detail to Susan Anspach that he's indeed serious—but not about music—but rather about the fact that a person can't be a person if he or she is living a life someone else has picked out for him or her. *Five Easy Pieces* (1970, Columbia).

9097 "When are you going to stop using the whole world as a straight man?" **Lee Remick** tells her ex-husband, publicity man Jack Lemmon, to stop being such a clown if he wants his son Robby Benson to take him seriously. *Tribute* (1980, Canada, 20th Century-Fox).

9098 "I mean, I write an excellent article and just because I'm cute no one takes me seriously. It's not fair." High school student **Joyce Hyser** believes her teachers have ignored her entry in a journalism competition because she's a girl. *Just One of the Guys* (1985, United Artists).

Servants and Servitude

see also SERVICES, WORK AND WORKERS

9099 PRASCOVIA: "A servant is not supposed to be a real man." ALBERT: "I understand. Sexless like the angels." **Dot Farley** doesn't mean that waiter **Adolphe Menjou** can't be real with her. *The Grand Duchess and the Waiter* (1926, silent, Paramount).

9100 "Very stupid to kill the servants: now we don't even know where to find the marmalade." It's the complaint of insensitive **Judith Anderson** after the second of two servants is found murdered. She'll soon get her comeuppance. *And Then There Were None* (1945, Popular Picture).

9101 "I'll wear your ring, I'll cook, and I'll wash, and I'll keep the land. But that is all. Until I've got my dowry safe about me, I'm no married woman. I'm the servant I've always been, without anything of my own!" **Maureen O'Hara** forcefully informs her husband John Wayne that she'll be having headaches every night until her brother Victor McLaglen is made to surrender her dowry to her. *The Quiet Man* (1952, Republic).

9102 LOUKA: "You have the soul of a servant, Nicola." NICOLA: "Yes, that's the secret of success in service." **Ellen Schwiers** talks down to servant **Manfred Inger** in George Bernard Shaw's witty, anti-militaristic satire. *Arms and the Man* (1962, Germany, Casino Films).

9103 "I die the king's good servant, but God's first." These are the last words of Thomas More, portrayed by **Paul Scofield**, before his execution at the chopping block. *A Man for All Seasons* (1966, GB, Columbia).

9104 "The world was changed by people with servants. I'll bet Marx had at least three." Wealthy, obnoxious, opinionated, beautiful **Mariangela Melato** believes that without someone to handle the routine tasks of life, a person doesn't have time or energy to do anything really significant—even communists. *Swept Away* (1974, Italy, Cinema 5).

Services

see also DUTIES, OCCUPATIONS, SERVANTS AND SERVITUDE, WORK

9105 "They also serve who only stand and. . . well, whatever it is they stand and do. I forget what it is." Four-F **Eddie Bracken** makes an impassioned defense of his value in the war effort. *The Miracle of Morgan's Creek* (1944, Paramount).

9106 "And you'll find me of great service, Mrs. King. I was also an obstetrician." **Clifton Webb**, genius and nanny-extraordinaire, assures Maureen O'Hara that she can count on his help when she finds she's pregnant once again. *Sitting Pretty* (1948, 20th Century-Fox).

9107 "There is only one way to deal with Rome. . . you must serve her. You must abase yourself before her. You must grovel at her feet. You must love her." Bisexual **Laurence Olivier** identifies with Rome, hinting to slave Tony Curtis what will be expected of him. Curtis runs away. *Spartacus* (1960, Universal).

9108 "Certainly, he can present a bill for such services; we're not communists, after all. But he has to let us draw water from the well." **Richard Conte**, head of a rival New York crime family, expects Marlon Brando to make his political clout available to the rackets of the other families. *The Godfather* (1972, Paramount).

9109 "If you want to do mankind a service, tell funnier jokes." This is the message filmmaker Woody Allen hears over and over in the movie. He even hears it from an alien in a spaceship. *Stardust Memories* (1980, United Artists).

9110 "Professional assassination is the highest form of public service." Ancient Korean martial arts expert **Joel Grey** instructs his pupil Fred Ward. *Remo Williams: The Adventure Begins* (1985, Orion).

9111 "Oh, sir, if I may say so, you're in the right store and in the right city for that matter." Rodeo Drive boutique manager **Larry Miller** fawns over wealthy Richard Gere, who wants clerks to suck up to him and Julia Roberts as they shop for an expensive wardrobe for her. *Pretty Woman* (1990, Touchstone-Buena Vista).

9112 "You are the lucky ones. You are going to serve God and country. I pronounce you handmaids. Shall we pray? I pledge allegiance to the Bible. . . . Oh God; make me fruitful." **Victoria Tennant** preaches to the women of the Republic of Gilead who can still bear children—only about one in three hundred. *The Handmaid's Tale* (1990, GB, Miramax).

9113 "Some day, and that day may never come, I may ask a service of you." Reminiscent of Marlon Brando's comment to the undertaker Salvatore Corsitto in "Godfather I," **Al Pacino** seeks a pledge from Franco Citti. Ultimately, Pacino asks Citti to perform a suicidal assassination of Immobiliare head Enzo Robutti, which Citti does. *The Godfather, Part III* (1991, Paramount).

Sex and Sexuality

see also APPEARANCES, ART AND ARTISTS, ATTENTION, ATTRACTIONS, BABIES, BACHELORS, BADNESS, BEAUTY, BEDS, BEHAVIOR, BODIES, BOYS, CHALLENGES, CHARM, CHILDREN AND CHILDHOOD, CLOSENESS, CLOTHES, CRUELTY, DANCING AND DANCERS, DATES AND DATING, DECENCY, DESIRES, DIVORCES, DOUBLE ENTENDRES, DREAMS, EMOTIONS, EXCITEMENTS, EYES, FACES, FAVORS, FLATTERY, GIRLS, GOOD AND EVIL, GUILT, HEART AND HEARTACHES, HOMOSEXUALITY, HONEYMOONS, IMAGINATION, IMPOTENCY, INNUENDOS, KISSES AND KISSING, LIKES AND DISLIKES, LOVE, LUST, MEN AND WOMEN, MODESTY, NAUGHTINESS, NUDITY, ORGASMS, PAINS, PARTIES, PARTNERS, PASSION, PERFUMES, PERVERSIONS, PREGNANCIES, PROMISCUITY, PROSTITUTION AND PROSTITUTES, RAPE, ROMANCES, SCANDALS, SPINSTERS, SURRENDER, TEMPTATIONS, VICES, VIRGINITY, WEDDINGS

9114 "Sex attraction and sex congeniality are two entirely different things." **Ruth Chatterton** makes an astute observation in an old-fashioned drawing room drama, whose like is unlikely to ever be seen again. *The Rich Are Always With Us* (1932, Warner Bros.).

9115 "Excuse me while I fix up the old sex appeal. The way I feel this morning I'll need a steam shovel." Showgirl **Aline MacMahon** has had a tough night before. *Gold Diggers of 1933* (1933, Warner Bros.).

9116 "They had IT all right, but they didn't photograph IT and put IT to the music." **Elizabeth Patterson** reflects on how sex appeal was handled when she was a girl. *Go West, Young Man* (1936, Paramount).

9117 "Oh, but of course it did, darling. I don't think he would have given it to me if I had. . . little short legs like an alligator. Sex always has something to do with it, dear. From the time you're about so big and wondering why your girl friends are starting to get so arch all of a sudden. Nothing wrong, just an overture to the opera that's coming. . . but from then on you get it [the sexual come-on look] from cops, taxi drivers, bell boys, delicatessen dealers. . . the 'how about this evening, babe?'" It's **Claudette Colbert**'s lengthy reply when her husband Joel McCrea asks if sex entered into elderly "wiener king" Robert Dudley's giving her enough money to pay all their numerous bills. *The Palm Beach Story* (1942, Paramount).

9118 "Well, I shall have to use a word I've never used in your presence. It seems the book is largely about sex." **Ronald Colman** reluctantly describes for his wife Edna Best the nature of the book he's discovered their daughter Peggy Cummins has been reading. *The Late George Apley* (1947, 20th Century-Fox).

9119 "Don't you think it's better for a girl to be pre-occupied with sex than occupied with it?" **Maggie McNamara** defends her frank talk about sex and seduction. *The Moon Is Blue* (1953, United Artists).

9120 RENATO: "You Americans get so disturbed about sex." JANE HUDSON: "We don't take it lightly." RENATO: "Take it. Don't talk it. . . . You are like a hungry child who is given ravioli to eat. My dear girl, you are hungry. Eat the ravioli." **Rossano Brazzi** tries to convince spinster **Katharine Hepburn**, in Venice on holiday, to have an affair with him. *Summertime* (1955, United Artists).

9121 "He says we're both scared of life and people and sex. There—I've said the word. He says I hate saying it even and he's right. I do. What's the matter with me? There must be something the matter with me?" Repressed spinster **Deborah Kerr** talks to Wendy Hiller about David Niven and her fear of men and sex. Kerr's problem would seem to be her domineering mother Gladys Cooper. *Separate Tables* (1958, United Artists).

9122 "With me, I always get to a certain point—listening to somebody's line and kissing and petting—then I get scared or disgusted and. . . do you think I've got a sex blockade or something?" Teenage **Carol Lynley** tells Brandon de Wilde she hasn't gone all the way with a boy yet. *Blue Denim* (1959, 20th Century-Fox).

9123 "I didn't know it could be so awful." **Lelia Goldoni** reacts to her first sexual experience. *Shadows* (1960, McEndree-Cassel-Lion).

9124 "Your father never laid a hand on me until we were married and then I just gave in because a wife has to. A woman doesn't enjoy these things the way a man does. She just lets her husband come near her in order to have children." **Audrey Christie** further confuses her troubled teenage daughter Natalie Wood, sexually aroused by boy friend Warren Beatty, who is making increasing demands on her. *Splendor in the Grass* (1961, Warner Bros.).

9125 "I used sex as you used alcohol." Promiscuous sculptor **Susan Hayward** compares herself to her alcoholic husband Michael Connors as their marriage falls apart. *Where Love Has Gone* (1964, Paramount).

9126 "We could do without sex. I don't really like it that much." **Julie Christie** wants a platonic affair with homosexual photographer Roland Curram. *Darling* (1965, GB, Anglo-Amalgamated).

9127 "Do you have good sex with your wife?" Outspoken Israeli freedom fighter **Senta Berger** will be happy to apply for duty if General Kirk Douglas's answer about Angie Dickinson is no—or even if it's yes. *Cast a Giant Shadow* (1966, United Artists).

9128 "My psychiatrist asked me if I thought sex was dirty and I said it is if you're doing it right." **Woody Allen** claims that a little guilt about sex makes it more exciting. *Take the Money and Run* (1969, Palomar).

9129 "Well, one thing you can say for masturbation. . . you don't have to look your best." Outrageous swishy gay **Cliff Gorman** finds an advantage in onanism. *The Boys in the Band* (1970, National General).

9130 "People like Hope accept what's been told them. . . . Then sex is the closest thing they have to flying." **Sally Kellerman** cautions Bud Cort, who plans to fly with man-made wings, about nymphomaniacal Jennifer Salt. *Brewster McCloud* (1970, MGM).

9131 "No, no food. I want sex. Bring me some sex. That one over there, the sultry bitch with the fire in her eyes. Take her clothes off and bring her to me." Newly arrived Army surgeon **Elliott Gould** is only half-kidding when he says he wants his appetite satisfied by a passing nurse. *M*A*S*H* (1970, 20th Century-Fox).

9132 "Is she better than self-abuse?. . . Does she lie there kind of quiet, or does she go 'oh-oh-oh'?" **Donald Sutherland** goads mentally unstable Robert Duvall over the edge with his questions about Sally Kellerman. *M*A*S*H* (1970, 20th Century-Fox).

9133 "If you're sexy, you can be sexy doing nothing. Sex is from inside." **Geri Miller** states her opinion on the matter in a sleazy, bizarre and funny film directed by Paul Morrissey. *Trash* (1970, Cinema 5-Warhol).

9134 "It's not as easy getting laid as it used to be." Now middle-aged, sexual athlete **Jack Nicholson** finds his life boring and empty, with women no longer falling for his questionable charm. *Carnal Knowledge* (1971, Avco Embassy).

9135 "There's nothing natural about sex and you'll find that out. Everything gets old if you do it often enough, so if you want to find out about monotony real quick, marry Duane." **Ellen Burstyn** advises her daughter Cybill Shepherd to sleep with Jeff Bridges, not marry him. *The Last Picture Show* (1971, Columbia).

9136 "No fornication of any kind with anyone ever." Crude prison warden **Andy Centenera** snarls the restrictions on sexual practices to new prisoners. *The Big Bird Cage* (1972, New World).

9137 LUNA SCHLOSSER: "You haven't had sex in 200 years?" MILES MONROE: "204—if you count my marriage." A bit of banter between 22nd century sexual animal **Diane Keaton** and 20th century nerd **Woody Allen** who has been re-animated after a 200-year sleep. *Sleeper* (1973, United Artists).

9138 "I'll bring the tea bags. We could run a quick check on your erogenous zones. . . ." **Woody Allen** slobbers over Countess Olga Georges-Picot. *Love and Death* (1975, United Artists).

9139 "Sex is the invention of a very clever venereal disease." A sign on the wall in the movie. *They Came from Within* (1975, Canada, AIP).

9140 "Sex is not funny; sex is serious." It's 1953 and Brooklyn College graduate **Lenny Baker** attempts to cheer up black homosexual Antonio Fargas. *Next Stop, Greenwich Village* (1976, 20th Century-Fox).

9141 "Sex is the most fun I've had without laughing." It's another of **Woody Allen**'s one-liners. *Annie Hall* (1977, United Artists).

9142 ALVY SINGER: "It's all mental masturbation." ANNIE HALL: "Oh, well, now we're finally getting to a subject you know something about." ALVY: "Hey, don't knock masturbation. It's sex with someone I love." **Woody Allen** believes **Diane Keaton** is having an affair with her college professor, who teaches a course Woody describes as "blue sky" nonsense. Her counter-accusation leads to his defense of the lonely sin. *Annie Hall* (1977, United Artists).

9143 "You know, there's not an hour goes by that I don't think of making love with you." Vietnam veteran **Jon Voight** may be paralyzed from the waist down, but it hasn't affected his desire for married Jane Fonda. *Coming Home* (1978, United Artists).

9144 "Can't you understand my feelings? I can't turn sex on and off. When I'm in the mood and you're in the mood, it's wonderful. . . . But it's not much fun when you make me feel like it's an obligation." **Jill Clayburgh** tells her husband Michael Murphy he needs to brush up on his seduction techniques. *An Unmarried Woman* (1978, 20th Century-Fox.)

9145 "Let's just get something straight right off the top, babe, huh? I don't get involved with my women. I'm a short-term guy. I don't fall in love. I don't want to get married. The only thing you can count on me for is sex. I am what I am. I make no bones about it." After **Cliff Gorman**'s ranting about his rules, it's a wonder that divorced Jill Clayburgh goes to bed with him—but then she also only wants to use him for sex. *An Unmarried Woman* (1978, 20th Century-Fox).

9146 "That's not music, that's masturbation." Music teacher **Albert Hague** doesn't appreciate Lee Curreri's high-tech compositions. *Fame* (1980, MGM-United Artists).

9147 "Could you tell me what some of the after-effects are?" Virgin **Tatum O'Neal** asks a camp counselor about sexual intercourse. *Little Darlings* (1980, Paramount).

9148 "Isn't empty sex better than no sex at all?" A groupie surprises movie maker Woody Allen in his bed. *Stardust Memories* (1980, United Artists).

9149 "SEX! That's the answer. We'll give them a $40 million porn epic. . . we gave them virtue. They wanted vice." Filmmaker **Richard Mulligan** has a flash of inspiration about what to do with his goody-two-shoes wife Julie Andrews and the sickly sweet movies she stars in that nobody wants to see anymore. *S.O.B.* (1981, Lorimar-Paramount).

9150 "Save me. Only you can stop this killing. You've got to make love with me as brother and sister. . . . Our parents were brother and sister. . . . Make love to me and save both of us. . . . We are an incestuous race and before we can become human again, we must kill." **Malcolm McDowell** insists to his sister Nastassja Kinski that only incest can mitigate their family curse of bestiality. *Cat People* (1982, RKO).

9151 "Before you get married, all there is is talk about the wedding—the plans, you know, and sex talk. You know, when can we Do It? Are your parents going to be out so we can Do It? Where do we Do It? Then after you get married, she's there all the time; when you wake up in the morning, she's there. When you come home from work, she's there. . . . There's no more sex talk. Nothing else to talk about. . . ." Married to Ellen Barkin, **Daniel Stern** discovers that an attraction based almost solely on sex doesn't make for a good marriage. *Diner* (1982, MGM).

9152 "Sex was all Sue Alabama ever needed and she used it the way some guys used a blackjack." **Frederic Forrest**, as Dashiell Hammett, writes about one of his female characters. *Hammett* (1982, Orion-Warner Bros.).

9153 "Everybody does everything in order to get laid." Cynical *People* magazine writer **Jeff Goldblum** has an interesting theory of motivation. *The Big Chill* (1983, Columbia).

9154 "Max Stein, the fornicating fiddler player—if you admire him as much as you say, you better see him tonight—it'll be his last performance." Orchestra conductor **Dudley Moore** tells private investigator Richard B. Shull that violinist Armand Assante may meet with a fatal accident. Moore believes that Assante is having an affair with Moore's young wife Nastassja Kinski. *Unfaithfully Yours* (1984, 20th Century-Fox).

9155 "Have you ever been felt up? Over the bra, under the blouse, shoes off, hopin' to God your parents don't walk in?. . . Over the panties, no bra, blouse unbuttoned, Calvins in a ball in the front seat, past 11 on a school night?" Hoodish **Judd Nelson** teases high school princess Molly Ringwald about a major scary teenage situation. *The Breakfast Club* (1985, Universal).

9156 "If this is foreplay, I'm a dead man!" **Steve Guttenberg** has outer-space, out-of-body sex with alien Tahnee Welch. *Cocoon* (1985, 20th Century-Fox.)

9157 "I like a little sex with my violence." On patrol in Israel, soft-hearted soldier **Amos Kollek** complains about the lack of women. *Goodbye, New York* (1985, U.S.-Israel-Castle Hill).

9158 "You give me this graphic harangue about the zipless fuck and then tell me you're just being honest. Well, you know what I think? I think you do that to try and keep a safe distance. . . all that jazz like you're just some poor slob who's getting led around by your cock. Well, I'm not buying it, so stop trying to sell me on it." **Brooke Adams** couldn't be more angry with her lover of the moment Ben Masters if they were married. *Key Exchange* (1985, 20th Century-Fox).

9159 "Well, Gilbert, I think sexual intercourse is in order." Domestic dominatrix **Maggie Smith** excites her sweet, weak husband Michael Palin. *A Private Function* (1985, GB, Handmade-Island Alive).

9160 "Have you ever considered a sexual encounter so intense it could conceivably change your political views?" Maybe it's his delivery, but **John Cusack** strikes out with this pickup line. *The Sure Thing* (1985, Embassy).

9161 "If I want to bump uglies with somebody, I've got plenty of places to go.... I can get tail any place." **Ed Harris** is hurt that Jessica Lange, as country and western singer Patsy Cline, misinterprets his pressing her for a date, assuming he's only after one thing. *Sweet Dreams* (1985, Tri-Star).

9162 "I happen to like uncomplicated sex." Post-doctorate student **Sigourney Weaver** augments her stipend by working for a London escort service. *Half Moon Street* (1986, 20th Century-Fox).

9163 "It's amazing, isn't it? You can handle any man as long as you know what his sexual trip is." Prostitute **Marusia Zach** agrees with colleague Louise Smith, who claims to have lost her fear of men by becoming a hooker. *Working Girls* (1986, Miramax).

9164 "I make it a policy never to have sex before the first date." If by a date, **Sally Field** means leaving her home to do something, she breaks her policy with writer Michael Caine. *Surrender* (1987, Warner Bros.).

9165 "I have a right to a little fornication after all that down time." Career criminal **Nick Nolte** tries to make up for his forced celibacy while in prison. *Weeds* (1987, Kingsgate).

9166 "Safe sex. Who would ever think those two words would exist in the same sentence?" Once promiscuous **Lea Thompson** is forced to lead a more celibate life because of herpes, AIDS, and other sexually transmitted diseases. *Casual Sex?* (1988, Universal).

9167 "Sex is like power—you can't help but leave a mess." It is the opinion of cafe regular Ernest Hemingway, portrayed by **Kevin J. O'Connor.** *The Moderns* (1988, Alive Film).

9168 "Once the sex goes, it all goes." **Woody Allen** comments on his rotten marriage to Joanna Gleason. *Crimes and Misdemeanors* (1989, Orion).

9169 "Well, I think someone in this house should be having sex with something that doesn't require batteries." **Martha Plimpton** justifies having sex with her boy friend Keanu Reeves and gets a dig in at her divorced mother Dianne Wiest at the same time. *Parenthood* (1989, Universal).

9170 "I've never been really that much into sex. I mean I like it and everything, but, you know, I just don't think it's such a big deal and I wouldn't miss it, you know, but lately I've been kind of curious about how things have slacked off.... He started not touching me before I started feeling like that...." **Andie MacDowell** wonders to her therapist why her husband Peter Gallagher hasn't tried to have sex with her for quite a while. He's getting all he can handle from Andie's sister Laura San Giacomo. *sex, lies and videotape* (1989, Miramax).

9171 "I think that sex is overrated. I think people place far too much importance on it, and I think that stuff about women wanting it just as bad as men is crap. I think that women want it, I just don't think they want it for the same reason that men think they do." In telling James Spader something "personal," **Andie MacDowell** may be partially correct, but as things progress it becomes clear that she's never had a man who satisfied her. *sex, lies and videotape* (1989, Miramax).

9172 HARRY BURNS: "No man can be friends with a woman he finds attractive. He always wants to have sex with her." SALLY ALBRIGHT: "So you're saying a man can be friends with a woman he finds unattractive." HARRY: "No. You pretty well want to nail them, too." **Billy Crystal**'s assertion that men want sex with every woman they meet appalls **Meg Ryan**. *When Harry Met Sally...* (1989, Columbia).

9173 "There's nothing sexier than a lapsed Catholic." It's **Joe Mantegna**'s questionable reason for having an affair with Mia Farrow. *Alice* (1990, Orion).

9174 "Women need sex as much as men do." **Robyn Stevan**, who married just before her husband went into the army and hasn't heard from him in over a year, justifies her numerous one-night stands. *Bye Bye Blues* (1990, Canada-U.S., Circle).

9175 "[I'm seeking] a spiritual substitute for sex." When **Ingrid Chavez** informs club-owner Morris Day of her search, he gives her a drug that knocks her out. It causes her to fall in love with the first man she sees when she revives. *Graffiti Bridge* (1990, Warner Bros.).

9176 "Selling art demands a certain sexuality." Stylish art gallery owner **Mark Hamill** can't keep his eyes off the ladies despite the pleadings of his longtime girl friend Amanda Wyss. It's lust at first sight when Hamill spots voluptuous beauty Apollonia. *Black Magic Woman* (1991, Vidmark).

9177 "All sex is the same; it leaves you more sad." **Vincent D'Onofrio**, who dresses as a gaucho, has a Valentino complex. *Naked Tango* (1991, New Line).

9178 "Check out the headlights on that blonde. How'd you like to play hide the salami with that for a week?" Blonde bombshell **Ellen Barkin**, the reincarnation of womanizer Perry King, is still trying to get his/her gender straightened out. She startles her date Jimmy Smits when she nudges him and cases a shapely girl walking by in a bar. *Switch* (1991, Warner Bros.).

The Sexes

see also MEN, MEN AND WOMEN, SEX AND SEXUALITY, WOMEN

9179 "We're caught like rats in a trap. . . . But I'm a boy rat and you're a girl rat." **Bob Hope** finds something positive about the dangerous situation he and Dorothy Lamour find themselves in. *My Favorite Brunette* (1947, Paramount).

9180 "I'm old fashioned. I like two sexes. All of a sudden I don't like being married to what's known as a 'new woman,' I want a wife, not a competitor." Prosecutor **Spencer Tracy** has a negative reaction to his wife Katharine Hepburn's feminism when she scores some legal points in a court case in which they are opposing counselors. *Adam's Rib* (1949, MGM).

9181 "I'd like a he to be a he and a she to be a she, five-0, five-0." Sports promoter **Spencer Tracy** tells Katharine Hepburn that he believes in the equality of the sexes, but believes that they shouldn't try to be like the other. *Pat and Mike* (1952, MGM).

Shadows

see also DARKNESS, HAPPINESS AND UNHAPPINESS, IMITATION, LIGHTS

9182 "Her shadow has been between us all the time—keeping us from one another. She knew this would happen." **Laurence Olivier** speaks of his deceased first wife to his second wife Joan Fontaine. *Rebecca* (1940, Selznick-United Artists).

9183 "You're like a shadow over our lives." **Tim Holt** begs Margaret Sullavan to end her long-time affair with his father Charles Boyer. *Back Street* (1941, Universal).

9184 "I am a shadowy reflection of you. It would take only a notch to make you more like me." Cynical French archaeologist **Paul Freeman**, in the employ of the Nazis, compares himself to hero Harrison Ford. *Raiders of the Lost Ark* (1981, Paramount).

9185 "But isn't that what all men are, the shadow of God?" Pregnant **Myriem Roussel** replies when her new husband Thierry Rode swears he will not touch her, only act as her protecting shadow. *Hail Mary* (1985, Fr.-Swiss, Pegace Films).

Shame

see also DISGRACES, EMOTIONS, GUILT, HONOR, HUMILITY AND HUMILIATION, MODESTY, RIDICULE AND RIDICULOUSNESS

9186 "Blackie is ashamed of his good deeds like other people are ashamed of their sins." Priest **Spencer Tracy** confides to Jeannette MacDonald about his atheistic friend Clark Gable, the owner of a Barbary Coast dive. *San Francisco* (1936, MGM).

9187 "I'm ashamed. And I hate being ashamed." **Ingrid Bergman** feels badly about her affair with her married musical mentor Leslie Howard. *Intermezzo* (1939, Selznick-United Artists).

9188 ELIZABETH BENNET: "Oh, Mr. Darcy. When I think of how I've misjudged you, the horrible things I said. . . I'm so ashamed." MR. DARCY: "Oh, no. It is I who should be ashamed. . . of my arrogance, of my stupid pride, of it all—except one thing: I'm not ashamed of having loved you. . . . Elizabeth, dare I ask you again?. . . Elizabeth, dear beautiful Lizzy. . . ." At the end of this exchange, **Greer Garson** and **Laurence Olivier** fall into an embrace and kiss. *Pride and Prejudice* (1940, MGM).

9189 "This thing must all along have been deep inside you. You've made me ashamed of my concept of superior and inferior. By what right did you decide that the boy in there was inferior and therefore could be killed?" Professor **James Stewart** is appalled that his students John Dall and Farley Granger have killed for the thrill of it, believing their superiority justified the action. Stewart must share some of the guilt. He proposed the theory that they acted upon. *Rope* (1948, Warner Bros.).

9190 "If you don't mind my saying so, I think it's a shame you let him take up tennis. That sort of thing would never happen to a cricketer." **Naunton Wayne** cuts right to the heart of the matter as he advises a distressed Basil Radford about his troublesome son, Jack Watling, a tennis player. *Quartet* (1949, GB, Rank-Eagle Lion).

9191 "An experienced caterer can make you ashamed of your house in fifteen minutes." At least that's how **Spencer Tracy** feels after his encounter with caterer Leo G. Carroll. *Father of the Bride* (1950, MGM).

9192 "Boy, if—if I had one day when I didn't have to feel that I was ashamed of everything—if I felt I belonged some place, you know. . . ." The movies first alienated teen, **James Dean**, tries to make himself understood by sympathetic juvenile officer Edward Platt. *Rebel Without a Cause* (1955, Warner Bros.).

9193 "Gentlemen of the court, there are times when I am ashamed to be a member of the human race. This is one such occasion. It's impossible for me to summarize a case for the defense when I have never been allowed a reasonable opportunity to present a defense." **Kirk Douglas** expresses his disgust after three of his men are sentenced to death by a firing squad to serve as object lessons for the other soldiers in a World War I French regiment. *Paths of Glory* (1957, United Artists).

9194 "I'm so ashamed, now I'm just somebody who's had an affair." **Diane Baker** is in a hospital after jumping out of her lover Bob Evans' speeding car. She's lost the baby she was carrying, which suits Evans. She thought he was taking her to a justice of the peace, but he was driving her to an abortionist. *The Best of Everything* (1959, 20th Century-Fox).

9195 "I will make the world so noisy and disgusting that even you will be ashamed of yourself." Devil **Peter Cook** makes a spiteful God laugh and laugh. *Bedazzled* (1967, GB, 20th Century-Fox).

9196 "I was more ashamed of being a homosexual than a murderer." Closeted homosexual murderer **William Windom** leaves a written confession before committing suicide. *The Detective* (1968, 20th Century-Fox).

9197 "Don't be ashamed, nothing is wrong, let it all hang out." Call girl **Jane Fonda** encourages a customer to tell her his fantasies. *Klute* (1971, Warner Bros.).

9198 "There's a lot of shit that I did over there that I find fucking hard to live with." Paralyzed from the waist down, Vietnam veteran **Jon Voight**'s voice trembles as he speaks to a group of high school students who are thinking of joining the armed forces. *Coming Home* (1978, United Artists).

9199 "There is no shame in being poor, only in dressing poor." Secret avenger **George Hamilton** plays the role of an effeminate dandy. *Zorro, the Gay Blade* (1981, 20th Century-Fox).

9200 BELLE STEINBERG CARROCA: "What are you ashamed of?" BENJY STONE: "Everything." **Lainie Kazan** and others of his Brooklyn family embarrass **Mark Linn-Baker** when he brings movie star Peter O'Toole home to dinner. *My Favorite Year* (1982, MGM-United Artists).

9201 "I think I already knew this one was going to be trouble. Still a person shouldn't be ashamed to wish for love." In voice-over, **Noni Hazelhurst**, a freewheeling single mother who frequently changes lovers, eyes a new prospect. *Monkey Grip* (1983, Australia, Cinecom).

9202 "What do you say we try something tonight that even we'll be ashamed of in the morning?" Brooklyn luncheonette owner **Elliott Gould** avoided marriage to his uncle Sid Caesar's choice, Jewish Carol Kane, a wild and kinky woman into spiked heels, whips and assorted other sexual gadgets. Gould ends up with the woman he's loved all along, shiksa Margaux Hemingway. *Over the Brooklyn Bridge* (1984, MGM-United Artists).

9203 "It's a damn shame when Russians can borrow money for their wheat but an American veteran can't borrow money for his boat." Bankrupt shrimp boat captain **Ed Harris** finds that appeals to patriotism don't win him any points in applying for a loan from a bank. *Alamo Bay* (1985, Tri-Star).

9204 "Isn't it a shame how you kill yourself getting a guy in shape so he can take care of you?" **Elaine May** comments on a woman's burden. *In the Spirit* (1990, Castle Hill).

9205 LUCY: "Tell me what you've done that's shameful, even though I've done worse." GEORGE: "I've done nothing." LUCY: "That's shameful." **Lil Taylor** is shocked by **Dermont Mulroney**'s confession. *Bright Angel* (1991, Hemdale).

Shape *see* APPEARANCES, BODIES, SIZE

Sharing *see* EQUALITY, GIFTS AND GIVING, PARTICIPATION

Shocks

see also DISTURBANCES, STIMULATION, SURPRISES, VIOLENCE

9206 "Afraid I'll shock the duchess? Don't you suppose she's ever seen a French postcard?" **Jean Harlow** teases Clark Gable about Mary Astor when he demands that Harlow let down the blinds while she's taking a bath in a rain barrel. *Red Dust* (1932, MGM).

9207 "I confess I find his whole attitude un-American." Wealthy **Henry Kolker** is shocked by the lack of ambition or interest in making money of his daughter Doris Nolan's fiancé Cary Grant *Holiday* (1938, Columbia).

9208 "Child, you're out of your mind. You can't wear red to the Olympus Ball." **Fay Bainter** is shocked by her head-strong niece Bette Davis' determination to wear the color of whores to a cotillion, rather than white, signifying purity and virginity. *Jezebel* (1938, Warner Bros.).

9209 "I'm used to being top banana in the shock department." **Audrey Hepburn** is jaded with George Peppard. *Breakfast at Tiffany's* (1961, Paramount).

9210 "You didn't! What if he beams it off some satellite?" **Andie MacDowell** is shocked when her sister Laura San Giacomo admits that she allowed James Spader to videotape her talking about sex, disrobing and masturbating. *sex, lies and videotape* (1989, Miramax).

9211 "Oh, look what's happened; I've got a run in my panty-hose. . . I'm not wearing panty hose." For the fun of it, streetwalker **Julia Roberts** shocks a well-to-do, middle-aged couple by giving them an eyeful of her beautiful legs and thighs in the lobby of the Regent Beverly Wilshire Hotel. The elegant looking grey-haired lady says to her husband, "Close your mouth, dear." *Pretty Woman* (1990, Touchstone-Buena Vista).

Shoes

see also CLOTHES, RUNNING AND RUNNERS

9212 "Fine thing when a horse can get shoes and humans can't." Stirring a kettle of soap, **Vivien Leigh** complains about the scarcity of things during Reconstruction. *Gone with the Wind* (1939, Selznick-MGM).

9213 "And remember, never let those ruby slippers off your feet for a moment, or you'll be at the mercy of the Wicked Witch of the West." **Billie Burke** warns Judy Garland about Margaret Hamilton. *The Wizard of Oz* (1939, MGM).

9214 "I walked my legs off. . . until my shoes were so thin I could count the cracks in the pavement through them." Survivor **Joan Crawford** recalls the frustration of trying to find work after her divorce, having no experience except as a mother and housekeeper. *Mildred Pierce* (1945, Warner Bros.).

9215 "Take off the red shoes." With her dying words, ballerina **Moira Shearer** demands to be rid of the accursed red ballet slippers that have brought her so much fame and unhappiness. *The Red Shoes* (1948, GB, The Archers-GFD).

9216 "I hate shoes, Mr. Dawes. I wear them to dance or to show myself, but I feel afraid in shoes and I feel safe with my feet in the dirt." Beautiful Spanish dancer **Ava Gardner** tells Humphrey Bogart about her own special foot fetish. *The Barefoot Contessa* (1954, United Artists).

9217 "They were Italian; now they're practical." **Michael Douglas** uses a machete to hack off the high heels of the shoes of complaining Kathleen Turner so she can maneuver better in the Colombian underbrush. *Romancing the Stone* (1984, 20th Century-Fox).

Shootings

see also DEATH AND DYING, EXPLOSIONS, KILLINGS, MILITARY, WEAPONS

9218 "Don't worry about me. I can shoot straight, if I don't have to shoot too far." **Vivien Leigh** ignores Clark Gable's warning and drives to her lumber mill via dangerous Shantytown. *Gone with the Wind* (1939, Selznick-MGM).

9219 HATFIELD: "Marshal, make room for one more! I'm offering my protection to this lady. I can shoot fairly straight if there's a need for it." CURLY WILCOX: "That's been proved too many times, Hatfield!" Gambler **John Carradine** steps into the stagecoach, telling sheriff **George Bancroft** that he will act as protector of pregnant passenger Louise Platt. *Stagecoach* (1939, United Artists).

9220 "Go ahead and shoot, you'll be doing me a favor." **Humphrey Bogart** doesn't care if he lives or dies as his one-time lover Ingrid Bergman tremblingly threatens to shoot him unless he gives her the Letters of Transit that will allow her husband, resistance leader Paul Henreid, to escape to Lisbon. *Casablanca* (1942, Warner Bros.).

9221 "Well, now, if you're going to shoot me, at—at least be honest about it. You don't give a hoot about Carol and you never have. I'd rather be shot by a jealous woman than a noble one anyway. Now don't you think we should sit down quietly and think up a little better reason to shoot me than that?" **Van Heflin** attempts to reason with jealous, obsessed, gun-toting Joan Crawford. *Possessed* (1947, Warner Bros.).

9222 "He was playing her fast and loose so she caught him out and popped him a few 32 calibers. Serves him right, the two-timer." **Katharine Hepburn** reads in the newspaper that Judy Holliday shot and wounded her philandering husband Tom Ewell in front of mistress Jean Hagen. *Adam's Rib* (1949, MGM).

9223 "Oh, yes. I have received quite a few appeals from resurrected Romanovs. It seems the Bolshevik firing squads were poor shots." Insensitive Empress **Helen Hayes** is unimpressed with Ingrid Bergman's claim to be her granddaughter. *Anastasia* (1956, 20th Century-Fox).

9224 "I remember hearing shots. But they didn't seem to be connected with me. They seemed far away. . . like somebody else was doing the shooting." **Ben Gazzara** gives a good impersonation of a man who didn't know what he was doing when he shot and killed his wife's rapist. *Anatomy of a Murder* (1959, Columbia).

9225 "Everything happens to me. Now I'm shot by a child." Outlaw and murderer **Jeff Corey** has no one to blame but himself. He told Kim Darby how to cock the old horse pistol she shoots him with. *True Grit* (1969, Paramount).

9226 "Nothing wrong with shooting as long as the right people get shot." **Clint Eastwood**, as Dirty Harry, believes he's one who knows who are the right people to shoot. *Magnum Force* (1973, Warner Bros.).

9227 KIT: "I shot him in the stomach." HOLLY: "Is he upset?" **Martin Sheen** and **Sissy Spacek** are quite matter-of-fact about the murder of her father Warren Oates. After all, Oates did shoot and kill her dog out of spite. *Badlands* (1974, Warner Bros.).

9228 "You have to think about one shot. One shot is what it's all about. The deer has to be taken with one shot. I try to tell people that. . . they don't listen." **Robert DeNiro** insists to his hunting companions that there's a right and wrong way to the ritual of taking the life of a deer. *The Deer Hunter* (1978, Universal).

9229 "I shot your pig. It tormented me. I shot it." **Mary Steenburgen** unashamedly confesses to farmer Rip Torn that she eliminated a swinish swine. *Cross Creek* (1981, Universal).

9230 "Honey, I've been shot at more times than you've been laid." We suppose that New York detective **Robert Urich** and lady sheriff JoBeth Williams can trade war stories. *Endangered Species* (1982, MGM-United Artists).

9231 "He was wearing a bulletproof vest." Professional hitman **Charles Bronson** casually explains why he blew the head off a particular victim. *The Evil That Men Do* (1984, Tri-Star).

9232 "Because it's very hard to shoot yourself while cleaning it." Top sergeant **James Garner** explains why he keeps a fully equipped, operable Sherman tank as a memento. *Tank* (1984, Universal).

9233 "After we rotate back to the real world, we're gonna miss not havin' anyone worth shootin'." **Kieron Jecchinis**, as Crazy Earl, poses for a photograph next to the bodies of dead Vietnamese troopers. *Full Metal Jacket* (1987, Warner Bros.).

9234 "If we join the union, they shoot us. If we don't join the union, you shoot us." Italian immigrant coal miner **Joe Grifasi** tells union organizer Chris Cooper that he doesn't see that he has much choice. Cooper replies, "Well, that's one way of looking at it." *Matewan* (1987, Cinecom).

9235 "Dad, it's not how many people you shoot, it's who you shoot." Black 20s mobster **Eddie Murphy** makes a distinction for Richard Pryor. *Harlem Nights* (1989, Paramount).

9236 "I wanted to shoot people." **Jamie Lee Curtis** has a tongue-in-cheek response to all the people who ask why a pretty peaceful young woman like her would want to become a New York cop. Of course on her first night of duty, she blows away a hold-up man. *Blue Steel* (1990, Vestron-MGM-United Artists).

9237 "Ya gonna shoot to death a deer? A sweet, innocent, leaf-eatin,' doe-eyed little deer? Imagine you're a deer. You're prancing along, ya get thirsty, ya spot a little brook, ya put ya little deer lips down to the clear water—Bam!—a fuckin' bullet rips off part of ya head, ya brains are lying in little bloody pieces. . . Now I ask ya, would ya give a fuck what kind of pants the son of a bitch who shot ya was wearin'?" Delightful **Marisa Tomei** lectures in her best Brooklyn accent when her boy friend Joe Pesci wonders what he should wear to go deer hunting. *My Cousin Vinny* (1992, 20th Century-Fox).

Shops and Shopping

see also BUYING AND SELLING, CUSTOMERS, SALESMEN

9238 "You know, I think we should take a stroll on Fifth Avenue and look at the shops. You'd be surprised at how reasonable things are these days." Show girl **Aline MacMahon** wants to take wealthy Guy Kibbee on a shopping spree for her. *Gold Diggers of 1933* (1933, Warner Bros.).

9239 "I've been shopping till I'm dropping." **Everley Gregg**, as Dolly Messiter, trills on as she interrupts the final farewell of Celia Johnson and Trevor Howard. *Brief Encounter* (1946, GB, Cineguild-Rank).

9240 "I think I'll go down to Solitary tonight and do some shopping." **Nick Benedict**, as Smiley, is a rapist guard in a woman's prison. *The Naked Cage* (1986, Cannon).

9241 "You were once smart and promising and funny, and I couldn't wait to see what you have made of that promise. What you have become is a compulsive shopper." **Craig T. Nelson** wants a divorce from his wife Shelley Long. She's proud of her specialty. See the next entry. *Troop Beverly Hills* (1989, Weintraub).

9242 "I may be a beginner in some things, but I'm a black-belt in shopping." **Shelley Long**, troop leader of the Beverly Hills chapter of the Wilderness Girls, leads her troop on a shopping spree on Rodeo Drive. *Troop Beverly Hills* (1989, Weintraub).

9243 "I lost my will to shop." Despairing **Shelley Long** has taken to her bed in her luxurious Beverly Hills home with several large bottles of imported mineral water. *Troop Beverly Hills* (1989, Weintraub).

9244 "What are they. . . shopping together?" Prostitute **Julia Roberts** sarcastically questions Richard Gere who admits to having both an ex-wife and an ex-girl friend back in New York. *Pretty Woman* (1990, Touchstone-Buena Vista).

Shows

see also DEMONSTRATIONS, ENTERTAINMENT, PERFORMANCES, THEATERS

9245 "Jones and Berry are doing a show." The news passes by word-of-mouth from one unemployed show girl to another that producers Robert McWade and Ned Sparks are planning to stage a Broadway musical despite the Depression. *42nd Street* (1933, Warner Bros.).

9246 "All right, everybody. Quiet and listen to me. Tomorrow morning, we're going to start a show. We're going to rehearse for five weeks, and I mean scheduled time. You're going to work and sweat and work some more. You're going to work days and you're going to work nights, and you're going to work between time when I think you need it. You're going to dance until your feet fall off and you're not able to stand up any longer. But five weeks from now, we're going to have a show." Theater director **Warner Baxter** gives a pep talk to his dancers. *42nd Street* (1933, Warner Bros.).

9247 "Are you kids willing to stick together and pull yourselves out of a hole? I've got an idea. Our folks think we're babes in arms, huh? Well, we'll show them whether we're babes in arms or not. I'm going to write a show for us, and put it on right here in Seaport. . . We'll get every kid in the town on our side, and we'll start right now. What do you say?" With **Mickey Rooney**'s speech, a cliché is born:

"Hey kids, let's put on a show." *Babes in Arms* (1939, MGM).

9248 "You've been all over the world and you've met all kinds of people. But you never write about them. You only write about yourself. You think the whole war's a show put on for you to cover like a Broadway play!" Socially conscious seaman **John Hodiak** accuses fashion writer Tallulah Bankhead of being a selfish, self-centered, useless individual. The two are among the handful of individuals thrown together in a lifeboat they used to escape from their ship which was sunk by a German U-boat. *Lifeboat* (1944, 20th Century-Fox).

9249 CHIP: "I've only got one day and I want to see all the famous landmarks of the city." BRUNHILDE: "Stick with me, kid. I'll show you plenty." Naïve sailor **Frank Sinatra** is taken in hand by man-hungry New York cabbie **Betty Garrett**. *On the Town* (1949, MGM).

9250 "It's show time." It's how pill-popping, chain-smoking, exhausted choreographer **Roy Scheider** gets himself going each morning. *All That Jazz* (1979, Columbia-20th Century-Fox).

9251 "Show business is dog eat dog. It's worse than dog eat dog. It's dog doesn't return dog's phone calls." Gloomy producer of unsold TV documentaries **Woody Allen** barely survives in show business. *Crimes and Misdemeanors* (1989, Orion).

Shyness *see* MODESTY, TRUST, VANITIES

Sickness

see also DISEASES, DOCTORS AND DENTISTS, HEALTH, MEDICINE, MINDS, NURSES, PSYCHOLOGY AND PSYCHIATRY, TREATS AND TREATMENT

9252 "When I think what goes on in the minds of these lice, I want to vomit!" Police Commissioner **Edwin Maxwell** is sickened by gangsters. *Scarface* (1932, United Artists).

9253 "[Is Cherry Chester] some new kind of soft drink?. . . marshmallow-faced movie stars make me sick." As "Anthony Amberton," big-time writer **Henry Fonda** expresses no interest in meeting movie star "Cherry Chester," played by Margaret Sullavan. But using his real name John Smith, he meets Sarah Brown, Sullavan's real name. They fall in love, get married and go on to honeymoon in a New England inn. *The Moon's Our Home* (1936, Paramount).

9254 WOLF VON FRANKENSTEIN: "But he's supposed to have been destroyed." YGOR: "No. Cannot be destroyed. Cannot die. Your father made him live for always. Now he's sick. Make him well, Frankenstein." **Basil Rathbone** is shocked when hunchback **Bela Lugosi** informs him that his father's monster is still alive. *Son of Frankenstein* (1939, Universal).

9255 ALBERTA MARLOW: "You make me sick, and if you stay here one minute longer I'll prove it to you." RICK LELAND: "Are you getting sick?" ALBERTA MARLOW: "How do girls usually act when you kiss them?" During a rough sea voyage, **Mary Astor** fumes at **Humphrey Bogart**. *Across the Pacific* (1941, Warner Bros.).

9256 SANDRA: "Why don't you tell me I'm smoking too much?" MAGGIE: "If it takes your mind off the weather. . . ." SANDRA: "That's right, humor me! Maggie the martyr! You make me sick!" Showing no gender prejudice, pregnant **Mary Astor** is sick of living with patient **Bette Davis** during her "confinement." *The Great Lie* (1941, Warner Bros.).

9257 "Maybe it's easier for the dying to be honest. I'm sick of you, sick of this house, sick of my unhappy life with you. I'm sick of your brothers and their dirty tricks to make a dime. There must be better ways of getting rich than building sweatshops and pounding the bones of the town to make dividends for you to spend. You'll wreck this town, you and your brothers. You'll wreck this country, you and your kind, if they let you. But not me. I'll die my own way, and I'll do it without making the world any worse. I leave that to you." Dying **Herbert Marshall** tells his greedy wife Bette Davis just what he thinks of her. *The Little Foxes* (1941, Goldwyn-RKO).

9258 "[She's] no more sick than a molting canary." Hateful **Gladys Cooper** dismisses the suggestion that her daughter Bette Davis needs psychological help. *Now, Voyager* (1942, Warner Bros.).

9259 "We are speaking about a schizophrenic, not a valentine." Psychiatrist **Michael Chekhov** wants to turn in Ingrid Bergman's patient Gregory Peck, wanted by the police for suspicion of murder. *Spellbound* (1945, United Artists).

9260 "You can have a hangover from other things than alcohol. I had one from women. Women make me sick." Maybe so, but private eye **Humphrey Bogart** doesn't avoid women. *The Big Sleep* (1946, Warner Bros.).

9261 "Terry's not well. She's sick inside. How it got started I don't know. An accident when you were babies, perhaps, that you've both forgotten." Psychiatrist **Lew Ayres** tells Olivia de Havilland, as Ruth, about Olivia de Havilland, as her twin sister Terry. *The Dark Mirror* (1946, Universal).

9262 "Sometimes I think I'm not as sick as the others. But they say that maybe if you think you're well, then you're really sick. If I say I'm sick, maybe that means I'm well." Mental patient **Olivia de Havilland** finds herself in a Catch 22 situation. *The Snake Pit* (1948, 20th Century-Fox).

9263 "You like to get hurt. Always picking the wrong guy. It's a sickness with a lot of women. Always looking for a new way to get hurt by a new man. Get smart. There hasn't been a new man since Adam." **Richard Conte** tells Susan Hayward to wise up. Seems the problem for some women is still around in the 90s. *House of Strangers* (1949, 20th Century-Fox).

9264 "Talk about dream worlds! You've got a pathological fix on a woman who's not only a criminal, but who screams if you come near her." **Tippi Hedren** accuses Sean Connery of being about as sick as she is. His reply is, "Well, I didn't say I was perfect." *Marnie* (1964, Universal).

9265 "You're so full of competition. You's so full of God knows what kind of sickness." Proletarian artist **George Segal** attacks his wealthy neurotic lover Elizabeth Ashley. *Ship of Fools* (1965, Columbia).

9266 LINDA CHRISTIE: "I got up, helped him pack, drove him to the airport and threw up in the United Airlines Terminal." ALLAN FELIX: "Yeah, that's a good terminal. I've thrown up there." Neglected **Diane Keaton** tells her troubles to **Woody Allen** after her husband Tony Roberts has left on another of his many business trips. *Play It Again, Sam* (1972, Paramount).

9267 ELLIOTT GARFIELD: "How do you feel?" LUCY MCFADDEN: "Did you see *The Exorcist*? Then you better leave the room." When **Richard Dreyfuss** asks about **Quinn Cumming**'s upset stomach, the pre-teen still breaks them off, even though sick enough to vomit. *The Goodbye Girl* (1977, MGM-United Artists).

9268 "I have terrible cramps, I'm bleeding profusely and I want to vomit on the table." **Frances Lee McCain** announces on camera that she's suffering with her period in this comedy about documentary filmmaker Albert Brooks, who moves in with a "typical" American family to record every aspect of their troubled lives. *Real Life* (1979, Paramount).

9269 "Fresh air makes me nauseous." National columnist **John Belushi** whines after he's been banished to the wilds with ornithologist Blair Brown, who's studying bald eagles. *Continental Divide* (1981, Universal).

9270 "Ladies are unwell. . . gentlemen vomit." **Peter O'Toole** corrects Mark Linn-Baker who announces he thinks he's going to be unwell. *My Favorite Year* (1982, MGM-United Artists).

9271 "I think I'm going to vomit on the floor." Two-bit gun-runner **Chevy Chase** shoots himself in the foot (twice). *Deal of the Century* (1983, Warner Bros.).

9272 "This is my ninth sick day of the semester. It's getting tough coming up with new illnesses. . . So I better make this one count." High school truant **Matthew Broderick** makes an aside to the camera. *Ferris Bueller's Day Off* (1986, Paramount).

9273 "Some people get fever blisters when they're sick. I get a long tail and lizard skin." As a result of a gypsy curse, **Scott Valentine** is transformed into a hideous creature anytime he's sexually aroused. *My Demon Lover* (1987, New Line).

9274 "I feel like I'm going to puke." With these words, narcotics agent **Jason Patric** bleeds to death from a shotgun blast to his thigh. *Rush* (1991, MGM-Path).

9275 "What won't make me vomit?" Snotty prep school brat **Ethan Randall** sarcastically replies to a fat waitress in a greasy spoon diner, who asks "What'd you like, honey?" *Dutch* (1992, 20th Century-Fox).

Sight and Sights

see also EYES, VISIONS AND VISUALIZATIONS

9276 "Be seeing you soon." **Humphrey Bogart**, as killer Duke Mantee, fatally wounds Leslie Howard, at the latter's request. Bogie knows his number is up, also. *The Petrified Forest* (1936, Warner Bros.).

9277 "How, by just closing my eyes and pretending it didn't happen? I wish it was as easy as that but it isn't. You see, I keep seeing that poor little sister of mine lying there with that fear still in her eyes and her pretty little head all twisted." Prostitute **Bette Davis** can't ignore the fact that mob boss Eduardo Ciannelli had her younger sister killed because she wouldn't work as a whore. *Marked Woman* (1937, Warner Bros.).

9278 "We all see with the same pair of eyes, but we don't see the same things." Kindly prison Chaplain **William Gargan** lectures the warden's skeptical wife. He believes there's goodness in even the most hardened con. *You Only Live Once* (1937, United Artists).

9279 "I guess when you're used to standing on the outside looking in, you can see a lot of things other people can't." Lonely loner **John Garfield** sounds sorry for himself. *Four Daughters* (1938, Warner Bros.).

9280 "Panic's a pretty sight, isn't it?" Pulling her into his carriage, **Clark Gable** rescues Vivien Leigh from the fleeing crowds in Atlanta streets. *Gone with the Wind* (1939, Selznick-MGM).

9281 GEORGE: "We're gonna have a little place. . . ." LENNY: "We gonna have a little place!" GEORGE: "We're gonna have a cow and a pig, and some chickens. . . a field of alfalfa. . . ." LENNY: "For the rabbits!. . . And I get to tend the rabbits. . . and we could live off the fat of the land!" GEORGE: "Just keep lookin' across the river. Like you can really see it. Just keep lookin'. . . It's gonna be nice there. . . There ain't gonna be trouble. No fights. There ain't gonna be nobody mean." LENNY: "Yeah—I can see it! Right over there! George! I can see it!" When childlike giant **Lon Chaney, Jr.** accidentally kills Betty Field, **Burgess Meredith** realizes he must kill his friend before he is caught by the authorities and locked up like an animal. While repeating their dream of a little farm, Meredith takes out a pistol and shoots Chaney. *Of Mice and Men* (1939, United Artists).

9282 "No one can really see what he loves." Blind pianist **Hans Yaray** composes an entire concerto as a "description" of Merle Oberon's beautiful face. *Lydia* (1941, Korda-United Artists).

9283 "You have each other, and a man and a woman in love have a gift of sight that is not granted to others." Housekeeper **Mildred Natwick** is one of only two people who understand that disfigured Robert Young and exceedingly plain Dorothy McGuire can see each other as handsome and beautiful, respectively, when they are alone in their cottage. *The Enchanted Cottage* (1945, RKO).

9284 WIFE: "I'll. . . never leave here. I'm part of Africa, and Africa is part of me." RONALD KORNBLOW: "Well, I'm certainly seeing the best part of Africa." When a local sheik leaves one of his wives behind at **Groucho Marx**'s Casablanca hotel, he asks her to run away with him as he leers at her décolletage. *A Night in Casablanca* (1946, United Artists).

9285 HOLLEY: "I didn't see that." JARVESS: "Well, I see it. I'll always see it and I don't want anyone to forget it." Wise-cracking GI **Van Johnson** turns away in disgust when he and conscientious **John Hodiak** spot an elderly woman picking through a garbage can for food in besieged Bastogne. *Battleground* (1949, MGM).

9286 "If you really want to see fireworks, it's better with the lights off. I have a feeling that tonight you're going to see one of the Riviera's most fascinating sights—I was talking about the fireworks." Sure she was. As she moves to switch off the light and turns to Cary Grant, **Grace Kelly** is certainly aware that he's admiring the loveliness of her low-cut gown and not the fireworks that can be seen from their window. *To Catch a Thief* (1955, Paramount).

9287 "We're all more or less blind; we can see precisely only the things we work with every day." Dutch painter **Hardy Kruger**, suspected of murdering his mistress, states the unifying theme of the film. *Blind Date* aka: *Chance Meeting* (1960, GB, Paramount).

9288 "You know what's wrong with you, Lewis? You've been sitting on a New Jersey porch for too long. You're out of touch. From my window here, I see everything that's going on in the world. Here I see old people, I see young people, nice people, bad people. I see holdups. I see drug addicts, ambulances, car crashes, jumpings from buildings. I see everything. You see a lawn mower and a milkman." **Walter Matthau** accuses his long-time comedy partner George Burns of being out of touch with life, whereas, he's kept vital and alive. *The Sunshine Boys* (1975, MGM).

9289 "When I broke the mirror of Sarah's existence, I became the first person outside of herself she had ever seen." One time nice guy, turned gangster-like tough guy **Jeff Bridges** refers to his over-sexed and self-absorbed wife Belinda Bauer. *The American Success Company* (1980, Columbia).

9290 "Golly! If the girls back home could see me now." **Bo Derek** thinks her friends would be impressed with her jungle conquest Miles O'Keeffe. *Tarzan, the Ape Man* (1981, MGM-United Artists).

9291 "I want to see more, more than any man has ever seen." Deranged scientist **Ted Sorel** develops a gruesome machine, called the Resonator, that activates a special sixth sense in the pineal gland, sometimes referred to as the third eye. Unfortunately, it also makes the possessor crave human brains. *From Beyond* (1986, Empire).

9292 "There's more to fighting than rest, sir. There's character, there's strength of heart. You should have seen us in action two days ago, sir. We were a sight to see. When do you want us?" **Matthew Broderick**, as gallant white Colonel Robert Gould Shaw, pleads with a senior officer to give his regiment of black civil war soldiers the honor of making a suicidal charge against a Confederate fort. *Glory* (1989, Tri-Star).

9293 "Do I have to see him?" At a party to celebrate the honor awarded him by the Catholic church, **Al Pacino** is annoyed that mobster Joe Mantegna intrudes and insists on seeing him. *The Godfather, Part III* (1991, Paramount).

Significance

see also CONSEQUENCES, IMPORTANCE

9294 "What does the war mean to me?" Adventuresome American **Gary Cooper** deserts the Italian ambulance corps during World War I to be with his love, English nurse Helen Hayes. *A Farewell to Arms* (1932, Paramount).

9295 JOE FABRINI: "I've always liked redheads." CASSIE HARTLEY: "Red means stop." JOE: "I'm color blind." Truck driver **George Raft** tries to make time with sassy waitress **Ann Sheridan**. *They Drive by Night* (1940, Warner Bros.).

9296 "The world has turned upside down, words don't mean what they're meant to mean. People are not what they should be." British agent **Nancy Coleman** warns New York intern John Garfield not to trust anyone. Unfortunately, he doesn't believe her until it's too late. *Dangerously They Live* (1942, Warner Bros.).

9297 "She was in the air I breathed and the food I ate." **Glenn Ford** tries to explain what title character Rita Hayworth means to him. *Gilda* (1946, Columbia).

9298 "A lot of women say no when they mean yes." Men like **Paul Newman** who won't take no for an answer from women like Joanne Woodward often are guilty of date-rape. *The Long, Hot Summer* (1958, 20th Century-Fox).

9299 "I think it means if I build a baseball field, Shoeless Joe Jackson will get to come back and play baseball again." **Kevin Costner** gives his inspired interpretation of the message of a bodiless voice in his corn field. *Field of Dreams* (1989, Universal).

Signs

see also EXISTENCE, INFORMATION AND INFORMERS, SYMBOLS

9300 "If it's a good picture, it's a Miracle." It's a sign at the entrance to Miracle Studios. *Hollywood Hotel* (1938, Warner Bros.).

9301 "Every werewolf is marked with that. He sees it in the palm of his next victim's hand." Winsome

Evelyn Ankers tells Lon Chaney, Jr. about the five-pointed star called the pentagram found on a silver-tipped cane with the head of a wolf. *The Wolf Man* (1941, Universal).

9302 "Your left hand shows your past. Your right hand shows your future. . . Go quickly. Go. . . I can't tell you anything tonight. . . Go quickly." As Fay Helm opens her right hand, gypsy fortune teller **Bela Lugosi**, who is a werewolf, sees the mark of the pentagram in her palm. She will be his next victim that night. *The Wolf Man* (1941, Universal).

9303 "I'm a Libra. What sign are you?" It's hard to believe that frightened **Jessica Lange** would wise-crack such a line to a giant ape with the hots for her. *King Kong* (1976, DeLaurentiis).

Silence

see also NOISES, QUIETNESS, SOUNDS, SPEECH AND SPEAKING, TALKS AND TALKING

9304 "I might say, sir, that I'm a Rolls-Royce for silence." A title card lets the audience know how **Clive Brook** gets his nickname. He also gets an employer when drunken Brook notices fearless burglar and killer George Bancroft at his work. *Underworld* (1927, silent, Paramount).

9305 "You, my dear, have the divine gift of silence." **Mary Forbes** speaks to her daughter Greta Garbo of a rare gift. *Anna Karenina* (1935, MGM).

9306 "There has never been such a silence." Title character **Elizabeth Taylor** reacts to the death of Richard Burton as Marc Antony. *Cleopatra* (1963, 20th Century-Fox).

9307 "You have the right to remain silent." Cop **Sylvester Stallone** solemnly intones as he prepares to silence a gasoline-soaked criminal by dropping a match on him. *Cobra* (1986, Warner Bros.)

Similarity *see* APPEARANCES, IDENTITIES, RESEMBLANCES

Simplicity

see also COMBINATIONS, EASE AND EASINESS, INNOCENCE, NAÏVETÉ, ORDINARINESS, PURITY

9308 "Ah, you can be had." **Mae West** believes it would be a simple thing to seduce undercover cop Cary Grant. *She Done Him Wrong* (1933, Paramount).

9309 "Well, wonderfully simple to buy a house, isn't it?" **Ray Milland** appears a bit dazed after he quickly strikes a deal for a mansion on a cliff with

Donald Crisp, even though he offered a low-ball price. *The Uninvited* (1944, Paramount).

9310 "I decided to look for a simple life. . . simple things." Young doctor **Lew Ayres** explains how he came to choose a small Nova Scotian village for his practice. *Johnny Belinda* (1948, Warner Bros.).

9311 "Less than a month ago, Santa Mira was like any other town. People with nothing but problems. Then out of the sky came a solution. Seeds drifting through space for years took root in a farmer's field. From the seeds came pods which had the power to reproduce themselves in the exact likeness of any form of life. Your new bodies are growing in there. They're taking you over cell for cell, atom for atom. There is no pain. Suddenly, while you're asleep, they'll absorb your minds, your memories and you're reborn into an untroubled world. Tomorrow you'll be one of them. There's no need for love. Love, desire, ambition, faith—without them life is so simple, believe me." Psychiatrist **Larry Gates**, who has already been changed over, ticks off the advantages to Kevin McCarthy of letting aliens take over his body. Filmed in the McCarthy era, the movie suggests some of the freedoms communist hunters would have American citizens give up. *Invasion of the Body Snatchers* (1956, Allied Artists).

9312 ELSA KNUDSEN: "My father says there's only right and wrong, good and evil, nothing in between. It isn't that simple, is it?" STEVE JUDD: "No, it isn't. It should be, but it isn't." **Mariette Hartley**, the repressed daughter of religious fanatic R.G. Armstrong, seeks some reassurance from aging, dignified, former lawman **Joel McCrea**. *Ride the High Country* (1962, MGM).

9313 "I think you are a very primitive people." Animal rights advocates would agree with alien **Jeff Bridges**, who is appalled when Karen Allen explains why a dead deer is tied to a hunter's car. Bridges proceeds to resurrect the animal. *Starman* (1984, Columbia).

Sincerity

see also HONESTY AND DISHONESTY, HYPOCRISY, INTEGRITY, TRUTH, TRUTH AND FALSEHOOD

9314 "I'm not always sincere—one can't be in this world, you know. But I am not sorry the mistake happened." Courtesan **Greta Garbo** flirts with handsome young Robert Taylor, whom she mistook for a rich man. *Camille* (1936, MGM).

9315 "When he's cockeyed drunk with sincerity, people can't resist him." **Katharine Hepburn** admires her estranged husband Spencer Tracy. *State of the Union* (1948, MGM).

9316 "There is no sincerity like a woman telling a lie." **Cecil Parker** speaks not unkindly about his sister-in-law, rich actress Ingrid Bergman. *Indiscreet* (1958, Warner Bros.).

9317 "Toadying is the sincerest form of contempt." Homosexual English lecturer **Alan Bates** is in position to know. *Butley* (1974, GB, Columbia).

9318 "A man is never lost as long as he keeps his eyes on the stars." Divorced **Jon Voight** expresses appalling sincerity in this slow, sentimental weeper. *Table for Five* (1983, Warner Bros.).

9319 JONATHAN: "I would kill or die to make love to you. . . That's not a lie." SASHA: "I know." **Anthony Edwards**' sincerity is recognized and rewarded by beautiful, mysterious **Linda Fiorentino**. *Gotcha!* (1985, Universal).

Singing and Singers *see* DANCING AND DANCERS, ENTERTAINMENTS AND ENTERTAINERS, MUSIC, PERFORMANCES, SONGS AND SINGING, VOICES

Sinister *see* DARKNESS, EVILNESS

Sins and Sinners

see also BADNESS, CONFESSIONS, CRIMES AND CRIMINALS, DEVILS, EVILNESS, FAULTS, FORGIVENESS, GOD, GOOD AND EVIL, GUILT, HEAVEN AND HELL, HELL, LAWS, LEGALITY AND ILLEGALITY, PUNISHMENTS, RELIGIONS

9320 "I'm hangin' on the edge of hell!. . . I've been a wicked woman! Don't let me sin no more!" Beautiful black woman **Nina Mae McKinney** lives among low lifes in a Tennessee community. She seeks forgiveness for her sins. The film is a daring all-black feature. *Hallelujah* (1929, MGM).

9321 "Well, sir, I suppose every train carries its cargo of sin, but this train is burdened with more than its share." Clergyman **Lawrence Grant** objects to the presence of shady-lady Marlene Dietrich and Anna May Wong as fellow passengers. *Shanghai Express* (1932, Paramount).

9322 "I am thinking of a woman who did wrong in the sight of God. Her name was Jezebel." Gracious and staunchly loyal **Fay Bainter** finally turns on her selfish, vicious niece Bette Davis. *Jezebel* (1938, Warner Bros.).

9323 "My son, she goes where there's no east or west, and she will be Judged by one who alone knows how great or how little were her sins." Priest **Ernest Cossart** comforts Robert Taylor after half-caste Hedy Lamarr kills Eurasian villain Joseph

Schildkraut and then herself. *Lady of the Tropics* (1939, MGM).

9324 "Jack, there's something on everybody. Man is conceived in sin and born in corruption." Politician **Broderick Crawford** employs John Ireland to collect useful dirt on just about everyone. Crawford believes that Ireland can find the sins of a political opponent, respected judge Raymond Greenleaf. Ireland doubts it, but Crawford is right. *All the King's Men* (1949, Columbia).

9325 "Why, yes, of course. Isn't that what we're all most concerned with? Sin." Wacky **Jennifer Jones** discusses sin with crooked Robert Morley. *Beat the Devil* (1954, GB, United Artists).

9326 "Do you take sinners here?" Seeking a place to hold his floating crap game, **Frank Sinatra** leads a group of Broadway gamblers into a Salvation Army-like mission. *Guys and Dolls* (1955, Goldwyn-MGM).

9327 "I was a sinner, but I didn't sin every day. Why do the gods punish me every day?" No Job he, blind prophet **Patrick Troughton** complains that the gods are petty. *Jason and the Argonauts* (1963, GB, Columbia).

9328 "If a woman sleeps alone, it puts a shame on all men. God has a very big heart, but there is one sin He will not forgive: if a woman calls a man to her bed and he will not go. I know because a very wise Turk told me." **Anthony Quinn** shares his own interpretation of God's will regarding sin. *Zorba the Greek* (1964, 20th Century-Fox).

9329 "I've lost all my sense of sin." Beatnik atheist artist **Elizabeth Taylor** confesses to minister Richard Burton. *The Sandpiper* (1965, MGM).

9330 "I want to confess today for the sins I will commit tomorrow." At confession, **Jean-Louis Trintignant** asks for absolution for his future sins. *The Conformist* (1970, Italy-Fr.-W. Ger., Mars-Marianne-Maran).

9331 "You don't make up for your sins in church—you do it in the streets." **Harvey Keitel**, who fancies himself a saint, knows that penance is not merely so many "Hail Marys." *Mean Streets* (1973, Warner Bros.).

9332 "I should have killed myself when he put it in me. . . After the first time. . . before we were married. Ralph promised never again. He promised. And I believed him. But sin never dies. Sin never dies." Fanatical, agitated **Piper Laurie** tells her suppressed daughter Sissy Spacek how the former's husband forced sex on her. *Carrie* (1976, United Artists).

9333 "In my family the biggest sin was to buy retail." **Woody Allen** is now involved in a bigger sin—all right, an injustice, then. He's fronting for blacklisted writers who can't sell their work on their own because of the communist witch hunts of the 1950s. *The Front* (1976, Columbia).

9334 "I have been with a man, which is a sin against nature." **Robby Benson** confesses having a homosexual encounter and throws himself off the Tallahatchie Bridge. *Ode to Billy Joe* (1976, Warner Bros.).

9335 "I cannot find hackers in the Ten Commandments." Priest **Judge Reinhold** hears Marianne Sagebrecht's confession of misusing credit cards and computer accounts. *Rosalie Goes Shopping* (1990, Germ.-Four Seasons).

9336 "It's a sin to kill an elephant. It's the only sin you can buy a license to do...I want to do it because it's a sin." John Huston–like director **Clint Eastwood** perversely explains why he wants to shoot a bull elephant while he's filming in Africa. *White Hunter, Black Heart* (1990, Warner Bros.).

Sizes

see also GREATNESS

9337 "You lost your size, Jerry, and I could never chase trains with a little man." **Carole Lombard** expresses her disappointment in her lover, con man Gary Cooper, when she learns he plans to sell his daughter Shirley Temple for $75,000. *Now and Forever* (1934, Paramount).

9338 "Small, small, we can make the whole world small." Wonderfully sinister **Rafaela Ottiano** continues the research of her deceased husband Henry B. Walthall and perfects his technique for miniaturizing people. *The Devil Doll* (1936, MGM).

9339 "Gee, it's—it's bigger than just a show. Say it's everybody in the country." **Mickey Rooney** gets all choked-up at the enormity of the show featuring the teenage sons and daughters of retired vaudevillians. *Babes in Arms* (1939, MGM).

9340 "Sure, I was all those things and more! When Rocco talked everybody shut up and listened. What Rocco said went! Nobody was as big as Rocco. It'll be like that again, only more so! I'll be back up there one of these days and then you're really going to see something." According to deported mobster **Edward G. Robinson**, he's a once and future Mr. Big in the rackets. *Key Largo* (1948, Warner Bros.).

9341 MARGO CHANNING: "You bought the new girdle a size smaller." BIRDIE: "Maybe somethin' else grew a size larger." Stage actress **Bette Davis** and her maid **Thelma Ritter** disagree about sizes. *All About Eve* (1950, 20th Century-Fox).

9342 "No one ever brings anything small to a bar." Lush **James Stewart** understands the desperation that drives people to sit at a bar night after night. *Harvey* (1950, Universal).

9343 "Professor Elwell, you're a little man. It's not that you're short. You're little, in the mind and in the heart. Tonight you tried to make a man little whose boots you couldn't touch if you stood on tiptoe on top of the highest mountain in the world. And, as it turned out, you're even littler than you were before." **Finlay Currie**, a murderer who twice spent time in jail, ridicules Hume Cronyn, who tried to discredit brilliant philosopher-physician Cary Grant, Currie's friend and employer. *People Will Talk* (1951, 20th Century-Fox).

9344 "It's a hard world on little things." Narrator **Lillian Gish** speaks as the camera pans over bunnies, birds, and other small creatures—but she's really thinking of children. *The Night of the Hunter* (1955, United Artists).

9345 "Big Daddy! Now what makes him so big? His big heart? His big belly? Or his big money?" Constantly whining and drinking, **Paul Newman** turns his acid tongue on to his dying tyrannical father Burl Ives. *Cat on a Hot Tin Roof* (1958, MGM).

9346 "When I was a little boy, I wouldn't even let my mother undress me." **Cary Grant** resists a bit when Eva Marie Saint helps him out of his soiled suit. She reminds him that he's a big boy now. *North by Northwest* (1959, MGM).

9347 "Michael, we're bigger than U.S. Steel!" Mobster **Lee Strasberg** informs Al Pacino that organized crime is the biggest business in the United States. *The Godfather, Part II* (1974, Paramount).

9348 "How did she wind up with a runt like me?" Realizing he's no great shakes in the looks or build department, **James Woods** is proud that he has a wife as beautiful as Sean Young. *The Boost* (1988, Hemdale).

9349 "I wish I were big." Twelve-year-old **David Moscow** makes the wish at a carnival booth and the next morning wakes up as adult Tom Hanks. *Big* (1988, 20th Century-Fox).

9350 "Adam and Eve are in the Garden of Eden and he says, 'Stand back! I don't know how big this thing gets.'" Aspiring stand-up comedian **Tom Hanks** gets off a raunchy one. *Punchline* (1989, Columbia).

9351 "I crap bigger than you." Rugged cowboy **Jack Palance** snarls at greenhorn Billy Crystal, who has just referred to Palance as a lunatic, not knowing he was right behind him at the time. *City Slickers* (1991, Columbia).

Skin

see also ANIMALS, BODIES, FACES

9352 "I swore I would skin him alive, but he died on me—damn him." **Hobart Bosworth** takes Wallace Beery "behind the door" to skin him alive. *Behind the Door* (1920, silent, Ince-Paramount).

9353 "I hate to tell you, dear, but your skin makes the Rocky Mountains look like velvet." Beauty parlor operator **Dennie Moore** breaks the bad news to an unfortunate customer. *The Women* (1939, MGM).

9354 "I wouldn't give you the skin off a grape." Maniacal gangster **Richard Widmark** makes it clear to assistant D.A. Brian Donlevy that he'll get no cooperation from him. *Kiss of Death* (1947, 20th Century-Fox).

9355 "Wild things leave skins behind, so that the fugitive kind can always follow their kind." **Joanne Woodward** finds Marlon Brando's snakeskin jacket in the smoking debris of a fire. *The Fugitive Kind* (1960, United Artists).

9356 GEORGE: "It's a bit odd becoming a school girl at your age." DORIS: "Listen, you think it's easy being the only one in the class with clear skin?" **Alan Alda** isn't so certain he approves of his once-a-year mistress **Ellen Burstyn** as a hippie college student. *Same Time, Next Year* (1978, Universal).

9357 "That's what my girl friend would look like without skin." Hoodish teen **Elias Koteas** points proudly to an original drawing he's made during detention class. *Some Kind of Wonderful* (1987, Paramount).

9358 "She lay there all day with her Sidney Sheldon novels and her coconut oil. The doctor said she had skin like a reptile." High-rolling mob figure **James Caan**, an incurable romantic, recalls his beloved wife who died of skin cancer. Nicolas Cage's girl friend Sarah Jessica Parker reminds Caan of the dearly deceased. *Honeymoon in Vegas* (1992, Columbia).

Slavery and Slaves

see also FREEDOMS, SERVANTS AND SERVITUDE

9359 JACK CLAYTON: "I could be your slave." TIRA: "Well, I guess that could be arranged." Since **Cary Grant**'s made the offer, **Mae West** supposes she could put up with having a handsome, virile and charming man fulfilling her every whim. *I'm No Angel* (1933, Paramount).

9360 "I resented you because you're beautiful and I'm a slave." Because he gave medical aid to rebels against the king, British surgeon **Errol Flynn** has been condemned to the life of a slave at the Caribbean plantation of Olivia de Havilland's uncle Lionel Atwill. *Captain Blood* (1935, Warner Bros.).

9361 ARABELLA BISHOP: "I don't wish to be bought by you." PETER BLOOD: "As a lady once said to a slave—you are hardly in a position to have anything to say about it." **Olivia de Havilland** is incensed that former slave **Errol Flynn** has purchased her from a pirate. *Captain Blood* (1935, Warner Bros.).

9362 "You've got to set Peggy free. You treat her like a slave." Coast Guardsman **Robert Ryan** warns blind artist Charles Bickford about his young wife Joan Bennett. *The Woman on the Beach* (1947, RKO)

9363 "We are opposed to slavery, but we do not believe it is right to kill one man to free another." Quaker **Dorothy McGuire** explains a belief in the greater of the two evils to Union officer Theodore Newton. *Friendly Persuasion* (1956, Allied Artists).

9364 NEFRETIRI: "Why aren't you kneeling at the feet of a princess?" MOSES: "I'm afraid the mud-pits have stiffened my knees, royal one." Princess **Anne Baxter** gets a double meaning reply from former prince, now a slave, **Charlton Heston**. *The Ten Commandments* (1956, Paramount).

9365 SUSAN GALE: "Trafficking in human lives is everyone's concern. Either you're for it or you're against it." AHMED: "Well, I'm for it." It shouldn't surprise **Barbara Eden** that slave trader **Peter Lorre** is "for it." *Five Weeks in a Balloon* (1962, 20th Century-Fox).

Sleep

see also BEDS, DREAMS, NIGHTS, UNCONSCIOUSNESS

9366 "Not with that alley cat squawking out there. I'm not used to sleeping nights anyway." **Jean Harlow**, wearing a cheap satin gown, walks into Clark Gable's room, announcing she can't sleep and also reminding him of her main occupation. *Red Dust* (1932, MGM).

9367 "Eleven o'clock in Grover's Corners. Everybody's resting. Tomorrow's going to be another day. You get a good rest, too. Good night." Stage manager **Frank Craven** directs the play's last line to the audience. *Our Town* (1940, Principal Arts).

9368 "Don't strain yourself. I can always sleep in a tree." Stranded **Ann Sheridan** responds to Helen Vinson's unenthusiastic offer to put her up for the night. *Torrid Zone* (1940, Warner Bros.).

9369 "You better go to bed, Hopsy, I think I can sleep peacefully now." Having aroused Henry Fonda, **Barbara Stanwyck** acts the innocent as she pours cold water on his expectations during their first shipboard tryst. *The Lady Eve* (1941, Paramount).

9370 "Get plenty of sleep." It's **W.C. Fields**' practical prescription for a huge Turkish passenger on an airplane who claims of being plagued with insomnia. *Never Give a Sucker an Even Break* (1941, Universal).

9371 "Benjamin, I want you to know I'm available to you. If you won't sleep with me this time—If you won't sleep with me this time, Benjamin, I want you to know you can call me up any time you want, and we'll make some kind of arrangement." **Anne Bancroft** very calmly tells a nervous young Dustin Hoffman that she wishes to have an affair with him. *The Graduate* (1967, Embassy).

9372 "Oh, my God—somebody's been sleeping in my dress!" **Beatrice Arthur**'s reacts upon awakening after a hard night of partying. *Mame* (1974, Warner Bros.).

9373 "Why don't you take some sodium pentothal? Then you could sleep through the whole thing." **Woody Allen** objects to Diane Keaton's need to smoke a joint each time before they have sex. *Annie Hall* (1977, United Artists).

9374 "If I were your sister, I wouldn't sleep on the same block with you." **Brian Drillinger** teases his younger brother Jonathan Silverman with whom he shares a room. Silverman is a very horny young teen. *Brighton Beach Memoirs* (1986, Universal).

9375 "I can't sleep anymore. It's too much like death." **Vincent Gardenia** tries to stave off old age by having an affair. *Moonstruck* (1987, MGM-United Artists).

9376 "That was great. . . . I'll call you tomorrow, o.k. Get some sleep." The tables are turned on womanizer Eddie Murphy, when his boss, beautiful **Robin Givens** compliments him on his prowess after their first sexual encounter, gets dressed and walks out on him lying bewildered in bed. *Boomerang* (1992, Paramount).

Slogans

see also MOTTOS

9377 "If you can't sleep at night it isn't the coffee, it's the bunk." It's the slogan thought up by **Dick Powell**. He mistakenly believes it has been chosen to receive the grand prize in a contest. *Christmas in July* (1940, Paramount).

9378 "If you ain't eatin' Wham, you ain't eatin' ham." Maid **Louise Beavers** solves her boss Cary Grant's problem by coming up with just the advertising slogan he needs. *Mr. Blandings Builds His Dream House* (1948, RKO).

9379 "No matter where you go, there you are." It's nuclear physicist, brain surgeon and rock 'n' roll singer **Peter Weller**'s slogan as he saves the world from domination by aliens from a distant galaxy. *The Adventures of Buckaroo Banzai: Across the 8th Dimension* (1984, 20th Century-Fox).

9380 "Fair is fair." It's the rallying cry of the kids who support folk hero **Helen Slater** who accidentally shoots a nasty man. She wants someone to pay for her brother's vandalized bike before she gives herself up. *The Legend of Billie Jean* (1985, Tri-Star).

Slowness

see also DULLNESS, SPEED

9381 "You think slow, Nick. You move fast, but you think slow." Scheming **Norman Lloyd** accuses impetuous John Garfield as they plan a payroll robbery. *He Ran All the Way* (1951, United Artists).

9382 "I'm slow, but you're slower." Con man **James Garner** mutters to simple-minded side-kick Jack Elam, who fancies himself handy with a six-shooter. *Support Your Local Gunfighter* (1971, United Artists).

9383 "Paulie may have moved slow but that's because Paulie didn't have to move for anybody." Narrator **Christopher Serrone** speaks admiringly of Mafia chief Paul Sorvino. *Goodfellas* (1990, Warner Bros.).

Smallness *see* GREATNESS, SIZES

Smartness *see* BRAINS, INTELLIGENCE, KNOWLEDGE

Smells

see also PERFUMES, SENSE AND SENSIBILITY

9384 "I could smell the honeysuckle again, only it was even stronger, now that it was night. . . . The machinery had started to move, and nothing could stop it." The smell from the flowers near Barbara Stanwyck's house reminds **Fred MacMurray** that the die is cast in the plan to kill her husband. *Double Indemnity* (1944, Paramount).

9385 "I didn't want any part of her, but I kept smelling that jasmine in her hair, and I wanted her in my arms. Yeah. . . I knew I was walking into something." **Humphrey Bogart** refers to Lizabeth Scott, the cool blonde ex-girlfriend of his buddy William Prince, who was killed because of her. *Dead Reckoning* (1947, Columbia).

9386 "Who wants perfume? Give me the fresh, wet smell of Iowa corn right after it rains." U.S. Army Captain **John Lund** pours on the phony charm for visiting Iowa Congresswoman Jean Arthur in post-war Berlin. *A Foreign Affair* (1948, Paramount).

9387 "Didn't anybody ever tell you before that you smell bad?" What does **Anne Baxter** expect of Gregory Peck? There's no bathtubs in a western ghost town. *Yellow Sky* (1948, 20th Century-Fox).

9388 "You stink! You stink with corruption. You're worse than a murderer. You're a grave robber." Crippled **Arthur Kennedy** lambasts his boxer brother Kirk Douglas when he discovers that the latter has seduced and then sent away his ex-wife Ruth Roman, whom Kennedy was planning to marry. *Champion* (1949, United Artists).

9389 "You never get out of Beaver Canal. The stink never gets out of you." **Linda Darnell** tells black doctor Sidney Poitier that she can never escape her low class beginnings. *No Way Out* (1950, 20th Century-Fox).

9390 "Sometimes I think I give off a scent or something. Arouses the females." **Dean Martin** speaks of a "curse" that some other guys would love to have. *The Young Lions* (1958, 20th Century-Fox).

9391 "And he takes about fifty baths a day. . . . I think a man should smell. . . at least a little bit." **Audrey Hepburn** refers to Vilallonga, a fabulously wealthy Brazilian landowner who has proposed marriage. *Breakfast at Tiffany's* (1961, Paramount).

9392 "You're beginning to smell. For a stud in New York that's a handicap." **Dustin Hoffman**, who's no violet himself, gives the needle to Jon Voight, whose career plan of servicing wealthy and appreciative women hasn't got off the ground for more reasons than just poor hygiene. *Midnight Cowboy* (1969, United Artists).

9393 "Hey, you know if you wanta make out you're such a fancy dude, you might wear something besides that cheap jockey club cologne. You think small." Brothel madam **Julie Christie** tells gambling western entrepreneur Warren Beatty that he smells bad. *McCabe and Mrs. Miller* (1971, Warner Bros.).

9394 "I love the smell of napalm in the morning. . . . It smells like. . . victory." Wacko helicopter squadron commander Colonel **Robert Duvall**'s copters fly on their raids to Wagner's "Ride of the Valkyries" because, as Duvall says, it "scares the hell out of the slopes." *Apocalypse Now* (1979, United Artists).

9395 "She makes the bench smell better." It's the opinion of one of the justices of the Supreme Court about its newest member Jill Clayburgh. *First Monday in October* (1981, Paramount).

9396 "You smell like the toasted cheese sandwiches my mother used to bring me." **Anthony Perkins** stands guard with an enormous knife over Meg Tilly, who awakens from sleep in the room that was his when he was a child. *Psycho II* (1983, Universal).

9397 "Oh, God, I love the smell of malamute in the morning." Executive turned survivalist **Robin Williams** mushes behind a dog team in the snow-covered wilds of New Hampshire. *The Survivors* (1983, Columbia).

9398 "You're my round, sweet-smellin' female." Taciturn **Gene Hackman** whispers sweet nothings to his new love Ann-Margret. *Twice in a Lifetime* (1985, Vestron).

9399 JOE FISK: "You smell great." LISA TAYLOR: "You're very observant." **Craig Sheffer**, a youngster from a minimum security reform school, compliments beautiful **Virginia Madsen**, a student in a girls' Catholic boarding school down the road. *Fire with Fire* (1986, Paramount).

9400 "I'm beginning to like the smell of paint thinner." Completely domesticated **Bonnie Bedelia** shares a secret with her husband Kevin Kline's ex-lover, famous photojournalist Sissy Spacek. *Violets Are Blue* (1986, Columbia).

9401 "I love the smell of cookies in the morning." Nasty girls' troop leader **Betty Thomas** is every bit as wacko and gung-ho as Robert Duvall in *Apocalypse Now*. *Troop Beverly Hills* (1989, Weintraub).

9402 "You smell good, like a bitch in her hothouse." One is forced to agree with **John Cusack** that at the moment in question, Annette Bening has a very steamy, sexy look to her. It is probably safe to assume that she smells good also. *The Grifters* (1990, Miramax-Cineplex-Odeon).

9403 "You use Evyan cream, and sometimes you wear L'Air du Temps, but not today." Dangerous mental institution prisoner **Anthony Hopkins** carefully addresses Jodie Foster's attire, sniffs and describes her scent. His next door neighbor was more elemental, claiming to Foster that he smelled her "cunt." *The Silence of the Lambs* (1991, Orion).

Smiles

see also FACES, LAUGHTER

9404 TRAMPAS: "You long-legged son of a...." THE VIRGINIAN: "When you want to call me that, smile." The line from Owen Wister's book is "When you call me that, smile," which is how **Joel McCrea** delivered it in the 1946 film. But the usually laconic **Gary Cooper** added a couple of words. **Walter Huston** was Trampas in the 1929 film, **Brian Donlevy** in the remake. *The Virginian* (1929, Famous Players-Paramount); (1946, Paramount).

9405 "Even your smile is crooked." **Jean Harlow** has Clark Gable pegged. *Hold Your Man* (1933, MGM).

9406 "Wipe that smile off your puss or I'll knock your teeth through the top of your head!" **Humphrey Bogart** gets tough with a captured Nazi pilot who calls Rex Ingram a "nigger." *Sahara* (1943, Columbia).

9407 "When you call me madam, smile." **Ethel Merman** repeats her stage hit as a Washington hostess who is appointed ambassador to Lichtenberg. *Call Me Madam* (1953, 20th Century-Fox).

9408 "Miss Clara, you slam the door in a man's face before he even knocks on it.... I can see you don't like me, but you're going to have me.... I'll tell you one thing, you're going to wake up smiling in the morning." **Paul Newman** won't take "no" for an answer from Joanne Woodward. *The Long Hot Summer* (1958, 20th Century-Fox).

9409 "The old man opened his eyes and for a moment he was coming back from a long way. Then he smiled." It's director **John Sturges** in voice-over as the screen is filled with a close up fisherman Spencer Tracy. *The Old Man and the Sea* (1958, Warner Bros.).

9410 "What's there to smile about?" Chosen to star in a new film, **Malcolm McDowell** finds it difficult to smile at the director Lindsay Anderson's request. However, when Anderson whacks McDowell across the face with the script, he smiles. *O Lucky Man!* (1973, GB, Warner Bros.).

9411 "Can I ask you a question? Do you smile all the time?" Jewish radical **Barbra Streisand** thinks WASPish Robert Redford might try to be a bit more serious now and then. *The Way We Were* (1973, Columbia).

9412 "Any idiot can have a long-term relationship; all you have to do is smile a lot." **Josh Mostel** wisecracks as he and Christine Estabrook announce their wedding after a long-time relationship. *Almost You* (1985, 20th Century-Fox).

9413 "Your sexy little smile isn't going to work this time." Having gotten wise to him, **Elisabeth Shue** rejects a renewal of her relationship with bartender Tom Cruise. *Cocktail* (1988, Touchstone).

9414 "What is it, Nick? You need some chapstick or some lip gloss or something?... 'Cause your lips keep getting stuck on your teeth; or is that your idea of a smile?" **Michelle Pfeiffer** puts down police detective Kurt Russell. *Tequila Sunrise* (1988, Warner Bros.).

9415 "Go and find your smile." Understanding **Patricia Wettig** sends her depressed 39-year-old husband Billy Crystal off to an actual cattle drive from New Mexico to Colorado, hoping it will bring back the man she knew and loved. *City Slickers* (1991, Columbia).

Smoking and Smokers

see also FIRES

9416 "Cigarette me, big boy." **Ginger Rogers'** come-on, asking for a smoke, caught on with the young crowd all over the country. *Young Man of Manhattan* (1930, Paramount).

9417 "That's a good quarter cigar. I smoked the other three-quarters myself." **Chico Marx** offers to share a smoke with his boss, Louis Calhern, the ambassador from the country of Sylvania. *Duck Soup* (1933, Paramount).

9418 DETECTIVE: "Say, what kind of cigarette is this?" DEGAR: "Oh, it's an Oriental cigarette." None-too-bright police detective **Matt McHugh** has been given a drugged cigarette by swami **Bela Lugosi**. *Night of Terror* aka: *He Lived to Kill* (1933, Columbia).

9419 "Wherever there's smoke, there must be. . . somebody smoking." Hat store proprietor **Franklin Pangborn** is suspicious when financier Edward Arnold brings young beautiful Jean Arthur into the store to buy a fur hat. *Easy Living* (1937, Paramount).

9420 "If my husband wouldn't let me smoke, I'd find me a way to get a husband that would." Maid **Hattie McDaniel** tells Beulah Bondi how she would handle Bondi's husband, college president Charles Coburn and his ban on cigarettes. *Vivacious Lady* (1938, RKO).

9421 "I think he wants her to give up smoking." **Bing Crosby** murmurs as he watches Anthony Quinn flick cigarettes from the mouth of his partner Dorothy Lamour with a whip. *Road to Singapore* (1940, Paramount).

9422 "Got a butt, buddy?" Delightfully trampy **Iris Adrian** is tough prisoner Two-Gun Gertie. *Roxie Hart* (1942, 20th Century-Fox).

9423 "I feel a lot better, too. Matter of fact, I never felt so good in my life. How about a cigarette?" Knowledgeable movie-goers know with a line like that, Marine **John Wayne** is a goner. A second later he's killed by a sniper's bullet. *Sands of Iwo Jima* (1949, Republic).

9424 "I can't stand cigarette smoke. . . cigarette smoking is both expensive and unhealthy. There should be a law against women smoking. . . . Now take the cigar. Cigars are an expression of the fundamental idea of smoking. A stimulant and a relaxation. A manly vice." **Victor Sjostrom** lectures his daughter-in-law Ingrid Thulin about smoking. *Wild Strawberries* (1957, Sweden, Svensk Filmindustri).

9425 "Back home in Boston, we don't grow tobacco, we just smoke it." **Troy Donahue** arrives to work on the Connecticut River Valley tobacco farm of Dean Jagger. *Parrish* (1961, Warner Bros.).

9426 "Anybody got a straight cigarette?" Pot-smoking motorcyclist **Bruce Dern** makes a dying request. *The Wild Angels* (1966, American International Pictures).

9427 "Where there's smoke, there's salmon?" **Joseph Wiseman** disapproves of his son Elliott Gould, as Billy Minsky, turning one of the family theaters into a burlesque house. *The Night They Raided Minsky's* (1968, United Artists).

9428 "You want to do me a really big favor? Smoke toward New Jersey." **David Sheiner** complains to poker playing crony Larry Haines. *The Odd Couple* (1968, Paramount).

9429 "Is there anywhere you don't smoke?" Non-smoker **Robert Redford** is tired of inhaling Dustin Hoffman's smoke. *All the President's Men* (1976, Warner Bros.).

9430 "I wish you wouldn't smoke during rehearsals. You don't act as if you're looking for your soul but for an ashtray" Eugene O'Neill, portrayed by **Jack Nicholson**, directs Louise Bryant, played by Diane Keaton, in one of O'Neill's early plays, "Thirst." *Reds* (1981, Paramount).

9431 "Here, you want a cigarette?. . . Come on, let's smoke. . . go on, taste it. Let's take our time and both die of cancer." Police detective **Mel Gibson** stands on a ledge of a building calming a "jumper." *Lethal Weapon* (1987, Warner Bros.).

9432 "Girls like guys who smoke. Let's smoke." **Jodie Foster** instructs her ten-year-old protégé Thatcher Goodwin. *Stealing Home* (1988, Warner Bros.).

Snakes and Reptiles

see also ANIMALS

9433 "I've never known a better seaman, but the man's a snake." **Clark Gable**, as Fletcher Christian, neatly summarizes the character of Charles Laughton, as Captain William Bligh. *Mutiny on the Bounty* (1935, MGM).

9434 "Making bedfellow of serpent no guarantee against snake bite." It seems title character **Sidney Toler** is warning that bad things happen to people with bad companions. *Charlie Chan in Honolulu* (1938, 20th Century-Fox).

9435 "See them down there, coiling and wiggling, sticking their pretty tongues out. . . ." Indian guru **Eduardo Ciannelli** shows his captives Cary Grant, Victor McLaglen, Douglas Fairbanks, Jr., and Sam Jaffe a snake pit to which they will be consigned if they aren't cooperative. *Gunga Din* (1939, RKO).

9436 "You know me, nothing but reptiles." Wealthy simpleton **Henry Fonda** doesn't have to work, but he'd love to spend his life studying reptiles in South America. *The Lady Eve* (1941, Paramount).

9437 "Hold on to your chair and don't step on no snakes." Alcoholic harridan **Esther Howard** welcomes private eye Dick Powell into her cluttered living room. *Murder, My Sweet* (1945, RKO).

9438 "Snakes—why does it always have to be snakes?" **Harrison Ford**, who hates snakes, must lower himself into an excavated Egyptian tomb filled with thousands of poisonous snakes. *Raiders of the Lost Ark* (1981, Paramount).

Snow *see* WEATHER.

Sobriety *see* ALCOHOL, DRINKING AND DRUNKENNESS, INSANITY AND SANITY

Societies

see also CIVILIZATIONS, CLASSES, GOVERNMENTS, PEOPLE

9439 "They've hounded us from the minute we were born. . . to the minute we walk in here. They hounded us when we were hungry and wanted to eat. . . . They hounded us when we didn't want to live no more in those dumps they call houses. . . . They hounded us when we found we couldn't get the fine things all around us. . .and took 'em for ourselves." In the death house, convicted murderer **James Cagney** rails against society and the law to his boyhood friend Priest Pat O'Brien. *Angels with Dirty Faces* (1938, Warner Bros.).

9440 "Cafe society. I'd rather read about the zoo!" Reporter Fred MacMurray's singer friend **Shirley Ross** has her druthers. *Cafe Society* (1939, Paramount).

9441 RINGO: "Looks like I got the plague, don't it?" DALLAS: "No, it's not you." RINGO: "Well, I guess you can't break out of prison and into society in the same week." Escaped prisoner **John Wayne** hasn't yet picked up on the fact that the other passengers on the stagecoach are avoiding both him and shady lady **Claire Trevor** during a meal. *Stagecoach* (1939, United Artists).

9442 "Your purchase of the property does not establish a social bond between us." **Donald Crisp** is unsociable to Ray Milland and his sister Ruth Hussey who have purchased a haunted house from the older man. Crisp doesn't want his daughter Gail Russell to have anything to do with them—or is it he doesn't want her to have anything to do with the house? *The Uninvited* (1944, Paramount).

9443 "It's a closed society. To get in, you have to be either beautiful or rich." **John Hurt**, as Dr. Stephen Ward, knows on which basis Joanne Whalley-Kilmer, as Christine Keeler, qualifies for membership. *Scandal* (1989, GB, Miramax).

9444 "All my life I kept trying to go up in society. Where everything higher up was legal. But the higher I go, the crookeder it becomes. Where the hell does it end?" **Al Pacino** tells his nephew Andy Garcia that it's very difficult to be a legitimate businessman because there are no legitimate businesses. *The Godfather, Part III* (1991, Paramount).

Soldiers *see* MILITARY, WARS, WEAPONS

Solitude

see also EXISTENCE, LONELINESS, RETIREMENT

9445 "I want to be alone." **Greta Garbo** did make the famous declaration credited to her, but it was as a weary, despairing, suicidal ballerina. *Grand Hotel* (1932, MGM).

9446 "Don't shoot. I got nobody. I'm all alone. My steel shutters don't work." Mobster **Paul Muni** pathetically surrenders to police after his sister Ann Dvorak is killed in a shoot-out with the police. *Scarface* (1932, United Artists).

9447 NICK CHARLES: "I think you better let us go alone." NORA CHARLES: "Catch me letting you go alone." When retired private detective **William Powell** is pulled into a murder case, his wife **Myrna Loy** counts herself in. *The Thin Man* (1934, MGM).

9448 "One day I shall find myself alone." Sadly, unfaithful wife **Greta Garbo**'s prediction is on target. *Anna Karenina* (1935, MGM).

9449 "I must go in now. No one must be here. . . Ann, be my best friend. Go now, please." Correctly sensing her end is near, **Bette Davis**, wishing to die alone, sends Geraldine Fitzgerald away. *Dark Victory* (1939, Warner Bros.).

9450 "You go into the arena alone. The lions are hungry for you." **Clark Gable** drops off Vivien Leigh at Olivia de Havilland's door the night of Leslie Howard's birthday party. *Gone with the Wind* (1939, Selznick-MGM).

9451 "Must I carry the weight—the agony—of the world alone?" **Bette Davis**, as England's Queen Elizabeth I, feels life would be more bearable if she had a consort like Errol Flynn. *The Private Lives of Elizabeth and Essex* (1939, Warner Bros.).

9452 "I don't like to be alone at night. I guess everybody in the world has a time they don't like. With me, it's right before I go to sleep. Now, it's going to be for always—all the rest of my life." With resignation, **Bette Davis** prepares to face life alone when her fascism-fighter husband Paul Lukas flees Washington for Mexico after killing Nazi sympathizer George Coulouris. *Watch on the Rhine* (1943, Warner Bros).

9453 "I wonder if you know what it means to stand all alone in a dark corner?" Recently released mental patient **Ray Milland** states an essential characteristic of film noir. *Ministry of Fear* (1945, Paramount).

9454 "We've got something in common. We're both alone." A down-on-his-luck middle-aged man speaks sadly to a despondent woman seated near him at a bus station. *Lady in the Lake* (1947, MGM).

9455 "I don't want to die alone." With just a few weeks to live, proud young Scottish soldier **Richard Todd** finally realizes he needs the friendship of his hospital mates. *The Hasty Heart* (1949, Warner Bros.).

9456 "Why all alone? Being exclusive? Being dramatic? Feeling blue?" Beautiful young **Elizabeth Taylor** tries to draw out working stiff Montgomery Clift, who feeling out of place at a fancy society party, has taken refuge in the billiards room. *A Place in the Sun* (1951, Paramount).

9457 "Georgia, I have to be alone tonight. After a picture is finished, something happens to me. The feeling of letdown, emptiness. It's bad. It gets worse. I can't help it." Having just come from a triumphant opening of her film, actress Lana Turner wants to celebrate with producer **Kirk Douglas**. He became her lover during the filming of the movie, not so much because he cared for her, but in order to get her best performance. She almost believes his story until starlet Elaine Stewart appears on the upstairs landing wearing a negligee. *The Bad and the Beautiful* (1952, MGM).

9458 "You are too much alone, dear Dr. Chasuble. You should get married. A misanthrope I can understand—a womanthrope, never." Spinster **Margaret Rutherford** encourages country parson Miles Malleson. *The Importance of Being Earnest* (1952, GB, Two Cities-Rank).

9459 BUNNY WATSON: "I've read every New York newspaper backward and forward for the past fifteen years. I don't smoke. I only drink champagne when I'm lucky enough to get it. My hair is naturally natural. I live alone and so do you." RICHARD SUMNER: "How do you know that?" BUNNY: "Because, you're wearing one brown sock and one black one. . . if you lived with anyone, they would've told you." RICHARD: "That's one of the advantages of living alone, no one tells you anything." TV network research expert **Katharine Hepburn** tells efficiency expert **Spencer Tracy** something about herself—and about him. *Desk Set* (1957, 20th Century-Fox).

9460 "You can be more alone in New York than in this hotel. . . being alone in a crowd is worse. It's more painful, more frightening—oh, so frightening, so frightening. I'm an awful coward, you see. I've never been able to face anything alone." **Rita Hayworth** confesses her fear of being alone to her ex-husband Burt Lancaster. She shows up at an English seaside resort run by his mistress Wendy Hiller. *Separate Tables* (1958, United Artists).

9461 "One shouldn't live alone, it's wrong." **Kim Novak** remarks sadly on awakening in James Stewart's apartment the morning after he rescued her from San Francisco Bay. *Vertigo* (1958, Paramount).

9462 "I haven't been alone ten minutes since I was 12." It's call-girl **Gina Lollobrigida**'s quip to a date who excuses himself at a restaurant, saying, "I don't like leaving you alone." *Go Naked in the World* (1960, MGM).

9463 "I want to go it alone." Former Western lawman **Joel McCrea** asks his old comrade Randolph Scott to allow him to die alone. *Ride the High Country* (1962, MGM).

9464 "Even when he's with somebody, he walks alone." **Marie Dubois** refers to melancholy piano player Charles Aznavour. *Shoot the Piano Player* (1960, Fr., Films de la Pleiade-Astor).

9465 "But you see—I don't want to be left alone—I don't think I could ever bear to be left alone." Widow **Jessica Tandy** begins to cry while talking to Tippi Hedren, who's interested in Tandy's son, Rod Taylor. *The Birds* (1963, Universal).

9466 "He craved anonymity." In voice-over, sea Captain **Jack Hawkins** speaks of mate Peter O'Toole who tries to lose himself in the farthest reaches of the earth after an act of cowardice at sea. *Lord Jim* (1965, GB, Columbia).

9467 "I like to be faceless and bodiless and be left alone." Part-time call-girl **Jane Fonda** updates Garbo's line. *Klute* (1971, Warner Bros.).

9468 "The creepy thing about battle is that you always feel alone." Narrator **Robert Carradine** speaks of a soldier's fear that he has no one to help him survive. *The Big Red One* (1980, United Artists).

9469 "We come alone and we leave alone. Everything else is a gift." Sensitive **Michael Brandon**'s soul is filled with rage because death has taken all of his loved ones. *A Change of Seasons* (1980, 20th Century-Fox).

9470 "Alone's kind of a nice place to be." **Albert Brooks** shares the thought with Bruno Kirby after the former breaks up with his lover Kathryn Harrold. He soon discovers that alone is a great place to visit, but he doesn't want to live there. *Modern Romance* (1981, Columbia).

9471 "A thousand people touching her all the time. . . to be alone all the time also." Joe DiMaggio-like ex-ballplayer **Gary Busey** describes what his Marilyn Monroe-like wife Theresa Russell needs. *Insignificance* (1985, GB, Zenith).

9472 HANNAH: "It seems so dark tonight. I feel so alone." ELLIOT: "You are not alone." Usually a rock, **Mia Farrow** displays vulnerability to her husband **Michael Caine** in bed one night. Perhaps she senses his plan to be unfaithful with her sister Barbara Hershey. *Hannah and Her Sisters* (1986, Orion).

9473 "She lives alone in a room, like a dog. . . . No matter how much money you got, if you're alone, you're sick." **Reizl Borzyk**, who lives alone, believes her unmarried granddaughter Amy Irving needs a husband. *Crossing Delancey* (1988, Warner Bros.).

9474 "I —I. . . it's always I. . . . There are three hundred teachers here. . . you did not do it alone." Long-suffering Vice Principal **Beverly Todd** has had it with Principal Morgan Freeman, who acts as if he alone has changed conditions at Eastside High School. *Lean on Me* (1989, Warner Bros.).

9475 "Alone in the dark with thousands of men—there is a God after all." **Bette Midler** is on a stage entertaining troops during World War II. *For the Boys* (1991, 20th Century-Fox).

Songs and Singing

see also ENTERTAINMENTS AND ENTERTAINERS, MUSIC AND MUSICIANS, PERFORMANCES, SHOWS

9476 "You spoke and all the world became a song. And all my heart a bird that heard its note." Via a title card, **Marguerite Clark** laments to a life-sized figure of Cupid, sculptured by the gardener who eloped with her mother. *Prunella* (1918, silent, Famous Players-Paramount).

9477 "This song of the Man and his Wife is of no place and every place; you might hear it anywhere at any time. Wherever the sun rises and sets in the city's turmoil or under the open sky on the farm life is much the same; sometimes bitter, sometimes sweet." It's a title card for the silent classic. *Sunrise* (1927, silent, Fox).

9478 "Wait a minute, wait a minute, you ain't heard nothin' yet! You wanna hear 'Toot, Toot, Tootsie'? All right, hold on, hold on. Lou listen, play 'Toot, Toot, Tootsie.' Three choruses, you understand. In the third chorus, I whistle. Now give it to 'em hard and heavy. Go right ahead!" The first words of **Al Jolson** in a movie, but not the first words heard in the movie. That honor goes to Bobby Gordon who played Jolson's role at 13. *The Jazz Singer* (1927, Part-Talkie, Warner Bros.).

9479 "Falling in love again/ Never wanted to,/What am I to do?/I can't help it." These are some of the lyrics of the famous song sung by tawdry nightclub entertainer **Marlene Dietrich**. *The Blue Angel* (1930, Ger., UFA).

9480 "What am I bid for my apples, the fruit that made Adam so wise?" Cabaret entertainer **Marlene Dietrich**'s seductive question in song, is meant especially for legionnaire Gary Cooper. *Morocco* (1930, Paramount).

9481 "Just wait a little while/ The nasty man in black will come/And with his little chopper/He will chop you up." Children standing in a circle recite a count-out song at the beginning of this classic film. *M* (1931, Ger., Nero Film).

9482 "If you wish a bird to sing, do not put it in cage." **Warner Oland**, as the Oriental detective Charlie Chan, believes more will be learned from a suspect on the loose than one in jail. *Charlie Chan's Courage* (1934, Fox).

9483 "Why don't you try that on the rustlers? You might sing them to sleep." Newspaper editor **Ann Rutherford** isn't impressed when Autry croons "The West Isn't What It Used To Be" to her. The modern day cattle rustlers use trucks and radios. *Public Cowboy Number One* (1937, Republic).

9484 "Singing is okay for those fellows, but I'm a man." **Fred MacMurray** refuses to sing for a living, believing that singers are sissies. *Sing You Sinners* (1938, Paramount).

9485 "Play it, Sam, play 'As Time Goes By'." **Ingrid Bergman** asks Dooley Wilson to play the song that was special to her and Humphrey Bogart when they were lovers in Paris. Later Bogie will order Wilson to play it for him, saying, "You played it for her. . . ." *Casablanca* (1942, Warner Bros.).

9486 "In about five minutes, I will introduce to you a young singer discovered by the United States Navy." Conductor **Jose Iturbi** promises a song by Kathryn Grayson, brought to his attention by sailor Gene Kelly. *Anchors Aweigh* (1945, MGM).

9487 "Listen—it's a song I hear—a melody that whispers all through these enchanted rooms." Hopelessly plain **Dorothy McGuire** tells her disfigured husband that she senses a magic in their small cottage. *The Enchanted Cottage* (1945, RKO).

9488 "One night she started to shimmy and shake/And that's what started the Frisco quake." Although Nan Wynn dubbed the singing for **Rita Hayworth** in her rendition of "Put The Blame On Mame," it was the fabulous redhead who caused a sensation with her sexy gyrations. *Gilda* (1946, Columbia).

9489 "And, Steve, when he gets home nights after the show, don't let him sing too long." As she leaves her husband Larry Parks, title character Al Jolson, **Evelyn Keyes** instructs his business manager William Demarest to take care of workaholic Parks. *The Jolson Story* (1946, Columbia).

9490 "Where I come from, nobody knows/And where I'm going, everything goes;/The wind blows/The sea flows/And nobody knows. . . ." **Jennifer Jones** sings the song each time she meets with Joseph Cotten—each time as a girl just a bit older than before. *Portrait of Jennie* (1948, Selznick).

9491 "French songs I cannot possibly allow. People always seem to think that they are improper and either looked shocked, which is vulgar, or laugh, which is worse." **Dame Edith Evans** speaks of the music her nephew Michael Denison is to help her select for one of her parties. *The Importance of Being Earnest* (1952, GB, Rank).

9492 "I didn't exactly fracture the people, did I?" Inferior nightclub singer **Jane Russell** hopes for some disagreement from wandering American Robert Mitchum. *Macao* (1952, RKO).

9493 "I somehow feel more alive when I'm singing." And **Judy Garland** could really sing. But her song wasn't enough to prevent her despondent, failing movie star husband James Mason from taking his own life. *A Star Is Born* (1954, Warner Bros.).

9494 "Got to give her credit. The girl can sing. . . . About that I was never wrong." **James Cagney**, as laundry racketeer Martin "The Gimp" Snyder, speaks admiringly and sorrowfully about the talent of his ex-wife Doris Day, as Ruth Etting. *Love Me or Leave Me* (1955, MGM).

9495 "The German people love to sing, no matter what the situation." **Marlene Dietrich** generalizes to Spencer Tracy about her musical countrymen. *Judgment at Nuremberg* (1961, United Artists).

9496 "In six years, I never sold one lousy song. Maybe they weren't lousy enough." Songwriter **Dick Van Dyke** really wants to be a chemist. He's just trying to please his overbearing mother, Maureen Stapleton. *Bye Bye Birdie* (1963, Columbia).

9497 "I hate a song makes you think that you're not any good. I hate a song makes you think you're just born to lose, bound to lose, no good to nobody, no good for nothing. Because you're either too old or too young or too fat or too thin, you're too ugly or too dead to do that. Songs that run you down, songs that poke fun at you on account of your bad luck or your hard traveling. I am out to fight those kinds of songs to my very last breath of air, to my last drop of blood. I'm out to sing songs that will prove to you that this is your world, and it has kicked you pretty hard and knocked you down for a dozen loops. No matter how hard it brung you down and rolled over you, no matter what color, what size you are, how you're built. I am out to sing the songs that will make you take pride in yourself." Woody Guthrie, portrayed by **David Carradine**, holds forth on songs. *Bound for Glory* (1976, United Artists).

9498 "Thank you. Thank you. You're, you're all making us feel real good up here. My friends and I want to sing this next song that goes back with me a long time. I'd like to sing it for my sister, no, I'd like to sing it for all my sisters, especially for my man, Stix. He's out there somewhere. I hope they can all hear me. Thank you." **Irene Cara** alone, of three sisters from Harlem has made it to the big time as a 50s rock 'n' roll singer, under the guidance of Philip M. Thomas. *Sparkle* (1976, Warner Bros.).

9499 "Translate the lyrics for me!" During a sexy seduction scene, **Paula Prentiss** makes the request of Robert Foxworth when he puts some instrumental Russian folk music on the stereo. *The Black Marble* (1980, Avco Embassy).

9500 "Piano wire. He [the murderer] must have heard her singing." It's **Vincent Price**'s unconcerned and unkind reaction upon finding the strangled body of his sister. *House of the Long Shadows* (1982, GB, Cannon).

9501 "There must be better songs to sing." With tears running down her face, **Patricia Jeffares** reflects on the emptiness of her life as she sits with her working class family, drinking beer and participating in a community sing in a pub. *Educating Rita* (1983, GB, Rank)

9502 "If I know a song of Africa, and the African new moon lying on her back, does Africa know a song of me?" **Meryl Streep** delivers the film's closing line. *Out of Africa* (1985, Universal).

9503 "Can you kiss me!/Baby, undress me." It's **Vanity**'s song. She dresses in outfits that appear more like part of her remarkable body than clothes. *Action Jackson* (1989, Lorimar).

9504 "When her muscles start relaxin'/Up the hill comes Michael Jackson." Title character **Robin Williams** adapts lyrics to Groucho Marx's song "Lydia, the Tattooed Lady." *The Fisher King* (1991, Tri-Star).

9505 "Men and women and love and pain—that's what songs are all about." So says small-time lounge singer **Santha Press**, who likes to live on the edge. *In Too Deep* (1991, Australia, Paramount).

9506 "Led Zeppelin didn't write songs everyone liked. They left that to the Bee Gees." Title character **Mike Myers** correctly observes that popularity isn't everything. *Wayne's World* (1992, Paramount).

Sons and Sons-in-law

see also BOYS, FATHERS, MEN, MOTHERS, PARENTS, YOUTH

9507 "Hello, my would-be ex-son-in-law. I've sent you a check for a hundred thousand." **Walter Connolly** is delighted to buy off Jameson Thomas when Connolly's daughter Claudette Colbert jilts Thomas to run off with Clark Gable. *It Happened One Night* (1934, Columbia).

9508 "You no good tramp. You dog. You dirty yella dog, you. Don't call me Mom. You ain't no son of mine. Go away, and leave us alone. Stay away, leave us alone to die, but leave us alone." Toil-worn **Marjorie Main** disowns her gangster son Humphrey Bogart when he returns to his old slum neighborhood. *Dead End* (1937, Goldwyn-United Artists).

9509 "It's almost like leaving a son—my own creation." As the ghost of **Constance Bennett** moves on to her reward, she admires the transformation of staid banker **Roland Young** into a new, confident and independent man. *Topper* (1937, MGM).

9510 "Your son was just here, Walter, he was so nice to me. He might have been my son, our son. I wonder what would have happened if I had met you that Sunday at the boat." For 28 years, **Margaret Sullavan** has been Charles Boyer's mistress. She refers to Boyer's son Tim Holt and to the fact that they once planned to marry, but she literally and figuratively missed the boat. *Back Street* (1941, Universal).

9511 "I don't like Leo. My own son and I don't like him. Isn't that funny? I even like Oscar better than Leo." **Patricia Collinge**, who drinks, refers to her son Dan Duryea and her husband Carl Benton Reid, two despicable characters. Where is it written that a mother must like her children if they don't deserve to be liked? *The Little Foxes* (1941, Goldwyn-RKO).

9512 "I haven't been richly blessed with friends or with sons—my eldest, a penny-grubbing trickster; my second, a proud illiterate. Strange, Regina, you turned out to be my only son." Tyrannical **Fredric March** degrades his sons Edmond O'Brien and Dan Duryea, preferring his pet Ann Blyth, who will become as ruthless as he is as she matures. *Another Part of the Forest* (1948, Universal).

9513 "I won't insist he be tough. I'll try to see that he's intelligent. And I won't insist that he read the Marine Corps manual. Instead, I'll get him a set of Shakespeare. In short, I don't want him to be a Sergeant John M. Stryker. I want him to be intelligent, considerate, cultured and a gentleman." **John Agar** lectures tough marine Sergeant John Wayne after the Duke congratulates Agar on becoming a father. Some people just can't accept things in the spirit they are offered. *Sands of Iwo Jima* (1949, Republic).

9514 "You have set the son-in-law business back fifty years." Washed-up, alcoholic, former silent screen star **Robert Warwick** gives a shot to bragging producer Lewis Howard, who owes his success to his famous and important father-in-law. *In a Lonely Place* (1950, Columbia).

9515 "There's a fly in the ointment. First, he steals my daughter, then he makes a grandpa out of me." **Spencer Tracy** refers to his son-in-law Don Taylor. *Father's Little Dividend* (1951, MGM).

9516 "My son, Sebastian and I constructed our days. Each day we—we would carve each day like a piece of sculpture, leaving behind us a trail of days like a gallery of sculpture until suddenly last summer." **Katharine Hepburn** regales psychiatrist Montgomery Clift with tales of her perfect poet son, who died on the previous summer. *Suddenly Last Summer* (1959, Columbia).

9517 "You know the drums carry a long distance. I hope one day they'll tell me you have a fine son." **David Farrar** says farewell to George Montgomery and Taina Elg who are leaving the African jungles. *Watusi* (1959, MGM).

9518 "A son is a poor substitute for a lover." **Anthony Perkins** speaks of his mother to Janet Leigh. *Psycho* (1960, Paramount).

9519 "All my sons are bastards." **Peter O'Toole**, as King Henry II of England, rages at Katharine Hepburn as his estranged queen, Eleanor of Aquitaine, about his three legitimate children Anthony Hopkins, John Castle and Nigel Terry. *The Lion in Winter* (1968, GB, Avco Embassy).

9520 "[He is] the bastard son of a hundred maniacs." According to **Ronee Blakley**, when a nursing nun became trapped in a ward for the criminally insane on one wicked weekend, she was repeatedly brutalized and raped. The result is Freddy Krueger, played by Robert Englund. *A Nightmare on Elm Street* (1984, New Line).

9521 "We are the sons of the sons of Michelangelo and Leonardo. Whose sons are you?" Master Italian craftsman **Vincent Spano**, who along with Joaquin de Almedia, have been brought to America to build movie sets for D.W. Griffith's classic *Intolerance*, loudly and defiantly shakes his fist at production manager David Brandon. *Good Morning, Babylon* (1987, Italy-Fr.-USA, Vestron.)

9522 "My son is going to be all right. If not, I'll have you killed." **Anjelica Huston** threatens a doctor as her son John Cusack is put in an ambulance. *The Grifters* (1990, Miramax).

9523 "I'll always be your son. But I will never have anything to do with your business." **Franc D'Ambrosio**, as Anthony Corleone, tells his father Al Pacino basically the same thing Pacino said to his father Marlon Brando. *The Godfather, Part III* (1991, Paramount).

9524 "[You are] nothing but a ball and chain of heartbreak and hurt." Domineering, female Archie Bunker, **Maureen O'Hara** belittles her doting 38-year-old son John Candy. *Only the Lonely* (1991, 20th Century-Fox).

Sophistication

see also CORRUPTION, EXPERIENCE, INNOCENCE, NAÏVETÉ, PERVERSIONS, TASTES

9525 TIRA: "I like sophisticated men to take me out." KIRK LAWRENCE: "Well, I'm not really sophisticated." TIRA: "You're not really out yet, either." **Mae West** toys with admirer **Kent Taylor**. At the time "sophisticated" meant sexually straight, i.e., heterosexual, and "out" of course, as in "gays coming out of the closet." *I'm No Angel* (1933, Paramount).

9526 "Guys in the army are just like us. . . just not as sophisticated." Aimless **Bill Murray** tries to convince his equally unambitious friend Harold Ramis to join the army. *Stripes* (1981, Columbia).

Sorrows

see also GRIEF, HAPPINESS AND UNHAPPINESS, JOY, SADNESS, SUFFERING AND SUFFERERS

9527 "I'm sorry for everybody in the world, I guess." South Seas prostitute **Joan Crawford** reverts to her wicked, wicked ways after missionary Walter Huston first reforms her and then rapes her, before taking his own life in remorse. *Rain* (1932, United Artists).

9528 "The sorrows of life are the joys of art." Broadway producer **John Barrymore** attempts profundity. *Twentieth Century* (1934, Columbia).

9529 "I'm sorry for you. Terribly, desperately sorry. You'll never make the big time, because you're small time in your heart." **Judy Garland** breaks up with her show business partner Gene Kelly after he deliberately smashes his hand to avoid the draft. *For Me and My Gal* (1942, MGM).

9530 ALEC: "I'm so sorry for boring you with long medical words." LAURA: "I'm so sorry for being so dull and stupid in not understanding them." Innocent lovers **Trevor Howard** and **Celia Johnson** constantly exchange apologies during lunch at The Kardomah. *Brief Encounter* (1946, GB, Cineguild).

9531 "She had doubts and that's why she was—just sorry. If you'd have been dragged off here instead of me, she wouldn't have been sorry, she'd have been furious. Belief makes you mad—doubt makes you sorry." **Edmund Gwenn** tells his attorney and friend John Payne that Maureen O'Hara is sorry for him, but she doesn't believe in him. He claims to be the real Santa Claus. *Miracle on 34th Street* (1947, 20th Century-Fox).

9532 "I'm sorry for what I done to Jess. I loved him." **John Ireland** portrays "the dirty little coward" Bob Ford who shot and killed Jesse James, played by Reed Hadley. According to this movie, Ford shot his friend James, hoping to win a pardon for himself and the reward money that would allow him to settle down with his childhood sweetheart. *I Shot Jesse James* (1949, Screen Guild).

9533 "Well, I ain't sorry no more, you crazy Psalm-singing skinny old maid." Tug Captain **Humphrey Bogart** is tired of apologizing for himself to missionary's sister Katharine Hepburn as they travel by tug down a dangerous African river. *The African Queen* (1951, IFD-Romulus-Horizon).

9534 "I don't like wars and I'm not crazy about armies and I'm sorry that we're such barbarians that the men we love have to go out and settle things with guns, but I'd be a lot sorrier if they hadn't gone. Now you get out of here." It's easy for **Dorothy McGuire** to scold her brother-in-law Farley Granger, who doesn't want to be drafted to fight in the Korean Police Action. He believes that if there must be a war, the U.S. should send atomic bombs, not boys. In hind-sight, neither view makes much sense. *I Want You* (1951, RKO).

9535 "If I die, I'm sorry for all the bad things I did to you. If I live, I'm sorry for all the bad things I'm going to do to you." Broadway choreographer **Roy Scheider** (Bob Fosse's alter-ego) makes the first statement to his ex-wife, dancer Leland Palmer, and the second to his new love, dancer Ann Reinking, as he's wheeled down a hospital corridor after suffering a heart attack. *All That Jazz* (1979, 20th Century-Fox).

9536 "We all have our little sorrows, Ducky. You're not the only one. The littler you are, the longer the sorrow. You think you loved him?. . . What about me?" Homosexual dresser **Tom Courtenay** addresses her Ladyship Zena Walker over the corpse of Shakespearean actor Albert Finney. *The Dresser* (1983, GB, Euro-American).

9537 "I felt sorry for you, dumped in your first overseas posting without contact, adrift, trying to bluff your way through. Could you be the unmet friend?" Mysterious dwarf Eurasian cameraman Billy Kwan, played by **Linda Hunt**, who keeps dossiers on all the people she knows, writes in her file on Mel Gibson. *The Year of Living Dangerously* (1983, Australian, MGM).

9538 PHILLIPPE GASTON: "Are you flesh or are you a spirit?" ISABEAU OF ANJOU: "I am sorrow." **Matthew Broderick** is awed when bewitched **Michelle Pfeiffer** changes from a hawk to a beautiful woman. *Ladyhawke* (1985, Warner Bros.).

9539 "I'm sorry, Lord. We stepped on your fucking territory." Medical student **Kevin Bacon** irreverently acknowledges that he and his friends have trod where no man was meant to walk. *Flatliners* (1990, Columbia).

9540 "I'm sorry about the other day. I must have had the book open to the wrong place." **Don Johnson** apologizes to Jennifer Connelly for kissing her, figuring he misread her interests. *The Hot Spot* (1990, Orion).

Souls

see also IMMORTALITY AND MORTALITY, NATURE AND NATURAL, SPIRIT AND SPIRITS

9541 REV. CARMICHAEL: "One of them is yellow, and the other is white—but both their souls are rotten."

CAPT. HARVEY: "You interest me, Mr. Carmichael. I'm not exactly irreligious, and, being a physician I sometimes wonder how a man like you can locate a soul and, having located it, diagnose its condition as rotten." Missionary **Lawrence Grant** criticizes prostitute Anna May Wong and Marlene Dietrich to British military doctor **Clive Brook**. *Shanghai Express* (1932, Paramount).

9542 LADY LOU: "Maybe I ain't got no soul." CAPT. CUMMINGS: "Oh, yes, you have, but you keep it hidden under a mask." Bowery saloon keeper **Mae West** has a run-in with **Cary Grant**, who runs a nearby mission. *She Done Him Wrong* (1933, Paramount).

9543 "You can burn my body but never my soul. That is in the keeping of the people of France." Title character **George Arliss** rages against injustice. *Voltaire* (1933, Warner Bros.).

9544 "I do. And may heaven have mercy on my soul." **William Powell** remarries Jean Arthur. *The Ex-Mrs. Bradford* (1936, MGM).

9545 "Not if I can stop you. . . . You can't take a woman in marriage and then sell her immortal soul!" Priest **Spencer Tracy** opposes Barbary Coast gambling hall and beer garden owner Clark Gable's plans for Jeanette MacDonald. *San Francisco* (1936, MGM).

9546 "Maybe it's like Casey says. A feller ain't got a soul, but only a piece of a big soul. . . ." **Henry Fonda** senses his destiny as a social activist after the death of his friend and model John Carradine. *The Grapes of Wrath* (1940, 20th Century-Fox).

9547 "That's enough to make a man sell his soul to the devil. And I would too for about two cents." Frustrated New Hampshire farmer **James Craig** loses his temper and finds two cents in his hand, just before Walter Huston as Mr. Scratch makes his appearance. *All That Money Can Buy* aka: *The Devil and Daniel Webster* (1941, RKO).

9548 "A soul? A soul is nothing. Can you see it? Smell it? Touch it? No. . . ." Devil **Walter Huston** assures farmer James Craig that the loss of his soul is nothing to become concerned about. Then why is Huston so all-fired intent on getting it? *All That Money Can Buy* aka: *The Devil and Daniel Webster* (1941, RKO).

9549 "There is something in the human soul that sets men above the animals." A voice-over in a film that tells the story of Spencer Tracy, an escapee from a Nazi concentration camp in Germany. Disillusioned and bitter, Tracy regains some of his humanity as he finds there are still good people who help him escape to neutral Holland. *The Seventh Cross* (1944, MGM).

9550 "If only the picture could change and I could be always what I am now. For that, I would give anything. Yes, there's nothing in the whole world I wouldn't give. I'd give my soul for that." Angelic looking, but evil incarnate **Hurd Hatfield** makes a mysterious supernatural pact with the devil while standing before his portrait. *The Picture of Dorian Gray* (1945, MGM).

9551 "Don't ask a dying man to send his soul to hell." Police detective **Sam Levene** makes a moralistic comment to Ava Gardner, who desperately beseeches dying mobster Albert Dekker to clear her name. *The Killers* (1946, Universal-International).

9552 "Your soul can undress in front of me." Charlatan hypnotist **Jose Ferrer** treats Gene Tierney for kleptomania. *Whirlpool* (1949, 20th Century-Fox).

9553 "I'd give my soul to take out my mind, hold it under a faucet and wash away the dirty pictures you put there today." Unforgiving police detective **Kirk Douglas** detests his wife Eleanor Parker when he learns he wasn't her first man; that she became pregnant by small-time criminal Gerald Mohr and had an abortion at the hands of butchering George Macready, a man Douglas hates. *Detective Story* (1951, Paramount).

9554 "Well, you were right, Carrington. Without a soul there's nothing but monstrousness. I only wish that heaven and Jeremy could forgive me for what I did." Demented **Otto Kruger** finally realizes his mistake in transplanting the brain of his deceased brother, brilliant scientist Ross Martin, into the body of a twelve-foot-tall robot. *The Colossus of New York* (1958, Paramount).

9555 "One long ball hitter, that's what we need. I'd sell my soul for one long ball hitter—hey, where did you come from?" In a baseball Faustian musical, die-hard Washington Senators' fan **Robert Shafer** says the magic words and devil Ray Walston shows up to oblige him. *Damn Yankees* (1958, Warner Bros.).

9556 "Listen to me, you wife-loving louse. You belong to me. You sold me your soul. You can't run out on me like this. Ya thief. Ya crook. You robbed me, that's what you did. You robbed me. You robbed me." At the end of the film, devil **Ray Walston** is outraged when Robert Shafer's soul slips through his hands as the middle-aged Washington Senators' fan returns to his wife Shannon Bolin. *Damn Yankees* (1958, Warner Bros.).

9557 "Oh, Richard, it profits man nothing to give his soul for the whole world—but for Wales?" **Paul Scofield**, as Thomas More, sadly confronts John Hurt, a former friend who has betrayed the honorable man for a political appointment. *A Man for All Seasons* (1966, GB, Columbia).

9558 "Never fear, brother, I'm always here to save the souls and heal the ills and cash the checks." Fast-talking bogus television evangelist **D'Urville Martin** repeats his favorite saying. *Black Caesar* (1973, American International).

9559 "We believe that after the human life is over, the soul lives on—in trees, in animals, in fire, in water. . . ." School teacher **Diane Cilento** explains the pagan philosophy of an island community to Edward Woodward, a devoutly Christian virgin middle-aged policeman, who is seeking a girl who has mysteriously disappeared. *The Wicker Man* (1974, GB, British Lion-Warner Bros.).

9560 "First, I will save your soul. Then I will destroy you." Hostile **Lincoln Maazel** accuses his cousin John Amplas of being an 84-year-old vampire from the old country. *Martin* (1978, Libra-Laurel).

9561 "There goes your soul, down the toilet." American expatriate **Charles Bronson** spits the words at corrupt Peruvian Police Captain Fernando Rey who has double-crossed Bronson. *Caboblanco* (1981, Avco Embassy).

9562 "For twelve years I've been forbidden to see my children, but I've seen the soul of D.H. Lawrence." German aristocrat **Janet Suzman** figures the price she had to pay when she eloped with Ian McKellen, as author D.H. Lawrence, is worth it. *Priest of Love* (1981, GB, Filmways).

9563 "Now, give it to me. Take my soul with your cock." Self-destructive floozie **Ornella Muti** offers herself to drunken poet Ben Gazzara, who stands in for writer Charles Bukowski. *Tales of Ordinary Madness* (1982, Italy-Fr., Giugno-Ginis-Miracle).

9564 "See, Daddy, sinners have souls too!" **Margaret Avery** speaks to her alienated preacher father when she switches from singing blues to singing gospel and commandeers the choir of his church. *The Color Purple* (1985, Warner Bros.).

9565 "We are each the keeper of our own souls." **Jeremy Irons**, as Claus von Bulow, tells his lawyer Ron Silver that no one can really know anyone else. *Reversal of Fortune* (1990, Warner Bros.).

Sounds

see also EXPLOSIONS, NOISES, SONGS AND SINGING, SPEECH AND SPEAKING, TALKS AND TALKING, VOICES

9566 TARZAN: "Aaaah-eei-aaaaah." JANE: "What was that?" RIANO: "Bwana—maybe hyena." PARKER: "But that was a human cry." The sound of **Johnny Weissmuller**'s soon-to-be famous yell frightens **Maureen O'Sullivan.** Native bearer **Curtis Nero** makes a suggestion regarding its origin, but **C. Aubrey Smith** knows better. *Tarzan, the Ape Man* (1932, MGM).

9567 "Five times!. . . Wedding bells must sound like an alarm clock to you." It's **Mae West**'s reaction when gentleman caller William B. Davidson tells her he's been married five times. *I'm No Angel* (1933, Paramount).

9568 "A woman who utters such depressing and disgusting sounds has no right to be anywhere." **Leslie Howard**, as Professor Henry Higgins, expresses disgust for flower seller Wendy Hiller as Eliza Doolittle. *Pygmalion* (1938, GB, Pascal-MGM).

9569 "South Bend. . . it sounds like dancing, doesn't it?" **Katharine Hepburn** gushes insincerity when she learns the hometown of unwelcome magazine writer James Stewart. *The Philadelphia Story* (1940, MGM).

9570 "Your American accent is coming along, Sidney—you sound like Bugs Bunny." Con man **Roger Moore** gives the needle to Michael Caine, who will have to impersonate an American scientist in their latest caper. *Bullseye!* (1991, Columbia).

Space

see also HEAVEN, PLACES, TIME, UNIVERSE

9571 "Just room for one inside, sir!" Hearse driver **Miles Malleson** offers a ride to Antony Baird who on a hunch has purposely missed a bus that then crashed. *Dead of Night* (1946, GB, Ealing-Rank-Universal).

9572 "You stifle me; I need some space." **Mia Farrow** can't churn up much enthusiasm for this cliche. *Avalanche* (1978, New World)

9573 "He's very deeply into his own space right now." Weird psychiatrist **Donald Pleasence**, director of a New Jersey mental hospital, refers to a raving murderous pyromaniac. *Alone in the Dark* (1982, New Line).

9574 GILLIAN TAYLOR: "Don't tell me. You're from outer space." CAPT. KIRK: "No, I'm from Iowa. I only work in outer space." **Catherine Hicks** and **William Shatner** share a pizza in 20th century San Francisco. *Star Trek IV: The Voyage Home* (1986, Paramount).

Spanking *see* PUNISHMENTS

Specialties

see also EDUCATION, EXCEPTIONS, PECULIARITIES, TRAINING, USES AND USING

9575 "Killers kill, squealers squeal." Petty thief **Jean-Paul Belmondo** explains how things are to whore-virgin Jean Seberg in this existentialist classic. *Breathless* (*A Bout de Souffle*) (1959, Fr., Imperia Films).

9576 "You enjoy the whole nun mystique, don't you, Mother, because it places you above the ordinary. It makes you something special!" **Stella Stevens**, as modern young Sister George, gives traditional Mother Superior Rosalind Russell some lip. *Where Angels Go, Trouble Follows* (1968, Columbia).

9577 "Besides getting knocked-up, what's your specialty?" **Jane Curtin** remarks snidely to fellow housewife Susan St. James, before the two team with Jessica Lange to take up robbery to balance their housekeeping budgets. *How to Beat the High Cost of Living* (1980, Filmways).

9578 "Special people deserve to be loved." Gay actor **James Coco** seeks acceptance and understanding. *Only When I Laugh* (1981, Columbia).

9579 "You're not special enough to overcome a bad marriage. I am totally convinced that if you marry Flap Horton tomorrow you will ruin your life and make wretched your destiny." **Shirley MacLaine** is so sure of her prediction of disaster for her daughter Debra Winger if she marries Jeff Daniels, that she doesn't show up for the wedding. *Terms of Endearment* (1983, Paramount).

Speech and Speaking

see also CONVERSATIONS, LANGUAGES, SOUNDS, TALKS AND TALKING, THINKING AND THOUGHTS

9580 "No, sir! And we might as well get together on this 'yielding' business right off the bat. I had some pretty good coaching last night and I find that if I yield only for a question, a point of order, or a personal privilege, I can hold this floor a little short of doomsday. In other words, I've got a piece to speak—and blow hot or cold, I'm going to speak it. " Naïve junior U.S. Senator **James Stewart** has learned how to hold a filibuster. He hopes to foil the plans of crooked politicians from his state. *Mr. Smith Goes to Washington* (1939, Columbia).

9581 "Why, they say that when he speaks, stars and stripes come right out of the sky. . . ." New Hampshire farmer **James Craig** joins the friendly competition of making a greater exaggeration about the oratory skills of Daniel Webster, portrayed by Edward Arnold. *All That Money Can Buy* aka: *The Devil and Daniel Webster* (1941, RKO).

9582 "Shove in your clutch." Burlesque queen Sugarpuss O'Shea, played by **Barbara Stanwyck**, gives lexicographer Bertram Potts, played by Gary Cooper, another example of slang for an encyclopedia entry he's working on. *Ball of Fire* (1941, Goldwyn-RKO).

9583 "To most of you, your neighbor is a stranger, a guy with a barking dog and a fence around him. Now you can't be a stranger to any guy who's on your own team. So tear down that fence that separates you. . . . You'll tear down a lot of hate and prejudices. . . . I know a lot of you are saying to yourself: 'He's asking for a miracle!'. . . Well, you're wrong. It's no miracle!. . . I see it happen once every year at Christmas time. . . . Why can't that spirit last the whole year round? Gosh, if it ever did—we'd develop such a strength that no human force could stand against it." Former vagrant **Gary Cooper** reads a speech prepared by reporter Barbara Stanwyck, but the sentiments belong to populist Frank Capra, the director, and Robert Riskin, the screenwriter. *Meet John Doe* (1941, Liberty Films).

9584 "He has a natural flair for politics. . . . That's as fine a political speech as I've heard since Bryan's Crown of Thorns." Judge **Jimmy Conlin** is impressed when Eddie Bracken confesses to the assembled townspeople that he's not a marine hero, but is a fraud. *Hail the Conquering Hero* (1944, Paramount).

9585 "Dr. Parry. . . come. . . it's I. . . Helen." **Dorothy McGuire** who is deaf and mute due to psychological trauma, finds the power of speech to use the phone to call Kent Smith for help at the end of the film. *The Spiral Staircase* (1945, RKO).

9586 "Listen, you hicks! I'm out for blood!" It's part of **Broderick Crawford**'s speech that rouses simple country folk to his banner of political populism. *All the King's Men* (1949, Columbia).

9587 "If we bring a little joy into your humdrum lives, it makes us feel our work ain't been in vain for nothin'." In her curtain call, movie actress **Jean Hagen** blows her cover, revealing that although a beautiful woman, she has a horrible speaking voice. *Singin' in the Rain* (1952, MGM).

9588 "No one speaks like that." **Jack Lemmon** reacts when he hears Tony Curtis parodying Cary Grant's speaking voice. The film is set in 1929, so Grant's voice has not yet been heard in a film. *Some Like It Hot* (1959, United Artists).

9589 "People of the Philippines: I have returned. By the grace of Almighty God, our forces stand again on Philippine soil—soil consecrated in the blood of two peoples. . . . Rally to me. Let the indomitable spirit of Bataan and Corregidor lead on. And the lines of battle roll forward to bring you within the zone of operation, rise and strike. Strike at every favorable opportunity! For your homes and hearths, strike! In the name of your sacred dead, strike! Let no heart be faint. Let every arm be steeled. The guidance of Divine God points the way. Follow in His name to the Holy Grail of righteous victory." Upon returning to the Philippines in World War II, General Douglas MacArthur, played by **Gregory Peck**, makes a radio address to the Philippine people urging them to rise up and destroy the conquering Japanese. *MacArthur* (1977, Universal).

9590 "How hard it is to say what there are no words for, but when a man speaks what's true and what's right, then his mouth is ten feet tall." Poor law student **Harry Hamlin** desperately tries to raise money so he can send his sister Kathleen Beller to Vienna to have an operation that will save her eyesight. *Movie, Movie* (1978, Warner Bros.).

9591 "[She]. . . speaks two languages—English and Gucci." **Anne Bancroft** refers to pretentious socially ambitious daughter-in-law Carrie Fisher. *Garbo Talks* (1984, MGM-United Artists).

Speed

see also HURRY AND HURRYING, RUNNING AND RUNNERS, SLOWNESS

9592 "I'm very quick in a slow way." Even this simple statement has levels and levels of meaning as meaningfully delivered by **Mae West** to Cary Grant. *I'm No Angel* (1933, Paramount).

9593 "He never heard that volley. Lead travels faster than sound." Imprisoned American pilot **Ray Milland** comments to a priest with whom he's playing cards. They are awaiting his execution in Spain and speak of one who has just met his end from a firing squad. *Arise, My Love* (1940, Paramount).

9594 "You'll have to work fast, son. They're hauling her in this Saturday—in a forty million dollar net!" **James Barton**, hoping that Bing Crosby will marry his daughter Jane Wyman, warns Der Bingle that he hasn't much time. Wyman is scheduled to merge with a wealthy playboy on the weekend. *Here Comes the Groom* (1951, Paramount).

9595 "Well, Howard, it all went by so fast, I just had no idea that it would be so quick." **Louise Lasser** responds to Howard Cosell, who covers the consummation of her marriage to Woody Allen as if it were a sporting event. *Bananas* (1971, United Artists).

9596 "God made me devout and—He made me fast." Serious Scottish Christian **Ian Charleson** tries to make his disapproving sister Cheryl Campbell understand that by using the gift God gave him as a competitive runner, he's not running for his glory—but for God's. *Chariots of Fire* (1981, GB, Enigma-20th Century-Fox).

9597 "I feel the need—the need for speed." No, **Tom Cruise** isn't yearning for a fix, he's speaking literally abut flying jet fighter planes. *Top Gun* (1986, Paramount).

9598 "Boy, that was fast! Probably helped that I had the hiccups." Cigarette girl **Mia Farrow**, trying to sleep her way to a career in radio broadcasting, has just completed a quick episode of rooftop romance with a famous radio personality. *Radio Days* (1987, Orion).

Spies

see also ENEMIES, INFORMATION AND INFORMERS, SECRETS

9599 "A spy in love is a tool that has outlived its usefulness." **Lewis Stone**, the head of a spy ring, refers to one of his agents, Karen Morley, who is eliminated by two of Stone's henchmen. *Mata Hari* (1932, MGM).

9600 "While nations have armies and navies, while there is greed, hatred and selfish ambition among men, there will be work for and great need of the spy. . . . While others receive the plaudits of those they have saved, the spy risks his or her all and lives or dies without glory." It's the foreword to a story of the World War I love affair of beautiful Russian spy Constance Bennett and dashing Austrian Captain Gilbert Roland. *After Tonight* (1933, RKO).

9601 "The 39 Steps is the name of an organization of foreign spies collecting information for. . . ." **Wylie Watson**, as Mr. Memory, instinctively reacts to Robert Donat's question, "What are the 39 Steps?" He is cut short by a shot fired by Godfrey Tearle. *The 39 Steps* (1935, GB, Gaumont-British).

9602 IRIS HENDERSON: "Then you are a spy?" MISS FROY: "I've always thought that was such a grim word." **Margaret Lockwood** questions British agent **Dame May Whitty** when she reappears after being captured by enemy agent Paul Lukas. *The Lady Vanishes* (1938, GB, Gaumont-MGM).

9603 "There was a time when I thought I wanted to be some kind of secret agent—I gave it up when I was eight." During World War II, American physicist **Gary Cooper** is about to revive his childhood ambition. *Cloak and Dagger* (1946, United Artists).

9604 "For men like us, there's no higher achievement than to be the master spy—the double agent." **O.E. Hasse** offers Clark Gable the chance to work as a double agent. When Gable declines, claiming it is a question of character, Hasse says, "The spy has no character. He only assumes one." *Betrayed* (1954, MGM).

9605 "A spy who came in from the cold cream." Cosmetics consultant **Doris Day** describes herself and her specialty, industrial espionage. *Caprice* (1967, 20th Century-Fox).

9606 "Don't think we didn't know. . . you're a fascist, you're lower than a worm, you revolt me, you disgust me, you're a spy." **Dominique Sanda** screams at Jean-Louis Trintignant, whose assignment, on the order of Mussolini's fascists, is to kill her husband Enzo Tarascio, a former friend and professor. *The Conformist* (1970, Italy-Fr.-W. Ger., Mars-Marianne-Maran).

9607 "Have you noticed that we are being replaced by young men with blank stupid faces. . .and a dedication to nothing more than efficiency? Keepers of machines, punchers of buttons, hardware men with highly complex toys, and except for language, not an iota of difference between the American model and the Soviet model." Soviet spy **Paul Scofield** sadly reflects on changes in spies to his American counterpart Burt Lancaster. *Scorpio* (1973, United Artists).

9608 "I'm a spy, and I don't care who knows it." Manchurian **Maggie Han**, as Eastern Jewel, confides to Empress Joan Chen that she's proud to be a Japanese spy. *The Last Emperor* (1987, Columbia).

Spinsters

see also BACHELORS, MARRIAGES, WEDDINGS, WIVES, WOMEN

9609 "She's had three husbands, and I'll be an old maid." **Evelyn Keyes** grumbles when her older sister Vivien Leigh marries Clark Gable. *Gone with the Wind* (1939, Selznick-MGM).

9610 "You needn't pity me, because she's really mine. And if she considers me an old maid, it's because I've deliberately made myself one in her eyes. I've done it from the beginning so she wouldn't have the least suspicion." **Bette Davis** has allowed Miriam Hopkins to raise the former's illegitimate daughter as her own. Davis refuses Hopkins' pity when the grown child Jane Bryan berates her "Aunt" Charlotte. *The Old Maid* (1939, Warner Bros.).

9611 "I'm what nature abhors—an old maid. A frozen asset." **Florence Nash** sadly reflects on her man-less existence. *The Women* (1939, MGM).

9612 "She's a perennial spinster." **John Halliday** makes an interesting and perhaps revealing assessment of his daughter, once married to Cary Grant and soon to be married to John Howard. *The Philadelphia Story* (1940, MGM).

9613 "Whenever a young man came and asked for my hand, if my mother said yes, my father said no. And when my father said yes, my mother said no. But Albert came in one of the rare moments when they were both on speaking terms. If I hadn't said yes, who knows when it might have happened again? I might have spent the rest of my life in Kansas. Don't misunderstand me. I love Kansas. I just don't like living there. And besides, I didn't want to be an old maid—not in Kansas!" **Gene Tierney** explains to Don Ameche how she came to be engaged to creep Allyn Joslyn. *Heaven Can Wait* (1943, 20th Century-Fox).

9614 "If you want the brutal truth, you're not the sort of wench men marry. You'll make a proper old maid, Maggie, if I ever saw one." **Charles Laughton** doesn't want his bright 30-year-old daughter Brenda De Banzie to find a husband because she is too valuable as an unpaid worker in his boot shop. *Hobson's Choice* (1954, GB, London Films-United Artists).

9615 "Not too late, you know. She's a well-preserved woman—yes, very well—preserved. And preserves have to be opened someday." **Edmund Gwenn** considers a romance with spinster Mildred Natwick. *The Trouble with Harry* (1955, Paramount).

9616 "I've got to see things the way they are and the way they will be. I've got to start thinking of myself as I am: old maid. Jim will get married, and one of these days even Noah will get married. I'll be the visiting aunt. I'll bring presents to their children to be sure I'm welcome. And Noah will say, 'Junior, be kind to your Aunt Lizzie. Her nerves aren't so good.' And Jim's wife will say, 'She's been visiting here a whole week. Why don't she ever go?' Go where? Go where?" **Katharine Hepburn** pitifully tells her loving and kindly father Cameron Prud'homme that she must accept that she'll spend the rest of her life as a spinster, unwelcome in the homes of her brothers, Lloyd Bridges and Earl Holliman. *The Rainmaker* (1956, Paramount).

9617 "Why not go on and love all the types I fancy, as Ursula Brangwen, spinster, school mistress?" **Sammi Davis** decides not to marry ever. *The Rainbow* (1989, GB, Vestron).

Spirit and Spirits

see also DEATH AND DYING, LIFE AND DEATH, LIVES AND LIVING, MINDS, MOODS, SOULS, SUPERNATURAL

9618 "What you call sins, Principal, I call the great spirit of love, which has thousands of forms." School mistresses **Dorothea Wieck** disagrees with Emilia Unda, who calls lonely and withdrawn student Hertha Thiele's affection for Wieck a sin. *Maedchen In Uniform* (1932, Germany, Deutsche Film-Gemeinschaft).

9619 "You haunted me like a nasty ghost. On rainy nights I could hear you moaning down the chimney." **Miriam Hopkins** relates to Fredric March what she felt about him while she was with her other lover Gary Cooper. *Design for Living* (1933, Paramount).

9620 "Why are you stalking about like Hamlet's ghost?" **May Robson** questions Cary Grant about his constant disappearances from the dinner table to look for a missing dinosaur bone. *Bringing Up Baby* (1938, RKO).

9621 "I have spirit, after all. I used to think you were all sugar water." **Bette Davis** is impressed with her daughter Teresa Wright, who finally rebels against her mother after her father's death. *The Little Foxes* (1941, Goldwyn-RKO).

9622 "No one would recognize me from that—doesn't catch the spirit." Suspected murderer **Cary Grant** doesn't care for his likeness on a wanted poster. *Talk of the Town* (1942, Columbia).

9623 "I am Matt Macauley; I have been dead for two years. But so much of me is still living that I know the end is really the beginning. . . my beliefs still live on in the lives of my loved ones." Omniscient spirit and story-teller **Ray Collins** pops in and out of the film when audiences need some assistance in understanding what's happening. *The Human Comedy* (1942, MGM).

9624 "There is a new spirit abroad in the land. The old days of grab and greed are on the way out. We're beginning to think of what we owe the other fellow, not just what we're compelled to give him. . . ." **Basil Rathbone**, as the great detective, muses to Nigel Bruce as Dr. Watson. *Sherlock Holmes Faces Death* (1943, Universal).

9625 "Build it as a monument to your spirit—which could have been mine!" Publisher **Raymond Massey** gives architect Gary Cooper a final commission before shooting himself. Massey realizes that his wife Patricia Neal loves Cooper. *The Fountainhead* (1949, Warner Bros.).

9626 "I'm a typical rare spirit. I was an orphan until I was twenty, then a rich and beautiful woman adopted me." **Humphrey Bogart** introduces himself. *Beat the Devil* (1954, GB, Romulus-United Artists).

9627 "He that hath no rule over his own spirit is like a city that is broken down and without walls." Torn by inner conflict Reverend **Richard Burton** lectures his Sunday flock. *The Night of the Iguana* (1964, MGM).

9628 "You cannot destroy a spirit. All you can do is drive it from one hell to another. . . ." Medium **Pamela Franklin** asserts that it's hopeless to try to destroy the spirit that is haunting an old mansion. *The Legend of Hell House* (1973, GB, 20th Century-Fox).

9629 "She had spoken out for Creb because she loved him. The sign had come. Finally she understood the vision. Durc was of the clan and one day he would be their leader. She must find her own people, she must walk alone. Everything she had lived through had prepared her for this journey and she was not afraid. For the first time Ayla felt the strength of her own spirit." Narrator **Salome Jens** speaks of Daryl Hannah, the outsider who joins a tribe of prehistoric Neanderthals but now wishes to find her own Cro-Magnon people. *The Clan of the Cave Bear* (1985, Warner Bros.).

9630 "Spirit ain't worth spit without experience." Preacher and gunman **Clint Eastwood** advises gold miner Michael Moriarty. *Pale Rider* (1985, Warner Bros.).

9631 "I hate to go anywhere near an open grave. . . . Besides I don't like to see people in their coffins. . . . They always look so much smaller without their spirits." **Lloyd Bridges** tells his son Ted Danson and grandson Keith Coogan why he didn't attend the funeral of his brother George Coe. *Cousins* (1989, Paramount).

9632 "Lou worked it out that there were seven spiritual planes, and the love we had was somewhere near the top." **Karen Colston** talks of the love she shares with Tom Lycos. *Sweetie* (1989, Australia, Filmpac).

9633 "The human spirit is more powerful than any drug and that's what needs to be nourished." Seeking more funds to help his catatonic patients, Bronx doctor **Robin Williams** optimistically makes a diagnosis for a board of doctors and patrons. *Awakenings* (1990, Columbia).

Sports

see also ENJOYMENTS, ENTERTAINMENTS AND ENTERTAINERS, GAMES, PLAYING AND PLAYERS

9634 GEORGE: "I was once second in an egg and spoon race." HECTOR: "How many runners?" GEORGE: "Two." **George Formby** claims that, like **Guy Middleton**, he is a sportsman. *Keep Fit* (1937, GB, Associated Talking Pictures).

9635 "A great thing, this baseball. It gets the legal cobwebs out of the brain." Law professor and Supreme Court nominee **Ronald Colman** takes some time off from defending Cary Grant on a charge of murder and rivalling him for the affections of Jean Arthur to comment on something trivial like baseball. *Talk of the Town* (1942, Columbia).

9636 "A golf course is nothing but a pool room moved outsides." Elderly pastor **Barry Fitzgerald** emphatically declines an invitation to a golf game with young clerics Bing Crosby and Frank McHugh. *Going My Way* (1944, Paramount).

9637 "But I'm too good a swimmer." Pregnant and unmarried **Betty Hutton** dismisses drowning as an answer to her problems. *The Miracle of Morgan Creek* (1944, Paramount).

9638 "My favorite sport is being kept prisoner." **Tom Neal** sarcastically speaks to Ann Savage, who blackmails him into being her virtual slave. *Detour* (1946, Producers Releasing Corporation).

9639 "I hate brutality, Mr. Anderson. The idea of two men beating each other to a pulp makes me sick." These are the first words of double-double-crossing **Ava Gardner** to boxer Burt Lancaster. *The Killers* (1946, Universal).

9640 "Prize fighting? That's a sport?" Most mothers would probably share **Anne Revere**'s disbelief in her son John Garfield's choice of a career. *Body and Soul* (1947, United Artists).

9641 "This is the only sport in the world where two guys get paid for doing something they'd be arrested for if they got drunk and did it for nothing." Fight manager **Paul Stewart** gives the low-down on the brutal game of boxing. *Champion* (1949, United Artists).

9642 "It's like any other business, only here the blood shows." Boxer **Kirk Douglas** jokes to his crippled brother Arthur Kennedy about his dangerous new occupation. *Champion* (1949, United Artists).

9643 "Two hours after the last fight you still didn't know who I was." **Audrey Totter** wants boxer Robert Ryan to give up the fight game before he becomes permanently damaged. *The Set-Up* (1949, RKO).

9644 "You'll never hit anyone with that hand again." Gambler **Alan Baxter** pounds Robert Ryan's hand to a pulp with a brick after Ryan wins a fight he was supposed to throw. *The Set-Up* (1949, RKO).

9645 "Golf is what I call a nice game. . . . I mean it, dignified and fresh air. Men and women both. Now you can take them lady rasslers. Now that's something I can't stomach. That's something that shouldn't ought to be allowed." Gangster **Sammy White** has some definite views on sports. *Pat and Mike* (1952, MGM).

9646 "A clean sweep for the United States provides a precious nineteen points, putting the Americans ahead in the team scores. With this victory, Bob Mathias joins the sports immortals, the only man to win the Olympic Decathlon twice. Honored in sports as a champion, he seeks further honor in accepting the responsibilities of his time and his generation. This is the kind of a boy a small town in America produced." The narrator brings to a close the sports biopic, starring Bob Mathias as himself. *The Bob Mathias Story* (1954, Allied Artists).

9647 "I won the kid in a crap game. I couldn't hock him, so I thought I'd do something with him." Fight manager **Gene Kelly**, referring to boxer Steve Mitchell, explains to Cyd Charisse how he got into the prize fighting business. *It's Always Fair Weather* (1955, MGM).

9648 "Fighters ain't human!" That's precisely how sleazy fight manager **Edward Andrews** treats the boxers in his stable. *The Harder They Fall* (1956, Columbia).

9649 "Professional boxing should be banned even if it takes an act of Congress to do it." Sports writer **Humphrey Bogart** (in his last film) begins an article on the "sport" at the end of the movie that deglamorizes boxing. *The Harder They Fall* (1956, Columbia).

9650 BIG DADDY: "But if you still got sports in your blood, go back to sports announcing." BRICK: "Sit in a glass box watchin' games I can't play. Describin' what I can't do while players are doing it? Sweatin' out their disgust and confusion in contests I'm not fit for? Drinkin' a Coke half bourbon, so I can stand it? That's no damn good anymore. Time just outran me, Big Daddy—got there first." **Burl Ives** doesn't understand that his son **Paul Newman**'s problems go a lot deeper than his inability to participate in sports anymore. *Cat on a Hot Tin Roof* (1958, MGM).

9651 "Small colleges and all. Musical beds is the faculty sport around here." History professor **Richard Burton** welcomes new faculty member George Segal. *Who's Afraid of Virginia Woolf?* (1966, Warner Bros.).

9652 "When you reach twenty-seven you know you'll never be a professional athlete—then you reach thirty and you watch others to see when they're going to give up." While riding in a subway, one-time athlete **John Cassavetes** shares his sadness for not making it big in sports with his friends Peter Falk and Ben Gazzara. *Husbands* (1970, Columbia).

9653 "Basketball. . . is staying in after school in your underwear." Trying to avoid the draft and being sent to Vietnam, **Michael Margotta**, a mad man who pretends he's mad (or one whose pretensons of madness drives him mad), makes a reasonably sane comment about his friend William Tepper's extra-curricular activity at an Ohio college. *Drive, He Said* (1971, Columbia).

9654 LINDA CHRISTIE: "Do you always think of baseball when you're making love?" ALLAN FELIX: "It keeps me going." LINDA: "Yea, I couldn't figure out why you kept yelling 'Slide.'" **Diane Keaton** and **Woody Allen** hold a post-coital discussion. *Play It Again, Sam* (1972, Paramount).

9655 "I've loved baseball since Arnold Rothstein fixed the World Series in 1919." **Lee Strasberg**, the head of the Jewish branch of organized crime, talks to Al Pacino about the national pastime. *The Godfather, Part II* (1974, Paramount).

9656 "I was a great athlete. I was all-school yard." **Woody Allen** makes a sentimental journey back to the Brooklyn neighborhood where he grew up with his lover Diane Keaton and friend Tony Roberts. *Annie Hall* (1977, United Artists).

9657 "If you can't be an athlete, be an athletic supporter." Speaking to the student body, Principal **Eve Arden** innocently repeats a very old joke. *Grease* (1978, Paramount).

9658 ROCKY BALBOA: "Apollo? You awake?" APOLLO CREED: "Yeah." ROCKY: "Can I ask you somethin'?" APOLLO: "Yeah." ROCKY: "Did you give me your best shot?" APOLLO: "Yeah, I did." ROCKY: "Thank you." After pummelling each other in the boxing match of the first Rocky movie, both bloodied challenger **Sylvester Stallone** and champion **Carl Weathers** are hospitalized. At the beginning of the sequel, in the middle of the night, Stallone enters Weathers' room to satisfy his curiosity and pride. *Rocky II* (1979, United Artists).

9659 "If nations could settle their differences on the football pitch, wouldn't that be a challenge?" Nazi Commandant **Max von Sydow** speaks hopefully to P.O.W. Michael Caine. Wonder what he'd think if he knew how many people have been killed in soccer stadium riots? *Victory* (1981, Paramount).

9660 ALAN SWANN: "Are you still in the fight game?" ROOKIE CARROCA: "In a way, I married Benjy's mother." Has-been movie star **Peter O'Toole** chats with one-time bantam weight **Ramon Sison**, now married to Mark Linn-Baker's mother Lainie Kazan. *My Favorite Year* (1982, MGM-United Artists).

9661 "Football is my shot, my way out." High school football star **Tom Cruise** hopes to escape the fate of his father and brother, stuck in the steel mills of a Pennsylvania town. *All the Right Moves* (1983, 20th Century-Fox).

9662 "I, I miss the cricket." **Rupert Everett**, loosely based on British traitor Guy Burgess, admits to a reporter that there is something he misses since he fled England for Russia. *Another Country* (1984, GB, Orion Classics).

9663 "There's never been a ball player who slept with me who didn't have the best year of his career... what I give them lasts a lifetime, what they give me lasts a hundred fifty-two games. Sometimes it seems like a bad trade, but bad trades are part of baseball." Intellectual groupie **Susan Sarandon** offers more than merely a great roll in the hay to her baseball lovers. *Bull Durham* (1988, Orion).

9664 "Getting thrown out of baseball...was like having part of me amputated.... I'd wake up at night with the smell of ballpark in my nose, the cool of the grass at my feet." Shoeless Joe Jackson was an illiterate country boy, but **Ray Liotta** makes him sound sensitive and poetic. *Field of Dreams* (1989, Universal).

9665 "The one constant through all the years, Ray, has been baseball. America has rolled by like an army of steam rollers. It's been erased like a blackboard, rebuilt and erased again.... Baseball has marked the time. This field, this game is part of our past.... It reminds us of all what once was good and can be again." J.D. Salinger—like author **James Earl Jones**—uses baseball as a metaphor for more innocent times when America believed in its dream for all of its people. *Field of Dreams* (1989, Universal).

9666 "Vaughn, a juvenile delinquent in the off-season, now pitching." Baseball announcer **Bob Uecker** gives some background dope on Cleveland Indians' pitcher Charlie Sheen. *Major League* (1989, Paramount).

9667 "I like to hit home runs." In 25 big league appearances in the film, **John Goodman**, appearing as Babe Ruth, hits 22 home runs, one single, and strikes out twice. That's an amazing batting average and slugging percentage. *The Babe* (1992, Universal).

9668 "Baseball is what gets inside you. It's what lights you up." Eccentric baseball manager **Tom Hanks** tells his female players for the Rockford Peaches that baseball goes deeper than what happens between the white lines. *A League of Their Own* (1992, Columbia).

Stars

see also ENTERTAINMENTS AND ENTERTAINERS, MOTION PICTURES, PERFORMANCES, SHOWS, THEATERS, UNIVERSE

9669 "You're going out a youngster—but you've got to come back a star." Theater director **Warner Baxter** heightens chorus girl Ruby Keeler's jitters with his last minute instructions as she is sent out on the stage, replacing the injured star Bebe Daniels. *42nd Street* (1933, Warner Bros.).

9670 "[They] took the idols and smashed them, the Fairbanks, the Gilberts, the Valentinos! Who've we got now? Just some nobodies." Silent screen star

Gloria Swanson doesn't believe that actors of the talkie era can compete with the stars of her day. *Sunset Boulevard* (1950, Paramount).

9671 "No one ever leaves a star. That's what makes one a star." **Gloria Swanson** makes an appeal with what she considers perfect logic to her kept man William Holden when he prepares to leave her. *Sunset Boulevard* (1950, Paramount).

9672 "They can't put me out to pasture. Why I'm an institution. Girls talked like me, imitated my make-up, my hair. . . . I was a star. I am a star!" Once famous Hollywood actress **Bette Davis'** career is in decline. Those girls probably also wished they had "Bette Davis" eyes. *The Star* (1952, 20th Century-Fox).

9673 "You've got that little something extra that Ellen Terry talked about. Ellen Terry, a great actress long before you were born. She said that that was what star quality was—that little something extra. Well, you've got it." While we're not certain Judy Garland's character in the movie has that "little something" extra that **James Mason** and Ellen Terry speak of, we're certain Garland had it. *A Star Is Born* (1954, Warner Bros.).

9674 "You look up at the sky and you cry for a star. You know you'll never get it. And then one night you look down—and there it is—shining in your hand." Plain spinster **Katharine Hepburn** tells con man Burt Lancaster that she's found happiness at last with Deputy Sheriff Wendell Corey. *The Rainmaker* (1956, Paramount).

9675 "Perseus and Andromeda will be happy together, have fine sons, rule wisely. And to perpetuate the story of his courage, I command that from henceforth he will be set among the stars and constellations. He, Perseus, the lovely Andromeda, the noble Pegasus, and even the vain Cassiopeia. Let the stars be named after them forever. As long as men shall walk the earth and search the night sky in wonder, they will remember the courage of Perseus forever. Even if we, the gods, are abandoned or forgotten, the stars will never fade, never. They will burn till the end of time." **Laurence Olivier**, as Zeus, honors Harry Hamlin, as Perseus, and Judi Bowker as Andromeda. *Clash of the Titans* (1981, ABC-MGM-United Artists).

9676 "God, I want to be a star so bad." Unemployed, gay actor **James Coco** has been trying, unsuccessfully, for twenty years to make it big in the entertainment industry. *Only When I Laugh* (1981, Columbia).

9677 "I just want to be in a swimming pool, eating tacos and signing autographs." **Susan Berman** has

a vague notion of her goals and fantasies of becoming a rock music star. *Smithereens* (1982, New Line).

Starvation *see* FOOD AND EATING, HUNGER

States *see* COUNTRIES, GOVERNMENTS, SOCIETIES

Statistics *see* PROBABILITY AND STATISTICS

Stealing *see* CRIMES AND CRIMINALS

Stimulation

see also ACTIONS AND ACTS, EXCITEMENTS

9678 "I hate cold showers. They stimulate me, then I don't know what to do." Comedy relief **Oscar Levant** lightens the mood of the melodrama. *Humoresque* (1947, Warner Bros.).

9679 "I've never caught a thief before. This is quite stimulating!" **Grace Kelly** is quite pleased with herself for deducing that Cary Grant is a cat burglar. As far as she's concerned, it makes him all the more desirable. *To Catch a Thief* (1955, Paramount).

9680 "Look, it happens to everybody. I mean, I love your mother, but, you know, sometimes you need a little stimulation, you know." Believing the only possible reason that Diane Keaton and his son Joseph Hindy would be getting a divorce is someone's infidelity, **Richard Castellano** confesses he once strayed, but he and Bea Arthur stayed married. *Lovers and Other Strangers* (1970, GB, Cinerama).

Stories

see also BOOKS, FICTION, LEGENDS, ROMANCES, TALKS AND TALKING, TRUTH AND FALSEHOOD, WRITING AND WRITERS

9681 "His story is like women's complexion—makes it up as she goes along." **Warner Oland**, as Charlie Chan, doesn't buy a suspect's story. *The Black Camel* (1931, Fox).

9682 "1847. . . in the gay half-world of Paris, the gentlemen of the day met the girls of the moment at certain theaters, balls and gambling clubs, where the code was discretion, but the game was romance. This is the story of one of those pretty creatures, living in the shifting sands of popularity—Marguerite Gautier, who brightened her wit with champagne and sometimes her eyes with tears." It's the opening subtitle of a romantic classic. *Camille* (1937, MGM).

9683 "I don't know what's wrong with Europe, but I do know a story when I see one, and I'll keep after it until I get it or it gets me." American crime reporter **Joel McCrea** is in Europe to get the low down on the events leading up to World War II. *Foreign Correspondent* (1940, United Artists).

9684 "This is the story of a ship." The foreword to a splendid British flagwaver about the survivors of the torpedoed destroyer Torrin. *In Which We Serve* (1942, GB, Two Cities-Rank).

9685 "There are eight million stories in the naked city. This has been one of them." Narrator **Mark Hellinger** ends the New York crime film. There are more stories today. *The Naked City* (1948, Universal).

9686 "You see, the story of the Red River D started this way. Along about August of 1851, Tom Dunston and me left St. Louis and joined a wagon train headed for Californy. After about three weeks in the trail we was to the northern border of Texas. . . ." Narrator **Walter Brennan** sets the stage for the beginning of a Western adventure classic. *Red River* (1948, United Artists).

9687 "Out of the shadows of knowledge, and out of a painting that hung on a museum wall, comes our story, the truth of which lies not on our screen but in your heart." The foreword to the romantic fantasy was written by Ben Hecht. *Portrait of Jennie* (1949, Selznick-Vanguard).

9688 "I thought this was going to be a 30-day stretch—maybe 60. Now it's a year. It looks like a life sentence. Where is it?. . . Where's that big story to get me out of here?" One-time big city reporter **Kirk Douglas** dreams of a story big enough to be his ticket off the small New Mexico newspaper he's working for. *Ace in the Hole* aka: *The Big Carnival* (1951, Paramount).

9689 "My story begins eleven years ago and two thousand miles away in my native Poland." Concentration camp survivor **Valentina Cortese** tells the story of how she assumed her dead friend's identity, so that on her release she would be sent to America. *The House on Telegraph Hill* (1951, 20th Century-Fox).

9690 "What a time we've had, Rosie. We'll never lack for stories to tell our grandchildren." **Humphrey Bogart** and Katharine Hepburn have survived a dangerous journey down river, being captured and sentenced to hang by the Germans, and the sinking of the Germans' boat by the wreckage of their tug. *The African Queen* (1952, United Artists).

9691 "My name is Johnny Barrett, and this is my story. . . as far as it went." Journalist **Peter Breck** narrates a film in which he gets himself admitted to a mental asylum to solve the murder of an inmate. *Shock Corridor* (1963, Allied Artists).

9692 "The old sad story, promising youth blighted, dragged down by money, position, noblesse oblige." It's **Sean Connery**'s self-mocking reply when Tippi Hedren asks, "What about your tough childhood, Mr. Rutland?" *Marnie* (1964, Universal).

9693 "This was the story of Howard Beale, the first known instance of a man who was killed because he had lousy ratings." Narrator **Lee Richardson** comments after news anchorman Peter Finch is gunned down on his show by radicals hired by the network. *Network* (1976, MGM-United Artists).

9694 "There is no way of telling his story without telling my own." Military assassin **Martin Sheen** refers to his target, out-of-control Colonel Marlon Brando. *Apocalypse Now* (1979, United Artists).

9695 "I've told these stories so many times that I've almost forgot it was me who had these things happen to him. It seems like somebody else." Ex-football star **Dennis Quaid**, once known as The Grey Ghost, talks to his wife Jessica Lange about his memories of his past glories on the gridiron. *Everybody's All-American* (1988, Warner Bros.).

9696 "It wasn't just a story, was it?" Young **Sarah Polley** questions John Neville about his adventures, which she thinks she's shared. *The Adventures of Baron Munchausen* (1989, Columbia).

9697 "One time there was this lake and it was right outside of town. . . . One November this big flock of ducks came and landed on the lake. Then the temperature dropped real low and the lake froze over. The ducks flew off and took the lake with them— and now they say that lake is somewhere over in Georgia." **Mary Stuart Masterson** repeats her dead brother's favorite story to Mary-Louise Parker as the latter dies of cancer. *Fried Green Tomatoes* (1991, Universal).

9698 "My version will be more interesting than yours." Evil nanny **Rebecca De Mornay** warns slightly retarded handyman Ernie Hudson that he won't be believed if he tells her employer Annabelle Sciorra and Matt McCoy that he saw her nursing their baby. To make certain, she sets up Hudson so it appears that he's molested the couple's young daughter. *The Hand That Rocks the Cradle* (1991, Hollywood Pictures-Buena Vista).

Strangeness and Strangers

see also ALIENS, ECCENTRICITIES, FOREIGNERS, FRIENDSHIP AND FRIENDS, GUESTS, KNOWLEDGE, UNKNOWNS, VISITS

9699 "All people who behave strangely are not insane." Psychiatrist **Fritz Feld** discusses irrational behavior with ditzy Katharine Hepburn while she nonchalantly stuffs her mouth with olives. *Bringing Up Baby* (1938, RKO).

9700 "There's something definitely queer in here." **Michael Redgrave**'s understatement is made on a train journeying across Europe filled with spies and other suspicious acting passengers. *The Lady Vanishes* (1938, GB, Gainsborough-Gaumont).

9701 "Twenty-two weeks the men were out, as the strike moved into winter. It was strange to go out onto the street and find men there in the day time. I had a feeling of fright in it, and always the mood of the men grew uglier." Narrator **Irving Pichel** recalls a coal miners' strike in his Welsh village that alienated his brothers from their father. *How Green Was My Valley* (1941, 20th Century-Fox).

9702 "My, my, it's strange how it's always cold in the winter and warm in the summer, isn't it?" **Billie Burke** appears in another of her flittering idiot roles. *Topper Returns* (1941, Roach-United Artists).

9703 "Ever strike you—that you're acting strangely? . . . You'll end up in a psychiatric ward. I don't think they've ever had a patient who fell in love with a corpse." **Clifton Webb** accuses Dana Andrews of obsessive behavior, bordering on necrophilia. *Laura* (1944, 20th Century-Fox).

9704 "It was strange. Here I was, among all those people, and at the same time, I felt as if I were looking at them from some place far away. The whole place seemed to me like a deep hole and the people down in it like strange animals, like—like snakes, and I'd been thrown in it. Yes, as though—as though I were in a snake pit." As the film shows it, **Olivia de Havilland** describes her vision of an insane asylum to her physician Leo Genn. *The Snake Pit* (1948, 20th Century-Fox).

9705 "It's funny how things turn out." Actress **Lana Turner** finds herself in competition with her daughter Sandra Dee for the affections of John Gavin. *Imitation of Life* (1959, Universal-International).

9706 "That's funny. . . . That plane's dustin' crops where there ain't no crops." Standing at the side of

the highway in northern Indiana, **Malcolm Atterbury**'s comment about a crop-dusting plane alerts Cary Grant to his danger. *North by Northwest* (1959, MGM).

9707 DR. SCHUMANN: "You're so strange—sometimes you're so bitter, then you're like a child, soft and warm." LA CONDESA: "I'm just a woman." **Oskar Werner** and **Simone Signoret** are absolutely brilliant as middle-aged partners in a doomed but beautiful ship-board love affair. *Ship of Fools* (1965, Columbia).

9708 "Mrs. Robinson, if you don't mind my saying so, this conversation is getting a little strange." Alone with Anne Bancroft, **Dustin Hoffman** begins to suspect she's trying to seduce him. *The Graduate* (1967, United Artists-Embassy).

9709 "We're all strangers, but after a while, you get used to it. You become deeper strangers. That's sort of love." With touching sincerity, **Richard Castellano** attempts to explain marriage to his son Joseph Hindy, who is planning a divorce from his wife Diane Keaton. *Lovers and Other Strangers* (1970, ABC-Cinerama).

9710 "Strange to have a daughter who wouldn't go through with her wedding night. When I was her age I'd go through with just 'bout any old night." **Ellen Burstyn** finds it hard to believe that her daughter Cybill Shepherd didn't sleep with Timothy Bottoms after the two ran off to be married. *The Last Picture Show* (1971, Columbia).

9711 "I think it's strange of you to think it's strange of me." Having been unsuccessful in his attempts to have just one passionate love affair in his life, **Alan Arkin** telephones his wife and asks her to meet him for a tryst. *Last of the Red Hot Lovers* (1972, Paramount).

9712 "With strangers, anything is possible." Melancholy **Yves Montand** holds out hope for something good to come of a relationship with equally despondent Romy Schneider. *Clair de Femme* (1980, Fr., Atlantic).

9713 "You can't handle mess. You need everything neat and easy. I don't know who you are. I don't know what we were playing at." Tearful **Donald Sutherland** questions his love for his wife Mary Tyler Moore, who has become a stranger, unable to express her love, since one of their sons was accidentally killed. *Ordinary People* (1980, Paramount).

9714 "After all these years, are you trying to tell me there's something strange about you?" **Candice**

Bergen is a bit suspicious when her life-long friend Jacqueline Bisset asks the former to kiss her at midnight on New Year's Eve. *Rich and Famous* (1981, MGM-United Artists).

9715 "What did we just do, become strangers?" **Keith Carradine** protests when Genevieve Bujold tells him that you don't know someone just because you slept with them. *Choose Me* (1984, Island Alive).

9716 "You are a strange species, not like any other. You are at your best when things are at their worst." Considering the small sample of humans alien **Jeff Bridges** has encountered, it's surprising that he would pay such a compliment to the human race. Perhaps earthling Karen Allen more than makes up for those who would capture Bridges and make him a specimen to be examined, dissected and destroyed. *Starman* (1984, Columbia).

9717 "I never did like two-faced women. It's amazing how greed and growing old make people act strange. At least those are two things I'll never have to worry about. By the way, what the hell was in those green bottles?" Unlicensed private investigator **Billy Dee Williams** is hired to kill the wife of a Wall Street tycoon, only to discover that murder's not the real crime. *Deadly Illusion* (1987, Cinetel).

9718 "I saw her drink the battery juice from your Honda!" **Alyson Hannigan** reports to her scientist father Dan Aykroyd that his new bride Kim Basinger, an alien from a distant galaxy, had a little pick-me-up. *My Stepmother Is an Alien* (1988, Columbia).

9719 "Be nice to strangers, 'cause sometimes you're a stranger too." Dimwitted escaped con **Sean Penn**, mistaken for an ecclesiastical monk, is asked to give a sermon and complies. *We're No Angels* (1989, Paramount).

Strengths

see also COURAGE, FORCE, POWER, WEAKNESS

9720 "The strength of the vampire is that people will not believe in him." **Edward Van Sloan**, as Professor Van Helsing, warns his fellow mortals. *Dracula* (1931, Universal).

9721 PRINCE SIRKI: "Now you see me as I really am." GRAZIA: "I've always seen you that way. I love you." SIRKI: "Now I know that Love is stronger than Death." **Fredric March** as Death relinquishes his human form and becomes a black apparition, but **Evelyn Venable** is not afraid and eagerly leaves with him. *Death Takes a Holiday* (1934, Paramount).

9722 "I'm well and strong and nothing can touch me." Wealthy playgirl **Bette Davis** holds this opinion until she is diagnosed as having a brain tumor. *Dark Victory* (1939, Warner Bros.).

9723 "Say it to America. Arise my love, and make yourself strong. Is it going to be their way of life, or ours?" **Claudette Colbert** and Ray Milland leave Europe for the safety of America after the fall of France to the Germans. *Arise, My Love* (1940, Paramount).

9724 "You thought you could be Mrs. de Winter—live in her house—walk in her steps—take the things that were hers. But she's too strong for you. You can't fight her. No one ever got the better of her—never—never. She was beaten in the end. But it wasn't a man—it wasn't a woman—it was the sea." Housekeeper **Judith Anderson** rages at Joan Fontaine about the first Mrs. de Winter. *Rebecca* (1940, United Artists).

9725 "I don't believe the Lord means for the strong to parade their strength, but I don't mind doing it if it has to be done." Ruthless, scheming, businessman **Charles Dingle** knows it's a dirty job, but someone has to do it. *The Little Foxes* (1941, Goldwyn).

9726 "In these times, we must be like steel." Norwegian patriot **Ann Sheridan** tells her lover Errol Flynn that they must be strong in their struggle against Nazi occupation. *Edge of Darkness* (1943, Warner Bros.).

9727 "Love is stronger than life—it reaches beyond the shadow of death." **Clifton Webb** has a sick fantasy that he will be able to hold onto Gene Tierney even if he kills her. *Laura* (1944, 20th Century-Fox).

9728 "Let me tell you all about making men strong: Einstein couldn't kick a football across the floor, but he changed the shape of the universe." Teacher **Kirk Douglas** has a no-win argument about the meaning of strength with brawny businessman Paul Douglas. *A Letter to Three Wives* (1949, 20th Century-Fox).

9729 "No, nothing can bring back the hour of splendor in the grass, glory in the flower. We will grieve not, rather find strength in what remains behind." **Natalie Wood** tested her recovery from a nervous collapse by seeing Warren Beatty again. She finds that he hasn't matched her maturity, and she can let go of the tragic love she felt for him. *Splendor in the Grass* (1961, Warner Bros.).

9730 "I wish I was a stronger person. . . . I lost my husband four years ago. . . . It's terrible how you depend on someone for strength." **Jessica Tandy** is terrified of being left alone as she talks to Tippi Hedren. *The Birds* (1963, Universal).

9731 "He's strong. Anyone who can get in front of an audience for 57 years has to be strong." **George Burns** expresses admiration and encouragement about his long-time partner Walter Matthau who has suffered a heart attack. *The Sunshine Boys* (1975, MGM).

Struggles

see also BATTLES AND BATTLEFIELDS, DIFFICULTIES, FIGHTS AND FIGHTING

9732 "You love me and you know it. There's no sense in struggling with a thing when it's got you." **Carole Lombard** tries to get William Powell to acknowledge that he loves her. *My Man Godfrey* (1936, Universal).

9733 "See these fingers, dear hearts! These fingers have veins that lead straight to the soul of man! The right hand, friends! The hand of love! Now watch and I'll show you the story of life. The fingers of these hands, dear hearts! They're always a-tuggin' and a-warin' one hand agin' th' other." Maniacal con man preacher **Robert Mitchum** has H-A-T-E tattooed on the fingers of his left hand and L-O-V-E on those of his right hand. *The Night of the Hunter* (1955, United Artists).

9734 "On the surface, she was all sex and devil-may-care, yet everything in her was struggling towards respectability. She never gave up trying." **Laurence Harvey** tells his wife Dina Merrill about his deceased mistress Elizabeth Taylor. *Butterfield 8* (1960, MGM).

9735 "There's a conflict within every human heart between the rational and the irrational, but the good does not always triumph." General **G.D. Spradlin** justifies his orders to have Martin Sheen assassinate renegade colonel Marlon Brando. *Apocalypse Now* (1979, United Artists).

9736 "As long as a single man is forced to cower under the iron fist of oppression, as long as a child cries out in the night or an actor can be elected president, we must continue to struggle." It's the opinion of **Lucy Gutteridge**, the daughter of a scientist held captive by the East Germans, in a boring spoof from the creators of *Airplane*. *Top Secret!* (1984, Paramount).

Stubbornness

see also DETERMINATION, REFUSALS AND REJECTIONS

9737 "Obstinate as a mule. . . . You got your nasty feet dug in the ground and you don't intend to budge an inch, do you?. . . If there is anything in the world that infuriates me, it's sheer wanton stubbornness. I should like to cut off your head with a meat ax." Out-of-control **Robert Montgomery** threatens his new bride Una Merkel on their wedding night when she won't give in to his demand that they vacate their hotel because his ex-wife Norma Shearer is at the same hotel on her honeymoon with her new husband Reginald Denny. *Private Lives* (1931, MGM).

9738 "I think I'll stick around. I had a friend once who collected postage stamps. Said the best thing about 'em was they stuck to one thing till they got there. I'm kinda like that too." Mild-mannered Deputy Sheriff **James Stewart** invents a little parable to demonstrate his stubbornness when it's suggested that he leave town. *Destry Rides Again* (1939, Universal).

Studies and Students

see also EDUCATION, LEARNING AND LESSONS, SCHOOLS, TEACHING AND TEACHERS

9739 "She's like she was studying you, like you were a play or a book or a set of blueprints." Maid **Thelma Ritter** is the first to suspect that shy Anne Baxter isn't what she seems. *All About Eve* (1950, 20th Century-Fox).

9740 "Medical students were described by the novelist Charles Dickens as a parcel of lazy, idle fellows, who are always smoking, drinking and lounging. That is, unfortunately, still true." Proper, ultra-conservative Dean **Geoffrey Keen** indifferently welcomes the new medical students to St. Swithan's Hospital. *Doctor in the House* (1954, GB, Rank).

9741 "Not until your grades improve." Pretty teen **Jill Schoelen** refuses to go all the way with Brad Pitt until he gets serious about his studies. *Cutting Class* (1989, Republic).

9742 "At Ruppert High, there are only two types of students, cooperative and life-threatening." Ruppert High teacher **Richard Libertini** reports his findings to newsman Bruce Willis, who is interviewing Libertini about one of his former students. *Bonfire of the Vanities* (1990, Warner Bros.).

9743 "At Ruppert High, a good student is one who comes to class every day and doesn't piss on the teacher." Teacher **Richard Libertini** answers when reporter Bruce Willis asks if a comatose mugger was a good student. *Bonfire of the Vanities* (1990, Warner Bros.).

Stupidity

see also DULLNESS, IGNORANCE, INTELLIGENCE, KNOWLEDGE, LEARNING AND LESSONS, SENSE AND SENSIBILITY, SLOWNESS, STUDIES AND STUDENTS, TEACHING AND TEACHERS, UNDERSTANDINGS AND MISUNDERSTANDINGS

9744 "A girl is a fool if she doesn't get ahead. It's just as easy to get a rich man as a poor man." **Jean Harlow** believes that the way for a woman to succeed is to marry well. *Red-Headed Woman* (1932, MGM).

9745 "Chicolini here may look like an idiot, he may speak like an idiot, but don't let that fool you—he really is an idiot." **Groucho Marx** defends Chico Marx, accused of being a traitor. *Duck Soup* (1933, Paramount).

9746 "The only crime punishable by death is stupidity." Egotistical criminal lawyer **Claude Rains** specializes in helping acquit murderers. *Crime Without Passion* (1934, Paramount).

9747 "You're an old idiot, but I can't help but love you." **Kathleen Howard** finally finds something nice to say about her husband W.C. Fields. *It's a Gift* (1934, Paramount).

9748 "We're all fools sometimes, only you choose such awkward times." **Katharine Hepburn** scolds her embezzler father Edmund Gwenn. *Sylvia Scarlett* (1935, RKO).

9749 "You weigh 163 pounds. You're a very stupid fellow and not likely to succeed. . . . You weigh 163 pounds. You're a very stupid fellow and not likely to succeed. . . . Save your money, sucker, I've told you twice already." Infuriated Arthur Lake invests three pennies in a fortune-telling scale to get insulting cards. *Blondie* (1938, Columbia).

9750 "You'll kiss me for this one. A dam!. . . I can see from the expression on your face you don't know what a dam is. A dam is something you put concrete in. You're kind of dumb this morning, aren't you, Dan?" Political boss **Akim Tamiroff** is an unexpected and unwelcomed visitor to the office of newly elected Governor Brian Donlevy. *The Great McGinty* (1940, Paramount).

9751 "He picks on me, too. The other day he called me an idiot. What could I do? I said, 'Yes, Mr. Matuschak, I'm an idiot.' I'm no fool." **Felix Bressart** tells James Stewart how he manages to get along with their bullying boss Frank Morgan. *The Shop Around the Corner* (1940, MGM).

9752 "Lady, the things I don't know, you could herd like cows." Using picturesque language, country doctor **Harry Carey** admits his limitations to Carole Lombard. *They Knew What They Wanted* (1940, RKO).

9753 "What a sap, going on a heist with a girl and a little dog." In a move out of character for an experienced robber, **Humphrey Bogart** lets Ida Lupino talk him into taking her and a mongrel dog with him on a caper at a resort hotel. *High Sierra* (1941, Warner Bros.).

9754 "Look, baby, you can't get away with it. . . . You want to knock him off, don't you?. . . what did you think I was anyway?. . . A guy who walks into a good lookin' dame's front parlor and says, 'Good afternoon, I sell accident insurance on husbands. You got one that's been around too long, one you'd like to turn into a little hard cash? Just give me a smile and I'll help you to collect.' Boy, what a dope you must think I am." Insurance salesman **Fred MacMurray** is outraged that Barbara Stanwyck would figure he's so stupid. She "innocently" asks him if it is possible to take out an insurance policy on her husband without him knowing it. He proves her right by devising just such a plan. *Double Indemnity* (1944, Paramount).

9755 "To regain one's youth one has merely to repeat one's follies." **George Sanders** offers Hurd Hatfield advice on how to stay eternally young. *The Picture of Dorian Gray* (1945, MGM).

9756 "I may be stupid, but I know when I'm licked." Private eye **Mark Stevens** is framed for murder. *The Dark Corner* (1946, 20th Century-Fox).

9757 "The boy has a fine mind, but it's overtaxed. That's the trouble. It's too good a mind. A weak mind isn't strong enough to hurt itself. Stupidity has saved many a man from going mad." Surgeon **Roger Livesey** views the intelligence of his patient David Niven with regret. *A Matter of Life and Death* aka: *Stairway to Heaven* (1946, GB, Archers-GFD-Universal).

9758 "We are protected by the enormity of your stupidity." **Leopoldine Konstantin** disparages her son Claude Rains when he confesses his discovery that his wife Ingrid Bergman is an American spy sent to infiltrate the organization of South American Nazi renegades to which he belongs. *Notorious* (1946, RKO).

9759 "Why did God make so many dumb fools and—Democrats?" We don't know if conservative businessman **William Powell** meant to be redundant or not. *Life with Father* (1947, Warner Bros.).

9760 "When I start out to make a fool of myself, there's very little can stop me." Narrator **Orson Welles** delivers the movie's first line. *The Lady from Shanghai* (1948, Columbia).

9761 "I am stupid and I like it. I got everything I want. I got two fur coats. . . . I tell you what I would like. I'd like to learn to talk good." Dumb blonde **Judy Holliday** proves to be an excellent student for William Holden, hired by Broderick Crawford to improve his mistress' manners. *Born Yesterday* (1950, Columbia).

9762 "I love that broad. Do you think we could find some one to make her dumb again?" Dishonest businessman **Broderick Crawford** regrets having hired William Holden to smooth off the rough edges of his mistress Judy Holliday. She's become too smart for Crawford's taste. *Born Yesterday* (1950, Columbia).

9763 "You couldn't play it smart, could you? All ya had to do was box. But no, not you, you hardhead!" Top Sergeant **Burt Lancaster** regrets the stubborn stupidity of Montgomery Clift, whose bucking the system indirectly leads to his death. *From Here to Eternity* (1953, Columbia).

9764 PETE PATTERSON: "How stupid can you get?" FREDDIE FRANKLIN: "How stupid do you want me to be?" **Bud Abbott**'s rhetorical question elicits one from **Lou Costello.** *Abbott and Costello Meet the Mummy* (1955, Universal-International).

9765 "Oh, darling, how could I have been so stupid? That's what I mean, you know, finesse, smooth stuff, god-like." **Barbara Rush** has caused her psychiatrist fiance David Niven a great deal of stress, because of her romantic flings with his patients. *Oh, Men! Oh, Women!* (1957, 20th Century-Fox).

9766 "Who do you think you're fooling? You've been around." Magazine editor **Brian Aherne** foists himself on unwed mother Martha Hyer. To Aherne, spoiled goods should be easy goods. *The Best of Everything* (1959, 20th Century-Fox).

9767 "Give thanks to God, Brighton, that when He made you a fool He gave you a fool's face." Nomadic Arab leader **Anthony Quinn** insults British Colonel Anthony Quayle. *Lawrence of Arabia* (1962, GB, Columbia).

9768 "I don't object to your headline-grabbing and crying 'wolf' all the time—that's standard stuff in politics—but it disturbs me you take yourself so seriously. It's par for the course, trying to fool the people, but it's downright dangerous when you start fooling yourself." Former president **Lee Tracy** advises presidential hopeful Cliff Robertson, a thoroughly dishonest and deceitful man. *The Best Man* (1964, United Artists).

9769 "My name is Karl Glocken and this is a ship of fools! I'm a fool. You'll meet more fools as we go along. This tub is packed with them. Emancipated ladies and ballplayers. Lovers. Dog lovers. Ladies of joy. Tolerant Jews. Dwarfs. All kinds. And who knows—if you look closely enough, you may even find yourself on board." Dwarf **Michael Dunn** operates as the narrator and Greek chorus. *Ship of Fools* (1965, Columbia).

9770 "We are the intelligent, civilized people who carry out orders we are given, no matter what they may be. Our biggest mission in life is to avoid being fools, and we wind up being the biggest fools of all." Ship's doctor **Oskar Werner** holds a low opinion of people and particularly himself. *Ship of Fools* (1965, Columbia).

9771 "Do you think I got off the bus from Stupidsville last night?" **Iris Adrian** is a suspicious landlady. *That Darn Cat!* (1965, Disney-Buena Vista).

9772 "Y'know every time I see 'Hole in the Wall' again, I ask myself the same question, 'How can I be so damn stupid as to keep coming back here?'" **Paul Newman** is disgusted with himself as he and fellow outlaw Robert Redford once again arrive at their hide-out. *Butch Cassidy and the Sundance Kid* (1969, 20th Century-Fox).

9773 "Don't be so dumb. No doctors. No cops. You ain't gonna send me to Bellevue. Once they get their hooks in you, you're dead. Don't be so goddamn dumb." Seriously ill, crippled New York hustler **Dustin Hoffman** yells at Jon Voight who thinks maybe he should go to a hospital. *Midnight Cowboy* (1969, United Artists).

9774 BENJIE: "My mother and father never did that." HERMIE: "Why not?" BENJIE: "Because it's stupid." **Oliver Conant** lets **Gary Grimes** know that he's ignorant of how he came to be, as he dismisses the sex act as stupid. *Summer of '42* (1971, Warner Bros.).

9775 "But I am a baseborn fool. I cannot screw above my station." Medieval court jester **Woody Allen** doubts if he can carry off the assignment given him by the ghost of his father, to seduce the queen. *Everything You Always Wanted to Know About Sex* (*but were afraid to ask)* (1972, United Artists).

9776 "I managed to fool one woman into loving me, and now she's gone." When his wife Susan

Anspach walks out on him, **Woody Allen** despairs of finding another. He tells his troubles to Diane Keaton, the wife of his best friend Tony Roberts. *Play It Again, Sam* (1972, Paramount).

9777 "That's the dumbest thing I've ever heard." **Ryan O'Neal** responds when Barbra Streisand mouths the famous line from his *Love Story*—"Love is never having to say you're sorry." *What's Up Doc?* (1972, Warner Bros.).

9778 FRANCES AMTHOR: "I think you're a very stupid person. You look stupid. You're in a stupid business. And you're on a stupid case." PHILIP MAR-LOWE: "I get it; I'm stupid." Vicious madam **Kate Murtagh** tells private eye **Robert Mitchum** what she thinks of him. *Farewell, My Lovely* (1975, Avco Embassy).

9779 "You got to be a moron to be a fighter." Rocky Balboa, played by **Sylvester Stallone**, is qualified. *Rocky* (1976, United Artists).

9780 "Clyde, sometimes I think you're not too tightly wrapped." Maybe so, but it's not **Clint Eastwood**'s best buddy, orangutan Clyde, who fights in bare-knuckle matches. *Any Which Way You Can* (1980, Warner Bros.).

9781 "Don't call me stupid." As throughout the movie, **Goldie Hawn** has done a long string of stupid things, she has little right to resent being called stupid. *Private Benjamin* (1980, Warner Bros.).

9782 "You're supposed to be stupid." It's what L.A. helicopter cop **Roy Scheider** expects of his novice co-pilot Daniel Stern, who obliges. *Blue Thunder* (1983, Columbia).

9783 SCARLET: "For a nigger, you're stupider than you look." TRACY: "You illiterate white trash whore." Both street smart white **Tatum O'Neal** and upper-class black **Irene Cara** display their stupidity. *Certain Fury* (1985, New World).

9784 "If a man looked at a woman's mouth before her eyes, he'd get fooled a lot less." Idealistic ex-cop **Kris Kristofferson** believes that women should be examined like horses. He falls in love with a fine looking filly, Lori Singer, in this film noir-like story set in the near future. *Trouble in Mind* (1985, Island Alive).

9785 "The London underground is not a political movement." **Jamie Lee Curtis** corrects stupid Kevin Kline, whose oft-repeated demand is, "Don't call me stupid." *A Fish Called Wanda* (1988, MGM-United Artists).

9786 "Fool, you're thirty cents away from a quarter. . . . You're raggedy as a roach. You eat holes out of doughnuts." For those who don't get it, **Robin Harris**, as Sweet Dick Willie, disparages the intelligence of Paul Benjamin as M.C. *Do the Right Thing* (1989, Universal).

9787 "You think I'm stupid, son?. . . Yes, you do. . . . You're trying to con a con man. . . . You're not even learning anything on the streets, are you?. . . " **Morgan Freeman**, as Principal Joe Clark, lectures Jermaine Hopkins as high school freshman Thomas Sams, who is trying to get reinstated after being expelled for truancy and smoking crack. *Lean on Me* (1989, Warner Bros.).

9788 "Do I have stupid written on my face?" Nineteen-year-old soldier **James Haig**, with a 48-hour pass, just realized that he's locked his condoms in a car and can't locate his keys—and Monica Sparrow is ready and willing. *The Big Dis* (1990, Olympia).

9789 "They're not bad, just stupid." **Ariana Richards** tells her father, Sheriff Douglas Barr, about short green Martians who have landed on Halloween night after picking up a rebroadcast of Orson Welles' "War of the Worlds." They assumed they were late for the invasion. *Spaced Invaders* (1991, Touchstone-Buena Vista).

Styles

see also APPEARANCES, CLOTHES, EXISTENCE, FASHIONS, IMAGINATION, WORDS, WRITING AND WRITERS

9790 "Lookee me! I'm da most stylish fella in da world." Fat California-Italian vineyard owner **Charles Laughton**, dressed in his Sunday suit and patent leather shoes, prepares to meet his mail-order bride Carole Lombard at the station. *They Knew What They Wanted* (1940, RKO).

9791 "Well, it's a new style of courting a pretty girl, I must say, for a young fellow to go deliberately out of his way to try and make an enemy of her father by attacking his business! By Jove! That's a new way of winning a woman." **Ray Collins** sarcastically chides his boorish nephew Tim Holt. Holt has criticized Anne Baxter's father Joseph Cotten for being in the automobile business—the business Holt believes has no future nor a right to one. *The Magnificent Ambersons* (1942, RKO).

9792 "Style is the answer to everything. . . a fresh way to approach a dull or dangerous thing with style is art. . . when Hemingway put his brains on the wall, that was style. . . Joan of Arc style. . . ." It's the opinion of **Ben Gazzara**, cast as writer Charles

Bukowski's alter ego. *Tales of Ordinary Madness* (1982, Italy-Fr., Ginguo-Gino-Miracle).

9793 "You don't just go out and pick a style off a tree one day—the tree is inside you, growing naturally." Jazz saxophonist **Dexter Gordon** narrates about his art. *'Round Midnight* (1986, Warner Bros.).

Successes

see also AMBITIONS, FAILURES, VICTORIES, WINNERS AND LOSERS

9794 "The last mass trials were a great success. There are going to be fewer but better Russians." **Greta Garbo**'s line drew laughs at the time, but considering all the Russians and other people murdered in the Stalinist purges, in hindsight it must be considered in bad taste. *Ninotchka* (1939, MGM).

9795 "I'm not a failure. I'm a success. You see, ambition is all right if it works, but no system could be right where one half of one percent were successes and the rest were failures. That wouldn't be right. I'm not a failure. I'm a success. And so are you if you earn your own living and pay your bills and look the world in the eye." **Harry Hayden** tries to make his employee Dick Powell realize that one can be a success even if he doesn't make a lot of money. *Christmas in July* (1940, Paramount).

9796 MAJOR STRASSER: "You have reached Casablanca—it is my duty to see that you stay in Casablanca." VICTOR LASZLO: "Whether or not you succeed is, of course, problematical." Nazi **Conrad Veidt** doesn't intimidate defiant Resistance leader **Paul Henreid**. *Casablanca* (1942, Warner Bros.).

9797 "Everybody's a flop until he's a success." It's these simple, insightful observations that makes wealthy, oft-married **Mary Astor** so appealing. *The Palm Beach Story* (1942, Paramount).

9798 "Success is no fun if you're alone. I'm tired of winning prizes. They're cold comfort." **Fay Bainter** tries to make her niece, career woman Katharine Hepburn understand why Bainter is marrying after a lifetime of spinsterhood. *Woman of the Year* (1942, MGM).

9799 "You don't know how important success is till you've had it." Divorced from her family, strong-willed **Barbara Stanwyck** comments when she returns to her home town to see her daughter in a school play. *All I Desire* (1953, Universal).

9800 "Success? That's a strange choice of word. Usually, newlyweds are wished happiness." Newlywed

Joan Crawford has good reason to be suspicious of the sentiments of her neighbor Jan Sterling. *Female on the Beach* (1955, Universal).

9801 "I gotta get somewhere in this world. I just gotta." Although it seems unlikely that he will find the kind of success he's seeking, **William Holden** sure wants it. *Picnic* (1955, Columbia).

9802 "You're successful as a call girl; you're not successful as an actress. . . ." Analyst **Vivian Nathan** replies when Jane Fonda asks, "Why do I still want to trick?" *Klute* (1971, Warner Bros.).

9803 "Nothing recedes like success." Playwright **Michael Caine** has lost his muse. *Deathtrap* (1982, Warner Bros.).

9804 "I'm no good at what I'm being a success at." **William Hurt** confesses that he's become a success as a TV journalist before he's learned his craft. *Broadcast News* (1987, 20th Century-Fox).

Suffering and Sufferers

see also HAPPINESS AND UNHAPPINESS, LOSSES AND LOSING, PAINS, PLEASURES, SADNESS, SORROWS

9805 "My lord, much as I desire to live, I'm not afraid to die. Since I first sailed on the Bounty over four years ago, I've known how men can be made to suffer worse things than death. Cruelty, beyond duty, beyond necessity." Midshipman **Franchot Tone** has his say at his court martial after being found guilty of mutiny. *Mutiny on the Bounty* (1935, MGM).

9806 "There is nothing wrong with suffering—if you suffer for a purpose. Our revolution didn't abolish danger or death. It simply made danger and death worthwhile." **Raymond Massey** preaches a message of sacrifice. *Things to Come* (1936, GB, London Films-United Artists).

9807 "He's more myself than I am. . . I am Heathcliff! Everything he has suffered, I've suffered." **Merle Oberon** believes that she and her love Laurence Olivier share one soul. *Wuthering Heights* (1939, Goldwyn-United Artists).

9808 "Dismiss your hearse. Live, little man, and suffer!" Alcoholic playwright **Thomas Mitchell** saves John Qualen from suicide. *Angels Over Broadway* (1940, Columbia).

9809 "As the rain enters the soil, the river enters the sea. So tears run to a predestined end. . . . Your suffering is over. Now you will find peace for eternity." Gypsy **Maria Ouspenskaya** adds her mystic thoughts to the scene after Claude Rains beats a werewolf to death with a silver-tipped handle. The beast undergoes a transformation in death and becomes the lifeless body of Rains' son Lon Chaney, Jr. Ouspenskaya misspoke. The film was popular enough to resurrect Chaney to play the role four more times. *The Wolf Man* (1941, Universal).

9810 "How's this, my holy sufferer?" **John Carradine**, as beastly Nazi Reinhard Heydrich, "the Hangman," grabs a sacred cloth from old village priest Al Shean and wipes his boots on it. *Hitler's Madman* (1943, MGM).

9811 "You've suffered enough, my child, for the heaven of heavens." Village Priest **Charles Bickford** recognizes Jennifer Jones' ordeal. *The Song of Bernadette* (1943, 20th Century-Fox).

9812 "He is suffering. He is more cruel to himself than he is to humans." **Josette Day** speaks of Jean Marais as the Beast to her father Marcel André. *La Belle et la Bête* aka: *Beauty and the Beast* (1947, Fr., Discina-Lopert).

9813 "It's like having a red hot buzz saw inside my head." **James Cagney** complains to his Ma, Margaret Wycherly, as he suffers from yet another of his severe, excruciating headaches. *White Heat* (1949, Warner Bros.).

9814 "So it wasn't enough to have suffered all that, the cellar, the asylum, the horror, the cruelty, the emptiness?. . . It was also necessary that I should meet you again—like this." **Ingrid Bergman**, who claims to be the surviving daughter of the last czar of Russia, is crushed that her grandmother, Empress Helen Hayes, doesn't believe her. *Anastasia* (1956, 20th Century-Fox).

9815 "Death is too easy for you, bitch. I want you to suffer." **Pam Grier** has special retribution in mind for Kathryn Loder, queen of a dope-prostitution-protection racket. *Foxy Brown* (1974, American International).

9816 "There were people sufferin' of pain and hunger. Such people. Their tongues were hangin' out of their mouths." Thirteen-year-old, world-weary narrator **Linda Manz** tells how it was in 1916 Texas. *Days of Heaven* (1978, Paramount).

9817 "The purpose of our suffering is only more suffering." Deranged scientist **William Hurt** desperately seeks God. *Altered States* (1980, Warner Bros.).

9818 "I don't want to make funny movies any more. I look around and all I see is human suffering. Didn't anyone else read that piece in the *New York*

Times how matter is decaying?" Fictional filmmaker **Woody Allen** is speaking for real filmmaker Woody Allen. Both should see the 1941 movie, *Sullivan's Travels*. *Stardust Memories* (1980, United Artists).

9819 "Suffer the little children. . . I want to suffer like a little child." Simple-minded novice nun **Meg Tilly** doesn't understand Christ's meaning any more than she understands where babies come from. *Agnes of God* (1985, Columbia).

9820 "My psychiatrist says I suffer from the halo effect." **Cybill Shepherd** explains her 23 years of chaste mooning over the memory of her deceased husband. *Chances Are* (1989, Tri-Star).

Sufficiency

see also NEEDS AND NECESSITIES

9821 "Sometimes I think being a great Broadway promoter isn't going to be enough for you." **Judy Garland** idolizes multi-talented Mickey Rooney. *Babes in Arms* (1939, MGM).

9822 "If I died tonight, would it have been enough?" Wealthy, intelligent mental patient **Jean Seberg** questions attendant Warren Beatty after they make love. *Lilith* (1964, Columbia).

Suicides

see also DEATH AND DYING, KILLINGS, LIFE AND DEATH, RUINATIONS AND RUINS

9823 LILY GARLAND: "What are you going to do?" OSCAR JAFFE: "Nothing. . . while you're here. New York. Ha! It received me once, when I came here a little farm boy. It will receive me again!. . . I remember many a winter's eve. . . . Lily Garland! I haven't finished yet!" Initially alarmed that **John Barrymore** might be planning to jump from a window, **Carole Lombard** decides to leave when his hammy suicide scene goes on too long. *Twentieth Century* (1934, Columbia).

9824 FREDDY EYNSFORD-HILL: "Where are you going?" ELIZA DOOLITTLE: "To the river." FREDDY: "What for?" ELIZA: "To make a hole in it." High society, penniless playboy **David Tree** isn't the man former flower girl **Wendy Hiller** needs to want to go on living. She needs her "creator," Leslie Howard, as Professor Henry Higgins. *Pygmalion* (1938, GB, MGM).

9825 "Suicide attempts are Frank's department." **Grace Kelly** assures William Holden that it's her alcoholic husband Bing Crosby, not she, who has suicidal tendencies. *The Country Girl* (1954, Paramount).

9826 "I kill myself because you have not loved me, because I haven't loved you. I kill myself because the bonds between us were loose, and to tighten those bonds, I will leave an indelible stain on you." Alcoholic writer **Maurice Ronet** finishes his book, then calmly shoots himself through the heart. He leaves behind the reason for his act to be read by his estranged wife. *The Fire Within* (1964, Fr.-Italy, Nouvelles Editions-Arco-Governor).

9827 "They went home and sat in a hot tub and opened their veins, and bled to death." **Michael V. Gazzo** describes the means of suicide used in ancient days to Robert Duvall. Gazzo uses the method himself. *The Godfather, Part II* (1974, Paramount).

9828 "Ladies and gentlemen, I would like at this moment to announce I will be retiring from this program in two week's time because of poor ratings. Since this show is the only thing I had going for me in my life, I have decided to kill myself. I'm going to blow my brains out right on this program a week from today." News anchorman **Peter Finch** calmly announces his intention to commit suicide on television to the few in his audience. *Network* (1976, United Artists).

9829 LARRY LAPINSKY: "I think about suicide once or twice a day." SARAH: "That's natural, thinking about suicide makes you feel talented." **Lenny Baker**'s girl friend **Ellen Greene** isn't too concerned with his suicidal thoughts. *Next Stop, Greenwich Village* (1976, 20th Century-Fox).

9830 "I'm not dead yet." **Gloria Grahame** mutters as she sits fully clothed in a filled bathtub, threatening to commit suicide. *Chilly Scenes of Winter* (1979, United Artists Classics).

9831 "I had a bad day." It's the perfect suicide note left by the mother of Diane Keaton, Jessica Lange and Sissy Spacek, who hanged herself and the family cat. *Crimes of the Heart* (1986, De Laurentiis).

9832 "Oh, what do you want to hear, man? Do you want to hear that sometimes I think about eating a bullet?... Well, I do... I even got a special one for the occasion with a hollow point. Look... make sure it blows the back of my goddamn head out, do the job right.... Every single day I wake up and think of a reason not to do it.... This is going to make you laugh.... You know why I don't do it?... The job, doing the job—now that's the reason." **Mel Gibson** responds emotionally to his new partner Danny Glover's question, "Do you want to die?" *Lethal Weapon* (1987, Warner Bros.).

9833 "Rattlesnakes don't commit suicide." **Gene Hackman** likens one of the suspects in the murder of three civil rights workers to a despised snake. *Mississippi Burning* (1988, Orion).

9834 "I've gone out the window." It's the self-evident suicide note left by Professor Levy, played by **Martin Bergmann**. *Crimes and Misdemeanors* (1989, Orion).

9835 "When I grew up in Brooklyn, no one committed suicide. They were all too unhappy." **Woody Allen** tries to mask his horror and grief when psychiatrist Martin Bergmann, the subject of the documentary Allen is working on, commits suicide. *Crimes and Misdemeanors* (1989, Orion).

9836 "Go on, jump.... Yes, you do.... You smoke crack, don't you?... You smoke crack, don't you?... Look at me, boy, don't you smoke crack?... You know what that does to you?... Huh?... It kills your brain cells, son, it kills your brain cells.... Now when you destroy your brain cells, you're doing the same thing as killing yourself, you're just doing it slower. Now I say if you want to kill yourself, don't fuck around with it, go ahead and do it expeditiously.... Now go ahead and jump. Jump!" On the roof of the school building, high school Principal **Morgan Freeman** uses an alternative to the "Just say no!" advice in dealing with fourteen-year-old Jermaine Hopkins, a user and pusher. *Lean on Me* (1989, Warner Bros.).

9837 "All is nothing, therefore nothing must end." It's the suicide note written by **Daniel Day-Lewis**, despondent over the engagement of the woman he loves, his teacher Fiona Shaw. *My Left Foot* (1989, GB, Miramax).

9838 "I do hope I haven't let people down too much.... The car needs oil in the gearbox." It's part of the suicide note left by Dr. Stephen Ward, played by **John Hurt**. *Scandal* (1989, GB, Miramax).

9839 "I'm contemplating suicide, or a seat in Parliament—No, suicide." **Roger Moore** tells a reporter of his plans when it is reported that his scientist partner Michael Caine's experiment with fusion is a failure. *Bullseye!* (1991, 21st Century Productions).

Superiority and Inferiority

see also AUTHORITIES, CONCEIT, QUALITIES, WORTH AND VALUES

9840 RUGGLES: "It just doesn't do for a gentleman's servant to sit with his superiors." EGBERT: "Superior, nothing. You're as good as I am and I'm as good as you are." British manservant **Charles Laughton** doesn't feel comfortable in his new role after being won in a poker game by a rough U.S.

rancher, **Charles Ruggles**. *Ruggles of Red Gap* (1935, Paramount).

9841 TERRY RANDALL: "You seem very superior, just what have you done in the theater?" EVE: "Everything but bust out of a pie at a Rotarian banquet." Would-be serious stage actress **Katharine Hepburn** feels superior to would-be actress **Eve Arden**, who uses wisecracking as a defense mechanism. *Stage Door* (1937, RKO).

9842 "Queer how the folks that lives on the bottom look down on the folks that lives on the top." **Margaret Wycherly** notes that Tennessee people who own good bottom land put on airs and feel superior to those who own rocky hill land. *Sergeant York* (1941, Warner Bros.).

9843 RUPERT CADELL: "Murder is—or should be—an art, and as such, the privilege of committing it should be reserved for the few who are really superior individuals." BRANDON: "And the victims are inferiors, whose lives are unimportant anyway!" CADELL: "Obviously!" Professor **James Stewart**'s questionable philosophy of right to kill inspires two of his students, **John Dall** and Farley Granger, to commit a murder. *Rope* (1948, Warner Bros.).

9844 "You're good, kid; but as long as I'm around, you're second best." Big time poker player **Edward G. Robinson** allows as how challenger Steve McQueen is good—but not good enough. *The Cincinnati Kid* (1965, MGM).

9845 "What makes you so high and mighty? Didn't you ever try to look at your own eyeballs in the mirror?" Twelve-year-old hooker **Jodie Foster** questions cabbie Robert De Niro's right to feel superior to her pimp Harvey Keitel. *Taxi Driver* (1971, Columbia).

9846 "It's been such a long time since I made love to a woman I didn't feel inferior to." **Richard Jordan** expresses this tender sentiment to Kristin Griffith just before he rapes her. *Interiors* (1978, United Artists).

9847 "Work is for people like Aiken. Not for you and me." Snotty **Virginia Madsen** confides to her sorority sister Ally Sheedy about Phoebe Cates. *Heart of Dixie* (1989, Orion).

9848 "Would you like to go to a land where there is no sadness?. . . Where everyone is fatter than you are and you can feel smug?" To cheer her up, when Jessica Lange tells him she's very sad, **Arliss Howard** takes her to a Polka Party. *Men Don't Leave* (1990, Warner Bros.).

Supernatural

see also GOD, HEAVEN, MIRACLES, SOULS, SPIRIT AND SPIRITS

9849 "Supernatural—perhaps; baloney—perhaps not." It's quite a treat to revengeful doctor **Bela Lugosi** to let this line trip over his lips when David Manners calls devil-worship cults, "supernatural baloney." *The Black Cat* (1934, Universal).

9850 "It has been written since the beginning of time, even unto these ancient stones, that evil supernatural creatures exist in a world of darkness; and that man, using the magic power of the ancient runic symbols can call forth these powers of darkness. . . the demons of hell." The foreword warns audiences to expect that some meddling human will call forth a medieval devil. *Curse of the Demon* aka: *Night of the Demon* (1957, GB, Columbia).

Superstitions *see* BELIEFS, CHANCES, FAITH AND FAITHFULNESS, LOGIC, MAGIC, REALITIES

Suppositions

see also ARGUMENTS, BELIEFS, CONDITIONS, EXPLANATIONS, REQUIREMENTS

9851 PHYLLIS DIETRICHSON: "There's a speed limit in this state, Mr. Neff. Forty-five miles per hour." WALTER NEFF: "How fast was I going, officer?" PHYLLIS: "I'd say around ninety." WALTER: "Suppose you get down from your motorcycle and give me a ticket?" PHYLLIS: "Suppose I let you off with a warning this time?" WALTER: "Suppose it doesn't take?" PHYLLIS: "Suppose I have to whack you on the knuckles?" WALTER: "Suppose I bust out crying and put my head on your shoulder?" PHYLLIS: "Suppose you try putting it on my husband's shoulder?" WALTER: "That tears it." **Barbara Stanwyck** pretends she's not interested in **Fred MacMurray**'s obvious interest in her. *Double Indemnity* (1944, Paramount).

9852 "I suppose a fuck's out of the question." It's blind **Richard Pryor**'s response when gorgeous murderess Joan Severance asks if he has any last requests before he's killed. *See No Evil, Hear No Evil* (1989, Tri-Star).

Surgery *see* DOCTORS AND DENTISTS, MEDICINE, NURSES, SICKNESS

Surprises

see also AMAZEMENT, SHOCKS, WONDERFULNESS AND WONDERS

9853 "Well, I'll be damned." The notable thing about this line, spoken by actress **Emma Dunn** in a bit role, is that it wasn't cut. Clark Gable *wasn't* the first one to say "damn" in a film. *Blessed Event* (1932, Warner Bros.).

9854 "This is unexpected as squirt from aggressive grapefruit." Charlie Chan, portrayed by **Warner Oland**, is surprised by developments in his case. *Charlie Chan's Chance* (1932, Fox).

9855 "You didn't know there was a woman aboard, did you?" Insanely jealous submarine Commander **Charles Laughton** shows his wife Tallulah Bankhead to her lover Gary Cooper. *Devil and the Deep* (1932, Paramount).

9856 BARBARA WILLIS: "I don't know how it happened. I didn't do anything." VANTINE: "I didn't hear you cry for help." **Mary Astor**'s expression of surprise after the evening her love affair with Clark Gable is consummated isn't bought by **Jean Harlow.** *Red Dust* (1932, MGM).

9857 "Gee whiz!" It's **Katharine Hepburn**'s surprised reaction when Fred MacMurray tells her he loves her despite her deceit. *Alice Adams* (1935, RKO).

9858 MICHEL MARNET: "I got scared. I said to myself, don't beautiful women travel any more? Evidently not. Then I saw you—and everything was all right. And I was saved. I hope. . . Cigarette?" TERRY MCKAY: "Have you been getting results with a line like that? Or would I be surprised?" MICHEL: "If you were surprised, that would surprise me." TERRY: "That sounds like a nasty crack." During a voyage, **Charles Boyer** flirts with **Irene Dunne.** Although they are both engaged to others, they fall in love. *Love Affair* (1939, RKO).

9859 "Gee, I never figured on that." Future director **Elia Kazan** as "Googi," a suave gangster, surprisingly gasps as he is fatally hit by a sniper's bullet. *City for Conquest* (1941, Warner Bros.).

9860 "I'm rather surprised myself, but perhaps it's because for the first time in my life I know what I want." It's **Joan Fontaine**'s response when Cary Grant states that he's surprised that she's not nervous while he certainly is. *Suspicion* (1941, RKO).

9861 "I am surprised but that is the way with you, you are always furnishing surprises." **Sydney Greenstreet** hadn't counted on Humphrey Bogart surviving an encounter with some murderous Japanese agents. *Across the Pacific* (1942, Warner Bros.).

9862 "You have no idea what a long-legged gal can do without doing anything." Confident **Claudette Colbert** assures her soon to be ex-husband Joel McCrea that she can attract a lot of wealthy men without any fuss on her part. *The Palm Beach Story* (1942, Paramount).

9863 "It wouldn't surprise me if she turned out to be a foreign agent. All she does around here is to come in and rearrange the dust." **Jack Benny** finds fault with the work of maid Hattie McDaniel. *George Washington Slept Here* (1942, Warner Bros.)

9864 LT. COOLEY: "You don't seem very surprised to hear that this Dr. Edwardes was a fake and may be guilty of murder." DR. CONSTANCE PETERSON: "I'm used to such surprises in my work." **Art Baker** thinks psychiatrist **Ingrid Bergman** takes the news that Gregory Peck is an imposter and maybe a murderer very casually. *Spellbound* (1945, United Artists).

9865 "They appear here and there, now and then. . . and how are you, Mr. Wilson?" Mental institution attendant **Jesse White** is taken aback when he reads the description of a pooka, an imaginary beast, in a dictionary. *Harvey* (1950, Universal-International).

9866 CHARLOTTE MANNING: "How could you?" MIKE HAMMER: "It was easy." Sexy murderer **Peggie Castle** is surprised when hard-boiled private eye **Biff Elliot** fatally shoots her, despite her seductive stripping away of her clothes for his benefit. Elliott allows her to finish stripping before letting her have it. *I, The Jury* (1953, 20th Century-Fox).

9867 "I thought you were only going to lean on him a little." **Marlon Brando** is surprised that he has set up a truculent union leader who was thrown to his death from a roof. *On the Waterfront* (1954, Columbia).

9868 "My young friend surprised me, however, by bending with the wind rather than breaking." By the end of the movie, editor **Robert Ryan** has modified his cynicism and Montgomery Clift has partly compromised his idealism. *Lonelyhearts* (1958, United Artists).

9869 "If you take my heart by surprise, the rest of my body has the right to follow." **Albert Finney** asserts that his relationship with Joan Greenwood should proceed to the next natural level. *Tom Jones* (1963, GB, Woodfall-United Artists).

9870 "Guess what I got for you? Baked potatoes. You can eat these with the jackets on them." Wounded **Mickey Rooney** waits for Japanese soldiers to approach, holding two grenades. *Ambush Bay* (1966, United Artists).

9871 "You mean to tell me she's not pregnant?" **Katherine Cassavetes** is incredulous that Gena Rowlands is marrying her son Seymour Cassel by her own choice. *Minnie and Moskowitz* (1971, Universal).

9872 "I don't know what's come over us." **Joan Collins** is the half-willing rape victim of her stepson Tom Marshall. *Terror from Under the House* aka: *Revenge* (1971, GB, Hemisphere).

9873 "Wait a minute, Doc. Are you trying to tell me you built a time machine out of a DeLorean?" Why is **Michael J. Fox** so surprised by Christopher Lloyd's accomplishment? The DeLorean automobile looks like something from another era. *Back to the Future* (1985, Universal).

9874 "How fascinating! You make love without fading away." Screen image **Jeff Daniels**, who has stepped down from the screen to be with Mia Farrow, is amazed after their first kiss. *The Purple Rose of Cairo* (1985, Orion).

9875 "You're the last person I thought would ever come through for me." Irascible, ill **Jackie Gleason** didn't expect much help from his self-centered son Tom Hanks, but he was surprised. *Nothing in Common* (1986, Tri-Star).

9876 "Come on, pal, tell me something I don't know. It's my birthday. Surprise me!" Vicious amoral trader **Michael Douglas** chides innocent young stock salesman, Charlie Sheen, who is looking to be corrupted by a master. *Wall Street* (1987, 20th Century-Fox).

9877 "I look at people's thoughts and see what they really mean. You do that a while and people stop surprising you. I just want to be surprised." Psychiatrist **Richard Gere** is bored with his patients and his problems. Things get a bit more interesting with sisters Kim Basinger and Uma Thurman on hand. *Final Analysis* (1992, Warner Bros.).

Surrender

see also CONTROL, GIFTS AND GIVING, POSSESSIONS, RESIGNATIONS

9878 "I'm lucky. I'm gifted. I have a talent for surrender." **Martin Balsam** confesses to his nonconformist brother Jason Robards. *A Thousand Clowns* (1965, United Artists).

9879 "I myself never surrendered, but they got my horse, and it surrendered." Old Cherokee Indian **Chief Dan George** tells Clint Eastwood why he ceased fighting in a battle with a white man. *The Outlaw Josey Wales* (1976, Warner Bros.).

9880 "Soon he no longer bothered to hide the real nature of his intentions towards me. Nor could I pretend surprise. My innocence was false from the moment I chose to stay. I could tell you that he overpowered me, that he drugged me. But it is not so. . . I gave myself to him." **Meryl Streep** describes to Jeremy Irons how she became the French lieutenant's whore. *The French Lieutenant's Woman* (1981, GB, United Artists).

9881 "Male or female, how do you compete with a body you've already surrendered to your opponent?" U.S. Olympic track team participant **Mariel Hemingway** has had a lesbian affair with her competitor Patrice Donnelly. *Personal Best* (1982, Warner Bros.).

9882 "Surrender, Dorothy!" This message to Judy Garland, written in the sky by Wicked Witch Margaret Hamilton in *The Wizard Of Oz,* is the exclamation Rosanna Arquette's ex-husband used each time they had sex. *After Hours* (1985, Warner Bros.).

9883 "You are right. I can't live either, unless I make you happy, so I promise, no more refusals, no more regrets." **Michelle Pfeiffer** finally surrenders herself to John Malkovich. *Dangerous Liaisons* (1988, Warner Bros.).

Survival

see also DEFENSES, LIVES AND LIVING, WEAPONS

9884 JAMES ALLEN: "They'll always be after me. No friends, no rest, no peace!" HELEN: "How do you get along?" JAMES: "I steal!" In the despairing final scene of the movie, **Paul Muni**, forced to go on the run to prevent being unjustly returned to a Georgia chain gang, has one last meeting with the woman he loves, **Helen Vinson**. *I Am a Fugitive from a Chain Gang* (1932, Warner Bros.).

9885 "I'm a survivor and I'm leaving these flats for the mile-high city. When I get there, baby—when I look down—I'll have few regrets." **Paul Newman** savagely addresses the grave of his girl friend Joanne Woodward, who has hanged herself. *WUSA* (1970, Paramount).

9886 "Surviving is the only glory in war." Narrator **Robert Carradine** delivers the last line of the film. *The Big Red One* (1980, United Artists).

9887 "Mr. Bond, you have a nasty habit of. . . surviving." Villainous Afghan Prince **Louis Jourdan** expresses his annoyance that Roger Moore, as James Bond, survives all of Jourdan's plans to kill him. *Octopussy* (1982, GB, MGM-United Artists).

9888 "For reasons long forgotten, two mighty warrior tribes went to war—and touched off a blaze which engulfed them all. Their world crumbled. Men began to feed on men. Only those mobile enough to pillage would survive." It is the spoken introduction to a post-apocalypse film that has achieved cult status. *The Road Warrior* aka: *Mad Max II* (1982, Australia, Warner Bros.).

9889 "Why are you living, fucking around while millions of Jews died?. . . What splendid little tricks and stratagems allowed you to survive?" Brooklyn Jew **Kevin Kline** viciously accuses his lover, Polish Catholic Auschwitz survivor Meryl Streep. *Sophie's Choice* (1982, Universal).

9890 "To endure thirty-two years of being distinguished. . . . I survived to see myself become extinct." Elderly Antonio Salieri, brilliantly portrayed by **F. Murray Abraham**, traces for his confessor Richard Frank the plunging of his musical star with the arrival in Vienna of Wolfgang Amadeus Mozart, played by Tom Hulce. *Amadeus* (1984, Orion).

9891 "I don't know how to fight. All I know is how to stay alive." It's part of **Whoopi Goldberg**'s letter to God. *The Color Purple* (1985, Warner Bros.).

9892 "To survive war, you gotta become war." A pearl of wisdom from **Sylvester Stallone**. *Rambo, First Blood, Part II* (1985, Tri-Star).

9893 "Survive! I've been doing that all my life. . . . Cut the self-pity crap, Bud. . . . If you make an enemy of Gordon Gekko, I can't be there to stand by you. . . ." Selfish, mercenary **Daryl Hannah** makes it clear to Charlie Sheen that without his mentor Michael Douglas, he won't have her. *Wall Street* (1987, 20th Century-Fox).

9894 "Some mad fucking minute, huh, Cherry. You survive 'Nam, you get to live forever, man." Veteran **Sean Penn** has just saved the life of new recruit Michael J. Fox. *Casualties of War* (1989, Columbia).

Suspense see Certainties, Decisions, Mysteries, Tensions, Terror, Unknowns

Suspicions and Suspects

see also Crimes and Criminals, Imagination, Probability and Statistics, Trust, Wrongs and Wrongdoings

9895 "There you are, always thinking, believing anybody. A Frenchman comes along with a violin case—locked, mind you—and we take it for granted it contains a violin—we never learn." **Lucien Littlefield**, as Herr Schultz, is suspicious of Frenchman Phillips Holmes who appears in a German village shortly after the end of World War I. *The Man I Killed* aka: *Broken Lullaby* (1932, Paramount).

9896 "The road to Reno is paved with suspicion. The first thing you know he'll end up in a divorce court." **Cary Grant** unwittingly predicts his own fate. *The Awful Truth* (1937, Columbia).

9897 "Toto, I have a feeling we're not in Kansas anymore." **Judy Garland** understates her suspicions and fears to her dog. *The Wizard of Oz* (1939, MGM).

9898 "Round up the usual suspects." It's a line that Casablanca French Police Captain **Claude Rains** uses several times, but it's best remembered when he announces that German Colonel Conrad Veidt has been killed and doesn't tell his men that it was Humphrey Bogart who did it. *Casablanca* (1942, Warner Bros.).

9899 "I'm a natural born suspect. It's because I'm not the conventional type." **Vincent Price** has never been conventional—bless him for that. *Laura* (1944, 20th Century-Fox).

9900 Amanda Bonner: "When did you suspect that you were losing your husband's affections?" Doris Attinger: "When he stopped batting me around." Defense Attorney **Katharine Hepburn** questions her client **Judy Holliday** about her philandering husband Tom Ewell, who Holliday is accused of trying to kill. *Adam's Rib* (1949, MGM).

9901 "Harry, we must beware of these men. They're desperate characters. Not one of them looked at my legs." **Jennifer Jones** warns her husband Edward Underwood about Robert Morley, Peter Lorre, Ivor Barnard and Marco Tulli. She not only knows she has a fine pair of legs, but she knows desperate characters when she sees them. *Beat the Devil* (1953, Romulus-Santana).

9902 "No wonder he was suspicious!. . . He turns around to get the key and this one says just loud enough for him to hear, 'Darling, are we doing the right thing? Maybe we ought to wait.'" **Barry Nelson** recalls a suspicious desk clerk at a motel where he and his then wife Debbie Reynolds once stayed. *Mary, Mary* (1963, Warner Bros.).

9903 "I suspect everyone, and I suspect no one." Incompetent Surete Inspector Clouseau, played for slapstick by **Peter Sellers**, fools no one. *The Pink Panther Strikes Again* (1976, GB, United Artists).

9904 "You aren't one of those women that get turned on by gimps?" Paralyzed from the waist down, angry Vietnam veteran **Jon Voight** is suspicious of the interest in him shown by married Jane Fonda. *Coming Home* (1978, United Artists).

9905 "You don't get suspicious when your analyst calls you at three in the morning and weeps into the telephone?" **Woody Allen** is amazed by the credulity of Diane Keaton. *Manhattan* (1979, United Artists).

9906 "When Aldo was a little boy, he must have wanted to grow up to be a suspect." Police Lieutenant **Steven Hill** refers to neurotic James Woods, who always looks guilty of something. *Eyewitness* (1981, 20th Century-Fox).

9907 "I've always been suspicious of neatness. . . . The most dangerous thing is to be cautious." Supreme Court Justice **Walter Matthau** lectures his law clerk James Stephens. *First Monday in October* (1981, Paramount).

9908 "Is it the habit of this community to be suspicious when a married man goes off with a married woman—especially when the woman happens to be the man's wife's best friend?" **Candice Bergen** huffily accuses Jacqueline Bisset, who has been given the rush by Bergen's husband David Selby. *Rich and Famous* (1981, MGM).

9909 "With all the psychos running around New York, you're trying to pin the rap on an endangered species?" Eccentric zoologist **Tom Noonan**, whose specialty is wolves, is outraged when authorities suspect that wolves are responsible for a series of mysterious mutilation deaths. *Wolfen* (1981, Warner Bros.).

9910 "A man who comes to a place like this, either he's runnin' away from something or he has nowhere else to go." **Barbara Hershey** is suspicious of Gene Hackman's reasons for taking a basketball coaching job in a small Indiana community. *Hoosiers* (1987, Orion).

9911 MICHAEL LAEMLE: "What are we eating?" LILY LAEMLE: "Leftovers." MICHAEL: "Leftovers from what?" Young **Bryan Madorsky** is suspicious of the mystery meat that his mother **Mary Beth Hurt** sets before him each night. *Parents* (1988, Vestron).

9912 "You're just suspicious of any woman who hasn't slept with you." **Michelle Pfeiffer** snaps disgustedly at police detective Kurt Russell, who hasn't slept with her—but is working on it. *Tequila Sunrise* (1988, Warner Bros.).

9913 "What you say in the mouthpiece is never what comes out the other end." **Kurtwood Smith**

strongly suspects that the phone company played a role in the John F. Kennedy assassination. *True Believer* (1989, Columbia).

Swearing *see* CURSES, OATHS, PLEDGES, PROFANITY

Sweetness

see also LOVE AND LOVERS

9914 "You were a sweet lover, like strawberries. . . ." **Gunn Walgren** fondly speaks of her aged lover Erland Josephson. *Fanny and Alexander* (1983, Sweden-Fr.-W. Germany, Swedish Film Institute).

9915 "You be sweet to your wife. My husband wasn't sweet to me and look how I turned out." **Geena Davis** instructs a sobbing policeman as she forces him into the trunk of her car. *Thelma & Louise* (1991, Pathe Entertainment).

Swords *see* WEAPONS

Symbols

see also SIGNS

9916 "All my life I have been a symbol. A symbol of eternal, changeless, an abstraction. A human being is mortal and changeable with desires and impulses. I'm tired of being a symbol. I long to be a human being. This longing I cannot suppress. . . . One must live life for one's self. After all, one's life is all one has." **Greta Garbo** abdicates the throne of Sweden. *Queen Christina* (1933, MGM).

9917 HAZEL FLAGG: "You mean they'll like me just because I'm dying?" WALLY COOK: "Oh, that's a cruel way to put it. No. They'll like you because you'd be a symbol of courage and heroism." **Carole Lombard** is not dying of radium poisoning but New York reporter **Fredric March** thinks she is. He plans to take her to the Big Apple to exploit her for his newspaper. *Nothing Sacred* (1937, Selznick-United Artists).

9918 "Sphinx, Sphinx: My way hither was the way of destiny; for I am he whose genius you are the symbol: part brute, part woman, and part god—nothing of man in me at all. Have I read your riddle, Sphinx?" **Claude Rains**, as Julius Caesar, is wrong in believing he is speaking to the Great Sphinx of Egypt. He is addressing one of its smaller kittens. *Caesar and Cleopatra* (1945, GB, Rank).

9919 "I'm tired, tired, tired of being a stupid sex symbol." Soft-core smut star **Karen Black** is aboard a skyjacked airplane. *Hostage* (1987, Columbia).

9920 "The knife is a phallic symbol." **Angela O'Neill**'s brother slaughtered the rest of their family 14 years earlier and now it seems he's slashing coeds in a deserted sorority house. *Sorority House Massacre* (1987, Concorde).

9921 "The gun is a penis. The safety means I'm ambivalent about my father's penis. The bullets are semen." Raped by her father, **Uma Thurman** interprets the symbolism of her gun and its safety which she checks ten times every morning for her analyst Richard Gere. Why bother paying his fees when she's got all the answers? *Final Analysis* (1992, Warner Bros.).

Sympathy

see also EMPATHY, PITY, SADNESS, SORROWS, UNDERSTANDINGS AND MISUNDERSTANDINGS

9922 "I hate to see you going the way of so many others." Sympathetic studio head **Adolphe Menjou** comforts falling star Fredric March who is drying-out in a small sanitarium. *A Star Is Born* (1937, Selznick-United Artists).

9923 "I say marriage with Max is not exactly a bed of roses, is it?" Poor relative **George Sanders** is insincerely sympathetic with Joan Fontaine. *Rebecca* (1940, Selznick-United Artists).

9924 "May a stranger offer condolences for your partner's unfortunate death?" It's the entry line of **Peter Lorre**, portraying Joel Cairo. He's talking to Humphrey Bogart, as private eye Sam Spade, about Bogie's partner Jerome Cowan, who has been murdered. *The Maltese Falcon* (1941, Warner Bros.).

9925 FRENCHY: "What are your sympathies?" HARRY MORGAN: "Minding my own business." French patriot **Marcel Dalio** is unable to convince American fishing boat skipper **Humphrey Bogart** to get involved with the politics of Vichy-controlled Martinique during World War II. *To Have and Have Not* (1944, Warner Bros.).

9926 "He doesn't want sympathy—he keeps saying that." Ballerina **Claire Bloom** refers to her protector, music hall comedian Charles Chaplin. She's wrong; he does want sympathy. *Limelight* (1952, United Artists).

Systems

see also OBJECTS, RULES, THEORIES

9927 "If something's good, that's OK, but if something's too good, it upsets the whole system." A racing official speaks of the phenomenal success of racehorse Phar Lap, the talk of the racing world in the early thirties. The horse is held in the same high regard in Australia as Man O' War or Secretariat is in the United States. It is suspected, but never has been proven, that gamblers were responsible for the animal's untimely death. *Phar Lap* (1984, Australia, 20th Century-Fox).

9928 "The system stinks, the insurance companies tell us what tests we can and cannot give." Physician **William Hurt** bemoans the influence of insurance companies on the practice of medicine. *The Doctor* (1991, Touchstone-Buena Vista).

Talents

see also ABILITIES AND CAPABILITIES, GENIUS, GIFTS AND POWER, SUPERIORITY AND INFERIORITY

9929 "I guess all talented people are a bit peculiar." **Katharine Hepburn** subtly tries to undermine Fred MacMurray's impression of another girl. *Alice Adams* (1935, RKO).

9930 "Back home everyone said I didn't have any talent. They might be saying the same thing over here, but it sounds better in French." American artist **Gene Kelly** finds failure easier to accept in Paris. *An American in Paris* (1951, MGM).

9931 "Some men can swing by their heels from a flying trapeze, some can become president of the republic. I can drink cognac." **Jose Ferrer**, portraying French artist Toulouse-Lautrec, mentions what he considers his major talent. *Moulin Rouge* (1952, GB, Romulus-United Artists).

9932 "She can't act, she can't sing, and she can't dance—a triple threat." **Donald O'Connor** belittles silent screen star Jean Hagen. *Singin' in the Rain* (1952, MGM).

9933 "We understand you got a lot of talent, and that's the only thing that could make Mr. Kirk Edwards fly all the way from Rome, all the way from California, you might say. Talent! Now where other men go for a pretty face or a pair of legs, talent is what Mr. Kirk Edwards worships. It's his religion, you might also say." Toadying press agent **Edmond O'Brien** fronts for Howard Hughes-like Warren Stevens, but he makes no impression with Madrid gypsy dancer Ava Gardner. *The Barefoot Contessa* (1954, United Artists).

9934 "I've been jinxed from the word go—first time I was ever kissed was in a cemetery. I was fifteen. We used to go there to smoke. His name was George. He threw me over for a drum majorette. I just have this talent for falling in love with the wrong guy in the wrong place at the wrong time." **Shirley MacLaine** admits to Jack Lemmon that she's a romantic patsy. He's just revived her after a suicide attempt in her apartment where she's had an argument with her married lover Fred MacMurray. *The Apartment* (1960, United Artists).

9935 "Because I can't sing or dance." It's the reason Italian Stallion **Sylvester Stallone** gives to Talia Shire when she asks why he became a boxer. He knows that through sports and the entertainment business a guy can escape from poverty. *Rocky* (1976, United Artists).

9936 "He could remember everybody's name. It was a real talent." Nightclub owner **Sidney Miller** admiringly remembers glib, narcissistic hustler Eric Roberts. *Star 80* (1983, Warner Bros.).

9937 "He would have cut a figure in any age, for he was an athlete, a musician, a lover of art and a fine sportsman." **Meryl Streep** praises her talented sometime lover Robert Redford. *Out of Africa* (1985, Universal).

9938 "My talent is survival." It's bum **Nick Nolte**'s major talent. *Down and Out in Beverly Hills* (1986, Touchstone-Buena Vista).

9939 "I don't know you, I don't know your work. . . but I think you're a very, very talented young man." Hollywood agent **Martin Short** wishes to represent directorial student Kevin Bacon because he's won an award at his school. *The Big Picture* (1989, Columbia).

9940 "You're good at singing. I'm good at inheriting money. I may be the best in the field." It's 1948, and wealthy playboy **Alec Baldwin** tries to impress Las Vegas lounge singer Kim Basinger with his talent. Although good at inheriting money, he's not equally adept at keeping it. *The Marrying Man* (1991, Hollywood Pictures-Buena Vista).

Talks and Talking

see also CONVERSATIONS, IMITATION, LANGUAGES, SPEECH AND SPEAKING, WORDS

9941 "Come on! Be brilliant! Talk yourself out of it! Bluff yourself in!" **Miriam Hopkins** angrily rebukes her partner-in-crime Herbert Marshall and demands he display the glibness that allows him to squirm out of trouble with the elegance of his speech. *Trouble in Paradise* (1932, Paramount).

9942 "Now let's talk it over from every angle, without any excitement, like a Disarmament confer-

ence." Having proposed to Fredric March and Gary Cooper that they enter into a non-sexual ménage à trois, **Miriam Hopkins** now wants to work out the details of this design for living. *Design for Living* (1933, Paramount).

9943 "We have ways of making men talk." Villain **Douglas Dumbrille** coins a now familiar cliché. *The Lives of a Bengal Lancer* (1935, Paramount).

9944 "Wouldn't have talked at all, if I'd known I was doin' it for nothing." Warsaw, Vermont baggage man **Olin Howland** reckons that providing New Yorker Fredric March with information as to where he can find Carole Lombard ought to be worth something. *Nothing Sacred* (1937, Selnick-United Artists).

9945 NINOTCHKA: "You are very talkative." LEON: "Was that talkative?" NINOTCHKA: "No, that was restful." **Greta Garbo** and **Melvyn Douglas** kiss for the first time. *Ninotchka* (1939, MGM).

9946 "When nobody shall talk more than is absolutely necessary." **Edmund Gwenn**, married and the father of five females of marriageable age, considers what heaven must be like. *Pride and Prejudice* (1940, MGM).

9947 "There was never any talk while we were eating. I never met anybody whose talk was better than good food." We disagree with never-seen narrator **Irving Pichel**. Good food and good talk complement each other. *How Green Was My Valley* (1941, 20th Century-Fox).

9948 "I'm a man who likes talking to a man who likes to talk. . . . I distrust a close-mouthed man. He generally picks the wrong time to talk, and says the wrong things. Talking is something you can't do judiciously unless you keep in practice." The "Fat Man," **Sydney Greenstreet** finds private eye Humphrey Bogart, a man who knows how to talk. *The Maltese Falcon* (1941, Warner Bros.).

9949 "I understand she doesn't like to talk to anyone who hasn't signed a non-aggression pact." Sports columnist **Spencer Tracy** accuses aggressive political columnist Katharine Hepburn of being stuck up. *Woman of the Year* (1942, MGM).

9950 "Only time a woman doesn't care to talk is when she's dead." Cranky **William Demarest** bases his opinion on his two talkative daughters. *The Miracle of Morgan's Creek* (1943, Paramount).

9951 "Sometimes people are where they can't talk— under six feet of dirt, maybe." **Fred MacMurray** muses out loud. *Double Indemnity* (1944, Paramount).

9952 "Money talks, they say. All it ever said to me was 'goodbye.'" Cockney drifter **Cary Grant** laments his lack of funds. *None but the Lonely Heart* (1944, RKO).

9953 "You'd better let me do the talking. The only thing that stands between you and eternity is my vocabulary." Dutchman **Sydney Greenstreet** advises Americans James Stewart and Spencer Tracy, posing as Irish sailors, to let him deal with a Japanese officer. *Malaya* (1949, MGM).

9954 "I'd like to learn how to talk good." Ex-chorus girl **Judy Holliday** tells writer William Holden there's an area in which she'd like to see self-improvement. *Born Yesterday* (1950, Columbia).

9955 "They're dead. They're finished. There was a time when this business had the eyes of the whole wide world. But that wasn't good enough. Oh, no! They wanted the ears of the world, too. So they opened their big mouths, and out came talk, talk, talk. . . ." Former silent screen star **Gloria Swanson** complains to out-of-work screenwriter William Holden about the decision to add sound to movies. *Sunset Boulevard* (1950, Paramount).

9956 "If you could possibly lift the needle from the long-playing record you got in your face!" Natural athlete **Katharine Hepburn** does not appreciate all the golfing advice her less-than-talented match partner is giving. Unsolicited advice on a golf course may prove dangerous to one's health. *Pat and Mike* (1952, MGM).

9957 "If you want to get a girl, you've got to learn to talk to them. You've got to act gentlemanly and well-spoken." Despite the good advice of their sister-in-law **Jane Powell**, six mountain men listen to her husband Howard Keel's advice and kidnap the girls of their choices. *Seven Brides for Seven Brothers* (1954, MGM).

9958 "When people are in trouble, they need to talk." **Cloris Leachman** is in trouble and needs to talk. Ralph Meeker, as private eye Mike Hammer, picks her up in his convertible when he finds her running barefoot down a dark highway. Shortly thereafter Meeker is knocked unconscious and Leachman is tortured to death with a pair of pliers. *Kiss Me Deadly* (1955, United Artists).

9959 "If thee talked as much to the Almighty as thee does to that horse, thee might stand more squarely in the light." Quaker **Dorothy McGuire** chides her husband Gary Cooper for his interest in racing his horse. *Friendly Persuasion* (1956, Allied Artists).

9960 "It's not so easy to raise my hand and send a boy to die without talking about it first." Juror **Henry Fonda** explains why he voted no in a show of hands in the first vote taken by a jury in the murder trial of a youngster accused of killing his father. The vote was 11 to 1. *12 Angry Men* (1957, United Artists).

9961 "Mr. Nazerman, a man gets hungry for talk, good talk." Lonely old **Juano Hernandez** visits Rod Steiger's pawnshop for conversation. *The Pawnbroker* (1965, Allied Artists-AIP).

9962 "It's like talking about current events at the dentist's to delay the drill." **Joan Hackett** confesses why she's arguing about modern architecture while being undressed by her first sexual partner Richard Mulligan. *The Group* (1966, United Artists).

9963 "I don't think we have much to say to each other." Older married woman **Anne Bancroft** sneeringly replies when her young lover Dustin Hoffman wonders if they might not talk to each other when they meet for sex. *The Graduate* (1967, Embassy).

9964 "I call that bold talk for a one-eyed fat man." Outlaw **Robert Duvall** backed by three members of his gang, shouts to John Wayne, who has given the former a chance to be taken back to be hanged by the authorities or to die on the spot. *True Grit* (1969, Paramount).

9965 "Y'know where we are right now, Harley?. . . We're in Wyoming territory, and you've been talkin' all the way since Texas. . . you say another word the rest of the day and I'm gonna kill ya." Cowpoke **James Stewart** intends to have the last word with his gregarious traveling companion Henry Fonda. *The Cheyenne Social Club* (1970, National General).

9966 "It's too bad about your dad. We're going to have to sit down and talk about that sometime." **Martin Sheen** speaks calmly to Sissy Spacek after the two have been captured following a murder spree which began with the killing of her father, Warren Oates. *Badlands* (1974, Columbia).

9967 "If there's something I can do for you, you come; we'll talk." **Robert De Niro** gains power by doing favors for people and then expecting them to pay him back when he decides the time is appropriate. *The Godfather, Part II* (1974, Paramount).

9968 "You talking to me?. . . Are you talking to me?. . . Who are you talking to?" Lonely taxi driver **Robert De Niro** is not talking to anyone in particular as he practices looking mean in front of a mirror. *Taxi Driver* (1976, Columbia).

9969 "Don't talk about it. Talk is dangerous. Sometimes it makes things happen. It makes them real." **Kathleen Turner** admonishes William Hurt not to talk about murdering her "small and mean and weak" husband Richard Crenna, lest he do something about it. Of course, the crafty Turner has put the idea in Hurt's mind. *Body Heat* (1981, Warner Bros.).

9970 "If you talk you always got the guys at the diner—you don't need a girl to talk." **Steve Guttenberg** tells his best man Timothy Daly that he is frightened by marriage and the changes it will bring in his life. *Diner* (1982, MGM).

9971 "I'm not talking mother to son, I'm talking shrink to shrink!" **Jessica Tandy** has a psychiatric conversation with her son Roy Scheider. *Still of the Night* (1982, MGM-United Artists).

9972 "I don't like talking about my past as much as you guys do." Naïve young outsider **Meg Tilly** doesn't have as much past to talk about as do the others who gather for her lover's funeral. *The Big Chill* (1983, Columbia).

9973 "Did you think I was all talk?" Terrorist **Harvey Keitel** casually knifes to death Pierre Clementi in front of aghast Nastassja Kinski. *Exposed* (1983, MGM-United Artists).

9974 "You don't talk, huh? Well, that's good. You don't talk, you don't talk people into things. You don't lie. My Bobby, you know, he's off living with this other girl. He's always talkin' people into things. He's great at that. You know, if they had it in the Olympics, he'd win a gold medal. Bobby. Bobby. I met him up at this place, you know, and he comes up to me an' he starts talkin'. Next thing you know, I'm big as a house with Little Earl here. Bobby's sweet, you know, if he doesn't get bored with you or see someone he likes better right across the street." White **Caroline Aaron** is pleased with the silence of Joe Morton, a mute, black alien, mostly indistinguishable from humans. She bends his ear about the father of her son. *The Brother from Another Planet* (1984, A-Train Films-Cinecom).

9975 BRUCE: "You have lovely breasts." PRUDENCE: "Do you wear contact lenses?" BRUCE: "I like the timbre of your voice—it's soft." PRUDENCE: "I love the smell of the Brut you're wearing." It's part of the chit-chat between bisexual **Jeff Goldblum** and uptight **Julie Hagerty** at their first date arranged through an ad in a newspaper personal column. *Beyond Therapy* (1987, New World).

9976 "No, no, no, on the contrary, one must talk, talk, talk. It is only by talking that we shall caper on the summit. Otherwise the mountain shall overshadow us." **Mark Tandy**, as Lord Risley, is right at home in this extremely talky film. *Maurice* (1987, GB, Cinecom).

9977 "Look, I don't want to be demanding here but do you think you can possibly say ten or twelve words before we get to the hotel? Consider it foreplay." **Valeria Golino** tries to get some attention from deep-in-thought Tom Cruise as they drive across country. *Rain Man* (1988, United Artists).

9978 "I'm talkin' about friendship. I'm talkin' about character. I'm talkin' about—hell, Leo, I ain't embarrassed to use the word—ethics." Rising Italian crime lord **Jon Polito** complains to Irish crime boss Albert Finney about that a Jewish bookie who is cheating Polito on fixed fights. *Miller's Crossing* (1990, 20th Century-Fox).

9979 "If there is half as much love in this old gal as talk I may be dead by the morning." Movie director **Clint Eastwood** leaves screenwriter Jeff Fahey to accompany Catherine Nielson to her room for the night. *White Hunter, Black Heart* (1990, Warner Bros.).

9980 VIRGINIA HILL: "Do you always talk this much before you do it?" BEN SIEGEL: "I only talk this much before I kill someone." **Annette Bening** and **Warren Beatty** are about to make love for the first time. *Bugsy* (1991, Tri-Star).

9981 FRANKIE: "I'm sorry. I'm not good at small talk." JOHNNY: "This isn't small talk. This is enormous talk." **Michelle Pfeiffer** tries to resist persistent suitor **Al Pacino**. *Frankie and Johnny* (1991, Paramount).

Tastes

see also DRINKING AND DRUNKENNESS, EXPERIENCES, FOOD AND EATING, MOUTHS, PREFERENCES, PROPRIETY, SENSE AND SENSIBILITY, SWEETNESS

9982 "Have caviar if you like, but it tastes like herring to me." Temporary typist **Joan Crawford** winces when she tries the caviar offered to her by Lionel Barrymore. *Grand Hotel* (1932, MGM).

9983 "Morals never bothered me too much but taste is so important." During the Russian Revolution, exiled aristocrat **Douglas Fairbanks, Jr.** has no concerns about correct behavior, but he feels it's important that he look just right. *Scarlet Dawn* (1932, Warner Bros.).

9984 "I feel as though somebody stepped on my tongue with muddy feet." **W.C. Fields** makes fun of his excessive drinking. *Never Give a Sucker an Even Break* (1941, Universal).

9985 "Power, yes, I want that as much as you want your job, or that girl. We all have different tastes as you can see, only I'm willing to back my tastes with the necessary force." Fifth columnist **Otto Kruger** prattles on to Robert Cummings. Kruger's explanations are to fill the gaps in the action and plot for the audience. *Saboteur* (1942, Universal).

9986 "You've tasted everything, you buzzard. But if you'd ever tasted Juan Castro, you'd have tasted a man." Soldier-of-fortune **Rory Calhoun** is almost buzzard food. *The Treasure of Pancho Villa* (1955, RKO).

9987 "You taste good like an orange drink should." **Montgomery Clift** makes points with Dolores Hart in front of a soft drink machine. *Lonelyhearts* (1958, United Artists).

9988 JAMES BOND: "Why do Chinese girls taste differently from all other girls?" CHINESE GIRL: "You think we better, yes?" BOND: "No, just different. Like Peking duck is different from Russian caviar." GIRL: "Darling, I give you very best duck." **Sean Connery**'s tasting **Tsai Chin** is interrupted when she jumps out of bed and presses a button. The bed, with Connery still in it, springs back into a recess in the wall. Men with tommy guns burst into the room, spray the closed bed, and rush out—leaving an apparently dead Connery. *You Only Live Twice* (1967, GB, United Artists).

9989 "There's no accounting for taste." Modeling magnate **Tammy Grimes** might be speaking of this silly movie, featuring the singing group, The Village People. *Can't Stop the Music* (1980, Associated Film Distribution).

9990 "Whadda ya gonna do if someone breaks in here? Stun them with your good taste?" Survivalist **Robin Williams** makes his point to his bewildered and appalled girl friend Annie McEnroe when he shows her his arsenal of grenades, knives and automatic rifles. *The Survivors* (1983, Columbia).

9991 "You're right, I married you." Wealthy **Rodney Dangerfield**, who gets no respect, snaps at his faithless second wife Adrienne Barbeau, who accuses him of having no taste. *Back to School* (1986, Orion).

9992 "Where's the cat? The one that shit in my mouth." It's tattooed, pistol-packing hell-raiser **Meg Ryan**'s question upon awakening. *Promised Land* (1988, Vestron).

9993 "Since when do you have to be hungry to eat a doughnut? It doesn't taste any better." Stock manipulator **Danny De Vito** has a weakness for Dunkin Donut doughnuts. He offers a doughnut to another weakness, beautiful Penelope Ann Miller, lawyer for a firm he's trying to take over. She declines his offer of a doughnut because she's not hungry. The script is so rich, that later Miller gets to repeat the line to De Vito. *Other People's Money* (1991, Warner Bros.).

Tattoos

see also SKIN

9994 "I never could understand the necessity of making a billboard out of the torso." Shipwrecked **Tallulah Bankhead** is both physically drawn to shirtless John Hodiak and repelled by the coarseness of his tattooed body. *Lifeboat* (1944, 20th Century-Fox).

9995 "See for yourself. His rose tattooed on my chest." **Virginia Grey** reveals to widow Anna Magnani that her late husband was unfaithful. *The Rose Tattoo* (1955, Paramount).

9996 "Navy don't take guys with tattoos." Boozy Navy career man **Robert Loggia** dismisses his son Richard Gere's chances of becoming a navy "flyboy." *An Officer and a Gentleman* (1982, Paramount).

9997 "You don't look like the type to be married to a man with a tattoo." **Loryn Locklin** has been sleeping with escaped con James Belushi, who has assumed the identity of Veronica Hamel's husband, obsessive businessman Charles Grodin. *Taking Care of Business* (1990, Hollywood Pictures-Buena Vista).

9998 "It's okay you killed that guy. He deserved it. He had tattoos and he was hairy." **Casey Siemaszko** comforts Leslie Hope when she shoots and kills a man. *The Big Slice* (1991, Canada, SC Entertainment Corporation).

Taunts

see also CONTEMPT, RIDICULE AND RIDICULOUSNESS

9999 "You don't like it, Rocco, the storm. Show it your gun, why don't you? If it doesn't stop, shoot it." **Humphrey Bogart** takes a big chance taunting mobster Edward G. Robinson during a hurricane. *Key Largo* (1948, Warner Bros.).

10000 "They got a little blue chair for little boys and a little pink chair for little girls." Loony old **Henry Jones** taunts sweet-looking little eight-year-old Patty McCormack, who just happens to be a murderess, about electric chairs. *The Bad Seed* (1956, Warner Bros.).

10001 "I don't call any of your cases crap—even when you worked a whole year on one for a non-dairy creamer, for God's sake." **Susan Sarandon** taunts her selfish husband Edward Herrmann for belittling her hopes and efforts as a writer. *Compromising Positions* (1985, Paramount).

10002 "Why don't you two go down to the gym and pump each other?" **Chevy Chase** taunts two burly cops who are pushing him around. *Fletch* (1985, Universal).

10003 "Better look out, I might break a nail." When a male heckler yells at the Rockford Peaches girls' professional baseball team members, he is quickly rewarded by being hit with a "stray" throw from Rosie O'Donnell. *A League of Their Own* (1992, Columbia).

Taxes

see also BUSINESS AND COMMERCE, GOVERNMENTS, LAWS, PEOPLE

10004 "Any objections to the new tax from our Saxon friends?" **Claude Rains**, as Norman Prince John, inquires without any real concern to Basil Rathbone, as Sir Guy of Gisbourne. *The Adventures of Robin Hood* (1938, Warner Bros.).

10005 "How could I know that income tax bill meant me too?" Incompetent U.S. Senator **William Powell** is unfit for anything except running for the presidency. *The Senator Was Indiscreet* (1947, Universal-International).

10006 "If you don't pay taxes, you're a liar. I'm not a liar. Liars are the second lowest form of human beings on the planet. . . [the first are] lawyers." **James Spader** reacts angrily when lawyer Peter Gallagher asks if he pays taxes. *sex, lies and videotape* (1989, Miramax).

Teaching and Teachers

see also EDUCATION, LEARNING AND LESSONS, SCHOOLS, STUDIES AND STUDENTS

10007 "In mixing the important thing is the rhythm. You should always have rhythm in your shaking. Now a Manhattan you shake to a fox trot; a Bronx to two-step time. A dry martini you always shake to waltz time." **William Powell** moves rhythmically to the music as he teaches an assemblage of bartenders and waitresses the proper way to mix drinks. *The Thin Man* (1934, MGM).

10008 "Say, where'd you learn to dunk, in finishing school? Twenty million dollars and you don't know how to dunk. . . . Dunking's an art. Don't let it soak so long. A dip and plot into your mouth. If you let it stay there too long, it'll get soft and fall off. It's all a matter of timing. I ought to write a book about it." **Clark Gable** corrects Claudette Colbert's doughnut dunking in coffee technique. *It Happened One Night* (1934, Columbia).

10009 RUPERT OF HENTZAU: "You're a man after my own heart, Rassendyl. Frankly, we're the only two worth saving out of this entire affair. . . . What did they teach you on the playing fields of England?" RUDOLPH RASSENDYL: "Chiefly not to throw knives at other people's backs. Bad-tempered fellow, aren't you, underneath the charm?" Villain **Douglas Fairbanks, Jr.** and hero **Ronald Colman** converse as they duel, not quite to the death. *The Prisoner of Zenda* (1937, Selznick-United Artists).

10010 "Oh, this is one of those days that the pages of history teach us are best spent in bed." **Roland Young** awakens much the worse for wear because of too much celebration the previous night. *The Philadelphia Story* (1940, MGM).

10011 "Why, Miss Hicks, I never knew that school teachers were human beings like everyone else. And better, too." Wonder if the second line of **Mickey Rooney**'s statement to teacher Mary Nash is to make up for the first line. *The Human Comedy* (1943, MGM).

10012 "You make a lot of people through the years a little more enlightened. You have contributed something." Suicidal professor **Edmund Gwenn**, commenting on teaching, tries to justify his existence. *Apartment for Peggy* (1948, 20th Century-Fox).

10013 "We had taught her to find glamour and excitement in faraway places and only boredom in the here and now." **James Mason**, as French author Gustave Flaubert, refers to his creation Emma Bovary, played in the film by Jennifer Jones. *Madame Bovary* (1949, MGM).

10014 "I've taught everyone from Nijinsky to Mickey Rooney." Dance instructor **Florence Bates** brags. *On the Town* (1949, MGM).

10015 "This is our last hour together. I'm not going to keep you for it. But I'll remember every one of your faces for the rest of my life. And I rather imagine you'll remember mine. Because we've gone on a journey together. There were times when I lost my way, and somewhere along the road you and others became the teacher and I the student. You taught me that as long as one man is without an answer, all men are without an answer. You taught me that only he who chooses to be alone is alone. And so even though our small journey is over and we go our separate ways, we'll never really be apart. Till the end of time we'll carry in our hearts the things that we've shared together. I'm sure someone somewhere said that much better than I, probably Shakespeare; surely the Bible. But I think it's something that a man should say at least to himself. As you know, I teach English, but there are some things very hard to say in it. So if you don't mind, I'll use my first-year Spanish. Vaya con Dios. Go with God. Let's all go with God." Having lost his wife and child in a gas explosion, university professor **Ray Milland** seeks solace in alcohol. He is prevented from committing suicide, an act of futility that shocks him back into reality. At the end of the movie, he takes leave of his students. *Night Into Morning* (1951, MGM).

10016 "What's the point of teaching if kids don't care about education? You were my professor in college. You should have taught me how to stop a fight in a classroom, how to deal with an I.Q. of 66. If I'm going to be a lion tamer, I should teach with a chair and a whip." **Glenn Ford** shouts his outrage to a former college professor about his unpreparedness for teaching in the public schools. At the time, many education professors wrote articles claiming that the movie overstated the problem. In fact, the school and the "students" depicted in the film are first-rate compared to some that teachers must deal with today. *The Blackboard Jungle* (1955, MGM).

10017 DADIER: "Who cares about teachers anyway? Teachers get two dollars an hour. A household cook gets more than we do. And they get room and board." MURDOCK: "You proved something—the kids can be taught—if you don't stop trying." Nearing the end of his first year of teaching, **Glenn Ford** is frustrated and depressed, but once cynical veteran teacher **Louis Calhern** declares Ford a success. *The Blackboard Jungle* (1955, MGM).

10018 "We teach them duty, honor, country and then send them out to die." **Tyrone Power**, the long-time athletic trainer at the U.S. Military Academy at West Point, muses on all the cadets he's seen. *The Long Gray Line* (1955, Columbia).

10019 "To 'Sir' with love. . . . We think we're better for having you as our teacher. We liked most the way you talked to us like grown-ups and not like brats." East End high school student **Lulu (Marie Lawre)** presents West Indian teacher Sidney Poitier with a gift on behalf of the class. *To Sir with Love* (1967, GB, Columbia).

10020 "I'm 26 and I'm single and I teach school and that's the bottom of the pit." **Katharine Ross** gives her reasons for teaming up with outlaws Paul Newman and Robert Redford. Teaching isn't all that bad—but in some places it is more dangerous than bank robbery. *Butch Cassidy and the Sundance Kid* (1969, 20th Century-Fox).

10021 "Destroy all values, conformity and morals. Throw away the pleasure of love, and realize the dream of eroticism." Elderly roue **Alain Cuny** earnestly instructs nineteen-year-old wife Sylvia Kristel in his sexual philosophy. *Emmanuelle* (1974, Fr., Columbia).

10022 "Yeah, I want to lie back on the grass and have you teach me some more about gardening." Having had enough adventure and excitement, **Jill Clayburgh** wants to take it easy with lover Gene Wilder. *Silver Streak* (1976, 20th Century-Fox).

10023 "I taught you everything you know." Malibu madam **Nina Van Pallandt** gives male hooker Richard Gere his assignments. *American Gigolo* (1980, Paramount).

10024 "Remember, kid, I taught you everything you know, but I didn't teach you everything I know." Pool shark **James Coburn** reminds his protégé Bruce Boxleitner that he can still beat him. *The Baltimore Bullet* (1980, Avco Embassy).

10025 "I found her when she was twelve. I taught her everything. . . and then she began to teach me." Underworld scum **Vittorio Gassman** speaks fondly of high-priced call girl Rachel Ward. *Sharky's Machine* (1981, Warner Bros.).

10026 "Teaching is something you do in spite of everything else." Principal **David Gardner** waxes idealistically to new music teacher Perry King in a violent and bloody reworking of *The Blackboard Jungle*. *Class of 1984* (1982, United Films Distribution).

10027 "Don't talk, OK, I'm a friend. A friend. I'll teach you a few very important things quickly and then I want you to meet a nice lady." After Christlike stranger Keir Dullea wanders off to sea, young **Jeremy Licht** hopes another like him will follow and want to meet his mother Adrienne Barbeau. *The Next One* (1982, US-Greek, Allstar).

10028 "I'm going to teach you to hate spending money." **Hume Cronyn** reaches from beyond the grave in a video cassette to his great nephew Richard Pryor. Cronyn offers Pryor the deal of spending $30 million without having anything to show for it, in order to inherit $300 million. *Brewster's Millions* (1985, Universal).

10029 "The war is over for me now, but it will always be there, for the rest of my days, as I'm sure Elias will be, fighting with Barnes. . . for the 'possession of my soul.' There are times since then I've felt like a child born of these two fathers. . . But be that as it may, those of us who did make it home are obligated to build again, to teach to others what we know and try with what's left of our lives to find a goodness and meaning to this life." Narrator **Charlie Sheen**, as he's evacuated from Vietnam, remembers the dead, the good Sergeant Willem Dafoe and the bad Sergeant Tom Berenger, who represent his personal Jekyll and Hyde. *Platoon* (1986, Orion).

10030 "I ain't no English teacher." **Mark Harmon** ideally makes his point to a summer school class of remedial students that "he can't learn them no English." *Summer School* (1987, Paramount).

10031 "He pulls a knife, you pull a gun. He sends one of yours to the hospital, you send one of his to the morgue. That's the Chicago way." Tough Irish cop **Sean Connery** instructs Federal Investigator Eliot Ness, portrayed by Kevin Costner, in how to deal with mobster Al Capone. *The Untouchables* (1987, Paramount).

10032 "I teach not only how to play, but how to live." Tyrannical piano teacher **Shirley MacLaine** preaches to her talented young pupil Navin Chowdhry. *Madame Sousatzka* (1988, Universal).

10033 "Never listen to your teachers. Just see what they look like." For many pupils, **Woody Allen**'s advice to his niece Jenny Nichols is unnecessary. *Crimes and Misdemeanors* (1989, Orion).

10034 "Con-gra-tu-la-tions to you and Peter. I'm glad you taught me how to speak so I can say that." **Daniel Day-Lewis**, in his bravo performance as Irish artist and writer Christy Brown, offers sarcastic congratulations to his beloved Fiona Shaw, a specialist in the treatment and education of cerebral palsy, when she announces her engagement to Adrian Dunbar. *My Left Foot* (1989, GB, Miramax).

10035 "My father taught me many things. . . .'Keep your friends close, but your enemies closer.'" Godfather **Al Pacino** recalls a lesson of his father that he quotes to his nephew Andy Garcia. *The Godfather, Part III* (1990, Paramount).

10036 "Teach me to read." Illiterate middle-aged **Robert De Niro** begs widow Jane Fonda to teach him to read. *Stanley & Iris* (1990, MGM).

Teams

see also SPORTS, TOGETHERNESS

10037 "In the nineteen-forties, it was Victor Mature and Judy Canova. In the fifties, Christine Jorgensen and James Dean. In the sixties, Smith and Wesson." **Arnold Johnson**, the token black on the executive board of an otherwise all white ad agency, makes an observation apropos of nothing very much. *Putney Swope* (1969, Cinema V Distributing-Herald).

10038 "Now an army is a team. It lives, eats, sleeps, fights as a team. This individuality stuff is a bunch of crap. The bilious bastards who wrote that stuff about individuality for the *Saturday Evening Post* don't know any more about real battle than they do about fornicating." Always outspoken, title character **George C. Scott** stresses the importance of teamwork. He should be reminded that Americans fight wars as teams to guarantee that in peace they may act as individuals. *Patton* (1970, 20th Century-Fox).

10039 "No, sir, don't thank me, warden. We're all part of the same team." **Christopher Reeve**, as Superman, hand-delivers Gene Hackman, as Lex Luthor, and Ned Beatty, as his simple-minded henchman Otis, to prison warden Roy Stevens at the end of the film. *Superman* (1978, Warner Bros.).

10040 "We're not the team. You're the team. We're only the equipment—like the jockstraps and the helmets." Professional passcatcher **Nick Nolte** has an attitude problem as far as football team owner Steve Forrest is concerned. *North Dallas Forty* (1979, Paramount).

10041 "We make a really good team. I think I'll ask her to marry me tonight. Together, I don't see how we can miss." Two-bit gunrunner **Chevy Chase** wants to make Sigourney Weaver his permanent partner. *Deal of the Century* (1983, Warner Bros.).

10042 "See, you got three or four good pals, why then you got yourself a tribe—there ain't nothin' stronger than that." **Emilio Estevez**, as Billy the Kid, talks Lou Diamond Phillips, as Indian Chevez Y Chavez, into joining Estevez's gang of young guns. *Young Guns* (1988, 20th Century-Fox).

10043 "Baby, I'm your ally against horse dung and fraud." Renowned painter **Nick Nolte** is obsessively in love with his inspiration Rosanna Arquette. *New York Stories (Life Lessons)* (1989, Touchstone-Buena Vista).

10044 TOMMY KORMAN: "If I were a medieval knight, I would have josted for you." BETSY/DONNA: "Jousted." TOMMY: "I mean, we're up there with Romeo and

Juliet, George and Grace, all the big ones." Sentimental mug **James Caan** flies **Sarah Jessica Parker** to Hawaii to woo her. *Honeymoon in Vegas* (1992, Columbia).

Tears see CRYING AND CRIES, LAUGHTER, PAINS, SADNESS, SORROWS, SYMPATHY

Technology see INVENTIONS, SCIENCE AND SCIENTISTS

Teenagers see CHILDREN AND CHILDHOOD, YOUTH

Teeth see MOUTHS

Telephones

see also TALKS AND TALKING

10045 "Whenever a day comes without an invitation, I pray to my telephone as though it were a little black god. I beg it to speak to me. . . to ask me out where ever there is champagne or caviar." Eternal guest **Rex O'Malley** lives for parties. *Midnight* (1939, Paramount).

10046 "Really, Papa, you'd think Mama had never seen a phone. She makes no allowance for science. She thinks she has to cover the distance by sheer lung power." **Edna Mae Wonacott** complains to her father Henry Travers that her mother Patricia Collinge misuses the telephone. Know-it-all children are a pain. *Shadow of a Doubt* (1943, Universal).

10047 "In the tangled networks of a great city, the telephone is the unseen link between a million lives. . . . It is the servant of our common needs— the confidence of our innermost secrets. . . life and happiness wait upon its ring. . . and horror. . . and loneliness. . . and death!" The narrator, in voice-over, in an excellent suspense film. *Sorry, Wrong Number* (1948, Paramount).

10048 "Marry me and I'll smother you with private phones." Wealthy **Tony Randall** makes an offer to Doris Day, who is desperate to get a private line— but not that desperate. *Pillow Talk* (1959, Universal).

10049 "Hello, is this someone with good news or money? No? Goodbye." **Jason Robards** has the right idea as he hangs up on an unwanted telephone caller. *A Thousand Clowns* (1965, United Artists).

10050 "If you need me, just call. You know how to call, don't you? You just put your finger in the hole and make tiny little circles." **Rachel Ward** parodies Lauren Bacall as she tells private detective Steve Martin he can phone her anytime. *Dead Men Don't Wear Plaid* (1982, Universal).

10051 "E.T. . . . phone home." It's the famous catchphrase from one of the all-time biggest box-office hits. *E.T. the Extra-Terrestrial* (1982, Universal).

10052 "You wouldn't have the wit to think of an obscene telephone call." Soon after **Patricia Charbonneau** chides her boy friend Sam Freed for his lack of imagination in turning her on, she receives an obscene call which she believes is from him. She agrees to meet the caller, with disastrous results. *Call Me* (1988, Vestron).

Television

see also ENTERTAINMENTS AND ENTERTAINERS, SHOWS

10053 "That's all television is, dear—just auditions." Theater critic **George Sanders** dismisses television for his new conquest, show girl Marilyn Monroe. *All About Eve* (1950, 20th Century-Fox).

10054 "You're television incarnate, Diana, indifferent to suffering, insensitive to joy. All life is reduced to the common rubble of banality, war, murder, death—all the same to you as bottles of beer, and the daily business of life is a corrupt comedy. You even shatter the sensation of time and space into split seconds and instant replays. You're madness, Diana. . . Like you, everything television touches is destroyed." Network news executive **William Holden** serves as Paddy Chayevsky's mouthpiece. He flays lover Faye Dunaway, who seems only interested in ratings. *Network* (1976, MGM-United Artists).

10055 "Television is not the truth. Television is a god-damned amusement park. Television is a circus, a carnival, a traveling troupe of acrobats, story tellers, dancers, singers, jugglers, sideshow freaks, lion tamers, and football players. We're in the boredom-killing business." Perhaps critics of television should take note of the function mad news anchorman **Peter Finch** has described for it, and be happy when it does alleviate boredom, rather than cause it. *Network* (1976, MGM-United Artists).

10056 "You dress like the tube, you eat like the tube, you raise your children like the tube. It's mass madness. You maniacs. You are the real thing—turn them off. Right in the middle of this sentence I am speaking." Mad television guru **Peter Finch** bites the hand that feeds him by encouraging his audience to turn away from television. *Network* (1976, MGM-United Artists).

10057 "They don't throw their garbage away. They make it into television shows." It's New Yorker **Woody Allen**'s cynical reaction when Diane Keaton admires the cleanliness of Beverly Hills. *Annie Hall* (1977, United Artists).

10058 "I'm gonna tell ya something. *Bonanza* is not an accurate depiction of the West." Aluminum siding salesman **Jackie Gayle** serves as TV critic at a breakfast with his cronies. *Tin Men* (1987, Touchstone-Buena Vista).

Telling *see* DESCRIPTIONS, TALKS AND TALKING

Temper *see* ANGER

Temperance *see* ALCOHOL, DRINKING AND DRUNKENNESS

Temperatures

see also HEAT, SICKNESS

10059 "Did you know that more murders are committed at 92 degrees than at any other temperature? At lower temperatures, people are easy-going; higher, it's too hot to move. But just at 92, people get irritable." A little more research might have led Sheriff **Charles Drake** to conclude it isn't the heat, it is the humidity (humanity?) that causes all the problems. *It Came from Outer Space* (1953, Universal-International).

10060 COLONEL: "Surely you've seen a temperature taken like this before?" MATRON: "Oh, yes, Colonel, many times, but never with a daffodil." The staff and socialized medicine patients have the last laugh on complaining paying patient **Wilfrid Hyde-White.** Matron **Hattie Jacques** finds a daffodil in the place where one usually finds a rectal thermometer. *Carry on Nurse* (1959, GB, Anglo-Amalgamated).

Temptations

see also CORRUPTION, IMMORALITY, MORALITY, SEDUCTIONS, SINS AND SINNERS

10061 "The only way to get rid of temptation is to yield to it." In a title card, **Brandon Hurst** encourages his prospective son-in-law John Barrymore, as Dr. Jekyll, to savor the fleshpots of London. *Doctor Jekyll and Mr. Hyde* (1920, silent, Famous Players-Lasky).

10062 "It's the things one can't do that always tempt me." **Fredric March** confesses to his friend Holmes Herbert. *Dr. Jekyll and Mr. Hyde* (1932, Paramount).

10063 "You don't want to be married to a mug like Westley. I can buy him off with a pot of gold, and you can make an old man happy, and you wouldn't

do so bad for yourself." As he escorts his daughter down the aisle to her marriage with Jameson Thomas, **Walter Connolly** tempts her with thoughts of the man he knows she really loves, Clark Gable. *It Happened One Night* (1934, Columbia).

10064 MRS. HUDSON: "Mr. Holmes, it's nearly midnight! You must eat something. Can I tempt you with a nice piece of haddock?" SHERLOCK HOLMES: "My dear Mrs. Hudson, you've always been a temptation to me, but haddock at this moment is not." Landlady **Minnie Rayner** frets about **Arthur Wontner**'s eating habits. *Silver Blaze* aka: *Murder at the Baskervilles* (1937, GB, Gaumont-British).

10065 "I generally avoid temptation, unless I can't resist it." Shady lady **Mae West** comes by her reputation honestly. *My Little Chickadee* (1940, Universal).

10066 "You have nothing to stay for. You have nothing to live for, really, have you? Look down there—it's easy, isn't it?" **Judith Anderson**, as housekeeper Mrs. Danvers, turns up the burner in her psychological campaign to get Joan Fontaine, as the second Mrs. de Winter, to commit suicide. *Rebecca* (1940, Selznick-United Artists).

10067 "Why worry about the people and their problems? Start thinking about your own. You want to be president of this country, don't you? And you ought to be.... Don't be a fool. Stop bothering with that speech and get busy promoting yourself instead of the people." An unseen **Walter Huston**, as the devil, whispers a temptation to Edward Arnold as Daniel Webster. *All that Money Can Buy* aka: *The Devil and Daniel Webster* (1941, RKO).

10068 "Pearl, you're curved in the flesh of temptation. Resistance is going to be a darn sight harder for you than females protected by the shapes of sows." Self-ordained preacher **Walter Huston** shares with shapely Jennifer Jones his theory that less voluptuous women feel less sexual temptation. *Duel in the Sun* (1946, Selznick).

10069 "Look down there. Would you really feel any pity if one of those dots stopped moving forever? If I said that you can have twenty thousand pounds for every dot that stops, would you really, old man, tell me to keep the money, or would you calculate how many dots you could afford to spare? Free of income tax, old man, free of income tax." Like Lucifer to Christ on the mountain, black marketeer **Orson Welles** tempts his friend, writer Joseph Cotten, from the top of a giant swaying Ferris wheel. *The Third Man* (1950, GB, London Films-Korda-Selznick).

10070 "How much longer are you going to be tempted by this firm young flesh?" **Pamela Franklin** puts it squarely on the line to art teacher Robert Stephens. *The Prime of Miss Jean Brodie* (1969, 20th Century-Fox).

10071 "No, I just find it hard to resist the temptation to take extreme closeups of myself." Filmmaker **Woody Allen** replies to the question, "Do you find it hard to direct yourself?" during a film seminar. *Stardust Memories* (1980, United Artists).

10072 "You are a temptress, my dear, and for an old man like me, that's dangerous." Shortly before he is assassinated, **Ben Kingsley**, as Mahatma Gandhi, confesses his attraction for Candice Bergen, as famed photographer Margaret Bourke-White. *Gandhi* (1982, GB-India, Columbia-Goldcrest).

10073 "I'm candy and it's very hard to get enough. . . ." Bragging **Debra Winger** is silkenly seductive with Richard Gere. *An Officer and a Gentleman* (1982, Paramount).

10074 "There's a certain someone here I want you to meet. . . . She's a very, very special person. . . . You're not going to strike out. . . . She was just released from parochial school; she's in her experimental stage. . . . She loves sex. . . . You remember the last snapshot I sent you?. . . The blonde in the string bikini?. . . Look at it. Fixate on it. . . . Are you fixating on it?. . . She's a 'sure thing,' Gib, a sure thing." **Anthony Edwards** entices his friend John Cusack to travel across continent at Christmas break to make it with Nicollette Sheridan. *The Sure Thing* (1985, Embassy).

10075 "I just happen to have access to one of the sexiest lasers in the entire free world." Nuclear scientist **John Lithgow** attempts to inveigle young Christopher Collet to arrange a date with the latter's mother Jill Eikenberry. *The Manhattan Project* (1986, 20th Century-Fox).

10076 "I know you have, but have you? Resist the temptation or you may end up like Pete and Mary and Ken." The last line of this silly film consisting of 20 different comedy sketches lampooning just about everything goes to Doctor **Paul Bartel**. *Amazon Women on the Moon* (1987, Universal).

Tenderness *see* CONSIDERATIONS, SENSE AND SENSIBILITY, SENSITIVITY AND INSENSITIVITY

Tensions

see also HOSTILITIES, RELATIONSHIPS

10077 "The ordinary person avoids tense situations. Repo man spends his life getting into tense situa-

tions. A repo man is always tense." Experienced car repossession man **Harry Dean Stanton** instructs neophyte Emilio Estevez in the trade. *Repo Man* (1984, Universal).

10078 "The tension was so thick you could cut it with a knife, which is more than I could say for the liver." Teenager **Jonathan Silverman** speaks of a family dinner. *Brighton Beach Memoirs* (1986, Universal).

Terror

see also FEARS, HORRORS, VIOLENCE

10079 "I guess if the unborn knew of the approach of life, they'd be just as terrified." **Charles Chaplin** philosophizes about death. *Monsieur Verdoux* (1947, Chaplin-United Artists).

10080 "We must make friends with mortal terror. . . it is judgment that defeats us." Mad martinet **Marlon Brando** lectures Martin Sheen who Brando knows has been sent to kill him. *Apocalypse Now* (1979, United Artists).

Thanks and Thankfulness

10081 "That will be all, thank you." It is **Norma Shearer**'s response to being kissed by Clark Gable. *A Free Soul* (1931, MGM).

10082 "Do give thee most humble and hearty thanks." **Flora Robson**, as Queen Elizabeth I, is thankful for the efforts of Laurence Olivier against the Spanish Armada. *Fire Over England* (1937, GB, United Artists).

10083 "Ladies and gentlemen, when something like this happens to you and you try to tell how you feel about it, you find that, out of all the words in the world, there are only two that really mean anything—thank you." How wonderful it would be if all Oscar winners were so elegant and brief in accepting their awards as is **Janet Gaynor**. **Judy Garland** piped in similarly in the remake. *A Star Is Born* (1937, Selznick-United Artists); (1954, Warner Bros).

10084 "You couldn't have done more for me if you'd been an adult my own age." It's **Mickey Rooney**'s inadequate way of thanking Judy Garland for saving him from the clutches of ruthless New York glamour girl Diana Lewis. *Andy Hardy Meets Debutante* (1940, MGM).

10085 "These are tears of gratitude. An old maid's gratitude. Nobody has ever called me 'darling' before." Once a repressed spinster, **Bette Davis** has found a man, Paul Henreid, who doesn't consider her an old maid. Unfortunately, her cruise-going lover is married. *Now, Voyager* (1942, Warner Bros.).

10086 "My mother thanks you, my father thanks you, my sister thanks you—and I thank you." **James Cagney** as George M. Cohan takes his usual curtain call. *Yankee Doodle Dandy* (1942, Warner Bros.).

10087 "I wasn't asleep, dear, I was just thinking of someone who loved us all very much and saying thank you." Elderly engineer **Myrna Loy** tells one of her twelve children that she was thinking of her long-deceased husband Clifton Webb. *Belles on Their Toes* (1952, 20th Century-Fox).

10088 "Lord, you sure knew what you was doing when you put me in this very cell at this very time. A man with $10,000 and a widow in the making." Psychopathic bogus preacher **Robert Mitchum** looks to the heavens from a window of the prison cell he shares with condemned Peter Graves, who has hidden the money he stole. *The Night of the Hunter* (1955, United Artists).

10089 "Dear Mr. Montgomery. There isn't much I can say with words, they always fail me when most needed. But please know that with all my heart, I appreciate everything you've done for me. Sincerely, Barbara." Shortly before her execution, **Susan Hayward** writes a letter of thanks to Simon Oakland. *I Want to Live!* (1958, United Artists).

10090 "My thanks to King Brian of Knocknasheega and his leprechauns, whose gracious co-operation made this picture possible. **Walt Disney.**" Opening card in the film. *Darby O'Gill and the Little People* (1959, Disney-Buena Vista).

10091 "I feel a great gratitude to my life, which gives me so much." After she dies from painful cancer, **Harriet Andersson**'s servant **Kari Sylwan** reads from the deceased's diary. *Cries and Whispers* (1973, Sweden, Cinematograph).

10092 "Thanks a lot for Josey Wales, who you changed from a murderin' bushwhacker on the side of Satan to a better man trying to deliver us from the Philistines." Covered wagon owner **Paula Trueman** thanks the Lord for Clint Eastwood. *The Outlaw Josey Wales* (1976, Warner Bros.).

10093 "I keep wanting to thank you—but then I keep wondering what for." Cowboy pitchman for a breakfast cereal **Robert Redford** says goodbye to TV reporter Jane Fonda after the two set free a twelve-million dollar thoroughbred horse. *The Electric Horseman* (1979, Columbia).

10094 "I saved the whole city, and what do I get for it?" Amicable, arrogant loser **Michael Moriarty** discovers the lair of a prehistoric Aztec deity that swoops down and rips the heads off rooftop sunbathers. *Q* aka: *Quetzalcoatl: The Winged Serpent* (1982, United Film Distributors).

10095 "Rohan, Rohan, it was a stray bomb. Thank you, Adolf." One of young Sebastian Rice-Edwards' chums cheers happily when their school is destroyed by a German bomb during the London Blitz. *Hope and Glory* (1987, GB, Columbia).

10096 "Thank God for lips. Thank God for necks, thank God for kneecaps, for elbows, for thighs." **Spike Lee** gives thanks to God as he rubs ice cubes over the body of Rosie Perez during a love scene. *Do the Right Thing* (1989, Universal).

10097 "I do everything I can to make you happy. You just better start showing some appreciation around here, Mr. Man." Crazy as a loon, **Kathy Bates** expects writer James Caan to be thankful that she rescued him from a car wreck, has crippled him and holds him captive. *Misery* (1990, Columbia).

Theaters

see also ACTING AND ACTORS, COMEDY AND COMEDIANS, DANCING AND DANCERS, DRAMA AND MELODRAMA, MOTION PICTURES, SHOWS, STARS, TRAGEDIES

10098 "We of the theater live apart from the outside world. We never open our mouths to speak, or our lips to kiss but to further our careers." Already a star, **Andrea King**, as Lillian Russell, instructs ambitious hopeful Dennis Morgan, as Irish tenor Chauncey Olcott. *My Wild Irish Rose* (1947, Warner Bros.).

10099 "There's nothing quite so mysterious and silent as a dark theater. A night without a star." It is **Grace Kelly**'s observation as she enters an empty theater. *The Country Girl* (1954, Paramount).

10100 "The theater's a stunted bleeding stump. Even stars have to wait years for one decent play." Movie actor **Jack Palance** is afraid to leave Hollywood and return to the Broadway stage. *The Big Knife* (1955, United Artists).

10101 "The theater is the most beautiful place on earth: the theater is—romance." **Anne Bancroft**, as British actress Mrs. Madge Kendal, gushes to John Hurt, as title character John Merrick. *The Elephant Man* (1980, GB, Paramount).

10102 "My only talent is that I love this little world inside the thick walls of the playhouse. . . . Outside is the big world, and sometimes the little world succeeds for a moment in reflecting the big world, so that we understand it better. Or is it perhaps that we give the people who come here the chance of forgetting for awhile the hard world outside?" Pretentiously, **Allan Edwall** addresses the cast of a theater group at a Christmas party. *Fanny and Alexander* (1982, Sweden, Swedish Film Institute-Embassy).

10103 "We draw the theater over our heads like a mantle of security." Actress **Ewa Froling**'s statement is more eloquent than Allan Edwall's (above). *Fanny and Alexander* (1982, Sweden, Swedish Film Institute-Embassy).

Theology *see* BELIEFS, FAITH AND UNFAITHFULNESS, GOD, RELIGIONS

Theories

see also ACTIONS AND ACTS, PHILOSOPHIES, SCIENCE AND SCIENTISTS, SYSTEMS

10104 "I just came to say goodbye. . . . You're the one that's going, baby, not me. I'm getting off a trolley car, right at this corner. . . . A friend of mine's got a funny theory. He says when two people commit a murder it's sorta like they're riding the trolley car together. One can't get off without the other. They have to go on riding together to the end of the line. The last stop's the cemetery. . . . Two people are going to ride to the end of the line, all right, but only I'm not going to be one of them. I've got another guy to finish my ride for me." **Fred Mac-Murray** explains Edward G. Robinson's theory to Barbara Stanwyck that the more people involved in a murder conspiracy, the more likely it will end in disaster for all concerned. MacMurray thinks he has a fall guy to take his place but Stanwyck shoots him. *Double Indemnity* (1944, Paramount).

10105 "I've always thought that the fourth dimension was neither philosophical nor mathematical, but purely intuitional." Escaped con **James Cagney** launches into an inexplicable discourse on a subject that he knows nothing about. *Kiss Tomorrow Goodbye* (1950, Warner Bros.).

10106 "That's what my ex-wife used to keep reminding me of. Tearfully. She had a theory that behind every great man there was a great woman. She was also thoroughly convinced that she was great and all I needed to qualify was guidance on her part. She worked hard at it—too hard." Theater director **William Holden** thinks he sees some similarities between his ex-wife and Bing Crosby's wife Grace Kelly. *The Country Girl* (1954, Paramount).

10107 "Well, I could tell you my latest theory." **Yahoo Serious** is Albert Einstein in this weird import from down-under. *Young Einstein* (1988, Australia, Warner Bros.).

10108 "I formed my own theory that you should never take advice from someone who doesn't know you intimately." **James Spader** tells Andie Mac-Dowell why he isn't in therapy. *sex, lies and videotape* (1989, Miramax).

Thieves *see* CRIMES AND CRIMINALS

Things

see also EVERYTHING, OBJECTS

10109 "I'm not a person to them, I'm a thing. . . hair and legs—no face, no feelings." **Carroll Baker** complains that it's a drag being a sex symbol. *Harlow* (1965, Paramount).

10110 "You keep throwing in your hand because you haven't got the whole thing. There is no whole thing." **Peggy Ashcroft** shares some wisdom with her daughter, executive Glenda Jackson. *Sunday, Bloody Sunday* (1971, GB, United Artists).

10111 "Why is any object we don't understand always called a 'thing'?" **DeForest Kelley**, as Dr. McCoy, poses an interesting question about an alien craft that seems to be on a threatening course toward earth—but no one answers it. *Star Trek: The Motion Picture* (1979, Paramount).

10112 "We didn't make a place for people, we made it for things. And when you make a place for things, things come." **John Glover**, a Donald Trump-Ted Turner clone, eulogizes his high-tech, high-rise after an invasion of gremlins. *Gremlins 2: The New Batch* (1990, Warner Bros).

10113 CHRISTINE HODGES: "It's more than an alligator; it's a mutation; it's. . . a thing." DAVID HODGES: "You're right, it's a thing." **Dee Wallace Stone** and **Joseph Bologna** agree that a giant alligator terrorizing some lake shore properties is a thing. *Alligator II: The Mutation* (1991, New Line).

Thinking and Thoughts

see also DETECTIVES AND DEDUCTION, IDEAS, INTELLIGENCE, LOGIC, MINDS, REASONS

10114 "You aren't kidding me? You aren't as red as you make out? You're just shooting off your face to those longhairs because you haven't found out yet what you want? You're not such a heavy thinker. Do you know how I know? Because a thinker is a dodo on the dance floor and you aren't." Soldier **Robert Young** lectures heiress Barbara Stanwyck, a turn-coat to her class, because she's fallen in love with a villainous radical student Hardie Albright. But she's not all bad—the kid can sure dance. *Red Salute* (1935, United Artists).

10115 BILL CHANDLER: "I thought that was rather clever of me." CONNIE ALLENBURY: "Yes, I thought you thought so." Devilish lawyer **William Powell** fails to impress heiress **Myrna Loy** with his clever-ness. *Libeled Lady* (1936, MGM).

10116 FAY CARTER: "And I thought I hated you. It's ridiculous. This is so sudden." DICK ORR: "Lightning never struck faster." FAY: "Don't talk. I want to think about us." Realizing their true feelings for each other, **Kay Francis** and **George Brent** talk between kisses. *Secrets of an Actress* (1938, Warner Bros.).

10117 "Think of her in my arms, my lips upon hers, and you'll be pleased to die." **Tod Slaughter** uses a bit of gamesmanship as he taunts John Warwick, his rival for Marjorie Taylor, into fighting an unfair duel. *The Face at the Window* (1939, GB, Pennant-Ambas-sador).

10118 "Don't think too hard, Robert. You might hurt yourself." Ancient father **Victor Moore** admonishes his none too bright youngest son Ray Mayer. *Make Way for Tomorrow* (1939, Paramount).

10119 "People will think what I tell them to think." Ego-maniacal newspaper tycoon **Orson Welles** believes he knows what is best for the masses. *Citizen Kane* (1941, RKO).

10120 "When I think of myself, I think of Uncle Charlie." **Teresa Wright** has a special affinity for Joseph Cotten with whom she identifies emotionally and telepathically. *Shadow of a Doubt* (1943, Uni-versal).

10121 "Women should not think at all. They are not equal to it." In this tribute to Chinese peas-ants fighting the Japanese, **Robert Bice** advises his son Turhan Bey, who has taken a thinking wife, Katharine Hepburn. *Dragon Seed* (1944, MGM).

10122 "If I don't talk I think. It's too late in life for me to start thinking." It is a bit of repartee at the first meeting in Acapulco of **Robert Mitchum** and Jane Greer. *Out of the Past* (1947, RKO).

10123 "Maybe we thought the world would end, or maybe we thought it was all dreams and we'd wake up with a hangover in Niagara Falls." **Robert Mitchum** recalls his evenings with Jane Greer when they had no past and no future—just the present. *Out of the Past* (1947, RKO).

10124 "I believe that man ought to be made to think about the things he says." Professor Wilington, played by **Barry Jones**, is sitting in a pub where a drunk loudly insists a bomb should be dropped on the Russians before they drop one on England. *Seven Days to Noon* (1950, GB, London Films).

10125 "It was as though all the time I could hear from her lips other words than she had spoken. . . our hidden thoughts poison the air." Poor, frail Priest **Claude Laydu** speaks of Countess Marie-Monique Arkell, whom he cures of her hatred for God before she dies. *Diary of a Country Priest* (1950, Fr., UGC).

10126 "You think slow, Nick. You move fast, but you think slow." Schemer **Norman Lloyd** puts his finger on the problem of impetuous thug John Garfield. *He Ran All the Way* (1951, United Artists).

10127 "I'm thinking now of. . . all the guys every-where who sail from tedium to apathy and back again with an occasional side trip to monotony." Title character **Henry Fonda** muses about what may be the most difficult part of war—dull routine. *Mister Roberts* (1955, Warner Bros.)

10128 "Then why did God plague us with the power to think, Mr. Brady? Why do you deny the one faculty of man that raises him above the other creatures of the earth, the power of his brain to rea-son?" Clarence Darrow-like attorney **Spencer Tracy** cross-examines William Jennings Bryan-like Fredric March at the infamous "monkey trial." *Inherit the Wind* (1960, United Artists).

10129 "Rome is an eternal thought in the mind of God." **Laurence Olivier** as Crassus, stresses the importance of imperial Rome. *Spartacus* (1960, Uni-versal-International).

10130 CATHERINE VAN OST: "One thing I don't under-stand—how you can have this fantastic background of music and just walk away from it without a sec-ond thought." ROBERT EROICA DUPEA: "I did give it a second thought." Perhaps it didn't occur to **Susan Anspach** that **Jack Nicholson** made a considered and thoughtful decision to give up his life as a musician. *Five Easy Pieces* (1970, Columbia).

10131 "Your thoughts drop from your brain to your tongue like a gumball machine." **Carol Burnett** shouts an insulting simile to her husband Alan Alda. *The Four Seasons* (1981, Universal).

10132 "Distance. Indifference. Boredom. Fear. Powerlessness. Helpless rage. Distance." Director **Erland Josephson** (Ingmar Bergman's artist-protagonist) has unspoken thoughts about his aversion to involving himself in demanding relationships. *After the Rehearsal* (1984, Sweden, Triumph).

10133 "If I say I know, I stop thinking, but so long as I think, I come to understand, I might approach the truth." **Michael Emil**, an Albert Einstein-like professor, aware that humans know very little and understand even less. *Insignificance* (1985, GB, Island Alive).

10134 "Well, since you're no longer director of CIA, and I am, it doesn't matter what you think." **Ed Herrmann** dismisses Charles Durning. *The Man with One Red Shoe* (1985, 20th Century-Fox).

10135 "Don't think. It can only hurt the ball club." Journeyman minor league baseball catcher **Kevin Costner** advises talented but not very bright pitcher Tim Robbins to rest his seldom-used brain. *Bull Durham* (1988, Orion).

10136 "I think, therefore you are." **Robin Williams**, in an uncredited appearance as the disembodied head of the King of the Moon, twists René Descartes' famous line. *The Adventures of Baron Munchausen* (1989, Columbia).

10137 "I'll think of something." The tag-line used by **Harrison Ford** in times of crisis. *Indiana Jones and the Last Crusade* (1989, Paramount).

10138 "I'm having a thought! It's coming! It's coming! It's gone!" Head mobster **Al Pacino** has difficulty using his grey cells. *Dick Tracy* (1990, Touchstone-Buena Vista).

10139 "Don't think of them as drug addicts. Think of them as killers." **Joan Plowright** advises her daughter Tracey Ullman who is outraged to discover that the two men she's hired to kill her philandering husband Kevin Kline, William Hurt and Keanu Reeves, are drug addicts. *I Love You to Death* (1990, Tri-Star).

10140 "Never let anyone know what you're thinking." **Al Pacino** gives some sage advice to his successor as Godfather, Andy Garcia. *The Godfather, Part III* (1991, Paramount).

10141 "You're the D.A. in New Orleans. Don't you think the Kennedy assassination is a little bit out of your domain?" **Sissy Spacek** doesn't believe that Dallas falls in her husband Kevin Costner's jurisdiction. *JFK* (1991, Warner Bros.).

Threats

see also DANGER, HARM, HURT AND HURTING, INTENTIONS, PAINS, PUNISHMENTS, WARNINGS

10142 "If you take the badge off, you muzzler, I'll make you eat it." Tough guy **Spencer Tracy** offers to fight cop Edgar Kennedy, who is chewing out Tracy in the film's first scene. A moment later Tracy flies out of his vehicle and tackles Kennedy. *Quick Millions* (1931, Fox).

10143 "Come out and take it, you dirty yellow-bellied rat, or I'll give it to you through the door." Taxi driver **James Cagney** screams at the cowering killer of his younger brother, who has barricaded himself in a bedroom. This is the basis for the Cagney impressionists' favorite line, "Come on out, ya dirty rat. Ya gave it to my brother and now I'm gonna give it to ya." *Taxi!* (1932, Warner Bros.).

10144 "Now if you write any more cracks about Lois Underwood I'll cut off your ears and mail them to your father." **James Cagney** corners a movie critic in a men's room and literally forces the wretch to eat some unkind words he's printed about Cagney's lady friend Margaret Lindsay. Cagney then shoves the writer's head into a toilet and flushes. *Lady Killer* (1933, Warner Bros.).

10145 "When I want you to sound off, Golden Bells, I'll pull your rope!" **Jean Harlow**'s violent reaction is aimed at an elegant Oriental woman who, seeing Harlow's outburst over Clark Gable, observes, "The more violent the storm, the sooner it subsides." *China Seas* (1935, MGM).

10146 "I'm sitting here, Mr. Cook, toying with the idea of cutting out your heart and stuffing it—like an olive!" Newspaper editor **Walter Connolly** has just about had it with reporter Fredric March and his phony news stories. *Nothing Sacred* (1937, Selznick-United Artists).

10147 "I'll get you, my pretty! And your little dog too!" It is bad enough that wicked witch **Margaret Hamilton** threatens Judy Garland, but to threaten a little dog—that's really low. *The Wizard of Oz* (1939, MGM).

10148 "Keep on ridin' me. They're gonna be pickin' iron out of your liver." Gunsel **Elisha Cook, Jr.** threatens Humphrey Bogart. *The Maltese Falcon* (1941, Warner Bros.).

10149 "Someday when your back is turned, I'll stab you!" **Carole Lombard** doesn't mean it. She and her husband Robert Montgomery are always teasing and bickering. But things get sticky when they discover their marriage ceremony wasn't legal. *Mr. and Mrs. Smith* (1941, RKO).

10150 "If that guy dies, I'll turn this place into a warehouse." Political boss **Brian Donlevy** threatens a doctor as he seeks information about his wounded right hand man, Alan Ladd. *The Glass Key* (1942, Paramount).

10151 "Serve the wine downwind, or so help me, I'll lay my cane across your shoulders." Evil squire **Dennis Price** threatens a malodorous Spanish waiter. *Caravan* (1946, GB, Gainsborough-GFD).

10152 "Down there, I sell whiskey and cards. All you can buy up here is a bullet in the head." Standing at the top of the stairs to her apartment in her saloon, **Joan Crawford** threatens a posse of townspeople who give her 24 hours to get out of town, when Mercedes McCambridge yells, "Go get her, drag her down." *Johnny Guitar* (1954, Republic).

10153 "You keep needlin' me, and if I want to, I'm gonna take this joint apart and you're not gonna know what hit you." Motorcyclist bum **Marlon Brando** snarls a threat at pretty Mary Murphy who has been asking too many questions. *The Wild One* (1954, Columbia).

10154 "If you pull anything, Hilliard, I'll let you watch me kick the kid's face in." Escaped con **Humphrey Bogart** keeps Fredric March in line by threatening the latter's feisty young son Richard Eyer. *The Desperate Hours* (1955, Paramount).

10155 "I'll have you torn in so many pieces even the vultures won't find them." **Anne Baxter** as Princess Nefretiri warns Judith Anderson as Maid Memnet to keep the secret of Moses' birth to herself. *The Ten Commandments* (1956, Paramount).

10156 "You bought me for a wife, not a whore. And if you ever come again at me like a slaverin' dog, I'll shoot you as you come." **Jean Seberg** threatens drunken prospector Lee Marvin, who has bought her and rips the clothes from her body. *Paint Your Wagon* (1969, Paramount).

10157 "You play that thing one more time, and I'm going to melt it down into hair spray." **Jack Nicholson** threatens Karen Black as she sings along with a record. *Five Easy Pieces* (1970, Columbia).

10158 "If you mess this up for me, I'll punch your heart out!" **George Segal** threatens his dotty mother Ruth Gordon when he invites his new love Trish Van Devere to their home. *Where's Poppa?* (1970, United Artists).

10159 "Touch my sister; I'll kill ya." **James Caan** beats up his brother-in-law Gianni Russo, who's slapped around his wife Talia Shire. *The Godfather* (1972, Paramount).

10160 "If you ever say another word about me or make another indecent proposal, I'm gonna get that gun of mine and I'll change you from a rooster to a hen with one shot." Secretary **Dolly Parton** threatens her womanizing, chauvinistic boss Dabney Coleman with a gun. *Nine to Five* (1980, 20th Century-Fox).

10161 "If you try to eat my face off, or take over my body, you're going to be very sorry, mister." Perplexed **Steve Guttenberg** has seen too many movies about horrible aliens. At the time, he's talking to nice alien Brian Dennehy. *Cocoon* (1985, 20th Century-Fox).

10162 "Freeze, hombre, or I'll be wearing your asshole for a garter." **Lainie Kazan** bursts into a saloon, leveling a gun at some varmints ready for a shoot-out. *Lust in the Dust* (1985, Fox Run).

10163 "You cross me and I'll personally grease the pole that slides you into a tub of shit." Chicago cop **Richard Gere** threatens a Cajun while in the New Orleans environs investigating the murder of his partner. *No Mercy* (1986, Tri-Star).

10164 "Keep it up, Arch, and I'll drill another hole in that chin of yours." Ex-con **Burt Lancaster** shares some friendly banter with his old partner in train robberies, Kirk Douglas. *Tough Guys* (1986, Touchstone-Buena Vista).

10165 "Feed one more bite of my food to your dogs, old man, and I'll kick you to death." Exasperated **Olympia Dukakis** threatens her ancient father-in-law Feodor Chaliapin, Jr., who feeds food from his plate to his dogs. *Moonstruck* (1987, MGM).

10166 "Gonna take you to the bank, Senator—the blood bank." **Steven Seagal** makes the announcement to a corrupt politician responsible for the death of Seagal's wife and his years in a coma. *Hard to Kill* (1990, Warner Bros.).

10167 "I'm gonna cut your balls off an' feed 'em to you." **Diane Ladd**, with an exaggerated southern drawl, threatens her would-be son-in-law Nicolas Cage. *Wild at Heart* (1990, Goldwyn).

Thrills

see also EMOTIONS, EXCITEMENTS, PLEASURES, SENSE
AND SENSIBILITY, SENSITIVITY AND INSENSITIVITY

10168 "A thrill a day keeps the chills away." It
is **Mae West**'s substitute for "An apple a day
keeps the doctor away." *Go West, Young Man* (1936,
Paramount).

10169 "I don't think I've ever been so thrilled in my
whole life!" Newly appointed U.S. Senator **James
Stewart** is elated upon seeing the Capitol and the
Lincoln Memorial. *Mr. Smith Goes to Washington*
(1939, Columbia).

10170 "Look at my investors now. . . . Hundreds of
little old ladies stopping off at Max Bialystock's
office to grab a last thrill on the way to the cemetery." Broadway producer **Zero Mostel** has been
reduced to conning money for his productions from
ancient, wealthy widows by romancing them. *The
Producers* (1966, MGM).

Throats

see also BODIES, HEADS AND HEADACHES, MOUTHS

10171 "Keep still, you young devil, or I'll cut your
throat." **Finlay Currie**, as the convict Magwitch,
threatens Anthony Wager, as young Pip, in a fog-
covered church graveyard. Currie appears as from
nowhere at the front of the screen in one of the
great fright scenes in movies. *Great Expectations*
(1946, GB, Cineguild-Rank).

10172 "I'll shove a grenade down your throat and
pull the pin." Platoon leader **Jack Palance** demands
back-up forces from sadistic Captain Eddie Albert or
else. *Attack!* (1956, United Artists).

10173 "Splitting a little girl's throat is like cutting
warm butter." It's the ominous observation of **Vernon
Wells**, one of the kidnappers of Arnold Schwarzenegger's 11-year-old daughter Alyssa Milano. *Commando*
(1985, 20th Century-Fox).

Time

see also DAYS, ETERNITY, FUTURE, LIVES AND LIVING,
PAST, YEARS

10174 "I dunno, but it sure saves time." **Mae West**
answers when asked if she believes in love at first
sight. *Night After Night* (1932, Paramount).

10175 "[We will be together]. . . not in my time, not
in yours, but in God's." **Heather Angel** assures her
lover, Leslie Howard, a visitor to her 18th century
London, who must now return to the 20th century.
Berkeley Square (1933, Fox).

10176 "I haven't time to die while there are thousands of people oppressed, tortured, starving."
George Arliss, in the title role, insists to his physician that his work is not ruining his health. *Voltaire*
(1933, Warner Bros.).

10177 "They were apes only yesterday. Give them
time." **George Sanders**, as a god, supports the theory of evolution in speaking of the human race. *The
Man Who Could Work Miracles* (1935, GB, London
Films-United Artists).

10178 "Now time is standing still!" Dying **Margaret
Sullavan** speaks after Robert Taylor (who makes a
habit of having the love of his life die in his arms)
destroys her watch when its ticking frightened her.
Three Comrades (1938, MGM).

10179 "I've done all the time I'm ever going to do."
Shortly before the end, mobster **Humphrey Bogart**
promises he'll never go back to prison. *High Sierra*
(1940, Warner Bros.).

10180 "Even ten minutes is a long time away
from you." **Ralph Bellamy**, who never gets the
girl, loses a grip on another when his fianceé,
reporter Rosalind Russell asks him for ten minutes
in order to get a news story. *His Girl Friday* (1940,
Columbia).

10181 "Me, I'm chairman of the board. I got nothing
but time." Elderly **Everett Sloane** welcomes an
interview about Charles Foster Kane (Orson Welles)
with reporter William Alland. *Citizen Kane* (1941,
RKO).

10182 "Six o'clock tomorrow morning, Euripi-
des." Munitions czar **Robert Morley** reminds his
industrial heir Rex Harrison that he must work
harder than he ever has before, starting the next
morning. *Major Barbara* (1941, GB, Pascal-Rank-
United Artists).

10183 JOHN L. SULLIVAN: "How can you talk about
musicals at a time like this, with the world committing suicide, with corpses piling up in the
street, with grim death gargling at you from
every corner, with people slaughtered like
sheep. . . . ?" MR. HADRIAN: "Maybe they'd like to
forget that." **Joel McCrea**, a Hollywood director
of lightweight films, has his pompous balloon,
filled with the hot air, punctured by astute studio
executive **Porter Hall**. *Sullivan's Travels* (1941,
Paramount).

10184 "I'll have a lot of time to read it where I'm going. . . ." As the police take smuggler **Sydney Greenstreet** away after he shoots and kills Zachary Scott, he asks Peter Lorre to send him a copy of the book he plans to write about scoundrel Scott. *The Mask of Dimitrios* (1944, Warner Bros.).

10185 "Okay, you cuckoo, talk and walk. . . I walked. I don't know how long. I didn't have a watch. They don't make that kind of time in watches anyway." Private eye **Dick Powell** tries to walk off the effects of being drugged. *Murder, My Sweet* (1945, RKO).

10186 "Punctuality is the thief of time." **George Sanders** said it, but Hurd Hatfield seems to be the real "thief of time" as his portrait, and not his body, ages with time. *The Picture of Dorian Gray* (1945, MGM).

10187 "Oh, Mr. Belinski! I don't think I'll have much time for plumbing." Maid and plumber **Jennifer Jones**, who can fix just about anything, has fallen in love with Czech author Charles Boyer, who has fled to England to escape the Nazis. *Cluny Brown* (1946, 20th Century-Fox).

10188 CAPT. BART COSGROVE: "Love—the way you think about it is a lifetime job. And I've got no lifetime." JOSEPHINE NORRIS: "How much time do you think I can be sure of? I have only till dawn, too." Worn out pilot **John Lund** is surprised that **Olivia de Havilland** is so willing to spend the night together—the only night they will ever have. *To Each His Own* (1946, Paramount).

10189 "Time is just a clock some sucker winds." As he leaves on what may be a suicidal mission, **Spencer Tracy** leaves a thought with his love Valentina Cortese. *Malaya* (1949, MGM).

10190 "Somehow I knew it would work out that way. Time is the great author. Always writes the perfect ending." **Charles Chaplin** resigns himself to having lost Claire Bloom to Sydney Chaplin. *Limelight* (1952, United Artists).

10191 "It wasn't the right time for us to meet just now. There'll be other nights, other stars for us to watch. They'll be back." **Richard Carlson** is wistful as an aliens' spaceship soars away from Earth. *It Came from Outer Space* (1953, Universal-International).

10192 "Time! Time! What is time? The Swiss manufacture it. The French hoard it. Italians want it. Americans say it is money. Hindus say it does not exist. Do you know what I say? I say time is a crook." **Peter Lorre**'s outburst about time sounds

great—but what does it mean? *Beat the Devil* (1954, Romulus-Santana).

10193 "A man sentenced to life imprisonment can always spare a few minutes." Devil's Island convict **Humphrey Bogart** puts himself at Joan Bennett's disposal. *We're No Angels* (1955, Paramount).

10194 CORA FLOOD: "What time is it?" RUBEN FLOOD: "It's the right time, honey." **Dorothy McGuire** awakens to find her amorous husband **Robert Preston** trying to arouse her. *The Dark at the Top of the Stairs* (1960, Warner Bros.).

10195 GLABRUS: "I don't know how I will ever be able to repay you." CRASSUS: "Time will solve that mystery." **John Dall** has just been made commander of the garrison of Rome by powerful and ambitious Roman General and Senator **Laurence Olivier**. *Spartacus* (1960, Universal).

10196 "One cannot choose but wonder. You see, he has all the time in the world." **Alan Young** can but speculate on where Victorian scientist Rod Taylor may have traveled to in his time machine. *The Time Machine* (1960, MGM).

10197 "Time is never reasonable. Time is our enemy, Caesar." Egyptian Queen **Elizabeth Taylor** expresses regret that she and Rex Harrison as Julius Caesar didn't have more time together. *Cleopatra* (1963, 20th Century-Fox).

10198 "Time is the enemy. It wounds us with its days." Former powerful British statesman **Maurice Evans** says a mouthful. *One of Our Spies Is Missing* (1966, MGM).

10199 "For us it's all been great, but you know what was the best time of all? Was in the beginning, when everything was a struggle, and you were working too hard and worried and sometimes frightened, and there were times when I felt, when I really knew, that I was a help to you. That was the very best time of all for me." **Katharine Hepburn** fondly remembers the years of struggle early in her marriage to Spencer Tracy. *Guess Who's Coming to Dinner* (1967, Columbia).

10200 "You know what the trouble is? The trouble is that probably all the good things in life take place no more than a minute—I mean, all added up. Especially at the end of 70 years, if you should live so long, you still haven't even figured it out. You spent 35 years of sleeping. You spent five years going to the bathroom. You spent 19 years doing some kind of work you absolutely hated. You spent 8,759 minutes blinking your eyes. And, after that, you got one minute of good things. So one day you wonder when you're minute's up." Beside some obvious problems with her life, lonely young **Liza Minnelli**'s figures don't add up. *The Sterile Cuckoo* (1969, Paramount).

10201 OLIVER BARRETT III: "If you marry her now, I'll not give you the time of day." OLIVER BARRETT IV: "Father, you don't know the time of day." **Ray Milland** intends to disinherit his son **Ryan O'Neal** if he marries Ali MacGraw. *Love Story* (1970, Paramount).

10202 "You lose some of the time what you go after, but you lose all the time what you don't go after." **Paul Winfield** and his son Kevin Hooks have a bond. *Sounder* (1972, 20th Century-Fox).

10203 "Time! Time happens, I suppose, to people. Everything becomes too late, finally. You know it's going on up the hill. You can see the dust and hear the cries. But you wait. Time happens." Aging Connecticut matriarch **Katharine Hepburn** heightens the tension. *A Delicate Balance* (1973, American Film Theater).

10204 "You couldn't have been gone only five minutes. . . . It took the seven Santini brothers two days to move everything in, three junkies aren't gonna move it all out in five minutes." **Jack Lemmon** makes what he considers a reasonable argument that his wife Anne Bancroft couldn't have been away from their burglarized unlocked New York City apartment only five minutes as she claims. *The Prisoner of Second Avenue* (1975, Warner Bros.).

10205 "You've been doin' time instead of usin' time." Intellectual con **Ron O'Neal** convinces his cellmate Bernie Casey of the need of an education. *Brothers* (1977, Warner Bros.).

10206 "Father Time has a way of just beating the shit out of us." It's something of a shock to hear distinguished actress **Jessica Tandy** deliver this line. *Best Friends* (1982, Warner Bros.).

10207 "Wake up. It's time to die." Replicant **Brion James**, one of a group of killer androids who mutinies on a space colony and returns to earth seeking to prolong his short life span by altering his programmed termination date, has the drop on Harrison Ford, a futuristic L.A. cop who is assigned the task of tracking down and killing the rebelling robots. *Blade Runner* (1982, Warner Bros.).

10208 "Days are years when it comes to sorrow—there's no such thing as time." Usually insensitive womanizer **Frederic Forrest** says a mouthful after the accidental death of his nephew. *The Stone Boy* (1984, 20th Century-Fox).

10209 "The time I lived with you is the best time of my life." It's the matter-of-fact suicide note left by **Jennifer Clay**, a refugee from a sexually abusive father, for her boy friend Wade Walston, the neglected son of a homosexual father. *Suburbia* (1984, New Horizon-New World).

10210 "Ladies and gentlemen, boys and girls, dyin' time is here." **Edwin Hodgeman** as hunchbacked emcee Dr. Dealgood introduces another fight to the finish in the Thunderdome arena. *Mad Max Beyond Thunderdome* (1985, Australia, Warner Bros.).

10211 "I do think I've put in the hours, don't you?" Selfish preppie **Tom Hanks** complains when Peace Corpswoman Rita Wilson refuses his blunt request that they have sex. He feels he's earned it by spending a day and a night on a plane being pleasant to her. *Volunteers* (1985, Tri-Star).

10212 "There's nothing to worry about, dear. You're just browsing through time." Long-dead **Maureen O'Sullivan** isn't surprised when her granddaughter Kathleen Turner reveals that she is visiting from the future. *Peggy Sue Got Married* (1986, Tri-Star).

10213 "I've got a galaxy to run. I don't have time for flatulence and orgasms." **Robin Williams**, as the King of the Moon, is very busy. *The Adventures of Baron Munchausen* (1989, GB, Columbia).

10214 "I have six hours to get home, get big and get to the mall." Teenager **Amy O'Neill** may have been shrunk by her father's formula, but she has her agenda set. *Honey, I Shrunk the Kids* (1989, Buena Vista).

10215 "If I had waited for another minute before I came here, would I have found you both on the floor?" Pompous and suspicious British resort manager **James Fox** fumes to his wife Mimi Rogers and black police officer Denzel Washington. *The Mighty Quinn* (1989, MGM).

10216 "Your first time. . . my last time." **Gregory Peck**, as the aging Ambrose Bierce, woos spinster Jane Fonda with his voice. *Old Gringo* (1989, Columbia).

10217 "How long do I have to lie here and hold her before I can get up and go home? Is 30 seconds enough?" Thinking to himself, **Billy Crystal** feels no afterglow following the sex act. *When Harry Met Sally. . .* (1989, Columbia).

10218 MARIE CURIE: "Oh, Albert, if only time could stand still." ALBERT EINSTEIN: "That's it! The theory of relativity!" And according to this farce from down under, that's how **Odile Le Clezio** as Madame Curie inspired **Yahoo Serious** as Albert Einstein. *Young Einstein* (1989, Australia, Warner Bros.).

10219 "It's time for a change, time to take a desperate chance for peace." **Sean Connery**, as Captain Marko Ramius, prepares to defect, taking with him a new advanced Russian nuclear submarine and its crew. *The Hunt for Red October* (1990, Paramount).

10220 "That should take fifteen minutes, and then what do we do?" British journalist **Victoria Tennant** reacts sarcastically when weatherman Steve Martin offers to take her on a cultural tour of Los Angeles. *L.A. Story* (1991, Tri-Star).

10221 "It's too late in the evening and too early in the relationship to be bringing a kid in." Chicago private eye **Kathleen Turner** complains to hockey player Stephen Meadows, who shows up at Turner's apartment with his 11-year-old daughter Angela Goethals in tow. *V.I. Warshawski* (1991, Hollywood Pictures-Buena Vista).

Tiredness *see* FATIGUE

Toasts

see also ALCOHOL, DRINKING AND DRUNKENNESS, PROPOSALS

10222 "We accept her, we accept her, one of us." The freaks toast trapeze artist Olga Baclanova after she's married dwarf Harry Eccles. When she poisons him for his money, they make her one of them. *Freaks* (1932, MGM).

10223 "To new worlds of gods and monsters." It's the toast of skeletal-looking black magician and weird scientist Dr. Praetorious, played by eccentric British actor **Ernest Thesiger**. *The Bride of Frankenstein* (1935, Universal).

10224 "Here's to the voyage of the Bounty. Still waters and the great golden sea. Flying fish like streaks of silver. Mermaids who sing in the night. The Southern Cross and all the stars on the other side of the world." Midshipman **Franchot Tone** toasts visitors and fellow officers at the bon voyage party for HMS Bounty. *Mutiny on the Bounty* (1935, MGM).

10225 "Here is my hope that Robert Conway will find his Shangri-La." **Hugh Buckler** lifts his glass in a toast to British diplomat Ronald Colman, whom Buckler trailed, as Colman struggled to return to his idyllic civilization in a Tibetan valley. *Lost Horizon* (1937, Columbia).

10226 "So stand by, your glass ready/The world is a world of lies./Here's a toast to the dead already:/Hur-

rah for the next man who dies!" It's the melancholy quatrain sung by young World War I British pilots between missions. *The Dawn Patrol* (1938, Warner Bros.).

10227 "A toast. Jedediah—to live on my terms. These are the only terms anybody ever knows, his own." Title character **Orson Welles** proposes a selfish toast to his only friend Joseph Cotten. *Citizen Kane* (1941, RKO).

10228 "Here's looking at you, kid!" **Humphrey Bogart** makes his classic toast to Ingrid Bergman more than once. *Casablanca* (1942, Warner Bros.).

10229 "I love her—I love her with ever fiber of my being, ladies and gentlemen—HMS Torrin." Chief Petty Officer **Bernard Miles** makes a Christmas toast to his ship. *In Which We Serve* (1942, GB, Rank).

10230 "I'm all for crime, Your Honor. May I propose a toast? Here's to crime." Shortly after proposing this toast, and downing his drink, **Mischa Auer** becomes the first victim of the unknown host who has sentenced his trapped guests to death for their supposed crimes. *And Then There Were None* (1945, 20th Century-Fox).

10231 "[Here's]. . . to the men we've loved—the stinkers." **Eve Arden**'s toast. *Mildred Pierce* (1945, Warner Bros.).

10232 "Here's looking at you, baby." Piano player **Bruce Bennett** uses his variation of Bogie's "Here's looking at you, kid!" toast with singer Ida Lupino. *The Man I Love* (1946, Warner Bros.).

10233 "Here's to the time when we were little girls and no one asked us to marry." Alone, **Joan Crawford** turns directly toward the camera and proposes a toast. *Humoresque* (1947, Warner Bros.).

10234 "To all the dumb chumps and all the crazy broads, past, present, and future, who thirst for knowledge and search for truth. . . and make it so tough for crooks like you and me." It's the toast offered by lawyer **Howard St. John** when it is clear that dishonest Broderick Crawford has been beaten by his former mistress Judy Holliday. *Born Yesterday* (1950, Columbia).

10235 "Gentlemen, to our wives." **Cameron Mitchell**, who has just informed his new wife Lauren Bacall that he's not just a grease monkey but is in fact a millionaire, proposes a toast for David Wayne and Rory Calhoun, newly married to Marilyn Monroe and Betty Grable, respectively. The three women faint at the announcement. *How to Marry a Millionaire* (1953, 20th Century-Fox).

10236 "I want to drink a toast to you, Mr. Keefer. From the beginning, you hated the navy. You thought up the whole idea, and you kept your skirts all starched and clean. Steve Maryk will be remembered as a mutineer—but you! You'll publish a novel, you'll make a million bucks, you'll marry a big movie star, and, for the rest of your life, you'll have to live with your conscience, if you have any. Now, here's to the real author of *The Caine Mutiny*. Here's to you, Mr. Keefer." At a victory party of the officers of the minesweeper Caine to celebrate the acquittal of Van Johnson for mutiny, drunken Defense Attorney **Jose Ferrer** accuses Fred Mac-Murray of being the evil influence in the whole rotten mess. At the end of his speech, Ferrer flings champagne in the face of MacMurray and offers to meet him outside for a fight. *The Caine Mutiny* (1954, Columbia).

10237 "Here's to men. Bless their clean-cut faces and their dirty little minds." **Suzy Parker** makes a toast for her friends Hope Lange and Diane Baker, all of whom are having man trouble. *The Best of Everything* (1959, 20th Century-Fox).

10238 "May the wind at your back never be your own." It's the flatulent toast **Charles Durning** makes for Jack Lemmon who is leaving the journalistic profession. *The Front Page* (1974, Universal).

10239 "Yeah, well, here's looking at you, kid." You'd think that Bogart impersonator **Robert Sacchi** would get it just right. *The Man with Bogart's Face* (1980, 20th Century-Fox).

10240 "Here's to us. . . . Here's to apple trees. . . to cheese. . . and wine. . . and bread. . . and life itself." **Alan Alda** raises his glass and makes a toast while enjoying life with his friends. *The Four Seasons* (1981, Universal).

10241 "To the Cubs winning the pennant—and big tits." **James Belushi**, a car thief who takes a furlough from prison just before he's to be released in order to go to the World Series, makes this toast twice. On the print released for showing on airplanes, the second part is amended to say, "and loose women." *Taking Care of Business* (1990, Hollywood-Buena Vista).

Togetherness

see also UNIONS

10242 "You're me, and I'm you. It has always been that way!" **Ann Dvorak** expresses more than mere sisterly love for her brother Paul Muni as together they face a shoot-out with the police. *Scarface* (1932, United Artists).

10243 "Spring isn't everything, is it, Essie? There's a lot to be said for autumn. That has beauty, too. And winter—if you're together." **Lionel Barrymore** is happy to grow old along with his wife Spring Byington. *Ah, Wilderness* (1935, MGM).

10244 "From tomorrow on, until death comes for one of us, we'll be sitting here alone together, beside the same lamp, in an empty house, with heaven knows what thoughts to keep us company." **Miriam Hopkins** promises not much future for her and cousin Bette Davis the day of the marriage of Jane Bryan, illegitimate daughter of Davis, who Hopkins raised as her own. *The Old Maid* (1939, Warner Bros.).

10245 "If I could only hold you until we were both dead!" As her strength ebbs, **Merle Oberon** expresses one last hope to her lover Laurence Olivier that they will be together in the after-life. *Wuthering Heights* (1939, Goldwyn-United Artists).

10246 "It'll be just the way you want it. Straight down the line." **Barbara Stanwyck** agrees to do anything Fred MacMurray asks of her in his plan to murder her husband in order to collect his insurance money. *Double Indemnity* (1944, Paramount).

10247 GREGORY: "What were you dreaming of?" PAULA: "Our life together." GREGORY: "And how do you see it?" PAULA: "I saw all the places where we'd be together. Lovely places." GREGORY: "I was thinking of our life together too, only I heard it in music. Something I want to write." PAULA: "Yes, what?" GREGORY: "The whole thing is alive with happiness. I want a feeling of the early morning." PAULA: "This morning." GREGORY: "Yes, with the sun rising in your hair, as it is now. I don't know how it ends. Perhaps it never ends until I write you." **Charles Boyer** and **Ingrid Bergman** are honeymooning. *Gaslight* (1944, MGM).

10248 "Shelby's no good, but he's what I want. We belong together because we're weak and we can't seem to help it." Wealthy **Judith Anderson** speaks of playboy Vincent Price. *Laura* (1944, 20th Century-Fox).

10249 "You and I are never going to be separated, as long as we live. You and I are going to be together. Always." Bad twin **Olivia de Havilland** speaks to her good twin, also de Havilland. *The Dark Mirror* (1946, Universal-International).

10250 "After all we've done together. After all we haven't done together." WAC **Ann Sheridan** is shocked when French Captain Cary Grant says he never wants to see her again after they spent an innocent night together on the last day of their mission. *I Was a Male War Bride* (1949, 20th Century-Fox).

10251 "With you around, Ma, nothing can stop me." Gangster **James Cagney**, with a mother fixation, salutes his partner and equally crooked mother Margaret Wycherly. *White Heat* (1949, Warner Bros.).

10252 "Where Ma goes, Cody goes." FBI Agent **John Archer** believes by following Margaret Wycherly, she will eventually lead them to her fugitive son James Cagney. *White Heat* (1949, Warner Bros.).

10253 "We go together. . . like guns and ammunition." Gun crazy **Peggy Cummins**, a Bonnie Parker–like thrill seeker, announces to John Dall, her Clyde Barrow. *Gun Crazy* (1950, United Artists).

10254 "But, Guy, you wanted it. . . we planned it together. You're just as much in it as I am. . . . You're a free man now." Psychotic **Robert Walker** tells tennis star Farley Granger that there is no backing out of their "deal" to exchange murders after Walker has disposed of Granger's unwanted wife. *Strangers on a Train* (1951, Warner Bros.).

10255 "Well, I don't know if I can lick you or you can lick me, but I do know one thing—together we can lick them all." **Spencer Tracy** tells Katharine Hepburn that they make an unbeatable team. *Pat and Mike* (1952, MGM).

10256 "You remember how it really was? You and me and booze—a threesome. . . . You and I were a couple of drunks on the sea of booze, and the boat sank. I got hold of something that kept me from going under, and I'm not going to let go of it. Not for you. Not for anyone. If you want to grab on, grab on. But there's just room for you and me—no threesome." Reformed alcoholic **Jack Lemmon** offers reconciliation to his dipsomaniac wife Lee Remick, but only if she gives up drinking. *Days of Wine and Roses* (1962, Warner Bros.)

10257 "We may not enjoy living together, but dying together isn't going to help." **Marilyn Eastman** tries to rouse her cowardly husband Karl Hardman to some kind of action after their daughter has been bitten by a ghoul. *Night of the Living Dead* (1968, Continental).

10258 "Look, I don't want somebody pointing to Joan and me in a couple of years, telling some miserable story ending with 'And they're still together.'" **Joseph Hindy** plans to go through with his divorce from Diane Keaton, despite the stories of his parent Bea Arthur and Richard Castellano of all their relatives, unhappily married, but still together. *Lovers and Other Strangers* (1970, Cinerama).

10259 "We have laughs together. I care about you. Your concerns are my concerns. We have great sex. Who could ask for more?" Seventeen-year-old **Mariel Hemingway** doesn't look very far in the future as she tries to reassure her fortyish lover Woody Allen that he's not too old for her. *Manhattan* (1979, United Artists).

10260 "A woman can ovulate and think at the same time." Supreme Court Justice **Jill Clayburgh** gives assurance that her gender will have no effect on her judicial duties. *First Monday in October* (1981, Paramount).

10261 "Oh, God, you're terrible. Wait till I tell Toby. I'll call her in a few minutes. Maybe we can all have lunch together. The whole world can go to hell as long as the three of us can have lunch together. I even reserved a nice little table in heaven. Italian, of course. Oh, thank God the three of us have each other to lean on." Homosexual actor **James Coco** has the film's last lines, planning a "lunch" for Marsha Mason, Joan Hackett and himself. *Only When I Laugh* (1981, Columbia).

10262 "Gaff had been there and let her live. Four years, he figured, he was wrong. Tyrell had told me Rachel was special, no termination date. I don't know how long we had together. who does?" As he brings his investigation to a close, futuristic L.A. cop **Harrison Ford** and replicant Sean Young fly away together to an uncertain life. *Blade Runner* (1982, Warner Bros).

10263 "Together we are more than the sum of our parts." Married **James Keach** declares his love to his mistress Jamie Lee Curtis in a letter. *Love Letters* (1984, New World).

10264 "We were altar boys together." **Timothy Hutton** responds to a question as to how he and fellow traitor Sean Penn came to be friends. *The Falcon and the Snowman* (1985, Orion).

10265 "When you testify, you'll be testifying for the both of us." Married **Isabelle Huppert** supports her lover Steve Guttenberg, who reports seeing, from his bedroom window, a killer assault a girl. Actually, he didn't see anything; she did but doesn't want to testify publicly. *The Bedroom Window* (1987, DEG).

10266 "I'm majorin' in Gavin and me." Southern belle **Jessica Lange** achieves her goal in attending college—football star Dennis Quaid. *Everybody's All-American* (1988, Warner Bros.).

10267 "If you men will take no pay, then none of us will." White officer **Matthew Broderick** joins his black troops in tearing up their pay chits, because the black soldiers are to be paid at a rate less than white soldiers. *Glory* (1989, Tri-Star).

10268 "I remember once we went out on some boats and I got to drive one by myself. That was good. Most of all I just remembered being together 'cause then I was saved." **Charlie Korsmo** has the last lines. It appears that he, his brother Chris O'Donnell and their mother Jessica Lange are finally recovering from the death of their father and husband. *Men Don't Leave* (1990, Warner Bros.).

10269 STEPHEN DALLAS: "What are you going to do?" STELLA CLAIRE: "Shouldn't there be a 'we' in that sentence somewhere?" Perhaps unconsciously **Stephen Collins** distances himself from the problem when Bette Midler announces she is pregnant with his baby. *Stella* (1990, Touchstone-Buena Vista).

Tongue Twisters

see also DOUBLE-TALK

10270 "Moses supposes his toes are roses/But Moses supposes erroneously./Moses he knows his toeses aren't roses/As Moses supposes his toeses to be." It's the tongue-twister diction coach **Bobby Watson** teaches to Gene Kelly and Donald O'Connor, which they put to music. *Singin' in the Rain* (1952, MGM).

10271 "I slit the sheet. The sheet I slit. And on the slitted sheet I sit. . . . I've never been relaxed enough around anyone to be able to say that." Wonder how many takes were necessary for **Steve Martin** to get it right? *The Jerk* (1979, Universal).

Tongues *see* MOUTHS

Tortures

see also CRUELTY, PAINS, PUNISHMENTS

10272 "In the East they have ways of shattering the strongest courage." **Lewis Stone**, as Nayland Smith of Scotland Yard, thinks of the cruelty of Fu Manchu. *The Mask of Fu Manchu* (1932, MGM).

10273 "The torture of the bell. It never stops. You will be frantically thirsty. You will be unspeakably foul. But there you will lie, day after day, until you tell. . . ." **Boris Karloff**, as Fu Manchu, straps Lawrence Grant to a bench located under a metal apparatus with a huge clapper. *The Mask of Fu Manchu* (1932, MGM).

10274 FAH LO SEE: "The whips. . . He is not entirely unhandsome, is he, my father?" FU MANCHU: "For a white man, no, but I must suggest a short delay in your customary procedures." **Boris Karloff** temporarily interrupts **Myrna Loy**'s sado-masochistic fun with Charles Starrett whose inert body she's fondling. *The Mask of Fu Manchu* (1932, MGM).

10275 "I'm going to tear the skin from your body—bit by bit!" Revengeful doctor **Bela Lugosi** announces the fate of his captive devil-worshipper Boris Karloff at the climax of the film that has nothing to do with a black cat or Edgar Allan Poe. *The Black Cat* (1934, Universal).

10276 "You know this? It's the rosary of pain. With this, it is possible to screw a man's eyes out of his head." Pirate Captain **Basil Rathbone** shows Errol Flynn a knotted rope. *Captain Blood* (1935, Warner Bros.).

10277 "What torture, what delicious torture. . . . Poe, you are avenged." In a moment of triumph, **Bela Lugosi** chuckles gleefully about his hero Edgar Allan Poe. *The Raven* (1935, Universal).

10278 "My lord, surely it's time to use the torture on this stubborn wench?" Prosecutor **George Zucco** anxiously asks Judge Cedric Hardwicke for permission to cause defendant Maureen O'Hara grievous pain. *The Hunchback of Notre Dame* (1939, RKO).

10279 "A totalitarian manicure." It is honeymooner **Joan Crawford**'s comment when German underground leader Conrad Veidt shows her a medieval torture device for removing fingernails in a Bavarian castle. *Above Suspicion* (1943, MGM).

10280 "They're not going to torture me. It hurts." Cowardly **Bob Hope** is afraid of what may be in store for him. *Road to Bali* (1952, Paramount).

10281 "There's no torture on earth to equal the torture which a cold woman inflicts on a man." **Karl Malden** complains about his uncooperative child-bride Carroll Baker. *Baby Doll* (1956, Warner Bros.).

10282 "I often wonder why people torture themselves as often as they can." **Bibi Andersson** is perplexed seeing people seemingly enjoy their suffering and relish martyrdom. *The Seventh Seal* (1957, Sweden, Svensk Filmindustri).

10283 "The Gestapo would take away your Bloomingdale's charge card; you'd tell them everything." **Woody Allen** makes a prediction when Diane Keaton wonders how she'd stand up under torture. *Annie Hall* (1977, United Artists).

10284 "Have you ever had your bones scraped, Mr. Roth?" Japanese Yakuza **Mako** captures and tortures Brent Huff. *Armed Response* (1986, Columbia).

10285 "Don't torture yourself, Gomez. That's my job." As she cuts the buds off roses, **Anjelica Huston** coos to her husband Raul Julia. *The Addams Family* (1991, Paramount).

Touches

see also BODIES, SENSITIVITY AND INSENSITIVITY, TREATS AND TREATMENTS

10286 "An icy wind seemed to touch me, only it wasn't a wind." **Evelyn Venable** is revived from a faint. She has had a premature visit from Death. *Death Takes a Holiday* (1934, Paramount).

10287 COLLECTION AGENT: "If you touch me, I'll call a cop." PAUL FABRINI: "If I touch you, you'll call an ambulance." **Jack Mower** is threatened by tough truck driver **Humphrey Bogart** when he tries to collect money owed him. *They Drive by Night* (1940, Warner Bros.).

10288 "Would you take your clammy hand off my chair? You have the touch of a love-starved cobra." In the play by George S. Kaufman and Moss Hart, dreadful house-guest **Monty Woolley** uses "sex-starved" rather than "love-starved" to insult his nurse, played in the film by Mary Wickes. *The Man Who Came to Dinner* (1941, Warner Bros.).

10289 "Well, there are some people that rarely touch it, but it touches them often." Despite his wife Kim Hunter's protests, **Marlon Brando** is convinced that his visiting sister-in-law Vivien Leigh is a secret drinker. *A Streetcar Named Desire* (1951, Warner Bros.-20th Century-Fox).

10290 "Don't you ever touch me again." **Kim Hunter** shouts at brutish husband Marlon Brando as she picks up her newborn baby and leaves him. He has raped her sister Vivien Leigh, driving her over the brink of sanity. *A Streetcar Named Desire* (1951, Warner Bros.-20th Century-Fox).

10291 "Odd, isn't it? The things you most want to touch in life, don't want you to touch them." Drunken, disgraced **Errol Flynn** speaks to prostitute Juliette Greco, who pulls back from Flynn's touch. *The Roots of Heaven* (1958, 20th Century-Fox).

10292 "I am quiet here alone. Sad, too. Touch me. Touch me." It is the words of **Maurice Roeves**, as Stephen Dedalus, the James Joyce-like character, in a pleasant enough attempt to film an unfilmable classic. *Ulysses* (1967, GB, Reade).

10293 "Take your stinking paws off me, you damn dirty ape." Astronaut **Charlton Heston**, caught in a time warp, is set down on a planet that is Earth of the future, ruled by apes. He surprises his captors with his ability to speak. *Planet of the Apes* (1968, 20th Century-Fox).

10294 "If you ever touch your husband or another man again, I'll kill you." Banker **Ray Sharkey** grabs his lover Ornella Muti, a financier's wife, on the street. *Love and Money* (1980, Lorimar).

10295 "Ooh, I've never touched a man before. Not bad." **Bo Derek** gropes title character Miles O'Keeffe, who lies exhausted after thrashing around with a boa constrictor. *Tarzan, the Ape Man* (1981, MGM).

10296 "When somebody touches you and you really don't want to be touched, you're not really being touched. You still have you inside you." **Dorsey Wright** comforts battered and bruised Jodie Foster as he carries her from the forest where she was gang-raped by members of the high school football team. *The Hotel New Hampshire* (1984, Orion).

10297 "It's time to get out. I want to touch Indians." Advertising executive **Albert Brooks** pesters his wife Julie Hagerty to give up their New York City lifestyle and hit the road to find the real America. *Lost in America* (1985, Warner Bros.).

10298 "They're fine. . . but I'm kinda going through this thing where I don't want him to touch me. Otherwise things are fine." **Andie MacDowell** resounds when therapist Ron Vawter asks her about her relationship with her husband Peter Gallagher. *sex, lies and videotape* (1989, Miramax).

10299 "That's the first time we've touched." **Tom Berenger** remarks after he slaps Elizabeth Perkins early in their troubled romance. *Love at Large* (1990, Orion).

10300 "Rose, can't I just touch it a little? Not a lot. To see what it's like?" Horny adolescent **Lukas Haas** asks to be allowed to explore Laura Dern's body. The girl, heartbroken over a rebuff by Haas' father Robert Duvall, climbs into bed with the 13-year-old, looking for a little comfort. *Rambling Rose* (1991, Seven Arts-New Line).

10301 "Oh, please, I wouldn't touch you to scratch you." **Michelle Pfeiffer**, as Catwoman, yawns when eager Danny De Vito as the Penguin propositions her. *Batman Returns* (1992, Warner Bros.).

Toughness

see also FIGHTS AND FIGHTING, STRENGTHS

10302 "I ain't so tough!" Mobster **James Cagney** collapses in an alley after being shot by rival gangsters. *The Public Enemy* (1931, Warner Bros.).

10303 "There can't be any gold, or he would have talked. Nobody can be that tough." Pirate leader **Wallace Beery** underestimates Clark Gable's ability to withstand torture. *China Seas* (1935, MGM).

10304 "Now, look, Whitey. In a pinch I can be tougher than you are and I guess maybe this is the pinch. You're coming with me to Boys Town because that's the way your brother wants it and that's the way I want it." To honor a promise to murderer Edward Norris, **Spencer Tracy**, as Father Flanagan, is taking Norris' younger brother Mickey Rooney to Boys Town, even if he doesn't want to go. *Boys Town* (1938, MGM).

10305 "Maybe he's a little tough but a kid's got to be tough in our neighborhood to survive. If you send him away he'll come out hard and mean and bitter. If you want to do something for these boys, why don't you clean up the slums?" Poor **Gale Page** pleads with the judge not to send her brother Billy Halop to reform school. She just doesn't understand that reform schools are cheaper to operate than cleaning up slums. *Crime School* (1938, Warner Bros.).

10306 "We're tougher than any truck ever come off an assembly line." Truck driver **George Raft** refers to himself and his brother Humphrey Bogart. *They Drive by Night* (1940, Warner Bros.).

10307 "You can't croak him—he's tough." Vicious goon **William Bendix**, grinning maniacally, reassures Eddie Marr that Alan Ladd can withstand the merciless beating Bendix is giving him. *The Glass Key* (1942, Paramount).

10308 "'Okay, Marlowe,' I said to myself. 'You're a tough guy. You've been sapped twice, choked, beaten silly with a gun, shot in the arm until you're as crazy as a couple of waltzing mice. Now let's see you do something really tough—like putting your pants on.'" Private eye Philip Marlowe, nicely defined by **Dick Powell**, challenges himself to get dressed after a difficult few days. *Murder, My Sweet* (1945, RKO).

10309 FIRST COWPOKE: "He don't look so tough to me." SECOND COWPOKE: "If he ain't tough, there's been an awful lot of sudden natural deaths in his vicinity." Two cowboys in a saloon eye gunslinger Jimmy Ringo, played by Gregory Peck. *The Gunfighter* (1950, 20th Century-Fox).

10310 "I've met some hard-boiled eggs in my time, but you, you're twenty minutes." **Jan Sterling**, who's been around the block a few times, tips her hat to self-seeking reporter Kirk Douglas. *Ace in the Hole* aka: *The Big Carnival* (1951, Paramount).

10311 "I can take anything you can dish out." Private **Montgomery Clift** defiantly challenges the non-coms who are giving him the "system" because he won't fight on the company boxing team. *From Here to Eternity* (1953, Columbia).

10312 "You haven't got tough, you've just got miserable." Trail boss **Glenn Ford** makes a distinction for one-time greenhorn Jack Lemmon, who has lost his idealism and compassion after a cattle drive. *Cowboy* (1958, Columbia).

10313 JOHNNY HOOKER: "He's not as tough as he thinks." HENRY GONDORFF: "Neither are we." **Robert Redford** and **Paul Newman** plan a con against mobster Robert Shaw to avenge the murder of Redford's former partner on the grift, Robert Earl Jones. *The Sting* (1973, Universal).

10314 "Do you think we've got it tough? How'd you like to work in there?" Professional wrestler **Laurene Landon** makes a good point as she and a colleague drive by a smelting plant. *All the Marbles* (1981, MGM).

10315 "Honey, if you call and I'm not home, I'll be at the gym or the gun club." Unemployed house-husband **Michael Keaton** wants to appear super-macho when his attractive wife, advertising executive Teri Garr is picked up at their house by her lustful boss Martin Mull. *Mr. Mom* (1983, 20th Century-Fox).

10316 "It's tough being a star. People think it's all tits and champagne." Rock singer **Rick Springfield** plays a super rock star with a problem. *Hard to Hold* (1984, Universal).

10317 "I eat Green Berets for breakfast." Super muscular **Arnold Schwarzenegger**, looking like a comic book super hero, snaps off a bit of macho bravado to a group of corrupt Green Berets. *Commando* (1985, 20th Century-Fox).

10318 "I don't step on toes, I step on necks." **Chuck Norris** is no one to mess with when he's intent on his mission. *Braddock: Missing in Action III* (1988, Cannon).

10319 "There is nothing tougher to remember than why you chased a dame after you've had her." John Huston-like movie director **Clint Eastwood** shares a chauvinistic reflection with screenwriter Jeff Fahey. *White Hunter, Black Heart* (1990, Warner Bros.).

Tours and Tourism

see also TRAVEL AND TRIPS

10320 "To the right, gentlemen, is Pneumonia Gulch. That is where we sleep. You fry by day and you freeze by night. To the left, just a little ways, about a mile and a half, is Ptomaine Towers. That is where we eat. The wheatcakes we leave are used by the navy as depth bombs." G.I. **Red Buttons** gives a guided tour of the facilities of an Air Force base to a group of new cadets. *Winged Victory* (1944, 20th Century-Fox).

10321 "I always say that my west window has all the endurance of Chaucer, without happily, any of the concomitant crudities of his period." Elderly parson **Alec Guinness** shows his murderer-to-be Dennis Price around his church. *Kind Hearts and Coronets* (1949, GB, Ealing).

10322 "Europe. What a drag! I've done the Coliseum bit and the Mona Lisa bit, but they never take me to any of those marvy places, like the Lido and the Crazy Horse and La Sexy." Nineteen-year-old **Pamela Tiffin** objects to the close chaperoning she's experienced when she arrives in Berlin for another leg of her European tour. *One, Two, Three* (1961, United Artists).

10323 "It's been too long since the Christie murders; a good colorful crime spree is good for tourism." Chief Inspector **Alec McCowen** finds something positive about a string of "necktie" murders in London. *Frenzy* (1972, GB, Universal).

Towns *see* CITIES AND TOWNS

Toys *see* CHILDREN AND CHILDHOOD, ENTERTAINMENTS AND ENTERTAINERS, GAMES, PLAYING AND PLAYERS

Trade *see* BUSINESS AND COMMERCE, BUYING AND SELLING

Tragedies

see also COMEDY AND COMEDIANS, DRAMA AND MELODRAMA, FAILURES, MORALITY, RUINATIONS AND RUINS

10324 "It's one of the tragedies of life that the people most in need of a good thrashing are usually enormous." Incredibly rich **Rudy Vallee**'s money won't buy him the muscle to take on men stronger and tougher than himself, such as Joel McCrea. *The Palm Beach Story* (1942, Paramount).

10325 "You must learn to see it in its proper perspective. You should look upon this tragedy as an episode in the wonderful spectacle of life." **George Sanders** encourages Hurd Hatfield to feel no regret when Angela Lansbury kills herself after being cruelly abandoned by Hatfield. *The Picture of Dorian Gray* (1945, MGM).

10326 "Wake up, Norma. You'll be killing yourself for an empty house. The audience left twenty years ago. You're a woman of fifty. There's nothing tragic about being fifty—not unless you try to be twenty-five." Writer **William Holden** tries to give suicidal aging former silent screen star Gloria Swanson a dose of reality. *Sunset Boulevard* (1950, Paramount).

10327 "Tragedy isn't Top Forty—which is just as well." Late night FM radio broadcaster **Jack Nicholson** refers to his own life. *The King of Marvin Gardens* (1972, Columbia).

10328 "The tragedy of war is that the horrors are committed by normal men in abnormal situations." Defense counsel **Jack Thompson** makes a keen observation. *Breaker Morant* (1980, Australia, South Australian Film Corporation).

10329 "You have stumbled upon a tragic story and now you are lost in it with the rest of us." **Leo McKern**, as Father Imperius, tells young thief Matthew Broderick how McKern is inadvertently responsible for the spell on Rutger Hauer and Michelle Pfeiffer. *Ladyhawke* (1985, Warner Bros.).

10330 RAY KINSELLA: "Fifty years ago, for five minutes you came this close. I mean it would kill some men to get that close to their dream and not touch it. . . . They'd consider it a tragedy." DR. "MOONLIGHT" GRAHAM: "If I'd only been a doctor for five minutes, now that would have been a tragedy." **Kevin Costner** offers deceased **Burt Lancaster** the opportunity to visit Costner's Iowa cornfield baseball field and fulfill Lancaster's dream of hitting against a major league pitcher. *Field of Dreams* (1989, Universal).

10331 "My personal tragedy will not interfere with my ability to do good hair." Cosmetologist **Daryl Hannah** shows the stuff she's made of, despite being deserted by her bigamist husband. *Steel Magnolias* (1989, Tri-Star).

Training

see also DISCIPLINE, EDUCATION, GROWTH AND DEVELOPMENT

10332 "You're a Hindu, and have been trained to sneak stealthily through a darkened room." Detective **Jack Mulhall** gives Indian swami Mischa Auer an assignment because of his supposed special expertise. *Sinister Hands* (1932, Capital Films).

10333 "They spent a lot of money training me how to use this and I'm gonna put it to good use when I get out." Bad-guy, bad-guy **Humphrey Bogart** tells good-guy, bad-guy James Cagney of his plans to live by a gun when he gets out of the army after World War I. *The Roaring Twenties* (1939, Warner Bros.).

10334 "I've never seen anyone leapfrog so fast—I've got the sore back to prove it." **Lily Tomlin** is put out that she trained Dabney Coleman and now he's her boss, only because he's a man. *Nine to Five* (1980, 20th Century-Fox).

10335 "I'm not trained for anything else." While in the Witness Protection Program, Italian-American mob informer **Steve Martin** justifies his own small crime wave to FBI agent Rick Moranis. *My Blue Heaven* (1990, Warner Bros.).

10336 "I'm afraid we haven't properly housebroken Miss Kyle." **Christopher Walken** unkindly speaks of his fumbling secretary Michelle Pfeiffer. *Batman Returns* (1992, Warner Bros.).

Trains

see also TRAVEL AND TRIPS

10337 "This is the twentieth century and we get to New York on time." Train conductor **James P. Burtis** proudly announces as his train pulls into the station. But that was when trains were a pleasant means of transportation. *Twentieth Century* (1934, Columbia).

10338 "I stood there and watched his train draw out of the station until its tail light had vanished into the darkness." **Celia Johnson** dashes to the edge of the tracks—but it's too late. Trevor Howard's train leaves her for the last time. *Brief Encounter* (1945, GB, Cineguild).

Transformations

see also CHANGES

10339 "Well, sir, in three months, I could pass her off as a duchess at an ambassador's reception. . . .

yes. . . I could even get her a job as a lady's maid or shop assistant, which requires better English." **Leslie Howard** as Professor Henry Higgins, tells Scott Sunderland, as Colonel Pickering, that he can transform Wendy Hiller, as Cockney flower girl Eliza Doolittle, into a real lady by teaching her to speak correctly. In the musical remake, **Rex Harrison** echoes the sentiments to Wilfrid Hyde White about Audrey Hepburn. *Pygmalion* (1938, GB, MGM); *My Fair Lady* (1964, Warner Bros.).

10340 "When I first came here I believed in justice. I believed that someday I'd be released. Then I began to figure in weeks and months and now I hate the whole world and everybody in it for lettin' me in for this. Buried in a black filthy hole because I was a good citizen, because I worked my head off to expose crime. And now I'm a convict! I act like a convict, smell like a convict! I think and hate like a convict! But I'll get out! I'll get out if I have to kill every screw in the joint." Framed reporter **James Cagney**, despairing of ever being cleared, has become a hardened con. *Each Dawn I Die* (1939, Warner Bros.).

10341 "I wasn't always a bitter old woman. I wasn't always a pest and a nuisance." James Stewart's meddling mother **Lucille Watson** lets her son and his wife Carole Lombard know that life has made her what she is. *Made for Each Other* (1939, United Artists).

10342 "Even the man who is pure in heart/And says his prayers by night/May become a wolf when the wolf bane blooms,/And the moon is pure and bright." Gypsy Maleva, played beautifully by **Maria Ouspenskaya**, quotes an ancient warning. She should know. Her own son was a werewolf. *The Wolf Man* (1940, Universal).

10343 "The kindest, gentlest, the most sympathetic man in the world. . . I should be sincerely sorry to see my neighbors' children devoured by wolves." It's the transformation that acerbic writer **Clifton Webb** claims he underwent for Gene Tierney. *Laura* (1944, 20th Century-Fox).

10344 LAWRENCE TALBOT: "You don't understand. Every night when the moon is full, I turn into a wolf." WILBUR GREY: "You and fifty million other guys." **Lon Chaney, Jr.**, repeating his role in *The Wolf Man* (1940), can't quite make **Lou Costello** understand his dilemma. *Abbott and Costello Meet Frankenstein* (1948, Universal).

10345 "He made you over just like I made you over—only better. Not only the clothes and the hair, but the looks and manner, and the words. And those beautiful phony trances. And then what did he do? Did he train you? Did he rehearse you? Did he tell you exactly what to do and what to say? You were a very apt pupil, weren't you? You were a very apt pupil." **James Stewart** finally stumbles onto the fact that Kim Novak was the instrument Tom Helmore used to get away with the murder of his wife. *Vertigo* (1958, Paramount).

10346 "Honey, you wouldn't believe what happened to me today." Sounding like Ozzie Nelson greeting Harriet, **Jack Nicholson**, grinning at his mistress Jerry Hall, announces his transformation into The Joker. *Batman* (1989, Warner Bros.).

Transportation *see* AUTOMOBILES, BOATS AND SHIPS, DRIVING AND DRIVERS, FLYING AND FLIERS, TRAINS

Transvestites *see* CLOTHES, PRETENSIONS, SEX AND SEXUALITY

Traps

see also ANIMALS, ESCAPES

10347 "I think I'm in a frame, [but] all I can see is the frame. I'm going in there now to look at the picture." **Robert Mitchum** tells friend Paul Valentine that he knows he's being set up, but he has to find out for what. *Out of the Past* (1947, RKO).

10348 "We're all in our private trap. We scratch and claw, but only at the air, at each other, and for all of it we never budge an inch." Amateur taxidermist **Anthony Perkins** shares his desperation with desperate Janet Leigh. *Psycho* (1960, Paramount).

10349 "To catch a lion, you need a goat." Leader of Israeli operatives **Klaus Kinski** tries to reel in lion Sami Frey, a Palestinian super-terrorist, with goat Diane Keaton. *The Little Drummer Girl* (1984, Warner Bros.).

Travels and Trips

see also AUTOMOBILES, BOATS AND SHIPS, DRIVING AND DRIVERS, FLYING AND FLIERS, TRAINS

10350 "Some people travel through life making friends wherever they go, while others—just travel through life." A title card introduces the film's hero "Friendless" Buster Keaton. *Go West* (1925, silent, MGM).

10351 FRED GILBERT: "Her mind must have been wandering." CAROL BALDWIN: "It's been on a Cook's tour." **George Brent** defends sexy secretary Dorothea Kent when **Jean Arthur** complains about

Kent's error-studded letters. *More Than a Secretary* (1936, Columbia).

10352 "We had a lovely trip. Nick was sober in Kansas City." **Myrna Loy** speaks lovingly of her husband William Powell, who is a real elbow-bender. *Another Thin Man* (1939, MGM).

10353 "You're soft, like a woman. This voyage ought to do you a lot of good." Maniacal sea captain **Edward G. Robinson** has taken a perverse liking to Alexander Knox, one of the survivors from a ferry accident in San Francisco Bay, picked up by Robinson's ship. *The Sea Wolf* (1941, Warner Bros.).

10354 ANGELA PHINLAY: "What about my trip, Uncle Lon?" ALONZO D. EMMERICH: "Don't worry, baby, you'll have plenty of trips." **Marilyn Monroe** is assured by crooked lawyer **Louis Calhern** that there will be other sugar daddies in her life. As for Calhern, suicide is his destination. *The Asphalt Jungle* (1950, MGM).

10355 "And she wanders—God knows where she wanders." **Tom Helmore** hires former classmate James Stewart to keep track of his strangely behaving wife Kim Novak. *Vertigo* (1958, Paramount).

10356 "I know about those airplane dolls. If we were traveling first class, we could get anything we want—and I mean anything!" A tourist-class passenger complains about the differential treatment of the stewardesses. *Come Fly with Me* (1963, MGM).

10357 "With joyous memories we leave the mystical city of Da Nang. What gay adventures lie ahead? Brother, this trip is going to make LSD feel like aspirin." **Jim Hutton** shouts over the roar of a helicopter that is to carry him to the combat zone. *The Green Berets* (1968, Warner Bros.).

10358 "I don't know about you, but next time, I'm taking a bus." At the end of an exciting train adventure, exhausted **Jill Clayburgh** tells Gene Wilder that she wants to get untracked. *Silver Streak* (1976, 20th Century- Fox).

10359 "Darlin', we're traveling on wit and grit." Ex-boxer **Tommy Lee Jones** encourages his hitchhiking companion, hooker Sally Field. *Back Roads* (1991, Meta Films).

Treason and Traitors

see also BETRAYALS, COUNTRIES, LOYALTIES, SPIES, TRUST, WARS

10360 MAID MARIAN: "Why, you speak treason." ROBIN HOOD: "Fluently." Ward of the throne **Olivia**

de Havilland is shocked by **Errol Flynn**'s attitude towards Claude Rains as Prince John. *The Adventures of Robin Hood* (1938, Warner Bros.)

10361 "I never discuss being a traitor with a man. You'll find it easier if you don't think about that part of it." Master spy **Sydney Greenstreet** recruits Humphrey Bogart to work for the goals of the Japanese prior to World War II. *Across the Pacific* (1942, Warner Bros.).

10362 "Why is it that you sneer every time you refer to this country? You've done pretty well here. I don't get it." Average Joe **Robert Cummings** can't figure out why wealthy American Otto Kruger would become a traitor to his country by supporting the Nazi cause in World War II. *Saboteur* (1942, Universal).

10363 "I think I'll go and join my comrades and talk a little treason." **Barry Fitzgerald**, probably a member of the IRA, takes his leave of John Wayne to go to the pub. *The Quiet Man* (1952, Republic).

Treats and Treatments

see also ACTIONS AND ACTS, BEHAVIOR, CARES AND CARING, DEALS AND DEALINGS, DOCTORS AND DENTISTS, ENTERTAINMENTS AND ENTERTAINERS, MEDICINE, NURSES, PLEASURES

10364 "If you come back to me, I shall treat you just the same as I have always treated you. I can't change my nature, and I don't intend to change my manners." Both **Leslie Howard** and **Rex Harrison** make it perfectly clear to Wendy Hiller and Audrey Hepburn, respectively, that they are set in their ways and are quite happy with their ways. *Pygmalion* (1938, GB, Pascal-Rank-MGM); *My Fair Lady* (1964, Warner Bros.).

10365 "Where the devil are my slippers, Eliza?" With the last line of the film, **Leslie Howard**, as Professor Henry Higgins, demonstrates that he has learned nothing about how to treat Wendy Hiller, the little flower girl, Eliza Doolittle, whom he has transformed into a lady, by teaching her to speak properly. *Pygmalion* (1938, GB, Pascal-Rank-MGM).

10366 "I don't want to be tied with a rope! Why can't I be handcuffed like the rest—I'm going to be hanged like the rest!...I'm going to die! I don't want to die, I'm only seventeen!" When a gang of cut throats are arrested for scuttling ships, adolescent **Stephen Haggard** is taken with them. His wrists are so slender that handcuffs slip from him, so they must be tied with a rope. When the lad realizes what he's said about his fate, he breaks down

and begins to weep. *Jamaica Inn* (1939, GB, Mayflower-Paramount).

10367 HILDY JOHNSON: "He treats me like a woman." WALTER BURNS: "How did I treat you? Like a water buffalo?" HILDY: "I dunno from water buffalos, but I do know about him. He's kind and sweet and he's considerate." WALTER: "He sounds like a guy I should marry." Reporter **Rosalind Russell** describes her fiancé Ralph Bellamy to her editor and ex-husband **Cary Grant**. *His Girl Friday* (1940, Columbia).

10368 "I'm told the sight of an eligible male is a rare treat in this part of the country." Eligible **Cary Grant** frightens mousy Joan Fontaine, for whom he's a rare sight. *Suspicion* (1941, RKO).

10369 RITTENHOUSE: "The more we quarrel and criticize and misunderstand each other, the bigger the ocean gets and the smaller the boat." KOVAC: "The boat's too small right now for me and this German!" RITTENHOUSE: "If we harm this man, we're guilty of the same tactics that you hate him for. On the other hand, if we treat him with kindness and consideration, we might be able to convert him to our way of thinking. That's the—uh—Christian way." Wealthy passenger **Henry Hull** argues with seaman **John Hodiak** over how to treat the prisoner in their lifeboat, German Walter Slezak. The survivors don't know that Slezak is the captain of the U-boat that sunk their ship before sinking itself. Hull wants to treat Slezak as a prisoner of war and Hodiak wants to feed him to the sharks. *Lifeboat* (1944, 20th Century-Fox).

10370 "Do it now. Mistreat me, make love to me, anything. Only get it over with." **Carroll Baker** resignedly offers herself to her stepson and former fiancé George Peppard after her husband, his father, Leif Erickson, dies. *The Carpetbaggers* (1964, Paramount).

10371 "Pills! I come to you in flames and you treat me for sunburn!" **Dustin Hoffman**, at the point of suicide, raves at his psychiatrist Jack Warden. *Who Is Harry Kellerman and Why Is He Saying Those Terrible Things About Me?* (1971, Cinema Center-National General).

10372 "I'm not used to being treated so well by a beautiful woman." Title character **John Hurt** is touched by the kindness of Hannah Gordon. *The Elephant Man* (1981, GB, EMI-Paramount).

10373 "I won't let you treat me like some slut you can bang a couple of times and then throw away like a piece of garbage." **Glenn Close** tears into her one-weekend stand Michael Douglas. *Fatal Attraction* (1987, Paramount).

10374 "Don't make me treat you like dogs." Would-be professional philosopher **Tim Robbins** tries to get rid of two unattractive girls who follow him into a pool hall. *Miss Firecracker* (1989, Corsair).

10375 "Actresses are treated like. . . well, shit! I remember when I was fifteen years old, Mr. Mayer called me into a meeting. He was sitting upon the toilet! On the toilet!. . . You can be sure he wouldn't do that to John Garfield." Flustered **Shirley MacLaine** does her version of Debbie Reynolds. *Postcards from the Edge* (1990, Columbia).

10376 "I'm sick and tired of being treated like a piece of meat." **Ellen Barkin**, the sexy reincarnation of womanizer Perry King, now knows how the pursuee feels. *Switch* (1991, Warner Bros.).

Trees

see also LAND AND FARMS, PLANTS

10377 "So that was once a tree? 'The Petrified Forest,' eh? A suitable haven for me. Well, perhaps that's what I'm destined for—to make an interesting fossil for future study." World-weary, wandering intellectual **Leslie Howard** muses. *The Petrified Forest* (1936, Warner Bros.).

10378 "Old trees, practicing curtsies in the wind, because they still think Louis XIV is king." American flyer **Ray Milland** makes a poetic description of the forest of Compiegne. *Arise, My Love* (1940, Paramount).

10379 "When I get through with you, you'll look like—well, what do you call beautiful? A tree? You'll look like a tree." Fashion photographer **Fred Astaire** convinces Audrey Hepburn to become his model. Actually because she's so thin, she looks more like a beautiful twig or branch. *Funny Face* (1957, Paramount).

10380 "Jonathan, before a man gets married, he's a—he's like a tree in the forest. He—he stands there independent, an entity unto himself. And then he's chopped down. His branches are cut off, and he's stripped of his bark, and he's thrown into the river with the rest of the logs. Then the tree is taken to the mill. Now, when it comes out, it's no longer a tree. It's a vanity table, a breakfast nook, a baby crib and the newspaper that lines the family garbage can." **Rock Hudson** uses an interesting analogy to explain why he resists getting married. Lumberjill Doris Day will change his mind. *Pillow Talk* (1959, Universal).

10381 "Trees are like people. If they know you don't care about them, they won't give you any-thing back." **Walter Matthau** muses about a stunted tree in his back yard. His daughter Dinah Manoff, who he deserted when she was a child, interjects, "I know." *I Ought to Be in Pictures* (1982, 20th Century-Fox).

10382 "When you plant a tree, you don't have a swing on it the next day." **Richard Crenna** uses this metaphor to explain to young Matt Dillon why he's working as a stock boy rather than an automobile salesman as Crenna promised. *The Flamingo Kid* (1984, 20th Century-Fox).

10383 "Trees scare me. They have human powers." At the beginning of the movie **Karen Colston** makes an assertion that suggests she may be a bit strange. *Sweetie* (1989, Australia, Filmpac).

10384 "I've always thought that trees were somehow disapproving of me." Burnt-out advertising man **Dudley Moore** confesses an irrational concern to beautiful, gentle mental patient Daryl Hannah. *Crazy People* (1990, Paramount).

Trials *see* CRIMES AND CRIMINALS, CROSS-EXAMINATIONS, JUDGMENTS, JUSTICE, LAWS, LAWYERS, LEGALITY AND ILLEGALITY, PROOFS

Tricks and Trickery

see also CARDS, DECEPTIONS, MAGIC, STUPIDITY

10385 NORA CHARLES: "I think it's a dirty trick to bring me all the way to New York just to make a widow out of me." NICK CHARLES: "You wouldn't be a widow long." NORA: "You bet I wouldn't." NICK: "Not with all your money." **Myrna Loy** expresses concern that husband **William Powell** will get himself killed working at his old profession as a detective. He's ungallant enough to suggest that it would be the money of smashing-looking Loy that would bring her suitors were he deceased. *The Thin Man* (1934, MGM).

10386 "I'm wiggling both my ears at the same time. It took me two solid years at the finest boy's school in the world to learn that trick. The fellow who taught me is now president of Venezuela." **Orson Welles** tries to take Dorothy Comingore's mind off her toothache. *Citizen Kane* (1941, RKO).

10387 "The trick is not minding that it hurts." It's **Peter O'Toole**'s masochistic reply to an officer's question, "Doesn't it hurt?" when O'Toole deliberately burns the palm of his hand with a match. *Lawrence of Arabia* (1962, GB, Columbia).

10388 "That's a neat trick, having a clear conscience when you work as a doctor on a ship which has

300 people living in an open deck." **Simone Signoret** questions Oskar Werner's medical ethics. No two performers ever worked better together than Signoret and Werner in this movie. *Ship of Fools* (1965, Columbia).

10389 "Thank God, I'm here. . . . You've been tricked. . . . My name is Katharine Parker and I'm an associate partner in mergers and acquisitions at Petty-Marsh—and this woman is my secretary." Hopping to the rescue like the cavalry on crutches, **Sigourney Weaver** arrives in the nick of time to blow the whistle on Melanie Griffith who has been putting together a big business deal while her boss is laid up. *Working Girl* (1988, 20th Century-Fox).

Triumph see LOSSES AND LOSING, VICTORIES, WINNERS AND LOSERS

Troubles

see also CONFUSION, DANGER, DIFFICULTIES, EFFORTS, NEEDS AND NECESSITIES, PAINS, PROBLEMS

10390 "I got mixed up in a little trouble and I thought I'd stay out of town till the gendarmes forget about it." **Jean Harlow** wishes to disappear when she shows up at Clark Gable's rubber plantation in Indo-China. *Red Dust* (1932, MGM).

10391 "I'm practically a married man. I'll be no trouble." Carole Lombard reluctantly takes on **Fred MacMurray** as a boarder in one-half of her apartment. *Hands Across the Table* (1935, Paramount).

10392 "Too many things occur to you, that's your trouble." Title character Paul Muni's severest critic is **Fritz Leiber**. *The Story of Louis Pasteur* (1936, Warner Bros.).

10393 "Savannah would be better for you. You'll just get in trouble in Atlanta." **Hattie McDaniel** knows why Vivien Leigh wishes to visit her aunt in Atlanta after Leigh's husband dies—she believes she'll get to see the man she really loves, Leslie Howard, married to Olivia de Havilland. *Gone with the Wind* (1939, Selznick-MGM).

10394 "You and trouble just naturally gravitate towards one another." **Judy Garland** certainly knows Mickey Rooney. *Andy Hardy Meets Debutante* (1940, MGM).

10395 "The trouble with you dames is you're always building castles in the air and trying to move into them." This is **James Cagney**'s great put-down of Ann Sheridan. *Torrid Zone* (1940, Warner Bros.).

10396 "I don't know where I'm going, but I'm not coming back till I know what trouble is." Only a Preston Sturges' character, Hollywood director **Joel McCrea** would have to go looking for trouble. *Sullivan's Travels* (1941, Paramount).

10397 "All the time you like trouble." **Lee Tung Foo** puts his finger on his friend Humphrey Bogart's problem. *Across the Pacific* (1942, Warner Bros.).

10398 "That's the trouble with Irish whiskey—you don't know you've been drinking until you're delirious." It is **James Mason**'s complaint after Michael Redgrave loses control and strikes him. *Thunder Rock* (1942, GB, Charter Films).

10399 "The trouble with the world is it has been seduced into listening to politicians instead of poets." It is **Lionel Stander**'s comment in the comedy-drama of a mentally unbalanced ballet dancer. *Spectre of the Rose* (1946, Republic).

10400 "You can't run from trouble—there isn't any place that far." **James Baskett**, as Uncle Remus, dispenses a bit of folk wisdom. *Song of the South* (1946, Disney-RKO).

10401 RIP: "You know the trouble with women is they ask too many questions. They should spend all that time just being beautiful." CORAL: "And let men do the worrying?" **Humphrey Bogart** has a prehistoric view of the function of women such as **Lizabeth Scott**. *Dead Reckoning* (1947, Columbia).

10402 ANNIE LAURIE STARR: "We're in real trouble this time." BART TARE: "Laurie, I wouldn't have it any other way." Bonnie- and Clyde-like **Peggy Cummins** and **John Dall** kiss passionately just before they are gunned down and lie dead, side by side. *Gun Crazy* (1949, United Artists).

10403 "George, I'm in trouble—real trouble, I think." **Shelley Winters** breaks the news to Montgomery Clift that she's pregnant with his child. At the time, being an unwed parent made one an outcast. *A Place in the Sun* (1951, Paramount).

10404 "Everyone has trouble at home. The only ones who deny it have had too much of it. I denied it for five years with the former Mrs. Dodd." **William Holden** notes that all marriages have troubles, some more than others. *The Country Girl* (1954, Paramount).

10405 "What good does it do you besides getting you in trouble?" **Marlon Brando** responds when Eva Marie Saint chides him for not having "a spark of sentiment or romance or human kindness." *On the Waterfront* (1954, Columbia).

10406 "I can smell trouble right here in this apartment.... Look out the window, see things you shouldn't see." Housekeeper **Thelma Ritter** warns James Stewart that his voyeurism will lead to trouble. *Rear Window* (1954, Paramount).

10407 "What seems to be the trouble, Captain?" Delightfully, **Mildred Natwick** is unperturbed by the sight of Edmund Gwenn dragging a dead body through the bushes. *The Trouble with Harry* (1955, Paramount).

10408 "If someone is in trouble, how can you not take them seriously?" Lovelorn columnist **Montgomery Clift** cares very much for suffering humanity—before disillusionment sets in. *Lonelyhearts* (1958, United Artists).

10409 "Sweetheart, you know what trouble is? I can't believe I'm here." In his screen debut, **Robert Redford** is a soldier who has just arrived at the forward area. He meets a Korean girl who announces she loves him and will fix all his troubles. *War Hunt* (1962, United Artists).

10410 "Boss, life is trouble. Only death is not. To be alive is to undo your belt and look for trouble." Greek peasant **Anthony Quinn** shares his vision of life with English writer Alan Bates. *Zorba, the Greek* (1964, U.S.-Greek, 20th Century-Fox).

10411 "Why does everyone have so much trouble in love?" **Romy Schneider** raises an impossible question to her fiancé Peter O'Toole. *What's New, Pussycat?* (1965, Famous Artists).

10412 "All this trouble to make up for your feelings of sexual inferiority. I'm beginning to think you may be a little neurotic." When Woody Allen is revealed to be the mastermind behind a plot of world domination, his uncle **David Niven** scolds him. *Casino Royale* (1967, GB, Columbia).

10413 "Oh, good. For a moment I thought we were in trouble." Seriously wounded bank robber **Paul Newman** is relieved when his equally wounded partner Robert Redford assures him that the posse that chased them out of the U.S West is not waiting outside with a detachment of Bolivian soldiers that have them surrounded. *Butch Cassidy and the Sundance Kid* (1969, 20th Century-Fox).

10414 "The trouble with some people is they work too hard." Observer of life, **Robert Redford** analyzes radical participant Barbra Streisand's problem. *The Way We Were* (1973, Columbia).

10415 "Real trouble comes in a dirty suit and a wrinkled collar." Ex-cop turned bounty hunter **John Saxon** speaks his piece on the sound track narration. *The Glove* (1978, Pro International).

10416 "I'm Jewish, my son is black and my lawyer smokes pot. Don't tell me I'm not in trouble." **George Segal** whines to his lawyer Dick Martin. *Carbon Copy* (1981, RKO).

10417 "I gather you are in a spot of bother." Supersleuth **Alan Shearman** deduces the situation klutzy Diz White, daughter of a kidnapped scientist, must deal with. *Bullshot* (1983, GB, Island Alive).

10418 "It's just some poor miner whose troubles are over." **Bob Gunton** prevents Jennie Cline from viewing a body that's been found in a hollow. *Matewan* (1987, Cinecom).

10419 GROUP LEADER: "Do you have a problem with your sexuality?" EVELYN COUCH: "No, ma'am, I have a problem with my girdle." When the instructor hands **Kathy Bates** a mirror and tells her and the other women in the group to take off their panties so they can look at their vaginas, Bates asks to be excused to go to the bathroom. *Fried Green Tomatoes* (1991, Universal).

10420 "You stroll around my apartment, touching my things. Do you know what trouble you've gotten me into? Do you?" Manhattan horticulturist **Andie MacDowell** tries to shift all the blame onto French composer Gerard Depardieu, whom she married in order to secure a desirable apartment and get him U.S. resident status. Now the government, suspecting fraud, is investigating their marriage. *Green Card* (1991, Touchstone-Buena Vista).

Trust

see also BELIEFS, BETRAYALS, CARES AND CARING, FAITH AND UNFAITHFULNESS, INTEGRITY

10421 "I think a girl knows instinctively when she can trust a man." Armed with that mistaken notion, **Anny Ondra** incautiously accepts artist Cyril Ritchard's invitation to visit his studio. *Blackmail* (1929, GB, BIP).

10422 CAPT. CUMMINGS: "If only I could trust you." LADY LOU: "Hundreds have." **Cary Grant** actually is the one flying under false colors. He's an undercover cop, posing as the captain of a Salvation Army-like bowery mission, trying to get the goods on saloon keeper **Mae West**. *She Done Him Wrong* (1933, Paramount).

10423 "You know, I've known people I've liked and some I've disliked. I've hated a few and thought I loved a couple, but I've never known anyone I could trust up to now." **Joan Crawford** makes her revelation after kissing Clark Gable. His kiss must have been very sincere. *Love on the Run* (1936, MGM).

10424 "When a Dillon gets polite, lock the henhouses and reach for the pitchfork." **Walter Brennan**'s family has been feuding with Moroni Olsen's family since the Civil War. *Kentucky* (1938, 20th Century-Fox).

10425 "I told you to forget that kootch. She's poison. Never trust a blue-eyed squaw." Sergeant **Preston Foster** attempts to indoctrinate constable Robert Preston with some of his hate of the Metis half-breeds, but Preston only sees how sexually available Paulette Goddard is. *Northwest Mounted Police* (1940, Paramount).

10426 "You begin well, sir. I distrust a man who says 'when.' He's got to be careful not to drink too much, because he's not to be trusted when he does. Well, sir, here's to plain speaking and clear understanding." **Sydney Greenstreet** toasts Humphrey Bogart, who can be trusted because he can hold his liquor. *The Maltese Falcon* (1941, Warner Bros.).

10427 "You're a very cynical person, Rick, and just because you despise me you're the only one I trust." Small-time operator **Peter Lorre** has a strange criterion for trusting a person. *Casablanca* (1942, Warner Bros.).

10428 "He keeps me on a leash so I can't breathe." **Barbara Stanwyck** complains to Fred MacMurray that her older husband Tom Powers doesn't trust her. *Double Indemnity* (1944, Paramount).

10429 "What is it about a man like that? Why does anyone trust him in the first place?" Writer **Peter Lorre** questions Kurt Katch, head of Turkey's secret police, about sinister criminal Zachary Scott. *The Mask of Dimitrios* (1944, Warner Bros.).

10430 "Never trust a woman." It's **Barry Fitzgerald**'s dying advice to Louis Hayward after the latter and June Duprez foil Fitzgerald's plans to kill all ten of his guests on a tiny isolated island. *And Then There Were None* (1945, Popular Pictures).

10431 "But you're a bishop. You, of all people, can trust the word of an angel." Bishop **David Niven** prayed for help, but he wasn't counting on it appearing in the form of Cary Grant, claiming to be an angel. *The Bishop's Wife* (1947, RKO).

10432 "Fred C. Dobbs, doesn't say nuthin' he don't mean." **Humphrey Bogart** is down on his luck, but he claims his word is his bond. *The Treasure of the Sierra Madre* (1948, Warner Brothers).

10433 "I won't let myself fall in love with a man who won't trust me, no matter what I do." Luscious sexpot **Marilyn Monroe** expects a great deal from her rich boyfriend Tommy Noonan, who sees her off as she prepares to sail by ocean liner to France. *Gentlemen Prefer Blondes* (1953, 20th Century-Fox).

10434 "Never trust anyone who functions from noble motives because they're never sure, and, in the end, they'll let you down." White Russian General **Yul Brynner** advises amnesiac Ingrid Bergman, whom he tries to pass off as the surviving daughter of the last czar of Russia. *Anastasia* (1956, 20th Century-Fox).

10435 "Never trust a patient!" **Joan Crawford**, the head nurse at a mental hospital, runs a judo class for her nurses. *The Caretakers* (1963, United Artists).

10436 "How can I trust a man who wears both a belt and suspenders? He doesn't even trust his own pants." Hired killer **Henry Fonda** confronts a man who has betrayed a confidence. *Once Upon a Time in the West* (1969, Italy-Paramount).

10437 "You came out of the blue to make us happy. And we made you happy, didn't we? We trusted you with our great treasure." At the end of the film, elderly **Julie Christie** reminisces with Michael Redgrave, who as a boy carried love letters back and forth from Christie and farmer Alan Bates. *The Go-Between* (1970, GB, EMI-World Film Services).

10438 "I don't dislike women, I merely mistrust them." **Robert Stephens**, as Sherlock Holmes, declares his position to Colin Blakely, as his companion Dr. Watson. *The Private Life of Sherlock Holmes* (1970, U.S., GB, United Artists).

10439 "Who can trust a cop who won't take money?" Crooked cop **Jack Kehoe** complains about honest cop Al Pacino. *Serpico* (1973, Paramount).

10440 "Never trust a mutant." Amazon queen **Sandahl Bergman** gives some sound advice. *She* (1982, Italy, Europix).

10441 "I don't trust that guy. Everything's too interesting to him." Swaggering war veteran **Nicolas Cage** refers to resident psychiatrist John Harkins. *Birdy* (1984, Tri-Star).

10442 "Never trust a man who says 'trust me.'" **Louanne Stephens** gives her daughter Lolita Davidovich wise advice as the latter leaves her backwoods homestead to seek her fortune in the world. *Blaze* (1989, Touchstone-Buena Vista).

10443 "Only if you trust the coins will you become a man of property; only then will you be happy. But beware the king of swords." Joseph Long's vision of a fanciful pig gives him good advice. *Queen of Hearts* (1989, GB, Cinecom).

10444 "If you can't trust a fix what can you trust?" Ambitious Italian mobster **Jon Polito** complains to big boss Irishman Albert Finney that a Jewish bookie has cheated him out of the winnings he expected from boxing matches that he fixes. *Miller's Crossing* (1990, 20th Century-Fox).

10445 "I trust too much, that's always been my fault. . . Michael, treachery's everywhere." Elderly criminal don **Eli Wallach** isn't to be trusted by Al Pacino, when Eli tells Al he was wrong about ambitious hood Joe Mantegna. *The Godfather, Part III* (1991, Paramount).

10446 "I've never trusted Klingons and I never will." **William Shatner** isn't impressed with the decision of the Klingons to join the Earth's Federation. *Star Trek VI: The Undiscovered Country* (1991, Paramount).

10447 MARTIN RIGGS: "Trust me." ROGER MURTAUGH: "That's usually my first mistake." Police detective **Mel Gibson** talks his partner **Danny Glover** into entering and investigating a building where it is suspected that a bomb is planted. Gibson assures Glover there's no bomb. Glover has made another mistake. *Lethal Weapon III* (1992, Warner Bros.).

Truth

see also HONESTY AND DISHONESTY, INTEGRITY, KNOWLEDGE, LIES AND LYING, LOGIC, PROOFS, REALITIES, SINCERITY, TRUTH AND FALSEHOOD

10448 "I'm going up there on that platform to tell people the truth. To tell what a liar and cheat I've been and neither you nor anybody else is going to stop me." **Barbara Stanwyck** yearns to confess that she's a religious con woman. *The Miracle Worker* (1931, Columbia).

10449 "I shall dare. I shall tell the truth, because if I did not, my nights would be haunted by the specter of an innocent being expiated, under the most frightful torture, a crime he never committed! It is impossible for honest people to read the iniquitous bill of accusation against Dreyfus without being overcome with indignation and crying out their revulsion." Title character **Paul Muni** reads his article, "J'Accuse" that states the truth about the railroading of Jewish officer Joseph Schildkraut for the crime of treason. For his efforts, the French writer is charged with libel, which he welcomes, because it gives him the opportunity to argue the case for Schildkraut's innocence. *The Life of Emile Zola* (1937, Warner Bros.).

10450 "They are a living truth written on my mind." Narrator **Irving Pichel** as the adult Huw, recalls his family in Wales. *How Green Was My Valley* (1941, 20th Century-Fox).

10451 "I'd like to tell you we've been sent out to bring back help, but that wouldn't be true." **Robert Montgomery**, the commander of six PT boats, refuses to lie to the men he and John Wayne must leave behind in the Philippines when they are ordered to leave before the Japanese arrive. *They Were Expendable* (1945, MGM).

10452 "There is truth in her story and a morality that has no truth in it is no morality at all. . . . Truth lives forever, men do not." **James Mason**, as French author Gustave Flaubert, claims that the truth gleaned from Emma Bovary's story compensates for her death. *Madame Bovary* (1949, MGM).

10453 "I know I fib a good deal. After all, a woman's charm is fifty percent illusion, but when a thing is important I tell the truth. . . ." **Vivien Leigh** assures Marlon Brando that veracity is important to her in important matters. *A Streetcar Named Desire* (1951, Warner Bros.-20th Century-Fox).

10454 "There are three sides to every story: yours, his and the truth." Wise Judge **Madge Kennedy** talks to Judy Holliday, who seeks a divorce from Aldo Ray. *The Marrying Kind* (1952, Columbia).

10455 "Truth is pain and sweat and paying back and making love to a woman that you don't love anymore. Truth is dreams that don't come true and nobody prints your name in the paper until you die." **Burl Ives**, as Big Daddy, has a bitter description of truth. *Cat on a Hot Tin Roof* (1958, MGM).

10456 "Nobody knows anybody. . . . That's a fact." Marine **Kerwin Mathews** responds to a general who asks about Ray Danton who died a hero's death in combat. *Tarawa Beachhead* (1958, Columbia).

10457 "Realizing that I may prejudice the case of my client, I must tell you that right has no meaning to me whatsoever—but truth has meaning, as a direction." Angry **Spencer Tracy**, as the Clarence Darrow-like lawyer, makes an important legal distinction in the famous Tennessee "Monkey Case." *Inherit the Wind* (1960, United Artists).

10458 "Miss Fellowes is a very moral person. If she ever found out the truth about herself, it would destroy her." Defrocked minister **Richard Burton** steps in to protect Grayson Hall, who Ava Gardner has knocked unconscious, calling her a "dyke." *The Night of the Iguana* (1964, MGM).

10459 "The 'Hole in the Wall Gang' led by Butch Cassidy and the Sundance Kid are all dead now. But once they ruled the world! Most of what follows is true." Written introduction. *Butch Cassidy and the Sundance Kid* (1969, 20th Century-Fox).

10460 "I'm not getting to the truth of our relationship. . . . I don't think there exists one truth." **Erland Josephson** speaks to his ex-wife Liv Ullmann. They are lovers again, years after their divorce. *Scenes from a Marriage* (1974, Sweden, Cinema 5).

10461 "Ultimate moment of nothing that is the beginning of life. . . the final truth is that there is no final truth. . . truth is transitory; only the human is real." It's the lesson that **William Hurt** learns while experimenting with psychedelic mushrooms. *Altered States* (1980, Warner Bros.).

10462 "As a matter of law, truth is irrelevant. If we prove we tried to contact him, there's absence of malice. . . . We may say whatever we like about Mr. Gallagher and be safe from harm. Democracy will be served." Cynical lawyer **John Harkins** gives a cavalier legal opinion, assuring his newspaper employers that they can safely continue their smear campaign against Miami businessman Paul Newman. *Absence of Malice* (1981, Columbia).

10463 "You don't write the truth. You write what people say. . . ." Businessman **Paul Newman** cautions reporter Sally Field to get her facts straight. *Absence of Malice* (1981, Columbia).

10464 "I don't see playing politics with the truth." Penologist **Robert Redford** has no luck getting the support of the rednecks who run the prison board to help him reform his prison. *Brubaker* (1981, 20th Century-Fox).

10465 "I feel like I'm lying even when I'm telling the truth. . . . I don't know what the truth is anymore." **Treat Williams** becomes an informant against fellow cops. *Prince of the City* (1981, Warner Bros.).

10466 "Even if you are a minority of one, truth is truth." **Ben Kingsley**, as Mahatma Gandhi, makes the point that truth doesn't necessarily belong to the majority. *Gandhi* (1982, GB, Goldcrest-Columbia).

10467 "I always tell the truth—even when I lie. . . . So, say goodnight to the bad guy." Cuban mobster **Al Pacino** addresses the patrons of an expensive Miami restaurant after Michelle Pfeiffer douses him with a drink and walks out on him. *Scarface* (1983, Universal).

10468 "If I wanted the truth, I'd hire '60 Minutes.'" Arab strong man **Spiros Focas** exclaims to romantic novelist Kathleen Turner whom he's hired to write his biography, that he wants a puff piece. *The Jewel of the Nile* (1985, 20th Century-Fox).

10469 "You got to get close to the truth. Get too close, you die." Combat photographer **James Woods** assesses the danger of his work. *Salvador* (1986, Hemdale).

10470 "Truth has no meaning in this house." **River Phoenix** screams at his parents Richard Jenkins and Caroline Kava, whom he has learned are Russian spies called sleepers. They were planted in the U.S. twenty years earlier and told to wait for the time when they will be called on to perform their duty to the U.S.S.R. The time has come. *Little Nikita* (1988, Columbia).

10471 "The truth is a virus." Teenage pirate radio station operator **Christian Slater** dispenses some teen wisdom to his listeners. *Pump Up the Volume* (1990, Canada-U.S., New Line).

10472 "I hope you're not being frivolous. . . my life now only has room for the truth." Russian **Michelle Pfeiffer** hopes that British publisher Sean Connery is telling the truth about his feelings for her. *The Russia House* (1991, MGM-United Artists).

Truth and Falsehood

see also LIES AND LYING, TRUTH

10473 "No, no! We've got to think of lies and tell them all the time, and stop them from finding the truth." Young **Bobby Henrey** believes that by lying he will save his friend, butler Ralph Richardson, from being accused of murdering his wife. Actually, his lies nearly incriminate the innocent man. *The Fallen Idol* (1948, GB, British Lion).

10474 "You tell the truth about a lie so beautifully." Psychiatrist **Art Garfunkel** upbraids troubled Theresa Russell with a demeaning compliment. *Bad Timing: A Sensual Obsession* (1980, GB, Rank).

Trying *see* EFFORTS

Tyranny and Tyrants

see also FORCE, POWER, REBELLIONS, REVOLUTIONS, SLAVERY AND SLAVES

10475 "That's not love, it's pure tyranny." Actress **Carole Lombard** wants to go to a nightclub and theatrical producer John Barrymore refuses to take her. *Twentieth Century* (1934, Columbia).

10476 "Sometimes tyranny masquerades as mother love." Renowned psychiatrist **Claude Rains** recognizes the nature of the problem his patient, repressed Bette Davis, has with her domineering mother Gladys Cooper. Davis will later repeat the line to Cooper. *Now, Voyager* (1942, Warner Bros.)

10477 "Resistance to tyrants is obedience to God." This romance set in Cuba opens with a quote from Thomas Jefferson. *We Were Strangers* (1949, Columbia).

10478 "Somoza? He's a tyrant too, of course, a butcher. But, finally, that is not the point, you see. If we wish to survive we might have a choice of tyrants. . . . In twenty years, we will know who's right." Government-fixer **Jean-Louis Trintignant** will never know if his crucial piece of political wisdom is right, because it is offered just before the rebels execute him. *Under Fire* (1983, Orion).

Ugliness

see also APPEARANCES, BEAUTY

10479 "Feast your eyes, glut your soul on my accursed ugliness." It is the title card after Mary Philbin snatches the mask from the face of horribly deformed **Lon Chaney, Sr**. *The Phantom of the Opera* (1925, silent, Universal).

10480 "Maybe if a man looks ugly, he does ugly things." Killer **Boris Karloff** begs surgeon Bela Lugosi to transform his appearance. He hopes his behavior will improve after plastic surgery. It is a premise that has been explored often in movies. *The Raven* (1935, Universal).

10481 "I was born ugly! Do you know how an ugly woman feels? Do you know what it is to be ugly all your life and feel in here that you are beautiful?" **Katina Paxinou** points to her head and heart as she asks her question. *For Whom the Bell Tolls* (1943, Paramount).

10482 "It was so ugly." **Judy Garland** finds her quick wedding ceremony to soldier Robert Walker, performed by a justice of the peace, not the thing young girls dream of. *The Clock* (1945, MGM).

10483 "How can an ugly man be so handsome?" **Marta Toren** asks an on target question about the appeal of Humphrey Bogart. *Sirocco* (1951, Columbia).

10484 "I'm just a fat little man. A fat ugly man. . . I'm ugly, I'm ugly, I'm ugly!" It's heartbreaking to see **Ernest Borgnine** speak of his appearance with bitter self-realization. *Marty* (1955, United Artists).

10485 "Most of them are ugly." **Paul Newman** snaps at Sally Field who asks him if he's ever heard of "women's liberation." *Absence of Malice* (1981, Columbia).

10486 "For the first time in my life, I've found something uglier than me." Seventeen-year-old **Keith Gordon** immediately falls in love with a red and white 1958 Plymouth Fury. *Christine* (1983, Columbia).

10487 "She was pale as something that had crawled out of a rotting log; her hair was quite gruesome, long and stringy and white as if she was very old; she was very big—you'd have to dig the whole day to find enough food to feed her." Nomadic bushman **N!xau**'s thoughts, as revealed by the narrator, upon seeing Sandra Prinsloo, who he feels is "the ugliest person" he's seen in his life. The audience sees a beautiful, shapely woman down to her skimpy bra and panties. Beauty is relative. *The Gods Must Be Crazy* (1984, South Africa, Momosa-CAT).

10488 "You've got the ugliest smile this side of creation." **Leonard Jackson** insults his stepdaughter Desreta Jackson, as the young Celie. *The Color Purple* (1985, Warner Bros).

10489 "Cecil doesn't mean to be uncivil. . . . He once explained, 'it's ugly things that upset him'—he's not uncivil to people." **Helena Bonham Carter** half-heartedly defends her uncivil fiancé Daniel Day-Lewis to her mother. *A Room with a View* (1985, GB, Merchant-Ivory-Goldcrest).

10490 "Look around you, Charlie, this place is a toilet." **Harrison Ford** tells his son River Phoenix that he's appalled at the ugliness as they drive down a fast-food-filled freeway. *The Mosquito Coast* (1986, Warner Bros.).

10491 "I look at it this way. I'll never have to see the ugliness of poverty or war or the Chevrolet Nova." Blind **Phoebe Legere** makes the best of things as she is befriended by Toxie (played by both Ron Fazio and John Altamura) who calls her his "beautiful blind buxom bimbo." *The Toxic Avenger Part III: The Last Temptation of Toxie* (1989, Troma).

Unconsciousness

see also SLEEP

10492 "Glory, baby—Glory!. . . Oh, God, don't let her die. She's wicked but I love her." Kentucky rube **Norman Foster** accidentally knocks out his wife, temperamental radio star Ginger Rogers, who has married him as a publicity stunt. *Professional Sweetheart* (1933, RKO).

10493 "I caught the blackjack right behind my ear. A black pool opened up at my feet. I dived in. It had no bottom." It's **Dick Powell**'s colorful way of describing being knocked unconscious. *Murder, My Sweet* (1945, RKO).

10494 "Wake up, little boy, I want you to see it coming." **Raymond Burr** revives Robert Mitchum, who he's been whipping with a belt, by pointing a gun between Mitchum's eyes. *His Kind of Woman* (1951, RKO).

Understandings and Misunderstandings

see also INTELLIGENCE, KNOWLEDGE, MINDS, SENSE AND SENSIBILITY, SYMPATHY, WISDOM

10495 "Oh, I think anybody's a sucker to tie up with those installment terms. Five years is too long. I pay cash for everything." Swelled-head boxer **James Cagney** attends a white-tie party where one of the guests asks his opinion of Russia's latest five-year plan. *Winner Take All* (1932, Warner Bros.).

10496 "Am I making myself clear now?" All the men watching **Mae West**'s shimmy understand her message. *I'm No Angel* (1933, Paramount).

10497 OTIS P. DRIFTWOOD: "That's what they call a sanity clause." FIORELLO: "You can't fool me. There ain't no Sanity Claus." Fast-talking promoter **Groucho Marx** negotiates a contract for opera singer Allan Jones with everybody's fool **Chico Marx**. *A Night at the Opera* (1935, MGM).

10498 "What do you mean illiterate? My mother and father were married at city hall." One of William Powell's underworld friends, **Joe Caits**, is a few letters off in his understanding of what he is called. *After the Thin Man* (1936, MGM).

10499 "I'm going to someone who understands me. I'm going to Dr. Hackenbush! Why, I never knew there was anything the matter with me until I met him!" Hypochondriac **Margaret Dumont** is indignant when the doctors at a sanitarium refuse to find anything wrong with her. Horse doctor Groucho Marx is happy to oblige her. *A Day at the Races* (1937, MGM).

10500 "They'll get to understand you after awhile." **Andrea Leeds**, a better actress who didn't get the part, wishes Katharine Hepburn well and assures her that the other girls at the theatrical boarding house will get over their dislike for Kate. The latter doesn't know that her father's money won her the part, nor that Leeds is about to take her own life in despair. *Stage Door* (1937, RKO).

10501 VAN DOON: "Won't you sit down?" PEACHES O'DAY: "What for? I ain't tired." VAN DOON (OFFERING HIS ARM)**:** "My arm." PEACHES: "What's the matter with it?" Gentlemen like **Charles Winninger** don't generally run in **Mae West**'s circle of acquaintances. She does not understand his consideration. *Every Day's a Holiday* (1938, Paramount).

10502 MICKEY MORAN: "Would you punch me right in the nose if I asked you to understudy?" PATSY BARTON: "Katharine Cornell did it. I would be proud." We wonder if the real **Judy Garland** would be so noble and understanding if **Mickey Rooney** gave her part to June Preisser. *Babes in Arms* (1939, MGM).

10503 "You've lived in dirt so long you can't understand anything else and you're jealous of something you can't understand." **Vivien Leigh** shouts at drunken Clark Gable in their dining room after Leslie Howard's birthday party. *Gone with the Wind* (1939, Selznick-MGM).

10504 "Oh, my goodness, I'm losing my finesse. If I don't watch out, everyone will understand me." Grand Duchess **Ina Claire** makes it very clear how she feels about Russian communist special emissary Greta Garbo. *Ninotchka* (1939, MGM).

10505 "I understand we understand each other." Spy magazine publisher **Henry Daniell** says it without saying it, that to protect the reputation of his ex-in-laws, Cary Grant has arranged to have reporter James Stewart and photographer Ruth Hussey cover the wedding of Grant's ex-wife Katharine Hepburn to stuffed-shirt John Howard. *The Philadelphia Story* (1940, MGM).

10506 "No, Candy Man. Now, for understanding you so well, what do I get?" **Lana Turner** takes back her reformed con artist husband Clark Gable. *Honky Tonk* (1941, MGM).

10507 "Can a nation that belches understand a nation that sings?" Happy-go-lucky Italian General

Fortunio Bonanova scornfully dismisses the Germans. *Five Graves to Cairo* (1943, Paramount).

10508 "You want him dead, don't you?" Suddenly understanding, insurance salesman **Fred MacMurray** gives words to the thought Barbara Stanwyck has about her husband Tom Powers. *Double Indemnity* (1944, Paramount).

10509 LANGUAGE COACH: "Can you name the consonants?" ALFRED MANFIELD: "Yes, sir: North America, South America and Patterson, New Jersey!" Old-time burlesque comic **Sid Fields** stands in for Bud Abbott in asking always confused **Lou Costello** a question he doesn't understand. *In Society* (1944, Universal).

10510 "I don't understand any of it. I don't understand people hurting each other and killing each other. I just don't understand it." When nurse **Mary Anderson** is asked by seaman John Hodiak what she is doing in uniform during World War II if she feels that way, she replies, "I'm doing the only thing I can, trying to put the wounded together again if they get hurt." *Lifeboat* (1944, 20th Century-Fox).

10511 "You mustn't think too harshly of my secretaries. They were kind and understanding when I came to the office after a hard day at home." Since his wife Bette Davis does not care for him, businessman **Claude Rains** has had numerous affairs with secretaries in his office. *Mr. Skeffington* (1944, Warner Bros.).

10512 PHILIP MARLOWE: "I don't get it." JULES AMTHOR: "You mean there are some things you do not understand. I've always credited the private detective with a high degree of omniscience. Or is that true only in rental fiction?" Private eye **Dick Powell** is sneered at by sinister **Otto Kruger**. *Murder, My Sweet* (1944, RKO).

10513 "I shall try to transplant a segment of the brain of a present day man into the skull of that prehistoric creature, endowing him with just enough understanding to make him obey my orders." Mad scientist **Bela Lugosi** uses the brain of unwilling John Carradine for his experiment. *Return of the Ape Man* (1944, Monogram).

10514 "I get it." Detective **Roland Young** figures out the mystery of the "Ten Little Indian" murders on a deserted island just a moment before he becomes the next victim. *And Then There Were None* (1945, Popular Pictures).

10515 "If I live to be a hundred, I shall never understand how any young man can come to Paris without evening clothes." Wealthy dilettante **Clifton Webb** is shocked at Tyrone Power's unpreparedness. *The Razor's Edge* (1946, 20th Century-Fox).

10516 "How do you get to be a geek? I can't understand how anybody can get so low." By the end of the picture, **Tyrone Power** will understand how a man can fall so low that he's willing to take the job of a side-show performer who engages in bizarre and disgusting acts such as biting the heads off live chickens. *Nightmare Alley* (1947, 20th Century-Fox).

10517 CLIENT: "I want you to help me.... Some men are following me." SAM GRUNION: "Really, I can't understand why!" In a small walk-on, **Marilyn Monroe** seeks protection from private eye **Groucho Marx**. *Love Happy* (1949, United Artists).

10518 PROF. BARNABY FULTON: "My, you're here early this morning." LOIS LAUREL: "Mr. Oxley complained about my punctuation, so I made sure I got here before nine." Chemist **Cary Grant** finds that sexy secretary **Marilyn Monroe** has vocabulary problems, but at least she's anxious to please her boss Charles Coburn. *Monkey Business* (1952, 20th Century-Fox).

10519 "I have loved with all my heart 100 women I never want to see again—and he's still after this one. It escapes me." **Anthony Quinn** doesn't understand his brother Marlon Brando's devotion to Jean Peters. *Viva Zapata!* (1952, 20th Century-Fox).

10520 "Yes, you understand. You're real bright. Well, see if you can understand this. I'm in love with Jeff and he walked out on me. You know why? Because I wanted him to kill you and he couldn't. You never knew me, you never bothered to figure me out. Well, I'm gonna tell you something. Owens did have something to do with me, but it was because I wanted him to. I wanted that big house he lived in. I wanted him to get rid of that wife of his. But he wasn't quite the fool you are. He knew what I was after. And you know what, I admired him for it. If I'd been a man, I'd of behaved exactly as he did. Now get out of here and let me unpack." In their train compartment, **Gloria Grahame** tells her hot-tempered husband Broderick Crawford about her sexual liaison with Glenn Ford, who she tried to get to kill Crawford. She also throws in his face her interest in Grandon Rhodes. Enraged, Crawford kills Grahame. *Human Desire* (1954, Columbia).

10521 "Why do you want to understand? The most beautiful things in life are things we don't understand." Married Italian **Rossano Brazzi** doesn't want American spinster Katharine Hepburn to intellectualize their love affair. *Summertime* (1955, Korda-Lopert).

10522 NOAH CULLEN: "Thanks for pulling me out." JOKER JACKSON: "Man, I didn't pull you out. I stopped you from pulling me in." Handcuffed together, escaped black prisoner **Sidney Poitier** falls into a stream, and red-necked **Tony Curtis** had no choice but to rescue him. *The Defiant Ones* (1958, United Artists).

10523 "I understand very well what he wants. Tell him I'm a married woman, that my husband is a great big official in the government, ready and willing to knock out all those pretty front teeth of his." **Janet Leigh** reacts to a young Mexican punk who has accosted her, using an old man as an interpreter. *Touch of Evil* (1958, Universal-International).

10524 "As many times as I'll be married, I'll never understand women." Millionaire **Tony Randall** loves and marries 'em, but doesn't understand 'em. *Pillow Talk* (1959, Universal).

10525 "I'll see you around, and if you don't say hello, I'll understand." Pretending that she doesn't care, **Gina Lollobrigida** breaks off her relationship with Tony Franciosa when she realizes that he can never forget her sordid past as a high paid prostitute. *Go Naked in the World* (1960, MGM).

10526 "You misunderstand me. I'm a civilian. I'm even more a civilian than most civilians." Cringing **Peter Ustinov** wants no part of a battle between escaped slaves and Roman soldiers. *Spartacus* (1960, Universal).

10527 "Did it ever occur to you that I don't understand you? You think of me as a child, as some kind of extension of yourself, but I'm me, Dad, myself. What am I gonna do? What am I gonna be? I'm going to be me, Dad!" Mama's boy **Richard Beymer** stands up to his intolerant businessman father Jack Hawkins. *Five Finger Exercise* (1962, Columbia).

10528 "I'm your Aryan and you're my Jewess. . . . Understand?" Carpenter **Josef Kroner** has been made the Aryan controller of Jewish shopkeeper Ida Kaminska by the Nazis occupying their Eastern European village. *The Shop on Main Street* (1965, Czech, Barrandov-Prominent).

10529 "My understanding of women goes only as far as the pleasure." Cockney Lothario **Michael Caine** has limited interest in women. *Alfie* (1966, GB, Paramount).

10530 "He told me he was a gynecologist. He couldn't speak any foreign languages. Who was he kidding?" **Louise Lasser** is interviewed about former boy friend, professional thief Woody Allen. *Take the Money and Run* (1969, Palomar).

10531 "I can understand her wanting to leave, but I can't understand her leaving." **Bea Arthur** is from a generation of wives that didn't divorce or leave their husbands no matter how bad the marriage was. Part of the reason was that they had no place to go and no prospects. *Lovers and Other Strangers* (1970, ABC-Cinerama).

10532 "Dames are simple. I never met one that didn't understand a slap in the mouth or a slug from a forty-five." **Jerry Lacy**, as the macho spirit of Humphrey Bogart, advises Woody Allen to treat women roughly. *Play It Again, Sam* (1972, Paramount).

10533 "I understand you want to marry my wife." **Laurence Olivier** gets right to the heart of the matter as he welcomes his visitor Michael Caine, his wife's lover. *Sleuth* (1972, GB, Palomar).

10534 MARIE: "I'm a cosmetologist." NAVIN JOHNSON: "It must be tough to handle weightlessness." The precise nature of **Bernadette Peters'** occupation escapes **Steve Martin**. *The Jerk* (1979, Universal).

10535 "No one can really understand what happens between a man and a woman—we communicate silently, like cockroaches have for 50 million years." **Hal Holbrook** has grown tired of his wife Louise Fletcher. *Natural Enemies* (1979, Cinema 5).

10536 "Why should I be gay? I'm miserable. I just lost my job." After spending twenty-five years in prison for train robbery, **Kirk Douglas** wanders into the wrong bar and misunderstands the suggestion that he's "gay." *Tough Guys* (1986, Touchstone-Buena Vista).

10537 "I have an IQ in the triple digits: what word do you think I didn't understand?" **Sean Young** replies testily to William Petersen who insistently asks if she understands when he insists she can't tell anyone about their affair. *Cousins* (1989, Paramount).

10538 "Naturally when Mr. Lewis leaves, I won't see you in this hotel again. I assume you have no other uncles here. . . Good, we understand each other. I also encourage you to dress a little more appropriately. . . ." Regent Beverly Wilshire Hotel manager **Hector Elizondo** accepts hooker Julia Roberts as Richard Gere's niece for the duration of his stay at the hotel only. *Pretty Woman* (1990, Touchstone-Buena Vista).

Underwear *see* CLOTHES

Unfairness *see* FAIRNESS AND UNFAIRNESS

Unhappiness *see* HAPPINESS AND UNHAPPINESS

Unions

see also WORK AND WORKERS

10539 "We've got men here who can break into a muck sweat merely by standing still." Management type **Terry-Thomas** complains about the do-nothing union workers. *I'm All Right, Jack* (1959, GB, British Lion).

10540 "Stone Mountain doesn't move one piece of coal unless it's a union man who moves it." Union organizer **Chris Cooper** shouts defiance, as the Italian and the black miners brought into West Virginia to be scabs join the union and the strike. *Matewan* (1987, Cinecom).

Uniqueness

see also EQUALITIES, INDIVIDUALISM, ORIGINALITY

10541 "Am I the only guy in the world that eats peanuts?" **Spencer Tracy** is baffled when he becomes a suspect in a murder because, like the murderer, he eats peanuts. *Fury* (1936, MGM).

10542 "Dr. Hackenbush tells me I'm the only case in history. I have high blood pressure on my right side and low blood pressure on my left side." Hypochondriac **Margaret Dumont** bursts with pride as she shares quack Groucho Marx's diagnosis. *A Day at the Races* (1937, MGM).

10543 "You're the one man in my life—right now." **Mae West** tells a masked bandit of his uniqueness, at least until someone better comes along. *My Little Chickadee* (1940, Universal).

10544 "I never knew it could be like this. Nobody ever kissed me the way you do." **Deborah Kerr**, who seeks to escape from her unhappiness in various meaningless sexual couplings, is thrilled by Burt Lancaster as they come up for air after their famous kiss in the surf. *From Here to Eternity* (1953, Columbia).

10545 "Only Capone kills like that." **Ralph Meeker**, as Bugs Moran, expresses his opinion as to who gave the orders for the slaughter of Moran's men in a north Chicago garage. *The St. Valentine's Day Massacre* (1967, 20th Century-Fox).

10546 "[You are] the only man in the world with clenched hair." **Walter Matthau** affectionately takes note of hypochondriac Jack Lemmon's tenseness. *The Odd Couple* (1968, Paramount).

10547 "Two things that come once in a lifetime." According to **Woody Allen**, they are sex and death. *Sleeper* (1973, United Artists).

10548 "You know, Tom, you are the only man I know that ignores the fact that the future becomes the present, the present the past, and the past turns into everlasting regret unless you plan for it." **Joanne Woodward** takes her son John Malkovich to task for his aimlessness. *The Glass Menagerie* (1987, Cineplex-Odeon).

United States *see* AMERICA AND AMERICANS

Unkindness *see* CRUELTY, KINDNESS

Universe

see also EXISTENCE, HEAVEN, MEN AND WOMEN, WORLD

10549 "It is this, or that—all the universe, or nothing. Which shall it be, Passworthy? Which shall it be?" It is **Raymond Massey**'s question of Edward Chapman when the former's daughter and the latter's son volunteer to be the first to travel to the moon to find man's true destiny in the vastness of outer space. *Things to Come* (1936, GB, London Films-United Artists).

10550 "[The universe] is all random, radiating aimlessly out of nothing and eventually vanishing forever. The universe, all space, all time, it's just a temporary convulsion. And I get paid to prove it." Physicist **Jack Warden** describes his profession. *September* (1987, Orion).

10551 "Our universe is vast, full of wonders. We'll explore, find strange new worlds, together." Having escaped from a prison galley spaceship, where they were serving a life sentence, beautiful **Elizabeth Cayton** and Cindy Beal have many dangerous adventures. *Slave Girls from Beyond Infinity* (1987, Urban Classics).

10552 "It is only we, with our capacity to love, that give meaning to the indifferent universe." **Martin Bergmann**, as Professor Louis Levy, tries to make sense out of a senseless world. *Crimes and Misdemeanors* (1989, Orion).

Unknowns

see also KNOWLEDGE, STRANGENESS AND STRANGERS, UNDERSTANDINGS AND MISUNDERSTANDINGS

10553 "I can't wait any longer. We shall go to Devon for our honeymoon and live on love and strawberries and the sight of the sea. . . . Oh, I love you so seriously, so seriously that it frightens me. You've opened a gate for me into another world. Before that, my work was everything. I was drawn to the mysteries of science, to the unknown. But now the unknown wears your face, looks back at me with your eyes." **Fredric March**'s pretty speech to his fiancée Rose Hobart suggests that if they were not forced to put off their marriage, he might not have experimented with the drug that brought forth the evil Mr. Hyde. *Dr. Jekyll and Mr. Hyde* (1932, Paramount).

10554 "Throughout the ages the heavens have unleashed their fury to make man tremble in the presence of the unknown. And as man has witnessed the power of nature's elements, so have some men sought desperately in this infinite ground on which they walk, the earth that will bury them remains to mock their existence." **Vincent Price** narrates the beginning of the "Dr. Heidegger's Experiment" segment. *Twice Told Tales* (1963, United Artists).

10555 "There is little one can do to prepare for the unknown." It is **Natasha Richardson**, as Patty Hearst, in voice-over as she and her then boyfriend Scott Kraft sit in their Berkeley apartment, from which she is about to be kidnapped by the Symbionese Liberation Army. *Patty Hearst* (1988, Atlantic).

10556 "No, I didn't, and I didn't know Shakespeare or Chaucer either." Name-dropper **Joan Plowright** snaps when one of her young companions asks if she knew Keats. *Enchanted April* (1992, GB, Miramax).

10557 "You won't be able to mention the name of a single person I know." Socialite **Polly Walker** is in need of respite from the attentions of male admirers. *Enchanted April* (1992, GB, Miramax).

Upsets and Upsetting *see* DEFEATS, DISTURBANCES

Uses and Using

see also ADVANTAGES, GOALS, HABITS, PRACTICES, PURPOSES, RITUALS, SERVICES, TREATS AND TREATMENTS

10558 "I love you, I worship you, I am used to you." **Robert Montgomery** gets to the bottom line as to why he would marry Carole Lombard again. *Mr. & Mrs. Smith* (1941, RKO).

10559 "Is that what love is? Using people? And maybe that's what hate is—not being able to use people." **Elizabeth Taylor** formulates a conclusion about love, based on her experience with her relatives who profess to love her, but really are only interested in using her. *Suddenly, Last Summer* (1959, Columbia).

10560 "They used me as you would use a woman." **Sal Mineo** confesses to Jewish terrorist leader David Opatoshu how he survived the Nazi death camps. *Exodus* (1960, United Artists).

10561 "It has fifty-eight functions. Fifty-nine if you want to light a cigarette." Secret agent **James Coburn** displays a gadgety cigarette lighter. *Our Man Flint* (1965, 20th Century-Fox).

10562 "I feel like a one-night stand." **Ryan O'Neal** feels used and complains when Barbra Streisand turns down his marriage proposal. *The Main Event* (1979, Warner Bros.).

10563 "By now we'd come to look at our replacements as dead men, and we temporarily had the use of their arms and legs." Narrator **Robert Carradine** has little hope that he, the other experienced foot-soldiers with whom he wars, or their replacements for the dead, will survive. *The Big Red One* (1980, United Artists).

10564 "They've used everybody else all up. They got to get around to guys like you and me sooner or later." **Willie Nelson** explains to his lead picker Slim Pickens how he became a nationwide super star after all these years. *Honeysuckle Rose* (1980, Warner Bros.).

10565 "Everybody's trying to get me, somebody with no face, and they're using you as a go-fer." Angry **Paul Newman** is correct. Federal investigator Bob Balaban uses naïve reporter Sally Field to nail Newman as someone who knows what's happened to a labor leader who's disappeared. *Absence of Malice* (1981, Columbia).

10566 "The most used piece of equipment in the gym." It's **Robin Samuel**'s cruel description of promiscuous health club devotee Laraine Newman who will sleep with anyone because no one will love her. *Perfect* (1985, Columbia).

10567 "Macon, are you really doing this? You mean to tell me you can just use a person up and move on—You think I'm some kind of bottle of something you don't need anymore. Is that the way you see me, Macon?" At least at the moment **Geena Davis** has correctly figured out William Hurt. He'd rather leave her than turn up his level of involvement with her. *The Accidental Tourist* (1988, Warner Bros.).

10568 CHARLES BABBITT: "Am I using you, Raymond?" RAYMOND BABBITT: "Yes." **Tom Cruise** doesn't know if his autistic brother **Dustin Hoffman** is responding to the current question or something earlier. *Rain Man* (1988, United Artists).

10569 "Well, I'm not trying to land him, I'm just using him for sex." **Julia Roberts** has a doubly-meaningful reply to a catty woman at a polo match, who refers to the former as Richard Gere's "flavor of the month," claiming all the girls are trying to land Gere. *Pretty Woman* (1990, Touchstone-Buena Vista).

10570 "Could it be we have both outlived our usefulness by being too inflexible?" Analytical as ever, **Leonard Nimoy**, as Mr. Spock, questions William Shatner as Admiral Kirk. *Star Trek VI: The Undiscovered Country* (1991, Paramount).

Vacations

see also PLEASURE, WORK

10571 "There are no crazy people here, we're all on vacation." Grinning shrink **Donald Pleasence** justifies his unusual therapy methods with dangerous mental patients. *Alone in the Dark* (1982, New Line Cinema).

10572 "Vacations are always a surprise—just like virgins." **Michael Caine** will be surprised by both in Rio de Janeiro. *Blame It on Rio* (1984, 20th Century-Fox).

10573 "I need a vacation." Things have been tough on **Arnold Schwarzenegger**. *Terminator 2: Judgment Day* (1991, Tri-Star).

10574 "How do you like your vacation so far?" **Susan Sarandon** asks good buddy Geena Davis. Why, the good times have barely begun. *Thelma & Louise* (1991, Pathe Entertainment-MGM).

Values *see* WORTH AND VALUES

Vampires

see also ANIMALS, BLOOD, DEATH AND DYING, MONSTERS, SEDUCTIONS, SEX AND SEXUALITY

10575 "How do you kill something already dead, or 'undead'?" **David Manners** puts the question to vampire hunter Edward Van Sloan about title character Bela Lugosi. *Dracula* (1931, Universal).

10576 "There just isn't room for two doctors and two vampires in one small town. . . ." Impeccable physician and bloodsucker **Max Adrian** arranges to be rid of his rivals, American doctor Donald Sutherland and the latter's vampire wife Jennifer Jayne. *Dr. Terror's House of Horrors* (1964, GB, Regal Films).

10577 "Hoi, have you got the wrong vampire!" Jewish vampire **Alfie Bass** scoffs at a potential victim trying to hold him off with a crucifix. *The Fearless Vampire Killers, or Pardon Me, Your Teeth Are in My Neck* (1967, GB, MGM).

10578 "Aw, man, you're jivin' me! Look, man, I don't mind bein' a vampire an' shit, but this really ain't hip." Super-cool ghetto youth **Don Mitchell** awakens vampire William Marshall from his eternal rest with a voodoo ceremony. Marshall sinks his fangs in the youth's neck, making him an apprentice vampire. *Scream, Blacula, Scream!* (1973, AIP).

10579 "The kids today don't have the patience for vampires. They want to see some weird slasher running around and chopping off heads." Host of a TV horror show **Roddy McDowall**, an avowed vampire killer, has a legitimate gripe. *Fright Night* (1985, Columbia).

10580 "Being a vampire in the 20th century is a nightmare." **Lauren Hutton**, a 390-year-old vampire, needs the blood of virgin males to maintain her good looks—but male virgins in L.A. are hard to come by. *Once Bitten* (1985, Goldwyn).

10581 "I don't want to be a vampire—I'm a day person." Teenager **Jim Carrey** would like to forego the honor offered him by beautiful vampiress Lauren Hutton, who needs the blood of a virgin male to keep a youthful appearance. *Once Bitten* (1985, Goldwyn).

10582 "One thing about living in Santa Clara I never could stomach was all the damn vampires." Grandpa **Barnard Hughes** refers to the gang of teenage vampire bikers, led by Kiefer Sutherland. *The Lost Boys* (1987, Warner Bros.).

10583 "There's worse things than being a vampire." Vampire mentor **Rene Auberjonois** encourages Robert Sean Leonard who has been bitten by a hot lady vamp and is beginning to notice some changes. *My Best Friend Is a Vampire* (1988, Kings Road).

10584 "I can't believe I'm in a graveyard hunting for vampires with a strange man—on a school night." Bubble-headed high school cheerleader **Kristy Swanson** and her cosmic coach Donald Sutherland are indeed in a graveyard looking for vampires—and on a school night. *Buffy, the Vampire Slayer* (1992, 20th Century-Fox).

Vanities

see also BOASTS AND BRAGGING, CONCEIT, EGOS AND EGOTISM, PRETENSIONS, SELF, VIRTUES

10585 "You're always mistaking your vanity for love." Femme fatale **Marlene Dietrich** accuses Lionel Atwill, one of her many "admirers." *The Devil Is a Woman* (1935, Paramount).

10586 "Vanities of vanities, all is vanity." So says **Charles Laughton** as Dutch painter Rembrandt Harmenszoon van Rijn with the film's last line. *Rembrandt* (1936, GB, London Films-United Artists).

10587 NINOTCHKA: "You see, it would have been very embarrassing for people of my sort to wear low-cut gowns in old Russia. The lashes of the Cossacks across our back were not very becoming, and you know how vain women are." GRAND DUCHESS SWANA: "Yes, you're quite right about the Cossacks. We made a great mistake when we let them use the whips. They had such reliable guns." It's a duel of bitter Russian cattiness between communist special envoy **Greta Garbo**, dressed attractively in a modest outfit, and exiled aristocrat **Ina Claire**, elegantly gowned. *Ninotchka* (1939, MGM)

10588 "Perhaps it offends my vanity to have anyone remotely my wife remarrying so obviously beneath her." **Cary Grant** states the reason he objects to his ex-wife Katharine Hepburn's marrying John Howard. *The Philadelphia Story* (1940, MGM).

10589 "Is it faith or just habit that compels a woman to put on fresh makeup before boarding a life raft?" Bitter nuclear scientist **Paul Kelly** expresses amazement that her appearance would still matter to shady lady Jan Sterling when their plane is in danger of going down over water. *The High and the Mighty* (1954, Warner Bros.).

Vegetables and Vegetarians

see also FOOD AND EATING

10590 "An intelligent carrot—the mind boggles." Reporter **Douglas Spencer** discovers that space alien James Arness is neither animal nor mineral. *The Thing* (1951, RKO).

10591 "Boil it. Boil it, stew it, bake it, fry it." **Margaret Sheridan** makes some culinary suggestions for getting rid of vegetable alien James Arness. *The Thing* (1951, RKO).

10592 GEORGE FIELDS: "You played a tomato for 30 seconds [in a television commercial]. They went a half day over schedule because you wouldn't sit down." MICHAEL DORSEY: "Yes, it wasn't logical." FIELDS: "You were a tomato. A tomato doesn't have logic. A tomato can't move." DORSEY: "If he can't move, how's he gonna sit down, George? I was a stand-up tomato, a juicy, sexy beefsteak tomato. Nobody else does vegetables like me. I did an evening of vegetables Off Broadway. I did the best tomato, the best cucumber. I did an endive salad that knocked the critics on their ass." Director **Sydney Pollack** appears as **Dustin Hoffman**'s agent as the latter spoofs method acting. *Tootsie* (1982, Columbia).

Vices

see also BADNESS, CRIMES AND CRIMINALS, IMMORALITY, SINS AND SINNERS, VIRTUES, WRONGS AND WRONGDOINGS

10593 "One way or another we all pay for our vices." Criminal mastermind **Sam Jaffe** has a deep sense of reality. *The Asphalt Jungle* (1950, MGM).

10594 MARIANNE: "What vices may a woman have?" ISAK: "Crying, bearing children, and gossiping about the neighbors." **Ingrid Thulin** is told by her elderly father-in-law **Victor Sjostrom** that she should not smoke because it is a vice for men only. *Wild Strawberries* (1957, Sweden, Svensk Filmindustri).

10595 "I'd rather have 50 unnatural vices than one unnatural virtue." Title character **Robert Morley** mockingly provokes a Victorian jury into finding him guilty of degeneracy. *Oscar Wilde* (1959, GB, Vantage).

10596 "It's my vocation, my vice." **John Hurt**, as Dr. Stephen Ward, tells Joanne Whalley-Kilmer as Christine Keeler, that she doesn't have to sleep with him to repay him for making her over and introducing her to wealthy and influential men. *Scandal* (1989, GB, Miramax).

Viciousness

see also CORRUPTION, CRUELTY, FAULTS, HARM, HURT AND HURTING

10597 "Rocks is a magnificent specimen of pure viciousness." Criminologist turned criminal mastermind **Edward G. Robinson** admires Humphrey Bogart, a mug who refuses to submit to Robinson's leadership. *The Amazing Dr. Clitterhouse* (1938, Warner Bros.).

10598 "These things are vicious: They've cut out our phone, they've cut out our power, it's only a matter of time till they get in here." In a moment dripping with drama and anticipation, farmer **Billy Green Bush** is trite. *Critters* (1986, New Line).

Victims

see also DEATH AND DYING, KILLINGS, LOSSES AND LOSING, SACRIFICES, SUFFERING AND SUFFERERS, TORTURES, TRICKS AND TRICKERY

10599 "Think how many times the lady with the camellias has lured her admirers on to become the victims of her seductive wiles!" It's a dialogue card in the story of the famous courtesan, played by Alla Nazimova, with Rudolph Valentino one of her victims. *Camille* (1921, silent, Metro).

10600 "I stayed at a hotel called the Tarantula Arms. . . . That's where I brought my victims." **Vivien Leigh** teases her brother-in-law Marlon Brando who says she's probably had countless young lovers. *A Streetcar Named Desire* (1951, Warner Bros.-20th Century-Fox).

10601 SHERMAN MCCOY: "Why me? Why was I singled out?" PETER FALLOW: "You're just lunch—and next week they're not gonna remember what they ate." **Tom Hanks** can't understand why the media and the public have made a circus of his misfortunes, but writer **Bruce Willis** understands. *The Bonfire of the Vanities* (1990, Columbia).

10602 "All victims are equal. . . none is more equal than others." British publisher **Sean Connery** holds forth with a group of Russian writers. *The Russia House* (1990, MGM-United Artists).

Victories

see also BATTLES AND BATTLEFIELDS, DEFEATS, ENEMIES, MILITARY, STRUGGLES, WARS, WINNERS AND LOSERS

10603 "Nothing can hurt us now. What we have can't be destroyed. That's our victory. Our victory over the dark." Even though she's dying of a brain tumor, former good-time society girl **Bette Davis** knows that her love shared with George Brent has made her life worthwhile. *Dark Victory* (1939, Warner Bros.).

10604 "We proved we can lick them. We showed them that they couldn't take the valley." After a hard-fought battle, militia man **Henry Fonda** is proud of their victory. *Drums Along the Mohawk* (1939, 20th Century-Fox).

10605 BRICK POLLITT: "What is the victory of a cat on a hot tin roof?" MAGGIE THE CAT: "Just staying on, I guess." It's an exchange between **Paul Newman** and his wife **Elizabeth Taylor** that gives the title to the Tennessee Williams play. *Cat on a Hot Tin Roof* (1958, MGM).

10606 "The Führer leads us from victory to victory. And each victory leads us further away from home. A few more such victories and we may never return." Hypochondriac German officer **Marius Goring** carefully complains about the war to Gestapo Chief Stanley Baker. *The Angry Hills* (1959, MGM).

10607 "Pork Chop Hill was held—bought and paid for at the same price we commemorate in monuments at Bunker Hill and Gettysburg. Yet you will find no monuments on Pork Chop Hill. Victory is a fragile thing and history does not linger long in our century. Pork Chop Hill is in North Korea now—but those who fought there know for what they died, and the meaning of it." In voice-over at the end of the film, Lieutenant **Gregory Peck** lectures the audience with a pretty speech. Too bad, that his words about an actual U.S. military event is nothing more than so much patriotic rhetoric that survivors always say about the unfortunate dead. *Pork Chop Hill* (1959, United Artists).

10608 "The room's a wreck, but her napkin is folded." **Anne Bancroft**, as Annie Sullivan, savors her victory. She has spent an entire afternoon of face-slapping, screaming, scratching and kicking, at the end of which Patty Duke, as young blind, deaf and mute Helen Keller, is finally taught some table manners. *The Miracle Worker* (1962, MGM).

10609 LYDIA: "I think the two of us are defeated in advance." MICHEL: "All victories start that way." **Romy Schneider** has her second meeting with **Yves Montand**, whose response is more interesting than meaningful. *Clair de Femme* (1980, Fr., Atlantic).

10610 "We came, we saw, we kicked ass." Parapsychologist **Bill Murray** enjoys the moment after vanquishing a powerful spirit. *Ghostbusters* (1984, Columbia).

Villains *see* BADNESS, EVILNESS, FICTION, HATE AND HATRED, HEROES, VICIOUSNESS

Violence

see also FORCE, KILLINGS, POWER, REBELLIONS, WARS, WRONGS AND WRONGDOINGS

10611 "Swordplay is such a violent business." **Tyrone Power** reinforces his image as a foppish sissy to hide his identity as the avenging Zorro. *The Mark of Zorro* (1940, 20th Century-Fox).

10612 "I hope she doesn't get too violent. I don't have the strength to knock her off the train." **W.C. Fields** refers to Margaret Hamilton in an aside to the audience. Hamilton is terribly upset by the appearance of shady lady Mae West. *My Little Chickadee* (1940, Universal).

10613 "I am not a violent man, Mr. Spade, but if you do not give me the black bird, I shall be compelled to murder you without mercy." Whiny **Peter Lorre** threatens private eye Humphrey Bogart. *The Maltese Falcon* (1941, Warner Bros.).

10614 "I tremble at the thought of such violence." Private eye **Dick Powell** responds when a new client, effeminate Douglas Walton, described by the elevator operator as "nice smelling," threatens to punch Powell in the nose. *Murder, My Sweet* (1945, RKO).

10615 "Women are weak. They have no place in society. You don't understand the criminal's need for violence." Hired assassin **Robert Keith** explains himself to a female hostage. *The Lineup* (1958, Columbia).

10616 "With you, living with violence is a way of life, living with violence and death." **Jacqueline Bisset** supposes that violence and death are old hat for San Francisco police detective Steve McQueen. *Bullitt* (1968, Warner Bros.).

10617 "I don't like violence, Tom. I'm a businessman. Murder's a big expense." Mobster **Al Lettieri** wants to make peace with consigliere Robert Duvall, shortly after having Duvall's boss Marlon Brando gunned down. *The Godfather* (1972, Paramount).

10618 "I've always noticed, it's you rich, soft, pampered people who are so in love with violence. You've never experienced it. You just want to see it done." Hitman **James Coburn** has another complaint against the privileged class. *Firepower* (1979, GB, ITC Entertainment).

10619 "Violence is contagious, like measles." **Malcolm McDowell**, as H.G. Wells, makes a pronouncement and a comparison. *Time After Time* (1979, Warner Bros.-Orion).

10620 "You know what the problem with you is? You're too violent." How can **Brigitte Nielsen** say that about cop Sylvester Stallone? He only kills thirty or forty people in the movie. *Cobra* (1986, Warner Bros.).

10621 JULIUS BENEDICT: "Actually, I hate violence." VINCENT BENEDICT: "But you're so good at it." **Arnold Schwarzenegger** wants to use his strength only for good, but his conniving twin **Danny De Vito** sees other possibilities. *Twins* (1988, Universal).

10622 "That's the problem with war. Too violent!" Short-timer radio operator **Nicholas Cascone** feels safe enough to make a quip about the madness of the war in Vietnam. *84 Charlie Mopic* (1989, New Century-Vista).

10623 "You realize your history of violent assault does not make your case any easier, but I can help you." Beautiful public defender **Theresa Russell** takes the case of hard-living policeman Burt Reynolds. While on temporary suspension from the police force, he is accused of murder. *Physical Evidence* (1989, Columbia).

Virginity and Virgins

see also INNOCENCE, MEN, NATURE AND NATURAL, PURITY, SEX AND SEXUALITY, SPINSTERS, WOMEN

10624 "I'm not the kind of girl you are, but there was a time I was." Streetwalker **Margot Grahame** humbly pleads for the life of Victor McLaglen to Heather Angel. *The Informer* (1935, RKO).

10625 "Men are usually bored with virgins. I'm so glad you're not. . . . Have you a mistress?" **Maggie McNamara**'s frank talk about sex intrigues womanizer David Niven. *The Moon Is Blue* (1953, Preminger-United Artists).

10626 "Is it that obvious that it's the first time for me?" Fortyish grade school teacher **Joanne Woodward** questions James Olson, who reacts to her sexual awkwardness when they make love by saying, "It's always hard the first time." *Rachel, Rachel* (1968, Warner Bros.)

10627 "A virgin. And it's her wish that one of you gentlemen be the first." Madam **Frances Faye** offers 12-year-old Brooke Shields to the highest bidder at the bordello where the child lives with her prostitute mother Susan Sarandon. *Pretty Baby* (1978, Warner Bros.).

10628 "It's not that bad. If it were, everybody wouldn't be doing it." One deflowered 15-year-old girl encourages a reluctant virgin to try intercourse. *Little Darlings* (1980, Paramount).

10629 "I'm still a virgin. I don't know whether that's good or bad. . . . Are you?" Provocatively underdressed **Bo Derek** asks naïvely as she runs her fingers up and down the body of Miles O'Keeffe as Tarzan. *Tarzan, the Ape Man* (1981, MGM-United Artists).

10630 "I've come all this way to give you something you may not even want—my virginity." An eighties version of a fifties Doris Day-like virgin, **Bo Derek**, has trouble finding a taker of her gift, even when offering it to a romantic Valentino-like Arab sheik, Greg Bensen. *Bolero* (1984, Cannon).

10631 "The fruit is so ripe, it's ready to fall off the tree." **Bo Derek** complains that her virginity may spoil if it is not taken soon. *Bolero* (1984, Cannon).

10632 "I never bagged a babe." Fourteen-year-old promoter **Anthony Michael Hall** shares his deepest dark secret with sixteen-year-old Molly Ringwald—he is a virgin. *Sixteen Candles* (1984, Universal).

10633 "You are a wirgin, yes. . . a wirgin, uh, you not yet being with woman?. . . I like wirgins. . . It's so exciting for me to touch boy in a way no woman ever touched before. . . it's a feeling of power." **Linda Fiorentino** makes Anthony Edwards sorry that he told her he has had thirty or forty women, when in fact he is a "wirgin." *Gotcha!* (1985, Universal).

10634 "I don't have to wallow in my virginity." Fifteen-year-old **Billy Jacoby** desperately wishes to lose his virginal status. *Just One of the Guys* (1985, Columbia).

10635 "I have to marry a virgin; I can't stand criticism." **Klaus Maria Brandauer** initially rejects Meryl Streep's suggestion that they marry, because she has been his brother's lover. *Out of Africa* (1985, Miramax-Universal).

10636 "Wait a minute, Connie Swail? Don't you mean the virgin Connie Swail?" **Tom Hanks** catches on when he picks up his police detective partner Dan Aykroyd in front of Alexandra Paul's house. Until now, Aykroyd always referred to her as "The Virgin Connie Swail." *Dragnet* (1987, Universal).

10637 "You'd still be a virgin if it weren't for me!" **Jeremy Irons**, as dominant twin Elliot, seduces women and then passes them along to his shy, retiring brother Beverly, also played by Irons. *Dead Ringers* (1988, Canada, 20th Century-Fox).

10638 "I came to him a wirgin [sic]." **Margaret Sophie Stein** is insulted when Anjelica Huston suggests that Stein had probably slept with their common husband Ron Silver before they were married. *Enemies, a Love Story* (1989, 20th Century-Fox).

10639 "Were you under the impression that I was a virgin?" Movie bit player **Annette Bening** snaps at mobster Warren Beatty when he alludes to her many former lovers. *Bugsy* (1991, Tri-Star).

10640 "There's really only a few places in the Amazon that could still be considered virgin." Documen-

tary filmmaker **Daryl Hannah** intones to Chevy Chase as she meaningfully sucks her finger. *Memoirs of an Invisible Man* (1992, Warner Bros.).

Virtues

see also GOODNESS, INTEGRITY, MORALITY, RIGHT AND WRONG, VICES

10641 "I don't know anything about charity. I never got any and I never handed any out." Crusty fan dancer **Carole Lombard** has no use for the virtue of charity until she adopts old rummy May Robson as a publicity stunt. *Lady by Choice* (1934, Columbia).

10642 "My deepest gratitude, brother, for virtue is its own reward." Title character **Miriam Hopkins** is a beautiful gold digger who rises from the depths of society to the side of the British throne. *Becky Sharp* (1935, RKO).

10643 "To put it simply, I would say that our general belief is in moderation. We preach the virtue of avoiding excess of all kind, even, if you will pardon the paradox, excess of virtue itself." **H.B. Warner** explains to Ronald Colman why things are so tranquil in Shangri-La. *Lost Horizon* (1937, Columbia).

10644 "And so they were married and went to Japan for their honeymoon, and had three lovely daughters, who grew up and were lectured by their father and of course me, their uncle, on the nice things that can happen to a girl, if she remains virtuous, even on a rainy Sunday in New York." Womanizing airline pilot **Cliff Robertson** has double-standard expectations of his nieces, offsprings of his sister Jane Fonda. He has also encouraged Fonda to hold out for marriage to Rod Taylor before going to bed with him. *Sunday in New York* (1963, MGM).

Visions and Visualizations

see also BEAUTY, EYES, IMAGINATION, SIGHT AND SIGHTS

10645 "I can see you bending over a hot stove—only I can't see the stove." **Groucho Marx** zings the perfect foil Margaret Dumont. *The Cocoanuts* (1929, Paramount).

10646 "I see a small Ohio farm boy become a great soldier. I see thousands of marching men. I see General Lee with a broken heart surrendering. And I can see the beginning of a new nation, like Abraham Lincoln said. And I can see that Ohio farm boy being inaugurated as president. Things like that can only happen in a country like America." **Gary Cooper** replies when Jean Arthur asks him what he sees as they visit U.S. General Grant's tomb. *Mr. Deeds Goes to Town* (1936, Columbia).

10647 "You've got to be able to visualize." With this phrase, sharp Yankee real estate agent **Ian Wolfe** clinches the deal of selling a ruined old Connecticut house to gullible New Yorkers Cary Grant and Myrna Loy. *Mr. Blandings Builds His Dream House* (1948, RKO).

10648 "I can see you now, with your cutlass in one hand and your. . . your compass in the other." Romantic **Judy Garland** imagines Gene Kelly as the fierce pirate he lets her think he is. *The Pirate* (1948, MGM).

10649 "I can't quite visualize it." Hollywood studio head **Millard Mitchell** reacts after Gene Kelly's description of a production number in a movie is presented as a ten-minute sequence of "Broadway Ballet." *Singin' in the Rain* (1952, MGM).

10650 "I've got vision; the rest of the world wears bifocals." **Paul Newman** defends the string of robberies he's master-minded. *Butch Cassidy and the Sundance Kid* (1969, 20th Century-Fox).

10651 "Don't you eyeball me, boy! Use your peripheral vision." Tough drill instructor **Lou Gossett, Jr.** shrieks at a recruit. *An Officer and a Gentleman* (1982, Paramount).

10652 "If you want a vision of the future, Winston, imagine a boot stamping on a human face forever." Interrogator **Richard Burton**, in his last role, talks almost kindly to his victim John Hurt. *1984* (1984, GB, Umbrella-Virgin-Atlantic).

10653 "Swamp makes a body see whatever they want to see." It's **Barbara Hershey**'s reaction to Jill Clayburgh's claim that she was rescued in the swamps of the bayou by a mysterious man, perhaps Hershey's long lost husband. *Shy People* (1987, Cannon).

Visits

see also GUESTS, HOSPITALITY

10654 "The aquarium was swell. If I lived in New York I'd go there every day." Speaking to wise-beyond-her-years reporter Jean Arthur, **Gary Cooper** delivers a line to indicate just how naïve and unimaginative a small-town hick he is. *Mr. Deeds Goes to Town* (1936, Columbia).

10655 SIR GUY OF GISBOURNE: "You've come to Nottingham once too often." ROBIN HOOD: "When this is over, my friend, there'll be no need to come

again." With drawn swords, **Basil Rathbone** and **Errol Flynn** taunt each other at the beginning of their duel to the death. *The Adventures of Robin Hood* (1938, Warner Bros.).

10656 "We came out to pay a call, a friendly call, and talk a little business with old friends." Scalawag **Victor Jory** and his wife Isabel Jewell arrive at Tara offering to buy the property from Vivien Leigh. The latter throws some dirt in the face of her father's former overseer, telling him that it's the only part of Tara he'll ever own. *Gone with the Wind* (1939, Selznick-MGM).

10657 "Your unexpected visit isn't connected by any chance with the Letters of Transit? It seems as long as I have those letters, I'll never be lonely." **Humphrey Bogart** sarcastically welcomes ex-lover Ingrid Bergman. He refers to letters that allow her and her resistance leader husband Paul Henreid escape from the Nazis. The Letters of Transit are pure fiction; there was nothing like them in World War II. *Casablanca* (1942, Warner Bros.).

10658 "Woman of the house. . . I've brought the brother to dinner." **John Wayne** stumbles into his house, yelling to his wife that he has dragged home his equally punchy brother-in-law, Victor McLaglen after the two had a donnybrook that took up half the afternoon. *The Quiet Man* (1952, Republic).

10659 "The visit is over." **Ingrid Bergman**, the richest woman in the world, leaves the small European village where she was born. She had returned with a deal for the financially desperate town—two million dollars if the town will murder Anthony Quinn, who years earlier had impregnated her and got some of his buddies to testify that she was a whore. The catch is that she wants her revenge on the town as well as Quinn. *The Visit* (1964, Ger.-Fr.-Italy-U.S., 20th Century-Fox).

10660 "You know something, Virgil? You're the first person who's been around to call. Nobody else has been here. . . nobody comes." Sparta, Mississippi Police Chief **Rod Steiger** sums up his unhappy existence when black Philadelphia police detective Sidney Poitier enters his home. When Poitier shows some spontaneous compassion, gently touching Steiger on the shoulder, the Southern lawman recoils and says, "Don't treat me like the nigger!" *In the Heat of the Night* (1967, United Artists).

10661 "Why should the Immaculate Conception wish to pay a visit?" Priest **Alec McCowen** sarcastically hears the confession of Karen Archer, who claims she has nothing to confess except for "perhaps the odd fleeting desire." *Forever Young* (1986, GB, Cinecom).

10662 "People will come." Little **Gaby Hoffman** tells her father Kevin Costner that he doesn't have to sell his farm, because people will come to see the baseball field he built in a cornfield. *Field of Dreams* (1989, Universal).

10663 "I was just 40 or 50 blocks from here. I thought I'd stop by. . . . Great box collection." Musician **Arliss Howard** drops in on Jessica Lange and notices that she hasn't unpacked a large number of boxes since moving to Baltimore. *Men Don't Leave* (1990, Warner Bros.).

Vocations *see* CAREERS, JOBS, TRAINING, WORK AND WORKERS

Voices

see also MUSIC AND MUSICIANS, SONGS AND SINGING, SOUNDS, SPEECHES AND SPEAKING

10664 "Look at this. I was in excellent voice, too." **Charles Laughton**, as Nero, pouts over a broken lyre. *The Sign of the Cross* (1932, Paramount).

10665 "You've got a pretty fair set of pipes, kid." Barbary Coast proprietor **Clark Gable** admires singer Jeanette MacDonald's voice. *San Francisco* (1936, MGM).

10666 "I guess mine is strictly a bathtub voice." **Claudette Colbert** is turned down time after time at Parisian clubs when she applies for a job as a blues singer. *Midnight* (1939, Paramount).

10667 "Hear from him? Every time we look across a river, we'll hear his voice, calling us through the wind. And he'll be within us, Elizabeth, no matter where we are or he may be, for that man will never die." Artist **Robert Young** has the last lines to his fiancée Ruth Hussey, as they watch Spencer Tracy, as Major Robert Rogers, set out with his rangers to find a northwest passage. *Northwest Passage* (1940, MGM).

10668 "A man thinks he has a voice. The truth is, the voice has a man." **Mario Lanza** stars as the great Italian tenor Enrico Caruso. *The Great Caruso* (1950, MGM).

10669 "You keep talking about my voice and yet it doesn't belong to me. . . . I'm only an instrument. A simple girl who lives in fear of a voice that has always obliged me to its will." Speaking to impresario Peter Cellier, **Janet Suzman**, the world's greatest soprano, is very humble about her gift of a miraculous voice. *And the Ship Sails On* (1983, Italy, Triumph).

10670 "It seemed to me that I heard the voice of God. . . . And it was the voice of an obscene child." **F. Murray Abraham**, as Antonio Salieri, describes his reaction upon first hearing a Mozart theme. *Amadeus* (1984, Orion).

10671 "I hear your voice all the time—every man has your voice." Sex club employee **Nastassja Kinski** dismisses her estranged husband Harry Dean Stanton. *Paris, Texas* (1984, Ger.-Fr., 20th Century-Fox).

10672 "Boys, you must strive to find your own voices. The longer you wait to begin, the less likely that you are of finding it at all." English teacher **Robin Williams** lectures his prep students. *Dead Poets Society* (1989, Touchstone-Buena Vista).

10673 "You are our voice." An ancient battered woman pleads respectfully to Raul Julia, archbishop of El Salvador. *Romano* (1989, Four Seasons-Vidmark).

Volunteers

see also FREE WILL, IMPULSES, PAYMENTS

10674 "While you're out there risking life and limb through shot and shell, we'll be in here thinking what a sap you are." **Groucho Marx** makes fun of Harpo Marx, who has volunteered to go for help. *Duck Soup* (1933, Paramount).

10675 MARTIN GREER: "What did you do that for?" HARVEY LANDRUM: "Oh, I don't know. Maybe I'm a boy scout at heart." **Dana Andrews** is surprised to learn that his friend **Jim Backus** has volunteered for service in Korea. *I Want You* (1951, Goldwyn-RKO).

10676 "There is another exercise I prefer, but it requires a volunteer." It's **Robert Urich**'s suggestive response when JoBeth Williams comments she's noticed him jogging in the evenings. *Endangered Species* (1982, MGM-United Artists).

Voting and Voters

see also DEMOCRACY, GOVERNMENTS, POLITICS AND POLITICIANS, RIGHTS

10677 "Do I get to vote too?" Black steward **Canada Lee** abstains when it comes time to decide what to do with German Walter Slezak pulled into a lifeboat from the water by the survivors of a ship sunk by Slezak's U-boat, before it sank itself. *Lifeboat* (1944, 20th Century-Fox).

10678 "Your face takes sides. . . as though you were

voting for or against." **Dorothy McGuire** looks into Gregory Peck's thoughtful face as he gives matters on his mind deep consideration. *Gentleman's Agreement* (1947, 20th Century-Fox).

10679 CHARLIE HALLORAN: "I'm telling you, if you rule there's no Santa Claus, you can count on getting just two votes—your own and that district attorney out there." JUDGE HARPER: "[No just one.] The district attorney's a Republican." Politician **William Frawley** warns Judge **Gene Lockhart**, who sadly holds up one finger. *Miracle on 34th Street* (1947, 20th Century-Fox).

10680 "I'm gong to run. You can't stop me. I'm going to run even if I don't get a single vote." **Broderick Crawford** shouts defiantly at night riders who have beaten up his boy and thrown a rock through his window to try to discourage him from running for elected office. *All the King's Men* (1949, Columbia).

10681 "He'll do or say anything to be loved—by all. People like Frank ought to have two votes. Then they could mark their ballots Democrat and Republican." **Grace Kelly** claims her husband Bing Crosby has an obsessive need to be loved. *The Country Girl* (1954, Paramount).

10682 "The story which you have just seen is a true one. In real life, Captain Alexander Holmes was brought to trial on a charge of murder. He was convicted and given the minimum sentence of six months because of the unusual circumstances surrounding the incident. If you had been a member of the jury, how would you have voted? Guilty or innocent?" The narrator sums up the case of a ship's officer, played by Tyrone Power, who had to make life and death decisions aboard a crammed life boat, after a luxury liner sunk. Realizing that not all can survive, he chose to save the fittest and cast the infirm into the sea. *Abandon Ship* (1957, GB, Columbia).

10683 "I wasn't the only chump in the city. It took a lot of you to elect me." Deposed Mayor Jimmy Walker, played by **Bob Hope,** bids farewell to his beloved New York as he leaves the country. *Beau James* (1957, Paramount).

10684 "[If I'm elected, I'd] repeal the 14th and 20th amendments—take the vote away from the women and make slaves of 'em." **Dean Martin** plans to use the money he gets from his part in robbing five Las Vegas casinos to run for public office. *Ocean's Eleven* (1960, Warner Bros.).

10685 "He never made the ten-most-wanted list. It's very unfair voting. It's who you know." **Janet Mar-**

golin is protective of her criminal husband Woody Allen. *Take the Money and Run* (1969, Palomar).

10686 "I'm a voter. Aren't you supposed to lie and kiss my butt?" **Bill Murray** questions a politician who's ignoring him. *Ghostbusters II* (1989, Columbia).

10687 "You're finished. The school board's going to be here this evening at seven o'clock and we're going to vote your black ass out." Black activist parent **Lynne Thigpen** is happy as black principal Morgan Freeman is led away in handcuffs for violating the fire code by chaining the doors of Eastside High to keep out drug dealers. The film would have been better if Thigpen's role represented legitimate concerns with Freeman's high-handed ways of dealing with the problems of his school. Instead, Thigpen portrays a vindictive, scheming woman with no other agenda than to frustrate Freeman's efforts. *Lean on Me* (1989, Warner Bros.).

Vows *see* OATHS, PLEDGES, PROMISES

Vulgarities

see also DECENCY, IGNORANCE, TASTES

10688 CARLOS MARGOLI: "Are you trying to double cross me?" MADELEINE DE BEAUPRE: "Don't be vulgar." Gentlemen jewel thief **John Halliday** becomes suspicious of his accomplice, **Marlene Dietrich**, in the theft of a valuable string of pearls. *Desire* (1936, Paramount).

10689 GRACE: "I won't have this vulgar talk in my house." DAWN: "It's only a joke, Mummy, I'm only sixteen. I'm still in school. I want to be a nun when I grow up." Mother **Sarah Miles** is justifiably concerned that World War II conditions have hastened the sexual awareness and activity of her teenage daughter **Sammi Davis**. *Hope and Glory* (1987, GB, Columbia).

Waits and Waiting

see also EXPECTATIONS, HOPES, PATIENCE AND IMPATIENCE

10690 "If I was a man like you, you know what I'd do? Well, I wouldn't sit around and wait for the undertaker." Brash young **James Cagney** advises retired and bored millionaire George Arliss to quit loafing and get back into life. *The Millionaire* (1931, Warner Bros.).

10691 MARY, DUCHESS OF TOWERS: "I fought my way back to bring you peace. . . . I'm waiting for you."

PETER IBBETSON: "Then there's something else beyond." MARY: "We've just begun to live, Peter. No more fears, no pain. . . ." PETER: "I'm coming to give it to you." The ghost of **Ann Harding** appears to her imprisoned lover **Gary Cooper** to comfort him in his final moments. Before he dies and joins her, he picks up the glove that the apparition dropped. *Peter Ibbetson* (1935, Paramount).

10692 "You know, Mary, I want to get a kick out of things I can see, like lights in the harbor, or a good fight, or a woman worth looking at. Did you ever taste the fog in your mouth like it was salt? Or take hold of someone and feel your blood rushing up like a river? What does a man need, or a woman either? You know I never tried to kid you, Mary. You take me as I am or you don't take me. Tim doesn't try to change me because he knows he can't. And you can't either. Nothing can. Do you know what I've been waiting for? I've been waiting to hear you say that I'm all right with the way I am. Maybe you're ready to say it now. Are you?" Like many a man before and since, amoral Barbary Coast saloon keeper **Clark Gable** waits for the woman he loves, Jeanette MacDonald, to accept him for what he is—not what he might become. It does not work for the King, either. *San Francisco* (1936, MGM).

10693 "Time will come, my friend, when the orgy must spend itself—when brutality and the lust for power must perish by its own sword. When that day comes, it is our hope that the doctrines of Shangri-La will spread throughout the world. Here we shall stay with our books and our music and our meditations. . . . Here will be found such wisdom as men will need when their passions are spent. Yes, my son, when the strong have devoured each other, the Christian ethic may at last be fulfilled and the meek shall inherit the earth." Dying High Lama **Sam Jaffe** instructs his chosen successor, Ronald Colman. Here's hoping that Shangri-La and some High Lama is still waiting for peace in the world. *Lost Horizon* (1937, Columbia).

10694 "The longer they wait, the better they like it." Entertainer **Marlene Dietrich** refers to the saloon customers and her singing. *Destry Rides Again* (1939, Universal).

10695 "What are you waiting for? A spectacle? You shall have it! Tell everyone how the Great Age ended!" **Charles Laughton** has climbed to the top mast of a ship and calls to the crowd below before hurling himself to his death in a mock heroic gesture. *Jamaica Inn* (1939, GB, Pommer-Mayflower-Paramount).

10696 "Let me look at the moors once more with you. I'll wait for you until you come." **Merle Oberon** dies, promising to wait for her love Laurence Olivier. *Wuthering Heights* (1939, Goldwyn-United Artists).

10697 "With the coming of the second World War, many eyes in imprisoned Europe turned hopefully, or desperately, toward the freedom of the Americas. Lisbon became the great embarkation point. But not everyone could get to Lisbon directly; and so a tortuous, roundabout refugee trail sprang up. Paris to Marseilles—across the Mediterranean to Oran—then by train, or auto, or foot, across the rim of Africa to Casablanca in French Morocco. Here, the fortunate ones through money, or influence, or luck, might obtain exit visas and scurry to Lisbon, and from Lisbon to the New World. But the others wait in Casablanca, and wait, and wait, and wait. . . ." Narrator **Lou Marcelle** speaks the foreword to the film as audiences are introduced to those who wait. *Casablanca* (1943, Warner Bros.).

10698 "OK, we'll be waiting for you." Marine **William Bendix** replies to a soldier who is marching onto Guadalcanal as the marines are leaving the island. The soldier says, "See you in Tokyo." *Guadalcanal Diary* (1943, 20th Century-Fox).

10699 "Here's the laundry waiting to be picked up." **Rita Hayworth** doesn't have a low opinion of herself—although it would be justified. It's an in-joke with her husband's employee Glenn Ford, who earlier told her he'll pick her up just like he picks up the boss's laundry. *Gilda* (1946, Columbia).

10700 "Tough monkey. Guys like you end up in the stockade sooner or later. Some day you'll walk in. I'll be waiting. I'll show you a couple of things." Sergeant of the stockade **Ernest Borgnine** licks his chops thinking of the fun he'll have when soldier Frank Sinatra is put in his tender, loving care. *From Here to Eternity* (1953, Columbia).

10701 "I waited and waited. . . . You were home? But last night was ours. One night a week is all we have. She did the same thing last week. How many headaches can she have? I will not be taken for granted. You and your rabbit-faced wife can go to hell." Tough boss lady **Joan Crawford** takes a phone call from her married lover. *The Best of Everything* (1959, 20th Century-Fox).

10702 "We'll wait and see what comes out of the river." Author **James Dickey** portrays a sheriff in the film version of his book. *Deliverance* (1972, Warner Bros.).

10703 "Where's Michael? I've got things to get straight with him and I can't wait on line." **Talia Shire** demands to see her brother Al Pacino without further delay. *The Godfather, Part II* (1974, Paramount).

10704 "Just think, a million years, waiting just for us." **Karen Robson** is in awe of the volcanic structure referred to as Hanging Rock. *Picnic at Hanging Rock* (1975, Australia, Australia Film Corporation).

10705 "To be on the wire is life—the rest is waiting." Choreographer and director **Roy Scheider** tells his Angel of Death Jessica Lange that he wishes to always live on the edge or not to live at all. *All That Jazz* (1979, 20th Century-Fox).

10706 "They say they always knew our boat, the divine vessel, was only dragged over the mountain so it could drift through the rapids. They say it was necessary, that they have been waiting for this since the time of their forefathers. It was necessary to reconcile the evil spirits of the rapids." Captain **Paul Hittscher** tells title character Klaus Kinski what the Indians think about the struggle to get a boat over a mountain. *Fitzcarraldo* (1982, W. Ger., Herzog/Project Filmproduktion).

10707 "All my life I've been waiting for someone, and when I find her she's a fish." **Tom Hanks** is in love with sexy mermaid Daryl Hannah. *Splash* (1984, Touchstone-Buena Vista).

10708 "Now their time was running out. Outside Shanghai, the Japanese dug in and waited—for Pearl Harbor." The narrator comments on the beginning of the end of British colonial life in China. *Empire of the Sun* (1987, Warner Bros.).

10709 "You tell me my life? I'll tell you yours. I'm a wolf? You run to the wolf in me, that don't make you no lamb! You're gonna marry my brother! Why you wanna sell your life short? Playing it safe is just about the most dangerous thing a woman like you could do. You waited for the right man the first time, why don't you wait for the right man again?" **Nicolas Cage** argues that he, not his brother Danny Aiello is the right man for widow Cher. *Moonstruck* (1987, MGM).

10710 "My love, I'm here. I'm waiting." If lovers Abelard and Heloise, played respectively by **Derek de Lint** and Kim Thompson, are to have any future, it has to be after death. Her family has him castrated. He retreats to a monastery and she to a convent. *Stealing Heaven* (1989, GB-Yugo, Scotti Bros.-Film Dallas).

10711 "I want us to marry. And I'll sit by your side till you're ready. If you tell me you're never ready, well, I'll just leave right now and never bother you again. Otherwise, I'm here, as long as it takes." Assistant D.A. **Timothy Hutton** is willing to wait for Jenny Lumet as long as it takes. *Q & A* (1990, Tri-Star).

Walks and Walking

10712 "He went out for a little walk." Half-mad young archaeologist **Bramwell Fletcher**, laughing insanely, tells his companions that a 3700-year-old mummy has walked away from his sarcophagus. *The Mummy* (1932, Universal).

10713 "One of the finest women who ever walked the streets." **Mae West** rolls her eyes and responds when a female says she's a fine woman. *She Done Him Wrong* (1933, Paramount).

10714 "Walk? Not bloody likely. I'm going to take a taxi." It's **Wendy Hiller**'s preferred means of transportation to Professor Henry Higgins' home when he chooses the flower girl for an experiment in phonetics. *Pygmalion* (1938, GB, Pascal-MGM).

10715 "I can't wait to get finished so I can walk on it." Gossip columnist Allyn Joslyn's mother **Jessie Ralph** is hooking a rug with his image at its center. *Cafe Society* (1939, Paramount).

10716 "Unless I can walk some day, he'll never know. . . . And I mean run." Crippled in an accident, **Irene Dunne** refuses to contact Charles Boyer, fearing his love will be replaced by pity because of her condition. *Love Affair* (1939, RKO).

10717 "A pastor's family walks a tightrope, balancing with one foot on earth and one foot already in heaven." **Fredric March**, as the Reverend William Spence, patiently acknowledges the special problems facing his children growing up in a minister's family. *One Foot in Heaven* (1941, Warner Bros.).

10718 "Walk. . . run and someone runs after you." Calm **Everett Sloane** advises nervous Ted de Corsia to stroll nonchalantly as they leave the site of a murder for hire. *The Enforcer* (1951, United States Pictures).

10719 "Did you notice the way Morris got up out of his chair suddenly and just walked away with no explanation at all? Well, something inside Morris did the same thing several years ago. Everything inside him just got up and went for a walk, and never came back." **Eve Arden** shares with her sister Dorothy McGuire her problems with her husband

Frank Overton. *The Dark at the Top of the Stairs* (1956, Warner Bros.).

10720 "Look how she moves. That's just like Jell-O with springs." **Jack Lemmon**'s description of Marilyn Monroe's wiggly walk seems accurate. *Some Like It Hot* (1959, United Artists).

10721 "Mein Führer, I can walk!" Mad invalid German scientist **Peter Sellers** rises from his wheelchair to give a Nazi salute to American President Peter Sellers as the doomsday device is triggered. *Dr. Strangelove: or How I Learned to Stop Worrying and Love the Bomb* (1964, Columbia).

10722 "Try to walk like a man." **Steve Martin** instructs Lily Tomlin, who shares his body, when their gait takes on an exaggerated feminine stride. *All of Me* (1984, Universal).

10723 "Looks like I'm walking." Bounty hunter **Robert De Niro** can't hire a cab to take him from an airport because all he has is the fortune given to him by Charles Grodin. The fortune is in $1000 bills. *Midnight Run* (1988, Universal).

10724 "If I walked like that, I'd walk everywhere." **Paul Newman**, as Louisiana Governor Earl Long, admires the way Lolita Davidovich, as Blaze Starr, struts her stuff. *Blaze* (1989, Touchstone-Buena Vista).

Walls

see also BUILDINGS, HOMES, HOUSES

10725 "Behold the walls of Jericho! Maybe not as thick as the ones that Joshua blew down, but a lot safer. You see, I have no trumpet." **Clark Gable** drapes a blanket over a clothes-line to divide the room in which he and Claudette Colbert will sleep. *It Happened One Night* (1934, Columbia).

10726 "You must be an iron man. From what I hear through the walls, you must have something going for you every night." Physician **Jack Kruschen** doesn't know that his next door neighbor Jack Lemmon is forced to lend out his apartment each night to one or another of his superiors at work, so they can participate in some hanky-panky with their mistresses. *The Apartment* (1960, United Artists).

10727 "I'm a brick wall, a rich brick wall." Wealthy WASP **Eddie Albert** is determined to prevent New York Jew Charles Grodin from marrying his daughter Cybill Shepherd—but the brick wall comes tumbling down. *The Heartbreak Kid* (1972, 20th Century-Fox).

Wants and Wanting

see also DESIRES, NEEDS AND NECESSITIES, WISHES

10728 "I get what I want—without the help of God or His holy book." Swaggering **Douglas Fairbanks, Sr.** brags to Padre Nigel De Brulier. *The Gaucho* (1927, silent, United Artists).

10729 "All my life I've wanted to go to the right places and get in with the right crowd." Slatternly **Barbara Stanwyck** is not allowed to rise above her station in life, but she makes certain her daughter Anne Shirley has her chance. *Stella Dallas* (1937, Goldwyn-United Artists).

10730 "There are some things I've been wantin' to tell you. . . . About what you've got and what you want. What a woman wants. A woman's supposed to lead the man's life. Her man's life. And women are made that way, occasionally. Woman's weakness is supposed to fit in a man's strength. Her respect pays for the security a man gives her. But not for you, Jessica, you've got strength of your own. You can do things. Not just dream about them like. . . like most women. Make a life for yourself. Always remember what it is you want. Get it. Any way you can. If you have to get it alone." Tight-lipped, grim and unsmiling, **Elizabeth Risdon** gives her daughter Joan Crawford a forceful feminist lecture. *Mannequin* (1938, MGM).

10731 ELIZABETH COTTON: "I want you to stay away from me." CANDY JOHNSON: "No, you don't. Why don't you jump in and get wet all over?" Cocky **Clark Gable** kisses **Lana Turner** for the first time. Does she really not know her own mind or is it that Gable just won't take no for an answer? Well, they do fall in love. *Honky Tonk* (1941, MGM).

10732 "If I can't have all there is, I don't want any of it." Despite having three other ardent suitors, **Merle Oberon** never marries after losing Alan Marshal. *Lydia* (1941, United Artists).

10733 "I want to get married. I want to have a house and children. I want to go to the market and cheat the grocer. I want to join the human race." Scarred and embittered **Joan Crawford** just wants to be an "ordinary" woman. *A Woman's Face* (1941, MGM).

10734 "WRECK": "Which way do you want the pleats turned?" RUTH SHERWOOD: "Towards Mecca." Dense ex-football player **Gordon Jones** does **Rosalind Russell**'s ironing. *My Sister Eileen* (1942, Columbia).

10735 "I go where I want to, with anybody I want. I just happen to be that kind of girl." **Doris Dowling**

defiantly informs returning World War II GI husband Alan Ladd that his wishes no longer mean anything to her. *The Blue Dahlia* (1946, Paramount).

10736 "It's not anybody's fault, it's just the way things are. It's what people want and how hard they want it and how hard it is for them to get it." Weakling **Kirk Douglas** finally stands up to his domineering wife Barbara Stanwyck, unhappy in not getting her way. *The Strange Love of Martha Ivers* (1946, Paramount).

10737 "Sometimes out of the worst comes the best. Mr. D'Angelo got what he wanted. Nick got what he wanted, and I got all I ever wanted. I got Nick." At the end of the movie, **Coleen Gray** claims she's happy with her man Victor Mature and the Assistant D.A. Brian Donlevy is happy because psychopath Richard Widmark has been eliminated. *Kiss of Death* (1947, 20th Century-Fox).

10738 "I want to walk out of the sun again and find you waiting. I want to sit in the same moonlight and tell you the things I never told you—till you don't hate me." **Jane Greer** wishes she could recapture the days in Acapulco when she and Robert Mitchum fell in love. *Out of the Past* (1947, RKO).

10739 "All I want to do is hang around someone on Sunday." **Ida Lupino** makes a futile effort to shake off spiritual isolation. *Road House* (1948, 20th Century-Fox).

10740 "What's a dame like you want with a guy like me." Working stiff **Burt Lancaster** can't understand the interest of wealthy neurotic Barbara Stanwyck. *Sorry, Wrong Number* (1948, Paramount).

10741 "I always wanted to be a man about town." It is **Bob Hope**'s wisecrack response to the prospect of dismemberment. *The Great Lover* (1949, Paramount).

10742 "A girl wants a man who is gentle and sweet and who doesn't run away." **Natalie Wood**'s dream of a man is influenced by her disappointment and shock when her father William Hopper rejects her physical expressions of affection—possibly because he has incestuous feelings for the blossoming teen. *Rebel Without a Cause* (1955, Warner Bros.).

10743 "Go find what you want somewhere else. Just don't tell me about it." Impotent **Jason Robards, Jr.** is too proud to ask for love from his wife Lana Turner, but he refuses to give her a divorce. *By Love Possessed* (1961, United Artists).

10744 "My check-out time in any hotel is when I— is when I want to check out." Rank has its privi-leges for aging glamour star **Geraldine Page**—at least she thinks so. *Sweet Bird of Youth* (1962, MGM).

10745 "I want. . . I want. . . everything I've ever seen in the movies." Accountant **Gene Wilder** succumbs to the temptation put before him by Broadway producer Zero Mostel. *The Producers* (1967, MGM).

10746 McClain: "Marrying me was the only real thing you ever did in your whole life that you really wanted to." Ellie: "Wrong! There were two things. . . . The second was divorcing you and there's about to be a third—telling you to get the hell out of here and never come back." Self-centered **Jim Brown** is told off by **Diahann Carroll**, the woman he deserted. *The Split* (1968, MGM).

10747 "Now you wouldn't want to do it just like that, with no feeling on my part." Disinclined to make love, **Dyan Cannon** is wrong in believing her husband Elliott Gould doesn't want sex just for his own gratification. *Bob & Carol & Ted & Alice* (1969, Columbia).

10748 "Norwood, do you know what I want? I want to live in a trailer and listen to you play and sing every day." **Kim Darby** thinks ex-Marine Glenn Campbell is just about perfect for her. *Norwood* (1969, Paramount).

10749 "I want you to be a merry widower." Dying **Ali MacGraw** doesn't want her husband Ryan O'Neal to throw himself on her funeral pyre. *Love Story* (1970, Paramount).

10750 "This one came so close to being what I wanted. Good pair of tits on her. Not a great pair. Almost no ass at all. And that bothered me. Sensational legs. I would have settled for the legs if she had two more inches here and there and three more here. Anyhow, that took two years out of my life." **Jack Nicholson** is one of those men who see women only as the sum of their body parts. *Carnal Knowledge* (1971, Columbia).

10751 "I love you, Miss, whoever you are. I want to have your child." **Woody Allen** is flustered when he meets blonde dancer Suzanne Zenor at a disco. *Play it Again, Sam* (1972, Paramount).

10752 "I never wanted to get married. I just wanted to get divorced." **Jessica Harper** wants to cut to the chase. *Love and Death* (1975, United Artists).

10753 "I was seized with an urge to love. All I could think of was Sonja. I wanted to hold her close to me, to weep tears on her shoulders and engage in oral sex." **Woody Allen** has both pure and profane desires for Diane Keaton. *Love and Death* (1975, United Artists).

10754 "When I want something I go get it." **Meryl Streep** wants to block a Supreme Court nomination, but she also wants married U.S. Senator Alan Alda—at least for awhile. *The Seduction of Joe Tynan* (1979, Universal).

10755 "I wanted to climb inside you and pull you around me like a blanket." **Richard Dreyfuss** confesses his love for Amy Irving, his competition in a piano festival that he needs to win. *The Competition* (1980, Columbia).

10756 GLORIA: "Whattaya have in mind?" ARTHUR: "VD, I'm really into penicillin." Eighth Avenue hooker **Anne De Salvo** asks what kind of "party" **Dudley Moore** wants. *Arthur* (1981, Orion).

10757 "I never wanted it like this before." At a particularly passionate moment in her love-making with William Hurt, **Kathleen Turner** updates Deborah Kerr's line to Burt Lancaster in the surf. *Body Heat* (1981, Warner Bros.).

10758 "I'm better than a human woman, because I can be what you want." **Dorothy Stratten**, the murdered former Playmate of the Year, portrays a virginal robot girl, perfect for a man in every way—at least according to the Playboy philosophy. *Galaxina* (1981, Crown International).

10759 "Daddy left you because he didn't want you; he wants me and Henry, but not you." **Henry Thomas** is hateful to his divorced mother Sissy Spacek. *Raggedy Man* (1981, Universal).

10760 "I want to marry a pilot and live overseas. Nobody DORs [Drops Out on Request] after eleven weeks." **Lisa Blount**'s ploy to marry a navy pilot backfires when David Keith quits Officers' Candidate School to marry her when she lies to him, telling him she's pregnant. *An Officer and a Gentleman* (1982, Paramount).

10761 "I don't want you to love me. I just want out." Having been effectively abandoned by both his parents, **Richard Gere**, fearful of a commitment, refuses to marry Debra Winger. *An Officer and a Gentleman* (1982, Paramount).

10762 ELIZABETH CARLSON: "What do you want?" RIVAS: "Clean sheets, women, good food, hot baths, Clint Eastwood movies. . . ." **Nastassja Kinski** is given terrorist **Harvey Keitel**'s order of favorite things. *Exposed* (1983, MGM-United Artists).

10763 "I fell in love with a gigolo, I don't want to grow old with the owner of a restaurant." Choosy streetwalker **Gudrun Landgrebe** opposes her male prostitute lover Mathieu Cariere's bourgeois plan of opening an art gallery restaurant. *A Woman in Flames* (1984, Germany, Libra).

10764 "What do you want from me? What have I done? I'm just a word processor, for Christ's sake. . . I just wanted to have my apartment, maybe meet a nice girl. . . and now I gotta die for it?" Sinking to his knees in a mean street of New York's Soho district, **Griffin Dunne** finds the price for his simple desires to be too dear. *After Hours* (1985, Warner Bros.).

10765 "If you can't see that I want you more than anything, then the hell with you." **Amy Madigan** yells at her married lover Ed Harris who is being difficult. *Alamo Bay* (1985, Tri-Star).

10766 "I don't want your gold, I want to touch human flesh. I want to kiss it, hold it." **Theresa Russell** complains to her father Gene Hackman, one of the world's richest men. They live like hermits on their own Caribbean island, oblivious to World War II. *Eureka* (1985, MGM-United Artists Classics).

10767 "People in hell want ice water." When Ed Harris tells **Jessica Lange**, as country singer Patsy Cline, that he wants her, she lets him know how likely he is to get what he wants. *Sweet Dreams* (1985, Tri-Star).

10768 "You want it. . .I want it. . .I want it, you know I want it. . .you don't have to bullshit me to get it. . .even if you're untruthful with me. . .you still get it." In his dream of her, "the sure thing" **Nicollette Sheridan** promises John Cusack everything. When he meets her, she's easier. *The Sure Thing* (1985, Embassy).

10769 "I wanted to meet some interesting, stimulating people from an ancient land. . .and kill them." **Matthew Modine**, as Private Joker, lives up to his nickname when he responds to a documentary news crew's request for personal comments on the Vietnam War. *Full Metal Jacket* (1987, Warner Bros.)

10770 "I'm a woman of the 80s. I can risk my life in armed combat. I can have empty sex with strangers, and all I want is to be loved." Dressed like Annie Hall, **Michelle Little** finds love with Scott Valentine. There's just one little problem. Whenever he becomes sexually aroused, he literally turns into a monster. *My Demon Lover* (1987, New Line).

10771 "I know what you really want. You want to do things to me. I know what you dream about." Hooker **Kathy Baker** talks trashy for a delighted customer. *Street Smart* (1987, Cannon).

10772 "I know you, and you just want to spread your wings and you want to kill something." **Sally Kirkland** humors near-psychotic Tom Waits. *Cold Feet* (1989, Avenue Pictures).

10773 "I want them to stop looking to me for answers. Wanting me to speak again, write again, be a leader. I want them to start thinking for themselves. I want privacy." Former 60s guru **James Earl Jones** responds bitterly when he misunderstands Kevin Costner's question, "What do you want?" referring to something to drink, at a baseball game. *Field of Dreams* (1989, Universal).

10774 "I want you to be better than you want yourself to be." Noble medical school professor **Christine Lahti** tries to rally wise-cracking medical student Matthew Modine with a tear-jerking emotional appeal. *Gross Anatomy* (1989, Touchstone-Buena Vista).

10775 "I don't want life to imitate art. I want life to be art." Struggling movie actress and former drug-user **Meryl Streep** asks for a lot, as she talks to director Gene Hackman. *Postcards from the Edge* (1990, Columbia).

10776 FRANKIE: "You don't know me." JOHNNY: "Of course, I don't know you. You don't know me either. We got off to a good start. Why do you want to stop? What do you want? What do you want from a guy?" FRANKIE: "I want a guy who'll love me no matter what." JOHNNY: "You got him." **Michelle Pfeiffer** isn't as sure that **Al Pacino** is right for her as he is. *Frankie and Johnny* (1991, Paramount).

10777 "It's not sex that she wants, it's love." **Diane Ladd**, the lady of a Southern family, takes a tolerant view of her promiscuous maid Laura Dern (Ladd's real life daughter). *Rambling Rose* (1991, Seven Arts-New World).

10778 "What do you want? Money? Jewelry? A big ball of string?" Industrialist **Christopher Walken** tries to bribe Michelle Pfeiffer, as Catwoman. *Batman Returns* (1992, Warner Bros.).

10779 "I don't know what you want, but I know that I can get it for you with a minimum of fuss." Smooth businessman **Christopher Walken** knows how to deal with a mortal enemy. *Batman Returns* (1992, Warner Bros.).

10780 "They don't want an old man." College professor **Woody Allen** admits to daydreaming about sexy young coeds, but doesn't do anything about them. *Husbands and Wives* (1992, Tri-Star).

Warnings

see also DANGER, EVILNESS, HARM, INFORMATION AND INFORMERS, THREATS

10781 "If by accident this door should open during the night, you would be greeted by six bullets—not one of which would miss its mark." Grand Duchess **Florence Vidor** warns amorous waiter Aldolphe Menjou that she is an excellent shot as she leaves him outside her bedroom. *The Grand Duchess and the Waiter* (1926, silent, Paramount).

10782 "From now on you will be No. 48642. You ran a man down with your car and killed him. You were drunk. Your sentence can be redeemed by good behavior. . . I want to warn you of evil influences. Prison does not give a man a yellow streak, but if he has one, it brings it out." Warden **Lewis Stone** greets new convict, playboy Robert Montgomery. He then assigns Montgomery to a cell with two of the prison's most dangerous cons, Chester Morris and Wallace Beery. *The Big House* (1930, MGM).

10783 "Just one word of warning, ladies and gentlemen—there are such things as vampires." Bela Lugosi shows up to prove the point of **Edward Van Sloan** as Professor Van Helsing. *Dracula* (1931, Universal).

10784 "Okay, now you're in the top spot where you've got twice as far to fall." Stage director **Clark Gable** warns the unwelcome new star of his show, former burlesque dancer Joan Crawford. *Dancing Lady* (1933, MGM).

10785 "Don't touch that lever—you'll blow us all to atoms." **Ernest Thesiger**, as Dr. Pretorious, warns about a lever that Frankenstein's monster will eventually pull, killing himself, his mate and the mad doctor. Why would anyone have a lever that would blow everyone to bits around anyway? *The Bride of Frankenstein* (1935, Universal).

10786 "You mustn't come between Irene and Godfrey. He's the only thing she's shown any affection for since her Pomeranian died last summer." **Alice Brady** warns her nasty daughter Gail Patrick not to ruin the relationship of her younger sister Carole Lombard and the butler William Powell. *My Man Godfrey* (1936, Universal).

10787 "Shooting and robbing—it'll just get in your blood, Jesse, you'll end up like a wolf!" **Nancy Kelly** warns title character Tyrone Power about where his thieving ways will lead him. *Jesse James* (1939, 20th Century-Fox).

10788 "Keep it cool, my girl, or I'll whisk you into a convent." **Gale Sondergaard** warns her niece Linda Darnell not to get uppity. *The Mark of Zorro* (1940, 20th Century-Fox).

10789 CAPT. RENAULT: "If you are thinking of warning him—don't put yourself out. He can't possibly escape." RICK BLAINE: "I stick my neck out for nobody." RENAULT: "A wise foreign policy." **Claude Rains** announces to **Humphrey Bogart** that he plans to arrest a murderer at Bogie's cafe later that night. *Casablanca* (1942, Warner Bros.).

10790 PAUL MADVIG: "I'm going to society. He's practically given me the key to his house." ED BEAUMONT: "Yeah, a glass key. Be sure it doesn't break in your hand." Political boss **Brian Donlevy** brags how in he is with Moroni Olsen, a reform candidate for governor. Donlevy's loyal aide **Alan Ladd** believes he's making a big mistake. *The Glass Key* (1942, Paramount).

10791 "Watch it with George. They won't let him pass the old ladies' home unless he's on a leash." **Joan Davis** warns Constance Moore about lecherous George Murphy. *Show Business* (1944, RKO).

10792 "There are no strings tied around you. . . not yet." **Lauren Bacall** gives Humphrey Bogart fair warning. *To Have and Have Not* (1945, Warner Bros.).

10793 "I'm giving you 'til sundown to get out of town." Villain **Brian Donlevy** wasn't the first to deliver this western cliché and he's not spooking Joel McCrea. *The Virginian* (1946, Paramount).

10794 "If you shoot, baby, you'll smear us all over the road." As Lizabeth Scott pulls a gun on **Humphrey Bogart**, he counters by pushing down the accelerator of the car they are riding in. *Dead Reckoning* (1947, RKO).

10795 "Fasten your seat belts, kids, it's going to be a bumpy night." Grumpy actress **Bette Davis**, upset with all the attention being paid her secretary Anne Baxter, gives fair warning to her party guests. *All About Eve* (1950, 20th Century-Fox).

10796 "North Pole, November third, Ned Scott reporting. One of the world's greatest battles was fought and won today by the human race. Here at the top of the world, a handful of American soldiers and civilians met the first invasion from another planet. A man by the name of Noah once saved our world with an ark of wood. Here at the North Pole, a few men performed a similar service with an arc of electricity. The flying saucer which landed here, and its pilot, have been destroyed. And now before giving you the details of the battle, I bring you a warning. Everyone of you listening to my voice, tell the world, tell this to everybody whomever they are. Watch the skies everywhere, keep looking, keep watching the skies." It's **Douglas Spencer**'s transmission to the world at the end of the film. *The Thing* (1951, RKO).

10797 "You better wake up or you'll find your women and your kids will be squeezed between barbed wire and fence posts!" **Mercedes McCambridge** riles up ranchers by implying that Joan Crawford wants the railroad because it will destroy their way of life. *Johnny Guitar* (1954, Republic).

10798 "I know myself extremely well. I'm just near the fighting stage at the moment, and if I don't get my way, I begin to break up people and things." Drunken movie star **James Mason** lets everyone know that he's about to turn mean. *A Star Is Born* (1954, Warner Bros.).

10799 "One of these days half the world will be in ruins from the air. I want this country to be in the other half." In the 1920s, U.S. General Billy Mitchell, portrayed by **Gary Cooper**, gives a warning that is tragically ignored. *The Court-Martial of Billy Mitchell* (1955, United States Pictures).

10800 "Never get crowded into a corner. Never let them get too close. . . ." Sexy showgirl **Cyd Charisse** instructs a young dancer on how to protect herself at parties from the men in attendance. *Party Girl* (1958, MGM).

10801 "You've got a hundred and thirty-five men, all of them thinking about the peace at Panmunjom— and it's a cinch they don't want to die in what may be the last battle of the war." General **Ken Lynch** warns Lieutenant Gregory Peck of what to expect from the men Peck must lead against a hill held by the enemy while peace talks are taking place. *Pork Chop Hill* (1959, United Artists).

10802 "Watch out for me, kid." **Jason Robards, Jr.** tells his younger brother Dean Stockwell that he's no one to emulate. *Long Day's Journey into Night* (1962, Landau-Embassy).

10803 "There's so much crap in the world; you're going to wallow in it sooner or later, like it or not!" At the end of the film, **Paul Newman** warns Brandon de Wilde as the latter walks off into the sunset, rejecting his Uncle Newman's standards. *Hud* (1963, Paramount).

10804 "I have a writ here that says for you to stop eating Chen Lee's cornmeal. It's a rat writ." Drunken Marshal **John Wayne** orders a rat to cease and desist just before he blows the rodent away. *True Grit* (1969, Paramount).

10805 "Watch out for your goodies, Hawkeye—that guy's a sex maniac. Hot Lips didn't satisfy him." **Elliott Gould** kibitzes as Donald Sutherland interrogates near-mad Robert Duvall about Sally Kellerman's skills in the sack. *M*A*S*H* (1970, 20th Century-Fox).

10806 "I am a superstitious man. And if some unlikely accident should befall my son, if my son is struck by a bolt of lightning, I will blame some of the people here. That bad luck I could never forgive. But aside from that, let me swear by the souls of my grandchildren that I will never break the peace we have made." **Marlon Brando** gives a friendly warning to the other dons. *The Godfather* (1972, Paramount).

10807 "Next time, I'll knock your damn head off." At the end of the movie, mysterious stranger **Clint Eastwood** warns cowardly Sheriff Gregory Walcott. *Joe Kidd* (1972, Universal).

10808 "In ten minutes you're going to have two hundred tons of locomotive smashing its way through Central Station on its way to Marshall Field." Police Chief **Len Birman** warns a Chicago "Amroad" official of a run-away train coming into the station. *Silver Streak* (1976, 20th Century-Fox).

10809 "Do not approach the nameless one, lest your soul be withered. Beware the one who comes from beneath northern skies and lets loose the nameless one." Archeologist **Susannah York** translates the hieroglyphic inscription on a queen's tomb. *The Awakening* (1980, GB, EMI-Orion).

10810 "I want the rest of you cowboys to know something. There's a new sheriff in town." Black con **Eddie Murphy**, temporarily free, waves Nick Nolte's police badge at a bunch of rednecks in an urban country and western bar. *48 Hours* (1982, Paramount).

10811 "If you don't keep down stage of me, I'll have you nailed to the orchestra pit." **Albert Finney** reminds another player who is the star of his traveling Shakespearean repertory troupe. *The Dresser* (1983, GB, Columbia).

10812 "Never stray from the path; never eat a windfall apple, and never trust a man whose eyebrows meet. . . a wolf may be more than he seems. He may come in many disguises. The wolf that ate your sister was hairy on the outside, but when she died she went straight to heaven. The worst kind of wolves are hairy on the inside. They drag you with them to hell." **Angela Lansbury** shares some old folk wisdom with her granddaughter Sarah Patterson. *The Company of Wolves* (1984, GB, ITC).

10813 "Keep passing open windows. Otherwise you might jump out." **Wallace Shawn**, as "Freud," repeats the admonition that a remarkable New England family live by. *The Hotel New Hampshire* (1984, Orion).

10814 "I'll tell you now, I see this trial degenerating and I'll hit you like a freight train coming down the High Sierra." Judge **John Dehner** admonishes trial lawyers Glenn Close and Peter Coyote, who are at each other's throats. *Jagged Edge* (1985, Columbia).

10815 "I have a meat cleaver and I know how to use it." Grandma **Fran Lopate** refuses to let in a young man who needs the powerful sleeping pills mistakenly delivered to her. They are meant to prevent him from becoming a werewolf. *Deadtime Stories* (1987, Bedford Entertainment).

10816 "Your grandfather is about to marry the Bermuda Triangle." **Gina DeAngelis'** Aunt Sofia, tells Keith Coogan about his grandfather Lloyd Bridges and twice-widowed Norma Aleandro. *Cousins* (1989, Paramount).

10817 "Keep a close watch on your, uh, valuables." Norwegian seaman **Trond Peter Stasmo Munch** warns 14-year-old Stian Smestad, who is being eyed by a London prostitute. *Shipwrecked* (1991, Norweigian, Walt Disney-Buena Vista).

10818 "Don't let Lecter get into your head." FBI agent **Scott Glenn** warns trainee Jodie Foster about cannibalistic killer Anthony Hopkins, who seems to enjoy messing with her mind, while she's trying to learn about a serial killer from him. *The Silence of the Lambs* (1991, Orion).

10819 "You lousy minx, I ought to have you spayed." **Danny De Vito** as the Penguin, warns his new partner Michelle Pfeiffer, as Catwoman. *Batman Returns* (1992, Warner Bros.).

Wars

see also BATTLES AND BATTLEFIELDS, BOATS AND SHIPS, BOMBS, DEATH AND DYING, DEFEATS, DEFENSES, EXPLOSIONS, FIGHTS AND FIGHTING, KILLINGS, MILITARY, PEACE, VICTORIES, VIOLENCE, WINNERS AND LOSERS

10820 "At the next war, let all the kaisers, presidents, generals and diplomats go into a big field and fight it out amongst themselves. This will satisfy them and keep us home." World War I German soldier **Louis Wolheim** makes a suggestion that the ordinary soldiers of every nation could probably endorse. *All Quiet on the Western Front* (1930, Universal).

10821 "War, war, war. This war talk's spoiling all the fun at every party this spring. I get so bored I could scream. . . . If either of you says 'war' once more, I'll go in the house and shut the door." **Vivien Leigh**'s first words as Scarlett O'Hara, are spoken to the Tarleton twins, Fred Crane and George Reeves. *Gone with the Wind* (1939, Selznick-MGM).

10822 "Most of the miseries of the world were caused by wars. And, when the wars were over, no one ever knew what they were about." **Leslie Howard** doesn't share the exhilaration and pride of other Southern gentlemen when it is announced that the South has fired on Fort Sumter, beginning the Civil War. *Gone with the Wind* (1939, Selznick-MGM).

10823 "Good heavens, woman, this is war, not a garden party." **Harry Davenport** responds sharply to Laura Hope Crews, who questions the propriety of Vivien Leigh and Olivia de Havilland remaining in Atlanta unchaperoned. *Gone with the Wind* (1939, Selznick-MGM).

10824 "We want to help humanity. We fight wars only because we crave peace so ardently and we pray that each war will be the last. But always in the strange scheme of things some maniac with a lust for power arises and. . . destroys the peace and tranquility we've created. . . . We hate war. . . but when war comes, we must and will fight on and on." In a stirring patriotic speech, **Holmes Herbert** addresses the camera at the end of the film. Of course, this justification of going to war, most reluctantly, can lead to "destroying a village to liberate it" rationale. *British Intelligence* (1940, Warner Bros.).

10825 "War is the last refuge of the capitalists." Mild-mannered Frenchman **Frank Readick**, pretending to be a communist, uses an insult whose last word can be a blank to be filled in by anyone with a different candidate. *Journey into Fear* (1942, RKO).

10826 "We can't sit around holding hands with all that going on!" Merchant Marine first mate **Humphrey Bogart** rejects his wife Julie Bishop's plea that he not go to sea during World War II. *Action in the North Atlantic* (1943, Warner Bros.).

10827 "Yes. It'd be different for us. Wars don't leave people as they were. All people will learn this and come to see that wars do not have to be. We'll make this the last war. We'll make a free world for all men. The earth belongs to us, the people, if we fight for it. And we will fight for it." Young Russian peasant **Anne Baxter** expresses a hopeful, but thus far unrealized, hope for the end of wars, and the need for wars. *The North Star* (1943, RKO).

10828 "This is your war. . . you wanted it. . . you asked for it. And now you're going to get it—and it won't be finished until your dirty little empire is wiped off the face of the earth." Condemned U.S. pilot **Dana Andrews** defiantly predicts the destruction of Japan. *The Purple Heart* (1944, 20th Century-Fox).

10829 "That's the trouble with wars—you've got to fight them by ear." Medic **Sterling Holloway** discovers that despite all the planning and strategies of generals, field soldiers must revise them on the spot. *A Walk in the Sun* (1945, 20th Century-Fox).

10830 "Was this trip necessary?. . . Nobody wanted this war but the Nazis. A great many people tried to deal with them. Millions have died for no other reason except that the Nazis wanted them dead. In the final showdown there was nothing left to do except to fight. There's a great lesson in this. And those of us who learned it the hard way aren't going to forget it. We must never again let any force dedicated to a super race or super idea or super anything become strong enough to impose itself upon a free world. We must be smart enough and tough enough in the beginning to put out the fire before it starts spreading. . . yes, this trip was necessary." Chaplain **Leon Ames** gives a sermon about the Battle of the Bulge. *Battleground* (1949, MGM).

10831 Pvt. McHugh: "What's war?" Cpl. Thomas: "Trading real estate for men." Young Marine **Martin Milner** is given a pretty fair answer to his query by veteran grunt **Forrest Tucker**. *The Sands of Iwo Jima* (1949, Republic).

10832 "Linda, war is the most malignant disease of the human race. It is an infection. It is contagious. When we doctors operate, we sometimes cut good tissue along with the bad because we cannot take a chance." Colonel **Robert Mitchum** rationalizes to Ann Blyth, who is shocked when she witnesses the slaughter of innocents in Korea. *One Minute to Zero* (1952, RKO).

10833 "Three world wars in one lifetime. Maybe whiskey's as much a part of our life as war." Heavy drinking military surgeon **Humphrey Bogart** believes there is much justification for his habit. *Battle Circus* (1953, MGM).

10834 "This is the testing grounds for the Reds, and if we don't stop him here, he'll use his arms somewhere else." Test pilot **Alan Ladd** is ready for the commies if it's war they want. *The McConnell Story* (1955, Warner Bros.).

10835 "Don't speak to me of rules. This is war. . . not a game of cricket. He is mad, your colonel, quite mad." Japanese POW Camp Commandant **Sessue Hayakawa** dismisses British doctor James Donald's insistence that Colonel Alec Guinness and his officers be treated according to the Geneva Treaty Accord. *The Bridge on the River Kwai* (1957, GB, Columbia).

10836 "I was wrong—this war's going to last a long time." **Robert Ryan** comes to the conclusion when his platoon is cut off from headquarters as they try to take an enemy hill in Korea in 1950. *Men in War* (1957, United Artists).

10837 "War is the most monstrous of man's illusions. Any idea worth anything is worth not fighting for." The Civil War and slavery causes **Walter Abel** to formulate this opinion. *Raintree County* (1957, MGM).

10838 KRISTINA: "Do you like the war?" MAJ. CLEVE SAVILLE: "It's the only war I've got." When she asks a stupid question, **May Britt** gets a smart-ass answer from regular-army **Robert Mitchum.** *The Hunters* (1958, 20th Century-Fox).

10839 "He's dead. I'm crippled. You're lost. I guess it's always like that. I mean war." Wounded British pilot **Richard Burton** talks to stranded American Private Richard Beymer near the body of a dead German soldier. *The Longest Day* (1962, 20th Century-Fox).

10840 CAPT. PRATT: "The war is over." PVT. ENDORE: "There'll be another." **Charles Aidman**'s news about the Korean conflict doesn't cheer **John Saxon.** *War Hunt* (1962, United Artists).

10841 "Do you recall what Clemenceau once said about war?. . . He said war was too important to be left to the generals. When he said that, fifty years ago, he might have been right. But today, war is too important to be left to politicians. They have neither the time, the training nor the inclination for strategic thought. I can no longer sit back and allow communist infiltration, communist subversion and the international communist conspiracy to sap and impurify our precious bodily fluids." **Sterling Hayden** justifies to Peter Sellers his ordering air force bombers loaded with nuclear weapons on a run over the U.S.S.R. *Dr. Strangelove: or How I Learned to Stop Worrying and Love the Bomb* (1963, GB, Columbia).

10842 "Nuclear combat, toe to toe with the Russkies." **Slim Pickens**, as Major Kong, drawls happily as his plane speeds toward the U.S.S.R. to drop atomic bombs. *Dr. Strangelove: or How I Learned to Stop Worrying and Love the Bomb* (1963, GB, Columbia).

10843 "We shall never get rid of war by pretending it's unreal. It's the virtue of war that's the fraud, not war itself. It's the valor and self-sacrifice and the goodness of war that need the exposing." **James Garner** expresses an opinion of war, often held between wars, until everyone has forgotten how horrible war really is. *The Americanization of Emily* (1964, MGM).

10844 "All wars are idiotic. I don't care who wins." Struggling to stay alive, wealthy German army deserter **Marlon Brando** states his bitterness and isolation as an unwilling undercover agent for the British to Janet Margolin. *Morituri* (1965, 20th Century-Fox).

10845 "Compared to war, all other forms of human endeavor shrink to insignificance. . . . God help me, I do love it so." **George C. Scott** is the title character. *Patton* (1970, 20th Century-Fox).

10846 "I guess we all died a little in that damn war." **Clint Eastwood** refers to the American Civil War. *The Outlaw Josey Wales* (1976, Warner Bros.).

10847 "It's going to be a long war." Such are the sentiments of General **Robert Stack** in this freewheeling ho-hum comedy about the beginning of World War II. *1941* (1979, Universal).

10848 "It's a new kind of war, a new war for a new century." Title character **Edward Woodward**, a valiant soldier and poet, refers to the Boer War in which no prisoners are taken. *Breaker Morant* (1980, Australia, South Australian Film Corporation).

10849 "I've declared war. That's what I've done. Declared war!" Having taken all he could stomach at the hands of the white race, half-breed Australian aborigine **Tommy Lewis**, axe in hand, brutally murders white women and children. *The Chant of Jimmie Blacksmith* (1980, Australia, Film House).

10850 "Now that they'll let you make an antiwar statement, you haven't got a war. Vietnam is long since gone, and it's too damn late." Writer **Allen Goorwitz (Garfield)** sees some irony for megalomaniacal movie director Peter O'Toole who is making a World War I epic on location. *The Stunt Man* (1980, 20th Century-Fox).

10851 "For reasons long forgotten, two mighty warrior tribes went to war—and touched off a blaze which engulfed them all. Their world crumbled. Men began to feed on men. Only those mobile enough to scavenge, brutal enough to pillage would survive." The narrator introduces the post-nuclear war scenario. *The Road Warrior* (1982, Australian-Warner Bros.).

10852 "You're gonna love this war—good guys, bad guys and cheap shrimp." **Joanna Cassidy** welcomes news photographer Nick Nolte to Nicaragua. *Under Fire* (1983, Orion).

10853 "There's plenty of war here for everybody." Platoon Sergeant **Richard Brooks** rejects the suggestion that a patrol go to the aid of some cut-off comrades. *84 Charlie Mopic* (1989, New Century-Vista).

10854 "Wars don't come along very often. It's the chance of a lifetime for a career officer. Combat duty is the foundation of a successful career." Officer **Jonathan Emerson** believes that in the military, the event of war is a golden opportunity. *84 Charlie Mopic* (1989, New Century-Vista).

10855 "I used to rate all the wars by their politics and their Saturday nights, but it's just not particularly true." CIA agent **Mel Gibson** responds when his partner Robert Downey, Jr., asks what's going on in his head. *Air America* (1990, Tri-Star).

10856 "I don't know when the war between my parents began, but the only prisoners they took were their children." Even before the title appears on the screen, narrator **Nick Nolte**, in a voice-over, sets the stage for this film about the effects of a family at war on the three children. *The Prince of Tides* (1991, Columbia).

10857 "But, Ed, what's a war for if not to hold on to what we love?" Beautiful **Melanie Griffith**, in her whiney little girl voice, takes her leave of her lover Michael Douglas in a scene meant to remind us of the airport farewell of Humphrey Bogart and Ingrid Bergman in *Casablanca. Shining Through* (1991, 20th Century-Fox).

Washing *see* CLEANLINESS

Waste and Wastefulness

see also DESTRUCTION, ENERGY, EXTRAVAGANCES, GARBAGE, LOSSES AND LOSING

10858 "You're not wasted away. You're just wasted!" Doctor **Joseph Cawthorn**'s prescription for young widowed Princess Jeannette MacDonald,

always weak and suffering from fainting spells, is that she needs a lover. *Love Me Tonight* (1932, Paramount).

10859 "I'm much too busy making sure you don't waste the money I married you for." Ex-detective **William Powell** explains his mercenary reason for not coming out of retirement to solve a murder case. *The Thin Man* (1934, MGM).

10860 "I hate overtures. Lovemaking is the red tape of marriage. It doesn't get you anywhere. I could take you out for three months and send you flowers and all that flapdoodle, and I wouldn't know any more about you than I do now." Wealthy American **Gary Cooper** wants to marry Claudette Colbert first and then get to know her. *Bluebeard's Eighth Wife* (1938, Paramount).

10861 "Not good enough. I say they're not good enough for him. Every Jane in the room is giving him the thermometer and he feels they're just a waste of time." Con woman **Barbara Stanwyck** surveys and dismisses the competition for wealthy naïve Henry Fonda aboard a luxury liner. *The Lady Eve* (1941, Paramount).

10862 CORBACCIO: "Hey, boss, you got a woman in there?" RONALD KORNBLOW: "If I haven't, I've been wasting thirty minutes of valuable time." **Chico Marx** tries to protect **Groucho Marx**, new manager of the Casablanca Hotel, from the wiles of Lisette Verea, one of a gang of Nazis who has killed the previous three hotel managers. *A Night in Casablanca* (1945, United Artists).

10863 "Did you ever want to possess something that was unattainable? These masters became everything to me. . . . Unfortunately, museums have a habit of wasting good art on dolts who can't distinguish between it and trash." Clever elitist art collector **Ray Collins** justifies his stealing art treasures. *Crack-Up* (1946, RKO).

10864 "All some of them need is a break. A little understanding and guidance, maybe we can salvage some of this waste." Psychiatrist **Lee J. Cobb**'s remote cabin is invaded by escaped killer William Holden, his girl friend Nina Foch, and two pals. Cobb spots Holden's mental illness and conquers him mentally. *The Dark Past* (1948, Columbia).

10865 "Sometimes I wonder whether it wasn't a great waste of money to import eleven thousand ping-pong tables for you men." General **Millard Mitchell** reprimands Captain John Lund for his affair with German singer Marlene Dietrich in post-war Berlin. *A Foreign Affair* (1948, Paramount).

10866 "I hate a tramp. . . you always gotta tell 'em, 'I love you, baby,'. . . a waste of time." **Richard Benedict** gasps to his faithful moll Gloria De Haven as he lies dying. *Scene of the Crime* (1949, MGM).

10867 "Sympathy? That's not what you're getting from me, baby. You don't deserve it. You're a great monument to Norman Maine, you are. He was a drunk, and he wasted his life, but he loved you. And he took enormous pride in the one thing in his life that wasn't a waste, you. His love for you and your success. That was the one thing in his life that wasn't a waste. And he knew it. Maybe he was wrong to do what he did, I don't know. But he didn't want to destroy that, destroy the only thing he took pride in. And now you're doing the one thing he was terrified of, you're wiping it out! You're tossing aside the one thing he had left. You're tossing it right back in the ocean after him. You're the only thing that remains of him now. And if you just kick it away, it's like he never existed, like there never was a Norman Maine at all." Old friend **Tommy Noonan** encourages movie star Judy Garland to go on with her career after her actor husband James Mason commits suicide by walking into the ocean. He realized that his behavior was not only ruining his life and career but hers as well. *A Star Is Born* (1954, Warner Bros.).

10868 "I had my chance, father, and I lost. If I lose without honor, if at the last moment I weaken, then it's all without meaning, wasted." To make up for the loss of the life of the son of a native chief, **Peter O'Toole** nobly offers up his life. *Lord Jim* (1965, GB, Columbia).

10869 "Don't waste your green years. Before you know it, your life's slipped down the drain." Not yet 30, boxer **Stacy Keach** advises young amateur boxer Jeff Bridges. *Fat City* (1972, Columbia).

10870 "Seven years down the drain." It's the disheartened comment of **John Belushi** after he's kicked out of college. *National Lampoon's Animal House* (1978, Universal).

10871 "If you're acting, you're wasting your time. If you're not, you're wasting mine." **Steve Forrest**, as lawyer Greg Savitt, is unimpressed with Faye Dunaway, portraying Joan Crawford. *Mommie Dearest* (1981, Paramount).

Watching and Watchers

see also ATTENTION, EYES, SIGHT AND SIGHTS, TIME

10872 COUNTESS VALENTINE: "The Baron will be down in a moment. He had to send to Paris for his costume, and it was late getting here. I've been watching him put it on." THE DUKE: "You've been what?" VICOMTE GILBERT DE VAREZE: "It's all right, Uncle. She has the room next to Maurice, and she's bored holes in the connecting door." THE DUKE: "Are you aware that that door has come down to us through generations?" VALENTINE: "So have my instincts." It's some delightfully naughty talk involving aristocratic **Myrna Loy**, her uncle **C. Aubrey Smith** and her penniless cousin **Charles Ruggles.** The object of their conversation is imposter Maurice Chevalier, thought to be a baron, but who in fact is a mere tailor. *Love Me Tonight* (1932, Paramount).

10873 "Sometimes it needs a lot of watching; seems to go crazy every now and then, like Uncle Charlie." Detective **Macdonald Carey** comforts Teresa Wright, who concludes the world is a terrible place after discovering that her beloved uncle Joseph Cotten is a psychopathic killer. *Shadow of a Doubt* (1943, Universal).

10874 "Even with her eyes shut she seems to be watching you like an evil spirit." Nurse **Sara Allgood** refers to her patient, dying Ethel Barrymore. *The Spiral Staircase* (1945, RKO).

10875 "You don't know what it's like to watch somebody you love just crumble away bit by bit, day by day, in front of your eyes, and stand there helpless. Love isn't enough. I thought it was." **Judy Garland** weeps to studio head Charles Bickford about the deterioration of her husband, alcoholic, fading movie idol James Mason. *A Star Is Born* (1954, Warner Bros.).

10876 "I'm paying you to watch her, ain't I? So why don't you get to work?" Chicago mobster **Harold J. Stone** commissions rock 'n' roll singer Elvis Presley to keep his eye on Stone's errant daughter Shelley Fabares in Fort Lauderdale during Easter week when all the collegians converge on the city for their annual spring break. *Girl Happy* (1965, MGM).

10877 "It's a little bit harder to watch what you did than it was for you to do what I was watching." **Robert Redford** defends himself in a domestic quarrel with his young wife Jane Fonda. She has hurt him to the quick, accusing him of being unable to have a good time. *Barefoot in the Park* (1967, Paramount).

10878 "Anything you ask me I'll do, except one thing. I won't watch you die. I'll miss that scene if you don't mind." **Katharine Ross** decides to leave outlaws Robert Redford and Paul Newman in Bolivia. *Butch Cassidy and the Sundance Kid* (1969, 20th Century-Fox).

10879 "I'm going to have to watch you from now on. You might just decide to cut off my other leg." **Clint Eastwood** curses school teacher Geraldine Page who admits that she amputated his wounded leg needlessly because he went to bed with student Jo Ann Harris instead of Page. *The Beguiled* (1971, Universal).

10880 "I like to watch!" Slow-witted gardener **Peter Sellers** means television. Shirley MacLaine thinks he means watching her masturbate. *Being There* (1979, United Artists).

10881 "Oh, we just go to the woods and watch the bark peel off the trees." It's **David Strathairn**'s response when asked what he does the rest of the year as he welcomes back classmates for a reunion. *The Return of the Secaucus 7* (1980, Libra).

10882 "I don't want crowds of people watching me grow old." Cranky **Henry Fonda** reacts when his daughter Jane Fonda shows up at Henry's lakeside summer home with her latest lover and his son just prior to Henry's 80th birthday. *On Golden Pond* (1981, Universal).

10883 "I can't pee—you're watching me because I'm Spanish." Adopted **Benjamin H. Carlin** complains to his father Al Pacino that he can't perform in an always crowded bathroom. *Author! Author!* (1982, 20th Century-Fox).

10884 "Look, there are two Guccis coming on to a Pierre Cardin." **Mary Woronov** resorts to brand names to point out the action at a party for swingers that she is attending with her husband Paul Bartel. *Eating Raoul* (1982, Bartel Films).

10885 "Other people are watching you. At home, at school, maybe even in the bathroom." Spooky father **Randy Quaid** stares down over his glasses at his youngest son Bryan Madorsky, who understandably has weird nightmares. *Parents* (1988, Vestron).

10886 "I can't believe I have a bunch of dead people watching videos in my living room." **Juliet Stevenson** delivers a memorable line when her beloved deceased husband comes back to watch video tapes with her. *Truly, Madly, Deeply* (1991, GB, Goldwyn).

Water

see also BATHING AND BATHROOMS, BOATS AND SHIPS, DRINKING AND DRUNKENNESS, SEAS, WEATHER

10887 "I'll send you an onion. That'll make your ice water!" Hotel manager **Groucho Marx** makes a little play on words to a guest who has called down to the front desk for some ice water. *The Cocoanuts* (1929, Paramount).

10888 "I never knew there was so much 'vater' in the 'vorld.'" Phony princess **Carole Lombard** gives her best Greta Garbo impersonation as she mournfully looks out to sea. *The Princess Comes Across* (1936, Paramount).

10889 "If they serve it again, I'm gonna bring a bar of soap to the table and wash out a few stockings." **Ginger Rogers** eyes the boardinghouse soup, which if it were a little thicker could pass for hot dish water. *Stage Door* (1937, RKO).

10890 "First drink of water he had in 20 years, and then he had to get it by accident. Bud, how do you wire congratulations to the Pacific Ocean?" Publicity director **Lionel Stander** sheds no tears with the news that difficult alcoholic actor Fredric March has drowned himself. *A Star Is Born* (1937, Selznick-United Artists).

10891 RICK: "I came to Casablanca for the waters." RENAULT: "But we're in the desert." RICK: "I was misinformed." It's our personal favorite exchange from the movie. **Humphrey Bogart** is evasive when police prefect **Claude Rains** speculates on what brought Bogart to Casablanca. *Casablanca* (1942, Warner Bros.).

10892 "Have you ever had your face close to the water and held your hand in it as you looked down in it?. . . Deep water is dark and restful and full of peace. I take my problems to the river." Mysterious **Laird Cregar**, a Jack the Ripper clone, confounds his intended victim, actress Merle Oberon. *The Lodger* (1944, 20th Century-Fox).

10893 "I don't hold with too much water, anyhow. Rusts the bones." **Percy Kilbride**, as Pa Kettle, doesn't bathe very often. *The Egg and I* (1947, Universal).

10894 "I used to hate water. I can't imagine why." Amity Island Police Chief **Roy Scheider** can joke now that he's survived the man-eating shark menacing the area, by jamming an air tank into the monster's mouth and exploding it. *Jaws* (1975, Universal).

10895 LIL: "Hey, this is for ladies!" ALAN SWANN: "So is this, madam, but every now and again I have to run some water through it." Wardrobe mistress **Selma Diamond**'s objection to **Peter O'Toole** using the women's lavatory is ignored. *My Favorite Year* (1982, MGM-United Artists).

Ways

see also ACTIONS AND ACTS, BEHAVIOR, EXPERIENCES, LIVES AND LIVING, MANNERS, PREFERENCES, PROGRESS, WISHES

10896 "That's the only way you get outta here. Serve your time or die." Old con **Edward Ellis** advises Paul Muni to forget about trying to escape as they watch freed Allen Jenkins ride out of the prison, sitting on the coffin of a prisoner who died. *I Am a Fugitive from a Chain Gang* (1932, Warner Bros).

10897 "There must be a way of getting that money back without getting in trouble with the Hays office." **Groucho Marx** makes an aside to the audience. He's referring to the Will Hays who oversees Hollywood's self-censorship office. Eve Arden has just grabbed Groucho's money and stuffed it into her bra. *At the Circus* (1939, MGM).

10898 "It's always been this way since Bible days. Every generation must make its own way—one way or another." Minister **Edwin Maxwell** confronts sobbing Clara Blandick as her daughter Claudette Colbert departs her wedding with her new husband Henry Fonda headed for New York's Mohawk Valley to make their new home. *Drums Along the Mohawk* (1939, 20th Century-Fox).

10899 "Don't think love can find a way. I know all the ways." **Donald Randolph** intercepts the love poems hotel clerk Jack Lemmon has written to Randolph's daughter Anna Kashfi. *Cowboy* (1958, Columbia).

10900 "The way of a woman is simple, my lord. It is always to follow the way of a man. . . ." Sheba, played by **Gina Lollobrigida**, says it to Solomon, portrayed by Yul Brynner. *Solomon and Sheba* (1959, United Artists).

10901 ELI LAPP: "It's not our way." JOHN BOOK: "But it's my way." When some boorish tourists make fun of the appearance and peaceful nature of the Amish, elder **Jan Rubes** tries to prevent **Harrison Ford**, a Philadelphia police detective posing as a member of the community, from reacting violently. Ford is not dissuaded. *Witness* (1985, Paramount).

Weakness

see also FAULTS, IMPOTENCY, LIMITS AND LIMITATIONS, STRENGTHS

10902 "My wife thinks I am a darling. My wife's best friend thinks I'm cute. It's a terrible situation. But I am determined not to weaken. [He shrugs.] We'll

see." Philandering Parisian doctor **Maurice Chevalier**, in an aside to the audience, refers to his lovely wife Jeanette MacDonald and the lustful Genevieve Tobin. *One Hour with You* (1932, Paramount).

10903 "Oh, I thought I was alone. Good evening! Have a cigar. It's my only weakness!" **Ernest Thesiger**, as Dr. Pretorius, plays the good host to Boris Karloff as Frankenstein's monster. At another point in the film, the flamboyant mad scientist and charlatan says, "Gin. It is my only weakness, you know." *The Bride of Frankenstein* (1935, Universal).

10904 "I've always had a weakness for size twelve." **John Barrymore** guesses Claudette Colbert's dress size. *Midnight* (1939, Paramount).

10905 "Tracy is a married maiden with no regard for human frailty." **Cary Grant** describes his ex-wife Katharine Hepburn. *The Philadelphia Story* (1940, MGM).

10906 "Laura, you have one tragic weakness. For you a lean, strong body is the measure of a man—and you always get hurt." Now if Gene Tierney would only dedicate herself to **Clifton Webb**, he knows she'd be okay. *Laura* (1944, 20th Century-Fox).

10907 "In every man lies the seed of destruction. . . a fatal weakness." Devil **Ray Milland** seeks such weaknesses to exploit. *Alias Nick Beal* (1949, Paramount).

10908 "Never apologize, Mister, it's a sign of weakness." Cavalry Captain **John Wayne** barks what sounds like an order to young Lieutenant Harry Carey, Jr. *She Wore a Yellow Ribbon* (1949, RKO).

10909 "You know this is my weak arm." **Arnold Schwarzenegger** warns David Patrick Kelly whom he's holding upside down with one arm over a cliff. Arnie gets tired. Later, when asked by Rae Dawn Chong as to what happened to Kelly, Schwarzenegger dryly says, "I had to let him go." *Commando* (1985, 20th Century-Fox).

10910 "I have a weakness. I like to lose control." **Meryl Streep** confesses as she sabotages her husband Charles Dance's political career. *Plenty* (1985, 20th Century-Fox-RKO).

Wealth and Riches

see also GOLD, GREED, JEWELRY, MONEY, POVERTY, WORTH AND VALUES

10911 "Enough ivory to supply the world. There's a million pounds for the man who finds it." Explorer

C. Aubrey Smith tells his daughter Maureen O'Sullivan that their safari seeks a legendary elephant ground containing a fortune in burial tusks. *Tarzan, the Ape Man* (1932, MGM).

10912 PETER WARNE: "To be a 'piggy-backer' it takes complete relaxation, a warm heart, and a loving nature." ELLIE ANDREWS: "And rich people have none of these qualifications, I suppose." PETER: "Not a one." **Clark Gable** argues with **Claudette Colbert** over the nature of people's "piggy-backing" skills. *It Happened One Night* (1934, Columbia).

10913 "I'm city people. I like great big shiny limousines and orchids in a vase. I love the cold wind whipping around a skyscraper—and a sable coat to keep it out." Sexy, vulnerable **Lana Turner** draws title character Lew Ayres away from his ethical practice and nearly wrecks his career. *Calling Dr. Kildare* (1939, MGM).

10914 "I guess rich people are only poor people with money." Salesgirl **Ginger Rogers** tries to be astute as she talks to complaining millionaire Walter Connolly. *Fifth Avenue Girl* (1939, RKO).

10915 "I know you don't like the rich, but I'm not a capitalist. I'm a victim of the capitalistic system. . . . All I wanted was a family and some fun." Millionaire **Walter Connolly** persuades unemployed Ginger Rogers to pose as a gold digger in order to upset his family. *Fifth Avenue Girl* (1939, RKO).

10916 "If true love carries any weight with you, you can be sure your sister will be rich in that." **Carroll Nye** asks Vivien Leigh, as the eldest of the surviving O'Haras, for her sister Evelyn Keyes' hand in marriage. When Leigh finds that Nye owns a prospering store and a lumber mill, she marries him herself. *Gone with the Wind* (1939, Selznick-MGM).

10917 "You have the sort of wealth no one can destroy." Soldier **John Hodiak** admires Anne Baxter and her poor, but loving family. *Sunday Dinner for a Soldier* (1944, 20th Century-Fox).

10918 "You're so dumb, you don't know the riches you're treading on. . . couple of jackasses for not seeing it. . . . But it's not rich enough. . . . Up there's where we got to go. . . . Up there. . . . Up there!" Prospector **Walter Huston** dances a little jig as he tells his partners Humphrey Bogart and Tim Holt that they are walking on gold and don't recognize it. But he claims the real riches are higher up in the mountains. *The Treasure of the Sierra Madre* (1948, Warner Bros.).

10919 "By golly, I'm the richest man in six counties." It's true, Professor **Ronald Reagan** has Diana Lynn and a chimpanzee brought up like a human baby. *Bedtime for Bonzo* (1951, Universal-International).

10920 "Bick, you should have shot that fella a long time ago. Now he's too rich to kill." **Chill Wills** regrets that rancher Rock Hudson didn't get rid of troublesome oil tycoon James Dean when he was just a hand on Hudson's ranch. *Giant* (1956, Warner Bros.).

10921 "I'm part of a minority group—millionaires. You outnumber us but you'll never get us. We'll fight for our rights to the bitter end. We've got the money to do it." It's difficult for Rock Hudson to have much sympathy for "minority" **Tony Randall**, as he stands up for his economic class. *Pillow Talk* (1959, Universal).

10922 FINIAN MCLONERGAN: "Everyone in America is rich." SHARON MCLONERGAN: "Are there no ill-housed and ill-clad?" FINIAN: "Yes, but they're the best ill-housed and ill-clad in all the world." Simple Irish immigrant **Fred Astaire** preaches the American dream to his daughter **Petula Clark.** Sadly, Astaire is wrong. *Finian's Rainbow* (1968, Warner Bros.).

10923 "Are you mountainously rich?" **Vanessa Redgrave**, as dancer Isadora Duncan, hopefully puts the question to Jason Robards, as sewing machine magnate Paris Singer. *Isadora* aka: *The Loves of Isadora* (1968, GB, Universal).

10924 JACY FARROW: "Mama, you married Daddy when he was poor and he got rich, didn't he?" LOIS FARROW: "I scared your daddy into getting rich, beautiful. You're not scary enough." **Cybill Shepherd** wants to marry penniless Jeff Bridges. Mama **Ellen Burstyn** doesn't think it's a good idea. *The Last Picture Show* (1971, Columbia).

10925 "All I am or was is rich, and that's all I ever wanted to be." **Walter Matthau**, the last of the New York playboys, is delighted that he's rich. *A New Leaf* (1971, Paramount).

10926 "Why, sure you will, honey pie. You've got used to me, didn't you? Anyways, first get used to being rich." After surviving a shoot-out with his former gang and the posse pursuing them, horse thief **Jack Nicholson** and weird Mary Steenburgen head south with their sacks of gold, moving toward the border and happiness. *Goin' South* (1978, Paramount).

10927 "Daddy does oil—and all that implies." **Madolyn Smith** boasts a bit when she takes John Travolta back to her luxurious Houston apartment. *Urban Cowboy* (1980, Paramount).

10928 "I've never seen such a vulgar display of wealth in my entire life. Where do I get one?" **Andrew McCarthy** is impressed with his first sight of his prep school roommate Rob Lowe's mansion home. Wait till he meets Lowe's mom, Jacqueline Bisset. *Class* (1983, Orion).

10929 "Wake up, will ya, pal? If you're not inside, you're outside, OK? And I'm not talking about some $400,000 a year working Wall Street stiff, flying first class and being comfortable. I'm talking about liquid. Rich enough to have your own jet. Rich enough to waste time. Fifty, a hundred million dollars, buddy. . . a player. . . or nothing." Player **Michael Douglas** is Mephistopheles to Charlie Sheen's Faust. *Wall Street* (1987, 20th Century-Fox).

Weapons

see also BATTLES AND BATTLEFIELDS, DEATH AND DYING, DEFENSES, KILLINGS, LIFE AND DEATH, MILITARY, SURVIVAL, WARS

10930 "What an awful way to kill a man with a knife! Now a good stiff whack over the 'ead with a brick is one thing—there's something British about that! But a knife? No, knives is not right! Now mind you, a knife is a difficult thing to handle. Not just any knife will do. . . a knife. . . and with a knife. . . . And if you come to Chelsea, you mustn't bring a knife." Gossipy neighbor **Phyllis Monkman** whines at a family breakfast about a murder reported in the morning newspaper. Anny Ondra, the daughter of the house, used the knife to kill artist Cyril Ritchard, when he tried to have his way with her after she foolishly went to his apartment. *Blackmail* (1929, GB, British International).

10931 "That's all I got between me and them, between me and the whole world." **Edward G. Robinson** has a wistful feeling for his gun. *Little Caesar* (1930, Warner Bros.)

10932 "Cute, isn't it? Did Santy Claus bring it for Christmas?. . . I got a fire engine." **Groucho Marx** taunts Harry Woods, who threatens Marx with a gun. *Monkey Business* (1931, Paramount).

10933 "Look at it, Johnny, you can carry it like a baby. . . . I'm goin' to write my name all over town in big letters. Outta my way, I'm spittin'." Mobster **Paul Muni** gleefully shows off his new toy to his boss Osgood Perkins. Muni is delighted with his first Thompson sub-machine gun. *Scarface* (1932, United Artists).

10934 "I unsheathed my Bowie knife and cut a path through the wa-a-all of human flesh dragging my canoe behind." **W.C. Fields** relates a tall tale of his battle against a bunch of savages. *Mississippi* (1935, Paramount).

10935 RASSENDYLL: "When did you give up knives for pistols?" RUPERT: "Oh, I left my knife in Michael. . . you may as well face it, Rassendyll, I'm not a gentleman." While dueling, British commoner **Ronald Colman** learns that **Douglas Fairbanks, Jr.** has killed Raymond Massey. The latter plotted to usurp the throne from his brother, the spitting image of Colman. When the heir to the throne was kidnapped, Colman was pressed into service to masquerade as the missing royal. *The Prisoner of Zenda* (1937, Selznick-United Artists).

10936 TERRY RANDALL: "I use the right knife and fork." JOAN MAITLAND: "All you need here is a knife." Smug **Katharine Hepburn** feels superior to the other girls living at the theatrical hotel for women, but her roommate **Ginger Rogers** warns her that things are pretty cutthroat. *Stage Door* (1937, RKO).

10937 "Aside from being nice ornaments, a fellow can have a whole lot of harmless amusement with these toys. . . ." Deputy Sheriff **James Stewart** demonstrates that though he doesn't personally pack six-shooters, he certainly can do some fancy shooting with them. *Destry Rides Again* (1939, Universal).

10938 "You handle your sword like a devil from hell." Still confident **Basil Rathbone** duels title character Tyrone Power to the death. *The Mark of Zorro* (1940, 20th Century-Fox).

10939 "He just touched the trigger and the gun went 'rat-tat-tat-tat.' And the rat fell out of his chair." To make a point for two young hoodlums Arthur Kennedy and Alan Curtis, graying gangster **Humphrey Bogart** taps rapidly on a table to simulate bullets spurting from a machine gun. Bogie tells the boys how a former partner dealt with a suspected informer. *High Sierra* (1941, Warner Bros.).

10940 "Was that cannon fire—or is it my heart pounding?" The audience isn't as close to **Ingrid Bergman** as is Humphrey Bogart, so all they can hear is the German cannon fire. *Casablanca* (1942, Warner Bros.).

10941 SAKIMA: "Your bullets are all gone, but I have one left." MASKED MARVEL: "Did it not occur to your Oriental mind that I might reload?" In a classic showdown, diabolical **Johnny Arthur**, head of enemy agents, gleefully notes that hero **William Forrest** has emptied his revolver in a frantic gun battle. As Arthur moves to shoot Forrest, the latter shoots the former with his reloaded gun. *The Masked Marvel* (1943, serial, Republic).

10942 "Oh, that, that's just part of my clothes. I hardly ever shoot anybody with it." Wisecracking at all times, private eye **Dick Powell** surrenders his gun to some bad guys. *Murder, My Sweet* (1944, RKO).

10943 "My, my, my. Such a lot of guns around town and so few brains." The most interesting private eyes such as **Humphrey Bogart** use their brains as weapons. *The Big Sleep* (1946, Warner Bros.).

10944 "Only a man who carries a gun needs one." There's something profound in **John Wayne**'s statement, but we're not sure what. *Angel and the Badman* (1947, Republic).

10945 "I must go and clean my pistol." **Michael Redgrave** has need of a weapon in this story of murder, doom and guilt. It's an unimaginative production of the Eugene O'Neill play based on the Greek tragedy "Oresteia." *Mourning Becomes Electra* (1947, RKO).

10946 "A dame with a rod is like a guy with a knitting needle." **Steve Brodie** has time to enjoy his little jab at Jane Greer, who has him covered with a gun—before she shoots and kills him, perhaps for bad taste. *Out of the Past* (1947, RKO).

10947 "My boy friend stabbed himself on a knife I was holding." Tough broad **Iris Adrian** matter of factly answers fellow inmate Joan Crawford's query as to why Adrian is in jail. *Flamingo Road* (1949, Warner Bros.).

10948 "I've just got to have a gun. [It makes me] feel good inside, like I'm somebody." **John Dall** tells a judge that a gun gives him some self-esteem. *Gun Crazy* (1949, King Brothers-United Artists).

10949 "Well, I don't know. If they can take off when the birds won't even fly, I guess the blockade isn't much of a weapon." **Paul Douglas** is one of the pilots involved in the Berlin airlift after World War II. *The Big Lift* (1950, 20th Century-Fox).

10950 "A gun is a tool, no better and no worse than the man using it." Gunslinger **Alan Ladd** defends weapons to Jean Arthur who tells him she doesn't want her son growing up using guns. *Shane* (1953, Paramount).

10951 "A man has to be what he is. . . . You can't break the mold. There's no living with a killing; it's a brand that sticks. . . . Go home now, Joey, and tell your mother that there are no more guns in the valley." After killing all the bad guys, who have been harassing the homesteaders, gunslinger **Alan Ladd** knows he can't just put his guns away and retire. He says his farewells to hero-worshiping young

Brandon de Wilde and then rides away, taking his gun out of the valley. *Shane* (1953, Paramount).

10952 "Without the gun I'm nothing, and I never had anything before I got one. First time I got one in my hands and killed a man I got some self-respect. I was somebody. Without the gun you would never have spit on me. You would never have even noticed me. But because of the gun, you'll remember me as long as you live." Hired assassin **Frank Sinatra** informs his hostages that a gun gets him the attention he seeks. *Suddenly* (1954, United Artists).

10953 "Don't tell me, you didn't know it was loaded." **Cary Grant** is almost done in by Audrey Hepburn. *Charade* (1963, Universal).

10954 ROOSTER COGBURN: "By God! A Colt's dragoon! Why you are no bigger than a corn nubbin! What are you doing with that pistol?" MATTIE ROSS: "It belonged to my father. I intend to kill Tom Chaney with it if the law fails to do so. I'm afraid nothing much is going to be done about him except if I do it myself." ROOSTER: "Well, that'll get the job done." **John Wayne** is impressed with the size of **Kim Darby**'s horse pistol and her intentions to kill Jeff Corey, who murdered her father. *True Grit* (1969, Paramount).

10955 "We've got to start thinking beyond our guns. Those days are closing fast." **William Holden** knows that his days as an outlaw leader are quickly coming to an end as civilization reaches further and further west. *The Wild Bunch* (1969, Warner Bros.).

10956 "Leave the gun, take the cannoli." **Richard Castellano** gives orders to the hood who shoots John Martino, Marlon Brando's bodyguard, who had absented himself when the godfather was shot down the street. *The Godfather* (1972, Paramount).

10957 "I knew one thing: as soon as anyone said you didn't need a gun, you'd better take one along that worked." Having been hired to do a job, private eye **Robert Mitchum** is careful. *Farewell, My Lovely* (1975, Avco Embassy).

10958 "He pulled a knife on me. A kitchen knife. It was still dirty from breakfast." **George Burns** believes his long-time comedy partner Walter Matthau is not only crazy but dangerous as well. *The Sunshine Boys* (1975, MGM).

10959 GENERAL BELLO: "Tell me what your favorite weapon is." ROBERT DAPES: "Brains." Venal, incompetent Cuban General **Martin Balsam** questions British mercenary **Sean Connery**. *Cuba* (1979, United Artists).

10960 "You mess with someone's blade, you mess with his soul." Fast-talking, foul-mouthed Japanese thug **Calvin Jung** warns American drifter Scott Glenn about the significance of a treasured ceremonial sword. *The Challenge* (1982, Embassy).

10961 "I always believed that mud is the best weapon." **Sylvester Stallone** is an untalented Victor Mature-like mercenary, who returns to Southeast Asia to continue the battle. *Rambo: First Blood Part II* (1985, Tri-Star).

10962 "That's not a knife. . . that's a knife." Australian **Paul Hogan** flashes a large Bowie knife to a would-be mugger wielding a switchblade. *"Crocodile" Dundee* (1986, Paramount).

10963 "Forty years and it's never been registered." **Paul Shenar** proudly displays his prize gun—a nickel-plated automatic once owned by gangster Ben "Bugsy" Siegel. *The Bedroom Window* (1987, DEG).

10964 "I suppose we'll have to register you as a lethal weapon." Police detective **Danny Glover** is half-serious about his new partner Mel Gibson, who has a tendency to kill people in the line of duty. *Lethal Weapon* (1987, Warner Bros.).

10965 "Where does he get those wonderful toys?" **Jack Nicholson**, as the Joker, is envious of Batman's special weapons. *Batman* (1989, Warner Bros.).

10966 "A clean weapon is a safe weapon." It's one of the aphorisms broadcast by **Claudia Wick**, the voice of Big Sister in this post-apocalyptic action film. *Aftershock* (1990, Spectrum).

10967 "[I don't know, but] the fourth war will be fought with stones." At the end of the film, **Harry Dean Stanton** repeats Albert Einstein's answer when he was asked what weapons will be used in a third World War. *The Fourth War* (1990, Cannon).

10968 "Why is it that there's a gun shop on almost every corner? You go to Beverly Hills, you don't see that shit. They want us to kill ourselves." Furious **Larry Fishburne** complains to some South Central L.A. residents. *Boyz N the Hood* (1991, Columbia).

10969 "God, I hate these things." Reporter **Jay O. Sanders** cringes when private eye Kathleen Turner tosses him a pistol. *V.I. Warshawski* (1991, Buena Vista-Hollywood Pictures).

10970 "My secret weapon is PMS." **Kristy Swanson** is able to detect bloodsucking vampires by using her menstrual cramps as a sort of radar. *Buffy, the Vampire Slayer* (1992, 20th Century-Fox).

10971 "I'm looking for a really big gun that holds a lot of bullets." Rookie law enforcement officer **Christian Slater** places an order in a gun shop. *Kuffs* (1992, 20th Century-Fox).

10972 LITTLE BILL DAGGETT: "You shot an unarmed man." BILL MUNNY: "Well, he should have armed himself." **Gene Hackman** is in danger of the same fate, as **Clint Eastwood** has him in his rifle's sights. *Unforgiven* (1992, Warner Bros.).

Weather ·

see also CLIMATES, SEASONS

10973 "The snow is like a wild sea. One could go out and be lost in it." Swedish Queen **Greta Garbo** compares the endless snow with the endless sea. *Queen Christina* (1933, MGM).

10974 "Strange things weather. Yesterday it was cool when the angels had charge of it. Today they must have an engagement somewhere else, so the devil took over and decided to move the equator to the North Pole, but by the time he got half way he must have thought of something else he wanted to do and left the equator right here on top of us. I wish he'd come back and get it." **Katharine Hepburn** desperately tries to make conversation about the extremely warm weather to society guest Fred Mac-Murray at a disastrous dinner party with her working class family. Her interpretation seems as good as the one given by today's clowning weather men and women. *Alice Adams* (1935, RKO).

10975 "When the clumsy cloud from here meets a fluffy little cloud from there, he billows towards her. She scurries away, and he runs right up to her. She cries a little, and then you have a shower. He comforts her. They spark. That's the lightning. They kiss. Thunder!" **Fred Astaire** pursues resistant Ginger Rogers with an amorous weather report. *Top Hat* (1935, RKO).

10976 "Well, it was raining and we were in Pittsburgh." **Helen Broderick** explains to Barbara Stanwyck why she married Ned Sparks with whom she is always bickering. *The Bride Walks Out* (1936, RKO).

10977 "It's a bit nippy tonight. You'll make a proper hot water bottle." It's the suggestion made by **Cary Grant** that sends Katharine Hepburn, posing as a boy, skedaddling. *Sylvia Scarlett* (1936, RKO).

10978 "We've been having a lot of weather lately." **Oliver Hardy** tries to strike up a conversation with fellow traveler Vivien Oakland. *Way Out West* (1937, MGM).

10979 "I think the whole world should be covered with snow; it would be so much more clean." **Norma Shearer** has a solution for world blight. *Idiot's Delight* (1939, MGM).

10980 "It always rains when Stephanie gives one of her dull parties—even Nature weeps." **Elaine Barrie** disparages Hedda Hopper's parties. *Midnight* (1939, Paramount).

10981 "It got a bit chilly uptown. I thought I'd come down here where it's warmer." **John Wayne** comes sniffling around Marlene Dietrich on the night he is wed to society woman Louise Allbritton. *Pittsburgh* (1942, Universal).

10982 "Nasty weather we're having, eh? And I so much hoped we could give you a white Christmas—just like the ones you used to know." Camp Commandant **Otto Preminger** makes a cruel little joke for American POWs. *Stalag 17* (1953, Paramount).

10983 "I love the rain. It washes off the sidewalks of life." **Woody Allen** is being pretentious. *Play It Again, Sam* (1972, Paramount).

10984 "You need the brain of a yak to go hunting robbers in this weather." Insurance investigator **Vittorio De Sica** refers to a bank heist at a resort carried out on skis and a snowmobile by real-life Olympic ski champion Jean-Claude Killy, who can ski, but can't act. *Snow Job* (1972, Warner Bros.)

10985 "I dunno. I suppose it's like two drops of rain that fall together and become one." **Burt Reynolds** makes a poetic explanation for Sarah miles of how two people fall in love. *The Man Who Loved Cat Dancing* (1973, MGM).

10986 "We had some money put aside for a rainy day, but we didn't know it was going to get this wet." **Jane Connell**, as Agnes Gooch, tells of the effects of the Depression on the household of Lucille Ball as Mame Dennis. *Mame* (1974, Warner Bros.).

10987 "Hi. You been down here before? Pretty funky. There's been some great storms; feels like everything's gonna blow away. I really like that feeling, you know? How old are you?" Seventeen-year-old **Melanie Griffith** questions private investigator Gene Hackman. He's been hired to find Griffith by her mother, blowzy actress Janet Ward. *Night Moves* (1975, Warner Bros.).

10988 "I've seen things people won't believe. . . attack ships on fire off the shoulders of Orion. . . .

All those moments will be lost in time. . . like tears in rain." Having murdered his creator Joe Turkel, replicant **Rutger Hauer** dies eloquently, lamenting the loss of his memories and experiences along with the loss of his life, with a metaphor on his lips as he notices rain moistening his face. *Blade Runner* (1982, Warner Bros.).

10989 "Just listen to the old Pork Chop Express here now, and take this advice on a dark and stormy night when the lightning's crashing and the thunder's roaring and the rain's coming down in sheets thick as lead. Just remember what old Jack Burton does when the earth quakes and the poison arrows fall from the sky and the pillars of heaven shake. Yeah, Jack Burton just looks that old big storm right square in the eye and he says, 'Give me your best shot, pal, I can take it.'" **Kurt Russell** is very macho. *Big Trouble in Little China* (1986, 20th Century-Fox).

10990 "Think of all those back in time. . . this solid world dwindling. . . snow falling in that lonely graveyard. . . . His soul swooned as he heard the snow falling through the universe and faintly falling, like the descent of their last end, upon all the living and the dead." In voice-over **Donal McCann** sadly delivers the last line of James Joyce's short story. *The Dead* (1987, Vestron).

10991 "Good mawning, Vietnam. The weather will be hot and wet, nice if you're a lady but not if you're a jungle." Outrageous Armed Forces radio disc jockey **Robin Williams** begins his broadcast in 1965 Saigon with the questionable taste that endears him to his military listeners and drives his superiors up the wall. *Good Morning, Vietnam* (1987, Touchstone-Buena Vista).

10992 "Kopa one hundred's advanced weather's got us trapped in a three-day heat streak with all intentions of breaking the one-eighteen mark wide open today. Just stay inside, forget the electric bill, turn up the air. Tomorrow a reprieve at one fifteen, low tonight seventy-seven, right now one sixteen in the valley of the sun, and Kopa, one hundred." A voice on the radio gives a blistering weather report at the end of the film featuring two rambunctious teens, Daniel H. Jenkins and Neill Barry, who are into acts of hard-core mayhem. *O.C. and Stiggs* (1987, MGM-United Artists).

10993 "So is acid rain." **Woody Allen** retorts when Mia Farrow describes crass and hugely successful TV producer Alan Alda as a "phenomenon of our time." *Crimes and Misdemeanors* (1989, Orion).

Weddings

see also CELEBRATIONS, ENGAGEMENTS, HAPPINESS AND UNHAPPINESS, HONEYMOONS, HUSBANDS, HUSBANDS AND WIVES, JOY, KISSES AND KISSING, LOVE AND LOVERS, MARRIAGES, PLEDGES, WIVES

10994 "Marry? Oh, wouldn't it be marvelous if we could. . . have a real wedding and be given away. . . with church bells, and champagne, and a white frock and orange blossoms and a wedding cake. That's one thing I won't have missed, and you're giving it to me. I can never love you enough!" Given less than a year to live, **Bette Davis** thanks her doctor George Brent, who has proposed marriage. *Dark Victory* (1939, Warner Bros.).

10995 "Will you try to be a little pleasant, at least until after the wedding?" Newspaper publisher **Robert Warwick** asks his daughter Susan Hayward to pull in her shrewish reins at least until she's legally married to politician Fredric March. *I Married a Witch* (1941, United Artists).

10996 "I would like to say a few words about weddings." **Spencer Tracy** gives the opening line of the film. It's reprised by **Steve Martin** in the remake. *Father of the Bride* (1950, MGM); (1991, Touchstone-Buena Vista).

10997 "Apparently, Kay had picked a day for her wedding when nobody within four hundred miles had anything else to do." **Spencer Tracy** is rather disappointed that everyone invited to his daughter Elizabeth Taylor's wedding can make it. *Father of the Bride* (1950, MGM).

10998 "They didn't have to go to all this trouble. A small wedding would have been all right." American **Fred Astaire**, who plans to marry English woman Sarah Churchill, quips about the preparations for the wedding of the future Queen Elizabeth II. *Royal Wedding* (1951, MGM).

10999 "Isn't it ironic? You're both so young and lovely, but of the three of us, I'm to be the bride." Secretary **Dorothy McGuire** tells her colleagues Jean Peters and Maggie McNamara that she's to wed her boss, writer Clifton Webb. *Three Coins in the Fountain* (1954, 20th Century-Fox).

11000 "You go listen to the moon and the waves. Until I hear wedding bells, I'm children, too." **Annette Funicello** knows what's on Frankie Avalon's mind. He tells her that all his girl friends before her had been "children," and urges her to accompany him to the beach for some moonlight romance. *Bikini Beach* (1964, AIP).

11001 "I want you there. The modern woman always has her lovers at her wedding." **Daphne Zuniga** invites Dermot Mulroney to her wedding to Keith Szarabajka after a night of love-making in a cabin. *Staying Together* (1989, Hemdale).

Weight *see* APPEARANCES, OBESITY, SIZES

Weirdness

see also FANTASIES, FATE AND DESTINY, MONSTERS, STRANGENESS AND STRANGERS, SUPERNATURAL, VAMPIRES

11002 "I've never hitchhiked before. Can I ask you something? Are you weird?" **Jamie Lee Curtis** climbs into Tommy Atkins' car even though his reply is, "Yeah, I am." *The Fog* (1980, Avco).

11003 "It's just to get the fish smell off of me. I don't want you to think it's weird or something." **Susan Sarandon**, a waitress in an oyster bar, is more concerned with what Burt Lancaster thinks than what he saw. He confesses that he nightly watches her through her window as she bathes her hands, arms and breasts with freshly cut lemons while listening to a tape of "Casta Diva" from *Norma*. *Atlantic City* (1981, US-Canada, Paramount).

11004 "Everybody's into weirdness right now." Auto yard weirdo **Tracey Walter** philosophizes. *Repo Man* (1984, Universal).

11005 "Yeah, my dad's weird. He gets like that when he's writing." **Chance Quinn** comments on his writer father Richard Dreyfuss to a friend. Dreyfuss has been writing about his friendships with three other boys when they were in their early teens. *Stand by Me* (1986, Columbia).

11006 "This has to be the weirdest thing that ever happened to me." It's the voice of **Bruce Willis**, as baby Mikey, who has just experienced birth. *Look Who's Talking* (1989, Tri-Star).

11007 "There's a lot of weird people in Baltimore. They found where we lived." Young **Charlie Korsmo** complains after he, his mother and brother have to move to Baltimore after the death of his father. *Men Don't Leave* (1990, Warner Bros.).

Welcomes

see also FRIENDSHIPS AND FRIENDS, GUESTS, HOSPITALITY, VISITS

11008 "I am Dracula. I bid you welcome." Only **Bela Lugosi** could make such an innocent welcome to Dwight Frye, as Renfield, drip with such foreboding. *Dracula* (1931, Universal).

11009 "Hello, Devil, welcome to Hell." Cynical Baltimore columnist **Gene Kelly** cynically welcomes lawyer Spencer Tracy, as he arrives at the small Tennessee town where the infamous "Monkey Trial" will be held. *Inherit the Wind* (1960, United Artists).

11010 "Wealthy people are hated and resented. Look what's written on the Statue of Liberty. Does it say 'send me your rich'? No, it says, 'send me your poor.' We're not even welcome in our own country." Millionaire **Tony Randall** complains to Rock Hudson about economic discrimination. *Lover Come Back* (1961, Universal).

11011 "We are here to turn you into industrious and honest citizens. If you'll play ball with us, we'll play ball with you." **Michael Redgrave**, the governor of a Borstal school (British reform school) welcomes newcomers. *The Loneliness of the Long Distance Runner* (1962, GB, British Lion).

11012 "Well, come on in. I've been sleeping too much anyway." **Karen Black** tells Tom Berenger he might as well come into her home when she finds the dirty young man on her doorstep in the middle of the night. *In Praise of Older Women* (1979, Canada, Avco Embassy).

11013 "You're going to love it here, Doc. You can drive drunk and get anybody killed for 50 bucks." Burnt-out photojournalist **James Woods** welcomes new arrival James Belushi to El Salvador. *Salvador* (1986, Hemdale).

11014 "Welcome to prime time, bitch." **Robert Englund**, as Freddy Krueger, dispatches another teenage victim. *A Nightmare on Elm Street 3: Dream Warriors* (1987, New Line Cinema).

Whales *see* FISH AND FISHING

Whistling and Whistlers

see also MUSIC AND MUSICIANS, NOISES, SOUNDS

11015 "You know you don't have to act with me, Steve. You don't have to say anything, and you don't have to do anything. Not a thing. Oh, maybe just whistle. You know how to whistle, don't you, Steve? You just put your lips together and blow." Giving him the "Look," **Lauren Bacall** slinks out of Humphrey Bogart's room. After she's gone, he smiles, and softly whistles. *To Have and Have Not* (1944, Warner Bros.).

11016 "You don't have to sing for me—just whistle." **Groucho Marx** pays tribute to Lauren Bacall's line in *To Have and Have Not* when vamp Lisette Verea says she'll sing for him at a cabaret. *A Night in Casablanca* (1946, United Artists).

11017 "I'm sorry, sir. I could never answer to a whistle. Whistles are for dogs and cats and other animals but not for children and definitely not for me. It would be too humiliating." New governess **Julie Andrews** indignantly tells Christopher Plummer that he must cease using a whistle to get his children to march like a group of young soldiers. *The Sound of Music* (1965, 20th Century-Fox).

11018 "The world is full of dames. All you gotta do is whistle." **Jerry Lacy,** as Humphrey Bogart's spirit, wises up romantic loser Woody Allen. *Play It Again, Sam* (1972, Paramount).

Widows

see also DEATH AND DYING, HUSBANDS, HUSBANDS AND WIVES, WIVES

11019 "A college widow stood for something in those days. In fact she stood for plenty." **Groucho Marx** recalls his college days and the promiscuous "widows" that taught the boys more than their professors. *Horse Feathers* (1932, Paramount).

11020 "My husband died three years ago. . . it was at sixteen I was wed. . . . Three years, the prince is dead. . . . He was the son of a noble house. . . . It was the happiness of great peace." Love-starved **Jeanette MacDonald** tells Maurice Chevalier of her marriage to a man old enough to be her grandfather. *Love Me Tonight* (1932, Paramount).

11021 "I'm too young to be a widow." **Vivien Leigh** ignores maid Hattie McDaniel, who disapproves when "Miss Scarlett" tries on a colorful bonnet when she's supposed to be in mourning for her recently deceased husband Rand Brooks. *Gone with the Wind* (1939, Selznick-MGM).

11022 "For a widow to appear in public at a social gathering—everytime I think of it, I feel faint." **Laura Hope Crews** is shocked when Vivien Leigh attends an Atlanta bazaar. *Gone with the Wind* (1939, Selznick-MGM).

11023 "Those widow weeds are hot. I hope I don't lose you in the summertime." Detective **Joan Blondell** is furious with her husband Melvyn Douglas, whose limp body tumbled out onto her from a closet. He was trying to frighten her. *There's Always a Woman* (1939, Columbia).

11024 "Widows make the best wives. If you are better than the first, they are grateful; if you are worse, they are not surprised." **Eugene Deckers** makes a sexist but perhaps sage observation. *Father Brown* (1954, GB, Columbia).

Wildness

see also CIVILIZATIONS, SAVAGERY, VIOLENCE

11025 "It's China Doll! The gal that drives men wild." It's how Gay Nineties saloon keeper **Mae West** bills herself. *She Done Him Wrong* (1933, Paramount).

11026 "We're going to carve a new majestic empire out of the wilderness." By the end of the film, wealthy **Joel McCrea** is happy to be fleeced by Miriam Hopkins, who falls in love with him in the process. *Woman Chases Man* (1937, United Artists).

11027 "Did you ever stop to think that it's you that brings out the wildness in me?" Sometime call girl **Elizabeth Taylor** assigns some of the blame for her behavior to her lover Laurence Harvey. *Butterfield 8* (1960, MGM).

11028 "It's a mistake you always made, Doc, trying to love a wild thing. You were always lugging home wild things. Once, it was a hawk with a broken wing, and—and that time it was a full-grown wildcat with a broken leg. Remember?. . . You mustn't give your heart to a wild thing. The more you do, the stronger they get until they're strong enough to run in the woods or fly to a tree and then a higher tree and then to the sky." Wild thing **Audrey Hepburn** speaks kindly to the older husband Buddy Ebsen whom she deserted when she was strong enough to fly away. *Breakfast at Tiffany's* (1961, Paramount).

11029 "The whole world is wild at heart and weird on top." **Laura Dern,** as Lulu, gives her opinion of the nature of things. *Wild at Heart* (1990, Goldwyn).

Will and Willingness *see* CHOICES, PURPOSES

Winds

see also WEATHER

11030 "There's an east wind, Watson. . . . Such a wind as never blew on England yet. It will be cold and bitter, Watson. And a good many of us may wither before its blast. But it's God's own wind, nonetheless. And a greener, better, stronger land will lie in the sunshine when the storm has cleared." **Basil Rathbone** quotes Arthur Conan Doyle directly from his story, "His Last Bow." Rathbone, as Sherlock Holmes, predicts that England will survive the threat of Nazi Germany. *Sherlock Holmes and the Voice of Terror* (1942, Universal).

11031 CAPTAIN OKANURA: "Your country is an overripe plum, it will be shaken from the earth by the wind sweeping from Japan." CAPT. ANDREW KENT: "We know how to handle big winds." Wily Japanese intelligence officer **Richard Loo**'s threats don't scare American POW **Michael St. Angel**. *First Yank in Tokyo* (1945, RKO).

11032 "One small wind can rain much dirt." With this aphorism, **Sidney Toler**, as Chinese detective Charlie Chan, says much by saying little. *Dark Alibi* (1946, Monogram).

11033 "You're like a leaf that the wind blows from one gutter to another." **Robert Mitchum**'s admiration for his former lover, untrustworthy Jane Greer, has taken a definite downward swing. *Out of the Past* (1947, RKO).

Wine *see* ALCOHOL

Winners and Losers

see also BATTLES AND BATTLEFIELDS, COMPETITION, CONTESTS, EFFORTS, GAMBLING, GAMES, LOSSES AND LOSING, SPORTS, SUCCESSES, VICTORIES

11034 "I don't care what they do to me back there. If I win, it'll be with you. And if I lose, it'll still be with you." Wealthy, married and successful lawyer **Clark Gable** runs for governor. His mistress Joan Crawford is a liability, but she's more important to him than winning, and he won't give her up. *Possessed* (1931, MGM).

11035 SHERLOCK HOLMES: "You came to see me professionally?" INSP. LESTRADE: "Well—er—unofficially." HOLMES: "I see. Heads, you win; tails, I lose." **Reginald Owen** welcomes puzzled Scotland Yard inspector **Alan Mowbray** to Baker Street. *A Study in Scarlet* (1933, Fox).

11036 "You'll win somebody's mother some night." **Myrna Loy** quips to her gangster-gambler boy friend Clark Gable, who is lucky beyond belief. *Manhattan Melodrama* (1934, MGM).

11037 "If I find a forgotten man first, I win." **Gail Patrick** tries to collect apparent bum William Powell in order to win a scavenger hunt. *My Man Godfrey* (1936, Universal).

11038 "A scavenger hunt is just like a treasure hunt, except in a treasure hunt you find something of value, and in a scavenger hunt, you find things you don't want and the one who wins gets a prize, only there really isn't any prize. It's just the honor of winning because all the money goes to charity, if there's any money left over, but there never is." Breathless **Carole Lombard** plaintively explains to "forgotten man" William Powell the purpose of a scavenger hunt in which he's one of the things nobody wants but must collect to win. *My Man Godfrey* (1936, Universal).

11039 "I wanted to conquer myself but instead I smashed myself." Violinist and prizefighter **William Holden** shares his despair with Barbara Stanwyck after winning his big fight but accidentally killing his opponent in the process. *Golden Boy* (1939, Columbia).

11040 "As a girl scout, I won three merit badges but I didn't mention it on the register." **Barbara Stanwyck** is irked by a hotel clerk's comment that she didn't register as a doctor. *You Belong to Me* (1941, Columbia).

11041 "However, man who ride on merry-go-round all the time sooner or later must catch brass ring." In the film's final aphorism, **Roland Winters**, as Charlie Chan, recommends persistence. *The Chinese Ring* (1947, Monogram).

11042 "I wouldn't do it! I won tonight! I won!" **Robert Ryan**, as boxer Stoker Thompson, is proud despite being badly beaten by hoods because he would not go into the tank as ordered. *The Set-Up* (1949, RKO).

11043 "So this is where the loser tells the winner she's making a terrible mistake. On the way out, think of something original, will you?" **Joan Crawford**, the winner in the Jeff Chandler sweepstakes, snarls at loser Jan Sterling. *Female on the Beach* (1955, Universal).

11044 "Like the man says, some days you win, some days you lose. Drinks on me." **Jack Lemmon** has lost Rita Hayworth to his buddy Robert Mitchum. *Fire Down Below* (1957, GB, Columbia).

11045 "The old man was right, only the farmers won. We'll always lose." Gunfighters **Yul Brynner** and Steve McQueen are about to ride away from the Mexican village which they helped defend from bandits. Five of their original seven, one alive and four dead, will remain behind. *The Magnificent Seven* (1960, United Artists).

11046 "The only way to win a war is to be just as nasty as the enemy. One thing that worries me is that we're liable to wake up one morning and find out we're even nastier than they are." It's the concern of **Gregory Peck**, head of the sabotage team sent to destroy two giant guns on a Turkish island. *The Guns of Navarone* (1961, GB, Columbia).

11047 "Look, you want to hustle, don't you? The game isn't like football. Nobody pays you for yardage. When you hustle, you keep score real simple. The end of the game you count your money. That's how you know who's best. It's the only way." Gambler **George C. Scott** offers pool hustler Paul Newman a proposition. Scott will pay all expenses and will get 75% of what Newman wins. Scott claims he's taking a big risk because so far all he's seen Newman do is lose to Jackie Gleason. *The Hustler* (1961, 20th Century-Fox).

11048 "We've got a funny kind of war here—a war we can't really win, because it's gotta be settled around a conference table." Company Commander **Charles Aidman** echoes the official line about the Korean Police Action. *War Hunt* (1962, United Artists).

11049 SIR WILLIAM WALKER: "It is inevitable that somebody has to lose. It's inevitable that it would be you, otherwise how could I have won?" JOSE DOLORES: "Fire does not destroy everything. Even after a fire, there will be one blade of grass." Aristocratic English agent **Marlon Brando** has defeated his old friend, revolutionary leader **Evaristo Marquez**, and orders the latter's execution. Marquez predicts that the revolutionary movement of the Caribbean island of Queimada is not over. As Brando prepares to leave the island after Marquez's death, a black dock hand stabs Brando to death. *Burn!* aka: *Queimada!* (1970, Ital.-Fr., United Artists).

11050 ACE BONNER: "If this world's all for the winners, what's for the losers?" JUNIOR BONNER: "Well, somebody's got to hold the horses." **Roger Preston**, a born loser, isn't looking for an answer, but his son **Steve McQueen**, another loser, provides one. *Junior Bonner* (1972, ABC-Cinerama).

11051 "It's not whether you win or lose; it's how many points you score that counts." **Moses Gunn**, who hopes to see his son Kevin Hooks escape the slums through professional basketball, doesn't emphasize team play. *Aaron Loves Angela* (1975, Columbia).

11052 "Ya suit yourself to the situation. When they want to kill ya, just livin' is winnin'." **Albert P. Hall**, as Dicklicker, shares some prison wisdom with his buddy, title character Roger E. Mosley. *Leadbelly* (1975, Paramount).

11053 "Now I know it's rough to leave your friends and move every year, but you are Marine kids and can chew nails while other kids are sucking cotton candy. And you are Meechums. A Meechum is a thoroughbred, a winner all the way. He gets the best grades, wins the most awards, and excels in sports. A Meechum never gives up. I want you hogs to let this burgh know you're here. I want these crackers to wake up and wonder what the hell blew into town." Gung-ho Marine Colonel **Robert Duvall** gives his kids a pep talk that would make Knute Rockne proud. *The Great Santini* (1979, Warner Bros.).

11054 "You've heard of a no-win situation? Vietnam. This. They're around. I think we're in one of them." **Albert Brooks** tells Kathryn Harrold that he wants to break up with her—again. *Modern Romance* (1981, Columbia).

11055 CLAIRE STRYDER: "Sure would be a prize winner, wouldn't it?" RUSSELL PRICE: "I've won every prize." CLAIRE: "But you've never won a war." Radio operator **Joanna Cassidy** encourages freelance photographer **Nick Nolte** to fake a photograph to help the rebels' cause in Nicaragua. *Under Fire* (1983, Orion).

11056 "Sir, do we get to win this time?" Vietnam ex-Green Beret, killing machine **Sylvester Stallone** questions his former commander Richard Crenna, as Stallone is sent back into the jungles of Vietnam to rescue American POWs. *Rambo: First Blood, Part II* (1985, Tri-Star).

11057 "You know what makes really good champagne? Winning!" Veteran Atlanta Braves manager **Martin Ritt** snarls after another loss. *The Slugger's Wife* (1985, Columbia).

11058 "When a couple starts keeping score. . . there isn't any winning, there's just degrees of losing." Divorce lawyer **Danny De Vito** knows when a marriage is doomed. *The War of the Roses* (1989, 20th Century-Fox).

11059 "This is Sherman, who started with so much, lost everything, but he gained his soul. Whereas I, you see, who started with so little, gained everything. But what does it profit a man if he gains the whole world and loses? Ah, well, there are compensations." Writer **Bruce Willis** gets the last words in the story of the decline of stockbroker Tom Hanks. *The Bonfire of the Vanities* (1990, Warner Bros.).

11060 "Make as much as you can for as long as you can. Whoever has the most when he dies is the winner." Corporate raider **Danny De Vito** tells opposing counselor, sexy Penelope Ann Miller that he loves the "game." *Other People's Money* (1991, Warner Bros.).

11061 "Black guys would rather look good and lose than look bad and win." Perhaps this racist remark by white hustler **Woody Harrelson** reproaching black partner Wesley Snipes is an answer to the racist message of the film's title. *White Men Can't Jump* (1992, 20th Century-Fox).

Winter *see* SEASONS

Wisdom

see also INTELLIGENCE, KNOWLEDGE, UNDERSTANDINGS AND MISUNDERSTANDINGS

11062 "The only way to grow wise is to get old." **Orson Welles** shares what he's learned with the last line of the movie. *The Lady from Shanghai* (1948, Columbia).

11063 "Little story now concluded, but history of world unfinished. Lovely ladies, kind gentlemen: go home and ponder. What was true at the beginning remains true. Play make man think. Thought make man wise. And wisdom makes life endurable." Narrator **Marlon Brando**, as Okinawan interpreter Sakini, brings the film to a close. *The Teahouse of the August Moon* (1956, MGM).

11064 "Six days does not a week make." **Jane Fonda** replies to her husband Robert Redford who had reminded her of their passionate six-day honeymoon at the Plaza hotel. Redford's mention of their honeymoon was in response to Fonda's demand for a divorce on the grounds they have nothing in common. *Barefoot in the Park* (1967, Paramount).

11065 "Me? When I look around me, I know I know nothing. I remember though once long ago in Persia, we met a wise man at the bazaar. He was a professional and used to sell his wisdom to anyone willing to pay. His specialty for tourists was a maxim engraved on the head of a pin: 'The wisest,' he said, 'the truest, the most instructive words for all men for all time.' Frederick bought one for me and back at the hotel if I peered through a magnifying glass to read the words, 'And this too shall pass.' And the wise man was right—if you remember that, you can't help but live fully." When young Bud Cort tells eighty-year-old **Ruth Gordon** that she's the wisest person he knows, she recalls an encounter she and her late husband had with a truly wise man, many years before. *Harold and Maude* (1971, Paramount).

11066 "The wise man shall be delivered into the hands of his enemies whether they can pay delivery charges or not." The meaning of **Woody Allen**'s line is not particularly significant to the plot of the film. *Love and Death* (1975, United Artists).

11067 "You learn by doing, that's wisdom, Mike, that's beautiful. Beautiful." **Jack Esformes** admires his prison buddy Casey Siemaszko, who has learned the burglary racket from 61-year-old pro Burt Reynolds. *Breaking In* (1989, Goldwyn).

11068 "You're a wise man, Don Altobello. I can learn a lot from you." It's not clear if **Andy Garcia** has convinced wise old Mafioso Eli Wallach that he's deserting Al Pacino to come over to Wallach's side. *The Godfather, Part III* (1991, Paramount).

Wishes

see also DESIRES, WANTS AND WANTING

11069 "There ya' go with that wishin' stuff again! I wish you was a wishin' well—so that I could tie a bucket t'ya and sink ya!" Sourpuss **James Cagney** lays some nasty verbal abuse on his mistress Mae Clarke. When this doesn't shut her up, he grinds half a grapefruit in her face. *The Public Enemy* (1931, Warner Bros.).

11070 "My father used to say that wishes are dreams we dream when we're awake. . . ." **Irene Dunne** quotes some parental wisdom to Charles Boyer. *Love Affair* (1939, RKO).

11071 LARRY WILSON: "You've turned my head." KAY WILSON: "I've often wished I could turn your head—on a spit over a fire." It's an exchange between old stick-in-the-mud businessman **William Powell** and his wife **Myrna Loy**, who is about to divorce him when a case of amnesia turns him into a new, desirable man. *I Love You Again* (1940, MGM).

11072 "Gosh, sometimes I wish a girl could have her face lifted upside down." **Judy Garland**'s frown is just a smile upside down. *Life Begins for Andy Hardy* (1941, MGM).

11073 "You ought not to express that wish in the presence of that cat: it is one of the seventy-three great gods of Egypt." **George Sanders** warns Hurd Hatfield about an objet d'art, when the latter wishes he could always look as young as he does in a portrait of him at 22. *The Picture of Dorian Gray* (1945, MGM).

11074 "I wish I could walk with Peggy through Central Park again and kiss the tip of her nose." Presumably doomed pilot **Fred MacMurray** is broadcasting his last message from his disabled aircraft. Peggy is his little dog. *Practically Yours* (1945, Paramount).

11075 "You've got your wish: you've never been born." Apprentice angel **Henry Travers** grants James Stewart's wish that he'd never been born. He wasn't really serious about the wish, but that's the thing about wishes; you have to watch them—sometimes you get what you wish for. *It's a Wonderful Life* (1946, RKO).

11076 TOM HANSEN: "You know. . . funny thing. . . I keep wishing for something to happen and it does." EDDIE BENDIX: "Like what?" TOM: "Like bustin' you in the nose." **Burt Lancaster** has a run-in with snide **John Hodiak**. *Desert Fury* (1947, Paramount).

11077 "I wish it could have been a tie, I really do." It is **Katharine Hepburn**'s wish after winning an acquittal for Judy Holliday on the charge of attempted murder, but it doesn't pacify the defeated prosecutor, her husband Spencer Tracy. *Adam's Rib* (1949, MGM).

11078 "You wished that you weren't here with me, didn't you? You wished that I was some place else where you'd never have to see me again. . . didn't you?. . . or maybe you wished that I was dead. Is that it? Do you wish that I was dead?" Pitiful, pregnant **Shelley Winters** has correctly read the mind of Montgomery Clift, who certainly would like a way out of marrying her. *A Place in the Sun* (1951, Paramount).

11079 "I wish I was in hell with my back broken." The reason for **James Cagney**'s strange wish is the shenanigans of Pamela Tiffin, daughter of his very conservative boss. Tiffin has been entrusted to Cagney's care while visiting Berlin, but she eludes Cagney long enough to be married and impregnated by German Communist Horst Buchholz. *One, Two, Three* (1961, United Artists).

11080 "I only wish it had been the knot of knots, there's no untying." **Terence Stamp** frees the hem of Julie Christie's gown from the spur on his boot. *Far from the Madding Crowd* (1967, GB, EMI).

11081 "Sometimes I wish my mother had taken the Pill." Depressed, unsuccessful playwright **Rick Lenz** shares a modern version of "I wish I had never been born" with Goldie Hawn. *Cactus Flower* (1969, Columbia).

11082 "Do you wish I wasn't your sister?. . . I wish you weren't my brother." Nude **Susanne Benton** taunts her brother Michael Burns. *That Cold Day in the Park* (1969, Canada, Commonwealth United Entertainment).

11083 "I just want to wish you well, both of you. I want you to have a good life, be happy. Salute." **Paul Mace** wishes street gang member Sylvester Stallone and his pregnant girl friend Maria Smith all the best. *The Lords of Flatbush* (1974, Columbia).

11084 "I wish I could stick my whole head in your mouth and have you suck out my eyeballs." A sicko policeman French-kisses heiress and murderer Mink Stole. *Desperate Living* (1977, Waters).

11085 "Just once I'd like to go out and eat. . . potato chips." Now and then **George Hamilton** wishes he wasn't a vampire limited to a blood diet. *Love at First Bite* (1979, Warner Bros.).

11086 "He reaches inside me and pulls me out. I only wish that I could love me as much as he does." **Talia Shire** describes her relationship with Richard Jordan. *Old Boyfriends* (1979, Avco Embassy).

11087 "Oh, God, I wish I was a loofah." Captain **John Larroquette** ogles a shower full of women soldiers through a telescope. *Stripes* (1981, Columbia).

11088 "I wish I could wake up tomorrow and it would be all over." Bright Seattle high school student **Matthew Broderick** accidentally plugs his home computer into a secret national defense terminal and has innocently triggered the prelude to World War III. *Wargames* (1983, MGM-United Artists).

11089 JAKE: "Happy birthday, Samantha. Make a wish." SAM: "It's already come true." Hunk **Michael Schoeffling** is the only gift **Molly Ringwald** wants for her sweet sixteenth birthday. *Sixteen Candles* (1984, Universal).

11090 LIBBY STRONG: "I wish we were back in Philadelphia." SARAH WEBBER: "But, dear, it would be hot in Philadelphia." LIBBY: "It would keep you from being so busy." While spending the summer on the Maine coast, elderly **Bette Davis** grows tired of the unrelenting saintliness of her sister **Lillian Gish**. *The Whales of August* (1987, Alive Films).

11091 "I wish I had some spurs." It is **Melanie Griffith**'s kinky preface as she initiates love-making with Matthew Modine. *Pacific Heights* (1990, 20th Century-Fox).

Witchcraft and Witches

see also DEVILS, MAGIC, UGLINESS, WOMEN

11092 "My devotion has made me a witch so I make myself hateful to my children." **Joanne Woodward** justifies her interference in the lives of her two children to son John Malkovich. *The Glass Menagerie* (1987, Cineplex-Odeon).

11093 "Witches are witches because they are extremely unhappy, viciously ugly and hate everybody." **Mai Zetterling** tells her grandson Jasen Fisher what makes a woman a witch. *The Witches* (1990, Warner Bros.).

11094 "Real witches look very much like ordinary women." **Mai Zetterling** warns her grandson Jasen Fisher. He is to encounter a whole convention of witches. He recognizes them because their eyes glow red, their wigs make their heads itch and they have no toes. *The Witches* (1990, Warner Bros.).

Wives

see also HUSBANDS, HUSBANDS AND WIVES, MARRIAGES, WEDDINGS

11095 "Well, come then. You'll have to go on teaching me, leading me. Sometime I'll know. Stay close. Give me your hand. I can't sing the hymn. I shan't look up either. I'll be looking at you and believing you're my wife." Rather than saving Christian Elissa Landi, Prefect of Rome **Fredric March** chooses to share her fate and goes to the lions with her. *The Sign of the Cross* (1932, Paramount).

11096 "Who do you think you're talkin' to, that first wife of yours out in Montana? The poor mealy-faced thing with her flat chest that didn't have enough nerve to talk up to ya', washin' out your greasy overalls and cookin' and slavin' in some mining shack? No wonder she died. Ya' big windbag." **Jean Harlow** takes none of husband Wallace Beery's guff. *Dinner at Eight* (1933, MGM).

11097 "My first wife was clever. My second wife was ambitious. My third—Thomas, if you want to be happy, marry a girl like my sweet little Jane. Marry a stupid woman." Title character **Charles Laughton** advises Robert Donat to marry a girl like Wendy Barrie. *The Private Life of Henry VIII* (1933, GB, London Films-United Artists).

11098 "For what I have done, Calpurnia, pardon. For what I am about to do, courage." Julius Caesar, portrayed by **Warren William**, speaks to his Roman wife, played by Gertrude Michael. *Cleopatra* (1934, Paramount).

11099 "If she was your wife, would you sleep on the porch?" **Lionel Stander** tells his boss Leo Carrillo that he doesn't believe that the new cook and butler, Jean Arthur and Herbert Marshall, are really married. *If You Could Only Cook* (1935, Columbia).

11100 "No man can support a wife and me at the same time." **Mae West** believes men will have to choose between her and their spouses. *Go West, Young Man* (1936, Paramount).

11101 "What they don't know won't hurt them." **Cary Grant** lies under a sunlamp to get a tan because his wife Irene Dunne believes he's been in Florida. He makes the mistake of presenting her a gift of citrus fruit stamped "California." *The Awful Truth* (1937, Columbia).

11102 "I never wanted to see you again. But you pulled me here with a two-inch cable. I'm taking you out of this side show.... You're coming with me as my wife... in the eyes of God, and man, and the United States Passport Bureau." American playboy **Robert Taylor** makes plans to marry half-caste Hedy Lamarr in Saigon. *Lady of the Tropics* (1939, MGM).

11103 "Did you ever know such a housewife?" **Rosalind Russell** states her disapproval of Norma Shearer's devotion to her home and family. *The Women* (1939, MGM).

11104 "I don't want to be ridden and driven, with her whip lashing me, and her spurs digging into me!" Title character **Raymond Massey** backs out of his marriage to Ruth Gordon as Mary Todd. We all know that eventually he married the lady. *Abe Lincoln in Illinois* (1940, RKO).

11105 ELLEN ARDEN: "You're sure you don't love her?" NICK ARDEN: "The moment I saw you downstairs, I knew...." ELLEN: "Oh, go on—I bet you say that to all your wives." NICK: "I could strangle you." **Irene Dunne** returns from a desert island after seven years. She's been declared legally dead, and her husband **Cary Grant** has married Gail Patrick. *My Favorite Wife* (1940, RKO).

11106 "I don't understand what kind of war you guys are fighting, dragging your wives around.... Don't you get enough of them at home?" **Humphrey Bogart** is dumbfounded to discover that the passengers he is rescuing from Devil's Island to transport to Martinique is a top French resistance leader and his wife. *To Have and Have Not* (1944, Warner Bros.).

11107 "That's the wife of the Austrian critic. She always looks like she's been out in the rain feeding the poultry." **Clifton Webb** points out a party guest to Kurt Kreuger. *The Dark Corner* (1946, 20th Century-Fox).

11108 "I wouldn't worry. Men are ten cents a dozen. I wish women were... he'd better hurry. The man-

agement is not responsible for wives left over thirty days...." Hotel desk clerk **Groucho Marx** comforts one of the twenty-eight wives of a local sheik who he left behind. She assures Marx that her husband will come back for her. *A Night in Casablanca* (1946, United Artists).

11109 "His words meant very little to me then, but as time passed, I came to know that the death of Sonseeahray had put a seal upon the peace. And from that day on wherever I went, in the cities, among the Apaches, in the mountains, I always remembered, my wife was with me." Frontiersman **James Stewart** speaks of the wisdom of the comforting words of his friend the great Apache chief, Cochise, played by Jeff Chandler, when white men kill Stewart's Indian wife Debra Paget. *Broken Arrow* (1950, 20th Century-Fox).

11110 "Can't you just see me, coming home from work to a nagging wife?" Speaking on the telephone, recuperating, globe-trotting photographer **James Stewart** expresses no interest in marriage. But with Grace Kelly as the wife, he might learn to live with a little nagging. *Rear Window* (1954, Paramount).

11111 "The wives of America will give me a medal." In another of his daydreaming fantasies, Tom Ewell imagines that his wife **Evelyn Keyes** finds him with model Marilyn Monroe and shoots him. *The Seven Year Itch* (1955, 20th Century-Fox).

11112 "One wife? One God, that I can understand—but one wife? That is not civilized. It is not generous." Rich sheik **Hugh Griffith** is shocked by Charlton Heston's monogamy. *Ben Hur* (1959, MGM).

11113 STANLEY FORD: "What do you call it when you hate the woman you love?" CHARLES: "A wife." Cartoonist **Jack Lemmon**'s man-servant **Terry-Thomas** loathes the thought of marriage. *How to Murder Your Wife* (1965, United Artists).

11114 JULIAN WINSTON: "My wife and I—why, I never even knew her." TONI SIMMONS: "How did the three children come? United Parcel?" Single dentist **Walter Matthau** has led his mistress **Goldie Hawn** to believe that he's married with three children. *Cactus Flower* (1969, Columbia).

11115 "Jesus H.! Goddamn hippies don't even marry women who look like wives." U.S. Senator **Rip Torn** is disappointed to discover that a sexy-looking blonde at a party, who he has bet Alan Alda is a screamer, is the wife of a freshman congressman. *The Seduction of Joe Tynan* (1979, Universal).

11116 "You've fallen in love with your wife." **Meryl Streep** suddenly understands the real reason U.S. Senator Alan Alda wishes to end their affair. *The Seduction of Joe Tynan* (1979, Universal).

11117 "I want you to start being a regular wife." **Leo Rossi** orders his wife Bonnie Bedelia to give up her career as a racing driver. *Heart Like a Wheel* (1981, 20th Century-Fox).

11118 "You said you'd be back Tuesday...I'm sounding like a boring, clinging, miserable wife." **Diane Keaton** recognizes that she is being petite bourgeoisie when she flings an accusation at her radical lover Warren Beatty. *Reds* (1981, Paramount).

11119 "I married a banana." **Jack Nicholson** whines to his grasping shrewish wife Valerie Perrine. *The Border* (1982, Universal).

11120 "I didn't marry any of them...they married me." Fading movie star **Peter O'Toole** has had a number of unsuccessful marriages. *My Favorite Year* (1983, MGM-United Artists).

Women

see also BEAUTY, CHARM, GIRLS, MEN, MEN AND WOMEN, SEX AND SEXUALITY

11121 "Are you not woman enough to know?" It's the title card that represents desert sheik **Rudolph Valentino**'s reply, nostrils flaring, when Agnes Ayres asks innocently, "Why have you brought me here?" *The Sheik* (1921, silent, Paramount).

11122 "Certain women should be struck regularly, like gongs." The carping of his new bride Una Merkel has led **Robert Montgomery** to coin the aphorism. *Private Lives* (1931, MGM).

11123 "The white woman stays with me." Rank has its privileges and preferences as Chinese revolutionary General **Warner Oland** confiscates prostitute Marlene Dietrich as his soldiers lead away her partner in sin Anna May Wong. *Shanghai Express* (1932, Paramount).

11124 "Women should be kept illiterate and clean, like canaries." **Roscoe Karns'** line got a big laugh in 1934. Today, it would probably get him tarred and feathered. *It Happened One Night* (1934, Columbia).

11125 "I wouldn't take that woman back if we were the last two people on earth and the future of the human race depended on us!" Broadway director **John Barrymore** insistently damns his former protégé Carole Lombard, who has left the stage to make movies. *Twentieth Century* (1934, Columbia).

11126 "I've loved as a woman loves, lost as a woman loses. But still, I win. You have no heir. My son will inherit your throne, my son will rule England. Still, still I win." In a meeting that never took place in history, thrice-married Mary, Queen of Scots, portrayed by **Katharine Hepburn**, accuses childless Elizabeth, played by Florence Eldridge, of not being a woman because she's unmarried and barren. *Mary of Scotland* (1936, RKO).

11127 "Does any man realize what the life of a woman is? How trivial we have to be. We have to please. We are obliged to please. If we attempt to take a serious share of life are we welcomed? And all the while—Men are so self-satisfied, so blind, so limited...I see things happening here! Injustice. Cruelty. There are things I should do for the poor—things I would do to make things better. I am not allowed. I have to pretend to be eaten up by my dresses, my jewels, my vanities. I make myself beautiful, often with an aching heart." **Margaretta Scott**, as Roxana, complains to Raymond Massey, as Cabal, of the empty life forced upon a woman. *Things to Come* (1936, GB, LFP-United Artists).

11128 "I can tell you what an Indian will do, but not a woman." Well, of course, Wild Bill Hickok, as played by **Gary Cooper**, has had more experience with the Indians than he has with women. It is not likely that the real Calamity Jane looked and acted like Jean Arthur. *The Plainsman* (1937, Paramount).

11129 "Don't make an issue of my womanhood." It's hard for Melvyn Douglas, Sig Rumann, Alexander Granach, Felix Bressart or any other male, to treat **Greta Garbo** just like any ordinary communist emissary. *Ninotchka* (1939, MGM).

11130 "Don't you know that we dames have got to be something more to the guy we marry than a school girl sweetheart? We've got to be a wife—a real wife—a mother too and a pal. And a nursemaid." **Paulette Goddard** describes the many roles a woman must play with a man. *The Women* (1939, MGM).

11131 "[She's] a simple, ordinary country woman. I've seen hundreds of women just like her, women who say nothing but do much." Title character **Henry Fonda** offers a stirring defense of Alice Brady, whose two sons Eddie Quillan and Richard Cromwell are on trial for murder. *Young Mr. Lincoln* (1939, 20th Century-Fox).

11132 "Gosh, how one's women do mount up." Title character **Mickey Rooney** has more "women" than he can handle. *Andy Hardy Meets Debutante* (1940, MGM).

11133 "I read about the guts of pioneer women or the women of the dust bowl and the gingham goddess of the covered wagon. What about the women of the covered typewriter?" **Ginger Rogers** champions a modern heroine. *Kitty Foyle* (1940, RKO).

11134 FAT WOMAN IN SUBWAY CAR: "What would people be without women?" SCHOLARLY MAN IN SUBWAY CAR: "Scarce, mighty scarce." Passengers on a subway car, **May Boley** and **Edward Fielding** exchange views on women. *Skylark* (1941, Paramount).

11135 "How extravagant you are, throwing away women like that. Some day they may become scarce." Womanizing police prefect **Claude Rains** witnesses **Humphrey Bogart** brushing off his French cutie Madeleine LeBeau. *Casablanca* (1942, Warner Bros.).

11136 "Women are strange little beasts. You can treat them like dogs, you can beat them until your arm aches—and they still love you. Of course, it's an absurd illusion that they have souls." **George Sanders** plays his caddish role to the hilt. *The Moon and Sixpence* (1942, United Artists).

11137 "I don't like women around the place." It's **James Mason**'s none too promising welcome to his ward Ann Todd, who has come to live with him after the death of her father. *The Seventh Veil* (1945, GB, GFD-Universal).

11138 "All women are fundamentally rivals." Shrink **Lew Ayres** make a huge generalization, based on his observation of two twins, both played by Olivia de Havilland. *The Dark Mirror* (1946, Universal).

11139 RIP: "You know, I've been thinking. Women ought to come capsule-size, about four inches high. When a man goes out for an evening, he just puts her in his pocket and takes her along with him, and that way, he knows exactly where she is. He gets to his favorite restaurant, he puts her on the table and lets her run among the coffee cups while he swaps a few lies with his pals. . . . Without chance of interruption. And when it comes to that time of the evening when he wants her full-sized and beautiful, he just waves his hand and she becomes full size." CORAL: "Why that's the most conceited statement I've ever heard." RIP: "And if she starts to interrupt, he just shrinks her back to pocket-size and puts her away." CORAL: "I understand. What you're saying is, women are made to be loved." RIP: "Is that what I'm saying?" CORAL: "Yes, it's a confession that. . . that a woman may drive you out of your mind. That. . . you wouldn't trust her. And because you couldn't put her in your pocket, you get mixed up." We do not know which is more outrageous, **Humphrey Bogart**'s notion of women or **Lizabeth**

Scott's interpretation of it. Wonder if the all male teams of screenwriters and the authors of the unpublished story on which the movie is based, believed the sentiments put in Bogie's mouth? *Dead Reckoning* (1947, Columbia).

11140 "A woman doesn't think. She gets stirred up. . . . Now you know all about women." **William Powell** holds a useless father-to-son chat about women with Jimmy Lydon. *Life with Father* (1947, Warner Bros.).

11141 "Once a woman betrays a man, she despises him. In spite of his goodness and position, she will give him up for someone inferior. . . if that someone is more physically attractive." **Charles Chaplin** tells Marilyn Nash, as the Girl, that he loves women but doesn't admire them. *Monsieur Verdoux* (1947, Chaplin-United Artists).

11142 "All women are wonders because they reduce all men to the obvious." Tax lawyer **Ken Niles** gives a gratis opinion. *Out of the Past* (1947, RKO).

11143 "Amanda, you've convinced me. I might even go out and become a woman!" After watching Katharine Hepburn and Spencer Tracy have a heated feminist debate, **David Wayne** is won over by Hepburn's arguments. *Adam's Rib* (1949, MGM).

11144 "This is not the great journey one undertakes with a. . . shall we say, overwrought woman." Great white hunter **Stewart Granger** tries to talk Deborah Kerr out of a trek into the African wilds to search for her missing husband. He had been trying to find a lost diamond mine. *King Solomon's Mines* (1950, MGM).

11145 "Salome—what a woman! What a part! The princess in love with a holy man. She dances the Dance of the Seven Veils. He rejects her, so she demands his head on a golden tray, kissing his cold, dead lips." Silent screen star **Gloria Swanson**, as Norma Desmond, recalls one of her screen triumphs for William Holden. *Sunset Boulevard* (1950, Paramount).

11146 "I never met a woman that didn't know if she was good looking or not, without being told, and some of them give themselves credit for more than they've got. I once went out with a doll who said to me: 'I am the glamorous type, I am the glamorous type!' I said, 'So what?'" **Marlon Brando** responds to Vivien Leigh when she tells him she's been fishing for a compliment about her looks. *A Streetcar Named Desire* (1951, Warner Bros.-20th Century-Fox).

11147 "No woman like her—fightin', scratchin', next moment, sweetest woman alive." **Charlton Heston** admires wild-spirited Carolina swamp girl Jennifer Jones. *Ruby Gentry* (1952, 20th Century-Fox).

11148 "Two women, each with half of the things a man wants." Bigamist **Alec Guinness** has a wife at each end of his steamer run between Gibraltar and Tangier. He's sure he has the best of two worlds with two wives of extremely different temperaments and interests. In Gibraltar, Celia Johnson is a reserved and refined homebody; while in Tangier, Yvonne De Carlo is a wild and sexy party animal. *The Captain's Paradise* (1953, GB, London Films-British Lion).

11149 "They all start out as Juliets and wind up as Lady Macbeths." **William Holden** holds a cynical view of women. *The Country Girl* (1954, Paramount).

11150 "Never seen a woman who was more like a man. Looks like one, acts like one and sometimes makes me feel like I'm not." **Paul Fix** is an employee in Joan Crawford's saloon. Miss Crawford dresses in black breeches, blouse and boots, and carries a six-gun she knows how to use. *Johnny Guitar* (1954, Republic).

11151 "Dignity? I'm talking about women, man, women! I like 'em fat and vicious and not too smart. Nothing spiritual, either. To have to say 'I love you' would break my teeth. I don't want to be loved." As usual, **Anthony Quinn**, as the painter Gauguin, lectures Kirk Douglas, as Vincent Van Gogh. For a more thorough exhibition of the painter's disdain of women as anything other than something to be used, see George Sanders in *The Moon and Sixpence*. (1943, United Artists). *Lust for Life* (1956, MGM).

11152 "You've got some foolish idea about me, Mr. Quick. I'm no trembling little rabbit full of smoldering unsatisfied desires. . . I'm a woman, full grown, very smart and not all bad to look at. . . . And I expect to live at the top of my head without help from you. . . . You are barking up the wrong girl." **Joanne Woodward** tells Paul Newman that she neither needs nor wants the like of him in her life. *The Long Hot Summer* (1958, 20th Century-Fox).

11153 "Women shouldn't be allowed to have lunch clubs. We've got to keep them off balance, disorganized—clawing and scratching at each other. Otherwise they might turn on us like mad dogs." **Jim Backus** has a very nasty view of women at a time when the "battle of the sexes" was all the rage in movies. *The Wheeler Dealers* (1963, MGM).

11154 "I thought you were sexless, but you've suddenly turned into a woman. Do you know how I know that? Because you, not me, are taking pleasure in my being tied up. All women, whether they want to face it or not, want to see a man in a tied-up situation. They spend their lives trying to get a man into a tied-up situation. They are fulfilled when they can get a man—or as many men as they can—into a tied-up situation." Defrocked minister **Richard Burton** lashes out at Deborah Kerr. *The Night of the Iguana* (1964, MGM).

11155 "As for women, you make fun of me that I love them. How can I not love them? They are such poor, weak creatures. They think so little. A man's hand on their breast, and they give you all they got." Title character **Anthony Quinn**'s approach to women may not work with the women Englishman Alan Bates knows. *Zorba the Greek* (1964, 20th Century-Fox).

11156 "Mrs. Treadwell, I am only a third-grade officer on a second-rate ship, but it has given me an opportunity to observe people. I have seen women like you before—46-year-old women who are still coquettes. They travel on boats often, and always searching for something. Do you know where that searching ends, Mrs. Treadwell? It ends by sitting in a nightclub with a paid escort who tells you the lies you must hear." Ship's officer **Werner Klemperer** presumptuously tells Vivien Leigh the truth. *Ship of Fools* (1965, Columbia).

11157 "My understanding of women goes only as far as the pleasures." **Michael Caine** candidly admits that he has no interest in women after he has had them. *Alfie* (1966, GB, Paramount).

11158 "We're always trying to fuck them. . . . They know it and they like it and they don't like it. . . that's just how it is. . . look, it's got nothing to do with you, man. It just happened." Womanizer **Warren Beatty** tries to make Jack Warden see that it was nothing personal that he slept with Warden's wife, mistress, and daughter, Lee Grant, Julie Christie and Carrie Fisher, respectively. *Shampoo* (1975, Columbia).

11159 "You can't handle a real woman—you want us all to be shy violets." Predatory **Beverly D'Angelo** reacts angrily when William Katt rejects her advances. *First Love* (1977, Paramount).

11160 "I'm a woman, not a trophy." **Candy Clark** is tired of being the prize for which Paul le Mat and Bruce McGill compete. *Handle with Care* (1977, Paramount).

11161 "If their hearts are free, their bodies are for the taking, and it seems to me I haven't the right to pass up the chance.... I look to everybody." **Charles Denner** devotes his life to the pursuit of women, and he's very successful at it. *The Man Who Loved Women* (1977, Fr., Les Films du Carrosse and Les Productions Artistes Associes).

11162 "I appeal to you as a woman, a desperate, helpless, single woman." Man-hungry divorcée **Cloris Leachman** throws herself at impassive Harvey Korman. *Herbie Goes Bananas* (1980, Buena Vista).

11163 "You don't want to kill me. I'm not a real woman." Smart-mouthed transvestite **Dick Shawn** struggles with hooker killer John Diehl, who makes an exception in Shawn's case. *Angel* (1983, New World).

11164 "Well, there you have it, it's finally over. And, David, these woman have walked for you for the last time. How I wish you were here to enjoy it. Your delight in women was so passionate, so generous, that miraculously we were all transformed, molded and sculpted by your love as if we were soft clay bent to your quiet will and then set firm in the fires of your passion, with the memories as powerful and rich and graceful as the sculpted images you created to beautify the world around us. Good-bye, David. God bless." Psychiatrist **Julie Andrews**, one of sculptor Burt Reynolds' many lovers, comments at the great womanizer's grave site. *The Man Who Loved Women* (1983, Columbia).

11165 "They don't yell, tell, or swell, and they're grateful as hell." Rich sexist strip miner **Paul Sorvino** favors married women for his dalliances. *That Championship Season* (1983, Cannon).

11166 "I'm a woman, not a flophouse. People don't just check in and out." **Glenn Close** is angered by the frequent invasion of her body by a dead 20s flapper, also played by Close. *Maxie* (1985, Orion).

11167 "Just because she's a thief and a hitter don't mean she ain't a good woman in all other departments.... She's a woman. She saw a way to make some dough." Godfather-like **William Hickey** assures loyal "soldier" Jack Nicholson that Kathleen Turner may be OK despite a few faults—such as being a killer for hire. *Prizzi's Honor* (1985, ABC).

11168 "Ah, all hens and no cocks. There are too many women in our family. They're a different species from us, Bill... I love them but don't try to understand them. That road leads to ruin." Elderly **Ian Bannen** passes on some familiar male advice to his grandson Sebastian Rice-Edwards. *Hope and Glory* (1987, GB, Columbia).

11169 "I'm a woman of the eighties. I can risk my life in armed combat; I can have empty sex with strangers, and I want to be loved." Annie Hall lookalike **Michelle Little** questions if she's come a long way, baby, in the right way. *My Demon Lover* (1987, New Line).

11170 "So what do you think? Women—a mistake? Or did He do it to us on purpose?" Devil **Jack Nicholson** sounds all too human in wondering why God created women. *The Witches of Eastwick* (1987, Warner Bros.).

11171 "Uh, arretez, stop for that woman." At the end of the film, **William Hurt** tells a French cabbie to pull over so he can pick up Geena Davis. *The Accidental Tourist* (1988, Warner Bros.).

11172 "On behalf of Janice and myself, I'd like to take this moment to thank all the instructors that voted for us. And I hope the people of the United States of America will be able to sleep better knowing that women like us have guns." **Rebecca De Mornay** and Mary Gross are new FBI agents. *Feds* (1988, Warner Bros.).

11173 "Cops were dying all over the place and all I could do was act like a woman." Undercover cop **Melanie Coll** loses her professional demeanor and runs away in tears when she sees her detective fiancé and partner gunned down in a botched drug bust. *Lust for Freedom* (1988, Troma).

11174 "If you don't run away, they'll suck the last drop of life out of you." **Ron Silver** should know. He is married to three women. *Enemies, a Love Story* (1989, 20th Century-Fox).

11175 HARRY: "You mean you'd leave the guy you had the best sex of your life with just because he's a bartender?" SALLY: "Yes, I would, and so would any woman. All women are practical." **Billy Crystal** is shocked with generalizing **Meg Ryan**'s priorities. *When Harry Met Sally. . .* (1989, Columbia).

11176 "I understand women in Hollywood enlarge their chests, vacuum their hips and barf on purpose." Southern small town businessman **Woody Harrelson** doesn't like anything about Michael J. Fox, a doctor stranded in the town while on the way to Hollywood. *Doc Hollywood* (1991, Warner Bros.).

11177 "That's why God made other women. Because no matter how good a woman is, just around the corner there may be a better one." A florist doesn't think his best customer, womanizer Kevin Bacon, should get hung up on just one woman, Elizabeth Perkins. *He Said, She Said* (1991, Touchstone-Buena Vista).

11178 "How could you? I'm a woman!" **Michelle Pfeiffer**, as Catwoman, rebukes Michael Keaton, as Batman, for clouting her—then she kicks him in the groin. *Batman Returns* (1992, Warner Bros.).

Wonderfulness and Wonders

see also AMAZEMENT, SURPRISES, THINKING AND THOUGHTS

11179 "I'm still beholdin' the wonders of the jungle that'll never grow old before your eyes, like a woman does." Great White Hunter **Harry Carey** rationalizes as he magnanimously gives up his claim to White Goddess Edwina Booth to Duncan Renaldo. *Trader Horn* (1931, MGM).

11180 "I was just wondering what makes dames like you so dizzy." Reporter **Clark Gable** is put off by the behavior of runaway heiress Claudette Colbert. *It Happened One Night* (1934, Columbia).

11181 "He's taken that ship beyond maps. I wonder if he's found his Island at last?" Back in England, **Franchot Tone** thinks of his friend, mutineer Clark Gable, who by this time has found and settled with the other mutineers on Pitcairn Island in the South Seas. *Mutiny on the Bounty* (1935, MGM).

11182 "I wonder why he left me all that money? I don't need it." Amicable small-town bumpkin **Gary Cooper** is not elated when informed that an uncle has left him an incredible fortune. *Mr. Deeds Goes to Town* (1936, Columbia).

11183 WILLIAM P. BROCK: "Now that it's over, Andy, I wonder if he really did it." ANDREW J. GRIFFIN: "I wonder." Reporter **Allyn Joslyn** and prosecutor **Claude Rains**'s actions inflamed a mob to lynch teacher Edward Norris, who probably wasn't guilty of the murder of school girl Lana Turner. *They Won't Forget* (1937, Warner Bros.).

11184 "You go tell them how wonderful I am, and I'll come over later." Nightclub singer **Ginger Rogers** urges biology professor James Stewart to break the news of their marriage gently to his parents. *Vivacious Lady* (1938, RKO).

11185 "My father taught me to see those things. He grew up with our state—an' he used to say to me, 'Son, don't miss the wonders that surround you. . . . Haven't you ever noticed how grateful you are to see daylight after going through a dark tunnel?' 'Well,' he'd say, 'open your eyes and always see life around you as if you'd just come out of a long tunnel.'" Junior U.S. Senator **James Stewart** quotes the great influence on his life, his deceased father. *Mr. Smith Goes to Washington* (1939, Columbia).

11186 "Oh, Walter, you're wonderful—in a loathsome sort of way." **Rosalind Russell** drops the other shoe on her ex-husband Cary Grant. *His Girl Friday* (1940, Columbia).

11187 "Oh, earth, you're too wonderful for anybody to realize you!" After dying in childbirth, **Martha Scott** is allowed to revisit one day in her life. She chooses her sixteenth birthday. *Our Town* (1940, United Artists).

11188 POMEROY WATSON: "Where do all the little bugs go this time of year?" TOMMY HALSTEAD: "Search me." POMEROY: "No, thanks, I was just wondering." An ancient routine is practiced by **Lou Costello** and **Dick Powell**. *In the Navy* (1941, Universal).

11189 "It's funny, but when I try to think of how I feel, I always come back to Uncle Charlie. . . . Are you trying to tell me I shouldn't think he's so wonderful?" That's precisely what young police detective Macdonald Carey is trying to tell **Teresa Wright.** Her "wonderful" uncle Joseph Cotten is suspected of killing several wealthy women. *Shadow of a Doubt* (1943, Universal).

11190 PHYLLIS DIETRICHSON: "I wonder if I know what you mean?" WALTER NEFF: "I wonder if you wonder." **Barbara Stanwyck** responds to one of **Fred MacMurray**'s double-entendres. *Double Indemnity* (1944, Paramount).

11191 "The window was open but the smoke didn't move; it was a gray web woven by a thousand spiders. I wondered how they got them to work together." Narrator **Dick Powell** speaks of private eye Dick Powell, who has visions, the result of being slugged too many times and injected with drugs. *Murder, My Sweet* (1945, RKO).

11192 "Ken, I'm going to tell you something. It had to happen the way it did. I needed to hit rock bottom before I could change. Now I, I'm never going to be afraid again. We're going to have a wonderful life together, darling. And, darling, it's wonderful to rise each day and fear not, to sleep each night and dream not, and to give one's heart and hurt not." Recovered alcoholic **Susan Hayward** tells her husband Lee Bowman that life is wonderful when not viewed from a drunken stupor. *Smash-Up, the Story of a Woman* (1947, Universal).

11193 "Could have had the whole world. Why did he do it to me? Why?" Dying politician **Broderick Crawford** wonders why his assassin would take his life. *All the King's Men* (1949, Columbia).

11194 "I was getting ready to take my tie off. . . wondering whether I should hang myself with it." Broke and with no prospects, **Robert Mitchum** is a bit despondent. *His Kind of Woman* (1951, RKO).

11195 "Why don't you love me, mother? I always wondered why you didn't." **Tippi Hedren** begs for understanding from her distant acting mother Louise Latham. *Marnie* (1964, Universal).

11196 "I wonder if Socrates and Plato took a house on Crete during the summer?" In 1812 Russia, **Woody Allen** ponders the special friendship of the two philosophers of ancient Greek. *Love and Death* (1975, United Artists).

11197 "I run in God's name, let the world stand back and wonder." **Ian Charleson**, as Eric Liddell, dedicates his competitive running to God, who has given him his talent. *Chariots of Fire* (1981, GB, 20th Century-Fox).

11198 "I'll tell you right now, it's going to be wonderful." Infatuated janitor **William Hurt** promises TV newscaster Sigourney Weaver that their love-making will be special as he finally gets her into bed. *Eyewitness* (1981, 20th Century-Fox).

11199 "You ever wondered what our lives down here must seem like to a bird?" Psychologically disturbed war veteran **Matthew Modine**, who has a fixation with flying like a bird, shares the thought with his friend Nicolas Cage. *Birdy* (1984, Tri-Star).

11200 "Kind of makes you wonder, doesn't it. . . whether she's naked under that toga." Weird **Bill Murray** refers to the Statue of Liberty. *Ghostbusters II* (1989, Columbia).

Words

see also BOOKS, LANGUAGES, SILENCE, SPEECH AND SPEAKING, TALKS AND TALKING, WRITING AND WRITERS

11201 "Words are but little thanks—yet let this speak volumes." Title character **Miriam Hopkins** hurls a cheap dictionary at Elspeth Dudgeon, the headmistress of Miss Pinkerton's Academy for Young Ladies, who has given an expensive copy of Dr. Johnson's dictionary to Hopkins' rival, wealthy Frances Dee. *Becky Sharp* (1935, Pioneer).

11202 NORA CHARLES: "What are you saying?" NICK CHARLES: "I'm trying to get all the bad words out of my system." **Myrna Loy** questions **William Powell**'s muttering outside her parents' palatial home. *After the Thin Man* (1936, MGM).

11203 "The words are all the same. It makes it so easy to remember. That's probably why the 'Star-Spangled Banner' is so confusing. Nobody seems to know the words." Bewildered **Alice Brady** likes the song "Otchi Tchornia!" that her protégé Mischa Auer sings at every opportunity. *My Man Godfrey* (1936, Universal).

11204 "I don't think any word can explain a man's life." Editor of the "March of Times" newsreel **Philip Van Zandt** remarks at the end of the film when all efforts to discover the significance of title character Orson Welles final word "Rosebud" fail. *Citizen Kane* (1941, RKO).

11205 "Always? That's a dreadful word. It makes me shudder to hear it. Women are so fond of using it, and they spoil every romance by trying to make it last forever." **George Sanders** holds forth once again on another subject for the edification of Hurd Hatfield. *The Picture of Dorian Gray* (1945, MGM).

11206 "'I love you' is such an inadequate way of saying 'I love you.'" Impassioned emotionally unstable **Joan Crawford** murmurs to engineer Van Heflin. *Possessed* (1947, Warner Bros.).

11207 "I did look it up and I still don't know." **Judy Holliday** complains to her tutor William Holden that the dictionary hasn't helped her understand the meaning of a word she doesn't know. *Born Yesterday* (1950, Columbia).

11208 "There's only two syllables, you know, from bank to bankruptcy." **Spencer Tracy** complains to his wife Joan Bennett as the bills for his daughter Elizabeth Taylor's wedding start piling up. *Father of the Bride* (1950, MGM).

11209 "You made a rope of words and strangled this business." Silent screen star **Gloria Swanson** addresses her remark to unemployed screenwriter William Holden, but she means everyone who had anything to do with bringing sound to movies. *Sunset Boulevard* (1950, Paramount).

11210 "I would have given anything this morning for one human word of compassion—or tenderness." Country priest **Claude Laydu** writes of his loneliness in his diary. *Diary of a Country Priest* (1951, Fr., UGC).

11211 "That is a B, darling—the first letter of a seven-letter word that means your late father." **Rosalind Russell** helps her young ward and nephew Jan Handzlik learn the alphabet. *Auntie Mame* (1958, Warner Bros.).

11212 "You don't know what the word love means. To you, it's just another four-letter word." **Paul Newman** accuses his father Burl Ives of having no concept of love—at least as far as it applies to his family. *Cat on a Hot Tin Roof* (1958, MGM).

11213 "Republic. . . I like the sound of the word. . . . Some words give the heart a warm feeling. 'Republic' is one of those words." Davy Crockett, portrayed by **John Wayne**, is taken with the Republic of Texas. *The Alamo* (1960, United Artists).

11214 "Gee, you sure know some terrific big words." Actress, model, exotic dancer and sometimes hooker **Barbra Streisand** is impressed with would-be writer George Segal. *The Owl and the Pussycat* (1970, Columbia).

11215 "Words with a K in it are funny. You didn't know that, did you?" Long-time comedy performer **Walter Matthau** tells his nephew Richard Benjamin this for the hundredth time. *The Sunshine Boys* (1975, United Artists).

11216 "That's a polite word for what you are." **Diane Keaton** zings Woody Allen when he admits he has an "anal" personality. *Annie Hall* (1977, United Artists).

11217 "I hadn't any words because you had taken charge of all the words at home. I loved you, it was a matter of life and death—I thought so anyway—but I distrusted your words. I knew instinctively that you hardly ever meant what you said. You have such a beautiful voice, Mother. When I was little I could feel it all over my body when you spoke to me, and often you were cross with me for not hearing what you said. It was because I was listening to your voice, but also because I didn't understand what you said. I didn't understand your words—they didn't match your intonation or the expression in your eyes." **Liv Ullmann** must have been a very precocious child to make such distinctions in her mother's words and her meanings. *Autumn Sonata* (1978, Sweden-W. Ger.-GB, Personafilm-ITC).

11218 "Words keep us afloat. They are balloons that keep us from sinking." It's **Yves Montand**'s unlikely aphorism when he bumps into Romy Schneider literally and figuratively. *Clair de Femme* (1980, Fr., Atlantic).

11219 "You obviously have a great economy with words. I look forward to your next syllable with eager anticipation." **John Gielgud** so stuns hooker Anne De Salvo when he finds her in bed with Dudley Moore one morning, that she can't say anything except, "Hi." *Arthur* (1981, Orion).

11220 "I don't believe there's such a word as 'aphrodisiacal.'" Hooker **Louise Smith** exclaims when one of her johns attempts to describe a particularly exciting experience. Well, there's such a word now. *Working Girls* (1987, Miramax).

11221 "Sticks and stones may break my bones, but words cause permanent damage." Talk show host **Eric Bogosian** provokes crazies in his audience. *Talk Radio* (1989, Universal).

11222 JOHNNY: "I bet you have a beautiful. . . ." FRANKIE: "I hate that word, Johnny." JOHNNY: "I wasn't going to say that one." FRANKIE: "I hate both of them." JOHNNY: "All right, thing! I'll look up a new word in my thesaurus. All I'm asking you is to open your robe so I can look at it. Just look. Fifteen seconds." Even though **Michelle Pfeiffer** and **Al Pacino** have already made love, she doesn't feel comfortable with his request that she exhibit herself to him. She does, but her discomfort is obvious. *Frankie and Johnny* (1991, Paramount).

Work and Workers

see also CAREERS, EFFORTS, INCOMPETENCE, JOBS, OCCUPATIONS, RETIREMENT, SPECIALTIES, UNIONS

11223 "My day's work has been useless as a life preserver for fish." We guess everyone has had days like **Walter Oland** as the title character. *Charlie Chan's Chance* (1932, Fox).

11224 "Since the world began, half of the female population has always been working women. The other half has been working men." It's a clever little play on words in the opening subtitle of a film that was renamed when censors forced "word" to be substituted for "name" in the title. *The Greeks Had a Word for Them* (1932, United Artists).

11225 "Forget it, kid, it's all in a day's work, as the road sweeper said to the elephant." **Aline MacMahon** tells Sidney Fox not to worry about the trouble she's causing the former. *The Mouthpiece* (1932, Warner Bros.).

11226 "I don't like work either." **Mae West** reacts when her guest William B. Davidson replies to her question about what he does for a living, by saying he's sort of a politician. *I'm No Angel* (1933, Paramount).

11227 "She hasn't worked in so long, if she does get a job it'll practically amount to a comeback." Wisecracking **Eve Arden** refers to would-be singer-dancer Ginger Rogers who has gone whooping out the door to a nightclub audition. *Stage Door* (1937, RKO).

11228 "I've been working since I was ten—I want to find out why I've been working." Having worked his way up from poverty into a career as an investment banker, **Cary Grant** is about to give it up to find out what makes him tick. *Holiday* (1938, Columbia).

11229 "Well, I reckon we'd better be gettin' back to work. There's gonna be a heap to do from now on." Back from the French and Indian War, farmer **Henry Fonda** wants to get back to his normal life. *Drums Along the Mohawk* (1939, 20th Century-Fox).

11230 JEAN HARRINGTON: "I don't see why I have to do all the dirty work. There must be plenty of rich old dames waiting for you to push them around." COL. HARRINGTON: "You find 'em, I'll push 'em." **Barbara Stanwyck** complains to her father and partner in swindling **Charles Coburn** that she shouldn't always have to entice men; he could work his charm on women, just as easily. *The Lady Eve* (1941, Paramount).

11231 "I was always in the kitchen. I felt as though I'd been born in a kitchen and lived there all my life, except for the few hours it took to get married. I married Bert when I was 17 and never knew any other life. Just cooking, washing, having children." **Joan Crawford** thinks back to simpler times when her only problems were that her work was never done. *Mildred Pierce* (1945, Warner Bros.).

11232 "[Your work] is brilliant but lifeless. There's no intuition in it. You approach all your problems with an ice pack on your head." Unsuccessful in trying to make love to psychiatrist Ingrid Bergman, her colleague **John Emery** suggests she may be frigid. *Spellbound* (1945, Selznick-United Artists).

11233 "It is very sad to love and lose somebody. But in a while you will forget, and you will take up the threads of your life where you left off not so long ago. And you will work hard. There is a lot of happiness in working hard, maybe the most." **Michael Chekhov** consoles Ingrid Bergman when the man she loves, Gregory Peck, is convicted of murder. *Spellbound* (1945, Selznick-United Artists).

11234 "Do you know how long it takes a working man to save five thousand dollars? Just remember this, Mr. Potter, that this rabble you're talking about. . . they do most of the working and paying and living and dying in this community. Well, is it too much to have them work and pay and live and die in a couple of decent rooms and a bath?" **James Stewart**'s inspired and inspiring address to the board of the savings and loan company founded by his father Samuel S. Hinds, after the latter's death, saves it from being closed as desired by Lionel Barrymore. *It's a Wonderful Life* (1946, RKO).

11235 "Work never hurt anyone. It's good for them. But if you're going to work, work hard. King Solomon had the right idea about work: 'Whatever thy hand findeth to do,' Solomon said, 'do thy doggonedest.'" **William Powell** invents a suitable Bible quote for his son James Lydon. *Life with Father* (1947, Warner Bros.).

11236 "I'd certainly like to go to New Orleans. I know a girl there. She has an embroidery shop on Royal Street. I'm good at embroidery. That's what I always wanted to do. . . . Yep. Instead of whoring. I just wanted to do fancy embroidery." Prostitute **Dona Drake** tells customer Dan Duryea that she'd like to try another line of work. *Another Part of the Forest* (1948, Universal-International).

11237 "I got home at midnight, intoxicated with an idea, and worked myself into a creative hangover." Writer **Clifton Webb** uses an alcoholic allegory to explain a writing spree to his secretary Dorothy McGuire. *Three Coins in the Fountain* (1954, 20th Century-Fox).

11238 "Just what is it that you do to earn your salary?" At a stockholder's meeting, guileless and extremely minor stockholder **Judy Holliday** bluntly but sweetly asks John Williams, the chairman of the board, what his duties are. *The Solid Gold Cadillac* (1956, Columbia).

11239 "I'm adamant. I will not have an officer from my battalion working as a coolie." British Colonel **Alec Guinness** defiantly refuses to surrender command of his troops to Japanese Commandant Sessue Hayakawa. *The Bridge on the River Kwai* (1957, GB, Columbia).

11240 "I'm tired of sweating for people who aren't there. I sweat to pay off my father's debt, and he's in his grave. I sweat to pay my ex-wife alimony and she's living on the other side of the world somewhere." **John Gavin** bitterly complains to his lover Janet Leigh about how hard he has to work. *Psycho* (1960, United Artists).

11241 "To work, my son." **Rex Harrison**, as an impatient Pope Julius II, exalts Charlton Heston, as Michelangelo, to finish the ceiling of the Sistine Chapel. *The Agony and the Ecstasy* (1965, 20th Century-Fox).

11242 "I never had a career—only work." **Andrew Keir** is Professor Bernard Quatermass. *Quatermass and the Pit* aka: *Five Million Years to Earth* (1968, GB, Hammer-20th Century-Fox).

11243 "Closest we ever came to ranch work was back in our rustling days. We weren't much at it even then, and it's hard. The hours are brutal. You got to be a kid to start a ranch." **Paul Newman** rejects Katharine Ross' suggestion that he and Robert Redford give up their outlaw ways and become ranchers. *Butch Cassidy and the Sundance Kid* (1969, 20th Century-Fox).

11244 "I'm workin' on my first million, and you're still workin' on eight seconds." Real estate developer **Joe Don Baker** compares his prospects with those of his brother, fading rodeo performer Steve McQueen. *Junior Bonner* (1972, ABC-Cinerama).

11245 "You gotta do what you gotta do." It's **Neville Brand**'s macho comment as he works at feeding women to a crocodile. *Eaten Alive* aka: *Death Trap; Starlight Slaughter; Horror Hotel Massacre; Legend of the Bayou* (1976, Virgo International).

11246 GLORIA: "What do you do for a living?" ARTHUR: "I race cars. I play tennis. . . . I fondle women. . . but I get weekends off and I'm my own boss." Hooker **Anne De Salvo** questions alcoholic millionaire **Dudley Moore** about his work. *Arthur* (1981, Orion-Warner Bros.).

11247 "Go throw yourself into your work. I've never seen a happily married man who was worth a damn." **Jack Warden**, George Segal's father-in-law and boss, advises the younger man to give up trying to make love to his frigid wife Susan St. James, and cheat discreetly. *Carbon Copy* (1981, RKO).

11248 "It's hard work being in love, especially when you don't know what girl it is." **Allison Forster**, who believes he should pay attention to her, sympathizes with Gordon John Sinclair, who is moping over Dee Hepburn. *Gregory's Girl* (1982, GB, Goldwyn).

11249 "I wasn't made to do work planned by other heads." **Richard Farnsworth**, known as "The Gentleman Bandit" in his younger days, originated the fundamental robbery command, "hands up." He tells his sister he has ambitions after being released from San Quentin where he spent thirty years. *The Grey Fox* (1983, Canada, United Artists Classics).

11250 BEN: "You see, the thing is I'm still working the place myself—it's my living, it supports me." GORDON: "You'd have lots of money; you wouldn't have to work." BEN: "Oh, we all have to work, Gordon. . . . And the beach. . . think of the state the place would get into. . . ." Delightful old Scottish beachcomber **Fulton MacKay** won't accept lawyer **Denis Lawson**'s arguments that he sell the beach, which gives him a meager living, to American oil interests for a fortune. *Local Hero* (1983, GB, Enigma-Goldcrest).

11251 "Now pay attention and concentrate on what I'm gonna say. This thing is going to work!" Unfulfilled **Bo Derek** bursts in on inconveniently gored matador Andrea Occhipinti. She believes with a little mind over matter, he'll be able to perform the way she wants. *Bolero* (1984, Cannon).

11252 "It's a real hoot. I wanna work and can't. You can and don't." Laid-off construction worker **Paul Newman** sees the irony in his situation and that of his son Robby Benson, who vaguely dreams of being a writer but really isn't very ambitious. *Harry and Son* (1984, Orion).

11253 "Never send a man to do a woman's work." Power-hungry sorceress **Faye Dunaway** is furious with the incompetence of her male henchmen. *Supergirl* (1984, Australia, Tri-Star).

11254 "Yeah, a good day's work for a good day's beating." It's ex-Chicago fireman **Robin Williams'** dry comment when a white racist visitor fondly recalls the productivity of the days of slavery in the Caribbean. *Club Paradise* (1986, Warner Bros.).

11255 "There are easier ways of making a living than being a drag queen, but try as I might. . . I can't get used to wearing flats." Gay female impersonator **Harvey Fierstein** makes an aside to the camera as he applies his make-up. *Torch Song Trilogy* (1988, New Line).

11256 "Is driving a UFO good work? Do you own or rent?" Valley girl **Geena Davis** questions alien Jeff Goldblum when she elects to take off with him for outer space. *Earth Girls Are Easy* (1989, Vestron).

World

see also LIVES AND LIVING, SPACE, UNIVERSE

11257 "The world is mine!" After discovering a fabulous fortune, **James O'Neill**, as recently escaped prisoner Edmund Dantes, shouts to the heavens, as he stands on a wave-washed rock, silhouetted against the sky. *The Count of Monte Cristo* (1913, silent, Famous Players-Paramount).

11258 "You live in a world where people are cheap and vulgar without knowing it." **Neil Hamilton** deserts his movie star wife Constance Bennett. *What Price Hollywood?* (1932, RKO).

11259 "This is how the Lord must have felt when He first beheld the finished world with all His creatures, breathing, living. . . ." **Greta Garbo** kisses John Gilbert in their private room. *Queen Christina* (1933, MGM).

11260 "It's the world against us and us against the world." Escaped slave **Errol Flynn** sizes up the odds for his gang of pirates. *Captain Blood* (1935, Warner Bros.).

11261 "The world as it is presently constituted stinks." It's the oft-stated philosophy of abrasive trumpeter **Jack Carson**. *Blues in the Night* (1941, Warner Bros.).

11262 "It's good to live among hopeful people again. I've escaped from a world I can't help. I'm building up one that I can. . . in my own head." Journalist **Michael Redgrave** explains to his friend James Mason why he chooses to retire to a light-house on Lake Michigan where he is haunted by the ghosts of immigrants who drowned a century before. *Thunder Rock* (1942, GB, Charter Films).

11263 "You're just an ordinary little girl living in an ordinary little town. You're a sleepwalker, you're blind. How do you know what the world is really like? Do you know the world is a foul sty? Do you know if you ripped the fronts off houses you'd find swine? The world's a hell. Wake up, Charlie, use your wits, learn something. . . . The same blood flows through our veins." Psychopathic killer **Joseph Cotten** rages at his once adoring niece Teresa Wright. *Shadow of a Doubt* (1943, Universal).

11264 "The world needs watching. . . . It seems to go a little crazy now and then." Police detective **Macdonald Carey** is on the trail of "The Merry Widow" murderer, Joseph Cotten. *Shadow of a Doubt* (1943, Universal).

11265 "This is the story of two worlds, the one we know and another which exists only in the mind of a young airman whose life and imagination have been violently shaped by war. Any resemblance to another world, known or unknown, is purely coincidental." It's the preface of a fantasy film in which brain damaged British pilot David Niven is torn between this world and the next. *A Matter of Life and Death* aka: *Stairway to Heaven* (1946, GB, Archers-General Film Distributors).

11266 HENRI VERDOUX: "It's a ruthless world, and one must be ruthless to cope with it." THE GIRL: "It's a blundering world and a very sad one, yet a little kindness can make it beautiful." VERDOUX: "You better go before your philosophy corrupts me." **Charles Chaplin** changes his mind about poisoning **Marilyn Nash** after exchanging views of the world. *Monsieur Verdoux* (1947, United Artists).

11267 MCNEAL: "It's a big thing when a sovereign state admits an error. And remember this, there aren't many governments in the world that would do it." FRANK WIECEK: "Yes, it's a good world—out-

side." Reporter **James Stewart**'s statement seems somewhat strange and insensitive. He has just successfully won a pardon for **Richard Conte**, who has spent 13 years in Statesville prison, losing his wife and child in the process, all for a crime he did not commit. Conte's mother, Kasia Orzazewski, newspaper editor Lee J. Cobb and Stewart are the only people who seem to care about justice for Conte. *Call Northside 777* (1948, 20th Century-Fox).

11268 "Now go out there and show 'em who's boss, son. . . . Remember, top of the world." **Margaret Wycherly** encourages her psychopathic killer and criminal son James Cagney as he recovers from another of his violent headache seizures. *White Heat* (1949, Warner Bros.).

11269 "When man entered the Atomic Age, he opened a door to a new world. What we'll eventually find in the new world nobody can predict." Scientist **Edmund Gwenn** is both profound and prophetic. *Them!* (1954, Warner Bros.).

11270 JACK BURNS: "Ever notice how many fences there are getting to be? Signs say 'No hunting. No admission, Private Property. Closed area.'. . . Paul just didn't naturally see the use of it. So he acted as if it weren't there. When people sneaked across, he felt they were just people. So he helped them." JERRI BONDI: "The world you and Paul live in doesn't exist. Maybe it never did. Out there is the real world. And it's got real borders and real fences. And real trouble. Either you play by the rules or you lose." Aging cowboy drifter **Kirk Douglas** and **Gena Rowlands** discuss his friend and her husband Michael Kane, who has been jailed for helping some Mexicans. She claims that the world the two men love no longer exists. *Lonely Are the Brave* (1962, Universal).

11271 "The world is so full of crap, a man's going to get into it sooner or later." **Paul Newman** defiantly shouts after his nephew Brandon de Wilde, who disgustedly leaves Newman at the end of the film. *Hud* (1963, Paramount).

11272 "We're playing with the end of the world." Banker **Kris Kristofferson** is caught up in a high-powered Arab investment plot. *Rollover* (1981, Warner Bros.).

11273 "Let me tell you the way the world is: nothing works right." It's world-weary cop **Tom Selleck**'s rule. *Runaway* (1984, Tri-Star).

11274 "It's a sad and beautiful world." Even though he's in a Louisiana prison, Italian **Roberto Benigni** is cheerful and constantly pleased with himself. *Down by Law* (1986, Island Pictures).

11275 "It's six a.m. on the island of Manhattan. In the dawn's early light you can imagine the first ship from the Old World sailing slowly up the biggest river they had ever seen. That was almost how you felt the first time you saw the city from the window of a Greyhound. Like you were looking at a new world waiting to be discovered. And that's how it looks to you now. But you have to go slowly. You'll have to learn everything all over again." It's the end of the movie in which **Michael J. Fox** tried to deal with his problems by turning to drink, sex and drugs in New York City's club scene. *Bright Lights, Big City* (1988, United Artists).

Worries

see also CONCERNS, DIFFICULTIES, PROBLEMS, TROUBLES

11276 "Now what's the use of worrying? It's silly to worry, isn't it? You're gone today and here tomorrow." **Groucho Marx**'s observation to young Oscar Shaw probably was a howl in 1929. *The Cocoanuts* (1929, Paramount).

11277 "I'm not going to bed till I have convulsions and my teeth start falling out. That's the time to worry, isn't it?" Mistakenly diagnosed as having a fatal disease, **Carole Lombard** tells reporter Fredric March, who is taking her to New York City for a final fling, that she's up to it until signs alert her that the end is near. *Nothing Sacred* (1937, Selznick-United Artists).

11278 "I was getting worried—afraid we'd have to hang the girl to make the old man crack." **Alan Ladd** is willing to sacrifice Veronica Lake to get a confession from Moroni Olsen that he killed his own son. *The Glass Key* (1942, Paramount).

11279 "I'm not going to worry about that until the Statue of Liberty goes by that porthole." On a ship sailing for the U.S., carrying war brides, male war bridegroom **Cary Grant** hasn't had a chance to be alone with his bride Ann Sheridan since they got married. He throws the key to the ship's brig in which he's confined out the porthole. Locked in with him, Sheridan wonders how they'll get out. *I Was a Male War Bride* (1949, 20th Century-Fox).

11280 "If a girl has to worry about all the money she doesn't have, how is she going to have time for love?" **Marilyn Monroe** offers her friend Jane Russell another reason for marrying a rich man—it will prevent a loveless marriage. *Gentlemen Prefer Blondes* (1953, 20th Century-Fox).

11281 "You know something, Doctor, I'm not going to worry about overpopulation just yet." Delivering the film's last line, charter boat captain **James Best** interrupts kissing bacteriologist Ingrid Goude to speak to her father Baruch Lumet. *The Killer Shrews* (1959, McLendon Radio Pictures).

11282 "I'm not worried about my virility, mate." Lovely **Susannah York** one-ups aging hippie James Coburn, who would like to get to know her better. *Duffy* (1968, GB, Columbia).

11283 "You want the place to look nice for the police?. . . You're worried they're going to put down in their books, 'bad housekeeper'. . . leave it alone. Maybe they'll find some clues." **Jack Lemmon** angrily snaps at his wife Anne Bancroft, who is straightening their burglarized apartment before the police arrive. *The Prisoner of Second Avenue* (1975, Warner Bros.).

11284 "The Boston gig's been canceled but I wouldn't worry about it, it's not a big college town." Inept **Tony Hendra**, manager of the unsuccessful British rock group Spinal Tap, is ignorant of the great number of colleges and universities in the Boston vicinity. *This Is Spinal Tap* (1984, Embassy).

11285 "I like being here. You get to do what you want, nobody fucks with you. The only worry you've got is dying. If that happens, you won't know about it anyway." **Kevin Dillon**, as Bunny, loud and not too bright, searches for something good about his stint in the jungles of Vietnam. *Platoon* (1986, Orion).

11286 "Don't worry about him. That's what he always does." **Christine Lahti** tells Sara Walker to take no mind of the owner of the rowboat they have "borrowed" who is chasing them. *Housekeeping* (1987, Columbia).

11287 "Don't worry about being loved. Worry about loving—it's far more important." Aging **Lynn Redgrave** shares some wisdom with young hairdresser Jesse Birdsall who has given his virginity to Redgrave. *Getting It Right* (1989, GB, MCEG).

11288 "Don't worry, if it's anything serious I'll come back for my driver." **Kurt Russell** jokes with his wife Madeleine Stowe as he arms himself with his putter before going downstairs to investigate a noise. *Unlawful Entry* (1992, 20th Century-Fox).

Worship

see also GOD, LOVE AND HATE, RELIGIONS

11289 "I love you as one adores sacred things." French officer **Ramon Novarro** worships beautiful German spy Greta Garbo. *Mata Hari* (1932, MGM).

11290 "You know, you'd soon get tired of a man who had nothing else to do but worship you. That's a dull kind of love, Gabrielle. It's the kind of love that makes people old too soon." As he does often in this movie, **Leslie Howard** lectures Bette Davis about what is good for her. *The Petrified Forest* (1936, Warner Bros.).

11291 "Oh, she worships me, sir, but it was no means an easy conquest. The young lady didn't believe in the institution of marriage." Butler **Ernest Cossart** speaks of his lady love to his master Herbert Marshall. *Angel* (1937, Paramount).

11292 "I don't want to be worshiped. I want to be loved." **Katharine Hepburn** tells fiancé John Howard that she doesn't want him to put her on a pedestal. Ditto for **Grace Kelly** to John Lund in the musical remake. *The Philadelphia Story* (1940, MGM); *High Society* (1956, MGM).

11293 "Adoring someone is certainly better than being adored. Being adored is a nuisance. You'll discover, Dorian, that women treat us just as humanity treats its gods; they worship us but keep bothering us to do something for them." **George Sanders** lectures Hurd Hatfield about women. *The Picture of Dorian Gray* (1945, MGM).

11294 "There was a maharajah who came all the way from India to beg one of her silk stockings. Later, he strangled himself with it." One-time movie director, now butler, **Erich von Stroheim** tells writer William Holden that his ex-wife and employer, silent screen star Gloria Swanson was worshipped by men. *Sunset Boulevard* (1950, Paramount).

11295 "They know I worship your body like a French cathedral." Ample-sized nurse **Lu Leonard** speaks to diminutive obstetrician Wallace Shawn. *Micki & Maude* (1984, Columbia).

Worth and Values

see also Costs, Prices, Wealth and Riches

11296 "A man in the house is worth three on the street." More words of wisdom from **Mae West**. *Belle of the Nineties* (1934, Paramount).

11297 "Living, I'm worth nothing to her. But dead, I can buy her the tallest cathedrals, golden vineyards and dancing in the streets." Wandering poet **Leslie Howard** explains to mad dog killer Humphrey Bogart why he has made waitress Bette Davis the beneficiary of his will. *The Petrified Forest* (1936, Warner Bros.).

11298 RHETT BUTLER: "You've been working like a field hand. What do you really want?" SCARLETT O'HARA: "[I need] $300 to pay the taxes to keep Tara." RHETT: "You're not worth $300. You'll never be anything but misery to any man." **Clark Gable** is visited in jail by **Vivien Leigh**, hoping he will lend her the money she needs to pay the taxes and keep Tara. His money is tied up in foreign banks, so he can't help her. He tells her, "So you see, my dear, you've abased yourself for nothing." *Gone with the Wind* (1939, Selznick-MGM).

11299 "The resale value of this car is going to be practically nil when we get through with this trip." A desperate bandit forces **W.C. Fields** to drive a getaway car. Fields runs into everything in the process. *The Bank Dick* (1940, Universal).

11300 "The only reason I took the job was my bank account was trying to crawl under a duck." Knowing his financial worth, private eye **Dick Powell** takes just about any job—because his "funds-arelow." *Murder, My Sweet* (1945, RKO).

11301 "It's not worth it, honey, no matter how much money that pig's got." Sarcastic **Humphrey Bogart** yells to a pretty young thing riding in a passing car with a much older man. *In a Lonely Place* (1950, Columbia).

11302 "No woman is worth the lives of eight men." The woman who, according to **Alan Ladd**, portraying Jim Bowie, is not worth the death of eight men, is Virginia Mayo, who directly or indirectly is responsible for the deaths of at least eight men. *The Iron Mistress* (1952, Warner Bros.).

11303 DR. STEWART MCIVER: "Since you mention my values, they include sitting here listening to the bull you throw at me and I don't say 'forget it'—because one of my values is not to toss in the sponge on human commitments." STEVEN W. HOLTE: "What a collection of junky platitudes." Shrink **Richard Widmark** gets a bit testy with difficult patient **John Kerr**. *The Cobweb* (1955, MGM).

11304 "You say that nothing's got a value except the value that men put upon it, and I don't know how men can put a higher value on something than by dying for it." Army Lieutenant **Rip Torn** figures his men must try and take Pork Chop Hill from the enemy to help peace negotiations at Panmunjom. *Pork Chop Hill* (1959, United Artists).

11305 "This, then, is what we stand for: truth, justice and the value of a single human being." American jurist **Spencer Tracy** reads from his decision in the war crimes trials of German judges. *Judgment at Nuremberg* (1961, United Artists).

11306 "Well, it seems we are to have a British waterworks with an Arab flag over it. Do you think it was worth it?" British civil servant **Claude Rains** muses near the end of the film. *Lawrence of Arabia* (1962, GB, Columbia).

11307 "I can't be spread so thin. . . it's just not worth all the deaths I have to die." **Judy Garland**, portraying herself to an uncomfortable degree, denounces her life as an entertainer. *I Could Go on Singing* (1963, GB, United Artists).

11308 "This is the story of passion, bloodshed, desire and death, everything, in fact, that makes life worth living." It's the written introduction to the story of a French streetwalker Shirley MacLaine and her pimp, ex-gendarme Jack Lemmon. *Irma la Douce* (1963, United Artists).

11309 "I'm worth something, ain't I?" Gold prospector **Jason Robards, Jr.** plots revenge against the men who robbed him. *The Ballad of Cable Hogue* (1970, Warner Bros.).

11310 "Gee, I've had men pay two hundred dollars for me—here, you're turning down a freebie. . . . You can get a perfectly good dishwasher for that." Part-time prostitute **Jane Fonda** exhibits mock dismay when Donald Sutherland refuses to do business with her—even gratis. *Klute* (1970, Warner Bros.).

11311 "If it hadn't been for him. . . I'd have missed it—whatever it is. . . . He's the only man I ever met who knew what I was worth. Sam the Lion. Sam the Lion. Nobody know where he got that name. I gave it to him—one night. Just came to me. He was so pleased. I was twenty-two then—can you imagine?. . . You know something, Sonny. It's terrible only to find one man in your whole life that knows what you're worth. It's just terrible—I wouldn't be tellin' you if it wasn't. I looked, too—you wouldn't believe how I've looked. When Sam. . . was sixty-five years old he could jus' walk into a room where I was and do more for me. . . nobody was like him." **Ellen Burstyn** tells Timothy Bottoms about Ben Johnson, the only man she has ever truly loved. *The Last Picture Show* (1971, Columbia).

11312 "Nothing worth knowing can be understood with the mind. . . the brain is man's most insignificant organ. . . everything really valuable has to enter through another opening." it sounds like **Woody Allen** is philosiphizing Diane Keaton. *Manhattan* (1979, United Artists).

11313 "A community with a juvenile crime problem is not a community with a high resale value." A pontificating Babbitt-like parent is more concerned with his property values than his kids. *Over the Edge* (1979, Orion-Warner Bros.)

11314 "Billy, you're the only son of bitch worth getting seriously drunk with." **Kris Kristofferson** has found a kindred soul in John Hurt. *Heaven's Gate* (1980, United Artists).

11315 "That library over there is worth millions and people keep telling me you're a piece of shit." Police Commissioner **James Cagney** gives his opinion of the relative worth of a building and Howard R. Rollins, who with other blacks have barricaded themselves in the J.P. Morgan Library. *Ragtime* (1981, Paramount).

11316 "At least once every show I try to put something of value in." **Tom Berenger** lamely protests about the quality of his work on a mindless escapism TV show. *The Big Chill* (1983, Columbia).

11317 "I don't know that I want to teach you; what you have is already too valuable." British Open University tutor **Michael Caine** fears that formal study of literature will tarnish the innate wisdom of cheerful young hairdresser Julie Walters. *Educating Rita* (1983, GB, Acorn-Rank).

11318 "You're black, you're poor, you're ugly, you're a woman. You're nothin' at all." **Danny Glover** cruelly tells Whoopi Goldberg that she is worthless. *The Color Purple* (1985, Warner Bros.).

11319 "He has rooms he does not value and he thinks you would value them." **Simon Callow**, as Reverend Beebe, takes a sensible approach while acting as intermediary in the exchange of rooms between Denholm Elliott and his son Julian Sands with Maggie Smith and her niece Helena Bonham Carter at a hotel in Florence. *A Room with a View* (1985, GB, Merchant-Ivory-Goldcrest).

11320 "Now what's worth doing, is worth doing for money. It's a bad bargain if nobody gains. . . ." **Michael Douglas** answers the accusation of Martin Sheen that his only interest in a deal is to make money. *Wall Street* (1987, 20th Century-Fox).

11321 "People down here feel some things are worth killing for." **Gene Hackman** responds to his FBI boss Willem Dafoe's observation that some people, like the missing civil rights workers they are seeking, feel some things are worth dying for. *Mississippi Burning* (1988, Orion).

11322 "It's a big man who knows the value of a small coin." Simple Italian shoemaker **Don Ameche**, masquerading as a Mafioso don, repeats to mob boss Robert Prosky the aphorism spoken to him by the man whom he is impersonating. The words seem to have great meaning for all involved. *Things Change* (1988, Columbia).

11323 "In fact, that Fred hated every human being except me really meant something." **Sara Gilbert** argues with Drew Barrymore for the affection of Gilbert's dog Fred. *Poison Ivy* (1992, New Line).

Wounds and Scars

see also HARM, HURT AND HURTING, PAINS, SKIN

11324 "Where I'll kick her, the camera will never pick up the scar." Studio publicity agent **Lee Tracy** makes a crack about blonde sexpot Jean Harlow, who is quite a pain in the neck—or somewhere. *Bombshell* (1933, MGM).

11325 NICK CHARLES: "I'm a hero. I was shot twice in the *Tribune*." NORA CHARLES: "I read you were shot five times in the tabloids." NICK: "It's not true. He didn't come anywhere near my tabloids." **William Powell**, who has been superficially wounded by a gunman, reads about the episode in the papers with his wife **Myrna Loy**. *The Thin Man* (1934, MGM).

11326 "If a man starts cutting you across the head, don't duck, let him keep cutting." **Ronald Colman** prefers death to the blindness that his World War I wound caused. *The Light That Failed* (1939, Paramount).

11327 "I'll bear the scar of this the rest of my life." Wealthy **Henry Fonda** whines when his physician wife Barbara Stanwyck leaves on an emergency call. *You Belong to Me* (1941, Columbia).

11328 "A severe wound, I hope." Parisian dress designer **Joan Crawford** snaps at an injured German officer, unwelcomingly billeted in her mansion. *Reunion in France* (1942, MGM).

11329 CATHERINE McDOWALL: "I hate you." CHAD BIXBY: "My papa cut me up better than that. You've seen my scars. Can you match them?" **Susan Kohner** goes crazy with frustration as she horsewhips **Robert Wagner**, who merely taunts her. *All the Fine Young Cannibals* (1960, MGM).

11330 "Wounds suffered in tropical climes can all too swiftly become nasty infections." Injured, would-be movie screenwriter **Jeff Bridges** talks like the stuff he writes when a motion picture crew res-

cues him in the desert. *Hearts of the West* (1975, MGM).

11331 "Yes, not a lot of scars." Sultry sculptress **Linda Fiorentino**, heavily into S&M, responds to Griffin Dunne's compliment on her great body. *After Hours* (1985, Warner Bros.).

11332 PAULA MURPHY: "I think it's going to go away someday." TIM MURPHY: "No, it won't go away. It will always be there." **Lisa Blount** and her husband **Don Johnson** are talking of both the physical and emotional scars he picked up in Vietnam. *Cease Fire* (1985, Cineworld).

Writing and Writers

see also BOOKS, CREATION AND CREATURES, FICTION, NEWS AND NEWSPAPERS, POETRY AND POETS, REPORTERS, STORIES, STYLES, WORDS

11333 "I came to find out whether writers make love out of fun or curiosity." Socialite **Ruth Chatterton** tests writer George Brent. *The Rich Are Always with Us* (1932, Warner Bros.).

11334 FIORELLO: "I forgot to tell you, I can't write." OTIS B. DRIFTWOOD: "Well, that's all right, there's no ink in the pen anyhow." **Chico Marx** rejects a pen offered to him by **Groucho Marx** to sign a contract. *A Night at the Opera* (1935, MGM).

11335 "We're not writers, we're hacks. . . . My God, I wrote once. I wrote a book—a darn good book. I was a promising novelist. . . . And now I'm writing dialogue for a horse." **James Cagney** echoes the complaint of many a Hollywood screenwriter. *Boy Meets Girl* (1938, Warner Bros.).

11336 "The fact is, you can't be a first-rate writer or a first-rate human being until you've learned to have some small regard for human frailty." **Katharine Hepburn** accuses magazine writer James Stewart, assigned to cover her society wedding, of being an "intellectual snob," because he has never seen her as a person, but only as a representative of her class. *The Philadelphia Story* (1940, MGM).

11337 "I don't use a pen, I write with a goose quill dipped in venom." Columnist and cynic **Clifton Webb** refuses Gene Tierney's request that he endorse a fountain pen in an advertisement. *Laura* (1944, 20th Century-Fox).

11338 "I'm going to put this whole weekend down, minute by minute." Alcoholic **Ray Milland** seeks salvation from his dipsomania by the public act of writing about his recent descent into a hell of booze. *The Lost Weekend* (1945, Paramount).

11339 "So you're a story writer too, huh? The detective business must be on the skids—what are you trying to do—elevate yourself?" Tough cop **Lloyd Nolan** doesn't think much of private eye Robert Montgomery. *Lady in the Lake* (1947, MGM).

11340 "I'd decided I'd write about a murder; it's safer. Besides they tell me the profits are good." Private detective **Robert Montgomery** doesn't mind explaining why he has turned to writing. *Lady in the Lake* (1947, MGM).

11341 "I don't make things happen. All I do is write them." Reporter **Kirk Douglas** is willing to risk the life of a man trapped in a cave to get the big story that will put him back on top as a journalist. *Ace in the Hole* aka: *The Big Carnival* (1951, Paramount).

11342 "Golly, to think you can put words down on paper like that and all I can do is hem brassieres!" Floozy **Shirley MacLaine** is impressed with failed writer Frank Sinatra. *Some Came Running* (1959, MGM).

11343 ELLA PETERSON: "He's not a playboy. He's a very talented playwright." GWYNNE: "But all he does is play—he never writes." Switchboard operators **Judy Holliday** and **Ruth Storey** have different opinions of subscriber Dean Martin. *Bells Are Ringing* (1960, MGM).

11344 "You never pushed a noun against a verb except to blow up something." Clarence Darrow-like lawyer **Spencer Tracy** accuses H.L. Mencken-like journalist Gene Kelly of being a rabble rouser with few real convictions. *Inherit the Wind* (1960, United Artists).

11345 "I'm trying to write good literature, but it always come out nightingales and roses." **Vanessa Redgrave**, as dancer Isadora Duncan, finds writing isn't easy. *Isadora* aka; *The Loves of Isadora* (1969, GB, Universal).

11346 "He writes like a housewife on the verge of the vapors." It's a hostile male's assessment of the literary achievements of Lord Byron, played by Richard Chamberlain. *Lady Caroline Lamb* (1972, GB-Italy, GEC Pulsar-Vides-United Artists).

11347 "I never did want the damn thing published while I was alive, anyway." Actress **Gloria Swanson** dictates the final touches on her autobiography aboard a plane that appears doomed. *Airport 75* (1974, Universal).

11348 "Don't whip me. . . not while I'm writing." Habitually irritable **Paolo Malio** as Dr. Leopold Von Sacher-Masoch snaps at his wife Francesco Sapio,

who beats him "daddy, eight to the bar." *Masoch* (1980, Italy, Difilm-Tierrepi).

11349 "This time, humor the writers. Say some of their lines." Television producer **Adolph Green** makes a request of his star Joseph Bologna. *My Favorite Year* (1982, MGM-United Artists).

11350 "There are no trashy writers—only trashy readers." Many writers might agree with poet **Tom Conti**, even though they might put it more diplomatically. Not! *Reuben, Reuben* (1983, 20th Century-Fox).

11351 "Gowan always maintained that what he hated most about writing was the paperwork." **Kara Wilson** is being interviewed by a reporter about her ex-husband, poet Tom Conti. *Reuben, Reuben* (1983, 20th Century-Fox).

11352 "When you sit down to write, forget you've got a mother!" *Rolling Stone* editor **Jann Wenner** barks instructions to feature reporter John Travolta, who has been known to trash his subjects. *Perfect* (1985, Columbia).

11353 "It's not a bad idea to get in the habit of writing down one's thoughts. It saves one having to bother anyone else with them." English aristocrat **James Mason** shares a thought with his granddaughter Rebecca Saire. *The Shooting Party* (1985, GB, Edenflow-European Classics).

11354 "This town is lousy with bookworms—everyone wants to be a ghostwriter." Highly assimilated rabbi **Alan King** threatens to fire Ron Silver as his ghostwriter. *Enemies, a Love Story* (1989, 20th Century-Fox).

11355 "Henry writes about fucking." Fred Ward, as novelist Henry Miller, is introduced to Maria de Medeiros as writer Anais Nin. *Henry & June* (1990, Universal).

11356 "You can crawl and kiss ass and write the happy endings." John Huston-like director **Clint Eastwood** accuses Peter Viertel-like writer Jeff Fahey of being hypocritical. *White Hunter, Black Heart* (1990, Warner Bros.).

11357 "Oh, just a little story about a man who wakes up and finds that he's become a giant insect." Title character **Jeremy Irons** replies when asked, "So what are you working on now, Kafka?" *Kafka* (1991, GB, Miramax).

11358 "I wouldn't mind writers so much if they didn't write books." Enchanting **Joan Plowright** has all the best lines. *Enchanted April* (1992, GB, Miramax).

Wrongs and Wrongdoings

see also CONSCIENCES, CORRUPTION, CRIMES AND CRIMINALS, EVILNESS, JUSTICE, MISTAKES, RIGHTS, SINS AND SINNERS, VICES

11359 "When women go wrong, men go right after them." **Mae West** speaks from experience, no doubt. *She Done Him Wrong* (1933, Paramount).

11360 "I'm on the wrong side of the road, outside looking in." Happy-go-lucky aviator **George Brent** is devastated when his parents and sister are killed in a crash of the plane he's piloting. *Living on Velvet* (1935, Warner Bros.).

11361 "We know in our hearts that love like ours is wrong." **Ingrid Bergman** feels great guilt because of her love affair with renowned married violinist Leslie Howard. *Intermezzo* (1939, Selznick-United Artists).

11362 "I can't undo the wrongs you have suffered. But I beg of you, let the dead past remain buried." Twenty-five years after his father's death, **Basil Rathbone**, as Wolf von Frankenstein, returns to his ancestral castle. He addresses an unhappy crowd of villagers, who rudely walk away while he's talking. *Son of Frankenstein* (1939, Universal).

11363 "I was never hooked on any guy that wasn't wrong." **Ida Lupino** wails about the men she falls in love with. *High Sierra* (1940, Warner Bros.).

11364 "I hope I'm not saying the wrong thing, but I love you." Protected wealthy spinster **Joan Fontaine** confesses her love to rogue Cary Grant. *Suspicion* (1941, RKO).

11365 "Because [our relationship] is wrong, it cannot bring happiness." **Vivien Leigh** tells her lover Laurence Olivier that they should part and never see each other again. *That Hamilton Woman* aka: *Lady Hamilton* (1941, London Films).

11366 JILL BAKER: "I'm sure there's absolutely nothing wrong with me." DR. VENGARD: "I'm sure you'll feel differently after you leave this office." **Merle Oberon** reluctantly visits psychoanalyst **Alan Mowbray** who caters to Park Avenue wives. *That Uncertain Feeling* (1941, United Artists).

11367 "What's wrong with Medicine Hat except that it's hot in summer and cold in winter and nothing ever happens there?" **Mary Astor** answers her rhetorical question as to why she left her home in Medicine Hat, Wyoming. *Across the Pacific* (1942, Warner Bros.).

11368 "You attack the wrong things in the wrong way. You attack the evil in men. We accept it. . . . Wherever you create misery and discontent there you will find us at work. . . ." High ranking Nazi **Luther Adler** brags to Canadian soldier Dick Powell about how evil the Nazis are. We believe there are no willing villains. Even the Nazis believed they were doing the right things. *Cornered* (1945, RKO).

11369 PHILIP MARLOWE: "What's wrong with you?" VIVIAN STERNWOOD: "Nothing you can't fix." **Humphrey Bogart** has his work set out for himself in the case of **Lauren Bacall**. *The Big Sleep* (1946, Warner Bros.).

11370 "He's suffered terribly. I've done him many and many wrongs. Wrong to love him. Wrong to marry him. No children. A burden when he was trying to save his soul in this new country. Why should he not hate me?" Dipsomaniac **Ingrid Bergman** feels she deserves her husband Joseph Cotten's cruelty. *Under Capricorn* (1949, GB, Warner Bros.).

11371 "I defended you, Steve, because I found the wrong man on trial—so I torpedoed Queeg for you." Tipsy military lawyer **Jose Ferrer** ashamedly tells Van Johnson that he destroyed Humphrey Bogart on the witness stand, because it was Fred MacMurray, not Johnson, who was the guilty party in a supposed mutiny. *The Caine Mutiny* (1954, Columbia).

11372 "Darwin was wrong. Man's still an ape." H.L. Menken-like cynic **Gene Kelly** has little respect for anyone other than himself—and maybe not even himself. *Inherit the Wind* (1960, United Artists).

11373 MARIANNE MOLLENDORF: "If I don't help, I lose my self-respect. Haven't you opposed something because it's wrong—morally wrong?" ERIC ERICKSON: "I suffer for them—but not with them." **Lilli Palmer**, the unhappy devout Catholic wife of a Nazi officer, and Swedish-American businessman **William Holden** have different reactions to the suffering of the victims of Nazi concentration camps. *The Counterfeit Traitor* (1962, Paramount).

11374 "This used to be a fine country. What went wrong?" Alcoholic lawyer **Jack Nicholson** moans his disillusionment. *Easy Rider* (1969, Columbia).

11375 "I don't know whether the men stars can help me as much as the women stars. From what I've seen lately I've been letting the wrong sex try and make me." Actress hopeful **Jane Fonda** contemplates a change of strategy. *They Shoot Horses, Don't They?* (1969, ABC-Cinerama).

11376 "So often we have to realize that our judgments and our interpretations and even our hopes have been wrong—wrong, that's all." Disillusioned **Marlon Brando** waxes philosophically. *Burn!* aka: *Queimada!* (1970, United Artists).

11377 "You're unhappy unless you do something. Because of me you've been trying to lay out, but that's wrong, wrong for you. . . . Commitment is part of you. Part of what makes you attractive, part of what attracted me to you." **Robert Redford** realizes that it was wrong of Barbra Streisand to trade in her Jewish activism for his WASP blandness in hopes of making their marriage work. *The Way We Were* (1973, Columbia).

11378 "I was a child! I was in love! It was wrong!" **Karen Allen** spits out her words at ex-lover Harrison Ford. *Raiders of the Lost Ark* (1981, Paramount).

11379 "The only thing we have in common is that we're both wrong for each other." Marine biologist and former baseball player **Nick Nolte** won't let that stop him from developing a relationship with drifter and part-time bordello employee Debra Winger. *Cannery Row* (1982, MGM-United Artists).

11380 "You have this exalted view of me and I hate it. if you think I'm that great then there must be something wrong with you." **Mary Beth Hurt** can't understand why John Heard likes her so much—she doesn't. *Chilly Scenes of Winter* (1982, United Artists Classics).

11381 "No matter. . . who you are. . . the pope or the president. . . something can always go wrong. What I know about is Texas, and down here you're on your own." Corrupt private detective **M. Emmet Walsh** narrates the opening of the movie. *Blood Simple* (1983, River Road).

11382 "For forty years I've been telling you when something will or will not happen. Have I ever been wrong?" Know-it-all **Paul Newman** snaps at his wife Joanne Woodward who dares have an independent thought. *Mr. & Mrs. Bridge* (1990, Mirimax-Cineplex Odeon).

Years

see also AGE AND AGING, TIME

11383 "Thirty years! You'll never love me thirty years. No one will." **Greta Garbo** exclaims when lover Robert Taylor shows her a photograph of his parents who have been married thirty years. *Camille* (1937, MGM).

11384 ANDY HARDY: "The next ten years of my life are the best." JUDGE HARDY: "The next ten years of anybody's life are the best." **Mickey Rooney** can never get the last word in any discussion with his wise father **Lewis Stone**. *Life Begins for Andy Hardy* (1941, MGM).

11385 "Well, things don't work out right, we'll do it all over again next year." Having taken a "furlough" from their Devil's Island prison, **Humphrey Bogart**, Peter Ustinov and Aldo Ray decide to go back—for now. *We're No Angels* (1955, Paramount).

11386 "Was I a good year?" Roman slave **Zero Mostel** considers a bottle of wine. *A Funny Thing Happened on the Way to the Forum* (1966, United Artists).

11387 "I didn't get my period, so I had a terrible year from 12 to 13. I thought there was something really wrong with me. I'd sort of. . . check and see." **Jill Clayburgh** discusses menstruation with her therapist Penelope Russianoff. *An Unmarried Woman* (1978, 20th Century—Fox).

11388 GLORIA: "My mother died when I was six. My father raped me when I was twelve." ARTHUR: "So you had six relatively good years." Hooker **Anne De Salvo** answers "sensitive" **Dudley Moore**'s question, "Why are you a hooker?" *Arthur* (1981, Orion).

11389 "Nineteen-fifty-four was a pretty good year all around. It was the year we finally got rid of Joe McCarthy." Narrator **Mark Linn-Baker** recalls one of the highlights of 1954—his favorite year. *My Favorite Year* (1983, MGM—United Artists).

11390 "[It's the] same as a regular year only it has less calories." Dumb fireman **Michael J. Pollard** answers the question of an even dumber fireman, "What's a light year?" *Roxanne* (1987, Columbia).

11391 "The 60s were ten years of phoniness, a decade long circle jerk. I didn't move to Marin County. I didn't drop out. I dropped in. I moved to Italy." American journalist **Andrew McCarthy** becomes involved with the terrorist activities of the Communist Red Brigade in the 70s. *Year of the Gun* (1991, Triumph).

Youth

see also AGE AND AGING, BABIES, BOYS, CHILDREN AND CHILDHOOD, GIRLS, MATURITY AND IMMATURITY

11392 "We older men supply the champagne—but when youth sings, the old fool stays home and pays the piper." Indiscreet Russian General **Lionel Bar-**

rymore reacts sadly when his mistress, German spy Greta Garbo, falls in love with lowly Lieutenant Ramon Novarro. *Mata Hari* (1931, MGM).

11393 "If that's the result of physical exercise, thank God I had a misspent youth." Passerby **C. Denier Warren** gets a look at weak barber George Formby, who has been mistaken for a famous athlete. *Keep Fit* (1937, GB, Associated Talking Pictures).

11394 "It's only natural to want to look young and be young when you are young." **Barbara O'Neil** comforts her daughter Vivien Leigh, who objects to wearing black mourning garments after the death of her first husband. *Gone with the Wind* (1939, Selznick-MGM).

11395 "This is the Land of Legend, where everything is possible when seen through the eyes of youth." Aged King **Morton Selten** welcomes young thief Sabu. *The Thief of Bagdad* (1940, GB, London Films).

11396 "Live! Let nothing be lost to you! As we grow older, our memories are haunted by the exquisite temptations we hadn't the courage to yield to. The world is yours for a season. It would be tragic if you realized too late, as many others do, that there is only one thing in this world worth having and that is youth. What the gods give, they quickly take away. Time is jealous of you, Mr. Gray. Don't squander the gold of your days. Live. Let nothing be lost upon you. Be afraid of nothing. There's such a little time that your youth will last. You can never get it back." **George Sanders** urges Hurd Hatfield not to waste his youth—but live it totally hedonistically. *The Picture of Dorian Gray* (1945, MGM).

11397 "You're in your green years, Robbie. You suffer the critical disease of being young. The Lord deliver me from ever having to go through that again!" **Charles Coburn** puts his finger on his great-grandson Tom Drake's problem. *The Green Years* (1946, MGM).

11398 "Her psyche will be scarred for the rest of her life. . . . It's just adolescence, dear, she'll live through it." **Maureen O'Hara** changes her tune when she sees her husband Fred MacMurray look as if he believes that in unintentionally mortifying his teenage daughter Betty Lynn, he's ruined her life. *Father Was a Fullback* (1949, 20th Century—Fox).

11399 "Do you know what I think when I see a pretty girl?. . . 'Oh, to be 80 again.'" **Louis Calhern**, as Supreme Court Justice Oliver Wendell Holmes, can take comfort that in aging there are so many more younger women. *The Magnificent Yankee* (1950, MGM).

11400 "Georgia, love is for the very young." Hollywood producer **Kirk Douglas** informs actress Lana Turner that he's too old to have time or need for love. *The Bad and the Beautiful* (1952, MGM).

11401 "Little Sheba should have stayed young forever. Some things should never grow old." Slovenly **Shirley Booth** thinks out loud about her missing little dog to her ex-alcoholic husband Burt Lancaster. *Come Back, Little Sheba* (1952, Paramount).

11402 "Youth is a series of low comedy disasters." Scientist **Cary Grant** will demonstrate his premise when he and wife Ginger Rogers accidentally drink an elixir of youth concocted by a laboratory chimpanzee. *Monkey Business* (1952, 20th Century-Fox).

11403 "I'm not going to die young at the top of the tower." Executive **William Holden** rejects the offer to become his company's new president because he realizes the price is just too high to pay. *Executive Suite* (1954, MGM).

11404 "Kids are people, and most people are worthwhile." **Anne Francis** offers words of encouragement to her English teacher husband Glenn Ford. He has to dig pretty deep to find worth in some of his pupils. *The Blackboard Jungle* (1955, MGM).

11405 "It's a heartbreaking time. They're no longer a boy and not yet a man, wondering what's going to be expected of them as men and how they'll measure up." Wife of a prep school coach, **Deborah Kerr** tries to make Edward Andrews understand the pain and pressure 17-year-olds like his son John Kerr experience. *Tea and Sympathy* (1956, MGM).

11406 "Youth! Stay close to the young, and a little rubs off." **Maurice Chevalier** gives excellent advice. *Gigi* (1958, MGM).

11407 BANKER: "I must say, Mr. Judd, I expected a much younger man." STEVE JUDD: "Well, I used to be. We all used to be." Banker **Byron Foulger** is taken aback by **Joel McCrea**'s age when the ex-lawman saunters into a bank and announces that he's the man who has been hired to escort a shipment of gold. *Ride the High Country* (1962, MGM).

11408 "Adolescence is a time when people worry about things there's no need to worry about." Kindly Jewish businessman **Heinz Ruehmann** consoles teenager Gila Golan, who despairs because she believes she's ugly. *Ship of Fools* (1965, Columbia).

11409 "I was never to see her again. Nor was I ever to learn what became of her. We were different then. Kids were different. It took us longer to understand the things we felt. Life is made up of small comings and goings, and for everything we take with us, there is something that we leave behind. In the summer of '42 we raided the Coast Guard station four times, we saw five movies and had nine days of rain. Benjie broke his watch. Oscy gave up the harmonica. And in a very special way, I lost Hermie—forever." Narrator and director **Robert Mulligan**, as the older Hermie, fondly recalls his love for an older woman, twentysomething Jennifer O'Neill, when he was adolescent Gary Grimes. *Summer of '42* (1971, Warner Bros.).

11410 "It's really different here. Back home, being young was just something you'd do until you grew up. Here. . . it's everything." Former Chicagoan **Patti D'Arbanville** is initiated into the beach life of Los Angeles. *Big Wednesday* (1978, Warner Bros.).

11411 "When I was young, I was tired and miserable." Envious **Paul Dooley** complains to his wife Barbara Barrie about their son Dennis Christopher's carefree life. *Breaking Away* (1979, 20th Century—Fox).

11412 "You guys were so all fired hopped-up to get out of the city, you turned your kids into what you were running away from." An uncredited Texas visitor blames the parents in a planned suburban community for their teenagers turning out so badly. The frustrated and alienated kids turn to booze and violence. *Over the Edge* (1979, Warner Bros.).

11413 "You look like kids, but you don't act like it. You're short 40-year-olds, and you're tough." Divorced **Sally Kellerman** fumes at her daughter Jodie Foster and her teenage friends. *Foxes* (1980, United Artists).

11414 "Young. I feel young." **William Shatner**, as Admiral Kirk, has the film's last line. *Star Trek II: The Wrath of Khan* (1982, Paramount).

11415 "They can kill but are too young to go to prison for life." **Marilia Pera** explains why she's a Fagin to a gang of 14-year-old drug dealers and killers. *Mixed Blood* (1985, Sara Films-Cinevista).

11416 "High school! I started out so hot. Sophomore year, two times. Junior year was excellent, four times. . . and not all with the same girl. . . . Senior year looked like the best. . . from the first day of classes. . . nothing." **John Cusack** tells of his sexual drought to his friend Anthony Edwards. *The Sure Thing* (1985, Embassy).

11417 "Take 'em from their momma when they're real young." It's **Dennis Quaid**'s, as rocker Jerry Lee Lewis, recipe for a happy marriage. He marries 13-year-old Winona Ryder. *Great Balls of Fire* (1989, Orion).

11418 "My teenage angst has a body count." **Winona Ryder** notes the growing number of teens she has helped Christian Slater kill. *Heathers* (1989, New World).

11419 "Now let me tell you something, the trouble with being a teenager is you don't know anything. . . . The trouble with teenagers is that you think you're smarter than people who've already been down the road you're traveling. . . ." High school principal **Morgan Freeman** lectures freshman druggie and truant Jermaine Hopkins. *Lean on Me* (1989, Warner Bros.).

11420 "Teenagers by definition are not fit for society." **Nick Nolte** tells Barbra Streisand she needn't apologize for her incredibly rude son Jason Gould. *The Prince of Tides* (1991, Columbia).

Index of Performers

Index of Movie Titles

Key to Abbreviations: *D-Director; W-Screenwriters, story writers, dialogue writers; T-Title card writers.*

1987, 2370, 3545, 5493, 7708, 10132

After the Thin Man (D: W.S. Van Dyke, W: Frances Goodrich, Albert Hackett based on story Dashiell Hammett) 189, 1609, 6992, 8692, 8696, 10498, 11202

After Tonight (D: George Archainbaud, W: Jane Murfin) 9600

Aftershock (D: Frank Harris, W: Michael Standing) 10966

Against All Odds (D: Taylor Hackford, W: Eric Hughes based on screenplay Daniel Mainwaring and novel William Morrow) 343

Age Isn't Everything (D, W: Douglas Katz) 2738

Agnes of God (D: Norman Jewison, W: John Pielmeier based on his play) 7, 595, 820, 2351, 2477, 3638, 4151, 5086, 6700, 8806, 9819

The Agony and the Ecstasy (D: Carol Reed, W: Philip Dunne based on novel Irving Stone) 2105, 2907, 7727, 11241

Ah, Wilderness (D: Clarence Brown, W: Albert Hackett, Frances Goodrich based on play Eugene O'Neill) 5668, 10243

Air America (D: Roger Spottiswoode, W: John Eskow, Richard Rush based on book Christopher Robbins) 3728, 10855

Air Force (D: Howard Hawks, W: Dudley Nichols) 2921

Airplane! (D, W: Jim Abrahams, David & Jerry Zucker) 2669, 6914, 7297

Airplane II: The Sequel (D, W: Ken Finkleman) 7875

Airport 75 (D: Jack Smight, W: Don Ingalls) 2581, 11347

Al Capone (D: Richard Wilson, W: Marvin Wald, Henry Greenberg) 3037

The Alamo (D: John Wayne, W: James Edward Grant) 5847, 8727, 11213

Alamo Bay (D: Louis Malle, W: Alice Arlen) 5660, 9203, 10765

Alexa (D: Sean Delgado, W: Peggy Bruen, Delgado) 8268

Alfie (D: Lewis Gilbert, W: Bill Naughton based on his play) 7651, 10529, 11157

Algiers (D: John Cromwell, W: John Howard Lawson) 2972, 5056

Alias Jimmy Valentine (D: Jack Conway, W: Sarah Y. Mason, A.P. Younger, Joe Farnham) 2108

Alias Nick Beal (D: John Farrow, W: Jonathan Latimer, Mindret Lord) 1613, 1809, 2467, 10907

Alice (D, W: Woody Allen) 2569, 3182, 3214, 6301, 7623, 9173

Alice Adams (D: George Stevens, W: Dorothy Yost, Mortimer Offner based on novel Booth Tarkington) 2052, 3558, 3709, 4706, 4721, 4960, 7594, 8911, 9857, 9929, 10974

Alice Doesn't Live Here Anymore (D: Martin Scorsese, W: Robert Getchell) 1449, 6368

Alice in Wonderland (D: Norman McLeod, W: Joseph L. Mankiewicz, William Cameron Menzies based on novels Lewis Carroll) 1182

Alien Nation (D: Graham Baker, W: Rockne S. O'Bannon) 7492

Aliens (D: James Cameron, W: Cameron, Walter Hill, David Gilder based on characters created Dan O'Bannon, Ronald Shusett) 4529, 6835

All About Eve (D, W: Joseph L. Mankiewicz based on story Mary Orr) 47, 48, 49, 136, 167, 462, 577, 720, 1059, 1189, 1272, 1273, 2858, 3894, 4191, 4488, 4543, 4579, 4984, 5579, 6108, 6354, 7230, 7608, 8020, 8102, 8506, 8632, 8743, 9341, 9739, 10053, 10795

The All-American Boy (D, W: Charles Eastman) 7696

All Fall Down (D: John Frankenheimer, W: William Inge based on novel James Leo Herlihy) 6875

All I Desire (D: Douglas Sirk, W: James Gunn, Robert Blees, Gina Kaus based on novel Carol Brink) 9799

All My Sons (D: Irving Reis, W: Chester Erskine based on play Arthur Miller) 3168, 5575

All Night Long (D: Jean-Claude Tramont, W: W.D. Richter) 3079, 3764, 6469, 7209, 7779

All of Me (D: Carl Reiner, W: Phil Alden Robinson, Henry Olek based on novel Ed Davis) 1640, 2107, 2241, 3323, 10722

All Quiet on the Western Front (D: Lewis Milestone, W: Del Andrews, Maxwell Anderson, George Abbott based on novel Erich Maria Remarque) 1721, 2163, 2164, 2485, 3729, 3831, 4563, 10820

All That Heaven Allows (D: Douglas Sirk, W: Peggy Fenwick based on story Edna & Harry Lee) 139, 6223

All That Jazz (D: Bob Fosse, W: Robert Alan Arthur, Fosse) 5823, 6000, 9250, 9535, 10705

All That Money Can Buy aka The Devil and Daniel Webster (D: William Dieterle, W: Dan Totheroh based on story Stephen Vincent Binet) 467, 1133, 3266, 3798, 3804, 5240, 8184, 9547, 9548, 9581, 10067

All the Fine Young Cannibals (D: Michael Anderson, W: Robert Thom based on story Rosamond Marshall) 5285, 11329

All the King's Men (D, W: Robert Rossen based on novel Robert Penn Warren) 772, 4646, 5920, 6782, 8859, 9324, 9586, 10680, 11193

... All the Marbles (D: Robert Aldrich, W: Mel Frohman) 2827, 10314

All the President's Men (D: Alan J. Pakula, W: William Goldman based on book Carl Bernstein, Bob Woodward) 4266, 6806, 9429

All the Right Moves (D: Michael Chapman, W: Michael Kane) 9661

All This and Heaven Too (D: Anatole Litvak, W: Casey Robinson based on novel Rachel Lyman Field) 3888, 6175

All Through the Night (D: Vincent Sherman, W: Leonard Spigelgass, Edwin Gilbert, Leonard Ross) 2337, 7106

Allan Quatermain and the Lost City of Gold (D: Gary Nelson & Newt Arnold, W: Gene Quintano, Lee Reynolds based on novel H. Rider Haggard) 86, 230, 5777

Alligator II: The Mutation (D: Jon Hess, W: Curt Allen) 10113

Almost You (D: Adam Brooks, W: Mark Horowitz based on story Brooks) 8598, 9412

Alone in the Dark (D, W: Jack Sholder) 2631, 5159, 7971, 9573, 10571

Along Came Jones (D: Stuart Heisler, W: Nunnally Johnson based on story Alan LeMay) 3566

Altered States (D: Ken Russell, W: Sidney Aaron (Paddy Chayefsky) based on his novel) 3149, 6003, 9817, 10461

Always (D: Steven Spielberg, W: Jerry Belson, Diane Thomas based on screenplay Dalton Trumbo and story Chandler Sprague, David Boehm) 824, 1598, 8640

Amadeus (D: Milos Forman, W: Peter Shaffer based on his play) 2421, 5901, 6482, 6981, 6982, 9890, 10670

The Amazing Dr. Clitterhouse (D: Anatole Litvak, W: John Wesley, John Huston based on play Barre Lyndon) 10597

Amazon Women on the Moon (D: Joe Dante, Carl Gottlieb, Peter Horton, John Landis, Robert K. Weiss, W: Michael Barrie, Jim Mulholland) 10076

Ambush (D: Sam Wood, W: Marguerite Roberts based on story Luke Short) 2464

Ambush Bay (D: Ron Winston, W: Marve Feinburg, Ib Melchoir) 9870

American Gigolo (D, W: Paul Schrader) 1725, 9080, 10023

American Gothic (D: John Hough, W: Bert Wetanson, Michael Vines) 4153

American Graffiti (D: George Lucas, W: Lucas, Gloria Katz, Willard Huyck) 563, 1265, 2990

An American in Paris (D: Vicente Minnelli, W: Alan Jay Lerner) 1044, 1466, 1467, 1560, 3237, 6966

American Madness (D: Frank Capra, W: Robert Riskin) 670, 6765

American Ninja 2: The Confrontation (D: Sam Firstenberg, W: Gary Conway, James Booth based on characters created Avi Kleinberger, Gideon Amir) 2331

American Rickshaw (d: Sergio Martino, w: Sauro Scavolini) 4433

The American Success Company aka: Success (D: William Richert, W: Richert, Larry Cohen) 4889, 7079, 9289

An American Werewolf in London (D, W: John Landis) 441, 1958, 3942, 6093

The Americanization of Emily (D: Arthur Hiller, W: Paddy Chayefsky) 1895, 1896, 6238, 10843

Amityville II: The Possession (D: Damiano Damiani, W: Tommy Lee Wallace based on book Hans Holzer) 552

Among the Living (D: Stuart Heisler, W: Lester Cole, Garrett Fort, Brian Marlowe) 1547, 5527

Anastasia (D: Anatole Litvak, W: Arthur Laurants based on play Marcelle Maurette adapted Guy Bolton) 3625, 4910, 7158, 7507, 9223, 9814, 10434

Anatomy of a Murder (D: Otto Preminger, W: Wendell Mayes based on novel John Traver (John D. Voelker)) 278, 750, 1971, 2314, 2315, 5013, 7001, 8450, 8479, 9224

Anchors Aweigh (D: George Sidney, W: Iso-

The Bed Sitting Room (*D:* Richard Lester, *D:* John Antrobus, Charles Wood based on play Antrobus, Spike Milligan) 531

Bedazzled (*D:* Stanley Donen, *W:* Peter Cook, Dudley Moore) 5123, 8481, 9195

The Bedroom Window (*D, W:* Curtis Hanson based on novel Anne Holden) 633, 4574, 5283, 6019, 10265, 10963

Bedtime for Bonzo (*D:* Frederick DeCordova, *W:* Val Burton, Lou Breslow based on story Raphael David Blau) 10919

The Beguiled (*D:* Don Siegel, *W:* John B. Sherry, Grimes Grice based on Thomas Cullinan's novel) 3357, 10879

Behind the Door (*D:* Irvin Willat, *W:* Luther A. Reed based on story Gouverneur Morris) 9352

Being There (*D:* Hal Ashby, *W:* Jerzy Kosinski based on his novel) 75, 9010, 10880

La Belle Noiseuse (*D:* Jacques Rivette, *W:* Rivette, Pascal Bonitzer, Christine Laurent adapted from a novel by Honore de Balzac) 1021

Belle of the Nineties (*D:* Leo Mccarey, *W:* Mae West) 395, 846, 884, 1208, 4179, 4505, 5023, 6548, 6719, 6758, 7541, 7850, 8223, 11296

Belles on Their Toes (*D:* Henry Levin, *W:* Phoebe & Henry Ephron based on book Frank B. Gilbreth, Jr., Ernestine Gilbreth Carey) 10087

Bells Are Ringing (*D:* Vincente Minnelli, *W:* Betty Comden, Adolph Green, Jule Styne) 8116, 11343

The Bells of St. Mary's (*D:* Leo McCarey, *W:* Dudley Nichols, McCarey) 6558

Ben-Hur (*D:* William Wyler, *W:* Karl Tunberg based on Lew Wallace's novel) 3424, 4416, 4547, 11112

Berkeley Square (*D:* Frank Lloyd, *W:* Sonya Levien, John L. Balderston based on Balderston's play) 10175

Best Friends (*D:* Norman Jewison, *W:* Valerie Curtin, Barry Levinson) 10206

The Best Intentions (*D:* Billie August, *W:* Ingmar Bergman) 4515

The Best Little Whorehouse in Texas (*D:* Colin Higgins, *W:* Larry L. King, Peter Masterson, Higgins based on Higgins' play) 341, 1760, 3845

The Best Man (*D:* Franklin Schaffner, *W:* Gore Vidal based on his play) 325, 1219, 7843, 7947, 9768

The Best of Everything (*D:* Jean Negulesco, *W:* Edith Sommer, Mann Rubin based on Rona Jaffe's novel) 779, 5169, 5752, 6231, 6232, 9194, 9766, 10237, 10701

The Best of Times (*D:* Roger Spottiswoode, *W:* Ron Shelton) 4128, 7404

The Best Years of Our Lives (*D:* William Wyler, *W:* Robert E. Sherwood based on novella MacKinlay Kantor) 614, 1401, 2472, 3515, 8901

Betrayal (*D:* David Jones, *W:* Harold Pinter based on his play) 5900, 6273

Betrayed (*D:* Gottfried Reinhardt, *W:* Ronald Miller, George Froeschel) 691, 835, 9604

Betrayed (*D:* Constantin Costa-Gavras, *W:* Joe Eszterhas) 6133

Betsy's Wedding (*D, W:* Alan Alda) 2521

Better Off Dead (*D, W:* Savage Steve Holland) 7855

Betty Blue (*D, W:* Jean-Jacques Beineix based on book Philippe Dijan) 445, 754, 1589, 2400

Between the Lines (*D:* Joan Micklin Silver, *W:* Fred Barron, David M. Halpern, Jr) 4362

Between Two Worlds (*D:* Edward A. Blatt, *W:* Daniel Fuchs based on Sutton Vane's play) 5952

Beverly Hills Cop (*D:* Martin Brest, *W:* Daniel Petrie, Jr., Danilo Bach) 1516, 6012

Beyond the Forest (*D:* King Vidor, *W:* Lenore Coffee based on novel Stuart Engstrand) 1058, 1909, 2978, 3035, 4726

Beyond the Valley of the Dolls (*D:* Russ Meyer, *W:* Rogert Ebert) 7355

Beyond Therapy (*D:* Robert Altman, *W:* Christopher Durang, Altman based on Durang's play) 9975

Bhowani Junction (*D:* George Cukor, *W:* Sonya Levien, Ivan Moffat based on John Master's novel) 1861, 8690

Big (*D:* Penny Marshall, *W:* Gary Ross, Anne Spielberg) 9349

The Big Bird Cage (*D, W:* Jack Hill) 8761, 9136

The Big Bounce (*D:* Alex March, *W:* Robert Dozier based on novel Elmore Leonard) 5986

The Big Broadcast of 1938 (*D:* Mitchell Leisen, *W:* Walter DeLeon, Francis Martin, Ken Englund adapted by Howard Lindsay, Russel Crouse of a story of Frederick Hazlitt Brennan) 5523

Big Business (*D:* Jim Abrahams, *W:* Dori Pierson, Marc Rubel) 4307

The Big Carnival *see* Ace in the Hole

The Big Chill (*D:* Lawrence Kasdan, *W:* Kasdan, Barbara Benedek) 3135, 3431, 4222, 4366, 6126, 7486, 8067, 9153, 9972, 11316

Big City Blues (*D:* Mervyn LeRoy, *W:* Ward Morehouse, Lillie Howard based on Morehouse's play) 5624

The Big Combo (*D:* Joseph H. Lewis, *W:* Philip Yordan) 6929

The Big Dis (*D, W:* Gordon Erickson, John O'Brien) 9788

The Big Doll House (*D:* Jack Hill, *W:* Don Spencer) 3649, 6334

The Big Heat (*D:* Fritz Lang, *W:* Sydney Boehm based on magazine serial William P. McGivern) 424, 3700, 3966, 7279, 8719

The Big House (*D:* George Hill, *W:* Frances Marion, Joe Farnham, Martin Flavin) 10782

Big Jake (*D:* George Sherman, *W:* Harry Julian Fink, R.M. Fink) 7651, 9018

The Big Knife (*D:* Robert Aldrich, *W:* James Poe based on Clifford Odets' play) 2955, 8213, 8960, 10100

The Big Lift (*D, W:* George Seaton) 10949

The Big Noise (*D:* Malcolm St. Clair, *W:* Scott Darling) 2833

The Big Parade (*D:* King Vidor, *W:* Harry Behn, *W:* Joseph W. Farnham) 1343

The Big Picture (*D:* Christopher Guest, *W:* Guest, Michael Varhol) 8202, 8542, 9939

The Big Red One (*D, W:* Samuel Fuller) 666, 2509 5453, 6265, 9468, 9886, 10663

The Big Sleep (*D:* Howard Hawks, *W:* William Faulkner, Jules Furthman, Leigh Brackett based on Raymond Chandler's novel) 198, 311, 1138, 2136, 2155, 2558, 2646, 2647, 5328, 5915, 10943, 11369

The Big Sleep (*D, W:* Michael Winner based on Raymond Chandler's novel) 3075, 7456, 9260

The Big Slice (*D, W:* John Bradshaw) 9998

The Big Stampede (*D:* Tenny Wright, *W:* Kurt Kempler based on story Marion Jackson) 8286

The Big Store (*D:* Charles Reisner, *W:* Sid Kuller, Hal Fimberg, Ray Golden based on Nat Perrin's story) 5670, 8370

The Big Street (*D:* Irving Reis, *W:* Leonard Spigelgass based on Damon Runyan story) 6776

The Big Sweat (*D:* Ulli Lommell, *W:* Max Bolt) 4434

Big Trouble (*D:* John Cassavetes, *W:* Warren Bogle, Andrew Bergman) 8931

Big Trouble in Little China (*D:* John Carpenter, *W:* W.D. Richter, Gary Goldman, David Z. Weinstein) 10989

Big Wednesday (*D:* John Milius, *W:* Milius, Dennis Aaberg) 11410

Bigger Than Life (*D:* Nicholas Ray, *W:* Cyril Hume, Richard Maibaum based on article Berton Roueche) 6646

The Biggest Bundle of Them All (*D:* Ken Annakin, *W:* Josef Shaftel, Sy Salkowitz, Riccardo Aragno) 843

Bikini Beach (*D:* William Asher, *W:* Asher, Leo Townsend, Robert Dillon) 11000

Bill and Ted's Bogus Journey (*D:* Pete Hewitt, *W:* Chris Matheson) 5835

Bill and Ted's Excellent Adventure (*D:* Stephen Herek, *W:* Chris Matheson, Ed Solomon) 3284, 4385, 6539, 8516

A Bill of Divorcement (*D:* George Cukor, *W:* Howard Estabrook, Harry Wagstaff Gribble based on Clemence Dane's play) 3442

Billy Budd (*D:* Peter Ustinov, *W:* Ustinov, Robert Rossen based on Herman Melville's novel) 2216, 2283

Billy Galvin (*D, W:* John Gray) 4472, 8045

Billy Jack (*D:* T.C. Frank (Tom Laughlin), *W:* Frank, Teresa Christina (Delores Taylor)) 280, 1794, 7705, 7730

Billy Jack Goes to Washington (*D:* T.C. Frank (Tom Laughlin), *W:* Frank, Teresa Christina (Delores Taylor)) 5775, 6639

Biloxi Blues (*D:* Mike Nichols, *W:* Neil Simon based on his play) 3678, 4375, 4503

Bird (*D:* Clint Eastwood, *W:* Joel Oliansky) 9094

Bird on a Wire (*D:* John Badham, *W:* David Seltzer, Louis Venosta, Eric Lerner) 1606, 3022, 6042, 7146

The Birds (*D:* Alfred Hitchcock, *W:* Evan Hunter based on story Daphne du Maurier) 3530, 9465, 9730

Birdy (*D:* Alan Parker, *W:* Sandy Kroopf, Jack Behr based on novel William Wharton) 1002, 10441, 11199

Birth of the Blues (*D:* Victor Schertzinger, *W:* Harry Tugend, Walter DeLeon based

play) 2694, 5886, 7255, 8700, 8930

Death on the Nile (*D:* John Guillermin, *W:* Anthony Shaffer based on novel Agatha Christie) 239

Death Takes a Holiday (*D:* Mitchell Leisen, *W:* Maxwell Anderson, Gladys Lehman, Walter Ferris based on play Alberto Casella) 6151, 9721, 10286

Death Wish II (*D:* Michael Winner, *W:* David Engelbach based on characters created by Brian Garfield) 5295

Death Wish 3 (*D:* Michael Winner, *W:* Michael Edmonds based on characters created by Brian Garfield) 3777, 5465

Death Wish 4: The Crackdown (*D:* J. Lee Thompson, *W:* Gail Morgan Hickman based on characters created by Brian Garfield) 2790

Deathtrap (*D:* Sidney Lumet, *W:* Jay Presson Allen based on play Ira Levin) 2675, 9803

Deception (*D:* Irving Rapper, *W:* John Collier, Joseph Than based on play Louis Verneuil) 4853, 5808, 6068

Defending Your Life (*D, W:* Albert Brooks) 4277, 4534

Deep in My Heart (*D:* Stanley Donen, *W:* Leonard Spigelgass based on book Elliott Arnold) 6969

The Deer Hunter (*D:* Michael Cimino, *W:* Deric Washburn based on story Cimino, Washburn, Louis Garfinkle, Quinn K. Redeker) 4801, 9228

The Defiant Ones (*D:* Stanley Kramer, *W:* Nathan E. Douglas, Harold Jacob Smith) 10522

A Delicate Balance (*D:* Tony Richardson, *W:* Edward Albee based on his play) 6581, 10203

The Delicate Delinquent (*D, W:* Don McGuire) 8114

Deliverance (*D:* John Boorman, *W:* James Dickey based on his novel) 5696, 6121, 8825, 10702

Demented (*W:* Arthur Jeffreys, *W:* Alex Rebar) 6530

Demon Seed (*D:* Donald Cammell, *W:* Robert Jaffe, Roger O. Hirson based on novel Dean R. Koontz) 2712

Desert Bloom (*D, W:* Eugene Corr based on story Linda Remy, Corr) 229, 1035, 1578, 1762, 8122

Desert Fury (*D:* Lewis Allen, *W:* Robert Rossen based on novel Ramona Stewart) 1255, 11076

Desert Hearts (*D:* Donna Deitch, *W:* Natalie Cooper based on novel Jane Rule) 3391, 3465

The Desert Rats (*D:* Robert Wise, *W:* Richard Murphy) 664

Design for Living (*D:* Ernst Lubitsch, *W:* Ben Hecht based on play Noel Coward) 1509, 2376, 3809, 4977, 6600, 8383, 9619, 9942

Designing Woman (*D:* Vicente Minnelli, *W:* George Wells based on suggestion Helen Rose) 470, 908, 3751

Desire (*D:* Frank Borzage, *W:* Edwin Justus Mayer, Waldemar Young, Samuel Hoffenstein based on story Hans Szekeley, R.A. Stemmle) 5564, 10688

Desk Set (*D:* Walter Lang, *W:* Phoebe &

Henry Ephron based on play William Marchant) 371, 572, 9459

Despair (*D:* Rainer Werner Fassbinder, *W:* Tom Stoppard based on novel Vladimir Nabokov) 1574, 5205, 6457

The Desperate Hours (*D:* William Wyler, *W:* Joseph Hayes based on his novel and play) 1085, 9095, 10154

Desperate Journey (*D:* Raoul Walsh, *W:* Arthur T. Horman based on story Horman) 3975

Desperate Living (*D, W:* John Waters) 11084

Destination Tokyo (*D:* Delmer Daves, *W:* Albert Maltz, Daves, based on story Steve Fisher) 2300, 5730

Destry Rides Again (*D:* George Marshall, *W:* Felix Jackson, Henry Meyers, Gertrude Purcell based on novel Max Brand) 2495, 2528, 2539, 2645, 3223, 4811, 4897, 5324, 9738, 10694, 10937

The Detective (*D:* Gordon Douglas, *W:* Abby Mann based on novel Roderick Thorp) 9196

Detective Story (*D:* William Wyler, *W:* Philip Yordan, Robert Wyler based on play Sidney Kingsley., 1770, 1944, 1979, 3099, 3666, 6404, 6729, 6828, 7963, 8056, 8165, 8190, 9553

Detour (*D:* Edgar G. Ulmer, *W:* Martin Goldsmith) 415, 687, 1043, 1082, 1667, 3410, 3411, 3978, 6780, 7274, 8111, 9638

The Devil and Daniel Webster *see* All That Money Can Buy

The Devil and Miss Jones (*D:* Sam Wood, *W:* Norman Krasna) 308, 6183, 8974

Devil and the Deep (*D:* Marion Gering, *W:* Benn Levy based on story Harry Hervey) 9855

The Devil Doll (*D:* Tod Browning, *W:* Garret Fort, Guy Endore, Erich von Stroheim based on novel Abraham Merritt) 9338

The Devil Is a Woman (*D:* Josef von Sternberg, *W:* John Dos Passos, S.K. Winston based on novel Pierre Louys) 2089, 2877, 10585

The Devil's Disciple (*D:* Guy Hamilton, *W:* Roland Kibbee, John Dighton based on play George Bernard Shaw) 3101

The Devil's Rain (*D:* Robert Fuest, *W:* Gabe Essoe, James Ashton, Gerald Hopman) 897

Dial M for Murder (*D:* Alfred Hitchcock, *W:* Frederick Knott based on play Knott) 224, 2812, 5431

Diamonds Are Forever (*D:* Guy Hamilton, *W:* Richard Maibaum, Tom Mankiewicz based on Ian Fleming's novel) 2649, 4298, 5304

Diary of a Country Priest (*D, W:* Robert Bresson based on novel George Bernanos) 5581, 10125, 11210

The Diary of Anne Frank (*D:* George Stevens, *W:* Frances Goodrich, Albert Hackett based on their play and Anne Frank's diary) 4185, 5231

Dick Tracy (*D:* Warren Beatty, *W:* Jim Cash Jack Epps, Jr. based on characters created by Chester Gould) 1602, 5910, 10138

Die Hard (*D:* John McTiernan, *W:* Jeb Stuart, Steven de Souza) 1451

Die Hard 2 aka Die Harder (*D:* Renny Harlin, *W:* Steven E. de Souza, Doug Richardson based on novel Walter Wager and characters created by Roderick Thorp) 3440

Diner (*D, W:* Barry Levinson) 709, 3322, 3590, 6433, 6811, 6977, 7261, 7438, 7733, 9151, 9970

Dinner at Eight (*D:* George Cukor, *W:* Frances Marion, Herman J. Mankiewicz, Donald Ogeden Stewart based on play George S. Kaufman, Edna Ferber) 392, 1295, 3332, 4200, 5610, 6547, 6900, 7831, 8134, 11096

Dirty Dancing (*D:* Emile Ardolino, *W:* Eleanor Bergstein) 449, 2081, 5829, 7065, 7191

Dirty Harry (*D:* Don Siegel, *W:* Harry Julian & Rita M. Fink, Dean Riesner based on story Finks) 6322

Dirty Rotten Scoundrels (*D:* Frank Oz, *W:* Dale Launer, Stanley Shapiro, Paul Henning) 3947

Dishonored (*D:* Josef von Sternberg, *W:* Daniel N. Rubin, von Sternberg) 81, 1529, 3502, 6483, 6597

A Dispatch from Reuters (*D:* William Dieterle, *W:* Milton Krims based on story Valentine Williams, Wolfgang Wilhelm) 8145

Diva (*D:* Jean-Jacques Beineix, *W:* Beineix, Jean Van Hamme based on novel Delacorta) 508

The Divorcee (*D:* Robert Z. Leonard, *W:* Nick Grinde, Zelda Sears, John Meehan based on novel Ursula Parrott) 937

Do the Right Thing (*D, W:* Spike Lee) 1626, 3784, 5067, 7200, 8046, 8478, 9786, 10096

Doc Hollywood (*D:* Michael Caton-Jones, *W:* Jeffrey Price, Peter S. Seaman, Daniel Pyne based on Laurian Leggett's adaptation of a book by Neil B. Shulman) 8839, 11176

The Doctor (*D:* Randa Haines, *W:* Robert Caswell based on novel Edward E. Rosenbaum) 7980, 9928

The Doctor and the Devils (*D:* Freddie Francis, *W:* Ronald Harwood based on screenplay Dylan Thomas) 46, 4272, 7996

Doctor Butcher M.D. (*D:* Frank Martin (Franco Martinelli), *W:* Martinelli, Fabrizio de Angelis, Walter Patriarca, Romano Scandariato) 1089

Dr. Ehrlich's Magic Bullet (*D:* William Dieterle, *W:* John Huston, Heinz Herald, Norman Burnside based on story Burnside and letters and notes of the Ehrlich family) 1398

Dr. Gillespie's Criminal Case (*D:* Willis Goldbeck, *W:* Martin Berkeley, Harry Ruskin, Lawrence P. Bachmann based on characters created by Max Brand) 3353

Doctor in Distress (*D:* Ralph Thomas, *W:* Nicholas Phipps, Ronald Scott Thorn based on characters created by Richard Gordon) 574

Doctor in the House (*D:* Ralph Thomas, *W:* Richard Gordon, Ronald Wilkins, Nicholas Phipps based on novel Gordon) 2625, 2626, 3288, 5168, 7177, 9740

Inside Daisy Clover (*D:* Robert Mulligan, *W:* Gavin Lambert based on his novel) 4034, 5039

Insignificance (*D:* Nicolas Roeg, *W:* Terry Johnson based on his play) 36, 4152, 4966, 5866, 6060, 9471, 10133

Inspiration (*D:* Calrence Brown, *W:* Gene Markey based on story Alphonse Daudet) 6756

Interiors (*D, W:* Woody Allen) 2231, 3113, 7134, 9846

Intermezzo (*D:* Gregory Ratoff, *W:* George O'Neil based on story Gosta Stevens, Gustav Molander) 4334, 4400 6486, 8289, 9187, 11361

Internal Affairs (*D:* Michael Figgis, *W:* Henry Bean) 757, 5048, 5363

International House (*D:* Edward Sutherland, *W:* Francis Martin, Walter DeLeon based on story Lou Heifetz, Neil Brant) 186, 2640, 6099

Internes Can't Take Money (*D:* Alfred Santell, *W:* Rian James, Theodore Reeves based on magazine story Max Brand) 6771

Into the Night (*D:* John Landis, *W:* Ron Koslow) 8776

Intruder in the Dust (*D:* Clarence Brown, *W:* Ben Maddow based on novel William Faulkner) 1768

Invaders from Mars (*D:* William Cameron Menzies, *W:* Richard Blake, John Tucker Battle, Menzies based on story Battle) 5200

Invasion of the Body Snatchers (*D:* Don Siegel, *W:* Daniel Mainwaring, Sam Peckinpah based on novel Jack Finney) 2094, 2606, 4748, 5009, 9311

The Invincible Six aka The Heroes (*D:* Jean Negulesco, *W:* Guy Elmes, Chester Erskine based on novel Michael Barrett) 2121, 5442

The Invisible Man (*D:* James Whale, *W:* R.C. Sheriff, Philip Wylie based on novel H.G. Wells) 2170, 2777, 3264, 3503 7891, 9011, 9012

Irene (*D:* Alfred E. Green, *W:* June Mathis, Rex Taylor, Mervyn LeRoy based on musical comedy James Montgomery, *T:* George Marion, Jr) 6545, 7864

The Irish in Us (*D:* Lloyd Bacon, *W:* Earl Baldwin) 6855

Irma La Douce (*D:* Billy Wilder, *W:* Wilder, I.A.L. Diamond based on play Alexandre Breffort) 6523, 7649, 8138, 11308

Iron Eagle (*D:* Sidney J. Furie, *W:* Kevin Elders, Furie) 284

The Iron Mistress (*D:* Gordon Douglas, *W:* James R. Webb based on story Paul I. Wellman) 11302

The Iron Triangle (*D:* Eric Weston, *W:* Weston, John Bushelman, Larry Hilbrand, Marshall Drazen) 1656

Ironweed (*D:* Hector Babenco, *W:* William Kennedy based on his novel) 3677

Irreconcilable Differences (*D:* Charles Shyer, *W:* Nancy Meyers, Shyer) 1661, 3773

Isaac Little Feathers (*D:* Les Rose, *W:* Rose, Barry Pearson) 1185

Isadora aka The Loves of Isadora (*D:* Karel Reisz, *W:* Melvyn Bragg, Clive Exton, Margaret Drabble based on autobiography Isadora Duncan) 2071, 2072, 7092, 7546, 10923, 11345

Island of Lost Souls (*D:* Erle C. Kenton, *W:* Philip Wylie, Waldemar Young based on novel H.G. Wells) 4129, 7081

It (*D:* Clarence Badger, *W:* Hope Loring, Louis D. Lighton, Elinor Glyn) 8175

It Came from Outer Space (*D:* Jack Arnold, *W:* Harry Essex based on story Ray Bradbury) 4322, 10059, 10191

It Happened on Fifth Avenue (*D:* Roy Del Ruth, *W:* Everett Freeman, Vick Knight based on story Herbert Clyde Lewis, Frederick Stephani) 556, 942, 2635

It Happened One Night (*D:* Frank Capra, *W:* Robert Riskin based on story Samuel Hopkins Adams) 1039, 1496, 1532, 1533, 2344, 3925, 4442, 4756, 4783, 4840, 4892, 5094, 5225, 5868, 6485, 6506, 6838, 7169, 7639, 8089, 8208, 8288, 8646, 9507, 10008, 10063, 10725, 10912, 11124, 11180

It Happened Tomorrow (*D:* Rene Clair, *D:* Dudley Nichols, Clair) 7172

It Should Happen to You (*D:* George Cukor, *W:* Garson Kanin) 1975, 5117

It's a Gift (*D:* Norman Z. McLeod, *W:* Jack Cunningham, W.C. Fields based on story Fields and J.P. McEvoy) 9747

It's a Wonderful Life (*D:* Frank Capra, *W:* Frances Goodrich, Albert Hackett, Capra, Jo Swerling based on story Philip Van Doren Stern) 266, 851, 1553, 1934, 5538, 5955, 6844, 7920, 11075, 11234

It's a Wonderful World (*D, W:* Val Guest) 7796

It's Always Fair Weather (*D:* Stanley Donen, Gene Kelly, *W:* Betty Comden, Adolph Green) 9647

It's My Turn (*D:* Claudia Weill, *W:* Eleanor Bergstein) 2909, 3327

Ivanhoe (*D:* Richard Thorpe, *W:* Noel Langley based on novel Sir Walter Scott) 1987

Jack and the Beanstalk (*D:* Jean Yarborough, *W:* Nat Curtis based on story Pat Costello, Felix Adler and fairy tales) 1084

Jacknife (*D:* David Jones, *W:* Stephen Metcalfe based on his play) 3785

Jagged Edge (*D:* Richard Marquand, *W:* Joe Estzerhas) 1642, 4273, 6834, 10814

Jail Bait aka Wild Game (*D, W:* Rainer Werner Fassbinder based on play Franz-Xaver Kroetz) 5318, 7286

Jamaica Inn (*D:* Alfred Hitchcock, *W:* Sidney Gilliat, Joan Harrison, J.B. Priestley, Alma Reville based on novel Daphne du Maurier) 8713, 10366

Jamaica Run (*D, W:* Lewis R. Foster, based on novel Max Murray) 4729, 10695

Jane Eyre (*D:* Robert Stevenson, *W:* Aldous Huxley, Stevenson, John Houseman based on novel Charlotte Brontë) 3198

Jason and the Argonauts (*D:* Don Chaffey, *W:* Jan Reed, Beverly Cross) 84, 896, 4548, 9327

Jassy (*D:* Bernard Knowles, *W:* Dorothy & Campbell Christie, Geoffrey Kerr based on novel Norah Lofts) 7032

Jaws (*D:* Steven Spielberg, *W:* Peter Benchley, Carl Gottlieb, Howard Sackler based on Benchley's novel) 934, 10894

The Jazz Singer (*D:* Alan Crosland, *W:* Jack Jamuth based on play Samson Raphaleson, *T:* Alred A. Cohn) 2484, 9478

The Jazz Singer (*D:* Richard Fleischer, *W:* Herbert Baker, Stephen H. Foreman based on Samuel Raphaelson's play) 1305

Jeremiah Johnson (*D:* Sydney Pollack, *W:* John Milius, Edward Anhalt based on novel Vardis Fisher and a story by Raymond W. Thorp, Robert Bunker) 4299, 4800

The Jerk (*D:* Carl Reiner, *W:* Steve Martin, Carl Gottlieb, Michael Elias based on story Martin & Gottlieb) 862, 4733, 10271, 10534

Jesse James (*D:* Henry King, *W:* Nunnally Johnson based on historical data assembled by Rosaline Schaeffer, Jo Frances James) 3003, 3091, 5704, 8150, 10787

Jewel of the Nile (*D:* Lewis Teague, *W:* Mark Rosenthal, Lawrence Konner based on characters created by Diane Thomas) 3495, 4931, 10468

Jezebel (*D:* William Wyler, *W:* Clements Ripley, Abem Finkel, John Huston, Robert Bruckner based on play Owen Davis, Sr.) 764, 4048, 9208, 9322

JFK (*D:* Oliver Stone, *W:* Stone, Zachary Sklar; based on books of Jim Garrison & Jim Marrs) 5387, 5518, 10141

The Jigsaw Man (*D:* Terence Young, *W:* Jo Eisinger) 1153

Jimmy the Gent (*D:* Michael Curtiz, *W:* Bertram Millhauser based on story Laird Doyle, Ray Nazarro) 2994, 6768

Jinxed! (*D:* Don Siegel, *W:* David Newman, Bert Blessing) 3673, 8753

Joe (*D:* John G. Avildsen, *W:* Norman Wexler) 4622

Joe Kidd (*D:* John Sturges, *W:* Elmore Leonard) 10807

Johnny Belinda (*D:* Jean Negulesco, *W:* Irmgard von Cube, Allen Vincent based on play Elmer Harris) 3336, 3449, 9310

Johnny Dangerously (*D:* Amy Heckerling, *W:* Norman Steinberg, Bernie Kukoff, Harry Colomby, Jeff Harris) 7061, 7734

Johnny Eager (*D:* Mervyn LeRoy, *W:* John Lee Mahin, James Edward Grant based on story Grant) 377, 3004, 3889, 7410, 8826

Johnny Guitar (*D:* Nicholas Ray, *W:* Philip Yordan based on novel Roy Chanslor) 2666, 3622, 3820, 5815, 8870, 10152, 10797, 11150

The Jolson Story (*D:* Alfred E. Green, *W:* Stephen Longstreet, Harry Chandlee, Andrew Solt) 9489

Jory (*D:* Jorge Fons, *W:* Gerald Herman, Robert Irving based on novel Milton R. Bass) 5639

Journey Into Fear (*D:* Norman Foster, *W:* Orson Welles, Joseph Cotten based on novel Eric Ambler) 2345, 10825

The Journey of Natty Gann (*D:* Jeremy Kagan, *W:* Jeanne Rosenberg) 3640

Joy of Living (*D:* Tay Garnett, *W:* Gene Towne, Graham Baker, Allan Scott based

Jerry Herman, Robert E. Lee from a novel by Patrick Dennis) 1303, 2125, 5549, 5970, 9372, 10986

A Man for All Seasons (*D:* Fred Zinnemann, *W:* Robert Bolt, Constance Willis based on Bolt's play) 3102, 9103, 9557

The Man I Killed aka Broken Lullaby (*D:* Ernst Lubitsch, *W:* Ernest Vadja, Samson Raphaleson based on play Maurice Rostand, adapted Reginald Berkeley) 1344, 3441, 9895

The Man I Love (*D:* Raoul Walsh, John Maxwell, *W:* Catherine Turney, Jo Pagano based on novel Maritta Wolff) 7349, 10232

The Man in Grey (*D:* Leslie Arliss, *W:* Margaret Kennedy, Doreen Montgomery, Arliss based on novel Lady Eleanor Smith) 6395, 7312

The Man in Half-moon Street (*D:* Ralph M. Murphy, *W:* Charles Kenyon, Garrett Fort based on play Barre Lyndon) 5106, 8976

The Man in the Grey Flannel Suit (*D, W:* Nunnally Johnson based on Sloan Wilson's novel) 5157

The Man in the Moon (*D:* Robert Mulligan, *W:* Jenny Wingfield) 715

The Man in the White Suit (*D:* Alexander Mackendrick, *W:* Roger MacDougall, John Dighton, Mackendrick based on MacDougall's play) 8981

Man Made Monster (*D:* George Waggner, *W:* Joseph West based on story H.J. Essex, Sid Schwartz, Len Golos) 5104, 9075

Man of a Thousand Faces (*D:* Joseph Pevney, *W:* Ivan Goff based on story Ralph Wheelwright) 1924

Man of Flowers (*D:* Paul Cox, *W:* Cox, Bob Ellis) 4630, 4965

Man of the West (*D:* Anthony Mann, *W:* Reginald Rose based on novel Will C. Brown) 7257

The Man on the Flying Trapeze (*D:* Clyde Bruckman, *W:* Ray Harris, Sam Hardy, Jack Cunningham, Bobby Vernon based on story Hardy, Charles Bogle [W.C. Fields]) 3738, 6100

Man Trouble (*D:* Bob Rafelson, *W:* Carole Eastman) 2663

The Man Who Came to Dinner (*D:* William Keighley, *W:* Julius J. & Philip G. Epstein based on play George S. Kaufman, Moss Hart) 409, 410, 542, 905, 2359, 2572, 3562, 7453, 8421, 8473, 9046, 10288

The Man Who Could Work Miracles (*D:* Lothar Mendes, *W:* H.G. Wells, Lajos Biro based on short story Wells) 1487, 1776, 4743, 10177

The Man Who Knew Too Much (*D:* Alfred Hitchcock, *W:* A.R. Rawlinson, Charles Bennett, D.B. Wyndham-Lewis, Emlyn Williams, Edwin Greenwood) 1348

The Man Who Knew Too Much (*D:* Alfred Hitchcock, *W: John Michael Hayes, Angus McPhail based on story Charles Bennett, D.B. Wyndham-Lewis)*) 370, 7703

The Man Who Loved Cat Dancing (*D:* Richard G. Sarafian, *W:* Eleanor Perry based on novel Marilyn Durham) 10985

The Man Who Loved Women (*D:* Francois Truffaut, *W:* Truffaut, Michel Femoayd,

Suzanne Schiffman) 993, 1368, 3956, 8996, 11161

The Man Who Loved Women (*D:* Blake Edwards, *W:* Edwards, Milton Wexler, Geoffrey Edwards based on French film Francois Truffaut) 11164

The Man Who Shot Liberty Valance (*D:* John Ford, *W:* Willis Goldbeck, James Warner Bellah based on story Dorothy M. Johnson) 5573

The Man Who Would Be King (*D:* John Huston, *W:* Huston, Gladys Hill based on story Rudyard Kipling) 1148, 3535 8139

The Man with Bogart's Face (*D:* Robert Day, *W:* Andrew J. Fenady based on his novel) 10239

The Man with One Red Shoe (*D:* Stan Dragoti, *W:* Robert Klane based on French film Francis Veber, Yves Robert) 10134

The Man with the Golden Arm (*D:* Otto Preminger, *W:* Walter Newman, Lewis Meltzer based on novel Nelson Algren) 2093, 2779, 4819

The Man with Two Brains (*D:* Carl Reiner, *W:* Reiner, Steve Martin, George Gipe) 283, 999, 3065, 4368, 4459, 5021

The Manchurian Candidate (*D:* John Frankenheimer, *W:* George Axelrod, Frankenheimer based on Richard Condon's novel) 2702, 4569, 5500

Mandalay (*D:* Michael Curtiz, *W:* Austin Parker, Charles Kenyon) 8989

Manhattan (*D:* Woody Allen, *W:* Allen, Marshall Brickman) 282, 583, 1478, 2126, 2396, 2411, 2674, 3309, 3494, 4195, 4248, 4655, 5042, 6466, 6467, 6749, 7078, 7421, 8119, 8579, 8928, 9052, 9905, 10259, 11312

Manhattan Melodrama (*D:* W.S. Van Dyke II, *W:* OLiver H.P. Garrett, Joseph L. Mankiewicz based on story Arthur Caesar) 847, 1389, 1666, 1836, 2173, 4395, 5840, 11036

The Manhattan Project (*D:* Marshall Brickman, *W:* Brickman, Thomas Baum) 1036, 10075

Mannequin (*D:* Michael Gottlieb, *W:* Edward Rugoff, Gottlieb) 512, 10730

The Manxman (*D:* Alfred Hitchcock, *W:* Eliot Stannard based on novel Hall Caine) 8433

Marie Antoinette (*D:* W.S. Vand Dyke II, Julien Duvivier, *W:* Claudine West, Donald Ogden Stewart, Ernest Vajda, F. Scott Fitzgerald based on book Stefan Zweig) 5508, 6691

Marius (*D:* Alexander Korda, *W:* Marcel Pagnol based on his play) 2047, 4669

The Mark of Zorro (*D:* Rouben Mamoulian, *W:* John Tainton Foote, Garrett Fort, Bess Meredyth based on novel Johnston McCulley) 3397, 5411, 6178, 6385, 7117, 7689, 7717, 7743, 8629, 10611, 10788, 10938

Marked Woman (*D:* Lloyd Bacon, *W:* Robert Rossen, Abem Finkel, Seton I. Miller) 1209, 5188, 8746, 8778, 9277

Marlowe (*D:* Paul Bogart, *W:* Stirling Silliphant based on novel Raymond Chan-

dler) 2527, 4855

Marnie (*D:* Alfred Hitchcock, *W:* Jay Presson Allen based on novel Winston Graham) 326, 327, 1179, 1365, 1949, 2278, 2279, 4914, 6239, 6755, 6878, 7354, 7967, 9264, 9692, 11195

Marriage on the Rocks (*D:* Jack Donohue, *W:* Cy Howard based on his story) 592

Married to It (*D, W:* Arthur Hiller) 3183

Married to the Mob (*D:* Jonathan Demme, *W:* Barry Strugatz, Mark R. Burns) 2518

The Marrying Kind (*D:* George Cukor, *W:* Ruth Gordon, Garson Kanin) 2848, 5016, 6076, 10454

The Marrying Man (*D:* Jerry Rees, *W:* Neil Simon) 1332, 1607, 2614, 3961, 5561, 6445, 8487, 9940

Martin (*D, W:* George A. Romero) 9560

Marty (*D:* Delbert Mann, *W:* Paddy Chayefsky based on his teleplay) 603, 2218, 2873, 4247, 5490, 5890, 7433, 7724, 10484

Mary, Mary (*D:* Mervyn LeRoy, *W:* Richard Breen based on play Jean Kerr) 1629, 1831, 2390, 3206, 4092, 7870, 8368, 8392, 9902

Mary of Scotland (*D:* John Ford, *W:* Dudley Nichols based on play Maxwell Anderson) 397, 7909, 11126

Mary Poppins (*D:* Robert Stevenson, *W:* Bill Walsh, Don DaGradi based on books by P.L. Travers) 7597, 9088

M*A*S*H (*D:* Robert Altman, *W:* Ring Lardner, Jr. based on novel Richard Hooker) 207, 1417, 4998, 5850, 6664, 7047, 8082, 8625, 9131, 9132, 10805

Mask (*D:* Peter Bogdanovich, *W:* Anna Hamilton Phelan based on true story Rocky Dennis) 4776, 5904, 7247

The Mask of Dimitrios (*D:* Jean Negulesco, *W:* Frank Gruber based on novel Eric Ambler) 1041, 1400, 2940, 5194, 5418, 5419, 5487, 6778, 10184, 10429

The Mask of Fu Manchu (*D:* Charles Brabin, King Vidor, *W:* Irene Kuhn, Edgar Allan Woolf, John Willard based on novel Sax Rohmer) 638, 2132, 2438, 2618, 7940, 8178, 10272, 10273, 10274

The Masked Marvel (*D:* Spencer Bennett, *W:* Royal K. Cole, Ronald Davidson, Basil Dickey, Albert Duffy, Grant Nelson, George Plympton, Joseph Poland) 10941

Masoch (*D, W:* Franco Brogi Taviani) 3539, 8341, 11349

Mass Appeal (*D:* Glenn Jordan, *W:* Bill C. Davis based on his play) 1431, 1614, 5130

Masters of Menace (*D:* Daniel Raskov, *W:* Tino Insana) 529

Mata Hari (*D:* George Fitzmaurice, *W:* Benjamin Glazer, Leo Birinski, Doris Anderson, Gilbert Emery) 6450, 8683, 9599, 11289, 11392

The Matchmaker (*D:* Joseph Anthony, *W:* John Michael Hayes based on play Thornton Wilder) 5969

Matewan (*D, W:* John Sayles) 1697, 2332, 2333, 5679, 8174, 9234, 10418, 10540

The Mating Season (*D:* Mitchell Leisen, *W:* Charles Brackett, Walter Reisch, Richard Breen) 3238

A Matter of Life and Death aka Stairway to

Conway, *W:* Laurence Stallings, Talbot Jennings based on novel Kenneth Roberts) 2415, 10667

Norwood (*D:* Jack Haley, Jr., *W:* Marguerite Roberts based on novel Charles Portis) 7618, 10748

Not as a Stranger (*D:* Stanley Kramer, *W:* Edna & Edward Anhalt based on novel Morton Thompson) 4546

Nothing but the Best (*D:* Clive Donner, *W:* Frederic Raphael based on short story Stanley Ellin) 8722

Nothing in Common (*D:* Garry Marshall, *W:* Rick Podell, Michael Preminger) 1883, 7199, 9875

Nothing Sacred (*D:* William Wellman, *W:* Ben Hecht, additional dialog Ring Lardner, Jr., Budd Schulberg based on story James H. Street) 295, 1385, 1547, 1802, 2379, 3368, 3611, 3927, 5942, 5943, 6473, 7787, 8649, 9917, 9944, 10146, 11277

Notorious (*D:* Alfred Hitchcock, *W:* Ben Hecht) 1738, 8669, 9758

Now and Forever (*D:* Henry Hathaway, *W:* Vincent Lawrence, Sylvia Thalliery based on story Jack Kirkland, Melville Baker) 9337

Now, Voyager (*D:* Irving Rapper, *W:* Casey Robinson based on novel Olive Higgins Prouty) 613, 848, 2896, 3123, 3352, 3374, 7157, 8030, 8305, 8438, 9258, 10085, 10476

The Nutty Professor (*D:* Jerry Lewis, *W:* Lewis, Bill Richmond based on story Lewis) 8798

O Lucky Man! (*D:* Lindsay Anderson, *W:* David Sherwin based on idea Malcolm McDowell) 9410

Objective, Burma (*D:* Raoul Walsh, *W:* Randal MacDougall, Lester Cole based on story Alvah Bessie) 1850, 5731, 6864, 8065, 8654

O.C. and Stiggs (*D:* Robert Altman, *W:* Donald Cantrel, Ted Mann) 10992

Ocean's Eleven (*D:* Lewis Milestone, *W:* Harry Brown, Charles Lederer based on story George Clayton Johnson, Jack Golden Russell) 4714, 10684

Octopussy (*D:* John Glen, *W:* George Maibaum, Michael G. Wilson based on stories by Ian Fleming) 386, 3433, 9887

The Odd Couple (*D:* Gene Saks, *W:* Neil Simon based on his play) 1202, 1233, 1514, 2120, 3633, 4886, 5221, 7093, 7267, 9428, 10546

Ode to Billy Joe (*D:* Max Baer, *W:* Herman Rauncher based on song Bobbie Gentry) 9334

The Odessa File (*D:* Ronald Neame, *W:* George Markstein, Kenneth Ross based on novel Frederick Forsyth) 3040

Of Mice and Men (*D:* Lewis Milestone, *W:* Eugene Solow based on novel John Steinbeck) 274

Of Mice and Men (*D:* Gary Sinise, *W:* Horton Foote based on John Steinbeck's novel) 9281

The Offense (*D:* Sidney Lumet, *W:* John Hopkins) 703

An Officer and a Gentleman (*D:* Taylor

Hackford, *W:* Douglas Day Stewart) 3133, 3461, 7137, 8730, 9996, 10073, 10651, 10760, 10761

The Official Story (*D:* Luis Puenzo, *W:* Puenzo, Aida Bortnik) 797

Oh, God! (*D:* Carl Reiner, *W:* Larry Gelbart based on novel Avery Corman) 1913, 4146, 6735

Oh, Men! Oh, Women! (*D, W:* Nunnally Johnson based on play Edward Chodorov) 7129, 9765

Oh, You Beautiful Doll (*D:* John M. Stahl, *W:* Arthur Lewis) 1140, 6784, 6964

Oklahoma! (*D:* Fred Zinnemann, *W:* Sonya Levien, William Ludwig based on musical Richard Rodgers, Oscar Hammerstein II from a play by Lynn Riggs) 6414

Old Acquaintance (*D:* Vincent Sherman, *W:* John Van Druten, Lenore Coffee based on Van Druten's play) 196, 1710, 7023

Old Boyfriends (*D:* Joan Tewkesbury, *W:* Paul & Leonard Schrader) 11086

The Old Dark House (*D:* James Whale, *W:* Benn W. Levy, R.C. Sherriff based on novel J.B. Priestley) 184, 4178

The Old-fashioned Way (*D:* William Beaudine, *W:* Garnett Weston, Jack Cunningham based on story Charles Bogle [W.C. Fields]) 1162

Old Gringo (*D:* Luis Puenzo, *W:* Aida Bortnik, Puenzo based on novel Carlos Fuentes) 6542, 10216

The Old Maid (*D:* Edmund Goulding, *W:* Casey Robinson based on play Zoe Akins from Edith Wharton's novel) 808, 6172, 6173, 6858, 6859, 8628, 9610, 10241

The Old Man and the Sea (*D:* John Sturges, *W:* Peter Viertel based on novella Ernest Hemingway) 2307, 2698, 3477, 3692, 9409

Old Yeller (*D:* Robert Stevenson, *W:* Fred Gipson, William Tunberg based on Gipson's novel) 317

Oliver's Story (*D:* John Korty, *W:* Erich Segal, Korty based on Segal's novel) 5854

On Approval (*D:* Clive Brook, *W:* Brook, Terence Young based on Frederick Lonsdale's play) 2346, 6033

On Golden Pond (*D:* Mark Rydell, *W:* Ernest Thompson based on his play) 156, 157, 863, 1372, 2140, 2630, 2853, 3460, 3907, 4627, 6495, 7363, 7437, 7465, 8921, 10882

On the Beach (*D:* Stanley Kramer, *W:* John Paxton, James Lee Barrett based on Nevil Shute's novel) 5272

On the Make (*D:* Samuel Hurwitz, *W:* Fred Carpenter, James McTernan) 6259, 6459

On the Road Again *see* Honeysuckle Rose

On the Town (*D:* Gene Kelly, Stanley Donen, *W:* Adolph Green, Betty Comden based on musical Comden, Green, Leonard Bernstein from ballet Jerome Robbins) 5884, 9249, 10014

On the Waterfront (*D:* Elia Kazan, *W:* Budd Schulberg based on series of articles Malcolm Johnson) 842, 1122, 1504, 2210, 2365, 3623, 5061, 5062, 5063, 5291, 6217, 7256, 9050, 9867, 10405

Once Bitten (*D:* Howard Storm, *W:* David Hines, Jeffrey Hause, Jonathan Roberts based on story Dimitir Villard) 8352,

10580, 10581

Once upon a Honeymoon (*D:* Leo McCarey, *W:* Sheridan Gibney) 1549, 5569, 6674

Once upon a Time (*D:* Alexander Hall, *W:* Lewis Meltzer, Oscar Saul, Irving Fineman based on radio play Norman Corwin, Lucille Fletcher Herrmann) 4019

Once upon a Time in the West (*D:* Sergio Leone *W:* Leone, Sergio Donati based on story Dario Argento, Bernardo Bertolucci, Leone) 329, 10436

One-Eyed Jacks (*D:* Marlon Brando, *W:* Guy Trosper, Calder Willingham based on novel Charles Neider) 3244

One Flew over the Cuckoo's Nest (*D:* Milos Forman, *W:* Laurence Hauben, Bo Goldman based on Ken Kesey's novel and play Dale Wasserman) 2393, 3053, 3174

One Foot in Heaven (*D:* Irving Rapper, *W:* Casey Robinson based on biography Hartzell Spence of his father) 10717

One Hour with You (*D:* Ernst Lubitsch, George Cukor, *W:* Samson Raphaelson based on play Lothar Schmidt) 289, 1723, 2406, 2946, 5684, 7218, 7478, 10902

100 Men and a Girl (*D:* Henry Koster, *W:* Bruce Manning, Charles Kenyon, James Mullhauser, Hans Kraly) 7424

One Minute to Zero (*D:* Tay Garnett, *W:* Milton Krims, William Wister Haines) 7039, 10832

One Night in the Tropics (*D:* A. Ed ward Sutherland, *W:* Gertrude Purcell, Charles Grayson, Kathryn Scola, Francis Martin based on novel Earl Derr Biggers) 3742

One of Our Spies Is Missing (*D:* E. Darrell Hallenbeck, *W:* Howard Rodman based on story of Henry Slesar) 1813, 10198

One Potato, Two Potato (*D:* Larry Peerce, *W:* Raphael Hayes, Orville H. Hampton based on Hampton's story) 1286

One, Two, Three (*D:* Billy Wilder, Andre Smagghe, *W:* Wilder, I.A.L. Diamond based on play Ferenc Molnar) 10322, 11079

The Onion Field (*D:* Harold Becker, *W:* Joseph Wambaugh based on his book) 4269, 63245

Only Angels Have Wings (*D:* Howard Hawks, *W:* Jules Furthman, William Rankin, Eleanor Griffin based on story Hawks) 571, 1095, 2145, 2819, 3511, 8331, 9061

The Only Game in Town (*D:* George Stevens, *W:* Frank P. Gilroy based on his play) 725, 4490, 6422

Only the Lonely (*D, W:* Chris Columbus) 1025, 5277, 6306, 7663, 8517, 9524

Only When I Laugh (*D:* Glenn Jordan, *W:* Neil Simon based on his play) 2141, 2764, 6430, 7466, 8572, 9578, 9676, 10261

Only Yesterday (*D:* John M. Stahl, *W:* William Hurlbut, Arthur Richman, George O'Neill based on book by Frederick Lewis Allen) 1615

Operation Pacific (*D, W:* George Waggner) 1299, 4240

Operation Petticoat (*D:* Blake Edwards, *W:* Stanley Shapiro, Maurice Richlin based on story Paul King, Joseph Stone) 1807, 8278

Roxanne (D: Fred Schepisi, W: Steve Martin based on play Edmond Rostand) 2769, 3254, 11390

Roxie Hart (D: William A. Wellman, W: Nunnally Johnson based on play Maurine Watkins) 2299, 2382, 3095, 5705, 8519, 9422

A Royal Scandal (D: Otto Preminger, W: Edwin Justus Mayer, Bruno Frank based on play Lajos Biro, Melchior Lengyell) 6067

Royal Wedding (D: Stanley Donen, W: Alan Jay Lerner) 10998

Ruby Gentry (D: King Vidor, W: Silvia Richards based on story Arthur Fitz-Richard) 7577, 11147

Rude Awakening (D: David Greenwalt, Aaron Russo, W: Neil Levy, Richard LaGravenese) 1823, 6711

Ruggles of Red Gap (D: Leo McCarey, W: Walter DeLeon, Harlan Thompson, Humphrey Pearson based on play & novel Harry Leon Wilson) 293, 9840

The Ruling Class (D: Peter Medak, W: Peter Barnes based on his play) 7788

Rumble Fish (D: Frances Ford Coppola, W: S.E. Hinton, Coppola based on novel Hinton) 4425, 5739, 8709

Run for Cover (D: Nicholas Ray, W: Winston Miller based on story Harriet Frank, Jr., Irving Ravetch) 2504

Run of the Arrow (D, W: Samuel Fuller) 8530

Runaway (D, W: Michael Crichton) 11273

Running (D, W: Stephen Hillard Stern) 8895

Rush (D: Lili Fini Zanuck, W: Pete Dexter based on novel Kim Wozencraft) 7494, 9274

The Russia House (W: Fred Schepisi, W: Tom Stoppard based on John le Carre's novel) 1676, 1865, 2967, 8205, 8543 10472, 10602

Ruthless People (D: Jim Abrahams, David & Jerry Zucker, W: Dale Launer) 4427, 4933, 5396

Saboteur (D: Alfred Hitchcock, W: Peter Viertel, Joan Harrison, Dorothy Parker based on an original story by Hitchcock) 769, 1057, 3166, 5074, 8018, 9985, 10362

Sahara (D: Zoltan Korda, W: John Howard Lawson, Korda, James O'Hanlon based on story Philip MacDonald) 1849, 2499, 3748 3863, 8770, 9406

The Sailor from Gibraltar (D: Tony Richardson, W: Christopher Isherwood, Don Magner based on novel Marguerite Duras) 5082, 6663

St. Elmo's Fire (D: Joel Schumacher, W: Schumacher, Carl Kurlander) 1857

The Saint Strikes Back (D: John Farrow, W: John Twist based on novel Leslie Charteris) 5409, 6174, 6605

The Saint Valentine's Day Massacre (D: Roger Corman, W: Howard Browne) 5439, 6638, 10545

Salvador (D: Oliver Stone, W: Georges Delerue) 7584, 7685, 8051, 10469, 11013

Same Time, Next Year (D: Robert Mulligan, W: Bernard Slade based on his play) 7777, 7983, 9356

Samson and Delilah (D: Cecil B. DeMille, W: Vladimir Jabotinsky, Harold Lamb, Jesse L. Lasky, Jr., Frederic M. Frank based on story from the Bible and book by Jabotinsky) 827, 4487, 8156

San Francisco (D: W.S. Van Dyke II, D.W. Griffith, W: Anita Loos, Erich von Stroheim based on story Robert Hopkins) 605, 1976, 3193, 3509, 4165, 6162, 7910, 9186, 9545, 10665, 10692

San Quentin (D: Lloyd Bacon, W: Peter Milne, Humphrey Cobb based on story Robert Tasker, John Bright) 3219

The Sand Pebbles (D: Robert Wise, W: Robert W. Anderson based on novel Richard McKenna) 2221

Sanders of the River (D: Zoltan Korda, W: Lajos Biro, Jeffrey Dell based on stories Edgar Wallace) 4197

The Sandpiper (D: Vincente Minnelli, W: Dalton Trumbo, Michael Wilson, Irene Kamp, Louis Kamp based on story Martin Ransohoff) 258, 3823, 7928, 9329

Sands of Iwo Jima (D: Allan Dwan, W: Harry Brown, James Edward Grant based on story Brown) 1141, 2302, 3522, 5245, 6727, 8101, 9423, 9513, 10831

Santa Fe Trail (D: Michael Curtiz, W: Robert Buckner) 7156, 8151

Saratoga Trunk (D: Sam Wood, W: Casey Robinson based on novel Edna Ferber) 685, 849

Saturday Night and Sunday Morning (D: Karel Reisz, W: Allan Sillitoe based on his novel) 3933, 5980, 6418, 8784

Saturday Night Fever (D: John Badham, W: Norman Wexler based on magazine article Nik Cohn) 2075, 2076, 2077, 7287, 7949

Savage Beach (D, W: Andy Sidaris) 2661

Save the Tiger (D: John G. Avildsen, W: Steve Shagan) 8740

The Saxon Charm (D, W: Claude Binyon based on novel Frederic Wakeman) 482

Say Anything. . . (D, W: Cameron Crowe) 2128, 4081, 4380, 5158, 6840, 8602

Sayonara (D: Joshua Logan, W: Paul Osborn based on novel James A. Michener) 6227, 7767

Scandal (D: Michael Caton-Jones, W: Michael Thomas) 935, 1919, 2354, 9443, 9838, 10596

Scandalous (D: Rob Cohen, W: Cohen, John Byrum based on story Byrum, Rob & Larry Cohen) 4494, 7232

The Scar see The Hollow Triumph

Scaramouche (D: George Sidney, W: Ronald Millar, George Froeschel based on story Rafael Sabatini) 857

Scarface (D: Howard Hawks, W: Ben Hecht, Seton I. Miller, John Lee Mahin, W.R. Burnett, Fred Pasley based on novel Armitage Trail) 1922, 5030, 6921, 7385, 7941, 9252, 9446, 10242, 10933

Scarface (D: Brian De Palma, W: Oliver Stone based on 1932 script Ben Hecht) 630, 2143, 3054, 7059, 7401, 10467

Scarlet Dawn (D: William Dieterle, W: Niven Busch, Erwin Gelsey, Douglas Fairbanks, Jr. based on novel Mary McCall, Jr) 9983

The Scarlet Empress (D: Josef von Stern-berg, W: Manuel Komroff based on diary of Catherine the Great) 3402, 8242

The Scarlet Pimpernel (D: Harold Young, Rowland V. Brown, Alexander Korda, W: S.N. Behrman, Robert Sherwood, Arthur Wimperis, Lajos Biro based on novel Baroness Emma Orczy) 1534, 1535, 2011

Scarlet Street (D: Fritz Lang, W: Dudley Nichols based on novel & play by Georges de la Fouchardiere, Mouezy-Eon) 489, 1805

Scene of the Crime (D: Roy Rowland, W: Charles Schnee based on story John Bartlow Martin) 10866

Scenes from a Mall (D: Paul Mazursky, W: Mazursky, Roger L. Simon) 1492, 8285

Scenes from a Marriage (D, W: Ingmar Bergman) 1304, 10460

Scenes from the Class Struggle in Beverly Hills (D: Paul Bartel, W: Bruce Wagner based on story Bartel, Wagner) 4497, 8884

Scorpio (D: Michael Winner, W: David W. Rintels, Gerald Wilson based on story Rintels) 4026, 9607

Scott of the Antarctic (D: Charles Frend, W: Walter Meade, Ivor Montagu, Mary Hayley Bell) 3573, 8903

The Scoundrel (D, W: Ben Hecht, Charles MacArthur) 1313, 7186, 7569, 8405

Scream Blacula Scream (D: Bob Kelljan, W: Joan Torres, Raymond Koenig, Maurice Jules based on story Koenig, Torres) 10578

Scrooge (D: Brian Desmond Hurst, W: Noel Langley based on Charles Dickens' story) 1143

Scrooged (D: Richard Donner, W: Mitch Glazer, Michael O'Donoghue) 1790

The Sea Chase (D: John Farrow, W: James Warner Bellah, John Twist based on novel Andrew Geer) 9003

The Sea Hawk (D: Michael Curtiz, W: Howard Koch, Seton I. Miller) 2799, 5615, 8369

Sea Wife (D: Bob McNaught, W: George K. Burke based on novel J.M. Scott) 3242

The Sea Wolf (D: Michael Curtiz, W: Robert Rossen based on novel Jack London) 4517, 10353

The Search (D: Fred Zinnemann, W: Richard Schweizer, David Wechsler, Paul Jarrico) 6867

The Searchers (D: John Ford, W: Frank S. Nugent based on novel Alan LeMay) 4602, 7309

Seconds (D: John Frankenheimer, W: Lewis John Carlino based on novel by David Ely) 2707

Secret Agent (D: Alfred Hitchcock, W: Charles Bennett, Ian Hay, Jesse Lasky, Jr., Alma Reville based on play Campbell Dixon from stories by W. Somerset Maugham) 1764, 5399, 5400, 5401

The Secret Beyond the Door (D: Fritz Lang, W: Silvia Richards based on story Rufus King) 2692

Secret Friends (D, W: Dennis Potter suggested by his novel) 3364, 8012

The Secret Life of Walter Mitty (D: Norman Z. McLeod, W: Ken Englund, Everett free-

ner, Bob Foss, Gaup, Nick Thiel) 10817

Shirley Valentine (*D:* Lewis Gilbert, *W:* Willy Russell based on his play) 1657, 6638

Shock Corridor (*D, W:* Samuel Fuller) 9691

Shoot the Moon (*D:* Alan Parker, *W:* Bo Goldman) 2369

Shoot the Piano Player (*D:* Francois Truffaut, *W:* Truffaut, Marcel Moussy based on novel David Goodis) 9464

Shoot to Kill (*D:* Roger Spottiswoode, *W:* Daniel Petrie, Jr, Harv Zimmel, Michael Burton) 877

The Shooting Party (*D:* Alan Bridges, *W:* Julian Bond based on novel Isabel Colegate) 4028, 11353

The Shootist (*D:* Don Siegel, *W:* Miles Hood Swarthout, Scott Hale based on novel by Glendon Swarthout) 1880, 3955, 4210, 8708, 9021

The Shop Around the Corner (*D:* Ernst Lubitsch, *W:* Samson Raphaelson based on play Nikolaus Laszlo) 3711, 4050, 5784, 6031 7004, 8015, 8933, 9751

The Shop on Main Street (*D:* Jan Kadar, Elmar Klos, *W:* Kadar, Klos, Ladislav Grossman based on story Grossman) 7281, 10528

A Shot in the Dark (*D:* Blake Edwards, *W:* Edwards, William Peter Blatty based on plays by Harry Kurnitz, Marcel Achard) 2446

Show Business (*D:* Edwin L. Marin, *W:* Joseph Quillan, Dorothy Bennett, Irving Elinson based on story Bert Granet) 1282, 3142, 4292, 5654, 5953, 10791

Shy People (*D:* Andrei Konchalovsky, *W:* Gerard Brach, Konchalovsky, Marjorie David) 1438, 1820, 6289, 10653

Sibling Rivalry (*D:* Carl Reiner, *W:* Martha Goldhirsh) 4228

Sid & Nancy (*D:* Alex Cox, *W:* Cox, Abbe Wool) 447, 8124

The Sign of the Cross (*D:* Cecil B. DeMille, *W:* Waldemar Young, Sidney Buchman based on play Wilson Barrett) 761, 1125, 2679, 4188, 7624, 10664, 11095

Signs of Life (*D:* John David Coles, *W:* Mark Malone) 2736

The Silence of the Lambs (*D:* Jonathan Demme, *W:* Ted Tally based on novel Thomas Harris) 645, 2662, 3347, 3470, 3794, 3923, 5004, 5608, 6544, 8317, 8855, 9403, 10818

Silk Stockings (*D:* Rouben Mamoulian, *W:* Leoanrd Gershe, Harry Kurnitz, Leoanrd Spigelgass based on musical George S. Kaufman, Lueeen McGrath, Abe Burrows and the screenplay by Billy Wilder Charles Brackett, Walter Reisch from the story by Melchior Lengyel) 651, 2067, 2561, 6970, 7768

Silkwood (*D:* Mike Nichols, *W:* Nora Ephron, Alice Arlen) 1000, 6884

Silver Blaze aka Murder at the Baskervilles (*D:* Thomas Bentley, *W:* Arthur Nacrae, H. Fowler Mear based on story Arthur Conan Doyle) 10064

Silver Streak (*D:* Arthur Hiller, *W:* Colin Higgins) 1065, 1234, 7052, 8373, 10022, 10358, 10808

Since You Went Away (*D:* John Cromwell, *W:* David O. Selznick based on novel Margaret Buell Wilder) 959, 4598, 7505, 9092

Sing You Sinners (*D:* Wesley Ruggles, *W:* Claude Binyon) 9484

Singin' in the Rain (*D:* Gene Kelly, Stanley Donen, *W:* Adolph Green, Betty Comden suggested by the song) 6904, 6928, 7220, 9587, 10270, 10649

Single White Female (*D:* Barbet Schroeder, *W:* Don Roos based on John Lutz's novel) 6596

Sinister Hands (*D:* Armand Schaefer, *W:* Norton Parker, Oliver Drake) 10332

Sinner's Holiday (*D:* John G. Adolfi, *W:* Harvey Thew, George Rosener based on play Marie Baumer) 3501

Siren of Bagdad (*D:* Richard Quine, *W:* Robert E. Kent) 5263

Sirocco (*D:* Curtis Bernhardt, *W:* A.I. Bezzerides, Hans Jacoby based on novel Joseph Kessel) 10483

Sister Kenny (*D:* Dudley Nichols, *W:* Nichols, Alexander Knox, Mary McCarthy, Milton Gunzburg based on book Elizabeth Kenny with Martha Ostenso) 2347

Sisters (*D:* Brian DePalma, *W:* DePalma, Louisa Rose based on DePalma story) 4194

Sitting Pretty (*D:* Walter Lang, *W:* F. Hugh Herbert based on novel Gwen Davenport) 4043, 5330, 6753, 7319, 8609, 9106

Six Weeks (*D:* Tony Bill, *W:* David Seltzer based on novel Fred Mustard Stewart) 3343, 6272, 7791

Sixteen Candles (*D, W:* John Hughes) 1585, 3361, 7139, 7854, 10632, 11089

Skin Deep (*D, W:* Blake Edwards) 2771

Skylark (*D:* Mark Sandrich, *W:* Zion Myers, Allan Scott based on novel and play by Samson Raphaelson) 11134

Slave Girls from Beyond Infinity (*D, W:* Ken Dixon) 10551

Sleeper (*D:* Woody Allen, *W:* Allen, Marshall Brickman) 148, 4455, 4571, 4772, 7159, 7196, 7610, 7630, 8595, 9137, 10547

Sleuth (*D:* Joseph L. Mankiewicz, *W:* Anthony Shaffer based on his play) 4024, 10533

Slightly Scarlett (*D:* Allan Dwan, *W:* Robert Blees based on novel James M. Cain) 619

Slow Dancing in the Big City (*D:* John G. Avildsen, *W:* Barra Grant) 7804

A Small Circle of Friends (*D:* Rob Cohen, *W:* Ezra Sacks) 2235

Smart Blonde (*D:* Frank McDonald, *W:* Don Ryan, Kenneth Gamer based on story Frederick Nebel) 8648

Smash-up, the Story of a Woman (*D:* Stuart Heisler, *W:* John Howard Lawson, Lionel Wiggam based on story Dorothy Parker, Frank Cavett) 11192

Smile (*D:* Michael Ritchie, *W:* Jery Belson) 6805

The Smiling Ghost (*D:* Lewis Seiler, *W:* Kenneth Stuart Palmer) 9068

The Smiling Lieutenant (*D:* Ernst Lubitsch, *W:* Ernest Vajda, Samson Raphaelson, Lubitsch based on operetta Leopold

Jacobson, Felix Doermann, and novel Hans Muller) 8502

Smithereens (*D:* Susan Seidelman, *W:* Ron Nyswaner, Peter Askin) 9677

Smokey and the Bandit II (*D:* Hal Needham, *W:* Jerry Belson, Brock Yates based on story Michael Kane and characters created by Needham, Robert L. Levy) 8364

Smooth Talk (*D:* Joyce Chopra, *W:* Tom Cole based on story Joyce Carol Oates) 2723

The Snake Pit (*D:* Anatole Litvak, *W:* Frank Partos, Millen Brand based on novel Mary Jane Ward) 1231, 1942 5111, 8990, 9262, 9704

Snow Job (*D:* George Englund, *W:* Ken Kolb, Jeffrey Bloom based on story Richard Gallagher) 10984

Snow White and the Seven Dwarfs (*D:* David Hand, *W:* Ted Sears, Otto Englander, Earl Hurd, Dorothy Ann Blank, Richard Creedon, Dick Richard, Merrill De Maris, Webb Smith based on Grimm Brothers' fairy tale) 677

The Snows of Kilimanjaro (*D:* Henry King, *W:* Casey Robinson based on short story Ernest Hemingway) 314, 380 3749

So Fine (*D, W:* Andrew Bergman) 8735

Soak the Rich (*D, W:* Ben Hecht, Charles MacArthur) 2335

Soapdish (*D:* Michael Hoffman, *W:* Robert Harling, Andrew Bergman based on story Harling) 458, 1026, 3496, 4755, 8207, 8613

S.O.B. (*D, W:* Blake Edwards) 9149

Soldier in the Rain (*D:* Ralph Nelson, *W:* Maurice Richlin, Blake Edwards based on novel William Goldman) 7077, 8099, 8914

Soldier of Fortune (*D:* Edward Dmytryk, *W:* Ernest K. Gann based on his novel) 6221

A Soldier's Story (*D:* Norman Jewison, *W:* Charles Fuller based on his play) 8805

The Solid Gold Cadillac (*D:* Richard Quine, *W:* Abe Burrows based on play George S. Kaufman, Howard Teichmann) 4067, 11238

Solomon and Sheba (*D:* King Vidor, *W:* Anthony Veillier, Paul Dudley, George Bruce based on story Crane Wilbur) 2282, 10900

Some Came Running (*D:* Vincente Minnelli, *W:* John Patrick, Arthur Sheekman based on novel James Jones) 11342

Some Kind of Wonderful (*D:* Howard Deutch, *W:* John Hughes) 1858, 5003, 7856, 9357

Some Like It Hot (*D:* Billy Wilder, *W:* Wilder, I.A.L. Diamond based on screenplay Robert Thoeron, M. Logan) 932, 975, 976, 1742, 2095, 3205, 4057, 4088, 4089, 5250, 5546, 6971, 6972, 7166, 8194, 8637, 9027, 9064, 9588, 10720

Somebody Has to Shoot the Picture (*D, W:* Frank Pierson) 3107, 5481, 5858

Somebody Loves Me (*D, W:* Irving Brecher suggested by the careers of Blossom Seeley & Benny Fields) 8423

Somebody Up There Likes Me (*D:* Robert Wise, *W:* Ernest Lehman based on autobiography Rocky Graziano written with Rowland Barber) 1285, 3627, 4414, 6416, 6520

Gordon & Mildred Gordon, Bill Walsh) 9771

That Hamilton Woman aka Lady Hamilton (*D:* Alexander Korda, *W:* Walter Reisch, R.C. Sheriff) 2281, 2985, 3373, 3973, 4538, 5036, 5530, 7556, 8016, 9091, 11365

That Touch of Mink (*D:* Delbert Mann, *W:* Stanley Shapiro, Nate Monaster) 5358

That Uncertain Feeling (*D:* Ernst Lubitsch, *W:* Donald Ogden Stewart) 129, 413, 4341, 6391, 5033, 6996, 9047, 11366

Theatre of Blood (*D:* Douglas Hickox, *W:* Anthony Greville-Bell) 54

Thelma & Louise (*D:* Ridley Scott, *W:* Callie Khouri) 2570, 3603, 5145, 6044, 9915, 10574

Them! (*D:* Gordon Douglas, *W:* Ted Sherdeman, Russell Hughes based on story George Worthing Yates) 8219, 11269

Theodora Goes Wild (*D:* Richard Boleslawski, *W:* Sidney Buchman based on story Mary E. McCarthy) 737, 1485, 2234, 3857, 4329, 4895, 5938

There's Always a Woman (*D:* Alexander Hall, *W:* Gladys Lehman, Joel Sayre, Philip Rapp, Morrie Ryskind based on short story Wilson Collison) 11023

There's Always Tomorrow (*D:* Douglas Sirk, *W:* Bernard C. Schoenfeld based on story Ursula Parrott) 5678

These Three (*D:* William Wyler, *W:* Lillian Hellman based on her play) 374, 7307, 9013

They All Kissed the Bride (*D:* Alexander Hall, *W:* P.J. Wolfson, Andrew P. Solt, Henry Altimus based on story Gina Kaus, Solt) 5192, 6344, 6724

They Call Me Mister Tibbs (*D:* Gordon Douglas, *W:* Alan R. Trustman, James R. Webb based on story Trustman and character created by John Ball) 4606

They Came from Within (*D, W:* David Cronenberg) 9139

They Died with Their Boots On (*D:* Raoul Walsh, *W:* Wally Klein, Aeneas MacKenzie) 1791, 3375, 4120

They Drive by Night (*D:* Raoul Walsh, *W:* Jerry Wald, Richard Macaulay based on novel A.I. Bezzerides) 811, 1848, 2634, 3472, 5412, 9045, 9295, 10287, 10306

They Gave Him a Gun (*D:* W.S. Van Dyke II, *W:* Cyril Hume, Richard Maibaum, Maurice Rapf based on William Joyce Cowen's novel) 6649

They Got Me Covered (*D:* David Butler, *W:* Harry Kurnitz based on story Leonard Q. Ross, Leonard Spigelgass) 7074

They Knew What They Wanted (*D:* Garson Kanin, *W:* Robert Ardrey based on Sidney Howard's play) 6387, 9752, 9790

They Live by Night (*D:* Nicholas Ray, *W:* Charles Schnee, Ray based on novel Edward Anderson) 5244

They Might Be Giants (*D:* Anthony Harvey, *W:* James Goldman based on his play) 2456

They Only Kill Their Masters (*D:* James Goldstone, *W:* Lane Slate) 4623

They Shoot Horses, Don't They? (*D:* Sydney Pollack, *W:* James Poe, Robert E. Thompson based on Horace McCoy's novel) 1724, 2074, 3173, 3986, 4654, 7592, 11375

They Were Expendable (*D:* John Ford, Robert Montgomery, *W:* Frank W. Wead based on book William L. White) 2059, 5882, 8444, 8900, 10451

They Won't Believe Me (*D:* Irving Pichel, *W:* Jonathan Latimer based on story Gordon McDonell) 419, 1361, 5077

They Won't Forget (*D:* Mervyn LeRoy, *W:* Robert Rossen, Aben Kandel based on novel Ward Greene) 870, 3221, 5070, 11183

Thief aka Violent Streets (*D, W:* Michael Mann based on book Frank Hohimer) 1959, 7248

The Thief of Bagdad (*D:* Ludwig Berger, Michael Powell, Tim Whelan, Zoltan Korda, William Cameron Menzies, Alexander Korda, *W:* Lajos Biro, Miles Malleson) 305, 1936, 2416, 3093, 3197, 3371, 3772, 3815, 5373, 5567, 6032, 7311, 7332, 7380, 7957, 8072, 8697, 11395

The Thin Man (*D:* W.S. Van Dyke, *W:* Albert Hackett, Frances Goodrich based on Dashiell Hammett's novel) 2743, 3962, 4061, 4062, 4201, 4252, 4288, 6153, 9447, 10007, 10385, 10859, 11325

The Thing (*D:* Christian Nyby, Howard Hawks, *W:* Charles Lederer based on story John Wood Campbell, Jr.) 216, 5582, 8982, 10590, 10591, 10796

Things Change (*D:* David Mamet, *W:* Mamet, Shel Silverstein) 11322

Things to Come (*D:* William Cameron Menzies *W:* H.G. Wells, Lajos Biro based on book Wells) 6601, 8144, 9806 10549, 11127

The Third Man (*D:* Carol Reed, *W:* Graham Greene) 18, 828, 1910, 2204, 4246, 6460, 10069

13 Rue Madeleine (*D:* Henry Hathaway, *W:* John Monks, Jr., Sy Bartlett) 8867

The Thirteenth Letter (*D:* Otto Preminger, *W:* Howard Koch based on story & screenplay Louis Chavance) 4168

The 39 Steps (*D:* Alfred Hitchcock, *W:* Charles Bennett, Alma Reville, Ian Hay based on John Buchan's novel) 3951, 4893, 4894, 7542, 9601

Thirty Seconds Over Tokyo (*D:* Mervyn LeRoy, *W:* Dalton Trumbo based on book Ted W. Lawson, Robert Considine) 1030

This Above All (*D:* Anatole Litvak, *W:* R.G. Sherriff based on Eric Knight's novel) 2460, 6105

This Angry Age (*D:* Rene Clement, *W:* Irwin Shaw, Clement based on novel Marguerite Duras) 2878

This Gun for Hire (*D:* Frank Tuttle, *W:* Albert Maltz, W.R. Burnett based on novel Graham Greene) 5416, 6318

This Is Spinal Tap (*D:* Rob Reiner, *W:* Christopher Guest, Michael McKean, Harry Shearer, Reiner) 794, 11284

This Land Is Mine (*D:* Jean Renoir, *W:* Dudley Nichols) 5689

This Thing Called Love (*D:* Paul L. Stein, *W:* Horace Jackson based on play Edwin Burke) 1648, 3316, 3663

A Thousand Clowns (*D:* Fred Coe, *W:* Herb Gardner based on his play) 859, 4033, 4418, 5790, 6637

Thousands Cheer (*D:* George Sidney, *W:* Paul Jarrico, Richard Collins based on their story) 4992, 9878, 10049

Three Blind Mice (*D:* William A. Seiter, *W:* Brown Holmes, Lynn Starling based on play Stephen Powys) 6379

Three Coins in the Fountain (*D:* Jean Negulesco, *W:* John Patrick based on John H. Secondari's novel) 496, 1628, 4021, 4112, 4648, 10999, 11237

Three Comrades (*D:* Frank Borzage, *W:* F. Scott Fitzgerald, Edward Paramore based on Erich Marie Remarque's novel) 2177, 10178

Three in the Attic (*D:* Richard Wilson, *W:* Stephen H. Yafa) 99, 7873, 8760

Three into Two Won't Go (*D:* Peter Hall, *W:* Edna O'Brien based on novel Andrea Newman) 3902

Three Men and a Baby (*D:* Leonard Nimoy, *W:* James Orr, Jim Cruickshank based on French film Coline Serreau) 53, 596, 7366

Three on a Match (*D:* Mervyn LeRoy, *W:* Lucien Hubbard, Kubec Glasmon, John Bright based on story Glasmon, Bright) 6852 3:10 to Yuma (*D:* Delmer Daves, *W:* Halsted Welles based on story Elmore Leonard) 5334

Thunder Alley (*D:* Richard Rush, *W:* Sy Salkowitz) 562

Thunder Rock (*D:* Roy Boulting, *W:* Jeffrey Dell, Bernard Miles based on Robert Ardrey's play) 7471, 10398, 11262

Thunderball (*D:* Terence Young, *W:* Richard Maibaum, John Hopkins based on characters created by Ian Fleming & story by Kevin McClory, Jack Whittingham, Fleming) 1201, 2220, 2949

Ticket to Heaven (*D:* Ralph L. Thomas, *W:* Thomas, Anne Cameron based on book Josh Freed) 4656

Tight Little Island *see* Whisky Galore

Tightrope (*D, W:* Richard Tuggle., 1662, 2114, 5131

Till the End of Time (1946, RKO), *D:* Edward Dmytryk, *W:* Allen Rivkin, based on novel Niven Busch) 5308

Tim (*D, W:* Michael Pate based on novel Colleen McCullough) 2237

Time After Time (*D, W:* Nicholas Meyer based on story Karl Alexander, Steve Hayes) 226, 817, 4609, 7053, 10169

Time Bandits (*D:* Terry Gilliam, *W:* Michael Palin, Gilliam) 4148

The Time Machine (*D:* George Pal, *W:* David Duncan based on H.G. Wells' novel) 10196

The Time of Your Life (*D:* H.C. Potter, *W:* Nathaniel Curtis based on William Saroyan's play) 2064

The Tin Drum (*D:* Volker Schlondorff, *W:* Franz Seitz, Schlondorff, Jean-Claude Carriere, Gunter Grass based on Grass' novel) 8940

Tin Men (*D, W:* Barry Levinson) 2285, 8611, 10058

Titanic (*D:* Jean Negulesco, *W:* Charles